The Top 6000 Companies in North West England

Companies with assets exceeding £6,500,000

John D Blackburn
Editor

dp

First Edition

Winter 2018

ISBN-13: 978-1-912736-09-6

ISBN-10: 1-912736-09-8

Printed in 8pt Nimbus Sans L

Designed by URW++ Design and Development GmbH

Dellam Publishing Limited

2 Heath Drive, Sutton, Surrey, SM2 5RP

Fax: 020 8770 7478 email: enquiries@dellam.com

SAN: 0177881 EAN/GLN: 5030670177882

Table of Contents

1 Acknowledgements iv

2 Introduction v

3 Total Assets League Table 1

- As a measure of size, total assets is preferable to turnover which is influenced by profit margins and whether companies are capital or labour intensive.

4 Company Profiles 45

- Full company name, date incorporated, net worth, total assets, registered office, activities, shareholders and parent company, directors (with date of birth, nationality and occupation) and number of employees (if available).

5 Standard Industrial Classification 587

- These codes are used to classify businesses by the type of economic activity in which they are engaged.

6 *finis* 620

Acknowledgements

This is a long and detailed publication containing thousands of facts and figures. It is only to be expected, despite continuous and repeated editing and checking, that errors may occur. In such cases, once we are aware of any, we publish a correction on our website.

Readers are encouraged to check regularly at www.dellam.com/books for any corrections and updates.

Although we take extreme care to ensure accuracy and being up-to-date, we cannot accept responsibility for any errors or omissions.

We appreciate your interest in our publications, and your comments and suggestions are always welcome. Please contact us at enquiries@dellam.com.

Introduction

This study looks at all companies registered in North West England and where their total assets are more than £6,500,000.

North West England consists of the five counties of Cheshire, Cumbria, Greater Manchester, Lancashire and Merseyside. The region has a population of 7 million and 3.5 million jobs.

There are two large conurbations centred on Liverpool and Manchester

The aim of this study is to provide an overview of the key movers and shakers in the corporate sector. Only key data has been isolated, particularly the company's net worth and total assets, but also their full name, date incorporated, registered office, activities, shareholders, directors (with date of birth, occupation and nationality) and number of employees.

Two indicators of size are used: net worth and total assets. These are preferable to turnover which is influenced by profit margins and whether the companies are capital or labour intensive.

A short summary of the corporate sector in North West England:

The region generated £165 billion GVA in 2016, exceeded only by London and the South East. This made the region the third-highest contributor of all the UK regions.

The region's growth was 1.3% but still below the national average of 1.6%.

There are many pockets of high growth within the region: parts of Cheshire and Greater Manchester, Warrington, and Blackburn and Darwen grew at a higher than average rate.

The region's strategic importance to the government's Northern Powerhouse programme has attracted public and private sector investment.

The value of construction work in the region jumped to more than £4.6 billion for the three months to August 2018, up £600m or 15% compared with the same period in 2017. Total construction output in Great Britain increased 1.5% for the period year on year, making the region's growth 10 times higher than the average.

Manchester is ranked number one for city centre growth and jobs: population growth (2002-2015) was 149%, and jobs growth (1998-2015) was 84%.

Greater Manchester has one of the highest number of business start-ups per 10,000 people out of all UK cities.

Standard cataloguing guidelines for company names in the profile section have been used, but there will be occurrences when the name may not be strictly alphabetical. A certain licence was adopted where it was felt that strictly alphabetical could lead to improper cataloguing. Some company names have been shortened in the league tables for aesthetic reasons.

John D Blackburn
Editor

This page is intentionally left blank

Total Assets League Table

Company	Value
GE Capital International Holdings Limited	£84,369,424,384
Unilever PLC	£52,728,942,592
The Co-operative Bank P.L.C.	£24,490,100,736
The Co-operative Bank Holdings Limited	£24,490,100,736
Accord Mortgages Limited	£19,933,483,008
UK Asset Resolution Limited	£19,812,999,168
IGE USA Investments	£17,594,382,336
United Utilities PLC	£14,702,900,224
United Utilities Group PLC	£13,003,499,520
United Utilities Water Limited	£12,622,799,872
Bradford & Bingley PLC	£11,857,000,448
GE Capital International Limited	£11,264,427,008
Kelda Eurobond Co Limited	£9,855,200,256
Wm Morrison Supermarkets P L C	£9,667,000,320
Kelda Finance (No.1) Limited	£9,222,899,712
Yorkshire Water Services Limited	£9,135,899,648
Chesnara PLC	£8,443,383,808
MBNA Limited	£8,066,458,112
Arris International PLC	£6,212,156,416
GE Capital European Treasury Services Limited	£6,137,605,120
Marks and Spencer Financial Services PLC	£5,785,147,904
AMEC Foster Wheeler Limited	£5,272,999,936
Mettler-Toledo Safeline Limited	£5,082,198,016
GE Industrial Sterling Treasury Services	£4,621,636,096
United Utilities North West Limited	£4,409,399,808
Safeway Stores Limited	£4,064,999,936
Erie Finance Limited	£4,045,488,896
NSG UK Enterprises Limited	£3,990,658,048
Peel Ports Limited	£3,942,200,064
Manchester Airport Group Investments Limited	£3,841,999,872
Safeway Limited	£3,827,000,064
Mortgage Express	£3,645,193,984
North West Electricity Networks (UK) Limited	£3,537,799,936
North West Electricity Networks (Finance) Limited	£3,514,800,128
North West Electricity Networks (Holdings) Limited	£3,514,500,096
North West Electricity Networks PLC	£3,502,400,000
Gollek UK Limited	£3,327,485,952
Manchester Airports Holdings Limited	£3,323,800,064
Electricity North West Limited	£3,305,600,000
Erie UK 1 Limited	£3,248,364,544
Manchester Airport Group Finance Limited	£3,146,976,000
GE Capital Investments	£3,137,901,056
Kellogg Group Limited	£3,128,271,360
Countrywide Assured PLC	£3,010,598,912
Provident Financial PLC	£2,965,900,032
Community Health Partnerships Limited	£2,904,972,032
Pilkington Group Limited	£2,860,486,912
The Manchester Airport Group PLC	£2,815,237,888
Shop Direct Limited	£2,814,299,904
SP Manweb PLC	£2,797,299,968
Iceland Foods Limited	£2,783,600,128
EG Group Limited	£2,782,296,832
EG Midco Limited	£2,782,296,832
Mondi UK Consumer Packaging Holding 1 Ltd	£2,689,036,032
NSG Holding (Europe) Limited	£2,624,506,624
Rathbone Investment Management Limited	£2,596,099,072
EG Finco Limited	£2,551,003,904
Auto Trader Holding Limited	£2,498,200,064
Manchester Airport Finance Holdings Limited	£2,494,245,888
Kellogg Latin America Holding Company (One) Ltd	£2,331,742,464
Redrow Homes Limited	£2,288,699,904
Redhill Famco Limited	£2,278,099,968
Together Financial Services Limited	£2,276,100,096
AFW Finance 2 Limited	£2,232,140,032
Redrow PLC	£2,200,999,936
Yorkshire Building Society Covered Bonds LLP	£2,124,420,992
Mettler-Toledo Finance (UK) Limited	£2,062,043,008
Manchester Airport PLC	£2,044,483,968
GE UK Group	£1,968,368,000
Red Football Limited	£1,966,028,032
IGE Dollar Treasury Services	£1,960,377,856
Peel Investments Holdings Limited	£1,956,715,008

Company	Value
Iceland Midco Limited	£1,908,524,032
Lookers PLC	£1,895,600,000
Inovyn Limited	£1,887,676,160
Vanquis Bank Limited	£1,855,100,032
Foster Wheeler Europe	£1,838,568,960
Peel Holdings (Land and Property) Limited	£1,820,209,024
Peel Ports Holdings Limited	£1,811,000,064
Shop Direct Finance Company Limited	£1,792,899,968
Peel Holdings Land and Property (UK) Limited	£1,792,530,048
Assura PLC	£1,784,400,000
AMEC Foster Wheeler Finance Limited	£1,783,597,056
Mere Plantations Limited	£1,770,506,624
Essar Oil (UK) Limited	£1,737,389,440
Thermo Fisher Scientific Life Holdings Limited	£1,730,966,016
Thermo Fisher Scientific Life Technologies Entr Hldg	£1,730,817,024
Thermo Fisher Scientific Life Technologies Invest UK I	£1,730,806,016
Stores Group Limited	£1,729,069,056
Iceland Topco Limited	£1,723,299,968
Attock Oil Company Limited (The)	£1,678,744,960
Emerson Developments (Holdings) Limited	£1,670,473,984
Peel Ports Group Limited	£1,629,400,064
JD Sports Fashion PLC	£1,626,200,064
Peel Ports Investments Limited	£1,618,700,032
Yorkshire Water Services Finance Limited	£1,614,727,040
Scoto Limited	£1,612,699,008
Bibby Line Group Limited	£1,599,224,064
Pets at Home No.1 Limited	£1,595,992,960
Inovyn Finance PLC	£1,575,259,392
Kingspan Group Limited	£1,506,569,856
Red Football Holdings Limited	£1,492,407,040
International General Electric (U.S.A.)	£1,468,855,040
Kellogg Company of Great Britain,Limited	£1,463,724,032
Iceland Acquico Limited	£1,444,409,984
Suncor Energy UK Limited	£1,441,472,000
Shop Direct Home Shopping Limited	£1,418,499,968
GE UK Holdings	£1,407,089,024
The Access Bank UK Limited	£1,402,475,520
GE Capital Corporation (Holdings)	£1,388,611,968
Auto Trader Limited	£1,385,799,936
Calvin Capital Group Holdings Limited	£1,371,025,024
Inovyn Group Treasury Limited	£1,339,896,704
Pets at Home Group PLC	£1,339,376,000
Manchester United Limited	£1,309,468,032
GE Infrastructure UK Limited	£1,307,286,016
Daisy Group Holdings Limited	£1,301,624,960
AMEC USA Holdings Limited	£1,301,336,960
Bruntwood Group Limited	£1,267,175,040
Bruntwood Limited	£1,266,897,024
Arysta LifeScience Global Limited	£1,264,946,688
Arrow Global Group PLC	£1,258,514,944
Moorland Covered Bonds LLLP	£1,252,491,008
Erie U.K. Limited	£1,247,760,000
Bodycote International Limited	£1,243,796,992
Ausurus Group Ltd	£1,216,000,000
Lambtrack Limited	£1,204,231,040
Together Commercial Finance Limited	£1,202,200,064
HBOS Social Housing Covered Bonds LLP	£1,200,316,032
IGE USA Holdings	£1,198,046,720
Cheselden Limited	£1,192,711,040
European Metal Recycling Limited	£1,174,000,000
Arysta LifeScience U.K. USD Limited	£1,173,585,920
PZ Cussons PLC	£1,168,999,936
Bentley Motors Limited	£1,147,800,064
Sellafield Limited	£1,132,999,936
Marlowe Holdings Limited	£1,122,835,968
The Mersey Docks and Harbour Co Ltd	£1,115,699,968
N Brown Group PLC	£1,067,000,000
Manchester City Limited	£1,060,785,984
Manchester City Football Club Limited	£1,060,782,016
Daisy Group Limited	£1,059,441,024
Suncor Energy UK Holdings Ltd	£1,057,889,984
B&M European Value Retail Holdco 4 Ltd	£1,053,468,032

Company	Value
Arris Global Ltd.	£1,051,807,232
Tyco Holdings (U.K.) Limited	£1,044,465,024
AMEC Foster Wheeler Group Limited	£1,036,699,008
United Utilities Water Finance PLC	£1,034,168,000
Federal-Mogul Global Growth Limited	£1,026,062,208
Princes Limited	£1,025,280,000
Kelda Group Limited	£1,011,601,024
B & M Retail Limited	£1,006,995,008
Bibby Financial Services Limited	£1,003,630,016
Peel Investments (U.K.) Limited	£1,000,734,976
Erie UK Senior Holding Limited	£988,092,992
GEH Holdings	£978,083,968
Kelda Finance (No.2) Limited	£977,777,024
Pets at Home Ltd	£977,363,008
J.D. Williams & Company Limited	£976,641,024
Bodycote PLC	£959,699,968
Iceland Foods Group Limited	£959,476,992
T. J. Morris Limited	£942,866,304
Urenco UK Limited	£940,801,984
Consolidated Investment Holdings Limited	£940,041,984
The Hut Group Limited	£938,947,968
Convatec Holdings U.K. Limited	£926,862,784
Turnstone Equityco 1 Limited	£926,257,984
Turnstone Midco 2 Limited	£926,113,984
Manchester United Football Club Limited	£924,396,032
Peel Land and Property Limited	£906,110,016
Survitec Eagle LLP	£898,955,008
VUR Village Hotels Limited	£897,494,976
Scusi Limited	£894,097,984
Iceland VInco Limited	£891,241,024
Arrow Global Limited	£887,430,976
Survitec Acquisition Company Limited	£879,286,016
Survitec Topco Limited	£879,206,016
Matalan Finance PLC	£877,400,000
Crown Packaging Manufacturing UK Limited	£873,489,984
Peel Ports UK Financeco Limited	£841,600,000
Bodycote Finance Limited	£830,894,016
Optimisation Investments Limited	£826,872,000
Certas Energy UK Limited	£812,454,976
Peel Land and Property Holdings Limited	£811,145,984
Iceland BondCo PLC	£808,902,016
Elli Finance (UK) PLC	£804,444,032
Manchester Airport Group Funding PLC	£803,134,976
Arrow Global Investments Holdings Limited	£802,820,992
Daisy Pikco Limited	£800,259,968
Daisy Midco Limited	£800,259,968
Daisy Finco Limited	£800,252,992
Turnstone Bidco 1 Limited	£799,016,000
Inovyn Holdings Limited	£792,772,992
Sigma Financial Facilities Limited	£785,697,024
Yorkshire Water Services Holdings Limited	£778,318,976
GE Capital Funding Services Limited	£776,398,016
Arrow Global Finance PLC	£774,785,024
DCC Energy UK Limited	£764,439,296
Littlewoods Limited	£763,294,976
Assura Financing PLC	£754,547,904
Daisy Holdings Limited	£741,721,024
Cott UK Acquisition Limited	£741,433,024
MM European Holdings LLP	£739,476,672
Exertis (UK) Ltd	£737,875,008
Amber Homeloans Limited	£733,560,000
Bracken Midco2 Limited	£729,900,032
Elders Glass Limited	£720,884,992
AECOM Global Holdings UK Limited	£716,993,536
Spectrum Brands (UK) Holdings Limited	£714,187,008
Westinghouse Electric UK Holdings Limited	£707,779,008
CMA CGM (UK) Shipping Limited	£704,617,984
Peel Property Holdings Limited	£696,974,016
Thermo Fisher Scientific Odyssey Holdings Ltd	£689,515,008
Euro Garages Limited	£685,812,992
Interactive Investor Limited	£685,499,008
Matalan Retail Ltd.	£684,099,968
Life Sciences International Limited	£683,062,016
Kingspan Holdings (Panels) Limited	£679,478,208
AMEC USA Finance Limited	£679,460,992
CF Industries (UK) Limited	£679,062,016
Warburtons Holdings Limited	£662,222,016
Thermo Fisher Scientific Life Technologies Invest UK	£659,313,024
Cott Retail Brands Limited	£654,153,024
Vita (Holdings) Limited	£651,651,200
Provident Personal Credit Limited	£650,200,000
MU Finance Limited	£648,092,032
Close Leasing Limited	£646,913,728
GE Capital Corporation Property Co Investments Ltd	£646,174,016
B&M European Value Retail Holdco 1 Ltd	£646,134,976
B&M European Value Retail Holdco 3 Ltd	£645,928,000
Dechra Pharmaceuticals PLC	£638,419,968
Warburtons 1876 Limited	£630,497,024
Smurfit Kappa UK Ltd	£629,680,000
James Fisher and Sons Public Limited Company	£618,600,000
Bibby Invoice Finance UK Limited	£606,417,024
Federal-Mogul Limited	£606,361,792
Farmers Boy Limited	£603,324,992
Edmundson Electrical Limited	£601,638,016
European Metal Recycling (USA) Limited	£598,723,008
Peel Land and Property Investments PLC	£595,198,016
Red Football Shareholder Limited	£590,684,032
Invista Textiles (U.K.) Limited	£587,708,352
Gusiute Holdings (UK) Limited	£584,490,944
Jerrold Finco PLC	£582,727,168
Bodycote America Treasury Limited	£565,867,264
Peel Holdings (Media) Limited	£560,156,032
IDH Finance PLC	£557,081,024
B&M European Value Retail Holdco 2 Ltd	£556,873,984
European Metal Recycling USA Holdings Limited	£549,810,624
HB (HDG) Limited	£548,300,032
Survitec Group Limited	£548,086,016
Daisy Intermediate Holdings Limited	£548,025,984
Peel Land Holdings Limited	£547,180,992
GE Capital UK Limited	£546,529,024
Lookers Motor Group Limited	£545,974,976
Dow Chemical Company Limited	£544,828,992
Catalyst Healthcare (Manchester) Holdings Ltd	£541,800,000
Catalyst Healthcare (Manchester) Limited	£541,800,000
Innospec Finance Limited	£540,846,976
Urenco Chemplants Limited	£540,230,976
Fisher Scientific UK Holding Company Limited	£539,284,992
SPX Clyde UK Limited	£539,089,024
Victrex PLC	£538,099,968
ENW Finance PLC	£536,478,016
UKSV Holdings Company Ltd.	£535,091,008
ABB Holdings Limited	£534,782,016
Hallmark Cards PLC	£533,958,016
GE Industrial (UK) Holdings	£533,316,992
Peel Media (Holdings) Limited	£528,332,000
Peel Media Limited	£528,153,984
Northern Trust Group Limited	£527,916,992
Northern Trust Company Limited	£524,923,008
Warburtons Limited	£524,440,992
Convatec International U.K. Limited	£523,712,256
Univar UK Limited	£522,735,008
JDW Finance Limited	£520,683,008
MKS Instruments Holdings Ltd	£518,402,816
AMEC USA Limited	£517,708,992
Novelis Europe Holdings Limited	£515,573,504
L.Rowland & Company (Retail) Limited	£514,232,000
Blemain Finance Limited	£508,900,000
Vita Industrial (UK) Limited	£508,399,488
Morris Homes Limited	£505,416,000
New Charter Homes Limited	£504,935,008
Hero Acquisitions Limited	£502,273,984
Johnsons Apparelmaster Limited	£500,208,000
Crane SC Holdings Limited	£496,038,880
INEOS Enterprises Holdings Limited	£493,921,120

Company	Turnover
Matalan Group Limited	£492,500,000
PZ Cussons (Holdings) Limited	£488,987,008
Brookhouse Properties Limited	£486,303,008
ABB Limited	£484,870,016
Liverpool Football Club and Athletic Grounds Ltd	£481,495,008
Innospec Limited	£481,140,992
Victrex Manufacturing Limited	£480,100,000
Vita (Group) Unlimited	£478,525,248
LF Europe Limited	£475,033,984
Northern Trust Group 1 Limited	£474,881,984
The Helping Foundation	£473,697,600
Phoenix Medical Supplies Limited	£470,598,016
Lex Vehicle Leasing (Holdings) Limited	£468,732,992
Terraform UK3 Intermediate Holdings Limited	£468,652,704
Micromass Holdings Limited	£465,121,984
Orbit Investments (Properties) Limited	£463,136,032
CAC Limited	£462,921,984
Peel Ports Intermediate Holdco Limited	£460,800,000
AECOM Intercontinental Holdings UK Limited	£458,256,960
Merseylink (Holdings) Limited	£456,398,016
Merseylink Limited	£456,398,016
Catalyst Healthcare (Manchester) Financing PLC	£454,084,992
Rubix Group International Limited	£452,700,000
Marlowe Holdings Investments Limited	£452,452,992
Shop Direct Group Financial Services Limited	£450,000,000
Phone-a-Loan Limited	£448,483,008
Nordic Packaging and Container (UK) Holdings Ltd	£447,019,008
Incommunities Group Limited	£445,289,984
AECOM GR1 Limited	£445,246,720
Erie UK 2 Limited	£440,196,992
LW Investments Limited	£439,295,008
Nufarm UK Limited	£438,000,992
AECOM GR2 Limited	£436,798,336
Peel South East Limited	£433,348,992
Mexichem Dura-Line UK, Ltd	£432,887,232
Phoenix Healthcare Distribution Limited	£431,857,984
HSS Hire Group PLC	£429,455,008
GD Global Holdings UK II Limited	£425,850,304
Nordic Packaging and Container Holdings Limited	£423,679,872
GE Capital Sigma Holding Ltd	£422,017,984
Pershing Securities Limited	£420,363,008
McBride PLC	£419,900,000
VUR Village Properties Limited	£418,200,992
Arrow Global Europe Limited	£417,588,192
Johnson Investment Limited	£417,553,984
Provident Financial Management Services Limited	£417,500,000
Assura Medical Centres Limited	£416,665,792
Morris Group Limited	£414,168,992
JCT600 Limited	£413,132,992
BASF Public Limited Company	£411,519,008
Turnstone Midco 1 Limited	£410,982,016
Moneysupermarket.Com Financial Group Holdings	£410,000,000
Neerock Limited	£405,451,008
Energy Assets Financing Limited	£400,620,992
Energy Assets Topco Limited	£399,286,016
Inovyn Chlorvinyls Limited	£398,700,000
Chubb Systems Limited	£397,779,008
FDML Holdings Limited	£396,963,264
Helmet Securities Limited	£396,355,008
Hexpol UK Limited	£394,505,376
Findel P.L.C.	£394,040,992
Auto Trader Group PLC	£390,500,000
Orbit Investments (Northern) Limited	£389,854,624
Wythenshawe Community Housing Group Limited	£387,544,992
Brother Finance (U.K.) PLC	£386,629,984
Wm Morrison Produce Limited	£386,352,000
UD-RD Holding Company Limited	£384,497,984
JDW Malta Limited	£383,476,800
Peel Property Limited	£379,475,008
Oxoid Limited	£379,332,000
EWM (Topco) Limited	£376,963,008
Verastar Holdings Limited	£375,977,984

Company	Turnover
NES Group Limited	£373,932,000
NCC Group PLC	£370,600,000
Saica Paper UK Limited	£369,121,984
Bracken Midco1 PLC	£367,900,000
Bestway National Chemists Limited	£367,407,008
Together Personal Finance Limited	£366,700,000
The Hut.Com Limited	£363,550,016
GE (Sigma) Holding Ltd	£363,456,992
Equity Solutions Asset Management Limited	£362,981,344
Johnson Service Group PLC	£361,800,000
NES Global Limited	£360,876,992
Peel Finance (UK) Limited	£357,115,200
Survitec Holdco Limited	£355,761,984
Survitec Interco Limited	£355,760,992
Survitec Midco Limited	£355,760,992
Peel Ports Operations Limited	£354,400,000
Survitec Group (Finance 2) Limited	£353,830,016
Radius Payment Solutions Limited	£352,200,000
Survitec Group (Finance 3) Limited	£351,913,984
Norcros Group (Holdings) Limited	£351,601,984
Hampshire Bidco Limited	£351,299,008
Rochpion Properties (4) LLP	£350,926,016
Speedy Hire PLC	£349,000,000
Arrow Global One Limited	£346,460,000
GE Capital EMEA Services Limited	£343,780,992
Nalco Acquisition One	£343,748,032
PZ Cussons (International) Limited	£341,307,008
NES Global Talent Limited	£340,754,048
CF Fertilisers UK Limited	£339,275,008
Innospec Trading Limited	£338,766,016
Kosa UK Limited	£338,248,544
Vetco Group Limited	£337,355,424
Pilkington Germany Finance Limited	£335,945,984
Peel Investments (Land and Property) No.1 Limited	£334,464,992
Moneysupermarket.Com Ltd	£333,984,000
UPL Europe Ltd	£330,768,000
Assura HC Limited	£330,372,544
Arysta LifeScience U.K. Holdings Limited	£328,626,240
Airswift Holdings Limited	£327,335,872
INEOS Runcorn (TPS) Holdings Limited	£326,771,008
INEOS Runcorn (TPS) Limited	£326,771,008
Pacific Nuclear Transport Limited	£326,464,000
Bibby Financial Services (Europe) Limited	£326,455,168
Wain Group Holdings Limited	£325,487,008
Novelis UK Ltd	£324,940,000
Spectrum Brands (UK) Limited	£324,267,008
Express Gifts Limited	£323,028,992
Kerling Newco 2 Limited	£321,454,016
Air Energi Group Holdings Limited	£319,816,288
Suncor Energy International Trading Limited	£319,183,008
Etihad Acquisitions Limited	£318,288,992
Dnata Catering Services Limited	£317,315,008
Kerling Newco 1 Limited	£317,214,688
Morris Homes (North) Limited	£316,044,992
Wienerberger Limited	£315,228,000
Norcros PLC	£313,000,000
Betfred Group Limited	£312,095,008
Lightcatch Limited	£312,062,016
Select Property Group (Holdings) Limited	£311,984,992
GE ESE UK Limited	£310,417,984
Hologic IP Ltd	£309,954,848
Bodycote Investments	£309,319,808
Daniel Thwaites Public Limited Company	£308,600,000
Done Brothers (Cash Betting) Limited	£306,571,008
K Europe Holding Company Limited	£304,532,448
USS Nero Limited	£302,112,320
TMD Friction Holdings (UK) Ltd	£301,074,112
Hexpol Finance UK Limited	£300,408,192
Innospec International Limited	£298,556,000
Peel Investments (North) Limited	£297,996,992
Azelis UK Holdings Limited	£294,186,976
North Yorkshire Mortgages Limited	£293,478,016

Company	Amount
Catalyst Healthcare (Romford) Limited	£292,990,016
Catalyst Healthcare (Romford) Holdings Limited	£292,990,016
Novelis Services Limited	£290,349,984
IDH Acquisitions Limited	£287,288,992
Luxfer Holdings PLC	£286,895,168
Thermo Shandon Limited	£286,577,984
Peel Land and Property (Ports No. 3) Limited	£285,598,016
Peel Chapel No.1 Limited	£281,931,424
Peel Chapel No.3 Limited	£281,915,232
Peel Chapel No.2 Limited	£281,915,104
SPX European Holding Limited	£281,107,008
St James's Oncology SPC Ltd	£280,543,008
Connells Limited	£280,401,984
Swinton Group Limited	£279,280,992
RT Lithium Limited	£278,060,352
Swinton (Holdings) Limited	£277,976,000
Speedy Asset Services Limited	£275,896,992
Bruntwood LG Limited	£274,444,000
Kellogg Marketing and Sales Company (UK) Ltd	£272,827,008
The Dutton-Forshaw Motor Company Limited	£269,392,992
IGE USA Group	£267,040,000
Edge Orbital Holdings Limited	£266,894,000
Innovia Group (Holding 3) Limited	£266,721,360
FMC Technologies Limited	£265,058,000
Smurfit Kappa Packaging UK Limited	£264,255,008
Kelda Water Services Limited	£264,054,000
AMEC Foster Wheeler Energy Limited	£262,700,000
AO World PLC	£260,500,000
Pilkington (US) Investments (No.3) Unlimited	£259,716,992
HSS Hire Service Group Limited	£259,423,008
URS Luxembourg LLP	£258,971,696
Britannia Hotels Limited	£258,372,000
Campus Living Villages (Bond Issuer) UK PLC	£256,702,000
Yodel Distribution Holdings Limited	£256,568,000
Mexichem Wavin UK Ltd	£256,499,216
Semara Group Limited	£254,644,992
Tip Holdings (UK) Limited	£254,462,656
Homefield PVT UK Ltd.	£253,656,992
Merseylink (Issuer) PLC	£253,608,992
NES Holdings Limited	£253,588,912
Clarke Energy Topco Limited	£252,658,000
Ulixes Limited	£252,019,008
International Nuclear Services Limited	£251,811,008
UK Fuels Limited	£250,243,008
Fircroft Engineering Services Holdings Limited	£250,128,000
First Ark Limited	£249,808,000
Dechra Limited	£249,604,000
Moneysupermarket.Com Group PLC	£249,524,000
Assura Properties PLC	£248,622,080
Tyco Fire & Integrated Solutions (UK) Limited	£247,256,000
Iggesund Paperboard (Workington) Limited	£246,662,000
Motors Insurance Company Limited	£246,604,000
Aviagen Turkeys Limited	£245,716,000
Paymentshield Limited	£245,044,000
Hologic GGO 3 LLP	£243,998,336
Meter Fit 5 Limited	£243,666,000
East Coast Main Line Company Limited	£243,446,000
Willow Park Housing Trust Limited	£242,342,000
Theo Topco Limited	£241,650,000
Survitec Group (Holdings) Limited	£241,502,000
Daisy Communications Ltd.	£241,436,000
Yodel Logistics Limited	£241,279,008
APV Overseas Holdings Limited	£240,248,992
Catalyst Healthcare (Romford) Financing PLC.	£239,495,008
CF Fertilisers UK Group Limited	£239,178,000
INEOS Enterprises Group Limited	£238,300,000
United Utilities Utility Solutions Holdings Limited	£237,597,680
L1 Renewables Limited	£237,263,808
Gardner Denver Holdings Limited	£236,491,392
Saica Pack UK Limited	£236,438,000
Four Seasons Health Care Holdings Limited	£236,339,008
WEX Europe Services Limited	£236,192,672
Trafford Housing Trust Limited	£234,340,992
Campus Living Villages (City Portfolio) UK Limited	£233,576,000
Examworks UK Ltd	£233,415,008
Car Benefit Holdings Limited	£233,287,328
GB Group PLC	£231,404,992
Whitecross Dental Care Limited	£230,768,992
AQA Education	£230,424,992
Assurant Group Limited	£228,616,992
Bet Security and Communications Limited	£228,491,008
Renold International Holdings Limited	£228,400,000
Peel Property (Investments) Limited	£227,752,000
Eddie Stobart Limited	£227,070,000
Scapa Group Public Limited Company	£227,000,000
Greenwhitestar Acquisitions Limited	£226,428,000
Vacation Rentals (UK) Ltd	£226,308,992
James Hall and Company (Holdings) Limited	£225,927,008
Blujay Topco Limited	£225,615,888
Car Benefit Car Schemes Limited	£225,076,576
Blujay Solutions Group Holdings Limited	£224,466,672
Fircroft Engineering Services Limited	£224,022,000
Wheatsheaf Group Limited	£223,842,000
Hologic Hub Ltd	£223,825,424
Bruntwood AV Limited	£223,604,992
Red Football Junior Limited	£222,447,696
Story Homes Limited	£221,285,376
Universe Holdco Limited	£221,107,344
AO Retail Limited	£220,856,992
Gardner Denver Industries Ltd	£220,029,664
Grattan Public Limited Company	£219,515,008
Pilkington Automotive Limited	£219,442,656
Gloucester Quays LLP	£219,231,008
Pershing Holdings (UK) Limited	£217,136,000
HSS Financing PLC	£217,047,008
LDF Group Holdco Limited	£216,731,408
Rainy City Investments Limited	£216,396,992
Theo Bidco Limited	£214,933,952
GHG Lubricants Holdings Limited	£213,939,088
Vita International Limited	£212,803,520
Corpacq Limited	£212,472,000
South Tyne & Wear Energy Recovery Ltd	£211,814,000
South Tyne & Wear Energy Recovery Holdings Ltd	£211,814,000
GGM Holdings Limited	£211,811,008
Dave Whelan Sports Limited	£211,063,424
MHC UK Limited	£210,812,992
Gorgemead Limited	£210,645,888
Graphic Packaging International Limited	£209,976,992
Carr's Group PLC	£209,040,000
Paymentshield Group Holdings Limited	£208,341,600
GE Capital Equipment Finance Ltd	£207,806,000
McJunkin Red Man UK Ltd	£206,370,944
Pilkington United Kingdom Limited	£206,364,000
Natrium Holdings Limited	£205,894,000
NCC Group (Solutions) Limited	£204,900,000
McBride Holdings Limited	£204,240,000
Henmead Limited	£203,330,000
Morris Homes (Midlands) Limited	£202,312,992
On The Beach Group PLC	£201,984,992
James Hall and Company Limited	£200,955,008
LW Finance Limited	£200,722,000
James Halstead PLC	£200,546,000
INEOS Fluor Limited	£199,824,000
Trust Inns Limited	£199,778,000
Star Academies	£199,164,992
Kelda Finance (No.3) PLC	£199,023,008
ALS Testing Services (UK) Limited	£198,990,000
Invibio Limited	£198,620,000
Energy Assets Micco Limited	£198,176,992
Everton Football Club Company, Limited	£198,087,008
Edward Billington and Son Limited	£197,552,992
Pilkington Italy Unlimited	£197,302,000
Wirral Partnership Homes Limited	£196,962,000
IKO U.K. Limited	£196,954,000

Company	Value
Catalyst Higher Education (Sheffield) PLC	£196,312,992
Catalyst Higher Education (Sheffield) Holdings Ltd	£196,312,992
Elior UK Holdings Limited	£195,818,000
GE Capital Information Technology Solutions Limited	£195,811,008
Acorn Care and Education Limited	£195,240,608
Kingspan Holdings (Insulation) Limited	£194,459,696
Smurfit Kappa Investments UK Ltd	£194,212,992
Tip Trailer Services UK Limited	£193,834,000
Bodycote America Finance Limited	£193,121,872
Swansway Group Limited	£192,532,688
Universe Bidco Limited	£192,395,008
NES Global Talent Finance Limited	£191,954,000
The Hospital Company (Liverpool) Limited	£191,839,008
The Hospital Company (Liverpool) Holdings Limited	£191,839,008
Lanxess Solutions UK Ltd	£191,760,000
Bestway Panacea Healthcare Limited	£191,066,000
NES Global Talent Holdings Ltd	£190,880,992
Kingspan Services (UK) Limited	£190,794,016
Radisson Hotels UK Ltd	£190,303,008
Renold Public Limited Company	£189,900,000
Yodel Delivery Network Limited	£189,203,008
Barrett Steel Limited	£188,474,000
Tote Bookmakers Limited	£188,362,000
Gartside Limited	£187,980,256
Eric Wright Group Limited	£187,952,000
NES Global Talent Holdco Limited	£187,772,992
Nugeneration Limited	£187,666,208
Thermo Electron Manufacturing Limited	£187,354,000
Scapa (No.2) Limited	£186,908,384
FW Investments Limited	£184,451,008
Energy Acquisitions UK Limited	£183,786,816
NWEN Finance PLC	£183,030,000
Morson Group Limited	£181,812,992
WJH Limited	£181,584,000
Warren James (Jewellers) Limited	£181,514,000
Survitec Group (Finance 1) Limited	£180,218,000
Ardagh Metal Beverage UK Limited	£179,163,008
Micromass UK Limited	£178,972,000
NWEN Group Limited	£178,700,000
Smurfit Corrugated Holdings	£178,682,000
Clarke Energy Limited	£178,200,992
The Nature's Bounty Co. Ltd.	£177,042,000
Kellogg U.K. Holding Company Limited	£176,026,000
Moneysupermarket.Com Financial Group Limited	£174,307,008
Network Space Holdings Limited	£174,198,000
Wayne Fueling Systems UK Holdco Ltd.	£174,184,016
Dow Chemical Services UK Limited	£174,096,000
Salford Van Hire Limited	£172,569,792
Bruntwood 2000 Alpha Portfolio Limited	£172,258,000
Daisy IT Group Limited	£172,186,000
Kingspan Limited	£171,430,512
Premex Group Limited	£170,972,992
Park Retail Limited	£170,882,432
Premex Services Limited	£170,532,992
Springfields Fuels Limited	£170,460,992
SGL (Holdings) Limited	£170,431,008
Meter Fit 4 Limited	£170,068,000
TSB (Investment Europe) Limited	£169,804,992
Pershing Limited	£169,334,000
Advanced Medical Solutions Group PLC	£168,718,000
Etihad Topco Limited	£168,560,992
East Midlands Airport Nottingham Derby Leicester Ltd	£168,442,000
UPM-Kymmene (UK) Holdings Limited	£167,718,000
Verastar Limited	£167,668,992
Dechra Investments Limited	£167,572,992
Addison Motors Limited	£167,236,992
GREP1 Limited	£167,053,040
Brother Holding (Europe) Ltd.	£167,051,200
Convatec Limited	£164,995,008
Brighterkind (MW) Limited	£164,800,000
Calvin Capital Group Limited	£164,728,000
Emerson International Limited	£164,634,224
Park Inn By Radisson UK Ltd	£163,810,000
FSHC (UK) Limited	£163,179,008
Oxoid 2000 Limited	£163,139,008
Exchequer Partnership (No.2) PLC	£162,264,000
Exchequer Partnership (No.2) Holdings Limited	£162,264,000
Calvin Capital UK Holdings Limited	£162,219,008
Wainhomes (North West) Limited	£161,487,008
MB South Limited	£161,475,008
Costcutter Supermarkets Group Limited	£161,472,000
Hologic UK Finance Ltd	£160,957,616
TVS Logistics Investment UK Limited	£160,567,008
GD Aria Holdings #2 Limited	£160,359,152
Assurant General Insurance Limited	£160,279,008
Ainscough Crane Hire Ltd	£160,270,000
Innovia Films Limited	£160,136,000
Peninsula Business Services Group Limited	£159,320,320
Fisher Clinical Services UK Limited	£159,240,992
Enrichment Technology Company Limited	£159,167,184
Eurocamp Limited	£159,148,000
Interfish Limited	£159,134,320
Glen Dimplex Home Appliances Limited	£159,123,008
Adidas (U.K.) Limited	£158,722,000
Robert McBride Ltd	£158,680,000
Ultima Acquisition GB Limited	£158,034,000
Matalan Limited	£157,782,000
Cork Street Properties Limited	£157,130,000
Brother International Europe Limited	£156,614,064
NNL Holdings Limited	£156,290,000
GEA Process Engineering Limited	£155,648,544
Brighterkind (CB) Limited	£155,172,992
International Motors Finance Limited	£155,079,008
West Wallasey Car Hire Limited	£154,926,800
Wood Nuclear Holdings Limited	£154,826,000
Alpha Flight Group Limited	£154,804,992
VUR Village Hotels & Leisure Limited	£154,620,992
Unifrax Limited	£154,347,600
Ultium Business Outsourcing Group Limited	£154,131,056
Calvin Capital Limited	£154,120,992
Knauf Insulation Limited	£153,748,992
Taurus Acquisition Limited	£153,282,832
Galaxy Bidco Limited	£153,196,000
E.H.Booth & Co.,Limited	£152,931,008
FSIR Holdings (UK) Limited	£152,841,392
Titan Telecom Limited	£152,463,088
Etihad Midco Limited	£152,459,008
Assura HC UK Limited	£151,791,232
Acepark Ltd	£151,513,008
Bibby Invoice Discounting Limited	£150,981,056
TMD Friction UK Limited	£150,936,000
Lloyd Motors Limited	£150,082,000
Galaxy Topco Limited	£149,954,000
Thermo Optek Limited	£149,866,000
Innospec Holdings Limited	£149,352,992
SGS United Kingdom Limited	£149,310,000
Riverside Finance PLC	£149,016,000
Acorn Care 4 Limited	£148,772,448
Alpla UK Limited	£147,975,008
Thermo Electron Limited	£147,974,000
The Land Restoration Trust	£147,739,008
Oboadler Company Limited	£147,440,992
Inovyn Chlorvinyls Holdings Limited	£147,362,800
Bond Street Real Estate Holdings Limited	£147,351,616
Medical Properties Limited	£147,174,976
Warren James Holdings Limited	£147,151,408
Energy Assets Group Limited	£146,360,000
Halewood Wines and Spirits PLC	£146,342,000
Hyde Industrial Holdings Limited	£145,986,624
Ecolab Limited	£145,591,008
Clean Energy and Infrastructure UK Limited	£144,728,992
Diamond Resorts (Europe) Limited	£144,704,992
Liverpool School of Tropical Medicine	£144,651,008
Bruntwood 2000 Beta Portfolio Limited	£144,330,000

Company	Value
Stagecoach Services Limited	£144,232,992
Porritts & Spencer Limited	£143,930,336
Acorn Care 2 Limited	£143,776,704
Park Group PLC	£143,580,992
Theo Midco Limited	£143,369,632
DWF LLP	£142,166,000
Unifrax Europe Holdings Limited	£141,992,560
Hunter Douglas (UK) Limited	£141,840,992
BASF U.K. Holdings Limited	£141,392,000
Calderdale Hospital SPC Ltd	£141,354,000
Community 1st Oldham Limited	£141,304,384
Wheatsheaf Group Finance Company	£141,282,816
Flowserve GB Limited	£140,902,000
Clarke Energy Operations Limited	£140,887,008
Oxoid Holdings Limited	£140,738,000
Fluidpower MIP Limited	£140,231,552
United Utilities International Limited	£139,886,000
Gladman Developments Limited	£139,868,240
NWF Group PLC	£139,600,000
The University of Cumbria	£139,442,000
Parkway Green Housing Trust	£139,384,000
Nalco Limited	£139,300,992
Amber Taverns Limited	£139,210,672
Thomas Armstrong (Holdings) Limited	£138,678,496
Morson Human Resources Limited	£138,671,008
Luxfer Group 2000 Limited	£138,516,000
Property Alliance Group Limited	£138,468,992
On The Beach Limited	£138,220,000
Lagonda Russell Propco Limited	£137,374,000
IGE Euro Treasury Services	£137,367,680
Williams Motor Co.(Holdings) Limited	£136,828,992
BBC Children in Need	£136,591,008
Thermo Cambridge Limited	£136,374,000
Eastlands Homes Partnership Limited	£136,162,000
Swissport UK Holding Limited	£136,019,008
Bruntwood Estates Holdings Limited	£135,980,000
Liverpool Hope University	£135,890,704
Armacell UK Limited	£135,864,000
Fisher Scientific UK Holding Company 2	£135,624,000
Milan Bidco Limited	£135,616,992
Boohoo.Com UK Limited	£135,472,992
National Nuclear Laboratory Limited	£135,432,000
MBNA Europe Holdings Limited	£135,152,000
CSM (United Kingdom) Limited	£134,867,008
Agilent Technologies Lda UK Limited	£134,176,256
Inovyn Enterprises Limited	£133,900,000
Allied London Properties Limited	£133,865,456
Armacell Insulation UK Holding Limited	£133,713,000
Acorn Care 3 Limited	£133,501,424
Exchequer Partnership Holdings Limited	£133,257,000
Exchequer Partnership PLC	£133,257,000
Bibby FS (Holdings) Limited	£133,038,000
Swansway Garages Limited	£132,942,968
Innovia Films (Holding) Limited	£132,879,952
Optimisation Developments Limited	£132,862,000
The Dean Trust	£132,233,000
Quest Bidco Limited	£132,129,904
PCT Healthcare (Holdings) Limited	£130,848,304
Network Space Limited	£130,726,000
GD Aria Holdings Limited	£130,660,352
Watts Blake Bearne and Company Limited	£130,431,608
Typhoo Tea Limited	£130,280,000
WIL Finco	£129,703,488
Clean Energy and Infrastructure UK Wind Limited	£129,605,000
Hampshire Topco Limited	£129,458,000
Alpha LSG Limited	£129,451,000
Costcutter Supermarkets Holdings Limited	£129,444,000
Monarch Assurance PLC	£129,183,338
Nalco Acquisition Two Limited	£128,740,200
Giti Tire Holdings (UK) Limited	£128,739,152
Consolidated Property Wilmslow Limited	£128,599,632
Arysta LifeScience European Investments Limited	£128,574,800
Morbaine Properties Limited	£128,493,744
PIMCO 2947 Topco Limited	£128,210,000
Trinity Medical Properties Limited	£128,185,872
Diamond Resorts (Holdings) Limited	£128,106,000
Thomas Cradley Holdings Limited	£127,946,032
F-M Motorparts Limited	£127,849,344
Taurus 3 Limited	£127,817,000
Brammer UK Limited	£127,344,000
Capcuest Investments Limited	£127,280,000
Geometric Results International Limited	£126,999,504
Storengy UK Limited	£126,986,000
Exertis (Holdings) Ltd	£126,723,000
Marubeni Auto Investment (UK) Limited	£126,348,000
Hoist Finance UK Limited	£126,261,872
Peel Land (Intermediate) Limited	£126,000,000
Real Good Food PLC	£125,974,000
Lanxess Holding UK Unlimited	£125,924,000
Hempel Decorative Paints Limited	£125,664,000
Urban Splash Holdings Limited	£125,094,480
Geometric Results Holdings Limited	£124,794,584
Peel Land and Property (Ports) Limited	£124,345,000
Vita Cellular Foams (UK) Limited	£124,123,664
Brightstar 20:20 UK Limited	£123,858,000
Tetrosyl Group Limited	£122,992,000
Praedius UK (No 1) Limited	£122,947,000
Wesco Aircraft Europe, Ltd	£122,749,000
One Manchester Treasury Limited	£122,653,000
JCT600 (Properties) Limited	£122,349,000
William Hare Group Limited	£122,335,000
Flowtech Fluidpower PLC	£122,026,000
K3 Business Technology Group PLC	£121,767,000
Port of Sheerness Limited	£121,300,000
Haydock Finance Holdings Limited	£121,074,000
Weir Minerals Europe Limited	£120,758,000
Flowserve International Limited	£120,290,000
Stella Travel Services (UK) Limited	£120,266,000
Wiggins Teape Group Limited (The)	£120,012,000
Terraform UK2 Intermediate Holdings, Ltd	£119,959,360
Nextgear Capital UK Limited	£119,864,000
Freemans Public Limited Company	£119,725,000
Tetrosyl Limited	£119,184,000
VUR Village Trading No 1 Limited	£118,998,000
Skipton Business Finance Limited	£118,995,400
S. Norton & Co Limited	£118,471,000
Arysta LifeScience U.K. EUR Limited	£118,397,832
Assura Health Investments Limited	£118,336,216
Timpson Group PLC	£117,543,000
Sustainable Communities for Leeds (Finance) PLC	£117,480,256
Skipton Group Holdings Limited	£117,420,000
MD Insurance Services Limited	£117,321,088
Great Yarmouth Port Company Ltd	£117,200,000
Hyde Group Holdings Limited	£117,070,736
Dixondale Limited	£117,022,816
Perstorp UK Ltd.	£116,955,000
Platform Funding Limited	£116,812,000
J.D. Williams Group Limited	£116,778,504
Sustainable Communities for Leeds Limited	£116,656,744
Nufarm Crop Products UK Limited	£116,646,000
Bolling Investments Limited	£116,497,000
Tote (Successor Company) Limited	£116,199,000
FSHC Properties (CH2) Limited	£115,918,000
Basell Polyolefins UK Limited	£115,806,000
Goldentree Financial Services PLC	£115,750,520
Bridgemere UK PLC	£115,706,000
J.W.Lees & Co.(Brewers) Limited	£115,451,720
SJM Holdings North Limited	£115,442,864
Senator International Limited	£115,418,000
Timpson Holdings Limited	£115,307,000
MHI Vestas Offshore Wind UK Ltd	£115,239,000
Group Auto Union UK and Ireland Limited	£115,125,920
Tangerine Confectionery Limited	£114,929,000
P&O Princess American Holdings	£114,848,640

Company	Value
Gardner Denver International Ltd	£114,827,320
Sustainable Communities for Leeds (Holdings) Ltd	£114,565,120
Sibelco UK Limited	£114,482,056
Bibby Holdings Limited	£114,383,000
Trouw (UK) Limited	£114,033,000
Thistle Devco LLP	£113,763,424
Galaxy Midco Limited	£113,753,000
Pure Leisure Group Limited	£113,507,000
Ardagh Metal Beverage Trading UK Limited	£113,472,000
Soogen Holdings Limited	£112,622,272
Solvay UK Holding Company Limited	£112,473,000
Peel Outlets (Gloucester) Limited	£112,333,000
Brookhouse Group Limited	£112,152,000
Travel Counsellors Group Limited	£111,983,000
CBL Finance (UK) Limited	£111,384,000
Ligna Biomass Limited	£111,100,000
Ligna Biomass Holdings Limited	£111,100,000
Joseph Holt Limited	£111,061,576
Magnesium Elektron Limited	£111,002,000
Park Group UK Limited	£110,856,816
The Co-operative Academies Trust	£110,595,000
Pets at Home Superstores Limited	£110,565,000
The Hollins Murray Group Limited	£110,098,000
AMEC Foster Wheeler (Holdings) Limited	£109,731,000
Borgwarner Limited	£109,260,000
Elior UK PLC	£109,246,848
Semara Investments Limited	£109,229,000
PQ Silicas UK Limited	£109,110,000
Freemans Grattan Holdings Limited	£109,073,000
Daytona JV Limited	£108,586,472
PAH Financial Services Limited	£108,533,000
Alderley Park Limited	£108,401,000
Jones Homes (North West) Limited	£108,264,648
Princes Dock Development Company Limited	£108,133,000
CFS Management Services Limited	£108,111,000
SGL (Finance) Limited	£107,973,000
Compass Minerals UK Limited	£107,856,000
Equity Solutions Lift Investments Limited	£107,713,968
CEP Biomass Limited	£107,271,952
Kondor Holdco Limited	£106,900,000
Gardner Denver Ltd	£106,573,000
Borgwarner Holdings Limited	£106,427,000
Drayton Group Limited	£106,405,000
BWA UK Holdco Limited	£106,049,312
Seddon Group Limited	£105,910,000
Uranium Asset Management Limited	£105,748,336
Mersey Bioenergy Holdings Limited	£105,708,000
John West Foods Limited	£105,623,000
Swissport GB Limited	£105,618,000
Cardinal Health Finance	£105,594,472
Joseph Holt Group Limited	£105,466,624
Blujay Solutions Holdings Limited	£105,282,752
Peabody Coaltrade International Limited	£105,097,784
Think Money Holdings Limited	£104,834,000
Libya Oil Eritrea Limited	£104,689,688
Nice-Pak International Limited	£104,617,560
Swift Technical Group Limited	£104,072,000
Rochdale Textile Supplies Limited	£103,841,000
Paymentshield Holdings Limited	£103,678,184
Worcestershire Hospital SPC PLC	£103,632,000
GGM Human Resources Limited	£103,505,000
Rubix International Limited	£103,107,560
The Calico Group Limited	£103,037,000
Pendleton Together Operating Limited	£103,022,000
Pace Distribution (Overseas) Limited	£102,970,624
Great Bear Distribution Limited	£102,823,976
Peel Real Estate Group Limited	£102,483,000
GE Capital Europe Limited	£102,482,000
Rubix Group Midco 4 Limited	£102,474,768
Bibby Financial Services (UK) Limited	£102,345,280
Regent Medical Limited	£102,209,000
Knights North West Limited	£101,951,000
Starlight Camping Limited	£101,414,000
OFS (DS) Holdings Limited	£101,384,000
Heron Foods Limited	£101,249,000
Roanza Limited	£101,184,096
Ecolab (U.K.) Holdings Limited	£101,172,000
Vabeld UK Limited	£101,104,688
NES UK Limited	£100,974,000
Haydock Finance Limited	£100,884,000
Peel Holdings (Real Estate) Limited	£100,665,000
North West Business Finance Limited	£100,516,312
Energy, Safety and Risk Consultants (UK) Limited	£100,373,000
Eddie Stobart Logistics PLC	£100,366,000
Tata Chemicals Europe Limited	£100,321,000
U F C Fund Management PLC	£100,292,088
Protec Fire and Security Group Limited	£99,986,552
Energy Assets Limited	£99,886,000
Granite Underwriting Limited	£99,665,424
Risol Imports Limited	£99,565,000
PSV Claims Bureau Limited	£99,555,000
S. Cartwright & Sons (Coachbuilders) Limited	£99,543,176
Life Technologies Bpd UK Limited	£99,384,000
Kondor Limited	£99,342,000
Abgene Limited	£99,212,000
SGS Holding UK Ltd	£99,058,000
Seatruck Ferries Holding Ltd	£98,825,416
Calico Homes Limited	£98,600,000
Brighterkind Limited	£98,156,000
Edible Oils Ltd	£97,979,000
Lookers Motor Holdings Limited	£97,977,000
Halewood International Limited	£97,916,000
Safran Nacelles Limited	£97,848,000
Lofthouse of Fleetwood Limited	£97,787,144
Carpenter Limited	£97,533,000
Project Daytona Limited	£97,511,432
PZ Cussons (UK) Limited	£97,408,000
Swift Technical Group Holdings Limited	£97,378,000
Crosslane Property Group UK Limited	£97,255,000
Compass Minerals (Europe) Limited	£96,954,000
Pro Investments Limited	£96,943,208
British Salt Limited	£96,892,000
Frederic Robinson Limited	£96,593,000
Hampshire Midco Limited	£96,510,000
Begbies Traynor Group PLC	£96,445,000
ALS Inspection UK Limited	£96,419,000
Cartwright Holdings Ltd	£96,390,624
Alterity Investments Limited	£96,055,264
Greater Manchester Buses South Limited	£95,970,000
Oakmore Investments Limited	£95,931,648
Ingleby (1952) Limited	£95,931,400
Regatta Ltd	£95,859,000
Anwyl Group Limited	£95,408,136
API Group PLC	£95,276,000
HMG Investments Limited	£95,113,872
Fortis UK Holdings Ltd	£94,898,080
Travelbag Limited	£94,883,000
Kerry Logistics Holding (Europe) Limited	£94,784,912
Norwich and Peterborough (LBS) Limited	£94,722,000
Promethean Limited	£94,557,000
Harpmanor Limited	£94,400,000
NRG Fleet Services Limited	£94,389,096
Saffil 2011 Limited	£94,358,472
P.E.Jones (Properties) Limited	£94,195,000
ICR Integrity (Group) Limited	£94,139,320
Mawdsleys Group Investments Limited	£94,026,000
Lex Vehicle Leasing Limited	£93,961,000
Bestway Panacea Holdings Limited	£93,951,000
Anwyl Construction Company Limited	£93,946,208
Meter Serve 4 Limited	£93,894,000
Heron Food Group Limited	£93,497,000
Forth Bidco Limited	£93,445,000
East Lancashire Building Partnership Limited	£93,267,472
The Challenge Academy Trust	£93,267,000

Company	Amount
GE Lighting Limited	£93,178,000
Shred-It Limited	£93,035,752
ESG-Utiligroup Intermediate Limited	£92,853,760
The First Milk Cheese Company Limited	£92,761,000
GE (Holdings)	£92,553,000
Calder Group Holdings Limited	£92,478,000
District Estates Limited (The)	£92,464,800
Lifestyle Services Group Limited	£92,444,000
Timpson Limited	£92,163,000
Daisy IT Continuity and Resilience Services Limited	£91,865,000
Fluidpower Group Limited	£91,745,104
Centre Island Hotels Limited	£91,672,888
Manchester Science Partnerships Limited	£91,531,000
Suttons International Limited	£91,073,520
William Hare Limited	£91,026,000
Acorn Care 1 Limited	£90,981,104
Peter Black Holdings Limited	£90,741,000
GA Pet Food Partners Group Limited	£90,715,000
Safeway (Overseas) Limited	£90,710,000
Graphic Packaging International Europe UK Limited	£90,676,000
Malcolm Properties Limited	£90,617,000
AMEC Foster Wheeler Property & Overseas Invest Ltd	£90,592,000
Bejam Group Limited	£90,537,000
Milk Ventures (UK) Limited	£90,301,000
X1 Media City Limited	£90,114,376
Tensar International Limited	£89,946,000
Riverside Truck Rental Limited	£89,606,728
City South Manchester Housing Trust Limited	£89,555,000
Pets at Home Holdings Limited	£89,423,000
Aramex (UK) Limited	£89,238,000
Harry Yearsley Limited	£89,163,200
Diodes Holdings UK Limited	£89,134,000
Holmen UK Limited	£89,084,000
JCT600 (South Yorkshire) Limited	£89,069,000
Monte Blackburn Limited	£89,022,248
Kindertons Topco Limited	£88,988,000
CBL Finance (Holdings) UK Limited	£88,906,000
Victrex USA Holdings Limited	£88,860,000
Shearings Group Limited	£88,844,000
First Manchester Limited	£88,840,000
Daisy IT Services Limited	£88,529,000
Mediacom North Limited	£88,494,000
Daisy Corporate Services Trading Limited	£88,133,000
CA-MC Acquisition UK Limited	£88,062,000
Brookhouse Retail Limited	£87,996,000
Aghoco 1079 Limited	£87,951,000
Hallmark Cards (Holdings) Limited	£87,926,000
East Midlands Airport Property Investments (Ind) Ltd	£87,779,000
Carpenter Holdings Limited	£87,504,000
RRG Group Limited	£87,199,000
The Manchester Ship Canal Company Limited	£86,900,000
Beauty Source Limited	£86,899,000
Vink Holdings Limited	£86,848,000
Bracken House Properties LLP	£86,818,576
JCT600 Vehicle Leasing Solutions Limited	£86,817,000
The Portman Travel Group Limited	£86,809,000
DS7 Limited	£86,570,696
Darwin Loan Solutions Limited	£86,006,000
Meter Fit 10 Limited	£85,960,000
Kinaxia Limited	£85,907,272
Peel Real Estate (Properties) Limited	£85,769,896
SJCF Investment Ltd	£85,719,544
The Fayrefield Group Limited	£85,382,368
Total Water Solutions Limited	£85,208,000
RSK Group Limited	£85,197,000
Ellis & Everard Distribution Limited	£85,000,000
Metro MRH Limited	£84,987,656
Beaverbrooks The Jewellers Ltd	£84,834,000
Metro MRI Limited	£84,799,696
Univar Limited	£84,777,000
Gold Medal Travel Group Limited	£84,692,000
Meadow Foods Limited	£84,681,000
Bruntwood Estates Alpha Portfolio Limited	£84,503,000
CPL Petroleum Limited	£84,446,000
A.G. Parfett & Sons Limited	£84,270,816
Bridgemere Land PLC	£84,035,312
J F Renshaw Ltd	£83,998,000
East London Bus & Coach Company Limited	£83,991,000
Celestica Limited	£83,818,064
Wood Nuclear Limited	£83,766,000
New Balance Athletic Shoes (U.K.) Limited	£83,677,136
Burnley FC Holdings Limited	£83,677,000
Pin Croft Dyeing and Printing Co. Limited	£83,569,000
S.A.N. Limited	£83,549,504
Marks and Spencer Retail Financial Services Hldgs	£83,464,000
Swift Worldwide Resources Midco Limited	£83,460,000
Lakeland Limited	£83,440,000
Rayovac (UK) Limited	£83,408,000
Diodes Zetex Limited	£83,386,000
Fluidpower Limited	£83,318,040
Salford Village Limited	£83,206,856
Emerson Automation Solutions SSC UK Limited	£83,107,000
Bibby Distribution Limited	£83,021,000
N Brown Foods Ltd	£82,888,000
Brookhouse Property Investments Limited	£82,744,000
Peel Holdings (Ports) Limited	£82,700,000
Southern Land Securities Limited	£82,675,856
Boutinot Limited	£82,608,976
S.J.M. Limited	£82,577,272
Kellogg Management Services (Europe) Limited	£82,476,000
Sebden Steel Service Centres Limited	£82,470,000
Alfred H. Knight Holdings Limited	£82,453,240
Manchester Metronet Limited	£82,196,000
FLSmidth (UK) Limited	£82,076,000
Football League Limited (The)	£82,027,536
Peel Property (No.2) Limited	£81,940,056
MGF Limited	£81,936,056
The Delivery Group Limited	£81,829,000
The Sebden Group Limited	£81,566,000
Bruntwood AV Holdings Limited	£81,323,320
Dixons Academies Charitable Trust Ltd	£81,120,000
Witherslack Group (Holdings) Limited	£81,108,952
Orbit Developments (Southern) Limited	£80,593,280
Cardinal Health U.K. Holding Limited	£80,504,000
Dechra Finance Sterling Limited	£80,432,000
Cuadrilla Resources Limited	£80,387,944
Energy Services Acquisitions Limited	£80,230,000
Berrymans Lace Mawer LLP	£80,159,000
Cardinal Health U.K. International Holding LLP	£79,966,000
Visage Limited	£79,962,000
Fives UK Holding Limited	£79,935,576
J.N. Bentley Limited	£79,753,416
Caesar Topco Limited	£79,753,000
Frodsham Wind Farm Limited	£79,675,192
Bridging Finance Limited	£79,363,000
Westmorland Limited	£79,230,000
Kingsland Drinks Limited	£79,140,000
Travel Counsellors Limited	£78,808,640
James Fisher Marine Services Limited	£78,675,328
Kingsclere Investments Ltd.	£78,544,128
Stonyhurst	£78,428,384
FMC Kongsberg Services Limited	£78,402,000
Anglia Telecom Centres Limited	£78,311,000
Andrew Industries Limited	£78,144,000
Renold Power Transmission Limited	£77,995,000
ADP Healthcare Services Limited	£77,690,000
W.H.Bowker Limited	£77,600,000
Blujay Solutions Ltd	£77,529,000
CarnaudMetalbox Engineering Limited	£77,520,000
Glanbia Cheese Limited	£77,509,000
MRC Transmark Holdings UK Limited	£77,447,384
Mawdsley-Brooks & Company Limited	£77,403,000
SMG Europe Holdings Limited	£77,385,000
Byrom Public Limited Company	£77,335,976

Company	Amount
Grayrentals Limited	£77,314,016
Arlington Industries Group Ltd	£77,310,000
AGC Chemicals Europe, Ltd.	£77,263,000
Atmore Developments Limited	£77,229,320
Danish Crown UK Limited	£77,085,160
Swift Worldwide Resources Bidco Limited	£76,988,000
Bibby Factors Limited	£76,968,128
Patrick Properties Group Ltd	£76,955,136
Colormatrix UK Holdings Limited	£76,929,000
Polyflor Limited	£76,925,664
Caesar Midco Limited	£76,895,928
Chiesi Limited	£76,823,000
PZ Cussons (International Finance) Limited	£76,594,000
Fitzwilton (U.K.) Limited	£76,560,000
Education and Leadership Trust	£76,522,232
South East London & Kent Bus Company Limited	£76,483,000
Ryman Group Limited	£76,429,000
Guenther Holdings Limited	£76,413,544
EV Retail Limited	£76,316,000
Hilti (Gt.Britain) Limited	£76,248,000
Get Motoring UK Limited	£76,195,000
Burnley Football & Athletic Company,Limited (The)	£76,186,000
Brunning and Price Limited	£76,150,000
Park Cakes Holdings Limited	£76,084,000
New Britain Oils Limited	£76,082,000
Stella Global UK Limited	£76,060,000
AJ Bell Holdings Limited	£76,032,000
Bramwell Pub Company Limited	£75,847,000
Concept Life Sciences (Holdings) Limited	£75,754,864
Ingredion UK Limited	£75,746,000
Revolution Bars Group PLC	£75,646,000
Taurus Bidco Limited	£75,423,000
AMEC Services Limited	£75,416,000
Firsdell Ltd	£75,400,000
ICR (Investment 1) Limited	£75,326,472
Footasylum PLC	£75,115,000
Carrs Billington Agriculture (Sales) Limited	£75,070,128
SHS International Ltd	£74,913,000
GE Transportation Systems Ltd	£74,880,000
Gemsupa Limited	£74,767,688
ICR (Investment 2) Limited	£74,709,280
P.J. Livesey Holdings Limited	£74,708,672
Acorn Insurance and Financial Services Limited	£74,365,256
In Vino Limited	£74,332,672
GE Capital Equipment Finance Holdings	£74,309,000
Milliken Industrials Limited	£74,131,000
Lancashire Schools SPC Phase 1 Ltd	£74,028,000
IESA Holdings Limited	£73,979,000
Colormatrix Europe Limited	£73,947,000
Arris International IP Ltd	£73,857,480
Licensed Wholesale Company Limited	£73,839,992
Azelis UK Limited	£73,789,000
Orica UK Limited	£73,661,000
PCT Healthcare Limited	£73,577,496
Ryman Limited	£73,545,000
Thor Specialities (UK) Limited	£73,526,000
TTC UK Holdings Limited	£73,468,000
Energy Assets (Meters) Limited	£73,212,000
MPM Bidco Limited	£73,040,000
Swizzels Matlow Limited	£73,036,000
Capquest Group Limited	£73,018,872
Arjo Wiggins Fine Papers Limited	£72,881,000
Fort Vale Limited	£72,710,544
Synexus Clinical Research Limited	£72,701,000
LWC Drinks Limited	£72,563,552
Daytona Holdco Limited	£72,562,360
Brunner Mond Group Limited	£72,544,000
Autosupply Holdings UK Limited	£72,515,000
NST Travel Group Limited	£72,503,096
Kellogg Manchester	£72,493,000
HDI Holdings (UK) Limited	£72,458,424
Findel Education Limited	£72,437,000
Blacks Outdoor Retail Limited	£72,151,000
Protec Fire Detection Public Limited Company	£72,027,312
Bibby Leasing Limited	£72,009,704
MPM Topco Limited	£71,920,000
Parasol Limited	£71,899,128
The Global Travel Group Limited	£71,841,000
FL 360 Limited	£71,780,408
Styles & Wood Limited	£71,738,000
Evolution Lending Limited	£71,706,456
Gradus Group Holdings Limited	£71,467,576
NDA Properties Limited	£71,258,000
Hyperlast Limited	£71,192,000
The London Property Partnership Limited	£71,083,176
Project Rock Equityco Limited	£71,032,000
Ingersoll - Rand Holdings Limited	£70,735,000
Accrol Papers Limited	£70,680,000
AECOM Worldwide Holdings UK Limited	£70,567,688
Brookhouse (Hamilton) Limited	£70,549,000
Meter Fit 3 Limited	£70,508,000
IESA Limited	£70,339,000
Great Academies Education Trust	£70,263,000
Ingenico (UK) Limited	£70,168,000
Nalco Holdings UK Limited	£70,060,000
CEP Teesside Biomass Limited	£69,967,736
Fargrace Limited	£69,753,512
Swift Worldwide Resources Holdco Limited	£69,680,152
Sistine Properties (Westbury) Limited	£69,596,000
TVS Supply Chain Solutions Limited	£69,554,000
Community Integrated Care	£69,508,000
Companion Care (Services) Limited	£69,444,000
Lookers Colborne Limited	£69,299,000
Dechra Finance Limited	£69,276,840
Bright Tribe Trust	£68,817,000
Gladman Commercial Properties	£68,745,336
Scapa UK Limited	£68,688,000
Christopher Topco Limited	£68,686,904
Thermo Fisher Diagnostics Limited	£68,658,000
Group First Global Limited	£68,582,328
Gedling Homes	£68,543,000
Seddon Construction Limited	£68,503,240
James Cropper Public Limited Company	£68,495,000
Per-Scent Limited	£68,473,864
Inenco Group Limited	£68,397,000
Project Ires Bidco Limited	£68,363,000
Maru Group Holdings Limited	£68,330,520
Project Ires Topco Limited	£68,290,000
Kingsland Drinks Group Limited	£68,237,000
Sovereign Health Care	£68,236,264
Go-Sykes Limited	£68,138,000
Peel Water Services Holdings Limited	£68,126,000
Keoghs Topco Limited	£68,040,000
Direct Rail Services Limited	£67,960,000
Bacchus Newco Limited	£67,946,376
INEOS Fluor Holdings Limited	£67,920,928
Express Cargo Forwarding Limited	£67,766,208
Hitachi Automotive Systems UK Ltd.	£67,753,328
Peel Water Services Limited	£67,598,176
Solvay Interox Limited	£67,404,000
The 1st Stop Group Limited	£67,380,160
Kindertons Limited	£67,299,000
Fitness First Clubs Limited	£67,292,752
Runcorn MCP Limited	£67,000,000
Keoghs Acquisition Limited	£66,951,000
Lyons Holiday Park Limited	£66,879,016
IKO PLC	£66,618,000
Associated Property Owners Limited	£66,555,048
IDH Limited	£66,434,000
Urban Splash Work Limited	£66,424,192
AMEC Nuclear Overseas Limited	£66,416,000
Mexichem UK Limited	£66,206,000
LRUK (Retail) Limited	£66,034,000
Norman 1985 Limited	£65,948,000

Company	Value
Egencia Holdings UK Ltd	£65,926,780
LDF Group Finance Limited	£65,734,732
Pulse Home Products (Holdings) Limited	£65,650,000
Caesar Bidco Limited	£65,567,220
VUR Village Hotel Holdings Limited	£65,458,000
Drive Devilbiss Healthcare Limited	£65,431,000
Wealth at Work Group Limited	£65,189,000
Frank Roberts & Sons Limited	£65,162,000
Manchester Diocesan Board of Finance	£65,095,000
Vertex Group Limited	£65,077,000
BNN Technology PLC	£65,059,000
Hall & Pickles 1812 Limited	£64,997,000
Rathbone Kear Limited	£64,992,000
Bruntwood Science Limited	£64,912,000
Weightmans LLP	£64,908,000
Peel Investment Properties Holdings Limited	£64,867,000
Blackburn Diocesan Board of Finance Limited	£64,826,000
Sune Green Holdco5 Limited	£64,775,396
Peninsula Business Services Limited	£64,650,040
Saffil Limited	£64,648,344
Contis Group Limited	£64,578,788
Medimmune U.K. Limited	£64,464,812
Alliedtropic Limited	£64,350,000
Project Daytona Bidco Limited	£64,320,912
Nexperia UK Ltd.	£64,309,000
Interfloor Operations Limited	£64,295,000
Mortgage Agency Services Number Five Limited	£64,242,000
Travel 2 Limited	£64,186,000
Cartoon (Holdings) Limited	£64,175,000
Morning Foods,Limited	£64,144,920
Bruntwood RB Limited	£63,961,000
Peel Investment Properties Limited	£63,748,000
Shoo 553 Limited	£63,580,000
Alma Atlas Investments Limited	£63,490,000
Ralawise Limited	£63,460,936
TFS Buying Limited	£63,456,000
Crown Paints Limited	£63,445,000
Cooper Topco Limited	£63,426,440
Wood Environment & Infrastructure Solutions UK Ltd	£63,304,000
Bliss Topco Limited	£63,271,120
Bibby Factors Leicester Limited	£63,224,100
Kingspan Investments Limited	£63,169,172
Original FS Holdings Limited	£63,160,000
Chess Limited	£63,069,000
Skirfare Investments Limited	£63,019,808
Pfaudler UK Ltd	£63,018,436
Rullion Limited	£62,970,860
Liverpool Airport Holdings Limited	£62,945,000
National Tyre Service Limited	£62,844,000
ICR Integrity (Holdings) Limited	£62,776,164
The Tensar Group Limited	£62,753,000
European Metal Recycling (Dormant) Limited	£62,717,000
Nos 2 Limited	£62,714,700
AMEC Foster Wheeler Earth & Environmental UK Ltd	£62,696,000
Henry Bath & Son Limited	£62,537,588
Bibby Marine Limited	£62,513,240
FW Chile Holdings 2 Limited	£62,390,000
Brahm Lift Limited	£62,302,664
Luxfer Group Limited	£62,291,000
Bolton School	£62,255,000
James Hall and Company (Properties) Limited	£62,205,004
Samuel Banner & Co. Limited	£62,182,052
Regency Factors PLC	£62,102,316
M.A.X. Funding Limited	£62,045,040
Northern Schools Trust	£61,943,000
Leeds Independent Living Accommodation Co Hldgs	£61,869,604
Leeds Independent Living Accommodation Co Ltd	£61,869,604
Bruntwood Estates Beta Portfolio Limited	£61,856,000
Sykes Cottages Holdings Limited	£61,827,000
James Dewhurst Limited	£61,731,000
Simonstone Estate Limited	£61,639,304
AGDC Holdings Limited	£61,603,000

Company	Value
INEOS Technologies (Holdings) Limited	£61,600,000
Gradus Limited	£61,466,784
CCL Secure (Holding) Limited	£61,363,636
NGF Europe Limited	£61,341,000
CEP Biomass Energy Limited	£61,312,988
F and N One Limited	£61,302,684
FMG (Holdings) Limited	£61,288,904
Shearings Holidays Limited	£61,265,000
Marlborough Fund Managers Ltd.	£61,237,784
Ball & Young Limited	£61,055,640
The Growth Company Limited	£61,044,000
NWF Fuels Limited	£60,992,000
Precision Technologies Group (PTG) Limited	£60,954,564
Compello Holdings Limited	£60,937,440
Newincco 1072 Limited	£60,840,000
A Pearson Holdings Limited	£60,836,000
The Heath Family (North West)	£60,833,184
Globe Union (UK) Limited	£60,723,000
Hill Dickinson LLP	£60,597,000
United Utilities Water Operations Holdings Limited	£60,428,944
Indutrade UK Limited	£60,359,708
Peel Property Intermediate Limited	£60,332,000
Morson Holdings Limited	£60,237,000
Mobica Holdings Limited	£60,203,652
Transdev PLC	£60,184,000
Contis Card Solutions Limited	£60,140,720
Fragrance Acquisitions Limited	£60,092,620
GE Capital Solutions Europe Limited	£60,030,000
VTX Holdings Limited	£59,976,000
Bibby Supply Chain Services Limited	£59,963,000
Co-operative Brands Limited	£59,957,000
Midland Red (South) Limited	£59,919,000
Burnhart Holdings Limited	£59,895,000
Lancashire Schools SPC Phase 2A Ltd	£59,865,000
Griffiths & Armour Global Risks Limited	£59,851,464
Deanbank Investments Limited	£59,818,752
JSSH Limited	£59,798,000
North of England Zoological Society (The)	£59,695,000
Acorn Mobility Services Ltd.	£59,685,564
Daisy Wholesale Limited	£59,607,000
Carrington Textiles Ltd	£59,599,000
The Lowry Centre Trust	£59,566,000
IS Pharma Ltd	£59,560,000
Stockport Homes Limited	£59,490,000
Christopher Bidco Limited	£59,458,448
INEOS Vinyls Holdings Limited	£59,400,000
On The Beach Travel Limited	£59,391,000
Specialist Leisure Group Limited	£59,293,000
E. C. M. (Vehicle Delivery Service) Limited	£59,239,928
Atlantic & Peninsula Marine Services Limited	£59,193,000
Clean Energy and Infrastructure 3 Limited	£59,047,736
Flextronics Europe Limited	£59,029,000
Cold Fell Group Limited	£58,939,432
Air Resources Limited	£58,924,000
Flextronics Global Services (Manchester) Limited	£58,858,980
Rowland Homes Limited	£58,815,852
Rowland Group Limited	£58,815,852
Fender Care Marine Ltd	£58,681,588
Sonoco Limited	£58,495,000
Kingspan Holdings (Structural & Offsite) Limited	£58,448,932
Speed Medical Examination Services Limited	£58,401,480
Conviviality Stores Ltd	£58,317,000
McCann-Erickson Network Limited	£58,316,000
Expert Logistics Ltd.	£58,253,000
MAN Energy Solutions UK Limited	£58,188,000
Stateside Foods Limited	£58,177,000
Billericay Dental Supply Co. Limited	£58,077,000
Underground Mining Services Limited	£57,899,552
Building Design Partnership Limited	£57,898,192
HB Fuller UK Operations Limited	£57,599,000
Amplifon United Kingdom Limited	£57,549,000
Diodes Zetex Semiconductors Limited	£57,480,000

Company	Value
Daisy IT Managed Services Limited	£57,268,000
Beaconsfield Footwear Limited	£57,228,000
Dean Property Group Limited	£57,174,888
The Professional Footballers' Association Charity	£57,029,508
CSA Group Capital UK Limited	£57,027,468
Basell UK Holdings Limited	£57,002,000
El Spa Holdings (UK) Limited	£56,985,704
Vital Holdings Limited	£56,884,952
Kondor Bidco Limited	£56,879,000
Foundation for Life Limited	£56,861,508
Granite Finance Ltd	£56,708,376
Brother U.K. Limited	£56,698,000
Fiserv (Europe) Limited	£56,625,000
WFEL Limited	£56,518,000
Graphic Packaging International Europe UK Hldgs	£56,483,000
Alfa Leisureplex Group Limited	£56,398,688
Begbies Traynor Limited	£56,336,496
On The Beach Bidco Limited	£56,284,000
Diamorph UK Limited	£56,264,032
Inspired Energy PLC	£56,236,228
Hammer PLC	£56,178,568
Concept Life Sciences (Midco) Limited	£56,142,456
Thermo Electron (Management Services) Limited	£56,118,000
Project Rock Bidco Limited	£56,082,000
Liverpool Airport Limited	£55,904,000
Axle Topco Limited	£55,847,728
Lucchini Unipart Rail Limited	£55,798,000
ScottishPower (DCL) Limited	£55,700,000
Jarden Consumer Solutions (Europe) Limited	£55,625,000
Styles & Wood Group Limited	£55,526,000
Praetura Asset Finance (Holdings) Limited	£55,455,752
VTX Subco Limited	£55,401,000
Angus International Safety Group Limited	£55,362,000
WGH UK Limited	£55,346,000
WGH UK Holdings Limited	£55,311,000
Hawkslease Finance Company Limited	£55,300,000
The Avalon Trustee Company Limited	£55,281,008
Calder Group Limited	£55,263,000
Healthcare Solutions (Hull) Holdings Limited	£55,244,000
INEOS Vinyls Limited	£55,214,724
Milan Midco Limited	£55,046,000
The Kay Group (UK Holdings) Ltd	£55,014,000
Rainy City Properties Limited	£54,990,004
Robert Scott & Sons Limited	£54,973,388
Nuvia Limited	£54,879,000
NWF Agriculture Limited	£54,862,000
Pipeline Induction Heat Limited	£54,823,488
Kingmoor Park Properties Limited	£54,670,880
Edam Group Limited	£54,602,480
Greif UK Ltd	£54,585,000
Fylde Coast Academy Trust	£54,559,000
McCann Manchester Limited	£54,526,000
Greenbank Holidays Limited	£54,458,000
Petro-Canada Europe Lubricants Limited	£54,421,124
MacDermid Canning Limited	£54,399,000
Revolution Bars Limited	£54,393,000
CLV Finance UK Limited	£54,362,000
Urenco Nuclear Stewardship Limited	£54,359,000
CHA Technologies Group Public Limited Company	£54,280,224
Prospect (GB) Limited	£54,266,000
Missguided Limited	£54,238,000
WFEL Holdings Limited	£54,214,000
Sabina Estates Group Holdings Limited	£54,167,684
Dnata Travel Holdings UK Limited	£54,065,000
SMG (UK) Limited	£54,039,000
Vynova Runcorn Limited	£54,007,456
American Golf Discount Centre Limited	£53,962,000
Fives Landis Limited	£53,962,000
The Wythenshawe Catholic Academy Trust	£53,936,076
Charles Street Commercial Investments Limited	£53,921,020
Healthcare Solutions (Hull) Limited	£53,893,000
Libra Textiles Limited	£53,879,416
Witherslack Group Limited	£53,845,576
Keoghs LLP	£53,822,000
Hologic Ltd.	£53,720,000
Sunsave 14 (Fenton) Limited	£53,641,008
Lancashire County Developments Limited	£53,618,908
Tustin Developments Limited	£53,613,432
New Co (Satellite) 2 Limited	£53,492,000
Cend Limited	£53,364,000
Electric Glass Fiber UK, Ltd.	£53,251,000
Merseyside Estates Limited	£53,214,456
Vita Ventures Limited	£53,175,000
F and N Holdings Limited	£53,160,048
Story Contracting Limited	£53,130,000
Pets at Home Vet Group Limited	£53,054,240
Mobica Bidco Limited	£53,031,932
BDP Holdings Limited	£52,980,016
Monitise Limited	£52,954,000
OFS (DS) Acquisitions Limited	£52,889,000
Brookfield Rose Limited	£52,837,764
Fender Care Limited	£52,821,108
Federal-Mogul Asia Investments Limited	£52,806,948
Advanced Medical Solutions (Europe) Limited	£52,777,516
Teamfurmanite Limited	£52,724,000
CSMB Limited	£52,692,320
Guenther 182 Limited	£52,668,112
P.J.H. Group Limited	£52,644,000
Elitetele.Com PLC	£52,610,400
Keoghs Midco Limited	£52,563,000
Glenvale Transport Limited	£52,535,000
Think Money Group Limited	£52,528,000
Consilium Academies	£52,518,000
Colebrook & Burgess Limited	£52,490,000
Bodycote Finance UK Limited	£52,427,192
Startech.Com Limited	£52,390,140
Equity Solutions Lift Investments Oldham Limited	£52,301,220
Western Buses Limited	£52,259,000
Hammer Consolidated Holdings Ltd	£52,245,692
Liverpool Diocesan Board of Finance (The)	£52,144,072
Glasdon Group Limited	£52,045,256
London & District Investments Limited	£52,023,892
Brightstar Mobility UK, Ltd.	£52,019,000
Peter Black International Limited	£51,902,000
Optimum Debtco Limited	£51,899,000
Denso Marston Ltd	£51,884,000
Cammell Laird Shiprepairers & Shipbuilders Limited	£51,876,000
Innovative Environmental Solutions UK Ltd	£51,753,000
Menta Redrow Limited	£51,729,808
Merseyrail Electrics 2002 Limited	£51,700,000
Stepan UK Limited	£51,685,000
Vital Energi Utilities Limited	£51,666,552
James Fisher Holdings UK Limited	£51,661,944
Wheelabrator Technologies (UK) Limited	£51,660,000
Eutelsat UK Limited	£51,656,912
Fort Vale Engineering Limited	£51,572,064
Crown Oil Limited	£51,563,784
Maple Grove Developments Limited	£51,523,804
Bilfinger UK Limited	£51,519,000
Blackburn Chemicals (Holdings) Limited	£51,476,044
Costcutter Holdings Limited	£51,475,000
St George Care UK Limited	£51,409,096
Merseyrail Services Holding Company Limited	£51,381,000
Halliwell Jones (Warrington) Limited	£51,263,612
Park Cakes Acquisition Limited	£51,217,000
Norcros Industry (International) Limited	£51,125,000
Orbit Developments (Manchester) Limited	£51,097,784
Proseal UK Limited	£51,042,792
Alliance Real Estate LLP	£51,006,600
Wigan Athletic Holdings Limited	£51,005,460
Network Space Developments Limited	£50,980,000
Magna Exteriors (Liverpool) Limited	£50,975,000
Citation Limited	£50,958,656
Fragrance Oils Limited	£50,919,432

Company	Value
Select Property Group Limited	£50,916,000
W2D2 Limited	£50,889,000
Hartley Investment Trust Limited	£50,704,000
Dutton-Forshaw Holdings Limited	£50,700,000
BAJ 1 Limited	£50,682,432
Lancashire County Developments (Property) Limited	£50,666,344
Ingersoll-Rand Company Limited	£50,621,000
Bruntwood Investments PLC	£50,609,000
Manchester Central Convention Complex Limited	£50,541,000
Louver-Lite Limited	£50,530,104
Promethean World Limited	£50,506,000
Denholm Logistics Group Limited	£50,455,296
Interfloor Limited	£50,400,000
W.R.Evans Healthcare Limited	£50,397,428
Modular Stock Limited	£50,364,000
Brookson Group Limited	£50,359,000
Park Cakes Limited	£50,059,000
Waterfall Elior Limited	£50,053,480
Great Bear Holdings Limited	£50,000,000
M. Sport Limited	£49,943,060
Ylem Group Limited	£49,897,000
Tenmat Limited	£49,887,000
Fresenius Kabi Limited	£49,875,000
Campus Living Villages (Goldsmiths) UK Limited	£49,832,000
Maru Group Finance Limited	£49,829,484
Peel Environmental Limited	£49,813,624
Cuadrilla Resources Holdings Limited	£49,762,712
Dorset Emergency Services PPP (Holdings) Limited	£49,696,020
PFF (Dorset) Limited	£49,696,020
0404 Investments Limited	£49,689,560
Bachy Soletanche Holdings (Europe) Limited	£49,680,000
Huntercombe (SP) Limited	£49,660,000
Nutreco Limited	£49,651,000
Universities Superannuation Scheme Limited	£49,646,000
Bridgehead Container Services Limited	£49,634,392
Bibby Factors Slough Limited	£49,632,400
Vita Student York Holding Company Limited	£49,541,000
Graham & Brown Limited	£49,424,000
Brightstar 20:20 Limited	£49,418,000
Turner Bianca PLC	£49,296,256
Shudehill Hotel Company Limited	£49,213,072
Contis Financial Services Limited	£49,082,088
Himor Group Limited	£49,006,000
Caribbean Biodiversity Fund	£48,932,020
MRC Transmark Limited	£48,901,844
Vine Mill Limited	£48,844,000
Heysham Port Limited	£48,700,000
Auction Finance Limited	£48,700,000
International Fibres Group (Holdings) Limited	£48,697,000
RM Property and Facilities Solutions Limited	£48,689,000
Futamura Chemical UK Limited	£48,607,972
Graphic Packaging International Gateshead Limited	£48,580,000
Middlewich Limited	£48,580,000
Sune Green Holdco3 Limited	£48,578,664
Leverhulme Academy Church of England Trust	£48,529,760
Emerald Group Holdings Limited	£48,496,000
Federal-Mogul Valvetrain Limited	£48,461,756
AMEC Investments Europe Limited	£48,450,000
Ferranti Technologies Limited	£48,392,000
Birmingham Schools SPC Phase 1A Limited	£48,392,000
Barrowway No. 1 Limited	£48,386,776
Maru Group Limited	£48,381,496
Fayrefield Foods Limited	£48,261,884
James Cropper Speciality Papers Limited	£48,188,000
Synexus Clinical Research Midco No 1 Limited	£48,157,000
Stagecoach (South) Limited	£48,108,000
Silentnight Group Limited	£47,994,000
Silentnight Holdings Limited	£47,994,000
Restaurant Bar and Grill Limited	£47,960,188
Whitecroft Lighting Limited	£47,939,584
George Hotel Investments Limited	£47,935,000
Birmingham Schools SPC Holdings Phase 1A Ltd	£47,899,000
JCT600 (Rawdon) Limited	£47,894,000
Vimto (Out of Home) Limited	£47,891,000
VIP (Group) Limited	£47,877,000
Bruntwood Scitech Limited	£47,822,000
Air Energi Newco Limited	£47,650,000
Bodycote Heat Treatments Limited	£47,634,000
Community 1st Sheffield Limited	£47,629,136
Pochin's Limited	£47,623,000
Barlows Holdings Limited	£47,610,400
Campus Living Villages (RCM 2) UK LLP	£47,574,000
TXM Plant Limited	£47,548,716
ICR Integrity Limited	£47,525,648
University of Chester Academies Trust	£47,426,000
Peel Ports Land and Property Investments Limited	£47,386,000
Bruntwood Estates Limited	£47,281,000
ANS Group Limited	£47,260,536
Sonoco Cores and Paper Limited	£47,242,000
What More UK Limited	£47,238,792
Ruia Trading Limited	£47,220,232
Accrol UK Limited	£47,202,000
Innospec Developments Limited	£47,116,000
Bright Futures Educational Trust	£47,092,000
Brookhouse (Lowestoft) Limited	£47,080,000
Ripat Limited	£47,079,000
Graphic Packaging International Bardon Limited	£47,038,000
JPTR Topco Limited	£47,001,000
UKFast.Net Limited	£46,891,560
G.R. & M.M. Blackledge PLC	£46,871,972
McDermott Developments Limited	£46,830,488
J Sykes & Sons (Manchester) Limited	£46,703,000
Gallagher Topco Limited	£46,692,384
Checkfree Solutions Limited	£46,622,320
Lookers Leasing Limited	£46,603,000
Bibby Factors Northwest Limited	£46,580,020
Damartex UK Limited	£46,514,000
Tata Chemicals Magadi Limited	£46,335,488
Cedar 2015 Limited	£46,331,000
Shearings Limited	£46,292,000
Sykes Seafoods Limited	£46,276,000
Easi-Drive Limited	£46,244,232
APS Group Limited	£46,223,452
Gweco 511 Limited	£46,217,224
WCF Ltd.	£46,217,000
OFS (DS) Finance Limited	£46,200,000
CDL Group Holdings Limited	£46,194,256
O.P.P. Investments Limited	£46,156,000
GKH Holdings Limited	£46,149,000
GNB Industrial Power (UK) Limited	£46,141,000
Sigma Capital Group PLC	£46,114,000
Centre Island Birmingham Limited	£46,045,164
Latium Roofing Systems Limited	£45,987,000
Airport City (Manchester) Limited	£45,901,000
Barrowway No. 2 Limited	£45,838,768
Waterfall Catering Group Limited	£45,836,052
Stokers Holdings Limited	£45,813,264
Carehome Medz Limited	£45,795,560
Kaman UK Holdings Limited	£45,795,000
St. Tropez Acquisition Co. Limited	£45,730,000
Leisureplex Hotels Limited	£45,726,120
Hyde Aero Products Limited	£45,692,692
Greenwood & Coope Limited	£45,642,000
Op Acquisitions Limited	£45,625,000
GE European Equipment Finance (Aircraft No. 2) Ltd	£45,588,304
Alliance Disposables Limited	£45,580,680
Air Energi Group Investments Limited	£45,491,000
Irwell Insurance Company Limited	£45,471,000
Quorum Estates Limited	£45,462,860
The St David's Hotel Cardiff Limited	£45,458,000
Lloyd Limited	£45,430,000
Vernacare Limited	£45,423,068
County Milk Products Limited	£45,409,044
Cooper Bidco Limited	£45,404,452

Company	Value
East London Bus Group Property Investments Limited	£45,381,000
McCann Health Medical Communications Limited	£45,376,000
European Diesel Card Limited	£45,376,000
Dairygold Food Ingredients (UK) Limited	£45,346,012
Optionis Bidco Limited	£45,339,740
Speedy Transport Limited	£45,336,000
Lake District Hotels Limited	£45,329,896
Tote Direct Limited	£45,311,000
OBG Finance Limited	£45,282,264
OBG Holding Limited	£45,243,748
Assystem UK Limited	£45,209,000
Wheelabrator Group Limited	£45,178,000
Bachy Soletanche Limited	£45,061,000
Pacific Shelf 1809 Limited	£45,026,000
Inception Point Systems Ltd	£45,002,456
Car Care Plan Limited	£44,982,000
Contitech United Kingdom Limited	£44,919,000
H.P.A.S. Limited	£44,841,000
Enterprise Healthcare Limited	£44,789,000
National Holidays Tours Limited	£44,783,000
Milan Swapco Limited	£44,738,000
Aintree Retail Park Limited	£44,711,616
Barnfield Group Limited	£44,682,844
UFP (UK) Limited	£44,503,432
Harrow Estates PLC	£44,497,780
GE Financial Investments	£44,495,940
Lomas Distribution Limited	£44,492,744
Deepdale PNE Holdings Limited	£44,436,000
Aspireplus Educational Trust	£44,421,044
Oxoid International Limited	£44,417,000
Vita Satellite 1 Limited	£44,402,000
Takeuchi Mfg. (U.K.) Limited	£44,326,052
JPTR Bidco Limited	£44,310,000
Elitetelecom Holdings PLC	£44,304,264
Stagecoach Devon Limited	£44,300,000
CuFe Investments Limited	£44,240,000
TESGL Limited	£44,111,224
New Co (Satellite) Limited	£44,066,000
Haydock Commercial Vehicles Limited	£44,049,528
Community 1st Sheffield (Tranche 2) Limited	£44,026,464
Enterprise Healthcare Holdings Limited	£44,008,000
H.I.G. Milan UK Midco Limited	£43,834,000
Kemira Chemicals (UK) Limited	£43,831,000
Preston North End Limited	£43,827,000
Matrix Technologies Corporation Limited	£43,776,000
Marcus Worthington Properties Limited	£43,756,252
Graphic Packaging International UK Finance Limited	£43,749,000
Prescot Business Park Limited	£43,727,040
Hargreave Hale Limited	£43,727,000
Stolle Europe Limited	£43,645,664
East Kent Road Car Company,Limited	£43,614,000
The Yorkshire Traction Company Limited	£43,541,000
Pearl Bidco Limited	£43,492,000
EPTA George Barker Ltd	£43,473,228
Burnden Leisure Limited	£43,332,000
Brand Addition Limited	£43,300,000
Lydiate Learning Trust	£43,265,000
Reddington Holdings Limited	£43,257,872
Metal & Waste Recycling Limited	£43,157,000
Sinclair Pharmaceuticals Limited	£43,112,000
Paybreak Limited	£43,061,992
Alternative Futures Group Limited	£43,058,000
LSC Finance Ltd	£43,016,840
Equipment and Track Solutions Limited	£42,959,528
Bollin Group Limited	£42,958,000
Kinaxia Transport and Warehousing Limited	£42,907,992
Mayr-Melnhof Packaging UK Limited	£42,898,000
Trac Precision Machining Limited	£42,893,000
JPTR Midco Limited	£42,866,000
Nycomm Limited	£42,864,704
Furmanite Limited	£42,851,000
Haynes International Ltd	£42,758,000
N.R.L. Group Limited	£42,733,168
Emerson & Renwick Limited	£42,705,232
Lincolnshire Road Car Company Limited	£42,697,000
Crane Payment Innovations Limited	£42,649,000
Renaker Build Limited	£42,625,240
Allergan Biologics Limited	£42,590,000
Amcare Limited	£42,582,000
Verna Group Equityco Limited	£42,523,120
Prinwest Limited	£42,520,968
Charities Trust	£42,488,072
Boulting Group Limited	£42,486,412
Qiagen Manchester Limited	£42,444,748
Capquest Debt Recovery Limited	£42,379,000
Bruntwood LG Holding Limited	£42,274,240
Thermo Onix Limited	£42,270,000
FQ Developments Limited	£42,260,840
APPH Limited	£42,233,000
English Provender Company Limited	£42,221,844
GE Capital Corporation (Funding) Limited	£42,193,000
Begbies Traynor (Central) LLP	£42,184,000
Sandhof Limited	£42,036,000
James Hargreaves (Plumbers' Merchants) Limited	£41,967,428
Axiom Education (Rochdale) Holdings Limited	£41,821,000
Thomas Hardie Commercials Limited	£41,818,848
North West Industrial Estates Limited	£41,806,336
National Holidays Limited	£41,804,000
Fanatics (International) Limited	£41,802,000
Peel Holdings (Overseas) Limited	£41,799,000
Otter Controls Limited	£41,790,000
O'Connor Utilities Limited	£41,663,036
Project Bullseye Topco Limited	£41,657,000
Empirical Property Group Limited	£41,643,916
Yanco Limited	£41,634,268
KELF	£41,608,000
FK Group Limited	£41,595,684
Medicash Health Benefits Limited	£41,591,000
Fairhome Group PLC	£41,583,796
Whispering Smith Group PLC	£41,534,004
OBG Pharmaceuticals Limited	£41,497,080
Salford Academy Trust	£41,495,000
IKO Holdings PLC	£41,493,000
P. & B. Foods Holdings Limited	£41,413,504
Cambus Limited	£41,400,000
Campus Living Villages (Goldsmiths) Issuer PLC	£41,382,000
Rowlinson Consolidated Ltd	£41,364,696
Tower Centre Hoddesdon Limited	£41,362,000
Visage Holdings (2010) Limited	£41,349,000
Nycomm Holdings Limited	£41,277,236
Monckton Properties Limited	£41,196,392
Fryett's Holdings Limited	£41,194,124
Sidhil Group Limited	£41,187,000
Bradford Diocesan Academies Trust	£41,066,000
Hydes' Brewery Limited	£41,063,348
Manchester Quays Two Limited	£41,061,600
Blackpool Football Club (Properties) Limited	£41,028,444
Chairs Limited	£40,944,384
Bents Holdings Limited	£40,938,528
Abney 2003 Limited	£40,882,000
Ferranti Technologies (Group) Limited	£40,778,000
Ultraframe (UK) Limited	£40,735,000
Axiom Education (Rochdale) Limited	£40,695,000
Himor (Carrington) Limited	£40,685,000
Werfen Limited	£40,647,524
Lendlock Group Limited	£40,628,148
Ventgrove Limited	£40,620,472
Vita First Street Limited	£40,589,000
Citation Holdings Limited	£40,582,072
Alpha Investments (North West) Ltd	£40,555,908
Countrywide Assured Life Holdings Limited	£40,506,668
Lazner Holdings Limited	£40,494,880
Fluidpower Shared Services Limited	£40,471,092
Plymouth Grove Residential LLP	£40,457,624

Company	Amount
Fragrance Oils (International) Limited	£40,403,152
Thompson and Capper Limited	£40,386,000
Merlin Ports Limited	£40,362,000
Lagonda Palace Propco Limited	£40,361,000
Elior UK Services Limited	£40,331,864
Electroimpact UK Limited	£40,289,124
Integrated Dental Holdings Limited	£40,124,000
Crerar Hotel Group Limited	£40,117,856
Elcometer Limited	£40,117,376
Inrix UK Ltd.	£40,090,804
Sune Green Holdco2 Ltd	£40,079,800
Patrick Properties Sterling Limited	£40,029,252
The Veterinary Defence Society Limited	£39,985,568
Lancaster Royal Grammar School	£39,921,000
Mardix Holdings Ltd	£39,883,604
Sigmatex (UK) Limited	£39,874,564
LSC Investments Limited	£39,870,280
Target Real Estate LLP	£39,849,856
Goldcrest Finance Limited	£39,815,820
Pearl Topco Limited	£39,798,000
Lhoist UK Limited	£39,783,000
Maryland Securities Limited	£39,737,192
Adi-Gardiner Limited	£39,652,000
Bridgewater High School	£39,568,976
Inspirepac Limited	£39,530,168
Meyer Group Limited	£39,529,000
Kingmoor Park Holdings Limited	£39,472,412
Potensial Limited	£39,464,772
Guenther Bakeries UK Limited	£39,434,640
Busways Travel Services Limited	£39,418,000
GP Premises Limited	£39,396,560
Conlon Holdings Limited	£39,388,000
Bespoke Supportive Tenancies Ltd	£39,332,016
Formidable Capital Assets Limited	£39,318,000
Chester Race Company Limited	£39,309,536
Paw Topco Limited	£39,269,000
International Seafoods Limited	£39,268,000
Allied Publicity Services (Manchester) Limited	£39,265,808
The Casey Group Limited	£39,265,068
The Blackburn Rovers Football and Athletic Limited	£39,172,248
Wolstenholme Square Developments Limited	£39,162,352
WEX Europe Services (UK) Limited	£39,148,000
Comfy Quilts Limited	£39,078,416
Peel Investments (Land and Property) No.2 Limited	£39,070,000
Standard Wool UK (Holdings) Limited	£39,020,504
Stax Trade Centres Limited	£39,003,024
Ossur UK Holding Limited	£38,989,972
Lancashire Schools SPC Phase 2 Ltd	£38,976,000
Henrob Limited	£38,928,064
Laser Quantum Limited	£38,887,000
Fostering Solutions Limited	£38,877,696
Cott Ventures UK Limited	£38,828,000
BASF Pharma (Callanish) Limited	£38,821,000
Derwent Lodge Estates Limited	£38,760,260
Cook (UK) Limited	£38,749,388
BC1.0 Ltd	£38,571,288
R.N. Wooler & Co (Holdings) Limited	£38,549,788
PIMCO 2947 Bidco Limited	£38,521,000
Avonside Roofing Limited	£38,458,792
Jones Homes (Southern) Limited	£38,458,660
Cole-Parmer Limited	£38,447,684
IFE Services Limited	£38,443,932
Promethean (Holdings) Limited	£38,378,000
William Strike Limited	£38,329,696
Quest Topco Limited	£38,275,400
Daisy No 1 Limited	£38,226,848
Kindertons 2013 Limited	£38,185,000
Inspiredspaces Rochdale (Holdings2) Limited	£38,131,000
Hive Bethnal Green Limited	£38,128,000
Jade Equity Limited	£38,107,000
PFP US JV LLP	£38,084,884
Nordex UK Limited	£38,032,128

Company	Amount
Daisy Computer Group Limited	£38,005,000
Lancashire Schools SPC Phase 3 Ltd	£37,925,000
Sandymere Limited	£37,910,440
Latium Plastics Enterprises Limited	£37,891,000
P B M Management Limited	£37,887,956
Liverpool Joint Catholic and CoE Academies Trust	£37,887,000
Comodo CA Limited	£37,859,000
Peel Investments (Intermediate) Limited	£37,839,000
Sherwin-Williams Protective & Marine Coatings	£37,814,504
North West Portfolio Limited	£37,789,296
Lowri Beck Services Limited	£37,768,336
Morbaine Limited	£37,759,736
UK Platforms Ltd	£37,753,000
Rayburn Trading Company Limited	£37,746,036
Anord Mardix (UK) Limited	£37,739,444
Sune Green Holdco7 Limited	£37,721,440
Flintbrook Limited	£37,713,000
Tygavac Advanced Materials Ltd	£37,657,548
Bridgewater Point Ltd	£37,465,080
1 Spinningfields Finance Two Ltd	£37,465,056
Merseyside Special Investment Fund Limited	£37,444,664
Gilkes Hydro Investments Limited	£37,429,784
Key Group Bidco Limited	£37,422,048
FocusEducation (Newcastle) Limited	£37,367,000
Flavour Warehouse Holdings Limited	£37,357,912
The Holchem Group Limited	£37,337,000
Bollinwater Estates LLP	£37,323,000
H.I.G. Milan UK Topco Limited	£37,320,000
Lagonda York Propco Limited	£37,296,000
Carden Park Hotel Limited	£37,268,000
Praetura Asset Finance (A) Limited	£37,266,592
Styles & Wood Investments Limited	£37,254,000
Bako North Western (Group) Limited	£37,241,000
Grangefern Properties Limited	£37,239,248
BHID Group Limited	£37,169,000
Kratos Group PLC	£37,162,000
Assura Primary Care Properties Limited	£37,160,104
Faiveley Transport Birkenhead Limited	£37,152,000
Arrow Global Accounts Management Limited	£37,137,000
Christopher Midco 1 Limited	£37,106,488
Commscare Group Limited	£37,065,276
FSUK Holdings Limited	£37,057,000
CLV (Bournemouth 1) UK LLP	£37,027,000
Manchester Airport Group Property Developments Ltd	£37,019,000
Inspiredspaces Rochdale (Projectco2) Limited	£36,956,000
M J Quinn Holdings Limited	£36,947,660
Quinn Infrastructure Services Limited	£36,941,928
Schoeller Allibert Limited	£36,857,000
Burnley General Hospital Phase V SPC Ltd	£36,825,000
WHP Telecoms Limited	£36,780,544
Labware Limited	£36,760,768
Campus Living Villages (Bedfordshire) UK Limited	£36,751,000
Thompson Motor Company (Preston) Limited	£36,744,392
Tennants Distribution Limited	£36,730,000
Pathway Care Group Limited	£36,673,048
Swift Technical Holdings Limited	£36,665,000
Regent Medical Americas Holdings Limited	£36,658,000
Ciceley Limited	£36,647,212
Trilogy (Leamington Spa) Limited	£36,617,000
Energy Assets (Meters) 2 Limited	£36,604,000
Emerson Automation Solutions Final Control UK Ltd	£36,596,000
Dickens 2014 Limited	£36,566,600
Maro Developments Limited	£36,532,208
J & J Ormerod PLC	£36,511,420
Distrupol Limited	£36,510,000
Whispering Smith Limited	£36,509,232
Hutt Investments Limited	£36,457,000
Seddon Homes Limited	£36,435,000
HT Forrest Holdings Limited	£36,412,000
James Fisher Fender Care Limited	£36,385,148
Manchester Airport Group Property Services Limited	£36,297,000
Vale Mill (Rochdale) Limited	£36,277,768

Company	Value
Oak Tyres UK Limited	£36,275,376
East Midlands Airport Property Investments Hotels	£36,275,000
Assura (SC 2) Limited	£36,274,016
TFS Stores Limited	£36,260,000
Sofology Limited	£36,239,000
Barlows Limited	£36,214,260
Emporia Leisure Limited	£36,200,496
Dale Farm (GB) Limited	£36,175,000
McManus Group Holdings Limited	£36,173,720
Peel Land and Property Investments (CL) Limited	£36,167,440
Bruntwood Cornwall Street Limited	£36,139,000
Micromass Limited	£36,079,000
Sunshine Cruise Holidays Limited	£36,064,180
Blackpool Pleasure Beach Limited	£36,023,000
Advanced Medical Solutions Limited	£35,996,000
BV Holdings Limited	£35,990,700
Farrel Limited	£35,986,620
M.G.F. (Trench Construction Systems) Limited	£35,941,648
Monitise International Limited	£35,941,000
Russells Limited	£35,904,348
Paradigm Burnley Holdings Ltd	£35,877,960
Greif UK Holding Ltd	£35,868,976
W. Maher & Sons Limited	£35,824,896
Blackpool Football Club.Limited (The)	£35,805,856
Thomas Hardie Truck & Bus Limited	£35,805,748
9 East Shipping Limited	£35,800,868
Kratos Analytical Limited	£35,791,000
Philip J Davies Holdings PLC	£35,789,420
Total Polyfilm Limited	£35,783,000
Brooks Automation Ltd	£35,781,000
Norkem Limited	£35,774,240
CCL Secure Limited	£35,711,000
Warwick Holdings Limited	£35,574,000
APS Produce Limited	£35,564,000
Timothy Taylor & Co.,Limited	£35,537,816
Zen Internet Limited	£35,533,320
Holroyd Precision Ltd	£35,513,416
Arlington Management Services Ltd	£35,438,000
Kaman Composites - UK Holdings Limited	£35,417,000
James Hargreaves Holdings Limited	£35,297,928
Hurstwood Properties (R) Limited	£35,269,360
Graves (Cumberland) Limited	£35,259,504
F. Duerr & Sons Limited	£35,220,380
Ungerer Limited	£35,211,000
Cumbria Education Trust	£35,210,336
VG Systems Limited	£35,210,000
Daisy Worldwide Limited	£35,157,000
Bestway Pharmacy NDC Limited	£35,142,000
Pets at Home Veterinary Specialist Group Limited	£35,132,000
Cartwright Rentals Limited	£35,130,632
McComb Property Company Limited	£35,118,648
Valtris Specialty Chemicals Limited	£35,106,512
J.F. and E. Hadwin Limited	£35,101,696
Affirmative Finance Limited	£35,095,668
Luxfer Gas Cylinders Limited	£35,073,000
Cequent UK Limited	£35,046,564
Verna Group Bidco Limited	£35,036,496
LDF Finance No. 1 Limited	£35,006,092
Inflight Productions Ltd	£34,971,668
Carrier Transicold (UK) Limited	£34,969,000
Airbags International Limited	£34,967,000
Brink's Limited	£34,935,000
Quintessential Brands UK Holdings Limited	£34,900,000
LVMH Watch & Jewellery (UK) Limited	£34,843,552
Heyrod Holdings Ltd	£34,829,324
The Port Sunlight Village Trust	£34,826,580
Metro MRM Limited	£34,795,244
Partington (Holdings) Limited	£34,774,372
Veka PLC	£34,771,000
Carrs Billington Agriculture (Operations) Limited	£34,743,384
Brighterkind (PC) Limited	£34,691,000
M2 Digital Limited	£34,688,000
Lydall UK Ltd	£34,651,852
Heyrod Construction Limited	£34,648,816
Audco Limited	£34,610,000
GP Strategies Limited	£34,601,000
Stonecroft Holdings PLC	£34,595,000
The Jesem Group Limited	£34,580,884
Barbican Investments Limited	£34,556,800
Kingsway Financial Group Holdings Limited	£34,546,804
Haydock Asset Finance Limited	£34,533,000
Bolton Wanderers Football & Athletic Company Ltd	£34,491,008
West Pennine Trucks Limited	£34,463,672
Bowker Preston Limited	£34,445,000
Anglo-Eastern Trust Limited (The)	£34,420,000
LA Holding Limited	£34,414,000
Liverpool College Independent School Trust	£34,350,296
European Care & Lifestyles (UK) Ltd	£34,291,000
Egencia UK Ltd	£34,256,000
SIL Holdings Limited	£34,232,000
Emerald Kalama Chemical Limited	£34,191,000
CRM Trading Limited	£34,182,176
Helical Industries Ltd.	£34,152,408
MKS Instruments UK Limited	£34,127,204
Thames Transit Limited	£34,126,000
Sambro International Limited	£34,107,692
Lakeland Leisure Estates Limited	£34,058,452
Bachy Soletanche Holdings Limited	£34,051,000
Morecambe Leisure 2 Limited	£34,020,000
Jesem Holdings Limited	£34,000,000
BYK Additives Limited	£33,995,000
Adesa Remarketing Limited	£33,987,600
Futaba Manufacturing U.K. Limited	£33,964,000
Discan Limited	£33,962,956
Greater Manchester Academies Trust	£33,949,000
Curtis Wool Direct Limited	£33,756,576
Synthite Limited	£33,743,568
Bents Property Limited	£33,707,968
Edina UK Limited	£33,693,240
Boxwood Leisure Limited	£33,692,444
Krones UK Limited	£33,628,000
Radisson Hotel Manchester Ltd	£33,610,000
Cotton Traders Limited	£33,595,000
GE Real Estate (Investment Property Company) Ltd	£33,595,000
Bibby Line Limited	£33,549,734
Sutton and Son (St.Helens) Limited	£33,523,190
Pexion Limited	£33,509,208
W. & G. Harrison Limited	£33,485,000
Standard Wool (UK) Limited	£33,444,970
Brookhouse (Prescot) Limited	£33,378,000
SLP Manufacturing Limited	£33,324,950
Blackpool Pleasure Beach (Holdings) Limited	£33,275,000
Red Rose Infrastructure Limited	£33,266,000
AMEC Hedge Co 1 Limited	£33,240,000
Hallco 1052 Limited	£33,202,072
Thumbs-Up (Bury) Limited	£33,180,576
The Fallibroome Trust	£33,159,614
Archibald Bathgate Group Limited	£33,136,736
Crown Promotional Packaging UK Limited	£33,136,000
Direct Accident Management Limited	£33,114,006
St Helens Rugby Football Club Limited	£33,099,576
Bibby Factors Manchester Limited	£33,093,720
Artech Reduction Technologies Limited	£33,088,016
Beauchamp Real Estate Holdings Limited	£33,059,130
LSC Holdings Limited	£33,034,996
Ifor Williams Trailers Limited	£32,995,860
Neuven Solutions Limited	£32,987,228
GE Intelligent Platforms Limited	£32,976,000
Ciceley Commercials Limited	£32,940,888
IVCC	£32,893,000
Darwin (Keswick Reach) Limited	£32,890,034
Broomco (3935) Limited	£32,882,000
Neuven Solutions Holdings Limited	£32,862,424
PFM Group Limited	£32,853,454

Company	Amount
Capital Bank Leasing 3 Limited	£32,847,000
Parkingeye Limited	£32,842,938
Enterprise Education Conwy Limited	£32,822,000
Enterprise Education Holdings Conwy Limited	£32,822,000
Peel Chapel No.4 Limited	£32,794,856
Realty Estates Limited	£32,778,008
Nilfisk Ltd.	£32,742,000
Gunn JCB Limited	£32,741,000
Halliwell Jones (Chester) Limited	£32,732,452
James Fisher (Aberdeen) Limited	£32,731,682
Verna Group International Limited	£32,718,306
Tithebarn Limited	£32,709,808
Seamark PLC	£32,695,992
Moduleco Healthcare Limited	£32,651,446
Peel Holdings (Environmental) Limited	£32,640,208
Curtis Wool Direct Holdings Limited	£32,609,206
H.B. Fuller Group Limited	£32,564,000
AECOM International Holdings UK Limited	£32,555,000
Joseph Heler Limited	£32,424,962
NCC Services Limited	£32,400,000
Pugh Davies Properties Limited	£32,377,356
Moortown Group Limited	£32,377,078
Edgefold Holdings Limited	£32,364,000
H.I.G Milan UK Bidco Limited	£32,335,000
Sune Green Holdco4 Limited	£32,329,892
Welspun UK Limited	£32,318,000
Select Sites Limited	£32,280,000
Huntercombe (BIR) Limited	£32,267,000
Bibby Maritime Limited	£32,261,536
Uren Food Group Limited	£32,250,000
USS Investment Management Limited	£32,188,000
Brink's (UK) Limited	£32,174,000
Brisbane House Limited	£32,166,712
Calachem Holding Limited	£32,157,000
Spectrum Living Solutions Ltd	£32,156,276
Vita Industrial (Poland) Limited	£32,137,180
Utopia Leisure Limited	£32,123,056
Himor (Property) Limited	£32,114,000
BES Utilities Holding Ltd	£32,094,384
Frank Marshall Estates Limited	£32,076,376
AJU2 Limited	£32,074,794
H&H Group PLC	£32,053,000
TSC Foods Limited	£32,043,482
Lewis's Home Retail Limited	£32,014,654
Natural Assets Investments Limited	£32,002,558
Tessuti Ltd	£31,980,000
LQ Developments Limited	£31,979,048
LLW Repository Limited	£31,968,000
1st Stop Home Loans Limited	£31,955,076
Albis (U.K.) Limited	£31,946,648
Halliwell Jones Holdings (Chester) Limited	£31,918,828
General All Purpose Plastics Limited	£31,861,260
Gott Agri Synergy Limited	£31,848,384
Bliss Bidco Limited	£31,831,276
Synexus Clinical Research Acquisitions Limited	£31,829,000
Stewart Holdings Management Limited	£31,807,000
Peel Airports (Liverpool) Limited	£31,804,586
Playnation Limited	£31,794,440
Birmingham Technology (Property) Limited	£31,756,710
Specialist People Services Group Limited	£31,714,868
Peel Media Studios Holdings Limited	£31,699,000
Total Fitness Health Clubs Limited	£31,696,000
Drayton Manor High School Academy Trust	£31,694,210
Pace Overseas Distribution Limited	£31,677,176
Abbey Logistics Group Limited	£31,655,304
Orbital Education Limited	£31,649,776
Blue Prism Group PLC	£31,643,000
Total Polyfilm (Holdings) Limited	£31,628,000
L F D Group Limited	£31,555,258
Ruia Group Limited	£31,553,252
Verdant Leisure 2 Limited	£31,553,000
Sporting Club St. Helens Limited	£31,550,352
Leasowe Community Homes	£31,550,000
Westinghouse Electric Company UK Limited	£31,540,000
Birmingham Schools PSP Phase 1B Limited	£31,519,000
Birmingham Schools SPC Holdings Phase 1B Limited	£31,514,000
Birmingham Schools SPC Phase 1B Limited	£31,514,000
Wright's Pies (Shelton) Limited	£31,428,768
Nuseed Global Innovation Ltd	£31,412,000
Dowbridge Limited	£31,374,000
Ruttle Plant Holdings Limited	£31,369,694
Debt Solutions (Holdings) Limited	£31,313,000
VIL Holdings Limited	£31,308,676
Emerald Publishing Limited	£31,308,000
Chester Diocesan Board of Finance	£31,244,000
Cuadrilla Bowland Limited	£31,219,586
WEC Group Limited	£31,217,000
E.Sutton & Son Limited	£31,205,056
Saltaire Water Limited	£31,156,000
Holt Holdings (UK) Limited	£31,154,000
Moneyplus Group Limited	£31,111,000
Manor Drug Company (Nottingham) Limited (The)	£31,097,928
Mondi Consumer Goods Packaging UK Ltd	£31,096,226
Calachem Ltd	£31,073,000
Barnfield Construction Limited	£31,071,618
Angus Holdings Safety Group Limited	£31,045,000
Kensington Developments Limited	£31,026,538
The Port of Mostyn Limited	£31,016,844
Little Raith Wind Farm Limited	£30,981,832
FMC Chemicals Limited	£30,971,000
Ascent Housing LLP	£30,947,000
Stonewell Property Company Limited	£30,918,182
Iconix MENA Ltd	£30,907,452
Highfield PFI SPV Limited	£30,882,390
Buttercup Topco Limited	£30,843,464
Flowgroup PLC	£30,838,000
Car Care Plan (Holdings) Limited	£30,757,000
Circle Leasing Limited	£30,704,000
Visage Group Limited	£30,692,000
Equity Solutions Lift Investments Cornwall Limited	£30,634,064
LRUK (Holdings) Limited	£30,609,000
ASICS UK Limited	£30,574,764
Jones Homes (Lancashire) Limited	£30,569,578
OMC Motor Holdings Limited	£30,567,012
Style Group Holdings Limited	£30,555,000
Aimia Foods Limited	£30,549,000
Clive Hurt (Plant Hire) Limited	£30,548,968
Little Greene (Holdings) Limited	£30,537,504
Christeyns UK Ltd	£30,519,140
Wigan Football Company Limited	£30,442,462
The Oak Trust	£30,441,000
Woodford Land Limited	£30,431,826
E.Park & Sons Limited	£30,407,784
Inovyn Newco 2 Limited	£30,400,000
Checkers Safety Group UK Ltd	£30,382,000
The Factory Shop Group Limited	£30,380,000
Wrather Group Limited	£30,369,512
Datac Adhesives Limited	£30,319,000
Fujifilm Imaging Colorants Limited	£30,305,000
W M L Industrial Holdings Limited	£30,287,716
Suttons Tankers Limited	£30,286,876
C.W.B.G Limited	£30,274,208
Driver Hire Group Services Limited	£30,246,044
Hyde Group Limited	£30,229,780
Cartwright Fleet Services Limited	£30,220,380
Hurt Plant Hire Limited	£30,132,500
Vita Industrial (Lithuania) Limited	£30,106,264
Daresbury SIC LLP	£30,091,326
G.I. Hadfield & Son Limited	£30,091,296
Kondor Midco Limited	£30,076,000
Hyde Group Tooling Limited	£30,044,060
Red & White Services Limited	£30,021,000
Day International (UK) Holdings	£30,004,000
Bristol Active Limited	£29,975,028

Company	Amount
Mann + Hummel Vokes Air Filtration Limited	£29,937,000
Garic Limited	£29,934,000
Character World Limited	£29,931,492
Driver Group PLC	£29,913,000
Orthoplastics Limited	£29,810,000
Craghoppers Limited	£29,807,000
Crabwall Claremont Limited	£29,788,000
Meter Serve 3 Limited	£29,753,000
International Travel Connections Limited	£29,739,000
New World Trading Company (UK) Limited	£29,721,588
Scalable Communications Limited	£29,675,000
Wrengate Holdings Limited	£29,625,656
Portcullis Oldham Limited	£29,622,436
Kerry Logistics (UK) Limited	£29,618,722
Singleton Trading Limited	£29,611,476
Eddie Stobart Group Limited	£29,603,000
Holt Lloyd International Limited	£29,601,000
Rullion IT Plus Limited	£29,567,088
Droylsden Academy	£29,555,552
JCT600 (Yorkshire) Ltd	£29,522,000
The Authentic Food Group Limited	£29,517,036
Castlefield Holdings Limited	£29,498,060
Bright Blue Foods Limited	£29,495,000
Speedy Support Services Limited	£29,426,000
Lagardere Sports UK Ltd	£29,390,632
Praedius Ltd.	£29,388,000
The Merchant Taylors' Schools,Crosby	£29,354,942
Highneal Limited	£29,354,444
The Altius Trust	£29,335,624
Kingdom Services Group Limited	£29,311,616
S J Bargh Group Limited	£29,307,152
New Kadampa Tradition - Kadampa Buddhist Union	£29,285,740
Edmund Rice Bicentennial Trust Limited	£29,283,510
Inrix Holdings UK Ltd	£29,258,212
Corporate Travel Management (North) Limited	£29,248,764
J K Ashbrook Holdings Limited	£29,223,382
Arrow XL Limited	£29,209,000
Iforce Limited	£29,199,000
Trak Global Group Limited	£29,188,332
J. Rose (Tyres) Limited	£29,187,814
Seddon Engineering Holdings Limited	£29,187,000
Gilbert Gilkes & Gordon Limited	£29,166,000
Burke Investments Limited	£29,096,808
Leeds Group PLC	£29,095,000
Calder Industrial Materials Limited	£29,058,000
AW Carbonless Papers Europe Limited	£29,056,000
Oakcrown Properties Limited	£29,051,744
JLG Industries (United Kingdom) Limited	£29,035,164
Convergys Holdings (GB) Limited	£29,017,000
Semara Contract Services Limited	£29,016,000
Rotary Building Services Ltd	£28,992,000
Park Inn By Radisson Hotels Management Ltd	£28,979,000
Mutley Properties (Holdings) Limited	£28,972,644
Domeline Limited	£28,971,674
Cringle Corporation Limited	£28,945,708
Tandom Metallurgical Group Limited	£28,904,314
Buoyant Upholstery Limited	£28,902,000
Wotton House Properties Limited	£28,901,000
Woodford Remediation Limited	£28,892,136
General All Purpose Plastics Group Limited	£28,890,646
Brine Multi Academy Trust	£28,856,336
Bruntwood Management Services Limited	£28,808,000
Recycling Lives Limited	£28,807,000
Ruberoid International Limited	£28,796,000
Wealth at Work Midco Limited	£28,784,000
The Together Trust	£28,747,000
Francis House Family Trust	£28,746,790
Sentinel Performance Solutions Limited	£28,729,000
Max Spielmann Limited	£28,668,000
Willan Group Limited	£28,620,186
Tratos (UK) Limited	£28,617,178
Henco (International) Limited	£28,616,104

Company	Amount
Wealth at Work Holdings Limited	£28,614,000
Commercial Regional Space Limited	£28,592,842
ADM Protexin Limited	£28,558,026
Zoe Group Limited	£28,556,940
Tangerine Holdings Limited	£28,526,288
Napoleons Leisure Limited	£28,515,618
Feversham Education Trust	£28,504,000
Marsh Finance Limited	£28,485,444
Healthcare Buying Group Limited	£28,469,000
G.G.R. Corporation Ltd	£28,428,264
Recycling Lives Holdings Limited	£28,423,000
Scan Computers International Limited	£28,416,828
International Paper Group (UK) Limited	£28,395,000
Gunn JCB Group Limited	£28,372,000
Cox Motor Group Limited	£28,364,952
Technical Fibre Products Limited	£28,362,000
K3 Business Systems Holdco Limited	£28,290,872
The Learning Trust	£28,273,000
D J Cox Limited	£28,240,468
Seneca Securities Ltd	£28,214,876
Dams Holdings Limited	£28,158,476
P.N.Daly Limited	£28,151,644
Northern Trust Group 2 Limited	£28,150,020
Secured Express Limited	£28,141,278
Laltex & Co.Limited	£28,134,300
MDS CEM Holdings Limited	£28,122,000
Cotton Traders Holdings Limited	£28,077,000
First Choice Dental Limited	£28,066,132
Principal Healthcare Finance (UK) No.2 Limited	£28,034,000
Moneyplus Holdings Limited	£28,033,000
Lymm High School	£28,013,970
AJ Bell Securities Limited	£27,992,000
Concept Life Sciences (Laboratories) Limited	£27,971,540
ASCO Joucomatic Limited	£27,970,000
K K Fine Foods Limited	£27,967,804
Ellis Whittam (Holdings) Limited	£27,961,552
In Vino Bidco Limited	£27,959,740
A.E.Yates,Limited	£27,929,802
EFS Los Guindos UK Limited	£27,925,324
D Wardle (Plant) Limited	£27,884,192
FEI UK Limited	£27,868,926
Wood Park Foods Limited	£27,841,000
Bellis Group Limited	£27,839,000
Community 1st Oldham (Werneth and Shaw) Limited	£27,830,698
Rethink Recruitment Solutions Limited	£27,819,810
Synexus Clinical Research Finance Limited	£27,813,000
Darwin (Woodside Bay) Limited	£27,778,866
Meter Fit (North West) Limited	£27,752,000
Brad Estates Limited	£27,736,000
Ruselco LLP	£27,716,540
Ashdowns Limited	£27,707,000
Jones Homes (Yorkshire) Limited	£27,703,854
Ansell Electrical Products Limited	£27,702,622
Redx Pharma PLC	£27,689,000
Please Hold (UK) Limited	£27,661,720
Rhodi Inc. Imports Limited	£27,660,596
Donald Wardle and Son Limited	£27,647,000
Grange School Hartford Limited (The)	£27,627,976
Wain Group Limited	£27,604,000
Paystream My Max Holdings Limited	£27,601,142
Kingspan Energy Limited	£27,556,426
Local Pensions Partnership Ltd	£27,549,000
Tom Martin & Company Limited	£27,539,568
Green Growth Power Ltd	£27,523,336
George Moss & Sons Limited	£27,522,104
Rayware Limited	£27,510,858
National Fed of Self Employed & Small Businesses	£27,503,854
Hanson Springs Limited	£27,476,004
Pyroguard UK Limited	£27,464,192
Bentley Global (UK) Limited	£27,455,908
Samjo Limited	£27,424,022
Sedbergh School	£27,403,000

Company	Turnover
Glasson Grain Limited	£27,394,434
West Lakes Multi Academy Trust	£27,392,000
T.K. Components Group Limited	£27,386,000
Joseph Parr Group Limited	£27,377,604
New Co (Beith Street) Limited	£27,369,000
King David and Harold House Foundation	£27,364,754
Mott MacDonald Bentley Ltd	£27,362,158
Stockport Grammar School	£27,352,796
The Hub Pharmacy Limited	£27,351,448
ARE II LLP	£27,343,908
VPG Systems UK Limited	£27,332,456
Cardinal Maritime Holdings Limited	£27,327,842
DCC Health & Beauty Solutions Limited	£27,321,000
DGD Properties Limited	£27,319,474
Houghton PLC	£27,316,000
Thomas Armstrong (Concrete Blocks) Limited	£27,291,642
Paradigm Precision Burnley Ltd	£27,278,000
J T Associates Limited	£27,267,310
FSHC Properties (Manor) Limited	£27,208,000
United Utilities Property Services Limited	£27,195,000
Uniroyal Global Limited	£27,193,000
Allied London Holdco Limited	£27,191,356
St Wilfrid's Church of England Academy	£27,165,384
Bondcare Willington Limited	£27,161,856
Bodycote H.I.P. Limited	£27,146,000
Rullion Engineering Limited	£27,139,054
Cavendish Investments (Manchester) Limited	£27,129,840
Bibby Factors Yorkshire Limited	£27,100,428
Brahm Fundco 1 Limited	£27,046,380
Wm. Nelstrop & Co. Ltd	£27,039,356
Pet City Holdings Limited	£27,034,000
Phil McIntyre Holdings Limited	£27,027,320
Fishawack Medical Communications Limited	£26,994,276
WTH (UK) Limited	£26,963,976
Holdsworth Holdings Limited	£26,963,476
GE Real Estate Finance Limited	£26,956,000
Altus Education Partnership	£26,925,000
Kamani Commercial Property Ltd	£26,923,870
G&J Distillers Ltd.	£26,892,000
Scantech Offshore Limited	£26,878,544
ABS Group Ltd.	£26,851,232
UK-2 Limited	£26,849,358
Cavalier Marketing Limited	£26,834,770
West Derby School	£26,831,222
Kirkby (Tyres) Limited	£26,827,396
SE Bury Lane Solar Limited	£26,819,332
Inspiredspaces Rochdale (Holdings1) Limited	£26,806,000
Millfield Estates (Bolton) Limited	£26,779,304
Emballator (UK) Limited	£26,766,700
Avocado Research Chemicals Limited	£26,725,000
Essa Foundation Academies Trust	£26,699,000
Icopal Limited	£26,687,000
RMS International Limited	£26,680,000
WB Developments (Salford) Limited	£26,669,248
Styles & Wood Property Management Limited	£26,654,000
Lookers Birmingham Limited	£26,625,000
Total Polyfilm Group Limited	£26,607,000
HTI Toys UK Limited	£26,594,000
AMEC Foster Wheeler International Limited	£26,582,000
Mistral Bus & Coach PLC	£26,571,872
Carrylift Materials Handling Limited	£26,571,364
Newton Abbot Health Limited	£26,562,860
Newton Abbot Health Holdings Limited	£26,562,860
Belle Engineering (Sheen) Limited	£26,525,952
Bradford College Education Trust	£26,506,000
Bibby Taurus Limited	£26,475,576
Paragon Hotels Limited	£26,472,000
Belden UK Limited	£26,440,948
Northbay Pelagic Limited	£26,433,542
National Refrigerants Ltd	£26,429,360
Sykes Cottages Ltd	£26,420,000
John Turner Construction Group Ltd	£26,400,494

Company	Turnover
Vita Lithuania (UK) Limited	£26,396,496
Citylabs Limited	£26,344,000
Bibby Wavemaster I Limited	£26,333,426
Compass Minerals UK Holdings Limited	£26,324,000
Red-D-Arc Limited	£26,310,284
St. Ambrose College Edmund Rice Academy Trust	£26,294,000
TIC Group Limited	£26,277,100
Boutique Hotel Group Limited	£26,270,208
Houghton Holdings Limited	£26,264,842
T.K. Components (Holdings) Limited	£26,260,000
YKK (U.K.) Limited	£26,232,768
Holgates (Caravan Parks) Limited	£26,230,654
Co-operative Legal Services Limited	£26,209,000
D.W. Armstrong Holdings Limited	£26,184,174
Windermere Educational Trust Limited	£26,166,776
Timetoken Limited	£26,162,606
Care Worldwide Limited	£26,154,222
Investment Fund Services Limited	£26,153,886
T I Midwood & Co Limited	£26,153,418
Network Space (Networkcentres) Limited	£26,142,344
Truecommerce Holdings Limited	£26,115,230
Alfred H. Knight International Limited	£26,111,640
Sanko Gosei UK Ltd	£26,094,320
Endress + Hauser Investments Limited	£26,048,000
Ensco 1090 Limited	£26,008,386
Bardsley Construction Limited	£26,004,510
Nikal Ltd	£25,970,180
TFHC Investments Limited	£25,957,000
Buckhurst Group Limited	£25,953,152
Luxfer Overseas Holdings Limited	£25,928,000
Jost (Great Britain) Limited	£25,921,000
Carr's Engineering Limited	£25,919,760
Optionis Management Limited	£25,913,240
Matchstick Men Limited	£25,905,808
Herbert T. Forrest Limited	£25,895,000
D.R.A. Ltd	£25,879,000
Axle Bidco Limited	£25,872,020
New Bridge Multi Academy Trust	£25,858,960
Inspiredspaces Rochdale (Projectco1) Limited	£25,841,000
The Oldham Motor Company Limited	£25,835,984
Dunbia (England)	£25,835,000
Nalco Energy Services Marketing Limited	£25,781,000
INX International UK Limited	£25,779,268
Swinton Properties Limited	£25,747,000
Krempel (UK) Holdings Limited	£25,740,360
AECOM E&C UK Limited	£25,735,000
V.I.P. Computer Centre Limited	£25,702,000
Assura (GHC) Ltd	£25,632,764
Quest Newco Limited	£25,630,838
Orica-GM Holdings Limited	£25,617,344
Beech Holdings (Manchester) Limited	£25,598,660
Icon Health & Fitness (Holdings) Limited	£25,592,130
Low Wood Hotel (1958) Limited	£25,571,836
Castlefield Estates Limited	£25,557,008
Special Piping Materials (Holdings) Limited	£25,541,926
Guarantee Protection Insurance Limited	£25,530,112
Greenergy Limited	£25,530,000
Wrengate Limited	£25,526,812
Blackburn Fundco Limited	£25,521,900
Novus Finance Ltd	£25,518,256
Keyland Developments Limited	£25,500,000
MMGG Acquisition Limited	£25,494,000
PKW Properties LLP	£25,493,240
Havwoods Global Holdings Limited	£25,491,988
Urban Splash (RWY) Limited	£25,465,630
Supreme Imports Ltd	£25,459,840
ROKPA Trust	£25,451,436
Moorcroft Group Public Limited Company	£25,449,926
Elegant Resorts Limited	£25,446,000
Budget Greeting Cards Limited	£25,441,412
MPM Products Limited	£25,438,000
The Outward Bound Trust	£25,435,000

Company	Amount
Bibby Factors Bristol Limited	£25,425,288
Buckhurst Plant Hire Limited	£25,410,896
Beckhall Properties Ltd	£25,408,084
Thomas Graham & Sons (Iron & Steel) Limited	£25,389,384
Banner Chemicals Limited	£25,379,964
T L Dallas Group Limited	£25,373,560
Manchester Innovation Limited	£25,365,496
Praedius (UK) Limited	£25,360,000
ADP Holdings Limited	£25,340,000
Evergreener Investments LLP	£25,334,834
J R Hutt Holdings Limited	£25,333,000
Budget Trading Limited	£25,317,342
Holgates Holdings Limited	£25,313,256
Focus Academy Trust (UK) Ltd	£25,304,000
CLV (St Andrews) UK LLP	£25,299,000
Talbot Deane Investments Limited	£25,292,428
Fortis Developments Ltd	£25,270,016
UP Global Sourcing Holdings PLC	£25,258,000
Alderley Park Holdings Limited	£25,252,000
UP Global Sourcing UK Limited	£25,208,000
BetterBathrooms (UK) Limited	£25,201,004
ISSA Foundation	£25,180,054
Exertis Continental Europe Holdings Limited	£25,176,574
Spectra-Physics Holdings Limited	£25,173,000
J & S Accessories Limited	£25,152,020
Jost UK Limited	£25,127,000
Makro Limited	£25,125,000
Becker Industrial Coatings Limited	£25,124,000
Gartside Investments Limited	£25,118,826
Project Play Midco 2 Limited	£25,116,000
R.S.Clare & Co.,Limited	£25,110,066
Fagan & Whalley Holdings Limited	£25,088,508
Huntapac Produce Limited	£25,085,786
Assura Properties UK Limited	£25,083,664
Blackpool Transport Services Limited	£25,064,712
Holchem Laboratories Limited	£25,057,000
FK Facades Limited	£25,052,544
Coral Products PLC	£25,029,000
AHL Anglia Limited	£25,028,000
Helium Sofa Group Limited	£25,014,000
Peel Media Studios Limited	£25,002,000
University of Liverpool Energy Company Limited	£25,000,000
Silkhouse Court Ltd	£24,990,746
Airedale Chemical Company Limited	£24,955,190
Presspart Manufacturing Limited	£24,946,000
NES Managed Services Limited	£24,945,000
M1 RE Manchester Limited	£24,941,078
Silver Cross (UK) Limited	£24,938,408
Bryden Capital Ltd	£24,927,084
Smiths Dock LLP	£24,922,164
Enesco Limited	£24,918,000
Cheltenham and Gloucester Omnibus Company Ltd	£24,915,000
Enterprise Civic Buildings Limited	£24,878,000
Enterprise Civic Buildings (Holdings) Limited	£24,878,000
Figurehead Homes Limited	£24,872,736
Abird Limited	£24,863,000
Bibliotheca Limited	£24,843,000
JD Roebuck Holdings Limited	£24,838,640
AKW Group Limited	£24,828,248
Stocks Bros. Limited	£24,827,122
Hamilton Heath Estates Limited	£24,826,608
Redrow Homes East Midlands Limited	£24,820,644
Bako North Western Limited	£24,818,000
Fletchers Solicitors Limited	£24,816,704
Rhenus Logistics Limited	£24,808,516
Park Inn By Radisson Hotel Heathrow Ltd	£24,802,000
Holt Lloyd Group Limited	£24,801,000
Centurion Truck Rental Ltd	£24,748,194
Urban Splash Group Limited	£24,734,864
R.N. Wooler & Company Limited	£24,726,868
UK Pharma Impex Limited	£24,679,384
Rodo Limited	£24,672,384
North West Water International Limited	£24,671,000
Mibelle Ltd	£24,631,000
Park Card Services Limited	£24,607,460
Husco International Holdings Three Ltd	£24,581,680
Sibelco Minerals and Chemicals (Holdings) Limited	£24,547,188
Education Partnership Trust	£24,497,440
Sidcot Group Ltd	£24,485,500
Stokers Limited	£24,483,780
Bibby Factors Sussex Limited	£24,458,466
The Authentic Food Company Limited	£24,447,944
2 Hardman Boulevard Investments Limited	£24,429,280
Payzone UK Limited	£24,394,270
Bradford Academy Trust	£24,389,000
Doosan International UK Limited	£24,364,000
C.G.I. Group Limited	£24,362,756
Formby Hall Golf Club Limited	£24,330,308
QMS International Limited	£24,323,732
Trinity Hospice and Palliative Care Services Ltd	£24,323,294
Just Childcare Consultancy Services Limited	£24,321,000
Oakes Millers Limited	£24,318,256
Telesign UK Limited	£24,307,822
Tote Media Limited	£24,292,260
Shurooq Limited	£24,284,686
M & I Materials Limited	£24,230,452
Univar Europe Limited	£24,229,000
Central Glass Europe Limited	£24,225,632
Gladman Retirement Living Limited	£24,194,868
Gresham Office Furniture Limited	£24,191,844
NCC Group Security Services Limited	£24,185,000
The Liverpool and Merseyside Theatres Trust Limited	£24,170,000
Pochin Construction Limited	£24,169,568
The Hub Community Healthcare Holdco Limited	£24,155,856
Trinity Church of England High School	£24,153,180
Colloids Limited	£24,120,310
Meridian Business Support Limited	£24,116,572
Brookhouse Residential Developments Limited	£24,087,000
Cheshire Salt Limited	£24,077,000
Woodland Assets Limited	£24,077,000
P. Casey & Co., Limited	£24,055,732
Marksans Pharma U.K. Limited	£24,043,708
Saxid Limited	£24,038,436
BES Commercial Electricity Ltd	£24,021,578
T.A. Weatherwear Holdings Limited	£24,010,522
M J Birtwistle & Co Limited	£24,008,528
GE Capital Limited	£23,989,000
Iconichem Widnes Limited	£23,985,756
Pinco 2223 Limited	£23,970,004
Brookhouse Helsby (Retail) Limited	£23,931,000
Wellacre Technology Academy Trust	£23,919,000
Fiserv Worldwide Holdings Limited	£23,887,068
Building Product Design Limited	£23,873,428
Halite Energy Group Limited	£23,871,038
Tensar Manufacturing Limited	£23,858,000
Good Night Vienna Productions Limited	£23,838,456
Gardner Denver Group Services Limited	£23,823,616
John Turner Holdings Limited	£23,804,788
Iceland Seafood Barraclough Ltd	£23,803,130
Birkenhead Port Limited	£23,800,000
Trilanco Limited	£23,781,000
Blackpool Multi Academy Trust	£23,771,846
Community 1st Stockport Limited	£23,755,348
Meter Fit (North East) Limited	£23,754,000
IDH Group Limited	£23,745,000
Armstrongs Aggregates Limited	£23,729,628
Cambi UK Limited	£23,727,000
Gusto Restaurants Group Limited	£23,709,000
Saica Natur UK Limited	£23,702,000
Northamptonshire Leisure Estates Limited	£23,685,732
Buxton Consortium Limited	£23,679,408
Crawford Healthcare Holdings Limited	£23,649,000
George Roberts (North West) Limited	£23,643,656
Clean Energy and Infrastructure UK Wind 2 Limited	£23,640,612

Company	Amount
AW-WS Group Limited	£23,633,000
Hero UK Limited	£23,606,000
Achievement Through Collaboration Trust	£23,599,000
Klash Holdings Limited	£23,585,742
Reich Insurance Brokers Limited	£23,571,792
Virgin Wines Holding Company Limited	£23,555,000
Deva Group Limited	£23,530,000
Akinika UK Limited	£23,525,000
Pathway Care Solutions Group Limited	£23,510,824
The City of Salford Community Stadium Limited	£23,499,016
Nationwide Produce Holdings PLC	£23,489,116
Bolton St Catherine's Academy	£23,482,000
Ventcroft Limited	£23,478,274
Assura Services Limited	£23,461,248
Nationwide Produce PLC	£23,444,392
Fragrance Oils (Purchasing) Limited	£23,442,802
Stanleybet Holdings Limited	£23,414,112
G.G.R. Group Ltd	£23,414,056
Stamptree Limited	£23,402,000
Deeside Cereals I Ltd	£23,399,000
UKapital Limited	£23,398,098
Chesterfield High School	£23,394,000
Foden Estates Ltd.	£23,393,548
Innovative Technology Limited	£23,379,000
Hollingsworth & Vose Air Filtration Limited	£23,373,000
Huntercombe (No 12) Limited	£23,360,000
Status International (UK) Ltd	£23,357,990
C & W Berry Limited	£23,348,356
Kermandine Limited	£23,348,058
Datum Finance Limited	£23,323,746
HSS Hire Service Finance Limited	£23,318,000
Gray Forklift Group (Holdings) Limited	£23,296,078
Texas Group PLC	£23,290,788
Autoliv U.K. Holding Limited	£23,283,000
Data Intensity Holdings Limited	£23,280,720
Nelson (Northwest) Hotels Limited	£23,261,198
Lake District Holdings Limited	£23,251,234
PMC Fluidpower Limited	£23,229,962
Eric Wright Construction Limited	£23,212,804
Atmore Centres Limited	£23,205,436
Searchlight Electric Limited	£23,197,760
Manchester Health Academy	£23,186,000
Mini-Cam Enterprises Limited	£23,184,402
Cornthwaite Holdings Limited	£23,091,424
Road Maintenance Services (Holdings) Limited	£23,078,252
Cardinal Limited	£23,069,344
Thomas Armstrong (Construction) Limited	£23,067,270
Thermal Ceramics UK Limited	£23,067,000
Robinson Way Limited	£23,053,208
Equilibrium Healthcare Limited	£23,049,322
ECG Holdings (UK) Limited	£23,036,536
Arrow Global (Holdings) Limited	£23,034,000
Eamar Development (UK) Limited	£23,024,084
Liberty Gas Group Limited	£23,021,000
Kelda Non-Reg Holdco Limited	£23,010,000
Just Childcare Holdings Limited	£23,007,000
Stephenson Multi Academy Trust	£23,005,152
Havwoods Limited	£22,962,686
BWA Water Additives UK Limited	£22,950,000
Bradbury & Son (Buxton) Limited	£22,941,862
Aus-Bore Estates Limited	£22,929,356
MacKnight Holdings Limited	£22,926,030
Ellis Brigham Holdings Limited	£22,925,816
Equity Solutions Lift Investments Sheffield Limited	£22,916,630
Northern Star Academies Trust	£22,902,000
Wren Properties Limited	£22,896,928
Husco International Four Ltd	£22,890,616
Remel Europe Limited	£22,864,000
Hammonds of Knutsford PLC	£22,859,692
Housing Units Group Ltd	£22,859,000
Pets Choice Limited	£22,848,892
Promat UK Limited	£22,828,000
Restore Scan Limited	£22,819,000
Archwood Limited	£22,791,000
Cardinal Health U.K. 418 Limited	£22,788,000
Winander Group Holdings Limited	£22,783,178
Campus Living Villages (Sutton Bonington) UK Ltd	£22,780,000
Bibby Factors International Limited	£22,779,700
Strainstall Group Limited	£22,776,506
Carpenter Investments Ltd	£22,773,652
P H Property Holdings Limited	£22,769,468
Conlon Construction Limited	£22,767,000
Airedale Chemical Holdings Limited	£22,757,900
Omega Multi-Academy Trust	£22,757,000
Rickerby Holdings Limited	£22,730,598
Cheshire Datasystems Limited	£22,721,498
Kingscrown Properties Limited	£22,713,448
GM Business Support Limited	£22,700,908
Alston Investments Limited	£22,699,000
Marcus Worthington and Company Limited	£22,683,696
Sosamja Holdings Limited	£22,650,238
James Briggs Limited	£22,645,000
Sussex Custodial Services (Holdings) Limited	£22,644,686
Lancaster Partners (Holdings) Limited	£22,638,000
Bardsley Group Limited	£22,628,084
Norwest Foods International Limited	£22,623,404
Tetra Pak Limited	£22,623,000
Air-Serv Limited	£22,610,064
Stagecoach (North West) Limited	£22,607,000
Norwest Foods International Group Limited	£22,606,492
The Partington Group Limited	£22,605,322
Airvending Limited	£22,603,360
Furness Academies Trust	£22,587,000
C.D. Medical Limited	£22,578,432
Michael I Holdsworth Limited	£22,577,952
Ashbury Leaseholds Limited	£22,555,456
Quality Save Limited	£22,543,928
BPS Developments Limited	£22,539,452
Seatruck Panorama Ltd	£22,537,616
KRS Finance Ltd	£22,530,532
The Sovereign Trust	£22,523,816
Derian House Childrens Hospice	£22,511,108
Amscreen Group Limited	£22,502,484
Fisher Scientific Holding U.K., Limited	£22,500,000
Plevin Holdings Limited	£22,486,000
BHG Nominee Co (2) Limited	£22,480,000
Bruntwood Development Holdings Limited	£22,459,308
Calea UK Limited	£22,459,000
R.B. Business Park Limited	£22,456,340
Scent Global Ltd	£22,454,032
Seashell Trust	£22,441,000
B.I.P. (Holdings) Limited	£22,436,136
Britannia Treasury Services Limited	£22,397,278
Accumuli Limited	£22,377,000
Entasis Therapeutics Limited	£22,365,656
Lendlock International Ltd	£22,339,692
Americhem Holdings International Limited	£22,313,000
Axis Manchester LLP	£22,309,000
The Great Schools Trust	£22,265,444
X1 Aire Leeds Limited	£22,249,900
Billing Aquadrome Limited	£22,243,904
Seabrook Crisps Holdings Limited	£22,242,000
James Briggs (Holdings) Limited	£22,216,000
Lehvoss UK Limited	£22,207,444
Just Childcare Limited	£22,200,000
C.G.I. Group Holdings Limited	£22,168,350
CHT Holdings Limited	£22,161,000
Valtris Advanced Organics Limited	£22,128,926
Bradford Hide Company Limited	£22,127,244
Lake District Estates Company Limited	£22,125,766
Iceland International Limited	£22,118,000
Homes By Woodford Limited	£22,117,410
GP Strategies Training Limited	£22,117,000
Inhoco 2952 Limited	£22,111,080

Company	Value
Meter Serve 10 Limited	£22,075,000
A. Schulman Thermoplastic Compounds Limited	£22,067,000
ELC (Tranche 1) Limited	£22,045,412
Diamond Resorts Financial Services Limited	£22,040,228
Piolax Ltd.	£22,039,398
The Laurus Trust	£22,038,000
Cartwright Properties Limited	£22,030,966
Viridis Energy (Norgen) Limited	£22,007,000
Dantex Group Limited	£21,973,000
Destination Manchester Limited	£21,930,576
Bibby Trade Factors Limited	£21,930,240
Tiger Tim Products Limited	£21,928,000
Skipton Properties Limited	£21,916,012
Roundel Limited	£21,908,034
Cleland McIver Limited	£21,908,004
Vision Support Services Group Limited	£21,891,284
Land & Lakes (Anglesey) Limited	£21,879,720
Sensormatic Commercial/Industrial Limited	£21,878,942
Brother Investments Limited	£21,878,430
Integra Insurance Solutions Limited	£21,860,000
Blue Prism Limited	£21,842,000
Prestigious Textiles Limited	£21,841,024
Cumbria Waste Management Ltd.	£21,830,000
Marsh Finance & Commercial Limited	£21,819,544
The Barton Grange Group Limited	£21,818,548
Bowker Blackburn Limited	£21,809,000
Zeus Capital Limited	£21,805,180
Billerudkorsnas Beetham Ltd	£21,797,196
Zeus Group Limited	£21,796,780
Moorcroft Debt Recovery Limited	£21,793,806
Centre Island Development Company Limited	£21,786,080
Qualtex Global Limited	£21,776,492
Harrison Leisure UK Limited	£21,775,240
M2 Smile Limited	£21,775,000
Eurogold Group Limited	£21,766,876
DRPT Properties Limited	£21,758,820
Yodel Properties Limited	£21,757,000
Inovyn Energy Limited	£21,736,100
AAG UK Parent Limited	£21,728,384
Perspective Financial Group Limited	£21,719,958
Hartley Property Trust Limited	£21,718,512
Sussex Custodial Services Limited	£21,718,344
Klash Clothing Co. Ltd	£21,696,224
Danbro Holdings Limited	£21,674,152
Stoves Group Ltd	£21,664,000
Shared Access Ltd	£21,660,852
Holmeswood Coaches Limited	£21,658,418
Acebench Limited	£21,656,416
Metcalfe Plant Hire Limited	£21,646,428
Verdant Leisure Limited	£21,637,000
BOI Trading Company Limited	£21,632,392
Seatruck Pennant Ltd	£21,631,652
The ACC Liverpool Group Ltd	£21,585,218
Borderway Finance Limited	£21,578,156
Reddington Developments Limited	£21,556,000
Medtrade Products Limited	£21,552,000
Gordon Moon Properties Limited	£21,541,124
Massey Bros (Feeds) Ltd.	£21,527,308
Great Leighs Estates Limited	£21,499,816
George Downing Construction Ltd.	£21,476,324
Harnage Estates Limited	£21,449,316
Eurogold Groundworks & Civil Engr Contractors	£21,447,376
Amerdale Investments LLP	£21,441,484
Bagnall & Morris (Waste Services) Ltd	£21,433,726
Meridian Business Support Group PLC	£21,418,750
Sheffield & Regional Properties Limited	£21,394,052
Iceland Manufacturing Limited	£21,394,000
Community Dental Centres Limited	£21,390,878
DCC Mobility & Rehab Limited	£21,382,000
Southernplus Limited	£21,368,364
More 2 Life Ltd	£21,366,620
St James's Oncology SPC Holdings Ltd	£21,350,000
First Travel Solutions Limited	£21,339,000
C-Mac Automotive Holding Limited	£21,330,024
TSC Engineering Limited	£21,319,394
Henty Capital Limited	£21,312,876
Petros Development Company Limited	£21,310,200
Brabners LLP	£21,304,000
The Mines Advisory Group	£21,282,000
Justrite Holdings Ltd	£21,264,324
WPI Civil Engineering Limited	£21,260,424
GE Capital Group Services Limited	£21,253,000
Sudlows Group Limited	£21,250,000
Brookhouse (Preston) Limited	£21,248,000
Whitford Limited	£21,247,000
Hyde Investments Limited	£21,241,024
K3 Business Technologies Limited	£21,190,744
Endress + Hauser Limited	£21,182,742
Late Rooms Limited	£21,177,104
Hope Capital Limited	£21,164,774
N.R.L. Limited	£21,156,628
D.A. Harrison and Company Wigton	£21,150,778
Migo Enterprises Limited	£21,145,928
Redhead Freight Limited	£21,135,844
Risktec Solutions Limited	£21,131,344
G2S Limited	£21,116,236
Ess-Gee Investments Limited	£21,110,184
Westex (Carpets) Limited	£21,104,000
Fishawack Communications Limited	£21,086,952
Calderdale Hospital SPC Holdings Ltd	£21,081,000
Apogent UK Limited	£21,067,326
Brahm Fundco 2 Limited	£21,054,320
Ylem Energy Limited	£21,027,872
Calder Finco UK Ltd	£21,017,870
Quint Holdings Ltd	£21,016,622
Music Tribe Brands UK Ltd.	£21,001,440
Ingleby (1951) Limited	£21,000,786
Agility Logistics Solutions Limited	£20,993,652
Berwin Rubber Company Limited	£20,986,660
Birch Park Investments Limited	£20,981,650
Sune Sundorne Grove Solar Limited	£20,978,220
P. & B. (Foods) Limited	£20,977,524
Parkwood Leisure Holdings Limited	£20,945,000
Newton Academy Trust	£20,937,000
Elle R Leisure Limited	£20,931,252
Amplifon Limited	£20,916,000
Belle Vue Girls' School	£20,896,596
H. Dawson Sons and Company (Wool) Limited	£20,891,972
API Laminates Limited	£20,886,000
Mancunian Mercantile Investments Ltd	£20,865,996
AEE Renewables UK 31 Limited	£20,865,964
IGT-UK Gaming Limited	£20,853,000
Manuli Hydraulics UK Limited	£20,852,292
Baywater Healthcare UK Limited	£20,840,000
Guenther Management Limited	£20,828,374
Nynas Limited	£20,825,000
Coed du Hall Limited	£20,811,360
St. Ann's Hospice	£20,796,334
Castle Metals UK Limited	£20,785,580
The Residence Manchester Limited	£20,769,216
Cheadle Hulme School	£20,768,000
Accumuli (Holdings) Limited	£20,751,000
Thermo Fisher Scientific Holdings Europe Limited	£20,727,000
Cascade Holdings Limited	£20,723,482
Bilfinger Construction UK Limited	£20,722,000
GA Pet Food Partners Milling Limited	£20,710,000
H.E. Simm & Son Limited	£20,705,406
2 Moto Limited	£20,694,122
P.F.D.(Carlisle) Limited	£20,667,552
Holmes Chapel Comprehensive School & Sixth Form	£20,662,328
Brookhouse (Christchurch) Limited	£20,662,000
Adviserplus Holdings Limited	£20,646,000
Specialist Anodising Company Limited	£20,642,336
James Fisher Nuclear Holdings Limited	£20,624,048

Company	Value
J S Fleet Services Limited	£20,616,500
The Harmony Trust Ltd	£20,600,000
Express Solicitors Limited	£20,595,256
Community 1st Oldham (Chadderton) Limited	£20,570,140
Printbetter Limited	£20,569,588
Frank Bird (Poultry) Limited	£20,561,806
Galaxy Optical Services Limited	£20,561,000
Woodall Nicholson Holdings Limited	£20,543,064
F Wilson (Holdings) Limited	£20,517,236
Skills and Work Solutions Limited	£20,511,982
Chase Templeton Limited	£20,506,080
The Kay Group (UK) Limited	£20,485,324
Sentinel Performance Solutions Group Limited	£20,483,000
P.J. Livesey Living Space Limited	£20,481,052
Kent Topco Limited	£20,478,000
MU RAML Limited	£20,468,000
Bold International Properties Limited	£20,453,088
Dechra Finance Australia Limited	£20,450,000
UK Biobank Limited	£20,438,514
Flightcare Multiservices UK Limited	£20,434,000
Firow Limited	£20,415,092
Corning Limited	£20,413,000
Grif051 Limited	£20,390,896
Cheshire Mouldings & Woodturnings Limited	£20,388,552
Bruntwood Albert Square Limited	£20,386,000
Mobica Limited	£20,385,598
FMC Agro Limited	£20,374,888
Winnington CHP Limited	£20,371,000
The Priestley Academy Trust	£20,369,740
Beva Investments Limited	£20,360,060
Sunsave 17 (Castle Combe) Limited	£20,352,284
Rural Concepts Construction Limited	£20,325,900
Arjo Wiggins Services Limited	£20,293,000
Harnbury Holdings Ltd	£20,278,138
Partnership Media Group Limited	£20,265,456
Belden UK Holdings Limited	£20,258,520
Safeguard World International Limited	£20,249,540
Marantomark Limited	£20,219,388
Evans Vanodine International PLC	£20,189,306
Sonova UK Limited	£20,183,000
Engenda Group Limited	£20,177,276
KHL Newco Limited	£20,174,304
P & A J Cattee (Wholesale) Ltd.	£20,173,056
Hinde Holdings Limited	£20,172,838
Wardle Storeys (Group) Limited	£20,157,000
Burnage Academy for Boys	£20,153,000
Taskers PLC	£20,146,866
Totally Wicked Group Limited	£20,144,188
Energy Coast West Cumbria (Properties) Limited	£20,106,840
Air Energi Investments Limited	£20,082,000
Sodajo Limited	£20,075,830
CGC Events Limited	£20,069,726
Countrywide Freight Group Limited	£20,054,244
Heathfield Holdings Limited	£20,050,068
Kalibrate Technologies Limited	£20,045,180
Autism Initiatives (UK)	£20,031,000
Project Bullseye Bidco Limited	£20,027,728
R. Plevin & Sons Limited	£20,018,000
Lawton Group Limited	£20,004,000
Parkwood Leisure Investments Limited	£20,000,000
KRL (LR) Hold Co Limited	£20,000,000
Rural Concepts (Libya) Limited	£20,000,000
Chalkfree Limited	£19,993,000
Cumbria Community Foundation	£19,988,192
Old Trafford Supporters Club Limited	£19,982,000
Kaman Composites - UK Limited	£19,941,000
Oxford Property Trading Ltd.	£19,904,000
Hobs Liver Limited	£19,901,692
Canvas Holidays Limited	£19,897,000
Prowell Ltd	£19,890,276
Boys Holdings PLC	£19,882,812
H.B. Fuller U.K. Limited	£19,873,486
Redwood TTM Ltd	£19,871,696
Liverpool Airport (Intermediate) No.1 Limited	£19,871,612
Simginuity Limited	£19,862,956
Paintfirst Limited	£19,841,608
GE Commercial Finance Limited	£19,840,000
The David Lewis Centre	£19,839,000
Mutley Group Limited	£19,834,296
Huntercombe Properties (Frenchay) Limited	£19,834,000
European Metal Recycling (International) Limited	£19,828,000
Making Space	£19,821,792
Topgrade Sportswear Limited	£19,820,000
Thomas Armstrong (Aggregates) Limited	£19,818,798
Greenhalgh's Craft Bakery Limited	£19,817,708
N.I.S. Holdings Limited	£19,816,000
Uniroyal Global (Europe) Limited	£19,801,000
James Fisher MFE Limited	£19,796,088
Safic-Alcan UK Limited	£19,779,556
Carole Nash Insurance Consultants Limited	£19,762,424
Willan Investments Limited	£19,760,412
Maltacourt Group Limited	£19,758,912
Wiggett Construction Group Limited	£19,757,920
James Fisher Subtech Group Limited	£19,753,288
Enhance Academy Trust	£19,751,000
Swift Technical (Europe) Limited	£19,749,000
PH Alderley Park LLP	£19,739,724
Fideliti Ltd	£19,733,244
Seneca Secured Lending Limited	£19,725,848
T L Dallas & Co Limited	£19,719,796
RSR Limited	£19,709,656
Bespoke Home Interior Design Limited	£19,696,000
Entertainment Magpie Limited	£19,683,000
Mullberry Homes Limited	£19,682,704
Stocks Hall Care Homes Limited	£19,679,560
FocusEducation (Lincolnshire) Limited	£19,664,000
Deckers Hospitality Group Limited	£19,656,108
Eurosonic Group Limited	£19,650,630
P H Holt Foundation	£19,649,758
Bugle Inn Motor Company (Holdings) Limited	£19,649,000
Bugle Inn Motor Company Limited	£19,648,000
S.J.Bargh Limited	£19,642,728
Peel Overseas Limited	£19,630,140
Houses for Homes Limited	£19,616,674
Multistar Container Transport Limited	£19,608,656
Tangerine Confectionery Group Limited	£19,608,000
Seddon Investments Limited	£19,601,600
Airedale Catering Equipment Group Limited	£19,598,000
Harry Peers & Co Limited	£19,574,806
Coffey Construction Limited	£19,551,872
WHT Holdings Limited	£19,529,420
Pemberton Park and Leisure Homes Limited	£19,527,592
Halliwell Jones (Wilmslow) Limited	£19,472,282
Ionics (U.K.) Limited	£19,456,000
Methven UK Limited	£19,455,964
Darwin (Cheddar Woods) Limited	£19,444,472
Thomas Hardy Holdings Limited	£19,423,000
Vinnolit Hillhouse Ltd	£19,421,000
Orthios Eco Parks (Anglesey) Limited	£19,418,656
Style Group UK Limited	£19,416,000
Urmston Grammar	£19,394,000
SPM Plastics U.K. Limited	£19,388,000
Kids Planet Day Nurseries Limited	£19,386,124
G.B.B.Estates Limited	£19,385,560
Rethink Professional Services Limited	£19,384,826
Ritrama (U.K.) Limited	£19,378,542
Community 1st Sheffield (Holdco) Limited	£19,369,812
Future Industrial Services Limited	£19,352,000
Eversheds Sutherland Legal Services Limited	£19,348,884
Oldham Property Partnerships Limited	£19,348,000
Liverpool Science Park Limited	£19,344,574
Brennan Enterprise Limited	£19,333,160
D. Morgan PLC	£19,321,476
James Fisher Everard Limited	£19,317,816

Powell (UK) Limited	£19,313,000	Templeton Holdings Limited	£18,660,856
Luby Group (UK) Limited	£19,288,472	McGoff Construction Limited	£18,660,260
Driver Consult Limited	£19,280,204	Oliver James Associates Group Limited	£18,650,536
Sunsave 10 (Fareham) Ltd	£19,271,636	Heritage Attractions Limited	£18,633,026
Liberty Group Investments Limited	£19,211,000	Cardinal Maritime Limited	£18,628,068
Parkwood Leisure Limited	£19,201,000	Affiniture Cards Limited	£18,614,308
Medway Ports Limited	£19,200,000	Future Heights Limited	£18,607,444
St Francis Xavier's College	£19,194,694	Assurant Life Limited	£18,603,000
Oliver James Associates Limited	£19,174,752	Co-operative Community Investment Foundation	£18,599,856
Thomas Milburn (Property) Limited	£19,170,704	Sune Prestop Park Limited	£18,595,744
Survitec Service & Distribution Limited	£19,154,000	BPD Holdings Limited	£18,593,720
William Loughran Limited	£19,147,836	Crosslane Investments Limited	£18,593,120
Chapel House Holdings Ltd	£19,114,972	Broker Direct PLC	£18,582,990
Kepak Kirkham Limited	£19,107,364	Fagan & Whalley Limited	£18,564,474
The University of Manchester Innovation Centre Ltd	£19,103,836	Tom Martin Metal Holdings 2011 Limited	£18,561,000
Cidari Education Limited	£19,102,192	Virtual Internet (UK) Limited	£18,558,026
Beesley & Fildes Limited	£19,101,092	Riverstone Properties Ltd	£18,552,748
Unifrax Emission Control Europe Ltd	£19,095,490	Renthal Limited	£18,546,718
API Foils Limited	£19,086,000	Soper Group Holdings Ltd	£18,536,928
Project Play Midco 1 Limited	£19,083,000	Precision Polymer Engineering Limited	£18,533,398
Vision Support Services Limited	£19,077,944	Courtesy Shoes Limited	£18,529,744
Compass Minerals Storage & Archives Limited	£19,054,000	Calder Holdings Limited	£18,520,000
Bruntwood Oxford Road Holdings Limited	£19,051,000	Cranmer Education Trust	£18,520,000
Sovereign Chemicals Limited	£19,046,000	Crawford Healthcare Limited	£18,508,578
Allscripts Healthcare (IT) UK Ltd	£19,046,000	Pfaudler Limited	£18,499,568
The Rowan Learning Trust	£19,043,000	Seatruck Ferries Ltd	£18,491,482
Career Connect	£19,042,668	Benteler Distribution Limited	£18,488,978
Leep Holdings (Utilities) Limited	£19,041,000	Jones Stroud Insulations Limited	£18,478,764
Forrest Corporate Limited	£19,041,000	Bridgemere Development Capital PLC	£18,476,788
Newtco Limited	£19,039,560	Safeguard World International Holdings Limited	£18,448,580
The King David High School	£19,023,328	Character World Bidco Limited	£18,448,112
Campus Living Villages (Salford) UK Limited	£19,015,724	Kverneland Group UK Limited	£18,444,000
The Hub Community Healthcare Limited	£19,004,344	Valdeco Ltd	£18,440,476
B & W Plant Hire and Sales Limited	£18,983,550	AJ Bell Management Limited	£18,434,000
Stoneygate 48 Limited	£18,966,416	Seabrook Crisps Limited	£18,430,000
Grade A Alternative Properties Limited	£18,957,604	Alan Howard (Stockport) Limited	£18,419,922
M & S Logistics Limited	£18,954,086	Lexington Catering Limited	£18,409,752
Harley Scott Holdings Limited	£18,954,078	Rowlinson Group Holdings Limited	£18,407,760
Brink's Global Services, Ltd.	£18,950,552	Lanxess Urethanes UK Ltd	£18,405,000
Frodsham Wind Farm Holdings Limited	£18,919,132	Mast Group Limited	£18,402,916
Entertainment Magpie Group Limited	£18,913,000	Hira Company Limited (The)	£18,394,568
Nesscoinvsat Limited	£18,895,942	The Queen Katherine School Multi Academy Trust	£18,388,988
House & Home (Lettings) Ltd	£18,888,938	XYZ Building Developments Limited	£18,373,920
Greenbank Technology Limited	£18,874,896	T&K Gallagher Limited	£18,358,408
Taylor Engineering & Plastics Limited	£18,872,644	Affymetrix, UK Ltd.	£18,346,982
Halliwell Jones Limited	£18,871,872	Univar Specialty Consumables Limited	£18,346,000
Jessgrove Limited	£18,870,960	ESPA International (UK) Limited	£18,342,870
O.P.P. (Westhulme) Limited	£18,870,000	John Hogg Technical Solutions Limited	£18,339,646
Phenomenex Limited	£18,864,320	Capital Bank Leasing 9 Limited	£18,327,000
Industrial Scientific Holdings UK Ltd	£18,863,642	Medlock Medical Limited	£18,326,000
Skelhurst Limited	£18,845,648	Sun Branding Solutions Ltd	£18,314,132
Oliver Ashworth Limited	£18,843,252	Dacsa Limited	£18,293,000
McGoff Group LLP	£18,840,634	Bolton Car Centre Limited	£18,291,746
The Bollington Group (Holdings) Limited	£18,838,636	Carefoot PLC	£18,282,460
Peel Property (Partnerships) Limited	£18,830,840	Penmarric Limited	£18,278,776
Sterilin Limited	£18,827,000	Mann + Hummel Vokes Air Treatment Holdings Limited	£18,276,000
Innospec Active Chemicals Limited	£18,812,000	Albany International Limited	£18,266,000
Community Windpower Limited	£18,778,364	Halewood International Holdings (Overseas) Limited	£18,261,000
Ginger Acquisition Company Limited	£18,777,776	Lowry Capital Limited	£18,256,702
Arlington Aerospace Limited	£18,774,000	Streason Limited	£18,234,796
ABS Consulting Ltd.	£18,773,348	Ashley Wilde Holdings Limited	£18,226,844
Classic Collection Holidays Limited	£18,768,408	M & A Pharmachem Limited	£18,205,124
Alfred Bagnall and Sons Limited	£18,765,400	Mitchells of Lancaster (Brewers) Limited	£18,203,000
Financial & Legal Insurance Company Ltd	£18,762,462	Melba Group Limited	£18,191,344
Focus International Limited	£18,735,000	Taylor Shaw Limited	£18,185,512
CSA Group Testing UK Limited	£18,731,916	Denholm Global Logistics Limited	£18,176,634
Halliwell Jones Holdings Limited	£18,725,984	Goodwood Holdings Limited	£18,176,472
The Liverpool Institute for Performing Arts	£18,711,086	Wetherby Building Systems Limited	£18,175,336
Laila's Fine Foods Limited	£18,704,530	James Robinson Fibres Limited	£18,164,164
Vogt Solar Ltd	£18,674,832	Skanem UK Limited	£18,159,000
Driver Hire Investments Group Limited	£18,666,760	PIMCO 2451 Limited	£18,126,056
Diverse Acquisitions Limited	£18,664,000	Vitaflo (International) Limited	£18,122,000

Rickerby Limited	£18,096,576	Street Crane Company Limited	£17,430,042
Melba Products Holdings Limited	£18,092,770	Computionics Group Limited	£17,394,176
Hive Topco Limited	£18,092,204	Four Seasons Homes No.4 Limited	£17,391,000
Phoenix Court Blackburn Limited	£18,089,118	Flairfax Limited	£17,377,288
Aptus Utilities Limited	£18,082,980	Fryett's Fabrics Limited	£17,363,228
Port of Sheerness Wind Farm Limited	£18,068,354	Richard Haworth Limited	£17,347,206
Scenic Tours (UK) Ltd	£18,060,896	Palace Chemicals Limited	£17,331,030
Harrison & Hetherington Limited	£18,013,592	Bilfinger Industrial Automation Services Limited	£17,327,970
Character World Holdco Limited	£18,007,836	Simon Jersey Ltd	£17,321,092
Welspun Home Textiles UK Limited	£18,003,000	Drillwave Limited	£17,320,000
Brynteg Solar Limited	£17,980,028	GP Strategies Holdings Limited	£17,316,000
William Rainford (Holdings) Limited	£17,936,008	151 Products Limited	£17,305,530
TSC Foods Group Limited	£17,932,432	FSHC Developments (Properties) Limited	£17,302,000
Trendsetter Home Furnishings Limited	£17,920,424	Qualtex UK Limited	£17,301,248
Doorway Holdings Limited	£17,910,860	Bobst Manchester Ltd	£17,289,000
Dantex Graphics Limited	£17,903,000	South Westmorland Multi Academy Trust	£17,286,044
Southport Learning Trust	£17,889,000	X1 The Gateway Limited	£17,275,498
Omnicell Limited	£17,871,000	Infinity 30 Limited	£17,273,974
The Hub Community Healthcare Ph Limited	£17,869,040	Taziker Industrial Limited	£17,268,000
Selden Research Limited	£17,866,424	OBG Finance Holding Limited	£17,267,776
Darwin (Hawkchurch Country Park) Ltd	£17,865,112	Inprova Group Ltd	£17,256,000
Regional & City Airports (Blackpool) Holdings Limited	£17,852,206	Sharples School A Multi Academy Trust	£17,250,852
Prisma Developments Limited	£17,845,944	Beneficial House (Birmingham) Regeneration LLP	£17,236,944
B. Dugdale & Son Limited	£17,839,244	IESA A & D Limited	£17,233,000
Key Group Midco 2 Limited	£17,836,558	Lunesdale Learning Trust	£17,229,258
Key Group Midco 1 Limited	£17,836,556	Bespoke Hotels Chester Limited	£17,223,894
Stevens Equipment Rental Limited	£17,824,864	Knutsford Multi Academy Trust	£17,214,748
Dixon Group Europe Ltd	£17,818,328	EDM Limited	£17,207,222
Cobaco Holdings Limited	£17,811,658	Birkenhead School	£17,191,044
Impact Development Training International Limited	£17,808,576	Foden Investments Limited	£17,181,414
Billington Foodservice Limited	£17,806,986	Molnlycke Health Care Limited	£17,174,000
Majorstage Limited	£17,762,692	Cancede Limited	£17,166,000
Edge Wear Properties Limited	£17,755,418	The Contact Specialists Ltd	£17,163,310
Cruden Group Limited	£17,744,246	Seven Scent Limited	£17,160,000
Sune Project1 Ltd	£17,726,316	Northwood Tissue (Disley) Limited	£17,158,760
Campus Living Villages (Portfolio Finance) UK Limited	£17,713,780	Qiagen Limited	£17,158,000
BMP Europe Limited	£17,712,656	Brookson Limited	£17,146,996
Eurostation Limited	£17,711,920	Z&D Property Investments Limited	£17,135,496
Accrol Holdings Limited	£17,691,000	Avecto Ltd	£17,129,292
System 3 Limited	£17,684,204	HPP Pinnacle Limited	£17,122,568
The Bury Grammar Schools Trustee Limited	£17,663,000	PCT Healthcare (Properties) Limited	£17,119,210
Assura Aspire UK Limited	£17,661,500	Coordination Group Publications Ltd	£17,107,764
On The Beach Beds Limited	£17,645,000	Project Finland Bidco Limited	£17,095,784
Kacoo Group Limited	£17,643,788	Advance Uranium Asset Management Limited	£17,094,438
The Flame Group Limited	£17,639,000	Exedy Clutch Europe Limited	£17,079,824
Local Pensions Partnership Investments Ltd	£17,622,000	Energy Coast West Cumbria Limited	£17,064,836
Pentre Group Limited	£17,598,776	Ribble Packaging Limited	£17,059,424
Deepstore Holdings Limited	£17,595,000	Fairfield High School for Girls	£17,049,000
Beechfield Brands Limited	£17,586,334	Eddie Rockers Limited	£17,044,480
Jacobson Group Limited	£17,584,000	Cornthwaite Agricultural Limited	£17,039,980
Domu Brands Limited	£17,577,632	Principal Healthcare Finance (UK) No.1 Limited	£17,022,000
Hurstwood Properties (A) Limited	£17,576,476	St Margaret's Church of England Academy	£17,018,000
Drive Devilbiss Sidhil Limited	£17,574,000	Rainbow Cosmetics (Manchester) Limited	£17,017,742
Kings Solutions Group Limited	£17,571,000	CRP Print & Packaging Limited	£17,000,000
Premaitha Health PLC	£17,563,234	Synexus Limited	£16,999,698
Pinco 2033 Limited	£17,556,760	Vita York 1 Limited	£16,993,000
Aptus Group Limited	£17,547,768	The Hub Community Healthcare Midco Limited	£16,985,912
Leyland Holding Company Limited	£17,544,000	Exoteric Metering Limited	£16,979,000
Withgill Farm Limited	£17,537,896	RMSpumptools Limited	£16,978,528
G.B.A. Services Limited	£17,535,516	Doric Group Limited	£16,957,156
Willan UK Limited	£17,532,252	Education Solutions Speke Limited	£16,954,286
Barron Wood Distribution Limited	£17,530,324	Bluethorn Developments Limited	£16,950,914
Computionics Limited	£17,521,100	Physical Properties Testing Ltd.	£16,950,818
Arthouse Midco Limited	£17,521,076	Amann Threads UK Limited	£16,949,362
Nitecrest Limited	£17,511,648	Whitecross Healthcare Limited	£16,942,000
This Is Protos LLP	£17,489,276	Whitecross Group Limited	£16,938,000
Altrad NSG Limited	£17,466,700	Retstone Limited	£16,927,542
Rainbow Cosmetics (Holdings) Limited	£17,450,658	Totally Local Company Limited	£16,927,000
William Fishwick & Son Limited	£17,448,492	AMEC Nuclear M & O Limited	£16,922,000
KRL (LR) Limited	£17,435,406	Johnson Group Properties PLC	£16,921,000
Pye Motors,Limited	£17,435,020	Primopost Limited	£16,920,000
Clear Business Limited	£17,432,500	J Moss Developments Limited	£16,908,624

Royal Liverpool Philharmonic Society (The) £16,906,000
Palletower (G.B.) Limited £16,904,396
The Little Greene Paint Company Limited £16,899,564
Kotug Smit Towage UK Limited £16,899,500
Associated Security Services Holdings Limited £16,889,640
Project One Consulting Limited £16,887,894
Robinrate Limited £16,876,960
Merry Fox Stud Limited £16,870,144
Bents Garden Centre Limited £16,865,520
MDS Global Ltd £16,863,000
S.R.G. Apparel PLC £16,856,166
QEGS Blackburn Academy Trust £16,854,918
EMC Properties Limited £16,849,620
William Kenyon & Sons Limited £16,848,080
Middleton Academy Limited £16,833,000
Caygill Holdings Limited £16,830,668
Harewood Venture Capital Ltd £16,825,344
Holland Shellfish International UK Ltd £16,822,644
Goodison Park Stadium Limited £16,817,132
GE Capital Corporation (Leasing) Limited £16,797,262
SPX Flow Technology London Limited £16,792,000
Barros Trading Ltd £16,790,036
Hollowood Chemists Limited £16,789,268
Warrant Group Limited £16,787,680
MCH Intermediate Limited £16,778,476
Ascot Properties UK Limited £16,775,223
Randomlight Limited £16,772,518
Deva Victrix Holdings Limited £16,769,000
Money Advice Group Limited £16,767,988
Knightsbridge Insolvency Services Limited £16,766,884
1 Spinningfields Developments Ltd £16,764,154
W.O.&J.Wilson Limited £16,750,725
E S Management Services Limited £16,747,939
Leach Holdings Limited £16,747,341
Centriq Group Limited £16,745,000
Curtins Group Limited £16,743,022
Crossco (1317) Limited £16,723,863
Oak Trees Multi Academy Trust £16,723,000
J. Holland & Sons Limited £16,719,031
Blackburn Chemicals Limited £16,714,472
Bernham Ltd £16,706,040
Curtins Consulting Limited £16,689,457
Survitec Aud Newco Limited £16,672,821
Survitec Global Solutions Limited £16,670,042
MBH Investments Ltd £16,664,193
The British Cycling Federation £16,662,272
Heritage Great Britain PLC £16,647,764
Gweco 510 Limited £16,644,015
John Shaw and Son Limited £16,643,836
Dorbiere Limited £16,638,210
Aim Engineering Limited £16,614,000
Benross Marketing Limited £16,611,392
Mitras Automotive (UK) Limited £16,600,847
Bibby Trade Services Limited £16,598,695
Shakespeare Monofilament UK Limited £16,595,713
Alsico Laucuba Ltd £16,592,218
Guyson (Holdings) Limited £16,584,154
IFG Drake Limited £16,570,000
Sysgroup PLC £16,569,000
Mortgage Agency Services Number One Limited £16,568,000
The Alchemist Bar & Restaurant Limited £16,564,286
New World Trading Company (UK) Holdings Limited £16,533,644
Four Seasons Health Care (Capital) Limited £16,524,000
Moto GB Limited £16,508,033
Waddicar Property Limited £16,504,883
Wentworth Miller Holdings Limited £16,500,002
Rutmark Properties Limited £16,494,702
W Howard Group Ltd £16,493,409
Texecom Limited £16,491,544
Hillfoot Steel Limited £16,486,624
J M Holdings Limited £16,482,789
Pentre Holdings Limited £16,476,874
Heatons Truck Group Ltd £16,466,000
The University of Manchester Worldwide Limited £16,461,644
Hardroad Limited £16,448,573
Scotts Hire Limited £16,444,590
Lyndhurst Shoe Company Limited £16,431,089
Styrene Packaging & Insulation Limited £16,424,709
Armstrong Pumps Limited £16,414,482
Camfil Limited £16,412,000
Carrylift Holdings Limited £16,410,755
Willowfox Limited £16,396,570
Gutteridge Haskins & Davey Limited £16,392,223
Prismo Road Markings Limited £16,392,036
Personalised Travel Services Limited £16,380,000
Project Finland Topco Limited £16,379,450
Road Maintenance Services Limited £16,378,064
Euroresins UK Limited £16,367,031
Ludgate Estates Limited (The) £16,366,241
Drighlington Fibres Limited £16,359,000
Akinika Limited £16,356,000
Surecalm Healthcare Ltd £16,355,513
Denim Merchants (UK) Limited £16,343,178
Armathwaite Hall Hotel Limited £16,339,886
Tipografic Limited £16,338,241
Interactive Investor Trading Limited £16,326,305
SMD (Holdings) Limited £16,324,236
Crest Oil Holdings Ltd £16,324,078
MUTV Limited £16,308,627
Simpsonhaugh and Partners Group LLP £16,301,034
Merchant Rentals Limited £16,289,851
Hopecrest Investments Limited £16,283,110
Clitheroe Royal Grammar School £16,279,000
Dams Furniture Limited £16,275,352
Akinika Debt Recovery Limited £16,269,000
HVF Limited £16,269,000
Mackintosh Limited £16,266,956
GE Real Estate European Finance Limited £16,265,017
Swift Engineering (Azerbaijan) Limited £16,265,000
Klinger Limited £16,253,460
Mistral Asset Finance Limited £16,242,043
Teesbay Retail Park (1) Limited £16,229,314
SPS (EU) Limited £16,224,000
Wellington School £16,222,000
Tetrosyl Express Limited £16,220,000
D P Williams Group Limited £16,215,751
Promocean No 1 Limited £16,190,604
Buxton Press Limited £16,188,802
Metronet (UK) Limited £16,179,000
Riverside Flooring Limited £16,177,162
Pario Leisure Group Limited £16,174,087
Brancaster Care Homes Limited £16,165,041
Chadwicks of Bury Limited £16,163,000
Brookhouse (Alexandra) Limited £16,161,000
Vodafone Automotive UK Limited £16,156,135
Brookhouse Chichester Limited £16,142,000
Allegro Corporation Limited £16,133,598
Bradley Topco Limited £16,129,720
Micrown Limited £16,121,408
Arthouse Limited £16,114,274
Abney Trust £16,106,212
Chariet Limited £16,094,281
The County High School, Leftwich £16,090,000
City Suites Manchester Limited £16,076,000
Icon Health and Fitness Limited £16,064,113
Michael Abakhan Limited £16,062,197
Airedale Catering Equipment Limited £16,058,000
Culimeta-Saveguard Limited £16,054,014
Pentagon HS Limited £16,052,570
Oliver Ashworth (Holdings) Limited £16,051,815
T.K. Components Limited £16,051,000
Melba Products Limited £16,042,222
Gusto Restaurants Limited £16,031,000
H. B. Projects Limited £16,024,207

Company	Value
Urban Splash Assets 2 Limited	£16,024,184
Omega Engineering Limited	£16,019,000
Proximo Limited	£16,015,868
Concept Life Sciences Analytical & Dev Services	£16,013,610
Dale Apartments LLP	£16,010,298
Shorrock Trichem Limited	£16,001,280
Patrick Properties Holdings Limited	£15,995,175
Meadow Foods (Holdings) Limited	£15,987,000
James Brearley & Sons Limited	£15,979,998
Arizonaco Limited	£15,954,986
SOG Limited	£15,929,833
SL Mortgage Funding No 1 Limited	£15,918,129
Woodall Nicholson Limited	£15,905,459
USS Heritors Limited	£15,892,850
Newhall Group Limited (The)	£15,887,766
The Saxon Crosses Mat	£15,886,000
Ainscough Investments Limited	£15,884,570
Daisy Corporate Services Limited	£15,884,000
W P I Surfacing Limited	£15,881,290
Princes Dock Hotel Limited	£15,880,000
Beechfield Brands Holdings Limited	£15,877,000
The Big Life Company Limited	£15,866,571
Peel Media Digital (Holdings) Limited	£15,856,000
Ikonic Technology Limited	£15,853,839
Harrison & Clough,Limited	£15,851,211
Digital World Centre Limited	£15,850,000
The British Millerain Company Limited	£15,818,310
Kadant UK Holdings Limited	£15,812,130
Telesign Mobile Limited	£15,797,375
Wm Morrison LP 2 Limited	£15,792,000
Community Foundations for Lancashire & Merseyside	£15,777,249
Lunar Holdings Limited	£15,768,404
Narbourne Limited	£15,767,233
Husco International Partners LLP	£15,755,942
Huyton Asphalt Limited	£15,749,946
Harry Peers Steelwork Limited	£15,746,789
TJA Motors Limited	£15,712,000
Meade-King,Robinson & Company Limited	£15,711,228
M53 Motors Limited	£15,711,000
NW Trading (Holdings) Limited	£15,707,827
Linteum (Lewisham) Limited	£15,695,591
Linteum (Lewisham) Holdings Limited	£15,695,591
E.S.A. Limited	£15,691,529
Olympic Oils Limited	£15,677,885
Worthington Mancap LLP	£15,671,756
Bentley & Bentley Limited	£15,660,874
Bardsley Construction Holdings Limited	£15,660,832
North West Lung Centre	£15,652,579
Surrenda-Link Mortgage Holdings Limited	£15,649,706
AJ Bell Limited	£15,649,000
Sefton Holdings Limited	£15,646,317
Congleton Multi-Academy Trust	£15,622,000
The Wordsworth Trust	£15,621,000
Darwin Contract Management Limited	£15,618,077
PTS Property Limited	£15,608,353
Nalco Manufacturing Ltd	£15,602,000
Ballyclare Limited	£15,589,548
Praetura Commercial Finance Limited	£15,587,967
James Cropper Converting Limited	£15,584,000
Aintree Plastics (Holdings) Limited	£15,583,511
Tensar Technologies Limited	£15,578,000
Longfield Chemicals Limited	£15,572,236
Bodycote Surface Technology Limited	£15,568,000
Olympus Engineering Limited	£15,555,891
Armstrong Integrated Limited	£15,535,477
Williams Tarr Holdings Ltd	£15,534,821
Outdoor & Sports Company Limited	£15,532,123
Ibco Limited	£15,526,153
Portable Foods Manufacturing Company Limited	£15,518,000
Bradley Bidco Limited	£15,507,133
Bradley Park Waste Management Limited	£15,503,794
Patterson and Rothwell Limited	£15,502,667
Hillcroft Ltd	£15,501,591
Invent and Invest	£15,487,964
North West Truck Services Limited	£15,485,000
F. Wilson (Insurance Brokers) Limited	£15,479,070
R N Wooler & Co (Developments) Limited	£15,478,157
LF Logistics Holdings (UK) Limited	£15,458,000
Loven Care Homes Limited	£15,456,962
Applethwaite Limited	£15,452,753
Business Energy Solutions Ltd	£15,438,703
Blue Machinery (Group) PLC	£15,437,232
Detrafford Sky Gardens Ltd	£15,431,956
Longfield Chemicals (Holdings) Limited	£15,430,588
Complete Medical Group Worldwide Limited	£15,427,000
Collinson Holdings Limited	£15,422,072
Glossop Caravans Limited	£15,420,527
Northern Rail Holdings Limited	£15,418,000
Hive Bidco Limited	£15,415,594
Claremont Group Interiors Limited	£15,409,669
Bibby Transport Limited	£15,398,170
Help Your Claim Limited	£15,387,739
Browallia Holdings Limited	£15,378,839
Warrington Sports Holdings Limited	£15,371,705
Arrow Global Receivables Management Limited	£15,371,000
Tytherington School	£15,369,000
Marbury Properties (Chester) LLP	£15,364,027
Granby Care Limited	£15,363,000
Holding Holding Company Limited	£15,354,417
David M. Robinson Limited	£15,351,624
Crosthwaite Hotels (Westmorland) Limited	£15,346,507
Ariens UK Limited	£15,344,201
CSA Group Europe Holdings Limited	£15,343,548
Proseat Limited Liability Partnership	£15,341,000
Sun Valley Limited	£15,332,031
Stanleybet International Limited	£15,323,000
Euro Options Limited	£15,320,533
Heads Recruitment Limited	£15,319,434
Sherborne Upholstery Limited	£15,311,740
Crawford Woundcare Limited	£15,308,622
Jaymel Limited	£15,305,492
Lonsdale Holdings Limited	£15,304,891
Mediterranean Projects Limited	£15,300,910
Liverpool Airport Hotel Limited	£15,289,295
J. Rosenthal and Son Limited	£15,286,267
Ensco 818 Limited	£15,278,350
Lancashire Schools PSP Limited	£15,262,000
Thinksmart Europe Limited	£15,260,971
MU Commercial Holdings Limited	£15,260,000
MU Commercial Holdings Junior Limited	£15,260,000
Guy Pilkington Memorial Home Limited (The)	£15,259,727
Rushcliffe (St Annes PCC) Limited	£15,253,249
VQ Developments Limited	£15,227,860
Ferratum UK Ltd	£15,223,117
Hamsard 3425 Limited	£15,203,299
Signature Shankly Limited	£15,200,638
Morson Projects Limited	£15,191,000
Czajka Properties Limited	£15,184,349
Grosvenor Farms Limited	£15,170,000
Cleveland Transit Ltd.	£15,159,000
RMS International UK Ltd	£15,154,831
Sale Grammar School	£15,135,000
Real Estate Two Limited	£15,118,845
Eldapoint Limited	£15,116,634
Forthright Finance Limited	£15,108,000
Knutsford Properties Limited	£15,106,000
Ridge Medical Limited	£15,102,414
Flanagan Group Limited	£15,099,109
Bunk-a-Bin Limited	£15,078,352
Trac Mexico Limited	£15,069,000
Hill's Panel Products Limited	£15,058,621
SPC Group Holdings Limited	£15,057,420
Boden & Davies Limited	£15,047,899
Fine Decor Wallcoverings Limited	£15,036,958

Company	Turnover
Kacoo Fashion Ltd	£15,032,962
Lunar Caravans Limited	£15,026,764
European Braking Systems Ltd	£15,017,663
Springhill Care Group Limited	£15,014,053
Grif040 Limited	£15,004,672
Innovation Birmingham Limited	£15,000,275
Advanced Biotechnologies Limited	£14,995,000
Fenwick Street Investments Limited	£14,986,649
Kingsway Leasing Limited	£14,981,897
Armstrong Brooks Limited	£14,975,103
Amelia Exports Ltd	£14,973,280
Zedra Trust Company (UK) Limited	£14,950,000
Atlantic Steel Processing Limited	£14,948,260
The Howells Group PLC	£14,927,537
The Bay Learning Trust	£14,926,000
BASF Agricultural Specialities Limited	£14,914,000
Expect Distribution Limited	£14,897,299
Mason & Vaughan Group Ltd	£14,895,344
Ormiston Bolingbroke Academy Trust	£14,883,000
Marblegrange Limited	£14,865,000
Allied London Leeds Holding Company Two Limited	£14,857,405
Sherwood Homes Limited	£14,844,865
Joloda (International) Limited	£14,841,714
Baas Construction Limited	£14,836,141
Bond Turner Limited	£14,831,736
Red Production Company Limited	£14,831,616
Imtech Engineering Services North Ltd	£14,830,000
Woodclay Limited	£14,824,865
Chrystal Consulting Limited	£14,824,460
Chrystal Holdings Limited	£14,824,360
South Craven Academy Trust	£14,819,000
The Hamblin Education Trust	£14,817,000
Eternity Capital Management Limited	£14,813,789
Key Group Topco Limited	£14,812,978
Preston Board and Packaging Limited	£14,809,000
Bollington Insurance Brokers Limited	£14,798,468
Wrendal Holdings Limited	£14,791,014
Sir Jacob Behrens & Sons,Limited	£14,771,391
Eric Wright Civil Engineering Limited	£14,769,274
Hiden Analytical Limited	£14,760,050
Community 1st Oldham Tranche 2 Limited	£14,758,338
Upton Hall School Fcj	£14,758,000
A.M. Seafoods Limited	£14,755,406
TFHC 2015 Limited	£14,752,000
Next Generation Health Limited	£14,740,946
N-Sea Offshore Ltd	£14,736,363
Micad Investments Holdings Limited	£14,733,218
Peter Black Footwear & Accessories Limited	£14,732,000
Red-D-Arc (UK) Limited	£14,731,390
Newstar Group Limited	£14,719,930
Digital Projection International Limited	£14,719,000
Merlin Diesel Systems Ltd	£14,713,502
Doncaster Sheffield Airport Limited	£14,710,565
Wiggett Homes Limited	£14,706,321
MRC Flangefitt Limited	£14,705,335
Secret Potions Limited	£14,694,470
Arthouse Holding Limited	£14,687,913
Postcode Anywhere Holdings Limited	£14,683,000
Boulting Environmental Services Limited	£14,681,393
The Grosvenor - Pulford Hotel Limited	£14,679,208
The Ticketline Network Limited	£14,678,566
Peel Media Management (Holdings) Limited	£14,675,000
Douglas Valley Finance Company Limited	£14,673,405
Bakers (Area 1) Limited	£14,667,000
M N Holdings Limited	£14,659,411
2020 Legal Limited	£14,638,069
Boels Rental Limited	£14,633,292
Supply UK Investments Limited	£14,633,292
BC21.0 Ltd	£14,627,137
Neenah Red Bridge International Limited	£14,623,313
Rigisystems Ltd	£14,621,008
Celtpower Limited	£14,616,000
Leisure Parks Limited	£14,615,296
S. L. L. Properties Limited	£14,612,609
Carman (Holdings) Limited	£14,601,339
Expalkan II Closed Scheme Limited	£14,590,000
Linmere Limited	£14,585,401
AMEC Nuclear Projects Limited	£14,584,000
Spellman & Walker Group Limited	£14,575,391
Kverneland Holding (UK) Limited	£14,570,000
Redrow Real Estate Limited	£14,558,662
LDF Operations Limited	£14,558,044
JWH Capital Limited	£14,551,459
Windermere Marina Village Limited	£14,551,028
CPUK Commercial Holdings Limited	£14,550,478
Communications Plus Ltd	£14,549,817
Liverpool Airport Property Holdings Limited	£14,546,000
British Mohair Holdings Limited	£14,544,173
Liverpool Airport Property Limited	£14,544,000
Nupharm Limited	£14,539,000
Van Centre (West Yorkshire) Limited	£14,537,523
Solomon Commercials Limited	£14,536,674
Beech Developments (Manchester) Limited	£14,523,410
Love Saving Group Limited	£14,521,392
Masshouse Developments Ltd	£14,513,995
Contract Chemicals Limited	£14,507,000
Quintessential Brands UK Group Limited	£14,502,000
Bolton Fundco 1 Limited	£14,489,943
Zebramarsh Limited	£14,489,532
W & A Casement Limited	£14,480,536
F X Leisure Limited	£14,473,608
Longside Properties Limited	£14,471,000
Housing Units Limited	£14,461,000
West Hill School	£14,461,000
Maraq Limited	£14,456,000
Roil Foods Limited	£14,452,525
ADP No.1 Limited	£14,452,000
GVS Filter Technology UK Ltd	£14,432,078
Belle Holdings Limited	£14,424,549
West & N Yorks Chamber of Commerce and Industry	£14,418,096
H C Slingsby P L C	£14,417,000
Globesign Limited	£14,407,290
Crest Medical Holdings Limited	£14,403,679
Queenscourt Hospice	£14,391,707
Red Gap Wind Farm Limited	£14,378,490
Priory Design Services Limited	£14,367,126
Kids Allowed Holdings Limited	£14,360,619
Airline Services Limited	£14,357,128
Pendle Education Trust	£14,357,000
Victorious Academies Trust	£14,340,435
Vita (Man 2) Limited	£14,338,000
Ainscough Industrial Services Limited	£14,329,103
IX Reach Ltd	£14,322,710
D. Jacobson & Sons Limited	£14,321,000
Matalan Holding Company Limited	£14,320,000
Baldwin Filters Limited	£14,314,776
Huhtamaki BCP Limited	£14,314,352
ELC (Barrow) Limited	£14,314,231
Key Retirement Solutions Limited	£14,314,150
Wm. Armstrong (Longtown) Limited	£14,313,054
Century Healthcare Limited	£14,294,034
Kudos Shower Products Limited	£14,292,851
Federation of Jewish Services	£14,292,365
HCRF Limited	£14,274,129
Emerson Management Services Limited	£14,271,940
Bolton Hospice	£14,263,925
OBG Property Holding Limited	£14,262,985
Arnold Stansby Holdings Limited	£14,253,985
Hope Street Properties Limited	£14,240,479
Dale Estates Limited (The)	£14,230,412
Makemore Limited	£14,201,478
University of Liverpool Construction Company Ltd	£14,170,000
X1 Developments Ltd	£14,168,276
Cavern City Tours Limited	£14,163,083

Company	Amount
Colin Appleyard Limited	£14,148,450
DQ Investments Limited	£14,147,855
Lancaster Girls' Grammar School	£14,135,000
E-Foods Limited	£14,130,643
Alma Products Limited	£14,125,821
Birkdale High School	£14,115,609
Joseph Gleave & Son Limited	£14,103,886
Hadwins (Lindale) Limited	£14,103,758
Expertband Limited	£14,103,657
CF Asset Finance Limited	£14,097,000
SPS (EU) Holdings Limited	£14,082,000
RMI Pressure Systems Limited	£14,071,831
Marks and Spencer Unit Trust Management Limited	£14,060,000
Peaspring Limited	£14,056,951
Jiffy Protective Packaging Limited	£14,049,000
Rowlinson Constructions Limited	£14,042,626
Health Care Resourcing Group Limited	£14,035,214
Six Town Housing Limited	£14,030,776
Johnston Ballantyne Holdings Limited	£14,029,000
J Rosenthal Holdings Limited	£14,010,957
Errigal Investments Limited	£14,007,547
The Bridgewater Canal Company Limited	£14,000,744
Poppies Europe Ltd	£13,996,929
Urban Splash Developments Limited	£13,996,696
Cogent Breeding Limited	£13,993,000
Exceed Academies Trust	£13,979,000
Carrs Agriculture Limited	£13,970,276
Greenbank Services Limited	£13,967,000
Salisbury Management Services Limited	£13,963,268
Brookhouse Northern Limited	£13,944,000
Niokem Limited	£13,941,631
Johoco 2029 Limited	£13,937,585
Ameon Limited	£13,937,349
Countrywide Property Lawyers Limited	£13,916,000
Creamline Dairies Limited	£13,913,017
Swallow Holdings Limited	£13,913,017
Bryken (Holdings) Limited	£13,911,629
Kunick (102) Limited	£13,910,000
Swift Technical (Azerbaijan) Limited	£13,904,000
Fichtner Consulting Engineers Limited	£13,900,118
Anderselite Holdings Ltd	£13,897,989
Anderselite Ltd	£13,895,741
Partingtons Holiday Centres Limited	£13,889,925
J.Stobart & Sons Limited	£13,880,877
Alam Investments Limited	£13,876,357
Synthetic Technologies Ltd	£13,870,788
G & A M Lawson Limited	£13,870,255
Here for You Hospitality Limited	£13,866,670
Glusburn Holdings Limited	£13,864,061
Texas Holdings Limited	£13,857,017
Atmore Investments Limited	£13,848,702
Trinity School, A Church of England Academy	£13,847,184
Dr Schar UK Limited	£13,842,617
Bell,Sons & Co.(Druggists) Limited	£13,834,928
Fairbanks Environmental Limited	£13,832,255
Adlington Welding Supplies Limited	£13,829,029
Park Lane Properties & Investments Limited	£13,828,169
Indespension Ltd	£13,801,000
Aegis Outsourcing UK Limited	£13,798,365
Furlong Flooring (Central) Ltd	£13,796,629
Latium Management Services Limited	£13,795,620
Ambassador (East Cliff) Limited	£13,792,000
Langdale Owners PLC	£13,780,889
MLM Ltd	£13,779,532
3B Construction Ltd	£13,777,165
Metropolitan Cathedral Services Limited	£13,774,699
Langdale Leisure Limited	£13,763,871
Voith Paper Limited	£13,760,902
Melli Limited	£13,735,753
Yeargate SPV Limited	£13,733,782
Sonomatic Limited	£13,733,616
J Clarke Investments Limited	£13,729,087
Oldham Hulme Grammar Schools	£13,722,610
Beauland Limited	£13,705,542
Lightning Management Limited	£13,695,841
Court Properties (Portugal) Limited	£13,695,417
R. Soper Limited	£13,694,710
Broome Management Co. Limited	£13,685,268
Bonfiglioli U.K. Limited	£13,680,604
Unomedical Limited	£13,679,000
Avonside Group Services Limited	£13,675,079
Clondalkin UK Newco Limited	£13,663,006
Althams Travel Services Limited	£13,657,891
Vita Student Southampton Portswood Limited	£13,648,000
Cruden Construction Limited	£13,634,697
William Kayley Limited	£13,627,003
Burton McCall Limited	£13,624,774
J.Mallinson (Ormskirk) Limited	£13,617,510
Swissport Stansted Ltd	£13,617,000
Howgill Holdings Limited	£13,612,362
Hobs Reprographics PLC	£13,605,388
Tellar Holdings Limited	£13,590,328
M J Quinn Integrated Services Limited	£13,587,806
Leigh Fundco Limited	£13,571,402
Goldhire Limited	£13,566,160
Medicines Evaluation Unit Limited	£13,564,496
Columbus McKinnon Corporation Limited	£13,563,463
Bekaert Bradford UK Limited	£13,544,197
Drew Brady & Co. Limited	£13,534,220
First Technical Recruitment Limited	£13,533,840
Ghekko Holdings Limited	£13,525,641
Pinco 2206 Limited	£13,510,549
Fords Cheshire Limited	£13,501,103
Smith Bateson Holdings Limited	£13,498,398
Millmead Optical Group Ltd	£13,489,368
The Bullen Healthcare Group Limited	£13,484,645
The Hub Community Healthcare P Finance Limited	£13,477,063
Daisy Partner Services Limited	£13,468,000
Engenda Properties Limited	£13,459,769
Markem-Imaje Limited	£13,455,003
Open Solutions (OsUK) Limited	£13,450,836
Linteum (Willesden) Limited	£13,448,676
Linteum (Willesden) Holdings Limited	£13,448,676
Dunkleys Limited	£13,447,079
Arnold Stansby & Co. Limited	£13,444,869
New Co (Newcastle) Limited	£13,444,000
CLS Finance Limited	£13,434,865
Thyson Group Limited	£13,426,000
Pilot Group Limited	£13,420,568
Pitcliffe Properties Limited	£13,414,113
MSP Fairwind Limited	£13,404,871
Queensland Place Limited	£13,401,338
P2G.com Worldwide Limited	£13,400,000
Pharmaserve (North West) Limited	£13,390,187
H.P. Chemie Pelzer (U.K.) Limited	£13,387,601
Urban Vision Partnership Limited	£13,386,914
Brit-European Transport Limited	£13,370,466
Ameon Holdings Limited	£13,365,905
Land Recovery Limited	£13,363,906
Darwin (Piran Meadows) Limited	£13,362,884
Wise Owl Trust	£13,359,345
P. Casey Enviro Limited	£13,357,368
Sage Automotive Interiors Limited	£13,353,348
Anglo European Group Ltd	£13,348,615
Think Money Holdings 1 Limited	£13,348,000
Airline Network Limited	£13,342,000
FocusEducation (Lambeth) Limited	£13,342,000
Solidagent Investment Limited	£13,335,714
Grant Leisure Group Limited	£13,335,572
Park Medical Services Limited	£13,332,420
Rock Chemicals Limited	£13,332,326
Select Group International Limited	£13,330,788
Sebden Steel Limited	£13,328,000
CHA Textiles Limited	£13,327,000

UK Wood Recycling Limited	£13,309,283	Amos Nelson,Limited	£12,893,315
Whelan Hotelco Limited	£13,307,800	Criddle & Co.Limited	£12,884,510
Shimadzu Europe Ltd.	£13,290,475	LHS (UK) Limited	£12,881,659
Blencathra Hydro Limited	£13,290,127	Ionix Aerospace Limited	£12,876,000
All About Food Limited	£13,287,562	Matthews Environmental Solutions Limited	£12,873,462
Glasdon (UK) Limited	£13,275,137	John Hargreaves,(Collyhurst and Stalybridge) Limited	£12,873,305
Cara Holdings Limited	£13,273,257	Flavourfresh Salads Limited	£12,867,750
Aintree Plastics Limited	£13,262,418	Sandymoor Free School	£12,861,127
Dilbag Cloth House Limited	£13,261,769	Choice Hotels Limited	£12,858,807
Craven Cattle Marts Limited	£13,260,178	Bacup and Rawtenstall Grammar School	£12,856,000
Monitise Group Limited	£13,260,000	Seaforth Power Limited	£12,854,000
Hope Street Hotel Limited	£13,256,353	Tranos (UK) Limited	£12,843,446
Ikon Hardware Limited	£13,243,334	Generation Two Limited	£12,834,540
TWP (Newco) 151 Limited	£13,243,121	Advancis Holdings Limited	£12,834,396
Joseph Gleave & Son (Holdings) Limited	£13,236,795	Burlington Slate Limited	£12,833,722
Heating Plumbing Supplies Group Limited	£13,228,371	G.Walker Properties Ltd	£12,827,012
Rittner Investments Limited	£13,228,279	Grif048 Limited	£12,821,485
EA Technology Limited	£13,222,000	Bethell Group Holdings Ltd	£12,804,000
Brand New Co (354) Limited	£13,217,967	Carlisle Refrigeration Limited	£12,800,422
Widdop Bingham & Co. Limited	£13,217,248	Streetlands Limited	£12,795,498
NW1.0 Ltd	£13,217,050	UK2M Limited	£12,790,317
SGS Ashby Ltd	£13,203,000	Hyde Details Limited	£12,789,330
Unity Homes Limited	£13,199,231	Rammon Group (Properties) Limited	£12,786,731
Cobco (450) Limited	£13,182,910	Ionix Systems Limited	£12,779,000
Postcode Anywhere (Europe) Limited	£13,180,000	Graham Engineering Limited	£12,774,533
Saica Flex UK Limited	£13,168,000	Russell Homes (UK) Limited	£12,773,635
Willem Properties Limited	£13,165,298	Eccleston Homes Limited	£12,762,795
Ryan Giggs Limited	£13,161,375	Brass Bank Limited	£12,760,171
Lyon Equipment Limited	£13,146,297	Valspar Powder Coatings Limited	£12,755,955
JMW Solicitors LLP	£13,137,958	Canda Copying Limited	£12,750,176
Selbourne Group Limited	£13,127,143	Rentsmart Limited	£12,745,466
The East Lancashire Hospice	£13,113,479	Frenkel Topping Group PLC	£12,740,926
John Morley (Importers) Limited	£13,108,436	Limitless Digital Group Ltd	£12,739,754
Sigma PRS Investments II Limited	£13,107,692	Brookhouse Estates Limited	£12,736,000
Endeavour Strategic Consulting Limited	£13,098,542	Dechra Veterinary Products Limited	£12,734,000
NW Build Limited	£13,092,140	Banks & Lloyd (Shipping) Limited	£12,732,897
Voiteq Limited	£13,084,000	Ravella Holdings Limited	£12,730,233
Peel Investments (Ljla) Limited	£13,077,948	Control Circle Limited	£12,710,000
ALS Life Sciences Limited	£13,076,000	Claims Advisory Group Limited	£12,708,071
Inprova Finance Ltd	£13,072,000	Tiger Trailers Limited	£12,706,099
WS Transportation Limited	£13,071,625	The Corbett Group Limited	£12,704,377
LCBSG Limited	£13,071,120	QED (KMC) Limited	£12,685,770
Dugdale Nutrition Limited	£13,067,725	ECBA Holdings Limited	£12,667,000
Windermere Lake Cruises Limited	£13,066,740	Andrew Brown Leisure Limited	£12,665,023
Pantheon Estates Limited	£13,061,616	Darwin (North West) Limited	£12,660,725
Cavalier Carpets Limited	£13,055,308	Promenade Baltic Limited	£12,660,697
A.P.S. Salads Limited	£13,047,000	Cybele Solutions Holdings Limited	£12,659,576
Equity Solutions Lift Investments Stockport Limited	£13,038,056	Gresham UK Holdings Limited	£12,658,284
Furnico Furniture Limited	£13,036,468	Howarth Group Limited	£12,652,233
Sudlows Limited	£13,036,000	Metamark (UK) Limited	£12,651,901
Bulman's Bulk & Haulage Limited	£13,026,001	Fenwall Investments Limited	£12,649,739
Four Seasons (DFK) Limited	£13,025,000	Protec International Limited	£12,649,709
PS 121 Limited	£13,024,978	Lumenpulse Alphaled Limited	£12,643,000
Total Glass Limited	£13,019,811	David Hayton Limited	£12,636,731
Affinity Living Trinity Holdco Limited	£13,017,000	EGI (UK) Limited	£12,635,000
Campbell Plant Hire (Holdings) Limited	£13,004,922	Centrelease Limited	£12,628,807
Mill Brow Worsley Limited	£13,004,314	The Blackpool Pier Company Limited	£12,622,123
Barnfield Investment Properties Limited	£12,983,363	JBA Group Limited	£12,621,534
Georgia GC Holdings Limited	£12,977,737	W. Howard Limited	£12,611,392
Ribble Investments Limited	£12,975,202	Zoll Medical UK Limited	£12,592,494
Carpenter Investments (Vine Street) Ltd	£12,960,136	Becker Holdings Limited	£12,585,000
Khan Estates Limited	£12,958,259	Grand Hotel (St. Annes) Limited	£12,584,185
Americhem Europe Limited	£12,958,201	H.J. Lea Oakes Limited	£12,583,010
A.M. Castle Metals UK, Limited	£12,954,898	Heritage Envelopes Limited	£12,581,233
Calbee (UK) Ltd	£12,953,842	Gordale Nurseries Limited	£12,575,778
Jon Richard Holdings Limited	£12,952,745	Gusto Restaurants UK Limited	£12,574,000
Jon Richard Limited	£12,952,727	Norkem Holdings PLC	£12,572,709
The Lancashire Wildlife Trust Ltd	£12,946,000	Huyton Asphalt Holdings Limited	£12,565,508
United Utilities Utility Solutions (Industrial) Limited	£12,935,000	Jonesco (Preston) Limited	£12,556,841
KHILG Ltd	£12,922,825	Williams Tarr Construction Limited	£12,555,299
L & K Group PLC	£12,902,260	Hope Technology Holdings Limited	£12,550,425
Zenith International Freight Limited	£12,895,635	Evergreen Energy Ltd	£12,548,930

Edge Worldwide Logistics Limited	£12,539,795
Falkirk Tod Hill Wind Limited	£12,522,063
Pendleton Together Holdings Limited	£12,518,000
IBI Group (UK) Limited	£12,515,000
Davane Holding Company Limited	£12,514,748
Cyclife UK Ltd	£12,505,640
O'Connor Holdings Limited	£12,502,160
PP O'Connor Contracting Limited	£12,502,160
J. Hopkins (Contractors) Limited	£12,498,855
J Hopkins (Contractors) Holdings Limited	£12,498,854
DBG (UK) Limited	£12,485,146
Rowleys of Northwich Limited	£12,484,363
Kirona Holdings Limited	£12,479,263
Noble Systems UK Limited	£12,477,339
CH Holding Limited	£12,466,447
Rowlinson Timber Limited	£12,463,684
Duo Packaging Group Limited	£12,456,924
Tarporley High School and Sixth Form College	£12,452,740
Starbank Holdings Limited	£12,450,378
Nurture Academies Trust	£12,449,863
Dent Steel Services (Yorkshire) Limited	£12,449,064
Landmarq LLP	£12,429,828
Caunce O'Hara & Company Limited	£12,421,125
Nanoco Group PLC	£12,419,000
Liverpool and Chester Property Company Limited	£12,417,708
ADI UK Limited	£12,411,976
Kadant U.K. Limited	£12,407,011
Michael W Halsall Solicitors Limited	£12,403,732
Aimia Foods Holdings Limited	£12,403,000
Coldham Windfarm Limited	£12,400,000
Elias Enterprises Limited	£12,389,391
AMEC Foster Wheeler Nuclear International Limited	£12,384,000
North West Air Ambulance	£12,373,341
The Villa (Wrea Green) Limited	£12,361,790
W H Real Estate Limited	£12,361,527
Buttercup Bidco Limited	£12,358,554
Frostall Limited	£12,356,046
Brook Taverner Limited	£12,350,939
West Kirby Grammar School	£12,350,000
Mitchell North West Limited	£12,349,250
Alfred Price & Sons,Limited	£12,346,721
Giggleswick School	£12,335,618
Jiffy Packaging Company Limited	£12,329,000
Kings Security Systems Limited	£12,329,000
Frankel Brow Limited	£12,322,887
University Technical College Warrington	£12,314,808
HI Global Holdings Ltd	£12,309,371
North Cheshire Developments Ltd	£12,309,196
Walter Carefoot & Sons (Construction) Limited	£12,308,278
Builders Supply (North West) Limited	£12,306,700
Kammac Limited	£12,306,000
Great British Botanical Limited	£12,299,646
Nimogen Limited	£12,296,352
Grove Business Park Limited	£12,294,085
YQ Developments Limited	£12,293,454
Sune Green Holdco9 Limited	£12,291,659
M.Markovitz Limited	£12,286,321
Seabrook Group Limited	£12,284,000
Fox Strategic Land and Property Limited	£12,275,827
JY Kinsha Limited Liability Partnership	£12,271,555
KME Yorkshire Limited	£12,271,000
Concept Life Sciences (Discovery) Limited	£12,269,398
Turley Associates Ltd	£12,268,083
NES Advantage Solutions Limited	£12,264,000
Dewlay Cheesemakers Limited	£12,260,973
East Midlands Airport Property Investments (Offices)	£12,253,000
Excalon Limited	£12,233,726
Peter Gilding & Co. Limited	£12,220,200
Erlsmere Investments Limited	£12,219,888
S M D Textiles Limited	£12,214,449
J.R. Webster and Company Limited	£12,209,266
Pinnacle Living 2 Ltd	£12,202,327
Love Brothers Limited	£12,196,332
Forrester (Sales) Limited	£12,190,192
Forresters of Cheshire Limited	£12,190,192
J.Dixon & Son,Limited	£12,188,388
Waterfall Services Limited	£12,179,623
Fender Care Marine Services Group Limited	£12,178,921
Whinmoor Estates Limited	£12,176,900
Betchton Limited	£12,174,319
Bossdean Properties Limited	£12,172,107
Panaz Holdings Limited	£12,170,122
Sheet Piling (UK) Limited	£12,166,134
Tearlach Limited	£12,160,779
Ascot Waterloo Limited	£12,159,724
Equitas Solicitors Limited	£12,159,619
Leonard Curtis Recovery Limited	£12,151,824
Makin Metal Powders (UK) Limited	£12,145,748
F.D. Sims Limited	£12,137,000
Marsylka Manufacturing Co.Limited	£12,135,005
Prolift Access Limited	£12,132,862
Metacre Limited	£12,111,000
JC Land (Investments) Ltd	£12,110,026
A. & B. Engineering (Mechanical Service Div) Ltd	£12,101,081
WHC01 Limited	£12,099,414
Starcrester Properties Limited	£12,097,463
Great John Street Hotel Limited	£12,092,578
G. & B. (North West) Limited	£12,091,270
Excel -a- Rate Business Services Limited	£12,087,573
Pharmacy Care Plus Limited	£12,084,689
Cheetham Hill Construction Limited	£12,084,000
NE Investments Limited	£12,083,000
Electric Systems Limited	£12,067,572
St. Catherine's Hospice (Lancashire) Limited	£12,063,000
Worldwide Connect Limited	£12,060,100
Parallel Parents Ltd	£12,058,528
Crossco (1318) Limited	£12,056,952
Link Learning Trust	£12,050,000
Genedrive PLC	£12,046,000
Kingsway Asset Finance Ltd	£12,043,525
Paw Structures Limited	£12,039,000
Oakbridge Financial Services Limited	£12,031,383
Wm Morrison LP 3 Limited	£12,028,000
Andrew Hillas Properties Limited	£12,021,830
Janson Computers PLC	£12,021,000
Dukefield Limited	£12,016,112
Faiveley Transport Tamworth Ltd	£12,015,564
Centre Island Development Company (1997) Limited	£12,009,493
Matryx Limited	£12,004,472
Keswick School Multi Academy Trust	£12,004,000
Neville Johnson Holdings Limited	£12,003,000
Roydon Group PLC	£12,002,292
Inciner8 Holdings Limited	£12,000,954
API Overseas Holdings Limited	£12,000,000
Cygnet Group Limited	£11,994,000
Construction Partnership UK Limited	£11,990,177
Wrapid Investments Limited	£11,987,472
Dewhurst Dent P.L.C.	£11,985,425
Select International Developments Limited	£11,977,001
LeadX Group Limited	£11,976,803
Sunsave 11 (Wrockwardine Farm) Limited	£11,976,380
Wirral Hospice St John's	£11,971,754
North West Cancer Research	£11,968,161
J.D. Hughes Group Limited	£11,967,614
Wool Growers (Great Britain) Limited	£11,967,000
I. W. T. Deeside Limited	£11,956,421
Meltham Properties Limited	£11,949,724
Avery House Healthcare Limited	£11,945,000
Radisson Hotel Edinburgh Ltd	£11,936,067
Armacell United Kingdom Holding Limited	£11,936,000
IGT (UK 1) Limited	£11,936,000
Cameolord Limited	£11,934,359
Petros (Truro) Limited	£11,931,933
YPG Developments Ltd	£11,928,777

Company	Value
Huggies Day Nursery Limited	£11,927,359
Thorneycroft Solicitors Limited	£11,927,345
W.H.Good Group Limited	£11,922,833
Ashbridge School Limited	£11,913,871
Audenshaw School Academy Trust	£11,899,000
BCW Engineering Ltd	£11,897,723
C.R. Laurence of Europe, Ltd	£11,874,381
Barwick Bathroom Distribution LLP	£11,872,946
Gilpin Lodge Country House Hotel Limited	£11,868,375
Bolton Whites Hotel Limited	£11,845,729
Wind Port of Liverpool Limited	£11,840,643
Haslebrow Finance Limited	£11,832,619
ACWA Services Limited	£11,831,576
Air Energi Group Limited	£11,827,000
Amerdale Ventures LLP	£11,821,932
116 Cardamon Limited	£11,818,086
GJ Creative Limited	£11,813,112
Rectella Limited	£11,808,101
Leck Group Ltd	£11,798,385
Lagonda Leeds Propco Limited	£11,794,000
Windermere Aquatic Limited	£11,792,409
W A Developments Holdings Limited	£11,785,000
O'Connor Container Transport Limited	£11,780,000
Bruntwood 2000 Fourth Properties Limited	£11,778,000
PJP (UK) Limited	£11,776,438
Berwin Industrial Polymers Limited	£11,776,199
Ainscough Brothers LLP	£11,774,856
BV PPT Holdings Ltd.	£11,774,340
J.Wareing & Son (Wrea Green) Limited	£11,774,029
Carron Lodge Limited	£11,769,393
De Trafford Property LLP	£11,768,811
Dovetail Systems Limited	£11,763,711
ASE PLC	£11,762,954
Formby High School	£11,751,711
Dunphy Technology Limited	£11,751,542
Silcoms Limited	£11,739,556
Thompsons Plant Hire Limited	£11,736,274
Radbourne Edge (Holdings) Limited	£11,735,021
Sky Building Ltd	£11,733,230
Thermo Fisher Scientific (China) Holding Limited	£11,721,000
Flair Flooring Group Limited	£11,719,315
Husco International Two Ltd	£11,717,033
Hubron (International) Limited	£11,714,347
Trutex Investments Limited	£11,711,000
Redrow Langley Limited	£11,709,642
Silver Cross Nurseries Limited	£11,697,000
J.P.S. Property Co. Limited	£11,693,861
Cyclesport North Limited	£11,692,150
Newport Spectra-Physics Limited	£11,689,917
Holker Holdings Limited	£11,685,730
Vista Engineering Limited	£11,681,752
MSS Products Limited	£11,675,609
The Coniston Hotel Limited	£11,673,084
Lappet Manufacturing Company Limited	£11,671,000
Blue Deer Limited	£11,669,975
Wilkinson Star Limited	£11,668,685
Western and Oriental Travel Limited	£11,667,000
Cavitech Solutions Limited	£11,666,523
Hermon Hodge Limited	£11,650,592
Home Products Group Limited	£11,646,765
F2 Chemicals Limited	£11,645,000
Lloyd & Jones Engineers (Holdings) Limited	£11,631,942
Launchrandom Limited	£11,631,290
Sadaqat Global Limited	£11,627,021
Promatic International Limited	£11,622,667
Husco International One Ltd	£11,618,854
Magellan Robotech Limited	£11,607,000
Brookhead Estate Limited	£11,580,085
Vertex Data Science Limited	£11,570,000
Solway Vehicle Distributors Limited	£11,560,137
Royal Exchange Theatre Company Limited	£11,558,000
Romaco SPV 2 Limited	£11,556,051
Vital Energi Solutions Limited	£11,551,834
Malling Health (UK) Limited	£11,549,537
PMC Fluidpower Group Limited	£11,535,557
The Blackburn Diocesan Board of Education	£11,530,000
Finbrook Limited	£11,529,992
Octapharma Limited	£11,529,855
Barnfield Developments Limited	£11,529,633
Value Catering Limited	£11,518,962
A K W Global Logistics Ltd	£11,518,460
Flair Flooring Supplies Limited	£11,517,975
Stephensons Solicitors LLP	£11,517,211
Edwards Cheshire Company Limited	£11,516,969
Graham Heath Group Limited	£11,515,237
Astonish Holdings Limited	£11,511,288
The London Oil Refining Co. Limited	£11,511,164
MLTS Holdings Limited	£11,496,809
Yemin Charitable Trust Ltd	£11,489,014
Doff Portland Limited	£11,488,071
Mercian Limited	£11,474,907
Smith & Bateson Limited,	£11,469,233
Helium Miracle 113 Limited	£11,468,731
South Shore Mutual Insurance Company Limited	£11,462,077
Centenary Property Developments LLP	£11,459,365
Cuerden Estates Ltd.	£11,459,199
Gavin Murray Limited	£11,457,137
Premier Textiles Limited	£11,455,563
Oxendale & Company Limited	£11,452,372
Deralam Laminates Limited	£11,450,394
Shawston Holdings Limited	£11,450,229
Glendale Foods Limited	£11,448,139
L.& W.Wilson (Endmoor) Limited	£11,448,025
Brookhouse Property Holdings Limited	£11,448,000
Miramar Investments Limited	£11,446,787
T.J. Morris Properties Limited	£11,443,163
SR Properties Manchester Limited	£11,440,908
NWM Holdings Limited	£11,440,278
Livbeth Investco Limited	£11,437,318
Peover Eye Investments Limited	£11,436,724
Money Controls Holdings Limited	£11,436,000
Bitrez Group Limited	£11,435,975
John Lord Holdings Limited	£11,433,380
UCFB College of Football Business Limited	£11,425,260
Create Construction Limited	£11,423,311
H.B. Fuller U.K. Manufacturing Limited	£11,421,911
Huber Packaging Limited	£11,418,040
T&M Property Investments Limited	£11,417,386
Crosslane Student Developments Limited	£11,415,915
Bromborough Paint & Building Supplies Limited	£11,411,283
Urban Splash Commercial 2017 Limited	£11,409,620
Granton Investments Limited	£11,408,860
Hurstwood Properties (Y) Limited	£11,406,271
Collinson PLC	£11,402,551
Dock 10 Limited	£11,402,000
Pagref Partner Ltd	£11,398,295
Sterling 2000 Group Limited	£11,396,245
Warrington Primary Academy Trust	£11,395,849
CPG 2016 Limited	£11,393,989
Hexpol Tpe Ltd	£11,390,000
A.C.Bacon Engineering Limited	£11,384,014
C & C Supplies Collinson Limited	£11,379,261
South Manchester Learning Trust	£11,372,000
Professional Disposables International Limited	£11,368,423
Sam Hagan Leisure (UK) Limited	£11,368,353
Chi Yip Holdings Limited	£11,366,116
Hope's Auction Company,Limited	£11,359,915
Eco Parks HNW Limited	£11,355,373
Carlisle Refrigeration (Holdings) Limited	£11,353,971
Peakdale Molecular Limited	£11,353,867
Cityblock Holdings Limited	£11,349,980
Hollinwood Homes Limited	£11,347,926
Daresbury Properties Limited	£11,347,496
Corbetts Support Solutions Limited	£11,345,376

Company	Value
H. Marcel Guest, Limited	£11,343,259
Chargepoint Technology Limited	£11,340,564
Charles S. Bullen Stomacare Limited	£11,339,069
Rushcliffe (Heysham) Limited	£11,338,080
Amscreen Public Limited Company	£11,337,826
PP O'Connor Group Limited	£11,336,854
Duni Limited	£11,336,000
L'Arche	£11,335,192
4L (Holdings) Limited	£11,334,054
Innospec Fuel Specialties Limited	£11,333,000
Wand Properties UK LLP	£11,330,193
Kingsley Asset Finance Limited	£11,324,693
IMCI (Services) Limited	£11,317,072
Bed Factory Hotels Limited	£11,316,265
John Roberts Holdings Limited	£11,313,177
Atul Europe Limited	£11,312,878
Wirral Grammar School for Boys	£11,305,000
Hale Country Club Limited	£11,302,000
DWL (Holdings) Limited	£11,301,415
Trek Diagnostic Systems Limited	£11,301,000
GPL Civil Engineering Limited	£11,299,812
H.I. Lime Street Limited	£11,285,349
Tablecheck Limited	£11,284,080
Alliance Family Foundation Limited	£11,282,795
Union Colours Limited	£11,279,744
Spencross Limited	£11,278,083
Paramount Estates (Lancashire) Limited (The)	£11,275,055
Bravo Inns II Limited	£11,273,350
RPW (Southampton) Limited	£11,273,209
Consolidated Insurance Holdings Limited	£11,271,000
Hensmill (SJR) LLP	£11,263,281
Hiden Instruments Limited	£11,260,034
Christy Home Textiles Limited	£11,252,000
Yokogawa United Kingdom Limited	£11,243,714
J & E Marshall Finance Limited	£11,241,074
Carrs Foods International Limited	£11,238,529
Czajka Group Holdings Limited	£11,231,666
Rix Motor Company Limited	£11,226,003
Concerted Academies Trust	£11,220,019
The Bolton Multi Academy Trust	£11,219,908
G.S. Cold Storage and Warehousing Limited	£11,214,168
Kids Allowed Group Limited	£11,202,959
Juristar Limited	£11,194,560
Safehands Group Limited	£11,191,694
Dawat-E-Islami UK	£11,190,818
The Enterprise Fund Limited	£11,170,064
Knossington Grange School Limited	£11,164,806
Carrs Foods Holdings Limited	£11,162,563
DRCT (PHPH) Ltd	£11,162,298
H&A Prestige Bottling Limited	£11,142,000
Oil Salvage Limited	£11,138,422
Imaan Healthcare Limited	£11,138,305
Bitrez Limited	£11,136,115
Ennis Paint U.K. Holding Company Limited	£11,135,170
Atmore Properties Limited	£11,134,801
Warrant Corporate Holdings Limited	£11,132,559
Sunsave 31 (Horam) Limited	£11,122,834
Breckland Leisure Limited	£11,120,818
Polytech International Limited	£11,118,967
Gaerwen Properties Limited	£11,117,040
London Luton Airport Parking Limited	£11,116,400
Chandos Civil Engineering Limited	£11,108,519
Wastdale Investments Limited	£11,090,412
Four Seasons (Bamford) Limited	£11,087,000
Duo Plastics Limited	£11,067,092
Tullis Russell Coaters Limited	£11,065,000
The Lingholm Estate Limited	£11,060,238
Comap UK Holdings Limited	£11,059,555
G E Robinson & Co Ltd	£11,050,667
Teresa Ball International Solidarity Fund	£11,048,181
Nutrition Group PLC	£11,045,936
Repic Limited	£11,043,654

Company	Value
GP Premises Holdings Limited	£11,041,715
J. S. Bailey Limited	£11,035,229
Peel Media Development (Holdings) Limited	£11,031,000
Security Window Shutters Limited	£11,030,905
Survey Supplies Limited	£11,029,610
Sterling Property Co. Limited	£11,019,545
V.A. Whitley & Co. Limited	£11,013,765
Garstang Community Academy Trust	£11,008,000
Kerax Limited	£11,001,512
Stagecoach Supertram Maintenance Ltd.	£10,999,000
Cash Converters UK Holdings PLC	£10,998,000
Cloverbrook Holdings Ltd	£10,997,959
Pomeroy IT Solutions UK Limited	£10,997,711
National Museum of Labour History (The)	£10,991,554
Goliath Footwear Limited	£10,990,135
Pilkington Finance Unlimited	£10,982,000
Blue Support Services Limited	£10,976,142
Kerax (Chorley) Limited	£10,971,213
CTI Data Solutions Limited	£10,969,617
Brookmann Home Manchester 1877 Ltd	£10,968,600
Medicina Limited	£10,956,102
Oxley Group Limited	£10,950,784
Agecroft Investment Co.Limited	£10,946,187
Cash Converters (UK) Limited	£10,946,000
Sunsave 43 (Epwell) Limited	£10,945,529
HKJ Investments (UK) Limited	£10,944,960
Chippindale Foods Limited	£10,942,273
Red Artificial Lift UK Limited	£10,942,000
Grandcross Limited	£10,940,000
Thomas Guy,Limited	£10,936,071
Westholme School Limited	£10,930,374
TS (UK) Limited	£10,929,792
Firstnet Data Centres (Leeds) LLP	£10,922,351
Lowe Clothing International Limited	£10,920,547
Claire House	£10,915,467
Moneta Communications Holdings Limited	£10,911,181
Sunsave 6 (Manston) Ltd	£10,910,274
Harewood Moor Estates Limited	£10,906,099
Seventh Continent Limited	£10,905,999
Kirkbie Kendal School Academy Trust	£10,896,320
Bishops' Blue Coat Church of England High School	£10,892,454
Altin Homes Limited	£10,890,781
Sandileaf Limited	£10,886,584
Paul Hartmann Limited	£10,883,824
The Keys Federation	£10,879,979
Generis Technology Limited	£10,879,505
O'Neill Patient Solicitors LLP	£10,877,970
Equilibrium Healthcare Group Limited	£10,877,364
Human Appeal	£10,875,143
Innospec Environmental Limited	£10,855,000
Tokyo Group Limited	£10,852,192
Synexus Clinical Research Midco No 2 Limited	£10,852,000
Synexus Clinical Research Midco No 3 Limited	£10,852,000
Wigan Athletic A.F.C. Limited	£10,850,155
Ferno (UK) Limited	£10,849,310
Genii Engineering & Technology Training Limited	£10,846,673
Cumbrian Homes Limited	£10,837,867
Liverpool Charity and Voluntary Services	£10,836,884
Drop & Collect Limited	£10,832,000
Portable Offices (Hire) Limited	£10,827,084
Smartpay Limited	£10,823,797
Narang Group Ltd	£10,818,853
Hopecrest Holdings Limited	£10,815,401
Unifrax UK Holdco Limited	£10,814,751
Acdoco Limited	£10,814,428
Regal Crown Logistics Limited	£10,810,707
Hosokawa Micron Limited	£10,802,889
Wigan and Leigh Hospice	£10,799,024
Royal Sanders (UK) Limited	£10,796,000
M C D Manchester Limited	£10,793,262
Bonarie Investments Limited	£10,788,335
Carrier Ltd	£10,786,877

Company	Value
Auk Investments Limited	£10,784,396
Bowdon Group Limited	£10,783,576
Condie Investments Limited	£10,773,749
Rowlinson Packaging Limited	£10,767,869
The Union Discount Company of London Limited	£10,767,850
Alphyra Payment Services Limited	£10,758,164
Bunton Plant Hire Limited	£10,754,281
Lingholm Private Trust Limited,(The)	£10,749,373
Estates and Leisure Holdings Limited	£10,749,232
W. M. Ewington & Company Limited	£10,748,215
Elastomerics Limited	£10,744,155
Eventmore Limited	£10,740,958
R. Bunton Limited	£10,732,973
Waitings Limited	£10,731,730
Blue Machinery (Southern) Limited	£10,726,327
Utilisoft Limited	£10,721,212
Cherry Tree Investments Limited	£10,718,974
Chester Diocesan Board of Education	£10,708,388
Port Salford Land Limited	£10,702,174
Centriforce Products Limited	£10,695,922
LPC Fresh Parks Limited	£10,691,914
C & C Catering Equipment Limited	£10,687,795
DSGPI 2015 Limited	£10,682,252
Adrian Francis Associates Ltd	£10,669,218
Trutex Limited	£10,668,000
M.& N.Textiles Limited	£10,667,536
Frank Armitt & Son Limited	£10,657,712
Eric Wright FM Limited	£10,646,981
Rotex Europe Ltd	£10,640,574
Gapp Developments Limited	£10,639,792
Fleetwood PPP Limited	£10,636,291
Brymau Estates Ltd	£10,626,804
Newbank Garden Centre Limited	£10,608,216
Ian Edgar (Liverpool) Limited	£10,604,746
M & A Beer Holdings Limited	£10,598,485
Fothergill Engineered Fabrics Limited	£10,594,277
Argus Fluidhandling Limited	£10,584,000
The Big Shed Limited	£10,583,545
Alder Hey Children's Charity	£10,583,000
Bolton Engineering (Holdings) Limited	£10,579,130
Gawith Hoggarth & Co.,Limited	£10,578,392
David Hermon Hodge Limited	£10,577,261
Cresta World Travel Limited	£10,575,196
Narang Wholesalers Limited	£10,567,236
Closomat Limited	£10,565,422
Frodsham Wind Farm Finance Limited	£10,564,667
Guyson International Limited	£10,560,488
Champion Limited	£10,559,570
Air Energi Holdings Limited	£10,553,000
Winander Leisure Limited	£10,549,857
Spiritel Mobile Limited	£10,548,000
Fresh Approach (UK) Holdings Limited	£10,538,494
Metrohm UK Limited	£10,533,190
Business & Enterprise Finance Ltd.	£10,529,806
Linatex Limited	£10,514,000
Hughes Safety Showers Limited	£10,510,938
E3G Limited	£10,502,316
Chums Limited	£10,501,409
Oliver Valves Limited	£10,491,625
Risedale Estates Limited	£10,490,206
Park Homes (UK) Limited	£10,489,844
Addison Project PLC	£10,489,573
Aidapt Bathrooms Limited	£10,488,273
Braecrest Limited	£10,486,154
Gecas UK Limited	£10,482,109
RW Jupe Limited	£10,469,139
Frenkel Topping Limited	£10,466,597
Sunsave 20 (Knowlton) Limited	£10,465,941
G.P.S. Holdings Limited	£10,463,362
Lancaster University Energy Services Ltd	£10,460,922
Tailored Fire & Security (London) Limited	£10,454,888
Emperors Gate Property Company Limited	£10,445,287
Birchwood Community Academy Trust	£10,445,000
Heimbach UK Limited	£10,437,837
Silicone Engineering Limited	£10,435,867
Legal Marketing Services Limited	£10,434,346
Warbrick Property Company Limited	£10,433,389
Hill Biscuits Limited	£10,431,896
Aviation Park Group Limited	£10,429,369
Washington Mills Electro Minerals Limited	£10,418,742
FHC (Holdings) Limited	£10,412,000
T D Partnership Investments LLP	£10,405,800
Brookhouse (Ashford) Limited	£10,404,000
R.E.Dawson,Limited	£10,399,369
Bowmore Investments Limited	£10,388,885
Satake Europe Limited	£10,388,034
Reays Coaches Limited	£10,383,706
Bleu Properties Ltd	£10,381,722
Topbonus Ltd	£10,380,448
Ouzledale Foundry Company Limited	£10,370,318
Sune Green Energy Ltd	£10,368,020
Kingfisher Learning Trust	£10,363,000
The Macclesfield Academy	£10,361,000
Bodycote Treasury Services Limited	£10,360,914
Apollo Scientific Ltd	£10,360,559
The Swinton High School Academy Trust	£10,359,000
Peelclose Properties Limited	£10,358,837
Arden Dies Limited	£10,357,879
G.D. Yarns Limited	£10,354,125
Redhead Holdings Limited	£10,350,670
Busi and Stephenson Limited	£10,348,849
Cardinal Shopfitting + Systems Limited	£10,347,988
Retail Property Investments Limited	£10,336,620
John Sylvester Engineering Company Limited	£10,335,115
Back Office Support Services Limited	£10,334,751
Contract Chemicals (Knowsley) Limited	£10,324,000
Datel Group PLC	£10,321,956
Beers Timber & Building Supplies Limited	£10,314,144
Nalco Services Limited	£10,310,000
Opus Bestpay Limited	£10,308,810
Datel Computing Limited	£10,307,404
INX Europe Limited	£10,299,779
Lateral Academy Trust	£10,296,000
Ledvance Ltd	£10,292,000
Workforce Holdings Limited	£10,283,309
Lydall Industrial Filtration Textile Mfg (EMEA) Ltd	£10,283,280
P J Livesey Living Space (North) Limited	£10,283,071
Deansgate Securities LLP	£10,281,028
Bathgate Silica Sand Limited	£10,278,982
Dormex Containers Limited	£10,275,685
Pantek Limited	£10,273,245
The Bluecoat	£10,267,001
Pendleside Hospice	£10,261,974
Ainscough Wind Energy Services Limited	£10,260,000
Bemis Limited	£10,248,432
Denholm UK Logistics Limited	£10,245,313
Praetura Asset Finance (L) Limited	£10,242,720
BHR Finance Limited	£10,239,000
Bolton UTC	£10,238,000
Vet Plus Limited	£10,230,443
North West Portfolio (No.3) Limited	£10,228,051
Silicone Holdings Limited	£10,226,741
Bender UK Limited	£10,225,942
Bibby Bulk Carriers Limited	£10,219,786
Coolair Equipment Limited	£10,217,886
Faci UK Chemicals Limited	£10,212,437
Gerber Technology Limited	£10,210,000
EDCAWI Limited	£10,207,133
Tom Howley Limited	£10,205,000
Ossur UK Limited	£10,201,494
Granada Material Handling Limited	£10,197,996
Elmwood Construction LLP	£10,196,313
SSCP Blink Bidco Limited	£10,195,861
Nederman Limited	£10,193,000

Company	Amount
Halle Concerts Society	£10,192,000
The Swan Hotel (Newby Bridge) Limited	£10,186,476
The Swan Hotel (Newby Bridge) Holdings Limited	£10,186,476
Thornsett Vale Limited	£10,186,243
Northcote Leisure Group Limited	£10,182,631
Leehand Limited	£10,174,102
Community First Academy Trust	£10,174,000
Ipackchem Limited	£10,172,771
Tarka Controls Limited	£10,172,765
Wrapid Group Limited	£10,171,620
A & M Energy Solutions Limited	£10,168,611
Dent Steel Holdings Limited	£10,167,203
Bethell Construction Limited	£10,155,000
Blenheim Land & Properties Ltd	£10,153,646
Switch2 Energy Limited	£10,152,013
Trewhiddle Village Limited	£10,147,474
Europlast (Blackburn) Limited	£10,141,254
Regional & City Airports (Blackpool) Limited	£10,135,946
Pulse Equipment Group Limited	£10,134,151
Delifresh Limited	£10,133,913
Osan Limited	£10,128,173
Broadway Halls Care Services Limited	£10,125,000
Oxoid (Ely) Limited	£10,124,000
Earnside Energy Limited	£10,123,000
New Charter Building Company Limited	£10,117,000
Cirteq Limited	£10,115,584
Rayrigg Estates Ltd	£10,113,785
Technical Demolition Services Limited	£10,112,483
Special Piping Materials Limited	£10,101,811
Neenah International UK Limited	£10,098,000
Reaper Limited	£10,097,391
Chorus Law Limited	£10,092,002
Aston Chemists Limited	£10,085,488
Four Seasons Estates Limited	£10,081,748
Eldapoint Investments Limited	£10,080,893
Eastern Green Limited	£10,079,555
Urban Regen Limited	£10,079,202
Dreambase Limited	£10,077,237
Newco Ventures Ltd	£10,067,684
Rodol Limited	£10,066,646
Armored Auto UK Limited	£10,065,709
Accrington St Christopher's CoE High School	£10,064,000
H.B. Panelcraft Limited	£10,062,682
Aztec Aerosols Limited	£10,050,363
Carden Croft (2012) Limited	£10,050,000
Concept Life Sciences Integrated Discovery	£10,048,659
Ashbury Freeholds Limited	£10,048,487
Business First Ltd	£10,041,547
Arighi Bianchi Holdings Limited	£10,039,831
Guildford Investments Limited	£10,038,594
Questport Limited	£10,038,401
Gas Control Equipment Limited	£10,033,000
Sonoco Products Company UK	£10,028,000
Quantil Agriculture Limited	£10,015,675
Rowlinson Garden Products Limited	£10,013,620
Blazing Productions Ltd	£10,010,379
Electrovision Limited	£10,008,937
Workshop Properties Limited	£10,008,290
Akcros Holdings Limited	£10,007,950
Speedy International Leasing Limited	£10,002,000
TFS London Holdings Limited	£10,000,999
1st Stop Funding Limited	£10,000,001
Enesco Holdings Limited	£10,000,000
Allied Filter Systems Holdings Limited	£10,000,000
Northern Packaging Limited	£9,997,598
Milo Properties Ltd	£9,993,587
The Lakes Freerange Egg Company Ltd.	£9,991,324
Lacy Roofing Company Limited	£9,985,936
Casterton Leisure Limited	£9,985,904
Oakdale Farms Limited	£9,981,802
Quadrant EPP UK Ltd.	£9,981,000
Forever Manchester	£9,976,265
Less Common Metals Limited	£9,973,976
Hurst Group (Northern) Limited	£9,973,000
Redstart Construction Limited	£9,969,045
Russell Armer Group Limited	£9,953,099
Barlows Childcare Properties Limited	£9,948,826
Involve Visual Collaboration Ltd	£9,945,305
Direct Tyre Management Limited	£9,944,302
Forty Limited	£9,940,815
Avery Lodge Limited	£9,930,000
Windsors (Wallasey) Limited	£9,929,296
Darwin (Bath Mill) Limited	£9,927,758
Hessle FT Holdings Limited	£9,923,207
Parklands High School	£9,922,000
Data Intensity Limited	£9,920,160
White Moss Horticulture Limited	£9,919,209
Byworth Boiler Hire Limited	£9,910,697
Ainscough Property Holdings Limited	£9,908,297
Monckton Properties (Holdings) Limited	£9,903,159
KVH Media Group Communication Limited	£9,899,000
Randle Brooks Limited	£9,896,855
NUS Services Limited	£9,893,195
Fiserv UK Holding Limited	£9,892,287
Principle Healthcare International Limited	£9,883,045
Elopak UK Limited	£9,882,477
Plant Health Care PLC	£9,881,733
Afgritech Limited	£9,874,832
Richminster Ltd	£9,867,520
The Waterside Hotel and Galleon Leisure Club Limited	£9,866,735
Hurstwood Properties (C) Limited	£9,866,567
Arysta LifeScience U.K. Limited	£9,864,709
Glenco Limited	£9,859,501
Zenith International Freight Holdings Ltd	£9,857,573
Ardale International Limited	£9,857,227
NUS Holdings Limited	£9,856,502
KS Brands Limited	£9,852,990
Milnes Investments Limited	£9,850,802
Finemere Limited	£9,850,761
Pentre Group Holdings Limited	£9,844,831
Reagens (UK) Limited	£9,844,189
Wigan Leisure and Culture Trust	£9,842,337
Rimape Ltd	£9,841,785
B S Stainless Limited	£9,840,874
Euro Wrap Limited	£9,840,000
HMG Paints Limited	£9,838,259
Hallmark Cards Property Company Limited	£9,833,000
Pure Leisure Estates Limited	£9,827,400
B.I. Properties Limited	£9,825,072
First Water Limited	£9,825,000
Pineapple Letting Ltd	£9,817,795
Martin Dawes Solutions Holdings Limited	£9,811,667
Sweet Dreams (Nelson) Limited	£9,803,579
Durham Tees Valley Airport Limited	£9,799,181
Hallmark Developments (North West) Limited	£9,798,501
C R Limited	£9,797,174
Albion Limited	£9,791,975
The Claims Guys Limited	£9,785,960
Platform Sales & Hire Limited	£9,780,415
Hexagon Care Services Limited	£9,778,060
H & S Restaurants Ltd	£9,777,647
Manchester Sale Rugby Club Limited	£9,776,859
Thrislington Cubicles Limited	£9,775,203
Luxury Fibres Limited	£9,774,231
Downtown Salford Limited	£9,768,874
Lawrence Hunt & Co Limited	£9,766,234
Potomac Capital Limited	£9,764,819
Information and Data Networks Supplies Limited	£9,764,068
Here for You Hospitality Middlesbrough Limited	£9,757,872
Treedown Investments Limited	£9,753,696
P J Livesey Country Homes (Eastern) Limited	£9,752,659
BB Legal Limited	£9,747,579
Gisburne Park Estates Limited	£9,745,806
I.C.S. (UK) Limited	£9,743,381

Company	Amount
Sheffield Investment Company Limited.(The)	£9,742,970
Mitchell's Brewery Limited	£9,737,000
Gilberts (Blackpool) Limited	£9,735,676
Chase Property Developments Limited	£9,727,828
Barton Park Estates Limited	£9,721,587
B&ESA Limited	£9,721,027
MRH Corporate Group Limited	£9,716,096
Hill's Salvage & Recycling Ltd	£9,712,992
Eaton Bank Academy	£9,711,000
Goldcrest Distribution Ltd	£9,710,810
Genix Healthcare Ltd	£9,710,633
S Evans & Sons Limited	£9,708,568
Manchester Urban Finance Corporation Limited	£9,708,437
Flameproofings Limited	£9,705,329
CRS Credit Ltd.	£9,703,209
Gemini Finance Ltd	£9,698,804
Tony Rampton Trust	£9,687,264
Mobius Motors Limited	£9,684,722
Kinetic Recruitment Services Limited	£9,683,549
M.J.C. Developments Limited	£9,680,337
Wardle Academy	£9,674,000
Rowlinson Investments Limited	£9,673,530
Bryken Limited	£9,673,093
Praedius UK (Industrial) Limited	£9,663,000
Leisureplan Projects Finance Limited	£9,658,270
UDP Group Limited	£9,653,810
Northern Industrial Properties Limited	£9,650,962
Atlantic Container Line UK Limited	£9,649,487
Total Glass Holdings Limited	£9,644,747
Meter Fit 2 Limited	£9,642,000
ESL Fuels Limited	£9,641,671
VIL Resins Ltd.	£9,632,801
Macmaster Properties Limited	£9,632,348
Illingworth Ingham (Manchester) Limited	£9,628,376
H. Mitton Limited	£9,626,578
X1 Management Limited	£9,614,742
Russell Armer Limited	£9,609,614
Carpenter Investments Brunswick Park 2 Ltd	£9,602,781
Nextdom Property Limited	£9,599,388
The Label Makers Limited	£9,598,212
C.P. Witter Limited	£9,594,012
The Forward Property Group Limited	£9,591,510
INEOS Technologies (Vinyls) Limited	£9,590,292
Car Transplants Limited	£9,585,822
Dunham Investments Limited	£9,584,877
Walshaw Moor Estate Limited	£9,584,787
Tamaris Healthcare (England) Limited	£9,584,000
P.J. Livesey Group Limited	£9,583,952
P. W. Greenhalgh Holdings Limited	£9,581,615
Ghekko Limited	£9,570,879
New City Vision (Liverpool) Limited	£9,565,435
Catford & Longford Limited	£9,565,344
Cragwood International Limited	£9,564,549
MacDermid Graphics Solutions UK Limited	£9,562,000
Ash Lea Cottage Nurseries Limited	£9,552,908
KS SPV 24 Limited	£9,550,246
H M Project Developments Ltd	£9,549,932
Barry Wood Plant Hire Limited	£9,547,574
Stirling Management Group Limited	£9,547,495
Rockfield Properties Limited	£9,542,184
Soho Flordis UK Limited	£9,538,450
Quercia Limited	£9,537,436
Wigan Boys & Girls Club	£9,534,678
Harrison Northern Limited	£9,534,195
J.Mills (Contractors) Limited	£9,533,083
Farmhouse Biscuits Limited	£9,528,859
Totally Wicked Limited	£9,526,915
Quintessential Brands Spirit Solutions Limited	£9,515,000
Computer Risk Management Limited	£9,514,448
Glendale S/S Limited	£9,512,211
Dennis Baldwin Group Ltd	£9,510,601
St George Healthcare Group Limited	£9,502,939

Company	Amount
Neville Johnson Limited	£9,501,000
Kinetic PLC	£9,496,917
Practice Services UK Limited	£9,486,000
Bulmer & Lumb Group Limited	£9,484,025
Bells of Lazonby (Holdings) Limited	£9,481,293
Barton and Redman Limited	£9,477,357
Blakedale Ltd	£9,472,451
Emeram Urbanics Ltd	£9,471,000
Newbridge (Healthcare) Limited	£9,470,864
Olympus Engineering (Holdings) Limited	£9,469,714
Graham (Commercials) Limited	£9,458,347
ISS Labour Group Limited	£9,457,848
Wax Lyrical Limited	£9,457,000
Glendale Grounds Management Limited	£9,451,000
Hyva (U.K.) Limited	£9,450,601
ModernUser Limited	£9,441,317
Hutchinson Engineering Limited	£9,440,814
C.P. Davidson & Sons Limited	£9,439,385
MGF Property Limited	£9,436,521
Paystream My Max Limited	£9,434,541
Blue Machinery (Central) Limited	£9,429,708
Engie Renewables Limited	£9,426,603
Risk Technology Limited	£9,424,086
T E Newsholme Limited	£9,422,945
Vegetarian Express Bidco Limited	£9,418,016
Perrers Properties Limited	£9,414,827
Zep UK Limited	£9,409,107
NSG Environmental Limited	£9,409,000
Speedy Products Limited	£9,408,875
Gaskells (North West) Limited	£9,402,223
The Contact Company Ltd	£9,393,881
Regency Glass (Holdings) Limited	£9,390,401
Chadderton Total-Care Unit Limited	£9,388,738
Valmet Limited	£9,378,000
R. McDowell Haulage and Distribution Limited	£9,375,206
Crompton House Church of England School	£9,369,344
Tonrose Limited	£9,368,887
Fourward Properties Limited	£9,366,086
ELE Advanced Technologies Limited	£9,365,250
Jeunesse Global (Europe) Limited	£9,360,452
Debmar Benevolent Trust Limited	£9,355,309
Future Energy Group Ltd	£9,354,597
X1 The Campus Limited	£9,354,495
TGC (2015) Limited	£9,353,488
CT Ice Limited	£9,353,000
Clear Law LLP	£9,352,574
Memhay Limited	£9,346,353
Capital & Centric (Cinnamon) Limited	£9,346,321
Silverburn Finance (U.K.) Limited	£9,341,876
mxData - Technologies Limited	£9,341,256
Flowflex Holdings Limited	£9,340,011
Movitex (UK) Limited	£9,336,000
GA Pet Food Partners Limited	£9,332,000
Cobco (236) Limited	£9,332,000
Washington Homes Limited	£9,330,634
Individual Restaurant Company Limited	£9,324,000
Star Tissue UK Limited	£9,319,869
Fairport Holdings Limited	£9,319,612
SZG Europe Limited	£9,318,840
Hussein Traders Limited	£9,315,361
Navagator Limited	£9,311,000
Khanjra International Foods Limited	£9,310,503
Bishop Rawstorne Church of England Academy Trust	£9,310,000
Lakeside Collection Limited	£9,309,025
West Wallasey Garages Limited	£9,308,246
Ellis Brigham Mountain Sports Limited	£9,308,156
Stamford Group Limited (The)	£9,308,000
In at The Side Limited	£9,296,717
Winfield Holdings Limited	£9,296,335
Queen Elizabeth Grammar School Penrith	£9,296,316
Concept Life Sciences (Environmental Consulting)	£9,288,976
Anfield (U.K.) Limited	£9,286,240

Company	Amount
Farralls Transport (Properties) Limited	£9,283,243
Paraplus (Holdings) Limited	£9,279,524
Partners Properties (UK) Ltd	£9,278,000
North Lancs. Training Group Limited (The)	£9,277,111
J. Parker Dutch Bulbs (Wholesale) Limited	£9,271,643
Brookes Bell LLP	£9,259,468
Holt Doctors Limited	£9,258,548
Bevie Partners Limited	£9,255,534
David Roberts & Partners (Insurance Brokers) Limited	£9,254,618
Abacus Estates Limited	£9,251,776
Metcalfe Holdings Limited	£9,249,531
The Market Village Company Limited	£9,247,804
Affinity Living 2 Limited	£9,241,000
Electricity North West (Construction and Maintenance)	£9,237,000
Mantank Environmental Services Limited	£9,228,834
Causeway Tractors Limited	£9,227,466
Fothergill Polycom Limited	£9,223,562
Inverco Limited	£9,222,979
Pinnacle Living Ltd	£9,219,738
Tom Barron Limited	£9,217,266
Gledhill Building Products Limited	£9,214,000
Regency Glass Limited	£9,212,697
Anderton Holdings Limited	£9,210,649
Keppel Healthcare Ltd.	£9,208,859
ASM Technologies Limited	£9,207,843
Amoria Bond Limited	£9,204,707
Cellbeam Limited	£9,203,000
Jade Solutions Limited	£9,200,874
Wire Regeneration Limited	£9,192,500
F.T. Patten (Holdings) Limited	£9,191,569
DBS Pochin LLP	£9,190,659
Omega Technologies Limited	£9,188,000
Mayfield Chicks Limited	£9,182,750
Kirkham Grammar School	£9,168,790
Lilytame Limited	£9,168,192
St. Rocco's Hospice	£9,167,670
Crossacres Primary Academy	£9,163,046
Vale UK Limited	£9,161,069
Abird Superior Limited	£9,161,000
R. D. Scott Limited	£9,159,000
Northcote Hotel Limited	£9,158,740
Milehouse Foods Limited	£9,156,419
Rhodi Group Limited	£9,149,862
Stainforth Construction LLP	£9,145,841
TMGH Limited	£9,143,232
Dawson Real Estates Limited	£9,141,952
Cerberus Holdings Limited	£9,137,558
Nick Brookes Recycling Limited	£9,130,298
Joe Davies (Manchester) Limited	£9,130,159
Challenger Text Limited	£9,128,525
Combine Asset Limited	£9,125,000
Aqua Fabrications Limited	£9,124,873
Positive Solutions Limited	£9,122,853
Egertons Recovery Group Limited	£9,122,073
Christian Property UK Ltd	£9,120,916
PTJ & R Limited	£9,115,855
British Muslim Heritage Centre	£9,110,934
Praetura Asset Finance (SB) Limited	£9,109,263
North West Logistics Ltd	£9,107,266
SJM Developments Limited	£9,105,993
Ocean Boulevard II Limited	£9,105,000
Oregon & Ratcliffe Ltd	£9,097,416
Promatic Holdings Limited	£9,091,151
Wealth at Work Limited	£9,091,000
L.T.D. Contractors Limited	£9,085,754
Grakon BMAC Holdings Limited	£9,081,758
San Marco Limited	£9,073,301
D C T Civil Engineering Limited	£9,069,000
Wilmslow PP Limited	£9,066,418
General Traffic Limited	£9,063,536
The James Group Limited	£9,060,219
Assystem Group UK Limited	£9,059,000
Robert Wright & Sons Limited	£9,058,339
Rectella International Limited	£9,053,443
Bawnbua Foods GB Ltd	£9,050,809
Fabrics & Yarns (Macclesfield) Ltd	£9,050,238
SmarDTV (UK) Limited	£9,049,656
Smith Brothers Holdings Limited	£9,049,644
Pitts Wilson Limited	£9,049,172
Wise Pharmacies Limited	£9,048,397
The James Mercer Group Limited	£9,044,429
Birtenshaw	£9,043,203
Plasto-Sac UK Limited	£9,041,943
Abbey Masterbatch Limited	£9,041,166
Inventive Service Company Limited	£9,041,000
Jones & Egan Estates Limited	£9,039,471
Country Park Foods Limited	£9,038,235
AVSL Group Limited	£9,033,193
Caterplus Services Limited	£9,032,106
Lex Vehicle Finance 2 Limited	£9,028,000
A.D.S. Graphics Limited	£9,024,639
The Wilkinson Corporation Limited	£9,006,531
Insert Ltd	£9,002,407
Crompton Lamps Limited	£9,002,155
Austin Friars	£9,001,479
Research & Development Tax Solutions (Holdings)	£9,000,000
Sports Tours International Limited	£8,994,823
Healthcare House Limited	£8,989,986
East Cheshire Hospice	£8,989,894
Ross Care Holdings Limited	£8,989,215
Mersey Waste Holdings Limited	£8,988,931
Hanes Holdings UK Limited	£8,988,930
Caldew School	£8,988,071
Tibst Limited	£8,984,223
Sunsave 15 (Westwood) Limited	£8,984,064
Jetchem Systems Limited	£8,982,836
St George Healthcare Limited	£8,982,012
GE Capital Corporation (Investment Properties) Ltd	£8,982,000
Elvaston Investments Limited	£8,980,586
St. Bede's College Limited	£8,978,678
Rowlinson Knitwear Limited	£8,976,103
TI Industrial Group Limited	£8,974,000
Range High School	£8,973,744
Highfield Farm LLP	£8,972,142
Sealand Commercial Properties Limited	£8,969,608
Luton Engineering Services (Southwest) Limited	£8,955,145
Forward Construction and Developments Limited	£8,954,496
Ralli Ltd.	£8,950,126
Rock House Investments Limited	£8,946,981
BCP Corporate Limited	£8,946,000
Moor Hall Holdings Limited	£8,945,466
The Pinnacle Learning Trust	£8,944,633
Big Life Schools	£8,944,000
Micad Systems (U.K.) Limited	£8,942,927
Wilson & Scott (Highways) Limited	£8,942,607
Daniel Johnston (1982) Limited	£8,941,590
P.J.D. (Holdings) Limited	£8,941,506
AC/DC LED Holdings Limited	£8,941,415
ATG Access Ltd	£8,939,917
NMU (Specialty) Ltd	£8,938,719
Walker Fire (UK) Limited	£8,938,108
HSL Group Holdings Limited	£8,932,740
John Chorley & Company,Limited	£8,932,422
A & D Transport (NW) Limited	£8,928,627
Sune Hill Farm Solar Limited	£8,927,345
Marchington Group Limited	£8,927,215
Marchington Stone Limited	£8,927,075
Mostyn Terminals Limited	£8,923,015
Drive Further Limited	£8,920,403
Jeremy Benn Associates Limited	£8,918,719
Cardinal Project Management Limited	£8,918,508
T. & J.T. Barton (Bottlers) Limited	£8,909,754
T & J T Barton (Holdings) Ltd	£8,909,754
Starbank Panel Products Limited	£8,909,587

Company	Amount
George Morgan Holdings Limited	£8,906,795
F.G.Whitley and Sons Co.Limited	£8,904,044
Cosmopolitan Textile Company Limited	£8,903,000
North East Convenience Stores Limited	£8,902,759
Baybutt Investments Limited	£8,901,221
Woodlands Care GRP Ltd	£8,896,242
Adlib Audio Limited	£8,895,126
P.E. Jones Contracts (Manchester) Limited	£8,886,206
Ripe Thinking Limited	£8,884,882
Mobiletron UK Limited	£8,874,319
James Industrial Limited	£8,868,668
CLV Investments UK Limited	£8,862,000
St. Johns Buildings Limited	£8,854,421
Alere Limited	£8,852,886
Yes Car Credit (Holdings) Limited	£8,847,000
The Monastery of St Francis and Gorton Trust	£8,842,688
McDermott Homes Limited	£8,831,743
Paragon Developments (Manchester) Limited	£8,831,111
Collier Industrial Waste Limited	£8,828,282
R & W Scott Ltd	£8,827,968
River Park Trading Estate Limited	£8,825,997
Co-operative Commercial Limited	£8,824,765
Deckers Restaurants Limited	£8,819,864
Piggott and Whitfield Limited	£8,812,756
Kintec Group Limited	£8,812,370
Provfin Limited	£8,811,000
Doric Anderton Limited	£8,810,284
CTI Billing Solutions Limited	£8,808,004
Travelworld International (Manchester) Limited	£8,805,278
Rigby Estates LLP	£8,802,552
Giti Tire (UK) Limited	£8,800,783
Oswaldtwistle Mills Limited	£8,794,909
Avantec Healthcare Limited	£8,794,068
Polcom UK Limited	£8,793,295
Kingswood Homes (UK) Ltd	£8,793,294
T.A. Weatherwear Limited	£8,787,397
Boughey Distribution Limited	£8,785,000
Plastic Recycling Limited	£8,784,401
Soil Engineering Geoservices Limited	£8,781,000
Raan Investments Ltd	£8,777,901
RG14 Limited	£8,776,467
Hallamshire Investments Limited	£8,775,271
Carlisle United Association Football Club (1921) Limited	£8,772,441
C.U.F.C. Holdings Limited	£8,772,441
1st Stop Reserve Limited	£8,770,019
Radioactive Waste Management Limited	£8,767,765
Tarncourt Investments LLP	£8,767,157
Raydex/CDT Limited	£8,766,000
K.R.M. U.K. Ltd	£8,762,646
AIS Vanguard Limited	£8,754,841
Apeks Marine Equipment Limited	£8,754,574
Siae Microelettronica Limited	£8,754,082
Pakeeza Dairies Limited	£8,753,882
Servicepower Business Solutions Limited	£8,753,000
Heaton Park Garage Limited	£8,752,239
Highland Smoked Salmon (Holdings) Limited	£8,749,526
Mudskipper Business Limited	£8,744,335
Shawston International Limited	£8,738,619
P. Casey (Developments) Limited	£8,737,922
Tower Hill Property Investments (10) Limited	£8,737,000
Bridge Insurance Brokers Limited	£8,727,099
Feralco (UK) Limited	£8,724,000
Laurus Living Space LLP	£8,722,834
Marpak Extrusions Limited	£8,719,237
Brooklyn Properties Limited	£8,711,995
SameTimeTomorrow Limited	£8,710,290
Barclay House Securities Limited	£8,709,519
Croner Taxwise Limited	£8,708,135
Crampton Bros (Coopers) Ltd	£8,706,037
Braymale Limited	£8,705,024
DSG 1988 Limited	£8,700,871
Leoron Investments Limited	£8,699,249
National Flexible Limited	£8,688,595
Reisser Limited	£8,684,943
Archbold Logistics Limited	£8,682,614
Dept UK Holding Limited	£8,679,531
Irmass Company Limited	£8,674,669
Assurant Intermediary Limited	£8,670,000
Westline Investments Limited	£8,667,017
Tom Martin Metal Holdings Limited	£8,666,262
Otto Simon Limited	£8,661,927
Montgomery Tomlinson Limited	£8,658,000
Interket Limited	£8,651,250
West Kirby Residential School	£8,647,981
Phillips & Cohen Associates International, Ltd	£8,647,195
Zoe Ashton Limited	£8,645,108
Servlite U.K. Limited	£8,644,061
Intervoice Limited	£8,635,000
ASE Group Limited	£8,634,879
HPO1 Nominees Limited	£8,633,000
Georgia GC Limited	£8,614,801
Bamfield Lodge Limited	£8,613,000
A Pearson & Sons (1949) LLP	£8,612,000
Acre Products Limited	£8,611,444
Daisytame Limited	£8,607,185
SW Golf Limited	£8,607,000
Young Foundations Limited	£8,602,534
Lightfooting Limited	£8,600,867
KRMCO Limited	£8,599,263
Vita (Sheff) 1 Limited	£8,598,000
M.A.C. (Roofing & Contracting) Limited	£8,593,269
JMU Property Development Company Limited	£8,593,098
Q Dental Care Limited	£8,592,517
Mini Gears Group Holdings Limited	£8,590,442
Equip4work Ltd	£8,587,059
Custom Glass Limited	£8,584,333
Methanex (UK) Limited	£8,584,000
Bux & Co. Limited	£8,583,130
Peel Leisure (Operations) Holdings Limited	£8,580,189
Greystone Financial Services (Holdings) Limited	£8,579,339
RPG Group Limited	£8,578,497
Total Care and Support Limited	£8,574,812
Carlson Filtration Limited	£8,573,461
Gee Lawson Limited	£8,573,294
Centre Island Preston Limited	£8,572,939
Harper Industries PLC	£8,572,719
Lee-Mar Estates Limited	£8,570,891
Thomas Hardy Kendal Limited	£8,570,000
Riverside Park Limited	£8,568,745
X1 Manchester Waters Limited	£8,565,247
Cox 22 Limited	£8,562,346
Ashton Agricultural and General Limited	£8,558,491
Medihealth Limited	£8,557,392
Bridge Brokers Limited	£8,554,012
RDG Foulridge Properties Limited	£8,554,011
C.N.T. Limited	£8,553,719
CRP Print & Packaging Holdings Limited	£8,553,000
Plantec Assist Limited	£8,552,000
Robert Tweddle (Timber Merchant & Haulage Contractor)	£8,546,419
Manchester and District Home for Lost Dogs Limited	£8,546,010
Wolfson Trago Limited	£8,543,000
Boardlink Limited	£8,542,573
Risebrook Properties Limited	£8,536,842
Geometric Furniture Limited	£8,534,579
Penman Estates Limited	£8,533,641
Penthouse Carpets Holdings Limited	£8,528,300
Penthouse Carpets Limited	£8,528,296
Warden Construction Limited	£8,527,079
JJC Hire Limited	£8,526,878
Precision Technologies Group (US) Limited	£8,524,833
G.F. Holding (Contractors) Limited	£8,519,397
S.P.L. Foods Limited	£8,507,483
FDC (Holdings) Limited	£8,505,047
Springhill Hospice (Rochdale)	£8,495,203

Company	Value
Swiscot Textiles Limited	£8,492,431
STB Holdings Limited	£8,489,000
Firwood Timber & Plywood Co. Limited	£8,485,025
J & K Confectionery Limited	£8,484,932
Clarke and Pulman Limited	£8,478,919
Adelphi Mill Properties Limited	£8,477,369
LMR Drilling UK Ltd	£8,476,078
Fairway (G.B.) Limited	£8,474,927
Parkhaven Trust	£8,474,109
Le-Fylde Estates Ltd	£8,471,635
Incorporate Travel Management Limited	£8,471,241
Holt Family (Holdings) Limited	£8,467,867
John Robson (Metals) Limited	£8,463,992
The Rosebery Group Limited	£8,457,487
J.Stell & Sons,Limited	£8,455,893
Berwin Group Limited	£8,455,177
Lawsons Haulage Limited	£8,445,787
MTX Holdings Limited	£8,443,605
Brookhouse Builders Limited	£8,443,000
Lifting Gear UK Group Limited	£8,435,378
Northern Diver (International) Ltd	£8,433,763
Bluebell (Crewe) Limited	£8,431,000
Dent Logistics Limited	£8,429,424
Tzortzis Limited	£8,417,787
Empire House Bradford Ltd	£8,416,613
Loop Customer Management Limited	£8,416,000
Sandown Property Company (Liverpool) Limited	£8,412,770
Kinaxia Logistics Limited	£8,410,170
Hewer-White Trust	£8,407,059
Impact Development Training Ltd.	£8,406,503
The Alternative Steel Group Limited	£8,404,231
PSC (Holdings) Limited	£8,399,770
Merlyn Industries U.K. Limited	£8,398,545
Manchester Rent A Home Limited	£8,395,303
BC3.01 Ltd	£8,394,424
Brampton View Limited	£8,387,000
Produmax Limited	£8,386,376
Lenagan Investments Limited	£8,379,953
Knowsley Contractors Limited	£8,379,457
Goyt Properties Limited	£8,378,265
Stell Cardboard Tubes Limited	£8,376,084
Flanagan Property Services Ltd.	£8,372,900
Medical Gas Solutions Limited	£8,370,000
Dobies Cumbria Finance Limited	£8,369,640
Revolution Direct Ltd	£8,363,938
Stavert Zigomala Limited	£8,362,864
Wigan and Leigh Homes Ltd	£8,362,696
Bulloughs Cleaning Services Limited	£8,355,123
Nextdom Roscoe Limited	£8,352,638
The Wings' CE Trust	£8,352,625
Business Computer Projects Limited	£8,351,858
K3 Syspro Limited	£8,346,808
API Foils Holdings Limited	£8,346,000
Pinnacle Student Developments (Egerton Street) Ltd	£8,344,138
Spindles Investment Limited	£8,344,126
Fleet and Plant Hire Limited	£8,344,000
Gunn JCB (Holdings) Limited	£8,343,000
C.M. Jefferies & Co. Limited	£8,339,671
Fibreforce Composites Limited	£8,333,000
The Valley Printing Company, Limited	£8,330,000
Sandbach School	£8,329,430
Tesni Properties Limited	£8,325,654
Fircroft Technical Services UK Limited	£8,324,561
Healthpoint 2016 Limited	£8,322,420
Cubby Construction Limited	£8,322,359
Hasgrove Limited	£8,322,156
Flowflex Components Limited	£8,321,655
NAT Flex Group Limited	£8,320,385
J.R. Bushell (Lowton) Limited	£8,317,973
Dorbcrest Homes Limited	£8,309,707
Blankstone Sington Limited	£8,309,196
Famevalley Limited	£8,305,922
Havencare Management Limited	£8,305,670
C J Services UK Limited	£8,305,598
Aidenhall Ltd	£8,305,015
Hodgson Academy	£8,305,000
K3 Business Solutions Limited	£8,304,735
Roy Hankinson (Holdings) Limited	£8,301,184
Amiculum Limited	£8,300,154
Ace Supply Company Limited (The)	£8,298,290
Widex UK Limited	£8,297,371
Aimia Foods Group Limited	£8,296,000
Patrick Properties Altrincham Holdings Limited	£8,291,081
Compass Seacare Holdings Limited	£8,288,502
Panaz Limited	£8,287,231
Maghull High School	£8,285,272
Kensington Developments Holdings Limited	£8,282,190
Smit Harbour Towage (UK) Limited	£8,280,000
Mansell Finishes Limited	£8,277,793
Jason Plastics Limited	£8,273,401
Transportation Infrastructure Group Limited	£8,271,246
Corkills Volkswagen Limited	£8,268,324
WSR Recycling Limited	£8,263,554
Equinox Properties Limited	£8,255,733
Holbeck Ghyll Hotel LLP	£8,253,351
Millbank Holdings Limited	£8,253,266
Per-Scent Group Limited	£8,250,005
Hurlston Hall Property Limited	£8,244,343
M-Hance Limited	£8,233,733
Tudorborne Limited	£8,229,193
Selmar Properties Ltd	£8,224,134
Staveley's Eggs Limited	£8,222,778
Bako South Eastern Limited	£8,221,000
Nutriad Ltd	£8,218,000
Performance Car Hire Limited	£8,217,304
Packed Chlorine Limited	£8,213,470
Penwortham Priory Academy Trust	£8,212,000
Victorguard Care PLC	£8,207,843
UPM Group Ltd	£8,207,050
Finsa UK Limited	£8,203,000
Bridstock Gate Limited	£8,197,300
Burnley Savings and Loans Limited	£8,197,265
Ultra Finance Limited	£8,189,000
Leisureplan Investments Limited	£8,188,682
Albany Products Limited	£8,187,000
Atlantic Tool Leasing U.K. Limited	£8,179,506
Ingot Portal Limited	£8,179,045
CMS Computers Limited	£8,173,000
Affordable Window Systems Limited	£8,172,906
Singleton's Dairy Limited	£8,171,929
Ling Properties Limited	£8,168,314
Infra Safety Services Labour Limited	£8,166,987
Global Equity Finance Ltd	£8,166,605
Caritas Diocese of Salford	£8,166,339
Hindle Group Limited	£8,165,647
Mardon Holdings Limited	£8,159,258
Lever Academy Trust	£8,159,082
RGFC Dust Limited	£8,157,000
The View Trust	£8,154,873
MPP Global Solutions Ltd	£8,150,009
Leisureplan Projects Limited	£8,150,004
AMR Textiles Limited	£8,146,792
IQRA Academy Education Trust	£8,145,994
Assura CVSK Limited	£8,144,408
The Christopher Harrison Group Limited	£8,140,831
Sanjeev 1979 Limited	£8,138,540
Earth's Crust Resources Limited	£8,138,215
Barton Park Homes Limited	£8,132,259
Hall Park Healthcare Limited	£8,131,000
Brand Search Limited	£8,129,112
Countrylass Ltd	£8,129,063
Alderley Urban Investments Limited	£8,128,048
53 King Street LLP	£8,123,078
Nuseed Europe Ltd	£8,122,000

Regency House Finance Limited	£8,120,118
Wigan Metropolitan Development Co (Investment) Ltd	£8,109,142
Nightjar Sustainable Power Limited	£8,106,106
Woodley Sports Centre Limited	£8,103,911
Genedrive Diagnostics Ltd	£8,103,000
St.Edward's College Edmund Rice Academy Trust	£8,099,447
Hadfield Wood Recyclers Limited	£8,097,758
Seamore Court Freehold Limited	£8,097,179
Stamford Products Limited	£8,097,000
Trigon Snacks Trading Limited	£8,096,892
Beesley Fuels Ltd	£8,095,292
H.H. Smith & Sons Co. Limited	£8,094,200
Driver Hire Investments Limited	£8,093,015
Boyton Solar Park Limited	£8,092,557
Healthy Learning Trust	£8,087,000
Penzance Leisure Limited	£8,083,349
Hough Green Garage Limited	£8,080,932
Komatsu Forest Limited	£8,080,784
Inspirepac Holdings Limited	£8,080,179
S Cooper Group Limited	£8,078,412
Schosween 6 Limited	£8,077,556
Trans - Continental Group Limited	£8,075,207
RSK Adas Limited	£8,073,000
E.C.A.M. Properties Limited	£8,072,089
C2 Investment Limited	£8,069,603
M-Hance Group Limited	£8,068,788
Motorplus Limited	£8,065,749
Becontree Limited	£8,064,431
Zabaxe Limited	£8,064,351
Arista (U.K.) Limited	£8,059,918
Refrigeration Norwest (Chester) Limited	£8,059,719
Wireless Holdings Limited	£8,059,098
Oxley Developments Company Limited	£8,057,874
James Galt & Co. Limited	£8,054,689
Graphic Packaging International Box Holdings Limited	£8,051,000
T.Anwyl & Son Limited	£8,047,449
Lloyd & Jones Engineers Limited	£8,047,087
Heat Trace Holdings Limited	£8,046,458
Harthill Wind Limited	£8,043,737
Bank Restaurant Company Limited	£8,040,000
Hilbre Estates Limited	£8,039,793
Heat Trace Limited	£8,034,357
Codecrest Limited	£8,033,808
Nanoco Technologies Limited	£8,031,000
PSS (UK)	£8,030,135
Exide Technologies (Transportation) Limited	£8,026,000
M2 Managed Document Services Ltd	£8,024,735
Capital Bank Leasing 5 Limited	£8,024,000
Hindle & Walker Limited	£8,023,078
Bowland (Holdings) Limited	£8,021,129
Rainbow Dust Colours Limited	£8,020,657
Wireless CCTV Limited	£8,019,831
Weltonhurst Limited	£8,016,419
Cepen Lodge Limited	£8,016,000
Millennium Care (U.K.) Limited	£8,010,889
Beamfeature Limited	£8,008,004
Holden Decor Limited	£8,000,764
Power Gems Holdings Limited	£8,000,000
Hearthcote Property Services Limited	£7,999,000
Saint-Gobain Industrial Ceramics Limited	£7,998,000
Liqui-Box UK Limited	£7,995,962
Alderley Edge School for Girls	£7,995,167
Federal Capital Limited	£7,993,418
XLR8 Sports Limited	£7,991,594
East Coast Concepts Group Limited	£7,990,243
Cutting Edge Investments Limited	£7,984,427
Gordon Rigg (Nurseries) Limited	£7,983,580
Cuerden Developments Ltd.	£7,982,214
Stockfis Holdings Limited	£7,981,761
Entwistle & Joynt Limited	£7,980,461
Lumenpulse UK Limited	£7,979,586
Liverpool Shipbrokers Benevolent Society Incorporated	£7,976,709
Bridging Finance Solutions Group Limited	£7,970,468
A.J.A. Smith Properties Limited	£7,968,700
Casartelli Buildings Limited	£7,968,016
Parry's Motor Parts Limited	£7,967,568
NCC Group Accumuli Security Limited	£7,965,000
Counterline Limited	£7,958,430
In Touch with Bricks Limited	£7,958,293
Bolton Lads' and Girls' Club	£7,952,196
Manchester Diocesan Board of Education	£7,951,279
AIS Projects Limited	£7,949,841
Eavesway Travel Limited	£7,928,586
Www.Rigby LLP	£7,924,782
Legacy Capital Limited	£7,924,673
The Rosebery Group Holdings Limited	£7,922,987
Autism Together	£7,918,000
Prorendita Five Limited	£7,917,683
PBM Debury Limited	£7,915,720
Furmanite 1986	£7,915,000
Ashaeve Limited	£7,909,124
NJK Clothing Ltd	£7,906,724
Whittle Eastern Europe Logistics Ltd.	£7,906,410
Advanced Medical Solutions (Plymouth) Limited	£7,906,000
United Reformed Church (North Western Province)	£7,904,109
Patrick Properties Crewe Limited	£7,898,767
Jacobi Carbons Limited	£7,889,220
JDS Trucks Limited	£7,882,301
Birkenhead Car and Van Hire Limited	£7,875,710
Mansfield, Pollard & Co. Limited	£7,875,562
Alderburgh Limited	£7,873,434
Sigma PRS Investments III Limited	£7,871,778
Irish Ferries (U.K.) Limited	£7,869,000
Warmwell Properties Limited	£7,868,384
Cascade (U.K.) Limited	£7,868,000
Nexus Telecommunications Limited	£7,864,910
Liverpool Streetscene Services Limited	£7,863,000
T G Cottam Limited	£7,858,707
The Ace Supply Holding Company Limited	£7,854,158
Jones & Brooks,Limited	£7,850,203
WA Casement Holdings Limited	£7,848,657
Golden Sunrise (Holdings) Limited	£7,845,257
Sean Louis Investments Limited	£7,843,527
Imperial Furniture Group Limited	£7,831,795
Energus	£7,830,721
Seacare Inverness Limited	£7,829,886
Lakeview Rest Homes Limited	£7,828,819
Orthoworld 2000 Limited	£7,825,000
Entwistle & Joynt Holdings Limited	£7,820,512
Harrington & Hallworth Limited	£7,818,527
Fortunelodge Limited	£7,810,060
Pinnacle Developments (NW) Limited	£7,806,805
South Yorkshire Supertram Limited	£7,803,000
Audas Project Management Limited	£7,800,011
LF Logistics (UK) Limited	£7,796,000
Kukri GB Limited	£7,785,208
Mardon Public Limited Company	£7,780,109
Cotton Estates Limited	£7,779,801
G & H Print Services Limited	£7,777,045
Multimedia International Services Limited	£7,776,512
Delamere Dairy Limited	£7,775,924
D. Stoker Group Limited	£7,775,774
P I H Holdings Limited	£7,775,541
CHP Supplies Limited	£7,774,864
Alfa Coaches Limited	£7,772,835
Salts Estates Limited	£7,770,405
Mediaco Limited	£7,765,647
Moore and Smalley LLP	£7,755,860
Cuadrilla Well Services Limited	£7,754,027
Whiskey Jack Developments Limited	£7,749,122
Peel Real Estate Developments Holdings Limited	£7,748,889
EHC Harnham House Limited	£7,748,751
NMS Logistics Limited	£7,746,125
Rowlinson Group Limited	£7,744,195

Company	Value
Warden Holdings Limited	£7,742,213
Vita Investments North America Limited	£7,735,073
Nova Group Limited	£7,731,918
Orchard House (MPS) Limited	£7,731,706
The Mansion Group Limited	£7,727,430
Uriah Woodhead & Son Limited	£7,727,050
Capital Bridging Finance Solutions Limited	£7,725,070
Warmer Energy Services Limited	£7,720,493
Incorez Limited	£7,718,884
TEF Transport Limited	£7,718,015
Spinney Garage Limited	£7,717,404
Burg-Wachter UK Limited	£7,716,947
Ortho-Care (U.K.) Limited	£7,716,896
I Care Extra Care Limited	£7,716,591
A. V. Group Limited	£7,713,502
Imperial Office Furniture Ltd	£7,711,690
Sartex Quilts & Textiles Limited	£7,698,270
Pattinson-Appleby Limited	£7,690,635
Ansell (Sales & Distribution) Limited	£7,685,256
Bibby Asset Finance Limited	£7,680,751
Gavco 188 Limited	£7,679,638
Manchester Diocesan Church House Company Ltd	£7,678,354
Haddow Group Limited	£7,676,344
ATG Airports Limited	£7,670,933
Rajan Trading Co. Limited	£7,663,597
Recipharm Limited	£7,659,000
Mortgage Agency Services Number Four Limited	£7,655,000
Plastic Formers Management Limited	£7,654,474
Ascot Road Watford Limited	£7,654,000
Scarisbrick Hall Limited	£7,653,881
Ainscough Strategic Land Limited	£7,653,856
Cole-Parmer UK Bibby Acquisition Limited	£7,647,870
L&D Real Estate Limited	£7,641,835
Brabant Limited	£7,639,098
Tuneside Limited	£7,630,562
Wrapid Manufacturing Limited	£7,629,174
Deliver Net Limited	£7,628,467
Armstrong Learning Limited	£7,618,913
The Formby Land Trust	£7,616,004
Underley Schools Limited	£7,613,648
Inns & Leisure Limited	£7,606,832
Brenrun Limited	£7,605,096
Titleabsolute Limited	£7,603,000
Spellman & Walker Direct Limited	£7,601,286
High Floor Rentals Ltd	£7,599,193
Kays Medical Limited	£7,595,987
Linco Care Limited	£7,592,742
Kiernan Construction Limited	£7,585,042
HSS Hire Service Holdings Limited	£7,584,000
PIMCO 2401 Limited	£7,578,506
Palmers Scaffolding UK Limited	£7,575,000
David Pluck (North West) Limited	£7,572,531
Consummate Investments Limited	£7,562,317
3Sixty Restaurants Limited	£7,561,780
Precision Parts UK Limited	£7,561,495
Baerlocher UK Limited	£7,560,886
Icknield Holdings Limited	£7,560,886
J.H.F. Limited	£7,559,234
Carrix Limited	£7,555,968
Cosatto Limited	£7,555,000
Contour Showers Limited	£7,554,858
Ian Armstrong (Carlisle) Limited	£7,553,194
Metaltek International (UK) Limited	£7,550,323
Ysgellog Wind Farm Limited	£7,549,941
Ethika Healthcare Investments Limited	£7,548,511
Sykes Chemists Limited	£7,547,824
Edge Hill Property Services Limited	£7,547,000
City Life Projects Limited	£7,546,333
Peel Wind Farms (Sheerness) Limited	£7,546,163
Red Rose Holdings Limited	£7,542,945
Thomas Higgins Limited	£7,537,267
J.S.M. Finance Limited	£7,535,365

Company	Value
St. Annes (Holdings) Limited	£7,532,134
Royal Greenland Limited	£7,531,517
Victor Manufacturing Limited	£7,524,692
S G Equipment Limited	£7,521,367
Ribble Valley Luxury Homes Limited	£7,518,516
Brinksway Tool Limited	£7,517,662
Dawsons Music Limited	£7,517,652
Care Worldwide (Southwell) Limited	£7,508,816
Northern Developments (Cumbria) Limited	£7,507,420
Browntree Properties Limited	£7,503,482
LB Europe Limited	£7,499,486
HO2 Management Limited	£7,499,390
Promatic Group Limited	£7,499,271
Sandown Property Holdings Limited	£7,494,739
Chesford Grange Estates LLP	£7,487,839
Fedex Trade Networks Transport & Brokerage (UK)	£7,487,246
C & W Berry Trading Limited	£7,484,647
SR Properties Nationwide Limited	£7,480,794
Setco Automotive (UK) Limited	£7,480,068
RSL Property Management Ltd	£7,478,935
Hilary Meredith Solicitors Limited	£7,476,874
Suez Water Technologies & Solutions United Kingdom	£7,476,000
Cumbria Waste Recycling Limited	£7,474,000
Zyex Group Limited	£7,473,694
Zyex Limited	£7,473,694
Calder International Holdings Limited	£7,473,000
Marplace (Number 754) Limited	£7,472,768
Yeargate Limited	£7,470,110
Ascent Ventures Limited	£7,465,848
Thermal Hire Ltd	£7,464,701
KH&GW Limited	£7,464,072
Martin Moore Furniture Limited	£7,460,138
Hill Ground Rents Limited	£7,456,386
Chain Link Holding Company Limited	£7,454,978
Bulmer & Lumb Holdings Limited	£7,453,764
Sovereign Group Limited	£7,451,685
Clive Hurt (Holdings) Limited	£7,450,184
Wilsons Contractors Limited	£7,446,816
Muraspec Limited	£7,442,467
F. Parkinson Limited	£7,440,773
Dr Kershaw's Hospice	£7,436,638
Maxilead Limited	£7,435,737
Kentmere Limited	£7,435,697
Monopol Holdings Limited	£7,434,107
Globe Enterprises Limited	£7,433,660
Cavitech Solutions (Holdings) Limited	£7,431,120
Mumtaz Food Products Limited	£7,425,491
NSX2 Management Co Limited	£7,424,031
Consensus Property Ltd	£7,420,494
Seddons (Plant and Engineers) Limited	£7,419,283
Botraco Holdings Limited	£7,418,703
Thomas Frederick & Company Limited	£7,416,229
Kintec Recruitment Limited	£7,415,424
The Franciscan Missionaries of St Joseph	£7,411,799
Town Head Farm Products Limited	£7,411,112
Joda Holdings Limited	£7,410,381
Midas Paper Converters Limited	£7,408,378
9CW04 Limited	£7,402,950
UAP Limited	£7,400,897
Northern Packaging Holdings Limited	£7,400,292
Mulard Renewables Limited	£7,395,972
Keysource Limited	£7,393,223
Mill Farm Ventures Limited	£7,391,329
Thomas Wright/Thorite Group Limited	£7,390,212
Regal Vehicle Rentals Limited	£7,388,270
McBride CE Holdings Limited	£7,386,000
Mastacab Assets LLP	£7,384,967
Thompson Management Services Blackpool Limited	£7,379,297
Patrick Properties Northampton Limited	£7,378,358
The Sisters Estate Limited	£7,376,252
Lockhurst Holdings Limited	£7,373,489
Cheetham Church of England Community Academy	£7,371,718

Personal Audit Systems Holdings Limited	£7,367,261
Adviserplus Business Solutions Limited	£7,367,000
Store First Midlands Limited	£7,366,670
Promenade Estates Limited	£7,362,180
UKFast Properties Limited	£7,359,741
Coral Products (Mouldings) Ltd	£7,358,069
Candelisa Limited	£7,354,347
Lock Inspection Systems Limited	£7,353,000
T.I.M. Co. (Didsbury) Limited	£7,349,534
Chi Yip Group Limited	£7,349,472
RRG (West Yorkshire) Limited	£7,346,000
Vision Multi Academy Trust	£7,344,000
Information and Data Networks Supplies Holdings	£7,343,697
Medlock FRB Limited	£7,332,759
First Pioneer Bus Limited	£7,329,000
Closomat (Great Britain) Limited	£7,325,719
MacKnight Limited	£7,322,963
Gutterline Services Limited	£7,321,768
Warrington Community Living	£7,321,473
Simba Smoby Toys (UK) Limited	£7,320,198
Egerton Investments Limited	£7,313,578
T.N.Robinson Limited	£7,311,707
Leep Utilities Electricity Limited	£7,311,016
Commercial Power Limited	£7,309,799
Parkhouse Lakeland LLP	£7,308,526
Summit Food Holdings Limited	£7,307,053
SAT Business Travel Management Limited	£7,305,548
North & Partners Technical Limited	£7,303,581
Sea Park (Apart) Hotel Limited	£7,303,444
Sellick Partnership Limited	£7,301,917
Snappy Snaps Franchises Limited	£7,300,959
Sandusky Limited	£7,299,151
I-Paye Limited	£7,290,923
H.T.Barnes & Sons Limited	£7,290,706
Bruntwood 2000 (NW Regen) Limited	£7,290,000
Hardscape Products Limited	£7,289,084
Custom Powders Limited	£7,288,233
The Funding Corporation (2) Limited	£7,285,547
Crest Plus Operations Limited	£7,284,852
Gresty Holdings Limited	£7,284,845
Whittle Programmed Maintenance Limited	£7,283,783
Allmand - Smith Limited	£7,273,299
Parkmount Estate Company (Allerton) Limited	£7,272,649
Revegate Limited	£7,269,249
Newfield Fabrications Company Limited	£7,264,739
St Helens Chamber Limited	£7,257,837
Bispham Green Brewery Company Limited	£7,256,332
Medline Stellar UK Limited	£7,252,965
M H & J Park and Son Limited	£7,249,908
Springhill House (Accrington) Limited	£7,245,318
Green Pastures North West Limited	£7,240,494
Concord Holdings Limited	£7,237,858
Ribble Property Developments Limited	£7,236,700
Harrisons Dairies Limited	£7,234,996
Wind Pol 2 Holding Limited	£7,230,316
Peel Environmental Holdings Limited	£7,226,480
Manchester Property & Development (No.2) Limited	£7,224,592
Hammer Group Limited	£7,220,847
Fleur Telecom Limited	£7,220,000
Multiplastics (Europe) Limited	£7,217,939
Bathgate Flooring Limited	£7,217,655
Schofields Limited	£7,207,921
Whitakers Chocolates Limited	£7,204,603
Agricultural Machinery (Nantwich) Limited	£7,195,644
Trinity Enterprise Centre Limited	£7,195,045
Manor Coating Systems (Holdings) Limited	£7,194,549
Brilie Properties Limited	£7,193,775
NST Transport Services Limited	£7,189,732
Talpole Limited	£7,187,587
Elterbeck Limited	£7,187,476
Arjowiggins Chartham Limited	£7,185,000
Univer Manufacturing Company Ltd	£7,179,782
Potter Rees Limited	£7,179,346
McGarr McCarrick Limited	£7,177,365
O.M.C. Motor Group Limited	£7,169,502
Alfa Travel Ltd.	£7,166,770
Intelling Group Limited	£7,165,741
Jo-Y-Jo Limited	£7,164,387
Jo-Y-Jo International Limited	£7,164,387
Obbligato Hotels Limited	£7,152,751
CMS Network (London) Ltd	£7,148,583
Micro Systems (UK) Limited	£7,143,041
Tyson H. Burridge Limited	£7,135,403
Primeur Limited	£7,130,508
BH (Manchester) Limited	£7,127,290
P J Livesey Living Space (11) Limited	£7,124,999
Grafenia Operations Limited	£7,118,000
Garden State Property Management Ltd	£7,108,553
Grafenia PLC	£7,105,000
Hen House (Wholesale) Limited	£7,104,908
K.M. Holmes (Bradford) Limited	£7,103,112
John Roberts Ventures Limited	£7,103,004
Adhan Homes Ltd	£7,097,598
Chorley Yamaha Centre Limited	£7,095,864
Nos 3 Limited	£7,095,289
Kingsoak Limited	£7,094,380
The Alternative Steel Company Limited	£7,087,460
Able2 UK Limited	£7,084,316
Edge Transport (Properties) Limited	£7,082,778
M.G.S. Estates Limited	£7,080,928
K M (Property Management) Limited	£7,077,190
S.M.D. Home Limited	£7,076,513
GPC Computer Software Limited	£7,071,794
The Oakes Business Park Development Company Ltd.	£7,069,790
Pet Food Brands (Holdings) Ltd	£7,069,027
Parkwood Community Leisure Limited	£7,065,000
1st International Limited	£7,063,513
Southport and Windsor Properties LLP	£7,063,336
Mitton Mechanical Services Limited	£7,063,150
Metalube Ltd	£7,061,554
Hexagon Solutions Limited	£7,054,248
Chiesi Healthcare Limited	£7,054,000
Bennett & Fountain Limited	£7,053,000
Cutwel Limited	£7,037,284
Hansengroup Limited	£7,035,819
Orford Investments Limited	£7,033,757
The Christian Trust	£7,030,859
Nalge (Europe) Limited	£7,030,000
Americk Advantage Limited	£7,022,000
Rothay Garden Hotel Limited	£7,017,113
Carrylift Group Finance Limited	£7,016,673
Holt Holdings North West Limited	£7,013,502
Black Cat Fireworks Limited	£7,007,000
Dana Sac UK Limited	£7,005,168
ADP Healthcare Acquisitions Limited	£7,005,000
Help Your Property Limited	£7,001,843
Ivan Ambrose and Company Limited	£6,996,825
Cloud Technology Solutions Ltd	£6,992,653
Baker Properties Limited	£6,992,455
Rotapoint Limited	£6,989,112
Simon Family Office Limited	£6,983,344
Imperial Corporate Events Ltd	£6,980,066
W W Hotels Limited	£6,975,428
Armcon Limited	£6,971,686
Park Card Marketing Services Limited	£6,970,948
Mathers Foundry Limited	£6,966,000
Medline Industries Limited	£6,963,746
Ironsides Lubricants Limited (The)	£6,961,492
The Chester Catholic Academies Partnership	£6,959,923
Johnston Developments Holdings Limited	£6,957,939
Calvin Capital Australia Holdings Limited	£6,955,932
Assurant Direct Limited	£6,949,000
Children of Success Schools Trust	£6,949,000
East Youlstone Wind Farm Limited	£6,932,728

Company	Amount
JCCO 387 Limited	£6,932,307
Peninsular Estates Limited	£6,931,959
Fresh Approach (UK) Limited	£6,929,772
Westcliffe Holdings Limited	£6,925,808
Cramer Properties Limited	£6,925,709
Q. R. I. Ltd	£6,920,941
Alpha Flight UK Limited	£6,920,000
The Grange Care Centre (Cheltenham) Limited	£6,916,491
Bradford Trident Limited	£6,914,799
Sayers The Bakers Limited	£6,908,000
Williams Tarr Developments Limited	£6,906,678
Manchester Drinks Company Ltd	£6,903,282
G & J Properties Limited	£6,900,959
Horizon Global European Holdings Limited	£6,900,895
Abbotsound Limited	£6,899,908
United Springs Limited	£6,895,573
API Group Services Limited	£6,893,000
Jiffy (UK) Holding I Limited	£6,891,000
Enza Group Limited	£6,889,562
Kindertons Holdings Limited	£6,887,000
Pfeifer Drako Ltd	£6,884,011
City of Liverpool Investment Company Limited (The)	£6,883,194
Alphacare Holdings Limited	£6,883,000
Gogar Services Limited	£6,880,436
Advanced Processing Limited	£6,877,619
Estuary Group Limited	£6,877,578
Rowcon Limited	£6,877,319
Mederco (Cardiff) Ltd	£6,876,821
System 3 Investments Limited	£6,876,577
Worldwide Procurement Limited	£6,875,001
Wm Morrison Bananas Limited	£6,875,000
Woodford Regeneration Limited	£6,870,083
Trac Group Limited	£6,868,000
Scotsland Limited	£6,865,356
Gladman Homes LLP	£6,862,869
SG World Limited	£6,862,820
Worldwide Foods (Rochdale) Limited	£6,860,578
M247 Ltd	£6,855,000
Keighley Fleece Mills Company Limited	£6,849,411
Meter Fit Assets Limited	£6,848,000
MPBM Limited	£6,844,194
Atkinson Homes Limited	£6,844,144
Cheshire Academies Trust	£6,842,594
Sam Learning Holdings Limited	£6,842,051
Wellington Shipping Services Ltd	£6,834,037
Parliment Place Limited	£6,832,558
Total Developments (NW) Ltd	£6,832,532
Bridgewater School	£6,830,687
Channon Holdings Limited	£6,825,512
Adhan Developments Limited	£6,823,617
Elstat Limited	£6,820,640
B. & E. Boys Limited	£6,819,557
Benmar Textiles Limited	£6,819,460
Elfreed Ltd	£6,815,486
SSH Property Investment Limited	£6,814,160
Alma Holdings Ltd	£6,811,383
Edgworth Developments Limited	£6,809,828
Peel Leisure (Operations) Limited	£6,809,201
Errigal Developments Limited	£6,807,977
Universal Steels and Aluminium Group Limited	£6,807,773
Graphic Packaging International Foodservice Europe	£6,804,624
IGT-UK Group Limited	£6,804,000
JH Estent Limited	£6,798,921
Discover Multi Academy Trust	£6,798,613
Hayes & Finch Limited	£6,786,583
Millfield Holdings Limited	£6,783,565
Qdos Developments Limited	£6,783,006
Arighi Bianchi & Co.Limited	£6,782,524
Comap UK Limited	£6,782,000
F.T.Everard & Sons Limited	£6,777,676
Johnson Cleaners UK Limited	£6,772,000
Dowhigh Limited	£6,768,248
J.A. Payne Limited	£6,760,269
James Hargreaves PM Limited	£6,759,551
Fenwell Estates Ltd	£6,755,049
Pattinson 3 Limited	£6,754,343
1st Technologies Ltd	£6,752,819
M. & W. Freight Limited	£6,752,356
Medicina Holdings Limited	£6,747,367
Arvo Sales Limited	£6,747,067
D R & P Holdings Limited	£6,743,240
Express Linen Services Limited	£6,737,444
First Water Ramsbury Limited	£6,734,000
Noble Nordmann Limited	£6,729,752
Oliver Valvetek Limited	£6,728,300
Rongxin Power Limited	£6,726,252
Peter Ramsey & Sons Limited	£6,723,840
Rhodi Suppliers Limited	£6,723,493
Eciffo Props No. 1 Limited	£6,722,585
Peel Holdings (Management) Limited	£6,722,327
Enterprise Solutions Holdings Limited	£6,721,533
A.J. Forster Limited	£6,721,525
Vita Liquid Polymers Limited	£6,719,617
Palletower Group Holdings Limited	£6,718,083
UBH International Limited	£6,715,416
Monitise Europe Limited	£6,713,000
Allen (Park Foot) Limited	£6,709,482
Almire Holdings Ltd	£6,702,000
Technology Rentals Limited	£6,701,636
W.L. Coller Limited	£6,698,364
Indace Limited	£6,698,219
Clarence Mill Limited	£6,690,977
Acuma Solutions Limited	£6,690,899
Platform Home Loans Limited	£6,690,000
Elmwood Property Investments Limited	£6,688,833
Workforce People Solutions Limited	£6,688,656
Deeside House Educational Trust Limited	£6,680,814
Gordons LLP	£6,671,277
Supremebase Limited	£6,670,326
ABS Brymar Floors Limited	£6,659,057
Nanoco Tech Limited	£6,652,000
Flightcare Limited	£6,647,856
Tarways Asphalte Co. Limited	£6,643,084
Hayes & Co Services Ltd	£6,642,602
Jarron Holdings Limited	£6,635,743
Gresty Holdings (Crewe) Limited	£6,634,346
Seafood Pub Company Group Limited	£6,633,504
M.B.C.Investments Limited	£6,632,983
Titan Leisure Group Limited	£6,630,618
James Killelea & Company Limited	£6,628,021
HTA Group Limited	£6,627,000
Lacey Green Primary Academy	£6,623,000
Knowsley S.K. Limited	£6,617,018
Pettra Limited	£6,614,345
Ellis Whittam Limited	£6,613,240
De La Salle Academy Trust	£6,613,000
Farinet Limited	£6,612,320
East Coast Concepts Holdings Limited	£6,606,458
Elnur UK Limited	£6,606,395
Core Education and Consulting Solutions (UK) Ltd.	£6,605,000
Three Sixty Water Limited	£6,605,000
Preston Plastics Limited	£6,603,235
Port Salford Holdings Limited	£6,591,619
Commercial Enterprises (Crewe) Limited	£6,590,621
DBG Acquisitions Limited	£6,585,000
Schilling Robotics Limited	£6,584,009
Glossop Carton and Print Limited	£6,580,151
Beis Yaakov Jewish High School Academy	£6,574,721
Begbies Traynor (London) LLP	£6,572,103
Furness Quay Ltd	£6,572,014
Thackeray Lettings Limited	£6,570,475
Mini-Gears (Stockport) Limited	£6,568,717
Ludgate Hill Developments Limited	£6,568,000
AW UK Holdings Limited	£6,567,151

Beyond Funding (Holdco) Ltd	£6,564,323
Gemcabin Limited	£6,560,783
J & K Henderson Enterprises Limited	£6,560,734
Griffiths & Armour Limited	£6,556,330
Sunsave 2 Limited	£6,549,156
Best International Limited	£6,548,594
Healthtrak (UK) Limited	£6,541,531
Singleton & Smart (Holdings) Limited	£6,540,113
Interket Holdings UK Limited	£6,533,668
Medlar Fruit Farms Ltd	£6,530,024
Brookshaw Developments Limited	£6,530,000
Corp Limited	£6,521,343
Broadstone Mill Ltd	£6,505,541

Company Profiles

0404 Investments Limited
Incorporated: 20 April 2004 *Employees:* 313
Net Worth: £20,860,612 *Total Assets:* £49,689,560
Registered Office: Pendle Court, Unit 4 Shuttleworth Mead Business Park, Mead Way, Padiham, Burnley, Lancs, BB12 7NG
Activities: Activities of head offices
Major Shareholder: Andrew Mark Holt
Officers: Virginia Hargreaves, Secretary; Andrew Mark Holt [1964] Director

1 Spinningfields Developments Ltd
Incorporated: 12 September 2006 *Employees:* 6
Net Worth: £697,696 *Total Assets:* £16,764,154
Registered Office: c/o Allied London, Level 12, No 1 Spinningfields, 1 Hardman Square, Manchester, M3 3EB
Activities: Other letting and operating of own or leased real estate
Parent: 1 Spinningfields Holdco Limited
Officers: Suresh Premji Gorasia [1974] Director; Frederick Paul Graham Watson [1957] Director; Michael Julian Ingall [1959] Director; Jonathan Raine [1981] Director

1 Spinningfields Finance Two Ltd
Incorporated: 1 December 2014 *Employees:* 5
Net Worth: £100 *Total Assets:* £37,465,056
Registered Office: c/o Allied London, Level 12, No 1 Spinningfields, 1 Hardman Square, Manchester, M3 3EB
Activities: Other letting and operating of own or leased real estate
Parent: Allied London Holdco Seven Limited
Officers: Suresh Premji Gorasia [1974] Director; Frederick Paul Graham-Watson [1957] Finance Director; Michael Julian Ingall [1959] Managing Director; Jonathan Raine [1981] Director

116 Cardamon Limited
Incorporated: 28 February 2008 *Employees:* 153
Net Worth: £223,123 *Total Assets:* £11,818,086
Registered Office: Speed Medical House, 16 Eaton Avenue, Matrix Park, Chorley, Lancs, PR7 7NA
Activities: Activities of head offices
Major Shareholder: Dr Rajnish Luthra
Officers: Graham Pulford [1969] Managing Director

151 Products Limited
Incorporated: 23 July 1987 *Employees:* 110
Net Worth: £9,183,223 *Total Assets:* £17,305,530
Registered Office: The Old School House, 39 Bengal Street, Manchester, M4 6AF
Activities: Wholesale of household goods (other than musical instruments) n.e.c
Parent: Eurostation Limited
Officers: Steven Martin Shonn, Secretary/Director; Ian Paul George [1958] Director/Accountant; Daniel Simon Shonn [1970] Director; Richard Lee Shonn [1977] Director; Steven Martin Shonn [1951] Director

1st Class Holidays (Holdings) Limited
Incorporated: 2 October 2015
Registered Office: Trafford House, Chester Road, Old Trafford, Manchester, M32 0RS
Activities: Activities of other holding companies n.e.c.
Parent: PHD (Nominees) Limited
Officers: Paul Ainsworth [1962] Director; Paul Neil Bland [1986] Finance Director; Andrew Graham Dodd [1973] Director/Chartered Accountant; Daniel Edward Gathercole [1983] Managing Director; Sharon Rose Mason [1968] Director

1st International Limited
Incorporated: 11 May 2015
Net Worth: £4,927,100 *Total Assets:* £7,063,513
Registered Office: Unit 15 Olympic Way, Longbarn Boulevard, Birchwood, Warrington, Cheshire, WA2 0XF
Activities: Other service activities n.e.c.
Major Shareholder: Brian John Manning
Officers: Brian John Manning [1957] Director

1st Stop Funding Limited
Incorporated: 16 October 2015
Net Worth: £1 *Total Assets:* £10,000,001
Registered Office: 10 Whitehills Business Park, Whitehills, Blackpool, Lancs, FY4 5LW
Activities: Financial intermediation not elsewhere classified
Parent: The 1st Stop Group Limited
Officers: Alexander John Mollart, Secretary; David Enright [1964] Director; Alexander John Mollart [1975] Director; Mark Allan Robins [1965] Director

The 1st Stop Group Limited
Incorporated: 27 April 2005 *Employees:* 116
Net Worth Deficit: £3,095,056 *Total Assets:* £67,380,160
Registered Office: 10 Whitehills Business Park, Whitehills, Blackpool, Lancs, FY4 5LW
Activities: Activities of financial services holding companies
Parent: 1st Stop Holdings Limited
Officers: Alexander John Mollart, Secretary; Stephen Paul Baker [1956] Director; David Enright [1964] Director; Philip Anthony George [1950] Director; Lindsey Villon McMurray [1971] Director; Alexander John Mollart [1975] Managing Director; Matthew James Gary Potter [1983] Director; Mark Allan Robins [1965] Director

1st Stop Home Loans Limited
Incorporated: 5 January 2006 *Employees:* 23
Net Worth Deficit: £648,341 *Total Assets:* £31,955,076
Registered Office: 10 Whitehills Business Park, Whitehills, Blackpool, Lancs, FY4 5LW
Activities: Financial intermediation not elsewhere classified
Parent: The 1st Stop Group Limited
Officers: Alexander John Mollart, Secretary; Stephen Paul Baker [1956] Director; Stephen John Beard [1977] Director; Philip Anthony George [1950] Director; Alexander John Mollart [1975] Director; Mark Allan Robins [1965] Director

1st Stop Reserve Limited
Incorporated: 28 August 2014 *Employees:* 1
Net Worth: £79,271 *Total Assets:* £8,770,019
Registered Office: 10 Whitehills Business Park, Whitehills, Blackpool, Lancs, FY4 5LW
Activities: Credit granting by non-deposit taking finance houses and other specialist consumer credit grantors
Parent: The 1st Stop Group Limited
Officers: Alexander John Mollart, Secretary; David Enright [1964] Director; Alexander John Mollart [1975] Director; Mark Allan Robins [1965] Director

1st Technologies Ltd
Incorporated: 7 November 1997 *Employees:* 38
Net Worth: £3,585,186 *Total Assets:* £6,752,819
Registered Office: Riverside House, Kings Reach Business Park, Yew Street, Stockport, Cheshire, SK4 2HD
Activities: Other information technology service activities
Officers: Benjamin Jude Craig [1989] Director; John Robert Graham [1966] Director

2 Hardman Boulevard Investments Limited
Incorporated: 9 June 2010 *Employees:* 5
Net Worth: £8,840,201 *Total Assets:* £24,429,280
Registered Office: c/o Allied London, Level 12, No 1 Spinningfields, 1 Hardman Square, Manchester, M3 3EB
Activities: Other letting and operating of own or leased real estate
Parent: XYZ Building Holdco Limited
Officers: Suresh Premji Gorasia [1974] Director; Frederick Paul Graham-Watson [1957] Director; Michael Julian Ingall [1959] Director; Jonathan Raine [1981] Director

2 Moto Limited
Incorporated: 27 September 2012 *Employees:* 137
Net Worth: £7,646,421 *Total Assets:* £20,694,122
Registered Office: White Bear Yard, Park Road, Adlington, Chorley, Lancs, PR7 4HZ
Activities: Sale, maintenance and repair of motorcycles and related parts and accessories
Shareholders: Keith James Mason; Eileen Mason
Officers: Keith James Mason [1955] Director

2020 Legal Limited
Incorporated: 11 May 2011 *Employees:* 235
Net Worth Deficit: £5,774,240 *Total Assets:* £14,638,069
Registered Office: No 1 Europa House, Conway Street, Birkenhead, Liverpool, CH41 4FT
Activities: Solicitors
Shareholders: Colin David Billing; Johanne Humphreys
Officers: Colin David Billing [1960] Director/Solicitor; Johanne Humphreys [1968] Director/Solicitor

3B Construction Ltd
Incorporated: 8 May 2003 *Employees:* 115
Net Worth: £5,555,038 *Total Assets:* £13,777,165
Registered Office: Fifteen Rosehill, Montgomery Way, Rosehill Estate, Carlisle, Cumbria, CA1 2RW
Activities: Development of building projects
Shareholders: Andrew Duncan Barr; Margaret Murray Barr
Officers: Stuart Duncan Barr, Secretary; Graeme Hamilton Barr [1975] Director/Construction; James Iain Barr [1970] Director/Construction; Stuart Duncan Barr [1973] Director/Construction

3Sixty Restaurants Limited
Incorporated: 23 February 2011 *Employees:* 597
Net Worth: £3,100,092 *Total Assets:* £7,561,780
Registered Office: 1st Floor, St Georges House, St Georges Road, Bolton, Lancs, BL1 2DD
Activities: Licenced restaurants
Shareholders: Andre Hoffman; Luke Johnson
Officers: Julie Nicole Leigh, Secretary; Adrian Mark Abbey [1965] Director; Nicholas Anthony Beart [1963] Director; Christian Hopkins [1965] Marketing and Commercial Director; James Michael Alexander Horler [1965] Director; Julie Nicole Leigh [1965] Finance Director; Martin Nelson [1977] Operations Director

4L (Holdings) Limited
Incorporated: 8 September 2014 *Employees:* 218
Net Worth: £6,510,985 *Total Assets:* £11,334,054
Registered Office: Bank Top Mill, Thompson Street Industrial Estate, Dixon Street, Blackburn, Lancs, BB2 1TX
Activities: Activities of production holding companies
Officers: Hans Anthony Lowe [1969] Director; Julian Amos Lowe [1972] Director; Nathan Symon Lowe [1978] Director

53 King Street LLP
Incorporated: 25 March 2009
Net Worth: £418,468 *Total Assets:* £8,123,078
Registered Office: 53 King Street, Manchester, M2 4LQ

9 East Shipping Limited
Incorporated: 29 April 2010 *Employees:* 6
Net Worth: £30,252,212 *Total Assets:* £35,800,868
Registered Office: Eversheds House, 70 Great Bridgewater Street, Manchester, M1 5ES
Activities: Other business support service activities n.e.c.
Parent: Peabody Coaltrace International Limited
Officers: Scott Jarboe, Secretary; David Richard Leslie Barham [1972] Managing Director of 9 East Shipping Limited; Bryan Galli [1960] Director/Executive [American]; Walter Leroy Hawkins Jr. [1958] Director/Senior VP Finance of Peabody Investments Corp [American]

9CW04 Limited
Incorporated: 19 May 2004 *Employees:* 2
Net Worth: £3,995,065 *Total Assets:* £7,402,950
Registered Office: Pendle Court, Unit 4 Shuttleworth Mead Business Park, Mead Way, Padiham, Burnley, Lancs, BB12 7NG
Activities: Other letting and operating of own or leased real estate
Officers: Virginia Hargreaves, Secretary; Virginia Hargreaves [1968] Director/Accountant; Andrew Mark Holt [1964] Director

A & D Transport (NW) Limited
Incorporated: 16 March 2006 *Employees:* 69
Net Worth: £1,200,131 *Total Assets:* £8,928,627
Registered Office: 60a Broad Lane, Collins Green, Warrington, Cheshire, WA5 4AB
Activities: Freight transport by road
Shareholders: Allan Stuart Brimble; Donna Brimble
Officers: Allan Stuart Brimble [1967] Director/Haulage Contractor

A & F Sprinklers Limited
Incorporated: 18 June 1986
Registered Office: Unit 4 Gorrels Way, Trans-Pennine Trading Estate, Rochdale, Lancs, OL11 2PX
Activities: Other specialised construction activities n.e.c.
Major Shareholder: Jonathan Mark Stansfield
Officers: Lesley Karen Stansfield, Secretary; Christopher Mooney [1957] Director; Duncan Lee Parker [1978] Director; Derrick Parr [1974] Director; Jonathan Mark Stansfield [1974] Director; Lesley Karen Stansfield [1969] Director/Office Manager; Michael Julian Stansfield [1971] Director; James Owen Whitlock [1980] Director

A & M Energy Solutions Limited
Incorporated: 13 June 1973 *Employees:* 212
Net Worth: £7,262,260 *Total Assets:* £10,168,611
Registered Office: Enviromental House, Sandwash Close, Rainford Industrial Estate, Rainford, St Helens, Merseyside, WA11 8LY
Activities: Other specialised construction activities n.e.c.
Parent: A & M Energy Group Ltd
Officers: Jason John Mansfield, Secretary; Simon Atherton [1968] Director; Ian Michael Holland [1975] Director/Accountant; Alexander Ross Laing [1946] Director; Gary Kevin Mollard [1974] Director A&M Insulations Ltd; Ian Langford Mollard [1969] Director/Manager; Sarah Louise Roldaan [1972] Director

A K W Global Logistics Ltd
Incorporated: 18 May 1983 *Employees:* 134
Net Worth: £2,141,021 *Total Assets:* £11,518,460
Registered Office: 26 Bond Europa Way, Trafford Park, Manchester, M17 1WF
Activities: Freight transport by road
Parent: AKW Group PLC
Officers: Michael James Lyons, Secretary; Michael James Lyons [1962] Director/Accountant; Julian Charles Richards [1961] Director; Paul Welsh [1970] Operations Director; Anthony Kevin Worthington [1958] Director/Chairman; Karen Lesley Worthington [1970] Director

A. & B. Engineering (Mechanical Service Division) Limited
Incorporated: 15 May 1978 *Employees:* 83
Net Worth: £1,569,207 *Total Assets:* £12,101,081
Registered Office: 9-17 Derby Lane, Liverpool, L13 6QA
Activities: Plumbing, heat and air-conditioning installation
Shareholders: Alexander John Currie; Michael Hart; Gary Dwyer
Officers: Michael Hart, Secretary/Director; Alexander John Currie [1963] Director; Gary Dwyer [1971] Director; Michael Hart [1964] Director

A. V. Group Limited
Incorporated: 24 November 1986 *Employees:* 38
Net Worth: £5,459,534 *Total Assets:* £7,713,502
Registered Office: Windmill Lane Industrial Estate, Denton, Manchester, M34 2JF
Activities: Renting and leasing of other machinery, equipment and tangible goods n.e.c.
Shareholders: Daniel Gareth Holloway; Willam Henry Holloway
Officers: Hedvig Ester Margareta Holloway, Secretary; Daniel Gareth Holloway [1964] Director/Area Manager; Hedvig Ester Margareta Holloway [1934] Director; John Yorke Holloway [1931] Director; William Henry Holloway [1960] Director; Helen Mary Scott [1964] Director

A.D.S. Graphics Limited
Incorporated: 22 March 1988 *Employees:* 159
Net Worth: £3,206,985 *Total Assets:* £9,024,639
Registered Office: 3-4 Apex Court, Bassendale Road, Wirral International Business Park, Bromborough, Wirral, Merseyside, CH62 3RE
Activities: Printing n.e.c.
Major Shareholder: Rudoplh David Patterson
Officers: David Hugh Patterson, Secretary; David Hugh Patterson [1965] Director/Marketing Manager; Rudolph David Patterson [1931] Director/Commercial Artist; Simon William Preston [1973] Operations Director; Barbara Thatcher [1970] Director/Company Accountant; Tamsyn Williams [1974] Director/Sales Person

A.M. Seafoods Limited
Incorporated: 16 December 2003 *Employees:* 240
Net Worth: £5,366,306 *Total Assets:* £14,755,406
Registered Office: Siding Road, Fleetwood, Lancs, FY7 6NS
Activities: Processing and preserving of fish, crustaceans and molluscs
Officers: Mark Peter Merrick, Secretary; Christine Falconer Merrick [1944] Director; Mark Peter Merrick [1969] Director/Accountant; Peter Maurice Merrick [1943] Director; Scott James Merrick [1973] Director/Factory Manager

A.P.S. Salads Limited
Incorporated: 23 October 2006 *Employees:* 48
Net Worth Deficit: £362,000 *Total Assets:* £13,047,000
Registered Office: Enterprise House, 97 Alderley Road, Wilmslow, Cheshire, SK9 1PT
Activities: Wholesale of fruit and vegetables
Parent: A Pearson & Sons (1949) LLP
Officers: Ashley Robert Haworth, Secretary; Ashley Robert Haworth [1979] Financial Director; Mark Pearson [1973] Director/Tomato Grower; John Edward Phibbs [1950] Director/Accountant; Steve Sadler [1968] Finance Director

AAG UK Parent Limited
Incorporated: 11 October 2010
Net Worth Deficit: £11,878,535 *Total Assets:* £21,728,384
Registered Office: Regent Mill, Fir Street, Failsworth, Manchester, M35 0HS
Activities: Activities of head offices
Parent: AAG UK Holding Limited
Officers: Christopher Berry [1954] Director; Anja Krueger [1967] Director of Legal Affairs [German]

Abacus Estates Limited
Incorporated: 14 May 1998
Net Worth: £2,585,916 *Total Assets:* £9,251,776
Registered Office: Linden Court House, 52 Liverpool Street, Salford, M5 4LT
Activities: Other letting and operating of own or leased real estate
Officers: Jonathan Choua Shasha, Secretary/Director; Alan Philip David Musry [1963] Director; Anil Kumar Ruia [1955] Director; Jonathan Choua Shasha [1956] Director

Michael Abakhan Limited
Incorporated: 3 April 1964 *Employees:* 409
Net Worth: £9,263,115 *Total Assets:* £16,062,197
Registered Office: Coast Road, Llanerch-Y-Mor, Mostyn, Flintshire, CH8 9DX
Activities: Other retail sale in non-specialised stores
Shareholders: Beth Abakhan; William Loudon Abakhan
Officers: Christopher James Hendy, Secretary; Antoinette Abakhan [1940] Director/Manager; George Abakhan [1941] Director/Chartered Accountant [Canadian]; Susan Elizabeth Abakhan [1950] Director/Manager; William Loudon Abakhan [1984] Director; David Malcolm Cordell [1940] Director; Amanda Jane Grahame [1968] Operations Director; Christopher James Hendy [1960] Director/Accountant; Nicholas Charles Powell [1953] Director; Beth Irina Pownall [1980] Marketing Director

ABB Holdings Limited
Incorporated: 28 April 1994
Net Worth: £439,056,992 *Total Assets:* £534,782,016
Registered Office: Daresbury Park, Daresbury, Warrington, Cheshire, WA4 4BT
Activities: Activities of head offices
Parent: ABB Ltd
Officers: Victoria Ann Mac Lean, Secretary; Lena Maria Andersson [1966] Director/Chief Financial Officer [Finnish]; Ian Grant Funnell [1957] Managing Director; Ian Donald Rennie [1961] Director

ABB Limited
Incorporated: 1 June 1999 *Employees:* 1,720
Net Worth: £211,486,000 *Total Assets:* £484,870,016
Registered Office: Daresbury Park, Daresbury, Warrington, Cheshire, WA4 4BT
Activities: Manufacture of electricity distribution and control apparatus
Parent: ABB Holdings Limited
Officers: Victoria Ann Mac Lean, Secretary; Lena Maria Andersson [1966] Director/Chief Financial Officer [Finnish]; Ian Grant Funnell [1957] Managing Director; Ian Donald Rennie [1961] Director

Abbey Logistics Group Limited
Incorporated: 22 March 1990 *Employees:* 579
Net Worth: £3,837,461 *Total Assets:* £31,655,304
Registered Office: Suite 11, Stone Cross Place, Stone Cross Lane North, Lowton, Warrington, Cheshire, WA3 2SH
Activities: Freight transport by road
Parent: Axle Bidco Limited
Officers: Tom Randle, Secretary; Christopher James Chambers [1972] Finance Director; David Coulson [1964] Commercial Director; Richard Michael Ellis [1963] Business Development Director; Steven Granite [1979] Managing Director

Abbey Masterbatch Limited
Incorporated: 22 February 1984 *Employees:* 48
Net Worth: £7,132,440 *Total Assets:* £9,041,166
Registered Office: Whitelands Mill, Whitelands Road, Ashton under Lyne, Lancs, OL6 6UG
Activities: Manufacture of plastics in primary forms
Parent: ATL Industries Limited
Officers: Louisa Carla Mather, Secretary; John Michael Shirt, Secretary; Louisa Carla Mather [1963] Director/Company Secretary; John Michael Shirt [1941] Director/Chemist; Mark Andrew Shirt [1965] Director/General Manager; Richard Julian Shirt [1969] Director/Quality Control Manager; Ruth Jennifer Shirt [1943] Director/Housewife

Abbotsound Limited
Incorporated: 19 January 1996 *Employees:* 52
Net Worth: £3,947,517 *Total Assets:* £6,899,908
Registered Office: The Links Resource Centre, 21 Cromwell Road, Eccles, Manchester, M30 0QT
Activities: Activities of other holding companies n.e.c.
Officers: Michael James Hampson, Secretary; Mark Leslie Hampson [1967] Director; Michael James Hampson [1982] Director; Nicholas Graham Waring [1966] Director

Abgene Limited
Incorporated: 7 September 2005 *Employees:* 179
Net Worth: £90,038,000 *Total Assets:* £99,212,000
Registered Office: 3rd Floor, 1 Ashley Road, Altrincham, Cheshire, WA14 2DT
Activities: Manufacture of other chemical products n.e.c.
Parent: Advanced Biotechnologies Limited
Officers: Rhona Gregg, Secretary; Lucie Mary Katja Grant [1976] Director/Solicitor; Nicholas Ince [1982] Director/Accountant; David John Norman [1960] Director/Chartered Accountant

Abird Limited
Incorporated: 16 November 1990 *Employees:* 80
Net Worth: £5,982,000 *Total Assets:* £24,863,000
Registered Office: Oakland House, 76 Talbot Road, Old Trafford, Manchester, M16 0PQ
Activities: Renting and leasing of construction and civil engineering machinery and equipment
Parent: Abird Superior Limited
Officers: Daniel James Joll, Secretary; Stephen Ashmore [1964] Director; Paul David Quested [1970] Financial Director

Abird Superior Limited
Incorporated: 16 November 1950
Net Worth: £1,440,000 *Total Assets:* £9,161,000
Registered Office: Oakland House, 76 Talbot Road, Old Trafford, Manchester, M16 0PQ
Activities: Activities of head offices
Parent: HSS Hire Service Group Limited
Officers: Daniel James Joll, Secretary; Stephen Ashmore [1964] Director; Paul David Quested [1970] Financial Director

Abito Limited
Incorporated: 4 June 2003
Registered Office: 4 Clippers Quay, Salford Quays, Manchester, M50 3BL
Activities: Buying and selling of own real estate
Parent: Levitt UK Real Estate Limited
Officers: Sarah Anne Butler [1976] Director; Philip Vickers [1961] Director

Able2 UK Limited
Incorporated: 29 August 2003 *Employees:* 40
Net Worth: £2,809,647 *Total Assets:* £7,084,316
Registered Office: Bridge Mill, Moorgate Street, Blackburn, Lancs, BB2 4PB
Activities: Manufacture of irradiation, electromedical and electrotherapeutic equipment
Parent: ADL Holdings Limited
Officers: Mark Diaj [1970] Director; Ian Stewart Reed [1967] Director

Abney 2003 Limited
Incorporated: 4 June 2003
Net Worth: £40,050,000 *Total Assets:* £40,882,000
Registered Office: Union, Albert Square, Manchester, M2 6LW
Activities: Other letting and operating of own or leased real estate
Major Shareholder: Jean Davies Oglesby
Officers: Christopher George Oglesby [1967] Director; Michael John Oglesby [1939] Director; Katharine Jane Vokes [1969] Director

Abney Trust
Incorporated: 1[illegible] December 2015 *Employees:* 198
Net Worth: £12,742,815 *Total Assets:* £16,106,212
Registered Office: The Kingsway School, Foxland Road, Cheadle, Cheshire, SK8 4QX
Activities: General secondary education
Officers: Caroline Ann Booth [1963] Director/Editor; Gary Keown [1965] Director/Editor; Joanne Sarah Lowe [1967] Director/Headteacher; Anne Thompson [1946] Director/Retired

ABS Brymar Floors Limited
Incorporated: 6 August 1984 *Employees:* 66
Net Worth: £913,596 *Total Assets:* £6,659,057
Registered Office: 1a The Moorings, Dane Road Industrial Estate, Sale, Cheshire, M33 7BH
Activities: Other specialised construction activities n.e.c.
Parent: Manchester Urban Finance Corporation
Officers: Nicholas Cable, Secretary; Nicholas Jon Cable [1976] Contracts Director

ABS Consulting Ltd.
Incorporated: 2 December 1987 *Employees:* 42
Net Worth: £1,880,207 *Total Assets:* £18,773,348
Registered Office: EQE House, The Beacons, Warrington Road, Birchwood, Cheshire, WA3 6WJ
Activities: Management consultancy activities other than financial management
Officers: Sarah Muriel Barton, Secretary/Lawyer; Michael Mannix, Secretary; Sarah Muriel Barton [1958] Director/Lawyer; Dr Bradley James Eccles [1972] Director/Civil Engineer; Malcolm Warren Goodwin [1957] Director/Consultant; Gary Graham [1967] Director/Vice President; David Alan Walker [1967] Director/Engineer [American]

ABS Group Ltd.
Incorporated: 26 November 1990
Net Worth Deficit: £2,003,027 *Total Assets:* £26,851,232
Registered Office: EQE House, The Beacons, Warrington Road, Birchwood, Warrington, Cheshire, WA3 6WJ
Activities: Other professional, scientific and technical activities n.e.c.
Officers: Sarah Muriel Barton, Secretary; Michael Mannix, Secretary; David Alan Walker [1967] Director/Engineer [American]

AC/DC LED Holdings Limited
Incorporated: 4 May 2012
Net Worth: £299,647 *Total Assets:* £8,941,415
Registered Office: Innovation Works, Gisburn Road, Barrowford, Lancs, BB9 8NB
Activities: Activities of other holding companies n.e.c.
Officers: Gareth Simeon Frankland [1974] Director; Andre Parcel Papoular [1955] Director/EVP Outdoor Lighting [French]; Georg Schaffgotch [1968] Director [Austrian]

The ACC Liverpool Group Ltd
Incorporated: 12 August 2004 *Employees:* 241
Net Worth Deficit: £7,433,346 *Total Assets:* £21,585,218
Registered Office: Kings Dock, Liverpool Waterfront, Liverpool, L3 4FP
Activities: Other business support service activities n.e.c.
Parent: Liverpool City Council
Officers: Joseph Vincent Anderson [1958] Director/Councillor; Generald Ernest Andrews [1954] Finance Director; Robert John Prattey [1955] Director; Antony Robert Reeves [1965] Director/Chief Executive; Cllr Wendy Ann Simon [1961] Director/Councillor

The Access Bank UK Limited
Incorporated: 10 September 2007 *Employees:* 113
Net Worth: £155,928,800 *Total Assets:* £1,402,475,520
Registered Office: 4 Royal Court, Gadbrook Way, Gadbrook Park, Rudheath, Northwich, Cheshire, CW9 7UT
Activities: Financial intermediation not elsewhere classified
Officers: Stephen Clark [1948] Director/Banker; Sean Patrick McLaughlin [1960] Finance Director; Roosevelt Ogbonna [1974] Director/Banker [Nigerian]; James Kevin Simmonds [1960] Director; Timothy Cardwell Wade [1959] Director [Australian]; Herbert Wigwe [1966] Director [Nigerian]

Accord Mortgages Limited
Incorporated: 11 June 1987
Net Worth: £340,607,008 *Total Assets:* £19,933,483,008
Registered Office: Yorkshire House, Yorkshire Drive, Bradford, W Yorks, BD5 8LJ
Activities: Activities of mortgage finance companies
Officers: Deborah Colley, Secretary; Charles Peter Canning [1963] Director; Jeremy Michael Duncombe [1969] Director of Intermediary Distribution; Paul Howley [1967] Director/Manager; Rob Andrew Purdy [1972] Director/Accountant; Richard Stephen Wells [1963] Director/General Manager - Risk; Mr Stephen White [1971] Chief Operating Officer & Executive Director

Accrington St Christopher's Church of England High School
Incorporated: 3 August 2011 *Employees:* 172
Net Worth: £6,327,000 *Total Assets:* £10,064,000
Registered Office: Queen's Road West, Accrington, Lancs, BB5 4AY
Activities: General secondary education
Officers: Pamela Jane Haralambos, Secretary; David Anderson [1945] Retired HR Director; Kathryn Baron [1972] Director/Teacher; Donna Bentley [1963] Director/Midwife; Lawrence William Carson-Featham [1953] Director/Vicar; Clare Carter [1956] Director/Teacher; Alex Nicholas John Cran [1971] Finance Director; David Crossland [1946] Director/Business Owner; Helen Fiona Davies [1966] Director/Teacher; Rev Ian Peter Enticott [1959] Director/Vicar; Linda Hargreaves [1961] Director/Education Officer; Helen Harker [1966] Director/Sales Manager; Vicky Howard [1969] Director/Head of HR; Peter Jones [1952] Retired Director of Social Services; Richard Jones [1966] Director/Headteacher; David Andrew Rogan [1961] Director/Teaching Assistant; Paul Stinchon [1970] Director/Manufacturing Engineer; Denise Taylor [1957] Director/Teaching Assistant; Rachel White [1971] Director; Frank Whitehead [1948] Director/Consultant Building Surveyor; Catherine Anne Wightman [1960] Director/Administrator

Accrol Holdings Limited
Incorporated: 9 October 2009
Net Worth: £7,691,000 *Total Assets:* £17,691,000
Registered Office: Delta Building, Roman Road, Blackburn, BB1 2LD
Activities: Manufacture of household and sanitary goods and of toilet requisites
Officers: Gareth Paul Jenkins [1967] Director/Chief Executive; Steven James Townsley [1967] Director/Chief Financial Officer

Accrol Papers Limited
Incorporated: 29 September 1998 *Employees:* 508
Net Worth: £29,903,000 *Total Assets:* £70,680,000
Registered Office: Delta Building, Roman Road, Blackburn, BB1 2LD
Activities: Manufacture of household and sanitary goods and of toilet requisites
Officers: Gareth Paul Jenkins [1967] Director/Chief Executive; Steven James Townsley [1967] Director/Chief Financial Officer

Accrol UK Limited
Incorporated: 24 April 2014
Net Worth: £32,810,000 *Total Assets:* £47,202,000
Registered Office: Delta Building, Roman Road, Blackburn, Lancs, BB1 2LD
Activities: Manufacture of household and sanitary goods and of toilet requisites
Parent: Accrol Group Holdings PLC
Officers: Gareth Paul Jenkins [1967] Director/Chief Executive; Steven James Townsley [1967] Director/Chief Financial Officer

Accumuli (Holdings) Limited
Incorporated: 13 March 2001
Net Worth Deficit: £17,184,000 *Total Assets:* £20,751,000
Registered Office: XYZ Building, 2 Hardman Boulevard, Spinningfields, Manchester, M3 3AQ
Activities: Activities of head offices
Parent: Accumuli Limited
Officers: Suzana Cross, Secretary; Edward Jonathan Williams, Secretary; Timothy John Kowalski [1958] Director; Roger Gary Rawlinson [1962] Director; Stuart James Sims [1981] Director

Accumuli Limited
Incorporated: 13 March 2001
Net Worth: £15,032,000 *Total Assets:* £22,377,000
Registered Office: XYZ Building, 2 Hardman Boulevard, Spinningfields, Manchester, M3 3AQ
Activities: Other information technology service activities
Parent: NCC Group PLC
Officers: Suzana Cross, Secretary; Edward Jonathan Williams, Secretary; Timothy John Kowalski [1958] Director; Roger Gary Rawlinson [1962] Director; Stuart James Sims [1981] Director

Acdoco Limited
Incorporated: 21 March 2007 *Employees:* 27
Net Worth: £1,999,270 *Total Assets:* £10,814,428
Registered Office: Mallison Street, Bolton, Lancs, BL1 8PP
Activities: Manufacture of soap and detergents
Shareholders: Heinrich Kurt Beckmann; Johann Gerhard Krauss; Brandon Pilling
Officers: Nigel Drinkwater, Secretary; Heinrich Kurt Beckman [1947] Director/General Manager [German]; Jeremy Guy Nicholas Bird [1961] Director/Management Consultant; Johann Gerhard Krauss [1961] Director/General Manager [German]; Brandon Pilling [1962] Director

Ace Supply Company Limited (The)
Incorporated: 18 November 1986 *Employees:* 49
Net Worth: £4,582,196 *Total Assets:* £8,298,290
Registered Office: Regency House, 45-51 Chorley New Road, Bolton, Lancs, BL1 4QR
Activities: Wholesale trade of motor vehicle parts and accessories
Parent: The Ace Supply Holding Company Limited
Officers: Murray Silverman, Secretary; David Davis [1976] Director; Dale Silverman [1978] Director; Murray Silverman [1950] Director/Motor Agent

The Ace Supply Holding Company Limited
Incorporated: 20 July 2016 *Employees:* 49
Net Worth: £2,246,919 *Total Assets:* £7,854,158
Registered Office: Regency House, 45-51 Chorley New Road, Bolton, Lancs, BL1 4QR
Activities: Wholesale trade of motor vehicle parts and accessories
Shareholders: David Davis; Loraine Silverman
Officers: David Davis [1976] Director; Dale Silverman [1978] Director; Murray Silverman [1950] Director

Acebench Limited
Incorporated: 2 June 1982
Net Worth: £5,434,607 *Total Assets:* £21,656,416
Registered Office: Oak House, Bank Parade, Preston, Lancs, PR1 3TA
Activities: Buying and selling of own real estate
Officers: Almas Yousuf Bhailok, Secretary; Yousuf Mohamed Ibrahim Bhailok [1956] Director

Acepark Ltd
Incorporated: 23 March 2010 *Employees:* 337
Net Worth: £35,755,792 *Total Assets:* £151,513,008
Registered Office: Botany Bay, Canal Mill, Botany Brow, Chorley, Lancs, PR6 9AF
Activities: Activities of other holding companies n.e.c.
Major Shareholder: Timothy John Peter Knowles
Officers: Claire Caroline Sharp, Secretary; Thomas Duncan Hopkinson [1956] Director; Timothy John Peter Knowles [1964] Managing Director; Claire Caroline Sharp [1973] Director

Achievement Through Collaboration Trust
Incorporated: 22 June 2011 *Employees:* 196
Net Worth: £19,795,000 *Total Assets:* £23,599,000
Registered Office: Bowland High, Riversmead, Grindleton, Clitheroe, Lancs, BB7 4QS
Activities: General secondary education
Officers: Jenny Louise Goy, Secretary; Michele Battersby [1962] Director/Teacher; Robert Duncan [1963] Director/Head of Commercial Systems at BAE; David John Hollings [1962] Director; John Robinson [1950] Director/Consultant; Siobhan Wignall [1976] Director/HR Manager

Acorn Care 1 Limited
Incorporated: 11 January 2010 *Employees:* 1,608
Net Worth Deficit: £189,956,400 *Total Assets:* £90,981,104
Registered Office: 1 Merchant's Place, River Street, Bolton, Lancs, BL2 1BX
Activities: Activities of other holding companies n.e.c.
Parent: SSCP Spring Bidco Limited
Officers: Jean-Luc Emmanuel Janet [1970] Director [French]; David Jon Leatherbarrow [1969] Director/Group Chief Executive Officer

Acorn Care 2 Limited
Incorporated: 11 January 2010
Net Worth: £56,215,256 *Total Assets:* £143,776,704
Registered Office: 1 Merchant's Place, River Street, Bolton, Lancs, BL2 1BX
Activities: Activities of other holding companies n.e.c.
Parent: Acorn Care 1 Limited
Officers: Jean-Luc Emmanuel Janet [1970] Director [French]; David Jon Leatherbarrow [1969] Director/Group Chief Executive Officer

Acorn Care 3 Limited
Incorporated: 11 January 2010
Net Worth: £19,549,976 *Total Assets:* £133,501,424
Registered Office: 1 Merchant's Place, River Street, Bolton, Lancs, BL2 1BX
Activities: Activities of other holding companies n.e.c.
Parent: Acorn Care 2 Limited
Officers: Jean-Luc Emmanuel Janet [1970] Director [French]; David Jon Leatherbarrow [1969] Director/Group Chief Executive Officer

Acorn Care 4 Limited
Incorporated: 11 January 2010
Net Worth Deficit: £119,054,308 *Total Assets:* £148,772,448
Registered Office: 1 Merchant's Place, River Street, Bolton, Lancs, BL2 1BX
Activities: Activities of other holding companies n.e.c.
Parent: Acorn Care 3 Limited
Officers: Jean-Luc Emmanuel Janet [1970] Director [French]; David Jon Leatherbarrow [1969] Director/Group Chief Executive Officer

Acorn Care and Education Limited
Incorporated: 19 January 2004 *Employees:* 48
Net Worth: £51,940,432 *Total Assets:* £195,240,608
Registered Office: 1 Merchant's Place, River Street, Bolton, Lancs, BL2 1BX
Activities: Activities of head offices
Shareholders: Acorn Care 4 Limited; Acorn Care 4 Limited
Officers: Helen Elizabeth Lecky, Secretary; Jean-Luc Emmanuel Janet [1970] Director [French]; David Jon Leatherbarrow [1969] Director/Group Chief Executive Officer

Acorn Insurance and Financial Services Limited
Incorporated: 18 May 1982 *Employees:* 346
Net Worth: £14,830,040 *Total Assets:* £74,365,256
Registered Office: 98 Liverpool Road, Formby, Merseyside, L37 6BS
Activities: Non-life insurance
Parent: Granite Underwriting Limited
Officers: Nicola Kate McLachlan, Secretary; Martin Richard Gowing [1970] Director; Alan Peter Keating [1967] Director/Insurance; Daniel Keating [1981] Director; Nicola Kate McLachlan [1971] Director/Insurance

Acorn Mobility Services Ltd.
Incorporated: 21 March 1991 *Employees:* 1,485
Net Worth: £17,524,536 *Total Assets:* £59,685,564
Registered Office: Telecom House, Millennium Business Park, Station Road, Steeton, Bradford, W Yorks, BD20 6RB
Activities: Other manufacturing n.e.c.
Major Shareholder: John Stewart Jakes
Officers: Graham John Moore, Secretary; Patrick Francis Bethell [1988] Global Systems Director [Bahamian]; John Stewart Jakes [1956] Director/Chairman; Michael Jonathan Oldham [1951] Director/Accountant; Joanne Amanda Richardson [1976] Director/Chartered Accountant; Nicholas Wilson [1973] Director/Operations Manager

Acre Products Limited
Incorporated: 26 October 1973
Net Worth: £7,434,582 *Total Assets:* £8,611,444
Registered Office: Dalton Lane, Keighley, W Yorks, BD21 4JH
Activities: Development of building projects
Shareholders: Robert Simon Smallwood; Andrew Charles Smallwood; David Mark Smallwood
Officers: Andrew Charles Smallwood, Secretary; Andrew Charles Smallwood [1961] Director/Purchasing; David Mark Smallwood [1967] Managing Director; Robert Simon Smallwood [1963] Director/Sales

Acuma Solutions Limited
Incorporated: 2 November 2000 *Employees:* 16
Net Worth: £2,664,630 *Total Assets:* £6,690,899
Registered Office: Applicon House, Exchange Street, Stockport, Cheshire, SK3 0EY
Activities: Information technology consultancy activities
Shareholders: Saksoft Solutions Limited; Saksoft Solutions Limited
Officers: Muthukrishnan Swaminathan, Secretary; Nirajkumar Ganeriwala [1978] Director/Service [Indian]; Aditya Krishna [1960] Director [Indian]

ACWA Services Limited
Incorporated: 3 June 1986 *Employees:* 28
Net Worth Deficit: £1,716,324 *Total Assets:* £11,831,576
Registered Office: ACWA House, Unit 9 Acorn Business Park, Skipton, N Yorks, BD23 2UE
Activities: Water collection, treatment and supply
Parent: Consolidated Contractors International (UK) Ltd
Officers: David Clegg, Secretary; Peter Brewer [1968] Director/General Manager; Yasser Adeeb Khalil Burgan [1964] Director/Assistant Vice President - CCC [Jordanian]; The Hon Stephen John Byers [1953] Director/Member of Parliament; Naji Mohammed El Moheb [1954] Director [Lebanese]; Gary Alan Jackson [1970] Director; Akl Jamal [1949] Director/Vice President-Estimation [Canadian]; Wail Said Khouri [1961] Director/Chairman/Area Manager [Belizean]

Addison Motors Limited
Incorporated: 8 February 1962 *Employees:* 1,021
Net Worth: £45,318,000 *Total Assets:* £167,236,992
Registered Office: Lookers House, 3 Etchells Road, West Timperley, Altrincham, Cheshire, WA14 5XS
Activities: Sale of new cars and light motor vehicles
Parent: Lookers Motor Group Limited
Officers: Glenda MacGeekie, Secretary; Andrew Campbell Bruce [1965] Director; Robin Anthony Gregson [1960] Director/Chartered Accountant; Nigel John McMinn [1968] Managing Director

Addison Project PLC
Incorporated: 9 January 1997 *Employees:* 31
Net Worth: £5,454,863 *Total Assets:* £10,489,573
Registered Office: Hillhouse Business Park, Bourne Road, Thornton Cleveleys, Lancs, FY5 4QD
Activities: Other engineering activities
Shareholder: Alan Wulstan Addison
Officers: Marcus Alan Addison, Secretary/Director; Marcus Alan Addison [1973] Director

Adelphi Mill Properties Limited
Incorporated: 15 December 1998 *Employees:* 6
Net Worth: £3,819,449 *Total Assets:* £8,477,369
Registered Office: The Adelphi Mill, Grimshaw Lane, Bollington, Cheshire, SK10 5JB
Activities: Development of building projects
Major Shareholder: Rupert Alexander Beckwith-Moore
Officers: Geoffrey Brian Claughton, Secretary; Rupert Alexander Beckwith-Moore [1967] Director; Kenneth Charles Moore [1938] Director/Retired; Sara Frances Moore [1941] Director/Historian

Adesa Remarketing Limited
Incorporated: 20 January 2016 *Employees:* 72
Net Worth Deficit: £1,411,432 *Total Assets:* £33,987,600
Registered Office: Deva House, The Office Village, Sandpiper Court, Chester Business Park, Chester, CH4 9QZ
Activities: Sale of used cars and light motor vehicles
Parent: KAR UK Holdings Limited
Officers: Jonathan Holland [1964] Director; Eric Michael Loughmiller [1959] Director [American]; Benjamin Skuy [1963] Director [Canadian]

Adhan Developments Limited
Incorporated: 7 May 2003 *Employees:* 1
Net Worth: £4,733,122 *Total Assets:* £6,823,617
Registered Office: 1st Floor, Adhan House, 52a Preston New Road, Blackburn, Lancs, BB2 6AH
Activities: Development of building projects
Parent: Adhan Properties Limited
Officers: Mohmed Salim Ismail Patel [1968] Director

Adhan Homes Ltd
Incorporated: 28 January 2005
Net Worth: £147,881 *Total Assets:* £7,097,598
Registered Office: 1st Floor, Adhan House, 52a Preston New Road, Blackburn, Lancs, BB2 6AH
Activities: Development of building projects
Major Shareholder: Salim Patel
Officers: Salim Patel [1968] Director

ADI UK Limited
Incorporated: 17 February 1997 *Employees:* 122
Net Worth: £3,573,338 *Total Assets:* £12,411,976
Registered Office: Regency House, 45-51 Chorley New Road, Bolton, Lancs, BL1 4QR
Activities: Renting and leasing of media entertainment equipment
Parent: Retstone Limited
Officers: Wendy Race [1974] Finance Director; James Robinson [1976] Operations Director; Nicholas Andrew Robinson [1974] Director; Geraint Edward Williams [1970] Director

Adi-Gardiner Limited
Incorporated: 20 July 1977 *Employees:* 262
Net Worth: £11,882,000 *Total Assets:* £39,652,000
Registered Office: Unit 7a-7b Transpennine Trading Estate, Gorrells Way, Rochdale, OL11 2PX
Activities: Wholesale of radio, television goods & electrical household appliances (other than records, tapes, CDs)
Parent: ADI-Gardiner EMEA Limited
Officers: Adrian Paul Connell [1965] Director; Colin McGinty [1972] Finance Director; Peter Joseph O'Toole [1959] Director; Hemant Trivedi [1962] Director

Adidas (U.K.) Limited
Incorporated: 10 October 1972 *Employees:* 1,136
Net Worth: £30,332,000 *Total Assets:* £158,722,000
Registered Office: The Adidas Centre, Pepper Road, Hazel Grove, Stockport, Cheshire, SK7 5SA
Activities: Wholesale of textiles
Parent: Adidas AG
Officers: Bhupinder Singh Sandhu, Secretary; Andrew Richard Hackett [1972] Finance Director; Arthur Anton Hoeld [1969] Managing Director [German]; Andreas Johannes Richter [1973] Director/Head of Group Accounting [German]; Gavin Preston Thomson [1965] Managing Director

Adlib Audio Limited
Incorporated: 29 April 1998 *Employees:* 122
Net Worth: £2,642,155 *Total Assets:* £8,895,126
Registered Office: Adlib House, Fleming Road, Speke, Liverpool, L24 9LS
Activities: Renting and leasing of media entertainment equipment
Major Shareholder: Andrew Paul Dockerty
Officers: Lynn Marie Dockerty, Secretary; Andrew Paul Dockerty [1961] Director; John Christopher Hughes [1983] Sales Director; David Andrew Jones [1976] P A Director; David Andrew Kay [1972] Director/Audio Electronic Engineer; Roger William Kirby [1971] Sales Director; Philip John Stoker [1979] Director/P.A Manager

Adlington Welding Supplies Limited
Incorporated: 17 August 1973 *Employees:* 64
Net Worth: £7,940,199 *Total Assets:* £13,829,029
Registered Office: North Street, Highfield Industrial Estate, Chorley, Lancs, PR7 1QD
Activities: Wholesale of wood, construction materials and sanitary equipment
Parent: Adlington Welding Supplies (Holdings) Limited
Officers: Mark Andrew Hunt, Secretary; Mark Andrew Hunt [1964] Director; Stephen James Scott [1978] Director; Howard Antony Turner [1966] Director; Nigel Andrew Turner [1964] Director

ADM Protexin Limited
Incorporated: 16 July 1973 *Employees:* 132
Net Worth: £22,746,428 *Total Assets:* £28,558,026
Registered Office: c/o Eversecretary Limited, Eversheds House, 70 Great Bridgewater Street, Manchester, M1 5ES
Activities: Manufacture of other food products n.e.c.
Parent: Archer Daniels Midland (U.K.) Limited
Officers: Emmanuel Njok Ayuk [1981] Director/Business Attorney [American]; Henri Massao Kanemaru [1973] Director/Financial Controller [Brazilian]; Aileen Angela Lockington [1975] Director [Irish]; Vikram Luthar [1967] Director/Executive Management [Indian]; Orla Margaret Muldoon [1969] Managing Director [Irish]; Jonathan Richard Sowler [1975] Director

ADP Healthcare Acquisitions Limited
Incorporated: 26 January 2007
Net Worth Deficit: £106,261,000 *Total Assets:* £7,005,000
Registered Office: Europa House, Europa Trading Estate, Stoneclough Road, Kearsley, Manchester, M26 1GG
Activities: Dental practice activities
Parent: ADP Healthcare Services Limited
Officers: Leo Damian Carroll, Secretary; Manish Prasad [1972] Clinical Director; Tom Riall [1960] Director; Mohammed Omar Shafi Khan [1974] Director/Chief Financial Officer; Krista Nyree Whitley [1970] Clinical Director

ADP Healthcare Services Limited
Incorporated: 30 January 2007
Net Worth: £66,183,000 *Total Assets:* £77,690,000
Registered Office: Europa House, Europa Trading Estate, Stoneclough Road, Kearsley, Manchester, M26 1GG
Activities: Dental practice activities
Parent: Turnstone Bidco 1 Limited
Officers: Leo Damian Carroll, Secretary; Tom Riall [1960] Director; Mohammed Omar Shafi Khan [1974] Director/Chief Financial Officer; Krista Nyree Whitley [1970] Clinical Director

ADP Holdings Limited
Incorporated: 3 October 2001
Net Worth Deficit: £4,874,000 *Total Assets:* £25,340,000
Registered Office: Europa House, Europa Trading Estate, Stoneclough Road, Kearsley, Manchester, M26 1GG
Activities: Activities of head offices
Parent: ADP Healthcare Acquisitions Limited
Officers: Leo Damian Carroll, Secretary; Tom Riall [1960] Director; Mohammed Omar Shafi Khan [1974] Director/Chief Financial Officer; Krista Nyree Whitley [1970] Clinical Director

ADP No.1 Limited
Incorporated: 24 October 2001
Net Worth: £9,422,000 *Total Assets:* £14,452,000
Registered Office: Europa House, Europa Trading Estate, Stoneclough Road, Kearsley, Manchester, M26 1GG
Activities: Dental practice activities
Parent: ADP Holdings Limited
Officers: Leo Damian Carroll, Secretary; Tom Riall [1960] Director; Mohammed Omar Shafi Khan [1974] Director/Chief Financial Officer; Krista Nyree Whitley [1970] Clinical Director

Advance Uranium Asset Management Limited
Incorporated: 25 February 2010
Net Worth Deficit: £24,769,004 *Total Assets:* £17,094,438
Registered Office: Springfields, Salwick, Preston, Lancs, PR4 0XJ
Activities: Wholesale of metals and metal ores
Shareholders: Westinghouse Electric UK Holdings Limited; Uranium Asset Management Limited; Toshiba Nuclear Energy Holdings (UK) Limited; Toshiba Corporation
Officers: Fiona Houghton, Secretary; Angela Darkey [1971] Managing Director UAM and AUAM Ltd; Yoshihiro Okada [1968] Director [Japanese]; Koichiro Yoshinio [1963] Director [Japanese]

Advanced Biotechnologies Limited
Incorporated: 28 December 1989
Net Worth: £14 995,000 *Total Assets:* £14,995,000
Registered Office: 3rd Floor, 1 Ashley Road, Altrincham, Cheshire, WA14 2DT
Activities: Manufacture of other chemical products n.e.c.
Parent: Erie UK Limited
Officers: Rhona Gregg, Secretary; Lucie Mary Katja Grant [1976] Director/Solicitor; Nicholas Ince [1982] Director/Accountant; David John Norman [1960] Director/Chartered Accountant

Advanced Medical Solutions (Europe) Limited
Incorporated: 18 December 2013
Net Worth: £52,451,088 *Total Assets:* £52,777,516
Registered Office: Premier Park, 33 Road One, Winsford Industrial Estate, Winsford, Cheshire, CW7 3RT
Activities: Non-trading company
Parent: Advanced Medical Solutions Group PLC
Officers: Mary Tavener, Secretary; Christopher Meredith [1966] Director/Chief Executive Officer; Mary Generaldine Tavener [1962] Finance Director

Advanced Medical Solutions (Plymouth) Limited
Incorporated: 23 July 1998 *Employees:* 74
Net Worth: £2,770,000 *Total Assets:* £7,906,000
Registered Office: Premier Park, 33 Road One, Winsford Industrial Estate, Winsford, Cheshire, CW7 3RT
Activities: Dormant company
Parent: Advanced Medical Solutions Group PLC
Officers: Mary Generaldine Tavener, Secretary; Christopher Meredith [1966] Director/Chief Executive Officer; Mary Generaldine Tavener [1962] Financial Director

Advanced Medical Solutions Group PLC
Incorporated: 1 November 1993 *Employees:* 603
Net Worth: £152,436,000 *Total Assets:* £168,718,000
Registered Office: Premier Park, 33 Road One, Winsford Industrial Estate, Winsford, Cheshire, CW7 3RT
Activities: Activities of head offices
Officers: Mary Generaldine Tavener, Secretary; Peter Vance Allen [1956] Director; Stephen Gerard Bellamy [1960] Director [New Zealander]; Penelope Anne Freer [1960] Director/Corporate Advisory; Christopher Meredith [1966] Director/Chief Executive Officer; Peter Maximilian Steinmann [1963] Director [Swiss]; Mary Generaldine Tavener [1962] Finance Director

Advanced Medical Solutions Limited
Incorporated: 29 November 1991 *Employees:* 231
Net Worth: £25,860,000 *Total Assets:* £35,996,000
Registered Office: Premier Park, 33 Road One, Winsford Industrial Estate, Winsford, Cheshire, CW7 3RT
Activities: Manufacture of basic pharmaceutical products
Parent: Advanced Medical Solutions Group PLC
Officers: Mary Generaldine Tavener, Secretary; Christopher Meredith [1966] Chief Executive Director; Mary Generaldine Tavener [1962] Finance Director

Advanced Processing Limited
Incorporated: 15 May 1997
Net Worth: £3,112,007 *Total Assets:* £6,877,619
Registered Office: 606 Building, Wharfedale Road, Euroway Trading Estate, Bradford, W Yorks, BD4 6SG
Activities: Freight transport by road
Shareholders: David Glyn Rogan; Michael David Danby; Mohsin Pervez Chohan; Advanced Supply Chain Group Limited
Officers: Michael David Danby, Secretary; Mohsin Pervez Chohan [1958] Director/Businessman; Michael David Danby [1960] Director; David Glyn Rogan [1964] Director

Advancis Holdings Limited
Incorporated: 21 July 2016
Net Worth: £850 *Total Assets:* £12,834,396
Registered Office: Alexandra Court, Carrs Road, Cheadle, Cheshire, SK8 2JY
Activities: Activities of other holding companies n.e.c.
Officers: Melih Sakir Basar [1978] Director [American]; David Cecil John Knevitt [1959] Director [Australian]; Robert Ian Templeton [1941] Director/Chartered Accountant; Bryan Joseph Unsworth [1968] Director [American]; Nicholas Adam Zapolski [1982] Director

Adviserplus Business Solutions Limited
Incorporated: 24 May 2001 *Employees:* 297
Net Worth: £5,380,000 *Total Assets:* £7,367,000
Registered Office: Woodcourt, Riverside Park, Southwood Road, Bromborough, Wirral, Merseyside, CH62 3QX
Activities: Information technology consultancy activities
Parent: Adviserplus Holdings Limited
Officers: Craig Fairey, Secretary; Nicholas Charles Bradley [1974] Director [Australian]; Simon Richard Downing [1965] Director; Craig Fairey [1969] Director; Julian Edward Harley [1957] Director; Joao Vicente Goncalves Rosa [1978] Director [Portuguese]

Adviserplus Holdings Limited
Incorporated: 20 October 2014 *Employees:* 296
Net Worth: £16,239,000 *Total Assets:* £20,646,000
Registered Office: Woodcourt, Riverside Park, Southwood Road, Bromborough, Wirral, Merseyside, CH62 3QX
Activities: Activities of other holding companies n.e.c.
Parent: Aplus Bidco Limited
Officers: Craig Fairey, Secretary; Nicholas Charles Bradley [1974] Director [Australian]; Simon Richard Downing [1965] Director; Craig Fairey [1969] Director; Julian Edward Harley [1957] Director; Joao Vicente Goncalves Rosa [1978] Director [Portuguese]

AECOM E&C UK Limited
Incorporated: 19 January 2000 *Employees:* 60
Net Worth: £16,410,000 *Total Assets:* £25,735,000
Registered Office: 3rd Floor, 401 Faraday Street, Birchwood Park, Warrington, Cheshire, WA3 6GA
Activities: Construction of commercial buildings
Parent: AECOM International Holdings UK Limited
Officers: Annette Bottaro-Walklet, Secretary; Gerard McGill [1955] Director/Businessman; Bernice Constance Lilian Philps [1959] Director/Chartered Accountant; David Wesley Swindle Jnr [1954] Director/Businessman [American]

AECOM Global Holdings UK Limited
Incorporated: 27 July 2009
Net Worth: £285,928,896 *Total Assets:* £716,993,536
Registered Office: 3rd Floor, 401 Faraday Street, Birchwood Park, Warrington, Cheshire, WA3 6GA
Activities: Activities of head offices
Parent: AECOM
Officers: Annette Bottaro-Walklet, Secretary; Bernice Constance Lilian Philps [1959] Director/Chartered Accountant; David John Price [1970] Director/Accountant

AECOM GR1 Limited
Incorporated: 30 October 2013
Net Worth: £13,603,013 *Total Assets:* £445,246,720
Registered Office: 3rd Floor, 401 Faraday Street, Birchwood Park, Warrington, Cheshire, WA3 6GA
Activities: Non-trading company
Parent: AECOM Intercontinental Holdings UK Limited
Officers: Annette Bottaro-Walklet, Secretary; Bernice Constance Lilian Philps [1959] Director/Chartered Accountant; David John Price [1970] Director/Accountant

AECOM GR2 Limited
Incorporated: 30 October 2013
Total Assets: £436,798,336
Registered Office: 3rd Floor, 401 Faraday Street, Birchwood Park, Warrington, Cheshire, WA3 6GA
Activities: Non-trading company
Parent: AECOM GR1 Limited
Officers: Annette Bottaro-Walklet, Secretary; Bernice Constance Lilian Philps [1959] Director/Chartered Accountant; David John Price [1970] Director/Accountant

AECOM Intercontinental Holdings UK Limited
Incorporated: 1 March 2012
Net Worth: £349,665,792 *Total Assets:* £458,256,960
Registered Office: 3rd Floor, 401 Faraday Street, Birchwood Park, Warrington, Cheshire, WA3 6GA
Activities: Activities of other holding companies n.e.c.
Parent: AECOM Worldwide Holdings UK Limited
Officers: Annette Bottaro-Walklet, Secretary; Bernice Constance Lilian Philps [1959] Director/Chartered Accountant; David John Price [1970] Director/Accountant

AECOM International Holdings UK Limited
Incorporated: 13 March 1954
Net Worth: £31,952,000 *Total Assets:* £32,555,000
Registered Office: 3rd Floor, 401 Faraday Street, Birchwood Park, Warrington, Cheshire, WA3 6GA
Activities: Activities of head offices
Parent: AECOM Intercontinental Holdings UK Limited
Officers: Annette Bottaro-Walklet, Secretary; David Charles Webb Barwell [1965] Director; William Jan Charles [1962] Director/Chief Operating Officer UK and Ireland; Cheryl Rosalind McCall [1974] Director/Accountant; Gerard McGill [1955] Director/Businessman; Bernice Constance Lilian Philps [1959] Director/Chartered Accountant; David Wesley Swindle Jr [1954] Director/Businessman [American]

AECOM Worldwide Holdings UK Limited
Incorporated: 22 March 2012
Net Worth: £70,483,272 *Total Assets:* £70,567,688
Registered Office: 3rd Floor, 401 Faraday Street, Birchwood Park, Warrington, Cheshire, WA3 6GA
Activities: Activities of other holding companies n.e.c.
Parent: AECOM Ghc1 Limited
Officers: Annette Bottaro-Walklet, Secretary; Bernice Constance Lilian Philps [1959] Director/Chartered Accountant; David John Price [1970] Director/Accountant

AEE Renewables UK 31 Limited
Incorporated: 24 January 2011
Net Worth: £313,199 *Total Assets:* £20,865,964
Registered Office: Eversheds House, 70 Great Bridgewater Street, Manchester, M1 5ES
Activities: Production of electricity
Parent: Sune Green Holdco2 Ltd
Officers: Carl Goran Dandanell [1959] Director [Swedish]

Aegis Outsourcing UK Limited
Incorporated: 28 March 2006 *Employees:* 116
Net Worth: £1,168,965 *Total Assets:* £13,798,365
Registered Office: 11th Floor, City Tower, Piccadilly Plaza, Manchester, M1 4BT
Activities: Other business support service activities n.e.c.
Officers: Ranjan Dalela [1966] Director/Service [Indian]

Affiniture Cards Limited
Incorporated: 19 December 2011 *Employees:* 7
Net Worth: £486,173 *Total Assets:* £18,614,308
Registered Office: International House, Kingsfield Court, Chester Business Park, Chester, CH4 9RF
Activities: Other credit granting n.e.c.
Officers: Jonathan David Back [1963] Director/Chartered Accountant; Peter Richard Murray [1960] Director

Affinity Living 2 Limited
Incorporated: 19 April 2016
Net Worth: £1,435,000 *Total Assets:* £9,241,000
Registered Office: The Box, Horseshoe Lane, Alderley Edge, Cheshire, SK9 7QP
Activities: Development of building projects
Parent: Affinity Living Limited
Officers: Giles Beswick, Secretary; Giles Peter Beswick [1974] Director; Mark Christopher Dawson [1973] Director; Mark David Stott [1972] Director

Affinity Living Trinity Holdco Limited
Incorporated: 24 February 2016
Net Worth Deficit: £4,000 *Total Assets:* £13,017,000
Registered Office: The Box, Horseshoe Lane, Alderley Edge, Cheshire, SK9 7QP
Activities: Development of building projects
Parent: Affinity Living Limited
Officers: Giles Beswick, Secretary; Giles Peter Beswick [1974] Director; Mark Christopher Dawson [1973] Director; Mark David Stott [1972] Director

Affirmative Finance Limited
Incorporated: 13 February 2004 *Employees:* 22
Net Worth: £10,606,630 *Total Assets:* £35,095,668
Registered Office: 7 St James Square, Manchester, M2 6XX
Activities: Credit granting by non-deposit taking finance houses and other specialist consumer credit grantors
Shareholders: Eugene Barry Esterkin; Lord David Alliance
Officers: Gary Scott Lederberg, Secretary; Eugene Barry Esterkin [1958] Director/Solicitor; Gary Scott Lederberg [1972] Director/Solicitor; Paul Edward Mitchell [1976] Director/Accountant

Affordable Window Systems Limited
Incorporated: 9 December 1992 *Employees:* 213
Net Worth: £1,644,200 *Total Assets:* £8,172,906
Registered Office: Aldon Road, Poulton Business Park, Poulton-le-Fylde, Lancs, FY6 8DU
Activities: Painting
Parent: Affordable Aluminium Limited
Officers: Michael Gaughan, Secretary; Paula Cocker [1975] Director; Edward Gaughan [1949] Director [Irish]; Michael Gaughan [1954] Production Director [Irish]; Andrew Hoop [1966] Director/Manager; Karen Mageean [1965] Director/Manager; Laurence Sydney George Myers [1969] Director/Manager; Nigel Stanton [1967] Director

Affymetrix, UK Ltd.
Incorporated: 25 June 1998 *Employees:* 64
Net Worth: £8,084,266 *Total Assets:* £18,346,982
Registered Office: 3rd Floor, 1 Ashley Road, Altrincham, Cheshire, WA14 2DT
Activities: Other business support service activities n.e.c.
Parent: Invitrogen Europe Limited
Officers: Rhona Gregg, Secretary; Lucie Mary Katja Grant [1976] Director/Solicitor; Nicholas Ince [1982] Director/Accountant; David John Norman [1960] Director/Chartered Accountant

Afgritech Limited
Incorporated: 14 October 2004 *Employees:* 13
Net Worth: £2,538,031 *Total Assets:* £9,874,832
Registered Office: Old Croft, Stanwix, Carlisle, Cumbria, CA3 9BA
Activities: Manufacture of prepared feeds for farm animals
Shareholder: Carr's Group PLC
Officers: Matthew Ratcliffe, Secretary; Neil Austin [1975] Finance Director; Timothy John Davies [1962] Director; Noel Geary [1973] Director [South African]; Anina Clarina Hunter [1977] Director [South African]

AFW Finance 2 Limited
Incorporated: 6 November 2015
Net Worth: £229,004,160 *Total Assets:* £2,232,140,032
Registered Office: Booths Park, Chelford Road, Knutsford, Cheshire, WA16 8QZ
Activities: Non-trading company
Parent: AMEC Foster Wheeler International Holdings Limited
Officers: Iain Angus Jones, Secretary; Carl Anthony Chatfield [1964] Director; William George Setter [1975] Director

AGC Chemicals Europe, Ltd.
Incorporated: 13 August 1999 *Employees:* 186
Net Worth: £12,248,000 *Total Assets:* £77,263,000
Registered Office: P O Box 4, York House, Hillhouse International, Thornton-Cleveleys, Lancs, FY5 4QD
Activities: Manufacture of plastics in primary forms
Parent: Asahi Glass Company Ltd
Officers: Stephen Howcroft, Secretary; Paul Desmond Davis [1959] Operations Director; Shin Kato [1967] Director [Japanese]; Hiroo Mori [1963] Director/Chairman and CEO [Japanese]; Nobuyasu Murahashi [1967] Director/Chief Technical Officer [Japanese]; Hiroaki Ono [1960] Director/General Manager [Japanese]; Yasunobu Yamada [1969] Commercial Director [Japanese]; Takashi Yukoshi [1961] Director/General Manager [Japanese]

AGDC Holdings Limited
Incorporated: 1 March 2004 *Employees:* 895
Net Worth Deficit: £1,559,000 *Total Assets:* £61,603,000
Registered Office: 1030 Europa Boulevard, Westbrook, Warrington, Cheshire, WA5 7YW
Activities: Other retail sale of new goods in specialised stores (not commercial art galleries and opticians)
Parent: WTS Bidco Limited
Officers: Lorraine Stringer, Secretary; Samantha Jane Tyrer [1970] Director/Chief Executive; Ian Robert Williams [1973] Director/Chief Financial Officer

Agecroft Investment Co.Limited
Incorporated: 5 March 1954 *Employees:* 1
Net Worth: £7,626,869 *Total Assets:* £10,946,187
Registered Office: 17 London Road, Alderley Edge, Cheshire, SK9 7JT
Activities: Development of building projects
Shareholder: Bollin Holdings Limited
Officers: Judith Jackson, Secretary; Robert Michael John Keene [1943] Director; Fraser Gowanloch Westbrook [1946] Director; Rachael Westbrook [1978] Director/Property Consultant

Aghoco 1079 Limited
Incorporated: 25 January 2012 *Employees:* 368
Net Worth Deficit: £9,604,000 *Total Assets:* £87,951,000
Registered Office: IESA Works, Daten Park, Birchwood, Warrington, Cheshire, WA3 6UT
Activities: Activities of head offices
Parent: Electrocomponents U.K. Limited
Officers: Deborah Catherine Ann Bowring [1963] Director; David John Egan [1967] Finance Director; Vanessa Elizabeth Gough [1967] Director/Group Financial Controller; Ian Peter Haslegrave [1968] Director/Group General Counsel; Andrew Bell Perry [1976] Finance Director

Agilent Technologies Lda UK Limited
Incorporated: 16 December 2013 *Employees:* 388
Net Worth: £82,652,896 *Total Assets:* £134,176,256
Registered Office: 5500 Lakeside, Cheadle Royal Business Park, Cheadle, Cheshire, SK8 3GR
Activities: Other professional, scientific and technical activities n.e.c.
Parent: Agilent Technologies Luxco S.A.R.L.
Officers: James Philip Wright, Secretary; Paul George Gourlay [1964] Director/Facilities Manager; Neil Watkin Rees [1966] Director/Business Executive; Karen Louise Waddell [1979] Director/HR Manager

Agility Logistics Solutions Limited
Incorporated: 10 February 2000
Net Worth: £7,683,563 *Total Assets:* £20,993,652
Registered Office: Number One Hurricane Court, Hurricane Drive, Speke, Liverpool, L24 8RL
Activities: Sea and coastal freight water transport
Officers: Amy Jane Elizabeth Bold, Secretary; Elizabeth Ann Preston [1960] Director; Howard Graham Sellers [1973] Director/Vice President

Agricultural Machinery (Nantwich) Limited
Incorporated: 2 February 1951 *Employees:* 26
Net Worth: £2,244,294 *Total Assets:* £7,195,644
Registered Office: Millstone Lane, Nantwich, Cheshire, CW5 5PJ
Activities: Sale of other motor vehicles
Parent: Cornthwaite Investments (AG) Limited
Officers: John Edwin Ashe, Secretary; John Edwin Ashe [1958] Director; Stuart Anthony Cornthwaite [1976] Director; Robert Charles Hughes [1971] Director/Manager

AHL Anglia Limited
Incorporated: 20 September 1996
Net Worth: £24,468,000 *Total Assets:* £25,028,000
Registered Office: Stretton Green Distribution Park, Langford Way, Appleton, Warrington, Cheshire, WA4 4TQ
Activities: Activities of head offices
Parent: Greenwhitestar Acquisitions Limited
Officers: Elaine Williams, Secretary; David Keith Meir [1970] Director; Rupert Henry Conquest Nichols [1949] Legal Director & Company Secretary; David Brian Pickering [1973] Director

Aidapt Bathrooms Limited
Incorporated: 26 January 1990 *Employees:* 70
Net Worth: £3,829,671 *Total Assets:* £10,488,273
Registered Office: Lancots Lane, Sutton Oak, St Helens, Merseyside, WA9 3EX
Activities: Other human health activities
Parent: Holmpatrick Ltd
Officers: Mark Benyon, Secretary/Director; Catherine Jane Benyon [1980] Director/Business Manager; Mark Benyon [1951] Director; Richard John Jeff Fox [1963] Director; Rebecca Louise Wilson [1980] Director/Manager

Aidenhall Ltd
Incorporated: 21 May 2009 *Employees:* 72
Net Worth: £2,191,072 *Total Assets:* £8,305,015
Registered Office: Priestley Road, Wardley Industrial Estate, Worsley, Manchester, M28 2LX
Activities: Management consultancy activities other than financial management
Major Shareholder: Paul Adam Abrahams
Officers: Paul Adam Abrahams, Secretary/Director; Paul Adam Abrahams [1960] Director

Aim Engineering Limited
Incorporated: 3 September 1992 *Employees:* 211
Net Worth: £4,822,000 *Total Assets:* £16,614,000
Registered Office: Southmoor Industrial Estate, Southmoor Road, Manchester, M23 9XD
Activities: Manufacture of other fabricated metal products n.e.c.
Parent: Arlington Aerospace Limited
Officers: Simon John Brazier [1963] Managing Director; Mark Bernard Franckel [1962] Director; Simon George Greenhalgh [1972] Director/Chief Financial Officer

Aimia Foods Group Limited
Incorporated: 10 August 2004
Net Worth: £8,296,000 *Total Assets:* £8,296,000
Registered Office: Penny Lane, Haydock, Merseyside, WA11 0QZ
Activities: Non-trading company
Shareholder: Aimia Foods Holdings Limited
Officers: Jason Robert Ausher [1973] Director [American]; Claire Duffy [1976] Director/Solicitor; Steven Kitching [1964] Director

Aimia Foods Holdings Limited
Incorporated: 3 April 2007
Net Worth: £12,403,000 *Total Assets:* £12,403,000
Registered Office: Penny Lane, Haydock, Merseyside, WA11 0QZ
Activities: Manufacture of other food products n.e.c.
Shareholder: Total Water Solutions Limited
Officers: Jason Robert Ausher [1973] Director [American]; Claire Duffy [1976] Director/Solicitor; Steven Kitching [1964] Director

Aimia Foods Limited
Incorporated: 28 January 1981 *Employees:* 322
Net Worth: £16,871,000 *Total Assets:* £30,549,000
Registered Office: Penny Lane, Haydock, Merseyside, WA11 0QZ
Activities: Tea processing
Shareholder: Aimia Foods Group Limited
Officers: Jason Robert Ausher [1973] Director [American]; Claire Duffy [1976] Director/Solicitor; Steven Kitching [1964] Director; Richard York [1971] Director/Head of Finance

Ainscough Brothers LLP
Incorporated: 20 November 2003
Net Worth: £11,454,295 *Total Assets:* £11,774,856
Registered Office: Centurion House, Leyland Business Park, Centurion Way, Leyland, Lancs, PR25 3GR
Officers: Brendan Ainscough [1954] Member; James Ainscough [1956] Member; Martin Ainscough [1952] Member

Ainscough Crane Hire Ltd
Incorporated: 3 September 1996 *Employees:* 987
Net Worth: £73,044,000 *Total Assets:* £160,270,000
Registered Office: Bradley Hall, Bradley Lane, Standish, Wigan, Lancs, WN6 0XQ
Activities: Other specialised construction activities n.e.c.
Parent: Accord Bidco Limited
Officers: Charles Peter Bithell [1968] Director/Chief Financial Officer; Janet Elizabeth Entwistle [1961] Managing Director

Ainscough Industrial Services Limited
Incorporated: 15 March 2013 *Employees:* 229
Net Worth: £3,289,551 *Total Assets:* £14,329,103
Registered Office: Vanguard House, Bradley Lane, Standish, Wigan, Lancs, WN6 0XF
Activities: Activities of head offices
Major Shareholder: Matthew Martin Ainscough
Officers: David Andrew Cheers, Secretary; Matthew Martin Ainscough [1978] Director/Chief Executive Officer; David Andrew Cheers [1966] Financial Director; Stephen William Edge [1973] Engineering Director; Robert McLemon [1964] Commercial Director

Ainscough Investments Limited
Incorporated: 9 July 2007 *Employees:* 14
Net Worth: £16,416 *Total Assets:* £15,884,570
Registered Office: Oakland House, 21 Hope Carr Road, Leigh, Wigan, Lancs, WN7 3ET
Activities: Activities of head offices
Parent: Ainscough Group Limited
Officers: Martin Ainscough [1952] Director; Rachael Eva Ainscough [1993] Director; David Philip Richard Watson [1978] Director/Accountant

Ainscough Property Holdings Limited
Incorporated: 24 November 2015
Net Worth: £9,908,297 *Total Assets:* £9,908,297
Registered Office: Centurion House, Leyland Business Park, Centurion Way, Leyland, Lancs, PR25 3GR
Activities: Other letting and operating of own or leased real estate
Shareholders: Brendan Ainscough; James Ainscough
Officers: Brendan Ainscough [1954] Director; James Ainscough [1956] Director; Aidan John Grimshaw [1964] Director

Ainscough Strategic Land Limited
Incorporated: 20 August 2007 *Employees:* 5
Net Worth Deficit: £1,579,614 *Total Assets:* £7,653,856
Registered Office: 21 Hope Carr Road, Leigh, Lancs, WN7 3ET
Activities: Buying and selling of own real estate
Parent: Ainscough Investments Limited
Officers: Martin Ainscough [1952] Director; Rachael Eva Ainscough [1993] Director; John Michael Brooks [1963] Director/Planning Professional; David Philip Richard Watson [1978] Director/Accountant

Ainscough Wind Energy Services Limited
Incorporated: 17 December 2010 *Employees:* 98
Net Worth: £8,716,000 *Total Assets:* £10,260,000
Registered Office: Bradley Hall, Bradley Lane, Standish, Wigan, Lancs, WN6 0XQ
Activities: Installation of industrial machinery and equipment
Shareholders: Westcountry Crane Hire Holdings Limited; JFHA Limited
Officers: Charles Peter Bithell [1968] Director/Chief Financial Officer; Janet Elizabeth Entwistle [1961] Managing Director

Aintree Plastics (Holdings) Limited
Incorporated: 2 February 2016 *Employees:* 1
Net Worth Deficit: £187,965 *Total Assets:* £15,583,511
Registered Office: Corpacq House, 1 Goose Green, Altrincham, Cheshire, WA14 1DW
Activities: Activities of head offices
Officers: Phillip Robert Millward [1962] Director

Aintree Plastics Limited
Incorporated: 30 November 1995 *Employees:* 25
Net Worth: £5,815,978 *Total Assets:* £13,262,418
Registered Office: 37 Stopgate Lane, Aintree, Liverpool, L9 6DX
Activities: Manufacture of plastic packing goods
Officers: Paul Edward Baylis [1969] Director/Manager; Stephen John Baylis [1967] Director/Manager; Phillip Robert Millward [1962] Director

Aintree Retail Park Limited
Incorporated: 15 July 1994
Net Worth: £39,254,516 *Total Assets:* £44,711,616
Registered Office: Emerson House, Heyes Lane, Alderley Edge, Cheshire, SK9 7LF
Activities: Development of building projects
Parent: Orbit Investments (Properties) Limited
Officers: Varun Maharaj, Secretary; Anthony Emerson Jones [1967] Director; Mark Emerson Jones [1964] Director; Peter Emerson Jones [1935] Director

Air Energi Group Holdings Limited
Incorporated: 2 August 2012 *Employees:* 679
Net Worth Deficit: £7,693,395 *Total Assets:* £319,816,288
Registered Office: 4th Floor, Delphian House, Riverside, New Bailey Street, Manchester M3 5FS
Activities: Activities of other holding companies n.e.c.
Officers: Duncan Alasdair Gregson [1964] Director; Matthew Harrison [1980] Director/Partner [Canadian]; Ian Michael Langley [1962] Director

Air Energi Group Investments Limited
Incorporated: 3 August 2012
Net Worth: £38,952,000 *Total Assets:* £45,491,000
Registered Office: 4th Floor, Delphian House, Riverside, New Bailey Street, Manchester, M3 5FS
Activities: Activities of other holding companies n.e.c.
Parent: Airswift Holdings Limited
Officers: Timothy Briant [1970] Director; Janette Bates Marx [1975] Director [American]; Peter William Courtis Searle [1962] Director

Air Energi Group Limited
Incorporated: 15 July 2005
Net Worth: £397,000 *Total Assets:* £11,827,000
Registered Office: 4th Floor, Delphian House, Riverside, New Bailey Street, Manchester, M3 5FS
Activities: Activities of head offices
Parent: Air Energi Investments Limited
Officers: Timothy Briant [1970] Director; Janette Bates Marx [1975] Director [American]; Peter William Courtis Searle [1962] Director

Air Energi Holdings Limited
Incorporated: 17 March 2009
Net Worth: £101,000 *Total Assets:* £10,553,000
Registered Office: 4th Floor, Delphian House, Riverside, New Bailey Street, Manchester, M3 5FS
Activities: Activities of other holding companies n.e.c.
Parent: Air Energi Group Investments Limited
Officers: Timothy Briant [1970] Director; Janette Bates Marx [1975] Director [American]; Peter William Courtis Searle [1962] Director

Air Energi Investments Limited
Incorporated: 17 March 2009
Net Worth Deficit: £5,703,000 *Total Assets:* £20,082,000
Registered Office: 4th Floor, Delphian House, Riverside, New Bailey Street, Manchester, M3 5FS
Activities: Activities of other holding companies n.e.c.
Parent: Air Energi Holdings Limited
Officers: Timothy Briant [1970] Director; Janette Bates Marx [1975] Director [American]; Peter William Courtis Searle [1962] Director

Air Energi Newco Limited
Incorporated: 26 November 2015
Net Worth Deficit: £4,674,000 *Total Assets:* £47,650,000
Registered Office: 4th Floor, Delphian House, Riverside, New Bailey Street, Manchester, M3 5FS
Activities: Activities of other holding companies n.e.c.
Parent: Air Energi Group Holdings Limited
Officers: Matthew Harrison [1980] Director/Partner [Canadian]; Ian Michael Langley [1962] Director; Peter William Courtis Searle [1962] Director

Air Resources Limited
Incorporated: 11 June 1979 *Employees:* 121
Net Worth: £30,081,000 *Total Assets:* £58,924,000
Registered Office: 4th Floor, Delphian House, Riverside, New Bailey Street, Manchester, M3 5FS
Activities: Other activities of employment placement agencies
Parent: Air Energi Group Ltd
Officers: Timothy Briant [1970] Director; Janette Bates Marx [1975] Director [American]; Peter William Courtis Searle [1962] Director; Gary Thomas Taylor [1966] Director

Air-Serv Limited
Incorporated: 19 December 1997 *Employees:* 114
Net Worth: £15,299,183 *Total Assets:* £22,610,064
Registered Office: Air-Serv, Redgate Road, South Lancashire Industrial Estate, Ashton in Makerfield, Wigan, Lancs, WN4 8DT
Activities: Other service activities n.e.c.
Officers: Jay Epstein [1970] Director/Chief Financial Officer [American]; Simon Paul Pope [1967] Director; Eric Anthony Robinson [1970] Director/Chief of Human Resources [American]

Airbags International Limited
Incorporated: 13 November 1985 *Employees:* 230
Net Worth: £23,393,000 *Total Assets:* £34,967,000
Registered Office: Viking Way, Congleton, Cheshire, CW12 1TT
Activities: Manufacture of other parts and accessories for motor vehicles
Parent: Autoliv UK Holding Limited
Officers: John Anthony Bonney, Secretary; Stuart Eustace [1979] Director/Plant Manager; Per Nielsen [1964] Director [Danish]

Airedale Catering Equipment Group Limited
Incorporated: 30 October 2012 *Employees:* 613
Net Worth: £2,574,000 *Total Assets:* £19,598,000
Registered Office: Airedale House, Victoria Road, Eccleshill, Bradford, W Yorks, BD2 2BN
Activities: Activities of head offices
Shareholders: Robert Howard Bywell; Rockpool Investment Nominee Limited
Officers: Andrew Wyatt Bristow [1962] Director; Robert Howard Bywell [1973] Director; Michael Gordge [1963] Director; Ian Richard Sisson [1958] Director; Paul Woodford [1971] Director

Airedale Catering Equipment Limited
Incorporated: 14 May 1985 *Employees:* 77
Net Worth: £8,067,000 *Total Assets:* £16,058,000
Registered Office: Airedale House, Victoria Road, Eccleshill, Bradford, W Yorks, BD2 2BN
Activities: Installation of industrial machinery and equipment
Parent: Airedale Catering Equipment Group Ltd
Officers: Robert Howard Bywell [1973] Commercial Director; Michael Gordge [1963] Contracts Director; Ian Richard Sisson [1958] Sales Director; Paul Woodford [1971] Director

Airedale Chemical Company Limited
Incorporated: 4 December 1973 *Employees:* 116
Net Worth: £5,736,443 *Total Assets:* £24,955,190
Registered Office: Airedale Mills, Skipton Road, Cross Hills, Keighley, W Yorks, BD20 7BX
Activities: Manufacture of other inorganic basic chemicals
Parent: Airedale Chemical Holdings
Officers: Craig Thomson, Secretary; Christopher John Chadwick [1983] Sales Director; Daniel Fox [1976] Operations Director; Brenda Malvina Hall [1929] Director/Retired; Martin Leighton [1964] Commercial Director; Craig Thomson [1974] Director/Accountant; Robert Mark Wolff [1968] Sales Director

Airedale Chemical Holdings Limited
Incorporated: 21 January 2013 *Employees:* 136
Net Worth: £2,374,289 *Total Assets:* £22,757,900
Registered Office: Airedale Mills, Skipton Road, Crosshills, Keighley, W Yorks, BD20 7BX
Activities: Manufacture of other inorganic basic chemicals
Officers: Chris John Chadwick [1983] Sales Director; David Michael Chadwick [1959] Director/Dyestuff Merchant; John Whitney Chadwick [1959] Director/Dyestuff Merchant; Craig Thomson [1974] Director/Accountant

Airline Network Limited
Incorporated: 27 June 1991 *Employees:* 125
Net Worth: £1,051,000 *Total Assets:* £13,342,000
Registered Office: The Trident Centre, Portway, Ribble Docklands, Preston, Lancs, PR2 2QA
Activities: Travel agency activities
Parent: Gold Medal International Ltd
Officers: Ryan James Cooke, Secretary; John Constantine Bevan [1965] Director; Asif Hamza Parkar [1974] Director

Airline Services Limited
Incorporated: 8 December 1982
Net Worth Deficit: £19,731,354 *Total Assets:* £14,357,128
Registered Office: Canberra House, Robeson Way, Sharston Green Business Park, Manchester, M22 4SX
Activities: Service activities incidental to air transportation
Parent: Airline Services Holdings Limited
Officers: Paul Dennis Carter [1952] Director; Lloyd Cromwell Griffiths [1945] Director; Christopher Peter Handy [1965] Investment Director

Airport City (Manchester) Limited
Incorporated: 1 February 2013
Net Worth Deficit: £7,678,000 *Total Assets:* £45,901,000
Registered Office: 6th Olympic House, Manchester Airport, Manchester, M90 1QX
Activities: Activities of head offices
Parent: Manchester Airport Holdings Limited
Officers: Charles Thomas Cornish [1959] Director; Neil Philip Thompson [1971] Director

Airswift Holdings Limited
Incorporated: 11 December 2015 *Employees:* 679
Net Worth: £118,905,792 *Total Assets:* £327,335,872
Registered Office: Delphian House, New Bailey Street, Salford, M3 5FS
Activities: Other activities of employment placement agencies
Shareholders: Air Energi Newco Limited; Swift Worldwide Resources Holdco Limited
Officers: Alexander Carles [1975] Director/Managing Partner [American]; Joshua Charles Cascade [1972] Director [American]; William Francis Dawson Jr. [1964] Director [American]; Matthew Harrison [1980] Director/Partner [Canadian]; Ian Michael Langley [1962] Director; Peter William Courtis Searle [1962] Director

Airvending Limited
Incorporated: 19 July 1984 *Employees:* 114
Net Worth: £12,155,221 *Total Assets:* £22,603,360
Registered Office: Air-Serv, Redgate Road, South Lancashire Industrial Estate, Ashton in Makerfield, Wigan, Lancs, WN4 8DT
Activities: Other service activities n.e.c.
Parent: Air Serv Limited
Officers: Jay Epstein [1970] Director/Chief Financial Officer [American]; Simon Paul Pope [1967] Director; Eric Anthony Robinson [1970] Director/Chief of Human Resources [American]

AIS Projects Limited
Incorporated: 8 August 2001 *Employees:* 6
Net Worth: £1,758,016 *Total Assets:* £7,949,841
Registered Office: Vanguard House, Bradley Lane, Standish, Wigan, Lancs, WN6 0XF
Activities: Installation of industrial machinery and equipment
Officers: David Andrew Cheers, Secretary; Brendan Ainscough [1954] Director; Matthew Martin Ainscough [1978] Director; David Andrew Cheers [1966] Financial Director

AIS Vanguard Limited
Incorporated: 28 March 2014 *Employees:* 121
Net Worth: £1,107,149 *Total Assets:* £8,754,841
Registered Office: Vanguard House, Bradley Lane, Standish, Wigan, Lancs, WN6 0XF
Activities: Installation of industrial machinery and equipment
Parent: Ainscough Industrial Services Ltd
Officers: Matthew Martin Ainscough [1978] Director; David Andrew Cheers [1966] Director; Stephen William Edge [1973] Director

AJU2 Limited
Incorporated: 25 November 2013
Net Worth: £9,319,341 *Total Assets:* £32,074,794
Registered Office: 7 Merseyway, Stockport, Cheshire, SK1 1PN
Activities: Other business support service activities n.e.c.
Shareholders: John Coulter; Ann Jones
Officers: Ann Jones, Secretary; John Coulter [1951] Director; Ann Jones [1954] Director; Uzi Katz [1960] Director

Akcros Holdings Limited
Incorporated: 17 January 2007 *Employees:* 5
Net Worth: £6,945,090 *Total Assets:* £10,007,950
Registered Office: Lankro Way, Eccles, Manchester, M30 0LX
Activities: Activities of head offices
Officers: Paul Alan Angus [1964] Director [Canadian]; Andy Gehrlein [1970] Director [American]; Dr Brian William Johnson [1965] Commercial and Marketing Director; Matthew Keshian [1988] Director/Private Equity Investor [American]; Keval Patel [1979] Director/Private Equity Investor [American]

Akinika Debt Recovery Limited
Incorporated: 30 January 1976 *Employees:* 304
Net Worth: £7,127,000 *Total Assets:* £16,269,000
Registered Office: 33-34 Winckley Square, Preston, Lancs, PR1 3EL
Activities: Activities of call centres
Parent: Akinika Limited
Officers: Adam Joseph Blake [1987] Director; Andrew John Bowman [1972] Director; Kevin Andrew Francis [1973] Director

Akinika Limited
Incorporated: 11 February 1982 *Employees:* 3
Net Worth: £7,952,000 *Total Assets:* £16,356,000
Registered Office: 33-34 Winckley Square, Preston, Lancs, PR1 3EL
Activities: Activities of head offices
Parent: Debt Solutions (Holdings) Limited
Officers: Francesca Anne Todd [1971] Director/Company Secretary; Robert David Tolfts [1962] Director

Akinika UK Limited
Incorporated: 13 July 1989 *Employees:* 208
Net Worth: £14,265,000 *Total Assets:* £23,525,000
Registered Office: 33-34 Winckley Square, Preston, Lancs, PR1 3EL
Activities: Activities of call centres
Parent: Akinika Debt Recovery Limited
Officers: Francesca Anne Todd [1971] Director/Company Secretary; Robert David Tolfts [1962] Director

AKW Group Limited
Incorporated: 19 December 2001 *Employees:* 349
Net Worth: £8,233,854 *Total Assets:* £24,828,248
Registered Office: 26 Bond, Europa Way, Trafford Park, Manchester, M17 1WF
Activities: Freight transport by road
Shareholder: Anthony Kevin Worthington
Officers: Michael James Lyons, Secretary; Rebecca Therese Davies [1969] Director; Michael James Lyons [1962] Finance Director; Paula Owens [1970] Director; Julian Charles Richards [1961] Director; Paul Welsh [1970] Operations Director; Anthony Kevin Worthington [1958] Director/Haulage Contractor; Karen Lesley Worthington [1970] Director

Alam Investments Limited
Incorporated: 15 July 1999 *Employees:* 1
Net Worth: £4,606,235 *Total Assets:* £13,876,357
Registered Office: Dean Bank House, Dean Bank Drive, Rochdale, Lancs, OL16 4RW
Activities: Other letting and operating of own or leased real estate
Major Shareholder: Pervez Alam
Officers: Pervez Alam [1956] Director/Businessman

Albany International Limited
Incorporated: 21 December 1907 *Employees:* 82
Net Worth: £16,776,000 *Total Assets:* £18,266,000
Registered Office: Pilsworth Road, Bury, Lancs, BL9 8RS
Activities: Manufacture of other technical and industrial textiles
Parent: Albany International Holdings (Switzerland) AG
Officers: Darren Christopher Johnson, Secretary; Daniel Albert Alphonse Halfter Meyer [1961] Managing Director [French]; Charles Joseph Silva [1959] Director/Vice President [American]

Albany Products Limited
Incorporated: 19 March 2002 *Employees:* 14
Net Worth: £1,494,000 *Total Assets:* £8,187,000
Registered Office: Ship Canal House, 98 King Street, Manchester, M2 4WU
Activities: Non-specialised wholesale of food, beverages and tobacco
Officers: Keith Courtney [1953] Director; Susan Courtney [1952] Director; Nigel Matthew Hunter [1962] Sales Director [Australian]

Albion Limited
Incorporated: 3 July 2007 *Employees:* 51
Net Worth: £4,054,245 *Total Assets:* £9,791,975
Registered Office: Paton House, Level One, Victoria Viaduct, Carlisle, CA3 8AN
Activities: Wholesale of clothing and footwear
Parent: Lowe Clothing International Ltd
Officers: Christopher Arthur Carlisle, Secretary; Simon Patrick Baker [1976] Commercial Director; Christopher Arthur Carlisle [1954] Finance Director; Clare Cukic [1966] Operations Director; Stephen Michael Gould [1960] Sales Director; Jonathan Adam Lowe [1981] Director/Chairman; Desmond Watkins [1960] Technical Director

Albis (U.K.) Limited
Incorporated: 2 September 1966 *Employees:* 117
Net Worth: £24,284,324 *Total Assets:* £31,946,648
Registered Office: Parkgate Industrial Estate, Knutsford, Cheshire, WA16 8XW
Activities: Manufacture of other plastic products
Officers: Tanya Michele Taylor, Secretary; Josephine Patricia Bagnall [1970] Managing Director; Balakrishnan Velayudhan Cheramparambil [1961] Operations Director; Frank Kriebisch [1961] Director/Chief Operating Officer [German]; Ian Richard Granville Mills [1963] Director/Chief Sales Officer; Tanya Michele Taylor [1972] Finance Director

The Alchemist Bar & Restaurant Limited
Incorporated: 9 July 2009 *Employees:* 420
Net Worth: £4,210,729 *Total Assets:* £16,564,286
Registered Office: The Alchemist, Chadsworth House, Wilmslow Road, Handforth, Cheshire, SK9 3HP
Activities: Licenced restaurants
Parent: Buttercup Bidco Td
Officers: Mark Francis Burville [1976] Operations Director; Simon Potts [1980] Managing Director; Jeremy Kevin Roberts [1962] Director; Victoria Stewart [1980] Finance Director

Alder Hey Children's Charity
Incorporated: 14 January 2015 *Employees:* 20
Net Worth: £8,235,000 *Total Assets:* £10,583,000
Registered Office: Eaton Road, West Derby, Liverpool, L12 2AP
Activities: Hospital activities
Officers: Shalni Arora [1971] Director; John Kendal Carson [1951] Director/Management Consultant; Nicola Susan Collins [1971] Director/Solicitor; Barbara Elizabeth Craig [1947] Director/Nurse Consultant; Helen Clare Dearden [1963] Director/Chartered Accountant; Jean Gaynor France-Hayhurst [1950] Barrister, Mediator, Director; Glynis Steen Johnston [1951] Director/Finance Manager; Eileen Frances Jones [1950] Director/Retired Civil Servant; Dame Josephine Williams [1948] Director

Alderburgh Limited
Incorporated: 11 June 1980 *Employees:* 60
Net Worth: £2,272,286 *Total Assets:* £7,873,434
Registered Office: Solutions House, Dane Street, Rochdale, Lancs, OL11 4EZ
Activities: Non-specialised wholesale trade
Major Shareholder: Peter Russell Davidson
Officers: Amanda Thirsk, Secretary; Gary Baker [1968] Director; Peter Russell Davidson [1956] Director; Karen Elizabeth Day [1968] Director

Alderley Edge School for Girls
Incorporated: 1 November 1991 *Employees:* 89
Net Worth: £6,922,282 *Total Assets:* £7,995,167
Registered Office: Wilmslow Road, Alderley Edge, Cheshire, SK9 7QE
Activities: Pre-primary education
Officers: Simon James Malkin, Secretary; Edward Peter Richard Ainsworth [1932] Director/Chartered Accountant Retired; Sister Janet Mary Arrowsmith [1947] Director; The Revd Canon Brendan David Clover [1958] Director/Senior Provost; Kathleen Margaret Doyle [1950] Director/University Lecturer - Retired; Anne Shirley Herring [1946] Director/Ofsted Inspector - Retired; Caroline Elizabeth Lowe [1962] Funeral Director; Keith Lowe [1952] Director/Management Consultant; Robert Dwyer Nolan [1943] Director [Irish]; Tracy Pollard [1966] Director/Headteacher; Joanna Claire Rostron [1964] Director; Deborah Jayne Summerfield [1964] Director/Consultant; Christopher Trueman [1945] Director/Retired

Alderley Park Holdings Limited
Incorporated: 14 January 2014 *Employees:* 6
Net Worth: £8,962,000 *Total Assets:* £25,252,000
Registered Office: Union, Albert Square, Manchester, M2 6LW
Activities: Other letting and operating of own or leased real estate
Shareholders: Bruntwood Science Limited; Manchester Science Partnerships Limited
Officers: Councillor Rachel Anne Bailey [1956] Director/Leader of The Council; Rowena May Burns [1953] Director; Peter Andrew Crowther [1972] Director; Dr Christopher Doherty [1961] Site Director; Kate Victoria Lawlor [1981] Director/Chartered Accountant; Christopher George Oglesby [1967] Director

Alderley Park Limited
Incorporated: 28 October 2013
Net Worth: £30,252,000 *Total Assets:* £108,401,000
Registered Office: Union, Albert Square, Manchester, M2 6LW
Activities: Other letting and operating of own or leased real estate
Parent: Alderley Park Holdings Limited
Officers: Councillor Rachel Anne Bailey [1956] Director/Leader of The Council; Rowena May Burns [1953] Director; Peter Andrew Crowther [1972] Director; Dr Christopher Doherty [1961] Site Director; Kate Victoria Lawlor [1981] Director/Chartered Accountant; Christopher George Oglesby [1967] Director

Alderley Urban Investments Limited
Incorporated: 29 November 1995
Net Worth Deficit: £5,381,450 *Total Assets:* £8,128,048
Registered Office: c/o Manchester United Limited, Sir Matt Busby Way, Old Trafford, Manchester, M16 0RA
Activities: Buying and selling of own real estate
Parent: Manchester United Limited
Officers: Patrick Charles Donald Stewart, Secretary; Avram Glazer [1960] Director [American]; Bryan Glazer [1964] Director [American]; Joel Glazer [1967] Director/Businessman [American]; Edward Gareth Woodward [1971] Director/Chief of Staff

Alere Limited
Incorporated: 20 April 1983 *Employees:* 45
Net Worth: £5,354,151 *Total Assets:* £8,852,886
Registered Office: Bio-Stat House, Pepper Road, Hazel Grove, Stockport, Cheshire, SK7 5BW
Activities: Manufacture of medical and dental instruments and supplies
Parent: Alere UK Holdings Limited
Officers: Trevor Fellows, Secretary; Tomas Blomquist [1970] Managing Director [Swedish]; Trevor Fellows [1969] Finance Director

Alfa Coaches Limited
Incorporated: 12 January 1996 *Employees:* 92
Net Worth: £3,279,490 *Total Assets:* £7,772,835
Registered Office: Alfa Building, Euxton Lane, Euxton, Chorley, Lancs, PR7 6AF
Activities: Other passenger land transport
Shareholders: Alfa Leisureplex Group Limited; Alfa Travel Limited
Officers: Emma Russell, Secretary; Paul Anthony Bull [1962] Operations Director; Lucia Danielle Maguire [1985] Tours Director; Emma Russell [1979] Finance Director; Karen Elizabeth Sawbridge [1965] Director

Alfa Leisureplex Group Limited
Incorporated: 27 May 2015 *Employees:* 687
Net Worth: £15,092,710 *Total Assets:* £56,398,688
Registered Office: Alfa Building, East Terrace, Euxton Lane, Euxton, Chorley, Lancs, PR7 6AF
Activities: Activities of other holding companies n.e.c.
Parent: Alfa Leisureplex Trustees Limited
Officers: Emma Russell, Secretary; Paul Anthony Bull [1962] Operations Director; Lucia Danielle Maguire [1985] Tours Director; Emma Russell [1979] Finance Director; Karen Elizabeth Sawbridge [1965] Operations Director; Peter George Sawbridge [1955] Director

Alfa Travel Ltd.
Incorporated: 8 December 1988 *Employees:* 34
Net Worth: £5,956,130 *Total Assets:* £7,166,770
Registered Office: Alfa Building, Euxton Lane, Euxton, Chorley, Lancs, PR7 6AF
Activities: Tour operator activities
Parent: Alfa Leisureplex Group Limited
Officers: Emma Russell, Secretary; Paul Anthony Bull [1962] Operations Director; Lucia Danielle Maguire [1985] Tours Director; Emma Russell [1979] Finance Director; Karen Elizabeth Sawbridge [1965] Director/Chartered Accountant

All About Food Limited
Incorporated: 30 July 1997 *Employees:* 40
Net Worth: £7,685,808 *Total Assets:* £13,287,562
Registered Office: The Tree House, Maple View, Whitemoss Business Park, Skelmersdale, Lancs, WN8 9TG
Activities: Wholesale of other food, including fish, crustaceans and molluscs
Officers: David Sefton, Secretary; Colin Curtis Hill [1969] Managing Director; Charles Francis Luyckx [1969] Director/Accountant [Italian]; Robert Adrian Graham T'hooft [1968] Director/Businessman [Dutch]

Allegro Corporation Limited
Incorporated: 12 April 1994 *Employees:* 3
Net Worth: £8,672,715 *Total Assets:* £16,133,598
Registered Office: Jupiter House, 1 Mercury Rise, Altham Business Park, Altham, Lancs, BB5 5BY
Activities: Development of building projects
Parent: McDermott Developments Limited
Officers: Catherine Davis, Secretary/Director; Catherine Davis [1963] Director; Richard Michael Kay [1962] Financial Director; Seamus McDermott [1964] Director [Irish]

Allen (Park Foot) Limited
Incorporated: 25 July 1985 *Employees:* 37
Net Worth: £4,733,855 *Total Assets:* £6,709,482
Registered Office: Park Foot, Pooley Bridge, Penrith, Cumbria, CA10 2NA
Activities: Recreational vehicle parks, trailer parks and camping grounds
Officers: Barbara Josephine Allen, Secretary; Barbara Josephine Allen [1958] Director/Caravan Park Proprietor; Thomas James Allen [1931] Director/Caravan Park; Fiona Jacqueline Bell [1961] Director/Caravan Park; Malcolm Edward Bell [1959] Director Caravan Park

Allergan Biologics Limited
Incorporated: 24 September 2002 *Employees:* 122
Net Worth Deficit: £77,956,000 *Total Assets:* £42,590,000
Registered Office: 12 Estuary Banks, Speke, Liverpool, L24 8RB
Activities: Manufacture of basic pharmaceutical products
Parent: Eden Biopharma Group Limited
Officers: Patricia Maria Haran, Secretary; Judith Tomkins, Secretary; Crawford David Brown [1962] Director/Scientist

Alliance Disposables Limited
Incorporated: 7 April 1999 *Employees:* 582
Net Worth: £10,327,103 *Total Assets:* £45,580,680
Registered Office: Alliance House, Marshfield Bank, Crewe, Cheshire, CW2 8UY
Activities: Other retail sale in non-specialised stores
Major Shareholder: David Henderson Elder
Officers: Steven Tew, Secretary; Paul Michael Bonson [1964] Director; David Henderson Elder [1959] Director; Aidan Francis Walker [1960] W&D Director

Alliance Family Foundation Limited
Incorporated: 11 December 1968
Net Worth: £1,137,494 *Total Assets:* £11,282,795
Registered Office: 4th Floor, Faulkner House, Faulkner Street, Manchester, M1 4DY
Activities: Other social work activities without accommodation n.e.c.
Shareholders: Lord David Alliance; Sara Dorn Esterkin
Officers: Lord David Alliance [1932] Director; Hon Graham Neil Alliance [1959] Director; Joshua Jacob Moshe Alliance [1989] Director; Sara Dorn Esterkin [1962] Director

Alliance Real Estate LLP
Incorporated: 12 June 2014
Net Worth: £21,113,348 *Total Assets:* £51,006,600
Registered Office: Alliance House, Westpoint Enterprise Park, Clarence Avenue, Trafford Park, Manchester, M17 1QS

Allied Filter Systems Holdings Limited
Incorporated: 11 May 2016 *Employees:* 2
Net Worth: £9,999,997 *Total Assets:* £10,000,000
Registered Office: Huntsman Drive, Northbank Industrial Park, Irlam, Manchester, M44 5EG
Activities: Dormant company
Shareholders: Daniel James Thompson; Christopher Howard Brian Thompson
Officers: Christopher Howard Brian Thompson [1977] Director; Daniel James Thompson [1974] Director

Allied London Holdco Limited
Incorporated: 8 October 2012 *Employees:* 5
Net Worth: £35,620 *Total Assets:* £27,191,356
Registered Office: c/o Allied London, Level 12, No 1 Spinningfields, 1 Hardman Square, Manchester, M3 3EB
Activities: Other letting and operating of own or leased real estate
Parent: Allied London Properties Limited
Officers: Suresh Premji Gorasia [1974] Director; Frederick Paul Graham-Watson [1957] Finance Director; Michael Julian Ingall [1959] Managing Director; Jonathan Raine [1981] Director

Allied London Leeds Holding Company Two Limited
Incorporated: 7 December 2015 *Employees:* 6
Net Worth Deficit: £2,437,600 *Total Assets:* £14,857,405
Registered Office: c/o Allied London, Level 12, No 1 Spinningfields, 1 Hardman Square, Manchester, M3 3EB
Activities: Other letting and operating of own or leased real estate
Parent: Allied London Leeds Holding Company One Limited
Officers: Suresh Premji Gorasia [1974] Director; Frederick Paul Graham-Watson [1957] Director; Michael Julian Ingall [1959] Director; Jonathan Raine [1981] Director

Allied London Properties Limited
Incorporated: 16 November 2012 *Employees:* 6
Net Worth: £19,308,444 *Total Assets:* £133,865,456
Registered Office: c/o Allied London, Level 12, No 1 Spinningfields, 1 Hardman Square, Manchester, M3 3EB
Activities: Other letting and operating of own or leased real estate
Parent: Capital DDB Holdco Limited
Officers: Suresh Premji Gorasia [1974] Director; Frederick Paul Graham-Watson [1957] Finance Director; Michael Julian Ingall [1959] Managing Director; Jonathan Raine [1981] Director

Allied Publicity Services (Manchester) Limited
Incorporated: 25 January 1961 *Employees:* 537
Net Worth: £17,056,544 *Total Assets:* £39,265,808
Registered Office: Chetham House, Bird Hall Lane, Stockport, Cheshire, SK3 0ZP
Activities: Other business support service activities n.e.c.
Parent: APS Group Limited
Officers: Gillian Mary Snelson, Secretary; John Holmes [1966] Executive Director; Gillian Mary Snelson [1942] Director/Secretary; Malcolm Snelson [1939] Director/Publicity Contractor; Nicholas John Snelson [1965] Director/Publicity Contractor; Richard Humphrey Snelson [1967] Director/Publicity Contractor

Alliedtropic Limited
Incorporated: 24 February 2003 *Employees:* 3
Net Worth: £49,072,000 *Total Assets:* £64,350,000
Registered Office: Back O' Th' Bank House, Hereford Street, Bolton, Lancs, BL1 8HJ
Activities: Manufacture of bread; manufacture of fresh pastry goods and cakes
Parent: Warburtons 1876 Limited
Officers: John Healey, Secretary; Jonathan Warburton [1957] Director; William Ross Warburton [1958] Director; William Brett Warburton [1955] Director

Allmand - Smith Limited
Incorporated: 12 August 1969
Net Worth: £2,020,334 *Total Assets:* £7,273,299
Registered Office: Georges Court, Chestergate, Macclesfield, Cheshire, SK11 6DP
Activities: Manufacture of metal structures and parts of structures
Shareholders: Martin Allmand-Smith; Oliver Timothy Allmand-Smith; Stephen Peter Allmand-Smith
Officers: Stephen Allmand Smith, Secretary/Director; Martin Allmand-Smith [1962] Sales Director; Oliver Allmand-Smith [1971] Production Director; Stephen Peter Allmand-Smith [1968] Director/Purchasing Manager

Allscripts Healthcare (IT) UK Ltd
Incorporated: 30 March 2011 *Employees:* 39
Net Worth Deficit: £11,518,000 *Total Assets:* £19,046,000
Registered Office: 15 Oxford Court, Manchester, M2 3WQ
Activities: Wholesale of computers, computer peripheral equipment and software
Parent: Allscripts Healthcare Solutions Inc.
Officers: Eric Lee Jacobson, Secretary; Dennis Olis [1962] Director Chief Financial Officer [American]

Alma Atlas Investments Limited
Incorporated: 16 March 1998
Net Worth: £60,000,000 *Total Assets:* £63,490,000
Registered Office: European Technical Centre, Hall Lane, Lathom, Ormskirk, Lancs, L40 5UF
Activities: Activities of head offices
Parent: Pilkington Finance Unlimited
Officers: Iain Michael Smith, Secretary; Judy Anne Massa [1967] Director/Accountant; Paul Joseph Ravenscroft [1970] Director/Head of Mergers & Acquisitions; Iain Michael Smith [1972] Director/Chartered Accountant

Alma Holdings Ltd
Incorporated: 9 January 2009 *Employees:* 55
Net Worth: £3,677,300 *Total Assets:* £6,811,383
Registered Office: 3rd Floor, Metropolitan House, Station Road, Cheadle Hulme, Cheadle, Cheshire, SK8 7AZ
Activities: Other business support service activities n.e.c.
Parent: Alma (Newco) Limited
Officers: Marshall John Doctors [1946] Director/Company Secretary; Ashok Mohanlal Karia [1959] Financial Director; Alison Mansell [1966] Design Director; Amanda Jane Seabourne [1964] Director/Sales Executive; Michele June Smith [1965] Production Director

Alma Products Limited
Incorporated: 21 September 1982 *Employees:* 83
Net Worth: £7,877,540 *Total Assets:* £14,125,821
Registered Office: 18b Evenwood Close, Daresbury Court, Runcorn, Cheshire, WA7 1LZ
Activities: Manufacture of plastic packing goods
Shareholders: David Blundell; James Stewart Dick
Officers: David Blundell, Secretary; David Blundell [1964] Director; James Stewart Dick [1957] Director

Almire Holdings Ltd
Incorporated: 22 June 2016 *Employees:* 82
Net Worth: £2,432,000 *Total Assets:* £6,702,000
Registered Office: The Courtyard, Green Lane, Heywood, Lancs, OL10 2EX
Activities: Roofing activities
Parent: Avonside Group Services Limited
Officers: Anthony Burke [1962] Director; Keith Kershaw [1957] Director; Andrew Morley [1967] Director; Simon Mark Smith [1966] Director; Nicholas Stephen Tappin [1971] Director

Alpha Flight Group Limited
Incorporated: 5 December 1994
Net Worth: £148,892,992 *Total Assets:* £154,804,992
Registered Office: Building 319, World Cargo Centre, Manchester Airport, Manchester, M90 5EX
Activities: Activities of head offices
Parent: Dnata Catering Services Limited
Officers: Mark Elly, Secretary; David John Loft [1961] Director/Vice President; Robin Brian Padgett [1968] Director/Divisional Senior Vice President; Carlo Federico Possa [1968] Director [Italian]

Alpha Flight UK Limited
Incorporated: 2 December 1996 *Employees:* 328
Net Worth: £38,000 *Total Assets:* £6,920,000
Registered Office: Building 319, World Cargo Centre, Manchester Airport, Manchester, M90 5EX
Activities: Other retail sale not in stores, stalls or markets
Parent: Alpha Flight Group Limited
Officers: Alexander John Forbes [1969] Business Director - Regional Airports UK&I; Ian Stanley Uren [1965] Director/Chartered Accountant

Alpha Investments (North West) Ltd
Incorporated: 10 July 1995
Net Worth: £16,078,464 *Total Assets:* £40,555,908
Registered Office: 78 Chorley New Road, Bolton, Lancs, BL1 4BY
Activities: Buying and selling of own real estate
Major Shareholder: James Stanley Caldwell
Officers: Margaret Elaine Caldwell, Secretary; James Stanley Caldwell [1944] Director; Mark James Caldwell [1973] Director

Alpha LSG Limited
Incorporated: 26 March 2012 *Employees:* 2,980
Net Worth: £8,766,000 *Total Assets:* £129,451,000
Registered Office: Building 319, World Cargo Centre, Manchester Airport, Manchester, M90 5EX
Activities: Other retail sale not in stores, stalls or markets
Shareholders: LSG/SKY Chefs Europe Holdings Limited; Alpha Flight Group Limited
Officers: Mark Elly, Secretary; Jochen Muller [1961] Director/Chief Operating Officer [German]; Robin Brian Padgett [1968] Director/Divisional Senior Vice President; Carlo Federico Possa [1968] Director [Italian]; Alexander Spahn [1967] Director [German]

Alphacare Holdings Limited
Incorporated: 13 June 2001 *Employees:* 83
Net Worth: £300,000 *Total Assets:* £6,883,000
Registered Office: Norcliffe House, Station Road, Wilmslow, Cheshire, SK9 1BU
Activities: Other business support service activities n.e.c.
Parent: Optimum Debtco Limited
Officers: Abigail Mattison, Secretary; Ryan Stuart MacAskill [1975] Director; Gregory Laurence Newman [1988] Director/Investment Professional; Jeremy Robert Arthur Richardson [1970] Director; Dr Maureen Claire Royston [1960] Director; Phillip Gary Thomas [1978] Director

Alphyra Payment Services Limited
Incorporated: 6 September 2001
Net Worth: £1,417,639 *Total Assets:* £10,758,164
Registered Office: Andmore House, Unit 4 Triangle Court, Cheshire Business Park, Manchester Road, Lostock Gralam, Cheshire, CW9 7YL
Activities: Other information technology service activities
Officers: Mark Dann [1972] Director; Clive Ian Kahn [1957] Director; James Rupert Lowery [1965] Director; Andrew McCann [1981] Director

Alpla UK Limited
Incorporated: 16 March 1990 *Employees:* 642
Net Worth: £114,355,000 *Total Assets:* £147,975,008
Registered Office: Unit 9 Yew Tree Way, Stonecross Business Park, Golborne, Warrington, Cheshire, WA3 3JD
Activities: Manufacture of other plastic products
Officers: Anthony John Corcoran, Secretary; Malcolm Finch [1955] Director; Stephen Robert Whitby [1975] Director/Finance Manager

ALS Inspection UK Limited
Incorporated: 3 July 1975 *Employees:* 115
Net Worth: £84,309,000 *Total Assets:* £96,419,000
Registered Office: Caddick Road, Knowsley Business Park, Prescot, Merseyside, L34 9HP
Activities: Other professional, scientific and technical activities n.e.c.
Parent: ALS Limited
Officers: Michael Paul Pearson, Secretary; Lubos Holy [1962] Director/Chemist [Czech]; John David Smyth [1965] Finance Director; Christopher David Walker [1972] Director

ALS Life Sciences Limited
Incorporated: 22 August 2000
Net Worth Deficit: £13,566,000 *Total Assets:* £13,076,000
Registered Office: Units 7-8 Hawarden Business Park, Manor Road, Deeside, Flintshire, CH5 3US
Activities: Other professional, scientific and technical activities n.e.c.
Officers: Neil Spencer, Secretary; Sten Rickard Olofsson [1974] Managing Director [Swedish]

ALS Testing Services (UK) Limited
Incorporated: 18 July 2011
Net Worth: £99,399,000 *Total Assets:* £198,990,000
Registered Office: Caddick Road, Knowsley Business Park, Prescot, Merseyside, L34 9HP
Activities: Support activities for other mining and quarrying
Parent: ALS Limited
Officers: Michael Paul Pearson, Secretary; Rajesh Naran [1961] Director/Chief Executive [American]; Christopher David Walker [1972] Director

Alsico Laucuba Ltd
Incorporated: 24 April 2007 *Employees:* 127
Net Worth: £12,878,845 *Total Assets:* £16,592,218
Registered Office: Pittman Way, Fulwood, Preston, Lancs, PR2 9ZD
Activities: Manufacture of workwear
Shareholders: David Robert Toon; Berphina NV
Officers: Emma Leanne Farmer [1988] Director/Accountant; Kevin John Mayes [1954] Director/Secretary; David Robert Toon [1961] Director; Daren Raymond Turner [1965] Operations Director; David Anthony Watson [1957] Director

Alston Investments Limited
Incorporated: 9 January 2014 *Employees:* 1,592
Net Worth: £3,610,000 *Total Assets:* £22,699,000
Registered Office: Parkwood House, Berkeley Drive, Bamber Bridge, Preston, Lancs, PR5 6BY
Activities: Activities of head offices
Major Shareholder: Mary Patricia Hewitt
Officers: Mary Patricia Hewitt [1950] Director/Teacher; Edwin Robert Lee [1949] Director; Mike John Quayle [1969] Director

Alterity Investments Limited
Incorporated: 28 October 1987
Net Worth: £94,442,136 *Total Assets:* £96,055,264
Registered Office: 3rd Floor, 1 Ashley Road, Altrincham, Cheshire, WA14 2DT
Activities: Buying and selling of own real estate
Officers: Ciaran Patrick Faloona, Secretary; Andrew James Carleton [1964] Director/Chartered Surveyor; Richard Faloon [1969] Director/Chartered Surveyor; Anne Teresa Lonergan [1950] Director; Edward Aidan Lonergan [1950] Director/Building Contractor [Irish]

Alternative Futures Group Limited
Incorporated: 22 January 1992 *Employees:* 7
Net Worth: £33,330,000 *Total Assets:* £43,058,000
Registered Office: Lion Court, Kings Drive, Kings Business Park, Prescot, Knowsley, Merseyside, L34 1BN
Activities: Hospital activities
Officers: Iain James Bell [1963] Director/Consultant; Daniel Chaffer [1977] Director/Finance Business Partner; Michael Clarke [1967] Director; Christine Margaret Hannah [1954] Director; Jonathan David Lloyd [1965] Director; Andrew Charles Lomas [1971] Managing Director; Jane McDonald [1966] Assistant Director; Professor Michael Henry Parkinson [1944] Director; Linda Whalley [1961] Director; Janet Wilkinson [1965] Director

The Alternative Steel Company Limited
Incorporated: 28 June 1994 *Employees:* 30
Net Worth: £5,325,672 *Total Assets:* £7,087,460
Registered Office: The Steel Service Centre, Dobson Park Way, Wigan, Lancs, WN2 2DY
Activities: Wholesale of metals and metal ores
Parent: The Alternative Steel Group Limited
Officers: David Graham Brown, Secretary; David Graham Brown [1960] Director; Stewart Outram [1969] Director/Steel Stockist; Gary Wake [1968] Director

The Alternative Steel Group Limited
Incorporated: 11 April 2003
Net Worth: £5,354,845 *Total Assets:* £8,404,231
Registered Office: Unit 6 Dobson Park Industrial Estate, Dobson Park Way, Ince, Wigan, Lancs, WN2 2DY
Activities: Dormant company
Shareholders: Stewart Outram; David Graham Brown
Officers: David Graham Brown, Secretary; David Graham Brown [1960] Director; Stewart Outram [1969] Director/Steel Stockist; Gary Wake [1968] Director

Althams Travel Services Limited
Incorporated: 16 November 1894 *Employees:* 230
Net Worth: £5,478,902 *Total Assets:* £13,657,891
Registered Office: Riverside Offices, Netherwood Road, Burnley, Lancs, BB10 2AN
Activities: Travel agency activities
Officers: Karen Blanche Mason, Secretary; John Michael Cook [1944] Director/Insurance Broker; Jacqueline Griffin [1964] Director/Travel Agent; Alfred David Knagg [1941] Director/Retired; Karen Blanche Mason [1959] Company Secretary/Director; Alison Sandra McAllister [1963] Director/Travel Agent

Altin Homes Limited
Incorporated: 19 April 2005 *Employees:* 9
Net Worth: £3,731,296 *Total Assets:* £10,890,781
Registered Office: 1a Woodlands Road, Altrincham, Cheshire, WA14 1HG
Activities: Development of building projects
Major Shareholder: Mohammad Zibandeh Khoy
Officers: Ali Sadigh Mostoufi, Secretary; Yousef Mousavi Aghdam [1973] Design Director; Mohammad Zibandeh Khoy [1958] Managing Director

The Altius Trust
Incorporated: 4 November 2008 *Employees:* 85
Net Worth: £26,646,844 *Total Assets:* £29,335,624
Registered Office: Manchester Enterprise Academy, Simonsway, Manchester, M22 9RH
Activities: General secondary education
Officers: Olivia Helen Clayton [1977] Group Reward Director; James Ross Eldon [1971] Director; Rodger Hill [1967] Director; Linda Jones [1961] Director/Headteacher; Rachael Marie Lees [1985] Finance Director; Sean McGonigle [1962] Director/Local Government Officer; Graham Whitham [1965] Director/Head of Programme Delivery, Banking IT; Nigel Peter Wilson [1963] Director/Group Chief Executive

Altrad NSG Limited
Incorporated: 6 May 2010 *Employees:* 433
Net Worth: £7,482,604 *Total Assets:* £17,466,700
Registered Office: Fourth Avenue, Deeside Industrial Park, Deeside, Flintshire, CH5 2NR
Activities: Repair of other equipment
Major Shareholder: Mohamed Altrad
Officers: Robert John Callaghan, Secretary; Robert John Callaghan [1971] Finance Director; Robert Trotter [1966] Commercial Director; Timothy Myerscough Walker [1977] Director/General Manager

Altus Education Partnership
Incorporated: 23 January 2017 *Employees:* 929
Net Worth: £6,056,000 *Total Assets:* £26,925,000
Registered Office: Rochdale Sixth Form College, College Road, Rochdale, Lancs, OL12 6HY
Activities: Primary education
Officers: Joy Bell, Secretary; Stephen Beckwith [1946] Director/Retired; Richard Frank Bramwell [1946] Director/Retired; Pamela Sarah Coward [1944] Director/Retired Headteacher; Kitsa Mavis Efthymiadis [1958] Director/Solicitor; Susan Janet Gettings [1960] Director/Teaching Assistant; Rodger Owen [1950] Director/Retired; John Patrick Menzies Rodger [1956] Director/Local Government Officer; Richard Ronksley [1968] Director/Principal/CEO; Professor Rupert Reginald Arthur Ward [1974] Director/Academic; Josephine Wiggans [1950] Director

Amann Threads UK Limited
Incorporated: 5 May 1953 *Employees:* 234
Net Worth: £10,572,745 *Total Assets:* £16,949,362
Registered Office: Guide Mill, South Street, Ashton under Lyne, Lancs, OL7 0PJ
Activities: Manufacture of other technical and industrial textiles
Officers: Jenine Margaret Stimpson, Secretary; Darren Roy Harding [1966] Managing Director; Ireneus Peter Morgalla [1965] Director/Chief Operating Officer [German]

Ambassador (East Cliff) Limited
Incorporated: 21 March 1958 *Employees:* 226
Net Worth Deficit: £2,807,000 *Total Assets:* £13,792,000
Registered Office: Halecroft, Hale Road, Hale, Cheshire, WA15 8RE
Activities: Hotels and similar accommodation
Parent: Ambassador Hotels Bournemouth Ltd
Officers: Robert Christopher Ferrari, Secretary/Financial Director; Robert Christopher Ferrari [1947] Financial Director

Amber Homeloans Limited
Incorporated: 19 May 1993
Net Worth: £8,185,000 *Total Assets:* £733,560,000
Registered Office: The Bailey, Skipton, N Yorks, BD23 1DN
Activities: Activities of mortgage finance companies
Parent: Skipton Building Society
Officers: John Joseph Gibson, Secretary; Ian Geoffrey Moore [1968] Director of Specialist Lending; Andrew Walter Nelson [1964] Director/Accountant; Henry Varney [1972] Director/General Manager

Amber Taverns Limited
Incorporated: 18 January 2005 *Employees:* 44
Net Worth: £78,496,744 *Total Assets:* £139,210,672
Registered Office: The Victory Offices, 112 Victory Road, Blackpool, Lancs, FY1 3NW
Activities: Public houses and bars
Parent: Melli Limited
Officers: Joanne Louise Jones, Secretary; James Edward Baer [1955] Director; Samuel Peter Frankland [1975] Director/Chartered Surveyor; Michael David George [1973] Director; Mark John Goddard [1970] Director; Joanne Louise Jones [1966] Director/Accountant; Gary Eric Roberts [1963] Director

Ivan Ambrose and Company Limited
Incorporated: 11 April 1957 *Employees:* 24
Net Worth: £6,193,825 *Total Assets:* £6,996,825
Registered Office: Rosemount Nurseries, Pygons Hill Lane, Lydiate, Sefton, Merseyside, L31 4JD
Activities: Growing of vegetables and melons, roots and tubers
Major Shareholder: Ian Thomas Lavelle
Officers: Marie Lavelle, Secretary; Ian Thomas Lavelle [1966] Director/Market Gardener; Kathleen Marion Lavelle [1944] Director/Market Gardener; Marie Lavelle [1966] Director/Secretary; Thomas Richard Lavelle [1941] Director/Market Gardener

Amcare Limited
Incorporated: 26 April 1996 *Employees:* 98
Net Worth: £37,163,000 *Total Assets:* £42,582,000
Registered Office: GDC, First Avenue, Deeside Industrial Park, Deeside, Flintshire, CH5 2NU
Activities: Other human health activities
Parent: Convatec Holdings U.K. Ltd
Officers: Clare Jane Bates [1976] Director/Solicitor; Sarah Jane Lewis [1970] Finance Director; Christopher John Sedwell [1976] Director/Chartered Accountant; Simon James Whitfield [1966] Business Director

AMEC Foster Wheeler (Holdings) Limited
Incorporated: 2 February 1920
Net Worth: £45,300,000 *Total Assets:* £109,731,000
Registered Office: Booths Park, Chelford Road, Knutsford, Cheshire, WA16 8QZ
Activities: Activities of head offices
Parent: Foster Wheeler Europe
Officers: Iain Angus Jones, Secretary; Carl Anthony Chatfield [1964] Director; William George Setter [1975] Director

AMEC Foster Wheeler Earth and Environmental (UK) Limited
Incorporated: 8 December 2003 *Employees:* 33
Net Worth Deficit: £16,519,000 *Total Assets:* £62,696,000
Registered Office: Booths Park, Chelford Road, Knutsford, Cheshire, WA16 8QZ
Activities: Support activities for other mining and quarrying
Parent: AMEC Nominees Limited
Officers: Iain Angus Jones, Secretary; Pier Luis Chiti [1965] Director/Mining Engineer [Italian]; Andrew William Winterbotham [1957] Director

AMEC Foster Wheeler Energy Limited
Incorporated: 3 April 1978 *Employees:* 1,118
Net Worth: £140,700,000 *Total Assets:* £262,700,000
Registered Office: Booths Park, Chelford Road, Knutsford, Cheshire, WA16 8QZ
Activities: Engineering design activities for industrial process and production
Parent: AMEC Foster Wheeler (Holdings) Limited
Officers: Iain Angus Jones Secretary; Roger Martin Cribb [1964] Director; Stephen James Nicol [1975] Director

AMEC Foster Wheeler Finance Limited
Incorporated: 30 September 1977
Net Worth: £255,943,008 *Total Assets:* £1,783,597,056
Registered Office: Booths Park, Chelford Road, Knutsford, Cheshire, WA16 8QZ
Activities: Other service activities n.e.c.
Parent: AMEC Foster Wheeler Limited
Officers: Iain Angus Jones, Secretary; Carl Anthony Chatfield [1964] Director William George Setter [1975] Director

AMEC Foster Wheeler Group Limited
Incorporated: 9 December 2002 *Employees:* 5,698
Net Worth: £452,780,000 *Total Assets:* £1,036,699,008
Registered Office: Booths Park, Chelford Road, Knutsford, Cheshire, WA16 8QZ
Activities: Other business support service activities n.e.c.
Parent: AMEC Foster Wheeler Limited
Officers: Iain Angus Jones Secretary; Stephen James Nicol [1975] Director; William George Setter [1975] Director; Mark James Watson [1964] Director

AMEC Foster Wheeler International Limited
Incorporated: 21 May 1996 *Employees:* 575
Net Worth: £319,000 *Total Assets:* £26,582,000
Registered Office: Booths Park, Chelford Road, Knutsford, Cheshire, WA16 8QZ
Activities: Support activities for petroleum and natural gas mining
Parent: AMEC Foster Wheeler Property and Overseas Investments Limited
Officers: Iain Angus Jones, Secretary; Matthew Nigel Plant [1968] Director

AMEC Foster Wheeler Limited
Incorporated: 2 November 1982 *Employees:* 30,900
Net Worth: £1,014,000,000 *Total Assets:* £5,272,999,936
Registered Office: Booths Park, Chelford Road, Knutsford, Cheshire, WA16 8QZ
Activities: Activities of head offices
Parent: John Wood Group P.L.C.
Officers: Iain Angus Jones, Secretary; Carl Anthony Chatfield [1964] Director; William George Setter [1975] Director

AMEC Foster Wheeler Nuclear International Limited
Incorporated: 8 October 1996
Net Worth: £11,749,000 *Total Assets:* £12,384,000
Registered Office: Booths Park, Chelford Road, Knutsford, Cheshire, WA16 8QZ
Activities: Engineering related scientific and technical consulting activities
Parent: Wood Nuclear Limited
Officers: Anthony Mark Thomas, Secretary; Ellen Lyons [1972] Director; Andrew John White [1966] Director/Business Management; Paul David Wood [1976] Commercial Director

AMEC Foster Wheeler Property and Overseas Investments Limited
Incorporated: 17 August 1981
Net Worth: £88,790,000 *Total Assets:* £90,592,000
Registered Office: Booths Park, Chelford Road, Knutsford, Cheshire, WA16 8QZ
Activities: Activities of head offices
Parent: AMEC Foster Wheeler Limited
Officers: Iain Angus Jones, Secretary; William George Setter [1975] Director

AMEC Hedge Co 1 Limited
Incorporated: 5 December 2011
Net Worth: £33,224,000 *Total Assets:* £33,240,000
Registered Office: Booths Park, Chelford Road, Knutsford, Cheshire, WA16 8QZ
Activities: Non-trading company
Parent: AMEC Foster Wheeler Property and Overseas Investments Limited
Officers: Iain Angus Jones, Secretary; William George Setter [1975] Director

AMEC Investments Europe Limited
Incorporated: 25 January 1999
Net Worth Deficit: £17,727,000 *Total Assets:* £48,450,000
Registered Office: Booths Park, Chelford Road, Knutsford, Cheshire, WA16 8QZ
Activities: Activities of head offices
Parent: AMEC Foster Wheeler Finance Limited
Officers: Iain Angus Jones, Secretary; William George Setter [1975] Director

AMEC Nuclear M & O Limited
Incorporated: 3 January 2006
Net Worth Deficit: £8,311,000 *Total Assets:* £16,922,000
Registered Office: Booths Park, Chelford Road, Knutsford, Cheshire, WA16 8QZ
Activities: Other business support service activities n.e.c.
Parent: Wood Nuclear Holdings Limited
Officers: Anthony Mark Thomas, Secretary; Michael John Hughes [1962] Director/VP Commercial; Nicola Jayne Okeeffe [1971] Director/Accountant; Clive Thomas White [1962] Director

AMEC Nuclear Overseas Limited
Incorporated: 20 July 2000
Net Worth: £66,416,000 *Total Assets:* £66,416,000
Registered Office: Booths Park, Chelford Road, Knutsford, Cheshire, WA16 8QZ
Activities: Non-trading company
Parent: Wood Nuclear Holdings Limited
Officers: Anthony Mark Thomas, Secretary; Michael John Hughes [1962] Director/VP Commercial; Clive Thomas White [1962] Director

AMEC Nuclear Projects Limited
Incorporated: 3 January 2006
Net Worth: £1,189,000 *Total Assets:* £14,584,000
Registered Office: Booths Park, Chelford Road, Knutsford, Cheshire, WA16 8QZ
Activities: Other business support service activities n.e.c.
Parent: AMEC Foster Wheeler Nuclear Holdings Limited
Officers: Anthony Mark Thomas, Secretary; Michael John Hughes [1962] Director/VP Commercial; Nicola Jayne Okeeffe [1971] Director/Accountant; Clive Thomas White [1962] Director

AMEC Services Limited
Incorporated: 26 March 1993 *Employees:* 49
Net Worth: £72,918,000 *Total Assets:* £75,416,000
Registered Office: Booths Park, Chelford Road, Knutsford, Cheshire, WA16 8QZ
Activities: Other engineering activities
Shareholders: AMEC Foster Wheeler Limited; AMEC Foster Wheeler Property and Overseas Investments Limited
Officers: Iain Angus Jones, Secretary; William George Setter [1975] Director

AMEC USA Finance Limited
Incorporated: 29 November 2004
Net Worth: £494,872,000 *Total Assets:* £679,460,992
Registered Office: Booths Park, Chelford Road, Knutsford, Cheshire, WA16 8QZ
Activities: Activities of head offices
Parent: AMEC USA Holdings Limited
Officers: Iain Angus Jones, Secretary; William George Setter [1975] Director

AMEC USA Holdings Limited
Incorporated: 26 July 2000
Net Worth: £513,230,016 *Total Assets:* £1,301,336,960
Registered Office: Booths Park, Chelford Road, Knutsford, Cheshire, WA16 8QZ
Activities: Activities of head offices
Parent: AMEC Foster Wheeler International Holdings Limited
Officers: Iain Angus Jones, Secretary; William George Setter [1975] Director

AMEC USA Limited
Incorporated: 27 July 2000
Net Worth: £365,503,008 *Total Assets:* £517,708,992
Registered Office: Booths Park, Chelford Road, Knutsford, Cheshire, WA16 8QZ
Activities: Activities of head offices
Parent: AMEC USA Finance Limited
Officers: Iain Angus Jones, Secretary; William George Setter [1975] Director

Amelia Exports Ltd
Incorporated: 16 August 2016
Net Worth: £14,873,610 *Total Assets:* £14,973,280
Registered Office: Unit 4 Hancock Road, Congleton, Cheshire, CW12 2AN
Activities: Other service activities n.e.c.
Major Shareholder: Brendon Williams
Officers: Brendon Williams [1971] Director

Ameon Holdings Limited
Incorporated: 5 March 2015 *Employees:* 216
Net Worth: £3,024,951 *Total Assets:* £13,365,905
Registered Office: Olympic Court, Boardmans Way, Blackpool, Lancs, FY4 5GU
Activities: Non-trading company
Officers: Rodney Bunce [1970] Contracts Director; Mark Court [1968] Director; Robin Charles Lawson [1970] Managing Director; Adam William Sutton [1977] Commercial Director

Ameon Limited
Incorporated: 4 March 1996 *Employees:* 216
Net Worth: £4,298,073 *Total Assets:* £13,937,349
Registered Office: 9-11 Olympic Court, Boardmans Way, Blackpool, Lancs, FY4 5GU
Activities: Electrical installation
Parent: Ameon Group Ltd
Officers: Jean O'Hagan, Secretary; Rodney Bunce [1970] Production Director; Mark Court [1968] Director; Robin Charles Lawson [1970] Director/Mechanical Engineer; Adam William Sutton [1977] Director; Paul Whitehead [1957] Director/Operations Manager

Amerdale Investments LLP
Incorporated: 2 June 2005
Net Worth: £5,634,742 *Total Assets:* £21,441,484
Registered Office: The Coach House, Arncliffe, Skipton, N Yorks, BD23 5QD
Officers: Joanne Haigh [1957] Member; David Richard Hood [1948] Member

Amerdale Ventures LLP
Incorporated: 12 December 2006 *Employees:* 28
Net Worth: £11,819,262 *Total Assets:* £11,821,932
Registered Office: The Coach House, Arncliffe, Skipton, N Yorks, BD23 5QD
Officers: Peter Allport [1955] Member; James Richard Elliott Andrew [1967] Member; Isobel Boissier [1967] Member; James Stanley Caldwell [1944] Member; Roger William Carey [1944] Member; Anthony Danaher [1955] Member; Dominic John Dinan [1966] Member; Robert Evans [1952] Member; Mark Edward Hancock [1965] Member; David Richard Hood [1948] Member; Nigel Justin Kempner [1956] Member; Adam Charles Kerr [1966] Member; Iain Cameron MacDonald [1974] Member; Christopher Michael Manning [1964] Member; Mark Nicholas Lewis Morgan [1962] Member; Andrew Richard Mullins [1964] Member; Geoffrey William Phillips [1961] Member; Mark Ridehalgh [1967] Member; Sir Malcolm Conrad Walker [1946] Member; Paul Ashley Williams [1962] Member

American Golf Discount Centre Limited
Incorporated: 5 May 1983 *Employees:* 895
Net Worth: £25,385,000 *Total Assets:* £53,962,000
Registered Office: Europa Boulevard, Gemini Business Park, Westbrook, Warrington, Cheshire, WA5 7YW
Activities: Retail sale of sports goods, fishing gear, camping goods, boats and bicycles
Parent: AGDC Holdings Limited
Officers: Lorraine Stringer, Secretary; Samantha Jane Tyrer [1970] Director/Chief Executive; Ian Robert Williams [1973] Director/Chief Financial Officer

Americhem Europe Limited
Incorporated: 28 April 1971 *Employees:* 71
Net Worth: £8,975,643 *Total Assets:* £12,958,201
Registered Office: Cawdor Street, Eccles, Manchester, M30 0QF
Activities: Manufacture of plastics in primary forms
Parent: Americhem Holdings International Limited
Officers: Richard Christian Juve, Secretary [American]; Richard Christian Juve [1956] Director [American]

Americhem Holdings International Limited
Incorporated: 12 May 1994 *Employees:* 152
Net Worth: £14,186,000 *Total Assets:* £22,313,000
Registered Office: Cawdor Street, Eccles, Manchester, M30 0QF
Activities: Activities of head offices
Officers: Richard Christian Juve, Secretary [American]; Richard Christian Juve [1956] Director [American]

Americk Advantage Limited
Incorporated: 11 March 1975 *Employees:* 99
Net Worth: £4,231,000 *Total Assets:* £7,022,000
Registered Office: 144 Manchester Road, Carrington, Manchester, M31 4QN
Activities: Printing n.e.c.
Officers: Steven Petty, Secretary; Angel Ramon Alejandro Balet [1961] Director [Spanish]; Susana Alejandro Balet [1970] Director [Spanish]; Thomas Anthony Rice [1966] Director [Irish]

Amiculum Limited
Incorporated: 28 July 2005 *Employees:* 156
Net Worth: £3,500,996 *Total Assets:* £8,300,154
Registered Office: The Boathouse, Clarence Mill, Clarence Road, Bollington, Cheshire, SK10 5JZ
Activities: Other business support service activities n.e.c.
Shareholders: Dr Richard John Allcorn; Dr Jennifer Claire Putin
Officers: Michael Putin, Secretary/Business Consultant; Dr Richard John Allcorn [1962] Director/Consultant; Doctor Jennifer Claire Putin [1963] Director; Michael Putin [1937] Director/Business Consultant; Jane Elizabeth Smith [1972] Director; Rebecca Thomas [1979] Director/Head of Finance

Amoria Bond Limited
Incorporated: 3 August 2006 *Employees:* 103
Net Worth: £622 062 *Total Assets:* £9,204,707
Registered Office: 14 Egerton House, Towers Business Park, Manchester, M20 2DX
Activities: Other activities of employment placement agencies
Shareholders: Nickolas Barrow; Daniel Georg Daw; Gareth Michael Lloyd
Officers: Nickolas Barrow [1974] Director/Consultant; Daniel Georg Daw [1977] Director/Consultant; Gareth Michael Lloyd [1978] Director/Consultant

Amplifon Limited
Incorporated: 31 May 1977 *Employees:* 506
Net Worth Deficit: £51,313,000 *Total Assets:* £20,916,000
Registered Office: Gateway House, Styal Road, Manchester, M22 5WY
Activities: Other human health activities
Parent: Amplifon United Kingdom Limited
Officers: Vicki Clare Milton, Secretary; Giuseppe Manzo [1973] Market Director [Italian]; Vicki Clare Milton [1984] Director; Iacopo Lorenzo Pazzi [1972] Director [Italian]

Amplifon United Kingdom Limited
Incorporated: 3 May 2006
Net Worth: £52,514,000 *Total Assets:* £57,549,000
Registered Office: Gateway House, Styal Road, Manchester, M22 5WY
Activities: Activities of head offices
Parent: Amplifon SpA
Officers: Vicki Clare Milton, Secretary; Gabriele Galli [1969] Director [Italian]; Giuseppe Manzo [1973] Market Director [Italian]; Vicki Clare Milton [1984] Director

AMR Textiles Limited
Incorporated: 15 January 2001 *Employees:* 135
Net Worth: £4,847,715 *Total Assets:* £8,146,792
Registered Office: Moss Rose Mill, Springfield Road, Kearsley, Bolton, Lancs, BL4 8JW
Activities: Manufacture of non-wovens and articles made from non-wovens, except apparel
Shareholders: Andrew Martin Sciama; Richard Nigel Sciama; Michael Ernest Sciama
Officers: Michael Ernest Sciama, Secretary; Andrew Martin Sciama [1956] Director; Michael Ernest Sciama [1958] Director; Richard Nigel Sciama [1961] Director

Amscreen Group Limited
Incorporated: 29 September 1992 *Employees:* 58
Net Worth: £3,388,716 *Total Assets:* £22,502,484
Registered Office: Amscreen House, Paragon Business Park, Chorley New Road, Horwich, Bolton, Lancs, BL6 6HG
Activities: Other professional, scientific and technical activities n.e.c.
Parent: Amscreen PLC
Officers: Sean Patrick Keenan, Secretary; Sean Patrick Keenan [1969] Finance Director; Michael Edward Ray [1963] Director; Simon Sugar [1969] Director

Amscreen Public Limited Company
Incorporated: 12 June 2008
Net Worth: £11,337,826 *Total Assets:* £11,337,826
Registered Office: Amscreen House, Paragon Business Park, Chorley New Road, Horwich, Lancs, BL6 6HG
Activities: Activities of head offices
Parent: Amshold Trading Limited
Officers: Sean Patrick Keenan, Secretary; Sean Patrick Keenan [1969] Director; Claude Manuel Littner [1949] Director [British/American]; Michael Edward Ray [1963] Director; Simon Sugar [1969] Director

Anderselite Holdings Ltd
Incorporated: 8 August 2016 *Employees:* 147
Net Worth: £2,937,038 *Total Assets:* £13,897,989
Registered Office: Adamson House, Centenary Way, Salford, M50 1RD
Activities: Activities of other holding companies n.e.c.
Parent: Morson Holdings Limited
Officers: Paul John Gilmour, Secretary; Paul John Gilmour [1964] Director/Accountant; Kevin Patrick Gorton [1964] Director; Gerard Anthony Mason [1964] Director

Anderselite Ltd
Incorporated: 16 March 1966 *Employees:* 141
Net Worth: £3,263,325 *Total Assets:* £13,895,741
Registered Office: Adamson House, Centenary Way, Salford, M50 1RD
Activities: Temporary employment agency activities
Parent: Anderselite Holdings Ltd
Officers: Paul John Gilmour, Secretary; Paul John Gilmour [1964] Director/Accountant; Kevin Patrick Gorton [1964] Director; Gerard Anthony Mason [1964] Director

Anderton Holdings Limited
Incorporated: 22 February 2002 *Employees:* 1
Net Worth: £7,160,157 *Total Assets:* £9,210,649
Registered Office: Cosgrove House, Cosgrove Business Park, Daisy Bank Lane, Anderton, Northwich, Cheshire, CW9 6AA
Activities: Other letting and operating of own or leased real estate
Shareholder: John Joseph Cosgrove
Officers: John Joseph Cosgrove [1948] Director [Irish]

Andrew Industries Limited
Incorporated: 29 March 1923 *Employees:* 736
Net Worth: £56,724,000 *Total Assets:* £78,144,000
Registered Office: Walton House, Syke Side Drive, Altham, Accrington, Lancs, BB5 5YE
Activities: Manufacture of other technical and industrial textiles
Shareholder: Edward Duxbury Andrew
Officers: Mark Robert Bennett, Secretary; Edward Duxbury Andrew [1936] Group Managing Director; Mark Roger Gaskell Andrew [1961] Director/V P Operations; Mark Robert Bennett [1964] Finance Director; Ian Frederick Leeder Kenyon [1951] Managing Director; Kathryn Susan Mitchell [1966] Director/Shop Proprietor; David Michael Neary [1957] Managing Director

Anfield (U.K.) Limited
Incorporated: 26 July 1993 *Employees:* 18
Net Worth: £6,911,169 *Total Assets:* £9,286,240
Registered Office: Stonepail Court, Stonepail Road, Gatley, Cheshire, SK8 4EX
Activities: Wholesale of textiles
Shareholders: Kaushik Pravinkumar Joshi; Tarla Pravinkumar Joshi
Officers: Vipasha Kaushik Joshi, Company Secretary; Kaushik Pravinkumar Joshi [1966] Director/Textile Merchant

Anglia Telecom Centres Limited
Incorporated: 24 March 1987 *Employees:* 74
Net Worth: £41,635,000 *Total Assets:* £78,311,000
Registered Office: Daisy House, Lindred Road Business Park, Nelson, Lancs, BB9 5SR
Activities: Wireless telecommunications activities
Parent: Daisy Intermediate Holdings Limited
Officers: David Lewis McGlennon, Secretary; Nathan Richard Marke [1970] Director; David Lewis McGlennon [1974] Director; Stephen Alan Smith [1963] Director

Anglo European Group Ltd
Incorporated: 23 September 2015 *Employees:* 58
Net Worth: £5,373,217 *Total Assets:* £13,348,615
Registered Office: 228 Briscoe Lane, Manchester, M40 2XG
Activities: Activities of production holding companies
Shareholders: Paul Marcus O'Sullivan; Octopus Apollo VCT PLC
Officers: Edward Keelan [1981] Director; Christopher Andrew O'Sullivan [1972] Director; Paul Marcus O'Sullivan [1970] Director; Peter Toland [1956] Director

Anglo-Eastern Trust Limited (The)
Incorporated: 23 December 1910 *Employees:* 2
Net Worth: £31,664,000 *Total Assets:* £34,420,000
Registered Office: 4th Floor, Faulkner House, Faulkner Street, Manchester, M1 4DY
Activities: Activities of other holding companies n.e.c.
Major Shareholder: Lord David Alliance
Officers: Lord David Alliance [1932] Director; Joshua Jacob Moshe Alliance [1989] Director

Angus Holdings Safety Group Limited
Incorporated: 12 March 2013 *Employees:* 8
Net Worth Deficit: £14,223,000 *Total Assets:* £31,045,000
Registered Office: Station Road, High Bentham, Lancaster, LA2 7NA
Activities: Activities of production holding companies
Parent: Angus International Safety Group Limited
Officers: Charles Delle-Case [1971] Director [French]; Lynda Michelle Guest [1962] Director; Christopher John Thomas [1955] Non-Executive Director Chairman; Paul Williams [1964] Director

Angus International Safety Group Limited
Incorporated: 12 March 2013 *Employees:* 324
Net Worth Deficit: £14,308,000 *Total Assets:* £55,362,000
Registered Office: Station Road, High Bentham, Lancaster, LA2 7NA
Activities: Activities of production holding companies
Shareholder: LDC II LP
Officers: Nicholas Edward Bridgmore Brown, Secretary; Nicholas John Barker [1970] Director; Charles Delle-Case [1971] Director [French]; Lynda Michelle Guest [1962] Director; Christopher Peter Handy [1965] Investment Director; Andrew Jack Leitch [1967] Director; Christopher Milburn [1966] Director; Christopher John Thomas [1955] Non-Executive Director Chairman; Paul Williams [1964] Director

Anord Mardix (UK) Limited
Incorporated: 7 January 1966 *Employees:* 467
Net Worth: £15,772,283 *Total Assets:* £37,739,444
Registered Office: Castle Mills, Aynam Road, Kendal, Cumbria, LA9 7DE
Activities: Manufacture of other electrical equipment
Parent: Mardix Holdings Ltd
Officers: Kevin Yamashita, Secretary; Jeffrey Mark Drazan [1958] Director [American]; Kevin Finegan [1960] Director [Irish]; David Andrew Gardner [1969] Director; Timothy Heston [1979] Director [American]; Shreyas Kataria [1991] Director [Indian]; Anthony Nordon [1946] Director [Irish]; James Peacock [1971] Director; Kevin Yamashita [1975] Director [American]

ANS Group Limited
Incorporated: 22 March 1996 *Employees:* 260
Net Worth: £15,941,323 *Total Assets:* £47,260,536
Registered Office: Synergy House, Manchester Science Park, Manchester, M15 6SY
Activities: Other telecommunications activities
Parent: Project Daytona Bidco Limited
Officers: Robert Nugent, Secretary; Andrew Phillip Barrow [1982] Director; Christopher James Hodgson [1983] Director/Chief Operating Officer; Paul Charles Shannon [1979] Director; Paul Patrick Sweeney [1970] Director/Executive Chairman

Ansell (Sales & Distribution) Limited
Incorporated: 28 May 1982 *Employees:* 18
Net Worth: £5,633,831 *Total Assets:* £7,685,256
Registered Office: Unit 6b Stonecross Industrial Park, Yew Tree Way, Golborne, Warrington, Cheshire, WA3 3JD
Activities: Wholesale of other machinery and equipment
Shareholder: Kunihiko Endo
Officers: Mark Stuart Abbott [1972] Managing Director; Michael Carson [1968] Director; Anish Chotai [1984] Financial Director; Kunihiko Endo [1974] Director/Businessman [Japanese]; Ryozo Endo [1943] Director/Businessman [Japanese]; Yoshiki Hirano [1970] Director [Japanese]; Ichiro Kikuchi [1955] Director [Japanese]; Yoshihiro Nakamura [1959] Director/Businessman [Japanese]

Ansell Electrical Products Limited
Incorporated: 2 January 2001 *Employees:* 111
Net Worth: £19,319,436 *Total Assets:* £27,702,622
Registered Office: Unit 6b Stonecross Industrial Park, Yew Tree Way, Golborne, Warrington, Cheshire, WA3 3JD
Activities: Wholesale of other machinery and equipment
Shareholder: Kunihiko Endo
Officers: Mark Stuart Abbott [1972] Managing Director; Michael Carson [1968] Director; Anish Chotai [1984] Financial Director; Kunihiko Endo [1974] Director/Businessman [Japanese]; Ryozo Endo [1943] Director/Businessman [Japanese]; Yoshiki Hirano [1970] Director [Japanese]; Ichiro Kikuchi [1955] Director [Japanese]; Yoshihiro Nakamura [1959] Director/Businessman [Japanese]

T.Anwyl & Son Limited
Incorporated: 18 July 1947
Net Worth: £5,072,545 *Total Assets:* £8,047,449
Registered Office: Anwyl House, St Davids Park, Ewloe, Deeside, Flintshire, CH5 3DT
Activities: Development of building projects
Officers: Graham Robert Anwyl, Secretary; Lucy Frances Wasdell, Secretary/Accountant; Ann Elizabeth Anwyl [1941] Director/Secretary; Graham Robert Anwyl [1943] Director/Builder; Mathew John Anwyl [1971] Director/Builder; Thomas James Anwyl [1967] Director/Builder; Lucy Frances Wasdell [1969] Director/Accountant

Anwyl Construction Company Limited
Incorporated: 16 May 1947 *Employees:* 158
Net Worth: £52,742,248 *Total Assets:* £93,946,208
Registered Office: Anwyl House, St Davids Park, Ewloe, Deeside, Flintshire, CH5 3DT
Activities: Development of building projects
Officers: Andrea Claire Anwyl, Secretary; Claire Alexandra Anwyl, Secretary; Graham Robert Anwyl, Secretary; Lucy Frances Wasdell, Secretary/Accountant; Timothy William Normand Wasdell, Secretary; Graham Robert Anwyl [1943] Director/Builder; Mathew John Anwyl [1971] Director/Builder; Thomas James Anwyl [1967] Director/Builder; Peter Joseph Townsend [1960] Director; Lucy Frances Wasdell [1969] Director/Accountant

Anwyl Group Limited
Incorporated: 15 February 2002 *Employees:* 158
Net Worth: £51,952,240 *Total Assets:* £95,408,136
Registered Office: Anwyl House, St Davids Park, Ewloe, Deeside, Flintshire, CH5 3DT
Activities: Development of building projects
Officers: Andrea Claire Anwyl, Secretary; Claire Alexandra Anwyl, Secretary; Graham Robert Anwyl, Secretary/Builder; Lucy Frances Wasdell, Secretary/Accountant; Timothy William Normand Wasdell, Secretary; Graham Robert Anwyl [1943] Director/Builder; Mathew John Anwyl [1971] Director/Builder; Thomas James Anwyl [1967] Director/Builder; Lucy Frances Wasdell [1969] Director/Accountant

AO Retail Limited
Incorporated: 28 January 2000 *Employees:* 761
Net Worth: £57,970,000 *Total Assets:* £220,856,992
Registered Office: Unit 5a The Parklands, Lostock, Bolton, Lancs, BL6 4SD
Activities: Retail sale of electrical household appliances in specialised stores
Parent: AO Limited
Officers: Julie Angela Louise Finnemore, Secretary; Daniel Anthony Emmett [1984] Operations Director; Jonathan Mark Stephen Higgins [1978] Director/Accountant; David Lawson [1984] E-Commerce Director

AO World PLC
Incorporated: 2 August 2005 *Employees:* 2,771
Net Worth: £81,200,000 *Total Assets:* £260,500,000
Registered Office: Unit 5a The Parklands, Lostock, Bolton, Lancs, BL6 4SD
Activities: Activities of head offices
Officers: Julie Angela Louise Finnemore, Secretary; Maria Luisa Cassoni [1951] Director; Stephen James Caunce [1969] Director; Geoffrey Ian Cooper [1954] Director; Jacqueline de Rojas [1962] Director; Jonathan Mark Stephen Higgins [1978] Director/Accountant; Christopher John Hopkinson [1959] Director; Brian James McBride [1955] Director; Shaun McCabe [1968] Director; John Charles Roberts [1973] Director

Apeks Marine Equipment Limited
Incorporated: 30 October 1975 *Employees:* 161
Net Worth: £6,494,836 *Total Assets:* £8,754,574
Registered Office: Neptune Way, Blackburn, Lancs, BB1 2BT
Activities: Other manufacturing n.e.c.
Shareholders: Montagu Private Equity LLP; MPE (General Partner V) Limited
Officers: Landon Helsby, Secretary; Jean-Luc Diainville [1956] Director/Department Manager [French]; Landon Helsby [1966] Managing Director; Angelika Kench [1962] Finance and Operations Director; Donald Robert Rockwell [1957] Director/Managerial [American]

API Foils Holdings Limited
Incorporated: 4 April 1990
Net Worth: £7,196,000 *Total Assets:* £8,346,000
Registered Office: Second Avenue, Poynton Industrial Estate, Poynton, Stockport, Cheshire, SK12 1ND
Activities: Manufacture of other paper and paperboard containers
Parent: API Group PLC
Officers: Claire Chadwick, Secretary; Claire Marie Chadwick [1982] Director/Group Legal Counsel; Peter Chapman [1960] Director; Robert Hall [1971] Director/Chief Financial Officer; Kostantinos Jim Kiriakopoulos [1970] Director [British/Canadian]

API Foils Limited
Incorporated: 28 November 1924 *Employees:* 122
Net Worth Deficit: £17,000 *Total Assets:* £19,086,000
Registered Office: Second Avenue, Poynton Industrial Estate, Poynton, Stockport, Cheshire, SK12 1ND
Activities: Manufacture of other paper and paperboard containers
Parent: API Foils Holdings Limited
Officers: Claire Chadwick, Secretary; Peter Chapman [1960] Director; Robert Hall [1971] Director/Chief Financial Officer; Kostantinos Jim Kiriakopoulos [1970] Director [British/Canadian]; William George Oldham [1961] Director

API Group PLC
Incorporated: 24 July 1920 *Employees:* 630
Net Worth: £26,580,000 *Total Assets:* £95,276,000
Registered Office: Second Avenue, Poynton Industrial Estate, Poynton, Stockport, Cheshire, SK12 1ND
Activities: Packaging activities
Parent: Cedar 2015 Limited
Officers: Claire Chadwick, Secretary; Jack Lawrence Howard [1961] Director [American]

API Group Services Limited
Incorporated: 16 January 2004 *Employees:* 27
Net Worth: £646,000 *Total Assets:* £6,893,000
Registered Office: Second Avenue, Poynton Industrial Estate, Poynton, Stockport, Cheshire, SK12 1ND
Activities: Combined office administrative service activities
Parent: API Group PLC
Officers: Claire Chadwick, Secretary; Peter Chapman [1960] Director; James Cunningham [1957] Director/UK Purchasing Manager; Robert Hall [1971] Director/Chief Financial Officer; Kostantinos Jim Kiriakopoulos [1970] Director [British/Canadian]

API Laminates Limited
Incorporated: 30 March 1921 *Employees:* 119
Net Worth: £6,935,000 *Total Assets:* £20,886,000
Registered Office: Second Avenue, Poynton Industrial Estate, Poynton, Stockport, Cheshire, SK12 1ND
Activities: Manufacture of plastic plates, sheets, tubes and profiles
Parent: API Group PLC
Officers: Claire Chadwick, Secretary; Peter Chapman [1960] Director; Robert Hall [1971] Director/Chief Financial Officer; Kostantinos Jim Kiriakopoulos [1970] Director [British/Canadian]

API Overseas Holdings Limited
Incorporated: 3 February 1998
Net Worth: £5,006,000 *Total Assets:* £12,000,000
Registered Office: Second Avenue, Poynton Industrial Estate, Poynton, Cheshire, SK12 1ND
Activities: Non-trading company
Shareholders: API Foils Holdings Limited; API Group PLC
Officers: Claire Chadwick, Secretary; Claire Marie Chadwick [1982] Director/Group Legal Counsel; Peter Chapman [1960] Director; Robert Hall [1971] Director/Chief Financial Officer; Kostantinos Jim Kiriakopoulos [1970] Director [British/Canadian]

Apogent UK Limited
Incorporated: 1 September 1993
Net Worth: £21,058,958 *Total Assets:* £21,067,326
Registered Office: 3rd Floor, 1 Ashley Road, Altrincham, Cheshire, WA14 2DT
Activities: Other business support service activities n.e.c.
Parent: Erie U.K. Limited
Officers: Rhona Gregg, Secretary; Lucie Mary Katja Grant [1976] Director/Solicitor; Nicholas Ince [1982] Director/Accountant; David John Norman [1960] Director/Chartered Accountant

Apollo Scientific Ltd
Incorporated: 24 September 1993 *Employees:* 73
Net Worth: £8,202,155 *Total Assets:* £10,360,559
Registered Office: Whitefield Road, Bredbury, Stockport, Cheshire, SK6 2QR
Activities: Manufacture of other inorganic basic chemicals
Parent: Central Glass Europe Limited
Officers: Jennifer Anne Holland, Secretary; Mitsuru Tanuma [1961] Director [Japanese]; Nobuyuki Tokunaga [1961] Director/General Manager [Japanese]

APPH Limited
Incorporated: 18 December 1985 *Employees:* 340
Net Worth: £24,558,000 *Total Assets:* £42,233,000
Registered Office: 8 Pembroke Court, Chancellor Road, Manor Park, Runcorn, Cheshire, WA7 1TG
Activities: Manufacture of fluid power equipment
Parent: HDI Holdings (UK) Limited
Officers: Julie Elizabeth Andrew [1963] Human Resources Director; Gaetan Roy [1959] Managing Director [Canadian]; Jon Stewart Sharrock [1969] Director/Accountant

Applethwaite Limited
Incorporated: 23 July 2004 *Employees:* 16
Net Worth: £1,565,803 *Total Assets:* £15,452,753
Registered Office: Sceptre House, Sceptre Way, Bamber Bridge, Preston, Lancs, PR5 6AW
Activities: Construction of domestic buildings
Parent: Eric Wright Developments Limited
Officers: Deborah Jane Rawlinson, Secretary; James Francis Carter [1955] Director/Chartered Surveyor; Allan Gundry [1958] Director; Jeremy Peter Hartley [1965] Director/Chartered Accountant; Colin Hetherington [1973] Director; Mark Smith [1965] Director

Colin Appleyard Limited
Incorporated: 29 March 1976 *Employees:* 143
Net Worth: £6,447,975 *Total Assets:* £14,148,450
Registered Office: Head Office, Cornmill Garage, Halifax Road, Keighley, W Yorks, BD21 1AH
Activities: Sale of new cars and light motor vehicles
Shareholders: Peggy Appleyard; Judith Carol Parker; Robin Michael Appleyard
Officers: Peggy Appleyard, Secretary; Peggy Appleyard [1939] Director/Secretary; Robin Michael Appleyard [1964] Director/Sales Manager; Antony Dodsworth [1971] Director/Accountant; Judith Carol Parker [1961] Director/Work Shop Manager

APS Group Limited
Incorporated: 28 February 2008 *Employees:* 779
Net Worth: £16,325,243 *Total Assets:* £46,223,452
Registered Office: Chetham House, Bird Hall Lane, Stockport, Cheshire, SK3 0ZP
Activities: Activities of head offices
Major Shareholder: Nicholas John Snelson
Officers: John Holmes [1966] Director; Kim Melita Naylor [1962] Director; Erica Snelson [1965] Director; Nicholas John Snelson [1965] Director

APS Produce Limited
Incorporated: 27 June 1997 *Employees:* 270
Net Worth: £12,094,000 *Total Assets:* £35,564,000
Registered Office: Enterprise House, 97 Alderley Road, Wilmslow, Cheshire, SK9 1PT
Activities: Growing of other non-perennial crops
Parent: A Pearson Holdings Ltd
Officers: Ashley Robert Haworth, Secretary; Andrew Patrick Burke [1962] Trading Director; Emma Rachel Burke [1973] Director; Ashley Robert Haworth [1979] Financial Director; Mark Alan Pearson [1973] Director; Philip Pearson [1963] Director; John Edward Phibbs [1950] Director/Chartered Accountant; Paul Robert Thomas [1979] Managing Director

Aptus Group Limited
Incorporated: 16 April 2012 *Employees:* 175
Net Worth: £3,413,086 *Total Assets:* £17,547,768
Registered Office: Aptus House, Barrs Fold Road, Westhoughton, Bolton, Lancs, BL5 3XP
Activities: Activities of construction holding companies
Shareholders: Andrew Wilson Reay; Norman Frederick Story
Officers: Jonathan Holden [1973] Director; Andrew Wilson Reay [1965] Director; Norman Frederick Story [1956] Director

Aptus Utilities Limited
Incorporated: 30 March 2010 *Employees:* 175
Net Worth: £3,948,298 *Total Assets:* £18,082,980
Registered Office: Aptus House, Barrs Fold Road, Westhoughton, Bolton, Lancs, BL5 3XP
Activities: Other specialised construction activities n.e.c.
Parent: Aptus Group Ltd
Officers: Susan Carol Wray, Secretary; Natasha Leanne Marie Clarke [1986] Support Services Director; Mark John Clegg [1975] Operations Director; Niall Gargan [1976] Commercial Director [Irish]; Andrea Susan Gerring [1976] Finance Director; Jonathan Holden [1973] Director; Lisa Joanne Kerford [1972] Operations Director; Andrew Wilson Reay [1965] Director; Norman Frederick Story [1956] Director

APV Overseas Holdings Limited
Incorporated: 27 February 1929
Net Worth Deficit: £23,997,000 *Total Assets:* £240,248,992
Registered Office: Ocean House, Towers Business Park, Wilmslow Road, Didsbury, Manchester, M20 2LY
Activities: Activities of head offices
Parent: SPX Flow Technology London Limited
Officers: Paul Andrew Cahill [1974] Director/Accountant; Mark Edward Shanahan [1970] Director; Jeremy Wade Smeltser [1975] Director/CFO, SPX Flow, Inc. [American]; Stephen Tsoris [1957] Director [American]

AQA Education
Incorporated: 30 September 1998 *Employees:* 1,262
Net Worth: £48,211,000 *Total Assets:* £230,424,992
Registered Office: Devas Street, Manchester, M15 6EX
Activities: General secondary education
Officers: Nicholas Martin Stevens, Secretary; Mark James Bramwell [1950] Director; Sir Michael Griffiths [1951] Director/Headmaster; Philippa Jane Hird [1964] Director/Consultant; Grenville William Jackson [1949] Director/Management Consultant; Elizabeth Kitcatt [1959] Director/Headteacher; Nadeem Maqsood Kiyani [1970] Director/Chartered Accountant; Susan Margaret Moore [1962] Director/Headteacher; Paul Anthony Nesbitt [1970] Director; Michael George Nicholson [1969] Director of Admissions University of Bath; Professor Jonathan Pitt Phillips [1965] Director; Professor Toby Dominic Brodigan Salt [1962] Director/Chief Executive Officer; Jan Eileen Smith [1947] Director; Professor Mark Edmund Smith [1963] Director/Vice-Chancellor; Jovan Trkulja [1968] Director/Examinations Officer; Martin Guy Turner [1957] Director; Justin James Van Wijngaarden [1967] Director/Chartered Accountant; Nigel David Walkey [1952] Director/Teacher

Aqua Fabrications Limited
Incorporated: 2 February 1988 *Employees:* 48
Net Worth: £3,448,539 *Total Assets:* £9,124,873
Registered Office: Belmont House, Garnett Place, East Gillibrands, Skelmersdale, Lancs, WN8 9UB
Activities: Manufacture of plastics in primary forms
Shareholders: Ian Thomas Smith; Lynda Christine Smith
Officers: Lynda Christine Smith, Secretary; Ian Thomas Smith [1947] Director; Lynda Christine Smith [1950] Director; Stuart Smith [1971] Sales Director

Aramex (UK) Limited
Incorporated: 4 June 1986 *Employees:* 222
Net Worth: £73,044,000 *Total Assets:* £89,238,000
Registered Office: Unit P6, Parklands, Heywood Distribution Park, Heywood, Lancs, OL10 2TT
Activities: Unlicensed carriers
Officers: Tariq Abdelghani Mah'd Kharouf, Secretary; Othman Tarik Al-Jeda [1970] Director; Bashar Issam Yousef Obeid [1972] Director [Jordanian]

Archbold Logistics Limited
Incorporated: 16 November 1973 *Employees:* 120
Net Worth: £1,238,024 *Total Assets:* £8,682,614
Registered Office: Unit H, Birch Business Park, Whittle Lane, Heywood, Lancs, OL10 2SX
Activities: Freight transport by road
Parent: Archbold Holdings Limited
Officers: Julie Holmes, Secretary; David Stuart Archbold [1941] Director; Yannis Christophe Archbold [1976] Director; Walter Murray Blackwood [1956] Director; Julie Holmes [1962] Director; Alan Maher [1968] Director

L'Arche
Incorporated: 18 May 1972 *Employees:* 257
Net Worth: £10,136,452 *Total Assets:* £11,335,192
Registered Office: 10 Briggate, Silsden, Keighley, W Yorks, BD20 9JT
Activities: Residential care activities for learning difficulties, mental health and substance abuse
Officers: John Francis Sargent, Secretary; Catherine Mary Baines [1941] Director/Retired; Dr Carole Glasson [1955] Director/Dr; Isobel Watson Gray [1953] Director/Retired; Benedict Robert Kirwan Moorhead [1958] Director/Lawyer; John Paul O'Brien [1961] Director/Accountant; David George Race [1949] Director/University Lecturer; Bernadette Elizabeth Ann Rijnenberg [1956] Director/Retired; Marie Roberts [1960] Director/Management Consultant; Peter James Whalley [1947] Director/Chartered Accountant; Susan Margaret Williams [1955] Director/Counsellor

Archibald Bathgate Group Limited
Incorporated: 10 August 1964 *Employees:* 170
Net Worth: £19,597,940 *Total Assets:* £33,136,736
Registered Office: c/o Langtons, The Plaza, 100 Old Hall Street, Liverpool, L3 9QJ
Activities: Other mining and quarrying n.e.c.
Shareholders: Roderick Hughes Walker; Barbara Ann Walker
Officers: Stephen Ian Bennett, Secretary; Gary Delaval Laverick [1959] Director; Barbara Ann Walker [1935] Director/Married Woman; Philip Hughes Walker [1968] Director; Roderick Hughes Walker [1935] Director/Chartered Accountant; Susan Elizabeth Walker [1965] Director/Property Developer

Archwood Limited
Incorporated: 15 July 1986 *Employees:* 254
Net Worth: £10,272,000 *Total Assets:* £22,791,000
Registered Office: Archwood House, Kingsfield Court, Chester Business Park, Chester, CH4 9RE
Activities: Sawmilling and planing of wood
Parent: Ripat Limited
Officers: Andrew Joseph Simms, Secretary; Josh Burbidge [1978] Director; Richard Henry Burbidge [1942] Director; Anthony Gerard Miles [1962] Director/Chief Executive; Marcus Moir [1965] Director

Ardagh Metal Beverage Trading UK Limited
Incorporated: 2 November 2011 *Employees:* 23
Net Worth: £20,286,000 *Total Assets:* £113,472,000
Registered Office: 1st Floor, Regus Offices, Herons Way, Chester Business Park, Chester, CH4 9QR
Activities: Combined office administrative service activities
Parent: Ardagh Metal Beverage Holdings UK Limited
Officers: Annemieke Bolt [1981] Director/General Counsel [Dutch]; Gary Anthony Brown [1977] Director/Manager; Mike Dick [1968] Sales Director; Simon John Gresty [1963] General Manager, Sales Director; Stefan Siebert [1968] Director [German]

Ardagh Metal Beverage UK Limited
Incorporated: 12 January 1990 *Employees:* 563
Net Worth: £167,163,008 *Total Assets:* £179,163,008
Registered Office: Regus, Herons Way, Chester Business Park, Chester, CH4 9QR
Activities: Manufacture of light metal packaging
Parent: Ardagh Metal Beverage Holdings UK Limited
Officers: David O'Brien, Secretary; Jody Clarke [1982] Director/Accountant; Michel Lemoyne [1950] Director/Plant Manager [Canadian]; Mark Rozmus [1962] Operations Director; Torsten Schoen [1969] Director/Chief Legal Officer [German]; Paul Tyas [1969] Director/Plant Manager

Ardale International Limited
Incorporated: 2 October 1997 *Employees:* 10
Net Worth: £4,659,084 *Total Assets:* £9,857,227
Registered Office: Suite H, Level 2, No 1 Booth Park, Chelford Road, Knutsford, Cheshire, WA16 8GS
Activities: Wholesale of household goods (other than musical instruments) n.e.c
Major Shareholder: Brian Gary Jones
Officers: Emma Louise Jones, Secretary/Administration; Darren Farmer [1974] Sales Director; Brian Gary Jones [1965] Director

Arden Dies Limited
Incorporated: 26 February 1965 *Employees:* 169
Net Worth: £6,708,676 *Total Assets:* £10,357,879
Registered Office: Shepley Lane Industrial Estate, Hawk Green, Marple, Stockport, Cheshire, SK6 7JW
Activities: Manufacture of other fabricated metal products n.e.c.
Shareholders: Peter Marbach; Martin Philip Poynter
Officers: Andrew Reece Hall, Secretary; Andrew Reece Hall [1965] Director/Chartered Accountant; Simon David Lynch [1967] Director/General Manager; Peter Marbach [1960] Director [German]; Martin Philip Poynter [1957] Director

ARE II LLP
Incorporated: 20 November 2014
Net Worth: £16,669,475 *Total Assets:* £27,343,908
Registered Office: Alliance House, Westpoint Enterprise Park, Clarence Avenue, Trafford Park, Manchester, M17 1QS

Argus Fluidhandling Limited
Incorporated: 19 August 2008 *Employees:* 179
Net Worth: £896,000 *Total Assets:* £10,584,000
Registered Office: 43 Wilcock Road, Haydock, St Helens, Merseyside, WA11 9TG
Activities: Other manufacturing n.e.c.
Parent: Hiflex Europe Limited
Officers: Enrico Gennasio [1958] Director [Italian]; Ian Whitley [1969] Director

Ariens UK Limited
Incorporated: 12 May 2010
Net Worth: £14,813,056 *Total Assets:* £15,344,201
Registered Office: Eversheds House, 70 Great Bridgewater Street, Manchester, M1 5ES
Activities: Activities of head offices
Officers: Daniel Timothy Ariens [1958] Director; Mark Rolaf Olsen [1953] Director/Chief Financial Officer, Treasurer [American]; Lawrence Joseph Weyers [1962] Director [American]

Arighi Bianchi & Co.Limited
Incorporated: 20 July 1900 *Employees:* 164
Net Worth: £924,510 *Total Assets:* £6,782,524
Registered Office: The Silk Road, Macclesfield, Cheshire, SK10 1LH
Activities: Other retail sale in non-specialised stores
Parent: Arighi Bianchi Holdings Limited
Officers: Sarah Bianchi, Secretary; John Bianchi [1964] Director/Retail; Paul Nicholas Ernesto Bianchi [1972] Director; Richard Enrico Bianchi [1961] Sales Director; Robert Anthony Bianchi [1970] Director; Robert Paul Bianchi [1937] Managing Director; Sarah Bianchi [1969] Director and Company Secretary

Arighi Bianchi Holdings Limited
Incorporated: 12 March 2012 *Employees:* 164
Net Worth: £3,165,174 *Total Assets:* £10,039,831
Registered Office: The Silk Road, Macclesfield, Cheshire, SK10 1LH
Activities: Other letting and operating of own or leased real estate
Officers: Sarah Bianchi, Secretary; John Bianchi [1964] Director; Paul Nicholas Ernesto Bianchi [1972] Director; Richard Enrico Bianchi [1961] Sales Director; Robert Anthony Bianchi [1970] Director; Robert Paul Bianchi [1937] Managing Director; Sarah Bianchi [1969] Director

Arista (U.K.) Limited
Incorporated: 27 November 1973 *Employees:* 31
Net Worth: £7,092,768 *Total Assets:* £8,059,918
Registered Office: Charter House, 18-20 Finsley Gate, Burnley, Lancs, BB11 2HA
Activities: Wholesale of textiles
Officers: Robert Edward Bank, Secretary/Director; John Jason Bank [1969] Director; Robert Edward Bank [1975] Director; Stephen Raoul Bank [1971] Director/Retail Sales

Arizonaco Limited
Incorporated: 4 August 2011
Net Worth: £15,920,618 *Total Assets:* £15,954,986
Registered Office: Shire House, Humboldt Street, Bradford, W Yorks, BD1 5HQ
Activities: Other service activities n.e.c.
Parent: Corporate Travel Management (UK) Limited
Officers: Stephen John Fleming, Secretary; Deborah Ann Carling [1963] Director/CEO CTM Travel Europe; Stephen John Fleming [1968] Director/Global CFO [Australian]; Jamie Michael Pherous [1968] Managing Director [Australian]

Arjo Wiggins Fine Papers Limited
Incorporated: 4 September 1969 *Employees:* 508
Net Worth: £15,896,000 *Total Assets:* £72,881,000
Registered Office: Eversheds House, 70 Great Bridgewater Street, Manchester, M1 5ES
Activities: Manufacture of paper and paperboard
Parent: The Wiggins Teape Group Limited
Officers: Alain Philippe Daniel Gourjon [1965] Group Accounts, Tax & Administrative Director [French]; Angus Lachlan Macsween [1965] Director/General Manager, Stoneywood Mill; Jonathan David Mitchell [1965] Managing Director Arjowiggins Creative Papers SAS; Martin John Newell [1957] Finance Director

Arjo Wiggins Services Limited
Incorporated: 15 June 2010 *Employees:* 660
Net Worth: £17,466,000 *Total Assets:* £20,293,000
Registered Office: Eversheds House, 70 Great Bridgewater Street, Manchester, M1 5ES
Activities: Other business support service activities n.e.c.
Parent: AW UK Holdings Limited
Officers: Alain Philippe Daniel Gourjon [1965] Group Accounts, Tax & Administrative Director [French]; Clive Mountford [1957] Director; Martin John Newell [1957] Director

Arjowiggins Chartham Limited
Incorporated: 29 September 2003 *Employees:* 90
Net Worth Deficit: £8,148,000 *Total Assets:* £7,185,000
Registered Office: Eversheds House, 70 Great Bridgewater Street, Manchester, M1 5ES
Activities: Manufacture of paper and paperboard
Parent: The Wiggins Teape Group Limited
Officers: Francois Gros [1960] Business Director [French]; Mark Hobday [1963] Director/Mill Manager; Jonathan David Mitchell [1965] Managing Director Arjowiggins Creative Papers SAS; Martin John Newell [1957] Finance Director

Arlington Aerospace Limited
Incorporated: 28 August 2007
Net Worth Deficit: £2,090,000 *Total Assets:* £18,774,000
Registered Office: Southmoor Industrial Estate, Southmoor Road, Manchester, M23 9XD
Activities: Activities of production holding companies
Parent: Arlington Industries Group Limited
Officers: Simon John Brazier [1963] Director; Mark Bernard Franckel [1962] Director; Simon George Greenhalgh [1972] Director/Chief Financial Officer

Arlington Industries Group Ltd
Incorporated: 21 October 2013 *Employees:* 682
Net Worth: £18,193,000 *Total Assets:* £77,310,000
Registered Office: Suite 15b, Manchester International Office Centre, Styal Road, Manchester, M22 5WB
Activities: Activities of production holding companies
Officers: Simon George Greenhalgh, Secretary; Mark Bernard Franckel [1962] Director/Chief Executive; Simon George Greenhalgh [1972] Director/Chief Financial Officer; Geoffrey Lee Hamlin [1960] Director [American]; Beth Michelson [1969] Director [American]; Professor Kevin Thomas Morley [1950] Director; Paul Gregory Pizzani [1960] Director [American]

Arlington Management Services Ltd
Incorporated: 16 November 2012 *Employees:* 6
Net Worth: £153,000 *Total Assets:* £35,438,000
Registered Office: Suite 15b, Manchester International Office Centre, Styal Road, Manchester, M22 5WB
Activities: Activities of production holding companies
Parent: Arlington Securities Limited
Officers: Mark Bernard Franckel [1962] Director; Simon George Greenhalgh [1972] Director/Chief Financial Officer; Geoffrey Lee Hamlin [1960] Director [American]; Beth Michelson [1969] Director [American]; Professor Kevin Thomas Morley [1950] Director; Paul Gregory Pizzani [1960] Director [American]

Armacell Insulation UK Holding Limited
Incorporated: 14 February 2012 *Employees:* 2
Net Worth: £26,809,000 *Total Assets:* £133,713,000
Registered Office: Mars Street, Oldham, Lancs, OL9 6LY
Activities: Financial intermediation not elsewhere classified
Shareholder: Ultima Acquisitions GB Ltd
Officers: Guillerme Huguen [1959] Commercial Director [French]; Stephen Clive Sturch [1958] Director/General Manager

Armacell UK Limited
Incorporated: 10 March 1999 *Employees:* 105
Net Worth: £36,945,000 *Total Assets:* £135,864,000
Registered Office: Mars Street, Oldham, Lancs, OL9 6LY
Activities: Manufacture of other rubber products
Parent: Armacell Insulation UK Holdings Ltd
Officers: Guillerme Huguen [1959] Commercial Director [French]; Stephen Clive Sturch [1958] Director/General Manager

Armacell United Kingdom Holding Limited
Incorporated: 19 May 2000 *Employees:* 2
Net Worth: £11,730,000 *Total Assets:* £11,936,000
Registered Office: Armacell UK Ltd, Mars Street, Oldham, Lancs, OL9 6LY
Activities: Financial intermediation not elsewhere classified
Officers: Guillerme Huguen [1959] Commercial Director [French]; Stephen Clive Sturch [1958] Director/General Manager

Armathwaite Hall Hotel Limited
Incorporated: 1 October 1976 *Employees:* 122
Net Worth: £8,201,358 *Total Assets:* £16,339,886
Registered Office: Armathwaite Hall, Bassenthwaite, Keswick, Cumbria, CA12 4RE
Activities: Hotels and similar accommodation
Officers: Charles John Graves, Secretary; Carolyn Elizabeth Graves [1951] Director/Hotel Proprietor; Charles John Graves [1949] Director/Hotel Proprietor

Armcon Limited
Incorporated: 20 January 1992 *Employees:* 45
Net Worth: £2,064,981 *Total Assets:* £6,971,686
Registered Office: Armcon Business Park, London Road South, Poynton, Cheshire, SK12 1LQ
Activities: Non-specialised wholesale trade
Shareholders: Armcon Trading Limited; Robert Armstrong
Officers: Robert Armstrong, Secretary/Director; Michael David Armitage [1950] Director; Robert Armstrong [1958] Director

Frank Armitt & Son Limited
Incorporated: 31 December 1962 *Employees:* 49
Net Worth: £4,769,155 *Total Assets:* £10,657,712
Registered Office: 26-30 South Road, Weston Point, Runcorn, Cheshire, WA7 4EZ
Activities: Freight transport by road
Major Shareholder: Paula Jayne Seedhouse
Officers: Allan Seedhouse, Secretary/General Admin Manager; Charles William Gray [1966] Finance Director; Paul Holden [1967] Financial Director; Nicholas John Marshall [1959] Commercial Director; Allan Seedhouse [1962] Director; Paula Jayne Seedhouse [1962] Director/Marine Fuel Trader

Armored Auto UK Limited
Incorporated: 17 March 1989 *Employees:* 53
Net Worth: £5,952,406 *Total Assets:* £10,065,709
Registered Office: Regent Mill, Fir Street, Failsworth, Manchester, M35 0HS
Activities: Manufacture of other chemical products n.e.c.
Parent: AAG UK Holding Limited
Officers: Christopher Berry [1954] Director; Anja Krueger [1967] Director of Legal Affairs [German]

Thomas Armstrong (Aggregates) Limited
Incorporated: 24 September 1976 *Employees:* 91
Net Worth: £12,045,856 *Total Assets:* £19,818,798
Registered Office: Workington Road, Flimby, Maryport, Cumbria, CA15 8RY
Activities: Freight transport by road
Officers: Paul Armstrong, Secretary; Paul Armstrong [1959] Director/Accountant; Anthony Robert Glover Denham [1960] Director; John Keith Denham [1943] Managing Director; Morrison Ian [1960] Transport Director

Ian Armstrong (Carlisle) Limited
Incorporated: 19 February 1985 *Employees:* 7
Net Worth: £7,159,685 *Total Assets:* £7,553,194
Registered Office: Lingy Close Road, Dalston, Carlisle, Cumbria, CA5 7LB
Activities: Freight transport by road
Major Shareholder: Ian Armstrong
Officers: Susan Grace Armstrong, Secretary; Ian Armstrong [1958] Director/Haulier; Susan Grace Armstrong [1959] Director

Thomas Armstrong (Concrete Blocks) Limited
Incorporated: 9 September 1964 *Employees:* 77
Net Worth: £19,792,108 *Total Assets:* £27,291,642
Registered Office: Workington Road, Flimby, Maryport, Cumbria, CA15 8RY
Activities: Manufacture of concrete products for construction purposes
Officers: Paul Armstrong, Secretary/Accountant; Paul Armstrong [1959] Director/Accountant; Anthony Robert Glover Denham [1960] Director; John Keith Denham [1943] Managing Director; Martin Home [1956] Sales Director; Mark Arthur Walker [1962] Director

Thomas Armstrong (Construction) Limited
Incorporated: 9 September 1964 *Employees:* 174
Net Worth: £12,094,892 *Total Assets:* £23,067,270
Registered Office: Workington Road, Flimby, Maryport, Cumbria, CA15 8RY
Activities: Construction of commercial buildings
Officers: Paul Armstrong, Secretary/Accountant; Paul Armstrong [1959] Director/Accountant; David Atkinson [1952] Director; Barry Raymond Denham [1963] Director; John Keith Denham [1943] Director; Philip Marcus Hoyles [1971] Commercial Director; Stuart Alexander Hoyles [1974] Director; Steven Park [1965] Director; Mark Hamilton Steele [1966] Director/Civil Engineer; Jonathan Maxwell Tibbitts [1960] Director

Thomas Armstrong (Holdings) Limited
Incorporated: 1 January 1930 *Employees:* 618
Net Worth: £112,085,504 *Total Assets:* £138,678,496
Registered Office: Workington Road, Flimby, Maryport, Cumbria, CA15 8RY
Activities: Construction of commercial buildings
Officers: Paul Armstrong, Secretary/Accountant; Paul Armstrong [1959] Director/Accountant; David Atkinson [1952] Director; Nikolos Clifford [1964] Director; Anthony Robert Glover Denham [1960] Director; John Keith Denham [1943] Managing Director; Raymond Glover Layton Denham [1935] Director/Secretary

Wm. Armstrong (Longtown) Limited
Incorporated: 19 October 1961 *Employees:* 262
Net Worth: £1,778,096 *Total Assets:* £14,313,054
Registered Office: Townfoot, Longtown, Carlisle, Cumbria, CA6 5LY
Activities: Freight transport by road
Shareholders: Jennifer Mary Whyberd; Geoffrey William Armstrong; Derek George Armstrong
Officers: Debbie Lisa Winter, Secretary; Derek George Armstrong [1963] Director; Geoffrey William Armstrong [1965] Director; Jennifer Mary Whyberd [1956] Managing Director

Armstrong Brooks Limited
Incorporated: 30 June 1988
Net Worth: £7,746,527 *Total Assets:* £14,975,103
Registered Office: Riverside House, Kings Reach Business Park, Yew Street, Stockport, Cheshire, SK4 2HD
Activities: Activities of other holding companies n.e.c.
Officers: Robert Cory [1944] Director

D.W. Armstrong Holdings Limited
Incorporated: 20 June 2005 *Employees:* 135
Net Worth: £9,496,294 *Total Assets:* £26,184,174
Registered Office: Horwich Recycling Centre, Chorley New Road, Horwich, Bolton, Lancs, BL6 5NJ
Activities: Other business support service activities n.e.c.
Major Shareholder: David William Armstrong
Officers: Susan Anne Ainsworth, Secretary/Financial Director; Susan Anne Ainsworth [1961] Financial Director; David William Armstrong [1961] Director/Haulage Contractor; Emma Maria Elizabeth Armstrong [1970] Director

Armstrong Integrated Limited
Incorporated: 7 November 2003 *Employees:* 160
Net Worth Deficit: £4,538,728 *Total Assets:* £15,535,477
Registered Office: 1 Wolverton Street, Manchester, M11 2ET
Activities: Manufacture of pumps
Parent: Armstrong Pumps Limited
Officers: James Cary Armstrong, Secretary; Charles Allan Armstrong [1950] Director/Business Executive [Canadian]; James Cary Armstrong [1946] Director/Business Executive [Canadian]

Armstrong Learning Limited
Incorporated: 7 April 2005
Net Worth: £2,738,961 *Total Assets:* £7,618,913
Registered Office: 26 Hulme Street, Manchester, M1 5BW
Activities: Other service activities n.e.c.
Parent: Martinez Investments Limited
Officers: Lisa Evelyn Armstrong, Secretary; Adrian Armstrong [1964] Director; Paul Stuart Ricketts [1947] Director

Armstrong Pumps Limited
Incorporated: 13 January 1977 *Employees:* 168
Net Worth Deficit: £7,193,181 *Total Assets:* £16,414,482
Registered Office: 1 Wolverton Street, Manchester, M11 2ET
Activities: Manufacture of pumps
Major Shareholder: Charles Allan Armstrong
Officers: James Cary Armstrong, Secretary; Charles Allan Armstrong [1950] Director/Business Executive [Canadian]; James Cary Armstrong [1946] Director/Business Executive [Canadian]

Armstrongs Aggregates Limited
Incorporated: 12 August 1986 *Employees:* 128
Net Worth: £8,000,144 *Total Assets:* £23,729,628
Registered Office: Horwich Recycling Centre, Chorley New Road, Horwich, Bolton, Lancs, BL6 5NJ
Activities: Other mining and quarrying n.e.c.
Major Shareholder: David William Armstrong
Officers: Susan Anne Ainsworth, Secretary/Accountant; Susan Anne Ainsworth [1961] Director/Group Accountant; David William Armstrong [1961] Director; Emma Maria Elizabeth Armstrong [1970] Director; John Shane Wallace [1968] Director

Arris Global Ltd.
Incorporated: 20 October 1982 *Employees:* 337
Net Worth: £290,888,544 *Total Assets:* £1,051,807,232
Registered Office: Victoria Road, Saltaire, W Yorks, BD18 3LF
Activities: Wireless telecommunications activities
Parent: Arris International PLC
Officers: Stephen McCaffery [1966] Director/Senior Vice President; David Bernard Potts [1957] Director/Executive Vice President [American]; Anthony Emilien Zuyderhoff [1971] Director [American]

Arris International IP Ltd
Incorporated: 28 August 2013 *Employees:* 2
Net Worth: £73,857,480 *Total Assets:* £73,857,480
Registered Office: Victoria Road, Saltaire, W Yorks, BD18 3LF
Activities: Financial management
Parent: Arris Global Ltd.
Officers: David Bernard Potts [1957] Director/Businessman [American]; Anthony Emilien Zuyderhoff [1971] Director [American]

Arris International PLC
Incorporated: 20 April 2015 *Employees:* 7,767
Net Worth: £2,553,299,712 *Total Assets:* £6,212,156,416
Registered Office: Victoria Road, Saltaire, W Yorks, BD18 3LF
Activities: Wired telecommunications activities
Officers: Patrick W. Macken, Secretary; Andrew McGregor Barron [1965] Director/Businessman; John Timothy Bryan [1961] Director [American]; James Alan Chiddix [1945] Director [American]; Andrew Todd Heller [1955] Director [American]; Dr. Jeong Hun Kim [1960] Director/Company Founder [American]; Bruce McClelland [1967] Director/Chief Executive Officer [Canadian]; Barton Shigemura [1959] Director [American]; Robert Stanzione [1948] Director/Executive Chairman [American]; Doreen Toben [1949] Director [American]; Debora Jane Wilson [1957] Director [American]; David Woodle [1955] Director/CEO and Chairman [American]

Arrow Global (Holdings) Limited
Incorporated: 28 October 2005
Net Worth: £6,772,000 *Total Assets:* £23,034,000
Registered Office: Belvedere, 12 Booth Street, Manchester, M2 4AW
Activities: Activities of head offices
Parent: Arrow Global Investments Holdings Limited
Officers: Stewart David Hamilton, Secretary; Paul David Cooper [1972] Director/Group Chief Financial Officer; Zachary Jason Lewy [1974] Director/Founder and Group Chief Investment Officer [British/American]; Lee Michael Rochford [1967] Director/Group Chief Executive Officer

Arrow Global Accounts Management Limited
Incorporated: 10 June 2005
Net Worth: £34,072,000 *Total Assets:* £37,137,000
Registered Office: Belvedere, 12 Booth Street, Manchester, M2 4AW
Activities: Activities of financial services holding companies
Parent: Arrow Global Limited
Officers: Stewart Hamilton, Secretary; Paul David Cooper [1972] Director/Group Chief Financial Officer; Zachary Jason Lewy [1974] Director/Founder and Group Chief Investment Officer [British/American]; Lee Michael Rochford [1967] Director/Group Chief Executive Officer

Arrow Global Europe Limited
Incorporated: 5 November 2014
Net Worth: £4,455 *Total Assets:* £417,588,192
Registered Office: Belvedere, 12 Booth Street, Manchester, M2 4AW
Activities: Other credit granting n.e.c.
Parent: Arrow Global Investments Holdings Limited
Officers: Stewart David Hamilton, Secretary; Paul David Cooper [1972] Director/Group Chief Financial Officer; Lee Michael Rochford [1967] Director/Group Chief Executive Officer

Arrow Global Finance PLC
Incorporated: 15 January 2013
Net Worth: £3,803,000 *Total Assets:* £774,785,024
Registered Office: Belvedere, 12 Booth Street, Manchester, M2 4AW
Activities: Activities of financial services holding companies
Parent: Arrow Global Investments Holdings Limited
Officers: Stewart David Hamilton, Secretary; Paul David Cooper [1972] Director/Group Chief Financial Officer; Zachary Jason Lewy [1974] Director/Founder and Group Chief Investment Officer [British/American]; Lee Michael Rochford [1967] Director/Group Chief Executive Officer

Arrow Global Group PLC
Incorporated: 14 August 2013 *Employees:* 1,464
Net Worth: £195,148,000 *Total Assets:* £1,258,514,944
Registered Office: Belvedere, 12 Booth Street, Manchester, M2 4AW
Activities: Activities of financial services holding companies
Officers: Stewart David Hamilton, Secretary; Maria Luis Albuquerque [1967] Director/Member of Portuguese Parliament [Portuguese]; Jonathan William Bloomer [1954] Director/Chairman; Paul David Cooper [1972] Director/Group Chief Financial Officer; Iain Charles Andrew Cornish [1960] Director; Andrew Charles Fisher [1958] Finance Director; Lee Michael Rochford [1967] Director/Group Chief Executive Officer; Thi Nhuoc Lan TU [1967] Director

Arrow Global Investments Holdings Limited
Incorporated: 17 April 2008
Net Worth: £7,287,000 *Total Assets:* £802,820,992
Registered Office: Belvedere, 12 Booth Street, Manchester, M2 4AW
Activities: Credit granting by non-deposit taking finance houses and other specialist consumer credit grantors
Parent: Arrow Global One Limited
Officers: Stewart David Hamilton, Secretary; Paul David Cooper [1972] Director/Group Chief Financial Officer; Zachary Jason Lewy [1974] Director/Founder and Group Chief Investment Officer [British/American]; Lee Michael Rochford [1967] Director/Group Chief Executive Officer

Arrow Global Limited
Incorporated: 28 October 2005 *Employees:* 166
Net Worth: £45,215,000 *Total Assets:* £887,430,976
Registered Office: Belvedere, 12 Booth Street, Manchester, M2 4AW
Activities: Credit granting by non-deposit taking finance houses and other specialist consumer credit grantors
Parent: Arrow Global (Holdings) Limited
Officers: Stewart David Hamilton, Secretary; Paul David Cooper [1972] Director/Group Chief Financial Officer; Zachary Jason Lewy [1974] Director/Founder and Group Chief Investment Officer [British/American]; Lee Michael Rochford [1967] Director/Group Chief Executive Officer

Arrow Global One Limited
Incorporated: 14 August 2013
Net Worth: £252,471,008 *Total Assets:* £346,460,000
Registered Office: Belvedere, 12 Booth Street, Manchester, M2 4AW
Activities: Activities of financial services holding companies
Parent: Arrow Global Group PLC
Officers: Stewart David Hamilton, Secretary; Paul David Cooper [1972] Director/Group Chief Financial Officer; Zachary Jason Lewy [1974] Director/Founder and Group Chief Investment Officer [British/American]; Lee Michael Rochford [1967] Director/Group Chief Executive Officer

Arrow Global Receivables Management Limited
Incorporated: 13 July 2006
Net Worth: £15,274,000 *Total Assets:* £15,371,000
Registered Office: Belvedere, 12 Booth Street, Manchester, M2 4AW
Activities: Credit granting by non-deposit taking finance houses and other specialist consumer credit grantors
Parent: Arrow Global (Holdings) Limited
Officers: Stewart David Hamilton, Secretary; Paul David Cooper [1972] Director/Group Chief Financial Officer; Zachary Jason Lewy [1974] Director/Founder and Group Chief Investment Officer [British/American]; Lee Michael Rochford [1967] Director/Group Chief Executive Officer

Arrow XL Limited
Incorporated: 23 January 2002 *Employees:* 1,095
Net Worth: £7,988,000 *Total Assets:* £29,209,000
Registered Office: 4 The Fort, Walthew House Lane, Martland Park, Wigan, Lancs, WN5 0LB
Activities: Freight transport by road
Parent: Yodel Logistics Limited
Officers: Aidan Stuart Barclay [1956] Director; Howard Myles Barclay [1959] Director; Richard John Neal [1976] Director/Accountant; Philip Leslie Peters [1957] Director; Michael Seal [1948] Director/Chartered Accountant; Charles Martin Shiels [1962] Director

Artech Reduction Technologies Limited
Incorporated: 13 March 2003 *Employees:* 7
Net Worth: £5,034,733 *Total Assets:* £33,088,016
Registered Office: Ground Floor, 177 Cross Street, Sale, Manchester, M33 7JQ
Activities: Manufacture of bodies (coachwork) for motor vehicles (except caravans)
Parent: Shred-It Limited
Officers: Robert John Guice [1966] Director/Manager

Arthouse Holding Limited
Incorporated: 6 July 2007 *Employees:* 1
Net Worth: £666,669 *Total Assets:* £14,687,913
Registered Office: St James Church, Bacup Road, Waterfoot, Rossendale, Lancs, BB4 7JU
Activities: Non-trading company
Parent: Arthouse Group Limited
Officers: Stephanie Avril Carroll [1967] Creative Director; Caryn Elizabeth Clarke [1969] Sales and Marketing Director; Anita Rae Kenyon [1963] Director

Arthouse Limited
Incorporated: 20 December 1999 *Employees:* 64
Net Worth: £10,618,532 *Total Assets:* £16,114,274
Registered Office: St James Church, Bacup Road, Waterfoot, Rossendale, Lancs, BB4 7JU
Activities: Manufacture of wallpaper
Parent: Arthouse Holding Limited
Officers: Stephanie Avril Carroll [1967] Creative Director; Caryn Elizabeth Clarke [1969] Sales and Marketing Director; Anita Rae Kenyon [1963] Director

Arthouse Midco Limited
Incorporated: 30 September 2015
Net Worth Deficit: £2,345,047 *Total Assets:* £17,521,076
Registered Office: St James Church, Bacup Road, Waterfoot, Rossendale, Lancs, BB4 7JU
Activities: Floor and wall covering
Parent: Arthouse Topco Limited
Officers: Anita Rae Kenyon [1963] Director; Nicola Helen McQuaid [1977] Director

Arvo Sales Limited
Incorporated: 19 October 1970 *Employees:* 1
Net Worth: £6,325,497 *Total Assets:* £6,747,067
Registered Office: 2nd Floor, Suite A, Kennedy House, 31 Stamford Street, Altrincham, Cheshire, WA14 1ES
Activities: Other letting and operating of own or leased real estate
Shareholders: Jaymal Jagdishchandra Amin; Shailesh Dollarrai Porecha
Officers: Sachin Rajendra Patel [1969] Director [American]; Shrujal Sachin Patel [1971] Director [American]; Priyanka Sailesh Porecha [1989] Director

Arysta LifeScience European Investments Limited
Incorporated: 7 March 2014 *Employees:* 1
Net Worth Deficit: £9,290,564 *Total Assets:* £128,574,800
Registered Office: Eversheds House, 70 Great Bridgewater Street, Manchester, M1 5ES
Activities: Activities of other holding companies n.e.c.
Parent: Arysta LifeScience U.K. Limited

Arysta LifeScience Global Limited
Incorporated: 24 May 2013 *Employees:* 1
Net Worth: £144,331,664 *Total Assets:* £1,264,946,688
Registered Office: Eversheds House, 70 Great Bridgewater Street, Manchester, M1 5ES
Activities: Activities of other holding companies n.e.c.
Parent: Platform Specialty Products Corporation

Arysta LifeScience U.K. EUR Limited
Incorporated: 20 May 2013 *Employees:* 1
Net Worth: £118,200,680 *Total Assets:* £118,397,832
Registered Office: Eversheds House, 70 Great Bridgewater Street, Manchester, M1 5ES
Activities: Financial management
Parent: Arysta LifeScience U.K. Holdings Limited

Arysta LifeScience U.K. Holdings Limited
Incorporated: 16 May 2013 *Employees:* 1
Net Worth: £75,353,664 *Total Assets:* £328,626,240
Registered Office: Eversheds House, 70 Great Bridgewater Street, Manchester, M1 5ES
Activities: Financial management
Parent: Arysta LifeScience European Investments Limited

Arysta LifeScience U.K. Limited
Incorporated: 19 November 2008 *Employees:* 5
Net Worth: £8,147,951 *Total Assets:* £9,864,709
Registered Office: Eversheds House, 70 Great Bridgewater Street, Manchester, M1 5ES
Activities: Management consultancy activities other than financial management
Parent: Arysta LifeScience Global Limited

Arysta LifeScience U.K. USD Limited
Incorporated: 20 May 2013 *Employees:* 1
Net Worth: £98,399,312 *Total Assets:* £1,173,585,920
Registered Office: Eversheds House, 70 Great Bridgewater Street, Manchester, M1 5ES
Activities: Financial management
Parent: Arysta LifeScience U.K. Holdings Limited

Ascent Housing LLP
Incorporated: 21 September 2010
Net Worth: £25,093,000 *Total Assets:* £30,947,000
Registered Office: 602 Aston Avenue, Birchwood Park, Birchwood, Warrington, Cheshire, WA3 6ZN

Ascent Ventures Limited
Incorporated: 7 January 2014 *Employees:* 2
Net Worth: £1,171,052 *Total Assets:* £7,465,848
Registered Office: The Edge Business Centre, The Edge, Clowes Street, Manchester, M3 5NA
Activities: Activities of venture and development capital companies
Major Shareholder: Anthony Stephen Critchlow
Officers: Anthony Stephen Critchlow [1960] Director/Chairman; Helen Claire Critchlow [1966] Director/Pharmacist

ASCO Joucomatic Limited
Incorporated: 12 October 1993 *Employees:* 133
Net Worth: £24,037,000 *Total Assets:* £27,970,000
Registered Office: Pit Hey Place, West Pimbo, Skelmersdale, Lancs, WN8 9PG
Activities: Other manufacturing n.e.c.
Parent: Emerson Holding Company Limited
Officers: Ivan Tejeda, Secretary; Ivan Tejeda [1977] Director/Vice President Finance EMEA [Spanish]; Jean Louis Tenu [1958] Director/President of Asco EMEA [French]; Harry Vicary [1959] Site Director

Ascot Properties UK Limited
Incorporated: 16 July 1996 *Employees:* 2
Net Worth: £4,749,739 *Total Assets:* £16,775,223
Registered Office: 122 South Road, Waterloo, Liverpool, L22 0ND
Activities: Buying and selling of own real estate
Parent: Ascot Waterloo Limited
Officers: Terence Patrick Michael Riley, Secretary; Lynda Susan Riley [1968] Director/Landlord; Terence Patrick Michael Riley [1969] Director/Landlord

Ascot Road Watford Limited
Incorporated: 31 January 2011
Net Worth Deficit: £499,000 *Total Assets:* £7,654,000
Registered Office: Hilmore House, Gain Lane, Bradford, W Yorks, BD3 7DL
Activities: Development of building projects
Parent: Optimisation Developments Limited
Officers: Jonathan James Burke, Secretary; Jonathan James Burke [1966] Director; Trevor John Strain [1975] Finance Director

Ascot Waterloo Limited
Incorporated: 15 February 2012 *Employees:* 2
Net Worth: £11,707,446 *Total Assets:* £12,159,724
Registered Office: 122 South Road, Waterloo, Liverpool, L22 0ND
Activities: Buying and selling of own real estate
Major Shareholder: Terence Patrick Michael Riley
Officers: Terence Patrick Michael Riley [1969] Director

ASE Group Limited
Incorporated: 28 November 1989 *Employees:* 272
Net Worth: £2,233,302 *Total Assets:* £8,634,879
Registered Office: Rowan Court, Concord Business Park, Threapwood Road, Manchester, M22 0RR
Activities: Activities of head offices
Shareholders: Robert Anthony Jones; Michael Andrew Jones
Officers: Michael James Sanchez Montes, Secretary; Michael Andrew Jones [1973] Director/Accountant; Robert Anthony Jones [1976] Director/Accountant

ASE PLC
Incorporated: 6 May 2009 *Employees:* 163
Net Worth: £2,059,910 *Total Assets:* £11,762,954
Registered Office: Rowan Court, Concord Business Park, Threapwood Road, Manchester, M22 0RR
Activities: Other information technology service activities
Parent: ASE Group Limited
Officers: Michael James Sanchez Montes, Secretary; Michael David Fazal [1971] Director; Michael Andrew Jones [1973] Director/Chartered Accountant; Robert Anthony Jones [1976] Director/Chartered Accountant; Michael James Sanchez Montes [1974] Director/Accountant

Ash Lea Cottage Nurseries Limited
Incorporated: 27 January 1976 *Employees:* 18
Net Worth: £8,025,300 *Total Assets:* £9,552,908
Registered Office: 1 Ashlea Cottage, St Michaels Road, Bilsborrow, Preston, Lancs, PR3 0RT
Activities: Plant propagation
Major Shareholder: John Nixon
Officers: Patricia Nixon, Secretary; John Nixon [1943] Director; Patricia Nixon [1944] Director/Company Secretary

Ashaeve Limited
Incorporated: 8 March 2006 *Employees:* 81
Net Worth: £1,368,556 *Total Assets:* £7,909,124
Registered Office: Units 7 & 8 Brookfield Trade Centre, Brookfield Drive, Liverpool, L9 7AS
Activities: Activities of head offices
Major Shareholder: Dr Sumit Kumar Kochhar
Officers: Kathryn Louise Kochhar, Secretary; Sumit Kumar Kochhar [1968] Director/Pharmacist

Ashbridge School Limited
Incorporated: 14 January 1999 *Employees:* 122
Net Worth: £4,196,493 *Total Assets:* £11,913,871
Registered Office: Ashbridge, Lindle Lane, Hutton, Preston, Lancs, PR4 4AQ
Activities: Primary education
Shareholders: Sarah Carr; Stuart Carr
Officers: Sarah Carr, Secretary/Director; Sarah Carr [1957] Director; Stuart Carr [1958] Director

J K Ashbrook Holdings Limited
Incorporated: 4 June 2014
Net Worth: £3,366,572 *Total Assets:* £29,223,382
Registered Office: 4 Poolwood Cottages, Holmes Chapel Road, Somerford, Congleton, Cheshire, CW12 4SN
Activities: Renting and leasing of agricultural machinery and equipment
Major Shareholder: James Keith Ashbrook
Officers: James Keith Ashbrook [1982] Managing Director; Michael Joseph Ashbrook [1984] Director

Ashbury Freeholds Limited
Incorporated: 3 October 2015
Net Worth: £7,988,137 *Total Assets:* £10,048,487
Registered Office: P O Box 58, Ashbury House, Liverpool, L19 9WX
Activities: Other letting and operating of own or leased real estate
Officers: Kenneth Carmichael [1963] Director

Ashbury Leaseholds Limited
Incorporated: 6 April 2016 *Employees:* 1
Net Worth: £502,394 *Total Assets:* £22,555,456
Registered Office: P O Box 58, Ashbury House, Liverpool, L19 9WX
Activities: Other letting and operating of own or leased real estate
Officers: Kenneth Carmichael [1963] Director

Ashdowns Limited
Incorporated: 7 April 1919
Net Worth: £22,115,000 *Total Assets:* £27,707,000
Registered Office: European Technical Centre, Hall Lane, Lathom, Ormskirk, Lancs, L40 5UF
Activities: Non-life insurance
Parent: NSG UK Enterprises Limited
Officers: Iain Michael Smith, Secretary; Julie Ann Brown [1968] Director/Accountant; John Andrew Burchill [1960] Director; Iain Michael Smith [1972] Director/Chartered Accountant

Ashton Agricultural and General Limited
Incorporated: 9 August 2000 *Employees:* 6
Net Worth: £3,476,362 *Total Assets:* £8,558,491
Registered Office: Ashlack Hall, Grizebeck, Kirkby in Furness, Cumbria, LA17 7XN
Activities: Raising of other animals
Parent: Leinster Asset Management Ltd
Officers: Michael William Barton [1957] Director; Mark Fitzpatrick Keegan [1948] Director; Thomas Patrick Keegan [1990] Director

Zoe Ashton Limited
Incorporated: 3 July 2002
Net Worth Deficit: £1,033,427 *Total Assets:* £8,645,108
Registered Office: 2nd Floor, Muskers Building, 1 Stanley Street, Liverpool, L1 6AA
Activities: Renting and operating of Housing Association real estate
Parent: Zoe Group Limited
Officers: Aneil Kumar Singh, Secretary; David Anastasiou [1962] Director; Eleftherios Eleftheriou [1959] Director

Oliver Ashworth (Holdings) Limited
Incorporated: 18 December 2014 *Employees:* 111
Net Worth: £398,203 *Total Assets:* £16,051,815
Registered Office: Oliver Ashworth Limited, Higher Ainsworth Road, Radcliffe, Manchester, M26 4AF
Activities: Non-specialised wholesale trade
Officers: Robbert Jan Alsem [1972] Director [Dutch]; James Langwade Gaby [1972] Director; Brian David Smithers [1971] Director

Oliver Ashworth Limited
Incorporated: 18 December 2014 *Employees:* 111
Net Worth: £3,355,891 *Total Assets:* £18,843,252
Registered Office: Oliver Ashworth Limited, Higher Ainsworth Road, Radcliffe, Manchester, M26 4AF
Activities: Non-specialised wholesale trade
Parent: Oliver Ashworth (Holdings) Ltd
Officers: Robbert Jan Alsem [1972] Director [Dutch]; James Langwade Gaby [1972] Director; Brian David Smithers [1971] Director; Leslie Sykes [1976] Director/Chartered Accountant

ASICS UK Limited
Incorporated: 2 March 1987 *Employees:* 257
Net Worth: £11,849,959 *Total Assets:* £30,574,764
Registered Office: 3 Clearwater, Lingley Mere, Lingey Green Avenue, Warrington, Cheshire, WA5 3UZ
Activities: Wholesale of clothing and footwear
Officers: Glen Paul Houston [1968] Director; Robert William Mitchell [1983] Director/Finance Manager

ASM Technologies Limited
Incorporated: 30 September 1992 *Employees:* 60
Net Worth: £1,549,083 *Total Assets:* £9,207,843
Registered Office: Meridian House, Winsford Industrial Estate, Winsford, Cheshire, CW7 3QG
Activities: Non-specialised wholesale trade
Shareholders: Roger Ian Smith; Graham John Aspinall
Officers: Christopher John Swallow, Secretary; Graham John Aspinall [1970] Director; Roger Ian Smith [1969] Director; Christopher John Swallow [1966] Director/Chartered Accountant; Iain James Tomkinson [1972] Sales Director

Aspireplus Educational Trust
Incorporated: 15 May 2017 *Employees:* 213
Net Worth: £41,853,348 *Total Assets:* £44,421,044
Registered Office: Longdendale High School, Spring Street, Hollingworth, Hyde, Cheshire, SK14 8LW
Activities: General secondary education
Officers: Louise Anne Hoyle, Secretary; Jane Barker [1971] Director; Matthew James Bowler [1971] Director; Barry John Harwood [1963] Director; Janet Anne Lambert [1965] Director; Dr Janet Nevin [1961] Director/College Principal; Jonathan Neil Reynolds [1980] Director; Kevin Taylor [1964] Director; Carol Thomas [1965] Director/School Improvement Consultant

Associated Property Owners Limited
Incorporated: 20 February 1904 *Employees:* 15
Net Worth: £45,614,532 *Total Assets:* £66,555,048
Registered Office: 32 Hamilton Square, Birkenhead, Merseyside, CH41 6AZ
Activities: Buying and selling of own real estate
Parent: Associated Property Holdings Limited
Officers: William Saville, Secretary; Elizabeth Anne Corke [1958] Director; Andrew Davenport Errington [1959] Director/Photographer; Anne Jacqueline Errington [1935] Director; Catherine Ann Errington [1957] Director [Australian]; Charles Stuart Errington [1961] Director; John Davenport Errington [1959] Director; Robin Davenport Errington [1957] Director; William Saville [1952] Director/Company Secretary

Associated Security Services Holdings Limited
Incorporated: 11 May 2009 *Employees:* 158
Net Worth: £11,373,463 *Total Assets:* £16,889,640
Registered Office: Security House, 25 Addington Street, Manchester, M4 5EU
Activities: Activities of head offices
Shareholders: Stephen John Turner; Roy Turner
Officers: Stephen John Turner [1963] Managing Director; Roy Turner Jr [1961] Director

Assura (GHC) Ltd
Incorporated: 24 June 1996 *Employees:* 7
Net Worth: £16,605,584 *Total Assets:* £25,632,764
Registered Office: The Brew House, Greenalls Avenue, Warrington, Cheshire, WA4 6HL
Activities: Development of building projects
Parent: Assura Financing Limited
Officers: Orla Ball [1970] Director; Paul Bryan Carroll [1969] Director/Accountant; Jayne Marie Cottam [1974] Finance Director; Simon Gould [1974] Director/Chartered Surveyor; Spencer Adrian Kenyon [1962] Director/Chartered Surveyor; Patrick William Lowther [1977] Director/Chartered Surveyor

Assura (SC 2) Limited
Incorporated: 9 October 2000 *Employees:* 7
Net Worth: £18,471,764 *Total Assets:* £36,274,016
Registered Office: The Brew House, Greenalls Avenue, Warrington, Cheshire, WA4 6HL
Activities: Other letting and operating of own or leased real estate
Parent: Assura Financing Limited
Officers: Orla Ball [1970] Director/Company Secretary; Paul Bryan Carroll [1969] Director/Accountant; Jayne Marie Cottam [1974] Finance Director; Simon Gould [1974] Director/Chartered Surveyor; Spencer Adrian Kenyon [1962] Director/Chartered Surveyor; Patrick William Lowther [1977] Director/Chartered Surveyor

Assura Aspire UK Limited
Incorporated: 5 May 2015
Net Worth: £2,116,579 *Total Assets:* £17,661,500
Registered Office: The Brewhouse, Greenalls Avenue, Warrington, Cheshire, WA4 6HL
Activities: Other letting and operating of own or leased real estate
Parent: Assura Financing Limited
Officers: Orla Ball [1970] Director/Company Secretary; Paul Bryan Carroll [1969] Director/Accountant; Jayne Marie Cottam [1974] Finance Director; Simon Gould [1974] Director/Chartered Surveyor; Spencer Adrian Kenyon [1962] Director/Chartered Surveyor; Patrick William Lowther [1977] Director/Chartered Surveyor

Assura CVSK Limited
Incorporated: 1[illegible] May 2011 *Employees:* 7
Net Worth: £8,090,428 *Total Assets:* £8,144,408
Registered Office: The Brew House, Greenalls Avenue, Warrington, Cheshire, WA4 6HL
Activities: Other letting and operating of own or leased real estate
Parent: Assura Primary Care Properties Limited
Officers: Orla Ball [1970] Director/Company Secretary

Assura Financing PLC
Incorporated: 24 February 2016 *Employees:* 6
Net Worth: £134,034,392 *Total Assets:* £754,547,904
Registered Office: The Brew House, Greenalls Avenue, Warrington, Cheshire, WA4 6HL
Activities: Activities of other holding companies n.e.c.
Parent: Assura IH Limited
Officers: Orla Ball [1970] Director/Company Secretary; Jayne Marie Cottam [1974] Finance Director; Jonathan Stewart Murphy [1972] Finance Director

Assura HC Limited
Incorporated: 31 July 2014
Net Worth: £30,055,848 *Total Assets:* £330,372,544
Registered Office: The Brew House, Greenalls Avenue, Warrington, Cheshire, WA4 6HL
Activities: Other letting and operating of own or leased real estate
Parent: Assura Financing Ltd
Officers: Orla Ball [1970] Director/Company Secretary; Paul Bryan Carroll [1969] Director/Accountant; Jayne Marie Cottam [1974] Finance Director; Simon Gould [1974] Director/Chartered Surveyor; Spencer Adrian Kenyon [1962] Director/Chartered Surveyor; Patrick William Lowther [1977] Director/Chartered Surveyor

Assura HC UK Limited
Incorporated: 31 July 2014
Net Worth: £8,301,446 *Total Assets:* £151,791,232
Registered Office: The Brew House, Greenalls Avenue, Warrington, Cheshire, WA4 6HL
Activities: Other letting and operating of own or leased real estate
Shareholders: Assura Financing Limited; Assura HC Limited
Officers: Orla Ball [1970] Director/Company Secretary; Paul Bryan Carroll [1969] Director/Accountant; Jayne Marie Cottam [1974] Finance Director; Simon Gould [1974] Director/Chartered Surveyor; Spencer Adrian Kenyon [1962] Director/Chartered Surveyor; Patrick William Lowther [1977] Director/Chartered Surveyor

Assura Health Investments Limited
Incorporated: 21 January 2010
Net Worth: £75,006,096 *Total Assets:* £118,336,216
Registered Office: The Brew House, Greenalls Avenue, Warrington, Cheshire, WA4 6HL
Activities: Other letting and operating of own or leased real estate
Parent: Assura Financing Limited
Officers: Orla Ball [1970] Director/Company Secretary; Paul Bryan Carroll [1969] Director/Accountant; Jayne Marie Cottam [1974] Finance Director; Simon Gould [1974] Director/Chartered Surveyor; Spencer Adrian Kenyon [1962] Director/Chartered Surveyor; Patrick William Lowther [1977] Director/Chartered Surveyor

Assura Medical Centres Limited
Incorporated: 24 October 2008
Net Worth: £81,985,664 *Total Assets:* £416,665,792
Registered Office: The Brew House, Greenalls Avenue, Warrington, Cheshire, WA4 6HL
Activities: Other letting and operating of own or leased real estate
Parent: Assura Financing Limited
Officers: Orla Ball [1970] Director/Company Secretary; Paul Bryan Carroll [1969] Director/Accountant; Jayne Marie Cottam [1974] Finance Director; Simon Gould [1974] Director/Chartered Surveyor; Spencer Adrian Kenyon [1962] Director/Chartered Surveyor; Patrick William Lowther [1977] Director/Chartered Surveyor

Assura PLC
Incorporated: 10 December 2014
Net Worth: £1,250,400,000 *Total Assets:* £1,784,400,000
Registered Office: The Brew House, Greenalls Avenue, Warrington, Cheshire, WA4 6HL
Activities: Activities of other holding companies n.e.c.
Officers: Orla Ball, Secretary; Jayne Marie Cottam [1974] Finance Director; Jonathan Owen Davies [1962] Finance Director; Jenefer Dawn Greenwood [1957] Director; Jonathan Stewart Murphy [1972] Finance Director; David Hedley Richardson [1951] Director; John Edward Kitson Smith [1954] Director

Assura Primary Care Properties Limited
Incorporated: 28 October 2013 *Employees:* 7
Net Worth: £20,297,958 *Total Assets:* £37,160,104
Registered Office: The Brew House, Greenalls Avenue, Warrington, Cheshire, WA4 6HL
Activities: Other letting and operating of own or leased real estate
Parent: Assura Financing Limited
Officers: Orla Ball [1970] Director/Company Secretary; Paul Bryan Carroll [1969] Director/Accountant; Jayne Marie Cottam [1974] Finance Director; Simon Gould [1974] Director/Chartered Surveyor; Spencer Adrian Kenyon [1962] Director/Chartered Surveyor; Patrick William Lowther [1977] Director/Chartered Surveyor

Assura Properties PLC
Incorporated: 20 September 2007
Net Worth: £85,263,544 *Total Assets:* £248,622,080
Registered Office: The Brew House, Greenalls Avenue, Warrington, Cheshire, WA4 6HL
Activities: Other letting and operating of own or leased real estate
Parent: Assura PLC
Officers: Orla Ball, Secretary; Orla Ball [1970] Director/Company Secretary; Paul Bryan Carroll [1969] Director/Accountant; Jayne Marie Cottam [1974] Finance Director; Simon Gould [1974] Director/Chartered Surveyor; Spencer Adrian Kenyon [1962] Director/Chartered Surveyor; Patrick William Lowther [1977] Director/Chartered Surveyor

Assura Properties UK Limited
Incorporated: 20 September 2007 *Employees:* 7
Net Worth: £23,338,036 *Total Assets:* £25,083,664
Registered Office: The Brew House, Greenalls Avenue, Warrington, Cheshire, WA4 6HL
Activities: Other letting and operating of own or leased real estate
Parent: Assura Properties PLC
Officers: Orla Ball [1970] Director/Company Secretary; Paul Bryan Carroll [1969] Director/Accountant; Jayne Marie Cottam [1974] Finance Director; Simon Gould [1974] Director/Chartered Surveyor; Spencer Adrian Kenyon [1962] Director/Chartered Surveyor; Patrick William Lowther [1977] Director/Chartered Surveyor

Assura Services Limited
Incorporated: 27 March 2003
Net Worth: £14,461,247 *Total Assets:* £23,461,248
Registered Office: The Brew House, Greenalls Avenue, Warrington, Cheshire, WA4 6HL
Activities: Activities of other holding companies n.e.c.
Parent: Assura PLC
Officers: Orla Ball [1970] Director/Company Secretary; Paul Bryan Carroll [1969] Director/Accountant; Jayne Marie Cottam [1974] Finance Director; Simon Gould [1974] Director/Chartered Surveyor; Spencer Adrian Kenyon [1962] Director/Chartered Surveyor; Patrick William Lowther [1977] Director/Chartered Surveyor

Assurant Direct Limited
Incorporated: 20 March 2005
Net Worth: £1,907,000 *Total Assets:* £6,949,000
Registered Office: Emerald Buildings, Westmere Drive, Crewe, Cheshire, CW1 6UN
Activities: Life insurance
Parent: Assurant, Inc.
Officers: Natalie Ann Paddock, Secretary; Michael John Carter [1981] Director; Keith Roland Meier [1970] Director/President, International Global Strategy & Merger [American]; Andrew James Morris [1971] Director/Chief Marketing Officer

Assurant General Insurance Limited
Incorporated: 30 January 1989
Net Worth: £72,327,000 *Total Assets:* £160,279,008
Registered Office: Emerald Buildings, Westmere Drive, Crewe, Cheshire, CW1 6UN
Activities: Non-life insurance
Parent: Assurant Group Limited
Officers: Natalie Ann Paddock, Secretary; George Derek Wilson Bartlett [1948] Director; Michael John Carter [1981] Director; Colin Martin Kersley [1956] Director; Keith Roland Meier [1970] Director/President, International Global Strategy & Merger [American]; Andrew James Morris [1971] Director/Chief Marketing Officer; Doris Rosario Vigo [1959] Director/Lawyer [American]

Assurant Group Limited
Incorporated: 17 October 1996
Net Worth: £164,168,000 *Total Assets:* £228,616,992
Registered Office: Emerald Buildings, Westmere Drive, Crewe, Cheshire, CW1 6UN
Activities: Activities of head offices
Parent: Assurant, Inc.
Officers: Natalie Ann Paddock, Secretary; George Derek Wilson Bartlett [1948] Director; Michael John Carter [1981] Director; Colin Martin Kersley [1956] Director; Keith Roland Meier [1970] Director/President, International Global Strategy & Merger [American]; Andrew James Morris [1971] Director/Chief Marketing Officer; Doris Rosario Vigo [1959] Director/Lawyer [American]

Assurant Intermediary Limited
Incorporated: 22 June 2000
Net Worth: £7,068,000 *Total Assets:* £8,670,000
Registered Office: Emerald Buildings, Westmere Drive, Crewe, Cheshire, CW1 6UN
Activities: Life insurance
Parent: Assurant Group Limited
Officers: Natalie Ann Paddock, Secretary; George Derek Wilson Bartlett [1948] Chairman and Non-Executive Director; Michael John Carter [1981] Director; Colin Martin Kersley [1956] Director; Keith Roland Meier [1970] Director/President, International Global Strategy & Merger [American]; Andrew James Morris [1971] Director/Chief Marketing Officer; Doris Rosario Vigo [1959] Director/Lawyer [American]

Assurant Life Limited
Incorporated: 17 October 1996
Net Worth: £10,940,000 *Total Assets:* £18,603,000
Registered Office: Emerald Buildings, Westmere Drive, Crewe, Cheshire, CW1 6UN
Activities: Life insurance
Parent: Assurant Group Limited
Officers: Natalie Ann Paddock, Secretary; George Derek Wilson Bartlett [1948] Chairman and Non-Executive Director; Michael John Carter [1981] Director; Colin Martin Kersley [1956] Director; Keith Roland Meier [1970] Director/President, International Global Strategy & Merger [American]; Andrew James Morris [1971] Director/Chief Marketing Officer; Doris Rosario Vigo [1959] Director/Lawyer [American]

Assystem Group UK Limited
Incorporated: 28 June 1996 *Employees:* 3
Net Worth: £8,700,000 *Total Assets:* £9,059,000
Registered Office: Club Court, Club St, Bamber Bridge, Preston, Lancs, PR5 6FN
Activities: Other professional, scientific and technical activities n.e.c.
Parent: Assystem Technologies SAS
Officers: David Christopher Caunce, Secretary; David Christopher Caunce [1964] Finance Director; Michael John Sheehan [1958] Director/Chief Executive Officer

Assystem UK Limited
Incorporated: 22 November 1973 *Employees:* 795
Net Worth: £12,617,000 *Total Assets:* £45,209,000
Registered Office: Club Street Works, Club Street, Bamber Bridge, Preston, Lancs, PR5 6FN
Activities: Engineering design activities for industrial process and production
Parent: Assystem Group UK Ltd
Officers: David Christopher Caunce, Secretary; David Christopher Caunce [1964] Finance Director; Jeffrey Lee Hoyle [1966] Director/Engineer; Michael John Sheehan [1958] Director/Chartered Engineer

Aston Chemists Limited
Incorporated: 24 February 1987 *Employees:* 69
Net Worth: £8,372,715 *Total Assets:* £10,085,488
Registered Office: Aston House, 387-391 Blackburn Road, Accrington, Lancs, BB5 1RP
Activities: Other human health activities
Parent: Astons Healthcare Limited
Officers: Mohammed Ayub, Secretary; Zafar Iqbal [1960] Director/Pharmacist

Astonish Holdings Limited
Incorporated: 20 August 1997 *Employees:* 72
Net Worth: £8,636,991 *Total Assets:* £11,511,288
Registered Office: Astonish House, Unit 1 Premier Point, Staithgate Lane, Bradford, W Yorks, BD6 1DW
Activities: Manufacture of cleaning and polishing preparations
Major Shareholder: Howard William Moss
Officers: Howard William Moss [1974] Managing Director

ATG Access Ltd
Incorporated: 6 September 1991 *Employees:* 72
Net Worth: £1,661,026 *Total Assets:* £8,939,917
Registered Office: Cobaco House, North Florida Road, Haydock Industrial Estate, Haydock, Merseyside, WA11 9TP
Activities: Other manufacturing n.e.c.
Parent: ATG Access Holdings Ltd
Officers: Robert Nicholas Ball [1961] Director; Glenn Charles Cooper [1957] Managing Director; Gavin Hepburn [1974] Sales and Marketing Director; Stephen Robert Purkis [1967] Director/Accountant

ATG Airports Limited
Incorporated: 12 March 1991 *Employees:* 95
Net Worth: £1,648,168 *Total Assets:* £7,670,933
Registered Office: Lowton Business Park, Newton Road, Lowton, Warrington, Cheshire, WA3 2AP
Activities: Manufacture of electric lighting equipment
Officers: David Michael Smith, Secretary; Robert Currie [1958] Director/Chartered Engineer; John Hodd [1950] Director/Consultant; Gerard Malachy McGuinness [1959] Director

Atkinson Homes Limited
Incorporated: 9 May 1989
Net Worth: £4,723,541 *Total Assets:* £6,844,144
Registered Office: 1 Brancana Court, East Lakes Business Park, Penrith, Cumbria, CA11 9BB
Activities: Development of building projects
Shareholder: Steve Atkinson
Officers: Steve Atkinson, Secretary; Steve Atkinson [1961] Director/Builder; Barry Mark Turner [1956] Director/Builder

Atlantic & Peninsula Marine Services Limited
Incorporated: 7 February 2011 *Employees:* 538
Net Worth: £15,371,000 *Total Assets:* £59,193,000
Registered Office: 5 Abbotts Quay, Monks Ferry, Birkenhead, Merseyside, CH41 5LH
Activities: Repair and maintenance of ships and boats
Officers: David Thomas McGinley [1955] Director; Jonathan Hugh Schofield [1961] Director/Accountant; Jean Raymond Syvret [1961] Managing Director; Steven Keith Underwood [1974] Director; Mark Whitworth [1966] Director

Atlantic Container Line UK Limited
Incorporated: 26 September 1990 *Employees:* 158
Net Worth: £2,342,956 *Total Assets:* £9,649,487
Registered Office: 90 Duke Street, Liverpool, L1 5AA
Activities: Freight transport by road
Parent: Atlantic Container Line AB
Officers: Christopher Stephens, Secretary; Andrew Abbott [1952] Director/Chief Executive Officer [American]; Ian Clinton Higby [1955] Managing Director; Chris John Leahy [1960] Director

Atlantic Steel Processing Limited
Incorporated: 15 January 2001 *Employees:* 38
Net Worth: £2,522,279 *Total Assets:* £14,948,260
Registered Office: Atlantic Quay, Vittoria Dock, Duke Street, Birkenhead, Merseyside, CH41 1EY
Activities: Wholesale of metals and metal ores
Major Shareholder: Karen Leslley Ann Hurst
Officers: Karen Lesley Ann Hurst, Secretary; Miles Battersby [1941] Director/Consultant; Matthew Ford [1976] Director; Karen Lesley Ann Hurst [1964] Director; Lorna Hurst [1989] Director; Philip McCabe [1980] Director; Kevin John Middis [1956] Director/Consultant

Atlantic Tool Leasing U.K. Limited
Incorporated: 10 October 1996
Net Worth: £7,079,506 *Total Assets:* £8,179,506
Registered Office: Calder Vale Park, Simonstone Lane, Simonstone, Burnley, Lancs, BB12 7ND
Activities: Activities of head offices
Major Shareholder: Edward Sagar Fort
Officers: Edward Martin Drury [1949] Director; Edward Sagar Fort OBE [1937] Director/Chairman

Atlantis Hedge Co 1 Limited
Incorporated: 10 November 2014
Registered Office: Booths Park, Chelford Road, Knutsford, Cheshire, WA16 8QZ
Activities: Non-trading company
Parent: AMEC Foster Wheeler PLC
Officers: Iain Angus Jones, Secretary; Carl Anthony Chatfield [1964] Director; William George Setter [1975] Director

Atlantis Hedge Co 2 Limited
Incorporated: 10 November 2014
Registered Office: Booths Park, Chelford Road, Knutsford, Cheshire, WA16 8QZ
Activities: Non-trading company
Parent: AMEC Foster Wheeler PLC
Officers: Iain Angus Jones, Secretary; Carl Anthony Chatfield [1964] Director; William George Setter [1975] Director

Atmore Centres Limited
Incorporated: 2 September 1998 *Employees:* 1
Net Worth: £3,384,824 *Total Assets:* £23,205,436
Registered Office: St John's House, Two Queen Square, Liverpool, L1 1RH
Activities: Other business support service activities n.e.c.
Parent: Atmore Properties Limited
Officers: Janet Margaret Geddes, Secretary; Anthony Nigel Carson [1960] Director; Charles Robert Leonard Shepherd [1970] Property Director

Atmore Developments Limited
Incorporated: 9 May 1989 *Employees:* 1
Net Worth: £22,730,346 *Total Assets:* £77,229,320
Registered Office: St John's House, Two Queen Square, Liverpool, L1 1RH
Activities: Renting and operating of Housing Association real estate
Parent: Atmore Properties Limited
Officers: Janet Margaret Geddes, Secretary; Anthony Nigel Carson [1960] Director; Charles Robert Leonard Shepherd [1970] Property Director

Atmore Investments Limited
Incorporated: 25 October 1989 *Employees:* 1
Net Worth: £9,102,721 *Total Assets:* £13,848,702
Registered Office: St John's House, Two Queen Square, Liverpool, L1 1RH
Activities: Development of building projects
Parent: Atmore Properties Limited
Officers: Janet Margaret Geddes, Secretary; Anthony Nigel Carson [1960] Director; Charles Robert Leonard Shepherd [1970] Property Director

Atmore Properties Limited
Incorporated: 1 August 1973 *Employees:* 7
Net Worth: £5,053,007 *Total Assets:* £11,134,801
Registered Office: St John's House, Two Queen Square, Liverpool, L1 1RH
Activities: Development of building projects
Shareholders: Daniel Lewis Grodner; Michael Maurice Grodner
Officers: Janet Margaret Geddes, Secretary; Anthony Nigel Carson [1960] Director; Daniel Lewis Grodner [1976] Director; Michael Maurice Grodner [1979] Director/Camera Operator; Charles Robert Leonard Shepherd [1970] Property Director

Attock Oil Company Limited (The)
Incorporated: 1 December 1913 *Employees:* 2,781
Net Worth: £471,751,008 *Total Assets:* £1,678,744,960
Registered Office: 4 Swan Street, Manchester, M4 5JN
Activities: Extraction of crude petroleum
Parent: Bay View International Group S.A.
Officers: Rehmat Ullah Bardaie, Secretary; Shuaib Anwer Malik [1952] Director/Senior Business Executive [Pakistani]; Laith Ghaith Pharaon [1968] Director/Investor Senior Business Executive [Saudi Arabian]; Wael Ghaith Pharaon [1978] Director/Investor Senior Business Executive [Saudi Arabian]

Atul Europe Limited
Incorporated: 29 January 1996 *Employees:* 49
Net Worth: £4,146,127 *Total Assets:* £11,312,878
Registered Office: 1st Floor, Office Suite 1c, Summerfields Village Centre, Wilmslow, Cheshire, SK9 2TB
Activities: Wholesale of chemical products
Officers: Jacques Collonge [1948] Director [French]; Satej Mahadeo Nabar [1963] Director/President - Polymer Division [Indian]; Dr Edward Sharkey [1947] Director

Auction Finance Limited
Incorporated: 31 October 2003
Net Worth: £1,200,000 *Total Assets:* £48,700,000
Registered Office: Lake View, Lakeside, Cheadle, Cheshire, SK8 3GW
Activities: Activities of mortgage finance companies
Parent: Together Financial Services Limited
Officers: Sarah Elizabeth Batt, Secretary; Gary Derek Beckett [1969] Director; Wayne Bowser [1952] Director; Marc Richard Goldberg [1971] Director; Robert Michael McTighe [1953] Director; Henry Neville Moser [1949] Director; Helga Clare Taylor [1969] Finance Director

Audas Project Management Limited
Incorporated: 16 January 2007 *Employees:* 48
Net Worth: £1,050,299 *Total Assets:* £7,800,011
Registered Office: Gemini House, Capricorn Park, Greenbank Business Park, Blakewater Road, Blackburn, Lancs, BB1 5QR
Activities: Other building completion and finishing
Parent: Audas Group Limited
Officers: Stephen John Bray [1960] Director; John Marland [1973] Director; Philip Dominic Sharp [1972] Director

Audco Limited
Incorporated: 30 July 1936
Net Worth: £34,610,000 *Total Assets:* £34,610,000
Registered Office: One St Peter's Square, Manchester, M2 3DE
Activities: Non-trading company
Officers: Martin Edwards, Secretary; Martin Edwards [1955] Director/Accountant; Christian Lawrence [1974] Director/Regional Controller

Audenshaw School Academy Trust
Incorporated: 2 August 2010 *Employees:* 118
Net Worth: £10,377,000 *Total Assets:* £11,899,000
Registered Office: Audenshaw School Academy Trust, Hazel Street, Audenshaw, Manchester, M34 5NB
Activities: Financial intermediation not elsewhere classified
Officers: Brian Atkin [1948] Director/Retired; Kenneth Brown [1972] Director/Financial Adviser; Timothy James Gartside [1961] Director/Headmaster; Terence John Hall [1954] Director; Neil Jackson [1976] Director; Brian Miller [1950] Director; Glynis Miller [1950] Director; Jane Roberts [1973] Director; William Stewart Thorpe [1947] Director/Court Warrant Officer

Auk Investments Limited
Incorporated: 15 December 1967 *Employees:* 52
Net Worth: £6,717,027 *Total Assets:* £10,784,396
Registered Office: 23 Princes Way, Fleetwood, Lancs, FY7 8PG
Activities: Retail sale of automotive fuel in specialised stores
Shareholders: Angus John Hockings; Marcus Benjamin Hockings; Simon Hockings
Officers: Hilda Hockings, Secretary; Angus John Hockings [1964] Director; Marcus Benjamin Hockings [1963] Director/Assistant; Simon Hockings [1962] Director/Assistant

Aus-Bore Estates Limited
Incorporated: 28 June 1995
Net Worth: £11,081,632 *Total Assets:* £22,929,356
Registered Office: Aus-Bore House, 19-25 Manchester Road, Wilmslow, Cheshire, SK9 1BQ
Activities: Development of building projects
Shareholders: Jonathon Scott Burgess; Elizabeth Jane Burgess
Officers: Elizabeth Jane Burgess, Secretary; Harriet Jane Burgess [1989] Director; James John Campbell Burgess [1987] Director; Jonathon Scott Burgess [1954] Managing Director

Austin Friars
Incorporated: 12 March 1985 *Employees:* 94
Net Worth: £5,313,390 *Total Assets:* £9,001,479
Registered Office: Austin Friars School, Etterby Scaur, Carlisle, CA3 9PB
Activities: Other education n.e.c.
Officers: Ewen Catanach Swinton, Secretary; Elizabeth Mary Bavidge [1945] Director; Stephen Joseph Bolger [1950] Director/Osteopath; Susan Claire Dymond [1978] Director/Executive Head; Neil Elsender [1964] Director/Consultant; Joanne Graham [1967] Director/Housewife; Stephen Paul Graham [1964] Director; Michael Higginbottom [1939] Director/Retired; John Little [1951] Director/Retired; Doctor Peter Tiplady [1942] Director/Retired; Michael James Walby [1976] Director/Solicitor; Ian Wilson [1954] Director/Priest

Ausurus Group Ltd
Incorporated: 9 July 2014 *Employees:* 3,000
Net Worth: £533,000,000 *Total Assets:* £1,216,000,000
Registered Office: Sirius House, Delta Crescent, Westbrook, Warrington, Cheshire, WA5 7NS
Activities: Activities of head offices
Officers: Christopher John Tinsley, Secretary; David Farrington Landless [1960] Director; Edwin Leijnse [1967] Director [Dutch]; Edward Scott Pysden [1948] Director/Solicitor; Christopher Phillip Sheppard [1974] Director; Robin Sheppard [1954] Director

The Authentic Food Company Limited
Incorporated: 3 July 1985 *Employees:* 195
Net Worth: £11,326,108 *Total Assets:* £24,447,944
Registered Office: 4-5 Robeson Way, Sharston Green Business Park, Manchester, M22 4SW
Activities: Manufacture of prepared meals and dishes
Shareholders: Kamal Basran; The Authentic Food Group Limited
Officers: Alexander Edward Stephens, Secretary; Kamaljit Kaur Basran [1951] Development Director; Nik Basran [1980] Managing Director; Simon Cowdroy [1961] HR Director; Sean Floyd [1962] Buying Director; Nicholas Harris [1983] Marketing Director; Alexander Edward Stephens [1976] Finance Director

The Authentic Food Group Limited
Incorporated: 6 April 1988 *Employees:* 482
Net Worth: £10,085,343 *Total Assets:* £29,517,036
Registered Office: 4-5 Robeson Way, Sharston Green Business Park, Manchester, M22 4SW
Activities: Manufacture of prepared meals and dishes
Major Shareholder: Kamal Basran
Officers: Alexander Edward Stephens, Secretary; Kamaljit Kaur Basran [1951] Development Director; Nik Basran [1980] Managing Director; Alexander Edward Stephens [1976] Finance Director

Autism Initiatives (UK)
Incorporated: 26 October 1989 *Employees:* 2,102
Net Worth: £13,346,000 *Total Assets:* £20,031,000
Registered Office: Sefton House, Bridle Road, Bootle, Merseyside, L30 4XR
Activities: Primary education
Officers: Andrew Grainger, Secretary; Rosario Veronica Buttery [1949] Director/Classroom Assistant S.E.N.; Sian Elizabeth Hiscock [1962] Director/Civil Servant; John McCarthy [1962] Director/Retired Police Officer; Carys Owen [1962] Director/Solicitor; Elizabeth Veronica Slater [1948] Director/Social Services Resource Centre; Brian Edward Williams [1943] Director/Social Work Manager

Autism Together
Incorporated: 29 October 1991 *Employees:* 936
Net Worth: £3,192,000 *Total Assets:* £7,918,000
Registered Office: Wirral Centre for Autism, Unit C Oak House, 6 Tebay Road, Bromborough, Wirral, Merseyside, CH62 3PA
Activities: Residential care activities for learning difficulties, mental health and substance abuse
Officers: Iain Cadman, Secretary; Catherine Louise Ames [1965] Director; Stephen Ashton [1954] Director; Carole Anne Forrester Battersby [1944] Director/Retired Special Needs Teacher; Edward Behan [1957] Director/Retired; Iain Nicholson Cadman [1954] Director/Accountant; John Callcott [1950] Director/Retired Engineer; Anthony Cragg [1947] Director; Andrew Derek Davies [1952] Director/Solicitor; Professor Hilary Dobson [1948] Director/Agricultural Scientist; Michael Gerard Fortune [1964] Director/Senior Behavioural Change Consultant; John Thomas Kennedy [1938] Director/Retired

Auto Trader Group PLC
Incorporated: 13 February 2015 *Employees:* 820
Net Worth Deficit: £21,400,000 *Total Assets:* £390,500,000
Registered Office: 1 Tony Wilson Place, Manchester, M15 4FN
Activities: Activities of head offices
Officers: Claire Baty, Secretary; Nathan James Coe [1978] Director/Chief Operating Officer [Australian]; Jill Easterbrook [1971] Director; David Keens [1953] Director; Trevor Nigel Mather [1967] Director; Jenifer Mary Mundy [1965] Director; Edmund Warren Williams [1962] Director

Auto Trader Holding Limited
Incorporated: 18 May 2003
Net Worth: £724,099,968 *Total Assets:* £2,498,200,064
Registered Office: 1 Tony Wilson Place, Manchester, M15 4FN
Activities: Activities of head offices
Parent: Auto Trader Group PLC
Officers: Claire Baty, Secretary; Nathan James Coe [1978] Director/Chief Operating Officer [Australian]; Trevor Nigel Mather [1967] Director/Chief Executive Officer

Auto Trader Limited
Incorporated: 19 January 2000 *Employees:* 786
Net Worth: £1,333,100,032 *Total Assets:* £1,385,799,936
Registered Office: 1 Tony Wilson Place, Manchester, M15 4FN
Activities: Publishing of consumer and business journals and periodicals
Parent: Auto Trader Holding Limited
Officers: Claire Baty, Secretary; Claire Baty [1976] Director/Company Secretary; Nathan James Coe [1978] Director/Chief Operating Officer [Australian]; Trevor Nigel Mather [1967] Director/Chief Executive Officer

Autoliv U.K. Holding Limited
Incorporated: 16 December 1998
Net Worth: £23,279,000 *Total Assets:* £23,283,000
Registered Office: Airbags International Limited, Viking Way, Congleton, Cheshire, CW12 1TT
Activities: Other business support service activities n.e.c.
Parent: Autoliv Inc.
Officers: John Anthony Bonney, Secretary; Christian Herbert Antero Hanke [1968] Director/Vice President Corporate Control [Swedish]; Zachariah Bronkhorst Miller [1979] Director/Attorney [American]

Autosupply Holdings UK Limited
Incorporated: 29 January 2016 *Employees:* 250
Net Worth: £10,036,000 *Total Assets:* £72,515,000
Registered Office: Holt Lloyd Services Ltd, Unit 100 Barton Dock Road, Stretford, Manchester, M32 0YQ
Activities: Activities of other holding companies n.e.c.
Officers: Michael Christopher Meehan [1954] Finance Director; Daniel Ricard [1961] Director [French]; Steven James Rudd [1964] President & Managing Director

The Avalon Trustee Company Limited
Incorporated: 15 July 1993 *Employees:* 111
Net Worth Deficit: £8,653,524 *Total Assets:* £55,281,008
Registered Office: Unit A2, Brooke Court, Handforth Dean, Wilmslow, Cheshire, SK9 3ND
Activities: Funeral and related activities
Parent: Nirvana Holdings Limited
Officers: Ben Evans, Secretary; Mark Dugdale [1968] Director; Jason Peter Gardner [1973] Operations Director; Peter Brian Leech [1983] Director

Avantec Healthcare Limited
Incorporated: 30 September 2004 *Employees:* 46
Net Worth: £2,722,692 *Total Assets:* £8,794,068
Registered Office: 2 Omega Way, Omega Drive, Irlam, Manchester, M44 5GR
Activities: Other human health activities
Parent: Omnicell Inc
Officers: Alan Patrick Clark, Secretary; Paul John O'Hanlon [1962] International Managing Director; Robert Gene Seim [1959] Director/Chief Financial Officer [American]; Arthur Van Dongen [1964] Director/General Manager [Dutch]

Avecto Ltd
Incorporated: 18 March 2008 *Employees:* 197
Net Worth Deficit: £2,083,267 *Total Assets:* £17,129,292
Registered Office: Building One, Trident Business Park, Styal Road, Manchester, M22 5XB
Activities: Business and domestic software development
Parent: Armour Bidco Limited
Officers: Matthew Dircks [1965] Director [American]; Janine Karyn Seebeck [1975] Director [American]

Avery House Healthcare Limited
Incorporated: 20 August 2007 *Employees:* 84
Net Worth: £3,026,000 *Total Assets:* £11,945,000
Registered Office: Norcliffe House, Station Road, Wilmslow, Cheshire, SK9 1BU
Activities: Other human health activities
Parent: Optimum FS Care Developments Limited
Officers: Abigail Mattison, Secretary; Ryan Stuart MacAskill [1975] Director; Gregory Laurence Newman [1988] Director/Investment Professional; Jeremy Robert Arthur Richardson [1970] Director; Dr Maureen Claire Royston [1960] Director; Phillip Gary Thomas [1978] Director

Avery Lodge Limited
Incorporated: 14 August 2007 *Employees:* 75
Net Worth: £3,378,000 *Total Assets:* £9,930,000
Registered Office: Norcliffe House, Station Road, Wilmslow, Cheshire, SK9 1BU
Activities: Other human health activities
Parent: Optimum Debtco Limited
Officers: Abigail Mattison, Secretary; Ryan Stuart MacAskill [1975] Director; Gregory Laurence Newman [1988] Director/Investment Professional; Jeremy Robert Arthur Richardson [1970] Director; Dr Maureen Claire Royston [1960] Director; Phillip Gary Thomas [1978] Director

Aviagen Turkeys Limited
Incorporated: 11 May 1962 *Employees:* 191
Net Worth: £161,176,992 *Total Assets:* £245,716,000
Registered Office: Chowley Five, Chowley Oak Business Park, Tattenhall, Cheshire, CH3 9GA
Activities: Raising of poultry
Parent: EW Malta Trading Limited
Officers: Wendrell Waller Dye, Secretary; Clay Michael Burrows [1969] Managing Director; Wendrell Waller Dye [1967] Director [American]; Christopher Paul Hill [1964] Director/Chief Financial Officer

Aviation Park Group Limited
Incorporated: 10 November 2004 *Employees:* 29
Net Worth: £5,098,663 *Total Assets:* £10,429,369
Registered Office: International House, Aviation Park, Flint Road, Saltney Ferry, Flintshire, CH4 0GZ
Activities: Service activities incidental to air transportation
Major Shareholder: Colin Charles Butt
Officers: Colin Charles Butt [1943] Director; Caroline Ann Gardner [1963] Director

Avocado Research Chemicals Limited
Incorporated: 29 January 1992 *Employees:* 130
Net Worth: £23,349,000 *Total Assets:* £26,725,000
Registered Office: 3rd Floor, 1 Ashley Road, Altrincham, Cheshire, WA14 2DT
Activities: Manufacture of other inorganic basic chemicals
Parent: Thermo Fisher (Heysham) Limited
Officers: Rhona Gregg, Secretary; Lucie Mary Katja Grant [1976] Director/Solicitor; Nicholas Ince [1982] Director/Accountant; David John Norman [1960] Director/Chartered Accountant

Avonside Group Services Limited
Incorporated: 13 May 2008 *Employees:* 5
Net Worth Deficit: £774,398 *Total Assets:* £13,675,079
Registered Office: The Courtyard, Green Lane, Heywood, Lancs, OL10 2EX
Activities: Other service activities n.e.c.
Parent: Burke Investments Limited
Officers: Anthony Burke [1962] Director; Vincent Hughes [1968] Director; Keith Kershaw [1957] Director; Andrew Morley [1967] Director; Nicholas Stephen Tappin [1971] Director/Accountant

Avonside Roofing Limited
Incorporated: 21 December 1988 *Employees:* 232
Net Worth: £20,781,852 *Total Assets:* £38,458,792
Registered Office: The Courtyard, Green Lane, Heywood, Lancs, OL10 2EX
Activities: Roofing activities
Parent: Avonside Group Services Limited
Officers: Keith Kershaw, Secretary; Anthony Burke [1962] Director; Vincent Hughes [1968] Director; Keith Kershaw [1957] Director/Accountant; Andrew Morley [1967] Director/Roofing Contractor; Nicholas Stephen Tappin [1971] Director/Accountant

AVSL Group Limited
Incorporated: 29 July 1998 *Employees:* 49
Net Worth: £4,302,520 *Total Assets:* £9,033,193
Registered Office: c/o Edwards Veeder (UK) Limited, Ground Floor, 4 Broadgate, Broadway Business Park, Chadderton, Oldham, Lancs, OL9 9XA
Activities: Non-specialised wholesale trade
Shareholders: AVSL Group (Holdings) Limited; AVSL Group (Holdings Limited
Officers: Caroline Diane Kelly, Secretary; Brian John Kelly [1946] Director/Consultant; Caroline Diane Kelly [1964] Director; Rachel Moran [1981] Director; Graham Stephen Purdy [1969] Director; Philip Williams [1968] Managing Director

AW Carbonless Papers Europe Limited
Incorporated: 30 July 1986
Net Worth: £6,401,000 *Total Assets:* £29,056,000
Registered Office: Eversheds House, 70 Great Bridgewater Street, Manchester, M1 5ES
Activities: Activities of head offices
Parent: AW UK Holdings Limited
Officers: Alain Philippe Daniel Gourjon [1965] Group Accounts, Tax & Administrative Director [French]; Clive Mountford [1957] Director/Accountant

AW UK Holdings Limited
Incorporated: 22 August 2000
Net Worth Deficit: £140,432,128 *Total Assets:* £6,567,151
Registered Office: Eversheds House, 70 Great Bridgewater Street, Manchester, M1 5ES
Activities: Activities of head offices
Parent: Sequana
Officers: Jonathan David Mitchell [1965] Managing Director Arjowiggins Creative Papers SAS; Martin John Newell [1957] Finance Director

AW-WS Group Limited
Incorporated: 13 March 1919
Net Worth: £23,633,000 *Total Assets:* £23,633,000
Registered Office: Eversheds House, 70 Great Bridgewater Street, Manchester, M1 5ES
Activities: Non-trading company
Parent: The Wiggins Teape Group Limited
Officers: Alain Philippe Daniel Gourjon [1965] Group Accounts, Tax & Administrative Director [French]; Clive Mountford [1957] Director/Accountant; Martin John Newell [1957] Finance Director

Axiom Education (Rochdale) Holdings Limited
Incorporated: 28 July 2005
Net Worth Deficit: £6,383,000 *Total Assets:* £41,821,000
Registered Office: Unit 18 Riversway Business Village, Navigation Way, Ashton on Ribble, Preston, Lancs, PR2 2YP
Activities: Activities of head offices
Parent: Aberdeen Infrastructure II Limited
Officers: Ion Bruce Balfour [1963] Director/Investment Manager; Kenneth John Simpson [1965] Director/Investment Manager

Axiom Education (Rochdale) Limited
Incorporated: 4 August 2005
Net Worth Deficit: £5,663,000 *Total Assets:* £40,695,000
Registered Office: Unit 18 Riversway Business Village, Navigation Way, Preston, Lancs, PR2 2YP
Activities: Other business support service activities n.e.c.
Parent: Axiom Education (Rochdale) Holdings Limited
Officers: Ion Bruce Balfour [1963] Director/Investment Manager; Kenneth John Simpson [1965] Director/Investment Manager

Axis Manchester LLP
Incorporated: 19 June 2008
Net Worth: £347,000 *Total Assets:* £22,309,000
Registered Office: Alliance House, Westpoint Enterprise Park, Clarence Avenue, Trafford Park, Manchester, M17 1QS

Axle Bidco Limited
Incorporated: 9 June 2016
Net Worth Deficit: £2,026,326 *Total Assets:* £25,872,020
Registered Office: Suite 11, Stone Cross Place, Stone Cross Lane North, Lowton, Warrington, Cheshire, WA3 2SH
Activities: Freight transport by road
Parent: Axle Topco Limited
Officers: Christopher James Chambers [1972] Finance Director; David Coulson [1964] Director; Steven Granite [1979] Director; Jon Pickering [1977] Director

Axle Topco Limited
Incorporated: 9 June 2016 *Employees:* 662
Net Worth Deficit: £2,460,333 *Total Assets:* £55,847,728
Registered Office: Suite 11, Stone Cross Place, Stone Cross Lane North, Lowton, Warrington, Cheshire, WA3 2SH
Activities: Activities of investment trusts
Parent: Northedge Capital Limited Fund LL LP
Officers: Christopher James Chambers [1972] Finance Director; David Coulson [1964] Director; Steven Granite [1979] Director; Ian Francis Kelly [1962] Director; Jon Pickering [1977] Director

Azelis UK Holdings Limited
Incorporated: 25 February 2002 *Employees:* 4
Net Worth: £15,175,408 *Total Assets:* £294,186,976
Registered Office: Alexander House, Crown Gate, Runcorn, Cheshire, WA7 2UP
Activities: Wholesale of chemical products
Parent: Azelis S.A.
Officers: Thijs Bakker [1974] Director; Anna Bertona [1967] Director [Italian]; Stephen Edward Roberts [1964] Director/Chartered Accountant; Joan Teresa Traynor [1959] Director/Sales & Marketing

Azelis UK Limited
Incorporated: 22 June 1998 *Employees:* 73
Net Worth: £12,030,000 *Total Assets:* £73,789,000
Registered Office: Alexander House, Crown Gate, Runcorn, Cheshire, WA7 2UP
Activities: Wholesale of chemical products
Parent: Azelis UK Holdings Limited
Officers: Thijs Bakker [1974] Commercial Director; Anna Bertona [1967] Director [Italian]; Stephen Edward Roberts [1964] Director/Chartered Accountant; Joan Teresa Traynor [1959] Director/Sales & Marketing

Aztec Aerosols Limited
Incorporated: 1 February 1983 *Employees:* 71
Net Worth: £1,322,006 *Total Assets:* £10,050,363
Registered Office: Gateway, Crewe, Cheshire, CW1 6YY
Activities: Manufacture of other chemical products n.e.c.
Parent: Instarmac Holdings Limited
Officers: Richard Anderson, Secretary; Paul Francis Butcher [1959] Director; Brady Michael Collins [1966] Director

B & M Retail Limited
Incorporated: 14 March 1978 *Employees:* 26,496
Net Worth: £606,552,000 *Total Assets:* £1,006,995,008
Registered Office: The Vault, Dakota Drive, Estuary Commerce Park, Speke, Liverpool, L24 8RJ
Activities: Other retail sale in non-specialised stores
Parent: E V Retail Limited
Officers: Simon Arora, Secretary; Bobby Arora [1972] Director; Robin Arora [1985] Director; Simon Arora [1969] Director; Paul Andrew McDonald [1966] Director/Accountant

B & W Plant Hire and Sales Limited
Incorporated: 9 October 2000 *Employees:* 73
Net Worth: £8,784,935 *Total Assets:* £18,983,550
Registered Office: Shorrocks Delf, Brandy House, Brow, Blackburn, Lancs, BB2 3EY
Activities: Non-specialised wholesale trade
Parent: B & W Plant Group Ltd
Officers: William Richard Whitwell [1970] Director/Plant Hire

B S Stainless Limited
Incorporated: 26 January 1998 *Employees:* 24
Net Worth: £7,270,199 *Total Assets:* £9,840,874
Registered Office: 360 Leach Place, Walton Summit Centre, Bamber Bridge, Preston, Lancs, PR5 8AS
Activities: Wholesale of metals and metal ores
Parent: B S Stainless Holdings Limited
Officers: Brian Shaw [1967] Director/Sales; Jacqueline Gail Shaw [1966] Director

B&ESA Limited
Incorporated: 28 June 1965 *Employees:* 88
Net Worth: £2,438,091 *Total Assets:* £9,721,027
Registered Office: Old Mansion House, Eamont Bridge, Penrith, Cumbria, CA10 2BX
Activities: Activities of business and employers membership organisations
Parent: Building Engineering Services Association
Officers: Skye Hardy, Secretary; David William Frise [1960] Director/Chief Executive; Timothy Hopkinson [1962] Managing Director

B&M European Value Retail Holdco 1 Ltd
Incorporated: 20 December 2012
Net Worth: £646,131,968 *Total Assets:* £646,134,976
Registered Office: B & M Retail, The Vault, Dakota Drive, Estuary Commerce Park, Speke, Liverpool, L24 8RJ
Activities: Non-trading company
Parent: B&M European Value Retail S.A.
Officers: Paul Andrew McDonald, Secretary; Simon Arora [1969] Director; Paul Andrew McDonald [1966] Director/Accountant

B&M European Value Retail Holdco 2 Ltd
Incorporated: 20 December 2012
Net Worth: £556,872,000 *Total Assets:* £556,873,984
Registered Office: B & M Retail Ltd, The Vault, Dakota Drive, Estuary Commerce Park, Speke, Liverpool, L24 8RJ
Activities: Non-trading company
Parent: B&M European Value Retail Holdco 1 Ltd
Officers: Paul Andrew McDonald, Secretary; Simon Arora [1969] Director; Paul Andrew McDonald [1966] Director/Accountant

B&M European Value Retail Holdco 3 Ltd
Incorporated: 27 November 2012
Net Worth: £645,926,016 *Total Assets:* £645,928,000
Registered Office: The Vault, Dakota Drive, Estuary Commerce Park, Speke, Liverpool, L24 8RJ
Activities: Non-trading company
Parent: B&M European Value Retail Holdco 2 Ltd
Officers: Paul Andrew McDonald, Secretary; Simon Arora [1969] Director; Paul Andrew McDonald [1966] Director/Accountant

B&M European Value Retail Holdco 4 Ltd
Incorporated: 27 November 2012
Net Worth: £418,575,008 *Total Assets:* £1,053,468,032
Registered Office: The Vault, Dakota Drive, Estuary Commerce Park, Speke, Liverpool, L24 8RJ
Activities: Non-trading company
Parent: B&M European Value Retail Holdco 3 Ltd
Officers: Paul Andrew McDonald, Secretary; Simon Arora [1969] Director; Paul Andrew McDonald [1966] Director/Accountant

B.I. Properties Limited
Incorporated: 24 October 1994 *Employees:* 4
Net Worth: £5,550,476 *Total Assets:* £9,825,072
Registered Office: 3 Roundhouse Court, South Rings Office Village, Bamber Bridge, Preston, Lancs, PR5 6DA
Activities: Other letting and operating of own or leased real estate
Major Shareholder: Janet Lefton
Officers: Harold Stanley Lefton, Secretary/Director; Harold Stanley Lefton [1956] Director/Accountant; Janet Lefton [1958] Director; Jeremy Harold Lefton [1986] Director/Surveyor; Michelle Karen Rothwell [1987] Director

B.I.P. (Holdings) Limited
Incorporated: 15 July 2015 *Employees:* 185
Net Worth: £12,453,235 *Total Assets:* £22,436,136
Registered Office: Pacific House, Pacific Way, Salford, M50 1DR
Activities: Other information service activities n.e.c.
Major Shareholder: Ronald Llewelyn Burges
Officers: Linda Andrews, Secretary; Carolyn Burges [1947] Director/Nurse; Ronald Llewellyn Burges [1947] Director; Simon Burges [1975] Director

Baas Construction Limited
Incorporated: 29 April 1982 *Employees:* 80
Net Worth: £10,830,408 *Total Assets:* £14,836,141
Registered Office: The Old Chapel, Brooklands Road, Burnley, Lancs, BB11 3PR
Activities: Development of building projects
Shareholders: Kevin O'Connell; Lindsey Leng
Officers: Carol Smith, Secretary; Lindsey Leng [1954] Director/Secretary; Adam O'Connell [1982] Director/Consultant; Kevin Oconnell [1948] Director/Builder; Haydn Williams [1970] Managing Director

Bacchus Newco Limited
Incorporated: 20 April 2016 *Employees:* 324
Net Worth Deficit: £5,657,991 *Total Assets:* £67,946,376
Registered Office: Park Lane Industrial Estates, Park Lane, off Wigan Road, Ashton in Makerfield, Wigan, Lancs, WN4 0BZ
Activities: Renting and leasing of construction and civil engineering machinery and equipment
Officers: John Charles Green [1967] Director; Robert Killen [1970] Director; Robin Clive Powell [1965] Director/Investment Manager; Brian Reynolds [1971] Director/Accountant; Gareth Winfield Richardson [1966] Director; Robin Michael Richardson [1959] Director/Chairman

Bachy Soletanche Holdings (Europe) Limited
Incorporated: 14 January 2003 *Employees:* 344
Net Worth: £20,310,000 *Total Assets:* £49,680,000
Registered Office: Henderson House, Langley Place, Higgins Lane, Burscough, Lancs, L40 8JS
Activities: Activities of construction holding companies
Officers: Graham James Trafford, Secretary; Mark Damien Deary [1962] Director/Accountant; Philip John Hines [1966] Managing Director; Graham James Trafford [1972] Director/Accountant

Bachy Soletanche Holdings Limited
Incorporated: 12 May 1986
Net Worth: £33,934,000 *Total Assets:* £34,051,000
Registered Office: Henderson House, Langley Place, Higgins Lane, Burscough, Lancs, L40 8JS
Activities: Activities of head offices
Officers: Graham James Trafford, Secretary; Philip John Hines [1966] Managing Director

Bachy Soletanche Limited
Incorporated: 4 March 1963 *Employees:* 330
Net Worth: £15,135,000 *Total Assets:* £45,061,000
Registered Office: Henderson House, Langley Place, Higgins Lane, Burscough, Lancs, L40 8JS
Activities: Construction of other civil engineering projects n.e.c.
Officers: Graham James Trafford, Secretary; Philip John Hines [1966] Director/Civil Engineer; Christopher James Merridew [1963] Director/Civil Engineer; Graham James Trafford [1972] Director/Accountant

Back Office Support Services Limited
Incorporated: 20 July 1998
Net Worth: £1,919,634 *Total Assets:* £10,334,751
Registered Office: 15 John Bradshaw Court, Alexandria Way, Congleton, Cheshire, CW12 1LB
Activities: Factoring
Major Shareholder: Ian Hewitt Humphrey
Officers: Ian Hewitt Humphrey, Secretary; Ian Hewitt Humphrey [1957] Director/Accountant

A.C.Bacon Engineering Limited
Incorporated: 27 December 1961 *Employees:* 103
Net Worth: £8,662,052 *Total Assets:* £11,384,014
Registered Office: 3 Hardman Street, Manchester, M3 3HF
Activities: Manufacture of metal structures and parts of structures
Parent: AC Bacon Engineering (Holdings) Ltd
Officers: Hazel Martha Bacon, Secretary; Andrew David Bacon [1978] Director/Manager; David Graham Bacon [1951] Managing Director; Colin Strugnell [1968] Technical Director

Bacup and Rawtenstall Grammar School
Incorporated: 6 September 2012 *Employees:* 146
Net Worth: £10,921,000 *Total Assets:* £12,856,000
Registered Office: Bacup and Rawtenstall Grammar School, Glen Road, Waterfoot, Rossendale, Lancs, BB4 7BJ
Activities: General secondary education
Officers: Amanda Jane Hughes, Secretary; Simon Bradshaw [1969] Director/Area Sales Engineer; David Cain [1958] Director/Management Consultant; Keith Harwood [1944] Director; David Sanders King [1953] Director/Retired; Barry John Lynch [1945] Director/Retired; Dr Caesar Merrifield [1948] Director/Retired; Alan Porteous [1965] Director/Headmaster; Donna Rawding [1960] Director; Patricia Heather Skilling [1943] Director/Retired; Mark Spencer [1975] Director/Teacher; Peter Terry [1954] Director/Retired; Mark Tomlinson [1966] Director; Angela Wardle [1966] Director/HR Officer; Malcolm Joseph White [1951] Director/Consultant; Natalie Ann Wild [1970] Director/Chartered Accountant

Baerlocher UK Limited
Incorporated: 25 April 1973 *Employees:* 36
Net Worth: £2,653,485 *Total Assets:* £7,560,886
Registered Office: Moss Hall Road, Bury, Lancs, BL9 7JJ
Activities: Manufacture of other organic basic chemicals
Parent: Baerlocher GmbH
Officers: David Hadfield, Secretary; Andrew Ian Jones [1965] Managing Director; Graeme Thomas Knox [1973] Operations Director; Andrew Tate [1965] Commercial Director

Bagnall & Morris (Waste Services) Ltd
Incorporated: 28 November 1997 *Employees:* 217
Net Worth: £8,930,139 *Total Assets:* £21,433,726
Registered Office: Iris House, Dock Road South, Bromborough, Wirral, Merseyside, CH62 4SQ
Activities: Collection of non-hazardous waste
Shareholders: Kenneth Curtis; Neil Curtis
Officers: Carol Curtis, Secretary; Michael Ashall [1966] Director; David Curtis [1977] Director; Graham Curtis [1972] Director; Kenneth Curtis [1947] Director; Neil Curtis [1974] Director; Paul Curtis [1983] Director; Amber Claire Greenhalgh [1983] Commercial Director; Grahame Henderson [1961] Finance Director; Graeme Martin Knight [1967] Major Accounts Director; Terence Milner [1950] Director

Alfred Bagnall and Sons Limited
Incorporated: 4 August 1911 *Employees:* 618
Net Worth: £8,976,226 *Total Assets:* £18,765,400
Registered Office: 6 Manor Lane, Shipley, W Yorks, BD18 3RD
Activities: Activities of head offices
Officers: John Charles Kirkham, Secretary; John Keith Bagnall [1941] Director/Chartered Accountant; Stephen John Bagnall [1968] Director/Painting Contractor; Stephen Bethell [1958] Director/Painting Contractor; Richard John Britten [1974] Director/Painting Contractor; Paul James Curry [1968] Director/Painting Contractor; Michael Graham Davenport [1965] Director/Chartered Accountant; Joanne Gualda [1968] Director/Painting Contractor; Elspeth Helen Jobes [1980] Director/Painting Contractor; John Charles Kirkham [1952] Director/Painting Contractor; Lindsay Mark Robertshaw [1960] Director/Painting Contractor

J. S. Bailey Limited
Incorporated: 14 June 1993 *Employees:* 73
Net Worth: £6,798,333 *Total Assets:* £11,035,229
Registered Office: 17 Alvaston Business Park, Middlewich Road, Nantwich, Cheshire, CW5 6PF
Activities: Wholesale of dairy products, eggs and edible oils and fats
Major Shareholder: John Bailey
Officers: John Stuart Bailey, Secretary; Gaynor Mary Bailey [1963] Director; John Stuart Bailey [1949] Company Secretary/Director

BAJ 1 Limited
Incorporated: 10 January 2006
Net Worth: £21,495,726 *Total Assets:* £50,682,432
Registered Office: 7 Merseyway, Stockport, Cheshire, SK1 1PN
Activities: Development of building projects
Shareholders: John Coulter; Ann Jones
Officers: Ann Jones, Secretary; John Coulter [1951] Director; Ann Jones [1954] Director; Uziel Zelig Katz [1960] Director

Baker Properties Limited
Incorporated: 14 January 2003 *Employees:* 3
Net Worth: £1,735,251 *Total Assets:* £6,992,455
Registered Office: 3a Bridgewater Street, Liverpool, L1 0AR
Activities: Buying and selling of own real estate
Major Shareholder: Damian Robin Baker
Officers: Damian Robin Baker [1975] Director/Property Manager

Bakers (Area 1) Limited
Incorporated: 6 June 1961 *Employees:* 99
Net Worth: £7,598,000 *Total Assets:* £14,667,000
Registered Office: 74 Roman Way Industrial Estate, Ribbleton, Preston, Lancs, PR2 5BE
Activities: Non-specialised wholesale of food, beverages and tobacco
Parent: Bako Northern (Holdings) Ltd
Officers: Kirti Hirani, Secretary; Joseph Hall [1965] Director/Master Baker; Janet Hill [1961] Director; Duncan Hindley [1956] Director/Baker; Philip Marshall [1974] Director/Master Baker; Alan Michael Moore [1961] Director; Martyn Anthony Taylor [1959] Director/Consultant; Dianne Gillian Davies Walker [1965] Director/Chartered Accountant; David Yates [1968] Director/Baker

Bako North Western (Group) Limited
Incorporated: 4 December 2013 *Employees:* 398
Net Worth: £6,499,000 *Total Assets:* £37,241,000
Registered Office: 74 Roman Way Industrial Estate, Longridge Road, Preston, Lancs, PR2 5BE
Activities: Other food services
Officers: Kirti Hirani, Secretary; Joseph Hall [1965] Director/Master Baker; Janet Hill [1961] Director; Duncan Hindley [1956] Director/Baker; Philip Marshall [1974] Director/Master Baker; Alan Michael Moore [1961] Director; Martyn Anthony Taylor [1959] Director/Consultant; Dianne Gillian Davies Walker [1965] Director/Chartered Accountant; David Yates [1968] Director/Baker

Bako North Western Limited
Incorporated: 28 December 1964 *Employees:* 203
Net Worth: £10,444,000 *Total Assets:* £24,818,000
Registered Office: 74 Roman Way Industrial Estate, Longridge Road, Preston, Lancs, PR2 5BE
Activities: Other food services
Parent: Bako North Western (Group) Limited
Officers: Kirti Hirani, Secretary; Joseph Hall [1965] Director/Master Baker; Janet Hill [1961] Director; Duncan Hindley [1956] Director/Baker; Philip Marshall [1974] Director/Master Baker; Alan Michael Moore [1961] Director; Martyn Anthony Taylor [1959] Director/Consultant; Dianne Gillian Davies Walker [1965] NED Director; David Yates [1968] Director/Baker

Bako South Eastern Limited
Incorporated: 22 March 2013 *Employees:* 83
Net Worth Deficit: £5,216,000 *Total Assets:* £8,221,000
Registered Office: 74 Roman Way Industrial Estate, Longridge Road, Preston, Lancs, PR2 5BE
Activities: Other food services
Parent: Bako North Western (Group) Limited
Officers: Kirti Hirani, Secretary; Joseph Hall [1965] Director/Master Baker; Janet Hill [1961] Director; Duncan Hindley [1956] Director/Baker; Philip Marshall [1974] Director/Master Baker; Alan Michael Moore [1961] Director; Martyn Anthony Taylor [1959] Director/Consultant; Dianne Gillian Davies Walker [1965] Director/Chartered Accountant; David Yates [1968] Director/Baker

Baldwin Filters Limited
Incorporated: 31 August 1949 *Employees:* 109
Net Worth: £1,252,094 *Total Assets:* £14,314,776
Registered Office: Baldwin Filters, Aston Lane North, Preston Brook, Runcorn, Cheshire, WA7 3GA
Activities: Other manufacturing n.e.c.
Parent: Parker Hannifin Corporation
Officers: Graham Mark Ellinor [1964] Finance Director; James Alan David Elsey [1970] Human Resources Director

Dennis Baldwin Group Ltd
Incorporated: 25 March 2008 *Employees:* 22
Net Worth: £7,423,842 *Total Assets:* £9,510,601
Registered Office: Number 3 Acorn Business Park, Airedale Business Centre, Skipton, N Yorks, BD23 2UE
Activities: Activities of head offices
Shareholders: Robert Peter Baldwin; Andrea Parkin
Officers: Robert Peter Baldwin [1985] Director; Andrea Parkin [1983] Director

Ball & Young Limited
Incorporated: 20 March 1967 *Employees:* 133
Net Worth: £54,292,736 *Total Assets:* £61,055,640
Registered Office: Oldham Road, Middleton, Manchester, M24 2DB
Activities: Manufacture of plastics in primary forms
Parent: Vita (Group) Unlimited
Officers: Jonathan Mark Cheele [1961] Director; Gilbert James Davids [1968] Director/Accountant; Daniel Joseph O'Riordan [1974] Director; Ann Southern Shaw [1948] Director; Thomas James Thorp [1960] Director

Teresa Ball International Solidarity Fund
Incorporated: 26 January 2000
Net Worth: £11,037,381 *Total Assets:* £11,048,181
Registered Office: Loreto Province Offices, 28 Hartley Road, Altrincham, Cheshire, WA14 4AY
Activities: Activities of religious organisations
Officers: Sister Therese Generaldine McMcleer, Secretary/Religious Sister; Sister Bernadette Boland [1943] Director/Religious Sister; Sister Anita Maria Braganza [1962] Director/Religious Sister [Indian]; Sister Mary Noelle Corscadden [1957] Director/Religious Sister [Irish]; Sister Brenda Eagan [1956] Director/Religious Sister [American]; Sister Macarena Fernandez de Bobadilla Lassaletta [1963] Director/Religious Sister [Spanish]; Sister Anne Patricia Grant [1945] Director/Religious Sister [Canadian]; Sister Therese Generaldine McMcleer [1959] Director/Religious Sister; Sister Nora Teresa Moynihan [1949] Director/Religious Sister [Irish]; Sister Judith Nekesa [1968] Director/Religious Sister [Kenyan]; Sister Igora Pinto [1965] Director/Religious Sister [Indian]

Ballyclare Limited
Incorporated: 8 December 2010 *Employees:* 81
Net Worth: £13,074,451 *Total Assets:* £15,589,548
Registered Office: The Forum, Hercules Business Park, Bird Hall Lane, Cheadle Hume, Stockport, Cheshire, SK3 0UX
Activities: Manufacture of workwear
Parent: Uniform Brands Limited
Officers: Carlton Greener [1966] Director; Philip John Kenny [1978] Director/Solicitor; Mirvet Russo [1968] Operations Director Group [Dutch]; Kieron Bartholemew Traynor [1960] Director; Glenn Robert Walker [1958] Director/Accountant

Bamfield Lodge Limited
Incorporated: 7 February 2007 *Employees:* 92
Net Worth: £3,519,000 *Total Assets:* £8,613,000
Registered Office: Norcliffe House, Station Road, Wilmslow, Cheshire, SK9 1BU
Activities: Other human health activities
Parent: Optimum FS Care Developments Limited
Officers: Abigail Mattison, Secretary; Ryan Stuart MacAskill [1975] Director; Gregory Laurence Newman [1988] Director/Investment Professional; Jeremy Robert Arthur Richardson [1970] Director; Dr Maureen Claire Royston [1960] Director; Phillip Gary Thomas [1978] Director

Bank Restaurant Company Limited
Incorporated: 14 October 2003
Total Assets: £8,040,000
Registered Office: 4th Floor, Ridgefield House, 14 John Dalton Street, Manchester, M2 6JR
Activities: Licenced restaurants
Parent: Individual Restaurant Company Ltd
Officers: Peter David McCulloch, Secretary; Vernon Lord [1966] Director; Peter David McCulloch [1978] Finance Director; Steven John Walker [1970] Director

Banks & Lloyd (Shipping) Limited
Incorporated: 4 August 1995 *Employees:* 36
Net Worth: £6,511,358 *Total Assets:* £12,732,897
Registered Office: Brook House, Church Street, Wilmslow, Cheshire, SK9 1AX
Activities: Other transportation support activities
Officers: Diane Elizabeth Verzijl, Secretary; Daria Mikhaylovna Banks [1987] Director; Philip Paul Lucas [1979] Director; Mark Edward Rahman [1967] Director; Diane Elizabeth Verzijl [1964] Director; Vincentius Verzijl [1966] Managing Director [Dutch]

Samuel Banner & Co. Limited
Incorporated: 22 July 1991 *Employees:* 99
Net Worth: £8,592,103 *Total Assets:* £62,182,052
Registered Office: 2M House, Sutton Quays Business Park, Clifton Road, Sutton Weaver, Runcorn, Cheshire, WA7 2EH
Activities: Manufacture of other chemical products n.e.c.
Officers: Brian Robert Perry, Secretary; Colin Richard Boyle [1962] Director/Accountant; David Robert John Dalton [1954] Compliance Director; Mordechai Kessler [1955] Director; Gal Maller [1977] Managing Director

Banner Chemicals Limited
Incorporated: 8 February 1902
Net Worth: £9,708,411 *Total Assets:* £25,379,964
Registered Office: 2M House, Sutton Quays Business Park, Clifton Road, Sutton Weaver, Runcorn, Cheshire, WA7 3EH
Activities: Activities of head offices
Officers: Brian Robert Perry, Secretary; Colin Richard Boyle [1962] Director/Accountant; David Robert John Dalton [1954] Compliance Director; Mordechai Kessler [1955] Director; Gal Maller [1977] Director

Barbican Investments Limited
Incorporated: 13 July 2015
Net Worth: £7,199,166 *Total Assets:* £34,556,800
Registered Office: 5th Floor, 196 Deansgate, Manchester, M3 3WF
Activities: Activities of financial services holding companies
Major Shareholder: Gareth O'Connell
Officers: Gareth O'Connell [1971] Director [Irish]

Barclay House Securities Limited
Incorporated: 31 January 1983
Net Worth: £4,249,547 *Total Assets:* £8,709,519
Registered Office: 91 Princess Street, Manchester, M1 4HT
Activities: Buying and selling of own real estate
Parent: Carlton House Group Ltd
Officers: Frances Feingold, Secretary; Elliot Feingold [1946] Director/Solicitor

Bardsley Construction Holdings Limited
Incorporated: 7 July 2009 *Employees:* 4
Net Worth: £4,787,015 *Total Assets:* £15,660,832
Registered Office: Globe Square, Dukinfield, Cheshire, SK16 4RG
Activities: Activities of construction holding companies
Parent: Project Gabriel Limited
Officers: Roland Bardsley [1964] Director; Robert Edmund Paul Bodnar-Horvath [1956] Director; Paul Strutt [1968] Director

Bardsley Construction Limited
Incorporated: 13 April 1964 *Employees:* 184
Net Worth: £10,041,690 *Total Assets:* £26,004,510
Registered Office: Globe Square, Dukinfield, Cheshire, SK16 4RG
Activities: Construction of commercial buildings
Parent: Bardsley Construction Holdings Limited
Officers: Emma Allsopp [1976] Director/Accountant; Jonathan Kingsley Cocker [1964] Director; Sean Andrew Kempley [1968] Director; Michael John Nevitt [1975] Director; Adrian Vincent Rooney [1973] Director; Gerard Rooney [1968] Director; Paul Strutt [1968] Director

Bardsley Group Limited
Incorporated: 1 November 2012 *Employees:* 184
Net Worth: £5,845,864 *Total Assets:* £22,628,084
Registered Office: Globe Square, Globe Lane, Dukinfield, Cheshire, SK16 4RG
Activities: Activities of construction holding companies
Major Shareholder: Roland Bardsley
Officers: Roland Bardsley [1964] Director; Robert Edmund Paul Bodnar-Horvath [1956] Director; Paul Strutt [1968] Director

S J Bargh Group Limited
Incorporated: 22 March 2016 *Employees:* 447
Net Worth: £17,460,068 *Total Assets:* £29,307,152
Registered Office: S J Bargh Ltd, Caton Road, Lancaster, LA1 3PE
Activities: Freight transport by road
Shareholders: Helen Elizabeth Lloyd; Rebecca Mary Towers; Rachel Kenyon Thomas
Officers: Tonnia Michelle Park, Secretary; Anthony Raymond Finlayson-Green [1961] Director; Thomas James Lloyd [1972] Director/Farmer; Tonnia Michelle Park [1982] Director/Chartered Accountant; Rachel Kenyon Thomas [1953] Director; Rebecca Mary Towers [1950] Director

S.J.Bargh Limited
Incorporated: 20 April 1954 *Employees:* 356
Net Worth: £12,284,492 *Total Assets:* £19,642,728
Registered Office: Head Office, S J Bargh Limited, Caton Road, Lancaster, LA1 3PE
Activities: Freight transport by road
Parent: S J Bargh Group Limited
Officers: Tonnia Michelle Park, Secretary; Anthony Raymond Finlayson-Green [1961] Managing Director; Thomas James Lloyd [1972] Director/Farmer; Tonnia Michelle Park [1982] Director/Chartered Accountant; Rachel Kenyon Thomas [1953] Director; Rebecca Mary Towers [1950] Director

Barlows Childcare Properties Limited
Incorporated: 23 July 2004 *Employees:* 2
Net Worth: £2,696,754 *Total Assets:* £9,948,826
Registered Office: Joshua House, Christie Way, Christie Fields Office Park, Manchester, M21 7QY
Activities: Other letting and operating of own or leased real estate
Parent: Kids Allowed Group Limited
Officers: Dawn Rochelle Wright, Secretary; Jennifer Ann Johnson [1971] Director; Kate Elizabeth Whistance [1974] Director

Barlows Holdings Limited
Incorporated: 6 November 1920 *Employees:* 4
Net Worth: £36,208,256 *Total Assets:* £47,610,400
Registered Office: Roughlow, Willington, Tarporley, Cheshire, CW6 0PG
Activities: Buying and selling of own real estate
Parent: Barlows Limited
Officers: Richard Fildes [1945] Director

Barlows Limited
Incorporated: 10 April 2001
Net Worth: £4,124,985 *Total Assets:* £36,214,260
Registered Office: Roughlow, Willington, Tarporley, Cheshire, CW6 0PG
Activities: Buying and selling of own real estate
Parent: Squire Bowker and Son Limited
Officers: David Christopher Fildes [1934] Director/Financial Journalist; Richard Fildes [1945] Director

H.T.Barnes & Sons Limited
Incorporated: 29 August 1931 *Employees:* 2
Net Worth: £7,117,801 *Total Assets:* £7,290,706
Registered Office: Lancaster House, 70-76 Blackburn Street, Radcliffe, Manchester, M26 2JW
Activities: Development of building projects
Parent: The Frank Barnes Settlement
Officers: Christine Pamela Brookes, Secretary; Anthony Frank Brookes [1940] Managing Director; Christine Pamela Brookes [1939] Director/Company Secretary

Barnfield Construction Limited
Incorporated: 28 March 1989 *Employees:* 126
Net Worth: £7,906,435 *Total Assets:* £31,071,618
Registered Office: 8 Kenyon Road, Brierfield, Nelson, Lancs, BB9 5SP
Activities: Construction of commercial buildings
Parent: Barnfield Nelson Ltd
Officers: Andrew John Couper, Secretary; Andrew John Couper [1976] Director/Accountant; Stephen John Riley [1955] Contracts Director; James Paul Webber [1978] Director/Contracts Manager; Sheila Webber [1957] Director/Secretary; Timothy John Henry Webber [1954] Director/Builder

Barnfield Developments Limited
Incorporated: 9 March 2004 *Employees:* 2
Net Worth: £712,430 *Total Assets:* £11,529,633
Registered Office: 8 Kenyon Road, Brierfield, Nelson, Lancs, BB9 5SP
Activities: Development of building projects
Parent: Barnfield Investment Properties Ltd
Officers: Andrew John Couper, Secretary; Andrew John Couper [1976] Director/Accountant; Timothy John Henry Webber [1954] Director

Barnfield Group Limited
Incorporated: 12 March 2012 *Employees:* 155
Net Worth: £14,987,854 *Total Assets:* £44,682,844
Registered Office: 8 Kenyon Road, Brierfield, Nelson, Lancs, BB9 5SP
Activities: Activities of head offices
Shareholders: James Paul Webber; Jonathan Webber
Officers: Andrew John Couper, Secretary; James Paul Webber [1978] Director/Contracts Manager; Sheila Webber [1957] Director/Secretary; Timothy John Henry Webber [1954] Director

Barnfield Investment Properties Limited
Incorporated: 20 December 2000 *Employees:* 3
Net Worth: £7,715,235 *Total Assets:* £12,983,363
Registered Office: 8 Kenyon Road, Brierfield, Nelson, Lancs, BB9 5SP
Activities: Other letting and operating of own or leased real estate
Shareholders: Timothy John Henry Webber; Dimehome Ltd
Officers: Andrew John Couper, Secretary; Andrew John Couper [1976] Director/Accountant; Sheila Webber [1957] Director/Secretary; Timothy John Henry Webber [1954] Director/Builder

Barrett Steel Limited
Incorporated: 14 October 1992 *Employees:* 1,026
Net Worth: £51,278,000 *Total Assets:* £188,474,000
Registered Office: Barrett House, Cutler Heights Lane, Dudley Hill, Bradford, BD4 9HU
Activities: Wholesale of metals and metal ores
Shareholders: Richard Braithwaite Barrett; James Stephenson Barrett
Officers: Marcus Tyldsley, Secretary; James Stephenson Barrett [1955] Director; Richard Braithwaite Barrett [1957] Director/Structural Engineer; Marcus Tyldsley [1980] Director/Chartered Accountant; Andrew Warcup [1965] Director

Tom Barron Limited
Incorporated: 24 March 1956 *Employees:* 123
Net Worth: £968,882 *Total Assets:* £9,217,266
Registered Office: The Poultry Farm, Square Lane, Catforth, Preston, Lancs, PR4 0HQ
Activities: Raising of poultry
Officers: Martin William Delaney, Secretary; David Harrison [1946] Director/Solicitor; Frank Barron Leeming [1954] Director/Farmer; Michael John Leeming [1982] Director/Farm Manager; Neil William Leeming [1957] Director/Farmer; Richard Neil William Leeming [1980] Director/General Manager; Martin Barron Tomlinson [1956] Director/Farmer

Barros Trading Ltd
Incorporated: 20 June 2014
Net Worth: £5,538,471 *Total Assets:* £16,790,036
Registered Office: 47 Bury New Road, Prestwich, Manchester, M25 9JY
Activities: Buying and selling of own real estate
Officers: Benjamin Daniel Rosenberg [1985] Director/Businessman; David Jonathan Rosenberg [1956] Director/Businessman

Barrowway No. 1 Limited
Incorporated: 18 November 2015
Net Worth: £8,760,851 *Total Assets:* £48,386,776
Registered Office: Canal Mill, Botany Brow, Chorley, Lancs, PR6 9AF
Activities: Activities of other holding companies n.e.c.
Parent: Acepark Limited
Officers: Claire Caroline Sharp, Secretary; Thomas Duncan Hopkinson [1956] Director/Chartered Accountant; Timothy John Peter Knowles [1964] Director; Claire Caroline Sharp [1973] Property Director

Barrowway No. 2 Limited
Incorporated: 18 November 2015
Net Worth: £8,000,000 *Total Assets:* £45,838,768
Registered Office: Canal Mill, Botany Brow, Chorley, Lancs, PR6 9AF
Activities: Activities of other holding companies n.e.c.
Parent: Barrowway No 1 Limited
Officers: Claire Caroline Sharp, Secretary; Thomas Duncan Hopkinson [1956] Director/Chartered Accountant; Timothy John Peter Knowles [1963] Director; Claire Caroline Sharp [1973] Property Director

T. & J.T. Barton (Bottlers) Limited
Incorporated: 19 January 1978 *Employees:* 39
Net Worth: £6,142,318 *Total Assets:* £8,909,754
Registered Office: 410 Bolton Road, Ashton in Makerfield, Wigan, Lancs, WN4 8UN
Activities: Wholesale of wine, beer, spirits and other alcoholic beverages
Parent: T. & J.T Barton (Holdings) Limited
Officers: John Thomas Barton, Secretary; John Thomas Barton [1947] Director; Margaret Gallagher [1943] Director

T & J T Barton (Holdings) Ltd
Incorporated: 22 March 2016 *Employees:* 39
Net Worth: £6,142,313 *Total Assets:* £8,909,754
Registered Office: 410 Bolton Road, Ashton in Makerfield, Wigan, Lancs, WN4 8UW
Activities: Activities of head offices
Shareholders: John Thomas Barton; Margaret Gallagher
Officers: John Thomas Barton [1947] Director; Margaret Gallagher [1943] Director

Barton and Redman Limited
Incorporated: 14 September 1964
Net Worth: £2,419,239 *Total Assets:* £9,477,357
Registered Office: Strawberry House, New Smithfield Market, Whitworth Street East, Manchester, M11 2WJ
Activities: Wholesale of fruit and vegetables
Officers: Paul Stewart Barton, Secretary/Manager; Matthew Paul Barton [1982] Director/Salesman; Paul Stewart Barton [1959] Director/Manager; Peter Barton [1968] Director/Salesman; Robert John Barton [1961] Director/Manager; Thomas Raymond Paul Barton [1985] Director/Salesman; Thomas Christopher Barton [1954] Director/Manager

The Barton Grange Group Limited
Incorporated: 17 February 1958 *Employees:* 403
Net Worth: £14,245,323 *Total Assets:* £21,818,548
Registered Office: Garstang Road, Brock, Preston, Lancs, PR3 0BT
Activities: Plant propagation
Shareholder: Edward George Topping
Officers: Jonathan Heaton [1954] Director/Chartered Accountant; Edward Peter Topping [1961] Director; Edward George Topping [1932] Director; Guy Topping [1965] Director

Barton Park Estates Limited
Incorporated: 26 March 2003 *Employees:* 6
Net Worth: £3,788,885 *Total Assets:* £9,721,587
Registered Office: Offices G12-G16, City Lab, 4-6 Dalton Square, Lancaster, LA1 1PP
Activities: Recreational vehicle parks, trailer parks and camping grounds
Shareholders: Charles Howard Barton Jnr; Charles Howard Barton
Officers: Anita Louise Barton, Secretary; Anita Louise Barton [1951] Director/Caravan Park Operator; Charles Howard Barton [1948] Director/Caravan Park Operator; Charles Howard Barton Jnr [1987] Director

Barton Park Homes Limited
Incorporated: 18 February 2000
Net Worth: £5,253,610 *Total Assets:* £8,132,259
Registered Office: Offices G12-G16, Citylab, 4-6 Dalton Square, Lancaster, LA1 1PP
Activities: Other retail sale not in stores, stalls or markets
Shareholders: Anita Louise Barton; Charles Howard Barton; Ian John Norman Gee
Officers: Anita Louise Barton, Secretary; Anita Louise Barton [1951] Director/Residential Park Home Operator; Charles Howard Barton [1948] Director/Residential Park Home Operator; Charles Barton Jnr [1987] Director/Mobile Home Salesman

Barwick Bathroom Distribution LLP
Incorporated: 30 November 2005 *Employees:* 96
Net Worth: £5,049,963 *Total Assets:* £11,872,946
Registered Office: 40 Wharfedale Road, Euroway Industrial Estate, Bradford, W Yorks, BD4 6SG
Officers: John Barwick [1953] Member; Michael Gabriel Barwick [1951] Member; Richard Brian Bower [1964] Member

Basell Polyolefins UK Limited
Incorporated: 21 April 1993 *Employees:* 150
Net Worth: £79,602,000 *Total Assets:* £115,806,000
Registered Office: Carrington Site, Urmston, Manchester, M31 4AJ
Activities: Manufacture of plastics in primary forms
Parent: Basell UK Holdings Limited
Officers: Ana Belen Campor Alegre [1966] Director [Spanish]; Muhammad Adil Quresh [1986] Director/Corporate Finance Manager UK

Basell UK Holdings Limited
Incorporated: 5 May 1995
Net Worth: £55,811,000 *Total Assets:* £57,002,000
Registered Office: Carrington Site, Urmston, Manchester, M31 4AJ
Activities: Activities of head offices
Parent: Lyondellbasell Industries N.V.
Officers: Benedictus Joseph Johannes Buckers [1964] Director, Polypropylene & Catalloy Europe [Dutch]; Muhammad Adil Qureshi [1986] Director/Corporate Finance Manager UK

BASF Agricultural Specialities Limited
Incorporated: 1 June 1982 *Employees:* 35
Net Worth: £12,471,000 *Total Assets:* £14,914,000
Registered Office: P O Box 4, Earl Road, Cheadle Hulme, Cheadle, Cheshire, SK8 6QG
Activities: Other manufacturing n.e.c.
Parent: Becker-Underwood (UK) Limited
Officers: Helen Victoria Koerner, Secretary; Richard John Carter [1962] Managing Director UK/Ireland; Karen Lois Harper [1964] Director/Head of HR UK & Ireland; Thomas Urwin [1966] Director/Finance Manager UK & Ireland

BASF Pharma (Callanish) Limited
Incorporated: 13 July 2005 *Employees:* 70
Net Worth Deficit: £19,648,000 *Total Assets:* £38,821,000
Registered Office: BASF, P O Box 4, Earl Road, Cheadle Hulme, Cheadle, Cheshire, SK8 6QG
Activities: Manufacture of oils and fats
Parent: BASF SE
Officers: Helen Victoria Koerner, Secretary; Richard John Carter [1962] Managing Director UK/Ireland; Karen Lois Harper [1964] Director/Head of HR UK & Ireland; Thomas Urwin [1966] Director/Finance Manager

BASF Public Limited Company
Incorporated: 18 August 1960 *Employees:* 1,128
Net Worth: £72,742,000 *Total Assets:* £411,519,008
Registered Office: Earl Road, Cheadle Hulme, Cheadle, Cheshire, SK8 6QG
Activities: Manufacture of other organic basic chemicals
Parent: BASF U.K. Holdings Limited
Officers: Helen Victoria Koerner, Secretary/Legal Counsel; Richard John Carter [1962] Managing Director UK/Ireland; Karen Lois Harper [1964] Director/Head of HR UK & Ireland; Geoffrey William Mackey [1965] Director/Head of Sustainable Development; Harald Pflanzl [1966] Director/Head of Subregion North West & Central Europe [Austrian]; Thomas Urwin [1966] Director/Finance Manager UK & Ireland

BASF U.K. Holdings Limited
Incorporated: 20 June 1997
Net Worth: £141,392,000 *Total Assets:* £141,392,000
Registered Office: P O Box 4, Earl Road, Cheadle Hulme, Cheadle, Stockport, Cheshire, SK8 6QG
Activities: Non-trading company
Parent: BASF SE
Officers: Helen Victoria Koerner, Secretary; Richard John Carter [1962] Managing Director UK/Ireland; Thomas Urwin [1966] Director/Accountant

Henry Bath & Son Limited
Incorporated: 1 January 1920
Net Worth: £20,777,452 *Total Assets:* £62,537,588
Registered Office: 12 Princes Parade, Liverpool, L3 1BG
Activities: Operation of warehousing and storage facilities for land transport activities
Officers: Phillip James Smith, Secretary; Jin Han [1964] Director/Board Member; Tielin Han [1958] Director/Chairman [Chinese]; Jianyun Sun [1984] Director/Investment Officer [Chinese]; Chiwei Wang [1955] Director/Senior Advisor [Chinese]; Haibin Wang [1968] Director/General Manager [Chinese]

Bathgate Flooring Limited
Incorporated: 25 February 2004 *Employees:* 73
Net Worth: £2,033,145 *Total Assets:* £7,217,655
Registered Office: c/o Langtons, The Plaza, 100 Hall Street, Liverpool, L3 9QJ
Activities: Manufacture of veneer sheets and wood-based panels
Parent: Archibald Bathgate Group Limited
Officers: Stephen Ian Bennett, Secretary; Stephen Ian Bennett [1969] Director/Accountant; Paul Freeman [1969] Manufacturing Director; Andrew John Hubbard [1957] Director; Karl Daniel Rye [1963] Contracts Director; Ernest Thomas Smyth [1960] Contracts Director; Roderick Hughes Walker [1935] Director

Bathgate Silica Sand Limited
Incorporated: 11 February 1916 *Employees:* 32
Net Worth: £7,422,517 *Total Assets:* £10,278,982
Registered Office: c/o Langtons, The Plaza, 100 Old Hall Street, Liverpool, L3 9QJ
Activities: Operation of gravel and sand pits; mining of clays and kaolin
Parent: Archibald Bathgate Group Limited
Officers: Stephen Ian Bennett, Secretary/Accountant; Stephen Ian Bennett [1969] Director/Accountant; David Robinson [1963] Director; Colin Sanders [1978] Commercial Director; Barbara Ann Walker [1935] Director/Married Woman; Ian Hughes Walker [1965] Director/Farmer; Roderick Hughes Walker [1935] Director/Chartered Accountant

Bawnbua Foods GB Ltd
Incorporated: 10 February 1987 *Employees:* 95
Net Worth: £3,873,819 *Total Assets:* £9,050,809
Registered Office: Ormside Close, Hindley Industrial Estate, Hindley, Wigan, Lancs, WN2 4HR
Activities: Production of meat and poultry meat products
Officers: Gary White, Secretary; David White [1976] Director [Irish]; Gary White [1973] Director/Marketing Manager [Irish]; Martin Patrick White [1979] Director/Operations Manager [Irish]; Martin Patrick White [1950] Director/Businessman [Irish]

The Bay Learning Trust
Incorporated: 1 April 2011 *Employees:* 190
Net Worth: £12,022,000 *Total Assets:* £14,926,000
Registered Office: The Lodge, Ripley St Thomas CE Academy, Ashton Road, Lancaster, LA1 4RR
Activities: General secondary education
Officers: Andrew McKinnell, Secretary; Peter Ballard [1955] Director/Chief Executive; Dawn Elizabeth Cheetham [1963] Director; Professor John David Crewdson [1942] Director; Michael Henry Dudfield [1947] Director/Solicitor; Jacqueline Gloria Garnett [1956] Director/Retired; Nicola Gomersall [1971] Director/Headteacher; Elizabeth Olive Nicholls [1953] Director/Principal; Jane Margaret Watson [1963] Managing Director; Robert Mitchel Webb [1950] Managing Director; Valerie Margaret Wilson [1947] Director/District Councillor

Baybutt Investments Limited
Incorporated: 15 January 2016 *Employees:* 93
Net Worth: £4,444,506 *Total Assets:* £8,901,221
Registered Office: Hodsons Farm, 467 Moss Lane, Hesketh Bank, Preston, Lancs, PR4 6XJ
Activities: Activities of other holding companies n.e.c.
Shareholders: Jamie Ross Baybutt; Robert Alan Baybutt; Ruth Baybutt
Officers: Jamie Ross Baybutt [1979] Director; Robert Alan Baybutt [1949] Director; Ruth Baybutt [1949] Director

Baywater Healthcare UK Limited
Incorporated: 1 March 2013 *Employees:* 219
Net Worth: £9,596,000 *Total Assets:* £20,840,000
Registered Office: 2 Millennium Gate, Westmere Drive, Crewe, Cheshire, CW1 6XB
Activities: Other human health activities
Parent: Kent Midco Limited
Officers: Vincent Bastide [1969] Director [French]; Arnaud Fayolle [1975] Director/Deputy CEO [French]; Howard Lee Jones [1957] Director; Olivier Jourdanney [1974] Director/Deputy CEO [French]; Adam Michael Sullivan [1968] Director

BB Legal Limited
Incorporated: 1 July 2010 *Employees:* 306
Net Worth: £1,708,759 *Total Assets:* £9,747,579
Registered Office: 20 Kennedy Street, Manchester, M2 4BY
Activities: Solicitors
Major Shareholder: Michael John Foxford
Officers: Paul Edward Pickering, Secretary; Michael John Foxford [1962] Director/Solicitor; Catherine Leah MacCracken [1969] Director/Solicitor; Jamie Patton [1970] Director/Solicitor; Paul Edward Pickering [1973] Director/Solicitor; Andrew Carberry Rattray [1965] Director/Accountant

BBC Children in Need
Incorporated: 4 April 2003 *Employees:* 136
Net Worth: £45,127,000 *Total Assets:* £136,591,008
Registered Office: Bridge House, Media City UK, Salford, M50 2BH
Activities: Other business support service activities n.e.c.
Officers: Peter Ranyard, Secretary; Matthew James Baker [1977] Director/TV Presenter; Joanna Berry [1968] Director/Solicitor (Non-Practising) and Author; Anne Christine Bulford [1959] Director; Christopher Luke Mayhew [1953] Director; Professor Peter Arthur James McBride [1964] Director; Rosemary Harriet Millard [1965] Director/Broadcaster/Journalist; Gillian Veronica Sheldon [1967] Director/Banking; Robert Duncan James Shennan [1962] Director/BBC Controller Radio 2; Alice Elizabeth Webb [1972] Director

BC1.0 Ltd
Incorporated: 18 November 2009
Net Worth Deficit: £572,551 *Total Assets:* £38,571,288
Registered Office: Building 2, 3rd Floor, Universal Square, Devonshire Street North, Manchester, M12 6JH
Activities: Other letting and operating of own or leased real estate
Major Shareholder: Naeem Kauser
Officers: Carol Allen [1963] Director; Graham Edward Lake [1944] Director/Solicitor

BC21.0 Ltd
Incorporated: 18 November 2009 *Employees:* 3
Net Worth Deficit: £1,262,020 *Total Assets:* £14,627,137
Registered Office: Building 2, 3rd Floor, Universal Square, Devonshire Street North, Manchester, M12 6JH
Activities: Other letting and operating of own or leased real estate
Major Shareholder: Naeem Kauser
Officers: Carol Allen [1963] Director; Graham Edward Lake [1944] Director/Solicitor

BC3.01 Ltd
Incorporated: 18 November 2009 *Employees:* 3
Net Worth Deficit: £1,583,747 *Total Assets:* £8,394,424
Registered Office: Building 2, 3rd Floor, Universal Square, Devonshire Street North, Manchester, M12 6JH
Activities: Other letting and operating of own or leased real estate
Major Shareholder: Naeem Kauser
Officers: Carol Allen [1963] Director; Graham Edward Lake [1944] Director/Solicitor

BCP Corporate Limited
Incorporated: 6 July 2004 *Employees:* 3
Net Worth: £5,098,000 *Total Assets:* £8,946,000
Registered Office: Crompton House, Nuttalls Way, Blackburn, Lancs, BB1 2JT
Activities: Activities of head offices
Parent: Huhtamaki Finance Limited UK
Officers: Philip John Covill [1970] Director/Financial Controller; Tarja Iitti [1959] Director/Group Controller [Finnish]

BCW Engineering Ltd
Incorporated: 21 November 2002 *Employees:* 134
Net Worth: £2,138,436 *Total Assets:* £11,897,723
Registered Office: 2 Innovation Drive, Burnley, Lancs, BB10 2FT
Activities: Other engineering activities
Parent: BCW Central Services Ltd
Officers: Andrew Whelan, Secretary/Director; Alec Gordon Stewart Cassie [1955] Director; Andrew Whelan [1949] Director

BDP Holdings Limited
Incorporated: 2 August 2000 *Employees:* 863
Net Worth: £18,202,288 *Total Assets:* £52,980,016
Registered Office: P O Box 85, 11 Ducie Street, Piccadilly Basin, Manchester, M60 3JA
Activities: Activities of head offices
Parent: Nippon Koei Co.,Ltd
Officers: Heather Olwyn Wells, Secretary; Ryuichi Arimoto [1952] Director/Business Management [Japanese]; Yoshikimi Inoue [1954] Director/Civil Engineer [Japanese]; John McManus [1957] Director/Architect; Takayasu Tsuyusaki [1956] Director/Business Management [Japanese]; Heather Olwyn Wells [1964] Finance Director

Beaconsfield Footwear Limited
Incorporated: 6 November 1959 *Employees:* 943
Net Worth: £37,075,000 *Total Assets:* £57,228,000
Registered Office: 2 Peel Road, Skelmersdale, Lancs, WN8 9PT
Activities: Manufacture of footwear
Officers: Andrew James Buckley [1970] Director/Chief Financial Officer; Robert Clive Perkins [1963] Operations Director; Sara Ellen Prowse [1969] Director/Chief Executive

Beamfeature Limited
Incorporated: 20 June 1986 *Employees:* 35
Net Worth: £6,348,992 *Total Assets:* £8,008,004
Registered Office: 3 Adbaston Road, Cobra Court, Stretford, Manchester, M32 0TP
Activities: manufacture of household textiles
Shareholders: Kevin Rylatt; James Rylatt
Officers: Anita Ruia, Secretary; Suresh Ruia [1954] Director/Textile Merchant; James Rylatt [1950] Director; Kevin Rylatt [1955] Director

Beauchamp Real Estate Holdings Limited
Incorporated: 30 April 2010
Net Worth: £18,839,880 *Total Assets:* £33,059,130
Registered Office: Cumberland House, Greenside Lane, Bradford, BD8 9TF
Activities: Activities of property unit trusts
Parent: Praxisifm Trustees (UK) Limited
Officers: Claire Marie Cain [1970] Director; Christopher Stephen Smith [1972] Director

Beauland Limited
Incorporated: 23 January 1981
Net Worth: £10,635,668 *Total Assets:* £13,705,542
Registered Office: 309 Bury New Road, Salford, M7 2YN
Activities: Other social work activities without accommodation n.e.c.
Officers: Pinchas Neumann, Secretary; Janet Bleier [1958] Director; Rebbecca de Lange [1962] Director; Miriam Friedlander [1951] Director; Esther Henry [1959] Director; Eli Neumann [1955] Director; Henry Neumann [1956] Director; Maurice Neumann [1949] Director; Pinchas Neumann [1952] Director; Hanna Roseman [1961] Director

Beauty Source Limited
Incorporated: 16 February 2000 *Employees:* 3
Net Worth: £74,828,000 *Total Assets:* £86,899,000
Registered Office: Manchester Business Park, 3500 Aviator Way, Manchester, M22 5TG
Activities: Other service activities n.e.c.
Parent: St. Tropez Acquisition Co. Limited
Officers: Simon Paul Plant, Secretary; Brandon Howard Leigh [1971] Director; Simon Paul Plant [1969] Director

Beaverbrooks The Jewellers Ltd
Incorporated: 11 December 1936 *Employees:* 916
Net Worth: £67,863,000 *Total Assets:* £84,834,000
Registered Office: Adele House, Park Road, St Annes on Sea, Lancs, FY8 1RE
Activities: Retail sale of watches and jewellery in specialised stores
Shareholders: Gerald David Adlestone; Andrew Brown
Officers: Susan Judith Graham, Secretary; Generald David Adlestone [1930] Director/Jeweller; Mark Isaac Adlestone [1959] Director/Jeweller; Anna Blackburn [1975] Managing Director; Andrew Brown [1946] Director/Jeweller

Becker Holdings Limited
Incorporated: 20 February 2002 *Employees:* 5
Net Worth: £2,978,000 *Total Assets:* £12,585,000
Registered Office: Goodlass Road, Speke, Liverpool, L24 9HJ
Activities: Activities of head offices
Major Shareholder: Jenny Linden Urnes
Officers: David Neale, Secretary; Anthony David Bowen [1957] Director/Accountant; Mats Nils Ole Hansson [1954] Director [Swedish]; Olivier Laune [1967] Director/Group Financial Controller [French]; David Neale [1963] Director/Accountant; Paul Stephen Thomas [1958] Managing Director

Becker Industrial Coatings Limited
Incorporated: 18 January 1961 *Employees:* 132
Net Worth: £8,044,000 *Total Assets:* £25,124,000
Registered Office: Goodlass Road, Speke, Liverpool, L24 9HJ
Activities: Manufacture of paints, varnishes and similar coatings, mastics and sealants
Parent: Becker Holdings Limited
Officers: David Neale, Secretary; Olivier Pierre Roger Laune [1967] Director/Financial Controller [French]; David Neale [1963] Director/Accountant; Johan Sandstrom [1961] Director/Coil Coatings Manager [Swedish]; Richard Harold Steele [1957] Director/Business Manager; Paul Stephen Thomas [1958] Managing Director; Christian Vogel [1973] Director/President Industrial Coatings [German]

Beckhall Properties Ltd
Incorporated: 27 May 1999 *Employees:* 3
Net Worth: £10,664,145 *Total Assets:* £25,408,084
Registered Office: c/o DBS, 40 Lower Hillgate, Stockport, Cheshire, SK1 1JE
Activities: Buying and selling of own real estate
Officers: Karl Nolan [1970] Director/Consultant

Becontree Limited
Incorporated: 17 January 2002
Net Worth: £1,380,065 *Total Assets:* £8,064,431
Registered Office: 39 Whittaker Lane, Prestwich, Manchester, M25 1HA
Activities: Buying and selling of own real estate
Officers: Roselyne Steinberg, Secretary/Director; Daniel Theodore Klein [1978] Director; Patrice Bernard Klein [1950] Director [French]; Karen Liss [1980] Director; Israel Steinberg [1967] Director Property Investment; Roselyne Steinberg [1968] Director

Bed Factory Hotels Limited
Incorporated: 18 June 1999 *Employees:* 57
Net Worth: £6,812,551 *Total Assets:* £11,316,265
Registered Office: c/o Edwards Veeder (UK) Limited, Ground Floor, 4 Broadgate, Broadway Business Park, Chadderton, Oldham, Lancs, OL9 9XA
Activities: Hotels and similar accommodation
Parent: Compass Hospitality Holdings (UK) Limited
Officers: Chye Teen Lim [1981] Director [Singaporean]; Harmil Singh [1962] Director/President & CEO [Singaporean]; Satkirath Singh [1993] Director [Singaporean]

Beech Developments (Manchester) Limited
Incorporated: 16 November 2015
Net Worth: £3,709,435 *Total Assets:* £14,523,410
Registered Office: 60 Oxford Street, Manchester, M1 5EE
Activities: Construction of commercial buildings
Parent: S B Holdings Manchester Ltd
Officers: Stephen Jonathan Beech [1977] Director

Beech Holdings (Manchester) Limited
Incorporated: 26 November 2014
Net Worth Deficit: £1,022,160 *Total Assets:* £25,598,660
Registered Office: 60 Oxford Street, Manchester, M1 5EE
Activities: Other letting and operating of own or leased real estate
Major Shareholder: Stehpen Beech
Officers: Stephen Beech [1977] Director

Beechfield Brands Holdings Limited
Incorporated: 22 December 2005 *Employees:* 35
Net Worth: £13,027,395 *Total Assets:* £15,877,000
Registered Office: Silverpoint, Moor Street, Bury, Lancs, BL9 5AQ
Activities: Wholesale of textiles
Major Shareholder: Roger McHugh
Officers: Roger McHugh, Secretary/Managing Director; Peter McHugh [1969] Logistics Director; Roger McHugh [1968] Managing Director

Beechfield Brands Limited
Incorporated: 28 July 1994 *Employees:* 34
Net Worth: £14,094,308 *Total Assets:* £17,586,334
Registered Office: Silverpoint, Moor Street, Bury, Lancs, BL9 5AQ
Activities: Wholesale of textiles
Parent: Beechfield Brands Holdings Limited
Officers: Shelley Jayne Bates, Secretary; Peter McHugh [1969] Logistics Director; Roger McHugh [1968] Managing Director

M & A Beer Holdings Limited
Incorporated: 1 August 2008 *Employees:* 120
Net Worth: £2,665,375 *Total Assets:* £10,598,485
Registered Office: Windrush, 15 Links Hey Road, Wirral, Merseyside, CH48 1NA
Activities: Activities of head offices
Shareholders: Michael John Thomas Beer; Alan James Beer
Officers: Alan James Beer [1966] Director; Michael John Thomas Beer [1958] Director

Beers Timber & Building Supplies Limited
Incorporated: 19 November 2001 *Employees:* 120
Net Worth: £3,895,093 *Total Assets:* £10,314,144
Registered Office: 1 Boundary Street, Liverpool, L5 9UD
Activities: Wholesale of wood, construction materials and sanitary equipment
Shareholders: Michael John Thomas Beer; Alan James Beer
Officers: Michelle Clare Moulds, Secretary; Alan James Beer [1966] Director; Michael John Thomas Beer [1958] Director; Paul Stephen Conboy [1967] Director; Simon Thomas Geering [1970] Director

Beesley & Fildes Limited
Incorporated: 10 August 1989 *Employees:* 223
Net Worth: £7,653,252 *Total Assets:* £19,101,092
Registered Office: Wilson Road, Huyton, Merseyside, L36 6AF
Activities: Agents involved in the sale of timber and building materials
Shareholders: John Francis Beesley; Paul Beesley
Officers: Lee Anthony Davies, Secretary/Managing Director; Jean Sanderson Beesley [1954] Director/Sales Administrator; John Francis Beesley [1956] Director/Builders Merchant; Julie Susan Beesley [1958] Director/Sales Administrator; Paul Beesley [1962] Director/Builders Merchant; Lee Anthony Davies [1972] Managing Director; Stephen Leslie Welch [1960] Director/Salesman

Beesley Fuels Ltd
Incorporated: 30 September 1997 *Employees:* 12
Net Worth: £6,135,693 *Total Assets:* £8,095,292
Registered Office: The Oil Centre, Bury New Road, Heap Bridge, Bury, Lancs, BL9 7HY
Activities: Wholesale of other fuels and related products
Parent: Crown Oil Ltd
Officers: Adrian John Greenhalgh, Secretary; Mark Christopher Andrews [1976] Director; Adrian John Greenhalgh [1968] Director/Accountant; Matthew Craig Greensmith [1973] Director

Begbies Traynor (Central) LLP
Incorporated: 16 January 2004 *Employees:* 232
Net Worth: £38,560,972 *Total Assets:* £42,184,000
Registered Office: 340 Deansgate, Manchester, M3 4LY
Officers: Paul Barber [1969] LLP Member; Brett Lee Barton [1974] LLP Member; Louise Baxter [1971] LLP Member; Jon Beard [1966] LLP Member; Lloyd Biscoe [1974] LLP Member; David Adam Broadbent [1975] LLP Member; Kenneth Robert Craig [1961] LLP Member; Mary Anne Currie-Smith [1961] LLP Member; Peter Richard Dewey [1958] LLP Member; Andrew David Dick [1965] LLP Member; Andrew James Dunn [1964] LLP Member; John Valentine Fairbrother [1962] LLP Member; Ian Soloman Robert Franses [1945] LLP Member; Jason Greenhalgh [1972] LLP Member; Simon Haskew [1959] LLP Member; David Hill [1953] LLP Member; William John Kelly [1953] LLP Member; Generald Maurice Krasner [1949] LLP Member; Gary Lee [1967] LLP Member; Adam David Livermore [1980] LLP Member; Andrew MacKenzie [1971] LLP Member; Mark Malone [1978] LLP Member; Robert Maxwell [1965] LLP Member; Thomas McKay [1982] LLP Member; Jonathan Peter Munnery [1959] LLP Member; Julie Anne Palmer [1965] LLP Member; Kenneth Wilson Pattullo [1964] LLP Member; Julian Nigel Richard Pitts [1961] LLP Member; Huw Morgan Powell [1979] LLP Member; Stephen Mark Powell [1971] LLP Member; Gareth Prince [1977] LLP Member; Richard Pugh [1965] LLP Member; Nicholas Edward Reed [1963] LLP Member; Paul Stanley [1962] LLP Member; Jamie Taylor [1960] LLP Member; David Geraint Thomas [1978] LLP Member; Richard William Traynor [1959] LLP Member; Keith Thomas Tully [1975] LLP Member; Neil Vinnicombe [1967] LLP Member; Ian Edward Walker [1951] LLP Member; John Alfred Waller [1959] LLP Member; John Walters [1969] LLP Member; Dean Watson [1973] LLP Member; Simon James Watson [1974] LLP Member; Paul David Wood [1974] LLP Member; Gareth John Woodward [1953] LLP Member; Joanne Sara Wright [1968] LLP Member

Begbies Traynor (London) LLP
Incorporated: 28 May 2016 *Employees:* 15
Net Worth: £5,489,798 *Total Assets:* £6,572,103
Registered Office: 340 Deansgate, Manchester, M3 4LY
Officers: David Neil Kenneth Abbott [1974] LLP Member; Mark Robert Fry [1967] LLP Member; Carla Dianne Matthews [1977] LLP Member; Kirstie Provan [1977] LLP Member; Gary Shankland [1979] LLP Member

Begbies Traynor Group PLC
Incorporated: 5 May 2004 *Employees:* 538
Net Worth: £58,100,000 *Total Assets:* £96,445,000
Registered Office: 340 Deansgate, Manchester, M3 4LY
Activities: Activities of head offices
Officers: John Ashton Humphrey, Secretary; Mark Robert Fry [1967] Director/Insolvency Practitioner; John Michael May [1955] Director; Randolf Graham McInnes [1952] Director/Corporate Financier; Mark Stupples [1962] Director/Chartered Surveyor; Edward Nicholas Taylor [1970] Director/Chartered Accountant; Richard William Traynor [1959] Director

Begbies Traynor Limited
Incorporated: 13 March 1995 *Employees:* 46
Net Worth Deficit: £2,352,900 *Total Assets:* £56,336,496
Registered Office: 340 Deansgate, Manchester, M3 4LY
Activities: Activities of head offices
Parent: Begbies Traynor Group PLC
Officers: John Ashton Humphrey, Secretary; Edward Nicholas Taylor [1970] Director/Chartered Accountant; Richard William Traynor [1959] Director/Chartered Accountant

Beis Yaakov Jewish High School Academy
Incorporated: 12 July 2012 *Employees:* 96
Net Worth: £6,2[illegible]3,804 *Total Assets:* £6,574,721
Registered Office: 69 Broom Lane, Salford, M7 4FF
Activities: General secondary education
Officers: Anthony Michael Brandeis [1944] Director; David Ziskind [1968] Director/Solicitor

Bejam Group Limited
Incorporated: 5 October 1967
Net Worth Deficit: £293,000 *Total Assets:* £90,537,000
Registered Office: Second Avenue, Deeside Industrial Park, Deeside, Flintshire, CH5 2NW
Activities: Activities of head offices
Parent: Iceland Midco Limited
Officers: Duncan Andrew Vaughan, Secretary; Tarsem Singh Dhaliwal [1963] Director; Duncan Andrew Vaughan [1972] Company Secretary & Legal Director

Bekaert Bradford UK Limited
Incorporated: 3 December 1907 *Employees:* 107
Net Worth: £10,126,969 *Total Assets:* £13,544,197
Registered Office: Park House Road, Low Moor, Bradford, W Yorks, BD12 0PX
Activities: Cold drawing of bars
Parent: NV Bekaert SA
Officers: David Charles Smith, Secretary; Jan Boelens [1965] Director [Belgian]; Serge Piceu [1976] Director [Belgian]; Piet Van Riet [1962] Director [Belgian]

Belden UK Holdings Limited
Incorporated: 20 November 2014 *Employees:* 3
Net Worth Deficit: £5,540,649 *Total Assets:* £20,258,520
Registered Office: Suite 13, Manchester International Office Centre, Styal Road, Manchester, M22 5WB
Activities: Activities of other holding companies n.e.c.
Parent: Belden, Inc.
Officers: Brian Edward Anderson [1974] Director/Attorney [American]; Holger Busch [1972] Director Legal EMEA [German]; Alec Thomas Lappe [1981] Director/Business Executive [American]; Anne La Belle Malyszko [1980] Director/Vice President [American]

Belden UK Limited
Incorporated: 20 December 1993
Net Worth: £7,480,648 *Total Assets:* £26,440,948
Registered Office: Suite 13, Manchester International Office Centre, Styal Road, Manchester, M22 5WB
Activities: Manufacture of other electronic and electric wires and cables
Parent: Belden, Inc.
Officers: Brian Edward Anderson [1974] Director/General Counsel [American]; Hendrikus Petrus Cornelis Derksen [1969] Director/Chief Financial Officer [Dutch]

AJ Bell Holdings Limited
Incorporated: 5 August 2002 *Employees:* 656
Net Worth: £61,362,000 *Total Assets:* £76,032,000
Registered Office: 4 Exchange Quay, Salford Quays, Manchester, M5 3EE
Activities: Activities of head offices
Shareholders: Andrew James Bell; Invesco Asset Management Limited
Officers: Christopher Bruce Robinson, Secretary; Andrew James Bell [1966] Director/Actuary; Laura Martine Carstensen [1960] Director; Eamonn Michael Flanagan [1963] Director; Leslie Michael Platts [1954] Director/Chartered Accountant; Michael Thomas Summersgill [1983] Director/Accountant; Simon Turner [1951] Director

AJ Bell Limited
Incorporated: 15 August 1995 *Employees:* 26
Net Worth: £4,173,000 *Total Assets:* £15,649,000
Registered Office: 4 Exchange Quay, Salford Quays, Manchester, M5 3EE
Activities: Activities auxiliary to financial intermediation n.e.c.
Parent: A J Bell Holdings Limited
Officers: Christopher Bruce Robinson, Secretary; Andrew James Bell [1966] Director/Actuary; Charles William Galbraith [1962] Managing Director; Fergus John Lyons [1961] Director [Irish]; Louis Petherick [1975] Director/Chief Risk Officer; Christopher Bruce Robinson [1956] Group Legal Services Director; Roger John Stott [1965] Finance Director; Michael Thomas Summersgill [1983] Director/Accountant

AJ Bell Management Limited
Incorporated: 15 March 2000 *Employees:* 432
Net Worth: £14,232,000 *Total Assets:* £18,434,000
Registered Office: 4 Exchange Quay, Salford Quays, Manchester, M5 3EE
Activities: Activities auxiliary to financial intermediation n.e.c.
Parent: A J Bell Holdings Limited
Officers: Christopher Bruce Robinson, Secretary; Andrew James Bell [1966] Director/Actuary; Charles William Galbraith [1962] Managing Director; Fergus John Lyons [1961] Director [Irish]; Louis Petherick [1975] Director/Chief Risk Officer; Christopher Bruce Robinson [1956] Group Legal Services Director; Roger John Stott [1965] Finance Director; Michael Thomas Summersgill [1983] Director/Accountant

AJ Bell Securities Limited
Incorporated: 16 June 1992 *Employees:* 795
Net Worth: £23,823,000 *Total Assets:* £27,992,000
Registered Office: 4 Exchange Quay, Salford Quays, Manchester, M5 3EE
Activities: Security and commodity contracts dealing activities
Parent: A J Bell Holdings Limited
Officers: Christopher Bruce Robinson, Secretary; Andrew James Bell [1966] Director/Actuary; Charles William Galbraith [1962] Managing Director; Fergus John Lyons [1961] Director [Irish]; Louis Petherick [1975] Director/Chief Risk Officer; Christopher Bruce Robinson [1956] Group Legal Services Director; Roger John Stott [1965] Finance Director; Michael Thomas Summersgill [1983] Director/Accountant

Bell,Sons & Co.(Druggists) Limited
Incorporated: 17 April 1939 *Employees:* 148
Net Worth: £5,039,008 *Total Assets:* £13,834,928
Registered Office: Gifford House, Slaidburn Crescent, Southport, Merseyside, PR9 9AL
Activities: Manufacture of basic pharmaceutical products
Parent: Marksans Holdings Limited
Officers: Gillian Jacks, Secretary; Sathish Kumar Konasagar Jayanna [1973] Managing Director; Mark Bosco Saldanha [1972] Director [Indian]; Sandra Saldanha [1971] Director [Indian]; Jitendra Mahavirprasad Sharma [1969] Director [Indian]; Russell David Williams [1968] Director

Belle Engineering (Sheen) Limited
Incorporated: 9 February 1961 *Employees:* 162
Net Worth: £15,733,632 *Total Assets:* £26,525,952
Registered Office: Sheen, Buxton, Derbys, SK17 0EU
Activities: Manufacture of other special-purpose machinery n.e.c.
Parent: Belle Holdings Limited
Officers: Raymond Kennedy Neilson, Secretary; Raymond Kennedy Neilson [1966] Director

Belle Holdings Limited
Incorporated: 23 June 1997
Net Worth: £3,879,086 *Total Assets:* £14,424,549
Registered Office: Sheen, Buxton, Derbys, SK17 0EU
Activities: Other manufacturing n.e.c.
Major Shareholder: Mohamed Altrad
Officers: Raymond Kennedy Neilson, Secretary; Raymond Kennedy Neilson [1966] Director

Belle Vue Girls' School
Incorporated: 28 February 2012 *Employees:* 204
Net Worth: £18,917,636 *Total Assets:* £20,896,596
Registered Office: Thorn Lane, Bingley Road, Bradford, BD9 6NA
Activities: General secondary education
Officers: Barbara Janet Edwards, Secretary; Vivianne Frances Brealey [1968] Director/Communications Manager; Ian Broadbent [1970] Director/Facilities Manager; Mary Copeland [1958] Director/Headteacher

Bellis Group Limited
Incorporated: 1 November 2006 *Employees:* 361
Net Worth: £20,350,000 *Total Assets:* £27,839,000
Registered Office: Innovative Business Park, Derker Street, Oldham, Lancs, OL1 4EQ
Activities: Activities of head offices
Major Shareholder: Robert David Bellis
Officers: Thomas Donald Pennington-Brookfield, Secretary; Robert David Bellis [1938] Director; Peter Ian Dunlop [1975] Director; Mustapha Hadj Ahmed [1960] Director [Spanish]; Thomas Donald Pennington-Brookfield [1979] Director/Certified Chartered Accountant

Bells of Lazonby (Holdings) Limited
Incorporated: 14 February 1990 *Employees:* 282
Net Worth: £5,773,630 *Total Assets:* £9,481,293
Registered Office: Edenholme Bakery, Lazonby, Penrith, Cumbria, CA10 1BG
Activities: Activities of head offices
Officers: David Simmons, Secretary; Eva Patricia Bell [1931] Director; John Suitor Bell [1924] Director; Michael John Bell [1960] Director; Jane Elizabeth Callaghan [1958] Managing Director

Bemis Limited
Incorporated: 17 October 1967 *Employees:* 61
Net Worth: £5,765,817 *Total Assets:* £10,248,432
Registered Office: Farrington Road, Rossendale Road Industrial Estate, Burnley, Lancs, BB11 5SW
Activities: Other manufacturing n.e.c.
Shareholder: Richard Albert Bemis
Officers: Lee William Oddie, Secretary; Norm Giertz [1950] Director/President, Proprietary [American]; Lee William Oddie [1968] Finance Director

Bender UK Limited
Incorporated: 18 December 1996 *Employees:* 46
Net Worth: £9,062,357 *Total Assets:* £10,225,942
Registered Office: J L Winder and Co, 125 Ramsden Square, Barrow in Furness, Cumbria, LA14 1XA
Activities: Non-specialised wholesale trade
Officers: Sabine Bender-Suhr, Secretary [German]; Sabine Bender-Suhr [1965] Director [German]; Gareth Brunton [1973] Director/Engineer; Steven John Mason [1972] Director/Engineer

Beneficial House (Birmingham) Regeneration LLP
Incorporated: 6 February 2013
Net Worth: £6,726,112 *Total Assets:* £17,236,944
Registered Office: Century House, Regent Road, Altrincham, Cheshire, WA14 1RR
Officers: Joel Matthew Adams [1972] Member; Gregory Spencer Caswill [1951] Member; Andrew Robert Mitchell [1954] Member; Sergio LeOnel Aguero [1988] LLP Member; Anthony Graham Lloyd Allan [1971] LLP Member; Graham David Bamping [1957] LLP Member; Dr Owen Alexander Bavinton [1948] LLP Member; Asmir Begovic [1987] LLP Member; Nigel Richard Bolton [1963] LLP Member; David James Boyle [1979] LLP Member; Paul John Boyle [1960] LLP Member; Dr John Templeton Bush [1956] LLP Member; Trevor Godfrey Carvey [1962] LLP Member; Anilsingh Chakowa [1954] LLP Member; Beebee Aziza Chakowa [1954] LLP Member; Veenay Surendra Chheda [1970] LLP Member; Richard Hamish Christie [1963] LLP Member; Dr Roderic Lawrance Clark [1960] LLP Member; Geoffrey Stephen Clarkson [1949] LLP Member; Scott Roger Cormack [1958] LLP Member; Andrew Michael Coxon [1949] LLP Member; Daniel John Cunliffe [1971] LLP Member; Andrew Paul Curley [1962] LLP Member; Philip Hywel Davies [1972] LLP Member; Dr Alan Joseph Dobkin [1943] LLP Member; Eamonn William Dunne [1967] LLP Member; John Ceredig Evans [1956] LLP Member; Stefana Ruxandra Fairholme [1982] LLP Member; Paul Maxwell Garvey [1958] LLP Member; Nigel Clive Gawthorpe [1960] LLP Member; Vincent Gray [1961] LLP Member; Simon Kenneth Grout [1964] LLP Member; Stephen James Groves [1975] LLP Member; Christopher Frederick Bernard Hadley [1973] LLP Member; Paul Brendan Hanratty [1961] LLP Member; Dr Esmail Fakirmohamed Harunani [1954] LLP Member; Dr Mohamed Nadeem Esmail Harunani [1987] LLP Member; Mark Christopher Henshall [1960] LLP Member; Gavin Michael Hill [1975] LLP Member; Dr Sacheen Hirani [1971] LLP Member; Prof Howard Saul Jacobs [1938] LLP Member; Jasvir Singh Jutla [1961] LLP Member; Dr Murtaza Kanani [1979] LLP Member; Mohib Ali Jaffer Kassamali [1967] LLP Member; Anthony David Lander [1959] LLP Member; Dr Eric David Livingstone [1948] LLP Member; Ian Keith MacLachlan [1958] LLP Member; Avnish Amritlal Malde [1965] LLP Member; Leena Avnish Malde [1966] LLP Member; Brian William Male [1967] LLP Member; Gerard Francis McDermott Q.C. [1956] LLP Member; Alister Hugh Mellor [1962] LLP Member; Alexander Jardine Millar [1960] LLP Member; Ashwin Bhagwanji Mody [1964] LLP Member; Paul Edward Mulholland [1964] LLP Member; Maxwell John Niser [1952] LLP Member; Rochelle Nisner [1953] LLP Member; James Gildon Harley Nott [1948] LLP Member; Michael John O'Brien [1963] LLP Member; Dr Parisima Pakzad [1961] LLP Member; Clement Robin Woodbine Parish [1950] LLP Member; Brian David Pengelly [1963] LLP Member; Vasily Petrenko [1976] LLP Member; Michael Henry Berkeley Portman [1962] LLP Member; Robert Stephen Preece [1956] LLP Member; Sir Steven Redgrave [1962] LLP Member; Graham Neil Reynolds [1964] LLP Member; Dr Kevin Michael Sadler [1966] LLP Member; Palvi Shah [1961] LLP Member; Vivak Shah [1980] LLP Member; Dr Gert Slaghuis [1960] LLP Member; Graeme Rennie Smith [1963] LLP Member; William Thomas Stockler [1945] LLP Member; Dr Ian David Strawford [1962] LLP Member; Archie James Struthers [1973] LLP Member; Dr Mark Sweeney [1960] LLP Member; Hina Tailor [1963] LLP Member; Dr Richard Kerr Thomson [1965] LLP Member; Antony Paul Tolson [1974] LLP Member; Hayley Anne Tolson [1978] LLP Member; Matthew Craig Toy [1977] LLP Member; Kamlesh Umeria [1964] LLP Member; Christopher Anthony Robert Wade [1968] LLP Member; Sir Stephen Harry Waley-Cohen [1946] LLP Member; Dr Graham John Walker [1962] LLP Member; Angela Claire Mary Watts [1975] LLP Member; Peter Welsh [1966] LLP Member; John Christopher Whitworth [1965] LLP Member; David Charles Wilkinson [1960] LLP Member; Dr Jeremy Mark Wilkinson [1968] LLP Member; Peter John Williamson [1966] LLP Member; Allister Gilbert Michael Wood [1963] LLP Member; Stephen Sagar Wood [1954] LLP Member; Piotr Zimmermann [1960] LLP Member

Benmar Textiles Limited
Incorporated: 6 January 1959 *Employees:* 12
Net Worth: £6,218,073 *Total Assets:* £6,819,460
Registered Office: 41 Greek Street, Stockport, Cheshire, SK3 8AX
Activities: Wholesale of textiles
Major Shareholder: Michael Philip Seitler
Officers: Michael Seitler, Secretary; Harold Doggett [1945] Director; Michael Philip Seitler [1966] Director

Jeremy Benn Associates Limited
Incorporated: 6 September 1996 *Employees:* 439
Net Worth: £4,911,528 *Total Assets:* £8,918,719
Registered Office: South Barn, Broughton Hall, Skipton, N Yorks, BD23 3AE
Activities: Engineering related scientific and technical consulting activities
Parent: JBA Group Ltd
Officers: Craig Robson, Secretary; David Graham Henry Bassett [1966] Director/Civil Engineer; Richard George Buck [1965] Director/Consulting Engineer; Alastair George Jervis Dale [1957] Director/Engineering Manager; Gary John Deakin [1960] Director/Engineering Manager; Andrew David Gubbin [1963] Director/Engineering Manager; Rachel Louise Huitson-Little [1980] Director/Hydrologist; Dr Mark Reuben Lawless [1974] Director [Canadian]; Stephen Maslen [1958] Director/Landscape Architect; Marc Graham Pinnell [1970] Director/Engineering Manager

Bennett & Fountain Limited
Incorporated: 3 September 1962
Net Worth Deficit: £12,827,000 *Total Assets:* £7,053,000
Registered Office: P O Box 1, Tatton Street, Knutsford, Cheshire, WA16 6AY
Activities: Activities of head offices
Parent: Marlowe Holdings Investments Limited
Officers: William Sones Woof, Secretary; Roger David Goddard [1953] Director/Chartered Accountant; Douglas Talbot McNair [1947] Director; William Sones Woof [1951] Director/Solicitor

Benross Marketing Limited
Incorporated: 23 March 1995 *Employees:* 56
Net Worth: £8,933,839 *Total Assets:* £16,611,392
Registered Office: Bridge Industrial Estate, Speke Hall Road, Liverpool, L24 9WD
Activities: Wholesale of household goods (other than musical instruments) n.e.c
Officers: Amit Juneja, Secretary; Amit Juneja [1982] Director/Buyer; Anil Juneja [1979] Director/Sales Manager; Dharam Vir Juneja [1957] Director

Benteler Distribution Limited
Incorporated: 29 June 1948 *Employees:* 83
Net Worth: £4,437,443 *Total Assets:* £18,488,978
Registered Office: New Progress Works, Crompton Way, Bolton, Lancs, BL1 8TY
Activities: Wholesale of metals and metal ores
Officers: Phillip Newberry, Secretary; Torsten Oliver Beer [1967] Director [German]; Robert Heath [1961] Director/Industrial Stockholder; Roger Higginbottom [1964] Director/Procurement

Bentley & Bentley Limited
Incorporated: 3 June 1993 *Employees:* 111
Net Worth: £4,478,864 *Total Assets:* £15,660,874
Registered Office: Airedale Business Centre, Millennium Road, Keighley Road, Skipton, N Yorks, BD23 2UB
Activities: Sale of new cars and light motor vehicles
Major Shareholder: Kevin Philip Bentley
Officers: Omer Khan, Secretary; Julie Mary Bentley [1943] Director; Kevin Philip Bentley [1945] Director

Bentley Global (UK) Limited
Incorporated: 5 August 2015
Net Worth: £27,399,514 *Total Assets:* £27,455,908
Registered Office: 20 Chapel Street, Liverpool, L3 9AG
Activities: Other information service activities n.e.c.
Shareholders: Terence Lee Leighton; Alan Ronald Bentley
Officers: Brian Raymond Bentley, Secretary; Alan Ronald Bentley [1962] Director; Brian Raymond Bentley [1963] Director

J.N. Bentley Limited
Incorporated: 7 December 1972 *Employees:* 1,218
Net Worth: £10,747,796 *Total Assets:* £79,753,416
Registered Office: Snaygill Industrial Estate, Keighley Road, Skipton, N Yorks, BD23 2QR
Activities: Construction of utility projects for fluids
Parent: Bentley Holdings Limited
Officers: Helen Marie Thompson, Secretary; David Mark Bentley [1969] Commercial Director; Paul Rogerson Bentley [1967] Managing Director; John Alastair Binns [1960] Commercial Director; Philip Robert Cundill [1977] Commercial Director; James Richard Fitton [1971] Operations Director North; John Matthew Greenwood [1975] Engineering Director; Michael David Haigh [1960] Director; James How Keir Harris [1968] Director; Judith Jeffery [1969] HR Director; Angus James Anderson Ridge [1966] Operations Director; Richard Risdon [1974] Operations Director South; Edwin George Roud [1963] Finance Director; Steven Christopher Tetlow [1966] Bidding & Estimating Director

Bentley Motors Limited
Incorporated: 28 October 1970 *Employees:* 4,192
Net Worth Deficit: £648,499,968 *Total Assets:* £1,147,800,064
Registered Office: Pym's Lane, Crewe, Cheshire, CW1 3PL
Activities: Manufacture of motor vehicles
Parent: Volkswagen Aktiengesellschaft
Officers: Andrew Thomas Armitage, Secretary; Dr Oliver Ingo Blume [1968] Director/Chairman of The Executive Board of Porsche AG [German]; Peter Bosch [1974] Manufacturing Director [German]; Christopher Noel Craft [1959] Sales & Marketing Director; Dr Astrid Angelika Fontaine [1969] Director/Board Member for People, Digitalisation & IT [German/American]; Adrian Michael Hallmark [1962] Director/Chairman & Chief Executive; Lutz Wolfgang Meschke [1966] Director/Member of The Executive Board of Porsche AG [German]; Dr Joerg Mull [1965] Finance Director [German]; Dr Werner Julius Tietz [1963] Engineering Director [German]

Bentleys Motor Group Ltd
Incorporated: 15 July 2003
Registered Office: 415-419 Manchester Road, Paddington, Warrington, Cheshire, WA1 3LR
Activities: Activities of head offices
Shareholders: Stephen Jonathan Langley; Anthony Francis Murray
Officers: Patricia Anne Langley, Secretary; Carl Keith Baldwin [1963] Sales Director; Stephen Hazlehurst [1969] Director; Stephen Jonathan Langley [1954] Director; Anthony Francis Murray [1956] Director

Bents Garden Centre Limited
Incorporated: 4 November 1993 *Employees:* 407
Net Worth: £12,816,583 *Total Assets:* £16,865,520
Registered Office: Bents Garden Centre, Warrington Road, Leigh End, Glazebury, Warrington, Cheshire, WA3 5NT
Activities: Other retail sale of new goods in specialised stores (not commercial art galleries and opticians)
Parent: Bents Holdings Limited
Officers: George James Brian Daniels, Secretary; Matthew Bent [1974] Director; Ronald Bent [1942] Director/Rose Grower; Wendy Bent [1945] Director; George James Brian Daniels [1953] Director/Chartered Accountant

Bents Holdings Limited
Incorporated: 11 January 2008 *Employees:* 400
Net Worth: £18,993,712 *Total Assets:* £40,938,528
Registered Office: Bents Garden Centre, Warrington Road, Leigh End, Glazebury, Warrington, Cheshire, WA3 5NT
Activities: Activities of head offices
Shareholder: Ronald Bent
Officers: George James Brian Daniels, Secretary; Matthew Bent [1974] Director; Ronald Bent [1942] Director; George James Brian Daniels [1953] Director/Chartered Accountant

Bents Property Limited
Incorporated: 11 January 2008
Net Worth: £10,310,433 *Total Assets:* £33,707,968
Registered Office: Bents Garden Centre, Warrington Road, Leigh End, Glazebury, Warrington, Cheshire, WA3 5NT
Activities: Renting and operating of Housing Association real estate
Parent: Bents Holdings Limited
Officers: George James Brian Daniels, Secretary; Matthew Bent [1974] Director; George James Brian Daniels [1953] Director/Chartered Accountant; Rachel Downton-Bent [1972] Director; Helen Heesom [1977] Director; Katherine Morris [1979] Director

Kevin Berkins Quality Meats Limited
Incorporated: 17 June 1977
Registered Office: Fence Gate, Wheatley Lane Road, Fence, Burnley, Lancs, BB12 9EE
Activities: Wholesale of meat and meat products
Major Shareholder: Kevin Berkins
Officers: Kevin Berkins, Secretary; Keeley Ann Beaumont [1976] Director; Kevin Berkins [1947] Director/Master Butcher; Michelle Berkins [1964] Director

Bernham Ltd
Incorporated: 16 September 2003
Net Worth: £5,072,430 *Total Assets:* £16,706,040
Registered Office: 73a Allerton Road, Mossley Hill, Liverpool, L18 2DA
Activities: Public houses and bars
Shareholders: Christian Julian Caine; Ian Frank Caine
Officers: Christian Julian Caine [1979] Director; Ian Frank Caine [1956] Director

C & W Berry Limited
Incorporated: 30 November 1979 *Employees:* 234
Net Worth: £21,250,800 *Total Assets:* £23,348,356
Registered Office: Wellfield Sawmills, King Street, Leyland, Preston, Lancs, PR25 2LE
Activities: Sawmilling and planing of wood
Parent: C.W.B.G Limited
Officers: Gary William Higham, Secretary; Colin Berry [1930] Director/Manager; David John Berry [1966] Director/Management Accountant; Susan Louise Berry [1962] Director; Gary William Higham [1965] Director/Accountant; Ian Richard Hunt [1967] Joinery Director; Peter Jones [1954] Director/Manager; Martin Lambert [1967] Director; Graham Charnley Parker [1955] Director/Manager

C & W Berry Trading Limited
Incorporated: 21 September 2000
Net Worth: £5,297,899 *Total Assets:* £7,484,647
Registered Office: Wellfield Sawmills, King Street, Leyland, Preston, Lancs, PR25 2LE
Activities: Other letting and operating of own or leased real estate
Shareholders: David John Berry; Susan Louise Berry
Officers: Gary William Higham, Secretary; David John Berry [1966] Director/Management Accountant; Susan Louise Berry [1962] Director; Gary William Higham [1965] Director/Accountant

Berrymans Lace Mawer LLP
Incorporated: 23 October 2008 *Employees:* 1,679
Net Worth: £30,269,000 *Total Assets:* £80,159,000
Registered Office: King's House, 42 King Street West, Manchester, M3 2NU
Officers: Matthew Harrington [1969] Member; Vivienne Elizabeth Williams [1965] Member; Mark Aitken [1963] LLP Member; Roger Ian Brooks [1958] LLP Member; Michael Jeremy Brown [1961] LLP Member; Gavin Francis Campbell [1959] LLP Member; Peter Gerard Campbell [1961] LLP Member; Fintan John Canavan [1969] LLP Member; Alison Mary Elizabeth Cassidy [1961] LLP Member; David Gwyn Caswell [1975] LLP Member; Clare Victoria Chapman [1976] LLP Member; Jonathan George Armstrong Clay [1958] LLP Member; Kerris Elizabeth Dale [1965] LLP Member; Karen Elizabeth Dance [1967] LLP Member; Helen Clare Devery [1968] LLP Member; Michael Francis Dobson [1972] LLP Member; Cormac Paul Fitzpatrick [1960] LLP Member; Christopher Michael Fletcher [1971] LLP Member; Matthew Ford [1978] LLP Member; Joanne Louise Francis [1970] LLP Member; Stuart John Furniss [1974] LLP Member; Louise Alison Gallagher [1963] LLP Member; Clare Helen Garnett [1970] LLP Member; Andrew Kenneth Gilmour [1974] LLP Member; Anne Ruth Graham [1959] LLP Member; Helen Elizabeth Grimberg [1969] LLP Member; James Edward Harvey [1972] LLP Member; Andrew Charles Hibbert [1969] LLP Member; Sarah Eloise Hill [1975] LLP Member; Paula Elizabeth Jefferson [1970] LLP Member; Simon William Jones [1965] LLP Member; Valerie Jane Jones [1963] LLP Member; Andrew James Kerr [1967] LLP Member; John Henry Austin Kirkup [1970] LLP Member; Luisa Claire Lamb [1970] LLP Member; Ian Paul Leach [1959] LLP Member; Nigel John Lock [1965] LLP Member; Keith Alan John Lonsdale [1964] LLP Member; Paul James MacAllister [1963] LLP Member; Gregory Andrew McEwen [1973] LLP Member; Simon Glyn Morrow [1964] LLP Member; Jason Miles Nash [1966] LLP Member; John O'Shea [1966] LLP Member; Nicholas Aidan Pargeter [1965] LLP Member; Ben Parks [1980] LLP Member; Michelle Annette Penn [1961] LLP Member; Michael Pether [1964] LLP Member; Elliot Andrew Pound [1970] LLP Member; Rachel Jane Rough [1978] LLP Member; Gillian Rushbury [1967] LLP Member; Michael Ike Salau [1964] LLP Member; Rosette Shapiro [1976] LLP Member; Andrew James Sherwood [1961] LLP Member; Julian Richard Berryman Smart [1972] LLP Member; Timothy George Edwin Smith [1969] LLP Member; Raymond Joseph Southern [1964] LLP Member; David James Spencer [1973] LLP Member; Victoria Ann Swanton [1970] LLP Member; Paul Charles Tarne [1979] LLP Member; Alexander Charles Traill [1975] LLP Member; Joseph Frederick Charles Wakeford [1956] LLP Member; Sarah Alison Woodwark [1963] LLP Member

Berwin Group Limited
Incorporated: 11 May 1983
Net Worth: £339,955 *Total Assets:* £8,455,177
Registered Office: Broadway, Globe Lane Industrial Estate, Broadway, Dukinfield, Cheshire, SK16 4UJ
Activities: Activities of head offices
Parent: Hexpol AB
Officers: Paul Michael Stevenson, Secretary; Mikael Fryklund [1963] Director [Swedish]; Karin Elisabeth Bachmann Gunnarsson [1962] Director [Swedish]; Carsten Ruter [1971] Director/President Technology [German]; Paul Michael Stevenson [1968] Director/Accountant; Ralph Joseph Wolkener [1971] Director/Employee [Belgian]

Berwin Industrial Polymers Limited
Incorporated: 29 October 1957 *Employees:* 73
Net Worth: £4,859,542 *Total Assets:* £11,776,199
Registered Office: Broadway, Globe Lane Industrial Estate, Dukinfield, Cheshire, SK16 4UJ
Activities: Manufacture of other rubber products
Parent: Berwin of Lydney
Officers: Paul Michael Stevenson, Secretary; Mikael Fryklund [1963] Director [Swedish]; Karin Elisabeth Bachmann Gunnarsson [1962] Director [Swedish]; Gareth Jefferson [1976] Director; Carsten Ruter [1971] Director/President Technology; Ralph Joseph Wolkener [1971] Director/Employee [Belgian]

Berwin Rubber Company Limited
Incorporated: 19 October 1953 *Employees:* 93
Net Worth: £11,687,709 *Total Assets:* £20,986,660
Registered Office: Broadway, Globe Lane Industrial Estate, Dukinfield, Cheshire, SK16 4UJ
Activities: Manufacture of other rubber products
Parent: Berwin Group
Officers: Paul Michael Stevenson, Secretary; Joseph Edmund Dowdall [1963] Director; Mikael Fryklund [1963] Director [Swedish]; Karin Elisabeth Bachmann Gunnarsson [1962] Director [Swedish]; Karin Elisabeth Bachmann Gunnarsson [1962] Director [Swedish]; Carsten Ruter [1971] Director/President Technology [German]; Ralph Joseph Wolkener [1971] Director/Employee [Belgian]

BES Commercial Electricity Ltd
Incorporated: 21 April 2009
Net Worth: £9,460,323 *Total Assets:* £24,021,578
Registered Office: Parkside Stand, Fleetwood Town Football Club, Park Avenue, Fleetwood, Lancs, FY7 6TX
Activities: Agents involved in the sale of fuels, ores, metals and industrial chemicals
Parent: BES Utilities Holding Ltd
Officers: Michelle Caron Davidson, Secretary; Michelle Caron Davidson [1973] Director; Andrew James Pilley [1970] Director

BES Utilities Holding Ltd
Incorporated: 15 April 2016 *Employees:* 191
Net Worth: £10,651,507 *Total Assets:* £32,094,384
Registered Office: Parkside Stand, Fleetwood Town Football Club, Park Avenue, Fleetwood, Lancs, FY7 6TX
Activities: Other business support service activities n.e.c.
Major Shareholder: Andrew James Pilley
Officers: Michelle Caron Davidson [1973] Director; Andrew James Pilley [1970] Director

Bespoke Home Interior Design Limited
Incorporated: 22 April 2014 *Employees:* 2
Net Worth Deficit: £2,953,000 *Total Assets:* £19,696,000
Registered Office: Broadoak Business Park, Ashburton Road West, Trafford Park, Manchester, M17 1RW
Activities: Manufacture of other furniture
Parent: BHID Ltd
Officers: William Keith Bennett [1953] Director; Nigel John Pailing [1958] Director

Bespoke Hotels Chester Limited
Incorporated: 6 February 2015 *Employees:* 212
Net Worth: £11,910,619 *Total Assets:* £17,223,894
Registered Office: Unit 5 Bankside, Crosfield Street, Warrington, Cheshire, WA1 1UP
Activities: Other business support service activities n.e.c.
Shareholders: Haydn Herbert James Fentum; Robin Michael Philpot Sheppard
Officers: Haydn Herbert James Fentum [1969] Director; Stephen Linton Littlefair [1965] Finance Director; Graham Marskell [1965] Director; Robin Michael Philpot Sheppard [1954] Director

Bespoke Supportive Tenancies Ltd
Incorporated: 14 September 2010 *Employees:* 23
Net Worth: £57,077 *Total Assets:* £39,332,016
Registered Office: 2a Sentinel House, Albert Street, Eccles, Manchester, M30 0NJ
Activities: Other residential care activities n.e.c.
Officers: Kevin Appleby [1969] Director/Chief Executive; Steven Boyd [1963] Commercial Director; Shelley Louise Hobbs [1977] Director/Chief Operations Officer; Hugh Charles McCaw [1952] Director; David Gerard Poppitt [1946] Director/Fund Raiser

Best International Limited
Incorporated: 6 October 1983 *Employees:* 1
Net Worth Deficit: £1,948,891 *Total Assets:* £6,548,594
Registered Office: 13-15 Brewery Yard, Deva City Office Park, Trinity Way, Salford, M3 7BB
Activities: Management consultancy activities other than financial management
Major Shareholder: Jacqueline Alexandra Punjabi
Officers: Sheila Isabelle Punjabi, Secretary; Suresh Punjabi, Secretary; Tarachand Utoomal Punjabi, Secretary; Jacqueline Alexandra Punjabi [1985] Director; Suresh Punjabi [1971] Director; Tarachand Utoomal Punjabi [1935] Director

Bestway National Chemists Limited
Incorporated: 18 September 2014
Net Worth: £161,211,008 *Total Assets:* £367,407,008
Registered Office: Merchants Warehouse, Castle Street, Castlefield, Manchester, M3 4LZ
Activities: Dispensing chemist in specialised stores
Parent: Bestway Panacea Holdings Limited
Officers: Tracy Jayne Barton [1967] HR Director; David Allen Hamilton [1974] Commercial Director; Lynette Gillian Krige [1966] Director/Chief Finance Officer [South African]; John Branson Nuttall [1963] Managing Director; Janice Margaret Perkins [1961] Director/Pharmacy Superintendent

Bestway Panacea Healthcare Limited
Incorporated: 18 September 2014
Net Worth: £162,724,992 *Total Assets:* £191,066,000
Registered Office: Merchants Warehouse, Castle Street, Castlefield, Manchester, M3 4LZ
Activities: Dispensing chemist in specialised stores
Parent: Bestway Panacea Holdings Limited
Officers: Tracy Jayne Barton [1967] HR Director; David Allen Hamilton [1974] Commercial Director; Lynette Gillian Krige [1966] Director/Chief Finance Officer [South African]; John Branson Nuttall [1963] Managing Director; Janice Margaret Perkins [1961] Director/Pharmacy Superintendent

Bestway Panacea Holdings Limited
Incorporated: 18 September 2014 *Employees:* 7,294
Net Worth Deficit: £4,837,000 *Total Assets:* £93,951,000
Registered Office: Merchants Warehouse, Castle Street, Castlefield, Manchester, M3 4LZ
Activities: Activities of head offices
Parent: Bestway UK Holdco Limited
Officers: Zameer Mohammed Choudrey [1958] Director; Lynette Gillian Krige [1966] Director/Chief Finance Officer [South African]; John Branson Nuttall [1963] Managing Director; Sir Mohammed Anwar Pervez [1935] Director

Bestway Pharmacy NDC Limited
Incorporated: 17 April 1972
Net Worth Deficit: £45,447,000 *Total Assets:* £35,142,000
Registered Office: Merchants Warehouse, Castle Street, Manchester, M3 4LZ
Activities: Wholesale of pharmaceutical goods
Parent: Bestway Panacea Holdings Limited
Officers: David Allen Hamilton [1974] Commercial Director; Lynette Gillian Krige [1966] Director/Chief Finance Officer [South African]; John Branson Nuttall [1963] Director/General Manager Health Care Group

Bet Security and Communications Limited
Incorporated: 21 March 1983
Net Worth: £21,278,000 *Total Assets:* £228,491,008
Registered Office: Shadsworth Road, Blackburn, Lancs, BB1 2PR
Activities: Other service activities n.e.c.
Parent: Chubb Group Security Limited
Officers: Robert Sloss, Secretary; Laura Wilcock, Secretary; Anthony Brennan [1966] Finance Director [Irish]; Robert John Sloss [1967] Director/Solicitor

Betchton Limited
Incorporated: 30 May 1990 *Employees:* 7
Net Worth: £8,028,807 *Total Assets:* £12,174,319
Registered Office: Lea House, Middlewich Road, Sandbach, Cheshire, CW11 1DH
Activities: Activities of head offices
Major Shareholder: Sidney Vaughan Gaskell
Officers: Nicholas Charlton Penrhys Bird, Secretary/Chartered Accountant; Nicholas Charlton Penrhys Bird [1952] Director/Chartered Accountant; Sidney Vaughan Gaskell [1938] Director; Henry Vaughan Wheeler [1961] Director

Betfred Group Limited
Incorporated: 25 July 2011 *Employees:* 6,124
Net Worth: £95,338,000 *Total Assets:* £312,095,008
Registered Office: The Spectrum, 56-58 Benson Road, Birchwood, Warrington, Cheshire, WA3 7PQ
Activities: Gambling and betting activities
Officers: Michael Rodney Hamilton, Secretary; Nicola Joan Barr [1977] Finance Director; Fred Done [1943] Director; Mark Warren Stebbings [1970] Managing Director

Bethell Construction Limited
Incorporated: 8 April 1932 *Employees:* 163
Net Worth: £2,172,000 *Total Assets:* £10,155,000
Registered Office: Dane House, Europa Park, Stoneclough Road, Kearsley, Manchester, M26 1GE
Activities: Construction of other civil engineering projects n.e.c.
Officers: Neil Hopkins-Coman, Secretary; Carl Robert Dixon [1971] Director/Civil Engineer; Patrick Donnellan [1972] Director/Quantity Surveyor [Irish]; Neil Hopkins-Coman [1962] Finance Director; Timothy Anthony Kilroe [1964] Director [Irish]; Ian Madden [1960] H&S Director; Gerard Patrick McCoy [1971] Contracts Director; Christopher Morley [1974] Director/Accountant; Vincent O'Dowd [1962] Contracts Director; Joseph Oleary [1970] Contracts Director [Irish]

Bethell Group Holdings Ltd
Incorporated: 2 February 2010 *Employees:* 167
Net Worth: £3,243,000 *Total Assets:* £12,804,000
Registered Office: Dane House, Europa Trading Estate, Stoneclough Road, Radcliffe, Manchester, M26 1GE
Activities: Construction of other civil engineering projects n.e.c.
Officers: Neil Hopkins-Coman [1962] Director; Cassie Marie Kilroe [1967] Director [Irish]; Timothy Anthony Kilroe [1964] Director [Irish]

BetterBathrooms (UK) Limited
Incorporated: 5 December 2003 *Employees:* 453
Net Worth: £7,875,479 *Total Assets:* £25,201,004
Registered Office: Horizon Park, Greenfold Way, Leigh, Lancs, WN7 3XH
Activities: Other retail sale of new goods in specialised stores (not commercial art galleries and opticians)
Shareholder: BGF GP Limited
Officers: George Miles Bramston Adams [1956] Director; Ben Julius Barker [1977] Director; Peter Alan Cowgill [1953] Director

Beva Investments Limited
Incorporated: 17 October 1980 *Employees:* 8
Net Worth: £11,466,195 *Total Assets:* £20,360,060
Registered Office: Chichester Business Centre, Chichester Street, Rochdale, OL16 2AU
Activities: Development of building projects
Shareholders: Frederick Chadwick; William Pascal Chadwick
Officers: William Chadwick, Secretary; Frederick Chadwick [1949] Director; William Pascal Chadwick [1978] Director

Bevie Partners Limited
Incorporated: 24 September 1992 *Employees:* 70
Net Worth: £5,585,791 *Total Assets:* £9,255,534
Registered Office: Philip Jones House, Poole Hall Industrial Estate, Ellesmere Port, Cheshire, CH66 1ST
Activities: Manufacture of other food products n.e.c.
Officers: Peter Richard Eastwood [1958] Director [New Zealander]; William Tucker Rahr [1968] Director [American]; Jeffrey Taylor [1965] Director [American]; Ian Ward [1967] Director [British/American]

Beyond Funding (Holdco) Ltd
Incorporated: 26 September 2016 *Employees:* 3
Net Worth Deficit: £89,162 *Total Assets:* £6,564,323
Registered Office: 1-7 Fallbarn Road, Rawtenstall, Rossendale, Lancs, BB4 7NT
Activities: Other credit granting n.e.c.
Parent: Beyond Funding (Topco) Ltd
Officers: Shaun Morley [1956] Director; Adam Mark Turner [1987] Director

BH (Manchester) Limited
Incorporated: 21 July 2016
Net Worth: £79 794 *Total Assets:* £7,127,290
Registered Office: 60 Oxford Street, Manchester, M1 5EE
Activities: Activities of other holding companies n.e.c.
Major Shareholder: Stephen Beech
Officers: Stephen Beech [1977] Director

BHG Nominee Co (2) Limited
Incorporated: 14 November 2007
Net Worth: £4,767,000 *Total Assets:* £22,480,000
Registered Office: Prospect House, 168-170 Washway Road, Sale, Cheshire, M33 6RH
Activities: Activities of other holding companies n.e.c.
Parent: Brookhouse Group Limited
Officers: Peter Chape, Secretary; Andrew Jeremy Gardner [1972] Director/Accountant; Emma Hindle [1975] Director

BHID Group Limited
Incorporated: 17 April 2014 *Employees:* 397
Net Worth Deficit: £1,223,000 *Total Assets:* £37,169,000
Registered Office: Broadoak Business Park, Ashburton Road West, Trafford Park, Manchester, M17 1RW
Activities: Manufacture of other furniture
Officers: William Keith Bennett [1953] Director; Jeffrey Forrester [1953] Director; Simon Patrick Meyrick [1962] Director; Dean Anthony Murray [1962] Director; Nigel John Pailing [1958] Director; Lisa Michelle Quinlan [1969] Group Marketing Director; Nick Richard Motum Seaman [1981] Director; Mark Henry Storey [1961] Director/Venture Capitalist

BHR Finance Limited
Incorporated: 24 April 2007
Net Worth: £10,239,000 *Total Assets:* £10,239,000
Registered Office: 98 King Street, Knutsford, Cheshire, WA16 6HQ
Activities: Activities of head offices
Parent: BH Restaurants Limited
Officers: Andrew Peter Haigh, Secretary/Accountant; Andrew Peter Haigh [1967] Financial Director; Jeremy Kevin Roberts [1962] Director

Bibby Asset Finance Limited
Incorporated: 1 August 2000
Net Worth: £7,665,368 *Total Assets:* £7,680,751
Registered Office: 105 Duke Street, Liverpool, L1 5JQ
Activities: Financial leasing
Parent: Bibby Financial Services (UK) Limited
Officers: Ian Downing [1958] Director/Accountant; Ian Stuart Ramsden [1970] Director; Ian John Wilkins [1967] Director

Bibby Bulk Carriers Limited
Incorporated: 23 December 1971
Net Worth Deficit: £216,470 *Total Assets:* £10,219,786
Registered Office: 105 Duke Street, Liverpool, L1 5JQ
Activities: Sea and coastal freight water transport
Parent: Bibby Line Limited
Officers: Ian Kenneth Crook [1970] Director/Accountant; Simon Jeremy Kitchen [1958] Director

Bibby Distribution Limited
Incorporated: 7 July 1999 *Employees:* 1,828
Net Worth: £34,909,000 *Total Assets:* £83,021,000
Registered Office: 105 Duke Street, Liverpool, L1 5JQ
Activities: Freight transport by road
Parent: Bibby Supply Chain Services Limited
Officers: Jacqueline Barker [1962] Director; John Harold Cresswell [1961] Director; Mark Joseph Lyons [1962] Director; Richard James Morson [1975] Director; Jonathan Osborne [1969] Director/Chartered Accountant; Nigel Leonard Douglas Tullett [1966] Director

Bibby Factors Bristol Limited
Incorporated: 12 March 1996 *Employees:* 7
Net Worth: £2,274,225 *Total Assets:* £25,425,288
Registered Office: 105 Duke Street, Liverpool, L1 5JQ
Activities: Factoring
Parent: Bibby Invoice Finance UK Limited
Officers: Ian Downing [1958] Director/Accountant; David John Postings [1960] Director; Ian Stuart Ramsden [1970] Director; Steven Vears Robinson [1968] Director; Stephen George Rose [1965] Director; Edward James Winterton [1975] Director

Bibby Factors International Limited
Incorporated: 29 September 2000 *Employees:* 33
Net Worth: £1,625,770 *Total Assets:* £22,779,700
Registered Office: 105 Duke Street, Liverpool, L1 5JQ
Activities: Factoring
Parent: Bibby Invoice Finance UK Limited
Officers: Ian Downing [1958] Director/Accountant; David John Postings [1960] Director; Ian Stuart Ramsden [1970] Director; Steven Vears Robinson [1968] Director; Stephen George Rose [1965] Director; Edward James Winterton [1975] Director

Bibby Factors Leicester Limited
Incorporated: 11 November 1994 *Employees:* 54
Net Worth: £4,932,893 *Total Assets:* £63,224,100
Registered Office: 105 Duke Street, Liverpool, L1 5JQ
Activities: Factoring
Parent: Bibby Invoice Finance UK Limited
Officers: Ian Downing [1958] Director/Accountant; David John Postings [1960] Director; Ian Stuart Ramsden [1970] Director; Steven Vears Robinson [1968] Director; Stephen George Rose [1965] Director; Edward James Winterton [1975] Director

Bibby Factors Limited
Incorporated: 21 May 1957 *Employees:* 56
Net Worth: £4,111,398 *Total Assets:* £76,968,128
Registered Office: 105 Duke Street, Liverpool, L1 5JQ
Activities: Factoring
Parent: Bibby Invoice Finance UK Limited
Officers: Ian Downing [1958] Director/Accountant; David John Postings [1960] Director; Ian Stuart Ramsden [1970] Director; Steven Vears Robinson [1968] Director; Stephen George Rose [1965] Director; Edward James Winterton [1975] Director

Bibby Factors Manchester Limited
Incorporated: 1 October 2001 *Employees:* 27
Net Worth: £2,398,014 *Total Assets:* £33,093,720
Registered Office: 105 Duke Street, Liverpool, L1 5JQ
Activities: Factoring
Parent: Bibby Invoice Finance UK Limited
Officers: Ian Downing [1958] Director/Accountant; David John Postings [1960] Director; Ian Stuart Ramsden [1970] Director; Steven Vears Robinson [1968] Director; Stephen George Rose [1965] Director; Edward James Winterton [1975] Director

Bibby Factors Northwest Limited
Incorporated: 10 November 1955 *Employees:* 33
Net Worth: £4,131,693 *Total Assets:* £46,580,020
Registered Office: 105 Duke Street, Liverpool, L1 5JQ
Activities: Factoring
Parent: Bibby Invoice Finance UK Limited
Officers: Ian Downing [1958] Director/Accountant; David John Postings [1960] Director; Ian Stuart Ramsden [1970] Director; Steven Vears Robinson [1968] Director; Stephen George Rose [1965] Director; Edward James Winterton [1975] Director

Bibby Factors Slough Limited
Incorporated: 6 June 1991 *Employees:* 59
Net Worth: £3,674,486 *Total Assets:* £49,632,400
Registered Office: 105 Duke Street, Liverpool, L1 5JQ
Activities: Factoring
Parent: Bibby Invoice Finance UK Limited
Officers: Ian Downing [1958] Director/Accountant; David John Postings [1960] Director; Ian Stuart Ramsden [1970] Director; Steven Vears Robinson [1968] Director; Stephen George Rose [1965] Director; Edward James Winterton [1975] Director

Bibby Factors Sussex Limited
Incorporated: 24 September 1999
Net Worth: £2,233,130 *Total Assets:* £24,458,466
Registered Office: 105 Duke Street, Liverpool, L1 5JQ
Activities: Factoring
Parent: Bibby Invoice Finance UK Limited
Officers: Ian Downing [1958] Director/Accountant; David John Postings [1960] Director; Ian Stuart Ramsden [1970] Director; Steven Vears Robinson [1968] Director; Stephen George Rose [1965] Director; Edward James Winterton [1975] Director

Bibby Factors Yorkshire Limited
Incorporated: 1 October 2003 *Employees:* 29
Net Worth: £2,408,674 *Total Assets:* £27,100,428
Registered Office: 105 Duke Street, Liverpool, L1 5JQ
Activities: Factoring
Parent: Bibby Invoice Finance UK Limited
Officers: Ian Downing [1958] Director/Accountant; David John Postings [1960] Director; Ian Stuart Ramsden [1970] Director; Steven Vears Robinson [1968] Director; Stephen George Rose [1965] Director; Edward James Winterton [1975] Director

Bibby Financial Services (Europe) Limited
Incorporated: 31 March 2015 *Employees:* 303
Net Worth: £23,460,724 *Total Assets:* £326,455,168
Registered Office: 105 Duke Street, Liverpool, L1 5JQ
Activities: Activities of financial services holding companies
Parent: Bibby FS (Holdings) Limited
Officers: Richard Andrew Carter [1961] Director; Kieran Mihkail Monteil [1979] Director [Trinidadian/American]; Christopher Parle [1974] Director/Chartered Accountant; Stephen George Rose [1965] Director; Paul Stack [1964] Director

Bibby Financial Services (UK) Limited
Incorporated: 4 December 2014
Net Worth: £92,249,072 *Total Assets:* £102,345,280
Registered Office: 105 Duke Street, Liverpool, L1 5JQ
Activities: Activities of financial services holding companies
Parent: Bibby FS (Holdings) Limited
Officers: Ian Downing [1958] Director/Accountant; David John Postings [1960] Director; Ian Stuart Ramsden [1970] Director; Steven Vears Robinson [1968] Director; Stephen George Rose [1965] Director; Edward James Winterton [1975] Director

Bibby Financial Services Limited
Incorporated: 13 March 1998 *Employees:* 1,196
Net Worth: £183,788,000 *Total Assets:* £1,003,630,016
Registered Office: 105 Duke Street, Liverpool, L1 5JQ
Activities: Activities of financial services holding companies
Parent: Bibby Line Group Limited
Officers: John Harold Cresswell [1961] Director; Michael Edward Fairey [1948] Director; Mark Joseph Lyons [1962] Director; David John Postings [1960] Director; Ian Stuart Ramsden [1970] Director; Steven Vears Robinson [1968] Director; Stephen George Rose [1965] Director; Edward James Winterton [1975] Director

Bibby FS (Holdings) Limited
Incorporated: 27 December 1995 *Employees:* 236
Net Worth: £125,921,000 *Total Assets:* £133,038,000
Registered Office: 105 Duke Street, Liverpool, L1 5JQ
Activities: Activities of financial services holding companies
Parent: Bibby Financial Services Limited
Officers: Sandra Jane Blackledge [1970] Director; Ian Downing [1958] Director/Accountant; Kieran Mihkail Monteil [1979] Director [Trinidadian/American]; David John Postings [1960] Director; Steven Vears Robinson [1968] Director; Stephen George Rose [1965] Director

Bibby Holdings Limited
Incorporated: 17 September 1970 *Employees:* 543
Net Worth: £56,930,000 *Total Assets:* £114,383,000
Registered Office: 105 Duke Street, Liverpool, L1 5JQ
Activities: Activities of other holding companies n.e.c.
Parent: Bibby Line Group Limited
Officers: Ian Kenneth Crook [1970] Director/Accountant; Andrew John Goody [1966] Director/Accountant; Mark Joseph Lyons [1962] Director

Bibby Invoice Discounting Limited
Incorporated: 10 November 2000 *Employees:* 29
Net Worth: £11,699,221 *Total Assets:* £150,981,056
Registered Office: 105 Duke Street, Liverpool, L1 5JQ
Activities: Factoring
Parent: Bibby Invoice Finance UK Limited
Officers: Ian Downing [1958] Director/Accountant; David John Postings [1960] Director; Ian Stuart Ramsden [1970] Director; Steven Vears Robinson [1968] Director; Stephen George Rose [1965] Director; Edward James Winterton [1975] Director

Bibby Invoice Finance UK Limited
Incorporated: 11 December 2014 *Employees:* 402
Net Worth: £55,891,000 *Total Assets:* £606,417,024
Registered Office: 105 Duke Street, Liverpool, L1 5JQ
Activities: Activities of financial services holding companies
Parent: Bibby Financial Services (UK) Limited
Officers: Ian Downing [1958] Director/Accountant; Kieran Mihkail Monteil [1979] Director [Trinidadian/American]; Ian Stuart Ramsden [1970] Director; Stephen George Rose [1965] Director

Bibby Leasing Limited
Incorporated: 12 August 1957 *Employees:* 32
Net Worth: £18,211,096 *Total Assets:* £72,009,704
Registered Office: 105 Duke Street, Liverpool, L1 5JQ
Activities: Financial leasing
Parent: Bibby Asset Finance Limited
Officers: Ian Downing [1958] Director/Accountant; Ian Stuart Ramsden [1970] Director; Ian John Wilkins [1967] Director

Bibby Line Group Limited
Incorporated: 1 June 1891 *Employees:* 4,934
Net Worth: £235,672,000 *Total Assets:* £1,599,224,064
Registered Office: 105 Duke Street, Liverpool, L1 5JQ
Activities: Activities of other holding companies n.e.c.
Shareholders: Mark Rupert Feeny; Philip Charles Okell; Lady Christine Maud Bibby
Officers: David John Lane Freer Anderson [1956] Director/Banker; Geoffrey Frank Harold Bibby [1965] Director; Sir Michael James Bibby [1963] Director; John Harold Cresswell [1961] Director; Paul Joseph Drechsler [1956] Director [Irish]; Caroline Dawn Hoare [1965] Director; Timothy Andrew Lebus [1951] Director; Mark Joseph Lyons [1962] Director

Bibby Line Limited
Incorporated: 20 December 2007 *Employees:* 3
Net Worth: £16 039,101 *Total Assets:* £33,549,734
Registered Office: 105 Duke Street, Liverpool, L1 5JQ
Activities: Sea and coastal freight water transport
Parent: Bibby Line Group Limited
Officers: John Harold Cresswell [1961] Director; Ian Kenneth Crook [1970] Director/Accountant; Simon Jeremy Kitchen [1958] Director; Mark Joseph Lyons [1962] Director; Jonathan Osborne [1969] Director/Chartered Accountant

Bibby Marine Limited
Incorporated: 8 December 1884 *Employees:* 144
Net Worth: £24,870,574 *Total Assets:* £62,513,240
Registered Office: 105 Duke Street, Liverpool, L1 5JQ
Activities: Sea and coastal freight water transport
Parent: Bibby Holdings Limited
Officers: Stephen Henry Bolton [1973] Director/Chartered Engineer; John Harold Cresswell [1961] Director; Ian Kenneth Crook [1970] Director/Accountant; John Howard Hughes [1955] Director; Simon Jeremy Kitchen [1958] Director; Mark Joseph Lyons [1962] Director; Jonathan Osborne [1969] Director/Chartered Accountant; Nigel Colin Patrick Quinn [1971] Director

Bibby Maritime Limited
Incorporated: 6 January 1975 *Employees:* 15
Net Worth: £27,228,984 *Total Assets:* £32,261,536
Registered Office: 105 Duke Street, Liverpool, L1 5JQ
Activities: Sea and coastal freight water transport
Parent: Bibby Marine Limited
Officers: Stephen Henry Bolton [1973] Director/Chartered Engineer; Ian Kenneth Crook [1970] Director/Accountant; John Howard Hughes [1955] Director; Carl Paul McLaughlin [1972] Director; Jonathan Osborne [1969] Director/Chartered Accountant

Bibby Supply Chain Services Limited
Incorporated: 2 April 1986 *Employees:* 1,981
Net Worth: £7,752,000 *Total Assets:* £59,963,000
Registered Office: 105 Duke Street, Liverpool, L1 5JQ
Activities: Activities of distribution holding companies
Parent: Bibby Line Group Limited
Officers: John Harold Cresswell [1961] Director; Richard James Morson [1975] Director

Bibby Taurus Limited
Incorporated: 12 September 2008
Net Worth: £12,517,057 *Total Assets:* £26,475,576
Registered Office: 105 Duke Street, Liverpool, L1 5JQ
Activities: Activities of other holding companies n.e.c.
Parent: Bibby Holdings Limited
Officers: Andrew John Goody [1966] Director/Accountant; Mark Joseph Lyons [1962] Director

Bibby Trade Factors Limited
Incorporated: 3 December 2004
Net Worth: £2,408,882 *Total Assets:* £21,930,240
Registered Office: 105 Duke Street, Liverpool, L1 5JQ
Activities: Factoring
Parent: Bibby Invoice Finance UK Limited
Officers: Ian Downing [1958] Director/Accountant; David John Postings [1960] Director; Ian Stuart Ramsden [1970] Director; Steven Vears Robinson [1968] Director; Stephen George Rose [1965] Director; Edward James Winterton [1975] Director

Bibby Trade Services Limited
Incorporated: 13 March 1998 *Employees:* 21
Net Worth: £7,943,521 *Total Assets:* £16,598,695
Registered Office: 105 Duke Street, Liverpool, L1 5JQ
Activities: Credit granting by non-deposit taking finance houses and other specialist consumer credit grantors
Parent: Bibby Financial Services (UK) Limited
Officers: Ian Downing [1958] Director/Accountant; David John Postings [1960] Director; Ian Stuart Ramsden [1970] Director; Steven Vears Robinson [1968] Director; Stephen George Rose [1965] Director; Edward James Winterton [1975] Director

Bibby Transport Limited
Incorporated: 17 September 1976
Net Worth Deficit: £5,163,375 *Total Assets:* £15,398,170
Registered Office: 105 Duke Street, Liverpool, L1 5JQ
Activities: Sea and coastal freight water transport
Parent: Bibby Line Limited
Officers: Ian Kenneth Crook [1970] Director/Accountant; Simon Jeremy Kitchen [1958] Director

Bibby Wavemaster I Limited
Incorporated: 24 November 2015
Net Worth Deficit: £368,338 *Total Assets:* £26,333,426
Registered Office: 105 Duke Street, Liverpool, L1 5JQ
Activities: Sea and coastal freight water transport
Parent: Bibby Marine Services Limited
Officers: Stephen Henry Bolton [1973] Director/Chartered Engineer; Alexei Robert Callender [1982] Director; Ian Kenneth Crook [1970] Director/Accountant; John Howard Hughes [1955] Director; Jonathan Osborne [1969] Director/Chartered Accountant

Bibliotheca Limited
Incorporated: 25 October 1994 *Employees:* 78
Net Worth: £9,359,000 *Total Assets:* £24,843,000
Registered Office: Landmark House, Station Road, Cheadle Hulme, Cheadle, Cheshire, SK8 7BS
Activities: Other information technology service activities
Parent: Bibliotheca Group GmbH
Officers: James Stephen Hopwood [1969] Managing Director & CTO; Darren Ratcliffe [1975] UK Managing Director; Phillip John Sykes [1974] Director Development

The Big Life Company Limited
Incorporated: 1 June 2001 *Employees:* 485
Net Worth: £11,215,252 *Total Assets:* £15,866,571
Registered Office: 1st Floor, 463 Stretford Road, Manchester, M16 9AB
Activities: Other human health activities
Officers: Regina McMorrow, Secretary; Maria Alavi [1973] Director/Banker; Allan Beswick [1948] Director/Broadcaster; Priti Butler [1964] Executive Director; Louise Grant [1983] Director/Doctor; Caroline Margaret Price [1958] Director; Edna Janet Robinson [1951] Director/Public Sector Advisor; Richard Scorer [1967] Director/Solicitor; Fay Lila Selvan [1959] Director/Chief Executive; Amit Shah [1981] Associate Director

Big Life Schools
Incorporated: 10 February 2012 *Employees:* 35
Net Worth: £8,538,000 *Total Assets:* £8,944,000
Registered Office: 1st Floor, 463 Stretford Road, Manchester, M16 9AB
Activities: Primary education
Officers: Regina McMorrow, Secretary; Karina Gay Carter [1963] Director/Senior Parenting Practitioner; Edward Gale [1985] Assistant Director Corporate Finance; Sandie Hayes [1968] Assistant Director; Andrea Heffernan [1970] Director of Corporate Support; Emma Elizabeth Perry [1975] Director/Operations Manager; Fay Lila Selvan [1959] Director/Chief Executive; Garry Shewan [1962] Director/Policeman; Philip Anthony Trohear [1972] Director/Deputy Headteacher

The Big Shed Limited
Incorporated: 8 April 2002 *Employees:* 100
Net Worth: £7,520,766 *Total Assets:* £10,583,545
Registered Office: Lancaster House, 70-76 Blackburn Street, Radcliffe, Manchester, M26 2JW
Activities: Activities of other holding companies n.e.c.
Major Shareholder: Michael Bernadine Murphy
Officers: Edward Elliot Murphy, Secretary; Michael Bernadine Murphy [1950] Director/Civil Engineer

Bilfinger Construction UK Limited
Incorporated: 30 August 1989 *Employees:* 4
Net Worth: £15,724,840 *Total Assets:* £20,722,000
Registered Office: One St Peter's Square, Manchester, M2 3DE
Activities: Construction of commercial buildings
Parent: Bilfinger SE
Officers: Paula Amesbury [1966] Director/Accountant; Philip Howard Maurer [1963] Director

Bilfinger Industrial Automation Services Limited
Incorporated: 25 October 1999 *Employees:* 347
Net Worth: £5,601,943 *Total Assets:* £17,327,970
Registered Office: Redwood House, Woodlands Park, Ashton Road, Newton-le-Willows, Merseyside, WA12 0HF
Activities: Manufacture of electricity distribution and control apparatus
Parent: Bilfinger SE
Officers: Paula Jill Amesbury, Secretary; Paula Jill Amesbury [1966] Finance Director; David Pickles [1962] Managing Director

Bilfinger UK Limited
Incorporated: 7 March 2005 *Employees:* 1,211
Net Worth: £28,049,000 *Total Assets:* £51,519,000
Registered Office: Axis House, Tudor Road, Manor Park, Runcorn, Cheshire, WA7 1BD
Activities: Construction of other civil engineering projects n.e.c.
Parent: Bilfinger Oil and Gas Limited
Officers: Paula Jill Amesbury, Secretary; Paula Jill Amesbury [1966] Finance Director; Duncan Michael Hall [1967] Director/Engineer; Phillip Howard Maurer [1963] Managing Director; Martin Richard Perry [1961] Commercial Director; David Pickles [1962] Managing Director

Billericay Dental Supply Co. Limited
Incorporated: 16 January 1975 *Employees:* 333
Net Worth: £22,733,000 *Total Assets:* £58,077,000
Registered Office: Europa House, Europa Trading Estate, Stoneclough Road, Kearsley, Manchester, M26 1GG
Activities: Non-specialised wholesale trade
Parent: HM Logistics Limited
Officers: Leo Damian Carroll, Secretary; Gervase Paul Adams [1958] Director; Tom Riall [1960] Director; Mohammed Omar Shafi Khan [1974] Director/Chief Financial Officer; Mark Wheatstone [1965] Technical & Equipment Sales Director

Billerudkorsnas Beetham Ltd
Incorporated: 18 March 1901 *Employees:* 152
Net Worth: £12,427,426 *Total Assets:* £21,797,196
Registered Office: Waterhouse Mills, Beetham, Milnthorpe, Cumbria, LA7 7AR
Activities: Manufacture of other articles of paper and paperboard n.e.c.
Parent: Billerudkorsnas AB
Officers: Sharon Peill, Secretary; Hakan Karl Krantz [1962] Mill Director [Swedish]; Susanne Karin Lithander [1961] Director/Chief Financial [Swedish]

Billing Aquadrome Limited
Incorporated: 10 February 1945
Net Worth: £15,558,509 *Total Assets:* £22,243,904
Registered Office: South Lakeland House, Main A6, Yealand Redmayne, Carnforth, Lancs, LA5 9RN
Activities: Other amusement and recreation activities n.e.c.
Officers: Paul Rossiter, Secretary; Paul Rossiter [1964] Director/Chartered Accountant; Trevor James White [1952] Director/Marketing Manager

Edward Billington and Son Limited
Incorporated: 12 December 1898 *Employees:* 1,783
Net Worth: £99,344,000 *Total Assets:* £197,552,992
Registered Office: Cunard Building, Liverpool, L3 1EL
Activities: Activities of head offices
Officers: David Marshall, Secretary; Gary Michael Blake [1973] Director; Stephen Glynn Hughes [1969] Finance Director; Aisling Kemp [1972] Director [Irish]; Andrew Saulez King [1966] Director; David Marshall [1961] Director; James Wiliam Noel Taylor [1966] Director; James Adrian Viner [1965] Director; Lloyd Leslie Russell Whiteley [1959] Director

Billington Foodservice Limited
Incorporated: 8 May 1987 *Employees:* 286
Net Worth: £12,002,366 *Total Assets:* £17,806,986
Registered Office: Cunard Building, Water Street, Liverpool, L3 1EL
Activities: Manufacture of other food products n.e.c.
Parent: Edward Billington & Son Ltd
Officers: David Marshall, Secretary; Gary Michael Blake [1973] Director

Birch Park Investments Limited
Incorporated: 28 March 1963 *Employees:* 5
Net Worth: £18,906,664 *Total Assets:* £20,981,650
Registered Office: 2nd Floor, Parkgates, Bury New Road, Prestwich, Manchester, M25 0TL
Activities: Other letting and operating of own or leased real estate
Shareholder: W Neumann Settlement
Officers: Pinchas Neumann, Secretary; Arnold Henry [1959] Director; Eli Neumann [1955] Director; Henry Neumann [1956] Director; Paul Mark Simon [1969] Director

Birchwood Community Academy Trust
Incorporated: 4 March 2013 *Employees:* 142
Net Worth: £8,802,000 *Total Assets:* £10,445,000
Registered Office: Brock Road, Birchwood, Warrington, Cheshire, WA3 7PT
Activities: General secondary education
Officers: Jane Calderbank, Secretary; Andrea Atherton [1948] Director/Retired Teacher; Colin Christopher Burrows [1956] Director/General Manager; Claire Doherty [1973] Director/Teacher; Andrew Campbell Lindsay [1958] Director; Deborah Jane Ost [1964] Director/Occupational Therapist; Rosemary Panting [1960] Director/Accountant; Alexander Paton [1949] Director/Retired; Mark Proctor [1964] Director; Nigel James Reeves [1966] Director/Consultant; Paul Taylor [1972] Managing Director; Jonathan Whaley [1968] Director/Teacher; Janet Wilson [1957] Director

Frank Bird (Poultry) Limited
Incorporated: 1 February 1997 *Employees:* 220
Net Worth: £10,423,994 *Total Assets:* £20,561,806
Registered Office: Underlyne, Langwathby, Penrith, Cumbria, CA10 1NB
Activities: Production of meat and poultry meat products
Parent: F & N Holdings Limited
Officers: Frank Bird, Secretary; Frank Bird [1936] Director; Mark Edward Bird [1969] Director

Birkdale High School
Incorporated: 6 July 2011 *Employees:* 61
Net Worth: £11,936,923 *Total Assets:* £14,115,609
Registered Office: Birkdale High School, Windy Harbour Road, Southport, Merseyside, PR8 3DT
Activities: General secondary education
Officers: Karen Marie Anslow, Secretary; Stuart Edward Bellerby [1965] Director/Local Government Senior Manager; Skender Berisha [1967] Director/Police Officer; Gil Bourgade [1966] Director/Headteacher [French]; Gillian Anne Carlisle-Collett [1970] Director/Lawyer; Annie Halina Gorski [1951] Director/Retired [French]; Bryan Guy Leece [1969] Director/Laboratory Technician; Pauline Marshall [1957] Director/Teacher; Angela Mulligan [1959] Director; Anita Margaret Sinnott [1977] Director/Teacher; Ian John Strom [1970] Director/School Business Manager; Mark Paul Sunderland [1971] Director; Christopher Simon Tait [1966] Director/Chartered Accountant; Elizabeth Wilson [1958] Director/Retired

Birkenhead Car and Van Hire Limited
Incorporated: 8 October 1993 *Employees:* 23
Net Worth: £1,448,812 *Total Assets:* £7,875,710
Registered Office: Hind Street, Birkenhead, Wirral, Merseyside, CH41 5DA
Activities: Renting and leasing of cars and light motor vehicles
Shareholders: Richard Joseph Houghton; Richard Michael Houghton
Officers: Richard Michael Houghton, Secretary; Richard Joseph Houghton [1941] Director/Vehicle Hirer; Richard Michael Houghton [1967] Director/Vehicle Hirer

Birkenhead Port Limited
Incorporated: 21 October 1994
Net Worth: £2,600,000 *Total Assets:* £23,800,000
Registered Office: Maritime Centre, Port of Liverpool, L21 1LA
Activities: Sea and coastal freight water transport
Parent: Peel Ports Operations Limited
Officers: Farook Akhtar Khan, Secretary; Caroline Ruth Marrison Gill, Secretary; Thomas Eardley Allison [1948] Director; Ian Graeme Lloyd Charnock [1962] Director; John Whittaker [1942] Director; Mark Whitworth [1966] Director

Birkenhead School
Incorporated: 23 July 2002 *Employees:* 146
Net Worth: £14,774,937 *Total Assets:* £17,191,044
Registered Office: The Lodge, 58 Beresford Road, Prenton, Merseyside, CH43 2JD
Activities: Pre-primary education
Officers: Mark Jonathan Turner, Secretary; Mark Richard Cashin [1953] Retired Director; Alasdair David Coates [1952] Director/Educational Consultant; Andrew James Cross [1954] Director/Solicitor; Lorraine Antonia Carrol Dodd [1955] Director Investment Management; Michael Stuart Furniss [1961] Director/IT Consultant; Judith Greeensmith [1954] Director/Business Executive; Dr Julia Moore [1956] Director/Medical Doctor; David Irvine Pottinger [1960] Director/Chief Executive; Edward Nicholas Rice [1949] Director/Chartered Surveyor; William David Crawford Rushworth [1943] Director/Regional Manager

Birmingham Schools PSP Phase 1B Limited
Incorporated: 13 April 2011
Net Worth: £55,000 *Total Assets:* £31,519,000
Registered Office: c/o Albany SPC Services Ltd, 3rd Floor, 3-5 Charlotte Street, Manchester, M1 4HB
Activities: Other education n.e.c.
Parent: Civis PFI/PPP Infrastructure Birmingham Schools Holdings Limited
Officers: Ailison Louise Mitchell, Secretary; Barry Paul Millsom [1974] Director

Birmingham Schools SPC Holdings Phase 1A Ltd
Incorporated: 26 May 2009
Net Worth: £367,000 *Total Assets:* £47,899,000
Registered Office: c/o Albany SPC Services Ltd, 3rd Floor, 3-5 Charlotte Street, Manchester, M1 4HB
Activities: Other education n.e.c.
Parent: Birmingham Schools PSP Phase 1A Limited
Officers: Ailison Louise Mitchell, Secretary; Jaswinder Didially [1964] Director/Head of Service; Kate Louise Flaherty [1980] Director; James William Lasseter [1965] Director/General Manager; Leo William McKenna [1966] Director [Irish]; Jasvinder Kaur Uppal [1971] Director

Birmingham Schools SPC Holdings Phase 1B Limited
Incorporated: 8 April 2011
Net Worth: £68,000 *Total Assets:* £31,514,000
Registered Office: c/o Albany SPC Services Ltd, 3rd Floor, 3-5 Charlotte Street, Manchester, M1 4HB
Activities: Other education n.e.c.
Parent: Birmingham Schools PSP Phase 1B Ltd
Officers: Ailison Louise Mitchell, Secretary; Jaswinder Didially [1964] Director/Head of Service; James William Lasseter [1965] Director/General Manager; Leo William McKenna [1966] Director [Irish]

Birmingham Schools SPC Phase 1A Limited
Incorporated: 27 May 2009
Net Worth: £178,000 *Total Assets:* £48,392,000
Registered Office: c/o Albany SPC Services Ltd, 3rd Floor, 3-5 Charlotte Street, Manchester, M1 4HB
Activities: Other education n.e.c.
Parent: Birmingham Schools SPC Holdings Phase 1A Ltd
Officers: Ailison Louise Mitchell, Secretary; Jaswinder Didially [1964] Director/Head of Service; Kate Louise Flaherty [1980] Director; James William Lasseter [1965] Director/General Manager; Leo William McKenna [1966] Director [Irish]; Jasvinder Kaur Uppal [1971] Director

Birmingham Schools SPC Phase 1B Limited
Incorporated: 11 April 2011
Net Worth: £68,000 *Total Assets:* £31,514,000
Registered Office: c/o Albany SPC Services Ltd, 3rd Floor, 3-5 Charlotte Street, Manchester, M1 4HB
Activities: Other education n.e.c.
Parent: Birmingham Schools SPC Holdings Phase 1B Ltd
Officers: Ailison Louise Mitchell, Secretary; Jaswinder Didially [1964] Director/Head of Service; James William Lasseter [1965] Director/General Manager; Leo William McKenna [1966] Director [Irish]

Birmingham Technology (Property) Limited
Incorporated: 5 November 1987
Net Worth: £2,753,839 *Total Assets:* £31,756,710
Registered Office: Union, Albert Square, Manchester, M2 6LW
Activities: Other letting and operating of own or leased real estate
Parent: Innovation Birmingham Limited
Officers: Kevin James Crotty [1976] Director/Chartered Accountant; Peter Andrew Crowther [1972] Director/Surveyor; Dr David John Hardman [1957] Director/Chief Executive; Philip Andrew Kemp [1964] Director/Chief Commercial Officer; Kate Victoria Lawlor [1981] Director/Chartered Accountant; Christopher George Oglesby [1967] Director

Birtenshaw
Incorporated: 13 October 1994 *Employees:* 278
Net Worth: £2,516,697 *Total Assets:* £9,043,203
Registered Office: Birtenshaw, Darwen Road, Bromley Cross, Bolton, Lancs, BL7 9AB
Activities: Other education n.e.c.
Officers: Ryan Armitage [1982] Director/Recruitment Consultant; Kathryn Brown [1954] Director/Safeguarding Consultant; Helen Kirk [1965] Director/Registered Nurse; Anthony Joseph Long [1959] Director/Professor of Child and Family Health; James Pilkington [1977] Director/Self Employed Copy Writer and Proof Reader; Deborah Joanne Sidebottom [1977] Sales Director; Glenn Andrew Tomison [1958] Director/Optician; Michael John Walmsley [1982] Director/Construction Manager

M J Birtwistle & Co Limited
Incorporated: 4 March 2003 *Employees:* 334
Net Worth: £1,743,711 *Total Assets:* £24,008,528
Registered Office: 1 Ferrous Way, Irlam, Manchester, M44 5FS
Activities: Wholesale of meat and meat products
Parent: Sosamja Holdings Limited
Officers: Elizabeth Watts, Secretary; Matthew John Birtwistle [1980] Director; Michael John Birtwistle [1952] Director; Mark Stephen Bradbury [1958] Director; Glenn Francis Eastwood [1965] Director; Michael Robert Gibson [1962] Director/Wholesale Meat Salesman; Steven James Woollands [1962] Director

Bishop Rawstorne Church of England Academy Trust
Incorporated: 16 June 2011 *Employees:* 86
Net Worth: £7,645,000 *Total Assets:* £9,310,000
Registered Office: Bishop Rawstorne Church of England Academy, Highfield Road, Croston, Leyland, Lancs, PR26 9HH
Activities: General secondary education
Officers: Lynn Eileen Hood, Secretary; Sian Louise Belfield [1973] Director; Reverend Andrew James Brown [1960] Director/Priest; Joanna Cast [1977] Director; Kathleen Cooper [1939] Director/Farmer/Retired Teacher; Sheila Cooper [1960] Director; Teresa Valerie Cowell [1949] Director; John Paul Cowley [1970] Director; Helen Suzanne Dixon [1952] Director; Wendy Marie Gibbons [1956] Director/Learning Support Special Needs; Stephen John Gregson [1970] Director; John Anthony Latham [1945] Director; Andrew Charles Marston [1954] Director/HR Consultant; Mark McNulty [1971] Director; Ellen Margaret Palmer [1988] Director; Paul Victor Phythian [1967] Sales Director; Karl Rhys Roberts [1976] Director; David Ernest Taylor [1947] Director/Quantity Surveyor; Warren Roy Websdell [1934] Director; Rev Michael Woods [1957] Director/Rector of Croston

The Bishops' Blue Coat Church of England High School
Incorporated: 18 March 2011 *Employees:* 112
Net Worth: £8,925,495 *Total Assets:* £10,892,454
Registered Office: Vaughans Lane, Great Boughton, Chester, CH3 5XF
Activities: General secondary education
Officers: Alison Beasley, Secretary; David Kenneth Abraham [1960] Director; Julian David Annison [1969] Director/Professional Engineer; David Richard Blackmore [1938] Director/Retired; Lynn Carstens [1961] Director; Eamonn Coffey [1956] Director/Teacher; John Cecil Davies [1940] Director; Haydn Michael Ebbrell [1965] Director/Teaching Assistant; Lindsay Anne Grundy [1959] Director/School Administration Officer; Dr. Elaine Hemmings [1962] Director/Tutor; John Hinnigan [1946] Director; Lesley Jane Ingram [1960] Director; Jane Jones [1947] Director/Retired Teacher; Dr Timothy Charles Quentin Noakes [1962] Director/Scientist; Helen Elizabeth Rowland [1969] Director/Primary School Teacher; Robert Edward Swettenham [1930] Director/Retired; David Walsh [1965] Director/Management Consultant [Irish]; Ian Wilson [1973] Director/Headteacher; Dr Timothy Gregory Arthur Wright [1949] Director

Bispham Green Brewery Company Limited
Incorporated: 27 February 1995 *Employees:* 91
Net Worth: £1,812,047 *Total Assets:* £7,256,332
Registered Office: Woodlands, Parbold, Wigan, Lancs, WN8 7AN
Activities: Licenced restaurants
Shareholder: Martin John Ainscough
Officers: Helen Mary Ainscough [1968] Director/Restaurant Owner; Martin John Ainscough [1966] Director

Bitrez Group Limited
Incorporated: 12 February 1982 *Employees:* 96
Net Worth: £8,963,791 *Total Assets:* £11,435,975
Registered Office: Unit 68 Bradley Hall Trading Estate, Bradley Lane, Standish, Wigan, Lancs, WN6 0XQ
Activities: Manufacture of other chemical products n.e.c.
Shareholders: Brian Allen; Paul Harry Jones
Officers: Brian Allen [1940] Director/Secretary; Paul Harry Jones [1966] Director

Bitrez Limited
Incorporated: 10 January 2001 *Employees:* 96
Net Worth: £8,865,887 *Total Assets:* £11,136,115
Registered Office: Bradley Hall Trading Estate, Bradley Hall, Standish, Wigan, Lancs, WN6 0XQ
Activities: Manufacture of other chemical products n.e.c.
Parent: Bitrez Group Limited
Officers: Brian Allen [1940] Managing Director; Paul Harry Jones [1966] Director

Black Cat Fireworks Limited
Incorporated: 29 March 1985 *Employees:* 23
Net Worth: £640,000 *Total Assets:* £7,007,000
Registered Office: Centenary House, Centenary Way, Salford, M50 1RF
Activities: Wholesale of household goods (other than musical instruments) n.e.c
Officers: Ulf Stefan Brettschneider [1964] Director [German]; Nicholas Andrew Cottrell [1960] Director; Robert Stephen Lister [1956] Director

Peter Black Footwear & Accessories Limited
Incorporated: 13 October 1947 *Employees:* 77
Net Worth: £1,994,000 *Total Assets:* £14,732,000
Registered Office: Centenary House, Centenary Way, Salford, M50 1RF
Activities: Wholesale of household goods (other than musical instruments) n.e.c
Parent: Peter Black Holdings Limited
Officers: Nicholas Andrew Cottrell [1960] Director; Robert Stephen Lister [1956] Director

Peter Black Holdings Limited
Incorporated: 19 August 1971
Net Worth: £76,930,000 *Total Assets:* £90,741,000
Registered Office: Centenary House, Centenary Way, Salford, M50 1RF
Activities: Activities of head offices
Parent: Peter Black International Limited
Officers: Robert Arthur Bacon, Secretary; Nicholas Andrew Cottrell [1960] Director; Robert Stephen Lister [1956] Director

Peter Black International Limited
Incorporated: 20 April 2006
Net Worth: £27,495,000 *Total Assets:* £51,902,000
Registered Office: Centenary House, Centenary Way, Salford, M50 1RF
Activities: Activities of head offices
Parent: LF Europe Limited
Officers: Robert Arthur Bacon, Secretary; Nicholas Andrew Cottrell [1960] Director; Robert Stephen Lister [1956] Director

Blackburn Chemicals (Holdings) Limited
Incorporated: 14 October 2004 *Employees:* 68
Net Worth: £45,577,204 *Total Assets:* £51,476,044
Registered Office: Cunliffe Road, Whitebirk Industrial Estate, Blackburn, Lancs, BB1 5SX
Activities: Renting and operating of Housing Association real estate
Major Shareholder: George Lamb
Officers: Amanda Susan Holt, Secretary; Katie Rebecca Connell [1982] Director; George Lamb [1935] Director; Maire Ciara Naessens [1963] Director [Irish]; Allan Whalley [1949] Director

Blackburn Chemicals Limited
Incorporated: 8 May 1973 *Employees:* 68
Net Worth: £9,527,096 *Total Assets:* £16,714,472
Registered Office: Cunliffe Road, Whitebirk Industrial Estate, Blackburn, BB1 5SX
Activities: Manufacture of other chemical products n.e.c.
Parent: Blackburn Chemicals (Holdings) Limited
Officers: Amanda Susan Holt, Secretary; Jack Bratt [1946] Director/Industrial Chemist; Dr Philip Andrew Cooper [1964] Director; John Andrew Covill [1962] Director; Amanda Susan Holt [1965] Director; George Lamb [1935] Director/Industrial Chemist; Steven George Lamb [1961] Director; Nicola Lord [1979] Director; Allan Whalley [1949] Director/Accountant

The Blackburn Diocesan Board of Education
Incorporated: 30 November 1955 *Employees:* 25
Net Worth: £6,253,000 *Total Assets:* £11,530,000
Registered Office: Diocesan Offices, Clayton House, Walker Office Park, Guide, Blackburn, BB1 2QE
Activities: Educational support services
Officers: Stephen Lawrence Whittaker, Secretary; Reverend David Alun Arnold [1978] Director/Vicar; Generald David Burrows [1942] Director/Retired; Natalie Esther Cox [1986] Director/Student; Timothy Daniel Cox [1980] Director/System Support; The Venerable Michael John Everitt [1968] Director/Religion; Jonathan Mark Phair Hewitt [1956] Director/Senior LEA Adviser; Andrew Holliday [1962] Director/Clerk in Holy Orders; Rev Timothy John Horobin [1960] Director/Clergyman; Mark Campbell Ireland [1960] Director/Archdeacon of Blackburn; Carolyn Ann Johnson [1952] Director/Barrister; Ruth Elizabeth Radford [1947] Director/Teacher; Joanne Snape [1966] Director/Headteacher; Reverend Philip Richard Meredith Venables [1958] Director/Clergyman

Blackburn Diocesan Board of Finance Limited
Incorporated: 29 October 1927 *Employees:* 42
Net Worth: £59,891,000 *Total Assets:* £64,826,000
Registered Office: Diocesan Offices, Clayton House, Walker Office Park, Guide, Blackburn, BB1 2QE
Activities: Activities of religious organisations
Officers: Graeme David Pollard, Secretary; Nicholas Peter Aves [1952] Director/Local Government Officer; David Lees Barlow [1951] Director/Retired; Generald David Burrows [1942] Director/Retired; Dr Awena Elizabeth Carter [1945] Director/Retired; Prof Richard Geoffrey Carter [1943] Director/Retired; Michael Leonard Chew [1948] Director/Retired; Robert John Collins [1947] Director/Site Administrator; Revd Dr Simon John Cox [1953] Director/Clergyman; Timothy Daniel Cox [1980] Director/System Support; Jillian Louise Calland Duff [1972] Director/Minister of Religion; Michael John Everitt [1968] Director/Minister of Religion; Rev Nancy Elisabeth Goodrich [1966] Director/Vicar; Julian Tudor Henderson [1954] Director/Minister of Religion; Andrew Holliday [1962] Director/Clerk in Holy Orders; Peter Howell-Jones [1962] Director/Dean; Mark Campbell Ireland [1960] Director/Archdeacon; Peter Jelley [1931] Director/Retired; Rev Peter Andrew Lillicrap [1965] Director/Vicar; Richard Arthur Howard Marshall [1966] Director; Philip John North [1966] Director/Bishop; Revd Canon Andrew George Sage [1958] Director/Clerk in Holy Orders; Colin Scott [1938] Director/Retired; Jacqueline Mary Stamper [1950] Director/Retired; David John Wilkinson [1951] Director/Farmer

Blackburn Fundco Limited
Incorporated: 24 October 2008 *Employees:* 5
Net Worth Deficit: £11,119,450 *Total Assets:* £25,521,900
Registered Office: Sceptre House, Sceptre Way, Bamber Bridge, Preston, Lancs, PR5 6AW
Activities: Development of building projects
Parent: Blackburn Holdco Limited
Officers: Deborah Jane Rawlinson, Secretary; Jeremy Peter Hartley [1965] Director/Chartered Accountant; Roger Martyn Parr [1970] Director; Neil Geoffrey Ward [1959] Director; Christine Desiree Winstanley [1966] Director; Mark Stuart Youlton [1963] Director

The Blackburn Rovers Football and Athletic Limited
Incorporated: 27 July 1897 *Employees:* 234
Net Worth Deficit: £75,787,456 *Total Assets:* £39,172,248
Registered Office: Ewood Park, Blackburn, BB2 4JF
Activities: Activities of sport clubs
Parent: Venkys London Limited
Officers: Ian David Silvester, Secretary; Michael Anthony Cheston [1961] Director/Accountant; Robert Duckworth Coar [1947] Director; Reddy Gandhi Babu [1963] Director [Indian]; Steven Waggott [1954] Director/Chief Executive Officer

G.R. & M.M. Blackledge PLC
Incorporated: 26 October 1983 *Employees:* 1,570
Net Worth: £27,688,020 *Total Assets:* £46,871,972
Registered Office: 9 Western Avenue, Matrix Park, Leyland, Lancs, PR7 7NB
Activities: Retail sale of cosmetic and toilet articles in specialised stores
Shareholders: Graham Richard Blackledge; Margaret Mary Blackledge
Officers: Roy McFarlane, Secretary; Daniel Richard Blackledge [1975] Managing Director; Graham Richard Blackledge [1949] Director/Chairman; Margaret Mary Blackledge [1949] Director/Secretary; Roy McFarlane [1949] IT Director

Blackpool Football Club (Properties) Limited
Incorporated: 12 December 1985 *Employees:* 164
Net Worth: £22,751,522 *Total Assets:* £41,028,444
Registered Office: The Blackpool Football Ground, Bloomfield Road, Blackpool, Lancs, FY1 6JJ
Activities: Activities of sport clubs
Major Shareholder: Owen John Oyston
Officers: Owen John Oyston [1934] Director

Blackpool Football Club.Limited (The)
Incorporated: 18 June 1896 *Employees:* 118
Net Worth: £33,670,144 *Total Assets:* £35,805,856
Registered Office: Bloomfield Road, Blackpool, Lancs, FY1 6JJ
Activities: Activities of sport clubs
Parent: Blackpool Football Club (Properties) Limited
Officers: Natalie Christopher [1985] Director; Owen John Oyston [1934] Director; Kaspars Varpins [1982] Director [Latvian]

Blackpool Multi Academy Trust
Incorporated: 4 July 2013 *Employees:* 244
Net Worth: £16,158,814 *Total Assets:* £23,771,846
Registered Office: 158 Whitegate Drive, Blackpool, Lancs, FY3 9HF
Activities: Primary education
Officers: Janet Lyn Ashbridge [1967] Director/Principal Lecturer; Kathryn Sarah Lord [1977] Director/Human Resource Manager; Lorraine Diane Stephen [1957] Director/Head Service; Paul Geoffrey Turner [1979] Director/School Safeguarding Advisor; David Leonard Wallbank [1966] Director/Chartered Civil Engineer

The Blackpool Pier Company Limited
Incorporated: 23 May 2015 *Employees:* 156
Net Worth: £3,588,093 *Total Assets:* £12,622,123
Registered Office: Empress Buildings, 97 Church Street, Blackpool, Lancs, FY1 1HU
Activities: Other amusement and recreation activities n.e.c.
Shareholders: Sue Sedgwick; Peter James Sedgwick
Officers: Peter James Sedgwick [1980] Director; Peter James Sedgwick [1945] Director; Renee Suezanka Sedgwick [1976] Director; Sue Sedgwick [1950] Director

Blackpool Pleasure Beach (Holdings) Limited
Incorporated: 30 July 1984 *Employees:* 669
Net Worth: £9,835,000 *Total Assets:* £33,275,000
Registered Office: Pleasure Beach, Ocean Boulevard, Promenade, Blackpool, Lancs, FY4 1EZ
Activities: Other amusement and recreation activities n.e.c.
Shareholders: Amanda Jean Thompson; Peter James Bates; Monitor and Merrimac Limited
Officers: Fiona Carolyn Gilje [1963] Director; Amanda Jean Thompson [1962] Director; Barbara Joan Thompson [1939] Director; Nicholas William Robert Thompson [1968] Director

Blackpool Pleasure Beach Limited
Incorporated: 10 January 1985 *Employees:* 565
Net Worth: £1,211,000 *Total Assets:* £36,023,000
Registered Office: Pleasure Beach, Ocean Boulevard, Promenade, Blackpool, Lancs, FY4 1EZ
Activities: Activities of amusement parks and theme parks
Parent: Blackpool Pleasure Beach (Holdings) Limited
Officers: Michael Brown [1956] Group Commercial Director; John Patrick Chamberlain Collins [1943] Director/Consultant; Fiona Carolyn Gilje [1963] Director; Jonathan Gray [1970] Finance Director; Craig John Hemmings [1962] Director; Nigel Peter Kilgallon [1959] Director/Legal Counsel; Robert Owen [1968] Director; Amanda Jean Thompson [1962] Director; Barbara Joan Thompson [1939] Director; Nicholas William Robert Thompson [1968] Director

Blackpool Transport Services Limited
Incorporated: 21 March 1986 *Employees:* 678
Net Worth: £7,319,641 *Total Assets:* £25,064,712
Registered Office: Rigby Road, Blackpool, Lancs, FY1 5DD
Activities: Other passenger land transport
Parent: Blackpool Council
Officers: Mark Towers, Secretary; James Carney [1958] Finance Director; Jane Cole [1961] Managing Director; James Thomson Elmes [1947] Director/Retired; Paul David Stuart Galley [1974] Managing Director; Neil Andrew Kimberley [1966] Director/Strategic Consultant; Robert Wayne Pinkett [1956] Director/Transport Planner [American]; Kathryn Helen Shane [1969] Director/Head of Blackpool Cluster - Merlin; Sally Marie Shaw [1975] Director of People and Stakeholders; Christine Elizabeth Wright [1948] Director/Councillor

Blacks Outdoor Retail Limited
Incorporated: 3 October 2011 *Employees:* 1,662
Net Worth Deficit: £30,679,000 *Total Assets:* £72,151,000
Registered Office: Hollinsbrook Way, Pilsworth, Bury, Lancs, BL9 8RR
Activities: Retail sale of clothing in specialised stores
Parent: JD Sports Fashion PLC
Officers: Siobhan Mawdsley, Secretary; Lee Paul Bagnall [1969] Managing Director; Peter Alan Cowgill [1953] Director; Brian Michael Small [1956] Director

Blakedale Ltd
Incorporated: 12 April 1995 *Employees:* 22
Net Worth: £1,722,910 *Total Assets:* £9,472,451
Registered Office: Sterling House, 2-4 Mill Lane, Whittle-le-Woods, Chorley, Lancs, PR6 7LX
Activities: Manufacture of other plastic products
Officers: Dominic James Horrocks, Secretary; Carmen Louise Bowley [1968] Director; Benjamin Edward Frederick Smith [1983] Director; Jonathan Charles Smith [1969] Director; Richard Anthony Smith [1966] Director

Blankstone Sington Limited
Incorporated: 2 May 1989 *Employees:* 35
Net Worth: £4,783,520 *Total Assets:* £8,309,196
Registered Office: Walker House, Exchange Flags, Liverpool, L2 3YL
Activities: Security and commodity contracts dealing activities
Officers: Christopher Anthony Dsouza, Secretary; Neil Simon Blankstone [1968] Director/Stockbroker; Kenneth John Conolly [1949] Director/Chartered Accountant; Christopher Anthony D'Souza [1962] Director/Chartered Accountant; Peter John Ellwood [1961] Director/Stockbroker; Benjamin Max Taxman [1972] Director/Investment Manager; Neil Patrick Turner [1976] Director/Investment Manager; Paul Raymond Williams [1964] Director/Research Analyst

Blazing Productions Ltd
Incorporated: 20 March 2014 *Employees:* 5
Net Worth: £4,597,368 *Total Assets:* £10,010,379
Registered Office: 6th Floor, Blackfrairs House, Parsonage, Manchester, M3 2JA
Activities: Motion picture production activities
Officers: Guy Stanley Collins [1944] Director/Film Producer; Fredrik Jan Hedman [1980] Director/Partner, GFM Films [Swedish]; Cherk Fung Sherman Lai [1984] Director/Media and Entertainment [Chinese]; Michael Patrick Ryan [1950] Director/Film Producer/Financier; Zhonglei Wang [1970] Director/Media and Entertainment [Chinese]; Ning Ye [1973] Director/Media and Entertainment [Chinese]

Blemain Finance Limited
Incorporated: 24 September 1974 *Employees:* 522
Net Worth: £7,500,000 *Total Assets:* £508,900,000
Registered Office: Lake View, Lakeside, Cheadle, Cheshire, SK8 3GW
Activities: Credit granting by non-deposit taking finance houses and other specialist consumer credit grantors
Parent: Together Financial Services Limited
Officers: Sarah Elizabeth Batt, Secretary; Peter Simon Ball [1968] Director; Ronald Baxter [1951] Director; Gary Derek Beckett [1969] Director; David Jonathan Bennett [1962] Director/Chairman; Wayne Bowser [1952] Director; Marcus John Joseph Reynolds Golby [1970] Executive Director; Robert Michael McTighe [1953] Director; Henry Neville Moser [1949] Director; Paul Antony Wilson [1971] Director

Blencathra Hydro Limited
Incorporated: 3 September 2015
Net Worth Deficit: £116,427 *Total Assets:* £13,290,127
Registered Office: Canal Head North, Kendal, Cumbria, LA9 7BZ
Activities: Production of electricity
Parent: Gilkes Hydro Investments Limited
Officers: Robert Henry Moffett Chaplin [1963] Director; Charles William Nepean Crewdson [1964] Director; Carl Peter Crompton [1973] Director

Blenheim Land & Properties Ltd
Incorporated: 28 March 2003 *Employees:* 4
Net Worth: £2,033,760 *Total Assets:* £10,153,646
Registered Office: Georges Court, Chestergate, Macclesfield, Cheshire, SK11 6DP
Activities: Buying and selling of own real estate
Shareholder: Christopher Jonathan Anderson
Officers: Christopher Jonathan Anderson [1984] Director/Commercial Letting Agent; Kevin Hatfield [1961] Director

Bleu Properties Ltd
Incorporated: 27 August 2004 *Employees:* 10
Net Worth: £1,591,923 *Total Assets:* £10,381,722
Registered Office: Suite 1, Buttershaw Works, Buttershaw Lane, Bradford, W Yorks, BD6 2DD
Activities: Buying and selling of own real estate
Officers: Anthony David Wormald [1961] Director

Bliss Bidco Limited
Incorporated: 20 June 2016 *Employees:* 13
Net Worth Deficit: £5,432,511 *Total Assets:* £31,831,276
Registered Office: Concorde House, Canal Street, Chester, CH1 4EJ
Activities: Tour operator activities
Shareholders: Northedge Capital LLP; Northedge Capital II GP LLP; Bliss Topco Limited
Officers: Jennifer Isobel Atkinson [1975] Managing Director; Mal Barritt [1972] Director; Judith Ellis Hinkson [1970] Director; Emma Victoria Pickering [1979] Finance Director; Sarah Louise Roberts [1979] Director; Raymond Stenton [1972] Director

Bliss Topco Limited
Incorporated: 20 June 2016 *Employees:* 201
Net Worth Deficit: £1,453,952 *Total Assets:* £63,271,120
Registered Office: Concorde House, Canal Street, Chester, CH1 4EJ
Activities: Tour operator activities
Shareholders: Jennifer Isobel Atkinson; Northedge Capital II GP LLP; Northedge Capital LLP
Officers: Jennifer Isobel Atkinson [1975] Managing Director; Mal Barritt [1972] Director; Judith Ellis Hinkson [1970] Director; Emma Victoria Pickering [1979] Finance Director; Sarah Louise Roberts [1979] Director; Raymond Stenton [1972] Director

Blue Deer Limited
Incorporated: 12 May 1997 *Employees:* 2
Net Worth: £6,948,557 *Total Assets:* £11,669,975
Registered Office: 31 Great King Street, Macclesfield, Cheshire, SK11 6PL
Activities: Development of building projects
Parent: Good Eyed Deer Company Limited
Officers: Lynne Turner, Secretary; Timothy Peter Turner [1958] Director

Blue Machinery (Central) Limited
Incorporated: 11 September 1992 *Employees:* 27
Net Worth: £1,767,849 *Total Assets:* £9,429,708
Registered Office: New Cheshire Business Park, Wincham Lane, Wincham, Northwich, Cheshire, CW9 6GG
Activities: Other retail sale not in stores, stalls or markets
Parent: McGeary Holdings Limited
Officers: Aidan Patrick McGeary, Secretary; Aidan Patrick McGeary [1980] Director; Patrick Oliver McGeary [1952] Director; Sean McGeary [1982] Director

Blue Machinery (Group) PLC
Incorporated: 15 August 2003 *Employees:* 89
Net Worth: £5,822,706 *Total Assets:* £15,437,232
Registered Office: New Cheshire Business Park, Wincham Lane, Wincham, Northwich, Cheshire, CW9 6GG
Activities: Other service activities n.e.c.
Officers: Eugene John Donnelly, Secretary/Director [Irish]; Austin Paul Daniel Carey [1970] Director; Eugene John Donnelly [1958] Director [Irish]; Brian Victor Maxwell [1959] Director; Patrick Oliver McGeary [1952] Director

Blue Machinery (Southern) Limited
Incorporated: 23 December 2003 *Employees:* 18
Net Worth: £4,168,705 *Total Assets:* £10,726,327
Registered Office: New Cheshire Business Park, Wincham Lane, Wincham, Northwich, Cheshire, CW9 6GG
Activities: Agents involved in the sale of machinery, industrial equipment, ships and aircraft
Major Shareholder: Brian Victor Maxwell
Officers: Brian Victor Maxwell [1959] Director

Blue Prism Group PLC
Incorporated: 2 September 2015 *Employees:* 134
Net Worth Deficit: £4,120,000 *Total Assets:* £31,643,000
Registered Office: Centrix House, Crow Lane East, Newton-le-Willows, St Helens, Merseyside, WA12 9UY
Activities: Business and domestic software development
Officers: John Warrick, Secretary; Alastair Douglas Bathgate [1964] Director; Christopher Michael Batterham [1955] Director; Charmaine Bridgette Eggberry [1970] Director; Dr Conrad Jason Kingdon [1962] Director; Kenneth Lever [1953] Director; Ijoma Patrick Tilowakuti Maluza [1979] Director/Accountant

Blue Prism Limited
Incorporated: 26 July 2001 *Employees:* 78
Net Worth Deficit: £3,533,000 *Total Assets:* £21,842,000
Registered Office: Centrix House, Crow Lane East, Newton-le-Willows, St Helens, Merseyside, WA12 9UY
Activities: Business and domestic software development
Parent: Blue Prism Group PLC
Officers: John Warrick, Secretary; Alastair Douglas Bathgate [1964] Director; Martin Flood [1957] Director of Sales; Patrick Geary [1965] Director; Dr Conrad Jason Kingdon [1962] Director; Ijoma Patrick Tilowakuti Maluza [1979] Director/Accountant; David William Moss [1974] Director; Neil Wright [1966] Director

Blue Support Services Limited
Incorporated: 4 November 2009 *Employees:* 116
Net Worth: £845,057 *Total Assets:* £10,976,142
Registered Office: Building 1000, Kings Reach, Yew Street, Stockport, Cheshire, SK4 2HG
Activities: Management of real estate on a fee or contract basis
Parent: E S Management Services Limited
Officers: Andrew Dwan [1965] Director; Michael Dwan [1959] Director

Bluebell (Crewe) Limited
Incorporated: 17 November 1987
Net Worth: £8,431,000 *Total Assets:* £8,431,000
Registered Office: Lookers House, 3 Etchells Road, West Timperley, Altrincham, Cheshire, WA14 5XS
Activities: Sale of new cars and light motor vehicles
Parent: Knights North West Limited
Officers: Glenda MacGeekie, Secretary; Andrew Campbell Bruce [1965] Director/Chief Executive Officer; Robin Anthony Gregson [1960] Director/Chartered Accountant; Nigel John McMinn [1968] Managing Director - Motor Division

The Bluecoat
Incorporated: 21 April 1988 *Employees:* 61
Net Worth: £9,958,172 *Total Assets:* £10,267,001
Registered Office: Bluecoat Chambers, School Lane, Liverpool, L1 3BX
Activities: Artistic creation
Officers: Edward Francis Berg [1958] Director of Arts Organisation; Dr Michael George Birchall [1985] Director/Curator; Ralph Hendrik Frank Bullivant [1964] Director/Solicitor; Robert Edward Corbett [1952] Director/Retired; Amy Louisa de Joia [1962] Museum Director [American]; Jamie Eastman [1972] Director/Arts Manager/Curator/Head of Dept, University; Dr Emmanuel Matan [1939] Director/Retired; Peter Malcolm Mearns [1950] Director/Retired; Cyril Harold Aston Powell [1948] Director/Retired; Kelly Susan Salvoni [1973] Director/Bank Manager; Sri Sarker [1980] Executive Director; Daniel Hugo Seton Stinson [1959] Director

Bluethorn Developments Limited
Incorporated: 25 October 2005
Net Worth: £87,958 *Total Assets:* £16,950,914
Registered Office: c/o Barlow Andrews, 78 Chorley New Road, Bolton, Lancs, BL1 4BY
Activities: Buying and selling of own real estate
Shareholder: Mark James Caldwell
Officers: Mark James Caldwell, Secretary; James Stanley Caldwell [1944] Director; Mark James Caldwell [1973] Director

Blujay Solutions Group Holdings Limited
Incorporated: 18 April 2012 *Employees:* 958
Net Worth Deficit: £58,978,728 *Total Assets:* £224,466,672
Registered Office: 4M Building, Malaga Avenue, Manchester Airport, Manchester, M90 3RR
Activities: Business and domestic software development
Parent: Kewill Topco Limited
Officers: Joy Burkholder Meier, Secretary; Douglas Arthur Braun [1960] Director/Chief Executive [American]; Deep Shah [1979] Director/Investment; Adam Alexi Solomon [1987] Director/Investor [American]

Blujay Solutions Holdings Limited
Incorporated: 18 April 2012
Net Worth Deficit: £2,339,008 *Total Assets:* £105,282,752
Registered Office: 4M Building, Malaga Avenue, Manchester Airport, Manchester, M90 3RR
Activities: Business and domestic software development
Parent: Kewill Group Holdings Ltd
Officers: Joy Burkholder Meier, Secretary; Douglas Arthur Braun [1960] Director/Chief Executive [American]; Deep Shah [1979] Director/Investment; Adam Alexi Solomon [1987] Director/Investor [American]

Blujay Solutions Ltd
Incorporated: 7 January 1972 *Employees:* 71
Net Worth: £42,708,000 *Total Assets:* £77,529,000
Registered Office: 4M Building, Malaga Avenue, Manchester Airport, Manchester, M90 3RR
Activities: Business and domestic software development
Parent: Kewill Holdings Limited
Officers: Joy Burkholder Meier, Secretary; Douglas Arthur Braun [1960] Director/Chief Executive [American]; Jonathan James Harston [1976] Director/Chief Financial Officer

Blujay Topco Limited
Incorporated: 25 April 2012 *Employees:* 958
Net Worth Deficit: £70,450,016 *Total Assets:* £225,615,888
Registered Office: 4M Building, Malaga Avenue, Manchester Airport, Manchester, M90 3RR
Activities: Business and domestic software development
Shareholder: Minister for Finance, Singapore
Officers: Joy Burkholder Meier, Secretary; Douglas Arthur Braun [1960] Director/Chief Executive [American]; Mukul Chawla [1975] Director [American]; Martin Andrew Hiscox [1960] Director; Deep Shah [1979] Director/Investment; Adam Alexi Solomon [1987] Director/Investor [American]

BMP Europe Limited
Incorporated: 5 September 1984 *Employees:* 138
Net Worth: £8,197,790 *Total Assets:* £17,712,656
Registered Office: Shorten Brook Drive, Altham Business Park, Accrington, Lancs, BB5 5YH
Activities: Other manufacturing n.e.c.
Parent: Andrew Industries Limited
Officers: Andrew Michael Worthington, Secretary/Financial Controller; Edward Duxbury Andrew [1936] Managing Director; Mark Athersmith [1961] Managing Director; Mark Robert Bennett [1964] Finance Director; Ian Frederick Leeder Kenyon [1951] Managing Director; Brian Malone [1957] Sales & Marketing Director; Allan Thompson [1979] Technical Director; Andrew Michael Worthington [1969] Director/Accountant

BNN Technology PLC
Incorporated: 19 June 2008 *Employees:* 285
Net Worth: £39,993,000 *Total Assets:* £65,059,000
Registered Office: First Floor, Mallory House, Goostrey Way, Mobberley, Knutsford, Cheshire, WA16 7GY
Activities: Data processing, hosting and related activities
Officers: Mark Anthony Crump Hanson [1953] Director [New Zealander]; Darren Christian Mercer [1963] Director; William Alan Grant Ramsay [1958] Director [Canadian]

Boardlink Limited
Incorporated: 3 June 1969 *Employees:* 88
Net Worth: £4,279,864 *Total Assets:* £8,542,573
Registered Office: Unit 10 KUS Industrial Estate, Manor Lane, Hawarden, Flintshire, CH5 3PJ
Activities: Manufacture of paper and paperboard
Parent: DWL Holdings Ltd
Officers: Sami Petteri Kasteniemi [1970] Director [Finnish]; Pamela Olga Lyon [1943] Director; Andrew David Morley [1974] Director/Chairman; Scarlett Victoria Richardson [1966] Finance Director; Paul John Shepherd [1969] Director; Benjamin William Still [1974] Director

Bobst Manchester Ltd
Incorporated: 15 September 1986 *Employees:* 98
Net Worth: £9,920,000 *Total Assets:* £17,289,000
Registered Office: Pennine Business Park, Pilsworth Road, Heywood, Lancs, OL10 2TL
Activities: Manufacture of other special-purpose machinery n.e.c.
Parent: Bobst UK Holdings Ltd
Officers: Thomas Henry McComb, Secretary; Erik Henri Eugene Bothorel [1962] Director/Executive [French]; Attilo Tissi [1968] Director/Executive [Swiss]

Boden & Davies Limited
Incorporated: 21 July 1961 *Employees:* 80
Net Worth: £4,848,907 *Total Assets:* £15,047,899
Registered Office: Boden House, Mellor Hall, Mellor, Stockport, Cheshire, SK6 5LU
Activities: Raising of other animals
Major Shareholder: Joan Boden
Officers: Joan Boden, Secretary; Charles Boden [1963] Director/Farmer; George Boden [1955] Director/General Manager; Joan Boden [1936] Director/Administrator; Wayne Boden [1956] Director/Production Manager

Bodycote America Finance Limited
Incorporated: 14 August 2009
Net Worth: £193,121,872 *Total Assets:* £193,121,872
Registered Office: Springwood Court, Springwood Close, Tytherington Business Park, Macclesfield, Cheshire, SK10 2XF
Activities: Financial intermediation not elsewhere classified
Parent: Bodycote International Limited
Officers: Ute Suse Ball, Secretary; Ute Suse Ball [1961] Director/Company Secretary [German]; Michael John Harkcom [1975] Director/Solicitor; Dominique Yates [1967] Director/Accountant

Bodycote America Treasury Limited
Incorporated: 11 September 2009
Net Worth: £556,047,296 *Total Assets:* £565,867,264
Registered Office: Springwood Court, Springwood Close, Tytherington Business Park, Macclesfield, Cheshire, SK10 2XF
Activities: Banks
Parent: Bodycote International Limited
Officers: Ute Suse Ball, Secretary; Ute Suse Ball [1961] Director/Company Secretary [German]; Michael John Harkcom [1975] Director/Solicitor; Dominique Yates [1967] Director/Accountant

Bodycote Finance Limited
Incorporated: 10 July 2007 *Employees:* 2
Net Worth Deficit: £67,290,000 *Total Assets:* £830,894,016
Registered Office: Springwood Court, Springwood Close, Tytherington Business Park, Macclesfield, Cheshire, SK10 2XF
Activities: Other business support service activities n.e.c.
Parent: Bodycote PLC
Officers: Ute Suse Ball, Secretary; Michael John Harkcom [1975] Director/Solicitor; Dominique Yates [1967] Director/Accountant

Bodycote Finance UK Limited
Incorporated: 16 June 2003
Net Worth: £52,280,536 *Total Assets:* £52,427,192
Registered Office: Springwood Court, Springwood Close, Tytherington Business Park, Macclesfield, Cheshire, SK10 2XF
Activities: Activities of head offices
Officers: Ute Suse Ball, Secretary; Michael John Harkcom [1975] Director/Solicitor; Dominique Yates [1967] Director/Accountant

Bodycote H.I.P. Limited
Incorporated: 9 September 1976 *Employees:* 44
Net Worth: £3,963,000 *Total Assets:* £27,146,000
Registered Office: Springwood Court, Springwood Close, Tytherington Business Park, Macclesfield, Cheshire, SK10 2XF
Activities: Treatment and coating of metals
Parent: Bodycote PLC
Officers: Ute Suse Ball, Secretary; Ute Suse Ball [1961] Director/Company Secretary [German]; Michael John Harkcom [1975] Director/Solicitor; Dominique Yates [1967] Director/Accountant

Bodycote Heat Treatments Limited
Incorporated: 29 September 1971 *Employees:* 280
Net Worth: £12,987,000 *Total Assets:* £47,634,000
Registered Office: Springwood Court, Springwood Close, Tytherington Business Park, Macclesfield, Cheshire, SK10 2XF
Activities: Treatment and coating of metals
Parent: Bodycote PLC
Officers: Ute Suse Ball, Secretary; Ute Suse Ball [1961] Director/Company Secretary [German]; Michael John Harkcom [1975] Director/Solicitor; Dominique Yates [1967] Director/Accountant

Bodycote International Limited
Incorporated: 4 January 1972
Net Worth: £290,372,992 *Total Assets:* £1,243,796,992
Registered Office: Springwood Court, Springwood Close, Tytherington Business Park, Macclesfield, Cheshire, SK10 2XF
Activities: Other business support service activities n.e.c.
Parent: Bodycote PLC
Officers: Ute Suse Ball, Secretary; Michael John Harkcom [1975] Director/Solicitor; Dominique Yates [1967] Director/Accountant

Bodycote Investments
Incorporated: 13 December 2006
Net Worth: £308,455,232 *Total Assets:* £309,319,808
Registered Office: Springwood Court, Springwood Close, Tytherington Business Park, Macclesfield, Cheshire, SK10 2XF
Activities: Activities of head offices
Parent: Bodycote International Limited
Officers: Anthony Noonan, Secretary; Simon Paul Blantern [1961] Director/Sales and New Business Development; Anthony Noonan [1983] Director/Financial Controller

Bodycote PLC
Incorporated: 27 April 1953 *Employees:* 5,594
Net Worth: £697,000,000 *Total Assets:* £959,699,968
Registered Office: Springwood Court, Springwood Close, Tytherington Business Park, Macclesfield, Cheshire, SK10 2XF
Activities: Activities of head offices
Officers: Ute Suse Ball, Secretary; Lili Chahbazi [1966] Director/Consultant [Canadian]; Ian Barnet Duncan [1961] Non-Executive Director; Stephen Clive Harris [1958] Director; Patrick Lawrence Larmon [1952] Director [American]; Eva Lindqvist [1958] Director [Swedish]; Anne Cecille Quinn [1951] Director [New Zealander]; Dominique Yates [1967] Director/Accountant

Bodycote Surface Technology Limited
Incorporated: 20 February 1923 *Employees:* 137
Net Worth: £10,946,000 *Total Assets:* £15,568,000
Registered Office: Springwood Court, Springwood Close, Tytherington Business Park, Macclesfield, Cheshire, SK10 2XF
Activities: Treatment and coating of metals
Parent: Bodycote PLC
Officers: Ute Suse Ball, Secretary; Ute Suse Ball [1961] Director/Company Secretary [German]; Michael John Harkcom [1975] Director/Solicitor; Dominique Yates [1967] Director/Accountant

Bodycote Treasury Services Limited
Incorporated: 3 January 2014 *Employees:* 3
Net Worth Deficit: £32,365 *Total Assets:* £10,360,914
Registered Office: Springwood Court, Springwood Close, Tytherington Business Park, Macclesfield, Cheshire, SK10 2XF
Activities: Other business support service activities n.e.c.
Parent: Bodycote Finance Limited
Officers: Ute Suse Ball, Secretary; Ute Suse Ball [1961] Director/Company Secretary [German]; Michael John Harkcom [1975] Director/Solicitor; Dominique Yates [1967] Director/Accountant

Boels Rental Limited
Incorporated: 7 April 1998 *Employees:* 163
Net Worth: £5,416,694 *Total Assets:* £14,633,292
Registered Office: Unit A8, Riverview, Embankment Business Park, Heaton Mersey, Stockport, Cheshire, SK4 3GN
Activities: Renting and leasing of construction and civil engineering machinery and equipment
Officers: Peter Bernard Marcel Boels [1962] Director [Dutch]; Elisabeth Petra Maria Boels-Van Kerkom [1967] Director [Dutch]; Piet Elisabeth Michiel Marie Donners [1962] Director [Dutch]

BOI Trading Company Limited
Incorporated: 4 March 1994 *Employees:* 34
Net Worth: £14,534,884 *Total Assets:* £21,632,392
Registered Office: Units 1-6 Euro Centre, 116-118 Bury New Road, Manchester, M8 8EB
Activities: Wholesale of clothing and footwear
Major Shareholder: Amarjit Singh Grewal
Officers: Amarjit Singh [1968] Director

Bold International Properties Limited
Incorporated: 30 May 1990 *Employees:* 3
Net Worth: £9,018,167 *Total Assets:* £20,453,088
Registered Office: 24 Oriel Chambers, Water Street, Liverpool, L2 8TD
Activities: Buying and selling of own real estate
Officers: Iain George Sharp, Secretary/Director; Mark Peter Griffiths [1959] Director; Peter Stephen Neumark [1949] Director; Iain George Sharp [1951] Director

Bollin Group Limited
Incorporated: 14 July 1989 *Employees:* 370
Net Worth: £19,954,000 *Total Assets:* £42,958,000
Registered Office: Bailey Court, Green Street, Macclesfield, Cheshire, SK10 1JQ
Activities: Activities of head offices
Shareholders: Alan David Walker; Herbert Anthony Cann; Carole Fahy; Hugh David Turner
Officers: Stephen James Cann, Secretary; Herbert Anthony Cann [1939] Director/Textile Technologist; Stephen James Cann [1965] Director

Bolling Investments Limited
Incorporated: 12 December 1908
Net Worth: £45,782,000 *Total Assets:* £116,497,000
Registered Office: Lookers House, 3 Etchells Road, West Timperley, Altrincham, Cheshire, WA14 5XS
Activities: Buying and selling of own real estate
Parent: Lookers Motor Holdings Limited
Officers: Glenda MacGeekie, Secretary; Andrew Campbell Bruce [1965] Director; Robin Anthony Gregson [1960] Director/Chartered Accountant; Nigel John McMinn [1968] Managing Director Motor Division

The Bollington Group (Holdings) Limited
Incorporated: 26 November 2002 *Employees:* 37
Net Worth Deficit: £829,837 *Total Assets:* £18,838,636
Registered Office: Adlington Court, Adlington Business Park, Adlington, Macclesfield, Cheshire, SK10 4NL
Activities: Non-life insurance
Parent: Talbot Deane Investments Limited
Officers: Patrick Francis McDonnell [1965] Finance Director [Irish]; Paul Christopher Moors [1962] Director/Insurance Broker; Christopher Mark Patterson [1971] Director/Insurance Broker

Bollington Insurance Brokers Limited
Incorporated: 14 April 1994 *Employees:* 168
Net Worth: £4,780,509 *Total Assets:* £14,798,468
Registered Office: Adlington Court, Adlington Business Park, Adlington, Macclesfield, Cheshire, SK10 4NL
Activities: Financial intermediation not elsewhere classified
Parent: The Bollington Group (Holdings) Limited
Officers: Karen Louise Adegoke [1969] Corporate Director; Rachel Aston [1978] Marketing Director; Patrick Francis McDonnell [1965] Finance Director [Irish]; Paul Christopher Moors [1962] Director/Insurance Broker; Paul O'Gorman [1967] Director/Insurance Broker; Christopher Mark Patterson [1971] Director/Insurance Broker; Carl David Shaw [1968] Director/Insurance Broker

Bollinwater Estates LLP
Incorporated: 7 December 2006
Net Worth: £5,496,000 *Total Assets:* £37,323,000
Registered Office: Chancery Place, Brown Street, Manchester, M2 2JT

Bolton Car Centre Limited
Incorporated: 17 May 1981 *Employees:* 143
Net Worth: £1,902,756 *Total Assets:* £18,291,746
Registered Office: BCC Group Administration, Hypatia Street, Bolton, Lancs, BL2 6AA
Activities: Sale of new cars and light motor vehicles
Major Shareholder: Michael John Holt
Officers: Michael John Holt [1946] Director

Bolton Engineering (Holdings) Limited
Incorporated: 17 January 2007 *Employees:* 152
Net Worth: £296,538 *Total Assets:* £10,579,130
Registered Office: Victoria Mill, Piggot Street, Farnworth, Bolton, Lancs, BL4 9QN
Activities: Manufacture of air and spacecraft and related machinery
Shareholders: Keith Alan Harrison; Keith Haworth Hindle
Officers: John Harry Cottam, Secretary; John Harry Cottam [1953] Director; John England [1948] Director; Keith Alan Harrison [1950] Director; Keith Haworth Hindle [1943] Director

Bolton Fundco 1 Limited
Incorporated: 24 April 2009
Net Worth Deficit: £4,933,105 *Total Assets:* £14,489,943
Registered Office: Sceptre House, Sceptre Way, Bamber Bridge, Preston, Lancs, PR5 6AW
Activities: Other letting and operating of own or leased real estate
Parent: Bolton Holdco Limited
Officers: Deborah Jane Rawlinson, Secretary; Jeremy Peter Hartley [1965] Director/Chartered Accountant; Annette Walker [1972] Public Sector Director; Neil Geoffrey Ward [1959] Director; Christine Desiree Winstanley [1966] Director

Bolton Hospice
Incorporated: 24 March 1987 *Employees:* 134
Net Worth: £13,714,007 *Total Assets:* £14,263,925
Registered Office: Queens Park Street, off Chorley New Road, Bolton, Lancs, BL1 4QT
Activities: Other human health activities
Officers: John Bramley Kirk, Secretary; Judith Bromley [1962] Director/Solicitor; Adrian Crook [1970] Assistant Director - (Social Care); Grace Hopps [1952] Director/Retired; Dr Robert Alan Hunt [1954] Director/General Medical Practitioner; John Bramley Kirk [1952] Director/Retired Solicitor; Patrick Anthony Lydon [1955] Director/Chartered Accountant; Dr Geoffrey McLardy [1953] Director/GP; Andrew Philip Morgan [1966] Director/Self Employed

Bolton Lads' and Girls' Club
Incorporated: 3 October 1995 *Employees:* 62
Net Worth: £7,034,169 *Total Assets:* £7,952,196
Registered Office: 18 Spa Road, Bolton, Lancs, BL1 4AG
Activities: Other social work activities without accommodation n.e.c.
Officers: Debbie Suzanne Sabini, Secretary; Professor George Edward Thomas Holmes [1961] Director/Vice Chancellor; David Rowland Jones [1953] Director; Brandon Pilling [1962] Director; Debbie Suzanne Sabini [1962] Director/Solicitor; David Singleton [1950] Director; Stuart Peter Stead [1973] Director/Chartered Accountant; Peter Vinden [1963] Director/Chartered Quantity Surveyor; Bernard Waldron [1955] Director

The Bolton Multi Academy Trust
Incorporated: 4 October 2013 *Employees:* 143
Net Worth: £7,967,322 *Total Assets:* £11,219,908
Registered Office: Smithills School, Smithills Dean Road, Bolton, Lancs, BL1 6JS
Activities: Educational support services
Officers: John Anthony William Austin [1944] Director/Retired; Michael William Crossley [1966] Director/Head of Manufacture; Nigel William Johnson [1942] Director; Ronald Allan Makins [1955] Director/Business Consultant; Anthony Purcell [1959] Director/Education Consultant; Michael Sidebottom [1973] Director/Principal; Councillor John Walsh [1951] Director/Planning and Transport Consultant

Bolton School
Incorporated: 20 May 2005 *Employees:* 60
Net Worth: £51,605,000 *Total Assets:* £62,255,000
Registered Office: Bolton School, Chorley New Road, Bolton, Lancs, BL1 4PA
Activities: Primary education
Officers: Catherine Lisa Fox, Secretary; George Robert Neville Apsion [1978] Director/Sound Engineer; Charles Anthony Cowling [1962] Director/Actuary; Helen Claire Critchlow [1966] Director/IT; Karen Wendy Diggle [1957] Director; Eric John Fairweather [1942] Director; Sheila Eunice Fisher [1952] Director/Surgeon; John Roger Beresford Gould [1940] Director/Retired; Michael Thomas Griffiths [1947] Director; Sally-Anne Huang [1971] Director/Teacher; Manjeet Kaur Hundle [1971] Director of a Medical Company; David Niaz Mohyuddin [1975] Director/Barrister; Robert Seton Ogilvie [1959] Director; Anthony Daykin Oldershaw [1945] Director/Retired; Andrew Russell Palmer [1958] Director/Accountant; Louise Relph [1957] Director/District Judge; Ian Riley [1963] Director/Private Equity; Caroline Elizabeth Topham [1958] Director; Amanda Jayne Valentine [1964] Director/Compliance Officer

Bolton St Catherine's Academy
Incorporated: 10 June 2009 *Employees:* 179
Net Worth: £20,793,000 *Total Assets:* £23,482,000
Registered Office: c/o Bolton St Catherine's Academy, Stitch Mi Lane, Bolton, Lancs, BL2 4HU
Activities: Primary education
Officers: Elaine Hodson, Secretary; Amanda Calcutt [1979] Director/Travel Agent; Alasdair David Coates [1952] Director/Retired; Marc Edward Crossland [1967] Director/Property Investor; Chris Hopkinson [1959] Director; Sir John Francis Jones [1950] Director/Presenter, Commentator and Author; Ainsley Leonard [1970] Director/Teacher; Rachael Lucas [1974] Director/Headteacher; Samantha Nicol [1966] Director/Management Consultant; Sarah Louise Williams [1978] Director/Office Manager - Education

Bolton UTC
Incorporated: 13 November 2012 *Employees:* 39
Net Worth: £9,255,000 *Total Assets:* £10,238,000
Registered Office: Senate House, Deane Road, Bolton, Lancs, BL3 5AB
Activities: Technical and vocational secondary education
Officers: Anthony Richard Unsworth, Secretary; John Dennis Baumber [1950] Director; Mark Victor Carriline [1961] Director/Consultant; Artis Mattheou [1969] Director of Marketing [Greek]; Christopher John McClelland [1971] Director; Liam McDaid [1985] Director/Principal (Acting); Dr Mustafa Tariq Mohammed [1969] Managing Director; Anne Elizabeth Pilling [1955] Director/Education Consultant; William Henry Charles Webster [1961] Director/Assistant Vice Chancellor

Bolton Wanderers Football & Athletic Company Limited (The)
Incorporated: 16 January 1895 *Employees:* 167
Net Worth: £7,327,953 *Total Assets:* £34,491,008
Registered Office: University of Bolton, Burnden Way, Lostock, Bolton, Lancs, BL6 6JW
Activities: Operation of sports facilities
Parent: Burnden Leisure Limited
Officers: Kenneth Anderson [1952] Director

Bolton Whites Hotel Limited
Incorporated: 27 November 1998 *Employees:* 66
Net Worth: £5,030,351 *Total Assets:* £11,845,729
Registered Office: Macron Stadium, Burnden Way, Lostock, Bolton, Lancs, BL6 6JW
Activities: Hotels and similar accommodation
Parent: Bolton Wanderers Football and Athletic Company Limited
Officers: Kenneth Anderson [1952] Director

Bonarie Investments Limited
Incorporated: 28 May 2013 *Employees:* 2
Net Worth: £2,002,600 *Total Assets:* £10,788,335
Registered Office: Little Birks Farm, Ballam Road, Lytham St Annes, Lancs, FY8 4NL
Activities: Security dealing on own account
Shareholders: Ann Denise Davies; Michael David Chandler Davies
Officers: David Michael Chandler Davies [1978] Director; Denise Ann Davies [1963] Director; Michael David Chandler Davies [1950] Director

Bond Street Real Estate Holdings Limited
Incorporated: 13 August 2010
Net Worth: £101,903,688 *Total Assets:* £147,351,616
Registered Office: Cumberland House, Greenside Lane, Bradford, BD8 9TF
Activities: Other business support service activities n.e.c.
Parent: Praxisifm Trustees (UK) Limited
Officers: Claire Marie Cain [1970] Director; Christopher Stephen Smith [1972] Director/Trust Manager

Bond Turner Limited
Incorporated: 5 April 2006 *Employees:* 152
Net Worth: £9,365,676 *Total Assets:* £14,831,736
Registered Office: The Plaza, Old Hall Street, Liverpool, L3 9QJ
Activities: Solicitors
Parent: Anexo Group PLC
Officers: Dawn O'Brien, Secretary; Joanne Elizabeth Allen [1980] Director/Solicitor; Samantha Ann Moss [1981] Director/Solicitor; Dawn Catherine O'Brien [1983] Director/Barrister

Bondcare Willington Limited
Incorporated: 11 August 2011 *Employees:* 366
Net Worth Deficit: £2,780,915 *Total Assets:* £27,161,856
Registered Office: 6th Floor, Cardinal House, 20 St Mary's Parsonage, Manchester, M3 2LG
Activities: Other business support service activities n.e.c.
Shareholders: Yael Levison; Arieh Leib Levison
Officers: Arieh Leib Levison [1965] Director

Bonfiglioli U.K. Limited
Incorporated: 27 August 1981 *Employees:* 26
Net Worth: £4,141,612 *Total Assets:* £13,680,604
Registered Office: 3-7 Grosvenor Grange, Woolston, Warrington, Cheshire, WA1 4SF
Activities: Manufacture of other fabricated metal products n.e.c.
Parent: Bon-Fi S.R.L.
Officers: John James Adair [1957] Sales Director; Sonia Bonfiglioli [1963] Director [Italian]; Fausto Carboni [1963] Director [Italian]; Michael McCann [1950] Director

Boohoo.Com UK Limited
Incorporated: 27 February 2006 *Employees:* 1,278
Net Worth: £48,403,000 *Total Assets:* £135,472,992
Registered Office: 49-51 Dale Street, Manchester, M1 2HF
Activities: Retail sale via mail order houses or via Internet
Officers: Keri Devine, Secretary; Neil James Catto [1967] Finance Director; Mahmud Abdullah Kamani [1964] Director; Carol Kane [1966] Design Director

E.H.Booth & Co.,Limited
Incorporated: 31 October 1896 *Employees:* 2,778
Net Worth: £46,822,000 *Total Assets:* £152,931,008
Registered Office: Booths Central Office, Longridge Road, Ribbleton, Preston, Lancs, PR2 5BX
Activities: Retail sale in non-specialised stores with food, beverages or tobacco predominating
Officers: John Adrian Vandermeer, Secretary [Australian]; David Graham Booth [1962] Director/Grocer; Edwin John Booth [1955] Director/Grocer; Simon Kenyon Booth [1957] Director/Grocer; Ross Anthony Faith [1971] Finance Director; Nigel Russell Murray [1970] Director; Kevin John Roberts [1949] Director

Borderway Finance Limited
Incorporated: 21 April 1995 *Employees:* 12
Net Worth: £1,345,989 *Total Assets:* £21,578,156
Registered Office: Cumberland House, Cooper Way, Parkhouse, Carlisle, Cumbria, CA3 0JF
Activities: Credit granting by non-deposit taking finance houses and other specialist consumer credit grantors
Parent: Cumberland Holdings Limited
Officers: John Paul Vines, Secretary; Michael Grant Deans [1970] Director; John Christopher Norman Kidd [1965] Finance Director; Patrick Desmond Moore [1962] Director/Chief Executive [Irish]; Susanne Jayne Parry [1972] Director/AGM Customer Service Development; Alex Windle [1976] Director/General Manager - Marketing

Borgwarner Holdings Limited
Incorporated: 17 November 1989 *Employees:* 337
Net Worth: £86,258,000 *Total Assets:* £106,427,000
Registered Office: Roydsdale Way, Euroway Industrial Estate, Bradford, W Yorks, BD4 6SE
Activities: Non-trading company
Parent: Borgwarner Inc.
Officers: Alan McMaken, Secretary; Dr. Bela Csonka [1968] Director/Plant Manager [Hungarian]; Thomas McGill [1966] Director/Treasurer [American]; Alan McMaken [1970] Tax Director [American]; Charles Polzin [1954] Director/Attorney [American]; Jeremiah Shives [1977] Director/European General Counsel [American]; Matthias Uhrig [1964] Director - Finance [German]

Borgwarner Limited
Incorporated: 10 February 1989 *Employees:* 337
Net Worth: £76,161,000 *Total Assets:* £109,260,000
Registered Office: Roydsdale Way, Euroway Industrial Estate, Bradford, W Yorks, BD4 6SE
Activities: Manufacture of other parts and accessories for motor vehicles
Parent: Borgwarner Inc.
Officers: Alan McMaken, Secretary; Dr. Bela Csonka [1968] Director/Plant Manager [Hungarian]; Thomas McGill [1966] Director/Treasurer [American]; Alan McMaken [1970] Tax Director [American]; Charles Polzin [1954] Director/Attorney [American]; Jeremiah Shives [1977] Director/European General Counsel [American]; Matthias Uhrig [1964] Director - Finance [German]

Bossdean Properties Limited
Incorporated: 25 January 2000
Net Worth: £5,166,203 *Total Assets:* £12,172,107
Registered Office: Suite 2, Morley Carr House, Morley Carr Road, Lowmoor, Bradford, BD12 0RA
Activities: Other letting and operating of own or leased real estate
Parent: Brunn SA
Officers: Richard Anthony Rowe, Secretary; David Francis Craven [1954] Sales Director; John de Jong [1954] Director/Steel Stockholder [Dutch]

Botraco Holdings Limited
Incorporated: 28 October 2010
Net Worth: £7,415,554 *Total Assets:* £7,418,703
Registered Office: 6th Floor, Cardinal House, St Marys Parsonage, Manchester, M3 2LG
Activities: Activities of head offices
Major Shareholder: Ankit Govind Ruia
Officers: Arun Desai, Secretary; Akhil Kumar Ruia [1981] Director; Anil Kumar Ruia [1955] Director

Boughey Distribution Limited
Incorporated: 23 March 1964 *Employees:* 460
Net Worth: £2,270,000 *Total Assets:* £8,785,000
Registered Office: Wardle, Nantwich, Cheshire, CW5 6BP
Activities: Freight transport by road
Parent: NWF Distribution Holdings Limited
Officers: Stephen Robert Andrew, Company Secretary; Stephen Robert Andrew [1962] Director/Company Secretary; Chris James Belsham [1975] Finance Director; Daniel Earp [1983] Director; Keith Graham Forster [1959] Director/Accountant; Ian Ronald Sherratt [1962] Finance Director; Neil Trotter [1984] Transport Operations Director; Richard Antony Whiting [1964] Director/Chief Executive

Boulting Environmental Services Limited
Incorporated: 11 July 2002 *Employees:* 72
Net Worth: £4,182,434 *Total Assets:* £14,681,393
Registered Office: Boulting House, Firecrest Court, Centre Park, Warrington, Cheshire, WA1 1RG
Activities: Other specialised construction activities n.e.c.
Parent: Boulting Limited
Officers: Joshua Groarke [1983] Director; Steve Marsh [1964] Director/Shareholder; John Richard Sugden [1960] Director/Chartered Engineer

Boulting Group Limited
Incorporated: 20 July 1994 *Employees:* 873
Net Worth: £12,109,074 *Total Assets:* £42,486,412
Registered Office: Boulting House, Firecrest Court, Centre Park, Warrington, Cheshire, WA1 1RG
Activities: Manufacture of electricity distribution and control apparatus
Parent: Acorn Holdco 2 Limited
Officers: David Friar [1953] Director; Peter Colin McLean [1956] Finance Director

Boutinot Limited
Incorporated: 25 November 1980 *Employees:* 140
Net Worth: £25,912,476 *Total Assets:* £82,608,976
Registered Office: Boundary House, Cheadle Point, Cheadle, Cheshire, SK8 2GG
Activities: Wholesale of wine, beer, spirits and other alcoholic beverages
Shareholders: Dennis Whiteley; Donna Whiteley; Araldica Castelvero SCA
Officers: Michael Joseph Moriarty, Secretary/Accountant; Antony Malcolm Brown [1957] Director; Iain Robert Davies [1970] Director; Claudio Manera [1963] Director [Italian]; Michael Joseph Moriarty [1965] Director/Accountant; Dennis Whiteley [1961] Deputy Managing Director

Boutique Hotel Group Limited
Incorporated: 28 March 2006 *Employees:* 195
Net Worth: £7,970,954 *Total Assets:* £26,270,208
Registered Office: Peckforton Castle, Stone House, Lane Peckforton, Tarporley, Cheshire, CW6 9TN
Activities: Activities of head offices
Shareholders: Christopher James Naylor; Kate Jayne Naylor
Officers: Kate Jayne Naylor, Secretary; Michael Auld [1981] Director; Christopher James Naylor [1978] Director; Georgina Ann Naylor [1951] Director; Kate Jayne Naylor [1982] Director; Matthew Richard Naylor [1979] Director; Richard Anthony Naylor [1948] Director

Bowdon Group Limited
Incorporated: 3 July 2007 *Employees:* 114
Net Worth: £2,560,894 *Total Assets:* £10,783,576
Registered Office: 78 Ashley Road, Hale, Altrincham, Cheshire, WA14 2UF
Activities: Activities of head offices
Shareholder: Brian Geoffrey Benson
Officers: Alistair Webb, Secretary; Brian Geoffrey Benson [1962] Director Secretary; Grant Michael Stuffins [1977] Commercial Director

Bowker Blackburn Limited
Incorporated: 24 April 1978 *Employees:* 101
Net Worth: £3,839,000 *Total Assets:* £21,809,000
Registered Office: Bowker BMW, Trident Way, Trident Park, Blackburn, Lancs, BB1 3NU
Activities: Sale of new cars and light motor vehicles
Parent: W H Bowker Limited
Officers: Darren Thomason, Secretary; Anthony Paul Bowker [1968] Director; Kenneth Neil Bowker [1965] Director/Transport Manager; Kenneth Neil Bowker [1944] Director; William Henry Bowker Jnr [1960] Director/Transport Manager; Christopher James Kojak Eccles [1975] Director/Dealer Principal; Darren Thomason [1969] Director

W.H.Bowker Limited
Incorporated: 8 January 1941 *Employees:* 461
Net Worth: £11,578,000 *Total Assets:* £77,600,000
Registered Office: Holme Road, Bamber Bridge, Preston, Lancs, PR5 6BP
Activities: Freight transport by road
Shareholder: William Henry Bowker Jnr
Officers: Darren Thomason, Secretary; Anthony Paul Bowker [1968] Director; Caroline Jennifer Bowker [1959] Director; Hilary Bowker [1963] Director; Kenneth Neil Bowker [1965] Director/Transport Manager; Kenneth Neil Bowker [1944] Director; Vicki Bowker [1969] Director; William Henry Bowker Jnr [1960] Director/Transport Manager; Elizabeth Helen Griffiths [1962] Director/Advertising Manager; Christopher Kay [1977] Finance Director

Bowker Preston Limited
Incorporated: 13 May 1964 *Employees:* 132
Net Worth: £6,419,000 *Total Assets:* £34,445,000
Registered Office: Channel Way, Ashton on Ribble, Preston, Lancs, PR2 2YA
Activities: Sale of new cars and light motor vehicles
Parent: W H Bowker Limited
Officers: Darren Thomason, Secretary; Anthony Paul Bowker [1968] Director/After Sales Manager; Kenneth Neil Bowker [1965] Director/Transport Manager; Kenneth Neil Bowker [1944] Director/Haulage Contractor; William Henry Bowker Jnr [1960] Director/Transport Manager; Thomas Bernard Fox [1965] Director/General Manager; Darren Thomason [1969] Director

Bowland (Holdings) Limited
Incorporated: 29 March 2007 *Employees:* 44
Net Worth: £6,727,717 *Total Assets:* £8,021,129
Registered Office: Richard House, Winckley Square, Preston, Lancs, PR1 3HP
Activities: Activities of head offices
Shareholders: James Henry Wood; Victoria Wood
Officers: Victoria Wood, Secretary; James Henry Wood [1956] Director/Meat Wholesaler; Victoria Wood [1961] Director/Secretary

Bowmore Investments Limited
Incorporated: 21 December 2015
Net Worth: £1,268,039 *Total Assets:* £10,388,885
Registered Office: Bowmore, Laurel Avenue, Lytham St Annes, Lancs, FY8 4LQ
Activities: Fund management activities
Shareholders: David Alan Halsall; Irene Halsall
Officers: Alan Halsall, Secretary; Alan Halsall [1954] Director; Irene Halsall [1953] Director

Boxwood Leisure Limited
Incorporated: 9 April 2001
Net Worth Deficit: £8,969,325 *Total Assets:* £33,692,444
Registered Office: Parkwood House, Cuerden Park, Bamber Bridge, Preston, Lancs, PR5 6BY
Activities: General public administration activities
Parent: Boxwood Holdings Limited
Officers: David John Harding [1980] Director/Chartered Accountant; Sion Laurence Jones [1974] Asset Management Director; Richard Daniel Knight [1974] Operations Director; Philip Arthur Would [1971] Director/Asset Manager

Boys Holdings PLC
Incorporated: 27 June 1969 *Employees:* 62
Net Worth: £12,379,240 *Total Assets:* £19,882,812
Registered Office: Todd Carr Road, Waterfoot, Rossendale, Lancs, BB4 9SJ
Activities: Buying and selling of own real estate
Officers: John Edward Lee, Secretary; Brian John Boys [1963] Quantity Surveyor/Director; Michael Adam Boys [1965] Projects Manager/Director; Peter Harvey Boys [1969] Contracts Manager/Director; John Edward Lee [1952] Finance Director

B. & E. Boys Limited
Incorporated: 2 December 1996 *Employees:* 57
Net Worth: £2,037,395 *Total Assets:* £6,819,557
Registered Office: Toddcarr Road, Waterfoot, Rossendale, Lancs, BB4 9SJ
Activities: Construction of commercial buildings
Officers: John Edward Lee, Secretary; Brian John Boys [1963] Quantity Surveyor/Director; Michael Adam Boys [1965] Projects Manager/Director; Peter Harvey Boys [1969] Contracts Manager/Director; John Edward Lee [1952] Finance Director

Boyton Solar Park Limited
Incorporated: 11 January 2011
Net Worth Deficit: £2,195,667 *Total Assets:* £8,092,557
Registered Office: Eversheds House, 70 Great Bridgewater Street, Manchester, M1 5ES
Activities: Production of electricity
Parent: Sune Green Holdco4 Limited
Officers: Carl Goran Dandanell [1959] Director [Swedish]

BPD Holdings Limited
Incorporated: 13 May 2002 *Employees:* 271
Net Worth: £13,224,997 *Total Assets:* £18,593,720
Registered Office: 2 Brooklands Road, Sale, Cheshire, M33 3SS
Activities: Activities of head offices
Major Shareholder: Linda Elizabeth Willan
Officers: Darren Richard Hill, Secretary; Keith Brian Alderson [1960] Director; Graham Leslie Dronfield [1964] Director; Darren Richard Hill [1966] Director/Accountant; Neil Murray Rideout [1962] Technical Director; Linda Elizabeth Willan [1949] Director

BPS Developments Limited
Incorporated: 21 September 1994
Net Worth: £12,828,937 *Total Assets:* £22,539,452
Registered Office: 1 Derby Building, Wavertree Road, Liverpool, L7 3ES
Activities: Development of building projects
Major Shareholder: David Michael Mahoney
Officers: Eric Mahoney, Secretary; David Michael Mahoney [1966] Director; Eric Mahoney [1941] Director

Brabant Limited
Incorporated: 17 April 1980 *Employees:* 13
Net Worth: £3,967,310 *Total Assets:* £7,639,098
Registered Office: Alexander House, Station Road, Cheadle Hulme, Cheadle, Cheshire, SK8 5AE
Activities: Wholesale of chemical products
Shareholders: Mir Saeed Razavi; Margaret Ann Razavi
Officers: Margaret Ann Razavi, Secretary; Margaret Ann Razavi [1951] Director/Computer Operator; Mir Saeed Razavi [1953] Director/Construction Engineer

Brabners LLP
Incorporated: 7 October 2004 *Employees:* 284
Net Worth: £10,984,000 *Total Assets:* £21,304,000
Registered Office: Horton House, Exchange Flags, Liverpool, L2 3YL
Officers: Nicholas Damian Campbell [1968] Member; Anthony James Harper [1959] Member; Rupert James Humphrey Jackson [1968] Member; Sam Grant Mabon [1974] Member; Helen Joan Marriott [1969] Member; Nicholas Giles White [1973] Member; Ian Bernard Alderson [1961] LLP Member; Steven James Appleton [1979] LLP Member; Nigel Duncan Lewis Bailey [1975] LLP Member; Peter Barlow [1961] LLP Member; Colin Philip Bell [1979] LLP Member; Christopher Mark Brandwood [1958] LLP Member; Stephen Mark Brodie [1961] LLP Member; Helen Mary Brown [1980] LLP Member; Matthew Brown [1974] LLP Member; Paul Chamberlain [1970] LLP Member; Stephen Claus [1956] LLP Member; Angela Margaret Clearkin [1960] LLP Member; Jonathon Miles Close [1971] LLP Member; Andrew James Cross [1954] LLP Member; Marcus Anthony Difelice [1971] LLP Member; Lydia Therese Edgar [1969] LLP Member; Mark Rupert Feeny [1955] LLP Member; Paul Nicholas Firth [1958] LLP Member; Alistair Graham Fletcher [1957] LLP Member; Iain Kenneth Gamble [1979] LLP Member; Rupert Edward Samuel Gill [1972] LLP Member; Jeffrey Andrew Gillbanks [1967] LLP Member; Barry Goodall [1968] LLP Member; Charlie Maurice Hansford [1969] LLP Member; Ian Gerrard Hardman [1971] LLP Member; John Richard Hepworth [1969] LLP Member; Richard John Hough [1969] LLP Member; Stuart John Irons [1962] LLP Member; Lee Jonathon Jeffcott [1970] LLP Member; Jeff Lewis [1965] LLP Member; Simon John Lewis [1979] LLP Member; Caroline Louise Litchfield [1972] LLP Member; Paul Graham Lunt [1972] LLP Member; David Samuel Maples [1959] LLP Member; Neil McBurney [1961] LLP Member; David Mark McGurnaghan [1979] LLP Member; Sarah Murphy [1975] LLP Member; Ian Mylrea [1977] LLP Member; Robert Nieri [1969] LLP Member; Lachlan Ross Nisbet [1974] LLP Member; Matthew Gerard O'Brien [1979] LLP Member; Andrew James O'Mahony [1971] LLP Member; Claire Joanne Petricca-Riding [1976] LLP Member; Joanne Rosa Radcliff [1983] LLP Member; Mark Edward Rathbone [1969] LLP Member; Richard Andrew Roberts [1975] LLP Member; Andrew Sion Rogers [1978] LLP Member; Louise Ann Scholes [1969] LLP Member; Philip Neil Sheard [1977] LLP Member; Joseph John Shelston [1974] LLP Member; Ross Shine [1963] LLP Member; Philip Richard Steele [1983] LLP Member; Robert Denis Turner [1974] LLP Member; Edward Maurice Watkins [1941] LLP Member; Mark Whiteside [1980] LLP Member; Nicola Joanne Whittle [1982] LLP Member; Nigel John Williams [1958] LLP Member

Bracken House Properties LLP
Incorporated: 6 June 2006 *Employees:* 28
Net Worth: £37,690,880 *Total Assets:* £86,818,576
Registered Office: Sterling House, Unit G, Waterfold Business Park, Bury, Lancs, BL9 7BR
Officers: Hayley Jayne Moser [1975] Member; Henry Neville Moser [1949] Member

Bracken Midco1 PLC
Incorporated: 7 June 2016
Net Worth: £82,400,000 *Total Assets:* £367,900,000
Registered Office: Lake View, Lakeside, Cheadle, Cheshire, SK8 3GW
Activities: Activities of financial services holding companies
Parent: Bracken Topco Limited
Officers: Gary Derek Beckett, Secretary; Gary Derek Beckett [1969] Director; Henry Neville Moser [1949] Director

Bracken Midco2 Limited
Incorporated: 4 May 2016
Net Worth: £511,100,000 *Total Assets:* £729,900,032
Registered Office: Lake View, Lakeside, Cheadle, Cheshire, SK8 3GW
Activities: Activities of financial services holding companies
Parent: Bracken Midco1 PLC
Officers: Gary Derek Beckett, Secretary; Gary Derek Beckett [1969] Director; Henry Neville Moser [1949] Director

Brad Estates Limited
Incorporated: 9 December 1994 *Employees:* 2
Net Worth: £18,382,000 *Total Assets:* £27,736,000
Registered Office: Lynton House, Ackhurst Park, Foxhole Road, Chorley, Lancs, PR7 1NY
Activities: Other business support service activities n.e.c.
Parent: Northern Trust Group Limited
Officers: Anne Kelleher, Secretary; John Clement Kay [1953] Director; Mark Lorimer Widders [1960] Director

Bradbury & Son (Buxton) Limited
Incorporated: 13 September 1940 *Employees:* 240
Net Worth: £5,629,820 *Total Assets:* £22,941,862
Registered Office: Unit 2 Staden Lane, Buxton, Derbys, SK17 9RZ
Activities: Wholesale of dairy products, eggs and edible oils and fats
Parent: G. & M. Paul Limited
Officers: George Paul, Secretary; Christopher Chisnall [1976] Director/Sales & Marketing Manager; Stephen Dillon [1977] Finance Director; Michelle Jackson Hanstock [1968] Procurement and Supply Chain Director; Brian Leonard Murrell [1947] Director; George Paul [1949] Director/Cheese and Diary Produce; Richard John Paul [1970] Director/Sales Executive; Steven John Pritchard [1973] Sales Director

Bradford & Bingley PLC
Incorporated: 28 February 2000 *Employees:* 175
Net Worth: £3,670,700,032 *Total Assets:* £11,857,000,448
Registered Office: Croft Road, Crossflatts, Bingley, W Yorks, BD16 2UA
Activities: Activities of mortgage finance companies
Parent: UK Asset Resolution Limited
Officers: John Gornall, Secretary; Ian John Hares [1958] Finance & Investment Director; Susan Carol Langley [1963] Director; Brendan Paul McDonagh [1958] Director [Irish]; Keith Charles William Morgan [1963] Director; Brendan John Russell [1961] Director; John Hartley Tattersall [1952] Director; Holger Randolph Vieten [1969] Director/Head of Banking and Capital Markets [German]

Bradford Academy Trust
Incorporated: 14 July 2005 *Employees:* 323
Net Worth: £19,267,000 *Total Assets:* £24,389,000
Registered Office: Teasdale Street, Bradford, W Yorks, BD4 7QJ
Activities: Pre-primary education
Officers: Andrew Blake, Secretary; Richard Keith Arnold [1953] Director/Retired; Bruce Berry [1946] Director/Consultant; Adrian Farley [1977] Director/Councillor; Nadine Good [1965] Assistant Director - Childrens Services; Manojkumar Narottam Liladhar Joshi [1952] Director/Healthcare Professional; Jagdeep Paul Singh Kainth [1984] Director/Operations Manager; Ruth Leetham [1964] Director/Parent Governor; Reverend Peter Mayo-Smith [1949] Director/Reverend; Darren Metcalfe [1971] Director/Businessman; Robert Ian Taylor [1968] Director/Minister; Rev Timothy Charles Rank Thomas [1975] Director/Reverend; Steve Walker [1970] Director/Teacher

Bradford College Education Trust
Incorporated: 12 December 2008 *Employees:* 289
Net Worth: £22,941,000 *Total Assets:* £26,506,000
Registered Office: Bradford College Further Education Corporation, Great Horton Road, Bradford, W Yorks, BD7 1AY
Activities: General secondary education
Officers: Kenneth Michael Cornforth [1955] Director/Education Consultant; Eve Gregory [1968] Director/Solicitor; Dawn Janice Leak [1967] Director; Christopher James Malish [1977] Director/Accountant; Huw Glyn Roberts [1963] People Services, Director, Bradford College

Bradford Diocesan Academies Trust
Incorporated: 18 October 2012 *Employees:* 1,080
Net Worth: £34,235,000 *Total Assets:* £41,066,000
Registered Office: 2nd Floor, Jade Building, Albion Mills, Albion Road, Greengates, Bradford, W Yorks, BD10 9TQ
Activities: Primary education
Officers: Nurjahan Ali Arobi [1974] Director/Patient and Public Involvement Manager; Ruby Khalid Bhatti [1970] Director/Solicitor; Roland Clark [1954] Director/Retired; Carol Ann Dewhurst [1981] Director/Executive Officer; Stephen James Emsley [1981] Managing Director; Pauline Mary Hagen [1958] Director/Principal; Bill Henry [1960] Director/Retired; Anthony Peter Hesselwood [1949] Director/Chartered Accountant; Judith Rosemary Kirk [1963] Deputy Director for Education and Skills; Theresa Mary Mason [1953] Director/DofE Consultant Adviser; Denise June Poole [1949] Director/Ordained Minister; Denise Averezene Sterling [1957] Director/Occupational Therapist; Catherine Mary Wilson [1966] Director/Solicitor

Bradford Hide Company Limited
Incorporated: 18 February 1982 *Employees:* 79
Net Worth: £14,135,492 *Total Assets:* £22,127,244
Registered Office: Dryden Street, Bradford, W Yorks, BD1 5ND
Activities: Wholesale of hides, skins and leather
Officers: Louise Roscoe, Secretary; John Anthony Woodward [1964] Director

Bradford Trident Limited
Incorporated: 5 October 2000 *Employees:* 48
Net Worth: £6,070,027 *Total Assets:* £6,914,799
Registered Office: Park Lane Centre, Park Lane, Bradford, W Yorks, BD5 0LN
Activities: Other letting and operating of own or leased real estate
Officers: Carlton James Smith, Secretary; Habib Rehman Afsar [1973] Director/Teacher; Mohammed Saeed Afsar [1987] Director/Family Support Worker; Yaqoob Ayoob [1971] Director; Ramenpreet Kaur Haire [1980] Director/Certified Chartered Accountant; Sarah Jane Hinton [1962] Director/Health Visitor; Hawarun Hussain [1974] Director/NHS Health Improvement Partnership Manager; Balaal Hussain Khan [1983] Director/Solicitor; Nasreen Khan [1967] Director/Health Worker; Sadaqat Ali Khan [1981] Director; Shahzada Meer [1957] Director/Telecoms Engineer; Fareeda Mir [1970] Director/NHS Public Health; Talat Sajawal [1979] Director/Family Support Worker; Taj Salam [1966] Director/PCV Driver; Imran Younis [1977] Director

Bradley Bidco Limited
Incorporated: 23 October 2015 *Employees:* 4
Net Worth Deficit: £1,385,873 *Total Assets:* £15,507,133
Registered Office: 363 Leach Place, Walton Summit Centre, Bamber Bridge, Preston, Lancs, PR5 8AS
Activities: Retail sale of sports goods, fishing gear, camping goods, boats and bicycles
Parent: Bradley Topco Limited
Officers: Paul Andrew Cocker [1979] Director; William James Pearson [1976] Director

Bradley Park Waste Management Limited
Incorporated: 24 July 2009 *Employees:* 23
Net Worth: £9,355,241 *Total Assets:* £15,503,794
Registered Office: One St Peter's Square, Manchester, M2 3DE
Activities: Other business support service activities n.e.c.
Major Shareholder: Robert McFarlane
Officers: Michelle Lappin, Secretary/Director; Michelle Lappin [1968] Director; Carol Thomson [1971] Director; Simon Towers [1968] Director

Bradley Topco Limited
Incorporated: 22 October 2015 *Employees:* 59
Net Worth Deficit: £2,672,199 *Total Assets:* £16,129,720
Registered Office: 363 Leach Place, Walton Summit Centre, Bamber Bridge, Preston, Lancs, PR5 8AS
Activities: Retail sale of sports goods, fishing gear, camping goods, boats and bicycles
Shareholder: True Capital Partners 1 LP
Officers: Paul Andrew Cocker [1979] Director; William James Pearson [1976] Director

Drew Brady & Co. Limited
Incorporated: 12 February 1947 *Employees:* 93
Net Worth: £7,923,187 *Total Assets:* £13,534,220
Registered Office: Kearsley Mill, Stoneclough, Radcliffe, Manchester, M26 1RH
Activities: Wholesale of clothing and footwear
Parent: Ruia Group Limited
Officers: Philip John Campbell, Secretary; Shane David Doughty [1972] Merchandising Director; Vimal Ruia [1959] Director

Braecrest Limited
Incorporated: 20 May 1998 *Employees:* 11
Net Worth: £5,749,745 *Total Assets:* £10,486,154
Registered Office: Unit 11 Mold Business Park, Wrexham Road, Mold, Flintshire, CH7 1XP
Activities: Renting and operating of Housing Association real estate
Major Shareholder: Damian James McGuinness
Officers: Bernard Owen McGuinness, Secretary/Self Employed; Bernard Owen McGuinness [1931] Director; Damian James McGuinness [1974] Director/Manager

Brahm Fundco 1 Limited
Incorporated: 17 November 2006 *Employees:* 4
Net Worth Deficit: £6,960,987 *Total Assets:* £27,046,380
Registered Office: Sceptre House, Sceptre Way, Bamber Bridge, Preston, Lancs, PR5 6AW
Activities: Development of building projects
Parent: Brahm Intermediate Holdco 1 Ltd
Officers: Deborah Jane Rawlinson, Secretary; Jeremy Peter Hartley [1965] Director; Annette Walker [1972] Public Sector Director; Neil Geoffrey Ward [1959] Director; Christine Desiree Winstanley [1966] Director

Brahm Fundco 2 Limited
Incorporated: 4 February 2008 *Employees:* 4
Net Worth Deficit: £2,445,662 *Total Assets:* £21,054,320
Registered Office: Sceptre House, Sceptre Way, Bamber Bridge, Preston, Lancs, PR5 6AW
Activities: Other letting and operating of own or leased real estate
Parent: Brahm Intermediate Holdco 2 Ltd
Officers: Deborah Jane Rawlinson, Secretary; Jeremy Peter Hartley [1965] Director; Annette Walker [1972] Public Sector Director; Neil Geoffrey Ward [1959] Director; Christine Desiree Winstanley [1966] Director

Brahm Lift Limited
Incorporated: 17 November 2006 *Employees:* 5
Net Worth Deficit: £13,755,670 *Total Assets:* £62,302,664
Registered Office: Sceptre House, Sceptre Way, Bamber Bridge, Preston, Lancs, PR5 6AW
Activities: Development of building projects
Shareholders: Community Health Partnerships Limited; Eric Wright Group Limited
Officers: Deborah Jane Rawlinson, Secretary; Jeremy Peter Hartley [1965] Director; Annette Walker [1972] Public Sector Director; Neil Geoffrey Ward [1959] Director; Christine Desiree Winstanley [1966] Director

Brammer UK Limited
Incorporated: 23 July 1956 *Employees:* 1,446
Net Worth: £35,204,000 *Total Assets:* £127,344,000
Registered Office: Claverton Court, Claverton Road, Wythenshawe, Manchester, M23 9NE
Activities: Wholesale of other machinery and equipment
Parent: Rubix International Limited
Officers: Mark Robert Graham Dixon [1964] Managing Director; Duncan Jonathan Magrath [1964] Director

Brampton View Limited
Incorporated: 7 February 2007 *Employees:* 108
Net Worth: £6,337,000 *Total Assets:* £8,387,000
Registered Office: Norcliffe House, Station Road, Wilmslow, Cheshire, SK9 1BU
Activities: Other human health activities
Parent: Optimum FS Care Developments Limited
Officers: Abigail Mattison, Secretary; Ryan Stuart MacAskill [1975] Director; Gregory Laurence Newman [1988] Director/Investment Professional; Jeremy Robert Arthur Richardson [1970] Director; Dr Maureen Claire Royston [1960] Director; Phillip Gary Thomas [1978] Director

Bramwell Pub Company Limited
Incorporated: 21 August 2012 *Employees:* 2,737
Net Worth: £164,000 *Total Assets:* £75,847,000
Registered Office: c/o Zolfo Cooper, The Zenith Building, 26 Spring Gardens, Manchester, M2 1AB
Activities: Activities of other holding companies n.e.c.
Officers: Jane Susan Holbrook, Secretary; Paul James Beadle [1957] Director; Ilfryn Cheyney Carstairs [1975] Director/Investment Professional [Australian]; Adam Peter Fowle [1959] Director/Chairman; Jane Susan Holbrook [1964] Director; Roger Timothy Moxham [1963] Director/Chief Executive Officer; Stephen Davis Seymour [1975] Director/Investment Professional [American]

Brancaster Care Homes Limited
Incorporated: 14 March 2005 *Employees:* 264
Net Worth: £7,410,733 *Total Assets:* £16,165,041
Registered Office: Genesis Centre, Garrett Field, Birchwood, Warrington, Cheshire, WA3 7BH
Activities: Residential nursing care facilities
Shareholder: Richard Alister Cook
Officers: Elaine Anne Bonnon, Secretary; Richard Alister Cook [1961] Director/Certified Chartered Accountant

Brand Addition Limited
Incorporated: 11 December 1986 *Employees:* 201
Net Worth: £26,710,000 *Total Assets:* £43,300,000
Registered Office: Broadway, Trafford Wharf Road, Manchester, M17 1DD
Activities: Other business support service activities n.e.c.
Parent: H.I.G Milan UK Bidco Limited
Officers: Claire Louise Thomson, Secretary; Christopher Lee [1971] Director; Claire Louise Thomson [1974] Finance Director

Brand New Co (354) Limited
Incorporated: 30 January 2007
Net Worth: £2,305,637 *Total Assets:* £13,217,967
Registered Office: 3-4 Tapton Way, Wavertree, Liverpool, L13 1DA
Activities: Roofing activities
Major Shareholder: Nick Hooper
Officers: Nick Hooper, Secretary; Keith Beck [1971] Director; Nick Hooper [1966] Director

Brand Search Limited
Incorporated: 28 November 2006 *Employees:* 12
Net Worth: £152,579 *Total Assets:* £8,129,112
Registered Office: Richard House, Winckley Square, Preston, Lancs, PR1 3HP
Activities: Wholesale of clothing and footwear
Parent: BS Property Holdings Limited
Officers: Beverley Wallington, Secretary; Andrew David Wallington [1965] Director

Brass Bank Limited
Incorporated: 2 October 2003 *Employees:* 2
Net Worth Deficit: £47,317 *Total Assets:* £12,760,171
Registered Office: Boundary Park, Furtherwood Road, Oldham, Lancs, OL1 2PA
Activities: Other letting and operating of own or leased real estate
Shareholders: Simon Blitz; Daniel Gazal
Officers: Simon Blitz, Secretary/Telecommunications Manager; Simon Blitz [1961] Director/Telecommunications Manager; Daniel Gazal [1962] Director/Telecommunications Manager [American]

Bravo Inns II Limited
Incorporated: 7 September 2007 *Employees:* 9
Net Worth: £4,466,790 *Total Assets:* £11,273,350
Registered Office: 44 Knutsford Road, Warrington, Cheshire, WA4 1AG
Activities: Public houses and bars
Officers: Philip John Dearden, Secretary/Director; Clive Anderson [1965] Director/Consultant; Kenneth Buckley [1948] Managing Director; William Thomas Fraser Allen [1970] Director

Braymale Limited
Incorporated: 2 May 1978 *Employees:* 558
Net Worth: £5,461,989 *Total Assets:* £8,705,024
Registered Office: Adelphi Chambers, 30 Hoghton Street, Southport, Merseyside, PR9 0NZ
Activities: Renting and leasing of trucks and other heavy vehicles
Shareholders: Carol Ellis; Barry Ellis.
Officers: Carol Ellis, Secretary; Barry Ellis [1939] Director/Haulier; Carol Ellis [1952] Director; Victoria Louise Swift [1969] Director/Office Manager

James Brearley & Sons Limited
Incorporated: 1 February 1999 *Employees:* 66
Net Worth: £5,634,492 *Total Assets:* £15,979,998
Registered Office: Walpole House, Unit 2 Burton Road, Blackpool, Lancs, FY4 4NW
Activities: Security and commodity contracts dealing activities
Shareholders: Roger William Brearley; Michael William Burnett
Officers: Roger William Brearley [1947] Director/Stockbroker; Nigel Christopher Corrie [1961] Director/Stockbroker; Richard Michael Dunsby [1974] Director/Stockbroker; David Vincent Hannis [1962] Director/Stockbroker; Simon Robert Trippier [1976] Director/Stockbroker

Breckland Leisure Limited
Incorporated: 21 January 2002
Net Worth Deficit: £2,225,395 *Total Assets:* £11,120,818
Registered Office: Parkwood House, Cuerden Park, Berkeley Drive, Bamber Bridge, Preston, Lancs, PR5 6BY
Activities: General public administration activities
Parent: Breckland Holdings Limited
Officers: David John Harding [1980] Director/Chartered Accountant; Richard Daniel Knight [1974] Operations Director; Philip Arthur Would [1971] Director/Asset Manager

Brennan Enterprise Limited
Incorporated: 17 December 2007 *Employees:* 158
Net Worth: £11,865,628 *Total Assets:* £19,333,160
Registered Office: Summit, Littleborough, Rochdale, Lancs, OL15 0LR
Activities: Non-trading company
Major Shareholder: Patrick Gerard Brennan
Officers: Patrick Gerard Brennan, Secretary/Director [Irish]; Patrick Gerard Brennan [1958] Director [Irish]; Veronica Anne Brennan [1959] Director [Irish]

Brenrun Limited
Incorporated: 21 January 1998 *Employees:* 2
Net Worth: £4,174,231 *Total Assets:* £7,605,096
Registered Office: Haresfield, Stockton Lane, Grappenhall, Warrington, Cheshire, WA4 3HQ
Activities: Other letting and operating of own or leased real estate
Shareholder: David John Critchley
Officers: Karen Jane Critchley, Secretary; David John Critchley [1963] Director/Off Licence Proprietor; Jack Peter Critchley [1988] Director

Bridge Brokers Limited
Incorporated: 24 February 1995 *Employees:* 95
Net Worth: £1,521,411 *Total Assets:* £8,554,012
Registered Office: Cobac House, 14-16 Charlotte Street, Manchester, M1 4FL
Activities: Non-trading company
Shareholder: Michael Backner
Officers: Michael Backner [1946] Director/Insurance Broker; Gilbert Daniel Cohen [1942] Director

Bridge Insurance Brokers Limited
Incorporated: 7 December 1970 *Employees:* 95
Net Worth: £1,693,496 *Total Assets:* £8,727,099
Registered Office: Cobac House, 14-16 Charlotte Street, Manchester, M1 4FL
Activities: Non-life insurance
Parent: Bridge Brokers Limited
Officers: Michael Backner [1946] Director/Insurance Broker; Gilbert Daniel Cohen [1942] Director/Insurance Broker; Roger Charles Potts [1956] Director; Philip Michael Webster [1960] Director/Insurance Broker

Bridgehead Container Services Limited
Incorporated: 19 May 1964 *Employees:* 15
Net Worth: £42,839,480 *Total Assets:* £49,634,392
Registered Office: Cunard Building, Water Street, Liverpool, L3 1DS
Activities: Other transportation support activities
Major Shareholder: Brian Robert Bibby
Officers: James Rudge, Secretary; Brian Robert Bibby [1937] Director; Joyce Hilary Bibby [1939] Director; Jane Hazel Marshall [1968] Operations Director

Bridgemere Development Capital PLC
Incorporated: 2 October 2007 *Employees:* 3
Net Worth: £17,592,208 *Total Assets:* £18,476,788
Registered Office: Bridgemere House, Chester Road, Preston Brook, Cheshire, WA7 3BD
Activities: Financial intermediation not elsewhere classified
Officers: Ashley Martin Lewis, Secretary/Chartered Accountant; Ashley Martin Lewis [1956] Director/Chartered Accountant; Peter Marsden [1979] Legal Director; Stephen Peter Morgan [1952] Director

Bridgemere Land PLC
Incorporated: 3 October 2001 *Employees:* 4
Net Worth: £80,006,728 *Total Assets:* £84,035,312
Registered Office: Bridgemere House, Chester Road, Preston Brook, Warrington, Cheshire, WA7 3BD
Activities: Buying and selling of own real estate
Officers: Ashley Martin Lewis, Secretary/Chartered Accountant; Ashley Martin Lewis [1956] Director/Chartered Accountant; Peter Marsden [1979] Legal Director; Jonathan Roderick Charles Masters [1959] Commercial Director; Stephen Peter Morgan [1952] Director

Bridgemere UK PLC
Incorporated: 7 December 2005 *Employees:* 270
Net Worth: £26,691,000 *Total Assets:* £115,706,000
Registered Office: Bridgemere House, Chester Road, Preston Brook, Cheshire, WA7 3BD
Activities: Activities of head offices
Officers: Ashley Martin Lewis, Secretary/Director; Ashley Martin Lewis [1956] Director; Peter Marsden [1979] Legal Director; Jonathan Roderick Charles Masters [1959] Commercial Director; Stephen Peter Morgan [1952] Director

The Bridgewater Canal Company Limited
Incorporated: 29 January 2009 *Employees:* 7
Net Worth: £10,906,621 *Total Assets:* £14,000,744
Registered Office: Peel Dome, intu Trafford Centre, Trafford City, Manchester, M17 8PL
Activities: Inland passenger water transport
Parent: Peel Land Holdings Limited
Officers: Neil Lees, Secretary; Peter John Hosker [1957] Director; Neil Lees [1963] Director; John Alexander Schofield [1968] Director/Accountant; Steven Keith Underwood [1974] Director; John Whittaker [1942] Director; Mark Whittaker [1969] Director

Bridgewater High School
Incorporated: 29 October 2014 *Employees:* 196
Net Worth: £36,395,304 *Total Assets:* £39,568,976
Registered Office: Bridgewater High School, Broomfields Road, Appleton, Warrington, Cheshire, WA4 3AE
Activities: General secondary education
Officers: Adrienne Laing, Secretary; Jonathan David Betts [1973] Director/Police Officer; Graham Peter Bratley [1963] Managing Director; Iain Alexander Deas [1967] Director/Lecturer; Amalia Gittins [1954] Director [Italian]; Dr Roger James Hayward [1945] Director/Retired Senior Education Manager; Timothy Mark Long [1964] Director/Headteacher; Mark Andrew Malam [1981] Director/Teacher; Anita Lorraine Pailing [1972] Director/Company Secretary; Michael William Thomas Palmer [1966] Director/Manager; Michele Scattergood [1968] Director/Chief Executive; Gary Fairfax Stuart [1967] Director/Police Officer; Janet Wells [1962] Director/Police Sergeant; Stephen Nicholas Whatmore [1953] Director; Ian Wilson [1973] Director/Teacher

Bridgewater Point Ltd
Incorporated: 12 June 2015
Net Worth: £84 *Total Assets:* £37,465,080
Registered Office: 300 St Marys Road, Garston, Liverpool, L19 0NQ
Activities: Other letting and operating of own or leased real estate
Parent: Fortis UK Holdings Ltd
Officers: Darren Kingsley McClellan [1972] Director/Manager; Kieran Stuart Moore [1975] Director/Manager; Gareth Morgan [1984] Director/Manager

Bridgewater School
Incorporated: 27 July 2004 *Employees:* 72
Net Worth: £3,367,593 *Total Assets:* £6,830,687
Registered Office: Drywood Hall, Worsley Road, Worsley, Manchester, M28 2WQ
Activities: Primary education
Officers: Elizabeth Fay Davenport, Secretary; Nicholas Robin Beesley [1951] Director/Retired Headmaster; Scott Alan Brenchley [1976] Managing Director; Craig Cheetham [1983] Director of Corporate Transactions; Amanda Elizabeth Dagg [1968] Director/Marketing Consultant; Michael Gatenby [1942] Director/Retired; Christopher Edmund Haighton [1969] Logistics Director; Jane Jones [1950] Director/Retired Teacher; Kathryn Sybil Mort [1977] Director/Deputy Headteacher; Dr Martin Christopher Moss [1962] Director/Chief Architect (IT Manager); Simon Christopher Ryan [1965] Director/Senior Manager; Kirstie Joanne Simpson [1973] Director/University Lecturer; Lisa Jayne Tyson [1968] Director/Solicitor

Bridging Finance Limited
Incorporated: 1 March 1996
Net Worth: £1,532,000 *Total Assets:* £79,363,000
Registered Office: Lake View, Lakeside, Cheadle, Cheshire, SK8 3GW
Activities: Credit granting by non-deposit taking finance houses and other specialist consumer credit grantors
Parent: Together Financial Services Limited
Officers: Sarah Elizabeth Batt, Secretary; Gary Derek Beckett [1969] Director; Wayne Bowser [1952] Director; Marc Richard Goldberg [1971] Director; Robert Michael McTighe [1953] Director; Henry Neville Moser [1949] Director; Helga Clare Taylor [1969] Finance Director

Bridging Finance Solutions Group Limited
Incorporated: 23 January 2006 *Employees:* 11
Net Worth: £1,094,436 *Total Assets:* £7,970,468
Registered Office: The Cottages, 86-88 Wallasey Road, Wallasey, Wirral, Merseyside, CH44 2AE
Activities: Other business support service activities n.e.c.
Major Shareholder: Steven Alex Barber
Officers: Diane Margaret McHugh, Secretary; Helen Louise Barber [1972] Director; Steven Alex Barber [1972] Director; Duncan Russell Cameron [1971] Director; Simon Justin Nixon [1967] Director; Guy Platt-Higgins [1971] Director/Costs Draftsman

Bridstock Gate Limited
Incorporated: 17 June 1975 *Employees:* 16
Net Worth: £7,055,496 *Total Assets:* £8,197,300
Registered Office: Helmet Street, off Fairfield Street, Manchester, M1 2NT
Activities: Wholesale of textiles
Parent: Evans Textile (Sales) Limited
Officers: Phillip Bailey [1960] Director; Carl Bennet [1969] Director; Paul Francis Callan [1965] Managing Director

James Briggs (Holdings) Limited
Incorporated: 18 February 2013 *Employees:* 280
Net Worth Deficit: £5,432,000 *Total Assets:* £22,216,000
Registered Office: Salmon Fields, Royton, Oldham, Lancs, OL2 6HZ
Activities: Manufacture of other chemical products n.e.c.
Shareholders: Endless LLP; Endless III General Partner LLP
Officers: Paul Richard Blackaby [1966] Director/Management Accountant; Mathew William Deering [1977] Director/Chartered Accountant; Thomas Andrew Jack [1973] Director; Richard Timothy Pugh [1965] Director

James Briggs Limited
Incorporated: 7 March 2013 *Employees:* 273
Net Worth Deficit: £4,904,000 *Total Assets:* £22,645,000
Registered Office: Salmon Fields, Royton, Oldham, Lancs, OL2 6HZ
Activities: Manufacture of other chemical products n.e.c.
Parent: James Briggs (Holdings) Limited
Officers: Paul Richard Blackaby [1966] Director/Management Accountant; Richard Timothy Pugh [1965] Director

Ellis Brigham Holdings Limited
Incorporated: 4 March 2009 *Employees:* 368
Net Worth: £14,599,724 *Total Assets:* £22,925,816
Registered Office: 47 Brunel Avenue, Salford, M5 4BE
Activities: Non-trading company
Shareholders: Margaret Elizabeth Brigham; Frederick Robert Brigham
Officers: Ellis Brigham [1944] Director; Mark Ellis Brigham [1975] Director; Robert Ellis Brigham [1974] Director

Ellis Brigham Mountain Sports Limited
Incorporated: 4 March 2009 *Employees:* 97
Net Worth: £4,359,744 *Total Assets:* £9,308,156
Registered Office: 47 Brunel Avenue, Salford, M5 4BE
Activities: Other retail sale of new goods in specialised stores (not commercial art galleries and opticians)
Parent: Ellis Brigham Holdings Limited
Officers: Ellis Brigham [1944] Director; Mark Ellis Brigham [1975] Director; Robert Ellis Brigham [1974] Director

Bright Blue Foods Limited
Incorporated: 12 September 2012 *Employees:* 911
Net Worth Deficit: £1,394,000 *Total Assets:* £29,495,000
Registered Office: Unit G, Sett End Road, Shadsworth Business Park, Blackburn, Lancs, BB1 2PT
Activities: Manufacture of bread; manufacture of fresh pastry goods and cakes
Parent: BBF (Holdings) Limited
Officers: Munaf Yusuf, Secretary; David Stephen Gallagher [1964] Operation Director; Peter Harold Hartshorn [1967] Director; Anthony Martin Hynes [1951] Director [Irish]; Mark Izzard [1979] Director; Jonathan Craig Lill [1968] Director; Diane Susan Walker [1972] Director; Munaf Yusuf [1971] Finance Director

Bright Futures Educational Trust
Incorporated: 6 July 2011 *Employees:* 635
Net Worth: £31,526,000 *Total Assets:* £47,092,000
Registered Office: Lodge House, Cavendish Road, Bowdon, Altrincham, Cheshire, WA14 2NJ
Activities: General secondary education
Officers: Joan Margaret Appleyard [1957] Director/Chief Executive Officer; Alan Foster [1944] Director/Retired; Lynn Nicholls [1960] Director/Headteacher; Yakub Patel [1953] Managing Director; Daniel Paul Rubin [1971] Director/Solicitor; Caroline Sarah Shaw [1967] Director; Dr John William Stephens [1964] Director/Chief Education Officer

Bright Tribe Trust
Incorporated: 16 July 2012 *Employees:* 564
Net Worth: £57,337,000 *Total Assets:* £68,817,000
Registered Office: Suite 9, 3rd Floor, Mansion House, 173-191 Wellington Road South, Stockport, Cheshire, SK1 3UA
Activities: Primary education
Shareholders: Kathryn Brunt; Teresa Margaret Tunnadine; Ruth Anne Dolan
Officers: Angela Jean Barry [1962] Director/Executive Headteacher; Sarah Margaret Brown [1963] Director; Ruth Anne Dolan [1959] Director/Governance Consultant; Nicolette King [1947] Director

Brighterkind (CB) Limited
Incorporated: 8 March 2013 *Employees:* 1,950
Net Worth: £61,219,000 *Total Assets:* £155,172,992
Registered Office: Norcliffe House, Station Road, Wilmslow, Cheshire, SK9 1BU
Activities: Other human health activities
Parent: Brighterkind (PC) Limited
Officers: Abigail Mattison, Secretary; Robert Nicolas Barr [1958] Director; Stephen Mark Julius [1959] Director; Ryan Stuart MacAskill [1975] Director; Gregory Laurence Newman [1988] Director/Investment Professional; Jeremy Robert Arthur Richardson [1970] Director; Dr Maureen Claire Royston [1960] Director; Phillip Gary Thomas [1978] Director

Brighterkind (MW) Limited
Incorporated: 8 March 2013
Net Worth: £34,123,000 *Total Assets:* £164,800,000
Registered Office: Norcliffe House, Station Road, Wilmslow, Cheshire, SK9 1BU
Activities: Other human health activities
Parent: Brighterkind (CB) Limited
Officers: Abigail Mattison, Secretary; Ryan Stuart MacAskill [1975] Director; Gregory Laurence Newman [1988] Director/Investment Professional; Jeremy Robert Arthur Richardson [1970] Director; Dr Maureen Claire Royston [1960] Director; Phillip Gary Thomas [1978] Director

Brighterkind (PC) Limited
Incorporated: 8 March 2013 *Employees:* 6
Net Worth: £34,691,000 *Total Assets:* £34,691,000
Registered Office: Norcliffe House, Station Road, Wilmslow, Cheshire, SK9 1BU
Activities: Other human health activities
Officers: Abigail Mattison, Secretary; Robert Nicolas Barr [1958] Director; Ryan Stuart MacAskill [1975] Director; Gregory Laurence Newman [1988] Director/Investment Professional; Dr Maureen Claire Royston [1960] Director; Benjamin Robert Taberner [1972] Director/Chartered Accountant

Brighterkind Limited
Incorporated: 7 February 2007 *Employees:* 20
Net Worth Deficit: £31,470,000 *Total Assets:* £98,156,000
Registered Office: Norcliffe House, Station Road, Wilmslow, Cheshire, SK9 1BU
Activities: Activities of head offices
Parent: Brighterkind (MW) Limited
Officers: Abigail Mattison, Secretary; Ryan Stuart MacAskill [1975] Director; Gregory Laurence Newman [1988] Director/Investment Professional; Jeremy Robert Arthur Richardson [1970] Director; Maureen Claire Royston [1960] Director; Phillip Gary Thomas [1978] Director

Brightstar 20:20 Limited
Incorporated: 20 February 2013 *Employees:* 61
Net Worth: £11,710,000 *Total Assets:* £49,418,000
Registered Office: Weston Road, Crewe, Cheshire, CW1 6BU
Activities: Activities of distribution holding companies
Parent: Chicago Group Limited
Officers: Andrew David Hancock [1971] Director; Noel Generald Marsden [1974] Director [American]; Stijn Piet Nijs [1975] Director [Belgian]; Michael David Eugene Singer [1971] Director/Senior Vice President [American]

Brightstar 20:20 UK Limited
Incorporated: 13 February 2013 *Employees:* 367
Net Worth: £26,209,000 *Total Assets:* £123,858,000
Registered Office: Weston Road, Crewe, Cheshire, CW1 6BU
Activities: Other telecommunications activities
Parent: Brightstar 20:20 Limited
Officers: Andrew David Hancock [1971] Director; Noel Generald Marsden [1974] Director [American]; Stijn Piet Nijs [1975] Director [Belgian]; Michael David Eugene Singer [1971] Director/Senior Vice President [American]

Brightstar Mobility UK, Ltd.
Incorporated: 31 August 2012
Net Worth: £46,592,000 *Total Assets:* £52,019,000
Registered Office: Weston Road, Crewe, Cheshire, CW1 6BU
Activities: Non-trading company
Parent: Brightstar Netherlands Cooperatief UA
Officers: Andrew David Hancock [1971] Director; Noel Generald Marsden [1974] Director [American]; Stijn Piet Nijs [1975] Director/Chief Financial Officer [Belgian]; Michael David Eugene Singer [1971] Director [American]

Brilie Properties Limited
Incorporated: 9 May 2005 *Employees:* 4
Net Worth: £2,164,146 *Total Assets:* £7,193,775
Registered Office: c/o E W Cartons Limited, Unit 5 Metcalf Drive, Altham Industrial Estate, Accrington, Lancs, BB5 5TU
Activities: Other letting and operating of own or leased real estate
Parent: Brilie Investments Limited
Officers: Adam Henry Clifton, Secretary/Director; Adam Henry Clifton [1969] Director; Julie Hazel Green-Jones [1963] Director; Brian Crompton Jones [1956] Director

Brine Multi Academy Trust
Incorporated: 12 August 2010 *Employees:* 191
Net Worth: £26,534,976 *Total Assets:* £28,856,336
Registered Office: Brine Leas School, Audlem Road, Nantwich, Cheshire, CW5 7DY
Activities: Other social work activities without accommodation n.e.c.
Shareholders: Anthony Frank Coxhill; Janet Mary Furber
Officers: Andrew Cliffe [1962] Director/Trustee; Anthony Frank Coxhill [1947] Director/School Governor; Julie Disney [1976] Director/Trustee; Janet Mary Furber [1949] Director/Agricultural Contractor; Brett Radford [1961] Director/Trustee; Andrew Robinson [1956] Director/Trustee

Brink's (UK) Limited
Incorporated: 2 March 1990 *Employees:* 213
Net Worth: £15,713,000 *Total Assets:* £32,174,000
Registered Office: Eversheds House, 70 Great Bridgewater Street, Manchester, M1 5ES
Activities: Other business support service activities n.e.c.
Parent: The Brink's Company
Officers: McAlister C Marshall [1970] Director [American]; Andrea Stina Sanchez [1966] Director - Human Resources

Brink's Global Services, Ltd.
Incorporated: 5 January 1999 *Employees:* 121
Net Worth Deficit: £822,563 *Total Assets:* £18,950,552
Registered Office: Eversheds House, 70 Great Bridgewater Street, Manchester, M1 5ES
Activities: Cargo handling for air transport activities
Parent: The Brink's Company
Officers: McAlister C Marshall [1970] Director [American]; Andrea Stina Sanchez [1966] Director - Human Resources

Brink's Limited
Incorporated: 6 August 1969 *Employees:* 211
Net Worth: £21,580,000 *Total Assets:* £34,935,000
Registered Office: Eversheds House, 70 Great Bridgewater Street, Manchester, M1 5ES
Activities: Freight transport by road
Parent: Brink's (UK) Limited
Officers: McAlister C Marshall [1970] Director [American]; Andrea Stina Sanchez [1966] Director - Human Resources; Mark Andrew Woolley [1966] Director

Brinksway Tool Limited
Incorporated: 17 June 1976 *Employees:* 45
Net Worth: £5,972,555 *Total Assets:* £7,517,662
Registered Office: Stamford House, 185 Stamford Street, Stalybridge, Cheshire, SK15 1QZ
Activities: Other engineering activities
Officers: Mark Vernon Haslam, Secretary; James Baker [1962] Director/Engineer; Michael Ford [1945] Director/Accountant; Mark Vernon Haslam [1968] Director; Carl Nickerson [1966] Director/Engineer; Malcolm O'Connor [1965] Director/Accountant

Brisbane House Limited
Incorporated: 12 February 2001
Net Worth: £11,258,083 *Total Assets:* £32,166,712
Registered Office: Springfield House, Water Lane, Wilmslow, Cheshire, SK9 5BG
Activities: Other letting and operating of own or leased real estate
Parent: Dean Property Group Limited
Officers: Michael Edward O'Donnell, Secretary; Jonathan Charles Patrick Beever [1963] Director/Property Manager; Michael Edward O'Donnell [1969] Director/Property Investment; James Anthony Wild [1941] Director/Property Investment

Bristol Active Limited
Incorporated: 14 August 2007
Net Worth Deficit: £5,469,944 *Total Assets:* £29,975,028
Registered Office: Parkwood House, Cuerden Park, Berkeley Drive, Bamber Bridge, Preston, Lancs, PR5 6BY
Activities: Construction of commercial buildings
Parent: Bristol Active Holdings Ltd
Officers: David John Harding [1980] Director/Chartered Accountant; Philip Arthur Would [1971] Director/Asset Manager

Brit-European Transport Limited
Incorporated: 13 May 1963 *Employees:* 196
Net Worth: £3,828,626 *Total Assets:* £13,370,466
Registered Office: The Courtyard, Radway Green, Crewe, Cheshire, CW2 5PR
Activities: Freight transport by road
Parent: Brit European Transport (Holdings) Limited
Officers: Andrew Jonathan Hodgson, Secretary; William Roderick Carman [1957] Director/Group Chairman; Andrew Jonathan Hodgson [1964] Director/Chartered Accountant; Graham David Lackey [1967] Group Managing Director; Robbie Andrew McNinch [1975] Commercial Director

Britannia Hotels Limited
Incorporated: 12 December 1977 *Employees:* 2,175
Net Worth: £143,740,000 *Total Assets:* £258,372,000
Registered Office: Halecroft, Hale Road, Hale, Cheshire, WA15 8RE
Activities: Hotels and similar accommodation
Officers: Robert Christopher Ferrari, Secretary; Robert Christopher Ferrari [1947] Director; Alexander Langsam [1938] Director/Hotelier

Britannia Treasury Services Limited
Incorporated: 7 August 1997
Net Worth: £2,868,891 *Total Assets:* £22,397,278
Registered Office: P O Box 101, 1 Balloon Street, Manchester, M60 4EP
Activities: Financial intermediation not elsewhere classified
Parent: The Co-operative Bank PLC
Officers: David Clive Whitehead, Secretary; Richard John Adnett [1974] Director/Head of Core Bank Business Partnering; David Michael Miller [1985] Director/Financial Performance Manager

The British Cycling Federation
Incorporated: 9 March 2000 *Employees:* 284
Net Worth: £4,323,697 *Total Assets:* £16,662,272
Registered Office: British Cycling Federation, Stuart Street, Manchester, M11 4DQ
Activities: Other sports activities
Officers: Rod Findlay, Secretary; Wendy Jean Cull [1966] Director/Environmental Health Officer; Graham Frank Elliott [1956] Director/Retired; Dr George Gilbert [1974] Director/Software Engineer; Julie Anne Harrington [1969] Director/Chief Executive; Peter Arthur King [1944] Director/Accountant; Marian Florence Lauder [1957] Director; Richard William Lodge [1962] Director/Tax Advisor; Alasdair MacLennan [1957] Director/Self Employed; Alexandra Libby Russell [1979] Director/Consultant; Francis Joseph Slevin [1963] Director; Nicholas Charles Smith [1961] Director/Retired

The British Millerain Company Limited
Incorporated: 24 November 1922 *Employees:* 102
Net Worth: £10,204,225 *Total Assets:* £15,818,310
Registered Office: Unit 1 Park Mill, Buckley Road, Rochdale, Lancs, OL12 9DJ
Activities: Finishing of textiles
Officers: Marie Louise Miller, Secretary; Dr Donna LEA Keeble [1982] Director; James Keeble [1983] Sales and Marketing Director; Marie Louise Miller [1962] Director; Michael Anthony Miller [1953] Director; Stephanie Anne Miller [1993] Director/Raw Material Buyer

British Mohair Holdings Limited
Incorporated: 19 October 1893
Net Worth Deficit: £1,108,179 *Total Assets:* £14,544,173
Registered Office: Old Mills, off Whitehall Grove, Drighlington, Bradford, W Yorks, BD11 1BY
Activities: Activities of head offices
Officers: Kathryn Anne Davenport, Secretary; Peter Jan Patrik Valentin Gyllenhammar [1953] Director [Swedish]

British Muslim Heritage Centre
Incorporated: 28 May 2003 *Employees:* 9
Net Worth: £7,978,782 *Total Assets:* £9,110,934
Registered Office: British Muslim Heritage Centre, College Road, Whalley Range, Manchester, M16 8BP
Activities: Other education n.e.c.
Officers: Farroukh Zaheer, Secretary/Charter Accountant Auditor; Whaid Ahmed [1957] Director; Dr Ahmad Al Dubayan [1957] Director General Islamic Cultural Centre [Saudi Arabian]; Dr Ghaith Mubarak Omran Al Kuwari [1969] Director/Manager [Qatari]; Mohammed Salim Al-Astewani [1961] Director/Property Manager; Dr Hamad Mohammad Algammas [1963] Director [Saudi Arabian]; Dr Hamad Abdullah Almajed [1959] Director/Lecturer [Saudi Arabian]; Dr Abdullah Mohammed Almajid [1960] Director/Lecturer [Saudi Arabian]; Dr Abdullah Almatouq [1957] Director/Manager; Saima Alvi [1968] Director/Educational Consultant; Elinor Mair Chohan [1965] Director Miri Roshni; Cllr Naeem Ul Hassan [1960] Director/Councillor; Abdulkadir Abdulrahim Othman Kawooya [1957] Director/Senior Lecturer; Nasar Mahmood [1952] Director/Self Employed; Adnan Abdul Rahman Saif [1961] Director; Doctor Mohammed Sarumi [1960] Director/Engineer; Sadiqbasha Thameembasha [1980] Director; Farroukh Zaheer [1955] Director/Accountant

British Salt Limited
Incorporated: 15 October 2007 *Employees:* 100
Net Worth: £92,693,000 *Total Assets:* £96,892,000
Registered Office: Mond House, Winnington, Northwich, Cheshire, CW8 4DT
Activities: Extraction of salt
Parent: Cheshire Salt Limited
Officers: David Philip William Davies, Secretary; Jonathan Laurence Abbotts [1964] Director; Dr Martin John Ashcroft [1969] Managing Director; David Philip William Davies [1971] Director/Solicitor; Peter Patrick Houghton [1963] Director; Dr Ladan Iravanian [1960] Director; Karen Lesley Lounds [1969] Director; Alan Neil Runciman [1964] Director

Broadstone Mill Ltd
Incorporated: 16 June 1997
Net Worth: £3,209,553 *Total Assets:* £6,505,541
Registered Office: Broadstone Mill, Broadstone Road, Stockport, Cheshire, SK5 7DL
Activities: Other letting and operating of own or leased real estate
Shareholders: Richard Ralph Sym; Richard Ralph Sym
Officers: Richard Ralph Sym [1955] Director

Broadway Halls Care Services Limited
Incorporated: 13 May 2008 *Employees:* 110
Net Worth: £2,374,000 *Total Assets:* £10,125,000
Registered Office: Norcliffe House, Station Road, Wilmslow, Cheshire, SK9 1BU
Activities: Other human health activities
Parent: Optimum Debtco Limited
Officers: Abigail Mattison, Secretary; Ryan Stuart MacAskill [1975] Director; Gregory Laurence Newman [1988] Director/Investment Professional; Jeremy Robert Arthur Richardson [1970] Director; Dr Maureen Claire Royston [1960] Director; Phillip Gary Thomas [1978] Director

Broker Direct PLC
Incorporated: 12 August 1994 *Employees:* 165
Net Worth: £1,689,255 *Total Assets:* £18,582,990
Registered Office: Deakins Park, Deakins Mill Way, Egerton, Bolton, Lancs, BL7 9RW
Activities: Activities auxiliary to financial intermediation n.e.c.
Officers: Iain Julian Gray, Secretary; Barbara Bradshaw [1951] Director; Joyce Ann Golder [1969] Operations Director; Iain Julian Gray [1962] Finance Director; Roy Green [1946] Non-Executive Director Chairman; John Kedric Rhodes [1944] Director; Terence Edward Stanley [1956] Director/Chief Executive Officer

Bromborough Paint & Building Supplies Limited
Incorporated: 31 December 1965 *Employees:* 130
Net Worth: £9,650,912 *Total Assets:* £11,411,283
Registered Office: 38 Bromborough Village Road, Bromborough, Wirral, Merseyside, CH62 7ET
Activities: Retail sale of hardware, paints and glass in specialised stores
Major Shareholder: Neville Wellings
Officers: Giuseppe Alfonso, Secretary; Giuseppe Giulio Alfonso [1965] Director/Accountant; John William Ferrington [1967] Director/Operations Manager; Philip Morris Samuel McCulloch [1953] Director/General Manager; Neville Wellings [1949] Director; David Hywel Williams [1948] Director/Sales Manager

Brook Taverner Limited
Incorporated: 9 March 1948 *Employees:* 113
Net Worth: £6,758,927 *Total Assets:* £12,350,939
Registered Office: Prospect Mill, Haincliffe Road, Ingrow, Keighley, W Yorks, BD21 5BU
Activities: Wholesale of clothing and footwear
Parent: Peaspring Limited
Officers: Andrew Philip Booth, Secretary/Chartered Accountant; Andrew Philip Booth [1968] Director/Chartered Accountant; Jo-Anne Booth [1969] Director; John Benjamin Jones [1969] Managing Director; Rachel Jones [1970] Director; Jason Edwin Russell Scott [1970] Director; Rebecca Scott [1970] Director

Brookes Bell LLP
Incorporated: 16 March 2005 *Employees:* 91
Net Worth: £5,416,857 *Total Assets:* £9,259,468
Registered Office: Walker House, Exchange Flags, Liverpool, L2 3YL

Nick Brookes Recycling Limited
Incorporated: 27 February 2007 *Employees:* 81
Net Worth: £3,291,642 *Total Assets:* £9,130,298
Registered Office: Nick Brookes Recycling Limited, Wardle Industrial Estate, Green Lane, Wardle, Nantwich, Cheshire, CW5 6DB
Activities: Recovery of sorted materials
Shareholders: Nicholas Duncan Brookes; Michael Rodney Brookes
Officers: Sarah Jane Howard Perry, Secretary; Michael Rodney Brookes [1943] Director; Nicholas Duncan Brookes [1971] Director; Sarah Jane Howard Perry [1964] Director

Brookfield Rose Limited
Incorporated: 9 June 2010
Net Worth: £11,436,988 *Total Assets:* £52,837,764
Registered Office: Booths Park 1, Chelford Road, Knutsford, Cheshire, WA16 8GS
Activities: Activities of head offices
Parent: Ultium Business Outsourcing Group Limited
Officers: Sam Richard Del Mar [1974] Director; Frederick Karl Minturn [1956] Director [American]; Andrew David Preston [1975] Director

Brookhead Estate Limited
Incorporated: 20 May 1937 *Employees:* 2
Net Worth: £5,373,870 *Total Assets:* £11,580,085
Registered Office: Clarke Nicklin House, Brooks Drive, Cheadle Royal Business Park, Cheadle, Cheshire, SK8 3TD
Activities: Buying and selling of own real estate
Parent: Broome Management Co. Limited
Officers: Rodney Ward, Secretary; David Karl McDonald [1966] Director/Property Management; Andrew John Robinson [1946] Director

Brookhouse (Alexandra) Limited
Incorporated: 16 March 2011
Net Worth: £4,392,000 *Total Assets:* £16,161,000
Registered Office: 168-170 Washway Road, Sale, Cheshire, M33 6RH
Activities: Development of building projects
Parent: Brookhouse Group Limited
Officers: Peter Chape, Secretary; Heath David Broadbent [1973] Construction Director; Andrew Jeremy Gardner [1972] Director; Emma Hindle [1975] Director; Michael Edward Nuttall [1964] Director/Surveyor

Brookhouse (Ashford) Limited
Incorporated: 15 August 2002
Net Worth: £10,404,000 *Total Assets:* £10,404,000
Registered Office: Prospect House, 168-170 Washway Road, Sale, Cheshire, M33 6RH
Activities: Buying and selling of own real estate
Parent: Brookhouse Property Holdings Limited
Officers: Peter Chape, Secretary; Heath David Broadbent [1973] Construction Director; Andrew Jeremy Gardner [1972] Director/Accountant; Emma Hindle [1975] Director; Michael Edward Nuttall [1964] Director/Surveyor

Brookhouse (Christchurch) Limited
Incorporated: 10 July 2003
Net Worth: £5,190,000 *Total Assets:* £20,662,000
Registered Office: Prospect House, 168-170 Washway Road, Sale, Cheshire, M33 6RH
Activities: Buying and selling of own real estate
Parent: Brookhouse Property Holdings Limited
Officers: Peter Chape, Secretary; Heath David Broadbent [1973] Construction Director; Andrew Jeremy Gardner [1972] Director/Accountant; Emma Hindle [1975] Director; Michael Edward Nuttall [1964] Director/Surveyor

Brookhouse (Hamilton) Limited
Incorporated: 28 May 2002
Net Worth: £23,418,000 *Total Assets:* £70,549,000
Registered Office: Prospect House, 168-170 Washway Road, Sale, Cheshire, M33 6RH
Activities: Buying and selling of own real estate
Parent: Brookhouse Group Limited
Officers: Peter Chape, Secretary; Heath David Broadbent [1973] Construction Director; Andrew Jeremy Gardner [1972] Director/Accountant; Emma Hindle [1975] Director; Michael Edward Nuttall [1964] Director/Surveyor

Brookhouse (Lowestoft) Limited
Incorporated: 31 May 2002
Net Worth: £24,071,000 *Total Assets:* £47,080,000
Registered Office: Prospect House, 168-170 Washway Road, Sale, Cheshire, M33 6RH
Activities: Buying and selling of own real estate
Parent: Brookhouse Group Limited
Officers: Peter Chape, Secretary; Heath David Broadbent [1973] Construction Director; Andrew Jeremy Gardner [1972] Director/Accountant; Emma Hindle [1975] Director; Michael Edward Nuttall [1964] Director/Surveyor

Brookhouse (Prescot) Limited
Incorporated: 11 July 2003
Net Worth: £18,842,000 *Total Assets:* £33,378,000
Registered Office: Prospect House, 168-170 Washway Road, Sale, Cheshire, M33 6RH
Activities: Buying and selling of own real estate
Parent: Brookhouse Group Limited
Officers: Peter Chape, Secretary; Heath David Broadbent [1973] Construction Director; Andrew Jeremy Gardner [1972] Director/Accountant; Emma Hindle [1975] Director; Michael Edward Nuttall [1964] Director/Surveyor

Brookhouse (Preston) Limited
Incorporated: 12 June 2009
Net Worth: £4,570,000 *Total Assets:* £21,248,000
Registered Office: 168-170 Washway Road, Sale, Cheshire, M33 6RH
Activities: Buying and selling of own real estate
Parent: Brookhouse Group Limited
Officers: Peter Chape, Secretary; Heath David Broadbent [1973] Construction Director; Andrew Jeremy Gardner [1972] Director; Emma Hindle [1975] Director; Michael Edward Nuttall [1964] Director/Surveyor

Brookhouse Builders Limited
Incorporated: 10 September 1990
Net Worth Deficit: £908,000 *Total Assets:* £8,443,000
Registered Office: Prospect House, 168-170 Washway Road, Sale, Cheshire, M33 6RH
Activities: Activities of head offices
Parent: Brookhouse Group Limited
Officers: Peter Chape, Secretary; James Peter Banfi [1953] Director/Solicitor; Heath David Broadbent [1973] Construction Director; Andrew Jeremy Gardner [1972] Director/Accountant; Emma Hindle [1975] Director; Michael Edward Nuttall [1964] Director/Chartered Surveyor

Brookhouse Chichester Limited
Incorporated: 5 December 2001
Net Worth: £7,663,000 *Total Assets:* £16,142,000
Registered Office: Prospect House, 168-170 Washway Road, Sale, Cheshire, M33 6RH
Activities: Buying and selling of own real estate
Parent: Brookhouse Group Limited
Officers: Peter Chape, Secretary; Heath David Broadbent [1973] Construction Director; Andrew Jeremy Gardner [1972] Director/Accountant; Emma Hindle [1975] Director; Michael Edward Nuttall [1964] Director/Surveyor

Brookhouse Estates Limited
Incorporated: 10 November 1933
Net Worth: £12,591,000 *Total Assets:* £12,736,000
Registered Office: Prospect House, 168-170 Washway Road, Sale, Cheshire, M33 6RH
Activities: Buying and selling of own real estate
Parent: Brookhouse Builders Limited
Officers: Peter Chape, Secretary; Heath David Broadbent [1973] Construction Director; Andrew Jeremy Gardner [1972] Director/Accountant; Emma Hindle [1975] Director; Michael Edward Nuttall [1964] Director/Surveyor

Brookhouse Group Limited
Incorporated: 16 February 1988
Net Worth: £101,603,000 *Total Assets:* £112,152,000
Registered Office: Prospect House, 168-170 Washway Road, Sale, Cheshire, M33 6RH
Activities: Buying and selling of own real estate
Parent: Brookhouse Properties Limited
Officers: Peter Chape, Secretary; James Peter Banfi [1953] Director; Heath David Broadbent [1973] Construction Director; Andrew Jeremy Gardner [1972] Director/Accountant; Emma Hindle [1975] Director; Michael Edward Nuttall [1964] Director/Surveyor

Brookhouse Helsby (Retail) Limited
Incorporated: 4 March 2011
Net Worth: £14,283,000 *Total Assets:* £23,931,000
Registered Office: 168-170 Washway Road, Sale, Cheshire, M33 6RH
Activities: Buying and selling of own real estate
Parent: Brookhouse Group Limited
Officers: Peter Chape, Secretary; Heath David Broadbent [1973] Construction Director; Andrew Jeremy Gardner [1972] Director; Emma Hindle [1975] Director; Michael Edward Nuttall [1964] Director/Surveyor

Brookhouse Northern Limited
Incorporated: 16 February 1989
Net Worth: £13,944,000 *Total Assets:* £13,944,000
Registered Office: Prospect House, 168-170 Washway Road, Sale, Cheshire, M33 6RH
Activities: Buying and selling of own real estate
Parent: Brookhouse Group Limited
Officers: Peter Chape, Secretary; Heath David Broadbent [1973] Construction Director; Andrew Jeremy Gardner [1972] Director/Accountant; Emma Hindle [1975] Director; Michael Edward Nuttall [1964] Director/Surveyor

Brookhouse Properties Limited
Incorporated: 23 September 1996 *Employees:* 20
Net Worth: £306,648,000 *Total Assets:* £486,303,008
Registered Office: Prospect House, 168-170 Washway Road, Sale, Cheshire, M33 6RH
Activities: Activities of other holding companies n.e.c.
Parent: Aggregate Company S.A.R.L.
Officers: Peter Chape, Secretary; Heather Ruth Cunningham [1963] Director/Chartered Accountant; Andrew Jeremy Gardner [1972] Director/Accountant; Emma Hindle [1975] Director; Alan Scanlan Murdoch [1949] Director/Chartered Surveyor

Brookhouse Property Holdings Limited
Incorporated: 5 December 2001
Net Worth: £11,448,000 *Total Assets:* £11,448,000
Registered Office: Prospect House, 168-170 Washway Road, Sale, Cheshire, M33 6RH
Activities: Activities of other holding companies n.e.c.
Parent: Brookhouse Group Limited
Officers: Peter Chape, Secretary; Andrew Jeremy Gardner [1972] Director/Accountant; Emma Hindle [1975] Director

Brookhouse Property Investments Limited
Incorporated: 3 September 1990
Net Worth Deficit: £5,524,000 *Total Assets:* £82,744,000
Registered Office: Prospect House, 168-170 Washway Road, Sale, Cheshire, M33 6RH
Activities: Buying and selling of own real estate
Parent: Brookhouse Group Limited
Officers: Peter Chape, Secretary; Heath David Broadbent [1973] Construction Director; Andrew Jeremy Gardner [1972] Director/Accountant; Emma Hindle [1975] Director; Michael Edward Nuttall [1964] Director/Surveyor

Brookhouse Residential Developments Limited
Incorporated: 1 March 1991
Net Worth: £18,897,000 *Total Assets:* £24,087,000
Registered Office: Prospect House, 168-170 Washway Road, Sale, Cheshire, M33 6RH
Activities: Buying and selling of own real estate
Parent: Brookhouse Group Limited
Officers: Peter Chape, Secretary; Heath David Broadbent [1973] Construction Director; Andrew Jeremy Gardner [1972] Director/Accountant; Emma Hindle [1975] Director; Michael Edward Nuttall [1964] Director/Surveyor

Brookhouse Retail Limited
Incorporated: 11 May 1998
Net Worth: £43,547,000 *Total Assets:* £87,996,000
Registered Office: Prospect House, 168-170 Washway Road, Sale, Cheshire, M33 6RH
Activities: Buying and selling of own real estate
Parent: Brookhouse Group Limited
Officers: Peter Chape, Secretary; Heath David Broadbent [1973] Construction Director; Andrew Jeremy Gardner [1972] Director/Accountant; Emma Hindle [1975] Director; Michael Edward Nuttall [1964] Director/Surveyor

Brooklea Meadows Leaseholds Limited
Incorporated: 17 September 2012
Registered Office: P O Box 58, Ashbury House, Garston, Liverpool, L19 9WX
Activities: Other letting and operating of own or leased real estate
Officers: Kenneth John Carmichael [1963] Director

Brooklyn Properties Limited
Incorporated: 17 May 1999 *Employees:* 4
Net Worth: £3,237,829 *Total Assets:* £8,711,995
Registered Office: 64a Cambridge Road, Seaforth, Liverpool, L21 1EY
Activities: Development of building projects
Shareholders: Laverne Hughes; Simone Jonas; Paul Hughes
Officers: Simone Jonas, Secretary; Laverne Hughes [1947] Director; Paul Hughes [1967] Director; Simone Jonas [1969] Director

Brookmann Home Manchester 1877 Ltd
Incorporated: 19 January 1877 *Employees:* 51
Net Worth: £3,501,548 *Total Assets:* £10,968,600
Registered Office: KPMG LLP, 1 St Peter's Square, Manchester, M2 3AE
Activities: Wholesale of textiles

Brooks Automation Ltd
Incorporated: 16 November 2000 *Employees:* 160
Net Worth: £2,131,000 *Total Assets:* £35,781,000
Registered Office: Gilchrist Road, Northbank Industrial Park, Irlam, Manchester, M44 5AY
Activities: Manufacture of electronic measuring, testing etc. equipment, not for industrial process control
Parent: Brooks Automation Inc
Officers: Jason W Joseph [1970] Director/Vice President, General Counsel and Secretary [American]; David Francis Pietrantoni [1972] Director/Vice President Finance and Controller [American]; Lindon Gene Robertson [1961] Director/Chief Financial Officer [American]

Brookshaw Developments Limited
Incorporated: 7 January 2010 *Employees:* 6
Net Worth Deficit: £11,113,000 *Total Assets:* £6,530,000
Registered Office: Etihad Stadium, Etihad Campus, Manchester, M11 3FF
Activities: Remediation activities and other waste management services
Parent: Abu Dhabi United Group Investment & Development Limited
Officers: Simon Richard Cliff, Secretary; Martin Lee Edelman [1941] Director/Strategic Advisor [American]; Alberto Galassi [1964] Director/Chief Executive [Italian]; John Theodore MacBeath [1956] Director/Chartered Accountant; Mohamed Mubarak Al Mazrouei [1977] Director/Civil Servant [Emirati]; Khaldoon Khalifa Al Mubarak [1976] Director/Chairman [Emirati]; Simon Pearce [1971] Director

Brookson Group Limited
Incorporated: 3 October 2006 *Employees:* 5,357
Net Worth: £21,089,000 *Total Assets:* £50,359,000
Registered Office: Brunel House, 340 Firecrest Court, Centre Park, Warrington, Cheshire, WA1 1RG
Activities: Accounting and auditing activities
Officers: Martin John Hesketh [1964] Director; Andrew Charles McGregor [1965] Director/Chairman; Carolyn Nevinson [1966] Director; Martin John Scott [1970] Director/Partner [Irish]; Thomas Jeremy Seddon [1985] Director/Private Equity

Brookson Limited
Incorporated: 21 November 1995 *Employees:* 241
Net Worth: £8,814,806 *Total Assets:* £17,146,996
Registered Office: Brunel House, 340 Firecrest Court, Centre Park, Warrington, Cheshire, WA1 1RG
Activities: Accounting and auditing activities
Officers: Martin John Hesketh [1964] Director/Accountant; Andrew Charles McGregor [1965] Director/Chairman; Carolyn Nevinson [1966] Director; Martin John Scott [1970] Director/Partner [Irish]; Thomas Jeremy Seddon [1985] Director/Private Equity

Broomco (3935) Limited
Incorporated: 15 November 2005
Net Worth: £32,882,000 *Total Assets:* £32,882,000
Registered Office: Sirius House, Delta Crescent, Westbrook, Warrington, Cheshire, WA5 7NS
Activities: Activities of other holding companies n.e.c.
Parent: CuFe Investments Limited
Officers: Christopher John Tinsley, Secretary; Christopher Phillip Sheppard [1974] Director; Neil Andrew Stinson [1970] Director/Accountant

Broome Management Co. Limited
Incorporated: 10 September 2013
Net Worth: £13,685,268 *Total Assets:* £13,685,268
Registered Office: Clarke Nicklin House, Brooks Drive, Cheadle Royal Business Park, Cheadle, Cheshire, SK8 3TD
Activities: Other letting and operating of own or leased real estate
Officers: Rodney Ward, Secretary; David Karl McDonald [1966] Director; Andrew John Robinson [1946] Director

Brother Finance (U.K.) PLC
Incorporated: 21 November 1989 *Employees:* 4
Net Worth: £6,838,313 *Total Assets:* £386,629,984
Registered Office: Brother House, 1 Tame Street, Audenshaw, Manchester, M34 5JE
Activities: Financial intermediation not elsewhere classified
Parent: Brother Industries Ltd
Officers: Misaki Iwata, Secretary; Toshihiro Ito [1962] Director [Japanese]; Isao Noji [1962] Director [Japanese]; Kenichiro Yagi [1974] Director [Japanese]

Brother Holding (Europe) Ltd.
Incorporated: 25 August 1994
Net Worth: £166,979,312 *Total Assets:* £167,051,200
Registered Office: Brother House, 1 Tame Street, Audenshaw, Manchester, M34 5JE
Activities: Wholesale of electronic and telecommunications equipment and parts
Parent: Brother Industries Ltd
Officers: Anthony Buxton, Secretary; Hiroyuki Kachi [1964] Director [Japanese]; Isao Noji [1962] Director [Japanese]

Brother International Europe Limited
Incorporated: 5 July 1960 *Employees:* 191
Net Worth: £75,954,808 *Total Assets:* £156,614,064
Registered Office: Brother House, 1 Tame Street, Audenshaw, Manchester, M34 5JE
Activities: Wholesale of electronic and telecommunications equipment and parts
Parent: Brother Industries Limited
Officers: Anthony Brian Buxton, Secretary; Hiroyuki Kachi [1964] Director [Japanese]; Ian Desmond Metcalfe [1966] Director; Isao Noji [1962] Director [Japanese]; Takeshi Yamada [1963] Director [Japanese]

Brother Investments Limited
Incorporated: 22 May 2000 *Employees:* 5
Net Worth: £3,086,744 *Total Assets:* £21,878,430
Registered Office: Block 1 & 2 Todd Carr Road, Waterfoot, Rossendale, Lancs, BB4 9SJ
Activities: Other letting and operating of own or leased real estate
Officers: John Edward Lee, Secretary; Brian John Boys [1963] Director/Quantity Surveyor; Michael Adam Boys [1965] Director/Projects Manager; Peter Harvey Boys [1969] Director/Contracts Manager; John Edward Lee [1952] Finance Director

Brother U.K. Limited
Incorporated: 5 July 1889 *Employees:* 198
Net Worth: £25,393,000 *Total Assets:* £56,698,000
Registered Office: Shepley Street, Guide Bridge, Audenshaw, Manchester, M34 5JD
Activities: Wholesale of household goods (other than musical instruments) n.e.c
Parent: Brother Industries Limited
Officers: Russell William Brown, Secretary; Phillip Stuart Jones [1968] Director; Ian Desmond Metcalfe [1966] Sales Director; Isao Noji [1962] Managing Director [Japanese]

Browallia Holdings Limited
Incorporated: 24 April 1883 *Employees:* 1
Net Worth: £8,490,339 *Total Assets:* £15,378,839
Registered Office: Old Mills, Moor Top, Drighlington, Bradford, W Yorks, BD11 1BY
Activities: Activities of head offices
Officers: Kathryn Davenport, Secretary; Peter Jan Patrik Valentin Gyllenhammar [1953] Director [Swedish]

N Brown Foods Ltd
Incorporated: 8 July 2003
Net Worth: £37,278,000 *Total Assets:* £82,888,000
Registered Office: 61 Stephenson Way, Wavertree, Liverpool, L13 1HN
Activities: Activities of head offices
Parent: Real Good Food PLC
Officers: Harveen Rai, Secretary; Hugh Charles Laurence Cawley [1956] Director; Harveen Rai [1974] Director; Patrick George Ridgwell [1946] Director; Christopher Owen Thomas [1945] Director

N Brown Group PLC
Incorporated: 29 July 1964 *Employees:* 2,644
Net Worth: £459,600,000 *Total Assets:* £1,067,000,000
Registered Office: Griffin House, 40 Lever Street, Manchester, M60 6ES
Activities: Activities of head offices
Officers: Theresa Casey, Secretary; Lord David Alliance [1932] Director; Gillian Carole Barr [1958] Director; Matthew Davies [1970] Director; Stephen Johnson [1972] Director; Margaret Lesley Jones [1954] Director; Craig Barry Lovelace [1973] Director/Accountant; Ronald Thomas McMillan [1952] Director; Richard Moross [1977] Director; Michael Alexander Nunes Ross [1969] Director; Angela Lesley Spindler [1962] Director

Andrew Brown Leisure Limited
Incorporated: 30 April 1999 *Employees:* 198
Net Worth: £6,727,991 *Total Assets:* £12,665,023
Registered Office: Crow Wood Leisure Centre, Royle Lane, Burnley, Lancs, BB12 0RT
Activities: Operation of sports facilities
Officers: Andrew Walter Brown, Secretary; Andrew Walter Brown [1958] Director; Oliver Andrew Brown [1988] Director; Susan Brown [1958] Director; Spencer Burge [1975] Director/Cook; Olivier Foucr&eacute [1973] Director [French]; Helen Ashley Lord [1986] Director

Browntree Properties Limited
Incorporated: 9 April 2002 *Employees:* 8
Net Worth: £3,171,338 *Total Assets:* £7,503,482
Registered Office: Legrams Commercial Centre, Legrams Lane, Bradford, W Yorks, BD7 1NH
Activities: Buying and selling of own real estate
Shareholder: Mozafar Gorji
Officers: Rida Gorji, Secretary; Zahra Daneshyar [1967] Director; Mozafar Gorji [1949] Managing Director; Nabil Gorji [1987] Director/Civil Engineer; Rida Gorji [1985] Director/Architect

Brunner Mond Group Limited
Incorporated: 10 March 1998
Net Worth: £72,544,000 *Total Assets:* £72,544,000
Registered Office: Mond House, Winnington, Northwich, Cheshire, CW8 4DT
Activities: Other business support service activities n.e.c.
Parent: Natrium Holdings Limited
Officers: Jonathan Laurence Abbotts, Secretary; Jonathan Laurence Abbotts [1964] Director; Dr Martin John Ashcroft [1969] Managing Director

Brunning and Price Limited
Incorporated: 3 February 1981 *Employees:* 1,927
Net Worth: £21,579,000 *Total Assets:* £76,150,000
Registered Office: Yew Tree Farm Buildings, Saighton, Chester, CH3 6EG
Activities: Public houses and bars
Parent: TRG (Holding) Ltd
Officers: Kirk Dyson Davis [1971] Director; Andrew McCue [1974] Director/Chief Executive Officer [Irish]; Mary Elizabeth Willcock [1972] Director

Bruntwood 2000 (NW Regen) Limited
Incorporated: 6 February 2007 *Employees:* 10
Net Worth Deficit: £1,009,000 *Total Assets:* £7,290,000
Registered Office: Union, Albert Square, Manchester, M2 6LW
Activities: Other letting and operating of own or leased real estate
Parent: Bruntwood Estates Holdings Limited
Officers: Richard Peter Burgess [1969] Director; Rowena May Burns [1953] Director; Andrew Charles Butterworth [1974] Director; Kevin James Crotty [1976] Director/Chartered Accountant; Peter Andrew Crowther [1972] Director/Surveyor; Philip Andrew Kemp [1964] Director/Chief Commercial Officer; John Roderick Marland [1967] Director/Surveyor; Christopher George Oglesby [1967] Director; Christopher Andrew Roberts [1971] Director/Surveyor; Katharine Jane Vokes [1969] Director

Bruntwood 2000 Alpha Portfolio Limited
Incorporated: 8 December 2006
Net Worth: £88,964,000 *Total Assets:* £172,258,000
Registered Office: Union, Albert Square, Manchester, M2 6LW
Activities: Other letting and operating of own or leased real estate
Parent: Bruntwood Estates Holdings Limited
Officers: Richard Peter Burgess [1969] Director; Rowena May Burns [1953] Director; Andrew Charles Butterworth [1974] Director; Kevin James Crotty [1976] Director/Chartered Accountant; Peter Andrew Crowther [1972] Director/Surveyor; Philip Andrew Kemp [1964] Director/Chief Commercial Officer; John Roderick Marland [1967] Director/Surveyor; Christopher George Oglesby [1967] Director; Christopher Andrew Roberts [1971] Director/Surveyor; Katharine Jane Vokes [1969] Director

Bruntwood 2000 Beta Portfolio Limited
Incorporated: 7 December 2006 *Employees:* 10
Net Worth: £65,525,000 *Total Assets:* £144,330,000
Registered Office: Union, Albert Square, Manchester, M2 6LW
Activities: Other letting and operating of own or leased real estate
Parent: Bruntwood Estates Holdings Limited
Officers: Richard Peter Burgess [1969] Director; Rowena May Burns [1953] Director; Andrew Charles Butterworth [1974] Director; Kevin James Crotty [1976] Director/Chartered Accountant; Peter Andrew Crowther [1972] Director/Surveyor; Philip Andrew Kemp [1964] Director/Chief Commercial Officer; John Roderick Marland [1967] Director/Surveyor; Christopher George Oglesby [1967] Director; Christopher Andrew Roberts [1971] Director/Surveyor; Katharine Jane Vokes [1969] Director

Bruntwood 2000 Fourth Properties Limited
Incorporated: 16 October 2003
Net Worth: £729,000 *Total Assets:* £11,778,000
Registered Office: Union, Albert Square, Manchester, M2 6LW
Activities: Other letting and operating of own or leased real estate
Parent: Bruntwood Development Holdings Limited
Officers: Richard Peter Burgess [1969] Director; Rowena May Burns [1953] Director; Andrew Charles Butterworth [1974] Director; Kevin James Crotty [1976] Director/Chartered Accountant; Peter Andrew Crowther [1972] Director/Surveyor; Philip Andrew Kemp [1964] Director/Chief Commercial Officer; John Roderick Marland [1967] Director/Surveyor; Christopher George Oglesby [1967] Director; Christopher Andrew Roberts [1971] Director/Surveyor; Katharine Jane Vokes [1969] Director

Bruntwood Albert Square Limited
Incorporated: 10 September 2015
Net Worth Deficit: £2,188,000 *Total Assets:* £20,386,000
Registered Office: Union, Albert Square, Manchester, M2 6LW
Activities: Other letting and operating of own or leased real estate
Parent: Bruntwood Estates Holdings Limited
Officers: Richard Peter Burgess [1969] Director; Andrew Charles Butterworth [1974] Director; Kevin James Crotty [1976] Director/Chartered Accountant; Peter Andrew Crowther [1972] Director/Surveyor; Philip Andrew Kemp [1964] Director/Chief Commercial Officer; John Roderick Marland [1967] Director/Surveyor; Christopher George Oglesby [1967] Director; Christopher Andrew Roberts [1971] Director/Surveyor; Katharine Jane Vokes [1969] Director

Bruntwood AV Holdings Limited
Incorporated: 20 October 2016
Net Worth: £1 *Total Assets:* £81,323,320
Registered Office: Union, Albert Square, Manchester, M2 6LW
Activities: Dormant company
Parent: Bruntwood Estates Limited
Officers: Richard Peter Burgess [1969] Director; Andrew Charles Butterworth [1974] Director; Kevin James Crotty [1976] Director/Chartered Accountant; Peter Andrew Crowther [1972] Director/Surveyor; Philip Andrew Kemp [1964] Director/Chief Commercial Officer; John Roderick Marland [1967] Director/Surveyor; Christopher George Oglesby [1967] Director; Christopher Andrew Roberts [1971] Director/Surveyor; Katharine Jane Vokes [1969] Director/Company Secretary

Bruntwood AV Limited
Incorporated: 20 October 2016
Net Worth: £7,916,000 *Total Assets:* £223,604,992
Registered Office: Union, Albert Square, Manchester, M2 6LW
Activities: Other letting and operating of own or leased real estate
Parent: Bruntwood AV Holdings Limited
Officers: Richard Peter Burgess [1969] Director; Andrew Charles Butterworth [1974] Director; Kevin James Crotty [1976] Director/Chartered Accountant; Peter Andrew Crowther [1972] Director/Surveyor; Philip Andrew Kemp [1964] Director/Chief Commercial Officer; John Roderick Marland [1967] Director/Surveyor; Christopher George Oglesby [1967] Director; Christopher Andrew Roberts [1971] Director/Surveyor; Katharine Jane Vokes [1969] Director/Company Secretary

Bruntwood Cornwall Street Limited
Incorporated: 10 October 2014
Net Worth: £5,[illegible]35,000 *Total Assets:* £36,139,000
Registered Office: Union, Albert Square, Manchester, M2 6LW
Activities: Other letting and operating of own or leased real estate
Parent: Bruntwood Estates Holdings Limited
Officers: Richard Peter Burgess [1969] Director; Andrew Charles Butterworth [1974] Director; Kevin James Crotty [1976] Director/Chartered Accountant; Peter Andrew Crowther [1972] Director/Surveyor; Philip Andrew Kemp [1964] Director/Chief Commercial Officer; John Roderick Marland [1967] Director/Surveyor; Christopher George Oglesby [1967] Director; Christopher Andrew Roberts [1971] Director/Surveyor; Katharine Jane Vokes [1969] Director/Company Secretary

Bruntwood Development Holdings Limited
Incorporated: 14 March 2014 *Employees:* 8
Net Worth: £1 *Total Assets:* £22,459,308
Registered Office: Union, Albert Square, Manchester, M2 6LW
Activities: Activities of construction holding companies
Parent: Bruntwood Limited
Officers: Richard Peter Burgess [1969] Director; Andrew Charles Butterworth [1974] Director; Kevin James Crotty [1976] Director/Chartered Accountants; Peter Andrew Crowther [1972] Director/Surveyor; Philip Andrew Kemp [1964] Director/Chief Commercial Officer; John Roderick Marland [1967] Director/Surveyor; Christopher George Oglesby [1967] Director; Christopher Andrew Roberts [1971] Director/Surveyor; Katharine Jane Vokes [1969] Director/Company Secretary

Bruntwood Estates Alpha Portfolio Limited
Incorporated: 8 December 2006 *Employees:* 10
Net Worth: £57,399,000 *Total Assets:* £84,503,000
Registered Office: Union, Albert Square, Manchester, M2 6LW
Activities: Other letting and operating of own or leased real estate
Parent: Bruntwood Estates Holdings Limited
Officers: Richard Peter Burgess [1969] Director; Rowena May Burns [1953] Director; Andrew Charles Butterworth [1974] Director; Kevin James Crotty [1976] Director/Chartered Accountant; Peter Andrew Crowther [1972] Director/Surveyor; Philip Andrew Kemp [1964] Director/Chief Commercial Officer; John Roderick Marland [1967] Director/Surveyor; Christopher George Oglesby [1967] Director; Christopher Andrew Roberts [1971] Director/Surveyor; Katharine Jane Vokes [1969] Director

Bruntwood Estates Beta Portfolio Limited
Incorporated: 7 December 2006
Net Worth: £33,468,000 *Total Assets:* £61,856,000
Registered Office: Union, Albert Square, Manchester, M2 6LW
Activities: Other letting and operating of own or leased real estate
Parent: Bruntwood Estates Holdings Limited
Officers: Richard Peter Burgess [1969] Director; Rowena May Burns [1953] Director; Andrew Charles Butterworth [1974] Director; Kevin James Crotty [1976] Director/Chartered Accountant; Peter Andrew Crowther [1972] Director/Surveyor; Philip Andrew Kemp [1964] Director/Chief Commercial Officer; John Roderick Marland [1967] Director/Surveyor; Christopher George Oglesby [1967] Director; Christopher Andrew Roberts [1971] Director/Surveyor; Katharine Jane Vokes [1969] Director

Bruntwood Estates Holdings Limited
Incorporated: 6 December 2006
Net Worth: £741,000 *Total Assets:* £135,980,000
Registered Office: Union, Albert Square, Manchester, M2 6LW
Activities: Other letting and operating of own or leased real estate
Parent: Bruntwood Estates Limited
Officers: Richard Peter Burgess [1969] Director; Rowena May Burns [1953] Director; Andrew Charles Butterworth [1974] Director; Kevin James Crotty [1976] Director/Chartered Accountant; Peter Andrew Crowther [1972] Director/Surveyor; Philip Andrew Kemp [1964] Director/Chief Commercial Officer; John Roderick Marland [1967] Director/Surveyor; Christopher George Oglesby [1967] Director; Christopher Andrew Roberts [1971] Director/Surveyor; Katharine Jane Vokes [1969] Director

Bruntwood Estates Limited
Incorporated: 5 December 2006
Net Worth: £4,101,000 *Total Assets:* £47,281,000
Registered Office: Union, Albert Square, Manchester, M2 6LW
Activities: Other letting and operating of own or leased real estate
Parent: Bruntwood Limited
Officers: Richard Peter Burgess [1969] Director; Rowena May Burns [1953] Director; Andrew Charles Butterworth [1974] Director; Kevin James Crotty [1976] Director/Chartered Accountant; Peter Andrew Crowther [1972] Director/Surveyor; Philip Andrew Kemp [1964] Director/Chief Commercial Officer; John Roderick Marland [1967] Director/Surveyor; Christopher George Oglesby [1967] Director; Christopher Andrew Roberts [1971] Director/Surveyor; Katharine Jane Vokes [1969] Director

Bruntwood Group Limited
Incorporated: 8 June 1993 *Employees:* 642
Net Worth: £513,167,008 *Total Assets:* £1,267,175,040
Registered Office: Union, Albert Square, Manchester, M2 6LW
Activities: Other letting and operating of own or leased real estate
Major Shareholder: Christopher George Oglesby
Officers: Christopher George Oglesby [1967] Director; Michael John Oglesby [1939] Director; Katharine Jane Vokes [1969] Director

Bruntwood Investments PLC
Incorporated: 16 May 2013
Net Worth: £50,000 *Total Assets:* £50,609,000
Registered Office: Union, Albert Square, Manchester, M2 6LW
Activities: Other letting and operating of own or leased real estate
Parent: Bruntwood Group Limited
Officers: Kevin James Crotty, Secretary; Kevin James Crotty [1976] Director/Chartered Accountants; Christopher George Oglesby [1967] Director

Bruntwood LG Holding Limited
Incorporated: 16 October 2012
Net Worth: £1 *Total Assets:* £42,274,240
Registered Office: Union, Albert Square, Manchester, M2 6LW
Activities: Other letting and operating of own or leased real estate
Parent: Bruntwood Estates Limited
Officers: Richard Peter Burgess [1969] Director; Andrew Charles Butterworth [1974] Director; Kevin James Crotty [1976] Director/Chartered Accountant; Peter Andrew Crowther [1972] Director/Surveyor; Philip Andrew Kemp [1964] Director/Chief Commercial Officer; John Roderick Marland [1967] Director/Surveyor; Christopher George Oglesby [1967] Director; Christopher Andrew Roberts [1971] Director/Surveyor; Katharine Jane Vokes [1969] Director/Company Secretary

Bruntwood LG Limited
Incorporated: 1 June 2012 *Employees:* 8
Net Worth: £76,633,000 *Total Assets:* £274,444,000
Registered Office: Union, Albert Square, Manchester, M2 6LW
Activities: Other letting and operating of own or leased real estate
Parent: Bruntwood LG Holding Limited
Officers: Richard Peter Burgess [1969] Director; Andrew Charles Butterworth [1974] Director; Kevin James Crotty [1976] Director/Chartered Accountant; Peter Andrew Crowther [1972] Director/Surveyor; Philip Andrew Kemp [1964] Director/Chief Commercial Officer; John Roderick Marland [1967] Director/Surveyor; Christopher George Oglesby [1967] Director; Christopher Andrew Roberts [1971] Director/Surveyor; Katharine Jane Vokes [1969] Director/Company Secretary

Bruntwood Limited
Incorporated: 4 December 2006 *Employees:* 642
Net Worth: £477,606,016 *Total Assets:* £1,266,897,024
Registered Office: Union, Albert Square, Manchester, M2 6LW
Activities: Other letting and operating of own or leased real estate
Parent: Bruntwood Group Limited
Officers: Richard Peter Burgess [1969] Director; Rowena May Burns [1953] Director; Andrew Charles Butterworth [1974] Director; Kevin James Crotty [1976] Director/Chartered Accountant; Peter Andrew Crowther [1972] Director/Surveyor; Philip Andrew Kemp [1964] Director/Chief Commercial Officer; John Roderick Marland [1967] Director/Surveyor; Christopher George Oglesby [1967] Director; Michael John Oglesby [1939] Director; Christopher Andrew Roberts [1971] Director/Surveyor; Katharine Jane Vokes [1969] Director

Bruntwood Management Services Limited
Incorporated: 6 December 2006 *Employees:* 642
Net Worth: £13,575,000 *Total Assets:* £28,808,000
Registered Office: Union, Albert Square, Manchester, M2 6LW
Activities: Management of real estate on a fee or contract basis
Parent: Bruntwood Limited
Officers: Richard Peter Burgess [1969] Director; Rowena May Burns [1953] Director; Andrew Charles Butterworth [1974] Director; Kevin James Crotty [1976] Director/Chartered Accountant; Peter Andrew Crowther [1972] Director/Surveyor; Philip Andrew Kemp [1964] Director/Chief Commercial Officer; John Roderick Marland [1967] Director/Surveyor; Christopher George Oglesby [1967] Director; Christopher Andrew Roberts [1971] Director/Surveyor; Katharine Jane Vokes [1969] Director

Bruntwood Oxford Road Holdings Limited
Incorporated: 5 February 2015
Total Assets: £19,051,000
Registered Office: The Box, Horseshoe Lane, Alderley Edge, Cheshire, SK9 7QP
Activities: Other letting and operating of own or leased real estate
Shareholder: Affinity Living 2 Limited
Officers: Mark Christopher Dawson [1973] Director; Kenneth John Knott [1959] Director; Michael Keith Slater [1974] Director

Bruntwood RB Limited
Incorporated: 16 May 2013 *Employees:* 9
Net Worth: £5,729,000 *Total Assets:* £63,961,000
Registered Office: Union, Albert Square, Manchester, M2 6LW
Activities: Other letting and operating of own or leased real estate
Parent: Bruntwood Limited
Officers: Richard Peter Burgess [1969] Director; Andrew Charles Butterworth [1974] Director; Kevin James Crotty [1976] Director/Chartered Accountant; Peter Andrew Crowther [1972] Director/Surveyor; Philip Andrew Kemp [1964] Director/Chief Commercial Officer; John Roderick Marland [1967] Director/Surveyor; Christopher George Oglesby [1967] Director; Christopher Andrew Roberts [1971] Director/Surveyor; Katharine Jane Vokes [1969] Director/Company Secretary

Bruntwood Science Limited
Incorporated: 11 August 2011 *Employees:* 9
Net Worth Deficit: £22,000 *Total Assets:* £64,912,000
Registered Office: Union, Albert Square, Manchester, M2 6LW
Activities: Other letting and operating of own or leased real estate
Parent: Bruntwood 2000 Limited
Officers: Kevin James Crotty [1976] Director/Chartered Accountant; Peter Andrew Crowther [1972] Director; Dr David John Hardman [1957] Managing Director; Philip Andrew Kemp [1964] Director/Chief Commercial Officer; Kate Victoria Lawlor [1981] Director/Chartered Accountant; Christopher George Oglesby [1967] Director; Thomas Peter Renn [1985] Managing Director

Bruntwood Scitech Limited
Incorporated: 27 July 1999
Net Worth: £3,118,000 *Total Assets:* £47,822,000
Registered Office: Union, Albert Square, Manchester, M2 6LW
Activities: Other letting and operating of own or leased real estate
Parent: Bruntwood Limited
Officers: Kevin James Crotty [1976] Director/Chartered Accountant; Christopher George Oglesby [1967] Director

Bryden Capital Ltd
Incorporated: 9 November 2005 *Employees:* 318
Net Worth: £13,181,133 *Total Assets:* £24,927,084
Registered Office: Bankfield Road, Tyldesley, Manchester, M29 8QH
Activities: Combined office administrative service activities
Major Shareholder: Brian Joseph Hall
Officers: Judith Dunn, Secretary; Judith Anne Dunn [1953] Director/Company Secretary; Brian Joseph Hall [1946] Director; Denise Hall [1959] Director; Mangesh Dattatraya Natal [1970] Director [Indian]; Laurence Whelehan [1970] Sales Director

Bryken (Holdings) Limited
Incorporated: 14 June 2010 *Employees:* 88
Net Worth: £11,355,864 *Total Assets:* £13,911,629
Registered Office: Randles Road, Knowsley Industrial Park, South Knowsley, Merseyside, L34 9HX
Activities: Activities of head offices
Parent: Bryken Group Holdings Limited
Officers: Brian Taylor [1952] Director

Bryken Limited
Incorporated: 15 October 1982 *Employees:* 99
Net Worth: £7,186,509 *Total Assets:* £9,673,093
Registered Office: Randles Road, Knowsley Industrial Park South, Knowsley, Merseyside, L34 9HX
Activities: Machining
Parent: Bryken (Holdings) Limited
Officers: Stewart Philip Taylor, Secretary; Brian Taylor [1952] Director; Phillip Taylor [1974] Director; Stewart Philip Taylor [1974] Director

Brymau Estates Ltd
Incorporated: 3 May 1971 *Employees:* 17
Net Worth: £8,233,607 *Total Assets:* £10,626,804
Registered Office: Riverside House, Brymau Three, River Lane, Saltney, Chester, CH4 8RQ
Activities: Other letting and operating of own or leased real estate
Shareholder: Denise Angela Lamont
Officers: Ramsay Lamont, Secretary; Denise Angela Lamont [1960] Director; Ramsay Lamont [1955] Director; Scott Lamont [1988] Director

Brynteg Solar Limited
Incorporated: 19 February 2013
Net Worth: £5,116,387 *Total Assets:* £17,980,028
Registered Office: Eversheds House, 70 Great Bridgewater Street, Manchester, M1 5ES
Activities: Other letting and operating of own or leased real estate
Parent: Sune Green Holdco7 Limited
Officers: Carl Goran Dandanell [1959] Director [Swedish]

BS Property Holdings Limited
Incorporated: 3 June 2009
Registered Office: Richard House, Winckley Square, Preston, Lancs, PR1 3HP
Activities: Activities of head offices
Major Shareholder: Andrew David Wallington
Officers: Beverley Wallington, Secretary; Andrew David Wallington [1965] Director

Buckhurst Group Limited
Incorporated: 25 August 2005 *Employees:* 104
Net Worth: £11,340,971 *Total Assets:* £25,953,152
Registered Office: Regency House, 45-51 Chorley New Road, Bolton, Lancs, BL1 4QR
Activities: Non-trading company
Major Shareholder: John Patrick Walsh
Officers: Andrea Walsh, Secretary; John Patrick Walsh [1964] Director

Buckhurst Plant Hire Limited
Incorporated: 10 April 1997 *Employees:* 104
Net Worth: £10,998,080 *Total Assets:* £25,410,896
Registered Office: Regency House, 45-51 Chorley New Road, Bolton, Lancs, BL1 4QR
Activities: Renting and leasing of construction and civil engineering machinery and equipment
Parent: Buckhurst Group Limited
Officers: Andrea Walsh, Secretary; John Patrick Walsh [1964] Director

Budget Greeting Cards Limited
Incorporated: 8 March 1984 *Employees:* 145
Net Worth: £19,233,898 *Total Assets:* £25,441,412
Registered Office: Prelude House, Chapter Street, Manchester, M40 2AY
Activities: Wholesale of other intermediate products
Parent: Budget Trading Limited
Officers: Attracta Mary Lavery, Secretary; Attracta Mary Lavery [1954] Director/Sales Assistant; Paul Declan Lavery [1956] Director/Wholesaler [Irish]

Budget Trading Limited
Incorporated: 1 May 2007 *Employees:* 145
Net Worth: £16,894,004 *Total Assets:* £25,317,342
Registered Office: Prelude House, Chapter Street, Manchester, M40 2AY
Activities: Activities of other holding companies n.e.c.
Major Shareholder: Paul Declan Lavery
Officers: Attracta Mary Lavery, Secretary; Paul Declan Lavery [1956] Director [Irish]

Bugle Inn Motor Company (Holdings) Limited
Incorporated: 21 October 1998 *Employees:* 231
Net Worth: £4,696,000 *Total Assets:* £19,649,000
Registered Office: Ackhurst Road, Chorley, Lancs, PR7 1NN
Activities: Activities of head offices
Major Shareholder: Andrew John Turner
Officers: Hilary Maria Nicol, Secretary; Hilary Maria Nicol [1961] Director/Chartered Accountant; Adam James Turner [1988] Sales Director; Andrew John Turner [1960] Managing Director; Pauline Mary Turner [1967] Sales Director; Stacey Turner [1985] Director/Solicitor

Bugle Inn Motor Company Limited
Incorporated: 11 November 1993 *Employees:* 231
Net Worth: £4,695,000 *Total Assets:* £19,648,000
Registered Office: Ackhurst Road, Chorley, Lancs, PR7 1NH
Activities: Sale of new cars and light motor vehicles
Parent: Bugle Inn Motor Company Holdings Limited
Officers: Hilary Maria Nicol, Secretary; Hilary Maria Nicol [1961] Director/Chartered Accountant; Adam James Turner [1988] Director; Andrew John Turner [1960] Managing Director; Pauline Mary Turner [1967] Director/Dealer Principal; Stacey Turner [1985] Director/Solicitor

Builders Supply (North West) Limited
Incorporated: 8 August 1975 *Employees:* 75
Net Worth: £7,167,037 *Total Assets:* £12,306,700
Registered Office: c/o Border Aggregates, Scotland Road, Carnforth, Lancs, LA5 9JZ
Activities: Agents specialised in the sale of other particular products
Parent: Hardroad Limited
Officers: Carolyn Elizabeth Masters, Secretary; Terry Billington [1944] Director; Thomas William Cross [1932] Director; Andrew Hetherington [1969] Finance Director; Stephen Pelter [1957] Director; Harold Donald Rogerson [1931] Director

Building Design Partnership Limited
Incorporated: 22 December 1987
Net Worth: £22,997,980 *Total Assets:* £57,898,192
Registered Office: P O Box 85, 11 Ducie Street, Piccadilly Basin, Manchester, M60 3JA
Activities: Architectural activities
Parent: BDP Holdings Limited
Officers: Heather Olwyn Wells, Secretary; David Michael Brennan [1961] Director/Building Services Engineer [Irish]; Gerard Couser [1966] Director/Architect; Nicholas Edwards [1966] Director/Landscape Designer; Gavin James Elliott [1963] Director/Architect; Suzanne Emms [1974] Director/Architect; Nicholas Stuart Fairham [1971] Director/Architect; Robert Ferry [1973] Director/Building Service Engineer; Stephen Gillham [1958] Director/Architect; Francis Peter Glare [1964] Director/Town Planner; Christopher Robert Harding [1962] Director/Architect; James Bothwell Hepburn [1974] Director/Building Services Engineer; Alistair William Kell [1968] Director/Architect; Christopher John Langston [1961] Director/Architect; Scott MacKenzie [1969] Director/Architect; Graham Stewart McClements [1958] Director/Chartered Architect; Michelle Janet McDowell [1963] Director/Structural Engineer; John McManus [1957] Director/Architect; Adrian Price [1970] Director/Architect; Stephen Barry Redfern [1961] Director/Architect; Simon Riley [1970] Director/Project Manager; John Seamus Roycroft [1974] Director/Structural Engineer; Mark Simpson [1964] Director/Interior Designer; Andrew Gerard Smith [1965] Director/Architect; Daniel Smyth [1965] Director/Architect [Irish]; Andrew Swain-Smith [1964] Director/Building Services Engineer; Jeremy Sweet [1964] Director/Architect; Heather Olwyn Wells [1964] Finance Director; Andrew James Whitehurst [1958] Director/Quantity Surveyor; Benedict Dominic Antony Zucchi [1964] Director/Architect

Building Product Design Limited
Incorporated: 9 March 2000 *Employees:* 217
Net Worth: £18,861,120 *Total Assets:* £23,873,428
Registered Office: 2 Brooklands Road, Sale, Cheshire, M33 3SS
Activities: Manufacture of builders ware of plastic
Shareholders: Linda Elizabeth Willan; BPD Holdings Limited
Officers: Darren Richard Hill, Secretary; Nicholas John Beswick [1965] Sales Director; Graham Leslie Dronfield [1964] Director; Darren Richard Hill [1966] Director/Accountant; Claire Michelle James [1970] Operations Director; Neil Murray Rideout [1962] Technical Director

The Bullen Healthcare Group Limited
Incorporated: 13 December 1995 *Employees:* 114
Net Worth: £3,250,990 *Total Assets:* £13,484,645
Registered Office: c/o DSG Chartered Accountants, Castle Chambers, 43 Castle Street, Liverpool, L2 9TL
Activities: Retail sale of clothing in specialised stores
Major Shareholder: Peter Francis Bullen
Officers: Paul Anthony Bullen [1970] Director; Peter Francis Bullen [1939] Director/Company Chairman; Ian Nicholas Burton [1969] Director; John Michael Charles [1949] Director; Louise Catherine Marsden [1973] Director

Bullen Plant Hire Limited
Incorporated: 19 August 1977
Registered Office: 45 Appley Lane North, Appley Bridge, Wigan, Lancs, WN6 9AD
Activities: Renting and leasing of construction and civil engineering machinery and equipment
Parent: Treebrook Ltd
Officers: Helen Jane Bullen, Secretary; Graham Peter Bullen [1967] Managing Director; Helen Jane Bullen [1944] Director/Company Secretary; John Robert Bullen [1976] Director

Charles S. Bullen Stomacare Limited
Incorporated: 13 December 1995 *Employees:* 106
Net Worth: £2,616,134 *Total Assets:* £11,339,069
Registered Office: c/o Duncan Sheard Glass, Castle Chambers, 43 Castle Street, Liverpool, L2 9TL
Activities: Retail sale of medical and orthopaedic goods in specialised stores (not incl. hearing aids) n.e.c.
Parent: The Bullen Healthcare Group Limited
Officers: Paul Anthony Bullen [1970] Director; Peter Francis Bullen [1939] Director/Company Chairman; Ian Nicholas Burton [1969] Director/Chartered Accountant; John Michael Charles [1949] Director; Louise Catherine Marsden [1973] Director

Bulloughs Cleaning Services Limited
Incorporated: 19 February 1987 *Employees:* 1,575
Net Worth: £6,282,534 *Total Assets:* £8,355,123
Registered Office: Craven House, Carleton New Road, Skipton, N Yorks, BD23 2DE
Activities: General cleaning of buildings
Shareholders: Duncan Scott Bullough; Frederick Bullough
Officers: Michael Bogg [1963] Director; Duncan Scott Bullough [1965] Managing Director

Bulman's Bulk & Haulage Limited
Incorporated: 3 February 1982 *Employees:* 70
Net Worth: £10,533,833 *Total Assets:* £13,026,001
Registered Office: Haweswater Road, Penrith Industrial Estate, Penrith, Cumbria, CA11 9EU
Activities: Freight transport by road
Major Shareholder: Peter James Housby
Officers: Peter James Housby, Secretary; Hilary Housby [1958] Managing Director; Peter James Housby [1956] Managing Director

Bulmer & Lumb Group Limited
Incorporated: 6 June 2001 *Employees:* 94
Net Worth: £5,151,908 *Total Assets:* £9,484,025
Registered Office: Bulmer & Lumb Group Limited, Royds Hall Lane, Buttershaw, Bradford, W Yorks, BD6 2NE
Activities: Preparation and spinning of textile fibres
Parent: Bulmer & Lumb Holdings Limited
Officers: Matthew Ian Whitehead, Secretary; Lee Darvill [1973] Export Sales Director; Paul Hamilton [1969] Group Technical Director; David William Midgley [1968] Managing Director; Matthew Ian Whitehead [1977] Financial Director

Bulmer & Lumb Holdings Limited
Incorporated: 19 November 2015 *Employees:* 95
Net Worth: £2,956,027 *Total Assets:* £7,453,764
Registered Office: Royds Hall Lane, Buttershaw, Bradford, W Yorks, BD6 2NE
Activities: Activities of head offices
Major Shareholder: David William Midgley
Officers: Doctor Elizabeth Jane Midgley, Secretary; David William Midgley [1968] Director; Matthew Ian Whitehead [1977] Finance Director

Bunk-a-Bin Limited
Incorporated: 19 December 1988 *Employees:* 12
Net Worth: £10,426,755 *Total Assets:* £15,078,352
Registered Office: Tweedale Way, Chadderton, Oldham, Lancs, OL9 7LD
Activities: Renting and leasing of other machinery, equipment and tangible goods n.e.c.
Parent: Portcullis Oldham Limited
Officers: Judith Rothwell, Secretary; Francis Leigh Rothwell [1950] Director/Engineer; Judith Rothwell [1949] Director/Secretary; Luke Rothwell [1975] Director/Operations; Susan Schofield [1977] Director/Invoice Clerk

R. Bunton Limited
Incorporated: 2 January 1979 *Employees:* 78
Net Worth: £3,781,851 *Total Assets:* £10,732,973
Registered Office: The Sidings, Station Road, Harecroft, Wilsden, Bradford, BD15 0BS
Activities: Renting and leasing of construction and civil engineering machinery and equipment
Parent: Bunton Plant Hire Limited
Officers: Tracey Bunton, Secretary; Andrew Bunton [1967] Director/Manager; Joyce Beryl Bunton [1948] Director/Secretary; Robert Leslie James Bunton [1948] Director/Builder; Robert Hall [1967] Director

Bunton Plant Hire Limited
Incorporated: 13 January 2011 *Employees:* 78
Net Worth: £4,708,699 *Total Assets:* £10,754,281
Registered Office: The Sidings, Station Road, Harecroft, Wilsden, Bradford, W Yorks, BD15 0BS
Activities: Activities of construction holding companies
Shareholders: Robert Leslie James Bunton; Joyce Beryl Bunton; Andrew Robert Bunton
Officers: Andrew Bunton [1967] Director/Manager; Joyce Beryl Bunton [1948] Director/Secretary; Robert Leslie James Bunton [1948] Director/Builder

Buoyant Upholstery Limited
Incorporated: 30 December 1998 *Employees:* 668
Net Worth: £19,285,000 *Total Assets:* £28,902,000
Registered Office: Oak Bank Mill, Hallam Road, Nelson, Lancs, BB9 8AJ
Activities: Manufacture of other furniture
Parent: Buoyant Holdings Limited
Officers: Antony Robert Darley, Secretary; Glen James Ainsworth [1969] Development Director; Michael Aramayo [1965] Sales Director; Stuart Bracewell [1964] Finance Director; Antony Robert Darley [1965] Finance Director; Hans Jansen [1965] Commercial Director [Dutch]; George Smith [1961] Production Director

Burg-Wachter UK Limited
Incorporated: 26 November 1987 *Employees:* 35
Net Worth: £6,779,950 *Total Assets:* £7,716,947
Registered Office: Unit 3 Eurocam Technology Park, Chase Way, Bradford, W Yorks, BD5 8HW
Activities: Wholesale of household goods (other than musical instruments) n.e.c
Officers: Reginald Charles Atkins [1962] Director/Manager; Andrew James Field [1977] Managing Director; Christopher Markus Lüling [1983] Director [German]; Dietmar Adalbert Lüling [1955] Director [German]; Harald Alfred Lüling [1958] Director [German]

Burke Investments Limited
Incorporated: 18 May 2015 *Employees:* 215
Net Worth: £10,394,971 *Total Assets:* £29,096,808
Registered Office: The Courtyard, Green Lane, Heywood, Lancs, OL10 2EX
Activities: Other service activities n.e.c.
Shareholders: Anthony Burke; Andrew Morley
Officers: Anthony Burke [1962] Director; Kyle Anthony Burke [1988] Director; Stephen Peter Edwards [1964] Director; Vincent Hughes [1968] Director; Keith Kershaw [1957] Director; Andrew Morley [1967] Director; Nicholas Stephen Tappin [1971] Finance Director

Burlington Slate Limited
Incorporated: 9 January 1984 *Employees:* 138
Net Worth: £5,628,860 *Total Assets:* £12,833,722
Registered Office: Cavendish House, Kirkby in Furness, Cumbria, LA17 7UN
Activities: Quarrying of ornamental and building stone, limestone, gypsum, chalk and slate
Shareholders: Peter Anthony Bostock; RBC Trustees (Ci) Ltd
Officers: Lucy Georgiana Cavendish [1973] Director/Painter; Lord Richard Hugh Baron Cavendish [1941] Director/Landowner; Michael Gerard Faughy [1958] Managing Director; Thomas Felix [1959] Quarries Director; Allen Joseph Gibb [1966] Director; Right Honourable Grania Mary Lady Cavendish [1947] Director; David Neil Sarti [1965] Director

Burnage Academy for Boys
Incorporated: 4 March 2014 *Employees:* 165
Net Worth: £18,653,000 *Total Assets:* £20,153,000
Registered Office: Burnage Academy for Boys, Burnage Lane, Burnage, Manchester, M19 1ER
Activities: General secondary education
Officers: Dr. Syed Ali Hassan Bokhari [1965] Director [Pakistani]; Erin Brown [1980] Director/Teacher; Nicole Elliott [1971] Director/Community [New Zealander]; Ian Douglas Fenn [1955] Director/Headteacher; Dr Jenny Fox [1977] Director/Community; Shagufta Ishaq [1974] Director/Parent; Kathryn McGuinness [1961] Director; Dr Colette Meyer [1987] Director/Community; Nasrullah Khan Moghal [1947] Director; Alan Scott [1949] Director; Jack Eric Leonard Shepherd [1987] Director/Teacher; Rosalyn Victoria Webster [1985] Director; Nagina Zafar [1981] Director/Parent

Burnden Leisure Limited
Incorporated: 11 January 1938 *Employees:* 234
Net Worth Deficit: £374,000 *Total Assets:* £43,332,000
Registered Office: University of Bolton Stadium, Burnden Way, Lostock, Bolton, Lancs, BL6 6JW
Activities: Operation of sports facilities
Shareholder: Kenneth Anderson
Officers: Kenneth Anderson [1952] Director

Burnhart Holdings Limited
Incorporated: 20 March 2013 *Employees:* 761
Net Worth: £25,978,000 *Total Assets:* £59,895,000
Registered Office: Britannia House, Junction Street, Darwen, Lancs, BB3 2RB
Activities: Activities of head offices
Parent: Vivoid Ltd
Officers: Andrew Barrington Sedgley, Secretary; James Stephen Hartley [1955] Director; Wayne Tierney [1962] Director/Chartered Accountant; Wayne Anthony Wild [1967] Director/Manager

Burnley FC Holdings Limited
Incorporated: 18 December 2012 *Employees:* 188
Net Worth: £40,036,000 *Total Assets:* £83,677,000
Registered Office: Turf Moor, Harry Potts Way, Burnley, Lancs, BB10 4BX
Activities: Operation of sports facilities
Shareholders: Michael Lee Garlick; John William Banaszkiewicz
Officers: Matthew Robert Williams, Secretary; John William Banaszkiewicz [1962] Managing Director; Terence Anthony David Crabb [1948] Director; Brendan Flood [1961] Director; Michael Lee Garlick [1963] Director; Clive John Holt [1943] Director; Barry Charles Kilby [1949] Director; Brian Thomas Nelson [1948] Director

Burnley Football & Athletic Company,Limited (The)
Incorporated: 29 September 1897 *Employees:* 188
Net Worth: £34,661,000 *Total Assets:* £76,186,000
Registered Office: Turf Moor, Burnley, Lancs, BB10 4BX
Activities: Operation of sports facilities
Parent: Burnley FC Holdings Ltd
Officers: Matthew Robert Williams, Secretary; John William Banaszkiewicz [1962] Director; Terence Anthony David Crabb [1948] Director; Brendan Flood [1961] Director; Michael Lee Garlick [1963] Managing Director; Clive John Holt [1943] Director; Barry Charles Kilby [1949] Director; Brian Thomas Nelson [1948] Director

Burnley General Hospital Phase V SPC Ltd
Incorporated: 26 October 2000
Net Worth Deficit: £8,234,000 *Total Assets:* £36,825,000
Registered Office: c/o Albany SPC Services Ltd, 3rd Floor, 3-5 Charlotte Street, Manchester, M1 4HB
Activities: Hospital activities
Parent: Burnley General Hospital Phase V SPC Holdings Ltd
Officers: Ailison Louise Mitchell, Secretary; Leo William McKenna [1966] Director/Strategic Advisor [Irish]; Barry Paul Millsom [1974] Director; Christopher Thomas Solley [1970] Director; Andrew Leslie Tennant [1958] Director

Burnley Savings and Loans Limited
Incorporated: 19 May 2011 *Employees:* 8
Net Worth: £274,076 *Total Assets:* £8,197,265
Registered Office: 30 Keirby Walk, Burnley, Lancs, BB11 2DE
Activities: Credit granting by non-deposit taking finance houses and other specialist consumer credit grantors
Major Shareholder: David John Fishwick
Officers: David John Fishwick [1971] Director

Tyson H. Burridge Limited
Incorporated: 7 March 1977 *Employees:* 52
Net Worth: £6,234,512 *Total Assets:* £7,135,403
Registered Office: Old Coach Works, Prospect Garage, Distington, Cumbria, CA14 5XJ
Activities: Freight transport by road
Shareholders: Tyson Hodgson Burridge; Audrey Burridge
Officers: Helen Mary Agnew, Secretary; Helen Mary Agnew [1965] Director; Andrew Tyson Burridge [1961] Director; Audrey Burridge [1935] Director; David Robert Burridge [1964] Director; Neil Alexander Robinson [1967] Director/Fleet Engineer

Burton McCall Limited
Incorporated: 24 September 1987 *Employees:* 72
Net Worth: £5,175,096 *Total Assets:* £13,624,774
Registered Office: 3 Bailey Court, Green Street, Macclesfield, Cheshire, SK10 1JQ
Activities: Non-specialised wholesale trade
Parent: Bollin Group Limited
Officers: Christopher Cooper, Secretary; Stephen James Cann [1965] Director/Accountant; Christopher Cooper [1972] Finance and Operations Director; Michelle Ann Dickinson [1964] Director

The Bury Grammar Schools Trustee Limited
Incorporated: 5 June 2008 *Employees:* 207
Net Worth: £14,721,000 *Total Assets:* £17,663,000
Registered Office: Farraday House, Bridge Road, Bury, Lancs, BL9 0HG
Activities: Pre-primary education
Officers: Jane Stevens, Secretary; David Joseph Baker [1959] Director/Building Services Consulting Engineer; Malcolm Clive Greenhalgh Edge [1952] Director/Chartered Accountant; Martin John Entwistle [1966] Director/Stockbroker; Suzanne Nicola Gauge [1970] Director/Housewife; Caroline Joanne Hulme-Mckibbin [1969] Director/Headmistress; Peter Francis Lee [1971] Director/Certified Accountant; Daniel James Long [1987] Director/Partner/Solicitor; Anthony Marshall [1964] Director/Chartered Accountant; Jagatjit Gurjeet Singh Rajasansir [1957] Director/Medical Practitioner; Antony Hugh Spencer [1962] Managing Director; Stephen John Wild [1970] Director; Gillian Winter [1953] Director/Educational Specialist

J.R. Bushell (Lowton) Limited
Incorporated: 28 November 1936
Net Worth: £2,978,621 *Total Assets:* £8,317,973
Registered Office: 6 Park Street, Lytham, Lancs, FY8 5LU
Activities: Other letting and operating of own or leased real estate
Shareholders: Stephen Alan Bushell; Richard Spencer Bushell
Officers: Stephen Alan Bushell, Secretary; Richard Spencer Bushell [1955] Director; Stephen Alan Bushell [1958] Director/Nurse

Busi and Stephenson Limited
Incorporated: 10 September 1919 *Employees:* 6
Net Worth: £1,954,371 *Total Assets:* £10,348,849
Registered Office: 4th Floor, Oriel Chambers, 14-16 Water Street, Liverpool, L2 8TD
Activities: Other business support service activities n.e.c.
Parent: Hawksford Nominees Jersey Limited
Officers: William Stephen Gilham, Secretary/Director; William Stephen Gilham [1951] Director; James Joseph Johnston [1960] Director; John Barrie Roberts [1947] Director

Business & Enterprise Finance Ltd.
Incorporated: 15 February 1984 *Employees:* 22
Net Worth: £8,448,721 *Total Assets:* £10,529,806
Registered Office: Devere House, Vicar Lane, Little Germany, Bradford, W Yorks, BD1 5AH
Activities: Other credit granting n.e.c.
Parent: West & North Yorkshire Chamber of Commerce
Officers: Julian Chima Abenbrook [1967] Director/Lawyer; Andrew Mark Caton [1963] Director; Malcolm John Lynch [1955] Director/Lawyer; Sandra Needham [1955] Director; Stephen John Nicholson [1963] Director; Kim Louise Rebecchi [1966] Director/Self Employed Advisor; Lee Ramon Underwood [1974] Managing Director; Stephen Arthur Waud [1968] Fund Director

Business Computer Projects Limited
Incorporated: 4 May 1984 *Employees:* 73
Net Worth: £5,839,126 *Total Assets:* £8,351,858
Registered Office: BCP House, 151 Charles Street, Stockport, Cheshire, SK1 3JY
Activities: Information technology consultancy activities
Shareholders: Peter Shield; Daryl Green
Officers: Zoe Michelle Halstead [1961] Development Operations Director; Richard Marshall [1967] Sales and Marketing Director; Peter Shield [1948] Managing Director; Timothy David Williams [1963] Director

Business Energy Solutions Ltd
Incorporated: 2 April 2002 *Employees:* 78
Net Worth: £7,262,097 *Total Assets:* £15,438,703
Registered Office: Parkside Stand, Fleetwood Town Football Club, Park Avenue, Fleetwood, Lancs, FY7 6TX
Activities: Agents involved in the sale of fuels, ores, metals and industrial chemicals
Parent: BES Utilities Holding Ltd
Officers: Philip Brown, Secretary; Michelle Caron Davidson [1973] Director; Andrew James Pilley [1970] Director

Business First Ltd
Incorporated: 16 September 2008
Net Worth Deficit: £1,428,162 *Total Assets:* £10,041,547
Registered Office: Group First House, Mead Way, Padiham, Lancs, BB12 7NG
Activities: Buying and selling of own real estate
Parent: Group First Global Limited
Officers: Sarah Fretwell [1980] Director; Leanne Marie Gregson [1979] Director; Christopher Parkinson [1985] Director

Busways Travel Services Limited
Incorporated: 12 September 1988 *Employees:* 1,121
Net Worth: £11,772,000 *Total Assets:* £39,418,000
Registered Office: c/o Stagecoach Services Limited, One Stockport Exchange, 20 Railway Road, Stockport, Cheshire, SK1 3SW
Activities: Other urban, suburban or metropolitan passenger land transport (not underground, metro or similar)
Parent: Stagecoach Bus Holdings Limited
Officers: Michael John Vaux, Secretary; Colin Brown [1968] Director/Accountant; Arnold Mark Threapleton [1954] Managing Director; Steven Walker [1971] Director

Buttercup Bidco Limited
Incorporated: 13 February 2015
Net Worth Deficit: £4,185,695 *Total Assets:* £12,358,554
Registered Office: The Alchemist, Chadsworth House, Wilmslow Road, Handforth, Cheshire, SK9 3HP
Activities: Licenced restaurants
Parent: Buttercup Topco Ltd
Officers: Simon Potts [1980] Managing Director; Jeremy Kevin Roberts [1962] Director; Victoria Stewart [1980] Finance Director

Buttercup Topco Limited
Incorporated: 13 February 2015 *Employees:* 607
Net Worth Deficit: £1,958,789 *Total Assets:* £30,843,464
Registered Office: The Alchemist, Chadsworth House, Wilmslow Road, Handforth, Cheshire, SK9 3HP
Activities: Licenced restaurants
Parent: Palatine Private Equity LLP
Officers: Paul Adam Campbell [1964] Director; Kieran Anthony Lawton [1978] Investment Director; Simon Potts [1980] Managing Director; Jeremy Kevin Roberts [1962] Director; Victoria Stewart [1980] Finance Director; Gary William Tipper [1963] Director

Bux & Co. Limited
Incorporated: 27 February 2012 *Employees:* 1
Net Worth: £429,887 *Total Assets:* £8,583,130
Registered Office: 141 Adelphi Street, Preston, Lancs, PR1 7BH
Activities: Dormant company
Shareholders: Yousuf Ayyub Bux; Nilufar Bux
Officers: Yousuf Ayyub Bux [1981] Director

Buxton Consortium Limited
Incorporated: 29 June 2005 *Employees:* 136
Net Worth: £18,474,532 *Total Assets:* £23,679,408
Registered Office: c/o Buxton Press Ltd, Palace Road, Buxton, Derbys, SK17 6AE
Activities: Activities of other holding companies n.e.c.
Major Shareholder: Bernard Galloway
Officers: Kirk Andrew Galloway, Secretary; Bernard Galloway [1936] Director

Buxton Press Limited
Incorporated: 20 June 1960 *Employees:* 136
Net Worth: £10,694,377 *Total Assets:* £16,188,802
Registered Office: Palace Road, Buxton, Derbys, SK17 6AE
Activities: Printing n.e.c.
Officers: Kirk Andrew Galloway, Secretary; Bernard Galloway [1936] Director; Kirk Andrew Galloway [1964] Director

BV Holdings Limited
Incorporated: 4 January 2002 *Employees:* 1,611
Net Worth: £2,751,479 *Total Assets:* £35,990,700
Registered Office: Clarke Nicklin House, Brooks Drive, Cheadle Royal Business Park, Cheadle, Cheshire, SK8 3TD
Activities: Other business support service activities n.e.c.
Major Shareholder: John Robert William Vernon
Officers: Lesley Jane Walker, Secretary; Eileen Vernon [1949] Director; John Robert William Vernon [1947] Director; Richard Andrew Vernon [1976] Director; Lesley Jane Walker [1975] Director

BV PPT Holdings Ltd.
Incorporated: 9 September 2014 *Employees:* 115
Net Worth: £6,360,773 *Total Assets:* £11,774,340
Registered Office: 3rd Floor, 1 Ashley Road, Altrincham, Cheshire, WA14 2DT
Activities: Manufacture of electronic measuring, testing etc. equipment, not for industrial process control
Officers: Jesse Feldman [1977] Director/Private Equity Investor [American]

BWA UK Holdco Limited
Incorporated: 7 June 2011 *Employees:* 88
Net Worth: £48,092,352 *Total Assets:* £106,049,312
Registered Office: 2 Brightgate Way, Manchester, M32 0TB
Activities: Activities of head offices
Shareholders: Amy Shapiro Ufberg; Joanna Berwind Creamer; Jessica Berwind Brummett; Richard Paul Wild; James Dwight Berwind; Charles Graham Berwind III
Officers: James Argyle, Secretary; James Alexander Argyle [1974] Director; Raymond John Baran [1967] Director [American]; Tim Callahan [1960] Director [American]; Joanna Creamer [1966] Director [American]; Graham Frederick Merfield [1962] Director

BWA Water Additives UK Limited
Incorporated: 19 December 2005 *Employees:* 55
Net Worth: £5,547,000 *Total Assets:* £22,950,000
Registered Office: 2 Brightgate Way, Manchester, M32 0TB
Activities: Manufacture of other chemical products n.e.c.
Parent: BWA UK Holdco Limited
Officers: James Alexander Argyle, Secretary/Director; James Alexander Argyle [1974] Director; Graham Frederick Merfield [1962] Director

BYK Additives Limited
Incorporated: 10 August 2000 *Employees:* 101
Net Worth: £28,698,000 *Total Assets:* £33,995,000
Registered Office: Moorfield Road, Widnes, Cheshire, WA8 3AA
Activities: Manufacture of other inorganic basic chemicals
Officers: Robin Byrne [1963] Managing Director; Stephan Christian Glander [1968] Director/Chemist [German]; Stefan Mossmer [1968] Director [German]; Albert Von Hebel [1961] Director/Bachelor of Business Administration [German]

Byrom Public Limited Company
Incorporated: 19 July 1991 *Employees:* 198
Net Worth: £20,300,316 *Total Assets:* £77,335,976
Registered Office: Seamos House, Brooks Drive, Cheadle, Cheshire, SK8 3SA
Activities: Activities of head offices
Officers: John Anthony Draper, Secretary; Enrique Byrom [1953] Director Economics Management [Mexican]; Jaime Byrom [1956] Director Management [Mexican]; Andrew David Jonathan Parker [1966] Marketing Director; Denis Anthony Robson [1934] Director

Byworth Boiler Hire Limited
Incorporated: 12 March 1973 *Employees:* 22
Net Worth: £8,799,799 *Total Assets:* £9,910,697
Registered Office: Beaconsfield House, Thwaites, Keighley, W Yorks, BD21 4NG
Activities: Renting and leasing of other machinery, equipment and tangible goods n.e.c.
Parent: Baldwin Holdings Limited
Officers: Allan Peter Baldwin [1953] Director/Boiler Manufacturer; Helen Baldwin [1960] Director/Accountant; Michael Anthony Rutter [1962] Sales Director

C & C Catering Equipment Limited
Incorporated: 9 May 1985 *Employees:* 59
Net Worth: £3,237,461 *Total Assets:* £10,687,795
Registered Office: Unit 1 Smithy Farm, Chapel Lane, Bruera, Chester, CH3 6EW
Activities: Wholesale of other machinery and equipment
Major Shareholder: Peter Nigel Kitchin
Officers: Heidi Cotton, Secretary; Ian Berrow [1962] Director; Peter Graham Farrell [1968] Sales Director; Peter Nigel Kitchin [1962] Managing Director; Paul Parry [1967] Contracts Director; Mark Anthony Roxburgh [1971] Director

C & C Supplies Collinson Limited
Incorporated: 15 July 1977 *Employees:* 52
Net Worth: £10,062,963 *Total Assets:* £11,379,261
Registered Office: Nateby Works, Longmoor Lane, Nateby, Garstang, Lancs, PR3 0JB
Activities: Agents involved in the sale of timber and building materials
Parent: Collinson Holdings Limited
Officers: Janet Doreen Collinson, Secretary/Director; David James Collinson [1961] Director/Driver; Ian Collinson [1963] Director/General Manager; Janet Doreen Collinson [1967] Director

C J Services UK Limited
Incorporated: 12 March 1997 *Employees:* 120
Net Worth: £1,484,051 *Total Assets:* £8,305,598
Registered Office: Sarus Court, Stuart Road, Manor Park, Runcorn, Cheshire, WA7 1TS
Activities: Other specialised construction activities n.e.c.
Major Shareholder: Christopher Leonard Langford
Officers: Ian Billington, Secretary; Ian Billington [1963] Director; Thomas Daniel Garner [1966] Director/Sales of Display; Christopher Leonard Langford [1959] Managing Director

C R Limited
Incorporated: 8 May 2000 *Employees:* 3
Net Worth: £7,347,275 *Total Assets:* £9,797,174
Registered Office: Brennand Mill, Bracewell Street, Burnley, Lancs, BB10 1TB
Activities: Development of building projects
Shareholders: Mohammed Yousaf; Qulsoom Akhtar Yousaf
Officers: Qulsoom Akhtar Yousaf, Secretary; Adnan Yousaf [1980] Director; Mohammed Yousaf [1954] Director

C-Mac Automotive Holding Limited
Incorporated: 16 April 2013 *Employees:* 298
Net Worth: £7,001,132 *Total Assets:* £21,330,024
Registered Office: 3rd Floor, 1 Ashley Road, Altrincham, Cheshire, WA14 2DT
Activities: Manufacture of loaded electronic boards
Officers: Yves Demeulemeester [1966] Director [Belgian]; Kenneth John Henderson [1949] Director

C.D. Medical Limited
Incorporated: 30 April 2015 *Employees:* 147
Net Worth: £16,254,864 *Total Assets:* £22,578,432
Registered Office: Unit 2002 Elland Close, Wingates Industrial Estate, Westhoughton, Bolton, Lancs, BL5 3XE
Activities: Wholesale of pharmaceutical goods
Shareholder: Elsie Maureen Armstrong
Officers: Lee Fairbrother, Secretary; Elsie Maureen Armstrong [1951] Director; Michael Gatenby [1942] Sales & Marketing Director; Gerard Michael Dominic Pessagno [1952] Director

C.G.I. Group Holdings Limited
Incorporated: 29 February 2008 *Employees:* 124
Net Worth Deficit: £5,509,595 *Total Assets:* £22,168,350
Registered Office: International House, Millfield Lane, Haydock, Merseyside, WA11 9GA
Activities: Activities of head offices
Parent: Pluto Bidco Limited
Officers: Matthew Robert Buxton, Secretary; Nicholas Paul Brayshaw [1955] Director; Matthew Robert Buxton [1972] Director/Accountant; Neil Andrew Tilsley [1967] Managing Director

C.G.I. Group Limited
Incorporated: 19 April 2004
Net Worth: £548,687 *Total Assets:* £24,362,756
Registered Office: International House, Millfield, Lane, Haydock, Merseyside, WA11 9GA
Activities: Activities of head offices
Parent: CGI Group Holdings Limited
Officers: Matthew Robert Buxton, Secretary; Matthew Robert Buxton [1972] Director/Accountant; Neil Andrew Tilsley [1967] Director

C.N.T. Limited
Incorporated: 19 June 1995 *Employees:* 2
Net Worth: £8,530,211 *Total Assets:* £8,553,719
Registered Office: Byron House, Green Lane, Heywood, Lancs, OL10 2DY
Activities: Non-trading company
Shareholders: Christopher Paul Mycock; Joanne Elizabeth Mycock
Officers: John Joseph Blackburn, Secretary; Christopher Paul Mycock [1957] Director

C.U.F.C. Holdings Limited
Incorporated: 27 January 1992 *Employees:* 223
Net Worth: £4,488,888 *Total Assets:* £8,772,441
Registered Office: Brunton Park, Warwick Road, Carlisle, Cumbria, CA1 1LL
Activities: Dormant company
Shareholders: Carlisle and Cumbria United Independent Supporters Society Limited; Herbert Andrew Jenkins
Officers: John Lee Nixon, Secretary/Managing Director; William Atkinson [1949] Director; Lord David George Clark of Windermere [1939] Director; John Robert Jackson [1968] Director; Andrew Jenkins [1936] Director; John Lee Nixon [1948] Managing Director; Steven Pattison [1954] Director

C.W.B.G Limited
Incorporated: 22 October 2012 *Employees:* 238
Net Worth: £28,011,052 *Total Assets:* £30,274,208
Registered Office: Wellfield Sawmills, King Street, Leyland, Preston, Lancs, PR25 2LE
Activities: Activities of head offices
Shareholders: Executors of Colin Berry; David John Berry
Officers: David John Berry [1966] Director/Accountant; Gary William Higham [1965] Finance Director

C2 Investment Limited
Incorporated: 16 October 2001 *Employees:* 117
Net Worth: £3,002,676 *Total Assets:* £8,069,603
Registered Office: Lancaster Leisure Park, Wyresdale Road, Lancaster, LA1 3LA
Activities: Public houses and bars
Shareholders: Matthew Scott Jackson; Phillip Anthony Simpson
Officers: Raluca Simpson, Secretary; Matthew Scott Jackson [1972] Director; Phillip Anthony Simpson [1971] Director

CA-MC Acquisition UK Limited
Incorporated: 16 November 1999
Net Worth: £10 959,000 *Total Assets:* £88,062,000
Registered Office: Coin House, New Coin Street, Royton, Oldham, Lancs, OL2 6JZ
Activities: Non-trading company
Parent: Crane SC Holdings Limited
Officers: Richard Wilkinson, Secretary; Richard Andrew Maue [1970] Director/Business Executive [American]; Max Homer Mitchell [1963] Director/Business Executive [American]; Edward Stephen Switter [1974] Director/Business Executive [American]; Richard Wilkinson [1967] Director

CAC Limited
Incorporated: 23 November 1996
Net Worth: £82,907,000 *Total Assets:* £462,921,984
Registered Office: 3rd Floor, 1 Ashley Road, Altrincham, Cheshire, WA14 2DT
Activities: Non-trading company
Parent: Onix Holdings Limited
Officers: Rhona Gregg, Secretary; Lucie Mary Katja Grant [1976] Director/Solicitor; Nicholas Ince [1982] Director/Accountant; David John Norman [1960] Director/Chartered Accountant

Caesar Bidco Limited
Incorporated: 5 December 2012 *Employees:* 3
Net Worth Deficit: £13,639,451 *Total Assets:* £65,567,220
Registered Office: Kings Court, Water Lane, Wilmslow, Cheshire, SK9 5AR
Activities: Activities of other holding companies n.e.c.
Parent: Caesar Midco Limited
Officers: Jenny Ingleby [1976] Sales & Marketing Director; Christopher Paul Morris [1972] Director; Eloise Wann [1977] Director/Chief Financial Officer

Caesar Midco Limited
Incorporated: 5 December 2012 *Employees:* 3
Net Worth Deficit: £2,392,516 *Total Assets:* £76,895,928
Registered Office: Kings Court, Water Lane, Wilmslow, Cheshire, SK9 5AR
Activities: Activities of other holding companies n.e.c.
Parent: Caesar Topco Limited
Officers: Jenny Ingleby [1976] Sales & Marketing Director; Christopher Paul Morris [1972] Director; Eloise Wann [1977] Director/Chief Financial Officer

Caesar Topco Limited
Incorporated: 5 December 2012
Net Worth: £853,000 *Total Assets:* £79,753,000
Registered Office: Kings Court, Water Lane, Wilmslow, Cheshire, SK9 5AR
Activities: Activities of other holding companies n.e.c.
Parent: HG Pooled Management Limited
Officers: Jenny Ingleby [1977] Sales and Marketing Director; Christopher Paul Morris [1972] Director; Eloise Wann [1977] Director/Chief Financial Officer

Calachem Holding Limited
Incorporated: 17 December 2015
Net Worth: £18,254,000 *Total Assets:* £32,157,000
Registered Office: One St Peters Square, Manchester, M2 3DE
Activities: Activities of production holding companies
Parent: Aurelius Equity Opportunities SE & Co KGaA
Officers: Gerhard Engleder [1968] Director/Vice President [Austrian]

Calachem Ltd
Incorporated: 18 February 2005 *Employees:* 178
Net Worth: £22,263,000 *Total Assets:* £31,073,000
Registered Office: One St Peters Square, Manchester, M2 3DE
Activities: Manufacture of pesticides and other agrochemical products
Parent: Aurelius Equity Opportunities SE & Co KGaA
Officers: Robert Huw Gair [1980] Director; Dr Neil Keith Partlett [1964] Managing Director

Calbee (UK) Ltd
Incorporated: 20 March 2014 *Employees:* 67
Net Worth: £1,018,831 *Total Assets:* £12,953,842
Registered Office: 3rd Floor, 1 Ashley Road, Altrincham, Cheshire, WA14 2DT
Activities: Manufacture of other food products n.e.c.
Parent: Calbee Inc
Officers: Koichi Kikuchi [1963] Director [Japanese]; Richard Anthony Robinson [1965] Managing Director; Keiei Sho [1966] Director [Japanese]

Calder Finco UK Ltd
Incorporated: 24 February 2006
Net Worth: £11,354,240 *Total Assets:* £21,017,870
Registered Office: Jupiter Drive, Chester West Employment Park, Chester, CH1 4EX
Activities: Activities of head offices
Parent: Caldergroup Swiss AG
Officers: Gregory Mark Andrews, Secretary; Gregory Mark Andrews [1973] Finance Director; Lee David Chaikin [1973] Managing Director [American]; Richard Benjamin Travers [1955] Director

Calder Group Holdings Limited
Incorporated: 25 February 2015 *Employees:* 731
Net Worth: £32,763,000 *Total Assets:* £92,478,000
Registered Office: Jupiter Drive, Chester West Employment Park, Chester, CH1 4EX
Activities: Activities of head offices
Shareholders: Latches Lane LLC; RCG IO Equity S.A.R.L
Officers: Greg Mark Andrews [1973] Finance Director; Matthew S Blank [1981] Director/Investor [American]; Lee D Chaikin [1973] Director/Investor [American]; Jeffrey Libshutz [1973] Director/Investor [American]; Richard Benjamin Travers [1955] Director/Chief Executive

Calder Group Limited
Incorporated: 12 January 1998 *Employees:* 5
Net Worth: £1,760,000 *Total Assets:* £55,263,000
Registered Office: c/o CIM Limited, Jupiter Drive, Chester West Employment Park, Chester, CH1 4EX
Activities: Non-trading company
Parent: Calder Holdings Limited
Officers: William Buist-Wells, Secretary/Director; Gregory Mark Andrews [1973] Finance Director; William Buist-Wells [1950] Director; Andrew Theodore Holt [1982] Director; Richard Benjamin Travers [1955] Director

Calder Holdings Limited
Incorporated: 12 January 1998
Net Worth: £1,375,000 *Total Assets:* £18,520,000
Registered Office: Number 1 Jupiter Drive, Chester West Employment Park, Chester, CH1 4EX
Activities: Non-trading company
Parent: Stamptree Limited
Officers: William Buist-Wells, Secretary/Director; Gregory Mark Andrews [1973] Finance Director; William Buist-Wells [1950] Director; Richard Benjamin Travers [1955] Director

Calder Industrial Materials Limited
Incorporated: 21 January 1889 *Employees:* 138
Net Worth: £10,928,000 *Total Assets:* £29,058,000
Registered Office: c/o Calder Industrial Materials, Jupiter Drive, Chester, CH1 4EX
Activities: Manufacture of other fabricated metal products n.e.c.
Parent: Calder Group Ltd
Officers: Martin Paul Henderson, Secretary; Russell John Adams [1961] Director; Gregory Mark Andrews [1973] Finance Director; Martin Paul Armour [1968] Commercial Director; Martin Paul Henderson [1970] Director; Richard Benjamin Travers [1955] Director; Paul Adrian Ward [1971] Managing Director

Calder International Holdings Limited
Incorporated: 12 January 1998
Net Worth: £7,441,000 *Total Assets:* £7,473,000
Registered Office: c/o CIM Limited, Jupiter Drive, Chester West Employment Park, Chester, CH1 4EX
Activities: Non-trading company
Parent: Calder Group Limited
Officers: Gregory Mark Andrews, Secretary; Gregory Mark Andrews [1973] Finance Director; William Buist-Wells [1950] Director; Richard Benjamin Travers [1955] Director

Calderdale Hospital SPC Holdings Ltd
Incorporated: 11 March 1998
Net Worth: £2,826,000 *Total Assets:* £21,081,000
Registered Office: c/o Albany SPC Services Ltd, 3rd Floor, 3-5 Charlotte Street, Manchester, M1 4HB
Activities: Other specialised construction activities n.e.c.
Parent: Consolidated Investment Holdings Limited
Officers: Ailison Louise Mitchell, Secretary; Leo William McKenna [1966] Director/Strategic Advisor [Irish]; Barry Paul Millsom [1974] Director; Peter John Sheldrake [1959] Director; Christopher Thomas Solley [1970] Director; Andrew Leslie Tennant [1958] Director

Calderdale Hospital SPC Ltd
Incorporated: 10 March 1998
Net Worth Deficit: £10,431,000 *Total Assets:* £141,354,000
Registered Office: c/o Albany SPC Services Ltd, 3rd Floor, 3-5 Charlotte Street, Manchester, M1 4HB
Activities: Other specialised construction activities n.e.c.
Parent: Calderdale Hospital SPC Holdings Ltd
Officers: Ailison Louise Mitchell, Secretary; Leo William McKenna [1966] Director/Strategic Advisor [Irish]; Barry Paul Millsom [1974] Director; Peter John Sheldrake [1959] Director; Christopher Thomas Solley [1970] Director; Andrew Leslie Tennant [1958] Director

Caldew School
Incorporated: 23 June 2011 *Employees:* 148
Net Worth: £6,112,732 *Total Assets:* £8,988,071
Registered Office: Caldew School, Carlisle Road, Dalston, Carlisle, Cumbria, CA5 7NN
Activities: General secondary education
Officers: David Foulkes, Secretary; Pamela Yvonne Abba [1968] Director/Occupational Therapist; Tazeem Zahra Abbas [1961] Director/Accountant; Louise Phyllis Atkinson [1980] Director/Teacher; Alexandria Denise Bradshaw [1982] Director/Teacher; Robert John Charlton [1972] Director/General Manager; David Bryan Craig [1947] Director/Retired; Johanne Elizabeth Doherty [1962] Director; Victoria Johanna Jackson [1970] Director/Headteacher; Rachael Thora Mason [1974] Director/Landlady; Brendan McArdle [1973] Director/Teacher; Kerry Richardson [1971] Director/Nursery Assistant; Keith Jonathan Ross [1973] Director/Crew Manager; Diane Shirvinton [1968] Director/Senior Teaching Assistant; Michael Smillie [1972] Director of Finance; Jennifer Margaret Wilkinson [1954] Director

Calea UK Limited
Incorporated: 30 May 1990 *Employees:* 430
Net Worth: £14,987,000 *Total Assets:* £22,459,000
Registered Office: Cestrian Court, Eastgate Way, Manor Park, Runcorn, Cheshire, WA7 1NT
Activities: Manufacture of pharmaceutical preparations
Parent: FHC (Holdings) Limited
Officers: Marc James Gerard Crouton [1959] Director [French]; Christopher Paul Harrison [1966] Managing Director; David Michael Kehoe [1984] Finance Director; Mark Henry Kirkup [1969] Director; Frank Lucassen [1972] Director [German]; Niamh Matic [1973] Director [Irish]

The Calico Group Limited
Incorporated: 24 October 2013 *Employees:* 653
Net Worth Deficit: £19,100,000 *Total Assets:* £103,037,000
Registered Office: Centenary Court, Croft Street, Burnley, Lancs, BB11 2ED
Activities: Activities of head offices
Officers: Steven Aggett, Secretary; Peter James Bevington [1952] Director/Consultant; Simon Howard Blackburn [1974] Managing Director; Lesley Hazel Burrows [1976] Director Education; Grahame Nicholas Elliott [1938] Director/Chartered Accountant; John Stewart Inglesfield [1959] Director/Head of Social Housing; Martin Gerard King [1971] Director; Paul Mayson [1970] Director/Solicitor; Carmel Therese McKeogh [1960] Director/HR Consultant; Sarah Jane Parr [1975] Consultancy Director; Philip Stuart Watson [1946] Director/Retired

Calico Homes Limited
Incorporated: 15 April 1999 *Employees:* 215
Net Worth Deficit: £20,696,000 *Total Assets:* £98,600,000
Registered Office: Centenary Court, Croft Street, Burnley, Lancs, BB11 2ED
Activities: Renting and operating of Housing Association real estate
Officers: Steve Aggett, Secretary; Victoria Appleton [1970] Director/Head of Growth and Investment; Peter James Bevington [1952] Director/Consultant; Gemma Mary Dyson [1979] Director/Head of Business Development; Adam Greenhalgh [1980] Director/Business Manager; John Stewart Inglesfield [1959] Director; William Kevin Lacey [1959] Development Director; Andrew James Mullen [1968] Director/Solicitor; Gregory Maxwell Robinson [1962] Director/Assistant Chief Executive; Paula Robinson [1965] Director; Stewart Michael Shaw [1949] Director/Self Employed; Christina MacKinnon Yates [1947] Director/Retired

Calvin Capital Australia Holdings Limited
Incorporated: 6 March 2017
Net Worth: £6,955,932 *Total Assets:* £6,955,932
Registered Office: 5th Floor, 1 Marsden Street, Manchester, M2 1HW
Activities: Activities of other holding companies n.e.c.
Parent: Calvin Capital Group Limited
Officers: Sarah Ann Blackburn, Secretary; Sarah Ann Blackburn [1980] Director/Solicitor; George Martin Donoghue [1974] Director; Sean Latus [1969] Director/Investment Officer; Henricus Lambertus Pijls [1965] Director/Chief Executive Officer [Dutch]

Calvin Capital Group Holdings Limited
Incorporated: 30 November 2016 *Employees:* 35
Net Worth: £583,843,968 *Total Assets:* £1,371,025,024
Registered Office: 5th Floor, 1 Marsden Street, Manchester, M2 1HW
Activities: Financial intermediation not elsewhere classified
Parent: CCH1 Limited
Officers: Sarah Ann Blackburn, Secretary; Sarah Ann Blackburn [1980] Director/Solicitor; Tara Courtney Davies [1977] Director; George Martin Donoghue [1974] Director; Sean Latus [1969] Director; James Thomas MacDonald [1959] Director; Henricus Lambertus Pijls [1965] Director/Chief Executive Officer [Dutch]; Oleg Igorevich Shamovsky [1982] Director [Canadian]

Calvin Capital Group Limited
Incorporated: 11 May 2016
Net Worth: £8,372,000 *Total Assets:* £164,728,000
Registered Office: 5th Floor, 1 Marsden Street, Manchester, M2 1HW
Activities: Activities of other holding companies n.e.c.
Parent: Calvin Capital Holdco Limited
Officers: Sarah Ann Blackburn, Secretary; Sarah Ann Blackburn [1980] Director/Solicitor; George Martin Donoghue [1974] Director; Sean Latus [1969] Director/Investment Officer; Henricus Lambertus Pijls [1965] Director/Chief Executive Officer [Dutch]

Calvin Capital Limited
Incorporated: 13 July 2007
Net Worth: £16,029,000 *Total Assets:* £154,120,992
Registered Office: 5th Floor, 1 Marsden Street, Manchester, M2 1HW
Activities: Activities of other holding companies n.e.c.
Parent: Calvin Capital UK Limited
Officers: Sarah Ann Blackburn, Secretary; Sarah Ann Blackburn [1980] Director/Solicitor; George Martin Donoghue [1974] Director; Sean Latus [1969] Director/Investment Officer; Henricus Lambertus Pijls [1965] Director/Chief Executive Officer [Dutch]

Calvin Capital UK Holdings Limited
Incorporated: 11 May 2016
Net Worth: £539,000 *Total Assets:* £162,219,008
Registered Office: 5th Floor, 1 Marsden Street, Manchester, M2 1HW
Activities: Activities of other holding companies n.e.c.
Parent: Calvin Capital Group Limited
Officers: Sarah Ann Blackburn, Secretary; Sarah Ann Blackburn [1980] Director/Solicitor; George Martin Donoghue [1974] Director; Sean Latus [1969] Director/Investment Officer; Henricus Lambertus Pijls [1965] Director/Chief Executive Officer [Dutch]

Cambi UK Limited
Incorporated: 7 December 1998 *Employees:* 40
Net Worth: £5,451,000 *Total Assets:* £23,727,000
Registered Office: Congleton Technology Park, Radnor Park Industrial Estate, First Avenue, Back Lane, Congleton, Cheshire, CW12 4XJ
Activities: Construction of water projects
Major Shareholder: Per Lillebo
Officers: Christian Isachsen, Secretary [Norwegian]; Christian Isachsen [1969] Director/Chief Financial Officer [Norwegian]; Per Lillebo [1955] Director [Norwegian]

Cambus Limited
Incorporated: 8 June 1984 *Employees:* 921
Net Worth: £20,825,000 *Total Assets:* £41,400,000
Registered Office: c/o Stagecoach Services Limited, One Stockport Exchange, 20 Railway Road, Stockport, Cheshire, SK1 3SW
Activities: Other urban, suburban or metropolitan passenger land transport (not underground, metro or similar)
Parent: Stagecoach Bus Holdings Limited
Officers: Michael John Vaux, Secretary; Colin Brown [1968] Director/Accountant; John Andrew Campbell [1953] Managing Director; Arnold Mark Threapleton [1954] Managing Director

Cameolord Limited
Incorporated: 16 March 1983 *Employees:* 76
Net Worth: £8,108,570 *Total Assets:* £11,934,359
Registered Office: 27 Aspinall Street, Rusholme, Manchester, M14 5UD
Activities: Dispensing chemist in specialised stores
Major Shareholder: Mohammad Aslam
Officers: Mohammed Bashir [1956] Director/Salesman

Camfil Limited
Incorporated: 8 December 1978 *Employees:* 193
Net Worth: £8,869,000 *Total Assets:* £16,412,000
Registered Office: Knowsley Road, Haslingden, Rossendale, Lancs, BB4 4EG
Activities: Other manufacturing n.e.c.
Parent: Camfil AB
Officers: Caroline Mansfield, Secretary; James Roy Dagnall [1981] Director; Dr Christopher Ecob [1958] Director; Tracy Joanne Hannon [1969] Director/Chartered Accountant; Caroline Mansfield [1966] Director/Accountant; David Moulton [1957] Commercial Director; Alan O'Connell [1957] Director [Irish]; Mark Ulrich Simmons [1975] Director [German]; Richard Mark Taylor [1962] Sales Director; William Harry Wilkinson [1957] Director

Cammell Laird Shiprepairers & Shipbuilders Limited
Incorporated: 4 May 2001 *Employees:* 639
Net Worth: £25,879,000 *Total Assets:* £51,876,000
Registered Office: Cammell Laird Shipyard, Campbeltown Road, Birkenhead, Wirral, Merseyside, CH41 9BP
Activities: Building of ships and floating structures
Parent: Peel Port Investments Limited
Officers: Jean Raymond Syvret, Secretary; John Kennedy [1958] Director/Engineer; Hamish MacPhail Massie MacKenzie [1969] Director; Michael Joseph Moran [1958] Director/Engineer; John Raymond Syvret [1961] Managing Director; Steven Keith Underwood [1974] Director; Mark Whitworth [1966] Director

Campbell Plant Hire (Holdings) Limited
Incorporated: 21 April 2016 *Employees:* 1
Net Worth Deficit: £182,372 *Total Assets:* £13,004,922
Registered Office: Corpacq House, 1 Goose Green, Altrincham, Cheshire, WA14 1DW
Activities: Activities of head offices
Officers: Benjamin David Hancock [1991] Director

Campus Living Villages (Bedfordshire) UK Limited
Incorporated: 16 March 2010
Net Worth Deficit: £6,257,000 *Total Assets:* £36,751,000
Registered Office: 7th Floor, Digital World Centre, 1 Lowry Plaza, Salford Quays, Manchester, M50 3UB
Activities: Other letting and operating of own or leased real estate
Officers: Lisa Jane Brown [1974] Director/Regional General Manager; Mathew Jason Panopoulos [1974] Director/Global Chief Financial Officer, CF Corporate Finance [Australian]

Campus Living Villages (Bond Issuer) UK PLC
Incorporated: 28 January 2014
Net Worth Deficit: £27,063,000 *Total Assets:* £256,702,000
Registered Office: 7th Floor, Digital World Centre, 1 Lowry Plaza, Salford Quays, Manchester, M50 3UB
Activities: Other letting and operating of own or leased real estate
Officers: Sean Thomas McKeown [1970] Commercial Director [Australian]; Mathew Jason Panopoulos [1974] Director/Global Chief Financial Officer, CF Corporate Finance [Australian]; George Nicholas Shweiry [1966] Director

Campus Living Villages (City Portfolio) UK Limited
Incorporated: 28 January 2014
Net Worth Deficit: £23,305,000 *Total Assets:* £233,576,000
Registered Office: 7th Floor, Digital World Centre, 1 Lowry Plaza, Salford Quays, Manchester, M50 3UB
Activities: Other letting and operating of own or leased real estate
Parent: Campus Living Villages (Bond Issuer) UK PLC
Officers: Lisa Jane Brown [1974] Director/Regional General Manager; Sean Thomas McKeown [1970] Commercial Director [Australian]; Mathew Jason Panopoulos [1974] Director/Global Chief Financial Officer, CF Corporate Finance [Australian]; George Nicholas Shweiry [1966] Director

Campus Living Villages (Goldsmiths) Issuer PLC
Incorporated: 27 July 2015
Net Worth: £50,000 *Total Assets:* £41,382,000
Registered Office: 7th Floor, Digital World Centre, 1 Lowry Plaza, Salford Quays, Manchester, M50 3UB
Activities: Other letting and operating of own or leased real estate
Officers: Sean Thomas McKeown [1970] Commercial Director [Australian]; Mathew Jason Panopoulos [1974] Director/Global Chief Financial Officer, CF Corporate Finance [Australian]; George Nicholas Shweiry [1966] Director

Campus Living Villages (Goldsmiths) UK Limited
Incorporated: 29 April 2015
Net Worth Deficit: £2,462,000 *Total Assets:* £49,832,000
Registered Office: 7th Floor, Digital World Centre, 1 Lowry Plaza, Salford Quays, Manchester, M50 3UB
Activities: Other letting and operating of own or leased real estate
Officers: Lisa Jane Brown [1974] Director/Regional General Manager; Sean Thomas McKeown [1970] Commercial Director [Australian]; Mathew Jason Panopoulos [1974] Director/Global Chief Financial Officer, CF Corporate Finance [Australian]; George Nicholas Shweiry [1966] Director

Campus Living Villages (Portfolio Finance) UK Limited
Incorporated: 23 January 2014
Net Worth: £8,687,551 *Total Assets:* £17,713,780
Registered Office: 7th Floor, Digital World Centre, 1 Lowry Plaza, Salford Quays, Manchester, M50 3UB
Activities: Activities of venture and development capital companies
Officers: Mathew Jason Panopoulos [1974] Director/Global Chief Financial Officer, CF Corporate Finance [Australian]

Campus Living Villages (RCM 2) UK LLP
Incorporated: 29 May 2014
Net Worth: £9,151,000 *Total Assets:* £47,574,000
Registered Office: 7th Floor, Digital World Centre, 1 Lowry Plaza, Salford Quays, Manchester, M50 3UB

Campus Living Villages (Salford) UK Limited
Incorporated: 11 September 2008
Net Worth: £680,787 *Total Assets:* £19,015,724
Registered Office: 7th Floor, Digital World Centre, 1 Lowry Plaza, Salford Quays, Manchester, M50 3UB
Activities: Other letting and operating of own or leased real estate
Officers: Aileen Goldspring [1959] Director/Regional General Manager; Mathew Jason Panopoulos [1974] Director/Global Chief Financial Officer, CF Corporate Finance [Australian]

Campus Living Villages (Sutton Bonington) UK Limited
Incorporated: 28 January 2014
Net Worth Deficit: £3,825,000 *Total Assets:* £22,780,000
Registered Office: 7th Floor, Digital World Centre, 1 Lowry Plaza, Salford Quays, Manchester, M50 3UB
Activities: Other letting and operating of own or leased real estate
Parent: Campus Living Villages (Bond Issuer) UK PLC
Officers: Aileen Goldspring [1959] Director/Regional General Manager; Sean Thomas McKeown [1970] Commercial Director [Australian]; Mathew Jason Panopoulos [1974] Director/Global Chief Financial Officer, CF Corporate Finance [Australian]; George Nicholas Shweiry [1966] Director

Cancede Limited
Incorporated: 13 November 2009
Net Worth: £2,066,000 *Total Assets:* £17,166,000
Registered Office: Hilmore House, Gain Lane, Bradford, W Yorks, BD3 7DL
Activities: Development of building projects
Parent: Optimisation Investments Limited
Officers: Jonathan James Burke, Secretary; Jonathan James Burke [1966] Director; Trevor John Strain [1975] Finance Director

Canda Copying Limited
Incorporated: 23 March 1982
Net Worth: £11,694,725 *Total Assets:* £12,750,176
Registered Office: 2nd Floor, Refuge House, 33-37 Watergate Row, Chester, CH1 2LE
Activities: Wholesale of other office machinery and equipment
Shareholders: Caroline Mary Elizabeth Mosley; Eileen Smith
Officers: Caroline Mary Elizabeth Mosley, Secretary; Caroline Mary Elizabeth Mosley [1971] Director; Eileen Smith [1942] Director; Nigel John Wyatt [1956] Director

Candelisa Limited
Incorporated: 2 April 2008 *Employees:* 18
Net Worth: £2,936,816 *Total Assets:* £7,354,347
Registered Office: Caroline House, Providence Place, Skipton, N Yorks, BD23 1FB
Activities: Construction of domestic buildings
Shareholders: Guy Alexander Taylor; Andrew John Phillip; Mirabelle Partners Limited
Officers: Dale Walter Chapman [1970] Director; Andrew John Phillip [1963] Director; Guy Alexander Taylor [1973] Director/Property Developer

Canvas Holidays Limited
Incorporated: 12 October 1970 *Employees:* 161
Net Worth: £13,196,000 *Total Assets:* £19,897,000
Registered Office: One St Peter's Square, Manchester, M2 3DE
Activities: Other accommodation
Parent: Canvas Holdings Limited
Officers: Philippe Jean Michel Mahouin [1970] COO Tohapi & Vacalians South Europe Director [French]

Capital & Centric (Cinnamon) Limited
Incorporated: 28 October 2015
Net Worth: £41,276 *Total Assets:* £9,346,321
Registered Office: Sun House, Little Peter Street, Manchester, M15 4PS
Activities: Buying and selling of own real estate
Parent: Genus Capital 3 Limited
Officers: Timothy Graham Heatley [1979] Director; Adam Stuart Higgins [1969] Director; Richard Mark Mathias [1971] Managing Director; David Francis Speakman [1946] Director

Capital Bank Leasing 3 Limited
Incorporated: 8 February 1965
Net Worth: £5,471,000 *Total Assets:* £32,847,000
Registered Office: Charterhall House, Charterhall Drive, Chester, CH88 3AN
Activities: Financial leasing
Parent: Bank of Scotland PLC
Officers: Alyson Elizabeth Mulholland, Secretary; Richard Andrew Jones [1972] Director; John Robert Turner [1964] Director

Capital Bank Leasing 5 Limited
Incorporated: 23 April 1959
Net Worth: £421,000 *Total Assets:* £8,024,000
Registered Office: Charterhall House, Charterhall Drive, Chester, CH88 3AN
Activities: Dormant company
Parent: Bank of Scotland PLC
Officers: David Dermot Hennessey, Secretary; Christopher Michael Adams [1982] Director; Richard Andrew Jones [1972] Director

Capital Bank Leasing 9 Limited
Incorporated: 31 October 1983
Net Worth: £2,172,000 *Total Assets:* £18,327,000
Registered Office: Charterhall House, Charterhall Drive, Chester, CH88 3AN
Activities: Dormant company
Parent: Bank of Scotland PLC
Officers: David Dermot Hennessey, Secretary; Christopher Michael Adams [1982] Director; Richard Andrew Jones [1972] Director

Capital Bridging Finance Solutions Limited
Incorporated: 24 January 2012 *Employees:* 1
Net Worth: £178,888 *Total Assets:* £7,725,070
Registered Office: 5 Glenn Buildings South, 10a Moor Lane, Crosby, Merseyside, L23 2UN
Activities: Activities of mortgage finance companies
Officers: Paul Dalton [1977] Director

Capquest Debt Recovery Limited
Incorporated: 18 May 1999 *Employees:* 355
Net Worth Deficit: £16,378,000 *Total Assets:* £42,379,000
Registered Office: Belvedere, 12 Booth Street, Manchester, M2 4AW
Activities: Other service activities n.e.c.
Parent: Capquest Group Limited
Officers: Stewart David Hamilton, Secretary; Paul David Cooper [1972] Director/Group Chief Financial Officer; Zachary Jason Lewy [1974] Director/Founder and Group Chief Investment Officer [British/American]; Lee Michael Rochford [1967] Director/Group Chief Executive Officer

Capquest Group Limited
Incorporated: 17 October 2003
Net Worth Deficit: £20,850,036 *Total Assets:* £73,018,872
Registered Office: Belvedere, 12 Booth Street, Manchester, M2 4AW
Activities: Financial intermediation not elsewhere classified
Parent: Quest Newco Limited
Officers: Stewart David Hamilton, Secretary; Paul David Cooper [1972] Director/Group Chief Financial Officer; Zachary Jason Lewy [1974] Director/Founder and Group Chief Investment Officer [British/American]; Lee Michael Rochford [1967] Director/Group Chief Executive Officer

Capquest Investments Limited
Incorporated: 29 September 2004
Net Worth: £71,510,000 *Total Assets:* £127,280,000
Registered Office: Belvedere, 12 Booth Street, Manchester, M2 4AW
Activities: Other business support service activities n.e.c.
Parent: Capquest Group Limited
Officers: Stewart David Hamilton, Secretary; Paul David Cooper [1972] Director/Group Chief Financial Officer; Zachary Jason Lewy [1974] Director/Founder and Group Chief Investment Officer [British/American]; Lee Michael Rochford [1967] Director/Group Chief Executive Officer

Car Benefit Car Schemes Limited
Incorporated: 2 April 2003 *Employees:* 81
Net Worth: £10,596,375 *Total Assets:* £225,076,576
Registered Office: The Barracks, 400 Bolton Road, Bury, Lancs, BL8 2DA
Activities: Other credit granting n.e.c.
Parent: Car Benefit Holdings Limited
Officers: Paul Stephen Taylor, Secretary; Neil Kevin Davies [1964] Director; Martin Joseph Maguire [1967] Director/Chartered Accountant; Dennis Studholme [1949] Director; Paul Stephen Taylor [1975] Director

Car Benefit Holdings Limited
Incorporated: 3 April 2003 *Employees:* 81
Net Worth: £32,363,684 *Total Assets:* £233,287,328
Registered Office: The Barracks, 400 Bolton Road, Bury, Lancs, BL8 2DA
Activities: Activities of head offices
Shareholders: Martin Joseph Maguire; Dennis Studholme; Gerry O'Neill
Officers: Paul Stephen Taylor, Secretary; Neil Kevin Davies [1964] Director; Martin Joseph Maguire [1967] Director/Chartered Accountant; Dennis Studholme [1949] Director; Paul Stephen Taylor [1975] Director

Car Care Plan (Holdings) Limited
Incorporated: 7 November 1977
Net Worth: £29,925,000 *Total Assets:* £30,757,000
Registered Office: Jubilee House, 5 Mid Point Business Park, Thornbury, W Yorks, BD3 7AG
Activities: Non-life insurance
Parent: Amtrust International Limited
Officers: Gavin William Work Tinch, Secretary; Jeremy Edward Cadle [1965] Director/Lawyer; Maximiliaan Gerard Caviet [1953] Director/Chief Executive Officer; Timothy John Heavisides [1959] Director/Chief Executive; John Anthony Levin [1963] Director; Paul Graeme Newton [1959] Director; Benjamin Seamus Russell [1972] Sales Director; Gary Whitelam [1959] Director; Simon Jonathan Wright [1966] Director/Chartered Accountant

Car Care Plan Limited
Incorporated: 26 May 1965 *Employees:* 307
Net Worth: £13,649,000 *Total Assets:* £44,982,000
Registered Office: Jubilee House, 5 Mid Point Business Park, Thornbury, W Yorks, BD3 7AG
Activities: Non-life insurance
Parent: Car Care Plan (Holdings) Limited
Officers: Gavin William Work Tinch, Secretary; Jeremy Edward Cadle [1965] Director/Lawyer; Maximiliaan Gerard Caviet [1953] Director/Chief Executive Officer; Timothy John Heavisides [1959] Director/Chief Executive; John Anthony Levin [1963] Director; Paul Graeme Newton [1959] Finance Director; Benjamin Seamus Russell [1972] Sales Director; Gary Whitelam [1959] Executive Director; Simon Jonathan Wright [1966] Director/Chartered Accountant

Car Transplants Limited
Incorporated: 20 June 1986 *Employees:* 61
Net Worth: £4,529,534 *Total Assets:* £9,585,822
Registered Office: Wharton Road, Winsford, Cheshire, CW7 3BQ
Activities: Recovery of sorted materials
Parent: Car Transplants (Holdings) Limited
Officers: John Anthony Schofield, Secretary; John Anthony Schofield [1954] Director; Mark Richard Malkin Schofield [1963] Director; Paul Alan Schofield [1956] Director

Cara Holdings Limited
Incorporated: 2 August 2002 *Employees:* 122
Net Worth: £7,450,089 *Total Assets:* £13,273,257
Registered Office: Victoria House, 1 Huntsman Drive, Irlam, Manchester, M44 5EG
Activities: Renting and leasing of construction and civil engineering machinery and equipment
Shareholder: John Thomas Grady
Officers: Patrick McGowan, Secretary; John Thomas Grady [1965] Director/Civil Engineer; Patrick Joseph Grady [1966] Director/Civil Engineer

Carden Croft (2012) Limited
Incorporated: 4 December 2012
Net Worth: £7,775,498 *Total Assets:* £10,050,000
Registered Office: c/o Allens Accountants, 123 Wellington Road South, Stockport, Cheshire, SK1 3TH
Activities: Activities of other holding companies n.e.c.
Shareholders: Simon Dennis Carden; David John Croft
Officers: David John Croft, Secretary; Simon Dennis Carden [1955] Director; David John Croft [1949] Director

Carden Park Hotel Limited
Incorporated: 15 September 2006 *Employees:* 262
Net Worth: £4,675,000 *Total Assets:* £37,268,000
Registered Office: Bridgemere House, Chester Road, Preston Brook, Warrington, Cheshire, WA7 3BD
Activities: Hotels and similar accommodation
Officers: Ashley Martin Lewis, Secretary; Vincent William Fairclough [1950] Director/Solicitor; Ashley Martin Lewis [1956] Director/Chartered Accountant; Stephen Peter Morgan [1952] Director

Cardinal Health Finance
Incorporated: 30 September 1999 *Employees:* 1
Net Worth: £105,550,208 *Total Assets:* £105,594,472
Registered Office: Eversheds House, 70 Great Bridgewater Street, Manchester, M1 5ES
Activities: Financial leasing
Parent: Cardinal Health, Inc
Officers: John Naughton [1965] Director/Accounting Executive [Irish]; Roddy Victor Stafford [1976] Director/Solicitor [Irish]; Scott Bryan Zimmerman [1976] Director/Executive [American]

Cardinal Health U.K. 418 Limited
Incorporated: 13 October 2003 *Employees:* 1
Net Worth: £22,756,000 *Total Assets:* £22,788,000
Registered Office: Eversheds House, 70 Great Bridgewater Street, Manchester, M1 5ES
Activities: Activities of other holding companies n.e.c.
Parent: Cardinal Health U.K. Holding Limited
Officers: Scott Bryan Zimmerman [1976] Director/Business Executive [American]

Cardinal Health U.K. Holding Limited
Incorporated: 12 March 2007 *Employees:* 1
Net Worth: £409,000 *Total Assets:* £80,504,000
Registered Office: Eversheds House, 70 Great Bridgewater Street, Manchester, M1 5ES
Activities: Activities of other holding companies n.e.c.
Parent: Cardinal Health U.K. International Holding LLP
Officers: Scott Bryan Zimmerman [1976] Director/Business Executive [American]

Cardinal Health U.K. International Holding LLP
Incorporated: 30 May 2008
Net Worth Deficit: £49,952,000 *Total Assets:* £79,966,000
Registered Office: Eversheds House, 70 Great Bridgewater Street, Manchester, M1 5ES

Cardinal Limited
Incorporated: 14 October 2008 *Employees:* 209
Net Worth: £10,941,086 *Total Assets:* £23,069,344
Registered Office: Fernhill House, Battye Street, Bradford, BD4 8AG
Activities: Activities of head offices
Officers: Mark Simpson, Secretary; Brian Considine [1938] Director; Timothy Brian Considine [1969] Director

Cardinal Maritime Holdings Limited
Incorporated: 5 April 2012 *Employees:* 207
Net Worth: £8,308,383 *Total Assets:* £27,327,842
Registered Office: Leestone Road, Sharston Industrial Estate, Sharston, Manchester, M22 4RB
Activities: Activities of distribution holding companies
Shareholder: Brian Peter Hay
Officers: Liam Anthony McGonagle, Secretary; Robert William Cross [1971] Managing Director; Brian Peter Hay [1971] Director; Charles Michael McGonagle [1978] Operations Director; Liam Anthony McGonagle [1979] Finance Director; James Matthew Whyatt [1974] Director

Cardinal Maritime Limited
Incorporated: 6 October 1997 *Employees:* 158
Net Worth: £7,881,104 *Total Assets:* £18,628,068
Registered Office: Leestone Road, Sharston Industrial Estate, Sharston, Manchester, M22 4RB
Activities: Sea and coastal freight water transport
Shareholder: Brian Peter Hay
Officers: Liam Anthony McGonagle, Secretary; Robert William Cross [1971] Managing Director; Brian Peter Hay [1971] Director/Group CEO; Charles Michael McGonagle [1978] Operations Director; Liam Anthony McGonagle [1979] Finance Director; James Matthew Whyatt [1974] Director

Cardinal Project Management Limited
Incorporated: 23 January 1998 *Employees:* 44
Net Worth: £3,897,261 *Total Assets:* £8,918,508
Registered Office: Fernhill House, Battye Street, Bradford, BD4 8AG
Activities: Other construction installation
Parent: Cardinal Ltd
Officers: Mark Simpson, Secretary; Brian Considine [1938] Director; Timothy Brian Considine [1969] Director/Systems; Richard Craig Johnson [1972] Director/Shopfitting

Cardinal Shopfitting + Systems Limited
Incorporated: 4 September 1989 *Employees:* 155
Net Worth: £5,079,883 *Total Assets:* £10,347,988
Registered Office: Fernhill House, Battye Street, Bradford, BD4 8AG
Activities: Manufacture of other fabricated metal products n.e.c.
Parent: Cardinal Ltd
Officers: Mark Simpson, Secretary; Brian Considine [1938] Director; Timothy Brian Considine [1969] Director

Care Worldwide (Southwell) Limited
Incorporated: 2 June 2011 *Employees:* 90
Net Worth: £1,753,228 *Total Assets:* £7,508,816
Registered Office: 6th Floor, Cardinal House, 20 St Mary's Parsonage, Manchester, M3 2LG
Activities: Residential care activities for the elderly and disabled
Parent: Care Worldwide Limited
Officers: Sarah Michelle Goldstein, Secretary; Alan Goldstein [1981] Director/Health Care Provider [Belgian]

Care Worldwide Limited
Incorporated: 5 March 1999 *Employees:* 458
Net Worth: £6,498,591 *Total Assets:* £26,154,222
Registered Office: 6th Floor, Cardinal House, 20 St Mary's Parsonage, Manchester, M3 2LG
Activities: Residential care activities for the elderly and disabled
Shareholders: James David Hassan; David Dennis Cuby; Subash Malkani; Adrian Gerard Olivero; Maurice Albert Perera; William Damian Cid de la Paz
Officers: Sarah Michelle Goldstein, Secretary; Alan Goldstein [1981] Director/Healthcare Regional Manager [Belgian]

Career Connect
Incorporated: 13 June 2001 *Employees:* 371
Net Worth: £16,221,776 *Total Assets:* £19,042,668
Registered Office: 7th Floor, Walker House, Exchange Flags, Liverpool, L2 3YL
Activities: Other education n.e.c.
Officers: Gillian Susan Holywell, Secretary; Ameena Ahmed [1961] Director; Nigel Edmund Bellamy [1952] Director/Voluntary Sector; Christine Mary Bennett [1961] Managing Director; Lorraine Antonia Carrol Dodd [1955] Retired Investment Director; Kieran Timothy Gordon [1958] Director/Chief Executive [Irish]; Martin John McEwan [1967] Marketing Director; Deborah Frances Shackleton [1952] Director/Retired; Kathleen Wyke [1966] Director/Enterprise Co-ordinator

Walter Carefoot & Sons (Construction) Limited
Incorporated: 17 April 1959 *Employees:* 58
Net Worth: £7,516,969 *Total Assets:* £12,308,278
Registered Office: Blackpool Road, Longridge, Lancs, PR3 3AL
Activities: Construction of commercial buildings
Parent: Carefoot PLC
Officers: Charles Douglas Carefoot [1952] Director; Colin William Clive Carefoot [1968] Managing Director

Carefoot PLC
Incorporated: 7 December 1992 *Employees:* 96
Net Worth: £10,231,924 *Total Assets:* £18,282,460
Registered Office: Blackpool Road, Longridge, Preston, Lancs, PR3 3AL
Activities: Activities of head offices
Shareholders: Charles Douglas Carefoot; Colin William Clive Carefoot
Officers: Colin William Clive Carefoot, Secretary; Charles Douglas Carefoot [1952] Director; Colin William Clive Carefoot [1968] Managing Director

Carehome Medz Limited
Incorporated: 2 December 2010 *Employees:* 1
Net Worth Deficit: £515,892 *Total Assets:* £45,795,560
Registered Office: Unit 28 Berkeley Business Park, Turner Lane, Ashton under Lyne, Lancs, OL6 8LB
Activities: Other human health activities
Shareholders: Narendra Kotecha; Carehome Medz Holdings Limited
Officers: Rakesh Govind Sawant [1974] Director [Indian]

Caribbean Biodiversity Fund
Incorporated: 6 September 2012
Net Worth: £48,668,880 *Total Assets:* £48,932,020
Registered Office: 3rd Floor, 1 Ashley Road, Altrincham, Cheshire, WA14 2DT
Activities: Other service activities n.e.c.
Officers: Roderick Patrick Cherry [1967] Director/COO, St Lucia Hotel and Tourism Association [Saint Lucian]; Garry Wendell Gore [1966] Director [Antiguan/Barbudan]; Sixto Joaquin Inchaustegui [1947] Director/Biologist [Dominican]; Dr. Jens MacKensen [1966] Director/Banker [German]; Eleanor Anna Phillips [1963] Director [Bahamian]

Caritas Diocese of Salford
Incorporated: 15 May 2008 *Employees:* 88
Net Worth: £7,934,541 *Total Assets:* £8,166,339
Registered Office: Cathedral Centre, 3 Ford Street, Salford, M3 6DP
Activities: Other social work activities without accommodation n.e.c.
Officers: Edward Nally, Secretary; Bishop John Stanley Kenneth Arnold [1953] Director/Roman Catholic Bishop; Alan Denneny [1938] Director/Roman Catholic Priest; Reverend David Glover [1950] Director/Roman Catholic Priest; Lorraine Jane Leonard [1969] Director/Youth Ministry Co-ordinator; Thomas Mulheran [1938] Director/Roman Catholic Priest; Anthony Murray [1938] Director/Retired; Edward Nally [1956] Director/Solicitor

Carlisle Refrigeration (Holdings) Limited
Incorporated: 20 April 2010 *Employees:* 110
Net Worth: £8,336,650 *Total Assets:* £11,353,971
Registered Office: Brunthill Road, Kingstown Industrial Estate, Carlisle, Cumbria, CA3 0EH
Activities: Repair of other equipment
Shareholders: Heather Joan Lowe; David Eric Lowe
Officers: David Robert Thompson, Secretary; David Eric Lowe [1955] Director; Heather Joan Lowe [1955] Director

Carlisle Refrigeration Limited
Incorporated: 30 August 1984 *Employees:* 110
Net Worth: £9,783,101 *Total Assets:* £12,800,422
Registered Office: Brunthill Road, Kingstown Industrial Estate, Carlisle, Cumbria, CA3 0EH
Activities: Repair of other equipment
Shareholders: Heather Joan Lowe; David Eric Lowe
Officers: David Robert Thompson, Secretary/Accountant; David Eric Lowe [1955] Director; Heather Joan Lowe [1955] Director

Carlisle United Association Football Club (1921) Limited
Incorporated: 20 June 1921 *Employees:* 223
Net Worth: £4,816,404 *Total Assets:* £8,772,441
Registered Office: Brunton Park, Warwick Road, Carlisle, Cumbria, CA1 1LL
Activities: Other sports activities
Parent: CUFC Holdings Limited
Officers: John Lee Nixon, Secretary; Nigel Clibbens [1968] Director/Chief Executive; Suzanne Catherine Kidd [1978] Finance Director; James Mitchell [1946] Director; John Lee Nixon [1948] Industrial Director

Carlson Filtration Limited
Incorporated: 20 June 1988 *Employees:* 62
Net Worth: £4,783,898 *Total Assets:* £8,573,461
Registered Office: Butts Mill, Barnoldswick, Lancs, BB18 5HP
Activities: Manufacture of paper and paperboard
Officers: Richard Matthew Bickley, Secretary; Richard Matthew Bickley [1960] Director/Accountant; Brian Robert Gabbett [1945] Director; Paul Martin Hirst [1965] Managing Director

Carman (Holdings) Limited
Incorporated: 14 February 2013 *Employees:* 254
Net Worth: £4,851,710 *Total Assets:* £14,601,339
Registered Office: The Courtyard, Radway Green, Crewe, Cheshire, CW2 5PR
Activities: Activities of head offices
Major Shareholder: Roderick William Carman
Officers: Andrew Jonathan Hodgson, Secretary; Sally Jane Carman [1964] Director; William Roderick Carman [1957] Director

CarnaudMetalbox Engineering Limited
Incorporated: 10 September 1949 *Employees:* 434
Net Worth: £24,528,000 *Total Assets:* £77,520,000
Registered Office: Dockfield Road, Shipley, W Yorks, BD17 7AY
Activities: Manufacture of machinery for food, beverage and tobacco processing
Parent: Crown Packaging Manufacturing UK Limited
Officers: Jennifer Patricia Simpson, Secretary; John Patrick Beardsley [1970] Director; Paul William Browett [1961] Director/Vice President/Treasurer; Robert Brown [1962] Director/Head of Finance; Richard Andrew Forti [1953] Director/SVP Business Support [American]; Andrew George Truelove [1973] Director/General Manager

Carpenter Holdings Limited
Incorporated: 22 August 2001 *Employees:* 335
Net Worth: £73,286,000 *Total Assets:* £87,504,000
Registered Office: Dinting Lodge Industrial Estate, Glossop, Derbys, SK13 6LE
Activities: Other business support service activities n.e.c.
Officers: Brian Messer, Secretary; David John Hulley [1962] Director; Brian Messer [1961] Director; Stanley Frank Pauley [1927] Director [American]

Carpenter Investments (Vine Street) Ltd
Incorporated: 30 May 2012
Net Worth: £688,539 *Total Assets:* £12,960,136
Registered Office: Seymour Chambers, 92 London Road, Liverpool, L3 5NW
Activities: Other letting and operating of own or leased real estate
Officers: Alan James Beer [1966] Director; David Charles Brewitt [1963] Director

Carpenter Investments Brunswick Park 2 Ltd
Incorporated: 22 November 2011
Net Worth: £1,957,175 *Total Assets:* £9,602,781
Registered Office: Seymour Chambers, 92 London Road, Liverpool, L3 5NW
Activities: Other service activities n.e.c.
Officers: Alan James Beer [1966] Director; David Charles Brewitt [1963] Director

Carpenter Investments Ltd
Incorporated: 30 May 2012 *Employees:* 6
Net Worth: £17,708,952 *Total Assets:* £22,773,652
Registered Office: Seymour Chambers, 92 London Road, Liverpool, L3 5NW
Activities: Other letting and operating of own or leased real estate
Officers: Alan James Beer [1966] Director; David Charles Brewitt [1963] Director

Carpenter Limited
Incorporated: 2 July 1926 *Employees:* 331
Net Worth: £79,753,000 *Total Assets:* £97,533,000
Registered Office: Dinting Lodge Industrial Estate, Glossop, Derbys, SK13 6LE
Activities: Manufacture of other plastic products
Officers: Brian Messer, Secretary; Jim Albert Hacker [1953] Director [American]; David John Hulley [1962] Managing Director; Brian Messer [1961] Director; Stanley Frank Pauley [1927] Director [American]

Carr's Engineering Limited
Incorporated: 19 December 1946 *Employees:* 191
Net Worth: £7,981,999 *Total Assets:* £25,919,760
Registered Office: Old Croft, Stanwix, Carlisle, Cumbria, CA3 9BA
Activities: Manufacture of other tanks, reservoirs and containers of metal
Parent: Carr's Group PLC
Officers: Matthew Ratcliffe, Secretary; Neil Austin [1975] Finance Director; Timothy John Davies [1962] Director; Graham Michael Hartley [1961] Director

Carr's Group PLC
Incorporated: 3 June 1908 *Employees:* 936
Net Worth: £91,482,000 *Total Assets:* £209,040,000
Registered Office: Old Croft, Stanwix, Carlisle, Cumbria, CA3 9BA
Activities: Activities of head offices
Officers: Matthew Ratcliffe, Secretary; Neil Austin [1975] Finance Director; Timothy John Davies [1962] Director; Christopher Nigel Couper Holmes [1951] Director; Alistair George Milne Wannop [1962] Director Ian Wood [1958] Director; John Graham Worby [1950] Director

Carrier Ltd
Incorporated: 13 December 1991 *Employees:* 84
Net Worth Deficit: £247,282 *Total Assets:* £10,786,877
Registered Office: One Didsbury Point, 2 The Avenue, Didsbury, Manchester, M20 2EY
Activities: Tour operator activities
Shareholders: DER Touristik UK Ltd; Kuoni Travel Ltd
Officers: Kevin Patrick O'Doherty, Secretary; Derek Jones [1963] Managing Director; Francis Torrilla [1960] Director

Carrier Transicold (UK) Limited
Incorporated: 6 November 1972 *Employees:* 35
Net Worth: £13,673,000 *Total Assets:* £34,969,000
Registered Office: Willis Carrier House, 260 Cygnet Court, Centre Park, Warrington, Cheshire, WA1 1RR
Activities: Wholesale of other machinery and equipment
Officers: John Ross, Secretary; Scott Thomas Dargan [1971] Operations Director; John Thomas Forster [1954] Sales Director; Paul Knight [1962] Operations Director; John William Joseph Ross [1977] Finance Director; Andrew Wainwright [1967] Service Director

Carrington Textiles Ltd
Incorporated: 27 November 1997 *Employees:* 39
Net Worth: £7,940,000 *Total Assets:* £59,599,000
Registered Office: Carrington Workwear Ltd, Market Street, Adlington, Lancs, PR7 4HJ
Activities: Wholesale of textiles
Parent: Pincroft Dyeing & Printing Co. Ltd
Officers: Nigel Andrew Bate, Secretary; Nigel Andrew Bate [1971] Director/Certified Chartered Accountant; Neil Jonathan Davey [1971] Sales Director; John Joseph Vareldzis [1972] Director

Carrix Limited
Incorporated: 18 May 2009 *Employees:* 11
Net Worth: £6,016,418 *Total Assets:* £7,555,968
Registered Office: Massey Hall, Half Acre Lane, Thelwall, Warrington, Cheshire, WA4 3JE
Activities: Management consultancy activities other than financial management
Shareholders: Carolyn Nevinson; Richard John Nevinson
Officers: Carolyn Nevinson [1966] Director; Richard John Nevinson [1963] Director

Carron Lodge Limited
Incorporated: 16 April 1996 *Employees:* 118
Net Worth: £7,749,477 *Total Assets:* £11,769,393
Registered Office: Parkhead Farm, Inglewhite, Preston, Lancs, PR3 2LN
Activities: Butter and cheese production
Shareholders: Robert Adrian Rhodes; Annette Suzanne Rhodes
Officers: Annette Suzanne Rhodes, Secretary; Annette Suzanne Rhodes [1967] Director/Farmer; Robert Adrian Rhodes [1964] Director/Farmer

Carrs Agriculture Limited
Incorporated: 31 March 1950 *Employees:* 77
Net Worth: £3,719,238 *Total Assets:* £13,970,276
Registered Office: Old Croft, Stanwix, Carlisle, Cumbria, CA3 9BA
Activities: Manufacture of prepared feeds for farm animals
Parent: Carr's Group PLC
Officers: Matthew Ratcliffe, Secretary; Neil Austin [1975] Finance Director; Timothy John Davies [1962] Director

Carrs Billington Agriculture (Operations) Limited
Incorporated: 2 June 1998 *Employees:* 173
Net Worth: £21,431,792 *Total Assets:* £34,743,384
Registered Office: Cunard Building, Water Street, Liverpool, L3 1EL
Activities: Manufacture of prepared feeds for farm animals
Parent: Edward Billington and Son Limited
Officers: David Marshall, Secretary; Gary Blake [1973] Director; Timothy John Davies [1962] Director; Kevin Dixon [1972] Director; David Marshall [1961] Director; Paul William Steeples [1957] Managing Director; Rae Tomlinson [1960] Director/Accountant; Lloyd Leslie Russell Whiteley [1959] Director

Carrs Billington Agriculture (Sales) Limited
Incorporated: 3 May 1923 *Employees:* 436
Net Worth: £27,833,266 *Total Assets:* £75,070,128
Registered Office: Old Croft, Stanwix, Carlisle, Cumbria, CA3 9BA
Activities: Manufacture of prepared feeds for farm animals
Shareholders: Billington Agriculture Holdings Ltd; Carr's Group PLC
Officers: Matthew Ratcliffe, Secretary; Gary Michael Blake [1973] Director/Chief Executive; Timothy John Davies [1962] Director; Kevin Dixon [1972] Director; Ian Gate [1962] Machinery Director Designate; Paul William Steeples [1957] Managing Director; Rae Tomlinson [1960] Director/Accountant; Lloyd Leslie Russell Whiteley [1959] Director

Carrs Foods Holdings Limited
Incorporated: 19 July 2004 *Employees:* 20
Net Worth: £2,549,691 *Total Assets:* £11,162,563
Registered Office: South Court, Sharston Road, Manchester, M22 4BB
Activities: Non-specialised wholesale of food, beverages and tobacco
Shareholders: Jeremy Philip Gilboy; Paul Baker
Officers: Jeremy Philip Gilboy, Secretary/Director; Paul Baker [1969] Director; Sally Ford [1968] Director; Jeremy Philip Gilboy [1958] Director

Carrs Foods International Limited
Incorporated: 4 October 1996 *Employees:* 23
Net Worth: £2,317,360 *Total Assets:* £11,238,529
Registered Office: South Court, Sharston Road, Manchester, M22 4BB
Activities: Non-specialised wholesale of food, beverages and tobacco
Parent: Carrs Foods Holdings Limited
Officers: Paul Baker [1969] Director; Sally Ford [1968] Director; Jeremy Philip Gilboy [1958] Finance Director

Carrylift Group Finance Limited
Incorporated: 21 January 2015 *Employees:* 1
Net Worth Deficit: £73,478 *Total Assets:* £7,016,673
Registered Office: Corpacq House, 1 Goose Green, Altrincham, Cheshire, WA14 1DW
Activities: Other business support service activities n.e.c.
Parent: Corpacq Finance Limited
Officers: Nicholas James Cattell [1974] Director/Chartered Accountant

Carrylift Holdings Limited
Incorporated: 1 December 2009
Net Worth: £10,000 *Total Assets:* £16,410,755
Registered Office: Corpacq House, 1 Goose Green, Altrincham, Cheshire, WA14 1DW
Activities: Other business support service activities n.e.c.
Parent: Carrylift Group Finance Limited
Officers: Nicholas James Cattell [1974] Director/Chartered Accountant

Carrylift Materials Handling Limited
Incorporated: 16 February 1988 *Employees:* 165
Net Worth: £11,396,225 *Total Assets:* £26,571,364
Registered Office: 3 Peel Road, West Pimbo, Skelmersdale, Lancs, WN8 9PT
Activities: Agents involved in the sale of machinery, industrial equipment, ships and aircraft
Parent: Carrylift Group (Holdings) Limited
Officers: Nicholas James Cattell [1974] Director; Stephen James Scott [1978] Director; Eamonn Paul Smyth [1966] Director/Accountant

Cartoon (Holdings) Limited
Incorporated: 12 October 2006 *Employees:* 1,162
Net Worth: £46,213,000 *Total Assets:* £64,175,000
Registered Office: Churchill Point, Lake Edge Green, Trafford Park Road, Manchester, M17 1BL
Activities: Retail sale of cosmetic and toilet articles in specialised stores
Officers: Vipul Jayantilal Vadera, Secretary; Sanjay Jayantilal Vadera [1967] Director; Vipul Jayantilal Vadera [1972] Director

S. Cartwright & Sons (Coachbuilders) Limited
Incorporated: 24 March 1961 *Employees:* 891
Net Worth: £17,239,480 *Total Assets:* £99,543,176
Registered Office: Head Office, Atlantic Street, Broadheath, Altrincham, Cheshire, WA14 5EW
Activities: Manufacture of motor vehicles
Parent: Cartwright Holdings
Officers: Peter Stanley Cartwright, Secretary; Christine Cartwright [1947] Director; Laura Kate Cartwright [1977] Director; Mark Robert Cartwright [1972] Director; Peter Stanley Cartwright [1945] Director; John Bernard Lee [1970] Director; Lisa Christina Lee [1974] Rentals Director; Robert Edward Ward [1953] Director/Accountant

Cartwright Fleet Services Limited
Incorporated: 12 April 1995 *Employees:* 150
Net Worth: £793,312 *Total Assets:* £30,220,380
Registered Office: Head Office, Atlantic Street, Broadheath, Altrincham, Cheshire, WA14 5EW
Activities: Manufacture of motor vehicles
Officers: Peter Stanley Cartwright, Secretary/Director; Mark Cartwright [1972] Director; Peter Stanley Cartwright [1945] Director; Christopher Delaney [1959] Director; Lisa Lee [1974] Director; Philip Anthony Rodman [1956] Director; Lawrence Todd [1967] Director; Robert Edward Ward [1953] Director

Cartwright Holdings Ltd
Incorporated: 20 March 2015 *Employees:* 891
Net Worth: £14,286,927 *Total Assets:* £96,390,624
Registered Office: 2nd Floor, 1 City Road East, Manchester, M15 4PN
Activities: Manufacture of trailers and semi-trailers
Shareholders: Peter Stanley Cartwright; Christina Cartwright
Officers: Christine Cartwright [1947] Director; Laura Kate Cartwright [1977] Director; Lisa Christina Cartwright [1974] Director; Mark Robert Cartwright [1972] Director; Peter Stanley Cartwright [1945] Director; John Bernard Lee [1970] Director; Robert Edward Ward [1953] Director

Cartwright Properties Limited
Incorporated: 7 November 1995 *Employees:* 1
Net Worth: £6,511,961 *Total Assets:* £22,030,966
Registered Office: Head Office, Atlantic Street, Broadheath, Altrincham, Cheshire, WA14 5EW
Activities: Renting and operating of Housing Association real estate
Officers: Peter Stanley Cartwright, Secretary; Laura Kate Cartwright [1977] Director; Mark Robert Cartwright [1972] Director; Peter Stanley Cartwright [1945] Director; John Bernard Lee [1970] Director; Lisa Christina Lee [1974] Director; Robert Edward Ward [1953] Director

Cartwright Rentals Limited
Incorporated: 30 March 1993 *Employees:* 13
Net Worth: £6,953,733 *Total Assets:* £35,130,632
Registered Office: Atlantic Street, Broadheath, Altrincham, Cheshire, WA14 5EW
Activities: Operation of warehousing and storage facilities for land transport activities
Shareholder: Peter Stanley Cartwright
Officers: Peter Stanley Cartwright, Secretary/Director; Paul Burn [1961] Director; Laura Kate Cartwright [1977] Director; Mark Robert Cartwright [1972] Director; Peter Stanley Cartwright [1945] Director; John Bernard Lee [1970] Director; Lisa Christina Lee [1974] Director; Philip Anthony Rodman [1956] Director; Robert Edward Ward [1953] Director/Accountant

Casartelli Buildings Limited
Incorporated: 31 October 1991
Net Worth: £3,052,653 *Total Assets:* £7,968,016
Registered Office: 1 Duke Street, Liverpool, L1 4AA
Activities: Hotels and similar accommodation
Officers: Cecilia Anne Gillbanks [1956] Director; Daniel Alexander Gillbanks [1994] Director

Cascade (U.K.) Limited
Incorporated: 6 February 1986 *Employees:* 89
Net Worth: £51,000 *Total Assets:* £7,868,000
Registered Office: 3 Kelbrook Road, Parkhouse Industrial Estate, Openshaw, Manchester, M11 2DD
Activities: Manufacture of lifting and handling equipment
Officers: Stephen David Flitcroft, Secretary; Richard Sibert John Anderson [1948] Director/Chief Operating Officer [American]; Peter David Drake [1967] Director/Vice President of North America [American]; Joseph George Pointer [1960] Director/Chief Financial Officer [American]; Davide Roncari [1973] Managing Director [Italian]; Robert Carlton Warren Jr [1948] Director/President and CEO [American]; Susan Chazin Wright [1952] Director/Vice President [American]

Cascade Holdings Limited
Incorporated: 16 November 1961 *Employees:* 81
Net Worth: £13,435,458 *Total Assets:* £20,723,482
Registered Office: Gorse Mill, Gorse Street, Chadderton, Oldham, Lancs, OL9 9RJ
Activities: Retail of furniture, lighting, and similar (not musical instruments or scores) in specialised store
Shareholders: Irvin Arran Abrahams; Malcolm David Stark; Alfred Tojarieh
Officers: Carol Evelyn Hyde, Secretary; Irvin Arran Abrahams [1949] Director; Jeanette Abrahams [1951] Director; Michael Smith Elsworth [1966] Director/Technical Manager; Andrew Eric Higginson [1968] Commercial Director; Peter John Kashem [1937] Director; Suzanne Keating [1970] Finance Director; Keith Slide [1964] IT Director

WA Casement Holdings Limited
Incorporated: 23 December 2014
Net Worth: £7,848,455 *Total Assets:* £7,848,657
Registered Office: 1211 Ashton Old Road, Manchester, M11 1AA
Activities: Activities of other holding companies n.e.c.
Parent: Nelcrest Limited
Officers: Maurice Moses Benady [1964] Director; Phillip Goldberg [1956] Director; Stephen Jonathan Goldberg [1953] Director/Solicitor; Maximilian Anthony Torres [1978] Director

W & A Casement Limited
Incorporated: 14 October 2014 *Employees:* 2
Net Worth: £7,023,787 *Total Assets:* £14,480,536
Registered Office: 1121 Ashton Old Road, Manchester, M11 1AA
Activities: Management of real estate on a fee or contract basis
Parent: WA Casement Holdings Limited
Officers: Maurice Moses Benady [1964] Director; Phillip Goldberg [1956] Director; Stephen Jonathan Goldberg [1953] Director/Solicitor; Maximilian Anthony Torres [1978] Director

P. Casey & Co., Limited
Incorporated: 28 September 1972 *Employees:* 121
Net Worth: £13,598,572 *Total Assets:* £24,055,732
Registered Office: Rydings Road, Wardle, Rochdale, OL12 9PS
Activities: Other construction installation
Parent: The Casey Group Limited
Officers: Jeremy Paul Warren, Secretary/Director; Anthony John Chell [1955] Director/Chartered Surveyor; Christopher Shaw Griffin [1946] Director/Chartered Surveyor; Paul Turner [1964] Health and Safety Director; Jeremy Paul Warren [1965] Director

P. Casey (Developments) Limited
Incorporated: 18 September 1974
Net Worth: £143,033 *Total Assets:* £8,737,922
Registered Office: Rydings Road, Wardle, Rochdale, OL12 9PS
Activities: Development of building projects
Parent: The Casey Group Limited
Officers: Jeremy Paul Warren, Secretary/Financial Director; Christopher Peter Casey [1974] Director/Quantity Surveyor; Christopher Shaw Griffin [1946] Director/Chartered Surveyor

P. Casey Enviro Limited
Incorporated: 27 May 1983 *Employees:* 43
Net Worth Deficit: £1,317,599 *Total Assets:* £13,357,368
Registered Office: c/o The Casey Group, Rydings Road, Rochdale, Lancs, OL12 9FS
Activities: Treatment and disposal of non-hazardous waste
Officers: Shane Harrison [1970] Director

The Casey Group Limited
Incorporated: 12 June 2001 *Employees:* 303
Net Worth: £17,895,020 *Total Assets:* £39,265,068
Registered Office: Rydings Road, Wardle, Rochdale, OL12 9PS
Activities: Activities of construction holding companies
Shareholders: Peter Casey; Patricia Anne Casey
Officers: Jeremy Paul Warren, Finance Director; Christopher Peter Casey [1974] Director/Quantity Surveyor; Peter Casey [1940] Director; Anthony John Chell [1955] Director/Quantity Surveyor; Christopher Shaw Griffin [1946] Director/Chartered Surveyor

Cash Converters (UK) Limited
Incorporated: 30 August 1995 *Employees:* 30
Net Worth: £1,226,000 *Total Assets:* £10,946,000
Registered Office: Innovation House, Aston Lane South, Whitehouse Industrial Estate, Runcorn, Cheshire, WA7 3FY
Activities: Retail sale of other second-hand goods in stores (not incl. antiques)
Officers: Bradley Edwards, Secretary; Peter Cumins [1951] Managing Director [Australian]; Martyn James Jenkins [1975] Director/Chief Operating Officer; Anthony Mark Richardson [1973] Marketing Director

Cash Converters UK Holdings PLC
Incorporated: 17 July 1996 *Employees:* 30
Net Worth: £1,278,000 *Total Assets:* £10,998,000
Registered Office: Innovation House, Aston Lane South, Whitehouse Industrial Estate, Runcorn, Cheshire, WA7 3FY
Activities: Retail sale of other second-hand goods in stores (not incl. antiques)
Officers: Bradley Edwards, Secretary; Peter Cumins [1951] Managing Director [Australian]; Martyn James Jenkins [1975] Director/Chief Operating Officer; Anthony Mark Richardson [1973] Managing Director

Casterton Leisure Limited
Incorporated: 1 September 1989 *Employees:* 105
Net Worth: £7,293,485 *Total Assets:* £9,985,904
Registered Office: Priory Close, St Mary's Gate, Lancaster, LA1 1XB
Activities: Hotels and similar accommodation
Major Shareholder: Eric Wildsmith
Officers: Claire Frances Wildsmith, Secretary; Andrew James Wildsmith [1977] Director; Claire Frances Wildsmith [1944] Director; Eric Wildsmith [1945] Director

Castle Metals UK Limited
Incorporated: 18 September 2002 *Employees:* 53
Net Worth Deficit: £11,511,516 *Total Assets:* £20,785,580
Registered Office: Unit 1 Commerce Way, Kiwi Park, Trafford Park, Manchester, M17 1HW
Activities: Wholesale of metals and metal ores
Parent: A.M. Castle Metals UK Limited
Officers: Marec Elden Edgar, Secretary; Patrick R Anderson [1972] Director/Executive Vice President Chief Financial Officer [American]; Marec Elden Edgar [1976] Director/Executive Vice President - General Counsel [American]; David Roges [1974] Managing Director Europe [French]; Steven William Scheinkman [1953] Director/President & Chief Executive Officer [American]

A.M. Castle Metals UK, Limited
Incorporated: 11 October 2007
Net Worth Deficit: £16,957,722 *Total Assets:* £12,954,898
Registered Office: Unit 1 Commerce Way, Kiwi Park, Trafford Park, Manchester, M17 1HW
Activities: Activities of head offices
Parent: A.M. Castle & Co
Officers: Marec Elden Edgar, Secretary; Patrick R Anderson [1972] Director/Executive Vice President, Chief Financial Officer [American]; Marec Elden Edgar [1976] Director/Executive Vice President - General Counsel [American]; David Roges [1974] Managing Director Europe [French]; Steven William Scheinkman [1953] Director/President & Chief Executive Officer [American]

Castlefield Estates Limited
Incorporated: 30 July 1981 *Employees:* 11
Net Worth: £15,279,169 *Total Assets:* £25,557,008
Registered Office: Eastgate, 2 Castle Street, Castlefield, Manchester, M3 4LZ
Activities: Management of real estate on a fee or contract basis
Shareholders: Sarah McDermott; James Ramsbottom; Anne Theresa Irwin
Officers: Jean Kathleen Ramsbottom, Secretary; Beth Adams [1969] Finance Director; James Ramsbottom [1939] Director/Bookmaker; Jean Kathleen Ramsbottom [1942] Director/S R Nurse; Sarah Caroline Ramsbottom [1973] Director

Castlefield Holdings Limited
Incorporated: 18 August 2015 *Employees:* 423
Net Worth: £25,392,060 *Total Assets:* £29,498,060
Registered Office: Eastgate, 2 Castle Street, Manchester, M3 4LZ
Activities: Activities of other holding companies n.e.c.
Major Shareholder: James Ramsbottom
Officers: Jean Kathleen Ramsbottom, Secretary; Beth Adams [1969] Director; Sarah McDermott [1967] Director; Kate McKenna [1968] Director; James Ramsbottom [1939] Director; James Ramsbottom [1970] Director; Jean Kathleen Ramsbottom [1942] Director; Lucy Ramsbottom [1980] Director

Catalyst Healthcare (Manchester) Financing PLC
Incorporated: 11 August 2004
Net Worth: £50,000 *Total Assets:* £454,084,992
Registered Office: c/o Albany SPC Services Ltd, 3rd Floor, 3-5 Charlotte Street, Manchester, M1 4HB
Activities: Hospital activities
Parent: Catalyst Healthcare (Manchester) Holdings Ltd
Officers: Ailison Louise Mitchell, Secretary; Jonathan Nigel Edward Cowdell [1966] Director; Mark Geoffrey David Holden [1957] Director; Barry Paul Millsom [1974] Director; Alastair Huw Page [1961] Commercial Director; Steven Marc Prior [1972] Director; Mark Christopher Wayment [1958] Director

Catalyst Healthcare (Manchester) Holdings Limited
Incorporated: 6 September 2002
Net Worth: £45,091,000 *Total Assets:* £541,800,000
Registered Office: c/o Albany SPC Services Ltd, 3rd Floor, 3-5 Charlotte Street, Manchester, M1 4HB
Activities: Activities of head offices
Officers: Ailison Louise Mitchell, Secretary; Jonathan Nigel Edward Cowdell [1966] Director; Mark Geoffrey David Holden [1957] Director; Barry Paul Millsom [1974] Director; Alastair Huw Page [1961] Commercial Director; Steven Marc Prior [1972] Director; Mark Christopher Wayment [1958] Director

Catalyst Healthcare (Manchester) Limited
Incorporated: 6 September 2002
Net Worth: £45,041,000 *Total Assets:* £541,800,000
Registered Office: c/o Albany SPC Services Ltd, 3rd Floor, 3-5 Charlotte Street, Manchester, M1 4HB
Activities: Other professional, scientific and technical activities n.e.c.
Parent: Catalyst Healthcare (Manchester) Holdings Ltd
Officers: Ailison Louise Mitchell, Secretary; Jonathan Nigel Edward Cowdell [1966] Director; Mark Geoffrey David Holden [1957] Director; Barry Paul Millsom [1974] Director; Alastair Huw Page [1961] Commercial Director; Steven Marc Prior [1972] Director; Mark Christopher Wayment [1958] Director

Catalyst Healthcare (Romford) Financing PLC.
Incorporated: 15 May 2003
Net Worth: £50,000 *Total Assets:* £239,495,008
Registered Office: c/o Albany SPC Services Ltd, 3rd Floor, 3-5 Charlotte Street, Manchester, M1 4HB
Activities: Hospital activities
Parent: Catalyst Healthcare (Romford) Holdings Ltd
Officers: Ailison Louise Mitchell, Secretary; Clement David Baptiste Leverd [1986] Director/Investment Executive [French]; Christopher Thomas Solley [1970] Director; Andrew Leslie Tennant [1958] Director; Mark Christopher Wayment [1958] Director

Catalyst Healthcare (Romford) Holdings Limited
Incorporated: 10 June 2003
Net Worth: £6,088,000 *Total Assets:* £292,990,016
Registered Office: c/o Albany SPC Services Ltd, 3rd Floor, 3-5 Charlotte Street, Manchester, M1 4HB
Activities: Hospital activities
Shareholders: Aberdeen Infrastructure Investments (No.3) Limited; Infrastructure Investment Holdings Limited
Officers: Ailison Louise Mitchell, Secretary; Clement David Baptiste Leverd [1986] Director/Investment Executive [French]; Christopher Thomas Solley [1970] Director; Andrew Leslie Tennant [1958] Director; Mark Christopher Wayment [1958] Director

Catalyst Healthcare (Romford) Limited
Incorporated: 10 June 2003
Net Worth: £6,038,000 *Total Assets:* £292,990,016
Registered Office: c/o Albany SPC Services Ltd, 3rd Floor, 3-5 Charlotte Street, Manchester, M1 4HB
Activities: Hospital activities
Parent: Catalyst Healthcare (Romford) Holdings Limited
Officers: Ailison Louise Mitchell, Secretary; Clement David Baptiste Leverd [1986] Director/Investment Executive [French]; Christopher Thomas Solley [1970] Director; Andrew Leslie Tennant [1958] Director; Mark Christopher Wayment [1958] Director

Catalyst Higher Education (Sheffield) Holdings Limited
Incorporated: 6 June 2005
Net Worth: £14,055,000 *Total Assets:* £196,312,992
Registered Office: c/o Albany SPC Services Ltd, 3rd Floor, 3-5 Charlotte Street, Manchester, M1 4HB
Activities: Management of real estate on a fee or contract basis
Shareholder: Infrastructure Investments Holdings Ltd
Officers: Ailison Louise Mitchell, Secretary; Mark Geoffrey David Holden [1957] Director; Leo William McKenna [1966] Director [Irish]; Barry Paul Millsom [1974] Director; Mark Christopher Wayment [1958] Director

Catalyst Higher Education (Sheffield) PLC
Incorporated: 6 June 2005
Net Worth: £14,055,000 *Total Assets:* £196,312,992
Registered Office: c/o Albany SPC Services Ltd, 3rd Floor, 3-5 Charlotte Street, Manchester, M1 4HB
Activities: Other education n.e.c.
Parent: Catalyst Higher Education (Sheffield) Holdings Limited
Officers: Ailison Louise Mitchell, Secretary; Mark Geoffrey David Holden [1957] Director; Leo William McKenna [1966] Director [Irish]; Barry Paul Millsom [1974] Director; Mark Christopher Wayment [1958] Director

Caterplus Services Limited
Incorporated: 25 March 1991 *Employees:* 884
Net Worth Deficit: £247,834 *Total Assets:* £9,032,106
Registered Office: The Courtyard, Catherine Street, Macclesfield, Cheshire, SK11 6ET
Activities: Other food services
Parent: Waterfall Services Limited
Officers: Jim Lovett [1969] Director; Vincent John Pearson [1959] Director; Catherine Margaret Roe [1960] Managing Director; Eleni Savva [1972] Finance Director

Catford & Longford Limited
Incorporated: 19 November 1985 *Employees:* 3
Net Worth: £1,756,639 *Total Assets:* £9,565,344
Registered Office: Abbey Road, Barrow in Furness, Cumbria, LA13 0PA
Activities: Hotels and similar accommodation
Officers: Brian Gerard Conroy [1971] Director/Hotel Manager; Neil Hopkins-Coman [1962] Director/Chartered Accountant; Timothy Anthony Kilroe [1964] Director [Irish]

P & A J Cattee (Wholesale) Ltd.
Incorporated: 29 April 1964
Net Worth: £5,362,525 *Total Assets:* £20,173,056
Registered Office: 11 Manchester Road, Walkden, Manchester, M28 3NS
Activities: Wholesale of pharmaceutical goods
Shareholders: Peter Cattee; Angela Jane Cattee; PCT Healthcare (Holdings) Limited
Officers: Angela Jane Cattee, Secretary/Pharmacist; Angela Jane Cattee [1953] Director/Pharmacist; Peter Cattee [1952] Director; Geoffrey Alan Tims [1943] Director/Pharmacist

Causeway Tractors Limited
Incorporated: 29 April 1994 *Employees:* 18
Net Worth: £4,521,669 *Total Assets:* £9,227,466
Registered Office: Lyon Road Industrial Estate, Moss Road, Kearsley, Bolton, Lancs, BL4 8NE
Activities: Agents involved in the sale of machinery, industrial equipment, ships and aircraft
Parent: Morris Leslie Ltd
Officers: Morris Young Leslie [1955] Director; Graham Robert Ogilvie [1972] Director; Craig Taylor [1968] Director [New Zealander]

Cavalier Carpets Limited
Incorporated: 21 October 1971 *Employees:* 218
Net Worth: £8,246,586 *Total Assets:* £13,055,308
Registered Office: Bank Top Mill, Dixon Street, Thompson Street Industrial Estate, Blackburn, Lancs, BB2 1TX
Activities: Manufacture of woven or tufted carpets and rugs
Parent: Ribble Valley (Holdings) Limited
Officers: Peter John Daniel Brierley, Secretary; Peter John Daniel Brierley [1979] Director/Accountant; Donald Giles [1951] Director/Designer; Stephen John Joyce [1959] Director; Hans Anthony Lowe [1969] Director; Julian Amos Lowe [1972] Director; Nathan Symon Lowe [1978] Director; Christopher John Sutton [1969] Services Director; Amanda Thompson [1975] Director

Cavalier Marketing Limited
Incorporated: 13 September 1988 *Employees:* 159
Net Worth: £13,284,770 *Total Assets:* £26,834,770
Registered Office: Cavalier Marketing, North Dean Road, Keighley, W Yorks, BD22 6QY
Activities: Manufacture of other furniture
Parent: Cavalier Marketing Holdings Limited
Officers: John Frazer Harrison [1971] Managing Director; Robert Hudson Harrison [1975] Managing Director

Cavendish Investments (Manchester) Limited
Incorporated: 2 August 1991
Net Worth: £671,896 *Total Assets:* £27,129,840
Registered Office: 2 Regency Chambers, Jubilee Way, Bury, Lancs, BL9 0JW
Activities: Financial intermediation not elsewhere classified
Parent: Regency Factors PLC
Officers: Jonathan Simon Myer Craft, Secretary; Hilary Susan Craft [1957] Director; Maurice Howard Craft [1955] Director; John Thomas Farrell [1965] Director

Cavern City Tours Limited
Incorporated: 4 August 1983 *Employees:* 100
Net Worth: £12,799,445 *Total Assets:* £14,163,083
Registered Office: Hanover Buildings, 11-13 Hanover Street, Liverpool, L1 3DN
Activities: Other amusement and recreation activities n.e.c.
Major Shareholder: William Heckle
Officers: William Heckle, Secretary; Julia Baird [1947] Director; George William Guinness [1956] Director; Kim Gunn [1972] Director; William Heckle [1956] Director; David Jones [1948] Director; Paul Robert Jones [1987] Assistant Director; Jon Keats [1966] Director

Cavitech Solutions (Holdings) Limited
Incorporated: 1 February 2016
Net Worth Deficit: £218,865 *Total Assets:* £7,431,120
Registered Office: Corpacq House, 1 Goose Green, Altrincham, Cheshire, WA14 1DW
Activities: Activities of head offices
Officers: Martyn Pearce Robinson [1969] Director; Stephen James Scott [1978] Director; Christopher Donald Smith [1959] Director

Cavitech Solutions Limited
Incorporated: 10 December 1990 *Employees:* 48
Net Worth: £6,976,668 *Total Assets:* £11,666,523
Registered Office: Corpacq House, 1 Goose Green, Altrincham, Cheshire, WA14 1DW
Activities: Manufacture of plastics and rubber machinery
Officers: Martyn Pearce Robinson [1969] Director/Engineer; Stephen James Scott [1978] Director; Christopher Donald Smith [1959] Director/Engineer

Caygill Holdings Limited
Incorporated: 27 April 2007 *Employees:* 48
Net Worth: £6,493,345 *Total Assets:* £16,830,668
Registered Office: LCW House, Chainbar Road, Cleckheaton, W Yorks, BD19 3QF
Activities: Sale of new cars and light motor vehicles
Shareholders: Andrew Martin Caygill; Susan Caroline Caygill
Officers: Susan Caroline Caygill, Secretary; Andrew Martin Caygill [1956] Director; Susan Caroline Caygill [1959] Director

CBL Finance (Holdings) UK Limited
Incorporated: 5 January 2012
Net Worth Deficit: £22,240,000 *Total Assets:* £88,906,000
Registered Office: Caddick Road, Knowsley Business Park, Prescot, Merseyside, L34 9HP
Activities: Dormant company
Parent: ALS Limited
Officers: Michael Paul Pearson, Secretary; John David Smyth [1965] Finance Director; Christopher David Walker [1972] Director

CBL Finance (UK) Limited
Incorporated: 5 January 2012
Net Worth: £111,343,000 *Total Assets:* £111,384,000
Registered Office: Caddick Road, Knowsley Business Park, Prescot, Merseyside, L34 9HP
Activities: Dormant company
Parent: ALS Limited
Officers: Michael Paul Pearson, Secretary; John David Smyth [1965] Finance Director; Christopher David Walker [1972] Director

CCL Secure (Holding) Limited
Incorporated: 4 September 2009
Net Worth: £61,363,636 *Total Assets:* £61,363,636
Registered Office: Station Road, Wigton, Cumbria, CA7 9BG
Activities: Activities of head offices
Parent: Innovia Group (Holding 3) Ltd
Officers: Dominic Mark Heaton [1972] Director; Geoffrey Thomas Martin [1954] Director/Chief Executive [American]; Neil Richard Sanders [1977] Director/General Manager

CCL Secure Limited
Incorporated: 4 November 2013 *Employees:* 60
Net Worth: £5,942,000 *Total Assets:* £35,711,000
Registered Office: Station Road, Wigton, Cumbria, CA7 9BG
Activities: Other manufacturing n.e.c.
Parent: CCL Secure (Holding) Ltd
Officers: Dominic Mark Heaton [1972] Director; Geoffrey Thomas Martin [1954] Director/Chief Executive [American]; Neil Richard Sanders [1977] Director/General Manager; James Sebastian Smith-Saville [1991] Director/Chartered Accountant

CDL Group Holdings Limited
Incorporated: 11 August 2000 *Employees:* 625
Net Worth: £37,146,620 *Total Assets:* £46,194,256
Registered Office: Strata House, Kings Reach Road, Stockport, Cheshire, SK4 2HD
Activities: Other information technology service activities
Officers: Melissa Fiona Johnson, Secretary; Thomas Harland Hogg [1935] Director; Gary Arthur Johnson [1966] Director; Melissa Fiona Johnson [1966] Director/HR Manager

Cedar 2015 Limited
Incorporated: 9 January 2015 *Employees:* 2
Net Worth: £46,331,000 *Total Assets:* £46,331,000
Registered Office: Second Avenue, Poynton Industrial Estate, Poynton, Cheshire, SK12 1ND
Activities: Non-trading company
Parent: Steel Partners Holdings L.P.
Officers: Jack Howard [1961] Director/President of Steel Partners LP [American]

Celestica Limited
Incorporated: 23 July 1996 *Employees:* 25
Net Worth Deficit: £43,285,480 *Total Assets:* £83,818,064
Registered Office: One St Peter's Square, Manchester, M2 3DE
Activities: Wholesale of computers, computer peripheral equipment and software
Shareholders: Celestica Inc; Celestica (UK) Holdings Limited
Officers: Robert Ellis, Secretary; Ioana Mariana Balint [1981] Finance Director [Romanian]; Kevin Walsh [1968] Director/VP AMS & Healthtech [Irish]

Cellbeam Limited
Incorporated: 20 February 2003 *Employees:* 42
Net Worth: £4,113,000 *Total Assets:* £9,203,000
Registered Office: Brandlesholme House, Brandlesholme Road, Bury, Lancs, BL8 1JJ
Activities: Manufacture of metal structures and parts of structures
Officers: David Michael William Hodgkiss [1948] Director; Susan Katrina Hodgkiss [1950] Director; Robert Redgate [1957] Finance Director; Gary Simmons [1959] Director/Structural Engineer

Celtpower Limited
Incorporated: 23 October 1991
Net Worth: £4,746,000 *Total Assets:* £14,616,000
Registered Office: 3 Prenton Way, Prenton, Birkenhead, Merseyside, CH43 3ET
Activities: Production of electricity
Parent: ScottishPower Renewables (UK) Limited
Officers: Andrew Philip, Secretary; Stuart Mason [1965] Construction Director; Robert David Pryce [1972] Director/Operations & Maintenance Manager; Roy Scott [1964] Director Control & Administration; Tetsuya Suwabe [1970] Managing Director [Japanese]

Cend Limited
Incorporated: 7 September 2000
Net Worth: £15,647,000 *Total Assets:* £53,364,000
Registered Office: 5th Floor, Voyager House, Chicago Avenue, Manchester Airport, Manchester, M90 3DQ
Activities: Other retail sale not in stores, stalls or markets
Parent: The Hut IHC Limited
Officers: James Pochin, Secretary; John Andrew Gallemore [1969] Director/Accountant; James Patrick Pochin [1976] Group Legal Director

Centenary Property Developments LLP
Incorporated: 20 March 2007
Net Worth: £6,464,762 *Total Assets:* £11,459,365
Registered Office: Clarendon Business Centre, 38 Clarendon Road, Eccles, Manchester, M30 9ES
Officers: Gerard Anthony Mason [1964] Member

Central Glass Europe Limited
Incorporated: 30 July 2003 *Employees:* 4
Net Worth: £22,600,654 *Total Assets:* £24,225,632
Registered Office: Whitefield Road, Bredbury, Stockport, Cheshire, SK6 2QR
Activities: Agents specialised in the sale of other particular products
Major Shareholder: Shuichi Sarasawa
Officers: Andrew James Hiett, Secretary; Minoru Irisawa [1960] Director [Japanese]; Mitsuru Tanuma [1961] Director [Japanese]; Nobuyuki Tokunaga [1961] Director/General Manager [Japanese]

Centre Island Birmingham Limited
Incorporated: 25 August 2005 *Employees:* 129
Net Worth: £7,776,363 *Total Assets:* £46,045,164
Registered Office: 62 Castle Street, Liverpool, L2 7LQ
Activities: Hotels and similar accommodation
Parent: Centre Island Hotels Limited
Officers: Mark Simon Sutton, Secretary; Mark Christopher Foster [1964] Director/Hotelier; Michael Peter O'Donoghue [1952] Director [Irish]; Mark Simon Sutton [1971] Director/Accountant

Centre Island Development Company (1997) Limited
Incorporated: 13 January 1997 *Employees:* 97
Net Worth: £8,824,690 *Total Assets:* £12,009,493
Registered Office: 62 Castle Street, Liverpool, L2 7LQ
Activities: Hotels and similar accommodation
Parent: Centre Island Hotels Limited
Officers: Mark Simon Sutton, Secretary; Mark Christopher Foster [1964] Director/Hotelier; Michael Peter Odonoghue [1952] Director [Irish]; Mark Simon Sutton [1971] Director/Accountant

Centre Island Development Company Limited
Incorporated: 19 June 1992 *Employees:* 121
Net Worth: £10,145,983 *Total Assets:* £21,786,080
Registered Office: 62 Castle Street, Liverpool, L2 7LQ
Activities: Hotels and similar accommodation
Parent: Centre Island Hotels Limited
Officers: Mark Simon Sutton, Secretary; Mark Christopher Foster [1964] Director/Hotelier; Michael Peter Odonoghue [1952] Director [Irish]; Mark Simon Sutton [1971] Director/Accountant

Centre Island Hotels Limited
Incorporated: 22 September 1998 *Employees:* 643
Net Worth: £35,680,088 *Total Assets:* £91,672,888
Registered Office: 62 Castle Street, Liverpool, L2 7LQ
Activities: Hotels and similar accommodation
Parent: Travan Services Limited
Officers: Mark Simon Sutton, Secretary; Mark Christopher Foster [1964] Director/Hotelier; Dennis Paul Kennedy [1943] Director [Irish]; Michael Peter O Donoghue [1952] Director [Irish]; Donal Ring [1946] Director [Irish]; Mark Simon Sutton [1971] Director/Accountant

Centre Island Preston Limited
Incorporated: 24 September 1999 *Employees:* 58
Net Worth: £2,996,346 *Total Assets:* £8,572,939
Registered Office: 62 Castle Street, Liverpool, L2 7LQ
Activities: Hotels and similar accommodation
Parent: Centre Island Hotels
Officers: Mark Simon Sutton, Secretary; Mark Christopher Foster [1964] Director/Hotelier; Michael Peter O Donoghue [1952] Director [Irish]; Mark Simon Sutton [1971] Director/Accountant

Centrelease Limited
Incorporated: 13 November 1982
Net Worth Deficit: £4,013,963 *Total Assets:* £12,628,807
Registered Office: 2 Mount Street, Manchester, M2 5WQ
Activities: Management of real estate on a fee or contract basis
Parent: Wrather Group Limited
Officers: Paul Robert Greenlees, Secretary; Patrick Franks [1965] Director/Architect; William Harry Wrather [1939] Director

Centriforce Products Limited
Incorporated: 9 April 1997 *Employees:* 138
Net Worth: £7,321,127 *Total Assets:* £10,695,922
Registered Office: Errington Works, 14-16 Derby Road, Bootle, Liverpool, L20 8EE
Activities: Manufacture of plastic plates, sheets, tubes and profiles
Parent: Plastic Recycling Limited
Officers: Simon John Carroll [1967] Managing Director; Dr David Wayne Cartmell [1961] Director/Chairman; Richard Nicholas Keighley [1959] Finance Director

Centriq Group Limited
Incorporated: 31 July 2009 *Employees:* 123
Net Worth: £7,505,000 *Total Assets:* £16,745,000
Registered Office: Neptune Court, Hallam Way, Whitehills, Blackpool, Lancs, FY4 5LZ
Activities: Other information technology service activities
Parent: Korber Logistics Systems GmbH
Officers: Chadwick Collins [1975] Director/Manager [American]; Bertram Rainer Salzinger [1959] Director [German]; David Raymond Stanhope [1964] Director

Centurion Truck Rental Ltd
Incorporated: 28 January 1948 *Employees:* 7
Net Worth: £7,975,344 *Total Assets:* £24,748,194
Registered Office: Stakehill Industrial Estate, Middleton, Manchester, M24 2RW
Activities: Renting and leasing of cars and light motor vehicles
Parent: Ballyvesey Holdings
Officers: Alan Thomson, Secretary; David Nigel Birkmyre [1952] Director; Harold Hugh Montgomery [1948] Director/Haulier; Alan William Thomson [1972] Director/Chartered Accountant

Century Healthcare Limited
Incorporated: 7 May 1987 *Employees:* 377
Net Worth: £9,772,639 *Total Assets:* £14,294,034
Registered Office: Temple Chambers, 296 Clifton Drive South, Lytham St Annes, Lancs, FY8 1LH
Activities: Other human health activities
Shareholders: Lorraine Matta; Jeremy Heney
Officers: Jeremy Heney, Secretary; Jeremy Heney [1966] Managing Director; Lorraine Matta [1943] Director/Chairman

CEP Biomass Energy Limited
Incorporated: 15 December 2014
Net Worth: £23,112,296 *Total Assets:* £61,312,988
Registered Office: Eversheds House, 70 Great Bridgewater Street, Manchester, M1 5ES
Activities: Activities of production holding companies
Officers: Joost Hessel Louis Bergsma [1965] Director/Fund Manager [Dutch]; Peter Robert Dickson [1964] Director/Chartered Engineer

CEP Biomass Limited
Incorporated: 19 May 2011
Net Worth: £101,094,336 *Total Assets:* £107,271,952
Registered Office: Eversheds House, 70 Great Bridgewater Street, Manchester, M1 5ES
Activities: Activities of production holding companies
Officers: Joost Hessel Louis Bergsma [1965] Director/Fund Manager [Dutch]; Peter Robert Dickson [1964] Director

CEP Teesside Biomass Limited
Incorporated: 13 August 2015
Net Worth: £25,318,722 *Total Assets:* £69,967,736
Registered Office: Eversheds House, 70 Great Bridgewater Street, Manchester, M1 5ES
Activities: Activities of production holding companies
Officers: Joost Hessel Louis Bergsma [1965] Director/Fund Manager [Dutch]; Peter Robert Dickson [1964] Director/Chartered Engineer

Cepen Lodge Limited
Incorporated: 19 May 2008 *Employees:* 75
Net Worth: £1,764,000 *Total Assets:* £8,016,000
Registered Office: Norcliffe House, Station Road, Wilmslow, Cheshire, SK9 1BU
Activities: Other human health activities
Parent: Optimum FS Care Developments Limited
Officers: Abigail Mattison, Secretary; Ryan Stuart MacAskill [1975] Director; Gregory Laurence Newman [1988] Director/Investment Professional; Jeremy Robert Arthur Richardson [1970] Director; Dr Maureen Claire Royston [1960] Director; Phillip Gary Thomas [1978] Director

Cequent UK Limited
Incorporated: 24 May 2012
Net Worth: £20,925,988 *Total Assets:* £35,046,564
Registered Office: Drome Road, Deeside Industrial Park, Deeside, Flintshire, CH5 2NY
Activities: Manufacture of other parts and accessories for motor vehicles
Parent: Horizon Global Corporation
Officers: Jay Samuel Goldbaum, Secretary; Paul Charles Caruso [1957] Director/Regional Vice President [American]; David Gerard Rice [1963] Director [American]

Cerberus Holdings Limited
Incorporated: 24 December 2008 *Employees:* 86
Net Worth: £4,575,608 *Total Assets:* £9,137,558
Registered Office: 26 Missouri Avenue, Salford, M50 2NP
Activities: Activities of head offices
Shareholders: Andrew William Roe; Simon Merrett
Officers: James Samuel Walker, Secretary/Chartered Certified Accountant; Simon Merrett [1975] Director; Andrew William Roe [1962] Director; Carol Patricia Roe [1963] Director; Sean William Roe [1990] Director; Sarah Ann Roscoe [1971] Director; James Samuel Walker [1967] Director/Chartered Certified Accountant; Andrew James Wilson [1950] Director/Solicitor

Certas Energy UK Limited
Incorporated: 26 February 2001 *Employees:* 2,348
Net Worth: £36,484,000 *Total Assets:* £812,454,976
Registered Office: 302 Bridgewater Place, Birchwood Park, Birchwood, Warrington, Cheshire, WA3 6XG
Activities: Wholesale of other fuels and related products
Parent: Energy Acquisitions UK Limited
Officers: Emma Louise Clark, Secretary; Daire Keating [1978] Director [Irish]; Daniel Stephen Paul Little [1976] Finance Director; Edward Gerard O'Brien [1970] Managing Director [Irish]; Stuart Sealey [1960] HSE Director; Steven Michael Taylor [1959] Managing Director; Paul John Williams [1968] Director; Emma Wordsworth-Higham [1971] HR Director

CF Asset Finance Limited
Incorporated: 19 May 1999
Net Worth Deficit: £279,000 *Total Assets:* £14,097,000
Registered Office: Charterhall House, Charterhall Drive, Chester, CH88 3AN
Activities: Credit granting by non-deposit taking finance houses and other specialist consumer credit grantors
Parent: Bank of Scotland Equipment Finance Limited
Officers: David Dermot Hennessey, Secretary; Christopher Michael Adams [1982] Director; Richard Andrew Jones [1972] Marketing Director; James Owen Trace [1963] Director/Senior Manager

CF Fertilisers UK Group Limited
Incorporated: 12 July 2007
Net Worth: £239,178,000 *Total Assets:* £239,178,000
Registered Office: Ince, Chester, CH2 4LB
Activities: Manufacture of fertilizers and nitrogen compounds
Parent: CF Industries (UK) Limited
Officers: John Braddock, Secretary; John Richard Braddock [1965] Director; Jennifer Margaret Halliday [1960] Finance Director; David Paul Hopkins [1956] Director

CF Fertilisers UK Limited
Incorporated: 27 October 1997 *Employees:* 597
Net Worth: £147,232,000 *Total Assets:* £339,275,008
Registered Office: Head Office Building, Ince, Chester, CH2 4LB
Activities: Manufacture of fertilizers and nitrogen compounds
Parent: CF Industries Holdings Inc.
Officers: John Braddock, Secretary; John Richard Braddock [1965] Director; Jennifer Margaret Halliday [1960] Finance Director; David Paul Hopkins [1956] Sales Director; David Timothy Little [1964] Manufacturing Director [American]

CF Industries (UK) Limited
Incorporated: 16 July 2015
Net Worth: £621,145,984 *Total Assets:* £679,062,016
Registered Office: Head Office, Ince, Chester, CH2 4LB
Activities: Manufacture of fertilizers and nitrogen compounds
Parent: CF Industries Holdings, Inc.
Officers: John Braddock, Secretary; John Richard Braddock [1965] Director/Solicitor; Jennifer Margaret Halliday [1960] Finance Director; David Paul Hopkins [1956] Managing Director

CFS Management Services Limited
Incorporated: 15 September 2005 *Employees:* 2,764
Net Worth: £46,447,000 *Total Assets:* £108,111,000
Registered Office: 1 Angel Square, Manchester, M60 0AG
Activities: Other business support service activities n.e.c.
Officers: Simon Andrew Bourne [1968] Director/Chief Information Officer; Andrew Philip Lee [1963] Director; Stuart Anthony Roberts [1962] Director of CFSMS; Jonathan Michael Wormald [1977] Financial Control Director

CGC Events Limited
Incorporated: 2 October 1944 *Employees:* 627
Net Worth: £14,629,950 *Total Assets:* £20,069,726
Registered Office: Manchester Arena, Hunts Bank Approach, Manchester, M3 1AR
Activities: Event catering activities
Officers: John Francis Burns, Secretary; John Francis Burns [1957] Director [American]; Harold Westley [1948] Director [American]

CH Holding Limited
Incorporated: 1 July 2015 *Employees:* 58
Net Worth: £319,140 *Total Assets:* £12,466,447
Registered Office: c/o Edwards Veeder (UK) Limited, Ground Floor, 4 Broadgate, Broadway Business Park, Chadderton, Oldham, Lancs, OL9 9XA
Activities: Other professional, scientific and technical activities n.e.c.
Major Shareholder: Harmil Singh
Officers: Harmil Singh [1962] Director/President & CEO [Singaporean]

CHA Technologies Group Public Limited Company
Incorporated: 20 July 2000 *Employees:* 280
Net Worth: £41 955,556 *Total Assets:* £54,280,224
Registered Office: Longshaw Industrial Park, Highfield Road, Blackburn, BB2 3AS
Activities: Manufacture of other textiles n.e.c.
Officers: Peter Roderick Martin, Secretary; Jacques Edmond Joseph Marie-Pierre Boubal [1949] Director/Manager [French]; Teddy Sou Inn [1941] Director/Manager [Chinese]; Peter Roderick Martin [1959] Director/Chief Financial Officer

CHA Textiles Limited
Incorporated: 2 April 1990 *Employees:* 9
Net Worth: £13,034,000 *Total Assets:* £13,327,000
Registered Office: Longshaw Industrial Park, Highfield Road, Blackburn, BB2 3AS
Activities: Manufacture of other textiles n.e.c.
Parent: CHA Technologies Group PLC
Officers: Jacques Edmond Joseph Marie-Pierre Boubal [1949] Director [French]; Michel Leon Louis Ghislain Gallez [1958] Director/Financial Controller [Belgian]; Teddy Sou-Yung Inn [1941] Director [American]; Peter Roderick Martin [1959] Director/Chief Financial Officer; Madeline May Lung Wong [1940] Director; Yue Shing Wong [1941] Director/Textile Technologist [Canadian]

Chadderton Total-Care Unit Limited
Incorporated: 30 September 1985 *Employees:* 239
Net Worth: £2,884,572 *Total Assets:* £9,388,738
Registered Office: 31 Sackville Street, Manchester, M1 3LZ
Activities: Other business support service activities n.e.c.
Parent: Alwen Holdings Ltd
Officers: Susan Rene Lomax, Secretary; Alan Miller [1948] Director/Property Developer

Chadwicks of Bury Limited
Incorporated: 1 July 1996 *Employees:* 112
Net Worth: £14,442,000 *Total Assets:* £16,163,000
Registered Office: Villiers Street, Bury, Lancs, BL9 6BS
Activities: Other manufacturing n.e.c.
Officers: John Chadwick [1955] Director

Chain Link Holding Company Limited
Incorporated: 14 March 2006
Net Worth: £2,927,460 *Total Assets:* £7,454,978
Registered Office: Suites 5 & 6, The Printworks, Hey Road, Barrow, Clitheroe, Lancs, BB7 9WB
Activities: Activities of other holding companies n.e.c.
Major Shareholder: Andrew Geoffrey Duckett
Officers: Andrew Geoffrey Duckett [1961] Director

Chairs Limited
Incorporated: 14 May 1992 *Employees:* 198
Net Worth: £35,524,484 *Total Assets:* £40,944,384
Registered Office: Metcalfe Drive, Altham Industrial Estate, Accrington, Lancs, BB5 5SS
Activities: Wholesale of household goods (other than musical instruments) n.e.c
Parent: Simonstone Estate Limited
Officers: Kathleen Murphy, Secretary; David Bovingdon [1946] Director/Business Executive; Diane Wendy Bovingdon [1954] Director/Business Executive

Chalkfree Limited
Incorporated: 10 September 2004 *Employees:* 3
Net Worth Deficit: £60,385,000 *Total Assets:* £19,993,000
Registered Office: Promethean House, Lower Philips Road, Whitebirk Industrial Estate, Blackburn, Lancs, BB1 5TH
Activities: Activities of head offices
Parent: Promethean World Limited
Officers: Ian David Curtis [1962] Sales Director

The Challenge Academy Trust
Incorporated: 24 March 2017 *Employees:* 23
Net Worth: £82,387,000 *Total Assets:* £93,267,000
Registered Office: Priestley College, Loushers Lane, Warrington, Cheshire, WA4 6RD
Activities: Primary education
Officers: Matthew William Grant [1957] Director/Principal; Jane Griffiths [1958] Director/Diocesan Schools Adviser; Paul Hinds [1969] Director; Gemma Victoria Elizabeth Johnson [1982] Cultural Director; Tobias Todd MacOrmac [1971] Director/Chairman & CEO; Maureen Kathleen Mellor [1947] Director; John Stephen Monaghan [1949] Director; Neil Pearson [1963] Director/Commercial Manager; Howard Wilson Platt [1955] Director; Stuart Norman Titchard [1969] Director/Head of Supply Chain; Linda Jane Waterson [1967] Director/Auditor; Stephen Nicholas Whatmore [1953] Director; Sheila Yates [1953] Director

Challenger Text Limited
Incorporated: 19 July 2005
Net Worth Deficit: £2,311,098 *Total Assets:* £9,128,525
Registered Office: 10 Riverview, The Embankment, Vale Road, Heaton Mersey, Stockport, Cheshire, SK4 3GN
Activities: Development of building projects
Parent: Windowhome Limited
Officers: Alan Philip David Musry, Secretary; Alan Philip David Musry [1963] Director/Chartered Accountant; Michael Shwartz [1952] Director

Champion Limited
Incorporated: 8 April 2003 *Employees:* 603
Net Worth: £4,291,935 *Total Assets:* £10,559,570
Registered Office: 1 Worsley Court, High Street, Worsley, Manchester, M28 3NJ
Activities: Activities of head offices
Shareholder: Gerard Cosgrove
Officers: Karen Lesley Baird, Secretary; Karen Lesley Baird [1971] Director/Accountant; Gerard Cosgrove [1958] Director/Accountant

Chandos Civil Engineering Limited
Incorporated: 16 December 2002 *Employees:* 23
Net Worth: £1,194,522 *Total Assets:* £11,108,519
Registered Office: Chandos House, Oak Green Business Park, Earl Road, Cheadle Hulme, Stockport, Cheshire, SK8 6QL
Activities: Construction of other civil engineering projects n.e.c.
Parent: Molloy Investments Limited
Officers: Daniel Molloy [1983] Director; David Molloy [1974] Director/Groundworker

Channon Holdings Limited
Incorporated: 20 March 2013 *Employees:* 12
Net Worth: £4,420,979 *Total Assets:* £6,825,512
Registered Office: Midland Buildings, 19a Briggate, Shipley, W Yorks, BD17 7BP
Activities: Financial management
Officers: Sharon Louise Wooler, Secretary; Gary Andrew Scott Channon [1967] Director/Investment Manager; Sedef Channon [1964] Director/Investment Manager [Turkish]; Steven David Tatters [1967] Director/Investment Manager

Chapel House Holdings Ltd
Incorporated: 7 December 1989 *Employees:* 221
Net Worth: £7,290,947 *Total Assets:* £19,114,972
Registered Office: 603 Liverpool Road, Ainsdale, Southport, Merseyside, PR8 3NG
Activities: Sale of new cars and light motor vehicles
Major Shareholder: Nicholas Coen
Officers: Julian Murray Edghill, Secretary; Nicholas Coen [1960] Director; Nicholas Greig Duffield [1965] Director/Group Accountant

Character World Bidco Limited
Incorporated: 31 March 2008 *Employees:* 2
Net Worth Deficit: £13,186,716 *Total Assets:* £18,448,112
Registered Office: c/o UHY Hacker Young, St James Building, 79 Oxford Street, Manchester, M1 6HT
Activities: Other business support service activities n.e.c.
Parent: Charater World Holdco Limited
Officers: Mark Alexander Harry Schweiger, Secretary; Daniel Eric Schweiger [1971] Director; Mark Alexander Harry Schweiger [1974] Director

Character World Holdco Limited
Incorporated: 25 March 2008 *Employees:* 2
Net Worth Deficit: £7,809,095 *Total Assets:* £18,007,836
Registered Office: c/o UHY Hacker Young, St James Building, 79 Oxford Street, Manchester, M1 6HT
Activities: Activities of head offices
Parent: Ensco 1089 Limited
Officers: Mark Alexander Harry Schweiger, Secretary; Daniel Eric Schweiger [1971] Director; Mark Alexander Harry Schweiger [1974] Director

Character World Limited
Incorporated: 14 February 2001 *Employees:* 77
Net Worth: £18,900,434 *Total Assets:* £29,931,492
Registered Office: c/o UHY Hacker Young, St James Building, 79 Oxford Street, Manchester, M1 6HT
Activities: Other business support service activities n.e.c.
Parent: Character World Bidco Limited
Officers: Mark Schweiger, Secretary; Karen Creed [1975] Director; Adam Howarth [1971] Director; Timothy Richard Kilby [1973] Brand Director; Andreas Niedergesaess [1969] Director [German]; Daniel Eric Schweiger [1971] Director; Mark Alexander Harry Schweiger [1974] Director

Chargepoint Technology Limited
Incorporated: 17 November 2008 *Employees:* 62
Net Worth: £7,228,427 *Total Assets:* £11,340,564
Registered Office: 58 Evans Road, Liverpool, L24 9PB
Activities: Manufacture of taps and valves
Parent: Chargepoint Technology Holdings Limited
Officers: John Goodwin, Secretary; Christopher Jan Pawel Eccles [1978] Director; Antony Peter O'Sullivan [1961] Director; Andrew Mark White [1968] Director

Chariet Limited
Incorporated: 1 May 1996 *Employees:* 131
Net Worth: £12,411,824 *Total Assets:* £16,094,281
Registered Office: c/o Edwards Veeder (UK) Limited, Ground Floor, 4 Broadgate, Broadway Business Park, Chadderton, Oldham, Lancs, OL9 9XA
Activities: Hotels and similar accommodation
Parent: Seacare Scarborough Limited
Officers: Sin How Choo [1957] Director [Singaporean]; Chye Teen Lim [1981] Director [Singaporean]; Thizi Chee Lim [1965] Director [Malaysian]; Ming Yee Mindy Wong [1976] Director [Singaporean]

Charities Trust
Incorporated: 24 June 1987 *Employees:* 31
Net Worth: £41,905,032 *Total Assets:* £42,488,072
Registered Office: Suite 22, Century Building, Tower Street, Brunswick Business Park, Liverpool, L3 4BJ
Activities: Other service activities n.e.c.
Officers: Sir Michael James Bibby [1963] Director; Mark John Blakeman [1970] Director/NHS Manager; John Jones [1956] Director; Graham John Morris [1949] Director/Management Consultant; Elizabeth Ann Perry [1950] Director; Leslie John Thomas [1962] Director

Chase Property Developments Limited
Incorporated: 3 December 1997 *Employees:* 3
Net Worth: £1,104,762 *Total Assets:* £9,727,828
Registered Office: The Corn Exchange, Brunswick Street, Liverpool, L2 0PJ
Activities: Buying and selling of own real estate
Shareholders: Andrew Peter Mason; Antonia Clare Goodall; Christopher Ian Mason; Peter Wild Bullivant; Paul Pearce
Officers: Ben Desmond Harvey, Secretary; Andrew Peter Mason [1965] Director/Chartered Surveyor; Geoffrey Owen Mason [1940] Director/Surveyor; Paul Pearce [1965] Director/Chartered Surveyor

Chase Templeton Limited
Incorporated: 8 January 1997 *Employees:* 118
Net Worth: £3,550,809 *Total Assets:* £20,506,080
Registered Office: 5 Arkwright Court, Blackburn Interchange, Darwen, Lancs, BB3 0FG
Activities: Non-life insurance
Officers: Iain Richard Picton Laws [1968] Director; Robert Laurance Worrell [1968] Director/Chartered Insurance Broker

Cheadle Hulme School
Incorporated: 10 August 1999 *Employees:* 277
Net Worth: £13,236,000 *Total Assets:* £20,768,000
Registered Office: Cheadle Hulme School, Claremont Road, Cheadle Hulme, Cheadle, Cheshire, SK8 6EF
Activities: Other education n.e.c.
Officers: Sue Kershaw, Secretary; Kamal Basran [1951] Director/Company Owner; Michael John Birchall [1967] Director/Solicitor; Joanne Elizabeth Birkett [1975] Director/Partner; Michael James Bolingbroke [1965] Director; Catherine Jane Boyd [1963] Director; Peter John Driver [1954] Director/Police Officer; Philip Robert Johnson [1946] Director/Chartered Accountant; Kay Marie Marshall [1959] Director/Head of Manchester Pharmacy School, University; Dr David Noel Riley [1958] Director/General Medical Practitioner; Christopher Andrew Roberts [1971] Director/Surveyor; Joanne Squire [1962] Director/HR Manager; Martin Gavin Tyley [1974] Director/Partner

Checkers Safety Group UK Ltd
Incorporated: 17 April 2015 *Employees:* 127
Net Worth Deficit: £9,706,000 *Total Assets:* £30,382,000
Registered Office: 3rd Floor, 1 Ashley Road, Altrincham, Cheshire, WA14 2DT
Activities: Manufacture of other plastic products
Officers: Jonathan Jacob Giardina [1970] Director/President & CEO - Checkers Safety Group [American]; Mark David McElhinny [1967] Director/President, CEO Justrite Mfg [American]; Douglas Waugaman [1958] Director/Accountant [American]

Checkfree Solutions Limited
Incorporated: 5 March 1992 *Employees:* 91
Net Worth: £28,305,416 *Total Assets:* £46,622,320
Registered Office: Eversheds House, 70 Great Bridgewater Street, Manchester, M1 5ES
Activities: Other information technology service activities
Parent: Fiserv Worldwide Holdings Limited
Officers: Derek John Dyamond [1962] Finance Director; David Gillingham [1974] Director, Finance; Peter Lincoln Holbrook [1969] Director/Chief Financial Officer, International Group, FISE [American]; John James Smith [1959] Managing Director, Fiserv EMEA

Cheetham Church of England Community Academy
Incorporated: 14 October 2011 *Employees:* 96
Net Worth: £6,782,883 *Total Assets:* £7,371,718
Registered Office: c/o Cheetham Church of England Community Academy, Halliwell Lane, Manchester, M8 9FR
Activities: Primary education
Officers: Sadaf Adeel [1985] Director/Student; Jawad Amin [1978] Director/Solicitor; Rachel Clare Bruno [1974] Director/Deputy Headteacher; Dr Maureen Elizabeth Cain [1947] Director/Education Tutor; Florence Karen Carter [1963] Director/Headteacher; Samuel Oladele Dada [1951] Director; Reverend Sarah Louise Fletcher [1972] Director/Vicar; Ray Riaz [1978] Director/Accounts Manager; Mary Upton [1935] Director/Retired Headteacher; Yau Jim Yip [1958] Director/Lecturer

Cheetham Hill Construction Limited
Incorporated: 23 March 1966 *Employees:* 119
Net Worth: £8,008,000 *Total Assets:* £12,084,000
Registered Office: Woodhill Road, Bury, Lancs, BL8 1AR
Activities: Construction of water projects
Parent: Drillwave Ltd
Officers: Katie Myers, Secretary; Claire Chamberlain [1973] HR Director; Howard Chamberlain [1946] Director/Construction Engineer; Sean Isherwood [1967] Director/Construction Plant Manager; Katie Myers [1975] Finance Director; Philip Ross [1952] Commercial Director

Cheltenham and Gloucester Omnibus Company Limited
Incorporated: 8 April 1983 *Employees:* 710
Net Worth: £11,723,000 *Total Assets:* £24,915,000
Registered Office: c/o Stagecoach Services Limited, One Stockport Exchange, 20 Railway Road, Stockport, Cheshire, SK1 3SW
Activities: Other urban, suburban or metropolitan passenger land transport (not underground, metro or similar)
Parent: Stagecoach Bus Holdings Limited
Officers: Michael John Vaux, Secretary; Colin Brown [1968] Director/Accountant; Rupert Miles Cox [1980] Managing Director; Arnold Mark Threapleton [1954] Managing Director

Cherry Tree Investments Limited
Incorporated: 9 August 1983 *Employees:* 4
Net Worth: £5,850,126 *Total Assets:* £10,718,974
Registered Office: 13-15 Brewery Yard, Deva City Office Park, Trinity Way, Salford, M3 7BB
Activities: Development of building projects
Officers: Evelyn Paul, Secretary/Director; Evelyn Paul [1954] Director; Gregory Mark Paul [1982] Director; Ian Simon Paul [1955] Director; Oliver Michael Paul [1981] Director

Cheselden Limited
Incorporated: 15 May 2007
Net Worth: £1,192,711,040 *Total Assets:* £1,192,711,040
Registered Office: Premex House, Futura Park, Middlebrook, Bolton, Lancs, BL6 6SX
Activities: Other professional, scientific and technical activities n.e.c.
Parent: Premex Group Limited
Officers: Caroline Emily Elizabeth Russell, Secretary; Donald Stuart Fowler [1973] Director; Doug Laver [1965] Finance Director

Chesford Grange Estates LLP
Incorporated: 10 December 2004
Net Worth: £4,040,702 *Total Assets:* £7,487,839
Registered Office: 18 Chesford Grange, Warrington, Cheshire, WA1 4RQ
Officers: Jane Walsh [1971] Member; Robert Edward Cheshire Walsh [1972] Member

Cheshire Academies Trust
Incorporated: 18 June 2012 *Employees:* 61
Net Worth: £5,846,395 *Total Assets:* £6,842,594
Registered Office: Kelsall Primary School, Flat Lane, Kelsall, Cheshire, CW6 0PU
Activities: Primary education
Officers: Alison Jean Ashley [1977] Director/Headteacher; Alison Brennan [1974] Director/Solicitor; Steven Michael Ellis [1978] Director/Headmaster; Robert Ford [1968] Director/Principal; Martin Huber [1964] Director/Retired; Jon Moorhouse [1966] Director/Architect; Janet Myers [1970] Director/Training Consultant; David Alan Wearing [1972] Director/Headteacher; Dr Harry John Ziman [1963] Director/Consultant

Cheshire Datasystems Limited
Incorporated: 11 May 2000 *Employees:* 578
Net Worth: £3,795,077 *Total Assets:* £22,721,498
Registered Office: Strata House, Kings Reach Road, Stockport, Cheshire, SK4 2HD
Activities: Other information technology service activities
Officers: Melissa Fiona Johnson, Secretary; Steven Aldred [1965] Finance Director; Stuart Bishop [1967] Director of Service; Thomas Harland Hogg [1935] Director; Gary Arthur Johnson [1966] Director; Melissa Fiona Johnson [1966] Director/HR Manager; Nigel Christopher Phillips [1969] Commercial Director; Frank Robinson [1958] Human Resources Director; Andrew Wormleighton [1972] Director of Software and Technology

Cheshire Mouldings & Woodturnings Limited
Incorporated: 29 November 1988 *Employees:* 67
Net Worth: £3,569,406 *Total Assets:* £20,388,552
Registered Office: Unit 7 Normans Road, Sutton, St Helens, Merseyside, WA9 4JQ
Activities: Other manufacturing n.e.c.
Officers: Joanne Graham, Company Secretary; John Carney [1968] Managing Director; Paul Carney [1969] Director/Works Manager; Philip Carney [1973] Director/Works Manager; Susan Carney [1945] Director/Secretary; Joanne Graham [1971] Director/Company Secretary

Cheshire Salt Limited
Incorporated: 1 June 2007
Net Worth: £24,077,000 *Total Assets:* £24,077,000
Registered Office: Mond House, Winnington, Northwich, Cheshire, CW8 4DT
Activities: Activities of head offices
Parent: Cheshire Salt Holdings Limited
Officers: David Philip William Davies, Secretary; Jonathan Laurence Abbotts [1964] Director; Dr Martin John Ashcroft [1969] Managing Director; Dr Ladan Iravanian [1960] Director

Chesnara PLC
Incorporated: 29 October 2003
Net Worth: £451,656,000 *Total Assets:* £8,443,383,808
Registered Office: 2nd Floor, Building 4, West Strand, Preston, Lancs, PR1 8UY
Activities: Activities of head offices
Officers: Alastair Lonie, Secretary; David Sheldon Brand [1954] Director/Actuary; Jane Dale [1960] Director/Chairman; John Vincent Deane [1958] Director; Peter William Mason [1950] Director; Veronica Susan Oak [1961] Director; David Anthony Rimmington [1968] Director/Accountant

Chess Limited
Incorporated: 10 March 1993 *Employees:* 528
Net Worth Deficit: £1,448,000 *Total Assets:* £63,069,000
Registered Office: Bridgford House, Heyes Lane, Alderley Edge, Cheshire, SK9 7JP
Activities: Other telecommunications activities
Major Shareholder: David Pollock
Officers: Tina Pollock, Secretary; John Richard Mark Btesh [1957] Finance Director; Stephen Dracup [1963] Director; Jessica Hughes [1988] Director; Mark Roy Lightfoot [1973] Financial Director; David Andrew Mason [1950] Director; Charles David Pollock [1960] Director; Charlie Pollock [1991] Director; Warren Andrew Pryer [1963] Director

The Chester Catholic Academies Partnership
Incorporated: 25 January 2013 *Employees:* 129
Net Worth Deficit: £891,989 *Total Assets:* £6,959,923
Registered Office: The Catholic High School, Old Wrexham Road, Handbridge, Chester, CH4 7HS
Activities: General secondary education
Officers: Stephen Alan Wlliam Gauller, Secretary; John Boggan [1961] Director/Deacon; Rev Jonathon Brandon [1976] Director/Priest; Jane Johnson [1959] Director/Teacher; Bernard Christopher Larkin [1953] Director/Retired; John Stephen Murray [1960] Director/Headteacher [Irish]

Chester Diocesan Board of Education
Incorporated: 7 July 1905
Net Worth: £9,689,530 *Total Assets:* £10,708,388
Registered Office: Church House, 5500 Daresbury Park, Daresbury, Warrington, Cheshire, WA4 4GE
Activities: Financial intermediation not elsewhere classified
Officers: Christopher Robert Penn, Secretary; Revd Lyndon Russell Bannon [1973] Director/Teacher; Paul Bowden [1955] Director/Defence Litigator; Revd Lynn Boyle [1958] Director/Vicar; Dr David John Scott Cumberland [1962] Director/Deputy Dean - University of Chester; Craig Hughes [1968] Director/HR Adviser; Elizabeth Jane Holden Lane [1966] Director/Bishop; Edward Charles Garnett Owen [1942] Director/Retired; Elizabeth Renshaw [1943] Director/Retired; Susan Riley [1967] Director/Headteacher; Ian Roberts [1940] Director/Retired

Chester Diocesan Board of Finance
Incorporated: 18 November 1873 *Employees:* 44
Net Worth: £25,311,000 *Total Assets:* £31,244,000
Registered Office: 5500 Daresbury Park, Daresbury, Warrington, Cheshire, WA4 4GE
Activities: Activities of religious organisations
Officers: George Beal Colville, Secretary; The Ven Ian Gregory Bishop [1962] Director/Clerk in Holy Orders; Revd Lynn Boyle [1958] Director/Clerk in Holy Orders; Dr John Graham Campbell [1942] Director/Chartered Accountant; Revd Elaine Chegwin Hall [1959] Director/Clerk in Holy Orders; Dr Alan Walter Dowen [1950] Director/Retired; Rev Simon Drew [1968] Director/Clerk in Holy Orders; David Rhys Felix [1955] Director/Clerk in Holy Orders; Peter Robert Forster [1950] Director/Bishop of Chester; John Jeremy Collier Freeman [1937] Director/Chemical Engineer; Revd Alison Fulford [1979] Director/Clerk in Holy Orders; Rev Simon Richard Gales [1959] Director/Clerk in Holy Orders; Michael Robert Gilbertson [1961] Director/Clerk in Holy Orders; Fiona Susan Goode [1962] Director/Solicitor; Reverend Andrew Quentin Greenhough [1968] Director/Clerk in Holy Orders; Jenny Kidd [1949] Director/Retired; Elizabeth Jane Holden Lane [1966] Director/Clerk in Holy Orders; Victor John Legg [1933] Director; David Anthony Marriott [1944] Director/Retired; Dr John Philip Mason [1959] Director/Retired; Reverend Robert Speight Munro [1963] Director/Clerk in Holy Orders; Rev David James Page [1962] Director/Clerk in Holy Orders; Elizabeth Renshaw [1943] Director/Bursar; Reverend Michael Laurence Ridley [1959] Director/Clerk in Holy Orders; Ian Roberts [1940] Director/Retired; Ian Neil Scott-Dunn [1951] Director/Retired; John Rupert Scrivener [1951] Director/University Lecturer; Revd Carol Seddon [1944] Director/Clerk in Holy Orders; Gordon Keith Sinclair [1952] Director/Clerk in Holy Orders; Reverend Michael Ian Antony Smith [1969] Director/Clerk in Holy Orders [British/Australian]; Timothy Richard Stratford [1961] Director/Dean of Chester Cathedral

Chester Race Company Limited
Incorporated: 21 November 1892 *Employees:* 129
Net Worth: £32,559,232 *Total Assets:* £39,309,536
Registered Office: The Racecourse, Chester, CH1 2LY
Activities: Hotels and similar accommodation
Officers: Marco John Garavello, Secretary; Richard Kenneth Aston [1954] Director; Kevin John Bacon [1959] Director; Charles Henry Barnett [1948] Director; Martin Dudley Beaumont [1949] Director/Businessman; Marco John Garavello [1977] Finance Director; John Sullivan O'Doherty [1962] Director/Financial Services [Irish]; Richard Gwyn Thomas [1969] Director/Chief Executive Chester Race Course; Jonathon Sloan Embree Turner [1951] Director/Shipbroker

Chesterfield High School
Incorporated: 5 September 2011 *Employees:* 105
Net Worth: £20,778,000 *Total Assets:* £23,394,000
Registered Office: Chesterfield High School, Chesterfield Road, Crosby, Liverpool, L23 9YB
Activities: General secondary education
Officers: Jacqueline Crampton, Secretary; Jeffrey William Bee [1962] Director/Businessman; Charlotte Bowers [1972] Director/Teacher; Stephen Peter Cowperthwaite [1967] Regional Senior Director; David Hird [1974] Director/Teacher; Paul Horwood [1968] Director/Business Intelligence Manager; Diane Elizabeth McCann [1964] Director/Student Support Manager; Claire Rebecca McDonough [1981] Director/Teacher; Derek Raymond McLoughlin [1933] Director; Simon Neil Penney [1959] Director/Headteacher; Janet Elizabeth Vicary [1963] Director/University Administrator; Leonie Therese Williams [1967] Director/Civil Servant

Chi Yip Group Limited
Incorporated: 2 April 1990 *Employees:* 67
Net Worth: £3,612,924 *Total Assets:* £7,349,472
Registered Office: Treasure House, Greengate Industrial Park, Greenside Way, Middleton, Manchester, M24 1SW
Activities: Wholesale of meat and meat products
Parent: Chi Yip Holdings Limited
Officers: Dorothy Fong Ching Yip, Secretary; Dorothy Fong Ching Yip [1960] Director; Jason Kan Wai Yip [1986] Director

Chi Yip Holdings Limited
Incorporated: 2 May 2007 *Employees:* 67
Net Worth: £8,279,808 *Total Assets:* £11,366,116
Registered Office: Tresure House, Greenside Way, Greengate Industrial Park, Middleton, Manchester, M24 1SW
Activities: Activities of head offices
Parent: Yip & Sons Limited
Officers: Dorothy Fong Ching Yip, Secretary; Dorothy Fong Ching Yip [1960] Director; Jason Kan Wai Yip [1986] Director

Chiesi Healthcare Limited
Incorporated: 30 December 1996
Net Worth: £6,364,000 *Total Assets:* £7,054,000
Registered Office: 333 Styal Road, Manchester, M22 5LG
Activities: Wholesale of pharmaceutical goods
Parent: Chiesi Farmaceutici SpA
Officers: Matthew Wiggetts, Secretary; Alberto Chiesi [1938] Director [Italian]; Alessandro Chiesi [1966] Director [Italian]; Paolo Chiesi [1940] Director [Italian]; Thomas Joseph Delahoyde [1958] Managing Director; Ugo di Francesco [1960] Director [Italian]; Andrew Philip Dickinson [1970] Director; Michael Jonathon Dixon [1965] Director; Danilo Piroli [1954] Director [Italian]; Marco Vecchia [1960] Director/Lawyer [Italian]

Chiesi Limited
Incorporated: 18 June 1987 *Employees:* 250
Net Worth: £20,020,000 *Total Assets:* £76,823,000
Registered Office: 333 Styal Road, Manchester, M22 5LG
Activities: Wholesale of pharmaceutical goods
Parent: Chiesi Healthcare Ltd
Officers: Matthew Wiggetts, Secretary; Alberto Chiesi [1938] Director [Italian]; Alessandro Chiesi [1966] Director [Italian]; Paolo Chiesi [1940] Director [Italian]; Thomas Joseph Delahoyde [1958] Managing Director; Ugo di Francesco [1960] Director [Italian]; Andrew Philip Dickinson [1970] Director; Michael Jonathon Dixon [1965] Director; Danilo Piroli [1954] Director [Italian]; Marco Vecchia [1960] Director/Lawyer [Italian]

Children of Success Schools Trust
Incorporated: 11 March 2013 *Employees:* 172
Net Worth: £5,208,000 *Total Assets:* £6,949,000
Registered Office: The Willows Primary School, Tayfield Road, Woodhouse Park, Manchester, M22 1BQ
Activities: Primary education
Officers: Professor Melvin Ainscow [1943] Director; Sheila Miriam Cairns [1948] Director; Richard George Dyson [1949] Director; Mark Glynn [1966] Director/Council Neighbourhood Manager; Linda Ann Hamilton [1953] Director; Rebecca Elizabeth Hodgkins [1975] Director/Solicitor; Alison Frances Jurkowski [1963] Director/Accountant; Stuart Victor Leeming [1954] Director/Education; Susan Spiteri [1971] Director/Headteacher; Daniel Stalford [1982] Director; Dr Paul Andrew Melland Thompson [1965] Director/Teacher

Chippindale Foods Limited
Incorporated: 17 August 1981 *Employees:* 52
Net Worth: £5,937,065 *Total Assets:* £10,942,273
Registered Office: Hilmore House, Gain Lane, Bradford, W Yorks, BD3 7DL
Activities: Wholesale of dairy products, eggs and edible oils and fats
Parent: Wm Morrison Supermarkets P L C
Officers: Jonathan Burke, Secretary; Darren Anthony Blackhurst [1966] Director; Mark Thomas Stitson [1976] Finance Director; Andrew Edward Thornber [1974] Managing Director

Choice Hotels Limited
Incorporated: 26 April 1978 *Employees:* 418
Net Worth: £4,960,246 *Total Assets:* £12,858,807
Registered Office: Choice House, 107 Dickson Road, Blackpool, Lancs, FY1 2ET
Activities: Hotels and similar accommodation
Officers: Sally Louise Carpenito, Secretary; Sally Louise Carpenito [1961] Director/Hotelier; Julian Edward Stefan Kollard [1961] Director/Hotelier; Anne Nelder [1933] Director/Hotelier; Edward Owen Nelder [1964] Director/Hotelier; Maureen Nelder [1940] Director/Hotelier; Owen William Nelder [1938] Director/Hotelier; Robert John Rowley Nelder [1958] Director/Hotelier; Neil Patrick Wilkinson [1962] Director/Hotelier

John Chorley & Company,Limited
Incorporated: 28 April 1924 *Employees:* 62
Net Worth: £1,708,226 *Total Assets:* £8,932,422
Registered Office: Dallam Lane, Warrington, Cheshire, WA2 7PZ
Activities: Manufacture of other fabricated metal products n.e.c.
Parent: Caldwells Limited
Officers: Christopher John Thomson, Secretary/Chartered Accountant; James Benedict Caldwell [1964] Director/General Executive; Nicholas Edward Caldwell [1960] Director; Terence Anthony Shanahan [1968] Director/Steel Stock Holding

Chorley Yamaha Centre Limited
Incorporated: 13 January 1998 *Employees:* 26
Net Worth: £1,513,956 *Total Assets:* £7,095,864
Registered Office: Chorley Yamaha Centre Ltd, Eaves Lane, Chorley, Lancs, PR6 0TB
Activities: Sale, maintenance and repair of motorcycles and related parts and accessories
Parent: 2 Moto Limited
Officers: Eileen Mason [1955] Director

Chorus Law Limited
Incorporated: 29 August 2003 *Employees:* 206
Net Worth Deficit: £588,208 *Total Assets:* £10,092,002
Registered Office: 1 Angel Square, Manchester, M60 0AG
Activities: Other business support service activities n.e.c.
Parent: Chorus Law Group Limited
Officers: Matthew Ian Howells [1978] Managing Director; Caoilionn Hurley [1965] Director/Accountant [Irish]

CHP Supplies Limited
Incorporated: 16 June 1980 *Employees:* 70
Net Worth: £5,019,371 *Total Assets:* £7,774,864
Registered Office: 55 Pottery Road, Wigan, Lancs, WN3 5AA
Activities: Wholesale of hardware, plumbing and heating equipment and supplies
Major Shareholder: Sean Peter Hollowed
Officers: Sean Peter Hollowed, Secretary; Barry Hodkinson [1970] Director; Sean Peter Hollowed [1969] Director; Joseph Thomas Shirley [1961] Director; Paul Harrison Wilding [1956] Director

Christeyns UK Ltd
Incorporated: 6 May 1965 *Employees:* 128
Net Worth: £22,950,100 *Total Assets:* £30,519,140
Registered Office: Rutland Street, East Bowling, Bradford, W Yorks, BD4 7EA
Activities: Manufacture of soap and detergents
Major Shareholder: Alain Joseph Andre Bostoen
Officers: Julie Susan Roberts, Secretary; David Peter Aveyard [1963] Director; Paul Gerrard Victor Camiel Bostoen [1939] Director [Belgian]; Elisabeth Josepha Margaretha Ghislenus Devos [1941] Director [Belgian]; Nicholas James Garthwaite [1957] Director; Daniel John Kilgallon [1956] Director Sales; Julie Susan Roberts [1969] Director/Chartered Accountant; Scott Alan Grant Wilson [1969] Sales Director; Jozef Maria Jaak Wittouck [1962] Director [Belgian]

Christian Property UK Ltd
Incorporated: 7 October 2016 *Employees:* 46
Net Worth: £1,886,850 *Total Assets:* £9,120,916
Registered Office: UHY-Hacker Young, St James Building, 79 Oxford Street, Manchester, M1 6HT
Activities: Other letting and operating of own or leased real estate
Major Shareholder: Mathew Kay
Officers: Mathew Kay [1979] Director

The Christian Trust
Incorporated: 24 December 1993 *Employees:* 84
Net Worth: £2,537,964 *Total Assets:* £7,030,859
Registered Office: Ellel Grange, Ellel, Lancaster, LA2 0HN
Activities: Other education n.e.c.
Officers: Robert John Hay, Secretary; David Malcolm Cross [1948] Centre Director; Gillian Fiona Horrobin [1949] Director/Centre Manager; Peter James Horrobin [1943] Director of Ellel Ministries; Roger Pook [1944] Director/Retired; Andrew James Taylor [1971] Director/Minister

Christopher Bidco Limited
Incorporated: 23 May 2016 *Employees:* 6
Net Worth Deficit: £429,677 *Total Assets:* £59,458,448
Registered Office: 2 Malt Street, Knutsford, Cheshire, WA16 6ES
Activities: Licenced restaurants
Officers: Justin Ash [1965] Director; Matthew Mark Bamber [1977] Director; Richard Thomas Barley [1978] Director; Christopher Hill [1980] Director; Timothy McCormac [1973] Property Director

Christopher Midco 1 Limited
Incorporated: 20 May 2016
Net Worth Deficit: £3,305,814 *Total Assets:* £37,106,488
Registered Office: 2 Malt Street, Knutsford, Cheshire, WA16 6ES
Activities: Licenced restaurants
Officers: Matthew Mark Bamber [1977] Director; Richard Thomas Barley [1978] Director; Christopher Hill [1980] Director; Timothy McCormac [1973] Property Director

Christopher Topco Limited
Incorporated: 20 May 2016 *Employees:* 1,091
Net Worth Deficit: £7,656,699 *Total Assets:* £68,686,904
Registered Office: 2 Malt Street, Knutsford, Cheshire, WA16 6ES
Activities: Licenced restaurants
Officers: Justin Ash [1965] Non-Executive Director Chairman; Matthew Mark Bamber [1977] Director; Richard Thomas Barley [1978] Director; Christopher Hill [1980] Director; Timothy McCormac [1973] Property Director

Christy Home Textiles Limited
Incorporated: 5 June 2000
Net Worth: £1,578,000 *Total Assets:* £11,252,000
Registered Office: Park Square, Bird Hall Lane, Stockport, Cheshire, SK3 0XF
Activities: Activities of head offices
Parent: CHT Holdings Ltd
Officers: Manish Bansal, Secretary; Manish Bansal [1972] Director/Accountant [Indian]; Dipali Balkrishan Goenka [1969] Director [Indian]; Leigh Antony Taylor [1961] Managing Director

Chrystal Consulting Limited
Incorporated: 23 September 1997 *Employees:* 8
Net Worth: £6,589,265 *Total Assets:* £14,824,460
Registered Office: 500 Styal Road, Manchester, M22 5HQ
Activities: Financial leasing
Parent: Chrystal Holdings Limited
Officers: Andrew Douglas Baker, Secretary; Andrew Douglas Baker [1968] Finance Director; Susanne Gayle Merrygold [1967] Operations Director; Ian Andrew Sinclair-Ford [1961] Director/Solicitor

Chrystal Holdings Limited
Incorporated: 22 January 2003 *Employees:* 8
Net Worth: £6,589,265 *Total Assets:* £14,824,360
Registered Office: 500 Styal Road, Manchester, M22 5HQ
Activities: Activities of financial services holding companies
Shareholders: Andrew Douglas Baker; Kevin Joseph Newsome
Officers: Andrew Douglas Baker, Secretary; Andrew Douglas Baker [1968] Director/Finance Company Manager; Kevin Joseph Newsome [1964] Director/Finance Company Manager

CHT Holdings Limited
Incorporated: 18 October 2002 *Employees:* 261
Net Worth: £4,484,000 *Total Assets:* £22,161,000
Registered Office: Park Square, Bird Hall Lane, Stockport, Cheshire, SK3 0XF
Activities: Retail sale of textiles in specialised stores
Parent: Welspun Home Textiles UK Ltd
Officers: Manish Bansal, Secretary; Manish Bansal [1972] Director/Accountant [Indian]; Dipali Balkrishan Goenka [1969] Director [Indian]; Leigh Antony Taylor [1961] Managing Director

Chubb Systems Limited
Incorporated: 12 February 1962 *Employees:* 227
Net Worth: £306,471,008 *Total Assets:* £397,779,008
Registered Office: United Technologies House, Shadsworth Road, Blackburn, BB1 2PR
Activities: Security systems service activities
Parent: Bet Security and Communications Limited
Officers: Robert Sloss, Secretary; Laura Wilcock, Secretary; Anthony Brennan [1966] Finance Director [Irish]; Craig Alexander Forbes [1963] Finance Director; Graeme Heanan [1960] Director

Chums Limited
Incorporated: 14 May 1981 *Employees:* 173
Net Worth: £4,850,526 *Total Assets:* £10,501,409
Registered Office: Unity Grove, Knowsley Business Park, Prescot, Merseyside, L34 9AR
Activities: Retail sale via mail order houses or via Internet
Officers: Graham Anthony Rubin, Secretary; Sarah Ann Nyman [1980] Director/Television Producer; Adam Rubin [1979] Director/Photographer; Graham Anthony Rubin [1951] Director; Joshua Max Rubin [1986] Director/Recruitment Consultant; Michelle Ruth Rubin [1954] Director

Ciceley Commercials Limited
Incorporated: 6 November 1992 *Employees:* 211
Net Worth: £6,594,648 *Total Assets:* £32,940,888
Registered Office: Ciceley Lane, Blackburn, Lancs, BB1 1HQ
Activities: Sale of other motor vehicles
Parent: Ciceley Limited
Officers: Russell Ian Morgan, Secretary; Colin Briggs [1957] Director; Michael Anton Wharton Lewis [1964] Director/Dealer Principal; Brian Morgan [1932] Director; Russell Ian Morgan [1962] Director; Simon David Wilson [1970] Finance Director

Ciceley Limited
Incorporated: 5 March 1941 *Employees:* 209
Net Worth: £12,934,188 *Total Assets:* £36,647,212
Registered Office: Ciceley Lane, Blackburn, Lancs, BB1 1HQ
Activities: Sale of other motor vehicles
Shareholders: Brian Morgan; Russell Ian Morgan; Sally Ann Morgan
Officers: Russell Ian Morgan, Secretary/Vice Chairman; Colin Briggs [1957] Director/General Manager; Brian Morgan [1932] Director; Russell Ian Morgan [1962] Director; Sally Ann Morgan [1961] Director/Freelance Production Assistant; Simon David Wilson [1970] Director/Accountant

Cidari Education Limited
Incorporated: 20 December 2013 *Employees:* 339
Net Worth: £12,394,252 *Total Assets:* £19,102,192
Registered Office: Clayton House, Walker Park, Blackburn, Lancs, BB1 2QE
Activities: Other education n.e.c.
Officers: Ronald Matthews, Secretary; Peter Nicholas Ashworth [1969] Director/Interim CEO and Head of Education; Michael John Everitt [1968] Director/Archdeacon of Lancaster; Carolyn Ann Johnson [1952] Director/Solicitor; Samuel Peter Johnson [1974] Deputy Director of Education; Angus MacLeod [1943] Director/Retired; Graeme Pollard [1960] Director/Diocesan Secretary/COO Charity; Helen Thomas [1961] Director/Headteacher; Josephine Miriam Venn [1954] Director/Retired; Graeme Warnock [1976] Director/Headteacher [Irish]; Stephen Lawrence Whittaker [1971] Director of Education

Circle Leasing Limited
Incorporated: 20 May 2002 *Employees:* 44
Net Worth: £7,413,000 *Total Assets:* £30,704,000
Registered Office: The Barracks, 400 Bolton Road, Bury, Lancs, BL8 2DA
Activities: Renting and leasing of cars and light motor vehicles
Shareholders: Dennis Studholme; Aidan Gerard Minogue; Mary Christine Studholme
Officers: Mary Christine Studholme, Secretary; Aidan Gerard Minogue [1962] Managing Director; Dennis Studholme [1949] Director; Mary Christine Studholme [1960] Director

Cirteq Limited
Incorporated: 30 May 1995 *Employees:* 235
Net Worth: £6,914,841 *Total Assets:* £10,115,584
Registered Office: Hayfield Colne Road, Glusburn, Keighley, W Yorks, BD20 8QP
Activities: Manufacture of wire products, chain and springs
Parent: Glusburn Holdings Limited
Officers: Andrew I'anson Crabtree, Secretary; Andrew I'anson Crabtree [195-] Director/Chartered Accountant; Angus McKay Meikle [1950] Director; Victor Elisabeth Alois Stevens [1957] Director [Belgian]

Citation Holdings Limited
Incorporated: 9 November 2000 *Employees:* 3
Net Worth: £5,599,805 *Total Assets:* £40,582,072
Registered Office: Kings Court, Water Lane, Wilmslow, Cheshire, SK9 5AR
Activities: Non-trading company
Parent: Caesar Bidco Limited
Officers: Jenny Ingleby [1976] Sales & Marketing Director; Christopher Paul Morris [1972] Director; Eloise Wann [1977] Director/Chief Financial Officer

Citation Limited
Incorporated: 1 September 1995 *Employees:* 367
Net Worth: £33,939,212 *Total Assets:* £50,958,656
Registered Office: Kings Court, Water Lane, Wilmslow, Cheshire, SK9 5AR
Activities: Management consultancy activities other than financial management
Parent: Citation Holdings Limited
Officers: Jenny Ingleby [1976] Sales & Marketing Director; Christopher Paul Morris [1972] Director; Andrew Charles Pumphrey [1965] Managing Director; Eloise Wann [1977] Director/Chief Financial Officer

City Life Projects Limited
Incorporated: 20 April 2000 *Employees:* 96
Net Worth: £574,262 *Total Assets:* £7,546,333
Registered Office: Atlantic House, 143 Sefton Street, Liverpool, L8 5SN
Activities: Hotels and similar accommodation
Officers: Kathleen Mary Flanagan, Secretary; Julian Flanagan [1971] Director/Builder; Kathleen Mary Flanagan [1942] Director/Manager; Paul Patrick Flanagan [1963] Director/Builder

City of Liverpool Investment Company Limited (The)
Incorporated: 28 April 1888 *Employees:* 3
Net Worth: £3,338,292 *Total Assets:* £6,883,194
Registered Office: 130 Buxton Road, Heaviley, Stockport, Cheshire, SK2 6PL
Activities: Other letting and operating of own or leased real estate
Parent: Tatton Land Limited
Officers: Elizabeth Mary Carson, Secretary/Partner Director; Anthony Nigel Carson [1960] Director

The City of Salford Community Stadium Limited
Incorporated: 16 April 2010 *Employees:* 8
Net Worth Deficit: £7,061,409 *Total Assets:* £23,499,016
Registered Office: Peel Dome, intu Trafford Centre, Trafford City, Manchester, M17 8PL
Activities: Operation of sports facilities
Shareholders: Christopher Eves; Sheila Greenwood; John Whittaker; The Council of The City of Salford
Officers: Paula Boshell [1951] Director; Miranda Lucy Mary Carruthers-Watt [1961] Director; David Jonathan Glover [1956] Director; Peter John Hosker [1957] Director of Corporate Affairs; David Anthony Lancaster [1944] Director

City South Manchester Housing Trust Limited
Incorporated: 10 October 2007
Net Worth: £5,396,000 *Total Assets:* £89,555,000
Registered Office: Lovell House, Archway 6, Hulme, Manchester, M15 5RN
Activities: Renting and operating of Housing Association real estate
Officers: Victor Hassan, Secretary; Nadim Ahmad [1970] Director; Graham Reynard Aitken [1956] Director; David Patrick Andrew Dennehy [1960] Director [Irish]; Alison Magdalene Gordon [1965] Director; John James Hughes [1975] Managing Director; Stephen Arthur Kinsey [1956] Director/Solicitor; Stephen Richard Mole [1956] Finance Director; Dr Slawomir Pawlik [1963] Director/National Health Service Manager [Polish]; Angela Bridie Robinson [1957] Director; Emily Rachel Rowles [1985] Director/Local Councillor/Research Assistant

City Suites Manchester Limited
Incorporated: 7 November 2013
Net Worth: £696,000 *Total Assets:* £16,076,000
Registered Office: The Box, Horseshoe Lane, Alderley Edge, Cheshire, SK9 7QP
Activities: Development of building projects
Parent: City Suites Ltd
Officers: Giles Peter Beswick, Secretary; Giles Peter Beswick [1974] Director; Mark Christopher Dawson [1973] Director; Mark David Stott [1972] Director

Cityblock Holdings Limited
Incorporated: 29 May 2002
Net Worth: £539,758 *Total Assets:* £11,349,980
Registered Office: 21 Castle Hill, Lancaster, LA1 1YN
Activities: Construction of domestic buildings
Parent: Cityblock Limited
Officers: Alison Jane Bargh, Secretary/Property Development & Management; Alison Jane Bargh [1961] Director/Property Development & Management; John Trevor Bargh [1958] Director

Citylabs Limited
Incorporated: 24 January 2011
Net Worth: £9,873,000 *Total Assets:* £26,344,000
Registered Office: Union, Albert Square, Manchester, M2 6LW
Activities: Other letting and operating of own or leased real estate
Parent: Manchester Science Partnerships Limited
Officers: Rowena May Burns [1953] Director/Chief Operating Officer; Kevin James Crotty [1976] Director/Chartered Accountant; Peter Andrew Crowther [1972] Director; Sean Martin Davies [1976] Finance Director; Kate Victoria Lawlor [1981] Director/Chartered Accountant; Thomas Peter Renn [1985] Managing Director; Edward Ashley Lote Smith [1960] Strategic Director

Claims Advisory Group Limited
Incorporated: 8 May 2007 *Employees:* 186
Net Worth: £1,354,231 *Total Assets:* £12,708,071
Registered Office: Unit 4 The Foundry, Ordsall Lane, Salford, M5 3LW
Activities: Other business support service activities n.e.c.
Major Shareholder: Terrence O'Neill
Officers: Jamie Tyler Alaise [1979] Director

The Claims Guys Limited
Incorporated: 17 February 2009 *Employees:* 527
Net Worth: £1,767,589 *Total Assets:* £9,785,960
Registered Office: Lynnfield House, Church Street, Altrincham, Cheshire, WA14 4DZ
Activities: Other business support service activities n.e.c.
Parent: LeadX Holdings
Officers: Mark Philip Simpkins, Secretary; Timothy Andrew Berry [1967] Director; Helen Mary Dwyer [1970] Director; Mark Philip Simpkins [1965] Director/Accountant

Claire House
Incorporated: 13 June 1991 *Employees:* 184
Net Worth: £10,389,816 *Total Assets:* £10,915,467
Registered Office: Claire House, Children's Hospice, Clatterbridge Road, Bebington, Wirral, Merseyside, CH63 4JD
Activities: Other human health activities
Officers: Janet Wallace, Secretary; Dr Eileen Baildam [1957] Director/Consultant Paediatrician; Dr Helen Jane Butterworth [1983] Director/GP; John Anthony Gittins [1960] Director; Valerie Ann Lawton [1971] Finance Director; Alan Rice [1953] Director/Retired; Dr Anne Briar Stewart [1954] Director/Retired; Mark William Thomas [1956] Director/Journalist; Helen Andrea Watson [1974] Director/Partner of an LLP Solicitor

R.S.Clare & Co.,Limited
Incorporated: 2 July 1902 *Employees:* 177
Net Worth: £18,625,712 *Total Assets:* £25,110,066
Registered Office: 8 Stanhope Street, Liverpool, L8 5RQ
Activities: Other treatment of petroleum products (excluding petrochemicals manufacture)
Officers: Neville Leslie Biddle [1951] Director/Barrister; Mattia Branca [1978] Director/Manager at Prudential Regulation Authority [Italian]; Roy Coldwell [1949] Director/Consultant; Rupert Sinclair Higgin [1964] Director/Self Employed; Robert Ian Shaw Meadows [1946] Director; Stephen David Scott [1952] Director; Paul Adrian Vann [1962] Managing Director

Claremont Group Interiors Limited
Incorporated: 20 November 1996 *Employees:* 104
Net Worth: £1,362,013 *Total Assets:* £15,409,669
Registered Office: The Breeze, 2 Kelvin Close, Birchwood, Warrington, Cheshire, WA3 7PB
Activities: Other building completion and finishing
Shareholder: Michael John Gardner
Officers: Matthew James Riley, Secretary; Kenneth Arthur Bundy [1959] Director; Simon David Campion [1960] Director; Ann Clarke [1960] Director; Lisa Marie Flannery [1969] Director; Timothy William Frankland [1965] Director; Michael John Gardner [1955] Director; Sarah Jane Osborne [1968] Director/Designer; Richard Lee Turner [1971] Director

Clarence Mill Limited
Incorporated: 28 September 1999 *Employees:* 1
Net Worth: £2,927,703 *Total Assets:* £6,690,977
Registered Office: Clarence Mill, Clarence Road, Bollington, Cheshire, SK10 2JZ
Activities: Development of building projects
Officers: Geoffrey Brian Claughton, Secretary; Rupert Alexander Beckwith-Moore [1967] Director; Kenneth Charles Moore [1938] Director; Sara Frances Moore [1941] Director

Clarke and Pulman Limited
Incorporated: 14 January 2003 *Employees:* 27
Net Worth: £1,354,331 *Total Assets:* £8,478,919
Registered Office: Langley Place, Burscough Industrial Estate, Burscough, Lancs, L40 8JS
Activities: Wholesale of agricultural machinery, equipment and supplies
Parent: Clarke and Pulman Holdings Limited
Officers: Sarah Clarke, Secretary; Generald Anthony Clarke [1968] Director

Clarke Energy Limited
Incorporated: 30 November 1977 *Employees:* 1,146
Net Worth: £93 935,000 *Total Assets:* £178,200,992
Registered Office: Power House, Senator Point, South Boundary Road, Knowsley Industrial Estate, Knowsley, Merseyside, L33 7RR
Activities: Production of electricity
Parent: Clarke Energy Holdings Limited
Officers: Kyle David Quinn, Secretary; Thomas Gerard Adler [1960] Director [American]; James Stuart Clarke [1979] Director; Thomas George Cromwell [1968] Director [American]; Peter John Holliday [1973] Director/Accountant; James McKee Robinson IV [1970] Director/General Counsel [American]

Clarke Energy Operations Limited
Incorporated: 25 May 2012
Net Worth Deficit: £29,028,000 *Total Assets:* £140,887,008
Registered Office: Power House, Senator Point, South Boundary Road, Knowsley Business Park, Knowsley, Merseyside, L33 7RR
Activities: Production of electricity
Parent: Clarke Energy Topco Limited
Officers: Kyle David Quinn, Secretary; Thomas Gerard Adler [1960] Director [American]; Thomas George Cromwell [1968] Director [American]; James McKee Robinson IV [1970] Director/General Counsel [American]

Clarke Energy Topco Limited
Incorporated: 25 May 2012 *Employees:* 1,057
Net Worth Deficit: £37,550,000 *Total Assets:* £252,658,000
Registered Office: Power House, Senator Point, South Boundary Road, Knowsley Business Park, Knowsley, Merseyside, L33 7RR
Activities: Production of electricity
Parent: KK Daytona Holding Limited
Officers: Kyle David Quinn, Secretary; Thomas George Cromwell [1968] Director [American]; Karger David Kohler [1966] Director [American]; Herbert Vollrath Kohler Jnr [1939] Director [American]; James McKee Robinson IV [1970] Director/General Counsel [American]

J Clarke Investments Limited
Incorporated: 5 November 2012
Net Worth: £2,455,119 *Total Assets:* £13,729,087
Registered Office: 98 Victoria Road, Freshfield, Formby, Merseyside, L37 1LP
Activities: Other letting and operating of own or leased real estate
Major Shareholder: James Clarke
Officers: James Clarke [1951] Director; Tanya Jane Clarke [1969] Director

Classic Collection Holidays Limited
Incorporated: 14 August 1980 *Employees:* 127
Net Worth: £8,376,469 *Total Assets:* £18,768,408
Registered Office: Park Square, Bird Hall Lane, Stockport, Cheshire, SK3 0XN
Activities: Tour operator activities
Parent: On The Beach Travel Limited
Officers: Kirsteen Vickerstaff, Secretary; Simon Matthew Cooper [1972] Director; Paul Meehan [1963] Director; Nicholas Harold Paul Munday [1957] Director/Travel Organiser; Matthew Damian Rice [1965] Director/Deputy MD

Clean Energy and Infrastructure 3 Limited
Incorporated: 18 November 2015
Net Worth: £9,975,462 *Total Assets:* £59,047,736
Registered Office: 1030 Slutchers Lane, Centre Park, Warrington, Cheshire, WA1 1QL
Activities: Activities of other holding companies n.e.c.
Officers: Elizabeth Oldroyd, Secretary; John William Breckenridge [1962] Managing Director [American]; Barnaby Alistair Coles [1984] Director/Fund Manager; Simon Richard Eaves [1967] Managing Director; Kirsty Louise Usher [1975] Director/Accountant

Clean Energy and Infrastructure UK Limited
Incorporated: 10 January 2013
Net Worth Deficit: £13,475,000 *Total Assets:* £144,728,992
Registered Office: 1030 Centre Park, Slutchers Lane, Warrington, Cheshire, WA1 1QL
Activities: Production of electricity
Officers: Elizabeth Alexandra Oldroyd, Secretary; Dario Bertagna [1984] Director/Fund Manager [Italian]; John William Breckenridge [1962] Managing Director [American]; Simon Richard Eaves [1967] Managing Director; Kirsty Louise Usher [1975] Director/Accountant

Clean Energy and Infrastructure UK Wind 2 Limited
Incorporated: 24 November 2015 *Employees:* 3
Net Worth: £3,484,449 *Total Assets:* £23,640,612
Registered Office: 1030 Centre Park, Slutchers Lane, Warrington, Cheshire, WA1 1QL
Activities: Activities of production holding companies
Officers: Elizabeth Oldroyd, Secretary; Dario Bertagna [1984] Director/Fund Manager [Italian]; John William Breckenridge [1962] Managing Director [American]; Simon Richard Eaves [1967] Managing Director; Kirsty Louise Usher [1975] Director/Accountant

Clean Energy and Infrastructure UK Wind Limited
Incorporated: 15 May 2014
Net Worth Deficit: £14,043,000 *Total Assets:* £129,605,000
Registered Office: 1030 Centre Park, Slutchers Lane, Warrington, Cheshire, WA1 1QL
Activities: Production of electricity
Officers: Elizabeth Alexandra Oldroyd, Secretary; Dario Bertagna [1984] Director/Fund Manager [Italian]; John William Breckenridge [1962] Managing Director [American]; Simon Richard Eaves [1967] Managing Director; Kirsty Louise Usher [1975] Director/Accountant

Clear Business Limited
Incorporated: 5 December 2007 *Employees:* 3
Net Worth: £15,376,065 *Total Assets:* £17,432,500
Registered Office: Universal House, Longley Lane, Manchester, M22 4SY
Activities: Other telecommunications activities
Parent: Verastar Limited
Officers: Gillian Elizabeth Hill, Secretary; Paul Doherty [1970] Director/Accountant; Christopher James Earle [1973] Operations Director; Janette Palmer [1968] Director

Clear Law LLP
Incorporated: 16 June 2004 *Employees:* 75
Net Worth: £2,275,715 *Total Assets:* £9,352,574
Registered Office: Units 115-119 Timber Wharf, 42-50 Worsley Street, Castlefield, Manchester, M15 4LD
Officers: Matthew John Corbett [1973] Member

Cleland McIver Limited
Incorporated: 24 December 1982 *Employees:* 142
Net Worth: £4,166,838 *Total Assets:* £21,908,004
Registered Office: Hollingworth Mill, Smithybridge Road, Littleborough, Rochdale, OL15 8QF
Activities: Wholesale of textiles
Shareholder: John James Richard McIver
Officers: Barbara Ann McIver, Secretary; Helen Louise Bostock [1974] Finance Director; Lisa Jayne Knight [1967] Personnel Director; Timothy John Knight [1967] Sales Director; Barbara Ann McIver [1942] Director/Secretary; John James Richard McIver [1965] Director; John Keith Willoughby McIver [1937] Director

Cleveland Transit Ltd.
Incorporated: 8 October 1990 *Employees:* 299
Net Worth: £8,411,000 *Total Assets:* £15,159,000
Registered Office: c/o Stagecoach Services Limited, One Stockport Exchange, 20 Railway Road, Stockport, Cheshire, SK1 3SW
Activities: Other urban, suburban or metropolitan passenger land transport (not underground, metro or similar)
Parent: Stagecoach Bus Holdings Limited
Officers: Michael John Vaux, Secretary; Colin Brown [1968] Director/Accountant; Arnold Mark Threapleton [1954] Managing Director; Steven Walker [1971] Director

Clitheroe Royal Grammar School
Incorporated: 6 December 2010 *Employees:* 136
Net Worth: £13,811,000 *Total Assets:* £16,279,000
Registered Office: York Street, Clitheroe, Lancs, BB7 2DJ
Activities: Other education n.e.c.
Officers: Lynne Carole Higginbottom, Secretary; James Oliver Alcock [1980] Director/Teacher; Michael John Blacklidge [1956] Director/Retired/Non-Practising Solicitor; Majella Margaret Brennan-Bargh [1967] Director/Lecturer [Irish]; Anthony Clavell Bate [1956] Director; Dr Andrew David Clayton [1952] Director/Partner in Skills Training Partnership; Jacqueline Janet Holden [1970] Director/Laboratory Technician; James Matthew Hendrik Keulemans [1970] Director/Headteacher; Judith Irene Pinder [1959] Director/Barrister; Andrew Frank Priory [1968] Director/School Teacher; Alan Edwin Rogers [1961] Director; Alan Frederick Scholfield [1947] Director/Retired Electrical Engineer; Amanda Elizabeth Singh [1967] Director/Head of Human Resources; Daljinder Singh [1966] Director/Accountant; Paul William Smalley [1973] Finance Director; Jonathan Stanley Sutton [1957] Director/Banker; Ann Lynda Taylor [1951] Director/Retired Educational Psychologist; Charles Peter Watson [1964] Director/Consulting Engineer; Judith Wenborn [1962] Director/Retired; Dr Hilary Frances Whitehead [1958] Director/Dentist

Clondalkin UK Newco Limited
Incorporated: 17 September 2014 *Employees:* 3
Net Worth: £5,857,286 *Total Assets:* £13,663,006
Registered Office: Villiers Street, Bury, Lancs, BL9 6BS
Activities: Other business support service activities n.e.c.
Parent: Yellow Newco 2 BV
Officers: Antonius Johannes Zoomers [1957] Director [Dutch]

Close Leasing Limited
Incorporated: 20 September 2007 *Employees:* 36
Net Worth: £10,796,331 *Total Assets:* £646,913,728
Registered Office: Olympic Court, Third Avenue, Trafford Park Village, Manchester, M17 1AP
Activities: Financial intermediation not elsewhere classified
Parent: Close Brothers Limited
Officers: Neil Geoffrey Davies [1957] Director; Adrian John Sainsbury [1968] Director/Banker; David Peter Thomson [1963] Director; Philip Townend [1960] Director/Head of Credit

Closomat (Great Britain) Limited
Incorporated: 1 May 1962 *Employees:* 9
Net Worth: £5,471,616 *Total Assets:* £7,325,719
Registered Office: Building 1, Brooklands Place, Brooklands Road, Sale, Cheshire, M33 3SD
Activities: Other manufacturing n.e.c.
Major Shareholder: Linda Elizabeth Willan
Officers: Keith Brian Alderson [1960] Director; Graham Leslie Dronfield [1964] Director; Brian John Hoare [1965] Director; Linda Elizabeth Willan [1949] Director

Closomat Limited
Incorporated: 5 April 1990 *Employees:* 57
Net Worth: £7,110,879 *Total Assets:* £10,565,422
Registered Office: Building 1, Brooklands Place, Brooklands Road, Sale, Cheshire, M33 3SD
Activities: Other retail sale not in stores, stalls or markets
Major Shareholder: Linda Elizabeth Willan
Officers: Keith Brian Alderson [1960] Director; Adele Entwistle [1975] Director/Office Manager; Brian John Hoare [1965] Managing Director; Mark Sadler [1977] Sales Director; Ian Tomlinson [1967] Commercial Director; Linda Elizabeth Willan [1949] Director

Cloud Technology Solutions Ltd
Incorporated: 3 November 2008 *Employees:* 65
Net Worth: £681,121 *Total Assets:* £6,992,653
Registered Office: Lowry House, 17 Marble Street, Manchester, M2 3AW
Activities: Other information technology service activities
Parent: Cloud Technology Solutions Investments Limited
Officers: Steven John Dobson [1966] Director; James Andrew Doggart [1971] Director

Cloverbrook Holdings Ltd
Incorporated: 24 February 2003 *Employees:* 295
Net Worth: £4,972,545 *Total Assets:* £10,997,959
Registered Office: Sandringham Court, Bentley Wood Way, Network 65 Business Park, Burnley, Lancs, BB11 5PY
Activities: Activities of other holding companies n.e.c.
Major Shareholder: Keith Chippendale
Officers: John Wilkinson, Secretary; Simon Chippendale [1958] Director/Textile Manufacturer; John Wilkinson [1952] Director/Accountant

CLS Finance Limited
Incorporated: 3 February 2004 *Employees:* 33
Net Worth: £1,635,569 *Total Assets:* £13,434,865
Registered Office: Unit 2 Alexandra Street, Hyde, Cheshire, SK14 1DX
Activities: Financial intermediation not elsewhere classified
Shareholders: Shaun Patrick Young; Charles Omar Holding
Officers: Shaun Patrick Young, Secretary; Charles Omar Holding [1969] Director; Shaun Patrick Young [1962] Director

CLV (Bournemouth 1) UK LLP
Incorporated: 5 September 2013
Net Worth Deficit: £1,501,000 *Total Assets:* £37,027,000
Registered Office: 7th Floor, Digital World Centre, 1 Lowry Plaza, Salford Quays, Manchester, M50 3UB

CLV (St Andrews) UK LLP
Incorporated: 12 June 2014
Net Worth: £734,000 *Total Assets:* £25,299,000
Registered Office: 7th Floor, Digital World Centre, 1 Lowry Plaza, Salford Quays, Manchester, M50 3UB

CLV Finance UK Limited
Incorporated: 24 November 2009
Net Worth: £53,006,000 *Total Assets:* £54,362,000
Registered Office: 7th Floor, Digital World Centre, 1 Lowry Plaza, Salford Quays, Manchester, M50 3UB
Activities: Other credit granting n.e.c.
Officers: Lisa Jane Brown [1974] Director/Regional General Manager; Aileen Goldspring [1959] Director/Regional General Manager; Mathew Jason Panopoulos [1974] Director/Global Chief Financial Officer, CF Corporate Finance [Australian]

CLV Investments UK Limited
Incorporated: 20 May 2014
Net Worth: £778,000 *Total Assets:* £8,862,000
Registered Office: 7th Floor, Digital World Centre, 1 Lowry Plaza, Salford Quays, Manchester, M50 3UB
Activities: Management of real estate on a fee or contract basis
Officers: Lisa Jane Brown [1974] Director/Regional General Manager; Mathew Jason Panopoulos [1974] Director/Global Chief Financial Officer, CF Corporate Finance [Australian]

CMA CGM (UK) Shipping Limited
Incorporated: 1 March 1990 *Employees:* 231
Net Worth: £115,027,000 *Total Assets:* £704,617,984
Registered Office: 12 Princes Parade, Princes Dock, Liverpool, L3 1BG
Activities: Sea and coastal freight water transport
Parent: CMA CGM (UK) Holdings Ltd
Officers: Lee Anthony Ward, Secretary; Ian Bassett [1964] Director/Chartered Accountant; Paul Haeri-Rohani [1966] Director/Vice President - Commercial & Agency Network [French]; Jean Philippe Thenoz [1954] Director [French]; Lee Anthony Ward [1977] Director/Chief Financial Officer - Agency; Robert Waterman [1968] Managing Director

CMS Computers Limited
Incorporated: 12 August 1996 *Employees:* 56
Net Worth: £156,000 *Total Assets:* £8,173,000
Registered Office: 4 Hardwick Grange, Woolston, Warrington, Cheshire, WA1 4RF
Activities: Manufacture of computers and peripheral equipment
Officers: Jitenderpal Singh Sahni, Secretary; Jitenderpal Singh Sahni [1966] Director; Michael Andrew Taylor [1959] Finance Director

CMS Network (London) Ltd
Incorporated: 26 February 1998 *Employees:* 107
Net Worth: £5,613,728 *Total Assets:* £7,148,583
Registered Office: Calver Road, Winwick Quay, Warrington, Cheshire, WA2 8UD
Activities: Licensed carriers
Parent: The Delivery Group Limited
Officers: Jason Jones, Secretary; Ian Patrick Brewer [1965] Director; Mark Calladine [1980] Director; Paul David Carvell [1955] Director; Stephen Leslie Stokes [1964] Managing Director

The Co-operative Academies Trust
Incorporated: 19 August 2011 *Employees:* 1,017
Net Worth: £96,518,000 *Total Assets:* £110,595,000
Registered Office: 1 Angel Square, Manchester, M60 0AG
Activities: Primary education
Officers: Gary Lagar, Secretary; Simon Andrew Bourne [1968] Director; Margaret Anne Bradbury [1975] Director/National Project Manager; Neil Braithwaite [1959] Director; Geoffrey Alan Clarke [1947] Director/Retired Solicitor; Jane Cowell [1953] Director/Civil Servant; Eric Sydney Craven [1953] Director/Education Consultant; Gillian Frances Gardner [1964] Director/Council Secretary of Co-operative Group Limited; Russell Mark Gill [1967] Director; Michael David Greenacre [1948] Director; Nicholas Anthony Lowry [1979] Director/Principal; Shaheen Akhtar Rasool [1976] Director/Trust Professional Development Lead [Pakistani/British]

The Co-operative Bank Holdings Limited
Incorporated: 13 July 2017 *Employees:* 3,965
Net Worth: £1,505,600,000 *Total Assets:* £24,490,100,736
Registered Office: P O Box 101, 1 Balloon Street, Manchester, M60 4EP
Activities: Non-trading company
Officers: David William John Bagley, Secretary; Andrew John Milton Bester [1965] Director [British/South African]; Laura Martine Carstensen [1960] Director; Paul David Copley [1975] Director; Robert Graham Dench [1950] Director; Glyn Michael Smith [1952] Director; William Gennydd Thomas [1959] Director; Christiaan Franciscus Henricus Herman Vogelzang [1962] Director [Dutch]; Derek James Weir [1966] Director

The Co-operative Bank P.L.C.
Incorporated: 5 October 1970 *Employees:* 3,965
Net Worth: £1,505,600,000 *Total Assets:* £24,490,100,736
Registered Office: P O Box 101, 1 Balloon Street, Manchester, M60 4EP
Activities: Banks
Parent: The Co-operative Bank Holdings Limited
Officers: David William John Bagley, Secretary; Andrew John Milton Bester [1965] Director [British/South African]; Laura Martine Carstensen [1960] Director; Paul David Copley [1975] Director; Robert Graham Dench [1950] Director; Glyn Michael Smith [1952] Director; William Gennydd Thomas [1959] Director; Christiaan Franciscus Henricus Herman Vogelzang [1962] Director [Dutch]; Derek James Weir [1966] Director

Co-operative Brands Limited
Incorporated: 5 November 2004
Net Worth Deficit: £60,386,000 *Total Assets:* £59,957,000
Registered Office: 1 Angel Square, Manchester, M60 0AG
Activities: Advertising agencies
Officers: Caroline Jane Sellers, Secretary; Anthony Philip James Crossland [1965] Director/Chartered Accountant; Andrew Paul Lang [1968] Director/Accountant

Co-operative Commercial Limited
Incorporated: 19 May 1969
Net Worth: £469,810 *Total Assets:* £8,824,765
Registered Office: P O Box 101, 1 Balloon Street, Manchester, M60 4EP
Activities: Other business support service activities n.e.c.
Parent: The Co-operative Bank PLC
Officers: David Clive Whitehead, Secretary; Richard John Adnett [1974] Director/Head of Core Bank Business Partnering; Ashley John William Lillie [1970] Director

Co-operative Community Investment Foundation
Incorporated: 27 November 2000 *Employees:* 4
Net Worth: £18,394,520 *Total Assets:* £18,599,856
Registered Office: 1 Angel Square, Manchester, M60 0AG
Activities: Other business support service activities n.e.c.
Officers: Steve Fowler, Secretary; Saleem Chowdhery [1969] Director of Internal Audit; Daniel Crowe [1975] Director/Actor; Sheila Jane Malley [1951] Director; Andrew Phelps [1981] Director; Jamie Ward-Smith [1966] Director

Co-operative Legal Services Limited
Incorporated: 10 January 2006 *Employees:* 321
Net Worth: £6,544,000 *Total Assets:* £26,209,000
Registered Office: 1 Angel Square, Manchester, M60 0AG
Activities: Solicitors
Officers: Steve Fowler, Secretary; Alison Joanne Close [1975] Commercial Director; Emma Kate Dimbylow [1975] Director/Head of Legal Practice/COLP; Helen Grantham [1965] Director/Company Secretary; Matthew Ian Howells [1978] Managing Director, Co-op Legal Services; Caoilionn Hurley [1965] Director/Accountant [Irish]

Cobaco Holdings Limited
Incorporated: 4 December 2012 *Employees:* 72
Net Worth Deficit: £10,947,048 *Total Assets:* £17,811,658
Registered Office: Cobaco House, North Florida Road, Haydock Industrial Estate, Haydock, Merseyside, WA11 9TP
Activities: Activities of head offices
Shareholder: LDC II LP
Officers: Robert Nicholas Ball [1961] Director; John Paul Clarke [1981] Director; Glenn Charles Cooper [1957] Director; Gerard Gould [1966] Director; Gavin Hepburn [1974] Director; Stephen Robert Purkis [1967] Director/Accountant

Cobco (236) Limited
Incorporated: 1 May 1998
Net Worth: £2,485,000 *Total Assets:* £9,332,000
Registered Office: Craven House, Craven Road, Broadheath, Altrincham, Cheshire, WA14 5HE
Activities: Other letting and operating of own or leased real estate
Parent: Cobco 939 Ltd
Officers: Ronald Edward Hill [1948] Director; Bradley John Sanders [1963] Director/Accountant [Australian]; Mark Philip Whitby [1958] Director

Cobco (450) Limited
Incorporated: 15 February 2002 *Employees:* 3
Net Worth Deficit: £203,980 *Total Assets:* £13,182,910
Registered Office: Sceptre House, Sceptre Way, Bamber Bridge, Preston, Lancs, PR5 6AW
Activities: Other business support service activities n.e.c.
Parent: Cobco (494) Limited
Officers: Deborah Jane Rawlinson, Secretary; Jeremy Peter Hartley [1965] Director; John Howard Wilson [1965] Director

Codecrest Limited
Incorporated: 23 February 1987 *Employees:* 49
Net Worth: £3,124,773 *Total Assets:* £8,033,808
Registered Office: Dalton House, 9 Dalton Square, Lancaster, LA1 1WD
Activities: Hotels and similar accommodation
Parent: Youngmight Limited
Officers: Diane Robinson, Secretary/Hotel Accountant; Geoffrey Goodyear Atkinson [1950] Director

Coed du Hall Limited
Incorporated: 19 November 1993 *Employees:* 138
Net Worth: £9,185,449 *Total Assets:* £20,811,360
Registered Office: 6-8 Old Hall Road, Gatley, Cheadle, Cheshire, SK8 4BE
Activities: Residential care activities for learning difficulties, mental health and substance abuse
Parent: Shogun Limited
Officers: Michael Denis Hartey [1956] Director

Coffey Construction Limited
Incorporated: 14 June 1988 *Employees:* 182
Net Worth: £10,955,493 *Total Assets:* £19,551,872
Registered Office: Unit 107 Mere Grange, Elton Head Road, Leaside, St Helens, Merseyside, WA9 5GG
Activities: Construction of roads and motorways
Shareholders: Olivia Coffey; Sean Coffey
Officers: Mark Coffey, Secretary; Mark Coffey [1971] Director/Civil Engineer [Irish]; Olivia Coffey [1974] Director [Irish]; Sean Coffey [1975] Director [Irish]; Simon Coffey [1974] Director/Civil Engineer [Irish]; Odran Madden [1977] Director/Civil Engineer [Irish]

Cogent Breeding Limited
Incorporated: 28 September 1992 *Employees:* 162
Net Worth: £4,264,000 *Total Assets:* £13,993,000
Registered Office: Beachin Stud, Lea Lane, Aldford, Chester, CH3 6JQ
Activities: Support activities for animal production (other than farm animal boarding)
Officers: Gregg Webber Bevier [1953] Director/Business Executive [American]; Juan Fernando Moreno [1966] Director/Business Executive [American]; Graham Paul Ramsbottom [1965] Director/Chief Executive

Cold Fell Group Limited
Incorporated: 30 January 2008 *Employees:* 752
Net Worth: £4,047,919 *Total Assets:* £58,939,432
Registered Office: The Airport, Carlisle, Cumbria, CA6 4NW
Activities: Activities of other holding companies n.e.c.
Shareholder: Grant MacDowall
Officers: Allen Blaney Stuart, Secretary; John Andrew Hope [1970] Director; Grant MacDowall [1962] Director; Raymond Gregory MacDowall [1954] Managing Director; Allen Blaney Stuart [1979] Director/Accountant

Coldham Windfarm Limited
Incorporated: 2 August 2004
Net Worth: £3,300,000 *Total Assets:* £12,400,000
Registered Office: 3 Prenton Way, Prenton, Birkenhead, Merseyside, CH43 3ET
Activities: Production of electricity
Parent: ScottishPower Renewables (UK) Limited
Officers: Andrew Philip, Secretary; Nigel Bryn Holden [1967] Director/Head of Energy and Environment; Stuart Mason [1965] Construction Director; Roy Scott [1964] Director Control & Administration

Cole-Parmer Limited
Incorporated: 25 September 2007 *Employees:* 123
Net Worth: £26,025,068 *Total Assets:* £38,447,684
Registered Office: 3rd Floor, 1 Ashley Road, Altrincham, Cheshire, WA14 2DT
Activities: Manufacture of medical and dental instruments and supplies
Parent: UK Boxer Midco 2 Limited
Officers: Bernd Brust [1967] Director/Chief Executive Officer [American]; Jamie Ronald Gallifant [1968] Managing Director; Jon Salkin [1970] Director [American]

Cole-Parmer UK Bibby Acquisition Limited
Incorporated: 5 October 2015
Net Worth: £4,387,812 *Total Assets:* £7,647,870
Registered Office: 3rd Floor, 1 Ashley Road, Altrincham, Cheshire, WA14 2DT
Activities: Non-trading company
Parent: Cole-Parmer Instrument Company Limited
Officers: Bernd Brust [1967] Director/President and CEO [American]; Jamie Ronald Gallifant [1968] Managing Director; Jon Salkin [1970] Director [American]

Colebrook & Burgess Limited
Incorporated: 29 July 1997 *Employees:* 330
Net Worth: £20,444,000 *Total Assets:* £52,490,000
Registered Office: Lookers House, 3 Etchells Road, West Timperley, Altrincham, Cheshire, WA14 5XS
Activities: Sale of new cars and light motor vehicles
Parent: Colebrook & Burgess Holdings Ltd
Officers: Glenda MacGeekie, Secretary; Andrew Campbell Bruce [1965] Director; Robin Anthony Gregson [1960] Director/Chartered Accountant; Nigel John McMinn [1968] Managing Director

W.L. Coller Limited
Incorporated: 6 October 1939 *Employees:* 31
Net Worth: £5,469,698 *Total Assets:* £6,698,364
Registered Office: Petersgate Mill, Unit 1-4 Holloway Drive, Wardley Industrial Estate, Worsley, Manchester, M28 2LA
Activities: Wholesale of other intermediate products
Officers: Caroline Mary Merry, Secretary; Alan Hulbert Merry [1930] Director/Paper Merchant; David Scott Hulbert Merry [1971] Factory Director; Paul Hulbert Merry [1969] Sales Director; Stuart David Hulbert Merry [1936] Director/Paper Merchant

Collier Industrial Waste Limited
Incorporated: 29 February 1980 *Employees:* 8
Net Worth: £1,457,417 *Total Assets:* £8,828,282
Registered Office: c/o Collier Disposal Group, Nash Road, Trafford Park, Manchester, M17 1SX
Activities: Treatment and disposal of non-hazardous waste
Shareholders: Philip John Collier; Sheena Collier; Philip John Collier; Sheena Collier
Officers: Philip John Collier, Secretary; Steven Nelson [1962] Operational Director; David Miller Wishart [1946] Technical Director

Collinson Holdings Limited
Incorporated: 14 September 1994 *Employees:* 74
Net Worth: £13,640,193 *Total Assets:* £15,422,072
Registered Office: Nateby Works, Longmoor Lane, Garstang, Preston, Lancs, PR3 0JB
Activities: Activities of other holding companies n.e.c.
Shareholders: Ian Collinson; David James Collinson
Officers: Janet Doreen Collinson, Company Secretary; David James Collinson [1961] Director/Driver; Ian Collinson [1963] Director/General Manager; Janet Doreen Collinson [1967] Director/Company Secretary

Collinson PLC
Incorporated: 22 October 1996 *Employees:* 139
Net Worth: £7,519,976 *Total Assets:* £11,402,551
Registered Office: Riverside Industrial Park, Catterall, Preston, Lancs, PR3 0HP
Activities: Manufacture of metal structures and parts of structures
Shareholders: Ernest Roger Collinson; Freda Collinson
Officers: Rebecca Jean Elizabeth Addis, Secretary; Daniel Collinson [1973] Managing Director; Ernest Roger Collinson [1951] Director/Chairman; Freda Collinson [1950] Director; Samuel Collinson [1979] Managing Director; John Frankiewicz [1955] Director; Paul James Hutton [1967] Agricultural Sales Director

Colloids Limited
Incorporated: 27 February 2004 *Employees:* 162
Net Worth: £9,663,752 *Total Assets:* £24,120,310
Registered Office: Kirkby Bank Road, Knowsley Industrial Park North, Kirkby, Merseyside, L33 7SY
Activities: Manufacture of other plastic products
Parent: Tosaf Compounds
Officers: Moshe Menachem Henig [1951] Director/International CFO [Israeli]; Russell David Livesey [1962] Director; Amos Megides [1953] Director [Israeli]

Colormatrix Europe Limited
Incorporated: 15 January 1993 *Employees:* 136
Net Worth: £58,352,000 *Total Assets:* £73,947,000
Registered Office: Units 9-11 Unity Grove, Knowsley Business Park, Knowsley, Merseyside, L34 9GT
Activities: Manufacture of dyes and pigments
Shareholders: Colormatrix Group Inc; Colormatrix Holdings Limited
Officers: Amanda Jayne Saal, Secretary; Gary James Fielding [1963] Director; Faye Marie Freeman [1975] Director/General Manager; Robert James [1979] Director [American]

Colormatrix UK Holdings Limited
Incorporated: 26 April 2006
Net Worth: £62,393,000 *Total Assets:* £76,929,000
Registered Office: Units 9-11 Unity Grove, Knowsley Business Park, Knowsley, Merseyside, L34 9GT
Activities: Non-trading company
Officers: Amanda Jayne Saal, Secretary; Gary James Fielding [1963] Director; Faye Marie Freeman [1975] Director/General Manager; Robert James [1979] Director [American]

Columbus McKinnon Corporation Limited
Incorporated: 6 February 1958 *Employees:* 67
Net Worth: £5,855,670 *Total Assets:* £13,563,463
Registered Office: Knutsford Way, Sealand Industrial Estate, Chester, CH1 4NZ
Activities: Manufacture of lifting and handling equipment
Parent: Columbus McKinnon EMEA GmbH
Officers: Steven Antony Sherwin, Secretary; Steven Antony Sherwin [1958] Director; Kurt Franklin Wozniak [1964] Director [American]

Comap UK Holdings Limited
Incorporated: 2 April 1991
Net Worth: £112,713 *Total Assets:* £11,059,555
Registered Office: 55 King Street, Manchester, M2 4LQ
Activities: Wholesale of hardware, plumbing and heating equipment and supplies
Parent: Comap SA
Officers: Vincent Grangier [1976] Director/Chief Executive [French]; Anne Palanque [1972] Financial Director [French]

Comap UK Limited
Incorporated: 25 July 1977 *Employees:* 60
Net Worth: £1,008,000 *Total Assets:* £6,782,000
Registered Office: Unit C6, William Way, Moss Industrial Estate, Leigh, Lancs, WN7 3PT
Activities: Wholesale of hardware, plumbing and heating equipment and supplies
Parent: Comap (UK) Limited
Officers: Vincent Grangier [1976] Director [French]; Nicholas Simon Horton [1966] Director; Arno Rudolf Monincx [1967] Director [Dutch]

Combine Asset Limited
Incorporated: 3 August 2016
Net Worth: £19,581 *Total Assets:* £9,125,000
Registered Office: 192 Altrincham Road, Manchester, M22 4RZ
Activities: Other letting and operating of own or leased real estate
Shareholders: Aurelius Eta UK Investments Limited; Aurelius Equity Opportunities SE & Co. KGaA
Officers: Jeremy Nicholas Rouch, Secretary; Tony Veverka [1961] Director

Comfy Quilts Limited
Incorporated: 22 January 1991 *Employees:* 332
Net Worth: £13,780,003 *Total Assets:* £39,078,416
Registered Office: 6th Floor, Cardinal House, 20 St Mary's Parsonage, Manchester, M3 2LG
Activities: manufacture of household textiles
Shareholders: James Moryoussef; Yves Robert Moryoussef
Officers: Gillian Ruth Moryoussef, Secretary; James Moryoussef [1975] Director; Max Moryoussef [1944] Director; Yves Robert Moryoussef [1968] Director/Solicitor

Commercial Enterprises (Crewe) Limited
Incorporated: 4 October 1977 *Employees:* 244
Net Worth: £4,585,999 *Total Assets:* £6,590,621
Registered Office: Alexandra Stadium, Gresty Road, Crewe, Cheshire, CW2 6EB
Activities: Other service activities n.e.c.
Parent: Gresty Holdings (Crewe) Limited
Officers: Michael Andrew Blakemore, Secretary; Edward John Bowler [1937] Director/Chairman; Dario Gradi [1941] Director/Football Coach; Charles Howard Grant [1954] Director; Catherine Ann Hassall [1945] Director; Clare Tracy Hassall [1972] Director/Accountant; Mark Andrew Hassall [1971] Director/Accountant; Norman Hassall [1943] Director; Julie Ann McEvoy [1967] Director; Steven McEvoy [1967] Business Development Director; Daniel Kenneth Dudley Potts [1973] Director/Property Developer; David Martin Rowlinson [1956] Director; Richard James Rowlinson [1954] Director; Ian Richard Williamson [1963] Director

Commercial Power Limited
Incorporated: 15 September 2004 *Employees:* 88
Net Worth: £1,596,037 *Total Assets:* £7,309,799
Registered Office: 3 Darwin Court, Hawking Place, Blackpool, Lancs, FY2 0JN
Activities: Other business support service activities n.e.c.
Parent: Jaymel Limited
Officers: Michelle Caron Davidson, Secretary; Michelle Caron Davidson [1973] Director; Andrew James Pilley [1970] Director

Commercial Regional Space Limited
Incorporated: 7 December 2015
Net Worth: £11,406,761 *Total Assets:* £28,592,842
Registered Office: 1st Floor, Adhan House, 52a Preston New Road, Blackburn, Lancs, BB2 6AH
Activities: Other letting and operating of own or leased real estate
Major Shareholder: Mohmed Salim Ismail Patel
Officers: Mohmed Salim Ismail Patel [1968] Director

Commscare Group Limited
Incorporated: 4 November 2002
Net Worth: £9,852,450 *Total Assets:* £37,065,276
Registered Office: 8 Cheshire Avenue, Lostock Gralam, Northwich, Cheshire, CW9 7UA
Activities: Other information service activities n.e.c.
Officers: Karel Victor Hubert Gabrielle Maria Everaet [1965] Director/Group Vice President & Associate General Counsel [Belgian]; Kris Emilie Paul Mees [1965] Director/International CFO [Belgian]; Matthew Sanderson [1971] Commercial Director

Communications Plus Ltd
Incorporated: 18 September 2006 *Employees:* 215
Net Worth: £6,389,387 *Total Assets:* £14,549,817
Registered Office: Comms House, 167a Ormskirk Road, Rainford, St Helens, Merseyside, WA11 8HR
Activities: Other telecommunications activities
Shareholders: Liza Marie Roberts; Stephen Michael Roberts
Officers: Nicholas John Burke, Secretary; Liza Marie Roberts [1971] Director; Stephen Michael Roberts [1970] Director/Manager

Community 1st Oldham (Chadderton) Limited
Incorporated: 29 March 2008
Net Worth: £5,994,308 *Total Assets:* £20,570,140
Registered Office: Building 1000, Kings Reach, Yew Street, Stockport, Cheshire, SK4 2HG
Activities: Other letting and operating of own or leased real estate
Parent: Community 1st Oldham Limited
Officers: Andrew Dwan [1965] Director; Michael Dwan [1959] Director; Edward Moores [1952] Director/Councillor

Community 1st Oldham (Werneth and Shaw) Limited
Incorporated: 28 October 2009
Net Worth: £12,178,838 *Total Assets:* £27,830,698
Registered Office: Building 1000, Kings Reach, Yew Street, Stockport, Cheshire, SK4 2HG
Activities: Other letting and operating of own or leased real estate
Parent: Community 1st Oldham Tranche 2 Limited
Officers: John Connolly [1961] Director; Andrew Dwan [1965] Director; Michael Dwan [1959] Director; Anthony Kane [1953] Director; Neil Geoffrey Ward [1959] Investment Director - CHP North

Community 1st Oldham Limited
Incorporated: 14 May 2004
Net Worth: £68,358,472 *Total Assets:* £141,304,384
Registered Office: Building 1000, Kings Reach, Yew Street, Stockport, Cheshire, SK4 2HG
Activities: Other letting and operating of own or leased real estate
Shareholders: Equity Solutions Lift Investments Oldham Limited; Community Health Partnerships Limited
Officers: John Connolly [1961] Director; Andrew Dwan [1965] Director; Michael Dwan [1959] Director; Anthony Kane [1953] Director; Neil Geoffrey Ward [1959] Investment Director - CHP North

Community 1st Oldham Tranche 2 Limited
Incorporated: 8 December 2009 *Employees:* 5
Net Worth: £14,758,338 *Total Assets:* £14,758,338
Registered Office: Building 1000, Kings Reach, Yew Street, Stockport, Cheshire, SK4 2HG
Activities: Other letting and operating of own or leased real estate
Parent: Community 1st Oldham Limited
Officers: John Connolly [1961] Director; Andrew Dwan [1965] Director; Michael Dwan [1959] Director; Anthony Kane [1953] Director; Neil Geoffrey Ward [1959] Investment Director - CHP North

Community 1st Sheffield (Holdco) Limited
Incorporated: 25 July 2011 *Employees:* 5
Net Worth: £19,369,812 *Total Assets:* £19,369,812
Registered Office: Building 1000, Kings Reach, Yew Street, Stockport, Cheshire, SK4 2HG
Activities: Other business support service activities n.e.c.
Parent: Community 1st Sheffield Limited
Officers: Richard John Coates [1966] CHP Investment Director; John Connolly [1961] Director; Andrew Dwan [1965] Director; Michael Dwan [1959] Director; Neil Geoffrey Ward [1959] Investment Director - CHP North

Community 1st Sheffield (Tranche 2) Limited
Incorporated: 26 July 2011
Net Worth: £15,397,303 *Total Assets:* £44,026,464
Registered Office: Building 1000, Kings Reach, Yew Street, Stockport, Cheshire, SK4 2HG
Activities: Other letting and operating of own or leased real estate
Parent: Community 1st Sheffield (Holdco) Limited
Officers: Richard John Coates [1966] CHP Investment Director; John Connolly [1961] Director; Andrew Dwan [1965] Director; Michael Dwan [1959] Director; Neil Geoffrey Ward [1959] Investment Director - CHP North

Community 1st Sheffield Limited
Incorporated: 14 May 2004
Net Worth: £31,332,052 *Total Assets:* £47,629,136
Registered Office: Building 1000, Kings Reach, Yew Street, Stockport, Cheshire, SK4 2HG
Activities: Other letting and operating of own or leased real estate
Shareholders: Equity Solutions Lift Investments Sheffield Limited; Community Health Partnerships Limited
Officers: Richard John Coates [1966] CHP Investment Director; John Connolly [1961] Director; Andrew Dwan [1965] Director; Michael Dwan [1959] Director; Neil Geoffrey Ward [1959] Investment Director - CHP North

Community 1st Stockport Limited
Incorporated: 16 February 2007
Net Worth: £9,970,319 *Total Assets:* £23,755,348
Registered Office: Building 1000, Kings Reach, Yew Street, Stockport, Cheshire, SK4 2HG
Activities: Other letting and operating of own or leased real estate
Parent: Equity Solutions Lift Investments Stockport Limited
Officers: Christopher Guy Rogan Pratt [1961] Director/Chartered Surveyor; Patrick John Smith [1965] Director/Chartered Accountant

Community Dental Centres Limited
Incorporated: 24 May 1955 *Employees:* 100
Net Worth: £19,727,224 *Total Assets:* £21,390,878
Registered Office: Europa House, Europa Trading Estate, Stoneclough Road, Kearsley, Manchester, M26 1GG
Activities: Dental practice activities
Parent: IDH Acquisitions Limited
Officers: Leo Damian Carroll, Secretary; Clifford Gwyn Davies [1966] Clinical Director; Bernard Moroney [1953] Clinical Director; Manish Prasad [1972] Clinical Director; Tom Riall [1960] Director; Mohammed Omar Shafi Khan [1974] Director/Chief Financial Officer; Krista Nyree Whitley [1970] Clinical Director

Community First Academy Trust
Incorporated: 14 January 2013 *Employees:* 178
Net Worth: £7,150,000 *Total Assets:* £10,174,000
Registered Office: Rivington Avenue, Platt Bridge, Wigan, Lancs, WN2 5NG
Activities: Primary education
Officers: Jane Elizabeth Chambers [1967] Director/Chief Executive/Headteacher; Susan Elizabeth Darbyshire [1965] Director/Headteacher; Ruth Rule Mullen [1975] Director/Solicitor; Jack Pugh [1939] Director/Retired Professional Engineer; Mark Rowlands [1968] Director/Fire Safety Trainer & Risk Assessor; Carl Sweeney [1975] Director/Local Councillor; Brenda Catharine Szwandt [1945] Director/Educational Consultant; Simeon Mark Woosey [1977] Director/Certified Chartered Accountant

Community Foundations for Lancashire and Merseyside
Incorporated: 20 August 1997 *Employees:* 13
Net Worth: £15,375,764 *Total Assets:* £15,777,249
Registered Office: Third Floor, Stanley Building, 43 Hanover Street, Liverpool, L1 3DN
Activities: Non-trading company
Officers: Christopher James Bliss [1968] Property Director; Miles Dunnett [1969] Estate Director; Carmel Anne Hall [1957] Director/Retired; Amanda Jane Meachin [1965] Director/Chief Executive; Carole Barbara Murphy [1954] Director/Chief Executive; Andrew John Myers [1956] Director/Retired; Arthur Roberts [1950] Director/Retired; Colin Charles Wardale [1956] Director/Retired; William David Wareing [1953] Director/Solicitor

Community Health Partnerships Limited
Incorporated: 21 May 2001 *Employees:* 172
Net Worth: £777,160,000 *Total Assets:* £2,904,972,032
Registered Office: Suite 12b, Manchester One, 53 Portland Street, Manchester, M1 3LD
Activities: General public administration activities
Officers: John William Bacon [1950] Director; Nigel Jonathan Beer [1954] Director/Business Consultant; Bernadette Sarah Conroy [1966] Non-Executive Director; Dr Susanna Mary Davidson [1956] Director/Medical Practitioner; Mark Day [1965] Director; Dr Anthony Herbert Everington [1957] Director; Gillian Muriel Hunt [1971] Finance Director; Benjamin Michael Patrick Masterson [1964] Director/Civil Servant; Malcolm Douglas Twite [1967] Director

Community Integrated Care
Incorporated: 1 March 1988 *Employees:* 5,610
Net Worth: £45,449,000 *Total Assets:* £69,508,000
Registered Office: 2 Old Market Court, Miners Way, Widnes, Cheshire, WA8 7SP
Activities: Other human health activities
Officers: David Hedley, Secretary; Fiona Kathryne Armstrong [1956] Director/Journalist; Lucy Ann Butler [1969] Director/Local Government Officer; Maria Juana Da Cunha Da Silva [1963] Director of People and Legal [Spanish]; Amanda de Ryk [1966] Director/Local Government Officer; Teresa Ester Fenech [1960] Director; Shaun Daniel Gallagher [1968] Director/Civil Servant; Peter Hay [1962] Strategic Director Adults and Communities; Simon Martin Learoyd [1959] Director/Retired; Nigel Fraser Lemmon [1965] Director; Brian James Logan [1971] Director; Stuart Lorimer [1966] Finance Director; David Dennis McIntosh [1963] Managing Director; Philip Jonathan Smyth [1954] Director/Business Consultant; Professor Dame Joan Kathleen Stringer [1948] Director/Businesswoman; Heather Louise Tierney-Moore [1960] Director/Chief Executive

Community Windpower Limited
Incorporated: 13 November 2002 *Employees:* 38
Net Worth: £8,364,205 *Total Assets:* £18,778,364
Registered Office: Godscroft House, Godscroft Lane, Frodsham, Warrington, Cheshire, WA6 6XU
Activities: Production of electricity
Officers: Diane Ailsa Wood, Secretary; Diane Ailsa Wood [1965] Director; Roderick Michael Haydn Wood [1963] Director

Comodo CA Limited
Incorporated: 23 August 2000 *Employees:* 24
Net Worth: £4,470,000 *Total Assets:* £37,859,000
Registered Office: 3rd Floor, Building 26, Office Village Exchange Quay, Trafford Road, Salford, M5 3EQ
Activities: Activities of head offices
Parent: Condor Buyer Limited
Officers: Brian James Decker [1982] Director [American]

Companion Care (Services) Limited
Incorporated: 15 January 2001 *Employees:* 229
Net Worth: £46,066,000 *Total Assets:* £69,444,000
Registered Office: Epsom Avenue, Stanley Green Trading Estate, Handforth, Cheshire, SK9 3RN
Activities: Other business support service activities n.e.c.
Parent: Pets at Home Vet Group Limited
Officers: Louise Ann Stonier, Secretary; Harvey Bertenshaw Ainley [1966] Director/Chief Financial Officer; Andrei Balta [1979] Director [Romanian]; Fiona Jayne Briault [1967] Director; Julie Ross [1978] Commercial Director

Compass Minerals (Europe) Limited
Incorporated: 27 September 1995
Net Worth: £31,144,000 *Total Assets:* £96,954,000
Registered Office: Astbury House, Bradford Road, Winsford, Cheshire, CW7 2PA
Activities: Activities of head offices
Parent: Compass Minerals International Inc
Officers: Richard Stewart Thomson, Secretary; Richard Stewart Thomson [1971] Director/Chartered Accountant

Compass Minerals Storage & Archives Limited
Incorporated: 29 September 1981 *Employees:* 51
Net Worth: £3,342,000 *Total Assets:* £19,054,000
Registered Office: Astbury House, Bradford Road, Winsford, Cheshire, CW7 2PA
Activities: Operation of warehousing and storage facilities for land transport activities
Parent: Deepstore Holdings Limited
Officers: Richard Stewart Thomson, Secretary; Christopher James Heywood [1978] Director/Sales Manager; Gary Sinclair [1961] Director/Mine Manager; Richard Stewart Thomson [1971] Director/Chartered Accountant

Compass Minerals UK Holdings Limited
Incorporated: 16 October 1991
Net Worth: £7,001,000 *Total Assets:* £26,324,000
Registered Office: Astbury House, Bradford Road, Winsford, Cheshire, CW7 2PA
Activities: Agents selling agricultural raw materials, livestock, textile raw materials and semi-finished goods
Parent: Compass Minerals Europe Ltd
Officers: Richard Stewart Thomson, Secretary; Richard Stewart Thomson [1971] Director/Chartered Accountant

Compass Minerals UK Limited
Incorporated: 16 October 1991 *Employees:* 119
Net Worth: £65,530,000 *Total Assets:* £107,856,000
Registered Office: Astbury House, Bradford Road, Winsford, Cheshire, CW7 2PA
Activities: Extraction of salt
Parent: Compass Minerals UK Holdings Limited
Officers: Richard Stewart Thomson, Secretary; Christopher James Heywood [1978] Director/Sales Manager; Gary Sinclair [1961] Director/Mine Manager; Richard Stewart Thomson [1971] Director/Chartered Accountant

Compass Seacare Holdings Limited
Incorporated: 19 June 2015
Net Worth Deficit: £578,550 *Total Assets:* £8,288,502
Registered Office: c/o Edwards Veeder (UK) Limited, Ground Floor, 4 Broadgate, Broadway Business Park, Chadderton, Oldham, Lancs, OL9 9XA
Activities: Hotels and similar accommodation
Officers: Chye Teen Lim [1981] Director [Singaporean]; Harmil Singh [1962] Director/President & CEO [Singaporean]; Satkirath Singh [1993] Director [Singaporean]

Compello Holdings Limited
Incorporated: 25 April 2012
Net Worth: £60,937,440 *Total Assets:* £60,937,440
Registered Office: Quays Reach, Carolina Way, Salford, M50 2ZY
Activities: Activities of financial services holding companies
Shareholders: Hoist Finance UK Limited; Hoist Finance AB
Officers: Ian McConnell [1968] Director/Accountant; Julian Michael Winfield [1970] Director/Chief Financial Officer

Complete Medical Group Worldwide Limited
Incorporated: 27 April 1992
Net Worth: £601,000 *Total Assets:* £15,427,000
Registered Office: CMC House, 19 King Edward Street, Macclesfield, Cheshire, SK10 1AQ
Activities: Activities of head offices
Parent: IPG Holdings (UK) Limited
Officers: Louise Bean, Secretary; Charles Edward George Buckwell [1964] Director; Phillip Sutcliffe [1968] Director/Chief Financial Officer

Computer Risk Management Limited
Incorporated: 26 January 1993 *Employees:* 48
Net Worth: £2,622,485 *Total Assets:* £9,514,448
Registered Office: 6 Edward Court, Altrincham Park, Altrincham, Cheshire, WA14 5GL
Activities: Wholesale of computers, computer peripheral equipment and software
Shareholders: Graham Leslie Vickers; James Robert Kight
Officers: Graham Leslie Vickers, Secretary/Manager; James Robert Kight [1979] Director/Manager; Susan Linda Kight [1967] Director; Graham Leslie Vickers [1962] Company Secretary/Director

Computionics Group Limited
Incorporated: 4 July 2005 *Employees:* 175
Net Worth: £11,291,194 *Total Assets:* £17,394,176
Registered Office: 54 Chorley Road, Hilldale, Parbold, Lancs, WN8 7AS
Activities: Activities of other holding companies n.e.c.
Major Shareholder: Andrew William Foster
Officers: Susana Jane Foster, Secretary; Andrew William Foster [1952] Director/Electrical Engineer

Computionics Limited
Incorporated: 1 May 1981 *Employees:* 160
Net Worth: £11,256,619 *Total Assets:* £17,521,100
Registered Office: The Barn, 54 Chorley Road, Hilldale, Parbold, Lancs, WN8 7AS
Activities: Manufacture of electronic components
Parent: Computionics Group Limited
Officers: Susana Jane Foster, Secretary; Andrew William Foster [1952] Director/Electrical Engineer; Susana Jane Foster [1955] Director

Concept Life Sciences (Discovery) Limited
Incorporated: 19 May 2014
Net Worth Deficit: £192,870 *Total Assets:* £12,269,398
Registered Office: One St Peter's Square, Manchester, M2 3DE
Activities: Dormant company
Parent: Concept Life Sciences (Midco) Limited
Officers: Mark Calderbank [1979] Director/Chief Financial Officer; Paul McCluskey [1963] Director

Concept Life Sciences (Environmental Consulting) Limited
Incorporated: 19 May 2014
Net Worth Deficit: £132,352 *Total Assets:* £9,288,976
Registered Office: One St Peter's Square, Manchester, M2 3DE
Activities: Dormant company
Parent: Concept Life Sciences (Midco) Limited
Officers: Mark Calderbank [1979] Director; Paul McCluskey [1963] Director

Concept Life Sciences (Holdings) Limited
Incorporated: 19 May 2014 *Employees:* 656
Net Worth Deficit: £10,091,045 *Total Assets:* £75,754,864
Registered Office: One St Peter's Square, Manchester, M2 3DE
Activities: Activities of other holding companies n.e.c.
Parent: Spectris Group Holdings Limited
Officers: Paul McCluskey [1963] Director; Eoghan Pol O'Lionaird [1966] Director [Irish]

Concept Life Sciences (Laboratories) Limited
Incorporated: 19 May 2014 *Employees:* 2
Net Worth Deficit: £438,385 *Total Assets:* £27,971,540
Registered Office: One St Peter's Square, Manchester, M2 3DE
Activities: Other professional, scientific and technical activities n.e.c.
Parent: Concept Life Sciences (Midco) Limited
Officers: Mark Calderbank [1979] Director/Chief Financial Officer; Paul McCluskey [1963] Director

Concept Life Sciences (Midco) Limited
Incorporated: 19 May 2014 *Employees:* 7
Net Worth Deficit: £16,613 882 *Total Assets:* £56,142,456
Registered Office: One St Peter's Square, Manchester, M2 3DE
Activities: Activities of other holding companies n.e.c.
Parent: Concept Life Sciences (Holdings) Limited
Officers: Mark Calderbank [1979] Director/Chief Financial Officer; Paul McCluskey [1963] Director

Concept Life Sciences Analytical & Development Services Limited
Incorporated: 22 June 1990 *Employees:* 340
Net Worth: £6,201,971 *Total Assets:* £16,013,610
Registered Office: One St Peter's Square, Manchester, M2 3DE
Activities: Other research and experimental development on natural sciences and engineering
Parent: Concept Life Sciences (Laboratories) Limited
Officers: John William Handley [1963] Director/Chief Operations Officer; Paul McCluskey [1963] Director/Consultant

Concept Life Sciences Integrated Discovery & Development Services Limited
Incorporated: 9 February 1989 *Employees:* 118
Net Worth: £7,275,376 *Total Assets:* £10,048,659
Registered Office: One St Peter's Square, Manchester, M2 3DE
Activities: Other research and experimental development on natural sciences and engineering
Parent: Concept Life Sciences (Discovery) Limited
Officers: Dr Paul Martin Doyle [1956] Director/Research Scientist; John William Handley [1963] Director/Chief Operations Officer; Paul McCluskey [1963] Director/Consultant

Concerted Academies Trust
Incorporated: 22 July 2013 *Employees:* 143
Net Worth: £7,967,433 *Total Assets:* £11,220,019
Registered Office: Smithills School, Smithills Dean Road, Bolton, Lancs, BL1 6JS
Activities: Educational support services
Officers: John Anthony William Austin [1944] Director/Retired; Nigel William Johnson [1942] Director; Ronald Allan Makins [1955] Director

Concord Holdings Limited
Incorporated: 23 July 1902 *Employees:* 59
Net Worth: £2,801,413 *Total Assets:* £7,237,858
Registered Office: 2 Hardman Street, Manchester, M60 2AT
Activities: Activities of head offices
Officers: Jeremy Alan Kemsley-Pein [1958] Managing Director [South African]; Christopher Stuart Knight [1952] Commercial Director; Paul Douglas McGreevy [1962] Financial Director

Condie Investments Limited
Incorporated: 28 October 2002 *Employees:* 3
Net Worth: £3,370,384 *Total Assets:* £10,773,749
Registered Office: Fairhurst House, 7 Acorn Business Park, Heaton Lane, Stockport, Cheshire, SK4 1AS
Activities: Buying and selling of own real estate
Major Shareholder: John Charles Thornley
Officers: Nigel Robert Blyth [1969] Director; Stephen John Cox [1957] Director/Consultant; John Charles Thornley [1957] Director

Congleton Multi-Academy Trust
Incorporated: 22 February 2011 *Employees:* 209
Net Worth: £13,191,000 *Total Assets:* £15,622,000
Registered Office: Congleton High School, Box Lane, Congleton, Cheshire, CW12 4NS
Activities: General secondary education
Officers: Sharon Clare Bowker, Secretary; Christopher Brislen [1959] Director/Business Executive; Victor John Croxson [1946] Director/Retired; Sharon Dempsey [1956] IT Director; John Ramon Gavin [1955] Director/Businessman; David Anthony Hermitt [1965] Director/Principal; Keith Hollins [1952] Director/Business Executive; Travis Scott Latham [1968] Director/Business Executive; Jane Millward [1966] Regional Education Director; Andrew Mark Pear [1963] Director; Daniel Adam Thomas [1979] Director/Business Executive; David Wootton [1956] Director/Business Executive

The Coniston Hotel Limited
Incorporated: 3 November 1997 *Employees:* 168
Net Worth: £2,094,958 *Total Assets:* £11,673,084
Registered Office: Coniston Hall, Coniston Cold, Skipton, N Yorks, BD23 4EB
Activities: Hotels and similar accommodation
Major Shareholder: Michael John Rennie Bannister
Officers: Michael John Rennie Bannister, Secretary; Michael John Rennie Bannister [1933] Director; Nicholas William Ayrton Bannister [1959] Director; Colin Blackett [1961] Director; Louise Bolton [1980] Director/General Manager; Duncan Storey Bowring [1954] Director

Conlon Construction Limited
Incorporated: 24 November 1961 *Employees:* 88
Net Worth: £5,073,000 *Total Assets:* £22,767,000
Registered Office: Charnley Fold Lane, Bamber Bridge, Preston, Lancs, PR5 6BE
Activities: Development of building projects
Parent: Conlon Holdings Limited
Officers: Nadine Loon Angela NG, Secretary; Maureen Boland [1959] Director/Human Resources; Michael Gerard Conlon [1960] Director/Contracts Manager; Darren Stuart Lee [1971] Director/Chartered Builder; Andrew Makinson [1966] Director/Chartered Builder; Nadine Loon Angela NG [1966] Director/Chartered Accountant; Guy Edward Parker [1974] Director/Chartered Builder

Conlon Holdings Limited
Incorporated: 22 January 2007 *Employees:* 100
Net Worth: £17,075,000 *Total Assets:* £39,388,000
Registered Office: Charnley Fold Lane, Bamber Bridge, Preston, Lancs, PR5 6BE
Activities: Activities of head offices
Officers: Nadine Loon Angela NG, Secretary; Maureen Boland [1959] Director; Michael Gerard Conlon [1960] Director/Chartered Builder; Nadine Loon Angela NG [1966] Director/Chartered Accountant; Guy Edward Parker [1974] Director/Chartered Builder

Connells Limited
Incorporated: 17 April 1996 *Employees:* 6,995
Net Worth: £140,179,008 *Total Assets:* £280,401,984
Registered Office: The Bailey, Skipton, N Yorks, BD23 1DN
Activities: Activities of financial services holding companies
Parent: Skipton Group Holdings Limited
Officers: John Joseph Gibson, Secretary; Amanda Jane Burton [1959] Director; David John Cutter [1962] Building Society Director; David Christopher Livesey [1959] Mortgage Services Director; Robert Samuel Duncan Mugenyi Ndawula [1974] Finance Director; David Kerry Plumtree [1969] Director/Chief Executive; Reginald Stephen Shipperley [1958] Director/Estate Agent; Richard John Twigg [1965] Director

Consensus Property Ltd
Incorporated: 2 September 1986
Net Worth: £3,648,646 *Total Assets:* £7,420,494
Registered Office: 6 The Downs, Altrincham, Cheshire, WA14 2PU
Activities: Other letting and operating of own or leased real estate
Shareholder: Paul Frederick Thompson
Officers: Karen Michelle Jones, Secretary; Derek Cyril Thompson [1944] Director/Chairman; Paul Frederick Thompson [1969] Director

Consilium Academies
Incorporated: 18 March 2015 *Employees:* 364
Net Worth: £46,232,000 *Total Assets:* £52,518,000
Registered Office: Room 418, Chadwick House, Birchwood Park, Warrington, Cheshire, WA3 6AE
Activities: General secondary education
Officers: Sonia Johnson, Secretary; Elizabeth Cresswell [1962] Director/Headteacher; Keith Arthur John Darch [1953] Director/Retired Chartered Civil Engineer; Professor Jonathan Glazzard [1971] Director/Professor; Benjamin John Peck [1981] Director; Joan Mary Pennington [1960] Director/Business Manager; Paul Woodmancy [1960] Director

Consolidated Insurance Holdings Limited
Incorporated: 29 December 1998
Net Worth: £9,056,000 *Total Assets:* £11,271,000
Registered Office: 3rd Floor, 1 Ashley Road, Altrincham, Cheshire, WA14 2DT
Activities: Activities of head offices
Parent: GE Capital Corporation (Holdings)
Officers: Vishal Gulati [1974] Director [Indian]; Shahryar Mufti [1976] Director/Chartered Accountant

Consolidated Investment Holdings Limited
Incorporated: 12 October 2005
Net Worth Deficit: £32,482,000 *Total Assets:* £940,041,984
Registered Office: c/o Albany SPC Services Ltd, 3rd Floor, 3-5 Charlotte Street, Manchester, M1 4HB
Activities: Activities of head offices
Shareholder: Aberdeen Infrastructure (No 3) Ltd
Officers: Ailison Louise Mitchell, Secretary; Leo William McKenna [1966] Director [Irish]; Barry Paul Millsom [1974] Director; Christopher Thomas Solley [1970] Director; Andrew Leslie Tennant [1958] Director/Banker

Consolidated Property Wilmslow Limited
Incorporated: 7 March 1986 *Employees:* 10
Net Worth: £88,486,096 *Total Assets:* £128,599,832
Registered Office: 56 London Road, Alderley Edge, Cheshire, SK9 7DZ
Activities: Development of building projects
Major Shareholder: Sally Jane Turner
Officers: William Marshall Smith, Secretary/Solicitor; Peter Stuart Dawson [1952] Director/Chartered Surveyor; William Marshall Smith [1955] Director/Company Solicitor; Martin Allan Ridgway [1968] Director/Chartered Surveyor; Sally Jane Turner [1984] Director/Chartered Surveyor

Construction Partnership UK Limited
Incorporated: 7 March 2000 *Employees:* 115
Net Worth: £1,222,088 *Total Assets:* £11,990,177
Registered Office: Chadwick House, Maple View, White Moss Business Park, Skelmersdale, Lancs, WN8 9TD
Activities: Construction of commercial buildings
Shareholders: Stuart John Whittle; Stephen Joseph Burke
Officers: Jane Elizabeth Burke, Secretary; Stephen Joseph Burke [1960] Director/Chartered Quantity Surveyor; Michael Joseph English [1970] Commercial Director; Stephen John Rees [1965] Operations Director; Stuart John Whittle [1960] Director/Chartered Accountant

Consummate Investments Limited
Incorporated: 4 December 2009 *Employees:* 54
Net Worth: £2,850,073 *Total Assets:* £7,562,317
Registered Office: 2b Maple Court, Maple View, White Moss Business Park, Skelmersdale, Lancs, WN8 9TW
Activities: Activities of head offices
Major Shareholder: Derek Ian Horrocks
Officers: Marian Horrocks, Secretary; Derek Ian Horrocks [1968] Director

The Contact Company Ltd
Incorporated: 30 August 2005 *Employees:* 588
Net Worth: £3,758,423 *Total Assets:* £9,393,881
Registered Office: Queensgate, Grange Road East, Birkenhead, Merseyside, CH41 5FD
Activities: Activities of call centres
Parent: The Contact Specialists Ltd
Officers: Alexi Luke Karolemeas, Secretary; Christopher Ramon Fry [1963] Director/Chartered Accountant; Asif Hamid [1968] Director; Alexi Luke Karolemeas [1981] Director/IT Manager; Anthony Tinker [1951] Director/Chartered Accountant

The Contact Specialists Ltd
Incorporated: 1 February 2006 *Employees:* 588
Net Worth: £3,283,782 *Total Assets:* £17,163,310
Registered Office: Queensgate, Grange Road East, Birkenhead, Merseyside, CH41 5FD
Activities: Activities of call centres
Major Shareholder: Asif Hamid
Officers: Alexi Luke Karolemeas, Secretary; Christopher Ramon Fry [1963] Director/Chartered Accountant; Asif Hamid [1968] Director; Alexi Luke Karolemeas [1981] Director/IT Manager; Anthony Tinker [1951] Director/Chartered Accountant

Contis Card Solutions Limited
Incorporated: 23 May 2002
Net Worth Deficit: £1,514,975 *Total Assets:* £60,140,720
Registered Office: Navigation House, Belmont Wharf, Skipton, N Yorks, BD23 1RL
Activities: Other business support service activities n.e.c.
Parent: Contis Group Limited
Officers: Lee Johnstone, Secretary; Flavia Alzetta [1966] Director/Chief Executive [Italian]; Peter John Cox [1945] Director/Company Executive; Lee Johnstone [1975] Finance & Commercial Director

Contis Financial Services Limited
Incorporated: 6 February 2007
Net Worth: £7,651,861 *Total Assets:* £49,082,088
Registered Office: Navigation House, Belmont Wharf, Skipton, N Yorks, BD23 1RL
Activities: Other business support service activities n.e.c.
Parent: Contis Group Limited
Officers: Lee Johnstone, Secretary; Flavia Alzetta [1966] Director/Chief Executive [Italian]; Peter John Cox [1945] Chairman/Director; Lee Johnstone [1975] Director/Chartered Accountant

Contis Group Limited
Incorporated: 11 February 2008 *Employees:* 86
Net Worth Deficit: £421,201 *Total Assets:* £64,578,788
Registered Office: Navigation House, Belmont Wharf, Skipton, N Yorks, BD23 1RL
Activities: Other business support service activities n.e.c.
Shareholder: Holger Bagger-Sorensen
Officers: Lee Johnstone, Secretary; Flavia Alzetta [1966] Director/Chief Executive [Italian]; Peter John Cox [1945] Director; Joseph Charles Dunne [1949] Director [Irish]; Michael Edward Wilson Jackson [1950] Director; Lee Johnstone [1975] Director/Chief Financial Officer; Fiona Barbara Wilkinson-Huckett [1960] Director

Contitech United Kingdom Limited
Incorporated: 17 October 1972 *Employees:* 161
Net Worth: £41,756,000 *Total Assets:* £44,919,000
Registered Office: Unit 1 Hindley Green Business Park, Leigh Road, Hindley Green, Wigan, Lancs, WN2 4TN
Activities: Manufacture of other rubber products
Parent: Contitech Holding Netherlands
Officers: Philip John Sheeran, Secretary; Philip Mark Griffin [1960] Director/Sales & Marketing; Ian Paul Jones [1962] Managing Director

Contour Showers Limited
Incorporated: 13 January 1978 *Employees:* 63
Net Worth: £5,455,637 *Total Assets:* £7,554,858
Registered Office: Siddorn Street, Winsford, Cheshire, CW7 2BA
Activities: Other manufacturing n.e.c.
Parent: Elfreed Ltd
Officers: David Whitehead, Secretary; Kevin Bower [1962] Commercial Director; Jeffrey Carver [1961] Operations Director; William Scott Hogg [1963] Managing Director; Fredric William Mendelsohn [1963] Director; David Whitehead [1961] Director

Contract Chemicals (Knowsley) Limited
Incorporated: 6 July 1983 *Employees:* 70
Net Worth: £1,403,000 *Total Assets:* £10,324,000
Registered Office: Penrhyn Road, Knowsley Business Park, Prescot, Merseyside, L34 9HY
Activities: Manufacture of other organic basic chemicals
Shareholders: Brian Trenbirth; Dr David Anthony Jones
Officers: Emma Elizabeth Bonner, Secretary; Dr Tony William Bastock [1948] Director/Sales Executive; Michael John Holding [1964] Director/Marketing Executive; Dr David Anthony Jones [1944] Director/Chemical Engineer; Brian William Trenbirth [1948] Director/Chemist

Contract Chemicals Limited
Incorporated: 3 January 1989 *Employees:* 85
Net Worth: £520,000 *Total Assets:* £14,507,000
Registered Office: Penrhyn Road, Knowsley Business Park, Prescot, Merseyside, L34 9HY
Activities: Manufacture of other organic basic chemicals
Shareholders: Dr David Anthony Jones; Brian Trenbirth
Officers: Emma Elizabeth Bonner, Secretary; Dr Tony William Bastock [1948] Director/Sales Executive; Michael John Holding [1964] Managing Director; Andrew David Jones [1971] Director; Dr David Anthony Jones [1944] Director/Chemical Engineer; Patricia Elizabeth Jones [1947] Director; Brian William Trenbirth [1948] Director/Chemist; Linda Trenbirth [1947] Director

Control Circle Limited
Incorporated: 18 April 2000
Net Worth: £5,498,000 *Total Assets:* £12,710,000
Registered Office: Daisy House, Lindred Road Business Park, Nelson, Lancs, BB9 5SR
Activities: Information technology consultancy activities
Parent: Daisy Corporate Services Trading Limited
Officers: David Lewis McGlennon, Secretary; David Lewis McGlennon [1974] Director; Stephen Alan Smith [1963] Director

Convatec Holdings U.K. Limited
Incorporated: 17 June 2008
Net Worth: £389,247,008 *Total Assets:* £926,862,784
Registered Office: GDC, First Avenue, Deeside Industrial Park, Deeside, Flintshire, CH5 2NU
Activities: Activities of head offices
Officers: Clare Jane Bates [1976] Director; Sarah Jane Lewis [1970] Finance Director; Mark Lee Muir [1964] Director Tax EMEA

Convatec International U.K. Limited
Incorporated: 17 June 2008
Net Worth: £523,697,920 *Total Assets:* £523,712,256
Registered Office: GDC, First Avenue, Deeside Industrial Park, Deeside, Flintshire, CH5 2NU
Activities: Activities of head offices
Officers: Clare Jane Bates [1976] Director; Sarah Jane Lewis [1970] Finance Director; Mark Lee Muir [1964] Director Tax EMEA

Convatec Limited
Incorporated: 21 April 1977 *Employees:* 844
Net Worth: £131,230,000 *Total Assets:* £164,995,008
Registered Office: GDC, First Avenue, Deeside Industrial Park, Deeside, Flintshire, CH5 2NU
Activities: Manufacture of medical and dental instruments and supplies
Parent: Convatec Holdings U.K. Ltd
Officers: Clare Jane Bates [1976] Director/Solicitor; Sarah Jane Lewis [1970] Finance Director; Christopher John Sedwell [1976] Director/Chartered Accountant; Simon James Whitfield [1966] Business Director

Convergys Holdings (GB) Limited
Incorporated: 23 July 2004
Net Worth Deficit: £15,184,000 *Total Assets:* £29,017,000
Registered Office: LBM House, Atlantic Street, Altrincham, Cheshire, WA14 5FY
Activities: Activities of head offices
Parent: Convergys Corporation
Officers: Andrew Albert Farwig, Secretary; Beth Evelyn Luciano [1964] Director [American]; Jarrod Blaine Pontius [1971] Director/General Counsel/Attorney [American]; Andre Scott Valentine [1963] Director [American]

Conviviality Stores Ltd
Incorporated: 7 July 2005
Net Worth: £20,095,000 *Total Assets:* £58,317,000
Registered Office: Weston Road, Crewe, Cheshire, CW1 6BP
Activities: Activities of head offices
Parent: Conviviality Brands Limited
Officers: Kenton Paul Burchell [1972] Director; Mark Moran [1960] Director/Group CFO

Cook (UK) Limited
Incorporated: 24 September 1982 *Employees:* 132
Net Worth: £24,612,632 *Total Assets:* £38,749,388
Registered Office: 3rd Floor, 1 Ashley Road, Altrincham, Cheshire, WA14 2DT
Activities: Non-specialised wholesale trade
Officers: Ian Edward Whitham, Secretary/Chartered Accountant; William Joseph Doherty [1956] Managing Director [Irish]; John Robert Kamstra [1953] Director/Chief Financial Officer [American]; Ian Edward Whitham [1964] Director/European Financial Controller

Coolair Equipment Limited
Incorporated: 22 December 1993 *Employees:* 93
Net Worth: £4,507,996 *Total Assets:* £10,217,886
Registered Office: Coolair House, Globe Lane, Broadway, Dukinfield, Cheshire, SK16 4UJ
Activities: Plumbing, heat and air-conditioning installation
Parent: Coolair Management Company Ltd
Officers: Helen Sharratt, Secretary; Adam Garstang [1968] Director/National General Manager; Jason Mark Garstang [1971] Director; Neil Simon Gibbard [1970] Sales Director; John James Otterson [1959] Director/Engineer; Helen Sharratt [1966] Director/Chartered Accountant; Steven Valentine [1972] Director

Cooper Bidco Limited
Incorporated: 5 March 2015
Net Worth Deficit: £2,949,731 *Total Assets:* £45,404,452
Registered Office: 401 Faraday Street, Birchwood, Warrington, Cheshire, WA3 6GA
Activities: Wireless telecommunications activities
Parent: Cooper Topco Limited
Officers: Martyn James Cheyne [1970] Commercial Director; Terrence Flanagan [1960] Director/Engineer; Paul Nicholas Hullah [1967] Operations Director; David Christopher Humphreys [1973] Director/Chartered Accountant; Robert Michael Potter [1972] Managing Director; Christopher Tracey [1971] Operations Director

S Cooper Group Limited
Incorporated: 14 January 2016 *Employees:* 146
Net Worth: £3,712,633 *Total Assets:* £8,078,412
Registered Office: Nat Lane, Winsford, Cheshire, CW7 3BS
Activities: Activities of other holding companies n.e.c.
Shareholders: Richard James Howarth; Jeremy Richard Howarth
Officers: Matthew Johnson, Secretary; Jeremy Richard Howarth [1936] Director; Kate Jane Howarth [1966] Director; Richard James Howarth [1963] Director

Cooper Topco Limited
Incorporated: 5 March 2015 *Employees:* 329
Net Worth Deficit: £2,344,242 *Total Assets:* £63,426,440
Registered Office: 401 Faraday Street, Birchwood, Warrington, Cheshire, WA3 6GA
Activities: Wireless telecommunications activities
Parent: Whistler Bidco Limited
Officers: Martyn James Cheyne [1970] Director; Terrence Flanagan [1960] Director/Engineer; Paul Nicholas Hullah [1967] Director; David Christopher Humphreys [1973] Director/Chartered Accountant; Robert Michael Potter [1972] Managing Director; Christopher Tracey [1971] Operations Director

Coordination Group Publications Ltd
Incorporated: 25 August 1999 *Employees:* 190
Net Worth: £9,995,731 *Total Assets:* £17,107,764
Registered Office: Broughton House, Griffin Street, Broughton in Furness, Cumbria, LA20 6HH
Activities: Book publishing
Major Shareholder: Richard Alan Parsons
Officers: Carla Michelle Little, Secretary; Leila Miller [1970] Director; Richard Alan Parsons [1966] Director; Jane Michelle Ross [1968] Director

Coral Products (Mouldings) Ltd
Incorporated: 24 February 2012 *Employees:* 95
Net Worth: £1,503,539 *Total Assets:* £7,358,069
Registered Office: North Florida Road, Haydock Industrial Estate, Haydock, Merseyside, WA11 9TP
Activities: Manufacture of plastic packing goods
Parent: Coral Products PLC
Officers: Sharon Adele Gramauskas, Secretary; Neil Ashurst [1968] Quality Director; Sharon Adele Gramauskas [1974] Finance Director; Joseph Grimmond [1948] Director/Chairman; Michael Boulton Wood [1963] Director/Chief Operating Officer

Coral Products PLC
Incorporated: 5 October 1989 *Employees:* 160
Net Worth: £13,797,000 *Total Assets:* £25,029,000
Registered Office: North Florida Road, Haydock Industrial Estate, Haydock, Merseyside, WA11 9TP
Activities: Other business support service activities n.e.c.
Officers: Sharon Adele Gramauskas, Secretary; Paul Joseph Freud [1965] Director; Sharon Adele Gramauskas [1974] Finance Director; Joseph Grimmond [1948] Director; David Low [1958] Director; Michael Boulton Wood [1963] Director/Chief Executive

The Corbett Group Limited
Incorporated: 11 February 2000 *Employees:* 217
Net Worth: £9,405,651 *Total Assets:* £12,704,377
Registered Office: 74-78 Welsh Road, Garden City Sealand, Deeside, Flintshire, CH5 2HU
Activities: Activities of head offices
Shareholders: William Christopher Corbett; Elizabeth Ann Corbett; Alastair Jonathan Newall; Michael Raymond Corbett; Nicholas Corbett
Officers: Michael Raymond Corbett [1960] Director; Nicholas Corbett [1962] Director; Maureen McKeon [1949] Director

Corbetts Support Solutions Limited
Incorporated: 17 March 2005 *Employees:* 36
Net Worth: £1,217,728 *Total Assets:* £11,345,376
Registered Office: Unit 10 Forward Works, Bridge Lane, Woolston, Warrington, Cheshire, WA1 4BA
Activities: Wholesale of other machinery and equipment
Parent: Corbetts Support Systems Limited
Officers: Diane May Corbett, Secretary; Christopher Thomas Corbett [1976] Sales Director; Daniel James Corbett [1978] Director/Salesman; Michelle Louise Corbett [1971] Director/Secretary

Core Education and Consulting Solutions (UK) Ltd.
Incorporated: 11 September 2007 *Employees:* 85
Net Worth Deficit: £8,054,000 *Total Assets:* £6,605,000
Registered Office: 53 King Street, Manchester, M2 4LQ
Activities: Information technology consultancy activities
Officers: Nikhil Morsawala, Secretary; Ashutosh Madhav Ghare [1968] Director [Indian]; Prakash Gupta [1955] Director [Indian]; Nikhil Morsawala [1959] Finance Director [Indian]

Cork Street Properties Limited
Incorporated: 5 June 2000 *Employees:* 5
Net Worth Deficit: £27,478,000 *Total Assets:* £157,130,000
Registered Office: c/o Allied London, Level 12, No 1 Spinningfields, 1 Hardman Square, Manchester, M3 3EB
Activities: Development of building projects
Shareholders: Michael Julian Ingall; Frederick Paul Graham-Watson
Officers: Suresh Premji Gorasia [1974] Director; Frederick Paul Graham Watson [1957] Director; Michael Julian Ingall [1959] Director; Jonathan Raine [1981] Director

Corkills Volkswagen Limited
Incorporated: 13 October 1993 *Employees:* 61
Net Worth: £2,119,154 *Total Assets:* £8,268,324
Registered Office: Corkills Wigan, Pennyhurst Street, Wigan, Lancs, WN3 4AS
Activities: Sale of new cars and light motor vehicles
Officers: Angela Cotton, Secretary; Angela Cotton [1966] Director/Accountant; Adrian Brian McGarth-Kermode [1958] Director/General Manager; Sally Victoria Wykeham Smith [1973] Director; Timothy Worrall [1946] Director/Consultant

Corning Limited
Incorporated: 21 February 1921 *Employees:* 63
Net Worth: £17,745,000 *Total Assets:* £20,413,000
Registered Office: Elwy House, Lakeside Business Village, St Davids Park, Ewloe, Flintshire, CH5 3XD
Activities: Other professional, scientific and technical activities n.e.c.
Parent: Corning Luxembourg SRL
Officers: Lucy Cunningham, Secretary; Stephen James Quartano Candler [1968] Director Commercial Operations EMEA; Alyson Jane Cowell [1966] Director/Chartered Accountant; Stephen Propper [1964] Director/Vice President and Treasurer [American]

Cornthwaite Agricultural Limited
Incorporated: 3 May 2007 *Employees:* 32
Net Worth: £5,297,910 *Total Assets:* £17,039,980
Registered Office: Hall Lane, Bispham Green, Ormskirk, Lancs, L40 3SB
Activities: Sale of other motor vehicles
Parent: Cornthwaite Holdings Limited
Officers: John Edwin Ashe, Secretary; John Edwin Ashe [1958] Finance Director; Stuart Anthony Cornthwaite [1976] Managing Director; Robert Charles Hughes [1971] Group Aftersales Director

Cornthwaite Holdings Limited
Incorporated: 25 July 2007 *Employees:* 58
Net Worth: £5,992,637 *Total Assets:* £23,091,424
Registered Office: Hall Lane, Bispham Green, Ormskirk, Lancs, L40 3SB
Activities: Activities of head offices
Major Shareholder: Stuart Anthony Cornthwaite
Officers: John Edwin Ashe, Secretary; Stuart Anthony Cornthwaite [1976] Director

Corp Limited
Incorporated: 11 February 2003 *Employees:* 1
Net Worth Deficit: £696,969 *Total Assets:* £6,521,343
Registered Office: Suite 1, No 3 Grove Street, Wilmslow, Cheshire, SK9 1DU
Activities: Other credit granting n.e.c.
Major Shareholder: Maria Prouost
Officers: John Eunny McGeechan, Secretary; Maria Prouost [1958] Director/Consultant

Corpacq Limited
Incorporated: 4 August 2006 *Employees:* 1,285
Net Worth: £22,913,000 *Total Assets:* £212,472,000
Registered Office: Corpacq House, 1 Goose Green, Altrincham, Cheshire, WA14 1DW
Activities: Activities of head offices
Parent: Orange UK Holdings Limited
Officers: Nicholas James Cattell [1974] Director; Fred Done [1943] Director; David Robert Martin [1964] Director/Accountant; Frédéric Méreau [1984] Director/Credit Analyst [French]; Simon Sebastian Orange [1967] Director; Stephen James Scott [1978] Director

Corporate Travel Management (North) Limited
Incorporated: 10 November 1950 *Employees:* 123
Net Worth: £5,914,503 *Total Assets:* £29,248,764
Registered Office: Shire House, Humboldt Street, Bradford, W Yorks, BD1 5HQ
Activities: Travel agency activities
Parent: Alpha-Omega Travel Ltd
Officers: Stephen John Fleming, Secretary; Deborah Ann Carling [1963] Director/CEO CTM Travel Europe; Stephen John Fleming [1968] Director/Global CFO [Australian]; Jamie Michael Pherous [1968] Managing Director [Australian]

Cosatto Limited
Incorporated: 11 March 2008 *Employees:* 64
Net Worth: £2,279,000 *Total Assets:* £7,555,000
Registered Office: Bentinck Mill, Bentinck Street, Farnworth, Bolton, Lancs, BL4 7EP
Activities: Wholesale of household goods (other than musical instruments) n.e.c
Major Shareholder: Andrew Stuart Kluge
Officers: Andrew Stuart Kluge [1963] Managing Director; Victoria Morley [1971] Director/Designer; Mark Swift [1967] Product Development Director

Cosmopolitan Textile Company Limited
Incorporated: 22 September 1960 *Employees:* 66
Net Worth: £5,770,000 *Total Assets:* £8,903,000
Registered Office: Longshaw Industrial Park, Highfield Road, Blackburn, BB2 3AS
Activities: Manufacture of other textiles n.e.c.
Parent: CHA Technologies Group PLC
Officers: Jessica Haslam, Secretary; Jacques Edmond Joseph Marie-Pierre Boubal [1949] Managing Director [French]; Peter Roderick Martin [1959] Director/Chief Financial Officer

Costcutter Holdings Limited
Incorporated: 7 May 2004 *Employees:* 5
Net Worth: £29,159,000 *Total Assets:* £51,475,000
Registered Office: 105 Duke Street, Liverpool, L1 5JQ
Activities: Activities of head offices
Parent: CSMB Limited
Officers: Huw Granville Edwards [1960] Director; Michael Charles Hollis [1968] Director; Matthias Alexander Seeger [1963] Director [German]; Darcy Willson-Rymer [1965] Director

Costcutter Supermarkets Group Limited
Incorporated: 30 September 1986 *Employees:* 300
Net Worth: £8,105,000 *Total Assets:* £161,472,000
Registered Office: 105 Duke Street, Liverpool, L1 5JQ
Activities: Other retail sale in non-specialised stores
Parent: Costcutter Holdings Limited
Officers: Huw Granville Edwards [1960] Director; Michael Charles Hollis [1968] Director; Matthias Alexander Seeger [1963] Director [German]; David Michael Thompson [1960] Director; Darcy Willson-Rymer [1965] Director

Costcutter Supermarkets Holdings Limited
Incorporated: 16 November 2005 *Employees:* 621
Net Worth Deficit: £74,703,000 *Total Assets:* £129,444,000
Registered Office: 105 Duke Street, Liverpool, L1 5JQ
Activities: Other retail sale in non-specialised stores
Parent: Bibby Line Group Limited
Officers: Lawrence Richard Christensen [1943] Director; Huw Granville Edwards [1960] Director; Michael Charles Hollis [1968] Director; Mark Joseph Lyons [1962] Director; Matthias Alexander Seeger [1963] Director [German]; David Michael Thompson [1960] Director; Darcy Willson-Rymer [1965] Director

Cott Retail Brands Limited
Incorporated: 25 October 1993
Net Worth: £566,537,024 *Total Assets:* £654,153,024
Registered Office: c/o Aimia Foods Limited, Penny Lane, Haydock, St Helens, Merseyside, WA11 0QZ
Activities: Activities of head offices
Shareholder: Cott UK Accquisition Limited
Officers: Jason Robert Ausher [1973] Director [American]; Claire Duffy [1976] Director/Solicitor; Steven Kitching [1964] Director

Cott UK Acquisition Limited
Incorporated: 4 August 2010
Net Worth: £623,139,968 *Total Assets:* £741,433,024
Registered Office: c/o Aimia Foods Limited, Penny Lane, Haydock, St Helens, Merseyside, WA11 0QZ
Activities: Activities of head offices
Shareholder: Cott Corporation
Officers: Claire Duffy [1976] Director/Solicitor; Steven Kitching [1964] Director; Earl Jay Wells [1962] Director/Vice President and Chief Financial Officer [American]

Cott Ventures UK Limited
Incorporated: 12 May 2014 *Employees:* 4
Net Worth: £12,908,000 *Total Assets:* £38,828,000
Registered Office: c/o Aimia Foods Limited, Penny Lane, Haydock, St Helens, Merseyside, WA11 0QZ
Activities: Manufacture of soft drinks; production of mineral waters and other bottled waters
Parent: Cott Retail Brands Limited
Officers: Jason Robert Ausher [1973] Director [American]; Claire Duffy [1976] Director/Solicitor; Steven Kitching [1964] Director

T G Cottam Limited
Incorporated: 9 September 1930
Net Worth: £6,812,827 *Total Assets:* £7,858,707
Registered Office: c/o Poulton Plaiz, Garstang Road West, Poulton-le-Fylde, Lancs, FY6 8AR
Activities: Recreational vehicle parks, trailer parks and camping grounds
Parent: UK Leisure Parks Limited
Officers: Kerry Ann McCarthy, Secretary/Caravan Park Owner [Irish]; Kerry Ann McCarthy [1965] Director/Caravan Park Owner [Irish]; Myles Patrick John McCarthy [1964] Director/Caravan Park Owner [Irish]

Cotton Estates Limited
Incorporated: 1 March 2001
Net Worth: £1,276,729 *Total Assets:* £7,779,801
Registered Office: 19 Chestergate, Macclesfield, Cheshire, SK11 6BX
Activities: Other letting and operating of own or leased real estate
Shareholders: Nicholas Brian Lewis; Simon William Edward Lewis; Lloyd Trevor Morgan
Officers: Nicholas Brian Lewis, Secretary/Director; Brian Edward Lewis [1942] Director; Nicholas Brian Lewis [1967] Director; Lloyd Trevor Morgan [1953] Director/Accountant

Cotton Traders Holdings Limited
Incorporated: 9 June 1994 *Employees:* 944
Net Worth: £13,658,000 *Total Assets:* £28,077,000
Registered Office: Cotton Traders House, Atlantic Street, Broadheath, Altrincham, Cheshire, WA14 5GZ
Activities: Retail sale of clothing in specialised stores
Parent: Beyondnewco105 Limited
Officers: Caroline Rhoda Allerton [1964] Director/Supply Chain [Irish]; Suzanne Jean Cadle Clark [1966] Brand Director; Francis Edward Cotton [1947] Director/Chairman; Jon Paul Dorsett [1963] Director; Nicholas Anthony Hamblin [1962] Managing Director; Paul Hawkins [1964] Buying Director; Mark Steven Howlings [1964] Finance Director; Shona Anne Jameson [1976] Marketing Director; Steven James Smith [1951] Director

Cotton Traders Limited
Incorporated: 24 April 1987 *Employees:* 972
Net Worth: £17,585,000 *Total Assets:* £33,595,000
Registered Office: Cotton Traders House, Atlantic Street, Broadheath, Altrincham, Cheshire, WA14 5GZ
Activities: Retail sale of clothing in specialised stores
Parent: Beyondnewco105 Limited
Officers: Francis Edward Cotton [1947] Director; Jonathan Paul Dorsett [1963] Director; Steven James Smith [1951] Director

Counterline Limited
Incorporated: 3 June 2005 *Employees:* 144
Net Worth: £3,487,780 *Total Assets:* £7,958,430
Registered Office: Unit 12 Randles Road, Knowsley Business Park, Knowsley, Merseyside, L34 9HZ
Activities: Other manufacturing n.e.c.
Shareholders: Simon Dutton; Andrew Perry; Timothy Joseph Christopher Flood
Officers: Simon Dutton, Secretary; Simon Dutton [1968] Director; Timothy Joseph Christopher Flood [1961] Director; Andrew Perry [1966] Director

Country Park Foods Limited
Incorporated: 30 May 1960 *Employees:* 177
Net Worth: £2,019,785 *Total Assets:* £9,038,235
Registered Office: The Snackhouse, St Georges Park, Kirkham, Preston, Lancs, PR4 2DZ
Activities: Production of meat and poultry meat products
Officers: Robert Grogan [1959] Finance Director [Irish]; John Horgan [1951] Managing Director [Irish]; Liam Keating [1969] Director/Chartered Accountant [Irish]

Countrylass Ltd
Incorporated: 4 March 2010
Net Worth: £606,002 *Total Assets:* £8,129,063
Registered Office: Lancaster House, 70-76 Blackburn Street, Radcliffe, Manchester, M26 2JW
Activities: Security dealing on own account
Major Shareholder: Gayle Halstead
Officers: Gayle Halstead [1960] Director

Countrywide Assured Life Holdings Limited
Incorporated: 12 November 1991
Net Worth: £40,506,412 *Total Assets:* £40,506,668
Registered Office: 2nd Floor, Building 4, West Strand, Preston, Lancs, PR1 8UY
Activities: Activities of financial services holding companies
Parent: Chesnara PLC
Officers: Alastair Lonie, Secretary; Kenneth Duncan Hogg [1965] Director; Peter William Mason [1950] Director/Actuary

Countrywide Assured PLC
Incorporated: 25 May 1988
Net Worth: £158,408,992 *Total Assets:* £3,010,598,912
Registered Office: 2nd Floor, Building 4, West Strand Road, Preston, Lancs, PR1 8UY
Activities: Life insurance
Parent: Countrywide Assured Life Holdings Limited
Officers: Alastair Lonie, Secretary; David Sheldon Brand [1954] Director/Actuary; Jane Dale [1960] Director/Chairman; John Vincent Deane [1958] Director; Kenneth Duncan Hogg [1965] Director; Peter William Mason [1950] Director/Actuary; Eithne Siobhan McManus [1964] Director/Actuary [Irish]; Veronica Susan Oak [1961] Director; Andrew James Richards [1977] Director/Certified Chartered Accountant; David Anthony Rimmington [1968] Director/Accountant

Countrywide Freight Group Limited
Incorporated: 20 October 1994 *Employees:* 326
Net Worth: £10,642,214 *Total Assets:* £20,054,244
Registered Office: Kestrel Road, Guinness Road, Trafford Park, Manchester, M17 1SF
Activities: Freight transport by road
Officers: Donal McAllister, Secretary; John Alexander Forsyth [1949] Director; Donal McAllister [1962] Finance Director; Simon John Rothwell [1965] Group Operations Director

Countrywide Property Lawyers Limited
Incorporated: 23 October 1986 *Employees:* 266
Net Worth: £10,341,000 *Total Assets:* £13,916,000
Registered Office: Lee House, 90 Great Bridgewater Street, Manchester, M1 5RR
Activities: Activities of patent and copyright agents; other legal activities n.e.c.
Parent: Balanus Limited
Officers: Gareth Rhys Williams, Secretary; Paul Robert Chapman [1969] Managing Director; Alison Jane Roberts [1959] Director/Lawyer James Robert Scott [1978] Director; Paul Anthony Wareham [1965] Director of Field Operations

The County High School, Leftwich
Incorporated: 2 July 2012 *Employees:* 135
Net Worth: £14,432,000 *Total Assets:* £16,090,000
Registered Office: The County High School, Granville Road, Leftwich, Northwich, Cheshire, CW9 8EZ
Activities: General secondary education
Officers: Alison Ayre Dunabin [1955] Director; Irena Anna El-Hoss [1956] Director; Christopher Worsley Penter [1949] Director; Graham Wilfred Scott [1944] Director; Gaynor Jean Sinar [1964] Director

County Milk Products Limited
Incorporated: 18 November 1993 *Employees:* 32
Net Worth: £10,090,100 *Total Assets:* £45,409,044
Registered Office: Dean Court, 85 Adlington Road, Wilmslow, Cheshire, SK9 2BT
Activities: Other retail sale of food in specialised stores
Major Shareholder: John Noel Langslow
Officers: Marie Elizabeth Langslow, Secretary; Steven James Howarth [1958] Director; John Noel Langslow [1941] Director; Mark David Langslow [1970] Director; Philip John Langslow [1967] Director; Timothy Daniel Lowth [1968] Director/Accountant; Peter David White [1966] Sales Director

Court Properties (Portugal) Limited
Incorporated: 15 November 1963 *Employees:* 13
Net Worth: £8,709,967 *Total Assets:* £13,695,417
Registered Office: Emerson House, Heyes Lane, Alderley Edge, Cheshire, SK9 7LF
Activities: Construction of domestic buildings
Shareholders: P.E. Jones (Properties) Limited; Deanbank Investments Limited
Officers: Varun Maharaj, Secretary; Anthony Emerson Jones [1967] Director; Audrey Jones [1936] Director; Mark Emerson Jones [1964] Director; Peter Emerson Jones [1935] Director; Maria Cidalia Serodio Rosa [1959] Director [Portuguese]

Courtesy Shoes Limited
Incorporated: 7 June 1956 *Employees:* 564
Net Worth: £11,303,980 *Total Assets:* £18,529,744
Registered Office: Parkside, Park Road Industrial Estate, Bacup, Lancs, OL13 0BW
Activities: Retail sale of footwear in specialised stores
Parent: E.Sutton & Son Ltd
Officers: Mark James Chalmers, Secretary; Mark James Chalmers [1974] Finance Director; Michael Stephen Kelly [1967] Director/Buyer; Mark Keith Richardson [1968] Managing Director

Cox 22 Limited
Incorporated: 3 June 1926
Net Worth: £8,460,135 *Total Assets:* £8,562,346
Registered Office: Woodlands, Gawthorpe Drive, Bingley, Bradford, W Yorks, BD16 4DQ
Activities: Buying and selling of own real estate
Officers: Ann Louise Leckenby, Secretary; Donald Richard Jaggar [1936] Director; Ann Louise Leckenby [1964] Financial Director

D J Cox Limited
Incorporated: 5 June 2000 *Employees:* 238
Net Worth: £8,359,794 *Total Assets:* £28,240,468
Registered Office: Lancaster Honda, Northgate, White Lund Industrial Estate, Morecambe, Lancs, LA3 3PA
Activities: Sale of new cars and light motor vehicles
Major Shareholder: David Johnathan Cox
Officers: Helen Hayton, Secretary/Group FD; David Johnathan Cox [1971] Director/Motor Retailer; Helen Hayton [1970] Director/Group FD

Cox Motor Group Limited
Incorporated: 20 November 2015 *Employees:* 233
Net Worth: £11,954,056 *Total Assets:* £28,364,952
Registered Office: Northgate, White Lund Industrial Estate, Morecambe, Lancs, LA3 3PA
Activities: Sale of new cars and light motor vehicles
Major Shareholder: David Johnathan Cox
Officers: Helen Hayton, Secretary; David Johnathan Cox [1971] Director/Motor Retailer; Helen Hayton [1970] Director/Group FD

CPG 2016 Limited
Incorporated: 18 March 2016 *Employees:* 2
Net Worth: £1,281,372 *Total Assets:* £11,393,989
Registered Office: 56 London Road, Alderley Edge, Cheshire, SK9 7DZ
Activities: Other letting and operating of own or leased real estate
Major Shareholder: Peter Stuart Dawson
Officers: William Marshall Smith, Secretary; Peter Stuart Dawson [1952] Director/Chartered Surveyor; William Marshall Smith [1955] Director/Solicitor

CPL Petroleum Limited
Incorporated: 21 December 1994
Net Worth: £58,427,000 *Total Assets:* £84,446,000
Registered Office: 2nd Floor, 302 Bridgewater Place, Birchwood Park, Birchwood, Warrington, Cheshire, WA3 6XG
Activities: Wholesale of other fuels and related products
Parent: Energy Acquisitions UK Limited
Officers: Emma Louise Clark, Secretary; Daniel Stephen Paul Little [1976] Finance Director; Edward Gerard O'Brien [1970] Director [Irish]; Steven Michael Taylor [1959] Managing Director

CPUK Commercial Holdings Limited
Incorporated: 9 September 2013 *Employees:* 125
Net Worth: £1,240,233 *Total Assets:* £14,550,478
Registered Office: Chadwick House, Maple View, White Moss Business Park, Skelmersdale, Lancs, WN8 9TD
Activities: Activities of construction holding companies
Officers: Jane Elizabeth Burke, Secretary; Stephen Joseph Burke [1960] Director/Chartered Quantity Surveyor; Michael Joseph English [1970] Commercial Director; Stephen John Rees [1965] Operations Director; Stuart John Whittle [1960] Director/Chartered Accountant

Crabwall Claremont Limited
Incorporated: 13 September 2005 *Employees:* 142
Net Worth Deficit: £1,773,000 *Total Assets:* £29,788,000
Registered Office: Norcliffe House, Station Road, Wilmslow, Cheshire, SK9 1BU
Activities: Other human health activities
Parent: Optimum Debtco Limited
Officers: Abigail Mattison, Secretary; Ryan Stuart MacAskill [1975] Director; Gregory Laurence Newman [1988] Director/Investment Professional; Jeremy Robert Arthur Richardson [1970] Director; Dr Maureen Claire Royston [1960] Director; Phillip Gary Thomas [1978] Director

Thomas Cradley Holdings Limited
Incorporated: 20 October 1977 *Employees:* 1,108
Net Worth: £50,023,004 *Total Assets:* £127,946,032
Registered Office: Gorsey Lane, Widnes, Cheshire, WA8 0GG
Activities: Activities of head offices
Officers: Nicola Wignall Jennings, Secretary; Timothy Nicholas Broadhurst [1975] Director; Keith Broom [1963] Finance Director; Alban Bede Denton [1964] Director; Dr Clare Michelle Kerry [1969] Director; Graeme McFaull [1961] Director; John Michael Sutton [1971] Managing Director

Craghoppers Limited
Incorporated: 17 May 1995 *Employees:* 326
Net Worth: £11,183,000 *Total Assets:* £29,807,000
Registered Office: Risol House, Mercury Way, Dumplington, Urmston, Manchester, M41 7RR
Activities: Wholesale of clothing and footwear
Shareholders: Keith Joseph Black; Joanne Black
Officers: David Michael Wynn Holt, Secretary; Joanne Black [1965] Buying Director; Keith Joseph Black [1959] Director/Chairman; David Michael Wynn Holt [1962] Operations Director; James Anthony McNamara [1954] Managing Director

Cragwood International Limited
Incorporated: 5 June 1985 *Employees:* 105
Net Worth: £4,991,427 *Total Assets:* £9,564,549
Registered Office: Cragwood House, Ecclerigg, Windermere, Cumbria, LA23 1LQ
Activities: Other service activities n.e.c.
Officers: Robert Bradbury, Secretary; David Hayden Williams [1956] Director/Outdoor Pursuits Manager

Cramer Properties Limited
Incorporated: 4 June 1999 *Employees:* 3
Net Worth: £1,463,193 *Total Assets:* £6,925,709
Registered Office: Rode Cottage, 69 Moss Road, Alderley Edge, Cheshire, SK9 7JB
Activities: Other letting and operating of own or leased real estate
Major Shareholder: Ian Howard Pollitt
Officers: Carole Pollitt, Secretary; Ian Howard Pollitt [1956] Director

Crampton Bros (Coopers) Ltd
Incorporated: 9 July 1958
Net Worth: £7,565,247 *Total Assets:* £8,706,037
Registered Office: Weaver Industrial Estate, Blackburne Street, Garston, Liverpool, L19 8JA
Activities: Operation of warehousing and storage facilities for land transport activities
Parent: Cramptons Ltd
Officers: Carole Ann Martin, Secretary; Harold Crampton [1964] Director

Crane Payment Innovations Limited
Incorporated: 21 December 1982 *Employees:* 302
Net Worth: £31,994,000 *Total Assets:* £42,649,000
Registered Office: Coin House, New Coin Street, Royton, Oldham, Lancs, OL2 6JZ
Activities: Other manufacturing n.e.c.
Parent: Coin Holdings Limited
Officers: Richard Wilkinson, Secretary; Nicholas John Aspinall [1969] Director; Kurt Franklin Gallo [1965] Director/Business Executive [American]; Leanne Holmes [1977] Director; Richard Andrew Maue [1970] Director/Business Executive [American]; Max Homer Mitchell [1963] Director/Business Executive [American]; Edward Stephen Switter [1974] Director/Business Executive [American]; Richard Wilkinson [1967] Director

Crane SC Holdings Limited
Incorporated: 29 October 2010 *Employees:* 3
Net Worth: £290,973,376 *Total Assets:* £496,038,880
Registered Office: Coin House, New Coin Street, Royton, Oldham, Lancs, OL2 6JZ
Activities: Activities of head offices
Parent: Crane International Capital SARL
Officers: Richard Wilkinson, Secretary; Richard Andrew Maue [1970] Director/Business Executive [American]; Max Homer Mitchell [1963] Director/Business Executive [American]; Edward Stephen Switter [1974] Director/Business Executive [American]

Cranmer Education Trust
Incorporated: 29 June 2011 *Employees:* 243
Net Worth: £14,815,000 *Total Assets:* £18,520,000
Registered Office: The Blue Coat School, Egerton Street, Oldham, Lancs, OL1 3SQ
Activities: Primary education
Officers: Janet Gregory [1953] Director/Retired; Julie Ann Hollis [1954] Director/Headteacher; Muzahid Khan [1970] Director/Marketing Consultant; Timothy Robert Mitchell [1955] Director/Retired; Eddie Moores [1952] Director/Councillor; Mary Tomlinson [1945] Director/Retired; Peter Bruce Hereward Winter [1968] Director/General Management

Craven Cattle Marts Limited
Incorporated: 2 July 1921 *Employees:* 47
Net Worth: £10,392,298 *Total Assets:* £13,260,178
Registered Office: Auction Mart, Gargrave Road, Skipton, N Yorks, BD23 1UD
Activities: Support activities for animal production (other than farm animal boarding)
Officers: Jeremy John Eaton, Secretary; Angus Dean [1975] Director/Farmer; Keith Downs [1947] Director/Farmer; John Anthony Hewetson [1960] Director/Farmer; Martyyn Paul Jennings [1979] Director; Generald Ernest Medcalf [1948] Director/Wholesale Meat Processor; Stuart Verity [1948] Director/Farmer; John Kevin Wilson [1959] Director

Crawford Healthcare Holdings Limited
Incorporated: 9 July 2009 *Employees:* 140
Net Worth: £5,179,000 *Total Assets:* £23,649,000
Registered Office: King Edward Court, King Edward Road, Knutsford, Cheshire, WA16 0BE
Activities: Activities of head offices
Parent: KCI UK Holdings Limited
Officers: John Thomas Bibb [1972] Director/General Counsel [American]; Simon James Peter Gilderson [1970] Director/VP, Commercial Operations; Jonathan Robert Lasparini [1980] Director/Vice President, Finance

Crawford Healthcare Limited
Incorporated: 11 October 1996 *Employees:* 38
Net Worth: £4,009,081 *Total Assets:* £18,508,578
Registered Office: King Edward Court, King Edward Road, Knutsford, Cheshire, WA16 0BE
Activities: Other professional, scientific and technical activities n.e.c.
Parent: Derms Development Limited
Officers: John Thomas Bibb [1972] Director/General Counsel [American]; Simon James Peter Gilderson [1970] Director/VP, Commercial Operations; Jonathan Robert Lasparini [1980] Director/Vice President, Finance

Crawford Woundcare Limited
Incorporated: 5 November 2010 *Employees:* 38
Net Worth Deficit: £1,385,780 *Total Assets:* £15,308,622
Registered Office: King Edward Court, King Edward Road, Knutsford, Cheshire, WA16 0BE
Activities: Manufacture of medical and dental instruments and supplies
Parent: Crawford Healthcare Holdings PLC
Officers: John Thomas Bibb [1972] Director/General Counsel [American]; Simon James Peter Gilderson [1970] Director/VP, Commercial Operations; Jonathan Robert Lasparini [1980] Director/Vice President, Finance

Creamline Dairies Limited
Incorporated: 21 June 1945 *Employees:* 267
Net Worth: £8,757,747 *Total Assets:* £13,913,017
Registered Office: Creamline Dairies, Mellors Road, Trafford Park, Manchester, M17 1PB
Activities: Liquid milk and cream production
Parent: Swallow Holdings Limited
Officers: Christopher David Swallow, Secretary/Management Executive; Robert Kenneth Berry Purvis [1969] Director/Management Executive; Anthony David Swallow [1940] Director/Executive; Christopher David Swallow [1970] Director/Management Executive; Helga Hildegard Gertrud Swallow [1935] Director/Housewife [German]

Create Construction Limited
Incorporated: 22 March 2006 *Employees:* 41
Net Worth: £877,901 *Total Assets:* £11,423,311
Registered Office: 15 Thompson Road, Whitehills Business Park, Blackpool, Lancs, FY4 5PN
Activities: Construction of commercial buildings
Shareholders: Paul Allan Mathison; Gillian Mathison
Officers: Gillian Mathison, Secretary; Lee Collyer [1967] Operations Director; Gillian Mathison [1967] PR & Marketing Director; Paul Allan Mathison [1975] Managing Director; Paul Mullaney [1979] Director; Claire Oakes [1969] Director; Adrian Ashley Tottey [1983] Development Director

Crerar Hotel Group Limited
Incorporated: 4 December 1902 *Employees:* 568
Net Worth: £25,165,592 *Total Assets:* £40,117,856
Registered Office: 16 Castle Park, Lancaster, LA1 1YG
Activities: Hotels and similar accommodation
Officers: Nigel Dearnley, Secretary; John Graham Crerar [1961] Director/Investment Manager; Patrick Lorne Crerar [1968] Director; John Nigel Dearnley [1964] Director/Accountant

Crest Medical Holdings Limited
Incorporated: 25 January 2008
Net Worth: £3,103,177 *Total Assets:* £14,403,679
Registered Office: Blue Dot House, 3 Chesford Grange, Woolston, Warrington, Cheshire, WA1 4RQ
Activities: Non-trading company
Officers: Matthew George Courtney, Secretary; Matthew George Courtney [1973] Director; Barry Cunningham [1979] Director/Accountant; John Humphrey Gunn [1942] Director; Peter James Mason [1968] Director; Alastair Generald Lees Maxwell [1970] Sales Director

Crest Oil Holdings Ltd
Incorporated: 25 June 2014 *Employees:* 99
Net Worth: £11,396,383 *Total Assets:* £16,324,078
Registered Office: Units 1 & 2 Fallows Way, Whiston, Prescot, Merseyside, L35 1RZ
Activities: Manufacture of margarine and similar edible fats
Shareholders: Tariq Sultan Ghani; Abeda Rashid Ghani
Officers: Abeda Rashid Ghani [1959] Director; Tariq Sultan Ghani [1955] Director

Crest Plus Operations Limited
Incorporated: 18 December 2002 *Employees:* 2,338
Net Worth: £1,431,909 *Total Assets:* £7,284,852
Registered Office: Office Village, Chester Business Park, Chester, CH4 9QP
Activities: Other professional, scientific and technical activities n.e.c.
Major Shareholder: Andrew Gordon Robertson
Officers: Derek John Harling, Secretary/Director; Derek John Harling [1956] Director; Valerie Ann Lawton [1971] Finance Director; Paul Anthony McDonnell [1970] Director/Businessman

Cresta World Travel Limited
Incorporated: 13 November 1991 *Employees:* 80
Net Worth: £3,060,024 *Total Assets:* £10,575,196
Registered Office: Cresta House, 32 Victoria Street, Altrincham, Cheshire, WA14 1ET
Activities: Travel agency activities
Shareholders: John William Bond; Hilary Bond
Officers: Hilary Bond, Secretary; Hilary Bond [1954] Director/Company Secretary; John William Bond [1948] Director/Travel Agent [Canadian]; Denise Kay Fraser [1962] Director; Susan Catherine Houldsworth [1951] Travel Agent & Director; Phillip Kendall [1974] Director; David Leonard Plume [1956] Accountant & Director; Adrian Smyth [1976] Sales Director

Criddle & Co.Limited
Incorporated: 28 February 1950
Net Worth: £5,761,565 *Total Assets:* £12,884,510
Registered Office: Cunard Buildings, Liverpool, L3 1EL
Activities: Wholesale of grain, unmanufactured tobacco, seeds and animal feeds
Parent: Edward Billington and Son Limited
Officers: David Marshall, Secretary; Stephen Glynn Hughes [1969] Director; Lloyd Leslie Russell Whiteley [1959] Director/Manager; Jason Young [1971] Director/Trader

Cringle Corporation Limited
Incorporated: 19 June 1946
Net Worth: £10,574,582 *Total Assets:* £28,945,708
Registered Office: Suite 17b, 111 Piccadilly, Manchester, M1 2HY
Activities: Other letting and operating of own or leased real estate
Officers: Morag Elizabeth Hoyland, Secretary; Nigel Alliance [1935] Director; Joshua Adam Senior [1990] Director

CRM Trading Limited
Incorporated: 22 June 1982 *Employees:* 47
Net Worth: £3,675,184 *Total Assets:* £34,182,176
Registered Office: 6th Floor, Cardinal House, 20 St Marys Parsonage, Manchester, M3 2LG
Activities: Wholesale of perfume and cosmetics
Parent: CRM Hdgs Limited
Officers: Matthew Pettit, Secretary; Simon Tennant Barker [1956] Finance Director; Charles Rodney Mathers [1956] Director [New Zealander]

Crompton House Church of England School
Incorporated: 21 July 2011 *Employees:* 178
Net Worth: £6,685,012 *Total Assets:* £9,369,344
Registered Office: Crompton House, C of E School, Rochdale Road, Shaw, Oldham, Lancs, OL2 7HS
Activities: General secondary education
Officers: Jacqueline Young, Secretary; Leon Ashton [1934] Director/Retired; Claire Louise Borthwick [1965] Director/Teacher; Jenny Louise Carr [1977] Director/Teacher; Irene Clark [1941] Director/Retired; Lindsey Sarah Clark [1978] Director/Finance Manager; Reverend Katy Cunliffe [1979] Director/Parish Priest; Yvonne Farrand [1966] Director/Self Employed Management Consultant; Christopher John Gloster [1963] Director; Frederick Hollingworth [1944] Director/Retired; Richard James Charles Lait [1958] Director/Headteacher; Sylviane Roberte Monique Lawrence [1969] Director [Belgian]; Paul Michael Needham [1969] Director/Engineering Manager; Karl Newell [1967] Director/Teacher; Catherine Elizabeth O'Gara [1981] Director/Teacher; Jonathan Scott Swift [1948] Director/Retired; David Taylor [1948] Director/Electrical Contractor; Cherry Elizabeth Vann [1958] Director/Church of England Archdeacon

Crompton Lamps Limited
Incorporated: 12 October 2005 *Employees:* 50
Net Worth: £5,388,514 *Total Assets:* £9,002,155
Registered Office: Unit 2 Marrtree Business Park, Bowling Back Lane, Bradford, W Yorks, BD4 8QE
Activities: Manufacture of electric lighting equipment
Parent: GCH Capital Limited
Officers: Andrew Glenn Hiscoe, Secretary; Andrew Glenn Hiscoe [1965] Director; Cassie Olivia Hutchings [1983] Director; Gregory Frederick Hutchings [1947] Director/Industrialist

Croner Taxwise Limited
Incorporated: 20 October 1995 *Employees:* 112
Net Worth: £3,961,361 *Total Assets:* £8,708,135
Registered Office: The Peninsula, Victoria Place, Manchester, M4 4FB
Activities: Activities of insurance agents and brokers
Parent: Peninsula Business Services Group Limited
Officers: Peter Nicholas Swift, Secretary; Benjamin Chaplin [1974] Director/Finance & Development; Peter Eric Done [1947] Director/Bookmaker; Desmond Shaw [1956] Operations Director; Peter Nicholas Swift [1958] Director/Chartered Accountant

James Cropper Converting Limited
Incorporated: 7 March 2003 *Employees:* 36
Net Worth: £3,045,000 *Total Assets:* £15,584,000
Registered Office: Burneside Mills, Kendal, Cumbria, LA9 6PZ
Activities: Manufacture of paper and paperboard
Parent: James Cropper PLC
Officers: James Francis Aldridge, Secretary; Stephen Anthony Adrian Adams [1964] Managing Director; Isabelle Marguerite Maddock [1968] Director/Financial Controller; Philip Ian Wild [1969] Director

James Cropper Public Limited Company
Incorporated: 29 November 1889 *Employees:* 553
Net Worth: £21,887,000 *Total Assets:* £68,495,000
Registered Office: Burneside Mills, Kendal, Cumbria, LA9 6PZ
Activities: Manufacture of paper and paperboard
Officers: James Francis Aldridge, Secretary; Stephen Anthony Adrian Adams [1964] Director; Mark Alexander James Cropper [1974] Director; Dr Andrew Joseph Hosty [1965] Director; Isabelle Marguerite Maddock [1968] Finance Director; James Edward Sharp [1967] Director/Private Equity Adviser; Martin Thompson [1959] Director; Karl David Watson [1964] Director; Philip Ian Wild [1969] Director; David Robert Wilks [1954] Director/Management Consultant; Patrick John Willink [1964] Director

James Cropper Speciality Papers Limited
Incorporated: 7 March 2003 *Employees:* 337
Net Worth: £5,871,000 *Total Assets:* £48,188,000
Registered Office: Burneside Mills, Kendal, Cumbria, LA9 6PZ
Activities: Manufacture of paper and paperboard
Parent: James Cropper PLC
Officers: James Francis Aldridge, Secretary; Stephen Anthony Adrian Adams [1964] Managing Director; Isabelle Marguerite Maddock [1968] Director/Financial Controller; Philip Ian Wild [1969] Director

Crossacres Primary Academy
Incorporated: 17 February 2014 *Employees:* 83
Net Worth: £8,381,812 *Total Assets:* £9,163,046
Registered Office: Crossacres Primary Academy, Crossacres Road, Manchester, M22 5AD
Activities: Primary education
Officers: David Bell [1972] Director/Headteacher; Suzanne Victoria Blay [1967] Director/Headteacher; Alistair David Fox [1972] Director/Health & Safety Manager; Catherine Leach [1957] Director/Registered Nurse; Helen Mary Rose [1967] Director

Crossco (1317) Limited
Incorporated: 15 April 2013
Net Worth: £1,585,467 *Total Assets:* £16,723,863
Registered Office: 242 Oxford Road, Gomersal, Cleckheaton, W Yorks, BD19 4RE
Activities: Activities of open-ended investment companies
Shareholders: Dean Hoyle; Janet Elizabeth Hoyle
Officers: Dean Hoyle [1967] Chairman/Director; Janet Elizabeth Hoyle [1967] Director

Crossco (1318) Limited
Incorporated: 15 April 2013
Net Worth: £760,018 *Total Assets:* £12,056,952
Registered Office: 242 Oxford Road, Gomersal, Cleckheaton, W Yorks, BD19 4RE
Activities: Activities of open-ended investment companies
Shareholders: Janet Elizabeth Hoyle; Dean Hoyle
Officers: Dean Hoyle [1967] Chairman/Director; Janet Elizabeth Hoyle [1967] Director

Crosslane Investments Limited
Incorporated: 26 September 2006 *Employees:* 29
Net Worth: £273,528 *Total Assets:* £18,593,120
Registered Office: Suite 3d, Manchester International Office Centre, Styal Road, Manchester, M22 5WB
Activities: Other professional, scientific and technical activities n.e.c.
Shareholders: James Metcalf; Michael Anthony James Sharples
Officers: Andrea Gerrish, Secretary; James Metcalf [1952] Director; Michael Anthony James Sharples [1962] Director

Crosslane Property Group UK Limited
Incorporated: 11 March 2016 *Employees:* 29
Net Worth: £18,664,508 *Total Assets:* £97,255,000
Registered Office: Suite 3d, Manchester International Office Centre, Styal Road, Manchester, M22 5WB
Activities: Activities of other holding companies n.e.c.
Shareholders: James Metcalf; Michael Anthony James Sharples
Officers: Anthony Richard Malkin, Secretary; James Metcalf [1952] Director; Michael Anthony James Sharples [1962] Director

Crosslane Student Developments Limited
Incorporated: 11 May 2012 *Employees:* 5
Net Worth: £2,412,968 *Total Assets:* £11,415,915
Registered Office: Suite 3d, Manchester International Office Centre, Styal Road, Manchester, M22 5WB
Activities: Development of building projects
Parent: Crosslane Property Group UK Limited
Officers: Andrea Gerrish, Secretary; James Metcalf [1952] Director; Michael Anthony James Sharples [1962] Director; David Ryder Smith [1962] Managing Director; Jonathan Alistair Gerard Stewart [1970] Director/Chartered Surveyor

Crosthwaite Hotels (Westmorland) Limited
Incorporated: 29 March 1947 *Employees:* 187
Net Worth: £6,369,125 *Total Assets:* £15,346,507
Registered Office: Low Wood, Windermere, Cumbria, LA23 1LP
Activities: Hotels and similar accommodation
Officers: Timothy Robert James Berry, Secretary/Leisure Director; Benjamin William James Berry [1988] Director; Simon Frederick Michael Berry [1959] Managing Director; Timothy Robert James Berry [1961] Leisure Director; Jonathan Alexander Noel Cook [1963] Director; Douglas Paterson Dale [1952] Director; Jonquil Anna Catherine Doremus Cook [1969] Director; David Huw Neale [1962] Commercial Director; Matthew John Wilkinson [1977] Financial Director

Crown Oil Limited
Incorporated: 31 May 1977 *Employees:* 258
Net Worth: £23,062,936 *Total Assets:* £51,563,784
Registered Office: The Oil Centre, Bury New Road, Heap Bridge, Bury, Lancs, BL9 7HY
Activities: Agents involved in the sale of fuels, ores, metals and industrial chemicals
Shareholders: Matthew Craig Greensmith; Andrew David Greensmith; Abigail Alicia Rayner; Norma Nanette Greensmith
Officers: Abigail Alicia Rayner, Secretary; Mark Christopher Andrews [1976] Director/Sales; Adrian John Greenhalgh [1968] Director/Accountant; Andrew David Greensmith [1970] Director/Plastics Distributor; Matthew Craig Greensmith [1973] Director/Fuel Consultant; Norma Nanette Greensmith [1946] Director/Fuel Oil Distributor; Abigail Alicia Rayner [1986] Director/Fuel Distributor

Crown Packaging Manufacturing UK Limited
Incorporated: 31 August 2016 *Employees:* 1,025
Net Worth: £673,724,992 *Total Assets:* £873,489,984
Registered Office: Crown Packaging Manufacturing UK Limited, Borland Avenue, Botcherby, Carlisle, Cumbria, CA1 2TL
Activities: Manufacture of light metal packaging
Shareholders: CarnaudMetalbox Group UK Ltd; CarnaudMetalbox Group UK Limited
Officers: Jenny Simpson, Secretary; Paul William Browett [1961] Director/VP/Treasurer; Jean-Francois Lelouch [1967] Director/Assistant General Counsel [French]; Mehmet Ziya Ozay [1963] Director [Turkish]; David Ray Underwood [1957] Director/Senior Vice President Food & Closures Europe [American]

Crown Paints Limited
Incorporated: 19 June 2008 *Employees:* 974
Net Worth: £17,436,000 *Total Assets:* £63,445,000
Registered Office: Crown House, Hollins Road, Darwen, Lancs, BB3 0BG
Activities: Manufacture of paints, varnishes and similar coatings, mastics and sealants
Parent: Crown Paints Holdings Limited
Officers: Graham John Haworth, Secretary; Joseph Devitt [1962] Director; Graham John Haworth [1963] Director; Philip James McDonald [1972] Director/Chartered Accountant; Darryl Lee Senior [1968] Purchasing Director

Crown Promotional Packaging UK Limited
Incorporated: 26 June 1989 *Employees:* 308
Net Worth: £23,220,000 *Total Assets:* £33,136,000
Registered Office: Crown Promotional Packaging UK Limited, P O Box 11, James Street, Carlisle, Cumbria, CA2 5AY
Activities: Manufacture of light metal packaging
Parent: Crown Packaging Manufacturing UK Limited
Officers: Jennifer Patricia Simpson, Secretary; Paul William Browett [1961] Director/VP & Treasurer; Jean-Francois Lelouch [1967] Director/Assistant General Counsel [French]; Laurent Watteaux [1972] Director/VP Aerosols & Promotional Packaging [French]

CRP Print & Packaging Holdings Limited
Incorporated: 11 June 2004
Net Worth: £494,000 *Total Assets:* £8,553,000
Registered Office: Cunard Building, Water Street, Liverpool, L3 1SF
Activities: Manufacture of other articles of paper and paperboard n.e.c.
Parent: Smurfit Kappa UK Limited
Officers: Nicky Pritchard, Secretary; Clive Bowers [1953] Director; Patrick McNeill [1959] Director

CRP Print & Packaging Limited
Incorporated: 28 October 1993
Net Worth: £17,000,000 *Total Assets:* £17,000,000
Registered Office: Cunard Building, Water Street, Liverpool, L3 1SF
Activities: Manufacture of other paper and paperboard containers
Shareholders: Howper 485 Limited; CRP Print & Packaging Holdings Limited
Officers: Nicky Pritchard, Secretary; Clive Bowers [1953] Director; Patrick McNeill [1959] Director; Nicky Pritchard [1975] Director/Chartered Accountant

CRS Credit Ltd.
Incorporated: 5 May 2011 *Employees:* 3
Net Worth: £1,200,113 *Total Assets:* £9,703,209
Registered Office: Enterprise House, 2 Pass Street, Oldham, Lancs, OL9 6HZ
Activities: Other business support service activities n.e.c.
Shareholders: Iva Necasova; Tomas Hlavnicka
Officers: Elizabeth Clare Woollam [1971] Director

Cruden Construction Limited
Incorporated: 10 April 1964 *Employees:* 93
Net Worth: £1,189,336 *Total Assets:* £13,634,697
Registered Office: Hillcrest, Knutsford Road, Grappenhall, Warrington, Cheshire, WA4 3LA
Activities: Construction of commercial buildings
Parent: Cruden Group Ltd
Officers: Carl Adrian Brian [1965] Director/Chartered Accountant; Simon Robert Burrows [1962] Director/Chartered Accountant; David Allen Dickie [1959] Director; Patrick Martin Treanor [1961] Director/Quantity Surveyor; Ian David Woolrich [1962] Director

Cruden Group Limited
Incorporated: 12 August 1994 *Employees:* 212
Net Worth: £1,036,432 *Total Assets:* £17,744,246
Registered Office: Hillcrest, Knutsford Road, Grappenhall, Warrington, Cheshire, WA4 3LA
Activities: Construction of domestic buildings
Parent: Hostone
Officers: Carl Adrian Brian [1965] Director/Chartered Accountant; Mark William Burns [1964] Director; Simon Robert Burrows [1962] Director/Chartered Accountant; Ian David Woolrich [1962] Director

CSA Group Capital UK Limited
Incorporated: 6 August 2010
Net Worth: £5,894,859 *Total Assets:* £57,027,468
Registered Office: Unit 6 Hawarden Industrial Park, Hawarden, Deeside, Flintshire, CH5 3US
Activities: Activities of head offices
Parent: CSA Group Europe Holdings Limited
Officers: Lee Markey [1978] Director/UK Financial Controller; James Andrew May [1983] Managing Director; Kathryn Anne Yung [1976] Managing Director [Canadian]

CSA Group Europe Holdings Limited
Incorporated: 29 June 2009
Net Worth Deficit: £15,015,043 *Total Assets:* £15,343,548
Registered Office: Unit 6 Hawarden Industrial Park, Hawarden, Deeside, Flintshire, CH5 3US
Activities: Technical testing and analysis
Officers: Lee Markey [1978] Director/UK Financial Controller; James Andrew May [1983] Managing Director; Kathryn Anne Yung [1976] Managing Director [Canadian]

CSA Group Testing UK Limited
Incorporated: 14 January 1994 *Employees:* 194
Net Worth Deficit: £67,923 *Total Assets:* £18,731,916
Registered Office: Unit 6 Hawarden Industrial Park, Hawarden, Deeside, Flintshire, CH5 3US
Activities: Engineering design activities for industrial process and production
Parent: CSA Group Europe Holdings Limited
Officers: Kathryn Anne Yung, Secretary; Lee Markey [1978] Director/UK Financial Controller; James Andrew May [1983] Managing Director; Kathryn Anne Yung [1976] Managing Director [Canadian]

CSM (United Kingdom) Limited
Incorporated: 11 February 1980 *Employees:* 1,775
Net Worth: £25,685,000 *Total Assets:* £134,867,008
Registered Office: Stadium Road, Bromborough, Wirral, Merseyside, CH62 3NU
Activities: Manufacture of other food products n.e.c.
Officers: Sarah Elaine McSherry, Secretary; Matthew Acheson [1983] Finance Director; Maarten Dirk Bok [1966] Finance Director [Dutch]; Marianne Kirkegaard [1966] Director [Danish]

CSMB Limited
Incorporated: 15 November 2005 *Employees:* 5
Net Worth Deficit: £18,141,412 *Total Assets:* £52,692,320
Registered Office: 105 Duke Street, Liverpool, L1 5JQ
Activities: Activities of head offices
Parent: CSMF Limited
Officers: Huw Granville Edwards [1960] Director; Michael Charles Hollis [1968] Director; Matthias Alexander Seeger [1963] Director [German]; Darcy Willson-Rymer [1965] Director

CT Ice Limited
Incorporated: 6 March 2001
Net Worth: £7,906,000 *Total Assets:* £9,353,000
Registered Office: Second Avenue, Deeside Industrial Park, Deeside, Flintshire, CH5 2NW
Activities: Other retail sale in non-specialised stores
Parent: CT Ice (Holdings) Limited
Officers: Duncan Andrew Vaughan, Secretary; Tarsem Singh Dhaliwhal [1963] Director; Sir Malcolm Conrad Walker [1946] Director

CTI Billing Solutions Limited
Incorporated: 30 October 1987 *Employees:* 32
Net Worth: £7,139,803 *Total Assets:* £8,808,004
Registered Office: Unit 504 Daisyfield Business Centre, Appleby Street, Blackburn, Lancs, BB1 3BL
Activities: Information technology consultancy activities
Parent: CTI Data Solutions Limited
Officers: Douglas Craig Bryson, Secretary; Stephen Sadler [1951] Director [Canadian]

CTI Data Solutions Limited
Incorporated: 20 September 1994 *Employees:* 16
Net Worth: £9,746,126 *Total Assets:* £10,969,617
Registered Office: Daisyfield Business Centre, Appleby Street, Blackburn, BB1 3BL
Activities: Business and domestic software development
Officers: Douglas Craig Bryson, Secretary; Stephen Sadler [1951] Director [Canadian]

Cuadrilla Bowland Limited
Incorporated: 24 December 2012
Net Worth Deficit: £63,277 *Total Assets:* £31,219,586
Registered Office: Cuadrilla House, Unit 6 Sceptre Court, Sceptre Way, Bamber Bridge, Preston, Lancs, PR5 6AW
Activities: Support activities for petroleum and natural gas mining
Parent: Cuadrilla Resources Limited
Officers: Francis Gerard Egan [1961] Director [Irish]; Mark Lappin [1961] Director

Cuadrilla Resources Holdings Limited
Incorporated: 4 February 2010 *Employees:* 24
Net Worth: £32,401,508 *Total Assets:* £49,762,712
Registered Office: Cuadrilla House, Unit 6 Sceptre Court, Sceptre Way, Bamber Bridge, Preston, Lancs, PR5 6AW
Activities: Activities of head offices
Officers: Rebecca Kate Henworth, Secretary; Philip James Arnall [1945] Director [Australian]; Robin Joseph Alexander Duggan [1966] Managing Director; Francis Gerard Egan [1961] Director [Irish]; Roy Alexander Franklin [1953] Director; Neville John Lancaster Jr [1968] Director [American]; Mark Lappin [1961] Director; Alfredo Antonio Marti [1976] Director [Venezuelan]; Ivor Raymond Orchard [1953] Director

Cuadrilla Resources Limited
Incorporated: 14 January 2008 *Employees:* 24
Net Worth Deficit: £6,386,441 *Total Assets:* £80,387,944
Registered Office: Cuadrilla House, Unit 6 Sceptre Court, Sceptre Way, Bamber Bridge, Preston, Lancs, PR5 6AW
Activities: Support activities for petroleum and natural gas mining
Parent: Cuadilla Resources Holdings Limited
Officers: Francis Gerard Egan [1961] Director [Irish]; Mark Lappin [1961] Director

Cuadrilla Well Services Limited
Incorporated: 5 February 2009
Net Worth Deficit: £33,046,778 *Total Assets:* £7,754,027
Registered Office: Cuadrilla House, Unit 6 Sceptre Court, Sceptre Way, Bamber Bridge, Preston, Lancs, PR5 6AW
Activities: Support activities for petroleum and natural gas mining
Parent: Cuadrilla Resources Limited
Officers: Francis Gerard Egan [1961] Director [Irish]; Mark Lappin [1961] Director

Cubby Construction Limited
Incorporated: 28 August 1991 *Employees:* 122
Net Worth: £4,587,567 *Total Assets:* £8,322,359
Registered Office: Units H and L Knights Drive, Kingmoor Park Central, Carlisle, Cumbria, CA6 4SG
Activities: Construction of commercial buildings
Shareholders: Sally Ann Cubby; John David Cubby; Thomas John Cubby
Officers: Sally Ann Cubby, Secretary; John David Cubby [1943] Director/Building Contractor; Sally Ann Cubby [1951] Director/Company Secretary; Thomas John Cubby [1973] Director/Contract Manager

Cuerden Developments Ltd.
Incorporated: 15 May 1996 *Employees:* 6
Net Worth Deficit: £108,101 *Total Assets:* £7,982,214
Registered Office: Unit 3 Beecham Court, Pemberton, Wigan, Lancs, WN3 6PR
Activities: Construction of other civil engineering projects n.e.c.
Parent: Launchrandom Limited
Officers: Richard James Lowe, Secretary; Kimberley Jane Cramant [1984] Director; Keith Lowe [1951] Director/Builder

Cuerden Estates Ltd.
Incorporated: 19 March 1992 *Employees:* 403
Net Worth: £5,262,135 *Total Assets:* £11,459,199
Registered Office: Unit 6 Beecham Court, Pemberton, Wigan, Lancs, WN3 6PR
Activities: Construction of other civil engineering projects n.e.c.
Parent: Launchrandom Limited
Officers: Richard James Lowe, Secretary; Kimberley Jane Cramant [1984] Director; Keith Lowe [1951] Director

CuFe Investments Limited
Incorporated: 21 January 2013 *Employees:* 240
Net Worth Deficit: £164,000 *Total Assets:* £44,240,000
Registered Office: Sirius House, Delta Crescent, Westbrook, Warrington, Cheshire, WA5 7NS
Activities: Activities of other holding companies n.e.c.
Parent: European Metal Recycling Limited
Officers: Christopher John Tinsley, Secretary; Christopher Phillip Sheppard [1974] Director; Neil Andrew Stinson [1970] Director/Accountant

Culimeta-Saveguard Limited
Incorporated: 24 September 1999 *Employees:* 244
Net Worth: £6,697,278 *Total Assets:* £16,054,014
Registered Office: Tame Valley Mill, Wainwright Street, Dukinfield, Cheshire, SK16 5NB
Activities: Manufacture of other transport equipment n.e.c.
Shareholders: Stephen Shaugnessy; Brendan Joseph McCormack; Vincent Cuylits; Diederik Cuylits
Officers: Paul Murphy, Secretary; Diederik Cuylits [1965] Director [German]; Vincent Cuylits [1963] Director [German]; Brendan Joseph McCormack [1961] Director/Textile Merchant; Stephen James Shaughnessy [1954] Director/Textile Consultant

Cumbria Community Foundation
Incorporated: 15 February 1999 *Employees:* 13
Net Worth: £19,151,940 *Total Assets:* £19,988,192
Registered Office: Dovenby Hall, Dovenby, Cockermouth, Cumbria, CA13 0PN
Activities: Other business support service activities n.e.c.
Officers: Timothy Henry Cartmell, Secretary; David George Beeby [1952] Director/Retired; Anthony James Hunter Burbridge [1947] Engineering Director; Timothy Henry Cartmell [1948] Director/Retired Solicitor; Steve Cockayne [1961] Director/Chief Engineer; Nicholas Coulson [1955] Director/Retired; Susan Claire Coulson [1974] Director; Katherine Anne Fairclough [1966] Director/Chief Executive; Catherine Anne Giel [1961] Director/Stakeholder Relations Manager; Jane Elizabeth Humpries [1946] Director; Jim Johnson [1946] Director/Retired; Alison Margaret Johnston [1968] Director/Chartered Accountant; Anthony Bryan Keen [1968] Managing Director; Dr Adam Charles Illingworth Naylor [1954] Director/Landowner and Antiquarian Bookseller; Richard Andrew Roberts [1958] Director/Solicitor; William Slavin [1939] Director; Michael John Starkie [1964] Director/Elected Mayor; Chris Tomlinson [1950] Director/Partner Langale Walking and Adventure Holidays; John Frank Whittle [1949] Director; John Stephen Robert Wilson [1963] Director/Solicitor; Valerie Young [1954] Director/Accountant

Cumbria Education Trust
Incorporated: 8 July 2011 *Employees:* 398
Net Worth: £26,907,384 *Total Assets:* £35,210,336
Registered Office: Cumbria Education Trust, Longtown Road, Brampton, Cumbria, CA8 1AR
Activities: General secondary education
Officers: James Pedlingham, Secretary; Michael Ian Burke [1956] Director; Deborah Anne Francis [1966] Managing Director; Stephen Phillip Holliday [1958] Director/Retired; Lorrayne McBeath Hughes [1968] Director/Headteacher; Clifford Ronald Lewis [1956] Director; Margaret Payne [1958] Director/Lecturer; Chris Sutcliffe [1965] Director/Training and Development Manager; Kathryn Rose Woolgar [1968] Director/Chartered Accountant

Cumbria Waste Management Ltd.
Incorporated: 20 November 1991 *Employees:* 148
Net Worth: £6,706,000 *Total Assets:* £21,830,000
Registered Office: Unit 5a Wavell Drive, Rosehill Industrial Estate, Carlisle, Cumbria, CA1 2ST
Activities: Treatment and disposal of non-hazardous waste
Parent: Cumbria County Holdings Limited
Officers: Andrew John Chant, Secretary/Accountant; Robert Michael Barltrop [1952] Director/Consultant; Andrew John Chant [1970] Director/Accountant; Marshall Charles Riddell [1962] Director/Valuer; Thomas Spaul [1953] Director; Ian Wood [1958] Director

Cumbria Waste Recycling Limited
Incorporated: 21 February 1996 *Employees:* 122
Net Worth: £3,223,000 *Total Assets:* £7,474,000
Registered Office: Unit 5a Wavell Drive, Rosehill Industrial Estate, Carlisle, Cumbria, CA1 2ST
Activities: Collection of non-hazardous waste
Parent: Cumbria Waste Management Limited
Officers: Andrew John Chant, Secretary/Accountant; Andrew John Chant [1970] Director/Accountant; Marshall Charles Riddell [1962] Director/Valuer

Cumbrian Homes Limited
Incorporated: 25 November 2002 *Employees:* 16
Net Worth: £8,251,076 *Total Assets:* £10,837,867
Registered Office: Castle View, Gillan Way, Penrith 40 Business Park, Penrith, Cumbria, CA11 9BP
Activities: Construction of commercial buildings
Shareholders: Nigel Anthony Pallister; Kenneth Wilson Pallister
Officers: Kenneth Wilson Pallister [1943] Director/Business Manager; Nigel Anthony Pallister [1969] Director/Graphic Designer

Curtins Consulting Limited
Incorporated: 10 September 1986 *Employees:* 389
Net Worth: £4,398,779 *Total Assets:* £16,689,457
Registered Office: 51-55 Tithebarn Street, Liverpool, L2 2SB
Activities: Engineering related scientific and technical consulting activities
Officers: Anthony Edward Dolan [1960] Director/Transport Planner; Daniel Robert Evans [1966] Director/Engineer; Robert James Melling [1964] Director/Consulting Engineer; Paul Menzies [1974] Director/Chartered Engineer; Jonathan Richard Moister [1976] Director/Chartered Engineer; Neil Parkinson [1972] Director/Consulting Engineer; Philip Paul Richardson [1962] Director/Engineer; David Strong [1974] Director/Chartered Engineer

Curtins Group Limited
Incorporated: 12 May 1997 *Employees:* 389
Net Worth: £4,962,300 *Total Assets:* £16,743,022
Registered Office: 51-55 Tithebarn Street, Liverpool, L2 2SB
Activities: Activities of head offices
Officers: Anthony Edward Dolan [1960] Director/Transport Planner; Daniel Robert Evans [1966] Director/Engineer; Robert James Melling [1964] Director/Consulting Engineer; Paul Menzies [1974] Director/Chartered Engineer; Jonathan Richard Moister [1976] Director/Chartered Engineer; Neil Parkinson [1972] Director/Consulting Engineer; Philip Paul Richardson [1962] Director/Engineer; David Strong [1974] Director/Chartered Engineer

Leonard Curtis Recovery Limited
Incorporated: 17 April 2001 *Employees:* 115
Net Worth: £10,373,200 *Total Assets:* £12,151,824
Registered Office: Tower 12, 18-22 Bridge Street, Spinningfields, Manchester, M3 3BZ
Activities: Accounting and auditing activities
Parent: LCBSG Limited
Officers: John Malcolm Titley, Secretary; Daniel John Booth [1978] Director; Jonathan Francis Mercer [1974] Director/Chartered Accountant; Andrew Poxon [1965] Director/Chartered Accountant; John Malcolm Titley [1959] Director/Insolvency Practitioner

Curtis Wool Direct Holdings Limited
Incorporated: 30 May 2002 *Employees:* 125
Net Worth: £16,702,992 *Total Assets:* £32,609,206
Registered Office: Lawrence House, Dowley Gap Business Park, Bingley, W Yorks, BD16 1WA
Activities: Activities of head offices
Parent: Nortura SA
Officers: Tim Holgate, Secretary; Knud Peder Daugaard [1950] Director/Vice President [Danish]; David Nigel Gisbourne [1961] Director; Timothy Lloyd Holgate [1966] Director; Erik Steinar Høeg [1976] Director [Norwegian]; Daniel Andre Isbecque [1964] Director; Kai Linnes [1953] Director [Norwegian]; Kristian Håvard SAEvik [1973] Director [Norwegian]

Curtis Wool Direct Limited
Incorporated: 4 January 1980 *Employees:* 17
Net Worth: £19,382,892 *Total Assets:* £33,756,576
Registered Office: Lawrence House, Dowley Gap Business Park, Bingley, W Yorks, BD16 1WA
Activities: Non-specialised wholesale trade
Parent: Curtis Wool Direct Holdings Limited
Officers: Tim Holgate, Secretary; Knud Peder Daugaard [1950] Managing Director [Danish]; David Nigel Gisbourne [1961] Director; Timothy Lloyd Holgate [1966] Director/Wool Merchant; Erik Steinar Høeg [1976] Director [Norwegian]; Daniel Andre Isbecque [1964] Sales Director; Kai Linnes [1953] Director [Norwegian]; Kristian Håvard SAEvik [1973] Director [Norwegian]

Custom Glass Limited
Incorporated: 26 April 1999 *Employees:* 132
Net Worth: £7,156,717 *Total Assets:* £8,584,333
Registered Office: Custom Complex, Yardley Road, Kirkby, Merseyside, L33 7SS
Activities: Manufacture of flat glass
Shareholders: Custom Glass Group Holdings Limited; Brabco 620 Limited
Officers: Jeffrey Robert Hooson, Secretary/Managing Director; Paul John Finnegan [1955] Director; Jeffrey Robert Hooson [1962] Director/Manager

Custom Powders Limited
Incorporated: 7 December 1979 *Employees:* 22
Net Worth: £6,553,171 *Total Assets:* £7,288,233
Registered Office: Gateway, Crewe, Cheshire, CW1 6YT
Activities: Manufacture of basic pharmaceutical products
Major Shareholder: Peter Colyer
Officers: Mark Ardern Chadwick [1965] Operations Director; Peter Colyer [1942] Director/Chemist; Nicholas David Kemp Hopper [1960] Director/Engineer; Pascal Jean Jacques Petronelle Van Wegberg [1967] Commercial Director [Dutch]

Cutting Edge Investments Limited
Incorporated: 22 April 1997 *Employees:* 140
Net Worth: £1,236,530 *Total Assets:* £7,984,427
Registered Office: Unit 8 Matrix Park, Western Avenue, Buckshaw Village, Chorley, Lancs, PR7 7NB
Activities: Activities of head offices
Major Shareholder: David Thomas Mook
Officers: Vanessa Hamer [1973] Director; David Thomas Mook [1960] Director

Cutwel Limited
Incorporated: 23 May 1996 *Employees:* 52
Net Worth: £4,578,155 *Total Assets:* £7,037,284
Registered Office: Unit A, Riverside Drive, Cleckheaton, W Yorks, BD19 4DH
Activities: Wholesale of machine tools
Parent: Crossco (1432) Limited
Officers: Adam Gillard [1980] Director/General Manager; Graham James Short [1971] Director/Accountant

Cybele Solutions Holdings Limited
Incorporated: 10 June 2011 *Employees:* 207
Net Worth: £4,270,973 *Total Assets:* £12,659,576
Registered Office: Bickerton House, Lloyd Drive, Ellesmere Port, Cheshire, CH65 9HQ
Activities: Activities of head offices
Shareholders: Connells Limited; LSL Property Services PLC
Officers: Peter David Clarkson, Secretary; Adam Robert Castleton [1964] Director; Nicholas Chadbourne [1977] Director; Peter David Clarkson [1966] Director; David Christopher Livesey [1959] Director

Cyclesport North Limited
Incorporated: 29 January 2001 *Employees:* 59
Net Worth: £9,680,276 *Total Assets:* £11,692,150
Registered Office: 363 Leach Place, Walton Summit Centre, Bamber Bridge, Preston, Lancs, PR5 8AS
Activities: Non-specialised wholesale trade
Parent: Bradley Bidco Limited
Officers: Matthew James Lawson [1983] Director/Chief Digital Officer; Liesl Potgieter [1970] Director; Andrew Smallwood [1975] Director; David Anthony Stacey [1986] Director

Cyclife UK Ltd
Incorporated: 20 May 2003 *Employees:* 24
Net Worth: £6,908,922 *Total Assets:* £12,505,640
Registered Office: 1 Joseph Noble Road, Lillyhall Industrial Estate, Lillyhall, Workington, Cumbria, CA14 4JX
Activities: Treatment and disposal of hazardous waste
Officers: Kevin James Dodd, Secretary; Generaldine Genevieve Marie Benoit [1973] Director/Head of Waste Operations [French]; Jean-Henri Culerier [1967] Director [Spanish]; Dr Kevin James Dodd [1966] Director; Helene Claire Loupes [1972] Director/Chief Financial & Administrative Officer [French]; Bertrand Martelet [1968] Director [French]; Simon Parsons [1970] Director/Head of Deconstruction; Joseph Spencer Robinson [1971] Sales Director

Cygnet Group Limited
Incorporated: 10 July 2006 *Employees:* 167
Net Worth: £5,254,000 *Total Assets:* £11,994,000
Registered Office: Swan House, Kimpton Drive, off Wincham Lane, Wincham, Northwich, Cheshire, CW9 6GG
Activities: Activities of head offices
Major Shareholder: Matthew James Kimpton-Smith
Officers: Janet Eileen Smith, Secretary; Matthew James Kimpton Smith [1967] Director/Accountant; Samantha Kimpton Smith [1968] Director; Colin Phillip Smith [1939] Director/Engineer; Janet Eileen Smith [1941] Director/Secretary; Julie Ann Trimble [1974] Finance Director

Czajka Group Holdings Limited
Incorporated: 15 December 2008
Net Worth: £10,047,001 *Total Assets:* £11,231,666
Registered Office: Victoria House, 66-70 Bingley Road, Saltaire, Shipley, W Yorks, BD18 4DJ
Activities: Activities of head offices
Parent: Redhall Limited
Officers: Janina Czajka, Secretary; Konrad Joseph Czajka [1949] Director

Czajka Properties Limited
Incorporated: 2 September 1977 *Employees:* 340
Net Worth: £11,004,546 *Total Assets:* £15,184,349
Registered Office: Victoria House, 66-70 Bingley Road, Saltaire, Shipley, W Yorks, BD18 4DJ
Activities: Residential nursing care facilities
Parent: Czajka Group Holdings Limited
Officers: Janina Czajka, Secretary; Janina Czajka [1951] Director; Konrad Joseph Czajka [1949] Director

D C T Civil Engineering Limited
Incorporated: 30 September 1980 *Employees:* 107
Net Worth: £1,567,000 *Total Assets:* £9,069,000
Registered Office: 100 Barbirolli Square, Manchester, M2 3EY
Activities: Construction of roads and motorways
Officers: Brian Frank Ashton [1954] Director/Civil Engineer; Peter Greenhalgh [1955] Director/Civil Engineer; John Charles Hensman [1965] Director; Lee Stringer [1973] Director/Quantity Surveyor; Paul Frederick Thompson [1969] Director/Chartered Accountant

D R & P Holdings Limited
Incorporated: 22 December 2005
Net Worth: £159,620 *Total Assets:* £6,743,240
Registered Office: Chancery House, Slaidburn Crescent, Southport, Merseyside, PR9 9YF
Activities: Non-life insurance
Major Shareholder: John David Page
Officers: John David Page, Secretary; John David Page [1966] Director

D.R.A. Ltd
Incorporated: 24 May 1996 *Employees:* 208
Net Worth: £14,503,000 *Total Assets:* £25,879,000
Registered Office: Paragon Business Park, Chorley New Road, Horwich, Bolton, Lancs, BL6 6HG
Activities: Manufacture of trailers and semi-trailers
Shareholders: Douglas Graham; Rosemary Anne Graham
Officers: Rosalynde Michelle Graham, Secretary; Anthony Edmund Graham [1967] Director; Douglas Graham [1946] Director/Engineer; Rosalynde Michelle Graham [1969] Director; Rosemary Anne Graham [1947] Director

Dacsa Limited
Incorporated: 11 August 2005 *Employees:* 27
Net Worth: £3,988,247 *Total Assets:* £18,293,000
Registered Office: Crosby Road South, Liverpool, L21 4PF
Activities: Grain milling
Parent: Maicerias Espanolas S A
Officers: Araceli Ciscar Garcia [1962] Director [Spanish]; Ricardo Ciscar Garcia [1958] Director [Spanish]; Ricardo Ciscar Martinez [1929] Director [Spanish]

Dairygold Food Ingredients (UK) Limited
Incorporated: 29 August 1980 *Employees:* 144
Net Worth: £7,182,772 *Total Assets:* £45,346,012
Registered Office: Lancaster Fields, Crewe Gates Farm Ind Estate, Crewe, Cheshire, CW1 6FU
Activities: Butter and cheese production
Parent: Dairygold Holdings (UK) Limited
Officers: Ann Nora Fogarty, Secretary; Edmund Lynch [1965] Director/Farmer [Irish]; John O'Gorman [1966] Director/Farmer [Irish]; Jim Woulfe [1960] Director/Chief Executive [Irish]

Daisy Communications Ltd.
Incorporated: 22 January 2001 *Employees:* 978
Net Worth Deficit: £30,648,000 *Total Assets:* £241,436,000
Registered Office: Daisy House, Lindred Road Business Park, Nelson, Lancs, BB9 5SR
Activities: Other telecommunications activities
Parent: Daisy Intermediate Holdings Limited
Officers: David Lewis McGlennon, Secretary; Nathan Richard Marke [1970] Director; David Lewis McGlennon [1974] Director; Stephen Alan Smith [1963] Director

Daisy Computer Group Limited
Incorporated: 30 November 1995 *Employees:* 13
Net Worth: £16,191,000 *Total Assets:* £38,005,000
Registered Office: Daisy House, Lindred Road Business Park, Nelson, Lancs, BB9 5SR
Activities: Other business support service activities n.e.c.
Parent: Daisy IT Group Limited
Officers: David Lewis McGlennon, Secretary; Nathan Richard Marke [1970] Director; David Lewis McGlennon [1974] Director; Stephen Alan Smith [1963] Director

Daisy Corporate Services Limited
Incorporated: 23 February 2001
Net Worth Deficit: £3,587,000 *Total Assets:* £15,884,000
Registered Office: Daisy House, Lindred Road Business Park, Nelson, Lancs, BB9 5SR
Activities: Other telecommunications activities
Parent: Daisy Intermediate Holdings Limited
Officers: David Lewis McGlennon, Secretary; Nathan Richard Marke [1970] Director; David Lewis McGlennon [1974] Director; Stephen Alan Smith [1963] Director

Daisy Corporate Services Trading Limited
Incorporated: 17 January 1994 *Employees:* 573
Net Worth: £46,743,000 *Total Assets:* £88,133,000
Registered Office: Daisy House, Lindred Road Business Park, Nelson, Lancs, BB9 5SR
Activities: Other telecommunications activities
Parent: Daisy Intermediate Holdings Limited
Officers: David Lewis McGlennon, Secretary; David Lewis McGlennon [1974] Director; Stephen Alan Smith [1963] Director

Daisy Finco Limited
Incorporated: 4 September 2014
Net Worth: £256,138,000 *Total Assets:* £800,252,992
Registered Office: Daisy House, Lindred Road Business Park, Nelson, Lancs, BB9 5SR
Activities: Activities of head offices
Parent: Daisy Midco Limited
Officers: David Lewis McGlennon, Secretary; David Lewis McGlennon [1974] Director; Stephen Alan Smith [1963] Director

Daisy Group Holdings Limited
Incorporated: 5 August 2014 *Employees:* 3,479
Net Worth Deficit: £227,736,992 *Total Assets:* £1,301,624,960
Registered Office: Daisy House, Lindred Road Business Park, Nelson, Lancs, BB9 5SR
Activities: Other telecommunications activities
Shareholder: Matthew Robinson Riley
Officers: David Lewis McGlennon, Secretary; Martin Brian Hughes [1961] Director; Nathan Richard Marke [1970] Director; Ian Robert McKenzie [1951] Director; Matthew Robinson Riley [1974] Director; Steven Scott [1965] Director; Stephen Alan Smith [1963] Director

Daisy Group Limited
Incorporated: 4 September 2014
Net Worth: £119,288,000 *Total Assets:* £1,059,441,024
Registered Office: Daisy House, Lindred Road Business Park, Nelson, Lancs, BB9 5SR
Activities: Activities of head offices
Parent: Daisy Finco Limited
Officers: David Lewis McGlennon, Secretary; David Lewis McGlennon [1974] Director; Stephen Alan Smith [1963] Director

Daisy Holdings Limited
Incorporated: 12 April 2000 *Employees:* 33
Net Worth: £379,048,992 *Total Assets:* £741,721,024
Registered Office: Daisy House, Lindred Road Business Park, Nelson, Lancs, BB9 5SR
Activities: Activities of head offices
Parent: Daisy Group Limited
Officers: David Lewis McGlennon, Secretary; David Lewis McGlennon [1974] Director; Stephen Alan Smith [1963] Director

Daisy Intermediate Holdings Limited
Incorporated: 1 February 2013
Net Worth: £85,088,000 *Total Assets:* £548,025,984
Registered Office: Daisy House, Lindred Road Business Park, Nelson, Lancs, BB9 5SR
Activities: Activities of head offices
Parent: Daisy Holdings Limited
Officers: David Lewis McGlennon, Secretary; Nathan Richard Marke [1970] Director; David Lewis McGlennon [1974] Director; Stephen Alan Smith [1963] Director

Daisy IT Continuity and Resilience Services Limited
Incorporated: 6 November 1992 *Employees:* 134
Net Worth: £43,945,000 *Total Assets:* £91,865,000
Registered Office: Daisy House, Lindred Road Business Park, Nelson, Lancs, BB9 5SR
Activities: Other information technology service activities
Parent: Daisy Computer Group Limited
Officers: David Lewis McGlennon, Secretary; Nathan Richard Marke [1970] Director; David Lewis McGlennon [1974] Director; Stephen Alan Smith [1963] Director

Daisy IT Group Limited
Incorporated: 4 December 1997
Net Worth: £112,158,000 *Total Assets:* £172,186,000
Registered Office: Daisy House, Lindred Road Business Park, Nelson, Lancs, BB9 5SR
Activities: Activities of head offices
Parent: Daisy Intermediate Holdings Limited
Officers: David Lewis McGlennon, Secretary; Nathan Richard Marke [1970] Director; David Lewis McGlennon [1974] Director; Stephen Alan Smith [1963] Director

Daisy IT Managed Services Limited
Incorporated: 29 January 1986 *Employees:* 297
Net Worth Deficit: £32,170,000 *Total Assets:* £57,268,000
Registered Office: Daisy House, Lindred Road Business Park, Nelson, Lancs, BB9 5SR
Activities: Other telecommunications activities
Parent: Daisy Computer Group Limited
Officers: David Lewis McGlennon, Secretary; Nathan Richard Marke [1970] Director; David Lewis McGlennon [1974] Director; Stephen Alan Smith [1963] Director

Daisy IT Services Limited
Incorporated: 11 December 1979 *Employees:* 1,306
Net Worth: £1,521,000 *Total Assets:* £88,529,000
Registered Office: Daisy House, Lindred Road Business Park, Nelson, Lancs, BB9 5SR
Activities: Other telecommunications activities
Parent: Daisy IT Group Limited
Officers: David Lewis McGlennon, Secretary; Nathan Richard Marke [1970] Director; David Lewis McGlennon [1974] Director; Stephen Alan Smith [1963] Director

Daisy Midco Limited
Incorporated: 15 October 2014
Net Worth: £256,144,992 *Total Assets:* £800,259,968
Registered Office: Daisy House, Lindred Road Business Park, Nelson, Lancs, BB9 5SR
Activities: Activities of head offices
Parent: Daisy Finco Limited
Officers: David Lewis McGlennon, Secretary; David Lewis McGlennon [1974] Director; Stephen Alan Smith [1963] Director

Daisy No 1 Limited
Incorporated: 17 April 2013
Net Worth: £7,873,435 *Total Assets:* £38,226,848
Registered Office: 70 Eversheds House, Great Bridgewater Street, Manchester, M1 5ES
Activities: Production of electricity
Parent: Sune Green Holdco7 Limited
Officers: Carl Goran Dandanell [1959] Director [Swedish]

Daisy Partner Services Limited
Incorporated: 14 February 1994 *Employees:* 119
Net Worth Deficit: £3,888,000 *Total Assets:* £13,468,000
Registered Office: Daisy House, Lindred Road Business Park, Nelson, Lancs, BB9 5SR
Activities: Other information technology service activities
Parent: Daisy Wholesale Limited
Officers: David Lewis McGlennon, Secretary; Nathan Richard Marke [1970] Director; David Lewis McGlennon [1974] Director; Stephen Alan Smith [1963] Director

Daisy Pikco Limited
Incorporated: 4 September 2014
Net Worth: £256,399,008 *Total Assets:* £800,259,968
Registered Office: Daisy House, Lindred Road Business Park, Nelson, Lancs, BB9 5SR
Activities: Activities of head offices
Parent: Daisy Group Holdings Limited
Officers: David Lewis McGlennon, Secretary; David Lewis McGlennon [1974] Director; Stephen Alan Smith [1963] Director

Daisy Wholesale Limited
Incorporated: 4 May 2001 *Employees:* 160
Net Worth: £2,738,000 *Total Assets:* £59,607,000
Registered Office: Daisy House, Lindred Road Business Park, Nelson, Lancs, BB9 5SR
Activities: Other telecommunications activities
Parent: Daisy Intermediate Holdings Limited
Officers: David Lewis McGlennon, Secretary; Nathan Richard Marke [1970] Director; David Lewis McGlennon [1974] Director; Stephen Alan Smith [1963] Director

Daisy Worldwide Limited
Incorporated: 19 September 2001 *Employees:* 18
Net Worth: £28,099,000 *Total Assets:* £35,157,000
Registered Office: Daisy House, Lindred Road Business Park, Nelson, Lancs, BB9 5SR
Activities: Other telecommunications activities
Parent: Worldwide Connect Limited
Officers: David Lewis McGlennon, Secretary; Nathan Richard Marke [1970] Director; David Lewis McGlennon [1974] Director; Stephen Alan Smith [1963] Director

Daisytame Limited
Incorporated: 26 May 2015 *Employees:* 4
Net Worth Deficit: £239,262 *Total Assets:* £8,607,185
Registered Office: Building 2, 3rd Floor, Universal Square, Devonshire Street North, Manchester, M12 6JH
Activities: Other letting and operating of own or leased real estate
Officers: Carol Allen [1963] Director/Accountant; Vikrant Bhargava [1972] Director; Benjamin Graham Eades [1981] Director/Solicitor; Dr Surbhi Virmani [1974] Director/Doctor

Dale Apartments LLP
Incorporated: 13 January 2010
Net Worth: £12,805,885 *Total Assets:* £16,010,298
Registered Office: 25 Rochdale Road, Manchester, M4 4HT
Officers: Jaleh Tishbi [1956] Member; Yousef Tishbi [1948] Member

Dale Estates Limited (The)
Incorporated: 8 September 1917 *Employees:* 6
Net Worth: £12,780,123 *Total Assets:* £14,230,412
Registered Office: 2 Friarsgate, Grosvenor Street, Chester, CH1 1XG
Activities: Other letting and operating of own or leased real estate
Officers: Nigel John Anderton [1954] Director/Chartered Surveyor; Ian James Davies [1966] Director/Chartered Surveyor; Peter James Hitchcock [1946] Director/Chartered Surveyor; Andrew Mills [1966] Director/Chartered Surveyor; Mark Guy Williams [1955] Director/Chartered Surveyor

Dale Farm (GB) Limited
Incorporated: 22 April 2003 *Employees:* 175
Net Worth: £6,072,000 *Total Assets:* £36,175,000
Registered Office: Lakeland Creamery, Shap Road Industrial Estate, Kendal, Cumbria, LA9 6NS
Activities: Manufacture of other milk products
Parent: Dale Farm Cooperative Ltd
Officers: Michael Anthony Dawson, Secretary; John Herbert Scott Dunlop [1956] Director/Farmer; Stephen John Elliott [1957] Finance Director; Nick Whelan [1972] Director/Chief Executive

T L Dallas & Co Limited
Incorporated: 23 December 1959 *Employees:* 75
Net Worth: £2,317,075 *Total Assets:* £19,719,796
Registered Office: Dallas House, Low Moor, Bradford, W Yorks, BD12 0HF
Activities: Non-life insurance
Parent: TL Dallas Group Limited
Officers: Jonathan William Hollowood, Secretary; Barry Battersby [1948] Director/Insurance Broker; John Derek Butterworth [1958] Director/Insurance Broker; MacKenzie John William Dallas [1976] Director; Jonathan William Hollowood [1979] Director/Chartered Accountant; Simon Darcy Hyde [1959] Credit Broking Director; Michael Peter Martin [1960] Director/Insurance Broker; Polly Eleanor Olivia Staveley [1975] Director/Insurance Broker

T L Dallas Group Limited
Incorporated: 20 October 1989 *Employees:* 122
Net Worth: £6,349,670 *Total Assets:* £25,373,560
Registered Office: Dallas House, Low Moor, Bradford, W Yorks, BD12 0HF
Activities: Activities of financial services holding companies
Officers: Jonathan William Hollowood, Secretary; Richard John Bottomley [1957] Non-Executive Director Chairman; John Derek Butterworth [1958] Director/Insurance Broker; Michael Peter Martin [1960] Director/Insurance Broker; Francis Clive Penton [1955] Director/Insurance Broker; Graham Hoy Reid [1951] Director/Insurance Broker; Polly Eleanor Olivia Staveley [1975] Director/Insurance Broker

P.N.Daly Limited
Incorporated: 18 February 1966 *Employees:* 549
Net Worth: £16,249,391 *Total Assets:* £28,151,644
Registered Office: Butterworth Hall Works, Charles Lane, Milnrow, Rochdale, Lancs, OL16 3PA
Activities: Other specialised construction activities n.e.c.
Shareholders: Fiona Anne Daly; Jennifer Anne Daly; Patrick Noel Daly; Sean Francis Daly
Officers: Jennifer Anne Daly, Secretary; Fiona Anne Daly [1965] Director [English/Irish]; Francis Paul Daly [1967] Director/Civil Engineer [Irish]; Jennifer Anne Daly [1943] Director/Secretary; Patrick John Daly [1966] Director/Manager; Patrick Noel Daly [1936] Director/Construction Contractor [Irish]; Sean Francis Daly [1975] Director; Neil Douglas Price [1955] Multi Utility Director

Damartex UK Limited
Incorporated: 28 June 1965 *Employees:* 454
Net Worth: £17,979,000 *Total Assets:* £46,514,000
Registered Office: Bowling Green Mills, Lime Street, Bingley, W Yorks, BD97 1AD
Activities: Retail sale via mail order houses or via Internet
Parent: Damartex
Officers: Stuart Creeley, Secretary; Lynn Cordall [1967] Merchandise Director; Stuart Creeley [1962] Finance Director; Andrew Ratcliffe Hill [1955] Managing Director; Linda Ann Montgomery [1958] HR Director; George Vasili [1960] IT and Logistics Director

Dams Furniture Limited
Incorporated: 10 September 2009 *Employees:* 247
Net Worth: £10,083,110 *Total Assets:* £16,275,352
Registered Office: Gores Road, Knowsley Industrial Park, Knowsley, Merseyside, L33 7XS
Activities: Manufacture of office and shop furniture
Parent: Dams Holdings Limited
Officers: Emma Jane Hibbs, Secretary; Matthew Aldcroft [1974] Sales Director; Emma Jane Hibbs [1979] Director/Accountant; Thomas William Hibbs [1977] Director/Warehouse & Logistics; Melissa Scott Moore [1973] Director; Christopher Scott [1975] Director; Michael Scott [1980] Director

Dams Holdings Limited
Incorporated: 8 March 2016 *Employees:* 247
Net Worth: £20,253,150 *Total Assets:* £28,158,476
Registered Office: Dams Furniture Ltd, Charleywood Road, Knowsley Industrial Park, Knowsley, Merseyside, L33 7SG
Activities: Activities of head offices
Shareholder: Christopher Scott
Officers: Emma Jane Hibbs, Secretary; Melissa Scott Moore [1973] Director; Christopher Scott [1975] Director; Michael Scott [1980] Director

Dana Sac UK Limited
Incorporated: 31 October 1986 *Employees:* 40
Net Worth: £4,612,888 *Total Assets:* £7,005,168
Registered Office: Kestrel Court, Lakeside Drive, Centre Park, Warrington, Cheshire, WA1 1QX
Activities: Manufacture of bearings, gears, gearing and driving elements
Officers: Russell Anthony Marsh, Secretary; Robin Nicholas Hillman [1968] Director; Christophe Dominique Francois Jouvensal-Lepere [1964] Director [French]; Russell Anthony Marsh [1969] Managing Director

Danbro Holdings Limited
Incorporated: 18 March 2008 *Employees:* 3,787
Net Worth: £8,477,681 *Total Assets:* £21,674,152
Registered Office: Jubilee House, East Beach, Lytham St Annes, Lancs, FY8 5FT
Activities: Activities of other holding companies n.e.c.
Shareholders: Damian John Broughton; Helen Broughton
Officers: Damian John Broughton, Secretary; Damian John Broughton [1961] Director/Accountant; Helen Broughton [1972] Director

Danish Crown UK Limited
Incorporated: 20 May 1986 *Employees:* 465
Net Worth: £10,292,569 *Total Assets:* £77,085,160
Registered Office: 57 Stanley Road, Whitefield, Manchester, M45 8GZ
Activities: Processing and preserving of meat
Parent: Danish Crown Holdings A/S
Officers: Martyn Robinson, Secretary; Lars Bech Albertsen [1962] Director [Danish]; Carl Beardshall [1969] Director; Thomas Brebol Christensen [1973] Director [Danish]; Soren Eriksen [1965] Director [Danish]; Jacob Lehrmann [1987] Managing Director [Danish]

Dantex Graphics Limited
Incorporated: 3 March 1967 *Employees:* 49
Net Worth: £11,253,383 *Total Assets:* £17,903,000
Registered Office: Danon House, 5 Kings Road, Bradford, BD2 1EY
Activities: Non-specialised wholesale trade
Officers: Torge Steffen, Secretary; Andrew David Abbott [1969] UK Sales Director; Benjamin Danon [1982] Director; Dorit Danon [1948] Director; Richard Danon [1945] Research & Development Director; Richard Hall [1966] R&D Director - Dantex Digital; Torge Steffen [1976] Finance Director [German]

Dantex Group Limited
Incorporated: 10 August 2006 *Employees:* 109
Net Worth: £12,256,000 *Total Assets:* £21,973,000
Registered Office: Danon House, 5 Kings Road, Bradford, W Yorks, BD2 1EY
Activities: Activities of head offices
Officers: Torge Steffen, Secretary; Benjamin Danon [1982] Director; Richard Danon [1945] Research & Development Director

Daresbury Properties Limited
Incorporated: 1 April 1963
Net Worth: £4,677,684 *Total Assets:* £11,347,496
Registered Office: 94 Wilderspool Causeway, Warrington, Cheshire, WA4 6PU
Activities: Mixed farming
Officers: Christine Susan Marsh, Secretary; The Hon. Thomas Edward Greenall [1984] Director; John Vivian Naunton Davies [1959] Director; Andrew Gererald Thomas [1942] Director

Daresbury SIC LLP
Incorporated: 16 September 2010 *Employees:* 2
Net Worth: £20,736,296 *Total Assets:* £30,091,326
Registered Office: St James Business Centre, Wilderspool Causeway, Warrington, Cheshire, WA4 6PS

Darwin (Bath Mill) Limited
Incorporated: 11 February 2009 *Employees:* 23
Net Worth: £5,309,790 *Total Assets:* £9,927,758
Registered Office: Talacre Beach Holiday Home Park, Station Road, Talacre, Flintshire, CH8 9RD
Activities: Recreational vehicle parks, trailer parks and camping grounds
Officers: Jonathan Curry, Secretary; Lindsey Ann Bamford [1971] Director; Andrew Campbell [1959] Operations Director; Anthony Geoffrey David Esse [1962] Director

Darwin (Cheddar Woods) Limited
Incorporated: 5 June 2008 *Employees:* 68
Net Worth: £4,218,056 *Total Assets:* £19,444,472
Registered Office: Talacre Beach Holiday Home Park, Station Road, Talacre, Flintshire, CH8 9RD
Activities: Holiday centres and villages
Officers: Lindsey Ann Bamford [1971] Director; Andrew Campbell [1959] Operations Director; Anthony Geoffrey David Esse [1962] Director

Darwin (Hawkchurch Country Park) Ltd
Incorporated: 27 November 2007 *Employees:* 30
Net Worth: £10,251,595 *Total Assets:* £17,865,112
Registered Office: Talacre Beach Holiday Home Park, Station Road, Talacre, Flintshire, CH8 9RD
Activities: Hotels and similar accommodation
Officers: Lindsey Ann Bamford [1971] Director; Andrew Campbell [1959] Operations Director; Anthony Geoffrey David Esse [1962] Director

Darwin (Keswick Reach) Limited
Incorporated: 1 May 2014 *Employees:* 33
Net Worth: £10,223,696 *Total Assets:* £32,890,034
Registered Office: Talacre Beach Caravan and Leisure Park, Station Road, Talacre, Flintshire, CH8 9RD
Activities: Hotels and similar accommodation
Officers: Jonathan Curry, Secretary; Lindsey Ann Bamford [1971] Director; Andrew Campbell [1959] Operations Director; Anthony Geoffrey David Esse [1962] Director

Darwin (North West) Limited
Incorporated: 25 March 2011 *Employees:* 145
Net Worth Deficit: £6,560,369 *Total Assets:* £12,660,725
Registered Office: Talacre Beach Caravan Park, Station Road, Talacre, Holywell, Flintshire, CH8 9RD
Activities: Recreational vehicle parks, trailer parks and camping grounds
Officers: Jonathan Peter Alexander Curry, Secretary; Lindsey Ann Bamford [1971] Director; Andrew Campbell [1959] Operations Director; Anthony Geoffrey David Esse [1962] Director; Christopher James Affleck Penney [1964] Director

Darwin (Piran Meadows) Limited
Incorporated: 15 June 2010 *Employees:* 46
Net Worth: £4,485,179 *Total Assets:* £13,362,884
Registered Office: Talacre Beach Holiday Home Park, Station Road, Talacre, Flintshire, CH8 9RD
Activities: Holiday centres and villages
Officers: Jonathan Curry, Secretary; Lindsey Ann Bamford [1971] Director; Andrew Campbell [1979] Operations Director; Anthony Geoffrey David Esse [1962] Director

Darwin (Woodside Bay) Limited
Incorporated: 15 June 2010 *Employees:* 30
Net Worth: £20,560,664 *Total Assets:* £27,778,866
Registered Office: Talacre Beach Holiday Home Park, Station Road, Talacre, Flintshire, CH8 9RD
Activities: Hotels and similar accommodation
Officers: Lindsey Ann Bamford [1971] Director; Andrew Campbell [1959] Operations Director; Anthony Geoffrey David Esse [1962] Director

Darwin Contract Management Limited
Incorporated: 3 July 2008
Net Worth Deficit: £9,612 *Total Assets:* £15,618,077
Registered Office: Talacre Beach Caravan Park, Station Road, Talacre, Holywell, Flintshire, CH8 9RD
Activities: Other business support service activities n.e.c.
Officers: Jonathan Curry, Secretary; Lindsey Ann Bamford [1971] Director; Andrew Campbell [1959] Operations Director; Anthony Geoffrey David Esse [1962] Director

Darwin Loan Solutions Limited
Incorporated: 27 February 2013 *Employees:* 156
Net Worth: £3,998,000 *Total Assets:* £86,006,000
Registered Office: 8 St John Street, Manchester, M3 4DU
Activities: Activities of financial services holding companies
Major Shareholder: Terence James O'Neill
Officers: Stephen Philip Brilus [1968] Director; Mathew James Montgomery [1980] Director; Robin John Russel-Fisher [1958] Finance Director

Data Intensity Holdings Limited
Incorporated: 27 October 2015 *Employees:* 415
Net Worth: £5,631,471 *Total Assets:* £23,280,720
Registered Office: 3rd Floor, 1 Ashley Road, Altrincham, Cheshire, WA14 2DT
Activities: Other information technology service activities
Officers: Kathleen Eastwood [1971] Director [American]; Antony Mark Sumpster [1966] Director

Data Intensity Limited
Incorporated: 30 October 1998 *Employees:* 97
Net Worth: £3,471,066 *Total Assets:* £9,920,160
Registered Office: 3rd Floor, 1 Ashley Road, Altrincham, Cheshire, WA14 2DT
Activities: Information technology consultancy activities
Parent: Red Stack Technology Group Limited
Officers: James Clifford Anthony [1975] Director; Kathleen Eastwood [1971] Director [American]; Alexander Benjamin Louth [1976] Director; Antony Mark Sumpster [1966] Director

Datac Adhesives Limited
Incorporated: 3 November 1980
Net Worth: £12,400,000 *Total Assets:* £30,319,000
Registered Office: Globe Lane Industrial Estate, Outram Road, Dukinfield, Cheshire, SK16 4XE
Activities: Manufacture of other chemical products n.e.c.
Parent: H. B. Fuller Company
Officers: Robert Joseph Martsching [1964] Director/Vice President and Corporate Controller [American]; Emilio Roque Vilas [1968] Business Director Hygiene [Spanish]; Heidi Ann Weiler [1966] Director/Vice President and Treasurer [American]

Datel Computing Limited
Incorporated: 9 April 1981 *Employees:* 178
Net Worth: £771,616 *Total Assets:* £10,307,404
Registered Office: Datel, Cinnamon Park, Warrington, Cheshire, WA2 0XP
Activities: Information technology consultancy activities
Parent: Datel Group PLC
Officers: Karen Alison Simpson, Secretary; Andrew Pritchard [1968] Director; Alan Keith Simpson [1956] Director; Nicholas Andrew Swarbrick [1968] Director

Datel Group PLC
Incorporated: 21 November 1989 *Employees:* 178
Net Worth: £710,759 *Total Assets:* £10,321,956
Registered Office: Cinnamon Park, Fearnhead, Warrington, Cheshire, WA2 0XP
Activities: Information technology consultancy activities
Major Shareholder: Alan Keith Simpson
Officers: Nicholas Andrew Swarbrick, Secretary; Andrew Pritchard [1968] Director; Alan Keith Simpson [1956] Director; Nicholas Andrew Swarbrick [1968] Director

Datum Finance Limited
Incorporated: 18 January 2005
Net Worth Deficit: £14,312,911 *Total Assets:* £23,323,746
Registered Office: Calder Vale Park, Simonstone Lane, Simonstone, Burnley, Lancs, BB12 7ND
Activities: Financial intermediation not elsewhere classified
Major Shareholder: Edward Sagar Fort
Officers: Edward Martin Drury [1949] Finance Director; Edward Sagar Fort OBE [1937] Director; Steven Derek Jelfs [1963] Director

Davane Holding Company Limited
Incorporated: 28 July 2010 *Employees:* 66
Net Worth: £4,302,748 *Total Assets:* £12,514,748
Registered Office: The Picturedrome, 102-104 Chestergate, Macclesfield, Cheshire, SK11 6DU
Activities: Activities of head offices
Shareholders: Karl David Massey; Susan Massey
Officers: Karl David Massey [1964] Director

C.P. Davidson & Sons Limited
Incorporated: 8 March 1991 *Employees:* 52
Net Worth: £2,735,650 *Total Assets:* £9,439,385
Registered Office: Lyons Lane, Chorley, Lancs, PR7 3BL
Activities: Manufacture of bodies (coachwork) for motor vehicles (except caravans)
Parent: P.J.D. (Holdings) Limited
Officers: Alison Lesley Davidson, Company Secretary; Alison Lesley Davidson [1955] Director; Philip James Davidson [1954] Director/Manager; Robert Andrew Davidson [1979] Operations Director; Stephen Anthony Davidson [1982] Director; Rebecca Jane Griffiths [1985] Director

Joe Davies (Manchester) Limited
Incorporated: 20 August 1971
Net Worth: £6,895,651 *Total Assets:* £9,130,159
Registered Office: 149 Broadstone Road, Reddish, Stockport, Cheshire, SK5 7GA
Activities: Wholesale of household goods (other than musical instruments) n.e.c
Parent: Joe Davies (Holdings) Limited
Officers: Stephen Joe Davies [1960] Director/Giftware Distributors Manager; Paul Martin Hooker [1969] Commercial Director

Philip J Davies Holdings PLC
Incorporated: 5 April 1966 *Employees:* 4
Net Worth: £26,836,828 *Total Assets:* £35,789,420
Registered Office: St Georges House, 215-219 Chester Road, Manchester, M15 4JE
Activities: Activities of head offices
Officers: Mark Steven Davies, Secretary/Solicitor; Elisabeth Josephine Davies [1965] Director; Mark Steven Davies [1961] Director

Dawat-E-Islami UK
Incorporated: 3 May 2005
Net Worth: £11,109,508 *Total Assets:* £11,190,818
Registered Office: Dawate E Islami UK Head Office, Cannon Street, Bolton, Lancs, BL3 5AP
Activities: Activities of religious organisations
Officers: Mohammad Jamil [1977] Director/Self Employed; Khalid Nazir Mirza [1966] Director; Basharat Mohammad [1980] Director/Tax Office Manager; Hasan Ali Safdar [1980] Director/Accountant

Martin Dawes Solutions Holdings Limited
Incorporated: 13 June 2002
Net Worth: £7,048,946 *Total Assets:* £9,811,667
Registered Office: Martin Dawes House, Europa Boulevard, Westbrook, Warrington, Cheshire, WA5 7WH
Activities: Activities of head offices
Shareholder: Martin Richard Dawes
Officers: Elizabeth Jane Dawes [1945] Director; Hayley Jane Dawes [1970] Director; Martin Richard Dawes [1943] Director; Paul Richard Dawes [1972] Director; Robert John Pasqualino [1965] Sales Director; Dewi Eifion Thomas [1957] Director

Dawson Real Estates Limited
Incorporated: 17 May 2013 *Employees:* 1
Net Worth: £4,251,482 *Total Assets:* £9,141,952
Registered Office: Glenfield Park, Philips Road, Blackburn, Lancs, BB1 5PF
Activities: Activities of other holding companies n.e.c.
Major Shareholder: Mustaq Ahmed Ismail Patel
Officers: Mustaq Ahmed Ismail Patel [1972] Director

H. Dawson Sons and Company (Wool) Limited
Incorporated: 27 March 1933 *Employees:* 131
Net Worth: £2,858,639 *Total Assets:* £20,891,972
Registered Office: Mercury House, Essex Street, Bradford, W Yorks, BD4 7PG
Activities: Other service activities incidental to land transportation, n.e.c.
Shareholders: Jo Harry Dawson; Andrew Gerrard Dawson
Officers: Jo Harry Dawson, Secretary; Andrew Gerrard Dawson [1941] Director/Wool Merchant; Jo Harry Dawson [1972] Director; Stuart Alan Greenwood [1947] Director

R.E.Dawson,Limited
Incorporated: 29 December 1947 *Employees:* 98
Net Worth: £6,136,542 *Total Assets:* £10,399,369
Registered Office: 56 King Street, Clitheroe, Lancs, BB7 2EU
Activities: Retail sale of hardware, paints and glass in specialised stores
Major Shareholder: Judith Mary Dawson
Officers: Simon Robin Dawson, Secretary/Director; Judith Mary Dawson [1949] Director/Shop Manageress; Simon Robin Dawson [1977] Director; Stephen Dawson [1984] Director; Amanda Jane Sutherland [1975] Director

Dawsons Music Limited
Incorporated: 27 May 1922 *Employees:* 104
Net Worth: £4,131,949 *Total Assets:* £7,517,652
Registered Office: 65 Sankey Street, Warrington, Cheshire, WA1 1SU
Activities: Retail sale of musical instruments and scores
Shareholders: Thomas David Briggs; Dr James Richard Briggs
Officers: Christopher Charles Hewson, Secretary; Dr James Richard Briggs [1948] Director/Doctor; Thomas David Briggs [1946] Director; Christopher Charles Hewson [1975] Director/Chartered Accountant; Mark Robert Siddiqui Taylor [1965] Director/Managing Director; Jesper Toft Christensen [1958] Director [Danish]

Day International (UK) Holdings
Incorporated: 8 August 1994
Net Worth: £4,743,000 *Total Assets:* £30,004,000
Registered Office: Varr House, Northbank Industrial Estate, Irlam, Salford, M44 5DL
Activities: Activities of head offices
Officers: Jayne Evelyn Williams, Secretary; Jeremy Theodore Berenzweig [1972] Director; Stephen Dryden [1968] Director/Chief Financial Officer; Anthony James Lord [1960] Director/General Manager; Georg Heinrich Johannes Strierath [1976] Director/Senior Counsel [German]

Daytona Holdco Limited
Incorporated: 4 December 2015
Net Worth: £24,329,296 *Total Assets:* £72,562,360
Registered Office: 3rd Floor, 1 Ashley Road, Altrincham, Cheshire, WA14 2DT
Activities: Other credit granting n.e.c.
Officers: Grant Bryce Bourke [1964] Director [Australian]; John James Cowin [1942] Director [Australian]; Donald Jeffrey Meij [1968] Director [Australian]; Andrew Charles Rennie [1968] Director [Australian]; Craig Ryan [1970] Director/General Counsel & Company Secretary [Australian]

Daytona JV Limited
Incorporated: 7 December 2015
Net Worth: £69,242,320 *Total Assets:* £108,586,472
Registered Office: 3rd Floor, 1 Ashley Road, Altrincham, Cheshire, WA14 2DT
Activities: Other credit granting n.e.c.
Shareholders: Domino's Pizza Group PLC; Daytona Holdco Limited
Officers: Grant Bryce Bourke [1964] Director [Australian]; John James Cowin [1942] Director [Australian]; Donald Jeffrey Meij [1968] Director [Australian]; Andrew Charles Rennie [1968] Director [Australian]; David James Wild [1955] Director

DBG (UK) Limited
Incorporated: 23 February 2010 *Employees:* 99
Net Worth: £9,185,628 *Total Assets:* £12,485,146
Registered Office: Europa House, Europa Trading Estate, Stoneclough Road, Kearsley, Manchester, M26 1GG
Activities: Repair of other equipment
Parent: DBG Acquisitions Limited
Officers: Leo Damian Carroll, Secretary; Gervase Paul Adams [1958] Director; Tom Riall [1960] Director; Mohammed Omar Shafi Khan [1974] Director/Chief Financial Officer

DBG Acquisitions Limited
Incorporated: 9 January 2010
Net Worth Deficit: £2,268,000 *Total Assets:* £6,585,000
Registered Office: Europa House, Europa Trading Estate, Stoneclough Road, Kearsley, Manchester, M26 1GG
Activities: Activities of head offices
Parent: DBG Topco Limited
Officers: Leo Damian Carroll, Secretary; Gervase Paul Adams [1958] Director; Tom Riall [1960] Director; Mohammed Omar Shafi Khan [1974] Director/Chief Financial Officer

DBS Pochin LLP
Incorporated: 25 July 2016
Net Worth: £9,176,957 *Total Assets:* £9,190,659
Registered Office: Brooks Lane, Middlewich, Cheshire, CW10 0JQ

DCC Energy UK Limited
Incorporated: 25 April 1985
Net Worth: £636,351,552 *Total Assets:* £764,439,296
Registered Office: 2nd Floor, 302 Bridgewater Place, Birchwood Park, Warrington, Cheshire, WA3 6XG
Activities: Activities of other holding companies n.e.c.
Parent: DCC Limited
Officers: Gerard Whyte, Secretary; James Henry Cubbon [1960] Director; Anthony Francis Levy [1957] Director; Edward Gerard O'Brien [1970] Director/Chartered Accountant [Irish]; Michael Steven Taylor [1959] Director

DCC Health & Beauty Solutions Limited
Incorporated: 23 December 1994 *Employees:* 6
Net Worth: £12,730,000 *Total Assets:* £27,321,000
Registered Office: 9-11 Hardwick Road, Astmoor Industrial Estate, Runcorn, Cheshire, WA7 1PH
Activities: Manufacture of other food products n.e.c.
Parent: DCC Healthcare UK Limited
Officers: Karen Michelle Leay, Secretary; Conor Francis Costigan [1971] Director [Irish]; Redmond McEvoy [1964] Director [Irish]; Stephen Clifford O'Connor [1964] Director/Chartered Accountant; Timothy Paul O'Connor [1968] Managing Director; Adrian Mark Williams [1965] Managing Director; Reginald Laurence Kenneth Witheridge [1941] Managing Director

DCC Mobility & Rehab Limited
Incorporated: 12 December 1990 *Employees:* 2
Net Worth: £12,222,000 *Total Assets:* £21,382,000
Registered Office: 9-12 Hardwick Road, Astmoor Industrial Estate, Runcorn, Cheshire, WA7 1PH
Activities: Other manufacturing n.e.c.
Parent: DCC Healthcare UK Limited
Officers: Karen Leay, Secretary; Conor Francis Costigan [1971] Director/Chartered Accountant [Irish]

De La Salle Academy Trust
Incorporated: 10 December 2010 *Employees:* 55
Net Worth: £5,263,000 *Total Assets:* £6,613,000
Registered Office: De La Salle Academy, Carr Lane East, Liverpool, L11 4SG
Activities: General secondary education
Officers: Susan Anne Pybis, Secretary; Jeremy David Barnes [1969] Director/Headteacher; Patricia Ann Cleworth [1963] Director/Business Analyst; Eileen Anne Davison [1955] Director/Bursar; David Mark Evans [1974] Director/Teacher; David Martin Hayes [1973] Director/Principal; Anthony Lavelle [1995] Director/Councillor; Sheelagh Mary McGovern [1954] Director/Teacher; Sang Taphou Mendy [1971] Director/Teacher; Generald Bernard Proctor [1951] Director/RC Priest

De Trafford Property LLP
Incorporated: 17 December 2009 *Employees:* 5
Net Worth: £2,297,885 *Total Assets:* £11,768,811
Registered Office: Suite 26g, Building 26, Alderley Park, Alderley Edge, Cheshire, SK10 4TG

Dean Property Group Limited
Incorporated: 22 March 1963 *Employees:* 5
Net Worth: £41,624,896 *Total Assets:* £57,174,888
Registered Office: Springfield House, Water Lane, Wilmslow, Cheshire, SK9 5BG
Activities: Other letting and operating of own or leased real estate
Shareholders: Michael Edward O'Donnell; Ludo Ventures Limited; Otto Ventures Limited; TEOD (1963) Limited
Officers: Jonathan Charles Patrick Beever, Secretary; Jonathan Charles Patrick Beever [1963] Director; Michael Edward O'Donnell [1969] Director; James Anthony Wild [1941] Director/Chartered Accountant

The Dean Trust
Incorporated: 12 April 2012 *Employees:* 358
Net Worth: £120,063,000 *Total Assets:* £132,233,000
Registered Office: Ashton on Mersey School, Cecil Avenue, Sale, Cheshire, M33 5BP
Activities: Other business support service activities n.e.c.
Officers: Sharon Bagshaw [1965] Director/Public Sector Leader, IBM UK; Anna Marie Beaumont [1979] Director; Jonathan Bowers [1975] Managing Director; Paul James Edwards [1980] Director/Solicitor; Tarun Kapur [1958] Director/Executive Headteacher; Damian McGann [1969] Director/Business and Financial Consultant; John Thomas Shiels [1959] Director/Chief Executive Officer

Deanbank Investments Limited
Incorporated: 2 July 1981
Net Worth: £23,776,324 *Total Assets:* £59,818,752
Registered Office: Emerson House, Heyes Lane, Alderley Edge, Cheshire, SK9 7LF
Activities: Development of building projects
Parent: P E Jones (Properties) Limited
Officers: Varun Maharaj, Secretary; Anthony Emerson Jones [1967] Director; Audrey Jones [1936] Director; Mark Emerson Jones [1964] Director; Peter Emerson Jones [1935] Director

Deansgate Securities LLP
Incorporated: 18 September 2006
Net Worth: £10,206,684 *Total Assets:* £10,281,028
Registered Office: 25 Rochdale Road, Manchester, M4 4HT

Debmar Benevolent Trust Limited
Incorporated: 4 July 1979
Net Worth: £6,258,005 *Total Assets:* £9,355,309
Registered Office: 2nd Floor, Parkgates, Bury New Road, Prestwich, Manchester, M25 0TL
Activities: Other social work activities without accommodation n.e.c.
Officers: Hilary Phyllis Olsberg, Secretary; Jacob Akiva Halpern [1964] Director; David Olsberg [1958] Director/Accountant

Debt Solutions (Holdings) Limited
Incorporated: 19 November 1998 *Employees:* 2
Net Worth: £16,102,000 *Total Assets:* £31,313,000
Registered Office: 33-34 Winckley Square, Preston, Lancs, PR1 3EL
Activities: Activities of head offices
Parent: Capita Holdings Limited
Officers: Francesca Anne Todd [1971] Director/Company Secretary; Robert David Tolfts [1962] Director

Dechra Finance Australia Limited
Incorporated: 29 September 2016 *Employees:* 3
Net Worth: £20,350,000 *Total Assets:* £20,450,000
Registered Office: 24 Cheshire Avenue, Cheshire Business Park, Lostock, Northwich, Cheshire, CW9 7UA
Activities: Activities of financial services holding companies
Parent: Dechra Limited
Officers: Melanie Jane Hall, Secretary; Richard John Cotton [1961] Director; Anthony Gerard Griffin [1963] Director [Irish]; Ian David Page [1961] Director

Dechra Finance Limited
Incorporated: 14 July 2014
Net Worth: £44,030,168 *Total Assets:* £69,276,840
Registered Office: 24 Cheshire Avenue, Cheshire Business Park, Lostock Gralam, Northwich, Cheshire, CW9 7UA
Activities: Activities of financial services holding companies
Parent: Dechra Pharmaceuticals PLC
Officers: Melanie Jane Hall, Secretary; Richard John Cotton [1961] Director; Ian David Page [1961] Director

Dechra Finance Sterling Limited
Incorporated: 22 June 2016 *Employees:* 4
Net Worth: £5,488,000 *Total Assets:* £80,432,000
Registered Office: 24 Cheshire Avenue, Cheshire Business Park, Lostock Gralam, Northwich, Cheshire, CW9 7UA
Activities: Activities of financial services holding companies
Parent: Dechra Pharmaceuticals PLC
Officers: Melanie Jane Hall, Secretary; Richard John Cotton [1961] Director; Anthony Gerard Griffin [1963] Director [Irish]; Ian David Page [1961] Director

Dechra Investments Limited
Incorporated: 7 January 2004 *Employees:* 2
Net Worth: £167,568,992 *Total Assets:* £167,572,992
Registered Office: 24 Cheshire Avenue, Cheshire Business Park, Lostock Gralam, Northwich, Cheshire, CW9 7UA
Activities: Activities of other holding companies n.e.c.
Parent: Dechra Pharmaceuticals PLC
Officers: Richard John Cotton [1961] Director; Ian David Page [1961] Director

Dechra Limited
Incorporated: 16 August 2002 *Employees:* 254
Net Worth: £204,227,008 *Total Assets:* £249,604,000
Registered Office: Snaygill Industrial Estate, Keighley Road, Skipton, N Yorks BD23 2RW
Activities: Manufacture of basic pharmaceutical products
Parent: Dechra Investments Limited
Officers: Melanie Jane Hall, Secretary; Richard John Cotton [1961] Director; Anthony Gerard Griffin [1963] Director [Irish]; Ian David Page [1961] Director

Dechra Pharmaceuticals PLC
Incorporated: 13 May 1997 *Employees:* 1,338
Net Worth: £301,073,984 *Total Assets:* £638,419,968
Registered Office: 24 Cheshire Avenue, Cheshire Business Park, Lostock Gralam, Northwich, Cheshire, CW9 7UA
Activities: Activities of head offices
Officers: Melanie Jane Hall, Secretary; Richard John Cotton [1961] Director; Anthony Gerard Griffin [1963] Director [Irish]; Julian Spenser Heslop [1954] Director; Dr Lawson MacArtney [1957] Director; Ishbel Jean Stewart Macpherson [1960] Director; Ian David Page [1961] Director; William Anthony Rice [1952] Director

Dechra Veterinary Products Limited
Incorporated: 8 March 2005 *Employees:* 76
Net Worth: £5,361,000 *Total Assets:* £12,734,000
Registered Office: 24 Cheshire Avenue, Lostock Gralam, Northwich, Cheshire, CW9 7UA
Activities: Wholesale of pharmaceutical goods
Parent: Dechra Pharmaceuticals PLC
Officers: Melanie Jane Hall, Secretary; Richard John Cotton [1961] Director; Anthony Gerard Griffin [1963] Director [Irish]; Ian David Page [1961] Director

Deckers Hospitality Group Limited
Incorporated: 17 February 2010 *Employees:* 238
Net Worth: £5,418,061 *Total Assets:* £19,656,108
Registered Office: Unit F, Royle Pennine Trading Estate, Lynroyle Way, Rochdale, OL11 3EX
Activities: Agents involved in the sale of food, beverages and tobacco
Major Shareholder: Clifford Brierley
Officers: Victoria Cosgrove, Secretary; Clifford Brierley [1950] Director/Chairman of Deckers; Maxwell James Brierley [1974] Managing Director of Deckers; Andrew Waller [1960] Managing Director

Deckers Restaurants Limited
Incorporated: 3 November 1987 *Employees:* 28
Net Worth: £2,138,238 *Total Assets:* £8,819,864
Registered Office: Unit F, Royle Pennine Trading Estate, Lynroyle Way, Rochdale, OL11 3EX
Activities: Production of meat and poultry meat products
Parent: Deckers Hospitality Group Ltd
Officers: Victoria Cosgrove, Secretary; Clifford Brierley [1950] Director/Restaurateur; Maxwell James Brierly [1974] Director/Hotelier; Andrew Waller [1960] Managing Director

Deepdale PNE Holdings Limited
Incorporated: 22 April 2010 *Employees:* 110
Net Worth: £5,320,000 *Total Assets:* £44,436,000
Registered Office: Deepdale Stadium, Sir Tom Finney Way, Deepdale, Preston, Lancs, PR1 6RU
Activities: Activities of head offices
Major Shareholder: Trevor James Hemmings
Officers: John Clement Kay [1953] Director; Kathryn Revitt [1964] Director

Deepstore Holdings Limited
Incorporated: 18 December 2008
Net Worth: £16,393,000 *Total Assets:* £17,595,000
Registered Office: Astbury House, Bradford Road, Winsford, Cheshire, CW7 2PA
Activities: Activities of other holding companies n.e.c.
Parent: Compass Minerals (Europe) Limited
Officers: Richard Stewart Thomson, Secretary; Richard Stewart Thomson [1971] Director/Chartered Accountant

Deeside Cereals I Ltd
Incorporated: 2 March 1976 *Employees:* 159
Net Worth: £8,660,000 *Total Assets:* £23,399,000
Registered Office: Fourth Avenue, Deeside Industrial Park, Deeside, Flintshire, CH5 2NR
Activities: Manufacture of breakfast cereals and cereals-based food
Major Shareholder: Rakesh Mahajan
Officers: Peter Thomas Robertson, Secretary; Charles Maurice Aston Botting [1955] Director/Manufacturing Consultant; Robert Hiscutt [1956] Director/Consultant; Rakesh Mahajan [1954] Director/Businessman [Indian]; Peter Thomas Robertson [1969] Managing Director; Ravikumar Sreenivasa [1957] Director/Consultant [Indian]

Deeside House Educational Trust Limited
Incorporated: 20 July 1976 *Employees:* 105
Net Worth: £4,723,728 *Total Assets:* £6,680,814
Registered Office: Saighton Grange, Saighton, Chester, CH3 6EN
Activities: General secondary education
Officers: Brian Desmond Wake, Secretary; Emma Alleyn Bunting [1966] Finance Director; Brian Michael Dawson [1952] Director/Solicitor; Jeremy Neil James Christopher Dussek [1970] Director/Canon Precentor; Ian Peter Dutton [1956] Director/Retired; Michelle Elizabeth Ellis [1956] Director/Retired; Richard Andrew Flood [1971] Director/Chartered Civil Engineer; Andrew Frederick Grime [1955] Director; Joanne Marie Lucy [1969] Director; William Giles Osmond [1945] Director/Retired; Dr Simon Timothy Stanley [1954] Director/Consultant Dentist; Felicity Ann Taylor [1954] Director; Anna Marie Tiplady [1966] Director; Edward Charles Harry Trevor-Barnston [1974] Director/Estate Manager

Delamere Dairy Limited
Incorporated: 28 April 1999 *Employees:* 23
Net Worth: £4,917,446 *Total Assets:* £7,775,924
Registered Office: Yew Tree Farm, Bexton Lane, Knutsford, Cheshire, WA16 9BH
Activities: Wholesale of dairy products, eggs and edible oils and fats
Parent: Delamere Dairy Holdings Ltd
Officers: Elizabeth Anne Sutton, Secretary; Patrick Dennis John Brunt [1963] Sales and Marketing Director; Edward John Salt [1977] Managing Director; Elizabeth Anne Sutton [1957] Director; Alan Whiston [1962] Operations Director

Delifresh Limited
Incorporated: 13 May 2002 *Employees:* 171
Net Worth: £4,662,645 *Total Assets:* £10,133,913
Registered Office: Paul Kershaw House, Essex Street, Bradford, W Yorks, BD4 7PG
Activities: Other food services
Major Shareholder: Noel Damian John Kershaw
Officers: Andrew Peter Nicholls, Secretary/Accountant; Noel Damian John Kershaw [1969] Director/Manager; Gerard Martin Morgan [1969] Operations Director; Andrew Peter Nicholls [1969] Director/Accountant; Reuben Buchanan Sutterby [1966] Sales Director

Deliver Net Limited
Incorporated: 28 February 2000 *Employees:* 71
Net Worth: £1,174,173 *Total Assets:* £7,628,467
Registered Office: Healthcare House, Keighley Road, Skipton, N Yorks, BD23 2QR
Activities: Non-specialised wholesale trade
Parent: Healthcare House Limited
Officers: Timothy James Lockett, Secretary; Adele Farquharson [1974] Director; Simon Jeremy Holt [1960] Director; Frances Lockett [1964] Director; Timothy James Lockett [1964] Director

The Delivery Group Limited
Incorporated: 4 May 2011 *Employees:* 391
Net Worth: £2,992,000 *Total Assets:* £81,829,000
Registered Office: Calver Road, Winwick Quay, Warrington, Cheshire, WA2 8RA
Activities: Licensed carriers
Parent: TDG 2018 Holdco Limited
Officers: Jason Jones, Secretary; Mark Stuart Bigley [1969] Managing Director; Ian Patrick Brewer [1965] Director; Paul David Carvell [1955] Director; Stephen Leslie Stokes [1964] Director; James Harvey Wilkins [1974] Director

Denholm Global Logistics Limited
Incorporated: 26 April 1994 *Employees:* 71
Net Worth: £6,687,297 *Total Assets:* £18,176,634
Registered Office: 2nd Floor, 5 St Paul's Square, Old Hall Street, Liverpool, L3 9SJ
Activities: Other transportation support activities
Parent: Denholm Logistics Group Limited
Officers: Gregory Albert Hanson, Group Company Secretary; James Niall William Denholm [1963] Director; Kieran Joseph Hall [1955] Director; Stephen Barrie Hughes [1973] Director; Michael Gerard McMahon [1962] Director; Tracey Newman [1961] Director

Denholm Logistics Group Limited
Incorporated: 30 July 2015 *Employees:* 24
Net Worth: £10,508,967 *Total Assets:* £50,455,296
Registered Office: 5 St Pauls Square, Old Hall Street, Liverpool, L3 9SJ
Activities: Activities of head offices
Parent: J. & J. Denholm Limited
Officers: Gregory Albert Hanson, Secretary; James Niall William Denholm [1963] Director; John Stephen Denholm [1956] Director/Chartered Accountant; The Rt Hon Lord Michael Bruce Forsyth [1954] Director/Banker; Kieran Joseph Hall [1955] Director; Martin Kieran Hall [1978] Director; Gregory Albert Hanson [1961] Director/Group Company Secretary; Stephen Barrie Hughes [1973] Director; Michael Gerard McMahon [1962] Director; John Watt [1965] Director

Denholm UK Logistics Limited
Incorporated: 3 November 2015 *Employees:* 117
Net Worth: £553,004 *Total Assets:* £10,245,313
Registered Office: 5 St Paul's Square, Old Hall Street, Liverpool, L3 9SJ
Activities: Operation of warehousing and storage facilities for land transport activities
Parent: Denholm Logistics Group Limited
Officers: Gregory Albert Hanson, Secretary; Mark Davies [1966] Director; James Niall William Denholm [1963] Director; Kieran Joseph Hall [1955] Director; Martin Kieran Hall [1978] Director; John Martin Harrison [1961] Director

Denim Merchants (UK) Limited
Incorporated: 26 July 2011 *Employees:* 6
Net Worth: £1,321,251 *Total Assets:* £16,343,178
Registered Office: 2nd Floor, 1 City Road East, Manchester, M15 4PN
Activities: Wholesale of clothing and footwear
Major Shareholder: Mariyah Farhan
Officers: Mariyah Farhan [1980] Director [Pakistani]

Denso Marston Ltd
Incorporated: 23 September 1935 *Employees:* 643
Net Worth: £35,344,000 *Total Assets:* £51,884,000
Registered Office: Marston House, Otley Road, Shipley, W Yorks, BD17 7JR
Activities: Manufacture of other fabricated metal products n.e.c.
Parent: Denso International UK Ltd
Officers: John Charles White, Secretary; Marco di Rao Marotta [1963] Director [Italian]; David Hanson [1971] Managing Director; Masami Taguchi [1961] Director/Deputy Head of Thermal Systems Business Unit [Japanese]

Dent Logistics Limited
Incorporated: 3 January 2014 *Employees:* 68
Net Worth: £213,412 *Total Assets:* £8,429,424
Registered Office: Barbary Plains, Edenhall, Penrith, Cumbria, CA11 8SR
Activities: Freight transport by road
Major Shareholder: Thomas Hugh Dent
Officers: Thomas Hugh Dent [1964] Director/Haulier

Dent Steel Holdings Limited
Incorporated: 4 January 2007
Net Worth: £10,070,431 *Total Assets:* £10,167,203
Registered Office: Low Moor Steel Works, New Works Road, Low Moor, Bradford, W Yorks, BD12 0QN
Activities: Activities of head offices
Major Shareholder: Gregory Frederick Hutchings
Officers: Cassie Olivia Hutchings, Secretary; Cassie Olivia Hutchings [1983] Director/Industrialist; Gregory Frederick Hutchings [1947] Director/Businessman; Andrew Peaty [1966] Director/Chief Operating Officer

Dent Steel Services (Yorkshire) Limited
Incorporated: 22 December 1976 *Employees:* 60
Net Worth: £5,932,982 *Total Assets:* £12,449,064
Registered Office: Low Moor Steel Works, New Works Road, Low Moor, Bradford, BD12 0QN
Activities: Agents involved in the sale of fuels, ores, metals and industrial chemicals
Major Shareholder: Gregory Frederick Hutchings
Officers: Cassie Olivia Hutchings, Secretary; Cassie Olivia Hutchings [1983] Director/Industrialist; Gregory Frederick Hutchings [1947] Director/Businessman; Andrew Peaty [1966] Director/Chief Operating Officer

Dept UK Holding Limited
Incorporated: 28 April 2016
Net Worth: £3,377,171 *Total Assets:* £8,679,531
Registered Office: 1 Portland Street, Manchester, M1 3BE
Activities: Activities of head offices
Parent: Dept Holding BV
Officers: Francois Louis Schmid, Secretary; Francois Louis Schmid [1981] Managing Director [Dutch]; Jasper Van de Luijtgaarden [1974] Director [Dutch]

Deralam Laminates Limited
Incorporated: 25 August 1983 *Employees:* 149
Net Worth: £2,524,340 *Total Assets:* £11,450,394
Registered Office: 68 Argyle Street, Birkenhead, Merseyside, CH41 6AF
Activities: Other business support service activities n.e.c.
Shareholders: Robert Ernest Andrew Stone; Kenneth Rimmer
Officers: Robert Ernest Andrew Stone, Secretary; David William Rimmer [1958] Director/Sales Manager; Robert Ernest Andrew Stone [1965] Director/Sales Manager

Derian House Childrens Hospice
Incorporated: 30 September 1991 *Employees:* 96
Net Worth: £22,303,980 *Total Assets:* £22,511,108
Registered Office: Derian House, Chancery Road, Astley Village, Chorley, Lancs, PR7 1DH
Activities: Other human health activities
Officers: Diane Heather McNally, Secretary; Andrew Chatterjee [1979] Regional Director; James Douglas Cole [1975] Director/Entrepreneur; Stephen Game [1959] Director/Retired; Christopher Monk [1975] Director/Accountant; Dr Ruth O'Connor [1965] Director/Doctor; Helen Rotheram [1973] Director/Accountant; Gretta Ariane Starks [1980] Director/Construction Manager; Karen Jane Swindley [1966] Director

Derwent Lodge Estates Limited
Incorporated: 5 September 1972 *Employees:* 6
Net Worth: £14,476,968 *Total Assets:* £38,760,260
Registered Office: 5th Floor, Melbourne Building, 21 North John Street, Liverpool, L2 5QU
Activities: Other letting and operating of own or leased real estate
Shareholder: Cytos Limited
Officers: Craig Robert Sneddon, Secretary; Jonathan Andrew Brown [1966] Director; Craig Robert Sneddon [1968] Director

Destination Manchester Limited
Incorporated: 10 February 2005
Net Worth: £10,186,450 *Total Assets:* £21,930,576
Registered Office: Town Hall, Albert Square, Manchester, M60 2LA
Activities: Activities of head offices
Parent: The Council of The City of Manchester
Officers: Carol Ann Culley [1968] Director/City Treasurer

Detrafford Sky Gardens Ltd
Incorporated: 15 April 2014
Net Worth Deficit: £1,891 *Total Assets:* £15,431,956
Registered Office: Suite 26g, Building 26, Alderley Park, Alderley Edge, Cheshire, SK10 4TG
Activities: Other business support service activities n.e.c.
Major Shareholder: Gary Thomas Jackson
Officers: Brian Lowndes, Secretary; Gary Thomas Jackson [1964] Director

Deva Group Limited
Incorporated: 20 November 1998
Net Worth: £23,475,000 *Total Assets:* £23,530,000
Registered Office: The Quarry, Hill Road, Eccleston, Chester, CH4 9HQ
Activities: Activities of head offices
Parent: Wheatsheaf Group Limited
Officers: Geoffrey Murray Chadwick, Secretary; Peter Lawrence Doyle [1952] Director/Accountant; Anthony William Searson James [1968] Director/Accountant; Graham Paul Ramsbottom [1965] Director/Surveyor

Deva Victrix Holdings Limited
Incorporated: 5 November 2013 *Employees:* 17
Net Worth: £5,443,000 *Total Assets:* £16,769,000
Registered Office: Eaton Estate Office, Eccleston, Chester, CH4 9ET
Activities: Activities of other holding companies n.e.c.
Shareholders: Mark Robin Preston; William Bruce Kendall; Michael George Alexander McLintock
Officers: Sarah Helen Carss, Secretary; Catherine Susan Fradley [1965] Director/Accountant; Helen Frances Jaquiss [1964] Director/Accountant; Mark Robin Preston [1968] Director/Chartered Surveyor

Dewhurst Dent P.L.C.
Incorporated: 1 December 1919 *Employees:* 134
Net Worth: £8,815,089 *Total Assets:* £11,985,425
Registered Office: Union Mill, Vernon Street, Bolton, Lancs, BL1 2PT
Activities: Wholesale of clothing and footwear
Officers: Stanley William Lee, Secretary; Faye Helena Herzberg [1958] Director; Linda Khalastchi [1950] Director; Alan Khazam [1955] Director/Solicitor; Anne Khazam [1967] Director; Deborah Moore [1958] Creative Director; Arran Kay Yentob [1982] Director; Robert Yentob [1947] Director

James Dewhurst Limited
Incorporated: 28 March 1952 *Employees:* 249
Net Worth: £49,249,000 *Total Assets:* £61,731,000
Registered Office: Altham Lane, Altham, Accrington, Lancs, BB5 5YA
Activities: Preparation and spinning of textile fibres
Parent: Jade Equity Limited
Officers: Geert Asselman [1961] Director [Belgian]; Malcolm Blackwell [1954] Director/Group CEO; Michèle Sioen [1965] Director [Belgian]; Frank Veranneman [1959] Director [Belgian]

Dewlay Cheesemakers Limited
Incorporated: 23 January 1961 *Employees:* 85
Net Worth: £8,528,519 *Total Assets:* £12,260,973
Registered Office: Garstang by Pass Road, Garstang, Preston, Lancs, PR3 0PR
Activities: Liquid milk and cream production
Shareholders: Richard William Kenyon; Nicholas John Kenyon
Officers: Dianne Mary Kenyon, Secretary; Conor Patrick Daunt [1974] Commercial Director [Irish]; Nicholas John Kenyon [1976] Director/Operations Manager; Richard William Kenyon [1980] Director/Production Manager

DGD Properties Limited
Incorporated: 20 June 2006
Net Worth: £1,385,397 *Total Assets:* £27,319,474
Registered Office: 208 Wilmslow Road, Manchester, M14 6LF
Activities: Development of building projects
Shareholders: Rachel Jane Cuthbert; Claudia Louise Cuthbert
Officers: Rachel Jane Cuthbert, Secretary/Surveyor; Claudia Louise Cuthbert [1979] Director/Physiotherapist; Rachel Jane Cuthbert [1974] Director/Surveyor

Diamond Resorts (Europe) Limited
Incorporated: 1 March 1989 *Employees:* 498
Net Worth Deficit: £3,538,000 *Total Assets:* £144,704,992
Registered Office: Citrus House, Caton Road, Lancaster, LA1 3UA
Activities: Other service activities n.e.c.
Parent: Diamond Resorts (Group Holdings) PLC
Officers: Susan Crook, Secretary/Solicitor; Susan Crook [1961] Director/Solicitor

Diamond Resorts (Holdings) Limited
Incorporated: 11 March 2004 *Employees:* 505
Net Worth Deficit: £32,533,000 *Total Assets:* £128,106,000
Registered Office: Citrus House, Caton Road, Lancaster, LA1 3UA
Activities: Activities of head offices
Parent: Apollo Global Management LLC
Officers: Susan Crook, Secretary/Solicitor; Susan Crook [1961] Director/Solicitor

Diamond Resorts Financial Services Limited
Incorporated: 29 July 1985
Net Worth: £5,883,076 *Total Assets:* £22,040,228
Registered Office: Citrus House, Caton Road, Lancaster, LA1 3UA
Activities: Activities of financial services holding companies
Parent: Diamond Resorts (Group Holdings) PLC
Officers: Susan Crook, Secretary/Solicitor; Susan Crook [1961] Director/Solicitor

Diamorph UK Limited
Incorporated: 16 May 2012 *Employees:* 2
Net Worth Deficit: £21,848,836 *Total Assets:* £56,264,032
Registered Office: c/o Tenmat Limited, Ashburton Road West, Trafford Park, Manchester, M17 1TD
Activities: Activities of other holding companies n.e.c.
Officers: Mark Andrew Hutchison [1970] Director

Dickens 2014 Limited
Incorporated: 17 January 2014
Net Worth: £29,411,400 *Total Assets:* £36,566,600
Registered Office: Cunard Building, Water Street, Liverpool, L3 1EL
Activities: Activities of head offices
Parent: Edward Billington and Son Limited
Officers: Gary Michael Blake [1973] Director/Chief Executive Officer; Simon Gamble [1961] Director; David Marshall [1961] Director; Matthew Wood [1969] Director

Digital Projection International Limited
Incorporated: 8 November 2001 *Employees:* 119
Net Worth: £1,069,000 *Total Assets:* £14,719,000
Registered Office: Greenside Way, Middleton, Manchester, M24 1XX
Activities: Activities of head offices
Officers: Roger Chih-Yuan Chu [1947] Director/Chief Finance Officer [Taiwanese]; Jeff Fu [1966] Director/General Manager [Chinese]; Tsai-Hsing Chang Jackie Chang [1967] Director; Kengo Ka [1971] Director/Chief Executive Officer [Taiwanese]; Michael Neil Levi [1960] Director [American]; Chiu-Hua Hao Maggie Hao [1970] Director [Chinese]; Dermot John Quinn [1963] Director

Digital World Centre Limited
Incorporated: 7 August 1998
Net Worth: £3,826,000 *Total Assets:* £15,850,000
Registered Office: Peel Dome, intu Trafford Centre, Trafford City, Manchester, M17 8PL
Activities: Other letting and operating of own or leased real estate
Parent: Peel Real Estate (Properties) Limited
Officers: Neil Lees, Secretary; Neil Lees [1963] Director; John Alexander Schofield [1968] Director/Accountant; Steven Keith Underwood [1974] Director; John Whittaker [1942] Director

Dilbag Cloth House Limited
Incorporated: 11 June 1993
Net Worth: £10,983,874 *Total Assets:* £13,261,769
Registered Office: Dilbag Building, Duncomb Road, Ingleby Road, Bradford, W Yorks, BD8 9AL
Activities: Wholesale of textiles
Officers: Dilbag Singh, Secretary; Gurmail Kaur [1945] Director; Harpreet Singh Makkar [1975] Marketing Director; Dilbag Singh [1939] Director; Jaswant Singh [1973] Sales Director

Diodes Holdings UK Limited
Incorporated: 16 January 2008 *Employees:* 2
Net Worth: £39,911,000 *Total Assets:* £89,134,000
Registered Office: Zetex Technology Park, Chadderton, Oldham, Lancs, OL9 9LL
Activities: Activities of head offices
Parent: Diodes Holding B.V
Officers: Keh-Shew Lu [1946] Director [American]; Richard Dallas White [1947] Director [American]

Diodes Zetex Limited
Incorporated: 17 July 1978 *Employees:* 4
Net Worth: £80,679,000 *Total Assets:* £83,386,000
Registered Office: Zetex Technology Park, Chadderton, Oldham, Lancs, OL9 9LL
Activities: Activities of head offices
Parent: Diodes Holdings UK Ltd
Officers: Dr Keh-Shew Lu [1946] Director [American]; Timothy Monaghan [1963] Director/European General Manager; Hans Rohrer [1949] Director [German]; Richard Dallas White [1947] Director [American]

Diodes Zetex Semiconductors Limited
Incorporated: 23 May 1989 *Employees:* 324
Net Worth: £22,865,000 *Total Assets:* £57,480,000
Registered Office: Zetex Technology Park, Chadderton, Oldham, Lancs, OL9 9LL
Activities: Manufacture of electronic components
Parent: Diodes Zetex Limited
Officers: Dr Keh-Shew Lu [1946] Director [American]; Richard Dallas White [1947] Director [American]

Direct Accident Management Limited
Incorporated: 7 October 1996 *Employees:* 160
Net Worth: £22,292,688 *Total Assets:* £33,114,006
Registered Office: 139 New Court Way, Ormskirk, Lancs, L39 2YT
Activities: Renting and leasing of cars and light motor vehicles
Officers: Valentina Slater, Secretary; Mark Andrew Bringloe [1972] Director/Chartered Accountant; James Graham Slater [1961] Director; Valentina Slater [1961] Sales Director

Direct Rail Services Limited
Incorporated: 13 February 1995 *Employees:* 420
Net Worth: £19,636,000 *Total Assets:* £67,960,000
Registered Office: Herdus House, Ingwell Drive, Westlakes Science & Technology Park, Moor Row, Cumbria, CA24 3HU
Activities: Freight rail transport
Officers: Helen Elizabeth Hodgson, Secretary; Alyson Noreen Armett [1966] Director/Head of Enterprise; Christopher Antony Peter Connelly [1967] Commercial and Business Development Director; Deborah Anne Francis [1966] Managing Director; Michael Charles Leckie [1965] Finance Director; Martin Claus Liefeith [1966] Director/Head of Finance; Jeffrey Marshall [1963] Operations and Compliance Director; Clive Richard Nixon [1969] Director/Head of Strategy; Geoffrey Michael Silson Spencer [1966] Director

Direct Tyre Management Limited
Incorporated: 19 May 2004 *Employees:* 40
Net Worth: £3,197,074 *Total Assets:* £9,944,302
Registered Office: Parkside Place, Oasis Business Park, Skelmersdale, Lancs, WN8 9RD
Activities: Other service activities incidental to land transportation, n.e.c.
Parent: NRG Fleet Services Limited
Officers: Martin Roy Ashcroft [1965] Director/Chief Financial Officer; Stephen Michael Richardson [1960] Sales Director; Muhammad Sadique [1963] Director; Christopher Snelson [1975] Fleet and Asset Director

Discan Limited
Incorporated: 2 March 2010 *Employees:* 243
Net Worth: £8,119,088 *Total Assets:* £33,962,956
Registered Office: 8 Cheshire Avenue, Lostock Gralam, Northwich, Cheshire, CW9 7UA
Activities: Non-trading company
Parent: Ingram Micro Holdings Limited
Officers: Karel Victor Hubert Gabrielle Maria Everaet [1965] Director/Group Vice President & Associate General Counsel [Belgian]; Kris Emilie Paul Mees [1965] Director/International CFO [Belgian]; Matthew Sanderson [1971] Director

Discover Multi Academy Trust
Incorporated: 10 July 2015
Net Worth: £5,576,101 *Total Assets:* £6,798,613
Registered Office: Upton Priory School, Berwick Close, Macclesfield, Cheshire, SK10 3ED
Activities: Primary education
Officers: Emma Burnage [1988] Director/Deputy Headteacher; Andrea Jane Cole [1973] Director/Medical Writer; Rachel Cragg [1989] Director; Peter Cresswell [1947] Director; Greeba Mary Jones [1939] Director/Retired Headteacher; Jane Knott [1967] Director/Assistant Principal; Joanna Clare Longman [1964] Director/Tax Accountant; Emma Newton [1980] Director; Dr Graeme Francis Wilkinson [1965] Director; Fiona Louise Williams [1972] Director/Finance Officer; Tim Williams [1976] Director/IT Consultant

District Estates Limited (The)
Incorporated: 12 April 1917 *Employees:* 6
Net Worth: £66,007,848 *Total Assets:* £92,464,800
Registered Office: 2 Friarsgate, Grosvenor Street, Chester, CH1 1XG
Activities: Buying and selling of own real estate
Officers: Nigel John Anderton [1954] Director/Chartered Surveyor; Ian James Davies [1966] Director/Chartered Surveyor; Peter James Hitchcock [1946] Director/Chartered Surveyor; Andrew Mills [1966] Director/Chartered Surveyor; Mark Guy Williams [1955] Director/Surveyor

Distrupol Limited
Incorporated: 22 March 1963 *Employees:* 53
Net Worth: £29,678,000 *Total Assets:* £36,510,000
Registered Office: Aquarius House, 6 Mid Point Business Park, Thornbury, Bradford, W Yorks, BD3 7AY
Activities: Manufacture of plastics in primary forms
Shareholders: Ellis & Everard (UK Holdings) Limited; Univar UK Limited
Officers: Paul Graham Bryant [1973] Director; Jeffrey William Carr [1956] Director/Global Counsel [American]; Sabine Duyfjes [1972] Director/VP & General Counsel EMEA [German]

Diverse Acquisitions Limited
Incorporated: 22 April 2004 *Employees:* 4
Net Worth: £18,000 *Total Assets:* £18,664,000
Registered Office: Europa House, Europa Trading Estate, Stoneclough Road, Kearsley, Manchester, M26 1GG
Activities: Activities of head offices
Parent: Diverse Holdings Limited
Officers: Leo Damian Carroll, Secretary; Tom Riall [1960] Director; Mohammed Omar Shafi Khan [1974] Director/Chief Financial Officer; Krista Nyree Whitley [1970] Clinical Director

J.Dixon & Son,Limited
Incorporated: 31 May 1957 *Employees:* 67
Net Worth: £8,371,868 *Total Assets:* £12,188,388
Registered Office: 10 Lowther Street, Whitehaven, Cumbria, CA28 7AL
Activities: Other retail sale in non-specialised stores
Shareholders: Donald Nelmes Dixon; Dr Elizabeth Helen Marie Dixon
Officers: Dr Elizabeth Helen Marie Dixon, Secretary; Donald Nelmes Dixon [1935] Director/Furnisher; Dr Elizabeth Helen Marie Dixon [1966] Director/Store Supervisor; William Robert Clive Spencer Dixon [1968] Director/Store Supervisor

Dixon Group Europe Ltd
Incorporated: 29 May 1937 *Employees:* 88
Net Worth: £8,494,534 *Total Assets:* £17,818,328
Registered Office: 350 Leach Place, Walton Summit Centre, Bamber Bridge, Preston, Lancs, PR5 8AS
Activities: Non-specialised wholesale trade
Parent: Dixon Valve & Coupling Company
Officers: Julie Ann Crowe [1968] Managing Director; Robert Steven Grace [1962] Director [American]; Johan Madison Trumpy [1965] Director/Senior Vice President [American]

Dixondale Limited
Incorporated: 7 September 1982 *Employees:* 165
Net Worth: £110,359,456 *Total Assets:* £117,022,816
Registered Office: 7 Robin Lane, High Bentham, Lancaster, LA2 7AB
Activities: Management of real estate on a fee or contract basis
Major Shareholder: Dr Bernard Rees-Smith
Officers: Jenny Louise Barwise, Secretary; Janet Bradbury [1966] Director/Scientist; Dr Shu Chen [1966] Director/Scientist; Dr Jadwiga Furmaniak [1951] Director/Scientist; Dr Michael Powell [1960] Director/Scientist; Dr Bernard Rees Smith [1944] Director/Scientist; Peter Rees-Smith [1950] Director/Solicitor; Dr Jane Sanders [1966] Director/Scientist

Dixons Academies Charitable Trust Ltd
Incorporated: 6 October 1988 *Employees:* 882
Net Worth: £73,693,000 *Total Assets:* £81,120,000
Registered Office: Dixons Academies Charitable Trust Ltd, Ripley Street, Bradford, W Yorks, BD5 7RR
Activities: General secondary education
Officers: Joanne Lynch, Secretary; Professor Grace Alderson [1950] Director/Retired University Professor; Lynn Barrett [1942] Director/Retired; Ruby Khalid Bhatti [1970] Director/Solicitor; John Bowers [1951] Director/Self Employed Consultant; David Hugh Clayton [1957] Director; Bryan Collins [1938] Director/Retired Head/CEO; Brent Fitzpatrick [1949] Director; Martin Joseph Gaskin [1959] Director/Accountant; Susan Richardson [1979] Qualified Accountant/Director

Dnata Catering Services Limited
Incorporated: 1 November 2010 *Employees:* 4,209
Net Worth: £130,852,000 *Total Assets:* £317,315,008
Registered Office: Building 319, World Cargo Centre, Manchester Airport, Manchester, M90 5EX
Activities: Non-trading company
Officers: Mark Elly, Secretary; David John Loft [1961] Director/Vice President; Robin Brian Padgett [1968] Director/Divisional Senior Vice President; Carlo Federico Possa [1968] Director [Italian]

Dnata Travel Holdings UK Limited
Incorporated: 31 October 2013 *Employees:* 3
Net Worth: £24,845,000 *Total Assets:* £54,065,000
Registered Office: The Trident Centre, Port Way, Ribble Docklands, Preston, Lancs, PR2 2QG
Activities: Tour operator activities
Officers: Paul Smith, Secretary; Iain Charles Richard Andrew [1965] Director/Chief Executive; John Constantine Bevan [1965] Director

Dobies Cumbria Finance Limited
Incorporated: 11 March 2013 *Employees:* 3
Net Worth: £8,253,737 *Total Assets:* £8,369,640
Registered Office: Dobies Business Park, Lillyhall West, Workington, Cumbria, CA14 4HX
Activities: Financial leasing
Officers: Emma Dobie [1975] Director/Mentor; William Dobie [1946] Director/Business Manager; Sarah Newton [1973] Director/Lecturer

Dock 10 Limited
Incorporated: 18 June 2010 *Employees:* 145
Net Worth: £2,276,000 *Total Assets:* £11,402,000
Registered Office: Peel Dome, intu Trafford Centre, Trafford City, Manchester, M17 8PL
Activities: Television programming and broadcasting activities
Parent: Peel Media Studios Limited
Officers: Jaqueline Ann Whalley, Secretary; Neil Lees [1963] Director; Mark Andrew Senior [1963] Director; Steven Keith Underwood [1974] Director; Malcolm Robert Wall [1956] Director; Jaqueline Ann Whalley [1963] Director; John Peter Whittaker [1982] Director

Doff Portland Limited
Incorporated: 18 October 1946 *Employees:* 95
Net Worth: £5,121,161 *Total Assets:* £11,488,071
Registered Office: The Old School House, 39 Bengal Street, Manchester, M4 6AF
Activities: Manufacture of pesticides and other agrochemical products
Parent: DP Bidco
Officers: Ian Paul George, Secretary; Christopher James Oswin [1980] Finance Director; Benjamin Jonathon Shapiro [1973] Director; Richard Lee Shonn [1977] Director

Domeline Limited
Incorporated: 22 March 1989
Net Worth: £9,436,274 *Total Assets:* £28,971,674
Registered Office: 6th Floor, Cardinal House, 20 St Mary's Parsonage, Manchester, M3 2LG
Activities: Buying and selling of own real estate
Officers: Joshua Halpern, Secretary; Joshua Halpern [1958] Director; Samuel Halpern [1960] Director

Domu Brands Limited
Incorporated: 17 October 2009 *Employees:* 104
Net Worth: £5,559,791 *Total Assets:* £17,577,632
Registered Office: Floors 4 & 5, The Tower, Deva City Office Park, Trinity Way, Salford, M3 7BF
Activities: Retail sale via mail order houses or via Internet
Shareholders: Craig Foster; Mark Richard Januszewski
Officers: Craig Foster [1981] Director; Mark Richard Januszewski [1981] Director

Doncaster Sheffield Airport Limited
Incorporated: 11 January 1999 *Employees:* 96
Net Worth Deficit: £27,315,588 *Total Assets:* £14,710,565
Registered Office: Peel Dome, intu Trafford Centre, Trafford City, Manchester, M17 8PL
Activities: Scheduled passenger air transport
Parent: Peel Investments (DSA) Limited
Officers: Neil Lees, Secretary; Peter John Hosker [1957] Director; Robert Eric Hough [1945] Director; Neil Lees [1963] Director/Company Secretary; Peter John Nears [1955] Director; Steven Keith Underwood [1974] Director; John Whittaker [1942] Director

Done Brothers (Cash Betting) Limited
Incorporated: 17 September 1976 *Employees:* 5,412
Net Worth: £29,016,000 *Total Assets:* £306,571,008
Registered Office: The Spectrum, 56-58 Benson Road, Birchwood, Warrington, Cheshire, WA3 7PQ
Activities: Gambling and betting activities
Parent: Lightcatch Limited
Officers: Michael Rodney Hamilton, Secretary; Nicola Joan Barr [1977] Finance Director; Fred Done [1943] Director/Bookmaker; Mark Warren Stebbings [1970] Managing Director

Doorway Holdings Limited
Incorporated: 4 February 2014
Net Worth: £3,322,857 *Total Assets:* £17,910,860
Registered Office: Eversheds House, 70 Great Bridgewater Street, Manchester, M1 5ES
Activities: Other business support service activities n.e.c.
Parent: Doorway Capital Limited
Officers: Gregory Francis Cox, Secretary; Gregory Francis Cox [1971] Director

Doosan International UK Limited
Incorporated: 18 September 2007 *Employees:* 33
Net Worth: £12,674,000 *Total Assets:* £24,364,000
Registered Office: Unit 20 Meadowcroft Way, Leigh Commerce Park, Leigh, Lancs, WN7 3XZ
Activities: Agents involved in the sale of machinery, industrial equipment, ships and aircraft
Officers: Andrew Hatton, Secretary; Andrew Michael Hatton [1965] Business Director

Dorbcrest Homes Limited
Incorporated: 29 September 1980 *Employees:* 15
Net Worth: £6,326,852 *Total Assets:* £8,309,707
Registered Office: The Old Carnegie Library, Ormskirk Road, Pemberton, Wigan, Lancs, WN5 9DQ
Activities: Construction of domestic buildings
Shareholder: James Boylan
Officers: Dympna Jane Mansfield, Secretary/Chartered Surveyor; James Boylan [1941] Director/Chairman [Irish]; Kierstan Julia Boylan [1975] Project Director; Dympna Jane Mansfield [1968] Managing Director

Dorbiere Limited
Incorporated: 2 November 1979 *Employees:* 52
Net Worth: £11,884,027 *Total Assets:* £16,638,210
Registered Office: Unit 3 Stainburn Road, Openshaw, Manchester, M11 2ER
Activities: Public houses and bars
Parent: Robinrate Limited
Officers: Peter Douglas Sumner, Secretary/Financial Controller; Amanda Jane Gray [1958] Director; Robin MacEwan Gray [1951] Director; Denise Mukadam [1957] Director; Ebrahim Kassam Mukadam [1957] Director

Doric Anderton Limited
Incorporated: 19 January 2004 *Employees:* 43
Net Worth: £4,239,183 *Total Assets:* £8,810,284
Registered Office: The Cooper Room, The Deva Centre, Trinity Way, Manchester, M3 7BG
Activities: Manufacture of paper and paperboard
Parent: Doric Group Limited
Officers: Robert David Ward, Secretary; Robert St John Brace [1962] Director; Bruce Alistair Ian Murray [1974] Director; Peter John Ward [1943] Director; Robert David Ward [1976] Director; Simon Jon Woodhouse [1971] Director

Doric Group Limited
Incorporated: 2 April 2013 *Employees:* 308
Net Worth: £4,759,071 *Total Assets:* £16,957,156
Registered Office: The Cooper Room, Deva Centre, Trinity Way, Manchester, M3 7BG
Activities: Activities of other holding companies n.e.c.
Officers: Bruce Murray, Secretary; Robert St John Brace [1962] Director; Bruce Alistair Ian Murray [1974] Director; Peter John Ward [1943] Director; Robert David Ward [1976] Director; Simon Jon Woodhouse [1971] Director

Dormex Containers Limited
Incorporated: 20 January 1993 *Employees:* 32
Net Worth: £7,475,796 *Total Assets:* £10,275,685
Registered Office: The Copper Room, Deva Centre, Trinity Way, Manchester, M3 7BG
Activities: Non-specialised wholesale trade
Major Shareholder: Kevin Desmond Murphy
Officers: Brenda Nuttall, Secretary; Kevin Desmond Murphy [1945] Director/Manager; Brenda Nuttall [1951] Director/Accounts Manager

Dorset Emergency Services PPP (Holdings) Limited
Incorporated: 26 April 2007
Net Worth: £437,108 *Total Assets:* £49,696,020
Registered Office: Unit 18 Riversway Business Village, Navigation Way, Ashton on Ribble, Preston, Lancs, PR2 2YP
Activities: Activities of head offices
Parent: CSES (Dorset) Ltd
Officers: Sally-Ann Ann Brooks [1966] Director/Project Manager; David Wyn Davies [1968] Director/Accountant; Angela Mills [1961] Director/Accountant

Douglas Valley Finance Company Limited
Incorporated: 17 March 1951 *Employees:* 4
Net Worth: £601,504 *Total Assets:* £14,673,405
Registered Office: 10 Station Court, 27-29 Station Road, Poulton-le-Fylde, Lancs, FY6 7HU
Activities: Management of real estate on a fee or contract basis
Shareholders: Anthony Stuart Brindle; Janet Sally Brindle
Officers: Rodney Stewart Howarth, Secretary; Anthony Stuart Brindle [1951] Director; Janet Sally Brindle [1950] Director; Rodney Stewart Howarth [1963] Company Secretary/Director

Dovetail Systems Limited
Incorporated: 21 September 2006 *Employees:* 79
Net Worth Deficit: £332,485 *Total Assets:* £11,763,711
Registered Office: Eversheds House, 70 Great Bridgewater Street, Manchester, M1 5ES
Activities: Information technology consultancy activities
Parent: Fiserv, Inc.
Officers: Erich Heinz Janzen [1969] Director/Accountant [American]; John James Smith [1959] Managing Director, Fiserv EMEA

Dow Chemical Company Limited
Incorporated: 20 August 1954
Net Worth: £320,286,016 *Total Assets:* £544,828,992
Registered Office: Station Road, Birch Vale, High Peak, Derbys, SK22 1BR
Activities: Manufacture of other inorganic basic chemicals
Officers: Cathrine Anne Jenkins, Secretary; Eduardo Antonio Gadea [1961] Operations Director UK & Nordic [Spanish]; Andrew Michael Jones [1966] Commercial Director; Gino Eduardus Angela Van Poorten [1973] EMEAI Tax Director [Dutch]

Dow Chemical Services UK Limited
Incorporated: 25 March 2010 *Employees:* 385
Net Worth: £14,399,000 *Total Assets:* £174,096,000
Registered Office: Station Road, Birch Vale, High Peak, Derbys, SK22 1BR
Activities: Human resources provision and management of human resources functions
Parent: Dow Chemical Company Limited
Officers: Cathrine Anne Jenkins, Secretary; Luis Antuna [1963] Director/Corporate Counsel [Spanish]; Alejandro Jose Farre Pelaez [1967] Finance Director [Spanish]; Eduardo Antonio Gadea [1961] Operations Director, UK & Nordic [Spanish]; Andrew Michael Jones [1966] Director; Gustavo Martinez de Lahidalga [1963] Director/HR Manager [Spanish]; Julie Emma Roberts [1970] Director/HR Leader/Nordic

Dowbridge Limited
Incorporated: 26 November 1971 *Employees:* 506
Net Worth: £18,597,000 *Total Assets:* £31,374,000
Registered Office: Ribby Hall Village, Ribby Road, Wrea Green, Preston, Lancs, PR4 2PR
Activities: Non-trading company
Shareholder: Paul Graham Harrison
Officers: Paul Graham Harrison, Secretary; Paul Graham Harrison [1958] Director

Dowhigh Limited
Incorporated: 2 May 1975 *Employees:* 60
Net Worth: £4,009,909 *Total Assets:* £6,768,248
Registered Office: Park Lane West, Netherton, Liverpool, L30 6UH
Activities: Construction of roads and motorways
Shareholders: Trevor Dominick Murray; Michael Murray
Officers: Peter Philip Allard [1955] Contracts Director; Brian William George Morrey [1974] Director/Civil Engineer; Michael Murray [1959] Director/Civil Engineer; Trevor Dominick Murray [1969] Plant/Transport Director

George Downing Construction Ltd.
Incorporated: 5 February 1988 *Employees:* 37
Net Worth: £6,224,324 *Total Assets:* £21,476,324
Registered Office: 5 Myrtle Street, Liverpool, L7 7DN
Activities: Construction of commercial buildings
Parent: Downing Construction Ltd
Officers: Ann Louise Lodge, Secretary; Ann Louise Lodge [1955] Director/Clerk; Sally Lynn O'Brien [1960] Director

Downtown Salford Limited
Incorporated: 30 September 2014
Net Worth Deficit: £250,725 *Total Assets:* £9,768,874
Registered Office: Mayfield House, Lyon Road, Altrincham, Cheshire, WA14 5EF
Activities: Buying and selling of own real estate
Officers: David Robert Foran [1974] Director; Christopher Andrew McGoff [1973] Director; David John Paul McGoff [1970] Director; Declan Thomas McGoff [1967] Director; James Matthew McGoff [1966] Director

DQ Investments Limited
Incorporated: 13 December 2013
Net Worth Deficit: £930,390 *Total Assets:* £14,147,855
Registered Office: 1st Floor, NQ Building, 47 Bengal Street, Ancoats, Manchester, M4 6BB
Activities: Development of building projects
Parent: XQ Developments Limited
Officers: Michael Shaw, Secretary; Daren Whitaker [1972] Director

Dr Kershaw's Hospice
Incorporated: 3 September 2004 *Employees:* 58
Net Worth: £7,333,156 *Total Assets:* £7,436,638
Registered Office: Dr Kershaws Hospice, Turf Lane, Royton, Oldham, Lancs, OL2 6EU
Activities: Other human health activities
Officers: Vernon Edward Cressey, Secretary; Susan Ann Briscall [1959] Director/Retired; Dr Paul Russell Cook [1955] Director/Retired; Vernon Edward Cressey [1945] Director; Sally Ann Deaville [1964] Director/Retired; Mirriam Lawton [1954] Director/Local Government; Jonathan Richard Lipton [1957] Director; Alan Moran [1951] Director/Consultant; Gordon Paige Russell [1947] Director/Retired; Anne Sykes [1945] Director; Paul Henry Vincent [1946] Director/Solicitor

Dr Schar UK Limited
Incorporated: 13 March 1998 *Employees:* 34
Net Worth: £9,085,684 *Total Assets:* £13,842,617
Registered Office: 401 Faraday Street, Birchwood Park, Birchwood, Warrington, Cheshire, WA3 6GA
Activities: Wholesale of other food, including fish, crustaceans and molluscs
Parent: Dr Schar SpA
Officers: Andrew Trevor Owens, Secretary; Bradley Ratcliffe Grimshaw [1972] Managing Director

Drayton Group Limited
Incorporated: 8 January 2001 *Employees:* 446
Net Worth: £10,056,000 *Total Assets:* £106,405,000
Registered Office: Lookers House, 3 Etchells Road, West Timperley, Altrincham, Cheshire, WA14 5XS
Activities: Sale of new cars and light motor vehicles
Parent: Warwick Holdings Limited
Officers: Glenda MacGeekie, Secretary; Andrew Campbell Bruce [1965] Director; Robin Anthony Gregson [1960] Director/Chartered Accountant; Nigel John McMinn [1968] Managing Director

Drayton Manor High School Academy Trust
Incorporated: 8 July 2011 *Employees:* 151
Net Worth: £28,673,076 *Total Assets:* £31,694,210
Registered Office: 3rd Floor, 1 Ashley Road, Altrincham, Cheshire, WA14 2DT
Activities: General secondary education
Officers: Sandra Scott, Secretary; Helena Auala [1983] Director/IT & Telecomms Asset Administrator; Professor Waljit Singh Dhillo [1969] Director/NHS Consultant; Sian Dowden [1962] Director/Teacher; Patricia Ann Eldred [1956] Director/Governor; Jonathan Eva [1968] Director/IT Consultant; Annette Alison Gormally [1956] Director/Finance and Senior Data Manager; Nicholas John Haymonds [1969] Director/Teacher; Trevor John Inns [1965] Director; Stella Louise MacAskill [1972] Director/Manager, Head of Professional Standards; Sahra Osman [1979] Director/Paediatric Nurse; Sir Pritpal Singh [1953] Director; Imelda Anne Wright [1952] Director/HR Manager

DRCT (PHPH) Ltd
Incorporated: 31 May 2016
Net Worth Deficit: £5,423 *Total Assets:* £11,162,298
Registered Office: 5 Clayton Court, Duke Street, Chester, CH1 1NE
Activities: Buying and selling of own real estate
Major Shareholder: Duncan Russell Cameron
Officers: Duncan Russell Cameron [1971] Director/Retired; Robert Gregory Thompson [1972] Director/Chartered Accountant

Dreambase Limited
Incorporated: 16 February 2009 *Employees:* 332
Net Worth: £3,951,835 *Total Assets:* £10,077,237
Registered Office: Primrose Mill, Martin Street, Burnley, Lancs, BB10 1SH
Activities: Activities of head offices
Major Shareholder: Riaz Ahmed
Officers: Adnan Farooq Ahmed, Secretary; Adnan Farooq Ahmed [1984] Director; Ghazala Ahmed [1982] Director; Riaz Ahmed [1949] Director

Drighlington Fibres Limited
Incorporated: 6 June 2001
Net Worth: £16,359,000 *Total Assets:* £16,359,000
Registered Office: Old Mills, Drighlington, Bradford, W Yorks, BD11 1BY
Activities: Non-trading company
Officers: Kathryn Anne Davenport, Secretary; Peter Jan Patrik Gyllenhammar [1953] Director [Swedish]; John Olof Hager [1964] Managing Director [Swedish]

Drillwave Limited
Incorporated: 2 October 2007 *Employees:* 119
Net Worth: £8,304,000 *Total Assets:* £17,320,000
Registered Office: c/o Cheetham Hill Construction Ltd, Woodhill Road, Bury, Lancs, BL8 1AR
Activities: Construction of other civil engineering projects n.e.c.
Shareholder: Katie Myers
Officers: Claire Chamberlain [1973] Director; Howard Chamberlain [1946] Director; Katie Myers [1975] Director

Drive Devilbiss Healthcare Limited
Incorporated: 8 October 2001 *Employees:* 478
Net Worth: £4,873,000 *Total Assets:* £65,431,000
Registered Office: Drive Devilbiss Healthcare Limited, Heathfield Lane, Birkenshaw, W Yorks, BD11 2HW
Activities: Non-specialised wholesale trade
Parent: Drive International, LLC
Officers: Amy O'Keefe, Secretary; Michael Thomas Waine, Secretary; Grant Abrahams [1979] Retail Director; Harvey Diamond [1953] Director [American]; Gemma Hartley [1978] Service Director; Richard James McGleenan [1970] Director; Timothy Newby [1963] Marketing Director; Jeffrey Schwarz [1960] Director [American]; Jeremy Paul Taylor [1969] Sales & Marketing Director; Mark Thompson [1964] Director; Graham Thomas Turner [1965] Business Support Director; Michael Thomas Waine [1951] Finance Director

Drive Devilbiss Sidhil Limited
Incorporated: 29 May 1951 *Employees:* 205
Net Worth: £6,756,000 *Total Assets:* £17,574,000
Registered Office: Drive Devilbiss Healthcare Limited, Heathfield Lane, Birkenshaw, W Yorks, BD11 2HW
Activities: Manufacture of other fabricated metal products n.e.c.
Parent: Sidhil Group Limited
Officers: Gemma Hartley [1978] Service Director; Richard James McGleenan [1970] Managing Director; Graham Thomas Turner [1965] Sales and Marketing Director; Michael Thomas Waine [1951] Finance Director

Drive Further Limited
Incorporated: 31 August 2012 *Employees:* 85
Net Worth: £1,437,702 *Total Assets:* £8,920,403
Registered Office: 1 Lakeside, Cheadle Royal Business Park, Cheadle, Stockport, Cheshire, SK8 3GW
Activities: Activities of head offices
Major Shareholder: Nicholas David Garner
Officers: Serena Angela Garner, Secretary; Nicholas David Garner [1978] Director/Chartered Accountant

Driver Consult Limited
Incorporated: 19 November 1999 *Employees:* 53
Net Worth: £3,153,406 *Total Assets:* £19,280,204
Registered Office: 4 St Crispin Way, Haslingden, Rossendale, Lancs, BB4 4PW
Activities: Support activities for petroleum and natural gas mining
Parent: Driver Group PLC
Officers: David John Kilgour, Secretary; David John Kilgour [1961] Director/Chartered Accountant

Driver Group PLC
Incorporated: 2 December 1997 *Employees:* 408
Net Worth: £16,134,000 *Total Assets:* £29,913,000
Registered Office: Driver House, 4 St Crispin Way, Haslingden, Rossendale, Lancs, BB4 4PW
Activities: Support activities for petroleum and natural gas mining
Officers: Tom Hugh Ferns, Secretary; Peter Mark Collini [1965] Director; John Bernard Gerard Horgan [1950] Director; David John Kilgour [1961] Director/Chartered Accountant; Steven John Norris [1945] Director; Mark Wheeler [1967] Director/Chief Operating Officer

Driver Hire Group Services Limited
Incorporated: 2 February 1988 *Employees:* 67
Net Worth: £26,583,542 *Total Assets:* £30,246,044
Registered Office: 7 Bradford Business Park, Kings Gate, Bradford, W Yorks, BD1 4SJ
Activities: Temporary employment agency activities
Parent: Driver Hire Holdings Ltd
Officers: Christopher Michael Chidley [1960] Director; Paul Howard McNulty [1970] Finance Director

Driver Hire Investments Group Limited
Incorporated: 23 July 2007
Net Worth: £2,332,082 *Total Assets:* £18,666,760
Registered Office: 7 Bradford Business Park, Kings Gate, Bradford, W Yorks, BD1 4SJ
Activities: Activities of head offices
Parent: Specialist People Services Group Limited
Officers: Christopher Michael Chidley [1960] Director; Paul Howard McNulty [1970] Director

Driver Hire Investments Limited
Incorporated: 10 August 2004
Net Worth Deficit: £21,886,846 *Total Assets:* £8,093,015
Registered Office: 7 Bradford Business Park, Kings Gate, Bradford, W Yorks, BD1 4SJ
Activities: Temporary employment agency activities
Parent: Driver Hire Investments Group Limited
Officers: Christopher Michael Chidley [1960] Director; Paul Howard McNulty [1970] Director

Drop & Collect Limited
Incorporated: 14 May 2008 *Employees:* 36
Net Worth: £6,074,000 *Total Assets:* £10,832,000
Registered Office: 2nd Floor, Atlantic Pavilion, Albert Dock, Liverpool, L3 4AE
Activities: Unlicensed carriers
Parent: Yodel Delivery Network Limited
Officers: Neil Henry Ashworth [1962] Commercial Director; Richard John Neal [1976] Director; Philip Leslie Peters [1957] Director; Stuart Andrew Winton [1964] Director

Droylsden Academy
Incorporated: 23 October 2008 *Employees:* 134
Net Worth: £28,579,616 *Total Assets:* £29,555,552
Registered Office: Droylsden Academy, Manor Road, Droylsden, Manchester, M43 6QD
Activities: General secondary education
Officers: Dr Nils Erik Elgar, Secretary; Leon Dowd [1973] Director/Vice Principal, Quality and Services to Learners; Stephen Michael Jackson [1968] Director/Teacher; Clare Lloyd [1973] Director/Chartered Accountant; John Albert Lyne [1962] Director/Practice Manager; Nakul Mohandas [1985] Director/Investment Manager; Jacqueline Victoria Moores [1967] Director/Principal/CEO; John Matthew Rogers [1955] Director/Retired; Philip James Wilson [1975] Director/Headteacher

DRPT Properties Limited
Incorporated: 3 March 2009 *Employees:* 40
Net Worth: £7,661,494 *Total Assets:* £21,758,820
Registered Office: 62 Castle Street, Liverpool, L2 7LQ
Activities: Hotels and similar accommodation
Parent: Hollfad Linited
Officers: Donal Ring, Secretary; Mark Christopher Foster [1964] Managing Director; Donal Ring [1946] Director [Irish]; Mark Simon Sutton [1971] Director/Accountant; Patrick Tobin [1941] Director [Irish]

DS7 Limited
Incorporated: 17 July 2014
Net Worth: £74,937,816 *Total Assets:* £86,570,696
Registered Office: 7 Empress Street, Old Trafford, Manchester, M16 9EN
Activities: Other business support service activities n.e.c.
Major Shareholder: Andrew John Camilleri
Officers: Charlie Alexander Clunie Cunningham [1978] Director

DSG 1988 Limited
Incorporated: 12 November 2015
Net Worth Deficit: £735,779 *Total Assets:* £8,700,871
Registered Office: Unity House, Hercules Office Park, Bird Hall Lane, Stockport, Cheshire, SK3 0UX
Activities: Financial intermediation not elsewhere classified
Parent: DSGPI 2015 Limited
Officers: Angus Moncrieff Burt [1984] Director/Entrepreneur; Mark Gow [1968] Director; Richard Matthew Hoggart [1971] Director; David Quate [1971] Director

DSGPI 2015 Limited
Incorporated: 12 November 2015 *Employees:* 61
Net Worth: £164,996 *Total Assets:* £10,682,252
Registered Office: Unity House, Hercules Office Park, Bird Hall Lane, Stockport, Cheshire, SK3 0UX
Activities: Financial intermediation not elsewhere classified
Shareholder: Promethean UK Opportunities Fund II LLP
Officers: Angus Moncrieff Burt [1984] Director/Entrepreneur; Mark Gow [1968] Director; Richard Matthew Hoggart [1971] Director; David Quate [1971] Director

F. Duerr & Sons Limited
Incorporated: 6 June 1924 *Employees:* 243
Net Worth: £21,764,080 *Total Assets:* £35,220,380
Registered Office: Floats House, Floats Road, Roundthorn Industrial Estate, Manchester, M23 9DR
Activities: Other processing and preserving of fruit and vegetables
Shareholder: Anthony Norman Duerr
Officers: Andrew John Collinson, Secretary; Andrew John Collinson [1952] Director; Anthony Norman Duerr [1937] Director; Mark Anthony Frederick Duerr [1964] Director; Richard Norman Andrew Duerr [1967] Director; David Keith Weatherhead [1970] Director

B. Dugdale & Son Limited
Incorporated: 13 January 2003 *Employees:* 76
Net Worth: £12,380,251 *Total Assets:* £17,839,244
Registered Office: Bellman Mill, Salthill, Clitheroe, Lancs, BB7 1QW
Activities: Activities of head offices
Shareholders: Stephen Benjamin Dugdale; John Roger Dugdale
Officers: Michael Townend, Secretary; John Roger Dugdale [1943] Director; Matthew Richard Dugdale [1978] Director; Stephen Benjamin Dugdale [1943] Director

Dugdale Nutrition Limited
Incorporated: 14 November 1934 *Employees:* 76
Net Worth: £1,995,160 *Total Assets:* £13,067,725
Registered Office: Bellman Mill, Salthill, Clitheroe, Lancs, BB7 1QW
Activities: Other manufacturing n.e.c.
Parent: B Dugdale & Son Ltd
Officers: Michael Townend, Secretary; Matthew Richard Dugdale [1978] Managing Director; Matthew Adam Tickle [1987] Operations Director; Michael Townend [1965] Director/Accountant; Peter Wormleighton [1955] Director

Dukefield Limited
Incorporated: 18 January 1977 *Employees:* 16
Net Worth: £11,276,646 *Total Assets:* £12,016,112
Registered Office: Parkside House, 167 Chorley New Road, Bolton, Lancs, BL1 4RA
Activities: Activities of other holding companies n.e.c.
Major Shareholder: Kenneth Andrew MacAulay
Officers: Kenneth Andrew MacAulay, Secretary; James Andrew Richard MacAulay [1989] Director/Civil Servant; Janet Elizabeth MacAulay [1951] Director; Kenneth Andrew MacAulay [1947] Director

Dunbia (England)
Incorporated: 8 March 1983 *Employees:* 530
Net Worth: £14,548,000 *Total Assets:* £25,835,000
Registered Office: Castill Laithe Abattoir, Gisburn Road, Sawley, Clitheroe, Lancs, BB7 4LH
Activities: Processing and preserving of meat
Parent: Dunbia Limited
Officers: Sean Breen [1958] Director [Irish]; Niall Browne [1972] Director [Irish]; James George Dobson [1953] Director; Matthew Samuel Dobson [1982] Managing Director; Michael Queally [1963] Director [Irish]

Dunham Investments Limited
Incorporated: 5 June 2003 *Employees:* 2
Net Worth: £178,888 *Total Assets:* £9,584,877
Registered Office: 11 Nicholas Street, Burnley, Lancs, BB11 2AL
Activities: Other letting and operating of own or leased real estate
Major Shareholder: Neil Crispin Gilson
Officers: Neil Crispin Gilson, Secretary/Haulier; Neil Crispin Gilson [1961] Director/Haulier; Neil Reginald Gilson [1940] Director; Karen Marise Parker [1960] Director

Duni Limited
Incorporated: 1 February 1967 *Employees:* 19
Net Worth: £2,235,000 *Total Assets:* £11,336,000
Registered Office: Chester Road, Preston Brook, Runcorn, Cheshire, WA7 3FR
Activities: Non-specialised wholesale trade
Parent: Duni Holding BV
Officers: Debra Jane Fabian [1964] Director; Paul Howard Fabian [1970] Director; Stig Mats Olof Lindroth [1960] Director/Group Chief Finance Officer [Swedish]

Dunkleys Limited
Incorporated: 26 March 1993 *Employees:* 245
Net Worth: £8,372,210 *Total Assets:* £13,447,079
Registered Office: Cunard Building, Water Street, Liverpool, L3 1EL
Activities: Production of meat and poultry meat products
Parent: Edward Billington & Son Limited
Officers: David Marshall, Secretary; Gary Michael Blake [1973] Director/Chief Executive; Stephen Glynn Hughes [1969] Director/Chief Financial Officer; Aisling Kemp [1972] Group Commercial Development Director [Irish]; Paul Andrew Richards [1968] Director

Dunphy Technology Limited
Incorporated: 2 December 2002 *Employees:* 87
Net Worth: £9,954,290 *Total Assets:* £11,751,542
Registered Office: Queensway, Rochdale, Lancs, OL11 2SL
Activities: Activities of head offices
Shareholders: Sharon Lorraine Kuligowski; Edward Peter Kuligowski
Officers: Sharon Lorraine Kuligowski, Secretary/Director; Bridget Dunphy [1943] Director; Edward Peter Kuligowski [1967] Director/Engineer; Sharon Lorraine Kuligowski [1966] Director

Duo Packaging Group Limited
Incorporated: 15 October 2014 *Employees:* 132
Net Worth: £1,749,974 *Total Assets:* £12,456,924
Registered Office: Vickers Street, Miles Platting, Manchester, M40 8PU
Activities: Manufacture of plastic packing goods
Shareholders: Anthony Michael Brimelow; Dale Barrington Brimelow
Officers: Anthony Michael Brimelow [1976] Director; Dale Barrington Brimelow [1979] Director; David Philip Brimelow [1954] Director; David Philip Brimelow [1954] Director; Zoe Anne Brimelow [1984] Director

Duo Plastics Limited
Incorporated: 20 May 1988 *Employees:* 98
Net Worth: £2,866,407 *Total Assets:* £11,067,092
Registered Office: Vickers Street, Miles Platting, Manchester, M40 8PU
Activities: Manufacture of plastic packing goods
Parent: Duo Packaging Group Limited
Officers: Anthony Michael Brimelow [1976] Director; Dale Barrington Brimelow [1979] Director; David Philip Brimelow [1954] Director; Zoe Anne Brimelow [1984] Director/Marketing Manager

Durham Tees Valley Airport Limited
Incorporated: 16 May 1986 *Employees:* 71
Net Worth Deficit: £8,836,076 *Total Assets:* £9,799,181
Registered Office: Peel Dome, intu Trafford Centre, Trafford City, Manchester, M17 8PL
Activities: Scheduled passenger air transport
Parent: Peel Investments (DTVA) Limited
Officers: Neil Lees, Secretary; Janice Brunton-Dobson [1953] Director; Cllr Michael Carr [1947] Director; Robert Wilfred Carson [1946] Director; Alan Ronald Clark [1986] Director; Councillor Brenda Forster [1940] Director; David Jonathan Glover [1956] Director; Cllr Raymond Norman Goddard [1938] Director; Peter John Hosker [1957] Director; Robert Eric Hough [1945] Director; Neil Lees [1963] Director/Company Secretary; Councillor Carl Marshall [1980] Director; Christopher Paul McEwan [1965] Director; Peter John Nears [1955] Director; Cllr Kevin Joseph Shaw [1958] Director; Steven Keith Underwood [1974] Director; John Whittaker [1942] Director; David Matthew Wilburn [1946] Director

Dutton-Forshaw Holdings Limited
Incorporated: 28 October 1997 *Employees:* 3
Net Worth: £37,462,000 *Total Assets:* £50,700,000
Registered Office: Lookers House, 3 Etchells Road, West Timperley, Altrincham, Cheshire, WA14 5XS
Activities: Activities of head offices
Parent: The Dutton-Forshaw Group Limited
Officers: Glenda MacGeekie, Secretary; Andrew Campbell Bruce [1965] Director; Robin Anthony Gregson [1960] Director/Chartered Accountant; Nigel John McMinn [1968] Managing Director Motor Division

The Dutton-Forshaw Motor Company Limited
Incorporated: 16 January 1961 *Employees:* 710
Net Worth: £24,146,000 *Total Assets:* £269,392,992
Registered Office: Lookers House, 3 Etchells Road, West Timperley, Altrincham, Cheshire, WA14 5XS
Activities: Sale of new cars and light motor vehicles
Parent: Dutton-Forshaw Holdings Limited
Officers: Glenda MacGeekie, Secretary; Andrew Campbell Bruce [1965] Director; Robin Anthony Gregson [1960] Director/Chartered Accountant; Nigel John McMinn [1968] Managing Director Motor Division

DWF LLP
Incorporated: 4 June 2007 *Employees:* 2,201
Net Worth: £42,097,000 *Total Assets:* £142,166,000
Registered Office: 1 Scott Place, 2 Hardman Street, Manchester, M3 3AA
Officers: Claire Bowler [1975] Member; Simon Jean Marie Christiaen [1964] Member; Andrew Richard Leaitherland [1969] Member; Stephen John Miles [1966] Member; Paul Robert Rimmer [1970] Member; Hilary Ross [1969] Member; Derek Paul Adamson [1956] LLP Member; Sabrina Ainouz [1978] LLP Member; Iftikhar Ali [1978] LLP Member; Laurence Hames Applegate [1974] LLP Member; Charles Robert James Ashmore [1967] LLP Member; Toby Jeremy James Askin [1973] LLP Member; Amanda Katherine Banister [1973] LLP Member; Paul Julian Banks [1962] LLP Member; Peter Thomas Barnes [1976] LLP Member; Andrew Robert MacKenzie Bautovich [1987] LLP Member; Damien Paul Bechelli [1978] LLP Member; John Matthew Benjamin [1973] LLP Member; John Bennett [1961] LLP Member; Stephen John Benson [1955] LLP Member; Paul Andrew Berry [1963] LLP Member; Jay Benedict Lennox Birch [1965] LLP Member; Richard Hugh Birks [1972] LLP Member; Oliver Bolthausen [1971] LLP Member; Ali Boroumand [1971] LLP Member; Jonathan Richard Branton [1970] LLP Member; Helga Alison Mary Breen [1959] LLP Member; Klaus Manuel Brisch [1966] LLP Member; Hamish Guy Broadbent [1972] LLP Member; Alice Victoria Broadfield [1973] LLP Member; Denise Brosnan [1963] LLP Member; Paul Andrew Brown [1959] LLP Member; Richard Burger [1974] LLP Member; Louis John Burke [1980] LLP Member; Richard Canon [1978] LLP Member; Lorraine Marcella Carolan [1965] LLP Member; Andrew John Carpenter [1961] LLP Member; Dermot Joseph Casserly [1973] LLP Member; Craig Chaplin [1971] LLP Member; Amanda Dawn Chapman [1972] LLP Member; Michele Cicchetti [1976] LLP Member; Eimear Patricia Collins [1970] LLP Member; Lisa Collins [1963] LLP Member; Robbie Constance [1975] LLP Member; Helen Mary Corner [1960] LLP Member; June Crombie [1962] LLP Member; Luca Cuomo [1981] LLP Member; Mark Andrew Curran [1968] LLP Member; Graham Dagnall [1964] LLP Member; Paul Dally [1963] LLP Member; Paul Richard Davies [1972] LLP Member; Gerard Graham Dickinson [1954] LLP Member; Paul James Donnelly [1985] LLP Member; Matthew Ian Doughty [1970] LLP Member; Abigail Catherine Dry [1973] LLP Member; Romain Serge Claude Robert Dupeyre [1979] LLP Member; Patrick James Eaton [1977] LLP Member; Sara-Jane Eaton [1969] LLP Member; Innes Elizabeth Ebert [1969] LLP Member; Andrew Charles John Edwards [1971] LLP Member; Robert John Edwards [1963] LLP Member; David Anthony Egan [1963] LLP Member; Derek George McNicoll Ellery [1961] LLP Member; Simon James Elphick [1977] LLP Member; Helen Robina Elsworth [1966] LLP Member; Michael Gunter Falter [1971] LLP Member; Edward Joseph Farrelly [1966] LLP Member; Andrew John Flounders [1958] LLP Member; Adrian Joseph Flynn [1979] LLP Member; Finella Fogarty [1978] LLP Member; Jason Alexander Ford [1967] LLP Member; John Robert Crosby Fox [1961] LLP Member; Trevor Jonathan Fox [1962] LLP Member; Christian Francis [1976] LLP Member; David John Frankland [1975] LLP Member; Martin Gallaher [1973] LLP Member; Pascale Gallien [1962] LLP Member; Nina Ruby Gaston [1961] LLP Member; Mark Adrian Gibson [1970] LLP Member; David William Gilchrist [1978] LLP Member; Peter Goodwill [1961] LLP Member; Jon Gould [1982] LLP Member; Carl Graham [1969] LLP Member; Jennifer Claire Graham [1973] LLP Member; Alison MacIntyre Grant [1960] LLP Member; Paul Nicholas Greaves [1968] LLP Member; Stephen Michael Green [1960] LLP Member; Dr Timothy Richard Green [1973] LLP Member; Steffan Groch [1971] LLP Member; John Edward Groome [1953] LLP Member; Anita Gupta [1971] LLP Member; Naveen Gupta [1978] LLP Member; Stephen Benjamin Hackett [1963] LLP Member; Catherine Louise Haslam [1972] LLP Member; Joel Heap [1975] LLP Member; Adam Tom Heather [1972] LLP Member; Damian John Hegarty [1988] LLP Member; Christian Hellmund [1979] LLP Member; Thomas Higson [1976] LLP Member

DWFCO 12 LLP
Incorporated: 26 June 2014
Registered Office: Knowsley House, Knowsley Street, Bolton, Lancs, BL1 2AH
Officers: Barbara Diane Gordon [1960] Member; James Neville Gordon [1982] Member

DWL (Holdings) Limited
Incorporated: 24 July 1995 *Employees:* 88
Net Worth: £4,846,431 *Total Assets:* £11,301,415
Registered Office: Nook House, Cliff Lane, Acton Bridge, Northwich, Cheshire, CW8 3QP
Activities: Manufacture of other articles of paper and paperboard n.e.c.
Major Shareholder: Pamela Olga Lyon
Officers: Pamela Olga Lyon [1943] Director/Psychologist

E S Management Services Limited
Incorporated: 27 July 2012 *Employees:* 157
Net Worth: £4,099,692 *Total Assets:* £16,747,939
Registered Office: Building 1000, Kings Reach, Yew Street, Stockport, Cheshire, SK4 2HG
Activities: Other business support service activities n.e.c.
Major Shareholder: Michael Dwan
Officers: Andrew Dwan [1965] Director; Michael Dwan [1959] Director; Marina Ann Guido [1985] Finance Director

E-Foods Limited
Incorporated: 8 January 2003 *Employees:* 47
Net Worth: £334,056 *Total Assets:* £14,130,643
Registered Office: Willow House, Orbital 24, Oldham Street, Denton, Manchester, M34 3SU
Activities: Agents involved in the sale of food, beverages and tobacco
Parent: EF Limited
Officers: Alexander Fisher [1955] Non-Executive Director; Stephen Peter McFall [1965] National Accounts Director; Paul Mizen [1959] Director; Andrew Neil Nation [1969] IT Director

E. C. M. (Vehicle Delivery Service) Limited
Incorporated: 5 September 1984 *Employees:* 752
Net Worth: £19,709,708 *Total Assets:* £59,239,928
Registered Office: The Airport, Carlisle, Cumbria, CA6 4NW
Activities: Freight transport by road
Officers: Allen Blaney Stuart, Secretary/Accountant; John Andrew Hope [1970] Director/Company Executive; Grant MacDowall [1962] Director/Transport Manager; Raymond Gregory MacDowall [1954] Director/Haulage Contractor; Allen Blaney Stuart [1979] Director/Accountant

E.C.A.M. Properties Limited
Incorporated: 20 July 1988
Net Worth: £5,364,619 *Total Assets:* £8,072,089
Registered Office: 15 Alexandra Drive, Liverpool, L17 8TA
Activities: Development of building projects
Parent: Ecam Holdings Limited
Officers: Christopher Amoo, Secretary; Chris Amoo [1952] Director; Sylvia Amoo [1946] Director

E.S.A. Limited
Incorporated: 5 July 1994 *Employees:* 76
Net Worth: £8,086,809 *Total Assets:* £15,691,529
Registered Office: Riverside, Newchurch Road, Bacup, Lancs, OL13 0DT
Activities: Activities of head offices
Parent: Sutton Group Trustee Ltd
Officers: Mark Alan Foster Butterworth, Secretary; Mark Alan Foster Butterworth [1974] Director/Accountant; Mark James Chalmers [1974] Director/Accountant; Simon Peter Lord Holding [1960] Director; Michael Stephen Kelly [1967] Director; Mark Keith Richardson [1968] Director

E3G Limited
Incorporated: 9 October 2001 *Employees:* 105
Net Worth: £5,704,682 *Total Assets:* £10,502,316
Registered Office: Bank Street, Clayton, Manchester, M11 4AS
Activities: Manufacture of other rubber products
Major Shareholder: Christopher Peter Turner
Officers: Paul Andrew Gorton, Secretary; Rachel Connerney [1986] Director; Paul Andrew Gorton [1968] Director; Keith O'Brien [1966] Managing Director; Christopher Peter Turner [1950] Director/Chairman

EA Technology Limited
Incorporated: 7 December 1990 *Employees:* 184
Net Worth: £1,232,000 *Total Assets:* £13,222,000
Registered Office: Capenhurst Technology Park, Capenhurst, Chester, CH1 6ES
Activities: Engineering related scientific and technical consulting activities
Shareholders: 20-20 Trustees Limited; EATL Group Covenantors Limited; Accuro Trust (Jersey) Ltd
Officers: Ceri Elisabeth Parry, Secretary; Robert Peter Davis [1965] Managing Director; Steven James Harvey [1972] Director/Solicitor; Ruth Hannah Percival [1973] Commercial Director; Jonathan Hugh Schofield [1961] Director; Julie Wynne [1971] Director/Accountant

Eamar Development (UK) Limited
Incorporated: 23 March 2012 *Employees:* 1
Net Worth: £5,027,648 *Total Assets:* £23,024,084
Registered Office: 14 Green Pastures, Stockport, Cheshire, SK4 3RA
Activities: Other letting and operating of own or leased real estate
Parent: Eamar Al-Khaleej Saudi Real Estate Co Ltd
Officers: Saleh Abdullah Alnaeem [1964] Director/Chartered Accountant [Saudi Arabian]

Earnside Energy Limited
Incorporated: 12 May 2010 *Employees:* 8
Net Worth Deficit: £101,000 *Total Assets:* £10,123,000
Registered Office: Suite 3, Chestnut House, 46 Halliwell Street, Chorley, Lancs, PR7 2AL
Activities: Treatment and disposal of non-hazardous waste
Officers: Tanja Willis, Secretary; James Alexander Waldorf Astor [1965] Director; Michael Fishwick [1965] Director/Chief Executive; Henry Julian Aglionby Stanford [1965] Director/Partner, Albion Ventures

Earth's Crust Resources Limited
Incorporated: 10 March 2003 *Employees:* 54
Net Worth: £2,573,069 *Total Assets:* £8,138,215
Registered Office: Eagley House, Deakins Business Park, Blackburn Road, Egerton, Bolton, Lancs, BL7 9RP
Activities: Agents involved in the sale of timber and building materials
Major Shareholder: Mathew James Haslam
Officers: Julie Haslam, Secretary; Mathew James Haslam [1962] Managing Director; David Michael Lowe [1974] Commercial Director; Alexander Peter Warren [1978] Operations Director; Christopher James Wood [1975] Finance Director

Easi-Drive Limited
Incorporated: 24 June 1999 *Employees:* 309
Net Worth: £12,876,138 *Total Assets:* £46,244,232
Registered Office: New Acre House, Shentonfield Road, Manchester, M22 4RW
Activities: Renting and leasing of cars and light motor vehicles
Parent: Edam Group Limited
Officers: Daniel James Bellamy [1976] Director; Simon Jon Bellamy [1972] Director; Gareth Robert Berry [1973] Director; Kenneth McPherson [1969] Director; Stephen Paul Turner [1974] Managing Director

East Cheshire Hospice
Incorporated: 10 April 1984 *Employees:* 126
Net Worth: £8,707,068 *Total Assets:* £8,989,894
Registered Office: East Cheshire Hospice, Millbank Drive, Macclesfield, Cheshire, SK10 3DR
Activities: Hospital activities
Officers: Robert Barrow [1949] Director/Retired; Dr Jonathan Samuel Beck [1963] Director; Annamarie Lisa Challinor [1975] Director/Macmillan End of Life Team Leader; Dr Louise Hastings [1969] Director/Doctor; Alastair Crawford Kennedy [1946] Director/Retired Accountant; James Robert Lovett [1969] Managing Director; Paul Gerard Morrissey [1953] Director; Stephen William Spinks [1958] Director/University Administrator; Eleanor Jane Stephens [1965] Director/Lecturer; Dr Alan Wills [1949] Director

East Coast Concepts Group Limited
Incorporated: 10 May 2016 *Employees:* 227
Net Worth Deficit: £1,598,946 *Total Assets:* £7,990,243
Registered Office: 1st Floor, Rational House, Bridge Street, Manchester, M3 3BN
Activities: Activities of other holding companies n.e.c.
Shareholders: Northedge Capital Nominee Limited; James Reginald Hitchen
Officers: Phillip Thomas Frame [1983] Director; John Hammond [1981] Director; James Reginald Hitchen [1983] Director; Harvey Smyth [1968] Director

East Coast Concepts Holdings Limited
Incorporated: 28 April 2016 *Employees:* 5
Net Worth Deficit: £670,014 *Total Assets:* £6,606,458
Registered Office: 1st Floor, Rational House, Bridge Street, Manchester, M3 3BN
Activities: Activities of other holding companies n.e.c.
Parent: East Coast Concepts Group Limited
Officers: Phillip Thomas Frame [1983] Director; John Hammond [1981] Director; James Reginald Hitchen [1983] Director; Nicola Margaret Sellers [1973] Operations Director

East Coast Main Line Company Limited
Incorporated: 7 February 2003 *Employees:* 3,044
Net Worth Deficit: £106,534,000 *Total Assets:* £243,446,000
Registered Office: One Stockport Exchange, 20 Railway Road, Stockport, Cheshire, SK1 3SW
Activities: Passenger rail transport, interurban
Parent: Inter City Railways Limited
Officers: Timothy Kavanagh, Secretary; Martin Andrew Griffiths [1966] Director; Timothy Brendan Kavanagh [1968] Director; Patrick Charles Kingdon McCall [1964] Director/Senior Partner; Neil Micklethwaite [1973] Director/Transport; Ross John Paterson [1971] Finance Director; Timothy Colin Shoveller [1972] Director; James Richard Rowland Tipple [1971] Director

East Kent Road Car Company,Limited
Incorporated: 11 August 1916 *Employees:* 1,329
Net Worth: £14,332,000 *Total Assets:* £43,614,000
Registered Office: c/o Stagecoach Services Limited, One Stockport Exchange, 20 Railway Road, Stockport, Cheshire, SK1 3SW
Activities: Other urban, suburban or metropolitan passenger land transport (not underground, metro or similar)
Parent: Stagecoach Bus Holdings Limited
Officers: Michael John Vaux, Secretary; Colin Brown [1968] Director/Accountant; Arnold Mark Threapleton [1954] Managing Director; Michael Watson [1973] Director

East Lancashire Building Partnership Limited
Incorporated: 4 June 2003 *Employees:* 5
Net Worth Deficit: £23,754,100 *Total Assets:* £93,267,472
Registered Office: Sceptre House, Sceptre Way, Bamber Bridge, Preston, Lancs, PR5 6AW
Activities: Development of building projects
Shareholders: Eric Wright Group Limited; Community Health Partnerships Limited
Officers: Deborah Jane Rawlinson, Secretary; Jeremy Peter Hartley [1965] Director/Chartered Accountant; Roger Martyn Parr [1970] Director; Neil Geoffrey Ward [1959] Director; Christine Desiree Winstanley [1966] Director; Mark Stuart Youlton [1963] Director

The East Lancashire Hospice
Incorporated: 20 April 1999 *Employees:* 108
Net Worth: £12,366,954 *Total Assets:* £13,113,479
Registered Office: The East Lancashire Hospice, Park Lee Road, Blackburn, Lancs, BB2 3NY
Activities: Other service activities n.e.c.
Officers: Anne Rachel Pallister, Secretary; Yusuf Jan-Virmani [1955] Director/Garage Proprietor; Tom Kennedy [1944] Director/Vice-Chair; Gillian Mary Leacy [1944] Director/Retired Headteacher; David McDonough [1961] Director/Retired; Anne Rachel Pallister [1945] Director/Retired; Frederick Graham Parr [1943] Retired NHS Estates Director; Richard John Sutlieff [1953] Director/Retired; Ian McGregor Willock [1934] Director/Retired

East London Bus & Coach Company Limited
Incorporated: 14 December 1988
Net Worth Deficit: £124,814,000 *Total Assets:* £83,991,000
Registered Office: c/o Stagecoach Services Limited, One Stockport Exchange, 20 Railway Road, Stockport, Cheshire, SK1 3SW
Activities: Other urban, suburban or metropolitan passenger land transport (not underground, metro or similar)
Parent: Stagecoach Bus Holdings Limited
Officers: Michael John Vaux, Secretary; Colin Brown [1968] Director/Accountant; Paul Graham Lynch [1962] Director; Arnold Mark Threapleton [1954] Managing Director

East London Bus Group Property Investments Limited
Incorporated: 9 May 2006
Net Worth: £29,070,000 *Total Assets:* £45,381,000
Registered Office: c/o Stagecoach Services Limited, One Stockport Exchange, 20 Railway Road, Stockport, Cheshire, SK1 3SW
Activities: Buying and selling of own real estate
Parent: Stagecoach Bus Holdings Limited
Officers: Michael John Vaux, Secretary; Colin Brown [1968] Director/Accountant; Paul Graham Lynch [1962] Director; Arnold Mark Threapleton [1954] Managing Director

East Midlands Airport Nottingham Derby Leicester Limited
Incorporated: 18 December 2000
Net Worth: £157,864,000 *Total Assets:* £168,442,000
Registered Office: 6th Floor, Olympic House, Manchester Airport, Manchester, M90 1QX
Activities: Activities of other holding companies n.e.c.
Parent: Manchester Airport Group Finance Limited
Officers: Charles Thomas Cornish [1959] Director/Chief Executive; John Kenneth O'Toole [1974] Director [Irish]; Neil Philip Thompson [1971] Director

East Midlands Airport Property Investments (Hotels) Limited
Incorporated: 26 November 2009
Net Worth: £8,757,000 *Total Assets:* £36,275,000
Registered Office: 4th Floor, Olympic House, Manchester Airport, Manchester, M90 1QX
Activities: Buying and selling of own real estate
Parent: East Midlands International Airport Limited
Officers: Charles Thomas Cornish [1959] Director; John Kenneth O'Toole [1974] Director [Irish]; Neil Philip Thompson [1971] Director

East Midlands Airport Property Investments (Industrial) Limited
Incorporated: 26 November 2009
Net Worth: £36,100,000 *Total Assets:* £87,779,000
Registered Office: 4th Floor, Olympic House, Manchester Airport, Manchester, M90 1QX
Activities: Buying and selling of own real estate
Parent: East Midlands International Airport Limited
Officers: Charles Thomas Cornish [1959] Director/Chief Executive; John Kenneth O'Toole [1974] Director [Irish]; Neil Philip Thompson [1971] Director

East Midlands Airport Property Investments (Offices) Limited
Incorporated: 26 November 2009
Net Worth: £2,807,000 *Total Assets:* £12,253,000
Registered Office: 4th Floor, Olympic House, Manchester Airport, Manchester, M90 1QX
Activities: Buying and selling of own real estate
Parent: East Midlands International Airport Limited
Officers: Charles Thomas Cornish [1959] Director/Chief Executive; John Kenneth O'Toole [1974] Director [Irish]; Neil Philip Thompson [1971] Director

East Youlstone Wind Farm Limited
Incorporated: 15 September 2011
Net Worth Deficit: £572,823 *Total Assets:* £6,932,728
Registered Office: 1030 Slutchers Lane, Centre Park, Warrington, Cheshire, WA1 1QL
Activities: Production of electricity
Officers: Elizabeth Alexandra Oldroyd, Secretary; John William Breckenridge [1962] Managing Director [American]; Simon Richard Eaves [1967] Managing Director; Adrian Waine Robinson [1961] Director/Chief Operating Officer; Kirsty Louise Usher [1975] Director/Accountant

Eastern Green Limited
Incorporated: 12 July 1995 *Employees:* 2
Net Worth: £6,769,245 *Total Assets:* £10,079,555
Registered Office: 2nd Floor, 1 Ashley Road, Altrincham, Cheshire, WA14 2DT
Activities: Other letting and operating of own or leased real estate
Major Shareholder: Stephen Edward Elias
Officers: Ernest Charles Elias [1955] Director; Stephen Edward Elias [1956] Director

Eastlands Homes Partnership Limited
Incorporated: 16 December 2002 *Employees:* 232
Net Worth Deficit: £19,691,000 *Total Assets:* £136,162,000
Registered Office: Lovell House, Archway 6, Hulme, Manchester, M15 5RN
Activities: Renting and operating of Housing Association real estate
Officers: Victor Hassan, Secretary; Graham Reynard Aitken [1956] Director; David Patrick Andrew Dennehy [1960] Director/Retired [Irish]; Alison Magdalene Gordon [1965] Director, Economic Development; John James Hughes [1975] Managing Director; Stephen Arthur Kinsey [1956] Director/Solicitor; Lyndsey McDonald [1985] Director/Project Supervisor - Civil Engineer; Stephen Richard Mole [1956] Finance Director; Dr Slawomir Pawlik [1963] Director/National Health Service Manager [Polish]; Angela Bridie Robinson [1957] Director; Sara Maria Todd [1968] Director/Deputy Chief Executive, Local Government

Eaton Bank Academy
Incorporated: 25 July 2012 *Employees:* 97
Net Worth: £7,541,000 *Total Assets:* £9,711,000
Registered Office: Eaton Bank Academy, Jackson Road, Congleton, Cheshire, CW12 1NT
Activities: General secondary education
Officers: Stuart David Carvell [1980] Director/Teacher; Christiana Caswell [1952] Director; Thomas Stephen Kennedy-Fowler [1985] Director/Teacher; Shelley Georgina Knott [1979] Director/Teacher; Martin John LEA [1965] Director/Farmer; Stephanie Lively [1977] Director/Charity Worker; Timothy Philip McCloud [1971] Director/Graphic Designer; Edward James O'Neill [1971] Director/Teacher; Professor David John Parsons [1941] Director/University Professor; Rebecca Elizabeth Simpson [1972] Director/Solicitor; Keith Smith [1957] Director/Business Consultant; Sonia Maria Smith [1969] Director/Project Manager; Glen Samuel Williams [1971] Director/Town Councillor; Wendy Wright [1946] Director/Retired

Eavesway Travel Limited
Incorporated: 27 March 1995 *Employees:* 48
Net Worth: £3,337,552 *Total Assets:* £7,928,586
Registered Office: Bryn Side, Bryn Road, Ashton in Makerfield, Wigan, Lancs, WN4 8BT
Activities: Other passenger land transport
Major Shareholder: Michael Eaves
Officers: Phillip Granville Rogers, Secretary; Lynne Eaves [1953] Director/Teacher; Michael Eaves [1952] Director/Coach Proprietor; Philip Granville Rogers [1963] Director/Coach Proprietor

ECBA Holdings Limited
Incorporated: 29 March 2016
Net Worth: £3,125,875 *Total Assets:* £12,667,000
Registered Office: Suite 1b, The Beehive, Lions Drive, Shadsworth Business Park, Blackburn, BB1 2QS
Activities: Activities of head offices
Shareholders: Michael Sturridge; Grace Sturridge
Officers: Cherelle Sturridge [1985] Director; Grace Gillian Sturridge [1963] Director; Michael Alexander Sturridge [1962] Director

Eccleston Homes Limited
Incorporated: 21 April 2011 *Employees:* 26
Net Worth: £2,596,142 *Total Assets:* £12,762,795
Registered Office: Cinnamon House, Cinnamon Park, Crab Lane, Fearnhead, Warrington, Cheshire, WA2 0XP
Activities: Construction of domestic buildings
Shareholder: Kevin John Marren
Officers: Alan Dingley [1969] Director; Kevin John Marren [1960] Director

ECG Holdings (UK) Limited
Incorporated: 20 April 2000
Net Worth: £11,822,886 *Total Assets:* £23,036,536
Registered Office: Albion Mills, Albion Road, Bradford, W Yorks, BD10 9TQ
Activities: Other business support service activities n.e.c.
Parent: Sun Chemical Ltd
Officers: Margaret Julia Pearce, Secretary; Paul Richard Bean [1960] Director/Business Manager; Gregory William Hayes [1962] Group Managing Director; Martjin Jan Charles Marie Schoonenberg [1977] Director/General Counsel [Dutch]

Eciffo Props No. 1 Limited
Incorporated: 23 March 2011
Net Worth Deficit: £837,410 *Total Assets:* £6,722,585
Registered Office: St John's House, Two Queen Square, Liverpool, L1 1RH
Activities: Other business support service activities n.e.c.
Parent: Atmore Properties Limited
Officers: Anthony Nigel Carson [1960] Director

Eco Parks HNW Limited
Incorporated: 18 November 2015
Net Worth: £1 *Total Assets:* £11,355,373
Registered Office: The Moorings, Rowton Bridge, Christleton, Chester, CH3 7AE
Activities: Activities of head offices
Parent: Orthios Eco Parks (Anglesey) Limited
Officers: Steven Hedley Haswell [1959] Director; Sean Michael McCormick [1965] Director

Ecolab (U.K.) Holdings Limited
Incorporated: 3 September 2002
Net Worth: £18,777,000 *Total Assets:* £101,172,000
Registered Office: Winnington Avenue, Northwich, Cheshire, CW8 4DX
Activities: Activities of head offices
Officers: Wendy Annette Joyce, Secretary; Carl Richmond Lee [1963] Finance Director; David Walker [1969] Director/Chartered Accountant

Ecolab Limited
Incorporated: 10 February 1960 *Employees:* 1,114
Net Worth: £79,304,000 *Total Assets:* £145,591,008
Registered Office: Winnington Avenue, Northwich, Cheshire, CW8 4DX
Activities: Manufacture of soap and detergents
Parent: Ecolab (U.K.) Holdings Limited
Officers: Wendy Annette Joyce, Secretary; Paul Hey [1964] Director; Carl Richmond Lee [1963] Finance Director; David Walker [1969] Director/Chartered Accountant

Edam Group Limited
Incorporated: 23 September 2008 *Employees:* 311
Net Worth: £16,680,105 *Total Assets:* £54,602,480
Registered Office: New Acre House, Shentonfield Road, Sharston Industrial Area, Manchester, M22 4RW
Activities: Other business support service activities n.e.c.
Parent: Commodore Limited
Officers: Daniel Bellamy [1976] Director; Simon Jon Bellamy [1972] Director; Gareth Robert Berry [1973] Director; Kenneth McPherson [1969] Director; Stephen Paul Turner [1974] Commercial Director

EDCAWI Limited
Incorporated: 3 June 2013 *Employees:* 97
Net Worth: £4,249,794 *Total Assets:* £10,207,133
Registered Office: 8 Sceptre Court, Sceptre Way, Walton Summit, Preston, Lancs, PR5 6AW
Activities: Other manufacturing n.e.c.
Shareholders: John Antony Wilkinson; Duncan Anthony Edwards
Officers: Duncan Anthony Edwards [1966] Director; Simon Christopher Edwards [1968] Director; John Antony Wilkinson [1972] Director

Eddie Rockers Limited
Incorporated: 13 January 1995 *Employees:* 227
Net Worth: £8,087,192 *Total Assets:* £17,044,480
Registered Office: Eleven Didsbury Park, Didsbury, Manchester, M20 5LH
Activities: Hotels and similar accommodation
Shareholders: Sally Victoria O'Loughlin; Edward Gerard Michael O'Loughlin
Officers: Howard Bayley Stubbings, Secretary; Edward Gerard Michael O'Loughlin [1958] Director/Hotel Group Owner [Irish]

Ian Edgar (Liverpool) Limited
Incorporated: 2 January 1957 *Employees:* 43
Net Worth: £3,135,177 *Total Assets:* £10,604,746
Registered Office: Units 2 & 3 Heather Close, Lyme Green Business Park, Macclesfield, Cheshire, SK11 0LR
Activities: Non-specialised wholesale trade
Shareholders: Allan Derek Edgar; Ian Edgar
Officers: Ian Edgar, Secretary; Ian Edgar [1939] Director; Ian Peter Gordon [1966] Director; Thea Susan Heapy [1984] Director; Thomas Jacob Timothy Heapy [1989] Director; Michael James Newman [1983] Director; Lisa Jane Riley [1966] Director

Edge Hill Property Services Limited
Incorporated: 29 March 1996
Net Worth: £7,183,000 *Total Assets:* £7,547,000
Registered Office: Edge Hill University, St Helens Road, Ormskirk, Lancs, L39 4QP
Activities: Other business support service activities n.e.c.
Officers: Stephen James Igoe, Secretary; John Charles Cater [1953] Director/University Vice Chancellor; Professor Clive Edwards [1949] Director

Edge Orbital Holdings Limited
Incorporated: 27 September 2016
Net Worth: £34,681,000 *Total Assets:* £266,894,000
Registered Office: c/o Albany SPC Services Limited, 3rd Floor, 3-5 Charlotte Street, Manchester, M1 4HB
Activities: Activities of construction holding companies
Shareholders: GCM Infrastructure Holdings II, LLC; Equitix Orbital Holdings Limited
Officers: Ailison Louise Mitchell, Secretary; Roger Georges Ammoun [1974] Managing Director; Achal Prakash Bhuwania [1979] Director; John Stephen Gordon [1962] Director; Richard Daniel Knight [1974] Director; Javier Dario Matallana Mendez [1979] Director/Principal; John McDonagh [1969] Director

Edge Transport (Properties) Limited
Incorporated: 7 February 2014 *Employees:* 67
Net Worth: £2,429,710 *Total Assets:* £7,082,778
Registered Office: Easter Park, Fourth Avenue, Deeside Industrial Park, Deeside, Flintshire, CH5 2NR
Activities: Freight transport by road
Shareholders: Anthea Claire Cleland; Jonathan Tyler Edge; Jennifer Lynn Pridding
Officers: Anthea Claire Cleland [1944] Director/Chairman; Jonathan Tyler Edge [1973] Managing Director; Nicola Edge [1973] Director; Jennifer Lynn Pridding [1969] Director; Richard Russell Pridding [1976] Director

Edge Wear Properties Limited
Incorporated: 26 March 1996
Net Worth: £13,948,587 *Total Assets:* £17,755,418
Registered Office: Emerson House, Heyes Lane, Alderley Edge, Cheshire, SK9 7LF
Activities: Other letting and operating of own or leased real estate
Shareholders: Milnes Investments Limited; P E Jones (Properties) Limited
Officers: Varun Maharaj, Secretary; Patricia Joyce Goddard [1944] Director; Mark Emerson Jones [1964] Director; Peter Emerson Jones [1935] Director; Amy Jade Kennedy [1990] Director/Business Executive

Edge Worldwide Logistics Limited
Incorporated: 17 October 1990 *Employees:* 51
Net Worth: £3,050,982 *Total Assets:* £12,539,795
Registered Office: Optimum House, Clippers Quay, Salford, M50 3XP
Activities: Other transportation support activities
Shareholder: Philip Adam Edge
Officers: Alan Joseph Edge, Secretary; Andrew Guy Davis [1970] Director/Chief Financial Officer; Alan Joseph Edge [1949] Director; Philip Adam Edge [1983] Director; James Vincent Postles [1971] Operations Director; Andrew Anthony Raglan [1979] Director

Edgefold Holdings Limited
Incorporated: 14 January 2014 *Employees:* 113
Net Worth: £27,324,000 *Total Assets:* £32,364,000
Registered Office: Units A2-A6 Edgefold Industrial Estate, Plodder Lane, Bolton, Lancs, BL4 0LR
Activities: Other letting and operating of own or leased real estate
Major Shareholder: Stephen John Seddon
Officers: Sarah Cook, Secretary; George Seddon [1939] Director; Stephen John Seddon [1966] Director

Edgworth Developments Limited
Incorporated: 14 April 1999
Net Worth Deficit: £8,400,926 *Total Assets:* £6,809,828
Registered Office: Lake View, Lakeside, Cheadle, Cheshire, SK8 3GW
Activities: Development of building projects
Major Shareholder: Henry Neville Moser
Officers: Gary Derek Beckett, Secretary/Director; Henry Neville Moser [1949] Director

Edible Oils Ltd
Incorporated: 10 December 2004 *Employees:* 195
Net Worth: £59,873,000 *Total Assets:* £97,979,000
Registered Office: 6th Floor, Royal Liver Building, Pier Head, Liverpool, L3 1NX
Activities: Manufacture of oils and fats
Shareholders: Princes Limited; Pura Foods Limited
Officers: Kazuhito Suematsu, Secretary; Martin Kropp [1965] Director [German]; Cameron John Mackintosh [1969] Director; Dermot O'Grady [1969] Director [Irish]; Craig Derek Price [1974] Director

Edina UK Limited
Incorporated: 21 December 2005 *Employees:* 125
Net Worth: £3,933,269 *Total Assets:* £33,693,240
Registered Office: 13 Rugby Park, Bletchley Road, Stockport, Cheshire, SK4 3EJ
Activities: Other manufacturing n.e.c.
Parent: Edina Acquisitions Limited
Officers: Ricardo Luis de Sousa Alves, Secretary; Neelima Jain [1981] Director [Indian]; Hugh Kerr Richmond [1962] Director/Head of Global Sales

EDM Limited
Incorporated: 2 February 1971 *Employees:* 186
Net Worth: £10,379,594 *Total Assets:* £17,207,222
Registered Office: Brunel House, 1 Thorpe Road, Newton Heath, Manchester, M40 5BJ
Activities: Other manufacturing n.e.c.
Parent: EDM Holdings Limited
Officers: Sarah Louise Ferguson, Secretary; Anthony Andrew Bermingham [1964] Commercial Director; Michael Bonney [1962] Director; Sarah Louise Ferguson [1971] Director; Nigel John Randall [1943] Director; Nigel Jeffrey Spring [1961] Operations Director

Edmundson Electrical Limited
Incorporated: 29 November 1991
Net Worth: £368,680,992 *Total Assets:* £601,638,016
Registered Office: P O Box 1, Tatton Street, Knutsford, Cheshire, WA16 6AY
Activities: Wholesale of radio, television goods & electrical household appliances (other than records, tapes, CDs)
Parent: Marlowe Holdings Investments Limited
Officers: Stuart Paul Newsum, Secretary; Philip Graham Elsegood [1958] Financial Director; Mark George Felber [1963] Managing Director; Roger David Goddard [1953] Director/Chartered Accountant; Gordon Alexander Love [1955] Director/Deputy Chairman; Douglas Talbot McNair [1947] Director/Executive Chairman; William Sones Woof [1951] Director/Solicitor

Education and Leadership Trust
Incorporated: 26 February 2014 *Employees:* 501
Net Worth: £71,773,496 *Total Assets:* £76,522,232
Registered Office: Whalley Range 11-18 High School, Wilbraham Road, Manchester, M16 8GW
Activities: General secondary education
Officers: Emma Jane Antrobus [1968] Director/Regional Manager; Matthew Stuart Begg [1978] Director/Data Manager; Jessica Catherine Bowles [1972] Strategy Director; Ronan Brindley [1966] Director/Museum Professional [Irish]; Michael Stuart Chidley [1946] Retired College Director; Patricia Denise Kane [1958] Director/Headteacher; Sandra Milne [1977] Director/Solicitor; Andrew Sean Mullen [1964] Deputy HR Director; Yvonne Eleanor Norton [1978] Director/Teacher; Richard Paver [1955] Director/Accountant

Education Partnership Trust
Incorporated: 15 February 2012 *Employees:* 258
Net Worth: £19,340,792 *Total Assets:* £24,497,440
Registered Office: Education Partnership Trust, Pleckgate Road, Blackburn, BB1 8QA
Activities: Other education n.e.c.
Officers: Angela Allen [1966] Director/Chief Executive; Ian Andrew Brown [1966] Director; Desmond John Callaghan [1959] Director/Headteacher; Michael Christopher Cartledge [1963] Director/Chief Executive; Harry Catherall [1963] Director/Chief Executive; John Luke Green [1982] Director/Solicitor; Julie Hughes [1958] Director/Assistant Principal; Ian Michael Kendrick [1954] Director/Semi Retired/School Consultancy; Hamid Patel [1979] Director/Headteacher; Sharon Roscoe [1969] Director/Chief Executive

Education Solutions Speke Limited
Incorporated: 6 March 2001
Net Worth Deficit: £2,370,893 *Total Assets:* £16,954,286
Registered Office: Building 1000, Kings Reach, Yew Street, Stockport, Cheshire, SK4 2HG
Activities: Management of real estate on a fee or contract basis
Parent: Equity Solutions Manchester Limited
Officers: Ian William Currie [1961] Director/Stockbroker; Alfred Michael Dwan [1959] Director; Richard Ian Hughes [1968] Director

Edwards Cheshire Company Limited
Incorporated: 27 August 1993 *Employees:* 64
Net Worth: £7,383,549 *Total Assets:* £11,516,969
Registered Office: 18 Chesford Grange, Woolston, Warrington, Cheshire, WA1 4RQ
Activities: Wholesale of wood, construction materials and sanitary equipment
Major Shareholder: Robert Edward Cheshire Walsh
Officers: Richard Lincoln, Secretary; Keith Brian Alderson [1960] Director; Tracey Bardell [1955] Director; David Cross [1971] Company Operations Director; Richard Oliver Lincoln [1975] Finance Director; Raymond Alexander Scott [1958] Managing Director; Jane Walsh [1971] Director; Robert Edward Cheshire Walsh [1972] Director

EFS Los Guindos UK Limited
Incorporated: 22 December 2015
Net Worth: £27,925,324 *Total Assets:* £27,925,324
Registered Office: 3rd Floor, 1 Ashley Road, Altrincham, Cheshire, WA14 2DT
Activities: Activities of head offices
Parent: EFS UK Holdings Limited
Officers: Mark Russell Hanson [1973] Director; Brian Peter Ward [1959] Director/Investment Professional [American]

EG Finco Limited
Incorporated: 15 October 2015 *Employees:* 5
Net Worth: £1,145,997,952 *Total Assets:* £2,551,003,904
Registered Office: Euro House, The Beehive Trading Park, Haslingden Road, Blackburn, Lancs, BB1 2EE
Activities: Activities of other holding companies n.e.c.
Officers: Imraan Musa Patel, Secretary; Mohsin Issa [1971] Director; Zuber Vali Issa [1972] Director

EG Group Limited
Incorporated: 15 October 2015 *Employees:* 10,752
Net Worth: £404,968,064 *Total Assets:* £2,782,296,832
Registered Office: Euro House, The Beehive Trading Park, Haslingden Road, Blackburn, BB1 2EE
Activities: Activities of other holding companies n.e.c.
Shareholders: Mohsin Issa Zuber Vali Issa
Officers: Imraan Musa Patel, Secretary; Mohsin Issa [1971] Director; Zuber Vali Issa [1972] Director

EG Midco Limited
Incorporated: 21 October 2016 *Employees:* 10,752
Net Worth: £404,968,064 *Total Assets:* £2,782,296,832
Registered Office: Euro House, The Beehive Trading Park, Haslingden Road, Blackburn, Lancs, BB1 2EE
Activities: Other service activities incidental to land transportation, n.e.c.
Officers: Imraan Musa Patel, Secretary; Mohsin Issa [1971] Director; Gary Lindsay [1979] Director/Investment Professional

Egencia Holdings UK Ltd
Incorporated: 22 February 2012
Net Worth Deficit: £136,756,640 *Total Assets:* £65,926,780
Registered Office: Egencia, 9th Floor, 3 Piccadilly Place, Manchester, M1 3BN
Activities: Activities of head offices
Parent: Expedia Group, Inc.
Officers: Robert John Dzielak [1971] Director/Business Executive [American]; Robert Greyber [1969] Director/Business Executive [American]; Hemanth Ramaswamy Munipalli [1969] Director/Chief Financial Officer [American]

Egencia UK Ltd
Incorporated: 11 May 1951 *Employees:* 377
Net Worth: £3,123,000 *Total Assets:* £34,256,000
Registered Office: 9th Floor, 3 Piccadilly Place, Manchester, M1 3BN
Activities: Travel agency activities
Parent: Expedia Group, Inc.
Officers: Robert Greyber [1969] Director/Business Executive [American]; Hemanth Ramaswamy Munipalli [1969] Director/Chief Financial Officer [American]

Egerton Investments Limited
Incorporated: 30 December 1997
Net Worth: £3,205,365 *Total Assets:* £7,313,578
Registered Office: 6th Floor, Cardinal House, 20 St Mary's Parsonage, Manchester, M3 2LG
Activities: Buying and selling of own real estate
Major Shareholder: Peter Eric Higginbottom
Officers: Heather Higginbottom, Secretary/Director; Claire Bothwick [1979] Director; Heather Higginbottom [1954] Director; Laura Jayne Higginbottom [1982] Director; Peter Eric Higginbottom [1948] Director/Chartered Surveyor

Egertons Recovery Group Limited
Incorporated: 1 June 2010 *Employees:* 238
Net Worth: £1,201,349 *Total Assets:* £9,122,073
Registered Office: Moss Lane, Mobberley, Cheshire, WA16 7BS
Activities: Activities of head offices
Parent: Egertons Holdings Limited
Officers: Diane Karen Egerton, Secretary; Diane Karen Egerton [1962] Director; Mark Jonathan Egerton [1960] Director

EGI (UK) Limited
Incorporated: 18 December 2006 *Employees:* 149
Net Worth: £9,656,000 *Total Assets:* £12,635,000
Registered Office: c/o Enesco Ltd, Brunthill Road, Kingstown, Carlisle, Cumbria, CA3 0EN
Activities: Activities of other holding companies n.e.c.
Major Shareholder: Jonathan Victor
Officers: Emily Kaye Brown, Secretary; Emily Kaye Brown [1965] Director [American]; Jonathan Victor [1957] Director/Managing Partner of a Private Equity Fund [American]

EHC Harnham House Limited
Incorporated: 27 April 2005 *Employees:* 75
Net Worth: £4,801,283 *Total Assets:* £7,748,751
Registered Office: Bollin House, Riverside Park, Bollin Link Road, Wilmslow, Cheshire, SK9 1DP
Activities: Other human health activities
Parent: Equilibrium Healthcare Group Limited
Officers: Harriet Jane Dudgeon [1959] Director; Patrick John Keely [1959] Director/Manager; David Phillip Madeley [1960] Director/Chartered Accountant

El Spa Holdings (UK) Limited
Incorporated: 18 November 2014 *Employees:* 199
Net Worth: £27,245,718 *Total Assets:* £56,985,704
Registered Office: 5th Floor, Voyager House, Chicago Avenue, Manchester Airport, Manchester, M90 3DQ
Activities: Activities of head offices
Parent: The Hut.Com Limited
Officers: James Pochin, Secretary; John Andrew Gallemore [1969] Director; Paul Jonathan Gedman [1981] Director

Elastomerics Limited
Incorporated: 5 November 1981 *Employees:* 11
Net Worth: £7,905,460 *Total Assets:* £10,744,155
Registered Office: London Road, Adlington, Macclesfield, Cheshire, SK10 4DU
Activities: Wholesale of chemical products
Parent: Caldic (UK) Ltd
Officers: Danielle Francesca Auton, Secretary; John Philip Robinson [1963] Director; Olav Van Caldenborgh [1968] Director [Dutch]

ELC (Barrow) Limited
Incorporated: 18 October 2016
Net Worth Deficit: £229,277 *Total Assets:* £14,314,231
Registered Office: Richard House, Winckley Square, Preston, Lancs, PR1 3HP
Activities: Development of building projects
Parent: ELC (Barrow) Holdco Limited
Officers: Nigel Anthony Bennett [1961] Director; Adam Mark Hearnden [1962] Director; Neil Geoffrey Ward [1959] Director

ELC (Tranche 1) Limited
Incorporated: 17 August 2011
Net Worth: £3,760,150 *Total Assets:* £22,045,412
Registered Office: Richard House, Winckley Square, Preston, Lancs, PR1 3HP
Activities: Development of building projects
Parent: Elift Cumbria Limited
Officers: Nigel Anthony Bennett [1961] Director; Adam Mark Hearnden [1962] Director; Ian James Tasker [1967] Director/Company Partner; Neil Geoffrey Ward [1959] Investment Director

Elcometer Limited
Incorporated: 7 June 1983 *Employees:* 271
Net Worth: £31,914,716 *Total Assets:* £40,117,376
Registered Office: Edge Lane, Manchester, M43 6BU
Activities: Manufacture of electronic measuring, testing etc. equipment, not for industrial process control
Shareholders: Nanette Patricia Everall Sellars; Michael Carrington Sellars
Officers: Michael Carrington Sellars [1972] Director; Nanette Patricia Everall Sellars [1943] Director

Eldapoint Investments Limited
Incorporated: 1 August 2013 *Employees:* 139
Net Worth: £673,568 *Total Assets:* £10,080,893
Registered Office: c/o A2E Industries Limited, 1 Marsden Street, Manchester, M2 1HW
Activities: Other business support service activities n.e.c.
Major Shareholder: Said Amin Amiri
Officers: Andrew John Blount [1966] Finance Director; Charles Stuart Chidley [1962] Director/General Manager

Eldapoint Limited
Incorporated: 15 February 1973 *Employees:* 139
Net Worth: £5,846,741 *Total Assets:* £15,116,634
Registered Office: Charleywood Road, Knowsley Industrial Park North, Knowsley, Merseyside, L33 7SG
Activities: Other service activities n.e.c.
Parent: Eldapoint Holdings Ltd
Officers: Andrew John Blount [1966] Director; Charles Stuart Chidley [1952] Director/General Manager

Elders Glass Limited
Incorporated: 6 December 1900
Net Worth: £720,884,992 *Total Assets:* £720,884,992
Registered Office: European Technical Centre, Hall Lane, Lathom, Ormskirk, Lancs, L40 5UF
Activities: Activities of head offices
Parent: NSG UK Enterprises Limited
Officers: Iain Michael Smith, Secretary; Judy Anne Massa [1967] Director/Accountant; Paul Joseph Ravenscroft [1970] Director/Head of Mergers & Acquisitions; Iain Michael Smith [1972] Director/Chartered Accountant

ELE Advanced Technologies Limited
Incorporated: 22 March 2000 *Employees:* 178
Net Worth: £4,400,210 *Total Assets:* £9,365,250
Registered Office: Cotton Tree Lane, Colne, Lancs, BB8 7BH
Activities: Manufacture of engines and turbines, except aircraft, vehicle and cycle engines
Shareholder: Crown Place VCT PLC
Officers: David Dudley [1970] Technical Director; Peter William Harrisson [1945] Director; Peter Palij [1956] Director; Manesh Pandya [1961] Director; Robert James Whitby Smith [1974] Director/Venture Capitalist

Electric Glass Fiber UK, Ltd.
Incorporated: 8 July 2016 *Employees:* 230
Net Worth: £35,304,000 *Total Assets:* £53,251,000
Registered Office: P O Box 132, Leigh Road, Hindley Green, Wigan, Lancs, WN2 4XZ
Activities: Manufacture of glass fibres
Parent: Nippon Electric Glass Co., Ltd.
Officers: Brian Keith Stewart [1965] Director/Manufacturing Manager

Electric Systems Limited
Incorporated: 24 January 2006 *Employees:* 45
Net Worth: £2,934,959 *Total Assets:* £12,067,572
Registered Office: 15 Carnarvon Street, Manchester, M3 1HJ
Activities: Wholesale of electronic and telecommunications equipment and parts
Parent: ESL Investco Limited
Officers: Wendy Littman, Secretary; Philip Isaac Hodari [1961] Director; Christopher Pearson [1971] Director; Simone Sara Peppi [1962] Director; Keith John Richardson [1959] Finance Director; Ruth Patricia Topham [1976] Finance Director

Electricity North West (Construction and Maintenance) Limited
Incorporated: 21 September 2010 *Employees:* 43
Net Worth: £3,436,000 *Total Assets:* £9,237,000
Registered Office: 304 Bridgewater Place, Birchwood, Warrington, Cheshire, WA3 6XG
Activities: Other specialised construction activities n.e.c.
Parent: North West Electricity Networks (UK) Limited
Officers: Richard Somerville, Secretary; David Graham Brocksom [1960] Director/Chief Finance Officer; Peter Richard Emery [1962] Director/Chief Executive Officer; Mark Philip Williamson [1966] Energy Solutions Director

Electricity North West Limited
Incorporated: 1 April 1989 *Employees:* 1,666
Net Worth: £764,600,000 *Total Assets:* £3,305,600,000
Registered Office: 304 Bridgewater Place, Birchwood Park, Warrington, Cheshire, WA3 6XG
Activities: Distribution of electricity
Parent: North West Electricity Networks PLC
Officers: Richard Somerville, Secretary; David Graham Brocksom [1960] Director/Chief Finance Officer; Alistair Buchanan [1961] Director; Susan Cooklin [1960] Director; Christopher Bruce Dowling [1953] Director [Australian]; Peter Richard Emery [1962] Director/Chief Executive Officer; Robert David Holden [1956] Director; Hamish Ambrose LEA-Wilson [1982] Director; John E Lynch [1970] Director [American]; Niall Patrick Mills [1968] Director/Senior Asset Manager; Tomas Pedraza [1977] Director [Spanish]; Dr John Edward Roberts [1946] Director; Mark Scarsella [1984] Director/Investment Principal [Australian]

Electroimpact UK Limited
Incorporated: 6 June 2000 *Employees:* 119
Net Worth: £32,534,752 *Total Assets:* £40,289,124
Registered Office: Electroimpact, Technology Park, Manor Lane, Hawarden, Deeside, Flintshire, CH5 3ST
Activities: Repair of machinery
Major Shareholder: Dr Peter Brian Zieve
Officers: Dr. Peter Zieve, Secretary/Director [American]; Michael Zieve [1989] Director/Vice President Electroimpart Inc [American]; Dr. Peter Zieve [1954] Director [American]

Electrovision Limited
Incorporated: 25 September 1980 *Employees:* 67
Net Worth: £3,639,169 *Total Assets:* £10,008,937
Registered Office: Lancots Lane, Sutton, St Helens, Merseyside, WA9 3EX
Activities: Wholesale of electronic and telecommunications equipment and parts
Parent: Holmpatrick Ltd
Officers: Mark Benyon, Secretary; Jill Allison Ball [1981] Director; Catherine Jane Benyon [1980] Director; Ian Robert Benyon [1981] Director; Mark Benyon [1951] Director/Business Manager; Simon Geoffrey Deeley [1967] Director/Manager; Richard John Jeff Fox [1963] Director/Business Manager

Elegant Resorts Limited
Incorporated: 18 February 1987 *Employees:* 123
Net Worth: £4,899,000 *Total Assets:* £25,446,000
Registered Office: Elegant House, Sandpiper Way, Chester Business Park, Chester, CH4 9QE
Activities: Travel agency activities
Parent: Portman Travel Group Limited
Officers: Abdullah Al Darwood [1981] Director [Saudi Arabian]; Mark Christopher Nevin [1957] Director; Redmond Gavin McGinty Walsh [1967] Director; Yousif Musa Yousif [1957] Director [American]

Elfreed Ltd
Incorporated: 10 March 2006 *Employees:* 63
Net Worth: £3,065,076 *Total Assets:* £6,815,486
Registered Office: Factory, Siddorn Street, Winsford, Cheshire, CW7 2BA
Activities: Other manufacturing n.e.c.
Shareholders: Fred Mendelsohn; Ken Terry; Patrick Smulders
Officers: David Whitehead, Secretary; Fredric William Mendelsohn [1963] Director

Elias Enterprises Limited
Incorporated: 12 June 1969 *Employees:* 14
Net Worth: £9,111,253 *Total Assets:* £12,389,391
Registered Office: 2nd Floor, 1 Ashley Road, Altrincham, Cheshire, WA14 2DT
Activities: Wholesale of textiles
Shareholders: Ernest Charles Elias; Stephen Edward Elias
Officers: Ernest Charles Elias [1955] Director; Stephen Edward Elias [1956] Director; Deborah Teasdale [1967] Director/Office Manager

Elior UK Holdings Limited
Incorporated: 24 February 1989 *Employees:* 12,244
Net Worth: £33,398,484 *Total Assets:* £195,818,000
Registered Office: The Courtyard, Catherine Street, Macclesfield, Cheshire, SK11 6ET
Activities: Activities of head offices
Parent: Elior SA
Officers: Esther Gaide [1961] Director/Group Chief Financial Officer [French]; Catherine Margaret Roe [1960] Managing Director; Eleni Savva [1972] Finance Director

Elior UK PLC
Incorporated: 6 April 1973 *Employees:* 7,172
Net Worth: £47,065,168 *Total Assets:* £109,246,848
Registered Office: The Courtyard, Catherine Street, Macclesfield, Cheshire, SK11 6ET
Activities: Event catering activities
Parent: Elior UK Holdings Limited
Officers: Joanna Luke, Secretary; Esther Gaide [1961] Director/Group Chief Financial Officer [French]; Catherine Margaret Roe [1960] Managing Director; Eleni Savva [1972] Finance Director; Thierry Thonnier [1966] Director [French]

Elior UK Services Limited
Incorporated: 3 February 2004 *Employees:* 212
Net Worth: £2,761,655 *Total Assets:* £40,331,864
Registered Office: The Courtyard, Catherine Street, Macclesfield, Cheshire, SK11 6ET
Activities: Other business support service activities n.e.c.
Parent: Elior UK Holdings Limited
Officers: Eleni Savva [1972] Finance Director

Elitetele.Com PLC
Incorporated: 24 July 1996 *Employees:* 91
Net Worth: £26,904,696 *Total Assets:* £52,610,400
Registered Office: Dawson House, Matrix Office Park, Buckshaw Village, Chorley, Lancs, PR7 7NA
Activities: Other telecommunications activities
Parent: Elitetelecom Holdings PLC
Officers: Robert William Burbidge, Secretary; Robert William Burbidge [1970] Director/Chartered Accountant; Alexandra Cliffe [1978] Director; Robert Christopher John Sims [1965] Director; Adam James Turton [1981] Director

Elitetelecom Holdings PLC
Incorporated: 6 August 2002 *Employees:* 146
Net Worth: £14,893,759 *Total Assets:* £44,304,264
Registered Office: Dawson House, Matrix Office Park, Buckshaw Village, Chorley, Lancs, PR7 7NA
Activities: Other telecommunications activities
Shareholders: Matthew John Newing; Robert Alexander Moulding
Officers: Robert William Burbidge, Secretary; Robert William Burbidge [1970] Director/Chartered Accountant; Alexandra Cliffe [1978] Director; Robert Christopher John Sims [1965] Director; Adam James Turton [1981] Director

Elle R Leisure Limited
Incorporated: 24 October 1966 *Employees:* 360
Net Worth: £18,190,188 *Total Assets:* £20,931,252
Registered Office: Lower Basement Office, Eastgate, 2 Castle Street, Manchester, M3 4LZ
Activities: Licenced restaurants
Parent: Castlefield Holdings Limited
Officers: Jean Kathleen Ramsbottom, Secretary; Beth Adams [1969] Financial Director; James Ramsbottom [1970] Director/General Manager; James Ramsbottom [1939] Director/Bookmaker; Jean Kathleen Ramsbottom [1942] Director/S R Nurse

Elli Finance (UK) PLC
Incorporated: 6 June 2012
Net Worth: £222,096,000 *Total Assets:* £804,444,032
Registered Office: Norcliffe House, Station Road, Wilmslow, Cheshire, SK9 1BU
Activities: Activities of head offices
Parent: Elli Group (UK) Limited
Officers: Abigail Mattison, Secretary; David Albert Edmonds [1944] Director; Timothy Richard William Hammond [1959] Director; Martin William Oliver Healy [1962] Director/Accountant [Irish]; Robert Iain Lynam [1952] Director; Dr Maureen Claire Royston [1960] Director; Benjamin Robert Taberner [1972] Director/Chartered Accountant

Ellis & Everard Distribution Limited
Incorporated: 18 May 1998
Net Worth: £47,209,000 *Total Assets:* £85,000,000
Registered Office: Aquarius House, 6 Mid Point Business Park, Thornbury, Bradford, BD3 7AY
Activities: Activities of head offices
Parent: Ellis & Everard (Overseas) Limited
Officers: Paul Graham Bryant [1973] Director; Sabine Duyfjes [1972] Director/VP & General Counsel EMEA [German]

Ellis Whittam (Holdings) Limited
Incorporated: 9 May 2016 *Employees:* 161
Net Worth Deficit: £3,120,140 *Total Assets:* £27,961,552
Registered Office: Woodhouse, Aldford, Chester, CH3 6JD
Activities: Activities of other holding companies n.e.c.
Shareholder: LDC GP LLP
Officers: Jonathan Scott Bell [1974] Director; Mark Generald Ellis [1967] Director; Andrew Digby Gunson [1975] Director; Richard Ibbett [1977] Director; Colin Kemp [1956] Director; Gavin John Snell [1965] Director; Andrew White [1966] Director; Nicholas Alan Wilson [1965] Director

Ellis Whittam Limited
Incorporated: 27 February 2002 *Employees:* 163
Net Worth: £897,691 *Total Assets:* £6,613,240
Registered Office: Woodhouse, Aldford, Chester, CH3 6JD
Activities: Activities of patent and copyright agents; other legal activities n.e.c.
Parent: Ellis Whittam (Holdings) Ltd
Officers: Mark Generald Ellis [1967] Director/Solicitor; Gavin John Snell [1965] Director; Andrew White [1965] Commercial Director; Nicholas Alan Wilson [1965] Director

Elmwood Construction LLP
Incorporated: 4 July 2006
Net Worth: £10,034,552 *Total Assets:* £10,196,313
Registered Office: Dalton House, 9 Dalton Square, Lancaster, LA1 1WD
Officers: Karl Michael Noblett [1963] Member; Paul Francis Noblett [1960] Member; Philip Andrew Noblett [1964] Member

Elmwood Property Investments Limited
Incorporated: 17 March 1999
Net Worth: £3,499,562 *Total Assets:* £6,688,833
Registered Office: Dalton House, 9 Dalton Square, Lancaster, LA1 1WD
Activities: Development of building projects
Shareholders: Philip Andrew Noblett; Paul Francis Noblett; Karl Michael Noblett
Officers: Phillip Andrew Noblett, Secretary; Karl Michael Noblett [1963] Director/Builder; Paul Francis Noblett [1960] Director/Builder; Phillip Andrew Noblett [1964] Director/Builder

Elnur UK Limited
Incorporated: 21 January 2000 *Employees:* 30
Net Worth: £1,374,940 *Total Assets:* £6,606,395
Registered Office: Douglas Bank House, Wigan Lane, Wigan, Lancs, WN1 2NB
Activities: Wholesale of electronic and telecommunications equipment and parts
Officers: Ricardo Javier Fernandez Tome, Secretary; Michael John Molyneux [1959] Sales Director; Alberto Fernandez Tome [1968] Sales Director [Spanish]; Ricardo Javier Fernandez Tome [1967] Director [Spanish]

Elopak UK Limited
Incorporated: 23 March 1961 *Employees:* 10
Net Worth Deficit: £4,426,416 *Total Assets:* £9,882,477
Registered Office: Cheadle Place, Stockport Road, Cheadle, Cheshire, SK8 2GL
Activities: Agents involved in the sale of machinery, industrial equipment, ships and aircraft
Shareholders: Elopak AS; Ferd Holding AS
Officers: Bjarke Ravn-Christensen, Secretary; Bjarke Ravn-Christensen [1974] Director [Danish]; Martin Shaw [1966] Director/General Manager

Elstat Limited
Incorporated: 27 September 1995 *Employees:* 38
Net Worth: £482,477 *Total Assets:* £6,820,640
Registered Office: A4 Astra Business Centre, Roman Way, Ribbleton, Preston, Lancs, PR2 5AP
Activities: Manufacture of electronic components
Officers: Andrew Joseph McCool, Secretary; Fabrice Bienfait [1974] Director/Investment Management [French]; Geoff Morley [1973] Director; Bengt Henrik Olof Olsen [1967] Director [Swedish]

Elterbeck Limited
Incorporated: 5 December 2009 *Employees:* 2
Net Worth: £7,023,818 *Total Assets:* £7,187,476
Registered Office: The Croft, Aglionby, Carlisle, Cumbria, CA4 8AQ
Activities: Other letting and operating of own or leased real estate
Major Shareholder: Esther Karis Nicholson-Gringinger
Officers: Dieter Maximilian Gringinger [1959] Director [Austrian]; Esther Karis Nicholson-Gringinger [1963] Director

Elvaston Investments Limited
Incorporated: 1 October 1982 *Employees:* 3
Net Worth: £6,249,009 *Total Assets:* £8,980,586
Registered Office: 3 Acorn Business Park, Airedale Business Centre, Skipton, N Yorks, BD23 2UE
Activities: Buying and selling of own real estate
Major Shareholder: Earl of Charles Henry Leicester Harrington
Officers: William Henry Leicester Stanhope, Company Secretary; Martin James Wynne Scriven [1945] Director/Chartered Accountant; William Henry Leicester Stanhope [1967] Director/Company Secretary

Emballator (UK) Limited
Incorporated: 12 October 1998 *Employees:* 125
Net Worth: £23,084,834 *Total Assets:* £26,766,700
Registered Office: Unit 1 City Link Industrial Park, Phoenix Way, Tyersal, Bradford, W Yorks, BD4 8JP
Activities: Manufacture of plastic packing goods
Major Shareholder: Agneta Lovisa Carolina Hamrin
Officers: Philip George Troop, Secretary; Tomas Bergdahl [1972] Director [Swedish]; Gerard Dibb [1962] Director/Packaging; Carl Johan Simonsson [1960] Director [Swedish]; Philip George Troop [1973] Finance Director

EMC Properties Limited
Incorporated: 21 November 2011 *Employees:* 118
Net Worth: £12,852,937 *Total Assets:* £16,849,620
Registered Office: 71-73 Hoghton Street, Southport, Merseyside, PR9 0PR
Activities: Other letting and operating of own or leased real estate
Major Shareholder: James Peter Clarke
Officers: James Peter Clarke [1957] Director

Emerald Group Holdings Limited
Incorporated: 17 July 1998 *Employees:* 374
Net Worth: £13,383,000 *Total Assets:* £48,496,000
Registered Office: Howard House, Wagon Lane, Bingley, W Yorks, BD16 1WA
Activities: Publishing of learned journals
Shareholder: Dr Keith Howard
Officers: Emma Jane Tregenza, Secretary; Richard Lloyd Bevan [1960] Director/Group CEO and Deputy Chairman; Peter Brian Casebow [1960] Director; Simon Guy Cox [1976] Director; Melissa Fojt [1991] Director/Social Responsibility Manager; Dr Keith Howard [1931] Director; Peter George Meredith [1942] Director/Company Auditor; John Roger Waterhouse [1945] Director; Victoria Caroline Williams [1976] Director

Emerald Kalama Chemical Limited
Incorporated: 13 March 2001 *Employees:* 86
Net Worth: £25,620,000 *Total Assets:* £34,191,000
Registered Office: Emerald Kalama Chemical Limited, Dans Road, Widnes, Cheshire, WA8 0RF
Activities: Manufacture of pesticides and other agrochemical products
Officers: Wayne Thomas Byrne [1963] Director/EVP/CFO [American]; Paul Lawrence Hogan [1969] Director/Vice President, General Manager [Irish]; Graham Robert Smith [1962] Site Director

Emerald Publishing Limited
Incorporated: 17 July 1995 *Employees:* 272
Net Worth: £9,852,000 *Total Assets:* £31,308,000
Registered Office: Howard House, Wagon Lane, Bingley, W Yorks, BD16 1WA
Activities: Publishing of learned journals
Parent: Emerald Group Holdings Limited
Officers: Emma Jane Tregenza, Secretary; Harriet Jane Bell [1973] Marketing Director; Richard Lloyd Bevan [1960] Director/Finance; Simon Guy Cox [1976] Finance Director; Dr Phillip Jones [1976] Director; Shariq Mumtaz [1976] Director; Tony Roche [1969] Publishing Director; Victoria Caroline Williams [1976] Director

Emeram Urbanics Holding Ltd
Incorporated: 20 February 2014
Registered Office: Tanzaro House, Ardwick Green North, Manchester, M12 6FZ
Activities: Manufacture of other wearing apparel and accessories n.e.c.
Officers: Dr Sven Oleownik [1964] Director/Managing Partner [German]

Emeram Urbanics Ltd
Incorporated: 20 February 2014
Net Worth Deficit: £9,936,000 *Total Assets:* £9,471,000
Registered Office: Tanzaro House, Ardwick Green North, Manchester, M12 6FZ
Activities: Manufacture of other wearing apparel and accessories n.e.c.
Officers: Dr Sven Oleownik [1964] Director/Managing Partner [German]

Emerson & Renwick Limited
Incorporated: 11 April 1925 *Employees:* 150
Net Worth: £9,019,186 *Total Assets:* £42,705,232
Registered Office: Peel Bank Works, Church Accrington, Lancs, BB5 4EF
Activities: Manufacture of metal forming machinery
Major Shareholder: David Bryant
Officers: David Alty [1963] Director; David Bryant [1969] Director/Chairman [American]; Benjamin Jon Clements [1972] Managing Director; Colin Hargreaves [1947] Director/Deputy Chairman; David Hargreaves [1947] Commercial Director; Andrew William McLaughlan [1963] Financial Director; Anthony Rowlands [1972] Director/Engineer; Ian Robert Westwell [1977] Technical Director

Emerson Automation Solutions Final Control UK Ltd
Incorporated: 1 November 1889 *Employees:* 273
Net Worth: £31,172,000 *Total Assets:* £36,596,000
Registered Office: P O Box 471, Sharp Street, Walkden, Manchester, M28 8BU
Activities: Manufacture of taps and valves
Parent: Emerson Automation Solutions SSC UK Limited
Officers: Sophie Katherine Grundy, Secretary; Philip Cox [1968] Director/Quality/EHS/Compliance Manager; Neale Preston Findley [1961] Finance Director; Susan Anne Greenway [1965] Director/HR Manager; Daniel John Lofthouse [1978] Director/Financial Controller; Nigel George William Petty [1963] Director/General Manager

Emerson Automation Solutions SSC UK Limited
Incorporated: 5 January 1999 *Employees:* 90
Net Worth: £27,511,000 *Total Assets:* £83,107,000
Registered Office: P O Box 471, Sharp Street, Walkden, Manchester, M28 8BU
Activities: Activities of head offices
Parent: Vulsub Holding Ltd
Officers: Sophie Katherine Grundy, Secretary; Neale Preston Findley [1961] Finance Director; Daniel John Lofthouse [1978] Director/Financial Controller

Emerson Developments (Holdings) Limited
Incorporated: 15 May 1974 *Employees:* 769
Net Worth: £816,326,016 *Total Assets:* £1,670,473,984
Registered Office: Emerson House, Heyes Lane, Alderley Edge, Cheshire, SK9 7LF
Activities: Buying and selling of own real estate
Officers: Varun Maharaj, Secretary; John Philip Allen [1953] Director; Jonathan Rodney Claber [1982] Director; Jonathan Haymer [1959] Director/Executive; Anthony Emerson Jones [1967] Director; Audrey Jones [1936] Director; Mark Emerson Jones [1964] Director; Peter Emerson Jones [1935] Director; Baron John Robert Louis Lee of Trafford [1942] Director; Mark Stephen Thomas Royle [1964] Director; Anne Catherine Weatherby [1954] Director/Solicitor; Simon Peter Wilson [1964] Director

Emerson International Limited
Incorporated: 6 April 1981
Net Worth: £28,686,774 *Total Assets:* £164,634,224
Registered Office: Emerson House, Heyes Lane, Alderley Edge, Cheshire, SK9 7LF
Activities: Activities of head offices
Parent: Emerson Developments (Holdings) Limited
Officers: Varun Marahaj, Secretary; Anthony Emerson Jones [1967] Director; Audrey Jones [1936] Director; Mark Emerson Jones [1964] Director; Peter Emerson Jones [1935] Director

Emerson Management Services Limited
Incorporated: 6 August 1971 *Employees:* 85
Net Worth: £3,009,428 *Total Assets:* £14,271,940
Registered Office: Emerson House, Heyes Lane, Alderley Edge, Cheshire, SK9 7LF
Activities: Other building completion and finishing
Parent: Emerson Developments (Holdings) Limited
Officers: Varun Maharaj, Secretary; Jonathan Clark [1968] Director/Business Executive; Michael James Drake [1971] Director/Business Executive; Anthony Emerson Jones [1967] Director; Audrey Jones [1936] Director; Mark Emerson Jones [1964] Director; Peter Emerson Jones [1935] Director; Peter John Shaw [1964] Director/Chartered Surveyor; Simon Peter Wilson [1964] Director; Carl Raymond Worthington [1967] Director/Chartered Surveyor

Emperors Gate Property Company Limited
Incorporated: 14 November 1994
Net Worth: £8,443,812 *Total Assets:* £10,445,287
Registered Office: Pacific Chambers, 11-13 Victoria Street, Liverpool, L2 5QQ
Activities: Other business support service activities n.e.c.
Parent: Homegate Properties Limited
Officers: Charles Hilary Harris [1952] Film Director; Elaine Rosamund Harris [1950] Director/Hospital and School Volunteer

Empire House Bradford Ltd
Incorporated: 13 September 2016
Net Worth: £56,704 *Total Assets:* £8,416,613
Registered Office: 2nd Floor, Parkgates, Bury New Road, Prestwich, Manchester, M25 0TL
Activities: Other letting and operating of own or leased real estate
Parent: JFJG Holdings Limited
Officers: Joseph Feldman [1971] Director [Canadian]; Joseph Grunfeld [1978] Director

Empirical Property Group Limited
Incorporated: 2 February 2011
Net Worth: £3,466,417 *Total Assets:* £41,643,916
Registered Office: 7 Empress Street, Old Trafford, Manchester, M16 9EN
Activities: Buying and selling of own real estate
Major Shareholder: Alan Paul John Pierce
Officers: Charles Alexander Clunie Cunningham [1978] Director; Phillip Wright [1958] Director

Emporia Leisure Limited
Incorporated: 31 January 1997
Net Worth: £13,136,526 *Total Assets:* £36,200,496
Registered Office: The Emporium, Moor Lane, Clitheroe, Lancs, BB7 1BE
Activities: Other letting and operating of own or leased real estate
Major Shareholder: James Peter Warburton
Officers: James Peter Warburton, Secretary; Helen Louise Warburton [1971] Director/Medical Sales Specialist; James Peter Warburton [1965] Director/Developer

Endeavour Strategic Consulting Limited
Incorporated: 3 July 2012 *Employees:* 4
Net Worth: £4,313,171 *Total Assets:* £13,098,542
Registered Office: 32 Crescent Crescent, Salford, M5 4PF
Activities: Buying and selling of own real estate
Officers: Stephen Robert Gray [1976] Director/Consultant; Jonathan Gareth Gwynne [1976] Director

Endress + Hauser Investments Limited
Incorporated: 24 June 1998 *Employees:* 3
Net Worth: £25,828,000 *Total Assets:* £26,048,000
Registered Office: Floats Road, Roundthorn Industrial Estate, Manchester, M23 9NF
Activities: Activities of head offices
Officers: James Howard Langford, Secretary; Steven Hans-Peter George Endress [1978] Director; Dr Luc Schultheiss [1962] Director/M.B.A. [Swiss]; Heiner Zehntner [1965] Director/Lawyer [Swiss]

Endress + Hauser Limited
Incorporated: 11 November 1968 *Employees:* 204
Net Worth: £17,122,420 *Total Assets:* £21,182,742
Registered Office: Floats Road, Manchester, M23 9NF
Activities: Manufacture of electronic industrial process control equipment
Parent: Endress + Hauser Investments Limited
Officers: James Howard Langford, Secretary; Steven Hans-Peter George Endress [1978] Managing Director; Craig Horan [1962] Director; Roger Stone [1963] Finance Director

Energus
Incorporated: 23 December 2005 *Employees:* 95
Net Worth: £1,135,462 *Total Assets:* £7,830,721
Registered Office: Herdus House, Ingwell Drive, Westlakes Science & Technology Park, Moor Row, Cumbria, CA24 3HU
Activities: Technical and vocational secondary education
Officers: Helen Elizabeth Hodgson, Secretary; Mike Barber [1974] Director/Head of Group People Strategy; Dr Lee Anthony Peck [1971] Director/Senior Technologist; Mehboob Gulam Vadiya [1978] Director/Solicitor; Gerard James Woodcock [1945] Director

Energy Acquisitions UK Limited
Incorporated: 18 June 2007
Net Worth: £74,198,848 *Total Assets:* £183,786,816
Registered Office: 2nd Floor, 302 Bridgewater Place, Birchwood Park, Warrington, Cheshire, WA3 6XG
Activities: Activities of other holding companies n.e.c.
Parent: DCC Energy UK Limited
Officers: Gerard Whyte, Secretary; James Henry Cubbon [1960] Director; Anthony Francis Levy [1957] Director; Edward Gerard O'Brien [1970] Director/Chartered Accountant [Irish]; Michael Steven Taylor [1959] Director

Energy Assets (Meters) 2 Limited
Incorporated: 22 June 2011
Net Worth: £5,896,000 *Total Assets:* £36,604,000
Registered Office: Ship Canal House, 98 King Street, Manchester, M2 4WU
Activities: Other business support service activities n.e.c.
Parent: Energy Assets Holdings Limited
Officers: Colin John Lynch [1966] Director; John McMorrow [1977] Director/Chief Financial Officer; David Sing [1966] Director

Energy Assets (Meters) Limited
Incorporated: 16 December 2008
Net Worth: £13,094,000 *Total Assets:* £73,212,000
Registered Office: Ship Canal House, 98 King Street, Manchester, M2 4WU
Activities: Other business support service activities n.e.c.
Parent: Energy Assets Holdings Limited
Officers: Colin John Lynch [1966] Director; John McMorrow [1977] Director/Chief Financial Officer; David Sing [1966] Director

Energy Assets Financing Limited
Incorporated: 6 April 2016 *Employees:* 380
Net Worth: £198,290,000 *Total Assets:* £400,620,992
Registered Office: Ship Canal House, 98 King Street, Manchester, M2 4WU
Activities: Activities of other holding companies n.e.c.
Parent: Energy Assets Midco Limited
Officers: Samuel Makepeace Coxe [1975] Director [American]; Read Fraser Gomm [1961] Director [Canadian]; Amy Caroline Sarah Gunning [1987] Director/Finance [Irish]; James Thomas MacDonald [1959] Director

Energy Assets Group Limited
Incorporated: 1 February 2012 *Employees:* 4
Net Worth: £43,061,000 *Total Assets:* £146,360,000
Registered Office: Ship Canal House, 98 King Street, Manchester, M2 4WU
Activities: Other business support service activities n.e.c.
Parent: Energy Assets Financing Limited
Officers: John McMorrow, Secretary; Colin John Lynch [1966] Director; John McMorrow [1977] Director/Chief Financial Officer

Energy Assets Limited
Incorporated: 7 April 2005 *Employees:* 187
Net Worth: £18,592,000 *Total Assets:* £99,886,000
Registered Office: Ship Canal House, 98 King Street, Manchester, M2 4WU
Activities: Other business support service activities n.e.c.
Parent: Energy Assets Holdings Limited
Officers: Stewart William Love [1968] Director; Colin John Lynch [1966] Director; John McMorrow [1977] Director/Chief Financial Officer; David Sing [1966] Director; Craig Philip Topley [1973] Director

Energy Assets Midco Limited
Incorporated: 6 April 2016
Net Worth: £7,148,000 *Total Assets:* £198,176,992
Registered Office: Ship Canal House, 98 King Street, Manchester, M2 4WU
Activities: Activities of other holding companies n.e.c.
Parent: Energy Assets Topco Limited
Officers: Samuel Makepeace Coxe [1975] Director [American]; Read Fraser Gomm [1961] Director [Canadian]; Amy Caroline Sarah Gunning [1987] Director/Finance [Irish]

Energy Assets Topco Limited
Incorporated: 6 April 2016 *Employees:* 380
Net Worth: £7,260,000 *Total Assets:* £399,286,016
Registered Office: Ship Canal House, 98 King Street, Manchester, M2 4WU
Activities: Activities of other holding companies n.e.c.
Officers: Samuel Makepeace Coxe [1975] Director [American]; Read Fraser Gomm [1961] Director [Canadian]; Amy Caroline Sarah Gunning [1987] Director/Finance [Irish]

Energy Coast West Cumbria (Properties) Limited
Incorporated: 17 August 1989
Net Worth: £8,038,641 *Total Assets:* £20,106,840
Registered Office: Ingwell Hall, Ingwell Drive, Westlakes Science & Technology Park, Moor Row, Cumbria, CA24 3JZ
Activities: Other letting and operating of own or leased real estate
Parent: Energy Coast West Cumbria Limited
Officers: Derek Joseph McHale, Secretary; Nigel Bruce Catterson [1949] Director; John Simon Clarke [1959] Director; Joy Noctor [1961] Director/Senior Lecturer, Nursing; Andrew Michael Colin Oldham [1959] Director/Head of Financial Operations; Michael Neville Pemberton [1966] Director/Chief Executive Officer; Alan Smith [1954] Director; David Edward Southward [1950] Director/Cumbria County Councillor; Michael John Starkie [1964] Director/Mayor

Energy Coast West Cumbria Limited
Incorporated: 23 March 1988 *Employees:* 22
Net Worth: £15,065,072 *Total Assets:* £17,064,836
Registered Office: Ingwell Hall, Ingwell Drive, Westlakes Science & Technology Park, Moor Row, Cumbria, CA24 3JZ
Activities: Activities of head offices
Officers: Derek Joseph McHale, Secretary; Nigel Bruce Catterson [1949] Chairman/Director; John Simon Clarke [1959] Director; Joy Noctor [1961] Director/Senior Lecturer, Nursing; Andrew Michael Colin Oldham [1959] Director/Head of Financial Operations; Michael Neville Pemberton [1966] Director/Chief Executive Officer; Alan Smith [1954] Director; David Edward Southward [1950] Director/Cumbria County Councillor; Michael John Starkie [1964] Director/Mayor

Energy Services Acquisitions Limited
Incorporated: 23 April 2013
Net Worth Deficit: £98,805,000 *Total Assets:* £80,230,000
Registered Office: Ribble House, Ballam Road, Lytham St Annes, Lancs, FY8 4TS
Activities: Activities of head offices
Parent: Igloo Investment Bidco Limited
Officers: Bernard Coady [1979] Director [Australian]; Gareth James Knight [1978] Director; Gary Martin Stokes [1961] Director/Chief Executive

Energy, Safety and Risk Consultants (UK) Limited
Incorporated: 27 October 2011 *Employees:* 461
Net Worth: £79,388,000 *Total Assets:* £100,373,000
Registered Office: Booths Park, Chelford Road, Knutsford, Cheshire, WA16 8QZ
Activities: Engineering related scientific and technical consulting activities
Parent: Wood Nuclear Holdings Limited
Officers: Anthony Mark Thomas, Secretary; David Hunter Boath [1960] Director; Ellen Lyons [1972] Director; Paul David Wood [1976] Commercial Director

Enesco Holdings Limited
Incorporated: 16 June 1994
Net Worth: £10,000,000 *Total Assets:* £10,000,000
Registered Office: Brunthill Road, Kingstown, Carlisle, Cumbria, CA3 0EN
Activities: Activities of other holding companies n.e.c.
Parent: EGI (UK) Limited
Officers: Emily Kaye Brown, Secretary; Robert Edward Freestone, Company Secretary; Emily Kaye Brown [1965] Director [American]; Jonathan Victor [1957] Director/Managing Partner of a Private Equity Fund [American]

Enesco Limited
Incorporated: 3 June 1987 *Employees:* 149
Net Worth: £16,980,000 *Total Assets:* £24,918,000
Registered Office: Brunthill Road, Kingstown, Carlisle, Cumbria, CA3 0EN
Activities: Printing n.e.c.
Parent: Enesco Holdings Limited
Officers: Emily Kaye Brown, Secretary; Robert Edward Freestone, Secretary; Emily Kaye Brown [1965] Director [American]; Jonathan Victor [1957] Director/Managing Partner of a Private Equity Fund [American]

Engenda Group Limited
Incorporated: 8 December 2009 *Employees:* 321
Net Worth: £2,244,173 *Total Assets:* £20,177,276
Registered Office: Dee House, Hampton Court, Manor Park, Runcorn, Cheshire, WA7 1TT
Activities: Other specialised construction activities n.e.c.
Major Shareholder: Leslie Arthur O'Hare
Officers: Paul Stuart Ashcroft [1965] Director/Chartered Accountant; Lee Grounsell Foundation [1965] Director/Engineer; Barry John O'Hare [1976] Manufacturing Director; Janet O'Hare [1956] Director; Leslie Arthur O'Hare [1954] Director; John Salkeld [1960] Operations Director

Engenda Properties Limited
Incorporated: 27 November 2014
Net Worth: £2,011,035 *Total Assets:* £13,459,769
Registered Office: Dee House, Hampton Court, Tudor Road, Manor Park, Runcorn, Cheshire, WA7 1TT
Activities: Other letting and operating of own or leased real estate
Major Shareholder: Leslie Arthur O'Hare
Officers: Paul Stuart Ashcroft, Secretary; Janet O'Hare [1956] Director; Leslie Arthur O'Hare [1954] Director

Engie Renewables Limited
Incorporated: 23 August 1995 *Employees:* 25
Net Worth: £8,172,414 *Total Assets:* £9,426,603
Registered Office: Mynydd Awel, Mold Business Park, Maes Gwern, Mold, Flintshire, CH7 1XN
Activities: Other business support service activities n.e.c.
Parent: Engie Renewables Holding UK Limited
Officers: Sarah Jane Gregory, Secretary; David George Alcock [1965] Director; Matteo Maria Maino [1965] Director [Italian]; Simon David Pinnell [1964] Director; Robert Paul Tate [1969] Director

English Provender Company Limited
Incorporated: 20 March 1991 *Employees:* 551
Net Worth: £21,351,220 *Total Assets:* £42,221,844
Registered Office: Cunard Building, Liverpool, L3 1EL
Activities: Manufacture of condiments and seasonings
Parent: Edward Billington and Son Limited
Officers: David Marshall, Secretary; Jason Belmont [1969] Director; Gary Michael Blake [1973] Managing Director; James Andrew Logan [1962] Managing Director; Lisa McCrystal [1978] Finance Director

Enhance Academy Trust
Incorporated: 10 January 2012 *Employees:* 396
Net Worth: £15,180,000 *Total Assets:* £19,751,000
Registered Office: Church Bank House, Church Bank, Bradford, W Yorks, BD1 4DY
Activities: Primary education
Officers: John Patrick Brady [1964] Director; Kevin Glyn Jones [1955] Director/Chief Executive Officer; Linda Margaret Maskill [1951] Director/Retired Headteacher; John Patrick McLeod [1954] Director; Fiona Anne McMahon [1976] Assistant Principal: Director of Sixth Form; Janet Margaret Milne [1957] Director/Teacher; Christopher Ernest Schofield [1962] Director/Solicitor; Katharine Olivia Helen Smith [1974] Director/Chartered Accountant; The Venerable Peter Kenneth Townley [1955] Director/Clerk in Holy Orders

Ennis Paint U.K. Holding Company Limited
Incorporated: 9 June 2006 *Employees:* 61
Net Worth Deficit: £10,451,020 *Total Assets:* £11,135,170
Registered Office: 5 Drumhead Road, Chorley North Industrial Park, Chorley, Lancs, PR6 7BX
Activities: Activities of head offices
Parent: Ennis Paint, Inc.
Officers: Daniel Louis Lang, Secretary; Daniel Louis Lang [1955] Managing Director [American]; Robert Steven Vetter [1956] Director/CEO of Ennis-Flint [American]

Enrichment Technology Company Limited
Incorporated: 29 January 2003 *Employees:* 531
Net Worth: £39,445,968 *Total Assets:* £159,167,184
Registered Office: Unit 6 South Capenhurst Technology Park, Capenhurst, Chester, CH1 6EH
Activities: Other manufacturing n.e.c.
Officers: Michael Llewellyn Wheldon Smith, Secretary; Patrick Pierre Champalaune [1959] Director [French]; Christopher Roy Chater [1968] Director; Pierre Fourrier [1967] Director [French]; Reinhard Hinterreither [1969] Director [Austrian]; Dirk Kalwei [1977] Director [German]; Olivier Jean Antoine Marques-Borras [1975] Chief Financial Director [French]

Ensco 1090 Limited
Incorporated: 19 September 2014 *Employees:* 77
Net Worth Deficit: £31,894,612 *Total Assets:* £26,008,386
Registered Office: St James Building, Oxford Street, Manchester, M1 6HT
Activities: Activities of other holding companies n.e.c.
Officers: Simon John Gardner [1960] Director; Andrew Lees [1964] Director; Daniel Eric Schweiger [1971] Director; Mark Alexander Harry Schweiger [1974] Director; James Winterbottom [1982] Director

Ensco 818 Limited
Incorporated: 3 December 2010
Net Worth: £1 *Total Assets:* £15,278,350
Registered Office: 5th Floor, Voyager House, Chicago Avenue, Manchester Airport, Manchester, M90 3DQ
Activities: Dormant company
Parent: The Hut IHC Limited
Officers: James Pochin, Secretary; John Andrew Gallemore [1969] Director; James Patrick Pochin [1976] Group Legal Director

Entasis Therapeutics Limited
Incorporated: 6 March 2015
Net Worth: £21,897,852 *Total Assets:* £22,365,656
Registered Office: 3rd Floor, 1 Ashley Road, Altrincham, Cheshire, WA14 2DT
Activities: Other business support service activities n.e.c.
Officers: Christian Plaza, Secretary; Michael John Gutch [1966] Director/Chief Financial & Chief Business Officer [American]; Dr Manoussos Perros [1967] Director [French]

Enterprise Civic Buildings (Holdings) Limited
Incorporated: 22 April 2002
Net Worth: £812,000 *Total Assets:* £24,878,000
Registered Office: Unit 18 Navigation Way, Ashton on Ribble, Preston, Lancs, PR2 2YP
Activities: Other business support service activities n.e.c.
Parent: Infrastructure Investments General Partner Limited
Officers: David Wyn Davies [1968] Director; Angela Mills [1961] Director/Accountant

Enterprise Civic Buildings Limited
Incorporated: 22 April 2002
Net Worth: £812,000 *Total Assets:* £24,878,000
Registered Office: Unit 18 Riverway Business Village, Navigation Way, Ashton on Ribble, Preston, Lancs, PR2 2YP
Activities: Financial intermediation not elsewhere classified
Parent: Enterprise Civic Buildings (Holdings) Limited
Officers: Jonathan Nigel Edward Cowdell [1966] Director; David Wyn Davies [1968] Director; Angela Mills [1961] Director/Accountant; Alastair Huw Page [1961] Commercial Director, Services Sector

Enterprise Education Conwy Limited
Incorporated: 16 August 2002
Net Worth Deficit: £2,613,000 *Total Assets:* £32,822,000
Registered Office: Unit 18 Riversway Business Village, Navigation Way, Ashton on Ribble, Preston, Lancs, PR2 2YP
Activities: Other business support service activities n.e.c.
Parent: Enterprise Education Holdings Conwy Limited
Officers: Sally-Ann Ann Brooks [1966] Director; Jonathan Nigel Edward Cowdell [1966] Director; Angela Mills [1961] Director; Alastair Huw Page [1961] Commercial Director, Services Sector

Enterprise Education Holdings Conwy Limited
Incorporated: 6 September 2002
Net Worth Deficit: £2,613,000 *Total Assets:* £32,822,000
Registered Office: Unit 18 Riversway Business Village, Navigation Way, Ashton on Ribble, Preston, Lancs, PR2 2YP
Activities: Activities of head offices
Parent: Infrastructure Investments General Partner Limited
Officers: Sally-Ann Ann Brooks [1966] Director; Jonathan Nigel Edward Cowdell [1966] Director; Angela Mills [1961] Director; Alastair Huw Page [1961] Commercial Director, Services Sector

The Enterprise Fund Limited
Incorporated: 13 June 2002 *Employees:* 34
Net Worth: £7,922,087 *Total Assets:* £11,170,064
Registered Office: Lee House, 90 Great Bridgewater Street, Manchester, M1 5JW
Activities: Credit granting by non-deposit taking finance houses and other specialist consumer credit grantors
Officers: Paul Anthony Simpson, Secretary; Simon Allport [1964] Director; Donna Elizabeth Edwards [1960] Managing Director; Bartholomew Flynn [1958] Director and Chartered Accountant; Mark Anthony Hughes [1966] Director/Chief Executive; Ronald Mason [1944] Director; Clive Allan James Memmott [1954] Director; Eric Allison Munro [1958] Director/Banker

Enterprise Healthcare Holdings Limited
Incorporated: 13 November 2003
Net Worth Deficit: £15,697,000 *Total Assets:* £44,008,000
Registered Office: Unit 18 Riversway Business Village, Navigation Way, Ashton on Ribble, Preston, Lancs, PR2 2YP
Activities: Activities of head offices
Parent: Infrastructure Investments General Partner Limited
Officers: John Philip George [1968] Director; David Geoffrey Lewis [1969] Director

Enterprise Healthcare Limited
Incorporated: 19 November 2003
Net Worth Deficit: £17,371,000 *Total Assets:* £44,789,000
Registered Office: Unit 18 Riversway Business Village, Navigation Way, Ashton on Ribble, Preston, Lancs, PR2 2YP
Activities: Other business support service activities n.e.c.
Parent: Enterprise Healthcare Holdings Limited
Officers: Jonathan Nigel Edward Cowdell [1966] Director; John Philip George [1968] Director; David Geoffrey Lewis [1969] Director; Alastair Huw Page [1961] Commercial Director, Services Sector

Enterprise Solutions Holdings Limited
Incorporated: 29 May 2012 *Employees:* 101
Net Worth: £2,244,713 *Total Assets:* £6,721,533
Registered Office: The Mission, Wellington Street, Stockport, Cheshire, SK1 3AH
Activities: Management consultancy activities other than financial management
Officers: Joseph James Blower [1960] Director; Joerg Jacques Sperling [1969] Director [German]; Paul Thomas Summers [1963] Director; Nicholas Adam Townend [1967] Director

Entertainment Magpie Group Limited
Incorporated: 14 September 2015 *Employees:* 850
Net Worth: £490,000 *Total Assets:* £18,913,000
Registered Office: Stockport Exchange, Railway Road, Stockport, Cheshire, SK1 3SW
Activities: Activities of head offices
Officers: Andrew William Leach [1957] Director; Steven Oliver [1971] Director; Ian Matthew Storey [1976] Director

Entertainment Magpie Limited
Incorporated: 13 June 2007 *Employees:* 778
Net Worth Deficit: £3,755,000 *Total Assets:* £19,683,000
Registered Office: Stockport Exchange, Railway Road, Stockport, Cheshire, SK1 3SW
Activities: Retail sale via mail order houses or via Internet
Parent: Entertainment Magpie Holdings Limited
Officers: Walter Scott Gleeson [1966] IT Director; Steven Oliver [1971] Director; Ian Matthew Storey [1976] Director

Entwistle & Joynt Holdings Limited
Incorporated: 12 June 2012 *Employees:* 51
Net Worth: £1,151,618 *Total Assets:* £7,820,512
Registered Office: 62 Darlington Street East, Wigan, Lancs, WN1 3AT
Activities: Wholesale of machine tools
Officers: David James Entwistle [1978] Director; Dorothy Entwistle [1953] Director; Iain Paul Entwistle [1976] Director; Paul Entwistle [1952] Director

Entwistle & Joynt Limited
Incorporated: 29 January 1971 *Employees:* 51
Net Worth: £4,211,467 *Total Assets:* £7,980,461
Registered Office: 62 Darlington Street East, Wigan, Lancs, WN1 3AT
Activities: Non-specialised wholesale trade
Parent: Entwistle & Joynt Holdings Limited
Officers: David James Entwistle [1978] Director; Iain Paul Entwistle [1976] Director

ENW Finance PLC
Incorporated: 12 March 2009
Net Worth: £11,222,000 *Total Assets:* £536,478,016
Registered Office: 304 Bridgewater Place, Birchwood Park, Warrington, Cheshire, WA3 6XG
Activities: Other business support service activities n.e.c.
Parent: North West Electricity Networks PLC
Officers: Richard Somerville, Secretary; David Graham Brocksom [1960] Director/Chief Finance Officer; Christopher Bruce Dowling [1953] Director [Australian]; Peter Richard Emery [1962] Director/Chief Executive Officer; John E Lynch [1970] Director [American]; Niall Patrick Mills [1968] Director/Senior Asset Manager

Enza Group Limited
Incorporated: 27 June 2006 *Employees:* 3
Net Worth: £340,856 *Total Assets:* £6,889,562
Registered Office: The Enza Building, Leacroft Road, Risley, Warrington, Cheshire, WA3 6NN
Activities: Activities of head offices
Parent: Roanza Limited
Officers: Michael Peter Jones, Secretary; Michael Peter Jones [1963] Finance Director; Roy Charles Reed [1958] Director

EPTA George Barker Ltd
Incorporated: 7 June 1962 *Employees:* 343
Net Worth: £14,955,185 *Total Assets:* £43,473,228
Registered Office: Highfield Works, Highfield Road, Idle, Bradford, W Yorks, BD10 8RU
Activities: Other manufacturing n.e.c.
Officers: Simon James Taylor, Secretary; Massimo Andrea Albertario [1966] Director [Italian]; Luca Lastella [1965] Director/General Manager [Italian]; Geoffrey Charles Mills [1965] Commercial Director; Enzo Santori [1959] Director [Italian]; Simon James Taylor [1968] Director/Accountant

Equilibrium Healthcare Group Limited
Incorporated: 15 June 2006 *Employees:* 136
Net Worth: £7,757,871 *Total Assets:* £10,877,364
Registered Office: Bollin House, Riverside Park, Bollin Link, Wilmslow, Cheshire, SK9 1DP
Activities: Other human health activities
Shareholders: Harriet Jane Dudgeon; Patrick John Keely
Officers: Harriet Jane Dudgeon, Secretary; Harriet Jane Dudgeon [1959] Director; Patrick John Keely [1959] Director; David Phillip Madeley [1960] Director/Chartered Accountant

Equilibrium Healthcare Limited
Incorporated: 15 February 1996 *Employees:* 116
Net Worth: £15,838,830 *Total Assets:* £23,049,322
Registered Office: Bollin House, Riverside Park, Bollin Link, Wilmslow, Cheshire, SK9 1DP
Activities: Hospital activities
Shareholders: Patrick John Keely; Harriet Jane Dudgeon
Officers: Patrick John Keely, Secretary/Manager; Harriet Jane Dudgeon [1959] Director; Patrick John Keely [1959] Director/Manager; David Phillip Madeley [1960] Director/Chartered Accountant

Equinox Properties Limited
Incorporated: 14 June 2011
Net Worth: £5,932,669 *Total Assets:* £8,255,733
Registered Office: 53 King Street, Manchester, M2 4LQ
Activities: Other letting and operating of own or leased real estate
Major Shareholder: Daniel Jebreel
Officers: Daniel Jebreel [1986] Director/Property Investor

Equip4work Ltd
Incorporated: 18 August 2004 *Employees:* 56
Net Worth: £4,918,856 *Total Assets:* £8,587,059
Registered Office: 2 Alstonby Court, Westlinton, Carlisle, CA6 6AF
Activities: Retail sale via mail order houses or via Internet
Parent: Takkt AG
Officers: Dr Heiko Hegwein [1974] Managing Director [German]; Martin Derek Hutchinson [1982] Director; Michael Anthony Hutchinson [1988] Director/IT Manager; Franzizkus Clemens Hermann Josten [1986] Director/Businessman [German]

Equipment and Track Solutions Limited
Incorporated: 12 September 2012 *Employees:* 310
Net Worth: £7,382,547 *Total Assets:* £42,959,528
Registered Office: Park Lane Industrial Estates, Park Lane, off Wigan Road, Ashton in Makerfield, Wigan, Lancs, WN4 0BZ
Activities: Activities of other holding companies n.e.c.
Parent: Bacchus Newco Limited
Officers: Robert Killen [1970] Director; Brian Reynolds [1971] Director/Accountant; Gareth Winfield Richardson [1966] Director

Equitas Solicitors Limited
Incorporated: 10 July 2006 *Employees:* 50
Net Worth: £8,281,681 *Total Assets:* £12,159,619
Registered Office: Muirfield Buildings, 5 Fairways Office Park, Pittman Way, Fulwood, Preston, Lancs, PR2 9LF
Activities: Solicitors
Major Shareholder: Mohsin Patel
Officers: Idris Yunus Natha [1978] Director/Solicitor; Mohsin Patel [1977] Director/Solicitor

Equity Solutions Asset Management Limited
Incorporated: 2 March 2012 *Employees:* 6
Net Worth: £91,631,384 *Total Assets:* £362,981,344
Registered Office: Building 1000, Kings Reach, Yew Street, Stockport, Cheshire, SK4 2HG
Activities: Other business support service activities n.e.c.
Major Shareholder: Michael Dwan
Officers: Amanda Jane Dwan [1969] Director; Michael Dwan [1959] Director; Marina Ann Guido [1985] Finance Director

Equity Solutions Lift Investments Cornwall Limited
Incorporated: 10 February 2004 *Employees:* 2
Net Worth: £28,075,868 *Total Assets:* £30,634,064
Registered Office: Building 1000, Kings Reach, Yew Street, Stockport, Cheshire, SK4 2HG
Activities: Other business support service activities n.e.c.
Parent: Equity Solutions Lift Investments Limited
Officers: Michael Dwan [1959] Director; Amanda Nottingham [1968] Director/Accountant

Equity Solutions Lift Investments Limited
Incorporated: 15 January 2003 *Employees:* 1
Net Worth: £107,713,568 *Total Assets:* £107,713,968
Registered Office: Building 1000, Kings Reach, Yew Street, Stockport, Cheshire, SK4 2HG
Activities: Activities of other holding companies n.e.c.
Parent: Equity Solutions Asset Management Limited
Officers: Michael Dwan [1959] Director

Equity Solutions Lift Investments Oldham Limited
Incorporated: 14 May 2004 *Employees:* 2
Net Worth: £47,029,140 *Total Assets:* £52,301,220
Registered Office: Building 1000, Kings Reach, Yew Street, Stockport, Cheshire, SK4 2HG
Activities: Other business support service activities n.e.c.
Parent: Equity Solutions Lift Investments Limited
Officers: Michael Dwan [1959] Director; Amanda Nottingham [1968] Director/Accountant

Equity Solutions Lift Investments Sheffield Limited
Incorporated: 14 May 2004 *Employees:* 2
Net Worth: £20,634,896 *Total Assets:* £22,916,630
Registered Office: Building 1000, Kings Reach, Yew Street, Stockport, Cheshire, SK4 2HG
Activities: Other business support service activities n.e.c.
Parent: Equity Solutions Lift Investments Limited
Officers: Michael Dwan [1959] Director; Amanda Nottingham [1968] Director/Accountant

Equity Solutions Lift Investments Stockport Limited
Incorporated: 16 February 2007
Net Worth: £11,974,067 *Total Assets:* £13,038,056
Registered Office: Building 1000, Kings Reach, Yew Street, Stockport, Cheshire, SK4 2HG
Activities: Other service activities n.e.c.
Parent: Equity Solutions Lift Investments Limited
Officers: Michael Dwan [1959] Director

Erie Finance Limited
Incorporated: 13 August 2014
Net Worth: £3,353,216,512 *Total Assets:* £4,045,488,896
Registered Office: 3rd Floor, 1 Ashley Road, Altrincham, Cheshire, WA14 2DT
Activities: Activities of other holding companies n.e.c.
Parent: Erie Finance Holding Limited
Officers: Rhona Gregg, Secretary; Lucie Mary Katja Grant [1976] Director/Solicitor; Nicholas Ince [1982] Director/Accountant; David John Norman [1960] Director/Chartered Accountant

Erie U.K. Limited
Incorporated: 28 February 2001
Net Worth: £319,958,016 *Total Assets:* £1,247,760,000
Registered Office: 3rd Floor, 1 Ashley Road, Altrincham, Cheshire, WA14 2DT
Activities: Activities of head offices
Parent: Thermo Fisher Scientific Inc.
Officers: Rhona Gregg, Secretary; Lucie Mary Katja Grant [1976] Director/Solicitor; Nicholas Ince [1982] Director/Accountant; David John Norman [1960] Director/Chartered Accountant

Erie UK 1 Limited
Incorporated: 14 October 2008
Net Worth: £230,739,584 *Total Assets:* £3,248,364,544
Registered Office: 3rd Floor, 1 Ashley Road, Altrincham, Cheshire, WA14 2DT
Activities: Activities of head offices
Parent: Thermo Fisher Scientific Inc.
Officers: Rhona Gregg, Secretary; Lucie Mary Katja Grant [1976] Director/Solicitor; Nicholas Ince [1982] Director/Accountant; David John Norman [1960] Director/Chartered Accountant

Erie UK 2 Limited
Incorporated: 14 October 2008
Net Worth Deficit: £46,379,000 *Total Assets:* £440,196,992
Registered Office: 3rd Floor, 1 Ashley Road, Altrincham, Cheshire, WA14 2DT
Activities: Activities of head offices
Parent: Lambtrack Limited
Officers: Rhona Gregg, Secretary; Lucie Mary Katja Grant [1976] Director/Solicitor; Nicholas Ince [1982] Director/Accountant; David John Norman [1960] Director/Chartered Accountant

Erie UK Senior Holding Limited
Incorporated: 14 October 2008
Net Worth: £451,051,008 *Total Assets:* £988,092,992
Registered Office: 3rd Floor, 1 Ashley Road, Altrincham, Cheshire, WA14 2DT
Activities: Activities of head offices
Parent: Erie U.K. Limited
Officers: Rhona Gregg, Secretary; Lucie Mary Katja Grant [1976] Director/Solicitor; Nicholas Ince [1982] Director/Accountant; David John Norman [1960] Director/Chartered Accountant

Erlsmere Investments Limited
Incorporated: 8 January 2009 *Employees:* 1
Net Worth: £3,782,704 *Total Assets:* £12,219,888
Registered Office: 17 Park Street, Lytham St Annes, Lancs, FY8 5LU
Activities: Other business support service activities n.e.c.
Parent: Erlsmere Holdings Limited
Officers: Matthew John Chadwick, Secretary; Matthew John Chadwick [1977] Director

Errigal Developments Limited
Incorporated: 14 November 2001 *Employees:* 3
Net Worth Deficit: £9,597,066 *Total Assets:* £6,807,977
Registered Office: 4 Lockside Office Park, Lockside Road, Riversway, Preston, Lancs, PR2 2YS
Activities: Buying and selling of own real estate
Parent: Errigal Investments Ltd
Officers: Justine Dowds, Secretary; Simon Andrew Lyons [1971] Director; Owen Gerard McLaughlin [1959] Director; Simon James Tomlinson [1967] Director/Chartered Accountant

Errigal Investments Limited
Incorporated: 8 November 2002 *Employees:* 6
Net Worth Deficit: £4,782,567 *Total Assets:* £14,007,547
Registered Office: 4 Lockside Office Park, Lockside Road, Riversway, Preston, Lancs, PR2 2YS
Activities: Other letting and operating of own or leased real estate
Shareholders: Owen Gerard McLaughlin; Sean Keogh
Officers: Justine Dowds, Secretary; Simon Andrew Lyons [1971] Director; Owen Gerard McLaughlin [1959] Director; Simon James Tomlinson [1967] Director/Chartered Accountant

ESG-Utiligroup Intermediate Limited
Incorporated: 4 April 2017
Net Worth: £92,853,752 *Total Assets:* £92,853,760
Registered Office: Utilihouse, East Terrace, Euxton Lane, Chorley, Lancs, PR7 6TE
Activities: Other business support service activities n.e.c.
Shareholders: Robert Palumbo; Thomas Barnds
Officers: Christopher Park Durrett [1976] Director [American]; Philip Galati [1964] Director [American]; Steven Paul Gosling [1967] Director; Matthew Christopher Hirst [1977] Director

ESL Fuels Limited
Incorporated: 5 June 2000 *Employees:* 12
Net Worth: £5,978,435 *Total Assets:* £9,641,671
Registered Office: High Growth Centre, Thornton Science Park, Pool Lane, Ince, Cheshire, CH2 4NU
Activities: Other manufacturing n.e.c.
Shareholders: Stephen David Whittaker; Janet Ann Whittaker
Officers: Janet Whittaker, Secretary/Director; Janet Whittaker [1958] Director; Stephen David Whittaker [1964] Director

ESPA International (UK) Limited
Incorporated: 21 August 1992 *Employees:* 199
Net Worth: £16,156,553 *Total Assets:* £18,342,870
Registered Office: 5th Floor, Voyager House, Chicago Avenue, Manchester Airport, Manchester, M90 3DQ
Activities: Wholesale of perfume and cosmetics
Parent: El Spa Holdings (UK) Limited
Officers: John Andrew Gallemore [1969] Director; Paul Jonathan Gedman [1981] Director

Ess-Gee Investments Limited
Incorporated: 28 October 1946
Net Worth: £8,159,031 *Total Assets:* £21,110,184
Registered Office: St John's House, Two Queen Square, Liverpool, L1 1RH
Activities: Development of building projects
Shareholders: David Albert Convisser; Howard Jonathan Wallis
Officers: Janet Margaret Geddes, Secretary; Anthony Nigel Carson [1960] Director; Michael Maurice Grodner [1979] Director/Camera Operator; Charles Robert Leonard Shepherd [1970] Property Director

Essa Foundation Academies Trust
Incorporated: 23 October 2008 *Employees:* 186
Net Worth: £23,873,000 *Total Assets:* £26,699,000
Registered Office: Lever Edge Lane, Bolton, Lancs, BL3 3HH
Activities: Pre-primary education
Officers: Charles Oluwaseyi Adegoroye [1974] Director/Accountant; Adam Collins [1984] Director/Accountant; Andrew Robert Cooper [1968] Director/Academies Trust Chief Executive; Lisa Fathers [1976] Director/Teacher; Kate Longworth [1978] Director/Solicitor; Anwer Ibrahim Patel [1954] Managing Director; Chris Read [1987] Director/Senior Advisor; Emily Reynard [1983] Director/Head of School; Dr Mohammed Sharif Salim [1946] Director/Retired; Nigel John Whittle [1951] Director/Financial Consultant

Essar Oil (UK) Limited
Incorporated: 10 November 2009 *Employees:* 971
Net Worth: £761,368,960 *Total Assets:* £1,737,389,440
Registered Office: 5th Floor, The Administration Building, Stanlow Manufacturing Complex, Ellesmere Port, Cheshire, CH65 4HB
Activities: Mineral oil refining
Parent: Essar Energy Limited
Officers: Samantha Chambers, Secretary; Prashant Ruia [1969] Managing Director [Indian]; Parthasarathy Sampath [1955] Director [Indian]; Thangapandian Srinivasalu [1961] Director [Indian]; Kuthoore Natarajan Venkatasubramanian [1938] Director [Indian]

Estates and Leisure Holdings Limited
Incorporated: 16 February 1990
Net Worth: £5,294,195 *Total Assets:* £10,749,232
Registered Office: 19 Chestergate, Macclesfield, Cheshire, SK11 6BX
Activities: Other letting and operating of own or leased real estate
Shareholders: Nicholas Brian Lewis; Brian Edward Lewis
Officers: Nicholas Brian Lewis, Secretary; Brian Edward Lewis [1942] Director; Nicholas Brian Lewis [1967] Director

Estuary Group Limited
Incorporated: 15 February 2001
Net Worth: £6,497,682 *Total Assets:* £6,877,578
Registered Office: Whitethorn, Chelford Road, Knutsford, Cheshire, WA16 8LY
Activities: Other credit granting n.e.c.
Shareholder: Thomas Stanley Davis
Officers: Thomas Stanley Davis, Secretary/Surveyor; Jane Caroline Davis [1969] Director/PR Manager; Thomas Stanley Davis [1960] Director/Surveyor; Howard Nicholas George [1965] Director/Surveyor; Melanie George [1963] Director/Teacher

Eternity Capital Management Limited
Incorporated: 22 May 2012
Net Worth Deficit: £4,511,537 *Total Assets:* £14,813,789
Registered Office: 4 Clippers Quay, Salford Quays, Manchester, M50 3BL
Activities: Other business support service activities n.e.c.
Major Shareholder: Alon Lanaido
Officers: Alon Laniado [1979] Director [Belgian]

Ethika Healthcare Investments Limited
Incorporated: 20 July 2016
Net Worth Deficit: £2,106,641 *Total Assets:* £7,548,511
Registered Office: 1.02 Boat Shed, 12 Exchange Quay, Salford, M5 3EQ
Activities: Other professional, scientific and technical activities n.e.c.
Major Shareholder: Gareth O'Connell
Officers: Gareth O'Connell [1971] Director/Barrister [Irish]

Etihad Acquisitions Limited
Incorporated: 29 December 2010 *Employees:* 915
Net Worth Deficit: £54,794,000 *Total Assets:* £318,288,992
Registered Office: Universal House, Longley Lane, Manchester, M22 4SY
Activities: Activities of other holding companies n.e.c.
Parent: Titan Telecom Limited
Officers: Gillian Elizabeth Hill, Secretary; Paul Doherty [1970] Director/Accountant; Christopher James Earle [1973] Director; Jayne Amanda Sutton [1970] Director

Etihad Midco Limited
Incorporated: 29 December 2010 *Employees:* 2
Net Worth: £1,437,000 *Total Assets:* £152,459,008
Registered Office: Universal House, Longley Lane, Manchester, M22 4SY
Activities: Activities of other holding companies n.e.c.
Parent: Etihad Topco Limited
Officers: Gillian Elizabeth Hill, Secretary; Paul Doherty [1970] Director/Accountant; Christopher James Earle [1973] Director

Etihad Topco Limited
Incorporated: 29 December 2010 *Employees:* 915
Net Worth Deficit: £52,995,000 *Total Assets:* £168,560,992
Registered Office: Universal House, Longley Lane, Manchester, M22 4SY
Activities: Activities of other holding companies n.e.c.
Parent: Vitruvian Partners LLP
Officers: Gillian Elizabeth Hill, Secretary; Zillah Ellen Byng-Thorne [1974] Director; Paul Doherty [1970] Director/Accountant; Paul Bernard Dollman [1956] Director; Christopher James Earle [1973] Director; Piotr Nowosad [1970] Director [Polish]; Eric Geoffrey Unwin [1942] Director

Euro Garages Limited
Incorporated: 4 July 2001 *Employees:* 3,701
Net Worth: £130,530,000 *Total Assets:* £685,812,992
Registered Office: Euro House, The Beehive Trading Park, Haslingden Road, Blackburn, Lancs, BB1 2EE
Activities: Retail sale of automotive fuel in specialised stores
Officers: Imraan Musa Patel, Secretary; Mohsin Issa [1971] Director; Zuber Vali Issa [1972] Managing Director

Euro Options Limited
Incorporated: 29 September 1998 *Employees:* 37
Net Worth: £8,317,911 *Total Assets:* £15,320,533
Registered Office: Unit 5a Greenvale Business Park, Todmorden Road, Littleborough, Rochdale, Lancs, OL15 9FG
Activities: Other information technology service activities
Officers: Peter Morley, Secretary; Paul Daniel Doherty [1979] Sales Director; Peter Morley [1968] Finance Director; Patricia Morris [1940] Director

Euro Wrap Limited
Incorporated: 15 November 1993 *Employees:* 54
Net Worth: £8,430,000 *Total Assets:* £9,840,000
Registered Office: Unit 2 Pikelaw Place, West Pimbo Industrial Estate, Skelmersdale, Lancs, WN8 9PP
Activities: Wholesale of other intermediate products
Parent: Eurowrap AS
Officers: Martin Bramley, Secretary/Manager; Martin Bramley [1963] Director/Manager; Anders Ditlev Jorgensen [1971] Director/Chief Executive Officer [Danish]

Eurocamp Limited
Incorporated: 4 September 1998
Net Worth: £132,002,000 *Total Assets:* £159,148,000
Registered Office: Chelford House, Rudheath Way, Rudheath, Northwich, Cheshire, CW9 7LN
Activities: Activities of head offices
Parent: Starlight Camping Limited
Officers: Alain Yvon Calme [1966] Director/Chief Executive [French]; Darren Paul Marsh [1975] Director

Eurogold Groundworks & Civil Engineering Contractors Ltd.
Incorporated: 6 July 2004 *Employees:* 40
Net Worth: £8,973,258 *Total Assets:* £21,447,376
Registered Office: 18 Paramount Business Park, Wilson Road, Huyton, Merseyside, L36 6AW
Activities: Construction of other civil engineering projects n.e.c.
Parent: Eurogold Holdings Limited
Officers: Bernard Damien Brickland, Secretary/Civil Engineer [Irish]; Bernard Damien Brickland [1955] Director [Irish]; Emma Louise Cassidy [1977] Director; Emma Ryan [1980] Director

Eurogold Group Limited
Incorporated: 8 October 2015 *Employees:* 40
Net Worth: £8,745,437 *Total Assets:* £21,766,876
Registered Office: 18 Paramount Business Park, Wilson Road, Huyton, Merseyside, L36 6AW
Activities: Construction of other civil engineering projects n.e.c.
Major Shareholder: Damien Bernard Brickland
Officers: Damien Bernard Brickland [1955] Director

European Braking Systems Ltd
Incorporated: 7 March 1995 *Employees:* 56
Net Worth: £5,031,781 *Total Assets:* £15,017,663
Registered Office: Unit 3 Westpoint Enterprise Park, Clarence Avenue, Trafford Park, Manchester, M17 1QS
Activities: Wholesale trade of motor vehicle parts and accessories
Parent: Luby Group (UK) Limited
Officers: Mark Peter Luby [1966] Director/Sales/Marketing

European Care & Lifestyles (UK) Ltd
Incorporated: 8 October 1999 *Employees:* 6,140
Net Worth Deficit: £26,045,000 *Total Assets:* £34,291,000
Registered Office: The Zenith Building, 26 Spring Gardens, Manchester, M2 1AB
Activities: Residential care activities for learning difficulties, mental health and substance abuse
Officers: David Lindsay Manson [1969] Director; Alan John Templer Pilgrim [1951] Director; Colin Rutherford [1959] Director/Chartered Accountant; Albert Edward Smith [1958] Director; Stephen Paul Webster [1952] Director

European Diesel Card Limited
Incorporated: 1 September 2005 *Employees:* 4
Net Worth: £14,677,000 *Total Assets:* £45,376,000
Registered Office: Eurocard Centre, Herald Park, Herald Drive, Crewe, Cheshire, CW1 6EG
Activities: Wholesale of other fuels and related products
Shareholder: William Stanley Holmes
Officers: Adrian Stuart Rushton, Secretary; Lee John Everett [1974] Sales Director; William Stanley Holmes [1964] Director

European Metal Recycling (Dormant) Limited
Incorporated: 24 February 2006
Net Worth Deficit: £44,851,000 *Total Assets:* £62,717,000
Registered Office: Sirius House, Delta Crescent, Westbrook, Warrington, Cheshire, WA5 7NS
Activities: Activities of head offices
Parent: European Metal Recycling Limited
Officers: Christopher John Tinsley, Secretary; Christopher Phillip Sheppard [1974] Director; Neil Andrew Stinson [1970] Director/Accountant

European Metal Recycling (International) Limited
Incorporated: 27 January 2006
Net Worth: £16,465,000 *Total Assets:* £19,828,000
Registered Office: Sirius House, Delta Crescent, Westbrook, Warrington, Cheshire, WA5 7NS
Activities: Activities of head offices
Parent: European Metal Recycling Limited
Officers: Christopher John Tinsley, Secretary; Christopher Phillip Sheppard [1974] Director; Neil Andrew Stinson [1970] Director/Accountant

European Metal Recycling (USA) Limited
Incorporated: 24 February 2006
Net Worth: £598,723,008 *Total Assets:* £598,723,008
Registered Office: Sirius House, Delta Crescent, Westbrook, Warrington, Cheshire, WA5 7NS
Activities: Activities of head offices
Parent: European Metal Recycling Limited
Officers: Christopher John Tinsley, Secretary; Christopher Phillip Sheppard [1974] Director; Neil Andrew Stinson [1970] Director/Accountant

European Metal Recycling Limited
Incorporated: 2 August 1994 *Employees:* 2,910
Net Worth: £584,000,000 *Total Assets:* £1,174,000,000
Registered Office: Sirius House, Delta Crescent, Westbrook, Warrington, Cheshire, WA5 7NS
Activities: Recovery of sorted materials
Parent: Ausurus Group Ltd
Officers: Christopher John Tinsley, Secretary; David Farrington Landless [1960] Director; Edwin Leijnse [1967] Director [Dutch]; Edward Scott Pysden [1948] Director/Solicitor; Christopher Phillip Sheppard [1974] Director; Robin Sheppard [1954] Director

European Metal Recycling USA Holdings Limited
Incorporated: 10 January 2013
Net Worth: £548,030,336 *Total Assets:* £549,810,624
Registered Office: Sirius House, Delta Crescent, Westbrook, Warrington, Cheshire, WA5 7NS
Activities: Activities of other holding companies n.e.c.
Officers: Christopher Phillip Sheppard [1974] Director/Group Chief Executive; Neil Andrew Stinson [1970] Finance Director

Europlast (Blackburn) Limited
Incorporated: 11 March 1993 *Employees:* 72
Net Worth: £4,792,130 *Total Assets:* £10,141,254
Registered Office: Euro House, Units 1 & 2 Shadsworth Business Park, Duttons Way, Blackburn, Lancs, BB1 2QR
Activities: Manufacture of plastic packing goods
Officers: Zakir Issa, Secretary; Zakir Issa [1969] Director

Euroresins UK Limited
Incorporated: 1 March 1988 *Employees:* 32
Net Worth: £9,699,416 *Total Assets:* £16,367,031
Registered Office: Cloister Way, Bridges Road, Ellesmere Port, Cheshire, CH65 4EL
Activities: Wholesale of chemical products
Parent: Cathay Investments Limited
Officers: Kevin Andrew Johnson, Secretary; Benjamin Ka Ping Chaing [1952] Director; Kevin Andrew Johnson [1969] Director/Accountant

Eurosonic Group Limited
Incorporated: 16 October 1978 *Employees:* 82
Net Worth: £4,974,047 *Total Assets:* £19,650,630
Registered Office: 11 Sherborne Street, Manchester, M3 1JS
Activities: Wholesale of radio, television goods & electrical household appliances (other than records, tapes, CDs)
Major Shareholder: Harpreet Singh Chadha
Officers: Jill Prendergast, Secretary; Harpreet Singh Chadha [1970] Director; Anthony Francis Dorgan [1962] Sales Director

Eurostation Limited
Incorporated: 20 July 2000 *Employees:* 115
Net Worth: £9,964,686 *Total Assets:* £17,711,920
Registered Office: The Old School Hose, 39 Bengal Street, Manchester, M4 6AF
Activities: Non-specialised wholesale trade
Shareholder: Richard Lee Shonn
Officers: Daniel Simon Shonn [1970] Director; Richard Lee Shonn [1977] Director; Steven Martin Shonn [1951] Director/Manager

Eutelsat UK Limited
Incorporated: 11 July 2003 *Employees:* 7
Net Worth: £45,694,900 *Total Assets:* £51,656,912
Registered Office: c/o PM+M, Greenbank Technology Park, Challenge Way, Blackburn, Lancs, BB1 5QB
Activities: Satellite telecommunications activities
Officers: Nicholas John Drew Daly, Secretary; Jean Francois Bureau [1953] Director [French]; Matthew Child [1961] Director/VP Global Government Sector; Nicholas John Drew Daly [1953] Managing Director; Joanna Trudi Darlington [1961] Director; Julien Jean-Baptiste Seligmann [1970] Director/Chief Executive Officer [French]; Sandrine Teran [1968] Director [French]

EV Retail Limited
Incorporated: 3 September 1996
Net Worth: £10,328,000 *Total Assets:* £76,316,000
Registered Office: The Vault, Dakota Drive, Estuary Commerce Park, Speke, Liverpool, L24 8RJ
Activities: Activities of head offices
Parent: B&M European Value Retail Holdco 4 Ltd
Officers: Simon Arora, Secretary; Bobby Arora [1972] Director; Robin Arora [1985] Director; Simon Arora [1969] Director; Paul Andrew McDonald [1966] Director/Accountant

S Evans & Sons Limited
Incorporated: 2 February 1999 *Employees:* 32
Net Worth: £8,651,767 *Total Assets:* £9,708,568
Registered Office: Demolition Contractors Site, Ditton Road, Widnes, Cheshire, WA8 0PJ
Activities: Demolition
Shareholder: Samuel Evans
Officers: Paul Barry Evans [1968] Director; Samuel Evans [1947] Director; Jordan Samuel Sumner [1992] Director; Sharon Amanda Sumner [1970] Director

W.R.Evans Healthcare Limited
Incorporated: 4 July 1960 *Employees:* 516
Net Worth: £12,881,040 *Total Assets:* £50,397,428
Registered Office: 11 Manchester Road, Walkden, Manchester, M28 3NS
Activities: Dispensing chemist in specialised stores
Parent: PCT Healthcare (Holdings) Limited
Officers: Angela Jane Cattee [1953] Director; Peter Cattee [1952] Director; Geoffrey Alan Tims [1943] Director

Evans Vanodine International PLC
Incorporated: 10 April 1953 *Employees:* 151
Net Worth: £15,935,064 *Total Assets:* £20,189,306
Registered Office: Brierley Road, Walton Summit Centre, Bamber Bridge, Preston, Lancs, PR5 8AH
Activities: Manufacture of soap and detergents
Shareholders: Peter David Evans; Anthony Ian Evans; Christopher John Evans
Officers: Christopher John Evans, Secretary; Anthony Ian Evans [1966] Systems Director; Christopher John Evans [1959] Operations Director; Derek Anthony Evans [1927] Director/Chairman; Peter David Evans [1955] Managing Director

Eventmore Limited
Incorporated: 18 December 2003
Net Worth: £1,862,849 *Total Assets:* £10,740,958
Registered Office: Brulimar House, Jubilee Road, Middleton, Manchester, M24 2LX
Activities: Buying and selling of own real estate
Shareholder: Maria Khaliq
Officers: Maria Yasmin Khaliq [1968] Director

F.T.Everard & Sons Limited
Incorporated: 1 April 1922
Net Worth: £1,105,790 *Total Assets:* £6,777,676
Registered Office: P O Box 4, Fisher House, Michaelson Road, Barrow in Furness, Cumbria, LA14 1HR
Activities: Sea and coastal freight water transport
Parent: James Fisher and Sons Public Limited Company
Officers: James Henry John Marsh, Secretary; Richard Douglas Burmeister [1956] Director; Nicholas Paul Henry [1961] Director; Stuart Charles Kilpatrick [1962] Director

Evergreen Energy Ltd
Incorporated: 1 April 2011
Net Worth: £11,173,014 *Total Assets:* £12,548,930
Registered Office: The Edge Business Centre, The Edge, Clowes Street, Manchester, M3 5NA
Activities: Activities of head offices
Major Shareholder: Anthony Stephen Critchlow
Officers: Anthony Stephen Critchlow [1960] Director; Andrew Kenneth Muir-Simpson [1978] Director/Accountant

Evergreener Investments LLP
Incorporated: 17 February 2006
Net Worth: £13 998,912 *Total Assets:* £25,334,834
Registered Office: 17 Alvaston Business Park, Middlewich Road, Nantwich, Cheshire, CW5 6PF
Officers: Stephen John Isherwood [1962] Member

Eversheds Sutherland Legal Services Limited
Incorporated: 28 September 1988 *Employees:* 2,171
Net Worth: £5,896,283 *Total Assets:* £19,348,884
Registered Office: Eversheds House, 70 Great Bridgewater Street, Manchester, M1 5ES
Activities: Other business support service activities n.e.c.
Parent: Eversheds Sutherland (International) LLP
Officers: Keith Froud [1970] Director/Solicitor; Lee Ranson [1964] Director/Solicitor; Paul Anthony Smith [1956] Director/Solicitor

Everton Football Club Company, Limited
Incorporated: 14 June 1892 *Employees:* 357
Net Worth: £91,688,000 *Total Assets:* £198,087,008
Registered Office: Goodison Park, Goodison Road, Liverpool, L4 4EL
Activities: Operation of sports facilities
Major Shareholder: Ardavan Farhad Moshiri
Officers: Denise Barrett-Baxendale [1971] Director; Keith Reginald Harris [1953] Director; William Kenwright [1945] Director; Alexander Ryazantsev [1974] Director; Jon Vincent Woods [1946] Director/Publisher

Evolution Lending Limited
Incorporated: 9 February 2007
Net Worth: £3,103,184 *Total Assets:* £71,706,456
Registered Office: 8 St John Street, Manchester, M3 4DU
Activities: Credit granting by non-deposit taking finance houses and other specialist consumer credit grantors
Parent: Darwin Loan Solutions Limited
Officers: Stephen Philip Brilus [1968] Director; Mathew James Montgomery [1980] Director; Robin John Russel-Fisher [1958] Finance Director; Kerriann Turtill [1979] Director

W. M. Ewington & Company Limited
Incorporated: 20 December 1976 *Employees:* 15
Net Worth: £7,418,378 *Total Assets:* £10,748,215
Registered Office: 92a Crewe Road, Nantwich, Cheshire, CW5 6JD
Activities: Other letting and operating of own or leased real estate
Major Shareholder: William Michael Ewington
Officers: Justine Shesha Turpin, Secretary; William Michael Ewington [1946] Director/Commercial Property Management; Justine Shesha Turpin [1966] Director/Property Management

EWM (Topco) Limited
Incorporated: 23 September 2002 *Employees:* 10,052
Net Worth: £268,324,992 *Total Assets:* £376,963,008
Registered Office: Site A, Queens Drive, Kingmoor Park South, Carlisle, CA6 4SB
Activities: Activities of head offices
Parent: The Edinburgh Woollen Mill (Group) Limited
Officers: June Carruthers, Secretary; Lauren Sarah Day [1990] Development Director; Philip Edward Day [1965] Director; Robert Neil Edmonds [1965] Finance Director; John Anthony Herring [1957] Director; David Oliver Houston [1953] Director; Carmel Leigh [1962] Director; Stephen Robert Simpson [1968] Commercial Director

Examworks UK Ltd
Incorporated: 31 August 2010 *Employees:* 858
Net Worth: £17,281,000 *Total Assets:* £233,415,008
Registered Office: Premex House, Futura Park, Horwich, Bolton, Lancs, BL6 6SX
Activities: Other human health activities
Parent: Examworks Europe Inc
Officers: Caroline Emily Elizabeth Russell, Secretary; Donald Fowler [1973] Director; Doug Laver [1965] Finance Director; Richard Elliot Perlman [1946] Director [American]; James Kerrick Price [1958] Director [American]

Excalon Limited
Incorporated: 29 May 2002 *Employees:* 222
Net Worth: £4,158,703 *Total Assets:* £12,233,726
Registered Office: 20 Modwen Road, Salford Quays, Manchester, M5 3EZ
Activities: Construction of utility projects for electricity and telecommunications
Shareholders: Michael Kevin O'Donnell; Brian Desmond Donnelly
Officers: Kevan Wakerley, Secretary; Desmond Brian Donnelly [1971] Director; Michael Kevin O'Donnell [1968] Director; Julie Anne Sutherland [1961] Director; Kevan Wakerley [1961] Finance Director; Daniel James Wilson [1974] Director

Exceed Academies Trust
Incorporated: 8 March 2016 *Employees:* 313
Net Worth: £10,858,000 *Total Assets:* £13,979,000
Registered Office: Horton Park Primary School, Dawnay Road, Bradford, W Yorks, BD5 9LQ
Activities: Primary education
Officers: Trevor Evans [1950] Director/Retired; Elaine Margaret Hughes [1976] Director/Chartered Management Accountant; Nadia Kauser Hussain [1981] Director/Project Manager; Carol Sharon Lambert [1956] Director/Retired; Dr Sandra Georgina Whitson [1938] Director/Retired; Ian Willoughby [1977] Director/Income Officer

Excel -a- Rate Business Services Limited
Incorporated: 21 November 1996 *Employees:* 17
Net Worth: £2,090,351 *Total Assets:* £12,087,573
Registered Office: Prospect House, 389-391 Ainsworth Road, Radcliffe, Manchester, M26 4HN
Activities: Financial intermediation not elsewhere classified
Major Shareholder: David Adrian Ballan
Officers: David Adrian Ballan, Secretary; David Adrian Ballan [1957] Director/Accountant; Zachary James Ballan [1990] Sales Director; Denise Pinder [1960] Director; Colin Jeffrey Samuels [1958] Director; Michael Brendan Slattery [1947] Director/Solicitor

Exchequer Partnership (No.2) Holdings Limited
Incorporated: 29 April 2002
Net Worth: £157,000 *Total Assets:* £162,264,000
Registered Office: c/o Albany SPC Services Ltd, 3rd Floor, 3-5 Charlotte Street, Manchester, M1 4HB
Activities: Activities of head offices
Shareholders: Consolidated Investment Holdings Limited; Aberdeen Sidecar LLP
Officers: Ailison Louise Mitchell, Secretary; Michael Andrew Donn [1972] Director; Karen Marie Hill [1977] Director/Investment Manager; Barry Paul Millsom [1974] Director; Steve Marc Prior [1972] Director; Christopher Thomas Solley [1970] Director; Andrew Leslie Tennant [1958] Director

Exchequer Partnership (No.2) PLC
Incorporated: 29 April 2002
Net Worth: £157,000 *Total Assets:* £162,264,000
Registered Office: c/o Albany SPC Services Ltd, 3rd Floor, 3-5 Charlotte Street, Manchester, M1 4HB
Activities: Activities of head offices
Parent: Exchequer Partnership (No. 2) Holdings Limited
Officers: Alison Louise Mitchell, Secretary; Michael Andrew Donn [1972] Director; Karen Marie Hill [1977] Director/Investment Manager; Barry Paul Millsom [1974] Director; Steve Marc Prior [1972] Director; Christopher Thomas Solley [1970] Director; Andrew Leslie Tennant [1958] Director

Exchequer Partnership Holdings Limited
Incorporated: 15 July 1999
Net Worth: £615,000 *Total Assets:* £133,257,000
Registered Office: c/o Albany SPC Services Ltd, 3rd Floor, 3-5 Charlotte Street, Manchester, M1 4HB
Activities: Management of real estate on a fee or contract basis
Shareholders: Consolidated Investment Holdings Limited; Aberdeen Sidecar LP
Officers: Ailison Louise Mitchell, Secretary; Michael Andrew Donn [1972] Director; Karen Marie Hill [1977] Director/Investment Manager; Barry Paul Millsom [1974] Director; Steve Marc Prior [1972] Director; Christopher Thomas Solley [1970] Director; Andrew Leslie Tennant [1958] Director

Exchequer Partnership PLC
Incorporated: 15 July 1999
Net Worth: £615,000 *Total Assets:* £133,257,000
Registered Office: c/o Albany SPC Services Ltd, 3rd Floor, 3-5 Charlotte Street, Manchester, M1 4HB
Activities: Management of real estate on a fee or contract basis
Parent: Exchequer Partnership Holdings Ltd
Officers: Ailison Louise Mitchell, Secretary; Michael Andrew Donn [1972] Director; Karen Marie Hill [1977] Director/Investment Manager; Barry Paul Millsom [1974] Director; Steven Marc Prior [1972] Director; Christopher Thomas Solley [1970] Director; Andrew Leslie Tennant [1958] Director

Exedy Clutch Europe Limited
Incorporated: 7 November 1989 *Employees:* 40
Net Worth: £5,327,102 *Total Assets:* £17,079,824
Registered Office: Unit 2 Rokeby Court, Manor Park, Runcorn, Cheshire, WA7 1RW
Activities: Wholesale trade of motor vehicle parts and accessories
Parent: Exedy Corporation
Officers: Kabel Davis [1973] Non Full Time Director [Australian]; Shogo Okamura [1947] Non Full Time Director, President [Japanese]; Shinsuke Seike [1974] Non Full Time Director [Japanese]; Koichi Suzuki [1971] Full Time Director [Japanese]

Exertis (Holdings) Ltd
Incorporated: 4 May 1989
Net Worth: £73,958,000 *Total Assets:* £126,723,000
Registered Office: Technology House, Magnesium Way, Hapton, Burnley, Lancs, BB12 7BF
Activities: Activities of head offices
Parent: DCC Technology Ltd
Officers: Richard Hinds, Secretary; Timothy David Griffin [1967] Director; Gerard Patrick O'Keeffe [1964] Director [Irish]

Exertis (UK) Ltd
Incorporated: 11 August 1980 *Employees:* 1,293
Net Worth: £153,096,000 *Total Assets:* £737,875,008
Registered Office: Technology House, Magnesium Way, Hapton, Burnley, Lancs, BB12 7BF
Activities: Wholesale of computers, computer peripheral equipment and software
Parent: Exertis (Holdings) Ltd
Officers: Richard Hinds, Secretary; Raj Kumar Advani [1959] Director; Paul William Bryan [1969] Managing Director; Stephen Casey [1980] Director [Irish]; Jason Martin Chibnall [1968] Director; Alexander Bernard James Croft [1973] Director; Nick Foster [1971] Director; Timothy David Griffin [1967] Director; Richard Hinds [1975] Finance Director; Mark Kahr [1966] Purchasing Director; Alan James Lynch [1969] Director; Fergal John O'Dwyer [1960] Director/Chartered Accountant [Irish]; Gerard Patrick O'Keeffe [1964] Group Managing Director [Irish]; Simon Anthony Woodman [1968] Director

Exertis Continental Europe Holdings Limited
Incorporated: 27 March 1997 *Employees:* 3
Net Worth Deficit: £2,031,943 *Total Assets:* £25,176,574
Registered Office: Technology House, Magnesium Way, Hapton, Burnley, Lancs, BB12 7BF
Activities: Activities of head offices
Parent: DCC Technology Ltd
Officers: Richard Hinds, Secretary; Paul John Donnelly [1956] Director; Timothy David Griffin [1967] Director; Gerard Patrick O'Keeffe [1964] Director [Irish]

Exide Technologies (Transportation) Limited
Incorporated: 14 November 1988 *Employees:* 21
Net Worth Deficit: £119,311,000 *Total Assets:* £8,026,000
Registered Office: Mansell House, Aspinall Close, Middlebrook, Horwich, Bolton, Lancs, BL6 6QQ
Activities: Wholesale trade of motor vehicle parts and accessories
Parent: Exide Transportation Holding Europe SL
Officers: Jayne Wynne Roy, Secretary; Nigel Jeremy Darke [1963] Senior Business Director; Brad Stewart Kalter [1967] Director [American]; Chi Wing Lam [1974] Finance Director [Dutch]; Stefan Alois Stubing [1962] Director [German]

Exoteric Metering Limited
Incorporated: 13 June 2008
Net Worth Deficit: £241,000 *Total Assets:* £16,979,000
Registered Office: Ship Canal House, 98 King Street, Manchester, M2 4WU
Activities: Distribution of gaseous fuels through mains
Parent: Energy Assets Limited
Officers: Colin John Lynch [1966] Director; John McMorrow [1977] Director/Chief Financial Officer; Craig Philip Topley [1973] Director

Expalkan II Closed Scheme Limited
Incorporated: 6 June 2013 *Employees:* 2
Net Worth: £6,698,000 *Total Assets:* £14,590,000
Registered Office: Eversheds House, 70 Great Bridgewater Street, Manchester, M1 5ES
Activities: Pension funding
Parent: Corbion N.V.
Officers: Harm Geert Noppers [1975] Director/Legal Counsel [Dutch]; Eduard Eric Van Rhede Van Der Kloot [1963] Director [Dutch]

Expect Distribution Limited
Incorporated: 25 September 1987 *Employees:* 249
Net Worth: £3,390,282 *Total Assets:* £14,897,299
Registered Office: Premier Point, Premier Gate, Staithgate Lane, Bradford, W Yorks, BD6 1DW
Activities: Freight transport by road
Shareholders: Robert Westwell Rushworth; Neil Wayne Rushworth
Officers: Robert Westwell Rushworth, Secretary; Elaine Rushworth [1943] Director; Neil Wayne Rushworth [1971] Director; Robert Westwell Rushworth [1944] Director; Andrew David Taylor [1982] Director of Transport; Steven Paul Wood [1955] Director/Consultant

Expert Logistics Ltd.
Incorporated: 1 October 1997 *Employees:* 964
Net Worth: £24,304,000 *Total Assets:* £58,253,000
Registered Office: Unit 5a The Parklands, Lostock, Bolton, Lancs, BL6 4SD
Activities: Freight transport by road
Parent: AO Limited
Officers: Julie Angela Louise Finnemore, Secretary; David Michael Ashwell [1967] Managing Director; Daniel Anthony Emmett [1984] Director; Stuart Mark Haynes [1983] Director/Accountant; Jonathan Mark Stephen Higgins [1978] Director/Accountant

Expertband Limited
Incorporated: 2 June 1992 *Employees:* 123
Net Worth: £6,123,812 *Total Assets:* £14,103,657
Registered Office: Charter House, Pittman Way, Fulwood, Preston, Lancs, PR2 9ZD
Activities: Non-trading company
Shareholders: Roy William Allen; Ruth Anne Hebden
Officers: Ruth Ann Hebden, Secretary; Roy William Allen [1947] Director & General Manager; Ruth Anne Hebden [1942] Director

Express Cargo Forwarding Limited
Incorporated: 4 May 1989 *Employees:* 22
Net Worth Deficit: £51,741,636 *Total Assets:* £67,766,208
Registered Office: Stretton Green Distribution Centre, Langford Way, Warrington, Cheshire, WA4 4TQ
Activities: Other service activities incidental to land transportation, n.e.c.
Officers: David Stewart, Secretary; Robert Michael McCafferty [1960] Director [American]; Mike Meades [1965] Director/General Manager; Stephanie Anne Shaw [1965] Director

Express Gifts Limited
Incorporated: 16 March 1962 *Employees:* 1,488
Net Worth: £67,137,000 *Total Assets:* £323,028,992
Registered Office: Church Bridge House, Henry Street, Accrington, Lancs, BB5 4EE
Activities: Retail sale via mail order houses or via Internet
Parent: Findel PLC
Officers: Mark Ashcroft, Secretary; Mark Ashcroft [1957] Director/Company Secretary; Mark Ashcroft [1957] Director/Company Secretary; Stuart Murdoch Caldwell [1972] Director; Richard John Hornby [1973] Finance Director; Paul Robert Kendrick [1967] Executive Director; Philip Binns Maudsley [1960] Director

Express Linen Services Limited
Incorporated: 20 November 2007 *Employees:* 134
Net Worth: £1,801,894 *Total Assets:* £6,737,444
Registered Office: 1 Brunel Way, Blackpool & Fylde Industrial Estate, Blackpool, Lancs, FY4 5ES
Activities: Washing and (dry-)cleaning of textile and fur products
Shareholders: Edward Bruce; Patricia Bruce
Officers: Carole Allan, Secretary; Edward Bruce [1941] Director/Engineer; Mark Anthony Bruce [1972] Sales Director; Patricia Bruce [1941] Director

Express Solicitors Limited
Incorporated: 22 March 2013 *Employees:* 178
Net Worth: £14,897,096 *Total Assets:* £20,595,256
Registered Office: Resolution House, 319 Palatine Road, Northenden, Manchester, M22 4HH
Activities: Solicitors
Shareholders: James Thomas Maxey; Robin Keith Patey
Officers: James Thomas Maxey [1970] Director/Solicitor; Robin Keith Patey [1975] Director/Solicitor; Daniel Adam Slade [1980] Director/Solicitor; Liam John Wynne [1979] Director

F and N Holdings Limited
Incorporated: 21 January 1971 *Employees:* 1
Net Worth: £51,232,008 *Total Assets:* £53,160,048
Registered Office: Underlyne, Langwathby, Penrith, Cumbria, CA10 1NB
Activities: Activities of head offices
Parent: F and N One Ltd
Officers: Frank Bird [1936] Director

F and N One Limited
Incorporated: 10 November 2008 *Employees:* 225
Net Worth: £56,093,384 *Total Assets:* £61,302,684
Registered Office: c/o The Old Court House, Clark Street, Morecambe, Lancs, LA4 5HR
Activities: Non-trading company
Parent: DWF (Trustee) Limited
Officers: Frank Bird [1936] Director

F X Leisure Limited
Incorporated: 7 November 1997 *Employees:* 85
Net Worth: £1,296,289 *Total Assets:* £14,473,608
Registered Office: FX Leisure, King Street, Leyland, Lancs, PR25 2LF
Activities: Fitness facilities
Shareholders: The Andrew Taylor Irrevocable Trust; The Stuart Taylor Irrevocable Trust
Officers: Kevin Joseph Carter, Secretary/Finance; Keith Belshaw [1970] Operations Director; Kevin Joseph Carter [1949] Director/Finance; Leonard Norman Latham [1944] Director/Development Consultant; Andrew John Taylor [1970] Director; Stuart James Taylor [1974] Director

F-M Motorparts Limited
Incorporated: 26 September 1972 *Employees:* 478
Net Worth: £112,839,288 *Total Assets:* £127,849,344
Registered Office: Suite 14, Manchester International Office Centre, Styal Road, Manchester, M22 5TN
Activities: Manufacture of other parts and accessories for motor vehicles
Parent: Icahn Enterprises L.P.
Officers: Beverley Ann Sutton, Secretary; Elaine Janet Milner [1962] Director/Finance Manager; Keith Power [1960] Director/President Asia Pacific Federal Mogul Motorparts

F2 Chemicals Limited
Incorporated: 23 January 1992 *Employees:* 43
Net Worth: £7,088,000 *Total Assets:* £11,645,000
Registered Office: F2 Chemicals Ltd, Lea Lane, Lea Town, Preston, Lancs, PR4 0RZ
Activities: Manufacture of other chemical products n.e.c.
Parent: Showa Denko K.K.
Officers: Toshitaka Hiro [1964] Director/Manager [Japanese]; Andrew James Penman [1972] Managing Director; Kazuhiro Sakurai [1963] Director/Manager [Japanese]; Hiroshi Ukita [1969] Director/Senior Manager and Prokurist [Japanese]; Takashi Usami [1963] Director/Manager [Japanese]; Masamichi Yagishita [1958] Director/Manager [Japanese]

Fabrics & Yarns (Macclesfield) Ltd
Incorporated: 29 October 1987 *Employees:* 10
Net Worth: £7,968,866 *Total Assets:* £9,050,238
Registered Office: Charter Way, Hurdsfield Industrial Estate, Macclesfield, Cheshire, SK10 2NG
Activities: Wholesale of textiles
Shareholder: Kaldoun Hussamy
Officers: Margaret Irene Comer, Secretary; David Jonathan Crowther [1958] Director; Mohamed Khaled Nashar [1975] Director

Faci UK Chemicals Limited
Incorporated: 9 April 2014 *Employees:* 18
Net Worth: £5,945,056 *Total Assets:* £10,212,437
Registered Office: Ashcroft Road, Knowsley Industrial Park, Knowsley, Merseyside, L33 7TW
Activities: Manufacture of other chemical products n.e.c.
Parent: Faci Corporate SpA
Officers: Modestino Cavaliere [1941] Managing Director of Faci Group [Italian]; Mark George Guilbert [1965] Director; Franco Rossi [1951] Director [Italian]; William Warnock [1959] Director/Sales Manager

The Factory Shop Group Limited
Incorporated: 24 February 2003
Net Worth: £2,768,000 *Total Assets:* £30,380,000
Registered Office: The Factory Shop Ltd, Orient Business Park, Billington Road, Burnley, Lancs, BB11 5UB
Activities: Dormant company
Parent: Original FS Holdings Limited
Officers: Carl Brian Allen [1966] Director; Timothy Richard Bettley [1966] Commercial Director; Stephen Andrew Cooke [1965] Director; Emma Louise Fox [1968] Director/Chief Executive Officer

Fagan & Whalley Holdings Limited
Incorporated: 15 August 2013 *Employees:* 307
Net Worth: £11,048,525 *Total Assets:* £25,088,508
Registered Office: Mead Way, Shuttleworth Mead Business Park, Padiham, Burnley, Lancs, BB12 7NG
Activities: Activities of other holding companies n.e.c.
Officers: Graham Michael Fagan [1959] Director; Stephen Alexander Fagan [1962] Director

Fagan & Whalley Limited
Incorporated: 24 April 1941 *Employees:* 307
Net Worth: £10,971,123 *Total Assets:* £18,564,474
Registered Office: St Crispin House, St Crispin Way, Haslingden, Rossendale, Lancs, BB4 4PW
Activities: Freight transport by road
Officers: Stephen Alexander Fagan, Secretary; Graham Michael Fagan [1959] Director; Stephen Alexander Fagan [1962] Director

Fairbanks Environmental Limited
Incorporated: 1 March 1995 *Employees:* 149
Net Worth: £11,178,533 *Total Assets:* £13,832,255
Registered Office: The Technology Management Centre, Moss Lane View, Skelmersdale, Lancs, WN8 9TN
Activities: Other business support service activities n.e.c.
Parent: Dover Fluids UK Limited
Officers: Susan Rebecca Boyle [1974] Finance Director; Jeroen Ludovicus Henricus de Gruijter [1965] Director [Dutch]; Kurt Rene Elisabeth Dillen [1965] Director/General Manager [Belgian]; Alistair Johnston [1972] Director; Andrew James Sullivan [1964] Director

Fairfield High School for Girls
Incorporated: 31 January 2011 *Employees:* 106
Net Worth: £15,555,000 *Total Assets:* £17,049,000
Registered Office: Fairfield High School for Girls, Fairfield Avenue, Droylsden, Manchester, M43 6AB
Activities: General secondary education
Officers: Julie Murphy, Secretary; Sharman Birtles [1951] Director/Retired; Rev Phillip James Cooper [1963] Director/Reverend; Barbara Derbyshire [1954] Director/Retired; Tom Doyle [1950] Director/Retired; Abigail Eyre [1973] Director/Senior Admin Assistant; Neil Gallagher [1964] Director/Retired; Brendan Hesketh [1972] Director/Headmaster; Roger Barry Lingard [1954] Director; Anne McGarry [1938] Director/Retired; Anglea Mutter [1961] Director/Librarian; Lisa Richards [1971] Director/Assistant Principal; Emily Rowland [1977] Director/Teacher; Anthony Colin Sever [1967] Director/Finance Manager; Peter Shackleton [1943] Director; Helen Weston [1954] Director/Retired; Bev Worthington [1960] Director/Retired

Fairhome Group PLC
Incorporated: 4 June 2014 *Employees:* 57
Net Worth: £17,171,966 *Total Assets:* £41,583,796
Registered Office: 16 Carolina Way, Quays Reach, Salford, M50 2ZY
Activities: Development of building projects
Shareholders: John Russell; Paul Stephen Green
Officers: Paul Stephen Green, Secretary; Ian Burgess [1971] Director; Colin Stewart Gore [1960] Director; Paul Stephen Green [1949] Director; John Russell [1964] Director

Fairport Holdings Limited
Incorporated: 11 June 1990 *Employees:* 95
Net Worth: £6,389,556 *Total Assets:* £9,319,612
Registered Office: No 1 Market Place, Adlington, Lancs, PR7 4EZ
Activities: Activities of head offices
Shareholders: Andrew Leonard John Porter; Christine Johnson
Officers: David Leslie Holden, Secretary; David Leslie Holden [1961] Finance Director; Andrew Leonard John Porter [1955] Group Chairman Managing Director

Fairway (G.B.) Limited
Incorporated: 13 January 1994 *Employees:* 37
Net Worth: £3,803,620 *Total Assets:* £8,474,927
Registered Office: 17 Crescent, Salford, M5 4PF
Activities: Wholesale of sugar and chocolate and sugar confectionery
Parent: Fairway Holdco Limited
Officers: Thomas James George Emmerton [1955] Director; Andrew James Goggins [1979] Sales Director; Ian Vaughan James [1962] Sales Director

Faiveley Transport Birkenhead Limited
Incorporated: 16 August 1984 *Employees:* 145
Net Worth: £5,390,000 *Total Assets:* £37,152,000
Registered Office: Morpeth Wharf, Twelve Quays, Birkenhead, Wirral, Merseyside, CH41 1LF
Activities: Repair and maintenance of other transport equipment n.e.c.
Parent: Faiveley Transport SA
Officers: William Patrick Costigan, Secretary; Simon Richard Charlesworth [1964] Director; William Patrick Costigan [1970] Finance Director; Xavier Bertrand Marie de Lavallade [1967] Director/Head of Legal Department [French]; Ian Stuart Dolman [1963] Managing Director; Lilian Mathieu Leroux [1971] Divisional Director [French]; Alexandre Vidal [1975] Director/Divisional CFO [French]

Faiveley Transport Tamworth Ltd
Incorporated: 8 September 1993 *Employees:* 54
Net Worth: £8,589,382 *Total Assets:* £12,015,564
Registered Office: Morpeth Wharf, Twelve Quays, Birkenhead, Wirral, Merseyside, CH41 1LF
Activities: Repair and maintenance of other transport equipment n.e.c.
Parent: Faiveley Transport SA
Officers: William Patrick Costigan, Secretary; Simon Richard Charlesworth [1964] Director; William Patrick Costigan [1970] Finance Director; Ian Stuart Dolman [1963] Managing Director; Stephane Michel Rambaud-Measson [1962] Director [French]; Alexandre Vidal [1975] Director/Divisional CFO [French]

Falkirk Tod Hill Wind Limited
Incorporated: 21 October 2010
Net Worth Deficit: £2,588,788 *Total Assets:* £12,522,063
Registered Office: 1030 Centre Park, Slutchers Lane, Warrington, Cheshire, WA1 1QL
Activities: Production of electricity
Officers: Liz Oldroyd, Secretary; John William Breckenridge [1962] Managing Director [American]; Simon Richard Eaves [1967] Managing Director; Adrian Waine Robinson [1961] Director/Chief Operating Officer; Kirsty Louise Usher [1975] Director/Accountant

The Fallibroome Trust
Incorporated: 16 August 2010 *Employees:* 456
Net Worth: £26,513,300 *Total Assets:* £33,159,614
Registered Office: The Fallibroome Academy, Priory Lane, Macclesfield, Cheshire, SK10 4AF
Activities: Pre-primary education
Officers: Alison Elizabeth Nuttall, Secretary; John Brooks [1956] Director/Businessman; Peter Cresswell [1947] Director/Retired; Geoffrey Michael Gorton [1956] Director/Farmer; Richard David Hipperson [1947] Director; Vivienne Meredith [1968] Director/Human Resources; Andrew Gary Naylor [1967] Director/Finance; Peter William Rubery [1957] Director/Academy Principal; Paul Thornber [1964] Bid Director for Infrastructure Investment Company; Joanne Watkins [1970] Director/Transformation Manager

Famevalley Limited
Incorporated: 21 September 2004 *Employees:* 79
Net Worth: £1,024,900 *Total Assets:* £8,305,922
Registered Office: Former Preston College, Moor Park Avenue, Preston, Lancs, PR1 6AS
Activities: Development of building projects
Major Shareholder: Ridwan Patel
Officers: Ridwan Patel [1985] Director

Fanatics (International) Limited
Incorporated: 13 September 2006 *Employees:* 534
Net Worth: £10,667,000 *Total Assets:* £41,802,000
Registered Office: Greengate, Middleton, Manchester, M24 1FD
Activities: Retail sale via mail order houses or via Internet
Parent: Fanatics UK Holdings Limited
Officers: Edward Philip Boardman [1980] Director; Lauren Levitan [1965] Director/Ecommerce Financial Management [American]; Douglas Mack [1969] Director/Business Management [American]; Martin James Smith [1970] Finance Director; Caren Yeamans [1975] Director/Attorney [American]

Fargrace Limited
Incorporated: 2 March 2001
Net Worth: £69,750,000 *Total Assets:* £69,753,512
Registered Office: Eaton Estate Office, Eaton Park, Eccleston, Chester, CH4 9ET
Activities: Other business support service activities n.e.c.
Shareholders: Mark Robin Preston; William Bruce Kendall; Michael George Alexander McLintock
Officers: Sarah Helen Carss, Secretary; Sarah Helen Dean [1977] Director/Accountant; Catherine Susan Fradley [1965] Director/Accountant; Helen Frances Jaquiss [1964] Director/Accountant

Farinet Limited
Incorporated: 18 June 2014
Net Worth: £6,331,585 *Total Assets:* £6,612,320
Registered Office: Archway, Birley Fields, Manchester, M15 5QJ
Activities: Hotels and similar accommodation
Shareholders: Lawrence Nigel Jones; Gail Suzanne Jones
Officers: Jonathan Bowers [1975] Director; Joseph Brian Cravagan [1977] Director; Catherine Laura Jane Greening [1971] Director

Farmers Boy Limited
Incorporated: 10 May 1972 *Employees:* 3,141
Net Worth: £255,788,992 *Total Assets:* £603,324,992
Registered Office: Hilmore House, Gain Lane, Bradford, W Yorks, BD3 7DL
Activities: Production of meat and poultry meat products
Parent: Wm Morrison Supermarkets Holdings Limited
Officers: Jonathan James Burke, Secretary; Darren Anthony Blackhurst [1966] Director; Andrew James Clappen [1965] Technical Director; Jonathan William Reed [1973] Director; Mark Thomas Stitson [1976] Finance Director; Andrew Edward Thornber [1974] Director

Farmhouse Biscuits Limited
Incorporated: 14 November 1973 *Employees:* 244
Net Worth: £6,179,452 *Total Assets:* £9,528,859
Registered Office: Brook Street Mill, Brook Street, Nelson, Lancs, BB7 9PX
Activities: Manufacture of rusks and biscuits; manufacture of preserved pastry goods and cakes
Shareholders: Ronald Philip McIvor; Dorothy May McIvor
Officers: Dorothy May McMcvor, Secretary; Dorothy May McIvor [1941] Director; Gillian McIvor [1962] Director/Office Manager; Ronald Philip McIvor [1936] Director; Wendy McIvor [1966] Director/Shop Manager

Farralls Transport (Properties) Limited
Incorporated: 19 May 2014 *Employees:* 84
Net Worth: £2,081,266 *Total Assets:* £9,283,243
Registered Office: Unit 2 Second Avenue, Deeside Industrial Park, Deeside, Flintshire, CH5 2NX
Activities: Operation of warehousing and storage facilities for land transport activities
Officers: Elaine Ann Farrall [1963] Director; Mark William Farrall [1964] Director; Michael Charles Farrall [1961] Director

Farrel Limited
Incorporated: 14 June 1985 *Employees:* 168
Net Worth: £5,318,441 *Total Assets:* £35,986,620
Registered Office: P O Box 27, Queensway Castleton, Rochdale, Lancs, OL11 2PF
Activities: Manufacture of plastics and rubber machinery
Officers: Peter Gaskell [1955] Director; Harald Wilhelm Friedrich Keuter [1967] Director [German]; Mark Meulbroek [1977] Director [Dutch]; Alan Newell [1962] Finance Director; Ian Wilson [1969] Business Unit Director

Fayrefield Foods Limited
Incorporated: 1 June 1982 *Employees:* 151
Net Worth: £21,034,008 *Total Assets:* £48,261,884
Registered Office: Englesea House, Barthomley Road, Crewe, Cheshire, CW1 5UF
Activities: Wholesale of dairy products, eggs and edible oils and fats
Parent: The Fayrefield Group Limited
Officers: Philip Anthony Austin, Secretary; Michelle Fenney [1974] Director; Daniel David Harper [1972] Director/Dairy Products Executive; Nicholas Anthony Hilton [1953] Director/Dairy Products Executive; John Douglas Kerr [1946] Director/Dairy Products Executive; Niel John Kerr [1977] Director/Executive; David Neil McFarlane [1962] Director; Michael Reade [1970] Food Services Director; Timothy Marcus Robinson [1964] Director/Dairy Products Executive; Ashley Weaver [1966] Group Financial Director; Leslie John Wright [1955] Director/Executive

The Fayrefield Group Limited
Incorporated: 28 November 1990 *Employees:* 193
Net Worth: £22,099,718 *Total Assets:* £85,382,368
Registered Office: Englesea House, Barthomley Road, Crewe Green, Crewe, Cheshire, CW1 5UF
Activities: Activities of head offices
Major Shareholder: John Douglas Kerr
Officers: Philip Anthony Austin, Secretary; Jens Bruun Haugstrup [1961] Director/Executive [Danish]; Nicholas Anthony Hilton [1953] Director/Dairy Products Executive; John Douglas Kerr [1946] Director/Dairy Products Executive; Wade Martin [1946] Director/Finance Executive; David Neil McFarlane [1962] Director; Markus Muhlbacher [1977] Director [German]; Peter Nielsen [1966] Director [Danish]; Timothy Marcus Robinson [1964] Director; Ashley Weaver [1966] Group Financial Director; Leslie John Wright [1955] Director/Executive

FDC (Holdings) Limited
Incorporated: 26 February 1997 *Employees:* 40
Net Worth: £4,872,198 *Total Assets:* £8,505,047
Registered Office: Charter House, Pittman Way, Preston, Lancs, PR2 9ZD
Activities: Operation of warehousing and storage facilities for land transport activities
Parent: Freight Distribution Consultants Limited
Officers: Carol Edith Allen, Secretary; Peter James Allen [1969] Managing Director; Stephen James Allen [1962] Director

FDML Holdings Limited
Incorporated: 5 December 1956
Net Worth: £396,963,264 *Total Assets:* £396,963,264
Registered Office: Manchester International Office Centre, Styal Road, Manchester, M22 5TN
Activities: Activities of other holding companies n.e.c.
Parent: Federal-Mogul Limited
Officers: Beverley Ann Sutton, Secretary; Elaine Janet Milner [1962] Director/Finance Manager

Federal Capital Limited
Incorporated: 6 March 2012 *Employees:* 4
Net Worth: £3,665,552 *Total Assets:* £7,993,418
Registered Office: 14a Old Marsh Farm Barns, Welsh Road, Sealand, Deeside, Flintshire, CH5 2LY
Activities: Financial intermediation not elsewhere classified
Major Shareholder: Matthew Charles Plumridge
Officers: Christopher Mark Angrave [1974] Director; Matthew Charles Plumridge [1978] Director

Federal-Mogul Asia Investments Limited
Incorporated: 29 August 2013
Net Worth: £52,806,948 *Total Assets:* £52,806,948
Registered Office: c/o Federal-Mogul Limited, Manchester International Office Centre, Styal Road, Manchester, M22 5TN
Activities: Activities of other holding companies n.e.c.
Parent: Icahn Enterprises L.P.
Officers: Beverley Ann Sutton, Secretary; Christoph Henrik Narten [1972] Director/General Counsel [German]

Federal-Mogul Global Growth Limited
Incorporated: 23 October 1997
Net Worth: £578,622,272 *Total Assets:* £1,026,062,208
Registered Office: Suite 14, Manchester International Office Centre, Styal Road, Manchester, M22 5TN
Activities: Activities of other holding companies n.e.c.
Parent: Icahn Enterprises L.P.
Officers: Beverley Ann Sutton, Secretary; Elaine Janet Milner [1962] Director/Finance Manager; Christoph Henrik Narten [1972] Director/General Counsel [German]

Federal-Mogul Limited
Incorporated: 12 February 1920 *Employees:* 596
Net Worth: £580,897,856 *Total Assets:* £606,361,792
Registered Office: Suite 14, Manchester International Office Centre, Styal Road, Manchester, M22 5TN
Activities: Manufacture of other parts and accessories for motor vehicles
Parent: Federal-Mogul Global Growth Limited
Officers: Beverley Ann Sutton, Secretary; Elaine Janet Milner [1962] Director/Finance Manager; Christoph Henrik Narten [1972] Director/General Counsel [German]

Federal-Mogul Valvetrain Limited
Incorporated: 28 November 2014
Net Worth: £38,363,536 *Total Assets:* £48,461,756
Registered Office: c/o Federal-Mogul Limited, Manchester International Office Centre, Styal Road, Manchester, M22 5TN
Activities: Manufacture of other parts and accessories for motor vehicles
Parent: Icahn Enterprises L.P.
Officers: Beverley Ann Sutton, Secretary; Elaine Janet Milner [1962] Director/Finance Manager; Christoph Henrik Narten [1972] Director/General Counsel [German]

Federation of Jewish Services
Incorporated: 27 June 2006 *Employees:* 375
Net Worth: £13,685,884 *Total Assets:* £14,292,365
Registered Office: Heathlands Drive, Prestwich, Manchester, M25 9SB
Activities: Residential care activities for the elderly and disabled
Officers: Leslie Kay, Secretary; Mark Isaac Adlestone [1959] Director; Julie Vanessa Besbrode [1971] Director/Business Consultant; David Howard Eventhall [1963] Director; Deborah Rachael Hamburger [1954] Director; Howard David Joseph [1961] Director/Self Employed; Leslie Kay [1933] Director/Retired; Michael Ernest Sciama [1958] Director; Bernard Max Yaffe [1954] Director/Retired

Fedex Trade Networks Transport & Brokerage (UK) Limited
Incorporated: 9 April 2009 *Employees:* 39
Net Worth: £4,887,136 *Total Assets:* £7,487,246
Registered Office: Unit 2, Building 303, World Freight Terminal, Manchester Airport, Manchester, M90 5UJ
Activities: Freight air transport
Parent: Fedex Corporation
Officers: Christian Blain [1960] Director/Business Executive [French]; Michael Edward Hagan [1958] Director/Business Executive [American]; Thomas Lawrence Holland [1957] Director/Business Executive [American]; Dr Udo Lange [1971] Director/Business Executive [German]; James Tierney [1960] Director/Business Manager

FEI UK Limited
Incorporated: 4 May 1989 *Employees:* 44
Net Worth: £4,427,111 *Total Assets:* £27,868,926
Registered Office: 3rd Floor, 1 Ashley Road, Altrincham, Cheshire, WA14 2DT
Activities: Repair of electronic and optical equipment
Parent: Thermo Fisher Scientific Inc.
Officers: Rhona Gregg, Secretary; Lucie Mary Katja Grant [1976] Director/Solicitor; Nicholas Ince [1982] Director/Accountant; David John Norman [1960] Director/Chartered Accountant; Rodrick John Shipley [1961] Director/VP Sales and Services Europe

Fender Care Limited
Incorporated: 14 June 1988 *Employees:* 79
Net Worth: £1,200,886 *Total Assets:* £52,821,108
Registered Office: P O Box 4, Fisher House, Barrow in Furness, Cumbria, LA14 1HR
Activities: Other business support service activities n.e.c.
Parent: Fender Care Marine Solutions Limited
Officers: James Henry John Marsh, Secretary; Paul Cansdale [1972] Finance Director; Lara Emma Elteb Griffin-Sparrow [1972] Director; Nicholas Paul Henry [1961] Director; Stuart Charles Kilpatrick [1962] Director; Martijn Hemmo Muntingh [1976] Director [Dutch]; Mark Charles Nicholls [1963] Director

Fender Care Marine Ltd
Incorporated: 4 July 1995 *Employees:* 15
Net Worth: £15,309,649 *Total Assets:* £58,681,588
Registered Office: P O Box 4, Fisher House, Barrow in Furness, Cumbria, LA14 1HR
Activities: Other business support service activities n.e.c.
Parent: Fender Care Marine Services Group Limited
Officers: James Henry John Marsh, Secretary; Paul Cansdale [1972] Financial Director; Nicholas Paul Henry [1961] Director; Stuart Charles Kilpatrick [1962] Finance Director; Martijn Hemmo Muntingh [1976] Director [Dutch]; Mark Charles Nicholls [1963] Director; Elizabeth Anne Skinner [1978] Director/Operations Manager

Fender Care Marine Services Group Limited
Incorporated: 16 August 2004
Net Worth: £349,109 *Total Assets:* £12,178,921
Registered Office: P O Box 4, Fisher House, Barrow in Furness, Cumbria, LA14 1HR
Activities: Activities of head offices
Parent: James Fisher Holdings UK Limited
Officers: James Henry John Marsh, Secretary; Nicholas Paul Henry [1961] Director; Stuart Charles Kilpatrick [1962] Finance Director; Mark Charles Nicholls [1963] Director

Fenwall Investments Limited
Incorporated: 30 April 1965 *Employees:* 5
Net Worth: £3,559,748 *Total Assets:* £12,649,739
Registered Office: c/o Newhall Group Ltd, Newhall Lane, Hoylake, Wirral, Merseyside, CH47 4BQ
Activities: Other letting and operating of own or leased real estate
Major Shareholder: Dr Andrew Kenneth Wissett Douglas
Officers: Christine Ann Blackford, Secretary; Christine Ann Blackford [1954] Finance Director; Dr Andrew Kenneth Wissett Douglas [1960] Director; Bryan Leon Douglas-Dala [1971] Marketing Director; Victoria Jane Jackson [1973] Director/Personnel Manager

Fenwell Estates Ltd
Incorporated: 2 April 2003
Net Worth: £2,328,094 *Total Assets:* £6,755,049
Registered Office: c/o Duncan Sheard Glass, Castle Chambers, 43 Castle Street, Liverpool, L2 9TL
Activities: Development of building projects
Major Shareholder: Damian Silverbeck
Officers: Damian Silverbeck [1976] Director/Surveyor

Fenwick Street Investments Limited
Incorporated: 29 January 1957 *Employees:* 3
Net Worth: £9,959,459 *Total Assets:* £14,986,649
Registered Office: 12 Molyneux Way, Aintree, Sefton, Merseyside, L10 2JA
Activities: Buying and selling of own real estate
Officers: Margaret Gough, Secretary; Marcus Julian Romaine Bleasdale [1962] Director

Feralco (UK) Limited
Incorporated: 14 August 2000 *Employees:* 27
Net Worth: £1,379,000 *Total Assets:* £8,724,000
Registered Office: Ditton Road, Widnes, Cheshire, WA8 0PH
Activities: Other business support service activities n.e.c.
Officers: Stephen Robert Childs [1961] Managing Director; Paul Hugh Foy [1965] Director

Ferno (UK) Limited
Incorporated: 8 April 1971 *Employees:* 60
Net Worth: £9,600,280 *Total Assets:* £10,849,310
Registered Office: Ferno House, Stubs Beck Lane, Cleckheaton, W Yorks, BD19 4TZ
Activities: Manufacture of medical and dental instruments and supplies
Officers: Elroy Edwin Bourgraf [1931] Director/Management [American]; Joseph George Bourgraf [1960] Director/Company President [American]; Jonathan Stewart Ellis [1968] Managing Director; Gary Hiles [1950] Director/Company Vice President [American]; Malgorzata Anna Nozykowska-Merkle [1969] Finance Director [Polish]; Paul Charles Riordan [1944] Director/Chief Financial Officer [American]

Ferranti Technologies (Group) Limited
Incorporated: 30 March 1999 *Employees:* 153
Net Worth: £9,488,000 *Total Assets:* £40,778,000
Registered Office: Cairo House, Greenacres Road, Waterhead, Oldham, Lancs, OL4 3JA
Activities: Activities of head offices
Parent: Elbit Systems UK Limited
Officers: Eliezer Brook [1953] Director [Israeli]; Paul Robert Owen [1968] Director; Tracey Louisa Pollinger [1970] Director

Ferranti Technologies Limited
Incorporated: 15 September 1994 *Employees:* 153
Net Worth: £19,102,000 *Total Assets:* £48,392,000
Registered Office: Cairo House, Greenacres Road, Waterhead, Oldham, Lancs, OL4 3JA
Activities: Other manufacturing n.e.c.
Parent: Ferranti Technologies (Holdings) Ltd
Officers: Martin Clifford St John Fausset [1957] Director; Shmuel Maman [1966] BU Senior Director Western Europe [Israeli]; Paul Robert Owen [1968] Director; Tracey Louisa Pollinger [1970] Director; Adi Raviv [1976] Programme Director [Israeli]; Yoram Shmuely [1960] Director/EVP & GM [Israeli]; Graham Robert Trevarthen [1955] Director

Ferratum UK Ltd
Incorporated: 18 August 2010 *Employees:* 29
Net Worth Deficit: £1,999,612 *Total Assets:* £15,223,117
Registered Office: Suite 318, 25 Goodlass Road, Liverpool, L24 9HJ
Activities: Credit granting by non-deposit taking finance houses and other specialist consumer credit grantors
Major Shareholder: Jorma Olavi Jokela
Officers: Anthony Stephen Gundersen [1960] Director; Saku Eero Juhana Timonen [1972] Director/Chief Operational Officer (COO) of JT Family [Finnish]

Feversham Education Trust
Incorporated: 7 July 2011 *Employees:* 257
Net Worth: £26,079,000 *Total Assets:* £28,504,000
Registered Office: Feversham Education Trust, Deanstones Lane, Queensbury, Bradford, BD13 2AS
Activities: General secondary education
Officers: Shakoor Ahmed [1983] Director; Waqas Ahmed [1984] Director/Accountant; John Geoffrey Ashton [1945] Director; Professor Irfan Awan [1967] Director; Ali Jan Haider [1963] Director; Sajjad Khan [1974] Director; Sarfraz Khan [1971] Director; Rahil Qasim [1985] Director/Accountant; Professor Ihtesham Rehman [1964] Director

FHC (Holdings) Limited
Incorporated: 1 September 1966 *Employees:* 6
Net Worth: £5,604,000 *Total Assets:* £10,412,000
Registered Office: Cestrian Court, Eastgate Way, Manor Park, Runcorn, Cheshire, WA7 1NT
Activities: Activities of head offices
Officers: Marc James Gerard Crouton [1959] Director [French]; Christopher Paul Harrison [1966] Managing Director; Mats Christer Henriksson [1967] Director [Swedish]; David Michael Kehoe [1984] Finance Director; Mark Henry Kirkup [1969] Director; Frank Lucassen [1972] Director [German]; Niamh Matic [1973] Director [Irish]

Fibreforce Composites Limited
Incorporated: 5 June 1929 *Employees:* 48
Net Worth: £4,711,000 *Total Assets:* £8,333,000
Registered Office: Fairoak Lane, Whitehouse, Runcorn, Cheshire, WA7 3DU
Activities: Manufacture of plastic plates, sheets, tubes and profiles
Parent: Exel Composites PLC
Officers: Richard Thomas, Secretary; Callum Anthony Gough [1960] Director/General Manager; John Robert Hartley [1959] Director/Group Technical Manager; Riku Kytömäki [1971] Director [Finnish]

Fichtner Consulting Engineers Limited
Incorporated: 25 April 1991 *Employees:* 119
Net Worth: £8,979,998 *Total Assets:* £13,900,118
Registered Office: Kingsgate, Wellington Road North, Stockport, Cheshire, SK4 1LW
Activities: Other engineering activities
Parent: Fichtner GmbH & Co KG
Officers: Elizabeth Edgley, Secretary; Duncan Stuart Abernethy [1977] Director/Business Development Manager; Phineas Mark Eddy [1960] Director/Consulting Engineer; Elizabeth Louise Edgley [1965] Finance Director; Nicholas Searle Gamble [1946] Director/Consulting Engineer; Robert John Hawcutt [1974] Director/Consultant Engineer; Tilman Herzig [1971] Director [German]; Hans Kalb [1951] Director/Engineer [German]; Stephen Mark Othen [1972] Director/Consultant; Dr Edmund John Weatherby [1959] Director/Consultant; Stuart Andrew Wilson [1970] Director/Senior Consultant [Australian]

Fideliti Ltd
Incorporated: 11 May 2005 *Employees:* 31
Net Worth: £893,197 *Total Assets:* £19,733,244
Registered Office: Unit 1a Birchwood One Business Park, Dewhurst Road, Birchwood, Warrington, Cheshire, WA3 7GB
Activities: Other business support service activities n.e.c.
Shareholders: Geoffrey Dennis Whittaker; Joanne Louise Whittaker
Officers: LEA Done-Jackson, Secretary; Geoffrey Dennis Whittaker [1970] Director; Joanne Louise Whittaker [1977] Director/Administrator

Figurehead Homes Limited
Incorporated: 5 February 2010 *Employees:* 4
Net Worth Deficit: £4,236,030 *Total Assets:* £24,872,736
Registered Office: Greenbank House, 152 Wigan Lane, Wigan, Lancs, WN1 2LA
Activities: Development of building projects
Officers: Christopher John Baybutt [1953] Director/Chartered Surveyor; David James Baybutt [1947] Director/Statutory Surveyor; John Melling [1949] Director

Financial & Legal Insurance Company Ltd
Incorporated: 17 March 1995 *Employees:* 24
Net Worth: £2,997,129 *Total Assets:* £18,762,462
Registered Office: 1 Lakeside, Cheadle Royal Business Park, Cheadle, Cheshire, SK8 3GW
Activities: Non-life insurance
Major Shareholder: Nicholas David Garner
Officers: Serena Angela Garner, Secretary; Susan Margaret Baldwin [1964] Director; Nicholas David Garner [1978] Director; Anthony Scott Hughes [1967] Director; Michael Francis Timmons [1956] Director

Finbrook Limited
Incorporated: 22 July 2009 *Employees:* 145
Net Worth: £4,637,451 *Total Assets:* £11,529,992
Registered Office: 28 Anglesey Drive, Poynton, Stockport, Cheshire, SK12 1BU
Activities: Residential care activities for the elderly and disabled
Officers: John Arthur Odell, Secretary; John Arthur Odell [1947] Director/Chartered Accountant; Kathryn Joan Odell [1946] Director/Care Home Proprietor

Findel Education Limited
Incorporated: 24 September 1973 *Employees:* 388
Net Worth: £720,000 *Total Assets:* £72,437,000
Registered Office: Church Bridge House, Henry Street, Accrington, Lancs, BB5 4EE
Activities: Retail sale via mail order houses or via Internet
Parent: Findel PLC
Officers: Mark Ashcroft, Secretary; Stuart Murdoch Caldwell [1972] Director; Chris David Mahady [1967] Operations Director; Philip Binns Maudsley [1960] Director; Mark Whittaker [1967] Director

Findel P.L.C.
Incorporated: 11 May 1955 *Employees:* 1,871
Net Worth: £39,681,000 *Total Assets:* £394,040,992
Registered Office: Church Bridge House, Henry Street, Accrington, Lancs, BB5 4EE
Activities: Activities of head offices
Officers: Mark Ashcroft, Secretary; Gregor Frank Ball [1963] Director; Ian Michael Burke [1956] Director; Stuart Murdoch Caldwell [1972] Director; Francois Regis Coumau [1971] Director/General Manager [French]; William Grimsey [1952] Director; Philip Binns Maudsley [1960] Director; Elaine Margaret O' Donnell [1970] Director

Fine Decor Wallcoverings Limited
Incorporated: 20 November 2000 *Employees:* 216
Net Worth Deficit: £281,920 *Total Assets:* £15,036,958
Registered Office: Victoria Mill, Macclesfield Road, Holmes Chapel, Crewe, Cheshire, CW4 7PA
Activities: Manufacture of wallpaper
Shareholder: James Grandberg
Officers: James Grandberg [1951] Director/President [American]; Kenneth Grandberg [1948] Director/President CEO [American]

Finemere Limited
Incorporated: 9 May 1972
Net Worth: £7,856,672 *Total Assets:* £9,850,761
Registered Office: Suite 17b, 111 Piccadilly, Manchester, M1 2HY
Activities: Other letting and operating of own or leased real estate
Officers: Nigel Alliance, Secretary/Director; Morag Elizabeth Hoyland, Secretary; Nigel Alliance [1935] Director; Joshua Adam Senior [1990] Director/Property Investments

Finsa UK Limited
Incorporated: 4 July 1990 *Employees:* 21
Net Worth: £2,686,000 *Total Assets:* £8,203,000
Registered Office: 15 Ocean Park, Dock Road, Birkenhead, Merseyside, CH41 1HW
Activities: Wholesale of wood, construction materials and sanitary equipment
Officers: Virgilio Romero, Secretary; Jose Carballo [1952] Director [Spanish]; Virgilio Romero [1957] Commercial Director [Spanish]; Rafael Federico Willisch [1957] Managing Director [Spanish]

Fircroft Engineering Services Holdings Limited
Incorporated: 22 May 2012 *Employees:* 642
Net Worth Deficit: £30,228,000 *Total Assets:* £250,128,000
Registered Office: Lingley House, 120 Birchwood Boulevard, Birchwood, Warrington, Cheshire, WA3 7QH
Activities: Activities of other holding companies n.e.c.
Officers: Louise Morrison, Secretary; Michael Cohen [1950] Director; Philip Allan Gore-Randall [1952] Director; Stuart Andrew Hall [1967] Director; Keith Hughes [1953] Director/Mechanical Engineer; John Morton Johnson [1939] Director; Johnathan James Johnson [1972] Director; Steve O'Hare [1975] Director/Private Equity

Fircroft Engineering Services Limited
Incorporated: 18 December 1978 *Employees:* 642
Net Worth: £66,034,000 *Total Assets:* £224,022,000
Registered Office: Lingley House, 120 Birchwood Boulevard, Birchwood, Warrington, Cheshire, WA3 7QH
Activities: Support activities for petroleum and natural gas mining
Parent: Fircroft Engineering Services Holdings Limited
Officers: Louise Morrison, Secretary; Michael Cohen [1950] Director/Chartered Accountant; Stuart Andrew Hall [1967] Director; Keith Hughes [1953] Recruitment Director; John Morton Johnson [1939] Director; Johnathan James Johnson [1972] Director/Manager

Fircroft Technical Services UK Limited
Incorporated: 30 March 2016
Net Worth: £39,940 *Total Assets:* £8,324,561
Registered Office: Lingley House, 120 Birchwood Point, Birchwood Boulevard, Birchwood, Warrington, Cheshire, WA3 7QH
Activities: Dormant company
Parent: Fircroft Engineering Services Limited
Officers: Stuart Andrew Hall [1967] Director; Johnathan James Johnson [1972] Director/Operations Manager

Firow Limited
Incorporated: 28 May 1982 *Employees:* 45
Net Worth: £6,533,402 *Total Assets:* £20,415,092
Registered Office: Firow House, Tarporley Road, Sandiway, Cheshire, CW8 2ES
Activities: Renting and leasing of trucks and other heavy vehicles
Major Shareholder: Paul Anthony Rowley
Officers: Andrew Bromley, Secretary/Director; Andrew Bromley [1961] Managing Director; Andrew John Rowley [1965] Director; Mark Rowley [1981] Director; Paul Anthony Rowley [1954] Director; Gary Steven Unsworth [1966] Director

Firsdell Ltd
Incorporated: 3 March 2011
Net Worth: £11,500,000 *Total Assets:* £75,400,000
Registered Office: Hilmore House, Gain Lane, Bradford, W Yorks, BD3 7DL
Activities: Development of building projects
Parent: Wm Morrison Supermarkets Holdings Limited
Officers: Jonathan James Burke, Secretary; Trevor John Strain [1975] Director/Chief Financial Officer

First Ark Limited
Incorporated: 25 June 2010 *Employees:* 444
Net Worth: £50,310,000 *Total Assets:* £249,808,000
Registered Office: Lakeview, Kings Business Park, Prescot, Merseyside, L34 1PJ
Activities: Activities of head offices
Officers: Sharon Marsh, Secretary; Philip Gerard Cusack [1954] Director/Chair; Tracey Johnson [1964] Executive Director - Customer Experience; John Anthony Mallalieu [1970] Director/Chief Executive Officer; Andrew Robert Orrey [1962] Director; Professor Peter Ward Roberts [1947] Professor Emeritus and Non-Executive Director; Helen White [1977] Director/Consultant

First Choice Dental Limited
Incorporated: 22 September 2006 *Employees:* 77
Net Worth: £17,642,064 *Total Assets:* £28,066,132
Registered Office: Europa House, Europa Trading Estate, Stoneclough Road, Kearsley, Manchester, M26 1GG
Activities: Dental practice activities
Parent: Integrated Dental Holdings Limited
Officers: Leo Damian Carroll, Secretary; Clifford Gwyn Davies [1966] Clinical Director; Manish Prasad [1972] Clinical Director; Tom Riall [1960] Director; Mohammed Omar Shafi Khan [1974] Director/Chief Financial Officer; Krista Nyree Whitley [1970] Clinical Director

First Manchester Limited
Incorporated: 12 May 1993 *Employees:* 1,839
Net Worth Deficit: £25,094,000 *Total Assets:* £88,840,000
Registered Office: Wallshaw Street, Oldham, Lancs, OL1 3TR
Activities: Other passenger land transport
Parent: First North West Limited
Officers: Michael Hampson, Secretary; David Brian Alexander [1965] Regional Managing Director; Ian Humphreys [1960] Director; Jeremy Peach [1960] Director/Bus Driver

The First Milk Cheese Company Limited
Incorporated: 2 August 2006 *Employees:* 227
Net Worth: £21,198,000 *Total Assets:* £92,761,000
Registered Office: The Lake District Creamery, Station Road, Aspatria, Wigton, Cumbria, CA7 2AR
Activities: Butter and cheese production
Officers: Angus John Somerville Waugh, Secretary; Shelagh Hancock [1967] Director/Chief Executive; Greg Stewart Iain Jardine [1976] Director

First Pioneer Bus Limited
Incorporated: 9 October 1984 *Employees:* 90
Net Worth: £984,000 *Total Assets:* £7,329,000
Registered Office: Wallshaw Street, Oldham, Lancs, OL1 3TR
Activities: Other passenger land transport
Parent: First Manchester Limited
Officers: Michael Hampson, Secretary; David Brian Alexander [1965] Regional Managing Director; Ian Humphreys [1960] Director; Jeremy Peach [1960] Director/Bus Driver

First Technical Recruitment Limited
Incorporated: 6 November 1997 *Employees:* 62
Net Worth: £1,462,803 *Total Assets:* £13,533,840
Registered Office: Parry House, Birchwood Boulevard, Birchwood, Warrington, Cheshire, WA3 7QU
Activities: Temporary employment agency activities
Shareholders: Andrew Cartledge; Stephen Farthing
Officers: Stephen Farthing, Secretary; Andrew Cartledge [1965] Director; Stephen Farthing [1969] Director; John Anthony Urpi [1955] Director/MD

First Travel Solutions Limited
Incorporated: 28 November 1985 *Employees:* 104
Net Worth: £14,671,000 *Total Assets:* £21,339,000
Registered Office: Unit 20 Time Technology Park, Blackburn Road, Simonstone, Burnley, Lancs, BB12 7TG
Activities: Other urban, suburban or metropolitan passenger land transport (not underground, metro or similar)
Parent: First Beeline Buses Limited
Officers: Michael Hampson, Secretary; Richard Kirk [1972] Director; Andrew Mark Scholey [1961] Director; Julia Michelle White [1977] Accountant/Director

First Water Limited
Incorporated: 19 April 2002 *Employees:* 3
Net Worth: £4,761,000 *Total Assets:* £9,825,000
Registered Office: 997 Manchester Road, Ashton under Lyne, Lancs, OL7 0ED
Activities: Other manufacturing n.e.c.
Parent: Scapa Group PLC
Officers: Wendy Baker, Secretary; Wendy Dickinson [1967] Director/Accountant; Oskar Zahn [1964] Director

First Water Ramsbury Limited
Incorporated: 19 April 2002 *Employees:* 68
Net Worth: £1,186,000 *Total Assets:* £6,734,000
Registered Office: 997 Manchester Road, Ashton under Lyne, Lancs, OL7 0ED
Activities: Other manufacturing n.e.c.
Parent: First Water Ltd
Officers: Wendy Baker, Secretary; Wendy Dickinson [1967] Director/Accountant; Oskar Zahn [1964] Director

Firstnet Data Centres (Leeds) LLP
Incorporated: 11 May 2007
Net Worth: £9,083,623 *Total Assets:* £10,922,351
Registered Office: City View House, 5 Union Street, Ardwick, Manchester, M12 4JD
Officers: Jason Charles Beresford [1971] Member; Stephen Leahy [1966] Member; Lisa Leahy [1974] LLP Member

Firwood Timber & Plywood Co. Limited
Incorporated: 20 May 1975 *Employees:* 81
Net Worth: £6,880,968 *Total Assets:* £8,485,025
Registered Office: Burscough Industrial Estate, Higgins Lane, Burscough, Ormskirk, Lancs, L40 8JS
Activities: Sawmilling and planing of wood
Major Shareholder: Peter Kenneth Booth
Officers: Robert Paul Owens, Secretary; Peter Kenneth Booth [1948] Director; Jane Margaret Johnson [1976] Director

Fiserv (Europe) Limited
Incorporated: 6 February 1990 *Employees:* 160
Net Worth: £4,533,000 *Total Assets:* £56,625,000
Registered Office: Eversheds House, 70 Great Bridgewater Street, Manchester, M1 5ES
Activities: Other information technology service activities
Parent: Checkfree Solutions Limited
Officers: Derek John Dyamond [1962] Finance Director; David Gillingham [1974] Director, Finance; Peter Lincoln Holbrook [1969] Director/Chief Financial Officer, International Group, FISE [American]; John James Smith [1959] Managing Director, Fiserv EMEA

Fiserv UK Holding Limited
Incorporated: 6 November 2014
Net Worth: £8,504,821 *Total Assets:* £9,892,287
Registered Office: Eversheds House, 70 Great Bridgewater Street, Manchester, M1 5ES
Activities: Other information technology service activities
Parent: Fiserv, Inc.
Officers: Derek John Dyamond [1962] Finance Director; David Gillingham [1974] Director, Finance; Peter Lincoln Holbrook [1969] Director/Chief Financial Officer, International Group, FISE [American]; John James Smith [1959] Managing Director, Fiserv EMEA

Fiserv Worldwide Holdings Limited
Incorporated: 6 November 2014
Net Worth: £22,490,268 *Total Assets:* £23,887,068
Registered Office: Eversheds House, 70 Great Bridgewater Street, Manchester, M1 5ES
Activities: Other information technology service activities
Parent: Fiserv UK Holding Limited
Officers: Derek John Dyamond [1962] Finance Director; David Gillingham [1974] Director, Finance; Peter Lincoln Holbrook [1969] Director/Chief Financial Officer, International Group, FISE [American]; John James Smith [1959] Managing Director, Fiserv EMEA

Fishawack Communications Limited
Incorporated: 25 October 2000 *Employees:* 91
Net Worth: £6,808,192 *Total Assets:* £21,086,952
Registered Office: 3 Booths Park, Booths Hall, Knutsford, Cheshire, WA16 8GS
Activities: Other professional, scientific and technical activities n.e.c.
Parent: Fishawack Holdings Limited
Officers: Jenifer Kirkland, Secretary; Dr Rachel Davies [1970] Director; Oliver John Dennis [1971] Director; Gail Louise Harvey [1964] Managing Director; Jenifer Kirkland [1976] Director; Dominic Thomas Miller [1970] Director

Fishawack Investment Limited
Incorporated: 2 November 2012
Registered Office: 3 Booths Park, Booths Hall, Knutsford, Cheshire, WA16 8GS
Activities: Activities of head offices
Parent: Fishawack Group Limited
Officers: Jenifer Kirkland, Secretary; Dr Rachel Davies [1970] Director; Oliver John Dennis [1971] Director/Chief Executive Officer; Gail Louise Flockhart [1964] Managing Director; Jenifer Kirkland [1976] Director; Dominic Thomas Miller [1970] Director/Chief Finance Officer

Fishawack Limited
Incorporated: 5 December 2007
Registered Office: 3 Booths Park, Booths Hall, Knutsford, Cheshire, WA16 8GS
Activities: Activities of head offices
Parent: Fishawack Investment Limited
Officers: Jenifer Kirkland, Secretary; Dr Rachel Davies [1970] Director; Oliver John Dennis [1971] Non-Executive Director; Gail Louise Flockhart [1964] Managing Director; Jenifer Kirkland [1976] Director; Dominic Thomas Miller [1970] Director

Fishawack Medical Communications Limited
Incorporated: 2 November 2012 *Employees:* 224
Net Worth Deficit: £6,239,771 *Total Assets:* £26,994,276
Registered Office: 3 Booths Park, Booths Hall, Knutsford, Cheshire, WA16 8GS
Activities: Activities of head offices
Parent: Aghoco 1476 Limited
Officers: Jenifer Kirkland, Secretary; Dr Rachel Davies [1970] Director; Oliver John Dennis [1971] Director/Chief Executive Officer; Gail Louise Flockhart [1964] Managing Director; Jenifer Kirkland [1976] Director; Dominic Thomas Miller [1970] Director/Chief Finance Officer

James Fisher (Aberdeen) Limited
Incorporated: 16 November 2005
Net Worth: £5,636,814 *Total Assets:* £32,731,682
Registered Office: P O Box 4, Fisher House, Michaelson Road, Barrow in Furness, Cumbria, LA14 1HR
Activities: Activities of head offices
Parent: James Fisher and Sons PLC
Officers: James Henry John Marsh, Secretary; Nicholas Paul Henry [1961] Director; Stuart Charles Kilpatrick [1962] Director

James Fisher and Sons Public Limited Company
Incorporated: 2 February 1926 *Employees:* 2,724
Net Worth: £285,000,000 *Total Assets:* £618,600,000
Registered Office: P O Box 4, Fisher House, Barrow in Furness, Cumbria, LA14 1HR
Activities: Sea and coastal freight water transport
Officers: James Henry John Marsh, Secretary; Justin Richard Atkinson [1960] Director; Aedamar Ita Comiskey [1967] Director/Solicitor [Irish]; Fergus Hugh Stirling Graham [1973] Director; Nicholas Paul Henry [1961] Director; Stuart Charles Kilpatrick [1962] Director; David George Moorhouse CBE [1947] Director; Malcolm Stephen Paul [1951] Director/Chartered Accountant; Michael John Lawrence Salter [1947] Director

Fisher Clinical Services UK Limited
Incorporated: 9 November 2004 *Employees:* 651
Net Worth: £130,726,000 *Total Assets:* £159,240,992
Registered Office: 3rd Floor, 1 Ashley Road, Altrincham, Cheshire, WA14 2DT
Activities: Packaging activities
Parent: Fisher Scientific UK Holding Company 2
Officers: Rhona Gregg, Secretary; Lucie Mary Katja Grant [1976] Director/Solicitor; Nicholas Ince [1982] Director/Accountant; David John Norman [1960] Director/Chartered Accountant

James Fisher Everard Limited
Incorporated: 14 March 1956 *Employees:* 16
Net Worth: £13,035,734 *Total Assets:* £19,317,816
Registered Office: P O Box 4, Fisher House, Barrow in Furness, Cumbria, LA14 1HR
Activities: Sea and coastal freight water transport
Parent: James Fisher Tankships Holdings Limited
Officers: James Henry John Marsh, Secretary; Richard Douglas Burmeister [1956] Director; Neil Burns [1970] Fleet Director; Fiona Caroline Everard [1981] Managing Director; Nicholas Paul Henry [1961] Director; Stuart Charles Kilpatrick [1962] Director

James Fisher Fender Care Limited
Incorporated: 21 February 2005
Net Worth: £538,118 *Total Assets:* £36,385,148
Registered Office: P O Box 4, Fisher House, Barrow in Furness, Cumbria, LA14 1HR
Activities: Activities of head offices
Parent: James Fisher and Sons Public Limited Company
Officers: James Henry John Marsh, Secretary; Paul Cansdale [1972] Finance Director; Nicholas Paul Henry [1961] Director; Stuart Charles Kilpatrick [1962] Director

James Fisher Holdings UK Limited
Incorporated: 12 November 2015
Net Worth: £414,697 *Total Assets:* £51,661,944
Registered Office: P O Box 4, Fisher House, Michaelson Road, Barrow in Furness, Cumbria, LA14 1HR
Activities: Activities of head offices
Parent: James Fisher and Sons PLC
Officers: James Henry John Marsh, Secretary; Nicholas Paul Henry [1961] Director; Stuart Charles Kilpatrick [1962] Director

James Fisher Marine Services Limited
Incorporated: 6 July 2004 *Employees:* 148
Net Worth: £26,998,676 *Total Assets:* £78,675,328
Registered Office: P O Box 4, Fisher House, Michaelson Road, Barrow in Furness, Cumbria, LA14 1HR
Activities: Other information technology service activities
Parent: James Fisher and Sons Public Limited Company
Officers: James Henry John Marsh, Secretary; Richard Douglas Burmeister [1956] Director; Nicholas Paul Henry [1961] Director; Stuart Charles Kilpatrick [1962] Director; Paul Adam Scullion [1979] Finance Director

James Fisher MFE Limited
Incorporated: 14 May 2014 *Employees:* 33
Net Worth Deficit: £387,011 *Total Assets:* £19,796,088
Registered Office: P O Box 4, Fisher House, Barrow in Furness, Cumbria, LA14 1HR
Activities: Other service activities n.e.c.
Parent: James Fisher Offshore Limited
Officers: James Henry John Marsh, Secretary; Aidan Andrew Douglas [1967] Director; Nicholas Paul Henry [1961] Director; Stuart Charles Kilpatrick [1962] Director; Kenneth Robert Mackie [1961] Director; Graham Ronald James Murdoch [1967] Director

James Fisher Nuclear Holdings Limited
Incorporated: 29 June 2004
Net Worth: £20,572,002 *Total Assets:* £20,624,048
Registered Office: P O Box 4, Fisher House, Barrow in Furness, Cumbria, LA14 1HR
Activities: Activities of head offices
Parent: James Fisher and Sons Public Limited Company
Officers: James Henry John Marsh, Secretary; Nicholas Paul Henry [1961] Director; Stuart Charles Kilpatrick [1962] Director; Paul Michael Read [1956] Director; Jason Nicholas Washington [1965] Director/Accountant

Fisher Scientific Holding U.K., Limited
Incorporated: 17 January 1994
Net Worth: £22,351,000 *Total Assets:* £22,500,000
Registered Office: 3rd Floor, 1 Ashley Road, Altrincham, Cheshire, WA14 2DT
Activities: Activities of head offices
Parent: Fisher Scientific UK Holding Company Limited
Officers: Rhona Gregg, Secretary; Lucie Mary Katja Grant [1976] Director/Solicitor; Nicholas Ince [1982] Director/Accountant; David John Norman [1960] Director/Chartered Accountant

Fisher Scientific UK Holding Company 2
Incorporated: 20 April 2000
Net Worth: £106,346,000 *Total Assets:* £135,624,000
Registered Office: 3rd Floor, 1 Ashley Road, Altrincham, Cheshire, WA14 2DT
Activities: Activities of head offices
Parent: Fisher Scientific UK Holding Company Limited
Officers: Rhona Gregg, Secretary; Lucie Mary Katja Grant [1976] Director/Solicitor; Nicholas Ince [1982] Director/Accountant; David John Norman [1960] Director/Chartered Accountant

Fisher Scientific UK Holding Company Limited
Incorporated: 14 March 2000 *Employees:* 3
Net Worth: £227,588,000 *Total Assets:* £539,284,992
Registered Office: 3rd Floor, 1 Ashley Road, Altrincham, Cheshire, WA14 2DT
Activities: Activities of head offices
Parent: Thermo Fisher Scientific Inc.
Officers: Rhona Gregg, Secretary; Lucie Mary Katja Grant [1976] Director/Solicitor; Nicholas Ince [1982] Director/Accountant; David John Norman [1960] Director/Chartered Accountant

James Fisher Subtech Group Limited
Incorporated: 25 February 2015
Net Worth: £17,179,232 *Total Assets:* £19,753,288
Registered Office: P O Box 4, Fisher House, Michaelson Road, Barrow in Furness, Cumbria, LA14 1HR
Activities: Activities of head offices
Parent: James Fisher and Sons Public Limited Company
Officers: James Henry John Marsh, Secretary; Nicholas Paul Henry [1961] Director; Stuart Charles Kilpatrick [1962] Director

William Fishwick & Son Limited
Incorporated: 5 April 1956 *Employees:* 12
Net Worth: £16,851,880 *Total Assets:* £17,448,492
Registered Office: 1 Stanley Street, Chester, CH1 2LR
Activities: Buying and selling of own real estate
Shareholders: Peter Nigel Edwards; Judith Ann Edwards
Officers: Nicola Clare Cannock-Edwards [1985] Director; Holly de Sylva Fishwick [1984] Director; Judith Ann Edwards [1954] Director; Peter Nigel Edwards [1954] Director; Simon William Harvey Edwards [1987] Director; Stephanie Kate Edwards [1989] Director

Fitness First Clubs Limited
Incorporated: 5 June 1996 *Employees:* 785
Net Worth: £28,564,002 *Total Assets:* £67,292,752
Registered Office: Whelco Place, Enfield Street, Wigan, Lancs, WN5 8DB
Activities: Fitness facilities
Parent: Dave Whelan Sports Ltd
Officers: Scott Barry Best [1976] Director; Daniel Andrew Cornes [1976] Director/Chartered Accountant; David Whelan [1936] Director

Fitzwilton (U.K.) Limited
Incorporated: 25 May 1977
Net Worth Deficit: £81,895,000 *Total Assets:* £76,560,000
Registered Office: c/o SL Investment Management, One City Place, Queens Road, Chester, CH1 3BQ
Activities: Activities of head offices
Major Shareholder: Peter John Goulandris
Officers: Raymond James Crilly, Secretary; Kevin McGoran [1935] Director/Businessman [Irish]; David William James Roxburgh [1963] Director/Accountant [Irish]

Fives Landis Limited
Incorporated: 28 September 2005 *Employees:* 327
Net Worth: £25,890,000 *Total Assets:* £53,962,000
Registered Office: Eastburn Works, Skipton Road, Cross Hills, Keighley, W Yorks, BD20 7SD
Activities: Manufacture of electronic measuring, testing etc. equipment, not for industrial process control
Parent: Fives UK Holding Limited
Officers: Thalie Benveniste, Secretary; Raphael Constantin [1969] Director [French]; Michael Hall [1961] Managing Director; Denis-René André Hugelmann [1958] Director/Deputy Chief Executive Officer [French]; Frederic Daniel Sanchez [1960] Director [French]

Fives UK Holding Limited
Incorporated: 4 November 2002
Net Worth: £31,618,304 *Total Assets:* £79,935,576
Registered Office: Eastburn Works, Skipton Road, Cross Hills, Keighley, W Yorks, BD20 7SD
Activities: Activities of head offices
Parent: Fives S.A.
Officers: Maud Valerie Tortu, Secretary; Suresh Johannes Abye [1979] Director/Group Chief Financial Officer [French]; Frederic Daniel Sanchez [1960] Director [French]

FK Facades Limited
Incorporated: 24 November 1993 *Employees:* 86
Net Worth: £8,860,659 *Total Assets:* £25,052,544
Registered Office: Keenan House, 22-26 Stockport Road, Altrincham, Cheshire, WA15 8EX
Activities: Development of building projects
Parent: Norney Holdings Limited
Officers: Mark Jonathan Brown, Secretary; Paul Graham Bentley [1972] Commercial Director; Stephen William Hall [1965] Construction Director; Francis Anthony Keenan [1978] Managing Director; Francis Keenan [1954] Director/Chairman [Irish]; Philip Mark Norris [1977] Finance Director

FK Group Limited
Incorporated: 8 August 2011 *Employees:* 160
Net Worth: £11,653,075 *Total Assets:* £41,595,684
Registered Office: Keenan House, 22-26 Stockport Road, Altrincham, Cheshire, WA15 8EX
Activities: Activities of construction holding companies
Shareholders: Francis Keenan; Francis Anthony Keenan
Officers: Francis Anthony Keenan [1978] Director; Francis Keenan [1954] Director [Irish]

FL 360 Limited
Incorporated: 24 June 2014 *Employees:* 347
Net Worth: £17,932,508 *Total Assets:* £71,780,408
Registered Office: Speed Medical House, Matrix Park, Chorley, Lancs, PR7 7NA
Activities: Activities of head offices
Shareholders: Dr Rajnish Luthra; NNN Investments Limited
Officers: Graham Pulford [1969] Director

Flair Flooring Group Limited
Incorporated: 3 October 2014 *Employees:* 99
Net Worth: £4,361,534 *Total Assets:* £11,719,315
Registered Office: Etherow Works, Etherow Industrial Estate, Woolley Bridge Road, Hadfield, Glossop, Derbys, SK13 2NS
Activities: Wholesale of textiles
Major Shareholder: Neel Shah
Officers: Priti Figgs, Secretary; Tina Ruth Carswell [1972] Director; Dineshkumar Premchand Shah [1950] Director; Neel Shah [1982] Director; Rekha Shah [1952] Director

Flair Flooring Supplies Limited
Incorporated: 10 September 1982 *Employees:* 99
Net Worth: £4,005,357 *Total Assets:* £11,517,975
Registered Office: Etherow Works, Etherow Industrial Estate, Woolley Bridge Road, Hadfield, Glossop, Derbys, SK13 2NS
Activities: Manufacture of woven or tufted carpets and rugs
Officers: Helen Shah, Secretary; Tina Ruth Carswell [1972] Director/Accountant; Dineshkumar Premchand Shah [1950] Director; Neel Shah [1982] Director; Rekha Shah [1952] Director

Flairfax Limited
Incorporated: 22 April 1983
Net Worth: £11,488,987 *Total Assets:* £17,377,288
Registered Office: 43 Singleton Road, Salford, M7 4NA
Activities: Buying and selling of own real estate
Officers: Antony Victor Hodari, Secretary; Antony Victor Hodari [1957] Director/Property Rentals

The Flame Group Limited
Incorporated: 16 June 2014 *Employees:* 124
Net Worth: £8,725,000 *Total Assets:* £17,639,000
Registered Office: Rhosesmor Industrial Estate, Rhosesmor, Mold, Flintshire, CH7 6PZ
Activities: Activities of production holding companies
Shareholder: Dutch Flame Onroerend Goed BV
Officers: Patricia Thomas, Secretary; Timothy Michael Blois [1967] Director; Jan Johan Kamps [1951] Director [Dutch]; Neil Rowland Popham [1950] Director/Chairman; Patricia Thomas [1970] Finance Director

Flameproofings Limited
Incorporated: 27 July 1995 *Employees:* 70
Net Worth: £5,681,549 *Total Assets:* £9,705,329
Registered Office: Moss Rose Mill, Springfield Road, Kearsley, Bolton, Lancs, BL4 8JW
Activities: Finishing of textiles
Shareholders: Michael Ernest Sciama; Richard Nigel Sciama; Andrew Martin Sciama
Officers: Michael Ernest Sciama, Secretary/Director; Andrew Martin Sciama [1956] Director; Michael Ernest Sciama [1958] Director; Richard Nigel Sciama [1961] Director

Flanagan Group Limited
Incorporated: 20 June 2000 *Employees:* 145
Net Worth: £68,734 *Total Assets:* £15,099,109
Registered Office: Atlantic House, 143 Sefton Street, Liverpool, L8 5SN
Activities: Activities of construction holding companies
Officers: Kathleen Mary Flanagan, Secretary; Julian Flanagan [1971] Director; Kathleen Mary Flanagan [1942] Director; Paul Patrick Flanagan [1963] Director

Flanagan Property Services Ltd.
Incorporated: 12 February 1998 *Employees:* 3
Net Worth Deficit: £826,721 *Total Assets:* £8,372,900
Registered Office: Atlantic House, 143 Sefton Street, Liverpool, L8 5SN
Activities: Other letting and operating of own or leased real estate
Officers: Kathleen Mary Flanagan, Secretary; Julian Flanagan [1971] Director/Builder; Paul Patrick Flanagan [1963] Director/Builder

Flavour Warehouse Holdings Limited
Incorporated: 12 February 2015 *Employees:* 75
Net Worth: £34,104,656 *Total Assets:* £37,357,912
Registered Office: Global Way, Darwen, Lancs, BB3 0RW
Activities: Management consultancy activities other than financial management
Shareholders: Philip Eamon Boyle; Nathan Lee Walton
Officers: Philip Eamon Boyle [1984] Director; Nathan Lee Walton [1982] Director

Flavourfresh Salads Limited
Incorporated: 20 June 1997 *Employees:* 375
Net Worth: £5,843,946 *Total Assets:* £12,867,750
Registered Office: Aldergrove Centre, Marsh Road, Banks, Southport, Merseyside, PR9 8DX
Activities: Growing of vegetables and melons, roots and tubers
Officers: Keith James Ball, Secretary; Keith James Ball [1951] Director/Grower; Michael John Fradsham [1953] Managing Director; Charmay Denise Prout [1985] Director; Kathryn Frances Wright [1975] Director; Leonard Wright [1942] Director/Grower

Fleet and Plant Hire Limited
Incorporated: 23 December 2009
Net Worth: £3,732,000 *Total Assets:* £8,344,000
Registered Office: The Matchworks, Pavillions 3 and 4, Garston, Liverpool, L19 2PH
Activities: Renting and leasing of cars and light motor vehicles
Parent: Enterprise Managed Services Limited
Officers: Andrew Lee Milner [1969] Director/Chartered Engineer; Andrew Latham Nelson [1959] Finance Director

Fleetwood PPP Limited
Incorporated: 2 March 2001
Net Worth: £2,027,919 *Total Assets:* £10,636,291
Registered Office: Sceptre House, Sceptre Way, Bamber Bridge, Preston, Lancs, PR5 6AW
Activities: Other business support service activities n.e.c.
Parent: Eric Wright Group Limited
Officers: Deborah Jane Rawlinson, Secretary; Jeremy Peter Hartley [1965] Director/Chartered Accountant; John Howard Wilson [1965] Director

Fletchers Solicitors Limited
Incorporated: 15 March 2006 *Employees:* 318
Net Worth: £4,467,139 *Total Assets:* £24,816,704
Registered Office: Dukes House, 34 Hoghton Street, Southport, Merseyside, PR9 0PU
Activities: Solicitors
Shareholders: Robert Arnold Fletcher; Edward Barron Fletcher
Officers: Gary Douglas Carrington, Secretary; Gary Douglas Carrington [1969] Director; Adrian Kevin Denson [1972] Director/Solicitor; Paul John Duncanson [1957] Director; Edward Barron Fletcher [1974] Director/Solicitor; Robert Arnold Fletcher [1954] Director/Solicitor; Alexandra Hatchman [1974] Director/Chief of Operations; Richard Nigel Savage [1950] Director; Vikas Shah [1981] Director; Stephen David Threlfall [1965] Director/Solicitor

Fleur Telecom Limited
Incorporated: 17 December 2014 *Employees:* 18
Net Worth: £2,831,000 *Total Assets:* £7,220,000
Registered Office: Daisy House, Lindred Road Business Park, Nelson, Lancs, BB9 5SR
Activities: Other telecommunications activities
Parent: Daisy Intermediate Holdings Limited
Officers: David Lewis McGlennon, Secretary; Nathan Richard Marke [1970] Director; David Lewis McGlennon [1974] Director; Stephen Alan Smith [1963] Director

Flextronics Europe Limited
Incorporated: 8 June 1992
Net Worth: £58,970,000 *Total Assets:* £59,029,000
Registered Office: Stretton Green Distribution Centre, Langford Way, Warrington, Cheshire, WA4 4TQ
Activities: Activities of head offices
Officers: David Stewart, Secretary; Micheal Meades [1965] Director/General Manager; Stephanie Anne Shaw [1965] Finance Director

Flextronics Global Services (Manchester) Limited
Incorporated: 10 June 1986 *Employees:* 233
Net Worth: £41,395,764 *Total Assets:* £58,858,980
Registered Office: Stretton Green Distribution Centre, Langford Way, Warrington, Cheshire, WA4 4TQ
Activities: Repair of computers and peripheral equipment
Parent: Flex Ltd
Officers: David Stewart, Secretary; Mike Meades [1965] Director/General Manager; Stephanie Anne Shaw [1965] Finance Director

Flightcare Limited
Incorporated: 14 May 1991 *Employees:* 296
Net Worth: £4,954,711 *Total Assets:* £6,647,856
Registered Office: Adminstration Office, 22-32 Flemington Avenue, Liverpool, L4 8UD
Activities: Residential nursing care facilities
Shareholders: Nurdin Gulamhusein Ajania; Shehnaz Nurdin Ajania
Officers: Amin Dhanjee, Secretary/Chartered Accountant; Amin Dhanjee [1959] Director/Chartered Accountant; Farah Samanani [1977] Director/Consultant [Canadian]

Flightcare Multiservices UK Limited
Incorporated: 17 August 1962 *Employees:* 811
Net Worth: £14,127,000 *Total Assets:* £20,434,000
Registered Office: Swissport House, Hampton Court, Manor Park, Runcorn, Cheshire, WA7 1TT
Activities: Activities of head offices
Parent: Swissport GB Limited
Officers: Benjamin Joseph Holme Kay [1974] Director; Anthony Tully [1967] Director/Chief Operating Officer [Irish]; Luzius Wirth [1974] Director [Swiss]

Flintbrook Limited
Incorporated: 6 December 1994
Net Worth: £8,134,000 *Total Assets:* £37,713,000
Registered Office: Lawrence House, Riverside Drive, Cleckheaton, W Yorks, BD19 4DH
Activities: Agents involved in the sale of machinery, industrial equipment, ships and aircraft
Shareholders: Wesco Aircraft International Holdings Limited; Wesco Holdings Inc
Officers: John Holland, Secretary; Jan Alexander Dobrucki [1964] Finance Director; John Generald Holland [1968] Director and Company Secretary [American]; Alexander Murray [1969] Director; Alun Phennah [1968] Supply Chain Director

Flowflex Components Limited
Incorporated: 9 March 1954 *Employees:* 87
Net Worth: £3,063,179 *Total Assets:* £8,321,655
Registered Office: Samuel Blaser Works, Tongue Lane Industrial Estate, Buxton, Derbys, SK17 7LR
Activities: Forging, pressing, stamping and roll-forming of metal; powder metallurgy
Major Shareholder: Terence Anthony Dickinson
Officers: Richard Thomas Wilcock, Secretary; David Bowers [1973] Director; Surya Dickinson [1963] Director; Terence Anthony Dickinson [1948] Director/Chairman; Neil Moses [1956] Director; Simon Payne [1964] Director; Richard Thomas Wilcock [1964] Director/Accountant

Flowflex Holdings Limited
Incorporated: 9 March 1987 *Employees:* 85
Net Worth: £4,182,411 *Total Assets:* £9,340,011
Registered Office: Samuel Blaser Works, Tongue Lane Industrial Estate, Buxton, Derbys, SK17 7LR
Activities: Manufacture of other fabricated metal products n.e.c.
Major Shareholder: Terence Anthony Dickinson
Officers: Richard Thomas Wilcock, Secretary; Surya Dickinson [1963] Director; Terence Anthony Dickinson [1948] Managing Director; Richard Thomas Wilcock [1964] Director/Accountant

Flowgroup PLC
Incorporated: 17 May 2006 *Employees:* 367
Net Worth Deficit: £14,746,000 *Total Assets:* £30,838,000
Registered Office: Castlefield House, Liverpool Road, Castlefield, Manchester, M3 4SB
Activities: Activities of head offices
Officers: Nigel Peter Canham, Secretary; James Dominic Brooke [1971] Director; Nigel Peter Canham [1968] Finance Director; Brian Farley Carroll [1971] Director [American]; David Kenneth Grundy [1968] Director; Alan Charles Lovell [1953] Director; Bradley Matthew Tirpak [1969] Director [American]

Flowserve GB Limited
Incorporated: 20 August 1992 *Employees:* 365
Net Worth: £99,508,000 *Total Assets:* £140,902,000
Registered Office: One St Peter's Square, Manchester, M2 3DE
Activities: Manufacture of pumps
Parent: Flowserve International Limited
Officers: Martin Edwards, Secretary; Martin Edwards [1955] Director/Accountant; Christian Lawrence [1974] Director/Regional Controller; Wynford Henri Meeke [1970] Marketing Director

Flowserve International Limited
Incorporated: 2 June 1998
Net Worth: £9,437,000 *Total Assets:* £120,290,000
Registered Office: One St Peter's Square, Manchester, M2 3DE
Activities: Machining
Officers: Martin Edwards, Secretary; Martin Edwards [1955] Director/Accountant; Wynford Henri Meeke [1970] Marketing Director; Akshar Chandrahas Patel [1985] Director/Attorney [American]

Flowtech Fluidpower PLC
Incorporated: 24 April 2014 *Employees:* 414
Net Worth: £74,864,000 *Total Assets:* £122,026,000
Registered Office: Pimbo Road, Skelmersdale, Lancs, WN8 9RB
Activities: Activities of head offices
Officers: Bryce Brooks, Secretary; Bryce Rowan Brooks [1965] Finance Director; Malcolm McDonald Diamond [1948] Director; Nigel Richens [1955] Director

FLSmidth (UK) Limited
Incorporated: 7 September 1925 *Employees:* 35
Net Worth: £34,365,000 *Total Assets:* £82,076,000
Registered Office: 3rd Floor, 1 Ashley Road, Altrincham, Cheshire, WA14 2DT
Activities: Other business support service activities n.e.c.
Officers: Stephen Harrington, Secretary; Stuart Alan Heley [1950] Director/Operations Manager; Liam MacNamara [1966] Director/General Manager

Fluidpower Group Limited
Incorporated: 16 May 2016
Net Worth: £100 *Total Assets:* £91,745,104
Registered Office: Flowtech, Pimbo Road, Skelmersdale, Lancs, WN8 9RB
Activities: Activities of distribution holding companies
Parent: Fluidpower MIP Limited
Officers: Bryce Rowan Brooks [1965] Director

Fluidpower Limited
Incorporated: 15 October 1982 *Employees:* 141
Net Worth: £48,241,176 *Total Assets:* £83,318,040
Registered Office: Pimbo Road, Skelmersdale, Lancs, WN8 9RB
Activities: Wholesale of hardware, plumbing and heating equipment and supplies
Parent: Fluidpower Group Limited
Officers: Bryce Rowan Brooks [1965] Finance Director; Alan Keith Dickinson [1957] Sales Director; John Farmer [1964] Director

Fluidpower MIP Limited
Incorporated: 6 May 2014 *Employees:* 2
Net Worth: £32,384,768 *Total Assets:* £140,231,552
Registered Office: Pimbo Road, Skelmersdale, Lancs, WN8 9RB
Activities: Activities of head offices
Parent: Flowtech Fluidpower PLC
Officers: Bryce Rowan Brooks [1965] Director; Sean Mark Fennon [1960] Director

Fluidpower Shared Services Limited
Incorporated: 17 August 2004 *Employees:* 15
Net Worth: £30,998,488 *Total Assets:* £40,471,092
Registered Office: Pimbo Road, Skelmersdale, Lancs, WN8 9RB
Activities: Activities of distribution holding companies
Parent: Fluidpower MIP Limited
Officers: Bryce Rowan Brooks [1965] Director/Accountant

FMC Agro Limited
Incorporated: 24 December 1985 *Employees:* 68
Net Worth: £14,550,348 *Total Assets:* £20,374,888
Registered Office: Rectors Lane, Pentre, Deeside, Flintshire, CH5 2DH
Activities: Manufacture of pesticides and other agrochemical products
Parent: FMC Corporation
Officers: Mandy Jones, Secretary; Peter John William Botham [1954] Director; Patrick Charles Day [1979] Finance Director [American]; Mandy Jones [1977] Finance Director

FMC Chemicals Limited
Incorporated: 2 October 2000 *Employees:* 55
Net Worth: £11,125,000 *Total Assets:* £30,971,000
Registered Office: Lithium Division, Commercial Road, Wirral, Merseyside, CH62 3NL
Activities: Manufacture of other organic basic chemicals
Parent: FMC Corporation
Officers: Samuel David Coleman, Secretary; Barbara Ann Fochtman [1970] Manufacturing Director [American]; Phil James Hardwick [1971] Director/Plant Manager; Sara Velazquez Ponessa [1971] Director/General Counsel [American]; Thomas Schneberger [1971] Global Business Director [American]

FMC Kongsberg Services Limited
Incorporated: 18 August 2003 *Employees:* 195
Net Worth: £22,867,000 *Total Assets:* £78,402,000
Registered Office: Eversheds House, 70 Great Bridgewater Street, Manchester, M1 5ES
Activities: Support activities for petroleum and natural gas mining
Parent: FMC Technologies Limited
Officers: Brenda Janette Mennie, Secretary; Ove Magne Kallestad [1960] Director Subsea [Norwegian]; Leonardo Ribeiro [1974] Director, Operations [Brazilian]; Brian James Wotherspoon [1969] Director/General Manager; Jan Christian Zahl [1969] Director/Finance Controller [Norwegian]

FMC Technologies Limited
Incorporated: 10 October 1931 *Employees:* 1,003
Net Worth: £51,751,000 *Total Assets:* £265,058,000
Registered Office: Eversheds House, 70 Great Bridgewater Street, Manchester, M1 5ES
Activities: Support activities for petroleum and natural gas mining
Parent: TechnipFMC Holdings Limited
Officers: Brenda Janette Mennie, Secretary; James Joseph Campbell [1960] Director/Financial Controller; Morven Forsyth [1970] Director/Human Resources Manager; Leonardo Ribeiro [1974] Director/Well Completions System Manager [Brazilian]; Michael Robert Tierney [1963] Technical Director

FMG (Holdings) Limited
Incorporated: 21 March 2016 *Employees:* 1
Net Worth Deficit: £112,892 *Total Assets:* £61,288,904
Registered Office: Corpacq House, 1 Goose Green, Altrincham, Cheshire, WA14 1DW
Activities: Activities of head offices
Officers: Stephen James Scott [1978] Director

Focus Academy Trust (UK) Ltd
Incorporated: 16 May 2012 *Employees:* 678
Net Worth: £13,940,000 *Total Assets:* £25,304,000
Registered Office: Talking Point Conference Centre, Huddersfield Road, Scouthead, Oldham, Lancs, OL4 4AG
Activities: Primary education
Officers: Paul Barry Leigh, Secretary; Greg Caiger [1982] Director/Regional Sales and Service Manager; Anthony Clive Davies [1951] Director; Helen Lee [1967] Director/Headteacher; Rosina Malik [1961] Director/Self Employed; Ross James Mather [1990] Associate Director; Matthew Milburn [1965] Director/Headteacher; Anne Sheila Redmond [1963] Director/Executive Principal; Helen Claire Rowland [1968] Director/Chief Executive; Daniel Gary Spencer [1977] Director/Facilities Manager; Simon Charles Willis [1948] Director/Retired

Focus International Limited
Incorporated: 16 November 1979 *Employees:* 205
Net Worth: £4,921,000 *Total Assets:* £18,735,000
Registered Office: Edinburgh House, Hollinsbrook Way, Pilsworth, Bury, Lancs, BL9 8RR
Activities: Non-specialised wholesale trade
Parent: Focus Group Holdings Limited
Officers: Siobhan Mawdsley, Secretary; Mark Harold Schaffer, Secretary; Philip Bryan [1963] Sales Director; Peter Alan Cowgill [1953] Director; Neil James Greenhalgh [1971] Director; Mark Harold Schaffer [1959] Director/Chartered Accountant; Brian Michael Small [1956] Director; David Guy Tolman [1958] Director; Michael David Tolman [1984] Director; Andrew Ward [1968] Director

FocusEducation (Lambeth) Limited
Incorporated: 23 July 2001
Net Worth Deficit: £1,808,000 *Total Assets:* £13,342,000
Registered Office: c/o Albany SPC Services Ltd, 3rd Floor, 3-5 Charlotte Street, Manchester, M1 4HB
Activities: Other education n.e.c.
Parent: FocusEducation Limited
Officers: Ailison Louise Mitchell, Company Secretary; Michael Andrew Donn [1972] Director/Banker; Leo William McKenna [1966] Director [Irish]; Christopher Thomas Solley [1970] Director

FocusEducation (Lincolnshire) Limited
Incorporated: 18 June 2001
Net Worth Deficit: £3,457,000 *Total Assets:* £19,664,000
Registered Office: c/o Albany SPC Services Ltd, 3rd Floor, 3-5 Charlotte Street, Manchester, M1 4HB
Activities: Other education n.e.c.
Parent: FocusEducation (Lincolnshire) Holdings Ltd
Officers: Ailison Louise Mitchell, Company Secretary; Michael Andrew Donn [1972] Director; Leo William McKenna [1966] Director [Irish]; Christopher Thomas Solley [1970] Director

FocusEducation (Newcastle) Limited
Incorporated: 25 March 2002
Net Worth Deficit: £3,754,000 *Total Assets:* £37,367,000
Registered Office: c/o Albany SPC Services Ltd, 3rd Floor, 3-5 Charlotte Street, Manchester, M1 4HB
Activities: Other education n.e.c.
Parent: FocusEducation (Newcastle) Holdings Ltd
Officers: Ailison Louise Mitchell, Company Secretary; Michael Andrew Donn [1972] Director/Banker; Leo William McKenna [1966] Director [Irish]; Christopher Thomas Solley [1970] Director

Foden Estates Ltd.
Incorporated: 26 May 2000 *Employees:* 1
Net Worth: £12,492,138 *Total Assets:* £23,393,548
Registered Office: Unit 1 Heatley Mere, Chaise Meadow, Lymm, Cheshire, WA13 9EL
Activities: Construction of commercial buildings
Major Shareholder: Robert Edward Foden
Officers: Debbie Cregan, Secretary; Robert Edward Foden [1962] Director

Foden Investments Limited
Incorporated: 15 December 1980
Net Worth: £10,269,269 *Total Assets:* £17,181,414
Registered Office: 78 Chorley New Road, Bolton, Lancs, BL1 4BY
Activities: Buying and selling of own real estate
Major Shareholder: James Stanley Caldwell
Officers: Margaret Elaine Caldwell, Secretary; James Stanley Caldwell [1944] Director; Margaret Elaine Caldwell [1945] Director; Mark James Caldwell [1973] Director

Footasylum PLC
Incorporated: 12 August 2005 *Employees:* 1,312
Net Worth: £42,210,000 *Total Assets:* £75,115,000
Registered Office: Sandbrook House, Sandbrook Park, Rochdale, Lancs, OL11 1RY
Activities: Retail sale of clothing in specialised stores
Shareholders: John Stephen Riches; John Carruthers Wardle
Officers: Nancy Kelsall, Secretary; Barry Colin Bown [1961] Director/Executive Chairman; Danielle Hazel Davies [1978] Director/Chief Financial Officer; Brendan Hynes [1960] Director; Clare Michelle Nesbitt [1987] Director/Deputy CEO; Stephen Peter Robertson [1954] Director

Football League Limited (The)
Incorporated: 11 April 1904 *Employees:* 75
Net Worth: £243,561 *Total Assets:* £82,027,536
Registered Office: EFL House, 10-12 West Cliff, Preston, Lancs, PR1 8HU
Activities: Other sports activities
Officers: Tadeusz Stephen Detko, Secretary; Mark Anthony Ashton [1971] Director/Chief Executive; Clifford Crown [1956] Finance Director; Stefan Gamble [1975] Director/Chief Executive; Shaun Antony Harvey [1970] Director/Chief Executive; Nigel Howe [1958] Director/Vice Chairman; Deborah Ann Jevans [1960] Director/Chief Executive; John Lee Nixon [1948] Director; James Richard Rodwell [1970] Director/Chief Executive; Ian Charles Watmore [1958] Director

Fords Cheshire Limited
Incorporated: 22 April 1999 *Employees:* 6
Net Worth: £4,043,177 *Total Assets:* £13,501,103
Registered Office: Fords of Winsford, Wharton Retail Park, Weaver Valley Road, Winsford, Cheshire, CW7 3AL
Activities: Sale of used cars and light motor vehicles
Officers: Paul Thomas Ford, Secretary/Director; Edward Ford [1989] Director; John William Ford [1989] Director; Paul Thomas Ford [1957] Director

Forever Manchester
Incorporated: 29 January 1993 *Employees:* 16
Net Worth: £9,765,950 *Total Assets:* £9,976,265
Registered Office: 2nd Floor, 8 Hewitt Street, Manchester, M15 4GB
Activities: Other social work activities without accommodation n.e.c.
Officers: Samantha Jane Booth [1981] Director/Deputy Chief Executive; Philip Richard Hogben [1949] Director/Retired; Sandra Lindsay [1965] Director/PR Consultant; Alan Owen Mackin [1978] Director; Louise Marshall [1967] Infrastructure and Shared Services Director; Michael Warner [1963] Director/Social Housing Regulator

Formby Hall Golf Club Limited
Incorporated: 19 May 1994 *Employees:* 237
Net Worth: £7,954,295 *Total Assets:* £24,330,308
Registered Office: Formby Hall Golf Resort & Spa, Southport Old Road, Formby, Southport, Merseyside, L37 0AB
Activities: Hotels and similar accommodation
Officers: Patrick Bamford, Secretary; Sanjoy Kumar Chattopadhyay [1974] Director; Simon James Laker [1967] Director

Formby High School
Incorporated: 1 August 2011 *Employees:* 114
Net Worth: £8,870,668 *Total Assets:* £11,751,711
Registered Office: Formby High School, Freshfield Road, Formby, Merseyside, L37 3HW
Activities: General secondary education
Officers: Lucy Forster, Secretary; Dr Colin Adams [1967] Director/Academic; Neil David Adshead [1971] Director/Architect; Mr David Luke Bennett [1974] Director/Business Manager; Fiona Grieveson [1964] Director/Headteacher; Christine Margaret Hanson [1947] Director/Retired; Allan Harris [1960] Director/Fire Officer; Ashleigh Harrison-Forsyth [1989] Director/Teacher; Gary Heatherington [1965] Director/Technician/Teacher; Stuart Alexander Jones [1968] Director/Solicitor; Isabel Ruth Jordan [1963] Director/Self Employed; Martine Jayne Lucas [1976] Director/Barrister; Dominic Andrew MacKenzie [1974] Director/Headteacher; Paul Edward McGrath [1977] Director/Engineer; Andrea Mitchell [1972] Director/Pharmacist; Francis James Murphy [1960] Director/Chartered Accountant; Professor Kenneth Ridings [1941] Director/Retired; Kathryn Helen Smith [1973] Director/Governor

The Formby Land Trust
Incorporated: 1 February 2001
Net Worth: £7,597,200 *Total Assets:* £7,616,004
Registered Office: BWMacfarlane, Castle Chambers, 43 Castle Street, Liverpool, L2 9SH
Activities: Fitness facilities
Officers: Patrick Appleton Moores, Secretary/Director; Paul Charles Kurthausen [1947] Director/Chartered Tax Advisor; Patrick Appleton Moores [1958] Director; David Vaughan Pugh [1961] Director/Consultant; Scott Wilkinson [1980] Director/Architect

Formidable Capital Assets Limited
Incorporated: 3 May 2005 *Employees:* 2
Net Worth: £24,983,000 *Total Assets:* £39,318,000
Registered Office: Tetrosyl Limited, Walmersley Old Road, Bury, Lancs, BL9 6RE
Activities: Other business support service activities n.e.c.
Parent: Tetrosyl Group Ltd
Officers: David James Rogers [1969] Director/Solicitor; Peter David Schofield [1961] Director

Forrest Corporate Limited
Incorporated: [illegible] April 2010 *Employees:* 2
Net Worth Deficit: £2,632,000 *Total Assets:* £19,041,000
Registered Office: The Yard, Dodd Lane, Westhoughton, Bolton, Lancs, BL5 3NU
Activities: Construction of commercial buildings
Parent: Ensco 995 Limited
Officers: Mark Nicholson [1966] Director; Keith Alan Reid [1980] Director

HT Forrest Holdings Limited
Incorporated: 20 June 2007 *Employees:* 2
Net Worth: £26,674,000 *Total Assets:* £36,412,000
Registered Office: The Yard, Dodd Lane, Westhoughton, Bolton, Lancs, BL5 3NU
Activities: Activities of head offices
Parent: Forrest Corporate Limited
Officers: Mark Nicholson [1966] Director; Keith Alan Reid [1980] Director

Herbert T. Forrest Limited
Incorporated: 10 July 1972 *Employees:* 443
Net Worth Deficit: £8,859,000 *Total Assets:* £25,895,000
Registered Office: The Yard, Dodd Lane, Westhoughton, Bolton, Lancs, BL5 3NU
Activities: Construction of domestic buildings
Parent: HT Forrest Holdings Limited
Officers: Mark Nicholson [1966] Director; Keith Alan Reid [1980] Director

Forrester (Sales) Limited
Incorporated: 7 December 1972 *Employees:* 208
Net Worth: £4,411,473 *Total Assets:* £12,190,192
Registered Office: Mill Lane, Kingsley, Frodsham, Cheshire, WA6 8HY
Activities: Production of meat and poultry meat products
Major Shareholder: Alan William Leslie Dilliway-Parry
Officers: Alan William Leslie Dilliway-Parry, Secretary; Timothy Mallalieu Diggle [1969] Director; Angus Alan Dilliway Parry [1979] Director; Heidi Elizabeth Lesley Dilliway-Nickson [1974] Director; Alan William Leslie Dilliway-Parry [1935] Director; Fay Deanne Dilliway-Parry [1940] Director

Forresters of Cheshire Limited
Incorporated: 13 March 2000 *Employees:* 208
Net Worth: £5,021,808 *Total Assets:* £12,190,192
Registered Office: Mill Lane, Kingsley, Frodsham, Cheshire, WA6 8HY
Activities: Processing and preserving of poultry meat
Major Shareholder: Alan William Leslie Dilliway-Parry
Officers: Alan William Leslie Dilliway-Parry, Secretary/Director; Heidi Elizabeth Lesley Dilliway-Nickson [1974] Director; Alan William Leslie Dilliway-Parry [1935] Director

A.J. Forster Limited
Incorporated: 10 September 1999 *Employees:* 10
Net Worth: £140,731 *Total Assets:* £6,721,525
Registered Office: Greengill Foot, Bowscar, Penrith, Cumbria, CA11 8RP
Activities: Raising of poultry
Shareholders: Mark Andrew Forster; Tracey Louise Forster; Christopher James Forster
Officers: Tracey Louise Forster, Secretary/Poultry Farmer; Christopher James Forster [1990] Production Director; Mark Andrew Forster [1965] Managing Director; Tracey Louise Forster [1965] Director/Company Secretary

Fort Vale Engineering Limited
Incorporated: 6 April 1967 *Employees:* 370
Net Worth: £18,670,384 *Total Assets:* £51,572,064
Registered Office: Calder Vale Park, Simonstone Lane, Simonstone, Burnley, Lancs, BB12 7ND
Activities: Manufacture of other fabricated metal products n.e.c.
Major Shareholder: Edward Sagar Fort
Officers: Edward Martin Drury, Finance Director; David Bailey [1968] Director; Andrew John Bishop [1963] Sales Director; Andrew Bryce [1962] Director; Edward Martin Drury [1949] Director; Edward Sagar Fort OBE [1937] Managing Director/Chairman; Sharon Hendleman [1970] Finance Director; John Horsfall [1963] Director; Shaun Laycock [1969] Director; Peter Anthony Staveley [1969] Director; Ian Wilson [1945] Director/General Manager

Fort Vale Limited
Incorporated: 14 February 1992 *Employees:* 524
Net Worth: £43,964,756 *Total Assets:* £72,710,544
Registered Office: Calder Vale Park, Simonstone Lane, Simonstone, Burnley, Lancs, BB12 7ND
Activities: Activities of head offices
Major Shareholder: Edward Sagar Fort
Officers: Edward Martin Drury, Secretary/Director; Edward Martin Drury [1949] Director; Edward Sagar Fort OBE [1937] Director; Ian Wilson [1945] Director

Forth Bidco Limited
Incorporated: 26 February 2016 *Employees:* 8
Net Worth: £31,470,000 *Total Assets:* £93,445,000
Registered Office: 6 Lodge Bank, Crown Lane, Horwich, Bolton, Lancs, BL6 5HY
Activities: Activities of other holding companies n.e.c.
Officers: Paolo Benedetto [1974] Director; Graham Philippe Bertwistle Moor [1967] Director; Jane Catherine Ratcliffe [1971] Director

Forthright Finance Limited
Incorporated: 21 February 1972
Net Worth: £14,139,000 *Total Assets:* £15,108,000
Registered Office: Charterhall House, Charterhall Drive, Chester, CH88 3AN
Activities: Financial intermediation not elsewhere classified
Parent: Bank of Scotland PLC
Officers: David Dermot Hennessey, Secretary; Richard Andrew Jones [1972] Marketing Director; Raymond Poole [1963] Director; Timothy Robin Smith [1966] Director

Fortis Developments Ltd
Incorporated: 11 September 2012
Net Worth: £4,143,416 *Total Assets:* £25,270,016
Registered Office: Suite 4, Richmond House, Heath Road, Hale, Altrincham, Cheshire, WA14 2XP
Activities: Development of building projects
Parent: Fortis UK Holdings Ltd
Officers: Darren Kingsley McClellan [1972] Director/Manager; Kieran Stuart Moore [1975] Director/Manager; Gareth Morgan [1984] Director

Fortis UK Holdings Ltd
Incorporated: 27 July 2015
Net Worth: £4,593,520 *Total Assets:* £94,898,080
Registered Office: 300 St Mary's Road, Garston, Liverpool, L19 0NQ
Activities: Activities of head offices
Shareholders: Direct Property Investments Ltd; DMC Estates Limited
Officers: Darren Kingsley McClellan [1972] Director/Manager; Kieran Stuart Moore [1975] Director/Manager; Gareth Morgan [1984] Director/Manager

Fortunelodge Limited
Incorporated: 31 December 1991 *Employees:* 2
Net Worth: £2,373,140 *Total Assets:* £7,810,060
Registered Office: 14 Kennedy Street, Manchester, M2 4BY
Activities: Other letting and operating of own or leased real estate
Parent: Parsonage Chambers Limited
Officers: Richard Christopher William Parkinson, Secretary; Linzi Sara Parkinson [1962] Director; Richard Christopher William Parkinson [1963] Director/Solicitor

Forty Limited
Incorporated: 5 January 1994
Net Worth: £7,533,430 *Total Assets:* £9,940,815
Registered Office: 6th Floor, Cardinal House, 20 St Marys Parsonage, Manchester, M3 2LG
Activities: Other letting and operating of own or leased real estate
Officers: Avrohom Schechter, Secretary; Richard Spitzer, Secretary; Hanna Gluck [1984] Director/Secretary; Jacob Gluck [1983] Director; Richard Spitzer [1944] Director

Forward Construction and Developments Limited
Incorporated: 1 December 1997 *Employees:* 4
Net Worth Deficit: £510,236 *Total Assets:* £8,954,496
Registered Office: The Old Laundry, Lady Mary Square, Rostherne Lane, Rostherne, Knutsford, Cheshire, WA16 6SA
Activities: Buying and selling of own real estate
Shareholders: Linda Shepherd; James Nelson Shepherd
Officers: Linda Shepherd, Secretary/Solicitor; James Nelson Shepherd [1963] Director/Builder; Linda Shepherd [1963] Director/Solicitor

The Forward Property Group Limited
Incorporated: 24 May 2006 *Employees:* 2
Net Worth: £1,294,030 *Total Assets:* £9,591,510
Registered Office: The Old Laundry, Lady Mary Square, Rostherne Lane, Rostherne, Knutsford, Cheshire, WA16 6SA
Activities: Other letting and operating of own or leased real estate
Parent: Forward Construction & Developments Ltd
Officers: Linda Shepherd, Secretary/Solicitor; James Nelson Shepherd [1963] Director/Builder; Linda Shepherd [1963] Director/Solicitor

Foster Wheeler Europe
Incorporated: 14 December 2000
Net Worth: £1,348,370,048 *Total Assets:* £1,838,568,960
Registered Office: Booths Park, Chelford Road, Knutsford, Cheshire, WA16 8QZ
Activities: Non-trading company
Parent: AFW Finance 2 Limited
Officers: Iain Angus Jones, Secretary; Carl Anthony Chatfield [1964] Director; William George Setter [1975] Director

Fostering Solutions Limited
Incorporated: 1 June 2000 *Employees:* 200
Net Worth: £16,678,192 *Total Assets:* £38,877,696
Registered Office: 1 Merchants Place, River Street, Bolton, Lancs, BL2 1BX
Activities: Other social work activities without accommodation n.e.c.
Parent: Acorn Care and Education Limited
Officers: Helen Elizabeth Lecky, Secretary; Antony Vincent Holt [1959] Director/Chartered Accountant; Isabella Mary Hutchison [1956] Managing Director; Jean-Luc Emmanuel Janet [1970] Director [French]; David Jon Leatherbarrow [1969] Director/Group Chief Executive Officer

Fothergill Engineered Fabrics Limited
Incorporated: 3 November 1994 *Employees:* 106
Net Worth: £6,459,678 *Total Assets:* £10,594,277
Registered Office: Summit, Littleborough, Rochdale, Lancs, OL15 0LR
Activities: Manufacture of other textiles n.e.c.
Major Shareholder: Patrick Gerard Brennan
Officers: Patrick Gerard Brennan [1958] Director/Chief Executive Officer [Irish]; Veronica Anne Brennan [1959] Director [Irish]; Trevor Alan Hopson [1962] Director/General Manager; Cheryl Mary Lamb [1964] Director/Corporate HR Manager; Nader Alan Midani [1977] Director

Fothergill Polycom Limited
Incorporated: 19 April 2000 *Employees:* 52
Net Worth: £5,405,946 *Total Assets:* £9,223,562
Registered Office: Admin Office, Summit, Littleborough, Rochdale, Lancs, OL15 0LR
Activities: Finishing of textiles
Major Shareholder: Patrick Gerard Brennan
Officers: Patrick Gerard Brennan [1958] Director [Irish]; Veronica Anne Brennan [1959] Director [Irish]; Trevor Alan Hopson [1962] Director; Cheryl Mary Lamb [1964] Director/Corporate HR Manager; Nader Alan Midani [1977] Director

Foundation for Life Limited
Incorporated: 16 October 2003 *Employees:* 4
Net Worth Deficit: £10,903,948 *Total Assets:* £56,861,508
Registered Office: Sceptre House, Sceptre Way, Bamber Bridge, Preston, Lancs, PR5 6AW
Activities: Development of building projects
Shareholders: Eric Wright Group Limited; Community Health Partnerships Limited
Officers: Deborah Jane Rawlinson, Secretary; Patricia Ann Anderson [1957] Director; Jeremy Peter Hartley [1965] Director/Chartered Accountant; Neil Geoffrey Ward [1959] Director; Christine Desiree Winstanley [1966] Director

Four Seasons (Bamford) Limited
Incorporated: 7 June 2006 *Employees:* 2,093
Net Worth Deficit: £14,548,000 *Total Assets:* £11,087,000
Registered Office: Norcliffe House, Station Road, Wilmslow, Cheshire, SK9 1BU
Activities: Other human health activities
Parent: Four Seasons Health Care Group Limited
Officers: Abigail Mattison, Secretary; Timothy Richard William Hammond [1959] Director Dr Maureen Claire Royston [1960] Director; Benjamin Robert Taberner [1972] Director/Chartered Accountant

Four Seasons (DFK) Limited
Incorporated: 13 August 1985 *Employees:* 257
Net Worth: £11,670,000 *Total Assets:* £13,025,000
Registered Office: Norcliffe House, Station Road, Wilmslow, Cheshire, SK9 1BU
Activities: Other human health activities
Parent: Four Seasons Health Care Group Limited
Officers: Abigail Mattison, Secretary; Timothy Richard William Hammond [1959] Director; Dr Maureen Claire Royston [1960] Director; Benjamin Robert Taberner [1972] Director/Chartered Accountant

Four Seasons Estates Limited
Incorporated: 21 February 2006
Net Worth: £1,590,037 *Total Assets:* £10,081,748
Registered Office: The Grange, Grange Avenue, Levenshulme, Manchester, M19 2EY
Activities: Renting and operating of Housing Association real estate
Shareholder: Bashir Ahmed Majid
Officers: Noreen Ahmed, Secretary; Bashir Ahmed Majid [1966] Sales Director; Abdul Rashid [1958] Director/Production Manager

Four Seasons Health Care (Capital) Limited
Incorporated: 26 June 2002
Net Worth: £16,524,000 *Total Assets:* £16,524,000
Registered Office: Norcliffe House, Station Road, Wilmslow, Cheshire, SK9 1BU
Activities: Activities of head offices
Parent: Four Seasons Health Care Limited
Officers: Abigail Mattison, Secretary; Timothy Richard William Hammond [1959] Director; Dr Maureen Claire Royston [1960] Director; Benjamin Robert Taberner [1972] Director/Chartered Accountant

Four Seasons Health Care Holdings Limited
Incorporated: 8 July 1999
Net Worth: £236,339,008 *Total Assets:* £236,339,008
Registered Office: Norcliffe House, Station Road, Wilmslow, Cheshire, SK9 1BU
Activities: Other human health activities
Parent: Mericourt Limited
Officers: Abigail Mattison, Secretary; Robert Nicolas Barr [1958] Director; Ryan Stuart MacAskill [1975] Director; Gregory Laurence Newman [1988] Director/Investment Professional; Dr Maureen Claire Royston [1960] Director; Benjamin Robert Taberner [1972] Director/Chartered Accountant

Four Seasons Homes No.4 Limited
Incorporated: 21 June 2000 *Employees:* 813
Net Worth: £14,799,000 *Total Assets:* £17,391,000
Registered Office: Norcliffe House, Station Road, Wilmslow, Cheshire, SK9 1BU
Activities: Other human health activities
Parent: Four Seasons Group Holdings Limited
Officers: Abigail Mattison, Secretary; Timothy Richard William Hammond [1959] Director; Dr Maureen Claire Royston [1960] Director; Benjamin Robert Taberner [1972] Director/Chartered Accountant

Fourward Properties Limited
Incorporated: 28 July 2003 *Employees:* 2
Net Worth: £7,590,162 *Total Assets:* £9,366,086
Registered Office: Gate House Farm, Jane Lane, Midge Hall, Leyland, Lancs, PR26 6TQ
Activities: Other letting and operating of own or leased real estate
Officers: Sally Mary Ward, Secretary; John Ward [1946] Director/Consultant

Fox Strategic Land and Property Limited
Incorporated: 21 May 2007
Net Worth: £12,203,939 *Total Assets:* £12,275,827
Registered Office: Gladman House, Alexandria Way, Congleton Business Park, Congleton, Cheshire, CW12 1LB
Activities: Buying and selling of own real estate
Officers: Jonathan Mark Stansfield Shepherd, Secretary; David John Gladman [1955] Director; Karen Jane Gladman [1957] Director; Geoffrey Lansbury [1951] Director; Jonathan Mark Stansfield Shepherd [1957] Director/Property Developer

FQ Developments Limited
Incorporated: 7 November 2014
Net Worth Deficit: £1,078,972 *Total Assets:* £42,260,840
Registered Office: 1st Floor, NQ Building, 47 Bengal Street, Ancoats, Manchester, M4 6BB
Activities: Other business support service activities n.e.c.
Parent: XQ Developments Limited
Officers: Michael Shaw, Secretary; Daren Whitaker [1972] Director

Fragrance Acquisitions Limited
Incorporated: 14 February 2005 *Employees:* 93
Net Worth: £44,612,192 *Total Assets:* £60,092,620
Registered Office: Churchill Point, Lake Edge Green, Trafford Park Road, Trafford Park, Manchester, M17 1BL
Activities: Wholesale of perfume and cosmetics
Officers: Sanjay Jayantilal Vadera, Secretary/Director; Sanjay Jayantilal Vadera [1967] Director; Vipul Jayantilal Vadera [1972] Director

Fragrance Oils (International) Limited
Incorporated: 12 August 1974 *Employees:* 31
Net Worth: £22,499,804 *Total Assets:* £40,403,152
Registered Office: Eton Hill Industrial Estate, Eton Hill Road, Radcliffe, Manchester, M26 2FR
Activities: Manufacture of perfumes and toilet preparations
Officers: John Morgan, Secretary; Barbara Carter [1951] Director; Malcolm Charles Hogan [1956] Director/Buyer; John Morgan [1955] Director/Accountant; Mark Peter Ogden [1957] Director/Export Sales Manager; Martin Christopher Francis Potts [1959] Director; Jacqueline Radovic [1956] Personnel Director; Jeffrey Robert Slavin [1952] Director/Chartered Accountant; Barry Starr [1950] Laboratory Director; Richard Jeremy Thomas [1960] Sales Director

Fragrance Oils (Purchasing) Limited
Incorporated: 20 September 1967 *Employees:* 168
Net Worth: £11,518,785 *Total Assets:* £23,442,802
Registered Office: Eton Hill Industrial Estate, Eton Hill Road, Radcliffe, Manchester, M26 2FR
Activities: Manufacture of perfumes and toilet preparations
Officers: John Morgan, Secretary; Malcolm Charles Hogan [1956] Director; John Morgan [1955] Director/Accountant; Martin Christopher Francis Potts [1959] Director; Jeffrey Robert Slavin [1952] Director/Chartered Accountant

Fragrance Oils Limited
Incorporated: 15 June 1994 *Employees:* 241
Net Worth: £43,669,680 *Total Assets:* £50,919,432
Registered Office: Eton Hill Industrial Estate, Eton Hill Road, Radcliffe, Manchester, M26 2FR
Activities: Activities of head offices
Major Shareholder: Barbara Carter
Officers: Jeffrey Robert Slavin, Secretary/Chartered Accountant; Barbara Carter [1951] Director/Personnel Officer; Martin Christopher Francis Potts [1959] Director; Jeffrey Robert Slavin [1952] Director/Chartered Accountant

Adrian Francis Associates Ltd
Incorporated: 13 August 2002 *Employees:* 10
Net Worth: £7,692,022 *Total Assets:* £10,669,218
Registered Office: Reedham House, 31 King Street West, Manchester, M3 2PJ
Activities: Trade of gas through mains
Parent: Adrian Francis (Holdings) Limited
Officers: Lisa Francis [1978] Director

Francis House Family Trust
Incorporated: 5 July 1990 *Employees:* 82
Net Worth: £28,560,566 *Total Assets:* £28,746,790
Registered Office: 390 Parrs Wood Road, Manchester, M20 5NA
Activities: Other service activities n.e.c.
Officers: Reverend David Stephen Ireland, Secretary; Judith Amosi-Khodadad [1953] Director [Israeli]; Bishop Terence John Brain [1938] Director/Roman Catholic Bishop; Dr Susan Kirk [1961] Director/Doctor; Charles Ledigo [1953] Director; Martin Lochery [1950] Director/Teacher; Thomas Mulheran [1938] Director/Catholic Priest; Dr Susan Mary O'Halloran [1954] Director/Doctor; Michael Redfearn [1964] Director; Christopher Roberts [1951] Director/Chartered Accountant; Michael Frederick Sainsbury [1948] Director; Vijay Andrew Kumar Srivastava [1964] Director; Dr Andrew Taylor [1947] Director

The Franciscan Missionaries of St Joseph
Incorporated: 7 September 2009 *Employees:* 37
Net Worth: £7,099,025 *Total Assets:* £7,411,799
Registered Office: St Joseph's Convent, Greenleach Lane, Worsley, Manchester, M28 2TS
Activities: Activities of religious organisations
Officers: Anne Moore, Secretary; Joan Kerley [1947] Director/Religious Sister [American]; Sister Brenda Makokha [1972] Director/Member of Religious Order [Kenyan]; Anne Moore [1950] Director/Religious Sister; Sister Maureen Theresa Murphy [1951] Director/Member of Religious Order; Sister Margaret Nyabongoye [1965] Director/Member of Religious Order [Kenyan]

Frankel Brow Limited
Incorporated: 10 April 1997
Net Worth: £230,254 *Total Assets:* £12,322,887
Registered Office: Spectrum, 56-58 Benson Road, Birchwood, Warrington, Cheshire, WA3 7PQ
Activities: Buying and selling of own real estate
Officers: Fred Done [1943] Director/Bookmaker

Thomas Frederick & Company Limited
Incorporated: 27 May 1940 *Employees:* 4
Net Worth: £2,487,706 *Total Assets:* £7,416,229
Registered Office: Linden Court House, 52 Liverpool Street, Salford, M5 4LT
Activities: Wholesale of textiles
Shareholders: Jonathan Choua Shasha; Roy Solomon Shasha
Officers: Jonathan Choua Shasha [1956] Director

Freemans Grattan Holdings Limited
Incorporated: 2 June 1999
Net Worth: £50,824,000 *Total Assets:* £109,073,000
Registered Office: 66-70 Vicar Lane, Little Germany, Bradford, W Yorks, BD99 2XG
Activities: Retail sale via mail order houses or via Internet
Officers: Andrew James Lord, Secretary; Markus Fuchshofen [1966] Director/Businessman [German]; John Hinchcliffe [1965] Director/Chief Executive Officer; Neill Lewis McDonald Moore [1966] Director/Chartered Accountant; Marc Erich Bernd Wolfgang Opelt [1962] Director/Businessman [German]

Freemans Public Limited Company
Incorporated: 8 December 1936 *Employees:* 179
Net Worth: £30,256,000 *Total Assets:* £119,725,000
Registered Office: 66-70 Vicar Lane, Little Germany, Bradford, W Yorks, BD99 2XG
Activities: Retail sale via mail order houses or via Internet
Parent: Freemans Grattan Holdings Limited
Officers: Andrew James Lord, Secretary; John Hinchcliffe [1965] Director/Chief Executive Officer; Neill Lewis McDonald Moore [1966] Director/Chartered Accountant; Marc Erich Bernd Wolfgang Opelt [1962] Director/Businessman [German]

Frenkel Topping Group PLC
Incorporated: 8 April 2003 *Employees:* 64
Net Worth: £11,722,205 *Total Assets:* £12,740,926
Registered Office: Frenkel House, 15 Carolina Way, Salford, M50 2ZY
Activities: Activities of head offices
Officers: Richard Cullen Fraser, Secretary; Stephen Graham Bentley [1953] Finance Director; Richard Cullen Fraser [1959] Director; Mark Stuart Holt [1976] Commercial Director; Timothy James Thornton Linacre [1958] Director; Paul Donald Richardson [1966] Director

Frenkel Topping Limited
Incorporated: 3 November 1988 *Employees:* 58
Net Worth: £7,959,930 *Total Assets:* £10,466,597
Registered Office: Frenkel House, 15 Carolina Way, Salford, M50 2ZY
Activities: Financial intermediation not elsewhere classified
Parent: Frenkel Topping Group Holdings Limited
Officers: Stephen Graham Bentley [1953] Finance Director; Richard Cullen Fraser [1959] Director; Mark Stuart Holt [1976] Commercial Director

Fresenius Kabi Limited
Incorporated: 22 October 1987 *Employees:* 326
Net Worth Deficit: £5,849,000 *Total Assets:* £49,875,000
Registered Office: Cestrian Court, Eastgate Way, Manor Park, Runcorn, Cheshire, WA7 1NT
Activities: Manufacture of pharmaceutical preparations
Parent: FHC (Holdings) Limited
Officers: Marc James Gerard Crouton [1959] Director [French]; John Robert Ducker [1960] Director; Christopher Paul Harrison [1966] Managing Director; David Michael Kehoe [1984] Finance Director; Mark Henry Kirkup [1969] Director; Frank Lucassen [1972] Director [German]; Niamh Matic [1973] Director [Irish]

Fresh Approach (UK) Holdings Limited
Incorporated: 22 April 2014 *Employees:* 78
Net Worth Deficit: £3,844,510 *Total Assets:* £10,538,494
Registered Office: Fin House, 1 Oakwater Avenue, Cheadle Royal, Cheadle, Cheshire, SK8 3SR
Activities: Management consultancy activities other than financial management
Officers: Karl Nicholas Cockwill [1965] Director; Lee Harris [1975] Director; Patrick Mathias Rhys Howells [1978] Director; Antony Peter Wilson [1976] Director

Fresh Approach (UK) Limited
Incorporated: 19 August 2004 *Employees:* 78
Net Worth: £2,399,525 *Total Assets:* £6,929,772
Registered Office: Fin House, 1 Oakwater Avenue, Cheadle Royal, Cheadle, Cheshire, SK8 3SR
Activities: Video production activities
Officers: Kathryn Clark [1985] Director; Karl Nicholas Cockwill [1965] Director; Lee Harris [1975] Director; Patrick Mathias Rhys Howells [1978] Director; Laura Lee [1978] Director; Michael McCabe [1978] Director; Stuart Whittle [1978] Director; Antony Peter Wilson [1976] Director

Frodsham Wind Farm Finance Limited
Incorporated: 8 July 2015 *Employees:* 4
Net Worth: £44 688 *Total Assets:* £10,564,667
Registered Office: Peel Dome, intu Trafford Centre, Trafford City, Manchester, M17 8PL
Activities: Other business support service activities n.e.c.
Parent: Peel Wind Farms (Frodsham) Limited
Officers: Neil Lees, Secretary; Neil Lees [1963] Director; David Muir Miller [1954] Director; Jack Christopher Steven [1986] Director; Charles Simon Wright [1983] Director

Frodsham Wind Farm Holdings Limited
Incorporated: 9 June 2014 *Employees:* 4
Net Worth: £8,354,465 *Total Assets:* £18,919,132
Registered Office: Peel Dome, intu Trafford Centre, Trafford City, Manchester, M17 8PL
Activities: Activities of other holding companies n.e.c.
Shareholders: Christopher Eves; John Whittaker; Sheila Greenwood; Second Generation Frodsham Limited
Officers: Neil Lees, Secretary; Neil Lees [1963] Director; David Muir Miller [1954] Director; Jack Christopher Steven [1986] Director; Charles Simon Wright [1983] Director

Frodsham Wind Farm Limited
Incorporated: 13 November 2009 *Employees:* 4
Net Worth: £4,943,369 *Total Assets:* £79,675,192
Registered Office: Peel Dome, intu Trafford Centre, Trafford City, Manchester, M17 8PL
Activities: Production of electricity
Parent: Frodsham Wind Farm Holdings Limited
Officers: Neil Lees, Secretary; Neil Lees [1963] Director; David Muir Miller [1954] Director; Jack Christopher Steven [1986] Director; Charles Simon Wright [1983] Director

Frostall Limited
Incorporated: 31 July 1997 *Employees:* 77
Net Worth: £9,651,710 *Total Assets:* £12,356,046
Registered Office: Wilson House, Cinnamon Park, Crab Lane, Fearnhead, Warrington, Cheshire, WA2 0XP
Activities: Other letting and operating of own or leased real estate
Shareholders: David Peter Verey; Louise Marie Lockley
Officers: Louise Marie Lockley [1981] Director; David Peter Verey [1977] Service Director; Peter Verey [1950] Managing Director

Fryett's Fabrics Limited
Incorporated: 12 January 2006 *Employees:* 46
Net Worth: £14,399,519 *Total Assets:* £17,363,228
Registered Office: Marshall House, Rake Lane, Clifton, Manchester, M27 8LJ
Activities: Wholesale of textiles
Parent: Fryett's Holdings Ltd
Officers: Nicholas John Marshall, Secretary; Simon John Baxendale [1964] Production Director; Christopher Robert Dew [1965] Director; Robin Johnston [1953] Finance Director; Henry Marshall [1931] Director/Chairman; Nicholas John Marshall [1970] Production Director; Paul Anthony Marshall [1969] Managing Director

Fryett's Holdings Limited
Incorporated: 28 October 2009
Net Worth: £29,277,616 *Total Assets:* £41,194,124
Registered Office: Marshall House, Rake Lake, Clifton, Manchester, M27 8LJ
Activities: Activities of head offices
Parent: PBM Management Ltd
Officers: Nicholas John Marshall, Secretary; Nicholas John Marshall [1970] Director; Paul Anthony Marshall [1969] Director

FSHC (UK) Limited
Incorporated: 30 June 1986
Net Worth: £163,179,008 *Total Assets:* £163,179,008
Registered Office: Norcliffe House, Station Road, Wilmslow, Cheshire, SK9 1BU
Activities: Activities of head offices
Parent: Four Seasons Group Holdings Limited
Officers: Abigail Mattison, Secretary; Timothy Richard William Hammond [1959] Director; Dr Maureen Claire Royston [1960] Director; Benjamin Robert Taberner [1972] Director/Chartered Accountant

FSHC Developments (Properties) Limited
Incorporated: 18 July 2005 *Employees:* 5
Net Worth Deficit: £10,482,000 *Total Assets:* £17,302,000
Registered Office: Norcliffe House, Station Road, Wilmslow, Cheshire, SK9 1BU
Activities: Other human health activities
Officers: Abigail Mattison, Secretary; Robert Nicolas Barr [1958] Director; Timothy Richard William Hammond [1959] Director; Ryan Stuart MacAskill [1975] Director; Gregory Laurence Newman [1988] Director/Investment Professional; Benjamin Robert Taberner [1972] Director/Chartered Accountant

FSHC Properties (CH2) Limited
Incorporated: 20 May 2005 *Employees:* 5
Net Worth Deficit: £266,226,000 *Total Assets:* £115,918,000
Registered Office: Norcliffe House, Station Road, Wilmslow, Cheshire, SK9 1BU
Activities: Other human health activities
Officers: Abigail Mattison, Secretary; Robert Nicolas Barr [1958] Director; Timothy Richard William Hammond [1959] Director; Ryan Stuart MacAskill [1975] Director; Gregory Laurence Newman [1988] Director/Investment Professional; Benjamin Robert Taberner [1972] Director/Chartered Accountant

FSHC Properties (Manor) Limited
Incorporated: 5 August 1987 *Employees:* 3
Net Worth: £24,258,000 *Total Assets:* £27,208,000
Registered Office: Norcliffe House, Station Road, Wilmslow, Cheshire, SK9 1BU
Activities: Other human health activities
Officers: Abigail Mattison, Secretary; Timothy Richard William Hammond [1959] Director; Dr Maureen Claire Royston [1960] Director; Benjamin Robert Taberner [1972] Director/Chartered Accountant

FSIR Holdings (UK) Limited
Incorporated: 9 November 2004
Net Worth Deficit: £88,985,168 *Total Assets:* £152,841,392
Registered Office: 3rd Floor, 1 Ashley Road, Altrincham, Cheshire, WA14 2DT
Activities: Activities of head offices
Parent: Thermo Fisher Scientific Inc.
Officers: Rhona Gregg, Secretary; Lucie Mary Katja Grant [1976] Director/Solicitor; Nicholas Ince [1982] Director/Accountant; David John Norman [1960] Director/Chartered Accountant

FSUK Holdings Limited
Incorporated: 9 November 2004
Net Worth: £37,012,000 *Total Assets:* £37,057,000
Registered Office: 3rd Floor, 1 Ashley Road, Altrincham, Cheshire, WA14 2DT
Activities: Activities of head offices
Parent: Fisher Scientific UK Holding Company Limited
Officers: Rhona Gregg, Secretary; Lucie Mary Katja Grant [1976] Director/Solicitor; Nicholas Ince [1982] Director/Accountant; David John Norman [1960] Director/Chartered Accountant

Fujifilm Imaging Colorants Limited
Incorporated: 18 February 2005 *Employees:* 121
Net Worth Deficit: £33,018,000 *Total Assets:* £30,305,000
Registered Office: 6th Floor, Acresfield, 8-10 Exchange Street, Manchester, M2 7HA
Activities: Manufacture of other chemical products n.e.c.
Parent: Fujifilm Ink Solutions Limited
Officers: Neil Llewellyn Denham, Secretary; Aiichiro Hiruma [1959] Director [Japanese]; Shinichiro Kuwabara [1963] Director/Manager [Japanese]; Robert Charles Platts [1975] Director/Chartered Accountant; Martin Wilhelm Schoeppler [1955] Director/Chief Executive Officer [American/German]; Tatsuo Suzuki [1964] Director/General Manager [Japanese]; Ian David Wilkinson [1964] Director/Chief Operating Officer; Masato Yamamoto [1963] Director [Japanese]

H.B. Fuller Group Limited
Incorporated: 7 September 2001
Net Worth: £22,480,000 *Total Assets:* £32,564,000
Registered Office: Globe Lane Industrial Estate, Outram Road, Dukinfield, Cheshire, SK16 4XE
Activities: Activities of head offices
Parent: Datac Adhesives Limited
Officers: Robert Joseph Martsching [1964] Director/Vice President and Corporate Controller [American]; Emilio Roque Vilas [1968] Business Director Hygiene [Spanish]; Heidi Ann Weiler [1966] Director/Vice President and Treasurer [American]

H.B. Fuller U.K. Limited
Incorporated: 20 November 1997 *Employees:* 28
Net Worth: £18,651,996 *Total Assets:* £19,873,486
Registered Office: Globe Lane Industrial Estate, Outram Road, Dukinfield, Cheshire, SK16 4XE
Activities: Other business support service activities n.e.c.
Parent: H.B. Fuller U.K. Operations Limited
Officers: Robert Joseph Martsching [1964] Director/Vice President and Corporate Controller [American]; Emilio Roque Vilas [1968] Business Director Hygiene [Spanish]

H.B. Fuller U.K. Manufacturing Limited
Incorporated: 15 March 2001 *Employees:* 22
Net Worth: £9,731,038 *Total Assets:* £11,421,911
Registered Office: Globe Lane Industrial Estate, Outram Road, Dukinfield, Cheshire, SK16 4XE
Activities: Manufacture of other chemical products n.e.c.
Parent: H.B. Fuller U.K. Operations Limited
Officers: Joseph Kijowski [1959] Director/Facility Manager; Heidi Ann Weiler [1966] Director/Vice President and Treasurer [American]

HB Fuller UK Operations Limited
Incorporated: 27 March 1998
Net Worth: £36,084,000 *Total Assets:* £57,599,000
Registered Office: Globe Lane Industrial Estate, Dukinfield, Cheshire, SK16 4XE
Activities: Manufacture of other chemical products n.e.c.
Parent: H.B. Fuller Group Limited
Officers: Robert Joseph Martsching [1964] Director/Vice President and Corporate Controller [American]; Emilio Roque Vilas [1968] Business Director Hygiene [Spanish]; Heidi Ann Weiler [1966] Director/Vice President and Treasurer [American]

The Funding Corporation (2) Limited
Incorporated: 8 May 2003
Net Worth: £950,274 *Total Assets:* £7,285,547
Registered Office: International House, Kingsfield Court, Chester Business Park, Chester, CH4 9RF
Activities: Financial leasing
Parent: The Funding Corporation Limited
Officers: David John Challinor [1962] Director; Gary Ernest Hutton [1959] Director

Furlong Flooring (Central) Ltd
Incorporated: 6 February 1996 *Employees:* 67
Net Worth: £6,905,218 *Total Assets:* £13,796,629
Registered Office: Unit 283 Carnfield Place, Walton Summit, Bamber Bridge, Preston, Lancs, PR5 8AN
Activities: Manufacture of woven or tufted carpets and rugs
Major Shareholder: Noel Furlong
Officers: Daryl Snape, Secretary; Karun Furlong [1965] Director [Irish]; Noel Furlong [1937] Director [Irish]; Muir O Loghlen [1950] Director [Irish]; Daryl Snape [1962] Finance Director; Neil Thomas Valentine [1962] Sales Director

Furmanite 1986
Incorporated: 26 March 1986
Net Worth: £5,421,000 *Total Assets:* £7,915,000
Registered Office: Furman House, Shap Road, Kendal, Cumbria, LA9 6RU
Activities: Repair of other equipment
Parent: Furmanite Limited
Officers: Rachel Dixon, Secretary; Greg Lee Boane [1963] Director/Chief Finance Officer [American]; Andre Charles Bouchard [1965] Director/Senior VP - Legal [American]; Jonathon Anthony Jarvis [1957] Director/Vice President

Furmanite Limited
Incorporated: 13 August 1990
Net Worth: £25,585,000 *Total Assets:* £42,851,000
Registered Office: Furman House, Shap Road, Kendal, Cumbria, LA9 6RU
Activities: Repair of other equipment
Parent: Furmanite Holding B.V.
Officers: Rachel Dixon, Secretary; Greg Lee Boane [1963] Director/Chief Finance Officer [American]; Andre Charles Bouchard [1965] Director/Senior VP - Legal [American]; Jonathon Anthony Jarvis [1957] Director/Vice President

Furness Academies Trust
Incorporated: 5 May 2009 *Employees:* 102
Net Worth: £17,132,000 *Total Assets:* £22,587,000
Registered Office: Furness Academy, Park Drive, Barrow in Furness, Cumbria, LA13 9BB
Activities: General secondary education
Officers: Andrew Robert Judd, Secretary; Gavin Edward Benbow [1978] Director/Head of Finance; Anthony James Hunter Burbridge [1947] Director/Consultant Engineer; Anne Burns [1948] Director/Cumbria County Councillor; Graeme Corkill [1972] Director/Chief Engineer; Edward William Creighton [1967] Director/Head of HR; Jane Dean-Wilcock [1971] Director/Accountant; Hilary Jane Ellam [1960] Director; David William Denning Graham [1974] Director/Solicitor; Adam Mark Hearnden [1962] Safety, Quality & Assurance Director; David Anthony Kelly [1950] Director/Education Consultant; John Austin Shields [1954] Director/Teacher; Mark Woodham [1961] Director/IT Manager

Furness Quay Ltd
Incorporated: 15 December 2015
Net Worth: £100 *Total Assets:* £6,572,014
Registered Office: 300 St Mary's Road, Garston, Liverpool, L19 0NQ
Activities: Development of building projects
Parent: Fortis UK Holdings Ltd
Officers: Darren Kingsley McClellan [1972] Director/Manager; Kieran Stuart Moore [1975] Director/Manager; Gareth Morgan [1984] Director/Manager

Furnico Furniture Limited
Incorporated: 15 July 1999 *Employees:* 331
Net Worth: £6,968,575 *Total Assets:* £13,036,468
Registered Office: Bradford House, Phillips Lane, Colne, Lancs, BB8 9PQ
Activities: Activities of head offices
Parent: Gavco 188 Limited
Officers: Paul Anthony Riding, Secretary/Director; David Mark Ellison [1966] Production Director; Paul Anthony Riding [1961] Finance Director; Stuart Shackleton [1969] Design Director; David Winter [1962] Sales Director

Futaba Manufacturing U.K. Limited
Incorporated: 13 September 2000 *Employees:* 214
Net Worth: £12,042,000 *Total Assets:* £33,964,000
Registered Office: Futaba Manufacturing UK Ltd, Liverpool Road, Burnley, Lancs, BB12 6HJ
Activities: Manufacture of other parts and accessories for motor vehicles
Parent: Futaba Industrial Co.,Ltd
Officers: Uichi Maeda [1961] Director [Japanese]; Tetsunori Matsuo [1961] Director/General Manager [Japanese]; Kevin Schofield [1958] Managing Director; Kenji Tsuyuguchi [1959] Director/General Manager [Japanese]

Futamura Chemical UK Limited
Incorporated: 3 March 2016 *Employees:* 281
Net Worth: £27,939,146 *Total Assets:* £48,607,972
Registered Office: Station Road, Wigton, Cumbria, CA7 9BG
Activities: Other manufacturing n.e.c.
Parent: Futamura Chemical Co., Ltd
Officers: Adrian Jon Cave, Secretary; Graeme Coulthard [1963] Director/General Manager - Europe; Nobuyoshi Goto [1971] Director/President [Japanese]; Yasuo Nagae [1961] Director/President [Japanese]; Takashi Sakamoto [1975] Director [Japanese]; Gen Sato [1961] Director [Japanese]

Future Energy Group Ltd
Incorporated: 15 October 2008 *Employees:* 148
Net Worth: £4,038,632 *Total Assets:* £9,354,597
Registered Office: Ship Canal House, 98 King Street, Manchester, M2 4WU
Activities: Construction of utility projects for fluids
Parent: Energy Assets Limited
Officers: Nigel Derek George Ford [1965] Director; Colin John Lynch [1966] Director; John McMorrow [1977] Director/Chief Financial Officer; Nathan Rhodes Schofield [1970] Director; Craig Philip Topley [1973] Director

Future Heights Limited
Incorporated: 12 June 1997 *Employees:* 27
Net Worth: £10,405,800 *Total Assets:* £18,607,444
Registered Office: 37 Stopgate Lane, Aintree, Liverpool, L9 6DX
Activities: Activities of head offices
Officers: Paul Edward Baylis [1969] Director; Stephen John Baylis [1967] Director; Phillip Robert Millward [1962] Director

Future Industrial Services Limited
Incorporated: 17 March 1999 *Employees:* 249
Net Worth Deficit: £685,000 *Total Assets:* £19,352,000
Registered Office: Image Business Park, Acornfield Road, Kirkby, Merseyside, L33 7UF
Activities: Remediation activities and other waste management services
Parent: Project Delorean Bidco Limited
Officers: John Scott Dunning [1973] Director; David Andrew Lusher [1966] Director/General Manager

FW Chile Holdings 2 Limited
Incorporated: 6 November 2015
Net Worth: £62,390,000 *Total Assets:* £62,390,000
Registered Office: Booths Park, Chelford Road, Knutsford, Cheshire, WA16 8QZ
Activities: Non-trading company
Parent: AMEC USA Holdings Limited
Officers: Iain Angus Jones, Secretary; Carl Anthony Chatfield [1964] Director; William George Setter [1975] Director

FW Investments Limited
Incorporated: 15 June 2009
Net Worth: £184,451,008 *Total Assets:* £184,451,008
Registered Office: Booths Park, Chelford Road, Knutsford, Cheshire, WA16 8QZ
Activities: Other business support service activities n.e.c.
Parent: AMEC Foster Wheeler International Holdings Limited
Officers: Iain Angus Jones, Secretary; William George Setter [1975] Director

Fylde Coast Academy Trust
Incorporated: 17 January 2013 *Employees:* 454
Net Worth: £44,274,000 *Total Assets:* £54,559,000
Registered Office: The Blackpool Sixth Form College, Blackpool Old Road, Blackpool, Lancs, FY3 7LR
Activities: Primary education
Officers: Jane Elizabeth McCumiskey, Secretary; Joel Matthew Arber [1974] Director/College Vice Chancellor; John Oswald Boyle [1955] Director/Financial Consultant; Alana Jane Frith [1955] Director/Leadership Skill Consultant; Jill Gray [1965] Director/College Principal; Mark Anthony Gutteridge [1960] Business Director; Lisa Knowles [1971] Director/Business Owner; Graham Brian Mawdsley [1971] Director/Education Manager - Offender Learning; Peter William Murphy [1956] Director/Boatmaster; Anthony Mark Nicholson [1961] Director/Headteacher

G & H Print Services Limited
Incorporated: 10 July 2006 *Employees:* 71
Net Worth: £434,226 *Total Assets:* £7,777,045
Registered Office: 3 Avocado Court, Commerce Way, Trafford Park, Manchester, M17 1HW
Activities: Printing n.e.c.
Major Shareholder: Earl Raymond Hawley
Officers: Earl Raymond Hawley, Secretary; Derek Clark [1951] Director/Certified Accountant; Earl Raymond Hawley [1946] Director; Ian Jeffrey Lamb [1965] Sales Director

G & J Properties Limited
Incorporated: 12 September 1994
Net Worth: £1,445,659 *Total Assets:* £6,900,959
Registered Office: 454 Darwen Road, Bromley Cross, Bolton, Lancs, BL7 9DX
Activities: Other letting and operating of own or leased real estate
Shareholders: Karen Flitcroft; Garry William Flitcroft
Officers: Garry William Flitcroft [1972] Director/Professional Footballer; Karen Flitcroft [1972] Director

G&J Distillers Ltd.
Incorporated: 14 April 2011 *Employees:* 118
Net Worth: £7,474,000 *Total Assets:* £26,892,000
Registered Office: Distribution Point, Melbury Park, Clayton Road, Birchwood, Warrington, Cheshire, WA3 6PH
Activities: Distilling, rectifying and blending of spirits
Parent: Quintessential Brands UK Group Limited
Officers: Michael Clifford, Secretary; Warren Michael Scott [1963] Director/Businessman; Vincenzo Visone [1955] Director/Businessman [Italian]

G. & B. (North West) Limited
Incorporated: 6 March 1984 *Employees:* 86
Net Worth: £8,896,112 *Total Assets:* £12,091,270
Registered Office: Giants Hall, Willow Road, Beech Hill, Wigan, Lancs, WN6 8RY
Activities: Other specialised construction activities n.e.c.
Shareholders: John Roger Gill; Christine Lesley Gill; Frank Brown
Officers: Christine Lesley Gill, Secretary; Ann Lovell Brown [1941] Director; Frank Brown [1941] Director; Roger Philip Brown [1969] Director/Operations Manager; Matthew Stratos Chialton [1980] Director; Christine Lesley Gill [1953] Director/Company Secretary; John Roger Gill [1950] Director

G.B.A. Services Limited
Incorporated: 2 March 2000 *Employees:* 286
Net Worth: £6,216,542 *Total Assets:* £17,535,516
Registered Office: 429 Moss Lane, Hesketh Bank, Preston, Lancs, PR4 6XJ
Activities: Freight transport by road
Officers: David Watson Birkbeck, Secretary/Director; Andrew John Birkbeck [1974] Director; David Watson Birkbeck [1942] Director; David James Birkbeck [1967] Director

G.B.B.Estates Limited
Incorporated: 10 January 1936 *Employees:* 3
Net Worth: £13,624,962 *Total Assets:* £19,385,560
Registered Office: 2 Friarsgate, Grosvenor Street, Chester, CH1 1XG
Activities: Other letting and operating of own or leased real estate
Shareholder: Mark Guy Williams
Officers: Nigel John Anderton, Secretary; Nigel John Anderton [1954] Director/Chartered Surveyor; Douglas Guy Meikle Williams [1992] Director/Chartered Surveyor; Guy Nicholas Williams [1957] Director/Investment Banker; Mark Guy Williams [1955] Director/Chartered Surveyor

G.D. Yarns Limited
Incorporated: 13 August 1985 *Employees:* 15
Net Worth: £9,961,256 *Total Assets:* £10,354,125
Registered Office: Pawan House, 200 Gorton Road, Manchester, M12 5DX
Activities: Wholesale of textiles
Shareholders: Artee Passi; Pardeep Kumar Passi
Officers: Artee Passi, Secretary/Director; Theresa Patricia Green [1962] Director; Artee Passi [1961] Director; Pardeep Kumar Passi [1956] Director

G.F. Holding (Contractors) Limited
Incorporated: 14 December 1972
Net Worth: £2,465,872 *Total Assets:* £8,519,397
Registered Office: St Andrew's Court, Lees Lane, Mottram St Andrew, Macclesfield, Cheshire, SK10 4LJ
Activities: Construction of commercial buildings
Parent: Holding Holding Company Limited
Officers: Liam Michael McKeever, Secretary; Jeffrey Thomas Barton [1957] Director/Quantity Surveyor; Geoffrey Egerton Holding [1939] Director; Simon Timothy Holding [1972] Director; James Howard Maltby [1961] Director/Contracts Manager; Liam Michael McKeever [1963] Director/Chartered Accountant

G.G.R. Corporation Ltd
Incorporated: 1 April 2010 *Employees:* 128
Net Worth: £20,961,706 *Total Assets:* £28,428,264
Registered Office: Presentation House, Broadgate, Broadway Business Park, Oldham, Lancs, OL9 0JA
Activities: Activities of head offices
Shareholders: Graeme David Riley; Gilliam Marie Riley
Officers: Barrie Michael Riches [1971] Finance Director; Gillian Riley [1971] Managing Director; Graeme Riley [1967] Managing Director

G.G.R. Group Ltd
Incorporated: 16 September 2003 *Employees:* 128
Net Worth: £15 947,499 *Total Assets:* £23,414,056
Registered Office: Presentation House, Broadgate, Broadway Business Park, Oldham, Lancs, OL9 0JA
Activities: Renting and leasing of construction and civil engineering machinery and equipment
Parent: GGR Corporation Ltd
Officers: Graeme David Riley, Secretary; Scott Edward Ainsworth [1970] Technical Support Director; Mia Jane Babb [1967] Customer Service Director; Michael Joseph Heneghan [1960] Sales Director; Christopher Kevin Lord [1958] Technical Director; Craig Phillip Parkin [1951] Technical Director [New Zealander]; Thomas Davidson Rae [1956] Director GGR Scotland; Barrie Michael Riches [1971] Finance Director; Gillian Riley [1971] Director; Graeme David Riley [1967] Director

G.P.S. Holdings Limited
Incorporated: 29 July 1986 *Employees:* 94
Net Worth: £3,152,561 *Total Assets:* £10,463,362
Registered Office: Unit 1-9 Carrington Business Park, Carrington, Urmston, Manchester, M31 4DD
Activities: Activities of head offices
Shareholder: Mark Ian Stephen
Officers: Robert Lee Scott, Secretary; Gavin Andrew Allen [1973] Director/Business Manager; Mark Ian Stephen [1968] Director

G.S. Cold Storage and Warehousing Limited
Incorporated: 7 December 1993 *Employees:* 2
Net Worth: £6,369,292 *Total Assets:* £11,214,168
Registered Office: Office 108, Admin Block, Riverpark Trading Estate, Riverpark Road, Manchester, M40 2XP
Activities: Development of building projects
Parent: Valuescene Limited
Officers: Andrew Birtwistle, Secretary/Director; Andrew Birtwistle [1953] Director; Sandra Birtwistle [1952] Director/Secretary

G2S Limited
Incorporated: 19 June 2009 *Employees:* 92
Net Worth: £4,379,522 *Total Assets:* £21,116,236
Registered Office: Green Bank Business Park, Swan Lane, Hindley Green, Wigan, Lancs, WN2 4EZ
Activities: Wholesale of radio, television goods & electrical household appliances (other than records, tapes, CDs)
Parent: Matchstick Men Limited
Officers: Lisa Marie Carroll, Secretary; Simone Paula Fisher [1973] Accounts Director; Gavin Hamer [1979] Managing Director; Olivia Paulette Hamer [1978] Director [New Zealander]; Stephen John Smith [1966] Director

GA Pet Food Partners Group Limited
Incorporated: 9 October 2000
Net Worth: £66,715,000 *Total Assets:* £90,715,000
Registered Office: The Albert Suite, Unit 2 Revolution Park, Buckshaw Avenue, Buckshaw Village, Chorley, Lancs, PR7 7DW
Activities: Activities of production holding companies
Major Shareholder: Roger Julian Thomas Acland Bracewell
Officers: Roger Julian Thomas Acland Bracewell, Secretary; David Hulme Bennison [1978] Sales Director; Giles Justin St John Acland Bracewell [1965] Director/Surveyor; Roger Julian Thomas Acland Bracewell [1930] Director/Surveyor; Dr Andrew Paul Kettle [1970] Managing Director; Diane Linda Metcalfe [1971] Cost Director; Jim Whittingham [1970] Operations Director

GA Pet Food Partners Limited
Incorporated: 6 September 1996 *Employees:* 31
Net Worth: £211,000 *Total Assets:* £9,332,000
Registered Office: The Albert Suite, Unit 2 Revolution Park, Buckshaw Avenue, Buckshaw Village, Chorley, Lancs, PR7 7DW
Activities: Manufacture of prepared pet foods
Parent: GA Pet Food Partners Group Ltd
Officers: Roger Julian Thomas Acland Bracewell, Secretary/Surveyor; David Hulme Bennison [1978] Sales Director; Giles Justin St John Acland Bracewell [1965] Director; Roger Julian Thomas Acland Bracewell [1960] Director; Dr Andrew Paul Kettle [1970] Managing Director

GA Pet Food Partners Milling Limited
Incorporated: 7 November 2000 *Employees:* 352
Net Worth: £263,000 *Total Assets:* £20,710,000
Registered Office: The Albert Suite, Unit 2 Revolution Park, Buckshaw Avenue, Buckshaw Village, Chorley, Lancs, PR7 7DW
Activities: Manufacture of prepared pet foods
Parent: GA Pet Food Partners Group Ltd
Officers: Roger Julian Thomas Acland Bracewell, Secretary; Giles Justin St John Acland Bracewell [1965] Director/Surveyor; Roger Julian Thomas Acland Bracewell [1960] Director/Surveyor; Dr Andrew Paul Kettle [1970] Managing Director; James Nicholas Whittingham [1970] Production Director

Gaerwen Properties Limited
Incorporated: 11 October 2012 *Employees:* 2
Net Worth: £2,947,642 *Total Assets:* £11,117,040
Registered Office: Rough Hill, Marlston-Cum-Lache, Chester, CH4 9JS
Activities: Other letting and operating of own or leased real estate
Officers: Catherine Jane Pickering [1969] Director/Property Developer; John Alec Pickering [1970] Director/Property Developer

Galaxy Bidco Limited
Incorporated: 12 December 2013
Net Worth Deficit: £7,955,000 *Total Assets:* £153,196,000
Registered Office: 2 Peel Road, Skelmersdale, Lancs, WN8 9PT
Activities: Activities of head offices
Officers: Andrew James Buckley [1970] Director/Chief Financial Officer; Neil Anthony Johnson [1949] Director; Gavin Maxwell Manson [1966] Director/Chief Financial Officer; Robert Clive Perkins [1963] Director; Sara Ellen Prowse [1969] Director/Chief Executive

Galaxy Midco Limited
Incorporated: 12 December 2013
Net Worth Deficit: £39,649,000 *Total Assets:* £113,753,000
Registered Office: 2 Peel Road, Skelmersdale, Lancs, WN8 9PT
Activities: Activities of head offices
Officers: Andrew James Buckley [1970] Director/Chief Financial Officer; Neil Anthony Johnson [1949] Director; Gavin Maxwell Manson [1966] Director/Chief Financial Officer; Robert Clive Perkins [1963] Director; Sara Ellen Prowse [1969] Director/Chief Executive

Galaxy Optical Services Limited
Incorporated: 13 December 1996 *Employees:* 271
Net Worth: £6,188,000 *Total Assets:* £20,561,000
Registered Office: Unit B3, Stuart Road, Altrincham Business Park, Altrincham, Cheshire, WA14 5GJ
Activities: Other manufacturing n.e.c.
Shareholders: Laura Weingarten; Nicole Miller Avni; Alexis Rosenthal
Officers: Sergio Weingarten, Secretary; Philip Johnston [1970] Director; Maurice Peter Miller [1945] Director/Optometrist; Rochelle Evelyn Miller [1953] Director; Sergio Weingarten [1981] Director of International Operations

Galaxy Topco Limited
Incorporated: 12 December 2013 *Employees:* 943
Net Worth Deficit: £52,560,000 *Total Assets:* £149,954,000
Registered Office: 2 Peel Road, Skelmersdale, Lancs, WN8 9PT
Activities: Activities of head offices
Officers: Andrew James Buckley [1970] Director/Chief Financial Officer; Neil Anthony Johnson [1949] Director; Gavin Maxwell Manson [1966] Director/Chief Financial Officer; Robert Clive Perkins [1963] Director; Sara Ellen Prowse [1969] Director/Chief Executive; Alan White [1955] Non-Executive Director Chairman

T&K Gallagher Limited
Incorporated: 22 August 2000 *Employees:* 331
Net Worth: £2,645,726 *Total Assets:* £18,358,408
Registered Office: Weaste Works, James Corbett Road, Salford, M50 1DE
Activities: Construction of other civil engineering projects n.e.c.
Parent: Gallagher Utility Services Group Limited
Officers: Michael Vincent O'Connor, Secretary; Stephen John Alderson [1958] Finance Director; Kathryn Anne Duckworth [1974] Commercial Director; Stuart Alan Fraser [1978] Managing Director; Thomas Joseph Gallagher [1970] Director; Daniel Lawrence Holland [1978] Director/Chief Executive Officer; Michael Vincent O'Connor [1972] Director [Irish]; Matthew Patrick O'Sullivan [1972] Compliance and Operations Director; Adam Robert Tilbrook [1968] Operations Director

Gallagher Topco Limited
Incorporated: 13 March 2016 *Employees:* 352
Net Worth: £1,821,058 *Total Assets:* £46,692,384
Registered Office: Weaste Works, James Corbett Road, Salford, M50 1DE
Activities: Activities of other holding companies n.e.c.
Shareholders: Daniel Lawrence Holland; Stuart Alan Fraser
Officers: Stephen John Alderson [1958] Director/Chartered Accountant; Stuart Alan Fraser [1978] Managing Director; Thomas Joseph Gallagher [1970] Director [Irish]; Daniel Lawrence Holland [1972] Director/Chief Executive Officer

James Galt & Co. Limited
Incorporated: 28 April 1914 *Employees:* 36
Net Worth: £1,985,076 *Total Assets:* £8,054,689
Registered Office: Sovereign House, Stockport Road, Cheadle, Cheshire, SK8 2EA
Activities: Manufacture of other games and toys, n.e.c.
Parent: Global Brand Investments Limited
Officers: John David Bolton, Secretary; John David Bolton [1957] Financial Director; David Elie Cicurel [1949] Director/Instrument Manufacturer; John Richard McDonnell [1957] Director; Guy Anthony Naggar [1940] Director/Merchant Banker [Italian]; Jonathan Naggar [1971] Director; Clive William Robinson [1961] UK Sales Director

Gapp Developments Limited
Incorporated: 30 July 2002
Net Worth: £3,193,039 *Total Assets:* £10,639,792
Registered Office: Beech House, Lancaster Gate, Leyland, Lancs, PR25 2EX
Activities: Other letting and operating of own or leased real estate
Shareholders: Sarah Carr; Stuart Carr
Officers: Sarah Carr, Secretary/School Manager; Sarah Carr [1957] Director; Stuart Carr [1958] Director

Garden State Property Management Ltd
Incorporated: 13 August 2012
Net Worth: £5,777,246 *Total Assets:* £7,108,553
Registered Office: 116 Duke Street, Liverpool, L1 5JW
Activities: Other accommodation
Major Shareholder: Sean Michael Lynch
Officers: Sean Michael Lynch [1967] Director/Security Consultant

Gardner Denver Group Services Limited
Incorporated: 13 November 1987 *Employees:* 500
Net Worth: £4,846,706 *Total Assets:* £23,823,616
Registered Office: c/o Gardner Denver International Ltd, Springmill Street, Bradford, W Yorks, BD5 7HW
Activities: Activities of head offices
Parent: Gardner Denver International Ltd
Officers: Mark Elliott Grummett, Secretary; Andrew Roger Schiesl [1971] Director/General Council [American]; Mark Robert Sweeney [1961] Director/Vice President and Corporate Controller [American]

Gardner Denver Holdings Limited
Incorporated: 25 September 2008
Net Worth: £2,073,180 *Total Assets:* £236,491,392
Registered Office: c/o Gardner Denver International Ltd, Springmill Street, Bradford, W Yorks, BD5 7HW
Activities: Activities of head offices
Parent: GD Global Holdings UK II Ltd
Officers: Mark Elliott Grummett, Secretary; Andrew Roger Schiesl [1971] Director/General Council [American]; Mark Robert Sweeney [1961] Director/Vice President and Corporate Controller [American]

Gardner Denver Industries Ltd
Incorporated: 10 April 1920
Net Worth: £206,976,544 *Total Assets:* £220,029,664
Registered Office: Gardner Denver Industries Ltd, Springmill Street, Bradford, W Yorks, BD5 7HW
Activities: Activities of head offices
Parent: GD Global Holdings UK II Ltd
Officers: Mark Elliott Grummett, Secretary; Andrew Roger Schiesl [1971] Director/General Council [American]; Mark Robert Sweeney [1961] Director/Vice President and Corporate Controller [American]

Gardner Denver International Ltd
Incorporated: 28 September 1962
Net Worth: £73,452,400 *Total Assets:* £114,827,320
Registered Office: Gardner Denver International Ltd, Springmill Street, Bradford, W Yorks, BD5 7HW
Activities: Activities of head offices
Parent: GD Global Holdings UK II Ltd
Officers: Mark Elliott Grummett, Secretary; Andrew Roger Schiesl [1971] Director/General Council [American]; Mark Robert Sweeney [1961] Director/Vice President and Corporate Controller [American]

Gardner Denver Ltd
Incorporated: 19 April 1995
Net Worth: £15,432,000 *Total Assets:* £106,573,000
Registered Office: c/o Gardner Denver International Ltd, Springmill Street, Bradford, W Yorks, BD5 7HW
Activities: Manufacture of compressors
Parent: Gardner Denver International Ltd
Officers: Mark Elliott Grummett, Secretary; Andrew Roger Schiesl [1971] Director/General Council [American]; Mark Robert Sweeney [1961] Director/Vice President and Corporate Controller [American]

Garic Limited
Incorporated: 12 February 1988 *Employees:* 227
Net Worth: £5,314,000 *Total Assets:* £29,934,000
Registered Office: 105 Duke Street, Liverpool, L1 5JQ
Activities: Renting and leasing of construction and civil engineering machinery and equipment
Parent: Bibby Taurus Limited
Officers: Mark Albiston [1971] Director; Jacqueline Barker [1962] Director; Peter John Bibby [1969] Director; John Harold Cresswell [1961] Director; Andrew John Goody [1966] Director/Accountant; Colin Archibald Hotchkiss [1970] Managing Director; Mark Joseph Lyons [1962] Director; Neil Robert Richardson [1983] Director

Garstang Community Academy Trust
Incorporated: 15 July 2011 *Employees:* 66
Net Worth: £9,552,000 *Total Assets:* £11,008,000
Registered Office: Garstang Community Academy, Bowgreave, Garstang, Preston, Lancs, PR3 1YE
Activities: General secondary education
Officers: Angela Rose Livesey, Secretary; Gordon Russell Alston [1945] Director/Ofsted Inspector; Philip Mark Birch [1963] Director/Headteacher; Anne Michele Green [1962] Director/Teaching Assistant Voluntary; Thomas Ibison [1937] Director/Partner-Garstang Golf Club; Peter William Murphy [1956] Director/Wyre Borough Councillor; Clare Michelle Whittingham [1973] Director/School Administrator; Cathryn Marie Wilkinson [1974] Director/Headteacher

Gartside Investments Limited
Incorporated: 21 April 2005 *Employees:* 3
Net Worth Deficit: £3,778,954 *Total Assets:* £25,118,826
Registered Office: c/o Allied London, Level 12, No 1 Spinningfields, 1 Hardman Square, Manchester, M3 3EB
Activities: Other letting and operating of own or leased real estate
Parent: Gartside Holdings Limited
Officers: Frederick Paul Graham Watson [1957] Director; Michael Julian Ingall [1959] Director

Gartside Limited
Incorporated: 25 January 2002 *Employees:* 3
Net Worth: £100,000 *Total Assets:* £187,980,256
Registered Office: c/o Allied London, Level 12, No 1 Spinningfields, 1 Hardman Square, Manchester, M3 3EB
Activities: Other letting and operating of own or leased real estate
Parent: Gartside Investments Limited
Officers: Frederick Paul Graham Watson [1957] Director; Michael Julian Ingall [1959] Director

Gas Control Equipment Limited
Incorporated: 24 March 1986 *Employees:* 25
Net Worth Deficit: £3,885,000 *Total Assets:* £10,033,000
Registered Office: 100 Empress Park, Penny Lane, Haydock, St Helens, Merseyside, WA11 9DB
Activities: Manufacture of other general-purpose machinery n.e.c.
Parent: GCE Holdings AB
Officers: Jeremy Matthew Pauline, Secretary; Michael Joseph Galvin [1960] Managing Director; Christophe Andre Raynaud de Fitte [1963] Director [French]

Gaskells (North West) Limited
Incorporated: 12 June 1995 *Employees:* 101
Net Worth: £1,945,442 *Total Assets:* £9,402,223
Registered Office: 17-21 Foster Street, Liverpool, L20 8EX
Activities: Treatment and disposal of hazardous waste
Major Shareholder: Jonathan David Gaskell
Officers: James Richard Gaskell, Secretary; Denise Banks [1971] Commercial Director; John Barlow Cushing [1943] Director; Jonathan David Gaskell [1971] Director/Waste Disposal Engineer

Gavco 188 Limited
Incorporated: 7 October 2016 *Employees:* 327
Net Worth: £4,328,339 *Total Assets:* £7,679,638
Registered Office: Bradford House, Phillips Lane, Colne, Lancs, BB8 9PQ
Activities: Non-trading company
Shareholders: David Winter; Paul Anthony Riding
Officers: Paul Anthony Riding [1961] Finance Director; David Winter [1962] Sales Director

GB Group PLC
Incorporated: 21 August 1989 *Employees:* 774
Net Worth: £157,752,000 *Total Assets:* £231,404,992
Registered Office: The Foundation, Herons Way, Chester Business Park, Chester, CH4 9GB
Activities: Information technology consultancy activities
Officers: John Henri Constantin, Secretary; Nicholas Richard Brown [1960] Director; Elizabeth Margaret Catchpole [1965] Director; Christopher Graham Clark [1969] Director/Chief Executive; Charmaine Bridgette Eggberry [1970] Director; David Anthony Rasche [1949] Director; David John Wilson [1962] Director/Accountant

GD Aria Holdings #2 Limited
Incorporated: 1 June 2012
Net Worth: £160,277,872 *Total Assets:* £160,359,152
Registered Office: Springmill Street, Bradford, W Yorks, BD5 7HW
Activities: Activities of head offices
Parent: GD Aria Holdings Ltd
Officers: Mark Elliott Grummett, Secretary; Andrew Roger Schiesl [1971] Director/General Council [American]; Mark Robert Sweeney [1961] Director/Vice President and Corporate Controller [American]

GD Aria Holdings Limited
Incorporated: 10 November 2011
Net Worth Deficit: £1,334,354 *Total Assets:* £130,660,352
Registered Office: Springmill Street, Bradford, W Yorks, BD5 7HW
Activities: Activities of head offices
Parent: U.S. Branch of GD Global Holdings II S.A.R.L.
Officers: Mark Elliott Grummett, Secretary; Andrew Roger Schiesl [1971] Director/General Council [American]; Mark Robert Sweeney [1961] Director/Vice President and Corporate Controller [American]

GD Global Holdings UK II Limited
Incorporated: 18 November 2014
Net Worth: £392,551,392 *Total Assets:* £425,850,304
Registered Office: Springmill Street, Bradford, W Yorks, BD5 7HW
Activities: Activities of head offices
Parent: GD Global Holdings II SARL
Officers: Mark Elliott Grummett, Secretary; Mark Elliott Grummett [1966] Director/Chartered Accountant; Andrew Roger Schiesl [1971] Director/General Counsel & Secretary [American]

GE (Holdings)
Incorporated: 3 March 1999
Net Worth Deficit: £60,000 *Total Assets:* £92,553,000
Registered Office: 3rd Floor, 1 Ashley Road, Altrincham, Cheshire, WA14 2DT
Activities: Activities of other holding companies n.e.c.
Parent: General Electric Company
Officers: Andrew Thomas Peter Budge [1973] Director/Chartered Accountant; Tristan Keith Chubb [1980] Director/Solicitor; Akhlesh Prasad Mathur [1972] Director/Chartered Accountant

GE (Sigma) Holding Ltd
Incorporated: 22 November 1993
Net Worth: £363,436,992 *Total Assets:* £363,456,992
Registered Office: 3rd Floor, 1 Ashley Road, Altrincham, Cheshire, WA14 2DT
Activities: Non-trading company
Parent: GE Capital Sigma Holding Ltd
Officers: Norris Andrew Geldard [1965] Director; Paul Stewart Girling [1978] Director

GE Capital Corporation (Funding) Limited
Incorporated: 11 December 1985 *Employees:* 7
Net Worth: £24,075,000 *Total Assets:* £42,193,000
Registered Office: 3rd Floor, 1 Ashley Road, Altrincham, Cheshire, WA14 2DT
Activities: Financial intermediation not elsewhere classified
Parent: GE Capital Corporation (Property Company Investments) Limited
Officers: Derek Carter [1983] Director/Portfolio Manager; Paul Stewart Girling [1978] Director

GE Capital Corporation (Holdings)
Incorporated: 28 August 1993
Net Worth: £290,552,000 *Total Assets:* £1,388,611,968
Registered Office: 3rd Floor, 1 Ashley Road, Altrincham, Cheshire, WA14 2DT
Activities: Activities of head offices
Parent: GE Capital Investments
Officers: Paul Stewart Girling [1978] Director

GE Capital Corporation (Investment Properties) Limited
Incorporated: 29 March 2000
Net Worth: £8,968,000 *Total Assets:* £8,982,000
Registered Office: 3rd Floor, 1 Ashley Road, Altrincham, Cheshire, WA14 2DT
Activities: Development of building projects
Parent: GE Capital Corporation (Property Company Investments) Limited
Officers: Derek Carter [1983] Director/Portfolio Manager; Paul Stewart Girling [1978] Director

GE Capital Corporation (Leasing) Limited
Incorporated: 11 December 1985
Net Worth: £12,286,801 *Total Assets:* £16,797,262
Registered Office: 3rd Floor, 1 Ashley Road, Altrincham, Cheshire, WA14 2DT
Activities: Financial leasing
Officers: Nina Mary Atkinson [1977] Director; Alan Evans [1968] Director; Lisa Farrell [1972] Director; Anita Kravos-Medimorec [1974] Director [British/Croatian]

GE Capital Corporation (Property Company Investments) Limited
Incorporated: 11 April 2000
Net Worth: £646,171,008 *Total Assets:* £646,174,016
Registered Office: 3rd Floor, 1 Ashley Road, Altrincham, Cheshire, WA14 2DT
Activities: Development of building projects
Parent: GE Capital Corporation (Holdings)
Officers: Derek Carter [1983] Director/Portfolio Manager; Paul Stewart Girling [1978] Director

GE Capital EMEA Services Limited
Incorporated: 1 January 1930 *Employees:* 397
Net Worth: £25,878,000 *Total Assets:* £343,780,992
Registered Office: 3rd Floor, 1 Ashley Road, Altrincham, Cheshire, WA14 2DT
Activities: Other service activities n.e.c.
Parent: GE Capital Sigma Holding Ltd
Officers: Claire Akehurst [1979] Director; Jonathan Lawrence John Gatt [1981] Director [Maltese]; Norris Andrew Geldard [1965] Director

GE Capital Equipment Finance Holdings
Incorporated: 31 October 1986
Net Worth: £72,713,000 *Total Assets:* £74,309,000
Registered Office: 3rd Floor, 1 Ashley Road, Altrincham, Cheshire, WA14 2DT
Activities: Activities of head offices
Parent: GE Capital Corporation (Holdings)
Officers: Nina Mary Atkinson [1977] Director; Alan Evans [1968] Director; Lisa Farrell [1972] Director

GE Capital Equipment Finance Ltd
Incorporated: 19 March 1973 *Employees:* 98
Net Worth: £55,396,000 *Total Assets:* £207,806,000
Registered Office: 3rd Floor, 1 Ashley Road, Altrincham, Cheshire, WA14 2DT
Activities: Financial intermediation not elsewhere classified
Parent: GE Capital Equipment Finance Holdings
Officers: Nina Mary Atkinson [1977] Director; Alan Evans [1968] Director; Lisa Farrell [1972] Director

GE Capital Europe Limited
Incorporated: 28 September 1990 *Employees:* 393
Net Worth: £32,244,000 *Total Assets:* £102,482,000
Registered Office: 3rd Floor, 1 Ashley Road, Altrincham, Cheshire, WA14 2DT
Activities: Other business support service activities n.e.c.
Parent: International General Electric (U.S.A.)
Officers: Christopher Lloyd Allcock [1972] Director; Akhlesh Prasad Mathur [1972] Director/Chartered Accountant; Anna Elizabeth Maxim [1976] Director/Sub Region Leader - North Europe, Global Operations

GE Capital European Treasury Services Limited
Incorporated: 21 July 1998
Net Worth: £88,132,000 *Total Assets:* £6,137,605,120
Registered Office: 3rd Floor, 1 Ashley Road, Altrincham, Cheshire, WA14 2DT
Activities: Financial intermediation not elsewhere classified
Parent: GE Capital Investments
Officers: Timothy Lane [1961] Director [American]; Akhlesh Prasad Mathur [1972] Director/Chartered Accountant

GE Capital Funding Services Limited
Incorporated: 11 March 1999 *Employees:* 198
Net Worth: £141,008,000 *Total Assets:* £776,398,016
Registered Office: 3rd Floor, 1 Ashley Road, Altrincham, Cheshire, WA14 2DT
Activities: Financial intermediation not elsewhere classified
Parent: GE Aircraft Engine Services Limited
Officers: Timothy Carfi [1968] Director [American]; Mark Kavanagh [1971] Director/Underwriting Pole Leader

GE Capital Group Services Limited
Incorporated: 21 May 1987
Net Worth: £50,000 *Total Assets:* £21,253,000
Registered Office: 3rd Floor, 1 Ashley Road, Altrincham, Cheshire, WA14 2DT
Activities: Financial intermediation not elsewhere classified
Parent: GE Capital Corporation (Holdings)
Officers: Anthony James Brown [1973] Director/Chartered Accountant; Matthew Smithart McClellan [1971] Director/Travel Expense Manager [American]

GE Capital Information Technology Solutions Limited
Incorporated: 16 January 1975
Net Worth: £195,811,008 *Total Assets:* £195,811,008
Registered Office: 3rd Floor, 1 Ashley Road, Altrincham, Cheshire, WA14 2DT
Activities: Other information technology service activities
Parent: GE ESE UK Limited
Officers: Jonathan Lawrence John Gatt [1981] Director/FP&A Leader [Maltese]; Paul Stewart Girling [1978] Director

GE Capital International Holdings Limited
Incorporated: 1 July 2015
Net Worth: £19,176,949,760 *Total Assets:* £84,369,424,384
Registered Office: 3rd Floor, 1 Ashley Road, Altrincham, Cheshire, WA14 2DT
Activities: Activities of head offices
Parent: General Electric Company
Officers: Jonathan Lawrence John Gatt [1981] Director [Maltese]; Norris Andrew Geldard [1965] Director; Paul Stewart Girling [1978] Director; Max Jessernigg [1974] Director [Austrian]

GE Capital International Limited
Incorporated: 1 July 2015
Net Worth: £11,264,392,192 *Total Assets:* £11,264,427,008
Registered Office: 3rd Floor, 1 Ashley Road, Altrincham, Cheshire, WA14 2DT
Activities: Activities of head offices
Parent: GE Capital International Holdings Limited
Officers: Jonathan Lawrence John Gatt [1981] Director [Maltese]; Norris Andrew Geldard [1965] Director; Paul Stewart Girling [1978] Director; Max Jessernigg [1974] Director [Austrian]

GE Capital Investments
Incorporated: 23 September 1996
Net Worth: £1,552,360,960 *Total Assets:* £3,137,901,056
Registered Office: 3rd Floor, 1 Ashley Road, Altrincham, Cheshire, WA14 2DT
Activities: Activities auxiliary to financial intermediation n.e.c.
Parent: IGE USA Investments
Officers: Norris Andrew Geldard [1965] Director/Accountant; Paul Stewart Girling [1978] Director

GE Capital Limited
Incorporated: 16 August 2000 *Employees:* 43
Net Worth: £17,126,000 *Total Assets:* £23,989,000
Registered Office: 3rd Floor, 1 Ashley Road, Altrincham, Cheshire, WA14 2DT
Activities: Other business support service activities n.e.c.
Parent: GE Capital Investments
Officers: Mark Russell Hanson [1973] Director; Raghuveer Kurada [1965] Director [American]; Bobby Psaradellis [1976] Director; Brian Peter Ward [1959] Director/Investment Professional [American]

GE Capital Sigma Holding Ltd
Incorporated: 26 February 1987
Net Worth: £229,440,992 *Total Assets:* £422,017,984
Registered Office: 3rd Floor, 1 Ashley Road, Altrincham, Cheshire, WA14 2DT
Activities: Renting and leasing of other machinery, equipment and tangible goods n.e.c.
Parent: GE Capital Corporation (Holdings)
Officers: Paul Stewart Girling [1978] Director

GE Capital Solutions Europe Limited
Incorporated: 6 November 1981 *Employees:* 2
Net Worth: £25,356,000 *Total Assets:* £60,030,000
Registered Office: 3rd Floor, 1 Ashley Road, Altrincham, Cheshire, WA14 2DT
Activities: Financial intermediation not elsewhere classified
Parent: GE Capital Equipment Finance Holdings
Officers: Norris Andrew Geldard [1965] Director; Paul Stewart Girling [1978] Director

GE Capital UK Limited
Incorporated: 17 October 1990 *Employees:* 231
Net Worth: £466,123,008 *Total Assets:* £546,529,024
Registered Office: 3rd Floor, 1 Ashley Road, Altrincham, Cheshire, WA14 2DT
Activities: Financial leasing
Parent: GE Capital Sigma Holding Ltd
Officers: Norris Andrew Geldard [1965] Director; Jennifer Anne Ross [1974] Director

GE Commercial Finance Limited
Incorporated: 5 November 1971 *Employees:* 56
Net Worth: £15,758,000 *Total Assets:* £19,840,000
Registered Office: 3rd Floor, 1 Ashley Road, Altrincham, Cheshire, WA14 2DT
Activities: Financial intermediation not elsewhere classified
Parent: GE Capital UK Limited
Officers: Norris Andrew Geldard [1965] Director; Jennifer Anne Ross [1974] Director

GE ESE UK Limited
Incorporated: 9 September 1977
Net Worth: £268,744,000 *Total Assets:* £310,417,984
Registered Office: 3rd Floor, 1 Ashley Road, Altrincham, Cheshire, WA14 2DT
Activities: Other business support service activities n.e.c.
Parent: IGE USA Investments
Officers: Jonathan Lawrence John Gatt [1981] Director/FP&A Leader [Maltese]; Paul Stewart Girling [1978] Director

GE European Equipment Finance (Aircraft No. 2) Limited
Incorporated: 20 July 1987
Net Worth: £44,379,376 *Total Assets:* £45,588,304
Registered Office: 3rd Floor, 1 Ashley Road, Altrincham, Cheshire, WA14 2DT
Activities: Renting and leasing of other machinery, equipment and tangible goods n.e.c.
Parent: GE Capital Investments
Officers: Nina Mary Atkinson [1977] Director; Alan Evans [1968] Director; Lisa Farrell [1972] Director

GE Financial Investments
Incorporated: 19 February 1997
Net Worth: £41,435,940 *Total Assets:* £44,495,940
Registered Office: 3rd Floor, 1 Ashley Road, Altrincham, Cheshire, WA14 2DT
Activities: Sale of new cars and light motor vehicles
Parent: General Electric Company
Officers: Jonathan Lawrence John Gatt [1981] Director/FP&A Leader [Maltese]

GE Industrial (UK) Holdings
Incorporated: 7 July 2006
Net Worth Deficit: £183,728,000 *Total Assets:* £533,316,992
Registered Office: 3rd Floor, 1 Ashley Road, Altrincham, Cheshire, WA14 2DT
Activities: Activities of other holding companies n.e.c.
Officers: Alasdair Murray Campbell Sloan [1967] Director/Chartered Accountant

GE Industrial Sterling Treasury Services
Incorporated: 21 October 2015
Net Worth: £71,599,000 *Total Assets:* £4,621,636,096
Registered Office: 3rd Floor, 1 Ashley Road, Altrincham, Cheshire, WA14 2DT
Activities: Financial intermediation not elsewhere classified
Parent: GE Industrial Treasury Holdings
Officers: Andrew Thomas Peter Budge [1973] Director/Chartered Accountant; Akhlesh Prasad Mathur [1972] Director/Chartered Accountant

GE Infrastructure UK Limited
Incorporated: 26 June 1958
Net Worth: £1,271,362,048 *Total Assets:* £1,307,286,016
Registered Office: 3rd Floor, 1 Ashley Road, Altrincham, Cheshire, WA14 2DT
Activities: Other information technology service activities
Parent: International General Electric (U.S.A.)
Officers: Andrew Thomas Peter Budge [1973] Director/Chartered Accountant; Akhlesh Prasad Mathur [1972] Director/Chartered Accountant

GE Intelligent Platforms Limited
Incorporated: 19 August 1999 *Employees:* 43
Net Worth: £30,683,000 *Total Assets:* £32,976,000
Registered Office: 3rd Floor, 1 Ashley Road, Altrincham, Cheshire, WA14 2DT
Activities: Manufacture of computers and peripheral equipment
Parent: GE UK Holdings
Officers: Huibert Cornelis Brouwer [1963] Tax Director [Dutch]; Deborah Lynn Sherry [1964] Director/GE Digital General Manager Europe

GE Lighting Limited
Incorporated: 10 November 1986 *Employees:* 71
Net Worth: £69,919,000 *Total Assets:* £93,178,000
Registered Office: 3rd Floor, 1 Ashley Road, Altrincham, Cheshire, WA14 2DT
Activities: Wholesale of radio, television goods & electrical household appliances (other than records, tapes, CDs)
Shareholders: IGE USA Holdings; General Electric Company
Officers: Lauren Maria Mierley Cramer [1984] Director/Chief Executive Officer [American]; Gary Lee Kimber [1958] Sales Director

GE Real Estate (Investment Property Company) Limited
Incorporated: 20 July 2005
Net Worth: £33,405,000 *Total Assets:* £33,595,000
Registered Office: 3rd Floor, 1 Ashley Road, Altrincham, Cheshire, WA14 2DT
Activities: Development of building projects
Parent: GE Capital Corporation (Property Company Investments) Limited
Officers: Derek Carter [1983] Director/Portfolio Manager; Paul Stewart Girling [1978] Director

GE Real Estate European Finance Limited
Incorporated: 25 March 2008
Net Worth: £14,627,936 *Total Assets:* £16,265,017
Registered Office: 3rd Floor, 1 Ashley Road, Altrincham, Cheshire, WA14 2DT
Activities: Development of building projects
Officers: Derek Carter [1983] Director/Portfolio Manager; Paul Stewart Girling [1978] Director

GE Real Estate Finance Limited
Incorporated: 7 November 2007
Net Worth: £22,840,000 *Total Assets:* £26,956,000
Registered Office: 3rd Floor, 1 Ashley Road, Altrincham, Cheshire, WA14 2DT
Activities: Development of building projects
Officers: Derek Carter [1983] Director/Portfolio Manager; Paul Stewart Girling [1978] Director

GE Transportation Systems Ltd
Incorporated: 25 November 1977 *Employees:* 14
Net Worth: £73,721,000 *Total Assets:* £74,880,000
Registered Office: 3rd Floor, 1 Ashley Road, Altrincham, Cheshire, WA14 2DT
Activities: Manufacture of computers and peripheral equipment
Parent: Altair Holdings UK Limited
Officers: Graham Barry Ellwood [1981] Director; Frederick Paul Camille Peeters [1975] Director/Tax Manager [Belgian]

GE UK Group
Incorporated: 29 January 2008
Net Worth: £980,089,984 *Total Assets:* £1,968,368,000
Registered Office: 3rd Floor, 1 Ashley Road, Altrincham, Cheshire, WA14 2DT
Activities: Activities of head offices
Parent: GE Industrial Consolidation Limited
Officers: Andrew Thomas Peter Budge [1973] Director/Chartered Accountant; Akhlesh Prasad Mathur [1972] Director/Chartered Accountant

GE UK Holdings
Incorporated: 16 November 2000
Net Worth: £1,070,540,032 *Total Assets:* £1,407,089,024
Registered Office: 3rd Floor, 1 Ashley Road, Altrincham, Cheshire, WA14 2DT
Activities: Activities of other holding companies n.e.c.
Parent: GE Industrial Consolidation Limited
Officers: Andrew Thomas Peter Budge [1973] Director/Chartered Accountant; Akhlesh Prasad Mathur [1972] Director/Chartered Accountant

GEA Process Engineering Limited
Incorporated: 27 August 1976 *Employees:* 155
Net Worth: £18,028,500 *Total Assets:* £155,648,544
Registered Office: Leacroft House, Leacroft Road, Birchwood, Warrington, Cheshire, WA3 6JF
Activities: Manufacture of machinery for food, beverage and tobacco processing
Officers: Ilija Aprcovic [1966] Director; Timothy John Donbavand [1967] Finance Director; Martin David Jackson [1966] Director/Head of Solutions Sales - UK; Tracey Ann O'Neill [1968] HR Director

Gecas UK Limited
Incorporated: 8 October 2004 *Employees:* 7
Net Worth: £7,547,269 *Total Assets:* £10,482,109
Registered Office: 3rd Floor, 1 Ashley Road, Altrincham, Cheshire, WA14 2DT
Activities: Other professional, scientific and technical activities n.e.c.
Parent: GE Capital International Holdings Limited
Officers: Paul Dominic James Wilson, Secretary; Michael Barry Jones [1963] Director/Risk Manager; Paul Dominic James Wilson [1964] Director/SVP, International Structured Finance

Gedling Homes
Incorporated: 23 October 2006 *Employees:* 91
Net Worth: £32,990,000 *Total Assets:* £68,543,000
Registered Office: 249 Cavendish Street, Ashton under Lyne, Lancs, OL6 7AT
Activities: Renting and operating of Housing Association real estate
Officers: Brian Paul Moran, Secretary; Councillor William John Clarke [1947] Director; Melvin Thomas Kenyon [1957] Director; Karen Lesley Potts [1964] Director; Hilary Catherine Roberts [1964] Director/Group Chief Executive; Michelle Rudkin [1972] Director/Teaching Assistant; Timothy Shaun Ryan [1964] Director/Web Designer; Emma Wilson [1974] Group Director of Neighbourhoods

Gee Lawson Limited
Incorporated: 16 October 1939 *Employees:* 29
Net Worth: £3,305,907 *Total Assets:* £8,573,294
Registered Office: Westminster House, 10 Westminster Road, Macclesfield, Cheshire, SK10 1BX
Activities: Wholesale of pharmaceutical goods
Parent: Gee Lawson Holdings Limited
Officers: Ivan Pennington [1972] Director

GEH Holdings
Incorporated: 5 April 2005
Net Worth Deficit: £585,190,976 *Total Assets:* £978,083,968
Registered Office: 3rd Floor, 1 Ashley Road, Altrincham, Cheshire, WA14 2DT
Activities: Activities of head offices
Parent: GE UK Group
Officers: Anthony Stephen Bowman [1963] Director; Andrew Thomas Peter Budge [1973] Director/Chartered Accountant; Susan Mary Henderson [1975] Director/Lawyer; Simone Dorothy Norma MacMillan-Binns [1962] Director/Pensions Manager; Akhlesh Prasad Mathur [1972] Director/Chartered Accountant; Kerrie Jane Rowland [1971] Human Resources Director

Gemcabin Limited
Incorporated: 23 January 1984 *Employees:* 43
Net Worth: £4,803,215 *Total Assets:* £6,560,783
Registered Office: 1 Cedar Square, Blackpool, Lancs, FY1 1BP
Activities: Other business support service activities n.e.c.
Shareholders: Nathan Kohler; Rosa Vivien Kohler
Officers: Dr Ava Lynn Lefton, Secretary; David Anthony Kohler [1959] Director; Nathan Kohler [1923] Director/Property Investor; Stephen Lefton [1949] Director

Gemini Finance Ltd
Incorporated: 17 May 2011
Net Worth: £3,711,070 *Total Assets:* £9,698,804
Registered Office: Oriel House, 2-8 Oriel Road, Bootle, Merseyside, L20 7EP
Activities: Activities auxiliary to financial intermediation n.e.c.
Major Shareholder: Simon Barnfather
Officers: Michael Alexander Barnfather [1947] Director; Simon Barnfather [1972] Director

Gemsupa Limited
Incorporated: 21 June 1994
Net Worth: £72,449,312 *Total Assets:* £74,767,688
Registered Office: 56 London Road, Alderley Edge, Cheshire, SK9 7DZ
Activities: Activities of other holding companies n.e.c.
Major Shareholder: Jennifer Louise Dawson
Officers: William Marshall Smith, Secretary/Solicitor; Jennifer Louise Dawson [1984] Director; Peter Stuart Dawson [1952] Director/Chartered Surveyor; William Marshall Smith [1955] Director/Company Solicitor; Martin Allan Ridgway [1968] Director/Chartered Surveyor

Genedrive Diagnostics Ltd
Incorporated: 4 January 2000 *Employees:* 79
Net Worth: £5,343,000 *Total Assets:* £8,103,000
Registered Office: The Incubator Building, Grafton Street, Manchester, M13 9XX
Activities: Research and experimental development on biotechnology
Parent: Genedrive PLC
Officers: Matthew John Fowler, Secretary; David Budd [1967] Director [Canadian]; Matthew John Fowler [1974] Director/Accountant

Genedrive PLC
Incorporated: 15 February 2007 *Employees:* 79
Net Worth: £3,441,000 *Total Assets:* £12,046,000
Registered Office: The Incubator Building, Grafton Street, Manchester, M13 9XX
Activities: Research and experimental development on biotechnology
Officers: Matthew John Fowler, Secretary; David Budd [1967] Director [Canadian]; Matthew John Fowler [1974] Director/Accountant; Dr Ian David Gilham [1960] Director; Thomas Lindsay [1957] Commercial Director; Dr David Roger Lloyd [1948] Director; Robert Dwyer Nolan [1943] Director

General All Purpose Plastics Group Limited
Incorporated: 24 November 2005 *Employees:* 636
Net Worth: £9,443,779 *Total Assets:* £28,890,646
Registered Office: Partnership Way, Shadsworth Business Park, Blackburn, Lancs, BB1 2QP
Activities: Activities of head offices
Shareholders: Andrew David Greensmith; Simon David Bird; Matthew Craig Greensmith; Abigail Alicia Rayner
Officers: Andrew David Greensmith, Secretary; Simon David Bird [1965] Director; Simon Martyn Terry Brayshaw [1962] Director; Barry John Elmer [1977] Financial Director; Andrew David Greensmith [1970] Director; Matthew Craig Greensmith [1973] Director; Abigail Alicia Rayner [1986] Director

General All Purpose Plastics Limited
Incorporated: 25 November 1992 *Employees:* 636
Net Worth: £11,416,383 *Total Assets:* £31,861,260
Registered Office: Partnership Way, Shadsworth Business Park, Blackburn, Lancs, BB1 2QP
Activities: Manufacture of other plastic products
Parent: General All Purpose Plastics Holdings Ltd
Officers: Andrew David Greensmith, Secretary; Simon David Bird [1965] Director/Plastics Distributor; Simon Martyn Terry Brayshaw [1962] Director; Barry John Elmer [1977] Financial Director; Andrew David Greensmith [1970] Director

General Traffic Limited
Incorporated: 9 June 1983 *Employees:* 322
Net Worth: £3,949,063 *Total Assets:* £9,063,536
Registered Office: Rutland Mill, Adelaide Street, Bolton, Lancs, BL3 3NZ
Activities: Wholesale trade of motor vehicle parts and accessories
Officers: Imtiaz Hassan Umarji, Secretary [Seychellois]; Adam Hassan Umarji [1957] Managing Director; Adil Imtiaz Umarji [1987] Director; Adnan Adam Umarji [1988] Director; Imtiaz Hassan Umarji [1961] Director [Seychellois]; Mohammed Hassan Umarji [1960] Director [Seychellois]

Generation Two Limited
Incorporated: 27 March 2012 *Employees:* 87
Net Worth: £7,357,379 *Total Assets:* £12,834,540
Registered Office: Coolair House, Globe Lane, Dukinfield, Cheshire, SK16 4UJ
Activities: Activities of head offices
Shareholder: John James Otterson
Officers: Adam Anthony Garstang [1968] Director; Mark Garstang [1971] Director; Neil Simon Gibbard [1970] Director; John James Otterson [1959] Director; Helen Sharratt [1966] Director/Chartered Accountant; Steven Valentine [1972] Director

Generis Technology Limited
Incorporated: 11 April 1995 *Employees:* 30
Net Worth: £7,857,310 *Total Assets:* £10,879,505
Registered Office: Suite 4a, Manchester International Office Centre, Styal Road, Manchester, M22 5WB
Activities: Business and domestic software development
Parent: Bayard Metering (UK)
Officers: Ralph Griewing [1965] Director/SVP BU Solutions [German]; Thomas Koutny [1964] Director [German]; Gavin Paul Anthony O'Neil [1965] Director

Genii Engineering & Technology Training Limited
Incorporated: 6 July 1999 *Employees:* 345
Net Worth: £5,974,410 *Total Assets:* £10,846,673
Registered Office: Centre for Advanced Manufacturing & Nuclear Skills, Blackwood Road, Lillyhall Industrial Estate, Workington, Cumbria, CA14 4JJ
Activities: Technical and vocational secondary education
Officers: Lesley Margaret Bowen [1964] Director/Head of Training; James Thomas Conybeare-Cross [1961] Director/Chief Financial Officer; Philip Thomas Ellaway [1956] Director of Strategy; Lord William Richard Fletcher Vane Inglewood [1951] Director/Member of The House of Lords; Christopher Eastland Jones [1965] Director/Chief Executive Officer; Christopher David Miller [1968] Director of Legal

Genix Healthcare Ltd
Incorporated: 21 July 2005 *Employees:* 228
Net Worth: £599,969 *Total Assets:* £9,710,633
Registered Office: Queen's Specialist Building, Queen Street, Farnworth, Bolton, Lancs, BL4 7AH
Activities: Dental practice activities
Major Shareholder: Dr Mustafa Tariq Mohammed
Officers: Wajid Mahmood Azam [1979] Director/Dentist; Professor Stephen Michael Dunne [1954] Director/Dentist; Hassnain Hamid [1976] Director/Dentist; Dr Mustafa Tariq Mohammed [1969] Director/Manager

Geometric Furniture Limited
Incorporated: 1 May 1972 *Employees:* 78
Net Worth: £4,313,198 *Total Assets:* £8,534,579
Registered Office: Geometric House, Lark Hill, Townley Street, Middleton, Manchester, M24 1AT
Activities: Manufacture of other furniture
Major Shareholder: James Broadbent
Officers: James Broadbent [1952] Director; David Carroll [1969] Director/Company Manager; Nicola Jane Whatmough [1970] Director/Company Manager

Geometric Results Holdings Limited
Incorporated: 19 May 2005 *Employees:* 133
Net Worth: £7,137,142 *Total Assets:* £124,794,584
Registered Office: Booths Park 1, Chelford Road, Knutsford, Cheshire, WA16 8GS
Activities: Management consultancy activities other than financial management
Parent: Brookfield Rose Limited
Officers: Sam Richard Del Mar [1974] Director; Frederick Karl Minturn [1956] Director [American]; Andrew David Preston [1975] Director

Geometric Results International Limited
Incorporated: 16 May 2003 *Employees:* 133
Net Worth: £6,342,064 *Total Assets:* £126,999,504
Registered Office: Booths Park 1, Chelford Road, Knutsford, Cheshire, WA16 8GS
Activities: Human resources provision and management of human resources functions
Parent: De Poel Holdings Limited
Officers: Sam Richard Del Mar [1974] Director; Frederick Karl Minturn [1956] Director [American]; Andrew David Preston [1975] Director

George Hotel Investments Limited
Incorporated: 12 May 2005 *Employees:* 4
Net Worth: £10,226,000 *Total Assets:* £47,935,000
Registered Office: c/o KPMG LLP, One St Peters Square, Manchester, M2 3AE
Activities: Other letting and operating of own or leased real estate
Parent: George Hotel Investments Holdco Limited
Officers: Patrick Bour [1978] Director [French]

Georgia GC Holdings Limited
Incorporated: 12 June 2015
Net Worth: £6,316,959 *Total Assets:* £12,977,737
Registered Office: Fremantle House, 2 Oakwater Avenue, Cheadle Royal Business Park, Cheadle, Cheshire, SK8 3SR
Activities: Activities of head offices
Shareholders: Stephen James Mort; Tracy Lynn Mort; Business Growth Fund PLC BGF Investments LP
Officers: Steven James Mort, Secretary; Benjamin James Armstrong [1975] Finance and Operations Director; Richard Cotter [1961] Director/Chairman; Neil Patrick Inskip [1980] Director; Tracy Lynn Mort [1974] Managing Director

Georgia GC Limited
Incorporated: 25 February 2013
Net Worth: £4,633,059 *Total Assets:* £8,614,801
Registered Office: Alex House, 260-268 Chapel Street, Salford, M3 5JZ
Activities: Activities of head offices
Parent: Georgia GC Holdings Limited
Officers: Tracy Lynn Mort, Secretary; Tracy Lynn Mort [1974] Director

Gerber Technology Limited
Incorporated: 6 April 1970 *Employees:* 19
Net Worth: £1,271,000 *Total Assets:* £10,210,000
Registered Office: Unit 7 Mercury Park, Mercury Way, Trafford Park, Manchester, M41 7LY
Activities: Wholesale of other machinery and equipment
Officers: James Condon Martin, Secretary; James Condon Martin [1957] Director/Vice President, Finance and Treasurer [American]; Theodor Hermann Ostendorf [1957] Managing Director [German]; Karen Lyn Watson [1974] Director/VP, Corporate Controller [American]

Get Motoring UK Limited
Incorporated: 4 April 2005 *Employees:* 35
Net Worth: £12 587,000 *Total Assets:* £76,195,000
Registered Office: Lookers House, 3 Etchells Road, West Timperley, Altrincham, Cheshire, WA14 5XS
Activities: Renting and leasing of cars and light motor vehicles
Parent: Lookers PLC
Officers: Glenda MacGeekie, Secretary; Mark Ronald Brandom [1959] Managing Director; Andrew Campbell Bruce [1965] Director; Liam Cahill [1978] Fleet Purchasing Director; Robin Anthony Gregson [1960] Director/Chartered Accountant; Ellen Marie Hylton [1966] Director/Accountant; Nigel John McMinn [1968] Managing Director Motor Division

GGM Holdings Limited
Incorporated: 13 November 2015 *Employees:* 1,615
Net Worth: £4,594,000 *Total Assets:* £211,811,008
Registered Office: Adamson House, Centenary Way, Salford, M50 1RD
Activities: Activities of head offices
Major Shareholder: Gerard Anthony Mason
Officers: Paulo Jacob Eapen [1976] Director/Finance Investor [Singaporean]; Paul John Gilmour [1964] Director; Kevin Patrick Gorton [1964] Director; Gerard Anthony Mason [1964] Director; Kevin Philbin [1959] Director/Solicitor

GGM Human Resources Limited
Incorporated: 10 November 2015
Net Worth: £7,394,000 *Total Assets:* £103,505,000
Registered Office: Adamson House, Centenary Way, Salford, M50 1RD
Activities: Activities of head offices
Parent: GGM Holdings Limited
Officers: Paul John Gilmour [1964] Director; Kevin Patrick Gorton [1964] Director; Gerard Anthony Mason [1964] Director; Kevin Philbin [1959] Director/Solicitor

Ghekko Holdings Limited
Incorporated: 4 December 2007 *Employees:* 63
Net Worth: £8,329,508 *Total Assets:* £13,525,641
Registered Office: Primary House, Spring Gardens, Macclesfield, Cheshire, SK10 2AP
Activities: Activities of head offices
Major Shareholder: Nigel Robin Skinner
Officers: Michael Andrew Taylor, Secretary; Nigel Robin Skinner [1967] Director

Ghekko Limited
Incorporated: 6 November 1991 *Employees:* 34
Net Worth: £307,760 *Total Assets:* £9,570,879
Registered Office: Amtri House, Hulley Road, Macclesfield, Cheshire, SK10 2NE
Activities: Wholesale of electronic and telecommunications equipment and parts
Major Shareholder: Nigel Robin Skinner
Officers: Michael Andrew Taylor, Secretary; Michael William Neillans [1980] Director; Nigel Robin Skinner [1967] Director/Secretary

GHG Lubricants Holdings Limited
Incorporated: 26 October 2012 *Employees:* 2
Net Worth Deficit: £17,235,092 *Total Assets:* £213,939,088
Registered Office: Houghton PLC, Beacon Road, Trafford Park, Manchester, M17 1AF
Activities: Other manufacturing n.e.c.
Parent: GHGL London Limited
Officers: Elizabeth Keller Arnold [1964] Director [American]; Peter Michael MacAluso [1975] Director/Lawyer [American]

Giggleswick School
Incorporated: 9 May 2005 *Employees:* 236
Net Worth: £8,198,661 *Total Assets:* £12,335,618
Registered Office: Settle, N Yorks, BD24 0DE
Activities: Other letting and operating of own or leased real estate
Officers: Matthew Zebedee Hodge, Secretary; Robert Andrew Palles Brocklehurst [1964] Director/Consultant; Ian Michael Cornelius [1969] Commercial Director; Mark Robert Corner [1958] Director/Retired; Thomas Coxon [1990] Art Director; Lee Michael Donner [1979] Director/Architect; John Lambert Ellacott [1963] Director/Chartered Accountant; Sarah Catherine Fox [1973] Director/Opera Singer; Heather Jane Hancock [1965] Director/Partner, Accountancy; Gillian Mary Harper [1968] Director/Televison and Video Production; Adele Louise Hudson [1965] Director/Chartered Surveyor; Andrew Miles Jarman [1957] Director/Teacher; Hon William James Kay-Shuttleworth [1979] Director/Teacher; Andrew Richard Mullins [1964] Director/Consultant; Alexander Vincent Thursby [1960] Director/Retired; Sir Gary Keith Verity [1964] Director/Business Consultant; Roderick Richard Waldie [1968] Director/Solicitor

Ryan Giggs Limited
Incorporated: 3 December 1993 *Employees:* 2
Net Worth: £11,753,589 *Total Assets:* £13,161,375
Registered Office: c/o Grant Thornton UK LLP, 4 Hardman Square, Spinningfields, Manchester, M3 3EB
Activities: Other sports activities
Officers: Lynne Kerry Johnson, Secretary; Ryan Joseph Giggs [1973] Director/Professional Footballer

Gilberts (Blackpool) Limited
Incorporated: 27 October 1960 *Employees:* 236
Net Worth: £5,311,591 *Total Assets:* £9,735,676
Registered Office: Clifton Road, Blackpool, Lancs, FY4 4QT
Activities: Manufacture of non-domestic cooling and ventilation equipment
Shareholders: Jonathan Joseph Haslam; Peter Gilbert Haslam; Michael John Wills
Officers: Neil Abbot, Secretary; Jonathan Joseph Haslam [1964] Director/Vice Chairman & MD; Peter Gilbert Haslam [1962] Director; Sheila Margaret Haslam [1929] Director; Roy George John Jones [1970] Technical Director; David Keith Matthews [1956] Operations Director; Ian Paul Rogers [1958] Sales Director; Michael John Wills [1954] Divisional Director

Peter Gilding & Co. Limited
Incorporated: 29 September 1986 *Employees:* 57
Net Worth: £3,885,112 *Total Assets:* £12,220,200
Registered Office: Caddick Road, Knowsley Business Park, Prescot, Merseyside, L34 9HP
Activities: Wholesale of fruit and vegetables
Major Shareholder: Peter Bernard Gilding
Officers: Lynne Penelope Gilding, Secretary; Nicholas Roger Dalfen [1972] Finance Director; Andrew Bernard Gilding [1966] Director; Lynne Penelope Gilding [1950] Director & Company Secretary; Peter Bernard Gilding [1938] Director; Marc William Hamilton Hughes [1966] Director

Gilbert Gilkes & Gordon Limited
Incorporated: 18 March 1921 *Employees:* 221
Net Worth: £16,355,000 *Total Assets:* £29,166,000
Registered Office: Canal Head North, Kendal, Cumbria, LA9 7BZ
Activities: Manufacture of engines and turbines, except aircraft, vehicle and cycle engines
Parent: Gilbert Gilkes & Gordon Holdings Limited
Officers: Charles William Nepean Crewdson [1964] Director/Retired Lt Col Armed Services; Victoria Lee Crewdson [1965] Director/Forester; Andrew William Poole [1961] Director; Katherine Louise Rowland [1968] Director

Gilkes Hydro Investments Limited
Incorporated: 20 June 2015
Net Worth: £8,791,757 *Total Assets:* £37,429,784
Registered Office: Canal Head North, Kendal, Cumbria, LA9 7BZ
Activities: Activities of financial services holding companies
Parent: GHI Bidco Limited
Officers: Robert Henry Moffett Chaplin [1963] Director; Charles William Nepean Crewdson [1964] Director; Bernd Michael Kussner [1971] Director [Swiss]

Gilpin Lodge Country House Hotel Limited
Incorporated: 11 February 1986 *Employees:* 127
Net Worth: £4,873,005 *Total Assets:* £11,868,375
Registered Office: Gilpin Lodge, Crook Road, Windermere, Cumbria, LA23 3NE
Activities: Hotels and similar accommodation
Shareholders: Christine Anne Cunliffe; John Anthony Clegg Cunliffe
Officers: John Anthony Clegg Cunliffe, Secretary; Zoe Cunliffe, Secretary; Barnaby Cunliffe [1968] Director/Hotel Manager; Benjamin Cunliffe [1971] Director/Architect; Christine Anne Cunliffe [1942] Director; John Anthony Clegg Cunliffe [1944] Hotel Director

Ginger Acquisition Company Limited
Incorporated: 24 October 2016 *Employees:* 357
Net Worth Deficit: £965,524 *Total Assets:* £18,777,776
Registered Office: Tudno Mill, Smith Street, Ashton under Lyne, Lancs, OL7 0DB
Activities: Manufacture of rusks and biscuits; manufacture of preserved pastry goods and cakes
Shareholder: LDC Nominees Limited
Officers: Mark John Bamber [1965] Director; Brendon James Banner [1973] Director; Simon Benjamin Braham [1975] Director; John Paul Clarke [1981] Director; Paul John Monk [1957] Director; Steven Wetherby [1955] Managing Director; Daniel Richard Woodwards [1977] Director

Gisburne Park Estates Limited
Incorporated: 17 September 1990 *Employees:* 32
Net Worth: £4,418,717 *Total Assets:* £9,745,806
Registered Office: The Estate Office, Mill Lane, Gisburn, Clitheroe, Lancs, BB7 4LP
Activities: Buying and selling of own real estate
Major Shareholder: Guy Reginald Hindley
Officers: Guy Reginald Alan Hindley, Secretary; Guy Reginald Alan Hindley [1975] Director

Giti Tire (UK) Limited
Incorporated: 22 January 2009 *Employees:* 27
Net Worth: £832,778 *Total Assets:* £8,800,783
Registered Office: 22 Cheshire Avenue, Cheshire Business Park, Lostock Gralam, Northwich, Cheshire, CW9 7UA
Activities: Non-specialised wholesale trade
Parent: Giti Tire Global Enterprise Pte. Limited
Officers: Huai Chin Lei [1964] Managing Director [Hong Kong]; Chia Hoong Tan [1972] Director/Financial Controller [Malaysian]; Dr Enk Ee Tan [1968] Director/Executive Chairman [Malaysian]; Zhi Min Wu [1971] Executive Director [Singaporean]

Giti Tire Holdings (UK) Limited
Incorporated: 8 May 2014
Net Worth: £128,721,128 *Total Assets:* £128,739,152
Registered Office: 22 Cheshire Avenue, Cheshire Business Park, Lostock, Gralam, Northwich, Cheshire, CW9 7UA
Activities: Dormant company
Parent: Giti Tire Global Enterprise Pte. Ltd
Officers: Chia Hoong Tan, Secretary; Huai Chin Lei [1964] Director [Chinese]; Chia Hoong Tan [1972] Director [Malaysian]; Enk Ee Tan [1968] Director [Malaysian]; Zhimin Wu [1971] Director [Singaporean]

GJ Creative Limited
Incorporated: 24 January 2012 *Employees:* 248
Net Worth: £9,264,167 *Total Assets:* £11,813,112
Registered Office: The Ragged School, School Street, Manchester, M4 4HD
Activities: Non-trading company
Officers: Brian Dixon Walters, Secretary; Joseph Carlo Bartolacci [1960] Director [American]; Steven Francis Nicola [1960] Director [American]; Brian Dixon Walters [1969] Director [American]

GKH Holdings Limited
Incorporated: 28 March 2000 *Employees:* 556
Net Worth: £3,522,000 *Total Assets:* £46,149,000
Registered Office: Suite 206, Group First House, 12a Mead Way, Padiham, Burnley, Lancs, BB12 7NG
Activities: Other business support service activities n.e.c.
Major Shareholder: Stephen Heys
Officers: Candice Louise Heys [1978] Director; Joseph Edward Heys [1989] Director/Production Manager; Richard Stephen Heys [1986] Director/Production Manager; Stephen Heys [1954] Director; Thomas Patrick Heys [1984] Director

Gladman Commercial Properties
Incorporated: 21 November 2005
Net Worth: £14,314,317 *Total Assets:* £68,745,336
Registered Office: Gladman House, Alexandria Way, Congleton, Cheshire, CW12 1LB
Activities: Other letting and operating of own or leased real estate
Officers: David John Gladman, Secretary/Director; David John Gladman [1955] Director; Karen Jane Gladman [1957] Director; Jonathan Mark Stansfield Shepherd [1957] Director

Gladman Developments Limited
Incorporated: 27 March 1997 *Employees:* 166
Net Worth: £46,194,912 *Total Assets:* £139,868,240
Registered Office: Gladman House, Alexandria Way, Congleton, Cheshire, CW12 1LB
Activities: Buying and selling of own real estate
Officers: Meryl Shepherd, Secretary; David John Gladman [1955] Director/Builder; Dr Edward John Alexander Gladman [1983] Director; Jenny Elizabeth Gladman [1985] Director; Karen Jane Gladman [1957] Director/Physiotherapist; Samuel David James Gladman [1987] Director; David James Stansfield Shepherd [1985] Director; James Daniel Stansfield Shepherd [1987] Director; Jonathan Mark Stansfield Shepherd [1957] Director/Builder; Rachael Jayne Stansfield Shepherd [1989] Director

Gladman Homes LLP
Incorporated: 17 October 2007 *Employees:* 9
Net Worth: £4,810,140 *Total Assets:* £6,862,869
Registered Office: Gladman House, Alexandria Way, Congleton Business Park, Congleton, Cheshire, CW12 1LB
Officers: David John Gladman [1955] Member; Karen Jane Gladman [1957] Member; Jonathan Mark Stansfield Shepherd [1957] Member; Josephine Ann Birchall [1959] LLP Member; Gregory Mark Limb [1967] LLP Member

Gladman Retirement Living Limited
Incorporated: 21 April 2004 *Employees:* 21
Net Worth: £18,552,200 *Total Assets:* £24,194,868
Registered Office: Gladman House, Alexandria Way, Congleton, Cheshire, CW12 1LB
Activities: Buying and selling of own real estate
Officers: Jonathan Mark Stansfield Shepherd, Secretary/Director; David John Gladman [1955] Director; Karen Jane Gladman [1957] Director; Jonathan Mark Stansfield Shepherd [1957] Director

Glanbia Cheese Limited
Incorporated: 25 March 1991 *Employees:* 360
Net Worth: £33,711,000 *Total Assets:* £77,509,000
Registered Office: 4 Royal Mews, Gadbrook Park, Rudheath, Northwich, Cheshire, CW9 7UD
Activities: Butter and cheese production
Shareholders: Waterford Foods International Limited; Leprino Foods Company
Officers: John Joseph Kiely Secretary [Irish]; Kevin James Burke [1966] Director/Senior VP Global Business Development Leprino [American]; George Michael Durkin [1959] Director/President Leprino Foods Company [American]; Lance Kevin Fitzsimmons [1977] Director/Chief Financial Office Leprino Foods Company [American]; Mark Anthony Garvey [1964] Finance Director [Irish]; Brian Anthony Phelan [1966] Director/Human Resources [Irish]; Hannah Josephine Talbot [1964] Director/Chartered Accountant [Irish]

Glasdon (UK) Limited
Incorporated: 2 September 1987 *Employees:* 202
Net Worth: £10,091,650 *Total Assets:* £13,275,137
Registered Office: Glasdon House, Preston New Road, Blackpool, Lancs, FY4 4WA
Activities: Manufacture of other plastic products
Parent: Glasdon Group Limited
Officers: Andrew Charles Jackson, Secretary; Michael Crofton Cooper [1945] Director; Philip Andrew Greenwood [1960] Director; John James Ward Hodgson [1966] Director; Roger Derek Mellor [1950] Director/Deputy Chairman; Donald Joseph Sidebottom [1937] Director/Group Chairman

Glasdon Group Limited
Incorporated: 4 September 1987 *Employees:* 322
Net Worth: £44,732,232 *Total Assets:* £52,045,256
Registered Office: Glasdon House, Preston New Road, Blackpool, Lancs, FY4 4WA
Activities: Activities of head offices
Officers: Andrew Charles Jackson, Secretary; Michael Crofton Cooper [1945] Director; Philip Andrew Greenwood [1960] Managing Director; John James Ward Hodgson [1966] Director; Andrew Charles Jackson [1970] Finance Director; Joy Kavanagh [1970] Director; Roger Derek Mellor [1950] Director/Deputy Chairman; Donald Joseph Sidebottom [1937] Director/Group Chairman; Adrian Matthew Steen [1970] Director

Glasson Grain Limited
Incorporated: 15 January 1979 *Employees:* 72
Net Worth: £16,585,044 *Total Assets:* £27,394,434
Registered Office: West Quay, Glasson Dock, Lancaster, LA2 0DB
Activities: Wholesale of grain, unmanufactured tobacco, seeds and animal feeds
Officers: Christopher Paul Leigh, Secretary; David Jonathan Chadwick [1967] Director/Trader; Gareth Wynn Davies [1963] Director/Chief Executive; Paul Jefferson Hayton [1971] Director/Trader; Robert James Kenyon Ingham [1961] Marketing Director; Christopher Paul Leigh [1966] Director/Accountant; Bryan Paul Roberts [1963] Financial Director

Joseph Gleave & Son (Holdings) Limited
Incorporated: 6 December 2011 *Employees:* 39
Net Worth: £10,353,188 *Total Assets:* £13,236,795
Registered Office: Beech House, 995 Chester Road, Stretford, Manchester, M32 0NB
Activities: Non-specialised wholesale trade
Major Shareholder: John Anthony Shaw
Officers: John Anthony Shaw [1963] Director

Joseph Gleave & Son Limited
Incorporated: 24 April 1957 *Employees:* 39
Net Worth: £11,518,547 *Total Assets:* £14,103,886
Registered Office: Beech House, 995 Chester Road, Stretford, Manchester, M32 0NB
Activities: Non-specialised wholesale trade
Major Shareholder: John Anthony Shaw
Officers: John Anthony Shaw, Secretary/Director; John Anthony Shaw [1963] Director

Gledhill Building Products Limited
Incorporated: 2 June 2003 *Employees:* 191
Net Worth: £4,265,000 *Total Assets:* £9,214,000
Registered Office: Sycamore Estate, Squires Gate, Blackpool, Lancs, FY4 3RL
Activities: Manufacture of other tanks, reservoirs and containers of metal
Parent: Atlantic Aquisition Holdings UK Ltd
Officers: Carol Lesley Wardle, Secretary; Emmanuel Philippe Antoine François Caille [1970] Director [French]; Shaun Barry Edwards [1968] Director; Steven Hairsine [1975] Director

Glen Dimplex Home Appliances Limited
Incorporated: 28 February 1992 *Employees:* 1,116
Net Worth: £61,481,000 *Total Assets:* £159,123,008
Registered Office: Stoney Lane, Prescot, Merseyside, L35 2XW
Activities: Manufacture of electric domestic appliances
Parent: Glen Electric Ltd
Officers: Stephen John Yarwood, Secretary; Jonathan Harvey Casley [1966] Director; Donal Francis Flynn [1973] Director [Irish]; Fergal John Naughton [1975] Director [Irish]; Martin Lawrence Naughton [1939] Director/Engineer [Irish]; Neil Naughton [1969] Director [Irish]; Stephen John Yarwood [1961] Director

Glenco Limited
Incorporated: 24 February 2016
Net Worth: £5,897,033 *Total Assets:* £9,859,501
Registered Office: 39 Broadway, Bramhall, Stockport, Cheshire, SK7 3BU
Activities: Other accommodation
Shareholders: Navin Patel; Rita Patel
Officers: Navin Kumar Patel [1953] Director/Dentist; Rita Patel [1955] Director/Pharmacist

Glendale Foods Limited
Incorporated: 19 April 1985 *Employees:* 136
Net Worth: £2,492,250 *Total Assets:* £11,448,139
Registered Office: Glendale House, Cobden Street, Pendleton, Salford, M6 6LX
Activities: Production of meat and poultry meat products
Shareholder: Paul Burkitt
Officers: Stephen Revill, Secretary; Paul Andrew Burkitt [1962] Director; Mark Jones [1965] Operations Director

Glendale Grounds Management Limited
Incorporated: 4 March 1983 *Employees:* 716
Net Worth: £5,449,000 *Total Assets:* £9,451,000
Registered Office: Parkwood House, Cuerden Park, Berkeley Drive, Bamber Bridge, Preston, Lancs, PR5 6BY
Activities: Landscape service activities
Parent: Glendale Managed Services Limited
Officers: Michael Harvey Brunskill [1966] Director; Erica Louise Oates [1969] Finance Director; Alexander Jeffrey Paterson [1978] Director; Mike John Quayle [1969] Director; Adrian Wickham [1973] Director

Glendale S/S Limited
Incorporated: 9 August 1979 *Employees:* 2
Net Worth: £2,267,187 *Total Assets:* £9,512,211
Registered Office: 6th Floor, Cardinal House, 20 St Marys Parsonage, Manchester, M3 2LG
Activities: Wholesale of perfume and cosmetics
Parent: Glendale Group Limited
Officers: Matthew Pettit, Secretary; Simon Tennant Barker [1956] Finance Director; Charles Rodney Mathers [1956] Director [New Zealander]

Glenvale Transport Limited
Incorporated: 11 May 2000 *Employees:* 1,191
Net Worth: £17,771,000 *Total Assets:* £52,535,000
Registered Office: c/o Stagecoach Services Limited, One Stockport Exchange, 20 Railway Road, Stockport, Cheshire, SK1 3SW
Activities: Other urban, suburban or metropolitan passenger land transport (not underground, metro or similar)
Parent: Stagecoach Bus Holdings Limited
Officers: Michael John Vaux, Secretary; Colin Brown [1968] Director/Accountant; Robert Jones [1974] Managing Director; Arnold Mark Threapleton [1954] Managing Director

Global Equity Finance Ltd
Incorporated: 20 March 2013
Net Worth: £543,658 *Total Assets:* £8,166,605
Registered Office: Ollerbarrow House, Ashley Road, Hale, Altrincham, Cheshire, WA15 9SQ
Activities: Management consultancy activities other than financial management
Officers: Natasha Marisa McCarthy, Secretary; Natasha McCarthy [1974] Finance Director

The Global Travel Group Limited
Incorporated: 14 December 1992 *Employees:* 318
Net Worth Deficit: £3,259,000 *Total Assets:* £71,841,000
Registered Office: Glendale House, Glendale Business Park, Sandycroft, Flintshire, CH5 2DL
Activities: Travel agency activities
Parent: Stella Global UK Limited
Officers: Ryan James Cooke, Secretary; Paul Smith [1975] Director

Globe Enterprises Limited
Incorporated: 18 January 1995 *Employees:* 6
Net Worth: £3,565,978 *Total Assets:* £7,433,660
Registered Office: The Globe Centre, St James Square, Accrington, Lancs, BB5 0RE
Activities: Development of building projects
Shareholders: Barnfield Contractors (UK) Ltd; Hyndburn Borough Council
Officers: Anthony Robert Martin Dobson, Secretary; Councillor Paul Ian Cox [1972] Director/Councillor; Anthony Robert Martin Dobson [1967] Director; James Stuart Nevison [1952] Director; Councillor Miles Parkinson [1967] Director/Councillor; Timothy John Henry Webber [1954] Director/Builder

Globe Union (UK) Limited
Incorporated: 2 February 2007 *Employees:* 486
Net Worth: £15,455,000 *Total Assets:* £60,723,000
Registered Office: Alder House, Slackey Brow, Kearsley, Bolton, Lancs, BL4 8SL
Activities: Non-trading company
Parent: Globe Union Industrial Corp
Officers: Jason David Shaw, Secretary; Yu-Li Chou [1966] Director/Vice President [Chinese]; Richard Ian George [1970] Director; Scott Ouyoung [1951] Chairman Director [Taiwanese]; Jason David Shaw [1971] Director; Andrew Yates [1961] Director/Chief Executive; Kuo-Chi Yen [1961] Director [Chinese]

Globesign Limited
Incorporated: 6 December 2004
Net Worth: £9,832,809 *Total Assets:* £14,407,290
Registered Office: Castle Mills, Moorend, Cleckheaton, W Yorks, BD19 3PS
Activities: Activities of head offices
Parent: Victoria Midco Holdings Limited
Officers: John Russell Shirt, Secretary; John Russell Shirt [1961] Director/Accountant; Geoffrey Brendon Wilding [1963] Director [New Zealander]

Glossop Caravans Limited
Incorporated: 13 February 2003 *Employees:* 165
Net Worth: £5,488,927 *Total Assets:* £15,420,527
Registered Office: c/o Freedman Frankl & Taylor, Reedham House, 31 King Street West, Manchester, M3 2PJ
Activities: Other business support service activities n.e.c.
Shareholders: Brian Laing; Stan Laing
Officers: Brian Laing, Secretary; Brian Laing [1957] Director/Caravan Retailer; Stanley a Laing [1944] Director/Caravan Retailer

Glossop Carton and Print Limited
Incorporated: 29 November 1982
Net Worth: £4,034,050 *Total Assets:* £6,580,151
Registered Office: Raymond Joseph Works, Unit 5 Haigh Avenue, Whitehill Industrial Estate, Stockport, Cheshire, SK4 1NU
Activities: Manufacture of other paper and paperboard containers
Shareholders: Jacqueline Cameron Sidebottom-Every; Brian Sidebottom
Officers: Jacqueline Cameron Sidebottom Every, Secretary; Brian Sidebottom [1961] Director/Printer; Jacqueline Cameron Sidebottom Every [1962] Director; Jillian Cameron Woodacre [1963] Director

Gloucester Quays LLP
Incorporated: 14 December 2006 *Employees:* 10
Net Worth: £149,396,992 *Total Assets:* £219,231,008
Registered Office: Peel Dome, intu Trafford Centre, Trafford City, Manchester, M17 8PL

Glusburn Holdings Limited
Incorporated: 23 January 2002 *Employees:* 238
Net Worth: £10,566,879 *Total Assets:* £13,864,061
Registered Office: Hayfield, Colne Road, Glusburn, Keighley, W Yorks, BD20 8QP
Activities: Manufacture of fasteners and screw machine products
Shareholders: Victor Elisabeth Alois Stevens; Andrew I'Anson Crabtree
Officers: Andrew I'anson Crabtree, Secretary; Andrew I'anson Crabtree [1951] Director; Victor Elisabeth Alois Stevens [1957] Director [Belgian]

GM Business Support Limited
Incorporated: 5 July 2012 *Employees:* 138
Net Worth: £387,387 *Total Assets:* £22,700,908
Registered Office: Lee House, 90 Great Bridgewater Street, Manchester, M1 5JW
Activities: Management consultancy activities other than financial management
Officers: Paul Anthony Simpson, Secretary; Donna Elizabeth Edwards [1960] Managing Director; Mark Anthony Hughes [1966] Director/Chief Executive

GNB Industrial Power (UK) Limited
Incorporated: 24 April 1989 *Employees:* 120
Net Worth: £43 842,000 *Total Assets:* £46,141,000
Registered Office: Mansell House, Aspinall Close, Middlebrook, Horwich, Bolton, Lancs, BL6 6QQ
Activities: Manufacture of batteries and accumulators
Shareholders: Euro Exide Corporation Limited; Exide Technologies SRL; Euro Exide Corporation Limited
Officers: Jayne Wynne Roy, Secretary; Nigel Jeremy Darke [1963] Director; Michael Geiger [1968] Director [German]; Brad Stewart Kalter [1967] Director [American]; Chi Wing Lam [1974] Director [Dutch]; Yvonne Russo [1959] Director [French]; Stefan Alois Stubing [1962] Director [German]

Go-Sykes Limited
Incorporated: 26 November 2014 *Employees:* 5
Net Worth Deficit: £12,063,000 *Total Assets:* £68,138,000
Registered Office: One St Peters Square, Manchester, M2 3DE
Activities: Activities of other holding companies n.e.c.
Parent: Sykes Cottages Holdings Limited
Officers: Simon James Taylor, Secretary; Graham Donoghue [1973] Director Mr Michael Steven Graham [1964] Director; Miles Geoffrey Hill [1968] Director; Clive Peter Sykes [1964] Director

Gogar Services Limited
Incorporated: 25 April 2016 *Employees:* 13
Net Worth: £387,644 *Total Assets:* £6,880,436
Registered Office: 139-143 Union Street, Oldham, Lancs, OL1 1TE
Activities: Other transportation support activities
Shareholder: Alison Snowie
Officers: Alison Snowie [1962] Director; Alistair Tait Snowie [1963] Director

Gold Medal Travel Group Limited
Incorporated: 29 June 1973 *Employees:* 310
Net Worth: £17,987,000 *Total Assets:* £84,692,000
Registered Office: The Trident Centre, Portway, Ribble Docklands, Preston, Lancs, PR2 2QG
Activities: Travel agency activities
Parent: Gold Medal International Limited
Officers: Paul Smith, Secretary; Iain Charles Richard Andrew [1965] Director/Chief Executive Officer; John Constantine Bevan [1965] Director

Goldcrest Distribution Ltd
Incorporated: 17 February 1993 *Employees:* 4
Net Worth: £7,739,030 *Total Assets:* £9,710,810
Registered Office: Unit 4 Trafalgar Business Park, Broughton Lane, Manchester, M8 9TZ
Activities: Wholesale of household goods (other than musical instruments) n e.c
Officers: Darshan Lal Chawla [1942] Director; Ranjit Kaur Chawla [1942] Director [Indian]; Ravinder Singh Chawla [1968] Director

Goldcrest Finance Limited
Incorporated: 19 February 1997 *Employees:* 10
Net Worth: £21,739,856 *Total Assets:* £39,815,820
Registered Office: Unit 4 Trafalgar Business Park, Broughton Lane, Manchester, M8 9TZ
Activities: Other credit granting n.e.c.
Officers: Ravinder Chawla, Secretary; Darshan Lal Chawla [1942] Director; Ranjit Kaur Chawla [1942] Director [Indian]; Ravinder Singh Chawla [1968] Director; Steven Mark Gildea [1979] Commercial Director; John Charles McGuire [1948] Director; Shaun James Rearden [1954] Director

Golden Sunrise (Holdings) Limited
Incorporated: 15 August 1963 *Employees:* 5
Net Worth: £7,525,204 *Total Assets:* £7,845,257
Registered Office: Gayton Wood, Gayton Farm Road, Gayton, Wirral, Merseyside, CH60 8NR
Activities: Buying and selling of own real estate
Major Shareholder: Demetrios Sergi
Officers: Maro Sergi, Secretary; Demetrios Sergi [1945] Director; Michael Demetrios Sergi [1973] Finance Director

Goldentree Financial Services PLC
Incorporated: 14 March 2001 *Employees:* 22
Net Worth Deficit: £1,993,821 *Total Assets:* £115,750,520
Registered Office: The Spectrum, 56-58 Benson Road, Birchwood, Warrington, Cheshire, WA3 7PQ
Activities: Financial intermediation not elsewhere classified
Shareholders: Fred Done; Peter Eric Done
Officers: Kathryn Elizabeth Clough, Secretary; Susan Catherine Bickerton [1963] Director/Certified Chartered Accountant; Philip John Derbyshire [1983] Managing Director; Fred Done [1943] Director; Steven Robert Marsh [1961] Director/Financier

Goldhire Limited
Incorporated: 28 August 1984 *Employees:* 112
Net Worth: £6,724,622 *Total Assets:* £13,566,160
Registered Office: Charter House, Pittman Way, Fulwood, Preston, Lancs, PR2 9ZD
Activities: Activities of head offices
Shareholders: Kirsty Cocker; James Robin Alexander; Dr Catherine Anne Alexander
Officers: Dr Catherine Anne Alexander, Secretary; Dr Catherine Anne Alexander [1949] Director; James Robin Alexander [1949] Director; Kirsty Cocker [1978] Director

Goliath Footwear Limited
Incorporated: 24 September 2003 *Employees:* 7
Net Worth: £2,764,736 *Total Assets:* £10,990,135
Registered Office: Goliath House, Chain Bar Road, Cleckheaton, W Yorks, BD19 3QF
Activities: Agents involved in the sale of textiles, clothing, fur, footwear and leather goods
Major Shareholder: Abdil Vedat Yakupoglu
Officers: Levent Gulcan, Secretary; Levent Gulcan [1968] Director [Turkish]; Abdil Vedat Yakupoglu [1961] Director [Turkish]

Gollek UK Limited
Incorporated: 9 April 2014
Net Worth: £2,998,362,368 *Total Assets:* £3,327,485,952
Registered Office: Orange Tower, Media City UK, Salford, M50 2HF
Activities: Other business support service activities n.e.c.
Parent: Kellogg Group Limited
Officers: Andrea Critchley [1973] Senior SC Director; Nigel David Jaynes [1966] Director/Environment, Health & Safety, Corporate Services; Philip David Knowles [1969] Finance Director; Ramesh Kollepara [1976] IT Director; Joel Alan Vanderkooi [1968] Director/Treasurer [American]

W.H.Good Group Limited
Incorporated: 1 April 2008 *Employees:* 68
Net Worth: £6,986,677 *Total Assets:* £11,922,833
Registered Office: WHGH Limited, Carrs Industrial Estate, Rossendale, Lancs, BB4 5JT
Activities: Activities of head offices
Major Shareholder: James Sumner
Officers: Paul John Sumner, Secretary/Director; David Patrick Sumner [1965] Director; James Sumner [1940] Director; Paul John Sumner [1969] Director; Philip Mark Sumner [1964] Director

Good Night Vienna Productions Limited
Incorporated: 22 December 1999 *Employees:* 2
Net Worth: £21,270,424 *Total Assets:* £23,838,456
Registered Office: Sterling House, 501 Middleston Road, Chadderton, Oldham, Lancs, OL9 9LY
Activities: Video production activities
Shareholders: Peter John Kay; Susan Rose Kay
Officers: Peter Kay [1973] Director/Writer; Susan Rose Kay [1971] Director

Goodison Park Stadium Limited
Incorporated: 17 January 2002
Net Worth Deficit: £22,992 *Total Assets:* £16,817,132
Registered Office: Goodison Park, Goodison Road, Liverpool, L4 4EL
Activities: Operation of sports facilities
Parent: The Everton Football Club Company Limited
Officers: William Kenwright [1945] Director; Jon Vincent Woods [1946] Director/Publisher

Goodwood Holdings Limited
Incorporated: 4 June 2014 *Employees:* 150
Net Worth: £11,205,611 *Total Assets:* £18,176,472
Registered Office: 223 Church Street, Blackpool, Lancs, FY1 3PB
Activities: Activities of production holding companies
Shareholder: Gladys Hacking
Officers: Christina Hilda Leigh Hacking [1966] Director; Gladys Hacking [1924] Director; James Joseph Park Hacking [1960] Sales Director; Thomas Henry Hacking [1955] Director; Frances Margaret Leigh Street [1953] Director; Geoffrey William Street [1949] Director; Kathryn Anne Leigh Thomas [1956] Director/Retired

Gordale Nurseries Limited
Incorporated: 27 September 1963 *Employees:* 93
Net Worth: £10,968,369 *Total Assets:* £12,575,778
Registered Office: Gordale Nurseries, Chester High Road, Burton, South Wirral, Merseyside, CH64 8TF
Activities: Other retail sale of new goods in specialised stores (not commercial art galleries and opticians)
Major Shareholder: Peter Alexander Nicholson
Officers: Gillian Deborah Nicholson, Secretary; Peter Alexander Nicholson [1955] Director

Gordons LLP
Incorporated: 25 April 2006 *Employees:* 198
Net Worth: £4,805,677 *Total Assets:* £6,671,277
Registered Office: Forward House, 8 Duke Street, Bradford, W Yorks, BD1 3QX
Officers: Paul Hugh Ayre [1964] Member; Nicholas James Chamberlain [1971] Member; Victoria Louise Davey [1971] Member; John Layfield Holden [1957] Member; Jonathan Asquez [1977] LLP Member; Andrew John Breckenridge [1966] LLP Member; Andrew Brian [1979] LLP Member; Richard Peter Cressall [1986] LLP Member; Graeme Edward Davy [1980] LLP Member; Gregory James Dixon [1986] LLP Member; James Anthony Fawcett [1976] LLP Member; Joanne Marie Fearnley [1969] LLP Member; Michael Andrew Finnett [1978] LLP Member; Duncan Mark Edward Firman [1981] LLP Member; Rachel Hudson [1971] LLP Member; Mark Francois Jones [1982] LLP Member; Anjon Mallik [1973] LLP Member; Stephen Andrew McVey [1979] LLP Member; Simon Terry Mydlowski [1979] LLP Member; John Edward Owen [1974] LLP Member; Phillip John Paget [1965] LLP Member; Wayne Matthew Parker [1959] LLP Member; Richard David Steuart Piper [1969] LLP Member; Sarah Jane Ratcliffe [1978] LLP Member; Diana Mary Smart [1964] LLP Member; Mary Katherine Charlotte Walker [1972] LLP Member; Paul Stephen Young [1970] LLP Member

Gorgemead Limited
Incorporated: 4 June 1979 *Employees:* 1,387
Net Worth: £57,020,688 *Total Assets:* £210,645,888
Registered Office: 2076 Lynstock House, Lynstock Way, Lostock, Bolton, Lancs, BL6 4SA
Activities: Dispensing chemist in specialised stores
Shareholders: Yakub Ibrahim Patel; Anwer Ibrahim Patel
Officers: Anwer Ibrahim Patel, Secretary; Stephen David Hall [1954] Director; Andrew Robert John [1967] Managing Director; Anwer Ibrahim Patel [1954] Director; Yakub Ibrahim Patel [1953] Director/Certified Accountant; Zoe Serrant [1973] Director/Pharmacist

Gott Agri Synergy Limited
Incorporated: 19 February 2016 *Employees:* 300
Net Worth: £2,117,393 *Total Assets:* £31,848,384
Registered Office: Addington Lodge, Addington Road, Nether Kellet, Carnforth, Lancs, LA6 1DZ
Activities: Dormant company
Major Shareholder: Adrian David Gott
Officers: Adrian David Gott [1981] Director

Goyt Properties Limited
Incorporated: 22 April 1988 *Employees:* 10
Net Worth: £5,289,754 *Total Assets:* £8,378,265
Registered Office: Incom House, Waterside, Trafford Park, Manchester, M17 1WD
Activities: Other letting and operating of own or leased real estate
Shareholder: Stonehill Ltd
Officers: Susan Monica Storfer, Secretary; Gordon Joseph Haynes [1946] Director; Stephen John Haynes [1977] Director; Michael Storfer [1950] Director/Chartered Accountant; Susan Monica Storfer [1952] Director

GP Premises Holdings Limited
Incorporated: 5 September 2012 *Employees:* 3
Total Assets: £11,041,715
Registered Office: The Brew House, Greenalls Avenue, Warrington, Cheshire, WA4 6HL
Activities: Buying and selling of own real estate
Parent: Assura Investments Ltd
Officers: Orla Ball [1970] Director/Company Secretary; Paul Bryan Carroll [1969] Director/Accountant; Jayne Marie Cottam [1974] Finance Director; Simon Gould [1974] Director/Chartered Surveyor; Spencer Adrian Kenyon [1962] Director/Chartered Surveyor; Patrick William Lowther [1977] Director/Chartered Surveyor

GP Premises Limited
Incorporated: 16 December 1998
Net Worth: £16,694,417 *Total Assets:* £39,396,560
Registered Office: The Brew House, Greenalls Avenue, Warrington, Cheshire, WA4 6HL
Activities: Development of building projects
Parent: GP Premises Holdings Limited
Officers: Orla Ball [1970] Director/Company Secretary; Paul Bryan Carroll [1969] Director/Accountant; Jayne Marie Cottam [1974] Finance Director; Simon Gould [1974] Director/Chartered Surveyor; Spencer Adrian Kenyon [1962] Director/Chartered Surveyor; Patrick William Lowther [1977] Director/Chartered Surveyor

GP Strategies Holdings Limited
Incorporated: 10 August 2007
Net Worth: £13,182,000 *Total Assets:* £17,316,000
Registered Office: 3rd Floor, 1 Ashley Road, Altrincham, Cheshire, WA14 2DT
Activities: Technical and vocational secondary education
Parent: General Physics (UK) Ltd.
Officers: Kenneth Lee Crawford, Secretary; Scott Neil Greenberg [1956] Director [American]; Adam Henry Stedham [1969] Director/Executive/President [American]

GP Strategies Limited
Incorporated: 23 March 2012 *Employees:* 443
Net Worth: £8,692,000 *Total Assets:* £34,601,000
Registered Office: 3rd Floor 1 Ashley Road, Altrincham, Cheshire, WA14 2DT
Activities: Other education n.e.c.
Parent: GP Strategies Holdings Limited
Officers: Kenneth Lee Crawford, Secretary; Scott Neil Greenberg [1956] Director [American]; Adam Henry Stedham [1969] Director/Executive/President [American]

GP Strategies Training Limited
Incorporated: 23 March 2012 *Employees:* 261
Net Worth: £19,836,000 *Total Assets:* £22,117,000
Registered Office: 3rd Floor, 1 Ashley Road, Altrincham, Cheshire, WA14 2DT
Activities: Technical and vocational secondary education
Parent: GP Strategies Holdings Limited
Officers: Kenneth Lee Crawford, Secretary; Scott Neil Greenberg [1956] Director [American]; Adam Henry Stedham [1969] Director/Executive/President [American]

GPC Computer Software Limited
Incorporated: 11 July 1991 *Employees:* 136
Net Worth: £3,745,355 *Total Assets:* £7,071,794
Registered Office: Cheadle Royal Business Park, Oakfield Road, Cheadle, Cheshire, SK8 3GX
Activities: Business and domestic software development
Major Shareholder: Haider Hossain Hadi
Officers: Dr Faiza Hadi, Secretary/Doctor; Hassan Abod [1992] Director

GPL Civil Engineering Limited
Incorporated: 20 June 2007 *Employees:* 19
Net Worth: £2,907,819 *Total Assets:* £11,299,812
Registered Office: Kennedy House, Cheltenham Street, Salford, M6 6WY
Activities: Construction of other civil engineering projects n.e.c.
Parent: GPL Group (Manchester) Limited
Officers: Bridget Mary Gallagher, Secretary [Irish]; Bridget Mary Gallagher [1945] Managing Director [Irish]; Sean Patrick Gallagher [1979] Director

Grade A Alternative Properties Limited
Incorporated: 25 October 2013 *Employees:* 2
Net Worth: £13,296,584 *Total Assets:* £18,957,604
Registered Office: 14 Kennedy Street, Manchester, M2 4BY
Activities: Other letting and operating of own or leased real estate
Major Shareholder: Linzi Sara Parkinson
Officers: Linzi Sara Parkinson [1962] Director; Richard Christopher William Parkinson [1963] Director/Solicitor

Gradus Group Holdings Limited
Incorporated: 31 October 2006
Net Worth Deficit: £12,213,399 *Total Assets:* £71,467,576
Registered Office: 3rd Floor, 1 Ashley Road, Altrincham, Cheshire, WA14 2DT
Activities: Activities of head offices
Officers: James Jack Collier, Secretary; James Jack Collier [1979] Director; Pierre Dominique Denis Convers [1968] Director [French]; Pierre Marc Lienhard [1967] Director [French]; Edouard Jean Michel Phelippeau [1967] Director [French]; Philippe Dominique Marie Puech [1974] Director [French]; Stephen Andrew Watt [1957] Director

Gradus Limited
Incorporated: 3 August 1987 *Employees:* 244
Net Worth: £42,799,416 *Total Assets:* £61,466,784
Registered Office: 3rd Floor, 1 Ashley Road, Altrincham, Cheshire, WA14 2DT
Activities: Manufacture of other plastic products
Parent: Gradus Group Limited
Officers: James Jack Collier, Secretary; James Jack Collier [1979] Director; Pierre Dominique Denis Convers [1968] Director [French]; Pierre Marc Lienhard [1967] Director [French]; Edouard Jean Michel Phelippeau [1967] Director [French]; Philippe Dominique Marie Puech [1974] Director [French]; Stephen Andrew Watt [1957] Director

Grafenia Operations Limited
Incorporated: 2 July 1992 *Employees:* 117
Net Worth Deficit: £182,000 *Total Assets:* £7,118,000
Registered Office: Third Avenue, The Village, Trafford Park, Manchester, M17 1FG
Activities: Other business support service activities n.e.c.
Shareholders: Grafenia PLC; Grafenia PLC
Officers: Richard Alan Lightfoot, Secretary; Gavin Graham Cockerill [1978] Director; Peter Robert Gunning [1975] Director

Grafenia PLC
Incorporated: 28 April 2000 *Employees:* 120
Net Worth: £4,613,000 *Total Assets:* £7,105,000
Registered Office: Third Avenue, The Village, Trafford Park, Manchester, M17 1FG
Activities: Other business support service activities n.e.c.
Officers: Richard Alan Lightfoot, Secretary; Simon Gregory Barrell [1959] Director; Conrad Christian Bona [1969] Director [Canadian]; Gavin Graham Cockerill [1978] Director; Peter Robert Gunning [1975] Director; Richard Alan Lightfoot [1972] Director and Company Secretary; Jan-Hendrik Markus Mohr [1989] Director/Fund Manager [German]

Graham & Brown Limited
Incorporated: 23 February 1942 *Employees:* 565
Net Worth: £22,740,000 *Total Assets:* £49,424,000
Registered Office: India Mill, Harwood Street, Blackburn, BB1 3DB
Activities: Manufacture of wallpaper
Officers: David Brown [1941] Director; Ian Andrew Brown [1966] Director; John Carter [1959] Director; Andrew Harold Graham [1970] Director; Roger Hugh Graham [1941] Director; Mark Jackson McCauley [1970] Commercial Director; Lisa Mitchell [1968] Director/Chartered Accountant

Thomas Graham & Sons (Iron & Steel) Limited
Incorporated: 20 April 1960 *Employees:* 175
Net Worth: £18,863,432 *Total Assets:* £25,389,384
Registered Office: 8 Spellar Way, Kingmoor Park East, Carlisle, CA6 4SQ
Activities: Non-specialised wholesale trade
Shareholder: Ian Davidson Smith
Officers: Phillip Sydney Barnes [1974] Director; Michael Charles Davidson [1954] Director; Gary Mark Smith [1969] Director; Ian Davidson Smith [1946] Director; Roger Duncan Smith [1972] Managing Director; Russell Mark Smith [1968] Contracts Director; Amanda Jane Ward [1971] Director/Chartered Accountant

Graham (Commercials) Limited
Incorporated: 9 August 1962 *Employees:* 45
Net Worth: £5,460,877 *Total Assets:* £9,458,347
Registered Office: Kingstown Broadway, Kingstown Industrial Estate, Carlisle, CA3 0HA
Activities: Sale of other motor vehicles
Shareholders: David Graham; Stuart Graham
Officers: Stuart Graham, Secretary; Colin Graham [1948] Director/Administrator; David Graham [1976] Director/Sales Executive; Kenneth Graham [1951] Director/Administrator; Stuart Graham [1974] Director/Accountant; Susan Dorothy Graham [1953] Director/Saleswoman; Stephen John Hogarth [1959] Director/Accountant

Graham Engineering Limited
Incorporated: 8 September 1977 *Employees:* 160
Net Worth: £8,597,338 *Total Assets:* £12,774,533
Registered Office: Unit 1a, Edward Street, Whitewalls Industrial Estate, Nelson, Lancs, BB9 8SY
Activities: Manufacture of other fabricated metal products n.e.c.
Major Shareholder: Corry Thomas Graham
Officers: Stuart Fraser [1956] Manufacturing Director; Pauline Graham [1945] Director/Married Woman; Frank Kelly [1960] Director/Accountant; Peter Manley [1946] Director/Engineer

Graham Heath Group Limited
Incorporated: 8 November 2010 *Employees:* 78
Net Worth: £5,583,556 *Total Assets:* £11,515,237
Registered Office: The Creamery, Wrenbury Industrial Estate, 2 Station Road, Wrenbury, Cheshire, CW5 8EX
Activities: Activities of construction holding companies
Major Shareholder: Graham James Thomas Heath
Officers: Graham James Thomas Heath [1972] Director

Grakon BMAC Holdings Limited
Incorporated: 28 September 2016
Net Worth: £3,369,866 *Total Assets:* £9,081,758
Registered Office: Units 13-14 Shepley Industrial Estate South, Audenshaw, Manchester, M34 5DW
Activities: Manufacture of other transport equipment n.e.c.
Officers: Christopher Dennis Butcher [1966] Director; Dave Paborsky [1967] Director [American]; Floris Spoel [1969] Director of Sales and Operation, Europe, Grakon [Dutch]

Granada Material Handling Limited
Incorporated: 30 December 1980 *Employees:* 119
Net Worth: £3,546,338 *Total Assets:* £10,197,996
Registered Office: Unit 1 Sherwood Industrial Park, Queensway, Rochdale, OL11 2NU
Activities: Manufacture of lifting and handling equipment
Officers: Margaret Anne Cantrell, Secretary; Andrew John Cantrell [1951] Sales Director; Jonathan Philip Hall [1968] Director; Mark Sidwell [1975] Sales Director; John Graham Smith [1950] Director; Lynda Vede [1968] Finance Director; Dave Wight [1962] Operations Director

Granby Care Limited
Incorporated: 29 October 1991 *Employees:* 5
Net Worth: £15,363,000 *Total Assets:* £15,363,000
Registered Office: Norcliffe House, Station Road, Wilmslow, Cheshire, SK9 1BU
Activities: Other human health activities
Parent: Brighterkind Health Care Group Limited
Officers: Abigail Mattison, Secretary; Robert Nicolas Barr [1958] Director; Ryan Stuart MacAskill [1975] Director; Gregory Laurence Newman [1988] Director/Investment Professional; Jeremy Robert Arthur Richardson [1970] Director; Phillip Gary Thomas [1978] Director

Grand Hotel (St. Annes) Limited
Incorporated: 22 June 1993 *Employees:* 89
Net Worth: £4,429,700 *Total Assets:* £12,584,185
Registered Office: South Promenade, Lytham St Annes, Lancs, FY8 1NB
Activities: Hotels and similar accommodation
Shareholders: Richard John Webb; Amanda Joy Webb
Officers: Amanda Joy Webb, Secretary; Amanda Joy Webb [1961] Director; Richard John Webb [1959] Director; Sam Webb [1989] Director; Thomas Webb [1992] Director

Grandcross Limited
Incorporated: 6 January 1998 *Employees:* 265
Net Worth: £9,394,000 *Total Assets:* £10,940,000
Registered Office: Norcliffe House, Station Road, Wilmslow, Cheshire, SK9 1BU
Activities: Other human health activities
Parent: Four Seasons Health Care Group Limited
Officers: Abigail Mattison, Secretary; Timothy Richard William Hammond [1959] Director; Dr Maureen Claire Royston [1960] Director; Benjamin Robert Taberner [1972] Director/Chartered Accountant

The Grange Care Centre (Cheltenham) Limited
Incorporated: 16 June 1982 *Employees:* 91
Net Worth: £3,486,016 *Total Assets:* £6,916,491
Registered Office: 6th Floor, Cardinal House, 20 St Mary's Parsonage, Manchester, M3 2LG
Activities: Residential care activities for the elderly and disabled
Parent: The Grange Care Centre UK Limited
Officers: Philip Klor, Secretary; Philip Klor [1984] Director [Swiss]; Solomon Klor [1959] Director [Swiss]

Grange School Hartford Limited (The)
Incorporated: 15 July 1958 *Employees:* 258
Net Worth: £20,736,540 *Total Assets:* £27,627,976
Registered Office: The Grange School, Bradburns Lane, Hartford, Northwich, Cheshire, CW8 1LU
Activities: Primary education
Officers: Deborah Jane Torjussen, Secretary; David Raoul Gerrard Akka [1971] Director; Ann Arthur [1946] Director; Simon George Batey [1953] Director/Retired; Susan Clare Briegal [1962] Director/Chief Executive; Neil Brougham [1966] Director/Actuary; Hannah Ruth Burgoyne [1981] Director/Solicitor; Sarah Jane Hudson [1965] Director/Solicitor; Nicola Irene Matthews [1959] Director/Retired Headteacher; Professor Catherine McCrohan [1955] Director/University Professor; Martin Harold Newsholme [1964] Director/Retired - Chartered Accountant; Christopher George Oglesby [1967] Director; Nigel Richard Parkinson [1956] Director/IT Project Manager; Jeremy Walker Simpson [1960] Director/Chartered Surveyor; Jurgen Stamer [1964] Director/NHS Doctor [German]; Catherine Elizabeth Stanton [1969] Director/Lecturer; Karen Michelle Williams [1966] Managing Director

Grangefern Properties Limited
Incorporated: 21 October 1991
Net Worth: £28,357,380 *Total Assets:* £37,239,248
Registered Office: Emerson House, Heyes Lane, Alderley Edge, Cheshire, SK9 7LF
Activities: Other letting and operating of own or leased real estate
Parent: Orbit Investments (Properties) Limited
Officers: Varun Maharaj, Secretary; Anthony Emerson Jones [1967] Director; Mark Emerson Jones [1964] Director; Peter Emerson Jones [1935] Director

Granite Finance Ltd
Incorporated: 1 March 2008 *Employees:* 11
Net Worth: £2,894,044 *Total Assets:* £56,708,376
Registered Office: 98 Liverpool Road, Formby, Merseyside, L37 6BS
Activities: Security and commodity contracts dealing activities
Parent: Granite Underwriting Limited
Officers: Nicola Kate McLachlan, Secretary; Alan Peter Keating [1967] Director/Insurance Broker; Nicola McLachlan [1971] Director/Insurance Broker

Granite Underwriting Limited
Incorporated: 19 September 2007 *Employees:* 558
Net Worth: £22 450,602 *Total Assets:* £99,665,424
Registered Office: The Lighthouse, 98 Liverpool Road, Formby, Merseyside, L37 6BS
Activities: Activities of head offices
Parent: Granite Investments One Limited
Officers: Nicola Kate McLachlan, Secretary; Martin Richard Gowing [1970] Director/Insurance Broker; Alan Peter Keating [1967] Director/Insurance Consultant; Coenraad Alexander Lugt [1973] Director [Dutch]

Grant Leisure Group Limited
Incorporated: 19 November 1982 *Employees:* 96
Net Worth: £10,006,411 *Total Assets:* £13,335,572
Registered Office: Blackpool Zoo, East Park Drive, Blackpool, Lancs, FY3 8PP
Activities: Botanical and zoological gardens and nature reserves activities
Parent: Parques Reunidos Servicios Centrales SA
Officers: Juan Jose Lopez Taracena, Secretary; Jesus Pablo Fernandez Moran [1966] Director/Animal Parks Division Manager [Spanish]; Juan Jose Lopez Taracena [1964] Northern Europe Division Director for Group [Spanish]

Granton Investments Limited
Incorporated: 14 February 2003 *Employees:* 1
Net Worth: £6,360,954 *Total Assets:* £11,408,860
Registered Office: c/o DSG Chartered Accountants, Castle Chambers, 43 Castle Street, Liverpool, L2 9TL
Activities: Renting and operating of Housing Association real estate
Shareholder: Ian Alan Douglas & Nigel John Williams
Officers: Generaldine Geaves, Secretary; Timothy Spencer Barlow [1967] Director/Surveyor; Robert Grant Sloss [1968] Director/Chartered Surveyor

Graphic Packaging International Bardon Limited
Incorporated: 21 June 1955 *Employees:* 321
Net Worth: £28,709,000 *Total Assets:* £47,038,000
Registered Office: Eversheds House, 70 Great Bridgewater Street, Manchester, M1 5ES
Activities: Manufacture of other paper and paperboard containers
Parent: Graphic Packaging International Box Holdings Limited
Officers: Stephen Richard Scherger [1964] Director [American]; Lauren Tashma [1966] Director/Business Executive [American]; Eveline Maria Van de Rovaart [1975] Director/Business Executive [Dutch]; Hilde Maria Willy Van Moeseke [1970] Director/Business Executive [Belgian]; Joseph Paul Yost [1967] Director/Business Executive [American]

Graphic Packaging International Box Holdings Limited
Incorporated: 22 March 2005 *Employees:* 53
Net Worth Deficit: £4,628,000 *Total Assets:* £8,051,000
Registered Office: Eversheds House, 70 Great Bridgewater Street, Manchester, M1 5ES
Activities: Manufacture of other paper and paperboard containers
Parent: Shoo 553 Limited
Officers: Stephen Richard Scherger [1964] Director [American]; Lauren Tashma [1966] Director/Business Executive [American]; Eveline Maria Van de Rovaart [1975] Director/Business Executive [Dutch]; Hilde Maria Willy Van Moeseke [1970] Director/Business Executive [Belgian]; Joseph Paul Yost [1967] Director/Business Executive [American]

Graphic Packaging International Europe UK Holdings Limited
Incorporated: 1 May 1940
Net Worth: £8,221,000 *Total Assets:* £56,483,000
Registered Office: Eversheds House, 70 Great Bridgewater Street, Manchester, M1 5ES
Activities: Activities of head offices
Parent: Graphic Packaging Holding Company, Inc.
Officers: Stephen Richard Scherger [1964] Director [American]; Lauren Tashma [1966] Director/Business Executive [American]; Eveline Maria Van de Rovaart [1975] Director/Business Executive [Dutch]; Hilde Maria Willy Van Moeseke [1970] Director/Business Executive [Belgian]; Joseph Paul Yost [1967] Director/Business Executive [American]

Graphic Packaging International Europe UK Limited
Incorporated: 27 November 1961 *Employees:* 437
Net Worth: £44,285,000 *Total Assets:* £90,676,000
Registered Office: Eversheds House, 70 Great Bridgewater Street, Manchester, M1 5ES
Activities: Manufacture of other paper and paperboard containers
Parent: Graphic Packaging International Europe UK Holdings Limited
Officers: Stephen Richard Scherger [1964] Director [American]; Lauren Tashma [1966] Director/Business Executive [American]; Eveline Maria Van de Rovaart [1975] Director/Business Executive [Dutch]; Hilde Maria Willy Van Moeseke [1970] Director/Business Executive [Belgian]; Joseph Paul Yost [1967] Director/Business Executive [American]

Graphic Packaging International Foodservice Europe Ltd
Incorporated: 30 June 1951 *Employees:* 30
Net Worth: £3,518,264 *Total Assets:* £6,804,624
Registered Office: Units 10 & 11 Navigation Park, Road One, Winsford Industrial Estate, Winsford, Cheshire, CW7 3RL
Activities: Manufacture of other paper and paperboard containers
Officers: Lauren Tashma, Secretary; Stephen Richard Scherger [1964] Director/Senior Vice President & Chief Financial Officer [American]; Lauren Tashma [1966] Director/Senior Vice President & General Counsel [American]; Eveline Van de Rovaart [1975] Director/Assistant General Counsel [Dutch]; Hilde Van Moeseke [1970] Director/Senior Vice President [Belgian]

Graphic Packaging International Gateshead Limited
Incorporated: 15 February 1977 *Employees:* 393
Net Worth: £31,398,000 *Total Assets:* £48,580,000
Registered Office: Eversheds House, 70 Great Bridgewater Street, Manchester, M1 5ES
Activities: Manufacture of other paper and paperboard containers
Parent: Graphic Packaging International Box Holdings Limited
Officers: Stephen Richard Scherger [1964] Director [American]; Lauren Tashma [1966] Director/Business Executive [American]; Eveline Maria Van de Rovaart [1975] Director/Business Executive [Dutch]; Hilde Maria Willy Van Moeseke [1970] Director/Business Executive [Belgian]; Joseph Paul Yost [1967] Director/Business Executive [American]

Graphic Packaging International Limited
Incorporated: 16 March 1988 *Employees:* 144
Net Worth: £62,829,000 *Total Assets:* £209,976,992
Registered Office: Eversheds House, 70 Great Bridgewater Street, Manchester, M1 5ES
Activities: Manufacture of other paper and paperboard containers
Parent: Graphic Packaging Holding Company, Inc.
Officers: Stephen Richard Scherger [1964] Director/Chief Financial Officer [American]; Lauren Tashma [1966] Director/Business Executive [American]; Eveline Maria Van de Rovaart [1975] Director/Business Executive [Dutch]; Hilde Maria Willy Van Moeseke [1970] Director/Business Executive [Belgian]; Joseph Paul Yost [1967] Director/Business Executive [American]

Graphic Packaging International UK Finance Limited
Incorporated: 19 May 2014
Total Assets: £43,749,000
Registered Office: Eversheds House, 70 Great Bridgewater Street, Manchester, M1 5ES
Activities: Other credit granting n.e.c.
Parent: Graphic Packaging International Limited
Officers: Stephen Richard Scherger [1964] Director [American]; Lauren Tashma [1966] Director/Business Executive [American]; Eveline Maria Van de Rovaart [1975] Director/Business Executive [Dutch]; Hilde Maria Willy Van Moeseke [1970] Director/Business Executive [Belgian]; Joseph Paul Yost [1967] Director/Business Executive [American]

Grattan Public Limited Company
Incorporated: 25 June 1930 *Employees:* 442
Net Worth: £106,491,000 *Total Assets:* £219,515,008
Registered Office: 66-70 Vicar Lane, Little Germany, Bradford, W Yorks, BD99 2XG
Activities: Retail sale via mail order houses or via Internet
Parent: Freemans Grattan Holdings Limited
Officers: Andrew James Lord, Secretary; John Hinchcliffe [1965] Director/Chief Executive Officer; Neill Lewis McDonald Moore [1966] Director/Chartered Accountant; Marc Erich Bernd Wolfgang Opelt [1962] Director/Businessman [German]

Graves (Cumberland) Limited
Incorporated: 16 March 1933 *Employees:* 138
Net Worth: £30,624,116 *Total Assets:* £35,259,504
Registered Office: 8 Falcon Place, Workington, Cumbria, CA14 2EX
Activities: Motion picture projection activities
Officers: Daryl Davidson, Secretary; Duncan Gilchrist Carter [1971] Director/Solicitor; Daryl Davidson [1962] Director/Accountant; Carolyn Elizabeth Graves [1951] Director/Hotelier; Charles John Graves [1949] Director/Hotelier; John Michael Graves [1947] Director; Peter Lawton [1952] Director/Retired; Nicholas Craig Smith [1958] Director/Chartered Surveyor

Gray Forklift Group (Holdings) Limited
Incorporated: 13 March 2015 *Employees:* 1
Net Worth Deficit: £645,576 *Total Assets:* £23,296,078
Registered Office: Corpacq House, 1 Goose Green, Altrincham, Cheshire, WA14 1DW
Activities: Other business support service activities n.e.c.
Officers: Stephen James Scott [1978] Director

Grayrentals Limited
Incorporated: 14 June 1991 *Employees:* 38
Net Worth: £40,448,148 *Total Assets:* £77,314,016
Registered Office: 3rd Floor, 1 Ashley Road, Altrincham, Cheshire, WA14 2DT
Activities: Renting and leasing of trucks and other heavy vehicles
Parent: Tip Trailer Services UK Limited
Officers: Scott Davies [1967] Director/Operations Leader; Robert Alain Fast [1956] Director [American]; Michael Robert Furnival [1963] Director; Susan Halsall [1969] Director; Malachy McEnroe [1965] Director [Irish]; Terry Stephen Moody [1956] Director

Great Academies Education Trust
Incorporated: 4 May 2007 *Employees:* 486
Net Worth: £61,858,000 *Total Assets:* £70,263,000
Registered Office: 249 Cavendish Street, Ashton under Lyne, Lancs, OL6 7AT
Activities: Other education n.e.c.
Officers: Christopher Graham Bowes [1972] Director/Partner; Allison Jean Crompton [1962] Director/Chief Executive; Helen Christina Curran [1967] Director/Accountant; Annette Hall [1955] Director/Executive Principal; Susan Jayne Hutchinson [1970] Director/Audit Partner; Ian Hamilton Munro [1954] Director/Chief Executive; Anthony Arthur Powell [1957] Executive Director; Gregory Thomas Suligowski [1983] Director/Senior Executive; Catherine Elizabeth Sullivan-Williams [1962] Director/People Consultant

Great Bear Distribution Limited
Incorporated: 17 February 1994 *Employees:* 1,879
Net Worth: £13,673,945 *Total Assets:* £102,823,976
Registered Office: Stellar House, Barbour Square, Field Lane, Tattenhall, Chester, CH3 9RF
Activities: Operation of warehousing and storage facilities for land transport activities
Parent: Culina Group Limited
Officers: Nigel Stephen Jury, Secretary; Alastair William Isbister [1965] Director; Nigel Stephen Jury [1950] Director; Christian Lee Price [1975] Director; Thomas Van Mourik [1963] Director [Dutch]; Liesl Janet Ward [1968] Director

Great Bear Holdings Limited
Incorporated: 2 September 2009
Net Worth: £42,543,728 *Total Assets:* £50,000,000
Registered Office: Stellar House, Barbour Square, Field Lane, Tattenhall, Chester, CH3 9RF
Activities: Operation of warehousing and storage facilities for land transport activities
Parent: Culina Group Limited
Officers: Nigel Stephen Jury, Secretary; Nigel Stephen Jury [1950] Director; Christian Lee Price [1975] Director; Thomas Van Mourik [1963] Director [Dutch]

Great British Botanical Limited
Incorporated: 21 April 2016 *Employees:* 65
Net Worth: £2,721,075 *Total Assets:* £12,299,646
Registered Office: 2 Wellington Road, Greenfield, Oldham, Lancs, OL3 7AG
Activities: Activities of head offices
Officers: Thomas Noel Barry [1961] Director; Martin Toogood [1946] Director

Great John Street Hotel Limited
Incorporated: 2 March 2012 *Employees:* 80
Net Worth: £5,008,078 *Total Assets:* £12,092,578
Registered Office: Eleven Didsbury Park, Didsbury, Manchester, M20 5LH
Activities: Hotels and similar accommodation
Officers: Edward Gerard Michael O'Loughlin [1958] Director [Irish]

Great Leighs Estates Limited
Incorporated: 18 July 2013 *Employees:* 123
Net Worth: £1,949,814 *Total Assets:* £21,499,816
Registered Office: The Spectrum, Benson Road, Birchwood, Warrington, Cheshire, WA3 7PQ
Activities: Event catering activities
Shareholders: Tote Media Limited; Bet Solutions International PLC
Officers: Paul James Kirszanek, Secretary; Simon Nicholas Bailey [1960] Director; Joseph Matthias Scanlon [1951] Director; Stephen Peter Shore [1966] Director; Philip Zenon Sierzputowski [1952] Director

The Great Schools Trust
Incorporated: 19 May 2011 *Employees:* 188
Net Worth: £18,590,004 *Total Assets:* £22,265,444
Registered Office: Hillock Lane, Woolston, Warrington, Cheshire, WA1 4PF
Activities: Educational support services
Officers: Robina Crowe [1953] Director/Retired; Aiden Thomas Christian Harper [1969] Director; Michael Ireland [1976] Director/Business Consultant; Kieran John McGing [1984] Director/Actuary; Colin Gary Scotland [1974] Managing Director; Joseph William Spencer [1959] Director/University Professor; Hilary Wilcock [1947] Director/Retired

Great Yarmouth Port Company Ltd
Incorporated: 18 October 2006 *Employees:* 54
Net Worth: £78,300,000 *Total Assets:* £117,200,000
Registered Office: Maritime Centre, Port of Liverpool, L21 1LA
Activities: Operation of warehousing and storage facilities for water transport activities
Parent: Peel Ports Investments Limited
Officers: Caroline Ruth Marrison Gill, Secretary; Farook Akhtar Khan, Secretary; Ian Graeme Lloyd Charnock [1962] Director; Mark Whitworth [1966] Director

Greater Manchester Academies Trust
Incorporated: 20 November 2008 *Employees:* 253
Net Worth: £32,205,000 *Total Assets:* £33,949,000
Registered Office: 3rd Floor, 1 Ashley Road, Altrincham, Cheshire, WA14 2DT
Activities: General secondary education
Officers: Carol Ann Culley [1968] Director/Accountant; Andrea Grant [1962] Director; Janice Hailwood [1959] Director/Client Industry Executive; Peter John Hale [1982] Director/Teacher; Lynne Jane Heath [1953] Director/Principal; Robin David Lawler [1954] Director/Chief Executive; Amanda Jacqueline Lund [1970] Director/Office Manager; Jonathan Andrew Thompson Putt [1968] Director/Educational Management; Victoria Susan Rosin [1952] Director/Local Government Officer; Helen Ruth Slinger [1973] Director; Susan Webster [1950] Project Director

Greater Manchester Buses South Limited
Incorporated: 12 May 1993 *Employees:* 2,371
Net Worth: £16 717,000 *Total Assets:* £95,970,000
Registered Office: c/o Stagecoach Services Limited, One Stockport Exchange, 20 Railway Road, Stockport, Cheshire, SK1 3SW
Activities: Other urban, suburban or metropolitan passenger land transport (not underground, metro or similar)
Parent: Stagecoach Bus Holdings Limited
Officers: Michael John Vaux, Secretary; Colin Brown [1968] Director/Accountant; Elisabeth Ann Tasker [1967] Director; Arnold Mark Threapleton [1954] Managing Director

Green Growth Power Ltd
Incorporated: 10 March 2016
Net Worth Deficit: £1,008,380 *Total Assets:* £27,523,336
Registered Office: Unit 5-6 Arbour Lane, Knowsley Industrial Park, Knowsley, Merseyside, L33 7XB
Activities: Sawmilling and planing of wood
Parent: Entrade Energy Corp.
Officers: Julien Felix Uhlig [1976] Director [German]

Green Pastures North West Limited
Incorporated: 2 September 2002
Net Worth: £948,828 *Total Assets:* £7,240,494
Registered Office: 9 Mornington Road, Southport, Merseyside, PR9 0TS
Activities: Buying and selling of own real estate
Shareholders: Andrew Mark Cunningham; Peter Cunningham; Ann Victoria Woodley
Officers: Ann Victoria Woodley, Secretary/Director; Andrew Mark Cunningham [1974] Director; Peter Cunningham [1942] Director; Ann Victoria Woodley [1947] Director

Greenbank Holidays Limited
Incorporated: 15 February 1974 *Employees:* 133
Net Worth: £21,940,000 *Total Assets:* £54,458,000
Registered Office: Chelford House, Rudheath Way, Rudheath, Northwich, Cheshire, CW9 7LN
Activities: Other service activities n.e.c.
Parent: Eurocamp Limited
Officers: Alain Yvon Calme [1966] Director [French]; Stijn Hendrik Marc Depraetere [1975] Director [Belgian]; Darren Paul Marsh [1975] Director

Greenbank Services Limited
Incorporated: 24 November 1980 *Employees:* 491
Net Worth: £797,000 *Total Assets:* £13,967,000
Registered Office: Chelford House, Rudheath Way, Rudheath, Northwich, Cheshire, CW9 7LN
Activities: Other service activities n.e.c.
Parent: Eurocamp Limited
Officers: Alain Yvon Calme [1966] Director [French]; Stijn Hendrik Marc Depraetere [1975] Director [Belgian]; Darren Paul Marsh [1975] Director

Greenbank Technology Limited
Incorporated: 7 December 1990 *Employees:* 27
Net Worth: £11,532,806 *Total Assets:* £18,874,896
Registered Office: Unit 3 Greenbank Business Park, Dyneley Road, Blackburn, BB1 3AB
Activities: Manufacture of ovens, furnaces and furnace burners
Parent: California Pellet Mills
Officers: Emma Louise Bachelor, Secretary; Erik Dean Carney [1966] Managing Director; Douglas Ostrich [1968] Director/Management [American]; Anna Louise Waugh [1974] Commercial Director

Greenergy Limited
Incorporated: 17 September 2016
Net Worth: £530,000 *Total Assets:* £25,530,000
Registered Office: 215a Centurion Park, Davyfield Road, Blackburn, BB1 2QY
Activities: Remediation activities and other waste management services
Major Shareholder: Naeem Abbass
Officers: Naeem Abbass, Secretary; Naeem Abbass [1979] Director/Engineer; Mohammed Arshed Khan [1968] Director/Waste Management

P. W. Greenhalgh Holdings Limited
Incorporated: 29 September 2005 *Employees:* 85
Net Worth: £5,963,486 *Total Assets:* £9,581,615
Registered Office: Newhey Bleach Works, Newhey, Rochdale, Lancs, OL16 3TH
Activities: Other letting and operating of own or leased real estate
Shareholders: Andrew Benjamin Greenhalgh; Simon Ross Greenhalgh
Officers: Andrew Benjamin Greenhalgh, Secretary; Andrew Benjamin Greenhalgh [1963] Director; Simon Ross Greenhalgh [1964] Director

Greenhalgh's Craft Bakery Limited
Incorporated: 14 March 1957 *Employees:* 860
Net Worth: £16,343,184 *Total Assets:* £19,817,708
Registered Office: Crescent Road, Lostock, Bolton, Lancs, BL6 4BU
Activities: Manufacture of bread; manufacture of fresh pastry goods and cakes
Officers: Raymond Desmond Lyons, Secretary; Anne Maria Busby [1956] Director; Raymond Desmond Lyons [1957] Director/Chartered Accountant; David Smart [1958] Director; Kathleen Mary Smart [1931] Director/Company Secretary; Helen Louise Smart-Torakis [1969] Director

Greenwhitestar Acquisitions Limited
Incorporated: 4 March 2014
Net Worth: £12,079,000 *Total Assets:* £226,428,000
Registered Office: Stretton Green Distribution Park, Langford Way, Appleton, Warrington, Cheshire, WA4 4TQ
Activities: Activities of other holding companies n.e.c.
Parent: Eddie Stobart Logistics PLC
Officers: Elaine Williams, Secretary; Damien Harte [1956] Director [Irish]; Alexander Laffey [1961] Director; Rupert Henry Conquest Nichols [1949] Director

Greenwood & Coope Limited
Incorporated: 11 October 1924 *Employees:* 270
Net Worth: £31,317,000 *Total Assets:* £45,642,000
Registered Office: Brookhouse Mill, Greenmount, Bury, Lancs, BL8 4HR
Activities: Manufacture of other carpets and rugs
Officers: Jonathan Charles Hill, Secretary; Thomas Barber [1947] Director/Management Consultant; Betty Winifred Cormack [1930] Director; David Neville Cormack [1965] Marketing Director; John Robert Cormack [1958] Director; Jonathan Charles Hill [1971] Finance Director; David James Judge [1956] Director; Helen Winifred Polito [1956] Director; Catherine Alison Wall [1960] Director

Greif UK Holding Ltd
Incorporated: 31 October 2008
Net Worth Deficit: £19,843,436 *Total Assets:* £35,868,976
Registered Office: Merseyside Works, Oil Sites Road, Ellesmere Port, Cheshire, CH65 4EZ
Activities: Activities of head offices
Parent: Greif UK International Holding Ltd
Officers: Andrew John Hall, Secretary; Graham Duerden [1959] Director; Andrew John Hall [1971] Finance Director

Greif UK Ltd
Incorporated: 30 June 2008 *Employees:* 176
Net Worth: £43,734,000 *Total Assets:* £54,585,000
Registered Office: Merseyside Works, Oil Sites Road, Ellesmere Port, Cheshire, CH65 4EZ
Activities: Manufacture of steel drums and similar containers
Parent: Greif UK Holding
Officers: Andrew John Hall, Secretary; Graham Duerden [1959] Managing Director; Andrew Hall [1971] Director

GREP1 Limited
Incorporated: 16 November 2006
Net Worth: £18,020,936 *Total Assets:* £167,053,040
Registered Office: Eversheds House, 70 Great Bridgewater Street, Manchester, M1 5ES
Activities: Production of electricity
Parent: CEP Biomass Limited
Officers: Joost Hessel Louis Bergsma [1965] Director/Fund Manager [Dutch]; Peter Robert Dickson [1964] Director/Chartered Engineer; Jordi Lopez Francesch [1977] Director/Asset Manager [Spanish]

Gresham Office Furniture Limited
Incorporated: 3 November 1976 *Employees:* 265
Net Worth: £17,714,500 *Total Assets:* £24,191,844
Registered Office: Platinum Park, Lynstock Way, Horwich, Bolton, Lancs, BL6 4SA
Activities: Manufacture of office and shop furniture
Parent: Gresham UK Holdings Limited
Officers: Craig Robert Turley, Secretary; Julian David Roebuck [1974] Managing Director; Richard Roebuck [1977] Director; Craig Robert Turley [1978] Finance Director

Gresham UK Holdings Limited
Incorporated: 4 October 2004
Net Worth: £1,489,357 *Total Assets:* £12,658,284
Registered Office: Platinum Park, Lynstock Way, Horwich, Bolton, Lancs, BL6 4SA
Activities: Other business support service activities n.e.c.
Parent: JD Roebuck Holdings Limited
Officers: Craig Robert Turley, Secretary; Julian David Roebuck [1974] Director/Manager; Richard Roebuck [1977] Director; Craig Robert Turley [1978] Director

Gresty Holdings (Crewe) Limited
Incorporated: 1 June 2006 *Employees:* 244
Net Worth: £3,048,635 *Total Assets:* £6,634,346
Registered Office: Cedarlea, 16 Barracks Lane, Ravensmoor, Nantwich, Cheshire, CW5 8PR
Activities: Non-trading company
Parent: Gresty Holdings Limited
Officers: Mark Andrew Hassall, Secretary; Catherine Ann Hassall [1945] Director; Clare Tracy Hassall [1972] Director/Certified Chartered Accountant; Mark Andrew Hassall [1971] Director/Accountant; Norman Hassall [1943] Finance Director; Julie Ann McEvoy [1967] Director; Daniel Kenneth Dudley Potts [1973] Director

Gresty Holdings Limited
Incorporated: 18 February 1977 *Employees:* 224
Net Worth: £2,030,621 *Total Assets:* £7,284,845
Registered Office: Cedarlea, 16 Barracks Lane, Ravensmoor, Nantwich, Cheshire, CW5 8PR
Activities: Management consultancy activities other than financial management
Shareholder: Norman Hassall
Officers: Mark Andrew Hassall, Secretary/Accountant; Catherine Ann Hassall [1945] Director; Mark Andrew Hassall [1971] Director/Accountant; Norman Hassall [1943] Director; Julie Ann McEvoy [1967] Director

Greystone Financial Services (Holdings) Limited
Incorporated: 15 August 2006 *Employees:* 69
Net Worth: £6,963,828 *Total Assets:* £8,579,339
Registered Office: Foundation House, Scott Drive, Altrincham, Cheshire, WA15 8AB
Activities: Activities of financial services holding companies
Parent: Focus Operating LLC
Officers: Neil Andrew Peden, Secretary; Neil Alexander [1961] Director; Neil Graeme Davidson [1961] Director; Stephen Paul Heap [1959] Director; Keith Horner [1951] Director/Chartered Accountant; Simon Ashley Lomas [1963] Director; Neil Andrew Peden [1960] Director

Grif040 Limited
Incorporated: 25 June 2013
Net Worth: £3,409,953 *Total Assets:* £15,004,672
Registered Office: c/o Brooks MacDonald, 10th Floor, No 1 Marsden Street, Manchester, M2 1HW
Activities: Other business support service activities n.e.c.
Parent: Ground Rents Income Fund PLC
Officers: Simon Paul Wombwell [1961] Director

Grif048 Limited
Incorporated: 19 November 2013
Net Worth: £2,516,838 *Total Assets:* £12,821,485
Registered Office: Brooks MacDonald, 10th Floor, No 1 Marsden Street, Manchester, M2 1HW
Activities: Other business support service activities n.e.c.
Parent: Ground Rents Income Fund PLC
Officers: Simon Paul Wombwell [1961] Director

Grif051 Limited
Incorporated: 19 November 2013
Net Worth: £289,540 *Total Assets:* £20,390,896
Registered Office: c/o Brooks MacDonald, 10th Floor, No 1 Marsden Street, Manchester, M2 1HW
Activities: Other business support service activities n.e.c.
Parent: Ground Rents Income Fund PLC
Officers: Simon Paul Wombwell [1961] Director

Griffiths & Armour (Holdings) Limited
Incorporated: 26 July 1993
Registered Office: 12 Princes Parade, Princes Dock, Liverpool, L3 1BG
Activities: Non-life insurance
Shareholder: Robin Mark Hill Griffiths
Officers: David John Darke, Secretary; Stephen Howard Bamforth [1964] Director/Insurance Broker; Paul Berg [1969] Director/Insurance Broker; Nicholas Adrian Brace [1959] Director/Insurance Broker; David John Darke [1947] Director/Accountant; Matthew Donnelly [1964] Director/Insurance Broker; Carl John Edwards [1971] Director/Insurance Broker; Carl Evans [1965] Director/Insurance Broker; Robin Mark Hill Griffiths [1941] Director; David John Haram [1964] Director/Insurance Broker; Simon Keenan [1979] Director/Insurance Broker; Richard Henry Trotter [1954] Director/Insurance Broker; David Johnson Whalley [1968] Director/Chartered Accountant

Griffiths & Armour Global Risks Limited
Incorporated: 15 March 2004 *Employees:* 12
Net Worth: £1,816,543 *Total Assets:* £59,851,464
Registered Office: 12 Princes Parade, Princes Dock, Liverpool, L3 1BG
Activities: Activities of insurance agents and brokers
Shareholder: Robin Mark Hill Griffiths
Officers: David Johnson Whalley, Secretary; Stephen Howard Bamforth [1964] Director/Insurance Broker; Nicholas Adrian Brace [1959] Director/Insurance Broker; Matthew Donnelly [1964] Director/Insurance Broker; Anthony James Dudgeon [1966] Director/Insurance Broker; Carl Evans [1965] Director/Insurance Broker; David John Haram [1964] Director/Insurance Broker; Michael Jonathan Stubbs [1967] Director/Insurance Broker; David Johnson Whalley [1968] Director/Chartered Accountant

Griffiths & Armour Limited
Incorporated: 1 December 1983 *Employees:* 12
Net Worth: £6,319,311 *Total Assets:* £6,556,330
Registered Office: 12 Princes Parade, Princes Dock, Liverpool, L3 1BG
Activities: Activities of financial services holding companies
Shareholder: Robin Mark Hill Griffiths
Officers: David John Darke, Secretary; Stephen Howard Bamforth [1964] Director/Insurance Broker; Paul Berg [1969] Director/Insurance Broker; Nicholas Adrian Brace [1959] Director/Insurance Broker; David John Darke [1947] Director/Accountant; Matthew Donnelly [1964] Director/Insurance Broker; Carl John Edwards [1971] Director/Insurance Broker; Carl Evans [1965] Director/Insurance Broker; Robin Mark Hill Griffiths [1941] Director; David John Haram [1964] Director/Insurance Broker; Simon Keenan [1979] Director/Insurance Broker; Richard Henry Trotter [1954] Director/Insurance Broker; David Johnson Whalley [1968] Director/Chartered Accountant

The Grosvenor - Pulford Hotel Limited
Incorporated: 26 November 1982 *Employees:* 265
Net Worth: £11,907,702 *Total Assets:* £14,679,208
Registered Office: The Grosvenor-Pulford Hotel, Wrexham Road, Pulford, Chester, CH4 9DG
Activities: Hotels and similar accommodation
Parent: Nelson (Northwest) Hotels Limited
Officers: Norman Andrew Howell, Secretary; Andrew Garner Nelson [1981] Director/Licencee; Harold Garner Nelson [1942] Director/Hotelier; Susan Marjorie Nelson [1953] Director/Hotelier

Grosvenor Farms Limited
Incorporated: 21 December 1973 *Employees:* 32
Net Worth: £9,124,000 *Total Assets:* £15,170,000
Registered Office: Aldford Hall Farm, Chester Road, Aldford, Chester, CH3 6HJ
Activities: Mixed farming
Parent: Deva Group Limited
Officers: Geoffrey Murray Chadwick, Secretary; Anthony William Searson James [1968] Director/Accountant; Graham Paul Ramsbottom [1965] Director/Chartered Surveyor; Mark Anthony Roach [1959] Farm Director; James Reginald Townshend [1954] Director; Angus Alexander Wielkopolski [1955] Director/Farmer

Group Auto Union UK and Ireland Limited
Incorporated: 21 February 1979 *Employees:* 73
Net Worth: £13,476,045 *Total Assets:* £115,125,920
Registered Office: Roydsdale House, Roydsdale Way, Euroway Trading Estate, Bradford, W Yorks, BD4 6SE
Activities: Other business support service activities n.e.c.
Parent: Alliance Automotive UK Limited
Officers: John Frederick Coombes, Secretary; Alistair Stuart Brown [1955] Director [New Zealander]; John Frederick Coombes [1965] Director; Jean-Jacques Mathieu Lafont [1959] Director [Belgian]

Group First Global Limited
Incorporated: 10 March 2006 *Employees:* 11
Net Worth Deficit: £30,610,264 *Total Assets:* £68,582,328
Registered Office: Group First House, Mead Way, Padiham, Lancs, BB12 7NG
Activities: Buying and selling of own real estate
Major Shareholder: Toby Scott Whittaker
Officers: John Slater [1978] Director; Toby Scott Whittaker [1977] Director

Grove Business Park Limited
Incorporated: 13 November 2015
Net Worth: £503,677 *Total Assets:* £12,294,085
Registered Office: Orchard House, Strawberry How Road, Cockermouth, Cumbria, CA13 9XQ
Activities: Other letting and operating of own or leased real estate
Parent: L F D Group Limited
Officers: Caroline Anne Cross, Secretary; David Robert Hill [1953] Director/Chartered Accountant; Ruth Elizabeth Hill [1954] Director

The Growth Company Limited
Incorporated: 17 November 1989 *Employees:* 1,081
Net Worth: £14,225,000 *Total Assets:* £61,044,000
Registered Office: Lee House, 90 Great Bridgewater Street, Manchester, M1 5JW
Activities: Other service activities n.e.c.
Officers: Paul Anthony Simpson, Secretary; Councillor Ebrahim Ayub Adia [1969] Director; Michael Blackburn [1959] Director; Jane Alexandra Boardman [1975] Director/Accountant; Paula Boshell [1951] Director/Deputy City Mayor of Salford; Paul Antony Dennett [1979] Director/City Mayor of Salford; Iwan James Lawrence Griffiths [1972] Director/Chartered Accountant; Mark Anthony Hughes [1966] Director/Chief Executive; Sir Richard Charles Leese [1951] Director; Vanda Murray [1960] Director; Richard Simon Topliss [1956] Director

Guarantee Protection Insurance Limited
Incorporated: 3 March 1997 *Employees:* 9
Net Worth: £4,676,607 *Total Assets:* £25,530,112
Registered Office: 14 Castle Street, Liverpool, L2 0NE
Activities: Non-life insurance
Parent: Kinnell Holdings Ltd
Officers: Jeremy MacDuff Brettell [1961] Non-Executive Director Chairman; Paul Byron Wakefield [1959] Director

Guenther 182 Limited
Incorporated: 14 April 1989
Net Worth: £32,457,516 *Total Assets:* £52,668,112
Registered Office: Hareshill Road, Heywood, Lancs, OL10 2TN
Activities: Activities of other holding companies n.e.c.
Parent: Guenther Holdings Limited
Officers: Thomas a McRae, Secretary; Thomas McRae [1957] Director [American]; Janelle M Sykes [1964] Director [American]; Dale W Tremblay [1958] Director [American]

Guenther Bakeries UK Limited
Incorporated: 10 February 2005 *Employees:* 143
Net Worth: £34,916,752 *Total Assets:* £39,434,640
Registered Office: Hareshill Road, Heywood, Lancs, OL10 2TN
Activities: Manufacture of bread; manufacture of fresh pastry goods and cakes
Parent: Guenther Holdings Limited
Officers: Thomas a McRae, Secretary; Melvyn Stewart Bugler [1956] Director; Justin Grubbs [1970] Director [American]; Thomas a McRae [1957] Director [American]; Janelle M Sykes [1964] Director [American]; Dale W Tremblay [1958] Director [American]

Guenther Holdings Limited
Incorporated: 1 April 2005 *Employees:* 615
Net Worth: £40,148,824 *Total Assets:* £76,413,544
Registered Office: Hareshill Road, Heywood, Lancs, OL10 2TN
Activities: Activities of head offices
Parent: CH Guenther & Son Inc
Officers: Thomas a McRae, Secretary; Thomas a McRae [1957] Director [American]; Janelle M Sykes [1964] Director [American]; Dale W Tremblay [1958] Director [American]

Guenther Management Limited
Incorporated: 6 November 2013
Net Worth: £20,828,374 *Total Assets:* £20,828,374
Registered Office: Hareshill Road, Heywood, Lancs, OL10 2TN
Activities: Activities of other holding companies n.e.c.
Parent: Guenther Holdings Limited
Officers: Thomas a McRae, Secretary; Thomas a McRae [1957] Director [American]; Janelle M Sykes [1964] Director [American]; Dale W Tremblay [1958] Director [American]

H. Marcel Guest, Limited
Incorporated: 4 October 1930 *Employees:* 173
Net Worth: £6,462,885 *Total Assets:* £11,343,259
Registered Office: Riverside Works, Collyhurst Road, Manchester, M40 7RU
Activities: Financial management
Shareholders: John Stuart Falder; Stephen Brian Falder; Katherine Jane Falder; Brian Falder
Officers: Kathrine Falder, Secretary; Brian Falder [1931] Director/Paint Manufacturer; Christine Jane Falder [1960] Director; Jane Elizabeth Falder [1955] Director; John Stuart Falder [1955] Managing Director; Stephen Brian Falder [1960] Managing Director

Guildford Investments Limited
Incorporated: 11 June 1959 *Employees:* 4
Net Worth: £8,605,589 *Total Assets:* £10,038,594
Registered Office: Fairview House, Victoria Place, Carlisle, Cumbria, CA1 1HP
Activities: Renting and operating of Housing Association real estate
Major Shareholder: William George Levi Marshall
Officers: Phoebe Marshall, Secretary; Clive David Marshall [1944] Director/Property Developer; Phoebe Marshall [1969] Director; William George Levi Marshall [1969] Director/Artist

Gunn JCB (Holdings) Limited
Incorporated: 13 April 2000 *Employees:* 3
Net Worth: £3,605,000 *Total Assets:* £8,343,000
Registered Office: Atlantic Street, Broadheath, Altrincham, Cheshire, WA14 5DN
Activities: Wholesale of agricultural machinery, equipment and supplies
Parent: Gunn JCB Group Limited
Officers: Paul Hartshorn [1964] Deputy Managing Director/Sales Director; Michael Stuart Hutchinson [1965] Director; Timothy Simcock [1967] Director

Gunn JCB Group Limited
Incorporated: 31 March 2014 *Employees:* 182
Net Worth: £6,333,000 *Total Assets:* £28,372,000
Registered Office: Gunn JCB Limited, Atlantic Street, Broadheath, Altrincham, Cheshire, WA14 5DN
Activities: Other retail sale not in stores, stalls or markets
Major Shareholder: Paul Hartshorn
Officers: Paul Hartshorn [1964] Director; Michael Stuart Hutchinson [1965] Director; Timothy Simcock [1967] Director; Gordon William Fraser Smith [1952] Director

Gunn JCB Limited
Incorporated: 7 January 1954 *Employees:* 180
Net Worth: £8,025,000 *Total Assets:* £32,741,000
Registered Office: Gunn JCB Limited, Atlantic Street, Broadheath, Altrincham, Cheshire, WA14 5DN
Activities: Other retail sale not in stores, stalls or markets
Parent: Gunn JCB (Holdings) Limited
Officers: Michael Stuart Hutchinson, Secretary; Paul Hartshorn [1964] Managing Director; Michael Stuart Hutchinson [1965] Finance Director; Mark Edward Patrick Roberts [1972] Sales Director; Timothy Simcock [1967] Service Director

Gusiute Holdings (UK) Limited
Incorporated: 4 December 2007 *Employees:* 2
Net Worth: £562,666,432 *Total Assets:* £584,490,944
Registered Office: Mond House, Winnington, Northwich, Cheshire, CW8 4DT
Activities: Activities of head offices
Officers: Dr Martin John Ashcroft [1969] Managing Director; John Mulhall [1968] Director/Chief Financial Officer; Mukundan Ramakrishnan [1966] Managing Director [Indian]

Gusto Restaurants Group Limited
Incorporated: 8 October 2013 *Employees:* 631
Net Worth Deficit: £3,673,000 *Total Assets:* £23,709,000
Registered Office: 98 King Street, Knutsford, Cheshire, WA16 6HQ
Activities: Licenced restaurants
Parent: Palatine Private Equity LLP
Officers: Paul Adam Campbell [1964] Director; Susan Jane Crimes [1972] Operations Director; Anthony James Griffin [1976] Director/Operations Manager; Kieran Anthony Lawton [1978] Investment Director; Gemma Marie Peel [1972] Finance Director; Jeremy Kevin Roberts [1962] Director; Matthew Adam Snell [1978] Managing Director; Gary William Tipper [1963] Director

Gusto Restaurants Limited
Incorporated: 13 October 1987 *Employees:* 631
Net Worth: £2,066,000 *Total Assets:* £16,031,000
Registered Office: 98 King Street, Knutsford, Cheshire, WA16 6HQ
Activities: Licenced restaurants
Parent: Gusto Restaurants UK Limited
Officers: Susan Jane Crimes [1972] Operations Director; Anthony James Griffin [1976] Director; Gemma Marie Peel [1972] Finance Director; Jeremy Kevin Roberts [1962] Director; Matthew Adam Snell [1978] Managing Director

Gusto Restaurants UK Limited
Incorporated: 8 October 2013
Net Worth Deficit: £4,145,000 *Total Assets:* £12,574,000
Registered Office: 98 King Street, Knutsford, Cheshire, WA16 6HQ
Activities: Licenced restaurants
Parent: Gusto Restaurants Group Limited
Officers: Susan Jane Crimes [1972] Operations Director; Anthony James Griffin [1976] Director/Operations Manager; Gemma Marie Peel [1972] Finance Director; Jeremy Kevin Roberts [1962] Director; Matthew Adam Snell [1978] Managing Director

Gutteridge Haskins & Davey Limited
Incorporated: 5 August 2005 *Employees:* 77
Net Worth: £10,204,604 *Total Assets:* £16,392,223
Registered Office: Level 1, Building 49, Thornton Science Park, Pool Lane, Ince, Chester, CH2 4NU
Activities: Engineering related scientific and technical consulting activities
Parent: GHD Holdings (UK) Pty Ltd
Officers: Lisa Maree Elbourne, Secretary; Michael Douglas Jennings, Secretary; Mark Charles Ingram [1962] Director/General Manager; Craig William Stockton [1970] Director/Mechanical Engineer

Gutterline Services Limited
Incorporated: 11 December 2013
Net Worth: £5,580,561 *Total Assets:* £7,321,768
Registered Office: High Peak Works, Chapel-en-le-Frith, High Peak, Derbys, SK23 0HW
Activities: Manufacture of builders ware of plastic
Parent: HD Sharman Group Limited
Officers: Mark Ian de Rozarieux, Secretary; Barry John Horgan [1971] Director [Irish]; Jakob Moeller-Jensen [1973] Director [Danish]

Thomas Guy,Limited
Incorporated: 11 November 1944 *Employees:* 10
Net Worth: £9,194,410 *Total Assets:* £10,936,071
Registered Office: 9 Osprey Place, Guys Industrial Estate, North Burscough, Ormskirk, Lancs, L40 8TG
Activities: Freight transport by road
Shareholder: Nigel Winston Guy
Officers: Julie Lesley Mitchell, Company Secretary; Nigel Winston Guy [1965] Director; Julie Lesley Mitchell [1961] Director/Company Secretary

Guyson (Holdings) Limited
Incorporated: 2 August 2011 *Employees:* 174
Net Worth: £10,294,907 *Total Assets:* £16,584,154
Registered Office: Snaygill Industrial Estate, Keighley Road, Skipton, N Yorks, BD23 2QR
Activities: Activities of head offices
Shareholders: James Robert Farquhar Thomson; Jane Thomson
Officers: James Robert Farquhar Thomson [1960] Director

Guyson International Limited
Incorporated: 9 March 1981 *Employees:* 124
Net Worth: £7,607,083 *Total Assets:* £10,560,488
Registered Office: Snaygill Industrial Estate, Keighley Road, Skipton, N Yorks, BD23 2QR
Activities: Other manufacturing n.e.c.
Shareholders: James Robert Farquhar Thomson; Jane Thomson
Officers: James Robert Farquhar Thomson [1960] Director

GVS Filter Technology UK Ltd
Incorporated: 23 September 1991 *Employees:* 339
Net Worth: £4,227,440 *Total Assets:* £14,432,078
Registered Office: NFC House, Vickers Industrial Estate, Mellishaw Lane, Morecambe, Lancs, LA3 3EN
Activities: Other manufacturing n.e.c.
Parent: Fenchurch Environmental Group Ltd
Officers: Mario Saccone, Secretary; John William Anthony Pike [1962] Director/Operations Manager; Massimo Scagliarini [1965] Director [Italian]

Gweco 510 Limited
Incorporated: 7 June 2011
Net Worth: £851,646 *Total Assets:* £16,644,015
Registered Office: 242 Oxford Road, Gomersal, Cleckheaton, W Yorks, BD19 4RE
Activities: Buying and selling of own real estate
Shareholders: Dean Hoyle; Janet Elizabeth Hoyle
Officers: Dean Hoyle [1967] Director; Janet Elizabeth Hoyle [1967] Director

Gweco 511 Limited
Incorporated: 24 June 2011 *Employees:* 2
Net Worth: £11,646,610 *Total Assets:* £46,217,224
Registered Office: 242 Oxford Road, Gomersal, Cleckheaton, W Yorks, BD19 4RE
Activities: Activities of open-ended investment companies
Shareholders: Dean Hoyle; Janet Elizabeth Hoyle
Officers: Dean Hoyle [1967] Director; Janet Elizabeth Hoyle [1967] Director

H & S Restaurants Ltd
Incorporated: 16 October 2006 *Employees:* 1,488
Net Worth: £2,149,746 *Total Assets:* £9,777,647
Registered Office: McDonald's Restaurant, Capitol Centre, Walton-le-Dale, Preston, Lancs, PR5 4AW
Activities: Unlicenced restaurants and cafes
Major Shareholder: Nigel Colin Dunnington
Officers: Lisa Dunnington, Secretary; Lisa Dunnington [1967] Director/Company Secretary; Nigel Colin Dunnington [1958] Director

H M Project Developments Ltd
Incorporated: 5 July 2006 *Employees:* 19
Net Worth Deficit: £1,764,907 *Total Assets:* £9,549,932
Registered Office: 21 Ben Nevis Drive, Little Sutton, Cheshire, CH66 4YZ
Activities: Support activities for other mining and quarrying
Shareholders: John Stephen Hornsby; Bindu Amritlal Bhatt
Officers: Lynne Marie Rathbone, Secretary/Solicitor; Bindu Amritlal Bhatt [1954] Director/Pharmacist; John Stephen Hornsby [1963] Director; Lynne Marie Rathbone [1966] Director/Solicitor

H&A Prestige Bottling Limited
Incorporated: 19 October 1983 *Employees:* 178
Net Worth: £2,822,000 *Total Assets:* £11,142,000
Registered Office: The Winery, Ackhurst Road, Ackhurst Business Park, Chorley, Lancs, PR7 1NH
Activities: Manufacture of cider and other fruit wines
Shareholders: Judith Margaret Halewood; Ian Alan Douglas; Halewood Wines and Spirits PLC
Officers: Ian Alan Douglas [1951] Director; Peter Gary Eaton [1960] Director; Graham Watt Gibson [1963] Sales Director; Stewart Andrew Hainsworth [1969] Director/Chief Executive; Judith Margaret Halewood [1951] Director; Alan William Robinson [1965] Director/Accountant; Lee Tayburn [1974] Director of Production

H&H Group PLC
Incorporated: 15 March 1892 *Employees:* 217
Net Worth: £17,753,000 *Total Assets:* £32,053,000
Registered Office: Borderway Mart, Rosehill Estate, Carlisle, CA1 2RS
Activities: Other business support service activities n.e.c.
Officers: Margaret Irving, Secretary; Andrew Douglas [1949] Director/Farmer; William Barr Hamilton [1959] Director/Farmer; Alasdair George Houston [1962] Director; Ian Callander Lancaster [1956] Director/Chartered Accountant; Dr Colin Lindsay [1966] Director/Veterinary Surgeon; Dawn Mary Harrison Livesey [1959] Director/Senior Lecturer; Richard Andrew Rankin [1973] Director/Chief Executive; Michael Leslie Scott [1951] Director/Farmer

H. B. Projects Limited
Incorporated: 18 December 1998 *Employees:* 204
Net Worth: £6,444,841 *Total Assets:* £16,024,207
Registered Office: Merrydale House, Roydsdale Way, Euroway Industrial Estate, Bradford, BD4 6SE
Activities: Construction of commercial buildings
Parent: H. B. Projects Group Limited
Officers: Carol Anne Watkinson, Secretary/Accountant; David Monro Baxter [1961] Director; Ed Beck [1970] Operations Director; Michael David Brace [1970] Regional Director; Beverley Peace [1973] Group Compliance Director; Carol Anne Watkinson [1953] Director/Accountant

H.B. Panelcraft Limited
Incorporated: 8 February 1978 *Employees:* 112
Net Worth: £7,802,905 *Total Assets:* £10,062,682
Registered Office: Richard House, Winckley Square, Preston, Lancs, PR1 3HP
Activities: Maintenance and repair of motor vehicles
Officers: David John Harwood [1974] Director/Motor Engineer; Gary Martin Harwood [1971] Director/Motor Engineer; Neil Andrew Harwood [1978] Director/Motor Engineer; M Paul Andrew Harwood [1965] Director/Chartered Accountant

H.I. Lime Street Limited
Incorporated: 27 September 1999 *Employees:* 95
Net Worth: £5,363,508 *Total Assets:* £11,285,349
Registered Office: 62 Castle Street, Liverpool, L2 7LQ
Activities: Hotels and similar accommodation
Parent: Centre Island Hotels Limited
Officers: Mark Simon Sutton, Secretary; Mark Christopher Foster [1964] Director/Hotelier; Michael Peter O Donoghue [1952] Director [Irish]; Mark Simon Sutton [1971] Director/Accountant

H.I.G Milan UK Bidco Limited
Incorporated: 17 January 2012
Net Worth Deficit: £14,935,000 *Total Assets:* £32,335,000
Registered Office: Broadway, Trafford Wharf Road, Manchester, M17 1DD
Activities: Activities of head offices
Parent: H.I.G. Milan UK Midco Limited
Officers: Christopher Lee [1971] Director; Claire Louise Thomson [1974] Finance Director

H.I.G. Milan UK Midco Limited
Incorporated: 6 February 2012
Net Worth: £1,465,000 *Total Assets:* £43,834,000
Registered Office: Broadway, Trafford Wharf Road, Manchester, M17 1DD
Activities: Activities of head offices
Parent: H.I.G. Milan UK Topco Limited
Officers: Christopher Lee [1971] Director; Claire Louise Thomson [1974] Finance Director

H.I.G. Milan UK Topco Limited
Incorporated: 17 January 2012
Net Worth Deficit: £3,630,000 *Total Assets:* £37,320,000
Registered Office: Broadway, Trafford Wharf Road, Manchester, M17 1DD
Activities: Activities of head offices
Parent: Project Amber Bidco Limited
Officers: Christopher Lee [1971] Director; Claire Louise Thomson [1974] Finance Director

H.P. Chemie Pelzer (U.K.) Limited
Incorporated: 24 November 1982 *Employees:* 85
Net Worth Deficit: £42,242,896 *Total Assets:* £13,387,601
Registered Office: Speke Hall Avenue, Speke, Liverpool, L24 1UU
Activities: Manufacture of other parts and accessories for motor vehicles
Parent: Adler Pelzer Holding GmbH
Officers: Gian Marco Romano, Secretary; Pietro Lardini [1963] Director [Italian]

H.P.A.S. Limited
Incorporated: 22 December 1992 *Employees:* 705
Net Worth: £29,858,000 *Total Assets:* £44,841,000
Registered Office: Style House, 14 Eldon Place, Bradford, BD1 3AZ
Activities: Other manufacturing n.e.c.
Parent: Style Group UK Limited
Officers: Richard Kenneth Short, Secretary; David Douglas Clarke [1963] Director; Mike Gallacher [1966] Director; Rob Neale [1978] Director; Giles Richell [1970] Director

Haddow Group Limited
Incorporated: 15 May 1987 *Employees:* 81
Net Worth: £5,440,764 *Total Assets:* £7,676,344
Registered Office: Listers Mill, Heaton Road, Bradford, W Yorks, BD9 4SH
Activities: Wholesale of textiles
Major Shareholder: Alan Frank Haddow
Officers: Nigel John Gould, Secretary; Alan Frank Haddow [1941] Director; Tristan Haigh James Haddow [1978] Director

G.I. Hadfield & Son Limited
Incorporated: 4 November 1980 *Employees:* 155
Net Worth: £14,433,111 *Total Assets:* £30,091,296
Registered Office: Lumm Farm, Lumb Lane, Littlemoss, Droylsden, Manchester, M43 7LB
Activities: Recovery of sorted materials
Major Shareholder: Geoff Isaac Louis Hadfield
Officers: Paul Darren Harrison, Secretary/Director; Geoffrey Isaac Louis Hadfield [1955] Director; Geoffrey Isaac Hadfield [1931] Director

Hadfield Wood Recyclers Limited
Incorporated: 7 December 2010 *Employees:* 109
Net Worth: £2,[illegible]00,765 *Total Assets:* £8,097,758
Registered Office: Lumm Farm, Littlemoss, Droylsden, Manchester, M43 7LB
Activities: Treatment and disposal of non-hazardous waste
Parent: G I Hadfield & Son Limited
Officers: Paul Harrison, Secretary; Geoffrey Isaac Louis Hadfield [1955] Director, Geoffrey Isaac Hadfield [1931] Director

J.F. and E. Hadwin Limited
Incorporated: 7 November 1986 *Employees:* 168
Net Worth: £11,752,237 *Total Assets:* £35,101,696
Registered Office: The Garage, Torver, Coniston, Cumbria, LA21 8BJ
Activities: Sale of new cars and light motor vehicles
Officers: Anne Doris Hadwin, Secretary; Anne Doris Hadwin [1941] Director; Eric Hadwin [1939] Director/Garage Proprietor; Jason Dean Hadwin [1966] Director

Hadwins (Lindale) Limited
Incorporated: 4 August 1970 *Employees:* 123
Net Worth: £6,119,221 *Total Assets:* £14,103,758
Registered Office: Charter House, Pittman Way, Fulwood, Preston, Lancs, PR2 9ZD
Activities: Sale of new cars and light motor vehicles
Parent: Expertoand Ltd
Officers: Ruth Ann Hebden, Secretary; Roy William Allen [1947] Managing Director; Ruth Anne Hebden [1942] Director

Sam Hagan Leisure (UK) Limited
Incorporated: 12 February 1992 *Employees:* 63
Net Worth: £4,052,027 *Total Assets:* £11,368,353
Registered Office: Solway Holiday Village, Skinburness Drive, Silloth on Solway, Cumbria, CA5 4QQ
Activities: Holiday centres and villages
Officers: Deborah Jane Hagan [1957] Director; Samuel John Hagan [1955] Director

Hale Country Club Limited
Incorporated: 22 July 2009 *Employees:* 82
Net Worth: £7,465,000 *Total Assets:* £11,302,000
Registered Office: 5th Floor, Voyager House, Chicago Avenue, Manchester Airport, Manchester, M90 3DQ
Activities: Operation of sports facilities
Officers: James Patrick Pochin, Secretary; John Andrew Gallemore [1969] Director; James Patrick Pochin [1976] Director

Halewood International Holdings (Overseas) Limited
Incorporated: 12 March 1999 *Employees:* 2
Net Worth: £17,678,000 *Total Assets:* £18,261,000
Registered Office: The Sovereign Distillery, Wilson Road, Huyton Business Park, Knowsley, Merseyside, L36 6AD
Activities: Activities of other holding companies n.e.c.
Parent: Halewood Wines and Spirits PLC
Officers: Stewart Andrew Hainsworth [1969] Director/Chief Executive; Alan William Robinson [1965] Director/Accountant

Halewood International Limited
Incorporated: 7 February 2000 *Employees:* 315
Net Worth: £13,086,000 *Total Assets:* £97,916,000
Registered Office: The Sovereign Distillery, Wilson Road, Huyton Business Park, Knowsley, Merseyside, L36 6AD
Activities: Manufacture of cider and other fruit wines
Parent: Halewood International Holdings (UK) Limited
Officers: John Andrew Bradbury [1971] Managing Director; Peter Gary Eaton [1960] Director; Timothy Robert Goff [1973] Purchasing Director; Stewart Andrew Hainsworth [1969] Director/Chief Executive Officer; Judith Margaret Halewood [1951] Director; Timothy Richard Hines [1979] Finance Director; Alan William Robinson [1965] Director/Accountant; Lee Tayburn [1974] Director of Production

Halewood Wines and Spirits PLC
Incorporated: 22 January 1999 *Employees:* 965
Net Worth: £63,031,000 *Total Assets:* £146,342,000
Registered Office: The Sovereign Distillery, Wilson Road, Huyton Business Park, Knowsley, Merseyside, L36 6AD
Activities: Activities of head offices
Shareholders: Judith Margaret Halewood; Ian Alan Douglas
Officers: John Andrew Bradbury [1971] Managing Director; Ian Alan Douglas [1951] Director; Peter Gary Eaton [1960] Director; Stewart Andrew Hainsworth [1969] Director/Group CEO; Judith Margaret Halewood [1951] Director; Alan William Robinson [1965] Director/Accountant

Halite Energy Group Limited
Incorporated: 23 January 2001 *Employees:* 5
Net Worth Deficit: £221,459,264 *Total Assets:* £23,871,038
Registered Office: Unit 5 St Georges Court, St Georges Park, Kirkham, Lancs, PR4 2EF
Activities: Other professional, scientific and technical activities n.e.c.
Parent: De Shaw Laminar Portfolios LLC
Officers: Keith Budinger [1965] Director; Ross Kenneth Hill [1940] Director [Australian]; John Edward Roberts [1946] Director

Hall & Pickles 1812 Limited
Incorporated: 21 February 1996 *Employees:* 257
Net Worth: £20,426,000 *Total Assets:* £64,997,000
Registered Office: Poynton Industrial Estate, London Road, Poynton, Stockport, Cheshire, SK12 1NB
Activities: Wholesale of metals and metal ores
Shareholder: Matthew Kindersley Hall
Officers: Arnold Hillier, Secretary/Chartered Accountant; Alexander Richard Congreve Hall [1966] Director; Matthew Kindersley Hall [1967] Director; Arnold Hillier [1930] Director/Chartered Accountant

James Hall and Company (Holdings) Limited
Incorporated: 14 February 1979 *Employees:* 3,092
Net Worth: £91,513,000 *Total Assets:* £225,927,008
Registered Office: Hoghton Chambers, Houghton Street, Southport, Merseyside, PR9 0TB
Activities: Activities of head offices
Shareholders: Andrew Nicholas Hall; Michael Dominic Wells Hall
Officers: Andrew Nicholas Hall, Secretary; Andrew Nicholas Hall [1949] Director; Ian Stuart Whittaker Hall [1942] Director; Michael Dominic Wells Hall [1972] Director

James Hall and Company (Properties) Limited
Incorporated: 6 March 1925
Net Worth: £14,558,269 *Total Assets:* £62,205,004
Registered Office: Hoghton Chambers, Hoghton Street, Southport, Merseyside, PR9 0TB
Activities: Development of building projects
Parent: James Hall and Company (Services) Limited
Officers: Christopher James Collins, Secretary; Andrew Nicholas Hall [1949] Director; Ian Stuart Whittaker Hall [1942] Director; Michael Dominic Wells Hall [1972] Director

James Hall and Company Limited
Incorporated: 25 August 1971 *Employees:* 907
Net Worth: £72,314,000 *Total Assets:* £200,955,008
Registered Office: Hoghton Chambers, Hoghton Street, Southport, Merseyside, PR9 0TB
Activities: Non-specialised wholesale trade
Parent: James Hall and Company (Holdings) Limited
Officers: Christopher James Collins, Secretary; Andrew Nicholas Hall [1949] Director; Ian Stuart Whittaker Hall [1942] Director; Michael Dominic Wells Hall [1972] Director

Hall Park Healthcare Limited
Incorporated: 20 August 2007 *Employees:* 75
Net Worth: £1,795,000 *Total Assets:* £8,131,000
Registered Office: Norcliffe House, Station Road, Wilmslow, Cheshire, SK9 1BU
Activities: Other human health activities
Parent: Optimum FS Care Developments Limited
Officers: Abigail Mattison, Secretary; Ryan Stuart MacAskill [1975] Director; Gregory Laurence Newman [1988] Director/Investment Professional; Jeremy Robert Arthur Richardson [1970] Director; Dr Maureen Claire Royston [1960] Director; Phillip Gary Thomas [1978] Director

Hallamshire Investments Limited
Incorporated: 2 February 1988
Net Worth: £8,775,271 *Total Assets:* £8,775,271
Registered Office: Roughlow, Willington, Tarporley, Cheshire, CW6 0PG
Activities: Buying and selling of own real estate
Parent: Barlows Holdings Limited
Officers: Richard Fildes [1945] Director

Hallco 1052 Limited
Incorporated: 27 May 2004
Net Worth: £4,245,062 *Total Assets:* £33,202,072
Registered Office: 2nd Floor, 1 Ashley Road, Altrincham, Cheshire, WA14 2DT
Activities: Other business support service activities n.e.c.
Shareholders: Ernest Charles Elias; Stephen Edward Elias
Officers: Stephen Edward Elias [1956] Director

Halle Concerts Society
Incorporated: 29 January 1899 *Employees:* 109
Net Worth Deficit: £2,555,000 *Total Assets:* £10,192,000
Registered Office: The Bridgewater Hall, Lower Moseley Street, Manchester, M1 5HA
Activities: Artistic creation
Officers: John Heath Summers, Secretary; Councillor Azra Gulshan Ali [1961] Director/Councillor; Eamonn John Boylan [1959] Director/Chief Executive; Alexander Michael Connock [1965] Digital Media Director; Timothy Edge [1968] Director/Chartered Accountant; Christine Ann Gaskell [1959] Director/Retired; Brandon Howard Leigh [1971] Finance Director; David William McKeith [1951] Director/Chartered Accountant; Jonathan Nicholas McLeod [1965] Director/Public Affairs Consultant; Professor Linda Joyce Merrick [1963] Director/Principal of Music College; Katrina Kerr Michel [1955] Director/Chief Executive; His Honour John Andrew Phillips [1950] Director/Retired; Merryl Webster [1959] Choral Director

Halliwell Jones (Chester) Limited
Incorporated: 25 November 1991 *Employees:* 139
Net Worth: £14,892,413 *Total Assets:* £32,732,452
Registered Office: Sealand Road, Chester, CH1 4LS
Activities: Sale of used cars and light motor vehicles
Parent: Halliwell Jones Holdings (Chester) Limited
Officers: Margaret Louise Clough, Secretary; James Mark Charles Houghton [1960] Director/Manager; Glyn Anthony Howes [1962] Finance Director; Phillip Jones [1950] Director

Halliwell Jones (Warrington) Limited
Incorporated: 24 February 1997 *Employees:* 232
Net Worth: £17,407,176 *Total Assets:* £51,263,612
Registered Office: BMW Showrooms, Winwick Road, Warrington, Cheshire, WA2 8HY
Activities: Sale of used cars and light motor vehicles
Shareholders: MJQ Trustees Limited; Phillip Jones; Michael Lowe Trustees Limited; Hill Dickinson Trust Corporation Limited
Officers: Margaret Louise Clough, Secretary; James Mark Charles Houghton [1960] Director; Glyn Anthony Howes [1962] Finance Director; Phillip Jones [1950] Director

Halliwell Jones (Wilmslow) Limited
Incorporated: 25 September 1945 *Employees:* 110
Net Worth: £2,834,832 *Total Assets:* £19,472,282
Registered Office: Manchester Road, Wilmslow, Cheshire, SK9 2LE
Activities: Sale of new cars and light motor vehicles
Parent: Roundel Limited
Officers: Margaret Louise Clough, Secretary; James Mark Charles Houghton [1960] Sales Director; Glyn Anthony Howes [1962] Director; Phillip Jones [1950] Director

Halliwell Jones Holdings (Chester) Limited
Incorporated: 17 March 2000 *Employees:* 139
Net Worth: £14,078,815 *Total Assets:* £31,918,828
Registered Office: Sealand Road, Chester, CH1 4LS
Activities: Activities of head offices
Shareholders: Phillip Jones; Michael James Quinn
Officers: Margaret Louise Clough, Secretary; Glyn Anthony Howes [1962] Director; Phillip Jones [1950] Director

Halliwell Jones Holdings Limited
Incorporated: 7 July 1993 *Employees:* 85
Net Worth: £7,011,105 *Total Assets:* £18,725,984
Registered Office: 59-61 Southport Road, Southport, Merseyside, PR8 5JF
Activities: Activities of head offices
Shareholders: Phillip Jones; Michael James Quinn
Officers: Margaret Louise Clough, Secretary; Glyn Anthony Howes [1962] Director; Phillip Jones [1950] Director

Halliwell Jones Limited
Incorporated: 5 August 1986 *Employees:* 85
Net Worth: £7,158,742 *Total Assets:* £18,871,872
Registered Office: 59-61 Southport Road, Scarisbrick, Southport, Merseyside, PR8 5JF
Activities: Sale of used cars and light motor vehicles
Parent: Halliwell Jones Holdings Limited
Officers: Margaret Louise Clough, Secretary; James Mark Charles Houghton [1960] Director; Glyn Anthony Howes [1962] Finance Director; Phillip Jones [1950] Director

Hallmark Cards (Holdings) Limited
Incorporated: 8 January 1987 *Employees:* 1,310
Net Worth: £41,307,000 *Total Assets:* £87,926,000
Registered Office: Hallmark Cards (Holdings) Limited, Dawson Lane, Bradford, W Yorks, BD4 6HN
Activities: Activities of head offices
Parent: HC Crown LLC
Officers: Phillipa Jane Dixon, Secretary; Donald Joyce Hall Jr [1955] Director/Business Executive [American]; James Cornelius Shay [1963] Director [American]; Ricky Roop Singh [1977] Director; Steven Paul Wright [1960] Director

Hallmark Cards PLC
Incorporated: 30 July 1997 *Employees:* 1,310
Net Worth: £74,777,000 *Total Assets:* £533,958,016
Registered Office: Hallmark Cards PLC, Dawson Lane, Bradford, W Yorks, BD4 6HN
Activities: Other publishing activities
Parent: Hallmark Cards UK
Officers: Phillipa Jane Dixson, Secretary; Matthew James Critchlow [1975] Commercial Director; Donald Joyce Hall Jr [1955] Director/Business Executive [American]; James Cornelius Shay [1963] Director [American]; Ricky Roop Singh [1977] Director; Steven Paul Wright [1960] Director

Hallmark Cards Property Company Limited
Incorporated: 22 December 1980
Net Worth: £1,967,000 *Total Assets:* £9,833,000
Registered Office: Hallmark Cards Property Company Limited, Dawson Lane, Bradford, W Yorks, BD4 6HN
Activities: Other letting and operating of own or leased real estate
Parent: Hallmark Cards (Holdings) Limited
Officers: Phillipa Jane Dixson, Secretary; Ricky Roop Singh [1977] Director; Steven Paul Wright [1960] Director

Hallmark Developments (North West) Limited
Incorporated: 2 February 2001 *Employees:* 5
Net Worth: £4,522,074 *Total Assets:* £9,798,501
Registered Office: Park House, 200 Drake Street, Rochdale, Lancs, OL16 1PJ
Activities: Development of building projects
Major Shareholder: Christopher David Grieves
Officers: Joanne Tracey Grieves, Secretary; Christopher David Grieves [1959] Director/Property Development

Michael W Halsall Solicitors Limited
Incorporated: 15 February 2013 *Employees:* 112
Net Worth: £5,519,429 *Total Assets:* £12,403,732
Registered Office: 11 The Parks, Newton-le-Willows, Merseyside, WA12 0JQ
Activities: Solicitors
Major Shareholder: Michael William Halsall
Officers: Nial Burke [1969] Director; Ian Halsall [1981] Director; Michael William Halsall [1947] Director/Solicitor; David William McDermott [1969] Director/Solicitor; Andrew John Simcott [1971] Director; Stephen Taylor [1966] Director

James Halstead PLC
Incorporated: 10 May 1915 *Employees:* 824
Net Worth: £114,060,000 *Total Assets:* £200,546,000
Registered Office: Beechfield, Hollinhurst Road, Radcliffe, Manchester, M26 1JN
Activities: Activities of head offices
Officers: David William Drillingcourt, Secretary; Stephen David Hall [1954] Director; Mark Halstead [1957] Director; Michael James Halstead [1957] Director; Gordon Richard Oliver [1958] Director/Chartered Accountant; Russell Peter Whiting [1966] Director; James Anthony Wild [1941] Director/Chartered Accountant

The Hamblin Education Trust
Incorporated: 6 January 2011 *Employees:* 197
Net Worth: £12,180,000 *Total Assets:* £14,817,000
Registered Office: Altrincham Grammar School for Boys, Marlborough Road, Bowdon, Altrincham, Cheshire, WA14 2RS
Activities: General secondary education
Officers: Duncan William Battman [1958] Director/Humanist Celebrant; Jill Yvonne Bottomley [1967] HR Director; Sharon Jane Heather Davies-Forster [1959] Director/Accountant; Timothy James Gartside [1961] Director/Headmaster; Richard Jonathan Green [1955] Director/Chartered Accountant; Andrew John Shaw [1955] Director/Chartered Surveyor

Hamilton Heath Estates Limited
Incorporated: 19 May 1999
Net Worth Deficit: £4,639,297 *Total Assets:* £24,826,608
Registered Office: Lester House, 19-21 Broad Street, Bury, Lancs, BL9 0DA
Activities: Other letting and operating of own or leased real estate
Officers: Andrew Jonathan Chaytow [1969] Managing Director; Mark Jonathan Clynes [1968] Property Director; Mark Rubens [1970] Director

Hammer Consolidated Holdings Ltd
Incorporated: 1 December 2004 *Employees:* 169
Net Worth: £24,640,702 *Total Assets:* £52,245,692
Registered Office: Technology House, Magnesium Way, Hapton, Burnley, Lancs, BB12 7BF
Activities: Other business support service activities n.e.c.
Shareholder: James Stidwill
Officers: Richard Hinds, Secretary; Jason Mark Beeson [1971] Director; Philip Brown [1975] Director; Paul William Bryan [1969] Director; Stephen Casey [1980] Director [Irish]; Matthew Steven Geoffrey Croucher [1979] Finance Director; Jason Goddard [1967] Director; Timothy David Griffin [1967] Director; Richard Hinds [1975] Director; Paul Simon Matravers [1973] Director; Gerard Patrick O'Keeffe [1964] Director [Irish]; James Stidwill [1970] Director

Hammer Group Limited
Incorporated: 23 August 1999
Net Worth: £665,668 *Total Assets:* £7,220,847
Registered Office: Technology House, Magnesium Way, Hapton, Burnley, Lancs, BB12 7BF
Activities: Other information technology service activities
Parent: Hammer Consolidated Holdings Limited
Officers: Richard Hinds, Secretary; Jason Mark Beeson [1971] Director; Philip Brown [1975] Director; Paul William Bryan [1969] Director; Stephen Casey [1980] Director [Irish]; Matthew Steven Geoffrey Croucher [1979] Finance Director; Jason Goodard [1967] Director; Timothy David Griffin [1967] Director; Richard Hinds [1975] Director; Paul Simon Matravers [1973] Director; Gerard Patrick O'Keeffe [1964] Director [Irish]; James Stidwill [1970] Director

Hammer PLC
Incorporated: 23 August 1991 *Employees:* 149
Net Worth: £21,036,256 *Total Assets:* £56,178,568
Registered Office: Technology House, Magnesium Way, Hapton, Burnley, Lancs, BB12 7BF
Activities: Information technology consultancy activities
Parent: Hammer Group Limited
Officers: Richard Hinds, Secretary; Jason Mark Beeson [1971] Director; Philip Brown [1975] Director; Paul William Bryan [1969] Managing Director; Stephen Casey [1980] Director [Irish]; Matthew Steven Geoffrey Croucher [1979] Finance Director; Jason Goddard [1967] Director; Timothy David Griffin [1967] Director; Paul Hickingbotham [1969] Group Technical Director; Richard Hinds [1975] Director; Paul Simon Matravers [1973] Director; Gerard Patrick O'Keeffe [1964] Managing Director [Irish]; James Stidwill [1970] Director

Hammonds of Knutsford PLC
Incorporated: 28 May 1999 *Employees:* 27
Net Worth: £12,739,735 *Total Assets:* £22,859,692
Registered Office: Warford Grange Farm, Pedley House Lane, Great Warford, Knutsford, Cheshire, WA16 7SP
Activities: Wholesale of wine, beer, spirits and other alcoholic beverages
Major Shareholder: Jonathan Hammond
Officers: Jonathan Hammond, Secretary; Jonathan Hammond [1970] Director/Wholesaler; Sarah Lucy Hancock Hammond [1971] Director

Hampshire Bidco Limited
Incorporated: 5 September 2012
Net Worth: £4,100,000 *Total Assets:* £351,299,008
Registered Office: Oakland House, 76 Talbot Road, Old Trafford, Manchester, M16 0PQ
Activities: Activities of head offices
Parent: Hampshire Midco Limited
Officers: Daniel James Joll, Secretary; Stephen Ashmore [1964] Director; Alan Edward Peterson [1947] Director; Paul David Quested [1970] Financial Director

Hampshire Midco Limited
Incorporated: 9 October 2012
Net Worth: £3,738,000 *Total Assets:* £96,510,000
Registered Office: Oakland House, 76 Talbot Road, Old Trafford, Manchester, M16 0PQ
Activities: Activities of head offices
Parent: Hampshire Topco Limited
Officers: Daniel James Joll, Secretary; Stephen Ashmore [1964] Director; Alan Edward Peterson [1947] Director; Paul David Quested [1970] Financial Director

Hampshire Topco Limited
Incorporated: 9 October 2012
Net Worth: £120,993,000 *Total Assets:* £129,458,000
Registered Office: Oakland House, 76 Talbot Road, Old Trafford, Manchester, M16 0PQ
Activities: Activities of head offices
Parent: HSS Hire Group PLC
Officers: Daniel James Joll, Secretary; Stephen Ashmore [1964] Director; Alan Edward Peterson [1947] Director; Paul David Quested [1970] Financial Director

Hamsard 3425 Limited
Incorporated: 27 July 2016 *Employees:* 43
Net Worth: £2,042,022 *Total Assets:* £15,203,299
Registered Office: Unit 7 Fairhills Industrial Estate, Woodrow Way, Irlam, Manchester, M44 6ZQ
Activities: Dormant company
Parent: Foresight Fund Managers Limited
Officers: Jocelyn Mary Morgan [1965] Finance Director; Matthew William Pomroy [1984] Director; Benjamin Paul Reeves [1989] Managing Director; Samuel Reeves [1991] Director; Richard Timothy Styles [1966] Director/Chairman

Hanes Holdings UK Limited
Incorporated: 4 September 2009
Net Worth: £8,461,259 *Total Assets:* £8,988,930
Registered Office: One St Peter's Square, Manchester, M2 3DE
Activities: Wholesale of textiles
Parent: Hanesbrands Inc
Officers: David Landt Bortolussi [1969] Director/Chief Financial Officer [Australian]; John Charles Grover [1961] Director [Australian]

Roy Hankinson (Holdings) Limited
Incorporated: 23 October 1975 *Employees:* 271
Net Worth: £2,983,298 *Total Assets:* £8,301,184
Registered Office: Cotton Place, 2 Ivy Street, Birkenhead, Merseyside, CH41 5EF
Activities: Painting
Major Shareholder: Stephen Roy Hankinson
Officers: Stephen Roy Hankinson, Secretary; Stephen Roy Hankinson [1957] Director; Ivor Arthur Thomas [1960] Contracts Director

Hansengroup Limited
Incorporated: 22 March 1993 *Employees:* 26
Net Worth: £737,447 *Total Assets:* £7,035,819
Registered Office: Cedar House, Sandbrook Business Park, Rochdale, OL11 1LQ
Activities: Activities of head offices
Officers: Kim Pedersen, Secretary; Hans Kolby Hansen [1946] Director [Danish]

Hanson Springs Limited
Incorporated: 26 July 1967 *Employees:* 200
Net Worth: £5,486,525 *Total Assets:* £27,476,004
Registered Office: Hanson Place, Gorrells Way, Rochdale, Lancs, OL11 2PX
Activities: Manufacture of wire products, chain and springs
Shareholders: Malcolm Hanson; Maureen Hanson
Officers: John Baldwin, Secretary; Roy Fox [1949] Director/Sales Manager; John Hanson [1973] Director/Engineer; Malcolm Hanson [1945] Managing Director; Maureen Hanson [1949] Director/Consultant; Lisa Jenkinson [1971] Marketing Director

Thomas Hardie Commercials Limited
Incorporated: 22 January 1985 *Employees:* 346
Net Worth: £10,884,756 *Total Assets:* £41,818,848
Registered Office: Newstet Road, Knowsley Industrial Park North, Knowsley, Merseyside, L33 7TJ
Activities: Sale of other motor vehicles
Parent: Thomas Hardie Truck & Bus Limited
Officers: Mark Alan Cunnew [1970] Aftermarket Director; Gerard William Keary [1958] Director; Stephen Bernard Kenyon [1966] Director; James Robson Murray [1965] Director; Chris Schofield [1957] Director of Used Trucks and Group Procurement; Steven Roger Wilson [1968] New Vehicle Sales & Marketing Director; Mark Owen Woosnam [1957] Managing Director

Thomas Hardie Truck & Bus Limited
Incorporated: 22 May 2006 *Employees:* 331
Net Worth: £6,280,272 *Total Assets:* £35,805,748
Registered Office: Thomas Hardie Commercials Ltd, Newstet Road, Knowsley Industrial Park, Knowsley, Merseyside, L33 7TJ
Activities: Activities of head offices
Parent: Rabor Limited
Officers: Mark Alan Cunnew [1970] Director; Stephen Bernard Kenyon [1966] Managing Director; James Robson Murray [1965] Director; Steven Roger Wilson [1968] Director; Mark Owen Woosnam [1957] Director

Hardroad Limited
Incorporated: 12 May 2011 *Employees:* 99
Net Worth: £10 500,125 *Total Assets:* £16,448,573
Registered Office: c/o Border Aggregates, Scotland Road, Carnforth, Lancs, LA5 9JZ
Activities: Other letting and operating of own or leased real estate
Major Shareholder: Terry Billington
Officers: Carolyn Elizabeth Masters, Secretary; Terry Billington [1944] Managing Director; Andrew Hetherington [1969] Finance Director; Stephen Pelter [1957] Director

Hardscape Products Limited
Incorporated: 2 November 1994 *Employees:* 54
Net Worth: £1,823,030 *Total Assets:* £7,289,084
Registered Office: Eagley House, Deakins Business Park, Blackburn Road, Egerton, Bolton, Lancs, BL7 9RP
Activities: Agents involved in the sale of timber and building materials
Parent: Earth's Crust Resources Ltd
Officers: Julie Haslam, Secretary; Mathew James Haslam [1962] Managing Director; David Michael Lowe [1974] Commercial Director; Alexander Peter Warren [1978] Operations Director; Christopher James Wood [1975] Finance Director

Thomas Hardy Holdings Limited
Incorporated: 27 December 1996 *Employees:* 114
Net Worth: £12,852,000 *Total Assets:* £19,423,000
Registered Office: Bold Lane, Burtonwood, Warrington, Cheshire, WA5 4TH
Activities: Manufacture of cider and other fruit wines
Officers: Neil Mark Voss [1969] Director; Jonathan Christopher Ward [1978] Director; Margaret Rae Ward [1944] Director

Thomas Hardy Kendal Limited
Incorporated: 29 December 1998 *Employees:* 63
Net Worth: £6,038,000 *Total Assets:* £8,570,000
Registered Office: Bold Lane, Burtonwood, Warrington, Cheshire, WA5 4TH
Activities: Manufacture of cider and other fruit wines
Officers: Peter Michael Armstrong [1965] Site Director; Neil Mark Voss [1969] Director; Jonathan Christopher Ward [1978] Director; Margaret Rae Ward [1944] Director

William Hare Group Limited
Incorporated: 31 May 1991 *Employees:* 1,761
Net Worth: £49,453,000 *Total Assets:* £122,335,000
Registered Office: Brandlesholme House, Brandlesholme Road, Bury, Lancs, BL8 1JJ
Activities: Activities of head offices
Officers: Robert Redgate, Secretary; David Michael William Hodgkiss [1948] Director; Sally Catherine Hodgkiss [1984] Director; Susan Katrina Hodgkiss [1950] Director; Thomas Bartle Hodgkiss [1980] Director; Robert John Redgate [1957] Finance Director

William Hare Limited
Incorporated: 8 October 1945 *Employees:* 591
Net Worth: £37,800,000 *Total Assets:* £91,026,000
Registered Office: Brandlesholme House, Brandlesholme Road, Bury, Lancs, BL8 1JJ
Activities: Manufacture of metal structures and parts of structures
Officers: Craig Arnold [1952] Director/Engineer; Hugo Alexandre Rato Camacho [1978] Chief Projects Director [Portuguese]; Nicholas John Day [1957] Commercial Director; Steven Duffield [1963] Sales Director; David Michael William Hodgkiss [1948] Director; Susan Katrina Hodgkiss [1950] Director; Thomas Bartle Hodgkiss [1980] Director; Nigel John Moss [1964] Director/Engineer; Robert John Redgate [1957] Finance Director; Gary Simmons [1959] Director/Engineer

Harewood Moor Estates Limited
Incorporated: 7 March 2016
Net Worth: £9,746,363 *Total Assets:* £10,906,099
Registered Office: Brookfield Hall, Manchester Road, Buxton, Derbys, SK17 6SU
Activities: Other letting and operating of own or leased real estate
Parent: The Harewood Moor Estates Limited Succession Trust
Officers: Stephen Matthew Richard Lamb [1975] Director

Harewood Venture Capital Ltd
Incorporated: 22 November 2012
Net Worth Deficit: £13,159,531 *Total Assets:* £16,825,344
Registered Office: 20 Chorley New Road, Bolton, Lancs, BL1 4AP
Activities: Buying and selling of own real estate
Officers: David Burnett Scott [1946] Director/Business Owner

Hargreave Hale Limited
Incorporated: 16 January 1996 *Employees:* 254
Net Worth: £12,785,000 *Total Assets:* £43,727,000
Registered Office: Talisman House, Boardmans Way, Blackpool, Lancs, FY4 5FY
Activities: Activities of financial services holding companies
Parent: Canaccord Genuity Wealth Group Holdings (Jersey) Limited
Officers: Stuart Neville Brookes [1969] Finance Director; David Esfandi [1978] Director/Chief Executive; Lee Finlayson [1971] Director/Stockbroker; John Richard Gulliver [1963] Director/Senior Executive, Finance; Peter Graham Hall [1963] Director/Head of IT & Operations; Terrence Allan Lyons [1949] Director [Canadian]; Stephen Leigh Massey [1957] Director/Chairman; Jill Patricia McAleenan [1950] Director

James Hargreaves (Plumbers' Merchants) Limited
Incorporated: 14 March 1923 *Employees:* 292
Net Worth: £25,727,928 *Total Assets:* £41,967,428
Registered Office: James Hargreaves, Todmorden Road, Burnley, Lancs, BB11 3JT
Activities: Wholesale of hardware, plumbing and heating equipment and supplies
Parent: James Hargreaves PM Ltd
Officers: Gordon John Rothwell, Secretary; Carl Andrew Bridge [1969] Director/Plumbers Merchant; William Davies [1958] Director/Merchanting Sales; David Eddison [1966] Director/Plumbers Merchant; Gordon John Rothwell [1959] Director; Chander Mohan Sharma [1977] Financial Director

James Hargreaves Holdings Limited
Incorporated: 9 March 2015 *Employees:* 292
Net Worth: £17,809,998 *Total Assets:* £35,297,928
Registered Office: c/o James Hargreaves PM, Todmorden Road, Burnley, Lancs, BB11 3JT
Activities: Wholesale of hardware, plumbing and heating equipment and supplies
Major Shareholder: Florence Rothwell
Officers: Carl Andrew Bridge [1969] Purchasing Director; William Davies [1958] Director; David Eddison [1966] Operations Director; Gordon John Rothwell [1959] Managing Director; Chander Mohan Sharma [1977] Financial Director

James Hargreaves PM Limited
Incorporated: 4 March 2008
Net Worth: £4,986,844 *Total Assets:* £6,759,551
Registered Office: Todmorden Road, Burnley, Lancs, BB11 3JT
Activities: Wholesale of hardware, plumbing and heating equipment and supplies
Officers: Gordon John Rothwell, Secretary; Carl Andrew Bridge [1969] Purchasing Director; William Davies [1958] Director; David Eddison [1966] Operations Director; Gordon John Rothwell [1959] Managing Director; Chander Mohan Sharma [1977] Financial Director

John Hargreaves,(Collyhurst and Stalybridge) Limited
Incorporated: 22 April 1924 *Employees:* 57
Net Worth: £1,006,172 *Total Assets:* £12,873,305
Registered Office: Tameside Paper Mills, Stalybridge, Cheshire, SK15 3AJ
Activities: Manufacture of paper and paperboard
Major Shareholder: John Michael Peter Hargreaves
Officers: Andrew Michael Robins, Secretary; Alistair Nicholas Hargreaves [1960] Director; John Michael Peter Hargreaves [1966] Director

The Harmony Trust Ltd
Incorporated: 10 January 2014 *Employees:* 261
Net Worth: £15,236,000 *Total Assets:* £20,600,000
Registered Office: Greenhill Academy, Harmony Street, Oldham, Lancs, OL4 1RR
Activities: Pre-primary education
Officers: Suzanne Angela Thompson, Secretary; Sajen Bakht [1970] Director/Category Specialist Manager; Sara Bashir [1983] Director; Ashley Forbes [1990] Director/Charity Worker [American]; Norman Hole [1955] Director/Retired; Antony Paul Hughes [1973] Director/Chief Executive; Paul Anthony Makin [1956] Executive Director; Graham William McGuffie [1949] Director/Consultant; Marian Evelyn Simmons [1955] Director/Independent Consultant; Christopher Thorne [1953] Director/Educational Consultant

Harnage Estates Limited
Incorporated: 23 March 1961 *Employees:* 138
Net Worth: £12,368,166 *Total Assets:* £21,449,316
Registered Office: c/o DSG Chartered Accountants, Castle Chambers, 43 Castle Street, Liverpool, L2 9TL
Activities: Growing of cereals (except rice), leguminous crops and oil seeds
Shareholder: Justin de Berkeley Scott
Officers: Ruth de Berkeley Scott, Secretary; Justin de Berkeley Scott [1960] Director; Ruth de Berkeley Scott [1935] Director; Simon David Scott [1958] Director/Farmer

Harnbury Holdings Ltd
Incorporated: 31 March 1992 *Employees:* 710
Net Worth: £8,628,440 *Total Assets:* £20,278,138
Registered Office: 1st Floor, Acresfield, 8-10 Exchange Street, Manchester, M2 7HA
Activities: Licenced restaurants
Officers: Marcello Guiseppe Distefano [1978] Director/Restaurateur [Italian]; Remigio Distefano [1944] Director [Italian]

Harper Industries PLC
Incorporated: 28 November 1995 *Employees:* 119
Net Worth: £2,811,644 *Total Assets:* £8,572,719
Registered Office: c/o Hallis Hudson Group Ltd, Unit B1 Redscar Business Park, Preston, Lancs, PR2 5NJ
Activities: Wholesale of household goods (other than musical instruments) n.e.c
Major Shareholder: John Winston Soper
Officers: Alastair John Soper, Secretary; Alastair John Soper [1977] Director/Operations; John Winston Soper [1945] Managing Director; Neil John Soper [1982] Director/Civil Engineer

Harpmanor Limited
Incorporated: 4 November 1985
Net Worth: £1,600,000 *Total Assets:* £94,400,000
Registered Office: Lake View, Lakeside, Cheadle, Cheshire, SK8 3GW
Activities: Credit granting by non-deposit taking finance houses and other specialist consumer credit grantors
Parent: Together Financial Services Limited
Officers: Sarah Elizabeth Batt, Secretary; Gary Derek Beckett [1969] Director; Wayne Bowser [1952] Director; Marc Richard Goldberg [1971] Director; Robert Michael McTighe [1953] Director; Henry Neville Moser [1949] Director; Helga Clare Taylor [1969] Finance Director

Harrington & Hallworth Limited
Incorporated: 2 September 1991 *Employees:* 30
Net Worth: £4,093,633 *Total Assets:* £7,818,527
Registered Office: 43 Grove Street, Wilmslow, Cheshire, SK9 1DT
Activities: Other retail sale of new goods in specialised stores (not commercial art galleries and opticians)
Shareholders: Alfred Hallworth; Peter Harrington; Alfred Hallworth; Peter Harrington
Officers: Peter Harrington, Secretary; Alfred Hallworth [1953] Director/Jeweller; Peter Harrington [1954] Director/Jeweller

Harrison & Clough,Limited
Incorporated: 8 May 1957 *Employees:* 148
Net Worth: £1,863,420 *Total Assets:* £15,851,211
Registered Office: P O Box 9, Harclo Road, off Aireworth Road, Keighley, W Yorks, BD21 4EG
Activities: Non-specialised wholesale trade
Parent: Heathfield Holdings Limited
Officers: Stuart James Holloway, Secretary; John Paul Aperghis [1973] Finance Director; Kelvin Ellison [1973] Commercial Director; Joyce Hutchinson [1935] Director/Company Secretary; Neville James Hutchinson [1935] Director/Chairman; Richard Mark Hutchinson [1961] Managing Director; Mark Edward Revak [1962] Operations Director

Harrison & Hetherington Limited
Incorporated: 31 August 1999 *Employees:* 78
Net Worth: £6,552,383 *Total Assets:* £18,013,592
Registered Office: Borderway Mart, Rosehill, Carlisle, Cumbria, CA1 2RS
Activities: Support activities for animal production (other than farm animal boarding)
Parent: H&H Group PLC
Officers: Margaret Irving, Secretary; Alasdair Scott Donaldson [1967] Director; David Henry James Pritchard [1955] Director/Auctioneer; Richard Andrew Rankin [1973] Director/Chief Executive; Michael Leslie Scott [1951] Director/Farmer

D.A. Harrison and Company Wigton
Incorporated: 11 June 1976
Net Worth: £16,211,549 *Total Assets:* £21,150,778
Registered Office: Solway House, Silloth Industrial Estate, The Airfield, Silloth, Wigton, Cumbria, CA7 4NS
Activities: Retail sale of automotive fuel in specialised stores
Officers: Sheila Margaret Paisley, Secretary; David Anthony Harrison [1965] Director; Mary Margaret Harrison [1942] Director; Richard Allan Harrison [1966] Director; William Henry Harrison [1962] Director; Judith Williamson [1968] Director

The Christopher Harrison Group Limited
Incorporated: 12 January 2009
Net Worth: £5,011,356 *Total Assets:* £8,140,831
Registered Office: Tannery House, Harraby Green Business Park, Carlisle, CA1 2SS
Activities: Other letting and operating of own or leased real estate
Major Shareholder: Christopher James Harrison
Officers: Julia Harrison, Secretary; Christopher James Harrison [1964] Director

Harrison Leisure UK Limited
Incorporated: 10 April 2001 *Employees:* 108
Net Worth: £4,342,081 *Total Assets:* £21,775,240
Registered Office: Riverside Leisure Centre, Southport New Road, Banks, Southport, Merseyside, PR9 8DF
Activities: Holiday centres and villages
Shareholder: George Harrison
Officers: George Harrison, Secretary; Ellen Harrison [1952] Director; George Harrison [1950] Director; William Harrison [1981] Director

W. & G. Harrison Limited
Incorporated: 29 November 1971 *Employees:* 532
Net Worth: £16,058,000 *Total Assets:* £33,485,000
Registered Office: Ribby Hall Village, Ribby Road, Wrea Green, Lancs, PR4 2PR
Activities: Holiday centres and villages
Parent: Dowbridge Limited
Officers: Paul Graham Harrison, Secretary/Builder; Paul Graham Harrison [1958] Director; Sylvia Holloway [1957] Director; Janet Patricia Livock [1955] Director; Mark Richard Partington [1956] Managing Director

Harrison Northern Limited
Incorporated: 19 October 1960 *Employees:* 21
Net Worth: £5,639,769 *Total Assets:* £9,534,195
Registered Office: Fairfield House, 105 Scotland Road, Carlisle, Cumbria, CA3 9HL
Activities: Real estate agencies
Parent: Harrison Northern Properties Limited
Officers: Michael Ferguson [1965] Facilities Director; Dominique Faith Harrison [1967] Director; Grace Elizabeth Harrison [1995] Director; Joseph James Harrison [1997] Director; Simon Nicholas Harrison [1967] Director; Thomas Jake Harrison [1999] Director; Nicola Ann Rayson [1968] Financial Director

Harrisons Dairies Limited
Incorporated: 9 August 1990 *Employees:* 188
Net Worth: £3,831,552 *Total Assets:* £7,234,996
Registered Office: Morton House, Kenyons Lane, Maghull, Merseyside, L31 0BP
Activities: Retail sale in non-specialised stores with food, beverages or tobacco predominating
Major Shareholder: Norman Harrison
Officers: John Stuart Walker, Secretary; Norman Harrison [1942] Director

Harrow Estates PLC
Incorporated: 20 February 2009 *Employees:* 14
Net Worth: £16,064,228 *Total Assets:* £44,497,780
Registered Office: Redrow House, St Davids Park, Ewloe, Flintshire, CH5 3RX
Activities: Development of building projects
Parent: HB (HDG) Limited
Officers: Graham Anthony Cope, Secretary; William Robert Heath [1979] Director/Chartered Surveyor; Julian Anthony Larkin [1967] Managing Director; Peter Marsden [1979] Director/Solicitor; Stephen Peter Morgan [1952] Director; Mark Leslie Nicholls [1972] Technical Director; Barbara Mary Richmond [1960] Director/Chartered Accountant

Harthill Wind Limited
Incorporated: 15 July 2011
Net Worth Deficit: £2,310,495 *Total Assets:* £8,043,737
Registered Office: 1030 Centre Park, Slutchers Lane, Warrington, Cheshire, WA1 1QL
Activities: Production of electricity
Officers: Liz Oldroyd, Secretary; John William Breckenridge [1962] Managing Director [American]; Simon Richard Eaves [1967] Managing Director; Adrian Waine Robinson [1961] Director/Chief Operating Officer; Kirsty Louise Usher [1975] Director/Accountant

Hartley Investment Trust Limited
Incorporated: 28 July 1983 *Employees:* 47
Net Worth: £36,417,000 *Total Assets:* £50,704,000
Registered Office: Cumberland House, Greenside Lane, Bradford, BD8 9TF
Activities: Other service activities n.e.c.
Major Shareholder: Alan James Lewis
Officers: Alan James Lewis [1938] Director/Chairman

Hartley Property Trust Limited
Incorporated: 13 October 1947 *Employees:* 2
Net Worth: £17,060,716 *Total Assets:* £21,718,512
Registered Office: Cumberland House, Greenside Lane, Bradford, BD8 9TF
Activities: Other service activities n.e.c.
Parent: Honeytree Trading Co. Limited
Officers: Alan James Lewis [1938] Director/Chairman

Paul Hartmann Limited
Incorporated: 17 October 1980 *Employees:* 97
Net Worth: £5,135,779 *Total Assets:* £10,883,824
Registered Office: Unit P2, Parklands, Heywood Distribution Park, Pilsworth Road, Heywood, Lancs, OL10 2TT
Activities: Wholesale of pharmaceutical goods
Parent: Paul Hartmann AG
Officers: Trevor John Coupe, Secretary; Richard Cornwell [1972] Managing Director; Trevor John Coupe [1963] Director/Accountant; Marc Perez [1974] Director [Spanish]

Hasgrove Limited
Incorporated: 1 October 2004 *Employees:* 104
Net Worth: £2,891,947 *Total Assets:* £8,322,156
Registered Office: 4th Floor, Station House, Stamford New Road, Altrincham, Cheshire, WA14 1EP
Activities: Activities of head offices
Shareholder: Godfrey Lionel Fozard Taylor
Officers: Paul Anthony Sanders, Secretary; Simon Dance [1981] Director; Dr Paul Antony Sanders [1964] Director/Chartered Accountant; Godfrey Lionel Fozard Taylor [1952] Director/Chartered Accountant

Haslebrow Finance Limited
Incorporated: 8 May 1964
Net Worth: £6,059,631 *Total Assets:* £11,832,619
Registered Office: Trident House, 31-33 Dale Street, Liverpool, L2 2HF
Activities: Other credit granting n.e.c.
Major Shareholder: Melville Morris
Officers: Melville Morris [1925] Director/Chartered Accountant

Havencare Management Limited
Incorporated: 1 March 1973 *Employees:* 69
Net Worth: £5,845,186 *Total Assets:* £8,305,670
Registered Office: 195a Bury Road, Rawtenstall, Rossendale, Lancs, BB4 6DJ
Activities: Funeral and related activities
Parent: Havencare Management Holdings Limited
Officers: John Winfield, Secretary/Director; Dawn Susan Winfield [1970] Director; John Winfield [1953] Director

Havwoods Global Holdings Limited
Incorporated: 30 July 2014 *Employees:* 119
Net Worth: £15,279,890 *Total Assets:* £25,491,988
Registered Office: Carnforth Business Park, Oakwood Way, Carnforth, Lancs, LA5 9FD
Activities: Activities of other holding companies n.e.c.
Shareholder: Oliver Muckle Whiley
Officers: Elizabeth Janette Whiley, Secretary; Elizabeth Janette Whiley [1956] Director; Jonathan Whiley [1984] Director; Nicholas Whiley [1974] Director; Oliver Muckle Whiley [1955] Director; Simon Whiley [1976] Director

Havwoods Limited
Incorporated: 4 September 1975 *Employees:* 71
Net Worth: £16,655,781 *Total Assets:* £22,962,686
Registered Office: Carnforth Business Park, Oakwood Way, Carnforth, Lancs, LA5 9FD
Activities: Wholesale of wood, construction materials and sanitary equipment
Parent: Havwoods Global Holdings Limited
Officers: Elizabeth Janette Whiley, Director/Secretary; Elizabeth Janette Whiley [1956] Director; Jonathan Whiley [1984] Director; Nicholas Whiley [1974] Director; Oliver Muckle Whiley [1955] Director; Simon Whiley [1976] Director

Hawkslease Finance Company Limited
Incorporated: 24 January 2002
Net Worth Deficit: £25,800,000 *Total Assets:* £55,300,000
Registered Office: P O Box 9, Runcorn Site HQ, South Parade, Runcorn, Cheshire, WA7 4JE
Activities: Activities of head offices
Parent: INEOS Vinyls Group Limited
Officers: Paul Frederick Nichols, Secretary; Michael John Maher [1968] Director; Christopher Edward Tane [1956] Director

Richard Haworth Limited
Incorporated: 19 July 1966 *Employees:* 148
Net Worth: £9,114,157 *Total Assets:* £17,347,206
Registered Office: Kearsley Mill, Stoneclough, Radcliffe, Manchester, M26 1RH
Activities: Wholesale of textiles
Parent: Ruia Group Limited
Officers: Philip John Campbell, Secretary; Rajendra Ruia [1962] Director; Sunil Ruia [1961] Managing Director

Haydock Asset Finance Limited
Incorporated: 13 January 1999
Net Worth: £3,136,000 *Total Assets:* £34,533,000
Registered Office: Challenge House, Challenge Way, Blackburn, BB1 5QB
Activities: Financial leasing
Parent: Haydock Finance Holdings Ltd
Officers: Jonathan Harper Wilkinson, Secretary; Ian Henry Barr [1964] Credit and Risk Director; Jonathan Harper Wilkinson [1952] Director; Steven Leslie Worrall [1971] Director

Haydock Commercial Vehicles Limited
Incorporated: 5 October 1984 *Employees:* 191
Net Worth: £8,788,636 *Total Assets:* £44,049,528
Registered Office: Unit 4 Lockheed Road, Burtonwood, Warrington, Cheshire, WA5 4AH
Activities: Sale of other motor vehicles
Parent: Cheshire 2 Holdings Limited
Officers: Graham Whittaker, Secretary; Gary Alan Bumford [1977] Director; Craig Anthony Hargreaves [1965] Director; Ian Hensall [1968] Director

Haydock Finance Holdings Limited
Incorporated: 8 December 2004 *Employees:* 45
Net Worth: £17,515,000 *Total Assets:* £121,074,000
Registered Office: Challenge House, Challenge Way, Blackburn, Lancs, BB1 5QB
Activities: Activities of head offices
Parent: HD Bidco Limited
Officers: Jonathan Harper Wilkinson, Secretary; Ian Henry Barr [1964] Credit & Risk Director; Jonathan Harper Wilkinson [1952] Director/Financier; Steven Leslie Worrall [1971] Director

Haydock Finance Limited
Incorporated: 7 November 1980 *Employees:* 45
Net Worth: £11,818,000 *Total Assets:* £100,884,000
Registered Office: Haydock Finance Ltd, Challenge House, Challenge Way, Blackburn, Lancs, BB1 5QB
Activities: Financial leasing
Parent: Haydock Finance Holdings Ltd
Officers: Jonathan Harper Wilkinson, Secretary; Ian Henry Barr [1964] Credit and Risk Director; Jonathan Harper Wilkinson [1952] Director/Financier; Steven Leslie Worrall [1971] Managing Director

Hayes & Co Services Ltd
Incorporated: 28 September 2009
Net Worth: £997,551 *Total Assets:* £6,642,602
Registered Office: Suite 21, 33 King Street, Blackburn, BB2 2DH
Activities: General medical practice activities
Officers: Sumayyabanu Patel [1979] Director [Indian]

Hayes & Finch Limited
Incorporated: 4 October 1905 *Employees:* 67
Net Worth: £5,937,142 *Total Assets:* £6,786,583
Registered Office: Hanson Road, Liverpool, L9 7BP
Activities: Other manufacturing n.e.c.
Officers: Andrew Peter Ware, Secretary; Karen Anne Reilly [1959] Director; Andrew Peter Ware [1971] Director/Church Furnisher

Haynes International Ltd
Incorporated: 29 April 1975 *Employees:* 64
Net Worth: £37 731,000 *Total Assets:* £42,758,000
Registered Office: Parkhouse Street, Openshaw, Manchester, M11 2ER
Activities: Manufacture of other fabricated metal products n.e.c.
Parent: Haynes International,Inc.
Officers: Jacqueline Anne Fairbrother, Secretary; Toni Barfoot [1958] Managing Director; Kenton David Cawley [1973] Director of Operations; Marlin Clarence Losch III [1960] Director/Vice President Sales [American]; Daniel Wayne Maudlin [1966] Director/Finance and Accounting [American]; Michael Shor [1959] Director/Chief Executive Officer [American]

David Hayton Limited
Incorporated: 3 November 1988 *Employees:* 121
Net Worth: £7,069,836 *Total Assets:* £12,636,731
Registered Office: Hillcrest Garage, Gilwilly Trading Estate, Penrith, Cumbria, CA11 9BF
Activities: Sale of new cars and light motor vehicles
Shareholders: David Hayton; Eleanor Hayton
Officers: Eleanor Hayton, Secretary; Christopher Richard Hayton [1967] Director/Motor Dealer; David Hayton [1940] Director/Motor Dealer; Eleanor Hayton [1942] Director/Motor Dealer; Phillip Adrian Hayton [1979] Director/Motor Dealer

HB (HDG) Limited
Incorporated: 18 February 1986
Net Worth: £472,600,000 *Total Assets:* £548,300,032
Registered Office: Redrow House, St David's Park, Deeside, Flintshire, CH5 3RX
Activities: Construction of domestic buildings
Parent: Redrow PLC
Officers: Graham Anthony Cope, Secretary/Legal Director; Barbara Mary Richmond [1960] Director/Chartered Accountant; John Frederick Tutte [1956] Director/Civil Engineer

HBOS Social Housing Covered Bonds LLP
Incorporated: 6 December 2004
Total Assets: £1,200,316,032
Registered Office: Charterhall House, Charterhall Drive, Chester, CH88 3AN

HCRF Limited
Incorporated: 1 May 2002
Net Worth: £14,269,929 *Total Assets:* £14,274,129
Registered Office: c/o Moore Stephens, Centurion House, 129 Deansgate, Manchester, M3 3WR
Activities: Buying and selling of own real estate
Parent: Arkow Investments Limited
Officers: Francis Joseph Dillon [1952] Director; Thomas McParland [1946] Director [Irish]

HDI Holdings (UK) Limited
Incorporated: 28 January 2014
Net Worth: £35,649,728 *Total Assets:* £72,458,424
Registered Office: 8 Pembroke Court, Chancellor Road, Manor Park, Runcorn, Cheshire, WA7 1TG
Activities: Activities of financial services holding companies
Officers: Julie Elizabeth Andrew [1963] Human Resources Director; Jon Stewart Sharrock [1969] Director/Accountant

Heads Recruitment Limited
Incorporated: 1 October 1997 *Employees:* 91
Net Worth: £9,775,185 *Total Assets:* £15,319,434
Registered Office: Kimada House, 442 Flixton Road, Flixton, Manchester, M41 6EY
Activities: Other activities of employment placement agencies
Parent: Proman Expansion SA
Officers: Patrick John Ramsdale, Secretary; Roland Joseph Gomez [1949] Director [French]; Roland Dominique Gomez [1972] Director [French]; Adam Bradley Gorton [1983] Director/Certified Chartered Accountant; Patrick John Ramsdale [1979] Director; Laurent Daniel Robert [1967] Director [French]

Health Care Resourcing Group Limited
Incorporated: 31 August 2007 *Employees:* 1,270
Net Worth: £1,057,081 *Total Assets:* £14,035,214
Registered Office: 8 Tiger Court, Kings Drive, Kings Business Park, Prescot, Merseyside, L34 1BH
Activities: Temporary employment agency activities
Shareholders: Twenty 20 Capital Limited; Ian James Munro
Officers: Ian James Munro [1977] Director; Tristan Nicholas Ramus [1972] Director/Chairman; Jamie Benjamin Webb [1974] Director/Chief Financial Officer

Healthcare Buying Group Limited
Incorporated: 25 March 2013
Net Worth Deficit: £9,705,000 *Total Assets:* £28,469,000
Registered Office: Europa House, Europa Trading Estate, Stoneclough Road, Kearsley, Manchester, M26 1GG
Activities: Activities of other holding companies n.e.c.
Parent: Turnstone Bidco 1 Limited
Officers: Leo Damian Carroll, Secretary; Gervase Paul Adams [1958] Director; Jean Michel Claude Bonnavion [1971] Director/Investment Manager [French]; Tom Riall [1960] Director; Mohammed Omar Shafi Khan [1974] Director/Chief Financial Officer

Healthcare House Limited
Incorporated: 6 April 2006 *Employees:* 72
Net Worth: £1,547,954 *Total Assets:* £8,989,986
Registered Office: c/o Deliver Net Limited, Snaygill Industrial Estate, Keighley Road, Skipton, N Yorks, BD23 2QR
Activities: Other service activities n.e.c.
Shareholders: Frances Lockett; Timothy James Lockett
Officers: Timothy James Lockett, Secretary/Director; Adele Farquharson [1974] Director; Simon Jeremy Holt [1960] Director; Beverley Jane Lockett [1965] Director; Frances Lockett [1964] Director; Timothy James Lockett [1964] Director

Healthcare Solutions (Hull) Holdings Limited
Incorporated: 28 July 2005
Net Worth Deficit: £23,835,000 *Total Assets:* £55,244,000
Registered Office: Unit 18 Riversway Business Village, Navigation Way, Ashton on Ribble, Preston, Lancs, PR2 2YP
Activities: Activities of head offices
Parent: Aberdeen Infrastructure II Limited
Officers: Ion Bruce Balfour [1963] Director/Investment Manager; Kenneth John Simpson [1965] Director/Investment Manager

Healthcare Solutions (Hull) Limited
Incorporated: 4 August 2005
Net Worth Deficit: £22,673,000 *Total Assets:* £53,893,000
Registered Office: Unit 18 Riversway Business Village, Navigation Way, Ashton on Ribble, Preston, Lancs, PR2 2YP
Activities: Other business support service activities n.e.c.
Parent: Healthcare Solutions (Hull) Holdings Limited
Officers: Ion Bruce Balfour [1963] Director/Investment Manager; Kenneth John Simpson [1965] Director/Investment Manager

Healthpoint 2016 Limited
Incorporated: 7 November 2016 *Employees:* 15
Net Worth: £214,334 *Total Assets:* £8,322,420
Registered Office: 11 Darwin Court, Hawking Place, Blackpool, Lancs, FY2 0JN
Activities: Non-trading company
Shareholder: Robin Neil Womersley
Officers: Ryan Scott Bevington [1976] Investment Director; Jacqueline Brooks [1977] Director; Jason Greenway [1964] Director; Amanda Parkinson [1983] Director; Michael Ryan [1965] Finance Director; Robert William Waling [1956] Director; Robin Neil Womersley [1971] Director

Healthtrak (UK) Limited
Incorporated: 22 May 2001 *Employees:* 2
Net Worth: £2,355,610 *Total Assets:* £6,541,531
Registered Office: 50 Brantwood Oval, Bradford, W Yorks, BD9 6QP
Activities: Development of building projects
Shareholder: Dr Mendhy Hussain Khan
Officers: Fatima Jaffar Shahid, Secretary; Dr Mendhy Hussain Khan [1968] Director/Doctor; Fatima Jaffar Shahid [1961] Director/Practice Manager

Healthy Learning Trust
Incorporated: 4 July 2011 *Employees:* 126
Net Worth: £6,729,000 *Total Assets:* £8,087,000
Registered Office: Flixton Girls' School, Flixton Road, Flixton, Urmston, Manchester, M41 5DR
Activities: General secondary education
Officers: Philip Deakin, Secretary; Anthony Paul Burke [1983] Director/Civil Servant; Professor Gerard John Byrne [1965] Director/Surgeon; John Douglas Byrne [1972] Director/Investment Banker; Damian Dallimore [1978] Director/Local Government Officer; Natalie Pearl Harling [1971] Director of Business Development; Julie Ann Hazeldine [1962] Director/Education Headteacher; Alison Mary Oliver [1970] Director/Charity CEO; Leo Pyrah [1984] Director/Project Manager; Bill Watkin [1958] Director/Education CEO

Hearthcote Property Services Limited
Incorporated: 10 April 1986
Net Worth: £1,837,000 *Total Assets:* £7,999,000
Registered Office: Henderson House, Langley Place, Higgins Lane, Burscough, Lancs, L40 8JS
Activities: Other letting and operating of own or leased real estate
Parent: Soletanche Freyssinet SAS
Officers: Graham James Trafford, Secretary; Mark Damien Deary [1962] Director/Accountant; Philip John Hines [1966] Director

Heat Trace Holdings Limited
Incorporated: 5 March 2008 *Employees:* 78
Net Worth: £6,040,782 *Total Assets:* £8,046,458
Registered Office: Meres Edge, Chester Road, Helsby, Frodsham, Cheshire, WA6 0DJ
Activities: Manufacture of other electronic and electric wires and cables
Shareholder: Neil Shaw Malone
Officers: Daniel Berrisford, Secretary; Daniel Berrisford [1971] Director/Accountant; Neil Shaw Malone [1945] Director/Engineer; Suzanne Malone [1969] Director/Accountant; Jason O'Connor [1975] Director/Technical Manager

Heat Trace Limited
Incorporated: 10 July 1981 *Employees:* 78
Net Worth: £6,065,519 *Total Assets:* £8,034,357
Registered Office: Meres Edge, Chester Road, Helsby, Frodsham, Cheshire, WA6 0DJ
Activities: Manufacture of other electronic and electric wires and cables
Parent: Heat Trace Holdings Limited
Officers: Daniel Berrisford, Secretary/Accountant; Daniel Berrisford [1971] Director/Accountant; Stephen Bonner [1956] Sales Director; Neil Shaw Malone [1945] Director/Engineer; Suzanne Malone [1969] Director/Accountant; Jason O'Connor [1975] Director/Technical Manager; Myung Soo Seo [1952] Managing Director [Korean]; Dean White [1970] Director

The Heath Family (North West)
Incorporated: 26 April 2011 *Employees:* 567
Net Worth: £48,524,076 *Total Assets:* £60,833,184
Registered Office: c/o Palace Fields Primary School, Badger Close, Palacefields, Runcorn, Cheshire, WA7 2QW
Activities: Primary education
Officers: Patricia Ann Roberts, Secretary; Jeremy David Barnes [1969] Director/Executive Headteacher; Morag Jennifer Davies [1973] Director/Consultant; Karl Smith [1964] Director/Teacher/Vice Principal; Helen Claire Stevenson [1972] Director/Consultant; Anantha Kumar Subramanayam [1981] Director/Head of Capital Developments; Edward Vitalis [1967] Director/Accountant; Laura Williams [1983] Director/Education Consultant

Heathfield Holdings Limited
Incorporated: 6 October 2003 *Employees:* 159
Net Worth: £8,765,840 *Total Assets:* £20,050,068
Registered Office: P O Box 9, Harclo Road, off Aireworth Road, Keighley, W Yorks, BD21 4EG
Activities: Other activities auxiliary to insurance and pension funding
Officers: Stuart James Holloway, Secretary; John Paul Aperghis [1973] Finance Director; Joyce Hutchinson [1935] Director; Neville James Hutchinson [1935] Director; Phillipa Ann Hutchinson [1963] Director; Richard Mark Hutchinson [1961] Director

Heating Plumbing Supplies Group Limited
Incorporated: 28 March 2011 *Employees:* 5
Net Worth: £13,217,300 *Total Assets:* £13,228,371
Registered Office: 1 Edmundson House, Tatton Street, Knutsford, Cheshire, WA16 6AF
Activities: Activities of head offices
Parent: Plumbing and Heating Investments Limited
Officers: William Sones Woof, Secretary; Douglas Brash Christie [1978] Director; Roger David Goddard [1953] Director; Douglas Talbot McNair [1947] Director; William Sones Woof [1951] Director/Solicitor

Heaton Park Garage Limited
Incorporated: 29 April 1996 *Employees:* 48
Net Worth: £6,853,423 *Total Assets:* £8,752,239
Registered Office: 396 Manchester Road, Oldham, Lancs, OL9 7PQ
Activities: Sale of new cars and light motor vehicles
Major Shareholder: Jonathan Herman
Officers: Victoria Maria Herman, Secretary; Jonathan Herman [1972] Director; Victoria Maria Herman [1976] Director/Admin Manager

Heatons Truck Group Ltd
Incorporated: 23 October 1950 *Employees:* 133
Net Worth: £2,506,000 *Total Assets:* £16,466,000
Registered Office: Griffiths Road, Lostock Gralam, Northwich, Cheshire, CW9 7NU
Activities: Maintenance and repair of motor vehicles
Major Shareholder: Robert William Heaton
Officers: Charles Pettingell, Secretary/Chartered Accountant; Robert William Heaton [1964] Director; Charles Pettingell [1946] Director/Chartered Accountant

Heimbach UK Limited
Incorporated: 24 January 1898 *Employees:* 93
Net Worth: £7,362,529 *Total Assets:* £10,437,837
Registered Office: Bradnor Road, Wythenshawe, Manchester, M22 4TS
Activities: Other manufacturing n.e.c.
Officers: Phillip John Burgess, Secretary; Phillip John Burgess [1971] Finance Director; Hans Hofmann [1960] Director/Corporate VP Manufacturing [German]; Russell Graeme Martin [1966] Director/Engineer; Peter Michels [1957] Sales Director [German]

Joseph Heler Limited
Incorporated: 12 September 1972 *Employees:* 137
Net Worth: £12,061,141 *Total Assets:* £32,424,962
Registered Office: Laurels Farm, Hatherton, Nantwich, Cheshire, CW5 7PE
Activities: Butter and cheese production
Officers: Mark Wilcox, Secretary; George Heler [1987] Director; Janet Heler [1937] Director; Michael Joseph Heler [1957] Director; Nick Shaw [1962] Director; Mark Wilcox [1965] Director/Accountant

Helical Industries Ltd.
Incorporated: 27 August 1962 *Employees:* 336
Net Worth: £21,521,852 *Total Assets:* £34,152,408
Registered Office: Unit 1 Dock Road, Lytham, Lancs, FY8 5AQ
Activities: Other information technology service activities
Officers: Elizabeth Ann Morris, Secretary; Alistair Matthew Morris [1960] Sales Director; Andrew Morris [1954] Director; Charles Mark Anthony Mills Morris [1955] Director/Engineer; Elizabeth Ann Morris [1934] Director/Secretary; James Mills Morris [1932] Director/Engineer

Helium Miracle 113 Limited
Incorporated: 17 November 2011 *Employees:* 4
Net Worth Deficit: £10,622,073 *Total Assets:* £11,468,731
Registered Office: Greenbank House, 152 Wigan Lane, Wigan, Lancs, WN1 2LA
Activities: Development of building projects
Officers: Christopher John Baybutt [1953] Director/Chartered Surveyor; David James Baybutt [1947] Director/Statutory Surveyor; John Melling [1949] Director; Jonathan Smith [1967] Developmental Director

Helium Sofa Group Limited
Incorporated: 3 April 2013 *Employees:* 793
Net Worth: £6,437,000 *Total Assets:* £25,014,000
Registered Office: Oak Bank Mill, Hallam Road, Nelson, Lancs, BB9 8AJ
Activities: Manufacture of other furniture
Officers: Antony Robert Darley, Secretary; Michael Aramayo [1965] Managing Director; Stuart Bracewell [1964] Finance Director; Karl Nicholas Cockwill [1965] Director; Antony Robert Darley [1965] Finance Director; Joel Simon Rosenblatt [1967] Director/Executive Chairman; George Smith [1961] Director

Helmet Securities Limited
Incorporated: 17 March 1958
Net Worth: £388,104,000 *Total Assets:* £396,355,008
Registered Office: 3rd Floor, 1 Ashley Road, Altrincham, Cheshire, WA14 2DT
Activities: Activities of head offices
Parent: Life Sciences International Limited
Officers: Rhona Gregg, Secretary; Lucie Mary Katja Grant [1976] Director/Solicitor; Nicholas Ince [1982] Director/Accountant; David John Norman [1960] Director/Chartered Accountant

Help Your Claim Limited
Incorporated: 17 April 2009 *Employees:* 466
Net Worth: £12,763,305 *Total Assets:* £15,387,739
Registered Office: 2nd Floor, 86 Deansgate, Manchester, M3 2ER
Activities: Activities of call centres
Major Shareholder: Kamran Ahmed
Officers: Peter Anwar [1980] Director

Help Your Property Limited
Incorporated: 11 June 2014 *Employees:* 1
Net Worth: £162,788 *Total Assets:* £7,001,843
Registered Office: 86 Deansgate, Manchester, M3 2ER
Activities: Management of real estate on a fee or contract basis
Major Shareholder: Kamran Ahmed
Officers: Kamran Ahmed [1979] Director; Michael Fairclough [1991] Director/Property Manager

The Helping Foundation
Incorporated: 11 March 2004
Net Worth: £268,912,608 *Total Assets:* £473,697,600
Registered Office: 59 Kings Road, Prestwich, Manchester, M25 0LQ
Activities: Activities of other membership organisations n.e.c.
Officers: Benny Stone, Secretary; David Neuwirth [1970] Director/Secretary; Benny Stone [1973] Director/Accountant; Aubrey Weis [1949] Director; Rachel Weis [1952] Director; Sir Weis [1981] Director

Hempel Decorative Paints Limited
Incorporated: 31 May 2011 *Employees:* 4
Net Worth: £63,069,000 *Total Assets:* £125,664,000
Registered Office: Crown House, Hollins Road, Darwen, Lancs, BB3 0BG
Activities: Activities of head offices
Shareholders: Briit Meelby Jensen; Lars Aaen; Richard Rudolf Sand; Birgitte Hagemann Snabe; Kim Allan Dam-Johansen; Anne Louise Kruger Kofoed; Claus Juul Petersen; Martin Bogsted; Leif Hansen
Officers: Graham John Haworth, Secretary; Henrik Andersen [1967] Director/Group President & CEO [Danish]; Joseph Devitt [1962] Director; Philip James McDonald [1972] Director/Chartered Accountant; Lars Johan Petersson [1969] Director/Group Executive Vice President [Swedish]

Hen House (Wholesale) Limited
Incorporated: 7 March 1990 *Employees:* 60
Net Worth: £2,331,049 *Total Assets:* £7,104,908
Registered Office: The Hen House, Elliott Street, Aqueduct Street, Preston, Lancs, PR1 7XN
Activities: Wholesale of meat and meat products
Major Shareholder: Peter Rayton
Officers: John Conlin Davis, Secretary; Caroline Louise Craven [1976] Director; John Conlin Davis [1948] Director/Poulterer; Peter Rayton [1953] Director/Poulterer; Stephen John Smith [1962] Director

Henco (International) Limited
Incorporated: 26 August 1983 *Employees:* 7
Net Worth: £14,677,024 *Total Assets:* £28,616,104
Registered Office: Unit 15 Olympic Court, Boardmans Way, Whitehills Business Park, Blackpool, Lancs, FY4 5GU
Activities: Development of building projects
Officers: Madeleine Jane Hibbert, Secretary [Dutch]; Christopher Hibbert [1984] Director/Chartered Surveyor; Madeleine Jane Hibbert [1959] Director/Manager [Dutch]; Johannes Jacobus Maria Staals [1930] Director [Dutch]

J & K Henderson Enterprises Limited
Incorporated: 4 December 1978 *Employees:* 38
Net Worth: £1,753,023 *Total Assets:* £6,560,734
Registered Office: Henderson House, Great Bank Road, Wingates Industrial Estate, Westhoughton, Bolton, Lancs, BL5 3XU
Activities: Wholesale of household goods (other than musical instruments) n.e.c
Officers: James Henderson [1958] Director; Richard James Henderson [1986] Director/Marketing Consultant

Henmead Limited
Incorporated: 30 January 1978 *Employees:* 644
Net Worth: £66,916,000 *Total Assets:* £203,330,000
Registered Office: Sceptre House, Sceptre Way, Bamber Bridge, Preston, Lancs, PR5 6AW
Activities: Activities of other holding companies n.e.c.
Shareholders: Bernard James Whewell; Alison Wright; Hugh MacDonald; Alan Douglas Sturrock; Michael Edward Collier
Officers: Manisha Kumar, Secretary; James Francis Carter [1955] Director; Jeremy Peter Hartley [1965] Director/Chartered Accountant; Richard Eric Wright [1937] Director

Henrob Limited
Incorporated: 19 December 1984 *Employees:* 229
Net Worth: £30,175,484 *Total Assets:* £38,928,064
Registered Office: Second Avenue, Deeside Industrial Park, Deeside, Flintshire, CH5 2NX
Activities: Manufacture of fasteners and screw machine products
Parent: Atlas Copco UK Holdings Limited
Officers: Mark Andrew Ayres [1966] Director; Daniela Ruggieri Baiochi [1982] Director/Business Controller [Brazilian]; Alex Christiaan Jan Bongaerts [1960] Director [Belgian]; Christopher James Clarke [1970] Director/Group Development and Engineering Manager; Arvid Gunnar Tobias Hahn [1965] Director [Swedish]; James Neilson McAllister [1971] Director/General Manager Customer Center UK & Ireland

Hensmill (SJR) LLP
Incorporated: 20 October 2015
Net Worth: £157,733 *Total Assets:* £11,263,281
Registered Office: 5 Clayton Court, Duke Street, Chester, CH1 1NE

Henty Capital Limited
Incorporated: 22 May 2012
Net Worth: £2,496,676 *Total Assets:* £21,312,876
Registered Office: Laxton House, 16 Goughs Lane, Knutsford, Cheshire, WA16 8QL
Activities: Activities of other holding companies n.e.c.
Shareholders: Paul Henty; Diane Henty
Officers: Diane Henty [1964] Director; Paul Henty [1949] Director

Here for You Hospitality Limited
Incorporated: 12 December 2006 *Employees:* 178
Net Worth: £3,468,738 *Total Assets:* £13,866,670
Registered Office: The Greyhound Hotel, Warrington Road, Leigh, Lancs, WN7 3XQ
Activities: Hotels and similar accommodation
Shareholders: Mark Victor Ashdown; Victor William Ashdown
Officers: Mark Victor Ashdown [1955] Director; Peter Michael Raven [1957] Director/Accountant

Here for You Hospitality Middlesbrough Limited
Incorporated: 3 October 2014 *Employees:* 93
Net Worth Deficit: £128,965 *Total Assets:* £9,757,872
Registered Office: The Greyhound Hotel, Warrington Road, Leigh, Lancs, WN7 3XQ
Activities: Hotels and similar accommodation
Parent: Here for You Hospitality Limited
Officers: Mark Victor Ashdown [1955] Director; Peter Michael Raven [1957] Director/Accountant

Heritage Attractions Limited
Incorporated: 26 March 1999 *Employees:* 213
Net Worth: £11,584,294 *Total Assets:* £18,633,026
Registered Office: 5th Floor, 88 Church Street, Liverpool, L1 3HD
Activities: Other amusement and recreation activities n.e.c.
Officers: Gary Johnson, Secretary; Peter Miles Johnson-Treherne, Secretary; Peter Miles Johnson-Treherne [1970] Director/Accountant; Allan James Stuart Leech [1972] Director

Heritage Envelopes Limited
Incorporated: 10 July 1986 *Employees:* 138
Net Worth: £6,442,800 *Total Assets:* £12,581,233
Registered Office: Heritage House, Davyfield Road, Blackburn, Lancs, BB1 2LU
Activities: Manufacture of paper stationery
Shareholders: Melanie Kirsten Withake; Stefanie Schwarz
Officers: Jean de Couespel [1964] Industrial Director [French]; Thomas Schwarz [1970] Director [German]; Mark Sears [1958] Director

Heritage Great Britain PLC
Incorporated: 5 April 1993 *Employees:* 245
Net Worth: £9,750,898 *Total Assets:* £16,647,764
Registered Office: 5th Floor, 88 Church Street, Liverpool, L1 3HD
Activities: Other business support service activities n.e.c.
Officers: Gary Johnson, Secretary; Peter Johnson-Treherne, Secretary; Peter Miles Johnson-Treherne [1970] Director; Allan James Stuart Leech [1972] Director

Hermon Hodge Limited
Incorporated: 5 March 1976 *Employees:* 57
Net Worth: £1,222,489 *Total Assets:* £11,650,592
Registered Office: 281 Carnfield Place, Walton Summit, Preston, Lancs, PR5 8AN
Activities: Wholesale of petroleum and petroleum products
Parent: David Hermon Hodge Ltd
Officers: David Hermon Hodge [1967] Managing Director; Mark Raymond McCaffery [1963] Finance Director

Hero Acquisitions Limited
Incorporated: 11 April 2007 *Employees:* 3,066
Net Worth Deficit: £200,615,008 *Total Assets:* £502,273,984
Registered Office: Oakland House, 76 Talbot Road, Old Trafford, Manchester, M16 0PQ
Activities: Activities of head offices
Parent: Hampshire Bidco Limited
Officers: Daniel James Joll, Secretary; Stephen Ashmore [1964] Director; Alan Edward Peterson [1947] Director; Paul David Quested [1970] Financial Director

Hero UK Limited
Incorporated: 13 March 2007 *Employees:* 18
Net Worth: £5,456,000 *Total Assets:* £23,606,000
Registered Office: 19 De Havilland Drive, Liverpool, L24 8RN
Activities: Manufacture of other food products n.e.c.
Major Shareholder: Dr Arend Oetker
Officers: Joseph Mitchell [1968] Finance Director

Heron Food Group Limited
Incorporated: 19 August 2002 *Employees:* 3,210
Net Worth: £28,107,000 *Total Assets:* £93,497,000
Registered Office: The Vault, Dakota Drive, Speke, Liverpool, L24 8RJ
Activities: Activities of head offices
Parent: EV Retail Limited
Officers: Paul Michael Robin Owen, Secretary; Bobby Arora [1972] Director; Simon Arora [1969] Director; David Charles Heuck [1961] Director; Paul Andrew McDonald [1966] Director/Accountant

Heron Foods Limited
Incorporated: 3 October 1978 *Employees:* 3,210
Net Worth: £36,857,000 *Total Assets:* £101,249,000
Registered Office: The Vault, Dakota Drive, Estuary Commerce Park, Speke, Liverpool, L24 8RJ
Activities: Retail sale in non-specialised stores with food, beverages or tobacco predominating
Parent: Heron Food Group Limited
Officers: Paul Michael Robin Owen, Secretary; Bobby Arora [1972] Director; Simon Arora [1969] Director; Anthony Kevin Dobbs [1969] Director; David Charles Heuck [1961] Director/Chartered Accountant; Jonathan Mark Laverack [1970] Director/Chartered Surveyor; Paul Andrew McDonald [1966] Director

Hessle FT Holdings Limited
Incorporated: 13 May 2011
Net Worth: £501 *Total Assets:* £9,923,207
Registered Office: Corpacq House, 1 Goose Green, Altrincham, Cheshire, WA14 1DW
Activities: Activities of other holding companies n.e.c.
Officers: Stephen James Scott [1978] Director

Hewer-White Trust
Incorporated: 15 February 1963 *Employees:* 4
Net Worth: £8,367,449 *Total Assets:* £8,407,059
Registered Office: Moor Park, 21-23 Heath Road, Stockport, Cheshire, SK2 6JJ
Activities: Other accommodation
Officers: Lindsey Patricia Webster, Secretary; Jane Louise Allen [1960] Director/Nurse; John Hanmer Allen [1958] Director/Precious Metals Executive; John Douglas Guillaume Crombie [1938] Director/Solicitor; Clare Freda Proctor Griffin [1939] Director/Chartered Accountant; Peter Julian Hale [1960] Director/Solicitor; Pamela Rose McGown [1955] Director/General Manager; Rodney Phillips [1944] Director/Retired; Cathryn Lee Smith [1959] Director/Housewife; John Thomas Edward Woodhead [1946] Managing Director; Ann Woolger [1949] Director/Accountant

Hexagon Care Services Limited
Incorporated: 11 February 2014 *Employees:* 454
Net Worth: £1,567,609 *Total Assets:* £9,778,060
Registered Office: Unit 1 Tustin Court, Riversway, Preston, Lancs, PR2 2YQ
Activities: Other residential care activities n.e.c.
Parent: HCS Group Limited
Officers: Francis Alan Ashcroft [1965] Care Director; Glenn Craig Bell [1969] Director; Tim Horrocks [1977] Finance Director; Peter Charles Hudson [1960] Director

Hexagon Solutions Limited
Incorporated: 31 March 2004
Net Worth: £1,686,325 *Total Assets:* £7,054,248
Registered Office: 10 The Edge, Clowes Street, Salford, M3 5NB
Activities: Other letting and operating of own or leased real estate
Shareholders: Paul Bell; Glenn Craig Bell
Officers: Paul Bell, Secretary/Accountant; Glenn Craig Bell [1969] Director/Property Developer; Paul Bell [1965] Director/Accountant

Hexpol Finance UK Limited
Incorporated: 9 August 2012
Net Worth: £300,358,080 *Total Assets:* £300,408,192
Registered Office: Unit 3 Fifth Avenue, Tameside Park, Dukinfield, Cheshire, SK16 4PP
Activities: Activities of production holding companies
Parent: Hexpol AB
Officers: Joseph Edmund Dowdall [1963] Director; Tracy Alan Garrison [1967] Director/Rubber Compounding-President & CEO [American]; Karin Elisabeth Bachmann Gunnarsson [1962] Director/Group Chief Financial Officer [Swedish]; David Andrew Hayes [1968] Director/Financial Controller

Hexpol Tpe Ltd
Incorporated: 9 March 2010 *Employees:* 45
Net Worth: £1,886,000 *Total Assets:* £11,390,000
Registered Office: Don Street, Middleton, Manchester, M24 2GG
Activities: Manufacture of other rubber products
Officers: Georg Brunstam [1957] Director/Chief Executive Officer [Swedish]; Karin Elisabeth Bachmann Gunnarsson [1962] Director/Chief Finance Officer [Swedish]; Per Goran Hellberg [1955] Director/Business Manager [Swedish]; Carsten Ruter [1971] Director/President Technology [German]; Ralph Wolkener [1979] Director/President Europe and Asia [Belgian]; Anthony Wood [1960] Managing Director

Hexpol UK Limited
Incorporated: 10 August 2012
Net Worth: £111,002,544 *Total Assets:* £394,505,376
Registered Office: Broadway, Globe Lane Industrial Estate, Dukinfield, Cheshire, SK16 4UJ
Activities: Activities of production holding companies
Officers: Joseph Edmund Dowdall [1963] Director; Tracy Alan Garrison [1967] Director/Rubber Compounding-President & CEO [American]; Karin Elisabeth Bachmann Gunnarsson [1962] Director/Group Chief Financial Officer [Swedish]; David Andrew Hayes [1968] Director/Financial Controller

Heyrod Construction Limited
Incorporated: 21 February 1978 *Employees:* 128
Net Worth: £16,466,393 *Total Assets:* £34,648,816
Registered Office: Albion Works, Clowes Street, Chadderton, Oldham, Lancs, OL9 7LY
Activities: Development of building projects
Major Shareholder: Francis Joseph Gillespie
Officers: Neil Timothy Harrison, Secretary/Accountant; Francis Joseph Gillespie [1943] Director/Chairman; Paul Francis Gillespie [1975] Managing Director; Neil Timothy Harrison [1968] Director/Accountant; Denis Quirke [1971] Director/Quantity Surveyor

Heyrod Holdings Ltd
Incorporated: 3 December 2015 *Employees:* 128
Net Worth: £16,571,121 *Total Assets:* £34,829,324
Registered Office: Albion Works, Clowes Street, Chadderton, Oldham, Lancs, OL9 7LY
Activities: Development of building projects
Major Shareholder: Francis Joseph Gillespie
Officers: Neil Timothy Harrison, Secretary; Francis Joseph Gillespie [1943] Director/Chairman; Paul Francis Gillespie [1975] Managing Director; Neil Timothy Harrison [1968] Director/Accountant

Heysham Port Limited
Incorporated: 29 November 1989 *Employees:* 75
Net Worth: £16,236,000 *Total Assets:* £48,700,000
Registered Office: Maritime Centre, Port of Liverpool, L21 1LA
Activities: Sea and coastal freight water transport
Parent: Merlin Ports Limited
Officers: Farook Akhtar Khan, Secretary; Caroline Ruth Marrison Gill, Secretary; Thomas Eardley Allison [1948] Director; Ian Graeme Lloyd Charnock [1962] Director; Mark Whitworth [1966] Director

HI Global Holdings Ltd
Incorporated: 26 April 2016 *Employees:* 1
Net Worth: £2,876,899 *Total Assets:* £12,309,371
Registered Office: Unit 2 Walnut Tree Farm, Walnut Tree Business Centre, Northwich Road, Lower Stretton, Warrington, Cheshire, WA4 4PG
Activities: Non-trading company
Shareholder: Lori Hogan
Officers: Paul Ross Hogan [1963] Director/Businessman [American]

Hiden Analytical Limited
Incorporated: 10 November 1981 *Employees:* 83
Net Worth: £12,661,259 *Total Assets:* £14,760,050
Registered Office: 420 Europa Boulevard, Gemini Business Park, Warrington, Cheshire, WA5 7UN
Activities: Manufacture of other special-purpose machinery n.e.c.
Parent: Hiden Instruments Limited
Officers: Robert William Blacas, Secretary; Lee James Ainscough [1973] Development Director; Robert William Blacas [1964] Finance Director; Peter John Hatton [1959] Managing Director; Paul Andrew Jones [1964] Director; Richard James Neale [1964] Director; Colin Robertson [1977] Sales Director

Hiden Instruments Limited
Incorporated: 12 October 2011 *Employees:* 106
Net Worth: £9,137,328 *Total Assets:* £11,260,034
Registered Office: 420 Europa Boulevard, Gemini Business Park, Warrington, Cheshire, WA5 7UN
Activities: Manufacture of other special-purpose machinery n.e.c.
Shareholders: Robert William Blacas; Peter John Hatton; Dr Michael John Benham
Officers: Robert William Blacas, Secretary; Dr Michael John Benham [1959] Director; Robert William Blacas [1964] Finance Director; Peter John Hatton [1959] Managing Director

Thomas Higgins Limited
Incorporated: 12 May 2016 *Employees:* 25
Net Worth: £1,197,711 *Total Assets:* £7,537,267
Registered Office: Lloyds Chambers, 19-21 Seaview Road, Wallasey, Merseyside, CH45 4TH
Activities: Solicitors
Shareholders: Barbara Higgins; Thomas Andrew Higgins
Officers: Barbara Higgins [1950] Director; Thomas Andrew Higgins [1949] Director/Solicitor

High Floor Rentals Ltd
Incorporated: 10 May 2010 *Employees:* 5
Net Worth: £7,464,065 *Total Assets:* £7,599,193
Registered Office: 21 Navigation Business Village, Navigation Way, Preston, Lancs, PR2 2YP
Activities: Buying and selling of own real estate
Shareholders: Roman Eroshin; Georgy Tretyak
Officers: Saad Ahmed, Secretary; Roman Eroshin [1970] Director [Russian]

Highfield Farm LLP
Incorporated: 2 August 2007 *Employees:* 8
Net Worth: £6,888,675 *Total Assets:* £8,972,142
Registered Office: Horwich Recycling Centre, Chorley New Road, Horwich, Bolton, Lancs, BL6 5NJ
Officers: David William Armstrong [1961] Member; Emma Maria Elizabeth Armstrong [1970] Member

Highfield PFI SPV Limited
Incorporated: 2 July 2010 *Employees:* 2
Net Worth Deficit: £7,215,498 *Total Assets:* £30,882,390
Registered Office: Sceptre House, Sceptre Way, Bamber Bridge, Preston, Lancs, PR5 6AW
Activities: Development of building projects
Parent: Highfield PFI Holdco Limited
Officers: Deborah Jane Rawlinson, Secretary; Jeremy Peter Hartley [1965] Director/Chartered Accountant; John Howard Wilson [1965] Director

Highland Smoked Salmon (Holdings) Limited
Incorporated: 19 April 2002 *Employees:* 77
Net Worth: £4,899,767 *Total Assets:* £8,749,526
Registered Office: Dalmar House, Barras Lane Estate, Dalston, Carlisle, Cumbria, CA5 7NY
Activities: Activities of head offices
Shareholders: Timothy Richard Oates; Timothy John Parsons
Officers: Timothy Richard Oates, Secretary; Timothy Richard Oates [1965] Director/Manager; Timothy John Parsons [1965] Director

Highneal Limited
Incorporated: 9 May 1985 *Employees:* 1
Net Worth: £11,257,000 *Total Assets:* £29,354,444
Registered Office: 7 Union Court, Liverpool, L2 4SJ
Activities: Other letting and operating of own or leased real estate
Officers: Joan Criss, Secretary; Kenneth Steele, Secretary; Anthony Peter Criss [1941] Director; Joan Criss [1946] Director

Hilary Meredith Solicitors Limited
Incorporated: 28 April 2011
Net Worth: £400,453 *Total Assets:* £7,476,874
Registered Office: Meredith House, 25-27 Water Lane, Wilmslow, Cheshire, SK9 5AR
Activities: Solicitors
Major Shareholder: Hilary Meredith
Officers: Sinead Maura Cartwright [1958] Director/Solicitor; Hilary Meredith [1959] Director/Senior Partner; Dianne Marie Yates [1961] Director/Solicitor

Hilbre Estates Limited
Incorporated: 3 March 2000 *Employees:* 4
Net Worth: £5,379,355 *Total Assets:* £8,039,793
Registered Office: Unit 1, Suite 4, Hilbre Business Park, Carr Lane, Hoylake, Wirral, Merseyside, CH47 4AZ
Activities: Other business support service activities n.e.c.
Shareholder: Stephen Hugh Roberts
Officers: Stephen Hugh Roberts, Secretary; Karl Joseph McKinney [1963] Director; Stephen Hugh Roberts [1960] Director

Hill Biscuits Limited
Incorporated: 26 April 1906 *Employees:* 369
Net Worth: £5,670,138 *Total Assets:* £10,431,896
Registered Office: Tudno Mill, Smith Street, Ashton under Lyne, Lancs, OL7 0DB
Activities: Manufacture of rusks and biscuits; manufacture of preserved pastry goods and cakes
Parent: Ginger Acquisition Company Limited
Officers: Mark John Bamber [1965] Manufacturing Director; Brendon James Banner [1973] Director; Steven Wetherby [1955] Managing Director

Hill Dickinson LLP
Incorporated: 8 July 2005 *Employees:* 1,098
Net Worth: £30,716,000 *Total Assets:* £60,597,000
Registered Office: No 1 St Paul's Square, Liverpool, L3 9SJ
Officers: Ian Francis Gillis [1973] Member; Peter William Jackson [1961] Member; James Edward Steward Lawson [1970] Member; William David Wareing [1953] Member; Anthony Charles Allen [1959] LLP Member; Peter Grant Anderson [1964] LLP Member; Graham Archibald [1969] LLP Member; Paul Baker [1959] LLP Member; Michael Louis Bennett [1971] LLP Member; Kirandeep Kaur Bhogal [1965] LLP Member; Michael Richard Blakey [1958] LLP Member; Philip Francis Bradbury [1966] LLP Member; Andrew Buchmann [1974] LLP Member; Ralph Hendrik Frank Bullivant [1964] LLP Member; Andrew John Caddies [1966] LLP Member; Robert Iain Campbell [1956] LLP Member; Jasel Chauhan [1979] LLP Member; Edwin Charles Cheyney [1960] LLP Member; David Simon Chinn [1962] LLP Member; Julian James Clark [1963] LLP Member; Claire Louise Cosgrove [1980] LLP Member; Andrew Craggs [1974] LLP Member; Iain Christopher Donaldson [1963] LLP Member; Jonathon Paul Dover [1964] LLP Member; Siiri Louise Duddington [1977] LLP Member; Andrew Dyer [1970] LLP Member; Philip Andrew Farrar [1966] LLP Member; Mark Fitzgibbon [1968] LLP Member; Emma Galland [1979] LLP Member; Ian Christopher Gardiner [1972] LLP Member; Russell St John Gardner [1957] LLP Member; James Garton [1964] LLP Member; Barry Scott Gibb [1980] LLP Member; Andrew Peter Gibson [1964] LLP Member; Jonathan Gillow [1982] LLP Member; Luke Green [1982] LLP Member; Philip Michael Haddon [1962] LLP Member; Darren Philip Hamer [1975] LLP Member; Patrick Henry Hawkins [1960] LLP Member; Jonathan Heap [1978] LLP Member; Joanne Hughes [1973] LLP Member; Amanda Hurst [1976] LLP Member; Jeffrey Edward Isaacs [1959] LLP Member; Christopher Johnston [1980] LLP Member; Gavin Lee Jones [1966] LLP Member; Michael Kenneth Jones [1966] LLP Member; Timon Karamanos [1979] LLP Member; Fionnuala Mary Rose Kenny [1967] LLP Member; Fred Robert Isambard Konynenburg [1969] LLP Member; Damien Aquinas Laracy [1967] LLP Member; Kevin Aidan Lee [1964] LLP Member; Andrew David Leslie [1975] LLP Member; David Locke [1979] LLP Member; Alasdair MacKinnon [1978] LLP Member; Ian Colin MacLean [1960] LLP Member; Adrian Peter Marsh [1972] LLP Member; Alexander James McCann [1972] LLP Member; Martyn Campbell McDonald [1961] LLP Member; Robert McGough [1972] LLP Member; Michael Joseph McKenna [1960] LLP Member; Janet McWhinney [1973] LLP Member; Jeff Middleton [1963] LLP Member; David Mkhitarian [1981] LLP Member; Maria Moisidou [1968] LLP Member; Tricia Marianne Morrison [1970] LLP Member; Philip Moy [1957] LLP Member; Michael Leo Murphy [1981] LLP Member; Matthew Leslie Noon [1976] LLP Member; David Robert Michael Oram [1959] LLP Member; Roderick James Palmer [1966] LLP Member; Jeff Park [1973] LLP Member; David Steven Parry [1979] LLP Member; Fiona Christine Parry [1969] LLP Member; David Christopher Pitlarge [1963] LLP Member; Panos Kyriakou Pourgourides [1970] LLP Member; Alan John Pugh [1973] LLP Member; James Watson Purves [1969] LLP Member; Nicholas Geoffrey Pye [1958] LLP Member; Ian Riggs [1972] LLP Member; Gareth Roberts [1974] LLP Member; Daniel Paul Rubin [1971] LLP Member; Generaldine Mary Ryan [1965] LLP Member; Craig Stephen Scott [1974] LLP Member; Jaspal Singh Sekhon [1981] LLP Member; Tracey Ann Sheehan [1966] LLP Member; Kerstina Mary Skeaping [1970] LLP Member; Paul Spence [1963] LLP Member; Emma Stockwell [1976] LLP Member; Paul Nicholas Taylor [1970] LLP Member; Richard Michael Taylor [1956] LLP Member; Sharon Claire Thomas [1969] LLP Member; Joanna Trewin [1976] LLP Member; Christopher Michael Tyrrell [1982] LLP Member; Mark Richard Walker [1979] LLP Member; Darren James Wall [1980] LLP Member; Paul Michael Walsh [1981] LLP Member; Paula Louise Warnock [1975] LLP Member; Richard Charles Watson [1966] LLP Member; Mark Weston [1972] LLP Member

Hill Ground Rents Limited
Incorporated: 15 February 2012
Net Worth: £2,243,175 *Total Assets:* £7,456,386
Registered Office: c/o Brooks MacDonald, 10th Floor, No 1 Marsden Street, Manchester, M2 1HW
Activities: Other business support service activities n.e.c.
Parent: Ground Rents Income Fund PLC
Officers: Simon Paul Wombwell [1961] Director

Hill's Panel Products Limited
Incorporated: 29 November 1990 *Employees:* 178
Net Worth: £10,478,554 *Total Assets:* £15,058,621
Registered Office: Scottfield Road, Oldham, Lancs, OL8 1LA
Activities: Manufacture of kitchen furniture
Shareholders: Stephen Michael Hill; Martin Stuart Hill
Officers: Richard George Mottram, Secretary; Alan Bolton [1962] Director; Martin Stuart Hill [1960] Director; Stephen Michael Hill [1958] Director; Richard George Mottram [1965] Finance Director; Keith Wardrope [1962] Sales Director

Hill's Salvage & Recycling Ltd
Incorporated: 29 November 1999 *Employees:* 132
Net Worth: £7,084,772 *Total Assets:* £9,712,992
Registered Office: 1-2 Gerrard Place, East Gillibrands, Skelmersdale, Lancs, WN8 9SU
Activities: Sale of used cars and light motor vehicles
Officers: Ian Maurice Hill [1970] Director/CD & Motor Repairer; Jeffrey Maurice Hill [1945] Director/CD & Motor Repairer

Andrew Hillas Properties Limited
Incorporated: 23 January 1996 *Employees:* 6
Net Worth: £7,981,737 *Total Assets:* £12,021,830
Registered Office: Tong Park Garage, Otley Road, Charlestown, Shipley, W Yorks, BD17 7QA
Activities: Other business support service activities n.e.c.
Parent: Hillas Group Limited
Officers: Charlotte Alice Annie Hillas [1988] Director; James Andrew Hillas [1989] Director; Victoria Elizabeth Hillas [1980] Director

Hillcroft Ltd
Incorporated: 2 April 1990 *Employees:* 358
Net Worth: £7,584,091 *Total Assets:* £15,501,591
Registered Office: Hillcroft Nursing Home, North Road, Carnforth, Lancs, LA5 9LX
Activities: Activities of other holding companies n.e.c.
Shareholders: John Paul Ayrton; Brian Alan Pinington; David Pinington
Officers: Louise Ann Mattinson, Secretary; John Paul Ayrton [1940] Director; Brian Alan Pinington [1946] Director; David Pinington [1949] Director

Hillfoot Steel Limited
Incorporated: 1 January 1958 *Employees:* 45
Net Worth: £9,048,444 *Total Assets:* £16,486,624
Registered Office: Lamba House, 5 Scholar Green Road, Stretford, Manchester, M32 0TR
Activities: Wholesale of metals and metal ores
Parent: Murray Metals Limited
Officers: Samuel William Peter Collard [1973] Financial Director; Graeme Everitt Hill [1964] Sales Director

Hilti (Gt.Britain) Limited
Incorporated: 18 March 1950 *Employees:* 781
Net Worth Deficit: £8,407,000 *Total Assets:* £76,248,000
Registered Office: 1 Trafford Wharf Road, Manchester, M17 1BY
Activities: Wholesale of other machinery and equipment
Officers: Amanda Louise Baxendale, Secretary; Felix Emanuel Hess [1975] Director/Business Executive [Swiss]; Dr Kyriaki Maurer [1971] Director/Lawyer [German]; Heinz Nett [1963] Director/Head of Tax Department [Swiss]

Himor (Carrington) Limited
Incorporated: 17 October 2013
Net Worth: £1,550,000 *Total Assets:* £40,685,000
Registered Office: Carrington Business Park, Manchester Road, Carrington, Manchester, M31 4DD
Activities: Buying and selling of own real estate
Major Shareholder: William Ainscough
Officers: Mark Booth, Secretary; William Ainscough [1948] Director; William Francis Ainscough [1977] Director; Andrew John Bain [1972] Director/Project Manager; Mark Austin Booth [1979] Director/Certified Chartered Accountant; Paul Wrigglesworth [1979] Director/Chartered Surveyor

Himor (Property) Limited
Incorporated: 30 June 2005
Net Worth: £25,877,000 *Total Assets:* £32,114,000
Registered Office: Carrington Business Park, Manchester Road, Carrington, Manchester, M31 4DD
Activities: Other letting and operating of own or leased real estate
Officers: Mark Booth, Secretary; William Ainscough [1948] Director; William Francis Ainscough [1977] Director/Surveyor; Mark Austin Booth [1979] Director/Certified Chartered Accountant; Paul Wrigglesworth [1979] Director/Chartered Surveyor

Himor Group Limited
Incorporated: 3 December 2008 *Employees:* 16
Net Worth: £47,733,000 *Total Assets:* £49,006,000
Registered Office: Carrington Business Park, Manchester Road, Carrington, Manchester, M31 4DD
Activities: Management of real estate on a fee or contract basis
Parent: Wain Group Holdings Ltd
Officers: Mark Austin Booth, Secretary; William Francis Ainscough [1977] Director; William Ainscough [1948] Director; Andrew John Bain [1972] Director/Project Manager; Mark Austin Booth [1979] Director/Certified Chartered Accountant; Paul Wrigglesworth [1979] Director/Chartered Surveyor

Hinde Holdings Limited
Incorporated: 11 September 2009 *Employees:* 122
Net Worth Deficit: £963,717 *Total Assets:* £20,172,838
Registered Office: Priory Close, St Mary's Gate, Lancaster, LA1 1XB
Activities: Activities of head offices
Major Shareholder: Stephen Kenneth Hinde
Officers: Rosemary Hinde, Secretary; Stephen Kenneth Hinde [1955] Director

Hindle & Walker Limited
Incorporated: 30 March 1971 *Employees:* 4
Net Worth: £6,808,295 *Total Assets:* £8,023,078
Registered Office: Haydock House, Pleckgate Road, Blackburn, BB1 8QW
Activities: Other credit granting n.e.c.
Shareholders: Mark Nicholas Hindle; Julian Charles Hindle
Officers: Leslie Hindle, Secretary; Julian Charles Hindle [1971] Director; Leslie Hindle [1941] Director; Mark Nicholas Hindle [1968] Director/Finance Executive

Hindle Group Limited
Incorporated: 9 December 1941 *Employees:* 38
Net Worth: £6,628,256 *Total Assets:* £8,165,647
Registered Office: Hapco Works, Caledonia Street, Bradford, BD5 0EL
Activities: Manufacture of other fabricated metal products n.e.c.
Shareholders: Techmotion Limited; Richard John Hindle
Officers: Steven Widdrington, Secretary; Peter Roy Bingham [1960] Director; David Hindle [1962] Director/Engineer; Richard John Hindle [1957] Managing Director; Steven Widdrington [1951] Director

Hira Company Limited (The)
Incorporated: 16 April 1959 *Employees:* 48
Net Worth: £8,086,768 *Total Assets:* £18,394,568
Registered Office: Elizabeth House, 1 Elizabeth Street, Manchester, M8 8JJ
Activities: Wholesale of household goods (other than musical instruments) n.e.c
Officers: Nari Shyam Hira, Secretary; Manohar Shyam Hira [1941] Director; Mohan Shyam Hira [1939] Director; Nari Shyam Hira [1946] Director; Shanker Shyam Hira [1944] Director

Hitachi Automotive Systems UK Ltd.
Incorporated: 15 January 1997 *Employees:* 119
Net Worth: £45,941,436 *Total Assets:* £67,753,328
Registered Office: Middlebrook Business Park, Aspinall Way, Horwich, Bolton, Lancs, BL6 6JH
Activities: Manufacture of other transport equipment n.e.c.
Officers: Sharon Rose Bryce [1960] Director/Head of HR Europe; Timothy Clark [1963] Director/President and GM Sales [American]; Samarth Gupta [1986] Managing Director [Indian]; Naotoshi Nishida [1967] Managing Director [Japanese]; Masayuki Oiwa [1961] Director/Chief Financial Officer [Japanese]; Masahiro Sasaki [1963] Director/General Manager Design [Japanese]

Hive Bethnal Green Limited
Incorporated: 19 December 2014
Total Assets: £38,128,000
Registered Office: Pension Fund Legal, Guardsman Tony Downes House, 5 Manchester Road, Droylsden, Manchester, M43 6SF
Activities: Buying and selling of own real estate
Parent: Tameside Metropolitan Borough Council
Officers: Neil Charnock [1962] Director/Chartered Legal Executive; Patrick George Dowdall [1975] Director/Accountant

Hive Bidco Limited
Incorporated: 9 October 2015
Net Worth Deficit: £1,228,693 *Total Assets:* £15,415,594
Registered Office: Grafton House, Grafton Street, Hyde, Cheshire, SK14 2AX
Activities: Activities of other holding companies n.e.c.
Parent: Hive Topco Limited
Officers: Daniel Charles Ball [1969] Director; Paul Anthony Ellis [1970] Director; Jonathan Kay [1969] Director; Mehul Patel [1980] Director; Christopher Smith [1971] Director

Hive Topco Limited
Incorporated: 9 October 2015 *Employees:* 72
Net Worth Deficit: £1,160,100 *Total Assets:* £18,092,204
Registered Office: Grafton House, Grafton Street, Hyde, Cheshire, SK14 2AX
Activities: Activities of other holding companies n.e.c.
Parent: August Equity Partners III GP Limited
Officers: Daniel Charles Ball [1969] Director; Mike Biddulph [1974] Director; Paul Anthony Ellis [1970] Director; Jonathan Kay [1969] Director; Mehul Patel [1980] Director; John Robert Edward Thompson [1971] Non-Executive Director Chairman

HKJ Investments (UK) Limited
Incorporated: 13 May 2013
Net Worth Deficit: £280,133 *Total Assets:* £10,944,960
Registered Office: 11th Floor, The Plaza, 100 Old Hall Street, Liverpool, L3 9HF
Activities: Activities of other holding companies n.e.c.
Shareholders: Adriana Dinte; Lawrence Jamieson Howie
Officers: Lawrence Jamieson Howie [1958] Director

HMG Investments Limited
Incorporated: 2 November 1948 *Employees:* 7
Net Worth: £34,902,016 *Total Assets:* £95,113,872
Registered Office: St John's House, Barrington Road, Altrincham, Cheshire, WA14 1TJ
Activities: Other letting and operating of own or leased real estate
Parent: HMG Investment Holdings Limited
Officers: Carol Ann Hall, Secretary; Joy Elizabeth Baggaley [1958] Director; Nicholas Peter Casson [1972] Director/Chartered Surveyor; Charles Hulme Hollins Murray [1962] Director; William John Howard Murray [1964] Director/Publisher

HMG Paints Limited
Incorporated: 8 September 1960 *Employees:* 184
Net Worth: £4,834,448 *Total Assets:* £9,838,259
Registered Office: Riverside Works, Collyhurst Road, Manchester, M40 7RU
Activities: Manufacture of paints, varnishes and similar coatings, mastics and sealants
Parent: H Marcel Guest Limited
Officers: Kathrine Falder, Secretary; Daniel Patrick Cleary [1963] Sales Director; Stephen Paul Crossman [1966] Business Development Director; Brian Falder [1931] Director; John Stuart Falder [1955] Director/Chief Executive; Stephen Brian Falder [1960] Marketing Director; John Gilbert Fenton [1961] Director; Leonard Peter Hutton [1956] Production Director

HO2 Management Limited
Incorporated: 9 June 2005 *Employees:* 29
Net Worth: £2,069,170 *Total Assets:* £7,499,390
Registered Office: Unit 317 India Mill Business Centre, Darwen, Lancs, BB3 1AE
Activities: Activities of head offices
Shareholder: Imran Hakim
Officers: Zubair Hakim, Secretary; Imran Hakim [1977] Director/Optician; Zubair Hakim [1982] Director/Dispensing Optician; Suaib Issa [1974] Director/Accountant

Hobs Liver Limited
Incorporated: 14 November 2014 *Employees:* 452
Net Worth: £7,216,859 *Total Assets:* £19,901,692
Registered Office: 14 Castle Street, Liverpool, L2 0NE
Activities: Activities of head offices
Officers: Peter Michael Bertram [1954] Director; James Jeffrey Duckenfield [1973] Director/Chief Executive; Neil Patrick Inskip [1980] Director; Steven Philip Walsh-Hill [1968] Finance Director

Hobs Reprographics PLC
Incorporated: 12 September 1952 *Employees:* 264
Net Worth: £4,637,670 *Total Assets:* £13,605,388
Registered Office: 14 Castle Street, Liverpool, L2 0NE
Activities: Other professional, scientific and technical activities n.e.c.
Parent: Hobs Liver Limited
Officers: Steven Philip Walsh-Hill, Secretary; James Jeffrey Duckenfield [1973] Director/Chief Executive; Brad Flook [1980] Director; David Gordon [1959] Director/Manager; Craig Horwood [1973] Managing Director; Steven Philip Walsh-Hill [1968] Finance Director

David Hermon Hodge Limited
Incorporated: 31 March 2011 *Employees:* 57
Net Worth: £115,729 *Total Assets:* £10,577,261
Registered Office: 281 Carnfield Place, Walton Summit, Preston, Lancs, PR5 8AN
Activities: Wholesale of other fuels and related products
Major Shareholder: David Hermon Hodge
Officers: David Hermon Hodge [1967] Director

Hodgson Academy
Incorporated: 14 April 2011 *Employees:* 128
Net Worth: £6,081,000 *Total Assets:* £8,305,000
Registered Office: Hodgson Academy, Moorland Road, Poulton-le-Fylde, Lancs, FY6 7EU
Activities: General secondary education
Officers: Martin John Pickles, Secretary; Stephanie Benson [1977] Director/Teacher; Helen Carmel Benwell [1959] Director/Retired; Charles Feeney [1966] Director/IT Service Manager; Nadine Galloway [1967] Director/Headteacher; Julie Glynn [1967] Director/HR/Daily Operations Manager; Colin David Jackson [1964] Director/Project Manager; Shabnam Khan [1983] Director/Teacher; Ian Mark Lindsay [1977] Managing Director; Christopher Robert McConnachie [1960] Director/Information Specialist/Computer; Anthony Mark Nicholson [1961] Director/Executive Principal; Andrea Louise Preston [1967] Director; Scott Smith [1968] Director/Academic Registrar; Jane Vila [1974] Director/Commercial Manager; Andrew James Walker [1963] Director/Social Worker; Derek Robert Yarwood [1963] Director/School Principal

John Hogg Technical Solutions Limited
Incorporated: 2 April 1917 *Employees:* 46
Net Worth: £13,907,957 *Total Assets:* £18,339,646
Registered Office: Mellors Road, Newbridge, Trafford Park, Manchester, M17 1PB
Activities: Manufacture of dyes and pigments
Parent: John Hogg & Co. Limited
Officers: Lynn Case, Secretary; Dr Philip John Double [1973] Technical Director; Ian Kenneth Webb [1973] Director; Robert Mitchel Webb [1950] Non-Executive Director Chairman; William Robert Webb [1979] Director/Chief Executive; Steven Wright [1977] Finance Director

Gawith Hoggarth & Co.,Limited
Incorporated: 10 October 1923 *Employees:* 36
Net Worth: £7,214,987 *Total Assets:* £10,578,392
Registered Office: Unit 16-22 Lake District Business Park, Mint Bridge Road, Kendal, Cumbria, LA9 6NH
Activities: Manufacture of tobacco products
Major Shareholder: Irene Mary Gawith
Officers: Christopher Steven Gawith [1980] Director; Irene Mary Gawith [1953] Director; Robert William Young [1962] Director

Hoist Finance UK Limited
Incorporated: 22 November 2012 *Employees:* 45
Net Worth: £11,913,696 *Total Assets:* £126,261,872
Registered Office: Quays Reach, Carolina Way, Salford, M50 2ZY
Activities: Management consultancy activities other than financial management
Shareholders: Hoist Kredit AB; Hoist Finance AB
Officers: Jan Christer Johansson [1979] Director [Swedish]; Ian McConnell [1968] Director/Accountant; Julian Michael Winfield [1970] Director/Chief Financial Officer

Holbeck Ghyll Hotel LLP
Incorporated: 25 November 2008
Net Worth Deficit: £111,127 *Total Assets:* £8,253,351
Registered Office: Holbeck Ghyll Country House Hotel, Holbeck Lane, Windermere, Cumbria, LA23 1LU
Officers: Stephen Leahy [1966] Member

The Holchem Group Limited
Incorporated: 10 April 2006 *Employees:* 236
Net Worth: £16,430,000 *Total Assets:* £37,337,000
Registered Office: Gateway House, Pilsworth Road, Pilsworth Industrial Estate, Bury, Lancs, BL9 8RD
Activities: Manufacture of soap and detergents
Shareholders: Simon Lee Bell; Samantha Jayne Hardman; Paul Allan Gold; Elizabeth Anne Bell
Officers: Samantha Jayne Hardman, Secretary/Administration Director; Stephen Charles Bagshaw [1954] Marketing Director; Simon Lee Bell [1972] Managing Director; Nicholas Quentin Edwards [1959] Sales Director; Katherine Emma Hallows [1968] Director; Samantha Jayne Hardman [1966] Administration Director; Dr John Trevor Holah [1958] Director/Microbiologist; Stuart Middleton [1959] Finance Director

Holchem Laboratories Limited
Incorporated: 14 December 1982 *Employees:* 188
Net Worth: £17,513,000 *Total Assets:* £25,057,000
Registered Office: Gateway House, Pilsworth Road, Pilsworth Industrial Estate, Bury, Lancs, BL9 8RD
Activities: Manufacture of soap and detergents
Parent: The Holchem Group Ltd
Officers: Samantha Jayne Hardman, Secretary; Stephen Charles Bagshaw [1954] Director; Simon Lee Bell [1972] Managing Director; Nicholas Quentin Edwards [1959] Sales Director; Samantha Jayne Hardman [1966] Administration Director; Dr John Trevor Holah [1958] Director/Microbiologist; Stuart Middleton [1959] Director/Chartered Accountant

Holden Decor Limited
Incorporated: 13 February 1991 *Employees:* 33
Net Worth: £5,833,547 *Total Assets:* £8,000,764
Registered Office: 10 Borough Road, Darwen, Lancs, BB3 1PL
Activities: Manufacture of wallpaper
Parent: D & V Holden Limited
Officers: Derek William Holden [1955] Managing Director

Holding Holding Company Limited
Incorporated: 11 December 2007 *Employees:* 58
Net Worth: £8,340,639 *Total Assets:* £15,354,417
Registered Office: St Andrews Court, Lees Lane, Mottram St Andrew, Macclesfield, Cheshire, SK10 4LJ
Activities: Other letting and operating of own or leased real estate
Shareholders: Simon Timothy Holding; Timothy Ronald Lovett; Geoffrey Egerton Holding
Officers: Simon Timothy Holding, Secretary/Director; Geoffrey Egerton Holding [1939] Director; Simon Timothy Holding [1972] Director

Holdsworth Holdings Limited
Incorporated: 7 October 1976 *Employees:* 423
Net Worth: £16,203,076 *Total Assets:* £26,963,476
Registered Office: Manchester Road, Tideswell, Buxton, Derbys, SK17 8LN
Activities: Other business support service activities n.e.c.
Major Shareholder: Michael Ian Holdsworth
Officers: Esther Victoria Trevethick, Secretary; Rupert Michael Ellis Holdsworth [1978] Director/Depot Manager; John Andrew Marriott [1950] Director; Esther Victoria Trevethick [1974] Director/Marketing Manager

Michael I Holdsworth Limited
Incorporated: 12 June 1986 *Employees:* 417
Net Worth: £12,652,102 *Total Assets:* £22,577,952
Registered Office: Manchester Road, Tideswell, Buxton, Derbys, SK17 8LN
Activities: Operation of warehousing and storage facilities for land transport activities
Shareholder: Michael Ian Holdsworth
Officers: Esther Victoria Trevethick, Secretary; Rupert Michael Ellis Holdsworth [1978] Director/Depot Manager; John Andrew Marriott [1950] Managing Director; Esther Victoria Trevethick [1974] Director/Marketing Manager; Rebecca Jane Christine Warhurst [1961] Director/Finance

Holgates (Caravan Parks) Limited
Incorporated: 22 August 1956 *Employees:* 120
Net Worth: £20,900,164 *Total Assets:* £26,230,654
Registered Office: Middlebarrow Plain, Silverdale, Carnforth, Lancs, LA5 0SH
Activities: Holiday centres and villages
Parent: Blue Brick UK Limited
Officers: Judith Margaret Holgate, Secretary; Judith Margaret Holgate [1944] Director/Secretary; Michael William Holgate [1966] Managing Director

Holgates Holdings Limited
Incorporated: 6 June 2007 *Employees:* 109
Net Worth: £13,328,694 *Total Assets:* £25,313,256
Registered Office: Middlebarrow Plain, Silverdale, Carnforth, Lancs, LA5 0SH
Activities: Activities of head offices
Major Shareholder: Michael William Holgate
Officers: Judith Margaret Holgate, Secretary; Judith Margaret Holgate [1944] Director; Michael William Holgate [1966] Director

Holker Holdings Limited
Incorporated: 1 September 1980 *Employees:* 136
Net Worth: £4,598,353 *Total Assets:* £11,685,730
Registered Office: Cavendish House, Kirkby in Furness, Cumbria, LA17 7UN
Activities: Activities of head offices
Shareholders: Richard William James Parry; Lord Charles Edward Vere Cecil
Officers: Peter Anthony Bostock [1953] Director/Solicitor; Lucy Georgiana Cavendish [1973] Director; Lord Richard Hugh Baron Cavendish [1941] Director/Landowner; Allen Joseph Gibb [1966] Director; Right Honourable Grania Mary Lady Cavendish [1947] Director; David Neil Sarti [1965] Director

J. Holland & Sons Limited
Incorporated: 29 October 1991 *Employees:* 64
Net Worth: £11,276,307 *Total Assets:* £16,719,031
Registered Office: Unit 3 St Georges Court, St Georges Park, Kirkham, Lancs, PR4 2EF
Activities: Gambling and betting activities
Shareholders: John Martin Holland; Jacqueline Elizabeth Holland
Officers: Jacqueline Elizabeth Holland, Secretary/Director; Charles John Holland [1982] Director; Jacqueline Elizabeth Holland [1954] Director; John Martin Holland [1953] Director

Holland Shellfish International UK Ltd
Incorporated: 24 February 1995 *Employees:* 1
Net Worth: £7,282,242 *Total Assets:* £16,822,644
Registered Office: 68 Argyle Street, Birkenhead, Merseyside, CH41 6AF
Activities: Activities of head offices
Major Shareholder: Simon Lenger
Officers: Nico de Wilde, Secretary [Dutch]; Simon Lenger [1947] Director [Dutch]

Hollingsworth & Vose Air Filtration Limited
Incorporated: 16 February 2000 *Employees:* 51
Net Worth: £20,399,000 *Total Assets:* £23,373,000
Registered Office: Waterford Bridge, Kentmere, Kendal, Cumbria, LA8 9JJ
Activities: Manufacture of other articles of paper and paperboard n.e.c.
Officers: Eileen Margaret Swain, Secretary; Jochem Hofstetter [1964] Director [German]; Joseph Kaiser [1962] Director of Operations [German]; John S Madej [1965] Director/Division President - EIF [American]

The Hollins Murray Group Limited
Incorporated: 30 October 2012 *Employees:* 20
Net Worth: £49,438,000 *Total Assets:* £110,098,000
Registered Office: St John's House, Barrington Road, Altrincham, Cheshire, WA14 1TJ
Activities: Other letting and operating of own or leased real estate
Officers: Carol Ann Hall, Secretary; Joy Elizabeth Baggaley [1958] Director; Nicholas Peter Casson [1972] Director/Chief Executive; Bill Murray [1964] Director; Bruce Alistair Ian Murray [1974] Director/Chartered Accountant; Charles Hulme Hollins Murray [1962] Director/Chartered Surveyor

Hollinwood Homes Limited
Incorporated: 2 December 2002 *Employees:* 4
Net Worth: £1,641,737 *Total Assets:* £11,347,926
Registered Office: Brockholes Pavilion, Brockholes, Way, Claughton on Brock, Preston, Lancs, PR3 0PZ
Activities: Development of building projects
Officers: Stephen Smith, Secretary; Stephen Smith [1959] Finance Director; Giles Matthew Worthington [1975] Construction Director; John Simeon Worthington [1973] Director; John Marcus Worthington [1946] Managing Director; Russell Edward Worthington [1979] Property Director

Hollowood Chemists Limited
Incorporated: 11 December 1958 *Employees:* 146
Net Worth: £3,229,863 *Total Assets:* £16,789,268
Registered Office: Navkar House, Ashbrook Office Park, 6 Longstone Road, Heald Green, Manchester, M22 5LB
Activities: Dispensing chemist in specialised stores
Major Shareholder: Rajesh Ramniklal Patel MBE
Officers: Manjari Patel, Secretary; Manjari Patel [1966] Director/Physiotherapist; Rajesh Ramniklal Patel [1964] Director/Pharmacist

Holmen UK Limited
Incorporated: 2 August 1979 *Employees:* 10
Net Worth: £87,366,000 *Total Assets:* £89,084,000
Registered Office: Holmen UK Limited, Siddick, Workington, Cumbria, CA14 1JX
Activities: Manufacture of paper and paperboard
Parent: Holmen Paper AB
Officers: Ulf Lennart Lofgren, Finance Director [Swedish]; Lars Gunnar Ericson [1959] Director; Anders Jernhall [1970] Director [Swedish]; Ulf Lennart Lofgren [1969] Finance Director [Swedish]; Anders Olsson [1959] Finance Director [Swedish]; Nils Ringborg [1958] Director/CEO and President [Swedish]; David Andrew Southwell [1970] Director/Head of Finance; Torsten Stjernschantz [1954] Director/Business Manager [Finnish]

K.M. Holmes (Bradford) Limited
Incorporated: 10 February 1978 *Employees:* 7
Net Worth: £6,388,768 *Total Assets:* £7,103,112
Registered Office: Valley Mills, Valley Road, Bradford, W Yorks, BD1 4RU
Activities: Other letting and operating of own or leased real estate
Officers: Adam Dale Gallagher, Secretary; Jenny Melissa Holmes [1960] Director; Julian Charles Holmes [1963] Director/Chartered Engineer; Peter Benson Holmes [1944] Director; Sally Kay Holmes [1945] Director; Ann Christine Howarth [1946] Director/Consultant

Holmes Chapel Comprehensive School & Sixth Form College
Incorporated: 20 July 2011 *Employees:* 164
Net Worth: £18,545,068 *Total Assets:* £20,662,328
Registered Office: Holmes Chapel Comprehensive School, Selkirk Drive, Holmes Chapel, Crewe, Cheshire, CW4 7DX
Activities: General secondary education
Officers: Anthony Halsall, Secretary; Jacqueline Beard [1951] Director; Peter Edward Black [1971] Managing Director; Helena Brealey Brealey [1985] Director/Teacher; Christina Marion Burgess [1950] Director/Retired; Michael Forsyth [1981] Director; Caroline Goodchild [1961] Director; James Colin Grace [1969] Director; Jan Hudson [1963] Director/Data and Communications Manager; Sarah Joanne Lawrence [1972] Director/Freelance Consultant; Christine Linda Lewis [1964] Director/Self Employed; Nicholas Ronald Lewis [1965] Managing Director; Denis Oliver [1949] Director; Michael Oliver [1943] Director; Jamie Edward Otter [1978] Director/Solicitor; Robert Campbell Parry [1941] Director; Gillian Andrea Preece [1976] Director; Philip Redford [1980] Director/Teacher; Rebecca Louise Rix [1966] Director/Marketing Consultant; Kate Woods [1971] Director/Police

Holmeswood Coaches Limited
Incorporated: 18 September 1947 *Employees:* 190
Net Worth: £4,055,425 *Total Assets:* £21,658,418
Registered Office: The Fallowfields, Sandy Way, Holmeswood, Rufford, Lancs, L40 1UB
Activities: Operation of warehousing and storage facilities for land transport activities
Shareholders: Colin Harold Aspinall; Duncan Edward Aspinall; Colin Harold Aspinall; Duncan Edward Aspinall; Mark Aspinall
Officers: Colin Harold Aspinall, Secretary; Colin Harold Aspinall [1965] Director/General Manager; Duncan Edward Aspinall [1962] Director/General Manager; James Francis Aspinall [1937] Director; Margaret Aspinall [1937] Director; Mark Aspinall [1965] Director; Michael John Forshaw [1954] Director/General Manager

Hologic GGO 3 LLP
Incorporated: 21 May 2015
Net Worth: £243,998,336 *Total Assets:* £243,998,336
Registered Office: Heron House, Oaks Business Park, Crewe Road, Wythenshawe, Manchester, M23 9HZ

Hologic Hub Ltd
Incorporated: 23 March 2015
Net Worth: £149,744,864 *Total Assets:* £223,825,424
Registered Office: Heron House, Oaks Business Park, Crewe Road, Wythenshawe, Manchester, M23 9HZ
Activities: Activities of head offices
Parent: Hologic IP Ltd
Officers: John Joseph O'Shea, Secretary; John Joseph O'Shea [1967] Director/Business Executive [Irish]; Michelangelo Stefani [1966] Director/International Counsel [Italian]; Jan Valeer Verstreken [1967] Director [Belgian]

Hologic IP Ltd
Incorporated: 11 March 2015 *Employees:* 7
Net Worth: £303,326,592 *Total Assets:* £309,954,848
Registered Office: Heron House, Oaks Business Park, Crewe Road, Wythenshawe, Manchester, M23 9HZ
Activities: Leasing of intellectual property and similar products, except copyright works
Parent: Hologic Holdings Limited
Officers: John Joseph O'Shea, Secretary; John Joseph O'Shea [1967] Director/Business Executive [Irish]; Michelangelo Stefani [1966] Director/International Counsel [Italian]; Jan Valeer Verstreken [1967] Director [Belgian]

Hologic Ltd.
Incorporated: 11 June 1992 *Employees:* 249
Net Worth: £35,520,000 *Total Assets:* £53,720,000
Registered Office: Heron House, Oaks Business Park, Crewe Road, Wythenshawe, Manchester, M23 9HZ
Activities: Manufacture of basic pharmaceutical products
Parent: Hologic Inc
Officers: John Joseph O'Shea, Secretary; John Joseph O'Shea [1967] Director/Business Executive [Irish]; Michelangelo Stefani [1966] Director/International Counsel [Italian]; Jan Valeer Verstreken [1967] Director [Belgian]

Hologic UK Finance Ltd
Incorporated: 16 October 2015
Net Worth: £160,116 *Total Assets:* £160,957,616
Registered Office: Heron House, Oaks Business Park, Crew Road, Wythenshawe, Manchester, M23 9HZ
Activities: Other business support service activities n.e.c.
Parent: Hologic GG0 4 Ltd
Officers: John Joseph O'Shea, Secretary; Marci Lerner [1964] Director/Vice President Treasurer [American]; John Joseph O'Shea [1967] Director/Business Executive [Irish]; Michelangelo Stefani [1966] Director/International Counsel [Italian]; Jan Valeer Verstreken [1967] Director [Belgian]

Holroyd Precision Ltd
Incorporated: 12 June 2006 *Employees:* 79
Net Worth: £6,724,469 *Total Assets:* £35,513,416
Registered Office: Holroyd, Harbour Lane North, Milnrow, Rochdale, Lancs, OL16 3LQ
Activities: Manufacture of other machine tools
Officers: Laurence John Neary, Secretary; Dr Antony James Bannan [1964] Director; Laurence John Neary [1971] Director/Chief Finance Officer; Wenguang Sun [1966] Director [Chinese]; Kai Wu [1970] Director [Chinese]; Mingzhi Zhang [1963] Director/Chairman [Chinese]

Holt Doctors Limited
Incorporated: 27 February 2009 *Employees:* 78
Net Worth: £3,544,300 *Total Assets:* £9,258,548
Registered Office: 4th Floor, 1 Belle Vue Square, Broughton Road, Skipton, N Yorks, BD23 1FJ
Activities: Temporary employment agency activities
Shareholders: Peter Andrew Gregory; Tracy Ward
Officers: Nina Catherine Learoyd, Secretary; Peter Andrew Gregory [1956] Director; Nina Catherine Learoyd [1955] Director/Financial Controller; Tracy Ward [1973] Director

Holt Family (Holdings) Limited
Incorporated: 8 August 2011 *Employees:* 109
Net Worth: £497,120 *Total Assets:* £8,467,867
Registered Office: Carlton House, Grammar School Street, Bradford, W Yorks, BD1 4NS
Activities: Dormant company
Officers: Damien Michael Holt [1981] Director; Daniel Brendan Holt [1981] Director; Robert Luke Holt [1985] Director; Elizabeth Louise Pix [1986] Director

P H Holt Foundation
Incorporated: 6 March 2006
Net Worth: £19,641,358 *Total Assets:* £19,649,758
Registered Office: 151 Dale Street, Liverpool, L2 2AH
Activities: Educational support services
Officers: Elspeth Victoria Christie, Secretary; Ian Bakewell [1958] Senior Investment Director; Elspeth Christie [1976] Director/Solicitor; Ann Crotty [1947] Director/Retired; Amy Louisa de Joia [1962] Director/Museum Consultant [American]; Chris Evered [1953] Director/Retired; Lesley Carol Martin-Wright [1957] Director/Chief Executive; Ian David Matthews [1950] Director/Retired; Kenneth James Ravenscroft [1939] Director/Retired

Joseph Holt Group Limited
Incorporated: 19 January 2000 *Employees:* 922
Net Worth: £77,161,888 *Total Assets:* £105,466,624
Registered Office: The Brewery, Empire Street, Manchester, M3 1JD
Activities: Manufacture of beer
Shareholders: Richard Peter Kershaw; Maxwell Mark Rushbroke; Rosemary Sarah Adams; Timothy Guy Page; David John Tully
Officers: Philip Adrian Rowan, Secretary; Thomas Leo Dempsey [1952] Director; Richard Peter Kershaw [1955] Director; Richard Neil Frederick Lee [1959] Director/Solicitor; Frank Nicholson [1954] Director; Philip Adrian Rowan [1961] Director/Chartered Accountant; Maxwell Mark Rushbrooke [1942] Director/Farmer

Holt Holdings (UK) Limited
Incorporated: 14 February 2011
Net Worth: £2,103,000 *Total Assets:* £31,154,000
Registered Office: Holt Lloyd International Limited, Unit 100 Barton Dock Road, Stretford, Manchester, M32 0YQ
Activities: Activities of other holding companies n.e.c.
Parent: Autosupply Holdings UK Limited
Officers: Steven Patrick Clancy [1962] Director [American]; Michael Christopher Meehan [1954] Director; Steven James Rudd [1964] Managing Director

Holt Holdings North West Limited
Incorporated: 11 August 2010 *Employees:* 4
Net Worth: £6,287,992 *Total Assets:* £7,013,502
Registered Office: Aston, Way, Leyland, Lancs, PR26 7UX
Activities: Other business support service activities n.e.c.
Major Shareholder: John Kershaw Holt
Officers: Gillian Margaret Holt [1959] Director; John Kershaw Holt [1953] Director

Joseph Holt Limited
Incorporated: 28 June 1922 *Employees:* 896
Net Worth: £95,358,392 *Total Assets:* £111,061,576
Registered Office: The Brewery, Empire Street, Cheetham, Manchester, M3 1JD
Activities: Manufacture of beer
Parent: Joseph Holt Group Limited
Officers: Philip Adrian Rowan, Secretary; Thomas Leo Dempsey [1952] Director/Administration Manager; Richard Peter Kershaw [1955] Director/Brewer; Philip Adrian Rowan [1961] Director/Chartered Accountant

Holt Lloyd Group Limited
Incorporated: 12 April 1994
Net Worth: £24,421,000 *Total Assets:* £24,801,000
Registered Office: Holt Lloyd International Ltd, Unit 100 Barton Dock Road, Stretford, Manchester, M32 0YQ
Activities: Activities of other holding companies n.e.c.
Parent: Holt Holdings (UK) Limited
Officers: Steven Patrick Clancy [1962] Director [American]; Michael Christopher Meehan [1954] Director; Steven James Rudd [1964] Managing Director

Holt Lloyd International Limited
Incorporated: 25 November 1975 *Employees:* 121
Net Worth: £1,268,000 *Total Assets:* £29,601,000
Registered Office: Holt Lloyd International Ltd, Unit 100 Barton Dock Road, Stretford, Manchester, M32 0YQ
Activities: Mineral oil refining
Parent: Holt Lloyd Group Limited
Officers: Steven Patrick Clancy [1962] Director [American]; Michael Christopher Meehan [1954] Director; Steven James Rudd [1964] Managing Director

Home Products Group Limited
Incorporated: 10 December 2013 *Employees:* 4
Net Worth Deficit: £5,218 *Total Assets:* £11,646,765
Registered Office: Astracast House, Wallis Street, Bradford, BD8 9RR
Activities: Activities of other holding companies n.e.c.
Parent: Astracast International Holdings Limited
Officers: Darren Cooper [1969] Managing Director

Homefield PVT UK Ltd.
Incorporated: 1 November 2005 *Employees:* 1,084
Net Worth Deficit: £287,606,016 *Total Assets:* £253,656,992
Registered Office: Mond House, Winnington, Northwich, Cheshire, CW8 4DT
Activities: Activities of head offices
Officers: David Philip William Davies, Secretary; Dr Martin John Ashcroft [1969] Managing Director; John Mulhall [1968] Director/Chief Financial Officer; Mukundan Ramakrishnan [1966] Managing Director [Indian]

Homes By Woodford Limited
Incorporated: 10 March 1998
Net Worth Deficit: £17,236,392 *Total Assets:* £22,117,410
Registered Office: 8d Lockside Office Park, Lockside Road, Preston, Lancs, PR2 2YS
Activities: Construction of domestic buildings
Officers: Jason Lee William Parkinson, Secretary; Anthony Francis Lochery [1960] Director

Hope Capital Limited
Incorporated: 23 September 2011
Net Worth: £1,545,417 *Total Assets:* £21,164,774
Registered Office: Suite B3, Switch House, Northern Perimeter Road, Netherton, Bootle, Merseyside, L30 7PT
Activities: Other credit granting n.e.c.
Major Shareholder: Jonathan Robert Sealey
Officers: Carol Diane Sealey [1958] Director/Investor; Jonathan Robert Sealey [1984] Director/Property Finance; Stephen Neville Sealey [1958] Director/Investment

Hope Street Hotel Limited
Incorporated: 7 October 2002 *Employees:* 101
Net Worth: £6,451,969 *Total Assets:* £13,256,353
Registered Office: Seymour Chambers, 92 London Road, Liverpool, L3 5NW
Activities: Hotels and similar accommodation
Officers: Dr Anthony Robert Harvey, Secretary; David Charles Brewitt [1963] Director; Mary Colston [1959] Director; Dr Anthony Robert Harvey [1961] Director

Hope Street Properties Limited
Incorporated: 28 October 1982 *Employees:* 20
Net Worth: £10,530,741 *Total Assets:* £14,240,479
Registered Office: 1 Derby Building, Wavertree Road, Liverpool, L7 3ES
Activities: Buying and selling of own real estate
Shareholders: Poven Developments Ltd; Eric Mahoney; Alfred Terence Worthington; Paul John Mahoney; Michael Thomas Kinsella; David Michael Mahoney
Officers: Eric Mahoney, Secretary; David Michael Mahoney [1966] Director/Builder; Eric Mahoney [1941] Director/Property Developer; Alfred Terence Worthington [1934] Director/Property Developer

Hope Technology Holdings Limited
Incorporated: 27 September 2007 *Employees:* 126
Net Worth: £7,209,219 *Total Assets:* £12,550,425
Registered Office: Hope Mill, Calf Hall Road, Barnoldswick, Lancs, BB18 5PX
Activities: Activities of head offices
Shareholders: Hope Too Holdings Limited; The Executors of The Estate of Mr S Sharp; Ian Christopher Weatherill
Officers: Alison Jayne Sharp [1965] Director; Ian Christopher Weatherill [1962] Director; Tracy Weatherill [1966] Director

Hope's Auction Company,Limited
Incorporated: 3 May 1897 *Employees:* 74
Net Worth: £4,629,877 *Total Assets:* £11,359,915
Registered Office: Hope's Auction House, Syke Road, Wigton, Cumbria, CA7 9NS
Activities: Other business support service activities n.e.c.
Officers: Barbara Christine Whitfield, Secretary; Gareth Paul Benson [1982] Director/Chartered Accountant; John Jeffrey Dixon [1946] Director/Farmer; John Benson Peile [1967] Director/Farmer; Ian Ritchie [1970] Director/Land Agent; Elizabeth Janet Wright [1956] Director/Farmer

Hopecrest Holdings Limited
Incorporated: 4 July 1988
Net Worth: £1,345,544 *Total Assets:* £10,815,401
Registered Office: Gateway, Crewe, Cheshire, CW1 6YY
Activities: Activities of head offices
Parent: Hopecrest Investments Limited
Officers: John Patrick Collins, Secretary/Manager; Brady Michael Collins [1966] Director/Manager; John Patrick Collins [1965] Director/Manager

Hopecrest Investments Limited
Incorporated: 13 February 1989 *Employees:* 148
Net Worth: £6,608,646 *Total Assets:* £16,283,110
Registered Office: Gateway, Crewe, Cheshire, CW1 6YY
Activities: Non-trading company
Shareholders: John Patrick Collins; Brady Michael Collins
Officers: John Patrick Collins, Secretary/Manager; Brady Michael Collins [1966] Director/Manager; John Patrick Collins [1965] Director/Manager

J Hopkins (Contractors) Holdings Limited
Incorporated: 19 September 1997 *Employees:* 66
Net Worth: £3,767,499 *Total Assets:* £12,498,854
Registered Office: 5 Denesway, Sale, Cheshire, M33 4PZ
Activities: Activities of head offices
Shareholders: John Hopkins; Maureen Hopkins
Officers: Maureen Hopkins, Secretary; John Hopkins [1935] Director; Maureen Hopkins [1937] Director

J. Hopkins (Contractors) Limited
Incorporated: 8 May 1973 *Employees:* 66
Net Worth: £7,699,225 *Total Assets:* £12,498,855
Registered Office: 5 Denesway, Sale, Cheshire, M33 4PZ
Activities: Construction of roads and motorways
Shareholders: J Hopkins (Contractors) Holdings Limited; Mary Maureen Hopkins as Trustee; John Hopkins as Trustee
Officers: John Hopkins [1935] Director; Noel Hopkins [1972] Director/Road Surfacing Contractor; Sean Hopkins [1960] Director

Horizon Global European Holdings Limited
Incorporated: 9 April 2013
Net Worth Deficit: £2,456,557 *Total Assets:* £6,900,895
Registered Office: Drome Road, Deeside Industrial Park, Deeside, Flintshire, CH5 2NY
Activities: Activities of other holding companies n.e.c.
Parent: Horizon Global Corporation
Officers: Paul Charles Caruso [1957] Director/Regional Vice President [American]; Jay Samuel Goldbaum [1981] Director [American]; Jason Cameron Kieseker [1975] Director [Australian]; David Gerard Rice [1963] Director [American]

Hosokawa Micron Limited
Incorporated: 19 October 1964 *Employees:* 66
Net Worth: £5,198,345 *Total Assets:* £10,802,889
Registered Office: Rivington Road, Whitehouse Industrial Estate, Runcorn, Cheshire, WA7 3DS
Activities: Manufacture of other special-purpose machinery n.e.c.
Officers: John Richard Cronshaw, Secretary; John Richard Cronshaw [1961] Director/Management Accountant; Iain Crosley [1958] Director; Hitoshi Kihara [1955] Company Officer and Director [Japanese]

The Hospital Company (Liverpool) Holdings Limited
Incorporated: 28 October 2013
Net Worth: £5,417,000 *Total Assets:* £191,839,008
Registered Office: Eversheds House, 70 Great Bridgewater Street, Manchester, M1 5ES
Activities: Activities of head offices
Shareholders: Carillion Private Finance (Health) 2013 Limited; Aberdeen Infrastructure Investments (No 5) Limited
Officers: Glynn Robert Thomas [1971] Director/Consultant

The Hospital Company (Liverpool) Limited
Incorporated: 24 October 2013
Net Worth: £5,417,000 *Total Assets:* £191,839,008
Registered Office: Eversheds House, 70 Great Bridgewater Street, Manchester, M1 5ES
Activities: Medical nursing home activities
Parent: The Hospital Company (Liverpool) Holdings Limited
Officers: Glynn Robert Thomas [1971] Director/Consultant

Hough Green Garage Limited
Incorporated: 25 April 2002 *Employees:* 100
Net Worth: £2,989,088 *Total Assets:* £8,080,932
Registered Office: Pickering Road, Halebank Industrial Estate, Halebank, Widnes, Cheshire, WA8 8XW
Activities: Maintenance and repair of motor vehicles
Shareholders: David Nigel Farrell; Joan Farrell
Officers: Joan Farrell, Secretary; Andrew James Farrell [1981] Director/Administration; David Andrew Farrell [1979] Director/Body Shop Engineer; David Nigel Farrell [1956] Director/Garage Proprietor; Joan Farrell [1949] Director/Office Administrator; Michael George Goodley [1957] Director/Vehicle Recovery

Houghton Holdings Limited
Incorporated: 25 July 2008 *Employees:* 2
Net Worth: £1,891,215 *Total Assets:* £26,264,842
Registered Office: Beacon Road, Trafford Park, Manchester, M17 1AF
Activities: Wholesale of chemical products
Parent: GHG Lubricants Holdings Limited
Officers: Peter Robert Gosnold, Secretary; Peter Michael MacAluso [1975] Director/Lawyer [American]

Houghton PLC
Incorporated: 11 October 1899 *Employees:* 252
Net Worth: £13,731,000 *Total Assets:* £27,316,000
Registered Office: Beacon Road, Trafford Park, Manchester, M17 1AF
Activities: Manufacture of other chemical products n.e.c.
Parent: Houghton Holding Limited
Officers: Peter Robert Gosnold, Secretary; Lee Bowditch [1974] Director; Stephen John Mayo [1959] Sales Director; Jonathan Richard Percival [1963] Operations and Supply Chain Director; Jon Tan [1980] Director

House & Home (Lettings) Ltd
Incorporated: 4 August 2016 *Employees:* 4
Net Worth: £5,148,233 *Total Assets:* £18,888,938
Registered Office: 26 Greek Street, Stockport, Cheshire, SK3 8AB
Activities: Other letting and operating of own or leased real estate
Shareholders: Alasdair MacDonald; Amanda MacDonald
Officers: Alasdair MacDonald [1967] Director; Amanda MacDonald [1972] Director

Houses for Homes Limited
Incorporated: 19 November 2002 *Employees:* 3
Net Worth: £9,922,354 *Total Assets:* £19,616,674
Registered Office: CT3 Building, Wigan Investment Centre, Waterside Drive, Wigan, Lancs, WN3 5BA
Activities: Other letting and operating of own or leased real estate
Officers: Philip Thomas Shanks, Secretary/Director; Ann Fairhurst [1961] Director; Philip Thomas Shanks [1961] Director

Housing Units Group Ltd
Incorporated: 24 March 1999 *Employees:* 289
Net Worth: £14,739,000 *Total Assets:* £22,859,000
Registered Office: Distribution and Administration Centre, Tweedale Way, Chadderton, Oldham, Lancs, OL9 7HU
Activities: Other retail sale in non-specialised stores
Major Shareholder: Harry Fox
Officers: Harry Fox [1951] Director; Jean Fox [1949] Director; Nicholas John Fox [1975] Director; Stuart James Fox [1978] Director; Richard James Newson [1968] Finance Director

Housing Units Limited
Incorporated: 24 November 1947 *Employees:* 289
Net Worth: £9,059,000 *Total Assets:* £14,461,000
Registered Office: Distribution and Administration Centre, Tweedale Way, Chadderton, Oldham, Lancs, OL9 7HU
Activities: Other retail sale in non-specialised stores
Parent: Housing Units Group Ltd
Officers: Harry Fox [1951] Director; Nicholas John Fox [1975] Director; Stuart James Fox [1978] Operations Director; Jeffrey Philip Hughes [1961] Director/Store Manager; Richard James Newson [1968] Finance Director; Stewart Gregory Smith [1982] Retail and Operations Director

Alan Howard (Stockport) Limited
Incorporated: 21 September 1973 *Employees:* 305
Net Worth: £8,943,895 *Total Assets:* £18,419,922
Registered Office: Section 12, Woodbank Industrial Estate, Turncroft Lane, Stockport, Cheshire, SK1 4AR
Activities: Non-specialised wholesale trade
Major Shareholder: Howard Littler
Officers: Anthony James Littler [1976] Director; Howard Littler [1944] Director/Chairman; Jonathan Mark Littler [1973] Director/Sales Manager

W Howard Group Ltd
Incorporated: 14 March 2001 *Employees:* 131
Net Worth: £5,067,557 *Total Assets:* £16,493,409
Registered Office: Phillips Sawmill, Lower Green Lane, Astley, Manchester, M29 7JZ
Activities: Activities of head offices
Officers: Jonathan Grant, Secretary; Frances Barbara Grant [1940] Director; Jonathan Alan Grant [1965] Managing Director

W. Howard Limited
Incorporated: 4 December 1970 *Employees:* 112
Net Worth: £4,343,865 *Total Assets:* £12,611,392
Registered Office: Lower Green Lane, Astley, Tyldesley, Manchester, M29 7JZ
Activities: Manufacture of other products of wood; manufacture of articles of cork, straw and plaiting materials
Officers: Jonathan Alan Grant, Secretary/Director of W Howard Ltd; Simon Fleet [1972] Commercial Director; Frances Barbara Grant [1940] Director; Jonathan Alan Grant [1965] Director of W Howard Ltd; David Graham McMconnell [1965] Director; Graham Thomas Williams [1964] Operations Director

Howarth Group Limited
Incorporated: 9 January 2007
Net Worth: £12,652,233 *Total Assets:* £12,652,233
Registered Office: c/o Edwards Veeder (UK) Limited, Ground Floor, 4 Broadgate, Broadway Business Park, Chadderton, Oldham, Lancs, OL9 9XA
Activities: Activities of other holding companies n.e.c.
Officers: Janet O'Neill, Secretary; Patricia Beaty [1962] Director; Annie Howarth [1935] Director; Janet O'Neill [1959] Director; Audrey Walker [1967] Director

The Howells Group PLC
Incorporated: 10 January 1990 *Employees:* 66
Net Worth: £13,319,641 *Total Assets:* £14,927,537
Registered Office: Longley Lane, Sharston Industrial Estate, Wythenshawe, Manchester, M22 4SS
Activities: Activities of production holding companies
Officers: Jennifer Bernadette Dudley, Secretary; Jennifer Bernadette Dudley [1967] Director/Secretary; David Peter Howells [1970] Director/Manager; Rebecca Louise Howells [1973] Director/Manager

Howgill Holdings Limited
Incorporated: 12 September 2003 *Employees:* 85
Net Worth: £11,981,438 *Total Assets:* £13,612,362
Registered Office: Units 3-7 Tebay Business Park, Old Tebay, Penrith, Cumbria, CA10 3SS
Activities: Activities of distribution holding companies
Shareholder: Malcolm Kensington Lyon
Officers: Francis Raymond Bennett [1951] Sales and Marketing Director; Tina Elizabeth Benson [1957] Finance Director; Jonathan Broughton Capper [1962] Director; Malcolm Kensington Lyon [1939] Director/Chairman; Carol Anne Nicholls [1958] Director

Tom Howley Limited
Incorporated: 5 January 2011 *Employees:* 183
Net Worth: £1,111,000 *Total Assets:* £10,205,000
Registered Office: Broadoak Business Park, Ashburton Road West, Trafford Park, Manchester, M17 1RW
Activities: Manufacture of kitchen furniture
Parent: Neville Johnson Holdings Ltd
Officers: William Keith Bennett, Secretary; William Keith Bennett [1953] Director; Jeffrey Forrester [1953] Director; Thomas Howley [1967] Director; Simon Patrick Meyrick [1962] Director; Nigel John Pailing [1958] Director; Lisa Michelle Quinlan [1969] Marketing Director

HPO1 Nominees Limited
Incorporated: 20 August 1976
Net Worth: £6,602,000 *Total Assets:* £8,633,000
Registered Office: Matalan Head Office, Perimeter Road, Knowsley Industrial Park, Knowsley, Merseyside, L33 7SZ
Activities: Retail sale of clothing in specialised stores
Parent: Matalan Limited
Officers: William George Lodder, Secretary; John Jason Hargreaves [1968] Managing Director; Stephen Mark Hill [1976] Finance Director; John Nicholas Mills [1955] Director; Gregory Vincent Pateras [1976] Director

HPP Pinnacle Limited
Incorporated: 1 April 2008 *Employees:* 166
Net Worth: £10,478,609 *Total Assets:* £17,122,568
Registered Office: Scottfield Road, Oldham, Lancs, OL8 1LA
Activities: Manufacture of kitchen furniture
Shareholders: Stephen Michael Hill; Martin Stuart Hill
Officers: Richard George Mottram, Secretary; Martin Stuart Hill [1960] Director; Stephen Michael Hill [1958] Director

HSL Group Holdings Limited
Incorporated: 8 February 2000 *Employees:* 49
Net Worth: £2,025,300 *Total Assets:* £8,932,740
Registered Office: Unit E & F, Glenfield Business Park, Phillips Road, Blackburn, Lancs, BB1 5PF
Activities: Renting and leasing of media entertainment equipment
Shareholders: David Jackson; Simon Walker Stuart
Officers: David Jackson, Secretary; Howard John Dean [1967] Managing Director; Simon Walker Stuart [1963] Director

HSS Financing PLC
Incorporated: 10 January 2014
Net Worth Deficit: £9,535,000 *Total Assets:* £217,047,008
Registered Office: Oakland House, Talbot Road, Old Trafford, Manchester, M16 0PQ
Activities: Activities of financial services holding companies
Parent: HSS Hire Service Group Limited
Officers: Daniel James Joll, Secretary; Stephen Ashmore [1964] Director; Paul David Quested [1970] Financial Director

HSS Hire Group PLC
Incorporated: 7 January 2015 *Employees:* 3,066
Net Worth: £73,572,000 *Total Assets:* £429,455,008
Registered Office: Oakland House, Talbot Road, Old Trafford, Manchester, M16 0PQ
Activities: Activities of head offices
Officers: Daniel James Joll, Secretary; Stephen Ashmore [1964] Director; Amanda Jane Burton [1959] Director; Alan Edward Peterson [1947] Director; Paul David Quested [1970] Financial Director; Douglas Grant Robertson [1953] Director; Thomas Sweet-Escott [1957] Director/Finance Company Partner

HSS Hire Service Finance Limited
Incorporated: 26 November 2003
Net Worth: £22,971,000 *Total Assets:* £23,318,000
Registered Office: Oakland House, 76 Talbot Road, Old Trafford, Manchester, M16 0PQ
Activities: Activities of head offices
Parent: HSS Hire Service Holdings Limited
Officers: Daniel James Joll, Secretary; Stephen Ashmore [1964] Director; Paul David Quested [1970] Financial Director

HSS Hire Service Group Limited
Incorporated: 15 December 1959 *Employees:* 2,771
Net Worth: £26,462,000 *Total Assets:* £259,423,008
Registered Office: Oakland House, Talbot Road, Old Trafford, Manchester, M16 0PQ
Activities: Renting and leasing of construction and civil engineering machinery and equipment
Parent: HSS Hire Service Finance Limited
Officers: Daniel James Joll, Secretary; Stephen Ashmore [1964] Director; Paul David Quested [1970] Financial Director

HSS Hire Service Holdings Limited
Incorporated: 25 March 2003
Net Worth: £7,182,000 *Total Assets:* £7,584,000
Registered Office: Oakland House, 76 Talbot Road, Old Trafford, Manchester, M16 0PQ
Activities: Activities of head offices
Parent: Hero Acquisitions Limited
Officers: Daniel James Joll, Secretary; Stephen Ashmore [1964] Director; Paul David Quested [1970] Financial Director

HTA Group Limited
Incorporated: 22 March 1989 *Employees:* 111
Net Worth: £2,211,000 *Total Assets:* £6,627,000
Registered Office: Britannia House, Junction Street, Darwen, Lancs, BB3 2RB
Activities: Manufacture of other fabricated metal products n.e.c.
Parent: HTA Group Holdings Ltd
Officers: Andrew Barrington Sedgley, Secretary; James Stephen Hartley [1955] Managing Director; Wayne Tierney [1962] Director; Wayne Anthony Wild [1967] Director/Manager

HTI Toys UK Limited
Incorporated: 6 December 1952 *Employees:* 92
Net Worth: £15,119,000 *Total Assets:* £26,594,000
Registered Office: Eastham House, Copse Road, Fleetwood, Lancs, FY7 7NY
Activities: Manufacture of other games and toys, n.e.c.
Parent: David Halsall International Holdings Limited
Officers: Colin Anthony Houlihan [1962] Director; David John Lord [1966] IT Director; Adam Miles Williams [1981] Director

The Hub Community Healthcare Holdco Limited
Incorporated: 12 November 2014 *Employees:* 214
Net Worth Deficit: £4,867,591 *Total Assets:* £24,155,856
Registered Office: Paddock Business Centre, 2 Paddock Road, Skelmersdale, Lancs, WN8 9PL
Activities: Activities of other holding companies n.e.c.
Parent: Bridges Ventures III (General Partner) Limited
Officers: David Atkinson [1973] Pharmacy Operations Director; Christopher Ball [1960] Director; Andrew Craig Butterworth [1972] Director; James Lewis Hurrell [1985] Director/Investment Manager; Stephen Thomas Jeffers [1956] Director; Oliver Quentin James Wyncoll [1969] Director/Investment Manager

The Hub Community Healthcare Limited
Incorporated: 11 November 2014 *Employees:* 4
Net Worth Deficit: £1,869,178 *Total Assets:* £19,004,344
Registered Office: Paddock Business Centre, 2 Paddock Road, Skelmersdale, Lancs, WN8 9PL
Activities: Activities of other holding companies n.e.c.
Parent: The Hub Community Healthcare Midco Limited
Officers: David Atkinson [1973] Pharmacy Operations Director; Christopher Ball [1960] Director; Andrew Craig Butterworth [1972] Director; James Lewis Hurrell [1985] Director/Investment Manager; Stephen Thomas Jeffers [1956] Director; Oliver Quentin James Wyncoll [1969] Director/Investment Manager

The Hub Community Healthcare Midco Limited
Incorporated: 6 May 2015
Net Worth: £24,506 *Total Assets:* £16,985,912
Registered Office: Paddock Business Centre, 2 Paddock Road, Skelmersdale, Lancs, WN8 9PL
Activities: Activities of other holding companies n.e.c.
Parent: The Hub Community Healthcare Holdco Limited
Officers: David Atkinson [1973] Pharmacy Operations Director; Christopher Ball [1960] Director; Andrew Craig Butterworth [1972] Director; James Lewis Hurrell [1985] Director/Investment Manager; Stephen Thomas Jeffers [1956] Director; Oliver Quentin James Wyncoll [1969] Director/Investment Manager

The Hub Community Healthcare P Finance Limited
Incorporated: 21 December 2010
Net Worth: £13,304,350 *Total Assets:* £13,477,063
Registered Office: Paddock Business Centre, 2 Paddock Road, Skelmersdale, Lancs, WN8 9PL
Activities: Activities of other holding companies n.e.c.
Parent: The Hub Community Healthcare Ph Limited
Officers: David Atkinson [1973] Pharmacy Operations Director; Christopher Ball [1960] Director; Andrew Craig Butterworth [1972] Director/Chartered Accountant; Stephen Thomas Jeffers [1956] Director

The Hub Community Healthcare Ph Limited
Incorporated: 21 December 2010
Net Worth: £11,132,840 *Total Assets:* £17,869,040
Registered Office: Paddock Business Centre, 2 Paddock Road, Skelmersdale, Lancs, WN8 9PL
Activities: Activities of other holding companies n.e.c.
Parent: The Hub Community Healthcare Limited
Officers: David Atkinson [1973] Pharmacy Operations Director; Christopher Ball [1960] Director; Andrew Craig Butterworth [1972] Director/Chartered Accountant; Stephen Thomas Jeffers [1956] Director

The Hub Pharmacy Limited
Incorporated: 19 November 2007 *Employees:* 195
Net Worth Deficit: £4,516,954 *Total Assets:* £27,351,448
Registered Office: Paddock Business Centre, 2 Paddock Road, West Pimbo Industrial Estate, Skelmersdale, Lancs, WN8 9PL
Activities: Dispensing chemist in specialised stores
Parent: The Hub Community Healthcare Ph Limited
Officers: David Atkinson [1973] Pharmacy Operations Director; Christopher Ball [1960] Director; Andrew Craig Butterworth [1972] Director/Chartered Accountant; Stephen Thomas Jeffers [1956] Director

Huber Packaging Limited
Incorporated: 21 November 2014 *Employees:* 85
Net Worth: £2,077,698 *Total Assets:* £11,418,040
Registered Office: Trinity Park, Orrell Lane, Bootle, Merseyside, L20 6BP
Activities: Manufacture of steel drums and similar containers
Parent: Huber Packaging Group GmbH
Officers: Lindsey Russell Mack, Secretary; Martin Luer [1970] Director/Chief Operation Officer [German]; Lindsey Russell Mack [1967] Director/Plant Manager

Hubron (International) Limited
Incorporated: 23 May 2004 *Employees:* 53
Net Worth: £1,441,808 *Total Assets:* £11,714,347
Registered Office: Ayrton House, Parliament Business Park, Commerce Way, Liverpool, L8 7BA
Activities: Manufacture of other plastic products
Officers: Philip Didlick, Secretary; Philip Didlick [1976] Director/Accountant; Generald Francis O'Brien [1949] Director/Chemist; Padraic Marc Obrien [1979] Director

Huggies Day Nursery Limited
Incorporated: 1 March 2005 *Employees:* 53
Net Worth: £2,510,400 *Total Assets:* £11,927,359
Registered Office: 3 Crewe Road, Sandbach, Cheshire, CW11 4NE
Activities: Other business support service activities n.e.c.
Officers: Edward Benjamin Twigge, Secretary; Julie Victoria Carson [1973] Director/Nursing Home Manager; Edward Benjamin Twigge [1972] Director/Nursing Home Manager; James Richard Twigge [1983] Director/Nursing Home Manager; Michael David Twigge [1970] Director/Nursing Home Manager

J.D. Hughes Group Limited
Incorporated: 24 September 1968 *Employees:* 108
Net Worth: £7,388,791 *Total Assets:* £11,967,614
Registered Office: Arden Works, Whitefield Road, Bredbury, Stockport, Cheshire, SK6 2SS
Activities: Other specialised construction activities n.e.c.
Parent: Justrite Holdings Ltd
Officers: Paul Darlington [1962] Director

Hughes Safety Showers Limited
Incorporated: 22 September 1995 *Employees:* 88
Net Worth: £2,378,533 *Total Assets:* £10,510,938
Registered Office: Arden Works, Whitefield Road, Bredbury, Stockport, Cheshire, SK6 2SS
Activities: Manufacture of other special-purpose machinery n.e.c.
Parent: J.D. Hughes Group Limited
Officers: Paul Darlington [1962] Managing Director

Huhtamaki BCP Limited
Incorporated: 21 June 1930 *Employees:* 146
Net Worth: £10 225,740 *Total Assets:* £14,314,352
Registered Office: Crompton House, Nuttalls Way, Blackburn, BB1 2JT
Activities: Manufacture of corrugated paper and paperboard, sacks and bags
Parent: 2 View Media
Officers: Philip John Covill [1970] Director/Financial Controller; Tarja Iitti [1959] Director/Group Controller [Finnish]

Human Appeal
Incorporated: 3 June 2013 *Employees:* 104
Net Worth: £6,421,506 *Total Assets:* £10,875,143
Registered Office: 1 Cheadle Point, Carrs Road, Cheadle, Cheshire, SK8 2BL
Activities: Other human health activities
Officers: Dr Hussein Mostafa Nagi [1958] Director [Irish]; Kamil Zakariyya Omoteso [1970] Director/Head of The School of Economics; Mohamad Hamed Yousef [1958] Director; Imad Zahidah [1959] Director

Lawrence Hunt & Co Limited
Incorporated: 1 October 1974 *Employees:* 530
Net Worth: £6,087,332 *Total Assets:* £9,766,234
Registered Office: 40b Liverpool Road, Penwortham, Preston, Lancs, PR1 0DQ
Activities: Retail sale in non-specialised stores with food, beverages or tobacco predominating
Officers: Philippa Bailey [1969] Director/Chartered Accountant; Andrea Hunt [1971] Director/Merchandising Administrator; Kevin Brian Hunt [1969] Director; Tony Miller [1963] Operations Director

Huntapac Produce Limited
Incorporated: 17 January 1979 *Employees:* 494
Net Worth: £13,693,193 *Total Assets:* £25,085,786
Registered Office: 293 Blackgate Lane, Holmes Tarleton, Preston, Lancs, PR4 6JJ
Activities: Growing of vegetables and melons, roots and tubers
Officers: Suzanne Harrison, Secretary; Suzanne Harrison [1963] Finance Director; Henry Hunter [1995] Director; Jason Charles Hunter [1971] Director/Manager; Joan Hunter [1943] Director; William Hunter [1994] Director; William Warren Hunter [1970] Managing Director; Steven William Kay [1969] Operations Director; Stephen Shields [1973] Technical Director

Hunter Douglas (UK) Limited
Incorporated: 30 May 1969 *Employees:* 421
Net Worth: £22,454,000 *Total Assets:* £141,840,992
Registered Office: c/o Hunter Douglas Limited, Mersey Industrial Estate, Battersea Road, Heaton Mersey, Stockport, Cheshire, SK4 3EQ
Activities: Other manufacturing n.e.c.
Officers: Robert Henry George Durston, Secretary; Harold Clement Fuller [1933] Director/Accountant; Adrianus Kuiper [1960] Director [Dutch]; Russell Mark Malley [1960] Managing Director; Leendert Reijtenbagh [1942] Financial Director [Dutch]

Huntercombe (BIR) Limited
Incorporated: 20 May 2005 *Employees:* 4
Net Worth: £12,674,000 *Total Assets:* £32,267,000
Registered Office: Norcliffe House, Station Road, Wilmslow, Cheshire, SK9 1BU
Activities: Other human health activities
Parent: Huntercombe (SP) Limited
Officers: Abigail Mattison, Secretary; Robert Nicolas Barr [1958] Director; Ryan Stuart MacAskill [1975] Director; Valerie Louise Michie [1975] Director; Gregory Laurence Newman [1988] Director/Investment Professional; Mark James Williamson [1973] Director

Huntercombe (No 12) Limited
Incorporated: 7 June 2006 *Employees:* 288
Net Worth: £22,141,000 *Total Assets:* £23,360,000
Registered Office: Norcliffe House, Station Road, Wilmslow, Cheshire, SK9 1BU
Activities: Other human health activities
Parent: The Huntercombe Group Limited
Officers: Abigail Mattison, Secretary; Valerie Louise Michie [1975] Director; Mark James Williamson [1973] Director

Huntercombe (SP) Limited
Incorporated: 20 May 2005 *Employees:* 5
Net Worth Deficit: £37,752,000 *Total Assets:* £49,660,000
Registered Office: Norcliffe House, Station Road, Wilmslow, Cheshire, SK9 1BU
Activities: Other human health activities
Parent: The Huntercombe Group Limited
Officers: Abigail Mattison, Secretary; Robert Nicolas Barr [1958] Director; Ryan Stuart MacAskill [1975] Director; Valerie Louise Michie [1975] Director; Gregory Laurence Newman [1988] Director/Investment Professional; Mark James Williamson [1973] Director

Huntercombe Properties (Frenchay) Limited
Incorporated: 12 January 2000 *Employees:* 512
Net Worth: £17,891,000 *Total Assets:* £19,834,000
Registered Office: Norcliffe House, Station Road, Wilmslow, Cheshire, SK9 1BU
Activities: Other human health activities
Parent: Huntercombe (No 12) Limited
Officers: Abigail Mattison, Secretary; Valerie Louise Michie [1975] Director; Mark James Williamson [1973] Director

Hurlston Hall Property Limited
Incorporated: 13 January 2016
Net Worth: £6,314,525 *Total Assets:* £8,244,343
Registered Office: Ayrton House, Commerce Way, Liverpool, L8 7BA
Activities: Other letting and operating of own or leased real estate
Officers: Philip Didlick, Secretary; Philip Didlick [1976] Director/Chartered Accountant; Generald Francis O'Brien [1949] Director; Padraic Marc O'Brien [1979] Director

Hurst Group (Northern) Limited
Incorporated: 23 March 1994 *Employees:* 301
Net Worth: £4,191,000 *Total Assets:* £9,973,000
Registered Office: Aynsley House, Common Road, Low Moor, Bradford, W Yorks, BD12 0UF
Activities: Other manufacturing n.e.c.
Officers: Leanne Hirst, Secretary; Leanne Jayne Hirst [1970] Director; Gary Stuart Hurst [1967] Director; Jeannie Hurst [1945] Director; Norman Robert Hurst [1938] Director; James Gerard Maye [1954] Director/Accountant

Hurstwood Properties (A) Limited
Incorporated: 16 December 2008 *Employees:* 3
Net Worth: £3,568,367 *Total Assets:* £17,576,476
Registered Office: Bridge Street Chambers, Bridge Street, Manchester, M3 2RJ
Activities: Other letting and operating of own or leased real estate
Officers: Julie Black, Secretary; Stephen John Ashworth [1967] Director; Henry Philip Hill [1974] Director/Chartered Surveyor; Andrew Charles Park [1967] Director

Hurstwood Properties (C) Limited
Incorporated: 16 December 2008
Net Worth: £2,538,589 *Total Assets:* £9,866,567
Registered Office: Bridge Street Chambers, 72 Bridge Street, Manchester, M3 2RJ
Activities: Other letting and operating of own or leased real estate
Officers: Julie Black, Secretary; Stephen John Ashworth [1967] Director; Henry Philip Hill [1974] Director/Chartered Surveyor; Andrew Charles Park [1967] Director

Hurstwood Properties (R) Limited
Incorporated: 16 December 2008 *Employees:* 3
Net Worth: £8,783,240 *Total Assets:* £35,269,360
Registered Office: Bridge Street Chambers, 72 Bridge Street, Manchester, M3 2RJ
Activities: Other letting and operating of own or leased real estate
Officers: Julie Black, Secretary; Stephen John Ashworth [1967] Director; Henry Philip Hill [1974] Director/Chartered Surveyor; Andrew Charles Park [1967] Director

Hurstwood Properties (Y) Limited
Incorporated: 16 December 2008
Net Worth: £3,037,161 *Total Assets:* £11,406,271
Registered Office: Bridge Street Chambers, 72 Bridge Street, Manchester, M3 2RJ
Activities: Other letting and operating of own or leased real estate
Officers: Julie Black, Secretary; Stephen John Ashworth [1967] Director; Henry Philip Hill [1974] Director/Chartered Surveyor; Andrew Charles Park [1967] Director

Clive Hurt (Holdings) Limited
Incorporated: 30 January 2003 *Employees:* 5
Net Worth: £4,590,442 *Total Assets:* £7,450,184
Registered Office: Sandham House, Redrose Drive, Lancashire Enterprise Business Park, Leyland, Lancs, PR26 6TJ
Activities: Activities of head offices
Parent: Hurt Plant Hire Ltd
Officers: Clive Edward Hurt, Secretary/Director; Clive Edward Hurt [1951] Director; Richard Hurt [1978] Director/Plant Manager

Clive Hurt (Plant Hire) Limited
Incorporated: 5 October 1984 *Employees:* 213
Net Worth: £23,629,700 *Total Assets:* £30,548,968
Registered Office: Sandham House, Redrose Drive, Lancashire Business Park, Leyland, Lancs, PR26 6TJ
Activities: Site preparation
Parent: Clive Hurt Holdings Ltd
Officers: Tina Lorraine Holland, Secretary; Caroline Elaine Barnes [1976] Director/Transport Manager; Mark Peter Gale [1969] Director/Manager; Clive Edward Hurt [1951] Director; Richard Hurt [1978] Director/Plant Manager

Hurt Plant Hire Limited
Incorporated: 17 October 2013
Net Worth: £21,184,372 *Total Assets:* £30,132,500
Registered Office: Richard House, Winckley Square, Preston, Lancs, PR1 3HP
Activities: Activities of other holding companies n.e.c.
Shareholders: Clive Edward Hurt; Richard Hurt
Officers: Clive Edward Hurt [1951] Director; Richard Hurt [1978] Director

Husco International Four Ltd
Incorporated: 22 June 2015
Net Worth: £22,807,762 *Total Assets:* £22,890,616
Registered Office: 6 Rivington Road, Whitehouse Industrial Estate, Runcorn, Cheshire, WA7 3DT
Activities: Financial intermediation not elsewhere classified
Major Shareholder: Agustin Alberto Ramirez
Officers: Gregg Donald Heller [1969] Director/General Manager [American]; Steven David Hough [1980] Finance Director; Austin Martin Ramirez [1978] Director [American]

Husco International Holdings Three Ltd
Incorporated: 17 June 2015
Net Worth: £469,269 *Total Assets:* £24,581,680
Registered Office: 6 Rivington Road, Whitehouse Industrial Estate, Runcorn, Cheshire, WA7 3DT
Activities: Financial intermediation not elsewhere classified
Major Shareholder: Agustin Alberto Ramirez
Officers: Gregg Donald Heller [1969] Director/General Manager [American]; Steven David Hough [1980] Finance Director; Austin Martin Ramirez [1978] Director [American]

Husco International One Ltd
Incorporated: 14 May 2015
Net Worth: £10 751,392 *Total Assets:* £11,618,854
Registered Office: 6 Rivington Road, Whitehouse Industrial Estate, Runcorn, Cheshire, WA7 3DT
Activities: Manufacture of fluid power equipment
Officers: Steven David Hough, Secretary; Gregg Donald Heller [1969] Director/General Manager [American]; Austin Martin Ramirez [1978] Director [American]

Husco International Partners LLP
Incorporated: 5 August 2015 *Employees:* 174
Net Worth Deficit: £671,595 *Total Assets:* £15,755,942
Registered Office: 6 Rivington Road, Whitehouse Industrial Estate, Runcorn, Cheshire, WA7 3DT

Husco International Two Ltd
Incorporated: 14 May 2015
Net Worth: £10,376,413 *Total Assets:* £11,717,033
Registered Office: 6 Rivington Road, Whitehouse Industrial Estate, Runcorn, Cheshire, WA7 3DT
Activities: Manufacture of fluid power equipment
Major Shareholder: Agustin Alberto Ramirez
Officers: Steven David Hough, Secretary; Gregg Donald Heller [1969] Director/General Manager [American]; Robert Christian Mortensen [1964] Director/Chief Operating Officer [American]

Hussein Traders Limited
Incorporated: 21 April 2009
Net Worth: £8,283,882 *Total Assets:* £9,315,361
Registered Office: Sterling House, 501 Middleton Road, Chadderton, Oldham, Lancs, OL9 9LY
Activities: Performing arts
Major Shareholder: Peter John Kay
Officers: Peter Kay [1973] Director/Comedian

The Hut Group Limited
Incorporated: 19 March 2008 *Employees:* 3,222
Net Worth: £319,225,984 *Total Assets:* £938,947,968
Registered Office: 5th Floor, Voyager House, Chicago Avenue, Manchester Airport, Manchester, M90 3DQ
Activities: Other retail sale not in stores, stalls or markets
Officers: James Patrick Pochin, Secretary; William Mark Evans [1957] Director [Canadian]; John Andrew Gallemore [1969] Director/Accountant; Paul Jonathan Gedman [1981] Director/Retailer; Nicolas Joseph Michel Gheysens [1976] Director [French]; Edward Johan Koopman [1962] Director/Member of Executive Committee [Dutch]; Bernard Liautaud [1962] Director/Venture Capitalist [French]; Iain McDonald [1971] Director; Angus Monro [1949] Director; Matthew John Moulding [1972] Director; Dominic Patrick Murphy [1967] Director; Richard John Pennycook [1964] Director; James Patrick Pochin [1976] Director

The Hut.Com Limited
Incorporated: 15 January 2004 *Employees:* 1,568
Net Worth: £18,489,000 *Total Assets:* £363,550,016
Registered Office: 5th Floor, Voyager House, Chicago Avenue, Manchester Airport, Manchester, M90 3DQ
Activities: Other retail sale not in stores, stalls or markets
Parent: The Hut IHC Limited
Officers: James Patrick Pochin, Secretary; John Andrew Gallemore [1969] Director/Accountant; Paul Jonathan Gedman [1981] Director/Retailer; James Patrick Pochin [1976] Legal Director

Hutchinson Engineering Limited
Incorporated: 2 July 1976 *Employees:* 133
Net Worth: £4,040,213 *Total Assets:* £9,440,814
Registered Office: 9th Floor, 3 Hardman Street, Manchester, M3 3HF
Activities: Manufacture of metal structures and parts of structures
Major Shareholder: Dean Clark Drinkwater
Officers: Stephen John Adams, Secretary; Stephen John Adams [1972] Director/Quantity Surveyor; Dean Clark Drinkwater [1965] Director/Construction Manager; Mark Madigan [1981] Commercial Director

J R Hutt Holdings Limited
Incorporated: 15 May 2006 *Employees:* 181
Net Worth: £6,304,000 *Total Assets:* £25,333,000
Registered Office: Eastham House, Copse Road, Fleetwood, Lancs, FY7 7NY
Activities: Other business support service activities n.e.c.
Major Shareholder: John Robert Hutt
Officers: Colin Anthony Houlihan [1962] Director; Adam Miles Williams [1981] Director

Hutt Investments Limited
Incorporated: 28 February 2011 *Employees:* 181
Net Worth Deficit: £1,914,000 *Total Assets:* £36,457,000
Registered Office: Eastham House, Copse Road, Fleetwood, Lancs, FY7 7NY
Activities: Other business support service activities n.e.c.
Major Shareholder: John Robert Hutt
Officers: Rebecca Jane Clinch, Secretary; Rebecca Jane Clinch [1963] Director/Solicitor; Colin Anthony Houlihan [1962] Director; Jacqueline Hutt [1964] Director; John Robert Hutt [1967] Director; Adam Miles Williams [1981] Director

Huyton Asphalt Holdings Limited
Incorporated: 5 June 2015 *Employees:* 69
Net Worth: £5,901,773 *Total Assets:* £12,565,508
Registered Office: Merton Bank Road, Parr, St Helens, Merseyside, WA9 1HZ
Activities: Construction of roads and motorways
Major Shareholder: James Blennerhassett
Officers: James Blennerhassett [1980] Commercial Director

Huyton Asphalt Limited
Incorporated: 28 May 1971 *Employees:* 69
Net Worth: £9,086,211 *Total Assets:* £15,749,946
Registered Office: Merton Bank Road, Parr, St Helens, Merseyside, WA9 1HZ
Activities: Construction of roads and motorways
Major Shareholder: James Blennerhassett
Officers: Lyndsey Toni Lythgoe, Secretary/Road Surfacing; Francis Blennerhassett [1950] Director; James Blennerhassett [1980] Commercial Director; Edward Paul Murray [1955] Director/Surveyor

HVF Limited
Incorporated: 4 April 1988
Net Worth: £16,210,000 *Total Assets:* £16,269,000
Registered Office: Charterhall House, Charterhall Drive, Chester, CH88 3AN
Activities: Other business support service activities n.e.c.
Parent: ACL Autolease Holdings Limited
Officers: David Dermot Hennessey, Secretary; Craig Cameron McNaughton [1964] Director; Carol Ann Parkes [1966] Finance Director; Timothy Revell Porter [1965] Director/Banker

Hyde Aero Products Limited
Incorporated: 16 December 1991 *Employees:* 359
Net Worth: £34,399,236 *Total Assets:* £45,692,692
Registered Office: Stamford House, 185 Stamford Street, Stalybridge, Cheshire, SK15 1QZ
Activities: Other engineering activities
Officers: Mark Vernon Haslam, Secretary; David Vincent Cooper [1950] Director; Michael Ford [1945] Director/Accountant; Darrin John Grant [1966] Director; Anthony Brendan Hammond [1970] Director/Engineer; Mark Vernon Haslam [1968] Director; Paul Mellor [1973] Director/Engineer; Malcolm O'Connor [1965] Director/Accountant; Matthew Smallman [1971] Director/Accountant; Steve Turner [1966] Director/Engineer

Hyde Details Limited
Incorporated: 8 October 1991 *Employees:* 59
Net Worth: £9,309,322 *Total Assets:* £12,789,330
Registered Office: Stamford House, 185 Stamford Street, Stalybridge, Cheshire, SK15 1QZ
Activities: Other engineering activities
Officers: Mark Vernon Haslam, Secretary; Steven James Brown [1987] Director; David Vincent Cooper [1950] Director; Michael Ford [1945] Director/Accountant; Andrew Harding [1971] Director; Mark Vernon Haslam [1968] Director; Malcolm Oconnor [1965] Director

Hyde Group Holdings Limited
Incorporated: 13 March 2000 *Employees:* 809
Net Worth: £92,293,128 *Total Assets:* £117,070,736
Registered Office: Stamford House, 185 Stamford Street, Stalybridge, Cheshire, SK15 1QZ
Activities: Accounting and auditing activities
Officers: Mark Vernon Haslam, Secretary; David Vincent Cooper [1950] Director/Engineer; Michael Ford [1945] Director/Accountant; Darrin John Grant [1966] Director; Malcolm O'Connor [1965] Director/Engineer

Hyde Group Limited
Incorporated: 21 October 1981 *Employees:* 30
Net Worth: £13,262,941 *Total Assets:* £30,229,780
Registered Office: Stamford House, 185 Stamford Street, Stalybridge, Cheshire, SK15 1QZ
Activities: Other engineering activities
Officers: Mark Vernon Haslam, Secretary; Graham Atkinson [1965] Director; Philip Beard [1965] Director; David Vincent Cooper [1950] Director; Paul Cox [1978] Director/Engineer; Michael Ford [1945] Director/Accountant; Mark Vernon Haslam [1968] Director; Michael Lynch [1966] Director; Malcolm Oconnor [1965] Director

Hyde Group Tooling Limited
Incorporated: 14 August 2013 *Employees:* 31
Net Worth: £14,796,509 *Total Assets:* £30,044,060
Registered Office: Stamford House, 185 Stamford Street, Stalybridge, Cheshire, SK15 1QZ
Activities: Machining
Officers: Mark Vernon Haslam, Secretary; Michael Ford [1945] Director; Mark Vernon Haslam [1968] Director; Malcolm O'Connor [1965] Director

Hyde Industrial Holdings Limited
Incorporated: 3 April 1974 *Employees:* 785
Net Worth: £121,153,944 *Total Assets:* £145,986,624
Registered Office: Stamford House, 185 Stamford Street, Stalybridge, Cheshire, SK15 1QZ
Activities: Activities of financial services holding companies
Officers: Mark Vernon Haslam, Secretary; Michael Ford [1945] Director/Accountant; Gary John Grant [1945] Director

Hyde Investments Limited
Incorporated: 18 September 1984 *Employees:* 1
Net Worth: £19,866,840 *Total Assets:* £21,241,024
Registered Office: Stamford House, 185 Stamford Street, Stalybridge, Cheshire, SK15 1QZ
Activities: Buying and selling of own real estate
Officers: Mark Vernon Haslam, Secretary; Michael Ford [1945] Director/Accountant

Hydes' Brewery Limited
Incorporated: 27 December 1912 *Employees:* 614
Net Worth: £18,011,352 *Total Assets:* £41,063,348
Registered Office: The Beer Studio, 30 Kansas Avenue, Salford, M50 2GL
Activities: Manufacture of beer
Officers: Charles Adam Hyde, Secretary; Brian Bagnall [1961] Director; Christopher Thomas Howard Hopkins [1961] Director/Chief Executive; Charles Adam Hyde [1954] Director/Chartered Accountant; Paul David Jefferies [1965] Director/Brewer; Peter Johnson [1942] Director/Chartered Accountant; Richard Mainon [1973] Director/Financial Adviser; Adam James Mayers [1975] Finance Director

Hyperlast Limited
Incorporated: 11 July 1994
Net Worth: £71,192,000 *Total Assets:* £71,192,000
Registered Office: Station Road, Birch Vale, High Peak, Derbys, SK22 1BR
Activities: Manufacture of plastics in primary forms
Officers: Cathrine Anne Jenkins, Secretary; Eduardo Antonio Gadea [1961] Operations Director UK & Nordic [Spanish]; Andrew Michael Jones [1966] Commercial Director

Hyva (U.K.) Limited
Incorporated: 25 August 1982 *Employees:* 45
Net Worth: £541,189 *Total Assets:* £9,450,601
Registered Office: Unit 2 Prince Mead Place, Trafford Park, Manchester, M17 1PN
Activities: Other transportation support activities
Shareholder: Andrew Liu
Officers: Carol Kirkman, Secretary; Martin Gerrit Christiaan Kolkman [1971] Regional Director [Dutch]; Lukasz Michalewski [1973] Director/Regional Controller [Polish]; Michael Christopher Taylor [1964] Managing Director

I Care Extra Care Limited
Incorporated: 22 December 2004 *Employees:* 12
Net Worth: £670,997 *Total Assets:* £7,716,591
Registered Office: Building 3, Kincraig Business Park, Kincraig Road, Blackpool, Lancs, FY2 0PJ
Activities: Residential care activities for learning difficulties, mental health and substance abuse
Major Shareholder: Stephen Vaseekaran Emmanuel
Officers: Wanitha Kamani Emmanuel, Secretary; Stephen Vaseekaran Emmanuel [1960] Director [Canadian]

I-Paye Limited
Incorporated: 10 March 2005 *Employees:* 125
Net Worth: £20,221 *Total Assets:* £7,290,923
Registered Office: Unit 10 Tiger Court, Kings Business Park, Knowsley, Merseyside, L34 1BH
Activities: Other business support service activities n.e.c.
Officers: Paul Colin Hughes, Secretary; Paul Colin Hughes [1970] Director/Tax Consultant; Shaun McGrail [1969] Director/Accountant

I. W. T. Deeside Limited
Incorporated: 11 July 2003 *Employees:* 85
Net Worth: £4,699,894 *Total Assets:* £11,956,421
Registered Office: One St Peter's Square, Manchester, M2 3DE
Activities: Manufacture of trailers and semi-trailers
Major Shareholder: John Owen Williams
Officers: Carole Ann Williams, Secretary; John Owen Williams [1962] Director

I.C.S. (UK) Limited
Incorporated: 11 November 1998 *Employees:* 124
Net Worth: £3,693,922 *Total Assets:* £9,743,381
Registered Office: Neville Road, Bradford, W Yorks, BD4 8TU
Activities: Non-specialised wholesale of food, beverages and tobacco
Parent: ICS UK (Holdings) Limited
Officers: Ismail Bhamji, Secretary; Ismail Bhamji [1966] Director/Salesman; Siddick Bhamji [1961] Director/Salesman

Ibco Limited
Incorporated: 15 July 2004 *Employees:* 96
Net Worth: £1,045,651 *Total Assets:* £15,526,153
Registered Office: Hulme Hall Lane, Lord North Street, Miles Platting, Manchester, M40 8AD
Activities: Wholesale of fruit and vegetables
Officers: Bilal Ahmed, Secretary; Bilal Ahmed [1964] Director; Iqbal Ahmed [1956] Managing Director; Kamal Ahmed [1960] Director

IBI Group (UK) Limited
Incorporated: 2 February 1996 *Employees:* 230
Net Worth: £5,344,000 *Total Assets:* £12,515,000
Registered Office: One Didsbury Point, The Avenue, Didsbury, Manchester, M20 2EY
Activities: Information technology consultancy activities
Parent: IBI Holdco Limited
Officers: Steven Ivan Kresak, Secretary; Dyfan Howells [1983] Finance Director; Scott Earle Stewart [1949] Director/Engineer Consultant [Canadian]; David Maxwell Thom [1950] Director/Architect [Canadian]

Iceland Acquico Limited
Incorporated: 7 February 2012
Net Worth: £253,754,000 *Total Assets:* £1,444,409,984
Registered Office: Second Avenue, Deeside Industrial Park, Deeside, Flintshire, CH5 2NW
Activities: Activities of head offices
Parent: Iceland Midco Limited
Officers: Duncan Andrew Vaughan, Secretary; Tarsem Singh Dhaliwal [1963] Director; Sir Malcolm Conrad Walker [1946] Director/Chief Executive

Iceland BondCo PLC
Incorporated: 12 June 2014
Net Worth: £50,000 *Total Assets:* £808,902,016
Registered Office: Second Avenue, Deeside Industrial Park, Deeside, Flintshire, CH5 2NW
Activities: Financial management
Parent: Iceland VLNCo Limited
Officers: Duncan Andrew Vaughan, Secretary; Nigel Martin Broadhurst [1959] Director; Tarsem Singh Dhaliwal [1963] Director; Sir Malcolm Conrad Walker [1946] Director/Chief Executive

Iceland Foods Group Limited
Incorporated: 29 January 2007
Net Worth: £826,000 *Total Assets:* £959,476,992
Registered Office: Second Avenue, Deeside Industrial Park, Deeside, Flintshire, CH5 2NW
Activities: Activities of head offices
Parent: Iceland Acquico Limited
Officers: Duncan Andrew Vaughan, Secretary; Tarsem Singh Dhaliwal [1963] Director; Sir Malcolm Conrad Walker [1946] Director

Iceland Foods Limited
Incorporated: 10 April 1973 *Employees:* 21,750
Net Worth: £805,000,000 *Total Assets:* £2,783,600,128
Registered Office: Second Avenue, Deeside Industrial Park, Deeside, Flintshire, CH5 2NW
Activities: Retail sale in non-specialised stores with food, beverages or tobacco predominating
Parent: Iceland Midco Limited
Officers: Duncan Andrew Vaughan, Secretary; Nigel Martin Broadhurst [1959] Director; Tarsem Singh Dhaliwal [1963] Director; Sir Malcolm Conrad Walker [1946] Director; Richard Malcolm Walker [1980] Director

Iceland International Limited
Incorporated: 3 March 1998 *Employees:* 11
Net Worth: £20,043,000 *Total Assets:* £22,118,000
Registered Office: Second Avenue, Deeside Industrial Park, Deeside, Flintshire, CH5 2NW
Activities: Other retail sale of food in specialised stores
Parent: Iceland Midco Limited
Officers: Duncan Andrew Vaughan, Secretary; Tarsem Singh Dhaliwal [1963] Director; Sir Malcolm Conrad Walker [1946] Director

Iceland Manufacturing Limited
Incorporated: 15 April 1985 *Employees:* 232
Net Worth Deficit: £12,625,000 *Total Assets:* £21,394,000
Registered Office: Second Avenue, Deeside Industrial Park, Deeside, Flintshire, CH5 2NW
Activities: Manufacture of prepared meals and dishes
Parent: Loxton Frozen Foods Limited
Officers: Duncan Andrew Vaughan, Secretary; Tarsem Singh Dhaliwal [1963] Director; Sir Malcolm Conrad Walker [1946] Director

Iceland Midco Limited
Incorporated: 17 January 2012
Net Worth: £22,528,000 *Total Assets:* £1,908,524,032
Registered Office: Second Avenue, Deeside Industrial Park, Deeside, Flintshire, CH5 2NW
Activities: Activities of head offices
Parent: Iceland VLNCo Limited
Officers: Duncan Andrew Vaughan, Secretary; Tarsem Singh Dhaliwal [1963] Director; Sir Malcolm Conrad Walker [1946] Director/Chief Executive

Iceland Seafood Barraclough Ltd
Incorporated: 10 December 1980 *Employees:* 150
Net Worth: £2,750,011 *Total Assets:* £23,803,130
Registered Office: 35 Essex Street, Bradford, W Yorks, BD4 7PG
Activities: Wholesale of other food, including fish, crustaceans and molluscs
Shareholder: Mark Holyoake
Officers: Peter Hawkins, Secretary; Lee Mark Camfield [1967] Director/Chief Operating Officer; Helgi Anton Eiriksson [1967] Director/Chief Executive Officer [Icelander]; Peter Hawkins [1967] Managing Director; Allen John Melville Townsend [1965] Managing Director

Iceland Topco Limited
Incorporated: 8 December 2011 *Employees:* 13,862
Net Worth: £317,600,000 *Total Assets:* £1,723,299,968
Registered Office: Second Avenue, Deeside Industrial Park, Deeside, Flintshire, CH5 2NW
Activities: Activities of head offices
Officers: Duncan Andrew Vaughan, Secretary; Nigel Martin Broadhurst [1959] Director; Tarsem Singh Dhaliwal [1963] Director; John Andrew Gnodde [1965] Director [South African]; Rolf Mark Hartmann [1974] Director/Investment Manager [South African]; Christopher Stefan Seabrooke [1953] Director [South African]; Sir Malcolm Conrad Walker [1946] Director/Chief Executive; Richard Malcolm Walker [1980] Director; Dr Christoffel Hendrik Wiese [1941] Director/Chairman [South African]

Iceland Vlnco Limited
Incorporated: 7 February 2012
Net Worth: £546,809,024 *Total Assets:* £891,241,024
Registered Office: Second Avenue, Deeside Industrial Park, Deeside, Flintshire, CH5 2NW
Activities: Activities of head offices
Parent: Iceland Topco Limited
Officers: Duncan Andrew Vaughan, Secretary; Tarsem Singh Dhaliwal [1963] Director; Sir Malcolm Conrad Walker [1946] Director/Chief Executive

Icknield Holdings Limited
Incorporated: 10 June 2016
Net Worth Deficit: £46,455 *Total Assets:* £7,560,886
Registered Office: c/o Grant Thornton UK LLP, 4 Hardman Square, Spinningfields, Manchester, M3 3EB
Activities: Non-trading company
Shareholders: Neil Mark Ostrer; Alison Ostrer
Officers: Alison Ostrer [1959] Director; Neil Mark Ostrer [1958] Director/Asset Manager

Icon Health & Fitness (Holdings) Limited
Incorporated: 24 October 1994
Net Worth Deficit: £3,824,829 *Total Assets:* £25,592,130
Registered Office: 3rd Floor, 1 Ashley Road, Altrincham, Cheshire, WA14 2DT
Activities: Other service activities n.e.c.
Officers: John McHale [1975] Director/Financial Controller; Everett Smith [1955] Director [American]

Icon Health and Fitness Limited
Incorporated: 29 November 1994 *Employees:* 18
Net Worth: £10,851,946 *Total Assets:* £16,064,113
Registered Office: 3rd Floor, 1 Ashley Road, Altrincham, Cheshire, WA14 2DT
Activities: Other service activities n.e.c.
Parent: Icon Health & Fitness (Holdings) Limited
Officers: Renaud Grout [1964] Director [French]; Everett Smith [1955] Director [American]

Icona Homes Limited
Incorporated: 3 October 2007
Registered Office: 2nd Floor, 9 Portland Street, Manchester, M1 3BE
Activities: Development of building projects
Shareholder: Waqar Ahmed
Officers: Waqar Ahmed, Secretary; Farhat Ahmed [1977] Commercial Director; Waqar Ahmed [1969] Director

Iconichem Widnes Limited
Incorporated: 23 October 2015 *Employees:* 58
Net Worth: £11,969,915 *Total Assets:* £23,985,756
Registered Office: Moss Bank Road, Widnes, Cheshire, WA8 0RU
Activities: Manufacture of other chemical products n.e.c.
Parent: Iconichem Group Limited
Officers: Francis Gary Jones, Secretary; Andrew William Garner [1964] Director/Chairman; Francis Gary Jones [1968] Director/Chartered Accountant; Trevor Middleton [1957] Director

Iconix MENA Ltd
Incorporated: 11 December 2014 *Employees:* 4
Net Worth: £28,615,416 *Total Assets:* £30,907,452
Registered Office: 29-31 Dale Street, Manchester, M1 1EY
Activities: Other professional, scientific and technical activities n.e.c.
Shareholders: Iconix Brand Group, Inc.; Global Brands Group Holding Limited
Officers: William Paul Burkhardt [1963] Director/Executive Vice President [American]; David Kevin Jones [1969] Director [American]; Jared Marshall Margolis [1974] Director/Executive VP of Business Development and Licensing [American]; Jason Rabin [1970] Director [American]

Icopal Limited
Incorporated: 21 February 1990 *Employees:* 132
Net Worth: £11,623,000 *Total Assets:* £26,687,000
Registered Office: Icopal Limited, Barton Dock Road, Stretford, Manchester, M32 0YL
Activities: Production of abrasive products
Parent: BMI Group Holdings UK Limited
Officers: Jason John Bradley [1963] Director/Accountant; Andrew John Dennis [1965] Managing Director; Alfons Horn [1970] Managing Director [German]; Klaus Sonne Ravn [1966] Finance Director [Danish]

ICR (Investment 1) Limited
Incorporated: 25 February 2014
Net Worth: £727,416 *Total Assets:* £75,326,472
Registered Office: Unit 10 Westmorland Business Park, Gilthwaiterigg Lane, Kendal, Cumbria, LA9 6NS
Activities: Activities of head offices
Parent: ICR Integrity (Holdings) Limited
Officers: William John Bayliss [1962] Director; Andrew Bruce [1958] Director; Mark Ritchie [1979] Finance Director

ICR (Investment 2) Limited
Incorporated: 25 February 2014 *Employees:* 2
Net Worth Deficit: £11,037 *Total Assets:* £74,709,280
Registered Office: Unit 10 Westmorland Business Park, Gilthwaiterigg Lane, Kendal, Cumbria, LA9 6NS
Activities: Activities of head offices
Parent: ICR (Investment 1) Limited
Officers: William John Bayliss [1962] Director; Mark Ritchie [1979] Finance Director

ICR Integrity (Group) Limited
Incorporated: 27 February 2014 *Employees:* 3
Net Worth Deficit: £25,851,652 *Total Assets:* £94,139,320
Registered Office: Unit 10 Westmorland Business Park, Gilthwaiterigg Lane, Kendal, Cumbria, LA9 6NS
Activities: Activities of head offices
Parent: ICR (Investment 2) Limited
Officers: William John Bayliss [1962] Director; Mark Ritchie [1979] Finance Director

ICR Integrity (Holdings) Limited
Incorporated: 25 February 2014 *Employees:* 165
Net Worth Deficit: £52,800,032 *Total Assets:* £62,776,164
Registered Office: Unit 10 Westmorland Business Park, Gilthwaiterigg Lane, Kendal, Cumbria, LA9 6NS
Activities: Activities of head offices
Shareholder: Graphite Capital General Partner VIII LLP
Officers: William John Bayliss [1962] Director; Maurice McBride [1954] Director; William George Rennie [1966] Director; Mark Ritchie [1979] Finance Director

ICR Integrity Limited
Incorporated: 13 April 2011 *Employees:* 4
Net Worth Deficit: £16,707,989 *Total Assets:* £47,525,648
Registered Office: Unit 10 Westmorland Business Park, Gilthwaiterigg Lane, Kendal, Cumbria, LA9 6NS
Activities: Activities of head offices
Parent: ICR Integrity (Group) Limited
Officers: William John Bayliss [1962] Director; Mark Ritchie [1979] Finance Director

IDH Acquisitions Limited
Incorporated: 19 December 2005
Net Worth: £4,334,000 *Total Assets:* £287,288,992
Registered Office: Europa House, Europa Trading Estate, Stoneclough Road, Kearsley, Manchester, M26 1GG
Activities: Non-trading company
Parent: IDH Group Limited
Officers: Leo Damian Carroll, Secretary; Clifford Gwyn Davies [1966] Director; Sharon Patricia Letters [1975] Clinical Director; Steven Andrew Melton [1962] Managing Director - Mydentist; Bernard Moroney [1953] Clinical Director; Manish Prasad [1972] Clinical Director Tom Riall [1960] Director; Mohammed Omar Shafi Khan [1974] Director/Chief Financial Officer; Krista Nyree Whitley [1970] Clinical Director

IDH Finance PLC
Incorporated: 7 May 2013
Net Worth: £1,234,000 *Total Assets:* £557,081,024
Registered Office: Europa House, Europa Trading Estate, Stoneclough Road, Kearsley, Manchester, M26 1GG
Activities: Financial intermediation not elsewhere classified
Parent: Turnstone Midco 2 Limited
Officers: Leo Damian Carroll, Secretary; Jean Michel Claude Bonnavion [1971] Director/Investment Manager [French]; Andrew Richard Burgess [1964] Director/Investment Professional; Karthic Jayaraman [1975] Director/Investment Professional; Tom Riall [1960] Director; Mohammed Omar Shafi Khan [1974] Director/Chief Financial Officer

IDH Group Limited
Incorporated: 19 December 2005
Net Worth: £21,200,000 *Total Assets:* £23,745,000
Registered Office: Europa House, Europa Trading Estate, Stoneclough Road, Kearsley, Manchester, M26 1GG
Activities: Non-trading company
Parent: Turnstone Bidco 1 Limited
Officers: Leo Damian Carroll, Secretary; Steven Andrew Melton [1962] Managing Director - Mydentist; Tom Riall [1960] Director; Mohammed Omar Shafi Khan [1974] Director/Chief Financial Officer; Krista Nyree Whitley [1970] Clinical Director

IDH Limited
Incorporated: 11 November 1929 *Employees:* 951
Net Worth: £7,119,000 *Total Assets:* £66,434,000
Registered Office: Europa House, Europa Trading Estate, Stoneclough Road, Kearsley, Manchester, M26 1GG
Activities: Dental practice activities
Parent: IDH Acquisitions Limited
Officers: Leo Damian Carroll, Secretary; Clifford Gwyn Davies [1966] Clinical Director; Bernard Moroney [1953] Clinical Director; Manish Prasad [1972] Clinical Director; Tom Riall [1960] Director; Mohammed Omar Shafi Khan [1974] Director/Chief Financial Officer; Krista Nyree Whitley [1970] Clinical Director

IESA A & D Limited
Incorporated: 18 December 2002 *Employees:* 39
Net Worth: £2,763,000 *Total Assets:* £17,233,000
Registered Office: IESA Works, Daten Park, Birchwood, Warrington, Cheshire, WA3 6UT
Activities: Other professional, scientific and technical activities n.e.c.
Parent: IESA A & D Group Limited
Officers: Deborah Catherine Ann Bowring [1963] Director; David John Egan [1967] Finance Director; Vanessa Elizabeth Gough [1967] Director/Group Financial Controller; Ian Peter Haslegrave [1968] Director/Group General Counsel; Andrew Bell Perry [1976] Director

IESA Holdings Limited
Incorporated: 8 August 2007 *Employees:* 392
Net Worth: £4,728,000 *Total Assets:* £73,979,000
Registered Office: IESA Works, Daten Park, Birchwood, Warrington, Cheshire, WA3 6UT
Activities: Activities of head offices
Parent: Aghoco 1079 Limited
Officers: David John Egan [1967] Finance Director; Vanessa Elizabeth Gough [1967] Director/Group Financial Controller; Andrew Bell Perry [1976] Commercial Director

IESA Limited
Incorporated: 28 March 2001 *Employees:* 377
Net Worth: £2,851,000 *Total Assets:* £70,339,000
Registered Office: IESA Works, Daten Park, Birchwood, Warrington, Cheshire, WA3 6UT
Activities: Wholesale of other intermediate products
Parent: IESA Holdings Limited
Officers: Andrew Bell Perry, Secretary; Deborah Catherine Ann Bowring [1963] Director; David John Egan [1967] Finance Director; Vanessa Elizabeth Gough [1967] Director/Group Financial Controller; Ian Peter Haslegrave [1968] Director/Group General Counsel; Andrew Bell Perry [1976] Finance Director

IFE Services Limited
Incorporated: 30 June 1997 *Employees:* 85
Net Worth: £15,049,210 *Total Assets:* £38,443,932
Registered Office: 3rd Floor, 1 Ashley Road, Altrincham, Cheshire, WA14 2DT
Activities: Motion picture distribution activities
Parent: IFE Holdings Limited
Officers: Paul Flowerday [1971] Director; Daniel Girard [1971] Director/VP Special Projects (Finance) [Canadian]

IFG Drake Limited
Incorporated: 15 May 1945 *Employees:* 106
Net Worth: £12,691,000 *Total Assets:* £16,570,000
Registered Office: Old Mills, Drighlington, Bradford, W Yorks, BD11 1BY
Activities: Manufacture of man-made fibres
Officers: Kathryn Anne Davenport, Secretary; John Olof Hager [1964] Managing Director [Swedish]; Stephen O'Neil [1961] Director; Geoffrey Rostron [1957] Director/Sales Manager

Iforce Limited
Incorporated: 30 September 1997 *Employees:* 962
Net Worth: £9,612,000 *Total Assets:* £29,199,000
Registered Office: Stretton Green Distribution Park, Langford Way, Appleton, Warrington, Cheshire, WA4 4TQ
Activities: Packaging activities
Parent: Iforce Group Limited
Officers: Elaine Williams, Secretary; Sebastien Robert Desreumaux [1972] Director [French]; Damien Harte [1956] Director [Irish]; Alexander Laffey [1961] Director; Rupert Henry Conquest Nichols [1949] Director

IGE Dollar Treasury Services
Incorporated: 7 July 1919
Net Worth: £122,845,712 *Total Assets:* £1,960,377,856
Registered Office: 3rd Floor, 1 Ashley Road, Altrincham, Cheshire, WA14 2DT
Activities: Financial intermediation not elsewhere classified
Parent: International General Electric (U.S.A.)
Officers: Andrew Thomas Peter Budge [1973] Director/Chartered Accountant; Akhlesh Prasad Mathur [1972] Director/Chartered Accountant

IGE Euro Treasury Services
Incorporated: 15 March 1995
Net Worth: £9,856,691 *Total Assets:* £137,367,680
Registered Office: 3rd Floor, 1 Ashley Road, Altrincham, Cheshire, WA14 2DT
Activities: Banks
Parent: International General Electric (U.S.A.)
Officers: Andrew Thomas Peter Budge [1973] Director/Chartered Accountant; Akhlesh Prasad Mathur [1972] Director/Chartered Accountant

IGE USA Group
Incorporated: 5 May 1995
Net Worth: £209,703,008 *Total Assets:* £267,040,000
Registered Office: 3rd Floor, 1 Ashley Road, Altrincham, Cheshire, WA14 2DT
Activities: Activities of other holding companies n.e.c.
Parent: IGE USA Holdings
Officers: Andrew Thomas Peter Budge [1973] Director/Chartered Accountant; Akhlesh Prasad Mathur [1972] Director/Chartered Accountant

IGE USA Holdings
Incorporated: 16 July 2015
Net Worth: £1,198,011,008 *Total Assets:* £1,198,046,720
Registered Office: 3rd Floor, 1 Ashley Road, Altrincham, Cheshire, WA14 2DT
Activities: Activities of other holding companies n.e.c.
Parent: General Electric Company
Officers: Andrew Thomas Peter Budge [1973] Director/Chartered Accountant; Akhlesh Prasad Mathur [1972] Director/Chartered Accountant

IGE USA Investments
Incorporated: 23 September 1996
Net Worth: £17,592,315,904 *Total Assets:* £17,594,382,336
Registered Office: 3rd Floor, 1 Ashley Road, Altrincham, Cheshire, WA14 2DT
Activities: Activities of head offices
Parent: GE Capital International Holdings Limited
Officers: Jonathan Lawrence John Gatt [1981] Director/FP&A Leader [Maltese]; Norris Andrew Geldard [1965] Director/Accountant; Paul Stewart Girling [1978] Director; Max Jessernigg [1974] Director/Risk Manager [Austrian/Swiss]

Iggesund Paperboard (Workington) Limited
Incorporated: 4 October 1902 *Employees:* 403
Net Worth: £151,208,992 *Total Assets:* £246,662,000
Registered Office: Iggesund Paperboard, Siddick, Workington, Cumbria, CA14 1JX
Activities: Manufacture of paper and paperboard
Parent: Holmen UK Ltd
Officers: Ulf Lennart Lofgren, Finance Director [Swedish]; Dr Ian Black [1967] Director/Head of Customer Service Development Centre; Lars Gunnar Ericson [1959] Director [Swedish]; Anders Jernhall [1970] Director/CFO - Holmen Paper [Swedish]; Ulf Lennart Lofgren [1969] Finance Director [Swedish]; Anders Olsson [1959] Finance Director [Swedish]; Daniel Peltonen [1971] Director/Head of Business Area [Finnish]; Nils Ringborg [1958] Director/CEO and President [Swedish]; Torsten Stjernschantz [1954] Director/Business Manager [Finnish]

IGT (UK 1) Limited
Incorporated: 21 July 2003 *Employees:* 22
Net Worth: £3,687,000 *Total Assets:* £11,936,000
Registered Office: Quay West, Trafford Wharf Road, Trafford Park, Manchester, M17 1HH
Activities: Gambling and betting activities
Parent: International Game Technology PLC
Officers: Matthew William Hughes [1969] Director [American]; Paul Anthony Mears [1966] Director; Anthony Lavaz Watson [1963] Director/Vice President [American]

IGT-UK Gaming Limited
Incorporated: 15 October 2002 *Employees:* 38
Net Worth Deficit: £648,000 *Total Assets:* £20,853,000
Registered Office: Quay West, Trafford Wharf Road, Trafford Park, Manchester, M17 1HH
Activities: Other business support service activities n.e.c.
Parent: IGT-UK Group Limited
Officers: Matthew William Hughes [1969] Director [American]; Paul Anthony Mears [1966] Director; Anthony Lavaz Watson [1963] Director/Vice President [American]

IGT-UK Group Limited
Incorporated: 19 August 2005
Net Worth: £1,673,000 *Total Assets:* £6,804,000
Registered Office: Quay West, Trafford Wharf Road, Trafford Park, Manchester, M17 1HH
Activities: Other manufacturing n.e.c.
Parent: International Game Technology PLC
Officers: Matthew William Hughes [1969] Director [American]; Paul Anthony Mears [1966] Director; Anthony Lavaz Watson [1963] Director/Vice President [American]

IKO Holdings PLC
Incorporated: 24 November 1989 *Employees:* 6
Net Worth: £39,417,000 *Total Assets:* £41,493,000
Registered Office: Appley Lane North, Appley Bridge, Wigan, Lancs, WN6 9AB
Activities: Activities of production holding companies
Parent: IKO UK Limited
Officers: Anthony Carlyle [1967] Commercial Director; Frank Hautman [1966] Director [Belgian]; Hartley Michael Koschitzky [1965] Director [Canadian]; Jonathan Koschitzky [1969] Director [Canadian]; Saul Koschitzky [1934] Director/President [Canadian]; David Patrick Maginnis [1963] Director

IKO PLC
Incorporated: 13 January 1992 *Employees:* 314
Net Worth: £32,657,000 *Total Assets:* £66,618,000
Registered Office: Appley Lane North, Appley Bridge, Wigan, Lancs, WN6 9AB
Activities: Other manufacturing n.e.c.
Parent: IKO Holdings PLC
Officers: Anthony Carlyle [1967] Director; Frank Hautman [1966] Director [Belgian]; Hartley Michael Koschitzky [1965] Director [Canadian]; Jonathan Koschitzky [1969] Director [Canadian]

IKO U.K. Limited
Incorporated: 13 December 1999 *Employees:* 1,060
Net Worth: £113,789,000 *Total Assets:* £196,954,000
Registered Office: Appley Lane North, Appley Bridge, Wigan, Lancs, WN6 9AB
Activities: Activities of production holding companies
Officers: Anthony Carlyle [1967] Director; Frank Hautman [1966] Director [Belgian]; Hartley Michael Koschitzky [1965] Director [Canadian]; Jonathan Koschitzky [1969] Director [Canadian]

Ikon Hardware Limited
Incorporated: 19 October 2009 *Employees:* 40
Net Worth: £2,191,555 *Total Assets:* £13,243,334
Registered Office: Sterling House, 3 Wavell Drive, Rosehill Industrial Estate, Carlisle, Cumbria, CA1 2SA
Activities: Other letting and operating of own or leased real estate
Major Shareholder: Robin George Graham
Officers: John Little, Secretary; Robin George Graham [1957] Director

Ikonic Technology Limited
Incorporated: 19 November 2008 *Employees:* 58
Net Worth: £6,386,688 *Total Assets:* £15,853,839
Registered Office: P16 Parklands, Heywood Distribution Park, Heywood, Lancs, OL10 2TT
Activities: Other information technology service activities
Shareholders: Jonathan Newman; Antony Richard Levene
Officers: Joshua David Goldstone [1981] Director; Anthony Richard Levene [1975] Director; Jonathan Antoni Newman [1974] Director; Christopher James Perry [1975] Managing Director

Illingworth Ingham (Manchester) Limited
Incorporated: 31 October 1929 *Employees:* 118
Net Worth: £5,802,763 *Total Assets:* £9,628,376
Registered Office: Village Way, Trafford Park, Manchester, M17 1AD
Activities: Sawmilling and planing of wood
Major Shareholder: Simon John Graveley
Officers: David Jarvis, Secretary; Colette Hazel Ford [1943] Director; Ralfe Graveley [1939] Director; Simon John Graveley [1962] Director/Chairman; Ian Keith Rawlings [1967] Director

Imaan Healthcare Limited
Incorporated: 14 June 2012 *Employees:* 255
Net Worth: £4,141,998 *Total Assets:* £11,138,305
Registered Office: Unit 18 Neills Road, Bold Industrial Park, Bold, St Helens, Merseyside, WA9 4TU
Activities: Dispensing chemist in specialised stores
Officers: Tahir Malik [1977] Director/Pharmacist; Zubair Malik [1975] Director/Pharmacist

IMCI (Services) Limited
Incorporated: 13 April 1987 *Employees:* 9
Net Worth: £7,470,052 *Total Assets:* £11,317,072
Registered Office: Progress House, Newby Road, Hazel Grove, Stockport, Cheshire, SK7 5DA
Activities: Other business support service activities n.e.c.
Shareholders: Charbel Youssef Faddoul; Avril Mairead O'Hanlon
Officers: Charbel Youssef Faddoul, Secretary; Avril Mairead O'Hanlon [1958] Director [Irish]

Impact Development Training International Limited
Incorporated: 27 November 2000
Net Worth: £6,099,142 *Total Assets:* £17,808,576
Registered Office: Cragwood House, Windermere, Cumbria, LA23 1LQ
Activities: Other service activities n.e.c.
Major Shareholder: David Hayden Williams
Officers: Robert Bradbury, Secretary; Adele Esther Blakebrough [1961] Director; Robert Bradbury [1956] Director/Chartered Accountant; Susan Jane Hunt [1959] Director; Derry John Newman [1957] Director; Thomas William Cyril Plimmer [1947] Director; Ann Elizabeth Williams [1957] Director; David Hayden Williams [1956] Director/Outdoor Training Manager

Impact Development Training Ltd.
Incorporated: 5 March 1990 *Employees:* 142
Net Worth: £3,888,965 *Total Assets:* £8,406,503
Registered Office: Cragwood House, Windermere, Cumbria, LA23 1LQ
Activities: Other service activities n.e.c.
Parent: Impact Development Training International Limited
Officers: Robert Bradbury, Secretary; Jeremy Benton [1973] Director; David Hayden Williams [1956] Director/Outdoor Training Manager

Imperial Corporate Events Ltd
Incorporated: 25 March 2002 *Employees:* 75
Net Worth: £1,776,116 *Total Assets:* £6,980,066
Registered Office: Bank House, Market Square, Congleton, Cheshire, CW12 1ET
Activities: Other sports activities
Shareholders: Glenn Michel Foston; Peter Leonard Frisby; Robert John Poutch
Officers: Michelle Tracy Shore, Secretary/Director; Glenn Michel Foston [1968] Director/General Manager; Peter Leonard Frisby [1973] Director; Amanda Hope-Richardson [1961] Director; Robert John Poutch [1978] Director

Imperial Furniture Group Limited
Incorporated: 12 January 2006 *Employees:* 127
Net Worth: £4,353,775 *Total Assets:* £7,831,795
Registered Office: The Exchange, 5 Bank Street, Bury, Lancs, BL9 0DN
Activities: Activities of head offices
Major Shareholder: Jeremy Bennett
Officers: Lindsay Bennett, Secretary; Jeremy Bennett [1970] Director; Lindsay Bennett [1982] Managing Director

Imperial Office Furniture Ltd
Incorporated: 14 October 1999 *Employees:* 133
Net Worth: £3,964,003 *Total Assets:* £7,711,690
Registered Office: The Exchange, 5 Bank Street, Bury, Lancs, BL9 0DN
Activities: Manufacture of office and shop furniture
Parent: Imperial Furniture Group Limited
Officers: Lindsay Bennett, Secretary; Richard Thomas Arnold [1962] Sales Director; Jeremy Bennett [1970] Director; Lindsay Bennett [1982] Finance Director

Imtech Engineering Services North Ltd
Incorporated: 12 November 1982
Net Worth Deficit: £118,000 *Total Assets:* £14,830,000
Registered Office: Calder House, St Georges Park, Kirkham, Preston, Lancs, PR4 2DZ
Activities: Electrical installation
Shareholders: EDF Energy Services Limited; ESSCI Engineering Services Limited
Officers: Michael Booth [1974] Director/Accountant; Neil Geoffrey Evans [1972] Director/Accountant; Anita Jean McFarlane [1973] Commercial Director

In at The Side Limited
Incorporated: 10 April 2014
Net Worth: £9,178,004 *Total Assets:* £9,296,717
Registered Office: Unit 3 Rugby Park, Battersea Road, Heaton Mersey, Stockport, Cheshire, SK4 3EB
Activities: Other professional, scientific and technical activities n.e.c.
Shareholders: Philip James Chong; Katharine Rachel Chong
Officers: Philip James Chong, Secretary; Joey Chong [2002] Director; Philip James Chong [1962] Director; Samuel James Chong [2000] Director/Administrator

In Touch with Bricks Limited
Incorporated: 8 March 1990 *Employees:* 24
Net Worth: £4,021,610 *Total Assets:* £7,958,293
Registered Office: Waters Green House, Sunderland Street, Waters Green, Macclesfield, Cheshire, SK11 6LF
Activities: Agents involved in the sale of timber and building materials
Shareholders: Barry Stephen Greening; Tracey Adele Greening
Officers: Barry Stephen Greening, Secretary/Managing Director; Barry Stephen Greening [1962] Managing Director; Tracey Adele Greening [1963] Director/Financial Administrator

In Vino Bidco Limited
Incorporated: 7 February 2013
Net Worth: £6,392,794 *Total Assets:* £27,959,740
Registered Office: Boundary House, Cheadle Point, Cheadle, Cheshire, SK8 2GG
Activities: Wholesale of wine, beer, spirits and other alcoholic beverages
Parent: In Vino Limited
Officers: Michael Joseph Moriarty, Secretary; Claudio Manera [1963] Director [Italian]; Michael Joseph Moriarty [1965] Director; Dennis Whiteley [1961] Director

In Vino Limited
Incorporated: 7 February 2013 *Employees:* 147
Net Worth: £14,220,430 *Total Assets:* £74,332,672
Registered Office: Boundary House, Cheadle Point, Cheadle, Cheshire, SK8 2GG
Activities: Wholesale of wine, beer, spirits and other alcoholic beverages
Shareholders: Dennis Whiteley; Donna Whiteley; Araldica Castelvero S.C.A.
Officers: Michael Joseph Moriarty, Secretary; Claudio Manera [1963] Director [Italian]; Michael Joseph Moriarty [1965] Director; Dennis Whiteley [1961] Director

Inception Point Systems Ltd
Incorporated: 25 July 2012 *Employees:* 2
Net Worth: £45,000,868 *Total Assets:* £45,002,456
Registered Office: Emerson Business Centre, Regent House, Heaton Lane, Stockport, Cheshire, SK4 1BS
Activities: Other professional, scientific and technical activities n.e.c.
Officers: Tzung Liang Lin [1964] Director/Chairman of VTC [Taiwanese]; Michael James Sheehan [1968] Director/CEO of VTC [American]

Inciner8 Holdings Limited
Incorporated: 17 January 2013
Net Worth: £11,841,000 *Total Assets:* £12,000,954
Registered Office: Unit 2 Canning Road Industrial Estate, Canning Road, Southport, Merseyside, PR9 7SN
Activities: Manufacture of other special-purpose machinery n.e.c.
Major Shareholder: Vincent Paul Ferguson
Officers: Vincent Paul Ferguson [1964] Director

Incommunities Group Limited
Incorporated: 22 May 2001 *Employees:* 998
Net Worth: £113,690,000 *Total Assets:* £445,289,984
Registered Office: The Quays, Victoria Street, Shipley, W Yorks, BD17 7BN
Activities: Other accommodation
Officers: Robert Terence Ward, Secretary; Kim Hilary Brear [1960] Assistant Director, Homes & Neighbourhoods; Ian Michael Cornelius [1969] Commercial Director; Judith Ann Crowther [1951] Director/Retired; Tansy Jane Hepton [1960] Director/Retired; Generaldine Lesley Howley [1957] Director/Chief Executive; Andrew James Kitchingman [1964] Finance Director; Janet Evelynne Ormondroyd [1954] Director/Retired Chief Executive; Keith Ramsay [1961] Director/Management Consultant; Matthew Alan Walker [1967] Director/Chief Executive; Simon Wilson [1971] Director/Chief Executive

Incorez Limited
Incorporated: 3 July 1986 *Employees:* 48
Net Worth: £2,598,533 *Total Assets:* £7,718,884
Registered Office: Sika House, Miller Street, Preston, Lancs, PR1 1EA
Activities: Manufacture of other chemical products n.e.c.
Parent: Sika AG
Officers: Daniel Emil Lang [1971] Director/Head Finance & Controlling Region EMEA [Swiss]; Paul Schuler [1955] Director/Head of Region EMEA [Swiss]

Incorporate Travel Management Limited
Incorporated: 20 March 2013 *Employees:* 40
Net Worth Deficit: £23,410 *Total Assets:* £8,471,241
Registered Office: 4th Floor, 2 Commercial Street, Manchester, M15 4RQ
Activities: Other service activities n.e.c.
Officers: Michael James Fletcher [1974] Director/Chartered Accountant; William Boyd Tannahill [1979] Director

Indace Limited
Incorporated: 30 September 1987 *Employees:* 3
Net Worth: £6,279,742 *Total Assets:* £6,698,219
Registered Office: 7-9 St Marys Place, Bury, Lancs, BL9 0DZ
Activities: Wholesale of chemical products
Major Shareholder: Asha Gautam Rawat
Officers: Gautam Rawat, Secretary; Asha Rawat [1952] Director/Service [Indian]; Gautam Rawat [1954] Director/Self Employed

Indespension Ltd
Incorporated: 23 April 1987 *Employees:* 186
Net Worth: £4,157,000 *Total Assets:* £13,801,000
Registered Office: Paragon Business Park, Chorley New Road, Horwich, Bolton, Lancs, BL6 6HG
Activities: Manufacture of other fabricated metal products n.e.c.
Parent: DRA Limited
Officers: Rosalynde Michelle Graham, Secretary; Paul Bonar [1970] Branch Director; Anthony Edmund Graham [1967] Joint Managing Director; Douglas Graham [1946] Director; Rosalynde Michelle Graham [1969] Operations Director; Lee Mangnall [1960] Technical Director; Heidi Maria Elizabeth Riley [1959] Finance Director; Steven Sadler [1968] Purchasing Director

Individual Restaurant Company Limited
Incorporated: 29 June 2000 *Employees:* 4
Net Worth: £8,324,000 *Total Assets:* £9,324,000
Registered Office: 4th Floor, Ridgefield House, 14 John Dalton Street, Manchester, M2 6JR
Activities: Licenced restaurants
Officers: Peter David McCulloch, Secretary; Tarsem Singh Dhaliwal [1963] Finance Director; Vernon Lord [1966] Director; Sir Malcolm Conrad Walker [1946] Director/Chief Executive; Steven John Walker [1970] Director

Industrial Scientific Holdings UK Ltd
Incorporated: 18 October 2016
Net Worth: £18,853,742 *Total Assets:* £18,863,642
Registered Office: Suite 1, Bollin House, Bollin Walk, Wilmslow, Cheshire, SK9 1DP
Activities: Activities of other holding companies n.e.c.
Officers: Todd Richard Lindemuth [1964] Director/Vice President, Finance & Chief Financial Officer [American]; Justin Kent McElhattan [1972] Director/President and Chief Executive Officer [American]

Indutrade UK Limited
Incorporated: 30 October 2014 *Employees:* 1
Net Worth: £3,840,982 *Total Assets:* £60,359,708
Registered Office: Ellard House, Floats Road, Roundthorn Industrial Estate, Wythenshawe, Manchester, M23 9WB
Activities: Activities of production holding companies
Parent: Indutrade AB
Officers: Geoffrey Charles Simonds, Secretary; Bo Gerhard Annvik [1965] Director [Swedish]; Peter Ian Rowlands [1968] Managing Director

Inenco Group Limited
Incorporated: 24 October 1989 *Employees:* 428
Net Worth: £51,929,000 *Total Assets:* £68,397,000
Registered Office: Ribble House, Ballam Road, Lytham St Annes, Lancs, FY8 4TS
Activities: Management consultancy activities other than financial management
Parent: Inenco Limited
Officers: Caroline Whalley-Hunter, Secretary; Bernard Coady [1979] Director [Australian]; Gareth James Knight [1978] Director; Gary Martin Stokes [1961] Director/Chief Executive; Caroline Whalley-Hunter [1959] Director/Chief Financial Officer

INEOS Enterprises Group Limited
Incorporated: 5 March 2003 *Employees:* 354
Net Worth: £93,400,000 *Total Assets:* £238,300,000
Registered Office: P O Box 9, Runcorn Site HQ, South Parade, Runcorn, Cheshire, WA7 4JE
Activities: Manufacture of other inorganic basic chemicals
Parent: INEOS Enterprises Holdings Limited
Officers: David John Wright Rey, Secretary; Andrew Brown [1981] Director/Chartered Accountant; Thomas Patrick Crotty [1956] Director [Irish]; John Allan Nicolson [1968] HR Director; Anthony White [1961] Director/Accountant

INEOS Enterprises Holdings Limited
Incorporated: 26 November 2014 *Employees:* 1,081
Net Worth: £175,894,336 *Total Assets:* £493,921,120
Registered Office: P O Box 9, Enterprises House, South Parade, Runcorn, Cheshire, WA7 4JE
Activities: Activities of head offices
Major Shareholder: James Arthur Ratcliffe
Officers: David John Wright Rey, Secretary; Andrew Brown [1981] Director; John Allan Nicolson [1968] HR Director; Anthony White [1961] Director

INEOS Fluor Holdings Limited
Incorporated: 9 August 2000
Net Worth Deficit: £259,781,328 *Total Assets:* £67,920,928
Registered Office: P O Box 9, Runcorn Site HQ, South Parade, Runcorn, Cheshire, WA7 4JE
Activities: Activities of head offices
Parent: INEOS Investments International Limited
Officers: David John Wright Rey, Secretary; Andrew Brown [1981] Director/Chartered Accountant; Jonathan Frank Ginns [1973] Director/Legal Manager; Anthony White [1961] Director/Accountant

INEOS Fluor Limited
Incorporated: 26 July 2000
Net Worth: £143,766,000 *Total Assets:* £199,824,000
Registered Office: P O Box 9, Runcorn Site HQ, South Parade, Runcorn, Cheshire, WA7 4JE
Activities: Manufacture of other inorganic basic chemicals
Parent: INEOS Fluor Holdings Limited
Officers: David John Wright Rey, Secretary; Yasin Stanley Ali [1974] Director/Company Secretary; Andrew Brown [1981] Director/Chartered Accountant; Dr Jill Christine Dolan [1960] Director/Manager; Jonathan Frank Ginns [1973] Director/Legal Manager; Debra Smeeton [1967] Director/Chartered Accountant; Anthony White [1961] Director/Accountant

INEOS Runcorn (TPS) Holdings Limited
Incorporated: 23 April 2008 *Employees:* 8
Net Worth Deficit: £57,230,000 *Total Assets:* £326,771,008
Registered Office: P O Box 9, Runcorn Site HQ, South Parade, Runcorn, Cheshire, WA7 4JE
Activities: Production of electricity
Shareholders: John Laing Investments Limited; Viridor Waste Management Limited
Officers: Paul Frederick Nichols, Secretary; Wouter Bleukx [1970] Director/Manager [Belgian]; Michael John Maher [1968] Director/Manager; Andrew Stephen Pearson [1964] Director; Elliot Arthur James Rees [1974] Director; Paul Michael Ringham [1969] Director; Francis Rourke [1964] Director; Julie Dawn Taylorson [1959] Purchasing Director

INEOS Runcorn (TPS) Limited
Incorporated: 24 April 2008
Net Worth Deficit: £57,230,000 *Total Assets:* £326,771,008
Registered Office: P O Box 9, Runcorn Site HQ, South Parade, Runcorn, Cheshire, WA7 4JE
Activities: Production of electricity
Parent: INEOS Runcorn (TPS) Holdings Limited
Officers: Paul Frederick Nichols, Secretary; Wouter Bleukx [1970] Director/Manager [Belgian]; Michael John Maher [1968] Director/Manager; Andrew Stephen Pearson [1964] Director; Elliot Arthur James Rees [1974] Director; Paul Michael Ringham [1969] Director; Francis Rourke [1964] Director; Julie Dawn Taylorson [1959] Purchasing Director

INEOS Technologies (Holdings) Limited
Incorporated: 6 October 2008 *Employees:* 89
Net Worth: £21,500,000 *Total Assets:* £61,600,000
Registered Office: P O Box 9, Runcorn Site HQ, South Parade, Runcorn, Cheshire, WA7 4JE
Activities: Activities of head offices
Major Shareholder: James Arthur Ratcliffe
Officers: Paul Frederick Nichols, Secretary; Michael John Maher [1968] Director/Manager; Christopher Edward Tane [1956] Director; Julie Dawn Taylorson [1959] Purchasing Director

INEOS Technologies (Vinyls) Limited
Incorporated: 24 November 2009 *Employees:* 19
Net Worth: £371,874 *Total Assets:* £9,590,292
Registered Office: P O Box 9, Runcorn Site HQ, South Parade, Runcorn, Cheshire, WA7 4JE
Activities: Manufacture of other chemical products n.e.c.
Parent: INEOS Vinyls Limited
Officers: Paul Frederick Nichols, Secretary; Luc Marie Georges Castin [1963] Director [Belgian]; Michael John Maher [1968] Director/Manager; Anthony Moorcroft [1959] HR Director; Francis Rourke [1964] Director; Christopher Edward Tane [1956] Director; Julie Dawn Taylorson [1959] Purchasing Director

INEOS Vinyls Holdings Limited
Incorporated: 19 January 2001
Net Worth: £59,400,000 *Total Assets:* £59,400,000
Registered Office: P O Box 9, Runcorn Site HQ, South Parade, Runcorn, Cheshire, WA7 4JE
Activities: Activities of head offices
Parent: Hawkslease Finance Company Limited
Officers: Paul Frederick Nichols, Secretary; Michael John Maher [1968] Director; Christopher Edward Tane [1956] Director

INEOS Vinyls Limited
Incorporated: 30 March 2005
Net Worth Deficit: £250,394,384 *Total Assets:* £55,214,724
Registered Office: P O Box 9, Runcorn Site HQ, South Parade, Runcorn, Cheshire, WA7 4JE
Activities: Manufacture of other organic basic chemicals
Parent: INEOS Vinyls Holdings Limited
Officers: Paul Frederick Nichols, Secretary; Thomas Patrick Crotty [1956] Director [Irish]; Michael John Maher [1968] Director; Christopher Edward Tane [1956] Director; Julie Dawn Taylorson [1959] Director

Infinity (MIOC) LLP
Incorporated: 10 February 2008
Registered Office: 4 Clippers Quay, Salford Quays, Manchester, M50 3BL

Infinity 30 Limited
Incorporated: 17 July 2012
Net Worth Deficit: £2,001,158 *Total Assets:* £17,273,974
Registered Office: 4 Clippers Quay, Salford Quays, Manchester, M50 3BL
Activities: Other business support service activities n.e.c.
Major Shareholder: Philip Vickers
Officers: Daniel John Finestein [1965] Director; Philip Vickers [1961] Director

Inflight Productions Ltd
Incorporated: 18 May 1979 *Employees:* 115
Net Worth Deficit: £34,595,884 *Total Assets:* £34,971,668
Registered Office: 3rd Floor, 1 Ashley Road, Altrincham, Cheshire, WA14 2DT
Activities: Motion picture, video and television programme post-production activities
Parent: IFE Holdings Limited
Officers: Paul Flowerday [1971] Director; Daniel Girard [1971] Director/VP Special Projects (Finance) [Canadian]

Information and Data Networks Supplies Holdings Limited
Incorporated: 21 February 1997 *Employees:* 73
Net Worth: £1,407,748 *Total Assets:* £7,343,697
Registered Office: 1b Springfield Court, Summerfield Road, Bolton, Lancs, BL3 2NT
Activities: Activities of head offices
Major Shareholder: Gareth Duncan Ashley Stocks
Officers: Gareth Duncan Ashley Stocks, Secretary; David John Shuttleworth [1968] Director; Gareth Duncan Ashley Stocks [1969] Director

Information and Data Networks Supplies Limited
Incorporated: 26 April 1988 *Employees:* 74
Net Worth: £3,547,885 *Total Assets:* £9,764,068
Registered Office: 1b Springfield Court, Summerfield Road, Bolton, Lancs, BL3 2NT
Activities: Other information technology service activities
Parent: Information and Data Networks Supplies Holdings Limited
Officers: David John Shuttleworth, Secretary; Gareth Duncan Ashley Stocks [1969] Director

Infra Safety Services Labour Limited
Incorporated: 21 May 2007 *Employees:* 100
Net Worth: £233,211 *Total Assets:* £8,166,987
Registered Office: 7 Bradford Business Park, Kings Gate, Bradford, W Yorks, BD1 4SJ
Activities: Other construction installation
Parent: ISS Labour Group Limited
Officers: Gary Beeston [1962] Managing Director; Christopher Michael Chidley [1960] Director; Paul Howard McNulty [1970] Director

Ingenico (UK) Limited
Incorporated: 29 May 1987 *Employees:* 338
Net Worth: £49,070,000 *Total Assets:* £70,168,000
Registered Office: Ingenico House, Rudheath Way, Gadbrook Park, Rudheath, Northwich, Cheshire, CW9 7LT
Activities: Manufacture of other electrical equipment
Parent: Ingenico Group SA
Officers: David Patrick McGuire, Secretary; Ian Timothy Benn [1964] Managing Director; Douglas Lindsay Hogg [1979] Director/Chief Financial Officer; Guillaume Pascal [1972] Managing Director [French]; Kashif Mohammed Sharif [1977] Director/Head of Finance

Ingersoll - Rand Holdings Limited
Incorporated: 27 May 1970
Net Worth: £67,403,000 *Total Assets:* £70,735,000
Registered Office: Sefton House, Northgate Close, Middlebrook Business Park, Bolton, Lancs, BL6 6PQ
Activities: Non-trading company
Parent: Ingersoll-Rand UK Limited
Officers: Mihaela Cristea, Secretary; Christopher Donohoe [1971] Treasury Director [Irish]; Stephen Vernon Taylor [1969] Regional Director Sales and Services Northern Europe

Ingersoll-Rand Company Limited
Incorporated: 24 August 1921
Net Worth: £50,621,000 *Total Assets:* £50,621,000
Registered Office: Sefton House, Northgate Close, Middlebrook Business Park, Bolton, Lancs, BL6 6PQ
Activities: Other business support service activities n.e.c.
Parent: Ingersoll-Rand Holdings Limited
Officers: Mihaela Cristea, Secretary; Christopher Donohoe [1971] Director/Treasury Manager [Irish]; Stephen Vernon Taylor [1969] Regional Director Sales and Services

Ingleby (1951) Limited
Incorporated: 2 April 2014
Net Worth: £21,000,786 *Total Assets:* £21,000,786
Registered Office: The Victory Offices, 112 Victory Road, Blackpool, Lancs, FY1 3NW
Activities: Activities of head offices
Parent: Kildale Bidco Limited
Officers: Joanne Jones, Secretary; James Edward Baer [1955] Director; Michael David George [1973] Director/Founding Partner; Mark John Goddard [1970] Director; Joanne Louise Jones [1966] Director/Accountant; Gary Eric Roberts [1963] Director

Ingleby (1952) Limited
Incorporated: 2 April 2014
Net Worth Deficit: £15,802,282 *Total Assets:* £95,931,400
Registered Office: The Victory Offices, 112 Victory Road, Blackpool, Lancs, FY1 3NW
Activities: Activities of head offices
Parent: Ingleby (1951) Limited
Officers: Joanne Jones, Secretary; James Edward Baer [1955] Director; Michael David George [1973] Director/Founding Partner; Mark John Goddard [1970] Director; Joanne Louise Jones [1966] Director/Accountant; Clive Henry Preston [1936] Director/Chairman; Gary Eric Roberts [1963] Director

Ingot Portal Limited
Incorporated: 16 January 2007 *Employees:* 15
Net Worth: £18,683 *Total Assets:* £8,179,045
Registered Office: 157 Regent Road, Liverpool, L5 9TF
Activities: Non-trading company
Parent: Warrant Corporate Holdings Limited
Officers: Ian Jones [1969] Director; Lynsey Morrison [1980] Finance Director

Ingredion UK Limited
Incorporated: 15 July 2010 *Employees:* 98
Net Worth: £17,337,000 *Total Assets:* £75,746,000
Registered Office: Ingredion House, Manchester Green, 339 Styal Road, Manchester, M22 5LW
Activities: Other business support service activities n.e.c.
Parent: Ingredion Incorporated
Officers: Shanin Terri Fuller [1970] Director/Attorney [American]; Richard John O'Shanna [1957] Director/Business Executive [American]

Inhoco 2952 Limited
Incorporated: 12 September 2003
Net Worth Deficit: £4,731,295 *Total Assets:* £22,111,080
Registered Office: Sceptre House, Sceptre Way, Bamber Bridge, Preston, Lancs, PR5 6AW
Activities: Other letting and operating of own or leased real estate
Parent: East Lancashire Building Partnership Ltd
Officers: Deborah Jane Rawlinson, Secretary; Jeremy Peter Hartley [1965] Director/Chartered Accountant; Roger Martyn Parr [1970] Director; Neil Geoffrey Ward [1959] Director; Christine Desiree Winstanley [1966] Director; Mark Stuart Youlton [1963] Director

Innospec Active Chemicals Limited
Incorporated: 16 March 2001
Net Worth: £18,259,000 *Total Assets:* £18,812,000
Registered Office: Innospec Manufacturing Park, Oil Sites Road, Ellesmere Port, Cheshire, CH65 4EY
Activities: Other business support service activities n.e.c.
Parent: Innospec Holdings Limited
Officers: Brian Robert Watt, Secretary; Ian Philip Cleminson [1965] Director; Philip Andrew Curran [1970] Director; Graeme Kay [1976] Director; Keri Louise Tither [1981] Director; Brian Robert Watt [1959] Director

Innospec Developments Limited
Incorporated: 25 February 1998
Net Worth: £47,116,000 *Total Assets:* £47,116,000
Registered Office: Innospec Manufacturing Park, Oil Sites Road, Ellesmere Port, Cheshire, CH65 4EY
Activities: Activities of head offices
Parent: Innospec International Limited
Officers: Brian Robert Watt, Secretary; Ian Philip Cleminson [1965] Director; Philip Andrew Curran [1970] Director; Graeme Kay [1976] Director; Keri Louise Tither [1981] Director; Brian Robert Watt [1959] Director

Innospec Environmental Limited
Incorporated: 11 May 2001 *Employees:* 4
Net Worth: £10,834,000 *Total Assets:* £10,855,000
Registered Office: Innospec Manufacturing Park, Oil Sites Road, Ellesmere Port, Cheshire, CH65 4EY
Activities: Remediation activities and other waste management services
Parent: Innospec Limited
Officers: Brian Robert Watt, Secretary; Philip John Boon [1959] Director; Ian Philip Cleminson [1965] Director; Philip Andrew Curran [1970] Director; Brian Robert Watt [1959] Director

Innospec Finance Limited
Incorporated: 12 January 2005
Net Worth: £51,857,000 *Total Assets:* £540,846,976
Registered Office: Innospec Manufacturing Park, Oil Sites Road, Ellesmere Port, Cheshire, CH65 4EY
Activities: Other business support service activities n.e.c.
Parent: Innospec Holdings Limited
Officers: Brian Robert Watt, Secretary; Ian Philip Cleminson [1965] Director; Philip Andrew Curran [1970] Director; Graeme Kay [1976] Director; Keri Louise Tither [1981] Director; Brian Robert Watt [1959] Director

Innospec Fuel Specialties Limited
Incorporated: 11 February 1997
Net Worth Deficit: £50,022,000 *Total Assets:* £11,333,000
Registered Office: Innospec Manufacturing Park, Oil Sites Road, Ellesmere Port, Cheshire, CH65 4EY
Activities: Other business support service activities n.e.c.
Parent: Innospec Holdings Limited
Officers: Brian Robert Watt, Secretary; Ian Philip Cleminson [1965] Director; Philip Andrew Curran [1970] Director; Graeme Kay [1976] Director; Keri Louise Tither [1981] Director; Brian Robert Watt [1959] Director

Innospec Holdings Limited
Incorporated: 13 November 2000 *Employees:* 6
Net Worth: £39,061,000 *Total Assets:* £149,352,992
Registered Office: Innospec Manufacturing Park, Oil Sites Road, Ellesmere Port, Cheshire, CH65 4EY
Activities: Activities of head offices
Parent: Innospec Developments Limited
Officers: Brian Robert Watt, Secretary; Ian Philip Cleminson [1965] Director; Philip Andrew Curran [1970] Director; Graeme Kay [1976] Director; Christopher John Parsons [1976] Director; Keri Louise Tither [1981] Director; Brian Robert Watt [1959] Director

Innospec International Limited
Incorporated: 11 February 1997
Net Worth: £19,893,000 *Total Assets:* £298,556,000
Registered Office: Innospec Manufacturing Park, Oil Sites Road, Ellesmere Port, Cheshire, CH65 4EY
Activities: Other business support service activities n.e.c.
Parent: Innospec Inc
Officers: Brian Robert Watt, Secretary; Ian Philip Cleminson [1965] Director; Philip Andrew Curran [1970] Director; David Bentley Jones Jr [1968] Director/General Counsel [American]; Graeme Kay [1976] Director; Keri Louise Tither [1981] Director; Brian Robert Watt [1959] Director

Innospec Limited
Incorporated: 16 September 1938 *Employees:* 505
Net Worth: £381,475,008 *Total Assets:* £481,140,992
Registered Office: Innospec Manufacturing Park, Oil Sites Road, Ellesmere Port, Cheshire, CH65 4EY
Activities: Manufacture of other inorganic basic chemicals
Parent: Innopsec Trading Limited
Officers: Brian Robert Watt, Secretary; Philip John Boon [1959] Director; Ian Philip Cleminson [1965] Director; Philip Andrew Curran [1970] Director; Graeme Kay [1976] Director; Christopher John Parsons [1976] Director; Keri Louise Tither [1981] Director; Brian Robert Watt [1959] Director

Innospec Trading Limited
Incorporated: 25 February 1998 *Employees:* 5
Net Worth: £85,137,000 *Total Assets:* £338,766,016
Registered Office: Innospec Manufacturing Park, Oil Sites Road, Ellesmere Port, Cheshire, CH65 4EY
Activities: Other business support service activities n.e.c.
Parent: Innospec Holdings Limited
Officers: Brian Robert Watt, Secretary; Ian Philip Cleminson [1965] Director; Philip Andrew Curran [1970] Director; Graeme Kay [1976] Director; Keri Louise Tither [1981] Director; Brian Robert Watt [1959] Director

Innovation Birmingham Limited
Incorporated: 4 May 1983 *Employees:* 37
Net Worth Deficit: £429,701 *Total Assets:* £15,000,275
Registered Office: Union, Albert Square, Manchester, M2 6LW
Activities: Other letting and operating of own or leased real estate
Parent: Birmingham Science Limited
Officers: Kevin James Crotty [1976] Director/Chartered Accountant; Peter Andrew Crowther [1972] Director/Surveyor; Dr David John Hardman [1957] Director/Chief Executive; Philip Andrew Kemp [1964] Director/Chief Commercial Officer; Kate Victoria Lawlor [1981] Director/Chartered Accountant; Christopher George Oglesby [1967] Director

Innovative Environmental Solutions UK Ltd
Incorporated: 2 May 2008
Net Worth Deficit: £110,244,000 *Total Assets:* £51,753,000
Registered Office: Sirius House, Delta Crescent, Westbrook, Warrington, Cheshire, WA5 7NS
Activities: Production of electricity
Parent: European Metal Recycling Limited
Officers: Christopher John Tinsley, Secretary; Anthony Rex Marrett [1970] Director; Christopher Phillip Sheppard [1974] Director

Innovative Technology Limited
Incorporated: 5 November 1985 *Employees:* 204
Net Worth: £18,898,000 *Total Assets:* £23,379,000
Registered Office: Innovative Business Park, Derker Street, Oldham, Lancs, OL1 4EQ
Activities: Other research and experimental development on natural sciences and engineering
Parent: Bellis Holdings Limited
Officers: Grenville Alun Evans, Secretary; Robert David Bellis [1938] Director; Timothy Jude Crowley [1963] Director/Operations [Irish]; Peter Ian Dunlop [1975] Director; Mustapha Hadj Ahmed [1960] Director [Spanish]; Anthony Edward Morrison [1965] Director; Thomas Donald Pennington-Brookfield [1979] Director/Certified Chartered Accountant; Christopher John Charles Robinson [1977] Director; John Edwin Robinson [1982] Development Director; Paul Andrew Smith [1980] Director; Marcus Tiedt [1968] Director [German]

Innovia Films (Holding) Limited
Incorporated: 15 March 2013
Net Worth: £132,879,952 *Total Assets:* £132,879,952
Registered Office: Lowther R & D Centre, West Road, Wigton, Cumbria, CA7 9XX
Activities: Activities of head offices
Parent: Innovia Group (Holding 3) Ltd
Officers: Dominic Mark Heaton [1972] Finance & Administration Director; Geoffrey Thomas Martin [1954] Director/Chief Executive [American]; Wayne Middleton Middleton [1969] Managing Director

Innovia Films Limited
Incorporated: 9 January 1933 *Employees:* 745
Net Worth: £49,053,000 *Total Assets:* £160,136,000
Registered Office: Lowther R & D Centre, West Road, Wigton, Cumbria, CA7 9XX
Activities: Other manufacturing n.e.c.
Parent: Innovia Films (Holding) Ltd
Officers: Dr Andrew Edward Bayliff [1961] R & D Director; Dominic Mark Heaton [1972] Finance Director; Geoffrey Thomas Martin [1954] Director/Chief Executive [American]; Wayne Middleton Middleton [1969] Managing Director

Innovia Group (Holding 3) Limited
Incorporated: 6 September 2004 *Employees:* 3
Net Worth: £266,538,464 *Total Assets:* £266,721,360
Registered Office: Lowther R & D Centre, West Road, Wigton, Cumbria, CA7 9XX
Activities: Activities of head offices
Parent: CCL Syrinx (UK) Ltd
Officers: Dominic Mark Heaton [1972] Finance & Administration Director; Geoffrey Thomas Martin [1954] Director/Chief Executive [American]; Wayne Middleton Middleton [1969] Managing Director

Inns & Leisure Limited
Incorporated: 15 October 1969 *Employees:* 94
Net Worth: £5,663,327 *Total Assets:* £7,606,832
Registered Office: 20-24 Leicester Road, Preston, Lancs, PR1 1PP
Activities: Public houses and bars
Officers: George David Clark [1946] Director; Peter Stephen Clark [1970] Director of Public House Operating Company; Stewart Charles Clark [1983] Director

Inovyn Chlorvinyls Holdings Limited
Incorporated: 24 November 2009 *Employees:* 3
Net Worth: £7,840,342 *Total Assets:* £147,362,800
Registered Office: P O Box 9, Runcorn Site HQ, South Parade, Runcorn, Cheshire, WA7 4JE
Activities: Activities of head offices
Parent: Inovyn Group Treasury Limited
Officers: Paul Frederick Nichols, Secretary; Michael John Maher [1968] Director; Christopher Edward Tane [1956] Director; Julie Dawn Taylorson [1959] Director

Inovyn Chlorvinyls Limited
Incorporated: 11 September 2000 *Employees:* 794
Net Worth Deficit: £353,400,000 *Total Assets:* £398,700,000
Registered Office: P O Box 9, Runcorn Site HQ, South Parade, Runcorn, Cheshire, WA7 4JE
Activities: Manufacture of industrial gases
Parent: Inovyn Newco 2 Limited
Officers: Paul Frederick Nichols, Secretary; Michael John Maher [1968] Director; Anthony Moorcroft [1959] HR Director; Francis Rourke [1964] Director; Christopher Edward Tane [1956] Director; Julie Dawn Taylorson [1959] Director

Inovyn Energy Limited
Incorporated: 20 November 1986 *Employees:* 3
Net Worth: £625,100 *Total Assets:* £21,736,100
Registered Office: P O Box 9, Runcorn Site HQ, South Parade, Runcorn, Cheshire, WA7 4JE
Activities: Distribution of electricity
Parent: Inovyn Chlorvinyls Limited
Officers: Paul Frederick Nichols, Secretary; Michael John Maher [1968] Director; Christopher Edward Tane [1956] Director; Julie Dawn Taylorson [1959] Director

Inovyn Enterprises Limited
Incorporated: 29 January 2003 *Employees:* 67
Net Worth: £68,900,000 *Total Assets:* £133,900,000
Registered Office: Runcorn Site HQ, South Parade, Runcorn, Cheshire, WA7 4JE
Activities: Manufacture of other inorganic basic chemicals
Parent: Inovyn Finance PLC
Officers: Paul Frederick Nichols, Secretary; Michael John Maher [1968] Director; Anthony Moorcroft [1959] HR Director; Francis Rourke [1964] Director; Christopher Edward Tane [1956] Director; Julie Dawn Taylorson [1959] Purchasing Director

Inovyn Finance PLC
Incorporated: 23 September 2009
Net Worth: £246,175,488 *Total Assets:* £1,575,259,392
Registered Office: P O Box 9, Runcorn Site HQ, South Parade, Runcorn, Cheshire, WA7 4JE
Activities: Activities of head offices
Parent: Inovyn Holdings Limited
Officers: Paul Frederick Nichols, Secretary; Michael John Maher [1968] Director; Christopher Edward Tane [1956] Director; Julie Dawn Taylorson [1959] Purchasing Director

Inovyn Group Treasury Limited
Incorporated: 23 March 2007 *Employees:* 3
Net Worth Deficit: £612,615,808 *Total Assets:* £1,339,896,704
Registered Office: P O Box 9, Runcorn Site HQ, South Parade, Runcorn, Cheshire, WA7 4JE
Activities: Activities of head offices
Parent: Inovyn Finance PLC
Officers: Paul Frederick Nichols, Secretary; Michael John Maher [1968] Director; Christopher Edward Tane [1956] Director; Julie Dawn Taylorson [1959] Director

Inovyn Holdings Limited
Incorporated: 28 May 2016
Net Worth: £453,226,656 *Total Assets:* £792,772,992
Registered Office: P O Box 9, Runcorn Site HQ, South Parade, Runcorn, Cheshire, WA7 4JE
Activities: Activities of head offices
Parent: Inovyn Limited
Officers: Paul Frederick Nichols, Secretary; Michael John Maher [1968] Director; Christopher Edward Tane [1956] Director; Julie Dawn Taylorson [1959] Director

Inovyn Limited
Incorporated: 18 September 2013 *Employees:* 3,922
Net Worth Deficit: £350,464,064 *Total Assets:* £1,887,676,160
Registered Office: P O Box 9, Runcorn Site HQ, South Parade, Runcorn, Cheshire, WA7 4JE
Activities: Activities of head offices
Parent: INEOS Group Investments Limited
Officers: Paul Frederick Nichols, Secretary; Filipe Manuel Ferreira Constant [1957] Director [Portuguese]; Paul Mark Daniels [1966] Director; Michael John Maher [1968] Director/Manager; Christopher Edward Tane [1956] Director; Julie Dawn Taylorson [1959] Purchasing Director

Inovyn Newco 2 Limited
Incorporated: 21 May 2003
Net Worth: £30,400,000 *Total Assets:* £30,400,000
Registered Office: Runcorn Site HQ, South Parade, Runcorn, Cheshire, WA7 4JE
Activities: Activities of head offices
Parent: Inovyn Chlorvinyls Holdings Limited
Officers: Paul Frederick Nichols, Secretary; Michael John Maher [1968] Director; Christopher Edward Tane [1956] Director; Julie Dawn Taylorson [1959] Purchasing Director

Inprova Finance Ltd
Incorporated: 21 October 2011 *Employees:* 3
Net Worth Deficit: £1,013,000 *Total Assets:* £13,072,000
Registered Office: Unit 2 Olympic Way, Birchwood, Warrington, Cheshire, WA2 0YL
Activities: Non-trading company
Parent: Inprova Group Ltd
Officers: Mohammed Ramzan, Secretary; Paul Alan Kennedy [1969] Director; Steven Malone [1969] Director; Mohammed Ramzan [1971] Director

Inprova Group Ltd
Incorporated: 17 February 2014 *Employees:* 152
Net Worth: £950,000 *Total Assets:* £17,256,000
Registered Office: Unit 2 Olympic Park, Woolston Grange Avenue, Warrington, Cheshire, WA2 0YL
Activities: Activities of head offices
Shareholders: Mohammed Ramzan; Paul Kennedy; LDC Parallel (Nominees) Limited
Officers: Robert Holt [1954] Director; Richard Michael Allan Ibbett [1977] Investment Director; Paul Alan Kennedy [1969] Director; Steven Malone [1969] Director; Mohammed Ramzan [1971] Director/Chief Financial Officer; Carl Edmund Wormald [1969] Director

Inrix Holdings UK Ltd
Incorporated: 15 July 2011 *Employees:* 200
Net Worth: £6,627,961 *Total Assets:* £29,258,212
Registered Office: Fifth Floor, Station House, Stamford New Road, Altrincham, Cheshire, WA14 1EP
Activities: Activities of other holding companies n.e.c.
Parent: Inrix Inc
Officers: Adrian James Beach [1956] Director/Chief Financial Officer [American]; Aileen Maria Holohan [1968] Director [Irish]; Bryan Peter Mistele [1968] Director/CEO - Inrix, Inc. [American]

Inrix UK Ltd.
Incorporated: 3 October 1996 *Employees:* 144
Net Worth: £17,822,050 *Total Assets:* £40,090,804
Registered Office: 5th Floor, Station House, Stamford New Road, Altrincham, Cheshire, WA14 1EP
Activities: Other service activities n.e.c.
Parent: Inrix Holdings UK Limited
Officers: Adrian James Beach [1956] Director/Chief Financial Officer [American]; Aileen Maria Holohan [1968] Director/Accountant [Irish]; Bryan Peter Mistele [1968] Director/CEO - Inrix, Inc. [American]

Insert Ltd
Incorporated: 22 December 2016
Net Worth: £8,866,499 *Total Assets:* £9,002,407
Registered Office: New Mount Business Centre, New Mount Street, Manchester, M4 4DE
Activities: Freight transport by road
Major Shareholder: Paul Sharp
Officers: Paul Sharp [1988] Director

Inspired Energy PLC
Incorporated: 19 May 2011 *Employees:* 266
Net Worth: £25,122,456 *Total Assets:* £56,236,228
Registered Office: 29 Progress Park, Orders Lane, Kirkham, Lancs, PR4 2TZ
Activities: Other professional, scientific and technical activities n.e.c.
Officers: Paul Anthony Connor [1984] Director/Chartered Accountant; Mark Dickinson [1972] Director; Michael James Fletcher [1974] Director; Richard Strachan Logan [1957] Director/Chartered Accountant; Gordon Richard Oliver [1958] Director/Chartered Accountant; Matthew Peter Thornton [1973] Director

Inspiredspaces Rochdale (Holdings1) Limited
Incorporated: 14 September 2009
Net Worth Deficit: £6,807,000 *Total Assets:* £26,806,000
Registered Office: c/o Albany SPC Services Ltd, 3rd Floor, 3-5 Charlotte Street, Manchester, M1 4HB
Activities: Activities of head offices
Parent: Dalmore Capital (Rochdale) Limited
Officers: Ailison Louise Mitchell, Secretary; Sandra Ann Bowness [1959] Service Director; Keith Joseph Edwards [1965] Operations Director; Peter Kenneth Johnstone [1965] Director; David Wilcock [1963] Director/Solicitor

Inspiredspaces Rochdale (Holdings2) Limited
Incorporated: 21 June 2012
Net Worth: £43,000 *Total Assets:* £38,131,000
Registered Office: c/o Albany SPC Services Ltd, 3rd Floor, 3-5 Charlotte Street, Manchester, M1 4HB
Activities: Activities of head offices
Parent: Inspiredspaces Rochdale (PSP3) Limited
Officers: Ailison Louise Mitchell, Secretary; Sandra Ann Bowness [1959] Service Director; Keith Joseph Edwards [1965] Operations Director; Mark Andrew Harding [1956] Director/Bid Manager; Peter Kenneth Johnstone [1965] Director; David Wilcock [1963] Director/Solicitor

Inspiredspaces Rochdale (Projectco1) Limited
Incorporated: 13 September 2009
Net Worth Deficit: £6,266,000 *Total Assets:* £25,841,000
Registered Office: c/o Albany SPC Services Ltd, 3rd Floor, 3-5 Charlotte Street, Manchester, M1 4HB
Activities: Other business support service activities n.e.c.
Parent: Inspiredspaces Rochdale (Holdings1) Limited
Officers: Ailison Louise Mitchell, Secretary; Sandra Ann Bowness [1959] Service Director; Keith Joseph Edwards [1965] Operations Director; Peter Kenneth Johnstone [1965] Director; David Wilcock [1963] Director/Solicitor

Inspiredspaces Rochdale (Projectco2) Limited
Incorporated: 21 June 2012
Net Worth: £20,000 *Total Assets:* £36,956,000
Registered Office: c/o Albany SPC Services Ltd, 3rd Floor, 3-5 Charlotte Street, Manchester, M1 4HB
Activities: Other business support service activities n.e.c.
Parent: Inspiredspaces Rochdale (Holdings2) Limited
Officers: Ailison Louise Mitchell, Secretary; Sandra Ann Bowness [1959] Service Director; Keith Joseph Edwards [1965] Operations Director; Peter Kenneth Johnstone [1965] Director; David Wilcock [1963] Director/Solicitor

Inspirepac Holdings Limited
Incorporated: 20 October 2009
Net Worth: £8,080,179 *Total Assets:* £8,080,179
Registered Office: Cunard Buildings, Water Street, Pier Head, Liverpool, L3 1SF
Activities: Activities of distribution holding companies
Parent: Smurfit Kappa 100 Ltd
Officers: Nicola Pritchard, Secretary; Clive Bowers [1953] Director; Christopher Marples [1965] Director; Hugh Patrick McNeill [1959] Director

Inspirepac Limited
Incorporated: 14 December 2006
Net Worth: £39,530,168 *Total Assets:* £39,530,168
Registered Office: Cunard Buildings, Water Street, Pier Head, Liverpool, L3 1SF
Activities: Manufacture of other paper and paperboard containers
Parent: Inspirepac Holdings Limited
Officers: Nicola Pritchard, Secretary; Clive Bowers [1953] Director; Christopher Marples [1965] Director/Manager; Hugh Patrick McNeill [1959] Director

Integra Insurance Solutions Limited
Incorporated: 27 November 2008
Net Worth: £4,859,000 *Total Assets:* £21,860,000
Registered Office: Currer House, Currer Street, Bradford, W Yorks, BD1 5BA
Activities: Non- ife insurance
Parent: Funis GmbH & Co KG
Officers: Maria Louise Bell, Secretary; Carlo Cavaliere [1969] Managing Director; Martin William Harry Cox [1971] Managing Director; Anders Larsson [1957] Director [Swedish]; Nicholas James Parr [1957] Director

Integrated Dental Holdings Limited
Incorporated: 17 January 1996
Net Worth: £18,263,000 *Total Assets:* £40,124,000
Registered Office: Europa House, Europa Trading Estate, Stoneclough Road, Kearsley, Manchester, M26 1GG
Activities: Dental practice activities
Parent: IDH Acquisitions Limited
Officers: Leo Damian Carroll, Secretary; Clifford Gwyn Davies [1966] Clinical Director; Sharon Patricia Letters [1975] Clinical Director; Steven Andrew Melton [1962] Managing Director - Mydentist; Bernard Moroney [1953] Clinical Director; Manish Prasad [1972] Clinical Director; Tom Riall [1960] Director; Mohammed Omar Shafi Khan [1974] Director/Chief Financial Officer; Krista Nyree Whitley [1970] Clinical Director

Intelling Group Limited
Incorporated: 30 November 2016 *Employees:* 392
Net Worth Deficit: £1,072,098 *Total Assets:* £7,165,741
Registered Office: Southmoor House, Southmoor Road, Manchester, M23 9XD
Activities: Data processing, hosting and related activities
Major Shareholder: Philip Morgan
Officers: Andrew William Leach [1957] Director/Partner; Philip Morgan [1972] Director; Ronald Allan MacLeod Pierce [1957] Director; Stephen Robert Taylor [1961] Director; Craig Winnard [1977] Director

Interactive Investor Limited
Incorporated: 2 May 2003 *Employees:* 319
Net Worth: £95,386,000 *Total Assets:* £685,499,008
Registered Office: 201 Deansgate, Manchester, M3 3NW
Activities: Activities of head offices
Officers: John Duncan Baines [1962] Director; Barry Michael Bicknell [1968] Finance Director; Alison Gail Bragg [1961] Director/Consultant; Jonathan James Cox [1980] Director; Tim John Hanford [1964] Director; Timothy Charles Levene [1973] Director; Hugo Henri Carel Van Vredenburch [1965] Director/Chairman [Dutch]; John Veichmanis [1973] Director; Richard Simon Wilson [1966] Director

Interactive Investor Trading Limited
Incorporated: 22 January 1999 *Employees:* 2
Net Worth: £15,351,055 *Total Assets:* £16,326,305
Registered Office: 201 Deansgate, Manchester, M3 3NW
Activities: Financial intermediation not elsewhere classified
Parent: Interactive Investor Limited
Officers: Barry Michael Bicknell [1968] Finance Director; Richard Simon Wilson [1966] Director

Interfish Limited
Incorporated: 17 October 1977 *Employees:* 336
Net Worth: £96,799,344 *Total Assets:* £159,134,320
Registered Office: Reedham House, 31 King Street West, Manchester, M3 2PJ
Activities: Processing and preserving of fish, crustaceans and molluscs
Officers: Rachel Anne Colam, Secretary; Johannus Jacobus Colam [1953] Director

Interfloor Limited
Incorporated: 19 January 1920 *Employees:* 319
Net Worth: £22,158,000 *Total Assets:* £50,400,000
Registered Office: Broadway, Haslingden, Rossendale, Lancs, BB4 4LS
Activities: Other manufacturing n.e.c.
Parent: Interfloor Operations Limited
Officers: Stephen Maurie Martin Byrne [1960] Director/Carpet Merchant; Gary Cowley [1960] Sales Director; Stephen Foster [1975] Director/Chartered Accountant; Mark Jennings [1968] Operations Director; John Joseph Snee [1962] Director/Textile Manager; Geoffrey Brendon Wilding [1963] Director [New Zealander]

Interfloor Operations Limited
Incorporated: 26 July 2005
Net Worth: £8,887,000 *Total Assets:* £64,295,000
Registered Office: Broadway, Haslingden, Rossendale, Lancs, BB4 4LS
Activities: Activities of head offices
Parent: Interfloor Group Llimited
Officers: Stephen Maurie Martin Byrne [1960] Director/Carpet Merchant; John Joseph Snee [1962] Director/Textile Manager; Geoffrey Brendon Wilding [1963] Director [New Zealander]

Interket Holdings UK Limited
Incorporated: 25 October 1995 *Employees:* 73
Net Worth: £2,046,240 *Total Assets:* £6,533,668
Registered Office: Unit 4 Bingswood Industrial Estate, Whaley Bridge, High Peak, Derbys, SK23 7SP
Activities: Other manufacturing n.e.c.
Officers: Carl Ekholm Parkander [1973] Director [Swedish]; Timothy John Pattison [1975] Sales Director; Andrew Paul Woodhouse [1964] Director

Interket Limited
Incorporated: 13 December 1976 *Employees:* 74
Net Worth: £4,497,289 *Total Assets:* £8,651,250
Registered Office: Bingswood Industrial Estate, Whaley Bridge, High Peak, Derbys, SK23 7SP
Activities: Other manufacturing n.e.c.
Parent: Stampiton Holdings Limited
Officers: Carl Ekholm Parkander [1972] Director [Swedish]; Timothy John Pattison [1975] Sales Director; Andrew Paul Woodhouse [1964] Director

International Fibres Group (Holdings) Limited
Incorporated: 18 May 1949 *Employees:* 4
Net Worth: £40,335,000 *Total Assets:* £48,697,000
Registered Office: Old Mills, Drighlington, Bradford, W Yorks, BD11 1BY
Activities: Activities of head offices
Major Shareholder: Peter Gyllenhammar
Officers: Kathryn Anne Davenport, Secretary; Peter Jan Patrik Gyllenhammar [1953] Director [Swedish]; John Olof Hager [1964] Managing Director [Swedish]; Jan Gustaf Lennart Holmstrom [1953] Director [Swedish]

International General Electric (U.S.A.)
Incorporated: 25 October 1983
Net Worth: £365,079,008 *Total Assets:* £1,468,855,040
Registered Office: 3rd Floor, 1 Ashley Road, Altrincham, Cheshire, WA14 2DT
Activities: Activities of other holding companies n.e.c.
Parent: General Electric Company
Officers: Andrew Thomas Peter Budge [1973] Director/Chartered Accountant; Akhlesh Prasad Mathur [1972] Director/Chartered Accountant; Kerrie Jane Rowland [1971] Human Resources Director

International Motors Finance Limited
Incorporated: 5 August 1994 *Employees:* 1
Net Worth: £12,189,000 *Total Assets:* £155,079,008
Registered Office: Charterhall House, Charterhall Drive, Chester, CH88 3AN
Activities: Credit granting by non-deposit taking finance houses and other specialist consumer credit grantors
Shareholders: Black Horse Group Limited; International Motors Limited
Officers: David Dermot Hennessey, Secretary; Christopher Michael Adams [1982] Director; Andrew Martin Edmiston [1969] Managing Director; Gary Ernest Hutton [1959] Director/Chartered Accountant; Richard Andrew Jones [1972] Marketing Director; Dr Nagla Thabet [1974] Director; Paul Graham Tunnicliffe [1953] Managing Director

International Nuclear Services Limited
Incorporated: 8 November 1973 *Employees:* 165
Net Worth: £38,766,000 *Total Assets:* £251,811,008
Registered Office: Herdus House, Ingwell Drive, Westlakes Science & Technology Park, Moor Row, Cumbria, CA24 3HU
Activities: Other professional, scientific and technical activities n.e.c.
Officers: Helen Elizabeth Hodgson, Secretary; Peter George Buchan [1970] Director; Katharine Jane Ellis [1965] Commercial Director; Jeremy Mark Gilmour [1966] Director/Head of Portfolio Office; Alaine Louise Greaves [1974] Director; Carole Ann Jones [1961] Director/Head of Financial Planning; Seth Kybird [1977] Managing Director; Charles Archibald Robertson [1953] Director

International Paper Group (UK) Limited
Incorporated: 6 November 1997
Net Worth: £28,395,000 *Total Assets:* £28,395,000
Registered Office: Units 10 and 11 Navigation Road, Road One, Winsford Industrial Estate, Winsford, Cheshire, CW7 3RL
Activities: Other business support service activities n.e.c.
Parent: International Paper Company Inc
Officers: Helen Jane Dickinson, Secretary; Micheal Philip Robertson [1965] Director/Sales Manager; Dominic Xenophon Gryffydh Turnbull [1957] Director/Manager

International Seafoods Limited
Incorporated: 7 November 2011 *Employees:* 485
Net Worth: £2,171,000 *Total Assets:* £39,268,000
Registered Office: Hilmore House, Gain Lane, Bradford, W Yorks, BD3 7DL
Activities: Processing and preserving of fish, crustaceans and molluscs
Parent: Wm Morrison Supermarkets Holdings Limited
Officers: Jonathan James Burke, Secretary; Darren Anthony Blackhurst [1966] Director; Andrew James Clappen [1965] Technical Director; Mark Thomas Stitson [1976] Finance Director; Andrew Edward Thornber [1974] Director

International Travel Connections Limited
Incorporated: 12 November 1971 *Employees:* 126
Net Worth: £8,023,000 *Total Assets:* £29,739,000
Registered Office: Concorde House, 6 Canal Street, Chester, CH1 4EJ
Activities: Tour operator activities
Shareholders: Northedge Capital II GP LLP; Northedge Capital LLP; Bliss Bidco Limited; Bliss Topco Limited; ITC Luxury Travel Group Ltd; Jennifer Isobel Atkinson
Officers: Jennifer Isobel Atkinson [1975] Director; Mal Barritt [1972] Director; Olga Fahey [1969] Director; Judith Ellis Hinkson [1970] Director; Lee Marshall [1969] Director; Emma Victoria Pickering [1979] Director; Sarah Roberts [1979] Director

Intervoice Limited
Incorporated: 16 April 1991 *Employees:* 75
Net Worth: £4,656,000 *Total Assets:* £8,635,000
Registered Office: Trident Business Park, Styal Road, Manchester, M22 5XB
Activities: Other service activities n.e.c.
Officers: Cameron Christie [1971] Director; Stuart Eveleigh [1957] Director [South African]; Andrew Albert Farwig [1981] Director [American]

Invent and Invest
Incorporated: 17 July 2001
Net Worth: £10,757,479 *Total Assets:* £15,487,964
Registered Office: Daresbury Point, Green Wood Drive, Manor Park, Runcorn, Cheshire, WA7 1UP
Activities: Management consultancy activities other than financial management
Major Shareholder: John Rowlinson
Officers: Joan Mary Barton, Secretary; John Rowlinson [1961] Director

Inventive Service Company Limited
Incorporated: 9 January 2014 *Employees:* 73
Net Worth: £204,000 *Total Assets:* £9,041,000
Registered Office: 21 Old Street, Ashton under Lyne, Lancs, OL6 6LA
Activities: Retail sale of beverages in specialised stores
Parent: Inventive Guaranteeco Limited
Officers: Michael Raymond Foster, Secretary; Michael Raymond Foster [1958] Director; Robert Anthony Pitcher [1974] Director

Inverco Limited
Incorporated: 17 March 2014
Net Worth: £1,704,099 *Total Assets:* £9,222,979
Registered Office: Saddleworth Business Centre, Huddersfield Road, Delph, Oldham, Lancs, OL3 5DF
Activities: Activities of agricultural holding companies
Officers: Massimo Felice Cavalli [1968] Director/Entrepreneur [Italian]; Allan Green [1958] Director; Keith Mumby Parker [1963] Director; Jonathan Mark Rees [1961] Technical Director

Investment Fund Services Limited
Incorporated: 16 February 2007 *Employees:* 105
Net Worth: £2,630,645 *Total Assets:* £26,153,886
Registered Office: Marlborough House, 59 Chorley New Road, Bolton, Lancs, BL1 4QP
Activities: Administration of financial markets
Parent: Marlborough Group Holdings Limited
Officers: Ryan Peter Barber, Secretary; Dom Clarke [1983] Finance Director; Nicholas Francis John Cooling [1964] Director; Helen Derbyshire [1982] Director/Compliance Officer; Wayne Daniel Green [1980] Joint Managing Director; Allan Hamer [1976] Joint Managing Director; Helen Redmond [1966] Director - Client Relations; Guy Russell William Sears [1961] Director; Andrew Staley [1955] Director

Invibio Limited
Incorporated: 11 October 2000 *Employees:* 28
Net Worth: £191,192,000 *Total Assets:* £198,620,000
Registered Office: Victrex Technology Centre, Hillhouse International, Thornton Cleveleys, Lancs, FY5 4QD
Activities: Manufacture of plastics in primary forms
Parent: Victrex PLC
Officers: Richard James Armitage [1965] Finance Director; Timothy John Cooper [1959] Director; Martin Court [1961] Director; Jakob Oskar Sigurdsson [1964] Director [Icelander]

Invista Textiles (U.K.) Limited
Incorporated: 9 October 2002 *Employees:* 680
Net Worth: £91,514,432 *Total Assets:* £587,708,352
Registered Office: One St Peter's Square, Manchester, M2 3DE
Activities: Preparation and spinning of textile fibres
Parent: Invista (U.K.) Holdings Limited
Officers: Reagan John Mathews [1974] Director/Vice President and Chief Financial Officer [American]; John Gibson Stewart [1965] Director/Vice President, Biotechnology; Andreas Samuel Westhuis [1980] Director/Controller [Dutch]

Involve Visual Collaboration Ltd
Incorporated: 12 May 1989 *Employees:* 124
Net Worth: £7,068,261 *Total Assets:* £9,945,305
Registered Office: Martin Dawes House, Europa Boulevard, Westbrook, Warrington, Cheshire, WA5 7WH
Activities: Wholesale of other office machinery and equipment
Shareholder: Martin Richard Dawes
Officers: Martin Richard Dawes [1943] Director; Robert John Pasqualino [1965] Director; Dewi Eifion Thomas [1957] Director; Jason Paul Ward [1970] Sales Director

INX Europe Limited
Incorporated: 16 March 2004 *Employees:* 4
Net Worth Deficit: £11,953,755 *Total Assets:* £10,299,779
Registered Office: Hareshill Distribution Park, Hilltop Road, off Hareshill Road, Heywood, Lancs, OL10 2TW
Activities: Manufacture of printing ink
Parent: INX International Ink Co.
Officers: Bryce Kristo, Secretary/Company Vice President [American]; Richard Clendenning [1950] Director/Company President [American]; Toshihiko Fukunaga [1961] Director [Japanese]; Ellaby Jonathan [1953] Director/VP International; Bryce Kristo [1964] Director/Company Vice President [American]

INX International UK Limited
Incorporated: 19 May 1992 *Employees:* 130
Net Worth: £19,403,152 *Total Assets:* £25,779,268
Registered Office: Hareshill Distribution Park, Hilltop Road, off Hareshill Road, Heywood, Lancs, OL10 2TW
Activities: Other manufacturing n.e.c.
Parent: INX Europe Limited
Officers: Peter Stanley Tresadern, Secretary/Printing Ink Manufacturer; Jonathan Ellaby [1953] Director/Vice President; Nicholas Sagalow [1963] Director [French]; Peter Stanley Tresadern [1948] Managing Director

Ionics (U.K.) Limited
Incorporated: 27 November 1985 *Employees:* 2
Net Worth: £18,185,000 *Total Assets:* £19,456,000
Registered Office: 3rd Floor, 1 Ashley Road, Altrincham, Cheshire, WA14 2DT
Activities: Activities of head offices
Parent: Ionics Ventures Limited
Officers: Richard James Brook [1974] Sales Director; Richard James Gray [1978] Commercial Director

Ionix Aerospace Limited
Incorporated: 4 February 2013 *Employees:* 221
Net Worth: £8,284,000 *Total Assets:* £12,876,000
Registered Office: Prospect House, Taylor Business Park, Risley, Warrington, Cheshire, WA3 6HP
Activities: Manufacture of wiring devices
Parent: Amphenol Limited
Officers: Lance Edward D'Amico, Secretary; Craig Anthony Lampo [1969] Director/Business Executive [American]; Richard Adam Norwitt [1969] Director [American]

Ionix Systems Limited
Incorporated: 29 October 1957 *Employees:* 58
Net Worth: £6,260,000 *Total Assets:* £12,779,000
Registered Office: Prospect House, Taylor Business Park, Risley, Warrington, Cheshire, WA3 6HP
Activities: Manufacture of wiring devices
Parent: Ionix Holdings Limited
Officers: Lance Edward D'Amico, Secretary; Craig Anthony Lampo [1969] Director/Business Executive [American]; Richard Adam Norwitt [1969] Director [American]

Ipackchem Limited
Incorporated: 17 May 1991 *Employees:* 86
Net Worth: £7,173,517 *Total Assets:* £10,172,771
Registered Office: Gateway, Crewe, Cheshire, CW1 6YA
Activities: Manufacture of plastic packing goods
Officers: Jean Philippe Morvan [1963] Managing Director [French]; Manfred Schneller [1965] Director [Austrian]

IQRA Academy Education Trust
Incorporated: 24 July 2013 *Employees:* 112
Net Worth: £7,113,993 *Total Assets:* £8,145,994
Registered Office: Iqra Academy, Drummond Road, Bradford, BD8 8DA
Activities: Primary education
Officers: Asama Javed, Secretary; Shahnaz Anwar-Bleem [1956] Director/Headteacher; Rizwan Aziz [1975] Director; Parwaiz Bashir [1965] Director/Accountant; Peter Anthony Cusack [1960] Director/Assistant Site Manager; Helen Dawson [1970] Director/Teacher; Asam Javed [1977] Director/Interpreter; Asama Javed [1974] Director/Solicitor; Ghazala Nosheen [1990] Director/Customer Registration/Operations; Faqir Rahman [1936] Director/Retired [Pakistani]; Emmerson Wayne Walgrove [1975] Director; Mohammed Younis [1971] Director

Irish Ferries (U.K.) Limited
Incorporated: 5 August 1971 *Employees:* 56
Net Worth: £5,582,000 *Total Assets:* £7,869,000
Registered Office: Suite 4d, 4th Floor, The Plaza, 100 Old Hall Street, Liverpool, L3 9QJ
Activities: Service activities incidental to water transportation
Parent: Irish Ferries Limited
Officers: Thomas Corcoran, Secretary; Declan Freeman [1975] Director/Accountant [Irish]; David Ledwidge [1980] Director/Accountant [Irish]; Eamonn Rothwell [1955] Director [Irish]; Andrew Paul Sheen [1972] Managing Director

Irmass Company Limited
Incorporated: 14 September 1984 *Employees:* 23
Net Worth: £6,199,081 *Total Assets:* £8,674,669
Registered Office: Trafford Park Road, Newbridge, Trafford Park, Manchester, M17 1AN
Activities: Sawmilling and planing of wood
Major Shareholder: Bertie Darius Herbert Livesey Morton
Officers: Amanda Bobo Livesey Morton Allwood, Secretary; Bertie Darius Herbert Livesey Morton [1962] Director

Ironsides Lubricants Limited (The)
Incorporated: 26 April 1940 *Employees:* 50
Net Worth: £4,417,507 *Total Assets:* £6,961,492
Registered Office: Shield Street, Stockport, Cheshire, SK3 0DS
Activities: Mineral oil refining
Shareholders: David Forrest Bell; Colin Forrest Bell
Officers: Ian Douglas Paterson, Secretary; Mark Andrew Barker [1967] Director; David Forrest Bell [1945] Director/Chairman; Neil Cork [1966] Operations Director

Irwell Insurance Company Limited
Incorporated: 13 January 1994
Net Worth: £17,922,000 *Total Assets:* £45,471,000
Registered Office: 2 Cheetham Hill Road, Manchester, M4 4FB
Activities: Non-life insurance
Shareholder: Peter Eric Done
Officers: Sarah Louise Hart, Secretary; Fred Done [1943] Director; Peter Eric Done [1947] Director; Sarah Louise Hart [1968] Director/Accountant; Clifford Leicester Houghton [1950] Director/Chartered Accountant; Stephen Brian Lewis [1956] Director; Keith William Wardell [1957] Director/Insurance Executive

IS Pharma Ltd
Incorporated: 21 March 1997
Net Worth: £28,124,000 *Total Assets:* £59,560,000
Registered Office: Eden House, Lakeside, Chester Business Park, Chester, CH4 9QT
Activities: Activities of head offices
Parent: Sinclair Pharma Holdings Limited
Officers: Jason Rodney Tate, Secretary; Jayne Katherine Burrell [1974] Director; Alan Musgrave Olby [1971] Director; Christopher Paul Spooner [1968] Director

ISS Labour Group Limited
Incorporated: 15 October 2013
Net Worth Deficit: £1,550,068 *Total Assets:* £9,457,848
Registered Office: 7 Bradford Business Park, Kings Gate, Bradford, BD1 4SJ
Activities: Activities of head offices
Parent: Specialist People Services Group Ltd
Officers: Gary Beeston [1962] Director; Christopher Michael Chidley [1960] Director; Paul Howard McNulty [1970] Director

ISSA Foundation
Incorporated: 2 February 2016 *Employees:* 3
Net Worth: £25,176,454 *Total Assets:* £25,180,054
Registered Office: Euro Garages Ltd, Beehive Trading Park, Haslingdon Road, Blackburn, BB1 2EE
Activities: Other service activities n.e.c.
Officers: Javid Patel, Secretary; Mohsin Issa [1971] Director; Zuber Vali Issa [1972] Director

IVCC
Incorporated: 9 October 2008 *Employees:* 14
Net Worth: £2,798,000 *Total Assets:* £32,893,000
Registered Office: Liverpool School of Tropical Medicine, Pembroke Place, Liverpool, L3 5QA
Activities: Research and experimental development on biotechnology
Officers: Lynn Meredith Byrne, Secretary; Karmen Coralie Bennett [1967] Director/Manager [Australian]; Professor Fred Newton Binka [1953] Director/Lecturer [Ghanaian]; Anthony David Brandling-Bennett [1943] Director/Senior Program Officer [American]; Martin James Paul Cooke [1947] Director/Finance; Pascal Housset [1949] Director/Retired [French]; Jeremy John Elton Lefroy [1959] Director/Member of Parliament; Professor Qiyong Liu [1963] Director/Professor CDC [Chinese]; Sir Mark Moody-Stuart [1940] Director; Stephen Rothwell O'Brien [1957] Director/Undersecretary General for Humanitarian Affairs; Richard Walter Steketee [1950] Director/Doctor [American]

IX Reach Ltd
Incorporated: 7 July 2004 *Employees:* 23
Net Worth Deficit: £3,574,541 *Total Assets:* £14,322,710
Registered Office: Southgate 2, 321 Wilmslow Road, Heald Green, Cheadle, Cheshire, SK8 3PW
Activities: Wired telecommunications activities
Shareholders: Stephen James Wilcox; Allegro Technology Investments Limited
Officers: Clare Tattersall [1979] Finance Director; Stephen James Wilcox [1978] Director

J & K Confectionery Limited
Incorporated: 27 January 2005 *Employees:* 17
Net Worth: £1,096,063 *Total Assets:* £8,484,932
Registered Office: 2a Maple View, White Moss Business Park, Skelmersdale, Lancs, WN8 9TW
Activities: Wholesale of sugar and chocolate and sugar confectionery
Shareholder: John Warburton Derbyshire
Officers: Kathleen Derbyshire, Secretary; John Warburton Derbyshire [1948] Director; Kathleen Derbyshire [1949] Director

J & S Accessories Limited
Incorporated: 15 May 1991 *Employees:* 232
Net Worth: £15,323,450 *Total Assets:* £25,152,020
Registered Office: J & S Accessories, Chester Road, Oakmere, Northwich, Cheshire, CW8 2HB
Activities: Sale, maintenance and repair of motorcycles and related parts and accessories
Shareholders: Peter Cook; Elisabeth Ann Cook
Officers: Sheila Cook, Secretary; Peter Cook [1953] Director/Supplier of Motorcycle Clothing; Sheila Cook [1932] Director/Secretary; Peter John Davenport Lynch [1956] Director/Accountant

J M Holdings Limited
Incorporated: 6 November 1996 *Employees:* 123
Net Worth: £12,835,489 *Total Assets:* £16,482,789
Registered Office: JM Holdings Limited, Morley Drive, Congleton, Cheshire, CW12 3LF
Activities: Activities of production holding companies
Shareholders: Paul Alan Roberts; Simon John Morley Roberts
Officers: Paul Alan Roberts, Secretary/Director; Paul Alan Roberts [1956] Director; Simon John Morley Roberts [1960] Director

J S Fleet Services Limited
Incorporated: 13 March 1995 *Employees:* 93
Net Worth: £4,056,299 *Total Assets:* £20,616,500
Registered Office: 1 Bridle Road, Bootle, Merseyside, L30 4UG
Activities: Other specialised construction activities n.e.c.
Shareholders: John Sutch; Elaine Sutch
Officers: Elaine Sutch, Secretary/Director; Andrea Lillian Lowrie [1975] Director; Elaine Sutch [1952] Director; John Sutch [1952] Director; Hayley Sutch-Ware [1977] Director

J T Associates Limited
Incorporated: 2 August 1996 *Employees:* 4
Net Worth: £14,336,991 *Total Assets:* £27,267,310
Registered Office: St Georges House, 215-219 Chester Road, Manchester, M15 4JE
Activities: Development of building projects
Shareholders: Menelaos Tsitsis; Jacqueline Tsitsis
Officers: Jacqueline Tsitsis, Secretary; Jacqueline Tsitsis [1960] Director; Menelaos Tsitsis [1957] Director

J.H.F. Limited
Incorporated: 13 June 1986 *Employees:* 47
Net Worth: £1,243,371 *Total Assets:* £7,559,234
Registered Office: 14th Floor, The Plaza, 100 Old Hall Street, Liverpool, L3 9QJ
Activities: Wholesale of fruit and vegetables
Parent: ASB Holdings Limited
Officers: Anthony Leo Fernandes [1961] Director/General Manager [Indian]; Johannes Charl Francois Holtzhausen [1949] Director/Chief Executive Officer [South African]

J.P.S. Property Co. Limited
Incorporated: 29 April 1974
Net Worth: £5,528,135 *Total Assets:* £11,693,861
Registered Office: Didsbury Business Centre, 137 Barlow Moor Road, Didsbury, Manchester, M20 2PW
Activities: Residents property management
Shareholders: Danny Samuels; Justin Paul Samuels
Officers: Justin Paul Samuels, Secretary; Danny Samuels [1944] Director/Property Management; Justin Paul Samuels [1974] Director/Property Developer

J.S.M. Finance Limited
Incorporated: 21 January 1991
Net Worth: £771,859 *Total Assets:* £7,535,365
Registered Office: 2 Regency Chambers, Jubilee Way, Bury, Lancs, BL9 0JW
Activities: Other business support service activities n.e.c.
Parent: Regency Factors PLC
Officers: Jonathan Simon Myer Craft, Secretary; Hilary Susan Craft [1957] Director; Maurice Howard Craft [1955] Director; John Thomas Farrell [1965] Director

J.V Investments (U.K.) Limited
Incorporated: 6 June 2013
Registered Office: 48-52 Penny Lane Mossley Hill, Liverpool, L18 1DG
Activities: Buying and selling of own real estate
Major Shareholder: David Ralph Campbell
Officers: David Ralph Campbell [1944] Director [Canadian]; Peter Leonard Llewellyn [1969] Director

Jacobi Carbons Limited
Incorporated: 12 April 1996 *Employees:* 24
Net Worth: £2,215,225 *Total Assets:* £7,889,220
Registered Office: Croft Court, Moss Estate, Leigh, Lancs, WN7 3PT
Activities: Manufacture of other chemical products n.e.c.
Parent: Jacobi Carbons AB
Officers: Allan Braid Royston, Secretary; Remko Goudappel [1965] Director/Chief Executive Officer [Dutch]

D. Jacobson & Sons Limited
Incorporated: 2 July 1982 *Employees:* 142
Net Worth: £879,000 *Total Assets:* £14,321,000
Registered Office: Clough Fold, Bacup Road, Rawtenstall, Rossendale, Lancs, BB4 7PA
Activities: Wholesale of clothing and footwear
Officers: David Green, Secretary; Anthony Michael Evans [1967] Director/Sales Executive; David Green [1956] Director/Certified Accountant; Harvey Jacobson [1956] Director; Jonathan Bernard Jacobson [1971] Director; Richard Sisson [1961] Director

Jacobson Group Limited
Incorporated: 1 August 2006 *Employees:* 238
Net Worth: £1,450,000 *Total Assets:* £17,584,000
Registered Office: c/o Jacobson & Sons Limited, Clough Fold, Bacup Road, Rawtenstall, Lancs, BB4 7PA
Activities: Activities of other holding companies n.e.c.
Major Shareholder: Harvey Jacobson
Officers: David Green, Secretary; Anthony Michael Evans [1967] Director; David Green [1956] Director/Certified Accountant; Harvey Jacobson [1956] Director; Jonathan Bernard Jacobson [1971] Director; Richard Sisson [1961] Director

Jade Equity Limited
Incorporated: 4 March 2008 *Employees:* 249
Net Worth Deficit: £3,469,000 *Total Assets:* £38,107,000
Registered Office: James Dewhurst Ltd, Altham Lane, Altham, Accrington, Lancs, BB5 5YA
Activities: Activities of production holding companies
Parent: Sioen Industries NV
Officers: Geert Asselman [1961] Director [Belgian]; Malcolm Blackwell [1954] Director/Group CEO; Michèle Sioen [1965] Director [Belgian]; Frank Veranneman [1959] Director [Belgian]

Jade Solutions Limited
Incorporated: 4 August 1993 *Employees:* 41
Net Worth: £6,580,614 *Total Assets:* £9,200,874
Registered Office: Beech House, Woodlands Park, Ashton Road, Newton-le-Willows, Merseyside, WA12 0HF
Activities: Wired telecommunications activities
Parent: Northern Technology Investments Group Limited
Officers: Peter Charles Thomson, Secretary/Director; Mark Brackley [1963] Sales and Marketing Director; Peter Charles Thomson [1961] Director

Warren James (Jewellers) Limited
Incorporated: 21 June 1979 *Employees:* 1,451
Net Worth: £93,036,000 *Total Assets:* £181,514,000
Registered Office: 7 Merseyway, Stockport, Cheshire, SK1 1PN
Activities: Other retail sale of new goods in specialised stores (not commercial art galleries and opticians)
Parent: WJH Limited
Officers: Ann Jones, Secretary; John Coulter [1951] Director/Jeweller; Ann Jones [1954] Director/Jeweller

Oliver James Associates Group Limited
Incorporated: 9 December 2015
Net Worth: £9,638,575 *Total Assets:* £18,650,536
Registered Office: No 1 Spinningfields, Hardman Square, Manchester, M3 3EB
Activities: Activities of head offices
Shareholders: Oliver Steven Castle; Nicholas James Wase Rogers
Officers: Oliver Steven Castle [1976] Director/Recruitment Consultant; Nicholas James Wase Rogers [1974] Director/Recruitment Consultant

Oliver James Associates Limited
Incorporated: 27 May 2002 *Employees:* 157
Net Worth: £10,378,096 *Total Assets:* £19,174,752
Registered Office: No 1 Spinningfields, Hardman Square, Manchester, M3 3EB
Activities: Other activities of employment placement agencies
Shareholders: Nicholas James Wase-Rogers; Oliver Steven Castle
Officers: Melissa Jane Wase Rogers, Secretary; Oliver Steven Castle [1976] Director/Recruitment Consultant; Nicholas James Wase Rogers [1974] Director/Recruitment Consultant

The James Group Limited
Incorporated: 25 November 2004 *Employees:* 267
Net Worth: £2,869,969 *Total Assets:* £9,060,219
Registered Office: Unit GF1, The Quad, Atherleigh Business Park, Gibfield Park Avenue, Atherton, Manchester, M46 0SY
Activities: Sale of new cars and light motor vehicles
Major Shareholder: Lee James Bootle
Officers: Lee James Bootle [1971] Director/Bodyshop Manager

Warren James Holdings Limited
Incorporated: 27 November 1996
Net Worth: £89,658,008 *Total Assets:* £147,151,408
Registered Office: 7 Merseyway, Stockport, Cheshire, SK1 1PN
Activities: Activities of head offices
Parent: WJA Limited
Officers: Ann Jones, Secretary; John Coulter [1951] Director/Jeweller; Ann Jones [1954] Director/Jeweller

James Industrial Limited
Incorporated: 29 July 1986 *Employees:* 7
Net Worth: £4,579,014 *Total Assets:* £8,868,668
Registered Office: Laurel House, 173 Chorley New Road, Bolton, Lancs, BL1 4QZ
Activities: Other business support service activities n.e.c.
Shareholders: Joanne Michelle James; Michael Stuart James
Officers: Michael Stuart James, Secretary/Director; Joanne Michelle James [1965] Director; Michael Stuart James [1958] Director

Janson Computers PLC
Incorporated: 26 August 1987
Net Worth: £12,021,000 *Total Assets:* £12,021,000
Registered Office: Technology House, Magnesium Way, Hapton, Burnley, Lancs, BB12 7BF
Activities: Information technology consultancy activities
Parent: Exertis (UK) Ltd
Officers: Richard Hinds, Secretary; Paul William Bryan [1969] Managing Director; Alexander Bernard James Croft [1973] Director; Antony John Taylor [1964] Director

Jarden Consumer Solutions (Europe) Limited
Incorporated: 25 January 1962 *Employees:* 121
Net Worth: £26,944,000 *Total Assets:* £55,625,000
Registered Office: 5400 Lakeside, Cheadle Royal Business Park, Cheadle, Cheshire, SK8 3GQ
Activities: Manufacture of electric domestic appliances
Parent: Vine Mill Limited
Officers: Ben Hartley [1976] Director/Attorney; Dasree Vishwamaryum Ramsammy [1961] Director/Attorney [American]

Jarron Holdings Limited
Incorporated: 29 July 2016
Net Worth: £6,635,193 *Total Assets:* £6,635,743
Registered Office: Scarisbrick Hall, Southport Road, Scarisbrick, Ormskirk, Lancs, L40 9RQ
Activities: Other business support service activities n.e.c.
Shareholders: Barry John Cackett; Lynda Ann Headley
Officers: Barry John Cackett [1969] Director; Lynda Ann Headley [1970] Director

Jason Plastics Limited
Incorporated: 24 July 1972 *Employees:* 54
Net Worth: £5,463,027 *Total Assets:* £8,273,401
Registered Office: Prettywood, Bury New Road, Heap Bridge, Bury, Lancs, BL9 7HZ
Activities: Manufacture of plastic packing goods
Shareholder: Dr Brenton Mark Walshaw
Officers: Dr Brenton Mark Walshaw [1963] Director

Jaymel Limited
Incorporated: 13 August 2009 *Employees:* 252
Net Worth Deficit: £630,011 *Total Assets:* £15,305,492
Registered Office: 17 St Peters Place, Fleetwood, Lancs, FY7 6EB
Activities: Activities of head offices
Major Shareholder: Andrew James Pilley
Officers: Andrew James Pilley [1970] Director

JBA Group Limited
Incorporated: 11 October 2007 *Employees:* 534
Net Worth: £8,289,727 *Total Assets:* £12,621,534
Registered Office: South Barn, Broughton Hall, Skipton, N Yorks, BD23 3AE
Activities: Engineering related scientific and technical consulting activities
Shareholder: Jeremy Richard Benn
Officers: Craig Robson, Secretary; Jeremy Richard Benn [1962] Director/Civil Engineer; William Albert Schlegel [1954] Director/Chartered Civil Engineer; Christopher Ernest Schofield [1962] Director/Solicitor

JC Land (Investments) Ltd
Incorporated: 8 June 2001 *Employees:* 1
Net Worth: £3,212,520 *Total Assets:* £12,110,026
Registered Office: 9 Winckley Square, Preston, Lancs, PR1 3HP
Activities: Other letting and operating of own or leased real estate
Major Shareholder: Jamie Robert Carter
Officers: Kellie Marie Carter, Secretary; Jamie Robert Carter [1968] Director

JCCO 387 Limited
Incorporated: 2 December 2015 *Employees:* 2
Net Worth: £797,207 *Total Assets:* £6,932,307
Registered Office: St Mary's Gate, Priory Close, Lancaster, LA1 1XB
Activities: Activities of other holding companies n.e.c.
Shareholders: Andrew Nigel Appleyard; Christine Doris Appleyard
Officers: Andrew Nigel Appleyard [1964] Director; Christine Doris Appleyard [1970] Director

JCT600 (Properties) Limited
Incorporated: 19 October 1987 *Employees:* 12
Net Worth: £45,022,000 *Total Assets:* £122,349,000
Registered Office: Tordoff House, Apperley Bridge, Bradford, W Yorks, BD10 0PQ
Activities: Development of building projects
Major Shareholder: Jack Crossley Tordoff
Officers: Nigel Martin Shaw, Secretary; Nigel Martin Shaw [1962] Finance Director; Jack Crossley Tordoff [1935] Director; John Cornel Tordoff [1963] Director/Chief Executive

JCT600 (Rawdon) Limited
Incorporated: 5 August 1988 *Employees:* 140
Net Worth: £29,094,000 *Total Assets:* £47,894,000
Registered Office: Tordoff House, Apperley Bridge, Bradford, W Yorks, BD10 0PQ
Activities: Sale of new cars and light motor vehicles
Major Shareholder: Jack Crossley Tordoff
Officers: Nigel Martin Shaw, Secretary; Nigel Martin Shaw [1962] Finance Director; Jack Crossley Tordoff [1935] Director; John Cornel Tordoff [1963] Director/Chief Executive

JCT600 (South Yorkshire) Limited
Incorporated: 28 January 1983 *Employees:* 245
Net Worth: £27,061,000 *Total Assets:* £89,069,000
Registered Office: Tordoff House, Apperley Bridge, Bradford, W Yorks, BD10 0PQ
Activities: Sale of new cars and light motor vehicles
Major Shareholder: Jack Crossley Tordoff
Officers: Nigel Martin Shaw, Secretary; Nigel Martin Shaw [1962] Finance Director; Jack Crossley Tordoff [1935] Director; John Cornel Tordoff [1963] Director/Chief Executive

JCT600 (Yorkshire) Ltd
Incorporated: 22 January 1960 *Employees:* 85
Net Worth: £7,847,000 *Total Assets:* £29,522,000
Registered Office: Tordoff House, Apperley Bridge, Bradford, W Yorks, BD10 0PQ
Activities: Sale of new cars and light motor vehicles
Major Shareholder: Jack Crossley Tordoff
Officers: Nigel Martin Shaw, Secretary; Nigel Martin Shaw [1962] Finance Director; Jack Crossley Tordoff [1935] Director; John Cornel Tordoff [1963] Director/Chief Executive

JCT600 Limited
Incorporated: 20 June 1946 *Employees:* 2,179
Net Worth: £154,056,000 *Total Assets:* £413,132,992
Registered Office: Tordoff House, Apperley Bridge, Bradford, W Yorks, BD10 0PQ
Activities: Sale of new cars and light motor vehicles
Major Shareholder: Jack Crossley Tordoff
Officers: Nigel Martin Shaw, Secretary; Nigel Martin Shaw [1962] Finance Director; Edward Ian Tordoff [1957] Director; Jack Crossley Tordoff [1935] Director; John Cornel Tordoff [1963] Director/Chief Executive

JCT600 Vehicle Leasing Solutions Limited
Incorporated: 18 July 1968 *Employees:* 43
Net Worth: £35,006,000 *Total Assets:* £86,817,000
Registered Office: Tordoff House, Apperley Bridge, Bradford, W Yorks, BD10 0PQ
Activities: Sale of new cars and light motor vehicles
Major Shareholder: Jack Crossley Tordoff
Officers: Nigel Martin Shaw, Secretary; Nigel Martin Shaw [1962] Finance Director; Edward Ian Tordoff [1957] Director; Jack Crossley Tordoff [1935] Director; John Cornel Tordoff [1963] Director/Chief Executive

JD Sports Fashion PLC
Incorporated: 21 February 1985 *Employees:* 30,292
Net Worth: £770,400,000 *Total Assets:* £1,626,200,064
Registered Office: Hollinsbrook Way, Pilsworth, Bury, Lancs, BL9 8RR
Activities: Retail sale of clothing in specialised stores
Officers: Siobhan Mawdsley, Secretary; Peter Alan Cowgill [1953] Director; Martin William Oliver Davies [1960] Director; Heather Louise Jackson [1965] Director; Andrew Marvin Leslie [1946] Director; Andrew Keith Rubin [1965] Director; Brian Michael Small [1956] Director

JDS Trucks Limited
Incorporated: 8 June 1965 *Employees:* 93
Net Worth: £3,377,213 *Total Assets:* £7,882,301
Registered Office: Navigation Garage, Forrest Street, Blackburn, Lancs, BB1 3BB
Activities: Sale of other motor vehicles
Parent: Rimape Limited
Officers: Mark Frank Griffiths, Secretary; Christopher Bell [1961] Sales Director Richard Neil Davies [1967] Director; Lee Duncan Drummond [1970] Director; Mark Frank Griffiths [1966] Director/Accountant

JDW Finance Limited
Incorporated: 18 November 2003 *Employees:* 2
Net Worth: £13,957,370 *Total Assets:* £520,683,008
Registered Office: Griffin House, 40 Lever Street, Manchester, M60 6ES
Activities: Other business support service activities n.e.c.
Parent: JD Williams & Company Limited
Officers: Daniel Michael Cropper, Secretary; Craig Barry Lovelace [1973] Director/Accountant; Ian James Somerset [1979] Director/Accountant

JDW Malta Limited
Incorporated: 24 February 2017 *Employees:* 1
Net Worth: £383,476,800 *Total Assets:* £383,476,800
Registered Office: Griffin House, 40 Lever Street, Manchester, M60 6ES
Activities: Activities of other holding companies n.e.c.
Parent: N Brown Group PLC
Officers: Daniel Michael Cropper, Secretary; Craig Barry Lovelace [1973] Director/Accountant

C.M. Jefferies & Co. Limited
Incorporated: 30 May 1950 *Employees:* 2
Net Worth: £7,906,460 *Total Assets:* £8,339,671
Registered Office: Aldford House, 8 Aldford Place, Alderley Edge, Cheshire, SK9 7RQ
Activities: Non-trading company
Shareholders: Elisabeth Penelope Anna Sinclair; Timothy Clarence Brandon Jefferies; Sara Catherine Barbara Wood
Officers: Barbara Jefferies, Secretary; Barbara Jefferies [1931] Director/Manager; Timothy Clarence Brandon Jefferies [1955] Director/Manager

Jerrold Finco PLC
Incorporated: 31 October 2003
Net Worth: £184,300 *Total Assets:* £582,727,168
Registered Office: Lake View, Lakeside, Cheadle, Cheshire, SK8 3GW
Activities: Activities of financial services holding companies
Parent: Together Financial Services Limited
Officers: Gary Derek Beckett, Secretary; Gary Derek Beckett [1969] Director; Marc Richard Goldberg [1971] Director; Henry Neville Moser [1949] Director

Simon Jersey Ltd
Incorporated: 26 March 1971 *Employees:* 141
Net Worth Deficit: £5,017,219 *Total Assets:* £17,321,092
Registered Office: The Forum, Hercules Business Park, Bird Hall Lane, Cheadle Hulme, Stockport, Cheshire, SK3 0UX
Activities: Wholesale of clothing and footwear
Parent: Simon Jersey Group Limited
Officers: Philip John Kenny, Secretary; Philip John Kenny [1978] Director/Solicitor; Mirvet Russo [1968] Operations Director Group [Dutch]; Kieron Bartholemew Traynor [1960] Director; Glenn Robert Walker [1958] Director/Accountant

The Jesem Group Limited
Incorporated: 11 May 2017 *Employees:* 170
Net Worth: £17,424,788 *Total Assets:* £34,580,884
Registered Office: KJG LLP, 1 City Road East, Manchester, M15 4PN
Activities: Activities of other holding companies n.e.c.
Shareholders: Howard Steven Goldman; Russell Stuart Goldman
Officers: Howard Steven Goldman [1978] Director; Michael David Goldman [1949] Director; Russell Stuart Goldman [1971] Director

Jesem Holdings Limited
Incorporated: 13 November 2012
Net Worth: £34,000,000 *Total Assets:* £34,000,000
Registered Office: 2nd Floor, 1 City Road East, Manchester, M15 4PN
Activities: Activities of other holding companies n.e.c.
Parent: The Jesem Group Limited
Officers: Howard Goldman [1978] Director; Michael David Goldman [1949] Director; Russell Stuart Goldman [1971] Director

Jessgrove Limited
Incorporated: 11 May 1979 *Employees:* 66
Net Worth: £10,050,841 *Total Assets:* £18,870,960
Registered Office: Cross Lane Mills, Cross Lane, Bradford, W Yorks, BD7 3JT
Activities: Wholesale of textiles
Officers: Molly Craven, Secretary; Lee Oliver Craven [1970] Director/General Manager; Molly Craven [1941] Director; Ronald Craven [1939] Director

Jetchem Systems Limited
Incorporated: 9 August 1991 *Employees:* 84
Net Worth: £5,358,903 *Total Assets:* £8,982,836
Registered Office: Unit 11 Cuba Industrial Estate, Bolton Road North, Stubbins, Ramsbottom, Bury, Lancs, BL0 0NE
Activities: Manufacture of pumps
Parent: JCS Holdings Limited
Officers: Mark Stephen Taylor, Secretary; Andrew Taylor [1961] Director; Mark Stephen Taylor [1969] Production Director; Paul Taylor [1962] Managing Director; Roland Howard Taylor [1930] Technical Director

Jeunesse Global (Europe) Limited
Incorporated: 8 December 2010
Net Worth: £1,885,247 *Total Assets:* £9,360,452
Registered Office: Frodsham Business Centre, Bridge Lane, Frodsham, Cheshire, WA6 7FZ
Activities: Retail sale via mail order houses or via Internet
Major Shareholder: Ogale Ray
Officers: Ogale Ray, Secretary; Ogale Ray [1941] Managing Director [American]

JFJG Properties Limited
Incorporated: 11 September 2013
Registered Office: 2nd Floor, Parkgates, Bury New Road, Prestwich, Manchester, M25 0TL
Activities: Other letting and operating of own or leased real estate
Shareholders: JFJG Holdings Ltd; JFJG Holdings Limited
Officers: Joseph Grunfeld [1978] Director

JH Estent Limited
Incorporated: 9 February 2017 *Employees:* 2
Net Worth: £178,932 *Total Assets:* £6,798,921
Registered Office: Nisiac House, 1 Cunningham Court, Lions Drive, Blackburn, Lancs, BB1 2QX
Activities: Other letting and operating of own or leased real estate
Major Shareholder: Jamal Udin Hussain
Officers: Jawid Hussain [1958] Director; Majid Hussain [1977] Director

Jiffy (UK) Holding I Limited
Incorporated: 1 July 2005
Net Worth Deficit: £8,522,000 *Total Assets:* £6,891,000
Registered Office: c/o Jiffy Packaging Company Ltd, Road Four, Industrial Estate, Winsford, Cheshire, CW7 3QR
Activities: Activities of production holding companies
Officers: Richard Gregg [1964] Managing Director; Markus Petrus Heinrich Kollmann [1964] Director [Dutch]; Michael Rathbone [1958] Director/Accountant

Jiffy Packaging Company Limited
Incorporated: 13 March 1964 *Employees:* 129
Net Worth: £524,000 *Total Assets:* £12,329,000
Registered Office: 9 Road Four, Winsford Industrial Estate, Winsford, Cheshire, CW7 3QR
Activities: Manufacture of corrugated paper and paperboard, sacks and bags
Officers: Michael Rathbone, Secretary; Richard Gregg [1964] Managing Director; Markus Petrus Heinrich Kollmann [1964] Director [Dutch]; Peter Lewis [1955] Director; Michael Rathbone [1958] Director/Accountant

Jiffy Protective Packaging Limited
Incorporated: 12 July 1909 *Employees:* 3
Net Worth: £13,585,000 *Total Assets:* £14,049,000
Registered Office: 9 Road Four, Winsford Industrial Estate, Winsford, Cheshire, CW7 3QR
Activities: Other business support service activities n.e.c.
Parent: Airpack S.P.A
Officers: Michael Rathbone, Secretary; Richard Gregg [1964] Managing Director; Marcus Petrus Heinrich Kollmann [1964] Director [Dutch]; Peter Lewis [1955] Director; Michael Rathbone [1958] Director/Accountant

JJC Hire Limited
Incorporated: 12 September 2007 *Employees:* 30
Net Worth: £1,739,426 *Total Assets:* £8,526,878
Registered Office: The Tower, Dalton Gate, Business Centre, Ulverston, Cumbria, LA12 7AJ
Activities: Collection of non-hazardous waste
Shareholders: Anne Armer; John Cooper
Officers: Robin James Walmsley [1959] Director

JLG Industries (United Kingdom) Limited
Incorporated: 18 August 1998 *Employees:* 100
Net Worth: £5,425,787 *Total Assets:* £29,035,164
Registered Office: Units 4 & 5 Bentley Avenue, Middleton, Manchester, M24 2GP
Activities: Manufacture of other general-purpose machinery n.e.c.
Parent: JLG EMEA B.V.
Officers: Robert Scott Grennier [1964] Director [American]; Marjorie Jirovec Griffing [1961] Director [American]; Carolus Hubertus Huijser [1961] Director [Dutch]

JMU Property Development Company Limited
Incorporated: 26 April 1995
Net Worth: £8,590,001 *Total Assets:* £8,593,098
Registered Office: c/o Liverpool John Moores University, Exchange Station, Tithebarn Street, Liverpool, L2 2QP
Activities: Management of real estate on a fee or contract basis
Officers: Christina Fitzpatrick, Secretary; Belinda Louise McGuiness [1961] Finance Director [Australian]; Mark Alan Power [1960] Director/Head of Institution and Chief Executive

JMW Solicitors LLP
Incorporated: 24 July 2008 *Employees:* 304
Net Worth: £9,326,330 *Total Assets:* £13,137,958
Registered Office: 1 Byrom Place, Spinningfields, Manchester, M3 3HG
Officers: Andrew Garvie [1970] Member; Ian Richard Gordon [1965] Member; George Edward Jones [1966] Member; Paul Martin Walker [1957] Member; Abigail Bennett [1975] LLP Member; Simon Barnet Bloch [1976] LLP Member; Michael James Blood [1968] LLP Member; Paul Kenneth Breen [1963] LLP Member; Gordon Paul Cartwright [1979] LLP Member; Stuart Cartwright [1974] LLP Member; Gerard William Chadwick [1963] LLP Member; Michael John Chapman [1978] LLP Member; Daniel David Clark [1978] LLP Member; Elizabeth Anne Cotton [1978] LLP Member; Thomas Edward Cressey [1976] LLP Member; Russel Forward [1976] LLP Member; Peter Joseph Grogan [1958] LLP Member; Claire Louise Hamilton [1974] LLP Member; Mark Michael Heppell [1981] LLP Member; Beverley Anne Jones [1982] LLP Member; Mark Jones [1963] LLP Member; Michael Kennedy [1965] LLP Member; Elspeth Rachel Kinder [1979] LLP Member; Joy Melanie Kingsley [1956] LLP Member; Ian Neal Lewis [1959] LLP Member; Andrew Robert Lilley [1970] LLP Member; Christopher Paul Albert Love [1978] LLP Member; Jodi Louise Lund [1982] LLP Member; Majid Mahmood [1979] LLP Member; Warren Scott Martin [1975] LLP Member; Ruth Carole McCarthy [1979] LLP Member; Derek James Millard-Smith [1974] LLP Member; Thomas Guy Lovett Pearson [1978] LLP Member; David Pickering [1955] LLP Member; Richard Matthew Powell [1969] LLP Member; Michael Derrick Purvis [1979] LLP Member; Michael Joseph Rainford [1957] LLP Member; Graham Paul Small [1963] LLP Member; Christopher John Sutton [1975] LLP Member; Ian Victor Keith Tranter [1955] LLP Member; Richard John Wolff [1968] LLP Member; Marc Simon Yaffe [1979] LLP Member

Jo-Y-Jo International Limited
Incorporated: 11 February 1987 *Employees:* 42
Net Worth: £4,872,934 *Total Assets:* £7,164,387
Registered Office: Basil Chambers, 4th Floor, 65 High Street, Manchester, M4 1FS
Activities: Wholesale of clothing and footwear
Major Shareholder: Stanley Arthur Fosbury
Officers: Timothy Robert Densem, Secretary; Timothy Robert Densem [1970] Director; Mark Fosbury [1963] Director/Sales Manager

Jo-Y-Jo Limited
Incorporated: 3 November 1967 *Employees:* 42
Net Worth: £4,872,934 *Total Assets:* £7,164,387
Registered Office: Basil Chambers, 4th Floor, 65 High Street, Manchester, M4 1FS
Activities: Wholesale of clothing and footwear
Major Shareholder: Stanley Arthur Fosbury
Officers: Timothy Robert Densem, Secretary; Mark Leslie Corness [1979] Director/Sales Person; Timothy Robert Densem [1970] Director; Mark Fosbury [1963] Director/Sales Manager; Paul Michael Fosbury [1966] Director; Stanley Arthur Fosbury [1935] Director/Chairman; Joanne Catherine Gaillard [1971] Director/Housewife; Andrew Darby Mitchell [1958] Director; Susan Katherine Walmsley [1969] Director/Sales Executive

Joda Holdings Limited
Incorporated: 17 March 2005 *Employees:* 110
Net Worth: £3,428,780 *Total Assets:* £7,410,381
Registered Office: Riparian Way, Cross Hills, Keighley, W Yorks, BD20 7BW
Activities: Operation of warehousing and storage facilities for land transport activities
Shareholders: David John Wareing; Johnathan Collett
Officers: David John Wareing, Secretary/Haulage Contractor; John Collett [1960] Director/Haulage Contractor; David John Wareing [1958] Director/Haulage Contractor

Johnson Cleaners UK Limited
Incorporated: 22 September 1994 *Employees:* 1,127
Net Worth Deficit: £4,586,000 *Total Assets:* £6,772,000
Registered Office: Timpson House, Claverton Road, Manchester, M23 9TT
Activities: Washing and (dry-)cleaning of textile and fur products
Parent: Timpson Group PLC
Officers: Roger Lane-Smith [1945] Director/Solicitor; Paresh Majithia [1967] Finance Director; Stephen Peter Robertson [1954] Director; James Timpson [1971] Director; Sir William John Anthony Timpson [1943] Director

Johnson Group Properties PLC
Incorporated: 31 August 1953 *Employees:* 1
Net Worth: £6,143,000 *Total Assets:* £16,921,000
Registered Office: Johnson House, Abbots Park, Monks Way, Preston Brook, Runcorn, Cheshire, WA7 3GH
Activities: Development of building projects
Parent: Johnson Service Group PLC
Officers: Yvonne May Monaghan, Secretary; Yvonne May Monaghan [1958] Director; Ian John Phillips [1960] Director; Christopher Sander [1958] Director

Neville Johnson Holdings Limited
Incorporated: 29 January 2008
Net Worth: £6,434,000 *Total Assets:* £12,003,000
Registered Office: Broadoak Business Park, Ashburton Road West, Trafford Park, Manchester, M17 1RW
Activities: Manufacture of other furniture
Parent: BHID Group Limited
Officers: William Keith Bennett, Secretary; William Keith Bennett [1953] Director; Jeffrey Forrester [1953] Director; Simon Patrick Meyrick [1962] Director; Nigel John Pailing [1958] Director

Johnson Investment Limited
Incorporated: 25 October 1999
Net Worth: £417,553,984 *Total Assets:* £417,553,984
Registered Office: Johnson House, Abbots Park, Monks Way, Preston Brook, Runcorn, Cheshire, WA7 3GH
Activities: Activities of head offices
Parent: Johnson Service Group PLC
Officers: Yvonne May Monaghan, Secretary; Yvonne May Monaghan [1958] Director; Timothy James Morris [1977] Director/Accountant

Neville Johnson Limited
Incorporated: 21 February 1983 *Employees:* 214
Net Worth: £1,846,000 *Total Assets:* £9,501,000
Registered Office: Broadoak Business Park, Ashburton Road West, Trafford Park, Manchester, M17 1RW
Activities: Manufacture of office and shop furniture
Parent: Neville Johnson Holdings Ltd
Officers: William Keith Bennett, Secretary; William Keith Bennett [1953] Director; Jeffrey Forrester [1953] Director; Simon Patrick Meyrick [1962] Director; Nigel John Pailing [1958] Sales Director; Lisa Michelle Quinlan [1969] Marketing Director

Johnson Service Group PLC
Incorporated: 4 September 1953 *Employees:* 5,119
Net Worth: £167,600,000 *Total Assets:* £361,800,000
Registered Office: Johnson House, Abbots Park, Monks Way, Preston Brook, Cheshire, WA7 3GH
Activities: Activities of head offices
Officers: Timothy James Morris, Secretary; Peter Egan [1972] Director/Chief Operating Officer; Christopher Francis Girling [1954] Director; Nicholas Mark Gregg [1963] Director; Yvonne May Monaghan [1958] Director; Christopher Sander [1958] Director; William Mervyn Frew Carey Shannon [1949] Director

Johnsons Apparelmaster Limited
Incorporated: 16 February 1949 *Employees:* 5,054
Net Worth: £254,792,000 *Total Assets:* £500,208,000
Registered Office: Pittman Way, Fulwood, Preston, Lancs, PR2 9ZD
Activities: Washing and (dry-)cleaning of textile and fur products
Parent: Semara Group Limited
Officers: Avijit Kar, Secretary; Gary Andrew Collis [1966] Director; Peter Egan [1972] Managing Director [Irish]; Avijit Kar [1961] Director; Yvonne May Monaghan [1958] Director; Gerard Moore [1964] Managing Director [Irish]; Mark Rue [1965] Director; Christopher Sander [1958] Director; Helen Wood [1968] Operations Director

Daniel Johnston (1982) Limited
Incorporated: 16 July 1982 *Employees:* 5
Net Worth: £8,438,695 *Total Assets:* £8,941,590
Registered Office: Dalmar House, Barras Lane Industrial Estate, Dalston, Carlisle, Cumbria, CA5 7NY
Activities: Development of building projects
Major Shareholder: Michael Connon
Officers: Alyson Richmond Connon, Secretary; Maxwell Clark Connon [1990] Director; Michael Connon [1945] Director

Johnston Ballantyne Holdings Limited
Incorporated: 26 September 2011
Net Worth: £14,025,000 *Total Assets:* £14,029,000
Registered Office: Eversheds House, 70 Great Bridgewater Street, Manchester, M1 5ES
Activities: Other business support service activities n.e.c.
Parent: SPX Flow, Inc.
Officers: Paul Andrew Cahill [1974] Director/Accountant; Mark Edward Shanahan [1970] Finance Director; Jeremy Wade Smeltser [1975] Director/CFO, SPX Flow, Inc. [American]; Stephen Tsoris [1957] Director [American]

Johnston Developments Holdings Limited
Incorporated: 17 December 2009 *Employees:* 69
Net Worth: £3,891,224 *Total Assets:* £6,957,939
Registered Office: Oakland House, 21 Hope Carr Road, Leigh, Lancs, WN7 3ET
Activities: Activities of head offices
Shareholders: Nigel Francis Johnston; Sandra Johnston
Officers: Nigel Francis Johnston [1963] Director; Sandra Johnston [1963] Director

Johoco 2029 Limited
Incorporated: 10 September 2014 *Employees:* 483
Net Worth: £644,953 *Total Assets:* £13,937,585
Registered Office: Suites G & H, Ground Floor, Steam Mill, Steam Mill Street, Chester, CH3 5AN
Activities: Licenced restaurants
Officers: Marita McDonnell, Secretary; Robert Alan Bacon [1976] Director; Paul Adam Campbell [1964] Director; Peter John Kemp-Welch [1969] Director; Neil Edward McDonnell [1969] Director; Matthew David Powell [1973] Finance Director; John William Welsh [1979] Director

Joloda (International) Limited
Incorporated: 19 October 1992 *Employees:* 107
Net Worth: £8,748,661 *Total Assets:* £14,841,714
Registered Office: 51 Speke Road, Liverpool, L19 2NY
Activities: Manufacture of lifting and handling equipment
Parent: Joloda International Holdings Limited
Officers: Michele Dematteis [1968] Director; Wojciech Joseph Kordel [1943] Director/Engineer; Alec McAndrew [1961] Operations Director; Wouter Satijn [1977] Director [Dutch]

Jones & Brooks,Limited
Incorporated: 29 April 1898 *Employees:* 54
Net Worth: £5,719,323 *Total Assets:* £7,850,203
Registered Office: Unit 13 Riverside Drive, Smallbridge Industrial Park, Rochdale, Lancs, OL16 2SH
Activities: Printing n.e.c.
Officers: Hilary June Blair, Secretary; Allan Blair [1974] Director; Andrew Blair [1980] Director; Caroline Blair [1980] Director; Hilary June Blair [1949] Director; Ronald Victor Blair [1949] Director; Victoria Kopczak [1980] Director; Rachel Squirrell [1976] Director

Jones & Egan Estates Limited
Incorporated: 21 August 2015 *Employees:* 3
Net Worth: £8,906,592 *Total Assets:* £9,039,471
Registered Office: 63 Rusland Park, Kendal, Cumbria, LA9 6AJ
Activities: Other letting and operating of own or leased real estate
Officers: David Egan [1979] Director; Laura Jean Egan [1982] Director; Susan Jane Jones [1952] Director

P.E.Jones (Properties) Limited
Incorporated: 10 August 1960 *Employees:* 19
Net Worth: £55,197,000 *Total Assets:* £94,195,000
Registered Office: Emerson House, Heyes Lane, Alderley Edge, Cheshire, SK9 7LF
Activities: Other letting and operating of own or leased real estate
Officers: Varun Maharaj, Secretary; Anthony Emerson Jones [1967] Director; Audrey Jones [1936] Director; Mark Emerson Jones [1964] Director; Peter Emerson Jones [1935] Director

P.E. Jones Contracts (Manchester) Limited
Incorporated: 14 August 1978 *Employees:* 10
Net Worth: £6,816,949 *Total Assets:* £8,886,206
Registered Office: Emerson House, Heyes Lane, Alderley Edge, Cheshire, SK9 7LF
Activities: Development of building projects
Parent: Orbit Developments (Manchester) Limited
Officers: Varun Maharaj, Secretary; Steven David Barnett [1961] Director; Audrey Jones [1936] Director; Mark Emerson Jones [1964] Director/Business Executive; Peter Emerson Jones [1935] Director; David Alan Quirk [1955] Director/Quantity Surveyor

Jones Homes (Lancashire) Limited
Incorporated: 17 May 1976 *Employees:* 33
Net Worth: £21,739,400 *Total Assets:* £30,569,578
Registered Office: Emerson House, Heyes Lane, Alderley Edge, Cheshire, SK9 7LF
Activities: Construction of domestic buildings
Parent: Emerson Developments (Holdings) Ltd
Officers: Varun Maharaj, Secretary; Ralph Bacon [1960] Director/Company Executive; Jonathan Rodney Claber [1982] Director; Gary John Hardy [1959] Director; Mark Emerson Jones [1964] Director/Business Executive; Peter Emerson Jones [1935] Director

Jones Homes (North West) Limited
Incorporated: 24 April 1959 *Employees:* 71
Net Worth: £69,006,632 *Total Assets:* £108,264,648
Registered Office: Emerson House, Heyes Lane, Alderley Edge, Cheshire, SK9 7LF
Activities: Construction of domestic buildings
Parent: Emerson Developments (Holdings) Limited
Officers: Varun Maharaj, Secretary; Jonathan Rodney Claber [1982] Director; Nigel John Galleymore [1955] Director; Gary John Hardy [1959] Director; Anthony Emerson Jones [1967] Director; Audrey Jones [1936] Director; Mark Emerson Jones [1964] Director; Peter Emerson Jones [1935] Director; Lee Sale [1973] Director/Business Executive

Jones Homes (Southern) Limited
Incorporated: 20 October 1995 *Employees:* 35
Net Worth: £21,109,576 *Total Assets:* £38,458,660
Registered Office: Emerson House, Heyes Lane, Alderley Edge, Cheshire, SK9 7LF
Activities: Construction of domestic buildings
Parent: Jones Homes (North West) Limited
Officers: Varun Maharaj, Secretary; Jeremy Paul Attwater [1969] Director/Business Executive; Terence Stephen Charles Brown [1961] Director/Business Executive; Jonathan Rodney Claber [1982] Director; Anthony Emerson Jones [1967] Director; Mark Emerson Jones [1964] Director; Peter Emerson Jones [1935] Director; Sara Jane Stanhope [1967] Director

Jones Homes (Yorkshire) Limited
Incorporated: 16 April 1996 *Employees:* 50
Net Worth: £24,034,104 *Total Assets:* £27,703,854
Registered Office: Emerson House, Heyes Lane, Alderley Edge, Cheshire, SK9 7LF
Activities: Construction of domestic buildings
Parent: Jones Homes (North West) Limited
Officers: Varun Maharaj, Secretary; Jonathan Rodney Claber [1982] Director Allan Glenn Cooke [1971] Technical Director; Gary John Hardy [1959] Director; Anthony Emerson Jones [1967] Director; Mark Emerson Jones [1964] Director; Peter Emerson Jones [1935] Director; David William Ruffley [1962] Director/Business Executive; Jayne Angela Swift [1973] Sales & Marketing Director

Jones Stroud Insulations Limited
Incorporated: 10 May 2000 *Employees:* 210
Net Worth: £14,744,338 *Total Assets:* £18,478,764
Registered Office: Queens Mill, Queen Street, Longridge, Preston, Lancs, PR3 3BS
Activities: Other manufacturing n.e.c.
Officers: Neil Robert Currie, Secretary; Robin Geoffrey Stenhouse [1959] Managing Director

Jonesco (Preston) Limited
Incorporated: 23 March 1967 *Employees:* 173
Net Worth: £8,318,864 *Total Assets:* £12,556,841
Registered Office: Pittman Way, Fulwood, Preston, Lancs, PR2 9ZD
Activities: Manufacture of other plastic products
Shareholders: Peter David Hine; Clifford Michael Shiers
Officers: Clifford Michael Shiers, Secretary; Andrew Richard Jones [1959] Joint Managing Director; Henry Rupert Jones [1960] Joint Managing Director; Peter Mark Williams [1961] Sales Director

Jost (Great Britain) Limited
Incorporated: 5 May 1969 *Employees:* 2
Net Worth: £3,283,000 *Total Assets:* £25,921,000
Registered Office: Edbro House, Nelson Street, Bolton, Lancs, BL3 2JJ
Activities: Wholesale trade of motor vehicle parts and accessories
Officers: Thilo Boeltink, Secretary; Lars Brorsen [1952] Director [Danish]; Paul Raymond Farthing [1962] Director/Sales & Marketing Executive

Jost UK Limited
Incorporated: 22 January 1934 *Employees:* 228
Net Worth: £5,612,000 *Total Assets:* £25,127,000
Registered Office: Edbro House, Nelson Street, Bolton, Lancs, BL3 2JJ
Activities: Manufacture of lifting and handling equipment
Parent: Jost GB Limited
Officers: Thilo Boeltink, Secretary; Lars Brorsen [1952] Director [Danish]; Neil Geldard Williams [1962] Managing Director

JPTR Bidco Limited
Incorporated: 11 August 2016
Net Worth: £1,370,000 *Total Assets:* £44,310,000
Registered Office: Spamedica House, 43 Churchgate, Bolton, Lancs, BL1 1HU
Activities: Activities of open-ended investment companies
Parent: JPTR Midco Limited
Officers: Anand Jagdishchandra Jain [1976] Director; Naveen Passi [1985] Director; Anil Kumar Pitalia [1967] Director; Paul Stout [1978] Director

JPTR Midco Limited
Incorporated: 10 August 2016
Net Worth Deficit: £509,000 *Total Assets:* £42,866,000
Registered Office: Spamedica House, 43 Churchgate, Bolton, Lancs, BL1 1HU
Activities: Activities of open-ended investment companies
Parent: JPTR Topco Limited
Officers: Anand Jagdishchandra Jain [1976] Director; Naveen Passi [1985] Director; Anil Kumar Pitalia [1967] Director; Paul Stout [1978] Director

JPTR Topco Limited
Incorporated: 10 August 2016 *Employees:* 115
Net Worth: £222,000 *Total Assets:* £47,001,000
Registered Office: Spamedica House, 43 Churchgate, Bolton, Lancs, BL1 1HU
Activities: Activities of open-ended investment companies
Parent: CBPE Nominees Limited
Officers: Anand Jagdishchandra Jain [1976] Director; Naveen Passi [1985] Director; Anil Kumar Pitalia [1967] Director; Paul Stout [1978] Director

JSSH Limited
Incorporated: 20 March 2013 *Employees:* 831
Net Worth: £43,922,000 *Total Assets:* £59,798,000
Registered Office: Manor House, Manor Lane, Holmes Chapel, Cheshire, CW4 8AF
Activities: Activities of other holding companies n.e.c.
Shareholder: John Stuart Seddon
Officers: Michelle Louise Owen, Secretary; Susan Claire Nuttall [1962] Director; Helen Mary Oakey [1959] Director; Michelle Louise Owen [1974] Finance Director; Neville Brian Richardson [1957] Director; John Stuart Seddon [1960] Director/Company Chairman; John Seddon [1935] Director

Juristar Limited
Incorporated: 23 August 2016 *Employees:* 111
Net Worth: £1,405,856 *Total Assets:* £11,194,560
Registered Office: Lockett Loveday McMahon, 4 Oxford Court, Manchester, M2 3WQ
Activities: Activities of other holding companies n.e.c.
Shareholders: Terence Peter Holland; Paul Ernest Clark
Officers: Robert Loveday, Secretary; Paul Ernest Clark [1967] Director; Terence Peter Holland [1966] Director

Just Childcare Consultancy Services Limited
Incorporated: 31 October 2014
Net Worth Deficit: £752,000 *Total Assets:* £24,321,000
Registered Office: Ridgway House, Progress Way, Denton, Manchester, M34 2GP
Activities: Pre-primary education
Parent: Project Play Midco 2 Limited
Officers: David William Johnson [1957] Director; Jacqueline Ann Johnson [1966] Director; Barry John Robinson [1979] Director/Private Equity; James Robert Thomas [1964] Director/Private Equity

Just Childcare Holdings Limited
Incorporated: 29 October 2014 *Employees:* 471
Net Worth Deficit: £11,330,000 *Total Assets:* £23,007,000
Registered Office: Ridgway House, Progress Way, Denton, Manchester, M34 2GP
Activities: Pre-primary education
Officers: David William Johnson [1957] Director; Jacqueline Ann Johnson [1966] Director; Vanda Murray [1960] Non-Executive Director; Barry John Robinson [1979] Director/Private Equity; James Robert Thomas [1964] Director/Private Equity

Just Childcare Limited
Incorporated: 5 April 2004 *Employees:* 417
Net Worth Deficit: £4,219,000 *Total Assets:* £22,200,000
Registered Office: Ridgway House, Progress Way, Denton, Manchester, M34 2GP
Activities: Pre-primary education
Parent: Just Childcare Consultancy Services Limited
Officers: David William Johnson, Secretary/Managing Director; David William Johnson [1957] Chairman Director; Jacqueline Ann Johnson [1966] Managing Director

Justrite Holdings Ltd
Incorporated: 12 April 2016 *Employees:* 108
Net Worth: £11,397,890 *Total Assets:* £21,264,324
Registered Office: Arden Works, Whitefield Road, Bredbury, Stockport, Cheshire, SK6 2SS
Activities: Activities of other holding companies n.e.c.
Officers: Paul Darlington [1962] Director; Mark David McElhinny [1967] Director/President, CEO Justrite Mfg [American]

JWH Capital Limited
Incorporated: 20 August 2015
Net Worth Deficit: £425,365 *Total Assets:* £14,551,459
Registered Office: Atlantic Pavillion, Albert Dock, Liverpool, L3 4AE
Activities: Non-trading company
Major Shareholder: John William Hughes
Officers: John William Hughes [1981] Director/Solicitor

JWS Holdings Limited
Incorporated: 14 July 2004
Registered Office: West Port House, 35 Frederick Road, Salford, M6 6LD
Activities: Treatment and disposal of non-hazardous waste
Major Shareholder: Robin Edwin Tweedale
Officers: Dr Paul Antony Sanders, Secretary/Accountant; Peter Duncan Lees Andrew [1952] Director; Kevin Philbin [1959] Director/Lawyer; Alan Rothwell [1956] Director; Dr Paul Antony Sanders [1964] Director; Robin Edwin Tweedale [1952] Director

JWS Waste & Recycling Services Limited
Incorporated: 6 May 1983
Registered Office: Westport House, 35 Frederick Road, Salford, M6 6LD
Activities: Treatment and disposal of non-hazardous waste
Parent: JWS Holdings Limited
Officers: Dr Paul Antony Sanders, Secretary/Accountant; Peter Duncan Lees Andrew [1952] Director; Robin Edwin Tweedale [1952] Director

JY Kinsha Limited Liability Partnership
Incorporated: 6 July 2006
Net Worth: £10,038,070 *Total Assets:* £12,271,555
Registered Office: 1st Floor, 120 Wigan Road, Ashton in Makerfield, Wigan, Lancs, WN4 9SU
Officers: Sanjay Kumar Pitalia [1960] Member; Shikha Pitalia [1964] Member

K Europe Holding Company Limited
Incorporated: 29 July 2015
Net Worth: £79,710,088 *Total Assets:* £304,532,448
Registered Office: Orange Tower, Media City UK, Salford, M50 2HF
Activities: Other business support service activities n.e.c.
Parent: Kellogg Company
Officers: Peter Headridge [1971] Director/Vice President; Philip David Knowles [1969] Finance Director; Ramesh Kollepara [1976] IT Director

K K Fine Foods Limited
Incorporated: 27 November 1986 *Employees:* 355
Net Worth: £9,425,757 *Total Assets:* £27,967,804
Registered Office: Estuary House, Tenth Avenue, Zone 3, Deeside Industrial Park, Deeside, Flintshire, CH5 2UA
Activities: Manufacture of other food products n.e.c.
Parent: Freshmeals N.V.
Officers: Dirk de Backer, Secretary; Christophe Bolsius [1969] Director [Belgian]; Wim Donaat Margriet de Cock [1961] Director [Belgian]; Samir Stephen James Edwards [1977] Director; Dirk Goeminne [1955] Director [Belgian]; René Stevens [1958] Director [Belgian]

K M (Property Management) Limited
Incorporated: 21 November 2001
Net Worth: £3,392,184 *Total Assets:* £7,077,190
Registered Office: Alabama House, 6 Rumford Place, Liverpool, L3 9BY
Activities: Other letting and operating of own or leased real estate
Officers: Andrew Generald Massie, Secretary; Stuart Nield Keppie [1953] Director/Surveyor; Andrew Generald Massie [1967] Director/Surveyor

K.R.M. U.K. Ltd
Incorporated: 3 December 1996 *Employees:* 3
Net Worth: £1,115,597 *Total Assets:* £8,762,646
Registered Office: 350 Leach Place, Walton Summit Centre, Bamber Bridge, Preston, Lancs, PR5 8AS
Activities: Construction of commercial buildings
Parent: Dixon Group Europe Limited
Officers: Julie Ann Crowe, Secretary; Julie Ann Crowe [1968] Managing Director; Richard Lewis Goodall [1943] Director [American]

K3 Business Solutions Limited
Incorporated: 15 March 2007 *Employees:* 69
Net Worth Deficit: £1,163,315 *Total Assets:* £8,304,735
Registered Office: Baltimore House, 50 Kansas Avenue, Manchester, M50 2GL
Activities: Information technology consultancy activities
Parent: K3 Business Systems Holdco Limited
Officers: Kevin Joseph Curry, Secretary; Robert David Price [1967] Director; Adalsteinn Valdimarsson [1969] Director [Icelander]

K3 Business Systems Holdco Limited
Incorporated: 16 May 2014
Net Worth: £594,465 *Total Assets:* £28,290,872
Registered Office: Baltimore House, 50 Kansas Avenue, Salford, M50 2GL
Activities: Activities of other holding companies n.e.c.
Parent: K3 Business Technology Group PLC
Officers: Kevin Joseph Curry, Secretary; Robert David Price [1967] Director; Adalsteinn Valdimarsson [1969] Director [Icelander]

K3 Business Technologies Limited
Incorporated: 10 December 2013 *Employees:* 162
Net Worth: £2,905,413 *Total Assets:* £21,190,744
Registered Office: Baltimore House, 50 Kansas Avenue, Salford, M50 2GL
Activities: Business and domestic software development
Parent: K3 Retail and Business Solutions Holdco Limited
Officers: Kevin Joseph Curry, Secretary; Robert David Price [1967] Director; Adalsteinn Valdimarsson [1969] Director [Icelander]

K3 Business Technology Group PLC
Incorporated: 28 August 1991 *Employees:* 762
Net Worth: £73,410,000 *Total Assets:* £121,767,000
Registered Office: Baltimore House, 50 Kansas Avenue, Manchester, M50 2GL
Activities: Activities of head offices
Officers: Kevin Joseph Curry, Secretary; Per Johan Claesson [1951] Director [Swedish]; Stuart Darling [1963] Director; Jonathan Paul Manley [1954] Director; Paul Gilmer Morland [1960] Director/Investment Banker; Robert David Price [1967] Director; Adalsteinn Valdimarsson [1969] Director [Icelander]

K3 Syspro Limited
Incorporated: 24 August 1983 *Employees:* 95
Net Worth: £2,562,996 *Total Assets:* £8,346,808
Registered Office: Baltimore House, 50 Kansas Avenue, Manchester, M50 2GL
Activities: Information technology consultancy activities
Parent: K3 Business Systems Holdco Limited
Officers: Kevin Joseph Curry, Secretary; Robert David Price [1967] Director; Adalsteinn Valdimarsson [1969] Director [Icelander]

Kacoo Fashion Ltd
Incorporated: 3 May 2007 *Employees:* 105
Net Worth: £4,150,702 *Total Assets:* £15,032,962
Registered Office: 269 Great Ancoats Street, Manchester, M4 7DB
Activities: Wholesale of clothing and footwear
Shareholders: Kacoo Group Ltd; Huan Huan Jin
Officers: Huan Huan Jin [1981] Director

Kacoo Group Limited
Incorporated: 22 July 2013 *Employees:* 121
Net Worth: £3,397,574 *Total Assets:* £17,643,788
Registered Office: Fabrica House, 269 Great Ancoats Street, Manchester, M4 7DB
Activities: Non-trading company
Major Shareholder: Huanhuan Huan Jin
Officers: Huanhuan Huan Jin [1981] Director

Kadant U.K. Limited
Incorporated: 25 July 1983 *Employees:* 78
Net Worth: £9,711,545 *Total Assets:* £12,407,011
Registered Office: Riverside Works, Woodhill Road, Bury, Lancs, BL8 1BD
Activities: Manufacture of machinery for paper and paperboard production
Parent: Kadant Inc
Officers: John Davidson, Secretary; Kevin John Joseph Callus [1959] Managing Director; John Davidson [1961] Director/Accountant; Eric Thomas Langevin [1962] Director/C.O.O. [American]; Jonathan Wood Painter [1959] Director/C.E.O. [American]

Kadant UK Holdings Limited
Incorporated: 18 July 2003
Net Worth: £2,438,497 *Total Assets:* £15,812,130
Registered Office: Riverside Works, Woodhill Road, Bury, Lancs, BL8 1BD
Activities: Activities of head offices
Parent: Kadant Inc
Officers: John Davidson, Secretary; Kevin John Joseph Callus [1959] Managing Director; Eric Thomas Langevin [1962] Director/Chief Operating Officer [American]; Jonathan Wood Painter [1959] Director [American]

Kalibrate Technologies Limited
Incorporated: 18 March 1993 *Employees:* 152
Net Worth: £12,383,283 *Total Assets:* £20,045,180
Registered Office: 196 Deansgate, Manchester, M3 3WF
Activities: Business and domestic software development
Officers: Ashley John Brown, Secretary; Ashley John Brown [1975] Director; Jog Dhody [1978] Director/Operating Partner; Mark Brian Hawtin [1965] Managing Director; Adam James Hutcheson [1979] Director [American]; Gary William McIlraith [1964] Director; Matthew Roy Peacock [1961] Director; Thomas Alexander Russell [1977] Director/Partner; Ian Raymond Thompson [1968] Managing Director

Kaman Composites - UK Holdings Limited
Incorporated: 16 January 2004 *Employees:* 25
Net Worth: £8,927,000 *Total Assets:* £35,417,000
Registered Office: India Mill Business Centre, Darwen, Lancs, BB3 1AD
Activities: Other business support service activities n.e.c.
Parent: Kaman UK Holdings Limited
Officers: Richard Roman Barnhart [1960] Director [American]; Michael Thomas Lafleur [1970] Director/Accountant [American]; Michael James Lyon [1956] Director/VP -Tax [American]; Robert Daniel Starr [1967] Director/Finance [American]

Kaman Composites - UK Limited
Incorporated: 25 March 1985 *Employees:* 235
Net Worth: £2,544,000 *Total Assets:* £19,941,000
Registered Office: India Mill, Darwen, Lancs, BB3 1AD
Activities: Manufacture of other plastic products
Parent: Brookhouse 2004 Limited
Officers: Richard Roman Barnhart [1960] Director [American]; Michael Thomas Lafleur [1970] Director/Accountant [American]; James Carl Larwood Jnr [1957] Director [American]; Michael James Lyon [1956] Director/VP - Tax [American]; Christopher John Morris [1968] Managing Director; Robert Daniel Starr [1967] Director/Finance [American]

Kaman UK Holdings Limited
Incorporated: 5 June 2008 *Employees:* 394
Net Worth Deficit: £22,467,000 *Total Assets:* £45,795,000
Registered Office: India Mill Business Centre, India Mill, Darwen, Lancs, BB3 1AD
Activities: Activities of head offices
Parent: Kaman Corporation
Officers: Richard Roman Barnhart [1960] Director [American]; Neal J Keating [1955] Director/Company Executive [American]; Robert Daniel Starr [1967] Director/Finance [American]

Kamani Commercial Property Ltd
Incorporated: 7 May 1999 *Employees:* 13
Net Worth: £14,352,008 *Total Assets:* £26,923,870
Registered Office: 49-51 Dale Street, Manchester, M1 2HF
Activities: Other letting and operating of own or leased real estate
Officers: Abdullah Bnanji Kamani [1935] Director/Business Consultant; Adam Mahmud Kamani [1989] Director; Mahmud Abdullah Kamani [1964] Director; Rabia Abdullah Kamani [1962] Director; Roshan Abdullah Kamani [1938] Director/Trader; Mahesh Patel [1965] Finance Director

Kammac Limited
Incorporated: 10 May 1988 *Employees:* 274
Net Worth: £1,810,000 *Total Assets:* £12,306,000
Registered Office: Bluebell House, Brian Johnson Way, Preston, Lancs, PR2 5PE
Activities: Freight transport by road
Shareholders: Paul Eric Kamel; Susan Kamel
Officers: Dawn Rosemary Taylor, Secretary/Accountant; Paul Eric Kamel [1953] Director; Susan Kamel [1953] Director/Accounts Manager

The Kay Group (UK Holdings) Ltd
Incorporated: 4 March 2016 *Employees:* 223
Net Worth: £40,385,764 *Total Assets:* £55,014,000
Registered Office: 1st Floor, Grimshaw Park, Blackburn, BB2 3AG
Activities: Activities of other holding companies n.e.c.
Shareholders: Kenneth Anthony Kay; Jean Kay
Officers: Jean Kay [1949] Director; Kenneth Anthony Kay [1946] Director

The Kay Group (UK) Limited
Incorporated: 8 March 1985 *Employees:* 176
Net Worth: £10,783,291 *Total Assets:* £20,485,324
Registered Office: 1st Floor, Grimshaw Park Service Station, Grimshaw Park, Blackburn, Lancs, BB2 3AG
Activities: Retail sale of automotive fuel in specialised stores
Parent: The Kay Group (UK Holdings) Ltd
Officers: Simon Lee Fielding, Secretary/Petrol Retail; Richard Stephen Cox [1962] Director; Robin Norman Entwistle [1959] Director; Simon Lee Fielding [1968] Director; Jean Kay [1949] Director; Kenneth Anthony Kay [1946] Director

William Kayley Limited
Incorporated: 25 September 1933 *Employees:* 4
Net Worth: £8,924,856 *Total Assets:* £13,627,003
Registered Office: 5 Brooklands Place, Brooklands Road, Sale, Cheshire, M33 3SD
Activities: Buying and selling of own real estate
Parent: Periodbond Limited
Officers: Valerie Ann Kayley, Secretary; Jonathan Benjamin James Kayley [1952] Director/Garage Proprietor; Valerie Ann Kayley [1940] Director/Property Developer; William Woodrow Kayley [1940] Director

Kays Medical Limited
Incorporated: 11 March 1976 *Employees:* 47
Net Worth: £3,258,606 *Total Assets:* £7,595,987
Registered Office: 1 Windward Drive, Speke, Liverpool, L24 8QR
Activities: Wholesale of pharmaceutical goods
Shareholders: David Henry Ludzker; Joyce Ludzker
Officers: Joyce Ludzker, Secretary; Benjamin Mathew Ludzker [1979] Director; David Henry Ludzker [1944] Director; Joyce Ludzker [1942] Director

Keighley Fleece Mills Company Limited
Incorporated: 14 August 1865
Net Worth: £4,876,741 *Total Assets:* £6,849,411
Registered Office: Old Mills, Moor Top, Drighlington, Bradford, W Yorks, BD11 1BY
Activities: Buying and selling of own real estate
Officers: Kathryn Davenport, Secretary; Peter Jan Patrik Valentin Gyllenhammar [1953] Director [Swedish]

Kelda Eurobond Co Limited
Incorporated: 21 November 2007 *Employees:* 3,773
Net Worth: £157,300,000 *Total Assets:* £9,855,200,256
Registered Office: Western House, Halifax Road, Bradford, W Yorks, BD6 2SZ
Activities: Financial intermediation not elsewhere classified
Officers: Kathy Smith, Secretary; Scott Auty [1978] Director/Fund Manager; Elizabeth Marian Barber [1965] Director/Accountant; Paul Johnstone Barr [1979] Director; Simon Daniel Beer [1980] Director/Asset Manager; Vicky Chan [1983] Director/Financier; Andrew James Dench [1969] Director; Richard David Flint [1968] Director; Mark Edwin Lorkin [1976] Managing Director [British/Australian]; Aparna Narain [1985] Director/Asset Management; Michael Peter Francis Osborne [1980] Director; Anthony Leon Philip Rabin [1955] Director

Kelda Finance (No.1) Limited
Incorporated: 11 May 2012 *Employees:* 2,681
Net Worth: £891,299,968 *Total Assets:* £9,222,899,712
Registered Office: Western House, Halifax Road, Bradford, BD6 2SZ
Activities: Financial management
Parent: Kelda Group Limited
Officers: Kathy Smith, Secretary; Elizabeth Marian Barber [1965] Director; Richard David Flint [1968] Director/Chief Executive; Kathy Smith [1974] Director/Company Secretary

Kelda Finance (No.2) Limited
Incorporated: 16 May 2012
Net Worth: £520,830,016 *Total Assets:* £977,777,024
Registered Office: Western House, Halifax Road, Bradford, BD6 2SZ
Activities: Financial management
Parent: Kelda Finance (No. 1) Limited
Officers: Kathy Smith, Secretary; Elizabeth Marian Barber [1965] Director; Richard David Flint [1968] Director/Chief Executive; Kathy Smith [1974] Director/Company Secretary

Kelda Finance (No.3) PLC
Incorporated: 26 October 2012
Net Worth Deficit: £2,595,000 *Total Assets:* £199,023,008
Registered Office: Western House, Halifax Road, Bradford, BD6 2SZ
Activities: Financial management
Parent: Kelda Finance (No. 2) Limited
Officers: Kathy Smith, Secretary; Elizabeth Marian Barber [1965] Director; Richard David Flint [1968] Director/Chief Executive; Anthony Leon Philip Rabin [1955] Director; Kathy Smith [1974] Director/Company Secretary

Kelda Group Limited
Incorporated: 1 April 1989 *Employees:* 101
Net Worth: £970,902,976 *Total Assets:* £1,011,601,024
Registered Office: Western House, Halifax Road, Bradford, W Yorks, BD6 2SZ
Activities: Water collection, treatment and supply
Parent: Kelda Eurobond Co Limited
Officers: Kathy Smith, Secretary; Elizabeth Marian Barber [1965] Director/Accountant; Richard David Flint [1968] Director; Kathy Smith [1974] Director/Company Secretary

Kelda Non-Reg Holdco Limited
Incorporated: 2- November 2007
Net Worth: £10,038,000 *Total Assets:* £23,010,000
Registered Office: Western House, Halifax Road, Bradford, W Yorks, BD6 2SZ
Activities: Financial intermediation not elsewhere classified
Parent: Kelda Eurobond Co Limited
Officers: Kathy Smith, Secretary; Elizabeth Marian Barber [1965] Director/Accountant; Richard David Flint [1968] Director; Kathy Smith [1974] Director/Company Secretary

Kelda Water Services Limited
Incorporated: 19 October 1987 *Employees:* 229
Net Worth Deficit: £9,351,000 *Total Assets:* £264,054,000
Registered Office: Western House, Halifax Road, Bradford, W Yorks, BD6 2SZ
Activities: Other business support service activities n.e.c.
Parent: Kelda Group Limited
Officers: Angela Wendy Miriam White, Secretary; Elizabeth Marian Barber [1965] Director/Accountant; Richard David Flint [1968] Director, Water Business; Thomas Hall [1979] Director; Charles Stewart Haysom [1957] Director/Civil Engineer; Benjamin Paul Raistrick [1979] Director/Commercial Manager

KELF
Incorporated: 5 November 2001
Net Worth: £41,553,000 *Total Assets:* £41,608,000
Registered Office: Orange Tower, Media City UK, Salford, M50 2HF
Activities: Other business support service activities n.e.c.
Parent: Kellogg Manchester
Officers: Nigel David Jaynes [1966] Director/Environment, Health & Safety, Corporate Services; Philip David Knowles [1969] Finance Director

Kellogg Company of Great Britain,Limited
Incorporated: 9 July 1924 *Employees:* 788
Net Worth: £1,288,546,944 *Total Assets:* £1,463,724,032
Registered Office: Orange Tower, Media City UK, Salford, M50 2HF
Activities: Manufacture of other food products n.e.c.
Parent: Kellogg U.K. Holding Company Limited
Officers: Andrea Critchley [1973] Senior SC Director; Nigel David Jaynes [1966] HR Director; Karen Lesley Thomas [1968] Plant Director

Kellogg Group Limited
Incorporated: 23 September 2004
Net Worth: £2,500,691,712 *Total Assets:* £3,128,271,360
Registered Office: Orange Tower, Media City UK, Salford, M50 2HF
Activities: Activities of head offices
Parent: Kellogg Company
Officers: Andrea Critchley [1973] Senior SC Director; Nigel David Jaynes [1966] Director/Environment, Health & Safety, Corporate Services; Philip David Knowles [1969] Finance Director; Ramesh Kollepara [1976] IT Director; Joel Alan Vanderkooi [1968] Director/Treasurer [American]

Kellogg Latin America Holding Company (One) Limited
Incorporated: 13 December 2010
Net Worth: £2,200,774,400 *Total Assets:* £2,331,742,464
Registered Office: Orange Tower, Media City UK, Salford, M50 2HF
Activities: Other business support service activities n.e.c.
Parent: Gollek UK Limited
Officers: Andrea Critchley [1973] Senior SC Director; Nigel David Jaynes [1966] Director/Environment, Health & Safety, Corporate Services; Philip David Knowles [1969] Finance Director; Ramesh Kollepara [1976] IT Director; Richard Wendell Schell [1963] Director/Finance/Tax [American]; Joel Alan Vanderkooi [1968] Director/Treasurer [American]

Kellogg Management Services (Europe) Limited
Incorporated: 2 August 1996 *Employees:* 326
Net Worth: £2,420,000 *Total Assets:* £82,476,000
Registered Office: Orange Tower, Media City UK, Salford, M50 2HF
Activities: Manufacture of other food products n.e.c.
Parent: Kellogg U.K. Holding Company Limited
Officers: Richard Ian Bradley [1975] IT - Director; Nigel David Jaynes [1966] Director/Environment, Health & Safety, Corporate Services; Susan Clare Platt [1965] HR Director; Wendy Wen-Lee Smith [1969] Director/VP Finance & CFO, Kellogg Europe [American]

Kellogg Manchester
Incorporated: 5 November 2001
Net Worth: £50,806,000 *Total Assets:* £72,493,000
Registered Office: Orange Tower, Media City UK, Salford, M50 2HF
Activities: Other business support service activities n.e.c.
Parent: Kellogg U.K. Holding Company Limited
Officers: Philip David Knowles [1969] Finance Director; Robert O'Sullivan [1977] Finance Director [Irish]

Kellogg Marketing and Sales Company (UK) Limited
Incorporated: 13 August 1996 *Employees:* 312
Net Worth: £110,164,000 *Total Assets:* £272,827,008
Registered Office: Orange Tower, Media City UK, Salford, M50 2HF
Activities: Manufacture of other food products n.e.c.
Parent: Kellogg U.K. Holding Company Limited
Officers: Gareth Patrick Maguire [1978] Marketing Director [Irish]; Oliver Richard Morton [1978] Sales Director; Robert O'Sullivan [1977] Finance Director [Irish]; Alexander Edward Weatherston Wilson [1979] Director/Head of Commercial Strategy

Kellogg U.K. Holding Company Limited
Incorporated: 25 June 1996 *Employees:* 18
Net Worth: £123,664,000 *Total Assets:* £176,026,000
Registered Office: Orange Tower, Media City UK, Salford, M50 2HF
Activities: Activities of head offices
Parent: Kellogg Company
Officers: Andrea Critchley [1973] Senior SC Director; Philip David Knowles [1969] Finance Director; Susan Clare Platt [1965] HR Director

Kemira Chemicals (UK) Limited
Incorporated: 7 June 1967 *Employees:* 167
Net Worth: £13,320,000 *Total Assets:* £43,831,000
Registered Office: Bowling Park Drive, West Bowling, Bradford, W Yorks, BD4 7TT
Activities: Manufacture of other chemical products n.e.c.
Officers: Linda Christine Crossland, Secretary; David John Normington [1972] Director Product Management; Anders Fredrik Nyren [1969] Director Sales [Swedish]; Elaine Wharton [1964] Director/Senior Manager Human Resources EMEA West

Kensington Developments Holdings Limited
Incorporated: 11 May 2006
Net Worth: £4,450,491 *Total Assets:* £8,282,190
Registered Office: 94 Park View Road, Lytham St Annes, Lancs, FY8 4JF
Activities: Activities of head offices
Officers: David Michael Tingle, Secretary; Denley Barrow [1944] Director; David Michael Tingle [1966] Director

Kensington Developments Limited
Incorporated: 13 March 1991 *Employees:* 34
Net Worth: £1,148,863 *Total Assets:* £31,026,538
Registered Office: 94 Park View Road, Lytham St Annes, Fylde, Lancs, FY8 4JF
Activities: Development of building projects
Parent: Kensington Developments Holdings Limited
Officers: David Michael Tingle, Secretary; Denley Barrow [1944] Managing Director; Peter Liversidge [1956] Director; David Michael Tingle [1966] Director

Kent Topco Limited
Incorporated: 25 September 2013 *Employees:* 219
Net Worth: £14,786,000 *Total Assets:* £20,478,000
Registered Office: 2 Millennium Gate, Westmere Drive, Crewe, Cheshire, CW1 6XB
Activities: Other human health activities
Parent: Souter Kent Limited
Officers: Vincent Bastide [1969] Director [French]; Arnaud Fayolle [1975] Director/Deputy CEO [French]; Howard Lee Jones [1957] Director; Olivier Jourdanney [1974] Director/Deputy CEO [French]; Adam Michael Sullivan [1968] Director

Kentmere Limited
Incorporated: 2 March 1906 *Employees:* 54
Net Worth: £5,802,163 *Total Assets:* £7,435,697
Registered Office: Staveley, Kendal, Cumbria, LA8 9PB
Activities: Manufacture of other paper and paperboard containers
Officers: Stephen William Hoyle, Secretary; Robert Holme Barker [1944] Director/Chartered Accountant; Nicholas Bramfitt [1972] Director/Factory Manager; Christopher John Chambers [1947] Director/Chartered Accountant; Penelope Anne Hanks [1952] Director; Stephen William Hoyle [1949] Director/Chartered Accountant; Shaun Patrick Mulvaney [1952] Managing Director

William Kenyon & Sons Limited
Incorporated: 27 July 1907 *Employees:* 105
Net Worth: £15,028,100 *Total Assets:* £16,848,080
Registered Office: P O Box 33, Chapel Field Works, Dukinfield, Cheshire, SK14 4RP
Activities: Activities of head offices
Officers: Piers Kenyon, Secretary/Managing Director; Christopher George Kenyon [1939] Director/Chairman; Helen Mary Kenyon [1966] Director; Margaret Kenyon [1940] Director; Piers Kenyon [1968] Managing Director; Sarah Ann Kenyon [1968] Director; William Kenyon [1965] Director/Chartered Accountant

Keoghs Acquisition Limited
Incorporated: 15 February 2012
Net Worth: £51,938,000 *Total Assets:* £66,951,000
Registered Office: 2 The Parklands, Bolton, Lancs, BL6 4SE
Activities: Activities of other holding companies n.e.c.
Parent: Keoghs Midco Limited
Officers: Asim Butt [1965] Director/Solicitor; Roger Donald Clarke [1963] Director/Solicitor; Gary Eugene Fitzpatrick [1970] Director/Solicitor; James Kenneth Heath [1971] Director/Solicitor; Alex Peter Hodgson [1979] Finance Director; Andrew Richard Underwood [1963] Director/Solicitor; Mark Andrew Whalley [1964] Director/Solicitor; John William Whittle [1967] Director/Solicitor

Keoghs LLP
Incorporated: 21 July 2006 *Employees:* 1,240
Net Worth: £33,000,000 *Total Assets:* £53,822,000
Registered Office: 2 The Parklands, Bolton, Lancs, BL6 4SE
Officers: John William Whittle [1967] Member; Jonathan David Anslow [1978] LLP Member; Andrew Auchterlounie [1977] LLP Member; Paul Andrew Baxter [1976] LLP Member; Stephanie Berry [1969] LLP Member; Matthew James Burfield [1969] LLP Member; Asim Butt [1965] LLP Member; Rada Campbell [1977] LLP Member; Allison Jane Carr [1970] LLP Member; Gregory Cave [1979] LLP Member; Roger Donald Clarke [1963] LLP Member; Louise Ann Clough [1970] LLP Member; Connie Cobb [1976] LLP Member; Rachel Sarah Coombs [1984] LLP Member; Douglas Cowan [1973] LLP Member; Daniel Crockford [1978] LLP Member; Stephen Croston [1973] LLP Member; Louise Cruise [1977] LLP Member; Anthony Dale [1970] LLP Member; Pamela Louise Davies [1974] LLP Member; Nina Dayal [1977] LLP Member; Howard Michael Dean [1965] LLP Member; Julian Maurice Dexter [1974] LLP Member; Suzanne Drinkwater [1969] LLP Member; Louise Edwards [1977] LLP Member; Daniel James Elder [1976] LLP Member; Elise Ellson [1978] LLP Member; Andrew David Evans [1975] LLP Member; Toby Evans [1980] LLP Member; Gary Eugene Fitzpatrick [1970] LLP Member; Lisa Fletcher [1973] LLP Member; Heather Ford [1980] LLP Member; Ewen Gardiner [1960] LLP Member; Aiden Geary [1964] LLP Member; Marise Gellert [1966] LLP Member; John Stuart Gibson [1982] LLP Member; Stuart William Giddings [1980] LLP Member; Alastair Gillespie [1969] LLP Member; Louise Clare Goble [1978] LLP Member; Robert Gray [1967] LLP Member; Richard Greer [1978] LLP Member; Mark Richard Hall [1968] LLP Member; Kari Hansen [1978] LLP Member; Katherine Harrison [1973] LLP Member; James Kenneth Heath [1971] LLP Member; David Hennessy [1980] LLP Member; Rachel Ann Hewitt [1973] LLP Member; Alex Peter Hodgson [1979] LLP Member; Caroline Ann Hoey [1973] LLP Member; Richard Thomas Houseago [1961] LLP Member; Elaine Ibbotson [1977] LLP Member; Emily Jeffrey [1981] LLP Member; Stefanie Johnston [1972] LLP Member; Lisa Kelly [1969] LLP Member; Peter Robert Kenworthy [1968] LLP Member; Ghazala Khalid [1975] LLP Member; Ruth Janet Lawrence [1966] LLP Member; Benjamin Leech [2012] LLP Member; Ivor Gerarde Long [1966] LLP Member; Graham Lynch [1965] LLP Member; Estelle Marie Machell [1976] LLP Member; Martin McAleer [1968] LLP Member; Fraser McAndry [1971] LLP Member; Helen Jayne McGovern [1973] LLP Member; Susan Nicola McLoughlin [1962] LLP Member; Melanie Louise Mooney [1970] LLP Member; Sarah Jane Naylor [1965] LLP Member; Ruth Needham [1979] LLP Member; Christopher Newton [1972] LLP Member; Amanda Jane Nuttall [1972] LLP Member; Peter James Oakes [1972] LLP Member; Julie Park [1974] LLP Member; Sarah Parker [1982] LLP Member; Nerys Lyn Parry [1971] LLP Member; Alex Penberthy [1977] LLP Member; Matthew James Perkins [1981] LLP Member; Andrew Pieri [1958] LLP Member; Michael Pope [1969] LLP Member; David Pugh [1967] LLP Member; Claire Quinn [1968] LLP Member; Michael Renshaw [1968] LLP Member; Matthew Howard Rogers [1968] LLP Member; Katie Rose [1984] LLP Member; Dene Rowe [1970] LLP Member; Kay Sanderson [1979] LLP Member; Andrew Schutte [1975] LLP Member; David Antony Scott [1963] LLP Member; Neena Sharma [1976] LLP Member; Darrell Smith [1971] LLP Member; Robert Smith [2009] LLP Member; Christopher Stanton [1971] LLP Member; Dragos Stoica [1980] LLP Member; Mike Suddards [1959] LLP Member; Andrew Temperley [1974] LLP Member; Avrom Samuel Topperman [1977] LLP Member; Neil McMurtry Trayhurn [1965] LLP Member; Andrew Richard Underwood [1963] LLP Member; Lucy Jane Walker [1973] LLP Member; David Mark Walton [1963] LLP Member

Keoghs Midco Limited
Incorporated: 15 February 2012 *Employees:* 5
Net Worth Deficit: £1,447,000 *Total Assets:* £52,563,000
Registered Office: 2 The Parklands, Bolton, Lancs, BL6 4SE
Activities: Activities of other holding companies n.e.c.
Parent: Keoghs Topco Limited
Officers: Simon Mark Beard [1963] Director; Roger Donald Clarke [1963] Director/Solicitor; James Kenneth Heath [1971] Director/Solicitor; Alex Peter Hodgson [1979] Finance Director; John William Whittle [1967] Director/Solicitor

Keoghs Topco Limited
Incorporated: 14 February 2012 *Employees:* 1,320
Net Worth: £4,909,000 *Total Assets:* £68,040,000
Registered Office: 2 The Parklands, Bolton, Lancs, BL6 4SE
Activities: Activities of other holding companies n.e.c.
Officers: Simon Mark Beard [1963] Director; Asim Butt [1965] Director/Solicitor; John Garner [1973] Director; Steven Richard Harrison [1956] Director; James Kenneth Heath [1971] Director/Solicitor; Alex Peter Hodgson [1979] Finance Director; John William Whittle [1967] Director/Solicitor

Kepak Kirkham Limited
Incorporated: 14 April 2004 *Employees:* 457
Net Worth: £3,260,371 *Total Assets:* £19,107,364
Registered Office: The Smackhouse, St Georges Park, Kirkham, Preston, Lancs, PR4 2DZ
Activities: Production of meat and poultry meat products
Officers: Liam Keating, Secretary/Accountant [Irish]; Robert Grogan [1959] Director [Irish]; John Horgan [1951] Director [Irish]; Liam Keating [1969] Director/Accountant [Irish]

Keppel Healthcare Ltd.
Incorporated: 27 March 1997 *Employees:* 2
Net Worth: £4,074,911 *Total Assets:* £9,208,859
Registered Office: 9 Retiro Street, Oldham, Lancs, OL1 1SA
Activities: Other letting and operating of own or leased real estate
Major Shareholder: John Patrick Kieran Kehoe
Officers: John Patrick Kieran Kehoe, Secretary; John Patrick Kieran Kehoe [1955] Director; Josephine Ann Kehoe [1956] Director/Solicitor

Kerax (Chorley) Limited
Incorporated: 14 February 2006 *Employees:* 85
Net Worth: £5,788,492 *Total Assets:* £10,971,213
Registered Office: Moorland Gate House, Cowling Road, Chorley, Lancs, PR6 9DR
Activities: Non-trading company
Parent: Kerax Holdings Limited
Officers: Paul Christopher Hebblethwaite, Secretary; Ian David Appleton [1959] Director; Lynne Carol Appleton [1966] Director

Kerax Limited
Incorporated: 18 November 2003 *Employees:* 85
Net Worth: £5,318,691 *Total Assets:* £11,001,512
Registered Office: Moorland Gate House, Cowling Road, Chorley, Lancs, PR6 9DR
Activities: Other treatment of petroleum products (excluding petrochemicals manufacture)
Parent: Kerax Holdings Limited
Officers: Paul Christopher Hebblethwaite, Secretary; Ian David Appleton [1959] Director; Lynne Carol Appleton [1966] Director; Christopher Bradley [1964] Director; Paul Christopher Hebblethwaite [1989] Finance Director; Graham Parker [1965] Director

Kerling Newco 1 Limited
Incorporated: 28 May 2015
Net Worth: £317,214,688 *Total Assets:* £317,214,688
Registered Office: P O Box 9, Runcorn Site HQ, South Parade, Runcorn, Cheshire, WA7 4JE
Activities: Activities of head offices
Parent: Kerling Newco 2 Limited
Officers: Paul Frederick Nichols, Secretary; Michael John Maher [1968] Director; Christopher Edward Tane [1956] Director; Julie Dawn Taylorson [1959] Director

Kerling Newco 2 Limited
Incorporated: 29 May 2015
Net Worth: £321,454,016 *Total Assets:* £321,454,016
Registered Office: P O Box 9, Runcorn Site HQ, South Parade, Runcorn, Cheshire, WA7 4JE
Activities: Activities of head offices
Parent: Inovyn Finance PLC
Officers: Paul Frederick Nichols, Secretary; Michael John Maher [1968] Director; Christopher Edward Tane [1956] Director; Julie Dawn Taylorson [1959] Director

Kermandine Limited
Incorporated: 14 May 1982 *Employees:* 195
Net Worth: £13,052,552 *Total Assets:* £23,348,058
Registered Office: 11 Birchley Avenue, Birchley, Billinge, Merseyside, WN5 7QW
Activities: Activities of production holding companies
Shareholder: Kevin Dermott McAdam
Officers: Sheila Maria McAdam, Secretary; Kevin Dermott McAdam [1942] Director; Sheila Maria McAdam [1942] Director; Nahill Asim Abdul Razak Younis [1968] Director/Management Consultant

Kerry Logistics (UK) Limited
Incorporated: 1 July 1981 *Employees:* 224
Net Worth: £11,110,031 *Total Assets:* £29,618,722
Registered Office: Kerry Logistics (UK) Limited, Broadoak Industrial Park, Ashburton Road West, Trafford Park, Manchester, M17 1RW
Activities: Freight air transport
Parent: Kerry Logistics Holding (Europe) Limited
Officers: Ian Fowler Dodsworth, Secretary; Thomas Alfred Blank [1961] Director/MD Europe [German]; Ian Fowler Dodsworth [1961] Director/Chief Financial Officer; David Thomas Gaughan [1971] Managing Director

Kerry Logistics Holding (Europe) Limited
Incorporated: 18 December 2012
Net Worth: £66,132,792 *Total Assets:* £94,784,912
Registered Office: Broadoak Industrial Park, Ashburton Road West, Trafford Park, Manchester, M17 1RW
Activities: Activities of head offices
Parent: Kerry Logistics Network Limited
Officers: Ian Fowler Dodsworth, Secretary; Thomas Alfred Blank [1961] Director/MD Europe [German]; Ian Fowler Dodsworth [1961] Executive Director; Wing Kai William Ma [1961] Director/Business Executive [Chinese]; George Yong-Boon Yeo [1954] Director/Business Executive [Singaporean]

Keswick School Multi Academy Trust
Incorporated: 9 June 2011 *Employees:* 168
Net Worth: £8,174,000 *Total Assets:* £12,004,000
Registered Office: Keswick School, Vicarage Hill, Keswick, Cumbria, CA12 5QB
Activities: General secondary education
Officers: Ruth Lawler, Secretary; Mark Ainsworth [1965] Director/Head of Bassenfell Christian Centre; Janice Lesley Boniface [1947] Director/Holiday Cottage Manager; Professor Robert Stewart Fowler [1932] Director/Retired; Tania Catherine Gibbin [1964] Director/Deputy Headteacher; David Simon Hammond [1961] Director/Company Secretary; Simon David Jackson [1974] Director/Headteacher; Susan Mary Leigh [1952] Director/Local Authority Officer; Sarah Fiona Peck [1957] Director/Educator; Steven Throp [1949] Director/Retired

Key Group Bidco Limited
Incorporated: 1 May 2013 *Employees:* 7
Net Worth: £9,105,861 *Total Assets:* £37,422,048
Registered Office: Baines House, Midgery Court, Pittman Way, Fulwood, Preston, Lancs, PR2 9ZH
Activities: Activities of financial services holding companies
Parent: Key Group Midco 2 Limited
Officers: Robert James Scott [1973] Director; Simon Christopher Thompson [1972] Director

Key Group Midco 1 Limited
Incorporated: 1 May 2013
Net Worth: £3,283,799 *Total Assets:* £17,836,556
Registered Office: Baines House, Midgery Court, Pittman Way, Fulwood, Preston, Lancs, PR2 9ZH
Activities: Activities of financial services holding companies
Parent: Key Group Topco Limited
Officers: Robert James Scott [1973] Director; Simon Christopher Thompson [1972] Director

Key Group Midco 2 Limited
Incorporated: 1 May 2013
Net Worth: £256,470 *Total Assets:* £17,836,558
Registered Office: Baines House, Midgery Court, Pittman Way, Fulwood, Preston, Lancs, PR2 9ZH
Activities: Activities of financial services holding companies
Parent: Key Group Midco 1 Limited
Officers: Robert James Scott [1973] Director; Simon Christopher Thompson [1972] Director

Key Group Topco Limited
Incorporated: 4 April 2013 *Employees:* 2
Net Worth Deficit: £1,523,222 *Total Assets:* £14,812,978
Registered Office: Baines House, Midgery Court, Pittman Way, Fulwood, Preston, Lancs, PR2 9ZH
Activities: Activities of other holding companies n.e.c.
Parent: Theo Bidco Limited
Officers: David Michael Harris [1967] Director; Robert James Scott [1973] Director; Simon Christopher Thompson [1972] Director

Key Retirement Solutions Limited
Incorporated: 9 January 1990 *Employees:* 164
Net Worth: £6,861,508 *Total Assets:* £14,314,150
Registered Office: Baines House, Midgery Court, Pittman Way, Fulwood, Preston, Lancs, PR2 9ZH
Activities: Financial intermediation not elsewhere classified
Parent: KRS Finance Ltd
Officers: Christopher Paul Bibby [1975] Director/Chief Marketing Officer; Lukas Martin Bucher [1976] Managing Director Value Creation [Swiss]; Andrew David Deakin [1973] Director/Private Equity Professional; Stephen James Groves [1975] Director/Actuary; William Hale [1975] Director; Robert James Scott [1973] Director; Simon Christopher Thompson [1972] Director; David Thomas McAree Young [1961] Director

Keyland Developments Limited
Incorporated: 19 October 1987 *Employees:* 4
Net Worth: £23,090,000 *Total Assets:* £25,500,000
Registered Office: Western House, Halifax Road, Bradford, W Yorks, BD6 2SZ
Activities: Development of building projects
Parent: Kelda Group Limited
Officers: Angela Wendy Miriam White, Secretary; Elizabeth Marian Barber [1965] Director/Accountant; Richard David Flint [1968] Director; Peter Garrett [1964] Director/Chartered Surveyor; Charles Stewart Haysom [1957] Director/Civil Engineer

The Keys Federation
Incorporated: 11 November 2014 *Employees:* 161
Net Worth: £8,787,367 *Total Assets:* £10,879,979
Registered Office: 682 Atherton Road, Hindley Green, Wigan, Lancs, WN2 4SQ
Activities: Primary education
Officers: Barend Philip Anthon [1957] Director/Pharmacist; Sharon Linda Bruton [1969] Director; Sheila Davidson [1946] Director; Katharine Mary Gore [1980] Director/Solicitor; Andrew Keith Meadows [1978] Director/Civil Servant; Julie Anne Reynolds [1970] Director/Company Secretary; Janet Victoria Anne Smith [1952] Director/Teaching Assistant; Lilian Worthington [1948] Director/Education Consultant

Keysource Limited
Incorporated: 2 November 1998 *Employees:* 71
Net Worth: £2,872,541 *Total Assets:* £7,393,223
Registered Office: Cavendish House, Cross Street, Sale, Cheshire, M33 7BU
Activities: Steam and air conditioning supply
Parent: Styles & Wood Group PLC
Officers: Philip Nicholas Lanigan [1964] Director; Anthony Stephen Lenehan [1959] Director/Chief Executive Officer; Michael Thomas West [1967] Director; Stephen Robert Whatling [1967] Director

KH&GW Limited
Incorporated: 30 January 2008 *Employees:* 27
Net Worth: £3,917,303 *Total Assets:* £7,464,072
Registered Office: Europa House, Europa Trading Estate, Stoneclough Road, Kearsley, Manchester, M26 1GG
Activities: Dental practice activities
Parent: IDH Acquisitions Limited
Officers: Leo Damian Carroll, Secretary; Bernard Moroney [1953] Director; Mohammed Omar Shafi Khan [1974] Director/Chief Financial Officer; Krista Nyree Whitley [1970] Clinical Director

Khan Estates Limited
Incorporated: 24 January 2013
Net Worth: £5,510,706 *Total Assets:* £12,958,259
Registered Office: 2nd Floor, 9 Portland Street, Manchester, M1 3BE
Activities: Buying and selling of own real estate
Parent: Khan Investment Holdings Ltd
Officers: Aneel Babar [1977] Director; Gwilym Bullock [1984] Director; Davinder Singh Sagoo [1961] Finance Director

Khanjra International Foods Limited
Incorporated: 16 April 1992 *Employees:* 7
Net Worth: £8,889,411 *Total Assets:* £9,310,503
Registered Office: Spices House, Greenbank Business Park, Blakewater Road, Blackburn, BB1 3HU
Activities: Non-specialised wholesale of food, beverages and tobacco
Shareholder: Yakub Khanjra
Officers: Yunus Patel, Secretary; Yakub Khanjra [1948] Director/Wholesaler; Yunus Patel [1956] Director/Wholesaler

KHILG Ltd
Incorporated: 5 January 2011
Net Worth: £6,532,424 *Total Assets:* £12,922,825
Registered Office: Parkgates, Bury New Road, Prestwich, Manchester, M25 0JW
Activities: Other building completion and finishing
Major Shareholder: Shabbir Khilji
Officers: Shabbir Khilji [1969] Director

KHL Newco Limited
Incorporated: 9 October 2014 *Employees:* 81
Net Worth Deficit: £2,647,102 *Total Assets:* £20,174,304
Registered Office: Barrington House, Heyes Lane, Alderley Edge, Cheshire, SK9 7LA
Activities: Business and domestic software development
Shareholder: Livingbridge VC LLP
Officers: Peter Clarke [1967] Director; Graham Mark Gilbert [1963] Director; Neil Harvey [1972] Director; Michael Anthony Marrison [1962] Director/Chartered Accountant; David John Murray [1970] Director

Kids Allowed Group Limited
Incorporated: 11 August 2008
Net Worth: £498,218 *Total Assets:* £11,202,959
Registered Office: Joshua House, Christie Way, Christie Fields Office Park, Manchester, M21 7QY
Activities: Activities of head offices
Parent: Kids Allowed Holdings Limited
Officers: Dawn Rochelle Wright, Secretary; Jennifer Ann Johnson [1971] Director; Kate Elizabeth Whistance [1974] Finance Director

Kids Allowed Holdings Limited
Incorporated: 13 January 2010 *Employees:* 365
Net Worth: £4,584,189 *Total Assets:* £14,360,619
Registered Office: Joshua House, Christie Way, Christie Fields Office Park, Manchester, M21 7QY
Activities: Activities of head offices
Shareholders: Jennifer Ann Johnson; Anthony Preston
Officers: Dawn Rochelle Wright, Secretary; Maureen Mary Bennett [1953] Director; Alison Haynes [1959] Director; Jennifer Ann Johnson [1971] Director; Kate Elizabeth Whistance [1974] Finance Director

Kids Planet Day Nurseries Limited
Incorporated: 19 May 2008 *Employees:* 588
Net Worth: £693,531 *Total Assets:* £19,386,124
Registered Office: 231 Higher Lane, Lymm, Cheshire, WA13 0RZ
Activities: Pre-primary education
Shareholder: Clare Roberts
Officers: Bernadette Hoban, Secretary; Rebecca Anne Green [1983] Finance Director; John Hoban [1952] Director/Chairman; Lucy Marie Kaczmarska [1986] Early Years Director; Mark McMenemy [1958] Director; Pinesh Mehta [1981] Director/Accountant; Clare Bernadette Roberts [1977] Director/Chief Executive

Kiernan Construction Limited
Incorporated: 30 March 1989 *Employees:* 60
Net Worth: £3,754,932 *Total Assets:* £7,585,042
Registered Office: Rowan House, 8 Rough Hey, Ribbleton, Preston, Lancs, PR2 5AR
Activities: Construction of commercial buildings
Parent: Kiernan Holdings Limited
Officers: Constance June Kiernan, Secretary; Paul Catterall [1955] Director/Accountant; John Damien Eccles [1964] Director/Civil Engineer; Constance June Kiernan [1940] Director/Administrator; Patrick Anthony Kiernan [1946] Director/Civil Engineer; Christopher Robert Ward [1971] Commercial Director

James Killelea & Company Limited
Incorporated: 1 July 1970 *Employees:* 102
Net Worth: £40,854 *Total Assets:* £6,628,021
Registered Office: Bold Venture Works, Stoneholme Road, Crawshawbooth, Rossendale, Lancs, BB4 8BA
Activities: Other specialised construction activities n.e.c.
Parent: Lonsdale Holdings Limited
Officers: Ellen Jane Killelea, Secretary; Patrick James Killelea [1955] Director; Robert Killelea [1945] Director

Kimpton Ltd
Incorporated: 20 November 1963
Registered Office: 5 Hawkshead Road, Greenfields Technology Park, Bromborough, Wirral, Merseyside, CH62 3RJ
Activities: Construction of commercial buildings
Major Shareholder: Richard Lawrence Kimpton
Officers: David Allan Kimpton, Secretary; David Allan Kimpton [1962] Director/Accountant; Richard Lawrence Kimpton [1965] Director; Colin Swanick [1964] Director/Service Manager; Ronald Tierney [1961] Director

Kinaxia Limited
Incorporated: 10 December 2010 *Employees:* 1,085
Net Worth: £9,719,482 *Total Assets:* £85,907,272
Registered Office: Kinaxia, Adlington Business Park, Adlington, Macclesfield, Cheshire, SK10 4NL
Activities: Activities of head offices
Shareholders: Peter Richard Fields; Graham Richard Norfolk
Officers: Peter Richard Fields [1960] Director; Graham Richard Norfolk [1961] Director

Kinaxia Logistics Limited
Incorporated: 18 February 2015 *Employees:* 4
Net Worth: £8,401,724 *Total Assets:* £8,410,170
Registered Office: Kinaxia, Adlington Business Park, Adlington, Macclesfield, Cheshire, SK10 4NL
Activities: Activities of head offices
Parent: Kinaxia
Officers: Peter Richard Fields [1960] Director; Barry John Germany [1968] Director; Thomas George Kyriakoudis [1975] Director; Graham Richard Norfolk [1961] Director

Kinaxia Transport and Warehousing Limited
Incorporated: 19 February 2015 *Employees:* 4
Net Worth: £9,037,570 *Total Assets:* £42,907,992
Registered Office: Kinaxia, Adlington Business Park, Adlington, Macclesfield, Cheshire, SK10 4NL
Activities: Activities of head offices
Parent: Kinaxia Logistics
Officers: Peter Richard Fields [1960] Director; Kevin Norman Johnson [1964] Managing Director; Graham Richard Norfolk [1961] Director; Benjamin James Warrillow [1974] Finance Director

Kindertons 2013 Limited
Incorporated: 1 May 2013
Net Worth: £7,825,000 *Total Assets:* £38,185,000
Registered Office: Kindertons House, Marshfield Bank, Crewe, Cheshire, CW2 8UY
Activities: Activities of head offices
Parent: Kindertons Topco Limited
Officers: Neil Simon Cox [1968] Director; Neil Lithgow Cunningham [1960] Director; Robert Douglas King [1982] Commercial Director; Jonathan Kim Walden [1953] Director; Nigel James Ward [1966] Finance Director

Kindertons Holdings Limited
Incorporated: 11 July 2005
Net Worth: £797,000 *Total Assets:* £6,887,000
Registered Office: Kindertons House, Marshfield Bank, Crewe, Cheshire, CW2 8UY
Activities: Other business support service activities n.e.c.
Parent: Kindertons 2013 Limited
Officers: Neil Lithgow Cunningham [1960] Director; Nigel James Ward [1966] Finance Director

Kindertons Limited
Incorporated: 10 February 1999 *Employees:* 603
Net Worth: £34,918,000 *Total Assets:* £67,299,000
Registered Office: Kindertons House, Marshfield Bank, Crewe, Cheshire, CW2 8UY
Activities: Renting and leasing of cars and light motor vehicles
Parent: Kindertons Holdings Limited
Officers: Neil Lithgow Cunningham [1960] Director; Nigel James Ward [1966] Director

Kindertons Topco Limited
Incorporated: 16 July 2013 *Employees:* 962
Net Worth: £3,671,000 *Total Assets:* £88,988,000
Registered Office: Kindertons House, Marshfield Bank, Crewe, Cheshire, CW2 8UY
Activities: Other business support service activities n.e.c.
Parent: Examworks UK Ltd
Officers: Neil Simon Cox [1968] Director; Neil Lithgow Cunningham [1960] Director; Donald Stuart Fowler [1973] Director; Heather Hayden [1967] Director; Robert Douglas King [1982] Director; Doug Laver [1965] Director; Richard Elliot Perlman [1946] Director [American]; James Kerrick Price [1958] Director [American]; Jonathan Kim Walden [1953] Director; Nigel James Ward [1966] Finance Director

Kinetic PLC
Incorporated: 27 March 2008 *Employees:* 66
Net Worth: £4,932,977 *Total Assets:* £9,496,917
Registered Office: Lancastrian Office Centre, Talbot Road, Stretford, Manchester, M32 0FP
Activities: Temporary employment agency activities
Major Shareholder: Neil Christian Smith
Officers: Neil Betton, Secretary; Neil Christian Smith [1960] Director; Susan Margaret Smith [1959] Director/Deputy Headteacher

Kinetic Recruitment Services Limited
Incorporated: 13 April 1982 *Employees:* 43
Net Worth: £7,459,915 *Total Assets:* £9,683,549
Registered Office: Lancastrian Office Centre, Talbot Road, Stretford, Manchester, M32 0FP
Activities: Temporary employment agency activities
Major Shareholder: Neil Christian Smith
Officers: Neil Betton, Secretary; Joanna Heseltine [1972] Operations Director; Neil Christian Smith [1960] Director/Accountant

King David and Harold House Foundation
Incorporated: 30 November 2010 *Employees:* 17
Net Worth: £27,304,984 *Total Assets:* £27,364,754
Registered Office: King David and Harold House Foundation, 120 Childwall Road, Liverpool, L15 6WU
Activities: Primary education
Officers: Sandra Heaps, Secretary; Michael Arthur Fraenkel [1945] Director; Michelle Hayward [1953] Director; Lauren Lesin-Davis [1963] Managing Director; Avril Kay Lewis [1948] Director; Max Marcus [1954] Director/Solicitor; Jonathan Reuben [1975] Director/Business Analyst; Paul Andrew Rosenblatt [1955] Director

The King David High School
Incorporated: 25 July 2011 *Employees:* 108
Net Worth: £17,847,448 *Total Assets:* £19,023,328
Registered Office: The King David High School, Eaton Road, Crumpsall, Manchester, M8 5DY
Activities: General secondary education
Officers: Andrew Spencer Berkeley [1971] Director/Property Developer; Jonathon Paul Dover [1964] Director/Solicitor; Joshua Rowe [1948] Director; Gidon Stemmer [1953] Director

Kingdom Services Group Limited
Incorporated: 2 March 1993 *Employees:* 3,560
Net Worth: £9,762,912 *Total Assets:* £29,311,616
Registered Office: Kingdom House, Woodlands Park, Ashton Road, Newton-le-Willows, St Helens, Merseyside, WA12 0HF
Activities: Private security activities
Shareholders: Terence Barton; Agnes Mary Barton
Officers: Terence Barton, Secretary/Director; Agnes Mary Barton [1954] Director; Terence Barton [1955] Director

Kingfisher Learning Trust
Incorporated: 7 March 2016 *Employees:* 137
Net Worth: £8,505,000 *Total Assets:* £10,363,000
Registered Office: Kingfisher Special School, Foxdenton Lane, Chadderton, Oldham, Lancs, OL9 9QR
Activities: Primary education
Officers: Anne Sheila Redmond, Secretary; Eileen Arthur [1949] Director/Retired; Helen Claire Crabtree [1949] Director/Retired; Ian Duncan [1956] Director/Retired; Deborah Jayne Lucas [1968] Director/Human Resources Manager; Melanie Rose McGuirk [1976] Director/Solicitor; Anne Sheila Redmond [1963] Director/Headteacher; Jeremy Michael Tweedale Sutcliffe [1945] Director/Retired

Kingmoor Park Holdings Limited
Incorporated: 21 March 2013 *Employees:* 18
Net Worth: £17,733,540 *Total Assets:* £39,472,412
Registered Office: The Marketing Suite, Baron Way, Kingmoor Business Park, Carlisle, CA6 4SJ
Activities: Other letting and operating of own or leased real estate
Officers: Neil McIntyre, Secretary; Geoffrey Dallimore [1966] Finance Director; Anthony William Goddard [1950] Director; Neil Stuart McIntyre [1981] Finance Director; Brian Kenneth Scowcroft [1956] Director

Kingmoor Park Properties Limited
Incorporated: 5 January 1999 *Employees:* 14
Net Worth: £25,196,024 *Total Assets:* £54,670,880
Registered Office: The Marketing Suite, Baron Way, Kingmoor Business Park, Carlisle, CA6 4SJ
Activities: Buying and selling of own real estate
Officers: Neil McIntyre, Secretary; Geoffrey Dallimore [1966] Finance Director; Neil Stuart McIntyre [1981] Finance Director; Brian Kenneth Scowcroft [1956] Director/Chartered Accountant

Kings Security Systems Limited
Incorporated: 15 April 1971 *Employees:* 515
Net Worth: £57,000 *Total Assets:* £12,329,000
Registered Office: 4 St Dunstans Technology Park, Ripley Street, Bradford, W Yorks, BD4 7HH
Activities: Security systems service activities
Parent: Kings Solutions Group Limited
Officers: Gaynor Amanda Kehoe, Secretary; Neil James Cossey [1970] Director; Kelly Fisher [1982] HR Director; Robin Charles Fisher [1951] Director [South African]; Robert David Forsyth [1969] Director; Darren Scott Gamage [1974] Director/Chief Operating Officer; Tim Goodwill [1979] Director; Emma Jane Shaw [1967] Director; Barry Abraham Stiefel [1949] Director [German]; Rocco Antonio Volpe [1971] Director; Geoffrey Peter Louis Zeidler [1962] Director

Kings Solutions Group Limited
Incorporated: 15 July 2011 *Employees:* 642
Net Worth: £3,050,000 *Total Assets:* £17,571,000
Registered Office: 4 St Dunstans Technology Park, Ripley Street, Bradford, W Yorks, BD4 7HH
Activities: Other business support service activities n.e.c.
Shareholders: Primekings Holding Limited; James Patrick King
Officers: Gaynor Amanda Kehoe, Secretary; Robin Charles Fisher [1951] Director [South African]; Emma Jane Shaw [1967] Director; Barry Abraham Stiefel [1949] Director [German]; Geoffrey Peter Louis Zeidler [1962] Director

Kingsclere Investments Ltd.
Incorporated: 23 February 1976
Net Worth: £78,424,768 *Total Assets:* £78,544,128
Registered Office: Eversheds House, 70-76 Great Bridgewater Street, Manchester, M1 5ES
Activities: Other business support service activities n.e.c.
Parent: Johnson Controls International PLC
Officers: David Grey Cooper [1947] Director/Attorney [British/Bermudian]; Ernest Angus Morrison [1957] Director/Attorney [British/Bermudian]

Kingscrown Properties Limited
Incorporated: 8 January 1997 *Employees:* 10
Net Worth: £7,191,868 *Total Assets:* £22,713,448
Registered Office: Suites 7-10, Prudential Buildings, 61 St Petersgate, Stockport, Cheshire, SK1 1DH
Activities: Development of building projects
Shareholders: Barrie Stephen Pollock; Paula Pollock
Officers: Laurie Sharples, Secretary; Barrie Stephen Pollock [1951] Director; Daniel Stefan Pollock [1984] Director

Kingsland Drinks Group Limited
Incorporated: 24 August 2004 *Employees:* 369
Net Worth: £10,493,000 *Total Assets:* £68,237,000
Registered Office: The Winery, Fairhills Road, Irlam, Manchester, M44 6BD
Activities: Other manufacturing n.e.c.
Officers: Edmund Anthony Baker, Secretary; Mark Dixon [1968] Director; Michael Forde [1964] Director; Andrew Jonathan Sagar [1959] Director; Karen Wilson [1967] Director

Kingsland Drinks Limited
Incorporated: 4 March 1994 *Employees:* 369
Net Worth: £15,792,000 *Total Assets:* £79,140,000
Registered Office: The Winery, Fairhills Road, Irlam, Manchester, M44 6BD
Activities: Other manufacturing n.e.c.
Parent: Kingsland Drinks Group Limited
Officers: Edmund Anthony Baker, Secretary; Mark Dixon [1968] Director; Michael Forde [1964] Director; Andrew Jonathan Sagar [1959] Director; Karen Wilson [1967] Director

Kingsley Asset Finance Limited
Incorporated: 28 March 2000 *Employees:* 9
Net Worth: £2,636,067 *Total Assets:* £11,324,693
Registered Office: Sterling House, 2-4 Mill Lane, Whittle-le-Woods, Chorley, Lancs, PR6 7LX
Activities: Financial leasing
Shareholders: Richard Ormisher; James Anthony Farrington
Officers: Lee James Knight, Secretary; James Anthony Farrington [1942] Commercial Director; Richard Ormisher [1955] Director; Charles Fred Smith [1943] Director; Jonathan Charles Smith [1969] Director

Kingsoak Limited
Incorporated: 16 May 1966
Net Worth: £6,569,581 *Total Assets:* £7,094,380
Registered Office: Woodlands, Gawthorpe Drive, Bingley, W Yorks, BD16 4DQ
Activities: Development of building projects
Shareholders: Pamela Susan Jaggar; Paul Richard Jaggar; Ann Louise Leckenby
Officers: Donald Richard Jaggar, Secretary; Donald Richard Jaggar [1936] Director; Pamela Susan Jaggar [1961] Director/Admin Manager; Paul Richard Jaggar [1967] Director; Ann Louise Leckenby [1964] Director

Kingspan Energy Limited
Incorporated: 1 September 1978 *Employees:* 15
Net Worth: £12,504,297 *Total Assets:* £27,556,426
Registered Office: Bagillt Road, Greenfield Business Park No 2, Greenfield, Holywell, Flintshire, CH8 7GJ
Activities: Construction of commercial buildings
Parent: Kingspan Holdings (Panels) Limited
Officers: Peter James Cameron Bullough [1967] Director

Kingspan Group Limited
Incorporated: 7 September 1979
Net Worth: £877,412,416 *Total Assets:* £1,506,569,856
Registered Office: Greenfield Business Park No 2, Greenfield, Holywell, Flintshire, CH8 7GJ
Activities: Activities of other holding companies n.e.c.
Parent: Kingspan Group PLC
Officers: Lorcan Dowd, Secretary/Solicitor [Irish]; Peter Charles Wilson [1956] Director [Irish]

Kingspan Holdings (Insulation) Limited
Incorporated: 14 February 1994
Net Worth: £194,459,152 *Total Assets:* £194,459,696
Registered Office: Greenfield Business Park No 2, Bagillt Road, Greenfield, Holywell, Flintshire, CH8 7GJ
Activities: Activities of other holding companies n.e.c.
Parent: Kingspan Group Limited
Officers: Peter Charles Wilson [1956] Director [Irish]

Kingspan Holdings (Panels) Limited
Incorporated: 14 August 2006
Net Worth: £667,170,368 *Total Assets:* £679,478,208
Registered Office: Greenfield Business Park No 2, Greenfield, Holywell, Flintshire, CH8 7GJ
Activities: Activities of other holding companies n.e.c.
Parent: Kingspan Group Limited
Officers: Peter Charles Wilson [1956] Director [Irish]

Kingspan Holdings (Structural & Offsite) Limited
Incorporated: 19 September 2006
Net Worth: £58,447,964 *Total Assets:* £58,448,932
Registered Office: Baggillt Road, Greenfield Business Park 2, Holywell, Flintshire, CH8 7GJ
Activities: Activities of other holding companies n.e.c.
Parent: Kingspan Group Limited
Officers: Peter Charles Wilson [1956] Director [Irish]

Kingspan Investments Limited
Incorporated: 5 April 2001
Net Worth: £61,022,152 *Total Assets:* £63,169,172
Registered Office: Greenfield Business Park No 2, Greenfield, Holywell, Flintshire, CH8 7HN
Activities: Activities of other holding companies n.e.c.
Parent: Kingspan Group Limited
Officers: Peter Charles Wilson [1956] Director [Irish]

Kingspan Limited
Incorporated: 7 January 1972 *Employees:* 885
Net Worth: £99,399,664 *Total Assets:* £171,430,512
Registered Office: Bagillt Road, Greenfield Business Park No 2, Greenfield, Holywell, Flintshire, CH8 7GJ
Activities: Manufacture of other fabricated metal products n.e.c.
Parent: Kingspan Holdings (Panels) Limited
Officers: Peter James Cameron Bullough [1967] Director; Mark Stanley Harris [1958] Divisional Building Technology Director; Philip Smith [1964] Sales Director

Kingspan Services (UK) Limited
Incorporated: 1 July 1998
Net Worth: £40,631,112 *Total Assets:* £190,794,016
Registered Office: Greenfield Business Park No 2, Greenfield, Holywell, Flintshire, CH8 7GJ
Activities: Financial management
Parent: Kingspan Holdings (Panels) Limited
Officers: Peter James Cameron Bullough [1967] Director

Kingsway Asset Finance Ltd
Incorporated: 27 June 1995 *Employees:* 14
Net Worth: £3,064,811 *Total Assets:* £12,043,525
Registered Office: Barons Court, Manchester Road, Wilmslow, Cheshire, SK9 1BQ
Activities: Financial leasing
Parent: Kingsway Financial Group Holdings Limited
Officers: Martin Basil Richards, Secretary/Accountant; Adrian James Anthon [1954] Director/Financier; Paul Nicholas Bradbury [1962] Director; Martin David Harrison [1951] Director; Martin Basil Richards [1952] Director/Accountant

Kingsway Financial Group Holdings Limited
Incorporated: 1 October 1997 *Employees:* 14
Net Worth: £2,085,973 *Total Assets:* £34,546,804
Registered Office: Barons Court, Manchester Road, Wilmslow, Cheshire, SK9 1BQ
Activities: Financial leasing
Shareholders: Martin David Harrison; Adrian James Anthon
Officers: Martin Basil Richards, Secretary; Adrian James Anthon [1954] Director/Financier; Paul Nicholas Bradbury [1962] Director; Martin David Harrison [1951] Director/Financier; Martin Basil Richards [1952] Finance Director

Kingsway Leasing Limited
Incorporated: 30 July 1997
Net Worth: £774,358 *Total Assets:* £14,981,897
Registered Office: Barons Court, Manchester Road, Wilmslow, Cheshire, SK9 1BQ
Activities: Financial leasing
Parent: Kingsway Financial Group Holdings Limited
Officers: Martin Basil Richards, Finance Director; Adrian James Anthon [1954] Director/Financier; Paul Nicholas Bradbury [1962] Director; Martin David Harrison [1951] Director/Financier; Martin Basil Richards [1952] Finance Director

Kingswood Homes (UK) Ltd
Incorporated: 31 March 2009
Net Worth: £1,921,886 *Total Assets:* £8,793,294
Registered Office: 8 Bridge Court, Liverpool New Road, Little Hoole, Preston, Lancs, PR4 5JT
Activities: Construction of domestic buildings
Shareholder: Alastair Bennett Fallows Salt
Officers: Andrea Mary Barrington-Fortune [1976] Director; Stephen Heaton [1975] Director; Leon Paul Jones [1980] Director; Alastair Bennett Fallows Salt [1948] Land & Commercial Property Director

Kintec Group Limited
Incorporated: 19 April 2008 *Employees:* 38
Net Worth: £3,972,364 *Total Assets:* £8,812,370
Registered Office: Floor 5 Building 4, Exchange Quay, Salford Quays, Manchester, M5 3EE
Activities: Activities of head offices
Major Shareholder: Neil Michael McCarthy
Officers: Rory Bowers, Secretary; Rory Bowers [1979] Director; Graeme Jones [1958] Finance Director; Neil McCarthy [1972] Director

Kintec Recruitment Limited
Incorporated: 10 January 2001 *Employees:* 27
Net Worth: £4,367,508 *Total Assets:* £7,415,424
Registered Office: Floor 5 Building 4, Exchange Quay, Salford Quays, Manchester, M5 3EE
Activities: Other activities of employment placement agencies
Major Shareholder: Neil Michael McCarthy
Officers: Rory Bowers, Secretary; Rory Bowers [1979] Director; Graeme Jones [1958] Director; Neil Michael McCarthy [1972] Director

Kirkbie Kendal School Academy Trust
Incorporated: 25 February 2011 *Employees:* 137
Net Worth: £8,613,259 *Total Assets:* £10,896,320
Registered Office: Kirkbie Kendal School, Lound Road, Kendal, Cumbria, LA9 7EQ
Activities: General secondary education
Officers: Lesley Jean Rudelhoff Scott, Secretary; William Robert Abram [1952] Director/Project Operations Manager; David Armstrong [1967] Director/Building Contractor; Paul Braithwaite [1964] Director/Postal Worker; Dr Naomi Brown [1960] Director/Charity Manager and Consultant; Graham Paul Duckworth [1968] Relationship Director Banking; Michael Duff [1959] Director/Telecommunications Consultant; David Peter Durnford [1968] Director; John Gee [1958] Director/Business Manager; Helen Herbert [1967] Director/Teacher; Philip David Hyman [1964] Director/Headteacher; Sally Parnaby [1957] Director/Retired; Jaki Summerfield [1969] Director/Lecturer; Sarah Vickers Tulley [1971] Director/Research and Compliance Manager Financial Services

Kirkby (Tyres) Limited
Incorporated: 9 June 1958 *Employees:* 80
Net Worth: £12,829,622 *Total Assets:* £26,827,396
Registered Office: 3rd Floor, 5 Temple Square, Temple Street, Liverpool, L2 5RH
Activities: Wholesale trade of motor vehicle parts and accessories
Parent: J. Rose (Tyres) Limited
Officers: Robin Walls, Secretary; Dave Dorrity [1963] Managing Director; Gordon Anthony Rosenthal [1951] Director/Chairman

Kirkham Grammar School
Incorporated: 2 April 2007 *Employees:* 193
Net Worth: £5,217,135 *Total Assets:* £9,168,790
Registered Office: Ribby Road, Kirkham, Preston, Lancs, PR4 2BH
Activities: Primary education
Officers: Christine Ellen Brown, Secretary; Dr Alan Raymond Berry [1949] Director/Retired; John Alastair Borradaile [1947] Director/Chartered Aeronautical Engineer; Rosemary Frances Cartwright [1944] Director/Retired; Larry Alan Fairclough [1954] Director/Retired; Thomas Andrew Lewis Greensmith [1959] Director/Judge; Dr James Barry Johnson [1945] Director/Retired; John Arthur Brooks Kelsall [1943] Director/Retired; Julian Edward Stefan Kollard [1961] Director; Barbara Elizabeth Lund [1955] Director/Retired Headmistress; Paul Robert Anthony Ribchester [1970] Sales Director; Lorraine Wareing [1967] Director/Accounts Clerk; Sean Antony Wilkinson [1969] Director/Businessman

Kirona Holdings Limited
Incorporated: 7 November 2011 *Employees:* 1
Net Worth Deficit: £90,458 *Total Assets:* £12,479,263
Registered Office: Barrington House, Heyes Lane, Alderley Edge, Cheshire, SK9 7LA
Activities: Business and domestic software development
Parent: KHL Newco Limited
Officers: Michael Anthony Marrison, Secretary; Neil Harvey [1972] Director; Michael Anthony Marrison [1962] Director/Chartered Accountant; David John Murray [1970] Director

Klash Clothing Co. Ltd
Incorporated: 26 October 1990 *Employees:* 2
Net Worth: £1,221,536 *Total Assets:* £21,696,224
Registered Office: Unit M, Arkwright Street, Westwood Industrial Estate, Oldham, Lancs, OL9 9LZ
Activities: Manufacture of other wearing apparel and accessories n.e.c.
Parent: Klash Holdings Limited
Officers: Mohammad Ashfaq, Secretary; Mohammad Ashfaq [1965] Director; Mohammad Shafiq [1962] Director

Klash Holdings Limited
Incorporated: 18 November 1998 *Employees:* 120
Net Worth: £8,152,685 *Total Assets:* £23,585,742
Registered Office: Unit M, Westwood Industrial Estate, Arkwright Street, Oldham, Lancs, OL9 9LZ
Activities: Activities of head offices
Shareholders: Mohammad Ashfaq; Mohammad Shafiq
Officers: Mohammad Ashfaq, Secretary/Director; Mohammad Haider Ashfaq [1998] Director; Mohammad Ashfaq [1965] Director; Mohammed Fahad Ashfaq [1994] Director; Mohammad Shafiq [1962] Director Mohammed Ali Shafiq [1992] Director; Omer Shafiq [1989] Director

Klinger Limited
Incorporated: 23 August 1971 *Employees:* 153
Net Worth: £12,374,489 *Total Assets:* £16,253,460
Registered Office: The Klinger Building, Wharfedale Road, Euroway Trading Estate, Bradford, W Yorks, BD4 6SG
Activities: Machining
Parent: Klinger Holdings Limited
Officers: Dominic Stephen Henry, Secretary; Oliver James Raymond Bache [1980] Projects Director; Stephen Brackstone [1982] Sales Director; Michael John Foulds [1968] Managing Director; Kevin Adrian Housam [1971] Director; David George Sorrie [1958] Business Development Director

KME Yorkshire Limited
Incorporated: 1[illegible] August 1986 *Employees:* 14
Net Worth: £11,559,000 *Total Assets:* £12,271,000
Registered Office: Yorkshire Copper Tube, East Lancashire Road, Kirkby, Merseyside, L33 7TU
Activities: Agents involved in the sale of fuels, ores, metals and industrial chemicals
Parent: KM Germany AG
Officers: John James Dodd, Secretary; John James Dodd [1962] Director/Accountant; Marco Miniati [1960] Director/Accountant [Italian]; Franz Thiele [1961] Director [German]

Knauf Insulation Limited
Incorporated: 27 June 1985 *Employees:* 609
Net Worth: £94,770,000 *Total Assets:* £153,748,992
Registered Office: P O Box 10, Stafford Road, St Helens, Merseyside, WA10 3NS
Activities: Manufacture of glass fibres
Officers: David Peter Justus Grimes, Secretary; Frédéric Marc Deslypere [1962] Director/Chief Financial Officer [Belgian]; Neil James Hargreaves [1976] Director/Chief Financial Officer; John Haydn Sinfield [1965] Managing Director

Alfred H. Knight Holdings Limited
Incorporated: 10 September 1985 *Employees:* 2,471
Net Worth: £62,291,528 *Total Assets:* £82,453,240
Registered Office: Alfred H Knight Group Headquarters (UK), Kings Business Park, Kings Drive, Prescot, Merseyside, L34 1PJ
Activities: Activities of head offices
Shareholders: David John Leslie Knight; Richard Kenneth Knight
Officers: Sandra Sadler, Secretary; Ian Anthony Baxter [1970] Director/Chief Financial Officer; David John Leslie Knight [1956] Director; Richard Kenneth Knight [1962] Director/Executive

Alfred H. Knight International Limited
Incorporated: 9 March 1967 *Employees:* 299
Net Worth: £8,877,546 *Total Assets:* £26,111,640
Registered Office: Alfred H Knight Group Headquarters (UK), Kings Business Park, Kings Drive, Prescot, Merseyside, L34 1PJ
Activities: Other professional, scientific and technical activities n.e.c.
Parent: Alfred H Knight UK Holdings Limited
Officers: Sandra Sadler, Secretary; Nigel Golborne [1962] Laboratory Director; David John Leslie Knight [1956] Director; Richard Kenneth Knight [1962] Director

Knights North West Limited
Incorporated: 29 November 2002 *Employees:* 288
Net Worth: £5,223,000 *Total Assets:* £101,951,000
Registered Office: Lookers House, 3 Etchells Road, West Timperley, Altrincham, Cheshire, WA14 5XS
Activities: Sale of new cars and light motor vehicles
Parent: Lookers Motor Group Limited
Officers: Glenda MacGeekie, Secretary; Andrew Campbell Bruce [1965] Director/Chief Executive Officer; Robin Anthony Gregson [1960] Director/Chartered Accountant; Nigel John McMinn [1968] Managing Director - Motor Division

Knightsbridge Insolvency Services Limited
Incorporated: 27 April 2010 *Employees:* 218
Net Worth: £3,893,974 *Total Assets:* £16,766,884
Registered Office: Thornley House, Carrington Business Park, Manchester, M31 4DD
Activities: Financial intermediation not elsewhere classified
Shareholders: Stuart Parkin; Shelly Parkin
Officers: Shelly Parkin [1979] Director; Stuart Parkin [1981] Director

Knossington Grange School Limited
Incorporated: 11 May 1977 *Employees:* 69
Net Worth: £8,563,741 *Total Assets:* £11,164,806
Registered Office: 1 Merchant's Place, River Street, Bolton, Lancs, BL2 1BX
Activities: General secondary education
Parent: Acorn Care and Education Limited
Officers: Helen Elizabeth Lecky, Secretary; Ryan David Edwards [1977] Finance Director; Jean-Luc Emmanuel Janet [1970] Director [French]; David Jon Leatherbarrow [1969] Director/Group Chief Executive Officer

Knowsley Contractors Limited
Incorporated: 12 November 2002 *Employees:* 116
Net Worth: £1,716,119 *Total Assets:* £8,379,457
Registered Office: Knowsley Contractors Ltd T/A King Construction, 18 Goodlass Road, Speke, Liverpool, L24 9HJ
Activities: Other building completion and finishing
Major Shareholder: Mark Neil Doyle
Officers: Adam McLean, Secretary; Matthew Corke [1992] Director/Quantity Surveyor; John Robert Carter Davies [1976] Director; Mark Neil Doyle [1979] Director; Benjamin Jones [1991] Director; Adam McLean [1971] Director/Health & Safety; Colin Pearce [1965] Director; David Prescott [1986] Director; Lee Randles [1971] Director; John Francis Shipley [1994] Director; Stuart Sidebottom [1966] Director; Michael John Taylor [1988] Director; Simon Warner [1980] Director

Knowsley S.K. Limited
Incorporated: 6 February 1984 *Employees:* 44
Net Worth: £2,553,450 *Total Assets:* £6,617,018
Registered Office: Centrepoint, Marshall Stevens Way, Trafford Park, Manchester, M17 1AE
Activities: Other manufacturing n.e.c.
Officers: Stephen John Masters, Secretary; Stephen John Masters [1973] Finance Director; Stephen James Wood [1963] Managing Director

Knutsford Multi Academy Trust
Incorporated: 9 March 2012 *Employees:* 126
Net Worth: £13,826,773 *Total Assets:* £17,214,748
Registered Office: Knutsford Academy, Bexton Road, Knutsford, Cheshire, WA16 0EA
Activities: General secondary education
Officers: Robert David Armstrong [1949] Director; Michael James Cladingbowl [1958] Director/Executive Principal; David Golden [1939] Director/Retired; Adam Seth Greenstein [1972] Director/Doctor; Robin McCluney [1975] Director/Computer Engineer; Catriona Jean Millson [1957] Director/School Governor; Valerie Jean Young [1942] Director

Knutsford Properties Limited
Incorporated: 16 June 1995
Net Worth: £12,792,000 *Total Assets:* £15,106,000
Registered Office: P O Box 1, Tatton Street, Knutsford, Cheshire, WA16 6AY
Activities: Buying and selling of own real estate
Parent: Marlowe Holdings Investments Limited
Officers: Philip Graham Elsegood, Secretary; Roger David Goddard [1953] Director/Chartered Accountant; Douglas Talbot McNair [1947] Director; William Sones Woof [1951] Director/Solicitor

Komatsu Forest Limited
Incorporated: 5 September 1996 *Employees:* 34
Net Worth: £1,778,061 *Total Assets:* £8,080,784
Registered Office: Unit 2 Longtown Industrial Estate, Longtown, Cumbria, CA6 5TJ
Activities: Support services to forestry
Parent: Komatsu Forest AB
Officers: Ian Stewart MacGregor, Secretary; Nils Ola Torbjorn Bostrom [1957] Director/Mechanical Engineer [Swedish]; David William McIlwraith [1975] Director; Mitsuru Ueno [1958] Company Secretary/Director [Japanese]

Kondor Bidco Limited
Incorporated: 7 February 2014
Net Worth Deficit: £18,982,000 *Total Assets:* £56,879,000
Registered Office: Technology House, Magnesium Way, Hapton, Burnley, Lancs, BB12 7BF
Activities: Activities of head offices
Parent: Kondor Midco Limited
Officers: Paul William Bryan [1969] Director; Stephen Casey [1980] Director [Irish]; Timothy David Griffin [1967] Director; Richard Hinds [1975] Director; Beatrice Madeleine Lafon [1959] Director [French]; Gerard Patrick O'Keeffe [1964] Director [Irish]

Kondor Holdco Limited
Incorporated: 5 February 2014 *Employees:* 295
Net Worth Deficit: £8,806,000 *Total Assets:* £106,900,000
Registered Office: Technology House, Magnesium Way, Hapton, Burnley, Lancs, BB12 7BF
Activities: Activities of head offices
Parent: Exertis (UK) Ltd
Officers: Paul William Bryan [1969] Director; Benjamin Charles Bushell [1975] Sales Director; Stephen Casey [1980] Director [Irish]; Desmond Joseph Duffy [1968] Director [Irish]; Timothy David Griffin [1967] Director; Richard Hinds [1975] Director; Beatrice Madeleine Lafon [1959] Director [French]; Gerard Patrick O'Keeffe [1964] Director [Irish]

Kondor Limited
Incorporated: 15 March 2000 *Employees:* 285
Net Worth: £55,715,000 *Total Assets:* £99,342,000
Registered Office: Technology House, Magnesium Way, Hapton, Burnley, Lancs, BB12 7BF
Activities: Agents specialised in the sale of other particular products
Parent: Kondor Bidco Limited
Officers: Paul William Bryan [1969] Director; Benjamin Charles Bushell [1975] Sales Director; Stephen Casey [1980] Director [Irish]; Desmond Joseph Duffy [1968] Director [Irish]; Timothy David Griffin [1967] Director; Richard Hinds [1975] Director; Beatrice Madeleine Lafon [1959] Director [French]; Gerard Patrick O'Keeffe [1964] Director [Irish]

Kondor Midco Limited
Incorporated: 6 February 2014 *Employees:* 4
Net Worth Deficit: £5,000 *Total Assets:* £30,076,000
Registered Office: Technology House, Magnesium Way, Hapton, Burnley, Lancs, BB12 7BF
Activities: Activities of head offices
Shareholders: Kondor Holdco Limited; Kondor Holdco Limited
Officers: Paul William Bryan [1969] Director; Stephen Casey [1980] Director [Irish]; Timothy David Griffin [1967] Director; Richard Hinds [1975] Director; Beatrice Madeleine Lafon [1959] Director [French]; Gerard Patrick O'Keeffe [1964] Director [Irish]

Kosa UK Limited
Incorporated: 20 October 2003
Net Worth Deficit: £314,646,400 *Total Assets:* £338,248,544
Registered Office: One St Peter's Square, Manchester, M2 3DE
Activities: Other business support service activities n.e.c.
Officers: Christopher Lee Crawshaw [1964] Director/Controller [American]; Reagan John Mathews [1974] Director/Vice President and Chief Financial Officer [American]; Andreas Samuel Westhuis [1980] Director/Controller [Dutch]

Kotug Smit Towage UK Limited
Incorporated: 18 March 2016 *Employees:* 3
Net Worth: £16,890,200 *Total Assets:* £16,899,500
Registered Office: Unit 40 Dunes Way, Wellington Employment Park, Liverpool, L5 9RJ
Activities: Activities of head offices
Officers: Harm Jan Van Der Meer [1964] Director [Dutch]; Rene Marie Raaijmakers [1968] Director [Dutch]

Kratos Analytical Limited
Incorporated: 22 March 1956 *Employees:* 201
Net Worth: £10,291,000 *Total Assets:* £35,791,000
Registered Office: Wharfside, Trafford Wharf Road, Manchester, M17 1GP
Activities: Manufacture of other special-purpose machinery n.e.c.
Officers: Tony Brooks, Secretary; Kozo Shimazu [1948] Director [Japanese]; Hiroaki Waki [1961] Managing Director [Japanese]

Kratos Group PLC
Incorporated: 6 November 1986 *Employees:* 201
Net Worth: £11,143,000 *Total Assets:* £37,162,000
Registered Office: Wharfside, Trafford Wharf Road, Manchester, M17 1GP
Activities: Activities of head offices
Officers: Tony Brooks, Secretary; Nakao Kosuke [1960] Director [Japanese]; Kozo Shimazu [1948] Director [Japanese]; David John Surman [1952] Director; Hiroaki Waki [1961] Managing Director [Japanese]; Yasunori Yamsmoto [1959] Managing Director [Japanese]

Krempel (UK) Holdings Limited
Incorporated: 26 April 2000 *Employees:* 329
Net Worth: £21,513,896 *Total Assets:* £25,740,360
Registered Office: Queens Mill, Queen Street, Longridge, Preston, Lancs, PR3 3BS
Activities: Activities of head offices
Officers: Neil Robert Currie, Secretary; Uwe Assmuth [1959] Joint Managing Director [German]; Christian Wolfgang Reh [1967] Joint Managing Director [German]

KRL (LR) Hold Co Limited
Incorporated: 3 June 2015
Net Worth: £1 *Total Assets:* £20,000,000
Registered Office: Hamilton House, Church Street, Altrincham, Cheshire, WA14 4DR
Activities: Production of electricity
Major Shareholder: Brian George Kennedy
Officers: Darren Karl Cornwall [1969] Director; Jonathon Steven Kennedy [1990] Managing Director; Adrian Christopher Kirk [1961] Finance Director

KRL (LR) Limited
Incorporated: 11 March 2010
Net Worth: £9,178,929 *Total Assets:* £17,435,406
Registered Office: Hamilton House, Church Street, Altrincham, Cheshire, WA14 4DR
Activities: Activities of head offices
Major Shareholder: Brian George Kennedy
Officers: Andrew Page, Secretary; Darren Karl Cornwall [1969] Director; Adrian Christopher Kirk [1961] Finance Director

KRMCO Limited
Incorporated: 17 July 2009
Net Worth: £8,469,220 *Total Assets:* £8,599,263
Registered Office: Units A2-A6 Edge Fold Industrial Estate, Plodder Lane, Farnworth, Bolton, Lancs, BL4 0LR
Activities: Activities of open-ended investment companies
Parent: KRMCO Holdings Limited
Officers: Sarah Jane Cock, Secretary; Karen Jean Ogden [1967] Director; Stephen John Seddon [1966] Director

Krones UK Limited
Incorporated: 16 July 1953 *Employees:* 128
Net Worth: £16,547,000 *Total Assets:* £33,628,000
Registered Office: Westregen House, Great Bank Road, Wingates Industrial Park, West Houghton, Bolton, Lancs, BL5 3XB
Activities: Manufacture of machinery for food, beverage and tobacco processing
Parent: Krones AG
Officers: Victoria Bridge, Secretary; Mark John Heath [1959] Sales Director; Thomas Ricker [1968] Director [German]; Andrew John Wilson [1964] Managing Director

KRS Finance Ltd
Incorporated: 16 November 2005
Net Worth: £3,398,318 *Total Assets:* £22,530,532
Registered Office: Baines House, Midgery Court, Pittman Way, Fulwood, Preston, Lancs, PR2 9ZH
Activities: Activities of financial services holding companies
Parent: Key Retirement Group Ltd
Officers: Robert James Scott [1973] Director; Simon Christopher Thompson [1972] Director

KS Brands Limited
Incorporated: 15 July 1971 *Employees:* 69
Net Worth: £5,225,951 *Total Assets:* £9,852,990
Registered Office: Laltex House, Leigh Commerce Park, Green Fold Way, Leigh, Lancs, WN7 3XH
Activities: Wholesale of household goods (other than musical instruments) n.e.c
Officers: Carl Price, Secretary; Rajan Jethanand Mulchand [1948] Director/General Merchant; Sanjay Rajan Mulchand [1975] Director

KS SPV 24 Limited
Incorporated: 20 July 2012
Net Worth Deficit: £1,726,542 *Total Assets:* £9,550,246
Registered Office: Eversheds House, 70 Great Bridgewater Street, Manchester, M1 5ES
Activities: Production of electricity
Parent: Sune Green Holdco4 Limited
Officers: Carl Goran Dandanell [1959] Director [Swedish]

Kudos Shower Products Limited
Incorporated: 19 May 1999 *Employees:* 116
Net Worth: £7,613,588 *Total Assets:* £14,292,851
Registered Office: Unit 1 Elmsfield Park, Holme, Carnforth, Lancs, LA6 1RJ
Activities: Other manufacturing n.e.c.
Major Shareholder: Bruce Raymond Ledwith
Officers: Nick Graville [1974] Sales Director; Mark Anthony Hill [1973] Finance Director; David Irwin [1966] Director; Bruce Raymond Ledwith [1952] Director

Kukri GB Limited
Incorporated: 3 December 2007 *Employees:* 69
Net Worth Deficit: £7,507,946 *Total Assets:* £7,785,208
Registered Office: Edinburgh House, Hollinsbrook Way, Pilsworth, Bury, Lancs, BL9 8RR
Activities: Retail sale of clothing in specialised stores
Parent: Kukri Sports Ltd.
Officers: Siobhan Mawdsley, Secretary; Peter Alan Cowgill [1953] Director; Andrew Ronnie [1968] Director/Business Consultant; Brian Michael Small [1956] Director

Kunick (102) Limited
Incorporated: 6 June 1963 *Employees:* 188
Net Worth Deficit: £8,251,000 *Total Assets:* £13,910,000
Registered Office: 4 Hardman Square, Spinningfields, Manchester, M3 3EB
Activities: Manufacture of other special-purpose machinery n.e.c.
Officers: Richard Matthew Still, Secretary; Julian Frederick Nicholls [1951] Director; Richard Matthew Still [1965] Director

Kverneland Group UK Limited
Incorporated: 16 March 1978 *Employees:* 49
Net Worth: £6,678,000 *Total Assets:* £18,444,000
Registered Office: Walkers Lane, Lea Green, St Helens, Merseyside, WA9 4AF
Activities: Manufacture of agricultural and forestry machinery other than tractors
Parent: Kubota Corporation
Officers: Jacqueline Raeburn, Secretary/Finance Controller; Joseph Bell [1954] Director; Arild Gjerde [1964] Director [Norwegian]

Kverneland Holding (UK) Limited
Incorporated: 29 November 1994 *Employees:* 2
Net Worth: £14,560,000 *Total Assets:* £14,570,000
Registered Office: Walkers Lane, Lea Green, St Helens, Merseyside, WA9 4AF
Activities: Manufacture of agricultural and forestry machinery other than tractors
Parent: Kubota Corporation
Officers: Jacqueline Raeburn, Secretary/Finance Controller; Joseph Bell [1954] Sales Director; Arild Gjerde [1964] Director [Norwegian]

KVH Media Group Communication Limited
Incorporated: 17 April 1985
Net Worth: £3,215,000 *Total Assets:* £9,899,000
Registered Office: Suite 1, 4th Floor, 1 Derby Square, Liverpool, L2 9XX
Activities: Other publishing activities
Parent: KVH Media Group Limited
Officers: Felise Feingold, Secretary; Mark Woodhead [1971] Director

L & K Group PLC
Incorporated: 29 June 1900 *Employees:* 73
Net Worth: £6,132,995 *Total Assets:* £12,902,260
Registered Office: J36 Rural Auction Centre, Crooklands, Milnthorpe, Cumbria, LA7 7FP
Activities: Activities of agricultural holding companies
Officers: Katie Louise Black, Secretary; Alan John Bargh [1953] Director/Farmer; Jill Marie Bargh [1969] Director/Farmer; David Herbert Barton [1961] Director/Farmer; Stuart Cornthwaite [1953] Director; James Anthony Dixon [1959] Director/Farmer; John Edward Drinkall [1955] Director/Farmer; John Addison Geldard [1951] Director/Farmer; Jonathan Walter Hodgson [1961] Director/Farmer; Professor Monica Mary Lee [1952] Director/Lecturer; Trevor William Wilson [1961] Director/Farmer

L F D Group Limited
Incorporated: 8 September 2006
Net Worth: £27,242,596 *Total Assets:* £31,555,258
Registered Office: Orchard House, Strawberry How Road, Cockermouth, Cumbria, CA13 9XQ
Activities: Other letting and operating of own or leased real estate
Shareholders: David Robert Hill; Ruth Elizabeth Hill
Officers: Caroline Anne Cross, Secretary; David Robert Hill [1953] Director; Ruth Elizabeth Hill [1954] Director

L&D Real Estate Limited
Incorporated: 11 June 2009
Net Worth: £348,126 *Total Assets:* £7,641,835
Registered Office: Charles Babbage Avenue, Kingsway Business Park, Rochdale, Lancs, OL16 4NW
Activities: Other letting and operating of own or leased real estate
Officers: Donald Friese Snr, Secretary; Simon John Boocock [1973] Director; Donald Friese Jr [1972] Director [American]; Donald Friese Sr [1940] Director [American]

L.T.D. Contractors Limited
Incorporated: 29 April 2015 *Employees:* 1
Net Worth: £124,401 *Total Assets:* £9,085,754
Registered Office: Kingsway House, Hatton Garden, Liverpool, L3 2AJ
Activities: Other building completion and finishing
Shareholders: Katie Christine Kenwright; Lawrence Kenwright
Officers: Katie Christine Kenwright [1977] Director

L1 Renewables Limited
Incorporated: 5 December 2014
Net Worth: £7,171,448 *Total Assets:* £237,263,808
Registered Office: c/o Universities Superannuation Scheme Limited, Royal Liver Building, Liverpool, L3 1PY
Activities: Other activities auxiliary to insurance and pension funding
Parent: Universities Superannuation Scheme Limited
Officers: Fiona Jackelin Achola Otika, Secretary; Damian Martin Holland [1977] Director/Head of Asset Management & Operations; Benjamin Mark Levenstein [1978] Director/Fund Manager; Emma Louise Singh [1988] Director/Associate

LA Holding Limited
Incorporated: 12 May 2011
Net Worth: £8,235,000 *Total Assets:* £34,414,000
Registered Office: Schoeller Alibert, Road 1 Winsford Industrial Estate, Winsford, Cheshire, CW7 3RA
Activities: Activities of head offices
Officers: Ian Alan Degnan [1965] Director/Chief Financial Officer

The Label Makers Limited
Incorporated: 28 October 1963 *Employees:* 69
Net Worth: £6,599,817 *Total Assets:* £9,598,212
Registered Office: Prince Street, Bradford, W Yorks, BD4 6HQ
Activities: Manufacture of other articles of paper and paperboard n.e.c.
Shareholders: David John Nocton Webster; Sarah Elizabeth Fletcher; Jane Katrina Jackson
Officers: Zenna Parfaniuk, Secretary; Sarah Elizabeth Fletcher [1959] Director/Counsellor; Jane Katrina Jackson [1964] Director/Learning Support Teacher; Kevin Lyons [1962] Sales Director; Zenna Parfaniuk [1965] Director/Company Secretary; Anthony John Bloye Webster [1932] Director/Chairman; David John Nocton Webster [1962] Managing Director

Labware Limited
Incorporated: 15 March 1995 *Employees:* 110
Net Worth: £25,683,978 *Total Assets:* £36,760,768
Registered Office: Denzell Lodge, Denzell Gardens, Dunham Road, Bowdon, Altrincham, Cheshire, WA14 4QF
Activities: Information technology consultancy activities
Officers: John Carlisle Peet Iii, Secretary/Attorney [American]; Mark David Gonzalez [1964] Director/Computing [American]; Robert William Alexander Hillhouse [1948] Director/Scientist; Vance Kershner [1953] Director/Laboratory Computer Programmer [American]; Nicholas John Townsend [1957] Managing Director

Lacey Green Primary Academy
Incorporated: 19 July 2011 *Employees:* 62
Net Worth: £6,212,000 *Total Assets:* £6,623,000
Registered Office: Lacey Green Primary Academy, Barlow Road, Wilmslow, Cheshire, SK9 4DP
Activities: Primary education
Officers: Brenda Acton [1949] Director/Retired; Sarah Jane Bacon [1967] Director/Trainer; Dr Darren Budd [1967] Managing Director; Lorraine Wendy Dooley [1948] Director/Headteacher; Cheryl Jones [1971] Director/Teacher; Kevin Michael Kelly [1951] Director/Retired; Christian Daniel Marner [1974] Director/Employee; Paul Scott [1975] Director/Project Manager; Steven Barry Shaw [1980] Director/Teacher; Peter Jeremy Robert Smith [1955] Director/Retired; Alison Taylor-Stokes [1972] Director/Architect; Jennifer Claire Unsworth [1980] Director

Lacy Roofing Company Limited
Incorporated: 28 September 1971 *Employees:* 17
Net Worth: £9,230,779 *Total Assets:* £9,985,936
Registered Office: 3-4 Tapton Way, Wavertree, Liverpool, L13 1DA
Activities: Roofing activities
Shareholders: Nicholas Hooper; Nick Hooper
Officers: Nick Hooper, Secretary/Director; Nick Hooper [1966] Managing Director

Lagardere Sports UK Ltd
Incorporated: 17 July 1998 *Employees:* 42
Net Worth: £12,528,328 *Total Assets:* £29,390,632
Registered Office: 2nd Floor, 40 Water Lane, Wilmslow, Cheshire, SK9 5AP
Activities: Advertising agencies
Parent: Lagardere Sports Germany GmbH
Officers: Tim Birt, Secretary; Tim Birt [1975] Director/Chartered Accountant; Andrew Georgiou [1974] Director/Chief Operating Officer [Greek]; Paul Michael O'Dowd [1972] Director/General Counsel; David Pearce [1967] Finance Director; Carl Woodman [1979] Director

Lagonda Leeds Propco Limited
Incorporated: 15 May 2001 *Employees:* 4
Net Worth Deficit: £4,240,000 *Total Assets:* £11,794,000
Registered Office: c/o KPMG LLP, One St Peters Square, Manchester, M2 3AE
Activities: Other letting and operating of own or leased real estate
Parent: Lagonda Leeds Holdco Limited
Officers: Patrick Bour [1978] Director [French]

Lagonda Palace Propco Limited
Incorporated: 15 May 2001 *Employees:* 4
Net Worth: £9,920,000 *Total Assets:* £40,361,000
Registered Office: c/o KPMG LLP, One St Peters Square, Manchester, M2 3AE
Activities: Other letting and operating of own or leased real estate
Parent: Lagonda Palace Holdco Limited
Officers: Patrick Bour [1978] Director [French]

Lagonda Russell Propco Limited
Incorporated: 15 May 2001 *Employees:* 4
Net Worth: £13,080,000 *Total Assets:* £137,374,000
Registered Office: c/o KPMG LLP, One St Peters Square, Manchester, M2 3AE
Activities: Other letting and operating of own or leased real estate
Parent: Lagonda Russell Holdco Limited
Officers: Patrick Bour [1978] Director [French]

Lagonda York Propco Limited
Incorporated: 15 May 2001 *Employees:* 4
Net Worth: £11,678,000 *Total Assets:* £37,296,000
Registered Office: c/o KPMG LLP, One St Peters Square, Manchester, M2 3AE
Activities: Other letting and operating of own or leased real estate
Parent: Lagonda York Holdco Limited
Officers: Patrick Bour [1978] Director [French]

Laila's Fine Foods Limited
Incorporated: 24 July 2002 *Employees:* 379
Net Worth: £2,910,862 *Total Assets:* £18,704,530
Registered Office: 91 Moor Park Avenue, Bispham, Blackpool, Lancs, FY2 0LZ
Activities: Manufacture of prepared meals and dishes
Shareholders: Laila Remtulla; Alnajir Bhurali Remtulla
Officers: Laila Remtulla, Secretary/Director; Natasha Beaver [1984] Purchasing Director; Alnajir Bhurali Remtulla [1953] Director; Laila Remtulla [1957] Director; Rishma Remtulla [1981] Sales and NPD Director; Zera Remtulla [1976] Technical Director

Lake District Estates Company Limited
Incorporated: 6 December 1938 *Employees:* 92
Net Worth: £8,552,162 *Total Assets:* £22,125,766
Registered Office: Maudlands, Maude Street, Kendal, Cumbria, LA9 4QD
Activities: Other retail sale of new goods in specialised stores (not commercial art galleries and opticians)
Parent: Lake District Holdings Ltd
Officers: Jonathan Ross Winter, Secretary; Ruth Isabel Adorian [1932] Director; Lady Julia Daphne Boyd [1948] Director; Edward James Clarkson Webb [1966] Director/Film Producer; Peter Richard Wavell Hensman [1948] Director/Chartered Accountant; Roger Hensman [1981] Director/Consultant; Lucinda Carolyn Barrett Langton [1978] Director/CRS Manager; Richard Wakefield Raynsford [1945] Director; Thomas Lindsay Wakefield Raynsford [1980] Director/Investment Banker; Carolyn Mary Seel [1958] Director; William Ian Simpson [1951] Director/Farmer; Georgina Anne Townsend [1957] Director; Alexandra Peard Wix [1984] Director/Tour Operator

Lake District Holdings Limited
Incorporated: 2 September 1987 *Employees:* 160
Net Worth: £12,424,977 *Total Assets:* £23,251,234
Registered Office: Maudlands, Maude Street, Kendal, Cumbria, LA9 4QD
Activities: Activities of other holding companies n.e.c.
Officers: Peter Richard Wavell Hensman, Secretary; Ruth Isabel Adorian [1932] Director; Lady Julia Daphne Boyd [1948] Director; Edward James Clarkson Webb [1966] Director; Peter Richard Wavell Hensman [1948] Director; Roger Hensman [1981] Director/Consultant; Lucinda Carolyn Barrett Langton [1978] Director/CRS Manager; Richard Wakefield Raynsford [1945] Director; Thomas Lindsay Wakefield Raynsford [1980] Director/Investment Banker; Carolyn Mary Seel [1958] Director; William Ian Simpson [1951] Director/Farmer; Georgina Anne Townsend [1957] Director; Alexandra Peard Wix [1984] Director/Tour Operator

Lake District Hotels Limited
Incorporated: 7 February 1983 *Employees:* 336
Net Worth: £34,098,824 *Total Assets:* £45,329,896
Registered Office: Armathwaite Hall Hotel, Bassenthwaite, Keswick, Cumbria, CA12 4RE
Activities: Hotels and similar accommodation
Shareholder: Charles John Graves
Officers: Charles John Graves, Secretary; Charles John Graves [1949] Director/Hotel Proprietor; Kit Berit Graves [1951] Director/Hotel Proprietor [Danish]; Daniella Charlene Hope [1984] Director

Lakeland Leisure Estates Limited
Incorporated: 10 May 1990 *Employees:* 97
Net Worth: £15,727,271 *Total Assets:* £34,058,452
Registered Office: The Studio, Station Road, Staveley, Kendal, Cumbria, LA8 9NB
Activities: Recreational vehicle parks, trailer parks and camping grounds
Shareholders: Phillip Trevor Morgan; Carol Morgan
Officers: Carol Morgan, Secretary; Carol Morgan [1953] Director/Caravan Park Operator; Phillip Trevor Morgan [1952] Director/Caravan Park Operator

Lakeland Limited
Incorporated: 19 June 1964 *Employees:* 1,668
Net Worth: £60,039,000 *Total Assets:* £83,440,000
Registered Office: Alexandra Buildings, Windermere, Cumbria, LA23 1BQ
Activities: Retail sale of hardware, paints and glass in specialised stores
Shareholders: William Martin Moorhouse Rayner; Samuel Alan Miles Rayner; Julian Anthony Rayner
Officers: William Martin Moorhouse Rayner, Secretary; Philip Robert Johnson [1946] Director/Chartered Accountant; Julian Anthony Rayner [1957] Director; Samuel Alan Miles Rayner [1953] Director; William Martin Moorhouse Rayner [1951] Director

The Lakes Freerange Egg Company Ltd.
Incorporated: 7 February 1997 *Employees:* 85
Net Worth: £7,139,366 *Total Assets:* £9,991,324
Registered Office: Meg Bank, Stainton, Penrith, Cumbria, CA11 0EE
Activities: Other business support service activities n.e.c.
Shareholders: Helen Brass; David John Brass
Officers: Helen Brass, Secretary; David John Brass [1959] Director/Farmer; Helen Brass [1963] Director/Farmer

Lakeside Collection Limited
Incorporated: 2 July 1993 *Employees:* 458
Net Worth: £2,031,546 *Total Assets:* £9,309,025
Registered Office: Stables Country Club, Bolholt Complex, off Walshaw Road, Bury, Lancs, BL8 1PU
Activities: Hotels and similar accommodation
Parent: Estate of Stefan Sikorski
Officers: Sarah Sikorski, Company Secretary; Jonathan David Butterworth [1977] Director; Natalie Jane Rogers [1979] Director; Sarah Elizabeth Sikorski [1967] Director

Lakeview Rest Homes Limited
Incorporated: 27 January 1997 *Employees:* 109
Net Worth: £2,916,214 *Total Assets:* £7,828,819
Registered Office: 93-99 St Andrews Road South, Lytham St Annes, Lancs, FY8 1PU
Activities: Residential care activities for learning difficulties, mental health and substance abuse
Shareholder: Peter Douglas Wood
Officers: Peter Wood [1967] Director; Peter Douglas Wood [1949] Director/Rest Home Proprietor

Laltex & Co.Limited
Incorporated: 15 November 1962 *Employees:* 140
Net Worth: £19,187,156 *Total Assets:* £28,134,300
Registered Office: Laltex House, Leigh Commerce Park, Greenfold Way, Leigh, Lancs, WN7 3XH
Activities: Wholesale of clothing and footwear
Officers: Carl Price, Secretary; Rajan Jethanand Mulchand [1948] Director/General Merchant; Sanjay Rajan Mulchand [1975] Director

Lambtrack Limited
Incorporated: 12 February 2007
Net Worth: £678,185,984 *Total Assets:* £1,204,231,040
Registered Office: 3rd Floor, 1 Ashley Road, Altrincham, Cheshire, WA14 2DT
Activities: Non-trading company
Parent: Erie UK Senior Holding Limited
Officers: Rhona Gregg, Secretary; Lucie Mary Katja Grant [1976] Director/Solicitor; Nicholas Ince [1982] Director/Accountant; David John Norman [1960] Director/Chartered Accountant

Lancashire County Developments (Property) Limited
Incorporated: 24 May 1983 *Employees:* 7
Net Worth: £45,465,332 *Total Assets:* £50,666,344
Registered Office: P O Box 78, County Hall, Preston, Lancs, PR1 8XJ
Activities: Other service activities n.e.c.
Parent: Lancashire County Developments Limited
Officers: Laura Sales, Secretary; Timothy Maxwell Ashton [1961] Director/Business Owner; Geoffrey Driver [1944] Director/Retired; Charles Edwards [1992] Director/County Councillor; Julie Patricia Gibson [1972] Director/Postwoman for Royal Mail; Michael Anthony Green [1973] Director/Non Practising Solicitor; Adrian Riggott [1976] Director/Operations Manager/County Councillor; David Thornton Smith [1944] Director/Retired

Lancashire County Developments Limited
Incorporated: 23 March 1982 *Employees:* 7
Net Worth: £41,608,152 *Total Assets:* £53,618,908
Registered Office: P O Box 78, County Hall, Preston, Lancs, PR1 8XJ
Activities: Other service activities n.e.c.
Officers: Laura Sales, Secretary; Timothy Maxwell Ashton [1961] Director/Business Owner; Geoffrey Driver [1944] Director/Retired; Charles Edwards [1992] Director/County Councillor; Julie Patricia Gibson [1972] Director/Postwoman for Royal Mail; Michael Anthony Green [1973] Director/Non Practising Solicitor; Adrian Riggott [1976] Director/Operations Manager/County Councillor; David Thornton Smith [1944] Director/Retired

Lancashire Schools PSP Limited
Incorporated: 24 October 2006
Net Worth: £164,000 *Total Assets:* £15,262,000
Registered Office: c/o Albany SPC Services Ltd, 3rd Floor, 3-5 Charlotte Street, Manchester, M1 4HB
Activities: Activities of head offices
Parent: Consolidated Investment Holdings Limited
Officers: Ailison Louise Mitchell, Secretary; Michael Andrew Donn [1972] Director; Barry Paul Millsom [1974] Director

Lancashire Schools SPC Phase 1 Ltd
Incorporated: 24 October 2006
Net Worth Deficit: £12,136,000 *Total Assets:* £74,028,000
Registered Office: c/o Albany SPC Services Ltd, 3rd Floor, 3-5 Charlotte Street, Manchester, M1 4HB
Activities: Other education n.e.c.
Parent: Lancashire Schools SPC Holdings Phase 1 Ltd
Officers: Ailison Louise Mitchell, Secretary; Michael Andrew Donn [1972] Director; Kate Louise Flaherty [1980] Investment Director; Steven Paul Fraser [1963] Director; Leo William McKenna [1966] Director [Irish]; Christopher Thomas Solley [1970] Director; Jasvinder Kaur Uppal [1971] Director

Lancashire Schools SPC Phase 2 Ltd
Incorporated: 9 August 2007
Net Worth Deficit: £8,377,000 *Total Assets:* £38,976,000
Registered Office: c/o Albany SPC Services Ltd, 3rd Floor, 3-5 Charlotte Street, Manchester, M1 4HB
Activities: Other education n.e.c.
Parent: Lancashire Schools SPC Holdings Phase 2 Ltd
Officers: Ailison Louise Mitchell, Secretary; Michael Andrew Donn [1972] Director; Kate Louise Flaherty [1980] Investment Director; Steven Paul Fraser [1963] Director; Leo William McKenna [1966] Director [Irish]; Christopher Thomas Solley [1970] Director; Jasvinder Kaur Uppal [1971] Director

Lancashire Schools SPC Phase 2A Ltd
Incorporated: 25 April 2008
Net Worth Deficit: £13,968,000 *Total Assets:* £59,865,000
Registered Office: c/o Albany SPC Services Ltd, 3rd Floor, 3-5 Charlotte Street, Manchester, M1 4HB
Activities: Other education n.e.c.
Parent: Lancashire Schools SPC Holdings Phase 2A Limited
Officers: Ailison Louise Mitchell, Secretary; Michael Andrew Donn [1972] Director; Kate Louise Flaherty [1980] Investment Director; Steven Paul Fraser [1963] Director; Leo William McKenna [1966] Director [Irish]; Christopher Thomas Solley [1970] Director; Jasvinder Kaur Uppal [1971] Director

Lancashire Schools SPC Phase 3 Ltd
Incorporated: 12 January 2009
Net Worth: £359,000 *Total Assets:* £37,925,000
Registered Office: c/o Albany SPC Services Ltd, 3rd Floor, 3-5 Charlotte Street, Manchester, M1 4HB
Activities: Other education n.e.c.
Parent: Lancashire Schools SPC Holdings Phase 3 Ltd
Officers: Ailison Louise Mitchell, Secretary; Michael Andrew Donn [1972] Director; Kate Louise Flaherty [1980] Investment Director; Steven Paul Fraser [1963] Director; Leo William McKenna [1966] Director [Irish]; Christopher Thomas Solley [1970] Director; Jasvinder Kaur Uppal [1971] Director

The Lancashire Wildlife Trust Ltd
Incorporated: 1 August 1962 *Employees:* 103
Net Worth: £11,919,000 *Total Assets:* £12,946,000
Registered Office: The Barn, Berkeley Drive, Bamber Bridge, Preston, Lancs, PR5 6BY
Activities: Activities of other membership organisations n.e.c.
Officers: Andrew Diccon James Royce, Secretary; Andrew John Martin Berry [1957] Director/Woodworker; Mustafa Ali Desai [1965] Director/Core Transmission Designer; John Michael Drury [1947] Director; James Ross Duggan [1956] Director/Circuit Judge; Dr Clive Harry Elphick [1956] Non-Executive Director & Senior Advisor; Steven Paul Garland [1956] Director/Chief Museums Officer; Gemma Louise Grady Hill [1979] Director/Membership Promotion Consultant; Geoffrey Higginbottom [1937] Director/Retired; Julian Boyd Jackson [1951] Non-Executive Director Company Chairman; Professor Philip James [1958] Director/Professor of Ecology; Stephen Niven [1946] Director/Manager; Andrew Diccon James Royce [1965] Director/Solicitor; Hazel Ann Ryan [1961] Risk and Operations Director; Deborah Frances Shackleton [1952] Business Leader & Non-Executive Director; Anthony Richard Thomas [1947] Retired Director; Ronald Wade [1957] Finance Director; John Michael Wells [1951] Director/Environment and Safety Manager

Lancaster Girls' Grammar School
Incorporated: 16 November 2010 *Employees:* 85
Net Worth: £12,489,000 *Total Assets:* £14,135,000
Registered Office: Lancaster Girls' Grammar School, Regent Street, Lancaster, LA1 1SF
Activities: General secondary education
Officers: Jane Louise Mason, Secretary; Sarah Katherine Bain [1967] Director of Banking; Jacqueline Shirley Cahalin [1961] Director/Teacher; Anthony James Capper [1971] Director/Trustee; Professor Amanda Chetwynd [1955] Director/Pro Vice Chancellor; Ian Paul Dodd [1966] Director/Firefighter; Dr Rachel Dyer [1972] Director/Trustee; Susan Elizabeth Hodgson [1952] Director/Solicitor; Dr Janet Margaret Lavelle [1958] Director/Doctor; Allison Jayne Norfolk [1968] Director/Bank Manager; Sarah Jane Randall-Paley [1968] Director/Chartered Accountant; Leanne Sharples [1986] Director/School Teacher; Julia Louise Stables [1962] Director/Administrator; Richard Parker Taylor [1962] Director/Chartered Surveyor; Alison Elaine Whittaker [1961] Director

Lancaster Partners (Holdings) Limited
Incorporated: 21 January 1970 *Employees:* 3
Net Worth: £22,607,000 *Total Assets:* £22,638,000
Registered Office: 6 Normanby Chase, Altrincham, Cheshire, WA14 4QP
Activities: Activities of head offices
Shareholders: John Malcolm Weldon Lockyear; Sandra Elizabeth Lockyear
Officers: John Malcolm Weldon Lockyear, Secretary; Helen Lockyear [1961] Director; John Malcolm Weldon Lockyear [1960] Director; Sandra Elizabeth Lockyear [1957] Director

Lancaster Royal Grammar School
Incorporated: 14 December 2010 *Employees:* 151
Net Worth: £36,390,000 *Total Assets:* £39,921,000
Registered Office: Lancaster Royal Grammar School, East Road, Lancaster, LA1 3EF
Activities: General secondary education
Officers: Richard Charles Gittins, Secretary; Professor Martin Alexander [1955] Director/Professor; Dr John Edward Bentham [1946] Director; Roderick Alexander Drake Burgess [1955] Director; Michael John Burrow [1965] Regional Managing Director; Douglas Howard Cameron [1930] Director; Hugh James Castle [1968] Director/Teacher; Paul Worrall Fitton [1949] Director/Accountant; Professor Anthony Michael Guenault [1937] Director; Ena Margaret Lund [1947] Director; Gillian Ruth Manklow [1958] Director; Richard Thomas Mellon [1971] Director/Teacher; Andrew Colin Neal [1964] Director/Self Employed; Wendy Preston [1955] Director/Accountant; Dr Christopher John Pyle [1972] Director/Headmaster; Howard Roberts [1949] Director; Kevin John Roberts [1949] Director; Denise Margaret Sinclair [1952] Director; Phillip Sycamore [1951] Director; Sarah Troughton [1972] Director/Teacher

Lancaster University Energy Services Ltd
Incorporated: 9 January 1989
Net Worth: £9,941,848 *Total Assets:* £10,460,922
Registered Office: University House, Lancaster University, Lancaster, LA1 4YW
Activities: Production of electricity
Officers: Geoffrey Peter Fielding, Secretary; Nicola Cheryl Banfield [1971] Director/Chief Administrative Officer; Paul Morris [1967] Director; Sarah Jane Randall-Paley [1968] Finance Director

Land & Lakes (Anglesey) Limited
Incorporated: 21 June 2010 *Employees:* 4
Net Worth: £7,263,672 *Total Assets:* £21,879,720
Registered Office: The Marketing Suite, Baron Way, Kingmoor Business Park, Carlisle, CA6 4SJ
Activities: Buying and selling of own real estate
Major Shareholder: Brian Kenneth Scowcroft
Officers: Neil McIntyre, Secretary; Geoffrey Dallimore [1966] Director/Chartered Accountant; Anthony William Goddard [1950] Director/Chartered Surveyor; Brian Kenneth Scowcroft [1956] Director; Richard Marcel Sidi [1964] Director

Land Recovery Limited
Incorporated: 5 July 1982
Net Worth: £6,820,786 *Total Assets:* £13,363,906
Registered Office: 128 Crewe Road, Haslington, Crewe, Cheshire, CW1 5RQ
Activities: Operation of gravel and sand pits; mining of clays and kaolin
Major Shareholder: David Neild Beecroft
Officers: David Nield Beecroft [1978] Director/Plant Operator; David Ernest Beecroft [1947] Director

The Land Restoration Trust
Incorporated: 18 March 2004 *Employees:* 37
Net Worth: £145,800,992 *Total Assets:* £147,739,008
Registered Office: 7 Birchwood One, Dewhurst Road, Birchwood, Warrington, Cheshire, WA3 7GB
Activities: Landscape service activities
Officers: Euan James Armstrong Hall, Secretary; Patrick Anthony Richard Aylmer [1963] Director/Chartered Accountant; Anthony Bickmore [1952] Director/Chartered Surveyor; Lady Jane Wight Garrett [1956] Director; Janet Haddock-Fraser [1963] Director/Professor; William John Hiscocks [1958] Director/Retired; Tom Keevil [1960] Director/Retired; Simon Gregor MacGillivray [1959] Director; Jeff Moore [1954] Director; Dinah Alison Nichols [1943] Director; Peter Alan Smith [1946] Director/Chartered Accountant; Sarah Jane Whitney [1963] Director

Landmarq LLP
Incorporated: 31 July 2003
Net Worth: £7,483,488 *Total Assets:* £12,429,828
Registered Office: 31 Wellington Road, Nantwich, Cheshire, CW5 7ED
Officers: Rachel Louise Collister [1972] Member; Suzanne Nicole Nicola Gauge [1970] Member; Jonathan Paul Nuttall [1969] Member; Marion Stock [1943] Member; Peter Alan Stock [1944] Member

Langdale Leisure Limited
Incorporated: 2 October 1986 *Employees:* 175
Net Worth: £4,704,218 *Total Assets:* £13,763,871
Registered Office: The Langdale Estate, Great Langdale, Ambleside, Cumbria, LA22 9JD
Activities: Hotels and similar accommodation
Parent: Langdale Owners PLC
Officers: Anne Louise Durnall, Secretary; Nicholas Owen Lancaster [1963] Managing Director; Dale Edward Watler [1948] Director/Accountant

Langdale Owners PLC
Incorporated: 2 January 1996 *Employees:* 180
Net Worth: £4,714,013 *Total Assets:* £13,780,889
Registered Office: Langdale Estate, Great Langdale, Ambleside, Cumbria, LA22 9JD
Activities: Hotels and similar accommodation
Officers: Anne Louise Durnall, Secretary; Don Camilleri [1949] Director [Maltese]; Michael Christopher Coletta [1968] Finance Director; Frederick Osborne Crouch [1938] Director/Lecturer; William Ian Robertson Hamilton [1955] Director/Manager; Nick Owen Lancaster [1963] Managing Director; Joseph Longmuir [1959] Managing Director; Dale Edward Watler [1948] Director/Chartered Accountant

Lanxess Holding UK Unlimited
Incorporated: 12 September 1930
Net Worth: £68,422,000 *Total Assets:* £125,924,000
Registered Office: UK Finance, 2nd Floor, Tenax Road, Trafford Park, Manchester, M17 1WT
Activities: Manufacture of other inorganic basic chemicals
Parent: Chemtura Europe GmbH
Officers: Christopher James Flett [1969] Director/Chief Financial Officer; Kiern Mark O'Connor [1951] Director/Country Speaker

Lanxess Solutions UK Ltd
Incorporated: 27 June 1991 *Employees:* 180
Net Worth: £177,668,992 *Total Assets:* £191,760,000
Registered Office: Accounts Department, Tenax Road, Trafford Park, Manchester, M17 1WT
Activities: Manufacture of other inorganic basic chemicals
Parent: Lanxess Holding UK Unlimited
Officers: Christopher James Flett [1969] Director/Chief Financial Officer; Kiern Mark O'Connor [1951] Director/Country Speaker; Anthony John Risino [1968] Director

Lanxess Urethanes UK Ltd
Incorporated: 24 May 1917 *Employees:* 77
Net Worth: £15,963,000 *Total Assets:* £18,405,000
Registered Office: Paragon Works, Baxenden, Accrington, Lancs, BB5 2SL
Activities: Manufacture of plastics in primary forms
Parent: Chemtura Corporation
Officers: Christopher James Flett [1969] Director/Chief Financial Officer; John Peter Lord [1958] Director/Operations Manager; Kiern Mark O'Connor [1951] Director/Country Speaker

Lappet Manufacturing Company Limited
Incorporated: 11 March 1996 *Employees:* 246
Net Worth Deficit: £4,292,000 *Total Assets:* £11,671,000
Registered Office: Vale Mill, Calder Vale, Garstang, Preston, Lancs, PR3 1SP
Activities: Weaving of textiles
Major Shareholder: Abdulaziz Al Ajlan
Officers: Robert Ian Williamson, Secretary; Abdulaziz Al Ajlan [1952] Director/Businessman [Saudi Arabian]; Robert John Quick [1955] Director

Laser Quantum Limited
Incorporated: 27 September 1994 *Employees:* 133
Net Worth: £34,215,000 *Total Assets:* £38,887,000
Registered Office: Emery Court, Vale Road, Stockport, Cheshire, SK4 3GL
Activities: Manufacture of optical precision instruments
Parent: Novanta Technologies UK Ltd
Officers: Doctor Steve Haydn Lane, Secretary; Robert John Buckley [1974] Director [American]; Doctor Alan Michael Cox [1972] Technical Director; Matthijs Glastra [1969] Director [Dutch]; Lawrence Anthony William Gloster [1969] Director/Chief Executive; Doctor Steve Haydn Lane [1971] Business Director; Philip Martin [1963] Director [American]; Brian Samuel Young [1969] Director [American]

Late Rooms Limited
Incorporated: 30 July 1999 *Employees:* 227
Net Worth: £5,293,939 *Total Assets:* £21,177,104
Registered Office: The Peninsula Building, Victoria Place, Manchester, M4 4FB
Activities: Other information technology service activities
Parent: Malvern Travel Limited
Officers: Abhishek Goenka [1979] Director [Indian]; Peter Ajit Ajay Kerkar [1963] Director [Indian]; Hugo Charles Kimber [1964] Director/Executive Chairman; John Daniel McLaughlin [1978] Director/Chief Financial Officer; Jonathan David Ross [1967] Director/Chief Technology Officer

Lateral Academy Trust
Incorporated: 8 August 2011 *Employees:* 162
Net Worth: £8,031,000 *Total Assets:* £10,296,000
Registered Office: Fred Longworth High School, Printshop Lane, Tyldesley, Manchester, M29 8JN
Activities: General secondary education
Officers: Alex Gallimore, Secretary; Anthony Fallows [1970] Director; Janet Helen Garretts [1961] Director; Carole Gradwell [1953] Director; Julian John Hartley [1957] Director/Minister of Religion - Vicar, Church of England; Tracy Lamb [1973] Director/Accountant; Elaine Marks-Parker [1953] Director/Retired; Jon McHugh [1986] Director/Teacher; Brian McPhail [1957] Director/School Master; Anita Mullineaux [1964] Director; Suzanne Partington [1969] Director; Samuel Charles Quigley [1975] Director; Ian Williams [1958] Director; Councillor Brian Malcolm Wilson [1949] Director; Andrew Wright [1970] Director/Police Officer

Latium Management Services Limited
Incorporated: 26 September 2001
Net Worth: £4,244,889 *Total Assets:* £13,795,620
Registered Office: Hamilton House, Church Street, Altrincham, Cheshire, WA14 4DR
Activities: Activities of head offices
Major Shareholder: Brian George Kennedy
Officers: Darren Karl Cornwall [1969] Director/Group CFO; Adrian Christopher Kirk [1961] Finance Director

Latium Plastics Enterprises Limited
Incorporated: 18 March 2010 *Employees:* 390
Net Worth: £9,778,000 *Total Assets:* £37,891,000
Registered Office: Hamilton House, Church Street, Altrincham, Cheshire, WA14 4DR
Activities: Activities of head offices
Major Shareholder: Brian George Kennedy
Officers: Adrian Christopher Kirk [1961] Finance Director

Latium Roofing Systems Limited
Incorporated: 18 May 2006
Net Worth: £22,450,000 *Total Assets:* £45,987,000
Registered Office: Enterprise Works, Salthill Road, Clitheroe, Lancs, BB7 1PE
Activities: Activities of head offices
Major Shareholder: Brian George Kennedy
Officers: Daniel Sean Kennedy [1993] Director; Jonathon Steven Kennedy [1990] Director; Jordan Robert Kennedy [1991] Director; Patrick Brian Kennedy [1984] Director; Adrian Christopher Kirk [1961] Finance Director; Julian Slade [1966] Managing Director

Launchrandom Limited
Incorporated: 30 January 1991 *Employees:* 407
Net Worth: £5,268,468 *Total Assets:* £11,631,290
Registered Office: Unit 6 Beecham Court, Pemberton, Wigan, Lancs, WN3 6PR
Activities: Development of building projects
Major Shareholder: Keith Lowe
Officers: Richard James Lowe, Secretary; Kimberley Jane Cramant [1984] Director; Keith Lowe [1951] Director

C.R. Laurence of Europe, Ltd
Incorporated: 18 April 1975 *Employees:* 59
Net Worth: £2,719,082 *Total Assets:* £11,874,381
Registered Office: C R Laurence of Europe Ltd, Charles Babbage Avenue, Kingsway Business Park, Rochdale, Lancs, OL16 4NW
Activities: Wholesale of machine tools
Parent: C.R. Laurence UK, Ltd
Officers: Gary Hickman, Secretary; Simon John Boocock [1973] Director; Stephen John Boocock [1950] Director; Nathan Bradley Creech [1975] Director [American]; Aristedes Feles [1967] Director [American]; Gaynor McIntosh [1971] Finance Director; Lloyd W Talbert [1960] Director [American]

Laurus Living Space LLP
Incorporated: 12 February 2016
Net Worth Deficit: £5,248 *Total Assets:* £8,722,834
Registered Office: Sale Point, 126-150 Washway Road, Sale, Manchester, M33 6AG

The Laurus Trust
Incorporated: 12 January 2012 *Employees:* 295
Net Worth: £17,959,000 *Total Assets:* £22,038,000
Registered Office: Cheadle Hulme High School, Woods Lane, Cheadle Hulme, Cheadle, Cheshire, SK8 7JY
Activities: General secondary education
Officers: Nicola Burgess, Secretary; Pauline Elizabeth Benton [1940] Director/Retired Teacher; David Brown [1967] Director/Teacher; Leonard James Elias [1950] Director/Retired; Catherine Dorothy Fisher [1949] Director/Retired; Dagmar Kent Kershaw [1968] Director/Chief Executive; Anthony Richard Morrell Little [1954] Director/Group Chief Education Officer; Linda Mary Magrath [1960] Director; Wendy Mason [1975] Director/Chief Financial Officer; Rev Charles John Nevin [1945] Director/Retired Methodist Minister; Jenny Louise Singleton [1969] Director/Principal and CEO; Lisa Woolley [1977] Director/Headteacher

G & A M Lawson Limited
Incorporated: 6 October 1992 *Employees:* 75
Net Worth: £12,220,247 *Total Assets:* £13,870,255
Registered Office: Whinbank Farm, Distington, Workington, Cumbria, CA14 4QH
Activities: Collection of non-hazardous waste
Officers: Barbara Thomson, Secretary; Alan Lawson [1964] Director/Plant Hire Contractor; Annie Mary Lawson [1938] Director/Plant Hire Contractor; David Lawson [1961] Director/Plant Hire Contractor; George Lawson [1936] Director/Plant Hire Contractor; John Langcake Lawson [1962] Director/Plant Hire Contractor; Barbara Thomson [1970] Director/Plant Hire Contractor; Mark Thomson [1965] Director

Lawsons Haulage Limited
Incorporated: 25 September 1992 *Employees:* 67
Net Worth: £5,292,680 *Total Assets:* £8,445,787
Registered Office: Gote Mill House, Gote Road, Cockermouth, Cumbria, CA13 0JQ
Activities: Freight transport by road
Parent: SameTimeTomorrow Limited
Officers: James Lawson, Secretary/Haulage Proprietor; James Lawson [1935] Director/Haulage Proprietor; Margaret Eileen Lawson [1941] Director/Haulage Proprietor; Pauline Lawson [1964] Director/Haulage Proprietor; Raymond John Lawson [1969] Director/Haulage Proprietor

Lawton Group Limited
Incorporated: 7 March 2000 *Employees:* 167
Net Worth: £4,896,000 *Total Assets:* £20,004,000
Registered Office: Norcliffe House, Station Road, Wilmslow, Cheshire, SK9 1BU
Activities: Other human health activities
Parent: Lawton Group Holdings Limited
Officers: Abigail Mattison, Secretary; Ryan Stuart MacAskill [1975] Director; Gregory Laurence Newman [1988] Director/Investment Professional; Jeremy Robert Arthur Richardson [1970] Director; Maureen Claire Royston [1960] Director; Phillip Gary Thomas [1978] Director

Lazner Holdings Limited
Incorporated: 23 March 2012 *Employees:* 78
Net Worth: £22,624,040 *Total Assets:* £40,494,880
Registered Office: 1 St Peters Square, Manchester, M2 3DE
Activities: Activities of distribution holding companies
Shareholders: Almar Holdings Limited; Alvest Limited
Officers: Alexander Samuel Lazarus [1977] Director; Marc Sivner [1969] Director

LB Europe Limited
Incorporated: 30 March 1993 *Employees:* 101
Net Worth: £2,568,896 *Total Assets:* £7,499,486
Registered Office: Southmoor Road, Wythenshawe, Manchester, M23 9XD
Activities: Manufacture of plastic packing goods
Officers: Michael Adams, Secretary; Michael Adams [1959] Director/Accountant; Leanne Michelle Parker [1972] Director/Certified Accountant [American]; Ken Swanson [1966] Director [American]

LCBSG Limited
Incorporated: 9 September 2014 *Employees:* 160
Net Worth: £9,952,160 *Total Assets:* £13,071,120
Registered Office: Tower 12, 18-22 Bridge Street, Spinningfields, Manchester, M3 3BZ
Activities: Activities of head offices
Officers: John Malcolm Titley, Secretary; Daniel John Booth [1978] Director; Jonathan Francis Mercer [1974] Director/Chartered Accountant; Andrew Poxon [1965] Director/Chartered Accountant; John Malcolm Titley [1959] Director/Chartered Accountant

LDF Finance No. 1 Limited
Incorporated: 10 September 2003 *Employees:* 8
Net Worth: £17,203,198 *Total Assets:* £35,006,092
Registered Office: Dee House, St David's Park, Ewloe, Flintshire, CH5 3XF
Activities: Financial leasing
Parent: LDF Group Finance Limited
Officers: Philip Michael Brereton, Secretary; Peter Stuart Alderson [1959] Director; Katherine Jane Applewhite [1980] Director; Philip Michael Brereton [1976] Director/Accountant; Raymond Anthony Corcoran [1971] Director; Thomas Andrew Davies [1971] Director; Christopher Heeley [1978] Director; Allan Warren Ross [1961] Director

LDF Group Finance Limited
Incorporated: 17 October 2013
Net Worth Deficit: £17,088,280 *Total Assets:* £65,734,732
Registered Office: Dee House, St David's Park, Ewloe, Flintshire, CH5 3XF
Activities: Activities of financial services holding companies
Parent: LDF Group Hold Co Limited
Officers: Peter Stuart Alderson [1959] Director; Katherine Jane Applewhite [1980] Director; Philip Michael Brereton [1976] Director; Raymond Anthony Corcoran [1971] Director; Thomas Andrew Davies [1971] Director; Christopher Heeley [1978] Director; Allan Warren Ross [1961] Director

LDF Group Holdco Limited
Incorporated: 17 October 2013 *Employees:* 204
Net Worth Deficit: £16,407,646 *Total Assets:* £216,731,408
Registered Office: Dee House, St David's Park, Ewloe, Flintshire, CH5 3XF
Activities: Activities of financial services holding companies
Parent: Cabot Square Capital Nominee Limited
Officers: Peter Stuart Alderson [1959] Director; Katherine Jane Applewhite [1980] Director; Philip Michael Brereton [1976] Director; Raymond Anthony Corcoran [1971] Director; Thomas Andrew Davies [1971] Director; Andre Hakkak [1973] Director/Managing Partner [American]; Christopher Heeley [1978] Director; Darius Joseph Mozaffarian [1977] Director [American]; Thomas Otte [1955] Managing Director [American]; Allan Warren Ross [1961] Director

LDF Operations Limited
Incorporated: 18 June 1986 *Employees:* 146
Net Worth: £7,547,506 *Total Assets:* £14,558,044
Registered Office: Dee House, St David's Park, Ewloe, Flintshire, CH5 3XF
Activities: Financial intermediation not elsewhere classified
Parent: LDF Group Finance Limited
Officers: Peter Stuart Alderson [1959] Director/Banker; Katherine Jane Applewhite [1980] Director; Philip Michael Brereton [1976] Director/Accountant; Raymond Anthony Corcoran [1971] Director; Thomas Andrew Davies [1971] Director; Christopher Heeley [1978] Director; Allan Warren Ross [1961] Director

Le-Fylde Estates Ltd
Incorporated: 13 August 2014 *Employees:* 24
Net Worth: £1,030,794 *Total Assets:* £8,471,635
Registered Office: P O Box 4, Hillhouse International Business Park, Thornton-Cleveleys, Lancs, FY5 4QD
Activities: Other service activities n.e.c.
Major Shareholder: Robert McFarlane
Officers: Michelle McFarlane [1968] Director; Robert McFarlane [1946] Director

H.J. Lea Oakes Limited
Incorporated: 13 January 1927 *Employees:* 90
Net Worth: £1,780,022 *Total Assets:* £12,583,010
Registered Office: Aston Mill, Aston, Nantwich, Cheshire, CW5 8DH
Activities: Wholesale of grain, unmanufactured tobacco, seeds and animal feeds
Parent: Oakes Millers Limited
Officers: Andrew Peter McLaren Rowe, Secretary; David Horace Fox [1946] Director/Manager; Keith Jamieson [1959] Director; Michael John Jepson [1950] Director/Mill Manager; Edward Philip LEA [1983] Director; James John LEA [1980] Director/Accountant; John Edward LEA [1946] Director; Arthur Preston [1940] Director; David Warr [1952] Company Secretary/Director

Leach Holdings Limited
Incorporated: 18 March 1997 *Employees:* 136
Net Worth: £8,043,265 *Total Assets:* £16,747,341
Registered Office: Brockholes Way, Garstang Road, Claughton on Brock, Preston, Lancs, PR3 0PZ
Activities: Activities of head offices
Major Shareholder: Eric Joseph Leach
Officers: Lynda Leach, Secretary; Eric Joseph Leach [1968] Director/Structural Engineer

LeadX Group Limited
Incorporated: 4 March 2016 *Employees:* 575
Net Worth: £1,137,749 *Total Assets:* £11,976,803
Registered Office: Lynnfield House, Church Street, Altrincham, Cheshire, WA14 4DZ
Activities: Activities of head offices
Shareholder: Timothy Andrew Berry
Officers: Timothy Andrew Berry [1967] Director; Helen Mary Dwyer [1970] Director; Mark Philip Simpkins [1965] Finance Director

The Learning Trust
Incorporated: 9 February 2011 *Employees:* 153
Net Worth: £25,703,000 *Total Assets:* £28,273,000
Registered Office: Christleton High School, Village Road, Christleton, Chester, CH3 7AD
Activities: Primary education
Officers: Jean Charlton [1962] Director; Nicholas John Edward Crowther [1960] Director; Michael Dempsey [1975] Director/Banker [Irish]; Paul Albury Heath [1958] Director/Consultant; Euan Imrie [1958] Director/Chief Operating Officer; Katrina Jane Worrall [1976] Marketing Director [Australian]

Leasowe Community Homes
Incorporated: 11 August 1998 *Employees:* 8
Net Worth: £27,342,000 *Total Assets:* £31,550,000
Registered Office: 8 Columbus Quay, Riverside Drive, Liverpool, L3 4DB
Activities: Renting and operating of Housing Association real estate
Officers: John Francis Grader, Secretary; Louise Carter [1984] Director/Carer; Anthony Michael Dunne [1956] Director/Self Employed; Marcus David Evans [1972] Director; Wendy Gooley [1971] Director/Carer; Martin John Latham [1954] Director/Retired; Anita Leech [1959] Director/Councillor; David Hugh McGaw [1949] Director

Leck Group Ltd
Incorporated: 22 May 1925 *Employees:* 93
Net Worth: £7,326,673 *Total Assets:* £11,798,385
Registered Office: 80 Deansgate Lane, Timperley, Cheshire, WA14 1SP
Activities: Activities of construction holding companies
Major Shareholder: Victor Barker
Officers: Dr David Russell Barker, Secretary; Catherine Mary Barker [1950] Director; Dr David Russell Barker [1976] Financial Director; Victor Barker [1939] Director

Ledvance Ltd
Incorporated: 19 November 1985 *Employees:* 44
Net Worth: £5,390,000 *Total Assets:* £10,292,000
Registered Office: Aquila House, Delta Crescent, Westbrook, Warrington, Cheshire, WA5 7NR
Activities: Manufacture of electric lighting equipment
Officers: Derek McMillan [1960] Director [Belgian]; Christoph Thalhammer [1977] Director [German]

Lee-Mar Estates Limited
Incorporated: 7 November 1977
Net Worth: £7,693,752 *Total Assets:* £8,570,891
Registered Office: Pear Industrial Estate, Stockport Road, Lower Bredbury, Stockport, Cheshire, SK6 2BP
Activities: Other letting and operating of own or leased real estate
Major Shareholder: David Lee
Officers: Peta Emma Blenkarn Williams, Secretary; David Lee [1945] Director; Peta Emma Blenkarn Williams [1973] Director

Leeds Group PLC
Incorporated: 21 November 1900 *Employees:* 186
Net Worth: £18,302,000 *Total Assets:* £29,095,000
Registered Office: Old Mills, Whitehall Grove, Drighlington, Bradford, W Yorks, BD11 1BY
Activities: Activities of other holding companies n.e.c.
Officers: Dawn Henderson, Secretary; Johan Claesson [1951] Managing Director [Swedish]; Jorg Helmut Hemmers [1967] Director [German]; Jan Gustaf Lennart Holmstrom [1953] Director [Swedish]

Leeds Independent Living Accommodation Company Holdings Limited
Incorporated: 11 December 2007 *Employees:* 6
Net Worth Deficit: £13,180,699 *Total Assets:* £61,869,604
Registered Office: Unit 18 Riversway Business Village, Navigation Way, Ashton on Ribble, Preston, Lancs, PR2 2YP
Activities: Activities of head offices
Shareholders: Jack Lunn (Properties) Limited; Civic PFI Investments Limited; Progress Care Housing Association
Officers: Robert John Austin [1964] Director; Mary Philomena Cunningham [1959] Director; Andrew Lunn [1967] Director; Peter McAteer [1954] Director/Company Secretary; Alexander Toby Shedden Parry [1976] Director; Andrew George Speer [1964] Finance Director

Leeds Independent Living Accommodation Company Limited
Incorporated: 11 December 2007 *Employees:* 6
Net Worth Deficit: £13,180,699 *Total Assets:* £61,869,604
Registered Office: Unit 18 Riversway Business Village, Navigation Way, Ashton on Ribble, Preston, Lancs, PR2 2YP
Activities: Other accommodation
Parent: Leeds Independent Living Accommodation Company Holdings Limited
Officers: Robert John Austin [1964] Director; Mary Philomena Cunningham [1959] Director; Andrew Lunn [1967] Director; Peter McAteer [1954] Director/Company Secretary; Alexander Toby Shedden Parry [1976] Director; Andrew George Speer [1964] Finance Director

Leehand Leisure Limited
Incorporated: 9 August 2002
Registered Office: Stanley House, off Preston New Road, Mellor, Lancs, BB2 7NP
Activities: Hotels and similar accommodation
Parent: Leehand Limited
Officers: Francis Michael Cochrane, Secretary; Francis Michael Cochrane [1950] Director; Andrew Simon Glassbrook [1960] Director

Leehand Limited
Incorporated: 25 September 2002 *Employees:* 132
Net Worth: £9,146,382 *Total Assets:* £10,174,102
Registered Office: Stanley House, off Preston New Road, Mellor, Lancs, BB2 7NP
Activities: Activities of head offices
Major Shareholder: Honora Elizabeth Walker
Officers: Francis Michael Cochrane, Secretary; Francis Michael Cochrane [1950] Director; Andrew Simon Glassbrook [1960] Director; Honora Elizabeth Walker [1928] Director

Leep Holdings (Utilities) Limited
Incorporated: 21 October 2008 *Employees:* 3
Net Worth: £2,201,000 *Total Assets:* £19,041,000
Registered Office: The Greenhouse, MediaCityUK, Salford, M50 2EQ
Activities: Activities of other holding companies n.e.c.
Parent: Leep Utilities Limited
Officers: David Jonathan Glover [1956] Director; Victoria Louise Manfredi [1971] Director; Timothy Michael Power [1986] Director [Australian]

Leep Utilities Electricity Limited
Incorporated: 29 August 2008
Net Worth: £1,801,122 *Total Assets:* £7,311,016
Registered Office: The Greenhouse, MediaCityUK, Salford, M50 2EQ
Activities: Activities of other holding companies n.e.c.
Parent: Leep Utilities Holdings Limited
Officers: David Jonathan Glover [1956] Director; Victoria Louise Manfredi [1971] Director; Timothy Michael Power [1986] Director [Australian]

J.W.Lees & Co.(Brewers) Limited
Incorporated: 11 November 1955 *Employees:* 1,227
Net Worth: £82,299,600 *Total Assets:* £115,451,720
Registered Office: Greengate Brewery, Middleton Junction, Manchester, M24 2AX
Activities: Manufacture of beer
Officers: Simon Cross, Secretary; Simon Cross [1972] Director; Anna Elizabeth Clare Griffin [1970] Director; Michael Christopher Lees Jones [1971] Director of Beer Quality; Simon Christopher Lees Jones [1966] Director; William George Richard Lees Jones [1964] Director/Manager; William Richard Lees Jones [1933] Director; Christina Francis Lees-Jones [1969] Director/Catering Manager; Christopher Peter Lees-Jones [1936] Director

Legacy Capital Limited
Incorporated: 26 November 2015
Net Worth Deficit: £81,513 *Total Assets:* £7,924,673
Registered Office: c/o Edwards Veeder (UK) Limited, Ground Floor, 4 Broadgate, Broadway Business Park, Chadderton, Oldham, Lancs, OL9 9XA
Activities: Hotels and similar accommodation
Parent: Excel Key International Limited
Officers: Rachan Singhpathom [1977] Director [Thai]; Suramit Singhpathom [1972] Director [Thai]

Legal Marketing Services Limited
Incorporated: 15 December 1994 *Employees:* 113
Net Worth: £4,017,605 *Total Assets:* £10,434,346
Registered Office: Bickerton House, Lloyd Drive, Ellesmere Port, Cheshire, CH65 9HQ
Activities: Other professional, scientific and technical activities n.e.c.
Parent: Cybele Solutions Limited
Officers: Peter David Clarkson, Secretary; Nicholas Chadbourne [1977] Director; Peter David Clarkson [1966] Director/Chartered Accountant

Lehvoss UK Limited
Incorporated: 27 February 1992 *Employees:* 48
Net Worth: £8,003,543 *Total Assets:* £22,207,444
Registered Office: Westminster House, 10 Westminster Road, Macclesfield, Cheshire, SK10 1BX
Activities: Wholesale of chemical products
Officers: Ivan Pennington, Secretary; Ivan Pennington [1972] Director

Leigh Fundco Limited
Incorporated: 27 October 2008 *Employees:* 4
Net Worth Deficit: £4,114,806 *Total Assets:* £13,571,402
Registered Office: Sceptre House, Sceptre Way, Bamber Bridge, Preston, Lancs, PR5 6AW
Activities: Development of building projects
Parent: Leigh Holdco Limited
Officers: Deborah Jane Rawlinson, Secretary; Patricia Ann Anderson [1957] Director; Jeremy Peter Hartley [1965] Director/Chartered Accountant; Neil Geoffrey Ward [1959] Director; Christine Desiree Winstanley [1966] Director

Leisure Parks Limited
Incorporated: 5 February 2003 *Employees:* 12
Net Worth: £8,506,740 *Total Assets:* £14,615,296
Registered Office: Fernbank, Crooklands, Milnthorpe, Cumbria, LA7 7PB
Activities: Recreational vehicle parks, trailer parks and camping grounds
Shareholders: Craig Ben Ellis; Tracy Louise Stevenson
Officers: Tracy Louise Stevenson, Secretary/Caravan Site Operator; Craig Ben Ellis [1961] Director/Civil Engineering Consultant; Tracy Louise Stevenson [1964] Director/Caravan Site Operator

Leisureplan Investments Limited
Incorporated: 6 December 2004
Net Worth: £7,402,735 *Total Assets:* £8,188,682
Registered Office: Parkwood House, Cuerden Park, Berkeley Drive, Bamber Bridge, Preston, Lancs, PR5 6BY
Activities: Activities of head offices
Parent: Equitix Leisure Ltd
Officers: David John Harding [1980] Director/Chartered Accountant; Richard Daniel Knight [1974] Operations Director; Philip Arthur Would [1971] Director/Asset Manager

Leisureplan Projects Finance Limited
Incorporated: 15 May 2007
Net Worth: £2 *Total Assets:* £9,658,270
Registered Office: Parkwood House, Cuerden Park, Berkeley Drive, Bamber Bridge, Preston, Lancs, PR5 6BY
Activities: Construction of commercial buildings
Parent: Equitix Leisure Limited
Officers: David John Harding [1980] Director/Chartered Accountant; Richard Daniel Knight [1974] Operations Director; Philip Arthur Would [1971] Director/Asset Manager

Leisureplan Projects Limited
Incorporated: 11 May 2007
Net Worth Deficit: £1,508,267 *Total Assets:* £8,150,004
Registered Office: Parkwood House, Cuerden Park, Berkeley Drive, Bamber Bridge, Preston, Lancs, PR5 6BY
Activities: Other building completion and finishing
Parent: Leisureplan Investments Limited
Officers: David John Harding [1980] Director/Chartered Accountant; Richard Daniel Knight [1974] Operations Director; Philip Arthur Would [1971] Director/Asset Manager

Leisureplex Hotels Limited
Incorporated: 21 March 1984 *Employees:* 561
Net Worth: £38,390,144 *Total Assets:* £45,726,120
Registered Office: Alfa Building, Euxton Lane, Euxton, Chorley, Lancs, PR7 6AF
Activities: Hotels and similar accommodation
Parent: Alfa Leisureplex Group Limited
Officers: Emma Russell, Secretary; Paul Anthony Bull [1962] Operations Director; Lucia Danielle Maguire [1985] Tours Director; Emma Russell [1979] Finance Director; Karen Elizabeth Sawbridge [1965] Director/Chartered Accountant

Lenagan Investments Limited
Incorporated: 4 July 2007 *Employees:* 98
Net Worth Deficit: £646,241 *Total Assets:* £8,379,953
Registered Office: Central Park, Montrose Avenue, Wigan, Lancs, WN5 9XL
Activities: Activities of head offices
Shareholders: Ann Lenagan; Simon Francis Lenagan
Officers: David John Moore, Secretary; Adrian Peter Lenagan [1975] Director; Ann Lenagan [1954] Director; Ian Francis Lenagan [1946] Director; Simon Francis Lenagan [1970] Director

Lendlock Group Limited
Incorporated: 8 May 2003 *Employees:* 339
Net Worth: £24,370,412 *Total Assets:* £40,628,148
Registered Office: 86 Guilden Sutton Lane, Guilden Sutton, Chester, CH3 7EX
Activities: Activities of other holding companies n.e.c.
Shareholders: Michael John Duffell; Valerie Ann Duffell
Officers: Michael John Duffell, Secretary; Andrew Michael Duffell [1969] Director; Matthew Samuel Michael Duffell [1976] Director; Michael John Duffell [1934] Director/Executive; Valerie Ann Duffell [1940] Director/Executive; Mark James Gwinnett [1968] Director; Victoria Ann Moody [1971] Director; Denys Taylor [1970] Director

Lendlock International Ltd
Incorporated: 28 February 1994 *Employees:* 22
Net Worth: £10,051,290 *Total Assets:* £22,339,692
Registered Office: 86 Guilden Sutton Lane, Guilden Sutton, Chester, CH3 7EX
Activities: Manufacture of other plastic products
Officers: Michael John Duffell, Secretary/Executive; Andrew Michael Duffell [1969] Director; Matthew Samuel Michael Duffell [1976] Director; Michael John Duffell [1934] Director/Executive; Valerie Ann Duffell [1940] Director/Executive; Mark James Gwinnett [1968] Director; Victoria Ann Moody [1971] Director; Denys Taylor [1970] Director

Leoron Investments Limited
Incorporated: 10 February 1961
Net Worth: £6,538,311 *Total Assets:* £8,699,249
Registered Office: 2nd Floor, 1 City Road East, Manchester, M15 4PN
Activities: Renting and operating of Housing Association real estate
Major Shareholder: Peter Ferbrache
Officers: Peter Butcher, Secretary; Peter Butcher [1951] Director/Company Secretary; Valerie Ann Butcher [1940] Director

Less Common Metals Limited
Incorporated: 24 February 1992 *Employees:* 27
Net Worth Deficit: £5,106,205 *Total Assets:* £9,973,976
Registered Office: Unit 2 Hooton Park, North Road, Ellesmere Port, Cheshire, CH65 1BL
Activities: Other non-ferrous metal production
Shareholder: Grant Hadyn Smith
Officers: Bridget Anne Bonehill, Secretary; Christopher William Hall [1954] Commercial Director; Dr Ian Higgins [1961] Managing Director; Muthurajan Jegadeesan [1985] Director [Indian]; Grant Haydn Smith [1959] Director [Australian]; Subramanian Vaikundarajan [1982] Director [Indian]

Lever Academy Trust
Incorporated: 8 July 2015 *Employees:* 106
Net Worth: £6,422,856 *Total Assets:* £8,159,082
Registered Office: Little Lever School, Church Street, Little Lever, Bolton, Lancs, BL3 1BT
Activities: General secondary education
Officers: Mandy Kelly, Secretary; John Adamopoulos [1970] Director/School Business Manager [Greek]; Dr Nicholas Browne [1971] Director/Doctor; Karina Carter [1963] Director/Commissioning Officer; Anthony Connell [1941] Director/Retired; Carleen Ann Fernside [1981] Director/Teacher; Rees Gibbon [1939] Director/Retired; Dominic McKeon [1980] Director/Principal; Dominic James McKeon [1980] Director/Headmaster; Jasmine Renold [1971] Director of Studies; Judith Twentyman [1948] Director/Retired

Leverhulme Academy Church of England and Community Trust
Incorporated: 7 December 2016 *Employees:* 383
Net Worth: £43,761,960 *Total Assets:* £48,529,760
Registered Office: Rivington and Blackrod High School, Rivington Lane, Horwich, Bolton, Lancs, BL6 7RU
Activities: General secondary education
Officers: Charles Robert Atkinson [1951] Director/School Improvement Professional; Sarah Horan [1965] Director/Head of Trustee Service; Christopher Knowles [1963] Director/Chartered Engineer; Judith Ann Marsden [1956] Director/Retired; Ethel Anne Quigley [1951] Director; Paul Roach [1972] Director/Headteacher; David Frederick Wakefield [1954] Director/Chairman NHS Trust [Irish]

The David Lewis Centre
Incorporated: 6 September 1990 *Employees:* 762
Net Worth: £11,852,000 *Total Assets:* £19,839,000
Registered Office: Mill Lane, Warford, Alderley Edge, Cheshire, SK9 7UD
Activities: Other education n.e.c.
Officers: Neil Alan Edwards, Secretary; Roisin Beressi [1965] Director/Solicitor; Darren Karl Cornwall [1969] Director/Group CFO; George Devlin [1952] Director/Retired; Stephen Devlin [1957] Director/Solicitor; Linda Feerick [1963] Director/Professional Coach; Alistair Vincent Hollows [1959] Director; Alastair Milne Imrie [1947] Director/Retired; Geoff Loughlin [1953] Director/Retired; Marie Elizabeth McLaughlin [1959] Director/Civil Servant; Marie Shahin [1956] Director/Registered Social Worker

Lewis's Home Retail Limited
Incorporated: 31 March 2009 *Employees:* 1,229
Net Worth: £6,402,396 *Total Assets:* £32,014,654
Registered Office: Hughes House, London Road, Liverpool, L3 8JA
Activities: Other retail sale in non-specialised stores
Shareholders: Right Inc Limited; Anil Juneja
Officers: Amit Juneja [1982] Director; Anil Juneja [1979] Director; Dharam Vir Juneja [1957] Director/Retail; Kulvinder Juneja [1979] Director/Retail; Kuldeep Singh [1968] Director [Chinese]

Lex Vehicle Finance 2 Limited
Incorporated: 6 May 2003
Net Worth: £9,027,000 *Total Assets:* £9,028,000
Registered Office: Charterhall House, Charterhall Drive, Chester, CH88 3AN
Activities: Renting and leasing of cars and light motor vehicles
Parent: ACL Autolease Holdings Limited
Officers: David Dermot Hennessey, Secretary; Andrew John Hartley [1969] Director; Carol Ann Parkes [1966] Finance Director

Lex Vehicle Leasing (Holdings) Limited
Incorporated: 27 July 1994
Net Worth: £350,784,992 *Total Assets:* £468,732,992
Registered Office: Charterhall House, Charterhall Drive, Chester, CH88 3AN
Activities: Activities of head offices
Parent: Halifax Vehicle Leasing (1998) Limited
Officers: David Dermot Hennessey, Secretary; Andrew John Hartley [1969] Director; Carol Ann Parkes [1966] Finance Director; Timothy Revell Porter [1965] Director/Banker

Lex Vehicle Leasing Limited
Incorporated: 26 July 1994
Net Worth: £93,959,000 *Total Assets:* £93,961,000
Registered Office: Charterhall House, Charterhall Drive, Chester, CH88 3AN
Activities: Other business support service activities n.e.c.
Parent: Lex Vehicle Leasing (Holdings) Limited
Officers: David Dermot Hennessey, Secretary; Andrew John Hartley [1969] Director; Carol Ann Parkes [1966] Finance Director; Timothy Revell Porter [1965] Director/Banker

Lexington Catering Limited
Incorporated: 3 September 1997 *Employees:* 851
Net Worth: £7,862,705 *Total Assets:* £18,409,752
Registered Office: The Courtyard, Catherine Street, Macclesfield, Cheshire, SK11 6ET
Activities: Other business support service activities n.e.c.
Parent: Elior UK Holdings Limited
Officers: Joanna Luke, Secretary; Julia Caroline Edmonds [1968] Managing Director; Pascal Lefebvre [1960] Director [French]; Catherine Margaret Roe [1960] Managing Director; Eleni Savva [1972] Finance Director; Michael Andrew Sunley [1959] Director/Contract Catering

Leyland Holding Company Limited
Incorporated: 8 February 2005 *Employees:* 119
Net Worth: £5,390,000 *Total Assets:* £17,544,000
Registered Office: 3 Centurion Court, Centurion Way, Leyland, Lancs, PR25 3UQ
Activities: Other letting and operating of own or leased real estate
Parent: Belcare Limited
Officers: Clare Kirkman, Secretary; Alnoor Jamal [1951] Director [Canadian]; Paul William Kirkman [1971] Director

LF Europe Limited
Incorporated: 4 September 1974 *Employees:* 32
Net Worth: £61,154,000 *Total Assets:* £475,033,984
Registered Office: Centenary House, Centenary Way, Salford, M50 1RF
Activities: Activities of head offices
Officers: Robert Arthur Bacon, Secretary; Ulf Stefan Brettschneider [1964] Director/Senior Vice President [German]; Nicholas Andrew Cottrell [1960] Director; Robert Stephen Lister [1956] Director

LF Logistics (UK) Limited
Incorporated: 17 July 1987 *Employees:* 35
Net Worth: £1,952,000 *Total Assets:* £7,796,000
Registered Office: Centenary House, Centenary Way, Salford, M50 1RF
Activities: Freight transport by road
Parent: LF Logistics Holdings (UK) Limited
Officers: James Alexander Circus [1975] Director; Nicholas Andrew Cottrell [1960] Director; Srinivasan Parthasarathy [1957] Director [Singaporean]

LF Logistics Holdings (UK) Limited
Incorporated: 8 August 2007
Net Worth Deficit: £28,293,000 *Total Assets:* £15,458,000
Registered Office: Centenary House, Centenary Way, Salford, M50 1RF
Activities: Activities of head offices
Officers: Nicholas Andrew Cottrell [1960] Director; Srinivasan Parthasarathy [1957] Director [Singaporean]

Lhoist UK Limited
Incorporated: 21 August 2000 *Employees:* 73
Net Worth: £4,285,000 *Total Assets:* £39,783,000
Registered Office: Lhoist UK Limited, Buxton Road, Hindlow, Buxton, Derbys, SK17 0EL
Activities: Manufacture of lime and plaster
Officers: Dirk Donck, Secretary; Axel Vincent Ampolini [1970] Vice President and Managing Director [American]; Cedric Joannes Rosa Georges de Vicq de Cumptich [1980] Director [Belgian]; Dirk Donck [1956] Director/Legal Advisor [Belgian]

LHS (UK) Limited
Incorporated: 12 February 1990
Net Worth: £12,881,659 *Total Assets:* £12,881,659
Registered Office: Winnington Avenue, Northwich, Cheshire, CW8 4DX
Activities: Dormant company
Parent: Nalco Asia Holding Company Pte. Ltd
Officers: Wendy Annette Joyce, Secretary; Carl Richmond Lee [1963] Finance Director; David Walker [1969] Director/Chartered Accountant

Liberty Gas Group Limited
Incorporated: 27 June 2001 *Employees:* 723
Net Worth: £3,078,000 *Total Assets:* £23,021,000
Registered Office: Garden Works, Charleywood Road, Knowsley Industrial Park, Knowsley, Merseyside, L33 7SG
Activities: Plumbing, heat and air-conditioning installation
Officers: David McGovern, Secretary; Derek Corbishley [1973] Managing Director; Timothy Charles Doyle [1965] Director; Martin John Joyce [1962] Director/Consultant; Colette McKune [1963] Director; Michael George Parkin [1971] Director

Liberty Group Investments Limited
Incorporated: 16 December 1969 *Employees:* 728
Net Worth: £1,720,000 *Total Assets:* £19,211,000
Registered Office: Garden Works, Charleywood Road, Knowsley Industrial Park, Knowsley, Merseyside, L33 7SG
Activities: Activities of head offices
Officers: David McGovern, Secretary; Derek Corbishley [1973] Managing Director; Timothy Charles Doyle [1965] Director; Martin John Joyce [1962] Director/Consultant; Colette McKune [1963] Director; Michael George Parkin [1971] Director

Libra Textiles Limited
Incorporated: 28 January 1971 *Employees:* 928
Net Worth: £28,143,764 *Total Assets:* £53,879,416
Registered Office: Head Office, Boundary Mill Stores, Vivary Way, Colne, Lancs, BB8 9NW
Activities: Retail sale of textiles in specialised stores
Major Shareholder: Richard Michael Rennie Bannister
Officers: Janine Elizabeth Bannister, Secretary; Janine Elizabeth Bannister [1960] Director; Richard Michael Rennie Bannister [1961] Managing Director; Annmarie McClintock [1963] Managing Director; George Richardson Middlemiss [1955] Finance Director

Libya Oil Eritrea Limited
Incorporated: 25 March 1993
Net Worth: £6,935,298 *Total Assets:* £104,689,688
Registered Office: Eversheds House, 70 Bridgewater Street, Manchester, M1 5ES
Activities: Other business support service activities n.e.c.
Parent: Libyan Investment Authority
Officers: Elmarimi Ali Kashim [1953] Director/Engineer [Libyan]; Omar Elfarok Samin [1956] Director/Engineer [Libyan]

Licensed Wholesale Company Limited
Incorporated: 5 September 1986 *Employees:* 724
Net Worth: £40,897,016 *Total Assets:* £73,839,992
Registered Office: Unit 3 Stainburn Road, Openshaw, Manchester, M11 2DN
Activities: Activities of head offices
Major Shareholder: Robin MacEwan Gray
Officers: Peter Douglas Sumner, Secretary/Financial Controller; Robin MacEwan Gray [1951] Director; Ebrahim Kassam Mukadam [1957] Director

Life Sciences International Limited
Incorporated: 27 February 1979
Net Worth: £140,614,000 *Total Assets:* £683,062,016
Registered Office: 3rd Floor, 1 Ashley Road, Altrincham, Cheshire, WA14 2DT
Activities: Activities of head offices
Parent: Thermo Fisher Scientific Inc.
Officers: Rhona Gregg, Secretary; Lucie Mary Katja Grant [1976] Director/Solicitor; Nicholas Ince [1982] Director/Accountant; David John Norman [1960] Director/Chartered Accountant

Life Technologies Bpd UK Limited
Incorporated: 25 February 1999 *Employees:* 144
Net Worth: £96,059,000 *Total Assets:* £99,384,000
Registered Office: 3rd Floor, 1 Ashley Road, Altrincham, Cheshire, WA14 2DT
Activities: Manufacture of basic pharmaceutical products
Parent: Thermo Fisher Scientific Inc.
Officers: Rhona Gregg, Secretary; Lucie Mary Katja Grant [1976] Director/Solicitor; Nicholas Ince [1982] Director/Accountant; David John Norman [1960] Director/Chartered Accountant

Lifestyle Services Group Limited
Incorporated: 28 April 2004 *Employees:* 1,000
Net Worth: £54,699,000 *Total Assets:* £92,444,000
Registered Office: Emerald Buildings, Westmere Drive, Crewe, Cheshire, CW1 6UN
Activities: Non-life insurance
Parent: Assurant Group Limited
Officers: Natalie Ann Paddock, Secretary; George Derek Wilson Bartlett [1948] Chairman and Non-Executive Director; Michael John Carter [1981] Director; Colin Martin Kersley [1956] Director; Keith Roland Meier [1970] Director/President, International Global Strategy & Merger [American]; Andrew James Morris [1971] Director/Chief Marketing Officer; Doris Rosario Vigo [1959] Director/Lawyer [American]

Lifting Gear UK Group Limited
Incorporated: 7 March 2016 *Employees:* 86
Net Worth: £3,785,644 *Total Assets:* £8,435,378
Registered Office: Unit 1d Maple Court, White Moss Business Park, Skelmersdale, Lancs, WN8 9TW
Activities: Activities of construction holding companies
Shareholders: Marina Alexandra Turner; Christopher Frederick Turner
Officers: Andrew Grant Stafford [1960] Director; Christopher Frederick Turner [1967] Director; Marina Alexandra Turner [1967] Director

Lightcatch Limited
Incorporated: 30 January 1991 *Employees:* 6,124
Net Worth: £95,305,000 *Total Assets:* £312,062,016
Registered Office: The Spectrum, 56-58 Benson Road, Birchwood, Warrington, Cheshire, WA3 7PQ
Activities: Activities of head offices
Parent: Betfred Group Limited
Officers: Michael Rodney Hamilton, Secretary; Nicola Joan Barr [1977] Finance Director; Fred Done [1943] Director; Joseph Matthias Scanlon [1951] Managing Director; Mark Warren Stebbings [1970] Managing Director

Lightfooting Limited
Incorporated: 5 December 2009 *Employees:* 4
Net Worth: £8,530,690 *Total Assets:* £8,600,867
Registered Office: Tarn House, Hallbankgate, Brampton, Cumbria, CA8 2PW
Activities: Renting and operating of Housing Association real estate
Shareholders: Eoin Hamish Nicholson; Christine Nicholson
Officers: Christine Nicholson, Secretary; Christine Nicholson [1961] Director [German]; Eoin Hamish Nicholson [1964] Director

Lightning Management Limited
Incorporated: 24 October 1990 *Employees:* 5
Net Worth: £11,252,931 *Total Assets:* £13,695,841
Registered Office: Bushbury House, 435 Wilmslow Road, Withington, Manchester, M20 4AF
Activities: Other letting and operating of own or leased real estate
Shareholders: Nighat Banu Awan; Rafique Ahmed Awan
Officers: Nighat Banu Awan, Secretary; Nighat Banu Awan [1955] Director/Secretary; Rafique Ahmed Awan [1941] Director/Restaurateur

Ligna Biomass Holdings Limited
Incorporated: 3 March 2014
Net Worth: £33,300,000 *Total Assets:* £111,100,000
Registered Office: Maritime Centre, Port of Liverpool, L21 1LA
Activities: Activities of other holding companies n.e.c.
Parent: Peel Ports Investments Limited
Officers: Farook Akhtar Khan, Secretary; Caroline Ruth Marrison Gill, Secretary; Thomas Eardley Allison [1948] Director; Ian Graeme Lloyd Charnock [1962] Director; Hamish MacPhail Massie MacKenzie [1969] Director; Steven Keith Underwood [1974] Director; Sundeep Vyas [1973] Director; John Whittaker [1942] Director; Mark Whitworth [1966] Director

Ligna Biomass Limited
Incorporated: 3 March 2014
Net Worth: £33,300,000 *Total Assets:* £111,100,000
Registered Office: Maritime Centre, Port of Liverpool, L21 1LA
Activities: Cargo handling for water transport activities
Parent: Ligna Biomass Holdings Limited
Officers: Farook Akhtar Khan, Secretary; Caroline Ruth Marrison Gill, Secretary; Thomas Eardley Allison [1948] Director; Ian Graeme Lloyd Charnock [1962] Director; Hamish MacPhail Massie MacKenzie [1969] Director; Steven Keith Underwood [1974] Director; Sundeep Vyas [1973] Director; John Whittaker [1942] Director; Mark Whitworth [1966] Director

Lilytame Limited
Incorporated: 27 April 2015 *Employees:* 4
Net Worth Deficit: £1,251,577 *Total Assets:* £9,168,192
Registered Office: Building 2, 3rd Floor, Universal Square, Devonshire Street North, Manchester, M12 6JH
Activities: Other letting and operating of own or leased real estate
Officers: Carol Allen [1963] Director/Accountant; Vikrant Bhargava [1972] Director; Benjamin Graham Eades [1981] Director/Solicitor; Dr Surbhi Virmani [1974] Director/Doctor

Limitless Digital Group Ltd
Incorporated: 23 March 2000 *Employees:* 196
Net Worth Deficit: £1,270,581 *Total Assets:* £12,739,754
Registered Office: Dawson Court, Billington Road Industrial Estate, Burnley, Lancs, BB11 5UB
Activities: Retail sale via mail order houses or via Internet
Major Shareholder: Stephen Heys
Officers: Nicholas Robert Hosker, Secretary; Steven Paul Cunliffe [1968] Director; Stephen Heys [1954] Director; Nicholas Robert Hosker [1973] Director; Thomas Charles Jones [1980] Commercial Director; Peter James Lilley [1975] Director

Linatex Limited
Incorporated: 21 March 1930
Net Worth: £9,719,000 *Total Assets:* £10,514,000
Registered Office: c/o Weir Minerals Europe, Halifax Road, Todmorden, Lancs, OL14 5RT
Activities: Non-trading company
Parent: The Weir Group PLC
Officers: Gillian Kyle, Secretary; John Brian Heasley [1974] Director/Chartered Accountant; Graham William Corbett Vanhegan [1964] Director/Chief Legal Officer and Company Secretary

Linco Care Limited
Incorporated: 17 May 1979 *Employees:* 57
Net Worth: £6,023,942 *Total Assets:* £7,592,742
Registered Office: Linco House, Manchester Road, Carrington, Manchester, M31 4BX
Activities: Other manufacturing n.e.c.
Officers: Farhad Sekaleshfar, Secretary [Iranian]; Farhad Sekaleshfar [1944] Director; Nasrin Sekaleshfar [1949] Director [Iranian]; Seena Sekaleshfar [1978] Director/Product Development

Lincolnshire Road Car Company Limited
Incorporated: 20 August 1928 *Employees:* 1,300
Net Worth: £25,919,000 *Total Assets:* £42,697,000
Registered Office: c/o Stagecoach Services Limited, One Stockport Exchange, 20 Railway Road, Stockport, Cheshire, SK1 3SW
Activities: Other urban, suburban or metropolitan passenger land transport (not underground, metro or similar)
Parent: The Yorkshire Traction Company Limited
Officers: Michael John Vaux, Secretary; Colin Brown [1968] Director/Accountant; Matthew James Cranwell [1981] Managing Director; Arnold Mark Threapleton [1954] Managing Director

Ling Properties Limited
Incorporated: 26 August 1988
Net Worth Deficit: £567,892 *Total Assets:* £8,168,314
Registered Office: 1 Allanadale Court, Waterpark Road, Salford, M7 4JN
Activities: Buying and selling of own real estate
Parent: Rowhurst Ltd
Officers: Rachel Weis, Secretary; David Neuwirth [1970] Director/Secretary; Aubrey Weis [1949] Director

The Lingholm Estate Limited
Incorporated: 11 July 2013 *Employees:* 31
Net Worth Deficit: £953,401 *Total Assets:* £11,060,238
Registered Office: c/o Clough Taxation Solutions, New Chartford House, Centurion Way, Cleckheaton, W Yorks, BD19 3QB
Activities: Holiday centres and villages
Officers: Jennifer Ann Seymour, Secretary; David Terry Seymour [1959] Director; Jane Pamela Seymour [1959] Director; Jennifer Ann Seymour [1985] Director

Lingholm Private Trust Limited,(The)
Incorporated: 29 March 1966 *Employees:* 3
Net Worth: £9,668,459 *Total Assets:* £10,749,373
Registered Office: Birbeck House, Duke Street, Penrith, Cumbria, CA11 7NA
Activities: Other service activities n.e.c.
Shareholders: Michael James Anderton; Elizabeth Norma Rochdale
Officers: Michael James Anderton, Secretary; Michael Anderton James [1970] Director; Simon Fairfax Knight [1950] Director/Chartered Surveyor; Elizabeth Norma Rochdale [1939] Director

Link Learning Trust
Incorporated: 8 March 2017 *Employees:* 124
Net Worth: £11,035,000 *Total Assets:* £12,050,000
Registered Office: Brookburn Primary School, Brookburn Road, Chorlton-Cum-Hardy, Manchester, M21 8EH
Activities: Primary education
Officers: Lord Keith Bradley [1950] Director/Member of The House of Lords; Lisa Schelene Ferris [1969] Director/Headteacher; Joan Marie Fye [1953] Director/Educational Consultant; Timothy Colin Naor Hilton [1973] Director/Senior Manager; Sonia Johnson [1968] Director/Chief Operations Officer; Jayne Kennedy [1965] Director/Headteacher; Trevor William Matthews [1956] Director; James Matthew Edward Shuttleworth [1976] Director/Town Planner; Catherine Ann Starbuck [1971] Assistant Director; Dr Adrian Rhys Young [1971] Director/Tax Manager

Linmere Limited
Incorporated: 23 April 1990
Net Worth: £6,802,273 *Total Assets:* £14,585,401
Registered Office: Cardinal House, 20 St Mary's Parsonage, Manchester, M3 2LG
Activities: Buying and selling of own real estate
Officers: Joshua Halpern, Secretary/Director; Joshua Halpern [1958] Director; Samuel Halpern [1960] Director

Linteum (Lewisham) Holdings Limited
Incorporated: 20 August 2004 *Employees:* 2
Net Worth Deficit: £3,539,779 *Total Assets:* £15,695,591
Registered Office: Unit 18 Riversway Business Village, Navigation Way, Ashton on Ribble, Preston, Lancs, PR2 2YP
Activities: Non-trading company
Parent: Aberdeen Infrastructure II Limited
Officers: Ion Bruce Balfour [1963] Director/Investment Manager; Kenneth John Simpson [1965] Director/Investment Manager

Linteum (Lewisham) Limited
Incorporated: 20 May 2004 *Employees:* 2
Net Worth Deficit: £3,539,779 *Total Assets:* £15,695,591
Registered Office: Unit 18 Riversway Business Village, Navigation Way, Ashton on Ribble, Preston, Lancs, PR2 2YP
Activities: Fitness facilities
Parent: Linteum (Lewisham) Holdings Limited
Officers: Ion Bruce Balfour [1963] Director/Investment Manager; Kenneth John Simpson [1965] Director/Investment Manager

Linteum (Willesden) Holdings Limited
Incorporated: 20 August 2004
Net Worth Deficit: £1,151,379 *Total Assets:* £13,448,676
Registered Office: Unit 18 Riversway Business Village, Navigation Way, Ashton on Ribble, Preston, Lancs, PR2 2YP
Activities: Non-trading company
Parent: Aberdeen Infrastructure II Limited
Officers: Ion Bruce Balfour [1963] Director/Investment Manager; Kenneth John Simpson [1965] Director/Investment Manager

Linteum (Willesden) Limited
Incorporated: 20 May 2004 *Employees:* 2
Net Worth Deficit: £1,151,379 *Total Assets:* £13,448,676
Registered Office: Unit 18 Riversway Business Village, Navigation Way, Ashton on Ribble, Preston, Lancs, PR2 2YP
Activities: Fitness facilities
Parent: Linteum (Willesden) Holdings Limited
Officers: Ion Bruce Balfour [1963] Director/Investment Manager; Kenneth John Simpson [1965] Director/Investment Manager

Liqui-Box UK Limited
Incorporated: 21 September 2011 *Employees:* 101
Net Worth Deficit: £2,561,002 *Total Assets:* £7,995,962
Registered Office: Southmoor Road, Wythenshawe, Manchester, M23 9XD
Activities: Other manufacturing n.e.c.
Officers: Michael Adams, Secretary; Michael Adams [1959] Director/Accountant; Lou Marmo [1972] Director [American]; Leanne Michelle Parker [1972] Director/Certified Accountant [American]; Ken Swanson [1966] Director [American]

Little Greene (Holdings) Limited
Incorporated: 13 January 2016 *Employees:* 109
Net Worth: £9,156,192 *Total Assets:* £30,537,504
Registered Office: The Coachworks, 420 Ashton Old Road, Openshaw, Manchester, M11 2DT
Activities: Activities of other holding companies n.e.c.
Shareholder: David Reginald Mottershead
Officers: John Stuart Falder, Secretary; John Stuart Falder [1955] Director; Stephen Brian Falder [1960] Director; Mohammed Naheed Hanif [1972] Director; Paul Raymond Mitchell [1951] Director; Benjamin David Reginald Mottershead [1983] Director; David Reginald Mottershead [1952] Director; Joanna Mottershead [1960] Director; Ruth Elizabeth Helen Mottershead [1985] Director; Remo Murray Ranken [1966] Director

The Little Greene Paint Company Limited
Incorporated: 22 May 1996 *Employees:* 104
Net Worth: £13,376,527 *Total Assets:* £16,899,564
Registered Office: The Coachworks, 420 Ashton Old Road, Openshaw, Manchester, M11 2DT
Activities: Manufacture of paints, varnishes and similar coatings, mastics and sealants
Parent: Little Greene Limited
Officers: Mohammed Naheed Hanif, Secretary; Mohammed Naheed Hanif [1972] Finance Director; Benjamin David Mottershead [1983] Director; David Reginald Mottershead [1952] Director; Ruth Elizabeth Helen Mottershead [1985] Director; Remo Murray Ranken [1966] Sales Director

Little Raith Wind Farm Limited
Incorporated: 1[illegible] March 2002 *Employees:* 2
Net Worth: £6,409,734 *Total Assets:* £30,981,832
Registered Office: Hamilton House, Church Street, Altrincham, Cheshire, WA14 4DR
Activities: Production of electricity
Major Shareholder: Brian George Kennedy
Officers: Andrew David Sibree Page, Secretary; Darren Karl Cornwall [1969] Director; Adrian Christopher Kirk [1961] Finance Director

Littlewoods Limited
Incorporated: 23 January 1932 *Employees:* 2
Net Worth: £256,030,000 *Total Assets:* £763,294,976
Registered Office: First Floor, Skyways House, Speke Road, Speke, Liverpool, L70 1AB
Activities: Activities of head offices
Officers: Aidan Stuart Barclay [1956] Director; Howard Myles Barclay [1959] Director/Financier Technical Consultant; Philip Leslie Peters [1957] Director; Michael Seal [1948] Director/Chartered Accountant

Livbeth Investco Limited
Incorporated: 3 October 2013 *Employees:* 1
Net Worth: £1,270,836 *Total Assets:* £11,437,318
Registered Office: 91 Walton Road, Stockton Heath, Warrington, Cheshire, WA4 6NR
Activities: Security dealing on own account
Major Shareholder: Stuart Middleton
Officers: Stuart Middleton [1963] Director

Liverpool Airport (Intermediate) No.1 Limited
Incorporated: 6 July 2015
Net Worth: £10,052,182 *Total Assets:* £19,871,612
Registered Office: Peel Dome, intu Trafford Centre, Trafford City, Manchester, M17 8PL
Activities: Other business support service activities n.e.c.
Parent: Liverpool Airport Holdings Limited
Officers: Neil Lees, Secretary; Joseph Vincent Anderson [1958] Director; Neil Lees [1963] Director; Steven Keith Underwood [1974] Director

Liverpool Airport Holdings Limited
Incorporated: 11 June 1997 *Employees:* 249
Net Worth Deficit: £36,239,000 *Total Assets:* £62,945,000
Registered Office: Peel Dome, intu Trafford Centre, Trafford City, Manchester, M17 8PL
Activities: Activities of other holding companies n.e.c.
Parent: Liverpool Airport Finance Limited
Officers: Neil Lees, Secretary; Peter John Hosker [1957] Director; Robert Eric Hough [1945] Director; Neil Lees [1963] Director

Liverpool Airport Hotel Limited
Incorporated: 21 May 2007
Net Worth: £14,504,557 *Total Assets:* £15,289,295
Registered Office: Peel Dome, intu Trafford Centre, Trafford City, Manchester, M17 8PL
Activities: Hotels and similar accommodation
Parent: Liverpool Airport Property Limited
Officers: Neil Lees, Secretary; Neil Lees [1963] Director; Steven Keith Underwood [1974] Director

Liverpool Airport Limited
Incorporated: 30 March 1987 *Employees:* 249
Net Worth Deficit: £28,264,000 *Total Assets:* £55,904,000
Registered Office: Peel Dome, intu Trafford Centre, Trafford City, Manchester, M17 8PL
Activities: Scheduled passenger air transport
Parent: Liverpool Airport (Intermediate) No.3 Limited
Officers: Neil Lees, Secretary; Peter John Hosker [1957] Director; Robert Eric Hough [1945] Director; John Andrew Irving [1978] Director; Neil Lees [1963] Director

Liverpool Airport Property Holdings Limited
Incorporated: 6 November 2015 *Employees:* 4
Net Worth: £3,451,000 *Total Assets:* £14,546,000
Registered Office: Peel Dome, intu Trafford Centre, Trafford City, Manchester, M17 8PL
Activities: Activities of construction holding companies
Parent: Peel Holdings Land and Property (UK) Limited
Officers: Neil Lees, Secretary; Neil Lees [1963] Director; Cllr James Edward Noakes [1976] Director; Cllr Wendy Ann Simon [1961] Director; Steven Keith Underwood [1974] Director

Liverpool Airport Property Limited
Incorporated: 9 November 2015
Net Worth: £3,735,000 *Total Assets:* £14,544,000
Registered Office: Peel Dome, intu Trafford Centre, Trafford City, Manchester, M17 8PL
Activities: Activities of construction holding companies
Parent: Liverpool Airport Property (Intermediate) Limited
Officers: Neil Lees, Secretary; Neil Lees [1963] Director; Steven Keith Underwood [1974] Director

Liverpool and Chester Property Company Limited
Incorporated: 1 November 1883 *Employees:* 7
Net Worth: £10,483,775 *Total Assets:* £12,417,708
Registered Office: 7 Union Court, Cook Street, Liverpool, L2 4SJ
Activities: Buying and selling of own real estate
Officers: Allan Douglas Pelan, Secretary; Geoffrey Robert Leece [1931] Director/Chartered Accountant; Colin Ewan McCaig [1948] Director/Chartered Surveyor; Allan Douglas Pelan [1968] Director/Chartered Surveyor; Keith Penny [1947] Director/Accountant; David Ian Renison [1944] Director/Solicitor; Paul Roberts [1960] Director/Chartered Surveyor; David Charles Bonar Watkins [1956] Director/Wholesaling

The Liverpool and Merseyside Theatres Trust Limited
Incorporated: 8 July 1999 *Employees:* 222
Net Worth: £23,056,000 *Total Assets:* £24,170,000
Registered Office: Everyman Theatre, 5-11 Hope Street, Liverpool, L1 9BH
Activities: Performing arts
Officers: Mark Elder Da Vanzo, Secretary; Peter Bennett-Jones [1955] Director/Theatre Producer; Paul Simon Bibby [1961] Director/Consultant; Michael Clarke [1967] Director; Paul Corcoran [1981] Managing Director; Claire Frances Dove [1952] Director/Chief Executive; Matthew Dunham [1964] Director/Financial Consultant; Bren Hutchinson [1967] Finance Director; Andrea Mary Nixon [1965] Director/Consultant; Gemma Samantha Redropp [1966] Theatre Director; Cllr Wendy Ann Simon [1961] Director/City Councillor

Liverpool Charity and Voluntary Services
Incorporated: 12 May 1922 *Employees:* 30
Net Worth: £6,706,938 *Total Assets:* £10,836,884
Registered Office: 151 Dale Street, Liverpool, L2 2AH
Activities: Other business support service activities n.e.c.
Officers: Graham Wright, Secretary; Heather Margaret Patricia Akehurst [1965] Director/Corporate Services Manager; Dorcas Olanike Akeju [1945] Director/Retired Midwife; Duncan Ian Brookes [1967] Director/Investment Manager; Michael Frederick James [1965] Director; Kenneth William Perry [1965] Director; John Anthony Price [1978] Director/Wealth Manager; Michael Salla [1983] Director of Health & Sport; Louise Ann Scholes [1969] Director/Solicitor; James Alexander Sloan [1985] Director/Chief Executive; Michael Thomas [1962] Director/Auditor; Andrew Mark Whitehead [1967] Director

Liverpool College Independent School Trust
Incorporated: 12 June 2013 *Employees:* 168
Net Worth: £33,451,480 *Total Assets:* £34,350,296
Registered Office: Liverpool College, Queens Drive, Mossley Hill, Liverpool, L18 8BG
Activities: Primary education
Officers: William Richard Edward Lisle Thompson, Secretary; Professor Katie Marie Atkinson [1979] Director/University Professor; Dr Owen Barden [1973] Director/University Lecturer; Johannes Bernardus Van Mourik Broekman [1966] Director/Principal [Dutch]; Dr Sally Alicea Carr [1955] Director/Retired; Alice Case [1968] Director/Self Employed; Kim Clarke [1963] Director/Company Secretary; Dr Hilary Irene Eccles [1964] Director/General Medical Practitioner; Tara Hallam [1975] Director/Specialist Palliative Social Worker; Professor Stephen Holloway [1952] Director/University Provost; Monica Lesley Mason [1947] Director/Chair of Governing Body; Roy Vincent Morgan [1955] Director/Headmaster; Timothy James Nichol [1961] Director/Dean; Dr Elizabeth Parr [1986] Director/Senior Professional Tutor; Collin Edmund Thompson [1947] Director/Retired; Conor Turbitt [1973] Director/Teacher

Liverpool Diocesan Board of Finance (The)
Incorporated: 10 May 1883 *Employees:* 68
Net Worth: £44,329,300 *Total Assets:* £52,144,072
Registered Office: St James House, St James Road, Liverpool, L1 7BY
Activities: Activities of religious organisations
Officers: Michael John Eastwood, Secretary; David Burgess [1941] Director/Retired; David Charles Greensmith [1953] Director/Consultant; Rev Hannah Margaret Lewis [1971] Director/Clerk in Holy Orders; Angela Michelle Matthewson [1962] Director/Customer Service Officer; Mike McGurk [1968] Director/Clerk in Holy Orders; The Venerable Jennifer McKenzie [1963] Director/Clerk in Holy Orders [American]; Doctor Peter Russell Owen [1947] Director; Dr Crispin Alexander Pailing [1975] Director/Clerk in Holy Orders; Michael Yate Pitts [1935] Director/Chartered Surveyor Consultant; The Venerable Roger Martin Howell Preece [1964] Director/Clerk in Holy Orders; The Venerable Peter Hendry Spiers [1981] Director/Clerk in Holy Orders; Rev Mark Stanford [1959] Director/Clerk in Holy Orders; Philip John Stott [1944] Director/Retired; Andrew John Orr Wilcockson [1954] Director/Retired

The Liverpool Football Club and Athletic Grounds Limited
Incorporated: 26 January 1892 *Employees:* 735
Net Worth: £98,542,000 *Total Assets:* £481,495,008
Registered Office: Anfield Road, Liverpool, L4 0TH
Activities: Operation of sports facilities
Parent: UKSV Holdings Company Limited
Officers: Joanne Roberts, Secretary; Kenneth Mathieson Dalglish [1951] Director/Former Professional Footballer and Manager; Michael Joseph Egan [1960] Director/Businessman [American]; Michael Gordon [1964] Director/Businessman [American]; John Henry [1949] Director/Businessman [American]; Andrew Lawrence Hughes [1967] Director/Chief Operating Officer; Peter Robert Moore [1955] Director/Chief Executive Officer; Thomas Charles Werner [1950] Director/Businessman [American]

Liverpool Hope University
Incorporated: 29 November 1996 *Employees:* 652
Net Worth: £102,719,088 *Total Assets:* £135,890,704
Registered Office: Hope Park, Liverpool, L16 9JD
Activities: First-degree level higher education
Officers: Derrick Nigel Dykins, Secretary; Sheryl Milanda Anderson [1953] Director/Minister of Religion; Paul Bayes [1953] Director/Bishop; Jane Ann Beever [1965] Director/Headteacher; Dr John Michael Bennett [1957] Director/University Lecturer; Sr Mary Charles-Murray [1939] Director/University Lecturer (Retired); Cllr Jane Mary Sandford Corbett [1957] Director/Councillor; Revd Christopher Anthony Fallon [1954] Director/Priest; Michael John Gilbertson [1951] Director/Accountant; Dr Simon Jeremy Hulme [1964] Director/Headteacher; Jack David Johnson [1996] Director/Students' Union President; Dr Winifred Joan McClelland [1943] Director/Retired; Christopher McCoy [1953] Director/Clergyman; Sr Maureen McKnight [1948] Director/Retired; Charles Gerard Mills [1953] Managing Director; Dr Arthur Naylor [1949] Director/Higher Education Advisor; John Douglas Norbury [1957] Director/Deputy Chairman, Tilney Bestinvest; Professor Generald John Pillay [1953] Director/Rector; Ultan Dominic Russell [1952] Director/Retired; Diane Susan Shaw [1954] Director/Headteacher; Margaret Anne Swinson [1957] Director/Chartered Accountant; Dr Sonja Tiernan [1968] Director/Lecturer [Irish]; Dr Ian Vandewalle [1953] Director/Pro Vice-Chancellor; Revd Peter Anthony Winn [1960] Director/Vicar; Graham Nash Wood [1957] Director/Judge

The Liverpool Institute for Performing Arts
Incorporated: 13 June 1990 *Employees:* 135
Net Worth: £14,626,049 *Total Assets:* £18,711,086
Registered Office: Mount Street, Liverpool, L1 9HF
Activities: First-degree level higher education
Officers: Katharine Anne Dimmock, Secretary; Isabel Begg [1967] Director/Management BBC; Julie Margaret Cullen [1965] Director/Editor; James Alexander Thomas Dow [1961] Director/Chartered Accountant; Louise Joyce Ellman [1945] Director/MP; Victoria Lucy Fea [1971] Director/TV Executive; Sir Mark Philip Featherstone-Witty [1946] Director/Administrator; Jonathon Robert Ford [1968] Director/Chartered Accountant; Simon Jeffrey Fowler [1965] Director; Geoffrey Michael Goodwin [1970] Director; Ian Malcolm Jones [1949] Director/Consultant; David Roger Morris [1947] Director/Administrator; Professor Frances Henry Sanderson [1946] Director/Retired; Kenneth James Webster [1944] Director/IT Manager; Prof Andrew William Westwood [1966] Director/Chief Executive; John Philip Wood [1956] Director/Lecturer; Claire Rosemary Workman [1970] Director/Management Consultant; Richard Young [1967] Director

The Liverpool Joint Catholic and Church of England Academies Trust
Incorporated: 2 September 2009 *Employees:* 199
Net Worth: £30,977,000 *Total Assets:* £37,887,000
Registered Office: 51 Horrocks Avenue, Garston, Liverpool, L19 5NY
Activities: General secondary education
Officers: Peter John Alcock [1946] Director/Retired; David Paul Clayton [1988] Director/Chief Executive Officer; Christopher Joseph Cleugh [1952] Director; Matthew Peter Elliott [1984] Director of Finance; Lady Erica Rosemary Hedley [1950] Director/Retired; Brynley John Marsh [1946] Director/Governor; Richard Charles Peers [1965] Director; Alexander Scott [1949] Director/Retired; Timothy Mark Warren [1958] Director of Schools and Colleges

Liverpool School of Tropical Medicine
Incorporated: 30 January 1905 *Employees:* 508
Net Worth: £45,801,000 *Total Assets:* £144,651,008
Registered Office: Pembroke Place, Liverpool, L3 5QA
Activities: Research and experimental development on social sciences and humanities
Officers: Robert Einion Holland, Secretary; Mark Allanson [1961] Director/Pro Vice Chancellor University; Dr Jenny Elisabeth Amery [1953] Director/LSTM Trustee; Nicholas Peter Francis Earlam [1958] Director/Executive Chairman of Plexus Cotton; Professor Janet Hemingway [1957] Director/Professor; Jeremy John Elton Lefroy [1959] Director/Member of Parliament; Dr Julian Peter Lob-Levyt [1956] Director/LSTM Trustee; Rebecca Nightingale [1983] Director/Student; John O'Brien [1959] Director/Retired; James Hood Ross [1938] Director; Susan Jane Russell [1960] Director/Solicitor; Jonathan Hugh Schofield [1961] Director/Chartered Accountant; Eileen Thornton [1947] Director/Retired; Professor Stephen Andrew Ward [1958] Director/Walter Myers Professor of Parisitology

Liverpool Science Park Limited
Incorporated: 13 June 2003 *Employees:* 16
Net Worth Deficit: £234,494 *Total Assets:* £19,344,574
Registered Office: Liverpool Science Park, 131 Mount Pleasant, Liverpool, L3 5TF
Activities: Other letting and operating of own or leased real estate
Parent: Liverpool City Council
Officers: Professor Janet Patricia Beer [1956] Director/Vice-Chancellor; Julie Elizabeth Bertolini [1963] Finance Director; Sarah Karen Jackson [1975] Director; Barbara Ann Murray [1954] Director/Councillor; Cllr Wendy Ann Simon [1961] Director/Deputy Mayor; Professor Nigel Peter Weatherill [1954] Director/Vice Chancellor

Liverpool Shipbrokers Benevolent Society Incorporated
Incorporated: 19 March 1919 *Employees:* 1
Net Worth: £7,970,567 *Total Assets:* £7,976,709
Registered Office: 4th Floor, Melbourne Buildings, 21 North John Street, Liverpool, L2 5QU
Activities: Other social work activities without accommodation n.e.c.
Officers: David Mark Galbraith, Secretary; Anthony Butler [1940] Director/Retired; Roy Cooke [1948] Director/Retired; John Day [1947] Director/Retired; David Gilmour [1942] Director/Chartered Shipbroker; Herbert William Jennings [1951] Director/Line Manager; Stuart George Lofthouse [1958] Director/Chartered Shipbroker; Joseph John McGuffie [1957] Director/Shipbroker; Paul Roxburgh Moss [1948] Director/Retired; Viorel Raducanescu [1967] Director/Chartered Shipbroker; Ian Robinson [1946] Director/Retired; Allan Seedhouse [1962] Director

Liverpool Streetscene Services Limited
Incorporated: 15 February 2001 *Employees:* 481
Net Worth Deficit: £10,295,000 *Total Assets:* £7,863,000
Registered Office: Newton Road, Liverpool, L13 3HS
Activities: Other business support service activities n.e.c.
Parent: Liverpool City Council
Officers: Cllr James Edward Noakes [1976] Director/Cabinet Member LCC; Ron Odunaiya [1968] Director Local Government; Cllr Wendy Ann Simon [1961] Director/Deputy Mayor

P J Livesey Country Homes (Eastern) Limited
Incorporated: 24 April 2001 *Employees:* 7
Net Worth: £350,764 *Total Assets:* £9,752,659
Registered Office: Ashburton Park, Beacon Road, Trafford Park, Manchester, M17 1AF
Activities: Construction of domestic buildings
Parent: P J Livesey South Limited
Officers: Dorothea Anne Livesey, Secretary/Interior Designer; John William Allcock [1957] Financial Director; Ralph Brocklehurst [1951] Technical Director; Dorothea Anne Livesey [1946] Director; Georgina Ann Livesey [1976] Director; Peter Joseph Livesey [1948] Managing Director; Paul Gerard Richardson [1956] Development Director; James Nicholas David Woodmansee [1973] Director

P.J. Livesey Group Limited
Incorporated: 21 September 2006
Net Worth: £1 *Total Assets:* £9,583,952
Registered Office: P J Livesey Group Ltd, Beacon Road, Ashburton Road West, Trafford Park, Manchester, M17 1AF
Activities: Construction of domestic buildings
Parent: P J Livesey Holdings
Officers: Dorothea Anne Livesey, Secretary/Director; John William Allcock [1957] Finance Director; Ralph Brocklehurst [1951] Technical Director; Dorothea Anne Livesey [1946] Director; Georgina Ann Livesey [1976] Director; Peter Joseph Livesey [1948] Managing Director; Paul Gerard Richardson [1956] Development Director; James Nicholas David Woodmansee [1973] Development Director

P.J. Livesey Holdings Limited
Incorporated: 7 May 1996 *Employees:* 150
Net Worth: £41,453,008 *Total Assets:* £74,708,672
Registered Office: Ashburton Park, Ashburton Road West, Trafford Park, Manchester, M17 1AF
Activities: Construction of domestic buildings
Major Shareholder: Peter Joseph Livesey
Officers: Dorothea Anne Livesey, Secretary/Director; John William Allcock [1957] Financial Director; Ralph Brocklehurst [1951] Technical Director; Mark Duckett [1964] Director; Gary Wayne Graves [1958] Director; Dorothea Anne Livesey [1946] Director; Georgina Ann Livesey [1976] Director; Peter Joseph Livesey [1948] Managing Director; Craig Daniel Lynch [1979] Director; Paul Gerard Richardson [1956] Development Director; James Nicholas David Woodmansee [1973] Director

P J Livesey Living Space (11) Limited
Incorporated: 2 June 2005 *Employees:* 7
Net Worth Deficit: £753,295 *Total Assets:* £7,124,999
Registered Office: Ashburton Park, Beacon Road, Trafford Park, Manchester, M17 1AF
Activities: Construction of domestic buildings
Parent: P J Livesey South Limited
Officers: Dorothea Anne Livesey, Secretary; John William Allcock [1957] Financial Director; Ralph Brocklehurst [1951] Technical Director; Dorothea Anne Livesey [1946] Director; Georgina Ann Livesey [1976] Director; Peter Joseph Livesey [1948] Director/Managing; Paul Gerard Richardson [1956] Director; James Nicholas David Woodmansee [1973] Director

P J Livesey Living Space (North) Limited
Incorporated: 27 August 2004 *Employees:* 7
Net Worth Deficit: £1,538,612 *Total Assets:* £10,283,071
Registered Office: Ashburton Park, Ashburton Road West, Trafford Park, Manchester, M17 1AF
Activities: Construction of domestic buildings
Parent: P J Livesey North Limited
Officers: Dorothea Anne Livesey, Secretary/Director; John William Allcock [1957] Financial Director; Ralph Brocklehurst [1951] Technical Director; Dorothea Anne Livesey [1946] Director; Georgina Ann Livesey [1976] Director; Peter Joseph Livesey [1948] Managing Director; Paul Gerard Richardson [1956] Director; James Nicholas David Woodmansee [1973] Director

P.J. Livesey Living Space Limited
Incorporated: 20 March 1996 *Employees:* 7
Net Worth: £111,939 *Total Assets:* £20,481,052
Registered Office: Ashburton Park, Ashburton Road West, Trafford Park, Manchester, M17 1AF
Activities: Construction of domestic buildings
Parent: P J Livesey North Limited
Officers: Dorothea Anne Livesey, Secretary/Director; John William Allcock [1957] Finance Director; Ralph Brocklehurst [1951] Technical Director; Dorothea Anne Livesey [1946] Director; Georgina Ann Livesey [1976] Director; Peter Joseph Livesey [1948] Managing Director; Paul Gerard Richardson [1956] Development Director; James Nicholas David Woodmansee [1973] Director

Lloyd & Jones Engineers (Holdings) Limited
Incorporated: 8 June 2001 *Employees:* 150
Net Worth: £6,057,860 *Total Assets:* £11,631,942
Registered Office: Langton House, 74 Regent Road, Bootle, Merseyside, L20 1BL
Activities: Other letting and operating of own or leased real estate
Major Shareholder: John Birch
Officers: Carol Ann Birch, Secretary; Jonathon Douglas Birch [1963] Managing Director

Lloyd & Jones Engineers Limited
Incorporated: 9 September 1983 *Employees:* 134
Net Worth: £4,356,567 *Total Assets:* £8,047,087
Registered Office: P O Box 29, Langton House, 74 Regent Road, Bootle, Merseyside, L20 1BL
Activities: Wholesale of other machinery and equipment
Parent: Lloyd & Jones Engineers Holdings Ltd
Officers: Jonathon Douglas Birch, Secretary; Carol Ann Birch [1967] Director; Jonathon Douglas Birch [1963] Director; Andrew Robert Boden [1964] Director; David Ian Nigel Lester [1965] Director; Stephen Ranson [1956] Director Purchasing

Lloyd Limited
Incorporated: 1 January 1964 *Employees:* 269
Net Worth: £14,322,000 *Total Assets:* £45,430,000
Registered Office: Kingstown Broadway, Kingstown Industrial Trading Estate, Carlisle, CA3 0EF
Activities: Wholesale of agricultural machinery, equipment and supplies
Officers: Howard Thomas Woolgar, Secretary; Beryl Lloyd [1932] Director; Bryan Lloyd [1956] Director; John Barry Lloyd [1952] Director

Lloyd Motors Limited
Incorporated: 4 August 1976 *Employees:* 932
Net Worth: £66,990,000 *Total Assets:* £150,082,000
Registered Office: Montgomery Way, Rosehill, Carlisle, Cumbria, CA1 2RP
Activities: Sale of new cars and light motor vehicles
Shareholders: Bryan Lloyd; John Barry Lloyd
Officers: Stuart Collins, Secretary; Bryan Lloyd [1956] Director; John Barry Lloyd [1952] Director

LLW Repository Limited
Incorporated: 1 November 2005 *Employees:* 230
Net Worth: £2,679,000 *Total Assets:* £31,968,000
Registered Office: Old Shore Road, Drigg, Holmrook, Cumbria, CA19 1XH
Activities: Other service activities n.e.c.
Parent: UK Nuclear Waste Management Limited
Officers: Neil Dennis Baldwin [1957] Director/Retired; Amy Gill-Weatherburn [1979] Business Director; Nigel Robert Lister [1967] Director/Head of Safety; Paul Pointon [1968] Deputy Managing Director; Alastair James Scrimgeour [1956] Director; Dennis Grey Thompson [1964] Director/Engineer/Manager [American]; Stephen William Topping [1965] Director; Martin Walkingshaw [1966] Director/Head of Commercial and Strategic Development

LMR Drilling UK Ltd
Incorporated: 5 May 1999 *Employees:* 7
Net Worth: £7,650,742 *Total Assets:* £8,476,078
Registered Office: Egerton House, 2 Tower Road, Birkenhead, Merseyside, CH41 1FN
Activities: Test drilling and boring
Officers: Jeremy Mark Seamans, Secretary; Ernst Georg Fengler [1969] Director/Engineer [German]; Heiko Franz Janz [1949] Director/Accountant [German]; Jeremy Mark Seamans [1969] Director/Engineer

Local Pensions Partnership Investments Ltd
Incorporated: 21 October 2015 *Employees:* 23
Net Worth: £10,530,000 *Total Assets:* £17,622,000
Registered Office: County Hall, Fishergate, Preston, Lancs, PR1 8XJ
Activities: Fund management activities
Parent: Local Pensions Partnership Limited
Officers: Greg Smith, Secretary; Sally Bridgeland [1964] Director/Management Consultant; Susan Christine Martin [1958] Director; Michael O'Higgins [1954] Director [Irish]; Thomas James Richardson [1975] Director/Chief Risk Officer; Christopher Paul Rule [1979] Director/Chief Investment Officer; Martin Andrew Tully [1962] Director/Consultant; Robert William Vandersluis [1972] Director [British/American]

Local Pensions Partnership Ltd
Incorporated: 19 October 2015 *Employees:* 226
Net Worth Deficit: £9,237,000 *Total Assets:* £27,549,000
Registered Office: County Hall, Fishergate, Preston, Lancs, PR1 8XJ
Activities: Activities of financial services holding companies
Shareholders: Lancashire County Council; London Pensions Fund Authority
Officers: Greg Smith, Secretary; Sally Bridgeland [1964] Director; Allister Jeffrey [1964] Director; Sarah Eileen Laessig [1968] Director [British/American]; Jill MacKenzie [1966] Director; Susan Christine Martin [1958] Director; Dermot John McMullan [1949] Director; Michael O'Higgins [1954] Director/Chairman [Irish]; Thomas James Richardson [1975] Director/Chief Risk Officer; Sir Peter Rogers [1949] Director; Alan Schofield [1946] Director/County Councillor; Robert William Vandersluis [1972] Director [British/American]

Lock Inspection Systems Limited
Incorporated: 28 January 1992 *Employees:* 77
Net Worth: £6,116,000 *Total Assets:* £7,353,000
Registered Office: Lock House, Neville Street, Chadderton, Oldham, Lancs, OL9 6LF
Activities: Manufacture of other special-purpose machinery n.e.c.
Officers: Giles Matthew Hudson [1972] Director/Chartered Accountant; Edward Ufland [1969] Director/Chartered Accountant

Lockhurst Holdings Limited
Incorporated: 12 March 1987 *Employees:* 4
Net Worth: £6,606,512 *Total Assets:* £7,373,489
Registered Office: Blaguegate Works, Stanley Way, Skelmersdale, Lancs, WN8 8EA
Activities: Activities of head offices
Parent: Blaguegate Limited
Officers: John Baron Rawcliffe, Secretary; David Richard Rawcliffe [1953] Director/Road Haulier; John Baron Rawcliffe [1945] Director/Road Haulier

Lofthouse of Fleetwood Limited
Incorporated: 18 November 1963 *Employees:* 385
Net Worth: £79,805,056 *Total Assets:* £97,787,144
Registered Office: Maritime Street, Fleetwood, Lancs, FY7 7LP
Activities: Manufacture of sugar confectionery
Shareholders: Doreen Wilson Lofthouse OBE; Duncan Charles Lofthouse
Officers: Duncan Charles Lofthouse, Secretary; Doreen Wilson Lofthouse [1930] Director; Duncan Charles Lofthouse [1951] Director

Lomas Distribution Limited
Incorporated: 28 January 1994 *Employees:* 256
Net Worth: £8,397,610 *Total Assets:* £44,492,744
Registered Office: 1 Waterswallows Industrial Park, Waterswallows Road, Buxton, Derbys, SK17 7JB
Activities: Freight transport by road
Shareholders: Lynne Beverley Lomas; Richard Anthony Lomas; Richard Lomas
Officers: Lynne Beverley Lomas, Company Secretary; Lynne Beverley Lomas [1961] Director/Company Secretary; Richard Lomas [1939] Director/Service Manager; Richard Anthony Lomas [1967] Managing Director

London & District Investments Limited
Incorporated: 12 November 1962 *Employees:* 6
Net Worth: £31,700,644 *Total Assets:* £52,023,892
Registered Office: The Copper Room, Deva Centre, Trinity Way, Manchester, M3 7BG
Activities: Development of building projects
Shareholders: Andrew Leslie Fisher; Roslyn Susanne Pine
Officers: Elliot Pine, Secretary; Andrew Leslie Fisher [1948] Director/Property Manager; Roslyn Susanne Pine [1945] Director

London Luton Airport Parking Limited
Incorporated: 18 May 2016 *Employees:* 4
Net Worth: £11,086,184 *Total Assets:* £11,116,400
Registered Office: Group First House, Mead Way, Padiham, Lancs, BB12 7NG
Activities: Buying and selling of own real estate
Parent: Group First Global Limited
Officers: Ruth Margaret Almond [1958] Director; Leanne Marie Gregson [1979] Director; John Slater [1978] Director; Toby Scott Whittaker [1977] Director

The London Oil Refining Co. Limited
Incorporated: 1 March 1991 *Employees:* 72
Net Worth: £8,636,911 *Total Assets:* £11,511,164
Registered Office: Astonish House, Unit 1 Premier Point, Staithgate Lane, Bradford, W Yorks, BD6 1DW
Activities: Manufacture of cleaning and polishing preparations
Officers: Alan Stanley Brian Moss, Secretary; Howard William Moss [1974] Managing Director

The London Property Partnership Limited
Incorporated: 13 March 2000
Net Worth: £33,544,826 *Total Assets:* £71,083,176
Registered Office: Regency House, 45-51 Chorley New Road, Bolton, Lancs, BL1 4QR
Activities: Buying and selling of own real estate
Shareholders: Dalveen Enterprises Limited; Huntingdon Group Limited
Officers: Matthew Patrick Kelly, Secretary; Matthew Patrick Kelly [1969] Director/Chartered Surveyor; William Ross Warburton [1958] Director

Longfield Chemicals (Holdings) Limited
Incorporated: 17 April 1986 *Employees:* 13
Net Worth: £2,485,600 *Total Assets:* £15,430,588
Registered Office: 125a King Street, Knutsford, Cheshire, WA16 6EH
Activities: Activities of head offices
Officers: Mark De-Ville Pepper, Secretary; Patricia Elizabeth Brian [1937] Director; Stuart John Forsyth [1969] Commercial Director; Stephen James Kilburn [1974] Marketing Director; Mark De-Ville Pepper [1960] Director/Chartered Accountant

Longfield Chemicals Limited
Incorporated: 3 January 1968 *Employees:* 15
Net Worth: £2,627,248 *Total Assets:* £15,572,236
Registered Office: 125a King Street, Knutsford, Cheshire, WA16 6EH
Activities: Wholesale of other intermediate products
Officers: Mark De-Ville Pepper, Secretary; Patricia Elizabeth Brian [1937] Director; Stuart John Forsyth [1969] Commercial Director; Stephen James Kilburn [1974] Marketing Director; Mark De-Ville Pepper [1960] Director/Chartered Accountant

Longside Properties Limited
Incorporated: 10 August 2004
Net Worth: £696,000 *Total Assets:* £14,471,000
Registered Office: Turf Moor, Harry Potts Way, Burnley, Lancs, BB10 4BX
Activities: Buying and selling of own real estate
Officers: Matthew Robert Williams, Secretary; John William Banaszkiewicz [1962] Managing Director; Terence Anthony Crabb [1948] Director; Brendan Flood [1961] Director; Michael Lee Garlick [1963] Director; Clive John Holt [1943] Director; Barry Charles Kilby [1949] Director; Brian Thomas Nelson [1948] Director

Lonsdale Holdings Limited
Incorporated: 9 October 2000 *Employees:* 106
Net Worth: £6,991,409 *Total Assets:* £15,304,891
Registered Office: Stoneholme Road, Rossendale, Lancs, BB4 8BA
Activities: Activities of head offices
Shareholders: Robert Killelea; Ellen Jane Killelea; Patrick James Killelea; Denise Killelea
Officers: Ellen Jane Killelea, Secretary; Patrick James Killelea [1955] Director; Robert Killelea [1945] Director

Lookers Birmingham Limited
Incorporated: 30 May 1997 *Employees:* 174
Net Worth: £2,565,000 *Total Assets:* £26,625,000
Registered Office: Lookers House, 3 Etchells Road, West Timperley, Altrincham, Cheshire, WA14 5XS
Activities: Sale of new cars and light motor vehicles
Parent: Lookers Motor Holdings Limited
Officers: Robin Anthony Gregson, Secretary; Andrew Campbell Bruce [1965] Managing Director Motors Division; Robin Anthony Gregson [1960] Director/Chartered Accountant; Nigel John McMinn [1968] Director

Lookers Colborne Limited
Incorporated: 5 March 2001 *Employees:* 427
Net Worth: £8,012,000 *Total Assets:* £69,299,000
Registered Office: Lookers House, 3 Etchells Road, West Timperley, Altrincham, Cheshire, WA14 5XS
Activities: Sale of new cars and light motor vehicles
Parent: Lookers Motor Group Limited
Officers: Glenda MacGeekie, Secretary; Andrew Campbell Bruce [1965] Director; Robin Anthony Gregson [1960] Director/Chartered Accountant; Nigel John McMinn [1968] Managing Director

Lookers Leasing Limited
Incorporated: 14 December 2005 *Employees:* 24
Net Worth: £5,443,000 *Total Assets:* £46,603,000
Registered Office: Lookers House, 3 Etchells Road, West Timperley, Altrincham, Cheshire, WA14 5XS
Activities: Sale of new cars and light motor vehicles
Parent: Bramall & Jones VW Ltd
Officers: Glenda MacGeekie, Secretary; Andrew Campbell Bruce [1965] Director; Robin Anthony Gregson [1960] Director/Chartered Accountant; Nigel John McMinn [1968] Managing Director Motor Division

Lookers Motor Group Limited
Incorporated: 30 March 1916 *Employees:* 2,216
Net Worth: £27,336,000 *Total Assets:* £545,974,976
Registered Office: Lookers House, 3 Etchells Road, West Timperley, Altrincham, Cheshire, WA14 5XS
Activities: Sale of new cars and light motor vehicles
Parent: Lookers Motor Holdings Limited
Officers: Glenda MacGeekie, Secretary; Andrew Campbell Bruce [1965] Director/Operations; Robin Anthony Gregson [1960] Director/Chartered Accountant; Nigel John McMinn [1968] Managing Director Motor Division

Lookers Motor Holdings Limited
Incorporated: 24 March 1958
Net Worth: £25,046,000 *Total Assets:* £97,977,000
Registered Office: Lookers House, 3 Etchells Road, West Timperley, Altrincham, Cheshire, WA14 5XS
Activities: Sale of new cars and light motor vehicles
Parent: Lookers PLC
Officers: Glenda MacGeekie, Secretary; Andrew Campbell Bruce [1965] Director; Robin Anthony Gregson [1960] Director/Chartered Accountant; Nigel John McMinn [1968] Managing Director Motor Division

Lookers PLC
Incorporated: 26 September 1910 *Employees:* 8,599
Net Worth: £385,000,000 *Total Assets:* £1,895,600,000
Registered Office: Lookers House, 3 Etchells Road, West Timperley, Altrincham, Cheshire, WA14 5XS
Activities: Sale of new cars and light motor vehicles
Officers: Glenda MacGeekie, Secretary; Douglas Charles Antony Bramall [1935] Director/Chartered Accountant; Andrew Campbell Bruce [1965] Managing Director Motor Division; Sally Joanne Cabrini [1964] Business Services Director; Stuart Robin Counsell [1950] Director/Chartered Accountant; Robin Anthony Gregson [1960] Director/Chartered Accountant; Nigel John McMinn [1968] Managing Director Motor Division; Richard Scott Walker [1966] Director; Philip Michael White [1949] Director

Loop Customer Management Limited
Incorporated: 29 July 1999 *Employees:* 726
Net Worth: £3,640,000 *Total Assets:* £8,416,000
Registered Office: Western House, Halifax Road, Bradford, W Yorks, BD6 2SZ
Activities: Other business support service activities n.e.c.
Parent: Kelda Group Limited
Officers: Angela Wendy Miriam White, Secretary; Elizabeth Marian Barber [1965] Director/Accountant; Richard David Flint [1968] Director; Jonathan Harding [1968] Director

John Lord Holdings Limited
Incorporated: 24 September 1996 *Employees:* 194
Net Worth: £8,270,816 *Total Assets:* £11,433,380
Registered Office: Wellington Cement Works, Ainsworth Road, Bury, Lancs, BL8 2RS
Activities: Activities of head offices
Major Shareholder: Edward Stephen Richard Lord
Officers: Kimberley Jayne Lord, Company Secretary; Edward Stephen Richard Lord [1952] Director

William Loughran Limited
Incorporated: 12 October 1978 *Employees:* 6
Net Worth: £13,544,133 *Total Assets:* £19,147,836
Registered Office: The Hawthornes, Gill Lane, Walmer Bridge, Preston, Lancs, PR4 5QN
Activities: Sale of used cars and light motor vehicles
Major Shareholder: George William Loughran
Officers: Patricia Nancy Diaz, Secretary/Retired; George William Loughran [1947] Director; Juliette Maria Loughran [1985] Director/Car Sales

Louver-Lite Limited
Incorporated: [illegible]7 May 197[illegible] *Employees:* 334
Net Worth: £46,821,216 *Total Assets:* £50,530,104
Registered Office: Ashton Road, Hyde, Cheshire, SK14 4BG
Activities: Other manufacturing n.e.c.
Major Shareholder: Reginald Charles Allsopp
Officers: Simon Jon Monk, Secretary; Reginald Charles Allsopp [1926] Director/Chairman; Antony Barnes [1964] Director; Stephen William Birtles [1955] Director; Simon Jon Monk [1966] Finance Director; David Peter Robinson [1958] Sales and Marketing Director

Love Brothers Limited
Incorporated: 6 November 1973 *Employees:* 6
Net Worth: £8,208,448 *Total Assets:* £12,196,332
Registered Office: Holcroft Hall, Holcroft Lane, Culcheth, Warrington, Cheshire, WA3 5AH
Activities: Growing of cereals (except rice), leguminous crops and oil seeds
Officers: James Douglas Love, Secretary; Angela Love [1972] Director; James Douglas Love [1970] Director/Farming & Quarrying

Love Saving Group Limited
Incorporated: 16 July 2015 *Employees:* 183
Net Worth: £1 001,386 *Total Assets:* £14,521,392
Registered Office: Unit 2 Springfield Court, Summerfield Road, Bolton, Lancs, BL3 2NT
Activities: Activities of head offices
Parent: Seahawk Bidco Limited
Officers: Phil Foster [1973] Director; Jonathan Charles King [1960] Director; Christopher Todd [1986] Director

Loven Care Homes Limited
Incorporated: 26 February 2013 *Employees:* 498
Net Worth: £1,220,316 *Total Assets:* £15,456,962
Registered Office: 6th Floor, Cardinal House, 20 St Marys Parsonage, Manchester, M3 2LG
Activities: Residential nursing care facilities
Officers: Joseph Abudarham [1978] Director/Solicitor; Daniel Theodore Klein [1978] Director; Francois Klein [1984] Director; Patrice Bernard Klein [1950] Director [French]

Low Wood Hotel (1958) Limited
Incorporated: 2 September 1958 *Employees:* 138
Net Worth: £11,378,609 *Total Assets:* £25,571,836
Registered Office: Low Wood, Windermere, Cumbria, LA23 1LP
Activities: Hotels and similar accommodation
Officers: Timothy Robert James Berry, Secretary/Leisure Director; Benjamin William James Berry [1988] Director; Simon Frederick Michael Berry [1959] Managing Director; Timothy Robert James Berry [1961] Leisure Director; Jonathan Alexander Noel Cook [1963] Director; Douglas Paterson Dale [1952] Director; Jonquil Anna Catherine Doremus Cook [1969] Director; David Huw Neale [1962] Commercial Director; Matthew John Wilkinson [1977] Financial Director

Lowe Clothing International Limited
Incorporated: 18 November 2004 *Employees:* 105
Net Worth: £1,077,793 *Total Assets:* £10,920,547
Registered Office: Paton House, Level One, Victoria Viaduct, Carlisle, CA3 8AN
Activities: Wholesale of clothing and footwear
Major Shareholder: Jonathan Adam Lowe
Officers: Christopher Arthur Carlisle, Secretary; Christopher Arthur Carlisle [1954] Finance Director; Jonathan Adam Lowe [1981] Director

Lowri Beck Services Limited
Incorporated: 2 May 1997 *Employees:* 1,474
Net Worth: £1,817,584 *Total Assets:* £37,768,336
Registered Office: Clarke Nicklin House, Brooks Drive, Cheadle Royal Business Park, Cheadle, Cheshire, SK8 3TD
Activities: Other professional, scientific and technical activities n.e.c.
Parent: BV Holdings Limted
Officers: David Barratt [1955] Director; Simon Paul Cuffin-Munday [1956] Finance Director; Jon Edward Parr [1966] Managing Director; Grant David Qualey [1984] Business Development Director; Tracy Anne Sanderson [1981] Director; John Robert William Vernon [1947] Director/Executive Chairman; Richard Andrew Vernon [1976] Director

Lowry Capital Limited
Incorporated: 5 December 2006 *Employees:* 7
Net Worth: £5,348,898 *Total Assets:* £18,256,702
Registered Office: 1st Floor, Kingston House, Towers Business Park, Wilmslow Road, Manchester, M20 2LX
Activities: Activities of mortgage finance companies
Shareholders: Richard Basso; Michael John Basso
Officers: Richard Basso, Secretary; Michael John Basso [1948] Director; Richard Basso [1973] Director/Property Investment

The Lowry Centre Trust
Incorporated: 4 March 1996 *Employees:* 7
Net Worth: £54,039,000 *Total Assets:* £59,566,000
Registered Office: The Lowry, Pier 8, Salford Quays, Salford, M50 3AZ
Activities: Performing arts
Officers: Jonathan Michael Brabbin, Finance Director; Sir Rodney Malcolm Aldridge [1947] Director/Chairman; Michael Blackburn [1959] Regional Director North West; Baroness Jane Mary Bonham-Carter [1957] Director/Politician; Ian William Currie [1961] Director; Angela Jane Frost [1957] Director; Richard Jeremy Glover [1953] Director/Chief Executive, Youth Charity; Charles William Victor Hinds [1945] Director/Councillor; Beverley June Hughes [1950] Director/Member of The House of Lords; Nadav Kander [1961] Director/Photographer [German]; John David Merry [1956] Director/Deputy City Mayor/Councillor; Thomas Burns Russell [1952] Director/Consultant (Urban Regeneration); James Thomas Taylor [1961] City Director, Salford City Council; Adrian Charles Vinken [1953] Director/Company MD

LPC Fresh Parks Limited
Incorporated: 10 June 2009
Net Worth Deficit: £3,206,482 *Total Assets:* £10,691,914
Registered Office: Optimum House, Clippers Quay, Salford, M50 3XP
Activities: Other letting and operating of own or leased real estate
Officers: Simon Richard Ashdown [1974] Director

LQ Developments Limited
Incorporated: 14 December 2012
Net Worth Deficit: £2,102,316 *Total Assets:* £31,979,048
Registered Office: 1st Floor, NQ Building, 47 Bengal Street, Manchester, M4 6BB
Activities: Development of building projects
Parent: KQ Developments Limited
Officers: Michael Shaw, Secretary; Daren Whitaker [1972] Director

LRUK (Holdings) Limited
Incorporated: 28 December 1909 *Employees:* 202
Net Worth: £16,899,000 *Total Assets:* £30,609,000
Registered Office: 2 Holdsworth Street, Bradford, W Yorks, BD1 4AH
Activities: Retail sale via mail order houses or via Internet
Shareholder: Ginette Moulin
Officers: Craig Roberts, Secretary; Nathalie Catherine Balla [1967] Director/Chief Executive [French]; Richard Burke [1971] Managing Director; Paul Kenworthy [1970] Finance Director; Michael Truluck [1980] Finance Director [South African]

LRUK (Retail) Limited
Incorporated: 28 June 1910 *Employees:* 75
Net Worth: £47,822,000 *Total Assets:* £66,034,000
Registered Office: 2 Holdsworth Street, Bradford, W Yorks, BD1 4AH
Activities: Retail sale via mail order houses or via Internet
Shareholders: Ginette Moulin; LRUK (Holdings) Limited
Officers: Richard Burke [1971] Managing Director; Paul Kenworthy [1970] Finance Director; Michael Truluck [1980] Finance Director [South African]

LSC Finance Ltd
Incorporated: 20 August 2012 *Employees:* 2
Net Worth: £10,783,255 *Total Assets:* £43,016,840
Registered Office: 1-7 Fallbarn Road, Rawtenstall, Lancs, BB4 7NT
Activities: Financial intermediation not elsewhere classified
Shareholder: Shaun Morley
Officers: Shaun Morley [1966] Director; Adam Mark Turner [1987] Director

LSC Holdings Limited
Incorporated: 9 April 2015
Net Worth: £33,034,996 *Total Assets:* £33,034,996
Registered Office: 1-7 Fallbarn Road, Rawtenstall, Rossendale, Lancs, BB4 7NT
Activities: Dormant company
Parent: LSC Group Limited
Officers: Shaun Morley [1966] Managing Director; Ashley Anne Morley-Doidge [1985] Director; Adam Mark Turner [1987] Director

LSC Investments Limited
Incorporated: 9 April 2015 *Employees:* 2
Net Worth: £38,510,552 *Total Assets:* £39,870,280
Registered Office: 1-7 Fallbarn Road, Rawtenstall, Rossendale, Lancs, BB4 7NT
Activities: Dormant company
Major Shareholder: Shaun Morley
Officers: Shaun Morley [1966] Managing Director; Ashley Anne Morley-Doidge [1985] Director; Adam Mark Turner [1987] Director

Luby Group (UK) Limited
Incorporated: 15 April 2008 *Employees:* 83
Net Worth: £14,556,082 *Total Assets:* £19,288,472
Registered Office: Unit 3 Westpoint Enterprise Park, Clarence Avenue, Trafford Park, Manchester, M17 1QS
Activities: Activities of head offices
Major Shareholder: Mark Peter Luby
Officers: Neil Patrick Inskip [1980] Director; Mark Peter Luby [1966] Director/Marketing; Michael John Molesworth [1956] Director

Lucchini Unipart Rail Limited
Incorporated: 1 November 1995 *Employees:* 340
Net Worth: £26,358,000 *Total Assets:* £55,798,000
Registered Office: Ashburton Park, Wheel Forge Way, Trafford Park, Manchester, M17 1EH
Activities: Manufacture of railway locomotives and rolling stock
Shareholders: Lucchini RS S.P.A.; Unipart Rail Limted
Officers: Victoria Helen Montgomery, Secretary; Christopher Stephen Fawdry [1953] Director; Richard Ian Jackson [1971] Director; Luigi Lucchini [1985] Director/Assistant General Manager [Italian]; Augusto Mensi [1975] Director [Italian]; George James Tillier [1955] Director

Ludgate Estates Limited (The)
Incorporated: 27 June 1923 *Employees:* 6
Net Worth: £14,113,977 *Total Assets:* £16,366,241
Registered Office: 2 Friarsgate, Grosvenor Street, Chester, CH1 1XG
Activities: Other letting and operating of own or leased real estate
Officers: Nigel John Anderton [1954] Director/Chartered Surveyor; Ian James Davies [1966] Director/Chartered Surveyor; Peter James Hitchcock [1946] Director/Chartered Surveyor; Andrew Mills [1966] Director/Chartered Surveyor; Mark Guy Williams [1955] Director/Surveyor

Ludgate Hill Developments Limited
Incorporated: 10 October 2000
Net Worth: £300,000 *Total Assets:* £6,568,000
Registered Office: KPMG LP, 1 St Peter's Square, Manchester, M2 3AE
Activities: Construction of domestic buildings
Parent: McInerney Group Limited (in Administration)
Officers: Philip Talbot, Secretary; Philip Talbot [1966] Director/Accountant

Lumenpulse Alphaled Limited
Incorporated: 23 June 2014 *Employees:* 70
Net Worth Deficit: £2,107,000 *Total Assets:* £12,643,000
Registered Office: 4th Avenue, The Village, Trafford Park, Manchester, M17 1DB
Activities: Manufacture of electric lighting equipment
Officers: Marilyn Mauricio, Secretary; Pierre Larochelle [1972] Director [Canadian]; Francois Xavier Souvay [1970] Director [Canadian]; Peter Timotheatos [1970] Director [Canadian]

Lumenpulse UK Limited
Incorporated: 12 September 2011
Net Worth: £4,531,555 *Total Assets:* £7,979,586
Registered Office: 4th Avenue, The Village, Trafford Park, Manchester, M17 1DB
Activities: Manufacture of electric lighting equipment
Officers: Marilyn Mauricio, Secretary; Pierre Larochelle [1972] Director [Canadian]; Francois Xavier Souvay [1970] Director [Canadian]; Peter Timotheatos [1970] Director [Canadian]

Lunar Caravans Limited
Incorporated: 16 July 1962 *Employees:* 258
Net Worth: £3,977,324 *Total Assets:* £15,026,764
Registered Office: Sherdley Road, Lostock Hall, Preston, Lancs, PR5 5JF
Activities: Manufacture of caravans
Parent: Lunar Holdings Limited
Officers: Lee Thomas Roberts, Secretary; Brian Stanley Mellor [1957] Managing Director; Darryl Brian Mellor [1982] Design & Development Director; Lee Thomas Roberts [1972] Financial Director

Lunar Holdings Limited
Incorporated: 23 October 2007 *Employees:* 258
Net Worth: £3,030,721 *Total Assets:* £15,768,404
Registered Office: Sherdley Road, Lostock Hall, Preston, Lancs, PR5 5JF
Activities: Other business support service activities n.e.c.
Major Shareholder: Brian Stanley Mellor
Officers: Lee Thomas Roberts, Secretary; Brian Stanley Mellor [1957] Managing Director; Susan Norma Mellor [1959] Director

Lunesdale Learning Trust
Incorporated: 12 November 2010 *Employees:* 257
Net Worth: £12,338,691 *Total Assets:* £17,229,258
Registered Office: Queen Elizabeth School, Kirkby Lonsdale, Cumbria, LA6 2HJ
Activities: General secondary education
Officers: Angela Clare Johnson, Secretary; Dr Sally Elizabeth Chalcraft [1962] Director/Lecturer; Christopher Clarke [1953] Director/Headteacher; Margaret Mary Cunningham [1947] Director; Walter Stewart Lawrenson [1951] Director/Self Employed Builder; Stephen Andrew Nelson [1966] Director/Bank Manager; Fenner James Pearson [1966] Director; Tyrone James Power [1941] Retired Director; Dr Richard Julian Shepherd [1944] Director

Luteaim Limited
Incorporated: 15 February 1989
Registered Office: 12-14a Bath Street, Hale, Cheshire, WA14 2EJ
Activities: Other service activities n.e.c.
Parent: County Car and Van Hire Manchester Limited
Officers: John Everett Briggs [1955] Finance Director; David Orritt [1960] Sales Director

Luton Engineering Services (Southwest) Limited
Incorporated: 31 January 2003
Net Worth: £1,738,598 *Total Assets:* £8,955,145
Registered Office: 16 Robert Street, Manchester, M3 1EY
Activities: Construction of other civil engineering projects n.e.c.
Major Shareholder: Henry Jones Awuku Aboagye
Officers: Mohammad Anwar, Secretary; Shirley Russell Aboagye [1986] Director/Student [Ghanaian]; Ofori Amaning [1952] Director/Manager; Mohammad Anwar [1944] Director; Mohammad Azhar [1955] Director

Luxfer Gas Cylinders Limited
Incorporated: 27 May 1997 *Employees:* 322
Net Worth: £11,620,000 *Total Assets:* £35,073,000
Registered Office: Lumns Lane, Manchester, M27 8LN
Activities: Manufacture of other tanks, reservoirs and containers of metal
Parent: Luxfer Group 2000 Limited
Officers: Jamie Mark Savage, Secretary; Andrew William John Butcher [1968] Director/Divisional President [American]; Alok Maskara [1971] Director/Chief Executive [American]; Stephen Mark Dale Webster [1971] Director/Group Financial Controller

Luxfer Group 2000 Limited
Incorporated: 4 July 2000
Net Worth: £124,180,000 *Total Assets:* £138,516,000
Registered Office: Lumns Lane, Manchester, M27 8LN
Activities: Activities of head offices
Parent: Luxfer Holdings PLC
Officers: Jamie Mark Savage, Secretary; Alok Maskara [1971] Director/Chief Executive [American]; Jamie Mark Savage [1978] Director/Company Secretary; Stephen Mark Dale Webster [1971] Director/Group Financial Controller

Luxfer Group Limited
Incorporated: 9 March 2000 *Employees:* 19
Net Worth: £19,751,000 *Total Assets:* £62,291,000
Registered Office: Lumns Lane, Manchester, M27 8LN
Activities: Activities of head offices
Parent: Luxfer Holdings PLC
Officers: Jamie Mark Savage, Secretary; Peter Nicholas Gibbons [1970] Director; Alok Maskara [1971] Director/Chief Executive [American]; Claire Louise Swarbrick [1974] Director/General Counsel; Stephen Mark Dale Webster [1971] Director/Group Financial Controller

Luxfer Holdings PLC
Incorporated: 31 December 1998 *Employees:* 1,658
Net Worth: £115,655,952 *Total Assets:* £286,895,168
Registered Office: Lumns Lane, Manchester, M27 8LN
Activities: Activities of head offices
Officers: Jamie Mark Savage, Secretary; Joseph Allison Bonn [1943] Director/Consultant [American]; Adam Cohn [1971] Director [American]; David Farrington Landless [1960] Director/Accountant; Alok Maskara [1971] Director/Chief Executive [American]; Clive John Snowdon [1953] Director

Luxfer Overseas Holdings Limited
Incorporated: 14 July 1995
Net Worth: £15,910,000 *Total Assets:* £25,928,000
Registered Office: Lumns Lane, Manchester, M27 8LN
Activities: Activities of head offices
Parent: Luxfer Group 2000 Limited
Officers: Jamie Mark Savage, Secretary; Alok Maskara [1971] Director/Chief Executive [American]; Jamie Mark Savage [1978] Director/Company Secretary; Stephen Mark Dale Webster [1971] Director/Group Financial Controller

Luxury Fibres Limited
Incorporated: 3 December 2007 *Employees:* 31
Net Worth: £32 *Total Assets:* £9,774,231
Registered Office: Ladywell Mills, Hall Lane, Bradford, W Yorks, BD4 7DF
Activities: Other business support service activities n.e.c.
Parent: SIL Holdings Limited
Officers: Andrew David Seal [1957] Director; Jeremy Charles Seal [1960] Director

LVMH Watch & Jewellery (UK) Limited
Incorporated: 5 March 1982 *Employees:* 147
Net Worth: £14,208,647 *Total Assets:* £34,843,552
Registered Office: Duval House, 16-18 Harcourt Street, Worsley, Manchester, M28 5GN
Activities: Retail sale of watches and jewellery in specialised stores
Parent: Timecrown Limited
Officers: Julie Jeanne Bourgeois, Secretary; Olivier Pierre Carrive [1955] Director [French]; Robert Diver [1965] Director; Michel Mousselon [1954] Director/Chief Financial Officer [French]

LW Finance Limited
Incorporated: 23 September 2002 *Employees:* 4
Net Worth: £200,722,000 *Total Assets:* £200,722,000
Registered Office: First Floor, Skyways House, Speke Road, Speke, Liverpool, L70 1AB
Activities: Activities of head offices
Parent: Shop Direct Limited
Officers: Aidan Stuart Barclay [1956] Director; Howard Myles Barclay [1959] Director/Financier Technical Consultant; Philip Leslie Peters [1957] Banker Director; Michael Seal [1948] Director/Chartered Accountant

LW Investments Limited
Incorporated: 2 August 2002 *Employees:* 4
Net Worth: £249,112,992 *Total Assets:* £439,295,008
Registered Office: First Floor, Skyways House, Speke Road, Speke, Liverpool, L70 1AB
Activities: Activities of head offices
Parent: LW Finance Limited
Officers: Aidan Stuart Barclay [1956] Director; Howard Myles Barclay [1959] Director/Financier Technical Consultant; Philip Leslie Peters [1957] Banker Director; Michael Seal [1948] Director/Chartered Accountant

LWC Drinks Limited
Incorporated: 21 June 2011 *Employees:* 724
Net Worth: £31,397,912 *Total Assets:* £72,563,552
Registered Office: Unit 3 Stainburn Road, Openshaw, Manchester, M11 2DN
Activities: Wholesale of wine, beer, spirits and other alcoholic beverages
Parent: Licensed Wholesale Company Limited
Officers: Peter Douglas Sumner, Secretary; Robin MacEwan Gray [1951] Director; Ebrahim Kassam Mukadam [1957] Director

Lydall Industrial Filtration Textile Manufacturing (EMEA) Limited
Incorporated: 17 December 1998 *Employees:* 82
Net Worth: £5,171,916 *Total Assets:* £10,283,280
Registered Office: 3rd Floor, 1 Ashley Road, Altrincham, Cheshire, WA14 2DT
Activities: Manufacture of non-wovens and articles made from non-wovens, except apparel
Parent: Lydall UK Ltd
Officers: Chad Allen McDaniel, Secretary; Dale Gregory Barnhart [1952] Director/Chief Executive Officer [American]; Andrew Victor Gibson [1967] Financial Director; David Noel Kirby [1962] Manufacturing Director

Lydall UK Ltd
Incorporated: 17 January 2014 *Employees:* 2
Net Worth: £18,429,696 *Total Assets:* £34,651,852
Registered Office: 3rd Floor, 1 Ashley Road, Altrincham, Cheshire, WA14 2DT
Activities: Activities of other holding companies n.e.c.
Parent: Lydall, Inc.
Officers: Chad Allen McDaniel, Secretary; Dale Gregory Barnhart [1952] Director/Chief Executive Officer [American]; Andrew Victor Gibson [1967] Financial Director

Lydiate Learning Trust
Incorporated: 8 August 2011 *Employees:* 340
Net Worth: £35,983,000 *Total Assets:* £43,265,000
Registered Office: Deyes High School, Deyes Lane, Maghull, Merseyside, L31 6DE
Activities: General secondary education
Officers: Deborah Jayne Moss, Secretary; John Graham [1961] Finance Director; Helen Ruth Heap [1966] Director; Graham Hewer [1951] Director/Retired Headteacher; John Malcolm Pearce [1956] Director/Senior Leader/Consultant; Louise Rooney [1979] HR Director; Ann Springford Stahler [1964] Director/Executive Headteacher

Lymm High School
Incorporated: 7 August 2012 *Employees:* 202
Net Worth: £25,519,926 *Total Assets:* £28,013,970
Registered Office: Lymm High School, Oughtrington Lane, Lymm, Cheshire, WA13 0RB
Activities: General secondary education
Officers: Helena Jayne Headon, Secretary; Ruth Isobel Ball [1962] Director/Head of Student Services; Cllr Kathryn Joan Buckley [1957] Director; Len Davies [1955] Director/Assistant Headteacher; Simon French [1957] Director/Engineer; Michael Adrian Gare [1970] Director; Julia Graham [1969] Director/Solicitor; Elizabeth Anne Green [1964] Voluntary Work/Non-Executive Director; David Winston Hester [1972] Director/Independent Financial Adviser; Emma Hutchison [1973] Director; Rev Beverley Jameson [1960] Director/Reverend; Ingolf Kirsten [1972] Director; Rebecca Knowles [1964] Director/Solicitor; Dr Christine Jane McLean [1967] Director; Yvonne Poskitt [1961] Director; Victoria Louise Proctor [1974] Director; Robin Spencer [1978] Director; Lauren Elizabeth Thomason [1975] Director; Dr Kieran Walshe [1964] Director/Academic; Gwyn Williams [1978] Director/Headteacher; Nicola Woodyatt [1968] Director/Forensic Scientist

Lyndhurst Shoe Company Limited
Incorporated: 18 November 1996 *Employees:* 13
Net Worth: £9,701,546 *Total Assets:* £16,431,089
Registered Office: 1-7 Fallbarn Road, Rawtenstall, Rossendale, Lancs, BB4 7NT
Activities: Non-specialised wholesale trade
Shareholders: Ashley Anne Morley-Doidge; Rumer Lauren Morley; LSC Group Limited
Officers: Lyn Hunter, Secretary; Anne Marie Morley [1956] Director; Rumer Lauren Morley [1991] Director; Shaun Morley [1966] Managing Director; Ashley Anne Morley-Doidge [1985] Director; Adam Mark Turner [1987] Director

Lyon Equipment Limited
Incorporated: 27 September 1995 *Employees:* 84
Net Worth: £11,923,247 *Total Assets:* £13,146,297
Registered Office: Units 3-7 Tebay Business Park, Old Tebay, Penrith, Cumbria, CA10 3SS
Activities: Manufacture of other wearing apparel and accessories n.e.c.
Shareholder: Malcolm Kensington Lyon
Officers: Francis Raymond Bennett [1951] Sales & Marketing Director; Tina Elizabeth Benson [1957] Finance Director; Jonathan Broughton Capper [1962] Managing Director - Technical; Malcolm Kensington Lyon [1939] Managing Director; Carol Anne Nicholls [1958] Commercial Director

Lyons Holiday Park Limited
Incorporated: 27 July 1981 *Employees:* 258
Net Worth: £42,986,600 *Total Assets:* £66,879,016
Registered Office: c/o Champion Allwoods Limited, 2nd Floor, Refuge House, 33-37 Watergate Row, Chester, CH1 2LE
Activities: Holiday centres and villages
Major Shareholder: Geoffery Lyons Mound
Officers: Laura Mound, Secretary; Joseph Frank Lyons Mound [1979] Director; Geoffrey Lyons Mound [1945] Director; Laura Mound [1949] Director; Geoffrey Frank Lyons Mound Jnr [1976] Director

M & A Pharmachem Limited
Incorporated: 1 February 1977 *Employees:* 119
Net Worth: £11,723,827 *Total Assets:* £18,205,124
Registered Office: Allenby Laboratories, Wigan Road, Westhoughton, Bolton, Lancs, BL5 2AL
Activities: Manufacture of basic pharmaceutical products
Shareholder: CD Medical Limited
Officers: Lee Fairbrother, Secretary; Elsie Maureen Armstrong [1951] Director; Michael Gatenby [1942] Sales & Marketing Director; Gerard Michael Dominic Pessagno [1952] Director

M & I Materials Limited
Incorporated: 11 December 1992 *Employees:* 146
Net Worth: £16,215,223 *Total Assets:* £24,230,452
Registered Office: Hibernia Way, Trafford Park, Manchester, M32 0ZD
Activities: Manufacture of other chemical products n.e.c.
Officers: Ellen Christina Maria Salt-Melis, Secretary [Dutch]; Colin John Salt [1942] Managing Director; Giles John Salt [1969] Managing Director; Ellen Christina Maria Salt-Melis [1944] Director and Company Secretary [Dutch]; Stephen Philip Sheard [1956] Finance Director

M & S Logistics Limited
Incorporated: 14 July 1998 *Employees:* 79
Net Worth: £1,786,244 *Total Assets:* £18,954,086
Registered Office: Hope Street Chapel, Hope Street, Sandbach, Cheshire, CW11 1BA
Activities: Sea and coastal freight water transport
Major Shareholder: David Frederick Jenkins
Officers: Wolfgang Gill [1957] Director [German]; David Richard Kew [1974] Director/Manager [South African]; John James Risbridger [1951] Director; Robert Neil Surman [1949] Director/Chartered Accountant; Louwrens Martinus Verwey [1983] Director [South African]

M C D Manchester Limited
Incorporated: 10 February 2010 *Employees:* 855
Net Worth: £2,642,040 *Total Assets:* £10,793,262
Registered Office: 243 Barlow Moor Road, Chorlton, Manchester, M21 7QL
Activities: Unlicenced restaurants and cafes
Major Shareholder: Roger Najib Khoryati
Officers: Jean Elizabeth Mary Khoryati [1969] Director; Roger Najib Khoryati [1964] Director

M N Holdings Limited
Incorporated: 23 February 2005 *Employees:* 127
Net Worth: £9,753,843 *Total Assets:* £14,659,411
Registered Office: Cromer Street, Newbridge Lane, Stockport, Cheshire, SK1 2NP
Activities: Activities of other holding companies n.e.c.
Shareholders: Gary Edwin Rhodes; Edwin Rhodes
Officers: Andrea Carole Rhodes, Secretary; Edwin Rhodes [1927] Director/Engineer; Gary Edwin Rhodes [1961] Director

M-Hance Group Limited
Incorporated: 25 March 2010 *Employees:* 140
Net Worth: £220,826 *Total Assets:* £8,068,788
Registered Office: Trinity House, Bredbury Park Way, Stockport, Cheshire, SK6 2SN
Activities: Activities of head offices
Major Shareholder: Jonathan Paul Moulton
Officers: Robert Alexander Asplin [1979] Director; Timothy Darbyshire [1963] Director; Simon Haigh [1966] Director; Alan John Moody [1970] Director

M-Hance Limited
Incorporated: 23 May 1978 *Employees:* 125
Net Worth Deficit: £5,379,417 *Total Assets:* £8,233,733
Registered Office: Trinity House, Bredbury Park Way, Stockport, Cheshire, SK6 2SN
Activities: Business and domestic software development
Parent: M-Hance Group Ltd
Officers: Robert Alexander Asplin [1979] Director; Timothy Darbyshire [1963] Director; Simon Haigh [1966] Director; Alan John Moody [1970] Director

M. & W. Freight Limited
Incorporated: 21 June 1979 *Employees:* 34
Net Worth: £2,663,276 *Total Assets:* £6,752,356
Registered Office: Northern Assurance Building, 9-21 Princess Street, Manchester, M2 4DN
Activities: Other transportation support activities
Shareholders: Samuel Brian Jones; Granville Parkinson
Officers: Deborah Presley, Secretary; Terry Humphrey [1942] Director/Chartered Accountant; Martin Roy Jones [1964] Director; Wayne Mather [1969] Director; Granville Parkinson [1960] Director; Kay Elisabeth Walsh [1971] Director

M. Sport Limited
Incorporated: 2 March 1987 *Employees:* 262
Net Worth: £35,983,076 *Total Assets:* £49,943,060
Registered Office: c/o Trevor Jones, Rowan Court, Concord Business Park, Threapwood Road, Manchester, M22 0RR
Activities: Other sports activities
Officers: Elaine Wilson, Secretary; John Steele [1955] Commercial Director; Elaine Wilson [1961] Director/Secretary; Malcolm Irving Wilson [1956] Director; Matthew James Wilson [1987] Director

M.& N.Textiles Limited
Incorporated: 23 July 1959 *Employees:* 16
Net Worth: £10,442,768 *Total Assets:* £10,667,536
Registered Office: 10 Riverview, The Embankment, Vale Road, Heaton Mersey, Stockport, Cheshire, SK4 3GN
Activities: Wholesale of textiles
Parent: Wrengate Limited
Officers: Souad Musry, Secretary; Alan Philip David Musry [1963] Director/Accountant; Ronald Musry [1935] Director; Souad Musry [1936] Director/Company Secretary

M.A.C. (Roofing & Contracting) Limited
Incorporated: 1 September 1975 *Employees:* 40
Net Worth: £2,645,285 *Total Assets:* £8,593,269
Registered Office: No 17 Moor Park Avenue, Preston, Lancs, PR1 6AS
Activities: Roofing activities
Parent: Chellaton Ltd
Officers: Peter Morana, Secretary; Lee Cavanagh [1986] Director; Terence Roy Cavanagh [1981] Director

M.A.X. Funding Limited
Incorporated: 15 January 2013 *Employees:* 2
Net Worth: £58,481,576 *Total Assets:* £62,045,040
Registered Office: Greylands, Macclesfield Road, Alderley Edge, Cheshire, SK9 7BS
Activities: Other credit granting n.e.c.
Shareholder: Myrna Madeleine Essayan
Officers: Beryl Essayan [1934] Director; Max Lucas Essayan [1933] Director; Myrna Madeleine Essayan [1937] Director; Jacqueline Clare Wortley [1961] Director

M.B.C.Investments Limited
Incorporated: 24 November 1927 *Employees:* 2
Net Worth: £5,708,423 *Total Assets:* £6,632,983
Registered Office: Unit 3a Lakeland Business Park, Lamplugh Road, Cockermouth, Cumbria, CA13 0QT
Activities: Other letting and operating of own or leased real estate
Major Shareholder: Peter William Bailey
Officers: Peter William Bailey, Secretary; Elizabeth Louise Bailey [1951] Director/Counsellor; Emma Jane Bailey [1979] Director/Chartered Surveyor; Peter William Bailey [1947] Director/Solicitor

M.G.F. (Trench Construction Systems) Limited
Incorporated: 18 February 1981 *Employees:* 322
Net Worth: £25,056,670 *Total Assets:* £35,941,648
Registered Office: Grant House, South Lancashire Ind Est, Lockett Road, Ashton in Makerfield, Wigan, Lancs, WN4 8DE
Activities: Renting and leasing of construction and civil engineering machinery and equipment
Parent: MGF Ltd
Officers: Generald Nowicki, Secretary; Kevin Laurence Clarke [1958] Director Northern; Stephen Douglas Hesketh [1963] Director; Ian David Jones [1958] Director; Simon James Littlewood [1972] Director; Generald Nowicki [1959] Director/Chartered Accountant; Michael O'Hara [1945] Director

M.G.S. Estates Limited
Incorporated: 17 August 1988 *Employees:* 3
Net Worth: £273,945 *Total Assets:* £7,080,928
Registered Office: 70 Barton Arcade Chambers, St Ann's Square, Manchester, M3 2BJ
Activities: Other letting and operating of own or leased real estate
Parent: U.K. Retail Investments Limited
Officers: John Simon Gradel [1962] Director; Robert Gradel [1968] Director/Solicitor

M.J.C. Developments Limited
Incorporated: 11 July 1991 *Employees:* 2
Net Worth: £8,004,465 *Total Assets:* £9,680,337
Registered Office: 15a School Street Trading Estate, Hazel Grove, Stockport, Cheshire, SK7 4RA
Activities: Development of building projects
Officers: Madalane Cundiff, Secretary; Keilly Jane Barnes [1976] Director; Richard James Cundiff [1979] Director

M1 RE Manchester Limited
Incorporated: 6 December 2013
Net Worth: £9,262,962 *Total Assets:* £24,941,078
Registered Office: Motel One Manchester-Royal Exchange, 11-15 Cross Street, Manchester, M2 1WD
Activities: Hotels and similar accommodation
Officers: Stefan Florian Lenze, Secretary; Stefan Florian Lenze [1974] Director/Lawyer [German]; Daniel Norman Müller [1978] Director [German]; Dieter Müller [1954] Director [German]; Armin Rödel [1971] Finance Director [German]; Ursula Sophie Schelle-Müller [1965] Director [German]; Franz Josef Wiessler [1950] Director [German]

M2 Digital Limited
Incorporated: 22 December 1992 *Employees:* 249
Net Worth: £16,847,000 *Total Assets:* £34,688,000
Registered Office: Brightgate House, Cobra Court, Brightgate Way, Manchester, M32 0TB
Activities: Other business support service activities n.e.c.
Parent: M2 Smile Limited
Officers: Damien Baker [1970] Director; John Patrick Higham [1966] Finance Director; James Peter Rigby [1971] Director; Steven Paul Rigby [1972] Director; Michael Joseph Swain [1964] Director; John Paul Taylor [1970] Managing Director

M2 Managed Document Services Ltd
Incorporated: 12 May 1999 *Employees:* 104
Net Worth: £6,903,346 *Total Assets:* £8,024,735
Registered Office: Brightgate House, Brightgate Way, Stretford, Manchester, M32 0TB
Activities: Other professional, scientific and technical activities n.e.c.
Shareholders: M2 Digital Limited; M2 Digital Limited
Officers: Simon Kelly [1972] Director/Business Manager; James Peter Rigby [1971] Director; Steven Paul Rigby [1972] Director; John Paul Taylor [1970] Director

M2 Smile Limited
Incorporated: 28 April 2006 *Employees:* 3
Net Worth: £6,752,000 *Total Assets:* £21,775,000
Registered Office: Brightgate House, Cobra Court, Brightgate Way, Manchester, M32 0TB
Activities: Other business support service activities n.e.c.
Parent: Specialist Computer Centres PLC
Officers: James Peter Rigby [1971] Director; Steven Paul Rigby [1972] Director; John Paul Taylor [1970] Managing Director

M247 Ltd
Incorporated: 18 November 2003 *Employees:* 33
Net Worth: £3,362,000 *Total Assets:* £6,855,000
Registered Office: Turing House, Archway 5, Manchester, M15 5RL
Activities: Information technology consultancy activities
Parent: Manchester Metronet Limited
Officers: Warren Ashcroft [1988] Director; Christopher George Byrd [1984] Director; Andrew Geoffrey Goldwater [1974] Director; Paul Pintiliescu [1987] Director [Romanian]; James Paul Smith [1986] Director

M53 Motors Limited
Incorporated: 10 August 1984 *Employees:* 75
Net Worth: £7,888,000 *Total Assets:* £15,711,000
Registered Office: Rossmore, Road East, Ellesmere Port, Cheshire, CH65 3BR
Activities: Sale of new cars and light motor vehicles
Officers: Carole Marsden, Secretary; Carole Marsden [1962] Director/Accountant; Carol Patricia McPhail [1953] Director/Company Secretary; Mark McPhail [1975] Director; Thomas James Allan McPhail [1954] Director; Philip Vaill [1965] Director/Sales Manager

The Macclesfield Academy
Incorporated: 8 April 2011 *Employees:* 72
Net Worth: £8,316,000 *Total Assets:* £10,361,000
Registered Office: Macclesfield College, Park Lane, Macclesfield, Cheshire, SK11 8LF
Activities: General secondary education
Officers: Jeremy John Green [1958] Director; Professor Alistair Gordon Sutcliffe [1951] Director/Retired; Anne Merle Thomson [1953] Director

MacDermid Canning Limited
Incorporated: 28 October 1955 *Employees:* 39
Net Worth: £14,532,000 *Total Assets:* £54,399,000
Registered Office: Cale Lane, New Springs, Wigan, Lancs, WN2 1JT
Activities: Manufacture of other chemical products n.e.c.
Parent: MacDermid Europe Limited
Officers: Simon Paul McManus [1966] Technical Director; Stephen Martin Oconnor [1968] Operations Director

MacDermid Graphics Solutions UK Limited
Incorporated: 17 December 2004 *Employees:* 41
Net Worth: £8,354,000 *Total Assets:* £9,562,000
Registered Office: Cale Lane, New Springs, Wigan, Lancs, WN2 1JT
Activities: Other manufacturing n.e.c.
Parent: MacDermid Canning Limited
Officers: John Edward Capps, Secretary; John Edward Capps [1964] Director [American]; Stephen Martin O'Connor [1968] Operations Director

Mackintosh Limited
Incorporated: 15 February 1974 *Employees:* 166
Net Worth: £11,982,784 *Total Assets:* £16,266,956
Registered Office: Mackintosh House, Waterford, Street, Nelson, Lancs, BB9 8AQ
Activities: Manufacture of other men's outerwear
Parent: Yagi Tsusho Limited
Officers: William John Burnett, Secretary; Kazuichi Nomura [1956] Managing Director [Japanese]; William Bryce Ross [1954] Director; Takayuki Seimiya [1976] Director [Japanese]; Satoshi Sumiyoshi [1956] Director [Japanese]; Yozo Yagi [1974] Director [Japanese]; Yuzo Yagi [1941] Director [Japanese]

MacKnight Holdings Limited
Incorporated: 19 March 2004 *Employees:* 132
Net Worth: £19,183,400 *Total Assets:* £22,926,030
Registered Office: Unit 14 Solway Industrial Estate, Maryport, Cumbria, CA15 8NF
Activities: Activities of head offices
Officers: Jonathan Seeker Reed Brown [1967] Director; Stephen Timothy Rose [1967] Director; Wayne Anthony Strudwick [1964] Director [American]

MacKnight Limited
Incorporated: 30 March 2010 *Employees:* 132
Net Worth: £4,625,899 *Total Assets:* £7,322,963
Registered Office: Unit 200, 17 Solway Industrial Estate, Maryport, Cumbria, CA15 8NF
Activities: Processing and preserving of fish, crustaceans and molluscs
Parent: MacKnight Holdings Limited
Officers: Jonathan Brown [1967] Director; Stephen Timothy Rose [1967] Director

Macmaster Properties Limited
Incorporated: 11 March 1981 *Employees:* 10
Net Worth: £3,944,693 *Total Assets:* £9,632,348
Registered Office: Incom House, Waterside, Trafford Park, Manchester, M17 1WD
Activities: Other letting and operating of own or leased real estate
Shareholders: Barbara Mary Shuttleworth; Linda Janet Macmaster
Officers: Linda Janet Macmaster, Secretary/Director; Douglas Alan Macmaster [1976] Director; Graham Ian Fergus Macmaster [1977] Director; Linda Janet Macmaster [1943] Director

Magellan Robotech Limited
Incorporated: 22 April 1997 *Employees:* 133
Net Worth: £1,648,000 *Total Assets:* £11,607,000
Registered Office: Exchange Station, Tithebarn Street, Liverpool, L2 2QP
Activities: Ready-made interactive leisure and entertainment software development
Parent: Interbets Limited
Officers: William Lymbery Bland [1950] Director/Chartered Accountant; Dr Giovanni Garrisi [1948] Director; John Samuel Whittaker [1950] Director

Maghull High School
Incorporated: 8 September 2011 *Employees:* 113
Net Worth: £5,258,577 *Total Assets:* £8,285,272
Registered Office: Maghull High School, Ormonde Drive, Maghull, Merseyside, L31 7AW
Activities: General secondary education
Officers: Valerie Ann Leatherbarrow, Secretary; Jacqueline Maria Aspinall [1976] Director/Teacher; Joanna Bailey [1963] Director/Higher Level Teaching Assistant; Victoria Garside [1974] Director/Investigations Officer; Councillor Geoffrey George Howe [1948] Director; Christopher Robert Hurst [1972] Director/Teacher; Carol Maudsley [1971] Director/HMRC Tax Officer; Julie McDowall [1973] Director/HMRC Tax Officer; Dorothy May Rigby [1939] Director; Karen Anne Rowlands [1961] Director/Administrative Assistant; Dorothy Margaret Thorne [1941] Director/Travel Assistant

Magna Exteriors (Liverpool) Limited
Incorporated: 12 October 1998 *Employees:* 382
Net Worth: £20,691,000 *Total Assets:* £50,975,000
Registered Office: Renaissance Way, Boulevard Industry Park, Liverpool, L24 9PL
Activities: Manufacture of other parts and accessories for motor vehicles
Parent: Magna International Inc
Officers: Alexej Seitz, Secretary; Grahame Keith Burrow [1963] Director [Canadian]; Alexej Seitz [1965] Director/Lawyer [German]; Mark John Smith [1968] Director

Magnesium Elektron Limited
Incorporated: 28 December 1995 *Employees:* 262
Net Worth: £77,722,000 *Total Assets:* £111,002,000
Registered Office: Lumns Lane, Manchester, M27 8LN
Activities: Manufacture of other inorganic basic chemicals
Parent: Luxfer Group Limited
Officers: Jamie Mark Savage, Secretary; Chris Allen Barnes [1955] Director/Divisional President [American]; Alok Maskara [1971] Director/Chief Executive [American]; Graham David Wardlow [1968] Managing Director; Stephen Mark Dale Webster [1971] Director/Group Financial Controller

W. Maher & Sons Limited
Incorporated: 25 July 1974 *Employees:* 85
Net Worth: £20,350,940 *Total Assets:* £35,824,896
Registered Office: Rixton Old Hall, Manchester Road, Rixton, Warrington, Cheshire, WA3 6EW
Activities: Other specialised construction activities n.e.c.
Officers: Brendan James Maher, Secretary; Brendan James Maher [1960] Director; Callum James Maher [1985] Director; Gerard Majella Maher [1959] Director/Civil Engineer; Matthew William Maher [1988] Director

Majorstage Limited
Incorporated: 1 May 1998 *Employees:* 146
Net Worth: £11,418,199 *Total Assets:* £17,762,692
Registered Office: Peckforton Castle, Stone House, Lane Peckforton, Tarporley, Cheshire, CW6 9TN
Activities: Hotels and similar accommodation
Parent: Boutique Hotel Group Limited
Officers: Kate Jayne Naylor, Secretary; Michael Auld [1981] Director/General Manager; Christopher James Naylor [1978] Director; Georgina Ann Naylor [1951] Director; Kate Jayne Naylor [1982] Director; Matthew Richard Naylor [1979] Sales Director; Richard Anthony Naylor [1948] Managing Director

Makemore Limited
Incorporated: 6 July 1998 *Employees:* 211
Net Worth: £5,222,159 *Total Assets:* £14,201,478
Registered Office: Bee Mill, Shaw Road, Royton, Oldham, Lancs, OL2 6EH
Activities: Non-trading company
Major Shareholder: Alan Rothwell
Officers: Robert Keith Anderson, Secretary; Alan Rothwell [1956] Director

Makin Metal Powders (UK) Limited
Incorporated: 25 August 2009 *Employees:* 44
Net Worth: £6,692,715 *Total Assets:* £12,145,748
Registered Office: Buckley Road, Rochdale, Lancs, OL12 9DT
Activities: Copper production
Officers: Stephen John Ellis [1963] Sales & Technical Director; Jonathan Rhys Hood [1961] Director; Songtao Huang [1963] Director/Vice President [Chinese]; Dr Limin Wang [1964] Director/General Manager [Chinese]; Philip Andrew Wilcock [1976] Director/Certified Chartered Accountant; Zhenyu Yan [1976] Marketing Director [Chinese]

Making Space
Incorporated: 8 June 1982 *Employees:* 995
Net Worth: £17,255,762 *Total Assets:* £19,821,792
Registered Office: 46 Allen Street, Warrington, Cheshire, WA2 7JB
Activities: Hospital activities
Officers: Anthony Wyn Jones, Secretary; Neil Allen [1977] Director/Barrister; Anne Josephine Broadhurst [1944] Director/Retired; John Heritage [1974] Director of Business Development; Stephen Allen Hull [1963] Director/Consultant; Elaine Johnstone [1966] Director/Senior Manager, NHS Commissioning Support Unit; Brian Robert Marshall [1955] Director; Edward Michael McGuinness [1948] Director; Alan Richard Teague [1947] Director/Retired

Makro Limited
Incorporated: 28 May 1946 *Employees:* 2
Net Worth: £2,386,000 *Total Assets:* £25,125,000
Registered Office: 1 Scott Place, 2 Hardman Street, Manchester, M3 3AA
Activities: Other business support service activities n.e.c.
Parent: Makro Cash & Carry UK Holding Limited
Officers: Imke Butefisch [1970] Director/Accounting Manager [German]; Juergen Schwarze [1967] Director [German]

Malcolm Properties Limited
Incorporated: 10 August 1921 *Employees:* 5
Net Worth: £34,719,000 *Total Assets:* £90,617,000
Registered Office: Unit B, Haydock Cross Industrial Estate, Kilbuck Lane, St Helens, Merseyside, WA11 9UX
Activities: Activities of head offices
Officers: Charles Roderick Stewart, Secretary/Chartered Accountant; David William Archer [1969] Finance Director; Martin Kiely [1963] Director/Civil Engineer; Andrew Buchanan Malcolm [1962] Managing Director; Walter Hattrick Malcolm [1960] Director/Haulage Contractor; Alan Charles Palmer [1962] Finance Director

Malling Health (UK) Limited
Incorporated: 30 September 2009 *Employees:* 378
Net Worth: £5,597,479 *Total Assets:* £11,549,537
Registered Office: 10th Floor, 1 City Approach, Albert Street, Eccles, Manchester, M30 0BG
Activities: Other business support service activities n.e.c.
Parent: Malling Health Limited
Officers: Dr Martyn David Diaper [1966] Director/General Practitioner; Jason Antony Zemmel [1971] Director/Chief Executive

J.Mallinson (Ormskirk) Limited
Incorporated: 9 June 1961 *Employees:* 43
Net Worth: £11,261,640 *Total Assets:* £13,617,510
Registered Office: Firtree Nurseries, Firswood Road, Lathom, Skelmersdale, Lancs, WN8 8UZ
Activities: Construction of other civil engineering projects n.e.c.
Shareholders: John Rowland Mallinson; Olive Mabel Mallinson
Officers: Olive Mabel Mallinson, Secretary; John Rowland Mallinson [1940] Director/Sport & Landscape Contractor; Olive Mabel Mallinson [1940] Director/Company Secretary

Maltacourt Group Limited
Incorporated: 13 April 2011 *Employees:* 155
Net Worth: £6,912,451 *Total Assets:* £19,758,912
Registered Office: Maltacourt House, Daresbury Court, Evenwood Close, Runcorn, Cheshire, WA7 1LZ
Activities: Activities of head offices
Major Shareholder: Matthew Paul Beech
Officers: Matthew Paul Beech [1970] Director

MAN Energy Solutions UK Limited
Incorporated: 1 May 1963 *Employees:* 228
Net Worth: £28,423,000 *Total Assets:* £58,188,000
Registered Office: 1 Mirrlees Drive, Hazel Grove, Stockport, Cheshire, SK7 5BP
Activities: Repair of machinery
Parent: MAN Energy Solutions SE
Officers: Ann Louise Durose, Secretary/Solicitor; Robin Wilhelm Sebastian Freiherr Von Plettenberg [1976] Sales Director [German]; Richard Colin Guest [1963] Managing Director; Wayne Jones [1966] Director; Per Rud Jorgensen [1965] Sales Director [Danish]; Michael Pfluger [1964] Finance Director [German]

Manchester Airport Finance Holdings Limited
Incorporated: 10 January 2013
Net Worth: £2,129,056,000 *Total Assets:* £2,494,245,888
Registered Office: 6th Floor, Olympic House, Manchester Airport, Manchester, M90 1QX
Activities: Activities of head offices
Parent: Manchester Airports Holdings Limited
Officers: Charles Thomas Cornish [1959] Director; Neil Philip Thompson [1971] Director/Accountant

Manchester Airport Group Finance Limited
Incorporated: 20 December 2012
Net Worth: £2,105,212,032 *Total Assets:* £3,146,976,000
Registered Office: 6th Floor, Olympic House, Manchester Airport, Manchester, M90 1QX
Activities: Activities of head offices
Parent: Manchester Airport Group Investments Limited
Officers: Charles Thomas Cornish [1959] Director; Neil Philip Thompson [1971] Director/Accountant

Manchester Airport Group Funding PLC
Incorporated: 27 December 2013
Net Worth: £63,000 *Total Assets:* £803,134,976
Registered Office: 6th Floor, Olympic House, Manchester Airport, Manchester, M90 1QX
Activities: Financial management
Parent: Manchester Airport Group Investments Limited
Officers: Brenda Louise Ruppel, Secretary; Charles Thomas Cornish [1959] Director; Neil Philip Thompson [1971] Director/Accountant

Manchester Airport Group Investments Limited
Incorporated: 20 December 2012 *Employees:* 5,184
Net Worth: £2,284,600,064 *Total Assets:* £3,841,999,872
Registered Office: 6th Floor, Olympic House, Manchester Airport, Manchester, M90 1QX
Activities: Activities of head offices
Parent: Manchester Airport Finance Holdings Limited
Officers: Charles Thomas Cornish [1959] Director; Neil Philip Thompson [1971] Director/Accountant

The Manchester Airport Group PLC
Incorporated: 28 November 2001 *Employees:* 506
Net Worth: £2,300,529,920 *Total Assets:* £2,815,237,888
Registered Office: Manchester Professional Services, P O Box 532, Town Hall, Manchester, M60 2LA
Activities: Service activities incidental to air transportation
Parent: Manchester Airport Group Investments Limited
Officers: Charles Thomas Cornish [1959] Director/Chief Executive; John Kenneth O'Toole [1974] Director [Irish]; Neil Philip Thompson [1971] Director

Manchester Airport Group Property Developments Limited
Incorporated: 26 November 2009 *Employees:* 16
Net Worth: £3,238,000 *Total Assets:* £37,019,000
Registered Office: 4th Floor, Olympic House, Manchester Airport, Manchester, M90 1QX
Activities: Development of building projects
Parent: Manchester Airport Group Finance Limited
Officers: Charles Thomas Cornish [1959] Director/Chief Executive; John Kenneth O'Toole [1974] Director [Irish]; Neil Philip Thompson [1971] Director

Manchester Airport Group Property Services Limited
Incorporated: 26 November 2009 *Employees:* 16
Net Worth: £2,168,000 *Total Assets:* £36,297,000
Registered Office: 4th Floor, Olympic House, Manchester Airport, Manchester, M90 1QX
Activities: Management of real estate on a fee or contract basis
Parent: Manchester Airport Group Finance Limited
Officers: Charles Thomas Cornish [1959] Director/Chief Executive; John Kenneth O'Toole [1974] Director [Irish]; Neil Philip Thompson [1971] Director

Manchester Airport PLC
Incorporated: 18 November 1985 *Employees:* 2,518
Net Worth: £1,237,216,000 *Total Assets:* £2,044,483,968
Registered Office: Sylvia Welsh, Professional Services Limited, P O Box 532, Town Hall, Manchester, M60 2LA
Activities: Scheduled passenger air transport
Parent: Manchester Airport Group Finance Limited
Officers: Charles Thomas Cornish [1959] Director/Chief Executive; Andrew David Cowan [1966] Director; John Kenneth O'Toole [1974] Director [Irish]; Neil Philip Thompson [1971] Director

Manchester Airports Holdings Limited
Incorporated: 9 January 2013 *Employees:* 5,188
Net Worth: £1,542,000,000 *Total Assets:* £3,323,800,064
Registered Office: 6th Floor, Olympic House, Manchester Airport, Manchester, M90 1QX
Activities: Activities of head offices
Shareholder: The Council of The City of Manchester
Officers: Brenda Louise Ruppel, Secretary; Charles Thomas Cornish [1959] Director; Andrew David Cowan [1966] Director; Sir Richard Charles Leese [1951] Director; Manoj Mehta [1970] Executive Director; Sir Adrian Alistair Montague [1948] Director; Vanda Murray [1960] Director; Robert Stewart Napier [1947] Director; John Kenneth O'Toole [1974] Director [Irish]; Councillor Bernard Priest [1949] Director/Councillor; Catherine Margaret Schefer [1968] Director; Christian Seymour [1964] Director/Investment Manager; Neil Philip Thompson [1971] Director/Accountant; Jonathan Leslie Wragg [1960] Director

Manchester and District Home for Lost Dogs Limited
Incorporated: 9 September 1966 *Employees:* 52
Net Worth: £8,443,410 *Total Assets:* £8,546,010
Registered Office: Crofters House, Moss Brook Road, Harpurhey, Manchester, M9 5PG
Activities: Veterinary activities
Officers: Terence James Askew, Secretary; Terence James Askew [1944] Director/Retired; Geoffrey Bridson [1941] Director/Retired; Jean Bridson [1938] Director; Maureen Fletcher [1939] Director/Retired; Josephine Jackson [1945] Director/Retired; Simon Stansfield [1978] Director/IT Governance Lead for a Bank; Clive Winterburn [1966] Director/Kennel Owner

Manchester Central Convention Complex Limited
Incorporated: 1 May 1969 *Employees:* 158
Net Worth: £31,565,000 *Total Assets:* £50,541,000
Registered Office: Manchester Central Convention Complex Limited, Windmill Street, Petersfield, Manchester, M2 3GX
Activities: Letting and operating of conference and exhibition centres
Parent: Destination Manchester Limited
Officers: Faye Laura Dyer, Secretary; Patricia Bartoli [1965] Director/Head of City Centre Regeneration; Charles Thomas Cornish [1959] Director/Chief Executive; Carol Ann Culley [1968] Director/City Treasurer; Faye Laura Dyer [1980] Finance Director; Shaun Charles Hinds [1968] Director/Chief Executive; Councillor Bernard Priest [1949] Director/Councillor

Manchester City Football Club Limited
Incorporated: 16 April 1894 *Employees:* 325
Net Worth: £678,204,032 *Total Assets:* £1,060,782,016
Registered Office: Etihad Stadium, Etihad Campus, Manchester, M11 3FF
Activities: Activities of sport clubs
Parent: Abu Dhabi United Group for Development & Investment
Officers: Simon Richard Cliff, Secretary; Abdulla Al Khouri [1974] Director/Government Employee [Emirati]; Mohamed Mubarak Al Mazrouei [1977] Director/Civil Servant [Emirati]; Khaldoon Khalifa Al Mubarak [1976] Director/Chairman [Emirati]; Martin Lee Edelman [1941] Director/Strategic Advisor [American]; Alberto Galassi [1964] Director/Chief Executive [Italian]; John Theodore MacBeath [1956] Director/Chartered Accountant; Simon Pearce [1971] Director

Manchester City Limited
Incorporated: 8 November 1994 *Employees:* 325
Net Worth: £678,208,000 *Total Assets:* £1,060,785,984
Registered Office: City Football HQ, 400 Ashton New Road, Manchester, M11 4TQ
Activities: Activities of sport clubs
Parent: Abu Dhabi United Group for Investment and Development
Officers: Simon Richard Cliff, Secretary; Mohamed Mubarak Al Mazrouei [1977] Director/Civil Servant [Emirati]; Khaldoon Khalifa Al Mubarak [1976] Director/Chairman [Emirati]; Martin Lee Edelman [1941] Director/Strategic Advisor [American]; Alberto Galassi [1964] Director/Chief Executive [Italian]; John Theodore MacBeath [1956] Director/Chartered Accountant; Simon Pearce [1971] Director

Manchester Diocesan Board of Education
Incorporated: 5 January 1959 *Employees:* 10
Net Worth: £4,818,296 *Total Assets:* £7,951,279
Registered Office: Church House, 90 Deansgate, Manchester, M3 2GH
Activities: Primary education
Officers: Maurice John Smith, Company Secretary; Marlene Armitage [1938] Director/Retired; The Revd Canon Dr Christopher Andrew Bracegirdle [1956] Director/Team Rector; The Right Reverend Mark Davies [1962] Director/Bishop of Middleton; Revd Edith Disley [1951] Director/Vicar; Dr Philip James Gooderson [1947] Director/Retired; Barbara Kellner [1953] Director/Headteacher; Richard James Charles Lait [1958] Director/Education Advisor; Karen Morris [1961] Director/Headmistress; Revd Karen Owen [1958] Director/Vicar; Revd Falak Sher [1965] Director/Vicar [Pakistani]; Nicholas Guy Smeeton [1974] Director/Parish Priest; David Stuart Walker [1957] Director/Diocesan Bishop; Harold Williams [1943] Director/Chief Education Officer; The Reverend Philip Howard Williamson [1959] Director/Headteacher; Peter Timothy Wright [1971] Director/Headmaster

Manchester Diocesan Board of Finance
Incorporated: 26 March 1918 *Employees:* 47
Net Worth: £57,040,000 *Total Assets:* £65,095,000
Registered Office: Church House, 90 Deansgate, Manchester, M3 2GH
Activities: Activities of religious organisations
Officers: David Weldon, Secretary; The Right Reverend Mark David Ashcroft [1954] Director/Clerk in Holy Orders; The Revd Canon Lisa Katherine Battye [1955] Director/Clerk in Holy Orders; Philip John Billson [1957] Director/Series Producer BBC; Phillip Steel Blinkhorn [1949] Director/Chartered Accountant; The Revd Canon Dr Christopher Andrew Bracegirdle [1956] Director/Team Rector; Jean Ann Burgess [1962] Director/Clerk in Holy Orders; The Right Reverend Mark Davies [1962] Director/Bishop of Middleton; Geoffrey Dent [1948] Director/Retired; Revd Canon Anne Joan Edwards [1967] Director/Clerk in Holy Orders; The Very Reverend Rogers Morgan Govender [1960] Director/Cathedral Dean; Barbara Ann Hodgson [1954] Director/Retired; Jane Ann Jones [1950] Director/Teaching Assistant; Keith Lewis [1955] Director/Retired; Richard Molyneux Lewis [1952] Director/Practice Manager; Hyacinth Elaine Lightbourne [1962] Director/Manager; Karen Belinda Lund [1962] Director/Priest in Holy Orders; Yvonne Muriel Mackereth [1947] Director/Retired; Reverend David Roy Penny [1967] Director/Clerk in Holy Orders; The Venerable David John Sharples [1958] Director/Clerk in Holy Orders; Barbara Christine Taylor [1951] Director/Tax Manager; Cherry Elizabeth Vann [1958] Director/Clerk in Holy Orders; David Stuart Walker [1957] Director/Diocesan Bishop

Manchester Diocesan Church House Company Limited (The)
Incorporated: 6 August 1908 *Employees:* 6
Net Worth: £6,348,922 *Total Assets:* £7,678,354
Registered Office: 90 Deansgate, Manchester, M3 2GP
Activities: Other letting and operating of own or leased real estate
Parent: Manchester Diocesan Board of Finance
Officers: David Weldon, Secretary; Phillip Steel Blinkhorn [1949] Director/Administrator; Richard John Byrom [1939] Director/Chartered Surveyor; Alan Cooper [1927] Director/Retired Headmaster; David William Millington [1940] Director/Chartered Surveyor; Paul Nott [1948] Director/Chartered Surveyor; Geoffrey Frank Tattersall [1947] Director/Barrister; David Weldon [1971] Finance Director

Manchester Drinks Company Ltd
Incorporated: 8 June 2005 *Employees:* 4
Net Worth: £3,931,489 *Total Assets:* £6,903,282
Registered Office: Suite 412, Warth Road, Bury, Lancs, BL9 9TB
Activities: Wholesale of fruit and vegetable juices, mineral water and soft drinks
Shareholders: Brian Colin Levine; Ricard Benjamin
Officers: Brian Colin Levine, Secretary/Director; Richard Marc Benjamin [1970] Director; Brian Colin Levine [1968] Director

Manchester Health Academy
Incorporated: 28 October 2008 *Employees:* 113
Net Worth: £21,550,000 *Total Assets:* £23,186,000
Registered Office: Manchester Health Academy, Moor Road, Wythenshawe, Manchester, M23 9BP
Activities: General secondary education
Officers: Louise Marie Staunton, Secretary; Margaret Anne Bradbury [1975] Director/Manager; David Cain [1958] Director/Manager National Health Service; Thomas Oliver Christie [1986] Director/Solicitor; Lorna Doyle [1957] Director/Teacher; Jeremy David Waddoup Green [1974] Director/Project Coordinator/Coach; Kevin John Green [1965] Director/Principal (Headteacher); Margot Johnson [1963] Executive Director of Human and Corporate Resource; Hannah Elenore Sarah Lowry [1975] Director/Provider Network Manager; Melanie Elizabeth Marshall [1971] Director; Steven John Oakes [1970] Director/Author; Samantha Simpson [1968] Director of Operational Finance; Sara Maria Todd [1968] Director/Local Government Officer

Manchester Innovation Limited
Incorporated: 29 October 1981
Net Worth: £17,925,864 *Total Assets:* £25,365,496
Registered Office: The Incubator Building, 48 Grafton Street, Manchester, M13 9XX
Activities: Other business support service activities n.e.c.
Officers: Claire Jane McKenzie, Secretary; Louise Virginia Anne Bissell [1963] Director/Accountant; Clive Gary Rowland [1954] Director/Businessman

Manchester Metronet Limited
Incorporated: 8 December 2011 *Employees:* 5
Net Worth: £148,000 *Total Assets:* £82,196,000
Registered Office: Turing House, Archway 5, Manchester, M15 5RL
Activities: Activities of other holding companies n.e.c.
Parent: PIMCO 2947 Bidco Limited
Officers: Steven Jon Axon [1981] Director; Nicola Jayne Beamish [1974] Director; Andrew Geoffrey Goldwater [1974] Director; Elliott McFarland Mueller [1968] Director

Manchester Property & Development (No.2) Limited
Incorporated: 6 January 2003
Net Worth Deficit: £1,092,313 *Total Assets:* £7,224,592
Registered Office: Metropolitan House, Station Road, Cheadle Hulme, Cheadle, Cheshire, SK8 7AZ
Activities: Buying and selling of own real estate
Parent: Maro Developments Limited
Officers: Christopher O'Brien, Secretary; John Nicholas Mills [1955] Director; Christopher O'Brien [1963] Director/Accountant

Manchester Quays Two Limited
Incorporated: 12 September 2013
Net Worth Deficit: £100,547 *Total Assets:* £41,061,600
Registered Office: c/o Allied London, Level 12, No 1 Spinningfields, 1 Hardman Square, Manchester, M3 3EB
Activities: Development of building projects
Parent: Manchester Quays Holding Limited
Officers: Suresh Premji Gorasia [1974] Director; Frederick Paul Graham-Watson [1957] Finance Director; Michael Julian Ingall [1959] Managing Director; Jonathan Raine [1981] Director

Manchester Rent A Home Limited
Incorporated: 27 July 1989
Net Worth: £2,835,466 *Total Assets:* £8,395,303
Registered Office: 11 Clothorn Road, Didsbury, Manchester, M20 6BF
Activities: Other letting and operating of own or leased real estate
Parent: Keaveney Holdings Limited
Officers: Christine Anne Keaveney, Secretary; Christine Anne Keaveney [1955] Director; Peter Barry Keaveney [1954] Director

Manchester Sale Rugby Club Limited
Incorporated: 14 March 1997 *Employees:* 87
Net Worth: £4,992,644 *Total Assets:* £9,776,859
Registered Office: Sale Sharks High Performance Centre, Carrington Lane, Sale, Cheshire, M31 4AE
Activities: Activities of sport clubs
Officers: Stephen Diamond [1966] Director; Jonathan Paul Dorsett [1963] Director; Gerard Anthony Mason [1964] Director; Simon Sebastian Orange [1967] Director

Manchester Science Partnerships Limited
Incorporated: 21 April 1983
Net Worth: £42,361,000 *Total Assets:* £91,531,000
Registered Office: Union, Albert Square, Manchester, M2 6LW
Activities: Other letting and operating of own or leased real estate
Parent: Bruntwood Science Limited
Officers: Councillor Rachel Anne Bailey [1956] Director/Leader of The Council; Rowena May Burns [1953] Director; Keith Thomas Chantler [1951] Director of Innovation; Sean Martin Davies [1976] Finance Director; Paul Antony Dennett [1979] Director/City Mayor; Jean-Noel Ezingeard [1968] Director/Deputy Vice Chancellor; Professor Luke Gregory Georghiou [1955] Director/Professor; Philip Andrew Kemp [1964] Director/Chief Commercial Officer; Kate Victoria Lawlor [1981] Director/Chartered Accountant; Christopher George Oglesby [1967] Director; Professor Malcolm Colin Press [1958] Director/Vice-Chancellor; Thomas Peter Renn [1985] Managing Director; Adrian Daniel Roberts [1963] Director of Finance; Edward Ashley Lote Smith [1960] Strategic Director; James Thomas Taylor [1961] City Director

The Manchester Ship Canal Company Limited
Incorporated: 12 November 2010 *Employees:* 47
Net Worth: £27,700,000 *Total Assets:* £86,900,000
Registered Office: Maritime Centre, Port of Liverpool, L21 1LA
Activities: Development of building projects
Parent: Peel Ports Investments Limited
Officers: Farook Akhtar Khan, Secretary; Caroline Ruth Marrison Gill, Secretary; Thomas Eardley Allison [1948] Director; Ian Graeme Lloyd Charnock [1962] Director; Neil Lees [1963] Director; Steven Keith Underwood [1974] Director; John Whittaker [1942] Director; Mark Whitworth [1966] Director

Manchester United Football Club Limited
Incorporated: 31 October 1907 *Employees:* 420
Net Worth Deficit: £214,186,000 *Total Assets:* £924,396,032
Registered Office: Old Trafford, Manchester, M16 0RA
Activities: Activities of sport clubs
Parent: Manchester United Limited
Officers: Patrick Charles Donald Stewart, Secretary; Richard Neil Arnold [1971] Commercial Director; Sir Robert Charlton [1937] Director/Travel; John Michael Edelson [1944] Director/Textiles; Sir Alexander Chapman Ferguson [1941] Director; David Alan Gill [1957] Director/Accountant; Avram Glazer [1960] Director/Businessman [American]; Bryan Glazer [1964] Director/Businessman [American]; Edward Glazer [1969] Director/Businessman [American]; Joel Glazer [1967] Director/Businessman [American]; Kevin Glazer [1962] Director/Businessman [American]; Darcie Glazer-Kassewitz [1968] Director/Businesswoman [American]; Edward Gareth Woodward [1971] Director/Executive Vice Chairman

Manchester United Limited
Incorporated: 21 December 1990 *Employees:* 329
Net Worth: £410,868,992 *Total Assets:* £1,309,468,032
Registered Office: Old Trafford, Manchester, M16 0RA
Activities: Activities of sport clubs
Shareholders: Red Football Limited; Red Football Junior Limited
Officers: Patrick Charles Donald Stewart, Secretary; Avram Glazer [1960] Director/Businessman [American]; Bryan Glazer [1964] Director/Businessman [American]; Darcie Glazer [1968] Director/Businesswoman [American]; Edward Glazer [1969] Director/Businessman [American]; Joel Glazer [1967] Director/Businessman [American]; Kevin Glazer [1962] Director/Businessman [American]

Manchester Urban Finance Corporation Limited
Incorporated: 22 December 1995 *Employees:* 67
Net Worth: £4,051,259 *Total Assets:* £9,708,437
Registered Office: 1a The Moorings, Dane Road Industrial Estate, Sale, Cheshire, M33 7BH
Activities: Activities of head offices
Officers: Nicholas Cable, Secretary; Nicholas Jon Cable [1976] Contracts Director

Mancunian Mercantile Investments Ltd
Incorporated: 3 June 1982 *Employees:* 7
Net Worth: £19,600,868 *Total Assets:* £20,865,996
Registered Office: Courtyard Lodge, The Courtyard, 283 Ashley Road, Hale, Altrincham, Cheshire, WA14 3NG
Activities: Activities of head offices
Major Shareholder: Michael John Bracegirdle
Officers: Brian Charles Milne, Secretary; Michael John Bracegirdle [1954] Director; Shirley Annette Bracegirdle [1957] Director; Sarah Louise Nichols [1980] Director

Mann + Hummel Vokes Air Filtration Limited
Incorporated: 10 October 2003
Net Worth: £25,136,000 *Total Assets:* £29,937,000
Registered Office: c/o Vokes Air Limited, Farrington Road, Burnley, Lancs, BB11 5SY
Activities: Activities of head offices
Officers: Berndt Hakan Ekberg [1967] Director/Businessman [Swedish]

Mann + Hummel Vokes Air Treatment Holdings Limited
Incorporated: 6 November 1919
Net Worth: £12,771,000 *Total Assets:* £18,276,000
Registered Office: c/o Vokes Air Limited, Farrington Road, Burnley, Lancs, BB11 5SY
Activities: Activities of head offices
Parent: Mann + Hummel Vokes Air Filtration Limited
Officers: Berndt Hakan Ekberg [1967] Director/Businessman [Swedish]

Manor Coating Systems (Holdings) Limited
Incorporated: 6 November 2013 *Employees:* 78
Net Worth: £5,099,678 *Total Assets:* £7,194,549
Registered Office: Otley Road, Charlestown, Shipley, W Yorks, BD17 7DP
Activities: Activities of production holding companies
Shareholders: Dale Smith; Martin Smith; Patrick Dale Smith
Officers: Patrick Dale Smith, Secretary; Michael Charles Brannan [1963] Director; Dale Smith [1940] Director; Martin Smith [1948] Director; Patrick Dale Smith [1969] Director

Manor Drug Company (Nottingham) Limited (The)
Incorporated: 22 November 1967 *Employees:* 63
Net Worth: £20,448,440 *Total Assets:* £31,097,928
Registered Office: 11 Manchester Road, Walkden, Manchester, M28 3NS
Activities: Wholesale of pharmaceutical goods
Parent: W R Evans Healthcare Ltd
Officers: Angela Jane Cattee [1953] Director; Peter Cattee [1952] Director; Geoffrey Alan Tims [1943] Director

Mansell Finishes Limited
Incorporated: 21 May 1990 *Employees:* 36
Net Worth: £4,995,208 *Total Assets:* £8,277,793
Registered Office: Unit 64 Boswell Way, Stakehill Industrial Estate, Middleton, Manchester, M24 2RW
Activities: Manufacture of metal structures and parts of structures
Parent: M & J Holdings (Manchester) Limited
Officers: Michael Andrew Foy [1980] Director; Stephen John Green [1967] Director; Stephanie Diane Mansell [1983] Director; Angela Jane Smethurst [1976] Director/Administration

Mansfield, Pollard & Co. Limited
Incorporated: 6 May 1914 *Employees:* 156
Net Worth: £4,251,205 *Total Assets:* £7,875,562
Registered Office: Edward House, Parry Lane, Bradford, W Yorks, BD4 8TL
Activities: Manufacture of non-domestic cooling and ventilation equipment
Parent: Mansfield Pollard (Holdings) Limited
Officers: Allison Jayne Howgate, Secretary; Shaun Gavin Cockcroft [1985] Technical Director; Louise Joanne Frankland [1982] Sales Director; Allison Jayne Howgate [1967] Finance Director; Richard Alan Pollard [1954] Director; Gary Mark Roberts [1973] Production Director; Joanna Zilta Robinson [1973] Managing Director

The Mansion Group Limited
Incorporated: 27 February 2007 *Employees:* 147
Net Worth Deficit: £14,568,698 *Total Assets:* £7,727,430
Registered Office: 1 Oakwood Square, Cheadle Royal Business Park, Cheadle, Cheshire, SK8 3SB
Activities: Other business support service activities n.e.c.
Parent: TMGH Limited
Officers: Eugene McTaggart [1957] Director [Irish]; Shankar Ramanathan [1964] Director/Banker

Mantank Environmental Services Limited
Incorporated: 30 January 1995 *Employees:* 89
Net Worth: £3,120,852 *Total Assets:* £9,228,834
Registered Office: Worsley Trading Estate, Lester Road, Little Hulton, Manchester, M38 0PT
Activities: Wholesale of waste and scrap
Major Shareholder: Ian Greenhalgh
Officers: Ian Greenhalgh, Secretary/Director; Ian Greenhalgh [1962] Director; David Royle [1965] Managing Director

Manuli Hydraulics UK Limited
Incorporated: 28 April 1989 *Employees:* 134
Net Worth: £2,891,890 *Total Assets:* £20,852,292
Registered Office: Nasmyth Business Centre, Green Lane, Patricroft, Manchester, M30 0SN
Activities: Manufacture of other rubber products
Parent: Manuli Rubber Industries S.P.A
Officers: Jason Wei Bing Tong, Secretary; Dardanio Mario Davide Manuli [1965] Director/Chief Executive Officer [Italian]; Mark Wood [1969] Director/Certified Chartered Accountant

Maple Grove Developments Limited
Incorporated: 30 July 1981 *Employees:* 6
Net Worth: £22,690,956 *Total Assets:* £51,523,804
Registered Office: Sceptre House, Sceptre Way, Bamber Bridge, Preston, Lancs, PR5 6AW
Activities: Development of building projects
Parent: Eric Wright Developments Limited
Officers: Deborah Jane Rawlinson, Secretary; James Francis Carter [1955] Director/Chartered Surveyor; Andrew Paul Dewhurst [1965] Director/Chartered Surveyor; Allan Gundry [1958] Director; Jeremy Peter Hartley [1965] Director/Accountant; Karen Jane Hirst [1968] Director; Richard Eric Wright [1937] Director

Marantomark Limited
Incorporated: 26 September 2000 *Employees:* 311
Net Worth: £5,186,695 *Total Assets:* £20,219,388
Registered Office: St Georges Nursing Home, Northgate Lane, Moorside, Oldham, Lancs, OL1 4RU
Activities: Residential nursing care facilities
Shareholders: Dr Joseph Sarkis Maximous; Isis Riad Maximous
Officers: Isis Riad Maximous [1961] Director/Housewife; Dr Joseph Sarkis Maximous [1950] Director/Manager of Long Term Care Home

Maraq Limited
Incorporated: 4 January 1995
Net Worth: £852,000 *Total Assets:* £14,456,000
Registered Office: Cavendish House, Cross Street, Sale, Cheshire, M33 7BU
Activities: Architectural activities
Parent: Styles and Wood Property Management Limited
Officers: Philip Nicholas Lanigan, Secretary/Director; Philip Nicholas Lanigan [1964] Director; Anthony Stephen Lenehan [1959] Director/Chief Executive Officer

Marblegrange Limited
Incorporated: 13 December 1996 *Employees:* 180
Net Worth: £6,387,000 *Total Assets:* £14,865,000
Registered Office: Arkwright Mill, Greenbank Street, Preston, Lancs, PR1 7JS
Activities: Activities of head offices
Shareholders: David John Hardman; Charles Stuart Ingham
Officers: Charles Stuart Ingham, Secretary/Director; David John Hardman [1945] Director; Charles Stuart Ingham [1950] Director

Marbury Properties (Chester) LLP
Incorporated: 26 November 2007 *Employees:* 1
Net Worth: £14,213,002 *Total Assets:* £15,364,027
Registered Office: 17 Alvaston Business Park, Middlewich Road, Nantwich, Cheshire, CW5 6PF
Officers: Simon Chantler [1959] Member; Neil John Duncan Lamont [1961] Member; Edward Charles Chantler [1984] LLP Member

Marchington Group Limited
Incorporated: 12 June 1980 *Employees:* 21
Net Worth: £4,050,149 *Total Assets:* £8,927,215
Registered Office: 105 Buxton Road, High Lane, Stockport, Cheshire, SK6 8DX
Activities: Activities of head offices
Officers: Lillian Marchington, Secretary; John Alan Marchington [1935] Director Lillian Marchington [1942] Director

Marchington Stone Limited
Incorporated: 16 April 1970 *Employees:* 21
Net Worth: £4,017,379 *Total Assets:* £8,927,075
Registered Office: 105 Buxton Road, High Lane, Stockport, Cheshire, SK6 8DX
Activities: Wholesale of other intermediate products
Parent: Marchington Group Limited
Officers: Lillian Marchington, Secretary; Simon Grenville Hughes [1952] Sales Director; Alan David Marchington [1971] Director; John Matthew Marchington [1970] Director; John Alan Marchington [1935] Director Lillian Marchington [1942] Director

Marcus Worthington and Company Limited
Incorporated: 20 October 1975 *Employees:* 85
Net Worth: £13,495,703 *Total Assets:* £22,683,696
Registered Office: Brockholes Pavilion, Brockholes Way, Claughton on Brock, Preston, Lancs, PR3 0PZ
Activities: Construction of commercial buildings
Shareholder: John Marcus Worthington
Officers: Graham Atkinson [1955] Director/Contracts Manager; Carl Brendan Bayliss [1971] Director/Quantity Surveyor; Peter Crook [1965] Director/Buyer; Barry Dickinson [1960] Director; David Kenneth Smart [1966] Contracts Director; Stephen Smith [1959] Director/Accountant; Angela Violet Worthington [1945] Director/Secretary; Giles Worthington [1975] Director/Site Agent; John Simeon Worthington [1973] Director; John Marcus Worthington [1946] Managing Director; Russell Edward Worthington [1979] Director/Property Developer

Marcus Worthington Properties Limited
Incorporated: 15 February 1989
Net Worth: £11,257,083 *Total Assets:* £43,756,252
Registered Office: Brockholes Pavilion, Brockholes Way, Claughton on Brock, Preston, Lancs, PR3 0PZ
Activities: Buying and selling of own real estate
Shareholder: John Marcus Worthington
Officers: Stephen Smith, Secretary; David Eric Boardman [1954] Director/Quantity Surveyor; Stephen Smith [1959] Director/Accountant; Giles Matthew Worthington [1975] Construction Director; John Simeon Worthington [1973] Director; John Marcus Worthington [1946] Director/Builder; Russell Edward Worthington [1979] Director/Property Developer

Mardix Holdings Ltd
Incorporated: 4 May 2006 *Employees:* 383
Net Worth: £15,174,860 *Total Assets:* £39,883,604
Registered Office: Castle Mills, Units 21 22 & 26 Aynam Road, Kendal, Cumbria, LA9 7DE
Activities: Other manufacturing n.e.c.
Parent: Anord Mardix Acquisitions Limited
Officers: Ingrid Swenson, Secretary; Jeffrey Mark Drazan [1958] Director [American]; Kevin Finegan [1960] Director [Irish]; David Andrew Gardner [1969] Director; Timothy Heston [1979] Director [American]; Shreyas Kataria [1991] Director [Indian]; Alan Nordon [1967] Director [Irish]; Kevin Yamashita [1975] Director [American]

Mardon Holdings Limited
Incorporated: 6 June 2007 *Employees:* 21
Net Worth: £380,922 *Total Assets:* £8,159,258
Registered Office: 10 Fenton Street, Lancaster, LA1 1TE
Activities: Activities of other holding companies n.e.c.
Major Shareholder: Mark John Donoghue
Officers: Mark John Donoghue, Secretary; Christine Marie Donoghue [1956] Director/Administrator; Mark John Donoghue [1958] Director

Mardon Public Limited Company
Incorporated: 8 October 1984 *Employees:* 21
Net Worth: £1,507,671 *Total Assets:* £7,780,109
Registered Office: Fenton House, 10 Fenton Street, Lancaster, LA1 1TE
Activities: Marine fishing
Major Shareholder: Mark John Donoghue
Officers: Mark John Donoghue, Secretary; Kevin John Bailey [1961] Sales Director; John Joseph Beamer [1964] Director/Manager; Mark John Donoghue [1958] Director; Anthony Turner [1955] Finance Director; Charles Stuart Wilson [1943] Director/Trader

Markem-Imaje Limited
Incorporated: 16 July 2013 *Employees:* 64
Net Worth: £1,445,000 *Total Assets:* £13,455,003
Registered Office: Brightgate House, Brightgate Way, Stretford, Manchester, M32 0TB
Activities: Repair of other equipment
Officers: Anne-Sophie Alric [1975] Director/Financial Controller [French]; Martin David Bailey [1968] Director/Operations Manager; Simon Wakeford [1971] Director/Management Accountant

The Market Village Company Limited
Incorporated: 2 November 1987
Net Worth: £2,714,604 *Total Assets:* £9,247,804
Registered Office: Management Suite, Prescot Centre, Eccleston Street, Prescot, Merseyside, L34 5GA
Activities: Other letting and operating of own or leased real estate
Major Shareholder: Monsieur Jean-Paul Joseph Bernard Auguste
Officers: Ambroise Marcel Cyrille Auguste [1988] Director [French]; Jean Paul Auguste [1954] Director [French]; Michel Distel [1946] Director/Lawyer [French]

M.Markovitz Limited
Incorporated: 6 May 1959 *Employees:* 166
Net Worth: £5,696,512 *Total Assets:* £12,286,321
Registered Office: Town End Yard, Richard Lane, Tideswell, Buxton, Derbys, SK17 8PZ
Activities: Agents involved in the sale of timber and building materials
Officers: Robert William Hopkins, Secretary; Audrey Hopkins [1934] Director/Manager; David John Brian Hopkins [1966] Director; Robert William Hopkins [1972] Director

Marks and Spencer Financial Services PLC
Incorporated: 24 November 1983 *Employees:* 1,595
Net Worth: £330,094,016 *Total Assets:* £5,785,147,904
Registered Office: Kings Meadow, Chester Business Park, Chester, CH99 9FB
Activities: Financial intermediation not elsewhere classified
Parent: HSBC UK Bank PLC
Officers: Christopher Meehan, Secretary; James Coyle [1956] Director; Suzanne Fox [1969] Director/Chief Executive Officer; Stuart Arthur Haire [1974] Director/Banker; Matthew Alexander Granger Handley [1979] Director/Chief Risk Officer; Dame Denise Mary Holt [1949] Director; Phillip William Scott [1976] Director/Chief Financial Officer; David Stewart [1965] Director; Andrew Douglas Van Den Aardweg [1954] Director/Chartered Accountant [South African/British]

Marks and Spencer Retail Financial Services Holdings Limited
Incorporated: 20 July 1988
Net Worth: £83,464,000 *Total Assets:* £83,464,000
Registered Office: Kings Meadow, Chester Business Park, Chester, CH99 9FB
Activities: Activities of head offices
Parent: HSBC Bank PLC
Officers: Christopher Meehan, Secretary; Suzanne Fox [1969] Director/Chief Executive Officer; Matthew Alexander Granger Handley [1979] Director/Chief Risk Officer; Phillip William Scott [1976] Director/Chief Financial Officer

Marks and Spencer Unit Trust Management Limited
Incorporated: 9 May 1988 *Employees:* 12
Net Worth: £6,786,000 *Total Assets:* £14,060,000
Registered Office: Kings Meadow, Chester Business Park, Chester, CH99 9FB
Activities: Financial intermediation not elsewhere classified
Parent: HSBC UK Bank PLC
Officers: Christopher Meehan, Secretary; James Coyle [1956] Director; Peter George Patrick Dew [1945] Non-Employee Non-Executive Director; Simon Charles Ellis [1959] Director/Banker; Suzanne Fox [1969] Director/Chief Executive Officer; Matthew Alexander Granger Handley [1979] Director/Chief Risk Officer; Phillip William Scott [1976] Director/Chief Financial Officer; David Stewart [1965] Director; Andrew Douglas Van Den Aardweg [1954] Director/Chartered Accountant [South African/British]

Marksans Pharma U.K. Limited
Incorporated: 31 May 2005 *Employees:* 167
Net Worth: £9,863,570 *Total Assets:* £24,043,708
Registered Office: Cheshire House, Gorsey Lane, Widnes, Cheshire, WA8 0RP
Activities: Activities of head offices
Parent: Marksans Pharma Limited
Officers: Gillian Jacks, Secretary; Sathish Kumar Konasagar Jayanna [1973] Director; Mark Bosco Saldanha [1972] Director [Indian]; Sandra Saldanha [1971] Director [Indian]; Jitendra Mahavirprasad Sharma [1969] Director/Service [Indian]; Russell David Williams [1968] Director

Marlborough Fund Managers Ltd.
Incorporated: 3 October 1986 *Employees:* 117
Net Worth: £23,076,560 *Total Assets:* £61,237,784
Registered Office: Marlborough House, 59 Chorley New Road, Bolton, Lancs, BL1 4QP
Activities: Financial intermediation not elsewhere classified
Parent: Marlborough Group Holdings Limited
Officers: Ryan Peter Barber, Secretary; Dom Clarke [1983] Finance Director; Nicholas Francis John Cooling [1964] Director/Fund Manager; Helen Derbyshire [1982] Director/Compliance Officer; Wayne Daniel Green [1980] Joint Managing Director; Allan Hamer [1976] Joint Managing Director; Geoffrey Robert Hitchin [1942] Director/Unit Trust Manager & Taxation; Guy Russell William Sears [1961] Director; Andrew Staley [1955] Director/Fund Manager

Marlowe Holdings Investments Limited
Incorporated: 17 December 1948
Net Worth: £372,596,000 *Total Assets:* £452,452,992
Registered Office: P O Box 1, Tatton Street, Knutsford, Cheshire, WA16 6AY
Activities: Activities of head offices
Parent: Marlowe Holdings Limited
Officers: William Sones Woof, Secretary; Keith Whiting Colburn [1948] Director [American]; Richard Whiting Colburn [1943] Director [American]; Roger David Goddard [1953] Director/Chartered Accountant; Carol Colburn Grigor [1944] Director

Marlowe Holdings Limited
Incorporated: 23 December 2009 *Employees:* 6,352
Net Worth: £763,662,016 *Total Assets:* £1,122,835,968
Registered Office: Edmundson House, Tatton Street, Knutsford, Cheshire, WA16 6AY
Activities: Activities of head offices
Officers: Keith Whiting Colburn [1948] Director/Executive [American]; Richard Whiting Colburn [1943] Director/Executive [American]; Roger David Goddard [1953] Director/Accountant; Carol Colburn Grigor [1944] Director; William Sones Woof [1951] Director/Solicitor

Maro Developments Limited
Incorporated: 13 June 2002 *Employees:* 4
Net Worth Deficit: £28,018,532 *Total Assets:* £36,532,208
Registered Office: Metropolitan House, Station Road, Cheadle Hulme, Cheadle, Cheshire, SK8 7AZ
Activities: Buying and selling of own real estate
Major Shareholder: John Hargreaves
Officers: Christopher O'Brien, Secretary; John Nicholas Mills [1955] Director; Christopher O'Brien [1963] Director/Accountant

Marpak Extrusions Limited
Incorporated: 12 January 2000 *Employees:* 24
Net Worth: £4,037,586 *Total Assets:* £8,719,237
Registered Office: 1 Parkview Court, St Pauls Road, Shipley, W Yorks, BD18 3DZ
Activities: Manufacture of plastic packing goods
Shareholders: Catherine Lynn Gibson; Richard Gary Gibson
Officers: James Gary Gibson [1976] Procurement Director; Richard Gary Gibson [1949] Managing Director; Matthew James White [1981] Director of Development; Peter Winterbottom [1964] Managing Director

Marplace (Number 754) Limited
Incorporated: 25 November 2009 *Employees:* 51
Net Worth: £3,840,098 *Total Assets:* £7,472,768
Registered Office: 8 Brindley Road, City Park, Old Trafford, Manchester, M16 9HQ
Activities: Other business support service activities n.e.c.
Officers: Peter Philip Noall, Secretary; Steven Gareth Hughes-Solomon [1969] Director/Contracts Manager; Dr Paul Reginald Noall [1950] Director

Marsh Finance & Commercial Limited
Incorporated: 19 February 1999
Net Worth: £4,593,950 *Total Assets:* £21,819,544
Registered Office: Crossfield Mill, Crawford Street, Rochdale, OL16 5RS
Activities: Other credit granting n.e.c.
Major Shareholder: Andrew James Marsh
Officers: Andrew James Marsh [1968] Director

Marsh Finance Limited
Incorporated: 5 October 1973 *Employees:* 46
Net Worth: £20,125,522 *Total Assets:* £28,485,444
Registered Office: Crossfield Mill, Crawford Street, Rochdale, OL16 5RS
Activities: Other credit granting n.e.c.
Officers: Wendy Joan Marsh, Secretary; Andrew James Marsh [1968] Director/I T Manager; Kevin Marsh [1939] Director; Wendy Joan Marsh [1941] Director

Frank Marshall Estates Limited
Incorporated: 25 May 2012
Net Worth: £14,334,187 *Total Assets:* £32,076,376
Registered Office: The East Wing, The Newhall, Newhall Way, Bradford, BD5 8FF
Activities: Other letting and operating of own or leased real estate
Shareholders: Frank Edward Marshall; James Ernest Marshall
Officers: Frank Edward Marshall [1978] Director; James Ernest Marshall [1979] Director

J & E Marshall Finance Limited
Incorporated: 26 April 2013
Net Worth: £6,037,638 *Total Assets:* £11,241,074
Registered Office: The East Wing, The Newhall, Newhall Way, Bradford, BD5 8FF
Activities: Financial management
Parent: Schosween 12 Ltd
Officers: Frank Edward Marshall [1978] Director; James Ernest Marshall [1979] Director

Marsylka Manufacturing Co.Limited
Incorporated: 11 December 1946 *Employees:* 1,334
Net Worth: £5,744,103 *Total Assets:* £12,135,005
Registered Office: 16 Roydsdale Way, Euroway Industrial Estate, Bradford, W Yorks, BD4 6SE
Activities: Manufacture of other women's outerwear
Officers: Robert Joseph Hainsworth, Secretary; Andrew Eric Hainsworth [1971] Director; John Simon Hainsworth [1969] Director; Robert Joseph Hainsworth [1967] Director; John Hammond Seller [1950] Director

Tom Martin & Company Limited
Incorporated: 1 October 1970 *Employees:* 77
Net Worth: £18,345,228 *Total Assets:* £27,539,568
Registered Office: Unit 123 Seedlee Road, Walton Summit Industrial Estate Preston, Lancs, PR5 8AE
Activities: Wholesale of waste and scrap
Parent: Majormobile Limited
Officers: Christopher Lowe, Secretary; George Edward Brettle [1974] Director; Christopher Lowe [1981] Finance Director; Colin McNeil [1965] Works Director; Alan Slater [1963] Director

Tom Martin Metal Holdings 2011 Limited
Incorporated: 23 March 2011 *Employees:* 74
Net Worth: £7,699,000 *Total Assets:* £18,561,000
Registered Office: 123 Seedlee Road, Walton Summit Centre, Preston, Lancs, PR5 8AE
Activities: Wholesale of waste and scrap
Parent: Tom Martin Metal Holdings 2017 Limited
Officers: Christopher Lowe, Secretary; George Brettle [1984] Director; Christopher Lowe [1981] Finance Director; Colin McNeil [1965] Director; Alan Slater [1953] Director

Tom Martin Metal Holdings Limited
Incorporated: 12 March 2008
Net Worth: £450,827 *Total Assets:* £8,666,262
Registered Office: 123 Seedlee Road, Walton Summit Centre, Preston, Lancs, PR5 8AE
Activities: Wholesale of waste and scrap
Parent: Tom Martin Metal Holdings 2011 Limited
Officers: Christopher Lowe, Secretary; George Brettle [1974] Director; Christopher Lowe [1981] Finance Director; Colin McNeill [1965] Director; Alan Slater [1963] Director

Maru Group Finance Limited
Incorporated: 23 November 2015
Net Worth Deficit: £51,697 *Total Assets:* £49,829,484
Registered Office: Eversheds House, 70 Great Bridgewater Street, Manchester, M1 5ES
Activities: Market research and public opinion polling
Parent: Maru Group Holdings Limited
Officers: Anthony Joseph Gahan [1966] Director; Graham John Heddle [1967] Director/Fund Manager; Heather Lyn McRae [1962] Director/Chartered Accountant; Generald Roger Parton [1965] Director; Neil Alan Wallace [1966] Director; Shane Alan Wright [1977] Director

Maru Group Holdings Limited
Incorporated: 23 November 2015 *Employees:* 341
Net Worth Deficit: £2,776,851 *Total Assets:* £68,330,520
Registered Office: Eversheds House, 70 Great Bridgewater Street, Manchester, M1 5ES
Activities: Market research and public opinion polling
Parent: Primary Capital IV (Nominees) Limited
Officers: Anthony Joseph Gahan [1966] Director; Graham John Heddle [1967] Director/Fund Manager; Heather Lyn McRae [1962] Director/Chartered Accountant; George Mrkonic [1952] Director/Investor [American]; Generald Roger Parton [1965] Director; Neil Alan Wallace [1966] Director; Shane Alan Wright [1977] Director

Maru Group Limited
Incorporated: 23 November 2015 *Employees:* 4
Net Worth Deficit: £2,326,447 *Total Assets:* £48,381,496
Registered Office: Eversheds House, 70 Great Bridgewater Street, Manchester, M1 5ES
Activities: Market research and public opinion polling
Parent: Maru Group Finance Limited
Officers: Anthony Joseph Gahan [1966] Director; Graham John Heddle [1967] Director/Fund Manager; Heather Lyn McRae [1962] Director/Chartered Accountant; Generald Roger Parton [1965] Director; Neil Alan Wallace [1966] Director; Shane Alan Wright [1977] Director

Marubeni Auto Investment (UK) Limited
Incorporated: 8 September 2000 *Employees:* 1,199
Net Worth: £36,403,000 *Total Assets:* £126,348,000
Registered Office: 173 Cross Lane, Salford, M5 4AP
Activities: Sale of new cars and light motor vehicles
Parent: Marubeni Corporation
Officers: Arran Bangham, Secretary; Tsugutoshi Akano [1974] Director [Japanese]; Arran Bangham [1968] Financial Director; Naonori Ishii [1967] Director [Japanese]; Kazuhiro Kondo [1967] Director [Japanese]; Takanori Tanaka [1963] Director [Japanese]

Maryland Securities Limited
Incorporated: 23 April 1986 *Employees:* 12
Net Worth: £18,352,604 *Total Assets:* £39,737,192
Registered Office: Ashfield House, Ashfield Road, Cheadle, Cheshire, SK8 1BB
Activities: Other letting and operating of own or leased real estate
Officers: Paul Nigel Manifold, Secretary; David Jebreel [1951] Director/Property Dealer; Ebrahim Jebreel [1954] Director; Jacob Jebreel [1962] Director

Mason & Vaughan Group Ltd
Incorporated: 25 July 2012
Net Worth Deficit: £159,780 *Total Assets:* £14,895,344
Registered Office: Ground Floor, Ocean House, Towers Business Park, Wilmslow Road, Manchester, M20 2LY
Activities: Activities of head offices
Parent: MVG Holdings Ltd
Officers: Carl William Mills [1979] Director

Massey Bros (Feeds) Ltd.
Incorporated: 28 March 1957 *Employees:* 172
Net Worth: £11,945,688 *Total Assets:* £21,527,308
Registered Office: Cranage Mills, Holmes Chapel, Crewe, Cheshire, CW4 8EE
Activities: Manufacture of prepared feeds for farm animals
Shareholder: Richard Thomas Massey
Officers: George Kynan Ardern Massey, Secretary; William Peter Harper [1955] Director/Animal Feed Nutritionist; Barbara Megan Hilary Massey [1948] Director & Secretary; George Kynan Ardern Massey [1969] Director/Animal Feed Manufacturer Manager; Richard Thomas Massey [1948] Director/Company Chairman; Thomas Auldan Ardern Massey [1974] Director; Dorothy Tamaran Ardern Massey-Ford [1979] Director; Philip Andrew Stirk [1964] Sales Director; Generald Neil Warburton [1965] Director

Masshouse Developments Ltd
Incorporated: 25 November 2002
Net Worth: £2,307,047 *Total Assets:* £14,513,995
Registered Office: Mynshulls House, 14 Cateaton Street, Manchester, M3 1SQ
Activities: Buying and selling of own real estate
Shareholders: Evora Developments Limited; Buro Services Limited
Officers: Stephen Paul Robinson, Secretary/Accountant; Nicholas Stuart Payne [1967] Director; Stephen Paul Robinson [1963] Director/Accountant

Mast Group Limited
Incorporated: 10 July 1959 *Employees:* 197
Net Worth: £11,848,065 *Total Assets:* £18,402,916
Registered Office: Mast House, Derby Road, Liverpool, L20 1EA
Activities: Other manufacturing n.e.c.
Shareholders: Margaret Oliver; Christopher John Oliver
Officers: Christopher John Oliver [1958] Director; Margaret Oliver [1926] Director

Mastacab Assets LLP
Incorporated: 5 March 2015
Net Worth: £7,371,717 *Total Assets:* £7,384,967
Registered Office: Park House, Pennine Way, Bredbury Park Industrial Estate, Stockport, Cheshire, SK6 2TF
Officers: Christopher John Coppock [1970] Member; Thomas Simon Coppock [1961] Member; Azadeh Coppock [1970] LLP Member; Dierdre Coppock [1934] LLP Member; Emma Coppock [1969] LLP Member; Michelle Coppock [1959] LLP Member; Thomas Michael John Coppock [1929] LLP Member

Matalan Finance PLC
Incorporated: 10 October 2006
Net Worth: £198,500,000 *Total Assets:* £877,400,000
Registered Office: Matalan Head Office, Perimeter Road, Knowsley Industrial Park, Knowsley, Merseyside, L33 7SZ
Activities: Activities of other holding companies n.e.c.
Parent: Matalan Group Limited
Officers: William George Lodder, Secretary; John Jason Hargreaves [1968] Managing Director; Stephen Mark Hill [1976] Finance Director; John Nicholas Mills [1955] Director; Gregory Vincent Pateras [1976] Director

Matalan Group Limited
Incorporated: 23 October 2006
Net Worth: £446,500,000 *Total Assets:* £492,500,000
Registered Office: Matalan Head Office, Perimeter Road, Knowsley Industrial Park, Knowsley, Merseyside, L33 7SZ
Activities: Activities of other holding companies n.e.c.
Shareholder: John Hargreaves
Officers: William George Lodder, Secretary; John Jason Hargreaves [1968] Managing Director; Stephen Mark Hill [1976] Finance Director; John Nicholas Mills [1955] Director; Gregory Vincent Pateras [1976] Director

Matalan Holding Company Limited
Incorporated: 11 July 2001
Net Worth: £5,187,000 *Total Assets:* £14,320,000
Registered Office: Matalan Head Office, Perimeter Road, Knowsley Industrial Park, Knowsley, Merseyside, L33 7SZ
Activities: Activities of other holding companies n.e.c.
Parent: Matalan Limited
Officers: William George Lodder, Secretary; John Jason Hargreaves [1968] Managing Director; Stephen Mark Hill [1976] Finance Director; John Nicholas Mills [1955] Director; Gregory Vincent Pateras [1976] Director

Matalan Limited
Incorporated: 13 August 1981
Net Worth: £96,385,296 *Total Assets:* £157,782,000
Registered Office: Matalan Head Office, Perimeter Road, Knowsley Industrial Park, Knowsley, Merseyside, L33 7SZ
Activities: Activities of other holding companies n.e.c.
Parent: Matalan Finance PLC
Officers: William George Lodder, Secretary; John Jason Hargreaves [1968] Managing Director; Stephen Mark Hill [1976] Finance Director; John Nicholas Mills [1955] Director; Gregory Vincent Pateras [1976] Director

Matalan Retail Ltd.
Incorporated: 25 February 1987 *Employees:* 14,098
Net Worth: £346,500,000 *Total Assets:* £684,099,968
Registered Office: Matalan Head Office, Perimeter Road, Knowsley Industrial Park, Knowsley, Merseyside, L33 7SZ
Activities: Retail sale of clothing in specialised stores
Parent: Matalan Limited
Officers: William George Lodder, Secretary; John Jason Hargreaves [1968] Managing Director; Stephen Mark Hill [1976] Finance Director; John Nicholas Mills [1955] Director; Gregory Vincent Pateras [1976] Commercial Director

Matchstick Men Limited
Incorporated: 3 June 2010 *Employees:* 152
Net Worth: £3,642,633 *Total Assets:* £25,905,808
Registered Office: Green Bank Business Park, Swan Lane, Hindley Green, Wigan, Lancs, WN2 4EZ
Activities: Activities of other holding companies n.e.c.
Officers: Simone Paula Fisher [1973] Director; Gavin Hamer [1979] Director; Olivia Paulette Hamer [1978] Director [New Zealander]; Stephen John Smith [1966] Director

Mathers Foundry Limited
Incorporated: 16 September 2008 *Employees:* 80
Net Worth Deficit: £557,367 *Total Assets:* £6,966,000
Registered Office: Park Works, Grimshaw Lane, Newton Heath, Manchester, M40 2BA
Activities: Casting of steel
Officers: Prakash Agarwal [1971] Director [Indian]; Krishina Kumar Ganeriwala [1963] Director [Indian]

Matrix Technologies Corporation Limited
Incorporated: 11 August 1998
Net Worth: £43,767,000 *Total Assets:* £43,776,000
Registered Office: 3rd Floor, 1 Ashley Road, Altrincham, Cheshire, WA14 2DT
Activities: Non-trading company
Parent: Apogent UK Limited
Officers: Rhona Gregg, Secretary; Lucie Mary Katja Grant [1976] Director/Solicitor; Nicholas Ince [1982] Director/Accountant; David John Norman [1960] Director/Chartered Accountant

Matryx Limited
Incorporated: 16 February 2005 *Employees:* 59
Net Worth: £910,569 *Total Assets:* £12,004,472
Registered Office: Unit 5 Woodstock Business Park, Meek Street, Royton, Oldham, Lancs, OL2 6HL
Activities: Manufacture of paper and paperboard
Officers: Susan Anne Samuel, Secretary; Robin Paul Andrews [1953] Finance Director; David Eccleston [1957] Director/Operations Manager; Nigel Huw Samuel [1965] Director; Susan Anne Samuel [1965] Director

Matthews Environmental Solutions Limited
Incorporated: 27 October 2011 *Employees:* 22
Net Worth: £1,759,651 *Total Assets:* £12,873,462
Registered Office: Unit 3 Dunkirk Lane, Hyde, Cheshire, SK14 4NL
Activities: Manufacture of other special-purpose machinery n.e.c.
Parent: Matthews Corporation Holding Company (UK) Limited
Officers: Joseph Carlo Bartolacci [1960] Director [American]; Paul Rahill [1956] Director [American]; Pier Luigi Romanelli [1964] Director [Italian]

Mawdsley-Brooks & Company Limited
Incorporated: 24 July 1895 *Employees:* 435
Net Worth: £22,218,000 *Total Assets:* £77,403,000
Registered Office: P O Box 18, Number Three, South Langworthy Road, Salford M50 2PW
Activities: Wholesale of pharmaceutical goods
Parent: Mawdsleys Group Investments Limited
Officers: Stephanie Joy Ellison, Secretary; Darren Robert Belcher [1966] Director; Ian Colin Brownlee [1948] Managing Director; Carol Currimjee [1946] Director; Stephanie Joy Ellison [1958] Director; Dr John Howard Mawdsley [1950] Director/Doctor of Medicine; William John Sanders [1966] Director; Gail Sanderson-Watts [1949] Director; Susan Penelope Westall [1944] Director

Mawdsleys Group Investments Limited
Incorporated: 7 December 2009 *Employees:* 532
Net Worth: £42,955,000 *Total Assets:* £94,026,000
Registered Office: P O Box 18, Number Three South Langworthy Road, Salford, M50 2PW
Activities: Activities of head offices
Shareholder: Dr John Mawdsley
Officers: Ian Colin Brownlee [1948] Director; Carole Currimjee [1946] Director; Stephanie Joy Ellison [1958] Director; Dr John Howard Mawdsley [1950] Director; William John Sanders [1966] Director; William James Westall [1975] Director

Maxilead Limited
Incorporated: 13 December 1985
Net Worth: £4,250,530 *Total Assets:* £7,435,737
Registered Office: Parr Bridge Works, Mosley Common Road, Tydesley, Lancs, M29 8PR
Activities: Wholesale of waste and scrap
Parent: Boxster Limited
Officers: Tom Clay, Secretary/Director; Lucy Butler [1985] Director; Peter Allan Clay [1957] Director; Tom Clay [1982] Director; Vera Lynne Clay [1958] Director; Anna Dagnall [1984] Director

Mayfield Chicks Limited
Incorporated: 8 April 1970 *Employees:* 5
Net Worth: £6,570,980 *Total Assets:* £9,182,750
Registered Office: 21 Union Street, Ramsbottom, Bury, Lancs, BL0 9AN
Activities: Raising of poultry
Major Shareholder: Peter Haslam
Officers: John Graham Clegg, Secretary; John Graham Clegg [1947] Director/Accountant; Nicholas Oliver Haslam [1970] Director/Teacher; Peter Haslam [1942] Director/Farmer; William Ernest Holt [1946] Director/Solicitor

Mayr-Melnhof Packaging UK Limited
Incorporated: 7 July 1992 *Employees:* 197
Net Worth: £16,114,000 *Total Assets:* £42,898,000
Registered Office: 4th Avenue, Deeside Industrial Estate, Deeside, Flintshire, CH5 2NR
Activities: Printing n.e.c.
Parent: Mayr-Melnhof Karton Aktiengesellschaft
Officers: Wayne Fitzpatrick [1973] Director/Sales Executive; Jose Antonio Rubio-Estrada [1975] Managing Director [Spanish]; Dr Peter Schneider [1970] Director [Austrian]

MB South Limited
Incorporated: 20 February 1973 *Employees:* 546
Net Worth: £18,660,000 *Total Assets:* £161,475,008
Registered Office: Lookers House, 3 Etchells Road, West Timperley, Altrincham, Cheshire, WA14 5XS
Activities: Sale of new cars and light motor vehicles
Parent: Lookers Motor Holdings Limited
Officers: Glenda MacGeekie, Secretary; Andrew Campbell Bruce [1965] Director; Robin Anthony Gregson [1960] Director/Chartered Accountant; Nigel John McMinn [1968] Managing Director Motor Division

MBH Investments Ltd
Incorporated: 16 January 1997
Net Worth: £9,080,880 *Total Assets:* £16,664,193
Registered Office: 2nd Floor, Parkgates, Bury New Road, Prestwich, Manchester, M25 0TL
Activities: Other letting and operating of own or leased real estate
Shareholders: Pearl Adler; Jacob Adler
Officers: Jacob Adler, Secretary/Property Manager; Jacob Adler [1969] Director/Property Manager; Pearl Adler [1968] Director

MBNA Europe Holdings Limited
Incorporated: 15 February 1994
Net Worth: £134,906,000 *Total Assets:* £135,152,000
Registered Office: Stansfield House, Chester Business Park, Chester, CH4 9QQ
Activities: Other business support service activities n.e.c.
Parent: MBNA Limited
Officers: Alyson Elizabeth Mulholland, Secretary; Jonathan Paul Metcalfe [1978] Director/Accountant; David James Walker [1967] Director/Accountant; Jonathan Bernard West [1972] Director/Treasury Manager

MBNA Limited
Incorporated: 25 January 1993 *Employees:* 1,698
Net Worth: £660,654,976 *Total Assets:* £8,066,458,112
Registered Office: Stansfield House, Chester Business Park, Chester, CH4 9QQ
Activities: Financial intermediation not elsewhere classified
Parent: Lloyds Bank PLC
Officers: Alyson Elizabeth Mulholland, Secretary; Elyn Jane Corfield [1969] Director/Chartered Accountant; Paul Andrew Gordon [1967] Managing Director; Israel Santos Perez [1972] Director [Spanish]

McBride CE Holdings Limited
Incorporated: 21 November 2002
Net Worth: £7,314,000 *Total Assets:* £7,386,000
Registered Office: McBride CE Holdings Limited, Middleton Way, Middleton, Manchester, M24 4DP
Activities: Non-trading company
Parent: McBride Holdings Ltd
Officers: Carol Williams, Secretary; Christopher Ian Charles Smith [1964] Director/Accountant; Rik Jean Pierre Dora Albert de Vos [1960] Director [Belgian]

McBride Holdings Limited
Incorporated: 31 March 1993
Net Worth: £6,416,000 *Total Assets:* £204,240,000
Registered Office: McBride Holdings Limited, Middleton Way, Middleton, Manchester, M24 4DP
Activities: Activities of head offices
Parent: McBride PLC
Officers: Carol Williams, Secretary; Christopher Ian Charles Smith [1964] Director/Accountant; Rik Jean Pierre Dora Albert de Vos [1960] Director [Belgian]

Robert McBride Ltd
Incorporated: 9 March 1927 *Employees:* 1,169
Net Worth: £12,255,000 *Total Assets:* £158,680,000
Registered Office: Middleton Way, Middleton, Manchester, M24 4DP
Activities: Manufacture of soap and detergents
Shareholders: McBride PLC; McBride Holdings Limited
Officers: Carol Williams, Secretary; David Thomas Rattigan [1969] Director/Accountant; Christopher Ian Charles Smith [1964] Director/Accountant; Rik Jean Pierre Dora Albert de Vos [1960] Director [Belgian]

McBride PLC
Incorporated: 11 March 1993 *Employees:* 4,125
Net Worth: £63,600,000 *Total Assets:* £419,900,000
Registered Office: Middleton Way, Middleton, Manchester, M24 4DP
Activities: Activities of head offices
Officers: Carol Williams, Secretary; John Coleman [1952] Director; Rik de Vos [1960] Director [Belgian]; Stephen John Hannam [1949] Director; Neil Simon Harrington [1963] Director/Accountant; Christopher Ian Charles Smith [1964] Director/Accountant; Sandra Turner [1952] Director

McCann Health Medical Communications Limited
Incorporated: 17 May 1990 *Employees:* 305
Net Worth: £25,932,000 *Total Assets:* £45,376,000
Registered Office: CMC House, 19 King Edward Street, Macclesfield, Cheshire, SK10 1AQ
Activities: Activities of head offices
Parent: McCann-Erickson UK Group Limited
Officers: Louise Bean, Secretary; Charles Edward George Buckwell [1964] Director; Phillip Sutcliffe [1968] Director/Accountant

McCann Manchester Limited
Incorporated: 28 February 1986 *Employees:* 346
Net Worth: £30,069,000 *Total Assets:* £54,526,000
Registered Office: Bonis Hall, Prestbury, Macclesfield, Cheshire, SK10 4EF
Activities: Advertising agencies
Parent: McCann-Erickson Network Limited
Officers: Louise Bean, Secretary; Martin James Jackson [1968] Director/Chartered Accountant; Susan Ann Little [1955] Director/Advertising Executive; Helen Denise Sullivan [1979] Director/Chartered Accountant

McCann-Erickson Network Limited
Incorporated: 14 January 1986
Net Worth: £58,248,000 *Total Assets:* £58,316,000
Registered Office: Bonis Hall, Prestbury, Macclesfield, Cheshire, SK10 4EF
Activities: Advertising agencies
Parent: McCann-Erickson UK Group Limited
Officers: Louise Bean, Secretary; Jane Ann Cottrill [1977] Director/Accountant; Martin James Jackson [1968] Director/Chartered Accountant; Helen Denise Sullivan [1979] Director/Chartered Accountant

McComb Property Company Limited
Incorporated: 18 May 1998 *Employees:* 7
Net Worth: £9,772,924 *Total Assets:* £35,118,648
Registered Office: Glenbourne House, 61 Burscough Street, Ormskirk, Lancs, L39 2EL
Activities: Other letting and operating of own or leased real estate
Shareholders: Michael William McComb; Sharon Michelle McComb
Officers: Sharon Michelle McComb, Secretary; Michael William McComb [1958] Director; Paul Michael McComb [1991] Director; Sharon Michelle McComb [1970] Director/Manager

McDermott Developments Limited
Incorporated: 30 March 1992 *Employees:* 45
Net Worth: £34,081,896 *Total Assets:* £46,830,488
Registered Office: Jupiter House, 1 Mercury Rise, Altham Business Park, Altham, Lancs, BB5 5BY
Activities: Development of building projects
Officers: Catherine Davis, Secretary/Computer Analyst; Catherine Davis [1963] Director; Richard Michael Kay [1962] Financial Director; Dr Beverley Kemp [1968] Sales Director; Seamus McDermott [1964] Director/Property Developer [Irish]; Robin Paul Rudkin [1971] Construction Director; Mark Wilkinson [1969] Technical Director

McDermott Homes Limited
Incorporated: 23 June 2006 *Employees:* 6
Net Worth: £2,593,445 *Total Assets:* £8,831,743
Registered Office: Jupiter House, 1 Mercury Rise, Altham Business Park, Altham, Lancs, BB5 5BY
Activities: Development of building projects
Parent: McDermott Developments Limited
Officers: Catherine Davis, Secretary/Director; Catherine Davis [1963] Director; Richard Michael Kay [1962] Financial Director; Dr Beverley Kemp [1968] Sales Director; Seamus McDermott [1964] Director [Irish]; Robin Paul Rudkin [1971] Construction Director; Mark Wilkinson [1969] Technical Director

R. McDowell Haulage and Distribution Limited
Incorporated: 16 February 1989 *Employees:* 138
Net Worth: £1,933,683 *Total Assets:* £9,375,206
Registered Office: Thunderbird Depot, Valley Road, Keighley, W Yorks, BD21 4LZ
Activities: Freight transport by road
Parent: McDowell H&D Limited
Officers: Joseph Clayton Balmforth [1963] Director/Transport Manager; Brian Christopher Dent [1962] Director; Nathan Jon Goodridge [1980] Director; Geoffrey David Hirst [1986] Director

McGarr McCarrick Limited
Incorporated: 19 November 2002 *Employees:* 1
Net Worth: £1,787,525 *Total Assets:* £7,177,365
Registered Office: 749-753 Oldham Road, Newton Heath, Manchester, M40 5AU
Activities: Hotels and similar accommodation
Major Shareholder: James McGarr
Officers: James McGarr [1959] Director

McGoff Construction Limited
Incorporated: 7 August 1973 *Employees:* 86
Net Worth: £1,378,461 *Total Assets:* £18,660,260
Registered Office: Mayfield House, Lyon Road, Atlantic Street, Broadheath, Altrincham, Cheshire, WA14 5EF
Activities: Construction of commercial buildings
Officers: David John Paul McGoff, Secretary/Director; Christopher Andrew McGoff [1973] Director/Builder; David John Paul McGoff [1970] Director; Declan Thomas McGoff [1967] Director/Builder; James Matthew McGoff [1966] Director/Builder

McGoff Group LLP
Incorporated: 14 June 2007 *Employees:* 86
Net Worth: £1,894,464 *Total Assets:* £18,840,634
Registered Office: Mayfield House, Lyon Road, Atlantic Street, Broadheath, Altrincham, Cheshire, WA14 5EF
Officers: Christopher Andrew McGoff [1973] Member; David John Paul McGoff [1970] Member; Declan Thomas McGoff [1967] Member; James Matthew McGoff [1966] Member

MCH Intermediate Limited
Incorporated: 19 December 2012
Net Worth: £3,745,172 *Total Assets:* £16,778,476
Registered Office: Solutions House, 39 Quayside, Grosvenor Wharf Road, Ellesmere Port, Cheshire, CH65 4AY
Activities: Activities of head offices
Parent: MCH Parent Ltd
Officers: Emily Bowers [1977] Director/Self Employed; Steven Bowers [1971] Director; Paul Stuart Rogers [1968] Director; Susan Caroline Rogers [1962] Director

Phil McIntyre Holdings Limited
Incorporated: 22 April 2003 *Employees:* 62
Net Worth: £6,491,822 *Total Assets:* £27,027,320
Registered Office: Richard House, Winckley Square, Preston, Lancs, PR1 3HP
Activities: Other amusement and recreation activities n.e.c.
Major Shareholder: Philip Charles McIntyre
Officers: John Peter McIntyre, Secretary; Philip Charles McIntyre [1950] Director/Promoter

McJunkin Red Man UK Ltd
Incorporated: 5 September 2009 *Employees:* 4
Net Worth: £105,649,960 *Total Assets:* £206,370,944
Registered Office: Heaton House, Riverside Drive, Cleckheaton, W Yorks, BD19 4DH
Activities: Activities of head offices
Parent: MRC Global Inc
Officers: Steinar Aasland [1966] Director [Norwegian]; Elton Ray Bond [1975] Director [American]; Claire Jane Hellmund [1983] Director/Solicitor; Adnan Velic [1980] Director

McManus Group Holdings Limited
Incorporated: 30 September 2015 *Employees:* 67
Net Worth: £14,283,992 *Total Assets:* £36,173,720
Registered Office: Lusteen House, 24 Roydsdale Way, Euroway Industrial Estate, Bradford, W Yorks, BD4 6SE
Activities: Activities of head offices
Major Shareholder: Aiden Thomas McManus
Officers: Graham Hunt [1956] Director/Chartered Accountant; Aiden Thomas McManus [1976] Director; Thomas John McManus [1949] Director

MD Insurance Services Limited
Incorporated: 1 October 1998 *Employees:* 347
Net Worth: £9,522,801 *Total Assets:* £117,321,088
Registered Office: 2 Shore Lines Building, Shore Road, Birkenhead, Wirral, Merseyside, CH41 1AU
Activities: Non-life insurance
Shareholders: Gary James Devaney; Bernadette Mary Devaney
Officers: Jacqueline Ann Goodman, Secretary; David Connolly [1972] Director/Accountant; Gary James Devaney [1956] Director; Jacqueline Ann Goodman [1959] Director/Human Resources; Ian Martin Turnick [1956] Director/Account Executive; Hywel Lyndon Williams [1974] Director

MDS CEM Holdings Limited
Incorporated: 22 December 2011 *Employees:* 227
Net Worth: £23,510,000 *Total Assets:* £28,122,000
Registered Office: The Point, 410 Birchwood Boulevard, Warrington, Cheshire, WA3 7WD
Activities: Business and domestic software development
Shareholder: Martin Richard Dawes
Officers: Simon Paul Blagden [1962] Director; Gary Douglas Bunney [1954] Director; Martin Richard Dawes [1943] Director; Russell James Hunt [1967] Director; William J Kelly [1941] Director [American]; Andrew George Taylor [1968] Director; Dewi Eifion Thomas [1957] Director

MDS Global Ltd
Incorporated: 27 May 1988 *Employees:* 223
Net Worth: £10,432,000 *Total Assets:* £16,863,000
Registered Office: The Point, 410 Birchwood Boulevard, Warrington, Cheshire, WA3 7WD
Activities: Business and domestic software development
Shareholder: Martin Richard Dawes
Officers: Helen Fitzsimmons, Secretary/Accountant; Gary Douglas Bunney [1954] Director; Elizabeth Jane Dawes [1945] Director/Consultant; Hayley Jane Dawes [1970] Director/Consultant; Martin Richard Dawes [1943] Director; Paul Richard Dawes [1972] Director/Consultant; Barry Michael Dowd [1965] Customer Support Director; Russell James Hunt [1967] Director; Dewi Eifion Thomas [1957] Director

Meade-King,Robinson & Company Limited
Incorporated: 23 February 1917 *Employees:* 32
Net Worth: £5,933,993 *Total Assets:* £15,711,228
Registered Office: Walker House, Exchange Flags, Liverpool, L2 3YL
Activities: Wholesale of chemical products
Officers: Philip Tarleton, Secretary/Managing Director; Andrew Clifford Roberts [1967] Commercial Director; Paul William James Rothery [1965] Sales Director; James Donald Cameron Smellie [1941] Director; Philip Tarleton [1960] Managing Director

Meadow Foods (Holdings) Limited
Incorporated: 4 May 1995
Net Worth: £2,269,000 *Total Assets:* £15,987,000
Registered Office: Rough Hill, Marlston-Cum-Lache, Chester, CH4 9JS
Activities: Liquid milk and cream production
Parent: P&P Green UK Holdings Limited
Officers: James Damian McDonald, Secretary/Accountant; Mark Henry Chantler [1986] Managing Director; Simon Chantler [1959] Director; James Damian McDonald [1962] Director/Accountant

Meadow Foods Limited
Incorporated: 5 June 1992 *Employees:* 269
Net Worth: £26,787,000 *Total Assets:* £84,681,000
Registered Office: Rough Hill, Marlston-Cum-Lache, Chester, CH4 9JS
Activities: Liquid milk and cream production
Parent: Meadow Foods Holdings Limited
Officers: James Damian McDonald, Secretary; Mark Henry Chantler [1986] Managing Director; Simon Chantler [1959] Director; Damian McDonald [1962] Director/Accountant

Mederco (Cardiff) Ltd
Incorporated: 9 March 2015
Net Worth Deficit: £2,389,449 *Total Assets:* £6,876,821
Registered Office: Unit 18 Cunningham Court, Lions Drive, Blackburn, Lancs, BB1 2QX
Activities: Buying and selling of own real estate
Major Shareholder: Stewart Day
Officers: Stewart Paul Day [1981] Director; Jennifer Anne Hamilton [1980] Director/Guesthouse Owner

Mediaco Limited
Incorporated: 7 December 1998 *Employees:* 82
Net Worth: £2,170,139 *Total Assets:* £7,765,647
Registered Office: Churchill Point, Churchill Way, Trafford Park, Manchester, M17 1BS
Activities: Printing n.e.c.
Shareholders: Mark Andrew Wardle; Arthur Wardle
Officers: Mark Andrew Wardle, Secretary/Advertising; Vincent Anthony Randall [1963] Director/Advertising; Arthur Edgeley Wardle [1929] Director/Advertising; Mark Andrew Wardle [1966] Director/Advertising

Mediacom North Limited
Incorporated: 5 June 1996 *Employees:* 275
Net Worth: £36,119,000 *Total Assets:* £88,494,000
Registered Office: 1 Hardman Street, Manchester, M3 3HF
Activities: Advertising agencies
Parent: WPP Samson Limited
Officers: Stephen David Allan [1963] Director/Chief Executive; Paul James Bramwell [1961] Managing Director; Paul Philip Cooper [1975] Managing Director; Erica Jane Ingham [1972] Director/Chief Financial Officer; Nicholas Alexander Lawson [1965] Director; Simon Paul Price [1973] Managing Director

Medical Gas Solutions Limited
Incorporated: 18 November 2003 *Employees:* 66
Net Worth: £3,954,000 *Total Assets:* £8,370,000
Registered Office: Unit 19 Manor Industrial Estate, Bagillt, Flint, CH6 5UY
Activities: Other human health activities
Parent: Flogas Britain Limited
Officers: Zarana Gandhi, Secretary; James Henry Cubbon [1960] Director; William Francis Gannon [1957] Director; Stephen Gullick [1964] Director/Chief Executive; Mark Edward Plyte [1961] Director

Medical Properties Limited
Incorporated: 9 September 1991
Net Worth: £44,944,952 *Total Assets:* £147,174,976
Registered Office: The Brew House, Greenalls Avenue, Warrington, Cheshire, WA4 6HL
Activities: Other letting and operating of own or leased real estate
Parent: Assura Medical Centres Limited
Officers: Orla Ball [1970] Director/Company Secretary; Paul Bryan Carroll [1969] Director/Accountant; Jayne Marie Cottam [1974] Finance Director; Simon Gould [1974] Director/Chartered Surveyor; Spencer Adrian Kenyon [1962] Director/Chartered Surveyor; Patrick William Lowther [1977] Director/Chartered Surveyor

Medicash Health Benefits Limited
Incorporated: 24 July 1931 *Employees:* 86
Net Worth: £36,555,000 *Total Assets:* £41,591,000
Registered Office: One Derby Square, Liverpool, L2 1AB
Activities: Non-life insurance
Officers: Andrew Roberts, Secretary; Rt Hon Frank Field [1942] Director/MP; Paul Gambon [1980] Sales Director; Robert Charles Hodson [1942] Director/Principal Robert Hodson Assoc; Andrew Roberts [1985] Finance Director; William Tubey [1947] Director/Consultant; Susan Jean Weir [1960] Director

Medicina Holdings Limited
Incorporated: 7 April 2011 *Employees:* 37
Net Worth Deficit: £519,538 *Total Assets:* £6,747,367
Registered Office: Unit 2 Rivington View Business Park, Station Road, Blackrod, Bolton, Lancs, BL6 5BN
Activities: Manufacture of medical and dental instruments and supplies
Parent: HMC Medical UK Limited
Officers: Andrea Bisi [1986] Director [Italian]; Giuseppe Bisi [1952] Director [Italian]; Kenneth George Harrison [1956] Director; Lesley Ann Harrison [1960] Director; Tracey Jane MacDonald [1974] Finance Director; Gianluca Masia [1961] Director [Italian]

Medicina Limited
Incorporated: 16 October 1991 *Employees:* 32
Net Worth: £5,830,938 *Total Assets:* £10,956,102
Registered Office: Unit 2 Rivington View Business Park, Station Road, Blackrod, Bolton, Lancs, BL6 5BN
Activities: Other business support service activities n.e.c.
Shareholders: HMC Medical UK Limited; Medicina Holdings Limited
Officers: Andrea Bisi [1986] Director [Italian]; Kenneth George Harrison [1956] Director

Medicines Evaluation Unit Limited
Incorporated: 28 May 1999 *Employees:* 97
Net Worth: £11,234,523 *Total Assets:* £13,564,496
Registered Office: The Langley Building, Southmoor Road, Wythenshawe, Manchester, M23 9QZ
Activities: Other research and experimental development on natural sciences and engineering
Parent: North West Lung Research Centre Charity
Officers: David Rogers, Secretary; Dr Philip Vernon Barber [1946] Director/Physician; Andrew Edward McNish [1966] Director/Solicitor; Dr Robert McLay Niven [1959] Director/Doctor of Medicine; Professor Charles Anthony Cary Pickering [1942] Director/Respiratory Physician; David Rogers [1962] Director of Operations Business; Professor Sukh Dave Singh [1967] Director/Doctor; Anthony Kevin Webb [1946] Director/Physician; Professor Ashley Arthur Woodcock [1951] Director/Professor of Medicine

Medihealth Limited
Incorporated: 10 August 1995
Net Worth: £6,112,029 *Total Assets:* £8,557,392
Registered Office: Unit 29 Devonshire Road, Worsley, Manchester, M28 3PT
Activities: Dormant company
Parent: Walkboost Limited
Officers: Craig Bernard Fishwick, Secretary; Anwer Ibrahim Patel [1954] Director; Jayanti Chimanbhai Patel Junior [1984] Director

Medimmune U.K. Limited
Incorporated: 6 October 1999 *Employees:* 280
Net Worth: £28 246,278 *Total Assets:* £64,464,812
Registered Office: Plot 6 Renaissance Way, Boulevard Industry Park, Speke, Liverpool, L24 9JW
Activities: Manufacture of other chemical products n.e.c.
Parent: AstraZeneca UK Limited
Officers: Matthew Ian Conacher, Secretary; Iain Alistair Collins [1970] Director; Katie Louise Jackson-Turner [1966] Director/Solicitor; Adrian Charles Noel Kemp [1966] Director

Mediterranean Projects Limited
Incorporated: 24 November 2008
Net Worth: £3,852,708 *Total Assets:* £15,300,910
Registered Office: 5 Brooklands Place, Brooklands Road, Sale, Cheshire, M33 3SD
Activities: Other business support service activities n.e.c.
Parent: Ritz Management Limited
Officers: Paul Michael Telfer [1970] Finance Director

Medlar Fruit Farms Ltd
Incorporated: 29 July 2002
Net Worth: £4,324,109 *Total Assets:* £6,530,024
Registered Office: Solarium Nurseries, Medlar Lane, Medlar with Wesham, Kirkham, Preston, Lancs, PR4 3HR
Activities: Growing of vegetables and melons, roots and tubers
Major Shareholder: Stephen Andrew Bell
Officers: Colin Edward Bell, Secretary; Rose Leighanda Bell [1989] Director/Horticulture; Stephen Andrew Bell [1963] Director and Soft Fruit Grower

Medline Industries Limited
Incorporated: 15 August 1996 *Employees:* 47
Net Worth: £2,777,719 *Total Assets:* £6,963,746
Registered Office: 3rd Floor, Quayside, Wilderspool Business Park, Greenalls Avenue, Warrington, Cheshire, WA4 6HL
Activities: Other business support service activities n.e.c.
Parent: Medline Stellar UK Ltd
Officers: James Abrams, Secretary; James Abrams [1962] Director/Chief Operating Officer of Medline Industries Inc [American]; Helene Marie Lienard [1982] Director/Financial Controller [French]; Carmen Victoria Martin-Hondarza Sobrino [1972] Finance Director [Spanish]

Medline Stellar UK Limited
Incorporated: 16 March 2011 *Employees:* 43
Net Worth: £1,502,123 *Total Assets:* £7,252,965
Registered Office: 3rd Floor, Quayside, Wilderspool Business Park, Greenalls Avenue, Warrington, Cheshire, WA4 6HL
Activities: Activities of distribution holding companies
Officers: James Abrams, Secretary; James D Abrams [1962] Director/Chief Executive Officer [American]; Helene Marie Lienard [1982] Director/Financial Controller [French]; Carmen Victoria Martin Hondarza Sobrino [1972] Finance Director [Spanish]

Medlock FRB Limited
Incorporated: 16 November 2006 *Employees:* 62
Net Worth: £1,686,496 *Total Assets:* £7,332,759
Registered Office: Medlock FRB Limited, Greengate Street, Oldham, Lancs, OL4 1DG
Activities: Development of building projects
Shareholders: Colin Thomas Drury; Andrew Dunster; Michael Peden
Officers: Colin Thomas Drury [1967] Director; Andrew Dunster [1961] Managing Director; Daniel Lewis [1989] Project Director; Michael Peden [1957] Director; David Robert Wheeler [1986] Commercial Director

Medlock Medical Limited
Incorporated: 26 November 2003 *Employees:* 184
Net Worth: £9,106,000 *Total Assets:* £18,326,000
Registered Office: Unity House, Medlock Street, Oldham, Lancs, OL1 3HS
Activities: Manufacture of basic pharmaceutical products
Parent: MHC UK Ltd
Officers: Christopher John Stubbs, Secretary; Stefan Ulf Fristedt [1966] Finance Director [Swedish]; Phil Anthony Hague [1962] Director/Factory Manager; Richard Twomey [1964] Director

Medtrade Products Limited
Incorporated: 10 September 1999 *Employees:* 64
Net Worth: £14,847,000 *Total Assets:* £21,552,000
Registered Office: Electra House, Electra Way, Crewe, Cheshire, CW1 6GL
Activities: Other manufacturing n.e.c.
Shareholders: Craig Julian Hardy; Melanie Ruth Hardy; The Summit Group Ltd
Officers: Stephen Collins, Secretary; Simon James Knevett Barratt [1958] Director; Stephen Philip Collins [1967] Finance Director; Craig Julian Hardy [1963] Director/Chief Executive; Melanie Ruth Hardy [1965] Technical Director; Philip Hogben [1963] Director/General Manager; Jonathan David Ranfield [1965] Regulatory Director

Medway Ports Limited
Incorporated: 2 October 1991
Net Worth: £19,200,000 *Total Assets:* £19,200,000
Registered Office: Maritime Centre, Port of Liverpool, L21 1LA
Activities: Activities of head offices
Parent: Peel Ports Operations Limited
Officers: Farook Akhtar Khan, Secretary; Caroline Ruth Marrison Gill, Secretary; Thomas Eardley Allison [1948] Director; Ian Graeme Lloyd Charnock [1962] Director; John Whittaker [1942] Director; Mark Whitworth [1966] Director

Melba Group Limited
Incorporated: 25 November 2015
Net Worth: £9,007,831 *Total Assets:* £18,191,344
Registered Office: Derby Works, Manchester Road, Bury, Lancs, BL9 9NX
Activities: Activities of head offices
Officers: Jonathan Gregg Dawson [1970] Director; Paul Lee Harrison [1960] Director

Melba Products Holdings Limited
Incorporated: 7 June 2011 *Employees:* 144
Net Worth: £9,621,992 *Total Assets:* £18,092,770
Registered Office: Derby Works, Manchester Road, Bury, Lancs, BL9 9NX
Activities: Manufacture of other plastic products
Parent: Melba Group Limited
Officers: Paul Lee Harrison, Secretary; Jonathan Gregg Dawson [1970] Director; Paul Lee Harrison [1960] Director

Melba Products Limited
Incorporated: 6 April 1982 *Employees:* 147
Net Worth: £8,285,102 *Total Assets:* £16,042,222
Registered Office: Derby Works, Manchester Road, Bury, Lancs, BL9 9NX
Activities: Manufacture of other plastic products
Officers: Paul Lee Harrison, Secretary; Jonathan Gregg Dawson [1970] Director/Production; Paul Lee Harrison [1960] Director; Phillip Roger Hyman [1965] Sales Director; Michael Shaun Todd [1973] Purchasing Director

Melli Limited
Incorporated: 4 October 2010
Net Worth Deficit: £3,563,548 *Total Assets:* £13,735,753
Registered Office: The Victory Offices, 112 Victory Road, Blackpool, Lancs, FY1 3NW
Activities: Public houses and bars
Parent: Apis Limited
Officers: Joanne Louise Jones, Secretary; James Edward Baer [1955] Director; Michael David George [1973] Director; Mark John Goddard [1970] Director; Joanne Louise Jones [1966] Director; Gary Eric Roberts [1963] Director

Meltham Properties Limited
Incorporated: 9 December 1999
Net Worth: £8,664,318 *Total Assets:* £11,949,724
Registered Office: Central Buildings, Richmond Terrace, Blackburn, Lancs, BB1 7AP
Activities: Other letting and operating of own or leased real estate
Parent: Meltham Properties (2012) Limited
Officers: Richard Collinge [1955] Managing Director; Timothy Benson Kay [1963] Director

Memhay Limited
Incorporated: 22 May 1989
Net Worth: £3,587,552 *Total Assets:* £9,346,353
Registered Office: 2nd Floor, Parkgates, Bury New Road, Prestwich, Manchester, M25 0TL
Activities: Other social work activities without accommodation n.e.c.
Officers: Chaim Shimen Lebrecht [1968] Director; Michael Yehuda Lebrecht [1964] Director/Manager; Susan Lebrecht [1943] Director

Menta Redrow Limited
Incorporated: 12 December 2012
Net Worth Deficit: £739,844 *Total Assets:* £51,729,808
Registered Office: Redrow House, St Davids Park, Ewloe, Deeside, Flintshire, CH5 3RX
Activities: Construction of domestic buildings
Shareholders: Menta Developments Limited; Redrow Homes Limited
Officers: Graham Anthony Cope, Secretary; Mark Robert Elson [1965] Director/Accountant; Helene Hjortland [1969] Director [Norwegian]; Craig Robert Marks [1963] Director; Keith Joseph Parrett [1955] Director

The James Mercer Group Limited
Incorporated: 1 February 2000 *Employees:* 204
Net Worth: £2,732,696 *Total Assets:* £9,044,429
Registered Office: Tulketh Hall Works, Hesketh Street, Ashton on Ribble, Preston, Lancs, PR2 2RB
Activities: Plumbing, heat and air-conditioning installation
Parent: James Mercer Holdings Limited
Officers: Jennifer Helen Mayor, Secretary; Paul Catterall [1960] Director; Jennifer Helen Mayor [1970] Director/Accountant; Andrew James Moxham [1977] Director; John Moxham [1949] Director; Susan Moxham [1949] Director; Stephen Michael George Potter [1961] Director

Merchant Rentals Limited
Incorporated: 21 May 2002 *Employees:* 57
Net Worth Deficit: £2,005,092 *Total Assets:* £16,289,851
Registered Office: Westway Park, Galway Crescent, Haydock, Merseyside, WA11 0GR
Activities: Financial leasing
Shareholder: Andrew John Peake
Officers: Michael Christopher Prendergast, Secretary; Kevin Leslie Adlam [1974] Director/Business Development; Graham Crabtree [1950] Director/Accountant; Mariel Lesley Crabtree [1948] Director; Simon MacAuley [1957] Director; Andrew John Peake [1969] Director

The Merchant Taylors' Schools,Crosby
Incorporated: 23 July 2008 *Employees:* 340
Net Worth: £26,360,106 *Total Assets:* £29,354,942
Registered Office: 186 Liverpool Road, Crosby, Liverpool, L23 0QP
Activities: General secondary education
Officers: Andrew David Norton, Secretary; Beverley Claire Bell [1959] Director/Senior Traffic Commissioner; John Paul Cartwright [1961] Director; Charles Anthony Cowling [1962] Director/Actuary; Kathryn Anne Crewe-Read [1968] Director/Headmistress; David Stephen Evans [1957] Director/Solicitor; Dr Jennifer Ann Fox [1959] Director/Medical Practitioner; Anna Gabriella Gervasoni [1975] Director/General Manager; Lesley Carol Martin-Wright [1957] Director/Chief Executive; David Yip [1967] Director/Management Consultant

Mercian Limited
Incorporated: 22 September 2004 *Employees:* 8
Net Worth: £5,329,094 *Total Assets:* £11,474,907
Registered Office: Units 3 & 4 The Barns, Highfield Farm, Mill Lane, Snelson, Macclesfield, Cheshire, SK11 9BN
Activities: Wholesale of fruit and vegetables
Shareholder: WHK Partnership Limited
Officers: Anthony Crawford Heal, Secretary; John Lee Carter [1970] Director; Anthony Crawford Heal [1963] Director; Phillip James Kemp [1966] Director; Martyn James Frank Read [1967] Director; Gary Thomas Stanier [1967] Director

Mere Plantations Limited
Incorporated: 4 January 2007 *Employees:* 4
Net Worth: £1,645,933,312 *Total Assets:* £1,770,506,624
Registered Office: Unit 1 Cherry Tree Lane, Rostherne, Altrincham, Cheshire, WA14 3RZ
Activities: Other business support service activities n.e.c.
Major Shareholder: Mark Andrew Hogg
Officers: Michael Anthony Steele, Secretary; Paul Forjoe [1957] Director [Ghanaian]; Mark Andrew Hogg [1970] Managing Director

Meridian Business Support Group PLC
Incorporated: 12 April 2005 *Employees:* 258
Net Worth: £3,733,064 *Total Assets:* £21,418,750
Registered Office: 1st Floor, Trident Business Park, 3 Styal Road, Manchester, M22 5XB
Activities: Dormant company
Shareholders: Rodney William Kavanagh; Sandra Beryl Kavanagh; Mark Mitchell
Officers: Jeanette Barrowcliffe, Secretary; Jeanette Barrowcliffe [1969] Finance Director; Rodney William Kavanagh [1945] Director; Mark Victor Mitchell [1963] Director

Meridian Business Support Limited
Incorporated: 19 May 1989 *Employees:* 322
Net Worth: £8,163,241 *Total Assets:* £24,116,572
Registered Office: 1st Floor, Trident Business Park, 3 Styal Road, Manchester, M22 5XB
Activities: Temporary employment agency activities
Officers: Jeanette Barrowcliffe, Secretary; Jeanette Barrowcliffe [1969] Finance Director; Richard Ewing [1974] Managing Director Built Environment; Derek Skelton [1963] Managing Director Industrial

Merlin Diesel Systems Ltd
Incorporated: 13 September 1990 *Employees:* 80
Net Worth: £7,030,389 *Total Assets:* £14,713,502
Registered Office: 189-191 Bradkirk Place, Walton Summit, Preston, Lancs, PR5 8AJ
Activities: Manufacture of other parts and accessories for motor vehicles
Parent: Merlin Diesel Holdings Limited
Officers: Emma Louise Bramley, Secretary; Kenneth Bramley [1946] Director/Engineer; Leigh Kenneth Bramley [1969] Director/Sales; Scott Bramley [1975] Director/Engineer; Michael Francis Brown [1972] Director; Michael Rawlinson [1962] Director/Engineer

Merlin Ports Limited
Incorporated: 27 October 1987
Net Worth: £1,498,000 *Total Assets:* £40,362,000
Registered Office: Maritime Centre, Port of Liverpool, L21 1LA
Activities: Activities of head offices
Parent: Peel Ports Operations Limited
Officers: Farook Akhtar Khan, Secretary; Caroline Ruth Marrison Gill, Secretary Thomas Eardley Allison [1948] Director; Ian Graeme Lloyd Charnock [1962] Director; John Whittaker [1942] Director; Mark Whitworth [1966] Director

Merlyn Industries U.K. Limited
Incorporated: 13 January 2000 *Employees:* 20
Net Worth: £2,387,521 *Total Assets:* £8,398,545
Registered Office: Ladyfield House, Station Road, Wilmslow, Cheshire, SK9 1BU
Activities: Wholesale of hardware, plumbing and heating equipment and supplies
Officers: Richard Hawke Collins, Secretary; Richard Hawke Collins [1962] Director; Nicholas Paul Kelsall [1956] Director; Robert James Sidell [1976] Director/Financial Controller; Shaun Michael Smith [1961] Director

Merry Fox Stud Limited
Incorporated: 13 September 2006
Net Worth: £16,678,514 *Total Assets:* £16,870,144
Registered Office: Mobberley Old Hall, Hall Lane, Mobberley, Knutsford, Cheshire, WA16 7AB
Activities: Raising of horses and other equines
Parent: Intertrust NV
Officers: Lisa Carr, Secretary; Craig Bennett [1963] Director; Gary Paul Hadden [1981] Managing Director [Irish]; Craig Anthony Hulme [1967] Finance Director

Mersey Bioenergy Holdings Limited
Incorporated: 9 September 2014
Net Worth Deficit: £2,931,000 *Total Assets:* £105,708,000
Registered Office: c/o Albany SPC Services Ltd, 3rd Floor, 3-5 Charlotte Street, Manchester, M1 4HB
Activities: Treatment and disposal of non-hazardous waste
Shareholders: Burmeister and Wain Scandanavian Contractor AS; Stobart Green Energy Ltd; UK Waste Resources and Energy Investments LP
Officers: Ailison Louise Mitchell, Secretary; Richard Edward Charles Butcher [1964] Director; Christian Andreas Grundtvig [1959] Director [Danish]; Robert Hamish McPherson [1976] Director; Andrew Street [1955] Director

The Mersey Docks and Harbour Company Limited
Incorporated: 12 November 2010 *Employees:* 408
Net Worth: £236,500,000 *Total Assets:* £1,115,699,968
Registered Office: Maritime Centre, Port of Liverpool, L21 1LA
Activities: Inland passenger water transport
Parent: Peel Ports Investments Limited
Officers: Farook Akhtar Khan, Secretary; Caroline Ruth Marrison Gill, Secretary; Thomas Eardley Allison [1948] Director; Ian Graeme Lloyd Charnock [1962] Director; Steven Keith Underwood [1974] Director; John Whittaker [1942] Director; Mark Whitworth [1966] Director

Mersey Waste Holdings Limited
Incorporated: 2 June 1992
Net Worth: £5,261,128 *Total Assets:* £8,988,931
Registered Office: 7th Floor, No 1 Mann Island, Liverpool, L3 1BP
Activities: Activities of head offices
Parent: Mersey Waste Disposal Authority
Officers: Carl David Beer [1962] Director/Chief Executive; Councillor Anthony Concepcion [1948] Director/Councillor; Michael John O'Brien [1949] Director/Retired; Dr Graham David Richard Parry [1945] Director; Councillor Charlie John Preston [1955] Director/Driver; Rex Keith Norman Russell [1944] Director; Peter Gwyn Williams [1963] Finance Director

Merseylink (Holdings) Limited
Incorporated: 18 November 2013
Net Worth Deficit: £43,936,000 *Total Assets:* £456,398,016
Registered Office: Forward Point, Tan House, Lane, Widnes, Cheshire, WA8 0SL
Activities: Construction of bridges and tunnels
Shareholders: MG Bridge Investments Limited; Wigg Investments Limited
Officers: Isela Bahena [1974] Director [American]; Jennifer Douglas [1976] Director [Irish]; Matthew James Edwards [1985] Director; Volker Ellenberg [1969] Director [German]; Alex Kornman [1982] Alternative Director [American]; Marietta Moshiashvili [1971] Director [Ukrainian]; Frank Manfred Schramm [1968] Director [German]

Merseylink (Issuer) PLC
Incorporated: 14 February 2014
Net Worth: £50,000 *Total Assets:* £253,608,992
Registered Office: Forward Point, Tan House, Lane, Widnes, Cheshire, WA8 0SL
Activities: Activities of construction holding companies
Parent: Merseylink (Finance) Limited
Officers: Alexander William Robert Fulcher, Secretary; Isela Bahena [1974] Director [American]; Jennifer Douglas [1976] Director [Irish]; Matthew James Edwards [1985] Director; Volker Ellenberg [1969] Director [German]; Alex Kornman [1982] Alternative Director [American]; Marietta Moshiashvili [1971] Director [Ukrainian]; Frank Manfred Schramm [1968] Director [German]

Merseylink Limited
Incorporated: 19 November 2013
Net Worth Deficit: £43,986,000 *Total Assets:* £456,398,016
Registered Office: Forward Point, Tan House, Lane, Widnes, Cheshire, WA8 0SL
Activities: Construction of bridges and tunnels
Parent: Merseylink (Finance) Limited
Officers: Isela Bahena [1974] Director [American]; Jennifer Douglas [1976] Director [Irish]; Matthew James Edwards [1985] Director; Volker Ellenberg [1969] Director [German]; Alex Kornman [1982] Alternative Director [American]; Marietta Moshiashvili [1971] Director [Ukrainian]; Frank Manfred Schramm [1968] Director [German]

Merseyrail Electrics 2002 Limited
Incorporated: 21 January 2002 *Employees:* 1,239
Net Worth: £12,640,000 *Total Assets:* £51,700,000
Registered Office: Rail House, Lord Nelson Street, Liverpool, L1 1JF
Activities: Passenger rail transport, interurban
Parent: Merseyrail Services Holding Company Limited
Officers: Dominic Daniel Gerard Booth [1963] Managing Director; Jeremy Paul Bowen [1972] Director/Accountant; Jane Christine English [1972] Human Resources Director; Christiaan Spencer Harris [1974] Finance Director; Andrew Joseph Heath [1964] Operations Director; John Michael Heron [1972] Director/Accountant; Andrew Brian Meadows [1963] Director; Peter Strachan [1959] Managing Director; John Anthony Richard Whitehurst [1971] Managing Director

Merseyrail Services Holding Company Limited
Incorporated: 18 December 2002 *Employees:* 1,239
Net Worth: £12,342,000 *Total Assets:* £51,381,000
Registered Office: Eversheds House, 70 Great Bridgewater Street, Manchester, M1 5ES
Activities: Activities of head offices
Shareholders: Serco Holdings Limited; Abellio Transport Holdings Ltd
Officers: Dominic Daniel Gerard Booth [1963] Managing Director; Alan Dingwall [1973] Director; Julian Edwards [1969] Finance Director; John Michael Heron [1972] Director/Accountant; Angelique Catherina Jannetje Magielse [1968] Finance Director [Dutch]; John Anthony Richard Whitehurst [1971] Managing Director

Merseyside Estates Limited
Incorporated: 21 May 1926 *Employees:* 7
Net Worth: £25,829,350 *Total Assets:* £53,214,456
Registered Office: c/o Guy Williams Layton, Solicitors, Pacific Chambers, 11-13 Victoria Street, Liverpool, L2 5QQ
Activities: Buying and selling of own real estate
Officers: Christine Sutton, Secretary; Andrew James Grey Atkinson [1956] Director; Christopher Mark Bolland [1978] Director/Architect; Neil Kemsley [1946] Director; Sean Timothy Seery [1964] Director/Estate Agent; Christine Sutton [1958] Director/Solicitor; Jason Wadeson [1972] Director/Chartered Surveyor

Merseyside Special Investment Fund Limited
Incorporated: 19 October 1994 *Employees:* 14
Net Worth: £8,804,169 *Total Assets:* £37,444,664
Registered Office: 2nd Floor, Exchange Court, 1 Dale Street, Liverpool, L2 2PP
Activities: Activities of financial services holding companies
Officers: Lisa Greenhalgh, Secretary/Director Finance; Neil Ashbridge [1955] Director/Retired; Mark Basnett [1960] Executive Director - Economic Development; Lisa Greenhalgh [1969] Director; John O'Brien [1959] Director/Retired; Elaine O'Donnell [1970] Director/Chartered Accountant [Irish]

Metacre Limited
Incorporated: 23 April 1987
Net Worth: £3,993,000 *Total Assets:* £12,111,000
Registered Office: Lynton House, Ackhurst Park, Foxhole Road, Chorley, Lancs, PR7 1NY
Activities: Other letting and operating of own or leased real estate
Parent: Northern Trust Company Limited
Officers: Anne Kelleher, Secretary; Michael John Grindrod [1958] Director; Patrick Lee Hemmings [1966] Director; Mark Lorimer Widders [1960] Finance Director

Metal & Waste Recycling Limited
Incorporated: 17 November 1971 *Employees:* 240
Net Worth: £4,163,000 *Total Assets:* £43,157,000
Registered Office: Sirius House, Delta Crescent, Westbrook, Warrington, Cheshire, WA5 7NS
Activities: Collection of non-hazardous waste
Shareholders: Ausurus Group Ltd; Gad Holdings Limited
Officers: Christopher John Tinsley, Secretary; Edwin Leijnse [1967] Director [Dutch]; Gary Samuel Mann [1957] Director/Metal Trader; Christopher Phillip Sheppard [1974] Director; Lee Peter Simmons [1963] Contracts Director; Neil Andrew Stinson [1970] Director/Accountant

Metaltek International (UK) Limited
Incorporated: 28 May 2008 *Employees:* 56
Net Worth Deficit: £649,751 *Total Assets:* £7,550,323
Registered Office: 64a Bridge Street, Manchester, M3 3BA
Activities: Casting of other non-ferrous metals
Parent: Metaltek International Inc
Officers: Richard M Danning, Secretary; Richard M Danning [1962] Director/Financial Management [American]; Summerfield Johnston Jr [1932] Director/Executive Manager [American]; Robert J Smickley [1951] Director/Executive Management [American]

Metalube Ltd
Incorporated: 31 May 1988 *Employees:* 29
Net Worth: £6,047,587 *Total Assets:* £7,061,554
Registered Office: 4 Huntsman Drive, Northbank Industrial Park, Irlam, Manchester, M44 5EG
Activities: Manufacture of other chemical products n.e.c.
Major Shareholder: Robert Peter Brown
Officers: Robert Peter Brown [1970] Director; Douglas Vivian Hunt [1966] Director/Sales Manager; Christopher John Nettleship [1970] Director/Chemist

Metamark (UK) Limited
Incorporated: 24 September 1992 *Employees:* 89
Net Worth: £6,295,795 *Total Assets:* £12,651,901
Registered Office: New Quay Road, Lancaster, LA1 5QP
Activities: Other manufacturing n.e.c.
Officers: Matthew Jonathan Enright [1978] Director/Chartered Accountant; Paul French [1972] Director/Chief Executive; Ian Geoffrey Simister [1968] Director

Metcalfe Holdings Limited
Incorporated: 31 March 2006 *Employees:* 1
Net Worth: £34,705 *Total Assets:* £9,249,531
Registered Office: Corpacq House, 1 Goose Green, Altrincham, Cheshire, WA14 1DW
Activities: Activities of other holding companies n.e.c.
Officers: Stephen James Scott [1978] Director

Metcalfe Plant Hire Limited
Incorporated: 26 January 1987 *Employees:* 103
Net Worth: £8,760,750 *Total Assets:* £21,646,428
Registered Office: Gilwilly Road, Gilwilly Industrial Estate, Penrith, Cumbria, CA11 9BL
Activities: Development of building projects
Officers: Leslie John Balmer [1956] Finance and Administration Director; Nigel John Clegg [1968] Director/Transport Manager; Elizabeth Fiona Dunn [1965] Director; Matthew Raymond Healey [1980] Director; Giles Keenan [1965] Director; Stephen James Scott [1978] Director

Meter Fit (North East) Limited
Incorporated: 5 April 2002
Net Worth: £11,001,000 *Total Assets:* £23,754,000
Registered Office: 5th Floor, 1 Marsden Street, Manchester, M2 1HW
Activities: Other business support service activities n.e.c.
Parent: Meter Serve (North East) Limited
Officers: Sarah Ann Blackburn, Secretary; Sarah Ann Blackburn [1980] Director/Solicitor; George Martin Donoghue [1974] Director; Sean Latus [1969] Director/Investment Officer; Henricus Lambertus Pijls [1965] Director/Chief Executive Officer [Dutch]

Meter Fit (North West) Limited
Incorporated: 28 December 2001
Net Worth: £8,729,000 *Total Assets:* £27,752,000
Registered Office: 5th Floor, 1 Marsden Street, Manchester, M2 1HW
Activities: Other business support service activities n.e.c.
Parent: Meter Serve (North West) Limited
Officers: Sarah Ann Blackburn, Secretary; Sarah Ann Blackburn [1980] Director/Solicitor; George Martin Donoghue [1974] Director; Sean Latus [1969] Director/Investment Officer; Henricus Lambertus Pijls [1965] Director/Chief Executive Officer [Dutch]

Meter Fit 10 Limited
Incorporated: 16 December 2015 *Employees:* 3
Net Worth: £15,000 *Total Assets:* £85,960,000
Registered Office: 5th Floor, 1 Marsden Street, Manchester, M2 1HW
Activities: Other business support service activities n.e.c.
Parent: Meter Serve 10 Limited
Officers: Sarah Ann Blackburn, Secretary; Sarah Ann Blackburn [1980] Director/Solicitor; George Martin Donoghue [1974] Director; Sean Latus [1969] Director/Investment Officer; Henricus Lambertus Pijls [1965] Director/Chief Executive Officer [Dutch]

Meter Fit 2 Limited
Incorporated: 22 January 2010 *Employees:* 3
Net Worth: £208,000 *Total Assets:* £9,642,000
Registered Office: 5th Floor, 1 Marsden Street, Manchester, M2 1HW
Activities: Other business support service activities n.e.c.
Parent: Meter Serve 2 Limited
Officers: Sarah Ann Blackburn, Secretary; Sarah Ann Blackburn [1980] Director/Solicitor; George Martin Donoghue [1974] Director; Sean Latus [1969] Director/Investment Officer; Henricus Lambertus Pijls [1965] Director/Chief Executive Officer [Dutch]

Meter Fit 3 Limited
Incorporated: 10 June 2010 *Employees:* 3
Net Worth: £4,242,000 *Total Assets:* £70,508,000
Registered Office: 5th Floor, 1 Marsden Street, Manchester, M2 1HW
Activities: Other business support service activities n.e.c.
Parent: Meter Serve 3 Limited
Officers: Sarah Ann Blackburn, Secretary; Sarah Ann Blackburn [1980] Director/Solicitor; George Martin Donoghue [1974] Director; Sean Latus [1969] Director/Investment Officer; Henricus Lambertus Pijls [1965] Director/Chief Executive Officer [Dutch]

Meter Fit 4 Limited
Incorporated: 19 September 2013 *Employees:* 3
Net Worth: £652,000 *Total Assets:* £170,068,000
Registered Office: 5th Floor, 1 Marsden Street, Manchester, M2 1HW
Activities: Other business support service activities n.e.c.
Parent: Meter Serve 4 Limited
Officers: Sarah Ann Blackburn, Secretary; Sarah Ann Blackburn [1980] Director/Solicitor; George Martin Donoghue [1974] Director; Sean Latus [1969] Director/Investment Officer; Henricus Lambertus Pijls [1965] Director/Chief Executive Officer [Dutch]

Meter Fit 5 Limited
Incorporated: 29 July 2015
Net Worth Deficit: £20,835,000 *Total Assets:* £243,666,000
Registered Office: 5th Floor, 1 Marsden Street, Manchester, M2 1HW
Activities: Other business support service activities n.e.c.
Parent: Meter Serve 5 Limited
Officers: Sarah Ann Blackburn, Secretary; Sarah Ann Blackburn [1980] Director/Solicitor; George Martin Donoghue [1974] Director; Sean Latus [1969] Director/Investment Officer; Henricus Lambertus Pijls [1965] Director/Chief Executive Officer [Dutch]

Meter Fit Assets Limited
Incorporated: 29 October 2010 *Employees:* 4
Net Worth: £1,632,000 *Total Assets:* £6,848,000
Registered Office: 5th Floor, 1 Marsden Street, Manchester, M2 1HW
Activities: Other business support service activities n.e.c.
Parent: Calvin Capital Limited
Officers: Sarah Ann Blackburn, Secretary; Sarah Ann Blackburn [1980] Director/Solicitor; George Martin Donoghue [1974] Director; Sean Latus [1969] Director/Investment Officer; Henricus Lambertus Pijls [1965] Director/Chief Executive Officer [Dutch]

Meter Serve 10 Limited
Incorporated: 16 December 2015
Net Worth: £5,000 *Total Assets:* £22,075,000
Registered Office: 5th Floor, 1 Marsden Street, Manchester, M2 1HW
Activities: Other business support service activities n.e.c.
Parent: Calvin Capital Limited
Officers: Sarah Ann Blackburn, Secretary; Sarah Ann Blackburn [1980] Director/Solicitor; George Martin Donoghue [1974] Director; Sean Latus [1969] Director/Investment Officer; Henricus Lambertus Pijls [1965] Director/Chief Executive Officer [Dutch]

Meter Serve 3 Limited
Incorporated: 10 June 2010
Net Worth: £5,000 *Total Assets:* £29,753,000
Registered Office: 5th Floor, 1 Marsden Street, Manchester, M2 1HW
Activities: Activities of other holding companies n.e.c.
Parent: Calvin Capital Limited
Officers: Sarah Ann Blackburn, Secretary; Sarah Ann Blackburn [1980] Director/Solicitor; George Martin Donoghue [1974] Director; Sean Latus [1969] Director/Investment Officer; Henricus Lambertus Pijls [1965] Director/Chief Executive Officer [Dutch]

Meter Serve 4 Limited
Incorporated: 19 September 2013
Net Worth: £7,788,000 *Total Assets:* £93,894,000
Registered Office: 5th Floor, 1 Marsden Street, Manchester, M2 1HW
Activities: Activities of other holding companies n.e.c.
Parent: Calvin Capital Limited
Officers: Sarah Ann Blackburn, Secretary; Sarah Ann Blackburn [1980] Director/Solicitor; George Martin Donoghue [1974] Director; Sean Latus [1969] Director/Investment Officer; Henricus Lambertus Pijls [1965] Director/Chief Executive Officer [Dutch]

Methanex (UK) Limited
Incorporated: 23 October 2000
Net Worth: £8,231,000 *Total Assets:* £8,584,000
Registered Office: Eversheds House, 70 Great Bridgewater Street, Manchester, M1 5ES
Activities: Manufacture of other chemical products n.e.c.
Parent: Methanex Corporation
Officers: Kevin Ian Price [1965] Director [Canadian]; David Paul Valembois [1971] Director/Finance Manager [Belgian]; Wade Wiggins [1968] Director/Vice President [Canadian]

Methven UK Limited
Incorporated: 22 June 2007 *Employees:* 49
Net Worth: £6,055,990 *Total Assets:* £19,455,964
Registered Office: Eversheds House, 70 Great Bridgewater Street, Manchester, M1 5ES
Activities: Wholesale of hardware, plumbing and heating equipment and supplies
Officers: David Banfield [1967] Director; Martin Stuart Walker [1968] Director

Metro MRH Limited
Incorporated: 4 February 1999
Net Worth: £38,355,432 *Total Assets:* £84,987,656
Registered Office: The Brew House, Greenalls Avenue, Warrington, Cheshire, WA4 6HL
Activities: Other letting and operating of own or leased real estate
Parent: Assura Financing Limited
Officers: Orla Ball [1970] Director/Company Secretary; Paul Bryan Carroll [1969] Director/Accountant; Jayne Marie Cottam [1974] Finance Director; Simon Gould [1974] Director/Chartered Surveyor; Spencer Adrian Kenyon [1962] Director/Chartered Surveyor; Patrick William Lowther [1977] Director/Chartered Surveyor

Metro MRI Limited
Incorporated: 4 February 2005 *Employees:* 7
Net Worth: £26,810,030 *Total Assets:* £84,799,696
Registered Office: The Brew House, Greenalls Avenue, Warrington, Cheshire, WA4 6HL
Activities: Other letting and operating of own or leased real estate
Parent: Assura Medical Centres Limited
Officers: Orla Ball [1970] Director/Company Secretary; Paul Bryan Carroll [1969] Director/Accountant; Jayne Marie Cottam [1974] Finance Director; Simon Gould [1974] Director/Chartered Surveyor; Spencer Adrian Kenyon [1962] Director/Chartered Surveyor; Patrick William Lowther [1977] Director/Chartered Surveyor

Metro MRM Limited
Incorporated: 16 June 2006
Net Worth: £7,746,052 *Total Assets:* £34,795,244
Registered Office: The Brew House, Greenalls Avenue, Warrington, Cheshire, WA4 6HL
Activities: Other letting and operating of own or leased real estate
Parent: Assura Financing Limited
Officers: Orla Ball [1970] Director/Company Secretary; Paul Bryan Carroll [1969] Director/Accountant; Jayne Marie Cottam [1974] Finance Director; Simon Gould [1974] Director/Chartered Surveyor; Spencer Adrian Kenyon [1962] Director/Chartered Surveyor; Patrick William Lowther [1977] Director/Chartered Surveyor

Metrohm UK Limited
Incorporated: 18 July 1994 *Employees:* 46
Net Worth: £7,524,919 *Total Assets:* £10,533,190
Registered Office: Metrohm House, Evenwood Close, Daresbury Court, Runcorn, Cheshire, WA7 1LZ
Activities: Non-specialised wholesale trade
Parent: Metrohm AG
Officers: Nicola Hough, Secretary; Dr Volker Jorg Frost [1966] Director [German]; Patrick Edgar Gruninger [1974] Director/Group CEO [Swiss]; Andrew Matthews [1962] Director; Daniel August Wager [1964] Director/Group Chief Financial Officer [Swiss]

Metronet (UK) Limited
Incorporated: 25 November 2003 *Employees:* 142
Net Worth: £8,503,000 *Total Assets:* £16,179,000
Registered Office: Turing House, Archway 5, Manchester, M15 5RL
Activities: Other telecommunications activities
Parent: Manchester Metronet Limited
Officers: Steven Jon Axon [1981] Director; Andrew Geoffrey Goldwater [1974] Director

Metropolitan Cathedral Services Limited
Incorporated: 17 October 1995
Net Worth: £12,627,102 *Total Assets:* £13,774,699
Registered Office: Lace, Croxteth Drive, Liverpool, L17 1AA
Activities: Other retail sale in non-specialised stores
Officers: John Paul McMahon, Secretary; The Right Reverend Peter Cookson [1939] Director/Roman Catholic Priest; Rev Sean Kirwin [1968] Director/RC Priest; Reverend Anthony O'Brien [1955] Director/Roman Catholic Priest

Mettler-Toledo Finance (UK) Limited
Incorporated: 15 November 2013
Net Worth: £1,695,831,040 *Total Assets:* £2,062,043,008
Registered Office: 520 Olympic Court, Montford Street, Salford, M50 2XD
Activities: Activities of head offices
Officers: Paul Colin Baines, Secretary; Paul Colin Baines [1962] Director; Marc Marie Bertrand Du Breuil-Helion de La Gueronniere [1964] Director [French]; Simon Richard Radcliffe Kirk [1959] Director; Mark Ronald Purle [1965] Director; Alan Lindsey Purvis [1950] Director

Mettler-Toledo Safeline Limited
Incorporated: 23 May 1988 *Employees:* 258
Net Worth: £5,067,652,096 *Total Assets:* £5,082,198,016
Registered Office: Olympic Court, Montford Street, Salford, M50 2XD
Activities: Machining
Parent: Mettler-Toledo Holdings LLC
Officers: Paul Colin Baines Secretary; Paul Colin Baines [1962] Director/Accountant; Alan Lindsey Purvis [1959] Managing Director

Mexichem Dura-Line UK, Ltd
Incorporated: 21 September 2015
Net Worth: £193,462,672 *Total Assets:* £432,887,232
Registered Office: c/o Andrea Ost, Mexichem Dura-Line UK Ltd, The Health Business and Technical Park, Runcorn, Cheshire, WA7 4QX
Activities: Manufacture of other plastic products
Officers: Andrea Ost [1968] Director/Downstream Controller

Mexichem UK Limited
Incorporated: 26 November 2009 *Employees:* 205
Net Worth: £41,184,000 *Total Assets:* £66,206,000
Registered Office: The Heath Business & Technical Park, Runcorn, Cheshire, WA7 4QX
Activities: Manufacture of industrial gases
Parent: Mexichem Fluor S.A. de C.V.
Officers: Paula Breden, Secretary; Simon Gardner [1969] Director/Medical Products General Manager; Andrea Ost [1968] Director

Mexichem Wavin UK Ltd
Incorporated: 22 September 2015
Net Worth: £252 709,952 *Total Assets:* £256,499,216
Registered Office: c/o Andrea Ost, Mexichem Wavin UK Ltd, The Health Business and Technical Park, Runcorn, Cheshire, WA7 4QX
Activities: Manufacture of builders ware of plastic
Officers: Andrea Ost [1968] Director/Downstream Controller

Meyer Group Limited
Incorporated: 14 August 1979 *Employees:* 113
Net Worth: £13,889,000 *Total Assets:* £39,529,000
Registered Office: Meyer Group Limited, Wirral International Business Park, Riverview Road, Bromborough, Wirral, Merseyside, CH62 3RH
Activities: Wholesale of household goods (other than musical instruments) n.e.c
Officers: Paul Burke, Secretary; Paul Burke [1965] Director/Certified Accountant; Geoffrey Thomas Gorst [1957] Sales Director; Mark Rossiter Ivory [1967] Managing Director; Sean Cameron Priest [1966] Operations Director; Carl James Wright [1979] Marketing Director

MGF Limited
Incorporated: 7 February 2001 *Employees:* 322
Net Worth: £69,736,032 *Total Assets:* £81,936,056
Registered Office: Grant House, South Lancashire Ind Est, Lockett Road, Ashton in Makerfield, Wigan, Lancs, WN4 8DE
Activities: Activities of head offices
Major Shareholder: Michael O'Hara
Officers: John Geoffrey Woodward, Secretary; Joanne Durr [1970] Director; Vanda Murray [1960] Director; Generald Nowicki [1959] Director/Chartered Accountant; Michael O'Hara [1945] Director; Catherine Whitworth [1969] Director

MGF Property Limited
Incorporated: 28 January 2005
Net Worth: £2,971,689 *Total Assets:* £9,436,521
Registered Office: Grant House, South Lancashire Industrial Estate, Lockett Road, Ashton in Makerfield, Wigan, Lancs, WN4 8DE
Activities: Other letting and operating of own or leased real estate
Parent: MGF Ltd
Officers: Generald Nowicki, Secretary/Chartered Accountant; Generald Nowicki [1959] Director/Chartered Accountant; Michael O'Hara [1945] Director

MHC UK Limited
Incorporated: 25 July 2006
Net Worth: £73,577,000 *Total Assets:* £210,812,992
Registered Office: Unity House, Medlock Street, Oldham, Lancs, OL1 3HS
Activities: Activities of head offices
Parent: Molnlycke Holding AB
Officers: Christopher John Stubbs, Secretary; Stefan Ulf Fristedt [1966] Finance Director [Swedish]; Nicholas Andrew Rothwell [1973] Director/General Manager; Richard Twomey [1964] Director

MHI Vestas Offshore Wind UK Ltd
Incorporated: 27 April 2006 *Employees:* 172
Net Worth: £19,166,000 *Total Assets:* £115,239,000
Registered Office: First Floor, 303 Bridgewater Place, Birchwood Park, Warrington, Cheshire, WA3 6XF
Activities: Manufacture of engines and turbines, except aircraft, vehicle and cycle engines
Officers: Flemming Obenhausen Andersen [1963] Director/Senior Vice President, Finance [Danish]; Tatsuichiro Honda [1964] Director [Japanese]; Flemming Ougaard [1963] Director/SVP Operations [Danish]

Mibelle Ltd
Incorporated: 4 November 2005 *Employees:* 194
Net Worth: £10,323,000 *Total Assets:* £24,631,000
Registered Office: Units 3-5 City Link Industrial Park, Phoenix Way, Tyersal, Bradford, W Yorks, BD4 8JP
Activities: Manufacture of perfumes and toilet preparations
Parent: Mibelle AG
Officers: Amanda Frances Louise Caldwell, Secretary; Amanda Frances Louise Caldwell [1971] Director/Chartered Accountant; Gary Brian Clarke [1968] Commercial Director; Massimiliano Costantini [1970] Commercial Director; Gregoire Filiatre [1976] Director/Chartered Accountant [French]; Walter Cornelio Huber [1957] Director [Swiss]; Dr Luigi Pedrocchi [1959] Director [Swiss]; Andrew Martin Sharp [1968] Operations Director

Micad Investments Holdings Limited
Incorporated: 4 March 2014 *Employees:* 21
Net Worth: £1,711,101 *Total Assets:* £14,733,218
Registered Office: 8 St Georges Court, Dairyhouse Lane, Broadheath, Altrincham, Cheshire, WA14 5UA
Activities: Activities of head offices
Parent: Young Associates Limited
Officers: Thomas Paul Johnson Ledson, Secretary; Simon Julian Alberga [1966] Director/Banker [Canadian]; Kenneth Christopher Gordon [1964] Director; Peter Anthony Harris [1973] Sales Director; Yoav Kurtzbard [1965] Director of Private Equity Firm; Thomas Paul Johnson Ledson [1975] Finance Director; Clifford Gilbert Wallworth [1966] Director/General Manager; Lord David Ivor Young of Graffham [1932] Director

Micad Systems (U.K.) Limited
Incorporated: 9 April 1987 *Employees:* 21
Net Worth: £5,438,126 *Total Assets:* £8,942,927
Registered Office: Ground Floor, 8 St George's Court, Altrincham Business Park, Dairy House Lane, Altrincham, Cheshire, WA14 5UA
Activities: Computer facilities management activities
Parent: Young Associates Limited
Officers: Thomas Paul Johnson Ledson, Secretary; Simon Julian Alberga [1966] Director/Banker [Canadian]; Kenneth Christopher Gordon [1964] Sales Director; Peter Anthony Harris [1973] Managing Director; Yoav Kurtzbard [1965] Director/Banker; Thomas Paul Johnson Ledson [1975] Finance Director; Clifford Gilbert Wallworth [1966] Director; Lord David Ivor Young of Graffham [1932] Director

Micro Systems (UK) Limited
Incorporated: 7 November 2002 *Employees:* 47
Net Worth: £3,163,227 *Total Assets:* £7,143,041
Registered Office: 101 Golborne Enterprise Park, Golborne, Warrington, Cheshire, WA3 3GR
Activities: Other manufacturing n.e.c.
Shareholders: Melanie Robinson; Gary Edward Clark
Officers: Gary Edward Clark, Secretary; Gary Edward Clark [1962] Director; Melanie Anne Robinson [1972] Director

Micromass Holdings Limited
Incorporated: 10 March 2000
Net Worth: £197,422,000 *Total Assets:* £465,121,984
Registered Office: Waters Wilmslow, Stamford Avenue, Altrincham Road, Wilmslow, Cheshire, SK9 4AX
Activities: Activities of head offices
Parent: Waters Corporation
Officers: Mark Tyrell Beaudouin, Secretary; Mark T Beaudouin [1955] Director/Attorney [American]; Andrew Aitchison Schoon [1970] Finance Director; Brian William Smith [1961] Director

Micromass Limited
Incorporated: 20 December 1995
Net Worth: £35,948,000 *Total Assets:* £36,079,000
Registered Office: Waters Wilmslow, Stamford Avenue, Altrincham Road, Wilmslow, Cheshire, SK9 4AX
Activities: Activities of head offices
Parent: Micromass Holdings Limited
Officers: Mark Tyrell Beaudouin, Secretary; Mark T Beaudouin [1955] Director/Attorney [American]; Andrew Aitchison Schoon [1970] Finance Director; Brian William Smith [1961] Director

Micromass UK Limited
Incorporated: 22 February 1996 *Employees:* 618
Net Worth: £127,584,000 *Total Assets:* £178,972,000
Registered Office: Waters Wilmslow, Stamford Avenue, Altrincham Road, Wilmslow, Cheshire, SK9 4AX
Activities: Manufacture of electronic measuring, testing etc. equipment, not for industrial process control
Parent: Micromass Limited
Officers: Mark Tyrell Beaudouin, Secretary; Susan Joy Robinson, Secretary; Mark T Beaudouin [1955] Director/Attorney [American]; Stephen Gary Curbishley [1963] Operations Director; Andrew Aitchison Schoon [1970] Finance Director; Brian William Smith [1961] Director; Stephen Mark Smith [1967] Senior Director Informatics

Micrown Limited
Incorporated: 16 August 1989 *Employees:* 80
Net Worth: £13,207,955 *Total Assets:* £16,121,408
Registered Office: Unit 49 Compass Industrial Park West, Speke, Liverpool, L24 1YA
Activities: Other manufacturing n.e.c.
Major Shareholder: Charles Clapham
Officers: Christopher John Sweeney, Secretary; Charles Clapham [1946] Managing Director; Christopher John Sweeney [1944] Finance Director

Midas Paper Converters Limited
Incorporated: 26 January 2001 *Employees:* 82
Net Worth: £4,156,726 *Total Assets:* £7,408,378
Registered Office: Stewart Close, Eccleshill, Bradford, W Yorks, BD2 2EE
Activities: Manufacture of paper stationery
Officers: Dominic Wilson de Luca, Secretary/Managing Director; John Paul Clemie [1950] Director; Dominic Wilson de Luca [1964] Managing Director; Margaret Ann Deluca [1940] Director; Robert John Kirkham [1946] Director

Middleton Academy Limited
Incorporated: 14 May 2007 *Employees:* 103
Net Worth: £15,439,000 *Total Assets:* £16,833,000
Registered Office: Bridge House, Ashley Road, Hale, Altrincham, Cheshire, WA14 2UT
Activities: General secondary education
Officers: Marc Edward Crossland [1967] Director/Governor; Stuart Ford [1946] Director/Retired Headteacher; Lisa Grundy [1980] Director/Area Manager Early Years; Julie Hollis [1954] Director/Chief Executive; Ellen Johnson [1975] Associate Director & Strategic Lead; Terence Linden [1956] Director; Yvonne Lorraine Mills [1972] Director/Parent Governor; Timothy Robert Mitchell [1955] Director/Retired; Caroline Preece [1958] Director/Headteacher; Elizabeth Schofield [1975] Director/English 6th Form & Literacy Mentor; Brenda Simpson [1940] Director/Retired

Middlewich Limited
Incorporated: 28 February 2014 *Employees:* 120
Net Worth: £6,978,000 *Total Assets:* £48,580,000
Registered Office: Brooks Lane, Middlewich, Cheshire, CW10 0JQ
Activities: Development of building projects
Parent: Kettley International Ltd
Officers: Nigel Keith Rawlings, Secretary; Richard Fildes [1945] Director; James William Pochin Nicholson [1965] Director; Robert Kenneth Heywood Nicholson [1997] Director; Sylvia Elizabeth Nicholson [1941] Director; Catherine Belinda Tuck [1963] Director/Operations Manager

Midland Red (South) Limited
Incorporated: 15 April 1981 *Employees:* 1,388
Net Worth Deficit: £5,989,000 *Total Assets:* £59,919,000
Registered Office: c/o Stagecoach Services Limited, One Stockport Exchange, 20 Railway Road, Stockport, Cheshire, SK1 3SW
Activities: Other urban, suburban or metropolitan passenger land transport (not underground, metro or similar)
Parent: Stagecoach Bus Holdings Limited
Officers: Michael John Vaux, Secretary; Colin Brown [1968] Director/Accountant; Stephen John Burd [1959] Managing Director; Philip Howard Medlicott [1962] Director; Arnold Mark Threapleton [1954] Managing Director; Mark Venables [1975] Director

T I Midwood & Co Limited
Incorporated: 23 April 1997 *Employees:* 117
Net Worth: £16 753,309 *Total Assets:* £26,153,418
Registered Office: c/o UHY Hacker Young, St Johns Chambers, Love Street, Chester, CH1 1QN
Activities: Non-specialised wholesale trade
Major Shareholder: Simon Ian Midwood
Officers: Simon Ian Midwood, Secretary; Yvonne Messenger [1965] Administration Director; Anne Victoria Ursula Midwood [1973] Director; Simon Ian Midwood [1972] Managing Director; Simon Rance [1970] Sales Director

Migo Enterprises Limited
Incorporated: 23 October 2014 *Employees:* 1
Net Worth: £2,638,854 *Total Assets:* £21,145,928
Registered Office: 91 Walton Road, Stockton Heath, Warrington, Cheshire, WA4 6NR
Activities: Security dealing on own account
Major Shareholder: Stuart Middleton
Officers: Stuart Middleton [1963] Director

Milan Bidco Limited
Incorporated: 1 June 2007
Net Worth: £85,447,000 *Total Assets:* £135,616,992
Registered Office: Think Park, Mosley Road, Trafford Park, Manchester, M17 1FQ
Activities: Activities of financial services holding companies
Officers: Ryan David Swann, Secretary; Simon David Kay [1968] Director/Manager; Stephen Andrew Stylianou [1969] Director/Manager; Jonathan Warr [1964] Director/Manager

Milan Midco Limited
Incorporated: 1 June 2007
Net Worth: £23,242,000 *Total Assets:* £55,046,000
Registered Office: Think Park, Mosley Road, Trafford Park, Manchester, M17 1FQ
Activities: Activities of financial services holding companies
Parent: Milan Swapco Limited
Officers: Ryan David Swann, Secretary; Simon David Kay [1968] Director/Manager; Stephen Andrew Stylianou [1969] Director/Manager; Jonathan Warr [1964] Director/Manager

Milan Swapco Limited
Incorporated: 6 July 2007
Net Worth: £40,263,000 *Total Assets:* £44,738,000
Registered Office: Think Park, Mosley Road, Trafford Park, Manchester, M17 1FQ
Activities: Activities of financial services holding companies
Officers: Ryan David Swann, Secretary; Simon David Kay [1968] Director/Manager; Stephen Andrew Stylianou [1969] Director/Manager; Jonathan Warr [1964] Director/Manager

Thomas Milburn (Property) Limited
Incorporated: 27 September 1974 *Employees:* 60
Net Worth: £16,737,632 *Total Assets:* £19,170,704
Registered Office: Seacote Park, St Bees, Cumbria, CA27 0ET
Activities: Hotels and similar accommodation
Shareholders: Thomas Milburn; Richard Thomas Milburn
Officers: Richard Thomas Milburn, Secretary; Richard Thomas Milburn [1974] Director/Engineer; Thomas Milburn [1939] Managing Director

Milehouse Foods Limited
Incorporated: 16 November 2015 *Employees:* 135
Net Worth: £1,163,664 *Total Assets:* £9,156,419
Registered Office: 45-49 Greek Street, Stockport, Cheshire, SK3 8AX
Activities: Activities of other holding companies n.e.c.
Shareholders: Paul Andrew Burkitt; Mark Jones
Officers: Paul Andrew Burkitt [1962] Director; Mark Jones [1965] Director

Milk Ventures (UK) Limited
Incorporated: 4 June 2003 *Employees:* 5
Net Worth: £27,605,000 *Total Assets:* £90,301,000
Registered Office: Manchester Business Park, 3500 Aviator Way, Manchester, M22 5TG
Activities: Other manufacturing n.e.c.
Parent: PZ Cussons (Holdings) Limited
Officers: Brandon Howard Leigh, Secretary; George Alexander Kanellis [1965] Director [Greek]; Brandon Howard Leigh [1971] Director; Simon Paul Plant [1969] Director/Company Secretary

Mill Brow Worsley Limited
Incorporated: 30 June 2010
Net Worth Deficit: £3,829,105 *Total Assets:* £13,004,314
Registered Office: The Spectrum, 56-58 Benson Road, Birchwood, Warrington, Cheshire, WA3 7PQ
Activities: Buying and selling of own real estate
Officers: Peter Daniel Done, Secretary; Peter Daniel Done [1974] Director; LEA Anne Done-Jackson [1976] Director; Nicola Anne Done-Orrell [1970] Director; Jacqueline Anne Siddons [1968] Director

Mill Farm Ventures Limited
Incorporated: 17 December 2012
Net Worth Deficit: £2,444,880 *Total Assets:* £7,391,329
Registered Office: Docklands, Dock Road, Lytham St Annes, Lancs, FY8 5AQ
Activities: Operation of sports facilities
Parent: Tangerine Holdings Ltd
Officers: David Alan Haythornthwaite [1953] Director; Stuart John King [1976] Finance Director

Millbank Holdings Limited
Incorporated: 8 March 1995 *Employees:* 992
Net Worth: £1,429,353 *Total Assets:* £8,253,266
Registered Office: Millbank House, Northway, Runcorn, Cheshire, WA7 2SX
Activities: Activities of head offices
Shareholders: David Hopley; Stuart Alan Faulkner; James Oskar Burton
Officers: James Oskar Burton [1949] Director; David Hopley [1965] Director

Millennium Care (U.K.) Limited
Incorporated: 7 November 1997 *Employees:* 231
Net Worth: £4,671,089 *Total Assets:* £8,010,889
Registered Office: Glebe Business Park, Lunts Heath Road, Widnes, Cheshire, WA8 5SQ
Activities: Other human health activities
Major Shareholder: Ghulam Haider
Officers: Nighat Shahleen Haider, Secretary; Ghulam Haider [1952] Director; Syma Haider [1983] Director

Millfield Estates (Bolton) Limited
Incorporated: 22 May 1981
Net Worth: £15,756,548 *Total Assets:* £26,779,304
Registered Office: Harewood House, Union Road, Bolton, Lancs, BL2 2HE
Activities: Other letting and operating of own or leased real estate
Parent: WML Industrial Holdings Ltd
Officers: John Matthew Farnworth, Secretary/Director; Paul Michael Dobson [1961] Director/Chartered Surveyor; Douglas John Farnworth [1939] Director; Joan Farnworth [1939] Director; John Matthew Farnworth [1970] Director

Millfield Holdings Limited
Incorporated: 7 March 2016 *Employees:* 220
Net Worth: £1,219,689 *Total Assets:* £6,783,565
Registered Office: B11 Broadlands, Heywood Distribution Park, Pilsworth Road, Heywood, Lancs, OL10 2TS
Activities: Activities of financial services holding companies
Major Shareholder: Shaun David Gent
Officers: Shaun David Gent [1962] Director

Milliken Industrials Limited
Incorporated: 17 December 1920 *Employees:* 603
Net Worth: £58,608,000 *Total Assets:* £74,131,000
Registered Office: Beech Hill Plant, Gidlow Lane, Wigan, Lancs, WN6 8RN
Activities: Manufacture of woven or tufted carpets and rugs
Officers: Martin John Haworth, Secretary; Jeremy Samuel Graham [1969] Lead Director; Martin John Haworth [1962] Director/Chartered Accountant; James John McNulty [1966] Director [American]

Millmead Optical Group Ltd
Incorporated: 18 December 2007 *Employees:* 90
Net Worth: £5,441,297 *Total Assets:* £13,489,368
Registered Office: 83 Sefton Lane, Maghull, Merseyside, L31 8BU
Activities: Activities of other holding companies n.e.c.
Shareholders: Daniel Matthew Thorn; James Gary Conway
Officers: David Graham, Secretary; Michael James Carberry [1974] Director; Paul Clapton [1968] Director; James Gary Conway [1978] Director; David Thomas Burton Graham [1964] Director; Daniel Matthew Thorn [1960] Director

J.Mills (Contractors) Limited
Incorporated: 17 July 1947 *Employees:* 51
Net Worth: £6,599,442 *Total Assets:* £9,533,083
Registered Office: 8 Brindley Road, City Park, Old Trafford, Manchester, M16 9HQ
Activities: Construction of other civil engineering projects n.e.c.
Officers: Peter Philip Noall, Secretary; Steven Gareth Hughes-Solomon [1969] Director/Contracts Manager; Dr Paul Reginald Noall [1950] Director

Milnes Investments Limited
Incorporated: 31 May 1960 *Employees:* 3
Net Worth: £8,679,800 *Total Assets:* £9,850,802
Registered Office: Unit 18 Turnstone Park, Mulberry Avenue, Widnes, Cheshire, WA8 0WN
Activities: Financial intermediation not elsewhere classified
Officers: Amy Jade Kennedy [1990] Director; Joanne Milnes [1970] Director

Milo Properties Ltd
Incorporated: 17 January 2003 *Employees:* 4
Net Worth: £7,573,585 *Total Assets:* £9,993,587
Registered Office: 8 St John Street, Manchester, M3 4DU
Activities: Development of building projects
Shareholders: John Bishop; Sarah Cornall Bishop
Officers: John Bishop [1966] Director; Sarah Cornall-Bishop [1966] Director

The Mines Advisory Group
Incorporated: 16 June 2000 *Employees:* 2,819
Net Worth: £2,279,000 *Total Assets:* £21,282,000
Registered Office: Suite 3a, South Central, 11 Peter Street, Manchester, M2 5QR
Activities: Other professional, scientific and technical activities n.e.c.
Officers: Sarah Louise Howell, Secretary; Karen Veronica Brown [1952] Director; Dr Tapera Knox Chitiyo [1961] Director/Africa Fellow Chatham House; Anthony Paul Collier [1980] Director/Accountant; Christopher Peter Kemp [1964] Director; Dominic Kendal-Ward [1980] Director/Solicitor; Jane Marriott [1976] Director/Diplomat (Crown Servant); Kathy Peach [1978] Director/Head of Innovation and Foresight; Diane Elizabeth Reid [1957] Director/Head of Outreach & Corporate Responsibility; Matthew Andrew Sherrington [1964] Director/Charity Sector Consultant; John Michael Shinnick [1956] Director/Entrepreneurial Advisor; Bertrand Oliver Taithe [1967] Director [French]; Neil Andrew Turton [1966] Trading Director

Mini Gears Group Holdings Limited
Incorporated: 5 May 2016 *Employees:* 82
Net Worth: £3,860,224 *Total Assets:* £8,590,442
Registered Office: Top Gear House, Bletchley Road, Heaton Mersey Industrial Estate, Stockport, Cheshire, SK4 3ED
Activities: Other business support service activities n.e.c.
Shareholder: Andrew Peter Darwent
Officers: Robert MacNeill, Secretary; Andrew Peter Darwent [1972] Director; Peter Samuel Durkin [1969] Director; Robert MacNeill [1979] Director; Nigel Walker [1967] Director

Mini-Cam Enterprises Limited
Incorporated: 22 May 2015 *Employees:* 51
Net Worth: £607,864 *Total Assets:* £23,184,402
Registered Office: Unit 4 Yew Tree Way, Golborne, Warrington, Cheshire, WA3 3FN
Activities: Manufacture of other electrical equipment
Parent: Halma Group PLC
Officers: Glenn Edward Cruger [1964] Director/General Manager [American]; Richard Anthony Paul Joynson [1967] Director; Colin Meadows White [1962] Finance Director; Nigel Jeremy Wilson [1970] Director/Engineer

Mini-Gears (Stockport) Limited
Incorporated: 26 April 1966 *Employees:* 82
Net Worth: £3,880,120 *Total Assets:* £6,568,717
Registered Office: Top Gear House, Bletchley Road, Heaton Mersey Industrial Estate, Stockport, Cheshire, SK4 3ED
Activities: Machining
Major Shareholder: Paul Reginald Darwent
Officers: Robert MacNeill, Secretary; Andrew Peter Darwent [1972] Director; Paul Reginald Darwent [1962] Director; Peter Samuel Durkin [1969] Technical Director; David Jobe [1965] Director; Robert MacNeill [1979] Director; Nigel Walker [1967] Director

Miramar Investments Limited
Incorporated: 22 October 1986 *Employees:* 129
Net Worth: £6,656,721 *Total Assets:* £11,446,787
Registered Office: Cunard Buildings, Water Street, Pier Head, Liverpool, L3 1SF
Activities: Manufacture of other paper and paperboard containers
Parent: Miramar Investments Holdings Limited
Officers: Nicola Pritchard, Secretary; Clive Bowers [1953] Director; Francois Christophe Eliet [1955] Director/Financial Executive [Irish]; Hugh Patrick McNeill [1959] Director; Anthony Smurfit [1963] Director/President & COO [Irish]

Missguided Limited
Incorporated: 9 August 1996 *Employees:* 436
Net Worth: £4,934,000 *Total Assets:* £54,238,000
Registered Office: 75 Trafford Wharf Road, Trafford Park, Manchester, M17 1ES
Activities: Other retail sale in non-specialised stores
Major Shareholder: Rajib Passi
Officers: Nitin Passi [1982] Director

Mistral Asset Finance Limited
Incorporated: 6 July 2004 *Employees:* 9
Net Worth: £454,836 *Total Assets:* £16,242,043
Registered Office: 139 Red Bank Road, Bispham, Blackpool, Lancs, FY2 9HZ
Activities: Financial leasing
Officers: Stephen Charles Priestley, Secretary; Stephen Charles Low [1969] Commercial Director; Tarunkumar Vallabhbhai Mistry [1969] Director/Financial Consultant; Guy Richard Wadsworth [1959] Commercial Director

Mistral Bus & Coach PLC
Incorporated: 21 May 1992 *Employees:* 15
Net Worth: £2,450,000 *Total Assets:* £26,571,872
Registered Office: 139 Red Bank Road, Bispham, Blackpool, Lancs, FY2 9HZ
Activities: Renting and leasing of trucks and other heavy vehicles
Officers: Stephen Charles Priestley, Secretary; Stephen Charles Low [1969] Commercial Director; Tarunkumar Vallabhbhai Mistry [1969] Director/Financial Consultant

Mitchell North West Limited
Incorporated: 23 August 1989 *Employees:* 112
Net Worth: £6,565,610 *Total Assets:* £12,349,250
Registered Office: Stanney Mill Lane, Cheshire Oaks, Chester, CH2 4RG
Activities: Retail trade of motor vehicle parts and accessories
Shareholders: Mark Steven Mitchell; Anita Louise Mitchell
Officers: Julie Oliver, Secretary; Neil Graham Crowden [1971] Sales Director; Anita Louise Mitchell [1967] Director; Mark Steven Mitchell [1962] Managing Director; Julie Oliver [1959] Finance Director

Mitchell's Brewery Limited
Incorporated: 25 August 1989 *Employees:* 278
Net Worth: £1,127,000 *Total Assets:* £9,737,000
Registered Office: 11 Moor Lane, Lancaster, LA1 1QB
Activities: Public houses and bars
Officers: Julia Hodge [1969] H R Director

Mitchells of Lancaster (Brewers) Limited
Incorporated: 30 March 1965 *Employees:* 216
Net Worth: £14,754,000 *Total Assets:* £18,203,000
Registered Office: 11 Moor Lane, Lancaster, LA1 1QB
Activities: Public houses and bars
Officers: Julia Hodge [1969] H R Director

Mitras Automotive (UK) Limited
Incorporated: 1 September 1993 *Employees:* 194
Net Worth Deficit: £2,139,690 *Total Assets:* £16,600,847
Registered Office: Road One, Winsford Industrial Estate, Winsford, Cheshire, CW7 3PZ
Activities: Other manufacturing n.e.c.
Parent: Senata GmbH
Officers: Joanne Mortimore, Secretary; Keith Worrall [1963] Managing Director

H. Mitton Limited
Incorporated: 8 June 2000 *Employees:* 275
Net Worth: £1,560,484 *Total Assets:* £9,626,578
Registered Office: MacKenzie House, 451 Cleckheaton Road, Low Moor, Bradford, W Yorks, BD12 0HS
Activities: Activities of head offices
Shareholder: Steven Taylor
Officers: Neil Burns [1963] Director; Graham Hawe [1958] Director; Steven Taylor [1976] Director

Mitton Mechanical Services Limited
Incorporated: 5 December 1957 *Employees:* 106
Net Worth: £2,909,038 *Total Assets:* £7,063,150
Registered Office: MacKenzie House, 451 Cleckheaton Road, Bradford, W Yorks, BD12 0HS
Activities: Plumbing, heat and air-conditioning installation
Parent: H Mitton Limited
Officers: Neil Burns [1963] Director; Graham Hawe [1958] Director; Jonathan Stuart Knowles [1982] Director; Steven Taylor [1976] Director

MKS Instruments Holdings Ltd
Incorporated: 1 November 2013
Net Worth: £496,990,784 *Total Assets:* £518,402,816
Registered Office: Units 3-4 Cowley Way, Weston Road, Crewe, Cheshire, CW1 6AG
Activities: Other service activities n.e.c.
Shareholders: MKS International Holdings Limited; MKS Instruments, Inc
Officers: Kathleen Burke, Secretary; Derek Pace D'Antilio [1972] Director [American]; Geoffrey Frederick Foxall [1960] Director/Financial Controller

MKS Instruments UK Limited
Incorporated: 5 October 2007 *Employees:* 111
Net Worth: £29,004,722 *Total Assets:* £34,127,204
Registered Office: Units 3-4 Cowley Way, Weston Road, Crewe, Cheshire, CW1 6AG
Activities: Manufacture of other fabricated metal products n.e.c.
Shareholders: MKS Instruments Holdings Ltd; MKS International Holdings Limited; MKS Instruments, Inc
Officers: Kathleen F Burke, Secretary [American]; Seth Bagshaw [1959] Director/Treasurer [American]; Derek D'Antilio [1972] Director [American]

MLM Ltd
Incorporated: 22 February 2005
Net Worth: £3,477,672 *Total Assets:* £13,779,532
Registered Office: Suite 10, Egerton House, Towers Business Park, Wilmslow Road, Didsbury, Manchester, M20 2DX
Activities: Recovery of sorted materials
Parent: America Chung Nam LLC
Officers: Guoxiang Zhao, Secretary; Wade Schuetzeberg [1968] Director [American]; Guoxiang Zhao [1959] Director [American]

MLTS Holdings Limited
Incorporated: 30 October 2015
Net Worth: £11,371,262 *Total Assets:* £11,496,809
Registered Office: The Old Shippon, Moseley Hall Farm, Chelford Road, Knutsford, Cheshire, WA16 8RB
Activities: Combined office administrative service activities
Major Shareholder: Matthew William Sanders
Officers: Mrs Louise Catherine Sanders [1979] Director; Matthew William Sanders [1973] Director

MM European Holdings LLP
Incorporated: 19 May 2003
Net Worth: £729,083,968 *Total Assets:* £739,476,672
Registered Office: Waters Wilmslow, Stamford Avenue, Altrincham Road, Wilmslow, Cheshire, SK9 4AX

MMGG Acquisition Limited
Incorporated: 5 March 2012
Net Worth: £11,406,000 *Total Assets:* £25,494,000
Registered Office: Adamson House, Centenary Way, Salford, M50 1RD
Activities: Human resources provision and management of human resources functions
Parent: GGM Human Resources Limited
Officers: Paul John Gilmour, Secretary; Paul John Gilmour [1964] Director; Kevin Patrick Gorton [1964] Director; Gerard Anthony Mason [1964] Director; Kevin Philbin [1959] Director/Solicitor

Mobica Bidco Limited
Incorporated: 23 September 2015 *Employees:* 5
Net Worth Deficit: £6,288,276 *Total Assets:* £53,031,932
Registered Office: Crown House, Manchester Road, Wilmslow, Cheshire, SK9 1BH
Activities: Other service activities n.e.c.
Parent: Mobica Holdings Limited
Officers: Jonathan Braddock Clayton [1958] Director; Andrew Neil Collis [1980] Director/Chief Financial Officer; Catherine Allingham Richards [1973] Director/Investment Professional; Nicholas Leet Stammers [1963] Director; David Alan Whileman [1972] Director; Simon John Wilkinson [1965] Director

Mobica Holdings Limited
Incorporated: 21 September 2015 *Employees:* 1,102
Net Worth: £2,710,197 *Total Assets:* £60,203,652
Registered Office: Crown House, Manchester Road, Wilmslow, Cheshire, SK9 1BH
Activities: Other service activities n.e.c.
Shareholder: Nicholas Leet Stammers
Officers: Jonathan Braddock Clayton [1958] Director; Andrew Neil Collis [1980] Director/Chief Financial Officer; Catherine Allingham Richards [1973] Director/Investment Professional; Nicholas Leet Stammers [1963] Director; David Alan Whileman [1972] Director; Simon John Wilkinson [1965] Director

Mobica Limited
Incorporated: 2 July 2004 *Employees:* 1,096
Net Worth: £15,500,413 *Total Assets:* £20,385,598
Registered Office: Crown House, Manchester Road, Wilmslow, Cheshire, SK9 1BH
Activities: Ready-made interactive leisure and entertainment software development
Parent: Mobica Bidco Limited
Officers: Nicholas Leet Stammers, Secretary; James Alexander Carroll [1971] Director; Jonathan Braddock Clayton [1958] Director; Andrew Neil Collis [1980] Director/Chief Financial Officer; Nicholas Leet Stammers [1963] Director; Simon John Wilkinson [1965] Director

Mobiletron UK Limited
Incorporated: 11 January 2000 *Employees:* 27
Net Worth: £6,506,477 *Total Assets:* £8,874,319
Registered Office: Unit 80 Roman Way Industrial Estate, Longridge Road, Preston, Lancs, PR2 5BE
Activities: Wholesale trade of motor vehicle parts and accessories
Parent: Mobiletron Electronics Company Limited
Officers: Linda Ann Hollings, Secretary; Edward Wen-Chin Ho [1966] Managing Director; Kim Yc Tsai [1956] Director/Company President [Taiwanese]; Chen-Ku Wei [1953] Technical Director [Taiwanese]

Mobius Motors Limited
Incorporated: 2 September 2010
Net Worth: £9,684,722 *Total Assets:* £9,684,722
Registered Office: Cliffe Barn, Church Lane, Tideswell, Derbys, SK17 8PD
Activities: Manufacture of motor vehicles
Shareholders: Ronald Lauder; Richard Parsons
Officers: Joel Alexander Jackson [1985] Director

ModernUser Limited
Incorporated: 26 April 1988 *Employees:* 133
Net Worth: £4,155,787 *Total Assets:* £9,441,317
Registered Office: 9th Floor, 3 Hardman Street, Manchester, M3 3HF
Activities: Other letting and operating of own or leased real estate
Officers: Stephen John Adams, Secretary; Stephen John Adams [1972] Director/Quantity Surveyor; Dean Clark Drinkwater [1965] Director; Joseph Edwin Drinkwater [1938] Director

Modular Stock Limited
Incorporated: 1 April 1997 *Employees:* 5
Net Worth: £5,877,000 *Total Assets:* £50,364,000
Registered Office: c/o Tenmat Limited, Ashburton Road West, Trafford Park, Manchester, M17 1TD
Activities: Activities of other holding companies n.e.c.
Parent: Diamorph UK Limited
Officers: Mark Andrew Hutchison [1970] Director

Moduleco Healthcare Limited
Incorporated: 23 June 2008 *Employees:* 4
Net Worth: £21,817,190 *Total Assets:* £32,651,446
Registered Office: Solutions House, 39 Quayside, Grosvenor Wharf Road, Ellesmere Port, Cheshire, CH65 4AY
Activities: Renting and leasing of other machinery, equipment and tangible goods n.e.c.
Parent: MCH Intermediate Ltd
Officers: Amanda Boote, Secretary; Michael William John Bailey [1953] Director/Chartered Accountant; Steven Bowers [1971] Director; Paul Stuart Rogers [1968] Director

Molnlycke Health Care Limited
Incorporated: 12 January 1998 *Employees:* 184
Net Worth: £2,604,000 *Total Assets:* £17,174,000
Registered Office: Unity House, Medlock Street, Oldham, Lancs, OL1 3HS
Activities: Manufacture of basic pharmaceutical products
Officers: Christopher John Stubbs, Secretary; Stefan Ulf Fristedt [1966] Finance Director [Swedish]; Nicholas Andrew Rothwell [1973] Director/General Manager; Richard Twomey [1964] Director

Monarch Assurance PLC
Incorporated: 26 October 1965 *Employees:* 5
Net Worth: £6,091,860 *Total Assets:* £129,183,368
Registered Office: 3rd Floor, 1 Portland Street, Manchester, M1 3BE
Activities: Life insurance
Parent: Soogen Holdings Limited
Officers: William Peter Andresen, Secretary; Johan Arthur Frans Cuypers [1960] Director [Belgian]; Alexander Roderick Jones [1955] Director; Alan Scott Morgan Moodie [1949] Director; Stephen Paul Robinson [1964] Director/Chartered Accountant; John Keith Tenconi [1953] Director/Barrister

The Monastery of St Francis and Gorton Trust
Incorporated: 19 September 1996 *Employees:* 50
Net Worth: £7,765,673 *Total Assets:* £8,842,688
Registered Office: The Monastery, Gorton Lane, Gorton, Manchester, M12 5WF
Activities: Operation of historical sites and buildings and similar visitor attractions
Officers: Paul Griffiths, Secretary; Jeremy Benjamin Cole [1960] Director/Corporate Financier; David John Dickinson [1952] Director/Management Consultant; Paul Griffiths [1953] Director/Business Consultant; Ray Hanks [1948] Director; Timothy Isherwood [1955] Director/Management Consultant; Claire Elizabeth Lewis [1974] Director; David Oliver [1957] Director/Management Consultant; Piers Anthony Sturridge [1954] Director/Consultant; Janet Louise Wallwork [1951] Director/Librarian

Monckton Properties (Holdings) Limited
Incorporated: 9 January 2002
Net Worth: £8,464,869 *Total Assets:* £9,903,159
Registered Office: Charles House, 2 Royal Court, Tatton Street, Knutsford, Cheshire, WA16 6EN
Activities: Activities of head offices
Officers: Henry Randle Brooks [1980] Director; Juliet Marit Gabriel Brooks [1945] Director; Randle Brooks [1941] Director; Franklyn Edward Jones [1940] Director/Bank Executive; Andrew Stuart D'Artois Rinker [1957] Director/Solicitor Attorney [American/British]

Monckton Properties Limited
Incorporated: 14 December 1960
Net Worth: £38,269,632 *Total Assets:* £41,196,392
Registered Office: Charles House, 2 Royal Court, Tatton Street, Knutsford, Cheshire, WA16 6EN
Activities: Other business support service activities n.e.c.
Officers: Henry Randle Brooks [1980] Director; Juliet Marit Gabriel Brooks [1945] Director; Randle Brooks [1941] Director; Franklyn Edward Jones [1940] Director/Bank Executive; Andrew Stuart D'Artois Rinker [1957] Director/Solicitor Attorney [American/British]

Mondi Consumer Goods Packaging UK Ltd
Incorporated: 23 July 2004 *Employees:* 234
Net Worth: £4,620,141 *Total Assets:* £31,096,226
Registered Office: Parkway, Deeside Industrial Park, Deeside, Flintshire, CH5 2NS
Activities: Packaging activities
Parent: Mondi UK Consumer Packaging Holding 2 Ltd
Officers: Ian Bragg, Secretary; Sandor Kardos [1970] Director [German]; Allan Martin Lock [1970] Director

Mondi UK Consumer Packaging Holding 1 Ltd
Incorporated: 6 March 2014
Net Worth: £2,689,036,032 *Total Assets:* £2,689,036,032
Registered Office: Parkway, Deeside Industrial Park, Deeside, Flintshire, CH5 2NS
Activities: Manufacture of plastic packing goods
Parent: Mondi Investments Limited
Officers: Ian Bragg, Secretary; Sandor Kardos [1970] Director [German]; Allan Martin Lock [1970] Director

Moneta Communications Holdings Limited
Incorporated: 3 September 2012
Net Worth: £4,334,297 *Total Assets:* £10,911,181
Registered Office: The Spectrum, 56-58 Benson Road, Birchwood, Warrington, Cheshire, WA3 7PQ
Activities: Activities of head offices
Officers: Michael Rodney Hamilton, Secretary; Fred Done [1943] Director/Bookmaker

Money Advice Group Limited
Incorporated: 11 May 2007 *Employees:* 218
Net Worth: £10,029,987 *Total Assets:* £16,767,988
Registered Office: Thornley House, Carrington Business Park, Manchester, M31 4DD
Activities: Financial intermediation not elsewhere classified
Shareholders: Stuart Parkin; Shelly Parkin
Officers: Shelly Parkin, Secretary; Shelly Parkin [1979] Director/Debt Management; Stuart Parkin [1981] Director

Money Controls Holdings Limited
Incorporated: 16 October 1990
Net Worth: £11,436,000 *Total Assets:* £11,436,000
Registered Office: Coin House, New Coin Street, Royton, Oldham, Lancs, OL2 6JZ
Activities: Non-trading company
Parent: CA-MC Acquisition UK Limited
Officers: Richard Wilkinson, Secretary; Patricia Ann Barrie [1956] Director/Financial Controller; Richard Andrew Maue [1970] Director/Business Executive [American]; Max Homer Mitchell [1963] Director [American]; Edward Stephen Switter [1974] Director/Business Executive [American]; Richard Wilkinson [1967] Director

Moneyplus Group Limited
Incorporated: 9 July 2010 *Employees:* 204
Net Worth: £7,391,000 *Total Assets:* £31,111,000
Registered Office: Riverside, New Bailey Street, Manchester, M3 5FS
Activities: Financial intermediation not elsewhere classified
Parent: Moneyplus Intermediary
Officers: Christopher Anthony Davis [1969] Director; Arnie Iversen [1947] Director/Consultant; Colin Marsden Jones [1970] Operations Director; Ben Miller [1982] Legal Director; Christopher David Williams [1979] Director

Moneyplus Holdings Limited
Incorporated: 28 March 2011 *Employees:* 204
Net Worth Deficit: £7,976,000 *Total Assets:* £28,033,000
Registered Office: Riverside, New Bailey Street, Manchester, M3 5FS
Activities: Activities of other holding companies n.e.c.
Shareholders: Christopher Anthony Davis; Zeus Private Equity Fund LP
Officers: Christopher Davis [1969] Director; Edmund Fazakerley [1969] Director; Arnie Iversen [1947] Director/Consultant; Colin Marsden Jones [1970] Operations Director; Christopher David Williams [1979] Director

Moneysupermarket.Com Financial Group Holdings Limited
Incorporated: 22 August 2012
Net Worth: £87,000,000 *Total Assets:* £410,000,000
Registered Office: Moneysupermarket House, St David's Park, Ewloe, Flintshire, CH5 3UZ
Activities: Activities of insurance agents and brokers
Parent: Moneysupermarket.Com Group PLC
Officers: Darren Paul Drabble, Secretary; Mark Peter Lewis [1969] Director; Matthew John Price [1969] Director/Chief Financial Officer

Moneysupermarket.Com Financial Group Limited
Incorporated: 9 February 1996 *Employees:* 523
Net Worth: £55,115,000 *Total Assets:* £174,307,008
Registered Office: Moneysupermarket House, St Davids Park, Ewloe, Flintshire, CH5 3UZ
Activities: Other information service activities n.e.c.
Parent: Moneysupermarket.Com Financial Group Holdings Limited
Officers: Darren Paul Drabble, Secretary; Mark Peter Lewis [1969] Director; Matthew John Price [1969] Director/Chief Financial Officer

Moneysupermarket.Com Group PLC
Incorporated: 14 March 2007 *Employees:* 598
Net Worth: £186,387,008 *Total Assets:* £249,524,000
Registered Office: Moneysupermarket House, St David's Park, Ewloe, Flintshire, CH5 3UZ
Activities: Activities of head offices
Officers: Darren Paul Drabble, Secretary; Bruce Neil Carnegie-Brown [1959] Director; Andrew Raymond Fisher [1969] Director; Robin Anthony David Freestone [1958] Director; Sally Ann James [1949] Director; Mark Peter Lewis [1969] Director; Matthew John Price [1969] Director/Chief Financial Officer; Genevieve Helen Shore [1969] Director; Sarah Warby [1971] Director

Moneysupermarket.Com Ltd
Incorporated: 13 March 2000
Net Worth: £145,830,000 *Total Assets:* £333,984,000
Registered Office: Moneysupermarket House, St Davids Park, Ewloe, Flintshire, CH5 3UZ
Activities: Other information service activities n.e.c.
Parent: Moneysupermarket.Com Financial Group Limited
Officers: Darren Paul Drabble, Secretary; Mark Peter Lewis [1969] Director; Matthew John Price [1969] Director/Chief Financial Officer

Monitise Europe Limited
Incorporated: 14 July 2003
Net Worth: £4,517,000 *Total Assets:* £6,713,000
Registered Office: Eversheds House, 70 Great Bridgewater Street, Manchester, M1 5ES
Activities: Activities of head offices
Parent: Monitise Group Limited
Officers: Thomas Hunter [1981] Finance Director; William Richard Jones [1964] Director; Richard Simon Waller [1969] Director

Monitise Group Limited
Incorporated: 12 October 2005 *Employees:* 168
Net Worth Deficit: £9,049,000 *Total Assets:* £13,260,000
Registered Office: Eversheds House, 70 Great Bridgewater Street, Manchester, M1 5ES
Activities: Activities of head offices
Parent: Monitise Limited
Officers: Thomas Hunter [1981] Finance Director; Richard Simon Waller [1969] Director

Monitise International Limited
Incorporated: 7 September 2005
Net Worth Deficit: £390,051,008 *Total Assets:* £35,941,000
Registered Office: Eversheds House, 70 Great Bridgewater Street, Manchester, M1 5ES
Activities: Activities of head offices
Parent: Monitise Group Limited
Officers: Thomas Hunter [1981] Finance Director; William Richard Jones [1964] Director; Richard Simon Waller [1969] Director

Monitise Limited
Incorporated: 28 November 2006 *Employees:* 428
Net Worth: £34,153,000 *Total Assets:* £52,954,000
Registered Office: Eversheds House, 70 Great Bridgewater Street, Manchester, M1 5ES
Activities: Activities of head offices
Parent: Fiserv UK Limited
Officers: Thomas Hunter [1981] Finance Director; Richard Simon Waller [1969] Director/Solicitor

Monopol Holdings Limited
Incorporated: 14 October 1988 *Employees:* 5
Net Worth: £4,647,483 *Total Assets:* £7,434,107
Registered Office: 1 Duke Street, Liverpool, L1 4AA
Activities: Other letting and operating of own or leased real estate
Officers: Cecilia Anne Gillbanks [1956] Director; Daniel Alexander Gillbanks [1994] Commercial Director

Monte Blackburn Limited
Incorporated: 4 March 2016
Net Worth: £218,253 *Total Assets:* £89,022,248
Registered Office: Euro House, Beehive Trading Park, Haslingden Road, Blackburn, Lancs, BB1 2EE
Activities: Development of building projects
Officers: Mohsin Issa [1971] Director; Zuber Vali Issa [1972] Director

Montgomery Tomlinson Limited
Incorporated: 20 June 1928 *Employees:* 583
Net Worth: £5,303,000 *Total Assets:* £8,658,000
Registered Office: KPMG LLP, 1 St Peter's Square, Manchester, M2 3AE
Activities: Manufacture of soft furnishings
Officers: Philip John Smith, Secretary; Barry Stephen Goodman-King [1966] Sales & Marketing Director; Cate Hulme [1973] Finance Director; Joanne McEwan [1970] Director; Grahame Montgomery Tomlinson [1936] Director; Louise Anne Tomlinson [1962] Director

Gordon Moon Properties Limited
Incorporated: 17 May 2016
Net Worth: £732,544 *Total Assets:* £21,541,124
Registered Office: Knowsley House, Knowsley Street, Bolton, Lancs, BL1 2AH
Activities: Other letting and operating of own or leased real estate
Officers: Barbara Diane Gordon [1960] Director; James Neville Gordon [1982] Director

Moor Hall Holdings Limited
Incorporated: 19 December 2014
Net Worth: £2,757,216 *Total Assets:* £8,945,466
Registered Office: Moor Hall, Prescot Road, Aughton, Ormskirk, Lancs, L39 6RT
Activities: Other service activities n.e.c.
Shareholders: Andrew James Bell; Tracey Anne Bell
Officers: Esther Ellen Martina Speksnijder, Secretary; Andrew James Bell [1966] Director; Tracey Anne Bell [1970] Director

Moorcroft Debt Recovery Limited
Incorporated: 2 March 1983
Net Worth: £12,868,213 *Total Assets:* £21,793,806
Registered Office: Moorcroft House, No 2 Spring Gardens, Stockport, Cheshire, SK1 4AA
Activities: Financial intermediation not elsewhere classified
Parent: Moorcroft Group PLC
Officers: Andrew James McRoberts, Secretary; Amanda Martin McRoberts [1970] Director; Andrew James McRoberts [1965] Director; Neil George McRoberts [1943] Director; Rodney Neil McRoberts [1967] Director

Moorcroft Group Public Limited Company
Incorporated: 3 March 1983 *Employees:* 456
Net Worth: £13,436,872 *Total Assets:* £25,449,926
Registered Office: Moorcroft House, No 2 Spring Gardens, Stockport, Cheshire, SK1 4AA
Activities: Financial intermediation not elsewhere classified
Major Shareholder: Neil George McRoberts
Officers: Andrew James McRoberts, Secretary; Amanda Martin-Mcroberts [1970] Director; Andrew James McRoberts [1965] Director; Neil George McRoberts [1943] Director; Rodney Neil McRoberts [1967] Director

Moore and Smalley LLP
Incorporated: 27 June 2005 *Employees:* 260
Net Worth: £4,513,806 *Total Assets:* £7,755,860
Registered Office: Richard House, Winckley Square, Preston, Lancs, PR1 3HP
Officers: Graham David Gordon [1968] Member; Karen Hain [1969] Member; Tony Medcalf [1969] Member; Damian John Walmsley [1966] Member; Christine Anne Wilson [1965] Member; Deborah Stuart Wood [1962] Member; David Alastair Bennett [1962] LLP Member; Ian Clark [1966] LLP Member; Virginia Teresa Louise Cooper [1975] LLP Member; Michael John Hardaker [1974] LLP Member; Daniel John Houghton [1974] LLP Member; Colin Johnson [1975] LLP Member; Tracey Nicole Johnson [1962] LLP Member; Jonathan James Main [1966] LLP Member; Rachel Helen Marsdin [1965] LLP Member; Jenny McCabe [1979] LLP Member; Adam Jerome Parton-Pickup [1975] LLP Member; Jonathan Mark Pinder [1966] LLP Member; Keith Porter [1966] LLP Member; Nicholas Raymond Stevenson [1969] LLP Member; Joseph William Sullivan [1984] LLP Member; Paul Andrew Williams [1984] LLP Member

Martin Moore Furniture Limited
Incorporated: 27 April 2011 *Employees:* 81
Net Worth: £2,351,677 *Total Assets:* £7,460,138
Registered Office: 36 Church Street, Altrincham, Cheshire, WA14 4DW
Activities: Activities of other holding companies n.e.c.
Officers: Richard Piers Moore, Secretary; Steven Peter Boygle [1959] Director; Gareth Martin Jinks [1972] Director; Barbara Moore [1943] Director; Martin Moore [1943] Director; Michael Moore [1970] Director; Richard Piers Moore [1971] Director

Moorland Covered Bonds Limited Liability Partnership
Incorporated: 12 March 2009
Net Worth Deficit: £8,097,000 *Total Assets:* £1,252,491,008
Registered Office: P O Box 101, 1 Balloon Street, Manchester, M60 4EP

Moortown Group Limited
Incorporated: 22 June 2012 *Employees:* 67
Net Worth: £14,375,982 *Total Assets:* £32,377,078
Registered Office: Lusteen House, 24 Roydsdale Way, Euroway Industrial Estate, Bradford, W Yorks, BD4 6SE
Activities: Construction of other civil engineering projects n.e.c.
Parent: McManus Group Holdings Limited
Officers: Michael John King [1974] Director/Business Development [Irish]; Aiden Thomas McManus [1976] Director; Thomas John McManus [1949] Director; Dean Jason Moxon [1970] Director/Head of Procurement

Morbaine Limited
Incorporated: 24 January 1977 *Employees:* 25
Net Worth: £1,143,221 *Total Assets:* £37,759,736
Registered Office: The Finlan Centre, Hale Road, Hale Bank, Widnes, Cheshire, WA8 8PU
Activities: Construction of commercial buildings
Shareholders: John Finlan; John Finlan
Officers: Stephen Paul Barnwell, Secretary; Alexander Brodie [1950] Director/Property Development Executive; Jean Connor [1947] Director/Personal Assistant; Annick Jean Lucienne Finlan [1941] Director [French]; John Finlan [1965] Director/Development Manager; John Finlan [1925] Director/Property Developer; Keith Leslie Nutter [1971] Director/Town Planner; John Parle [1942] Director/Designer; Keith Thomas Williams [1955] Director/Chartered Surveyor

Morbaine Properties Limited
Incorporated: 15 May 1963 *Employees:* 28
Net Worth: £72,591,680 *Total Assets:* £128,493,744
Registered Office: The Finlan Centre, Hale Road, Hale Bank, Widnes, Cheshire, WA8 8PU
Activities: Development of building projects
Shareholders: John Finlan; John Finlan
Officers: Stephen Paul Barnwell, Secretary; Jean Connor [1947] Director/Personal Assistant; Annick Jean Lucienne Finlan [1941] Director [French]; John Finlan [1925] Director/Property Developer; John Parle [1942] Director

More 2 Life Ltd
Incorporated: 11 March 2005 *Employees:* 43
Net Worth: £15,066,452 *Total Assets:* £21,366,620
Registered Office: Baines House, Midgery Court, Fulwood, Preston, Lancs, PR2 9ZH
Activities: Activities of mortgage finance companies
Parent: KRS Finance Ltd
Officers: Lukas Martin Bucher [1976] Managing Director Value Creation [Swiss]; Andrew David Deakin [1973] Director/Private Equity Professional; Stephen James Groves [1975] Director/Actuary; David Michael Harris [1967] Director; Robert James Scott [1973] Director; Simon Christopher Thompson [1972] Director; David Thomas McAree Young [1961] Director

Morecambe Leisure 2 Limited
Incorporated: 9 August 2010
Net Worth Deficit: £11,615,000 *Total Assets:* £34,020,000
Registered Office: 10 Mannin Way, Lancaster Business Park, Lancaster, LA1 3SW
Activities: Holiday centres and villages
Parent: Palatine Private Equity LLP
Officers: Andrew Jonathan Wall, Secretary; Beverley Jayne Dixon [1969] Director; Graham Robert Hodgson [1960] Director; Andrew Wall [1960] Director

George Morgan Holdings Limited
Incorporated: 23 September 2015 *Employees:* 166
Net Worth: £3,371,758 *Total Assets:* £8,906,795
Registered Office: Mold Industrial Estate, Wrexham Road, Mold, Flintshire, CH7 4HE
Activities: Manufacture of other products of wood; manufacture of articles of cork, straw and plaiting materials
Major Shareholder: Steven George Morgan
Officers: Andrew Baker [1976] Director; Rhys Hywel Hughes [1970] Director; Steven George Morgan [1969] Director

D. Morgan PLC
Incorporated: 23 March 1964 *Employees:* 218
Net Worth: £8,091,016 *Total Assets:* £19,321,476
Registered Office: 68 Argyle Street, Birkenhead, Merseyside, CH41 6AF
Activities: Construction of other civil engineering projects n.e.c.
Major Shareholder: Denis Morgan
Officers: Victoria Leigh Morgan, Secretary; Denis Morgan [1952] Director; Victoria Leigh Morgan [1984] Company Secretary/Director

John Morley (Importers) Limited
Incorporated: 5 August 1944 *Employees:* 112
Net Worth: £4,283,084 *Total Assets:* £13,108,436
Registered Office: Morley Drive, Hightown, Congleton, Cheshire, CW12 3LF
Activities: Other processing and preserving of fruit and vegetables
Parent: JM Holdings Limited
Officers: Simon Jon Brown [1969] Director/Manager; Paul Alan Roberts [1956] Director; Vivienne Marie Ryan [1956] Director; Alan John Wright [1959] Commercial Director

Morning Foods,Limited
Incorporated: 31 August 1942 *Employees:* 363
Net Worth: £41,346,760 *Total Assets:* £64,144,920
Registered Office: North Western Mills, Gresty Road, Crewe, Cheshire, CW2 6HP
Activities: Grain milling
Major Shareholder: John Edward Lea
Officers: David Warr, Secretary/Accountant; John Borrowdale [1983] Director; Derek Charles Croucher [1966] Technical Director; Edward LEA [1983] Director; James John LEA [1980] Director; John Edward LEA [1946] Director/Chartered Accountant; Alan Meikle [1961] Director; David Warr [1952] Director/Accountant

Morris Group Limited
Incorporated: 27 January 2004 *Employees:* 249
Net Worth: £103,132,000 *Total Assets:* £414,168,992
Registered Office: Morland House, Altrincham Road, Wilmslow, Cheshire, SK9 5NW
Activities: Activities of head offices
Officers: Joanne Iddon, Secretary; Michael Norman Carruthers [1980] Director; Martin Paul Edmunds [1961] Director; Michael John Gaskell [1962] Director/Chartered Accountant; David Peter Hesson [1972] Director; Joanne Iddon [1969] Director/Accountant; Bernard Robert Norman [1941] Director; Mark Rutledge [1986] Director [Canadian]; Andrew Marmaduke Lane Tuckey [1943] Director

Morris Homes (Midlands) Limited
Incorporated: 28 September 1922 *Employees:* 75
Net Worth: £12,697,000 *Total Assets:* £202,312,992
Registered Office: Morland House, Altrincham Road, Wilmslow, Cheshire, SK9 5NW
Activities: Construction of domestic buildings
Officers: Joanne Iddon, Secretary; Martin Paul Edmunds [1961] Director; Michael John Gaskell [1962] Director/Chartered Accountant; David Peter Hesson [1972] Director; Joanne Iddon [1969] Director/Accountant

Morris Homes (North) Limited
Incorporated: 25 March 1964 *Employees:* 92
Net Worth: £95,006,000 *Total Assets:* £316,044,992
Registered Office: Morland House, Altrincham Road, Wilmslow, Cheshire, SK9 5NW
Activities: Construction of domestic buildings
Officers: Joanne Iddon, Secretary; Martin Paul Edmunds [1961] Land Director; Michael John Gaskell [1962] Director/Chartered Accountant; David Peter Hesson [1972] Director; Joanne Iddon [1969] Director/Accountant

Morris Homes Limited
Incorporated: 7 July 1998 *Employees:* 249
Net Worth: £150,424,000 *Total Assets:* £505,416,000
Registered Office: Morland House, Altrincham Road, Wilmslow, Cheshire, SK9 5NW
Activities: Construction of domestic buildings
Officers: Joanne Iddon, Secretary; Martin Paul Edmunds [1961] Land Director; Michael John Gaskell [1962] Director/Chartered Accountant; David Peter Hesson [1972] Director; Joanne Iddon [1969] Director/Accountant

T. J. Morris Limited
Incorporated: 30 June 1980 *Employees:* 18,048
Net Worth: £747,814,464 *Total Assets:* £942,866,304
Registered Office: T J Morris Limited, Portal Way, Axis Business Park, Gillmoss, Liverpool, L11 0JA
Activities: Other retail sale in non-specialised stores
Major Shareholder: Thomas Joseph Morris
Officers: Graeme Peter McLoughlin, Secretary; Joseph Lawrence Morris [1959] Operations Director; Thomas Joseph Morris [1954] Managing Director

T.J. Morris Properties Limited
Incorporated: 9 January 1995
Net Worth: £4,021,502 *Total Assets:* £11,443,163
Registered Office: T J Morris Limited, Portal Way, Axis Business Park, Gillmoss, Liverpool, L11 0JA
Activities: Buying and selling of own real estate
Major Shareholder: Thomas Joseph Morris
Officers: Graeme Peter McLoughlin, Secretary; Thomas Joseph Morris [1954] Director

Wm Morrison Bananas Limited
Incorporated: 15 July 2013
Net Worth: £5,532,000 *Total Assets:* £6,875,000
Registered Office: Hilmore House, Gain Lane, Bradford, BD3 7DL
Activities: Other processing and preserving of fruit and vegetables
Parent: Wm Morrison Produce Limited
Officers: Jonathan James Burke, Secretary; Darren Anthony Blackhurst [1966] Director; Jonathan Paul Hornby [1972] Director; Mark Thomas Stitson [1976] Finance Director; Andrew Edward Thornber [1974] Managing Director

Wm Morrison LP 2 Limited
Incorporated: 17 September 2014
Net Worth: £15,261,000 *Total Assets:* £15,792,000
Registered Office: Hilmore House, Gain Lane, Bradford, W Yorks, BD3 7DL
Activities: Other business support service activities n.e.c.
Parent: Wm Morrison Supermarkets Holdings Limited
Officers: Jonathan James Burke, Secretary; Jonathan James Burke [1966] Director; Trevor John Strain [1975] Director/Accountant

Wm Morrison LP 3 Limited
Incorporated: 17 September 2014
Net Worth: £11,708,000 *Total Assets:* £12,028,000
Registered Office: Hilmore House, Gain Lane, Bradford, W Yorks, BD3 7DL
Activities: Other business support service activities n.e.c.
Parent: Wm Morrison Supermarkets Holdings Limited
Officers: Jonathan James Burke, Secretary; Jonathan James Burke [1966] Director; Trevor John Strain [1975] Director/Accountant

Wm Morrison Produce Limited
Incorporated: 4 October 1963 *Employees:* 2,651
Net Worth: £271,550,016 *Total Assets:* £386,352,000
Registered Office: Hilmore House, Gain Lane, Bradford, W Yorks, BD3 7DL
Activities: Other processing and preserving of fruit and vegetables
Parent: Wm Morrison Supermarkets Holdings Limited
Officers: Jonathan James Burke, Secretary; Darren Anthony Blackhurst [1966] Director; Andrew James Clappen [1965] Technical Director; Jonathan Paul Hornby [1972] Director; Mark Thomas Stitson [1976] Finance Director; Andrew Edward Thornber [1974] Director

Wm Morrison Supermarkets P L C
Incorporated: 22 January 1940 *Employees:* 105,487
Net Worth: £4,544,999,936 *Total Assets:* £9,667,000,320
Registered Office: Hilmore House, Gain Lane, Bradford, W Yorks, BD3 7DL
Activities: Retail sale in non-specialised stores with food, beverages or tobacco predominating
Officers: Jonathan James Burke, Secretary; Rooney Anand [1964] Director/Chief Executive Officer; Belinda Carew Jones [1958] Director; Richard Colin Neil Davidson [1951] Director; Kevin John Havelock [1957] Director; Andrew Thomas Higginson [1957] Director; Tony Van Kralingen [1958] Director [South African]; David Tom Potts [1957] Director/Chief Executive; Trevor John Strain [1975] Finance Director; The Reverend Paula Anne Vennells [1959] Director/Chief Executive Officer The Post Office

Morson Group Limited
Incorporated: 26 April 2004 *Employees:* 1,410
Net Worth: £87,115,000 *Total Assets:* £181,812,992
Registered Office: Adamson House, Centenary Way, Salford, M50 1RD
Activities: Human resources provision and management of human resources functions
Parent: MMG3 Acquisition Limited
Officers: Paul John Gilmour, Secretary/Director; Paul John Gilmour [1964] Director; Kevin Patrick Gorton [1964] Director; Gerard Anthony Mason [1964] Director; Kevin Philbin [1959] Director

Morson Holdings Limited
Incorporated: 21 September 1999 *Employees:* 14
Net Worth: £234,000 *Total Assets:* £60,237,000
Registered Office: Adamson House, Centenary Way, Salford, M50 1RD
Activities: Human resources provision and management of human resources functions
Parent: Morson Group Limited
Officers: Paul John Gilmour, Secretary/Accountant; Paul John Gilmour [1964] Director/Accountant; Kevin Patrick Gorton [1964] Director; Gerard Anthony Mason [1964] Director

Morson Human Resources Limited
Incorporated: 14 May 1992 *Employees:* 1,190
Net Worth: £57,410,000 *Total Assets:* £138,671,008
Registered Office: Adamson House, Centenary Way, Salford, M50 1RD
Activities: Human resources provision and management of human resources functions
Parent: Morson Holdings Limited
Officers: Paul John Gilmour, Secretary; Paul John Gilmour [1964] Director; Kevin Patrick Gorton [1964] Director; Gerard Anthony Mason [1964] Director

Morson Projects Limited
Incorporated: 26 October 1979 *Employees:* 167
Net Worth: £4,143,000 *Total Assets:* £15,191,000
Registered Office: Adamson House, Centenary Way, Salford, M50 1RD
Activities: Manufacture of electricity distribution and control apparatus
Parent: Morson Holdings Limited
Officers: Paul John Gilmour, Secretary; Paul John Gilmour [1964] Director; Kevin Patrick Gorton [1964] Director; Gerard Anthony Mason [1964] Director

Mortgage Agency Services Number Five Limited
Incorporated: 19 April 2002
Net Worth: £49,343,000 *Total Assets:* £64,242,000
Registered Office: 1 Angel Square, Manchester, M60 0AG
Activities: Financial intermediation not elsewhere classified
Parent: The Co-operative Bank PLC
Officers: David Clive Whitehead, Secretary; Ashley John William Lillie [1970] Director; Caroline Jane Richardson [1974] Director/Accountant

Mortgage Agency Services Number Four Limited
Incorporated: 19 April 2002
Net Worth: £6,058,000 *Total Assets:* £7,655,000
Registered Office: 1 Angel Square, Manchester, M60 0AG
Activities: Financial intermediation not elsewhere classified
Parent: The Co-operative Bank PLC
Officers: David Clive Whitehead, Secretary; Ashley John William Lillie [1970] Director; Caroline Jane Richardson [1974] Director/Accountant

Mortgage Agency Services Number One Limited
Incorporated: 16 November 1988
Net Worth: £12,815,000 *Total Assets:* £16,568,000
Registered Office: 1 Angel Square, Manchester, M60 0AG
Activities: Financial intermediation not elsewhere classified
Parent: The Co-operative Bank PLC
Officers: David Clive Whitehead, Secretary; Ashley John William Lillie [1970] Director; Caroline Jane Richardson [1974] Director/Accountant

Mortgage Express
Incorporated: 18 July 1989
Net Worth: £508,660,000 *Total Assets:* £3,645,193,984
Registered Office: P O Box 88, Croft Road, Crossflatts, Bingley, W Yorks, BD16 2UA
Activities: Activities of mortgage finance companies
Parent: Bradford & Bingley PLC
Officers: Claire Louise Craigie, Secretary; Ian John Hares [1958] Director/Banker; Martin Andrew Scott [1962] Finance Director

George Moss & Sons Limited
Incorporated: 13 September 1920 *Employees:* 8
Net Worth: £18,923,736 *Total Assets:* £27,522,104
Registered Office: Unit C4, 1 Centre Court, Moss Industrial Estate, St Helens Road, Leigh, Lancs, WN7 3PT
Activities: Development of building projects
Parent: Moss Holdings Limited
Officers: Anita Felicity May Moss [1956] Director; Philip Hanbidge Moss [1955] Director; Sebastian Hanbidge Moss [1984] Director

J Moss Developments Limited
Incorporated: 9 May 1994
Net Worth: £9,707,046 *Total Assets:* £16,908,624
Registered Office: Hanover Buildings, 11-13 Hanover Street, Liverpool, L1 3DN
Activities: Construction of commercial buildings
Major Shareholder: Julian Moss
Officers: Adele Moss, Secretary; Adele Moss [1963] Director/Retail Manager; Julian Moss [1962] Director/Property Developer

Mostyn Terminals Limited
Incorporated: 2 July 2003
Net Worth: £5,168,550 *Total Assets:* £8,923,015
Registered Office: The Port of Mostyn, Coast Road, Mostyn, Holywell, Flintshire, CH8 9HE
Activities: Sea and coastal freight water transport
Shareholders: Carole Brazier; James Peter O'Toole; Susan Kim Parker; Rachael Julie Byrne
Officers: Fiona Jane Wynne-Jones, Secretary; James Peter O'Toole [1942] Director

Moto GB Limited
Incorporated: 10 May 2000 *Employees:* 95
Net Worth: £4,700,417 *Total Assets:* £16,508,033
Registered Office: White Bear Yard, Park Road, Adlington, Chorley, Lancs, PR7 4HZ
Activities: Sale, maintenance and repair of motorcycles and related parts and accessories
Parent: 2 Moto Limited
Officers: Eileen Mason [1955] Director; Keith James Mason [1955] Director

Motorplus Limited
Incorporated: 18 August 1995 *Employees:* 153
Net Worth: £1,543,220 *Total Assets:* £8,065,749
Registered Office: Speed Medical House, Eaton Avenue, Buckshaw Village, Chorley, Lancs, PR7 7NA
Activities: Non-life insurance
Parent: 116 Cardamon Limited
Officers: Graham Pulford [1969] Director; Jason Myles Tripp [1973] Director

Motors Insurance Company Limited
Incorporated: 16 January 1992 *Employees:* 18
Net Worth: £90,435,000 *Total Assets:* £246,604,000
Registered Office: Jubilee House, 5 Mid Point Business Park, Thornbury, W Yorks, BD3 7AG
Activities: Non-life insurance
Parent: Car Care Plan (Holdings) Limited
Officers: Gavin William Work Tinch, Secretary; Jeremy Edward Cadle [1965] Director/Lawyer; Maximiliaan Gerard Caviet [1953] Director/Chief Executive Officer; Timothy John Heavisides [1959] Managing Director; John Anthony Levin [1963] Director; Paul Graeme Newton [1959] Director; Benjamin Seamus Russell [1972] Sales Director; Gary Whitelam [1959] Managing Director; Simon Jonathan Wright [1966] Finance Director

Mott MacDonald Bentley Ltd
Incorporated: 17 August 1999
Net Worth: £1,000 *Total Assets:* £27,362,158
Registered Office: Keighley Road, Skipton, N Yorks, BD23 2QR
Activities: Construction of water projects
Parent: J N Bentley Limited
Officers: Helen Marie Thompson, Secretary; David Mark Bentley [1969] Commercial Director; Paul Rogerson Bentley [1967] Contracts Director; Richard Risdon [1974] Operations Director; Paul Smedley [1971] Director/Consultant Engineer; Steven Christopher Tetlow [1966] Director

Movitex (UK) Limited
Incorporated: 13 November 1945 *Employees:* 17
Net Worth: £3,520,000 *Total Assets:* £9,336,000
Registered Office: 2 Holdsworth Street, Bradford, W Yorks, BD1 4AH
Activities: Retail sale via mail order houses or via Internet
Shareholder: Monsieur Jean-Joel Huber
Officers: Jean Joel Huber [1963] Managing Director [French]

MPBM Limited
Incorporated: 9 April 2008 *Employees:* 2
Net Worth: £1,093,247 *Total Assets:* £6,844,194
Registered Office: Clint Mill, Cornmarket, Penrith, Cumbria, CA11 7HW
Activities: Development of building projects
Shareholders: Paula Boak; Martyn Howard Boak
Officers: Martyn Howard Boak, Secretary; Martyn Howard Boak [1964] Managing Director; Paula Boak [1967] Director

MPM Bidco Limited
Incorporated: 8 March 2016 *Employees:* 58
Net Worth Deficit: £3,604,000 *Total Assets:* £73,040,000
Registered Office: Floor 2, Trident 3, Trident Business Park, Styal Road, Manchester, M22 5XB
Activities: Other business support service activities n.e.c.
Parent: MPM Topco Limited
Officers: Julian Bambridge [1972] Director; James Bracewell [1978] Director; Jonathan Robert Kinsey [1960] Director; Peter William Thornton [1965] Director

MPM Products Limited
Incorporated: 6 December 2002 *Employees:* 60
Net Worth: £10,362,000 *Total Assets:* £25,438,000
Registered Office: Floor 2, Trident 3, Trident Business Park, Styal Road, Manchester, M22 5XB
Activities: Agents specialised in the sale of other particular products
Parent: MPM Bidco Limited
Officers: Julian Bambridge [1972] Director; James Bracewell [1978] Director

MPM Topco Limited
Incorporated: 7 March 2016 *Employees:* 68
Net Worth Deficit: £9,208,000 *Total Assets:* £71,920,000
Registered Office: Floor 2, Trident 3, Trident Business Park, Styal Road, Manchester, M22 5XB
Activities: Non-trading company
Parent: ECI Ventures Nominees Limited
Officers: Julian Bambridge [1972] Director; James Bracewell [1978] Director; Mark Daniel Keeley [1978] Director/Venture Capitalist; Jonathan Robert Kinsey [1960] Director; Peter William Thornton [1965] Director

MPP Global Solutions Ltd
Incorporated: 20 March 2000 *Employees:* 57
Net Worth: £6,800,663 *Total Assets:* £8,150,009
Registered Office: 401 Faraday Street, Birchwood Park, Warrington, Cheshire, WA3 6GA
Activities: Other information technology service activities
Officers: James Patrick Johnson, Secretary/Engineer; Christopher Charles Cheney [1972] Director/Engineer; Paul William Johnson [1972] Director/Engineer; Edward William Anthony Lascelles [1975] Director/Investment Manager; Jonathan Mathew Strudwick [1965] Director/Chief Financial Officer; Oliver Glyn Thomas [1980] Director/Investor; Keith Wallington [1972] Director

MRC Flangefitt Limited
Incorporated: 13 June 1985 *Employees:* 23
Net Worth: £4,957,643 *Total Assets:* £14,705,335
Registered Office: Heaton House, Riverside Drive, Cleckheaton, W Yorks, BD19 4DH
Activities: Wholesale of metals and metal ores
Parent: MRC Transmark Limited
Officers: Claire Jane Hellmund [1983] Director/Solicitor; Stephen Bradley Smith [1967] Director; Adnan Velic [1980] Director

MRC Transmark Holdings UK Limited
Incorporated: 26 April 2005 *Employees:* 57
Net Worth: £66,087,836 *Total Assets:* £77,447,384
Registered Office: Heaton House, Riverside Drive, Cleckheaton, W Yorks, BD19 4DH
Activities: Activities of head offices
Parent: MRC Transmark Group BV
Officers: Steinar Aasland [1966] Director [Norwegian]; Elton Ray Bond [1975] Director [American]; Claire Jane Hellmund [1983] Director/Solicitor; Adnan Velic [1980] Director

MRC Transmark Limited
Incorporated: 25 November 1997 *Employees:* 74
Net Worth: £18,170,534 *Total Assets:* £48,901,844
Registered Office: Heaton House, Riverside Drive, Cleckheaton, W Yorks, BD19 4DH
Activities: Other retail sale not in stores, stalls or markets
Parent: MRC Transmark Holdings UK Limited
Officers: Sarah Jayne Rawcliffe, Secretary; Claire Jane Hellmund [1983] Director/Solicitor; Stephen Bradley Smith [1967] Managing Director; Adnan Velic [1980] Director

MRH Corporate Group Limited
Incorporated: 4 May 2016 *Employees:* 69
Net Worth: £4,236,641 *Total Assets:* £9,716,096
Registered Office: Caroline House, 115-125 Bradshawgate, Bolton, Lancs, BL2 1BJ
Activities: Activities of other holding companies n.e.c.
Major Shareholder: Ashiq Husen Patel
Officers: Ashiq Husen Patel [1976] Director/Solicitor; Mohammed Yusuf Patel [1978] Director

MSP Fairwind Limited
Incorporated: 30 April 2013
Net Worth: £2,639,337 *Total Assets:* £13,404,871
Registered Office: Eversheds House, 70 Great Bridgewater Street, Manchester, M1 5ES
Activities: Production of electricity
Parent: Sune Green Holdco5 Limited
Officers: Carl Goran Dandanell [1959] Director [Swedish]

MSS Products Limited
Incorporated: 28 January 2002 *Employees:* 21
Net Worth: £3,584,638 *Total Assets:* £11,675,609
Registered Office: Bankfield Road, Tyldesley, Manchester, M29 8QH
Activities: Wholesale of metals and metal ores
Major Shareholder: Liam Gregory Hall
Officers: Michael Camilus Dinneen [1969] Director; Gerard Francis Hall [1980] Director; Liam Gregory Hall [1969] Director

MTX Holdings Limited
Incorporated: 12 November 2015 *Employees:* 36
Net Worth: £2,591,463 *Total Assets:* £8,443,605
Registered Office: Innovation House, Lower Meadow Road, Handforth, Wilmslow, Cheshire, SK9 3ND
Activities: Activities of other holding companies n.e.c.
Officers: David James Hartley [1976] Director; Generald Hartley [1954] Director; Steven Thomas Hartley [1978] Director

MU Commercial Holdings Junior Limited
Incorporated: 24 June 2015
Net Worth: £15,260,000 *Total Assets:* £15,260,000
Registered Office: Sir Matt Busby Way, Old Trafford, Manchester, M16 0RA
Activities: Activities of sport clubs
Parent: MU Commercial Holdings Limited
Officers: Patrick Charles Donald Stewart, Secretary; Richard Neil Arnold [1971] Group Managing Director; Avram Glazer [1960] Director/Businessman [American]; Bryan Glazer [1964] Director/Businessman [American]; Joel Glazer [1967] Director/Businessman [American]; Edward Gareth Woodward [1971] Director/Executive Vice Chairman

MU Commercial Holdings Limited
Incorporated: 24 June 2015
Net Worth: £15,260,000 *Total Assets:* £15,260,000
Registered Office: Sir Matt Busby Way, Old Trafford, Manchester, M16 0RA
Activities: Activities of sport clubs
Parent: Manchester United Limited
Officers: Patrick Charles Donald Stewart, Secretary; Richard Neil Arnold [1971] Group Managing Director; Avram Glazer [1960] Director/Businessman [American]; Bryan Glazer [1964] Director/Businessman [American]; Joel Glazer [1967] Director/Businessman [American]; Edward Gareth Woodward [1971] Director/Executive Vice Chairman

MU Finance Limited
Incorporated: 26 November 2009
Net Worth: £19,000,000 *Total Assets:* £648,092,032
Registered Office: Old Trafford, Sir Matt Busby Way, Manchester, M16 0RA
Activities: Activities of sport clubs
Parent: Manchester United Limited
Officers: Patrick Charles Donald Stewart, Secretary; Avram Glazer [1960] Director/Businessman [American]; Joel Glazer [1967] Director/Businessman [American]

MU RAML Limited
Incorporated: 25 June 2015 *Employees:* 32
Net Worth: £11,176,000 *Total Assets:* £20,468,000
Registered Office: Sir Matt Busby Way, Old Trafford, Manchester, M16 0RA
Activities: Activities of sport clubs
Parent: MU Commercial Holdings (Junior) Limited
Officers: Patrick Charles Donald Stewart, Secretary; Richard Neil Arnold [1971] Group Managing Director; Avram Glazer [1960] Director/Businessman [American]; Bryan Glazer [1964] Director/Businessman [American]; Joel Glazer [1967] Director/Businessman [American]; Edward Gareth Woodward [1971] Director/Executive Vice Chairman

Mudskipper Business Limited
Incorporated: 12 June 2001 *Employees:* 38
Net Worth: £6,024,431 *Total Assets:* £8,744,335
Registered Office: The Boathouse, Clarence Mill, Clarence Road, Bollington, Cheshire, SK10 5JZ
Activities: Public relations and communications activities
Parent: Amiculum Limited
Officers: Michael Putin, Secretary; Dr Richard John Allcorn [1962] Director/Consultant; Doctor Jennifer Claire Putin [1963] Director; Michael Putin [1937] Director/Business Consultant

Mulard Renewables Limited
Incorporated: 4 November 2013
Net Worth: £7,165,767 *Total Assets:* £7,395,972
Registered Office: Canal Head North, Kendal, Cumbria, LA9 7BZ
Activities: Production of electricity
Parent: TT Nominees Limited
Officers: Charles William Nepean Crewdson [1964] Director; David Benjamin Freeder [1981] Investment Director; Robert Charles Peter Troughton [1982] Director

Mullberry Homes Limited
Incorporated: 16 December 1980 *Employees:* 19
Net Worth: £16,229,231 *Total Assets:* £19,682,704
Registered Office: Old Hall House, Old Hall Lane, Pleasington, Blackburn, Lancs, BB2 6RJ
Activities: Construction of domestic buildings
Officers: Catherine Lesley Eastham, Secretary/Accounts Executive; Alistair Christian Wilcock [1973] Director/General Manager

Multimedia International Services Limited
Incorporated: 1 September 1999 *Employees:* 75
Net Worth Deficit: £1,231,243 *Total Assets:* £7,776,512
Registered Office: Premier House, Premier Way, Poulton Business Park, Poulton-le-Fylde, Lancs, FY6 8JP
Activities: Advertising agencies
Parent: Media International Holdings Limited
Officers: Angela Margaret Darnell, Secretary; Angela Margaret Darnell [1959] Director Secretary; David Ravenscroft [1963] Director; Adrian John Reed [1980] Director

Multiplastics (Europe) Limited
Incorporated: 8 June 1989 *Employees:* 29
Net Worth: £6,067,854 *Total Assets:* £7,217,939
Registered Office: Columbus House, 30 Manchester Road, Northwich, Cheshire, CW9 5ND
Activities: Manufacture of other plastic products
Officers: Amanda Adderley, Secretary; Paul Frith [1952] Managing Director; John Robert Parsio [1939] Director/Company President [American]

Multistar Container Transport Limited
Incorporated: 10 December 1986 *Employees:* 2
Net Worth: £7,667,652 *Total Assets:* £19,608,656
Registered Office: Hope Chapel, Hope Street, Sandbach, Cheshire, CW11 1BA
Activities: Renting and leasing of other machinery, equipment and tangible goods n.e.c.
Major Shareholder: David Frederick Jenkins
Officers: David Richard Kew [1974] Director [South African]; Robert Neil Surman [1949] Director/Chartered Accountant; Louwrens Martinus Verwey [1983] Director [South African]

Mumtaz Food Products Limited
Incorporated: 14 May 2008
Net Worth: £2,221,701 *Total Assets:* £7,425,491
Registered Office: 42 Legrams Lane, Bradford, W Yorks, BD7 1ND
Activities: Activities of other holding companies n.e.c.
Shareholder: Kauser Gul-Nawaz Akbar
Officers: Kauser Gul-Nawaz Akbar, Secretary; Bilal Akbar [1988] Director; Ismail Akbar [1995] Director

Muraspec Limited
Incorporated: 9 January 2012
Net Worth: £30,000 *Total Assets:* £7,442,467
Registered Office: c/o A2E Industries Limited, 1 Marsden Street, Manchester, M2 1HW
Activities: Activities of head offices
Shareholders: Said Amin Amiri; Tariq Rashid
Officers: Said Amin Amiri [1956] Director/Financier; Tariq Rashid [1958] Director

Gavin Murray Limited
Incorporated: 20 July 1961 *Employees:* 123
Net Worth: £3,493,129 *Total Assets:* £11,457,137
Registered Office: 61 Boundary Road, St Helens, Merseyside, WA10 2LX
Activities: Other passenger land transport
Parent: Ellisons Travel Services Limited
Officers: Michael Gavin Magowan, Secretary; Andrew John Magowan [1966] Managing Director; Michael Gavin Magowan [1963] Finance Director

Music Tribe Brands UK Ltd.
Incorporated: 10 November 2009
Net Worth Deficit: £14,859,435 *Total Assets:* £21,001,440
Registered Office: Quay House, City Park Business Village, 5 Brindley Road, Old Trafford, Manchester, M16 9UN
Activities: Other research and experimental development on natural sciences and engineering
Officers: Cheryl Saldana de Leon [1978] Director/Lawyer [Filipino]; Raul Guevara Gerodias [1963] Director/Lawyer [Filipino]

Mutley Group Limited
Incorporated: 8 April 2016
Net Worth: £14,133,565 *Total Assets:* £19,834,296
Registered Office: Suite 308, Lester House, 21 Broad Street, Bury, Lancs, BL9 0DA
Activities: Activities of other holding companies n.e.c.
Shareholder: Ann Marilyn Marks
Officers: Margaret Cicely Alice Ford, Secretary; Ann Marilyn Marks [1947] Director; Ashley Hardy Marks [1979] Director; David Leonard Marks [1950] Director

Mutley Properties (Holdings) Limited
Incorporated: 11 February 1999
Net Worth: £20,239,700 *Total Assets:* £28,972,644
Registered Office: Suite 308, Lester House, 21 Broad Street, Bury, Lancs, BL9 0DA
Activities: Buying and selling of own real estate
Officers: Margaret Cicely Alice Ford, Secretary; Ann Marilyn Marks [1947] Director; Ashley Hardy Marks [1979] Director; David Leonard Marks [1950] Director; Geoffrey Robert Marks [1941] Director/Solicitor; Dr Gillian Marks [1976] Director/Doctor; Marcelle Palmer [1987] Director

MUTV Limited
Incorporated: 13 August 1997 *Employees:* 90
Net Worth: £309,981 *Total Assets:* £16,308,627
Registered Office: Sir Matt Busby Way, Old Trafford, Manchester, M16 0RA
Activities: Television programming and broadcasting activities
Parent: Manchester United Commercial Holdings Junior Limited
Officers: Patrick Charles Donald Stewart, Secretary; Richard Neil Arnold [1971] Director; Avram Glazer [1960] Director [American]; Bryan Glazer [1964] Director [American]; Joel Glazer [1967] Director/Businessman [American]; Edward Gareth Woodward [1971] Director

mxData - Technologies Limited
Incorporated: 17 August 2000 *Employees:* 2
Net Worth: £8,424,340 *Total Assets:* £9,341,256
Registered Office: Atlantic House, Atlas Business Park, Simonsway, Manchester, M22 5PR
Activities: Other information technology service activities
Parent: mxData Holdings Limited
Officers: Anne-Marie Marie Alexander [1969] Director; David Ian Nicholson James [1970] Director; David Brian Thomas [1974] Director

N-Sea Offshore Ltd
Incorporated: 19 December 2013 *Employees:* 36
Net Worth: £1,148,084 *Total Assets:* £14,736,363
Registered Office: Eversheds House, 70 Great Bridgewater Street, Manchester, M1 5ES
Activities: Support activities for petroleum and natural gas mining
Parent: N-Sea Holding BV
Officers: Jarrod David James [1969] Director/C.O.O; Gerardus Antonius Keser [1965] General Director N-Sea Group [Dutch]

N.I.S. Holdings Limited
Incorporated: 3 December 1982 *Employees:* 246
Net Worth: £8,983,000 *Total Assets:* £19,816,000
Registered Office: Ackhurst Road, Chorley, Lancs, PR7 1NH
Activities: Activities of head offices
Major Shareholder: Dr Ching Chih Chen
Officers: Howard Entwistle, Secretary/Director; Chih Yuan Chen [1962] Director/Merchant [Chinese]; Ching Chih Chen [1938] Director [Taiwanese]; Shea Daniel Chen [1985] Director [American]; Howard Entwistle [1956] Director; Norman Ian Meffan [1928] Non-Executive Director Chairman; John Morris [1952] Director; James Stephen Porter [1965] Director

N.R.L. Group Limited
Incorporated: 28 August 1991 *Employees:* 110
Net Worth: £13,639,354 *Total Assets:* £42,733,168
Registered Office: Building 5, Glass House Road, Glass House Business Park, Wigan, Lancs, WN3 6GL
Activities: Activities of head offices
Major Shareholder: Andrew Paul Redmayne
Officers: Benjamin Humpage, Secretary; Benjamin Mark Humpage [1974] Director/Accountant; Donald Livingston [1956] Director/Business Development; Andrew Paul Redmayne [1958] Director; David Redmayne [1985] Director; Hugh Geoffrey Redmayne [1960] Director

N.R.L. Limited
Incorporated: 15 November 1982 *Employees:* 75
Net Worth: £7,283,003 *Total Assets:* £21,156,628
Registered Office: Building 5, Glass House Road, Glass House Business Park, Wigan, Lancs, WN3 6GL
Activities: Other activities of employment placement agencies
Parent: NRL Group Limited
Officers: Benjamin Humpage, Secretary; Mhairi Brown [1967] Director/Recruitment Business; Neil David Campbell [1972] Director; Greg Compton [1972] Director; William John Fossey [1977] Director; Gillian Gomersall [1966] Director/Recruitment Business; Rebecca Graves [1983] Regional Director; Benjamin Mark Humpage [1974] Director/Accountant; Philip Jennings [1959] Director/Recruitment Business; Donald Livingston [1956] Director/Recruitment Business; Andrew Paul Redmayne [1958] Director; Hugh Geoffrey Redmayne [1960] Director; James Douglas Taylor [1956] Director/Recruitment Business

Nalco Acquisition One
Incorporated: 24 October 2003
Net Worth: £343,748,032 *Total Assets:* £343,748,032
Registered Office: P O Box 11, Winnington Avenue, Northwich, Cheshire, CW8 4DX
Activities: Manufacture of other organic basic chemicals
Officers: Wendy Annette Joyce, Secretary; Paul Hey [1964] Director; Carl Richmond Lee [1963] Director/Chartered Accountant

Nalco Acquisition Two Limited
Incorporated: 23 October 2003
Net Worth: £128,740,200 *Total Assets:* £128,740,200
Registered Office: P O Box 11, Winnington Avenue, Northwich, Cheshire, CW8 4DX
Activities: Manufacture of other organic basic chemicals
Parent: Nalco Acquisition One
Officers: Wendy Annette Joyce, Secretary; Paul Hey [1964] Director; Carl Richmond Lee [1963] Director

Nalco Energy Services Marketing Limited
Incorporated: 13 April 1994 *Employees:* 15
Net Worth: £21,497,000 *Total Assets:* £25,781,000
Registered Office: P O Box 11, Winnington Avenue, Northwich, Cheshire, CW8 4DX
Activities: Manufacture of other inorganic basic chemicals
Parent: Nalco Energy Services Limited
Officers: Wendy Annette Joyce, Secretary; John Denman Gamble [1962] Director/VP Europe Customer Service; Carl Richmond Lee [1963] Finance Director

Nalco Holdings UK Limited
Incorporated: 14 March 1967
Net Worth: £70,060,000 *Total Assets:* £70,060,000
Registered Office: Winnington Avenue, Northwich, Cheshire, CW8 4DX
Activities: Non-trading company
Parent: Nalco Acquisition Two Limited
Officers: Wendy Annette Joyce, Secretary; John Denman Gamble [1962] Director/VP Europe Customer Service; Carl Richmond Lee [1963] Finance Director

Nalco Limited
Incorporated: 25 November 1958 *Employees:* 502
Net Worth: £52,822,000 *Total Assets:* £139,300,992
Registered Office: Winnington Avenue, Northwich, Cheshire, CW8 4DX
Activities: Manufacture of other inorganic basic chemicals
Parent: Nalco Holdings UK Limited
Officers: Wendy Annette Joyce, Secretary; Paul Hey [1964] Director; Carl Richmond Lee [1963] Director/Chartered Accountant; David Walker [1969] Director/Chartered Accountant

Nalco Manufacturing Ltd
Incorporated: 14 October 2010 *Employees:* 131
Net Worth: £9,547,000 *Total Assets:* £15,602,000
Registered Office: Winnington Avenue, Northwich, Cheshire, CW8 4DX
Activities: Manufacture of other inorganic basic chemicals
Parent: Nalco Limited
Officers: Peter James Hussey [1959] Director/Business Executive

Nalco Services Limited
Incorporated: 29 April 1998 *Employees:* 2
Net Worth: £10,310,000 *Total Assets:* £10,310,000
Registered Office: P O Box No 11, Winnington Avenue, Northwich, Cheshire, CW8 4DX
Activities: Other business support service activities n.e.c.
Parent: Nalco Limited
Officers: Wendy Annette Joyce, Secretary; John Denman Gamble [1962] Director/VP Europe Customer Service; Carl Richmond Lee [1963] Finance Director

Nalge (Europe) Limited
Incorporated: 7 August 1985
Net Worth: £7,027,000 *Total Assets:* £7,030,000
Registered Office: 3rd Floor, 1 Ashley Road, Altrincham, Cheshire, WA14 2DT
Activities: Non-specialised wholesale trade
Parent: Apogent UK Limited
Officers: Rhona Gregg, Secretary; Lucie Mary Katja Grant [1976] Director/Solicitor; Nicholas Ince [1982] Director/Accountant; David John Norman [1960] Director/Chartered Accountant

Nanoco Group PLC
Incorporated: 9 March 2004 *Employees:* 110
Net Worth: £10,447,000 *Total Assets:* £12,419,000
Registered Office: 46 Grafton Street, Manchester, M13 9NT
Activities: Research and experimental development on biotechnology
Officers: Brian Thomas Tenner, Secretary; Brendan Matthew Cummins [1957] Director/Consultant [Irish]; Dr Michael Albert Edelman [1964] Director [British/American]; Dr Alison Margaret Fielding [1964] Director; Dr Nigel Leroy Pickett [1969] Director; Dr Christopher Gareth Joseph Richards [1953] Director; Brian Thomas Tenner [1968] Director

Nanoco Tech Limited
Incorporated: 21 June 2006 *Employees:* 3
Net Worth: £6,652,000 *Total Assets:* £6,652,000
Registered Office: 46 Grafton Street, Manchester, M13 9NT
Activities: Other research and experimental development on natural sciences and engineering
Parent: Nanoco Group PLC
Officers: Brian Thomas Tenner, Secretary; Dr Michael Albert Edelman [1964] Director [British/American]; Dr Nigel Leroy Pickett [1969] Director/Researcher; Brian Thomas Tenner [1968] Director

Nanoco Technologies Limited
Incorporated: 26 April 2001 *Employees:* 107
Net Worth Deficit: £50,057,000 *Total Assets:* £8,031,000
Registered Office: 46 Grafton Street, Manchester, M13 9NT
Activities: Other research and experimental development on natural sciences and engineering
Officers: Brian Thomas Tenner, Secretary; Dr Michael Albert Edelman [1964] Director [British/American]; Andrew Halford Gooda [1963] Director/Engineer; Dr Nigel Leroy Pickett [1969] Director/Researcher; Brian Thomas Tenner [1968] Director

Napoleons Leisure Limited
Incorporated: 23 February 1984 *Employees:* 177
Net Worth: £23,913,900 *Total Assets:* £28,515,618
Registered Office: One St Peters Square, Manchester, M2 3DE
Activities: Gambling and betting activities
Parent: Mayfair Casino Limited
Officers: Christian Huot [1984] Director [French]; Vanthan Huot [1941] Director [French]

Narang Group Ltd
Incorporated: 21 July 2009 *Employees:* 98
Net Worth: £5,310,861 *Total Assets:* £10,818,853
Registered Office: Narang House, 121 City Road, Bradford, W Yorks, BD8 8JR
Activities: Activities of head offices
Shareholders: Jasbir Singh Narang; Ravinder Singh Narang
Officers: Jasbir Singh Narang [1966] Director; Ravinder Singh Narang [1969] Director

Narang Wholesalers Limited
Incorporated: 25 July 1995
Net Worth: £5,068,795 *Total Assets:* £10,567,236
Registered Office: Narang House, 121 City Road, Bradford, W Yorks, BD8 8JR
Activities: Wholesale of wine, beer, spirits and other alcoholic beverages
Parent: Narang Group Limited
Officers: Jagjeet Singh Kalsi, Secretary; Mohammed Younis Hussain [1971] Director/Wholesalers; Jagjeet Singh Kalsi [1951] Director/Wholesalers; Jasbir Singh Narang [1966] Director

Narbourne Limited
Incorporated: 7 October 2004 *Employees:* 2
Net Worth Deficit: £2,846,157 *Total Assets:* £15,767,233
Registered Office: Cumberland House, Greenside Lane, Bradford, BD8 9TF
Activities: Development of building projects
Parent: Hartley Investment Trust Limited
Officers: Alan James Lewis [1938] Director/Chairman

Carole Nash Insurance Consultants Limited
Incorporated: 12 April 1991 *Employees:* 404
Net Worth: £13,815,617 *Total Assets:* £19,762,424
Registered Office: Trafalgar House, 110 Manchester Road, Altrincham, Cheshire, WA14 1NU
Activities: Non-life insurance
Parent: Atlanta Investment Holdings A Limited
Officers: Clive Timothy Roberts, Secretary; Craig David Ball [1972] Director; Jennifer Victoria Lee Devaney [1967] Compliance Director; Ian James Donaldson [1974] Director; Philip Frank Evans [1976] Operations and Sales Director; James Richard Fairhurst [1974] Director/Chief Information Officer; Clive Timothy Roberts [1965] Finance Director

NAT Flex Group Limited
Incorporated: 5 April 2011 *Employees:* 47
Net Worth: £3,387,516 *Total Assets:* £8,320,385
Registered Office: 2 Battlefield View, Birkenshaw, Bradford, W Yorks, BD11 2PT
Activities: Dormant company
Officers: Julia Davys, Secretary; Julia Davys [1966] Finance Director; George Slack [1973] Managing Director; William Barry Twigg [1939] Director

National Federation of Self Employed and Small Businesses Limited
Incorporated: 17 June 1976 *Employees:* 209
Net Worth: £12,777,307 *Total Assets:* £27,503,854
Registered Office: Sir Frank Whittle Way, Blackpool Business Park, Blackpool, Lancs, FY4 2FE
Activities: Activities of professional membership organisations
Officers: Michael Hugh Cherry [1953] Director/Woodwork Engineer; Melanie Dawn Coley [1970] Director; Peter Brian Charles Davys [1965] Managing Director; Alexis Lesey Lay [1951] Director; Gary Lovatt [1959] Director/Partner in Guest House; Gillian Margaret MacEwan [1972] Director/Event Management; Martin Gerard McTague [1956] Director; David John Miles [1976] Director; Ian Douglas O'Donnell [1976] Director; David Anthony Stallon [1954] Director/Proprietor-Engineer; Veronika Weisweiller [1949] Director/Business Proprietor

National Flexible Limited
Incorporated: 19 December 1997 *Employees:* 47
Net Worth: £3,886,617 *Total Assets:* £8,688,595
Registered Office: 2 Battlefield View, Birkenshaw, Bradford, BD11 2PT
Activities: Packaging activities
Officers: Julia Davys, Secretary; Carol Abigail Burdett [1959] Director; David Daniels [1977] Technical Director; Julia Davys [1966] Finance Director; George Slack [1973] Managing Director; Mark Alan Thompson [1973] Sales & Marketing Director; William Barry Twigg [1939] Director

National Holidays Limited
Incorporated: 17 February 1987 *Employees:* 219
Net Worth: £34,796,000 *Total Assets:* £41,804,000
Registered Office: Waterside House, Waterside Drive, Wigan, Lancs, WN3 5AZ
Activities: Other urban, suburban or metropolitan passenger land transport (not underground, metro or similar)
Parent: National Holidays Tours Limited
Officers: Richard James Calvert [1967] Director; Vincent Flower [1960] Director; Martin Stuart Lock [1970] Director; Graham John Rogers [1963] Director; Gary Speakman [1961] Finance Director

National Holidays Tours Limited
Incorporated: 19 June 1996 *Employees:* 126
Net Worth Deficit: £1,242,000 *Total Assets:* £44,783,000
Registered Office: Waterside House, Waterside Drive, Wigan, Lancs, WN3 5AZ
Activities: Other passenger land transport
Parent: Shearings Group Limited
Officers: Carl Allan Brackenbury [1968] Director/Holidays Manager; Richard James Calvert [1967] Director; Vincent Flower [1960] Director; Martin Stuart Lock [1970] Director/General Manager; Graham John Rogers [1963] Director; Gary Speakman [1961] Finance Director

National Museum of Labour History (The)
Incorporated: 28 July 1986 *Employees:* 30
Net Worth: £10,889,924 *Total Assets:* £10,991,554
Registered Office: Peoples History Museum, Left Bank, Spinningfields, Manchester, M3 3ER
Activities: Archives activities
Officers: Catherine Vivien Birchall, Secretary; Councillor Derek Antrobus [1954] Director/Lecturer; Lord John Steve Bassam [1953] Director/Chief Whip Labour Lords; Kay Carberry [1950] Director/Trade Union Official; Martin Alexander Carr [1965] Managing Director; Bernard Donoghue [1969] Director; Dr Wayne Garvie [1963] Director/Television Executive; Russell Mark Gill [1967] Director/Co-operative Official; John Hannett [1953] Director/Union General Secretary; Maziar Jamnejad [1984] Director/Solicitor; Thomas Patrick Russell Jones [1965] Director/Lawyer; Beth Maria Knowles [1988] Director/Councillor; Steven James Lindsay [1962] Director/Accountant; Alveena Malik [1973] Charity Director; Paul Nowak [1972] Director/Trade Union Official; Lucy Maria Powell [1974] Director/Member of Parliament; Michael John Pye [1937] Director/Retired; Janet Anne Royall of Blaisdon [1955] Director/Politician

National Nuclear Laboratory Limited
Incorporated: 7 October 1999 *Employees:* 798
Net Worth: £55,077,000 *Total Assets:* £135,432,000
Registered Office: Chadwick House, Warrington Road, Birchwood Park, Warrington, Cheshire, WA3 6AE
Activities: Engineering related scientific and technical consulting activities
Parent: NNL Holdings Limited
Officers: David Barry Dukes, Secretary; David John Beacham [1968] Director/Chief Customer Officer; Ruth Marie Dunphy [1973] Director; Claire Louise Flint [1964] Director; Dr Paul John Arton Howarth [1970] Director; John Malcolm Lanaghan [1955] Director; Andrew David Hugh Mathews [1958] Director/Engineering Consultant; Anna Charlotte Payton [1978] Director/Civil Servant; Professor Andrew Hamilton Sherry [1961] Director/Chief Science and Technology Officer; Dr Michael William Weightman [1949] Director/Engineering Consultant

National Refrigerants Ltd
Incorporated: 8 December 1988 *Employees:* 41
Net Worth: £16,167,450 *Total Assets:* £26,429,360
Registered Office: Granite Building, 6 Stanley Street, Liverpool, L1 6AF
Activities: Manufacture of other chemical products n.e.c.
Officers: Paul Mottram, Secretary; Carmen Carosella [1951] Director [American]; John Harvey Reilly III [1970] Director [American]

National Tyre Service Limited
Incorporated: 12 August 1970 *Employees:* 1,176
Net Worth: £12,177,000 *Total Assets:* £62,844,000
Registered Office: c/o National Tyres, Regent House, Heaton Lane, Stockport, Cheshire, SK4 1BS
Activities: Maintenance and repair of motor vehicles
Parent: Axle Group Limited
Officers: John Alexander Taylor, Secretary/Accountant; John Irvine Caldwell [1956] Director/Sales & Marketing; Alan Livingstone Revie [1959] Director; John Alexander Taylor [1964] Director/Accountant

Nationwide Produce Holdings PLC
Incorporated: 5 November 1996 *Employees:* 74
Net Worth: £5,385,007 *Total Assets:* £23,489,116
Registered Office: The Business Centre, 164 Lord Street, Southport, Merseyside, PR9 0HQ
Activities: Other food services
Officers: Patrick O'Malley, Secretary/Director; Philip Martin Johnson [1969] Director; John Paul Mann [1965] Director; David Michael Noton [1977] Director; Anthony O'Malley [1963] Director; Bernard Joseph Patrick O'Malley [1936] Director/Chairman; Patrick O'Malley [1968] Director; Timothy O'Malley [1966] Director

Nationwide Produce PLC
Incorporated: 18 December 1985 *Employees:* 91
Net Worth: £5,439,312 *Total Assets:* £23,444,392
Registered Office: 164 Lord Street, Southport, Merseyside, PR9 0QA
Activities: Other food services
Officers: Anthony O'Malley, Secretary; Steven John Armstrong [1964] Director; Scott Hollins [1983] Sales Director; Philip Martin Johnson [1969] Director; Rafael Lopez Lopez [1977] Director [Spanish]; John Paul Mann [1965] Director/Produce Broker; Michael John Murray [1968] Financial Director; David Noton [1977] Sales Director; Anthony O'Malley [1963] Director/Produce Broker; Bernard Joseph Patrick O'Malley [1936] Director/Produce Broker; Timothy O'Malley [1966] Director; Patrick Omalley [1968] Director/Produce Broker; Ian Paul Thornhill [1963] Director; Robert Voskamp [1981] Sales Director [Dutch]

Natrium Holdings Limited
Incorporated: 7 December 2010 *Employees:* 386
Net Worth Deficit: £83,866,000 *Total Assets:* £205,894,000
Registered Office: Mond House, Winnington, Northwich, Cheshire, CW8 4DT
Activities: Activities of production holding companies
Parent: TCE Group Limited
Officers: Jonathan Laurence Abbotts, Secretary; David Philip William Davies, Secretary; Jonathan Laurence Abbotts [1964] Director; Dr Martin John Ashcroft [1969] Director; David Philip William Davies [1971] Director/Solicitor

Natural Assets Investments Limited
Incorporated: 24 February 2011 *Employees:* 142
Net Worth Deficit: £32,283,324 *Total Assets:* £32,002,558
Registered Office: 1st Floor, Whitecroft House, 51 Water Lane, Wilmslow, Cheshire, SK9 5BQ
Activities: Other accommodation
Officers: Umar Mark Aziz [1979] Director/Solicitor; Timothy Dennis [1975] Director; Fraser MacDonald Douglas [1950] Director/Retired; David Michael Gorton [1963] Director/Fund Manager; Ewan James Kearney [1971] Director; Matthew Dawson Spence [1963] Director; Anthony Wild [1974] Director

The Nature's Bounty Co. Ltd.
Incorporated: 19 July 2005 *Employees:* 156
Net Worth Deficit: £5,502,000 *Total Assets:* £177,042,000
Registered Office: Eversheds House, 70 Great Bridgewater Street, Manchester, M1 5ES
Activities: Other human health activities
Officers: Stephen Conboy [1960] Director/Chief Financial Officer [American]; Stephen Kelsey Ford [1968] Finance Director; Ryan Kiran Standen [1979] Director/Finance Manager

Navagator Limited
Incorporated: 27 January 2012 *Employees:* 175
Net Worth: £7,773,000 *Total Assets:* £9,311,000
Registered Office: Stamford Works, Bayley Street, Stalybridge, Cheshire, SK15 1QQ
Activities: Non-trading company
Officers: Katie Jane Ferris [1971] Director; Stephen Keith Picot [1950] Director; Alan Reay [1938] Director

NBTY (2015) Limited
Incorporated: 30 July 2015
Registered Office: Eversheds House, 70 Great Bridgewater Street, Manchester, M1 5ES
Activities: Non-trading company
Parent: The Nature's Bounty Co. Ltd.
Officers: Nicholas John Heywood Collins [1962] Director/Chief Strategy & Product Supply Officer International; Stephen Kelsey Ford [1968] Finance Director; Stephen John Quinn [1962] Director/Business Executive; Frederick Francis Whitcomb [1955] Director/Business Executive

NCC Group (Solutions) Limited
Incorporated: 29 March 1999
Net Worth: £10,000,000 *Total Assets:* £204,900,000
Registered Office: XYZ Building, 2 Hardman Boulevard, Spinningfields, Manchester, M3 3AQ
Activities: Other information technology service activities
Parent: NCC Group PLC
Officers: Suzana Cross, Secretary; Edward Jonathan Williams, Secretary; Timothy John Kowalski [1958] Director; Dr Adam Howard Palser [1975] Director; Roger Gary Rawlinson [1962] Director

NCC Group Accumuli Security Limited
Incorporated: 24 May 1996 *Employees:* 103
Net Worth Deficit: £5,127,000 *Total Assets:* £7,965,000
Registered Office: XYZ Building, 2 Hardman Boulevard, Spinningfields, Manchester, M3 3AQ
Activities: Information technology consultancy activities
Parent: Accumuli (Holdings) Limited
Officers: Suzana Cross, Secretary; Edward Jonathan Williams, Secretary; Timothy John Kowalski [1958] Director; Dr Adam Howard Palser [1975] Director; Roger Gary Rawlinson [1962] Director

NCC Group PLC
Incorporated: 2 January 2003 *Employees:* 1,697
Net Worth: £212,100,000 *Total Assets:* £370,600,000
Registered Office: XYZ Building, 2 Hardman Boulevard, Spinningfields, Manchester, M3 3AQ
Activities: Other professional, scientific and technical activities n.e.c.
Officers: Suzana Cross, Secretary; Christopher Michael Batterham [1955] Director; Jonathan Brooks [1956] Director; Jennifer Susan Duvalier [1969] Director; Michael Ernest Ettling [1964] Director [British/South African]; Timothy John Kowalski [1958] Director; Dr Adam Howard Palser [1975] Director/Chief Executive Officer; Christopher Michael Renwick Stone [1962] Director

NCC Group Security Services Limited
Incorporated: 1 July 2002 *Employees:* 482
Net Worth: £4,308,000 *Total Assets:* £24,185,000
Registered Office: XYZ Building, 2 Hardman Boulevard, Spinningfields, Manchester, M3 3AQ
Activities: Information technology consultancy activities
Parent: NCC Group (Solutions) Limited
Officers: Suzana Cross, Secretary; Edward Jonathan Williams, Secretary; Timothy John Kowalski [1958] Director; Dr Adam Howard Palser [1975] Director; Roger Gary Rawlinson [1962] Director

NCC Services Limited
Incorporated: 22 March 1993 *Employees:* 228
Net Worth: £7,400,000 *Total Assets:* £32,400,000
Registered Office: XYZ Building, 2 Hardman Boulevard, Spinningfields, Manchester, M3 3AQ
Activities: Information technology consultancy activities
Parent: NCC Group (Solutions) Limited
Officers: Suzana Cross, Secretary; Edward Jonathan Williams, Secretary; Timothy John Kowalski [1958] Director; Daniel Adam Liptrott [1972] Director; Dr Adam Howard Palser [1975] Commercial Director

NDA Properties Limited
Incorporated: 16 September 1994
Net Worth: £15,909,000 *Total Assets:* £71,258,000
Registered Office: Herdus House, Ingwell Drive, Westlakes Science & Technology Park, Moor Row, Cumbria, CA24 3HU
Activities: Management of real estate on a fee or contract basis
Officers: Helen Elizabeth Hodgson, Secretary; David Mark Atkinson [1962] Director/Chartered Surveyor; Michael Westland Glass [1962] Director/Head of Revenues and Services; Heather McAtear [1967] Director/Accountant; Anthony Edward Smithers [1968] Director/Chartered Surveyor

NE Investments Limited
Incorporated: 1 August 2007
Net Worth Deficit: £254,000 *Total Assets:* £12,083,000
Registered Office: Hamilton House, Church Street, Altrincham, Cheshire, WA14 4DR
Activities: Activities of head offices
Major Shareholder: Brian George Kennedy
Officers: Brian George Kennedy [1960] Director; Patrick Brian Kennedy [1984] Sales Director; Shaun Kennedy [1976] Director; Adrian Christopher Kirk [1961] Finance Director; Angus Roderick Morison [1980] Sales Director

Nederman Limited
Incorporated: 11 October 1978 *Employees:* 92
Net Worth: £4,974,000 *Total Assets:* £10,193,000
Registered Office: 91 Seedlee Road, Walton Summit Centre, Bamber Bridge, Preston, Lancs, PR5 8AE
Activities: Installation of industrial machinery and equipment
Parent: Nederman Holding AB
Officers: Philip James Bamforth, Secretary; Philip James Bamforth [1975] Finance Director; Sven Kristensson [1962] Director/Chairman [Swedish]; Paul Rowlands [1963] Director

Neenah International UK Limited
Incorporated: 23 November 2007
Net Worth: £1,858,966 *Total Assets:* £10,098,000
Registered Office: Red Bridge Offices, Ainsworth, Bolton, Lancs, BL2 5PD
Activities: Other manufacturing n.e.c.
Officers: Michael Hughes, Secretary; Noah Benz [1973] Director [American]; Michael Hughes [1962] Director; Bonnie Lind [1958] Finance Director [American]; Byron Racki [1977] Director [American]; Jonathan Paul Robson [1967] Director

Neenah Red Bridge International Limited
Incorporated: 30 October 2000 *Employees:* 64
Net Worth: £3,446,020 *Total Assets:* £14,623,313
Registered Office: Ainsworth, Bolton, Lancs, BL2 5PD
Activities: Other manufacturing n.e.c.
Officers: Michael Hughes, Secretary; Noah Benz [1973] Director [American]; Michael Hughes [1962] Director; Bonnie Lind [1958] Director [American]; Byron Racki [1977] Director [American]; Jonathan Paul Robson [1967] Director

Neerock Limited
Incorporated: 10 January 1991 *Employees:* 1,600
Net Worth: £181,280,000 *Total Assets:* £405,451,008
Registered Office: Hilmore House, Gain Lane, Bradford, W Yorks, BD3 7DL
Activities: Production of meat and poultry meat products
Parent: Wm Morrison Supermarkets Holdings Limited
Officers: Jonathan James Burke, Secretary; Darren Anthony Blackhurst [1966] Director; Andrew James Clappen [1965] Technical Director; Jonathan William Reed [1973] Director; Mark Thomas Stitson [1976] Finance Director; Andrew Edward Thornber [1974] Director

Nelson (Northwest) Hotels Limited
Incorporated: 1 April 1982 *Employees:* 264
Net Worth: £12,106,005 *Total Assets:* £23,261,198
Registered Office: The Grosvenor-Pulford Hotel, Wrexham Road, Pulford, Chester, CH4 9DG
Activities: Activities of head offices
Shareholders: Harold Garner Nelson; Susan Marjorie Nelson
Officers: Norman Andrew Howell, Secretary; Andrew Garner Nelson [1981] Director/Licencee; Harold Garner Nelson [1942] Director/Hotelier; Susan Marjorie Nelson [1953] Director/Hotelier

Amos Nelson,Limited
Incorporated: 28 June 1921 *Employees:* 7
Net Worth: £11,763,048 *Total Assets:* £12,893,315
Registered Office: Old Gledstone, Skipton, N Yorks, BD23 3JR
Activities: Support services to forestry
Officers: Armorel Brandreth Nelson, Secretary; Lucinda Harriet Mullins [1966] Director/Property Manager; Armorel Brandreth Nelson [1941] Director; David George Hargreaves Nelson [1933] Director/Textile Merchant; James Matthew Ryves Nelson [1971] Director/Farmer; Victoria Jane Sandars [1968] Director/P R Consultant; Geoffrey Arnold Shindler [1942] Director/Solicitor

Wm. Nelstrop & Co. Ltd
Incorporated: 2 November 1931 *Employees:* 46
Net Worth: £21,132,300 *Total Assets:* £27,039,356
Registered Office: Albion Flour Mills, Stockport, Cheshire, SK4 1TZ
Activities: Grain milling
Shareholder: Conrad Jarlath Nelstrop
Officers: Alexander Paul Fraser Nelstrop [1975] Director/Flour Miller; Conrad Jarlath Nelstrop [1939] Director/Chairman; Dr George Anthony Nelstrop [1938] Director; Matthew Benjamin Nelstrop [1974] Director/Flour Miller; Paul Alan Roberts [1956] Director; Simon John Morley Roberts [1960] Director; Conrad Huw Syers [1961] Director

NES Advantage Solutions Limited
Incorporated: 9 December 2004 *Employees:* 115
Net Worth: £10,551,000 *Total Assets:* £12,264,000
Registered Office: Station House, Stamford New Road, Altrincham, Cheshire, WA14 1EP
Activities: Temporary employment agency activities
Officers: Stephen William Buckley [1968] Finance Director; Simon Francis Coton [1974] Managing Director

NES Global Limited
Incorporated: 25 February 1992 *Employees:* 33
Net Worth: £95,881,000 *Total Assets:* £360,876,992
Registered Office: Station House, Stamford New Road, Altrincham, Cheshire, WA14 1EP
Activities: Temporary employment agency activities
Officers: Stephen William Buckley [1968] Finance Director; Simon Francis Coton [1974] Director

NES Global Talent Finance Limited
Incorporated: 4 October 2012
Net Worth Deficit: £22,875,000 *Total Assets:* £191,954,000
Registered Office: Station House, Stamford New Road, Altrincham, Cheshire, WA14 1EP
Activities: Temporary employment agency activities
Officers: Stephen William Buckley [1968] Director; Simon Francis Coton [1974] Director

NES Global Talent Holdco Limited
Incorporated: 4 October 2012
Total Assets: £187,772,992
Registered Office: Station House, Stamford New Road, Altrincham, Cheshire, WA14 1EP
Activities: Temporary employment agency activities
Officers: Stephen William Buckley [1968] Director; Simon Francis Coton [1974] Director

NES Global Talent Holdings Ltd
Incorporated: 28 September 2012
Net Worth Deficit: £45,693,000 *Total Assets:* £190,880,992
Registered Office: Station House, Stamford New Road, Altrincham, Cheshire, WA14 1EP
Activities: Temporary employment agency activities
Officers: Stephen William Buckley [1968] Director; Simon Francis Coton [1974] Director

NES Global Talent Limited
Incorporated: 4 October 2012 *Employees:* 610
Net Worth Deficit: £183,474,208 *Total Assets:* £340,754,048
Registered Office: Station House, Stamford New Road, Altrincham, Cheshire, WA14 1EP
Activities: Temporary employment agency activities
Officers: Stephen William Buckley [1968] Finance Director; Brendan Wynne Derek Connolly [1956] Director/Investor; Simon Francis Coton [1974] Director; Theron Idol Gilliam [1964] Director/Investor [American]; Alexander James William Hoffman [1975] Director/Investor; Karl Erik Kjelstad [1966] Director [Norwegian]; Andreas Constantinos Kramvis [1952] Director [American]; Thomas Joseph Pryma [1973] Director/Private Equity [American]

NES Group Limited
Incorporated: 18 December 1998 *Employees:* 48
Net Worth: £116,214,000 *Total Assets:* £373,932,000
Registered Office: Station House, Stamford New Road, Altrincham, Cheshire, WA14 1EP
Activities: Other activities of employment placement agencies
Officers: Stephen William Buckley [1968] Finance Director; Simon Francis Coton [1974] Managing Director

NES Holdings Limited
Incorporated: 8 August 2006 *Employees:* 2
Net Worth Deficit: £44,995,856 *Total Assets:* £253,588,912
Registered Office: Station House, Stamford New Road, Altrincham, Cheshire, WA14 1EP
Activities: Temporary employment agency activities
Officers: Stephen William Buckley [1968] Finance Director; Simon Francis Coton [1974] Director

NES Managed Services Limited
Incorporated: 14 August 2009 *Employees:* 6
Net Worth Deficit: £703,000 *Total Assets:* £24,945,000
Registered Office: Station House, Stamford New Road, Altrincham, Cheshire, WA14 1EP
Activities: Temporary employment agency activities
Officers: Stephen William Buckley [1968] Finance Director; Simon Francis Coton [1974] Managing Director

NES UK Limited
Incorporated: 14 August 1979 *Employees:* 76
Net Worth: £40,531,000 *Total Assets:* £100,974,000
Registered Office: Station House, Stamford New Road, Altrincham, Cheshire, WA14 1EP
Activities: Temporary employment agency activities
Officers: Stephen William Buckley [1968] Finance Director; Simon Francis Coton [1974] Director

Nesscoinvsat Limited
Incorporated: 19 November 1998 *Employees:* 48
Net Worth: £12,454,723 *Total Assets:* £18,895,942
Registered Office: 3rd Floor, 1 Ashley Road, Altrincham, Cheshire, WA14 2DT
Activities: Other telecommunications activities
Parent: Rignet UK Holdings Limited
Officers: Egbert Clarke [1960] Director/VP Global Operations Operations [American]; John Mark Cope [1966] Director/Accountant; Danielle Edwards [1978] Director/VP IoT and Apps; Oyvind Folge [1968] Director [Norwegian]; Jay Hilbert [1959] Sales Director [American]; Steven Pickett [1964] Director/CEO - President [American]; Edward Paul Traupman [1950] Director/VP - Systems Integration [American]

Network Space (Networkcentres) Limited
Incorporated: 26 November 1998
Net Worth: £12,712,163 *Total Assets:* £26,142,344
Registered Office: Centrix House, Crow Lane East, Newton-le-Willows, Merseyside, WA12 9UY
Activities: Management of real estate on a fee or contract basis
Parent: Network Space Ltd
Officers: Daniel Manus Adamson [1974] Finance Director; Richard James Ainscough [1978] Director; Nicola Jones [1973] Director; Martin John Mellor [1964] Director/Surveyor

Network Space Developments Limited
Incorporated: 16 December 1981 *Employees:* 9
Net Worth: £46,346,000 *Total Assets:* £50,980,000
Registered Office: Centrix House, Crow Lane East, Newton-le-Willows, St Helens, Merseyside, WA12 9UY
Activities: Development of building projects
Parent: Network Space Holdings Ltd
Officers: Daniel Manus Adamson [1974] Finance Director; Richard James Ainscough [1978] Director/Accountant; Stephen Frank Barnes [1970] Director/Chartered Surveyor; Nicola Jones [1973] Director; Martin John Mellor [1964] Director

Network Space Holdings Limited
Incorporated: 12 April 2012 *Employees:* 43
Net Worth: £121,239,000 *Total Assets:* £174,198,000
Registered Office: Centrix House, Crow Lane East, Newton-le-Willows, St Helens, Merseyside, WA12 9UY
Activities: Development of building projects
Parent: Datum Edge Limited
Officers: Daniel Manus Adamson [1974] Finance Director; Richard James Ainscough [1978] Director/Accountant; Stephen Frank Barnes [1970] Director; Nicola Jones [1973] Director; Martin John Mellor [1964] Director

Network Space Limited
Incorporated: 14 April 2012 *Employees:* 16
Net Worth: £66,932,000 *Total Assets:* £130,726,000
Registered Office: Centrix House, Crow Lane East, Newton-le-Willows, Merseyside, WA12 9UY
Activities: Buying and selling of own real estate
Parent: Network Space Holdings Limited
Officers: Daniel Manus Adamson [1974] Finance Director; Richard James Ainscough [1978] Director/Accountant; Nicola Jones [1973] Director; Martin John Mellor [1964] Director

Neuven Solutions Holdings Limited
Incorporated: 28 March 2012 *Employees:* 28
Net Worth: £504,807 *Total Assets:* £32,862,424
Registered Office: Manchester International Office Centre, Styal Road, Manchester, M22 5WB
Activities: Activities of head offices
Major Shareholder: John Charles Richard Simmonds
Officers: Edward Gilbert Cobb, Secretary; Martin Lee Shaw [1980] Finance Director; John Charles Richard Simmonds [1966] Director

Neuven Solutions Limited
Incorporated: 5 July 2007 *Employees:* 28
Net Worth: £629,609 *Total Assets:* £32,987,228
Registered Office: Manchester International Office Centre, Styal Road, Manchester, M22 5WB
Activities: Management consultancy activities other than financial management
Parent: Neuven Solution Holdings Ltd
Officers: Edward Gilbert Cobb, Secretary; Martin Lee Shaw [1980] Finance Director; John Charles Richard Simmonds [1966] Director/Chief Executive

New Balance Athletic Shoes (U.K.) Limited
Incorporated: 23 February 1982 *Employees:* 599
Net Worth Deficit: £18,250,228 *Total Assets:* £83,677,136
Registered Office: Appleton House, 430 Birchwood Boulevard, Birchwood, Warrington, Cheshire, WA3 7WD
Activities: Manufacture of footwear
Major Shareholder: James Spiro Davis
Officers: Paul Gauron, Secretary; Francis Allen [1954] Director/Vice President, EMEA, New Balance [American]; James Spiro Davis [1943] Director/Company Owner [American]; Robert Demartini [1961] Director/Executive [American]; John Withee [1955] Director/Executive [American]

New Bridge Multi Academy Trust
Incorporated: 5 July 2012 *Employees:* 366
Net Worth: £20,324,930 *Total Assets:* £25,858,960
Registered Office: New Bridge School, Roman Road, Hollinwood, Oldham, Lancs, OL8 3PH
Activities: Other education n.e.c.
Officers: Rita Kay Righini, Secretary; Alison Michelle Nield [1968] Director; Phil Palmer [1966] Director/Finance Manager; Graham Quinn [1963] Director/Headteacher; Margaret Jean Ramsbottom [1941] Director; Joan Readyhough [1932] Director; Valerie Shaw [1951] Director; Stephen Williams [1957] Director/Factory Worker

New Britain Oils Limited
Incorporated: 24 June 2008 *Employees:* 75
Net Worth: £27,977,000 *Total Assets:* £76,082,000
Registered Office: 45 Derby Road, Liverpool, L20 8DY
Activities: Other business support service activities n.e.c.
Parent: New Britain Palm Oil Ltd
Officers: Yusef Bin Basiran [1948] Director [Malaysian]; Franki Anthony Dass [1956] Director [Malaysian]; Philip Ko Kunjappy [1957] Director [Malaysian]; Mohd Haris Mohd Arshad [1972] Director [Malaysian]; Mohd Bakke Bin Salleh [1954] Director [Malaysian]; Andrew Timothy Worrall [1967] Commercial Director

New Charter Building Company Limited
Incorporated: 9 July 1999 *Employees:* 188
Net Worth: £4,840,000 *Total Assets:* £10,117,000
Registered Office: 249 Cavendish Street, Ashton under Lyne, Lancs, OL6 7AT
Activities: Other building completion and finishing
Officers: Brian Paul Moran, Secretary; Gillian Brown [1960] Executive Director; Mark Ian Dunford [1969] Executive Director; Geoffrey William Durbin [1961] Director/Chief Commercial Officer; Carole Ruth Green [1965] Director/Health Care Management Consultant & Advisor; Paul Thomas Hoey [1964] Director; Steven Normansell [1954] Director; Anthony Arthur Powell [1957] Executive Director; Michael Stewart Taylor [1966] Director/External Affairs Advisor; Paul Alfred Woodcock [1971] Managing Director

New Charter Homes Limited
Incorporated: 9 July 1999 *Employees:* 60
Net Worth: £166,210,000 *Total Assets:* £504,935,008
Registered Office: 249 Cavendish Street, Ashton under Lyne, Lancs, OL6 7AT
Activities: Renting and operating of Housing Association real estate
Officers: Brian Paul Moran, Secretary; Shoab Akhtar [1969] Director/Manager [Pakistani]; Madan Lal Jassi [1958] Director; Andrew Peter Leah [1957] Director/Retired; Janet Mutch [1961] Director/Retail Manager; Michael Richmond [1946] Director/Retired

New City Vision (Liverpool) Limited
Incorporated: 24 April 2002
Net Worth Deficit: £619,957 *Total Assets:* £9,565,435
Registered Office: Site Office, Porchester Road, Liverpool, L11 1EB
Activities: Construction of domestic buildings
Shareholders: Owen Kirk; Michael Cannon
Officers: Michael Canon [1956] Director/Accountant [Irish]; Owen Kirk [1952] Director/House Builder [Irish]; Harry Joseph O'Donnell [1954] Director/Developer [Irish]

New Co (Beith Street) Limited
Incorporated: 18 March 2016
Net Worth Deficit: £4,000 *Total Assets:* £27,369,000
Registered Office: The Box, Horseshoe Lane, Alderley Edge, Cheshire, SK9 7QP
Activities: Development of building projects
Parent: Vita Glasgow 1 Limited
Officers: Giles Beswick, Secretary; Giles Peter Beswick [1974] Director; Mark Christopher Dawson [1973] Director; Michael Keith Slater [1974] Director; Mark David Stott [1972] Director

New Co (Newcastle) Limited
Incorporated: 18 March 2016
Net Worth Deficit: £4,000 *Total Assets:* £13,444,000
Registered Office: The Box, Horseshoe Lane, Alderley Edge, Cheshire, SK9 7QP
Activities: Development of building projects
Parent: Vita Ventures Limited
Officers: Giles Beswick, Secretary; Giles Peter Beswick [1974] Director; Mark Christopher Dawson [1973] Director; Michael Keith Slater [1974] Director; Mark David Stott [1972] Director

New Co (Satellite) 2 Limited
Incorporated: 18 March 2016
Net Worth Deficit: £347,000 *Total Assets:* £53,492,000
Registered Office: The Box, Horseshoe Lane, Alderley Edge, Cheshire, SK9 7QP
Activities: Development of building projects
Parent: New Co (Satellite) Limited
Officers: Giles Beswick, Secretary; Giles Peter Beswick [1974] Director; Mark Christopher Dawson [1973] Director; Michael Keith Slater [1974] Director; Mark David Stott [1972] Director

New Co (Satellite) Limited
Incorporated: 18 March 2016
Net Worth Deficit: £4,000 *Total Assets:* £44,066,000
Registered Office: The Box, Horseshoe Lane, Alderley Edge, Cheshire, SK9 7QP
Activities: Development of building projects
Parent: Vita Satellite 1 Limited
Officers: Giles Beswick, Secretary; Giles Peter Beswick [1974] Director; Mark Christopher Dawson [1973] Director; Michael Keith Slater [1974] Director; Mark David Stott [1972] Director

New Kadampa Tradition - International Kadampa Buddhist Union
Incorporated: 22 October 1992 *Employees:* 34
Net Worth: £25,356,564 *Total Assets:* £29,285,740
Registered Office: Conishead Priory, Priory Road, Ulverston, Cumbria, LA12 9QQ
Activities: Activities of religious organisations
Officers: Stephen Paul Cowing, Secretary; Jennifer Jane Andrews [1984] Director/Charity Administrator; Paul Anthony Philip Boseley [1955] Director/Charity Administration; Henry Freymueller Shefveland [1969] Director/Minister of Religion [American]; Heather Carolyn Wright [1957] Director/Minister of Religion

New World Trading Company (UK) Holdings Limited
Incorporated: 21 February 2013
Net Worth: £2,835,201 *Total Assets:* £16,533,644
Registered Office: 2 Malt Street, Knutsford, Cheshire, WA16 6ES
Activities: Licenced restaurants
Officers: Matthew Mark Bamber [1977] Operations Director; Richard Thomas Barley [1978] Finance Director; Christopher Hill [1980] Managing Director; Timothy McCormac [1973] Property Director

New World Trading Company (UK) Limited
Incorporated: 28 June 2011 *Employees:* 1,087
Net Worth: £6,611,164 *Total Assets:* £29,721,588
Registered Office: 2 Malt Street, Knutsford, Cheshire, WA16 6ES
Activities: Public houses and bars
Parent: Graphite Capital General Partner VIII LP
Officers: Matthew Mark Bamber [1977] Operations Director; Richard Thomas Barley [1978] Finance Director; Christopher Hill [1980] Director; Timothy McCormac [1973] Property Director

Newbank Garden Centre Limited
Incorporated: 8 April 1981 *Employees:* 129
Net Worth: £8,871,465 *Total Assets:* £10,608,216
Registered Office: Prince of Wales House, 18-19 Salmon Fields Business Village, Royton, Oldham, Lancs, OL2 6HT
Activities: Other retail sale of new goods in specialised stores (not commercial art galleries and opticians)
Shareholder: John Lees Hartle
Officers: Jean Isobelle Hartle, Secretary; Frances Mary Bottomley [1955] Director; Christopher John Hartle [1961] Director; John Lees Hartle [1927] Director

Newbridge (Healthcare) Limited
Incorporated: 2 July 2003 *Employees:* 62
Net Worth: £3,155,470 *Total Assets:* £9,470,864
Registered Office: St Crispin House, St Crispin Way, Haslingden, Rossendale, Lancs, BB4 4PW
Activities: Dispensing chemist in specialised stores
Shareholders: Erez Haim Bar-Ilan; Vivake Bhatia
Officers: Erez Haim Bar-Ilan, Secretary; Erez Haim Bar-Ilan [1974] Director; Vivake Bhatia [1974] Director

Newco Ventures Ltd
Incorporated: 12 February 2015 *Employees:* 167
Net Worth: £9,594 *Total Assets:* £10,067,684
Registered Office: Bredbury Hall Hotel & Country Club, Osborne Street, Bredbury, Stockport, Cheshire, SK6 2DH
Activities: Hotels and similar accommodation
Major Shareholder: Golam Sarwar
Officers: Golam Sarwar [1954] Director [Bangladeshi]; Sabera Sarwar Nina [1959] Director [Bangladeshi]

Newfield Fabrications Company Limited
Incorporated: 13 January 1965 *Employees:* 146
Net Worth: £5,443,987 *Total Assets:* £7,264,739
Registered Office: Hall Lane Works, Elton, Sandbach, Cheshire, CW11 3TU
Activities: Manufacture of metal structures and parts of structures
Shareholders: Henbury Engineering Limited; Henbury Engineering Co Ltd
Officers: Joshua Dudley-Toole [1990] Director; John Brian Fowler [1968] Director; Paul Robert Morgan [1973] Director

Newhall Group Limited (The)
Incorporated: 12 February 1987 *Employees:* 102
Net Worth: £14,297,542 *Total Assets:* £15,887,766
Registered Office: Newhall Lane, Hoylake, Wirral, Merseyside, CH47 4BQ
Activities: Publishing of consumer and business journals and periodicals
Major Shareholder: Dr Andrew Kenneth Wissett Douglas
Officers: Christine Ann Blackford, Secretary; Christine Ann Blackford [1954] Finance Director; Dr Andrew Kenneth Wissett Douglas [1960] Director/Chairman; Bryan Leon Douglas-Dala [1971] Marketing Director

Newincco 1072 Limited
Incorporated: 7 January 2011
Net Worth: £20,942,000 *Total Assets:* £60,840,000
Registered Office: Hilmore House, Gain Lane, Bradford, W Yorks, BD3 7DL
Activities: Development of building projects
Parent: Ascot Road Watford Limited
Officers: Jonathan James Burke, Secretary; Jonathan James Burke [1966] Director; Trevor John Strain [1975] Finance Director

Newport Spectra-Physics Limited
Incorporated: 5 February 1987 *Employees:* 11
Net Worth: £8,725,952 *Total Assets:* £11,689,917
Registered Office: Units 3-4 Cowley Way, Weston Road, Crewe, Cheshire, CW1 6AG
Activities: Manufacture of optical precision instruments
Parent: MKS Instruments Holdings Ltd
Officers: Alain Dudouit, Secretary; Kathleen Burke [1965] Director/VP, GC & Assistant Secretary-MKS Instruments, Inc. [American]; Derek Pace D'Antilio [1972] Director/VP & Corporate Controller-MKS Instruments, Inc. [American]

T E Newsholme Limited
Incorporated: 1 February 2001 *Employees:* 195
Net Worth: £2,377,780 *Total Assets:* £9,422,945
Registered Office: The Snackhouse, St Georges Park, Kirkham, Preston, Lancs, PR4 2DZ
Activities: Activities of head offices
Officers: Robert Grogan [1959] Finance Director [Irish]; John Horgan [1951] Managing Director [Irish]; Liam Keating [1969] Director/Chartered Accountant [Irish]

Newstar Group Limited
Incorporated: 12 July 2006 *Employees:* 22
Net Worth: £2,509,943 *Total Assets:* £14,719,930
Registered Office: Caxton House, Caxton Road, Fulwood, Preston, Lancs, PR2 9ZB
Activities: Wholesale of clothing and footwear
Officers: Imran Bargit [1976] Director/Businessman

Newtco Limited
Incorporated: 10 September 2010
Net Worth: £6,085,003 *Total Assets:* £19,039,560
Registered Office: National House, 80-82 Wellington Road North, Stockport, Cheshire, SK4 1HW
Activities: Activities of head offices
Major Shareholder: Michael David Noblett
Officers: Michael David Noblett [1972] Director

Newton Abbot Health Holdings Limited
Incorporated: 3 January 2007
Net Worth Deficit: £10,989,191 *Total Assets:* £26,562,860
Registered Office: Unit 18 Riverway Business Village, Navigation Way, Ashton on Ribble, Preston, Lancs, PR2 2YP
Activities: Activities of other holding companies n.e.c.
Parent: New Intermediate Care Limited
Officers: David Wyn Davies [1968] Director/Accountant; Angela Mills [1961] Director/Accountant

Newton Abbot Health Limited
Incorporated: 8 September 2006
Net Worth Deficit: £10,989,192 *Total Assets:* £26,562,860
Registered Office: Unit 18 Riversway Business Village, Navigation Way, Ashton on Ribble, Preston, Lancs, PR2 2YP
Activities: Hospital activities
Parent: Newton Abbot Health Holdings Limited
Officers: David Wyn Davies [1968] Director/Accountant; Angela Mills [1961] Director/Accountant

Newton Academy Trust
Incorporated: 18 January 2008 *Employees:* 107
Net Worth: £17,387,000 *Total Assets:* £20,937,000
Registered Office: Hope Academy, Ashton Road, Newton-le-Willows, St Helens, Merseyside, WA12 0AQ
Activities: General secondary education
Officers: Donna Worthington, Secretary; Marie Jane Adams [1975] Director/Vice Principal; Michael Joseph Boland [1965] Director/Headteacher; Martin Francis Cogley [1944] Director; Sue Cronin [1963] Director; Patrick Hugh Ferguson [1952] Director/Principal; Jane Griffiths [1958] Director/Headteacher; Bridget Greta Byrne Leek [1966] Director/Data Manager; Frances McCaul [1964] Director; John Paul McMahon [1974] Director/Chartered Accountant [Irish]; Barbara Naylor [1957] Director/Retired; Victoria Margaret Roberts [1973] Director/FE College Manager; Christopher James Stafford [1967] Director/Clerk in Holy Orders; Karen Lesley White [1968] Director

Nexperia UK Ltd.
Incorporated: 11 May 2006 *Employees:* 591
Net Worth: £45,810,000 *Total Assets:* £64,309,000
Registered Office: Bramhall Moor Lane, Hazel Grove, Stockport, Cheshire, SK7 5BJ
Activities: Manufacture of electronic components
Parent: China Jianyin Investment Ltd
Officers: Rachel Whittaker, Secretary; Michael Julian Humphreys [1962] Director/Vice-President & General Manager; Ruben Everard Gerard Lichtenberg [1967] Director/Senior Legal Counsel [Dutch]; Rachel Whittaker [1975] Financial Director

Next Generation Health Limited
Incorporated: 18 January 2005 *Employees:* 104
Net Worth: £3,159,848 *Total Assets:* £14,740,946
Registered Office: St Johns Chambers, Love Street, Chester, CH1 1QN
Activities: Non-trading company
Shareholders: Rajesh Mansulhial Morjaria; Purnima Rajesh Morjaria
Officers: Purnima Rajesh Morjaria, Secretary/Systems Analyst; Purnima Rajesh Morjaria [1964] Director/Systems Analyst; Rajesh Mansulhial Morjaria [1964] Director/Pharmacist

Nextdom Property Limited
Incorporated: 11 January 2016 *Employees:* 12
Net Worth Deficit: £209,573 *Total Assets:* £9,599,388
Registered Office: Ayrton House, Commerce Way, Liverpool, L8 7BA
Activities: Other letting and operating of own or leased real estate
Officers: Philip Didlick, Secretary; Philip Didlick [1976] Director/Chartered Accountant; Generald Francis O'Brien [1949] Director; Padraic Marc O'Brien [1979] Director

Nextdom Roscoe Limited
Incorporated: 11 January 2016 *Employees:* 3
Net Worth: £373,917 *Total Assets:* £8,352,638
Registered Office: Ayrton House, Commerce Way, Liverpool, L8 7BA
Activities: Other letting and operating of own or leased real estate
Officers: Philip Didlick, Secretary; Philip Didlick [1976] Director/Chartered Accountant; Generald Francis O'Brien [1949] Director; Padraic Marc O'Brien [1979] Director

Nextgear Capital UK Limited
Incorporated: 18 September 2013 *Employees:* 77
Net Worth: £6,160,000 *Total Assets:* £119,864,000
Registered Office: Nextgear House, Kingsfield Court, Chester Business Park, Chester, CH4 9RE
Activities: Other information service activities n.e.c.
Officers: Michael Buxton [1965] Director/Chief Operating Officer - International; Martin Leigh Forbes [1976] Director/Chief Operating Officer; Darren Paul Mornin [1968] Finance Director; Juliette Williams Pryor [1965] Director/Senior Vice President, General Counsel & Corporate [American]; Sanford H Schwartz [1953] Director/President [American]

Nexus Telecommunications Limited
Incorporated: 16 December 1999 *Employees:* 30
Net Worth: £4,715,164 *Total Assets:* £7,864,910
Registered Office: Dawson House, Matrix Office Park, Buckshaw Village, Chorley, Lancs, PR7 7NA
Activities: Wired telecommunications activities
Parent: Nexus Telecom Limited
Officers: Robert William Burbidge, Secretary; Robert William Burbidge [1970] Director/Chartered Accountant; Alexandra Cliffe [1978] Director; Adam James Turton [1981] Director

NGF Europe Limited
Incorporated: 27 February 1991 *Employees:* 225
Net Worth: £53,427,000 *Total Assets:* £61,341,000
Registered Office: Lea Green Road, Lea Green, St Helens, Merseyside, WA9 4PR
Activities: Other manufacturing n.e.c.
Officers: David Anthony Farmer, Secretary; Mitsuharu Akiyama [1967] Director/General Manager [Japanese]; David Anthony Farmer [1961] Financial Director; Gerrard Lee Farnworth [1968] Operations Director; Colin Arthur Hamand [1960] Commercial Director; Alistair George Richard Poole [1965] Director; Dr Chris Stevens [1958] Technical Director

Nice-Pak International Limited
Incorporated: 3 April 1987 *Employees:* 932
Net Worth: £63,603,672 *Total Assets:* £104,617,560
Registered Office: Aber Park, Aber Road, Flint, CH6 5EX
Activities: Manufacture of non-wovens and articles made from non-wovens, except apparel
Officers: David John Cowell, Secretary; Robert Picker Julius [1939] Director [American]; Michael Alexander Staton [1947] Director

Nightjar Sustainable Power Limited
Incorporated: 14 April 2014
Net Worth: £6,123,738 *Total Assets:* £8,106,106
Registered Office: Canal Head North, Kendal, Cumbria, LA9 7BZ
Activities: Other specialised construction activities n.e.c.
Parent: TT Nominees Limited
Officers: Charles William Nepean Crewdson [1964] Director; Carl Peter Crompton [1973] Director; David Benjamin Freeder [1981] Investment Director; Matthew Justin Hazell [1971] Director

Nikal Ltd
Incorporated: 16 November 1998 *Employees:* 11
Net Worth Deficit: £6,299,925 *Total Assets:* £25,970,180
Registered Office: Mynshulls House, 14 Cateaton Street, Manchester, M3 1SQ
Activities: Buying and selling of own real estate
Parent: Nikal Jersey Limited
Officers: Stephen Paul Robinson, Secretary/Accountant; Michael Cochrane [1950] Director; Alan George Murphy [1948] Director; Nicholas Stuart Payne [1967] Director; Stephen Paul Robinson [1963] Director/Accounting

Nilfisk Ltd.
Incorporated: 23 March 1926 *Employees:* 150
Net Worth: £20,917,000 *Total Assets:* £32,742,000
Registered Office: Nilfisk House, Units 18 & 19 Bowerbank Way, Gilwilly Industrial Estate, Penrith, Cumbria, CA11 9BQ
Activities: Wholesale of other machinery and equipment
Officers: Gary Keith Edmondson, Secretary; Karina Kjaer Deacon [1969] Director/Chief Financial Officer [Danish]; Stewart James Dennett [1965] Director; Steen Lindbo [1965] Director [Danish]

Nimogen Limited
Incorporated: 16 October 1991 *Employees:* 66
Net Worth: £4,310,258 *Total Assets:* £12,296,352
Registered Office: The Picturedrome, Chestergate, Macclesfield, Cheshire, SK11 6DU
Activities: Retail sale of watches and jewellery in specialised stores
Parent: Rollerpen
Officers: Karl David Massey [1964] Director/Jeweller; Natasha Jane Massey [1988] Director/Jeweller

Niokem Limited
Incorporated: 23 June 2010
Net Worth: £4,351,832 *Total Assets:* £13,941,631
Registered Office: St George's House, 215-219 Chester Road, Manchester, M15 4JE
Activities: Wholesale of chemical products
Major Shareholder: Lynne Smith
Officers: Alan Nicholson [1949] Director; David John Robinson [1978] Director/Chartered Accountant

Nitecrest Limited
Incorporated: 24 June 1996 *Employees:* 190
Net Worth: £12,994,476 *Total Assets:* £17,511,648
Registered Office: 32 Marathon Place, Moss Side Industrial Estate, Leyland, Lancs, PR26 7QN
Activities: Manufacture of paper stationery
Major Shareholder: Executors of Ronald Anthony Hart (Deceased)
Officers: Susan Hart, Secretary; Joseph Aoun [1964] Sales Director [American]; Hilary Ann Bradley [1976] Director; John Michael Hart [1954] Director; Ronald Michael Hart [1970] Director; Susan Hart [1949] Director; Kathryn Mary Jeffers [1972] Director; Leeroy Pye [1978] Sales Director; Wendy Slater [1973] Director/Company Secretary

NJK Clothing Ltd
Incorporated: 30 July 2009 *Employees:* 17
Net Worth: £7,286,690 *Total Assets:* £7,906,724
Registered Office: NJK House, Unit B1, Haslingden Road, Blackburn, BB1 2EE
Activities: Wholesale of clothing and footwear
Shareholders: ZDK & Company Ltd; SLB Investments LLP
Officers: Serena Louise Bellamy [1989] Director; Zaynul Keshani [1960] Director; Rafiq Daud Patel [1973] Director

NMS Logistics Limited
Incorporated: 3 November 2004 *Employees:* 38
Net Worth: £2,394,129 *Total Assets:* £7,746,125
Registered Office: The Exchange, 5 Bank Street, Bury, Lancs, BL9 0DN
Activities: Other business support service activities n.e.c.
Major Shareholder: Natasa Sabanovic
Officers: Marko Sabanovic, Secretary [Bosnia/Herzegovina]; Natasa Sabanovic [1970] Director

NMU (Specialty) Ltd
Incorporated: 11 June 1976 *Employees:* 115
Net Worth: £144,187 *Total Assets:* £8,938,719
Registered Office: The Exchange, New York Street, Manchester, M1 4HN
Activities: Non-life insurance
Officers: Lisa Michelle Fairbairn, Secretary; Thomas Eduard Artmann [1962] Director [German]; Charles Anthony Edward Burgess [1970] Director; Timur Coskun [1959] Director/Chartered Accountant; Greg Guelfand [1974] Financial Director [Australian]; Paul David Hiscoe [1961] Director; Nicholas Limb [1971] Director; Duncan Thomas McClean [1967] Director; Anthony Aidan O'Dwyer [1978] Director/Underwriter; David Antony Perfect [1967] Director

NNL Holdings Limited
Incorporated: 25 March 2009 *Employees:* 798
Net Worth: £75,852,000 *Total Assets:* £156,290,000
Registered Office: Chadwick House, Warrington Road, Birchwood Park, Birchwood, Warrington, Cheshire, WA3 6AE
Activities: Other professional, scientific and technical activities n.e.c.
Parent: Office for The Secretary of State for Business, Energy and Industrial Strategy
Officers: David Barry Dukes, Secretary; Ruth Marie Dunphy [1973] Director/Chief Finance Officer; Craig Douglas Lester [1966] Director/Civil Servant; Anna Charlotte Payton [1978] Director/Civil Servant

Noble Nordmann Limited
Incorporated: 19 March 2005
Net Worth: £423,522 *Total Assets:* £6,729,752
Registered Office: c/o Brabners Chaffe Street, 3rd Floor, Horton House, Exchange Flags, Liverpool, L2 3YL
Activities: Growing of cereals (except rice), leguminous crops and oil seeds
Officers: Jimm Enevoldsen [1959] Director [Danish]; Marie Janderup Lundgaard Enevoldsen [1962] Director/Freelance [Danish]; Peter Arndrup Poulsen [1962] Director/Chairman [Danish]

Noble Systems UK Limited
Incorporated: 8 November 1999 *Employees:* 43
Net Worth: £8,979,530 *Total Assets:* £12,477,339
Registered Office: 11 Commerce Way, Westinghouse Road, Manchester, M17 1HW
Activities: Other telecommunications activities
Officers: Sara Andrews, Secretary; Christopher Grey Hodges [1962] Director [American]; James Kerr Noble [1958] Director/President CEO [American]

Norcros Group (Holdings) Limited
Incorporated: 29 May 1956 *Employees:* 1,044
Net Worth: £146,726,000 *Total Assets:* £351,601,984
Registered Office: Ladyfield House, Station Road, Wilmslow, Cheshire, SK9 1BU
Activities: Activities of head offices
Officers: Richard Hawke Collins, Secretary; Richard Hawke Collins [1962] Director/Company Secretary and Group Counsel; Nicholas Paul Kelsall [1956] Director; Robert James Sidell [1976] Director/Financial Controller; Shaun Michael Smith [1961] Finance Director

Norcros Industry (International) Limited
Incorporated: 6 January 1936 *Employees:* 3
Net Worth: £43,672,000 *Total Assets:* £51,125,000
Registered Office: Ladyfield House, Station Road, Wilmslow, Cheshire, SK9 1BU
Activities: Non-trading company
Officers: Richard Hawke Collins, Secretary; Richard Hawke Collins [1962] Director/Company Secretary & Group Counsel; Nicholas Paul Kelsall [1956] Director; Shaun Michael Smith [1961] Finance Director

Norcros PLC
Incorporated: 5 January 1999
Net Worth: £104,600,000 *Total Assets:* £313,000,000
Registered Office: Ladyfield House, Station Road, Wilmslow, Cheshire, SK9 1EU
Activities: Activities of head offices
Officers: Richard Hawke Collins, Secretary; Joanna Christine Hallas [1970] Director; Nicholas Paul Kelsall [1956] Director; David William McKeith [1951] Director; Shaun Michael Smith [1961] Finance Director; Martin George Towers [1952] Director

Nordex UK Limited
Incorporated: 16 May 2001 *Employees:* 162
Net Worth: £4,534,917 *Total Assets:* £38,032,128
Registered Office: Suite 4, Egerton House, The Towers Business Park, Wilmslow Road, Didsbury, Manchester, M20 2DX
Activities: Electrical installation
Officers: David Marsh, Secretary; Ralph Patrick Max Boettcher [1981] Director [German]; Dr Ilya Taka Hartmann [1973] Director [German]; Nigel James Hayes [1978] Director [Irish]; Ibrahim Ozarslan [1972] Director [Danish]

Nordic Packaging and Container (UK) Holdings Limited
Incorporated: 30 August 2016 *Employees:* 922
Net Worth: £80,720,816 *Total Assets:* £447,019,008
Registered Office: One St Peter's Square, Manchester, M2 3DE
Activities: Packaging activities
Officers: Richard Harris Copans [1976] Director/Investor [American]; Thomas S. Souleles [1968] Director [American]

Nordic Packaging and Container Holdings Limited
Incorporated: 30 August 2016 *Employees:* 1
Net Worth: £94,724,752 *Total Assets:* £423,679,872
Registered Office: One St Peters Square, Manchester, M2 3DE
Activities: Packaging activities
Officers: Marco Casiraghi [1947] Director [Italian]; Richard Harris Copans [1976] Director/Investor [American]; Thomas Andrew MacHa [1986] Director/Investor [American]; Thomas S. Souleles [1968] Director [American]; David Andrew Walton [1965] Director

Norkem Holdings PLC
Incorporated: 30 November 1987
Net Worth: £12,048,101 *Total Assets:* £12,572,709
Registered Office: Norkem House, Bexton Lane, Knutsford, Cheshire, WA16 9FB
Activities: Activities of head offices
Shareholders: Alan Nicholson; Lynne Patricia Smith
Officers: Lynne Patricia Colling, Secretary; Lynne Patricia Colling [1950] Director; Alan Nicholson [1949] Director; David John Robinson [1978] Director/Chartered Accountant

Norkem Limited
Incorporated: 18 January 1973 *Employees:* 61
Net Worth: £8,828,475 *Total Assets:* £35,774,240
Registered Office: Norkem House, Bexton Lane, Knutsford, Cheshire, WA16 9FB
Activities: Wholesale of chemical products
Officers: Lynne Patricia Colling, Secretary; Lynne Patricia Colling [1950] Director; Paul Ian Connolly [1954] Development Director; Mark Gregory [1967] Commercial Director; Graham Lewis [1964] Director/Manager; David John Miller [1968] Commercial Director; Alan Nicholson [1949] Director; David John Robinson [1978] Director/Chartered Accountant

Norman 1985 Limited
Incorporated: 24 November 2015
Net Worth Deficit: £886,000 *Total Assets:* £65,948,000
Registered Office: 1030 Centre Park, Slutchers Lane, Warrington, Cheshire, WA1 1QL
Activities: Activities of production holding companies
Officers: Elizabeth Oldroyd, Secretary; Dario Bertagna [1984] Director/Vice President [Italian]; Simon Richard Eaves [1967] Managing Director; Kirsty Louise Usher [1975] Director/Accountant

North & Partners Technical Limited
Incorporated: 1 February 2013 *Employees:* 6
Net Worth: £460,178 *Total Assets:* £7,303,581
Registered Office: Building 1000, Kings Reach, Yew Street, Stockport, Cheshire, SK4 2HG
Activities: Construction of commercial buildings
Parent: E S Management Services Limited
Officers: Andrew Dwan [1965] Director; Michael Dwan [1959] Director

North Cheshire Developments Ltd
Incorporated: 3 March 2008 *Employees:* 9
Net Worth: £450,448 *Total Assets:* £12,309,196
Registered Office: 145-147 Liverpool Road, Cadishead, Manchester, M44 5BT
Activities: Other letting and operating of own or leased real estate
Major Shareholder: Neil McArthur
Officers: Anne McArthur, Secretary; Christopher John Chisnall [1985] Director/Property Surveyor; Neil McArthur [1955] Director/Professional Engineer

North East Convenience Stores Limited
Incorporated: 13 September 2001 *Employees:* 379
Net Worth: £2,995,212 *Total Assets:* £8,902,759
Registered Office: Hoghton Chambers, Hoghton Street, Southport, Merseyside, PR9 0TB
Activities: Retail sale in non-specialised stores with food, beverages or tobacco predominating
Parent: James Hall and Company Limited
Officers: Chris Collins, Secretary; Andrew Nicholas Hall [1949] Director; Ian Stuart Whittaker Hall [1942] Director; Michael Dominic Wells Hall [1972] Director; Naveen Vadhera [1971] Director; Sanjeev Vadhera [1980] Director

North Lancs. Training Group Limited (The)
Incorporated: 18 September 1985 *Employees:* 220
Net Worth: £7,995,326 *Total Assets:* £9,277,111
Registered Office: Bradshawgate House, Oak Street, Accrington, Lancs, BB5 1EQ
Activities: Technical and vocational secondary education
Major Shareholder: James William Harkness
Officers: David Baron [1962] Director; Mark Andrew Durr [1969] Director; James William Harkness [1939] Director; Collette Humphreys [1970] Director; Gareth Lindsay [1971] Director; Phillip George Mills [1952] Director; David Monks [1953] Director; Stephen Graham Simpson [1957] Managing Director

North of England Zoological Society (The)
Incorporated: 9 May 1934 *Employees:* 555
Net Worth: £47,641,000 *Total Assets:* £59,695,000
Registered Office: Cedar House, Zoological Gardens, Caughall Road, Upton-by-Chester, Chester, CH2 1LH
Activities: Veterinary activities
Officers: Malcolm Stephen Ardron [1962] Proprietor Director; William John Beale [1970] Director/Charity Manager; Catherine Margaret Buckley [1948] Director/Headmistress; Edwin Paul Collis Christmas [1977] Director/Chartered Surveyor; Penny Ann Coates [1963] Non-Executive Director and Trustee; Sandra Donnelly [1974] Director/Teacher; Professor Richard Alun Griffiths [1957] Director/Professor; Professor David MacDonald [1951] Director; Professor Russell Newton [1946] Director/Trustee; Angela Pinnington [1957] Director/Trustee; Bruce Anthony Ursell [1942] Director; Simon Peter Venables [1978] Director/Chartered Accountant

North West Air Ambulance
Incorporated: 12 April 1999 *Employees:* 29
Net Worth: £10,917,237 *Total Assets:* £12,373,341
Registered Office: North Mersey Business Centre, Woodward Road, Knowsley, Merseyside, L33 7UY
Activities: Other human health activities
Officers: Peter Michael George Douglas, Secretary; Dr Rachel Christine Hall [1982] Director/Doctor; Daniel Robert Head [1974] Director/Tax Consultant; Allan George Jude [1951] Finance Director; Stewart Edward Meehan [1946] Director/Consultant; Dorothy Jane Marie Smith [1969] Associate Director Healthcare; Kim Jayne Spencer [1977] Director/Solicitor; Simon John Williams [1982] Director/Solicitor

North West Business Finance Limited
Incorporated: 24 September 2009 *Employees:* 9
Net Worth: £39,100,272 *Total Assets:* £100,516,312
Registered Office: The Maltings, 98 Wilderspool Causeway, Warrington, Cheshire, WA4 6PU
Activities: Fund management activities
Officers: Clive Matthew Brook [1950] Director; Rory Earley [1958] Director; Edge Malcolm [1951] Director/Chartered Accountant; Clifford Gary Maylor [1961] Director/Chartered Accountant; Michael John Prince [1954] Director

North West Cancer Research (incorporating Clatterbridge Cancer Research CCR)
Incorporated: 16 September 1987 *Employees:* 10
Net Worth: £5,657,940 *Total Assets:* £11,968,161
Registered Office: North West Cancer Research Centre, 200 London Road, Liverpool, L3 9TA
Activities: Other human health activities
Officers: Alastair David Richards, Secretary; Hilary Anne Atherton [1958] Director/Founder and MD of Management Consultancy; Catherine Bond [1956] Director/Retired; Stephen Claus [1956] Director/Solicitor; Mark Haig [1959] Director; Catherine Mary Jones [1960] Director/Retired; Nigel Stuart Lanceley [1949] Regional Director; Moira Jane Owen [1957] Director/Retired; Dr Philip Charles Robertshaw [1959] Director/Fundraiser; Professor David Ross Sibson [1958] Director/Professor of Applied Cancer Biology; Steven Ward Smith [1971] Director/MD Software Architect; Frances Margaret Leigh Street [1953] Director/Chairman, Wirral Community NHS Trust

North West Electricity Networks (Finance) Limited
Incorporated: 15 November 2007 *Employees:* 1,666
Net Worth: £123,300,000 *Total Assets:* £3,514,800,128
Registered Office: 304 Bridgewater Place, Birchwood Park, Warrington, Cheshire, WA3 6XG
Activities: Activities of head offices
Parent: North West Electricity Networks (UK) Limited
Officers: Richard Somerville, Secretary; David Graham Brocksom [1960] Director/Chief Finance Officer; Peter Richard Emery [1962] Director/Chief Executive Officer

North West Electricity Networks (Holdings) Limited
Incorporated: 15 November 2007 *Employees:* 1,666
Net Worth: £123,000,000 *Total Assets:* £3,514,500,096
Registered Office: 304 Bridgewater Place, Birchwood Park, Warrington, Cheshire, WA3 6XG
Activities: Activities of head offices
Parent: North West Electricity Networks (Finance) Limited
Officers: Richard Somerville, Secretary; David Graham Brocksom [1960] Director/Chief Finance Officer; Peter Richard Emery [1962] Director/Chief Executive Officer

North West Electricity Networks (UK) Limited
Incorporated: 15 November 2007 *Employees:* 1,718
Net Worth: £260,200,000 *Total Assets:* £3,537,799,936
Registered Office: 304 Bridgewater Place, Birchwood Park, Warrington, Cheshire, WA3 6XG
Activities: Activities of head offices
Officers: Richard Somerville, Secretary; David Graham Brocksom [1960] Director/Chief Finance Officer; Peter Richard Emery [1962] Director/Chief Executive Officer; John E Lynch [1970] Director [American]; Niall Patrick Mills [1968] Director/Senior Asset Manager

North West Electricity Networks PLC
Incorporated: 15 November 2007 *Employees:* 1,666
Net Worth: £122,400,000 *Total Assets:* £3,502,400,000
Registered Office: 304 Bridgewater Place, Birchwood Park, Warrington, Cheshire, WA3 6XG
Activities: Activities of head offices
Parent: NWEN Group Limited
Officers: Richard Somerville, Secretary; David Graham Brocksom [1960] Director/Chief Finance Officer; Christopher Bruce Dowling [1953] Director [Australian]; Peter Richard Emery [1962] Director/Chief Executive Officer; Robert David Holden [1956] Director; John E Lynch [1970] Director [American]; Niall Patrick Mills [1968] Director/Senior Asset Manager

North West Industrial Estates Limited
Incorporated: 7 December 1995 *Employees:* 3
Net Worth: £15 877,453 *Total Assets:* £41,806,336
Registered Office: The Corn Exchange, Brunswick Street, Liverpool, L2 0PJ
Activities: Buying and selling of own real estate
Shareholders: Peter Wild Bullivant; Tarsem Singh Dhaliwal
Officers: Ben Desmond Harvey, Secretary; Peter Wild Bullivant [1939] Director/Solicitor; Andrew Peter Mason [1965] Director; Geoffrey Owen Mason [1940] Director/Chartered Surveyor; Lee Randle [1970] Director/Chartered Surveyor

North West Logistics Ltd
Incorporated: 5 May 2009 *Employees:* 70
Net Worth: £2,176,648 *Total Assets:* £9,107,266
Registered Office: Unit 4 Shorten Brook Drive, Altham Business Park, Altham, Lancs, BB5 5YH
Activities: Freight transport by road
Major Shareholder: Stephen Dunn
Officers: Jacqueline Dunn, Secretary; Stephen Dunn [1955] Managing Director; John Walker [1954] Finance Director

North West Lung Centre
Incorporated: 29 February 2000 *Employees:* 97
Net Worth: £14,456,450 *Total Assets:* £15,652,579
Registered Office: North West Lung Research Centre, Wythenshawe Hospital, Southmoor Road, Manchester, M23 9LT
Activities: Other human health activities
Officers: Professor Charles Anthony Cary Pickering, Secretary/Physician; John Herbert Alcock [1947] Director/Solicitor; Dr Andrew Mark Jones [1968] Director; Dr Clare Suzanne Murray [1966] Director; Professor Charles Anthony Cary Pickering [1942] Director/Physician; Dr Angela Simpson [1966] Director/Medical Practitioner; Dr Yvonne Jane Summers [1970] Director/Oncologist; Anthony Kevin Webb [1946] Director/Respiratory Physician; Professor Ashley Arthur Woodcock [1951] Director/Consultant of Respiratory Medicine; Professor Mark Andrew Woodhead [1954] Director/Doctor of Medicine

North West Portfolio (No.3) Limited
Incorporated: 23 March 2016
Net Worth: £74,772 *Total Assets:* £10,228,051
Registered Office: Emerson House, Heyes Lane, Alderley Edge, Cheshire, SK9 7LF
Activities: Development of building projects
Parent: Emerson Developments (Holdings) Limited
Officers: Varun Maharaj, Secretary; Paul James Hubball [1973] Director/Business Executive; Anthony Emerson Jones [1967] Director; Mark Emerson Jones [1964] Director; Peter Emerson Jones [1935] Director

North West Portfolio Limited
Incorporated: 12 August 1992
Net Worth: £13,102,124 *Total Assets:* £37,789,296
Registered Office: Emerson House, Heyes Lane, Alderley Edge, Cheshire, SK9 7LF
Activities: Development of building projects
Parent: Emerson Developments (Holdings) Limited
Officers: Varun Maharaj, Secretary; Paul James Hubball [1973] Director; Anthony Emerson Jones [1967] Director; Mark Emerson Jones [1964] Director; Peter Emerson Jones [1935] Director

North West Truck Services Limited
Incorporated: 16 July 1987 *Employees:* 105
Net Worth: £2,797,000 *Total Assets:* £15,485,000
Registered Office: Griffiths Road, Lostock Gralam, Northwich, Cheshire, CW9 7NU
Activities: Sale of other motor vehicles
Officers: Charles Pettingell, Secretary/Director; Robert William Heaton [1964] Director; Charles Pettingell [1946] Director

North West Water International Limited
Incorporated: 21 April 1989
Net Worth Deficit: £89,333,000 *Total Assets:* £24,671,000
Registered Office: Haweswater House, Lingley Mere Business Park, Lingley Green Avenue, Great Sankey, Warrington, Cheshire, WA5 3LP
Activities: Non-trading company
Parent: United Utilities PLC
Officers: Darren Antony Hill [1964] Director/Group Claims and Litigation Manager

North Yorkshire Mortgages Limited
Incorporated: 30 March 1988
Net Worth: £11,820,000 *Total Assets:* £293,478,016
Registered Office: The Bailey, Skipton, N Yorks, BD23 1DN
Activities: Activities of mortgage finance companies
Parent: Skipton Building Society
Officers: John Joseph Gibson, Secretary; Ian Geoffrey Moore [1968] Director of Specialist Lending; Andrew Walter Nelson [1964] Director/Accountant; Henry Varney [1972] Director/General Manager

Northamptonshire Leisure Estates Limited
Incorporated: 14 December 2005
Net Worth Deficit: £374 *Total Assets:* £23,685,732
Registered Office: South Lakeland House, Main A6, Yealand Redmayne, Carnforth, Lancs, LA5 9RN
Activities: Activities of amusement parks and theme parks
Parent: Pure Leisure Group Limited
Officers: Paul Rossiter, Secretary; Paul Rossiter [1964] Director/Chartered Accountant; Trevor James White [1952] Director/Marketing Manager

Northbay Pelagic Limited
Incorporated: 11 December 2013 *Employees:* 85
Net Worth: £14,561,960 *Total Assets:* £26,433,542
Registered Office: Reedham House, 31 King Street West, Manchester, M3 2PJ
Activities: Processing and preserving of fish, crustaceans and molluscs
Shareholders: Interfish Limited; Cool Seas (Seafood) Limited
Officers: Johannus Jacobus Colam [1953] Director

Northcote Hotel Limited
Incorporated: 20 March 1986 *Employees:* 210
Net Worth Deficit: £4,869,429 *Total Assets:* £9,158,740
Registered Office: Northcote Manor, Northcote Road, Langho, Blackburn, BB6 8BE
Activities: Hotels and similar accommodation
Parent: Northcote Leisure Group Limited
Officers: Craig John Bancroft [1961] Director/Hotel Manager; Matthew Charles Bye [1962] Director/Accountant

Northcote Leisure Group Limited
Incorporated: 14 May 2013 *Employees:* 375
Net Worth Deficit: £7,368,063 *Total Assets:* £10,182,631
Registered Office: Northcote Manor, Northcote Road, Langho, Blackburn, Lancs, BB6 8BE
Activities: Licenced restaurants
Major Shareholder: Nigel Hall
Officers: Craig John Bancroft [1961] Hospitality Director; Matthew Charles Bye [1962] Director/Accountant

Northern Developments (Cumbria) Limited
Incorporated: 7 November 1996 *Employees:* 7
Net Worth: £218,243 *Total Assets:* £7,507,420
Registered Office: Oakvale House, Thomas Lane, Burgh Road Industrial Estate, Carlisle, Cumbria, CA2 7ND
Activities: Development of building projects
Parent: MPBM Limited
Officers: Martyn Howard Boak, Secretary/Building Contractor; Martyn Howard Boak [1964] Managing Director

Northern Diver (International) Ltd
Incorporated: 7 October 1985
Net Worth: £6,919,591 *Total Assets:* £8,433,763
Registered Office: Appley Lane North, Appley Bridge, Wigan, Lancs, WN6 9AE
Activities: Non-specialised wholesale trade
Parent: AHML Limited
Officers: Ian Daniel McLeod, Secretary; Paul Case [1964] Director/Mechanical Engineer; Melanie Jane Simm [1975] Director; Neil Tordoff [1982] Sales Director

Northern Industrial Properties Limited
Incorporated: 5 September 2001 *Employees:* 4
Net Worth: £3,764,175 *Total Assets:* £9,650,962
Registered Office: c/o Mason & Partners Ltd, The Corn Exchange, Brunswick Street, Liverpool, L2 7TP
Activities: Development of building projects
Major Shareholder: Geoffrey Owen Mason
Officers: Ben Desmond Harvey, Secretary; Andrew Dean Kelly [1972] Director/Surveyor; Andrew Peter Mason [1965] Director; Geoffrey Owen Mason [1940] Director/Chart Surveyor; Lee Randle [1970] Director/Chart Surveyor

Northern Packaging Holdings Limited
Incorporated: 15 January 2015 *Employees:* 1
Net Worth Deficit: £330,790 *Total Assets:* £7,400,292
Registered Office: Corpacq House, 1 Goose Green, Altrincham, Cheshire, WA14 1DW
Activities: Manufacture of corrugated paper and paperboard, sacks and bags
Officers: Phillip Robert Millward [1962] Director

Northern Packaging Limited
Incorporated: 7 January 1980 *Employees:* 86
Net Worth: £6,403,599 *Total Assets:* £9,997,598
Registered Office: Corpacq House, 1 Goose Green, Altrincham, Cheshire, WA14 1DW
Activities: Manufacture of corrugated paper and paperboard, sacks and bags
Officers: Joycelyn McEvoy, Secretary; Benjamin Michael Dack [1965] Director; Joycelyn McEvoy [1953] Director/Accountant; Phillip Robert Millward [1962] Director

Northern Rail Holdings Limited
Incorporated: 5 June 2000 *Employees:* 5,193
Net Worth: £4,940,000 *Total Assets:* £15,418,000
Registered Office: Eversheds House, 70 Great Bridgewater Street, Manchester, M1 5ES
Activities: Activities of head offices
Shareholders: Abellio Transport Holdings Ltd; Serco Holdings Limited
Officers: Dominic Daniel Gerard Booth [1963] Managing Director; Alan Dingwall [1973] Director; Julian Edwards [1969] Finance Director; John Michael Heron [1972] Director/Accountant; Angelique Catherina Jannetje Magielse [1968] Finance Director [Dutch]; John Anthony Richard Whitehurst [1971] Managing Director

Northern Schools Trust
Incorporated: 9 March 2004 *Employees:* 389
Net Worth: £53,168,000 *Total Assets:* £61,943,000
Registered Office: 120 Heyworth Street, Liverpool, L5 0SQ
Activities: General secondary education
Officers: Louise Mary Hughes, Secretary; John Geoffrey Ashton [1945] Director/Education Adviser; Louise Mary Hughes [1982] Director of Finance; Stephen McKeown [1961] Director/Local Authority Manager; Ian Paul Joseph Mooney [1963] Director; Dr Geoffrey Wainwright [1968] Director; Nigel Maurice Ward [1962] Director

Northern Star Academies Trust
Incorporated: 7 March 2011 *Employees:* 264
Net Worth: £17,765,000 *Total Assets:* £22,902,000
Registered Office: 77 Gargrave Road, Skipton, N Yorks, BD23 1QN
Activities: General secondary education
Officers: Beverley Dawn Ashby [1958] Director; Ian Andrew Curtis [1950] Director/Retired; Howard Geoffrey Cutler [1943] Director/HR Consultant; Helen Catherine Flynn [1963] Director/Company Secretary; Martin Paul Kelly [1957] Chairman/Director; Stuart Phillips [1981] Director/Accountant; Jennifer Plews [1972] Director/Headteacher; Steven Scott [1971] Director/Banker

Northern Trust Company Limited
Incorporated: 17 September 1962 *Employees:* 39
Net Worth: £205,336,992 *Total Assets:* £524,923,008
Registered Office: Lynton House, Ackhurst Park, Foxhole Road, Chorley, Lancs, PR7 1NY
Activities: Other letting and operating of own or leased real estate
Parent: Northern Trust Group Limited
Officers: Anne Kelleher, Secretary; Michael John Grindrod [1958] Director; Patrick Lee Hemmings [1966] Director; Peter Graham Hemmings [1955] Director; John Clement Kay [1953] Director; Thomas Robert Parkinson [1966] Director/Surveyor; Kathryn Revitt [1964] Director/Solicitor; Mark Lorimer Widders [1960] Finance Director

Northern Trust Group 1 Limited
Incorporated: 9 May 2014 *Employees:* 88
Net Worth: £204,716,992 *Total Assets:* £474,881,984
Registered Office: Lynton House, Ackhurst Park, Foxhole Road, Chorley, Lancs, PR7 1NY
Activities: Activities of head offices
Major Shareholder: Trevor James Hemmings
Officers: Patrick Lee Hemmings [1966] Director; John Clement Kay [1953] Director; Kathryn Revitt [1964] Director/Solicitor; Mark Lorimer Widders [1960] Finance Director

Northern Trust Group 2 Limited
Incorporated: 9 May 2014
Net Worth: £28,150,020 *Total Assets:* £28,150,020
Registered Office: Lynton House, Ackhurst Park, Foxhole Road, Chorley, Lancs, PR7 1NY
Activities: Activities of head offices
Parent: Northern Trust Group 1 Limited
Officers: Patrick Lee Hemmings [1966] Director; John Clement Kay [1953] Director; Kathryn Revitt [1964] Director/Solicitor; Mark Lorimer Widders [1960] Finance Director

Northern Trust Group Limited
Incorporated: 4 January 1993 *Employees:* 87
Net Worth: £244,904,000 *Total Assets:* £527,916,992
Registered Office: Lynton House, Ackhurst Park, Foxhole Road, Chorley, Lancs, PR7 1NY
Activities: Activities of head offices
Parent: Northern Trust Group 2 Limited
Officers: Anne Kelleher, Secretary; Patrick Lee Hemmings [1966] Director; Trevor James Hemmings [1935] Director; John Clement Kay [1953] Director/Chartered Accountant; Kathryn Revitt [1964] Director/Solicitor; Mark Lorimer Widders [1960] Director

Northwood Tissue (Disley) Limited
Incorporated: 17 September 2009 *Employees:* 62
Net Worth: £7,337,198 *Total Assets:* £17,158,760
Registered Office: Waterside, Disley, Stockport, Cheshire, SK12 2HW
Activities: Manufacture of household and sanitary goods and of toilet requisites
Major Shareholder: Paul Fecher
Officers: Paul Edward King, Secretary; Christopher John Davies [1965] Director; Adam Scott Fecher [1974] Director; Marc Darren Fecher [1971] Director; Paul Fecher [1946] Director/Paper Agent; David Bryn Harries [1978] Director; Paul Edward King [1974] Director/Accountant

S. Norton & Co Limited
Incorporated: 29 October 1984 *Employees:* 155
Net Worth: £91,876,000 *Total Assets:* £118,471,000
Registered Office: Bankfield House, Bankfield Mill, Regent Road, Liverpool, L20 8RQ
Activities: Collection of non-hazardous waste
Shareholders: John Anthony Harry; Charles Thomas Harry; Matthew Paul Harry
Officers: Charles Thomas Harry, Secretary; Graham William Donohue [1967] Finance Director; Charles Thomas Harry [1949] Director; John Anthony Harry [1946] Director; Margaret Harry [1948] Director/Manager; Matthew Paul Harry [1950] Director; Norman William Jones [1953] Director/Solicitor; Roger John Morton [1960] Director

Norwest Foods International Group Limited
Incorporated: 11 September 2014 *Employees:* 11
Net Worth: £5,635,491 *Total Assets:* £22,606,492
Registered Office: 3 Haig Court, Haig Road, Knutsford, Cheshire, WA16 8XZ
Activities: Activities of head offices
Shareholders: Simon Thomas Rowe; Claddagh Foods Limited
Officers: Simon Rowe, Secretary; Ray McSharry [1964] Director [Irish]; Simon Thomas Rowe [1968] Director

Norwest Foods International Limited
Incorporated: 18 June 1998 *Employees:* 11
Net Worth: £6,177,414 *Total Assets:* £22,623,404
Registered Office: 3 Haig Court, Haig Road, Knutsford, Cheshire, WA16 8XZ
Activities: Other business support service activities n.e.c.
Shareholders: Simon Thomas Rowe; Claddagh Foods Ltd
Officers: Ray John McSharry Jnr [1964] Director [Irish]; Simon Thomas Rowe [1968] Director

Norwich and Peterborough (LBS) Limited
Incorporated: 12 December 1991
Net Worth: £2,200,000 *Total Assets:* £94,722,000
Registered Office: Yorkshire House, Yorkshire Drive, Bradford, W Yorks, BD5 8LJ
Activities: Financial intermediation not elsewhere classified
Officers: Helen Clare Nellist, Secretary; Charles Peter Canning [1963] Director; Rob Andrew Purdy [1972] Director/Accountant

Nos 2 Limited
Incorporated: 8 April 2005
Net Worth: £7,538,688 *Total Assets:* £62,714,700
Registered Office: Alliance House, Westpoint Enterprise Park, Clarence Avenue, Trafford Park, Manchester, M17 1QS
Activities: Buying and selling of own real estate
Parent: Farraday Limited
Officers: Justin Seers, Secretary; John Slater, Secretary; Anthony Clifford Iannazzo [1976] Director [American]; Timothy Mooney [1975] Director [American]; Matthew Patrick Scannell [1978] Director/Accountant

Nos 3 Limited
Incorporated: 7 February 2006
Net Worth: £4,443,527 *Total Assets:* £7,095,289
Registered Office: Alliance House, Westpoint Enterprise Park, Clarence Avenue, Trafford Park, Manchester, M17 1QS
Activities: Buying and selling of own real estate
Parent: Farraday Ltd
Officers: Justin Seers, Secretary; John Slater, Secretary; Anthony Clifford Iannazzo [1976] Director [American]; Timothy Mooney [1975] Director [American]; Matthew Patrick Scannell [1978] Director/Accountant

Nova Group Limited
Incorporated: 1 July 1980 *Employees:* 185
Net Worth: £3,437,820 *Total Assets:* £7,731,918
Registered Office: Nova Group Ltd, Norman Road, Altrincham, Cheshire, WA14 4EN
Activities: Manufacture of other plastic products
Parent: Nova Double Glazing Systems Limited
Officers: Simon Michael Felstein, Secretary; Paul Corrie [1962] Director; Rosina Lesley Felstein [1967] Director; Simon Michael Felstein [1965] Finance Director; Stephen William Ridgard [1958] Director; Ian Wootton [1965] Director

Novelis Europe Holdings Limited
Incorporated: 8 December 2004
Net Worth: £321,918,368 *Total Assets:* £515,573,504
Registered Office: Latchford Locks Works, Thelwell Lane, Warrington, Cheshire, WA4 1NN
Activities: Activities of head offices
Officers: Fortunato Lucido, Secretary; Steven Kenneth Clarke [1971] Director/VP Operations; Steve Hedar [1968] Director; Fortunato Lucido [1971] Director/Lawyer [American]

Novelis Services Limited
Incorporated: 24 June 2008
Net Worth: £288,191,840 *Total Assets:* £290,349,984
Registered Office: Latchford Locks Works, Thelwell Lane, Warrington, Cheshire, WA4 1NN
Activities: Other business support service activities n.e.c.
Parent: Novelis UK Ltd
Officers: Fortunato Lucido, Secretary/Lawyer [American]; Steven Kenneth Clarke [1971] Director/VP Operations; Christopher Courts [1977] Director/Attorney [American]; Fortunato Lucido [1971] Director/Lawyer [American]

Novelis UK Ltd
Incorporated: 13 September 1933 *Employees:* 207
Net Worth: £219,847,008 *Total Assets:* £324,940,000
Registered Office: Latchford Lock Works, Thelwall Lane, Warrington, Cheshire, WA4 1NN
Activities: Cold rolling of narrow strip
Parent: Novelis Europe Holdings Limited
Officers: Fortunato Lucido, Secretary/Lawyer [American]; Steven Kenneth Clarke [1971] Director/General Manager, Foil Value Stream; Daniel James Haydon [1979] Director/Senior Accounting Officer; Steve Hedar [1968] Director; Fortunato Lucido [1971] Director/Lawyer [American]

Novus Finance Ltd
Incorporated: 18 March 2008
Net Worth: £13,992,119 *Total Assets:* £25,518,256
Registered Office: Hunsworth Lane, Cleckheaton, W Yorks, BD19 3UJ
Activities: Activities of production holding companies
Officers: Michael Boardman, Secretary; Mark Nicholas Horton [1965] Director; Gerardus Christiaan Paulus Jacobus Maters [1967] Director/Global Chief Financial Officer [Dutch]; Jon Stokes [1965] Director [American]

NRG Fleet Services Limited
Incorporated: 16 February 2006 *Employees:* 390
Net Worth: £8,430,928 *Total Assets:* £94,389,096
Registered Office: Oasis Business Park, Parkside Place, Skelmersdale, Lancs, WN8 9RD
Activities: Renting and leasing of trucks and other heavy vehicles
Parent: NRG Fleet Holdings Limited
Officers: Martin Roy Ashcroft [1965] Director/Chief Financial Officer; Stephen Michael Richardson [1960] Director; Muhammad Sadique [1963] Director

NSG Environmental Limited
Incorporated: 30 November 1992 *Employees:* 117
Net Worth: £6,454,000 *Total Assets:* £9,409,000
Registered Office: NIS Limited, Ackhurst Road, Chorley, Lancs, PR7 1NH
Activities: Machining
Parent: N.I.S. Holdings Limited
Officers: Howard Entwistle, Secretary/Director; Mark Raymond Coles [1965] Director; Andrew John Deall [1972] Director; Howard Entwistle [1956] Director; Norman Ian Meffan [1928] Non-Executive Director Chairman; John Morris [1952] Director; James Stephen Porter [1965] Director; Michelle Wise [1966] Director

NSG Holding (Europe) Limited
Incorporated: 9 August 2001
Net Worth: £2,364,988,416 *Total Assets:* £2,624,506,624
Registered Office: European Technical Centre, Hall Lane, Lathom, Ormskirk, Lancs, L40 5UF
Activities: Activities of head offices
Parent: Nippon Sheet Glass Co., Limited
Officers: Iain Michael Smith, Secretary; Shirley Ruth Anderson [1960] Director/Chief HR Officer; Koichi Hiyoshi [1959] Director/Manager [Japanese]; Dr Clemens Miller [1959] Director/President Building Products Worldwide [German]; Shigeki Mori [1958] Director [Japanese]; Kenichi Morooka [1956] Director/Deputy CFO [Japanese]; Iain Michael Smith [1972] Director/Chartered Accountant; Philip Douglas Wilkinson [1967] Director/Chief Information Officer

NSG UK Enterprises Limited
Incorporated: 6 October 2005
Net Worth: £1,818,131,968 *Total Assets:* £3,990,658,048
Registered Office: European Technical Centre, Hall Lane, Lathom, Ormskirk, Lancs, L40 5UF
Activities: Activities of head offices
Parent: NSG Holding (Europe) Limited
Officers: Iain Michael Smith, Secretary; Shirley Ruth Anderson [1960] Director/Chief HR Officer; Timothy Peter Bolas [1960] Finance Director; Koichi Hiyoshi [1959] Director/Legal Adviser/Company Secretary [Japanese]; Judy Anne Massa [1967] Director/Group Treasurer; Kenichi Morooka [1956] Director/Deputy CFO [Japanese]; Paul Joseph Ravenscroft [1970] Director/Head of Mergers & Acquisitions; Iain Michael Smith [1972] Director/Group Financial Controller

NST Transport Services Limited
Incorporated: 24 November 1995 *Employees:* 4
Net Worth: £740,820 *Total Assets:* £7,189,732
Registered Office: Discovery House, Brooklands Way, Whitehills Business Park, Blackpool, Lancs, FY4 5LW
Activities: Other urban, suburban or metropolitan passenger land transport (not underground, metro or similar)
Parent: NST Travel Group Limited
Officers: Navneet Bali [1956] Director; Peter John Churchus [1954] Director; Abhishek Goenka [1979] Director/General Manager [Indian]; Timothy William May [1960] Director/Treasurer

NST Travel Group Limited
Incorporated: 21 November 1991 *Employees:* 153
Net Worth: £8,566,113 *Total Assets:* £72,503,096
Registered Office: Discovery House, Brooklands Way, Whitehills Business Park, Blackpool, Lancs, FY4 5LW
Activities: Travel agency activities
Parent: HB Education Limited
Officers: Navneet Bali [1956] Director; Peter John Churchus [1954] Director; Stephen Craven [1967] Director; Abhishek Goenka [1979] Director/General Manager [Indian]; Timothy William May [1960] Director/Treasurer; Anthony Graham Sadler [1959] IT Director

NSX2 Management Co Limited
Incorporated: 8 October 2015 *Employees:* 121
Net Worth: £1,124,022 *Total Assets:* £7,424,031
Registered Office: Junction Business Park, Rake Lane, Swinton, Manchester, M27 8LR
Activities: Activities of head offices
Shareholder: Neil Michael Harrison
Officers: Sabin Ali, Secretary; Sabin Chistee Ali [1977] Director/Chartered Accountant; Neil Michael Harrison [1973] Director; Nathan Kingdon [1985] Director; Sherrie Lubeck [1966] Director

Nufarm Crop Products UK Limited
Incorporated: 21 June 2004
Net Worth: £110,433,000 *Total Assets:* £116,646,000
Registered Office: Nufarm Wyke Lane, Wyke, Bradford, W Yorks, BD12 9EJ
Activities: Other research and experimental development on natural sciences and engineering
Parent: Nufarm UK Limited
Officers: Paul Andrew Binfield [1965] Director [New Zealander]; John Paul Else [1970] Director/Operations Manager; Christopher John Karoly Fazekas [1969] Director/Management [Australian]; Hugo Wilhelm Schweers [1957] Director/Business Executive [German]; Peter Johannes Josef Van Sloun [1959] Director/Financial Controller [German]

Nufarm UK Limited
Incorporated: 21 December 1993 *Employees:* 335
Net Worth: £218,700,992 *Total Assets:* £438,000,992
Registered Office: Nufarm, Wyke Lane, Wyke, Bradford, W Yorks, BD12 9EJ
Activities: Manufacture of pesticides and other agrochemical products
Parent: Medisup Securities Limited
Officers: Paul Andrew Binfield [1965] Director [New Zealander]; John Paul Else [1970] Director/Operations Manager; Mark Joseph Joyce [1968] Director/Regional Supply Chain Manager - EUMEA; Elbert Prado [1957] Director/Group Executive Supply Chain Operations [American]; Hugo Wilhelm Schweers [1957] Director/Business Executive [German]; Peter Johannes Josef Van Sloun [1959] Director/Financial Controller [German]

Nugeneration Limited
Incorporated: 25 February 2009 *Employees:* 179
Net Worth: £155,182,400 *Total Assets:* £187,666,208
Registered Office: 7th Floor, 3 Piccadilly Place, Manchester, M1 3BN
Activities: Production of electricity
Parent: Advance Energy UK Limited
Officers: Mamoru Hatazawa [1959] Director [Japanese]; Kei Kawamura [1960] Director/General Manager [Japanese]; Thomas Samson [1968] Director; Takayuki Shibano [1962] Director/Vice President [Japanese]

Nupharm Limited
Incorporated: 12 September 2003 *Employees:* 55
Net Worth: £559,000 *Total Assets:* £14,539,000
Registered Office: Rivington Road, Whitehouse Industrial Estate, Runcorn, Cheshire, WA7 3DJ
Activities: Wholesale of pharmaceutical goods
Officers: Michael Peter Blakeman, Secretary; Stephen William Anderson [1966] Director; Kenneth John Black [1965] Director; Kevin Robert Hudson [1963] Director

Nurture Academies Trust
Incorporated: 1 March 2016 *Employees:* 230
Net Worth: £9,929,701 *Total Assets:* £12,449,863
Registered Office: Lapage Primary School, Barkerend Road, Bradford, W Yorks, BD3 8QX
Activities: Primary education
Officers: Paul Bailey [1952] Director/Retired; Chris Bem [1951] Director/Consultant Surgeon; Gareth Davies [1969] Director; Nasreen Karim [1969] Director/Solicitor; Paul Martin [1965] Director; William John Nunes Nabarro [1955] Director/Consultant; Jeremy Leslie Townend [1963] Director/Consultant; Wahid Zaman [1969] Director/Chief Executive Officer

NUS Holdings Limited
Incorporated: 1 February 1974 *Employees:* 33
Net Worth: £4,816,672 *Total Assets:* £9,856,502
Registered Office: Ian King House, Snape Road, Macclesfield, Cheshire, SK10 2NZ
Activities: Management consultancy activities other than financial management
Officers: Shakira Cotcheta Martin [1988] Director/NUS National President; Ali Reza Milani [1994] Director/NUS Officer; Peter Jerome Robertson [1963] Managing Director; Douglas Taylor [1954] Director/General Manager NUS

NUS Services Limited
Incorporated: 1 June 1982 *Employees:* 56
Net Worth Deficit: £403,442 *Total Assets:* £9,893,195
Registered Office: Snape Road, Macclesfield, Cheshire, SK10 2NZ
Activities: Non-specialised wholesale trade
Officers: Audrey Clare Burns [1966] Director/Chief Executive; Melanie Kee [1995] Director/SU Elected Officer; Ahtesham Mahmood [1993] Director/Volunteer; Ali Reza Milani [1994] Director/NUS Officer; Patricia Anne O'Neill [1972] Director/Chief Executive; Daryl John Ormerod [1981] Director; Chisomo Phiri [1996] Director/Womens Officer; David Gavin Redpath [1978] IT Director; Graeme Wood [1970] Commercial Director

Nuseed Europe Ltd
Incorporated: 2 August 2013 *Employees:* 5
Net Worth Deficit: £3,340,000 *Total Assets:* £8,122,000
Registered Office: Barnett House, 53 Fountain Street, Manchester, M2 2AN
Activities: Seed processing for propagation
Parent: Nuseed Europe Holding Company Ltd
Officers: Damien Grundy, Secretary; Gary Anthony Barber [1961] Director/Executive; Andrew Bruce Thomas [1968] Director/President of Nuseed Americas [Australian]; Brent Evan Zacharias [1971] Director/General Manager, Nuseed [Canadian]

Nuseed Global Innovation Ltd
Incorporated: 2 October 2013 *Employees:* 2
Net Worth: £8,393,000 *Total Assets:* £31,412,000
Registered Office: Barnett House, 53 Fountain Street, Manchester, M2 2AN
Activities: Seed processing for propagation
Parent: Nuseed Europe Holding Company Ltd
Officers: Damien Grundy, Secretary; Gary Anthony Barber [1961] Director/Executive; Damien Paul Grundy [1972] Director/NGI General Manager; Leon George Streit [1963] Director/Global Manager R&D [American]; Andrew Bruce Thomas [1968] Director/President of Nuseed Americas [Australian]

Nutreco Limited
Incorporated: 11 July 1994
Net Worth: £3,958,000 *Total Assets:* £49,651,000
Registered Office: Minsal Works, Winham, Northwich, Cheshire, CW9 6DF
Activities: Marine aquaculture
Officers: Janine Bolton, Secretary; Janine Bolton [1965] Director/Chartered Accountant; John Mark Williamson [1967] Director/General Manager

Nutriad Ltd
Incorporated: 24 June 1963 *Employees:* 16
Net Worth: £5,470,000 *Total Assets:* £8,218,000
Registered Office: 1 Telford Court, Chester Gates, Dunkirk Lea, Chester, CH1 6LT
Activities: Other manufacturing n.e.c.
Officers: Hubertus Antonius Henricus Maria Janssen [1966] Finance Director [Dutch]; Erik Robert Visser [1969] Director/Business Manager [Dutch]

Nutrition Group PLC
Incorporated: 11 December 2007 *Employees:* 105
Net Worth: £7,240,842 *Total Assets:* £11,045,936
Registered Office: 316 Blackpool Road, Fulwood, Preston, Lancs, PR2 3AE
Activities: Manufacture of basic pharmaceutical products
Major Shareholder: Peter Greathead
Officers: John Hartley Smith, Secretary; John David Atkinson [1966] Director; Sean Anthony Carey [1966] Director [Irish]; Peter Greathead [1943] Director; Richard Lewis Greathead [1984] Director; John Hartley Smith [1955] Director/Accountant

Nuvia Limited
Incorporated: 13 October 1986 *Employees:* 659
Net Worth Deficit: £13,943,000 *Total Assets:* £54,879,000
Registered Office: Chadwick House, Birchwood Park, Risley, Warrington, Cheshire, WA3 6AE
Activities: Remediation activities and other waste management services
Parent: Soletanche Freyssinet SA
Officers: Michael David Roberts, Secretary; Keith Frederick Collett [1956] Director; Herve Pierre Robert Contamin [1964] Director/Accountant [French]; Mark Damien Deary [1962] Finance Director; Bruno Lancia [1966] Director/Chartered Engineer [French]; Manuel Claude Peltier [1969] Director [French]; Michael David Roberts [1970] Director/Accountant

NW Build Limited
Incorporated: 6 November 2012
Net Worth: £1,501,852 *Total Assets:* £13,092,140
Registered Office: 3a Bridgewater Street, Liverpool, L1 0AR
Activities: Other business support service activities n.e.c.
Major Shareholder: Kerrie Marie Baker
Officers: Kerrie Marie Baker [1975] Director

NW Trading (Holdings) Limited
Incorporated: 24 February 2006 *Employees:* 78
Net Worth: £3,200,268 *Total Assets:* £15,707,827
Registered Office: Cavendish Wharf, off Duke Street, Birkenhead, Wirral, Merseyside, CH41 1HN
Activities: Activities of other holding companies n.e.c.
Major Shareholder: Colin Joseph Littler
Officers: Anthony Woolrich, Secretary/Director; Andrew Forker [1957] Director/Shipbroker; Dean Mark Hammond [1962] Director; Mark Hatfield [1956] Director; Colin Joseph Littler [1947] Director/Shipbroker; Anthony Woolrich [1963] Director

NW1.0 Ltd
Incorporated: 5 February 2010 *Employees:* 3
Net Worth Deficit: £96,202 *Total Assets:* £13,217,050
Registered Office: Building 2, 3rd Floor, Universal Square, Devonshire Street North, Manchester, M12 6JH
Activities: Activities of head offices
Major Shareholder: Naeem Kauser
Officers: Carol Allen [1963] Director; Graham Edward Lake [1944] Director/Solicitor

NWEN Finance PLC
Incorporated: 24 January 2013
Net Worth: £84,000 *Total Assets:* £183,030,000
Registered Office: 304 Bridgewater Place, Birchwood Park, Warrington, Cheshire, WA3 6XG
Activities: Activities of other holding companies n.e.c.
Parent: North West Electricity Networks (Holdings) Limited
Officers: Richard Somerville, Secretary; David Graham Brocksom [1960] Director/Chief Finance Officer; Christopher Bruce Dowling [1953] Director [Australian]; Peter Richard Emery [1962] Director/Chief Executive Officer; John E Lynch [1970] Director [American]; Niall Patrick Mills [1968] Director/Senior Asset Manager

NWEN Group Limited
Incorporated: 7 April 2009
Net Worth: £178,700,000 *Total Assets:* £178,700,000
Registered Office: 304 Bridgewater Place, Birchwood Park, Warrington, Cheshire, WA3 6XG
Activities: Activities of head offices
Officers: Richard Somerville, Secretary; David Graham Brocksom [1960] Director/Chief Finance Officer; Peter Richard Emery [1962] Director/Chief Executive Officer

NWF Agriculture Limited
Incorporated: 7 June 1973 *Employees:* 206
Net Worth: £5,947,000 *Total Assets:* £54,862,000
Registered Office: Wardle, Nantwich, Cheshire, CW5 6BP
Activities: Manufacture of prepared feeds for farm animals
Parent: NWF Agriculture Holdings Limited
Officers: Stephen Robert Andrew, Company Secretary; Stephen Robert Andrew [1962] Director/Company Secretary; Chris James Belsham [1975] Finance Director; Andrew Downie [1968] Managing Director; George Franks [1975] National Sales Director; Robert John Thomas [1979] Finance Director; Robert Warrington [1982] Director; Richard Antony Whiting [1964] Director/Chief Executive

NWF Fuels Limited
Incorporated: 7 June 1973 *Employees:* 211
Net Worth: £5,446,000 *Total Assets:* £60,992,000
Registered Office: Wardle, Nantwich, Cheshire, CW5 6BP
Activities: Agents involved in the sale of fuels, ores, metals and industrial chemicals
Parent: NWF Fuels Holdings Limited
Officers: Stephen Robert Andrew, Company Secretary; Mark Adcock [1969] Sales Director; Stephen Robert Andrew [1962] Director/Company Secretary; Chris James Belsham [1975] Finance Director; Richard Huxley [1968] Director; Mark Nicholls [1964] Director/Operations Manager; Erica Parkinson [1971] Finance Director; Richard Antony Whiting [1964] Director/Chief Executive

NWF Group PLC
Incorporated: 1 June 1988 *Employees:* 901
Net Worth: £37,700,000 *Total Assets:* £139,600,000
Registered Office: Wardle, Nantwich, Cheshire, CW5 6BP
Activities: Activities of head offices
Officers: Stephen Robert Andrew, Company Secretary; Thomas Philip Acton [1958] Director; Chris James Belsham [1975] Finance Director; David Stewart Downie [1965] Director; Yvonne May Monaghan [1958] Finance Director; Richard Antony Whiting [1964] Director/Chief Executive

NWM Holdings Limited
Incorporated: 8 February 2000 *Employees:* 120
Net Worth Deficit: £556,141 *Total Assets:* £11,440,278
Registered Office: 501 Green Place, Walton Summit Centre, Bamber Bridge, Preston, Lancs, PR5 8AY
Activities: Activities of head offices
Major Shareholder: Francesco Gaetano Caltagirone
Officers: Annalisa Costantini [1976] Director/Lawyer [Italian]; Patrick Franchomme [1961] Director [French]; Enrico Friz [1962] Managing Director [Italian]; Massimo Angelo Sala [1961] Director [Italian]

Nycomm Holdings Limited
Incorporated: 3 May 1996 *Employees:* 319
Net Worth: £12,894,364 *Total Assets:* £41,277,236
Registered Office: Agecroft Road, Pendlebury, Swinton, Manchester, M27 8SB
Activities: Other telecommunications activities
Major Shareholder: Julian Howard Niman
Officers: Christopher Philip Gee, Secretary; David Richard Bennett [1966] Executive Director - Financial; Susan Yvonne Niman [1958] Director/Investors in People Manager; Andrew John Roberts [1960] Director

Nycomm Limited
Incorporated: 11 January 1985
Net Worth: £15,939,131 *Total Assets:* £42,864,704
Registered Office: Nycomm, Agecroft Road, Pendlebury, Swinton, Manchester, M27 8SB
Activities: Other telecommunications activities
Major Shareholder: Julian Howard Niman
Officers: Christopher Philip Gee, Secretary; David Richard Bennett [1966] Executive Director - Financial; Christopher Philip Gee [1952] Director/Chartered Accountant; Andrew John Roberts [1960] Director

Nynas Limited
Incorporated: 10 March 1989
Net Worth: £20,814,000 *Total Assets:* £20,825,000
Registered Office: North Road, Ellesmere Port, Cheshire, CH65 1AJ
Activities: Activities of head offices
Officers: Scott Austin Kirkness, Secretary; James Cunningham Christie [1960] Business Area Director; Maria Lundin Olandersson [1963] Finance Director [Swedish]

O'Connor Container Transport Limited
Incorporated: 18 March 1988 *Employees:* 157
Net Worth: £5,104,000 *Total Assets:* £11,780,000
Registered Office: c/o Eddie Stobart Limited, Stretton Distribution Park, Langford Way, Appleton, Warrington, Cheshire, WA4 4TQ
Activities: Freight transport by road
Parent: Greenwhitestar Acquisitions Limited
Officers: Elaine Williams, Secretary; Alexander Laffey [1961] Director; David Keith Meir [1970] Director; Rupert Henry Conquest Nichols [1949] Director; David Brian Pickering [1973] Director

PP O'Connor Contracting Limited
Incorporated: 5 October 2016
Net Worth: £2,228,764 *Total Assets:* £12,502,160
Registered Office: The Exchange, 5 Bank Street, Bury, Lancs, BL9 0DN
Activities: Renting and leasing of construction and civil engineering machinery and equipment
Shareholders: O'Connor Holdings Limited; Christine O'Connor
Officers: Charmaine O'Connor [1978] Director; Justin Patrick O'Connor [1973] Director; Peter Paul O'Connor [1971] Director

PP O'Connor Group Limited
Incorporated: 3 October 1990 *Employees:* 179
Net Worth: £4,326,314 *Total Assets:* £11,336,854
Registered Office: The Exchange, 5 Bank Street, Bury, Lancs, BL9 0DN
Activities: Demolition
Shareholder: Christine O'Connor
Officers: Christine O'Connor, Secretary; Charmaine Mary O'Connor [1978] Director; Justin Patrick O'Connor [1973] Director; Peter Paul Oconnor [1971] Director/Excavation Contractor

O'Connor Holdings Limited
Incorporated: 5 October 2016
Net Worth: £2,228,764 *Total Assets:* £12,502,160
Registered Office: The Exchange, 5 Bank Street, Bury, Lancs, BL9 0DN
Activities: Activities of other holding companies n.e.c.
Shareholder: Christine O'Connor
Officers: Charmaine O'Connor [1978] Director; Justin Patrick O'Connor [1973] Director; Peter Paul O'Connor [1971] Director

O'Connor Utilities Limited
Incorporated: 8 April 1994 *Employees:* 107
Net Worth: £21,626,874 *Total Assets:* £41,663,036
Registered Office: 10 Sandfold Lane, Manchester, M19 3BJ
Activities: Other specialised construction activities n.e.c.
Parent: OCU Group Limited
Officers: Breda O'Connor, Secretary; Lisa Moran [1976] Financial Director; Thomas Joseph O'Connor [1961] Director [Irish]; Timothy Gerard O'Connor [1960] Director [Irish]

Caunce O'Hara & Company Limited
Incorporated: 1 December 1998 *Employees:* 42
Net Worth: £6,958,065 *Total Assets:* £12,421,125
Registered Office: 82 King Street, Manchester, M2 4WQ
Activities: Activities of insurance agents and brokers
Shareholders: Christopher Thomas David Caunce; Sun Alliance Insurance Overseas Ltd
Officers: Martin Stephen O'Hara, Secretary; Christopher Thomas David Caunce [1968] Director/Insurance Broker; Martin Stephen O'Hara [1958] Director/Insurance Broker

O'Neill Patient Solicitors LLP
Incorporated: 26 September 2006 *Employees:* 253
Net Worth: £7,777,348 *Total Assets:* £10,877,970
Registered Office: Chester House, 2 Chester Road, Hazel Grove, Stockport, Cheshire, SK7 5NT
Officers: Suzanne Elizabeth Brown [1957] Member; Adam Kevin Ronald Forshaw [1985] LLP Member; Amanda Claire Grundy [1967] LLP Member; Warren Elliot Kaye [1972] LLP Member; Michael Stephen Lennon [1976] LLP Member; Steven Thomas [1974] LLP Member

O.M.C. Motor Group Limited
Incorporated: 12 December 1907 *Employees:* 3
Net Worth: £6,110,445 *Total Assets:* £7,169,502
Registered Office: 1 Manchester Road, Oldham, Lancs, OL8 4AU
Activities: Activities of head offices
Parent: OMC Motor Holdings Limited
Officers: Jonathan James Eglin [1971] Director/Manager; Robin Mellor Eglin [1945] Director; Sally Hoyles [1975] Director/Manager

O.P.P. (Westhulme) Limited
Incorporated: 14 July 1999
Net Worth: £8,558,000 *Total Assets:* £18,870,000
Registered Office: Prospect House, 168-170 Washway Road, Sale, Cheshire, M33 6RH
Activities: Buying and selling of own real estate
Parent: Oldham Property Partnerships Limited
Officers: Peter Chape, Secretary; James Peter Banfi [1953] Director; Heath David Broadbent [1973] Construction Director; Andrew Jeremy Gardner [1972] Director/Accountant; Michael Edward Nuttall [1964] Director/Surveyor; Benjamin William Scandrett [1977] Director/Estates Surveyor; Jean Mary Stretton [1958] Director/Councillor

O.P.P. Investments Limited
Incorporated: 14 January 1998
Net Worth: £13,595,000 *Total Assets:* £46,156,000
Registered Office: Prospect House, 168-170 Washway Road, Sale, Cheshire, M33 6RH
Activities: Buying and selling of own real estate
Parent: Oldham Property Partnerships Limited
Officers: Peter Chape, Secretary; James Peter Banfi [1953] Director; Heath David Broadbent [1973] Construction Director; Andrew Jeremy Gardner [1972] Director/Accountant; Michael Edward Nuttall [1964] Director/Surveyor; Benjamin William Scandrett [1977] Director/Estates Surveyor; Jean Mary Stretton [1958] Director/Councillor

Oak Trees Multi Academy Trust
Incorporated: 27 February 2017 *Employees:* 197
Net Worth: £13,094,000 *Total Assets:* £16,723,000
Registered Office: Stanton Road Primary School, Stanton Road, Bebington, Wirral, Merseyside, CH63 3HW
Activities: Primary education
Officers: Tony Bignold [1965] Director; Dr Adam David Boddison [1981] Director; Sue Cotton [1949] Director/Retired; Tony Lacey [1972] Director; Carole Molyneux [1946] Director; Jane Helen Owens [1953] Director/Education Consultant; Simon Pritchard [1970] Director; Richard Taylor [1976] Director; Alan Wilson [1954] Director

The Oak Trust
Incorporated: 28 July 2014 *Employees:* 179
Net Worth: £27,284,000 *Total Assets:* £30,441,000
Registered Office: North Chadderton School, Chadderton Hall Road, Chadderton, Oldham, Lancs, OL9 0BN
Activities: General secondary education
Officers: Lisa Brierley [1973] Director/HR Consultant; Philip Eaton Carnell [1956] Director/Driving Instructor; Alison Claire Cheetham [1958] Director/Retired; Joy Alison Clark [1958] Director/Headteacher; Garvin Crabtree [1950] Director/Printing; Judith Ann Rainford [1957] Director/Headteacher; Maurice Scott [1957] Director/Accountant; Iain Windeatt [1951] Director/Teacher

Oak Tyres UK Limited
Incorporated: 17 March 1986 *Employees:* 273
Net Worth: £16,609,708 *Total Assets:* £36,275,376
Registered Office: Oak House, Woodlands Park, Ashton Road, Newton-le-Willows, St Helens, Merseyside, WA12 0HF
Activities: Wholesale trade of motor vehicle parts and accessories
Parent: Oak Group Holdings Ltd
Officers: Lawrence Cross, Secretary; Debra Cross [1964] Director; Lawrence Cross [1960] Director/Tyre Distributor

Oakbridge Financial Services Limited
Incorporated: 1 November 2004 *Employees:* 6
Net Worth: £3,806,411 *Total Assets:* £12,031,383
Registered Office: 10 Riverview, The Embankment, Vale Road, Heaton Mersey, Stockport, Cheshire, SK4 3GN
Activities: Financial intermediation not elsewhere classified
Parent: Wrengate Holdings Limited
Officers: Andrew Michael Grimshaw [1957] Director/Chartered Accountant; Wyn Morrell [1953] Director; Alan Philip David Musry [1963] Director/Chartered Accountant; Ronald Musry [1935] Director

Oakcrown Properties Limited
Incorporated: 5 December 2000
Net Worth: £15,866,262 *Total Assets:* £29,051,744
Registered Office: Richard House, 9 Winckley Square, Preston, Lancs, PR1 3HP
Activities: Buying and selling of own real estate
Shareholders: Oana Crisan; Oliver Paul Egerton-Vernon; Willaim James Garfield-Bennett; Michael Anthony Collins
Officers: Michael Anthony Collins [1968] Director/Accountant [Irish]; Oliver Paul Egerton-Vernon [1982] Director/Solicitor; William James Garfield-Bennett [1963] Director/Solicitor

Oakdale Farms Limited
Incorporated: 14 May 2003 *Employees:* 2
Net Worth: £5,152,215 *Total Assets:* £9,981,802
Registered Office: Clint Mill, Cornmarket, Penrith, Cumbria, CA11 7HW
Activities: Other letting and operating of own or leased real estate
Major Shareholder: Dr Leon Roger Furlong
Officers: Sally Elvina Furlong, Secretary; Dr Leon Roger Furlong [1956] Director; Sally Elvina Furlong [1953] Director

The Oakes Business Park Development Company Ltd.
Incorporated: 13 May 1992
Net Worth Deficit: £898,414 *Total Assets:* £7,069,790
Registered Office: 78 Chorley New Road, Bolton, Lancs, BL1 4BY
Activities: Buying and selling of own real estate
Major Shareholder: Mark James Caldwell
Officers: James Stanley Caldwell [1944] Director (Property); Mark James Caldwell [1973] Director

Oakes Millers Limited
Incorporated: 8 November 1937 *Employees:* 161
Net Worth: £10,266,945 *Total Assets:* £24,318,256
Registered Office: Aston Mill, Aston, Nantwich, Cheshire, CW5 8DH
Activities: Manufacture of prepared feeds for farm animals
Shareholders: John Edward Lea; Anne Arden Borrowdale
Officers: Andrew Peter McLaren Rowe, Secretary; John Mark Borrowdale [1983] Director; David Horace Fox [1946] Director/Manager; Andrew George Hebditch Jackson [1975] Director; Keith Jamieson [1959] Director; Michael John Jepson [1950] Director/Mill Manager; Edward Philip LEA [1983] Director; James John LEA [1980] Director/Accountant; John Edward LEA [1946] Director/Chartered Accountant; Arthur Preston [1940] Director; David Warr [1952] Company Secretary/Director

Oakmore Investments Limited
Incorporated: 9 August 2016 *Employees:* 3
Net Worth Deficit: £537,265 *Total Assets:* £95,931,648
Registered Office: 116 Duke Street, Liverpool, L1 5JW
Activities: Credit granting by non-deposit taking finance houses and other specialist consumer credit grantors
Officers: Christopher Lathey [1969] Director

Obbligato Hotels Limited
Incorporated: 23 September 2002
Net Worth: £1,376,892 *Total Assets:* £7,152,751
Registered Office: c/o Edwards Veeder (UK) Limited, Ground Floor, 4 Broadgate, Broadway Business Park, Chadderton, Oldham, Lancs, OL9 9XA
Activities: Hotels and similar accommodation
Parent: Legacy Capital Limited
Officers: Rachan Singhpathom [1977] Director [Thai]; Suramit Singhpathom [1972] Director [Thai]

OBG Finance Holding Limited
Incorporated: 11 January 2016
Net Worth: £17,267,776 *Total Assets:* £17,267,776
Registered Office: Ayrton House, Commerce Way, Liverpool, L8 7BA
Activities: Activities of financial services holding companies
Officers: Philip Didlick, Secretary; Philip Didlick [1976] Director/Chartered Accountant; Generald Francis O'Brien [1949] Director; Padraic Marc O'Brien [1976] Director

OBG Finance Limited
Incorporated: 12 January 2016 *Employees:* 3
Net Worth: £17,132,802 *Total Assets:* £45,282,264
Registered Office: Ayrton House, Commerce Way, Liverpool, L8 7BA
Activities: Financial intermediation not elsewhere classified
Officers: Philip Didlick, Secretary; Philip Didlick [1976] Director/Chartered Accountant; Generald Francis O'Brien [1949] Director; Padraic Marc O'Brien [1979] Director

OBG Holding Limited
Incorporated: 11 January 2016 *Employees:* 382
Net Worth: £16,410,583 *Total Assets:* £45,243,748
Registered Office: Ayrton House, Commerce Way, Liverpool, L8 7BA
Activities: Manufacture of basic pharmaceutical products
Shareholder: Gerald Francis Obrien
Officers: Philip Didlick, Secretary; Philip Didlick [1976] Director/Chartered Accountant; Generald Francis O'Brien [1949] Director; Padraic Marc O'Brien [1979] Director; Brigid Christina Obrien [1946] Director

OBG Pharmaceuticals Limited
Incorporated: 21 October 1996 *Employees:* 21
Net Worth: £22,955,388 *Total Assets:* £41,497,080
Registered Office: Ayrton Saunders House, Parliament Business Park, Commerce Way, Liverpool, L8 7BA
Activities: Other business support service activities n.e.c.
Officers: Philip Didlick, Secretary; Philip Didlick [1976] Director/Accountant; Generald Francis O'Brien [1949] Director/Retail Pharmacist; Padraic Marc Obrien [1979] Director

OBG Property Holding Limited
Incorporated: 11 January 2016
Net Worth: £454,540 *Total Assets:* £14,262,985
Registered Office: Ayrton House, Commerce Way, Liverpool, L8 7BA
Activities: Other letting and operating of own or leased real estate
Officers: Philip Didlick, Secretary; Philip Didlick [1976] Director/Chartered Accountant; Generald Francis O'Brien [1949] Director; Padraic Marc O'Brien [1979] Director

Oboadler Company Limited
Incorporated: 23 April 1999
Net Worth: £121,585,000 *Total Assets:* £147,440,992
Registered Office: Innospec Manufacturing Park, Oil Sites Road, Ellesmere Port, Cheshire, CH65 4EY
Activities: Activities of other holding companies n.e.c.
Parent: Innospec Finance Limited
Officers: Brian Robert Watt Secretary; Ian Philip Cleminson [1965] Director; Brian Robert Watt [1959] Director

Ocean Boulevard II Limited
Incorporated: 14 June 2002 *Employees:* 81
Net Worth: £5,695,000 *Total Assets:* £9,105,000
Registered Office: Pleasure Beach, Ocean Boulevard, Promenade, Blackpool, Lancs, FY4 1EZ
Activities: Hotels and similar accommodation
Parent: Blackpool Pleasure Beach Limited
Officers: Michael Brown [1956] Director; Jonathan Gray [1970] Finance Director; Martin Jackson [1956] Hotel Director; Nigel Peter Kilgallon [1959] Director/Legal Counsel; Amanda Jean Thompson [1962] Director

Octapharma Limited
Incorporated: 17 April 1989 *Employees:* 21
Net Worth: £10,685,428 *Total Assets:* £11,529,855
Registered Office: The Zenith Building, 26 Spring Gardens, Manchester, M2 1AB
Activities: Manufacture of basic pharmaceutical products
Shareholder: Wolfgang Marguerre
Officers: Cornelius Marguerre, Secretary; Cornelius Marguerre [1958] Director/General Counsel [German]; Wolfgang Marguerre [1941] Director/General Manager [German]

OFS (DS) Acquisitions Limited
Incorporated: 26 November 2007
Net Worth Deficit: £3,738,000 *Total Assets:* £52,889,000
Registered Office: c/o The Factory Shop Limited, Orient Business Park, Billington Road, Burnley, Lancs, BB11 5UB
Activities: Activities of other holding companies n.e.c.
Parent: OFS (DS) Finance Limited
Officers: Carl Brian Allen [1966] Director; Timothy Richard Bettley [1966] Commercial Director; Stephen Andrew Cooke [1965] Director; Emma Louise Fox [1968] Director/Chief Executive Officer

OFS (DS) Finance Limited
Incorporated: 26 November 2007
Net Worth Deficit: £16,554,000 *Total Assets:* £46,200,000
Registered Office: c/o The Factory Shop Limited, Orient Business Park, Billington Road, Burnley, Lancs, BB11 5UB
Activities: Activities of other holding companies n.e.c.
Parent: OFS (DS) Holdings Limited
Officers: Carl Brian Allen [1966] Director; Timothy Richard Bettley [1966] Commercial Director; Stephen Andrew Cooke [1965] Director; Emma Louise Fox [1968] Director/Chief Executive Officer

OFS (DS) Holdings Limited
Incorporated: 26 November 2007 *Employees:* 2,819
Net Worth Deficit: £67,349,000 *Total Assets:* £101,384,000
Registered Office: c/o The Factory Shop Limited, Orient Business Park, Billington Road, Burnley, Lancs, BB11 5UB
Activities: Activities of other holding companies n.e.c.
Parent: Duke Street General Partner Limited
Officers: Carl Brian Allen [1966] Director; Timothy Richard Bettley [1966] Commercial Director; Stephen Andrew Cooke [1965] Director; Emma Louise Fox [1968] Director/Chief Executive Officer; Alistair Kenneth McGeorge [1959] Director; Peter Lance Taylor [1964] Director/Investor; David Gay Williams [1946] Director; Matthew Thomas Mathieson Williams [1974] Director/Chief Executive

Oil Salvage Limited
Incorporated: 22 October 1984 *Employees:* 61
Net Worth: £7,701,387 *Total Assets:* £11,138,422
Registered Office: Seymour Chambers, 92 London Road, Liverpool, L3 5NW
Activities: Other treatment of petroleum products (excluding petrochemicals manufacture)
Officers: Linzi Vernon, Secretary; James Vernon [1974] Director; Linzi Vernon [1968] Director; Vincent Robert Vernon [1966] Director/Dealer in Waste Oil; Vincent Vernon [1934] Director/Dealer in Waste Oil

Old Trafford Supporters Club Limited
Incorporated: 25 January 2011 *Employees:* 202
Net Worth Deficit: £521,000 *Total Assets:* £19,982,000
Registered Office: St Andrews Chambers, 21 Albert Square, Manchester, M2 5PE
Activities: Hotels and similar accommodation
Major Shareholder: Eng Hock Lim
Officers: Ryan Joseph Giggs [1973] Director/Professional Footballer; Hasan Malik [1963] Director/Company Secretary Rowsley Ltd [Singaporean]; Gary Alexander Neville [1975] Director; Wee Tuck Tan [1969] Director/Group CFO Rowsley Ltd [Singaporean]

Oldham Hulme Grammar Schools
Incorporated: 23 February 2007 *Employees:* 184
Net Worth: £11,824,209 *Total Assets:* £13,722,610
Registered Office: The Oldham Hulme Grammar Schools, Chamber Road, Oldham, Lancs, OL8 4BX
Activities: Primary education
Officers: Ian Martin, Secretary/Chartered Accountant; Dr Zahid Mahmood Chauhan [1976] Director/Doctor; John David Greenwood [1969] Director; Robert Stuart Illingworth [1957] Director; Richard Brian Lobley [1951] Director/Chartered Surveyor; David Mark Meredith [1962] Bank Director; Andrew Milnes [1963] Director/Chartered Accountant; Ann Susan Richards [1949] Director/Retired; Kevin Charles Sanders [1961] Director; Vijay Andrew Kumar Srivastava [1964] Director/Solicitor; Valerie Stocker [1961] Director/Solicitor; Jeremy Michael Tweedale Sutcliffe [1945] Director/Retired; John David Williams [1973] Director/Teacher

The Oldham Motor Company Limited
Incorporated: 6 April 1988 *Employees:* 142
Net Worth: £8,845,710 *Total Assets:* £25,835,984
Registered Office: 1 Manchester Road, Oldham, Lancs, OL8 4AU
Activities: Sale of new cars and light motor vehicles
Parent: OMC Motor Holdings Limited
Officers: Jonathan James Eglin [1971] Director/Manager; Robin Mellor Eglin [1945] Director; Sally Hoyles [1975] Director/Customer Operations Manager

Oldham Property Partnerships Limited
Incorporated: 18 March 1994
Net Worth: £12,121,000 *Total Assets:* £19,348,000
Registered Office: Prospect House, 168-170 Washway Road, Sale, Cheshire, M33 6RH
Activities: Development of building projects
Parent: Brookhouse Group Limited
Officers: Peter Chape, Secretary; James Peter Banfi [1953] Director; Heath David Broadbent [1973] Construction Director; Andrew Jeremy Gardner [1972] Director/Accountant; Michael Edward Nuttall [1964] Director/Surveyor; Benjamin William Scandrett [1977] Director/Estates Surveyor; Jean Mary Stretton [1958] Director/Councillor

Oliver Valves Limited
Incorporated: 22 May 1979 *Employees:* 112
Net Worth: £4,904,528 *Total Assets:* £10,491,625
Registered Office: Parkgate Industrial Estate, Knutsford, Cheshire, WA16 8DX
Activities: Manufacture of taps and valves
Shareholder: Michael Roderick Oliver
Officers: Lynn Kathryn Goryl, Secretary; Richard James Bedford [1974] Sales Director; Colm Kane [1959] Operations Director [Irish]; Mark Roderick Oliver [1968] Director; Doctor Michael Roderick Oliver [1938] Director/Chairman

Oliver Valvetek Limited
Incorporated: 14 June 1994 *Employees:* 68
Net Worth: £3,400,004 *Total Assets:* £6,728,300
Registered Office: Parkgate Industrial Estate, Knutsford, Cheshire, WA16 8DX
Activities: Manufacture of taps and valves
Major Shareholder: Michael Roderick Oliver
Officers: Lynn Kathryn Goryl, Secretary; Richard James Bedford [1974] Sales Director; Colm Kane [1959] Operations Director [Irish]; Mark Roderick Oliver [1968] Director; Michael Roderick Oliver [1938] Director; Paul Edgcumbe Shillito [1963] Director/Engineering Manager

Olympic Oils Limited
Incorporated: 11 September 1985 *Employees:* 97
Net Worth: £10,933,538 *Total Assets:* £15,677,885
Registered Office: Olympic Foods, Fallows Way, Whiston, Merseyside, L35 1RZ
Activities: Manufacture of oils and fats
Parent: Crest Oil Holdings Limited
Officers: Abeda Rashid Ghani, Secretary; Abeda Rashid Ghani [1959] Director; Tariq Sultan Ghani [1955] Director; Kevin Rimmer [1968] Director

Olympus Engineering (Holdings) Limited
Incorporated: 24 April 2014 *Employees:* 144
Net Worth: £5,016,607 *Total Assets:* £9,469,714
Registered Office: Corpacq House, 1 Goose Green, Altrincham, Cheshire, WA14 1DW
Activities: Machining
Officers: Benjamin David Hancock [1991] Director

Olympus Engineering Limited
Incorporated: 11 August 2000 *Employees:* 144
Net Worth: £11,102,684 *Total Assets:* £15,555,891
Registered Office: Corpacq House, 1 Goose Green, Altrincham, Cheshire, WA14 1DW
Activities: Machining
Officers: Christopher Mark Hammond [1958] Director; Benjamin David Hancock [1991] Director; Jacqueline Elizabeth Williamson [1963] Finance Director

OMC Motor Holdings Limited
Incorporated: 5 April 2000 *Employees:* 161
Net Worth: £15,238,040 *Total Assets:* £30,567,012
Registered Office: 1 Manchester Road, Oldham, Lancs, OL8 4AU
Activities: Activities of head offices
Officers: Christine Eglin [1944] Director; Jonathan James Eglin [1971] Director/Manager; Robin Mellor Eglin [1945] Director; Sally Hoyles [1975] Director/Manager

Omega Engineering Limited
Incorporated: 30 November 1990 *Employees:* 69
Net Worth: £9,989,000 *Total Assets:* £16,019,000
Registered Office: One Omega Drive, Northbank Irlam, Manchester, M44 5BD
Activities: Manufacture of non-electronic industrial process control equipment
Parent: Spectris US Holdings Limited
Officers: Andrea Lorraine Howard, Secretary; Joanna Christine Hallas [1970] Director/Management; David Geoffrey Tipton [1957] Director/Chartered Engineer; Joseph Vorih [1967] Director [American]; Clive Graeme Watson [1958] Director

Omega Multi-Academy Trust
Incorporated: 29 November 2012 *Employees:* 172
Net Worth: £19,873,000 *Total Assets:* £22,757,000
Registered Office: Great Sankey High School, Barrow Hall Lane, Great Sankey, Warrington, Cheshire, WA5 3AA
Activities: General secondary education
Officers: Andrew James Bent [1984] Director/Business Analyst; Paul Gerard Goodwin [1965] Director/Teacher; Richard Hannibal [1977] Director/Senior Regional Manager; John Joyce [1939] Retired Financial Analyst/Director; Naheem Shafiq [1976] Director/Chartered Accountant; Jonathan Andrew Wright [1962] Director/Executive Headteacher

Omega Technologies Limited
Incorporated: 4 January 1993
Net Worth: £8,592,000 *Total Assets:* £9,188,000
Registered Office: One Omega Drive, River Bend Technology Centre, Northbank, Irlam, Manchester, M44 5BD
Activities: Other letting and operating of own or leased real estate
Parent: Omega Engineering Limited
Officers: Andrea Lorraine Howard, Secretary; David Geoffrey Tipton [1957] Director/Engineer; Joseph Vorih [1967] Director [American]

Omnicell Limited
Incorporated: 15 October 2002 *Employees:* 52
Net Worth: £14,534,000 *Total Assets:* £17,871,000
Registered Office: Two Omega Drive, River Bend Technology Centre, Irlam, Manchester, M44 5GR
Activities: Wholesale of pharmaceutical goods
Parent: Omnicell Inc
Officers: Alan Clark, Secretary; Jeroen Peter Johan Kuipers [1971] Director/Executive [Dutch]; Paul John O'Hanlon [1962] Director/Pharmacist; Rob Seim [1959] Director/Chief Financial Officer [American]

On The Beach Beds Limited
Incorporated: 27 June 2007 *Employees:* 34
Net Worth: £7,975,000 *Total Assets:* £17,645,000
Registered Office: Park Square, Bird Hall Lane, Cheadle Heath, Stockport, Cheshire, SK3 0XN
Activities: Travel agency activities
Parent: On The Beach Travel Limited
Officers: Kirsteen Vickerstaff, Secretary; Simon Matthew Cooper [1972] Director; Paul Alan Meehan [1963] Director/Chief Financial Officer

On The Beach Bidco Limited
Incorporated: 24 September 2013
Net Worth Deficit: £11,570,000 *Total Assets:* £56,284,000
Registered Office: Park Square, Bird Hall Lane, Cheadle Heath, Stockport, Cheshire, SK3 0XN
Activities: Travel agency activities
Parent: On The Beach Topco Limited
Officers: Kirsteen Vickerstaff, Secretary; Simon Matthew Cooper [1972] Director; Paul Alan Meehan [1963] Director/Chief Financial Officer

On The Beach Group PLC
Incorporated: 17 August 2015 *Employees:* 337
Net Worth: £96,560,000 *Total Assets:* £201,984,992
Registered Office: Park Square, Bird Hall Lane, Cheadle Heath, Cheshire, SK3 0XN
Activities: Travel agency activities
Officers: Kirsteen Vickerstaff, Secretary; Simon Cooper [1972] Director; Lee Dale Ginsberg [1957] Director; David Thomas Kelly [1963] Director; Paul Alan Meehan [1963] Director/Chief Financial Officer; Elaine Margaret O'Donnell [1970] Director

On The Beach Limited
Incorporated: 22 February 1996 *Employees:* 293
Net Worth: £55,035,000 *Total Assets:* £138,220,000
Registered Office: Park Square, Bird Hall Lane, Stockport, Cheshire, SK3 0XN
Activities: Travel agency activities
Parent: On The Beach Travel Limited
Officers: Kirsteen Vickerstaff, Secretary; Simon Matthew Cooper [1972] Director; Paul Alan Meehan [1963] Director/Chief Financial Officer

On The Beach Travel Limited
Incorporated: 20 June 2007
Net Worth: £1,617,000 *Total Assets:* £59,391,000
Registered Office: Park Square, Bird Hall Lane, Cheadle Heath, Stockport, Cheshire, SK3 0XN
Activities: Travel agency activities
Parent: On The Beach Bidco Limited
Officers: Kirsteen Vickerstaff, Secretary; Simon Matthew Cooper [1972] Director; Paul Alan Meehan [1963] Director/Chief Financial Officer

One Manchester Treasury Limited
Incorporated: 24 February 2015
Net Worth: £106,000 *Total Assets:* £122,653,000
Registered Office: Lovell House, Archway 6, Hulme, Manchester, M15 5RN
Activities: Renting and operating of Housing Association real estate
Parent: One Manchester Limited
Officers: Victor Hassan, Secretary; Graham Reynard Aitken [1956] Director; John Joseph McGrail [1966] Director of Finance and Resources; David James Power [1957] Director/Chief Executive

Op Acquisitions Limited
Incorporated: 25 September 2013 *Employees:* 150
Net Worth: £33,773,000 *Total Assets:* £45,625,000
Registered Office: Grove Mill, Todmorden Road, Bacup, Lancs, OL13 9EF
Activities: Manufacture of plastic plates, sheets, tubes and profiles
Parent: Medplast LLC
Officers: Daniel Agroskin [1976] Managing Director JLL Partners LLC; Harold Joseph Faig [1948] Director [American]; Anthony Gilarde [1970] Director [American]; Brian Douglas King [1967] Director [American]; Peter Maurice Strothman [1977] Director/Partner, Water Street Healthcare Partners [American]

Open Solutions (OsUK) Limited
Incorporated: 1 November 2012
Net Worth: £6,616,509 *Total Assets:* £13,450,836
Registered Office: Waterfront Point, Warrington Road, Widnes, Cheshire, WA8 0TD
Activities: Other letting and operating of own or leased real estate
Parent: Halton Housing Trust
Officers: Neil Mark McGrath, Secretary; Nicholas St.John Atkin [1968] Director/Chief Executive; Mark Patrick Forrest [1951] Director; David John Hughes [1957] Director/Chief Executive; Robert Alan Poole [1975] Managing Director; Judith Margaret Winterbourne [1955] Housing Association Director

Optimisation Developments Limited
Incorporated: 22 July 2008
Net Worth Deficit: £168,900,000 *Total Assets:* £132,862,000
Registered Office: Hilmore House, Gain Lane, Bradford, W Yorks, BD3 7DL
Activities: Other business support service activities n.e.c.
Parent: Wm Morrison Supermarkets Holdings Limited
Officers: Jonathan James Burke, Secretary; Jonathan James Burke [1966] Director; Trevor John Strain [1975] Finance Director

Optimisation Investments Limited
Incorporated: 22 July 2008
Net Worth Deficit: £78,578,000 *Total Assets:* £826,872,000
Registered Office: Hilmore House, Gain Lane, Bradford, W Yorks, BD3 7DL
Activities: Other business support service activities n.e.c.
Parent: Wm Morrison Supermarkets Holdings Limited
Officers: Jonathan James Burke, Secretary; Jonathan James Burke [1966] Director; Trevor John Strain [1975] Finance Director

Optimum Debtco Limited
Incorporated: 24 January 2007
Net Worth Deficit: £22,606,000 *Total Assets:* £51,899,000
Registered Office: Norcliffe House, Station Road, Wilmslow, Cheshire, SK9 1BU
Activities: Activities of other holding companies n.e.c.
Parent: Brighterkind Limited
Officers: Abigail Mattison, Secretary; Ryan Stuart MacAskill [1975] Director; Gregory Laurence Newman [1988] Director/Investment Professional; Jeremy Robert Arthur Richardson [1970] Director; Dr Maureen Claire Royston [1960] Director; Phillip Gary Thomas [1978] Director

Optionis Bidco Limited
Incorporated: 28 October 2013 *Employees:* 2
Net Worth Deficit: £8,893,677 *Total Assets:* £45,339,740
Registered Office: Optionis House, 840 Ibis Court, Centre Park, Warrington, Cheshire, WA1 1RL
Activities: Activities of other holding companies n.e.c.
Parent: Optionis Midco Ltd
Officers: Kevin John Budge [1961] Director; Derek Andrew Kelly [1972] Director

Optionis Management Limited
Incorporated: 7 December 2005 *Employees:* 343
Net Worth: £20,535,548 *Total Assets:* £25,913,240
Registered Office: Optionis House, 840 Ibis Court, Centre Park, Warrington, Cheshire, WA1 1RL
Activities: Management consultancy activities other than financial management
Parent: Optionis Bidco Limited
Officers: Derek Andrew Kelly, Secretary; Kevin John Budge [1961] Commercial Director; Derek Andrew Kelly [1972] Technical Director

Opus Bestpay Limited
Incorporated: 29 December 2010
Net Worth Deficit: £249,074 *Total Assets:* £10,308,810
Registered Office: Drake House, Gadbrook Park, Rudheath, Northwich, Cheshire, CW9 7RA
Activities: Other business support service activities n.e.c.
Major Shareholder: Morris Adam Quinton Hazell
Officers: Adrian Benedict Sacco [1966] Director

Orbit Developments (Manchester) Limited
Incorporated: 4 May 1971
Net Worth: £45,675,512 *Total Assets:* £51,097,784
Registered Office: Emerson House, Heyes Lane, Alderley Edge, Cheshire, SK9 7LF
Activities: Development of building projects
Parent: Emerson Developments (Holdings) Limited
Officers: Varun Maharaj, Secretary; Simon Gavin Clarke-Williams [1951] Marketing Director; Giles Ivan Hardern [1967] Director/Chartered Surveyor; Anthony Emerson Jones [1967] Director; Audrey Jones [1936] Director; Mark Emerson Jones [1964] Director; Peter Emerson Jones [1935] Director; Paul Robert McLeman [1963] Director/Chartered Surveyor; Mark Stephen Thomas Royle [1964] Director/Architect; Simon Peter Wilson [1964] Director

Orbit Developments (Southern) Limited
Incorporated: 10 March 1987 *Employees:* 5
Net Worth: £13,929,681 *Total Assets:* £80,593,280
Registered Office: Emerson House, Heyes Lane, Alderley Edge, Cheshire, SK9 7LF
Activities: Development of building projects
Parent: Emerson Developments (Holdings) Limited
Officers: Varun Maharaj, Secretary; Anthony Emerson Jones [1967] Director; Audrey Jones [1936] Director; Mark Emerson Jones [1964] Director; Peter Emerson Jones [1935] Director; Simon Peter Wilson [1964] Director

Orbit Investments (Northern) Limited
Incorporated: 31 May 1996
Net Worth: £220,674,736 *Total Assets:* £389,854,624
Registered Office: Emerson House, Heyes Lane, Alderley Edge, Cheshire, SK9 7LF
Activities: Development of building projects
Parent: Emerson Developments (Holdings) Limited
Officers: Varun Maharaj, Secretary; Robert Anthony Hallworth [1968] Director/Business Executive; Giles Ivan Hardern [1967] Director/Chartered Surveyor; Anthony Emerson Jones [1967] Director; Mark Emerson Jones [1964] Director; Peter Emerson Jones [1935] Director; Mark Stephen Thomas Royle [1964] Director/Architect

Orbit Investments (Properties) Limited
Incorporated: 6 July 1988
Net Worth: £127,762,168 *Total Assets:* £463,136,032
Registered Office: Emerson House, Heyes Lane, Alderley Edge, Cheshire, SK9 7LF
Activities: Development of building projects
Parent: Emerson Developments (Holdings) Limited
Officers: Varun Maharaj, Secretary; Giles Ivan Hardern [1967] Director/Chartered Surveyor; Anthony Emerson Jones [1967] Director; Audrey Jones [1936] Director; Mark Emerson Jones [1964] Director; Peter Emerson Jones [1935] Director; Mark Stephen Thomas Royle [1964] Director/Architect; Simon Peter Wilson [1964] Director

Orbital Education Limited
Incorporated: 25 January 2008 *Employees:* 444
Net Worth: £2,811,493 *Total Assets:* £31,649,776
Registered Office: Landmark House, Station Road, Cheadle Hulme, Cheadle, Cheshire, SK8 7BS
Activities: Activities of head offices
Major Shareholder: Kevin Joseph McNeany
Officers: James William Stewart, Secretary; Kevin Joseph McNeany [1943] Director; Myles Antony McNeany [1986] Director/Group Head of IT; David Irvine Pottinger [1960] Director; James William Stewart [1965] Director

Orchard House (MPS) Limited
Incorporated: 26 November 2015 *Employees:* 408
Net Worth: £3,864,699 *Total Assets:* £7,731,706
Registered Office: 12-16 Pitcliffe Way, West Bowling, Bradford, W Yorks, BD5 7SG
Activities: Activities of head offices
Parent: Mailway Packaging Solutions Group Limited
Officers: Elizabeth Alice Astin [1967] Director; Richard Bramma [1967] Director

Oregon & Ratcliffe Ltd
Incorporated: 30 May 2012
Net Worth: £1,493,645 *Total Assets:* £9,097,416
Registered Office: Seymour Chambers, 92 London Road, Liverpool, L3 5NW
Activities: Other letting and operating of own or leased real estate
Officers: Alan James Beer [1966] Director; David Charles Brewitt [1963] Director

Orford Investments Limited
Incorporated: 29 September 1998
Net Worth: £3,130,311 *Total Assets:* £7,033,757
Registered Office: Orford Barn, Lady Lane, Croft, Warrington, Cheshire, WA3 7AY
Activities: Construction of commercial buildings
Major Shareholder: Trevor Lloyd
Officers: Trevor Lloyd [1963] Director/Builder

Orica UK Limited
Incorporated: 26 January 1998 *Employees:* 39
Net Worth: £50,382,000 *Total Assets:* £73,661,000
Registered Office: 4 Stonecrop, North Quarry Business Park, Appley Bridge, Wigan, Lancs, WN6 9DL
Activities: Manufacture of explosives
Officers: Richard Ian Brown [1968] Director/Vice President Europe; John Ferguson [1956] Director/Commercial Lead Western Europe

Orica-GM Holdings Limited
Incorporated: 14 March 2000
Net Worth: £24,491,442 *Total Assets:* £25,617,344
Registered Office: 3rd Floor, 1 Ashley Road, Altrincham, Cheshire, WA14 2DT
Activities: Activities of head offices
Officers: Andres Alejandro Fuentes Angarita [1964] Director/Administrator [Venezuelan]; Sebastián Felipe Pinto Fernández [1966] Director/Mining Services [Chilean]; Felix Torres Segui Junior [1969] Director/General Manager [Brazilian]

Original FS Holdings Limited
Incorporated: 16 September 2004
Net Worth: £9,578,000 *Total Assets:* £63,160,000
Registered Office: c/o The Factory Shop Ltd, Orient Business Park, Billington Road, Burnley, Lancs, BB11 5UB
Activities: Activities of head offices
Parent: OFS (DS) Acquisitions Ltd
Officers: Carl Brian Allen [1966] Director; Timothy Richard Bettley [1966] Commercial Director; Stephen Andrew Cooke [1965] Director; Emma Louise Fox [1968] Director/Chief Executive Officer

J & J Ormerod PLC
Incorporated: 30 April 1968 *Employees:* 365
Net Worth: £26,326,546 *Total Assets:* £36,511,420
Registered Office: Colonia House, Bacup, Lancs, OL13 0EA
Activities: Other manufacturing n.e.c.
Shareholders: Stephen Ellis Greenhalgh; Lee Greenhalgh; Gillian Burke
Officers: Stephen Gerard Ashton [1960] Director/Salesman; Gillian Burke [1968] Director/Purchasing Manager; Lee Greenhalgh [1961] Director/Property Developer; Stephen Ellis Greenhalgh [1966] Director/Property Developer; Robert Myers [1962] Director/Production; John Pollitt [1965] Sales Director

Ormiston Bolingbroke Academy Trust
Incorporated: 18 August 2010 *Employees:* 184
Net Worth: £13,868,000 *Total Assets:* £14,883,000
Registered Office: Ormiston Bolingbroke Academy, Barnfield Avenue, Runcorn, Cheshire, WA7 6EP
Activities: General secondary education
Officers: Samantha Crane [1972] Director/Attendance Officer; Michael Cunliffe [1958] Director/Electrical Engineer; Philip Healey [1961] Director/Retired; Christine Heffernan [1977] Director/Teaching Assistant; James Miller [1973] National Director of Estates and Technology; Robert Andrew Pritchard [1968] Regional Director West; Kris Reid [1974] Director/Teacher; Emlyn Wright [1976] Director/Principal

Orthios Eco Parks (Anglesey) Limited
Incorporated: 29 April 2013
Net Worth Deficit: £15,504,590 *Total Assets:* £19,418,656
Registered Office: The Moorings, Rowton Bridge, Christleton, Chester, CH3 7AE
Activities: Growing of vegetables and melons, roots and tubers
Parent: Orthios Group (Holdings) Limited
Officers: Charles Ian Hodgkinson, Secretary; Steven Hedley Haswell [1959] Director; Charles Ian Hodgkinson [1960] Director/Solicitor; Lewis H Levasseur [1953] Director [Canadian]; Michael David Masters [1944] Director; Philip McCormick [1947] Director/Chief Development Office; Sean Michael McCormick [1965] Director/Chartered Architect

Ortho-Care (U.K.) Limited
Incorporated: 26 November 1981 *Employees:* 47
Net Worth: £7,200,341 *Total Assets:* £7,716,896
Registered Office: 1 Riverside Estate, Saltaire, W Yorks, BD17 7DR
Activities: Dental practice activities
Shareholders: Richard Garford; Kelvin George Scott
Officers: Richard Garford, Secretary; Richard Garford [1957] Director; Kelvin George Scott [1956] Director

Orthoplastics Limited
Incorporated: 8 November 2005 *Employees:* 150
Net Worth: £22,511,000 *Total Assets:* £29,810,000
Registered Office: Grove Mill, Todmorden Road, Bacup, Lancs, OL13 9EF
Activities: Manufacture of plastic plates, sheets, tubes and profiles
Parent: Orthoproducts Ltd
Officers: Anthony Gilarde, Secretary; Daniel Agroskin [1976] Managing Director [American]; Mark Allen [1969] Managing Director; Darren Close [1965] Director; Harold Joseph Faig [1948] Director/Chief Executive [American]; Anthony Gilarde [1970] Director [American]; Brian Douglas King [1967] Director [American]; Peter Maurice Strothman [1977] Director/Partner, Water Street Healthcare Partners [American]

Orthoworld 2000 Limited
Incorporated: 4 April 1952 *Employees:* 126
Net Worth: £6,613,000 *Total Assets:* £7,825,000
Registered Office: Europa House, Europa Trading Estate, Stoneclough Road, Kearsley, Manchester, M26 1GG
Activities: Dental practice activities
Parent: IDH Acquisitions Limited
Officers: Leo Damian Carroll, Secretary; Clifford Gwyn Davies [1966] Director; Sharon Patricia Letters [1975] Clinical Director; Bernard Moroney [1953] Director; Manish Prasad [1972] Clinical Director; Tom Riall [1960] Director; Mohammed Omar Shafi Khan [1974] Director/Chief Financial Officer; Krista Nyree Whitley [1970] Clinical Director

Osan Limited
Incorporated: 21 December 1993 *Employees:* 69
Net Worth: £7,334,119 *Total Assets:* £10,128,173
Registered Office: Premier House, 2nd Avenue, Crewe Gates Industrial Estate, Crewe, Cheshire, CW1 6BZ
Activities: Wholesale of clothing and footwear
Parent: Ruia Group Limited
Officers: Philip John Campbell, Secretary; Amit Ruia [1970] Managing Director; Vimal Ruia [1959] Director

Ossur UK Holding Limited
Incorporated: 28 November 2005
Net Worth: £1,200,367 *Total Assets:* £38,989,972
Registered Office: Unit No 1 S:Park, Hamilton Road, Stockport, Cheshire, SK1 2AE
Activities: Activities of head offices
Parent: Ossur Europe B.V.
Officers: Emlyn Lewis, Secretary; Jos Van Poorten [1964] Finance Director [Dutch]

Ossur UK Limited
Incorporated: 16 November 1990 *Employees:* 44
Net Worth: £7,126,335 *Total Assets:* £10,201,494
Registered Office: Unit 1 S:Park, Hamilton Way, Stockport, Cheshire, SK1 2AE
Activities: Wholesale of other intermediate products
Parent: Innovative Medical Products Holdings Ltd
Officers: Emlyn Lewis, Secretary; Emlyn Huw Elystan Lewis [1971] Managing Director; Jos Van Poorten [1964] Director/Chief Financial Officer [Dutch]

Oswaldtwistle Mills Limited
Incorporated: 13 May 1994 *Employees:* 96
Net Worth: £3,642,345 *Total Assets:* £8,794,909
Registered Office: Clifton Mill, Pickup Street, Oswaldtwistle, Lancs, BB5 0EY
Activities: Other retail sale in non-specialised stores
Parent: Nfield Holdings Limited
Officers: Boyd Michael Hargreaves, Secretary; Russell Justin Booth [1969] Director; Boyd Michael Hargreaves [1975] Managing Director

Otter Controls Limited
Incorporated: 26 March 1946 *Employees:* 994
Net Worth: £23,949,912 *Total Assets:* £41,790,000
Registered Office: Tongue Lane Industrial Estate, Dew Pond Lane, Fairfield, Buxton, Derbys, SK17 7LF
Activities: Manufacture of electronic measuring, testing etc. equipment, not for industrial process control
Officers: Graeme Thomas Brown, Secretary; Paul Boundy [1960] Director/Mechanical Engineer; Michael Leonard Colling [1962] Director/Chartered Accountant; Johannes Joesphus Berendinus Maria Derksen [1960] Director [Dutch]; William Ross Jolliffe [1965] Director; Brian Smith [1952] Director; Dr David Andrew Smith [1964] Director/Chartered Certified Accountant; Simon Mark Whiteley [1960] Director/Mechanical Engineer

Otto Simon Limited
Incorporated: 5 February 2003 *Employees:* 89
Net Worth: £5,899,591 *Total Assets:* £8,661,927
Registered Office: Churchfield House, 5 The Crescent, Cheadle, Cheshire, SK8 1PS
Activities: Other professional, scientific and technical activities n.e.c.
Officers: Christine Haywood, Secretary; Christopher Richard Bridgland [1965] Director/Engineer; Richard Allen Buckley [1974] Director/Engineer; Paul Michael Cooper [1975] Finance Director; Peter Creer [1968] Director/Engineer; Stephen Patrick Haywood [1957] Director; Nicolas Peter Shaw [1970] Director/Engineer

Outdoor & Sports Company Limited
Incorporated: 9 September 1970 *Employees:* 125
Net Worth: £4,877,067 *Total Assets:* £15,532,123
Registered Office: 3 Bailey Court, Green Street, Macclesfield, Cheshire, SK10 1JQ
Activities: Manufacture of other wearing apparel and accessories n.e.c.
Parent: Outdoor & Sports Company (Holdings) Limited
Officers: Stephen James Cann, Secretary/Director; Paul Anthony Allison [1961] Director/Certified Chartered Accountant; Stephen James Cann [1965] Director/Chartered Accountant

The Outward Bound Trust
Incorporated: 13 November 2008 *Employees:* 308
Net Worth: £22,100,000 *Total Assets:* £25,435,000
Registered Office: Hackthorpe Hall, Hackthorpe, Penrith, Cumbria, CA10 2HX
Activities: General secondary education
Officers: David Kim Parry, Secretary; Ian Campbell Ashman [1956] Director/College Principal; Andrew Martin Cartwright [1948] Director/Retired Banker; Mbe Gair [1957] Director/Association Chief Executive; Leo Houlding [1980] Director & Professional Climber; Philippa Lisa Kramer [1973] HR Director; Jonathan Wayne Lewis [1967] Director/Investment Banker; Farajollah Farshad Mahjoor [1952] Director/Businessman/Architect [American]; Dame Pamela Louise Makin [1960] Director/Chief Executive Officer; Colin James Maund [1958] Director; Terence Charles Mordaunt [1947] Director/Chairman; Charles Edward Laurence Philipps [1959] Director/Chief Executive; HRH Andrew Albert Christian Prince Andrew The Duke of York KG KCVO ADC [1960] Director; Caroline Sarah Jane Sellar [1974] Commercial Director; Paul Marcus George Voller [1955] Director/Solicitor; Christine Mary Walker [1966] Director/Head of Development at a Charitable Trust; Guy Hampson Williams [1967] Managing Director

Ouzledale Foundry Company Limited
Incorporated: 22 August 1936 *Employees:* 70
Net Worth: £9,189,733 *Total Assets:* £10,370,318
Registered Office: Ouzledale Foundry, Long Ing, Barnoldswick, Lancs, BB18 6BJ
Activities: Casting of iron
Shareholders: Martin Ashby; Jeremy Ashby
Officers: Amanda Louise Ashby, Secretary; Charlotte Ashby [1973] Director; Jeremy Ashby [1971] Director; Martin Ashby [1965] Director/Company Secretary

Oxendale & Company Limited
Incorporated: 1 March 1919
Net Worth: £732,912 *Total Assets:* £11,452,372
Registered Office: Griffin House, 40 Lever Street, Manchester, M60 6ES
Activities: Other service activities n.e.c.
Parent: J.D. Williams & Company Limited
Officers: Daniel Michael Cropper, Secretary; Craig Barry Lovelace [1973] Director/Accountant; Ralph Eric Tucker [1974] Director

Oxford Property Trading Ltd.
Incorporated: 28 March 2011 *Employees:* 3
Net Worth: £4,360,000 *Total Assets:* £19,904,000
Registered Office: The Box, Horseshoe Lane, Alderley Edge, Cheshire, SK9 7QP
Activities: Development of building projects
Parent: Select Charles Street Residential (Holdings) Limited
Officers: Mark Christopher Dawson [1973] Director; Kenneth John Knott [1959] Director; Michael Keith Slater [1974] Director

Oxley Developments Company Limited
Incorporated: 12 September 1942 *Employees:* 156
Net Worth: £2,043,007 *Total Assets:* £8,057,874
Registered Office: Priory Park, Ulverston, Cumbria, LA12 9QG
Activities: Manufacture of electronic components
Parent: Oxley Group Limited
Officers: Darren Mark Cavan [1972] Director; Jacqueline Kelly [1967] Finance Director; Garnet Lindsay North [1954] Director

Oxley Group Limited
Incorporated: 27 October 1969 *Employees:* 194
Net Worth: £4,533,584 *Total Assets:* £10,950,784
Registered Office: Priory Park, Ulverston, Cumbria, LA12 9QG
Activities: Activities of head offices
Major Shareholder: Ann Shirley Oxley
Officers: Peter Graham Wilson Bedwin [1943] Director; Darren Mark Cavan [1972] Director; Jacqueline Kelly [1967] Finance Director; Murielle Thuy-Kieu Madrona [1970] Director/Consultant [French]; Garnet Lindsay North [1954] Director; Martin Edward Sloan [1955] Director [American]

Oxoid (Ely) Limited
Incorporated: 26 October 1987
Net Worth Deficit: £2,616,000 *Total Assets:* £10,124,000
Registered Office: 3rd Floor, 1 Ashley Road, Altrincham, Cheshire, WA14 2DT
Activities: Non-trading company
Parent: I Q (Bio) Limited
Officers: Rhona Gregg, Secretary; Lucie Mary Katja Grant [1976] Director/Solicitor; Nicholas Ince [1982] Director/Accountant; David John Norman [1960] Director/Chartered Accountant

Oxoid 2000 Limited
Incorporated: 20 April 2000
Net Worth: £117,218,000 *Total Assets:* £163,139,008
Registered Office: 3rd Floor 1 Ashley Road, Altrincham, Cheshire, WA14 2DT
Activities: Activities of head offices
Parent: Thermo Fisher Scientific Inc.
Officers: Rhona Gregg, Secretary; Lucie Mary Katja Grant [1976] Director/Solicitor; Nicholas Ince [1982] Director/Accountant; David John Norman [1960] Director/Chartered Accountant

Oxoid Holdings Limited
Incorporated: 9 December 1996
Net Worth: £111,250,000 *Total Assets:* £140,738,000
Registered Office: 3rd Floor 1 Ashley Road, Altrincham, Cheshire, WA14 2DT
Activities: Activities of head offices
Parent: Oxoid 2000 Limited
Officers: Rhona Gregg, Secretary; Lucie Mary Katja Grant [1976] Director/Solicitor; Nicholas Ince [1982] Director/Accountant; David John Norman [1960] Director/Chartered Accountant

Oxoid International Limited
Incorporated: 10 December 1996
Net Worth: £42,539,000 *Total Assets:* £44,417,000
Registered Office: 3rd Floor, 1 Ashley Road, Altrincham, Cheshire, WA14 2DT
Activities: Other manufacturing n.e.c.
Parent: Oxoid Holdings Limited
Officers: Rhona Gregg, Secretary; Nicholas Ince [1982] Director/Accountant; David John Norman [1960] Director/Chartered Accountant

Oxoid Limited
Incorporated: 9 December 1996 *Employees:* 355
Net Worth: £350,252,992 *Total Assets:* £379,332,000
Registered Office: 3rd Floor, 1 Ashley Road, Altrincham, Cheshire, WA14 2DT
Activities: Other manufacturing n.e.c.
Parent: Oxoid Holdings Limited
Officers: Rhona Gregg, Secretary; Lucie Mary Katja Grant [1976] Director/Solicitor; Nicholas Ince [1982] Director/Accountant; David John Norman [1960] Director/Chartered Accountant

P B M Management Limited
Incorporated: 10 February 2003 *Employees:* 15
Net Worth: £26,586,112 *Total Assets:* £37,887,956
Registered Office: 116 Duke Street, Liverpool, L1 5JW
Activities: Buying and selling of own real estate
Major Shareholder: Paul Anthony Marshall
Officers: Paul Anthony Marshall [1969] Director

P H Property Holdings Limited
Incorporated: 16 February 1996 *Employees:* 36
Net Worth: £6,984,208 *Total Assets:* £22,769,468
Registered Office: Bollin House, Oakfield Road, Cheadle Royal Business Park, Cheadle, Cheshire, SK8 3GX
Activities: Development of building projects
Shareholders: Philip Nigel Hughes; Paul Henry Hogarth
Officers: Philip Nigel Hughes, Secretary; Daniel Richard Gale [1965] Director/Chartered Surveyor; James Randle Heyworth [1968] Director/Chartered Surveyor; Paul Henry Hogarth [1959] Director; Philip Nigel Hughes [1965] Director/Self Employed; John McKelvey [1964] Construction Director; Lee Francis Wood [1972] Technical Director

P I H Holdings Limited
Incorporated: 19 March 1997
Net Worth: £7,774,791 *Total Assets:* £7,775,541
Registered Office: Farrington Road, Rossendale Road Industrial Estate, Burnley, Lancs, BB11 5SW
Activities: Activities of construction holding companies
Parent: Bandhart
Officers: Steven John Costello, Secretary; Caroline Allen [1979] Finance Director; Adam Rhys Wynne Hughes [1965] Managing Director

P&O Princess American Holdings
Incorporated: 10 October 1979
Net Worth: £114,848,640 *Total Assets:* £114,848,640
Registered Office: 3rd Floor, 1 Ashley Road, Altrincham, Cheshire, WA14 2DT
Activities: Activities of head offices
Parent: Carnival PLC
Officers: Arnaldo Perez, Secretary/Executive & Attorney [American]; Simon Charles Walters [1969] Director/Solicitor; Paul Robert Wilkinson [1974] Director/Accountant

P. & B. (Foods) Limited
Incorporated: 27 August 1970 *Employees:* 123
Net Worth: £13,354,607 *Total Assets:* £20,977,524
Registered Office: Prologis Park, Newhall Way, Bradford, W Yorks, BD5 8LZ
Activities: Non-specialised wholesale of food, beverages and tobacco
Parent: P. & B. Foods Holdings Limited
Officers: Mohinder Singh Bhatoa, Secretary/Sales Director [Indian]; Mohinder Singh Bhatoa [1950] Sales Director [Indian]; Chandra Patel [1973] Director; Thakorbhai Vitthalbhai Patel [1940] Director

P. & B. Foods Holdings Limited
Incorporated: 12 November 2010 *Employees:* 123
Net Worth: £27,295,254 *Total Assets:* £41,413,504
Registered Office: Prologis Park, Newhall Way, Bradford, W Yorks, BD5 8LZ
Activities: Non-trading company
Officers: Mohinder Singh Bhatoa [1950] Sales Director [Indian]; Chandra Patel [1973] Director; Thakorbhai Vitthalbhai Patel [1940] Director

P.F.D.(Carlisle) Limited
Incorporated: 11 November 1955 *Employees:* 311
Net Worth: £17,081,164 *Total Assets:* £20,667,552
Registered Office: P O Box 30, Pioneer House, Rosehill Estate, Carlisle, Cumbria, CA1 2RR
Activities: Wholesale of meat and meat products
Shareholders: David Andrew Jenkins; Nigel Graham Jenkins
Officers: Katrina Elizabeth Abbott, Secretary; David Andrew Jenkins [1973] Director/Food Wholesaler; Herbert Andrew Jenkins [1936] Director/Chairman; Nigel Graham Jenkins [1971] Managing Director; Pamela Diane Jenkins [1948] Director

P.J.D. (Holdings) Limited
Incorporated: 6 October 2004 *Employees:* 52
Net Worth: £2,235,671 *Total Assets:* £8,941,506
Registered Office: Lyons Lane, Chorley, Lancs, PR7 3BL
Activities: Non-trading company
Shareholders: Philip James Davidson; Alison Lesley Davidson
Officers: Alison Lesley Davidson, Secretary/Director; Alison Lesley Davidson [1955] Director; Philip James Davidson [1954] Managing Director

P.J.H. Group Limited
Incorporated: 26 May 1972 *Employees:* 484
Net Worth: £9,419,000 *Total Assets:* £52,644,000
Registered Office: Alder House, Kearsley, Bolton, Lancs, BL4 8SL
Activities: Operation of warehousing and storage facilities for land transport activities
Parent: Globe Union Industrial Corp
Officers: Jason David Shaw, Secretary; Yu-Li Chou [1966] Director/Vice President [Chinese]; Richard Ian George [1970] Director/Chief Executive Officer; Scott Ouyoung [1951] Chairman Director [Taiwanese]; Jason David Shaw [1971] Director/Chief Financial Officer; Andrew Yates [1961] Director/Group Chief Executive Officer; Kuo-Chi Yen [1961] Director [Chinese]

P2G.com Worldwide Limited
Incorporated: 13 September 2012 *Employees:* 151
Net Worth: £3,049,000 *Total Assets:* £13,400,000
Registered Office: The Cube, Coe Street, Bolton, Lancs, BL3 6BU
Activities: Activities of head offices
Officers: Harry Phillip Anthony Adams-Mercer [1953] Director; Richard Harry Phillip Adams-Mercer [1980] Director; James Brett Greenbury [1961] Director; Steven Joseph Kramer [1976] Commercial Director; Mark Jonathan Charles Livingstone [1966] Director; Christopher Alfred Simpson [1952] Director

Pace Distribution (Overseas) Limited
Incorporated: 2 August 1996
Net Worth: £101,999,384 *Total Assets:* £102,970,624
Registered Office: Victoria Road, Saltaire, W Yorks, BD18 3LF
Activities: Satellite telecommunications activities
Shareholders: Arris Global Ltd; Arris Global Ltd.
Officers: David Bernard Potts [1957] Director/Businessman [American]; Anthony Emilien Zuyderhoff [1971] Director [American]

Pace Overseas Distribution Limited
Incorporated: 9 November 2006
Net Worth: £31,677,176 *Total Assets:* £31,677,176
Registered Office: Victoria Road, Saltaire, W Yorks, BD18 3LF
Activities: Satellite telecommunications activities
Parent: Pace Distribution (Overseas) Limited
Officers: David Bernard Potts [1957] Director/Businessman [American]; Anthony Emilien Zuyderhoff [1971] Director [American]

Pacific Nuclear Transport Limited
Incorporated: 29 September 1975 *Employees:* 134
Net Worth: £6,150,000 *Total Assets:* £326,464,000
Registered Office: Herdus House, Ingwell Drive, Westlakes Science & Technology Park, Moor Row, Cumbria, CA24 3HU
Activities: Sea and coastal freight water transport
Officers: Helen Elizabeth Hodgson, Secretary; Peter George Buchan [1970] Director; Frederic de Agostini [1964] Director/Chief Executive [French]; Atsushi Fujioka [1965] Director/General Manager [Japanese]; Alaine Louise Greaves [1974] Director; Seth Kybird [1977] Managing Director; David Keith Peattie [1954] Director/Chief Executive Officer; Hiroaki Takiue [1963] Director/Acting General Manager

Pacific Shelf 1809 Limited
Incorporated: 26 June 2015 *Employees:* 134
Net Worth Deficit: £2,664,000 *Total Assets:* £45,026,000
Registered Office: Seabrook House, Duncombe Street, Bradford, BD8 9AJ
Activities: Activities of production holding companies
Parent: Calbee (UK) Ltd
Officers: Jonathan Bye [1963] Director; Makoto Ehara [1958] Director/Executive Vice President [Japanese]; Koichi Kikuchi [1963] Director/Senior Managing Executive Officer [Japanese]; Richard Anthony Robinson [1965] Director; Keiei Sho [1966] Director/Executive Officer [Japanese]; Jonathan Nigel Wood [1976] Commercial Director; Daniel Richard Woodwards [1977] Director

Packed Chlorine Limited
Incorporated: 20 August 2012 *Employees:* 6
Net Worth: £129,671 *Total Assets:* £8,213,470
Registered Office: 2M House, Sutton Quays Business Park, Clifton Road, Sutton Weaver, Runcorn, Cheshire, WA7 3EH
Activities: Wholesale of chemical products
Officers: Brian Robert Perry, Secretary; Colin Richard Boyle [1962] Director; Mordechai Kessler [1955] Director; Gal Maller [1977] Director

Pagref Partner Ltd
Incorporated: 10 June 2014
Net Worth: £1,224,079 *Total Assets:* £11,398,295
Registered Office: Alliance House, Westpoint Enterprise Park, Clarence Avenue, Trafford Park, Manchester, M17 1QS
Activities: Activities of other holding companies n.e.c.
Shareholders: David Russell; Property Alliance Group Ltd
Officers: David Russell [1956] Director

PAH Financial Services Limited
Incorporated: 13 January 2003
Net Worth Deficit: £1,672,000 *Total Assets:* £108,533,000
Registered Office: Epsom Avenue, Stanley Green Trading Estate, Handforth, Cheshire, SK9 3RN
Activities: Other business support service activities n.e.c.
Parent: Pet at Home Ltd
Officers: Louise Ann Stonier, Secretary; Michael James Iddon [1965] Director; Peter Pritchard [1970] Director; Louise Ann Stonier [1973] Director/Company Secretary

Paintfirst Limited
Incorporated: 27 December 2000
Net Worth: £12,986,992 *Total Assets:* £19,841,608
Registered Office: The Zenith Building, 26 Spring Gardens, Manchester, M2 1AB
Activities: Other letting and operating of own or leased real estate
Officers: Rivka Niederman, Secretary; Rivka Gross [1947] Director; David Schreiber [1952] Director; Jacob Schreiber [1974] Director

Pakeeza Dairies Limited
Incorporated: 26 January 2010 *Employees:* 188
Net Worth: £5,218,353 *Total Assets:* £8,753,882
Registered Office: Kingsway West Business Park, Moss Bridge Road, Rochdale, OL16 5LX
Activities: Liquid milk and cream production
Shareholders: Ghulam Qadir Zouq; Mohammed Azhar Zouq
Officers: Ghulam Qadir Zouq [1941] Director; Mohammed Azhar Zouq [1971] Director

Palace Chemicals Limited
Incorporated: 5 July 1978 *Employees:* 80
Net Worth: £14,417,577 *Total Assets:* £17,331,030
Registered Office: Unit 49 Compass Industrial Park West, Speke, Liverpool, L24 1YA
Activities: Manufacture of other chemical products n.e.c.
Major Shareholder: Charles Clapham
Officers: Christopher John Sweeney, Secretary; Steven Ball [1977] Commercial Director; Charles Clapham [1946] Managing Director; Wayne Clapham [1967] Production Director; Simon Clough [1960] Sales Director; James Percival [1962] Technical Director; Christopher John Sweeney [1944] Finance Director

Palletower (G.B.) Limited
Incorporated: 9 June 1967 *Employees:* 48
Net Worth: £10,542,635 *Total Assets:* £16,904,396
Registered Office: Pallet Centre Europe, Dane Road Industrial Estate, Sale, Cheshire, M33 7BH
Activities: Other transportation support activities
Major Shareholder: Matthew Robert Palmer
Officers: Matthew Robert Palmer [1972] Director; Russell John Palmer [1975] Director; Lee Spratt [1977] Director

Palletower Group Holdings Limited
Incorporated: 4 May 2001
Net Worth: £6,718,083 *Total Assets:* £6,718,083
Registered Office: Pallet Centre Europe, Dane Road Industrial Estate, Sale, Cheshire, M33 7BH
Activities: Dormant company
Officers: Matthew Robert Palmer [1972] Director; Russell John Palmer [1975] Director; Lee Spratt [1977] Director

Palmers Scaffolding UK Limited
Incorporated: 26 September 1919 *Employees:* 239
Net Worth: £2,473,000 *Total Assets:* £7,575,000
Registered Office: Business Aviation Centre, Aviation Park, Flint Road, Saltney Ferry, Chester, CH4 0GZ
Activities: Scaffold erection
Major Shareholder: Colin Charles Butt
Officers: Catherine Meighan, Secretary; Adam Colin Butt [1995] Director; Colin Charles Butt [1943] Director/Chief Executive; Lindsay Harle [1961] Director; Donald Morrison [1966] Managing Director

Panaz Holdings Limited
Incorporated: 15 September 2008 *Employees:* 87
Net Worth: £5,829,471 *Total Assets:* £12,170,122
Registered Office: Panaz HQ, Bentley Wood Way, Network 65 Business Park, Hapton, Burnley, Lancs, BB11 5ST
Activities: Manufacture of soft furnishings
Major Shareholder: Anthony John William Attard
Officers: Anthony John William Attard [1958] Director; Patricia Margaret Attard [1959] Director; Rollie Sebastian Attard [1988] Director/Panaz Ltd Chief Operating Officer; Simon James Attard [1983] Director/Panaz Ltd Product Development Co-ordinator

Panaz Limited
Incorporated: 5 September 1985 *Employees:* 82
Net Worth: £4,305,443 *Total Assets:* £8,287,231
Registered Office: Panaz HQ, Bentley Wood Way, Network 65 Business Park, Hapton, Burnley, Lancs, BB11 5ST
Activities: Manufacture of other technical and industrial textiles
Parent: Panaz Holdings Ltd
Officers: Patricia Margaret Attard, Secretary; Anthony John William Attard [1958] Managing Director; Patricia Margaret Attard [1959] Director; Carmel Marie Satterthwaite [1957] Sales & Marketing Director

Pantek Limited
Incorporated: 16 April 1997 *Employees:* 103
Net Worth: £5,778,716 *Total Assets:* £10,273,245
Registered Office: Unit 1 Oakfield Road, Cheadle Royal Business Park, Cheadle, Cheshire, SK8 3GX
Activities: Activities of head offices
Shareholders: Christine Bailey; John Edward Bailey
Officers: Christine Bailey [1954] Director; Ian Bailey [1980] Director; John Edward Bailey [1953] Director

Pantheon Estates Limited
Incorporated: 5 October 1999
Net Worth: £6,540,041 *Total Assets:* £13,061,616
Registered Office: 161 and 163-165 Picton Road, Liverpool, L15 4LG
Activities: Development of building projects
Officers: Michael Anthony Hughes, Secretary/Accountant; Michael Anthony Hughes [1964] Director/Accountant; David Peter Walker [1952] Retired Director

Paradigm Burnley Holdings Ltd
Incorporated: 21 August 2013
Net Worth: £7,913,532 *Total Assets:* £35,877,960
Registered Office: 1 Bentley Wood Way, Network 65 Business Park, Hapton, Burnley, Lancs, BB11 5TG
Activities: Activities of other holding companies n.e.c.
Officers: Ian William Bushell [1965] Director; Steven Croke [1959] Director/President and CEO [American]; Raymond Bernard Grochowski [1954] Director/General Counsel and Secretary [American]; Charles Quentin Hughes [1959] Director

Paradigm Precision Burnley Ltd
Incorporated: 26 May 2004 *Employees:* 271
Net Worth: £14,914,000 *Total Assets:* £27,278,000
Registered Office: 1 Bentley Wood Way, Network 65 Business Park, Hapton, Burnley, Lancs, BB11 5TG
Activities: Manufacture of electronic components
Parent: Paradigm Burnley Limited
Officers: Ian William Bushell [1965] Director; Steven Croke [1959] Director/President and CEO [American]; Raymond Bernard Grochowski [1954] Director/General Counsel and Secretary [American]; Charles Quentin Hughes [1959] Managing Director

Paragon Developments (Manchester) Limited
Incorporated: 27 January 2012
Net Worth: £5,639,180 *Total Assets:* £8,831,111
Registered Office: 1st Floor, NQ Building, 47 Bengal Street, Manchester, M4 6BB
Activities: Development of building projects
Major Shareholder: Daren Whitaker
Officers: Michael Shaw, Secretary; Daren Whitaker [1972] Director

Paragon Hotels Limited
Incorporated: 3 November 2015 *Employees:* 450
Net Worth: £17,691,000 *Total Assets:* £26,472,000
Registered Office: Blenheim House, Ackhurst Park, Foxhole Road, Chorley, Lancs, PR7 1NY
Activities: Activities of head offices
Major Shareholder: Trevor James Hemmings
Officers: Craig John Hemmings [1962] Director; John Clement Kay [1953] Director; Kathryn Revitt [1964] Director; Mark Lorimer Widders [1960] Finance Director

Parallel Parents Ltd
Incorporated: 26 October 2001
Net Worth: £10,828,034 *Total Assets:* £12,058,528
Registered Office: 2nd Floor, Lansdowne House, 85 Buxton Road, Heaviley, Stockport, Cheshire, SK3 8LZ
Activities: Other social work activities without accommodation n.e.c.
Shareholders: Dr Sean Anthony Fitzpatrick; Ellen Fitzpatrick
Officers: Ellen Fitzpatrick, Secretary; Dr Sean Anthony Fitzpatrick [1948] Director/Residential Childcare

Paramount Estates (Lancashire) Limited (The)
Incorporated: 26 June 1963 *Employees:* 3
Net Worth: £4,181,079 *Total Assets:* £11,275,055
Registered Office: 1 Abbots Quay, Monks Ferry, Birkenhead, Merseyside, CH41 5LH
Activities: Other letting and operating of own or leased real estate
Major Shareholder: Glyn Trevor Owens
Officers: Glyn Trevor Owens, Secretary; George Henry Edward Birch [1938] Director; Glyn Trevor Owens [1963] Director

Paraplus (Holdings) Limited
Incorporated: 30 November 2010 *Employees:* 3,360
Net Worth Deficit: £3,624,055 *Total Assets:* £9,279,524
Registered Office: Booths Park 1, Chelford Road, Knutsford, Cheshire, WA16 8GS
Activities: Temporary employment agency activities
Parent: Brookfield Rose Limited
Officers: Sam Richard Del Mar [1974] Director; Frederick Karl Minturn [1956] Director [American]; Andrew David Preston [1975] Director

Parasol Limited
Incorporated: 6 March 2000 *Employees:* 6,914
Net Worth: £10,805,736 *Total Assets:* £71,899,128
Registered Office: Optionis House, 840 Ibis Court, Centre Park, Warrington, Cheshire, WA1 1RL
Activities: Activities of head offices
Parent: Optionis Management Limited
Officers: Derek Andrew Kelly, Secretary; Kevin John Budge [1961] Director; Derek Andrew Kelly [1972] Technical Director

A.G. Parfett & Sons Limited
Incorporated: 15 January 1980 *Employees:* 558
Net Worth: £21,921,970 *Total Assets:* £84,270,816
Registered Office: Didsbury Road, Stockport, Cheshire, SK4 2JP
Activities: Non-specialised wholesale of food, beverages and tobacco
Parent: Parfetts Employee Trust Limited
Officers: David Grimes, Secretary; Barbara Anne Ashcroft [1960] Director; David Grimes [1965] Director/Chartered Accountant; Alan Godfrey Parfett [1929] Director/Wholesaler; Judith Marian Parfett [1968] Director; Patricia Ann Parfett [1948] Director; Patricia Marian Parfett [1929] Director; Stephen Parfett [1956] Director/Wholesaler; Gregory Suszczenia [1966] Director; Andrew Whitworth [1971] Director

Pario Leisure Group Limited
Incorporated: 14 March 2005
Net Worth: £3,297,288 *Total Assets:* £16,174,087
Registered Office: c/o Duncan Sheard Glass, Castle Chambers, 43 Castle Street, Liverpool, L2 9TL
Activities: Buying and selling of own real estate
Shareholders: David Wyn Williams; Samantha Flora Mollie Williams
Officers: Samantha Flora Mollie Williams, Secretary; David Wyn Williams [1966] Director; Flora Rio Ross Angharad Williams [1995] Director; Paris Mollie Jennifer Williams [1992] Director; Samantha Flora Mollie Williams [1965] Director/Secretary

E.Park & Sons Limited
Incorporated: 24 February 1972 *Employees:* 170
Net Worth: £25,328,264 *Total Assets:* £30,407,784
Registered Office: Bentworth, Lees Lane, Newton Adlington, Macclesfield, Cheshire, SK10 4LL
Activities: Processing and preserving of potatoes
Major Shareholder: Richard Park
Officers: Lynne Patricia Arnot, Secretary; Richard Park [1954] Director; Stephen Richard Park [1972] Operations Director

M H & J Park and Son Limited
Incorporated: 24 April 2006 *Employees:* 56
Net Worth: £4,602,757 *Total Assets:* £7,249,908
Registered Office: Caton Road, Lancaster, LA1 3PE
Activities: Freight transport by road
Shareholders: Simon Andrew Park; Martyn Harris Park
Officers: Joyce Park, Secretary; David Edmund Park [1970] Director/Solicitor; Joyce Park [1949] Director; Martyn Harris Park [1948] Director; Simon Andrew Park [1977] Director/Manager

Park Cakes Acquisition Limited
Incorporated: 14 November 2006 *Employees:* 1,429
Net Worth Deficit: £6,405,000 *Total Assets:* £51,217,000
Registered Office: Ashton Road, Oldham, Lancs, OL8 2ND
Activities: Other manufacturing n.e.c.
Officers: Paul Morton, Secretary; Anne Allen [1957] Director; Ken Andrew McGill [1958] Director; Paul Morton [1974] Finance Director; Gareth John Voyle [1959] Director

Park Cakes Holdings Limited
Incorporated: 21 December 2016 *Employees:* 1,447
Net Worth: £1,335,000 *Total Assets:* £76,084,000
Registered Office: Park Cakes Holdings, Ashton Road, Oldham, Lancs, OL8 2ND
Activities: Activities of head offices
Major Shareholder: Gareth Voyle
Officers: Anne Allen [1957] Director; John Edward Dutton [1954] Director; Ken Andrew McGill [1958] Director; Paul Morton [1974] Director; Gareth Voyle [1959] Director

Park Cakes Limited
Incorporated: 14 November 2006 *Employees:* 1,429
Net Worth Deficit: £5,267,000 *Total Assets:* £50,059,000
Registered Office: Ashton Road, Oldham, Lancs, OL8 2ND
Activities: Manufacture of bread; manufacture of fresh pastry goods and cakes
Officers: Paul Morton, Secretary; Anne Patricia Allen [1957] Director; Ken Andrew McGill [1958] Director; Paul Morton [1974] Finance Director; Andrew Parsons [1975] Director; Gareth John Voyle [1959] Director

Park Card Marketing Services Limited
Incorporated: 6 January 2005 *Employees:* 24
Net Worth: £2,621,044 *Total Assets:* £6,970,948
Registered Office: c/o Park Group Limited, Valley Road, Birkenhead, Merseyside, CH41 7ED
Activities: Other business support service activities n.e.c.
Parent: Park Group PLC
Officers: Timothy Patrick Clancy [1968] Finance Director; John Sullivan O'Doherty [1962] Director [Irish]

Park Card Services Limited
Incorporated: 18 November 1996
Net Worth: £1,895,582 *Total Assets:* £24,607,460
Registered Office: Valley Road, Birkenhead, Merseyside, CH41 7ED
Activities: Financial intermediation not elsewhere classified
Parent: Park Group PLC
Officers: Timothy Patrick Clancy [1968] Finance Director; John Sullivan O'Doherty [1962] Director [Irish]

Park Group PLC
Incorporated: 5 April 1983
Net Worth: £12,425,000 *Total Assets:* £143,580,992
Registered Office: Valley Road, Birkenhead, Merseyside, CH41 7ED
Activities: Activities of head offices
Officers: Russell Fairbrother, Secretary; Laura Martine Carstensen [1960] Director; Timothy Patrick Clancy [1968] Finance Director; Michael Dekare Silver [1956] Director; John Anthony Gittins [1960] Director/Accountant; John Sullivan O'Doherty [1962] Director/Chief Executive [Irish]

Park Group UK Limited
Incorporated: 29 March 2006
Net Worth: £13,427,015 *Total Assets:* £110,856,816
Registered Office: Valley Road, Birkenhead, Wirral, Merseyside, CH41 7ED
Activities: Activities of head offices
Parent: Park Group PLC
Officers: Russell Fairbrother, Secretary; Timothy Patrick Clancy [1968] Finance Director; John Sullivan O'Doherty [1962] Director [Irish]

Park Homes (UK) Limited
Incorporated: 10 April 1997 *Employees:* 331
Net Worth: £6,557,727 *Total Assets:* £10,489,844
Registered Office: 50 Brantwood Oval, Bradford, W Yorks, BD9 6QP
Activities: Other business support service activities n.e.c.
Major Shareholder: Dr Mendhy Hussain Khan
Officers: Fatima Jaffar Shahid, Secretary; Munawar Hussain [1972] Marketing Director; Dr Mendhy Hussain Khan [1968] Director/Doctor; Fatima Jaffar Shahid [1961] Director

Park Inn By Radisson Hotel Heathrow Ltd
Incorporated: 4 March 2004 *Employees:* 195
Net Worth Deficit: £18,442,000 *Total Assets:* £24,802,000
Registered Office: Chicago Avenue, Manchester, M90 3RA
Activities: Hotels and similar accommodation
Officers: Kevin John Greenwood, Secretary; Eva-Maria Margaretha Erauw [1977] Director/SVP & General Counsel, Legal [Belgian]; Sven Gosta Andreas Fondell [1973] Director/VP Group Accounting [Swedish]; Kevin John Greenwood [1957] Director/Financial Controller; Knut Jan Kleiven [1954] Director/Executive VP CFO [Norwegian]; Richard John Moore [1965] Director

Park Inn By Radisson Hotels Management Ltd
Incorporated: 22 April 2005 *Employees:* 416
Net Worth Deficit: £59,859,000 *Total Assets:* £28,979,000
Registered Office: Chicago Avenue, Manchester, M90 3RA
Activities: Hotels and similar accommodation
Officers: Kevin John Greenwood, Secretary; Eva-Maria Margaretha Erauw [1977] Director/SVP & General Counsel, Legal [Belgian]; Sven Gosta Andreas Fondell [1973] Director/VP Group Accounting [Swedish]; Kevin John Greenwood [1957] Director/Financial; Knut Jan Kleiven [1954] Director/Deputy President & CFO [Norwegian]; Richard John Moore [1965] Director

Park Inn By Radisson UK Ltd
Incorporated: 4 March 2004 *Employees:* 5
Net Worth: £110,689,000 *Total Assets:* £163,810,000
Registered Office: Chicago Avenue, Manchester, M90 3RA
Activities: Hotels and similar accommodation
Officers: Kevin John Greenwood, Secretary; Eva-Maria Margaretha Erauw [1977] Director/SVP & General Counsel Legal [Belgian]; Sven Gosta Andreas Fondell [1973] Director/VP Group Accounting [Swedish]; Kevin John Greenwood [1957] Director/Financial Controller; Knut Jan Kleiven [1954] Director/Executive VP CFO [Norwegian]; Richard John Moore [1965] Director

Park Lane Properties & Investments Limited
Incorporated: 10 March 1972
Net Worth: £11,354,307 *Total Assets:* £13,828,169
Registered Office: 6th Floor, Cardinal House, 20 St Marys Parsonage, Manchester, M3 2LG
Activities: Other letting and operating of own or leased real estate
Shareholders: Martin Gross; Leah Pearl Gross
Officers: Claire Patiniott, Secretary; Leah Pearl Gross [1944] Director; Martin Gross [1929] Director/Accountant

Park Medical Services Limited
Incorporated: 12 March 2001
Net Worth: £4,297,287 *Total Assets:* £13,332,420
Registered Office: The Brew House, Greenalls Avenue, Warrington, Cheshire, WA4 6HL
Activities: Other letting and operating of own or leased real estate
Parent: Assura Financing Limited
Officers: Orla Ball [1970] Director/Company Secretary; Paul Bryan Carroll [1969] Director/Accountant; Jayne Marie Cottam [1974] Finance Director; Simon Gould [1974] Director/Chartered Surveyor; Spencer Adrian Kenyon [1962] Director/Chartered Surveyor; Patrick William Lowther [1977] Director/Chartered Surveyor

Park Retail Limited
Incorporated: 17 December 1945 *Employees:* 281
Net Worth: £54,865,072 *Total Assets:* £170,882,432
Registered Office: Valley Road, Birkenhead, Merseyside, CH41 7ED
Activities: Other business support service activities n.e.c.
Parent: Park Group UK Limited
Officers: Timothy Patrick Clancy [1968] Finance Director; John Sullivan O'Doherty [1962] Director [Irish]

J. Parker Dutch Bulbs (Wholesale) Limited
Incorporated: 18 December 1979 *Employees:* 210
Net Worth: £5,550,571 *Total Assets:* £9,271,643
Registered Office: 14-16 Hadfield Street, Old Trafford, Manchester, M16 9FG
Activities: Retail sale of flowers, plants, seeds, fertilizers, pet animals and pet food in specialised stores
Shareholder: Christopher Anthony Martin Herman Duiker-Parker
Officers: Paul Herman Duiker Parker [1977] Managing Director; Christopher Anthony Martin Herman Duiker-Parker [1949] Director/Chairman; Daniel Christopher Duiker-Parker [1973] Director/Manager; Richard George Liversage [1961] Operations Director

Parkhaven Trust
Incorporated: 29 May 1940 *Employees:* 201
Net Worth: £8,002,618 *Total Assets:* £8,474,109
Registered Office: Administration Office, Liverpool Road South, Maghull, Merseyside, L31 8BR
Activities: Residential care activities for the elderly and disabled
Officers: Katherine Joanne Randall, Secretary; Kevin Fairclough [1983] Director/Chartered Accountant; Charles James Flynn [1953] Director; Elizabeth Rosemary Kitt [1942] Director/Volunteer; Rory McDonnell [1988] Director; John Samuel Parry [1944] Director/Retired; Hilary Torpey [1958] Director/Headteacher; Dr Julie Williams [1960] Director of Nursing Education

Parkhouse Lakeland LLP
Incorporated: 25 May 2010 *Employees:* 2
Net Worth: £3,817,267 *Total Assets:* £7,308,526
Registered Office: Houghtons Parkhouse Coachworks, Grisleymires Lane, Milnthorpe, Cumbria, LA7 7RF
Officers: Michael John Houghton [1954] Member; Pamela Audrey Houghton [1956] Member

Parkingeye Limited
Incorporated: 21 May 2004 *Employees:* 330
Net Worth: £13,429,262 *Total Assets:* £32,842,938
Registered Office: 40 Eaton Avenue, Buckshaw Village, Chorley, Lancs, PR7 7NA
Activities: Other service activities incidental to land transportation, n.e.c.
Parent: Capita Business Services Ltd
Officers: Christopher Stuart Ashburn [1968] Director; Philip Neil Boynes [1965] Director; Raja Taj [1985] Director

F. Parkinson Limited
Incorporated: 15 December 1947 *Employees:* 95
Net Worth: £873,636 *Total Assets:* £7,440,773
Registered Office: 50 Mowbray Drive, Blackpool, Lancs, FY3 7UN
Activities: Construction of commercial buildings
Officers: Robert Wilson, Secretary; Raymond John Eyre [1966] Managing Director; Stephen Robert Jackson [1970] Regional Director; Steven David Williamson [1971] Regional Director; Robert Wilson [1970] Financial Director

Parklands High School
Incorporated: 20 July 2012 *Employees:* 119
Net Worth: £8,309,000 *Total Assets:* £9,922,000
Registered Office: Parklands High School, Southport Road, Chorley, Lancs, PR7 1LL
Activities: General secondary education
Officers: Doreen Astin, Secretary; Briony Mary Boardman-Owen [1962] Director; Elizabeth Cathey [1977] Director; Fiona Rachel Eastham [1972] Director; Keith Robert Fielding [1950] Director/Head of Advertising; Daniel James Gosling [1974] Director; Julie Andrea Green [1973] Director; Judith Mary Hagarty [1937] Director/Retired; Ian Andrew Hamer [1966] Director/Distribution Manager; Marie Hunt [1959] Director; Linda Kinnaird [1958] Director; Peter Malpas [1954] Director/Retired; Steven James Mitchell [1971] Director/Deputy Headteacher; Geoffrey O'Donoghue [1954] Director [Irish]; Mark Perks [1957] Director/Teacher; Elisabeth Jane Williams [1971] Director

Parkmount Estate Company (Allerton) Limited
Incorporated: 30 October 1968
Net Worth: £7,206,465 *Total Assets:* £7,272,649
Registered Office: Keighley Business Centre, South Street, Knowle Mill, Keighley, W Yorks, BD21 1SY
Activities: Other letting and operating of own or leased real estate
Parent: Arthington Estates Limited
Officers: Elaine Kunz, Secretary; Elaine Kunz [1950] Director; Karl Antony Kunz [1957] Director/Farmer

Parkway Green Housing Trust
Incorporated: 2 September 2004 *Employees:* 160
Net Worth: £79,209,000 *Total Assets:* £139,384,000
Registered Office: 8 Poundswick Lane, Wythenshawe, Manchester, M22 9TA
Activities: Renting and operating of Housing Association real estate
Officers: Shahida Latif-Haider, Secretary; Robert William Cressey [1962] Director/Accountant; Councillor Glynn Evans [1950] Director/Retired; Clare Flynn [1959] Director/Civil Servant; Bernadette Mary Heanue [1963] Director/Events Promoter [Irish]; Ian George Hilton [1961] Director/Principal Housing Manager, Salix Homes; Sarah Alison Russell [1981] Director/Solicitor; Sam Wilson [1980] Director/Systems Analyst

Parkwood Community Leisure Limited
Incorporated: 16 January 2007 *Employees:* 851
Net Worth: £305,000 *Total Assets:* £7,065,000
Registered Office: Parkwood House, Cuerden Park, Berkeley Drive, Bamber Bridge, Preston, Lancs, PR5 6BY
Activities: Activities of sport clubs
Officers: Glen Alan Hall [1973] Leisure Director; William Giles Rawlinson [1967] Finance Director

Parkwood Leisure Holdings Limited
Incorporated: 5 March 2014 *Employees:* 1,235
Net Worth: £2,506,000 *Total Assets:* £20,945,000
Registered Office: Parkwood House, Berkeley Drive, Bamber Bridge, Preston, Lancs, PR5 6BY
Activities: Activities of head offices
Major Shareholder: Mary Patricia Hewitt
Officers: Lara Hewitt [1982] Director/Teacher; Mary Patricia Hewitt [1950] Director/Teacher; Edwin Robert Lee [1949] Director; Mike John Quayle [1969] Director; Amy Rachel Sinacola [1975] Director/Nurse

Parkwood Leisure Investments Limited
Incorporated: 17 July 2008
Net Worth: £20,000,000 *Total Assets:* £20,000,000
Registered Office: Parkwood House, Cuerden Park, Berkeley Drive, Bamber Bridge, Preston, Lancs, PR5 6BY
Activities: Management consultancy activities other than financial management
Parent: Parkwood Holdings Ltd
Officers: Mike John Quayle [1969] Director; William Giles Rawlinson [1967] Director

Parkwood Leisure Limited
Incorporated: 2 August 1996 *Employees:* 323
Net Worth: £4,242,000 *Total Assets:* £19,201,000
Registered Office: Parkwood House, Cuerden Park, Berkeley Drive, Bamber Bridge, Preston, Lancs, PR5 6BY
Activities: Other business support service activities n.e.c.
Parent: Parkwood Leisure Investments Ltd
Officers: Peter Thomas Fitzboydon [1976] Managing Director; Glen Alan Hall [1973] Operations Director; Mary Patricia Hewitt [1950] Director; William Giles Rawlinson [1967] Finance Director

Parliment Place Limited
Incorporated: 27 May 2015
Net Worth Deficit: £900 *Total Assets:* £6,832,558
Registered Office: 116 Duke Street, Liverpool, L1 5JW
Activities: Management of real estate on a fee or contract basis
Major Shareholder: Elliot Philip Lawless
Officers: Elliot Philip Lawless [1987] Director

Joseph Parr Group Limited
Incorporated: 30 December 1911 *Employees:* 249
Net Worth: £17,940,112 *Total Assets:* £27,377,604
Registered Office: Parr Building Centre, Dunnings Bridge Road, Liverpool, L30 6UU
Activities: Activities of other holding companies n.e.c.
Major Shareholder: Robert Allen Lomas
Officers: Paul Welch, Secretary; Christine Janet Jones [1970] Director/Manager; Robert Allen Lomas [1929] Director

Parry's Motor Parts Limited
Incorporated: 12 April 1965 *Employees:* 39
Net Worth: £7,610,757 *Total Assets:* £7,967,568
Registered Office: 104 Frog Lane, Wigan, Lancs, WN6 7DA
Activities: Other retail sale in non-specialised stores
Parent: Parry's Holding Limited
Officers: Norman Parry, Secretary; Barbara Parry [1932] Director/Housewife; Norman Parry [1930] Director/Engineer

Partington (Holdings) Limited
Incorporated: 28 October 2014 *Employees:* 240
Net Worth: £14,797,576 *Total Assets:* £34,774,372
Registered Office: 204 Fleetwood Road North, Thornton-Cleveleys, Lancs, FY5 4BJ
Activities: Dormant company
Shareholders: Andrea Margaret Challis; Robert Partington Kearsley
Officers: Andrea Margaret Challis [1967] Director; Robert Partington Kearsley [1969] Director

The Partington Group Limited
Incorporated: 1 February 1950
Net Worth: £6,844,216 *Total Assets:* £22,605,322
Registered Office: 204 Fleetwood Road North, Thornton-Cleveleys, Lancs, FY5 4BJ
Activities: Recreational vehicle parks, trailer parks and camping grounds
Parent: Partington Holdings
Officers: Andrea Margaret Challis [1967] Director; Robert Partington Kearsley [1969] Director

Partingtons Holiday Centres Limited
Incorporated: 13 November 1944 *Employees:* 240
Net Worth: £2,890,215 *Total Assets:* £13,889,925
Registered Office: 204 Fleetwood Road North, Thornton-Cleveleys, Lancs, FY5 4BJ
Activities: Recreational vehicle parks, trailer parks and camping grounds
Parent: The Partington Group
Officers: Andrea Margaret Challis [1967] Director; Robert Partington Kearsley [1969] Director

Partners Properties (UK) Ltd
Incorporated: 14 January 2003 *Employees:* 6
Net Worth: £5,380,000 *Total Assets:* £9,278,000
Registered Office: Ryman House, Savoy Road, Crewe, Cheshire, CW1 6NA
Activities: Other letting and operating of own or leased real estate
Shareholders: Ryman Group Limited; Sevenfathers Limited
Officers: Kirsten Lawton, Secretary; Ian Michael Childs [1956] Director; Malcolm Stanley Cooke [1942] Director; Kypros Kyprianou [1968] Commercial Director; Simon John Lakin [1967] Director/Accountant; Theodoros Paphitis [1959] Director; Richard Edward Towner [1936] Director/Solicitor

Partnership Media Group Limited
Incorporated: 20 January 1997 *Employees:* 159
Net Worth: £9,289,646 *Total Assets:* £20,265,456
Registered Office: 1 Byrom Place, Manchester, M3 3HG
Activities: Advertising agencies
Major Shareholder: Joanne Walsh
Officers: Joanne Walsh [1961] Business Director

Pathway Care Group Limited
Incorporated: 2 September 2005 *Employees:* 4
Net Worth Deficit: £16,782,772 *Total Assets:* £36,673,048
Registered Office: 1 Merchants Place, River Street, Bolton, Lancs, BL2 1BX
Activities: Activities of head offices
Parent: Fostering Solutions Limited
Officers: Helen Elizabeth Lecky, Secretary; Antony Vincent Holt [1959] Director/Chartered Accountant; Isabella Mary Hutchison [1956] Managing Director; Jean-Luc Emmanuel Janet [1970] Director [French]; David Jon Leatherbarrow [1969] Director/Group Chief Executive Officer

Pathway Care Solutions Group Limited
Incorporated: 11 May 2001 *Employees:* 43
Net Worth: £487,896 *Total Assets:* £23,510,824
Registered Office: 1 Merchants Place, River Street, Bolton, Lancs, BL2 1BX
Activities: Residential care activities for learning difficulties, mental health and substance abuse
Parent: Acorn Care and Education Limited
Officers: Helen Elizabeth Lecky, Secretary; Ryan David Edwards [1977] Finance Director; Jean-Luc Emmanuel Janet [1970] Director [French]; David Jon Leatherbarrow [1969] Director/Group Chief Executive Officer

Patrick Properties Altrincham Holdings Limited
Incorporated: 8 July 2015
Net Worth: £1,877,627 *Total Assets:* £8,291,081
Registered Office: Hamilton House, Church Street, Altrincham, Cheshire, WA14 4DR
Activities: Buying and selling of own real estate
Parent: Patrick Properties Group Ltd
Officers: Darren Karl Cornwall [1969] Director/Group CFO; Adrian Christopher Kirk [1961] Finance Director

Patrick Properties Crewe Limited
Incorporated: 20 February 2012
Net Worth: £767,289 *Total Assets:* £7,898,767
Registered Office: Hamilton House, Church Street, Altrincham, Cheshire, WA14 4DR
Activities: Other letting and operating of own or leased real estate
Parent: Patrick Properties Group Limited
Officers: Darren Karl Cornwall [1969] Director/Group CFO; Adrian Christopher Kirk [1961] Finance Director

Patrick Properties Group Ltd
Incorporated: 25 September 2013 *Employees:* 4
Net Worth: £16,698,020 *Total Assets:* £76,955,136
Registered Office: Hamilton House, Church Street, Altrincham, Cheshire, WA14 4DR
Activities: Buying and selling of own real estate
Major Shareholder: Brian George Kennedy
Officers: Darren Karl Cornwall [1969] Director/Group CFO; Adrian Christopher Kirk [1961] Finance Director

Patrick Properties Holdings Limited
Incorporated: 25 April 2003
Net Worth: £4,205,218 *Total Assets:* £15,995,175
Registered Office: Hamilton House, Church Street, Altrincham, Cheshire, WA14 4DR
Activities: Development of building projects
Officers: Timothy John Halpin, Secretary; Darren Karl Cornwall [1969] Director; Steven John Kennedy [1957] Director/Consultant; Adrian Christopher Kirk [1961] Finance Director

Patrick Properties Northampton Limited
Incorporated: 20 February 2012
Net Worth: £1,141,728 *Total Assets:* £7,378,358
Registered Office: Hamilton House, Church Street, Altrincham, Cheshire, WA14 4DR
Activities: Other letting and operating of own or leased real estate
Parent: Patrick Properties Group Limited
Officers: Darren Karl Cornwall [1969] Director/Group CFO; Adrian Christopher Kirk [1961] Finance Director

Patrick Properties Sterling Limited
Incorporated: 23 January 2009
Net Worth: £10,113,240 *Total Assets:* £40,029,252
Registered Office: Hamilton House, Church Street, Altrincham, Cheshire, WA14 4DR
Activities: Buying and selling of own real estate
Major Shareholder: Brian George Kennedy
Officers: Timothy John Halpin, Secretary; Darren Karl Cornwall [1969] Director/Group CFO; Adrian Christopher Kirk [1961] Finance Director

F.T. Patten (Holdings) Limited
Incorporated: 8 February 1993
Net Worth: £6,949,734 *Total Assets:* £9,191,569
Registered Office: 6th Floor, Cardinal House, 20 St Mary's Parsonage, Manchester, M3 2LG
Activities: Other letting and operating of own or leased real estate
Parent: Straits Holdings Limited
Officers: Susan Patten, Secretary; Neil Clifford Patten [1969] Director/Civil Engineer; Susan Patten [1971] Director/Property Surveyor

Patterson and Rothwell Limited
Incorporated: 14 September 1984 *Employees:* 211
Net Worth: £6,523,561 *Total Assets:* £15,502,667
Registered Office: Bee Mill, Shaw Road, Royton, Oldham, Lancs, OL2 6EH
Activities: Manufacture of other plastic products
Parent: Makemore Limited
Officers: Robert Keith Anderson, Secretary; Alan Rothwell [1956] Director; Lee Frederick Tilley [1960] Director

Pattinson 3 Limited
Incorporated: 5 December 2009 *Employees:* 5
Net Worth: £6,040,352 *Total Assets:* £6,754,343
Registered Office: Applegarth Middleton, Kirkby Lonsdale, Carnforth, Cumbria, LA6 2LX
Activities: Other letting and operating of own or leased real estate
Major Shareholder: Christopher Jeth Nicholson
Officers: Freya Nicholson, Secretary; Alison Nicholson [1948] Director; Christopher Jeth Nicholson [1958] Director; Freya Christobel Nicholson [1990] Director/Brand Builder; Hebe Calypso Nicholson [1992] Director/Student; Nancy Viola Nicholson [1988] Director/Theatre Set Design

Pattinson-Appleby Limited
Incorporated: 5 December 2009 *Employees:* 2
Net Worth: £7,580,901 *Total Assets:* £7,690,635
Registered Office: Low Wall, Walton, Brampton, Cumbria, CA8 2JR
Activities: Other letting and operating of own or leased real estate
Shareholders: Rafaele Mary Appleby; Timothy Appleby
Officers: Rafaele Mary Appleby [1961] Director; Timothy Appleby [1956] Director

Paw Structures Limited
Incorporated: 21 August 2002 *Employees:* 69
Net Worth: £6,251,000 *Total Assets:* £12,039,000
Registered Office: Birkbecks, Water Street, Skipton, N Yorks, BD23 1PB
Activities: Manufacture of metal structures and parts of structures
Parent: Paw Holdings Limited
Officers: Matthew Jowett [1979] Director; Paul Smith [1968] Director; James Matthew Walker [1979] Commercial Director; Clive Webberley [1967] Director; Marcus Wood [1972] Director

Paw Topco Limited
Incorporated: 31 May 2016 *Employees:* 121
Net Worth: £319,000 *Total Assets:* £39,269,000
Registered Office: Birbecks, Water Street, Skipton, N Yorks, BD23 1PB
Activities: Activities of head offices
Shareholder: LDC V LP
Officers: Dale Brent Alderson [1979] Director; Robert Edmund Paul Bodnar-Horvath [1956] Director; Matthew Jowett [1979] Director; Martyn John Vitty [1975] Director; James Matthew Walker [1979] Director; Peter Alan Walker [1948] Director; Marcus Wood [1972] Director

Paybreak Limited
Incorporated: 16 November 2010 *Employees:* 18
Net Worth: £21,307,816 *Total Assets:* £43,061,992
Registered Office: The Bloc, Ashley Road, Altrincham, Cheshire, WA14 2DW
Activities: Financial intermediation not elsewhere classified
Shareholder: Contentis B.V.
Officers: Simon Paul Evetts Dawson [1973] Technology Director; Victor Juttmann [1977] Director/Financial Advisor [Dutch]; Andrew Joseph Moore [1965] Director/Chief Executive [American]; Julie Sands [1958] Sales Director; Joost Schuijff [1962] Director [Dutch]; Julia Throop [1964] Managing Director

Paymentshield Group Holdings Limited
Incorporated: 30 August 2006
Net Worth: £96,947,920 *Total Assets:* £208,341,600
Registered Office: Paymentshield House, Wight Moss Way, Southport, Merseyside, PR8 4HQ
Activities: Activities of financial services holding companies
Parent: Towergate Insurance Limited
Officers: Geoffrey Costerton Gouriet, Secretary; Antonios Erotocritou [1971] Director/Deputy CFO [Cypriot]; Kay Alison Martin [1967] Director

Paymentshield Holdings Limited
Incorporated: 18 May 2004
Net Worth: £34,906,580 *Total Assets:* £103,678,184
Registered Office: Paymentshield House, Wight Moss Way, Southport, Merseyside, PR8 4HQ
Activities: Non-trading company
Parent: Paymentshield Group Holdings Limited
Officers: Geoffrey Costerton Gouriet, Secretary; Antonios Erotocritou [1971] Director/Deputy CFO [Cypriot]; Kay Alison Martin [1967] Director

Paymentshield Limited
Incorporated: 6 July 1992 *Employees:* 250
Net Worth: £177,403,008 *Total Assets:* £245,044,000
Registered Office: Paymentshield House, Wight Moss Way, Southport, Merseyside, PR8 4HQ
Activities: Financial intermediation not elsewhere classified
Parent: Paymentshield Holdings Limited
Officers: Geoffrey Costerton Gouriet, Secretary; Antonios Erotocritou [1971] Director/Deputy CFO [Cypriot]; Kay Alison Martin [1967] Director

J.A. Payne Limited
Incorporated: 13 November 1963 *Employees:* 5
Net Worth: £1,712,375 *Total Assets:* £6,760,269
Registered Office: 80 Deansgate Lane, Timperley, Altrincham, Cheshire, WA14 1SP
Activities: Development of building projects
Parent: Leck Group Limited
Officers: Dr David Russell Barker, Secretary; Claire Louise Barker [1978] Director/Company Publicity; Dr David Russell Barker [1976] Director; Victor Barker [1939] Director

Paystream My Max Holdings Limited
Incorporated: 11 April 2011 *Employees:* 6,152
Net Worth: £8,061,436 *Total Assets:* £27,601,142
Registered Office: Mansion House, Manchester Road, Altrincham, Cheshire, WA14 4RW
Activities: Activities of other holding companies n.e.c.
Shareholders: Paul Malley; EV Management Ltd
Officers: Clare Baker, Secretary; Jayne Louise Stirrup, Secretary; Julian Alastair Ball [1968] Legal Director; Paul Malley [1964] Director

Paystream My Max Limited
Incorporated: 5 January 2007 *Employees:* 3,278
Net Worth: £561,364 *Total Assets:* £9,434,541
Registered Office: Mansion House, Manchester Road, Altrincham, Cheshire, WA14 4RW
Activities: Temporary employment agency activities
Parent: Paystream My Max Holdings Ltd
Officers: Clare Baker, Secretary; Jayne Louise Stirrup, Secretary; Julian Alistair Bal [1968] Legal Director

Payzone UK Limited
Incorporated: 14 September 1995 *Employees:* 341
Net Worth Deficit: £12,410,735 *Total Assets:* £24,394,270
Registered Office: Andmore House, Unit 4 Triangle Court, Cheshire Business Park, Manchester Road, Lostock Gralam, Cheshire, CW9 7YL
Activities: Other information technology service activities
Officers: Mark Dann [1972] Director; Clive Ian Kahn [1957] Director; James Rupert Lowery [1965] Director; Andrew McCann [1981] Director

PBM Debury Limited
Incorporated: 27 May 2011
Net Worth: £2,573,324 *Total Assets:* £7,915,720
Registered Office: 45-51 Chorley New Road, Bolton, Lancs, BL1 4QR
Activities: Development of building projects
Shareholders: PBM Management Limited; Debury Limited
Officers: Jeremy Walker Banks [1968] Director; Paul Anthony Marshall [1969] Director

PCT Healthcare (Holdings) Limited
Incorporated: 15 October 2007 *Employees:* 1,338
Net Worth: £8,490,763 *Total Assets:* £130,848,304
Registered Office: 11 Manchester Road, Walkden, Manchester, M28 3NS
Activities: Activities of other holding companies n.e.c.
Shareholders: Peter Cattee; Angela Jane Cattee; Geoffrey Alan Tims
Officers: Angela Jane Cattee, Secretary; Angela Jane Cattee [1953] Director/Pharmacist; Peter Cattee [1952] Director/Pharmacist; Geoffrey Alan Tims [1943] Director/Pharmacist

PCT Healthcare (Properties) Limited
Incorporated: 15 January 2008
Net Worth: £3,021,596 *Total Assets:* £17,119,210
Registered Office: 11 Manchester Road, Walkden, Manchester, M28 3NS
Activities: Other letting and operating of own or leased real estate
Parent: PCT Healthcare (Holdings) Limited
Officers: Angela Jane Cattee, Secretary; Angela Jane Cattee [1953] Director/Pharmacist; Peter Cattee [1952] Director/Pharmacist; Geoffrey Alan Tims [1943] Director/Pharmacist

PCT Healthcare Limited
Incorporated: 10 November 1983 *Employees:* 951
Net Worth: £15,723,071 *Total Assets:* £73,577,496
Registered Office: 11 Manchester Road, Walkden, Manchester, M28 3NS
Activities: Dispensing chemist in specialised stores
Shareholders: Peter Cattee; Angela Jane Cattee; PCT Healthcare (Holdings) Limited
Officers: Angela Jane Cattee, Secretary; Angela Jane Cattee [1953] Director/Pharmacist; Joseph Cattee [1985] Director/Operations Manager; Peter Cattee [1952] Director/Pharmacist; Geoffrey Alan Tims [1943] Director/Pharmacist

Peabody Coaltrade International Limited
Incorporated: 2 January 2007
Net Worth Deficit: £8,567,438 *Total Assets:* £105,097,784
Registered Office: Eversheds House, 70 Great Bridgewater Street, Manchester, M1 5ES
Activities: Other business support service activities n.e.c.
Officers: Scott Jarboe, Secretary; David Richard Leslie Barham [1972] Managing Director of 9 East Shipping Limited; Bryan Galli [1960] Director/Executive [American]; Walter Leroy Hawkins Jr. [1958] Director/Senior VP Finance of Peabody Investments Corp [American]

Peakdale Molecular Limited
Incorporated: 17 June 2015
Net Worth: £231,961 *Total Assets:* £11,353,867
Registered Office: One St Peter's Square, Manchester, M2 3DE
Activities: Other research and experimental development on natural sciences and engineering
Parent: Concept Life Sciences Integrated Discovery & Development Services Limited
Officers: Michael John Fort [1959] Director; Paul McCluskey [1963] Director

Pearl Bidco Limited
Incorporated: 16 January 2008
Net Worth: £39,798,000 *Total Assets:* £43,492,000
Registered Office: Europa House, Europa Trading Estate, Stoneclough Road, Kearsley, Manchester, M26 1GG
Activities: Non-trading company
Parent: Pearl Topco Limited
Officers: Leo Damian Carroll, Secretary; Tom Riall [1960] Director; Mohammed Omar Shafi Khan [1974] Director/Chief Financial Officer

Pearl Topco Limited
Incorporated: 16 January 2008
Net Worth: £39,798,000 *Total Assets:* £39,798,000
Registered Office: Europa House, Europa Trading Estate, Stoneclough Road, Kearsley, Manchester, M26 1GG
Activities: Non-trading company
Parent: Turnstone Bidco 1 Limited
Officers: Leo Damian Carroll, Secretary; Tom Riall [1960] Director; Mohammed Omar Shafi Khan [1974] Director/Chief Financial Officer

A Pearson & Sons (1949) LLP
Incorporated: 11 May 2012 *Employees:* 48
Net Worth: £4,581,000 *Total Assets:* £8,612,000
Registered Office: Enterprise House, 97 Alderley Road, Wilmslow, Cheshire, SK9 1PT
Officers: David Pearson [1966] Member; Mark Alan Pearson [1973] Member; Philip Pearson [1963] Member; William Alan Pearson [1947] Member; Wendy Lowther [1943] LLP Member; George Raymond Pearson [1940] LLP Member; Matthew Jack Pearson [1990] LLP Member

A Pearson Holdings Limited
Incorporated: 12 March 2008 *Employees:* 652
Net Worth: £5,868,000 *Total Assets:* £60,836,000
Registered Office: Enterprise House, 97 Alderley Road, Wilmslow, Cheshire, SK9 1PT
Activities: Activities of head offices
Officers: John Edward Phibbs, Secretary; Paul Raymond Mitchell [1951] Director; Mark Pearson [1973] Director; John Edward Phibbs [1950] Director/Accountant; Matthew Joseph Widdall [1972] Director/Investor

Peaspring Limited
Incorporated: 8 February 2000 *Employees:* 124
Net Worth: £10,274,928 *Total Assets:* £14,056,951
Registered Office: c/o Brook Taverner & Co Ltd, Haincliffe Road, Ingrow, Keighley, W Yorks, BD21 5BU
Activities: Activities of head offices
Shareholders: Jo-Anne Booth; Rebecca Scott; Rachel Jones
Officers: Andrew Philip Booth, Secretary/Chartered Accountant; Andrew Philip Booth [1968] Director/Chartered Accountant; Jo-Anne Booth [1969] Director; John Benjamin Jones [1969] Managing Director; Rachel Jones [1970] Director; Jason Edwin Russell Scott [1970] Production Director; Rebecca Scott [1970] Director

Peel Airports (Liverpool) Limited
Incorporated: 18 May 1989
Net Worth: £31,641,448 *Total Assets:* £31,804,586
Registered Office: Peel Dome, intu Trafford Centre, Trafford City, Manchester, M17 8PL
Activities: Development of building projects
Parent: Peel Land Holdings Limited
Officers: Neil Lees, Secretary; Peter John Hosker [1957] Director; Neil Lees [1963] Director; John Alexander Schofield [1968] Director/Accountant

Peel Chapel No.1 Limited
Incorporated: 23 September 2013
Net Worth: £135,783,136 *Total Assets:* £281,931,424
Registered Office: Peel Dome, intu Trafford Centre, Trafford City, Manchester, M17 8PL
Activities: Other business support service activities n.e.c.
Shareholders: Sheila Greenwood; Christopher Eves; John Whittaker
Officers: Neil Lees, Secretary; Peter John Hosker [1957] Director; Neil Lees [1963] Director; Steven Keith Underwood [1974] Director; John Whittaker [1942] Director

Peel Chapel No.2 Limited
Incorporated: 23 September 2013
Net Worth: £135,783,424 *Total Assets:* £281,915,104
Registered Office: Peel Dome, intu Trafford Centre, Trafford City, Manchester, M17 8PL
Activities: Other business support service activities n.e.c.
Shareholders: Sheila Greenwood; John Whittaker; Christopher Eves
Officers: Neil Lees, Secretary; Peter John Hosker [1957] Director; Neil Lees [1963] Director; Steven Keith Underwood [1974] Director; John Whittaker [1942] Director

Peel Chapel No.3 Limited
Incorporated: 23 September 2013
Net Worth: £135,783,024 *Total Assets:* £281,915,232
Registered Office: Peel Dome, intu Trafford Centre, Trafford City, Manchester, M17 8PL
Activities: Other business support service activities n.e.c.
Shareholders: Christopher Eves; Sheila Greenwood; John Whittaker
Officers: Neil Lees, Secretary; Peter John Hosker [1957] Director; Neil Lees [1963] Director; Steven Keith Underwood [1974] Director; John Whittaker [1942] Director

Peel Chapel No.4 Limited
Incorporated: 1 June 2015
Net Worth Deficit: £28,718,188 *Total Assets:* £32,794,856
Registered Office: Peel Dome, intu Trafford Centre, Trafford City, Manchester, M17 8PL
Activities: Other business support service activities n.e.c.
Shareholders: John Whittaker; Christopher Eves; Sheila Greenwood
Officers: Neil Lees, Secretary; Peter John Hosker [1957] Director; Neil Lees [1963] Director; Steven Keith Underwood [1974] Director; John Whittaker [1942] Director

Peel Environmental Holdings Limited
Incorporated: 23 January 2006
Net Worth: £135,410 *Total Assets:* £7,226,480
Registered Office: Peel Dome, intu Trafford Centre, Trafford City, Manchester, M17 8PL
Activities: Activities of other holding companies n.e.c.
Parent: Peel Holdings (Environmental) Limited
Officers: Neil Lees, Secretary; Peter John Hosker [1957] Director; Myles Howard Kitcher [1967] Director; Neil Lees [1963] Director/Company Secretary; John Alexander Schofield [1968] Director/Accountant; Steven Keith Underwood [1974] Director; John Whittaker [1942] Director

Peel Environmental Limited
Incorporated: 9 July 2002
Net Worth: £35,872,128 *Total Assets:* £49,813,624
Registered Office: Peel Dome, intu Trafford Centre, Trafford City, Manchester, M17 8PL
Activities: Other business support service activities n.e.c.
Parent: Peel Environmental Holdings Limited
Officers: Neil Lees, Secretary; Peter John Hosker [1957] Director; Myles Howard Kitcher [1967] Director; Neil Lees [1963] Director/Company Secretary; John Alexander Schofield [1968] Director/Accountant; Steven Keith Underwood [1974] Director; John Whittaker [1942] Director

Peel Finance (UK) Limited
Incorporated: 26 June 2009
Net Worth: £2,798,702 *Total Assets:* £357,115,200
Registered Office: Peel Dome, intu Trafford Centre, Trafford City, Manchester, M17 8PL
Activities: Other business support service activities n.e.c.
Shareholders: Sheila Greenwood; Christopher Eves; John Whittaker
Officers: Neil Lees, Secretary; Peter John Hosker [1957] Director; Neil Lees [1963] Director/Company Secretary; Steven Keith Underwood [1974] Director; John Whittaker [1942] Director; Ruth Helen Woodhead [1967] Director

Peel Holdings (Environmental) Limited
Incorporated: 1 August 2006
Net Worth: £27,048,908 *Total Assets:* £32,640,208
Registered Office: Peel Dome, intu Trafford Centre, Trafford City, Manchester, M17 8PL
Activities: Activities of other holding companies n.e.c.
Parent: Peel Property Limited
Officers: Neil Lees, Secretary; Peter John Hosker [1957] Director; Neil Lees [1963] Director/Company Secretary; John Alexander Schofield [1968] Director/Accountant; Steven Keith Underwood [1974] Director; John Whittaker [1942] Director

Peel Holdings (Land and Property) Limited
Incorporated: 13 October 2005 *Employees:* 10
Net Worth: £686,060,992 *Total Assets:* £1,820,209,024
Registered Office: Peel Dome, intu Trafford Centre, Trafford City, Manchester, M17 8PL
Activities: Development of building projects
Parent: Peel Holdings Land and Property (UK) Limited
Officers: Neil Lees, Chartered Secretary; Peter John Hosker [1957] Director; Neil Lees [1963] Director/Company Secretary; John Alexander Schofield [1968] Director/Accountant; Steven Keith Underwood [1974] Director; John Whittaker [1942] Director

Peel Holdings (Management) Limited
Incorporated: 13 April 2006 *Employees:* 67
Net Worth Deficit: £598,732 *Total Assets:* £6,722,327
Registered Office: Peel Dome, intu Trafford Centre, Trafford City, Manchester, M17 8PL
Activities: Activities of head offices
Shareholders: Christopher Eves; Sheila Greenwood; John Whittaker
Officers: Neil Lees, Secretary; David Jonathan Glover [1956] Director; Peter John Hosker [1957] Director; Robert Eric Hough [1945] Director; Neil Lees [1963] Director/Company Secretary; Louise Helen Morrissey [1959] Director; Peter John Nears [1955] Director; Steven Keith Underwood [1974] Director; James Whittaker [1971] Director; John Peter Whittaker [1982] Director; John Whittaker [1942] Director; Mark Whittaker [1969] Director; Ruth Helen Woodhead [1967] Director

Peel Holdings (Media) Limited
Incorporated: 4 December 2006
Net Worth: £116,178,000 *Total Assets:* £560,156,032
Registered Office: Peel Dome, intu Trafford Centre, Trafford City, Manchester, M17 8PL
Activities: Development of building projects
Shareholders: Christopher Eves; Sheila Greenwood; John Whittaker; Legal & General Capital Investments Limited
Officers: Neil Lees, Company Secretary; Gordon Clark Aitchison [1964] Director; Catherine Laura Mason [1976] Director; Steven Keith Underwood [1974] Director; Mark Whittaker [1969] Director

Peel Holdings (Overseas) Limited
Incorporated: 7 February 2008
Net Worth: £34,078,000 *Total Assets:* £41,799,000
Registered Office: Peel Dome, intu Trafford Centre, Trafford City, Manchester, M17 8PL
Activities: Activities of other holding companies n.e.c.
Parent: Peel Holdings Land and Property (UK) Limited
Officers: Neil Lees, Secretary/Director; Peter John Hosker [1957] Director; Neil Lees [1963] Director; John Alexander Schofield [1968] Director/Accountant; Steven Keith Underwood [1974] Director; John Whittaker [1942] Director

Peel Holdings (Ports) Limited
Incorporated: 6 September 2004
Net Worth: £82,700,000 *Total Assets:* £82,700,000
Registered Office: Maritime Centre, Port of Liverpool, L21 1LA
Activities: Activities of head offices
Parent: Peel Ports UK Financeco Limited
Officers: Farook Akhtar Khan, Secretary; Caroline Ruth Marrison Gill, Secretary; Thomas Eardley Allison [1948] Director; Ian Graeme Lloyd Charnock [1962] Director; Hamish MacPhail Massie MacKenzie [1969] Director; Sundeep Vyas [1973] Director; John Whittaker [1942] Director; Mark Whitworth [1966] Director

Peel Holdings (Real Estate) Limited
Incorporated: 1 August 2006
Net Worth: £37,269,000 *Total Assets:* £100,665,000
Registered Office: Peel Dome, intu Trafford Centre, Trafford City, Manchester, M17 8PL
Activities: Development of building projects
Parent: Peel Real Estate Group Limited
Officers: Neil Lees, Secretary; Peter John Hosker [1957] Director; Neil Lees [1963] Director/Company Secretary; John Alexander Schofield [1968] Director/Accountant; Steven Keith Underwood [1974] Director; John Whittaker [1942] Director

Peel Holdings Land and Property (UK) Limited
Incorporated: 7 February 2008 *Employees:* 148
Net Worth: £499,360,000 *Total Assets:* £1,792,530,048
Registered Office: Peel Dome, intu Trafford Centre, Trafford City, Manchester, M17 8PL
Activities: Development of building projects
Shareholders: Christopher Eves; Sheila Greenwood; John Whittaker
Officers: Neil Lees, Secretary; Peter John Hosker [1957] Director; Neil Lees [1963] Director; John Alexander Schofield [1968] Director/Accountant; Steven Keith Underwood [1974] Director; John Whittaker [1942] Director

Peel Investment Properties Holdings Limited
Incorporated: 23 May 2012 *Employees:* 6
Net Worth Deficit: £17,902,000 *Total Assets:* £64,867,000
Registered Office: Peel Dome, intu Trafford Centre, Trafford City, Manchester, M17 8PL
Activities: Other business support service activities n.e.c.
Parent: Peel Investments (Land & Property) No.2 Limited
Officers: Neil Lees, Secretary; Peter John Hosker [1957] Director; Neil Lees [1963] Director; John Alexander Schofield [1968] Director/Accountant; Steven Keith Underwood [1974] Director; John Whittaker [1942] Director

Peel Investment Properties Limited
Incorporated: 28 July 1998 *Employees:* 6
Net Worth Deficit: £12,936,000 *Total Assets:* £63,748,000
Registered Office: Peel Dome, intu Trafford Centre, Trafford City, Manchester, M17 8PL
Activities: Other business support service activities n.e.c.
Parent: Peel Investment Properties Holdings Limited
Officers: Neil Lees, Secretary; Peter John Hosker [1957] Director; Neil Lees [1963] Director/Company Secretary; John Alexander Schofield [1968] Director/Accountant; Steven Keith Underwood [1974] Director; John Whittaker [1942] Director

Peel Investments (Intermediate) Limited
Incorporated: 6 February 2008
Net Worth Deficit: £54,523,000 *Total Assets:* £37,839,000
Registered Office: Peel Dome, intu Trafford Centre, Trafford City, Manchester, M17 8PL
Activities: Development of building projects
Parent: Peel Holdings Land and Property (UK) Limited
Officers: Neil Lees, Secretary/Director; Peter John Hosker [1957] Director; Neil Lees [1963] Director; John Alexander Schofield [1968] Director/Accountant; Steven Keith Underwood [1974] Director; John Whittaker [1942] Director; Mark Whittaker [1969] Director

Peel Investments (Land and Property) No.1 Limited
Incorporated: 1 March 2011 *Employees:* 7
Net Worth: £117,351,000 *Total Assets:* £334,464,992
Registered Office: Peel Dome, intu Trafford Centre, Trafford City, Manchester, M17 8PL
Activities: Development of building projects
Parent: Peel Investments Holdings Limited
Officers: Neil Lees, Secretary; Peter John Hosker [1957] Director; Neil Lees [1963] Director; John Alexander Schofield [1968] Director/Accountant; Steven Keith Underwood [1974] Director; John Whittaker [1942] Director; Mark Whittaker [1969] Director

Peel Investments (Land and Property) No.2 Limited
Incorporated: 21 May 2012 *Employees:* 6
Net Worth: £23,127,000 *Total Assets:* £39,070,000
Registered Office: Peel Dome, intu Trafford Centre, Trafford City, Manchester, M17 8PL
Activities: Activities of other holding companies n.e.c.
Parent: Peel Property Limited
Officers: Neil Lees, Secretary; Peter John Hosker [1957] Director; Neil Lees [1963] Director; John Alexander Schofield [1968] Director/Accountant; Steven Keith Underwood [1974] Director; John Whittaker [1942] Director

Peel Investments (Ljla) Limited
Incorporated: 18 March 2014 *Employees:* 2
Net Worth Deficit: £1,475,820 *Total Assets:* £13,077,948
Registered Office: Peel Dome, intu Trafford Centre, Trafford City, Manchester, M17 8PL
Activities: Other business support service activities n.e.c.
Shareholders: Christopher Eves; Sheila Greenwood; John Whittaker
Officers: Neil Lees, Secretary; Steven Keith Underwood [1974] Director; John Whittaker [1942] Director

Peel Investments (North) Limited
Incorporated: 10 February 1923
Net Worth: £260,020,000 *Total Assets:* £297,996,992
Registered Office: Peel Dome, intu Trafford Centre, Trafford City, Manchester, M17 8PL
Activities: Development of building projects
Parent: Peel Land Holdings Limited
Officers: Neil Lees, Secretary; Peter John Hosker [1957] Director; Neil Lees [1963] Director/Company Secretary; John Alexander Schofield [1968] Director/Accountant; Steven Keith Underwood [1974] Director; John Whittaker [1942] Director; Mark Whittaker [1969] Director

Peel Investments (U.K.) Limited
Incorporated: 2 March 2004 *Employees:* 6
Net Worth: £662,049,984 *Total Assets:* £1,000,734,976
Registered Office: Peel Dome, intu Trafford Centre, Trafford City, Manchester, M17 8PL
Activities: Activities of other holding companies n.e.c.
Parent: Peel Land and Property Limited
Officers: Neil Lees, Secretary; Peter John Hosker [1957] Director; Neil Lees [1963] Director/Company Secretary; John Alexander Schofield [1968] Director/Accountant; Steven Keith Underwood [1974] Director; John Whittaker [1942] Director

Peel Investments Holdings Limited
Incorporated: 6 February 2008 *Employees:* 10
Net Worth: £825,692,032 *Total Assets:* £1,956,715,008
Registered Office: Peel Dome, intu Trafford Centre, Trafford City, Manchester, M17 8PL
Activities: Development of building projects
Parent: Peel Investments (U.K.) Limited
Officers: Neil Lees, Secretary/Director; Peter John Hosker [1957] Director; Neil Lees [1963] Director; John Alexander Schofield [1968] Director/Accountant; Steven Keith Underwood [1974] Director; John Whittaker [1942] Director

Peel Land (Intermediate) Limited
Incorporated: 6 February 2008
Net Worth: £8,735,000 *Total Assets:* £126,000,000
Registered Office: Peel Dome, intu Trafford Centre, Trafford City, Manchester, M17 8PL
Activities: Development of building projects
Parent: Peel Land Holdings Limited
Officers: Neil Lees, Secretary/Director; Peter John Hosker [1957] Director; Neil Lees [1963] Director; John Alexander Schofield [1968] Director/Accountant; Steven Keith Underwood [1974] Director; John Whittaker [1942] Director; Mark Whittaker [1969] Director

Peel Land and Property (Ports No. 3) Limited
Incorporated: 7 February 2008
Net Worth: £57,115,000 *Total Assets:* £285,598,016
Registered Office: Peel Dome, intu Trafford Centre, Trafford City, Manchester, M17 8PL
Activities: Development of building projects
Parent: Peel Investments (Land and Property) No.1 Limited
Officers: Neil Lees, Secretary/Director; Peter John Hosker [1957] Director; Neil Lees [1963] Director; John Alexander Schofield [1968] Director/Accountant; Steven Keith Underwood [1974] Director; John Whittaker [1942] Director; Mark Whittaker [1969] Director

Peel Land and Property (Ports) Limited
Incorporated: 1 August 2006 *Employees:* 7
Net Worth: £112,354,000 *Total Assets:* £124,345,000
Registered Office: Peel Dome, intu Trafford Centre, Trafford City, Manchester, M17 8PL
Activities: Development of building projects
Parent: Peel Land Holdings Limited
Officers: Neil Lees, Secretary; Peter John Hosker [1957] Director; Neil Lees [1963] Director/Company Secretary; John Alexander Schofield [1968] Director/Accountant; Steven Keith Underwood [1974] Director; John Whittaker [1942] Director; Mark Whittaker [1969] Director

Peel Land and Property Holdings Limited
Incorporated: 25 January 2006 *Employees:* 6
Net Worth: £329,620,992 *Total Assets:* £811,145,984
Registered Office: Peel Dome, intu Trafford Centre, Trafford City, Manchester, M17 8PL
Activities: Activities of other holding companies n.e.c.
Parent: Peel Holdings (Land and Property) Limited
Officers: Neil Lees, Secretary; Peter John Hosker [1957] Director; Neil Lees [1963] Director/Company Secretary; John Alexander Schofield [1968] Director/Accountant; Steven Keith Underwood [1974] Director; John Whittaker [1942] Director

Peel Land and Property Investments (CL) Limited
Incorporated: 28 April 2006
Net Worth Deficit: £7,090,427 *Total Assets:* £36,167,440
Registered Office: Peel Dome, intu Trafford Centre, Trafford City, Manchester, M17 8PL
Activities: Non-trading company
Parent: Peel Land and Property Holdings (CL) Limited
Officers: Neil Lees, Secretary; Peter John Hosker [1957] Director; Neil Lees [1963] Director/Company Secretary; John Alexander Schofield [1968] Director/Accountant; Steven Keith Underwood [1974] Director John Whittaker [1942] Director; Mark Whittaker [1969] Director

Peel Land and Property Investments PLC
Incorporated: 30 April 1920 *Employees:* 10
Net Worth: £299,001,984 *Total Assets:* £595,198,016
Registered Office: Peel Dome, intu Trafford Centre, Trafford City, Manchester, M17 8PL
Activities: Development of building projects
Parent: Peel Investments Holdings Limited
Officers: Neil Lees, Secretary; David Jonathan Glover [1956] Director; Peter John Hosker [1957] Director; Neil Lees [1963] Director/Company Secretary; John Alexander Schofield [1968] Director/Accountant; Steven Keith Underwood [1974] Director; John Whittaker [1942] Director; Mark Whittaker [1969] Director

Peel Land and Property Limited
Incorporated: 2 March 2004 *Employees:* 6
Net Worth: £666,654,976 *Total Assets:* £906,110,016
Registered Office: Peel Dome, intu Trafford Centre, Trafford City, Manchester, M17 8PL
Activities: Activities of other holding companies n.e.c.
Parent: Peel Land and Property Holdings Limited
Officers: Neil Lees, Secretary; Peter John Hosker [1957] Director; Neil Lees [1963] Director/Company Secretary; John Alexander Schofield [1968] Director/Accountant; Steven Keith Underwood [1974] Director; John Whittaker [1942] Director

Peel Land Holdings Limited
Incorporated: 6 February 2008
Net Worth: £155,328,000 *Total Assets:* £547,180,992
Registered Office: Peel Dome, intu Trafford Centre, Trafford City, Manchester, M17 8PL
Activities: Activities of other holding companies n.e.c.
Parent: Peel Property Limited
Officers: Neil Lees, Secretary/Director; Peter John Hosker [1957] Director; Neil Lees [1963] Director; John Alexander Schofield [1968] Director/Accountant; Steven Keith Underwood [1974] Director; John Whittaker [1942] Director

Peel Leisure (Operations) Holdings Limited
Incorporated: 17 March 2014 *Employees:* 5
Net Worth Deficit: £28,070 *Total Assets:* £8,580,189
Registered Office: Peel Dome, intu Trafford Centre, Trafford City, Manchester, M17 8PL
Activities: Activities of other holding companies n.e.c.
Shareholders: John Whittaker; Christopher Eves; Sheila Greenwood
Officers: Neil Lees, Secretary; Peter John Hosker [1957] Director; Neil Lees [1963] Director; Steven Keith Underwood [1974] Director; John Whittaker [1942] Director

Peel Leisure (Operations) Limited
Incorporated: 4 September 2008
Net Worth Deficit: £2,556,491 *Total Assets:* £6,809,201
Registered Office: Peel Dome, intu Trafford Centre, Trafford City, Manchester, M17 8PL
Activities: Activities of other holding companies n.e.c.
Parent: Peel Leisure (Operations) Holdings Limited
Officers: Neil Lees, Secretary; Peter William de La Perrelle [1951] Director; Peter John Hosker [1957] Director; Neil Lees [1963] Director; Steven Keith Underwood [1974] Director; John Whittaker [1942] Director

Peel Media (Holdings) Limited
Incorporated: 4 December 2006
Net Worth: £102,755,000 *Total Assets:* £528,332,000
Registered Office: Peel Dome, intu Trafford Centre, Trafford City, Manchester, M17 8PL
Activities: Development of building projects
Parent: Peel Holdings (Media) Limited
Officers: Neil Lees, Company Secretary; Gordon Clark Aitchison [1964] Director; Catherine Laura Mason [1976] Director; Steven Keith Underwood [1974] Director; Mark Whittaker [1969] Director

Peel Media Development (Holdings) Limited
Incorporated: 21 January 2014 *Employees:* 4
Net Worth Deficit: £4,000 *Total Assets:* £11,031,000
Registered Office: Peel Dome, intu Trafford Centre, Trafford City, Manchester, M17 8PL
Activities: Activities of construction holding companies
Parent: Peel Holdings (Media) Limited
Officers: Neil Lees, Secretary; Gordon Clark Aitchison [1964] Director; Catherine Laura Mason [1976] Director; Steven Keith Underwood [1974] Director; Mark Whittaker [1969] Director

Peel Media Digital (Holdings) Limited
Incorporated: 2 December 2013
Net Worth: £3,319,000 *Total Assets:* £15,856,000
Registered Office: Peel Dome, intu Trafford Centre, Trafford City, Manchester, M17 8PL
Activities: Other business support service activities n.e.c.
Shareholders: Christopher Eves; Sheila Greenwood; John Whittaker
Officers: Neil Lees, Secretary; Neil Lees [1963] Director; John Alexander Schofield [1968] Director/Accountant; Steven Keith Underwood [1974] Director; John Whittaker [1942] Director

Peel Media Limited
Incorporated: 14 November 2006 *Employees:* 4
Net Worth: £138,538,000 *Total Assets:* £528,153,984
Registered Office: Peel Dome, intu Trafford Centre, Trafford City, Manchester, M17 8PL
Activities: Development of building projects
Parent: Peel Media (Holdings) Limited
Officers: Neil Lees, Company Secretary; Gordon Clark Aitchison [1964] Director; Catherine Laura Mason [1976] Director; Steven Keith Underwood [1974] Director; Mark Whittaker [1969] Director

Peel Media Management (Holdings) Limited
Incorporated: 25 November 2011
Net Worth Deficit: £9,104,000 *Total Assets:* £14,675,000
Registered Office: Peel Dome, intu Trafford Centre, Trafford City, Manchester, M17 8PL
Activities: Other business support service activities n.e.c.
Shareholders: Christopher Eves; Sheila Greenwood; John Whittaker
Officers: Neil Lees, Secretary; Neil Lees [1963] Director; John Alexander Schofield [1968] Director/Accountant; Steven Keith Underwood [1974] Director; John Whittaker [1942] Director

Peel Media Studios Holdings Limited
Incorporated: 17 March 2014 *Employees:* 160
Net Worth Deficit: £18,137,000 *Total Assets:* £31,699,000
Registered Office: Peel Dome, intu Trafford Centre, Trafford City, Manchester, M17 8PL
Activities: Other letting and operating of own or leased real estate
Shareholders: Christopher Eves; Sheila Greenwood; John Whittaker
Officers: Neil Lees, Secretary; Peter John Hosker [1957] Director; Neil Lees [1963] Director; Steven Keith Underwood [1974] Director; John Whittaker [1942] Director

Peel Media Studios Limited
Incorporated: 4 December 2006 *Employees:* 5
Net Worth Deficit: £18,935,000 *Total Assets:* £25,002,000
Registered Office: Peel Dome, intu Trafford Centre, Trafford City, Manchester, M17 8PL
Activities: Television programme distribution activities
Parent: Peel Media Studios Holdings Limited
Officers: Neil Lees, Company Secretary; David Jonathan Glover [1956] Director; Neil Lees [1963] Director/Company Secretary; Steven Keith Underwood [1974] Director; John Whittaker [1942] Director

Peel Outlets (Gloucester) Limited
Incorporated: 7 February 2008 *Employees:* 6
Net Worth: £48,234,000 *Total Assets:* £112,333,000
Registered Office: Peel Dome, intu Trafford Centre, Trafford City, Manchester, M17 8PL
Activities: Activities of other holding companies n.e.c.
Shareholders: Christopher Eves; Sheila Greenwood; John Whittaker
Officers: Neil Lees, Secretary/Director; Peter John Hosker [1957] Director; Neil Lees [1963] Director; John Alexander Schofield [1968] Director/Accountant; Steven Keith Underwood [1974] Director; John Whittaker [1942] Director; Mark Whittaker [1969] Director

Peel Overseas Limited
Incorporated: 27 May 1986 *Employees:* 7
Net Worth Deficit: £497,189 *Total Assets:* £19,630,140
Registered Office: Peel Dome, intu Trafford Centre, Trafford City, Manchester, M17 8PL
Activities: Activities of other holding companies n.e.c.
Parent: Peel Holdings (Overseas) Limited
Officers: Neil Lees, Secretary; David Jonathan Glover [1956] Director; Peter John Hosker [1957] Director; Neil Lees [1963] Director/Company Secretary; John Alexander Schofield [1968] Director/Accountant; Steven Keith Underwood [1974] Director; John Whittaker [1942] Director

Peel Ports Group Limited
Incorporated: 12 October 2006 *Employees:* 2,344
Net Worth Deficit: £1,680,800,000 *Total Assets:* £1,629,400,064
Registered Office: Maritime Centre, Port of Liverpool, L21 1LA
Activities: Activities of head offices
Shareholders: Christopher Eves; John Whittaker; Sheila Greenwood
Officers: Farook Akhtar Khan, Secretary; Caroline Ruth Marrison Gill, Secretary; Thomas Eardley Allison [1948] Director; Ian Graeme Lloyd Charnock [1962] Director; Hamish MacPhail Massie MacKenzie [1969] Director; Steven Keith Underwood [1974] Director; Sundeep Vyas [1973] Director; John Whittaker [1942] Director; Mark Whitworth [1966] Director

Peel Ports Holdings Limited
Incorporated: 11 October 2002
Net Worth Deficit: £158,500,000 *Total Assets:* £1,811,000,064
Registered Office: Maritime Centre, Port of Liverpool, L21 1LA
Activities: Activities of head offices
Parent: Peel Holdings (Ports) Limited
Officers: Farook Akhtar Khan, Secretary; Caroline Ruth Marrison Gill, Secretary; Thomas Eardley Allison [1948] Director; Ian Graeme Lloyd Charnock [1962] Director; John Whittaker [1942] Director; Mark Whitworth [1966] Director

Peel Ports Intermediate Holdco Limited
Incorporated: 26 October 2006
Net Worth: £337,800,000 *Total Assets:* £460,800,000
Registered Office: Maritime Centre, Port of Liverpool, L21 1LA
Activities: Activities of head offices
Parent: Peel Ports Group Limited
Officers: Farook Akhtar Khan, Secretary; Caroline Ruth Marrison Gill, Secretary; Thomas Eardley Allison [1948] Director; Ian Graeme Lloyd Charnock [1962] Director; Peter John Hosker [1957] Director; John Whittaker [1942] Director; Mark Whitworth [1966] Director

Peel Ports Investments Limited
Incorporated: 22 April 2005 *Employees:* 138
Net Worth: £292,200,000 *Total Assets:* £1,618,700,032
Registered Office: Maritime Centre, Port of Liverpool, L21 1LA
Activities: Activities of head offices
Parent: Peel Ports Holdings Limited
Officers: Farook Akhtar Khan, Secretary; Caroline Ruth Marrison Gill, Secretary; Thomas Eardley Allison [1948] Director; Ian Graeme Lloyd Charnock [1962] Director; John Whittaker [1942] Director; Mark Whitworth [1966] Director

Peel Ports Land and Property Investments Limited
Incorporated: 22 April 2005
Net Worth: £1,761,000 *Total Assets:* £47,386,000
Registered Office: Maritime Centre, Port of Liverpool, L21 1LA
Activities: Activities of head offices
Parent: Peel Holdings (Ports) Limited
Officers: Farook Akhtar Khan, Secretary; Caroline Ruth Marrison Gill, Secretary; Thomas Eardley Allison [1948] Director; Ian Graeme Lloyd Charnock [1962] Director; John Whittaker [1942] Director; Mark Whitworth [1966] Director

Peel Ports Limited
Incorporated: 11 October 2002
Net Worth: £82,200,000 *Total Assets:* £3,942,200,064
Registered Office: Maritime Centre, Port of Liverpool, L21 1LA
Activities: Activities of head offices
Parent: Peel Ports Holdings Limited
Officers: Farook Akhtar Khan, Secretary; Caroline Ruth Marrison Gill, Secretary; Thomas Eardley Allison [1948] Director; Ian Graeme Lloyd Charnock [1962] Director; Steven Keith Underwood [1974] Director; John Whittaker [1942] Director; Mark Whitworth [1966] Director

Peel Ports Operations Limited
Incorporated: 13 March 2005
Net Worth: £10,900,000 *Total Assets:* £354,400,000
Registered Office: Maritime Centre, Port of Liverpool, L21 1LA
Activities: Activities of head offices
Parent: Peel Ports Investments Limited
Officers: Farook Akhtar Khan, Secretary; Caroline Ruth Marrison Gill, Secretary; Thomas Eardley Allison [1948] Director; Ian Graeme Lloyd Charnock [1962] Director; Steven Keith Underwood [1974] Director; John Whittaker [1942] Director; Mark Whitworth [1966] Director

Peel Ports UK Financeco Limited
Incorporated: 15 August 2006
Net Worth: £333,500,000 *Total Assets:* £841,600,000
Registered Office: Maritime Centre, Port of Liverpool, L21 1LA
Activities: Activities of head offices
Parent: Peel Ports Intermediate Holdco Limited
Officers: Farook Akhtar Khan, Secretary; Caroline Ruth Marrison Gill, Secretary; Thomas Eardley Allison [1948] Director; Ian Graeme Lloyd Charnock [1962] Director; Peter John Hosker [1957] Director; John Whittaker [1942] Director; Mark Whitworth [1966] Director

Peel Property (Investments) Limited
Incorporated: 1 March 2011
Net Worth: £61,514,000 *Total Assets:* £227,752,000
Registered Office: Peel Dome, intu Trafford Centre, Trafford City, Manchester, M17 8PL
Activities: Development of building projects
Parent: Peel Investments (Land and Property) No.1 Limited
Officers: Neil Lees, Secretary; Peter John Hosker [1957] Director; Neil Lees [1963] Director; John Alexander Schofield [1968] Director/Accountant; Steven Keith Underwood [1974] Director; John Whittaker [1942] Director; Mark Whittaker [1969] Director

Peel Property (No.2) Limited
Incorporated: 2 March 2004 *Employees:* 6
Net Worth: £10,695,771 *Total Assets:* £81,940,056
Registered Office: Peel Dome, intu Trafford Centre, Trafford City, Manchester, M17 8PL
Activities: Activities of other holding companies n.e.c.
Parent: Peel Investments (U.K.) Limited
Officers: Neil Lees, Secretary; Peter John Hosker [1957] Director; Neil Lees [1963] Director/Company Secretary; John Alexander Schofield [1968] Director/Accountant; Steven Keith Underwood [1974] Director; John Whittaker [1942] Director

Peel Property (Partnerships) Limited
Incorporated: 16 January 2008 *Employees:* 6
Net Worth Deficit: £3,674,477 *Total Assets:* £18,830,840
Registered Office: Peel Dome, intu Trafford Centre, Trafford City, Manchester, M17 8PL
Activities: Activities of other holding companies n.e.c.
Parent: Peel Holdings Land and Property (UK) Limited
Officers: Neil Lees, Secretary; Peter John Hosker [1957] Director; Neil Lees [1963] Director/Company Secretary; John Alexander Schofield [1968] Director/Accountant; Steven Keith Underwood [1974] Director; John Whittaker [1942] Director

Peel Property Holdings Limited
Incorporated: 18 June 2013
Net Worth: £178,340,000 *Total Assets:* £696,974,016
Registered Office: Peel Dome, intu Trafford Centre, Trafford City, Manchester, M17 8PL
Activities: Activities of construction holding companies
Parent: Peel Investments Holdings Limited
Officers: Neil Lees, Secretary; Peter John Hosker [1957] Director; Neil Lees [1963] Director; John Alexander Schofield [1968] Director/Accountant; Steven Keith Underwood [1974] Director; John Whittaker [1942] Director

Peel Property Intermediate Limited
Incorporated: 30 November 2012 *Employees:* 7
Net Worth: £16,225,000 *Total Assets:* £60,332,000
Registered Office: Peel Dome, intu Trafford Centre, Trafford City, Manchester, M17 8PL
Activities: Development of building projects
Parent: Peel Property Limited
Officers: Neil Lees, Secretary; Peter John Hosker [1957] Director; Neil Lees [1963] Director; John Alexander Schofield [1968] Director/Accountant; Steven Keith Underwood [1974] Director; John Whittaker [1942] Director; Mark Whittaker [1969] Director

Peel Property Limited
Incorporated: 20 June 2013 *Employees:* 6
Net Worth: £5,532,000 *Total Assets:* £379,475,008
Registered Office: Peel Dome, intu Trafford Centre, Trafford City, Manchester, M17 8PL
Activities: Activities of construction holding companies
Parent: Peel Property Holdings Limited
Officers: Neil Lees, Secretary; Peter John Hosker [1957] Director; Neil Lees [1963] Director; John Alexander Schofield [1968] Director/Accountant; Steven Keith Underwood [1974] Director; John Whittaker [1942] Director

Peel Real Estate (Properties) Limited
Incorporated: 11 April 2006
Net Worth: £16,797,700 *Total Assets:* £85,769,896
Registered Office: Peel Dome, intu Trafford Centre, Trafford City, Manchester, M17 8PL
Activities: Development of building projects
Parent: Peel Holdings (Real Estate) Limited
Officers: Neil Lees, Company Secretary; Peter John Hosker [1957] Director; Neil Lees [1963] Director/Company Secretary; John Alexander Schofield [1968] Director/Accountant; Steven Keith Underwood [1974] Director; John Whittaker [1942] Director

Peel Real Estate Developments Holdings Limited
Incorporated: 22 June 2009
Net Worth: £7,720,933 *Total Assets:* £7,748,889
Registered Office: Peel Dome, intu Trafford Centre, Trafford City, Manchester, M17 8PL
Activities: Activities of other holding companies n.e.c.
Parent: Peel Real Estate Group Limited
Officers: Neil Lees, Secretary; Peter John Hosker [1957] Director; Neil Lees [1963] Director/Company Secretary; John Alexander Schofield [1968] Director/Accountant; Steven Keith Underwood [1974] Director; John Whittaker [1942] Director

Peel Real Estate Group Limited
Incorporated: 17 February 2010
Net Worth: £39,494,000 *Total Assets:* £102,483,000
Registered Office: Peel Dome, intu Trafford Centre, Trafford City, Manchester, M17 8PL
Activities: Activities of other holding companies n.e.c.
Shareholders: John Whittaker; Christopher Eves; Sheila Greenwood
Officers: Neil Lees, Secretary; Peter John Hosker [1957] Director; Neil Lees [1963] Director; John Alexander Schofield [1968] Director/Accountant; Steven Keith Underwood [1974] Director; John Whittaker [1942] Director

Peel South East Limited
Incorporated: 15 September 1926
Net Worth: £276,584,000 *Total Assets:* £433,348,992
Registered Office: Peel Dome, intu Trafford Centre, Trafford City, Manchester, M17 8PL
Activities: Development of building projects
Parent: Peel Investments Holdings Limited
Officers: Neil Lees, Secretary; Peter John Hosker [1957] Director; Neil Lees [1963] Director/Company Secretary; John Alexander Schofield [1968] Director/Accountant; Steven Keith Underwood [1974] Director; John Whittaker [1942] Director; Mark Whittaker [1969] Director

Peel Water Services Holdings Limited
Incorporated: 24 August 2011
Net Worth: £43,962,000 *Total Assets:* £68,126,000
Registered Office: Peel Dome, intu Trafford Centre, Trafford City, Manchester, M17 8PL
Activities: Other service activities n.e.c.
Shareholders: Sheila Greenwood; Christopher Eves; John Whittaker
Officers: Neil Lees, Secretary; David Jonathan Glover [1956] Director; Peter John Hosker [1957] Director; Neil Lees [1963] Director/Company Secretary; John Alexander Schofield [1968] Director/Accountant; Steven Keith Underwood [1974] Director; John Whittaker [1942] Director

Peel Water Services Limited
Incorporated: 22 August 2008 *Employees:* 7
Net Worth: £43,467,720 *Total Assets:* £67,598,176
Registered Office: Peel Dome, intu Trafford Centre, Trafford City, Manchester, M17 8PL
Activities: Water collection, treatment and supply
Parent: Peel Water Services Holdings Limited
Officers: Neil Lees, Secretary; David Jonathan Glover [1956] Director; Peter John Hosker [1957] Director; Neil Lees [1963] Director/Secretary; John Alexander Schofield [1968] Director/Accountant; Steven Keith Underwood [1974] Director; John Whittaker [1942] Director

Peel Wind Farms (Sheerness) Limited
Incorporated: 12 November 2009
Net Worth: £4,910,210 *Total Assets:* £7,546,163
Registered Office: Peel Dome, intu Trafford Centre, Trafford City, Manchester, M17 8PL
Activities: Production of electricity
Shareholders: Christopher Eves; Sheila Greenwood; John Whittaker
Officers: Neil Lees, Secretary; Neil Lees [1963] Director; David Muir Miller [1954] Director; John Alexander Schofield [1968] Director/Accountant; Steven Keith Underwood [1974] Director; John Whittaker [1942] Director

Peelclose Properties Limited
Incorporated: 10 November 1971
Net Worth: £6,090,748 *Total Assets:* £10,358,837
Registered Office: 71-73 Hoghton Street, Southport, Merseyside, PR9 0PR
Activities: Renting and operating of Housing Association real estate
Major Shareholder: Louis Isaac Silverbeck
Officers: Stella Lyn Silverbeck, Secretary; Louis Isaac Silverbeck [1944] Director

Harry Peers & Co Limited
Incorporated: 30 April 1934 *Employees:* 60
Net Worth: £7,561,586 *Total Assets:* £19,574,806
Registered Office: Elton Street, Bolton, Lancs, BL2 2BS
Activities: Other specialised construction activities n.e.c.
Major Shareholder: Michael Harry Peers
Officers: Jean Dorothy June Peers [1928] Director/Design Consultant; Michael Harry Peers [1954] Director/Engineer

Harry Peers Steelwork Limited
Incorporated: 10 September 1982 *Employees:* 59
Net Worth: £3,556,556 *Total Assets:* £15,746,789
Registered Office: Elton Street, Mill Hill, Bolton, Lancs, BL2 2BS
Activities: Other specialised construction activities n.e.c.
Parent: Harry Peers & Co Limited
Officers: Michael Harry Peers [1954] Director/Engineer

Pemberton Park and Leisure Homes Limited
Incorporated: 3 July 1980 *Employees:* 203
Net Worth: £13,677,179 *Total Assets:* £19,527,592
Registered Office: Woodhouse Lane, Wigan, Lancs, WN6 7NF
Activities: Manufacture of caravans
Parent: Pemberton Caravans Limited
Officers: John Peter Finch, Secretary; John Peter Finch [1968] Director/Chartered Accountant; Nahill Asim Abdul Razak Haj Younis [1968] Director/Treasurer Investment Banking; Kevin Dermott McAdam [1942] Director

Pendle Education Trust
Incorporated: 22 October 2012 *Employees:* 237
Net Worth: £9,965,000 *Total Assets:* £14,357,000
Registered Office: Nelson and Colne College, Scotland Road, Nelson, Lancs, BB9 7YT
Activities: Primary education
Officers: David John Franklin [1948] Director/Retired; Dean Edwin Langton [1969] Director Strategic Services; Amanda Jane Melton [1963] Director/Headteacher; Robert Michael Pheasey [1967] Director/Chairman; David Nigel Roberts [1963] Director/Management Consultant; Susan Jane Scott [1966] Managing Director; David Michael Whatley [1965] Director/Auditor; Waseem Yasin [1969] Director/Chartered Accountant

Pendleside Hospice
Incorporated: 27 July 1988 *Employees:* 87
Net Worth: £10,047,046 *Total Assets:* £10,261,974
Registered Office: Pendleside, Colne Road, Reedley, Burnley, Lancs, BB10 2LW
Activities: Other human health activities
Officers: Roger Cornes, Secretary; Nicola Alden [1983] Director/Commercial Management; David Harold Brown [1952] Director; Mary Angela Brown [1952] Retired Nurse and NHS Director; Francesca Chapman [1965] Director/Career Development Adviser Business; Roger Langford Cornes [1947] Director/Retired Chartered Accountant; Matthew Davies [1971] Director; Dianne Sarah Evans [1973] Director/HR Manager; Margaret Hynes [1952] Director/Retired; David Robert Walker [1986] Managing Director; Giles Scott Williams [1962] Director/Physiotherapist

Pendleton Together Holdings Limited
Incorporated: 26 July 2013
Net Worth: £1,000 *Total Assets:* £12,518,000
Registered Office: Brotherton House, Loganberry Avenue, Salford, M6 5UX
Activities: Activities of extraterritorial organisations and bodies
Parent: Together Housing Association Limited
Officers: Peter Emsden, Secretary; Mark Ian Dunford [1969] Group Services Director; Peter Clare Emsden [1961] Director; Thomas Michael Miskell [1955] Director

Pendleton Together Operating Limited
Incorporated: 26 July 2013
Net Worth Deficit: £1,831,000 *Total Assets:* £103,022,000
Registered Office: Brotherton House, Loganberry Avenue, Salford, M6 5UX
Activities: Other accommodation
Parent: Pendleton Together Holdings Limited
Officers: Peter Emsden, Secretary; Mark Ian Dunford [1969] Group Services Director; Peter Clare Emsden [1961] Director; Thomas Michael Miskell [1955] Director

Peninsula Business Services Group Limited
Incorporated: 12 December 1990 *Employees:* 2,250
Net Worth: £82,748,584 *Total Assets:* £159,320,320
Registered Office: The Peninsula, Victoria Place, Manchester, M4 4FB
Activities: Non-trading company
Parent: Rainy City Investments Limited
Officers: Peter Nicholas Swift, Secretary; Fred Done [1943] Director; Peter Eric Done [1947] Director

Peninsula Business Services Limited
Incorporated: 25 February 1983 *Employees:* 895
Net Worth: £43,345,272 *Total Assets:* £64,650,040
Registered Office: The Peninsula, Victoria Place, Manchester, M4 4FB
Activities: Activities of patent and copyright agents; other legal activities n.e.c.
Parent: Peninsula Business Services Group Limited
Officers: Peter Nicholas Swift, Secretary; Nicholas Anthony Babington [1972] Sales Director; Darren Stuart Chadwick [1970] Sales Training and Development Director; Russell Corlett [1965] Health & Safety Director; Peter Eric Done [1947] Director/Bookmaker; Geoffrey Ford [1969] Sales Director; Alan Price [1978] Director; Bertrand Quentin Stern-Gillet [1980] Director; Peter Nicholas Swift [1958] Director/Chartered Accountant; Dennis Walter Upfold [1960] Sales Director

Peninsular Estates Limited
Incorporated: 26 March 2008 *Employees:* 241
Net Worth: £2,815,896 *Total Assets:* £6,931,959
Registered Office: Thornton Hall Hotel, Neston Road, Thornton Hough, Wirral, Merseyside, CH63 1JF
Activities: Activities of head offices
Officers: Andrew Lloyd Thompson, Secretary; Andrew Lloyd Thompson [1961] Director/Company Secretary; Nancy Thompson [1930] Director

Penman Estates Limited
Incorporated: 4 December 1996 *Employees:* 56
Net Worth: £7,012,610 *Total Assets:* £8,533,641
Registered Office: Imperial Point, Express Trading Estate, Stone Hill Road, Farnworth, Bolton, Lancs, BL4 9TN
Activities: Wholesale of hardware, plumbing and heating equipment and supplies
Major Shareholder: Ronald John Ricketts
Officers: Roger Derek Booth, Secretary/Assistant Manager; William Henry Martin Allan [1960] Director/Facilities Manager; Roger Derek Booth [1959] Director; Stephen Andrew Cumberlidge [1969] Director/Purchaser; Ronald John Gambles [1973] Director/Accountant; John Paul Humphreys [1972] Sales Director; Andrew Mulligan [1965] Director/Sales Manager; Ronald John Ricketts [1960] Director/Salesman

Penmarric Limited
Incorporated: 27 September 1979
Net Worth Deficit: £3,239,723 *Total Assets:* £18,278,776
Registered Office: Suite One, Courthill House, 66 Water Lane, Wilmslow, Cheshire, SK9 5AP
Activities: Other business support service activities n.e.c.
Shareholder: Joseph Claude Dwek
Officers: Joseph Claude Dwek [1940] Managing Director; Linda Rosalind Dwek [1945] Director

Pentagon HS Limited
Incorporated: 8 January 2009 *Employees:* 7
Net Worth: £6,618,444 *Total Assets:* £16,052,570
Registered Office: The Brew House, Greenalls Avenue, Warrington, Cheshire, WA4 6HL
Activities: Other letting and operating of own or leased real estate
Parent: Assura Financing Limited
Officers: Orla Ball [1970] Director/Company Secretary; Paul Bryan Carroll [1969] Director/Accountant; Jayne Marie Cottam [1974] Finance Director; Simon Gould [1974] Director/Chartered Surveyor; Spencer Adrian Kenyon [1962] Director/Chartered Surveyor; Patrick William Lowther [1977] Director/Chartered Surveyor

Penthouse Carpets Holdings Limited
Incorporated: 21 October 1994 *Employees:* 81
Net Worth: £5,636,077 *Total Assets:* £8,528,300
Registered Office: Buckley Carpet Mill, Buckley Road, Rochdale, Lancs, OL12 9DU
Activities: Activities of head offices
Shareholders: Stephen Ingram; Michael Muschamp; Brian Holmes Taylor
Officers: Steven Cheuk Ying Yu, Secretary; Jonathan Robert Gamble [1971] Sales Director; Shirley Anne Jackson [1965] Production Director; Michael Muschamp [1954] Director/Chartered Accountant; Steven Cheuk Ying Yu [1965] Finance Director

Penthouse Carpets Limited
Incorporated: 22 June 1972 *Employees:* 81
Net Worth: £5,517,747 *Total Assets:* £8,528,296
Registered Office: Buckley Carpet Mill, Buckley Road, Rochdale, Lancs, OL12 9DU
Activities: Manufacture of woven or tufted carpets and rugs
Shareholders: Stephen Ingram; Michael Muschamp; Brian Holmes Taylor
Officers: Steven Cheuk Ying Yu, Secretary; Jonathan Robert Gamble [1971] Sales Director; Shirley Anne Jackson [1965] Production Director; Michael Muschamp [1954] Director/Chartered Accountant; Steven Cheuk Ying Yu [1965] Financial Director

Pentre Group Holdings Limited
Incorporated: 6 November 2015 *Employees:* 196
Net Worth: £7,339,989 *Total Assets:* £9,844,831
Registered Office: Unit 2 Penfield Road, Leigh, Lancs, WN7 3PG
Activities: Other manufacturing n.e.c.
Major Shareholder: Michael Frederick Seymour
Officers: Richard Peter Johnstone [1968] Director/Manager; Sean Andrew Kilgallon [1970] Director/Manager; Julie Ann Meal [1967] Director/Accountant; Jeremy Peter Orrell [1957] Director/Solicitor; Howard Wilson Platt [1955] Director; Michael Frederick Seymour [1947] Director

Pentre Group Limited
Incorporated: 21 June 1990 *Employees:* 126
Net Worth: £11,736,830 *Total Assets:* £17,598,776
Registered Office: Unit 2 Penfield Road, Leigh, Lancs, WN7 3PG
Activities: Other manufacturing n.e.c.
Major Shareholder: Michael Frederick Seymour
Officers: Julie Meal, Secretary; Richard Peter Johnstone [1968] Director/Manager; Sean Andrew Kilgallon [1970] Director/General Manager; Julie Ann Meal [1967] Director/Management Accountant; Michael Frederick Seymour [1947] Director/Accountant

Pentre Holdings Limited
Incorporated: 1 October 2003 *Employees:* 196
Net Worth: £13,972,032 *Total Assets:* £16,476,874
Registered Office: Unit 2 Penfield Road, Leigh, Lancs, WN7 3PG
Activities: Activities of head offices
Major Shareholder: Michael Frederick Seymour
Officers: Julie Meal, Secretary; Richard Peter Johnstone [1968] Director/Manager; Sean Andrew Kilgallon [1970] Director/Manager; Julie Ann Meal [1967] Director/Accountant; Jeremy Peter Orrell [1957] Director/Solicitor; Howard Wilson Platt [1955] Director; Michael Frederick Seymour [1947] Director

Penwortham Priory Academy Trust
Incorporated: 6 July 2012 *Employees:* 90
Net Worth: £6,697,000 *Total Assets:* £8,212,000
Registered Office: Penwortham Priory Academy, Crow Hills Road, Penwortham, Preston, Lancs, PR1 0JE
Activities: General secondary education
Officers: Susan Paula Spencer, Secretary; Cheryl Kathleen Barker [1977] Director/Assistant Business Manager; Professor Gordon Becket [1948] Director/University Professor; Kevin Stephen Burke [1958] Director/DFE, Further Education Workforce Policy; Matthew Eastham [1974] Director/Headteacher; Peter Faulkner [1966] Director/Teacher; Georgina Eugenee Clowence Herd [1977] Director/Business Support Leader; Rachel Ann Lancaster [1982] Director/Head of Product and Channels Micro:Bit Educational; Christopher David Martin [1974] Director; Dr Philip Kenneth Range [1953] Director/Retired; Darren Robert Taylor [1969] Director/Engineer; Kathryn Elizabeth Thornton [1981] Director/Teacher; Michaela Catherine Turner [1967] Director/Business Support Engineer; Atiquah Vohra [1980] Director/Company Secretary/Legal

Penzance Leisure Limited
Incorporated: 11 January 2002
Net Worth Deficit: £1,987,511 *Total Assets:* £8,083,349
Registered Office: Parkwood House, Cuerden Park, Berkeley Drive, Bamber Bridge, Preston, Lancs, PR5 6BY
Activities: General public administration activities
Parent: Penzance Holdings Limited
Officers: David John Harding [1980] Director/Chartered Accountant; Philip Arthur Would [1971] Director/Asset Manager

Peover Eye Investments Limited
Incorporated: 28 November 2014 *Employees:* 116
Net Worth: £5,599,828 *Total Assets:* £11,436,724
Registered Office: Kudos Shower Products Ltd, Elmsfield Park, Holme, Cumbria, LA6 1RJ
Activities: Activities of other holding companies n.e.c.
Major Shareholder: Bruce Raymond Ledwith
Officers: David Irwin [1966] Director; Bruce Raymond Ledwith [1952] Director

Per-Scent Group Limited
Incorporated: 16 December 1994
Net Worth: £4,338,857 *Total Assets:* £8,250,005
Registered Office: Churchill Point, Lake Edge Green, Trafford Park Road, Manchester, M17 1BL
Activities: Wholesale of perfume and cosmetics
Parent: Fragrance Acquisitions Ltd
Officers: Sanjay Jayantilal Vadera, Secretary; Sanjay Jayantilal Vadera [1967] Managing Director; Vipul Jayantilal Vadera [1972] Director

Per-Scent Limited
Incorporated: 29 September 2004 *Employees:* 93
Net Worth: £51,893,132 *Total Assets:* £68,473,864
Registered Office: Churchill Point, Lake Edge Green, Trafford Park Road, Manchester, M17 1BL
Activities: Wholesale of perfume and cosmetics
Parent: Per-Scent Group Ltd
Officers: Sanjay Jayantila Vadera, Secretary; Sanjay Jayantilal Vadera [1967] Director; Vipul Jayantilal Vadera [1972] Director

Performance Car Hire Limited
Incorporated: 12 September 1997
Net Worth: £3,042,668 *Total Assets:* £8,217,304
Registered Office: 850 Ibis Court, Centre Park, Warrington, Cheshire, WA1 1RL
Activities: Renting and leasing of cars and light motor vehicles
Officers: Michael Allen [1971] Director/Accountant; Beverley Jayne Specter [1963] Director

Perrers Properties Limited
Incorporated: 17 October 1996
Net Worth: £3,110,188 *Total Assets:* £9,414,827
Registered Office: The Corn Exchange, Brunswick Street, Liverpool, L2 7TP
Activities: Buying and selling of own real estate
Shareholders: Peter Wild Bullivant; Antonia Clare Goodall; Andrew Peter Mason; Christopher Ian Mason
Officers: Ben Desmond Harvey, Secretary; Geoffrey Owen Mason [1940] Director/Surveyor

Pershing Holdings (UK) Limited
Incorporated: 7 February 2003
Net Worth: £217,123,008 *Total Assets:* £217,136,000
Registered Office: Royal Liver Building, Pier Head, Liverpool, L3 1LL
Activities: Activities of financial services holding companies
Officers: Elizabeth Mary Canning [1958] Director/Chief Administrative Officer [Canadian/British]; Janet Mary Johnstone [1963] Director/Bank Official [Irish/South African]; Margaret Anne McPhail [1957] Director; Sophie Jane O'Connor [1970] Director; Geoffrey Charles Towers [1960] Director

Pershing Limited
Incorporated: 10 November 1986 *Employees:* 394
Net Worth: £158,091,008 *Total Assets:* £169,334,000
Registered Office: Royal Liver Building, Pier Head, Liverpool, L3 1LL
Activities: Financial intermediation not elsewhere classified
Parent: Pershing Holdings (UK) Limited
Officers: Elizabeth Mary Canning [1958] Director/Chief Administrative Officer [Canadian/British]; Janet Mary Johnstone [1963] Director/Bank Official [Irish/South African]; Margaret Anne McPhail [1957] Director; Sophie Jane O'Connor [1970] Director; Geoffrey Charles Towers [1960] Director

Pershing Securities Limited
Incorporated: 27 February 1990
Net Worth: £123,943,000 *Total Assets:* £420,363,008
Registered Office: Royal Liver Building, Pier Head, Liverpool, L3 1LL
Activities: Financial intermediation not elsewhere classified
Parent: Pershing Limited
Officers: Elizabeth Mary Canning [1958] Director/Chief Administrative Officer [Canadian/British]; Janet Mary Johnstone [1963] Director/Bank Official [Irish/South African]; Margaret Anne McPhail [1957] Director; Sophie Jane O'Connor [1970] Director; Geoffrey Charles Towers [1960] Director

Personal Audit Systems Holdings Limited
Incorporated: 13 September 2010
Net Worth: £7,312,214 *Total Assets:* £7,367,261
Registered Office: Britannic House, 657 Liverpool Road, Irlam, Manchester, M44 5XD
Activities: Activities of head offices
Major Shareholder: Matthew Beech
Officers: Matthew Charles Beech [1966] Director

Personalised Travel Services Limited
Incorporated: 11 October 1999 *Employees:* 34
Net Worth: £3,351,000 *Total Assets:* £16,380,000
Registered Office: Glendale House, Glendale Business Park, Glendale Avenue, Sandycroft, Deeside, Flintshire, CH5 2DL
Activities: Other reservation service activities n.e.c.
Parent: The Global Travel Group Limited
Officers: Ryan James Cooke, Secretary; Paul Smith [1975] Director

Perspective Financial Group Limited
Incorporated: 18 December 2007 *Employees:* 171
Net Worth Deficit: £5,448,664 *Total Assets:* £21,719,958
Registered Office: Paradigm House, Lower Meadow Road, Handforth, Wilmslow, Cheshire, SK9 3ND
Activities: Financial intermediation not elsewhere classified
Shareholder: Paul Henry Hogarth
Officers: David John Philip Hesketh, Secretary; Julie Suzanne Hepworth [1974] Compliance Director; David John Philip Hesketh [1981] Director/Accountant; Paul Henry Hogarth [1959] Director; Paul Michael Newton [1964] Director/Accountant; Michael Peter Rogan [1968] Director; Ian Mitcheal Wilkinson [1970] Financial Adviser Director

Perstorp UK Ltd.
Incorporated: 18 May 1992 *Employees:* 83
Net Worth: £14,325,000 *Total Assets:* £116,955,000
Registered Office: Perstorp, Baronet Road, Warrington, Cheshire, WA4 6HA
Activities: Manufacture of other chemical products n.e.c.
Officers: David Philip Turner, Secretary; Olof Magnus Lanner [1969] Director/Operations Manager [Swedish]; Paul Shelley [1961] Director/Chemical Engineer; David Philip Turner [1964] Director

Pet City Holdings Limited
Incorporated: 1 February 1989
Net Worth: £27,034,000 *Total Assets:* £27,034,000
Registered Office: Epsom Avenue, Stanley Green Trading Estate, Handsforth, Wilmslow, Cheshire, SK9 3RN
Activities: Non-trading company
Parent: Pets at Home Holdings Limited
Officers: Louise Ann Stonier, Secretary; Michael James Iddon [1965] Director; Peter Pritchard [1970] Director; Louise Ann Stonier [1973] Director/Company Secretary

Pet Food Brands (Holdings) Ltd
Incorporated: 2 July 2013
Net Worth: £3,780,995 *Total Assets:* £7,069,027
Registered Office: Brentwood House, Lower Philips Road, Whitebirk Industrial Estate, Blackburn, Lancs, BB1 5UD
Activities: Activities of other holding companies n.e.c.
Shareholders: Anthony Paul Goodwin Raeburn; P.F.I. Vitakraft GmbH
Officers: Hans-Jurgen Jurgen Deuerer [1964] Director [German]; Anthony Paul Goodwin Raeburn [1959] Director

Petro-Canada Europe Lubricants Limited
Incorporated: 7 February 2005 *Employees:* 24
Net Worth: £47,171,412 *Total Assets:* £54,421,124
Registered Office: 3rd Floor, 1 Ashley Road, Altrincham, Cheshire, WA14 2DT
Activities: Wholesale of other fuels and related products
Parent: Hollyfrontier Corporation
Officers: Denise Clark McWatters [1959] Director/Attorney [American]; Mark Allen Plake [1958] Director/President, Petro-Canada Lubricants Inc. [American]; Martin Philip Benjamin Wright [1956] Managing Director

Petros (Truro) Limited
Incorporated: 5 October 1999
Net Worth: £658,088 *Total Assets:* £11,931,933
Registered Office: The Copper Room, Deva Centre, Trinity Way, Manchester, M3 7BG
Activities: Development of building projects
Parent: Petros Development Company Limited
Officers: Peter Collins, Secretary/Director; Catherine Ann Collins [1963] Director; David John Collins [1963] Director; Lise Jane Collins [1964] Director/Surveyor; Peter Collins [1934] Director

Petros Development Company Limited
Incorporated: 24 August 1964 *Employees:* 6
Net Worth: £11,551,489 *Total Assets:* £21,310,200
Registered Office: The Copper Room, Deva Centre, Trinity Way, Manchester, M3 7BG
Activities: Other business support service activities n.e.c.
Major Shareholder: Peter Collins
Officers: Peter Collins, Secretary; David John Collins [1963] Director; Lise Jane Collins [1964] Director/Surveyor; Peter Collins [1934] Director/Chartered Secretary

Pets at Home Group PLC
Incorporated: 10 February 2014 *Employees:* 6,701
Net Worth: £906,352,000 *Total Assets:* £1,339,376,000
Registered Office: Epsom Avenue, Stanley Green Trading Estate, Handforth, Cheshire, SK9 3RN
Activities: Activities of head offices
Officers: Louise Ann Stonier, Secretary; Dr Susan Dawson [1961] Director; Antonio Denunzio [1960] Non-Executive Director/Consultant; Sharon Emma Flood [1965] Director; Theresa Mary Green [1964] Director; Michael James Iddon [1965] Director; Stanislas Marie Laurent [1968] Director [French]; Dennis Henry Millard [1949] Director; Paul Stephen Moody [1957] Director; Peter Pritchard [1970] Director

Pets at Home Holdings Limited
Incorporated: 25 October 1999
Net Worth: £18,972,000 *Total Assets:* £89,423,000
Registered Office: Pets at Home Ltd, Epsom Avenue, Stanley Green Trading Estate, Handforth, Cheshire, SK9 3RN
Activities: Non-trading company
Parent: Pets at Home No.1 Limited
Officers: Louise Ann Stonier, Secretary; Michael James Iddon [1965] Director; Peter Pritchard [1970] Director; Louise Ann Stonier [1973] Director/Company Secretary

Pets at Home Ltd
Incorporated: 7 June 1984 *Employees:* 6,036
Net Worth: £686,972,032 *Total Assets:* £977,363,008
Registered Office: Epsom Avenue, Stanley Green Trading Estate, Handforth, Cheshire, SK9 3RN
Activities: Other retail sale of new goods in specialised stores (not commercial art galleries and opticians)
Parent: Pets at Home Superstores Limited
Officers: Louise Ann Stonier, Secretary; Michael James Iddon [1965] Director; Peter Pritchard [1970] Director; Louise Ann Stonier [1973] Director/Company Secretary

Pets at Home No.1 Limited
Incorporated: 11 February 2014
Net Worth: £670,284,032 *Total Assets:* £1,595,992,960
Registered Office: Epsom Avenue, Stanley Green Trading Estate, Handforth, Cheshire, SK9 3RN
Activities: Non-trading company
Parent: Pets at Home Group PLC
Officers: Louise Ann Stonier, Secretary; Michael James Iddon [1965] Director; Peter Pritchard [1970] Director; Louise Ann Stonier [1973] Director/Company Secretary

Pets at Home Superstores Limited
Incorporated: 30 October 1995
Net Worth: £5,940,000 *Total Assets:* £110,565,000
Registered Office: Epsom Avenue, Stanley Green Trading Estate, Handforth, Cheshire, SK9 3RN
Activities: Non-trading company
Parent: Pets at Home Holdings Limited
Officers: Louise Ann Stonier, Secretary; Michael James Iddon [1965] Director; Peter Pritchard [1970] Director; Louise Ann Stonier [1973] Director/Company Secretary

Pets at Home Vet Group Limited
Incorporated: 3 July 2013
Net Worth: £53,054,240 *Total Assets:* £53,054,240
Registered Office: Epsom Avenue, Stanley Green Trading Estate, Handforth, Cheshire, SK9 3RN
Activities: Non-trading company
Parent: Pets at Home Holdings Limited
Officers: Louise Stonier, Secretary; Harvey Bertenshaw Ainley [1966] Director/Chief Financial Officer; Andrei Balta [1979] Director [Romanian]; Fiona Jayne Briault [1967] Director; Michael James Iddon [1965] Director; Peter Pritchard [1970] Director; Julie Ross [1978] Commercial Director

Pets at Home Veterinary Specialist Group Limited
Incorporated: 25 March 2015
Net Worth Deficit: £1,411,000 *Total Assets:* £35,132,000
Registered Office: Pets at Home Limited, Epsom Avenue, Stanley Green Trading Estate, Handforth, Wilmslow, Cheshire, SK9 3RN
Activities: Non-trading company
Parent: Pets at Home Holdings Limited
Officers: Louise Stonier, Secretary; Harvey Bertenshaw Ainley [1966] Director/Chief Financial Officer; Andrei Balta [1979] Director [Romanian]; Fiona Jayne Briault [1967] Director; Peter Pritchard [1970] Director; Julie Ross [1978] Commercial Director

Pets Choice Limited
Incorporated: 20 October 1987 *Employees:* 171
Net Worth: £11,014,357 *Total Assets:* £22,848,892
Registered Office: Brentwood House, Lower Philips Road, Whitebirk Industrial Estate, Blackburn, Lancs, BB1 5UD
Activities: Manufacture of prepared pet foods
Parent: Pet Food Brands Limited
Officers: Scott William Francis Campbell, Secretary; Hans-Jurgen Jurgen Deuerer [1964] Director [German]; Anthony Paul Goodwin Raeburn [1959] Director

Pettra Limited
Incorporated: 1 October 2014 *Employees:* 78
Net Worth: £831,674 *Total Assets:* £6,614,345
Registered Office: 4th Floor, 1 Belle Vue Square, Broughton Road, Skipton, N Yorks, BD23 1FJ
Activities: Temporary employment agency activities
Shareholders: Peter Andrew Gregory; Tracy Ward
Officers: Peter Andrew Gregory [1956] Director; Nina Catherine Learoyd [1955] Director; Tracy Ward [1973] Director

Pexion Limited
Incorporated: 1 July 1986 *Employees:* 345
Net Worth: £4,302,346 *Total Assets:* £33,509,208
Registered Office: Crosses Barn, Shaw Brow, Whittle-le-Woods, Chorley, Lancs, PR6 7HG
Activities: Other business support service activities n.e.c.
Shareholders: Darren James Turner; David James Brindle
Officers: David James Brindle [1970] Director; Darren James Turner [1973] Director

Pfaudler Limited
Incorporated: 20 November 1987 *Employees:* 130
Net Worth: £12,156,363 *Total Assets:* £18,499,568
Registered Office: Unit 5 Lyon Road Industrial Estate, Kearsley, Bolton, Lancs, BL4 8TG
Activities: Manufacture of other special-purpose machinery n.e.c.
Parent: Pfaudler UK Ltd
Officers: Pauline Dunn, Secretary; Dr Jonathan Andrew Drury [1962] Sales Director; Mark Goldsmith [1961] Director/Manager; Kathryn Patricia McCann [1963] Director/Financial Controller

Pfaudler UK Ltd
Incorporated: 20 October 2014 *Employees:* 4
Net Worth: £47,351,872 *Total Assets:* £63,018,436
Registered Office: Unit 5 Lyon Road Industrial Estate, Kearsley, Bolton, Lancs, BL4 8TG
Activities: Activities of head offices
Officers: Pauline Dunn, Secretary; Dr Dominic Thilo Deller [1969] Director/Chief Financial Officer [German]; Mark Goldsmith [1961] Director/Chief Operations Officer; Thomas Otto Kehl [1960] Director/Chief Executive Officer [German]; Kathryn Patricia McCann [1963] Director/Financial Controller

Pfeifer Drako Ltd
Incorporated: 4 September 1980 *Employees:* 72
Net Worth: £3,797,649 *Total Assets:* £6,884,011
Registered Office: Marshfield Bank, Woolstanwood, Crewe, Cheshire, CW2 8UY
Activities: Manufacture of wire products, chain and springs
Officers: Sandra Mary Dutton Jones, Secretary/Accountant; Eduard Hermann Gehard Pfeifer [1955] Director [German]; Daniel Michael Polec [1967] Managing Director

PFF (Dorset) Limited
Incorporated: 26 April 2007
Net Worth: £437,108 *Total Assets:* £49,696,020
Registered Office: Unit 18 Riversway Business Village, Navigation Way, Ashton on Ribble, Preston, Lancs, PR2 2YP
Activities: Activities of head offices
Parent: Dorset Emergency Services PPP (Holdings) Limited
Officers: Sally-Ann Ann Brooks [1966] Director/Project Manager; David Wyn Davies [1968] Director/Accountant; Angela Mills [1961] Director/Accountant

PFM Group Limited
Incorporated: 2 April 2004 *Employees:* 3
Net Worth Deficit: £589,669 *Total Assets:* £32,853,454
Registered Office: Paradigm House, Brooke Court, Wilmslow, Cheshire, SK9 3ND
Activities: Other business support service activities n.e.c.
Parent: Perspective Financial Group Ltd
Officers: David John Philip Hesketh, Secretary; Julie Suzanne Hepworth [1974] Director; David John Philip Hesketh [1981] Director; Ian Mitcheal Wilkinson [1970] Director

PFP US JV LLP
Incorporated: 2 December 2013
Net Worth: £2,676,569 *Total Assets:* £38,084,884
Registered Office: Timber Wharf, 16-22 Worsley Street, Manchester, M15 4LD

PH Alderley Park LLP
Incorporated: 17 June 2016
Net Worth: £11,166,222 *Total Assets:* £19,739,724
Registered Office: Bollin House, Oakfield Road, Cheadle Royal Business Park, Cheadle, Cheshire, SK8 3GX

Pharmacy Care Plus Limited
Incorporated: 3 March 2008 *Employees:* 127
Net Worth: £4,818,116 *Total Assets:* £12,084,689
Registered Office: Suite M, No 2 The Courtyard, Earl Road, Stanley Green, Cheadle Hulme, Cheadle, Cheshire, SK8 6GN
Activities: Other human health activities
Officers: Michael Niblock, Secretary; Dr Robert George Andrew [1961] Director; Michael Niblock [1981] Director; Dr Devendra Shah [1967] Director

Pharmaserve (North West) Limited
Incorporated: 12 September 2007 *Employees:* 111
Net Worth: £2,139,060 *Total Assets:* £13,390,187
Registered Office: Ayrton House, Parliament Business Park, Commerce Way, Liverpool, L8 7BA
Activities: Manufacture of pharmaceutical preparations
Officers: Philip Didlick, Secretary; Philip Didlick [1976] Director/Accountant; Padraic Marc O'Brien [1979] Director; Generald Francis Obrien [1949] Director [Irish]

Phenomenex Limited
Incorporated: 12 May 1987 *Employees:* 78
Net Worth: £17,046,296 *Total Assets:* £18,864,320
Registered Office: Melville House, Queens Avenue, Hurdsfield Industrial Estate, Macclesfield, Cheshire, SK10 2BN
Activities: Wholesale of chemical products
Parent: AB Sciex UK Limited
Officers: Michelle Elizabeth Caron [1967] Director [American]; Dennis Shane Lyons [1957] Director [American]; Keith Graham Ward [1953] Director

Phillips & Cohen Associates International, Ltd
Incorporated: 16 August 2012
Net Worth: £5,855,406 *Total Assets:* £8,647,195
Registered Office: Building 5, Exchange Quay, Salford, M5 3EF
Activities: Activities auxiliary to financial intermediation n.e.c.
Shareholders: Matthew Philips; Adam Cohen
Officers: Christine Wigham, Secretary; Nicholas John Cherry [1974] Director; Adam Scott Cohen [1971] Director [American]; Howard Alan Enders [1971] Director [American]; Matthew Mark Phillips [1970] Director [American]

Phoenix Court Blackburn Limited
Incorporated: 12 May 2010 *Employees:* 3
Net Worth: £8,359,521 *Total Assets:* £18,089,118
Registered Office: Nisiac House, 1 Cunningham Court, Lions Drive, Blackburn, Lancs, BB1 2QX
Activities: Other letting and operating of own or leased real estate
Parent: Epoch Estates Limited
Officers: Majid Hussain [1977] Director; Mozam Hussain [1983] Director; Wajid Hussain [1980] Director

Phoenix Healthcare Distribution Limited
Incorporated: 4 June 1913 *Employees:* 1,419
Net Worth: £197,451,008 *Total Assets:* £431,857,984
Registered Office: Rivington Road, Whitehouse Industrial Estate, Runcorn, Cheshire, WA7 3DJ
Activities: Wholesale of pharmaceutical goods
Officers: Michael Peter Blakeman, Secretary; Stephen William Anderson [1966] Director; Kenneth John Black [1965] Director; Alan David Fairfield [1966] Director; Kevin Robert Hudson [1963] Finance Director; Jeremy David Meader [1966] Sales Director Pharmacy

Phoenix Medical Supplies Limited
Incorporated: 23 July 1998 *Employees:* 117
Net Worth: £88,456,000 *Total Assets:* £470,598,016
Registered Office: Rivington Road, Whitehouse, Runcorn, Cheshire, WA7 3DJ
Activities: Wholesale of pharmaceutical goods
Shareholders: Ludwig Merckle; Jutta Breu
Officers: Michael Peter Blakeman, Secretary; Stephen William Anderson [1966] Director; Kenneth John Black [1965] Director; Helmut Karl Fisher [1970] Director [German]; Frank Grobe-Natrop [1961] Director [German]; Stefan Herfeld [1967] Director [German]; Kevin Robert Hudson [1963] Director; Oliver Thomas Windholz [1966] Director [German]

Phone-a-Loan Limited
Incorporated: 21 June 1983
Net Worth: £448,483,008 *Total Assets:* £448,483,008
Registered Office: Lake View, Lakeside, Cheadle, Cheshire, SK8 3GW
Activities: Financial intermediation not elsewhere classified
Parent: Together Financial Services Limited
Officers: Gary Derek Beckett, Secretary; Gary Derek Beckett [1969] Director; Marc Richard Goldberg [1971] Director; Henry Neville Moser [1949] Director

Physical Properties Testing Ltd.
Incorporated: 9 September 2014 *Employees:* 4
Net Worth: £6,553,306 *Total Assets:* £16,950,818
Registered Office: 3rd Floor, 1 Ashley Road, Altrincham, Cheshire, WA14 2DT
Activities: Manufacture of electronic measuring, testing etc. equipment, not for industrial process control
Parent: BV PPT Holdings Ltd.
Officers: Jesse Feldman [1977] Director/Private Equity Investor [American]; Adam Dean Markin [1966] Director; Zachary Smotherman [1983] Director/Private Equity Investor [American]; Donald Edward Templeman [1960] Director/Management [American]

Piggott and Whitfield Limited
Incorporated: 2 July 1947 *Employees:* 99
Net Worth: £1,681,737 *Total Assets:* £8,812,756
Registered Office: Exemplar House, Station View, Hazel Grove, Stockport, Cheshire, SK7 5ER
Activities: Electrical installation
Major Shareholder: John Richard Whitfield
Officers: Victoria Rachel Gee, Secretary; Shaun Christopher Lappin [1964] Commercial Director; Kara Poyser [1981] Director; Robert Speakman [1968] Director/Engineer; Gareth Michael White [1972] Director; John Richard Whitfield [1949] Director/Electrical Engineer; Laraine Whitfield [1949] Director; Mark Lawrence Whitfield [1986] Director

Pilkington (US) Investments (No.3) Unlimited
Incorporated: 9 April 2002
Net Worth: £136,988,000 *Total Assets:* £259,716,992
Registered Office: European Technical Centre, Hall Lane, Lathom, Ormskirk, Lancs, L40 5UF
Activities: Activities of head offices
Parent: Pilkington Germany Finance Limited
Officers: Iain Michael Smith, Secretary; Herr Wolfgang Endemann [1966] Director/Manufacturing Manager/Plant Manager [German]; Herr Michael Kiefer [1966] Director/Lawyer/General Counsel Europe [German]; Herr Marcus Mosner [1965] Director/HR Manager [German]; Dr. Christian Quenett [1964] Director/General Manager [German]; Paul Joseph Ravenscroft [1970] Director/Head of Mergers & Acquisitions; Iain Michael Smith [1972] Director/Chartered Accountant

Pilkington Automotive Limited
Incorporated: 25 March 1993 *Employees:* 587
Net Worth: £95,789,424 *Total Assets:* £219,442,656
Registered Office: European Technical Centre, Hall Lane, Lathom, Ormskirk, Lancs, L40 5UF
Activities: Manufacture of flat glass
Parent: Pilkington Group Limited
Officers: Iain Michael Smith, Secretary; Shirley Ruth Anderson [1960] Human Resources Director; Timothy Peter Bolas [1960] Director/Global Financial Controller; Rachael Elizabeth Dorey [1978] Human Resources Director, UK Operations; Michael James Farrow [1985] Finance Director; Anthony Kevin Fradgley [1968] Director/Accountant; Christopher Hanley [1967] European Regional Director; Koichi Hiyoshi [1959] Director/Head of Legal Department [Japanese]; Jukichi Kuboi [1963] Director/General Manager [Japanese]; Robert James Purcell [1966] Managing Director; Paul Joseph Ravenscroft [1970] Director/Head of Mergers and Acquisitions; Iain Michael Smith [1972] Director/Chartered Accountant; Katsunori Tatemoto [1961] Director/Senior Corporate Officer [Japanese]; Peter John Watters [1965] Director/Business Manager

Pilkington Finance Unlimited
Incorporated: 9 March 1987
Net Worth: £10,982,000 *Total Assets:* £10,982,000
Registered Office: European Technical Centre, Hall Lane, Lathom, Ormskirk, Lancs, L40 5UF
Activities: Financial intermediation not elsewhere classified
Parent: NSG UK Enterprises Limited
Officers: Iain Michael Smith, Secretary; Judy Anne Massa [1967] Director/Accountant; Paul Joseph Ravenscroft [1970] Director/Head of Mergers & Acquisitions; Iain Michael Smith [1972] Director/Chartered Accountant

Pilkington Germany Finance Limited
Incorporated: 26 January 2001
Net Worth: £140,768,000 *Total Assets:* £335,945,984
Registered Office: European Technical Centre, Hall Lane, Lathom, Ormskirk, Lancs, L40 5UF
Activities: Activities of head offices
Parent: Pilkington Holding GmbH
Officers: Iain Michael Smith, Secretary; Herr Wolfgang Endemann [1966] Director/Manufacturing Manager/Plant Manager [German]; Herr Michael Kiefer [1966] Director/Lawyer/General Counsel Europe [German]; Herr Marcus Mosner [1965] Director/HR Manager [German]; Dr. Christian Quenett [1964] Director/General Manager [German]; Paul Joseph Ravenscroft [1970] Director/Head of Mergers & Acquisitions; Iain Michael Smith [1972] Director/Chartered Accountant

Pilkington Group Limited
Incorporated: 30 June 1894 *Employees:* 228
Net Worth: £1,843,795,968 *Total Assets:* £2,860,486,912
Registered Office: European Technical Centre, Hall Lane, Lathom, Ormskirk, Lancs, L40 5UF
Activities: Manufacture of flat glass
Parent: NSG UK Enterprises Limited
Officers: Iain Michael Smith, Secretary; Timothy Peter Bolas [1960] Finance Director; Koichi Hiyoshi [1959] Director/Legal Adviser [Japanese]; Jukichi Kuboi [1963] Director/General Manager [Japanese]; Judy Anne Massa [1967] Director/Group Treasurer; Richard John Mercer [1963] Procurement Director; Paul Joseph Ravenscroft [1970] Director/Head of Mergers & Acquisitions; Nicholas Anthony Lithgow Shore [1964] Director BP Engineering & Sustainability; Iain Michael Smith [1972] Director/Group Financial Controller

Pilkington Italy Unlimited
Incorporated: 4 July 1947
Net Worth: £197,302,000 *Total Assets:* £197,302,000
Registered Office: European Technical Centre, Hall Lane, Lathom, Ormskirk, Lancs, L40 5UF
Activities: Activities of head offices
Parent: NSG UK Enterprises Limited
Officers: Iain Michael Smith, Secretary; Julie Ann Brown [1968] Director/Accountant; Judy Anne Massa [1967] Director/Accountant; Paul Joseph Ravenscroft [1970] Director/Head of Mergers & Acquisitions; Iain Michael Smith [1972] Director/Chartered Accountant

Guy Pilkington Memorial Home Limited (The)
Incorporated: 25 October 1973 *Employees:* 196
Net Worth: £13,411,407 *Total Assets:* £15,259,727
Registered Office: Fairfield Hospital, Crank Rd, St Helens, Merseyside, WA11 7RS
Activities: Hospital activities
Officers: Cheryl Nolan, Secretary/CEO; Cyril David Barratt [1947] Managing Director; Carl Andrew Bridge [1966] Director/Self Employed Consultant; Carolyn Ann Dodwell [1959] Director; Geoffrey Hammond [1950] Director/Self Employed Consultant; Colin Stuart Ince [1944] Director/Consultant; Leonard Barry Marlow [1943] Retired Managing Director; Khushroo Suraliwala [1955] Director/Consultant Orthopaedic Surgeon [Indian]; Sharon Watson [1972] Director/Healthcare Inspector; John David Watts [1947] Director/Insurance Broker

Pilkington United Kingdom Limited
Incorporated: 27 February 1979 *Employees:* 911
Net Worth: £52,165,000 *Total Assets:* £206,364,000
Registered Office: European Technical Centre, Hall Lane, Lathom, Ormskirk, Lancs, L40 5UF
Activities: Manufacture of flat glass
Parent: Pilkington Group Limited
Officers: Iain Michael Smith, Secretary; Emma Louise Ballantyne [1982] HR Director; Matthew Alexander Buckley [1966] Commercial Director; Gary Charlton [1962] Operations Director; Michael James Farrow [1985] Finance Director; Andrew David McDowell [1967] Commercial Director; Paul Joseph Ravenscroft [1970] Director/Head of Mergers & Acquisitions; Iain Michael Smith [1972] Director/Chartered Accountant

Pilot Group Limited
Incorporated: 29 July 2010 *Employees:* 49
Net Worth: £8,098,832 *Total Assets:* £13,420,568
Registered Office: 15 Carnarvon Street, Manchester, M3 1HJ
Activities: Activities of head offices
Shareholder: Simone Sara Peppi
Officers: Wendy Littman, Secretary; Philip Isaac Hodari [1961] Director; Simone Sara Peppi [1962] Director; Keith John Richardson [1959] Finance Director

PIMCO 2401 Limited
Incorporated: 16 December 2005
Net Worth Deficit: £1,298,631 *Total Assets:* £7,578,506
Registered Office: Sceptre House, Sceptre Way, Bamber Bridge, Preston, Lancs, PR5 6AW
Activities: Development of building projects
Parent: Foundation for Life Limited
Officers: Deborah Jane Rawlinson, Secretary; Patricia Ann Anderson [1957] Director; Jeremy Peter Hartley [1965] Director; Neil Geoffrey Ward [1959] Director; Christine Desiree Winstanley [1966] Director

PIMCO 2451 Limited
Incorporated: 13 March 2006
Net Worth Deficit: £5,221,935 *Total Assets:* £18,126,056
Registered Office: Sceptre House, Sceptre Way, Bamber Bridge, Preston, Lancs, PR5 6AW
Activities: Other business support service activities n.e.c.
Parent: East Lancashire Building Partnership Ltd
Officers: Deborah Jane Rawlinson, Secretary; Jeremy Peter Hartley [1965] Director; Roger Martyn Parr [1970] Director; Neil Geoffrey Ward [1959] Director; Christine Desiree Winstanley [1966] Director; Mark Stuart Youlton [1963] Director

PIMCO 2947 Bidco Limited
Incorporated: 21 May 2014
Net Worth Deficit: £12,657,000 *Total Assets:* £38,521,000
Registered Office: Turing House, Archway 5, Manchester, M15 5RL
Activities: Other information service activities n.e.c.
Parent: PIMCO 2947 Topco Limited
Officers: Steven Jon Axon [1981] Director; Matthew Caffrey [1974] Director; Jenny Elizabeth Davies [1977] Director; Andrew Geoffrey Goldwater [1974] Director

PIMCO 2947 Topco Limited
Incorporated: 21 May 2014 *Employees:* 197
Net Worth Deficit: £11,191,000 *Total Assets:* £128,210,000
Registered Office: Turing House, Archway 5, Manchester, M15 5RL
Activities: Other information service activities n.e.c.
Shareholders: Livingbridge GP Company Limited; Livingbridge EP LLP
Officers: Matthew Caffrey [1974] Director; Jenny Elizabeth Davies [1977] Director; Andrew Geoffrey Goldwater [1974] Director; James Nicholas McCall [1971] Director; Kevin Raymond Paige [1965] Director; Mark Robert James Turner [1970] Director

Pin Croft Dyeing and Printing Co. Limited
Incorporated: 28 March 1953 *Employees:* 204
Net Worth: £42,707,000 *Total Assets:* £83,569,000
Registered Office: Adlington Works, Market Street, Adlington, Chorley, Lancs, PR7 4HJ
Activities: Finishing of textiles
Parent: Rochdale Textiles Supplies Limited
Officers: Nigel Andrew Bate, Secretary; Nigel Andrew Bate [1971] Director/Certified Chartered Accountant; Neil Jonathan Davey [1971] Sales Director; John Joseph Vareldzis [1972] Managing Director

Pinco 2033 Limited
Incorporated: 21 October 2003 *Employees:* 5
Net Worth Deficit: £4,163,270 *Total Assets:* £17,556,760
Registered Office: Sceptre House, Sceptre Way, Bamber Bridge, Preston, Lancs, PR5 6AW
Activities: Development of building projects
Parent: Foundation for Life Limited
Officers: Deborah Jane Rawlinson, Secretary; Patricia Ann Anderson [1957] Director; Jeremy Peter Hartley [1965] Director; Neil Geoffrey Ward [1959] Director; Christine Desiree Winstanley [1966] Director

Pinco 2206 Limited
Incorporated: 29 September 2004
Net Worth Deficit: £2,861,423 *Total Assets:* £13,510,549
Registered Office: Sceptre House, Sceptre Way, Bamber Bridge, Preston, Lancs, PR5 6AW
Activities: Other letting and operating of own or leased real estate
Parent: Foundation for Life Limited
Officers: Deborah Jane Rawlinson, Secretary; Patricia Ann Anderson [1957] Director; Jeremy Peter Hartley [1965] Director; Neil Geoffrey Ward [1959] Director; Christine Desiree Winstanley [1966] Director

Pinco 2223 Limited
Incorporated: 10 November 2004
Net Worth Deficit: £5,333,867 *Total Assets:* £23,970,004
Registered Office: Sceptre House, Sceptre Way, Bamber Bridge, Preston, Lancs, PR5 6AW
Activities: Development of building projects
Parent: East Lancashire Building Partnership Ltd
Officers: Deborah Jane Rawlinson, Secretary; Jeremy Peter Hartley [1965] Director; Roger Martyn Parr [1970] Director; Neil Geoffrey Ward [1959] Director; Christine Desiree Winstanley [1966] Director; Mark Stuart Youlton [1963] Director

Pineapple Letting Ltd
Incorporated: 22 December 2008
Net Worth: £1,074,037 *Total Assets:* £9,817,795
Registered Office: 24 Manchester Road, Wilmslow, Cheshire, SK9 1BG
Activities: Other letting and operating of own or leased real estate
Officers: Arthur John Abercromby [1943] Director; Judith Abercromby [1941] Director/Company Secretary; Marie-Louise Abercromby [1978] Director; Mark Lhind Abercromby [1975] Director

Pinnacle Developments (NW) Limited
Incorporated: 17 May 2012
Net Worth: £2,480 *Total Assets:* £7,806,805
Registered Office: 1st Floor, NQ Building, 47 Bengal Street, Manchester, M4 6BB
Activities: Other business support service activities n.e.c.
Parent: KQ Developments Limited
Officers: Michael Shaw, Secretary; Daren Whitaker [1972] Director

The Pinnacle Learning Trust
Incorporated: 29 June 2011 *Employees:* 172
Net Worth: £6,455,243 *Total Assets:* £8,944,633
Registered Office: The Hathershaw College, Bellfield Avenue, Hathershaw, Oldham, Lancs, OL8 3EP
Activities: Other education n.e.c.
Officers: Danielle Sarah Hunt, Secretary; Jayne Louise Clarke [1971] Director/Principal; Mike David Gibbons [1967] Director; Andrew Kilburn [1973] Director/Retired; David Jack McEntee [1964] Director/Principal; John Andrew Christian Porter [1964] Director/Solicitor; Ateeque Ur-Rehman [1969] Director; Alan Christopher Wilson [1958] Director/Financial Consultant

Pinnacle Living 2 Ltd
Incorporated: 2 June 2004 *Employees:* 2
Net Worth Deficit: £52,709 *Total Assets:* £12,202,327
Registered Office: 2 Heap Bridge, Bury, Lancs, BL9 7HR
Activities: Development of building projects
Major Shareholder: Brent Heaton Miller
Officers: Julie Ann Miller, Secretary; Brent Heaton Miller [1962] Director

Pinnacle Living Ltd
Incorporated: 2 June 2004 *Employees:* 7
Net Worth: £2,045,197 *Total Assets:* £9,219,738
Registered Office: 2 Heap Bridge, Bury, Lancs, BL9 7HR
Activities: Other letting and operating of own or leased real estate
Parent: Pinnacle Living 2 Ltd
Officers: Julie Ann Miller, Secretary; Brent Heaton Miller [1962] Director

Pinnacle Student Developments (Egerton Street) Limited
Incorporated: 28 January 2014
Net Worth Deficit: £309,222 *Total Assets:* £8,344,138
Registered Office: Suite 410, Courthill House, 60 Water Lane, Wilmslow, Cheshire, SK9 5AJ
Activities: Development of building projects
Parent: MVG Holdings Limited
Officers: Carl William Mills [1979] Director/Accountant

Piolax Ltd.
Incorporated: 25 October 1994 *Employees:* 123
Net Worth: £19,084,556 *Total Assets:* £22,039,398
Registered Office: Shorten Brook Drive, Altham Business Park, Altham, Accrington, Lancs, BB5 5YH
Activities: Manufacture of other parts and accessories for motor vehicles
Parent: Piolax Incorporated
Officers: Andrew Duncan Cornwall, Secretary; Andrew Duncan Cornwall [1963] Director/Accountant; Peter England [1962] Director/Engineer; Shigeo Hoshino [1958] Marketing Director [Japanese]; Seiichi Sato [1955] Director/Designer [Japanese]; Paul Whelan [1965] Director

Pipeline Induction Heat Limited
Incorporated: 11 February 1980 *Employees:* 147
Net Worth: £30,444,080 *Total Assets:* £54,823,488
Registered Office: The Pipeline Centre, Farrington Road, Rossendale Road Industrial Estate, Burnley, Lancs, BB11 5SW
Activities: Treatment and coating of metals
Parent: PIH Holdings Limited
Officers: Steven John Costello, Secretary; Caroline Allen [1979] Finance Director; Paul Joseph McShane [1978] Director of Operations & Service Delivery; Adam Rhys Wynne Hughes [1965] Managing Director

Pitcliffe Properties Limited
Incorporated: 19 November 1959 *Employees:* 9
Net Worth: £12,719,669 *Total Assets:* £13,414,113
Registered Office: 183 Paradise Shopping Precinct, Pasture Lane, Clayton, Bradford, W Yorks, BD7 2SB
Activities: Development of building projects
Parent: Pitcliffe (Holdings) Limited
Officers: David Blyth [1959] Director/Builder; Graham Blyth [1950] Director/Builder

Pitts Wilson Limited
Incorporated: 4 February 1997 *Employees:* 87
Net Worth: £6,712,731 *Total Assets:* £9,049,172
Registered Office: Cutler House, Wakefield Road, Bradford, W Yorks, BD4 7LU
Activities: Repair of electrical equipment
Parent: Pitts Wilson Holdings Limited
Officers: Jeremy Harrison, Secretary/Accountant; Paul Nicholas Bottomley [1979] Director; Mark Flude [1960] Director/Electrical Engineer; Jeremy Harrison [1958] Director/Accountant; Christopher Paul Hepworth [1966] Contracts Director; David Hooley [1959] Director/Electrical Engineer; Geoffrey Mountain [1957] Director; Stuart Sinclair Reid [1970] Director/Mechanical Engineer

PJP (UK) Limited
Incorporated: 24 March 1983 *Employees:* 21
Net Worth: £1,815,945 *Total Assets:* £11,776,438
Registered Office: 15 Mill Bank, Mill Street, Radcliffe, Manchester, M26 1AJ
Activities: Renting and leasing of construction and civil engineering machinery and equipment
Major Shareholder: Colin Francis Power
Officers: Diane Foster, Secretary; Colin Francis Power [1960] Managing Director; Evelyn Carole Power [1961] Director

PKW Properties LLP
Incorporated: 29 May 2012
Net Worth: £24,855,880 *Total Assets:* £25,493,240
Registered Office: Ash House, Ash Lane, Ollerton, Knutsford, Cheshire, WA16 8RQ
Officers: Andrew Simon Pritchard [1958] Member

Plant Health Care PLC
Incorporated: 30 April 2004 *Employees:* 37
Net Worth: £7,706,968 *Total Assets:* £9,881,733
Registered Office: c/o DWF LLP, 1 Scott Place, 2 Hardman Street, Manchester, M3 3AA
Activities: Activities of head offices
Officers: Christine Mazzone, Secretary; Michael James Higgins [1956] Director; William Martin Lewis [1960] Director [American]; Dr Christopher Gareth Joseph Richards [1953] Director; Dr Richard Hannam Webb [1959] Director/Management Consultant

Plantec Assist Limited
Incorporated: 19 September 2013 *Employees:* 114
Net Worth: £3,520,000 *Total Assets:* £8,552,000
Registered Office: Kindertons House, Marshfield Bank, Crewe, Cheshire, CW2 8UY
Activities: Renting and leasing of cars and light motor vehicles
Parent: Kindertons Holdings Limited
Officers: Neil Lithgow Cunningham [1960] Director; Paul Taylor [1974] Operations Managing Director; Nigel James Ward [1966] Finance Director

Plastic Formers Management Limited
Incorporated: 12 March 1990
Net Worth: £5,224,855 *Total Assets:* £7,654,474
Registered Office: Unit 1 Crown Point South Industrial Park, King Street, Denton, Manchester, M34 6PF
Activities: Other letting and operating of own or leased real estate
Shareholders: Daniel Stuart Jepson; Alexandra Clare Rhodes
Officers: Daniel Stuart Jepson [1976] Director/Industrial Designer; Stuart William Jepson [1945] Director/Engineer; Alexandra Clare Rhodes [1974] Director/Secretary

Plastic Recycling Limited
Incorporated: 9 October 2013 *Employees:* 141
Net Worth: £2,496,654 *Total Assets:* £8,784,401
Registered Office: 14-16 Derby Road, Bootle, Liverpool, L20 8EE
Activities: Manufacture of plastic plates, sheets, tubes and profiles
Shareholders: Simon John Carroll; Merseyside Loan and Equity Fund LLP
Officers: Simon John Carroll [1967] Director; Dr David Wayne Cartmell [1961] Director/Chairman; Richard Nicholas Keighley [1959] Finance Director

Plasto-Sac UK Limited
Incorporated: 14 April 1999 *Employees:* 27
Net Worth: £867,373 *Total Assets:* £9,041,943
Registered Office: 23 Leek Road, Mossley, Congleton, Cheshire, CW12 3HU
Activities: Manufacture of plastic packing goods
Parent: Plasto-Sac Limited
Officers: James Michael Whitehead, Secretary/Sales Executive; Gabriel Nagar [1960] Director [Israeli]; James Michael Whitehead [1969] Director/Sales Executive

Platform Funding Limited
Incorporated: 28 October 1997
Net Worth: £43,152,000 *Total Assets:* £116,812,000
Registered Office: P O Box 101, 1 Balloon Street, Manchester, M60 4EP
Activities: Non-trading company
Parent: The Co-operative Bank PLC
Officers: David Clive Whitehead, Secretary; Ashley John William Lillie [1970] Director; Caroline Jane Richardson [1974] Director/Accountant

Platform Home Loans Limited
Incorporated: 12 January 1989
Net Worth: £60,000 *Total Assets:* £6,690,000
Registered Office: P O Box 101, 1 Balloon Street, Manchester, M60 4EP
Activities: Financial intermediation not elsewhere classified
Parent: The Co-operative Bank PLC
Officers: David Clive Whitehead, Secretary; Ashley John William Lillie [1970] Director; Caroline Jane Richardson [1974] Director/Accountant

Platform Sales & Hire Limited
Incorporated: 21 September 1999 *Employees:* 59
Net Worth: £2,209,420 *Total Assets:* £9,780,415
Registered Office: Chase House, 16 The Parks, Newton-le-Willows, Merseyside, WA12 0JQ
Activities: Other business support service activities n.e.c.
Parent: Speedy Asset Services Limited
Officers: Neil John Hunt, Secretary; Russell Down [1965] Director; Thomas Christopher Morgan [1966] Director

Playnation Limited
Incorporated: 18 October 2012 *Employees:* 466
Net Worth: £24,849,684 *Total Assets:* £31,794,440
Registered Office: Unit 17 Berkeley Court, Manor Park, Runcorn, Cheshire, WA7 1TQ
Activities: Gambling and betting activities
Parent: Novomatic UK Ltd
Officers: Andrew Brown [1971] Director; Peter John Davies [1970] Director; Zane Cedomir Mersich [1972] Managing Director; Neil Paramore [1962] Financial Director

Please Hold (UK) Limited
Incorporated: 17 November 1998 *Employees:* 465
Net Worth: £7,301,213 *Total Assets:* £27,661,720
Registered Office: Oakland House, Talbot Road, Old Trafford, Manchester, M16 0PQ
Activities: Advertising agencies
Shareholders: Grant Lawrence Reed; Jason Peter Clarke
Officers: Christopher John Berisford, Secretary; Grant Lawrence Reed [1962] Director

R. Plevin & Sons Limited
Incorporated: 1 May 1974 *Employees:* 193
Net Worth: £3,113,000 *Total Assets:* £20,018,000
Registered Office: Cheshire Street, Mossley, Ashton under Lyne, Lancs, OL5 9NG
Activities: Sawmilling and planing of wood
Parent: Plevin Holdings Limited
Officers: Graham Hobson [1963] Financial Director; Jamie Plevin [1971] Director; Simon Plevin [1966] Director

Plevin Holdings Limited
Incorporated: 16 February 2009 *Employees:* 193
Net Worth: £7,741,000 *Total Assets:* £22,486,000
Registered Office: Cheshire Street, Mossley, Ashton under Lyne, Lancs, OL5 9NG
Activities: Activities of head offices
Major Shareholder: Jamie Plevin
Officers: Jamie Plevin [1971] Director; Simon Plevin [1966] Director

David Pluck (North West) Limited
Incorporated: 5 February 1980 *Employees:* 171
Net Worth: £4,626,943 *Total Assets:* £7,572,531
Registered Office: c/o DSG Chartered Accountants, Castle Chambers, 43 Castle Street, Liverpool, L2 9TL
Activities: Gambling and betting activities
Major Shareholder: David Leslie Pluck
Officers: Nicholas Francis Thompson, Secretary; David Leslie Pluck [1950] Director/Turf Accountant; Nicholas Francis Thompson [1975] Director/General Manager

Plymouth Grove Residential LLP
Incorporated: 1 October 2007
Net Worth Deficit: £43,812,884 *Total Assets:* £40,457,624
Registered Office: Landmark House, Station Road, Cheadle Hulme, Cheadle, Cheshire, SK8 7BS
Officers: Julie Anne Everton [1968] Member; Richard Albert Everton [1952] Member; Charles Everton [1988] LLP Member

PMC Fluidpower Group Limited
Incorporated: 19 April 2005 *Employees:* 9
Net Worth: £1,482,560 *Total Assets:* £11,535,557
Registered Office: Flowtech Fluidpower, Pimbo Road, Skelmersdale, Lancs, WN8 9RB
Activities: Activities of other holding companies n.e.c.
Parent: Fluidpower MIP Limited
Officers: Jon Burke, Secretary/Financial Manager; Bryce Rowan Brooks [1965] Director

PMC Fluidpower Limited
Incorporated: 1 February 1968 *Employees:* 70
Net Worth: £7,778,978 *Total Assets:* £23,229,962
Registered Office: Flowtech Fluidpower PLC, Pimbo Road, Skelmersdale, Lancs, WN8 9RB
Activities: Manufacture of fluid power equipment
Parent: PMC Fluidpower Limited
Officers: Jon Burke, Secretary/Financial Manager; Bryce Rowan Brooks [1965] Director; Anthony Browne [1958] Director; Jon Burke [1972] Director; Paul Andrew McGrady [1970] Director

Pochin Construction Limited
Incorporated: 21 June 1945 *Employees:* 96
Net Worth: £6,413,236 *Total Assets:* £24,169,568
Registered Office: Brooks Lane, Middlewich, Cheshire, CW10 0JQ
Activities: Development of building projects
Parent: Pochin's Limited
Officers: Nigel Keith Rawlings, Secretary; Jonathan Henry Adams [1964] Director; Eduard Willem Bredenhann [1971] Director [South African]; Richard Fildes [1945] Director; Raymond Mark Hatton [1966] Director/Surveyor; James William Pochin Nicholson [1965] Director; Robert Kenneth Heywood Nicholson [1967] Director; Nigel Keith Rawlings [1956] Director/Chartered Accountant

Pochin's Limited
Incorporated: 9 May 1935 *Employees:* 120
Net Worth: £9,983,000 *Total Assets:* £47,623,000
Registered Office: Brooks Lane, Middlewich, Cheshire, CW10 0JQ
Activities: Buying and selling of own real estate
Parent: Middlewich Limited
Officers: Nigel Keith Rawlings, Secretary; Richard Fildes [1945] Director; James William Pochin Nicholson [1965] Director; Robert Kenneth Heywood Nicholson [1967] Director; Sylvia Elizabeth Nicholson [1941] Director/Company Secretary; Nigel Keith Rawlings [1956] Director/Chartered Accountant

Polcom UK Limited
Incorporated: 26 November 2004 *Employees:* 4
Net Worth: £376,790 *Total Assets:* £8,793,295
Registered Office: The Moorings, Dane Road Industrial Estate, Sale, Cheshire, M33 7BH
Activities: Other building completion and finishing
Shareholders: Eugeniusz Slominski; Gabriella Slominska
Officers: Anwyl Richard Whitehead, Secretary; Lukasz Wojciech Slominski [1982] Director [Polish]; Marcin Mateusz Slominski [1986] Director [Polish]

Polyflor Limited
Incorporated: 10 December 1962 *Employees:* 489
Net Worth: £25,087,592 *Total Assets:* £76,925,664
Registered Office: Beechfield, Hollinhurst Road, Radcliffe, Manchester, M26 1JN
Activities: Manufacture of builders ware of plastic
Parent: James Halstead PLC
Officers: David William Drillingcourt, Secretary; Mark Halstead [1957] Director; Steven Roger Mulholland [1974] Manufacturing Director; Michael John O'Connor [1967] Finance Director; Gordon Richard Oliver [1958] Director/Chartered Accountant; Thomas Gareth Rollo [1983] UK & International Marketing Director; Mark Anthony Scull [1969] Sales Director; Robert Nathan Bancroft Smith [1956] Technical Director; David Vincent Southern [1952] Director

Polytech International Limited
Incorporated: 26 February 1996 *Employees:* 22
Net Worth: £5,674,474 *Total Assets:* £11,118,967
Registered Office: 7 St Petersgate, Stockport, Cheshire, SK1 1EB
Activities: Manufacture of synthetic rubber in primary forms
Officers: David Alan Bell [1977] Director/Commercial; Paul Alexander Crellin [1971] Operations Director; Christopher Simon Nicholls [1955] Director; Karen Wells [1973] Director/Sales

Pomeroy IT Solutions UK Limited
Incorporated: 3 May 1996 *Employees:* 231
Net Worth: £9,181,129 *Total Assets:* £10,997,711
Registered Office: 3rd Floor, 1 Ashley Road, Altrincham, Cheshire, WA14 2DT
Activities: Other information technology service activities
Officers: Paul David Yeomans, Secretary; Keith Bradley [1963] Director [American]; Paul David Yeomans [1958] IT Director

Poppies Europe Ltd
Incorporated: 16 March 2010 *Employees:* 144
Net Worth: £1,350,054 *Total Assets:* £13,996,929
Registered Office: Poppies House, Unit 7 Parr Industrial Estate, Cornwall Street, St Helens, Merseyside, WA9 1QT
Activities: Manufacture of paper and paperboard
Shareholder: Masoud Khadem-Ahmadabadi
Officers: Axel Dehy [1971] Director [French]; John-Simon Fearns [1986] Director; Masoud Khadem-Ahmadabadi [1956] Director [Iranian]; Armindo Marques [1975] Director [Portuguese]; Anthony Gerard Pye [1968] Director; Robert Thorniley [1988] Director

Porritts & Spencer Limited
Incorporated: 16 March 1914
Net Worth: £12,951,04· *Total Assets:* £143,930,336
Registered Office: Manchester Road, Ashton under Lyne, Lancs, OL7 0ED
Activities: Non-trading company
Parent: Scapa Group PLC
Officers: Wendy Baker, Secretary; Wendy Dickinson [1967] Director/Accountant; Oskar Zahn [1964] Director

The Port of Mostyn Limited
Incorporated: 29 March 1993 *Employees:* 15
Net Worth: £18,177,048 *Total Assets:* £31,016,844
Registered Office: The Port of Mostyn, Coast Road, Mostyn, Holywell, Flintshire, CH8 9HE
Activities: Sea and coastal freight water transport
Shareholders: Carole Brazier; Rachael Julie Byrne; Susan Kim Parker; James Peter O'Toole
Officers: Fiona Jane Wynne-Jones, Secretary; John Howard Kearsley [1948] Director/Accountant; James Peter O'Toole [1942] Managing Director

Port of Sheerness Limited
Incorporated: 14 August 1991 *Employees:* 154
Net Worth: £7,600,000 *Total Assets:* £121,300,000
Registered Office: Maritime Centre, Port of Liverpool, L21 1LA
Activities: Sea and coastal freight water transport
Parent: Medway Ports Limited
Officers: Farook Akhtar Khan, Secretary; Caroline Ruth Marrison Gill, Secretary; Thomas Eardley Allison [1948] Director; Ian Graeme Lloyd Charnock [1962] Director; Gary Edward Hodgson [1958] Director; Steven Keith Underwood [1974] Director; John Whittaker [1942] Director; Mark Whitworth [1966] Director

Port of Sheerness Wind Farm Limited
Incorporated: 4 December 2007
Net Worth: £191,743 *Total Assets:* £18,068,354
Registered Office: Peel Dome, intu Trafford Centre, Trafford City, Manchester, M17 8PL
Activities: Production of electricity
Parent: Peel Wind Farms (Sheerness) Limited
Officers: Neil Lees, Secretary; Neil Lees [1963] Director/Company Secretary; David Muir Miller [1954] Director; John Alexander Schofield [1968] Director/Accountant; Steven Keith Underwood [1974] Director; John Whittaker [1942] Director

Port Salford Holdings Limited
Incorporated: 5 March 2013
Net Worth: £7,678 *Total Assets:* £6,591,619
Registered Office: Peel Dome, intu Trafford Centre, Trafford City, Manchester, M17 8PL
Activities: Activities of other holding companies n.e.c.
Parent: Peel Holdings Land and Property (UK) Limited
Officers: Neil Lees, Secretary; Peter John Hosker [1957] Director; Neil Lees [1963] Director; John Alexander Schofield [1968] Director/Accountant; Steven Keith Underwood [1974] Director; John Whittaker [1942] Director

Port Salford Land Limited
Incorporated: 17 December 2014 *Employees:* 6
Net Worth Deficit: £4,836,001 *Total Assets:* £10,702,174
Registered Office: Peel Dome, intu Trafford Centre, Trafford City, Manchester, M17 8PL
Activities: Development of building projects
Parent: Port Salford Holdings Limited
Officers: Neil Lees, Secretary; Peter John Hosker [1957] Director; Neil Lees [1963] Director; John Alexander Schofield [1968] Director/Accountant; Steven Keith Underwood [1974] Director; John Whittaker [1942] Director

The Port Sunlight Village Trust
Incorporated: 25 February 1999
Net Worth: £33,462,156 *Total Assets:* £34,826,580
Registered Office: 23 King George's Drive, Port Sunlight, Wirral, Merseyside, CH62 5DX
Activities: Other letting and operating of own or leased real estate
Officers: Paul Patrick Harris, Secretary; Emma Rachael Chaplin [1971] Director/Museum Consultant; John Robert Cocker [1942] Director/Retired Town Planner; Stephen Connolly [1953] Managing Director; Peter David de Figueiredo [1947] Director/Historic Buildings Consultant; John Jones [1956] Director/Retired; Robert Clive Young [1955] Director/Chief Executive

Portable Foods Manufacturing Company Limited
Incorporated: 18 March 1998 *Employees:* 166
Net Worth: £12,120,000 *Total Assets:* £15,518,000
Registered Office: Orange Tower, Media City UK, Salford, M50 2HF
Activities: Manufacture of other food products n.e.c.
Parent: Kellogg Company
Officers: Andrea Critchley [1973] Senior SC Director; Albert Roch Dosaiguas [1976] Portable Foods Plant Director [Spanish]; Nigel David Jaynes [1966] Director/Environment, Health & Safety, Corporate Services

Portable Offices (Hire) Limited
Incorporated: 19 April 2001 *Employees:* 70
Net Worth: £6,078,142 *Total Assets:* £10,827,084
Registered Office: c/o Duncan Sheard Glass, Castle Chambers, 43 Castle Street, Liverpool, L2 9TL
Activities: Renting and leasing of other machinery, equipment and tangible goods n.e.c.
Parent: Harnage Estates Limited
Officers: Simon David Scott, Secretary/Farmer; Andrew John Rattray Sayer [1957] Director; Justin de Berkeley Scott [1960] Director/Farmer; Simon David Scott [1958] Director/Farmer; Stephen Brian Ward [1978] Director; Adrian Richard Witty [1955] Managing Director

Portcullis Oldham Limited
Incorporated: 19 April 2002
Net Worth: £25,546,316 *Total Assets:* £29,622,436
Registered Office: Tweedale Way, Chadderton, Oldham, Lancs, OL9 7LD
Activities: Activities of other holding companies n.e.c.
Shareholders: Judith Rothwell; Francis Leigh Rothwell
Officers: Judith Rothwell, Secretary; Francis Leigh Rothwell [1950] Director/Plant Engineer; Judith Rothwell [1949] Director/Secretary; Luke Rothwell [1975] Director/Operations; Susan Schofield [1977] Director/Manageress

The Portman Travel Group Limited
Incorporated: 3 January 2014 *Employees:* 739
Net Worth: £6,107,000 *Total Assets:* £86,809,000
Registered Office: Elegant House, Sandpiper Way, Chester Business Park, Chester, CH4 9QE
Activities: Tour operator activities
Officers: Abdullah Al Dawood [1981] Director [Saudi Arabian]; Mark Christopher Nevin [1957] Director; Redmond Gavin McGinty Walsh [1967] Director; Yousif Musa Yousif [1957] Director [American]

Positive Solutions Limited
Incorporated: 10 August 1993 *Employees:* 76
Net Worth: £6,120,437 *Total Assets:* £9,122,853
Registered Office: P O Box 18, Number Three, South Langworthy Road, Salford, M50 2PW
Activities: Other information technology service activities
Parent: Mawdsleys Group Investments Limited
Officers: Stephanie Joy Ellison, Secretary/Director; Ian Colin Brownlee [1948] Director; Stephanie Joy Ellison [1958] Director; William John Sanders [1966] Director

Postcode Anywhere (Europe) Limited
Incorporated: 9 April 1997 *Employees:* 49
Net Worth: £3,818,000 *Total Assets:* £13,180,000
Registered Office: The Foundation, Herons Way, Chester Business Park, Chester, CH4 9GB
Activities: Data processing, hosting and related activities
Parent: Postcode Anywhere (Holdings) Ltd
Officers: John Henri Constantin, Secretary; Nicholas Richard Brown [1960] Director; Christopher Graham Clark [1969] Director; David John Wilson [1962] Director

Postcode Anywhere Holdings Limited
Incorporated: 26 July 2002 *Employees:* 52
Net Worth: £5,644,000 *Total Assets:* £14,683,000
Registered Office: The Foundation, Herons Way, Chester Business Park, Chester, CH4 9GB
Activities: Other information technology service activities
Parent: GB Group PLC
Officers: John Henri Constantin, Secretary; Nicholas Richard Brown [1960] Director; Christopher Graham Clark [1969] Director; David John Wilson [1962] Director

Potensial Limited
Incorporated: 14 June 2006 *Employees:* 1,175
Net Worth: £12,926,309 *Total Assets:* £39,464,772
Registered Office: 68 Grange Road West, Birkenhead, Merseyside, CH41 4DB
Activities: Other residential care activities n.e.c.
Shareholders: John Farragher; Rachel Farragher
Officers: John Farragher, Secretary; Thomas George Arnold [1961] Finance Director; John Farragher [1958] Director; Rachel Farragher [1963] Director; Nicki Jane Stadames [1973] Director/Chief Operating Officer

Potomac Capital Limited
Incorporated: 4 February 2005 *Employees:* 1
Net Worth: £9,701,799 *Total Assets:* £9,764,819
Registered Office: c/o Booth Ainsworth LLP, Alpha House, 4 Greek Street, Stockport, Cheshire, SK3 8AB
Activities: Development of building projects
Parent: New Potomac Limited
Officers: Steven Alfred Hurrell, Secretary; Warren Hill McInteer [1959] Director

Potter Rees Limited
Incorporated: 6 February 2012 *Employees:* 44
Net Worth: £4,961,659 *Total Assets:* £7,179,346
Registered Office: 12 Commercial Street, Manchester, M15 4PZ
Activities: Solicitors
Shareholders: Jonathan Hugh Conwy Potter; Helen Sarah Dolan
Officers: Helen Sarah Dolan [1966] Director; Jonathan Hugh Conwy Potter [1962] Director

Powell (UK) Limited
Incorporated: 26 May 2005 *Employees:* 215
Net Worth: £13,842,000 *Total Assets:* £19,313,000
Registered Office: Factory Site, Ripley Road, Bradford, W Yorks, BD4 7EH
Activities: Manufacture of electricity distribution and control apparatus
Parent: Powell International BV
Officers: Don Rhea Madison, Secretary/Director [American]; Michael John Galley [1948] Managing Director; Eileen Lynn Howell [1957] Director/Accountant [American]; Don Rhea Madison [1957] Director [American]

Power Gems Holdings Limited
Incorporated: 16 July 2015
Net Worth: £8,000,000 *Total Assets:* £8,000,000
Registered Office: Britannic House, 657 Liverpool Road, Irlam, Manchester, M44 5XD
Activities: Activities of other holding companies n.e.c.
Shareholder: Patrick McGuane
Officers: Dr Phillip Ellams [1967] Director; Patrick McGuane [1953] Director

PQ Silicas UK Limited
Incorporated: 20 December 2007 *Employees:* 244
Net Worth: £56,034,000 *Total Assets:* £109,110,000
Registered Office: Bank Quay, 4 Liverpool Road, Warrington, Cheshire, WA5 1AQ
Activities: Manufacture of other inorganic basic chemicals
Officers: William James Sichko, Secretary [American]; Joseph Steven Koscinski [1965] Director [American]; Nicolaas Theodorus Oostveen [1975] Director [Dutch]; Scott Howard Randolph [1962] Director [American]; William James Sichko [1954] Director/Businessman [American]

Practice Services UK Limited
Incorporated: 23 February 2005 *Employees:* 47
Net Worth: £8,792,000 *Total Assets:* £9,486,000
Registered Office: Phoenix, Rivington Road, Whitehouse Industrial Estate, Runcorn, Cheshire, WA7 3DJ
Activities: Other business support service activities n.e.c.
Parent: Phoenix Healthcare Distribution Limited
Officers: Michael Peter Blakeman, Secretary; Stephen William Anderson [1966] Director; Kevin Robert Hudson [1963] Director; Paul Jonathan Smith [1962] Director

Praedius (UK) Limited
Incorporated: 14 August 2014
Net Worth: £25,360,000 *Total Assets:* £25,360,000
Registered Office: Capella House, Delta Crescent, Westbrook, Warrington, Cheshire, WA5 7NS
Activities: Buying and selling of own real estate
Parent: Praedius Ltd.
Officers: Christopher John Tinsley, Secretary; Andrew Dolman [1977] Finance Director; Christopher Phillip Sheppard [1974] Director; Robin Sheppard [1954] Director

Praedius Ltd.
Incorporated: 9 July 2014
Net Worth: £28,762,000 *Total Assets:* £29,388,000
Registered Office: Capella House, Delta Crescent, Westbrook, Warrington, Cheshire, WA5 7NS
Activities: Activities of head offices
Parent: Ausurus Group Ltd
Officers: Christopher John Tinsley, Secretary; Andrew Dolman [1977] Finance Director; Christopher Phillip Sheppard [1974] Director; Robin Sheppard [1954] Director

Praedius UK (Industrial) Limited
Incorporated: 20 June 2016
Net Worth: £1,977,000 *Total Assets:* £9,663,000
Registered Office: Capella House, Delta Crescent, Westbrook, Warrington, Cheshire, WA5 7NS
Activities: Other letting and operating of own or leased real estate
Parent: Praedius (UK) Limited
Officers: Christopher John Tinsley, Secretary; Andrew Dolman [1977] Director; Christopher Phillip Sheppard [1974] Director; Robin Sheppard [1954] Director

Praedius UK (No 1) Limited
Incorporated: 3 October 2014
Net Worth: £36,516,000 *Total Assets:* £122,947,000
Registered Office: Sirius House, Delta Crescent, Westbrook, Warrington, Cheshire, WA5 7NS
Activities: Other letting and operating of own or leased real estate
Parent: Praedius (UK) Limited
Officers: Christopher John Tinsley, Secretary; Andrew Dolman [1977] Finance Director; Christopher Phillip Sheppard [1974] Director; Robin Sheppard [1954] Director

Praetura Asset Finance (A) Limited
Incorporated: 2 July 2014
Net Worth: £139,043 *Total Assets:* £37,266,592
Registered Office: Giants Basin, Potato Wharf, Manchester, M3 4NB
Activities: Other service activities n.e.c.
Parent: Praetura Asset Finance Limited
Officers: Daryl Lee Johnson, Secretary; Michael Ian Dalzell [1962] Director; Michael Christopher Hartley [1965] Director; Daryl Lee Johnson [1958] Director; Jack Daniel Summers [1984] Director

Praetura Asset Finance (Holdings) Limited
Incorporated: 6 November 2013 *Employees:* 21
Net Worth Deficit: £3,060,384 *Total Assets:* £55,455,752
Registered Office: Giants Basin, Potato Wharf, Manchester, M3 4NB
Activities: Activities of financial services holding companies
Officers: Daryl Lee Johnson, Secretary; Michael Ian Dalzell [1962] Director; Michael Christopher Hartley [1965] Director/Financier; Daryl Lee Johnson [1958] Director; Peadar James O'Reilly [1976] Director; Stephen Neville Sealey [1958] Director/Chairman; Jack Daniel Summers [1984] Director

Praetura Asset Finance (L) Limited
Incorporated: 16 January 2014
Net Worth Deficit: £1,176,585 *Total Assets:* £10,242,720
Registered Office: Giants Basin, Potato Wharf, Manchester, M3 4NB
Activities: Financial leasing
Parent: Praetura Asset Finance Limited
Officers: Daryl Lee Johnson, Secretary; Michael Ian Dalzell [1962] Director; Michael Christopher Hartley [1965] Director; Daryl Lee Johnson [1958] Director; Jack Daniel Summers [1984] Director

Praetura Asset Finance (SB) Limited
Incorporated: 7 November 2013
Net Worth Deficit: £712,540 *Total Assets:* £9,109,263
Registered Office: Giants Basin, Potato Wharf, Manchester, M3 4NB
Activities: Financial leasing
Parent: Praetura Asset Finance Limited
Officers: Daryl Lee Johnson, Secretary; Michael Ian Dalzell [1962] Director; Michael Christopher Hartley [1965] Director/Financier; Daryl Lee Johnson [1958] Director; Jack Daniel Summers [1984] Director

Praetura Commercial Finance Limited
Incorporated: 19 September 2016 *Employees:* 6
Net Worth Deficit: £1,883,435 *Total Assets:* £15,587,967
Registered Office: Ground Floor, Giants Basin, Potato Wharf, Manchester, M3 4NB
Activities: Financial intermediation not elsewhere classified
Parent: Praetura Commercial Finance Holdings Limited
Officers: Stuart James Bates [1973] Commercial Director North; Jack Daniel Summers [1984] Finance Director; Lisa Marie Wood [1968] Deputy Managing Director

Precision Parts UK Limited
Incorporated: 1 March 2004 *Employees:* 36
Net Worth: £6,248,873 *Total Assets:* £7,561,495
Registered Office: Corner House, 28 Huddersfield Road, Milnrow, Rochdale, Lancs, OL16 3QF
Activities: Manufacture of medical and dental instruments and supplies
Parent: ESI Process U.K. Limited
Officers: Gregory Collins, Secretary; Morgan O'Brien [1961] Director [Irish]; Robert David Parry [1973] Director

Precision Polymer Engineering Limited
Incorporated: 1 February 1980 *Employees:* 257
Net Worth: £8,906,515 *Total Assets:* £18,533,398
Registered Office: Greenbank Road, Blackburn, Lancs, BB1 3EA
Activities: Other manufacturing n.e.c.
Parent: Seals Limited
Officers: Lisa Michelle Anderson, Secretary; Brian Patrick Hanigan, Secretary; Eric Shawn McKinley [1984] Director/Business Executive [American]; Neil Thompson [1965] Director/Business Executive; Marc Arthur Uleman [1963] Director/Manager

Precision Technologies Group (PTG) Limited
Incorporated: 1 August 2011 *Employees:* 160
Net Worth: £13,838,594 *Total Assets:* £60,954,564
Registered Office: Harbour Lane North, Milnrow, Rochdale, Lancs, OL16 3LQ
Activities: Activities of head offices
Parent: Chongqing Machinery & Electric Co Ltd
Officers: Laurence John Neary, Secretary; Dr Antony James Bannan [1964] Director; Wenguang Sun [1966] Director [Chinese]; Kai Wu [1970] Director [Chinese]; Mingzhi Zhang [1963] Director [Chinese]

Precision Technologies Group (US) Limited
Incorporated: 9 April 2015 *Employees:* 1
Net Worth Deficit: £364,566 *Total Assets:* £8,524,833
Registered Office: Harbour Lane North, Milnrow, Rochdale, Lancs, OL16 3LQ
Activities: Other manufacturing n.e.c.
Officers: Dr Antony James Bannan [1964] Director; Laurence John Neary [1971] Director; Mingzhi Zhang [1963] Director [Chinese]

Premaitha Health PLC
Incorporated: 13 April 2000 *Employees:* 52
Net Worth: £5,844,800 *Total Assets:* £17,563,234
Registered Office: Enterprise House, Manchester Science Park, Lloyd Street North, Manchester, M15 6SE
Activities: Manufacture of medical and dental instruments and supplies
Officers: Barry Kenneth Hextall, Secretary; Bill Chang [1975] Director [Taiwanese]; Peter Collins [1958] Director/Healthcare; Barry Kenneth Hextall [1967] Finance Director; Keng Hsu [1977] Director [Taiwanese]; Dr Stephen Little [1957] Director/Healthcare; Nicholas Mustoe [1961] Director; Lyn Dafydd Rees [1973] Director; Adam Reynolds [1962] Director

Premex Group Limited
Incorporated: 21 September 2003 *Employees:* 666
Net Worth: £50,994,000 *Total Assets:* £170,972,992
Registered Office: Premex House, Futura Park, Middlebrook, Bolton, Lancs, BL6 6SX
Activities: Other human health activities
Parent: Examworks UK Limited
Officers: Caroline Emily Elizabeth Russell, Secretary; Donald Stuart Fowler [1973] Director; Doug Laver [1965] Finance Director; Simon Margolis [1961] Director; Richard Elliot Perlman [1946] Director [American]; James Kerrick Price [1958] Director [American]

Premex Services Limited
Incorporated: 20 November 1996 *Employees:* 537
Net Worth: £52,082,000 *Total Assets:* £170,532,992
Registered Office: Premex House, Futura Park, Middlebrook, Bolton, Lancs, BL6 6SX
Activities: Other human health activities
Parent: Premex Group Limited
Officers: Caroline Emily Elizabeth Russell, Secretary; Michael Philip Cutler [1973] Director; Peter Sleigh [1966] Director; Christopher Wheatley [1974] Director

Premier Textiles Limited
Incorporated: 14 December 1981 *Employees:* 25
Net Worth: £10,009,692 *Total Assets:* £11,455,563
Registered Office: Green Lane Industrial Estate, Green Lane, Stockport, Cheshire, SK4 2JR
Activities: Wholesale of textiles
Major Shareholder: Ashok Abraham Kallumpram
Officers: Anna Eapen Kallumpram, Secretary; Anna Eapen Kallumpram [1961] Director/Lawyer; Ashok Abraham Kallumpram [1958] Director/Businessman; Nicholas Peter Smith [1971] Director

Prescot Business Park Limited
Incorporated: 13 August 2010
Net Worth: £2,486,951 *Total Assets:* £43,727,040
Registered Office: Laurel House, 173 Chorley New Road, Bolton, Lancs, BL1 4QZ
Activities: Development of building projects
Major Shareholder: Thomas Joseph Morris
Officers: Michael Stuart James [1958] Director

Presspart Manufacturing Limited
Incorporated: 26 November 1970 *Employees:* 159
Net Worth: £9,174,000 *Total Assets:* £24,946,000
Registered Office: Whitebirk Estate, Blackburn, Lancs, BB1 5RF
Activities: Machining
Shareholders: Heitkamp & Thumann KG; Presspart Verwaltungs GmbH
Officers: Tracey Elizabeth Catlow, Secretary; Antony Cross [1964] Operations Pharmaceutical Director; Julian Napier Hemy [1962] Commercial Director; Peter Schmelzer [1970] Director/Chairman of The Managing Board [German]

Prestigious Textiles Limited
Incorporated: 9 February 1988 *Employees:* 120
Net Worth: £17,321,262 *Total Assets:* £21,841,024
Registered Office: 4 Cross Lane, Westgate Hill Street, Bradford, W Yorks, BD4 0SG
Activities: Wholesale of textiles
Shareholders: Nicola Brumfitt; Matthew Simon Helliwell; Trevor Allen Helliwell
Officers: Nicola Brumfit, Secretary; Graham Richard Bateman [1957] Director; Nicola Brumfit [1977] Director; Andrew David Gautry [1956] Director/Chartered Accountant; Matthew Simon Helliwell [1974] Director; Trevor Allen Helliwell [1947] Textile Director

Preston Board and Packaging Limited
Incorporated: 12 June 1981 *Employees:* 172
Net Worth: £6,350,000 *Total Assets:* £14,809,000
Registered Office: Arkwright Mill, Greenbank Street, Preston, Lancs, PR1 7JS
Activities: Manufacture of paper and paperboard
Parent: Marblegrange Limited
Officers: Charles Richard Ingham, Secretary; David John Hardman [1945] Director; Nicholas David Hardman [1967] Director; Charles Richard Ingham [1980] Director; Charles Stuart Ingham [1950] Director; Christopher James Ingham [1976] Director

Preston North End Limited
Incorporated: 10 March 1982 *Employees:* 110
Net Worth: £35,369,000 *Total Assets:* £43,827,000
Registered Office: Sir Tom Finney Way, Deepdale, Preston, Lancs, PR1 6RU
Activities: Activities of sport clubs
Parent: Deepdale PNE Holdings Ltd
Officers: Kevin Mark Abbott, Secretary/Chartered Accountant; Kevin Mark Abbott [1973] Director/Chartered Accountant; Anthony Scott Hughes [1967] Director/Solicitor; John Clement Kay [1953] Director/Chief Executive; David Robsinson [1960] Director/Chartered Surveyor; David Wilson Taylor [1950] Director

Preston Plastics Limited
Incorporated: 29 May 1997 *Employees:* 27
Net Worth: £5,746,314 *Total Assets:* £6,603,235
Registered Office: Charter Hosue, Pittman Way, Fulwood, Preston, Lancs, PR2 9ZD
Activities: Recovery of sorted materials
Major Shareholder: Edgar Wallace
Officers: Michelle Ann Alston, Secretary; Wayne Emerson Clark [1969] Director/Plastics Recycling; Edgar Wallace [1962] Director

Alfred Price & Sons,Limited
Incorporated: 15 August 1938 *Employees:* 59
Net Worth: £8,201,942 *Total Assets:* £12,346,721
Registered Office: Penrhyn Road, Knowsley Business Park, Prescot, Merseyside, L34 9HY
Activities: Wholesale of fruit and vegetables
Shareholders: David Anthony Price; Alfred Price & Sons Trustees Ltd
Officers: Elaine Ann Arnold, Secretary; Marcus Guerrero [1972] Director/Sales Executive; Philip Alexander McCaughrean [1969] Director/Sales Executive; David Anthony Price [1940] Director/Chairman; Simon Charles Price [1969] Managing Director

The Priestley Academy Trust
Incorporated: 5 October 2016
Net Worth: £16,256,632 *Total Assets:* £20,369,740
Registered Office: Green Lane Primary School, Green Lane, Bradford, W Yorks, BD8 8HT
Activities: Primary education
Officers: Javed Kausar Ahmed [1957] Director/Finance Manager; Ros Garside [1949] Director/Education Consultant; Kevin Paul Holland [1957] Director; Sam Keighley [1967] Director/Chief Executive of a Charity; Ashfaq Ahmed Rahman [1970] Director/Executive Headteacher; Margaret Mercedes Smith [1947] Director/Retired

Primeur Limited
Incorporated: 23 March 1990 *Employees:* 66
Net Worth: £912,213 *Total Assets:* £7,130,508
Registered Office: Castlefields, Cross Flats, Bingley, W Yorks, BD16 2AF
Activities: Non-specialised wholesale trade
Shareholders: James Alexander Holcroft Keighley; Stephen Fearnley
Officers: Ian Brazier, Secretary; Ian Brazier [1956] Finance Director; Jennifer Douthwaite [1981] Sales Director; Stephen Fearnley [1945] Director; James Alexander Holcroft Keighley [1964] Buying Director

Primopost Limited
Incorporated: 7 July 1986 *Employees:* 114
Net Worth: £8,109,000 *Total Assets:* £16,920,000
Registered Office: 144 Manchester Road, Carrington, Manchester, M31 4QN
Activities: Other manufacturing n.e.c.
Parent: Americk NI Limited
Officers: Steven Petty, Secretary; Angel Ramon Alejandro Balet [1961] Director [Spanish]; Susana Alejandro Balet [1970] Director [Spanish]; Thomas Anthony Rice [1966] Director [Irish]

Princes Dock Development Company Limited
Incorporated: 6 February 1997
Net Worth: £100,027,000 *Total Assets:* £108,133,000
Registered Office: Peel Dome, intu Trafford Centre, Trafford City, Manchester, M17 8PL
Activities: Develoment of building projects
Parent: Peel Land Holdings Limited
Officers: Neil Lees, Secretary; Peter John Hosker [1957] Director; Neil Lees [1963] Director/Company Secretary; John Alexander Schofield [1968] Director/Accountant; Steven Keith Underwood [1974] Director; John Whittaker [1942] Director; Mark Whittaker [1969] Director

Princes Dock Hotel Limited
Incorporated: 6 February 1997 *Employees:* 7
Net Worth: £15,822,000 *Total Assets:* £15,880,000
Registered Office: Peel Dome, intu Trafford Centre, Trafford City, Manchester, M17 8PL
Activities: Non-trading company
Parent: Mersey Docks Property Holdings Limited
Officers: Neil Lees, Secretary; Peter John Hosker [1957] Director; Neil Lees [1963] Director/Company Secretary; John Alexander Schofield [1968] Director/Accountant; Steven Keith Underwood [1974] Director; John Whittaker [1942] Director; Mark Whittaker [1969] Director

Princes Limited
Incorporated: 15 December 1988 *Employees:* 6,900
Net Worth: £284,547,008 *Total Assets:* £1,025,280,000
Registered Office: Royal Liver Building, Pier Head, Liverpool, L3 1NX
Activities: Non-specialised wholesale of food, beverages and tobacco
Parent: Mitsubishi Corporation
Officers: Kazuhito Suematsu, Secretary; Takeshi Arakawa [1963] Director [Japanese]; Stephen David Cardall [1971] Director; Kazuo Ito [1968] Director [Japanese]; Isao Kano [1960] Director [Japanese]; Cameron John Mackintosh [1969] Director; Manabu Oda [1970] Director [Japanese]; Craig Derek Price [1974] Director; Yoshihiro Shimazu [1968] Director [Japanese]; Nicholas John Spruyt [1964] Director; Kazuhito Suematsu [1977] Director [Japanese]

Principal Healthcare Finance (UK) No.1 Limited
Incorporated: 10 October 1997
Net Worth Deficit: £63,059,000 *Total Assets:* £17,022,000
Registered Office: Norcliffe House, Station Road, Wilmslow, Cheshire, SK9 1BU
Activities: Renting and operating of Housing Association real estate
Parent: Principal Healthcare Finance (UK) No 2 Limited
Officers: Abigail Mattison, Secretary; Robert Nicolas Barr [1958] Director; Timothy Richard William Hammond [1959] Director; Ryan Stuart MacAskill [1975] Director; Gregory Laurence Newman [1988] Director/Investment Professional; Benjamin Robert Taberner [1972] Director/Chartered Accountant

Principal Healthcare Finance (UK) No.2 Limited
Incorporated: 10 October 1997 *Employees:* 5
Net Worth: £28,034,000 *Total Assets:* £28,034,000
Registered Office: Norcliffe House, Station Road, Wilmslow, Cheshire, SK9 1BU
Activities: Renting and operating of Housing Association real estate
Parent: Principal Healthcare Ltd
Officers: Abigail Mattison, Secretary; Robert Nicolas Barr [1958] Director; Timothy Richard William Hammond [1959] Director; Ryan Stuart MacAskill [1975] Director; Gregory Laurence Newman [1988] Director/Investment Professional; Benjamin Robert Taberner [1972] Director/Chartered Accountant

Principle Healthcare International Limited
Incorporated: 20 January 2004 *Employees:* 148
Net Worth: £4,134,937 *Total Assets:* £9,883,045
Registered Office: Principle Healthcare International Ltd, Airedale Business Centre, Millennium Road, Skipton, N Yorks, BD23 2TZ
Activities: Manufacture of basic pharmaceutical products
Major Shareholder: Michael John Davies
Officers: Richard Howard Doyle, Secretary/Chartered Accountant; Andrew Michael Davies [1982] Director; Michael John Davies [1951] Director; Philip Benjamin Davies [1977] Director

Printbetter Limited
Incorporated: 15 October 1990 *Employees:* 346
Net Worth: £15,113,702 *Total Assets:* £20,569,588
Registered Office: Unit 2 Roman Court, Roman Way, Preston, Lancs, PR2 5BB
Activities: Activities of other holding companies n.e.c.
Shareholders: David Patrick Cosgrove; Andrew John Cosgrove
Officers: David Patrick Cosgrove, Secretary/Director; Andrew John Cosgrove [1978] Director/Accountant [Irish]; David Patrick Cosgrove [1975] Director

Prinwest Limited
Incorporated: 10 December 1998
Net Worth: £21,763,100 *Total Assets:* £42,520,968
Registered Office: 2076 Lynstock House, Lynstock Way, Lostock, Bolton, Lancs, BL6 4SA
Activities: Wholesale of pharmaceutical goods
Shareholders: Anwer Ibrahim Patel; Yakub Ibrahim Patel
Officers: Anwar Ibrahim Patel, Secretary; Anwer Ibrahim Patel [1954] Director; Yakub Ibrahim Patel [1953] Director

Priory Design Services Limited
Incorporated: 3 October 1985 *Employees:* 689
Net Worth: £556,148 *Total Assets:* £14,367,126
Registered Office: Millbank House, Northway, Runcorn, Cheshire, WA7 2SX
Activities: Temporary employment agency activities
Parent: Millbank Holdings Limited
Officers: James Oskar Burton [1949] Director; David Hopley [1965] Director/Technical Recruitment

Prisma Developments Limited
Incorporated: 26 January 2000
Net Worth Deficit: £15,101,018 *Total Assets:* £17,845,944
Registered Office: 53 Rodney Street, Liverpool, L1 9ER
Activities: Other business support service activities n.e.c.
Officers: Richard Peter Hazzard [1987] Director/Accountant

Prismo Road Markings Limited
Incorporated: 15 August 2006 *Employees:* 59
Net Worth Deficit: £5,535,359 *Total Assets:* £16,392,036
Registered Office: 5 Drumhead Road, Chorley North Industrial Park, Chorley, Lancs, PR6 7BX
Activities: Other manufacturing n.e.c.
Parent: Ennis Paint UK Holding Company Limted
Officers: Daniel Louis Lang, Secretary; Daniel Louis Lang [1955] Director/Vice President of Ennis-Flint [American]; Matthew Louis Soule [1969] Director/CFO of Ennis-Flint [American]; Robert Steven Vetter [1956] Director/President and CEO of Ennis-Flint [American]

Pro Investments Limited
Incorporated: 14 July 2006
Net Worth: £16,619,783 *Total Assets:* £96,943,208
Registered Office: Canal Mill, Botany Brow, Chorley, Lancs, PR6 9AF
Activities: Other letting and operating of own or leased real estate
Parent: Barrowway No 2 Limited
Officers: Claire Caroline Sharp, Secretary/Property Director; Thomas Duncan Hopkinson [1956] Director/Accountant; Timothy John Peter Knowles [1964] Director; Claire Caroline Sharp [1973] Director/Administration Manager

Produmax Limited
Incorporated: 28 April 1966
Net Worth: £5,177,211 *Total Assets:* £8,386,376
Registered Office: Unit 2 Sapper Jordan Rossi Park, Baildon, Shipley, W Yorks, BD17 7AX
Activities: Manufacture of other fabricated metal products n.e.c.
Shareholders: Jeremy Paul Ridyard; Mandy Ridyard
Officers: Mandy Ridyard, Secretary; Jeremy Paul Ridyard [1967] Director/Engineer; Mandy Ridyard [1966] Director

Professional Disposables International Limited
Incorporated: 14 June 2007 *Employees:* 87
Net Worth: £1,849,036 *Total Assets:* £11,368,423
Registered Office: Aber Park, Aber Road, Flint, CH6 5EX
Activities: Non-specialised wholesale trade
Major Shareholder: Zachary Thornton Julius
Officers: David John Cowell, Secretary; David Cowell [1964] Director/Accountant; Michael Alexander Staton [1947] Director

The Professional Footballers' Association Charity
Incorporated: 8 January 2013
Net Worth: £53,399,144 *Total Assets:* £57,029,508
Registered Office: 20 Oxford Court, Bishopsgate, Manchester, M2 3WQ
Activities: Technical and vocational secondary education
Officers: Brendon Martin Batson [1953] Director/Sports Management Consultant; Garth Anthony Crooks [1958] Director/Sports Management Consultant; Paul Marcellous Ellion [1964] Director; Gareth John Griffiths [1970] Director/Independent Financial Advisor; Simon Charles Morgan [1966] Director/Head of Football Relations; Christopher George Robin Powell [1969] Director/First Team Manager Charlton Athletic; David Gillespie Weir [1970] Director/Reserve Team Coach Everton Football Club; Darren Anthony Wilson [1971] Director of Finance

Project Bullseye Bidco Limited
Incorporated: 30 November 2015 *Employees:* 9
Net Worth Deficit: £3,180,246 *Total Assets:* £20,027,728
Registered Office: Hardys Gate, Dumers Lane, Bury, Lancs, BL9 9UE
Activities: Activities of other holding companies n.e.c.
Shareholders: Project Bullseye Topco Limited; Elysian Capital LLP
Officers: Jeremy Paul Clynes [1974] Director; Thomas John Duffy [1973] Director; Thomas William Falcon [1969] Director; Brian Andrew Robinson [1965] Director/Accountant; Nicholas Michael Samuels [1974] Director

Project Bullseye Topco Limited
Incorporated: 30 November 2015
Net Worth Deficit: £1,753,000 *Total Assets:* £41,657,000
Registered Office: Hardys Gate, Dumers Lane, Bury, Lancs, BL9 9UE
Activities: Activities of other holding companies n.e.c.
Shareholders: Elysian Capital GP II LLP; Elysian Capital LLP
Officers: Jeremy Paul Clynes [1974] Director; David James Colclough [1971] Director/Private Equity Partner; Thomas John Duffy [1973] Director; Thomas William Falcon [1969] Director; Brian Andrew Robinson [1965] Director/Accountant; Nicholas Michael Samuels [1974] Director

Project Daytona Bidco Limited
Incorporated: 11 March 2016 *Employees:* 3
Net Worth Deficit: £3,665,550 *Total Assets:* £64,320,912
Registered Office: 9th Floor, Neo Building, Charlotte Street, Manchester, M1 4ET
Activities: Information technology consultancy activities
Parent: Project Daytona Limited
Officers: Scott Jonathan Fletcher [1973] Director; Ian Richardson Hogg [1949] Director; Robert Nugent [1982] Director; Paul Patrick Sweeney [1970] Director

Project Daytona Limited
Incorporated: 9 February 2016 *Employees:* 263
Net Worth: £848,871 *Total Assets:* £97,511,432
Registered Office: 9th Floor, Neo Building, Charlotte Street, Manchester, M1 4ET
Activities: Information technology consultancy activities
Shareholder: Scott Jonathan Fletcher
Officers: Robert Nugent, Secretary; Scott Jonathan Fletcher [1973] Director; Ian Richardson Hogg [1949] Director; Robert Nugent [1982] Director; Paul Patrick Sweeney [1970] Director

Project Finland Bidco Limited
Incorporated: 20 January 2016
Net Worth Deficit: £1,717,206 *Total Assets:* £17,095,784
Registered Office: Laurel House, 173 Chorley New Road, Bolton, Lancs, BL1 4QZ
Activities: Activities auxiliary to financial intermediation n.e.c.
Parent: Project Finland Topco Limited
Officers: Stuart Lee Almond [1964] Director; Ben Joseph Cartwright [1987] Director; Paul Ford [1977] Director; Kevin Hindley [1964] Director; Mark Kilgallon [1973] Director; Andrew Neil Marsh [1970] Director; Simon Andrew Moore [1973] Director; Garry Peter Lee Taylor [1978] Director; Timothy Allen Wheeldon [1966] Director

Project Finland Topco Limited
Incorporated: 20 January 2016 *Employees:* 117
Net Worth Deficit: £3,343,321 *Total Assets:* £16,379,450
Registered Office: Laurel House, 173 Chorley New Road, Bolton, Lancs, BL1 4QZ
Activities: Activities auxiliary to financial intermediation n.e.c.
Shareholder: Beech Tree Private Equity Partners (GP) Limited as General Partner of Beech Tree Private Equity Partners, L.P.
Officers: Stuart Lee Almond [1964] Director; Ben Joseph Cartwright [1987] Director; Paul Ford [1977] Director; Kevin Hindley [1964] Director; Mark Kilgallon [1973] Director; Andrew Neil Marsh [1970] Director; Simon Andrew Moore [1973] Director; Garry Peter Lee Taylor [1978] Director; Timothy Allen Wheeldon [1966] Director

Project Ires Bidco Limited
Incorporated: 3 July 2014
Net Worth Deficit: £21,344 000 *Total Assets:* £68,363,000
Registered Office: Eversheds House, 70 Great Bridgewater Street, Manchester, M1 5ES
Activities: Activities of head offices
Parent: Project Ires Topco Limited
Officers: Francis Herlihy [1966] Director; Matthew Edward McKinlay [1988] Director/Investment Executive; Alan James Proctor [1950] Director; Catherine Allingham Richards [1973] Director; Simon Rio [1976] Managing Director

Project Ires Topco Limited
Incorporated: 2 July 2014 *Employees:* 86
Net Worth Deficit: £32,972,000 *Total Assets:* £68,290,000
Registered Office: Eversheds House, 70 Great Bridgewater Street, Manchester, M1 5ES
Activities: Activities of head offices
Officers: Francis Herlihy [1966] Director; Matthew Edward McKinlay [1988] Director/Investment Executive; Alan James Proctor [1950] Director; Catherine Allingham Richards [1973] Director; Simon Rio [1976] Managing Director

Project One Consulting Limited
Incorporated: 30 September 1998 *Employees:* 111
Net Worth: £10,387,854 *Total Assets:* £16,887,894
Registered Office: The Clocktower, Manor Lane, Holmes Chapel, Crewe, Cheshire, CW4 8DJ
Activities: Management consultancy activities other than financial management
Parent: Gulltech Ltd
Officers: Robert Loveday, Secretary; Paul Ernest Clark [1967] Director/Chairman; Terence Peter Holland [1966] Managing Director; Timothy John Newman [1967] Director/Management Consultant; James O'Sullivan [1973] Director/Management Consultant

Project Play Midco 1 Limited
Incorporated: 30 October 2014
Net Worth Deficit: £4,934,000 *Total Assets:* £19,083,000
Registered Office: Ridgway House, Progress Way, Denton, Manchester, M34 2GP
Activities: Pre-primary education
Parent: Just Childcare Holdings Ltd
Officers: David William Johnson [1957] Director; Jacqueline Ann Johnson [1966] Director

Project Play Midco 2 Limited
Incorporated: 30 October 2014 *Employees:* 2
Net Worth: £58,000 *Total Assets:* £25,116,000
Registered Office: Ridgway House, Progress Way, Denton, Manchester, M34 2GP
Activities: Pre-primary education
Parent: Project Play Midco 1 Limited
Officers: David William Johnson [1957] Director; Jacqueline Ann Johnson [1966] Director

Project Rock Bidco Limited
Incorporated: 25 January 2016 *Employees:* 4
Net Worth Deficit: £3,487,000 *Total Assets:* £56,082,000
Registered Office: 10 Mannin Way, Lancaster Business Park, Lancaster, LA1 3SW
Activities: Holiday centres and villages
Parent: Palatine Private Equity
Officers: Beverley Jayne Dixon [1969] Operations Director; Graham Robert Hodgson [1960] Director/Chief Executive Officer; Ronald John Peters [1974] Director/Sales Manager; Andrew Jonathan Wall [1960] Finance Director

Project Rock Equityco Limited
Incorporated: 25 January 2016 *Employees:* 172
Net Worth: £138,000 *Total Assets:* £71,032,000
Registered Office: 10 Mannin Way, Lancaster Business Park, Lancaster, LA1 3SW
Activities: Holiday centres and villages
Parent: Palatine Private Equityllp
Officers: Beverley Jayne Dixon [1969] Operations Director; Edmund Fazakerley [1969] Director; Graham Robert Hodgson [1960] Director/Chief Executive Officer; George Hope [1962] Director; James Painter [1989] Director/Investment Manager; Ronald John Peters [1974] Director/Sales Manager; Andrew Jonathan Wall [1960] Finance Director

Prolift Access Limited
Incorporated: 5 November 2009 *Employees:* 67
Net Worth: £2,303,504 *Total Assets:* £12,132,862
Registered Office: Chase House, 16 The Parks, Newton-le-Willows, Merseyside, WA12 0JQ
Activities: Renting and leasing of construction and civil engineering machinery and equipment
Parent: Speedy Asset Services Limited
Officers: Neil John Hunt, Secretary; Russell Down [1965] Director; Thomas Christopher Morgan [1966] Director

Promat UK Limited
Incorporated: 23 January 1984 *Employees:* 95
Net Worth: £15,212,000 *Total Assets:* £22,828,000
Registered Office: B1 Heywood Distribution Park, Heywood, Lancs, OL10 2TS
Activities: Manufacture of plaster products for construction purposes
Officers: Danielle Christine Worthington, Secretary; Ian Cowley [1966] Director/General Manager; Frankie Alfons Flecijn [1969] Director [Belgian]; Steven Achiel Alice Heytens [1969] Director [Belgian]

Promatic Group Limited
Incorporated: 6 July 2007
Net Worth: £732,027 *Total Assets:* £7,499,271
Registered Office: Station Works, Hooton Road, Hooton, Ellesmere Port, Cheshire, CH66 7NF
Activities: Manufacture of other special-purpose machinery n.e.c.
Parent: Promatic Holdings Limited
Officers: John Peter Lamb, Secretary; Jonathan Luke Henry Goodhart [1965] Director; Brian Jardine [1953] Director; John Peter Lamb [1964] Director/Company Accountant; James Darwin Moses [1955] Director/CEO, Promatic Inc [American]

Promatic Holdings Limited
Incorporated: 1 August 2014 *Employees:* 87
Net Worth: £3,292,514 *Total Assets:* £9,091,151
Registered Office: Station Works, Hooton Road, Hooton, Ellesmere Port, Cheshire, CH66 7NF
Activities: Manufacture of other special-purpose machinery n.e.c.
Shareholders: Brian Jardine; Ram (102) Limited
Officers: Charles Giles Clarke [1953] Director/Chairman; Jonathan Luke Henry Goodhart [1965] Director; Brian Jardine [1953] Director; John Peter Lamb [1964] Director; James Darwin Moses [1955] Director [American]

Promatic International Limited
Incorporated: 16 December 1996 *Employees:* 64
Net Worth: £5,893,337 *Total Assets:* £11,622,667
Registered Office: Station Works, Hooton Road, Hooton, South Wirral, Merseyside, CH66 7NF
Activities: Manufacture of other special-purpose machinery n.e.c.
Parent: Promatic Group Limited
Officers: John Peter Lamb, Secretary; Graham Stephen Fair [1954] Group Technical Director; Jonathan Luke Henry Goodhart [1965] Director; Brian Jardine [1953] Director; John Peter Lamb [1964] Director/Company Accountant; Iain Thomas McDonald Duncan Petrie [1950] International Sales Director Group; Martin John Sambrook [1955] Manufacturing Director - Group

Promenade Baltic Limited
Incorporated: 10 September 2013
Net Worth: £10,404,926 *Total Assets:* £12,660,697
Registered Office: 2nd Floor, 2 Queen Square, Liverpool, L1 1RH
Activities: Development of building projects
Officers: Daniel Peter Hynd [1984] Director; Peter James Hynd [1981] Director; Peter Hynd [1951] Director; Simon Peter Hynd [1977] Director; Brian Meharg [1952] Director; Elizabeth Jane Spencer [1987] Director

Promenade Estates Limited
Incorporated: 18 September 2002 *Employees:* 7
Net Worth: £1,015,202 *Total Assets:* £7,362,180
Registered Office: 2nd Floor, 2 Queen Square, Liverpool, L1 1RH
Activities: Management of real estate on a fee or contract basis
Shareholders: Peter Hynd; Jennifer Elizabeth Hynd
Officers: Daniel Peter Hynd, Secretary; Daniel Peter Hynd [1984] Director; Jennifer Elizabeth Hynd [1951] Director; Peter Hynd [1951] Director; Brian Meharg [1952] Director

Promethean (Holdings) Limited
Incorporated: 10 March 1989 *Employees:* 3
Net Worth: £18,384,000 *Total Assets:* £38,378,000
Registered Office: Promethean House, Lower Philips Road, Whitebirk Industrial Estate, Blackburn, Lancs, BB1 5TH
Activities: Activities of head offices
Parent: Chalkfree Limited
Officers: Ian David Curtis [1962] Sales Director

Promethean Limited
Incorporated: 15 April 1977 *Employees:* 194
Net Worth Deficit: £24,930,000 *Total Assets:* £94,557,000
Registered Office: Promethean House, Lower Philips Road, Whitebirk Industrial Estate, Blackburn, Lancs, BB1 5TH
Activities: Manufacture of telegraph and telephone apparatus and equipment
Parent: Promethean (Holdings) Limited
Officers: Ian David Curtis [1962] Sales Director; Simon Leung Lim Kin [1954] Director [Canadian]

Promethean World Limited
Incorporated: 6 January 2010 *Employees:* 572
Net Worth Deficit: £29,662,000 *Total Assets:* £50,506,000
Registered Office: Promethean House, Lower Philips Road, Whitebirk Industrial Estate, Blackburn, Lancs, BB1 5TH
Activities: Activities of head offices
Shareholder: Dejian Liu
Officers: Ian David Curtis [1962] Sales Director; Simon Leung Lim Kin [1954] Director [Canadian]

Promocean No 1 Limited
Incorporated: 15 November 2004 *Employees:* 2
Net Worth Deficit: £8,842,568 *Total Assets:* £16,190,604
Registered Office: Centenary House, Centenary Way, Salford, M50 1RF
Activities: Activities of head offices
Officers: Nicholas Andrew Cottrell [1960] Director; Robert Stephen Lister [1956] Director

Property Alliance Group Limited
Incorporated: 5 June 2002 *Employees:* 32
Net Worth: £61,688,000 *Total Assets:* £138,468,992
Registered Office: Alliance House, Westpoint Enterprise Park, Clarence Avenue, Trafford Park, Manchester, M17 1QS
Activities: Buying and selling of own real estate
Major Shareholder: David Russell
Officers: Ian Hunter [1957] Director; Ella Magill [1974] Director/Chartered Surveyor; Alexander James Russell [1982] Director; David Russell [1956] Director

Property North West Ltd
Incorporated: 20 May 2002
Registered Office: Mentor House, Ainsworth Street, Blackburn, Lancs, BB1 6AY
Activities: Development of building projects
Shareholders: Stephen Robert Ashton; Christopher David Grieves
Officers: Christopher David Grieves, Secretary; Stephen Robert Ashton [1969] Director; Christopher David Grieves [1959] Director

Prorendita Five Limited
Incorporated: 13 July 2007 *Employees:* 3
Net Worth: £17,000 *Total Assets:* £7,917,683
Registered Office: One City Place, Queens Road, Chester, CH1 3BQ
Activities: Life insurance
Parent: Prorendita Funf GmbH & Co KG
Officers: Karen Cathrall, Secretary; Robert Ireland [1978] Director/Fund Manager; Roman Wiktora [1985] Director/Fund Manager [Austrian]

Proseal UK Limited
Incorporated: 15 January 1998 *Employees:* 292
Net Worth: £33,922,016 *Total Assets:* £51,042,792
Registered Office: Unit B, Adlington Industrial Estate, Adlington, Cheshire, SK10 4NL
Activities: Manufacture of other special-purpose machinery n.e.c.
Officers: Stephen Mark Malone, Secretary/Engineer; Robert Julian Hargreaves [1963] Director/Engineer; Stephen Mark Malone [1960] Director/Engineer

Proseat Limited Liability Partnership
Incorporated: 3 November 2006 *Employees:* 142
Net Worth: £13,166,000 *Total Assets:* £15,341,000
Registered Office: Unit A, Stakehill Industrial Estate, Manchester, M24 2SJ

Prospect (GB) Limited
Incorporated: 2 April 2001 *Employees:* 39
Net Worth: £11,749,000 *Total Assets:* £54,266,000
Registered Office: 2 Estuary Boulevard, Estuary Commerce Park, Liverpool, L24 8RF
Activities: Other business support service activities n.e.c.
Parent: The Riverside Group Limited
Officers: Anne-Marie Owens, Secretary; Simon Maxwell Bennett [1963] Director; David William Broadbent [1954] Director/Residential Consultancy Work; John Henry Graham [1955] Relationship Director; Ian Andrew Gregg [1970] Executive Director of Asset Services; Carol Mary Matthews [1960] Director/Group Chief Executive; Cristy-Ann McGuinness [1976] Director

Protec Fire and Security Group Limited
Incorporated: 21 July 1986 *Employees:* 1,039
Net Worth: £66,709,688 *Total Assets:* £99,986,552
Registered Office: Protec House, Churchill Way, Nelson, Lancs, BB9 6RT
Activities: Wholesale of radio, television goods & electrical household appliances (other than records, tapes, CDs)
Shareholder: Barrie Russell
Officers: Thomas Reginald Fairnie, Secretary; Barrie Russell [1947] Director/Company Chairman

Protec Fire Detection Public Limited Company
Incorporated: 16 May 1974 *Employees:* 796
Net Worth: £43,818,212 *Total Assets:* £72,027,312
Registered Office: Protec House, Churchill Way, Lomeshaye Industrial Estate, Nelson, Lancs, BB9 6RT
Activities: Manufacture of electronic components
Parent: Protec Fire & Security Group Limited
Officers: Thomas Reginald Fairnie, Secretary; Gawin James Davies [1971] Service Director; Peter Anthony Doyle [1961] Director/Contracts Manager; David Michael Firth [1964] Business Development Director; Stuart Craig Hore [1964] Sales Director; Dermot McArdle [1962] Director; Margaret Mary Merrin [1943] Director/Company Secretary; Robert Anthony Royle [1968] Project Director; Barrie Russell [1947] Director; Kathleen Russell [1949] Director; David Francis Scaife [1953] Service Director

Protec International Limited
Incorporated: 21 December 1998 *Employees:* 56
Net Worth: £4,124,104 *Total Assets:* £12,649,709
Registered Office: 45-49 Greek Street, Stockport, Cheshire, SK3 8AX
Activities: Agents involved in the sale of timber and building materials
Major Shareholder: James Daintry Harrison
Officers: Catherine Sarah Harrison, Secretary; Stephen Alan Cox [1964] Director; Malcolm Paul Ginn [1947] Director; James Daintry Harrison [1965] Director; Darren Anthony Moore [1974] Director

Provfin Limited
Incorporated: 22 January 1985
Net Worth: £8,807,000 *Total Assets:* £8,811,000
Registered Office: No 1 Godwin Street, Bradford, W Yorks, BD1 2SU
Activities: Other business support service activities n.e.c.
Parent: Yes Car Credit (Holdings) Limited
Officers: Andrew Charles Fisher [1958] Director; Kenneth John Mullen [1958] Director/Scottish Solicitor

Provident Financial Management Services Limited
Incorporated: 18 June 1937 *Employees:* 1,046
Net Worth: £198,700,000 *Total Assets:* £417,500,000
Registered Office: No 1 Godwin Street, Bradford, W Yorks, BD1 2SU
Activities: Financial intermediation not elsewhere classified
Parent: Provident Financial PLC
Officers: David George Whincup, Secretary; Andrew Charles Fisher [1958] Director; Christopher Donald Gillespie [1963] Director; Malcolm John Le May [1958] Director; Eleanor Thornhill [1974] Director; David George Whincup [1987] Director/Company Secretary

Provident Financial PLC
Incorporated: 31 August 1960 *Employees:* 4,684
Net Worth: £535,100,000 *Total Assets:* £2,965,900,032
Registered Office: No 1 Godwin Street, Bradford, W Yorks, BD1 2SU
Activities: Activities of financial services holding companies
Officers: Kenneth John Mullen, Secretary; Robert William Anderson [1958] Director; Andrea Margaret Blance [1964] Director; Elizabeth Grace Chambers [1962] Director [American]; Andrew Charles Fisher [1958] Director; Paul William Hewitt [1956] Director; Angela Ann Knight [1950] Director; Malcolm John Le May [1958] Director; Patrick Joseph Robert Snowball [1950] Director; John Coleman Straw [1959] Director

Provident Personal Credit Limited
Incorporated: 20 February 1917 *Employees:* 2,056
Net Worth: £211,000,000 *Total Assets:* £650,200,000
Registered Office: No 1 Godwin Street, Bradford, W Yorks, BD1 2SU
Activities: Credit granting by non-deposit taking finance houses and other specialist consumer credit grantors
Parent: Provident Financial Management Services Limited
Officers: David George Whincup, Secretary; Christopher Donald Gillespie [1963] Director; Malcolm John Le May [1958] Director; Eleanor Thornhill [1974] Director; David George Whincup [1987] Director/Company Secretary

Prowell Ltd
Incorporated: 4 December 2006 *Employees:* 59
Net Worth: £16,195,742 *Total Assets:* £19,890,276
Registered Office: Pioneer 210, North Road, Ellesmere Port, Cheshire, CH65 1AQ
Activities: Other business support service activities n.e.c.
Major Shareholder: Karl Juergen Heindl
Officers: Karl Juergen Heindl [1955] General Manager/Director [German]; Philipp Kosloh [1973] Director [German]; Volker Metz [1975] Director [German]

Proximo Limited
Incorporated: 26 November 2002 *Employees:* 46
Net Worth: £8,054,920 *Total Assets:* £16,015,868
Registered Office: Park House, Chantry Court, Sovereign Way, Chester, CH1 4QN
Activities: Other urban, suburban or metropolitan passenger land transport (not underground, metro or similar)
Parent: Proximo Holdings Limited
Officers: Eliane Margherite Chadwick, Secretary; Eliane Marguerite Chadwick [1962] Finance Director; Gavin Scott Cooper [1967] Sales Director; Peter Fairhurst [1969] Engineering and Network Director; Mary Ann Murphy [1986] Director [Irish]; Gunna Von Doneck [1968] Director

PS 121 Limited
Incorporated: 1 May 2015
Net Worth: £5,986,818 *Total Assets:* £13,024,978
Registered Office: 60 Oxford Street, Manchester, M1 5EE
Activities: Development of building projects
Parent: Beech Holdings (Manchester) Limited
Officers: Stephen Beech [1977] Director

PSC (Holdings) Limited
Incorporated: 20 February 2016
Net Worth: £4,337,713 *Total Assets:* £8,399,770
Registered Office: Charter House, Pittman Way, Fulwood, Preston, Lancs, PR2 9ZD
Activities: Dormant company
Shareholders: Peter James Allen; Christopher Andrew Swarbrick
Officers: Peter James Allen [1969] Director; Stephen James Allen [1962] Director; Christopher Andrew Swarbrick [1973] Director

PSS (UK)
Incorporated: 31 May 1926 *Employees:* 382
Net Worth: £5,324,706 *Total Assets:* £8,030,135
Registered Office: 18 Seel Street, Liverpool, L1 4BE
Activities: Other social work activities without accommodation n.e.c.
Officers: Hilary Andrea Berg [1962] Director/Communications Consultant; Julie Cooke [1967] Director/Civil Servant; Veronica Ann Jackson [1950] Director/Retired; Angela Alison Jones [1939] Director/Retired; John Andrew Kellaway [1946] Director/Consultant Chartered Surveyor; Geoffrey John Vernon Manning [1943] Director/Retired; Samantha Louise Proffitt [1970] Finance Director; Mark Edward Rathbone [1969] Director/Solicitor

PSV Claims Bureau Limited
Incorporated: 26 July 1988 *Employees:* 5
Net Worth: £313,000 *Total Assets:* £99,555,000
Registered Office: c/o Stagecoach Services Limited, One Stockport Exchange, 20 Railway Road, Stockport, Cheshire, SK1 3SW
Activities: Other activities auxiliary to insurance and pension funding
Parent: Stagecoach Bus Holdings Limited
Officers: Michael John Vaux, Secretary; Robert Gervase Andrew [1963] Director; Colin Brown [1968] Director/Accountant; Samuel Derek Greer [1968] Director; Malcolm Marwick [1971] Managing Director; Michael John Vaux [1971] Director/Solicitor

PTJ & R Limited
Incorporated: 17 November 2009 *Employees:* 116
Net Worth: £4,156,249 *Total Assets:* £9,115,855
Registered Office: 3-5 Paddock Road, West Pimbo, Skelmersdale, Lancs, WN8 9PL
Activities: Activities of head offices
Shareholders: Glyn Robert Jones; Margaret Elizabeth Jones
Officers: Marie Elizabeth Molyneux, Secretary; Glyn Robert Jones [1970] Director; Charles Joseph Molyneux [1946] Director; Marie Elizabeth Molyneux [1947] Director

PTS Property Limited
Incorporated: 8 June 2001
Net Worth: £11,056,747 *Total Assets:* £15,608,353
Registered Office: Daresbury Point, Green Wood Drive, Manor Park, Runcorn, Cheshire, WA7 1UP
Activities: Management consultancy activities other than financial management
Major Shareholder: John Rowlinson
Officers: Joan Mary Barton, Secretary; Joan Mary Barton [1956] Director/Company Secretary; John Rowlinson [1961] Director

Pugh Davies Properties Limited
Incorporated: 25 April 1972 *Employees:* 2
Net Worth: £19,465,172 *Total Assets:* £32,377,356
Registered Office: 6th Floor, Cardinal House, 20 St Mary's Parsonage, Manchester, M3 2LG
Activities: Other letting and operating of own or leased real estate
Parent: Pugh, Davies & Company Limited
Officers: Ian Peter Stoner, Secretary; Andrew Jeremy Joseph [1963] Director; Jonathan Michael Joseph [1947] Director

Pulse Equipment Group Limited
Incorporated: 6 October 2008 *Employees:* 107
Net Worth: £360,790 *Total Assets:* £10,134,151
Registered Office: Pulse Fitness, Radnor Park Industrial Estate, Back Lane, Congleton, Cheshire, CW12 4YA
Activities: Activities of sport clubs
Parent: Mig 1 Limited
Officers: Johnson Christopher [1965] Director; David Mark Johnson [1962] Director

Pulse Home Products (Holdings) Limited
Incorporated: 24 July 2007
Net Worth: £65,650,000 *Total Assets:* £65,650,000
Registered Office: 5400 Lakeside, Cheadle Royal Business Park, Cheadle, Cheshire, SK8 3GQ
Activities: Agents involved in the sale of furniture, household goods, hardware and ironmongery
Parent: Holmes Products (Europe) Limited
Officers: Raj Bhalchandra Dave [1974] Director/Attorney [American]; Ben Hartley [1976] Director/Attorney

Pure Leisure Estates Limited
Incorporated: 5 June 2006 *Employees:* 36
Net Worth Deficit: £7,535,997 *Total Assets:* £9,827,400
Registered Office: South Lakeland House, Main A6, Yealand Redmayne, Carnforth, Cumbria, LA5 9RN
Activities: Other amusement and recreation activities n.e.c.
Parent: Pure Leisure Group Limited
Officers: Paul Rossiter, Secretary; Paul Rossiter [1964] Director/Chartered Accountant; Trevor James White [1952] Director/Marketing Manager

Pure Leisure Group Limited
Incorporated: 27 April 2004 *Employees:* 378
Net Worth: £53,707,000 *Total Assets:* £113,507,000
Registered Office: South Lakeland House, Main A6, Yealand Redmayne, Carnforth, Lancs, LA5 9RN
Activities: Activities of other membership organisations n.e.c.
Major Shareholder: John Charles Morphet
Officers: Paul Rossiter, Secretary; Matthew David Morphet [1974] Director/Logistics Manager; Paul Rossiter [1964] Director/Chartered Accountant; Trevor James White [1952] Marketing Director

Pye Motors,Limited
Incorporated: 23 March 1925 *Employees:* 127
Net Worth: £2,780,069 *Total Assets:* £17,435,020
Registered Office: Ovangle Road, Morecambe, Lancs, LA3 3PF
Activities: Sale of new cars and light motor vehicles
Shareholder: Helen Joyce Morley-Pye
Officers: Helen Joyce Morley Pye [1962] Director/Motor Trader; Anthony Payne [1936] Director/Motor Trader; Nicholas Payne [1964] Director/Motor Trader; David Lomax Pye [1927] Director/Motor Trader; James Marsland Pye [1931] Director/Motor Trader

Pyroguard UK Limited
Incorporated: 12 October 1998 *Employees:* 56
Net Worth: £24,338,300 *Total Assets:* £27,464,192
Registered Office: International House, Millfield Lane, Haydock, Merseyside, WA11 9GA
Activities: Manufacture of flat glass
Parent: C.G.I. Group Ltd
Officers: Matthew Robert Buxton, Secretary; Matthew Robert Buxton [1972] Finance Director; Neil Andrew Tilsley [1967] Director

PZ Cussons (Holdings) Limited
Incorporated: 9 May 1936 *Employees:* 3
Net Worth: £93,385,000 *Total Assets:* £488,987,008
Registered Office: Manchester Business Park, 3500 Aviator Way, Manchester, M22 5TG
Activities: Activities of head offices
Parent: PZ Cussons PLC
Officers: Martyn John Campbell, Secretary; Andrew Bowie [1966] Director; George Alexander Kanellis [1965] Director [Greek]; Simon Paul Plant [1969] Director/Company Secretary

PZ Cussons (International Finance) Limited
Incorporated: 28 June 2013
Net Worth: £75,702,000 *Total Assets:* £76,594,000
Registered Office: Manchester Business Park, 350 Aviator Way, Manchester, M22 5TG
Activities: Other business support service activities n.e.c.
Parent: PZ Cussons (Holdings) Limited
Officers: Martyn John Campbell, Secretary; Andrew Bowie [1966] Director; Brandon Howard Leigh [1971] Director; Simon Paul Plant [1969] Director/Company Secretary

PZ Cussons (International) Limited
Incorporated: 26 October 1961 *Employees:* 129
Net Worth: £271,944,992 *Total Assets:* £341,307,008
Registered Office: Manchester Business Park, 3500 Aviator Way, Manchester, M22 5TG
Activities: Activities of head offices
Parent: PZ Cussons PLC
Officers: Martyn John Campbell, Secretary; Andrew Bowie [1966] Director; Brandon Howard Leigh [1971] Director; Simon Paul Plant [1969] Director

PZ Cussons (UK) Limited
Incorporated: 25 January 1963 *Employees:* 246
Net Worth: £47,675,000 *Total Assets:* £97,408,000
Registered Office: Manchester Business Park, 3500 Aviator Way, Manchester, M22 5TG
Activities: Other manufacturing n.e.c.
Parent: PZ Cussons (Holdings) Limited
Officers: Martyn John Campbell, Secretary; Andrew Bowie [1966] Director; Neill James Craigie [1961] Director; Brandon Howard Leigh [1971] Director; Simon Paul Plant [1969] Director; Frazer Yeomans [1972] Director

PZ Cussons PLC
Incorporated: 20 February 1884 *Employees:* 4,520
Net Worth: £492,700,000 *Total Assets:* £1,168,999,936
Registered Office: Manchester Business Park, 3500 Aviator Way, Manchester, M22 5TG
Activities: Other manufacturing n.e.c.
Officers: Simon Paul Plant, Secretary; George Alexander Kanellis [1965] Director/Chief Executive [Greek]; Dariusz Kucz [1961] Director [Polish]; Brandon Howard Leigh [1971] Finance Director; Jeremy Kim Maiden [1961] Director; Tamara Lee Minick-Scokalo [1959] Director [American]; John Ross Nicolson [1953] Director; Helen Owers [1963] Director; Caroline Louise Silver [1962] Director/Investment Banker

Q Dental Care Limited
Incorporated: 27 March 2008 *Employees:* 103
Net Worth: £7,889,862 *Total Assets:* £8,592,517
Registered Office: Europa House, Europa Trading Estate, Stoneclough Road, Kearsley, Manchester, M26 1GG
Activities: Dental practice activities
Parent: IDH Acquisitions Limited
Officers: Leo Damian Carroll, Secretary; Clifford Gwyn Davies [1966] Clinical Director; Mohammed Omar Shafi Khan [1974] Director/Chief Financial Officer; Krista Nyree Whitley [1970] Clinical Director

Q. R. I. Ltd
Incorporated: 23 December 1999 *Employees:* 38
Net Worth: £5,772,249 *Total Assets:* £6,920,941
Registered Office: 40 Stockhill Road, Greengates, Bradford, BD10 9AX
Activities: Manufacture of other women's outerwear
Officers: Christine Ann Rankin, Secretary; Michael Kelly [1958] Managing Director

Qdos Developments Limited
Incorporated: 10 October 2006
Net Worth Deficit: £2,283,794 *Total Assets:* £6,783,006
Registered Office: Stone Cottage, Summerhill Road, Prestbury, Macclesfield, Cheshire, SK10 4AH
Activities: Construction of domestic buildings
Major Shareholder: Howard Wyndham Bilton
Officers: Howard Wyndham Bilton [1955] Director/Property Developer

QED (KMC) Limited
Incorporated: 30 December 2004 *Employees:* 3
Net Worth Deficit: £1,601,934 *Total Assets:* £12,685,770
Registered Office: Unit 18 Riversway Business Village, Navigation Way, Ashton on Ribble, Preston, Lancs, PR2 2YP
Activities: Other business support service activities n.e.c.
Parent: QED (KMC) Holdings Limited
Officers: Alastair William Hopps [1986] Director/Accountant; Alexander Toby Shedden Parry [1976] Director/Chartered Accountant; Cllr Habiban Zaman [1968] Director/Councillor

QEGS Blackburn Academy Trust
Incorporated: 14 December 2012 *Employees:* 127
Net Worth: £14,795,378 *Total Assets:* £16,854,918
Registered Office: Queen Elizabeth's Grammar School, West Park Road, Blackburn, Lancs, BB2 6DF
Activities: Other education n.e.c.
Officers: Paul Anthony Atkinson, Secretary; Simon Timothy Brown [1964] Director/National Account Sales Manager; Dr Zuber Mohammed Bux [1970] Director/Doctor; David John Clark [1958] Director/Retired Headmaster; Ann Letitia Dean [1948] Director; Claire Yvette Gammon [1977] Director/Teacher; Peter Howell-Jones [1962] Director/Dean of Blackburn Cathedral; Ian Albert Liddle [1969] Director/Solicitor; Neil McMillan [1978] Director/Chartered Accountant; David Alan Peat [1948] Director/Retired; Professor Iqbal Singh [1951] Director/Doctor; Gregory Turner [1948] Director; Kathleen Anne Whyte [1950] Retired University Admissions Director

Qiagen Limited
Incorporated: 4 October 1993 *Employees:* 89
Net Worth: £9,990,087 *Total Assets:* £17,158,000
Registered Office: Skelton House, Lloyd Street North, Manchester, M15 6SH
Activities: Other human health activities
Parent: Qiagen NV
Officers: Paul Jonathan Birch, Secretary; Dr Andrew David Critchley [1967] Director/Vice President, Head of Global Technical Service; Roland Sackers [1968] Director/Chief Financial Officer [German]; Peer Michael Schatz [1965] Director/Chief Executive Officer [Austrian]

Qiagen Manchester Limited
Incorporated: 14 February 2001 *Employees:* 227
Net Worth: £20,971,748 *Total Assets:* £42,444,748
Registered Office: Skelton House, Lloyd Street North, Manchester, M15 6SH
Activities: Manufacture of basic pharmaceutical products
Parent: Qiagen NV
Officers: Paul Jonathan Birch, Secretary; Thierry Bernard [1964] Director/Senior VP Head of Business Area Molecular Diagnostics [French]; Roland Sackers [1968] Director [German]; Peer Michael Schatz [1965] Director [Austrian]; Thomas Schweins [1967] Director/Senior Vice President Life Sciences [German]

QMS International Limited
Incorporated: 26 March 2015 *Employees:* 69
Net Worth: £2,710,589 *Total Assets:* £24,323,732
Registered Office: Kings Court, Water Lane, Wilmslow, Cheshire, SK9 5AR
Activities: Other business support service activities n.e.c.
Parent: Citation Holdings Limited
Officers: Christopher Paul Morris [1972] Director; Matthew Brian Stacey [1977] Finance Director; Eloise Wann [1977] Director/Chief Financial Officer

Quadrant EPP UK Ltd.
Incorporated: 15 October 1962 *Employees:* 41
Net Worth: £8,018,000 *Total Assets:* £9,981,000
Registered Office: Quadrant, Woodhouse Road, Todmorden, Lancs, OL14 5TP
Activities: Manufacture of plastic plates, sheets, tubes and profiles
Shareholders: Quadrant Holding UK Ltd; The Board of The Pension Protection Fund
Officers: Sian Emily Ruddy, Secretary; Ronald Engelbertink [1966] Director [Dutch]; David Lively [1970] Director; Joe Norwood [1956] Area Sales Director; Stefan Willing [1971] Director [German]

Quality Save Limited
Incorporated: 1 June 2009 *Employees:* 519
Net Worth: £16,914,662 *Total Assets:* £22,543,928
Registered Office: 5 Brooklands Place, Brooklands Road, Sale, Cheshire, M33 3SD
Activities: Other retail sale in non-specialised stores
Shareholders: Diane Rudkin; Robert Bernard Rudkin; Robert Bernard Rudkin; Diane Rudkin
Officers: Paul Austin Rudkin, Secretary; Diane Rudkin [1946] Director; Paul Austin Rudkin [1971] Director; Richard Rudkin [1976] Director; Robert Bernard Rudkin [1940] Director

Qualtex Global Limited
Incorporated: 12 December 2013 *Employees:* 187
Net Worth: £5,162,343 *Total Assets:* £21,776,492
Registered Office: Unit 1 Denton Hall Farm Road, Denton, Manchester, M34 2SX
Activities: Activities of other holding companies n.e.c.
Major Shareholder: Philip Hulme
Officers: Richard Storah, Secretary; John Hughes [1962] Director/Chairman; Caroline Hulme [1965] Director; Philip Hulme [1965] Director; Richard Storah [1977] Director

Qualtex UK Limited
Incorporated: 24 November 1961 *Employees:* 159
Net Worth: £6,516,692 *Total Assets:* £17,301,248
Registered Office: Unit 1 Denton Hall Farm Road, Denton, Manchester, M34 2SX
Activities: Wholesale of household goods (other than musical instruments) n.e.c
Officers: Richard Storah, Secretary; John Hughes [1962] Director/Chairman; Caroline Hulme [1965] Director; Philip Hulme [1965] Director; Richard Storah [1977] Director

Quantil Agriculture Limited
Incorporated: 13 March 1997 *Employees:* 13
Net Worth: £5,731,623 *Total Assets:* £10,015,675
Registered Office: New Park Gates, Cranes Lane, Lathom, Ormskirk, Lancs, L40 5UJ
Activities: Growing of cereals (except rice), leguminous crops and oil seeds
Major Shareholder: David Warwick Symondson
Officers: Fiona Mary Symondson, Secretary; Stephen David Lewis [1940] Director/Chartered Accountant; John Barry Pape [1954] Director; David Warwick Symondson [1955] Director/Chartered Accountant; Fiona Mary Symondson [1961] Director/Manager; Lucy Symondson [1987] Director/Consultant

Queen Elizabeth Grammar School Penrith
Incorporated: 30 March 2011 *Employees:* 116
Net Worth: £7,495,715 *Total Assets:* £9,296,316
Registered Office: Queen Elizabeth Grammar School, Ullswater Road, Penrith, Cumbria, CA11 7EG
Activities: General secondary education
Officers: David James Chappell, Secretary; Michael Robert Frederick Bauer [1970] Director/Lawyer; Tine Boving-Foster [1963] Director/Bed and Breakfast Owner [Danish]; Paul Edward Buckland [1963] Director/Headteacher; Dr Tyrone Castles [1961] Director/Hotelier; Gail Katherine Gravett [1959] Business Director; Charlie Maurice Hansford [1969] Director/Solicitor; Joanne Mills [1968] Director/Chief Officer; Judith Anne Nicol [1962] Director/Leadership Development Consultant; Karen Anne Rae [1973] Director/Accountant; Robert James Shephard [1968] Director; Susan Warner [1956] Director/Cover Manager; Alastair Craig Worth [1970] Director/Teacher

The Queen Katherine School Multi Academy Trust
Incorporated: 17 December 2010 *Employees:* 361
Net Worth: £11,043,127 *Total Assets:* £18,388,988
Registered Office: The Queen Katherine School, Appleby Road, Kendal, Cumbria, LA9 6PJ
Activities: General secondary education
Officers: Michael James Walby, Secretary; Beth Curl [1954] Director/Consultant; Anna Catherine Gregg [1991] Director/Trainee Solicitor; Jennifer Mitchell [1955] Director/Teacher/Senco; Elizabeth Ann Moffatt [1950] Director; Anthony Sinton [1957] Director/Former Headteacher; Stephen Wilkinson [1955] Director/Executive Headteacher

Queenscourt Hospice
Incorporated: 23 February 1987 *Employees:* 157
Net Worth: £13,663,541 *Total Assets:* £14,391,707
Registered Office: Town Lane, Southport, Merseyside, PR8 6RE
Activities: Other human health activities
Officers: Debra Jane Lawson, Secretary; Carol Bernard [1961] Director/Retired Nurse; Dr Generaldine Rose Boocock [1953] Director/Retired Doctor; Yvonne Burns [1957] Director/Shopping Centre Manager; Anthony Damian Crewe [1964] Director/HMRC Enquiry Co-ordinator; Christopher Paul Cutner [1955] Director/Retired; Peter Andrew Downham [1948] Director/Retired; Thomas Fairclough [1959] Director/NHS Manager; Richard Jacklin [1946] Director/Solicitor; Christopher Downing Leather [1950] Director/Retired; Keith Carr Mitchell [1944] Director/Retired; Steven Simpson [1976] Director/Pharmacist; Margaret Helen Tarpey [1946] Managing Director; Dr David John Unwin [1958] Director/Doctor

Queensland Place Limited
Incorporated: 10 September 2014
Net Worth Deficit: £19,941 *Total Assets:* £13,401,338
Registered Office: 116 Duke Street, Liverpool, L1 5JW
Activities: Buying and selling of own real estate
Parent: Parliment Place Limited
Officers: Elliot Philip Lawless [1987] Director

Quercia Limited
Incorporated: 17 April 1973 *Employees:* 35
Net Worth Deficit: £33,876 *Total Assets:* £9,537,436
Registered Office: 501 Green Place, Walton Summit Centre, Bamber Bridge, Preston, Lancs, PR5 8AY
Activities: Treatment and disposal of non-hazardous waste
Parent: NWM Holdings Ltd
Officers: Annalisa Costantini [1976] Director/Lawyer [Italian]; Enrico Friz [1962] Managing Director [Italian]; Massimo Angelo Sala [1961] Director [Italian]

Quest Bidco Limited
Incorporated: 1 June 2011
Net Worth: £1,875,423 *Total Assets:* £132,129,904
Registered Office: Belvedere, 12 Booth Street, Manchester, M2 4AW
Activities: Financial intermediation not elsewhere classified
Parent: Quest Topco Limited
Officers: Stewart David Hamilton, Secretary; Paul David Cooper [1972] Director/Group Chief Financial Officer; Zachary Jason Lewy [1974] Director/Founder and Group Chief Investment Officer [British/American]; Lee Michael Rochford [1967] Director/Group Chief Executive Officer

Quest Newco Limited
Incorporated: 22 July 2011
Net Worth: £19,036,448 *Total Assets:* £25,630,838
Registered Office: Belvedere, 12 Booth Street, Manchester, M2 4AW
Activities: Financial intermediation not elsewhere classified
Parent: Quest Bidco Limited
Officers: Stewart David Hamilton, Secretary; Paul David Cooper [1972] Director/Group Chief Financial Officer; Zachary Jason Lewy [1974] Director/Founder and Group Chief Investment Officer [British/American]; Lee Michael Rochford [1967] Director/Group Chief Executive Officer

Quest Topco Limited
Incorporated: 1 June 2011
Net Worth: £34,487,764 *Total Assets:* £38,275,400
Registered Office: Belvedere, 12 Booth Street, Manchester, M2 4AW
Activities: Financial intermediation not elsewhere classified
Parent: Arrow Global Investments Holdings Limited
Officers: Stewart David Hamilton, Secretary; Paul David Cooper [1972] Director/Group Chief Financial Officer; Zachary Jason Lewy [1974] Director/Founder and Group Chief Investment Officer [British/American]; Lee Michael Rochford [1967] Director/Group Chief Executive Officer

Questport Limited
Incorporated: 16 July 2004
Net Worth Deficit: £1,524,928 *Total Assets:* £10,038,401
Registered Office: 10 Riverview, The Embankment, Vale Road, Heaton Mersey, Stockport, Cheshire, SK4 3GN
Activities: Financial intermediation not elsewhere classified
Shareholders: Ronald Musry; Alan Philip David Musry
Officers: Alan Philip David Musry, Secretary/Director; Alan Philip David Musry [1963] Director/Chartered Accountant; Ronald Musry [1935] Director

M J Quinn Holdings Limited
Incorporated: 29 September 2008 *Employees:* 392
Net Worth Deficit: £10,945,700 *Total Assets:* £36,947,660
Registered Office: Oak House, Overbrook Lane, Knowsley Business Park, Knowsley, Merseyside, L34 9FB
Activities: Wired telecommunications activities
Parent: Zeus Private Equity Fund LLP
Officers: Michael John Quinn, Secretary/Electrical Contractor; Edmund Fazakerley [1969] Director/Venture Capitalist; Gary Nigel Howse [1960] Director; Karl Monaghan [1963] Operations Director; Michael William Orme [1958] Finance Director; Michael John Quinn [1954] Director/Electrical Contractor; Neil John Shearwood [1968] Operations Director; Gary William Tipper [1963] Director/Venture Capitalist

Quinn Infrastructure Services Limited
Incorporated: 12 May 1989 *Employees:* 392
Net Worth Deficit: £8,860,367 *Total Assets:* £36,941,928
Registered Office: Oak House, Overbrook Lane, Knowsley Business Park, Knowsley, Merseyside, L34 9FB
Activities: Wired telecommunications activities
Parent: MJ Quinn Group Ltd
Officers: Michael John Quinn, Secretary/Electrical Contractor; Karl Monaghan [1963] Operations Director; Michael William Orme [1958] Finance Director; Michael John Quinn [1954] Director/Electrical Contractor; Neil Shearwood [1968] Operations Director

M J Quinn Integrated Services Limited
Incorporated: 29 September 2008
Net Worth Deficit: £91,623 *Total Assets:* £13,587,806
Registered Office: Oak House, Overbrook Lane, Knowsley Business Park, Knowsley, Merseyside, L34 9FB
Activities: Other specialised construction activities n.e.c.
Parent: MJ Quinn Holdings Ltd
Officers: Michael John Quinn, Secretary/Electrical Contractor; Gary Nigel Howse [1960] Director; Karl Monaghan [1963] Operations Director; Michael William Orme [1958] Finance Director; Michael John Quinn [1954] Director/Electrical Contractor; Neil John Shearwood [1968] Operations Director

Quint Holdings Ltd
Incorporated: 11 April 2013 *Employees:* 110
Net Worth: £2,790,748 *Total Assets:* £21,016,622
Registered Office: Cottage Street Mill, Cottage Street, Macclesfield, Cheshire, SK11 8DZ
Activities: Activities of financial services holding companies
Major Shareholder: Gregory Charles Cox
Officers: Gregory Charles Cox [1981] Director; Kate Jowitt [1978] Director/Personal Assistant

Quintessential Brands Spirit Solutions Limited
Incorporated: 14 April 2011 *Employees:* 12
Net Worth: £254,000 *Total Assets:* £9,515,000
Registered Office: Distribution Point, Melbury Park, Clayton Road, Birchwood, Warrington, Cheshire, WA3 6PH
Activities: Wholesale of wine, beer, spirits and other alcoholic beverages
Parent: Quintessential Brands UK Group Limited
Officers: Michael Clifford, Secretary; Warren Michael Scott [1963] Director/Businessman; Vincenzo Visone [1955] Director/Businessman [Italian]

Quintessential Brands UK Group Limited
Incorporated: 14 April 2011 *Employees:* 33
Net Worth: £4,910,000 *Total Assets:* £14,502,000
Registered Office: Distribution Point, Melbury Park, Clayton Road, Birchwood, Warrington, Cheshire, WA3 6PH
Activities: Activities of other holding companies n.e.c.
Parent: Quintessential Brands UK Holdings Limited
Officers: Michael Clifford, Secretary; Warren Michael Scott [1963] Director/Businessman; Vincenzo Visone [1955] Director/Businessman [Italian]

Quintessential Brands UK Holdings Limited
Incorporated: 14 April 2011 *Employees:* 179
Net Worth: £3,233,000 *Total Assets:* £34,900,000
Registered Office: Distribution Point, Melbury Park, Clayton Road, Birchwood, Warrington, Cheshire, WA3 6PH
Activities: Activities of other holding companies n.e.c.
Shareholders: Warren Michael Scott; Vincenzo Visone
Officers: Michael Clifford, Secretary; Warren Michael Scott [1963] Director/Businessman; Vincenzo Visone [1955] Director/Businessman [Italian]

Quorum Estates Limited
Incorporated: 4 June 1993 *Employees:* 10
Net Worth: £22,053,564 *Total Assets:* £45,462,860
Registered Office: 3rd Floor, 1 Ashley Road, Altrincham, Cheshire, WA14 2DT
Activities: Development of building projects
Officers: Ann Christine Slater, Secretary; John David Slater [1947] Director; Paul Martin Wardle [1960] Director/Property Investment & Dealing

R.B. Business Park Limited
Incorporated: 10 May 2001 *Employees:* 1
Net Worth: £10,610,658 *Total Assets:* £22,456,340
Registered Office: Head Office, Boundary Mill Stores, Vivary Way, Colne, Lancs, BB8 9NW
Activities: Buying and selling of own real estate
Parent: R.B. Business Park Holdings Limited
Officers: Janine Elizabeth Bannister, Secretary; Janine Elizabeth Bannister [1960] Director; Richard Michael Rennie Bannister [1961] Director

Raan Investments Ltd
Incorporated: 15 October 2003
Net Worth: £3,861,452 *Total Assets:* £8,777,901
Registered Office: Unit 1A, Empress Business Centre, Chester Road, Manchester, M16 9EA
Activities: Buying and selling of own real estate
Shareholder: Aarti Takiar
Officers: Aarti Takiar, Secretary/Director [Indian]; Aarti Takiar [1972] Director [Indian]; Anu Takiar [1970] Director; Neeraj Takiar [1968] Director [Indian]; Pankaj Takiar [1966] Director

Radbourne Edge (Holdings) Limited
Incorporated: 17 October 2013 *Employees:* 5
Net Worth: £5,193,220 *Total Assets:* £11,735,021
Registered Office: Redrow House, St David's Park, Deeside, Flintshire, CH5 3RX
Activities: Activities of construction holding companies
Parent: Redrow Homes Limited
Officers: Graham Anthony Cope, Secretary; Helen Davies [1966] Director/Accountant; Warren Thompson [1974] Director/Regional Chief Executive; John Frederick Tutte [1956] Director/Civil Engineer; Robert Paul Wilson [1960] Director/Surveyor

Radioactive Waste Management Limited
Incorporated: 3 March 2014 *Employees:* 117
Net Worth: £1 *Total Assets:* £8,767,765
Registered Office: Herdus House, Ingwell Drive, Westlakes Science & Technology Park, Moor Row, Cumbria, CA24 3HU
Activities: Other professional, scientific and technical activities n.e.c.
Officers: Helen Elizabeth Hodgson, Secretary; Dr Michael Byron John Bowman [1953] Director/Professor; Dr Nia Melanie Brownridge [1971] Director/Head of R&D; John Roger Corderoy [1966] Director/Engineer; Peter John Lock [1966] HSSEQ Director; Ann Marie McCall [1962] Director/Professional Engineer; Bruce John McKirdy [1958] Director/Radioactive Waste Management; Professor Malcolm Morley [1955] Director; Dr David Michael Prout [1963] Director/Pro-Vice Chancellor; Claes Thegerstrom [1947] Director/Senior Adviser [Swedish]; Andrew Cornelis Van Der Lem [1972] Director/Public Servant; Karen Wheeler [1956] Director/Civil Servant

Radisson Hotel Edinburgh Ltd
Incorporated: 8 June 2001 *Employees:* 125
Net Worth: £2,195,169 *Total Assets:* £11,936,067
Registered Office: Chicago Avenue, Manchester, M90 3RA
Activities: Hotels and similar accommodation
Officers: Kevin John Greenwood, Secretary; Eva-Maria Margaretha Erauw [1977] Director/SVP & General Counsel, Legal [Belgian]; Sven Gosta Andreas Fondell [1973] Director/VP Group Accounting [Swedish]; Kevin John Greenwood [1957] Director/Financial Controller; Knut Jan Kleiven [1954] Director/Chief Financial Officer [Norwegian]; Richard John Moore [1965] Director

Radisson Hotel Manchester Ltd
Incorporated: 27 September 1996 *Employees:* 160
Net Worth: £21,109,000 *Total Assets:* £33,610,000
Registered Office: Chicago Avenue, Manchester, M90 3RA
Activities: Hotels and similar accommodation
Parent: Radisson Hotels UK Ltd.
Officers: Kevin John Greenwood, Secretary; Eva-Maria Margaretha Erauw [1977] Director/SVP & General Counsel, Legal [Belgian]; Sven Gosta Andreas Fondell [1973] Director/VP Group Accounting [Swedish]; Kevin John Greenwood [1957] Director/Regional Controller; Knut Jan Kleiven [1954] Director/VP & Finance Officer [Norwegian]; Richard John Moore [1965] Director

Radisson Hotels UK Ltd
Incorporated: 28 November 1988 *Employees:* 105
Net Worth: £122,797,000 *Total Assets:* £190,303,008
Registered Office: Chicago Avenue, Manchester, M90 3RA
Activities: Hotels and similar accommodation
Officers: Kevin John Greenwood, Secretary; Eva-Maria Margaretha Erauw [1977] Director/SVP & General Counsel Legal [Belgian]; Sven Gosta Andreas Fondell [1973] Director/VP Group Accounting [Swedish]; Kevin John Greenwood [1957] Director/Financial Controller; Knut Jan Kleiven [1954] Director/Group Controller of SAS A/S Denmark [Norwegian]; Richard John Moore [1965] Director

Radius Payment Solutions Limited
Incorporated: 19 October 2012 *Employees:* 847
Net Worth: £117,100,000 *Total Assets:* £352,200,000
Registered Office: Euro Card Centre, Herald Park, Herald Drive, Crewe, Cheshire, CW1 6EG
Activities: Wholesale of other fuels and related products
Major Shareholder: William Stanley Holmes
Officers: Adrian Stuart Rushton, Secretary; Lee John Everett [1974] Director; William Stanley Holmes [1964] Director; Timothy Simon Oldfield [1964] Director/Certified Chartered Accountant; David Frederick Price Roberts [1976] Director/Chief Information Officer; Roy Alfred Sciortino [1958] Director

Rainbow Cosmetics (Holdings) Limited
Incorporated: 10 June 1999 *Employees:* 53
Net Worth: £7,472,003 *Total Assets:* £17,450,658
Registered Office: 61 Stanley Road, Whitefield, Manchester, M45 8GZ
Activities: Activities of head offices
Shareholders: Heather Jean Sharman; Howard Clague
Officers: Heather Sharman, Secretary; Howard Clague [1954] Director; John William Sharman [1955] Director; Stephen John Sharman [1980] Director

Rainbow Cosmetics (Manchester) Limited
Incorporated: 11 January 2002 *Employees:* 48
Net Worth: £1,243,996 *Total Assets:* £17,017,742
Registered Office: 61 Stanley Road, Whitefield, Manchester, M45 8GZ
Activities: Wholesale of perfume and cosmetics
Parent: Rainbow Cosmetics (Holdings) Ltd
Officers: Heather Sharman, Secretary; Heather Sharman [1957] Director/Company Secretary; John William Sharman [1955] Director; Stephen John Sharman [1980] Director

Rainbow Dust Colours Limited
Incorporated: 31 July 2008 *Employees:* 32
Net Worth: £7,115,510 *Total Assets:* £8,020,657
Registered Office: 61 Stephenson Way, Wavertree, Liverpool, L13 1HN
Activities: Other professional, scientific and technical activities n.e.c.
Parent: RGFC Dust Ltd
Officers: Harveen Rai, Secretary; Hugh Charles Laurence Cawley [1956] Director; Harveen Rai [1974] Director; Patrick George Ridgwell [1946] Director; Christopher Owen Thomas [1945] Director

William Rainford (Holdings) Limited
Incorporated: 10 July 1970 *Employees:* 31
Net Worth: £13,063,340 *Total Assets:* £17,936,008
Registered Office: Workington Road, Flimby, Maryport, Cumbria, CA15 8RY
Activities: Manufacture of concrete products for construction purposes
Officers: Paul Armstrong, Secretary/Accountant; Paul Armstrong [1959] Director/Accountant; Mark Billows [1964] Director; Anthony Robert Glover Denham [1960] Director; John Keith Denham [1943] Director

Rainy City Investments Limited
Incorporated: 15 January 2008 *Employees:* 2,149
Net Worth: £111,456,440 *Total Assets:* £216,396,992
Registered Office: The Peninsula, Victoria Place, Manchester, M4 4FB
Activities: Activities of head offices
Shareholders: Peter Eric Done; Fred Done
Officers: Peter Nicholas Swift, Secretary; Fred Done [1943] Director; Peter Eric Done [1947] Director

Rainy City Properties Limited
Incorporated: 27 October 2006
Net Worth: £7,158,506 *Total Assets:* £54,990,004
Registered Office: The Peninsula, Victoria Place, Manchester, M4 4FB
Activities: Other letting and operating of own or leased real estate
Officers: Peter Nicholas Swift, Secretary; Fred Done [1943] Director/Managing Executive; Peter Eric Done [1947] Director/Managing Executive

Rajan Trading Co. Limited
Incorporated: 16 August 1973
Net Worth: £4,011,304 *Total Assets:* £7,663,597
Registered Office: The Exchange, 5 Bank Street, Bury, Lancs, BL9 0DN
Activities: Buying and selling of own real estate
Officers: Rajan Kumar, Secretary/Director; Ashok Kumar [1947] Director; Rajan Kumar [1961] Director; Sanjay Kumar [1969] Director

Ralawise Limited
Incorporated: 13 April 1978 *Employees:* 527
Net Worth: £38,913,660 *Total Assets:* £63,460,936
Registered Office: Unit 112 Tenth Avenue, Zone 3, Deeside Industrial Park, Deeside, Flintshire, CH5 2UA
Activities: Other retail sale not in stores, stalls or markets
Shareholders: Jonathan Peter Batson; Jeoffrey Paul Batson; Edna Violet Batson
Officers: Edna Violet Batson, Secretary; Edna Violet Batson [1932] Director; Jeffrey Paul Batson [1964] Director; Jonathon Peter Batson [1964] Director; Alistair Malcolm McPherson [1974] Director

Ralli Ltd.
Incorporated: 14 August 2001 *Employees:* 32
Net Worth: £2,593,892 *Total Assets:* £8,950,126
Registered Office: Jackson House, Sibson Road, Sale, Cheshire, M33 7RR
Activities: Solicitors
Shareholders: Martin James Coyne; Stephen Howard Fox; Adrian Ernest Anderson
Officers: Adrian Ernest Anderson, Secretary; Adrian Ernest Anderson [1949] Director/Solicitor; Martin James Coyne [1956] Director/Solicitor; Stephen Howard Fox [1948] Director/Lawyer; Farhanah Ismail [1974] Director/Solicitor; James Douglas Reilly [1975] Director/Solicitor

Rammon Group (Properties) Limited
Incorporated: 31 May 1996 *Employees:* 5
Net Worth: £2,705,263 *Total Assets:* £12,786,731
Registered Office: The Mews, 189b Ashley Road, Hale, Altrincham, Cheshire, WA15 9SQ
Activities: Other letting and operating of own or leased real estate
Shareholder: David Weusberg
Officers: David Weisberg [1956] Director; Philip Weisberg [1951] Director

Tony Rampton Trust
Incorporated: 13 February 1974
Net Worth: £9,680,746 *Total Assets:* £9,687,264
Registered Office: Centre of Excellence, Hope Park, Trevor Foster Way, Bradford, W Yorks, BD5 8HH
Activities: Other business support service activities n.e.c.
Officers: Sandra Lingwood, Secretary; Debra Ali [1984] Director/Marketing Campaign Manager; Robert Stephen Colledge [1945] Director/Human Resources Manager; Norman Finnigan [1944] Director/Retired; Mary Priestman Johnston [1948] Director/Retired; Angela Kennedy [1968] Director; Andrew John Langridge [1962] Director; Graham Marshall [1948] Director; John Jeremy Pearmund [1953] Director; Phillip Robert Poole [1949] Director/Retired; John Richard Anthony Rampton [1941] Director/Barrister; Dawn Redman [1959] Director/Business Consultant; Christine Noella Southam [1956] Director; Jonathan Stratford Tinning [1969] Director; Dilys Mary Ashton Ward [1940] Director/Retired

Peter Ramsey & Sons Limited
Incorporated: 11 November 2002 *Employees:* 153
Net Worth: £4,087,872 *Total Assets:* £6,723,840
Registered Office: Wellington Street Sawmills, Sticker Lane, Bradford, W Yorks, BD4 8BW
Activities: Other letting and operating of own or leased real estate
Shareholders: Michael Jonathan Stobbart Ramsey; Patricia Elaine Ramsey
Officers: Michael Jonathan Stobbart Ramsey, Secretary/Timber Merchant; Michael Jonathan Stobbart Ramsey [1962] Director/Timber Merchant; Nicholas Peter Robertshaw Ramsey [1960] Director/Timber Merchant; Patricia Elaine Ramsey [1965] Director; Peter Richard Hattersley Ramsey [1935] Director/Timber Merchant

Randle Brooks Limited
Incorporated: 6 February 1957
Net Worth: £9,655,444 *Total Assets:* £9,896,855
Registered Office: Charles House, 2 Royal Court, Tatton Street, Knutsford, Cheshire, WA16 6EN
Activities: Other letting and operating of own or leased real estate
Officers: Juliet Marit Gabriel Brooks [1945] Director; Richard Edward Thomas Sanders [1961] Director/Agricultural Consultant

Randomlight Limited
Incorporated: 10 March 1989 *Employees:* 101
Net Worth: £3,690,143 *Total Assets:* £16,772,518
Registered Office: 6-8 Old Hall Road, Gatley, Cheadle, Cheshire, SK8 4BE
Activities: Hospital activities
Parent: Ovalseal Limited
Officers: Michael Denis Hartey [1956] Director

Range High School
Incorporated: 12 September 2011 *Employees:* 158
Net Worth: £5,249,319 *Total Assets:* £8,973,744
Registered Office: Range High School, Stapleton Road, Formby, Merseyside, L37 2YN
Activities: General secondary education
Officers: Graham Andrew Aldridge [1966] Director/Headteacher; Ian Michael Burton [1959] Director/Accountant; Michele Gallen [1968] Director/Teaching Assistant; Gillian Gentles [1960] Director/Teacher; Kevin Patrick Grimes [1962] Director/Art Consultant; Roderick Hugh McGreevy [1960] Director/Retired; Jane Philippa McNeice [1966] Director/Housewife; Catherine Morris [1963] Director/Banker; Paul Povey [1981] Director/Teacher; Jim Rimmer [1947] Director/Retired; Dr Richard Lewis Snowdon [1973] Director/Doctor; Paul Steiger [1969] Director/Advertising Consultant; Dr Mervyn Thomas [1949] Director/Retired

Rathbone Investment Management Limited
Incorporated: 17 September 1979 *Employees:* 1,035
Net Worth: £269,497,984 *Total Assets:* £2,596,099,072
Registered Office: Port of Liverpool Building, Pier Head, Liverpool, L3 1NW
Activities: Fund management activities
Parent: Rathbone Brothers PLC
Officers: Ali Johnson, Secretary; James William Dean [1957] Director/Chartered Accountant; Terri Lynn Duhon [1972] Director [American]; Sarah Felicity Gentlemen [1970] Director; Philip Luard Howell [1955] Director Financial Services; Mark Patrick Nicholls [1949] Director; James Neilson Pettigrew [1958] Director; Robert Paul Stockton [1965] Director/Chartered Accountant

Rathbone Kear Limited
Incorporated: 7 April 2005 *Employees:* 345
Net Worth: £39,811,000 *Total Assets:* £64,992,000
Registered Office: Hilmore House, Gain Lane, Bradford, W Yorks, BD3 7DL
Activities: Manufacture of bread; manufacture of fresh pastry goods and cakes
Parent: Wm Morrison Supermarkets Holdings Limited
Officers: Jonathan James Burke, Secretary; Darren Anthony Blackhurst [1966] Director; Andrew James Clappen [1965] Technical Director; Jonathan Paul Hornby [1972] Director; Mark Thomas Stitson [1976] Finance Director; Andrew Edward Thornber [1974] Director

Ravella Holdings Limited
Incorporated: 25 October 2016
Net Worth: £2,008,396 *Total Assets:* £12,730,233
Registered Office: No 1 Universal Square, Devonshire Street North, Manchester, M12 6JH
Activities: Activities of other holding companies n.e.c.
Shareholders: Kenneth Edward Corness; Daryl Neil Norvock
Officers: Kenneth Edward Corness [1955] Director; Daryl Neil Norvock [1981] Director

Rayburn Trading Company Limited
Incorporated: 8 August 1957 *Employees:* 170
Net Worth: £20,589,942 *Total Assets:* £37,746,036
Registered Office: 2nd Floor, 1 City Road East, Manchester, M15 4PN
Activities: Wholesale of pharmaceutical goods
Parent: Jesem Holdings Limited
Officers: Tony Hobson, Secretary/Accountant; Howard Goldman [1978] Director; Michael David Goldman [1949] Director; Russell Stuart Goldman [1971] Director; Tony Hobson [1961] Director/Accountant; Simon Weiner [1956] Director

Raydex/CDT Limited
Incorporated: 24 April 1995 *Employees:* 62
Net Worth: £6,841,000 *Total Assets:* £8,766,000
Registered Office: c/o Carlisle IT, Unit 9 Walker Industrial Estate, Walker Road, Guide, Blackburn, BB1 2QE
Activities: Manufacture of other electronic and electric wires and cables
Officers: Titus Ball [1973] Director/Business Executive [American]; Steven Joseph Ford [1959] Director/Vice President [American]; Michael L Roberson [1955] Director/Attorney [American]

Rayovac (UK) Limited
Incorporated: 4 March 1983
Net Worth: £83,408,000 *Total Assets:* £83,408,000
Registered Office: Regent Mill, Fir Street, Failsworth, Manchester, M35 0HS
Activities: Dormant company
Parent: Spectrum Brands (UK) Limited
Officers: Christopher Berry [1954] Director

Rayrigg Estates Ltd
Incorporated: 6 September 2001 *Employees:* 3
Net Worth: £8,932,227 *Total Assets:* £10,113,785
Registered Office: Rayrigg Road, Windermere, Cumbria, LA23 1BW
Activities: Other letting and operating of own or leased real estate
Shareholder: Diana Ruth Matthews
Officers: Diana Ruth Matthews, Secretary; Diana Ruth Matthews [1946] Director; Montague Gordon Pattinson Matthews [1977] Director/Social Worker; Rachael Ruth Matthews [1974] Director/Designer

Rayware Limited
Incorporated: 12 December 1975 *Employees:* 160
Net Worth: £802,757 *Total Assets:* £27,510,858
Registered Office: c/o Grant Thornton, 1st Floor, Royal Liver Building, Liverpool, L3 1PS
Activities: Wholesale of household goods (other than musical instruments) n.e.c
Major Shareholder: Raymond Hilton Endfield
Officers: Anthony Elton Endfield [1954] Director/Wholesale Distributor

RDG Foulridge Properties Limited
Incorporated: 26 October 2011 *Employees:* 3
Net Worth: £810,443 *Total Assets:* £8,554,011
Registered Office: Cat Fold Stable House, Cat Fold, Foulridge, Colne, Lancs, BB8 7PJ
Activities: Buying and selling of own real estate
Shareholders: Richard Herbert John Sutton; Anthony Patrick Hall; Ruth Eileen Sutton
Officers: James Robert Sutton [1964] Director; Richard Herbert John Sutton [1961] Managing Director

Reagens (UK) Limited
Incorporated: 13 March 1996 *Employees:* 10
Net Worth: £4,048,792 *Total Assets:* £9,844,189
Registered Office: Unit 7 St Georges Court, Dairyhouse Lane, Broadheath, Altrincham, Cheshire, WA14 5UA
Activities: Other business support service activities n.e.c.
Parent: Reagens SpA
Officers: Roger McKie, Secretary; Nino Robert Mann [1959] Director

Real Estate Two Limited
Incorporated: 4 July 2013
Net Worth: £7,327,210 *Total Assets:* £15,118,845
Registered Office: 4 Clippers Quay, Salford Quays, Manchester, M50 3BL
Activities: Other business support service activities n.e.c.
Shareholders: Daniel John Finestein; Sarah Anne Butler
Officers: Sarah Anne Butler [1976] Director/Accountant; Daniel John Finestein [1965] Director/Accountant; Philip Vickers [1961] Director/Accountant

Real Good Food PLC
Incorporated: 13 February 2003 *Employees:* 1,045
Net Worth: £86,718,000 *Total Assets:* £125,974,000
Registered Office: 61 Stephenson Way, Wavertree, Liverpool, L13 1HN
Activities: Manufacture of bread; manufacture of fresh pastry goods and cakes
Shareholder: NB. Ingredients Limited
Officers: Harveen Rai, Secretary; Hugh Charles Laurence Cawley [1956] Director; Jacques D'Unienville [1968] Director [Mauritian]; Steve Dawson [1959] Director; Michael John Holt [1960] Director; Judith Anne MacKenzie [1972] Director; Harveen Rai [1974] Finance Director; Patrick George Ridgwell [1946] Director; Christopher Owen Thomas [1945] Director

Realty Estates Limited
Incorporated: 17 August 1984 *Employees:* 40
Net Worth: £22,554,232 *Total Assets:* £32,778,008
Registered Office: 25 Rochdale Road, Manchester, M4 4HT
Activities: Development of building projects
Shareholders: Yousef Tishbi; Lord David Alliance
Officers: Jaleh Tishbi, Secretary; Yousef Tishbi [1948] Director/Architect

Reaper Limited
Incorporated: 3 May 1962 *Employees:* 4
Net Worth: £6,804,658 *Total Assets:* £10,097,391
Registered Office: The Albert Suite, Unit 2 Revolution Park, Buckshaw Avenue, Buckshaw Village, Chorley, Lancs, PR7 7DW
Activities: Other letting and operating of own or leased real estate
Shareholders: Roger Julian Thomas Acland Bracewell; Acland Bracewell Limited
Officers: Roger Julian Thomas Acland Bracewell, Secretary/Land Agent; James Henry George Acland Bracewell [1990] Director/Chartered Surveyor; Roger Julian Thomas Acland Bracewell [1960] Director/Chartered Surveyor; Mark Vernon Powys [1975] Director

Reays Coaches Limited
Incorporated: 20 January 2000 *Employees:* 141
Net Worth: £2,700,370 *Total Assets:* £10,383,706
Registered Office: Strawberry Fields, Syke Park, Wigton, Cumbria, CA7 9NE
Activities: Other urban, suburban or metropolitan passenger land transport (not underground, metro or similar)
Shareholders: Nicola Reay; Christopher Walter Reay
Officers: Nicola Reay, Secretary; Stephen John Crossley [1967] Director; Christopher Walter Reay [1972] Director; Nicola Reay [1971] Director

Recipharm Limited
Incorporated: 10 August 2012 *Employees:* 140
Net Worth Deficit: £482,000 *Total Assets:* £7,659,000
Registered Office: Bardsley Vale Mills, Oldham Road, Ashton under Lyne, Lancs, OL7 9RR
Activities: Manufacture of basic pharmaceutical products
Parent: Recipharm Holdings Limited
Officers: Thomas Bengt Eldered [1960] Director [Swedish]; Mark Royston Quick [1966] Director

Rectella International Limited
Incorporated: 6 June 1974 *Employees:* 52
Net Worth: £3,328,598 *Total Assets:* £9,053,443
Registered Office: The Copper Room, Deva Centre, Trinity Way, Manchester, M3 7BG
Activities: Other specialised construction activities n.e.c.
Parent: Tellar Holdings Limited
Officers: John Paul Keighley, Secretary; Julia Louise Eventhall [1968] Sales Director

Rectella Limited
Incorporated: 27 February 1947 *Employees:* 297
Net Worth: £4,669,133 *Total Assets:* £11,808,101
Registered Office: 6th Floor, Cardinal House, 20 St Mary's Parsonage, Manchester, M3 2LG
Activities: Wholesale of textiles
Parent: Julian Charles Group Limited
Officers: Anthony Wilfred Graham [1969] Sales Director; Charles Fredric Greibach [1950] Director

Recycling Lives Holdings Limited
Incorporated: 3 January 2006 *Employees:* 238
Net Worth: £5,609,000 *Total Assets:* £28,423,000
Registered Office: Recycling Lives Centre, Essex Street, Preston, Lancs, PR1 1QE
Activities: Activities of head offices
Major Shareholder: Steven Terence Jackson
Officers: Paul Finnerty, Secretary; Paul Finnerty [1968] Finance Director; William Thomas Fletcher [1979] Managing Director

Recycling Lives Limited
Incorporated: 2 June 1999 *Employees:* 213
Net Worth: £8,827,000 *Total Assets:* £28,807,000
Registered Office: Recycling Lives Centre, Essex Street, Preston, Lancs, PR1 1QE
Activities: Recovery of sorted materials
Officers: Paul Finnerty [1968] Director/Solicitor; William Thomas Fletcher [1979] Managing Director; Daniel Scott Jackson [1972] Operations Director

Red & White Services Limited
Incorporated: 6 November 1990 *Employees:* 931
Net Worth: £15,325,000 *Total Assets:* £30,021,000
Registered Office: c/o Stagecoach Services Limited, One Stockport Exchange, 20 Railway Road, Stockport, Cheshire, SK1 3SW
Activities: Other urban, suburban or metropolitan passenger land transport (not underground, metro or similar)
Parent: Stagecoach Bus Holdings Limited
Officers: Michael John Vaux, Secretary; Colin Brown [1968] Director/Accountant; Arnold Mark Threapleton [1954] Managing Director; Nigel Winter [1963] Director

Red Artificial Lift UK Limited
Incorporated: 16 October 2013
Net Worth: £10,903,000 *Total Assets:* £10,942,000
Registered Office: 3rd Floor, 1 Ashley Road, Altrincham, Cheshire, WA14 2DT
Activities: Activities of other holding companies n.e.c.
Parent: General Electric Company
Officers: Andrew Thomas Peter Budge [1973] Director/Chartered Accountant; Akhlesh Prasad Mathur [1972] Director/Chartered Accountant

Red Football Holdings Limited
Incorporated: 24 July 2012
Net Worth: £1,079,689,984 *Total Assets:* £1,492,407,040
Registered Office: Old Trafford, Manchester, M16 0RA
Activities: Activities of sport clubs
Parent: Manchester United PLC
Officers: Avram Glazer [1960] Director [American]; Joel Glazer [1967] Director [American]

Red Football Junior Limited
Incorporated: 18 February 2005
Net Worth: £222,447,696 *Total Assets:* £222,447,696
Registered Office: Old Trafford, Manchester, M16 0RA
Activities: Activities of sport clubs
Parent: Red Football Limited
Officers: Avram Glazer [1960] Director/Businessman [American]; Bryan Glazer [1964] Director/Businessman [American]; Darcie Glazer [1968] Director/Businesswoman [American]; Edward Glazer [1969] Director/Businessman [American]; Joel Glazer [1967] Director/Businessman [American]; Kevin Glazer [1962] Director/Businessman [American]

Red Football Limited
Incorporated: 18 February 2005 *Employees:* 865
Net Worth: £861,808,000 *Total Assets:* £1,966,028,032
Registered Office: Old Trafford, Manchester, M16 0RA
Activities: Activities of sport clubs
Parent: Red Football Joint Venture Limited
Officers: Avram Glazer [1960] Director/Businessman [American]; Bryan Glazer [1964] Director/Businessman [American]; Darcie Glazer [1968] Director/Businesswoman [American]; Edward Glazer [1969] Director/Businessman [American]; Joel Glazer [1967] Director/Businessman [American]; Kevin Glazer [1962] Director/Businessman [American]

Red Football Shareholder Limited
Incorporated: 24 December 2004
Net Worth: £564,964,992 *Total Assets:* £590,684,032
Registered Office: Old Trafford, Manchester, M16 0RA
Activities: Activities of sport clubs
Parent: Red Football Holdings Limited
Officers: Avram Glazer [1960] Director/Businessman [American]; Bryan Glazer [1964] Director/Businessman [American]; Darcie Glazer [1968] Director/Businesswoman [American]; Edward Glazer [1969] Director/Businessman [American]; Joel Glazer [1967] Director/Businessman [American]; Kevin Glazer [1962] Director/Businessman [American]

Red Gap Wind Farm Limited
Incorporated: 22 September 2015
Net Worth: £40,520 *Total Assets:* £14,378,490
Registered Office: 1030 Centre Park, Slutchers Lane, Warrington, Cheshire, WA1 1QL
Activities: Production of electricity
Officers: Elizabeth Oldroyd, Secretary; John William Breckenridge [1962] Managing Director [American]; Simon Richard Eaves [1967] Managing Director; Adrian Waine Robinson [1961] Director/Chief Operating Officer; Kirsty Louise Usher [1975] Director/Accountant

Red Production Company Limited
Incorporated: 24 December 1997 *Employees:* 29
Net Worth: £3,685,676 *Total Assets:* £14,831,616
Registered Office: Level 2, White, Media City UK, Salford, M50 2NT
Activities: Television programme production activities
Officers: Andrew Brian Critchley, Secretary/Accountant; Elisabeth Anne Marie de Vigouroux D'Arvieu [1977] Director [French]; Didier Lupfer [1964] Director [French]; Nicola Shindler [1968] Director/Producer

Red Rose Holdings Limited
Incorporated: 22 July 2005 *Employees:* 24
Net Worth: £3,183,714 *Total Assets:* £7,542,945
Registered Office: Riverside House, Branch Road, Lower Darwen, Lancs, BB3 0PR
Activities: Non-trading company
Shareholders: Mark John Holden; Michael John Anderson
Officers: Mark John Holden, Secretary/Director; Michael John Anderson [1957] Director; Mark Thomas Edgar [1976] Director; Mark John Holden [1966] Director

Red Rose Infrastructure Limited
Incorporated: 28 June 2011 *Employees:* 67
Net Worth Deficit: £2,698,000 *Total Assets:* £33,266,000
Registered Office: 1030 Centre Park, Slutchers Lane, Warrington, Cheshire, WA1 1QL
Activities: Production of electricity
Officers: Elizabeth Alexandra Oldroyd, Secretary; John William Breckenridge [1962] Managing Director [American]; Simon Richard Eaves [1967] Managing Director; Kirsty Louise Usher [1975] Director/Accountant

Red-D-Arc (UK) Limited
Incorporated: 13 March 2008
Net Worth: £139,396 *Total Assets:* £14,731,390
Registered Office: Unit 9 Station Road Industrial Estate, Station Road, Sutton, St Helens, Merseyside, WA9 3JG
Activities: Renting and leasing of other machinery, equipment and tangible goods n.e.c.
Parent: L'Air Liquide S.A.
Officers: Lola Lin, Secretary; Nicolas Droin [1974] Director/Chief Financial Officer [French]

Red-D-Arc Limited
Incorporated: 31 March 1987 *Employees:* 35
Net Worth: £16,368,367 *Total Assets:* £26,310,284
Registered Office: Unit 9 Station Road Industrial Estate, Station Road, Sutton, St Helens, Merseyside, WA9 3JG
Activities: Renting and leasing of other machinery, equipment and tangible goods n.e.c.
Parent: Red-D-Arc (UK) Limited
Officers: Lola Lin, Secretary; Nicolas Droin [1974] Director/Chief Financial Officer [French]; Ross Alfred McCrorie [1978] Director/General Manager

Reddington Developments Limited
Incorporated: 16 June 2004 *Employees:* 7
Net Worth: £21,477,000 *Total Assets:* £21,556,000
Registered Office: Peel Dome, intu Trafford Centre, Trafford City, Manchester, M17 8PL
Activities: Non-trading company
Parent: Reddington Holdings Limited
Officers: Neil Lees, Secretary; Peter John Hosker [1957] Director; Neil Lees [1963] Director/Company Secretary; John Alexander Schofield [1968] Director/Accountant; Steven Keith Underwood [1974] Director; John Whittaker [1942] Director; Mark Whittaker [1969] Director

Reddington Holdings Limited
Incorporated: 17 November 2004 *Employees:* 7
Net Worth: £1,166,064 *Total Assets:* £43,257,872
Registered Office: Peel Dome, intu Trafford Centre, Trafford City, Manchester, M17 8PL
Activities: Activities of other holding companies n.e.c.
Parent: Peel Land and Property Investments (CL) Limited
Officers: Neil Lees, Secretary; Peter John Hosker [1957] Director; Neil Lees [1963] Director/Company Secretary; John Alexander Schofield [1968] Director/Accountant; Steven Keith Underwood [1974] Director; John Whittaker [1942] Director; Mark Whittaker [1969] Director

Reddish Vale Academy Trust
Incorporated: 22 December 2011
Registered Office: Reddish Vale Technology College, Reddish Vale Road, Reddish, Stockport, Cheshire, SK5 7HD
Activities: General secondary education
Officers: Jill Lewins [1964] Director/Teacher; Malcolm Stansfield [1951] Director/Retired; Tony Mark Walker [1967] Director

Redhead Freight Limited
Incorporated: 3 March 1978 *Employees:* 367
Net Worth: £4,499,578 *Total Assets:* £21,135,844
Registered Office: Freightspeed House, Woodroyd Industrial Estate, Dealburn Road, Low Moor, Bradford, BD12 0RG
Activities: Freight transport by road
Officers: Keith Michael Shackleton, Secretary; Philip Andrew Baxter [1967] Operations Director; Robert Michael Cockroft [1961] Sales Director; Mark Spencer Cosgrove [1966] Irish Region Director; Reiner Heiken [1962] Director/Chief Executive [German]; Paul Anthony Suggitt [1961] Managing Director

Redhead Holdings Limited
Incorporated: 26 September 2000
Net Worth: £729,365 *Total Assets:* £10,350,670
Registered Office: Freightspeed House, Woodroyd Industrial Estate, Dealburn Road, Low Moor, Bradford, BD12 0RG
Activities: Other letting and operating of own or leased real estate
Parent: Schenker Aktiengesellschaft
Officers: Keith Michael Shackleton, Secretary; Philip Andrew Baxter [1967] Operations Director; Mark Spencer Cosgrove [1966] Irish Region Director; Reiner Heiken [1962] Director/Chief Executive [German]; Paul Anthony Suggitt [1961] Managing Director

Redhill Famco Limited
Incorporated: 4 May 2016 *Employees:* 514
Net Worth: £316,900,000 *Total Assets:* £2,278,099,968
Registered Office: Lake View, Lakeside, Cheadle, Cheshire, SK8 3GW
Activities: Activities of financial services holding companies
Shareholders: Dorah Leah Moser; Henry Neville Moser
Officers: Gary Derek Beckett, Secretary; Gary Derek Beckett [1969] Director; Henry Neville Moser [1949] Director

Redrow Homes East Midlands Limited
Incorporated: 18 May 2001 *Employees:* 74
Net Worth: £16,214,635 *Total Assets:* £24,820,644
Registered Office: Redrow House, St David's Park, Deeside, Flintshire, CH5 3RX
Activities: Construction of domestic buildings
Parent: Redrow Homes Limited
Officers: Graham Anthony Cope, Secretary; Helen Davies [1966] Director/Accountant; Warren Thompson [1974] Director/Regional Chief Executive; John Frederick Tutte [1956] Director/Civil Engineer; Robert Paul Wilson [1960] Director/Surveyor

Redrow Homes Limited
Incorporated: 18 February 1986 *Employees:* 2,076
Net Worth: £456,000,000 *Total Assets:* £2,288,699,904
Registered Office: Redrow House, St David's Park, Deeside, Flintshire, CH5 3RX
Activities: Construction of domestic buildings
Parent: HB (HDG) Limited
Officers: Graham Anthony Cope, Secretary/Legal Director; Graham Anthony Cope [1964] Director/Solicitor; Helen Davies [1966] Director/Accountant; William Robert Heath [1979] Director/Chartered Surveyor; Keith Joseph Parrett [1955] Director; Matthew John Pratt [1975] Director/Quantity Surveyor; Barbara Mary Richmond [1960] Director/Chartered Accountant; Warren Thompson [1974] Director; John Frederick Tutte [1956] Director/Civil Engineer

Redrow Langley Limited
Incorporated: 7 July 2010
Net Worth: £5,174,932 *Total Assets:* £11,709,642
Registered Office: Redrow House, St David's Park, Deeside, Flintshire, CH5 3RX
Activities: Construction of domestic buildings
Parent: Redrow Homes Limited
Officers: Graham Anthony Cope, Secretary; Helen Davies [1966] Director/Accountant; Warren Thompson [1974] Director/Regional Chief Executive; John Frederick Tutte [1956] Director/Civil Engineer; Robert Paul Wilson [1960] Director/Surveyor

Redrow PLC
Incorporated: 2 December 1993 *Employees:* 2,130
Net Worth: £1,235,000,064 *Total Assets:* £2,200,999,936
Registered Office: Redrow House, St David's Park, Deeside, Flintshire, CH5 3RX
Activities: Construction of domestic buildings
Officers: Graham Anthony Cope, Secretary/Legal Director; Alison Deborah Hewitt [1963] Director; Andrew Nicholas Hewson [1958] Director/Chartered Accountant; Sir Michael Thomas Lyons [1949] Director/Company Chairman; Stephen Peter Morgan [1952] Director; Vanda Murray [1960] Director; Barbara Mary Richmond [1960] Director/Chartered Accountant; John Frederick Tutte [1956] Director/Civil Engineer

Redrow Real Estate Limited
Incorporated: 18 May 2000
Net Worth: £6,067,588 *Total Assets:* £14,558,662
Registered Office: Redrow House, St David's Park, Deeside, Flintshire, CH5 3RX
Activities: Construction of domestic buildings
Parent: Redrow Regeneration PLC
Officers: Graham Anthony Cope, Secretary/Solicitor; Graham Anthony Cope [1964] Director/Solicitor; Helen Davies [1966] Director/Chartered Accountant; John Richard Mann [1968] Director; Barbara Mary Richmond [1960] Director/Chartered Accountant; John Frederick Tutte [1956] Director/Civil Engineer

Redstart Construction Limited
Incorporated: 3 December 1991 *Employees:* 2
Net Worth: £5,064,686 *Total Assets:* £9,969,045
Registered Office: HLB House, 68 High Street, Tarporley, Cheshire, CW6 0AT
Activities: Development of building projects
Major Shareholder: John Robert Gwilliam
Officers: John Robert Gwilliam, Secretary; Alison Jane Gwilliam [1968] Director/Receptionist; John Robert Gwilliam [1956] Director/Building Contractor

Redwood TTM Ltd
Incorporated: 9 December 1993 *Employees:* 199
Net Worth: £14,154,480 *Total Assets:* £19,871,696
Registered Office: c/o Grant Thornton, 1st Floor, Royal Liver Building, Liverpool, L3 1PS
Activities: Wholesale of textiles
Parent: Redwood Group Holdings Limited
Officers: Brian John Lyde Atherton, Secretary/Sales Manager; Brian John Lyde Atherton [1944] Managing Director; John Alexander Lyde Atherton [1976] Sales Director; Maureen Helen Atherton [1944] Director; Darren Rose [1971] Finance Director

Redx Pharma PLC
Incorporated: 7 September 2010 *Employees:* 131
Net Worth: £14,327,000 *Total Assets:* £27,689,000
Registered Office: Block 33 Mereside, Alderley Park, Macclesfield, Cheshire, SK10 4TG
Activities: Research and experimental development on biotechnology
Officers: Andrew William Booth, Secretary; Lisa Mary Whewell Anson [1968] Director/Pharmaceuticals Executive; Dominic Nicholas Jackson [1981] Director/Private Equity; Dr Bernhard Jurgen Kirschbaum [1958] Director [German]; Peter Eric Presland [1950] Director/Chartered Accountant; Iain Gladstone Ross [1954] Director

Refrigeration Norwest (Chester) Limited
Incorporated: 18 May 1970 *Employees:* 27
Net Worth: £5,870,195 *Total Assets:* £8,059,719
Registered Office: Hawarden Industrial Park, Manor Lane, Hawarden, Deeside, Flintshire, CH5 3PZ
Activities: Wholesale of radio, television goods & electrical household appliances (other than records, tapes, CDs)
Major Shareholder: James Dudley Lloyd Hughes
Officers: James Dudley Lloyd Hughes, Secretary/Company Sales Director; James Dudley Lloyd Hughes [1939] Company Sales Director; Kathryn Susan Hughes [1972] Director/Teacher; Paul James Hughes [1969] Director; Susan Margaret Hughes [1942] Director

Regal Crown Logistics Limited
Incorporated: 8 February 1993 *Employees:* 22
Net Worth: £2,971,248 *Total Assets:* £10,810,707
Registered Office: 8 Eastway, Sale, Cheshire, M33 4DX
Activities: Other service activities n.e.c.
Major Shareholder: Roy Edward Crossley
Officers: Paul Crossley, Secretary; Paul Crossley [1972] Operations Director; Roy Edward Crossley [1955] Director/Logistics

Regal Vehicle Rentals Limited
Incorporated: 12 November 1997 *Employees:* 100
Net Worth: £449,816 *Total Assets:* £7,388,270
Registered Office: Kingfisher Court, Parkgate Road, Mollington, Chester, CH1 6RR
Activities: Renting and leasing of cars and light motor vehicles
Major Shareholder: Jamie Harold Frost
Officers: Jamie Harold Frost [1971] Managing Director; Ian Stuart Horton [1975] Finance Director

Regatta Ltd
Incorporated: 31 July 1972 *Employees:* 638
Net Worth: £44,708,000 *Total Assets:* £95,859,000
Registered Office: Risol House, Mercury Way, Urmston, Manchester, M41 7RR
Activities: Wholesale of clothing and footwear
Officers: David Michael Wynn Holt, Secretary; Joanne Black [1965] Buying Director; Keith Joseph Black [1959] Managing Director; David Michael Wynn Holt [1962] Operations Director; Graham Jonothan Rickard [1966] Marketing Director; Bernard Max Yaffe [1954] Director

Regency Factors PLC
Incorporated: 28 October 1991 *Employees:* 50
Net Worth: £4,342,227 *Total Assets:* £62,102,316
Registered Office: 2 Regency Chambers, Jubilee Way, Bury, Lancs, BL9 0JW
Activities: Other business support service activities n.e.c.
Shareholders: Hilary Susan Craft; Maurice Howard Craft
Officers: Jonathan Simon Myer Craft, Secretary; Stephen Clague [1949] Director/Chairman; Hilary Susan Craft [1957] Director; Maurice Howard Craft [1955] Director/Business Consultant; Paresh Devchand Dusara [1959] Director; John Thomas Farrell [1965] Director; Peter Ratcliffe [1949] Director/Chartered Accountant

Regency Glass (Holdings) Limited
Incorporated: 15 January 2016 *Employees:* 94
Net Worth: £3,032,313 *Total Assets:* £9,390,401
Registered Office: Hope Carr Industrial Estate, Butts Street, Leigh, Lancs, WN7 3AE
Activities: Activities of other holding companies n.e.c.
Shareholders: Darren Beazant; Simon Sebastian Orange
Officers: Mr Darren Beazant [1965] Director; Simon Sebastian Orange [1967] Director

Regency Glass Limited
Incorporated: 7 August 2006 *Employees:* 94
Net Worth: £4,626,057 *Total Assets:* £9,212,697
Registered Office: Hope Carr Industrial Estate, Butts Street, Leigh, Lancs, WN7 3AE
Activities: Shaping and processing of flat glass
Parent: Regency Glass (Holdings) Limited
Officers: Mr Darren Beazant [1965] Director; Wayne Lee Fitzmartin [1969] Director; Simon Sebastian Orange [1967] Director

Regency House Finance Limited
Incorporated: 12 April 1994
Net Worth: £1 *Total Assets:* £8,120,118
Registered Office: 2 Regency Chambers, Jubilee Way, Bury, Lancs, BL9 0JW
Activities: Other business support service activities n.e.c.
Parent: Regency Factors PLC
Officers: Jonathan Simon Myer Craft, Secretary; Hilary Susan Craft [1957] Director; Maurice Howard Craft [1955] Director; John Thomas Farrell [1965] Director

Regent Medical Americas Holdings Limited
Incorporated: 23 June 2004
Net Worth: £36,658,000 *Total Assets:* £36,658,000
Registered Office: Unity House, Medlock Street, Oldham, Lancs, OL1 3HS
Activities: Activities of head offices
Parent: Regent Medical Ltd
Officers: Christopher John Stubbs, Secretary; Stefan Ulf Fristedt [1966] Finance Director [Swedish]; Nicholas Andrew Rothwell [1973] Director/General Manager; Richard Twomey [1964] Director

Regent Medical Limited
Incorporated: 16 April 2004
Net Worth: £38,960,000 *Total Assets:* £102,209,000
Registered Office: Unity House, Medlock Street, Oldham, Lancs, OL1 3HS
Activities: Other human health activities
Parent: MHC UK Ltd
Officers: Christopher John Stubbs, Secretary; Stefan Ulf Fristedt [1966] Finance Director [Swedish]; Nicholas Andrew Rothwell [1973] Director/General Manager; Richard Twomey [1964] Director

Regional & City Airports (Blackpool) Holdings Limited
Incorporated: 30 April 2008
Net Worth: £15,732,153 *Total Assets:* £17,852,206
Registered Office: Number One Bickerstaffe Square, Talbot Road, Blackpool, Lancs, FY1 3AH
Activities: Activities of head offices
Parent: Blackpool Council
Officers: Mark Adrian Towers, Secretary; Neil Anthony Jack [1972] Director; Steven Thompson [1963] Director

Regional & City Airports (Blackpool) Limited
Incorporated: 11 December 2003
Net Worth Deficit: £1,163,786 *Total Assets:* £10,135,946
Registered Office: Number One Bickerstaffe Square, Talbot Road, Blackpool, Lancs, FY1 3AH
Activities: Activities of head offices
Officers: Mark Adrian Towers, Secretary; Neil Anthony Jack [1972] Director; Steven Thompson [1963] Director

Reich Insurance Brokers Limited
Incorporated: 19 January 1999 *Employees:* 25
Net Worth: £10,600,037 *Total Assets:* £23,571,792
Registered Office: 197 Chapel Street, Salford, M3 5EQ
Activities: Non-life insurance
Officers: Simon Paul Taylor, Secretary/Insurance Broker; Daniel Akiva Lopian [1963] Director/Insurance Broker; Simon Paul Taylor [1963] Director/Insurance Broker; Andrew James Tidey [1967] Director

Reisser Limited
Incorporated: 9 November 1981 *Employees:* 19
Net Worth: £1,456,895 *Total Assets:* £8,684,943
Registered Office: Bramhall Moor Industrial Estate, Pepper Road, Hazel Grove, Stockport, Cheshire, SK7 5BW
Activities: Non-specialised wholesale trade
Shareholders: Jane O'Neill; Charles Ledigo
Officers: Jane O'Neill, Secretary; Charles Ledigo [1953] Director/Sales Executive; Patrick Brian Meads [1971] Director; Jane O'Neill [1964] Director/Accountant

Remel Europe Limited
Incorporated: 4 July 2001 *Employees:* 127
Net Worth: £19,832,000 *Total Assets:* £22,864,000
Registered Office: 3rd Floor, 1 Ashley Road, Altrincham, Cheshire, WA14 2DT
Activities: Non-specialised wholesale trade
Parent: Erie Finance Limited
Officers: Rhona Gregg, Secretary; Lucie Mary Katja Grant [1976] Director/Solicitor; Nicholas Ince [1982] Director/Accountant; David John Norman [1960] Director/Chartered Accountant

Renaker Build Limited
Incorporated: 22 May 2008 *Employees:* 137
Net Worth: £7,863,857 *Total Assets:* £42,625,240
Registered Office: 1st Floor, NQ Building, 47 Bengal Street, Manchester, M4 6BB
Activities: Other business support service activities n.e.c.
Major Shareholder: Daren Whitaker
Officers: Michael Shaw, Secretary; Daren Whitaker [1972] Director/Construction

Renold International Holdings Limited
Incorporated: 17 December 1907 *Employees:* 1,752
Net Worth: £28,800,000 *Total Assets:* £228,400,000
Registered Office: Trident 2, Trident Business Park, Styal Road, Wythenshawe, Manchester, M22 5XB
Activities: Activities of head offices
Parent: Renold Public Limited Company
Officers: Antony Kenneth Edwards [1963] Corporate Development Director; Philip Mark Robinson [1967] Group Human Resources Director; Lynne Joan Rosser [1962] Director/Group Pensions Manager; Ian Lloyd Scapens [1974] Director; Michael Peter Wallwork [1971] Managing Director

Renold Power Transmission Limited
Incorporated: 9 June 1922 *Employees:* 317
Net Worth Deficit: £38,885,000 *Total Assets:* £77,995,000
Registered Office: Trident 2, Trident Business Park, Styal Road, Wythenshawe, Manchester, M22 5XB
Activities: Manufacture of wire products, chain and springs
Parent: Renold Public Limited Company
Officers: Antony Kenneth Edwards [1963] Corporate Development Director; Philip Mark Robinson [1967] Group Human Resources Director; Lynne Joan Rosser [1962] Director/Group Pensions Manager; Ian Lloyd Scapens [1974] Director; Michael Peter Wallwork [1971] Managing Director

Renold Public Limited Company
Incorporated: 23 July 1930 *Employees:* 2,044
Net Worth Deficit: £900,000 *Total Assets:* £189,900,000
Registered Office: Trident 2, Trident Business Park, Styal Road, Wythenshawe, Manchester, M22 5XB
Activities: Manufacture of wire products, chain and springs
Officers: Andrew John Bachelor, Secretary; Ian Roy Griffiths [1950] Director; Mark Jeremy Harper [1956] Director; David Farrington Landless [1960] Director; John Robert Purcell [1961] Director; Ian Lloyd Scapens [1974] Director

J F Renshaw Ltd
Incorporated: 21 September 1982 *Employees:* 310
Net Worth: £63,909,000 *Total Assets:* £83,998,000
Registered Office: 61 Stephenson Way, Wavertree, Liverpool, L13 1HN
Activities: Manufacture of sugar
Parent: N Brown Foods Ltd
Officers: Harveen Rai, Secretary; Hugh Charles Laurence Cawley [1956] Director; Harveen Rai [1974] Director; Patrick George Ridgwell [1946] Director; Christopher Owen Thomas [1945] Director

Renthal Limited
Incorporated: 29 August 1975 *Employees:* 67
Net Worth: £12,064,368 *Total Assets:* £18,546,718
Registered Office: Bredbury Park Way, Bredbury, Stockport, Cheshire, SK6 2SN
Activities: Manufacture of other fabricated metal products n.e.c.
Parent: Race Valley Limited
Officers: Laura May Birchall, Secretary; Thomas David Wade [1973] Director/Accountant; Paul James Watkins [1961] Operations Director; Rees Whittal-Williams [1981] Director

Rentsmart Limited
Incorporated: 24 December 1998 *Employees:* 78
Net Worth: £4,670,394 *Total Assets:* £12,745,466
Registered Office: 7th Floor, Oakland House, Talbot Road, Old Trafford, Manchester, M16 0PQ
Activities: Other credit granting n.e.c.
Parent: Thinksmart Europe Limited
Officers: Gary Robert Halton, Secretary/Chief Financial Officer; Gary Robert Halton [1968] Director/European CFO; Natale Ronald Montarello [1961] Director/Executive Chairman [Australian]

Repic Limited
Incorporated: 15 January 2004 *Employees:* 18
Net Worth: £349,207 *Total Assets:* £11,043,654
Registered Office: Repic House, Waterfold Business Park, Waterfold, Bury, Lancs, BL9 7BR
Activities: Activities of other membership organisations n.e.c.
Officers: Louise Christine Grantham, Secretary; Michael David Birch [1959] Director; Abrar Hussain Bokhari [1968] Director; Mark Burrows Smith [1967] Director/Chief Executive; Wayne Karl Copley [1959] Procurement Director; Geoffrey Ivor Edwards [1957] Director; Louise Christine Grantham [1963] Finance Director; Sebastian Timothy Robin Hardy [1982] Director/Solicitor; Andrew Mullen [1963] Director; Paul Mulvenna [1967] Director; Joseph Francis O'Sullivan [1960] Director

Research & Development Tax Solutions (Holdings) Limited
Incorporated: 24 March 2016
Net Worth: £1,589,412 *Total Assets:* £9,000,000
Registered Office: c/o Eba, 253 Manchester Business Park, 3000 Aviator Way, Manchester, M22 5TG
Activities: Activities of other holding companies n.e.c.
Shareholder: Mark John Tighe
Officers: Daniel James Alcock [1980] Director; Jonathan Thomas Anderson [1974] Director; Mark John Tighe [1963] Director

The Residence Manchester Limited
Incorporated: 25 February 2016
Net Worth Deficit: £5,322 *Total Assets:* £20,769,216
Registered Office: 116 Duke Street, Liverpool, L1 5JW
Activities: Buying and selling of own real estate
Parent: 1DOM Limited
Officers: Elliot Philip Lawless [1987] Director/Developer

Restaurant Bar and Grill Limited
Incorporated: 31 July 1998 *Employees:* 1,539
Net Worth: £1,435,330 *Total Assets:* £47,960,188
Registered Office: 4th Floor, Ridgefield House, 14 John Dalton Street, Manchester, M2 6JR
Activities: Licenced restaurants
Parent: Individual Restaurant Company Limited
Officers: Peter David McCulloch, Secretary; Vernon Lord [1966] Director; Peter David McCulloch [1978] Finance Director; Steven John Walker [1970] Director

Restore Scan Limited
Incorporated: 23 December 2002 *Employees:* 294
Net Worth: £16,025,000 *Total Assets:* £22,819,000
Registered Office: Unit 2 Tally Close, Agecroft Commerce Park, Swinton, Manchester, M27 8WJ
Activities: Other business support service activities n.e.c.
Parent: Restore PLC
Officers: Sarah Waudby, Secretary; Adam Thomas Councell [1978] Director; Paul Edmund Moonan [1961] Director; Charles Antony Lawrence Skinner [1960] Director

Retail Property Investments Limited
Incorporated: 23 November 1962 *Employees:* 6
Net Worth: £3,022,360 *Total Assets:* £10,336,620
Registered Office: 4 The Cottages, Deva Centre, Trinity Way, Manchester, M3 7BE
Activities: Buying and selling of own real estate
Shareholder: Leonard Daniel Seitler
Officers: Sandra Seitler, Secretary; Benjamin Seitler [1933] Director; Leonard Daniel Seitler [1968] Director/Surveyor; Sandra Seitler [1938] Director

Rethink Professional Services Limited
Incorporated: 29 April 2008 *Employees:* 24
Net Worth: £491,144 *Total Assets:* £19,384,826
Registered Office: 19 Spring Gardens, Manchester, M2 1FB
Activities: Human resources provision and management of human resources functions
Parent: Rethink Group Limited
Officers: Benjamin Felton, Secretary; Benjamin Thomas Felton [1981] Director; Graeme Paxton [1977] Sales Director

Rethink Recruitment Solutions Limited
Incorporated: 26 March 2007 *Employees:* 117
Net Worth: £349,989 *Total Assets:* £27,819,810
Registered Office: 19 Spring Gardens, Manchester, M2 1FB
Activities: Human resources provision and management of human resources functions
Parent: The Rethink Group Limited
Officers: Benjamin Felton, Secretary; Benjamin Thomas Felton [1981] Director; Robert O'Callaghan [1973] Director; John Osullivan [1956] Director

Retstone Limited
Incorporated: 19 September 2001 *Employees:* 141
Net Worth: £5,548,558 *Total Assets:* £16,927,542
Registered Office: Regency House, 45-51 Chorley New Road, Bolton, Lancs, BL1 4QR
Activities: Activities of other holding companies n.e.c.
Shareholders: Geraint Edward Williams; John Stephen Payne
Officers: Geraint Edward Williams [1970] Director

Revegate Limited
Incorporated: 30 October 1979 *Employees:* 7
Net Worth: £4,464,329 *Total Assets:* £7,269,249
Registered Office: 2nd Floor, 1 City Road East, Manchester, M15 4PN
Activities: Development of building projects
Major Shareholder: Terry Malcolm Krell
Officers: Hilary Jan Krell, Secretary; Hilary Jan Krell [1956] Director; Imogen Cara Krell [1994] Director; Terry Malcolm Krell [1953] Director

Revolution Bars Group PLC
Incorporated: 9 January 2014 *Employees:* 2,743
Net Worth: £40,002,000 *Total Assets:* £75,646,000
Registered Office: 21 Old Street, Ashton under Lyne, Lancs, OL6 6LA
Activities: Retail sale of beverages in specialised stores
Officers: Michael Raymond Foster, Secretary; Jemima Chloe Bird [1972] Marketing Director; Keith Graeme Edelman [1950] Director; Michael Raymond Foster [1958] Director; Robert Antony Pitcher [1974] Director; Michael St John Shallow [1954] Director/Chartered Accountant

Revolution Bars Limited
Incorporated: 9 January 2014 *Employees:* 1,993
Net Worth: £34,565,000 *Total Assets:* £54,393,000
Registered Office: 21 Old Street, Ashton under Lyne, Lancs, OL6 6LA
Activities: Retail sale of beverages in specialised stores
Parent: Inventive Guaranteeco Limited
Officers: Michael Raymond Foster, Secretary; Michael Raymond Foster [1958] Director; Robert Anthony Pitcher [1974] Director

Revolution Direct Ltd
Incorporated: 3 August 2012 *Employees:* 48
Net Worth Deficit: £7,429,845 *Total Assets:* £8,363,938
Registered Office: 3rd Floor, 1 Ashley Road, Altrincham, Cheshire, WA14 2DT
Activities: Activities of distribution holding companies
Officers: Michael Scott Kronenfeld [1962] Director/Chief Financial Officer [American]; Joseph Sclafani [1961] Director [American]

RG14 Limited
Incorporated: 21 July 2008 *Employees:* 5
Net Worth: £3,843,029 *Total Assets:* £8,776,467
Registered Office: 327 Clifton Drive South, Lytham St Annes, Lancs, FY8 1HN
Activities: Activities of other holding companies n.e.c.
Shareholders: Derek Anthony Byrne; Dermot Gerard Byrne
Officers: Dermot Gerard Byrne [1957] Director [Irish]; Mark Henderson [1959] Director

RGFC Dust Limited
Incorporated: 5 December 2014
Net Worth Deficit: £98,000 *Total Assets:* £8,157,000
Registered Office: 61 Stephenson Way, Wavertree, Liverpool, L13 1HN
Activities: Activities of head offices
Parent: Real Good Food PLC
Officers: Harveen Rai, Secretary; Hugh Charles Laurence Cawley [1956] Director; Harveen Rai [1974] Director; Patrick George Ridgwell [1946] Director; Christopher Owen Thomas [1945] Director

Rhenus Logistics Limited
Incorporated: 22 March 2002 *Employees:* 289
Net Worth: £10,855,321 *Total Assets:* £24,808,516
Registered Office: Rhenus Logistics, Liverpool Road, Eccles, Manchester, M30 7RF
Activities: Freight transport by road
Parent: Rhenus Beteiligunen International GmbH
Officers: Richard Kennerley, Secretary/Accountant; Tobias Bartz [1977] Director [German]; Richard Kennerley [1973] Director/Accountant; Graham Thomas Miller [1954] Director/Freight Forwarder; David John Williams [1965] Managing Director

Rhodi Group Limited
Incorporated: 24 March 1995
Net Worth: £2,376,149 *Total Assets:* £9,149,862
Registered Office: 1 Fishwick Park, Mercer Street, Preston, Lancs, PR1 4LZ
Activities: Other letting and operating of own or leased real estate
Shareholder: Rizwan Ibrahim Bux
Officers: Ibrahim Vali Bux, Secretary; Hamida Ibrahim Bux [1945] Director; Ibrahim Vali Bux [1942] Director; Rizwan Ibraham Bux [1979] Director

Rhodi Inc. Imports Limited
Incorporated: 25 July 1995
Net Worth: £1,584,503 *Total Assets:* £27,660,596
Registered Office: 1 Fishwick Park, Mercer Street, Preston, Lancs, PR1 4LZ
Activities: Wholesale of clothing and footwear
Officers: Hamida Ibrahim Bux, Secretary; Ibrahim Vali Bux [1942] Director; Rizwan Ibraham Bux [1979] Director

Rhodi Limited
Incorporated: 8 June 2001
Registered Office: 1 Fishwick Park, Mercer Street, Preston, Lancs, PR1 4LZ
Activities: Other business support service activities n.e.c.
Major Shareholder: Ibrahim Vali Bux
Officers: Hamida Ibrahim Bux, Secretary; Ibrahim Vali Bux [1942] Director; Rizwan Ibraham Bux [1979] Director

Rhodi Suppliers Limited
Incorporated: 10 September 2008
Net Worth: £237,381 *Total Assets:* £6,723,493
Registered Office: 1 Fishwick Park, Mercer Street, Preston, Lancs, PR1 4LZ
Activities: Wholesale of clothing and footwear
Officers: Hamida Ibrahim Bux, Secretary; Ibrahim Vali Bux [1942] Director; Rizwan Ibraham Bux [1979] Director

Ribble Investments Limited
Incorporated: 14 March 2003 *Employees:* 107
Net Worth: £1,592,556 *Total Assets:* £12,975,202
Registered Office: Greengate Street, Oldham, Lancs, OL4 1DF
Activities: Manufacture of corrugated paper and paperboard, sacks and bags
Major Shareholder: Stephen Rector
Officers: Michael Gerard Kernaghan, Secretary; Stephen Edward Phineas Isaacs [1961] Director; Michael Gerard Kernaghan [1966] Director; Stephen Rector [1965] Director; Graham Souter [1970] Director

Ribble Packaging Limited
Incorporated: 16 July 1953 *Employees:* 107
Net Worth: £5,676,786 *Total Assets:* £17,059,424
Registered Office: Greengate Street, Oldham, Lancs, OL4 1DF
Activities: Manufacture of corrugated paper and paperboard, sacks and bags
Major Shareholder: Stephen Rector
Officers: Michael Gerard Kernaghan, Secretary; Stephen Edward Phineas Isaacs [1961] Director; Michael Gerard Kernaghan [1966] Director; Stephen Rector [1965] Director; Graham Souter [1970] Director

Ribble Property Developments Limited
Incorporated: 29 January 1999
Net Worth: £1,491,060 *Total Assets:* £7,236,700
Registered Office: Ribble Court, 1 Mead Way, Shuttleworth Mead Business Park, Padiham, Lancs, BB12 7NG
Activities: Construction of commercial buildings
Shareholders: Tahir Mohsin; Howard Rigg
Officers: Deborah Jane Benedetto, Secretary; Christopher Holgate [1945] Director/Building Contractor; Howard Rigg [1944] Director/Property Developer; Timothy John Henry Webber [1954] Director

Ribble Valley Luxury Homes Limited
Incorporated: 12 October 1998 *Employees:* 4
Net Worth: £3,979,438 *Total Assets:* £7,518,516
Registered Office: Eastham House Farm, Clitheroe Road, Mitton, Clitheroe, Lancs, BB7 9PH
Activities: Construction of commercial buildings
Major Shareholder: Stanley Ainsworth
Officers: Stanley Ainsworth [1946] Director/Builder; Gwen Skillings [1967] Director

Edmund Rice Bicentennial Trust Limited
Incorporated: 5 June 2001
Net Worth: £29,253,448 *Total Assets:* £29,283,510
Registered Office: Woodeaves, Wicker Lane, Hale Barns, Altrincham, Cheshire, WA15 0HF
Activities: Activities of religious organisations
Officers: Kieran Timothy Gordon [1958] Director [Irish]; Patrick George Gordon [1942] Director/Retired Teacher [Irish]; Paul Griffiths [1952] Director/Chartered Secretary; Mark Vincent Holland [1961] Director/Business Owner; Joseph Johnson [1970] Director/Religious Brother [Indian]; Julian McDonald [1942] Director/Religious Brother [Australian]; Clement Mukuka Sindazi [1965] Director/Religious Brother [Zambian]

Jon Richard Holdings Limited
Incorporated: 25 January 2010 *Employees:* 622
Net Worth: £7,402,121 *Total Assets:* £12,952,745
Registered Office: Tilson Road, Roundthorn Industrial Estate, Manchester, M23 9GF
Activities: Activities of head offices
Major Shareholder: Malcolm David Stark
Officers: Sarah Frew [1963] Director; Malcolm David Stark [1947] Director; Louise Anne Yates [1974] Director/Chartered Accountant

Jon Richard Limited
Incorporated: 28 July 1992 *Employees:* 622
Net Worth: £7,398,787 *Total Assets:* £12,952,727
Registered Office: Tilson Road, Roundthorn Industrial Estate, Wythenshawe, Manchester, M23 9GF
Activities: Retail sale of watches and jewellery in specialised stores
Parent: Jon Richard Holdings Limited
Officers: Louise Anne Yates, Secretary; Sarah Frew [1963] Director; Malcolm David Stark [1947] Director; Louise Anne Yates [1974] Director/Chartered Accountant

Richminster Ltd
Incorporated: 10 March 2010
Net Worth: £224,125 *Total Assets:* £9,867,520
Registered Office: Lancaster House, 70-76 Blackburn Street, Radcliffe, Manchester, M26 2JW
Activities: Security dealing on own account
Officers: Colette Halstead, Secretary; Mark Halstead [1957] Director

Rickerby Holdings Limited
Incorporated: 21 February 1918 *Employees:* 138
Net Worth: £10,246,601 *Total Assets:* £22,730,598
Registered Office: Currock Road, Carlisle, Cumbria, CA2 4AU
Activities: Other letting and operating of own or leased real estate
Shareholder: Dr Elizabeth Jane Rickerby
Officers: Neil Platton, Secretary; Neil Platton [1969] Director/Accountant; Patrick Rutherford David Rickerby [1955] Director; William Maxwell Rickerby [1979] Director

Rickerby Limited
Incorporated: 4 December 2003 *Employees:* 135
Net Worth: £7,024,817 *Total Assets:* £18,096,576
Registered Office: Currock Road, Carlisle, Cumbria, CA2 4AU
Activities: Sale of other motor vehicles
Parent: Rickerby Holdings Limited
Officers: Neil Platton, Secretary; Kenneth Michael Conley [1961] Managing Director; Martyn William Henderson [1961] Sales Director; Neil Platton [1969] Director/Management Accountant; Colin Hugh Potts [1959] Sales Director; Patrick Rutherford David Rickerby [1955] Director

Ridge Medical Limited
Incorporated: 10 August 2007 *Employees:* 4
Net Worth: £5,088,674 *Total Assets:* £15,102,414
Registered Office: Ridge Medical Centre, Cousen Road, Bradford, W Yorks, BD7 3JX
Activities: Other letting and operating of own or leased real estate
Officers: Nicholas Nurden, Secretary; Dr Andrew Timothy Hansen [1967] Director/GP; Dr Christopher Paul Harris [1962] Director/GP; Nicholas Stuart Nurden [1967] Director/Business Manager; Dr Susan Marie Towers [1962] Director/Doctor

Rigby Estates LLP
Incorporated: 16 September 2009
Net Worth: £839,487 *Total Assets:* £8,802,552
Registered Office: 4 Croft Court, Whitehills Business Park, Blackpool, Lancs, FY4 5PR
Officers: Linda Rigby [1961] Member; William Simon Rigby [1961] Member

Gordon Rigg (Nurseries) Limited
Incorporated: 18 January 1977 *Employees:* 208
Net Worth: £5,908,430 *Total Assets:* £7,983,580
Registered Office: Calderbank Nurseries, Walsden, Todmorden, Lancs, OL14 7TJ
Activities: Retail sale of flowers, plants, seeds, fertilizers, pet animals and pet food in specialised stores
Officers: Pauline Rigg [1961] Director/Nurseryman; Peter Rigg [1950] Director/Nurseryman

Rigisystems Ltd
Incorporated: 9 January 2001 *Employees:* 66
Net Worth: £7,116,905 *Total Assets:* £14,621,008
Registered Office: Grant Thornton UK LLP, 4 Hardman Square, Spinningfields, Manchester, M3 3EB
Activities: Manufacture of other fabricated metal products n.e.c.
Officers: Simon Charles Neale, Secretary; Simon Charles Neale [1965] Financial Director; Grahame Rankin [1958] Sales Director; Peter Taylor [1951] Managing Director; Mark Walder [1955] Commercial Director; John Raymond Williams [1949] Director/Engineer

Rimape Ltd
Incorporated: 18 August 2009 *Employees:* 93
Net Worth: £4,701,858 *Total Assets:* £9,841,785
Registered Office: Navigation Garage, Forrest Street, Blackburn, Lancs, BB1 3BB
Activities: Activities of head offices
Shareholder: Mark Frank Griffiths
Officers: Mark Frank Griffiths, Secretary; Christopher Bell [1961] Director; Richard Neil Davies [1967] Director; Mark Frank Griffiths [1966] Director/Chartered Accountant

Ripat Limited
Incorporated: 5 November 2009 *Employees:* 305
Net Worth: £33,067,000 *Total Assets:* £47,079,000
Registered Office: Archwood House, Kingsfield Court, Chester Business Park, Chester, CH4 9RE
Activities: Activities of head offices
Shareholder: Richard Henry Burbidge
Officers: Andrew Joseph Simms, Secretary; Joshua Burbidge [1978] Director; Richard Henry Burbidge [1942] Director

Ripe Thinking Limited
Incorporated: 22 June 2015 *Employees:* 52
Net Worth: £5,874,332 *Total Assets:* £8,884,882
Registered Office: The Royals, Altrincham Road, Manchester, M22 4BJ
Activities: Activities of other holding companies n.e.c.
Shareholders: Colin Whitehead; John Robert Woosey
Officers: Colin Whitehead, Secretary; Colin Whitehead [1959] Director; Paul Michael Williams [1968] Director; John Robert Woosey [1969] Director

Risebrook Properties Limited
Incorporated: 1 September 1986 *Employees:* 11
Net Worth: £5,401,537 *Total Assets:* £8,536,842
Registered Office: Freedman Frankl & Taylor, 31 King Street West, Manchester, M3 2PJ
Activities: Buying and selling of own real estate
Major Shareholder: Gary Hodgkinson
Officers: Gary Hodgkinson, Secretary; Ruth Slattery, Secretary; Gary Hodgkinson [1962] Director/Consultant

Risedale Estates Limited
Incorporated: 30 December 1985 *Employees:* 585
Net Worth: £5,252,060 *Total Assets:* £10,490,206
Registered Office: Risedale at Abbey Meadow, Duchy Court, Barrow in Furness, Cumbria, LA13 0BF
Activities: Residential nursing care facilities
Shareholders: Paul Albert Fraser; Charles Threlfall Dent
Officers: Barbara Anne Hetherington, Secretary; Charles Threlfall Dent [1961] Director; John George Edmond [1953] Director; Paul Albert Fraser [1951] Director; Barbara Anne Hetherington [1960] Director/Secretary

Risk Technology Limited
Incorporated: 28 May 2012
Net Worth: £1,698,385 *Total Assets:* £9,424,086
Registered Office: Matrix House, Merlin Court, Atlantic Street, Altrincham, Cheshire, WA14 5NL
Activities: Retail trade of motor vehicle parts and accessories
Shareholders: Wayne Thomas Shillito; Deborah Ann Shillito
Officers: Stephen Brian Eastwell [1966] Director; Mark Frederick Packman [1961] Director; Deborah Ann Shillito [1967] Director; Wayne Thomas Shillito [1967] Director

Risktec Solutions Limited
Incorporated: 1 December 2000 *Employees:* 252
Net Worth: £13,213,047 *Total Assets:* £21,131,344
Registered Office: Wilderspool Park, Greenalls Avenue, Warrington, Cheshire, WA4 6HL
Activities: Other professional, scientific and technical activities n.e.c.
Officers: Graham Peter Wallace, Secretary; Gareth John Book [1974] Director/Safety Consultant; Gordon Robert Dixon [1964] Director/Safety Consultant; Martin Gary Fairclough [1966] Director/Safety Consultant; Alan James Hoy [1960] Director/Consultant; Stephen John Lewis [1963] Director/Consultant; Dr John Manuel Llambias [1960] Director/Chartered Engineer; Graham Peter Wallace [1965] Director/Chartered Accountant

Risol Imports Limited
Incorporated: 7 July 1939 *Employees:* 1,040
Net Worth: £46,041,000 *Total Assets:* £99,565,000
Registered Office: Risol House, Mercury Way, Urmston, Manchester, M41 7RR
Activities: Activities of distribution holding companies
Major Shareholder: Keith Joseph Black
Officers: David Michael Wynn Holt, Secretary; Joanne Black [1965] Director; Keith Joseph Black [1959] Director; Tania Henrietta Black [1968] Director; David Michael Wynn Holt [1962] Operations Director; Nicholas John Young [1961] Director

Ritrama (U.K.) Limited
Incorporated: 27 February 1981 *Employees:* 67
Net Worth: £7,348,233 *Total Assets:* £19,378,542
Registered Office: Unit 2 Fifth Avenue, Dukinfield, Cheshire, SK16 4PP
Activities: Other manufacturing n.e.c.
Officers: Peter Burton, Secretary; Dr Martin David Attwood [1963] Technical Director; Peter Lawrence Burton [1966] Finance Director; Mark Leonard Evans [1969] Managing Director; Ricardo Rink [1968] Director [Italian]; Ronald Rink [1971] Director [Italian]; Tomas Fredrico Rink [1944] Director [Venezuelan]; Lee Peter Ward [1969] Sales Director

Rittner Investments Limited
Incorporated: 18 February 2016
Net Worth: £381,872 *Total Assets:* £13,228,279
Registered Office: Seymour Chambers, 92 London Road, Liverpool, L3 5NW
Activities: Other business support service activities n.e.c.
Shareholders: Alan James Beer; David Charles Brewitt
Officers: Alan James Beer [1966] Director; David Charles Brewitt [1963] Director

River Park Trading Estate Limited
Incorporated: 6 April 2000 *Employees:* 4
Net Worth: £4,999,635 *Total Assets:* £8,825,997
Registered Office: 25 Rochdale Road, Manchester, M4 4HT
Activities: Other letting and operating of own or leased real estate
Parent: Realty Estates Limited
Officers: Jaleh Tishbi, Secretary; Yousef Tishbi [1948] Director

Riverside Finance PLC
Incorporated: 18 September 2014
Net Worth: £50,000 *Total Assets:* £149,016,000
Registered Office: 2 Estuary Boulevard, Estuary Commerce Park, Liverpool, L24 8RF
Activities: Other credit granting n.e.c.
Parent: The Riverside Group Limited
Officers: Thomas Richard John Ferguson, Secretary; Devan Bala [1982] Director/Group Treasurer [Australian]; Susan Jee [1955] Director/Chartered Accountant; Nigel Robin Perryman [1958] Director/Accountant

Riverside Flooring Limited
Incorporated: 3 September 2010 *Employees:* 72
Net Worth: £5,051,353 *Total Assets:* £16,177,162
Registered Office: Beechfield, Hollinhurst Road, Radcliffe, Manchester, M26 1JN
Activities: Floor and wall covering
Parent: James Halstead PLC
Officers: David William Drillingcourt, Secretary; Mark Halstead [1957] Director; Gordon Richard Oliver [1958] Director; Mark Raine [1974] Production Director; Alan Turner [1957] Director

Riverside Park Limited
Incorporated: 21 January 2002
Net Worth Deficit: £753,840 *Total Assets:* £8,568,745
Registered Office: Bank House, Market Square, Congleton, Cheshire, CW12 1ET
Activities: Development of building projects
Major Shareholder: John David Henley
Officers: John David Henley, Secretary/Director; John David Henley [1962] Director; Carl Alexander Lewis [1951] Director

Riverside Truck Rental Limited
Incorporated: 25 April 1996 *Employees:* 264
Net Worth: £10,919,331 *Total Assets:* £89,606,728
Registered Office: Oasis Business Park, Parkside Place, Skelmersdale, Lancs, WN8 9RD
Activities: Renting and leasing of trucks and other heavy vehicles
Parent: NRG Fleet Services Limited
Officers: Martin Roy Ashcroft [1965] Director/Chief Financial Officer; Stephen Michael Richardson [1960] Managing Director; Muhammad Sadique [1963] Director; Christopher Snelson [1975] Operations Director

Riverstone Properties Ltd
Incorporated: 14 July 2010 *Employees:* 1
Net Worth: £5,458,216 *Total Assets:* £18,552,748
Registered Office: 2-4 Wigan Road, Hindley, Wigan, Lancs, WN2 3BE
Activities: Other letting and operating of own or leased real estate
Parent: Heaton 2014 Limited
Officers: John Heaton [1973] Director

Rix Motor Company Limited
Incorporated: 31 July 1984 *Employees:* 51
Net Worth: £2,178,475 *Total Assets:* £11,226,003
Registered Office: Rix Motor Co Ltd, Hawleys Lane, Warrington, Cheshire, WA2 8JP
Activities: Sale of used cars and light motor vehicles
Major Shareholder: Reginald Rix
Officers: Jane Rix, Secretary; Charles Jessie James Rix [1989] Director; Henry Trevor Rix [1990] Director; Jane Rix [1954] Director; Reginald Rix [1959] Director

RM Property and Facilities Solutions Limited
Incorporated: 15 June 2001 *Employees:* 2,884
Net Worth: £16,585,000 *Total Assets:* £48,689,000
Registered Office: Highbank House, Exchange Street, Stockport, Cheshire, SK3 0ET
Activities: Other engineering activities
Parent: Royal Mail Group Limited
Officers: Kulbinder Kaur Dosanjh, Secretary; Dr Shaun Paul Davis [1974] Director; Martin David Gafsen [1961] Director; Jayesh Patel [1974] Director

RMI Pressure Systems Limited
Incorporated: 16 February 2006 *Employees:* 44
Net Worth Deficit: £977,055 *Total Assets:* £14,071,831
Registered Office: 1 Wolverton Street, Manchester, M11 2ET
Activities: Manufacture of pumps
Major Shareholder: Charles Allan Armstrong
Officers: James Cary Armstrong, Secretary; Charles Allan Armstrong [1950] Director/Business Executive [Canadian]; James Cary Armstrong [1946] Director/Business Executive [Canadian]

RMS International Limited
Incorporated: 6 April 1994 *Employees:* 147
Net Worth: £8,153,000 *Total Assets:* £26,680,000
Registered Office: Grafix House, 6 Boundary Road, Pendlebury, Swinton, Manchester, M27 4EQ
Activities: Activities of head offices
Shareholder: Tyrone Stuart Farber
Officers: Yonni Leslie Spiero Abramson [1984] Director; Tyrone Stuart Farber [1957] Director; James Paul Flude [1974] Director/Chief Financial Officer; Stuart Rose [1949] Director/Chairman; Matthew Widdall [1972] Director

RMS International UK Ltd
Incorporated: 26 February 1974 *Employees:* 77
Net Worth: £5,803,800 *Total Assets:* £15,154,831
Registered Office: Grafix House, 6 Boundary Road, Pendlebury, Swinton, Manchester, M27 4EQ
Activities: Wholesale of other intermediate products
Shareholders: RMS International Limited; RMS International Holdings Limited
Officers: Jackie Farber, Secretary; Tyrone Stuart Farber [1957] Director; James Paul Flude [1974] Director/Chief Financial Officer; Michael Taylor [1974] Director

RMSpumptools Limited
Incorporated: 12 August 1983 *Employees:* 76
Net Worth: £2,029,007 *Total Assets:* £16,978,528
Registered Office: P O Box 4, Fisher House, Barrow in Furness, Cumbria, LA14 1HR
Activities: Manufacture of other electrical equipment
Parent: James Fisher Holdings UK Limited
Officers: James Henry John Marsh, Secretary; Stanley James Foster Rooke [1954] Director; Douglas Marion Harwell [1975] Director/Engineer [American]; Nicholas Paul Henry [1961] Director; Stuart Charles Kilpatrick [1962] Director; Martin Graham Marsh [1977] Director

Road Maintenance Services (Holdings) Limited
Incorporated: 26 June 1947 *Employees:* 149
Net Worth: £13,518,307 *Total Assets:* £23,078,252
Registered Office: Road Maintenance Services (Holdings) Ltd, Mowpen Brow High Legh, Knutsford, Cheshire, WA16 6PB
Activities: Activities of construction holding companies
Officers: Stephen John Barlow, Secretary; Gregory William Barlow [1953] Director/Engineer; Stephen John Barlow [1956] Director/Company Secretary; Jonathan Harry Chorlton [1956] Director/Personnel & Training Manager; Andrew Peter Holland [1962] Director/Manager

Road Maintenance Services Limited
Incorporated: 29 October 1987 *Employees:* 145
Net Worth: £9,138,625 *Total Assets:* £16,378,064
Registered Office: Road Maintenance Services Ltd, Mowpen Brow, High Legh, Knutsford, Cheshire, WA16 6PB
Activities: Construction of roads and motorways
Parent: Road Maintenance Services (Holdings) Ltd
Officers: Stephen John Barlow, Secretary; Gregory William Barlow [1953] Engineer - Director; Stephen John Barlow [1956] Director; Jonathan Harry Chorlton [1956] Director/Personnel & Training Manager; Andrew Peter Holland [1962] Director/Manager

Roanza Limited
Incorporated: 28 January 2014 *Employees:* 446
Net Worth: £7,825,442 *Total Assets:* £101,184,096
Registered Office: The Enza Building, Leacroft Road, Birchwood, Warrington, Cheshire, WA3 6NN
Activities: Activities of head offices
Shareholder: Roy Charles Reed
Officers: Michael Peter Jones, Secretary; Michael Peter Jones [1963] Director/Accountant; Roy Charles Reed [1958] Managing Director

David Roberts & Partners (Insurance Brokers) Limited
Incorporated: 9 September 1977 *Employees:* 50
Net Worth: £6,429,043 *Total Assets:* £9,254,618
Registered Office: Chancery House, Slaidburn Crescent, Southport, Merseyside, PR9 9YF
Activities: Non-life insurance
Parent: DR&P Holdings Ltd
Officers: John David Page, Secretary/Managing Director; David Brian Chorley [1953] Director; John David Page [1966] Director

Frank Roberts & Sons Limited
Incorporated: 8 September 1920 *Employees:* 920
Net Worth: £26,283,000 *Total Assets:* £65,162,000
Registered Office: Rudheath, Northwich, Cheshire, CW9 7RQ
Activities: Manufacture of bread; manufacture of fresh pastry goods and cakes
Officers: Byron Lloyd Cooper, Secretary; Byron Lloyd Cooper [1974] Finance Director; Robert Charles Higginson [1961] Director; Margaret Lindsay Occleston [1961] Director; Julia Clare Roberts [1955] Director; Michael Frank Roberts [1954] Director; Paul William Roberts [1956] Director; Amelia Anne Wright [1962] Director

George Roberts (North West) Limited
Incorporated: 2 July 1992 *Employees:* 62
Net Worth: £11,432,798 *Total Assets:* £23,643,656
Registered Office: Unit D, Wakefield Road, Netherton, Liverpool, L30 6TZ
Activities: Agents involved in the sale of timber and building materials
Shareholders: George William Roberts; David Thomas Cawley; Robert Charles Tyler
Officers: Mark Roach, Secretary; David Thomas Cawley [1954] Director; Philip Gorton [1953] Sales Director; Mark Roach [1963] Director/Management Accountant; George William Roberts [1952] Director/Scaffolding Salesman; Andrew Roscoe [1968] Director/Operations Manager; Robert Charles Tyler [1945] Director

John Roberts Holdings Limited
Incorporated: 16 July 1996 *Employees:* 60
Net Worth: £6,552,770 *Total Assets:* £11,313,177
Registered Office: Christies High Mill, Settle, N Yorks, BD24 9LX
Activities: Manufacture of paper and paperboard
Shareholder: Paul Adrian Nelson
Officers: Jeremy William Smith, Secretary; Claire Louise Beresford [1976] Sales Director; Scott John Littlewood [1979] Operations Director; Paul Adrian Nelson [1959] Managing Director; Timothy Denzil Pryce [1966] Director; Jeremy William Smith [1961] Finance Director

John Roberts Ventures Limited
Incorporated: 10 August 2012 *Employees:* 60
Net Worth: £1,744,406 *Total Assets:* £7,103,004
Registered Office: Christies High Mill, Settle, N Yorks, BD24 9LX
Activities: Manufacture of corrugated paper and paperboard, sacks and bags
Officers: Jeremy William Smith, Secretary; Paul Adrian Nelson [1959] Sales Director; Timothy Denzil Pryce [1966] Director; Jeremy William Smith [1961] Finance Director

Robinrate Limited
Incorporated: 6 December 1993 *Employees:* 52
Net Worth: £12,543,196 *Total Assets:* £16,876,960
Registered Office: Unit 3 Stainburn Road, Openshaw, Manchester, M11 2DN
Activities: Activities of head offices
Major Shareholder: Robin MacEwan Gray
Officers: Peter Douglas Sumner, Secretary/Financial Controller; Robin MacEwan Gray [1951] Director; Ebrahim Kassam Mukadam [1957] Director

G E Robinson & Co Ltd
Incorporated: 20 June 1994 *Employees:* 155
Net Worth: £6,138,719 *Total Assets:* £11,050,667
Registered Office: Thurlow Sawmills, Montford Street, Salford, M50 2XD
Activities: Sawmilling and planing of wood
Parent: Haldane Shiells & Company Ltd
Officers: Andrew Spencer Gerrard, Secretary; Gareth Pinder Foster [1968] Sales Director; Andrew Spencer Gerrard [1964] Director; David Owen Haldane [1971] Director; Ian McGregor Haldane [1963] Director; Paul Thomas Kavanagh [1954] Director; Carol Ann Murphy [1961] Director; Duncan Mark Rossall [1960] Director; Craig Anthony Sidlow [1971] Director; Simon Walling [1978] Merchanting Director

James Robinson Fibres Limited
Incorporated: 31 July 1944 *Employees:* 43
Net Worth: £13,958,351 *Total Assets:* £18,164,164
Registered Office: Millersdale Close, Euroway Industrial Estate, Bradford, BD4 6SG
Activities: Preparation and spinning of textile fibres
Major Shareholder: Christopher John Frederick Taylor
Officers: Nicholas James Batty [1969] Finance Director; Mark Andrew Longley [1961] Director/Sales Executive; Adrian William Tate [1964] Director/Operations; Christopher John Fredrick Taylor [1948] Director/Textile Fibre Manufacturer; Eileen Mary Taylor [1949] Director/Housewife; James Maxwell Taylor [1973] Director/Textile Fibre Manufacturer; Andrew David Thornton [1967] Director/Export Manager

T.N.Robinson Limited
Incorporated: 30 June 1939 *Employees:* 97
Net Worth: £2,939,789 *Total Assets:* £7,311,707
Registered Office: 94-98 Daw Bank, Stockport, Cheshire, SK3 0EH
Activities: Wholesale of electronic and telecommunications equipment and parts
Major Shareholder: Michael Robinson Drake
Officers: Ian William Gregory, Secretary; Margaret Christine Anderson [1950] Director/School Teacher; Anthony Paul Drake [1957] Director/Manager; Christopher John Drake [1975] Purchasing Director; Janet Elizabeth Drake [1959] Director; Michael Robinson Drake [1948] Managing Director; Ian William Gregory [1965] Finance Director; Simon Mark Stanley Thwaite [1965] Director/Manager; Patricia Mary Yates [1947] Director

Frederic Robinson Limited
Incorporated: 7 October 1920 *Employees:* 487
Net Worth: £77,876,000 *Total Assets:* £96,593,000
Registered Office: Unicorn Brewery, Lower Hillgate, Stockport, Cheshire, SK1 1JJ
Activities: Manufacture of beer
Shareholders: Dennis William Robinson; Peter Bryan Robinson; David John Robinson
Officers: Sara Xanthe Robinson, Secretary; John Edwards [1957] Director; David John Robinson [1937] Director; Dennis William Robinson [1933] Director; Oliver John Robinson [1971] Director; Paul Andrew Robinson [1969] Director; Peter Bryan Robinson [1931] Director; Veronica Helen Robinson [1969] Director; William Joseph Robinson [1971] Director; Neil Robinson-Stanier [1966] Director

David M. Robinson Limited
Incorporated: 24 July 1969 *Employees:* 86
Net Worth: £8,406,933 *Total Assets:* £15,351,624
Registered Office: 14 Railway Street, Altrincham, Cheshire, WA14 2RE
Activities: Retail sale of watches and jewellery in specialised stores
Major Shareholder: David Michael Robinson
Officers: Joanna Kate Irwin, Secretary; David Michael Robinson [1943] Director; John Michael Robinson [1968] Director

Robinson Way Limited
Incorporated: 29 July 2009 *Employees:* 369
Net Worth: £4,078,751 *Total Assets:* £23,053,208
Registered Office: Quays Reach, Carolina Way, Salford, M50 2ZY
Activities: Financial intermediation not elsewhere classified
Shareholders: Hoist Finance UK Limited; Hoist Finance AB
Officers: Jan Christer Johansson [1979] Director [Swedish]; Ian McConnell [1968] Director/Accountant; Julian Michael Winfield [1970] Director/Chief Financial Officer

John Robson (Metals) Limited
Incorporated: 5 December 1973 *Employees:* 64
Net Worth: £6,251,058 *Total Assets:* £8,463,992
Registered Office: Stump Cross Farm, Goosnargh, Preston, Lancs, PR3 2FE
Activities: Wholesale of waste and scrap
Major Shareholder: Elizabeth Slater
Officers: Elizabeth Slater, Secretary; Mark Eastham [1977] Director; Elizabeth Slater [1970] Director

Rochdale Textile Supplies Limited
Incorporated: 24 October 2001 *Employees:* 257
Net Worth: £44,748,000 *Total Assets:* £103,841,000
Registered Office: Adlington Works, Market Street, Adlington, Chorley, Lancs, PR7 4HJ
Activities: Activities of head offices
Parent: Rochdale Textiles (Jersey) Ltd
Officers: Nigel Andrew Bate, Secretary; Nigel Andrew Bate [1971] Director/Certified Chartered Accountant; Neil Jonathan Davey [1971] Sales Director; John Joseph Vareldzis [1972] Managing Director

Rochpion Properties (4) LLP
Incorporated: 20 June 2008
Net Worth: £84,686,000 *Total Assets:* £350,926,016
Registered Office: 1 Angel Square, Manchester, M60 0AG

Rock Chemicals Limited
Incorporated: 26 January 1965 *Employees:* 80
Net Worth: £4,641,674 *Total Assets:* £13,332,326
Registered Office: 90 Priestley Street, Warrington, Cheshire, WA5 1ST
Activities: Other manufacturing n.e.c.
Officers: Barbara Hewitt, Secretary; Barbara Hewitt [1933] Director/Secretary; Charles Edward Hewitt [1953] Director/Chairman; Gregory Edward Hewitt [1979] Managing Director; Martyn Alan Waterhouse [1984] Director

Rock House Investments Limited
Incorporated: 5 July 1976 *Employees:* 2
Net Worth: £2,456,010 *Total Assets:* £8,946,981
Registered Office: Estate Office, Dunscar Business Park, Blackburn Road, Bolton, Lancs, BL7 9PQ
Activities: Other letting and operating of own or leased real estate
Officers: Nigel Harry Moon [1963] Director

Rockfield Properties Limited
Incorporated: 5 March 1991 *Employees:* 1
Net Worth: £4,856,150 *Total Assets:* £9,542,184
Registered Office: Rockfield, Cuckoo Lane, Liverpool, L25 3PL
Activities: Development of building projects
Shareholders: James Paul Parry; Angela Mary Parry
Officers: Angela Mary Parry, Secretary; Angela Mary Parry [1944] Director; James Paul Parry [1945] Director

Rodo Limited
Incorporated: 13 July 1984 *Employees:* 118
Net Worth: £18,719,722 *Total Assets:* £24,672,384
Registered Office: Lumb Lane, Droylsden, Manchester, M43 7BU
Activities: Wholesale of other intermediate products
Shareholders: Peter William Brierley; Jack Brierley
Officers: Peter William Brierley, Secretary; Jack Brierley [1946] Sales Director; Peter William Brierley [1953] Managing Director; Darryl Andrew Williamson [1953] Director/Chartered Accountant

Rodol Limited
Incorporated: 24 December 1937 *Employees:* 29
Net Worth: £9,661,241 *Total Assets:* £10,066,646
Registered Office: Richmond Row, Liverpool, L3 3BP
Activities: Manufacture of other inorganic basic chemicals
Shareholder: Roland Keith Brough Robinson
Officers: Deborah Jane Robinson, Secretary; Deborah Jane Robinson [1966] Director/Financial Controller; Gregory Brough Robinson [1970] Director/Technical Executive; Roland Keith Brough Robinson [1942] Director/Chemist

JD Roebuck Holdings Limited
Incorporated: 21 November 2012 *Employees:* 266
Net Worth: £13,019,545 *Total Assets:* £24,838,640
Registered Office: Platinum Park, Lynstock Way, Horwich, Bolton, Lancs, BL6 4SA
Activities: Non-trading company
Major Shareholder: Julian David Roebuck
Officers: Julian David Roebuck [1974] Director

Roil Foods Limited
Incorporated: 27 May 1993 *Employees:* 48
Net Worth: £4,473,311 *Total Assets:* £14,452,525
Registered Office: Rough Hill, Marlston-Cum-Lache, Chester, CH4 9JS
Activities: Manufacture of oils and fats
Parent: Roilvest Limited
Officers: Damian McDonald, Secretary; Mark Henry Chantler [1986] Director; Simon Chantler [1959] Director; Damian McDonald [1962] Director

ROKPA Trust
Incorporated: 7 October 1996 *Employees:* 11
Net Worth: £24,393,132 *Total Assets:* £25,451,436
Registered Office: Fifteen Rosehill, Montgomery Way, Rosehill Estate, Carlisle, CA1 2RW
Activities: Other human health activities
Officers: Kenneth MacKenzie, Secretary; Karma Lhamo Cosgrove [1970] Director/Chartered Company Secretary; Tsultim Palbar Lama [1977] Director/Buddhist Monk; Ani Lhamo [1956] Director/Personal Assistant; Lama Yeshe Losal [1950] Director/Teacher; John Frederick Michael Maxwell [1943] Director/Retired; Lama Zangmo [1952] Director/Teacher [Danish]

Romaco SPV 2 Limited
Incorporated: 13 May 2016 *Employees:* 1
Net Worth: £227,617 *Total Assets:* £11,556,051
Registered Office: 15 Carnarvon Street, Manchester, M3 1HJ
Activities: Financial intermediation not elsewhere classified
Parent: Romaco Limited
Officers: Wendy Littman, Secretary; Philip Isaac Hodari [1961] Director; Scott James Marshall [1974] Managing Director; Keith John Richardson [1959] Finance Director

Rongxin Power Limited
Incorporated: 23 November 2015
Net Worth: £4,339,980 *Total Assets:* £6,726,252
Registered Office: Suite 4, Mansion House, Manchester Road, Altrincham, Cheshire, WA14 4RW
Activities: Construction of utility projects for electricity and telecommunications
Officers: Graeme Noel Bathurst [1973] Director [New Zealander]; Haitao Zhang [1979] Director [Chinese]

J. Rose (Tyres) Limited
Incorporated: 17 March 1952 *Employees:* 86
Net Worth: £15,475,097 *Total Assets:* £29,187,814
Registered Office: 3rd Floor, 5 Temple Square, Temple Street, Liverpool, L2 5RH
Activities: Wholesale trade of motor vehicle parts and accessories
Major Shareholder: Gordon Anthony Rosenthal
Officers: Robin Walls, Secretary; Gordon Anthony Rosenthal [1951] Director/Chairman

The Rosebery Group Holdings Limited
Incorporated: 18 February 2015 *Employees:* 122
Net Worth: £913,808 *Total Assets:* £7,922,987
Registered Office: Hastings House, 79-83 Station Road, Ellesmere Port, Cheshire, CH65 4BN
Activities: Activities of construction holding companies
Parent: The Rosebery Trustee Company Limited
Officers: Peter Geoffrey Arnold [1969] Director; Stuart James Lockwood [1979] Director; Thomas James Topping [1946] Director; Colin Charles Woodward [1950] Director

The Rosebery Group Limited
Incorporated: 8 June 1987 *Employees:* 126
Net Worth: £6,718,191 *Total Assets:* £8,457,487
Registered Office: Hastings House, 79-83 Station Road, Ellesmere Port, Cheshire, CH65 4BN
Activities: Electrical installation
Parent: The Rosebery Group Holdings Limited
Officers: Thomas James Topping [1946] Director; Colin Charles Woodward [1950] Director

J. Rosenthal and Son Limited
Incorporated: 21 August 1989 *Employees:* 166
Net Worth: £4,206,989 *Total Assets:* £15,286,267
Registered Office: P O Box 54, 158 Bury Road, Radcliffe, Manchester, M26 2JR
Activities: Wholesale of textiles
Officers: Gillian Denise Crolla, Secretary; Gillian Denise Crolla [1959] Director/H R Manager; Jacqueline Anne McLoughlin [1962] Design Director; John Steven Potter [1973] Director; Harry Ralph Rosenthal [1944] Managing Director

J Rosenthal Holdings Limited
Incorporated: 11 September 2007 *Employees:* 166
Net Worth Deficit: £481,023 *Total Assets:* £14,010,957
Registered Office: Britannia House, 158 Bury Road, Radcliffe, Manchester, M26 2JR
Activities: Wholesale of textiles
Shareholders: Andrew Peter Rigby; Harry Ralph Rosenthal
Officers: Andrew Peter Rigby, Secretary/Accountant; Andrew Peter Rigby [1957] Director/Accountant; Jennifer Ann Rigby [1957] Director/Accountant

Ross Care Holdings Limited
Incorporated: 20 July 1995 *Employees:* 198
Net Worth: £5,211,718 *Total Assets:* £8,989,215
Registered Office: Hoghton Chambers, Hoghton Street, Southport, Merseyside, PR9 0TB
Activities: Activities of head offices
Shareholders: John Michael Norton Turner; Peter Antony Smith
Officers: Peter Antony Smith, Secretary; Peter Antony Smith [1963] Finance Director; John Michael Norton Turner [1942] Managing Director

Rotapoint Limited
Incorporated: 19 October 1989 *Employees:* 2
Net Worth: £1,067,453 *Total Assets:* £6,989,112
Registered Office: St George's House, 215-219 Chester Road, Manchester, M15 4JE
Activities: Development of building projects
Major Shareholder: Anthony Leslie Wood-Robinson
Officers: Anthony Leslie Wood Robinson [1949] Director/Property Consultant

Rotary Building Services Ltd
Incorporated: 19 September 1979 *Employees:* 155
Net Worth Deficit: £745,000 *Total Assets:* £28,992,000
Registered Office: Phoenix House, Lakeside Drive, Centre Park, Warrington, Cheshire, WA1 1RX
Activities: Electrical installation
Parent: LSRM Holdings Ltd
Officers: Inbaraj Rajakumar, Secretary; Tarek Fuad Abuzayyad [1969] Director; Gary Heitmann [1970] Group Business Development Director; Paul James Hughes [1956] Group Commercial and Legal Director; Jacob Kurian [1958] Director/Group Financial Controller [Australian]; Puliyelethu Mathai Mathew [1952] Director/Group Vice Chairman [Indian]; Ramesh Krishna Murthy [1962] Director/Group Chief Financial Officer [Indian]; Simon Roopchand [1972] Director/Group Chief Executive Officer; Gary Worrall [1959] Director/CEO - Contracting

Rotex Europe Ltd
Incorporated: 19 October 2001 *Employees:* 68
Net Worth: £4,982,615 *Total Assets:* £10,640,574
Registered Office: Aston Lane North, Whitehouse Vale, Runcorn, Cheshire, WA7 3FA
Activities: Manufacture of other special-purpose machinery n.e.c.
Officers: Kristina a Cerniglia [1966] Director/Senior Vice President and Chief Financial Officer [American]; Robert William Dieckman Jr [1964] Director/Group CFO [American]

Rothay Garden Hotel Limited
Incorporated: 27 October 1989 *Employees:* 25
Net Worth: £3,120,804 *Total Assets:* £7,017,113
Registered Office: Rothay Garden Hotel, Broadgate, Grasmere, Cumbria, LA22 9RJ
Activities: Hotels and similar accommodation
Major Shareholder: Christopher Morton Carss
Officers: Christopher Morton Carss [1957] Director/Hotelier; Jillian Wilson [1967] Director/Hotel Front of House Manager

Roundel Limited
Incorporated: 23 December 2013 *Employees:* 126
Net Worth Deficit: £243,198 *Total Assets:* £21,908,034
Registered Office: Hoghton Chambers, Hoghton Street, Southport, Merseyside, PR9 0TB
Activities: Activities of head offices
Major Shareholder: Phillip Jones
Officers: Margaret Louise Clough, Secretary; James Mark Charles Houghton [1960] Sales Director; Glyn Anthony Howes [1962] Director; Phillip Jones [1950] Director

The Rowan Learning Trust
Incorporated: 28 March 2012 *Employees:* 364
Net Worth: £10,430,000 *Total Assets:* £19,043,000
Registered Office: Hawkley Hall High School, Carr Lane, Hawkley Hall, Wigan, Lancs, WN3 5NY
Activities: Primary education
Officers: Elizabeth Roberts, Secretary; Anthony Robert Ball [1973] Director/Chartered Accountant; Melanie Jayne Chadwick [1962] Director/Vice Principal: Winstanley College; Alison Foster [1962] Director/Housewife; Royston William Halford [1959] Director/CEO/Executive Headteacher; Anne Isherwood [1969] Director/Headteacher; David Joseph Leonard [1964] Director/Manager; George Andrew Wilson [1957] Director/Contracts Co-ordinator; Margaret Mary Philomena Woodhouse [1952] Director

Rowcon Limited
Incorporated: 24 July 2014 *Employees:* 63
Net Worth: £60,511 *Total Assets:* £6,877,319
Registered Office: London House, London Road South, Poynton, Stockport, Cheshire, SK12 1YP
Activities: Activities of head offices
Officers: David Simon Chilton [1969] Director; Nigel Keith Rawlings [1956] Director; David Jonathan Roberts [1957] Director; Adrian Charles Simpson [1959] Finance Director; Stephen Joseph Weir [1972] Director

L.Rowland & Company (Retail) Limited
Incorporated: 23 August 1988 *Employees:* 4,770
Net Worth: £63,370,000 *Total Assets:* £514,232,000
Registered Office: L Rowland & Co (Retail) Limited, Rivington Road, Whitehouse Industrial Estate, Runcorn, Cheshire, WA7 3DJ
Activities: Dispensing chemist in specialised stores
Parent: L Rowland & Co Limited
Officers: Michael Peter Blakeman, Secretary; Stephen William Anderson [1966] Director; Kenneth John Black [1965] Director/Pharmacist; Ian Campbell Cowan [1943] Director/Pharmacist; Kevin Robert Hudson [1963] Director; Margaret Elizabeth MacRury [1960] Director/Superintendent Pharmacist

Rowland Group Limited
Incorporated: 12 July 2006 *Employees:* 56
Net Worth: £34,097,284 *Total Assets:* £58,815,852
Registered Office: Farington House, Stanifield Business Park, Stanifield Lane, Leyland, Lancs, PR25 4UA
Activities: Construction of domestic buildings
Major Shareholder: Paul Keith Rowley
Officers: Christopher James Sams, Secretary; Paul Rowley [1966] Director/Developer; Christopher James Sams [1970] Director/Accountant

Rowland Homes Limited
Incorporated: 17 February 1993 *Employees:* 56
Net Worth: £34,097,284 *Total Assets:* £58,815,852
Registered Office: Farington House, Stanifield Business Park, Stanifield Lane, Leyland, Lancs, PR25 4UA
Activities: Construction of domestic buildings
Shareholders: Paul Keith Rowley; Rowland Group Ltd
Officers: Christopher James Sams, Finance Director; Stephen John Grant [1967] Sales & Marketing Director; Clive Mellings [1963] Technical Director; Jonathan Pickthall [1980] Land Director; Paul Rowley [1966] Director/Developer; Christopher James Sams [1970] Finance Director

Rowleys of Northwich Limited
Incorporated: 29 September 1981 *Employees:* 40
Net Worth: £6,050,014 *Total Assets:* £12,484,363
Registered Office: Wincham Lane, Wincham, Northwich, Cheshire, CW9 6DE
Activities: Renting and leasing of trucks and other heavy vehicles
Shareholders: Paul Anthony Rowley; Paul Anthony Rowley
Officers: Richard Rowley, Secretary; Paul Anthony Rowley [1954] Director; Richard Rowley [1972] Director

Rowlinson Consolidated Ltd
Incorporated: 28 March 2015 *Employees:* 274
Net Worth: £16,731,827 *Total Assets:* £41,364,696
Registered Office: Group Offices, Green Lane, Wardle, Nantwich, Cheshire, CW5 6BN
Activities: Activities of head offices
Major Shareholder: Richard James Rowlinson
Officers: Alistair Richard Norris Sharman, Secretary; Lynda Jean Rowlinson [1955] Director; Richard James Rowlinson [1954] Director

Rowlinson Constructions Limited
Incorporated: 31 March 1991 *Employees:* 59
Net Worth: £8,410,039 *Total Assets:* £14,042,626
Registered Office: London House, London Road South, Poynton, Stockport, Cheshire, SK12 1YP
Activities: Development of building projects
Officers: Adrian Charles Simpson, Secretary; David Simon Chilton [1969] Director; David Jonathan Roberts [1957] Director; Adrian Charles Simpson [1959] Director; Stephen Joseph Weir [1972] Director

Rowlinson Garden Products Limited
Incorporated: 6 August 1946 *Employees:* 71
Net Worth: £2,553,308 *Total Assets:* £10,013,620
Registered Office: Group Offices, Green Lane, Wardle, Nantwich, Cheshire, CW5 6BN
Activities: Sawmilling and planing of wood
Parent: Rowlinson Timber Limited
Officers: Alistair Richard Norris Sharman, Secretary; Charles David Firth [1966] Managing Director; Michael John Lightfoot [1973] Sales Director; Richard James Rowlinson [1954] Director; Peter Charles Woolley [1970] Commercial Director

Rowlinson Group Holdings Limited
Incorporated: 21 February 2008
Net Worth: £18,407,760 *Total Assets:* £18,407,760
Registered Office: Group Offices, Green Lane, Wardle, Nantwich, Cheshire, CW5 6BN
Activities: Activities of head offices
Parent: Rowlinson Consolidated Ltd
Officers: Alistair Richard Norris Sharman, Secretary; Richard James Rowlinson [1954] Director

Rowlinson Group Limited
Incorporated: 31 January 1961 *Employees:* 22
Net Worth: £2,788,627 *Total Assets:* £7,744,195
Registered Office: Group Offices, Green Lane, Wardle, Nantwich, Cheshire, CW5 6BN
Activities: Other letting and operating of own or leased real estate
Parent: Rowlinson Group Holdings Limited
Officers: Alistair Richard Norris Sharman, Secretary; John McCormack Brodie [1952] Director; Richard James Rowlinson [1954] Director; Alistair Richard Norris Sharman [1961] Finance Director; John Derek Williams [1952] Director

Rowlinson Investments Limited
Incorporated: 8 June 2000 *Employees:* 2
Net Worth: £3,591,754 *Total Assets:* £9,673,530
Registered Office: London House, London Road South, Poynton, Stockport, Cheshire, SK12 1YP
Activities: Other letting and operating of own or leased real estate
Major Shareholder: David Jonathan Roberts
Officers: Adrian Charles Simpson, Secretary; David Jonathan Roberts [1957] Director

Rowlinson Knitwear Limited
Incorporated: 20 September 1972 *Employees:* 42
Net Worth: £5,553,786 *Total Assets:* £8,976,103
Registered Office: Unit 1a Discovery Park, Crossley Road, Stockport, Cheshire, SK4 5DZ
Activities: Manufacture of other knitted and crocheted apparel
Shareholders: Rowlinson Knitwear Employee Ownership Trustees Ltd; Moira Sylvia Rowlinson
Officers: Daniel Sheng-Niann Chan [1973] Director; Kenneth Edgar [1967] Technical Director; Andrew McConnell [1961] Sales Director; Donald Campbell Moore [1958] Managing Director; Christopher Sean Rowlinson [1978] Director; Moira Sylvia Rowlinson [1944] Director; Ian Paul Smith [1970] Planning Director; Neil Ward [1981] Commercial Director

Rowlinson Packaging Limited
Incorporated: 4 July 1974 *Employees:* 135
Net Worth: £6,109,289 *Total Assets:* £10,767,869
Registered Office: Rowlinson Packaging Limited, Green Lane, Wardle, Nantwich, Cheshire, CW5 6BN
Activities: Manufacture of wooden containers
Parent: Rowlinson Group Limited
Officers: Alistair Richard Norris Sharman, Secretary; Matthew James Brown [1966] Sales Director; John Carter [1957] Director; Andrew Clive King [1965] Managing Director; Richard James Rowlinson [1954] Director

Rowlinson Timber Limited
Incorporated: 6 August 1946 *Employees:* 16
Net Worth: £4,949,843 *Total Assets:* £12,463,684
Registered Office: Group Offices, Green Lane, Wardle, Nantwich, Cheshire, CW5 6BN
Activities: Wholesale of wood, construction materials and sanitary equipment
Parent: Rowlinson Group Limited
Officers: Alistair Richard Norris Sharman, Secretary; Darren James Hill [1973] Sales Director; Richard James Rowlinson [1954] Director; Richard Smith [1966] Managing Director

Royal Exchange Theatre Company Limited
Incorporated: 12 February 1968 *Employees:* 130
Net Worth: £10,021,000 *Total Assets:* £11,558,000
Registered Office: St Ann's Square, Manchester, M2 7DH
Activities: Performing arts
Officers: Barry Christopher James, Secretary; Tania Black [1968] Director/Housewife; James Benedict Caldwell [1964] Director; Anthony Noel Gordon [1964] Director/Consultant; Sinead Greenaway [1971] Director; Councillor Ann-Marie Humphreys [1965] Director/Elected Member/Councillor and Assistant Mayor; Nicole May [1991] Director/Producer; Jean Davies Oglesby [1939] Director/Housewife; Sally Penni [1977] Director/Barrister; Jennifer Maria Raffle [1964] Director/Chartered Accountant; Aziz Din Rashid [1966] Director/Head of Programmes - BBC; Caroline Roberts Cherry [1965] Director/TV Executive Producer; David Roscoe [1959] Director/Head of Planning; Davina Shah [1980] Director/Theatrical Agent; Councillor Bernard Sharp [1936] Director/Councillor; Geoffrey Arnold Shindler [1942] Director/Solicitor; Martyn Philip Torevell [1967] Director/Independent Financial Adviser

Royal Greenland Limited
Incorporated: 28 October 1986 *Employees:* 10
Net Worth: £4,708,477 *Total Assets:* £7,531,517
Registered Office: Gateway House, Styal Road, Manchester, M22 5WY
Activities: Wholesale of other food, including fish, crustaceans and molluscs
Officers: Michael Derek Horne, Secretary; Randall John Jennings [1968] Managing Director; Bruno Olesen [1957] Sales & Marketing Director [Danish]; Mikael Thinguus [1962] Director [Danish]

Royal Liverpool Philharmonic Society (The)
Incorporated: 31 March 1906 *Employees:* 223
Net Worth: £8,230,000 *Total Assets:* £16,906,000
Registered Office: Philharmonic Hall, Hope Street, Liverpool, L1 9BP
Activities: Performing arts
Officers: Dr Tony Harvey, Secretary; Jon Anthony Corner [1959] Director; Michael Eakin [1954] Director; Melvyn Grodner [1944] Director/Retired; Alexander James Nicolas Holladay [1981] Director/Musician; Susanna Jordan [1974] Director/Musician; Estelle Morris [1952] Director/Politician; David William Nicholls [1962] Director/Certified Chartered Accountant; Vanessa Caroline Reed [1974] Director; Cllr Wendy Ann Simon [1961] Director/Councillor; Professor Nigel Peter Weatherill [1954] Director/Chief Executive

Royal Sanders (UK) Limited
Incorporated: 19 September 2008 *Employees:* 106
Net Worth: £4,746,000 *Total Assets:* £10,796,000
Registered Office: Unit A4, Red Scar Industrial Estate, Longridge Road, Ribbleton, Preston, Lancs, PR2 5NA
Activities: Manufacture of soap and detergents
Parent: UKPC B.V.
Officers: Mark Christiaan de Lange [1967] Finance Director [Dutch]; Bart Otger Hullegie [1971] Director [Dutch]; Gavin Patrick McNally [1962] Managing Director

Roydon Group PLC
Incorporated: 28 April 2009 *Employees:* 85
Net Worth: £6,263,013 *Total Assets:* £12,002,292
Registered Office: Units 1-3 Junction Eco Park, Rake Lane, Swinton, Manchester, M27 8LU
Activities: Manufacture of plastics in primary forms
Parent: Roydon Holdings Limited
Officers: Sarah Patricia Sumner, Secretary; Sarah Patricia Sumner [1961] Director; Wilfred Sumner [1958] Director; Gareth Roy Wallwork [1982] Director

RPG Group Limited
Incorporated: 10 March 2015 *Employees:* 53
Net Worth: £545,551 *Total Assets:* £8,578,497
Registered Office: The Copper Room, Deva Centre, Trinity Way, Manchester, M3 7BG
Activities: Accounting and auditing activities
Shareholder: Christopher Michael Poston
Officers: John Julian Redmond, Secretary; Jonathan Selwyn Brownson [1962] Director; Peter John Buckley [1956] Director; Martin Andrew Chatten [1968] Director; Alan Brian Coleman [1971] Director; Phillip Rees Owen [1969] Director; Christopher Michael Poston [1967] Director; Christopher Mark Slater [1958] Director

RPW (Southampton) Limited
Incorporated: 10 September 2013 *Employees:* 3
Net Worth: £413,422 *Total Assets:* £11,273,209
Registered Office: Eversheds House, 70 Great Bridgewater Street, Manchester, M1 5ES
Activities: Development of building projects
Officers: Ernest Stephen Battey [1959] Director/Operations Manager; Kevin Anthony Mudd [1957] Director/Chief Executive Officer

RRG (West Yorkshire) Limited
Incorporated: 19 September 2003 *Employees:* 105
Net Worth Deficit: £1,556,000 *Total Assets:* £7,346,000
Registered Office: 173 Cross Lane, Salford, M5 4AP
Activities: Sale of new cars and light motor vehicles
Parent: RRG Group Limited
Officers: Arran Bangham, Secretary; Arran Bangham [1968] Managing Director; Anthony Robert Cliff [1969] Managing Director

RRG Group Limited
Incorporated: 5 May 1972 *Employees:* 775
Net Worth: £29,747,000 *Total Assets:* £87,199,000
Registered Office: 173 Cross Lane, Salford, M5 4AP
Activities: Sale of new cars and light motor vehicles
Parent: Marubeni Auto Investment (UK) Limited
Officers: Arran Bangham, Secretary/Accountant; Tsugutoshi Akano [1974] Director [Japanese]; Arran Bangham [1968] Managing Director; Anthony Robert Cliff [1969] Managing Director; Naonori Ishii [1967] Director [Japanese]; Kazuhiro Kondo [1967] Director [Japanese]; Takanori Tanaka [1963] Director [Japanese]

RSK Adas Limited
Incorporated: 18 November 2016
Net Worth Deficit: £414,000 *Total Assets:* £8,073,000
Registered Office: Spring Lodge, 172 Chester Road, Helsby, Cheshire, WA6 0AR
Activities: Environmental consulting activities
Shareholders: RSK Group PLC; R.W. Management (Holdings) Ltd
Officers: Steven Geoffrey Mills, Secretary; Abigail Sarah Draper [1970] Director; Dr Alasdair Alan Ryder [1961] Director; Ian Harry Strudwick [1969] Director

RSK Group Limited
Incorporated: 28 April 1999 *Employees:* 1,131
Net Worth Deficit: £5,832,000 *Total Assets:* £85,197,000
Registered Office: Spring Lodge, 172 Chester Road, Helsby, Cheshire, WA6 0AR
Activities: Activities of head offices
Shareholder: Dr Alasdair Alan Ryder
Officers: Steven Geoffrey Mills, Secretary; Stefan Bangels [1964] Director [Belgian]; Nigel Paul Board [1963] Director/Environmental Scientist; Garry Charnock [1954] Director; Abigail Sarah Draper [1970] Director; Michael William Mason [1964] Director/Environmental Consultant; Dr Alasdair Alan Ryder [1961] Director/Environmental Consultant; Susan Sljivic [1961] Director/Environmental Consultant; Dr Mary Ann Elizabeth Smyth [1962] Director; Ian Harry Strudwick [1969] Director/Environmental Consultant; Dr Paul Stewart Upton [1956] Director; Peter John Witherington [1951] Director

RSL Property Management Ltd
Incorporated: 17 September 2013
Net Worth: £2,912,654 *Total Assets:* £7,478,935
Registered Office: Suite 4102, Charlotte House, QD Business Centre, 67-83 Norfolk Street, Liverpool, L1 0BG
Activities: Other letting and operating of own or leased real estate
Shareholders: Robert William McPartland; Mark Anthony Robinson
Officers: Robert William McPartland [1974] Director; Mark Anthony Robinson [1970] Director

RSR Limited
Incorporated: 7 May 1999 *Employees:* 117
Net Worth: £17,973,888 *Total Assets:* £19,709,656
Registered Office: 7 Robin Lane, High Bentham, Lancaster, LA2 7AB
Activities: Manufacture of basic pharmaceutical products
Major Shareholder: Dr Bernard Rees-Smith
Officers: Jenny Louise Barwise, Secretary; Janet Bradbury [1966] Director/Scientist; Dr Shu Chen [1966] Director/Scientist; Dr Jadwiga Furmaniak [1951] Director/Scientist; Dr Michael Powell [1960] Director/Scientist; Dr Bernard Rees Smith [1944] Director; Dr Jane Sanders [1966] Director/Scientist

RT Lithium Limited
Incorporated: 21 November 2013
Net Worth: £276,923,488 *Total Assets:* £278,060,352
Registered Office: Eversheds LLP, Eversheds House, 70 Great Bridgewater Street, Manchester, M1 5ES
Activities: Activities of other holding companies n.e.c.
Parent: Albemarle Corporation
Officers: Karen Goldthwaite Narwold [1960] Director/Lawyer [American]; Hugh David Wilson [1969] Director/Accountant

Ruberoid International Limited
Incorporated: 11 October 1993
Net Worth: £14,069,000 *Total Assets:* £28,796,000
Registered Office: Appley Lane North, Appley Bridge, Wigan, Lancs, WN6 9AB
Activities: Activities of production holding companies
Parent: IKO Holdings PLC
Officers: Anthony Carlyle [1967] Director; Frank Hautman [1966] Director [Belgian]; Hartley Michael Koschitzky [1965] Director [Canadian]

Rubix Group International Limited
Incorporated: 16 January 1920 *Employees:* 3,862
Net Worth: £148,300,000 *Total Assets:* £452,700,000
Registered Office: St Ann's House, 1 Old Market Place, Knutsford, Cheshire, WA16 6PD
Activities: Activities of head offices
Parent: Rubix Group Midco 3 Limited
Officers: Daniel Pierre Bruno Freches [1988] Director/Investment Professional [French/Portuguese]; Duncan Jonathan Magrath [1964] Director/Accountant; Hermann Josef Maier [1960] Director/Chief Executive [German]; Yves Pascal Michel Saunier [1966] Legal Director [French]

Rubix Group Midco 4 Limited
Incorporated: 19 January 2000
Net Worth: £44,520,944 *Total Assets:* £102,474,768
Registered Office: St Ann's House, 1 Old Market Place, Knutsford, Cheshire, WA16 6PD
Activities: Dormant company
Parent: Rubix Group International Limited
Officers: Paul Finnigan [1975] Director/Tax Manager; Duncan Jonathan Magrath [1964] Director; Yves Pascal Michel Saunier [1966] Legal Director [French]

Rubix International Limited
Incorporated: 19 January 2000
Net Worth: £6,226,636 *Total Assets:* £103,107,560
Registered Office: St Ann's House, 1 Old Market Place, Knutsford, Cheshire, WA16 6PD
Activities: Dormant company
Parent: Rubix Group Midco 4 Limited
Officers: Paul Finnigan [1975] Director/Tax Manager; Duncan Jonathan Magrath [1964] Director; Yves Pascal Michel Saunier [1966] Legal Director [French]

Ruia Group Limited
Incorporated: 30 September 1993
Net Worth: £3,473,309 *Total Assets:* £31,553,252
Registered Office: Kearsley Mill, Stoneclough, Radcliffe, Manchester, M26 1RH
Activities: Activities of head offices
Parent: Ruia Trading Limited
Officers: Philip John Campbell, Secretary; Alok Ruia [1964] Director; Amit Ruia [1970] Director; Rajendra Ruia [1962] Director; Sunil Ruia [1961] Director; Vimal Ruia [1959] Director

Ruia Trading Limited
Incorporated: 16 November 2016
Net Worth: £18,518,460 *Total Assets:* £47,220,232
Registered Office: Kearsley Mill, Crompton Road, Stoneclough, Radcliffe, Manchester, M26 1RH
Activities: Activities of head offices
Officers: Philip John Campbell, Secretary; Amit Ruia [1970] Director; Vimal Ruia [1959] Director

Rullion Engineering Limited
Incorporated: 19 December 1973 *Employees:* 710
Net Worth: £5,730,812 *Total Assets:* £27,139,054
Registered Office: P O Box 47, Trafalgar House, Altrincham, Cheshire, WA14 1FG
Activities: Temporary employment agency activities
Parent: Rullion Limites
Officers: Matthew Hart, Secretary; Philip James Higgins [1959] Director; James Socrates Saoulli [1978] Director; Themistocles Mathew Socrates Saoulli [1941] Director; Robert Scott [1958] Director/Accountant

Rullion IT Plus Limited
Incorporated: 11 November 1987 *Employees:* 107
Net Worth: £11,478,176 *Total Assets:* £29,567,088
Registered Office: P O Box 47, Trafalgar House, 110 Manchester Road, Altrincham, Cheshire, WA14 1FG
Activities: Temporary employment agency activities
Parent: Rullion Ltd
Officers: Matthew Hart, Secretary; James Socrates Saoulli [1978] Director; Themistocles Mathew Socrates Saoulli [1941] Director; Robert Scott [1958] Director/Accountant

Rullion Limited
Incorporated: 17 February 1993 *Employees:* 1,830
Net Worth: £16,627,677 *Total Assets:* £62,970,860
Registered Office: P O Box 47, Trafalgar House, 110 Manchester Road, Altrincham, Cheshire, WA14 1FG
Activities: Activities of head offices
Major Shareholder: Rose Marie Jean Saoulli
Officers: Matthew Hart, Secretary; Philip Higgins [1959] Director/General Manager; James Basil Saoulli [1978] Director/Finance Analyst; Rose Maria Jean Teresa Saoulli [1950] Director [Irish/Cypriot]; Themistocles Mathew Socrates Saoulli [1941] Director; Robert Scott [1958] Director/Accountant

Runcorn MCP Limited
Incorporated: 7 July 2014 *Employees:* 92
Net Worth: £51,200,000 *Total Assets:* £67,000,000
Registered Office: P O Box 9, Runcorn Site HQ, South Parade, Runcorn, Cheshire, WA7 4JE
Activities: Manufacture of industrial gases
Shareholders: Inovyn Chlorvinyls Limited; Vynova Runcorn Limited
Officers: Paul Frederick Nichols, Secretary; Paul Mark Daniels [1966] Director; Luc Eduard Maria Leunis [1959] Director [Belgian]; James David Morrison [1962] Director/Manager; Stefan Sommer [1957] Director [German]

Rural Concepts (Libya) Limited
Incorporated: 1 July 2015
Net Worth: £100 *Total Assets:* £20,000,000
Registered Office: The Estate Office, Broughton Hall, Skipton, N Yorks, BD23 3AE
Activities: Dormant company
Parent: Rural Concepts Limited
Officers: Roger Henry Tempest [1963] Director

Rural Concepts Construction Limited
Incorporated: 30 June 1998
Net Worth: £20,000,002 *Total Assets:* £20,325,900
Registered Office: Estate Office, Broughton Hall, Broughton, Skipton, N Yorks, BD23 3AE
Activities: Development of building projects
Parent: Rural Concepts (Libya) Limited
Officers: Roger Henry Tempest [1963] Director/Landowner

Ruselco LLP
Incorporated: 15 June 2004
Net Worth: £27,712,224 *Total Assets:* £27,716,540
Registered Office: Eversheds House, 70 Great Bridgewater Street, Manchester, M1 5ES

Rushcliffe (Heysham) Limited
Incorporated: 2 February 2010 *Employees:* 2
Net Worth: £1,108,091 *Total Assets:* £11,338,080
Registered Office: Old Bank Chambers, 43 Woodlands Road, Lytham St Annes, Lancs, FY8 1DA
Activities: Other letting and operating of own or leased real estate
Officers: James Henry Ashworth [1947] Director

Rushcliffe (St Annes PCC) Limited
Incorporated: 24 May 2005
Net Worth Deficit: £288,304 *Total Assets:* £15,253,249
Registered Office: 43 Woodlands Road, Ansdell, Lytham St Annes, Lancs, FY8 1DA
Activities: Other letting and operating of own or leased real estate
Officers: James Henry Ashworth [1947] Director

Russell Armer Group Limited
Incorporated: 14 February 2005 *Employees:* 69
Net Worth: £6,754,260 *Total Assets:* £9,953,099
Registered Office: Mintsfeet Place, Mintsfeet Road North, Kendal, Cumbria, LA9 6LL
Activities: Activities of head offices
Shareholders: David Martyn Nicholson; Andrew Christopher Taylor
Officers: Karen Patricia Cowgill, Secretary; David Martyn Nicholson [1956] Director; Andrew Christopher Taylor [1960] Director

Russell Armer Limited
Incorporated: 17 January 1961 *Employees:* 69
Net Worth: £6,202,354 *Total Assets:* £9,609,614
Registered Office: Mintsfeet Place, Mintsfeet Road North, Kendal, Cumbria, LA9 6LL
Activities: Construction of commercial buildings
Parent: Russell Armer Group Limited
Officers: Karen Patricia Cowgill, Secretary; David Martyn Nicholson [1956] Director/Quantity Surveyor; Andrew Christopher Taylor [1960] Director

Russell Homes (UK) Limited
Incorporated: 16 March 2004 *Employees:* 13
Net Worth: £1,596,052 *Total Assets:* £12,773,635
Registered Office: 13 Westpoint Enterprise Park, Clarence Avenue, Trafford Park, Manchester, M17 1QS
Activities: Construction of domestic buildings
Shareholders: WBHO UK Limited; Andrew Scott Russell; Gareth Mark Russell
Officers: Lee David Downs, Secretary; Paul Joseph Foley [1967] Director [South African]; Charles Victor Henwood [1963] Director [South African]; Daniel Kershaw [1974] Director/Housing; Andrew Scott Russell [1969] Director; Gareth Mark Russell [1972] Director

Russells Limited
Incorporated: 29 October 1993 *Employees:* 110
Net Worth: £15,792,170 *Total Assets:* £35,904,348
Registered Office: 13 Westpoint Enterprise Park, Clarence Avenue, Trafford Park, Manchester, M17 1QS
Activities: Construction of commercial buildings
Parent: WBHO UK Limited
Officers: Lee David Downs, Secretary; Lee David Downs [1971] Director/Accountant; Paul Joseph Foley [1967] Director [South African]; Christopher Raymond Harper [1977] Director/Estimator [New Zealander]; Charles Victor Henwood [1963] Director [South African]; John Charles Millward [1972] Director/Construction Professional; Andrew Scott Russell [1969] Director; Gareth Mark Russell [1972] Construction Director

Rutmark Properties Limited
Incorporated: 26 October 2000
Net Worth: £8,422,016 *Total Assets:* £16,494,702
Registered Office: Unit A, Kingmoor Park South Industrial Estate, Queens Drive, Carlisle, CA6 4SB
Activities: Other letting and operating of own or leased real estate
Parent: Equorium Property Company Limited
Officers: June Carruthers, Secretary; Stephen Robert Simpson [1968] Commercial Director

Ruttle Plant Holdings Limited
Incorporated: 10 October 1977
Net Worth: £17,556,550 *Total Assets:* £31,369,694
Registered Office: Lancaster House, Ackhurst Road, Chorley, Lancs, PR7 1NH
Activities: Activities of head offices
Officers: George Henry Ruttle [1945] Director/Agricultural Contractor

RW Jupe Limited
Incorporated: 30 July 2012 *Employees:* 48
Net Worth: £3,575,778 *Total Assets:* £10,469,139
Registered Office: Pallet Centre Europe, Dane Road Industrial Estate, Sale, Cheshire, M33 7BH
Activities: Activities of head offices
Major Shareholder: Matthew Robert Palmer
Officers: Matthew Robert Palmer [1972] Commercial Director; Russell John Palmer [1975] Director; Lee Spratt [1977] Director

Ryman Group Limited
Incorporated: 13 May 1992 *Employees:* 1,461
Net Worth: £55,857,000 *Total Assets:* £76,429,000
Registered Office: Ryman House, Savoy Road, Crewe, Cheshire, CW1 6NA
Activities: Activities of head offices
Parent: Sevenfathers Limited
Officers: Kirsten Lawton, Secretary; Ian Michael Childs [1956] Director/Marketing Executive; Malcolm Stanley Cooke [1942] Director; Kypros Kyprianou [1968] Commercial Director; Simon John Lakin [1967] Director/Accountant; Theodoros Paphitis [1959] Director; Richard Edward Towner [1936] Director/Consultant

Ryman Limited
Incorporated: 9 January 1995 *Employees:* 1,393
Net Worth: £53,390,000 *Total Assets:* £73,545,000
Registered Office: Ryman House, Savoy Road, Crewe, Cheshire, CW1 6NA
Activities: Retail sale of newspapers and stationery in specialised stores
Parent: Ryman Group Limited
Officers: Kirsten Lawton, Secretary; Ian Michael Childs [1956] Director; Malcolm Stanley Cooke [1942] Director; Kypros Kyprianou [1968] Commercial Director; Simon John Lakin [1967] Director/Accountant; Theodoros Paphitis [1959] Director; Richard Edward Towner [1936] Director/Consultant

S G Equipment Limited
Incorporated: 9 October 2001 *Employees:* 61
Net Worth: £5,605,868 *Total Assets:* £7,521,367
Registered Office: Stamford House, 185 Stamford Street, Stalybridge, Cheshire, SK15 1QZ
Activities: Other engineering activities
Officers: Mark Vernon Haslam, Secretary; Andrew Dobson [1958] Director/Engineer; Michael Ford [1945] Director/Accountant; Mark Vernon Haslam [1968] Director; Malcolm O'Connor [1965] Director/Accountant; Paul Waine [1969] Director

S M D Textiles Limited
Incorporated: 19 March 1987 *Employees:* 54
Net Worth: £5,655,146 *Total Assets:* £12,214,449
Registered Office: Unit F2, Pittman Way, Preston North Employment Industrial Estate, Fulwood, Preston, Lancs, PR2 9ZD
Activities: Wholesale of textiles
Parent: SMD (Holdings) Limited
Officers: Neil Anderson [1963] Sales Director; Richard John Hargreaves [1968] Director/Chartered Accountant; Robert Jason Kenworthy [1969] Director; Jonathan Edward Pink [1982] Operations Director

S. L. L. Properties Limited
Incorporated: 27 December 1996 *Employees:* 4
Net Worth: £3,620,774 *Total Assets:* £14,612,609
Registered Office: Regency House, Regent Road, Kirkdale, Liverpool, L5 9SR
Activities: Buying and selling of own real estate
Major Shareholder: David Alan Day
Officers: Paul Edmund Day, Secretary/Director; David Alan Day [1954] Director; Paul Edmund Day [1957] Director/Property Management

S.A.N. Limited
Incorporated: 20 December 1963 *Employees:* 5
Net Worth: £18,964,472 *Total Assets:* £83,549,504
Registered Office: 42 Bloom Street, Manchester, M1 3HR
Activities: Manufacture of other textiles n.e.c.
Shareholders: Deborah Essayan; Steven Essayan; Jacqueline Clare Wortley
Officers: Max Lucas Essayan, Secretary; Beryl Essayan [1934] Director; Max Lucas Essayan [1933] Director; Myrna Madeleine Essayan [1937] Director; Jacqueline Clare Wortley [1961] Director

S.J.M. Limited
Incorporated: 12 February 1992 *Employees:* 56
Net Worth: £7,842,762 *Total Assets:* £82,577,272
Registered Office: 3rd Floor, Colwyn Chambers, 19 York Street, Manchester, M2 3BA
Activities: Other amusement and recreation activities n.e.c.
Parent: SJM Holdings North Limited
Officers: Robert Kevin Ballantine, Secretary; Robert Kevin Ballantine [1962] Director/Leisure Consultant; Simon James Moran [1965] Director/Music Promoter; Glenn Alan Tyrrell [1967] Director/Accountant; Christopher John York [1969] Director/Leisure Consultant

S.M.D. Home Limited
Incorporated: 25 October 1979 *Employees:* 31
Net Worth: £3,345,252 *Total Assets:* £7,076,513
Registered Office: Pittman Way, Fulwood, Preston, Lancs, PR2 9ZD
Activities: Wholesale of textiles
Officers: Richard John Hargreaves [1968] Director/Chartered Accountant; Robert Jason Kenworthy [1969] Director; Jonathan Edward Pink [1982] Operations Director

S.P.L. Foods Limited
Incorporated: 4 February 1991 *Employees:* 44
Net Worth: £1,335,581 *Total Assets:* £8,507,483
Registered Office: SPL Ltd, Drury Lane, Chadderton, Oldham, Lancs, OL9 7PH
Activities: Activities of head offices
Officers: Raymond Butler [1951] Director; Graham Knight [1974] Commercial Director; Harold Simon [1944] Director; Robert Andrew Simon [1966] Director; Lyndsey Jane Winstanley [1966] Director

S.R.G. Apparel PLC
Incorporated: 29 December 1998 *Employees:* 82
Net Worth: £8,613,402 *Total Assets:* £16,856,166
Registered Office: Unit 14 Park Seventeen, Whitefield, Manchester, M45 8FJ
Activities: Wholesale of clothing and footwear
Major Shareholder: Rajesh Kumar Passi
Officers: Andrew William Spence, Secretary; Nita Passi [1956] Director/Administrator; Rajesh Kumar Passi [1954] Managing Director; Rohit Passi [1980] Design Director; Andrew William Spence [1965] Finance Director

Sabina Estates Group Holdings Limited
Incorporated: 16 November 2015
Net Worth Deficit: £312,891 *Total Assets:* £54,167,684
Registered Office: 3rd Floor, 1 Ashley Road, Altrincham, Cheshire, WA14 2DT
Activities: Management of real estate on a fee or contract basis
Officers: Jonathan James Mark Olav Gray [1966] Director/Investment Banker; Giles Leo Rabbetts [1971] Director

Sadaqat Global Limited
Incorporated: 4 June 2008 *Employees:* 15
Net Worth: £702,545 *Total Assets:* £11,627,021
Registered Office: Unit 6 Westpoint Enterprise Park, Clarence Avenue, Trafford Park, Manchester, M17 1QS
Activities: Weaving of textiles
Shareholders: Khurram Mukhtar; Shoaib Mukhtar
Officers: Khurram Mukhtar [1972] Director [Pakistani]; Shoaib Mukhtar [1976] Director [Pakistani]

Safeguard World International Holdings Limited
Incorporated: 20 November 2015 *Employees:* 518
Net Worth Deficit: £17,295,496 *Total Assets:* £18,448,580
Registered Office: Edwin Foden Business Centre, Moss Lane, Sandbach, Cheshire, CW11 3AE
Activities: Activities of head offices
Officers: Jonathan Edgar Coker [1981] Director/Venture Capitalist; John Giles [1954] Director/Chief Operating Officer; Patrick Francis Goepel [1961] Director/CEO of Assure Software [American]; Bjorn Reynolds [1975] Director; Bruce John Thew [1958] Director

Safeguard World International Limited
Incorporated: 28 November 2007
Net Worth Deficit: £14,371,910 *Total Assets:* £20,249,540
Registered Office: Edwin Foden Business Centre, Moss Lane, Sandbach, Cheshire, CW11 3AE
Activities: Financial intermediation not elsewhere classified
Parent: Safeguard World International Holdings Ltd
Officers: John Giles, Secretary; Bjorn Reynolds, Secretary/Managing Director; Jonathan Edgar Coker [1981] Director/Venture Capital; John Giles [1954] Director/Chief Operating Officer; Patrick Francis Goepel [1961] Director/CEO of Assure Software [American]; Bjorn Reynolds [1975] Director; Bruce John Thew [1958] Director/Chief Executive Officer

Safehands Group Limited
Incorporated: 24 August 2010 *Employees:* 430
Net Worth: £1,688,853 *Total Assets:* £11,191,694
Registered Office: 4 Croft Court, Whitehills Business Park, Blackpool, Lancs, FY4 5PR
Activities: Activities of other holding companies n.e.c.
Officers: Thomas Adam Flack [1985] Finance Director; Paul Dixon Manning [1954] Director; Linda Rigby [1961] Director; William Simon Rigby [1961] Director

Safeway (Overseas) Limited
Incorporated: 3 October 1924 *Employees:* 304
Net Worth: £85,742,000 *Total Assets:* £90,710,000
Registered Office: Hilmore House, Gain Lane, Bradford, W Yorks, BD3 7DL
Activities: Retail sale in non-specialised stores with food, beverages or tobacco predominating
Parent: Safeway Stores Limited
Officers: Jonathan James Burke, Secretary; Jonathan James Burke [1966] Director/Company Secretary; Trevor John Strain [1975] Finance Director

Safeway Limited
Incorporated: 23 February 1977 *Employees:* 44,819
Net Worth: £1,804,999,936 *Total Assets:* £3,827,000,064
Registered Office: Hilmore House, Gain Lane, Bradford, W Yorks, BD3 7DL
Activities: Retail sale in non-specialised stores with food, beverages or tobacco predominating
Parent: Wm Morrison Supermarkets Holdings Limited
Officers: Jonathan James Burke, Secretary; Jonathan James Burke [1966] Director; Trevor John Strain [1975] Finance Director

Safeway Stores Limited
Incorporated: 15 January 1963 *Employees:* 48,133
Net Worth: £650,000,000 *Total Assets:* £4,064,999,936
Registered Office: Hilmore House, Gain Lane, Bradford, W Yorks, BD3 7DL
Activities: Retail sale in non-specialised stores with food, beverages or tobacco predominating
Parent: Stores Group Limited
Officers: Jonathan James Burke, Secretary; Jonathan James Burke [1966] Director; Alison Charnock [1969] Director/Solicitor; Gary William Mills [1966] Director; Trevor John Strain [1975] Finance Director

Saffil 2011 Limited
Incorporated: 7 July 2011
Net Worth Deficit: £21,920,720 *Total Assets:* £94,358,472
Registered Office: Mill Lane, Rainford, St Helens, Merseyside, WA11 8LP
Activities: Activities of head offices
Officers: John Charles Dandolph IV [1976] Director/Chief Financial Officer [American]; Anthony Bret Greene [1959] Director/Accountant [American]; Daniel Thomas Liebel [1963] Finance Director [American]; Edward Duncan Barton Yardley [1959] Director/Senior Vice-President

Saffil Limited
Incorporated: 7 October 1998 *Employees:* 85
Net Worth: £10,837,374 *Total Assets:* £64,648,344
Registered Office: Mill Lane, Rainford, St Helens, Merseyside, WA11 8LP
Activities: Other manufacturing n.e.c.
Officers: John Charles Dandolph IV [1976] Director/Chief Financial Officer [American]; Anthony Bret Greene [1959] Director/Accountant [American]; Daniel Thomas Liebel [1963] Finance Director [American]; Edward Duncan Barton Yardley [1959] Director/Senior Vice-President

Safic-Alcan UK Limited
Incorporated: 15 March 1957 *Employees:* 58
Net Worth: £8,224,657 *Total Assets:* £19,779,556
Registered Office: 812 Fountain Court, Birchwood Boulevard, Birchwood, Warrington, Cheshire, WA3 7QZ
Activities: Wholesale of chemical products
Parent: Safic-Alcan Espana SA
Officers: Deanne Michelle Davies, Secretary; Philippe Combette [1962] Director [French]; Martial Gaston Maurice Lecat [1951] Director [French]; Barry James McDonnell [1968] Director

Safran Nacelles Limited
Incorporated: 8 February 1989 *Employees:* 777
Net Worth Deficit: £11,000 *Total Assets:* £97,848,000
Registered Office: Bancroft Road, Burnley, Lancs, BB10 2TQ
Activities: Manufacture of air and spacecraft and related machinery
Parent: Safran Nacelles SA
Officers: Claire Stanley, Secretary; Cedric Goubet [1971] Director [French]; Cedric Hale [1976] Director/VP Human Resources [French]; Simon Hallas [1975] Director of Human Resources; Bertrand Hugueny [1962] Director/VP Industrial [French]; Gilles Poilvet [1967] Director/VP Programs [French]; Michael Rigalle [1971] Managing Director [French]; Claire Stanley [1977] Finance Director

Sage Automotive Interiors Limited
Incorporated: 8 July 2009 *Employees:* 217
Net Worth: £7,646,564 *Total Assets:* £13,353,348
Registered Office: Unit 1 Phoenix Park, Blakewater Road, Blackburn, BB1 5SJ
Activities: Manufacture of other technical and industrial textiles
Officers: David Neil Campbell [1958] Director/Accountant; Dirk Raymond Pieper [1957] Director/Chief Executive Officer [American]

Saica Flex UK Limited
Incorporated: 26 March 1990 *Employees:* 128
Net Worth: £8,813,000 *Total Assets:* £13,168,000
Registered Office: 144 Manchester Road, Carrington, Manchester, M31 4QN
Activities: Manufacture of paper and paperboard
Parent: Saica Paper UK Limited
Officers: Steven Petty, Secretary; Angel Ramon Alejandro Balet [1961] Director [Spanish]; Susana Alejandro Balet [1970] Director [Spanish]; Thomas Anthony Rice [1966] Director [Irish]

Saica Natur UK Limited
Incorporated: 23 July 1994 *Employees:* 201
Net Worth: £11 856,000 *Total Assets:* £23,702,000
Registered Office: 144 Manchester Road, Carrington, Manchester, M31 4QN
Activities: Recovery of sorted materials
Officers: Steven Petty, Secretary; Angel Ramon Alejandro Balet [1961] Director [Spanish]; Pedro Jose Gascon Munio [1957] Managing Director [Spanish]; Thomas Anthony Rice [1966] Finance Director [Irish]; Victor Manuel Sanz Martinez [1963] Director [Spanish]

Saica Pack UK Limited
Incorporated: 4 July 1975 *Employees:* 1,516
Net Worth: £198,922,000 *Total Assets:* £236,438,000
Registered Office: 144 Manchester Road, Carrington, Manchester, M31 4QN
Activities: Manufacture of other paper and paperboard containers
Officers: Steven Petty, Secretary; Angel Ramon Alejandro Balet [1961] Director/Manager Corrugated Board Division [Spanish]; Susana Alejandro Balet [1970] Director/Saica Embalaje Manager [Spanish]; Pascal Giraud [1958] Director/General Manager [French]; Brian Lister [1964] Director/Country Manager; Thomas Anthony Rice [1966] Finance Director [Irish]

Saica Paper UK Limited
Incorporated: 17 April 2008 *Employees:* 104
Net Worth: £286,183,008 *Total Assets:* £369,121,984
Registered Office: 144 Manchester Road, Carrington, Manchester, M31 4QN
Activities: Manufacture of paper and paperboard
Officers: Steven Petty, Secretary; Angel Ramon Alejandro Balet [1961] Director/Manager Corrugated Board Division [Spanish]; Pedro Jose Gascon Munio [1957] Managing Director [Spanish]; Thomas Anthony Rice [1966] Finance Director [Irish]

Saint-Gobain Industrial Ceramics Limited
Incorporated: 30 June 1967 *Employees:* 48
Net Worth: £7,998,000 *Total Assets:* £7,998,000
Registered Office: Mill Lane, Rainford, St Helens, Merseyside, WA11 8LP
Activities: Manufacture of refractory products
Officers: Alun Roy Oxenham, Secretary; Michael Strickland Chaldecott [1960] Managing Director; Stephane Heraud [1965] Director [French]

Sale Grammar School
Incorporated: 22 February 2011 *Employees:* 118
Net Worth: £13,775,000 *Total Assets:* £15,135,000
Registered Office: Sale Grammar School, Marsland Road, Sale, Cheshire, M33 3NH
Activities: General secondary education
Officers: Alison Jane McPartland, Secretary; Sara Ashan [1963] Director/University Teacher; Philippa Elizabeth Barron [1964] Director/Chartered Surveyor; Christopher James Brindley [1981] Director/Assistant Editor; Alan Neil Budenberg [1966] Director/Portfolio Manager; David Peter Citrine [1970] Director/Head of Customer Services; Alastair John Cutteridge [1965] Director/Associate Pastor; Nicola Jane Harrison [1968] Director/Head of Operations; Victoria Kelly Morgan Hole [1971] Business Manager/Director; David Charles Holland [1970] Director; Teresa Hopley [1965] Director/Manager [Chinese]; Dr Sirfraz Hussain [1975] Director/Doctor; Aileen Isabelle Joan Kirkham [1954] Director/Auditor; John Rodney Lund [1951] Director/Solicitor; Dr Jonathan Paul McNamara [1975] Director/Teacher; Phiip Roberts [1975] Director/Teacher; Caroline Rose Royle [1964] Director/Retired; Dr Donna Sager [1959] Deputy Director Public Health; Mark Stephen Smallwood [1961] Director/Headteacher

Salford Academy Trust
Incorporated: 21 June 2012 *Employees:* 234
Net Worth: £38,668,000 *Total Assets:* £41,495,000
Registered Office: Frontier House, Merchants Quay, Salford, M50 3SR
Activities: General secondary education
Officers: Gilda Kaseke, Secretary; Kimberley Cash [1980] Director/Centre Principal; Tracy Anne Kitchingman [1970] Director of Finance; Ruth Osborne-Thompson [1977] Director/Education; Paul Stephen Renshaw [1970] NHS Director; Michael John Sheehan [1956] Director/College Principal; Catherine Ann Starbuck [1971] Assistant Director (Education); Professor Richard Christopher Stephenson [1960] Director/Deputy Vice-Chancellor; Paul Ward [1970] Deputy Director of The University of Salford

Salford Van Hire Limited
Incorporated: 22 November 1965 *Employees:* 209
Net Worth: £56,191,768 *Total Assets:* £172,569,792
Registered Office: Sherborne Street, Manchester, M3 1EJ
Activities: Renting and leasing of trucks and other heavy vehicles
Major Shareholder: Raffaello Bacci
Officers: Graziella Ernesta Bacci, Secretary; Alessandro Bacci [1977] Director/Manager; Eda Bacci [1937] Director [Italian]; Patrizia Bacci [1966] Director; Raffaello Bacci [1937] Director [Italian]; Graziella Ernesta Bacci-Evers [1961] Director; Nicholas Marius Evers [1954] Director

Salford Village Limited
Incorporated: 13 May 2013
Net Worth Deficit: £2,877 *Total Assets:* £83,206,856
Registered Office: 7th Floor, Digital World Centre, 1 Lowry Plaza, Salford Quays, Manchester, M50 3UB
Activities: Management of real estate on a fee or contract basis
Shareholders: Campus Living Villages (Peel Park) UK Limited; Equitix Education 2 Limited
Officers: Charlotte Sophie Ellen Douglass [1978] Director/Chartered Surveyor; Mark Jonathan Fowkes [1970] Director/Investment Manager; Aileen Goldspring [1959] Director/Regional General Manager; Mathew Jason Panopoulos [1974] Director/Global Chief Financial Officer, CF Corporate Finance [Australian]

Salisbury Management Services Limited
Incorporated: 28 April 1998 *Employees:* 45
Net Worth: £4,728,062 *Total Assets:* £13,963,268
Registered Office: Enterprise House, The Courtyard, Old Courthouse Road, Bromborough, Wirral, Merseyside, CH62 4UE
Activities: Residential nursing care facilities
Shareholders: Russell Michael Canner; Marika Elonka Canner
Officers: Russell Michael Canner, Secretary/Director; Marika Elonka Canner [1953] Director; Russell Michael Canner [1958] Director

Saltaire Water Limited
Incorporated: 21 November 2007
Net Worth Deficit: £156,324,992 *Total Assets:* £31,156,000
Registered Office: Western House, Halifax Road, Bradford, W Yorks, BD6 2SZ
Activities: Financial intermediation not elsewhere classified
Parent: Kelda Group Limited
Officers: Kathy Smith, Secretary; Elizabeth Marian Barber [1965] Director/Accountant; Richard David Flint [1968] Director; Kathy Smith [1974] Director/Company Secretary

Salts Estates Limited
Incorporated: 15 April 1987 *Employees:* 104
Net Worth: £6,995,294 *Total Assets:* £7,770,405
Registered Office: Salts Mill, Victoria Road, Saltaire, Shipley, W Yorks, BD18 3LB
Activities: Retail sale of books in specialised stores
Officers: Linda Wilkinson, Secretary; Maurice Miller [1947] Director; Davina Silver [1979] Director; Margaret Silver [1949] Director; Robin Jeremy Silver [1951] Director; Zoe Silver [1976] Director/Producer

Sam Learning Holdings Limited
Incorporated: 4 July 2007
Net Worth: £5,592,671 *Total Assets:* £6,842,051
Registered Office: 3rd Floor, 1 Ashley Road, Altrincham, Cheshire, WA14 2DT
Activities: Activities of head offices
Major Shareholder: David Asher Jaffa
Officers: Maxine Jaffa, Secretary; David Asher Jaffa [1965] Director; Malcolm Jaffa [1941] Director

Sambro International Limited
Incorporated: 13 October 1989 *Employees:* 160
Net Worth: £12,738,765 *Total Assets:* £34,107,692
Registered Office: Sambro International Limited, Hardys Gate, Dumers Lane, Bury, Lancs, BL9 9UE
Activities: Wholesale of household goods (other than musical instruments) n.e.c
Parent: Project Bullseye Bidco Ltd
Officers: Brian Andrew Robinson, Secretary; Jeremy Paul Clynes [1974] Director; Thomas John Duffy [1973] Director; Brian Andrew Robinson [1965] Director/Accountant; Nicholas Michael Samuels [1974] Director

SameTimeTomorrow Limited
Incorporated: 28 July 2015 *Employees:* 67
Net Worth: £5,659,180 *Total Assets:* £8,710,290
Registered Office: Gote Mill House, Gote Road, Cockermouth, Cumbria, CA13 0JQ
Activities: Activities of head offices
Shareholders: Raymond John Lawson; Pauline Lawson
Officers: James Lawson [1935] Director; Margaret Eileen Lawson [1941] Director; Pauline Lawson [1964] Director/Haulage Proprietor; Raymond John Lawson [1969] Director

Samjo Limited
Incorporated: 13 May 2002
Net Worth: £15,534,098 *Total Assets:* £27,424,022
Registered Office: 6th Floor, Cardinal House, 20 St Mary's Parsonage, Manchester, M3 2LG
Activities: Buying and selling of own real estate
Shareholders: Joshua Halpern; Samuel Halpern
Officers: Samuel Halpern, Secretary/Director; Israel Friedman [1971] Director/Rabbi; Joshua Halpern [1958] Director; Samuel Halpern [1960] Director

San Marco Limited
Incorporated: 10 March 1987 *Employees:* 148
Net Worth: £3,162,324 *Total Assets:* £9,073,301
Registered Office: Chandler House, 7 Ferry Road Office Park, Riversway, Preston, Lancs, PR2 2YH
Activities: Licenced restaurants
Major Shareholder: Ivan Bragagnini
Officers: Louise Bragagnini, Secretary; Carlo Bragagnini [1979] Director/Restaurateur; Ivan Bragagnini [1953] Director/Restaurateur [Italian]; Louise Bragagnini [1953] Director/Restaurateur

Sandbach School
Incorporated: 28 January 2008 *Employees:* 159
Net Worth: £6,350,139 *Total Assets:* £8,329,430
Registered Office: Sandbach School, Crewe Road, Sandbach, Cheshire, CW11 3NS
Activities: General secondary education
Officers: David Osborne, Secretary; Stewart Brotherston [1981] Director/Design Manager; Sarah Irene Burns [1964] Director/Headteacher; John Duncan Cargill [1951] Director; Stephen Christopher Davies [1982] Director/Solicitor; Stuart Charles Dodds [1961] Director/School Teacher; Robert David England [1948] Director; David Anthony Evans [1985] Director/Teacher; Susan Ann Kennerley [1960] Director; Louise Lewis [1975] Director/Marketing Consultant; Clare Elizabeth Longden [1962] Director/Consultant HR; Gillian Mary Merry [1942] Director/Retired Consultant; Adrian Paul Mitchell [1972] Director/IT Consultant; Claire Louise Reel [1973] Director of Pharmacy Business; Michael Frank Roberts [1954] Director; Peter John Sherrat [1955] Director/Management Consultant; Dominic David Surry [1969] Director/Training Provider; Dr Jennifer Wells [1968] Director/Lecturer

Sandhof Limited
Incorporated: 25 June 1991
Net Worth: £26,859,000 *Total Assets:* £42,036,000
Registered Office: Direct House, Lancaster Way, Westhoughton, Bolton, Lancs, BL5 3XY
Activities: Manufacture of other food products n.e.c.
Parent: Freiberger Lebensmittel GmbH
Officers: Timothy Jones, Secretary; Uwe Berndt [1970] Director/Accountant [German]; Oliver Carsten Heinisch [1969] Director [German]; Michael Ian Kent [1962] Director; Jonathan Alan Lucas [1960] Director/Chartered Accountant; Robert Marnell [1964] Director; Herr Hans Detlev Schulz [1953] Director [German]; Siegfried Weber [1963] Director/NPD Manager [German]

Sandileaf Limited
Incorporated: 13 January 1977
Net Worth: £7,674,350 *Total Assets:* £10,886,584
Registered Office: 17 St Anns Square, Manchester, M2 7PW
Activities: Other letting and operating of own or leased real estate
Shareholders: Harold Maurice Baron; Heather Rochelle Baron
Officers: Heather Rochelle Baron, Secretary/Director; Harold Maurice Baron [1952] Director; Heather Rochelle Baron [1952] Director

Sandown Property Company (Liverpool) Limited
Incorporated: 6 June 1951
Net Worth: £8,303,879 *Total Assets:* £8,412,770
Registered Office: Pacific Chambers, 11-13 Victoria Street, Liverpool, L2 5QQ
Activities: Renting and operating of Housing Association real estate
Officers: Michael Arthur Fraenkel, Secretary; Rachael Marie Coleman [1973] Director; Beatrice Lesser Fraenkel [1945] Director; Michael Arthur Fraenkel [1945] Director

Sandown Property Holdings Limited
Incorporated: 26 February 2016
Net Worth: £7,395,239 *Total Assets:* £7,494,739
Registered Office: Pacific Chambers, 11-13 Victoria Street, Liverpool, L2 5QQ
Activities: Activities of other holding companies n.e.c.
Officers: Rachael Marie Coleman [1973] Director; Beatrice Lesser Fraenkel [1945] Director; Dr Michael Arthur Fraenkel [1974] Director

Sandusky Limited
Incorporated: 4 October 1962 *Employees:* 56
Net Worth Deficit: £941,756 *Total Assets:* £7,299,151
Registered Office: 64a Bridge Street, Manchester, M3 3BA
Activities: Casting of steel
Parent: Metaltek International (UK) Limited
Officers: Andrew Garden Cope [1941] Director/Executive Management [American]; Richard M Danning [1962] Director/Financial Management [American]; Thomas Graeme Gibb [1965] Managing Director; Robert James Smickley [1951] Director/Executive Management [American]

Sandymere Limited
Incorporated: 16 January 1937
Net Worth: £36,394,564 *Total Assets:* £37,910,440
Registered Office: Timpson House, Claverton Road, Roundthorn Industrial Estate, Manchester, M23 9TT
Activities: Non-trading company
Parent: Timpson Group PLC
Officers: Paresh Majithia, Secretary; Paresh Majithia [1967] Finance Director; William James Timpson [1971] Director; Sir William John Anthony Timpson [1943] Director

Sandymoor Free School
Incorporated: 16 May 2011 *Employees:* 63
Net Worth: £11,921,193 *Total Assets:* £12,861,127
Registered Office: Sandymoor School, Wharford Lane, Sandymoor, Runcorn, Cheshire, WA7 1QU
Activities: General secondary education
Officers: Nevin Julia Deakin [1970] Director/Headteacher; Dr David Francis Dennison [1951] Director/School Governor; Richard Melvyn Eastburn [1974] Director; Chris Fenelon [1963] Director/Physiotherapist; Moira Frances Griffiths-Parr [1951] Director/Associate Member of The Trust; Simon Hurst [1965] Director/Scientist; Bryan Jones [1971] Director/University Lecturer; Sally Jones [1979] Director/School Principal; Deborah Kinsella [1982] Director/Teacher; Andrew Lockyer [1971] Director/Architect; Linda Mary Needham [1965] Director; Joanne Wakefield [1976] Director/Project Manager

Sanjeev 1979 Limited
Incorporated: 30 May 1996 *Employees:* 88
Net Worth: £733,734 *Total Assets:* £8,138,540
Registered Office: 140 Cheetham Hill Road, Manchester, M8 8PZ
Activities: Wholesale of clothing and footwear
Shareholders: Rajeev Kumar; Sanjeev Kumar
Officers: Sanjeev Kumar, Secretary; Bimal Kumar [1949] Director [Indian]; Rajeev Kumar [1981] Director/Businessman; Sanjeev Kumar [1979] Director; Saroj Kumar [1950] Director

Sanko Gosei UK Ltd
Incorporated: 31 August 1987 *Employees:* 243
Net Worth: £8,733,866 *Total Assets:* £26,094,320
Registered Office: 15-17 Seddon Place, Stanley Industrial Estate, Skelmersdale, Lancs, WN8 8EB
Activities: Manufacture of other plastic products
Parent: Sanko Gosei Ltd
Officers: Karen Maria Houghton, Secretary; Hideyuki Aoki [1967] Technical Director [Japanese]; Wayne Ash [1966] Sales Director; David Hughes [1969] Operations Director; Amen Kusumi [1962] Director [Japanese]; Yoichi Sawada [1960] Production Engineering Director [Japanese]; Tatsuo Shibata [1953] Director [Japanese]; Yoshiaki Shibata [1961] Director/European President [Japanese]; Laurence Paul Tabner [1969] Director

Sartex Quilts & Textiles Limited
Incorporated: 15 May 1992 *Employees:* 87
Net Worth: £2,675,578 *Total Assets:* £7,698,270
Registered Office: Castle Mill, Queensway, Rochdale, Lancs, OL11 2NY
Activities: Manufacture of soft furnishings
Officers: Maqbool Ahmed, Secretary/Textile Manufacturer; Maqbool Ahmed [1952] Director/Textile Manufacturer; Maqsood Ahmed [1961] Director/Administration; Zulfiqar Ali [1953] Director/Textile Manufacturer; Shahnawaz Gauhar [1979] Director; Saleem Khalid [1962] Director; Iftikhar Ahmed Randhawa [1963] Director

SAT Business Travel Management Limited
Incorporated: 3 September 2001 *Employees:* 16
Net Worth: £3,113,301 *Total Assets:* £7,305,548
Registered Office: 4th Floor, 2 Commercial Street, Manchester, M15 4RQ
Activities: Other transportation support activities
Parent: Strandhall Management Ltd
Officers: William Boyd Tannahill [1979] Director

Satake Europe Limited
Incorporated: 6 March 1984 *Employees:* 40
Net Worth: £8,533,266 *Total Assets:* £10,388,034
Registered Office: Satake Europe Ltd, Horsfield Way, Bredbury Park Industrial Estate, Bredbury, Stockport, Cheshire, SK6 2SU
Activities: Installation of industrial machinery and equipment
Major Shareholder: Toshiko Satake
Officers: Yoshihiro Kunimitsu, Secretary; Hajime Harada [1954] Director/Manager [Japanese]; Kazuyuki Kihara [1949] Director [Japanese]; Yoshihiro Kunimitsu [1960] Director/General Manager [Japanese]

Saxid Limited
Incorporated: 5 December 2013
Net Worth: £24,038,436 *Total Assets:* £24,038,436
Registered Office: Manchester International Office Centre, Styal Road, Manchester, M22 5TN
Activities: Activities of other holding companies n.e.c.
Parent: Icahn Enterprises L.P.
Officers: Beverley Ann Sutton, Secretary; Michael Andrew Bagguley [1956] Director/Plant Manager; Elaine Janet Milner [1962] Finance Director

The Saxon Crosses Mat
Incorporated: 12 October 2010 *Employees:* 159
Net Worth: £14,038,000 *Total Assets:* £15,886,000
Registered Office: Sandbach High School and Sixth Form College, Middlewich Road, Sandbach, Cheshire, CW11 3NT
Activities: General secondary education
Officers: Alan Edwin Bell [1957] Director/Accounts Manager; Ella Brett [1965] Director/Headteacher; Deborah Jane Broad [1967] Director/Registered Health Visitor; Anna Joy Condliffe [1975] Director/Landlady; David Graham [1970] Director/Health & Safety Consultant; Sara Halstead [1974] Director/Teacher; Gerard William Heath [1957] Director/Self Employed; Catherine Houghton [1962] Director/Teacher; Helen Hulse [1985] Director/Finance Manager; Ben Hunt [1965] Director/Head of Property; Thomas Price Jones [1935] Director/Retired School Teacher; Sharon Joyce [1969] Director/Accountant; John Leigh [1959] Director/Headteacher; Harriet O'Rourke [1992] Director/Teacher; Stephanie Owen [1966] Director/Manager; Joanne Wilkins [1970] Director/Mature Student; Jeanette Wynn [1953] Director/Retired Teacher

Sayers The Bakers Limited
Incorporated: 1 May 2008 *Employees:* 1,582
Net Worth: £55,000 *Total Assets:* £6,908,000
Registered Office: The Bakery, Sidney Street, Bolton, Lancs, BL3 6BG
Activities: Manufacture of bread; manufacture of fresh pastry goods and cakes
Parent: STB Holdings Ltd
Officers: Alexander Peter Birnie [1960] Director; Mark Stephen James [1970] Commercial Director; David Silvester [1966] Director/Chief Operating Officer - Retail; Isabella May Stroud Williams [1980] Director/Financial Consultant

Scalable Communications Limited
Incorporated: 30 September 1997
Net Worth: £9,708,000 *Total Assets:* £29,675,000
Registered Office: Daisy House, Lindred Road Business Park, Nelson, Lancs, BB9 5SR
Activities: Other telecommunications activities
Parent: Daisy Corporate Services Trading Limited
Officers: David Lewis McGlennon, Secretary; David Lewis McGlennon [1974] Director; Stephen Alan Smith [1963] Director

Scan Computers International Limited
Incorporated: 13 June 1991 *Employees:* 228
Net Worth: £10,540,388 *Total Assets:* £28,416,828
Registered Office: 56 Chorley New Road, Bolton, Lancs, BL1 4AP
Activities: Retail sale of computers, peripheral units and software in specialised stores
Officers: Nilendra Pratap Raja, Secretary; Nilendra Pratap Raja [1966] Director/Salesman; Shailendra Raja [1964] Director/Salesman

Scantech Offshore Limited
Incorporated: 26 October 1998 *Employees:* 61
Net Worth: £5,206,494 *Total Assets:* £26,878,544
Registered Office: P O Box 4, Fisher House, Barrow in Furness, Cumbria, LA14 1HR
Activities: Renting and leasing of other machinery, equipment and tangible goods n.e.c.
Parent: James Fisher and Sons PLC
Officers: James Henry John Marsh, Secretary; Nicholas Paul Henry [1961] Director; Stuart Charles Kilpatrick [1962] Director; Shaun Colin Ryan [1962] Director

Scapa (No.2) Limited
Incorporated: 30 May 2000
Net Worth: £112,258,432 *Total Assets:* £186,908,384
Registered Office: Manchester Road, Ashton under Lyne, Lancs, OL7 0ED
Activities: Non-trading company
Parent: Porritts & Spencer Ltd
Officers: Wendy Baker, Secretary; Wendy Dickinson [1967] Director/Accountant; Oskar Zahn [1964] Director

Scapa Group Public Limited Company
Incorporated: 5 November 1964 *Employees:* 32
Net Worth: £100,400,000 *Total Assets:* £227,000,000
Registered Office: Manchester Road, Ashton under Lyne, Lancs, OL7 0ED
Activities: Activities of head offices
Officers: Wendy Baker, Secretary; David Charles Blackwood [1959] Director; Heejae Richard Chae [1969] Director [American]; Pierre Roger Michel Guyot [1964] Director [French]; Brendan Patrick McAtamney [1962] Director [Irish]; Laurence Craig Pentz [1955] Director [American]; Martin Trevor Sawkins [1955] Director; Oskar Zahn [1964] Director

Scapa UK Limited
Incorporated: 10 October 1996 *Employees:* 233
Net Worth: £14,970,000 *Total Assets:* £68,688,000
Registered Office: 997 Manchester Road, Ashton under Lyne, Lancs, OL7 0ED
Activities: Other manufacturing n.e.c.
Parent: Porritts & Spencer Ltd
Officers: Wendy Baker, Secretary; Wendy Dickinson [1967] Director/Accountant; Oskar Zahn [1964] Director

Scarisbrick Hall Limited
Incorporated: 14 August 2006
Net Worth Deficit: £189,862 *Total Assets:* £7,653,881
Registered Office: Scarisbrick Hall, Southport Road, Ormskirk, Lancs, L40 9RQ
Activities: Development of building projects
Parent: Scarisbrick Hall Developments Limited
Officers: Michael Headley, Secretary/Director; Gregory Aylmer [1966] Director; Susan Jane Aylmer [1972] Director; Barry John Cackett [1966] Director; Linda Carol Headley [1952] Director; Lynda Ann Headley [1970] Director; Michael Headley [1949] Director

Scenic Tours (UK) Ltd
Incorporated: 5 April 2006 *Employees:* 61
Net Worth Deficit: £6,731,835 *Total Assets:* £18,060,896
Registered Office: Level 13, 111 Piccadilly, Manchester, M1 2HY
Activities: Travel agency activities
Major Shareholder: Glendon Mark Moroney
Officers: Colin John Downing [1963] Managing Director; Glendon Mark Moroney [1962] Director [Australian]

Scent Global Ltd
Incorporated: 20 May 2009 *Employees:* 48
Net Worth: £174,829 *Total Assets:* £22,454,032
Registered Office: 6th Floor, Cardinal House, 20 St Mary's Parsonage, Manchester, M3 2LG
Activities: Wholesale of perfume and cosmetics
Major Shareholder: Atul Thakrar
Officers: Atul Thakrar [1967] Director

Schilling Robotics Limited
Incorporated: 28 July 2003
Net Worth: £5,980,762 *Total Assets:* £6,584,009
Registered Office: Eversheds House, 70 Great Bridgewater Street, Manchester, M1 5ES
Activities: Manufacture of other special-purpose machinery n.e.c.
Parent: FMC Technologies Limited
Officers: George Lee Shirreffs [1973] Managing Director

Schoeller Allibert Limited
Incorporated: 12 May 2011 *Employees:* 230
Net Worth: £21,277,000 *Total Assets:* £36,857,000
Registered Office: Road One Winsford Industrial Estate, Winsford, Cheshire, CW7 3RA
Activities: Manufacture of other plastic products
Parent: LA Holding Ltd
Officers: Ian Alan Degnan [1965] Director/Chief Financial Officer

Schofields Limited
Incorporated: 23 April 1984 *Employees:* 9
Net Worth: £6,522,837 *Total Assets:* £7,207,921
Registered Office: Trinity House, 7 Institute Street, Bolton, Lancs, BL1 1PZ
Activities: Activities of insurance agents and brokers
Shareholders: Barbara Mary Schofield; Keith Schofield
Officers: Barbara Mary Schofield, Secretary; Barbara Mary Schofield [1947] Director/Secretary; Jonathan Paul Schofield [1974] Director/Insurance Consultant; Keith Schofield [1946] Director; Mark James Schofield [1973] Director/Construction Manager; Philip David Schofield [1977] Director/Insurance Broker

Schosween 6 Limited
Incorporated: 25 May 2012
Net Worth: £8,068,402 *Total Assets:* £8,077,556
Registered Office: The East Wing, The Newhall, Newhall Way, Bradford, BD5 8FF
Activities: Financial management
Parent: Frank Marshall Estates Ltd
Officers: Frank Edward Marshall [1978] Director; James Ernest Marshall [1979] Director

A. Schulman Thermoplastic Compounds Limited
Incorporated: 20 July 1971 *Employees:* 102
Net Worth: £13,939,000 *Total Assets:* £22,067,000
Registered Office: 1 Kingsland Grange, Woolston, Warrington, Cheshire, WA1 4RA
Activities: Manufacture of plastics in primary forms
Parent: A. Schulman, Inc.
Officers: Kevin Jude Blake, Secretary; Sean Layton Bishop [1966] Director/General Manager; Heinrich Lingnau-Schneider [1962] Director [German]

Scoto Limited
Incorporated: 24 June 1999
Net Worth: £1,019,246,016 *Total Assets:* £1,612,699,008
Registered Office: c/o Stagecoach Services Limited, One Stockport Exchange, 20 Railway Road, Stockport, Cheshire, SK1 3SW
Activities: Activities of head offices
Parent: Stagecoach Transport Holdings Limited
Officers: Michael John Vaux, Secretary; Colin Brown [1968] Director/Accountant; John Connor Hamilton [1967] Director/Tax Accountant

Scotsland Limited
Incorporated: 5 October 1990
Net Worth: £1,156,182 *Total Assets:* £6,865,356
Registered Office: 6th Floor, Cardinal House, 20 St Mary's Parsonage, Manchester, M3 2LG
Activities: Other letting and operating of own or leased real estate
Shareholders: Arnold Henry; Alizah Neumann; Pinchas Neumann
Officers: Arnold Henry, Secretary; Arnold Henry [1959] Director; Esther Henry [1959] Director; Alizah Neumann [1960] Director; Henry Neumann [1956] Director; Judith Neumann [1952] Director

Robert Scott & Sons Limited
Incorporated: 27 February 1973 *Employees:* 228
Net Worth: £47,735,752 *Total Assets:* £54,973,388
Registered Office: Oak View Mills, Manchester Road, Greenfield, Oldham, Lancs, OL3 7HG
Activities: Manufacture of other textiles n.e.c.
Shareholders: Alastair Matthew Scott; Daniel Peter Scott
Officers: Daniel Peter Scott, Secretary; Frank Murphy [1955] Purchasing Director; Alastair Matthew Scott [1963] Sales Director; Ann Katherine Scott [1947] Director; Daniel Peter Scott [1973] Production Director; James Anthony Scott [1937] Director/Textile Manufacturer; Margaret Joyce Scott [1936] Director; Peter Robert Scott [1943] Director/Textile Manufacturer; Mark Smith [1964] Works Director

Harley Scott Holdings Limited
Incorporated: 3 January 2003 *Employees:* 48
Net Worth: £73,444 *Total Assets:* £18,954,078
Registered Office: Group First House, Mead Way, Padiham, Lancs, BB12 7NG
Activities: Other letting and operating of own or leased real estate
Parent: Group First Global Limited
Officers: Leanne Gregson [1979] Director/Completions Manager; John Slater [1978] Director; Toby Scott Whittaker [1977] Director

R. D. Scott Limited
Incorporated: 12 July 1983 *Employees:* 105
Net Worth: £7,943,000 *Total Assets:* £9,159,000
Registered Office: Hollinsbrook Way, Pilsworth, Bury, Lancs, BL9 8RR
Activities: Retail sale of clothing in specialised stores
Parent: JD Sports Fashion PLC
Officers: Siobhan Mawdsley, Secretary; Peter Alan Cowgill [1953] Director; Brian Michael Small [1956] Director

R & W Scott Ltd
Incorporated: 15 March 2004 *Employees:* 96
Net Worth: £1,891,108 *Total Assets:* £8,827,968
Registered Office: 61 Stephenson Way, Wavertree, Liverpool, L13 1HN
Activities: Other processing and preserving of fruit and vegetables
Parent: Real Good Food PLC
Officers: Harveen Rai, Secretary; Hugh Charles Laurence Cawley [1956] Director; Harveen Rai [1974] Director; Patrick George Ridgwell [1946] Director; Christopher Owen Thomas [1945] Director

ScottishPower (DCL) Limited
Incorporated: 7 January 1992
Net Worth: £55,600,000 *Total Assets:* £55,700,000
Registered Office: 3 Prenton Way, Prenton, Birkenhead, Merseyside, CH43 3ET
Activities: Production of electricity
Parent: Scottish Power Generation Holdings Limited
Officers: Alistair Orr, Secretary; Heather Chalmers White [1964] Director/Accountant; Oscar Fortis Pita [1970] Director [Spanish]

Scotts Hire Limited
Incorporated: 1 July 2008 *Employees:* 32
Net Worth: £4,477,790 *Total Assets:* £16,444,590
Registered Office: Alpha House, 4 Greek Street, Stockport, Cheshire, SK3 8AB
Activities: Renting and leasing of construction and civil engineering machinery and equipment
Shareholders: Martin Robert Smithson; Jane Elizabeth Smithson
Officers: Wayne Roberts [1975] Director; Martin Robert Smithson [1963] Director

Scusi Limited
Incorporated: 11 June 1999
Net Worth: £702,707,968 *Total Assets:* £894,097,984
Registered Office: c/o Stagecoach Services Limited, One Stockport Exchange, 20 Railway Road, Stockport, Cheshire, SK1 3SW
Activities: Activities of head offices
Parent: Scoto Limited
Officers: Michael John Vaux, Secretary; Colin Brown [1968] Director/Accountant; Bruce Dingwall [1983] Director/Accountant; John Connor Hamilton [1967] Director/Tax Manager; Andrew Jacques Levy [1963] Legal Director

SE Bury Lane Solar Limited
Incorporated: 8 May 2013
Net Worth: £6,377,387 *Total Assets:* £26,819,332
Registered Office: Eversheds House, 70 Great Bridgewater Street, Manchester, M1 5ES
Activities: Production of electricity
Parent: Sune Green Holdco7 Limited
Officers: Carl Goran Dandanell [1959] Director [Swedish]

Sea Park (Apart) Hotel Limited
Incorporated: 20 July 1979 *Employees:* 5
Net Worth: £2,230,351 *Total Assets:* £7,303,444
Registered Office: Unit 11 Mold Business Park, Wrexham Road, Mold, Flintshire, CH7 1XP
Activities: Hotels and similar accommodation
Parent: W.J. Limited
Officers: Damian James McGuinness, Secretary; Bernard Owen McGuinness [1931] Director/Property Manager; Damian James McGuinness [1974] Director/Property Manager

Seabrook Crisps Holdings Limited
Incorporated: 18 December 2002
Net Worth: £20,305,000 *Total Assets:* £22,242,000
Registered Office: Seabrook House, Duncombe Street, Bradford, W Yorks, BD8 9AJ
Activities: Other business support service activities n.e.c.
Parent: Seabrook Group Limited
Officers: Daniel Richard Woodwards, Secretary; Jonathan Bye [1963] Director/Chief Executive Officer; Makoto Ehara [1958] Director/Executive Vice President [Japanese]; Koichi Kikuchi [1963] Director/Senior Managing Executive Officer [Japanese]; Richard Anthony Robinson [1965] Director; Keiei Sho [1966] Director/Executive Officer [Japanese]; Jonathan Nigel Wood [1976] Commercial Director; Daniel Richard Woodwards [1977] Finance Director

Seabrook Crisps Limited
Incorporated: 31 August 1949 *Employees:* 134
Net Worth: £13,842,000 *Total Assets:* £18,430,000
Registered Office: Seabrook House, Duncombe Street, Bradford, W Yorks, BD8 9AJ
Activities: Processing and preserving of potatoes
Parent: Seabrook Crisps Holdings Limited
Officers: Daniel Richard Woodwards, Secretary; Jonathan Bye [1963] Director/Chief Executive Officer; Makoto Ehara [1958] Director/Executive Vice President [Japanese]; Koichi Kikuchi [1963] Director/Senior Managing Executive Officer [Japanese]; Richard Anthony Robinson [1965] Director; Keiei Sho [1966] Director/Executive Officer [Japanese]; Jonathan Nigel Wood [1976] Commercial Director; Daniel Richard Woodwards [1977] Finance Director

Seabrook Group Limited
Incorporated: 9 February 2006 *Employees:* 3
Net Worth Deficit: £3,647,000 *Total Assets:* £12,284,000
Registered Office: Seabrook House, Duncombe Street, Bradford, W Yorks, BD8 9AJ
Activities: Manufacture of other food products n.e.c.
Parent: Pacific Shelf 1809 Limited
Officers: Daniel Richard Woodwards, Secretary; Jonathan Bye [1963] Director/Chief Executive Officer; Makoto Ehara [1958] Director/Executive Vice President [Japanese]; Koichi Kikuchi [1963] Director/Senior Managing Executive Officer [Japanese]; Richard Anthony Robinson [1965] Director; Keiei Sho [1966] Director/Executive Officer [Japanese]; Jonathan Nigel Wood [1976] Commercial Director; Daniel Richard Woodwards [1977] Finance Director

Seacare Inverness Limited
Incorporated: 7 March 2016 *Employees:* 50
Net Worth: £62,976 *Total Assets:* £7,829,886
Registered Office: c/o Edwards Veeder (UK) Limited, Ground Floor, 4 Broadgate, Broadway Business Park, Chadderton, Oldham, Lancs, OL9 9XA
Activities: Hotels and similar accommodation
Parent: Seacare Hospitality (UK) Limited
Officers: Jee Hwee Foo [1967] Director/Chairman [Singaporean]; Soo Lee Koh [1971] Director [Singaporean]; Yingying Li [1983] Director [Singaporean]; Chui Hoon Neo [1968] Director [Singaporean]

Seafood Pub Company Group Limited
Incorporated: 15 June 2016
Net Worth Deficit: £157,172 *Total Assets:* £6,633,504
Registered Office: 8 Vantage Court, Riverside Way, Barrowford, Lancs, BB9 6BP
Activities: Public houses and bars
Parent: SPC Group Holdings Ltd
Officers: Ian Edward [1959] Director; William Torquil MacNaughton [1962] Director; William Andrew McLean [1960] Director; Joycelyn Rebecca Neve [1985] Director

Seaforth Power Limited
Incorporated: 20 July 1988
Net Worth: £3,292,000 *Total Assets:* £12,854,000
Registered Office: Maritime Centre, Port of Liverpool, L21 1LA
Activities: Transmission of electricity
Parent: Port of Sheerness Limited
Officers: Farook Akhtar Khan, Secretary; Caroline Ruth Marrison Gill, Secretary; Thomas Eardley Allison [1948] Director; Ian Graeme Lloyd Charnock [1962] Director; Mark Whitworth [1966] Director

Sealand Commercial Properties Limited
Incorporated: 22 September 2006
Net Worth Deficit: £2,454,859 *Total Assets:* £8,969,608
Registered Office: 68 Derby Street, Manchester, M8 8AT
Activities: Buying and selling of own real estate
Parent: Grasslake Ltd
Officers: James Andrew Dempsey, Secretary/Director; James Andrew Dempsey [1948] Director; Philip Maurice Estry [1936] Director

Seamark PLC
Incorporated: 22 January 1991 *Employees:* 181
Net Worth: £17,254,090 *Total Assets:* £32,695,992
Registered Office: Hulme Hall Lane, Lord North Street, Miles Platting, Manchester, M40 8AD
Activities: Processing and preserving of poultry meat
Shareholders: Bilal Ahmed; Iqbal Ahmed; Kamal Ahmed
Officers: Bilal Ahmed, Secretary; Bilal Ahmed [1964] Director; Iqbal Ahmed [1956] Managing Director; Kamal Ahmed [1960] Deputy Managing Director

Seamore Court Freehold Limited
Incorporated: 29 March 2007 *Employees:* 2
Net Worth: £5,223,007 *Total Assets:* £8,097,179
Registered Office: Cumberland House, Greenside Lane, Bradford, BD8 9TF
Activities: Management of real estate on a fee or contract basis
Major Shareholder: Alan James Lewis
Officers: Alan James Lewis [1938] Director/Chairman

Sean Louis Investments Limited
Incorporated: 24 June 1999
Net Worth: £2,278,543 *Total Assets:* £7,843,527
Registered Office: 1 Abbots Quay, Monks Ferry, Birkenhead, Merseyside, CH41 5LH
Activities: Renting and leasing of trucks and other heavy vehicles
Major Shareholder: Sean Ian Munro
Officers: Patricia Ann Beckett, Secretary; Sean Ian Munro [1985] Director

Searchlight Electric Limited
Incorporated: 8 May 1974 *Employees:* 165
Net Worth: £17,992,856 *Total Assets:* £23,197,760
Registered Office: Sidney House, 900 Oldham Road, Manchester, M40 2BS
Activities: Wholesale of household goods (other than musical instruments) n.e.c
Shareholders: Daniel Sigmund Hamburger; Herzl Eric Hamburger; David Martin Hamburger; Morris Emanuel Hamburger
Officers: David Martin Hamburger, Secretary; Daniel Sigmund Hamburger [1973] Business Development Director; David Martin Hamburger [1945] Director; Herzl Eric Hamburger [1941] Director/Chairman; Morris Emanuel Hamburger [1952] Sales Director; David Stuart Joyce [1960] Managing Director; David John Metcalfe [1966] Director/Accountant

Seashell Trust
Incorporated: 15 May 2001 *Employees:* 441
Net Worth: £19,783,000 *Total Assets:* £22,441,000
Registered Office: Stanley Road, Cheadle Hulme, Stockport, Cheshire, SK8 6RQ
Activities: Other education n.e.c.
Officers: Mark John Ascroft, Secretary; Edward Baines [1951] Director/Solicitor; Julie Vanessa Besbrode [1971] Director; Nicola Jane Bottley [1968] Director/Accountant; Gwen Carr [1955] Deputy Director Research Group University; Stephen Paul Gillingham [1969] Director of Property and Consultancy Group; Nicholas John Gower [1959] Director/Chartered Accountant; Doctor Afshan Naseem Khawaja [1970] Director/Doctor; Dr David Sanders [1949] Director/Local Government; David Charles Shipley [1943] Director; Christopher Luke Smale [1954] Director/Retired

Seatruck Ferries Holding Ltd
Incorporated: 15 September 2005 *Employees:* 86
Net Worth: £16,093,949 *Total Assets:* £98,825,416
Registered Office: North Quay, Port of Heysham, Morecambe, Lancs, LA3 2UH
Activities: Activities of head offices
Parent: Clipper Group A/S
Officers: Karen Elizabeth Donaldson, Secretary; Benjamin Simon Coppack [1960] Fleet Director; Karen Elizabeth Donaldson [1960] Director/Accountant; Alistair James Eagles [1970] Director; Jesper Kjaedegaard [1958] Director/Consultant [Danish]; Peter Lybecker [1953] Director/Chairman [Danish]; Peter Norborg [1966] Director/Group CEO [Danish]

Seatruck Ferries Ltd
Incorporated: 12 December 2005 *Employees:* 69
Net Worth: £6,020,779 *Total Assets:* £18,491,482
Registered Office: North Quay, Port of Heysham, Morecambe, Lancs, LA3 2UH
Activities: Sea and coastal freight water transport
Parent: Seatruck Ferries Holding Ltd
Officers: Karen Elizabeth Donaldson, Secretary; Karen Elizabeth Donaldson [1960] Director/Accountant; Alistair James Eagles [1970] Director; Peter Norborg [1966] Director/Group CEO [Danish]

Seatruck Panorama Ltd
Incorporated: 15 September 2005 *Employees:* 5
Net Worth: £2,699,418 *Total Assets:* £22,537,616
Registered Office: North Quay, Port of Heysham, Morecambe, Lancs, LA3 2UH
Activities: Sea and coastal freight water transport
Parent: Clipper Group A/S
Officers: Karen Elizabeth Donaldson, Secretary; Karen Elizabeth Donaldson [1960] Director; Alistair James Eagles [1970] Director; Peter Norborg [1966] Director/Group CEO [Danish]

Seatruck Pennant Ltd
Incorporated: 15 September 2005 *Employees:* 5
Net Worth: £6,196,607 *Total Assets:* £21,631,652
Registered Office: North Quay, Port of Heysham, Morecambe, Lancs, LA3 2UH
Activities: Sea and coastal freight water transport
Parent: Clipper Group A/S
Officers: Karen Elizabeth Donaldson, Secretary; Karen Elizabeth Donaldson [1960] Director/Accountant; Alistair James Eagles [1970] Director; Peter Norborg [1966] Director/Group CEO [Danish]

The Sebden Group Limited
Incorporated: 30 April 1996 *Employees:* 241
Net Worth: £18,465,000 *Total Assets:* £81,566,000
Registered Office: Craven House, Craven Road, Broadheath, Altrincham, Cheshire, WA14 5HE
Activities: Wholesale of metals and metal ores
Officers: Ronald Edward Hill [1948] Director; Bradley John Sanders [1963] Director [Australian]; Martin Christopher Weisselberg [1942] Director; Mark Philip Whitby [1958] Director

Sebden Steel Limited
Incorporated: 24 February 1995 *Employees:* 3
Net Worth: £4,120,000 *Total Assets:* £13,328,000
Registered Office: Craven House, Craven Road, Broadheath, Altrincham, Cheshire, WA14 5HE
Activities: Activities of head offices
Parent: The Sebden Group Ltd
Officers: Ronald Edward Hill [1948] Director; Bradley John Sanders [1963] Director/Accountant [Australian]; Martin Christopher Weisselberg [1942] Director

Sebden Steel Service Centres Limited
Incorporated: 30 October 1990 *Employees:* 186
Net Worth: £23,359,000 *Total Assets:* £82,470,000
Registered Office: Craven House, Craven Road, Broadheath, Altrincham, Cheshire, WA14 5HE
Activities: Wholesale of metals and metal ores
Parent: Sebden Steel Ltd
Officers: Ronald Edward Hill [1948] Director; Steven Hill [1971] Director; Craig Hodson [1969] Director; Mark McCausland [1969] Director; Bradley John Sanders [1963] Director/Accountant [Australian]; Anthony David Thomas Smith [1960] Director/Steel Stockholder; Mark Philip Whitby [1958] Director

Secret Potions Limited
Incorporated: 29 April 1999 *Employees:* 104
Net Worth: £2,656,586 *Total Assets:* £14,694,470
Registered Office: St Johns Chambers, Love Street, Chester, CH1 1QN
Activities: Dispensing chemist in specialised stores
Parent: Next Generation Health Limited
Officers: Purnima Rajesh Morjaria, Secretary/Systems Analyst; Purnima Rajesh Morjaria [1964] Director/Systems Analyst; Rajesh Mansulhial Morjaria [1964] Director/Pharmacist

Secured Express Limited
Incorporated: 16 July 2003 *Employees:* 257
Net Worth Deficit: £9,595,096 *Total Assets:* £28,141,278
Registered Office: Calver Road, Winwick Quay, Warrington, Cheshire, WA2 8UD
Activities: Licensed carriers
Parent: Delivery Group Holdings Limited
Officers: Jason Jones, Secretary; Ian Patrick Brewer [1965] Director; Paul David Carvell [1955] Director; Stephen Leslie Stokes [1964] Director; James Harvey Wilkins [1974] Director

Security Window Shutters Limited
Incorporated: 24 April 1987 *Employees:* 114
Net Worth: £7,696,221 *Total Assets:* £11,030,905
Registered Office: Hornby Road, Claughton, Lancaster, LA2 9LA
Activities: Manufacture of other fabricated metal products n.e.c.
Parent: CRH (UK) Limited
Officers: David Edmondson [1966] Director/Management Accountant; Kevin Russell-Lindeque [1973] Managing Director

Sedbergh School
Incorporated: 13 March 2000 *Employees:* 410
Net Worth: £17,839,000 *Total Assets:* £27,403,000
Registered Office: Sedbergh School, Malim Lodge, Sedbergh, Cumbria, LA10 5RY
Activities: Primary education
Officers: Peter Stephen Marshall, Secretary; The Venerable Nicholas John Willoughby Barker [1949] Director/Clerk in Holy Orders; Louise Bates [1959] Director/Retired Solicitor; Adrian Jeremy Norville Bedford [1968] Director/Investment Management; Hugh McGill Blair [1954] Director/Management Consultant; John Donington Campbell [1959] Director/Financial Services; Anna Louise Denney [1961] Director/Barrister; Ian Willcox Durrans [1958] Director/Consultant; Sir Michael Roger Gifford [1955] Director/Banker; Richard John Gledhill [1954] Director/Climate Change Consultant; Sir Andrew Richard Gregory [1957] Director/Chief Executive; Claire Theresa Hensman [1948] Non-Executive Director (Voluntary); Richard Noel Papworth [1964] Director/Retired Solicitor; Michael Ronald Piercy [1962] Director/Headmaster; John Henry Bernard Warburton-Lee [1963] Director/Photographer & Farmer; Dr Emma Jane Louise Waring [1977] Director/Academic

Seddon Construction Limited
Incorporated: 9 June 1998 *Employees:* 595
Net Worth: £35,674,376 *Total Assets:* £68,503,240
Registered Office: Plodder Lane, Edge Fold, Bolton, Lancs, BL4 0NN
Activities: Development of building projects
Parent: Seddon Group Ltd
Officers: Christopher John Wilcox, Secretary; Nicola Jane Hodkinson [1967] Director; Peter James Francis Jackson [1970] Director; Ian Alan William McGillivary [1970] Director; Ian Bruce Scott [1943] Director/Business Consultant; Jonathan Frank Seddon [1972] Director; Keith Waddington [1960] Director; Christopher John Wilcox [1977] Director; Duncan Richard Williams [1970] Director; Edward Charles Wootton [1971] Director

Seddon Engineering Holdings Limited
Incorporated: 25 March 2013 *Employees:* 113
Net Worth: £24,179,000 *Total Assets:* £29,187,000
Registered Office: Units A2-A6 Edge Fold Industrial Estate, Plodder Lane, Farnworth, Bolton, Lancs, BL4 0LR
Activities: Activities of head offices
Parent: Edgefold Holdings Limited
Officers: Sarah Jane Cook, Secretary; George Seddon [1939] Director; Stephen John Seddon [1966] Director; Kenton Lloyd Whitaker [1971] Director

Seddon Group Limited
Incorporated: 25 March 2013 *Employees:* 11
Net Worth: £58,828,000 *Total Assets:* £105,910,000
Registered Office: Seddon Building, Plodder Lane, Farnworth, Bolton, Lancs, BL4 0NN
Activities: Activities of head offices
Shareholders: Jonathan Frank Seddon; James Christopher Bruce Seddon; Nicola Jane Hodkinson
Officers: Colin William Edward Graham [1964] Director/Chartered Accountant; Jonathan Hugh Schofield [1961] Director; Ian Bruce Scott [1943] Director; Jonathan Frank Seddon [1972] Director; Keith Waddington [1960] Commercial Director

Seddon Homes Limited
Incorporated: 12 April 1995 *Employees:* 76
Net Worth: £12,661,000 *Total Assets:* £36,435,000
Registered Office: Birchwood One Business Park, Dewhurst Road, Birchwood, Warrington, Cheshire, WA3 7GB
Activities: Construction of domestic buildings
Parent: Seddon Group Limited
Officers: Stuart McLaughlin, Secretary; Colin William Edward Graham [1964] Director/Chartered Accountant; Michael Robert Jefferson [1974] Managing Director; Stuart McLaughlin [1962] Director/Accountant; Jonathan Frank Seddon [1972] Director

Seddon Investments Limited
Incorporated: 29 June 2016
Net Worth: £220 *Total Assets:* £19,601,600
Registered Office: Arden Lea, 470 Chorley New Road, Heaton, Bolton, Lancs, BL1 5AZ
Activities: Buying and selling of own real estate
Shareholder: Wayne Seddon
Officers: Wayne Seddon [1958] Director

Seddons (Plant and Engineers) Limited
Incorporated: 8 September 1951 *Employees:* 82
Net Worth: £5,212,743 *Total Assets:* £7,419,283
Registered Office: Units A2-A6 Edge Fold Industrial Estate, Plodder Lane, Farnworth, Bolton, Lancs, BL4 0LR
Activities: Wholesale of other machinery and equipment
Parent: Seddon Engineering Holdings Limited
Officers: Sarah Jane Cook, Secretary; Stephen Charles Brown [1963] Director/Engineer; Paul Alan Goulbourne [1953] Director; Stephen John Seddon [1966] Director; Lee Robert Wright [1971] Commercial Director

Sefton Holdings Limited
Incorporated: 25 January 1957 *Employees:* 1
Net Worth: £10,529,304 *Total Assets:* £15,646,317
Registered Office: 12 Molyneux Way, Aintree, Sefton, Merseyside, L10 2JA
Activities: Buying and selling of own real estate
Officers: Margaret Gough, Secretary; Marcus Julian Romaine Bleasdale [1962] Director

Selbourne Group Limited
Incorporated: 5 January 1998 *Employees:* 10
Net Worth: £6,149,956 *Total Assets:* £13,127,143
Registered Office: 6th Floor, Cardinal House, 20 St Mary's Parsonage, Manchester, M3 2LG
Activities: Other letting and operating of own or leased real estate
Major Shareholder: Rita Dorothy de Massey
Officers: Rita Dorothy de Massey, Secretary/Director; Michael Charles de Massey [1979] Director/Chartered Surveyor; Rita Dorothy de Massey [1945] Director

Selden Research Limited
Incorporated: 10 July 1970 *Employees:* 172
Net Worth: £11,502,559 *Total Assets:* £17,866,424
Registered Office: Staden Business Park, Staden Lane, Buxton, Derbys, SK17 9RZ
Activities: Manufacture of soap and detergents
Shareholders: Sandra Buchanan Woodhead; Denis Edwin Woodhead
Officers: Sandra Buchanan Woodhead, Secretary; David Alexander Woodhead [1967] Works Director; Denis Edwin Woodhead [1937] Director Industrial Chemist; Mark Andrew Woodhead [1963] Sales Director; Peter Philip Woodhead [1975] Technical Director; Sandra Buchanan Woodhead [1942] Director Secretary

Select Group International Limited
Incorporated: 3 October 2001
Net Worth: £5,970,483 *Total Assets:* £13,330,788
Registered Office: The Box, Horseshoe Lane, Alderley Edge, Cheshire, SK9 7QP
Activities: Activities of head offices
Parent: Select Group International (Holdings) Limited
Officers: Giles Peter Beswick, Secretary/Director; Giles Peter Beswick [1974] Director; Mark Stephen Littlewood [1977] Director; Mark David Stott [1972] Director

Select International Developments Limited
Incorporated: 10 June 2005
Net Worth: £11,025 *Total Assets:* £11,977,001
Registered Office: The Box, Horseshoe Lane, Alderley Edge, Cheshire, SK9 7QP
Activities: Development of building projects
Parent: Select International Developments (Holdings) Limited
Officers: Giles Peter Beswick, Secretary; Giles Peter Beswick [1974] Director; Mark Stephen Littlewood [1977] Director; Mark David Stott [1972] Managing Director

Select Property Group (Holdings) Limited
Incorporated: 25 March 2014 *Employees:* 226
Net Worth: £11,229,000 *Total Assets:* £311,984,992
Registered Office: The Box, Horseshoe Lane, Alderley Edge, Cheshire, SK9 7QP
Activities: Buying and selling of own real estate
Major Shareholder: Mark David Stott
Officers: Giles Beswick, Secretary; Mark Christopher Dawson [1973] Director; Natalia Alexandrovna Markelova [1979] Director [Russian]; Angus Monro [1949] Director; Trevor Philip Moore [1969] Director; Mark Jonathan Oakes [1971] Director; Michael Keith Slater [1974] Director; Mark David Stott [1972] Director

Select Property Group Limited
Incorporated: 12 March 2004 *Employees:* 183
Net Worth Deficit: £22,079,000 *Total Assets:* £50,916,000
Registered Office: The Box, Horseshoe Lane, Alderley Edge, Cheshire, SK9 7QP
Activities: Management of real estate on a fee or contract basis
Officers: Giles Peter Beswick, Secretary/Director; Giles Peter Beswick [1974] Operations Director; Mark Christopher Dawson [1973] Director; Mark Stephen Littlewood [1977] Director; Mark David Stott [1972] Director

Select Sites Limited
Incorporated: 18 March 1955
Net Worth: £901,000 *Total Assets:* £32,280,000
Registered Office: Chelford House, Rudheath Way, Rudheath, Northwich, Cheshire, CW9 7LN
Activities: Other service activities n.e.c.
Parent: Eurocamp Limited
Officers: Alain Yvon Calme [1966] Director [French]; Stijn Hendrik Marc Depraetere [1975] Director [Belgian]; Darren Paul Marsh [1975] Director

Sellafield Limited
Incorporated: 16 February 1971 *Employees:* 10,959
Total Assets: £1,132,999,936
Registered Office: Hinton House, Birchwood Park Avenue, Risley, Warrington, Cheshire, WA3 6GR
Activities: Other service activities n.e.c.
Officers: Andrew Michael Carr, Secretary; Lorraine Ingrid Baldry [1949] Director; John Baxter [1951] Director/Retired Chartered Engineer; Dr Dolores Byrne [1950] Director; Dr Anne-Marie Françoise Jeanne Choho [1965] Director/Industry Executive [French]; Martin John Chown [1971] Supply Chain Director; Alan Douglas Cumming [1962] Director/Civil Engineer; Paul Foster [1967] Director/Chief Executive Officer; Jonathan Michael Seddon [1956] Finance Director; Nigel Watkin Roberts Smith [1954] Director; Duncan Michael Thompson [1967] Director

Sellick Partnership Limited
Incorporated: 7 February 2001 *Employees:* 81
Net Worth: £618,203 *Total Assets:* £7,301,917
Registered Office: Queens Court, 24 Queen Street, Manchester, M2 5HX
Activities: Other business support service activities n.e.c.
Parent: Sellick Partnership Group Limited
Officers: Hannah Cottam [1974] Director; Marianne Jane Sellick [1975] Director; Thomas Jolyon Letts Sellick [1970] Director/Recruitment Consultant; Ray Wareing [1970] Director

Selmar Properties Ltd
Incorporated: 2 March 2005 *Employees:* 6
Net Worth: £3,524,662 *Total Assets:* £8,224,134
Registered Office: 20 St Marys Parsonage, Manchester, M3 2LG
Activities: Development of building projects
Major Shareholder: Terry Malcolm Krell
Officers: Hilary Jan Krell, Secretary; Georgia Megan Krell [1990] Director/Trainee Solicitor; Terry Malcolm Krell [1953] Director/Chartered Surveyor

Semara Contract Services Limited
Incorporated: 15 October 1964
Net Worth: £28,380,000 *Total Assets:* £29,016,000
Registered Office: Johnson House, Abbots Park, Monks Way, Preston Brook, Runcorn, Cheshire, WA7 3GH
Activities: Activities of head offices
Parent: Semara Group Limited
Officers: Yvonne May Monaghan, Secretary; Yvonne May Monaghan [1958] Director; Timothy James Morris [1977] Director/Accountant

Semara Group Limited
Incorporated: 14 August 1984
Net Worth: £243,012,992 *Total Assets:* £254,644,992
Registered Office: Johnson House, Abbots Park, Monks Way, Preston Brook, Runcorn, Cheshire, WA7 3GH
Activities: Non-trading company
Parent: Johnson Investment Limited
Officers: Yvonne May Monaghan, Secretary; Yvonne May Monaghan [1958] Director; Timothy James Morris [1977] Director/Accountant

Semara Investments Limited
Incorporated: 29 October 1965
Net Worth: £109,229,000 *Total Assets:* £109,229,000
Registered Office: Johnson House, Abbots Park, Monks Way, Preston Brook, Runcorn, Cheshire, WA7 3GH
Activities: Activities of head offices
Parent: Johnson Investment Limited
Officers: Yvonne May Monaghan, Secretary; Yvonne May Monaghan [1958] Director; Timothy James Morris [1977] Director/Accountant

Senator International Limited
Incorporated: 1 August 1977 *Employees:* 1,403
Net Worth: £65,809,000 *Total Assets:* £115,418,000
Registered Office: Syke Side Drive, Altham Business Park, Accrington, Lancs, BB5 5YE
Activities: Manufacture of other furniture
Major Shareholder: Colin Mustoe
Officers: Robert James Mustoe, Secretary/Company Executive; Julia Elizabeth Davies [1979] Director; Colin George Mustoe [1945] Director; Janice Mustoe [1946] Director/Secretary; Robert James Mustoe [1972] Director/Company Executive; Kristian Roberts [1979] Finance Director

Seneca Secured Lending Limited
Incorporated: 16 October 2013 *Employees:* 7
Net Worth: £19,412,236 *Total Assets:* £19,725,848
Registered Office: 12 The Parks, Haydock, Newton-le-Willows, Merseyside, WA12 0JQ
Activities: Financial intermediation not elsewhere classified
Officers: Richard Edward Manley [1979] Director; Timothy Daniel Murphy [1965] Director

Seneca Securities Ltd
Incorporated: 12 November 2012
Net Worth: £71,725 *Total Assets:* £28,214,876
Registered Office: 12 The Parks, Haydock, Merseyside, WA12 0JQ
Activities: Financial intermediation not elsewhere classified
Parent: Seneca Finance Limited
Officers: Mark Alan Hopton [1966] Director/Chartered Accountant; Richard Edward Manley [1979] Director

Sensormatic Commercial/Industrial Limited
Incorporated: 27 April 1992 *Employees:* 7
Net Worth: £2,725,999 *Total Assets:* £21,878,942
Registered Office: Tyco Park, Grimshaw Lane, Newton Heath, Manchester, M40 2WL
Activities: Other business support service activities n.e.c.
Parent: Johnson Controls International PLC
Officers: Mark Ayre [1963] Finance Director; Philip Dashey [1971] Director/VP & General Manager

Sentinel Performance Solutions Group Limited
Incorporated: 17 November 2010 *Employees:* 68
Net Worth Deficit: £851,000 *Total Assets:* £20,483,000
Registered Office: 7650 Daresbury Park, Daresbury, Warrington, Cheshire, WA4 4BS
Activities: Manufacture of other chemical products n.e.c.
Shareholder: Epiris Managers LLP
Officers: Nicholas Paul Brayshaw [1955] Director; Charles Edward Nicholas Elkington [1970] Director; Steve Mark Goodwin [1961] Director/Chief Executive; Arvind Tewari [1985] Director/Investment Manager

Sentinel Performance Solutions Limited
Incorporated: 22 April 2005 *Employees:* 66
Net Worth: £17,916,000 *Total Assets:* £28,729,000
Registered Office: 7650 Daresbury Park, Daresbury, Warrington, Cheshire, WA4 4BS
Activities: Manufacture of other chemical products n.e.c.
Shareholder: Epiris Managers LLP
Officers: Steve Mark Goodwin [1961] Director/Chief Executive; Gary James Roebuck [1968] Director/C O O

Servicepower Business Solutions Limited
Incorporated: 14 October 1996 *Employees:* 42
Net Worth Deficit: £14,925,000 *Total Assets:* £8,753,000
Registered Office: Petersgate House, St Petersgate, Stockport, Cheshire, SK1 [illegible]HE
Activities: Other information technology service activities
Parent: Diversis Capital Ltd
Officers: Kevin Daekyung Ma [1985] Director [American]; Ron Nayot [1978] Director [Canadian]

Servlite U.K. Limited
Incorporated: 22 July 1991 *Employees:* 66
Net Worth: £1,958,840 *Total Assets:* £8,644,061
Registered Office: Wardley Industrial Estate, Priestly Road, Worsley, Manchester, M28 2LX
Activities: Wholesale of furniture, carpets and lighting equipment
Parent: Aidenhall Ltd
Officers: Paul Adam Abrahams, Secretary/Salesman; Paul Adam Abrahams [1960] Director/Salesman; Paul Isaacs [1960] Director/Accountant; Dean Barnett Miller [1964] Sales Director

Setco Automotive (UK) Limited
Incorporated: 18 November 2005 *Employees:* 29
Net Worth: £90[illegible],088 *Total Assets:* £7,480,068
Registered Office: Lipe Clutch Division, York Avenue, Haslingden, Rossendale, Lancs, BB4 4HU
Activities: Manufacture of other parts and accessories for motor vehicles
Officers: John Clement Wibberley, Secretary; Udit Harish Sheth [1979] Director/General Manager [Indian]; John Barry Sumner [1959] Director

Seven Scent Limited
Incorporated: 16 June 1960 *Employees:* 38
Net Worth: £1,585,000 *Total Assets:* £17,160,000
Registered Office: Agecroft Commerce Park, Lamplight Way, Swinton, Manchester, M27 8UJ
Activities: Other manufacturing n.e.c.
Parent: PZ Cussons (Holdings) Limited
Officers: Martyn John Campbell, Secretary; Andrew Bowie [1966] Director; Brandon Howard Leigh [1971] Director; Simon Paul Plant [1969] Director/Company Secretary

Seventh Continent Limited
Incorporated: 17 June 2010
Net Worth Deficit: £6,033 *Total Assets:* £10,905,999
Registered Office: Suite 2, 5th Floor, Marshall House, Ring Way, Preston, Lancs, PR1 2QD
Activities: Ready-made interactive leisure and entertainment software development
Major Shareholder: Dr Gergely Adam Harmati
Officers: Gergely Adam Harmati [1969] Director [Hungarian]

SG World Limited
Incorporated: 20 October 1997 *Employees:* 149
Net Worth: £2,119,163 *Total Assets:* £6,862,820
Registered Office: Arnold Haase House, Duchy Road, Crewe, Cheshire, CW1 6ND
Activities: Manufacture of paper stationery
Major Shareholder: Mark Paul Haase
Officers: Debbie Brandon-Sweeney, Secretary; Mark Paul Haase [1961] Director/Chief Executive Officer; Douglas Hayes Kinsman [1970] Operations Director; Richard Nichols [1983] UK Sales & Marketing Director

SGL (Finance) Limited
Incorporated: 7 July 2004 *Employees:* 3
Net Worth Deficit: £94,582,000 *Total Assets:* £107,973,000
Registered Office: 1-5 Beaufort Road, Birkenhead, Merseyside, CH41 1HQ
Activities: Activities of head offices
Officers: Sally Lewis, Secretary; John Cyril George Stocker [1967] Director/Chief Operations Officer; Brian Mark Stringer [1963] Director/Chief Operating Officer

SGL (Holdings) Limited
Incorporated: 7 July 2004
Net Worth: £18,097,000 *Total Assets:* £170,431,008
Registered Office: 1-5 Beaufort Road, Birkenhead, Merseyside, CH41 1HQ
Activities: Activities of head offices
Officers: Sally Lewis, Secretary; John Cyril George Stocker [1967] Director/Chief Operations Officer; Brian Mark Stringer [1963] Director/Chief Operating Officer

SGS Ashby Ltd
Incorporated: 18 November 2008 *Employees:* 183
Net Worth: £10,125,000 *Total Assets:* £13,203,000
Registered Office: c/o SGS United Kingdom Limited, Rossmore Business Park, Inward Way, Ellesmere Port, Wirral, Merseyside, CH65 3EN
Activities: Technical testing and analysis
Parent: SGS Holding UK Ltd
Officers: Catherine Anne Aldag, Secretary; Catherine Jane Griffiths [1970] Director/Chartered Accountant; James McGurk [1972] Managing Director

SGS Holding UK Ltd
Incorporated: 5 November 1998
Net Worth: £88,079,000 *Total Assets:* £99,058,000
Registered Office: Rossmore Business Park, Ellesmere Port, Cheshire, CH65 3EN
Activities: Other professional, scientific and technical activities n.e.c.
Parent: SGS Group Management SA
Officers: Catherine Anne Aldag, Secretary; Catherine Jane Griffiths [1970] Director/Accountant; James McGurk [1972] Managing Director

SGS United Kingdom Limited
Incorporated: 16 December 1974 *Employees:* 1,255
Net Worth: £26,828,000 *Total Assets:* £149,310,000
Registered Office: Rossmore Business Park, Ellesmere Port, Cheshire, CH65 3EN
Activities: Other professional, scientific and technical activities n.e.c.
Parent: SGS Holding UK Ltd
Officers: Catherine Anne Aldag, Secretary; Catherine Jane Griffiths [1970] Director/Accountant; James McGurk [1972] Managing Director

Shakespeare Monofilament UK Limited
Incorporated: 15 December 1989 *Employees:* 26
Net Worth: £14,248,942 *Total Assets:* £16,595,713
Registered Office: Enterprise Way, Venture Road, Fleetwood, Lancs, FY7 8RY
Activities: Manufacture of man-made fibres
Parent: Newell Brands
Officers: Benjamin James Sturgell [1981] Director/Attorney [American]

Shared Access Ltd
Incorporated: 16 August 2007 *Employees:* 43
Net Worth Deficit: £13,961,431 *Total Assets:* £21,660,852
Registered Office: Eversheds LLP, Eversheds House, 70 Great Bridgewater Street, Manchester, M1 5ES
Activities: Other telecommunications activities
Parent: The Goldman Sachs Group, Inc
Officers: Stephen Harl Clark [1944] Director [American]; Christopher Leslie Jackman [1951] Director

Sharples School A Multi Academy Trust
Incorporated: 8 July 2015 *Employees:* 99
Net Worth: £15,038,937 *Total Assets:* £17,250,852
Registered Office: Sharples School, Hill Cot Road, Sharples, Bolton, Lancs, BL1 8SN
Activities: General secondary education
Officers: Catherine Ingram, Secretary; Lesley Ann Hart [1966] Director/Vice Principal - Finance & Resources; Lesley Ann Hart [1966] Director/Vice Principal - Finance & Resources; James Heyes [1967] Director/Driver; John Kirk Shepley [1944] Director/Retired; Dr Leigh Vallance [1961] Director/Charity Worker; Ann Webster [1966] Director/Headteacher; Christine Wild [1945] Director/Retired

John Shaw and Son Limited
Incorporated: 1 February 1972 *Employees:* 194
Net Worth: £10,166,277 *Total Assets:* £16,643,836
Registered Office: The Coach and Travel Centre, Scotland Road, Carnforth, Lancs, LA5 9RQ
Activities: Other urban, suburban or metropolitan passenger land transport (not underground, metro or similar)
Parent: Zircon Holdings Limited
Officers: Pamela Shaw, Secretary; John Paul Shaw [1970] Operations Director; Mark Robert Shaw [1979] Director; Pamela Shaw [1958] Director; Robert Richard Shaw [1948] Director

Shawston Holdings Limited
Incorporated: 7 July 2005 *Employees:* 114
Net Worth: £3,086,396 *Total Assets:* £11,450,229
Registered Office: Suite 35, The Forum, Tameside Business Park, Windmill Lane, Denton, Manchester, M34 3QS
Activities: Manufacture of metal structures and parts of structures
Shareholders: Christopher Borkett; Robert George Davenport; Michelle Denise Davenport
Officers: Christopher Borkett [1954] Director; Michelle Denise Davenport [1971] Director; Robert George Davenport [1969] Director; Graham Wilkins [1969] Director

Shawston International Limited
Incorporated: 12 July 2001
Net Worth: £2,651,020 *Total Assets:* £8,738,619
Registered Office: Suite 35, The Forum, Tameside Business Park, Windmill Lane, Denton, Manchester, M34 3QS
Activities: Wholesale of hardware, plumbing and heating equipment and supplies
Parent: Shawston Holdings Limited
Officers: Michelle Denise Davenport [1971] Director; Robert George Davenport [1969] Director; Graham Wilkins [1969] Director

Shearings Group Limited
Incorporated: 28 October 2004 *Employees:* 4
Net Worth: £12,283,000 *Total Assets:* £88,844,000
Registered Office: Waterside House, Waterside Drive, Wigan, Lancs, WN3 5AZ
Activities: Activities of head offices
Parent: Specialist Leisure Group Limited
Officers: Richard James Calvert [1967] Director; Vincent Flower [1960] Director; Graham John Rogers [1963] Director; Gary Speakman [1961] Finance Director

Shearings Holidays Limited
Incorporated: 30 December 1926
Net Worth Deficit: £5,544,000 *Total Assets:* £61,265,000
Registered Office: Waterside House, Waterside Drive, Wigan, Lancs, WN3 5AZ
Activities: Other service activities incidental to land transportation, n.e.c.
Parent: Shearings Group Limited
Officers: Richard James Calvert [1967] Director; Vincent Flower [1960] Director; Graham John Rogers [1963] Director; Gary Speakman [1961] Finance Director

Shearings Limited
Incorporated: 12 March 1963 *Employees:* 529
Net Worth: £34,107,000 *Total Assets:* £46,292,000
Registered Office: Waterside House, Waterside Drive, Wigan, Lancs, WN3 5AZ
Activities: Other urban, suburban or metropolitan passenger land transport (not underground, metro or similar)
Parent: Shearings Holidays Limited
Officers: Christopher Brown [1967] Operations Director; Richard James Calvert [1967] Director; Vincent Flower [1960] Director; Graham John Rogers [1963] Director; Gary Speakman [1961] Finance Director

Sheet Piling (UK) Limited
Incorporated: 20 November 2012 *Employees:* 44
Net Worth: £1,780,261 *Total Assets:* £12,166,134
Registered Office: Oakfield House, Rough Hey Road, Grimsargh, Preston, Lancs, PR2 5AR
Activities: Other specialised construction activities n.e.c.
Major Shareholder: Andrew Cotton
Officers: Andrew John Cotton, Secretary; Andrew John Cotton [1976] Director/Engineer; Andrew James Foy [1973] Construction Director; John Oliver Hull [1946] Director/Chairman; Jonathan Charles Mitchell [1964] Commercial Director; Imran Patel [1982] Finance Director

Sheffield & Regional Properties Limited
Incorporated: 15 February 2006 *Employees:* 5
Net Worth: £4,087,628 *Total Assets:* £21,394,052
Registered Office: Warth Business Centre, Warth Industrial Park, Warth Road, Bury, Lancs, BL9 9TB
Activities: Buying and selling of own real estate
Major Shareholder: Bernard Christopher Norman Roger Holmes
Officers: Richard Harvey James Nuttall, Secretary; Ian Elliott [1969] Director; Bernard Christopher Norman Roger Holmes [1945] Director; Richard Harvey James Nuttall [1965] Director; Paul Raymond Williams [1956] Director

Sheffield Investment Company Limited.(The)
Incorporated: 17 December 1919 *Employees:* 3
Net Worth: £9,234,558 *Total Assets:* £9,742,970
Registered Office: The Copper Room, Deva Centre, Trinity Way, Manchester, M3 7BG
Activities: Other letting and operating of own or leased real estate
Officers: Robert Michael Peasegood, Secretary; Charles Roland John Dewhurst [1953] Director; Margaret Joan Peasegood [1951] Director; Robert Michael Peasegood [1954] Director and Company Secretary

Sherborne Upholstery Limited
Incorporated: 6 June 1953 *Employees:* 258
Net Worth: £13,255,365 *Total Assets:* £15,311,740
Registered Office: Pasture Lane, Clayton, Bradford, W Yorks, BD14 6LT
Activities: Manufacture of other furniture
Shareholders: Christopher David Fort; Kathleen Fort
Officers: Daniel Edward Atkinson, Secretary; Daniel Edward Atkinson [1970] Financial Director; Christopher David Fort [1954] Managing Director; Kathleen Fort [1929] Director/Married Woman; Christopher Walker [1967] Production Director

Sherwin-Williams Protective & Marine Coatings
Incorporated: 30 November 1966 *Employees:* 233
Net Worth: £17,994,754 *Total Assets:* £37,814,504
Registered Office: Tower Works, Kestor Street, Bolton, Lancs, BL2 2AL
Activities: Manufacture of paints, varnishes and similar coatings, mastics and sealants
Parent: The Sherwin-Williams Company
Officers: Ezio Nicola Giacomo Braggio [1956] Director/President EMEAI, Corporate Vice President [Italian]; Jeffrey James Miklich [1974] Director/Business Executive [American]; Allen Joseph Mistysyn [1968] Director/Business Executive [American]; Matthew Palmer [1972] Finance Director; Ian Walker [1963] Director/General Manager

Sherwood Homes Limited
Incorporated: 10 January 2013 *Employees:* 7
Net Worth Deficit: £6,813,019 *Total Assets:* £14,844,865
Registered Office: Houldsworth Mill Business and Arts Centre, Houldsworth Street, Stockport, Cheshire, SK5 6DA
Activities: Buying and selling of own real estate
Officers: David Burnett Scott [1946] Director

Shimadzu Europe Ltd.
Incorporated: 25 July 1997
Net Worth: £13,277,799 *Total Assets:* £13,290,475
Registered Office: Wharfside, Trafford Wharf Road, Manchester, M17 1GP
Activities: Activities of other holding companies n.e.c.
Parent: Shimadzu Corporation
Officers: Izumi Nakai [1965] Director [Japanese]; Kozo Shimazu [1948] Director [Japanese]; Jiro Takashima [1960] Director [Japanese]

Shoo 553 Limited
Incorporated: 30 September 2011
Net Worth: £57,284,000 *Total Assets:* £63,580,000
Registered Office: Eversheds House, 70 Great Bridgewater Street, Manchester, M1 5ES
Activities: Manufacture of other paper and paperboard containers
Parent: Graphic Packaging International Limited
Officers: Stephen Richard Scherger [1964] Director [American]; Lauren Tashma [1966] Director/Business Executive [American]; Eveline Maria Van de Rovaart [1975] Director/Legal Secretary [Dutch]; Hilde Maria Willy Van Moeseke [1970] Director/Business Executive [Belgian]; Joseph Paul Yost [1967] Director/Vice President [American]

Shop Direct Finance Company Limited
Incorporated: 10 February 2003 *Employees:* 772
Net Worth: £250,300,000 *Total Assets:* £1,792,899,968
Registered Office: Aintree Innovation Centre, Park Lane, Netherton, Bootle, Merseyside, L30 1SL
Activities: Other credit granting n.e.c.
Parent: Shop Direct Group Financial Services Limited
Officers: Richard Lee Banks [1951] Director; Neil Chandler [1971] Director/Financial Services Executive; Katrina Jane Machin [1966] Director/VP General Manager American Express Global Business; Graham Lloyd Singleton [1963] Director

Shop Direct Group Financial Services Limited
Incorporated: 9 August 2004 *Employees:* 5
Net Worth: £375,000,000 *Total Assets:* £450,000,000
Registered Office: First Floor, Skyways House, Speke Road, Speke, Liverpool, L70 1AB
Activities: Financial intermediation not elsewhere classified
Parent: Shop Direct Limited
Officers: Aidan Stuart Barclay [1956] Director; Howard Myles Barclay [1959] Director; Philip Leslie Peters [1957] Director; Michael Seal [1948] Director; Stuart Andrew Winton [1964] Director

Shop Direct Home Shopping Limited
Incorporated: 11 February 2003 *Employees:* 2,792
Net Worth: £317,800,000 *Total Assets:* £1,418,499,968
Registered Office: First Floor, Skyways House, Speke Road, Speke, Liverpool, L70 1AB
Activities: Retail sale via mail order houses or via Internet
Parent: Littlewoods Limited
Officers: Aidan Stuart Barclay [1956] Director; Howard Myles Barclay [1959] Director; Philip Leslie Peters [1957] Director; Michael Seal [1948] Director; Stuart Andrew Winton [1964] Director

Shop Direct Limited
Incorporated: 11 April 2003 *Employees:* 3,869
Net Worth: £199,900,000 *Total Assets:* £2,814,299,904
Registered Office: First Floor, Skyways House, Speke Road, Speke, Liverpool, L70 1AB
Activities: Activities of head offices
Parent: Shop Direct Holdings Limited
Officers: Aidan Stuart Barclay [1956] Director; Howard Myles Barclay [1959] Director; Philip Leslie Peters [1957] Director/Businessman; Michael Seal [1948] Director; Stuart Andrew Winton [1964] Director

Shorrock Trichem Limited
Incorporated: 14 March 2001 *Employees:* 277
Net Worth: £9,309,733 *Total Assets:* £16,001,280
Registered Office: Chanters Industrial Estate, Atherton, Manchester, M46 9SD
Activities: Manufacture of soap and detergents
Shareholder: Keith Entwistle Shorrock
Officers: Joel Howard Lewis, Secretary; David Paul Allison [1964] Technical Director; Caron Michelle Darlington [1966] Director; Malcolm Denning [1939] Director; Ian James Eckersley [1959] Managing Director; Duncan Fishwick [1966] Sales Director; Joel Howard Lewis [1941] Managing Director; David Lee Oliver [1976] Finance Director; Keith Entwistle Shorrock [1936] Director

Shred-It Limited
Incorporated: 4 August 2000 *Employees:* 709
Net Worth: £63,683,968 *Total Assets:* £93,035,752
Registered Office: Ground Floor, 177 Cross Street, Sale, Cheshire, M33 7JQ
Activities: Other business support service activities n.e.c.
Parent: Stericycle International Holdings Ltd
Officers: John Schetz, Secretary; Charles Anthony Alutto [1965] Director [American]; Brent Arnold [1968] Director/Employee and Officer of Stericycle, Inc [American]; Daniel Ginnetti [1968] Director [American]; Robert John Guice [1966] Director/Manager

SHS International Ltd
Incorporated: 6 October 1910 *Employees:* 332
Net Worth: £52,173,000 *Total Assets:* £74,913,000
Registered Office: 100 Wavertree Boulevard, Liverpool, L7 9PT
Activities: Manufacture of homogenized food preparations and dietetic food
Parent: Scientific Hospital Supplies Holdings Limited
Officers: Paul Michael Bromilow [1980] Director/Accountant; Tanya Selma Hene [1975] Director/Chemical Engineer [Dutch]

Shudehill Hotel Company Limited
Incorporated: 10 March 2005 *Employees:* 102
Net Worth: £21,150,096 *Total Assets:* £49,213,072
Registered Office: 62 Castle Street, Liverpool, L2 7LQ
Activities: Hotels and similar accommodation
Parent: Foremount Company
Officers: Mark Simon Sutton, Secretary; Mark Christopher Foster [1964] Managing Director; Dennis Paul Kennedy [1943] Director [Irish]; Donal Ring [1946] Director [Irish]; Mark Simon Sutton [1971] Director/Accountant

Shurooq Limited
Incorporated: 12 August 2016 *Employees:* 73
Net Worth Deficit: £150,610 *Total Assets:* £24,284,686
Registered Office: RMI Accountancy, Blue Tower, Media City, Manchester, M50 2ST
Activities: Hotels and similar accommodation
Officers: Ahmed Elgharib, Secretary; Khalaf Ahmed Al Otaiba [1941] Director/Investor [Emirati]

Siae Microelettronica Limited
Incorporated: 21 December 1995 *Employees:* 60
Net Worth: £2,442,356 *Total Assets:* £8,754,082
Registered Office: Ramsbrook Farm, Ramsbrook Lane, Widnes, Cheshire, WA8 8NZ
Activities: Wireless telecommunications activities
Parent: SIAE Microelettronica SpA
Officers: Kenneth O'Neil Anderson, Secretary; Alberto Mascetti [1959] Director/Chairman [Italian]; Enrico Mascetti [1963] Director [Italian]; Giovanni Mascetti [1965] Director [Italian]

Sibelco Minerals and Chemicals (Holdings) Limited
Incorporated: 15 May 1951
Net Worth: £12,912,627 *Total Assets:* £24,547,188
Registered Office: Brookside Hall, Congleton Road, Sandbach, Cheshire, CW11 4TF
Activities: Other mining and quarrying n.e.c.
Parent: Watts Blake Bearne & Co. Limited
Officers: Mark Christopher James [1959] Director; John Willem Van Put [1962] Director/Chief Executive Officer Sibelco Europe [Dutch]

Sibelco UK Limited
Incorporated: 18 February 1957 *Employees:* 407
Net Worth: £16,840,402 *Total Assets:* £114,482,056
Registered Office: Brookside Hall, Congleton Road, Sandbach, Cheshire, CW11 4TF
Activities: Operation of gravel and sand pits; mining of clays and kaolin
Parent: Sibelco Minerals and Chemicals (Holdings) Limited
Officers: Mark Peter Addiscott [1976] Finance Director; Kurt Jean-Emile Elise Decat [1965] Director/Group Chief Financial Officer Sibelco [Belgian]; Jean-Luc Andre Victor Deleersnyder [1961] Director [Belgian]; Jacques Emsens [1963] Director [Belgian]; Mark Christopher James [1959] Director; Felix Moreno Diaz [1962] Director [Spanish]; John Willem Van Put [1962] Director/Chief Executive Officer Sibelco Europe [Dutch]

Sidcot Group Ltd
Incorporated: 16 February 2005 *Employees:* 103
Net Worth: £4,200,716 *Total Assets:* £24,485,500
Registered Office: Unit 5 Woodstock Business Park, Meek Street, Royton, Oldham, Lancs, OL2 6HL
Activities: Activities of head offices
Shareholder: Nigel Huw Samuel
Officers: Susan Anne Samuel, Secretary; Robin Paul Andrews [1953] Finance Director; Julian Bartholet [1966] Commercial Director; Patrick John Collins [1949] Director/Holding Company; Nigel Huw Samuel [1965] Director; Susan Anne Samuel [1965] Director

Sidhil Group Limited
Incorporated: 21 April 2015 *Employees:* 205
Net Worth: £27,173,000 *Total Assets:* £41,187,000
Registered Office: Drive Devilbiss Healthcare Limited, Heathfield Lane, Birkenshaw, W Yorks, BD11 2HW
Activities: Activities of head offices
Parent: Drive Devilbiss Healthcare Limited
Officers: Richard James McGleenan [1970] Managing Director; Graham Thomas Turner [1965] Director; Michael Thomas Waine [1951] Finance Director

Sigma Capital Group PLC
Incorporated: 2 March 2000 *Employees:* 26
Net Worth: £40,035,000 *Total Assets:* £46,114,000
Registered Office: Floor 3, 1 St Ann Street, Manchester, M2 7LR
Activities: Activities of other holding companies n.e.c.
Officers: Malcolm Douglas Briselden, Secretary; Graham Fleming Barnet [1963] Director; Malcolm Douglas Briselden [1967] Director/Accountant; Graeme Ronald Rae Hogg [1965] Director; James Cairns McMahon [1949] Director; David Sigsworth [1946] Director; Duncan William Sutherland [1951] Regeneration Director; Gwynn Galloway Thomson [1967] Director

Sigma Financial Facilities Limited
Incorporated: 22 October 1999
Net Worth: £717,100,992 *Total Assets:* £785,697,024
Registered Office: Booths Park, Chelford Road, Knutsford, Cheshire, WA16 8QZ
Activities: Activities of other holding companies n.e.c.
Parent: Sigma 2 AFW Limited
Officers: Iain Angus Jones, Secretary; William George Setter [1975] Director

Sigma PRS Investments II Limited
Incorporated: 15 April 2016
Net Worth: £1,109,851 *Total Assets:* £13,107,692
Registered Office: Floor 3, 1 St Ann Street, Manchester, M2 7LR
Activities: Management of real estate on a fee or contract basis
Parent: The PRS REIT Holding Company Limited
Officers: David Steffan Francis [1955] Director; Roderick MacLeod MacRae [1964] Director; Stephen Paul Smith [1953] Director

Sigma PRS Investments III Limited
Incorporated: 22 April 2016
Net Worth: £100 *Total Assets:* £7,871,778
Registered Office: Floor 3, 1 St Ann Street, Manchester, M2 7LR
Activities: Management of real estate on a fee or contract basis
Parent: The PRS REIT Holding Company Limited
Officers: David Steffan Francis [1955] Director; Roderick MacLeod MacRae [1964] Director; Stephen Paul Smith [1953] Director

Sigmatex (UK) Limited
Incorporated: 20 October 1986 *Employees:* 205
Net Worth: £11,086,573 *Total Assets:* £39,874,564
Registered Office: 1 Manor Farm Road, Runcorn, Cheshire, WA7 1TE
Activities: Manufacture of other technical and industrial textiles
Major Shareholder: Erik David Ian Ehnimb
Officers: Anthony John Eaden, Secretary; Jonathan Charles Coleman [1965] Director/Chartered Accountant; Anthony John Eaden [1950] Director; Erik David Ian Ehnimb [1957] Director [Swiss]; Leonardo Nastagio Erik Ehnimb [1997] Director [Swiss]; Scott Justin Tolson [1963] Director

Signature Shankly Limited
Incorporated: 3 February 2015
Net Worth: £4,576,718 *Total Assets:* £15,200,638
Registered Office: Kingsway House, Hatton Garden, Liverpool, L3 2AJ
Activities: Hotels and similar accommodation
Parent: Signature Living Hotel Limited
Officers: Katie Christine Kenwright [1977] Director; Lawrence Kenwright [1965] Director

SIL Holdings Limited
Incorporated: 1 October 2001 *Employees:* 221
Net Worth: £2,792,000 *Total Assets:* £34,232,000
Registered Office: Ladywell Mills, Hall Lane, Bradford, W Yorks, BD4 7DF
Activities: Activities of other holding companies n.e.c.
Parent: Stonecroft Holdings PLC
Officers: John Andrew Bradley [1967] Finance Director; Andrew David Seal [1957] Director; Jeremy Charles Seal [1960] Director

Silcoms Limited
Incorporated: 23 March 1939 *Employees:* 152
Net Worth: £1,456,964 *Total Assets:* £11,739,556
Registered Office: Piggott Street, Farnworth, Bolton, Lancs, BL4 9QN
Activities: Manufacture of air and spacecraft and related machinery
Officers: John Harry Cottam, Secretary; John Harry Cottam [1953] Director/Accountant; John England [1948] Director; David John Hamilton [1956] Director; Keith Alan Harrison [1950] Director; James Hill [1957] Operations Director; Keith Haworth Hindle [1943] Director; Alfred Clive Winby [1959] Commercial Director

Silentnight Group Limited
Incorporated: 10 February 2011 *Employees:* 1,132
Net Worth: £1,866,000 *Total Assets:* £47,994,000
Registered Office: Long Ing Business Park, Long Ing Lane, Barnoldswick, Lancs, BB18 6BJ
Activities: Manufacture of mattresses
Officers: Adrian John Fawcett [1968] Director/Chairman; Stephen David Freeman [1956] Director; Mark Kelly [1967] Director [Irish]; Richard Joseph Logan [1958] Director; Paul Seth McKoen [1961] Director; Neil McLlroy [1979] Director/Private Equity Professional [Irish]

Silentnight Holdings Limited
Incorporated: 9 May 2011 *Employees:* 1,132
Net Worth: £1,866,000 *Total Assets:* £47,994,000
Registered Office: Long Ing Business Park, Long Ing Lane, Barnoldswick, Lancs, BB18 6BJ
Activities: Manufacture of mattresses
Officers: Paul Seth McKoen, Secretary; Adrian John Fawcett [1968] Director/Chairman; Stephen David Freeman [1956] Director; Mark Kelly [1967] Director [Irish]; Richard Joseph Logan [1958] Director; Paul Seth McKoen [1961] Director; Neil McLlroy [1979] Director/Private Equity Professional [Irish]

Silicone Engineering Limited
Incorporated: 17 December 2001 *Employees:* 136
Net Worth: £5,578,662 *Total Assets:* £10,435,867
Registered Office: Greenbank Business Park, Blakewater Road, Blackburn, Lancs, BB1 3HU
Activities: Manufacture of other rubber products
Parent: Silicone Holdings Ltd
Officers: Clarissa Beadman [1959] Director; Steven Hadlington [1971] Director/Quality Assurance; Paul Robert Kinsella [1968] Director/Manufacturing; Mustaq Patel [1968] Director/Production Manager

Silicone Holdings Limited
Incorporated: 8 April 2005 *Employees:* 136
Net Worth: £5,368,536 *Total Assets:* £10,226,741
Registered Office: Greenbank Business Park, Blakewater Road, Blackburn, Lancs, BB1 3HU
Activities: Manufacture of other rubber products
Major Shareholder: Clarissa Beadman
Officers: Clarissa Beadman [1959] Director; Steven Hadlington [1971] Director; Paul Robert Kinsella [1968] Director; Mustaq Patel [1968] Director

Silkhouse Court Ltd
Incorporated: 14 January 2016
Net Worth: £100 *Total Assets:* £24,990,746
Registered Office: 300 St Mary's Road, Garston, Liverpool, L19 0NQ
Activities: Development of building projects
Shareholder: Fortis UK Holdings Ltd
Officers: Darren Kingsley McClellan [1972] Director/Manager; Kieran Stuart Moore [1975] Director/Manager; Gareth Morgan [1984] Director/Manager

Silver Cross (UK) Limited
Incorporated: 6 December 2002 *Employees:* 54
Net Worth: £13,069,790 *Total Assets:* £24,938,408
Registered Office: Micklethorn, Broughton, Skipton, N Yorks, BD23 3JA
Activities: Wholesale of household goods (other than musical instruments) n.e.c
Major Shareholder: Guangchang Guo
Officers: William John Lockwood, Secretary; Jonathan David Halsall [1985] Director/Chartered Accountant; Qian Jiabei [1979] Director/Finance [Chinese]; William John Lockwood [1951] Director/Chartered Accountant; Samantha Anne Newton [1962] Sales and Marketing Director; Nicholas John Paxton [1967] Director/Chief Executive; Philip Jeffrey Taylor [1965] Director/Product Designer; Song Xiaoting [1990] Director [Chinese]; Wei Zhang [1978] Director/Finance [Chinese]; Xueqing Zhang [1966] Director [Chinese]

Silver Cross Nurseries Limited
Incorporated: 23 December 2009
Net Worth: £7,045,000 *Total Assets:* £11,697,000
Registered Office: Micklethorn, Broughton, Skipton, N Yorks, BD23 3JA
Activities: Activities of head offices
Major Shareholder: Guangchang Guo
Officers: William John Lockwood, Secretary; Jonathan David Halsall [1985] Director/Chartered Accountant; Nicholas John Paxton [1967] Director/Buyer; Wei Zhang [1978] Director/Finance [Chinese]; Xueqing Zhang [1966] Director [Chinese]

Silverburn Finance (U.K.) Limited
Incorporated: 9 January 1962 *Employees:* 6
Net Worth: £3,219,453 *Total Assets:* £9,341,876
Registered Office: 76 Winter Hey Lane, Horwich, Bolton, Lancs, BL6 7PQ
Activities: Factoring
Parent: Rosedean Investments Limited
Officers: Irene Mary Boundy, Secretary; Irene Mary Boundy [1946] Director; Mary-Rose Boundy [1975] Director

Simba Smoby Toys (UK) Limited
Incorporated: 27 July 2009 *Employees:* 14
Net Worth: £1,949,897 *Total Assets:* £7,320,198
Registered Office: Broomfield House, Bolling Road, Bradford, W Yorks, BD4 7BG
Activities: Non-specialised wholesale trade
Shareholders: Anthony Belford; Simba Toys GmbH & Co KG
Officers: Anthony Belford [1947] Director; Richard Adam Belford [1985] Director/Sales Manager; Manfred Duschl [1955] Director/Merchant [German]; Uwe Weiler [1959] Director/Merchant [German]

Simginuity Limited
Incorporated: 26 January 2015 *Employees:* 186
Net Worth: £10,005,773 *Total Assets:* £19,862,956
Registered Office: 1 Thorp Road, Manchester, M40 5BJ
Activities: Other manufacturing n.e.c.
Major Shareholder: Anthony Andrew Bermingham
Officers: Anthony Bermingham, Secretary; Anthony Andrew Bermingham [1964] Managing Director; Fiona Bird [1962] Director; Nigel John Randall [1943] Director

H.E. Simm & Son Limited
Incorporated: 21 February 1936 *Employees:* 294
Net Worth: £3,830,342 *Total Assets:* £20,705,406
Registered Office: Spinnaker House, 141 Sefton Street, Liverpool, L8 5SN
Activities: Electrical installation
Shareholders: Raymond Simm; Wendy Anne Simm; Jennifer Simm
Officers: Jean Simm, Secretary; Anthony Simm [1958] Director/Plumber; Gareth Simm [1971] Director/Business Development Manager; Graham Simm [1951] Director/Surveyor; Gregory Maddocks Simm [1975] Director/Contract Manager; Jean Simm [1952] Director/Office Manager; Lawrence Simm [1946] Director/Surveyor; Martyn Robert Simm [1981] Director/IT/Fleet Manager

Simon Family Office Limited
Incorporated: 7 July 2011 *Employees:* 2
Net Worth: £88,395 *Total Assets:* £6,983,344
Registered Office: Second Floor, Shipgate House, Shipgate Street, Chester, CH1 1RT
Activities: Financial management
Major Shareholder: Simon Justin Nixon
Officers: Simon Justin Nixon, Secretary; Robert Gregory Thompson, Secretary; Simon Justin Nixon [1967] Director

Simonstone Estate Limited
Incorporated: 28 January 2015 *Employees:* 198
Net Worth: £50,311,648 *Total Assets:* £61,639,304
Registered Office: Simonstone Hall, Padiham Road, Simonstone, Burnley, Lancs, BB12 7HN
Activities: Activities of other holding companies n.e.c.
Major Shareholder: Diane Wendy Bovingdon
Officers: Kathleen Murphy, Secretary; David Bovingdon [1946] Director/Business Executive; Diane Wendy Bovingdon [1954] Director

Simpsonhaugh and Partners Group LLP
Incorporated: 7 May 2008 *Employees:* 121
Net Worth: £11,076,138 *Total Assets:* £16,301,034
Registered Office: Riverside, 4 Commercial Street, Manchester, M15 4RQ
Officers: Rachel Jane Haugh [1961] Member; Richard Spencer Banks Jackson [1971] Member; Ian Robert Simpson [1955] Member; Matthew Ayres [1974] LLP Member; Nick Fleming [1975] LLP Member; Dave Green [1966] LLP Member; David MacDonald [1973] LLP Member; Christian Male [1963] LLP Member; David Moyes [1971] LLP Member; Nick Owen [1975] LLP Member; Kalpana Patel [1969] LLP Member; Mark Savage [1967] LLP Member; Helen Trott [1967] LLP Member

F.D. Sims Limited
Incorporated: 11 January 2001 *Employees:* 36
Net Worth: £6,105,000 *Total Assets:* £12,137,000
Registered Office: Lions Drive, Shadsworth Business Park, Blackburn, BB1 2QS
Activities: Manufacture of wire products, chain and springs
Major Shareholder: Filippo Casadio
Officers: Filippo Casadio [1948] Director [Italian]; Robert Andrew Jones [1953] Director/General Manager; Gianfranco Sepriano [1946] Director [Italian]

Sinclair Pharmaceuticals Limited
Incorporated: 6 April 1971 *Employees:* 79
Net Worth: £13,659,000 *Total Assets:* £43,112,000
Registered Office: Eden House, Lakeside, Chester Business Park, Chester, CH4 9QT
Activities: Manufacture of basic pharmaceutical products
Parent: Sinclair Pharma Holdings Ltd
Officers: Jason Rodney Tate, Secretary; Jayne Katherine Burrell [1974] Director; Alan Musgrave Olby [1971] Director; Christopher Paul Spooner [1968] Director

Singleton & Smart (Holdings) Limited
Incorporated: 2 October 1973 *Employees:* 4
Net Worth: £5,328,122 *Total Assets:* £6,540,113
Registered Office: c/o Singleton & Smart Ltd, 71 Chorley Road, Blackpool, Lancs, FY3 7XQ
Activities: Development of building projects
Major Shareholder: Graham Smart
Officers: Christine Pettitt, Secretary; Alan Smart [1956] Director/Joiner; Graham Smart [1948] Director/Joiner; Kevan Smart [1950] Director/Joiner

Singleton Trading Limited
Incorporated: 29 May 2003 *Employees:* 78
Net Worth: £12,881,660 *Total Assets:* £29,611,476
Registered Office: One St Peters Square, Manchester, M2 3DE
Activities: Other business support service activities n.e.c.
Officers: Alexander Samuel Lazarus [1977] Director; Marc Sivner [1969] Director

Singleton's Dairy Limited
Incorporated: 3 March 1945 *Employees:* 76
Net Worth: £5,829,019 *Total Assets:* £8,171,929
Registered Office: c/o Bishops, Phoenix Park, Blakewater Road, Blackburn, BB1 5BG
Activities: Butter and cheese production
Parent: Singleton's Dairy 2010 Limited
Officers: Julia Watson, Secretary; Tracy Maria Carefoot [1964] Director; Gary Brian Johnson [1970] Managing Director

Sir Jacob Behrens & Sons,Limited
Incorporated: 20 May 1948 *Employees:* 59
Net Worth: £12,807,194 *Total Assets:* £14,771,391
Registered Office: Centrepoint, Marshall Stevens Way, Trafford Park, Manchester, M17 1PP
Activities: Wholesale of textiles
Shareholders: Christopher David Maxwell Hughes; Christopher David Maxwell Hughes
Officers: Christopher David Maxwell Hughes, Secretary; Christopher David Maxwell Hughes [1957] Director; George Christopher John Hughes [1989] Director

The Sisters Estate Limited
Incorporated: 10 February 2017 *Employees:* 2
Net Worth: £229,863 *Total Assets:* £7,376,252
Registered Office: 141 Adelphi Street, Preston, Lancs, PR1 7BH
Activities: Buying and selling of own real estate
Shareholders: Fatima Holdings Limited; Shehla Holdings Limited; Fawziyah Holdings Limited
Officers: Ayyub Vali Bux [1955] Director; Yousuf Ayyub Bux [1981] Director

Sistine Properties (Westbury) Limited
Incorporated: 26 February 2008
Net Worth Deficit: £14,222,000 *Total Assets:* £69,596,000
Registered Office: Norcliffe House, Station Road, Wilmslow, Cheshire, SK9 1BU
Activities: Development of building projects
Parent: Brighterkind Health Care Group Limited
Officers: Abigail Mattison, Secretary; Robert Nicolas Barr [1958] Director; Ryan Stuart MacAskill [1975] Director; Gregory Laurence Newman [1988] Director/Investment Professional; Jeremy Robert Arthur Richardson [1970] Director; Phillip Gary Thomas [1978] Director

Six Town Housing Limited
Incorporated: 30 October 2003 *Employees:* 240
Net Worth Deficit: £56,440 *Total Assets:* £14,030,776
Registered Office: 6 Knowsley Place, Angouleme Way, Bury, Lancs, BL9 0EL
Activities: Residents property management
Parent: Bury Council
Officers: Alison Jayne Leach, Secretary; Hugh Broadbent [1952] Director/Semi-Retired; Jacqueline Maureen Harris [1943] Director/Councillor for Bury Council; David Howell [1959] Director/Retired; Clare Louise King [1965] Director/Consultant; Sharon McCambridge [1961] Director/Chief Executive; Anthony Philip Noblet [1942] Director/Retired; Beryl Power Park [1948] Director/Retired; Philip Anthony Saxton [1958] Director/Accountant; Sarah Jane Louise Southworth [1967] Director/Accountant; Susan Joy Southworth [1948] Director/Councillor/Business Owner; Sasha Wayne [1980] Director/Legal Counsel; Steven David Wright [1965] Director/General Manager

SJCF Investment Ltd
Incorporated: 24 July 2015
Net Worth: £4,411,043 *Total Assets:* £85,719,544
Registered Office: Hollingworth Manor, Peanock Lane, Littleborough, Rochdale, Lancs, OL15 0AD
Activities: Activities of investment trusts
Shareholders: Noel Francis William McKee; Catherine Ann McKee
Officers: Catherine Ann McKee [1966] Director; Noel Francis William McKee [1969] Director

SJM Developments Limited
Incorporated: 18 December 1997 *Employees:* 3
Net Worth: £2,976,259 *Total Assets:* £9,105,993
Registered Office: The Brew House, Greenalls Avenue, Warrington, Cheshire, WA4 6HL
Activities: Development of building projects
Parent: Assura Financing Limited
Officers: Orla Ball [1970] Director/Company Secretary; Paul Bryan Carroll [1969] Director/Accountant; Jayne Marie Cottam [1974] Finance Director; Simon Gould [1974] Director/Chartered Surveyor; Spencer Adrian Kenyon [1962] Director/Chartered Surveyor; Patrick William Lowther [1977] Director/Chartered Surveyor

SJM Holdings North Limited
Incorporated: 7 November 2013 *Employees:* 184
Net Worth: £12,419,249 *Total Assets:* £115,442,864
Registered Office: 3rd Floor, Colwyn Chambers, 19 York Street, Manchester, M2 3BA
Activities: Activities of other holding companies n.e.c.
Major Shareholder: Simon James Moran
Officers: Simon James Moran [1965] Director/Music Promoter

Skanem UK Limited
Incorporated: 25 October 1984 *Employees:* 175
Net Worth: £10,737,000 *Total Assets:* £18,159,000
Registered Office: Skanem Liverpool, Bassendale Road, Croft Business Park, Bromborough, Wirral, Merseyside, CH62 3QL
Activities: Manufacture of printed labels
Major Shareholder: Ole Rugland
Officers: Duncan Raper, Secretary; Dag Gundersen [1963] Group Contract Director [Norwegian]; Ole Kristian Rugland [1983] Director/Chief Financial Officer [Norwegian]; Ole Rugland [1945] Director/Businessman [Norwegian]

Skelhurst Limited
Incorporated: 11 December 1968 *Employees:* 6
Net Worth: £11,149,875 *Total Assets:* £18,845,648
Registered Office: The Copper Room, Deva Centre, Trinity Way, Manchester, M3 7BG
Activities: Other letting and operating of own or leased real estate
Shareholders: David Pine; Roslyn Susanne Pine
Officers: David Pine, Secretary; Alexander Pine [1982] Director/Research Fellow; Daniel Pine [1977] Director; David Pine [1942] Solicitor/Director; Elliot Pine [1980] Director; Roslyn Susanne Pine [1945] Director/Pharmacist

Skills and Work Solutions Limited
Incorporated: 2 February 2000 *Employees:* 623
Net Worth Deficit: £483,950 *Total Assets:* £20,511,982
Registered Office: Lee House, 90 Great Bridgewater Street, Manchester, M1 5JW
Activities: Technical and vocational secondary education
Parent: The Growth Company Limited
Officers: Paul Anthony Simpson, Secretary; Mark Anthony Hughes [1966] Director/Chief Executive; Michelle Victoria Leeson [1976] Director; Jayne Worthington [1969] Director

Skipton Business Finance Limited
Incorporated: 2 March 2001 *Employees:* 89
Net Worth: £4,747,671 *Total Assets:* £118,995,400
Registered Office: The Bailey, Skipton, N Yorks, BD23 1DN
Activities: Factoring
Parent: Skipton Group Holdings Limited
Officers: John Joseph Gibson, Secretary; Gregory Mark Bell [1969] Director; Andrew Paul Grantham [1966] Director; Andrew David Hill [1972] Operations Director; Andrew Walter Nelson [1964] Director/Accountant; Fiona Wlizabeth Nightingale [1970] Director/Chartered Accountant; Alexander Charles Robinson [1969] Director; Ralph Anthony Walker [1946] Director

Skipton Group Holdings Limited
Incorporated: 20 December 2000
Net Worth: £82,868,000 *Total Assets:* £117,420,000
Registered Office: The Bailey, Skipton, N Yorks, BD23 1DN
Activities: Activities of financial services holding companies
Parent: Skipton Building Society
Officers: John Joseph Gibson, Secretary; Andrew Paul Bottomley [1965] Director; Amanda Jane Burton [1959] Director; Maria Luisa Cassoni [1951] Director; John Richard Coates [1951] Director; Denise Patricia Cockrem [1962] Director; Ian Michael Cornelius [1969] Commercial Director; David John Cutter [1962] Building Society Director; Robert David East [1960] Director; Denis Arthur Hall [1955] Director; Mark Joseph Lund [1957] Director; Robert Samuel Duncan Mugenyi Ndawula [1974] Finance Director; Alexander Charles Robinson [1969] Director; Helen Claire Stevenson [1960] Director

Skipton Properties Limited
Incorporated: 27 August 1987 *Employees:* 73
Net Worth: £10,125,520 *Total Assets:* £21,916,012
Registered Office: Skipton House, Riparian Court, Riparian Way, Crosshills, N Yorks, BD20 7BW
Activities: Development of building projects
Officers: Linda Mary Verity, Secretary; Sarah Louise Barraclough [1981] Sales Director; Luke Alan Woodrow Davis [1984] Director/Accountant; Brian Verity [1949] Director; Caroline Elizabeth Verity [1984] Director; Linda Mary Verity [1953] Director

Skirfare Investments Limited
Incorporated: 20 September 2011
Net Worth: £10,952,645 *Total Assets:* £63,019,808
Registered Office: Throstles Nest, Conistone with Kilnsey, Skipton, N Yorks, BD23 5HT
Activities: Fund management activities
Major Shareholder: David Richard Hood
Officers: David Richard Hood [1948] Director/Entrepreneur

Sky Building Ltd
Incorporated: 10 February 2015
Net Worth Deficit: £5,303,179 *Total Assets:* £11,733,230
Registered Office: 24 Queen Avenue, Queen Insurance Buildings, Dale Street, Liverpool, L2 4TZ
Activities: Development of building projects
Parent: Daisy Property Investments Ltd
Officers: Kerry Tomlinson [1969] Director/Property Developer; Pauline Elizabeth Tomlinson [1969] Director

SL Mortgage Funding No 1 Limited
Incorporated: 14 May 2004
Net Worth Deficit: £332,675 *Total Assets:* £15,918,129
Registered Office: One City Place, Queens Road, Chester, CH1 3BQ
Activities: Activities auxiliary to financial intermediation n.e.c.
Parent: Surrenda Link Mortgage Holdings Limited
Officers: David William James Roxburgh, Secretary; David William James Roxburgh [1963] Director/Accountant [Irish]; Michael Semple [1945] Director/Chartered Accountant [Irish]

H C Slingsby P L C
Incorporated: 19 April 1948 *Employees:* 105
Net Worth: £384,000 *Total Assets:* £14,417,000
Registered Office: H C Slingsby PLC, Otley Road, Baildon, Shipley, W Yorks, BD17 7LW
Activities: Retail sale via mail order houses or via Internet
Officers: Morgan Lawn Morris, Secretary; Morgan Lawn Morris [1971] Financial Director; Dominic Stanley Slingsby [1961] Director

SLP Manufacturing Limited
Incorporated: 24 August 2015 *Employees:* 17
Net Worth: £26,148,788 *Total Assets:* £33,324,950
Registered Office: 3 St Mary's Parsonage, Manchester, M3 2RD
Activities: Other business support service activities n.e.c.
Parent: H&K Distribution Limited
Officers: Catherine Gallagher [1969] Director [Irish]; Edward Hudson [1962] Director [Irish]; Nick Scallan [1968] Director [Irish]; David Spain [1969] Director [Irish]; Paul Gavin Waterfield [1972] Director/VP of European Operations

SmarDTV (UK) Limited
Incorporated: 19 January 1988 *Employees:* 94
Net Worth: £4,207,793 *Total Assets:* £9,049,656
Registered Office: Beckside Design Centre, Millennium Business Park, Station Road, Steeton, Keighley, W Yorks, BD20 6QW
Activities: Other research and experimental development on natural sciences and engineering
Parent: SmarDTV SA
Officers: Mark Beariault [1971] Director/General Counsel [American]; Pascal Lenoir [1960] Director [French]; Wouter Naessens [1978] Director [Belgian]

Smartpay Limited
Incorporated: 10 November 2005 *Employees:* 35
Net Worth: £595,636 *Total Assets:* £10,823,797
Registered Office: Blackpool Technology Management Centre, Faraday Way, Blackpool, Lancs, FY2 0JW
Activities: Other business support service activities n.e.c.
Major Shareholder: Paul George Ruocco
Officers: Christopher Joseph Futcher [1977] Director; Rebecca Joanne Ward [1987] Director

SMD (Holdings) Limited
Incorporated: 19 November 2002 *Employees:* 95
Net Worth: £5,984,497 *Total Assets:* £16,324,236
Registered Office: Unit F2, Pittman Way, Preston North Employment Industrial Estate, Fulwood, Preston, Lancs, PR2 9ZD
Activities: Wholesale of textiles
Major Shareholder: Robert Jason Kenworthy
Officers: Richard John Hargreaves [1968] Director/Chartered Accountant; Robert Jason Kenworthy [1969] Director; Jonathan Edward Pink [1982] Operations Director

SMG (UK) Limited
Incorporated: 29 September 1964 *Employees:* 797
Net Worth: £12,718,000 *Total Assets:* £54,039,000
Registered Office: Manchester Arena, Hunts Bank Approach, Manchester, M3 1AR
Activities: Other food services
Officers: John Francis Burns, Secretary; John Francis Burns [1957] Director [American]; Harold Westley [1948] Director [American]

SMG Europe Holdings Limited
Incorporated: 8 September 2005 *Employees:* 1,979
Net Worth: £27,889,000 *Total Assets:* £77,385,000
Registered Office: Manchester Arena, Hunts Bank, Manchester, M3 1AR
Activities: Activities of head offices
Officers: John Burns, Secretary; John Burns [1957] Director [American]; Harold Westley [1948] Director [American]

Smit Harbour Towage (UK) Limited
Incorporated: 9 December 1986 *Employees:* 43
Net Worth: £6,758,000 *Total Assets:* £8,280,000
Registered Office: Unit 40 Dunes Way, Wellington Employment Park, Liverpool, L5 9RJ
Activities: Other professional, scientific and technical activities n.e.c.
Parent: Kotug Smit Towage UK Ltd
Officers: Rene Marie Raaijmakers [1968] Director [Dutch]; Harm Jan Van Der Meer [1964] Director [Dutch]

Smith & Bateson Limited,
Incorporated: 4 September 1953 *Employees:* 48
Net Worth: £7,468,003 *Total Assets:* £11,469,233
Registered Office: Stronghold House, Kitling Road, Knowsley Business Park, Knowsley, Merseyside, L34 9HQ
Activities: Wholesale of other intermediate products
Parent: Smith Bateson Holdings Limited
Officers: Graeme Hurst, Secretary/Director; Graeme Hurst [1960] Operations Director; Adrian Mark Kennerley [1966] Purchasing Director; Stephen Vincent McKuhen [1961] Managing Director; Peter John Smith [1968] Logistics Director

H.H. Smith & Sons Co. Limited
Incorporated: 31 May 1962 *Employees:* 82
Net Worth: £2,850,977 *Total Assets:* £8,094,200
Registered Office: 95 Bury Old Road, Whitefield, Bury, Lancs, M45 7AY
Activities: Development of building projects
Shareholder: David Harold Smith
Officers: Fiona Smith, Secretary; David Harold Smith [1951] Director; Fiona Smith [1954] Director; Philip John Smith [1977] Director/Contract Manager; Robert Nathaniel Smith [1972] Director

Smith Bateson Holdings Limited
Incorporated: 30 July 2008 *Employees:* 48
Net Worth: £8,917,609 *Total Assets:* £13,498,398
Registered Office: Stronghold House, Kitling Road, Knowsley Business Park, Prescot, Merseyside, L34 9HQ
Activities: Wholesale of other intermediate products
Major Shareholder: Stephen Vincent McKuhen
Officers: Stephen Vincent McKuhen [1961] Managing Director

Smith Brothers Holdings Limited
Incorporated: 2[illegible] February 1990 *Employees:* 2
Net Worth: £8,628,003 *Total Assets:* £9,049,644
Registered Office: 216 Dowson Road, Hyde, Cheshire, SK14 5BP
Activities: Activities of head offices
Major Shareholder: John Albert Smith
Officers: Julia Wibberley, Secretary; John Albert Smith [1940] Director

A.J.A. Smith Properties Limited
Incorporated: 26 January 2005 *Employees:* 4
Net Worth: £2,686,809 *Total Assets:* £7,968,700
Registered Office: c/o AJA Smith Transport, Heys Lane, Great Harwood, Blackburn, BB6 7UA
Activities: Other letting and operating of own or leased real estate
Officers: Anthony James Smith [1972] Director; James Anthony Smith [1971] Director; Lorraine Smith [1965] Director; Nicola Smith [1967] Director

Smiths Dock LLP
Incorporated: 18 March 2014
Total Assets: £24,922,164
Registered Office: Timber Wharf, 16-22 Worsley Street, Manchester, M15 4LD

Smurfit Corrugated Holdings
Incorporated: 21 October 1983
Net Worth: £13,926,000 *Total Assets:* £178,682,000
Registered Office: Cunard Buildings, Water Street, Liverpool, L3 1SF
Activities: Other business support service activities n.e.c.
Parent: Smurfit Kappa Packaging UK Limited
Officers: Nicola Hales, Secretary; Nicola Hales [1975] Director/Accountant; Patrick McNeill [1959] Director

Smurfit Kappa Investments UK Ltd
Incorporated: 25 April 1986
Net Worth Deficit: £11,067,000 *Total Assets:* £194,212,992
Registered Office: Cunard Buildings, Water Street, Pier Head, Liverpool, L3 1SF
Activities: Manufacture of corrugated paper and paperboard, sacks and bags
Parent: Smurfit Kappa Group PLC
Officers: Nicola Hales, Secretary; Clive Bowers [1953] Director; Patrick McNeill [1959] Director; John Moody [1978] Director/Chartered Accountant

Smurfit Kappa Packaging UK Limited
Incorporated: 19 May 1998
Net Worth: £164,124,000 *Total Assets:* £264,255,008
Registered Office: Cunard Buildings, Water Street, Pier Head, Liverpool, L3 1SF
Activities: Financial intermediation not elsewhere classified
Shareholders: Smurfit Kappa Investments UK Limited; Smurfit Kappa Group PLC
Officers: Nicola Hales, Secretary; Clive Bowers [1953] Director; Patrick McNeill [1959] Director; John Moody [1978] Director/Chartered Accountant; Colin Shepherd [1970] Director/Finance

Smurfit Kappa UK Ltd
Incorporated: 8 July 1971 *Employees:* 3,442
Net Worth: £92,003,000 *Total Assets:* £629,680,000
Registered Office: Cunard Buildings, Water Street, Pier Head, Liverpool, L3 1SF
Activities: Manufacture of corrugated paper and paperboard, sacks and bags
Parent: Smurfit Kappa Packaging UK Limited
Officers: Nicola Hales, Secretary; Clive Bowers [1953] Director; Ken Byrne [1963] Director [Irish]; Richard Andrew Coventry [1979] Director/Chartered Accountant; Patrick McNeill [1959] Director; John Moody [1978] Director/Chartered Accountant; Michael O Riordan [1957] Director/Company Secretary [Irish]; Colin Shepherd [1970] Director/Finance

Snappy Snaps Franchises Limited
Incorporated: 24 July 1991 *Employees:* 30
Net Worth: £4,683,046 *Total Assets:* £7,300,959
Registered Office: Timpson House, Claverton Road, Roundthorn Industrial Estate, Manchester, M23 9TT
Activities: Activities of head offices
Parent: Cedric Services Limited
Officers: Paresh Majithia, Secretary; Paresh Majithia [1967] Finance Director; Sir William John Anthony Timpson [1943] Director/Chairman; William James Timpson [1971] Managing Director

Sodajo Limited
Incorporated: 5 November 2009
Net Worth: £19,445,154 *Total Assets:* £20,075,830
Registered Office: Archwood House, Kingsfield Court, Chester Business Park, Chester, CH4 9RE
Activities: Other business support service activities n.e.c.
Parent: Ripat Limited
Officers: Andrew Joseph Simms, Secretary; Daniel Henry Anderson Burbidge [1971] Director/Solicitor; Joshua Richard Burbidge [1978] Director/Customer Services and Logistics Manager; Patricia Anderson Burbidge [1945] Director/Magistrate; Richard Henry Burbidge [1942] Director; Sophie Anne Peach [1968] Director

Sofology Limited
Incorporated: 16 December 1983 *Employees:* 912
Net Worth Deficit: £13,185,000 *Total Assets:* £36,239,000
Registered Office: Sofology Limited, Ashton Road, Golborne, Warrington, Cheshire, WA3 3UL
Activities: Retail of furniture, lighting, and similar (not musical instruments or scores) in specialised store
Parent: DFS Furniture Company Limited
Officers: Jonathan Hugh Massey [1949] Director/Chairman; Neil Kamal Sharma-Burford [1966] Director/Chief Financial Officer; Jason Brian Tyldesley [1973] Director/Chief Executive Officer

SOG Limited
Incorporated: 10 December 1999 *Employees:* 17
Net Worth: £11,931,064 *Total Assets:* £15,929,833
Registered Office: The Heath Business and Technical Park, The Heath, Runcorn, Cheshire, WA7 4QF
Activities: Combined facilities support activities
Parent: Lionlike Management Limited
Officers: John Stephen Lewis [1962] Director; Carol Mary Thomas [1959] Director/Accountant [Irish]

Soho Flordis UK Limited
Incorporated: 22 June 2015 *Employees:* 46
Net Worth: £3,832,280 *Total Assets:* £9,538,450
Registered Office: Douglas Bank House, Wigan Lane, Wigan, Lancs, WN1 2TB
Activities: Wholesale of pharmaceutical goods
Officers: Robert Charles Gerard Hendriks [1963] Director [Dutch]

Soil Engineering Geoservices Limited
Incorporated: 1 July 1992 *Employees:* 160
Net Worth: £581,000 *Total Assets:* £8,781,000
Registered Office: Henderson House, Langley Place, Higgins Lane, Burscough, Lancs, L40 8JS
Activities: Construction of other civil engineering projects n.e.c.
Parent: Soletenche Freyssinet SAS
Officers: Graham James Trafford, Secretary; Philip John Hines [1966] Director; Tristan Paul Llewellyn [1973] Director/Civil Engineer; Graham James Trafford [1972] Director/Accountant

Solidagent Investment Limited
Incorporated: 27 February 1996
Net Worth: £2,111,227 *Total Assets:* £13,335,714
Registered Office: 433 Wilmslow Road, Withington, Manchester, M20 4AF
Activities: Development of building projects
Major Shareholder: Peter Lie Ming Yuan
Officers: Eliza Kar Lai Yim, Company Secretary; Gen Cheung Goh [1947] Director/Merchant; Peter Ka Leung Yim [1957] Director/Consultant

Solomon Commercials Limited
Incorporated: 13 April 1981 *Employees:* 338
Net Worth: £1,969,214 *Total Assets:* £14,536,674
Registered Office: Knowsley Road Industrial Estate, Haslingden, Rossendale, Lancs, BB4 4RX
Activities: Manufacture of bodies (coachwork) for motor vehicles (except caravans)
Parent: Solcomm Limited
Officers: Michael John Solomon, Secretary; Mark Christopher Solomon [1974] Director/Motor Body Builder; Michael John Solomon [1969] Director/Motor Body Builder; Raymond Solomon [1948] Director/Motor Body Builder; Susan Ellen Solomon [1950] Director/Motor Body Builder

Solvay Interox Limited
Incorporated: 18 March 1971 *Employees:* 93
Net Worth: £6,607,000 *Total Assets:* £67,404,000
Registered Office: Solvay House, Baronet Road, Warrington, Cheshire, WA4 6HA
Activities: Manufacture of other inorganic basic chemicals
Parent: Solvay UK Holding Company Limited
Officers: Alison Murphy, Secretary; Jean Allen [1958] Director/Human Resources Manager; Craig Robert Barraclough [1974] Director; Alison Murphy [1965] Director; Henricus Lambertus Johannes Venbrux [1958] Director/Chemical Engineer [Dutch]

Solvay UK Holding Company Limited
Incorporated: 23 November 1992 *Employees:* 5
Net Worth: £68,960,000 *Total Assets:* £112,473,000
Registered Office: Solvay House, Baronet Road, Warrington, Cheshire, WA4 6HA
Activities: Activities of other holding companies n.e.c.
Parent: Solvay S.A.
Officers: Alison Murphy, Secretary; Craig Robert Barraclough [1974] Director; Alexis Michel Brouhns [1955] Director [Belgian]; Melvin John Dawes [1967] Director/Solicitor; Alison Murphy [1965] Director

Solway Vehicle Distributors Limited
Incorporated: 12 October 1978 *Employees:* 75
Net Worth: £7,670,889 *Total Assets:* £11,560,137
Registered Office: Kingstown Broadway, Kingstown Industrial Estate, Carlisle, Cumbria, CA3 0HD
Activities: Sale of other motor vehicles
Major Shareholder: Peter Fullelove
Officers: David Smith, Secretary; Ernest William Coulthard [1953] Service Director; Peter Fullelove [1952] Managing Director

Sonoco Cores and Paper Limited
Incorporated: 20 May 2004 *Employees:* 185
Net Worth: £40,022,000 *Total Assets:* £47,242,000
Registered Office: Station Road, Milnrow, Rochdale, OL16 4HQ
Activities: Manufacture of paper and paperboard
Officers: Helen Elizabeth Rees, Secretary; Vicki Brock Arthur [1958] Finance Director [American]; Clayton Beck [1958] Director [American]; Angela Clayton [1960] HR Director; Antonius Johannes Maria Mutsaers [1963] Director [Dutch]; Helen Elizabeth Rees [1984] Director; Adam Wood [1968] Director

Sonoco Limited
Incorporated: 4 October 1904 *Employees:* 550
Net Worth: £25,027,000 *Total Assets:* £58,495,000
Registered Office: Station Road, Milnrow, Rochdale, Lancs, OL16 4HQ
Activities: Manufacture of paper and paperboard
Officers: Helen Elizabeth Rees, Secretary; Clayton Beck [1958] Director [American]; Robert Frank Carroll [1950] Director/General Manager; Angela Clayton [1960] HR Director; Timothy John Nash [1972] Director/Finance Manager; Helen Elizabeth Rees [1984] Director; Adam Wood [1968] Director

Sonoco Products Company UK
Incorporated: 4 November 1993 *Employees:* 5
Net Worth Deficit: £24,069,000 *Total Assets:* £10,028,000
Registered Office: Station Road, Milnrow, Rochdale, Lancs, OL16 4HQ
Activities: Activities of head offices
Officers: Helen Elizabeth Rees, Secretary; Clayton Beck [1958] Director [American]; Angela Clayton [1960] HR Director; Timothy John Nash [1972] Director/Finance Manager; Helen Elizabeth Rees [1984] Director; Adam Wood [1968] Director

Sonomatic Limited
Incorporated: 16 September 2003 *Employees:* 120
Net Worth: £2,741,227 *Total Assets:* £13,733,616
Registered Office: One City Place, Queens Road, Chester, CH1 3BQ
Activities: Technical testing and analysis
Officers: Dr Charles Becht IV [1954] Director/Engineer [American]; Esteban Cesan [1982] Director/General Manager, Australia [American]; Raul Elbio Cesan [1947] Director/Investor [Argentinian]

Sonova UK Limited
Incorporated: 11 August 1997 *Employees:* 97
Net Worth: £3,459,000 *Total Assets:* £20,183,000
Registered Office: Sonova House, Lakeside Drive, Centre Park, Warrington, Cheshire, WA1 1RX
Activities: Manufacture of medical and dental instruments and supplies
Parent: Sonova Holding AG
Officers: Tim John Clark, Secretary/Accountant; Jonathan Matthew Billings [1973] Managing Director; Alessandra Perego [1959] Director/Tax Manager [Swiss]

Soogen Holdings Limited
Incorporated: 3 February 2015 *Employees:* 7
Net Worth: £4,985,293 *Total Assets:* £112,622,272
Registered Office: 3rd Floor, 1 Portland Street, Manchester, M1 3BE
Activities: Activities of financial services holding companies
Major Shareholder: Johan Arthur Frans Cuypers
Officers: Johan Arthur Frans Cuypers [1960] Director [Belgian]

Soper Group Holdings Ltd
Incorporated: 16 September 2016 *Employees:* 205
Net Worth: £6,698,792 *Total Assets:* £18,536,928
Registered Office: Grane Road Mill, Grane Road, Haslingden, Rossendale, Lancs, BB4 5BT
Activities: Non-trading company
Major Shareholder: Marilyn Jane Soper
Officers: James Anthony Jones [1977] Director; Benjamin Soper [1977] Director; Marilyn Jane Soper [1953] Director

R. Soper Limited
Incorporated: 1 July 1943 *Employees:* 99
Net Worth: £6,477,210 *Total Assets:* £13,694,710
Registered Office: Grane Road Mill, Grane Road, Haslingden, Rossendale, Lancs, BB4 5ET
Activities: Manufacture of soft furnishings
Major Shareholder: Marilyn Jane Soper
Officers: Jessica Mary Fell [1978] Director; James Anthony Jones [1977] Director/Accountant; Benjamin David Soper [1977] Director/Sales Executive; Joshua Thomas Soper [1985] Director; Marilyn Jane Soper [1953] Director

Sosamja Holdings Limited
Incorporated: 16 December 2011 *Employees:* 334
Net Worth: £258,785 *Total Assets:* £22,650,238
Registered Office: 1 Ferrous Way, Irlam, Manchester, M44 5FS
Activities: Wholesale of meat and meat products
Major Shareholder: Steven James Woollands
Officers: Michael John Birtwistle [1952] Director; Steven James Woollands [1962] Director

South Craven Academy Trust
Incorporated: 5 April 2011 *Employees:* 203
Net Worth: £9,188,000 *Total Assets:* £14,819,000
Registered Office: South Craven School, Holme Lane, Cross Hills, Keighley, W Yorks, BD20 7RL
Activities: General secondary education
Officers: Marie Brook, Secretary; Joy Adamson [1972] Director/University Lecturer; Emma Louise Benn [1977] Director/Sales Office Manager; Roy Burgin [1947] Director/Retired; Joan Fleming [1944] Director/Retired; Wendy Caroline Hamilton [1971] Director/Teacher; Stephen Hanson [1958] Director/Policeman; David Harvey [1955] Director; Terry Hawley [1953] Director/Retired; Martyn Paul Hill [1974] Director/Headmaster; Katherine Mary Lloyd [1971] Director/Support Worker; Kika Masters [1965] Director/Premises & Contracts Manager; Paul Morrison [1984] Director/Teacher; Christopher James Pomery [1958] Director/Mature Student

South East London & Kent Bus Company Limited
Incorporated: 14 December 1988 *Employees:* 1,448
Net Worth: £52,784,000 *Total Assets:* £76,483,000
Registered Office: c/o Stagecoach Services Limited, One Stockport Exchange, 20 Railway Road, Stockport, Cheshire, SK1 3SW
Activities: Other urban, suburban or metropolitan passenger land transport (not underground, metro or similar)
Parent: Stagecoach Bus Holdings Limited
Officers: Michael John Vaux, Secretary; Colin Brown [1968] Director/Accountant; Paul Graham Lynch [1962] Director; Arnold Mark Threapleton [1954] Managing Director

South Manchester Learning Trust
Incorporated: 10 July 2012 *Employees:* 127
Net Worth: £10,130,000 *Total Assets:* £11,372,000
Registered Office: Altrincham College, Green Lane, Timperley, Altrincham, Cheshire, WA15 8QW
Activities: General secondary education
Officers: Danielle Nicola Taylor, Secretary; Peter Richard Brooks [1958] Director/Headteacher; Jane Elizabeth Brophy [1963] Director/Councillor; Pam Dunham [1963] Director/Local Government Officer; Alison Gaynor Hewitt [1967] Finance Director; Margo Mary Kane [1965] Director; Jenny Louise Singleton [1969] Director/Principal and CEO; Malcolm Stansfield [1951] Director/Retired; Susan Gwenda Wildman [1960] Director

South Shore Mutual Insurance Company Limited
Incorporated: 25 October 1945
Net Worth: £10,550,923 *Total Assets:* £11,462,077
Registered Office: 525 Ocean Boulevard, Promenade, Blackpool, Lancs, FY4 1EZ
Activities: Non-life insurance
Parent: Blackpool Pleasure Beach Limited
Officers: James Graham Freeman [1935] Director; Jonathan Gray [1970] Director/Accountant; Nigel Peter Kilgallon [1959] Director/Legal Counsel; Amanda Jean Thompson [1962] Director

South Tyne & Wear Energy Recovery Holdings Ltd
Incorporated: 25 October 2010
Net Worth Deficit: £35,222,000 *Total Assets:* £211,814,000
Registered Office: c/o Albany SPC Services Ltd, 3rd Floor, 3-5 Charlotte Street, Manchester, M1 4HB
Activities: Treatment and disposal of non-hazardous waste
Shareholder: Sita UK Ltd
Officers: Ailison Mitchell, Secretary; Florent Thierry Antoine Duval [1976] Director/Chief Finance Officer [French]; Gregor Scott Jackson [1974] Director; Belinda Faith Knox [1972] Director; Graham Arthur McKenna-Mayes [1968] Director/Chief Operating Officer; Barry Paul Millsom [1974] Director; Ian Anthony Sexton [1956] Director; Yuji Suzuki [1970] Director [Japanese]

South Tyne & Wear Energy Recovery Ltd
Incorporated: 25 October 2010
Net Worth Deficit: £35,222,000 *Total Assets:* £211,814,000
Registered Office: c/o Albany SPC Services Ltd, 3rd Floor, 3-5 Charlotte Street, Manchester, M1 4HB
Activities: Treatment and disposal of non-hazardous waste
Parent: South Tyne & Wear Energy Recovery Holdings Ltd
Officers: Ailison Mitchell, Secretary; Florent Thierry Antoine Duval [1976] Director/Chief Finance Officer [French]; Gregor Scott Jackson [1974] Director; Belinda Faith Knox [1972] Director; Graham Arthur McKenna-Mayes [1968] Director/Chief Operating Officer; Barry Paul Millsom [1974] Director; Ian Anthony Sexton [1956] Director; Yuji Suzuki [1970] Director [Japanese]

South Westmorland Multi Academy Trust
Incorporated: 25 May 2011 *Employees:* 224
Net Worth: £10,472,245 *Total Assets:* £17,286,044
Registered Office: Dallam School, Milnthorpe, Cumbria, LA7 7DD
Activities: General secondary education
Officers: Joanne Hamer, Secretary; Enid Joy Fraser [1948] Director/Retired Headteacher; Roy James Pirie [1947] Director/Retired and Part Time Consultant; Sarah Catherine Swindley [1972] Director; Rupert Timothy Villiers-Smith [1967] Director; Stephen William Wetton [1960] Director/Educational Consultant; Nigel James Whittle [1984] Director/Headteacher; Reverend Susan Elizabeth Wilson [1952] Director/Retired Vicar

South Yorkshire Supertram Limited
Incorporated: 2 August 1991 *Employees:* 229
Net Worth: £4,813,000 *Total Assets:* £7,803,000
Registered Office: c/o Stagecoach Services Limited, One Stockport Exchange, 20 Railway Road, Stockport, Cheshire, SK1 3SW
Activities: Urban and suburban passenger railway transportation by underground, metro and similar systems
Officers: Michael John Vaux, Secretary; Timothy David Bilby [1972] Director/Accountant; Martin Andrew Griffiths [1966] Finance Director; Timothy Colin Shoveller [1972] Director; James Norton Stewart [1974] Director; Michael John Vaux [1971] Director/Solicitor; Nigel Wragg [1967] Director

Southern Land Securities Limited
Incorporated: 30 November 1993 *Employees:* 9
Net Worth: £49,175,416 *Total Assets:* £82,675,856
Registered Office: 13-15 Brewery Yard, Deva City Office Park, Trinity Way, Salford, M3 7BB
Activities: Other service activities n.e.c.
Major Shareholder: Ruth Diane Taube
Officers: Ruth Diane Taube, Secretary; Barrie Jonathan Taube [1976] Director; Raymond Taube [1949] Director; Ruth Diane Taube [1954] Director/Company Secretary

Southernplus Limited
Incorporated: 2 November 1994 *Employees:* 10
Net Worth: £10,316,417 *Total Assets:* £21,368,364
Registered Office: 467a Smithdown Road, Liverpool, L15 5AE
Activities: Renting and operating of Housing Association real estate
Shareholders: Gregory David Ormesher; Simon David Hanson
Officers: Gregory David Ormesher, Secretary/Property Development; Simon David Hanson [1966] Director/Property Developer; Gregory David Ormesher [1962] Director/Property Development

Southport and Windsor Properties LLP
Incorporated: 22 June 2004 *Employees:* 4
Net Worth: £2,727,305 *Total Assets:* £7,063,336
Registered Office: Clint Mill, Cornmarket, Penrith, Cumbria, CA11 7HW
Officers: Celine Hilary Elizabeth Carney [1966] Member; Gerard Paul Carney [1967] Member; Paula Carney [1974] Member; Philip Andrew Carney [1961] Member

Southport Learning Trust
Incorporated: 28 September 2011 *Employees:* 90
Net Worth: £14,839,000 *Total Assets:* £17,889,000
Registered Office: Greenbank High School, Hastings Road, Southport, Merseyside, PR8 2LT
Activities: General secondary education
Officers: Stuart Bellerby [1965] Director/Education Officer; Richard Cottier [1965] Director/Business Development Manager; Dr Richard Hadji [1977] Director/Audit Manager; Victoria Karen Keeley [1970] Director; Ian David Raikes [1972] Director/Headteacher; Carol Sharman [1951] Director/Teacher/Data Manager; Anna Josephine Smith [1962] Director of Business and Finance; Ruth Marion Williams [1957] Director

Sovereign Chemicals Limited
Incorporated: 20 November 1996
Net Worth: £16,744,000 *Total Assets:* £19,046,000
Registered Office: Park Road, Barrow in Furness, Cumbria, LA14 4EQ
Activities: Manufacture of other chemical products n.e.c.
Parent: Arkema Ltd
Officers: Paul Anthony Hudson, Secretary; Roland Albers [1968] Director/Senior Vice President [Dutch]; Gary Jonathan Dee [1964] Managing Director; Frederique Marie-Pierre Lepinay [1960] Director/Corporate Finance Analyst [French]; Jason Walker [1971] Director/Finance Controller, Europe

Sovereign Group Limited
Incorporated: 5 January 1973 *Employees:* 183
Net Worth: £4,194,510 *Total Assets:* £7,451,685
Registered Office: Vale Street Mill, Nelson, Lancs, BB9 0TA
Activities: Other manufacturing n.e.c.
Parent: Austhall Holdings Limited
Officers: Lorraine Kluczniak, Secretary; Frances Anne Austin [1965] Director; David James Fitton [1964] Director; Jason Gibson [1975] Construction Director; Mark Johnston [1981] Finance Director; Glenn Milligan [1958] Sales Director

Sovereign Health Care
Incorporated: 17 August 1905 *Employees:* 48
Net Worth: £65,389,776 *Total Assets:* £68,236,264
Registered Office: Royal Standard House, 26 Mannningham Lane, Bradford, BD1 3DN
Activities: Non-life insurance
Officers: Julian Scott Sellars, Secretary; Michael Stuart Bower [1960] Director/Solicitor; Stewart Michael Cummings [1977] Director/HR Business Partner; Simon Rhys Davies [1958] Director; Dr Robert Eddy Dugdale [1949] Director/Retired; Janet Christine Fortune [1958] Director; Christopher Mark Hudson [1957] Retired Financial Director; Russell Steven Piper [1959] Director/Chief Executive; Julian Scott Sellars [1973] Director/Chartered Accountant

The Sovereign Trust
Incorporated: 1 July 2015 *Employees:* 183
Net Worth: £20,906,136 *Total Assets:* £22,523,816
Registered Office: Pictor Academy, Grove Lane, Timperley, Altrincham, Cheshire, WA15 6PH
Activities: Pre-primary education
Officers: Maurice John French [1947] Director/Retired; Nicholas Spear Gill [1957] Director/Consultant; Shirley Cathryn Jones [1967] Director/Accountant; Ian Patrick McGrath [1967] Director [Irish]; Dilys Morgan [1956] Director/Education Consultant; Paul Francis Nolan [1962] Director/Business Manager; Beverley Owens [1955] Director/Headteacher; David Ashley Rowntree [1982] Director/Head of Underwriting

SP Manweb PLC
Incorporated: 1 April 1989 *Employees:* 12
Net Worth: £990,899,968 *Total Assets:* £2,797,299,968
Registered Office: 3 Prenton Way, Prenton, Birkenhead, Merseyside, CH43 3ET
Activities: Production of electricity
Parent: Scottish Power Energy Networks Holdings Limited
Officers: Seumus O'Gorman, Secretary; Wendy Jacqueline Barnes [1957] Director; Suzanne Fox [1969] Director; Scott Hamilton Mathieson [1972] Regulation Director; Frank Mitchell [1964] Director/Engineer; Stephen Alexander Stewart [1965] Director

SPC Group Holdings Limited
Incorporated: 15 June 2016 *Employees:* 340
Net Worth Deficit: £481,150 *Total Assets:* £15,057,420
Registered Office: 8 Vantage Court, Riverside Way, Barrowford, Lancs, BB9 6BF
Activities: Public houses and bars
Parent: Tosca Penta Pubco Limited Partnership
Officers: Ian Edward [1959] Director; William Torquil MacNaughton [1962] Director; William Andrew McLean [1960] Director; Joycelyn Rebecca Neve [1985] Director; Graham Hilton Price [1961] Director

Special Piping Materials (Holdings) Limited
Incorporated: 20 September 2013 *Employees:* 54
Net Worth: £18,375,212 *Total Assets:* £25,541,926
Registered Office: Unit 26 Globe Lane Industrial Estate, Broadway, Dukinfield, Cheshire, SK16 4UU
Activities: Wholesale of metals and metal ores
Shareholders: Leslie Buckley; Mary Linda Buckley
Officers: Anne Michelle King, Secretary; Leslie Buckley [1950] Director; Mary Linda Buckley [1949] Director

Special Piping Materials Limited
Incorporated: 20 October 1988 *Employees:* 18
Net Worth: £8,389,175 *Total Assets:* £10,101,811
Registered Office: Unit 26 Globe Industrial Estate, Dukinfield, Cheshire, SK16 4UU
Activities: Non-specialised wholesale trade
Parent: Special Piping Materials (Holdings) Limited
Officers: Mary Linda Buckley, Secretary; Leslie Buckley [1950] Director; Mary Linda Buckley [1949] Director/Secretary; Paul Leslie Buckley [1975] Director

Specialist Anodising Company Limited
Incorporated: 21 September 1984 *Employees:* 245
Net Worth: £17,194,072 *Total Assets:* £20,642,336
Registered Office: 86 Guilden Sutton Lane, Guilden Sutton, Chester, CH3 7EX
Activities: Manufacture of light metal packaging
Officers: Michael John Duffell, Secretary/Director; Andrew Michael Duffell [1969] Director; Matthew Samuel Michael Duffell [1976] Director; Michael John Duffell [1934] Director; Valerie Ann Duffell [1940] Director; Mark James Gwinnett [1968] Manufacturing Director; Victoria Ann Moody [1971] Sales & Commercial Director; Denys Taylor [1970] Director

Specialist Leisure Group Limited
Incorporated: 24 April 2014 *Employees:* 2,489
Net Worth: £15,103,000 *Total Assets:* £59,293,000
Registered Office: Waterside House, Waterside Drive, Wigan, Lancs, WN3 5AZ
Activities: Activities of head offices
Officers: Mark William Anderson [1978] Director; Richard James Calvert [1967] Director; Rob Edward Gray [1977] Director; Grant David Hearn [1958] Director; James Hendry Riddell [1979] Investment Director; Gary Speakman [1961] Finance Director; William David Young [1960] Director/Counsel [American]

Specialist People Services Group Limited
Incorporated: 21 April 2011 *Employees:* 227
Net Worth Deficit: £1,291,125 *Total Assets:* £31,714,868
Registered Office: 7 Bradford Business Park, Kings Gate, Bradford, W Yorks, BD1 4SJ
Activities: Activities of head offices
Parent: Lloyds Development Capital (Holdings) Ltd
Officers: Christopher Michael Chidley [1960] Director; Steven Richard Harrison [1956] Venture Capitalist/Director; Paul Howard McNulty [1970] Finance Director; Anthony William Rieger [1945] Director

Spectra-Physics Holdings Limited
Incorporated: 28 July 1987
Net Worth: £25,169,000 *Total Assets:* £25,173,000
Registered Office: 3rd Floor, 1 Ashley Road, Altrincham, Cheshire, WA14 2DT
Activities: Financial intermediation not elsewhere classified
Parent: Thermo Fisher Scientific Inc.
Officers: Rhona Gregg, Secretary; Lucie Mary Katja Grant [1976] Director/Solicitor; Nicholas Ince [1982] Director/Accountant; David John Norman [1960] Director/Chartered Accountant

Spectrum Brands (UK) Holdings Limited
Incorporated: 29 November 2010
Net Worth: £275,864,000 *Total Assets:* £714,187,008
Registered Office: Regent Mill, Fir Street, Failsworth, Manchester, M35 0HS
Activities: Activities of head offices
Parent: Spectrum Brands Lux II SARL
Officers: Christopher Berry [1954] Director; Anja Krueger [1967] Director [German]; Matthias Schiller [1962] Director [German]; Timothy John Wright [1962] Director

Spectrum Brands (UK) Limited
Incorporated: 13 June 1989 *Employees:* 582
Net Worth: £236,930,000 *Total Assets:* £324,267,008
Registered Office: Regent Mill, Fir Street, Failsworth, Manchester, M35 0HS
Activities: Manufacture of batteries and accumulators
Parent: Spectrum Brands (UK) Holdings Limited
Officers: Christopher Berry [1954] Director; Glen Alfred Rutherford [1969] Director/General Manager; Timothy John Wright [1962] Director

Spectrum Living Solutions Ltd
Incorporated: 17 February 2015 *Employees:* 1
Net Worth: £1,725,606 *Total Assets:* £32,156,276
Registered Office: 26 Regent Road, Altrincham, Cheshire, WA14 1RP
Activities: Other letting and operating of own or leased real estate
Shareholders: David Lockhart; Oliver Peter Patrick MacFarlane
Officers: David Lockhart [1962] Director; Oliver Peter Patrick MacFarlane [1967] Director

Speed Medical Examination Services Limited
Incorporated: 19 May 1998 *Employees:* 224
Net Worth: £19,303,634 *Total Assets:* £58,401,480
Registered Office: Speed Medical House, Matrix Park, Chorley, Lancs, PR7 7NA
Activities: Other human health activities
Parent: FL 360 Limited
Officers: Susan Henry [1975] Operations Director; Ian David Robins [1966] Finance Director

Speedy Asset Services Limited
Incorporated: 16 March 2009 *Employees:* 2,867
Net Worth: £41,008,000 *Total Assets:* £275,896,992
Registered Office: Chase House, 16 The Parks, Newton-le-Willows, Merseyside, WA12 0JQ
Activities: Renting and leasing of other machinery, equipment and tangible goods n.e.c.
Parent: Speedy Hire PLC
Officers: Neil John Hunt, Secretary; Russell Down [1965] Finance Director; Thomas Christopher Morgan [1966] Director

Speedy Hire PLC
Incorporated: 22 February 1968 *Employees:* 3,641
Net Worth: £189,600,000 *Total Assets:* £349,000,000
Registered Office: Chase House, 16 The Parks, Newton-le-Willows, Merseyside, WA12 0JQ
Activities: Renting and leasing of other machinery, equipment and tangible goods n.e.c.
Officers: Neil John Hunt, Secretary; Jan Gunnar Astrand [1947] Director [Swedish]; Robert Barclay [1969] Director; Robert Leonard Contreras [1962] Director; Russell Down [1965] Finance Director; David Noel Christopher Garman [1951] Director; Thomas Christopher Morgan [1966] Director; David James Buchanan Shearer [1959] Director

Speedy International Leasing Limited
Incorporated: 2 March 2010
Net Worth Deficit: £9,954,000 *Total Assets:* £10,002,000
Registered Office: Chase House, 16 The Parks, Newton-le-Willows, Merseyside, WA12 0JQ
Activities: Renting and leasing of other machinery, equipment and tangible goods n.e.c.
Parent: Speedy International Asset Services (Holdings) Limited
Officers: Neil John Hunt, Secretary; Russell Down [1965] Finance Director; Thomas Christopher Morgan [1966] Director

Speedy Products Limited
Incorporated: 28 January 1976 *Employees:* 226
Net Worth: £4,996,833 *Total Assets:* £9,408,875
Registered Office: Speedy House, Cheltenham Street, Manchester, M6 6WY
Activities: Wholesale of household goods (other than musical instruments) n.e.c
Major Shareholder: Ivor Henry Seddon
Officers: Dean Jeremy Seddon, Secretary; Dean Jeremy Seddon [1979] Managing Director; Ivor Henry Seddon [1952] Director

Speedy Support Services Limited
Incorporated: 9 March 1990 *Employees:* 233
Net Worth Deficit: £82,839,000 *Total Assets:* £29,426,000
Registered Office: Chase House, 16 The Parks, Newton-le-Willows, Merseyside, WA12 0JQ
Activities: Renting and leasing of other machinery, equipment and tangible goods n.e.c.
Parent: Speedy Hire PLC
Officers: Neil John Hunt, Secretary; Russell Down [1965] Finance Director; Thomas Christopher Morgan [1966] Director

Speedy Transport Limited
Incorporated: 3 April 2002
Net Worth: £1,488,000 *Total Assets:* £45,336,000
Registered Office: Chase House, 16 The Parks, Newton-le-Willows, Merseyside, WA12 0JQ
Activities: Renting and leasing of other machinery, equipment and tangible goods n.e.c.
Parent: Speedy Hire PLC
Officers: Neil John Hunt, Secretary; Russell Down [1965] Finance Director; Thomas Christopher Morgan [1966] Director

Spellman & Walker Direct Limited
Incorporated: 6 October 2005 *Employees:* 98
Net Worth: £5,610,808 *Total Assets:* £7,601,286
Registered Office: Graphica House, Chase Way, Bradford, W Yorks, BD5 8SW
Activities: Activities of head offices
Shareholders: Susan Jane Hirst; Michael Owen Hirst
Officers: Nigel Stuart Risby, Secretary; Michael Owen Hirst [1961] Director; Nigel Stuart Risby [1957] Sales Director

Spellman & Walker Group Limited
Incorporated: 10 October 2005
Net Worth: £13,806,481 *Total Assets:* £14,575,391
Registered Office: Graphica House, Chase Way, Bradford, W Yorks, BD5 8SW
Activities: Printing n.e.c.
Parent: Spellman & Walker Direct Limited
Officers: Nigel Stuart Risby, Secretary; Michael Owen Hirst [1961] Director; Nigel Stuart Risby [1957] Sales Director

Spencross Limited
Incorporated: 28 November 1997 *Employees:* 98
Net Worth: £2,454,122 *Total Assets:* £11,278,083
Registered Office: 46 Fountain Street, Manchester, M2 2BE
Activities: Activities of head offices
Shareholders: Raymond Roberts; Allabe SARL
Officers: Nathan Duke Chuwen, Secretary; Dr Dorothy Joan Clayton [1950] Director/Historical Researcher; Raymond Roberts [1951] Director/Solicitor

Max Spielmann Limited
Incorporated: 18 December 2008 *Employees:* 1,061
Net Worth: £9,566,000 *Total Assets:* £28,668,000
Registered Office: Timpson House, Claverton Road, Wythenshawe, Manchester, M23 9TT
Activities: Other service activities n.e.c.
Parent: Timpson Group PLC
Officers: Paresh Majithia, Secretary; Paresh Majithia [1967] Finance Director; Sir William John Anthony Timpson [1943] Director; William James Timpson [1971] Managing Director

Spindles Investment Limited
Incorporated: 9 January 2015 *Employees:* 2
Net Worth: £926,517 *Total Assets:* £8,344,126
Registered Office: 4 Hardman Square, Spinningfields, Manchester, M3 3EB
Activities: Financial intermediation not elsewhere classified
Officers: David Alan Gill [1957] Director; Victoria Jane Gill [1957] Director/Housewife

Spinney Garage Limited
Incorporated: 14 September 1977 *Employees:* 59
Net Worth: £3,757,891 *Total Assets:* £7,717,404
Registered Office: Knutsford Road, Cranage, Crewe, Cheshire, CW4 8HJ
Activities: Sale of other motor vehicles
Major Shareholder: Gillian Diane Holland
Officers: Benjamin Edward Holland [1984] Director; Charles Douglas Holland [1989] Director; Gillian Diane Holland [1958] Director

Spiritel Mobile Limited
Incorporated: 12 June 2001 *Employees:* 26
Net Worth: £7,336,000 *Total Assets:* £10,548,000
Registered Office: Daisy House, Lindred Road Business Park, Nelson, Lancs, BB9 5SR
Activities: Other telecommunications activities
Parent: Anglia Telecom Centres Limited
Officers: David Lewis McGlennon, Secretary; Nathan Richard Marke [1970] Director; David Lewis McGlennon [1974] Director; Stephen Alan Smith [1963] Director

SPM Plastics U.K. Limited
Incorporated: 29 August 2000 *Employees:* 358
Net Worth Deficit: £36,265,000 *Total Assets:* £19,388,000
Registered Office: Grove Mill, Todmorden Road, Bacup, Lancs, OL13 9EF
Activities: Manufacture of other plastic products
Parent: Medplast LLC
Officers: Anthony Gilarde, Secretary; Daniel Agroskin [1976] Managing Director, JLL Partners, LLC [American]; Harold Faig [1948] Director/Business Executive [American]; Brian Douglas King [1967] Director [American]; Peter Maurice Strothman [1977] Director/Partner Water Street Healthcare Partners [American]

Sporting Club St. Helens Limited
Incorporated: 11 November 1999 *Employees:* 560
Net Worth: £12,848,546 *Total Assets:* £31,550,352
Registered Office: St Helens RFC Stadium, McManus Drive, St Helens, Merseyside, WA9 3AL
Activities: Non-trading company
Officers: Colin Roy Whitehead, Secretary; Dermot John Coleman [1962] Director; Michael Coleman [1960] Director; James Alexander George Hartley [1951] Director/Antique Dealer; Kevin John Marren [1960] Director; Robert Keith McCormack [1946] Director; Eamonn McManus [1956] Director; Joseph Nicholl [1964] Managing Director

Sports Tours International Limited
Incorporated: 22 December 1987 *Employees:* 26
Net Worth: £2,240,198 *Total Assets:* £8,994,823
Registered Office: The Spectrum, 56-58 Benson Road, Birchwood, Warrington, Cheshire, WA3 7PQ
Activities: Tour operator activities
Officers: Michael Rodney Hamilton, Secretary/Accountant; Christopher Matthew Bird [1963] Director; Fred Done [1943] Director

Springfields Fuels Limited
Incorporated: 7 October 1999 *Employees:* 1,016
Net Worth: £40,159,000 *Total Assets:* £170,460,992
Registered Office: Springfields, Salwick, Preston, Lancs, PR4 0XJ
Activities: Processing of nuclear fuel
Parent: Westinghouse Electric UK Holdings Limited
Officers: Fiona Anne Houghton, Secretary; Kirsty Armer [1970] Director Business and Product Delivery; Linda Aylmore [1970] Director; Michael Robert Gornall [1964] Operations Director; David Mills [1965] Director/Head of Communications & Marketing; Brian Nixon [1976] Managing Director UK Fuel Operations

Springhill Care Group Limited
Incorporated: 10 June 1998 *Employees:* 381
Net Worth: £2,333,493 *Total Assets:* £15,014,053
Registered Office: 11 Cannon Street, Accrington, Lancs, BB5 1NJ
Activities: Activities of head offices
Major Shareholder: Kenneth Anthony Nolan
Officers: Nicola Jean Nolan, Secretary; Donna Margaret Briggs [1968] Managing Director; Kaitlyn Elizabeth Nolan [2001] Director; Kenneth Anthony Nolan [1960] Director/Nursing Home Proprietor; Luke Anthony Nolan [1996] Director; Matthew Joseph Nolan [1993] Director; Nicola Jean Nolan [1972] Director/Company Secretary

Springhill Hospice (Rochdale)
Incorporated: 7 December 1988 *Employees:* 107
Net Worth: £8,023,434 *Total Assets:* £8,495,203
Registered Office: The Springhill Hospice, Broad Lane, Rochdale, Lancs, OL16 4PZ
Activities: Other human health activities
Officers: Sultan Ali [1956] Director/Probation Officer; Susan Ann Blundell [1959] HR Director; Robert Clegg [1951] Director/Retired Health Manager; John Frederick Dafforne [1940] Director/Retired Bank Official; The Right Reverend Mark Davies [1962] Director/Bishop; Kitsa Mavis Efthymiadis [1958] Director/Solicitor; Carol Hopkins [1965] Director/Business Consultant; Lesley Ann Mort [1954] Director/Retired; Ratna Mukherjee [1949] Director/Civil Servant; Robert Namushi Namushi [1955] Director/Consultant; Steven Charles Price [1952] Director/Solicitor

Springhill House (Accrington) Limited
Incorporated: 5 March 1987 *Employees:* 182
Net Worth: £1,051,136 *Total Assets:* £7,245,318
Registered Office: 11 Cannon Street, Accrington, Lancs, BB5 1NJ
Activities: Residential nursing care facilities
Parent: Springhill Care Group Limited
Officers: Nicola Jean Nolan, Secretary; Donna Margaret Briggs [1968] Managing Director; Kenneth Anthony Nolan [1960] Director; Nicola Jean Nolan [1972] Director; Kathleen Annis Parkinson [1947] Director

SPS (EU) Holdings Limited
Incorporated: 21 November 2013 *Employees:* 303
Net Worth: £2,585,000 *Total Assets:* £14,082,000
Registered Office: Neptune House, Sycamore Trading Estate, Squires Gate Lane, Blackpool, Lancs, FY4 3RL
Activities: Activities of other holding companies n.e.c.
Parent: PF Concept International BV
Officers: Scott Barnett [1974] Director/Chief Financial Officer [American]; Ralf Oster [1961] Director/Chief Executive Officer [German]

SPS (EU) Limited
Incorporated: 4 July 1990 *Employees:* 298
Net Worth: £4,099,000 *Total Assets:* £16,224,000
Registered Office: Neptune House, Sycamore Trading Estate, Squires Gate Lane, Blackpool, Lancs, FY4 3RL
Activities: Manufacture of other plastic products
Parent: SPS (EU) Holdings Limited
Officers: Adriaan Willem Hartog [1970] Managing Director [Dutch]; Philip John Morgan [1971] Director/Chief Executive; Ralf Oster [1961] Director/Chief Executive Officer [German]; Tracey Elizabeth Street [1962] Director

SPX Clyde UK Limited
Incorporated: 27 September 2011
Net Worth Deficit: £83,405,000 *Total Assets:* £539,089,024
Registered Office: Eversheds House, 70 Great Bridgewater Street, Manchester, M1 5ES
Activities: Other business support service activities n.e.c.
Parent: Johnston Ballantyne Holdings Limited
Officers: Paul Andrew Cahill [1974] Director/Accountant; Mark Edward Shanahan [1970] Finance Director; Jeremy Wade Smeltser [1975] Director/CFO, SPX Flow, Inc. [American]; Stephen Tsoris [1957] Director [American]

SPX European Holding Limited
Incorporated: 20 April 2015
Net Worth: £139,900,992 *Total Assets:* £281,107,008
Registered Office: Eversheds House, 70 Great Bridgewater Street, Manchester, M1 5ES
Activities: Other service activities n.e.c.
Parent: SPX Corporation
Officers: Kevin Paul Lench [1961] Managing Director; John Nurkin [1969] Director [American]; Scott William Sproule [1969] Director/Vice President, Treasurer & CFO [American]; Lynn Williams [1956] Director/Accountant

SPX Flow Technology London Limited
Incorporated: 10 June 1910
Net Worth: £13,825,000 *Total Assets:* £16,792,000
Registered Office: Ocean House, Towers Business Park, Wilmslow Road, Didsbury, Manchester, M20 2LY
Activities: Activities of head offices
Parent: SPX Clyde UK Limited
Officers: Paul Andrew Cahill [1974] Director/Accountant; Mark Edward Shanahan [1970] Director; Jeremy Wade Smeltser [1975] Director/CFO, SPX Flow, Inc. [American]; Stephen Tsoris [1957] Director [American]

SR Properties Manchester Limited
Incorporated: 10 September 2012 *Employees:* 4
Net Worth: £1,420,495 *Total Assets:* £11,440,908
Registered Office: Warth Business Centre, Warth Industrial Park, Warth Road, Bury, Lancs, BL9 9TB
Activities: Buying and selling of own real estate
Parent: Sheffield and Regional Properties Limited
Officers: Richard Harvey James Nuttall, Secretary; Ian Elliott [1969] Director; Bernard Christopher Norman Roger Holmes [1945] Director; Richard Harvey James Nuttall [1965] Director; Paul Raymond Williams [1956] Director

SR Properties Nationwide Limited
Incorporated: 29 July 2010 *Employees:* 4
Net Worth: £429,231 *Total Assets:* £7,480,794
Registered Office: Warth Business Centre, Warth Industrial Park, Warth Road, Bury, Lancs, BL9 9TB
Activities: Buying and selling of own real estate
Parent: Sheffield & Regional Properties Limited
Officers: Richard Harvey James Nuttall, Secretary; Ian Elliott [1969] Director; Bernard Christopher Norman Roger Holmes [1945] Director; Richard Harvey James Nuttall [1965] Director; Paul Raymond Williams [1956] Director

SSCP Blink Bidco Limited
Incorporated: 19 April 2015 *Employees:* 31
Net Worth Deficit: £1,254,176 *Total Assets:* £10,195,861
Registered Office: Fernbank House, Springwood Way, Tytherington Business Park, Macclesfield, Cheshire, SK10 2XA
Activities: Wholesale of pharmaceutical goods
Officers: Ian Martin Snelson, Secretary; Christian Reichenberger [1979] Finance Director [German]; Ian Martin Snelson [1967] Director/Chartered Accountant

SSH Property Investment Limited
Incorporated: 25 September 2015
Net Worth: £16,022 *Total Assets:* £6,814,160
Registered Office: The Robert Street Hub, 12-14 Robert Street, Manchester, M3 1EY
Activities: Buying and selling of own real estate
Shareholders: Suleman Nurez Kamani; Hannah Nurez Kamani; Sara Nurez Kamani
Officers: Hannah Nurez Kamani [1991] Director; Sara Nurez Kamani [1995] Director; Suleman Nurez Kamani [1989] Director

The St David's Hotel Cardiff Limited
Incorporated: 6 January 1997 *Employees:* 209
Net Worth: £37,668,000 *Total Assets:* £45,458,000
Registered Office: c/o KPMG LLP, One St Peters Square, Manchester, M2 3AE
Activities: Hotels and similar accommodation
Parent: The St David's Hotel Cardiff Holdco Limited
Officers: Patrick Bour [1978] Director [French]

St Francis Xavier's College
Incorporated: 10 July 2012 *Employees:* 130
Net Worth: £15,691,461 *Total Assets:* £19,194,694
Registered Office: Woolton Hill Road, Liverpool, L25 6EG
Activities: General secondary education
Officers: Donna Victoria Banks, Secretary; Andrew Robert Austin [1965] Director; Daniel Karl Bowers [1980] Director; Genevieve Butcher [1969] Director/Attendance Officer; Sandra Ann Coleman [1977] Director/Teacher; Anthony Joseph Crilly [1967] Director/HR Professional; David Delaney [1980] Director/Teacher; Michael James Edwards [1952] Director/Retired; Andrew John Emmott [1983] Director/Civil Engineer; Amy Clare Fitzsimons [1992] Director/Teacher; Pauline Cecilia Formela [1955] Director; Moira Gormely [1951] Director/Childminder; Dr Andrew Keeley [1962] Director/Research Scientist; Stephen MacNally [1963] Director; Joanne Murphy [1970] Director/Project Manager; Nicholas O'Hare [1969] Director; Francis Patterson [1938] Director/Retired; Paul Rawlinson [1960] Director/IT Consultant; David Reynolds [1945] Director/Groundsman; Lisa Riccio-Jones [1971] Director/Civil Servant; Louis Seite [1948] Director/Retired [French]; David Michael Yates [1973] Director/Headmaster

St George Care UK Limited
Incorporated: 20 February 2008
Net Worth: £11,574,423 *Total Assets:* £51,409,096
Registered Office: The Old Rectory, Rectory Lane, Winwick, Warrington, Cheshire, WA2 8LE
Activities: Activities of head offices
Officers: Hala Elnarshy-Fouad, Secretary/Accountant; Hala Elnarshy-Fouad [1969] Director/Accountant; Dr Naser Michel Fouad [1964] Director/Doctor

St George Healthcare Group Limited
Incorporated: 7 February 2005 *Employees:* 23
Net Worth: £3,189,934 *Total Assets:* £9,502,939
Registered Office: The Old Rectory, Rectory Lane, Winwick, Warrington, Cheshire, WA2 8LE
Activities: Activities of head offices
Officers: Hala Elnarshy Fouad, Secretary/Accountant; Hala Elnarshy Fouad [1969] Director/Accountant; Dr Naser Michel Fouad [1964] Director/Doctor

St George Healthcare Limited
Incorporated: 26 July 1999 *Employees:* 128
Net Worth: £873,771 *Total Assets:* £8,982,012
Registered Office: Floyd Drive, Warrington, Cheshire, WA2 8DB
Activities: Hospital activities
Officers: Hala Elnarshy Fouad, Secretary; Hala Elnarshy Fouad [1969] Director/Accountant; Naser Michel Fouad [1964] Director/Doctor Medical

St Helens Chamber Limited
Incorporated: 18 December 1989 *Employees:* 109
Net Worth: £5,558,797 *Total Assets:* £7,257,837
Registered Office: St Helens Chamber, Salisbury Street, off Chalon Way, St Helens, Merseyside, WA10 1FY
Activities: Other information service activities n.e.c.
Officers: Clare Maria Gravener, Secretary; Kathleen Elizabeth Boullen [1963] Director/Chief Executive; Andrew John Bowden [1964] Director/Office Manager; Caroline Elizabeth Haworth [1960] Director; Hazel Marion James [1961] Managing Director; Jackie Mafi [1957] Director/Business Administration Manager; Andrew McMinnis [1973] Director/Accountant; Michael MacKay Palin [1981] Director/Chief Executive, St Helens Council; Andrew Smith [1960] Director; William Graham Worsley [1954] Managing Director

St Helens Rugby Football Club Limited
Incorporated: 24 September 1937 *Employees:* 603
Net Worth: £7,900,028 *Total Assets:* £33,099,576
Registered Office: St Helens RFC Stadium, McManus Drive, St Helens, Merseyside, WA9 3AL
Activities: Operation of sports facilities
Parent: Sporting Club St Helens Limited
Officers: Colin Roy Whitehead, Secretary; Dermot Coleman [1962] Director; Michael Coleman [1960] Director; James Alexander George Hartley [1951] Director/Antique Dealer; Kevin John Marren [1960] Director; Robert Keith McCormack [1946] Director; Eamonn McManus [1956] Director; Joseph Nicholl [1964] Managing Director

St James's Oncology SPC Holdings Ltd
Incorporated: 5 April 2004
Net Worth: £50,000 *Total Assets:* £21,350,000
Registered Office: c/o Albany SPC Services Ltd, 3rd Floor, 3-5 Charlotte Street, Manchester, M1 4HB
Activities: Hospital activities
Parent: Consolidated Investment Holdings Ltd
Officers: Ailison Louise Mitchell, Secretary; Barry Paul Millsom [1974] Director; Christopher Thomas Solley [1970] Director; Andrew Leslie Tennant [1958] Director

St James's Oncology SPC Ltd
Incorporated: 27 April 2004
Net Worth Deficit: £22,141,000 *Total Assets:* £280,543,008
Registered Office: c/o Albany SPC Services Ltd, 3rd Floor, 3-5 Charlotte Street, Manchester, M1 4HB
Activities: Other human health activities
Parent: St James's Oncology SPC Holdings Ltd
Officers: Ailison Louise Mitchell, Secretary; Barry Paul Millsom [1974] Director; Christopher Thomas Solley [1970] Director; Andrew Leslie Tennant [1958] Director

St Margaret's Church of England Academy
Incorporated: 30 July 2012 *Employees:* 130
Net Worth: £14,514,000 *Total Assets:* £17,018,000
Registered Office: St Margaret's Church of England Academy, Aigburth Road, Liverpool, L17 6AB
Activities: General secondary education
Officers: Mark Robert D'Arcy, Secretary; Stephen Jon Bray [1976] Director/Governor; Stephen Clifford Brierley [1967] Director/Headmaster; Stephanie Davidson [1971] Director/Governor; Nuala Dunne [1981] Director/Teacher; Celine Duzant [1946] Director/Governor; Terence Van Eker [1958] Director/Governor; Mark Andrew Fidler [1989] Director/Governor; John Owen Foulkes [1951] Director/Governor; Rev Ian Greenwood [1974] Director/Governor; Jane Griffiths [1958] Director/Governor; Deana Ann Hughes [1975] Director/Governor; Andrew David McCaldon [1989] Director/Student; Janet Anne McCall [1959] Director/Governor; Victoria Merriman [1972] Director/Governor; Revd David Michael Morris [1959] Director/Governor; Peter Oliver [1979] Director/Governor; Helen Jane Schluter [1975] Director/Governor; Christopher John Ward [1973] Director/Governor

St Wilfrid's Church of England Academy
Incorporated: 15 June 2011 *Employees:* 198
Net Worth: £23,283,616 *Total Assets:* £27,165,384
Registered Office: St Wilfred's Church of England Academy, Duckworth Street, Blackburn, Lancs, BB2 2JR
Activities: General secondary education
Officers: Caroline Holt, Secretary; Alison Jane Crompton [1967] Director/Assistant Principal; Aileen Jill Cross [1955] Director/Medical Secretary; Tymika Louise Duffy [1982] Director/Student; Valerie Margaret Edge [1948] Director/Part Time Tutor; Heather Henderson [1956] Director/Bishops Wife; Mark Adrian Hodson [1961] Director/Marketing Manager; Jamila Hounslow [1967] Director/Church Community Worker; Catherine Huddleston [1965] Director/Acting Principal; John Leigh [1944] Director/Solicitor; Gordon Frank Moulding [1955] Director/Local Government Corporate Appointee/Deputy; Mark Power [1967] Director/Deputy Headteacher; David Rintoul [1967] Director/Quality & Performance Manager NHS; Andrew Robinson [1971] Director/Engineer; Jean Margaret Sherwood-Hartley [1952] Director/Teaching Assistant; John Henry Venables [1948] Director/Retired; Janet Vials [1960] Director/Teacher; Michael Joseph White [1967] Director/Local Government Officer; Judith Margaret Wilcock [1971] Director/Occupational Therapist

St. Ambrose College Edmund Rice Academy Trust
Incorporated: 28 October 2011 *Employees:* 97
Net Worth: £25,501,000 *Total Assets:* £26,294,000
Registered Office: St Ambrose College, Hale Barns, Altrincham, Cheshire, WA15 0HE
Activities: General secondary education
Officers: Dr Peter Charles Goodwin [1968] Director; Patrick George Gordon [1942] Director/Retired Headmaster [Irish]; Margaret Anne Kerr [1940] Director/Retired; Matthew Thomas Lalley [1966] Director; Helen Rosemary Norwood [1950] Director; Pauline Margaret Ridgway [1957] Director; Councillor Bernard Sharp [1936] Director/Solicitor (Retired)

St. Ann's Hospice
Incorporated: 3 February 1969 *Employees:* 241
Net Worth: £14,788,818 *Total Assets:* £20,796,334
Registered Office: St Ann's Road North, Heald Green, Cheadle, Cheshire, SK8 3SZ
Activities: Hospital activities
Officers: Dr Paul Jarvis, Secretary; Allan William Beardsworth [1962] Director/Chartered Tax Adviser, Chartered Accountant; Alan John Bond [1943] Director/Accountant; Christopher Michael Brown [1946] Director/Management Consultant; Luke Dillon [1955] Director/Educational Consultant; Dr Stephanie Gomm [1950] Director/Retired Medical Doctor; Professor Jacqueline Oldham [1961] Director/Professor; Kate Squire [1962] Director/BBC Manager; Fiona Taylor [1964] Director/Chief Executive, NHS; Steve Wilson [1973] Director/Executive Lead

St. Annes (Holdings) Limited
Incorporated: 23 March 2017
Net Worth: £6,787 *Total Assets:* £7,532,134
Registered Office: c/o HRC Law LLP, Acresfield, 8-10 Exchange Street, Manchester, M2 7HA
Activities: Construction of other civil engineering projects n.e.c.
Officers: Paul Tomlinson, Secretary; Jonathan Bracegirdle [1973] Director; Jamie Brian Foster [1977] Director; Russell James Hitchin [1978] Director; Liam Peter Melly [1981] Director; Paul Tomlinson [1970] Director; Thomas Wood [1981] Director

St. Bede's College Limited
Incorporated: 14 July 1988 *Employees:* 149
Net Worth: £6,497,845 *Total Assets:* £8,978,678
Registered Office: St Bede's College, Alexandra Park, Manchester, M16 8HX
Activities: Pre-primary education
Officers: Mark Michael Lynch, Secretary; Rev Paul Daly [1965] Director/Priest; David Harold Frost [1956] Director/College Principal; Clare Kathryn Hopton [1970] Director/IT Manager [British/Australian]; Rebecca Mary Kennedy [1966] Director/Counsellor; Zofia Kwiatkowska [1955] Director/Retired; Terence Walsh [1983] Director/Solicitor

St. Catherine's Hospice (Lancashire) Limited
Incorporated: 7 December 1981
Net Worth: £11,063,000 *Total Assets:* £12,063,000
Registered Office: Lostock Lane, Lostock Hall, Preston, Lancs, PR5 5XU
Activities: Other education n.e.c.
Officers: Stephen Greenhalgh, Secretary; John Anthony Bonser [1945] Director/Retired; John George Chesworth [1971] Director/Solicitor; Lesley Anne Doxsey [1962] Director/NHS Manager; Dr Fiona Margaret Duncan [1956] Director/Nurse; Peter Austin Franks [1956] Director/Retired; Timothy Roger Frier [1979] Marketing Director; Anthony Ernest Harrisson [1946] Director/Retired Chief Executive; Jonathan Holden [1980] Director/Solicitor; Philip Robert Jones [1954] Director/Retired; Michael James Lough [1975] Director; Rachael Elaine Moses [1979] Director/Consultant Physiotherapist; Lorraine Norris [1958] Director/Retired; Doctor Stephen Thomas Ward [1954] Medical Director

St. Johns Buildings Limited
Incorporated: 18 May 1995 *Employees:* 76
Net Worth: £5,755,775 *Total Assets:* £8,854,421
Registered Office: 24a-28 St John Street, Manchester, M3 4DJ
Activities: Other business support service activities n.e.c.
Officers: David Anderson, Secretary; David Berkley [1955] Director/Barrister; Andrew James Green [1970] Director/Barrister; Peter John Harrison [1960] Director/Barrister; Sally Harrison [1968] Director/Barrister; Frances Heaton [1961] Director/Barrister; Benjamin Lawrence [1981] Director/Barrister; Richard Norton [1969] Director/Barrister; Joseph Patrick Anthony Peter O'Brien [1966] Director; Andrew John Martin O'Byrne [1950] Director/Barrister [Irish]; Karl Rowley [1969] Director/Barrister; David Christopher Taylor [1975] Director/Barrister

St. Rocco's Hospice
Incorporated: 2 June 1981 *Employees:* 122
Net Worth: £8,738,072 *Total Assets:* £9,167,670
Registered Office: St Rocco's Hospice, Lockton Lane, Warrington, Cheshire, WA5 0BW
Activities: Other human health activities
Officers: John Alan Farquharson, Secretary; Zack Clements [1986] Director/Recruitment Consultant; Ian Dennis Currie [1963] Director/Retired; Guy Hindle [1966] Director/Retired; David Kendrick [1955] Director/Premises Manager; Andrew William Mellor [1967] Director/IT Consultant; The Venerable Roger Martin Howell Preece [1964] Director/Minister of Religion; Jennifer Sophie Elizabeth Roulston [1979] Director/Solicitor; Mary Rudkin [1963] Director/HR Specialist; Lyn Sanchez [1959] Director/Retired; Dr Catherine Elizabeth Walshe [1965] Director/University Academic; Michael Watson [1960] Director/Retired

St. Tropez Acquisition Co. Limited
Incorporated: 13 February 2006
Net Worth Deficit: £13,507,000 *Total Assets:* £45,730,000
Registered Office: Manchester Business Park, 3500 Aviator Way, Manchester, M22 5TG
Activities: Other business support service activities n.e.c.
Parent: St. Tropez Holdings Limited
Officers: Simon Paul Plant, Secretary; Brandon Howard Leigh [1971] Director; Simon Paul Plant [1969] Director

St.Edward's College Edmund Rice Academy Trust
Incorporated: 8 April 2011 *Employees:* 125
Net Worth: £4,356,891 *Total Assets:* £8,099,447
Registered Office: St Edward's College, North Drive, Sandfield Park, Liverpool, L12 1LF
Activities: General secondary education
Officers: Dr Philip Henry Doyle [1947] Director/Retired; Nicholas John Melville [1961] Director/Solicitor; Stephen Morris [1969] Director/Principal

Stagecoach (North West) Limited
Incorporated: 8 August 1912 *Employees:* 745
Net Worth: £6,688,000 *Total Assets:* £22,607,000
Registered Office: c/o Stagecoach Services Limited, One Stockport Exchange, 20 Railway Road, Stockport, Cheshire, SK1 3SW
Activities: Other urban, suburban or metropolitan passenger land transport (not underground, metro or similar)
Parent: Stagecoach Bus Holdings Limited
Officers: Michael John Vaux, Secretary; Colin Brown [1968] Director/Accountant; Arnold Mark Threapleton [1954] Managing Director; Mark Thomas Whitelocks [1982] Managing Director

Stagecoach (South) Limited
Incorporated: 22 October 1982 *Employees:* 1,227
Net Worth: £23,113,000 *Total Assets:* £48,108,000
Registered Office: c/o Stagecoach Services Limited, One Stockport Exchange, 20 Railway Road, Stockport, Cheshire, SK1 3SW
Activities: Other urban, suburban or metropolitan passenger land transport (not underground, metro or similar)
Parent: Stagecoach Bus Holdings Limited
Officers: Michael John Vaux, Secretary; Colin Brown [1968] Director/Accountant; Edward Leonard Hodgson [1970] Managing Director; Arnold Mark Threapleton [1954] Managing Director

Stagecoach Devon Limited
Incorporated: 21 December 1995 *Employees:* 1,221
Net Worth: £14,406,000 *Total Assets:* £44,300,000
Registered Office: c/o Stagecoach Services Limited, One Stockport Exchange, 20 Railway Road, Stockport, Cheshire, SK1 3SW
Activities: Other urban, suburban or metropolitan passenger land transport (not underground, metro or similar)
Parent: Stagecoach Bus Holdings Limited
Officers: Michael John Vaux, Secretary; Colin Brown [1968] Director/Accountant; Robert Dennison [1976] Managing Director [New Zealander]; Arnold Mark Threapleton [1954] Managing Director

Stagecoach Services Limited
Incorporated: 9 May 1989 *Employees:* 230
Net Worth Deficit: £5,749,000 *Total Assets:* £144,232,992
Registered Office: c/o Stagecoach Services Limited, One Stockport Exchange, 20 Railway Road, Stockport, Cheshire, SK1 3SW
Activities: Other transportation support activities
Parent: Stagecoach Bus Holdings Limited
Officers: Michael John Vaux, Secretary; Robert Gervase Andrew [1963] Director; Lesley Ashman [1961] Director; Colin Brown [1968] Director/Accountant; Mark Stuart Edwin Haberfield [1963] Managing Director; Ross John Paterson [1971] Director/Accountant; Arnold Mark Threapleton [1954] Managing Director

Stagecoach Supertram Maintenance Ltd.
Incorporated: 30 June 1986 *Employees:* 80
Net Worth Deficit: £1,414,000 *Total Assets:* £10,999,000
Registered Office: c/o Stagecoach Services Limited, One Stockport Exchange, 20 Railway Road, Stockport, Cheshire, SK1 3SW
Activities: Repair and maintenance of other transport equipment n.e.c.
Parent: South Yorkshire Supertram Limited
Officers: Michael John Vaux, Secretary; Timothy David Bilby [1972] Director/Accountant Martin Andrew Griffiths [1966] Finance Director; James Norton Stewart [1974] Director; Michael John Vaux [1971] Director/Solicitor; Nigel Wragg [1967] Director

Stainforth Construction LLP
Incorporated: 17 December 2010 *Employees:* 41
Net Worth: £2,501,037 *Total Assets:* £9,145,841
Registered Office: 1 Butterfield Park, Otley Road, Shipley, W Yorks, BD17 7HE
Officers: Lee Terence Barnes [1973] Member; Dean Martyn Slingsby [1964] Member; Christopher Daniel Wilson [1962] Member; Alison Marie Barnes [1972] LLP Member; Michelle Ann Slingsby [1972] LLP Member; Kathleen Wilson [1962] LLP Member

Stamford Group Limited (The)
Incorporated: 29 June 1982 *Employees:* 175
Net Worth: £7,769,000 *Total Assets:* £9,308,000
Registered Office: Stamford Works, Bayley Street, Stalybridge, Cheshire, SK15 1QQ
Activities: Activities of head offices
Parent: Navagator Ltd
Officers: Stephen Keith Picot, Secretary; Stephen Dubyl [1959] Director; Katie Jane Ferris [1971] Director/Teacher; Stephen Keith Picot [1950] Director/Chartered Accountant; Alan Reay [1938] Director

Stamford Products Limited
Incorporated: 19 July 1982 *Employees:* 175
Net Worth: £6,197,000 *Total Assets:* £8,097,000
Registered Office: Stamford Works, Bayley Street, Stalybridge, Cheshire, SK15 1QQ
Activities: Manufacture of other plastic products
Parent: The Stamford Group Ltd
Officers: Dawn Marie Lee, Secretary; Stephen Dubyl [1959] Director; Katie Jane Ferris [1971] Director; Stephen McKenna [1943] Sales and Marketing Director; Stephen Keith Picot [1950] Director/Chartered Accountant; Alan Reay [1938] Director; Allison Kay Seabourne [1961] Director; David Robert Sergeant [1960] Director

Stamptree Limited
Incorporated: 25 November 2005
Net Worth Deficit: £1,402,000 *Total Assets:* £23,402,000
Registered Office: c/o Calder Industrial Materials Limited, Jupiter Drive, Chester, CH1 4EX
Activities: Activities of head offices
Parent: Calder Finco UK Limited
Officers: William Buist-Wells, Secretary/Director; Gregory Mark Andrews [1973] Finance Director; William Buist-Wells [1950] Director; Richard Benjamin Travers [1955] Director

Standard Wool (UK) Limited
Incorporated: 29 January 1962 *Employees:* 80
Net Worth: £12,135,573 *Total Assets:* £33,444,970
Registered Office: Standard House, Trevor Foster Way, Bradford, W Yorks, BD5 8HB
Activities: Other manufacturing n.e.c.
Parent: Standard Wool UK (Holdings) Limited
Officers: Mark Andrews [1963] Production Director; Paul Stuart Hughes [1985] Trading Director; Paul Thomas Hughes [1948] Managing Director; Ian Ralph Marwood [1961] Director

Standard Wool UK (Holdings) Limited
Incorporated: 1 March 2004 *Employees:* 156
Net Worth: £6,416,964 *Total Assets:* £39,020,504
Registered Office: Standard House, Trevor Foster Way, Bradford, W Yorks, BD5 8HB
Activities: Preparation and spinning of textile fibres
Major Shareholder: Paul Thomas Hughes
Officers: Kathryn Hughes [1959] Director; Paul Stuart Hughes [1985] Trading Director; Paul Thomas Hughes [1948] Managing Director; Ian Ralph Marwood [1961] Director

Stanleybet Holdings Limited
Incorporated: 1 February 2007 *Employees:* 319
Net Worth: £3,844,440 *Total Assets:* £23,414,112
Registered Office: Exchange Station, Tithebarn Street, Liverpool, L2 2QP
Activities: Activities of other holding companies n.e.c.
Major Shareholder: Dr Giovanni Garrisi
Officers: William Lymbery Bland [1950] Director/Accountant; Dr Giovanni Garrisi [1948] Director; John Samuel Whittaker [1950] Director

Stanleybet International Limited
Incorporated: 23 July 2002 *Employees:* 3
Net Worth: £9,269,000 *Total Assets:* £15,323,000
Registered Office: Exchange Station, Tithebarn Street, Liverpool, L2 2QP
Activities: Other business support service activities n.e.c.
Parent: Europe Business Limited
Officers: William Lymbery Bland [1950] Director/Accountant; Dr Giovanni Garrisi [1948] Director; John Samuel Whittaker [1950] Director

Arnold Stansby & Co. Limited
Incorporated: 4 July 2011 *Employees:* 8
Net Worth: £400,653 *Total Assets:* £13,444,869
Registered Office: 3rd Floor, Alexandra Buildings, 28 Queen Street, Manchester, M2 5JJ
Activities: Activities of financial services holding companies
Parent: Arnold Stansby Holdings Limited
Officers: Karl Townsend, Secretary; Benjamin Robert Pearce [1977] Director/Accountant; Jeremy Ward Stockton [1960] Director; Nicholas Gerard Stockton [1957] Director; Karl David Townsend [1987] Director/Stockbroker

Arnold Stansby Holdings Limited
Incorporated: 24 May 2012 *Employees:* 8
Net Worth: £1,030,668 *Total Assets:* £14,253,985
Registered Office: 3rd Floor, Alexandra Buildings, 28 Queen Street, Manchester, M2 5JJ
Activities: Activities of financial services holding companies
Shareholders: Jeremy Ward Stockton; Nicholas Gerard Stockton
Officers: Karl Townsend, Secretary; Jeremy Ward Stockton [1960] Director/Stockbroker; Nicholas Gerard Stockton [1957] Director/Stockbroker

Star Academies
Incorporated: 23 August 2010 *Employees:* 1,126
Net Worth: £185,087,008 *Total Assets:* £199,164,992
Registered Office: Star Academies, Shadsworth Road, Blackburn, Lancs, BB1 2HT
Activities: Primary education
Officers: Carol Theresa Costello [1962] Director of Human Resources; Faruk Dasu [1969] Director/Pharmaceutical Account Manager; Harry Devonport [1953] Director/Retired; Mohamed Isap [1973] Director; Afzal Sadik Ismail [1966] Finance Director; Kevin Jaquiss [1958] Director; Fiona Jean Jordan [1956] Director/Retired; Kamruddin Isap Kothia [1963] Director; Hamid Patel [1979] Director/Chief Executive; Imraan Musa Patel [1978] Director/Solicitor; Rt Hon Jack John Whitaker Straw [1946] Director/Consultant

Star Tissue UK Limited
Incorporated: 27 June 2006 *Employees:* 89
Net Worth: £3,330,788 *Total Assets:* £9,319,869
Registered Office: Unit K, Princess Street, Star Industrial Estate, Blackburn, Lancs, BB2 2QR
Activities: Manufacture of paper and paperboard
Parent: Star Tissue Holdings Limited
Officers: Abid Saifullah Ditta, Secretary; Abid Saifullah Ditta [1977] Director; Khalid Saifullah [1974] Director; Sajid Saifullah [1980] Director

Starbank Holdings Limited
Incorporated: 1 June 2004 *Employees:* 91
Net Worth: £4,576,531 *Total Assets:* £12,450,378
Registered Office: Unit 2 Anglezarke Road, Sankey Valley Industrial Estate, Newton-le-Willows, Merseyside, WA12 8DJ
Activities: Activities of head offices
Shareholder: Philip Gordon Darbyshire
Officers: Mary Kathleen Darbyshire, Secretary; Mary Kathleen Darbyshire [1942] Director/Company Secretary; Wendy Kathleen Elsworthy [1973] Finance Director

Starbank Panel Products Limited
Incorporated: 3 July 1996 *Employees:* 91
Net Worth: £4,388,697 *Total Assets:* £8,909,587
Registered Office: Unit 2 Anglezarke Road, Sankey Valley Industrial Estate, Newton-le-Willows, Merseyside, WA12 8DJ
Activities: Manufacture of veneer sheets and wood-based panels
Parent: Starbank Holdings Limited
Officers: Wendy Kathleen Elsworthy, Secretary; Paul Atkinson [1961] Director; Michael Dennis Durham [1970] Director; Wendy Kathleen Elsworthy [1973] Director; John Derek Roper [1955] Director

Starcrester Properties Limited
Incorporated: 8 September 1972
Net Worth: £7,600,808 *Total Assets:* £12,097,463
Registered Office: 12 Vaughan Street, Manchester, M12 5FQ
Activities: Residents property management
Shareholder: Roslyn Susanne Pine
Officers: Elliot Pine, Secretary; David Pine [1942] Director/Solicitor; Joshua Pine [1956] Director; Simon Pine [1947] Director

Starlight Camping Limited
Incorporated: 21 May 2014 *Employees:* 829
Net Worth: £46,030,000 *Total Assets:* £101,414,000
Registered Office: 1st Floor, Chelford House, Rudheath Way, Rudheath, Northwich, Cheshire, CW9 7LN
Activities: Activities of head offices
Officers: Alain Calm&eacute [1966] Director [French]; Philippe de Tremiolles [1967] Director [French]

Startech.Com Limited
Incorporated: 10 December 2003 *Employees:* 37
Net Worth: £4,644,156 *Total Assets:* £52,390,140
Registered Office: Eversheds House, 70 Great Bridgewater Street, Manchester, M1 5ES
Activities: Wholesale of radio, television goods & electrical household appliances (other than records, tapes, CDs)
Major Shareholder: Paul Seed
Officers: Kenrick Kalopsis, Secretary; Kenrick Kalopsis [1957] Director/Business Owner; Paul Seed [1960] Director/Business Owner [Canadian]

Stateside Foods Limited
Incorporated: 12 October 1989 *Employees:* 1,018
Net Worth: £14,343,000 *Total Assets:* £58,177,000
Registered Office: Direct House, Lancaster Way, Westhoughton, Bolton, Lancs, BL5 3XY
Activities: Manufacture of other food products n.e.c.
Parent: Sandhof Ltd
Officers: Timothy Jones, Secretary; Uwe Berndt [1970] Director/Accountant [German]; Oliver Carsten Heinisch [1969] Director [German]; Michael Ian Kent [1962] Director; Jonathan Alan Lucas [1960] Director/Chartered Accountant; Robert Marnell [1964] Director; Herr Hans Detlev Schulz [1953] Director [German]; Siegfried Weber [1963] Director/NPD Manager [German]

Status International (UK) Ltd
Incorporated: 22 November 1990 *Employees:* 85
Net Worth: £16,122,958 *Total Assets:* £23,357,990
Registered Office: Pennine House, Mortimer Street, Cleckheaton, W Yorks, BD19 5AR
Activities: Wholesale of household goods (other than musical instruments) n.e.c
Shareholders: Peter Barre McVeigh; Nicholas John McVeigh
Officers: Nicholas John McVeigh, Secretary; Nicholas John McVeigh [1967] Director; Peter Barre McVeigh [1938] Director; Andrew Myatt [1969] Director; Jonathan Mark Sheard [1971] Director

Staveley's Eggs Limited
Incorporated: 14 November 1978 *Employees:* 109
Net Worth: £6,107,819 *Total Assets:* £8,222,778
Registered Office: Coppull Moor Farm, Preston Road, Coppull, Chorley, Lancs, PR7 5EB
Activities: Raising of poultry
Shareholders: David James Staveley; Helen Louise Staveley
Officers: Helen Staveley, Secretary; David James Staveley [1973] Director/Salesman; Kenneth Thomas Staveley [1942] Director/Farmer; Mary Staveley [1944] Director/Farmer

Stavert Zigomala Limited
Incorporated: 28 November 1923
Net Worth: £7,354,906 *Total Assets:* £8,362,864
Registered Office: 2-4 Primrose Avenue, Urmston, Manchester, M41 0TY
Activities: Financial intermediation not elsewhere classified
Officers: Roger Myles Cooper, Secretary; Edward Nigel Cooper [1951] Director/Solicitor; Alicia Christine Sullivan [1972] Director/Solicitor

Stax Trade Centres Limited
Incorporated: 25 March 1983 *Employees:* 627
Net Worth: £17,260,460 *Total Assets:* £39,003,024
Registered Office: Holloway Drive, Wardley Industrial Estate, Worsley, Manchester, M28 2LA
Activities: Non-specialised wholesale trade
Shareholder: David George Hibbert
Officers: David George Hibbert, Secretary; Tim Ball [1958] Director; Edward James Brady [1949] Director; Della Butler [1963] Director; Anne Gardiner [1941] Director; Angela Hibbert [1957] Director; David George Hibbert [1956] Director; Helen Louise Mayers [1974] Director; Nigel John Wright [1965] Director; Simon James Wright [1968] Director

STB Holdings Limited
Incorporated: 23 May 2008 *Employees:* 1,582
Net Worth Deficit: £1,100,000 *Total Assets:* £8,489,000
Registered Office: The Bakery, Sidney Street, Bolton, Lancs, BL3 6BG
Activities: Activities of head offices
Major Shareholder: Alexander Peter Birnie
Officers: Alexander Peter Birnie [1960] Director

J.Stell & Sons,Limited
Incorporated: 11 March 1930 *Employees:* 95
Net Worth: £2,793,004 *Total Assets:* £8,455,893
Registered Office: Riverside Business Park, Royd Ings Avenue, Keighley, W Yorks, BD21 4AF
Activities: Manufacture of other articles of paper and paperboard n.e.c.
Major Shareholder: Samuel Vaughan Stell
Officers: Samuel Vaughan Stell, Secretary; Richard Ian Guest [1970] Director; Samuel Adrian Stell [1978] Director; Samuel Vaughan Stell [1947] Director/Paper Tube Manufacturer

Stell Cardboard Tubes Limited
Incorporated: 21 February 2014 *Employees:* 95
Net Worth: £2,713,195 *Total Assets:* £8,376,084
Registered Office: Riverside Business Park, Royd Ings Avenue, Keighley, W Yorks, BD21 4AF
Activities: Manufacture of other articles of paper and paperboard n.e.c.
Major Shareholder: Samuel Vaughan Stell
Officers: Richard Ian Guest [1970] Director; Samuel Adrian Stell [1978] Director; Samuel Vaughan Stell [1947] Director

Stella Global UK Limited
Incorporated: 30 October 2007 *Employees:* 318
Net Worth Deficit: £22,234,000 *Total Assets:* £76,060,000
Registered Office: Glendale House, Glendale Business Park, Glendale Avenue, Sandycroft, Flintshire, CH5 2DL
Activities: Travel agency activities
Parent: Dnata Travel Holdings UK Limited
Officers: Ryan James Cooke, Secretary; Iain Charles Richard Andrew [1965] Director/Divisional Senior Vice President; Asif Hamza Parkar [1974] Director/Finance Manager

Stella Travel Services (UK) Limited
Incorporated: 19 October 2004 *Employees:* 341
Net Worth: £43,166,000 *Total Assets:* £120,266,000
Registered Office: Glendale House, Glendale Business Park, Glendale Avenue, Sandycroft, Flintshire, CH5 2DL
Activities: Tour operator activities
Parent: Dnata Travel Holdings UK Limited
Officers: Ryan James Cooke, Secretary; Iain Charles Richard Andrew [1965] Director/Divisional Senior Vice President; Asif Hamza Parkar [1974] Director/Finance Manager

Stepan UK Limited
Incorporated: 17 October 1996 *Employees:* 116
Net Worth: £26,791,000 *Total Assets:* £51,685,000
Registered Office: Bridge House, Bridge Street, Stalybridge, Cheshire, SK15 1PH
Activities: Manufacture of soap and detergents
Parent: Stepan Europe S.A
Officers: Stephen David Smales, Secretary; Wojciech Mazurek [1966] Director [Polish]; Didier Ray [1962] Commercial Director [French]; Stephen Smales [1974] Director/Accountant

Stephenson Multi Academy Trust
Incorporated: 16 January 2017 *Employees:* 154
Net Worth: £19,965,500 *Total Assets:* £23,005,152
Registered Office: Rainhill High School, Warrington Road, Rainhill, Prescot, Merseyside, L35 6NY
Activities: General secondary education
Officers: Steven John Anderson [1957] Director/Talent Manager; David Thomas Boyer [1965] Director/Civil Engineer; John Peter Boyer [1962] Director/Chartered Electrical Engineer; Lisa Flaherty [1978] HR Director; Maureen Kathleen Mellor [1947] Director/Retired College Principal; Michaela Peers-Zilkova [1978] Director/Finance Manager [Slovak]; Derek Jonathon Pout [1963] Director/Headteacher

Stephensons Solicitors LLP
Incorporated: 6 October 2006 *Employees:* 456
Net Worth: £5,796,851 *Total Assets:* £11,517,211
Registered Office: Wigan Investment Centre, Waterside Drive, Wigan, Lancs, WN3 5BA
Officers: David Baybut [1971] Member; Jonathan Paul Chadwick [1975] Member; Michael Dominic Devlin [1953] Member; Ann Elizabeth Harrison [1956] Member; Andrew Welch [1965] Member; Victoria Clare Gethin [1976] LLP Member; Louise Bernadette Griffiths [1971] LLP Member; Sean Adrian Joyce [1972] LLP Member; Andrew Christopher Leakey [1972] LLP Member

Sterilin Limited
Incorporated: 25 February 2008 *Employees:* 234
Net Worth: £9,025,000 *Total Assets:* £18,827,000
Registered Office: 3rd Floor, 1 Ashley Road, Altrincham, Cheshire, WA14 2DT
Activities: Manufacture of other plastic products
Parent: FSUK Holdings Limited
Officers: Rhona Gregg, Secretary; Lucie Mary Katja Grant [1976] Director/Solicitor; Nicholas Ince [1982] Director/Accountant; David John Norman [1960] Director/Chartered Accountant

Sterling 2000 Group Limited
Incorporated: 19 September 2016 *Employees:* 3,929
Net Worth: £1,695,904 *Total Assets:* £11,396,245
Registered Office: Sterling House, 810 Mandarin Court, Centre Park, Warrington, Cheshire, WA1 1GG
Activities: Activities of other holding companies n.e.c.
Major Shareholder: Ian Alexander Black
Officers: Ian Alexander Black [1966] Director; Simon Andrew McClean [1966] Director/Accountant; Sarah Ann McIver [1968] Director; Karen O'Neill [1972] Director/Accountant; Janene Lisa Rudge [1969] Director/Accountant

Sterling Property Co. Limited
Incorporated: 16 May 1996 *Employees:* 28
Net Worth: £7,893,763 *Total Assets:* £11,019,545
Registered Office: Sterling House, Unit G, Waterfold Business Park, Bury, Lancs, BL9 7BR
Activities: Management of real estate on a fee or contract basis
Parent: Bracken House Properties LLP
Officers: Henry Neville Moser [1949] Director; Matthew Laurence Settle [1984] Operations Director

Stevens Equipment Rental Limited
Incorporated: 20 April 2005 *Employees:* 21
Net Worth: £10,055,637 *Total Assets:* £17,824,864
Registered Office: Causeway Head, Silloth, Wigton, Cumbria, CA7 4PE
Activities: Other specialised construction activities n.e.c.
Shareholders: Andrew Stevens; Michael Stevens
Officers: Alan Rennie Dickson, Secretary; Andrew Stevens [1975] Director; Michael Stevens [1977] Director

Stewart Holdings Management Limited
Incorporated: 11 September 2006 *Employees:* 6
Net Worth Deficit: £34,542,000 *Total Assets:* £31,807,000
Registered Office: Caddick Road, Knowsley Business Park, Prescot, Merseyside, L34 9HP
Activities: Support activities for other mining and quarrying
Parent: ALS Limited
Officers: Michael Paul Pearson, Secretary; John David Smyth [1965] Finance Director; Christopher David Walker [1972] Director

Stirling Management Group Limited
Incorporated: 10 September 1982
Net Worth: £7,914,115 *Total Assets:* £9,547,495
Registered Office: 24 Manchester Road, Wilmslow, Cheshire, SK9 1BG
Activities: Construction of domestic buildings
Officers: Arthur John Abercromby, Secretary; Arthur John Abercromby [1943] Director; Judith Abercromby [1941] Director; Marie-Louise Abercromby [1978] Director; Mark Lhind Abercromby [1975] Director

J.Stobart & Sons Limited
Incorporated: 6 December 1963 *Employees:* 22
Net Worth: £11,831,869 *Total Assets:* £13,880,877
Registered Office: Newlands Mill, Hesket New Market, Wigton, Cumbria, CA7 8HP
Activities: Manufacture of prepared feeds for farm animals
Major Shareholder: Ronald John Stobart
Officers: Celia Margaret Stobart, Secretary; Linda Elizabeth Rigg [1960] Director; Peter John Stobart [1965] Director; Richard Andrew Stobart [1962] Managing Director; Ronald John Stobart [1936] Director

Eddie Stobart Group Limited
Incorporated: 20 April 1995
Net Worth: £21,330,000 *Total Assets:* £29,603,000
Registered Office: Stretton Green Distribution Park, Langford Way, Appleton, Warrington, Cheshire, WA4 4TQ
Activities: Activities of head offices
Parent: Stobart Transport & Distribution Limited
Officers: Elaine Williams, Secretary; Alexander Laffey [1961] Director; David Keith Meir [1970] Director; Rupert Henry Conquest Nichols [1949] Company Secretary/Director; David Brian Pickering [1973] Director

Eddie Stobart Limited
Incorporated: 23 November 1970 *Employees:* 3,823
Net Worth: £93,353,000 *Total Assets:* £227,070,000
Registered Office: Stretton Green Distribution Park, Langford Way, Appleton, Warrington, Cheshire, WA4 4TQ
Activities: Freight transport by road
Parent: Eddie Stobart Group Limited
Officers: Elaine Williams, Secretary; Damien Harte [1956] Director [Irish]; Alexander Laffey [1961] Director; David Keith Meir [1970] Finance Director; Rupert Henry Conquest Nichols [1949] Company Secretary/Director; David Brian Pickering [1973] Director

Eddie Stobart Logistics PLC
Incorporated: 4 March 2014
Net Worth: £65,095,000 *Total Assets:* £100,366,000
Registered Office: Stretton Green Distribution Park, Langford Way, Appleton, Warrington, Cheshire, WA4 4TQ
Activities: Activities of other holding companies n.e.c.
Officers: Elaine Williams, Secretary; Christopher Michael Casey [1955] Director; Stephen John Harley [1951] Managing Director; Damien Harte [1956] Director [Irish]; Alexander Laffey [1961] Director; Philip Hilary Swatman [1949] Director

Stockfis Holdings Limited
Incorporated: 7 April 1983 *Employees:* 3
Net Worth: £7,354,203 *Total Assets:* £7,981,761
Registered Office: 4 Osborne Close, Wilmslow, Cheshire, SK9 2EE
Activities: Other letting and operating of own or leased real estate
Major Shareholder: Kenneth Robert Stockfis
Officers: Eileen Stockfis, Secretary; Roberta Mary Cresswell [1953] Director/Insurance Claims Officer; Avril Reynolds [1946] Director; Susan Smith [1948] Director/Company Secretary; Eileen Stockfis [1950] Director; Kenneth Robert Stockfis [1924] Director

Stockport Grammar School
Incorporated: 29 May 2007 *Employees:* 224
Net Worth: £25,465,288 *Total Assets:* £27,352,796
Registered Office: Stockport Grammar School, Buxton Road, Stockport, Cheshire, SK2 7AF
Activities: Pre-primary education
Officers: Christopher Watson, Secretary; Philip John Britton [1969] Director/Headmaster; Anthony Paul Carr [1952] Director/Lawyer; Sarah Elizabeth Carroll [1965] Director/Banker; Philip Adrian Cuddy [1952] Director/Solicitor Consultant; Christopher Frank Dunn [1957] Director/Solicitor; Peter Laban Giblin [1949] Director/Retired; Samantha Lansbury [1970] Director/Solicitor; Jonathan Mark Round Lee [1964] Property Director; Paul Milner [1957] Director/Retired; Doctor Elizabeth Margaret Morris [1948] Director/Pediatrician; Christine Suzanne Muscutt [1954] Director/Retired; John Anthony Shackleton [1954] Director/Retired; Adrian Charles Simpson [1959] Finance Director

Stockport Homes Limited
Incorporated: 29 August 2002 *Employees:* 443
Net Worth: £5,968,000 *Total Assets:* £59,490,000
Registered Office: Cornerstone, 2 Edward Street, Stockport, Cheshire, SK1 3NQ
Activities: Management of real estate on a fee or contract basis
Parent: Stockport Metropolitan Borough Council
Officers: David Ronald Beckett [1970] Director/Chief Executive; Robin Barry Burman [1952] Director/Lawyer; Peter Fitzhenry [1958] Director/Consultant; Josephine Teresa Hague [1958] Director/Receptionist; Jamie MacLean Hirst [1978] Director/IT Professional; Sarah Leigh Keenan [1982] Director/Tenancy Enforcement Officer; Jenny Osbourne [1973] Director/Chief Executive; Stephen Brian Partridge [1963] Director/Management Consultant; Alanna Hourie Vine [1948] Director/Retired; Christine Woolridge [1945] Director/Retired

Stocks Bros. Limited
Incorporated: 11 June 1952 *Employees:* 24
Net Worth: £11,127,522 *Total Assets:* £24,827,122
Registered Office: Workington Road, Flimby, Maryport, Cumbria, CA15 8RY
Activities: Manufacture of other articles of concrete, plaster and cement
Officers: Paul Armstrong Secretary; Paul Armstrong [1959] Director; Ainsley Paul Calvert [1967] Sales Director; Anthony Robert Glover Denham [1960] Director; John Keith Denham [1943] Director

Stocks Hall Care Homes Limited
Incorporated: 7 October 1987 *Employees:* 635
Net Worth: £7,712,393 *Total Assets:* £19,679,560
Registered Office: Stocks House, 50c White Moss Road, Skelmersdale, Lancs, WN8 8BL
Activities: Residential nursing care facilities
Officers: Susan Elizabeth Lace, Secretary; Gareth Brian Thomas Jones [1950] Director; Stuart Henderson Lace [1946] Director/Retailer; Susan Elizabeth Lace [1947] Director

D. Stoker Group Limited
Incorporated: 31 August 1961 *Employees:* 67
Net Worth: £3,477,906 *Total Assets:* £7,775,774
Registered Office: 1 Ironworks Road, Barrow in Furness, Cumbria, LA14 2PG
Activities: Sale of new cars and light motor vehicles
Major Shareholder: Iain Leslie Stoker
Officers: Margaret Elizabeth Stoker, Secretary; Iain Leslie Stoker [1954] Managing Director; Margaret Elizabeth Stoker [1955] Director

Stokers Holdings Limited
Incorporated: 24 June 2004 *Employees:* 223
Net Worth: £32,417,404 *Total Assets:* £45,813,264
Registered Office: 277 Wennington Road, Southport, Merseyside, PR9 7TW
Activities: Retail of furniture, lighting, and similar (not musical instruments or scores) in specialised store
Shareholders: Jonathan Nigel Stoker; Steven Graham Schofield
Officers: Jonathan Nigel Stoker, Secretary/Chartered Accountant; Steven Graham Schofield [1960] Director/Buyer; Jonathan Nigel Stoker [1967] Director/Chartered Accountant

Stokers Limited
Incorporated: 23 November 1935 *Employees:* 222
Net Worth: £14,627,481 *Total Assets:* £24,483,780
Registered Office: 277 Wennington Road, Southport, Merseyside, PR9 7TW
Activities: Retail of furniture, lighting, and similar (not musical instruments or scores) in specialised store
Major Shareholder: Jonathan Nigel Stoker
Officers: Jonathan Nigel Stoker, Secretary/Chartered Accountant; Steven Graham Schofield [1960] Director/Buyer; Jonathan Nigel Stoker [1967] Director/Chartered Accountant

Stolle Europe Limited
Incorporated: 1 August 1988 *Employees:* 46
Net Worth: £11,735,969 *Total Assets:* £43,645,664
Registered Office: Kingstown Broadway, Kingstown Industrial Estate, Carlisle, CA3 0HA
Activities: Machining
Officers: Stephen Leigh Higginson [1954] Director; Gus Reall [1960] Director [American]

Stonecroft Holdings PLC
Incorporated: 20 July 2001 *Employees:* 221
Net Worth: £14,260,000 *Total Assets:* £34,595,000
Registered Office: Ladywell Mills, Hall Lane, Bradford, W Yorks, BD4 7DF
Activities: Activities of head offices
Shareholders: Andrew David Seal; Jeremy Charles Seal
Officers: Jayne Stephanie Woodthorpe, Secretary; Lucci Dammone [1957] Director/Solicitor; Andrew David Seal [1957] Director; Jeremy Charles Seal [1960] Director; Jayne Stephanie Woodthorpe [1963] Director/Chartered Accountant

Stonewell Property Company Limited
Incorporated: 9 December 1988 *Employees:* 87
Net Worth: £7,343,735 *Total Assets:* £30,918,182
Registered Office: Brockholes Pavilion, Brockholes Way, Claughton on Brock, Preston, Lancs, PR3 0PZ
Activities: Development of building projects
Shareholder: John Marcus Worthington
Officers: Stephen Smith, Secretary; Stephen Smith [1959] Director/Accountant; Angela Violet Worthington [1945] Director/Secretary; Giles Matthew Worthington [1975] Construction Director; John Simeon Worthington [1973] Director; John Marcus Worthington [1946] Managing Director; Russell Edward Worthington [1979] Director/Property Developer

Stoneygate 48 Limited
Incorporated: 22 February 2002 *Employees:* 7
Net Worth: £17,209,468 *Total Assets:* £18,966,416
Registered Office: Great Oak Farm Offices, Mag Lane, Lymm, Cheshire, WA13 0TF
Activities: Other business support service activities n.e.c.
Major Shareholder: Wayne Mark Rooney
Officers: Paul Stretford, Secretary; Wayne Mark Rooney [1985] Director/Professional Footballer; Paul Stretford [1958] Director

Stonyhurst
Incorporated: 27 June 2008 *Employees:* 378
Net Worth: £68,601,624 *Total Assets:* £78,428,384
Registered Office: Stonyhurst, Clitheroe, Lancs, BB7 9PZ
Activities: Pre-primary education
Officers: Simon Peter Marsden, Secretary; Mark Joseph Belderboss [1942] Director/Retired Solicitor; Richard Francis Brumby [1947] Director/Investment Banker; Anthony Michael Chitnis [1964] Director/Recruitment Consultant; John Cowdall [1940] Director; Michael Ian Davis [1945] Director; Roger Dawson [1960] Director/Priest; David Augustine Finn [1949] Director/Retired; Simon Glassbrook [1960] Director; Doctor Maria Alicia Josephine Guzkowska [1957] Director/Deputy Vice Chancellor; Christine Margaret Keunen [1959] Director/Solicitor; Dr Nuala Brigid Mary Mellows [1955] Director/GP; Reverend Matthew John Power [1961] Director/Minister of Religion; John Edmund Stoer [1954] Director/Retired; Stephen Withnell [1980] Managing Director

Store First Midlands Limited
Incorporated: 6 April 2006 *Employees:* 4
Net Worth Deficit: £7,916,869 *Total Assets:* £7,366,670
Registered Office: Group First House, Mead Way, Padiham, Lancs, BB12 7NG
Activities: Buying and selling of own real estate
Parent: Harley Scott Holdings Limited
Officers: Ruth Margaret Almond [1958] Director; Leanne Gregson [1979] Director/Completion Manager; John Slater [1978] Director; Toby Scott Whittaker [1977] Director

Storengy UK Limited
Incorporated: 13 July 2007 *Employees:* 44
Net Worth: £41,590,000 *Total Assets:* £126,986,000
Registered Office: Stublach Site, King Street, Northwich, Cheshire, CW9 7SE
Activities: Trade of gas through mains
Parent: Engie S.A.
Officers: Caroline Martine Bony-Vivien, Secretary; Raphaelle Castillon [1973] Asset Management Director [French]; Catherine Marguerite Gras [1970] Deputy Managing Director [French]; Nelly Nicoli [1975] Director/Commercial [French]; Cecile Previeu [1971] Director [French]; Ben Watts [1974] Innovation & Solutions Director UK & Ireland

Stores Group Limited
Incorporated: 7 February 1983
Net Worth: £264,500,000 *Total Assets:* £1,729,069,056
Registered Office: Hilmore House, Gain Lane, Bradford, W Yorks, BD3 7DL
Activities: Activities of head offices
Parent: Safeway Limited
Officers: Jonathan James Burke, Secretary; Jonathan James Burke [1966] Director; Trevor John Strain [1975] Finance Director

Story Contracting Limited
Incorporated: 3 February 1999 *Employees:* 518
Net Worth: £20,891,000 *Total Assets:* £53,130,000
Registered Office: Burgh Road Industrial Estate, Carlisle, Cumbria, CA2 7NA
Activities: Construction of commercial buildings
Major Shareholder: Norman Frederick Story
Officers: Roger Neil Gass, Secretary; Jason Butterworth [1967] Director/Chief Executive; Lindsey Jane Pownall [1962] Director/Consultant; John Frederick Story [1986] Director/Accountant; Norman Frederick Story [1956] Managing Director

Story Homes Limited
Incorporated: 8 July 1988 *Employees:* 354
Net Worth: £91,081,520 *Total Assets:* £221,285,376
Registered Office: Story House, Lords Way, Kingmoor Business Park, Carlisle, CA6 4SL
Activities: Construction of commercial buildings
Officers: Roger Neil Gass, Secretary; Lindsey Jane Pownall [1962] Director; John Frederick Story [1986] Director/Accountant; Norman Frederick Story [1956] Director

Stoves Group Ltd
Incorporated: 24 February 1989
Net Worth: £17,869,000 *Total Assets:* £21,664,000
Registered Office: Stoney Lane, Prescot, Merseyside, L35 2XW
Activities: Manufacture of electric domestic appliances
Parent: Glen Electric Ltd
Officers: Stephen John Yarwood, Secretary; Donal Francis Flynn [1973] Director/Chartered Accountant [Irish]; Fergal John Naughton [1975] Director [Irish]; Martin Lawrence Naughton [1939] Director/Engineer [Irish]; Stephen John Yarwood [1961] Director

Strainstall Group Limited
Incorporated: 21 July 2000
Net Worth: £2,180,883 *Total Assets:* £22,776,506
Registered Office: P O Box 4, Fisher House, Barrow in Furness, Cumbria, LA14 1HR
Activities: Activities of head offices
Parent: James Fisher and Sons Public Limited Company
Officers: James Henry John Marsh, Secretary; Nicholas Paul Henry [1961] Director; Stuart Charles Kilpatrick [1962] Director

Streason Limited
Incorporated: 24 August 1962 *Employees:* 165
Net Worth: £9,661,704 *Total Assets:* £18,234,796
Registered Office: Townend Works, Chapel-en-le-Frith, Derbys, SK23 0PH
Activities: Activities of head offices
Officers: Jocelyn Sarah Street, Secretary; Martin Street, Secretary; Simon James Eastwood [1963] Director; Martin Street [1955] Director/Crane Manufacturer

Charles Street Commercial Investments Limited
Incorporated: 15 July 1983
Net Worth: £17,114,168 *Total Assets:* £53,921,020
Registered Office: Lake View, Lakeside, Cheadle, Cheshire, SK8 3GW
Activities: Credit granting by non-deposit taking finance houses and other specialist consumer credit grantors
Major Shareholder: Henry Neville Moser
Officers: Gary Derek Beckett, Secretary; Gary Derek Beckett [1969] Director; Henry Neville Moser [1949] Director; Mark Mulgrew [1978] Finance Director

Street Crane Company Limited
Incorporated: 2 May 1958 *Employees:* 165
Net Worth: £9,041,198 *Total Assets:* £17,430,042
Registered Office: Town End Works, Chapel-en-le-Frith, Derbys, SK23 0PH
Activities: Manufacture of lifting and handling equipment
Officers: Martin Street, Secretary; Michael Andrew Husbands [1963] Finance Director; Christopher Mark Lindley-Smith [1972] Sales Director; Eric Andrew Pimblett [1953] Non-Executive - Director; Christopher Russell [1971] Director/Design Engineer; Martin Street [1955] Director; Augusto Zona [1971] Managing Director [Italian]

Streetlands Limited
Incorporated: 9 January 1979 *Employees:* 2
Net Worth Deficit: £14,701,614 *Total Assets:* £12,795,498
Registered Office: 2 Mount Street, Manchester, M2 5WQ
Activities: Management of real estate on a fee or contract basis
Parent: Wrather Group Limited
Officers: Paul Robert Greenlees, Secretary; Patrick Franks [1965] Director/Architect; William Harry Wrather [1939] Director

William Strike Limited
Incorporated: 7 January 1908 *Employees:* 873
Net Worth: £27,896,578 *Total Assets:* £38,329,696
Registered Office: c/o Houghton Hall Garden Centre, Houghton, Carlisle, CA6 4JB
Activities: Other retail sale of new goods in specialised stores (not commercial art galleries and opticians)
Parent: Strikes Holdings Limited
Officers: Dorothy Agnes Dickson Gault, Secretary/Director; David Abbott [1970] Retail Operations Director; Sharon Allan [1971] Financial Director; Keren Feeney [1969] Director/Catering and Food Sales; Dorothy Agnes Dickson Gault [1945] Director; Robert John Hewitt [1956] Director/Chief Executive; David Alan Robb [1960] Director/Chartered Accountant; William David Yardley [1964] Director

Style Group Holdings Limited
Incorporated: 5 April 2005
Net Worth: £12,250,000 *Total Assets:* £30,555,000
Registered Office: Style House, 14 Eldon Place, Bradford, W Yorks, BD1 3AZ
Activities: Activities of head offices
Officers: Richard Kenneth Short, Secretary; Mike Gallacher [1966] Director; Rob Neale [1978] Director

Style Group UK Limited
Incorporated: 25 February 2000 *Employees:* 6
Net Worth: £3,058,000 *Total Assets:* £19,416,000
Registered Office: Style House, 14 Eldon Place, Bradford, BD1 3AZ
Activities: Activities of head offices
Parent: Safestyle UK PLC
Officers: Richard Kenneth Short, Secretary; Mike Gallacher [1966] Director; Rob Neale [1978] Director

Styles & Wood Group Limited
Incorporated: 14 November 2005 *Employees:* 328
Net Worth: £3,412,000 *Total Assets:* £55,526,000
Registered Office: Cavendish House, Cross Street, Sale, Cheshire, M33 7BU
Activities: Activities of head offices
Officers: Philip Nicholas Lanigan, Secretary/Director; Philip Nicholas Lanigan [1964] Director; Anthony Stephen Lenehan [1959] Director/Chief Executive Officer

Styles & Wood Investments Limited
Incorporated: 29 March 2004
Net Worth: £4,970,000 *Total Assets:* £37,254,000
Registered Office: Cavendish House, Cross Street, Sale, Cheshire, M33 7BU
Activities: Non-trading company
Parent: Styles & Wood Group PLC
Officers: Philip Nicholas Lanigan, Secretary/Director; Philip Nicholas Lanigan [1964] Director; Anthony Stephen Lenehan [1959] Director/Chief Executive Officer

Styles & Wood Limited
Incorporated: 15 June 1981 *Employees:* 312
Net Worth: £14,970,000 *Total Assets:* £71,738,000
Registered Office: Cavendish House, Cross Street, Sale, Cheshire, M33 7BU
Activities: Development of building projects
Parent: Maraq Limited
Officers: Philip Nicholas Lanigan, Secretary/Director; Philip Nicholas Lanigan [1964] Director; Anthony Stephen Lenehan [1959] Director/Chief Executive Officer; Paul Richard Lonsdale [1964] Operations Director; Karen Morley [1977] Director; Andrew James Shaw [1969] Director; Martin Ward [1971] Director

Styles & Wood Property Management Limited
Incorporated: 8 May 2001
Net Worth: £1,528,000 *Total Assets:* £26,654,000
Registered Office: Cavendish House, Cross Street, Sale, Cheshire, M33 7BU
Activities: Non-trading company
Parent: Styles & Wood Investments Limited
Officers: Philip Nicholas Lanigan, Secretary/Director; Philip Nicholas Lanigan [1964] Director; Anthony Stephen Lenehan [1959] Director/Chief Executive Officer

Styrene Packaging & Insulation Limited
Incorporated: 16 March 1984 *Employees:* 104
Net Worth: £5,405,458 *Total Assets:* £16,424,709
Registered Office: Morley Carr Road, Low Moor, Bradford, W Yorks, BD12 0RA
Activities: Other manufacturing n.e.c.
Officers: Maria Edge, Secretary; Joseph William Edge [1981] Director; Maria Edge [1955] Director/Secretary; Michael Edge [1952] Director/Engineer; Paul Edge [1955] Director/Engineer

Sudlows Group Limited
Incorporated: 8 March 2006 *Employees:* 176
Net Worth: £4,304,000 *Total Assets:* £21,250,000
Registered Office: Ducie Works, 107 Hulme Hall Lane, Manchester, M40 8HH
Activities: Activities of head offices
Shareholders: John Anthony Collins; Christopher William Dummett
Officers: Debra Taylor, Secretary; Collette Jean Collins [1965] Director; John Anthony Collins [1966] Director; Christopher William Dummett [1972] Director; Gail Hurst Dummett [1973] Director; Andrew David Hirst [1966] Director/Accountant; Philip Roy Nield [1963] Director/Accountant

Sudlows Limited
Incorporated: 9 May 1988 *Employees:* 61
Net Worth: £4,658,000 *Total Assets:* £13,036,000
Registered Office: Ducie Works, Hulme Hall Lane, Manchester, M40 8HH
Activities: Other professional, scientific and technical activities n.e.c.
Parent: Sudlows Group Ltd
Officers: Philip Roy Nield, Secretary; John Anthony Collins [1966] Managing Director; Christopher William Dummett [1972] Commercial Director; Andrew David Hirst [1966] Global Director; Philip Roy Nield [1963] Director/Accountant

Suez Water Technologies & Solutions United Kingdom
Incorporated: 20 March 1969
Net Worth: £7,476,000 *Total Assets:* £7,476,000
Registered Office: 3rd Floor, 1 Ashley Road, Altrincham, Cheshire, WA14 2DT
Activities: Manufacture of other chemical products n.e.c.
Parent: Ondeo Industrial Solutions UK Limited
Officers: Richard James Brook [1974] Sales Director; Christopher Michael Alan Jeffery [1973] Sales Director (ES) - Europe

Summit Food Holdings Limited
Incorporated: 24 June 1994 *Employees:* 174
Net Worth: £4,913,400 *Total Assets:* £7,307,053
Registered Office: 170 Walton Summit Road, Bamber Bridge, Preston, Lancs, PR5 6SY
Activities: Activities of head offices
Parent: Abbeydale Food Group Limited
Officers: Jonathan Stuart Beach [1975] Director; Richard Miles Firth [1970] Director; Andrew Patrick Hayes [1962] Director; Colin Vincent Wright [1962] Director

Sun Branding Solutions Ltd
Incorporated: 9 March 1966 *Employees:* 250
Net Worth: £11,864,073 *Total Assets:* £18,314,132
Registered Office: Albion Mills, Albion Road, Bradford, W Yorks, BD10 9TQ
Activities: Other business support service activities n.e.c.
Parent: ECG Holdings (UK) Ltd
Officers: Margaret Julia Pearce, Secretary; Paul Richard Bean [1960] Director/Business Manager; Charles Allen Heynes [1958] Finance Director; Martjin Jan Charles Marie Schoonenberg [1977] Director/General Counsel [Dutch]

Sun Valley Limited
Incorporated: 27 April 1955 *Employees:* 150
Net Worth: £8,420,543 *Total Assets:* £15,332,031
Registered Office: Georgia Avenue, Bromborough, Wirral, Merseyside, CH62 3RD
Activities: Manufacture of other food products n.e.c.
Parent: Goodwood Holdings Limited
Officers: James Joseph Park Hacking, Secretary; Christine Hilda Leigh Hacking [1967] Director; Gladys Hacking [1924] Director; James Joseph Park Hacking [1960] Sales Director; Thomas Henry Hacking [1955] Director/Sales Representative; Frances Margaret Leigh Street [1953] Director; Geoffrey William Street [1949] Managing Director; Kathryn Anne Leigh Thomas [1956] Director

Suncor Energy International Trading Limited
Incorporated: 15 April 2002
Net Worth: £37,841,000 *Total Assets:* £319,183,008
Registered Office: 3rd Floor, 1 Ashley Road, Altrincham, Cheshire, WA14 2DT
Activities: Non-specialised wholesale trade
Parent: Suncor Energy UK Holdings Ltd
Officers: Gabriella La Guardia [1975] Director/Crude Oil Trader [Italian]; Mark William Townley [1962] Director/VP Supply & Trading [Canadian/British]; Caroline Mary Britt Watkins [1968] Director/Oil Trader

Suncor Energy UK Holdings Ltd
Incorporated: 12 April 2002
Net Worth: £697,139,008 *Total Assets:* £1,057,889,984
Registered Office: 3rd Floor, 1 Ashley Road, Altrincham, Cheshire, WA14 2DT
Activities: Activities of head offices
Parent: Suncor Energy Inc.
Officers: Ronald Davie [1959] Director/Accountant; Steven Trueman [1969] Director/Geologist; Dwayne Zeller [1954] Director/Engineer [Canadian]

Suncor Energy UK Limited
Incorporated: 17 February 1970 *Employees:* 31
Net Worth: £586,356,992 *Total Assets:* £1,441,472,000
Registered Office: 3rd Floor, 1 Ashley Road, Altrincham, Cheshire, WA14 2DT
Activities: Extraction of crude petroleum
Parent: Suncor Energy UK Holdings Ltd
Officers: Ronald Davie [1959] Director/Accountant; Steven Trueman [1969] Director/Geologist; Dwayne Zeller [1954] Director/Engineer [Canadian]

Sune Green Energy Ltd
Incorporated: 15 April 2013
Net Worth: £2,171,022 *Total Assets:* £10,368,020
Registered Office: Eversheds House, 70 Great Bridgewater Street, Manchester, M1 5ES
Activities: Production of electricity
Parent: Sune Green Holdco7 Limited
Officers: Carl Goran Dandanell [1959] Director [Swedish]

Sune Green Holdco2 Ltd
Incorporated: 27 November 2013
Net Worth: £3,149,395 *Total Assets:* £40,079,800
Registered Office: Eversheds House, 70 Great Bridgewater Street, Manchester, M1 5ES
Activities: Production of electricity
Parent: Terraform UK3 Intermediate Holdings Limited
Officers: Carl Goran Dandanell [1959] Director [Swedish]

Sune Green Holdco3 Limited
Incorporated: 18 February 2014
Net Worth: £4,521,829 *Total Assets:* £48,578,664
Registered Office: Eversheds House, 70 Great Bridgewater Street, Manchester, M1 5ES
Activities: Production of electricity
Parent: Terraform UK3 Intermediate Holdings Limited
Officers: Carl Goran Dandanell [1959] Director [Swedish]

Sune Green Holdco4 Limited
Incorporated: 28 April 2014
Net Worth Deficit: £5,642,254 *Total Assets:* £32,329,892
Registered Office: Eversheds House, 70 Great Bridgewater Street, Manchester, M1 5ES
Activities: Activities of financial services holding companies
Parent: Terraform UK3 Intermediate Holdings Limited
Officers: Carl Goran Dandanell [1959] Director [Swedish]

Sune Green Holdco5 Limited
Incorporated: 28 March 2014
Net Worth Deficit: £8,605,757 *Total Assets:* £64,775,396
Registered Office: Eversheds House, 70 Great Bridgewater Street, Manchester, M1 5ES
Activities: Activities of financial services holding companies
Parent: Terraform UK3 Intermediate Holdings Limited
Officers: Carl Goran Dandanell [1959] Director [Swedish]

Sune Green Holdco7 Limited
Incorporated: 30 April 2014
Net Worth Deficit: £7,227,328 *Total Assets:* £37,721,440
Registered Office: Eversheds House, 70 Great Bridgewater Street, Manchester, M1 5ES
Activities: Activities of financial services holding companies
Parent: Terraform UK3 Intermediate Holdings Limited
Officers: Carl Goran Dandanell [1959] Director [Swedish]

Sune Green Holdco9 Limited
Incorporated: 29 April 2014
Net Worth Deficit: £2,723,564 *Total Assets:* £12,291,659
Registered Office: Eversheds House, 70 Great Bridgewater Street, Manchester, M1 5ES
Activities: Activities of financial services holding companies
Parent: Terraform UK3 Intermediate Holdings Limited
Officers: Carl Goran Dandanell [1959] Director [Swedish]

Sune Hill Farm Solar Limited
Incorporated: 24 June 2014
Net Worth: £1,581,183 *Total Assets:* £8,927,345
Registered Office: Eversheds House, 70 Great Bridgewater Street, Manchester, M1 5ES
Activities: Production of electricity
Parent: Terraform UK3 Intermediate Holdings Limited
Officers: Carl Goran Dandanell [1959] Director [Swedish]

Sune Prestop Park Limited
Incorporated: 20 June 2014
Net Worth: £4,453,904 *Total Assets:* £18,595,744
Registered Office: Eversheds House, 70 Great Bridgewater Street, Manchester, M1 5ES
Activities: Production of electricity
Parent: Sune Green Holdco13 Limited
Officers: Carl Goran Dandanell [1959] Director [Swedish]

Sune Project1 Ltd
Incorporated: 8 May 2013
Net Worth Deficit: £125,830 *Total Assets:* £17,726,316
Registered Office: Eversheds House, 70 Great Bridgewater Street, Manchester, M1 5ES
Activities: Production of electricity
Parent: Sune Green Holdco2 Ltd
Officers: Carl Goran Dandanell [1959] Director [Swedish]

Sune Sundorne Grove Solar Limited
Incorporated: 4 October 2013
Net Worth: £8,937,320 *Total Assets:* £20,978,220
Registered Office: Eversheds House, 70 Great Bridgewater Street, Manchester, M1 5ES
Activities: Production of electricity
Parent: Terraform UK3 Intermediate Holdings Limited
Officers: Carl Goran Dandanell [1959] Director [Swedish]

Sunsave 10 (Fareham) Ltd
Incorporated: 2 August 2012
Net Worth: £213,435 *Total Assets:* £19,271,636
Registered Office: Eversheds House, 70 Great Bridgewater Street, Manchester, M1 5ES
Activities: Production of electricity
Parent: Sune Green Holdco3 Limited
Officers: Carl Goran Dandanell [1959] Director [Swedish]

Sunsave 11 (Wrockwardine Farm) Limited
Incorporated: 10 August 2012
Net Worth Deficit: £279,218 *Total Assets:* £11,976,380
Registered Office: Eversheds House, 70 Great Bridgewater Street, Manchester, M1 5ES
Activities: Production of electricity
Parent: Terraform UK3 Intermediate Holdings Limited
Officers: Carl Goran Dandanell [1959] Director [Swedish]

Sunsave 14 (Fenton) Limited
Incorporated: 14 March 2013
Net Worth: £24 246,320 *Total Assets:* £53,641,008
Registered Office: Eversheds House, 70 Great Bridgewater Street, Manchester, M1 5ES
Activities: Production of electricity
Parent: Sune Green Holdco5 Limited
Officers: Carl Goran Dandanell [1959] Director [Swedish]

Sunsave 15 (Westwood) Limited
Incorporated: 20 February 2013
Net Worth: £231,615 *Total Assets:* £8,984,064
Registered Office: Eversheds House, 70 Great Bridgewater Street, Manchester, M1 5ES
Activities: Production of electricity
Parent: Sune Green Holdco3 Limited
Officers: Carl Goran Dandanell [1959] Director [Swedish]

Sunsave 17 (Castle Combe) Limited
Incorporated: 15 March 2013
Net Worth Deficit: £1,795,630 *Total Assets:* £20,352,284
Registered Office: Eversheds House, 70 Great Bridgewater Street, Manchester, M1 5ES
Activities: Production of electricity
Parent: Terraform UK3 Intermediate Holdings Limited
Officers: Carl Goran Dandanell [1959] Director [Swedish]

Sunsave 2 Limited
Incorporated: 22 June 2011
Net Worth: £574,902 *Total Assets:* £6,549,156
Registered Office: 5th Floor, One City Place, Queens Road, Chester, CH1 3BQ
Activities: Production of electricity
Major Shareholder: Dagmar Vogt
Officers: Anton Charles Milner [1961] Director; Dagmar Vogt [1964] Director [German]

Sunsave 20 (Knowlton) Limited
Incorporated: 25 March 2013
Net Worth: £52,009 *Total Assets:* £10,465,941
Registered Office: Eversheds House, 70 Great Bridgewater Street, Manchester, M1 5ES
Activities: Production of electricity
Parent: Sune Green Holdco3 Limited
Officers: Carl Goran Dandanell [1959] Director [Swedish]

Sunsave 31 (Horam) Limited
Incorporated: 4 April 2014
Net Worth: £175,286 *Total Assets:* £11,122,834
Registered Office: Eversheds House, 70 Great Bridgewater Street, Manchester, M1 5ES
Activities: Production of electricity
Parent: Terraform UK3 Intermediate Holdings Limited
Officers: Carl Goran Dandanell [1959] Director [Swedish]

Sunsave 43 (Epwell) Limited
Incorporated: 19 June 2014
Net Worth: £2,587,715 *Total Assets:* £10,945,529
Registered Office: Eversheds House, 70 Great Bridgewater Street, Manchester, M1 5ES
Activities: Production of electricity
Parent: Sune Green Holdco6 Limited
Officers: Carl Goran Dandanell [1959] Director [Swedish]

Sunsave 6 (Manston) Ltd
Incorporated: 26 July 2012
Net Worth Deficit: £2,170,066 *Total Assets:* £10,910,274
Registered Office: Eversheds House, 70 Great Bridgewater Street, Manchester, M1 5ES
Activities: Production of electricity
Parent: Sune Green Holdco4 Limited
Officers: Carl Goran Dandanell [1959] Director [Swedish]

Sunshine Cruise Holidays Limited
Incorporated: 22 February 2000 *Employees:* 140
Net Worth: £2,034,982 *Total Assets:* £36,064,180
Registered Office: Unit F1A Lowry Outlet Mall, Salford Quays, Salford, M50 3AH
Activities: Travel agency activities
Shareholders: Travel 1st Limited; RCL Investments Ltd.
Officers: Caspar Moore, Secretary; Martin Betzwieser [1983] Director/Chief Financial Officer [German]; Carl Frier [1967] Director [Australian]; Dr Stefan Peter Gutberlet [1984] Director/Business Executive [German]; Caspar Moore [1968] Finance Director; Felix Benjamin Schneider [1981] Director [German]; Danyal Taj Taraghi [1985] Director/Business Executive [German]; Daniel Robert Townsley [1971] Director

Supply UK Investments Limited
Incorporated: 7 April 2015 *Employees:* 163
Net Worth: £5,416,694 *Total Assets:* £14,633,292
Registered Office: Unit 8 Riverview, Embankment Business Park, Heaton Mersey, Stockport, Cheshire, SK4 3GN
Activities: Renting and leasing of construction and civil engineering machinery and equipment
Officers: Peter Bernard Marcel Boels [1962] Director [Dutch]; Elisabeth Petra Maria Boels-Van Kerkom [1967] Director [Dutch]; Piet Elisabeth Michiel Marie Donners [1962] Director [Dutch]

Supreme Imports Ltd
Incorporated: 19 November 2004 *Employees:* 96
Net Worth: £13,400,000 *Total Assets:* £25,459,840
Registered Office: 4 Beacon Road, Trafford Park, Manchester, M17 1AF
Activities: Wholesale of household goods (other than musical instruments) n.e.c
Major Shareholder: Sandeep Singh Chadha
Officers: Michael Generald Clinch, Finance Director; Aditi Chadha [1975] Director; Sandeep Singh Chadha [1968] Director; Michael Generald Clinch [1961] Director

Supremebase Limited
Incorporated: 12 July 1994
Net Worth: £16,843 *Total Assets:* £6,670,326
Registered Office: Allerton Golf Course, Allerton Road, Mossley Hill, Liverpool, L18 3JT
Activities: Activities of construction holding companies
Shareholders: Michael Hanlon; James Mutch
Officers: James Mutch, Secretary/Mechanical Director; Michael Hanlon [1946] Director/Mechanical Engineer; James Mutch [1945] Mechanical Director

Surecalm Healthcare Ltd
Incorporated: 19 January 2010 *Employees:* 17
Net Worth: £8,110,811 *Total Assets:* £16,355,513
Registered Office: GDC, First Avenue, Deeside Industrial Park, Deeside, Flintshire, CH5 2NU
Activities: Other human health activities
Parent: Surecalm Healthcare Holdings Limited
Officers: Clare Jane Bates [1976] Director/Solicitor; Sarah Jane Lewis [1970] Finance Director; Christopher John Sedwell [1976] Director/Chartered Accountant

Surrenda-Link Mortgage Holdings Limited
Incorporated: 5 July 2004 *Employees:* 1
Net Worth Deficit: £6,806,424 *Total Assets:* £15,649,706
Registered Office: One City Place, Queens Road, Chester, CH1 3BQ
Activities: Activities of head offices
Parent: Surrenda Link (Investors) Limited
Officers: David William James Roxburgh, Secretary; David William James Roxburgh [1963] Director/Accountant [Irish]; Cuthbert Paul Sands [1943] Director; Michael Semple [1945] Director/Chartered Accountant [Irish]

Survey Supplies Limited
Incorporated: 10 November 1969 *Employees:* 66
Net Worth: £6,297,817 *Total Assets:* £11,029,610
Registered Office: 34-44 Mersey View, Waterloo, Liverpool, L22 6QB
Activities: Other specialised construction activities n.e.c.
Parent: Precise Construction Instruments (UK) Ltd
Officers: David Sydney Hodkinson, Secretary; Alan Charles Browne [1967] Director [Irish]; David Sydney Hodkinson [1970] Finance Director

Survitec Acquisition Company Limited
Incorporated: 28 November 2014 *Employees:* 2,320
Net Worth Deficit: £96,637,000 *Total Assets:* £879,286,016
Registered Office: 1-5 Beaufort Road, Birkenhead, Merseyside, CH41 1HQ
Activities: Activities of head offices
Officers: John Cyril George Stocker [1967] Director/Chief Operations Officer; Brian Mark Stringer [1963] Director/Chief Operating Officer

Survitec Aud Newco Limited
Incorporated: 16 March 2015 *Employees:* 3
Net Worth: £16,672,821 *Total Assets:* £16,672,821
Registered Office: 1-5 Beaufort Road, Birkenhead, Merseyside, CH41 1HQ
Activities: Activities of head offices
Officers: Cyril Stocker [1967] Director/Chief Operating Officer; Brian Mark Stringer [1963] Director/Chief Executive Officer

Survitec Eagle LLP
Incorporated: 15 December 2014 *Employees:* 2,320
Net Worth: £217,878,000 *Total Assets:* £898,955,008
Registered Office: 1-5 Beaufort Road, Merseyside, CH41 1HQ

Survitec Global Solutions Limited
Incorporated: 24 January 2013 *Employees:* 9
Net Worth Deficit: £724,642 *Total Assets:* £16,670,042
Registered Office: 1-5 Beaufort Road, Birkenhead, Merseyside, CH41 1HQ
Activities: Activities of head offices
Officers: Sally Lewis, Secretary; John Cyril George Stocker [1967] Director/Chief Operating Officer; Brian Mark Stringer [1963] Director/Chief Operating Officer

Survitec Group (Finance 1) Limited
Incorporated: 9 November 2009
Net Worth: £180,218,000 *Total Assets:* £180,218,000
Registered Office: 1-5 Beaufort Road, Birkenhead, Merseyside, CH41 1HQ
Activities: Activities of head offices
Parent: Survitec Acquisition Company Limited
Officers: Sally Lewis, Secretary; John Cyril George Stocker [1967] Director/Chief Operations Officer; Brian Mark Stringer [1963] Director/Chief Operating Officer

Survitec Group (Finance 2) Limited
Incorporated: 1 December 2009 *Employees:* 3
Net Worth Deficit: £6,610,000 *Total Assets:* £353,830,016
Registered Office: 1-5 Beaufort Road, Birkenhead, Merseyside, CH41 1HQ
Activities: Activities of head offices
Officers: Sally Lewis, Secretary; John Cyril George Stocker [1967] Director/Chief Operations Officer; Brian Mark Stringer [1963] Director/Chief Operating Officer

Survitec Group (Finance 3) Limited
Incorporated: 1 December 2009 *Employees:* 3
Net Worth: £1,520,000 *Total Assets:* £351,913,984
Registered Office: 1-5 Beaufort Road, Birkenhead, Merseyside, CH41 1HQ
Activities: Activities of head offices
Officers: Sally Lewis, Secretary; John Cyril George Stocker [1967] Director/Chief Operations Officer; Brian Mark Stringer [1963] Director/Chief Operating Officer

Survitec Group (Holdings) Limited
Incorporated: 23 November 2009 *Employees:* 3
Net Worth Deficit: £118,401,000 *Total Assets:* £241,502,000
Registered Office: 1-5 Beaufort Road, Birkenhead, Merseyside, CH41 1HQ
Activities: Activities of head offices
Parent: Survitec Acquisition Company Limited
Officers: Sally Lewis, Secretary; John Cyril George Stocker [1967] Director/Chief Operating Officer; Brian Mark Stringer [1963] Director/Chief Operating Officer

Survitec Group Limited
Incorporated: 3 May 1967 *Employees:* 573
Net Worth: £124,986,000 *Total Assets:* £548,086,016
Registered Office: 1-5 Beaufort Road, Birkenhead, Merseyside, CH41 1HQ
Activities: Other manufacturing n.e.c.
Parent: Survitec Holdings 1 Limited
Officers: Sally Lewis, Secretary; John Cyril George Stocker [1967] Director/Chief Operations Officer; Brian Mark Stringer [1963] Director/Chief Operating Officer

Survitec Holdco Limited
Incorporated: 15 December 2014 *Employees:* 5
Net Worth Deficit: £3,925,000 *Total Assets:* £355,761,984
Registered Office: 1-5 Beaufort Road, Birkenhead, Merseyside, CH41 1HQ
Activities: Activities of head offices
Officers: John Cyril George Stocker [1967] Director/Chief Operations Officer; Brian Mark Stringer [1963] Director/Chief Operating Officer

Survitec Interco Limited
Incorporated: 12 December 2014
Net Worth Deficit: £3,654,000 *Total Assets:* £355,760,992
Registered Office: 1-5 Beaufort Road, Birkenhead, Merseyside, CH41 1HQ
Activities: Activities of head offices
Officers: John Cyril George Stocker [1967] Director/Chief Operations Officer; Brian Mark Stringer [1963] Director/Chief Operating Officer

Survitec Midco Limited
Incorporated: 12 December 2014
Net Worth Deficit: £3,654,000 *Total Assets:* £355,760,992
Registered Office: 1-5 Beaufort Road, Birkenhead, Merseyside, CH41 1HQ
Activities: Activities of head offices
Officers: John Cyril George Stocker [1967] Director/Chief Operations Officer; Brian Mark Stringer [1963] Director/Chief Operating Officer

Survitec Service & Distribution Limited
Incorporated: 27 August 1955
Net Worth: £6,649,000 *Total Assets:* £19,154,000
Registered Office: 1-5 Beaufort Road, Birkenhead, Merseyside, CH41 1HQ
Activities: Other manufacturing n.e.c.
Officers: Sally Lewis, Secretary; Johan Denis [1962] Director/Vice President [Belgian]; Joanne Sarah Rugman [1978] Finance Director; John Cyril George Stocker [1967] Director/Chief Operating Officer; Brian Mark Stringer [1963] Director/Chief Operating Officer

Survitec Topco Limited
Incorporated: 12 December 2014 *Employees:* 2,320
Net Worth Deficit: £96,521,000 *Total Assets:* £879,206,016
Registered Office: 1-5 Beaufort Road, Birkenhead, Merseyside, CH41 1HQ
Activities: Activities of head offices
Officers: Sir Jonathon Band [1950] Director; Stefan Miesner [1986] Director/Principal [German]; Anthony David Morgan [1972] Managing Director; Simon Arthur Davidson Morse [1952] Director; Erik Nyheim [1972] Director/Chief Commercial Officer [Norwegian]; Mark Robertshaw [1968] Director; John Cyril George Stocker [1967] Director/Chief Operations Officer; Brian Mark Stringer [1963] Director/Chief Executive Officer; Warren Tucker [1962] Director

Sussex Custodial Services (Holdings) Limited
Incorporated: 21 February 2001
Net Worth: £1,402,048 *Total Assets:* £22,644,686
Registered Office: Unit 18 Riversway Business Village, Navigation Way, Ashton on Ribble, Preston, Lancs, PR2 2YP
Activities: Development of building projects
Parent: Infrastructure Investments General Partner Limited
Officers: Sally-Ann Ann Brooks [1966] Director; Angela Mills [1961] Director

Sussex Custodial Services Limited
Incorporated: 20 February 2001
Net Worth: £2,030,917 *Total Assets:* £21,718,344
Registered Office: Unit 18 Riversway Business Village, Navigation Way, Ashton on Ribble, Preston, Lancs, PR2 2YP
Activities: Development of building projects
Parent: Sussex Custodial Services (Holdings) Limited
Officers: Sally-Ann Ann Brooks [1966] Director; Angela Mills [1961] Director

Sustainable Communities for Leeds (Finance) PLC
Incorporated: 2 July 2013
Net Worth: £84,847 *Total Assets:* £117,480,256
Registered Office: Unit 18 Navigation Way, Ashton on Ribble, Preston, Lancs, PR2 2YP
Activities: Other accommodation
Parent: Sustainable Communities for Leeds (Holdings) Limited
Officers: Paul Ellis Gill [1975] Director/Investment Manager; Robert Alistair Martin Gillespie [1990] Director/Chartered Accountant; Daniel Marinus Maria Vermeer [1981] Director/Senior Manager [Dutch]; Edward Arthur Wilson [1965] Director/Chief Investment Officer

Sustainable Communities for Leeds (Holdings) Limited
Incorporated: 5 December 2012
Net Worth Deficit: £10,315,852 *Total Assets:* £114,565,120
Registered Office: Unit 18 Riversway Business Village, Navigation Way, Ashton on Ribble, Preston, Lancs, PR2 2YP
Activities: Activities of head offices
Shareholders: Aberdeen Infrastructure Investments (No 5) Limited; Equitix Housing II Limited
Officers: Paul Ellis Gill [1975] Director/Investment Manager; Robert Alistair Martin Gillespie [1990] Director/Chartered Accountant; Daniel Marinus Maria Vermeer [1981] Director/Senior Manager [Dutch]; Edward Arthur Wilson [1965] Director/Chief Investment Officer

Sustainable Communities for Leeds Limited
Incorporated: 6 December 2012
Net Worth Deficit: £10,496,124 *Total Assets:* £116,656,744
Registered Office: Unit 18 Navigation Way, Ashton on Ribble, Preston, Lancs, PR2 2YP
Activities: Other accommodation
Parent: Sustainable Communities for Leeds (Holdings) Limited
Officers: Paul Ellis Gill [1975] Director/Investment Manager; Robert Alistair Martin Gillespie [1990] Director/Chartered Accountant; Daniel Marinus Maria Vermeer [1981] Director/Senior Manager [Dutch]; Edward Arthur Wilson [1965] Director/Chief Investment Officer

E.Sutton & Son Limited
Incorporated: 10 May 1945 *Employees:* 576
Net Worth: £21,209,418 *Total Assets:* £31,205,056
Registered Office: Riverside, Newchurch Road, Bacup, Lancs, OL13 0DT
Activities: Activities of head offices
Shareholders: Riverside Charitable Trust Ltd; ESA Ltd
Officers: Mark Alan Foster Butterworth, Secretary; Mark Alan Foster Butterworth [1974] Director; Michael Stephen Kelly [1967] Director/Chairman

Sutton and Son (St.Helens) Limited
Incorporated: 1 January 1954 *Employees:* 26
Net Worth: £11,742,150 *Total Assets:* £33,523,190
Registered Office: Gorsey Lane, Widnes, Cheshire, WA8 0GG
Activities: Freight transport by road
Parent: Suttons Transport Group Limited
Officers: Nicola Wignall Jennings, Secretary; Keith Broom [1963] Finance Director; Michael Paul Cundy [1977] Director; Christopher Charles Orger [1975] Finance Director; John Michael Sutton [1971] Managing Director

Suttons International Limited
Incorporated: 25 August 1967 *Employees:* 47
Net Worth: £23,730,978 *Total Assets:* £91,073,520
Registered Office: Gorsey Lane, Widnes, Cheshire, WA8 0GG
Activities: Other transportation support activities
Parent: Suttons Transport Group Limited
Officers: Nicola Wignall Jennings, Secretary; Keith Broom [1963] Finance Director; Ian David Daines [1964] Finance Director; Barry McNally [1972] Director/International Operations [Irish]; John Michael Sutton [1971] Managing Director

Suttons Tankers Limited
Incorporated: 11 November 1988 *Employees:* 820
Net Worth: £7,502,162 *Total Assets:* £30,286,876
Registered Office: Gorsey Lane, Widnes, Cheshire, WA8 0GG
Activities: Freight transport by road
Parent: Sutton & Son (St Helens) Limited
Officers: Nicola Wignall Jennings, Secretary; Keith Broom [1963] Finance Director; Michael Paul Cundy [1977] Director; Stephen Barry Hassall [1969] Director/Operations Manager; Chrisi Lloyd Roberts [1977] Director/Procurement and Projects Manager; Gregan Trevor Lofts [1970] Director; Christopher Charles Orger [1975] Director/Accountant; Roger Martin Parr [1969] Director/Operations Manager; John Michael Sutton [1971] Managing Director

SW Golf Limited
Incorporated: 26 February 2001 *Employees:* 30
Net Worth Deficit: £1,096,000 *Total Assets:* £8,607,000
Registered Office: Europa Boulevard, Gemini Business Park, Westbrook, Warrington, Cheshire, WA5 7YW
Activities: Other retail sale of new goods in specialised stores (not commercial art galleries and opticians)
Parent: American Golf Discount Centre Limited
Officers: Lorraine Stringer, Secretary; Samantha Jane Tyrer [1970] Director/Chief Executive; Ian Robert Williams [1973] Director/Chief Financial Officer

Swallow Holdings Limited
Incorporated: 14 October 1994 *Employees:* 267
Net Worth: £8,757,254 *Total Assets:* £13,913,017
Registered Office: Creamline Dairies, Mellors Road, Trafford Park, Manchester, M17 1PB
Activities: Liquid milk and cream production
Shareholders: Christopher David Swallow; Robert Kenneth Berry Purvis
Officers: Christopher David Swallow, Secretary/Management Executive; Robert Kenneth Berry Purvis [1969] Director/Management Executive; Anthony David Swallow [1940] Director/Executive; Christopher David Swallow [1970] Director/Management Executive; Helga Hildegard Gertrud Swallow [1935] Director/Housewife [German]

The Swan Hotel (Newby Bridge) Holdings Limited
Incorporated: 8 February 2006 *Employees:* 119
Net Worth: £2,788,189 *Total Assets:* £10,186,476
Registered Office: Newby Bridge, Ulverston, Cumbria, LA12 8NB
Activities: Hotels and similar accommodation
Shareholders: Audrey Campbell Robertson; Sharon Anne Bardsley
Officers: Lisa Jayne Gray-Joyce, Secretary; Anne Bardsley [1942] Director; Sharon Anne Bardsley [1969] Director/Chairman; Sarah Gibbs [1981] Managing Director; Audrey Campbell Robertson [1969] Director/Secretary

The Swan Hotel (Newby Bridge) Limited
Incorporated: 14 May 1996 *Employees:* 119
Net Worth: £2,788,189 *Total Assets:* £10,186,476
Registered Office: Newby Bridge, Ulverston, Cumbria, LA12 8NB
Activities: Hotels and similar accommodation
Shareholders: Sharon Anne Bardsley; Audrey Campbell Robertson
Officers: Lisa Jayne Gray-Joyce, Secretary; Anne Bardsley [1942] Director; Ottilie India Bardsley [2000] Director; Sharon Anne Bardsley [1969] Director; Claire Anne Dickinson [1977] Director; Sarah Gibbs [1981] Director/General Manager; Craig Jeffrey Hadfield [1977] Food & Beverage Director; Audrey Campbell Robertson [1969] Director

Swansway Garages Limited
Incorporated: 8 August 2002 *Employees:* 803
Net Worth: £23,692,856 *Total Assets:* £132,942,968
Registered Office: Swansway Group, Gateway, Crewe, Cheshire, CW1 6YY
Activities: Sale of new cars and light motor vehicles
Parent: Swansway Group Limited
Officers: Richard Marsland, Secretary; Richard Marsland [1962] Finance Director; David Smyth [1962] Director; John Smyth [1967] Director; Michael Smyth [1939] Director; Peter Smyth [1964] Director

Swansway Group Limited
Incorporated: 15 December 2009 *Employees:* 895
Net Worth: £24,383,160 *Total Assets:* £192,532,688
Registered Office: Swansway Group, Gateway, Crewe, Cheshire, CW1 6YY
Activities: Activities of head offices
Officers: Richard Marsland, Secretary; Richard Marsland [1962] Finance Director; David Smyth [1962] Director; John Smyth [1967] Director; Michael Smyth [1939] Director; Peter Smyth [1964] Director

Sweet Dreams (Nelson) Limited
Incorporated: 28 November 1988 *Employees:* 331
Net Worth: £1,890,063 *Total Assets:* £9,803,579
Registered Office: Primrose Mill, Martin Street, Burnley, Lancs, BB10 1SH
Activities: Other manufacturing n.e.c.
Parent: Dreambase Limited
Officers: Adnan Farooq Ahmed, Secretary; Adnan Farooq Ahmed [1984] Director; Majid Ahmed [1976] Director; Riaz Ahmed [1949] Director

Swift Engineering (Azerbaijan) Limited
Incorporated: 15 November 2002 *Employees:* 26
Net Worth: £482,000 *Total Assets:* £16,265,000
Registered Office: 4th Floor, Delphian House, Riverside, New Bailey Street, Salford, M3 5FS
Activities: Other activities of employment placement agencies
Parent: Swift Technical Group Limited
Officers: Timothy Briant [1970] Director; Janette Bates Marx [1975] Director [American]; Peter William Courtis Searle [1962] Director; Norman Young [1945] Director

Swift Technical (Azerbaijan) Limited
Incorporated: 3 December 2002 *Employees:* 3
Net Worth: £13,258,000 *Total Assets:* £13,904,000
Registered Office: 4th Floor, Delphian House, Riverside, New Bailey Street, Salford, M3 5FS
Activities: Other activities of employment placement agencies
Parent: Swift Technical Group Limited
Officers: Timothy Briant [1970] Director; Ford David Garrard [1983] Director; Janette Bates Marx [1975] Director [American]; Peter William Courtis Searle [1962] Director; Norman Young [1945] Director

Swift Technical (Europe) Limited
Incorporated: 20 January 2003 *Employees:* 57
Net Worth: £13,571,000 *Total Assets:* £19,749,000
Registered Office: 4th Floor, Delphian House, Riverside, New Bailey Street, Salford, M3 5FS
Activities: Other activities of employment placement agencies
Parent: Swift Technical Group Limited
Officers: Timothy Briant [1970] Director; Ford David Garrard [1983] Director; Janette Bates Marx [1975] Director [American]; Peter William Courtis Searle [1962] Director

Swift Technical Group Holdings Limited
Incorporated: 20 June 2006
Net Worth: £97,378,000 *Total Assets:* £97,378,000
Registered Office: 4th Floor, Delphian House, Riverside, New Bailey Street, Salford, M3 5FS
Activities: Other activities of employment placement agencies
Parent: Swift Worldwide Resources Bidco Limited
Officers: Timothy Briant [1970] Director; Joshua Charles Cascade [1972] Director [American]; Janette Bates Marx [1975] Director [American]; Peter William Courtis Searle [1962] Director

Swift Technical Group Limited
Incorporated: 30 January 2003
Net Worth: £104,064,000 *Total Assets:* £104,072,000
Registered Office: 4th Floor, Delphian House, Riverside, New Bailey Street, Salford, M3 5FS
Activities: Other activities of employment placement agencies
Parent: Swift Technical Holdings Limited
Officers: Timothy Briant [1970] Director; Janette Bates Marx [1975] Director/Businesswoman [American]; Peter William Courtis Searle [1962] Director

Swift Technical Holdings Limited
Incorporated: 23 May 2006
Net Worth: £23,085,000 *Total Assets:* £36,665,000
Registered Office: 4th Floor, Delphian House, Riverside, New Bailey Street, Salford, M3 5FS
Activities: Other activities of employment placement agencies
Parent: Swift Techinical Group Holdings Limited
Officers: Timothy Briant [1970] Director; Joshua Charles Cascade [1972] Director [American]; Janette Bates Marx [1975] Director [American]; Peter William Courtis Searle [1962] Director

Swift Worldwide Resources Bidco Limited
Incorporated: 7 October 2013 *Employees:* 6
Net Worth Deficit: £39,704,000 *Total Assets:* £76,988,000
Registered Office: 4th Floor, Delphian House, Riverside, New Bailey Street, Salford, M3 5FS
Activities: Other activities of employment placement agencies
Parent: Swift Worldwide Resources Midco Limited
Officers: Timothy Briant [1970] Director; Alexander Edward Carles [1975] Director [American]; Joshua Charles Cascade [1972] Director [American]; William Francis Jr Dawson [1964] Director [American]; Janette Bates Marx [1975] Director [American]; Peter William Courtis Searle [1962] Director

Swift Worldwide Resources Holdco Limited
Incorporated: 7 October 2013
Net Worth: £66,778,488 *Total Assets:* £69,680,152
Registered Office: 4th Floor, Delphian House, Riverside, New Bailey Street, Salford, M3 5FS
Activities: Other activities of employment placement agencies
Officers: Timothy Briant [1970] Director; Alexander Edward Carles [1975] Director [American]; Joshua Charles Cascade [1972] Director [American]; William Francis Jr Dawson [1964] Director/United States [American]; Peter William Courtis Searle [1962] Director

Swift Worldwide Resources Midco Limited
Incorporated: 7 October 2013
Net Worth: £78,463,000 *Total Assets:* £83,460,000
Registered Office: 4th Floor, Delphian House, Riverside, New Bailey Street, Salford, M3 5FS
Activities: Other activities of employment placement agencies
Parent: Swift Worldwide Resources Holdco Limited
Officers: Timothy Briant [1970] Director; Alexander Edward Carles [1975] Director [American]; Joshua Charles Cascade [1972] Director [American]; William Francis Jr Dawson [1964] Director [American]; Janette Bates Marx [1975] Director [American]; Peter William Courtis Searle [1962] Director

Swinton (Holdings) Limited
Incorporated: 25 July 1983 *Employees:* 3,090
Net Worth: £157,296,992 *Total Assets:* £277,976,000
Registered Office: Embankment West Tower, 101 Cathedral Approach, Salford, M3 7FB
Activities: Activities of head offices
Parent: MMA Holdings UK PLC
Officers: Annabel Felicity Wilson, Secretary; David Robert Harding [1974] Director; Bertrand Lefebvre [1963] Director [French]; Dominique Salvy [1957] Director [French]; Steven Whittaker [1958] Director

Swinton Group Limited
Incorporated: 5 April 1963 *Employees:* 2,304
Net Worth: £168,203,008 *Total Assets:* £279,280,992
Registered Office: Embankment West Tower, 101 Cathedral Approach, Salford, M3 7FB
Activities: Non-life insurance
Parent: Swinton (Holdings) Limited
Officers: Annabel Felicity Wilson, Secretary; Alain Chaumeret [1956] Director [French]; Angela Doreen Crawford-Ingle [1952] Director; David Robert Harding [1974] Director; Scott Stewart Kennedy [1979] Director; Ashley John Machin [1964] Independent Non-Executive Director; Christopher Moat [1968] Director; Jerome Roncoroni [1956] Director [French]; Clare Leslie Salmon [1963] Independent Non-Executive Director

The Swinton High School Academy Trust
Incorporated: 13 May 2011 *Employees:* 85
Net Worth: £8,400,000 *Total Assets:* £10,359,000
Registered Office: Sefton Road, Swinton, Manchester, M27 6JU
Activities: General secondary education
Officers: Brian Briggs [1938] Director/Retired; Neil Andrew D'Arcy [1976] Director/Civil Engineer; Patricia Louise Dalton-Bunker [1969] Director/Teacher; Lesley Jacqueline Davies [1952] Director/Education Manager; Councillor James Brian Dawson [1941] Director; Kevin James Hardwidge [1981] Director/Church Leader; George Harrison [1941] Director; Mark Francis Harrison [1975] Director/Headteacher; Geoffrey Henry Hubbard [1946] Director; Andrew Robert Hyde [1967] Director/Transport Planner; Rachel Elizabeth Knight [1980] Director/Teacher; Kathrine Lewis [1966] Director/Homemaker; Valerie Elsie Meredith [1945] Director; Timothy Alastair Rackham [1971] Director/Chief Quantity Surveyor; John Ridyard [1948] Director

Swinton Properties Limited
Incorporated: 17 November 1983
Net Worth: £25,149,000 *Total Assets:* £25,747,000
Registered Office: Embankment West Tower, 101 Cathedral Approach, Salford, M3 7FB
Activities: Buying and selling of own real estate
Parent: Swinton (Holdings) Limited
Officers: Annabel Felicity Wilson, Secretary; David Robert Harding [1974] Director

Swiscot Textiles Limited
Incorporated: 28 March 1967 *Employees:* 22
Net Worth: £3,039,824 *Total Assets:* £8,492,431
Registered Office: Swiscot House, Unit 5 Pacific Way, Salford, M50 1DL
Activities: Wholesale of textiles
Major Shareholder: Vikas Shah
Officers: Mona Sejal Shah, Secretary; Christina Patricia Kittos [1957] Operations Director; Nirav Patel [1972] Financial Director; Mark Seddon [1968] Director; Chandravadan Harilal Shah [1937] Director [Indian]; Kalpana Chandravadan Shah [1949] Director [Indian]; Mona Sejal Shah [1975] Director/Secretary; Vikas Sagar Shah [1981] Director/Textile Merchant; Richard Yates [1971] Director

Swissport GB Limited
Incorporated: 7 July 1952 *Employees:* 7,304
Net Worth: £551,000 *Total Assets:* £105,618,000
Registered Office: Swissport House, Hampton Court, Manor Park, Runcorn, Cheshire, WA7 1TT
Activities: Service activities incidental to air transportation
Parent: Swissport Group UK Limited
Officers: Jason Gaskell [1971] Director; Darren Harding [1971] Director; Benjamin Joseph Holme Kay [1974] Director; Luzius Wirth [1974] Director [Swiss]

Swissport Stansted Ltd
Incorporated: 17 December 2001 *Employees:* 613
Net Worth: £6,896,000 *Total Assets:* £13,617,000
Registered Office: Swissport House, Hampton Court, Manor Park, Runcorn, Cheshire, WA7 1TT
Activities: Non-scheduled passenger air transport
Parent: Swissport GB Limited
Officers: Benjamin Joseph Holme Kay [1974] Director; Luzius Wirth [1974] Director [Swiss]

Swissport UK Holding Limited
Incorporated: 10 December 2010
Net Worth Deficit: £77,644,000 *Total Assets:* £136,019,008
Registered Office: Swissport House, Hampton Court, Manor Park, Runcorn, Cheshire, WA7 1TT
Activities: Freight air transport
Officers: Dr Christian Goseke [1967] Director/CFO of Swissport International Limited [German]; Benjamin Joseph Holme Kay [1974] Director; Luzius Wirth [1974] Director [Swiss]

Switch2 Energy Limited
Incorporated: 31 July 1989 *Employees:* 145
Net Worth: £6,121,505 *Total Assets:* £10,152,013
Registered Office: The Waterfront, Salts Mill Road, Shipley, W Yorks, BD17 7EZ
Activities: Plumbing, heat and air-conditioning installation
Shareholders: Martin Lothar Ernst Hornig; Dr Thomas Martin Joseph Wilhelm
Officers: Christopher John Hull [1966] Director/Chief Financial Officer; Kirsty Jane Lambert [1970] Director; Samantha Jane Scott [1980] Director; Timothy Hays Scott [1950] Director; Anthony Peter Roy Ward [1978] Director

Swizzels Matlow Limited
Incorporated: 6 March 1956 *Employees:* 634
Net Worth: £41,499,000 *Total Assets:* £73,036,000
Registered Office: Carlton House, Albion Road, New Mills, High Peak, Derbys, SK22 3HA
Activities: Manufacture of sugar confectionery
Officers: Ian Walker, Secretary; Brian Neiman Dee [1945] Director/Manufacturing Confectioner; Jeremy Adam Dee [1975] Director; Jonathan Mark Dee [1976] Director; Trevor Jack Leslie William Matlow [1935] Director/Manufacturing Confectioner; Nicola Ruth Wertheim [1970] Director

J Sykes & Sons (Manchester) Limited
Incorporated: 24 August 1988 *Employees:* 55
Net Worth: £6,085,000 *Total Assets:* £46,703,000
Registered Office: New Smithfield Market, Whitworth Street East, Manchester, M11 2WP
Activities: Wholesale of other food, including fish, crustaceans and molluscs
Parent: Sykes Seafoods Ltd
Officers: Gordon John Blackshaw [1960] Director; Alan David Dale [1980] Director; Andrew David Pickup [1970] Director; David Samwell [1974] National Accounts Director; Daniel John Wright [1980] Director

Sykes Chemists Limited
Incorporated: 20 November 1998 *Employees:* 146
Net Worth: £1,436,945 *Total Assets:* £7,547,824
Registered Office: 328 St Helens Road, Bolton, Lancs, BL3 3RP
Activities: Dispensing chemist in specialised stores
Shareholders: Chimanlal Govind Patel; Utamkumar Govind Patel
Officers: Chimanlal Govind Patel, Secretary/Pharmacist; Chimanlal Govind Patel [1953] Director/Pharmacist; Suresh Govind Patel [1955] Director/Chemical Engineer; Utamkumar Govind Patel [1957] Director/Pharmacist

Sykes Cottages Holdings Limited
Incorporated: 8 December 2014 *Employees:* 254
Net Worth Deficit: £6,178,000 *Total Assets:* £61,827,000
Registered Office: One St Peter's Square, Manchester, M2 3DE
Activities: Activities of other holding companies n.e.c.
Parent: FIS Nominee Limited
Officers: Simon James Taylor, Secretary; Graham Donoghue [1973] Director; Paul John Thomas Gilbert [1962] Director; Michael Steven Graham [1964] Director; Adam Stuart Holloway [1967] Director; Matthew Woolfe Jacobs [1987] Director; Laurence Roy Marlor [1974] Director; Michael Charles Rivis [1970] Director; James Martin Shaw [1979] Director; Clive Peter Sykes [1964] Director

Sykes Cottages Ltd
Incorporated: 25 June 2002 *Employees:* 247
Net Worth: £16,555,000 *Total Assets:* £26,420,000
Registered Office: Sykes Cottages Ltd, One City Place, Queens Road, Chester, CH1 3BQ
Activities: Other reservation service activities n.e.c.
Parent: Go-Sykes Limited
Officers: Simon James Taylor, Secretary; Graham Donoghue [1973] Director; Mr Michael Steven Graham [1964] Director; Clive Peter Sykes [1964] Director

Sykes Seafoods Limited
Incorporated: 13 February 1998 *Employees:* 102
Net Worth: £8,809,000 *Total Assets:* £46,276,000
Registered Office: New Smithfield Market, Whitworth Street East, Manchester, M11 2WP
Activities: Wholesale of other food, including fish, crustaceans and molluscs
Major Shareholder: Alan David Dale
Officers: Gordon John Blackshaw [1960] Director; Alan David Dale [1980] Director; Andrew David Pickup [1970] Director/Chartered Accountant; Daniel Wright [1980] Director

John Sylvester Engineering Company Limited
Incorporated: 13 July 1964 *Employees:* 19
Net Worth: £9,432,706 *Total Assets:* £10,335,115
Registered Office: Vulcan Street, Dudley Hill, Bradford, W Yorks, BD4 9QU
Activities: Wholesale of machine tools
Officers: Arthur Sylvester, Secretary; Andrew Charles Sylvester [1975] Director/Company Manager; Arthur Sylvester [1933] Director

Synexus Clinical Research Acquisitions Limited
Incorporated: 24 October 2007
Net Worth: £27,799,000 *Total Assets:* £31,829,000
Registered Office: Sandringham House, Ackhurst Park, Chorley, Lancs, PR7 1NY
Activities: Other professional, scientific and technical activities n.e.c.
Parent: Synexus Clinical Research Finance Limited
Officers: Brainerd Judd Hartman [1963] Director [American]; Julia Mary James [1974] Director; Christopher David Neild [1962] Director

Synexus Clinical Research Finance Limited
Incorporated: 24 October 2007
Net Worth: £6,216,000 *Total Assets:* £27,813,000
Registered Office: Sandringham House, Ackhurst Park, Chorley, Lancs, PR7 1NY
Activities: Other professional, scientific and technical activities n.e.c.
Parent: Synexus Clinical Research Midco No 4 Limited
Officers: Brainard Judd Hartman [1963] Director [American]; Julia Mary James [1974] Director; Christopher David Neild [1962] Director

Synexus Clinical Research Limited
Incorporated: 27 September 2005 *Employees:* 84
Net Worth: £19,613,000 *Total Assets:* £72,701,000
Registered Office: Sandringham House, Ackhurst Park, Chorley, Lancs, PR7 1NY
Activities: Other professional, scientific and technical activities n.e.c.
Parent: Synexus Clinical Research Midco No 1 Limited
Officers: Marcin Gondek [1979] Director [Polish]; Brainard Judd Hartman [1963] Director [American]; Julia Mary James [1974] Director; Christopher David Neild [1962] Director

Synexus Clinical Research Midco No 1 Limited
Incorporated: 14 January 2015
Net Worth: £24,197,000 *Total Assets:* £48,157,000
Registered Office: Sandringham House, Ackhurst Business Park, Foxhole Road, Chorley, Lancs, PR7 1NY
Activities: Other professional, scientific and technical activities n.e.c.
Parent: PPD International Investments Limited
Officers: Brainard Judd Hartman [1963] Director [American]; Julia Mary James [1974] Director; Christopher David Neild [1962] Director

Synexus Clinical Research Midco No 2 Limited
Incorporated: 21 May 2010
Net Worth: £9,480,000 *Total Assets:* £10,852,000
Registered Office: Sandringham House, Ackhurst Business Park, Foxhole Road, Chorley, Lancs, PR7 1NY
Activities: Other information service activities n.e.c.
Parent: Synexus Clinical Research Midco No 1 Limited
Officers: Brainard Judd Hartman [1963] Director [American]; Julia Mary James [1974] Director; Christopher David Neild [1962] Director

Synexus Clinical Research Midco No 3 Limited
Incorporated: 23 June 2010
Net Worth: £10,852,000 *Total Assets:* £10,852,000
Registered Office: Sandringham House, Ackhurst Business Park, Foxhole Road, Chorley, Lancs, PR7 1NY
Activities: Other professional, scientific and technical activities n.e.c.
Parent: Synexus Clinical Research Midco No 2 Limited
Officers: Brainard Judd Hartman [1963] Director [American]; Julia Mary James [1974] Director; Christopher David Neild [1962] Director

Synexus Limited
Incorporated: 2 March 1999 *Employees:* 195
Net Worth Deficit: £510,304 *Total Assets:* £16,999,698
Registered Office: Sandringham House, Ackhurst Park, Chorley, Lancs, PR7 1NY
Activities: Other professional, scientific and technical activities n.e.c.
Parent: Synexus Clinical Research Limited
Officers: Marcin Gondek [1979] Director [Polish]; Radoslaw Michal Janiak [1972] President and COO/Executive Director [Polish]

Synthetic Technologies Ltd
Incorporated: 2 July 1997 *Employees:* 82
Net Worth: £10,139,979 *Total Assets:* £13,870,788
Registered Office: Unit 14 Graphite Way, Hadfield, Glossop, Derbys, SK13 1QH
Activities: Wholesale of chemical products
Major Shareholder: Douglas Birch
Officers: Douglas Birch, Secretary; Douglas Birch [1957] Director/Chartered Accountant; Gregory Butler [1957] Director/Chemist [American]; Dr Martin Fraser Woolley [1967] Director/Chemical Sales

Synthite Limited
Incorporated: 28 February 1920 *Employees:* 109
Net Worth: £26,405,336 *Total Assets:* £33,743,568
Registered Office: Alyn Works, Denbigh Road, Mold, Flintshire, CH7 1BT
Activities: Manufacture of other organic basic chemicals
Parent: Chemical Petroleum Investments
Officers: David John Kelso, Company Secretary; William Paul Alexander [1954] Director; Kevin Garth Jones [1956] Managing Director; David John Kelso [1963] Director; Sana Ullah Niazi [1959] Director; Keith James Polden [1972] Director

Sysgroup PLC
Incorporated: 20 March 2007 *Employees:* 74
Net Worth: £11,337,000 *Total Assets:* £16,569,000
Registered Office: Walker House, Exchange Flags, Liverpool, L2 3YL
Activities: Data processing, hosting and related activities
Officers: Martin Richard Audcent, Secretary; Martin Audcent [1973] Director; Adam Binks [1983] Director/Chief Executive Officer; John Michael Edelson [1944] Non-Executive Director Chairman; Michael James Fletcher [1974] Director; Robert Khalastchy [1962] Director; Mark Richard Quartermaine [1963] Director

System 3 Investments Limited
Incorporated: 18 May 2012
Net Worth: £73,245 *Total Assets:* £6,876,577
Registered Office: Denton Hall Farm Road, Denton, Manchester, M34 2SY
Activities: Management of real estate on a fee or contract basis
Shareholders: Michael Brown; Allan Brown
Officers: Allan Brown [1957] Director; Michael Brown [1963] Director

System 3 Limited
Incorporated: 27 October 2015 *Employees:* 232
Net Worth: £14,296,693 *Total Assets:* £17,684,204
Registered Office: Denton Hall Farm Road, Denton, Manchester, M34 2SY
Activities: Shaping and processing of flat glass
Shareholders: Michael Brown; Allan Brown
Officers: Michael Brown, Secretary; Allan Brown [1957] Director; Michael Brown [1963] Director

SZG Europe Limited
Incorporated: 18 June 2014
Net Worth Deficit: £615,096 *Total Assets:* £9,318,840
Registered Office: Eversheds House, 70 Great Bridgewater Street, Manchester, M1 5ES
Activities: Wholesale of radio, television goods & electrical household appliances (other than records, tapes, CDs)
Shareholders: Blaine Rusy Renfert; U.S. Bank Trust National Association SD
Officers: Blaine Rusy Renfert, Secretary; Anthony Frank Ascione [1969] Director/Business Executive [American]; James John Bakke [1954] Director/Business Owner [American]; Anthony Stafford Fox [1970] Director/Vice President - Finance [American]; Scott Steven Lafleur [1958] Director/Chief Operations Officer, Sub-Zero Group, Inc. [American]; Blaine Rusy Renfert [1951] Director/General Counsel [American]

T D Partnership Investments LLP
Incorporated: 11 December 2006
Net Worth: £958,332 *Total Assets:* £10,405,800
Registered Office: 28 Eaton Avenue, Matrix Office Park, Buckshaw Village, Chorley, Lancs, PR7 7NA
Officers: Andrew David Dick [1965] Member; Richard William Traynor [1959] Member

T&M Property Investments Limited
Incorporated: 20 November 2014
Net Worth: £279,307 *Total Assets:* £11,417,386
Registered Office: The Robert Street Hub, 12-14 Robert Street, Manchester, M3 1EY
Activities: Other letting and operating of own or leased real estate
Shareholders: Tayyab Jalaludin Kamani; Mustafa Jalaludin Kamani
Officers: Mustafa Jalaludin Kamani [1994] Director; Tayyab Jalaludin Kamani [1992] Director; Mohammad Marzouk [1969] Finance Director

T.A. Weatherwear Holdings Limited
Incorporated: 25 March 2011 *Employees:* 19
Net Worth: £21,222,550 *Total Assets:* £24,010,522
Registered Office: Unit 3 Trafalgar Business Park, Broughton Lane, Manchester, M7 9TZ
Activities: Other business support service activities n.e.c.
Major Shareholder: Arun Kumar Anand
Officers: Arun Kumar Anand, Secretary; Arun Kumar Anand [1969] Director

T.A. Weatherwear Limited
Incorporated: 14 June 1989 *Employees:* 19
Net Worth: £7,217,015 *Total Assets:* £8,787,397
Registered Office: Unit 3 Trafalgar Business Park, Broughton Lane, Manchester, M7 9TZ
Activities: Wholesale of clothing and footwear
Parent: T.A. Weatherwear Holdings Limited
Officers: Arun Kumar Anand, Secretary; Arun Kumar Anand [1969] Director/Retailer Textiles; Nandjit Anand [1937] Director

T.I.M. Co. (Didsbury) Limited
Incorporated: 10 December 1992 *Employees:* 1
Net Worth: £1,628,510 *Total Assets:* £7,349,534
Registered Office: 634 Wilmslow Road, Manchester, M20 3QR
Activities: Combined office administrative service activities
Shareholders: Charles Greenwood; Tim Greenwood
Officers: Timothy Sandiford Greenwood [1959] Director/Chartered Accountant

T.K. Components (Holdings) Limited
Incorporated: 30 November 2015 *Employees:* 122
Net Worth Deficit: £1,162,000 *Total Assets:* £26,260,000
Registered Office: Unit 3 Cranberry Drive, Denton, Manchester, M34 3UL
Activities: Wholesale of household goods (other than musical instruments) n.e.c
Officers: Ian Philip Plumb [1978] Director/Accountant; Roy Saunders [1958] Director/Chief Executive; Peter John Williamson [1966] Director

T.K. Components Group Limited
Incorporated: 30 November 2015
Net Worth Deficit: £4,051,000 *Total Assets:* £27,386,000
Registered Office: Unit 3 Cranberry Drive, Denton, Manchester, M34 3UL
Activities: Wholesale of household goods (other than musical instruments) n.e.c
Parent: T.K Components (Holdings) Limited
Officers: Roy Saunders [1958] Director/Chief Executive; Peter John Williamson [1966] Director

T.K. Components Limited
Incorporated: 21 November 1988 *Employees:* 135
Net Worth: £11 870,000 *Total Assets:* £16,051,000
Registered Office: Unit 3 Cranberry Drive, Denton, Manchester, M34 3UL
Activities: Wholesale of household goods (other than musical instruments) n.e.c
Parent: T.K Components Group Limited
Officers: Philip Joseph Foster [1966] Finance Director; Adam Haydon [1974] Supply Chain Director; Roy Saunders [1958] Director/Chief Executive; Brian Wade [1959] Supply Chain Director

Tablecheck Limited
Incorporated: 12 June 1996 *Employees:* 9
Net Worth: £5,215,014 *Total Assets:* £11,284,080
Registered Office: 159 Smithdown Road, Wavertree, Liverpool, L15 2HD
Activities: Other letting and operating of own or leased real estate
Shareholders: Andrew Lee Skeete; Anthony James Skeete
Officers: Andrew Lee Skeete [1984] Director/Housing Manager; Anthony James Skeete [1986] Director/Property Manager; Leopold Anthony Skeete [1949] Director

Tailored Fire & Security (London) Limited
Incorporated: 30 April 2015 *Employees:* 8
Net Worth: £9,922,998 *Total Assets:* £10,454,888
Registered Office: Unit 4 Howarth Court, Broadway Business Park, Oldham, Lancs, OL9 9XB
Activities: Fire service activities
Parent: TFS London Holdings Limited
Officers: Anthony Ernest Whittle [1970] Director

Takeuchi Mfg. (U.K.) Limited
Incorporated: 23 August 1996 *Employees:* 24
Net Worth: £16 291,872 *Total Assets:* £44,326,052
Registered Office: Unit E2B Kingsway Business Park, John Boyd Dunlop Drive, Rochdale, Lancs, OL16 4NG
Activities: Other business support service activities n.e.c.
Parent: Takeuchi Mfg. Co., Ltd.
Officers: Tomonori Tamaru, Secretary; Akio Takeuchi [1933] Director/President [Japanese]; Toshiya Takeuchi [1963] Director [Japanese]; Tomonori Tamaru [1968] Managing Director [Japanese]

Talbot Deane Investments Limited
Incorporated: 2 January 2013 *Employees:* 219
Net Worth Deficit: £6,315,489 *Total Assets:* £25,292,428
Registered Office: Adlington Court, Adlington Business Park, Adlington, Macclesfield, Cheshire, SK10 4NL
Activities: Activities of financial services holding companies
Parent: Bollington Wilson Limited
Officers: Patrick Francis McDonnell [1965] Finance Director [Irish]; Paul Christopher Moors [1962] Director; Christopher Mark Patterson [1971] Director

Talpole Limited
Incorporated: 20 July 1999
Net Worth: £3,560 *Total Assets:* £7,187,587
Registered Office: Cumberland House, Greenside Lane, Bradford, BD8 9TF
Activities: Agents specialised in the sale of other particular products
Major Shareholder: Franco Grottoli
Officers: Claire Marie Cain [1970] Director/Company Secretary; Christopher Stephen Smith [1972] Director/Trust Manager

Tamaris Healthcare (England) Limited
Incorporated: 6 March 1997 *Employees:* 1,760
Net Worth Deficit: £4,604,000 *Total Assets:* £9,584,000
Registered Office: Norcliffe House, Station Road, Wilmslow, Cheshire, SK9 1BU
Activities: Other human health activities
Parent: Four Seasons Group Holdings Limited
Officers: Abigail Mattison, Secretary; Timothy Richard William Hammond [1959] Director; Dr Maureen Claire Royston [1960] Director; Benjamin Robert Taberner [1972] Director/Chartered Accountant

Tandom Metallurgical Group Limited
Incorporated: 31 July 2008 *Employees:* 109
Net Worth: £3,969,078 *Total Assets:* £28,904,314
Registered Office: Third Avenue, Radnor Park Industrial Estate, Congleton, Cheshire, CW12 4XE
Activities: Other service activities n.e.c.
Shareholder: Andrew Gordon Lumsden
Officers: Robert John Charles [1971] Director; Peter Michael Dines [1958] Director; Liam James McMcelis [1980] Director; Thomas Muir [1956] Director; Darren John Ponsonby [1976] Director [Irish]; Nicholas Alan Rose [1970] Director

Tangerine Confectionery Group Limited
Incorporated: 21 December 2005
Net Worth Deficit: £11,482,000 *Total Assets:* £19,608,000
Registered Office: Quality House, Vicarage Lane, Blackpool, Lancs, FY4 4NQ
Activities: Activities of production holding companies
Parent: Taurus Bidco Limited
Officers: Antony Francheterre [1970] Director [French]; Andrew Hawley [1965] Director; Maria Elza Marleen Van Troys [1965] Director [Belgian]

Tangerine Confectionery Limited
Incorporated: 4 June 1986 *Employees:* 1,278
Net Worth: £76,967,000 *Total Assets:* £114,929,000
Registered Office: Quality House, Vicarage Lane, Blackpool, Lancs, FY4 4NQ
Activities: Manufacture of sugar confectionery
Parent: Tangerine Confectionery Group Limited
Officers: Antony Francheterre [1970] Director [French]; Andrew Hawley [1965] Director; Maria Elza Marleen Van Troys [1965] Director [Belgian]

Tangerine Holdings Limited
Incorporated: 7 October 1994 *Employees:* 219
Net Worth: £10,019,551 *Total Assets:* £28,526,288
Registered Office: Animal House, Boundary Road, Lytham St Annes, Lancs, FY8 5LT
Activities: Activities of head offices
Major Shareholder: David Alan Haythornthwaite
Officers: David Alan Haythornthwaite, Secretary; David Alan Haythornthwaite [1953] Director; Sharon Haythornthwaite [1962] Director

Target Real Estate LLP
Incorporated: 5 January 2015
Net Worth: £9,878,428 *Total Assets:* £39,849,856
Registered Office: One St Peters Square, Manchester, M2 3DE

Tarka Controls Limited
Incorporated: 8 March 1971
Net Worth: £9,663,075 *Total Assets:* £10,172,765
Registered Office: Unit 12 Tongue Lane Industrial Estate, Dew Pond Lane, Fairfield, Buxton, Derbys, SK17 7LF
Activities: Activities of head offices
Parent: Otter Controls Limited
Officers: Michael Leonard Colling, Secretary; Michael Leonard Colling [1962] Director/Chartered Accountant; Dr David Andrew Smith [1964] Director

Tarncourt Investments LLP
Incorporated: 23 December 2007 *Employees:* 4
Net Worth: £5,421,954 *Total Assets:* £8,767,157
Registered Office: Richard House, Winckley Square, Preston, Lancs, PR1 3HP
Officers: Charles Edward Dickson [1982] Member

Tarporley High School and Sixth Form College
Incorporated: 11 June 2012 *Employees:* 89
Net Worth: £10,246,040 *Total Assets:* £12,452,740
Registered Office: Eaton Road, Tarporley, Cheshire, CW6 0BL
Activities: General secondary education
Officers: Jonathan Neil Hayes, Secretary; James Edward Bowland [1987] Director/Teacher; Trudy Boyle [1945] Director/Retired Headteacher; Roger Spencer Craig [1968] Director/Police Officer; Andrew Christopher Joseph Davies [1981] Director/Headteacher; Alison Jane Dodwell-Cooke [1974] Director/Teaching Assistant; Jane Alison Hough [1964] Director/Teaching Assistant; Michael Geoffrey Hutchinson [1968] Director/Teacher; Dawn Carol Joyce [1961] Director/Company Secretary; Michael Ian Lomas [1958] Director/Chartered Quantity Surveyor; Jason Lowe [1970] Director/Headteacher; Rachel Sims [1967] Director/Teaching Assistant; Bethany Althea Spray [1973] Director; Jane Sarah Stephens [1962] Finance Director; Nigel Andrew Taylor [1956] Sales Research and Development Director; Sharon Maria Varey [1963] Director/Researcher, Editor, Writer and Tutor; Dr Harry John Ziman [1963] Director/Consultant

Tarways Asphalte Co. Limited
Incorporated: 26 September 1973 *Employees:* 73
Net Worth: £2,329,008 *Total Assets:* £6,643,084
Registered Office: Goodlass Road, Speke, Liverpool, L24 9HJ
Activities: Construction of roads and motorways
Parent: Directscale Limited
Officers: Tracey Jane Batterton, Secretary/Director; David Walter Batterton [1963] Director; Tracey Jane Batterton [1964] Director; Robert William Lowe [1969] Director/Estimator; Darren Lee Robinson [1971] Director/Quantity Surveyor

Taskers PLC
Incorporated: 9 July 1976 *Employees:* 244
Net Worth: £10,320,457 *Total Assets:* £20,146,866
Registered Office: Unit G1 & G3, Liver Industrial Estate, Long Lane, Walton, Liverpool, L9 7ES
Activities: Other retail sale in non-specialised stores
Major Shareholder: John Stephen Tasker
Officers: Paul Schwartz, Secretary; Paul Schwartz [1970] Director/Accountant; John Stephen Tasker [1956] Director/Executive; Karen Louise Tasker [1960] Director

Tata Chemicals Europe Limited
Incorporated: 2 May 1991 *Employees:* 286
Net Worth Deficit: £71,481,000 *Total Assets:* £100,321,000
Registered Office: Mond House, Winnington, Northwich, Cheshire, CW8 4DT
Activities: Manufacture of other chemical products n.e.c.
Parent: Brunner Mond Group Limited
Officers: David Philip William Davies, Secretary; Jonathan Laurence Abbotts [1964] Director; Dr Martin John Ashcroft [1969] Managing Director; David Philip William Davies [1971] Director/Solicitor; Peter Patrick Houghton [1963] Director; Dr Ladan Iravanian [1960] Director; Karen Lesley Lounds [1969] Director; Alan Neil Runciman [1964] Director

Tata Chemicals Magadi Limited
Incorporated: 29 December 1924 *Employees:* 663
Net Worth Deficit: £22,223,660 *Total Assets:* £46,335,488
Registered Office: Mond House, Winnington, Northwich, Cheshire, CW8 4DT
Activities: Manufacture of other inorganic basic chemicals
Parent: Gusiute Holdings (UK) Limited
Officers: Zarir Noshir Langrana [1959] Director [Indian]; Stephen Santamo Moiko [1974] Director/Social Scientist [Kenyan]; Jackson Mbui Michael Muchira [1958] Managing Director [Kenyan]; John Mulhall [1968] Director/Chief Financial Officer; Titus Tukero Naikuni [1953] Director [Kenyan]; Mukundan Ramakrishnan [1966] Managing Director [Indian]; Dr Yashwantrao Shankarrao Patil Thorat [1947] Director/Retired [Indian]

Taurus 3 Limited
Incorporated: 24 May 2011 *Employees:* 1,448
Net Worth: £61,148,000 *Total Assets:* £127,817,000
Registered Office: Quality House, Vicarage Lane, Blackpool, Lancs, FY4 4NQ
Activities: Activities of production holding companies
Parent: Rowse Honey Limited
Officers: Antony Francheterre [1970] Director [French]; Andrew Hawley [1965] Director; Maria Elza Marleen Van Troys [1965] Director [Belgian]

Taurus Acquisition Limited
Incorporated: 14 July 2011
Net Worth: £18,855,976 *Total Assets:* £153,282,832
Registered Office: 3rd Floor, 1 Ashley Road, Altrincham, Cheshire, WA14 2DT
Activities: Activities of financial services holding companies
Officers: Wiley Howard Cooper [1958] Director/President of Amwins Group, Inc. [American]; Michael Steven Decarlo [1958] Director/Executive Chairman of Amwins Group, Inc. [American]; Scott Michael Purviance [1970] Director/CEO of Amwins Group, Inc. and its Subsidiaries [American]

Taurus Bidco Limited
Incorporated: 24 May 2011
Net Worth: £53,599,000 *Total Assets:* £75,423,000
Registered Office: Quality House, Vicarage Lane, Blackpool, Lancs, FY4 4NQ
Activities: Activities of production holding companies
Parent: Taurus 3 Limited
Officers: Antony Francheterre [1970] Director [French]; Andrew Hawley [1965] Director; Maria Elza Marleen Van Troys [1965] Director [Belgian]

Timothy Taylor & Co.,Limited
Incorporated: 16 November 1929 *Employees:* 123
Net Worth: £31,732,548 *Total Assets:* £35,537,816
Registered Office: Knowle Spring Brewery, Keighley, W Yorks, BD21 1AW
Activities: Manufacture of beer
Officers: John Edward Thomas Varley, Secretary; Michael Lloyd Bramley [1951] Director; Timothy Clarke [1957] Director; Benjamin Thomas Dent [1984] Director/Partner; Diana Mary Dent [1953] Director; Sarah Louise Dent [1984] Director/Advertising & Sponsorship Manager; Timothy William Dewey [1958] Director/Chief Executive; Claire Hodgson [1985] Director/Marketing Manager; John Edward Thomas Varley [1966] Director/Chartered Accountant

Taylor Engineering & Plastics Limited
Incorporated: 2 June 1977 *Employees:* 173
Net Worth: £13,206,352 *Total Assets:* £18,872,644
Registered Office: Molesworth Street, Rochdale, Lancs, OL16 2BD
Activities: Manufacture of other plastic products
Major Shareholder: Rodney Taylor
Officers: Alan Dennis Worth, Secretary; Ian Barnes Taylor [1970] Director; Jean Margaret Taylor [1945] Director; John Scott Taylor [1967] Director; Rodney Taylor [1944] Director/Chairman

Taylor Shaw Limited
Incorporated: 24 April 2008 *Employees:* 2,375
Net Worth Deficit: £2,295,406 *Total Assets:* £18,185,512
Registered Office: The Courtyard, Catherine Street, Macclesfield, Cheshire, SK11 6ET
Activities: Other food services
Parent: Waterfall Services Limited
Officers: Jim Lovett [1969] Director; Vincent John Pearson [1959] Director; Catherine Margaret Roe [1960] Managing Director; Eleni Savva [1972] Finance Director

Taziker Industrial Limited
Incorporated: 23 November 1992 *Employees:* 291
Net Worth: £8,750,000 *Total Assets:* £17,268,000
Registered Office: 6 Lodge Bank, Crown Lane, Horwich, Bolton, Lancs, BL6 5HY
Activities: Painting
Parent: TI Industrial Group Limited
Officers: Paolo Benedetto [1974] Director; Neil Christian Harrison [1975] Director; Graham Philippe Bertwistle Moor [1967] Director/Estimating Surveyor; Jane Catherine Ratcliffe [1971] Director; Michael Stuart Taziker [1970] Operations Director; Nigel Thomas Taziker [1975] Director; Jason Pearce Worrall [1975] Director

Teamfurmanite Limited
Incorporated: 15 April 1929 *Employees:* 320
Net Worth: £25,702,000 *Total Assets:* £52,724,000
Registered Office: Furman House, Shap Road, Kendal, Cumbria, LA9 6RU
Activities: Repair of other equipment
Parent: Furmanite 1986
Officers: Rachel Dixon, Secretary; Greg Lee Boane [1963] Director/Chief Finance Officer [American]; Andre Charles Bouchard [1965] Director/Senior VP - Legal [American]; Jonathon Anthony Jarvis [1957] Director/Vice President

Tearlach Limited
Incorporated: 21 July 2015
Net Worth: £2,145,862 *Total Assets:* £12,160,779
Registered Office: Brabners LLP, Exchange Flags, Liverpool, L2 3YL
Activities: Fund management activities
Shareholder: Donald Roderick MacLean
Officers: Donald Roderick MacLean [1955] Director; Sylvia June MacLean [1960] Director

Technical Demolition Services Limited
Incorporated: 3 December 1982 *Employees:* 83
Net Worth: £6,132,253 *Total Assets:* £10,112,483
Registered Office: Dock Road South, Bromborough, Wirral, Merseyside, CH62 4SQ
Activities: Demolition
Officers: Victoria Margaret Evans [1975] Marketing Director; Julie Ann Hitchen [1966] Finance Director; Austin Anthony Taperell [1966] Managing Director; Tony Geoffrey Taperell [1946] Chief Executive Director; Craig Wilson [1965] Commercial Director

Technical Fibre Products Limited
Incorporated: 5 September 1986 *Employees:* 89
Net Worth: £10,076,000 *Total Assets:* £28,362,000
Registered Office: Burneside, Kendal, Cumbria, LA9 6PZ
Activities: Other manufacturing n.e.c.
Parent: James Cropper PLC
Officers: James Francis Aldridge, Secretary; Isabelle Marguerite Maddock [1968] Director/Financial Controller; Martin Thompson [1959] Director; Philip Ian Wild [1969] Director

Technology Rentals Limited
Incorporated: 27 January 2004 *Employees:* 4
Net Worth: £2,807,746 *Total Assets:* £6,701,636
Registered Office: 2nd Floor, Parkgates, Bury New Road, Prestwich, Manchester, M25 0TL
Activities: Financial leasing
Major Shareholder: Leslie Woolf
Officers: Kevin Lovett, Secretary; Howard Henoch Moher [1963] Director

Techtex Holdings Limited
Incorporated: 11 April 2006
Registered Office: Units 7 & 8 Rhodes Business Park, Silburn Way, Middleton, Manchester, M24 4NE
Activities: Activities of head offices
Shareholders: David John Beardsworth; Brian John Whitney
Officers: Stephen John Oldfield, Secretary/Accountant; David John Beardsworth [1960] Director; Stephen John Oldfield [1963] Director/Accountant; Brian John Whitney [1967] Director

Teesbay Retail Park (1) Limited
Incorporated: 28 September 1998 *Employees:* 1
Net Worth: £7,423,475 *Total Assets:* £16,229,314
Registered Office: c/o Mason & Partners, The Corn Exchange, Brunswick House, Liverpool, L2 7TP
Activities: Buying and selling of own real estate
Parent: Chase Property Developments Limited
Officers: Ben Desmond Harvey, Secretary/Director; Paul Pearce [1965] Director/Surveyor

TEF Transport Limited
Incorporated: 1 November 1973 *Employees:* 100
Net Worth: £2,895,119 *Total Assets:* £7,718,015
Registered Office: Unit 1 City Link Industrial Park, Phoenix Way, Tyersal, Bradford, W Yorks, BD4 8JP
Activities: Freight transport by road
Shareholders: Andrew McLaughlin; Linda McLaughlin
Officers: Linda McLaughlin, Secretary; Gerard Dibb [1962] Managing Director; Andrew McLaughlin [1967] Director/Transport Manager; Linda McLaughlin [1963] Director/Secretary; Philip George Troop [1973] Finance Director

Telesign Mobile Limited
Incorporated: 26 September 2002 *Employees:* 5
Net Worth: £9,616,060 *Total Assets:* £15,797,375
Registered Office: Eversheds House, 70 Great Bridgewater Street, Manchester, M1 5ES
Activities: Wireless telecommunications activities
Officers: Philipp Gast [1974] Director/Chief Financial Officer - Telesign Corp, USA [Swiss]

Telesign UK Limited
Incorporated: 21 March 2011 *Employees:* 164
Net Worth: £4,385,468 *Total Assets:* £24,307,822
Registered Office: Eversheds House, 70 Great Bridgewater Street, Manchester, M1 5ES
Activities: Other information technology service activities
Officers: Philipp Gast [1974] Director/Chief Financial Officer - Telesign Corp, US Parent [Swiss]

Tellar Holdings Limited
Incorporated: 19 July 1983 *Employees:* 68
Net Worth: £10,262,636 *Total Assets:* £13,590,328
Registered Office: The Copper Room, Deva Centre, Trinity Way, Manchester, M3 7BG
Activities: Activities of head offices
Major Shareholder: David Howard Eventhall
Officers: Julia Louise Eventhall, Secretary; David Howard Eventhall [1963] Director

Templeton Holdings Limited
Incorporated: 2 January 2003 *Employees:* 892
Net Worth: £7,765,376 *Total Assets:* £18,660,856
Registered Office: 1st Floor, Acresfield, 8-10 Exchange Street, Manchester, M2 7HA
Activities: Activities of head offices
Officers: Marcello Guiseppe Distefano [1978] Director/Restaurateur [Italian]; Remigio Distefano [1944] Director/Restaurateur [Italian]

Tenmat Limited
Incorporated: 1 April 1997 *Employees:* 210
Net Worth: £42,068,000 *Total Assets:* £49,887,000
Registered Office: Ashburton Road West, Trafford Park, Manchester, M17 1TD
Activities: Manufacture of other plastic products
Parent: Modular Stock Limited
Officers: Kapil Chopra [1981] Director; Mark Andrew Hutchison [1970] Director

Tennants Distribution Limited
Incorporated: 28 November 1995 *Employees:* 158
Net Worth: £30,580,000 *Total Assets:* £36,730,000
Registered Office: Tennants Distribution Ltd, Hazelbottom Road, Cheetham, Manchester, M8 0GR
Activities: Wholesale of chemical products
Parent: Tennants Consolidated Limited
Officers: Barry David Price, Secretary; Duncan James Alexander [1956] Director; William Paul Alexander [1954] Director; Timothy Griffiths [1974] Director; Maria Elaine Kelly [1979] Director; Mark Lawrence [1964] Director; Andrew Fraser John Mitchell [1953] Director

The Tensar Group Limited
Incorporated: 24 March 1994
Net Worth Deficit: £46,715,000 *Total Assets:* £62,753,000
Registered Office: Units 2-4 Cunningham Court, Shadsworth Business Park, Blackburn, Lancs, BB1 2QX
Activities: Activities of production holding companies
Parent: TTC UK Holdings Limited
Officers: Thierry Georges Yves Emile Amat [1960] Director/Chief Financial Officer [French/American]; Michael David Lawrence [1957] Director/Chief Executive Officer [American]; Luc Jozef Mechelaere [1961] Director/Executive Vice President [Belgian]

Tensar International Limited
Incorporated: 5 January 1952 *Employees:* 73
Net Worth: £54,358,000 *Total Assets:* £89,946,000
Registered Office: Units 2-4 Cunningham Court, Shadsworth Business Park, Blackburn, Lancs, BB1 2QX
Activities: Manufacture of other plastic products
Parent: The Tensar Group Limited
Officers: Thierry Georges Yves Emile Amat [1960] Director/Chief Financial Officer [French/American]; Michael David Lawrence [1957] Director/Chief Executive Officer [American]; Luc Jozef Mechelaere [1961] Director/Executive Vice President [Belgian]

Tensar Manufacturing Limited
Incorporated: 30 December 2004 *Employees:* 86
Net Worth: £3,938,000 *Total Assets:* £23,858,000
Registered Office: Sett End Road West, Shadsworth Business Park, Blackburn, Lancs, BB1 2PU
Activities: Manufacture of builders ware of plastic
Parent: The Tensar Group Limited
Officers: Thierry Georges Yves Emile Amat [1960] Director/Chief Financial Officer [French/American]; Michael David Lawrence [1957] Director/Chief Executive Officer [American]

Tensar Technologies Limited
Incorporated: 15 March 2005
Net Worth: £11,792,000 *Total Assets:* £15,578,000
Registered Office: Sett End Road West, Shadsworth Business Park, Blackburn, Lancs, BB1 2PU
Activities: Other research and experimental development on natural sciences and engineering
Parent: The Tensar Group Limited
Officers: Thierry Georges Yves Emile Amat [1960] Director/Chief Financial Officer [French/American]; Michael David Lawrence [1957] Director/Chief Executive Officer [American]; Luc Jozef Mechelaere [1961] Director/Executive Vice President [Belgian]

Terraform UK2 Intermediate Holdings, Ltd
Incorporated: 23 October 2015
Net Worth: £92,076,208 *Total Assets:* £119,959,360
Registered Office: Eversheds House, 70 Great Bridgewater Street, Manchester, M1 5ES
Activities: Activities of other holding companies n.e.c.
Parent: Vortex Solar UK Limited
Officers: Carl Goran Dandanell [1959] Director [Swedish]

Terraform UK3 Intermediate Holdings Limited
Incorporated: 18 March 2015
Net Worth: £48 034,588 *Total Assets:* £468,652,704
Registered Office: Eversheds House, 70 Great Bridgewater Street, Manchester, M1 5ES
Activities: Activities of other holding companies n.e.c.
Parent: Terraform UK2 Intermediate Holdings, Ltd
Officers: Carl Goran Dandanell [1959] Director [Swedish]

TESGL Limited
Incorporated: 23 March 2013 *Employees:* 285
Net Worth: £13,550,036 *Total Assets:* £44,111,224
Registered Office: Ocean Court, Caspian Road, Atlantic Street, Altrincham, Cheshire, WA14 5HH
Activities: Other building completion and finishing
Parent: The Energy Solutions Group Bidco Limited
Officers: Brian Dominic Sharma, Secretary; Kevin David Andrew Greenhorn [1967] Managing Director; Aled Robert Humphreys [1979] Commercial Director

Tesni Properties Limited
Incorporated: 14 August 2006 *Employees:* 11
Net Worth Deficit: £351,434 *Total Assets:* £8,325,654
Registered Office: Linden House, Unit 4 Mold Business Park, Wrexham Road, Mold, Flintshire, CH7 1XP
Activities: Development of building projects
Shareholders: Paula Marian Jewson; Geraint Keith Jewson
Officers: Paula Marian Jewson, Secretary; James Martin Hennie [1973] Director; Geraint Keith Jewson [1958] Director/Chartered Surveyor; Paula Marian Jewson [1963] Director/Accountant; Sarah Louise Smith [1969] Director/Accountant

Tessuti Ltd
Incorporated: 30 November 2005 *Employees:* 354
Net Worth: £3,457,000 *Total Assets:* £31,980,000
Registered Office: Hollinsbrook Way, Pilsworth, Bury, Lancs, BL9 8RR
Activities: Retail sale of clothing in specialised stores
Parent: Tessuti Group Limited
Officers: Siobhan Mawdsley, Secretary; Peter Alan Cowgill [1953] Director; David Arthur Light [1955] Director/Accountant; Brian Michael Small [1956] Director

Tetra Pak Limited
Incorporated: 1 July 1955 *Employees:* 99
Net Worth: £8,476,000 *Total Assets:* £22,623,000
Registered Office: The Foundation, Herons Way, Chester Business Park, Chester, CH4 9QS
Activities: Non-specialised wholesale trade
Officers: Benjamin Cutts [1981] Director; Carl Johan Olof Rabe [1969] Director [Swedish]; Goran Lars Soderstrom [1960] Finance Director [Swecish]

Tetrosyl Express Limited
Incorporated: 26 April 2013 *Employees:* 25
Net Worth Deficit: £3,693,000 *Total Assets:* £16,220,000
Registered Office: Bevis Green Works, Mill Road, Walmersley, Bury, Lancs, BL9 6RE
Activities: Wholesale trade of motor vehicle parts and accessories
Parent: Tetrosyl Group Limited
Officers: Michael Green [1962] Director; David James Rogers [1969] Director/Solicitor; Peter David Schofield [1961] Director

Tetrosyl Group Limited
Incorporated: 12 August 2004 *Employees:* 850
Net Worth: £63,506,000 *Total Assets:* £122,992,000
Registered Office: Bevis Green Works, Walmersley, Bury, Lancs, BL9 6RE
Activities: Activities of head offices
Major Shareholder: Peter David Schofield
Officers: David James Rogers [1969] Director/Solicitor; Peter David Schofield [1961] Director

Tetrosyl Limited
Incorporated: 8 September 1954 *Employees:* 557
Net Worth: £64,170,000 *Total Assets:* £119,184,000
Registered Office: Bevis Green Works, Walmersley, Bury, Lancs, BL9 6RE
Activities: Manufacture of cleaning and polishing preparations
Parent: Tetrosyl Group Limited
Officers: David James Rogers [1969] Director/Solicitor; Peter David Schofield [1961] Director

Texas Group PLC
Incorporated: 4 June 1958 *Employees:* 13
Net Worth: £15,416,537 *Total Assets:* £23,290,788
Registered Office: Barton Hall, Hardy Street, Eccles, Manchester, M30 7NB
Activities: Other letting and operating of own or leased real estate
Officers: Stuart James Mollekin, Secretary; Thomas Jones [1944] Director/Solicitor; James Mark McDonald [1973] Director; Robert Kean McDonald [1963] Director; Stuart James Mollekin [1960] Director/Accountant; Robin Slinger [1953] Director

Texas Holdings Limited
Incorporated: 4 June 1973
Net Worth: £13,850,903 *Total Assets:* £13,857,017
Registered Office: Barton Hall, Hardy Street, Eccles, Manchester, M30 7NB
Activities: Activities of head offices
Officers: Stuart James Mollekin, Secretary; Thomas Jones [1944] Director/Solicitor; James Mark McDonald [1973] Director; Robert Kean McDonald [1963] Director; Stuart James Mollekin [1960] Director/Accountant

Texecom Limited
Incorporated: 15 December 1986 *Employees:* 321
Net Worth: £8,299,729 *Total Assets:* £16,491,544
Registered Office: Bradwood Court, St Crispin Way, Haslingden, Rossendale, Lancs, BB4 4PW
Activities: Manufacture of other electrical equipment
Parent: Halma PLC
Officers: Richard Anthony Paul Joynson, Secretary; James Daniel Ashton [1972] Supply Chain Director; Clym Brown [1976] Director; Steven Malcolm Brown [1966] Director; Mark Douglas [1961] Director; Richard Anthony Paul Joynson [1967] Finance Director; James Ernest Ludwig [1973] Director [American]; Michael Stembridge [1969] Director

TFHC 2015 Limited
Incorporated: 26 November 2014
Net Worth: £772,000 *Total Assets:* £14,752,000
Registered Office: Total Fitness, Wilmslow Way, Handforth, Cheshire, SK9 3PW
Activities: Management consultancy activities other than financial management
Officers: Jasvir Sanghera, Secretary; Brian Joseph Davidson [1963] Director; Sophie Lawler [1978] Director/Chief Executive; Warwick John Ley [1972] Director [Australian/British]; Keven David Parker [1969] Director/PE Partner; Jasvir Singh Sanghera [1966] Finance Director

TFHC Investments Limited
Incorporated: 3 February 2015 *Employees:* 597
Net Worth: £1,662,000 *Total Assets:* £25,957,000
Registered Office: Total Fitness, Wilmslow Way, Handforth, Wilmslow, Cheshire, SK9 3PE
Activities: Activities of head offices
Shareholders: Northedge Capital I GP LLP; Northedge Capital LLP
Officers: Jasvir Sanghera, Secretary; Brian Joseph Davidson [1963] Director; Sophie Lawler [1978] Director/Chief Executive; Warwick John Ley [1972] Director [Australian/British]; Keven David Parker [1969] Director/PE Partner; Jasvir Singh Sanghera [1966] Finance Director

TFS Buying Limited
Incorporated: 13 January 2009 *Employees:* 1,146
Net Worth: £34,933,000 *Total Assets:* £63,456,000
Registered Office: Churchill Point, Lake Edge Green, Trafford Park Road, Manchester, M17 1BL
Activities: Retail sale of cosmetic and toilet articles in specialised stores
Parent: Cartoon (Holdings) Ltd
Officers: Julian Holt [1963] Operations Director; Sanjay Jayantilal Vadera [1967] Director/Chief Executive; Vipul Jayantilal Vadera [1972] Non-Executive Director

TFS London Holdings Limited
Incorporated: 2 March 2005
Net Worth: £999 *Total Assets:* £10,000,999
Registered Office: Unit 4 Howarth Court, Broadway Business Park, Oldham, Lancs, OL9 9XB
Activities: Activities of other holding companies n.e.c.
Parent: Tailored Fire & Security Group Limited
Officers: Zoe Clare Whittle, Secretary; Anthony Ernest Whittle [1970] Sales Director

TFS Stores Limited
Incorporated: 13 January 2009 *Employees:* 1,023
Net Worth: £19,557,000 *Total Assets:* £36,260,000
Registered Office: Churchill Point, Lake Edge Green, Trafford Park Road, Manchester, M17 1BL
Activities: Retail sale of cosmetic and toilet articles in specialised stores
Parent: Cartoon (Holdings) Ltd
Officers: Sanjay Jayantilal Vadera [1967] Director/Chief Executive; Vipul Jayantilal Vadera [1972] Non-Executive Director

TGC (2015) Limited
Incorporated: 28 January 2015 *Employees:* 147
Net Worth Deficit: £237,084 *Total Assets:* £9,353,488
Registered Office: Tong Garden Centre, Tong Lane, Bradford, W Yorks, BD4 0RY
Activities: Retail sale of flowers, plants, seeds, fertilizers, pet animals and pet food in specialised stores
Parent: Birch Valley Holdings Limited
Officers: Charles Peter Barker [1979] Director/Chartered Accountant; Mark William Farnsworth [1977] Director/Retailer; Thomas Alan Taylor Megginson [1974] Director

Thackeray Lettings Limited
Incorporated: 31 August 2016
Net Worth Deficit: £14,205 *Total Assets:* £6,570,475
Registered Office: Ram Mill, Gordon Street, Chadderton, Oldham, Lancs, OL9 9RH
Activities: Other letting and operating of own or leased real estate
Parent: Thackeray Trading Limited
Officers: Jahid Akbar [1972] Director; Mohammed Pervez Akbar [1980] Director; Saeed Akbar [1972] Director

Thames Transit Limited
Incorporated: 28 June 1988 *Employees:* 515
Net Worth: £10,889,000 *Total Assets:* £34,126,000
Registered Office: c/o Stagecoach Services Limited, One Stockport Exchange, 20 Railway Road, Stockport, Cheshire, SK1 3SW
Activities: Other urban, suburban or metropolitan passenger land transport (not underground, metro or similar)
Parent: Stagecoach Bus Holdings Limited
Officers: Michael John Vaux, Secretary; Colin Brown [1968] Director/Accountant; Christopher Sean Lee Coleman [1970] Managing Director; Arnold Mark Threapleton [1954] Managing Director

Theo Bidco Limited
Incorporated: 12 April 2017
Net Worth Deficit: £2,534,787 *Total Assets:* £214,933,952
Registered Office: Baines House, Midgery Court, Pittman Way, Fulwood, Preston, Lancs, PR2 9ZH
Activities: Activities of other holding companies n.e.c.
Parent: Theo Midco Limited
Officers: Lukas Martin Bucher [1976] Director [Swiss]; Andrew David Deakin [1973] Director; Robert James Scott [1973] Director; Simon Christopher Thompson [1972] Director

Theo Midco Limited
Incorporated: 5 May 2017
Net Worth Deficit: £2,094,240 *Total Assets:* £143,369,632
Registered Office: Baines House, Midgery Court, Pittman Way, Fulwood, Preston, Lancs, PR2 9ZH
Activities: Activities of other holding companies n.e.c.
Parent: Theo Topco Limited
Officers: Robert James Scott [1973] Director; Simon Christopher Thompson [1972] Director

Theo Topco Limited
Incorporated: 5 May 2017 *Employees:* 409
Net Worth: £66,864,000 *Total Assets:* £241,650,000
Registered Office: Baines House, Midgery Court, Pittman Way, Fulwood, Preston, Lancs, PR2 9ZH
Activities: Activities of other holding companies n.e.c.
Officers: Lukas Martin Bucher [1976] Managing Director Value Creation [Swiss]; Andrew David Deakin [1973] Director/Private Equity Professional; Steve Groves [1975] Non-Executive Director Chairman; Robert James Scott [1973] Director; Simon Christopher Thompson [1972] Director; David Thomas McAree Young [1961] Director

Thermal Ceramics UK Limited
Incorporated: 26 October 1966 *Employees:* 59
Net Worth Deficit: £7,621,000 *Total Assets:* £23,067,000
Registered Office: Tebay Road, Bromborough, Wirral, Merseyside, CH62 3PH
Activities: Manufacture of other ceramic products n.e.c.
Parent: Morgan Europe Holding Limited
Officers: Matthew John Price, Secretary; Andrew Robert Bloomer [1981] Director/General Manager; Matthew John Price [1981] Director; Dr Michael Gwyn Thomas [1965] Director/Engineering Manager

Thermal Hire Ltd
Incorporated: 19 June 1974 *Employees:* 79
Net Worth: £5,659,117 *Total Assets:* £7,464,701
Registered Office: 1st Floor, 8-12 London Street, Southport, Merseyside, PR9 0UE
Activities: Treatment and coating of metals
Major Shareholder: James Bernard Riley
Officers: Benjamin Daniel Riley [1976] Director; James Bernard Riley [1947] Director/Engineer

Thermo Cambridge Limited
Incorporated: 10 October 2006
Net Worth: £136,354,000 *Total Assets:* £136,374,000
Registered Office: 3rd Floor, 1 Ashley Road, Altrincham, Cheshire, WA14 2DT
Activities: Activities of head offices
Parent: Thermo Optek Limited
Officers: Rhona Gregg, Secretary; Lucie Mary Katja Grant [1976] Director/Solicitor; Nicholas Ince [1982] Director/Accountant; David John Norman [1960] Director/Chartered Accountant

Thermo Electron (Management Services) Limited
Incorporated: 31 January 1996
Net Worth: £19,208,000 *Total Assets:* £56,118,000
Registered Office: 3rd Floor, 1 Ashley Road, Altrincham, Cheshire, WA14 2DT
Activities: Activities of head offices
Parent: Life Sciences International Limited
Officers: Rhona Gregg, Secretary; Lucie Mary Katja Grant [1976] Director/Solicitor; Nicholas Ince [1982] Director/Accountant; David John Norman [1960] Director/Chartered Accountant

Thermo Electron Limited
Incorporated: 30 June 1983 *Employees:* 134
Net Worth: £119,416,000 *Total Assets:* £147,974,000
Registered Office: 3rd Floor, 1 Ashley Road, Altrincham, Cheshire, WA14 2DT
Activities: Manufacture of electronic measuring, testing etc. equipment, not for industrial process control
Parent: Life Sciences International Limited
Officers: Rhona Gregg, Secretary; Lucie Mary Katja Grant [1976] Director/Solicitor; Nicholas Ince [1982] Director/Accountant; David John Norman [1960] Director/Chartered Accountant

Thermo Electron Manufacturing Limited
Incorporated: 30 August 1947 *Employees:* 280
Net Worth: £119,568,000 *Total Assets:* £187,354,000
Registered Office: 3rd Floor, 1 Ashley Road, Altrincham, Cheshire, WA14 2DT
Activities: Manufacture of electronic measuring, testing etc. equipment, not for industrial process control
Parent: Thermo Shandon Limited
Officers: Rhona Gregg, Secretary; Lucie Mary Katja Grant [1976] Director/Solicitor; Nicholas Ince [1982] Director/Accountant; David John Norman [1960] Director/Chartered Accountant

Thermo Fisher Diagnostics Limited
Incorporated: 19 January 2004 *Employees:* 92
Net Worth Deficit: £3,701,000 *Total Assets:* £68,658,000
Registered Office: 3rd Floor, 1 Ashley Road, Altrincham, Cheshire, WA14 2DT
Activities: Other human health activities
Parent: Thermo Fisher Scientific Inc.
Officers: Rhona Gregg, Secretary; Lucie Mary Katja Grant [1976] Director/Solicitor; Nicholas Ince [1982] Director/Accountant; Mark Kelly [1976] Director/Country Manager; David John Norman [1960] Director/Chartered Accountant; Anthony Hugh Smith [1962] Director/Vice President, Tax and Treasury [American]

Thermo Fisher Scientific (China) Holding Limited
Incorporated: 31 January 1996
Net Worth: £4,522,000 *Total Assets:* £11,721,000
Registered Office: 3rd Floor, 1 Ashley Road, Altrincham, Cheshire, WA14 2DT
Activities: Activities of head offices
Parent: Thermo Fisher Scientific Inc.
Officers: Rhona Gregg, Secretary; Lucie Mary Katja Grant [1976] Director/Solicitor; Nicholas Ince [1982] Director/Accountant; David John Norman [1960] Director/Chartered Accountant

Thermo Fisher Scientific Holdings Europe Limited
Incorporated: 23 December 2009
Net Worth: £20,727,000 *Total Assets:* £20,727,000
Registered Office: 3rd Floor, 1 Ashley Road, Altrincham, Cheshire, WA14 2DT
Activities: Activities of head offices
Parent: Thermo Fisher Scientific Inc.
Officers: Rhona Gregg, Secretary; Lucie Mary Katja Grant [1976] Director/Solicitor; Nicholas Ince [1982] Director/Accountant; David John Norman [1960] Director/Chartered Accountant

Thermo Fisher Scientific Life Holdings Limited
Incorporated: 27 November 2013
Net Worth: £490,087,008 *Total Assets:* £1,730,966,016
Registered Office: 3rd Floor, 1 Ashley Road, Altrincham, Cheshire, WA14 2DT
Activities: Manufacture of basic pharmaceutical products
Parent: Thermo Fisher Scientific Life Technologies Investment UK II Limited
Officers: Rhona Gregg, Secretary; Lucie Mary Katja Grant [1976] Director/Solicitor; Nicholas Ince [1982] Director/Accountant; David John Norman [1960] Director/Chartered Accountant; Janet Sutherland [1968] Director/Finance Leader

Thermo Fisher Scientific Life Technologies Enterprise Holding Limited
Incorporated: 10 October 2014
Net Worth: £1,730,807,040 *Total Assets:* £1,730,817,024
Registered Office: 3rd Floor, 1 Ashley Road, Altrincham, Cheshire, WA14 2DT
Activities: Activities of head offices
Parent: Invitrogen Europe Limited
Officers: Rhona Gregg, Secretary; Lucie Mary Katja Grant [1976] Director/Solicitor; Nicholas Ince [1982] Director/Accountant; David John Norman [1960] Director/Chartered Accountant

Thermo Fisher Scientific Life Technologies Investment UK I Limited
Incorporated: 8 October 2014
Net Worth: £1,730,806,016 *Total Assets:* £1,730,806,016
Registered Office: 3rd Floor, 1 Ashley Road, Altrincham, Cheshire, WA14 2DT
Activities: Activities of head offices
Parent: Thermo Fisher Scientific Life Technologies Enterprise Holding Limited
Officers: Rhona Gregg, Secretary; Lucie Mary Katja Grant [1976] Director/Solicitor; Nicholas Ince [1982] Director/Accountant; David John Norman [1960] Director/Chartered Accountant

Thermo Fisher Scientific Life Technologies Investment UK II Limited
Incorporated: 8 October 2014
Net Worth: £659,313,024 *Total Assets:* £659,313,024
Registered Office: 3rd Floor, 1 Ashley Road, Altrincham, Cheshire, WA14 2DT
Activities: Activities of head offices
Parent: Thermo Fisher Scientific Inc.
Officers: Rhona Gregg, Secretary; Lucie Mary Katja Grant [1976] Director/Solicitor; Nicholas Ince [1982] Director/Accountant; David John Norman [1960] Director/Chartered Accountant

Thermo Fisher Scientific Odyssey Holdings Limited
Incorporated: 4 September 2012 *Employees:* 3
Net Worth: £87,440,632 *Total Assets:* £689,515,008
Registered Office: 3rd Floor, 1 Ashley Road, Altrincham, Cheshire, WA14 2DT
Activities: Non-trading company
Parent: Thermo Fisher Scientific Inc.
Officers: Rhona Gregg, Secretary; Lucie Mary Katja Grant [1976] Director/Solicitor; Nicholas Ince [1982] Director/Accountant; David John Norman [1960] Director/Chartered Accountant

Thermo Onix Limited
Incorporated: 26 November 1996 *Employees:* 51
Net Worth: £31,585,000 *Total Assets:* £42,270,000
Registered Office: 3rd Floor, 1 Ashley Road, Altrincham, Cheshire, WA14 2DT
Activities: Manufacture of electronic measuring, testing etc. equipment, not for industrial process control
Parent: Onix Holdings Limited
Officers: Rhona Gregg, Secretary; Lucie Mary Katja Grant [1976] Director/Solicitor; Nicholas Ince [1982] Director/Accountant; David John Norman [1960] Director/Chartered Accountant

Thermo Optek Limited
Incorporated: 26 March 1991
Net Worth: £138,104,992 *Total Assets:* £149,866,000
Registered Office: 3rd Floor, 1 Ashley Road, Altrincham, Cheshire, WA14 2DT
Activities: Activities of head offices
Parent: Life Sciences International Limited
Officers: Rhona Gregg, Secretary; Lucie Mary Katja Grant [1976] Director/Solicitor; Nicholas Ince [1982] Director/Accountant; David John Norman [1960] Director/Chartered Accountant

Thermo Shandon Limited
Incorporated: 24 August 1937 *Employees:* 149
Net Worth: £270,440,992 *Total Assets:* £286,577,984
Registered Office: 3rd Floor, 1 Ashley Road, Altrincham, Cheshire, WA14 2DT
Activities: Manufacture of medical and dental instruments and supplies
Parent: Thermo Fisher Scientific Inc.
Officers: Rhona Gregg, Secretary; Lucie Mary Katja Grant [1976] Director/Solicitor; Nicholas Ince [1982] Director/Accountant; David John Norman [1960] Director/Chartered Accountant

Think Money Group Limited
Incorporated: 2 November 2006 *Employees:* 355
Net Worth: £4,947,000 *Total Assets:* £52,528,000
Registered Office: Think Park, Mosley Road, Trafford Park, Manchester, M17 1FQ
Activities: Activities of financial services holding companies
Parent: Milan Bidco Limited
Officers: Ryan David Swann, Secretary; Michael Christopher Dennis [1976] Director; William David Grout [1984] Director; Simon David Kay [1968] Director; Richard Price [1961] Director; Patrick Desmond Storey [1958] Director; Stephen Andrew Stylianou [1969] Director; Jonathan Warr [1964] Director

Think Money Holdings 1 Limited
Incorporated: 31 May 2005
Net Worth: £600,000 *Total Assets:* £13,348,000
Registered Office: Think Park, Mosley Road, Trafford Park, Manchester, M17 1FQ
Activities: Activities of financial services holding companies
Parent: Think Money Group Limited
Officers: Ryan David Swann, Secretary; Simon David Kay [1968] Director; Stephen Andrew Stylianou [1969] Director; Jonathan Warr [1964] Director

Think Money Holdings Limited
Incorporated: 18 October 2001 *Employees:* 610
Net Worth: £11,249,000 *Total Assets:* £104,834,000
Registered Office: Think Park, Mosley Road, Trafford Park, Manchester, M17 1FQ
Activities: Activities of financial services holding companies
Parent: Think Money Holdings 1 Limited
Officers: Ryan David Swann, Secretary; Simon David Kay [1968] Director; Stephen Andrew Stylianou [1969] Director; Jonathan Gavin Warr [1964] Director

Thinksmart Europe Limited
Incorporated: 6 December 2002
Net Worth: £48,193 *Total Assets:* £15,260,971
Registered Office: 7th Floor, Oakland House, Talbot Road, Old Trafford, Manchester, M16 0PQ
Activities: Activities of head offices
Parent: Thinksmart Limited
Officers: Gary Robert Halton, Secretary; Gary Robert Halton [1968] Director/Chief Financial Officer; Natale Ronald Montarello [1961] Director/Chairman & CEO [Australian]

This Is Protos LLP
Incorporated: 10 May 2010
Net Worth: £11,659,496 *Total Assets:* £17,489,276
Registered Office: Peel Dome, intu Trafford Centre, Trafford City, Manchester, M17 8PL

Thistle Devco LLP
Incorporated: 1 August 2014
Net Worth: £46,599,012 *Total Assets:* £113,763,424
Registered Office: Floor 3, 1 St Ann Street, Manchester, M2 7LR

Thompson and Capper Limited
Incorporated: 21 December 1928
Net Worth: £32,854,000 *Total Assets:* £40,386,000
Registered Office: 9-12 Hardwick Road, Astmoor Industrial Estate, Runcorn, Cheshire, WA7 1PH
Activities: Manufacture of basic pharmaceutical products
Parent: DCC Health & Beauty Solutions Limited
Officers: Karen Michelle Leay, Secretary; Conor Francis Costigan [1971] Director [Irish]; John Downey [1952] Director; Matthew Richard Dyal [1963] Operations Director; Karen Michelle Leay [1972] Director/Accountant; Redmond McEvoy [1964] Director [Irish]; Stephen Clifford O'Connor [1964] Director/Chartered Accountant; Reginald Laurence Kenneth Witheridge [1941] Director

Thompson Management Services Blackpool Limited
Incorporated: 21 October 2013 *Employees:* 2
Net Worth: £5,343,704 *Total Assets:* £7,379,297
Registered Office: Saxon House, Great Plumpton, Preston, Lancs, PR4 3NE
Activities: Development of building projects
Major Shareholder: Joseph Thompson
Officers: Joseph Thompson [1983] Director; Kelly Thompson [1987] Director

Thompson Motor Company (Preston) Limited
Incorporated: 26 June 2000 *Employees:* 222
Net Worth: £8,889,928 *Total Assets:* £36,744,392
Registered Office: Swansway Group, Gateway, Crewe, Cheshire, CW1 6YY
Activities: Sale of new cars and light motor vehicles
Parent: Swansway Garages Limited
Officers: Richard Marsland, Secretary; Richard Marsland [1962] Finance Director; David Smyth [1962] Director; John Smyth [1967] Director; Michael Smyth [1939] Director; Peter Smyth [1964] Director

Thompsons Plant Hire Limited
Incorporated: 20 December 1994 *Employees:* 81
Net Worth: £4,145,086 *Total Assets:* £11,736,274
Registered Office: Carleton House, 136 Gray Street, Workington, Cumbria, CA14 2LU
Activities: Recovery of sorted materials
Major Shareholder: Kevin Victor Thompson
Officers: Linda Mary Porter, Secretary; Linda Mary Porter [1971] Director; Kevin Victor Thompson [1970] Director

Thor Specialities (UK) Limited
Incorporated: 14 October 1983 *Employees:* 82
Net Worth: £66 937,000 *Total Assets:* £73,526,000
Registered Office: Wincham Avenue, Wincham, Northwich, Cheshire, CW9 6GB
Activities: Manufacture of other chemical products n.e.c.
Parent: Tato Holdings Ltd
Officers: John David Sykes, Secretary; Scott Raymond Betts [1967] Technical & Regulatory Director [American]; Stephen Charlton [1966] Sales Director; David Alain Hewitt [1960] Director/Accountant

Thorneycroft Solicitors Limited
Incorporated: 15 October 2003 *Employees:* 143
Net Worth: £4,721,889 *Total Assets:* £11,927,345
Registered Office: Bridge Street Mills, Bridge Street, Macclesfield, Cheshire, SK11 6QA
Activities: Solicitors
Shareholders: TSG Professional Services Ltd; TSGroup Ltd
Officers: Mark David Belfield [1970] Director/Lawyer; Susan Patricia Carnwell [1966] Director/Chartered Accountant; Rachel Leonie Stow [1969] Director/Solicitor; Robert Patrick Thorneycroft [1958] Director

Thornsett Vale Limited
Incorporated: 11 January 1995 *Employees:* 110
Net Worth: £3,029,729 *Total Assets:* £10,186,243
Registered Office: Abbey Road, Barrow in Furness, Cumbria, LA13 0PA
Activities: Hotels and similar accommodation
Officers: Brian Gerard Conroy [1971] Director/Hotel Manager; Neil Hopkins-Coman [1962] Director/Chartered Accountant; Cassie Marie Kilroe [1967] Director [Irish]; Martin Gerard Kilroe [1970] Sales Director [Irish]; Timothy Anthony Kilroe [1964] Director [Irish]; Andrew Langwallner [1966] Director [Irish]

Three Sixty Water Limited
Incorporated: 16 December 2015 *Employees:* 39
Net Worth Deficit: £82,000 *Total Assets:* £6,605,000
Registered Office: Western House, Halifax Road, Bradford, W Yorks, BD6 2SZ
Activities: Activities of other holding companies n.e.c.
Parent: Kelda Group Limited
Officers: Angela Wendy Miriam White, Secretary; Elizabeth Marian Barber [1965] Director/Accountant; Richard David Flint [1968] Director; Nicholas Richard Topham [1966] Managing Director

Thrislington Cubicles Limited
Incorporated: 10 February 1995 *Employees:* 63
Net Worth: £7,020,125 *Total Assets:* £9,775,203
Registered Office: Prince William Avenue, Sandycroft, Flintshire, CH5 2QZ
Activities: Manufacture of veneer sheets and wood-based panels
Parent: Bobrick Washroom Equipment Ltd.
Officers: Michael Elwine [1970] Director; Tuan SI Ho [1965] Director/Manager [American]; Mark Sandel Louchheim [1955] Director/Manager [American]; Matthew Sandel Louchheim [1982] Director/Manager [American]; Jeffrey Robert Orme [1963] Director/General Manager

Thumbs-Up (Bury) Limited
Incorporated: 13 November 1978 *Employees:* 223
Net Worth: £22,758,256 *Total Assets:* £33,180,576
Registered Office: Greenfields, Dumers Lane, Bury, Lancs, BL9 9UT
Activities: Manufacture of other plastic products
Officers: Angela Antonietta Merotto, Secretary/Solicitor; Richard John McMcuinness [1972] Managing Director

Daniel Thwaites Public Limited Company
Incorporated: 17 March 1897 *Employees:* 819
Net Worth: £174,200,000 *Total Assets:* £308,600,000
Registered Office: Myerscough Road, Mellor Brook, Blackburn, Lancs, BB2 7LB
Activities: Manufacture of beer
Officers: Susan Irene Woodward, Secretary; Richard Anthony John Bailey [1973] Director/Investment Banker; Michael John Barnes [1949] Director; Nicholas Stephen MacKenzie [1968] Director; Kevin David Wood [1966] Finance Director; Ann Jean Mary Yerburgh [1947] Director; Oscar Guy Hamlyn Yerburgh [1983] Director

Thyson Group Limited
Incorporated: 15 April 2016 *Employees:* 101
Net Worth: £278,000 *Total Assets:* £13,426,000
Registered Office: Unit 2 Burnell Road, Thornton Industrial Estate, Ellesmere Port, Cheshire, CH65 5EX
Activities: Activities of other holding companies n.e.c.
Officers: Matthew Robert Allen [1976] Director; Michael James Braddock [1968] Director; Andrew William Leach [1957] Director; Ronald Smith [1952] Non-Executive Director Chairman

TI Industrial Group Limited
Incorporated: 30 June 2009
Net Worth: £2,368,000 *Total Assets:* £8,974,000
Registered Office: 6 Lodge Bank, Crown Lane, Horwich, Bolton, Lancs, BL6 5HY
Activities: Activities of other holding companies n.e.c.
Parent: Forth Bidco Limited
Officers: Paolo Benedetto [1974] Director; Neil Christian Harrison [1975] Director; Graham Philippe Bertwistle Moor [1967] Director; Jane Catherine Ratcliffe [1971] Director; Michael Stuart Taziker [1970] Director; Nigel Thomas Taziker [1975] Director; Jason Pearce Worrall [1975] Director

Tibst Limited
Incorporated: 11 May 2016
Net Worth Deficit: £291,475 *Total Assets:* £8,984,223
Registered Office: The Spectrum, 56-58 Benson Road, Birchwood, Warrington, Cheshire, WA3 7PQ
Activities: Development of building projects
Shareholders: Fred Done; Secret City Investments Ltd
Officers: Christopher Michael Bowman [1980] Director; Fred Done [1943] Director; John Haynes [1969] Commercial Director; Naushad Islam [1970] Commercial Director; Simon Anthony Ismail [1976] Commercial Director

TIC Group Limited
Incorporated: 18 November 1997 *Employees:* 7
Net Worth: £14,351,909 *Total Assets:* £26,277,100
Registered Office: Matrix House, Merlin Court, Atlantic Street, Altrincham, Cheshire, WA14 5NL
Activities: Development of building projects
Major Shareholder: Wayne Thomas Shillito
Officers: Thomas Shillito, Secretary; Wayne Thomas Shillito [1967] Managing Director

The Ticketline Network Limited
Incorporated: 14 September 1993 *Employees:* 47
Net Worth: £3,747,598 *Total Assets:* £14,678,566
Registered Office: Queens Chambers, 5 John Dalton Street, Manchester, M2 6ET
Activities: Other service activities n.e.c.
Parent: Ticketline Group Ltd
Officers: Linda Rachel Betesh, Secretary/Director/Ticket Agent; Linda Rachel Betesh [1966] Director; Paul Abraham Betesh [1968] Director/Chief Executive Officer; Susan Ellen Betesh [1966] Director; Colin Paul Mableson [1972] Managing Director

Tiger Tim Products Limited
Incorporated: 12 October 1978 *Employees:* 102
Net Worth: £14,892,000 *Total Assets:* £21,928,000
Registered Office: Rhosesmor Industrial Estate, Rhosesmor, Mold, Flintshire, CH7 6PZ
Activities: Manufacture of other chemical products n.e.c.
Parent: SHOO786AA Ltd
Officers: Patricia Thomas, Secretary; Timothy Michael Blois [1967] Director; Jan Johan Kamps [1951] Managing Director [Dutch]; Neil Rowland Popham [1950] Director/Chairman; Patricia Thomas [1970] Director

Tiger Trailers Limited
Incorporated: 13 March 2014 *Employees:* 179
Net Worth: £2,730,078 *Total Assets:* £12,706,099
Registered Office: 16 Road One, Winsford Industrial Estate, Winsford, Cheshire, CW7 3RL
Activities: Manufacture of trailers and semi-trailers
Officers: Alan John Cartwright [1965] Director; Steven Cartwright [1968] Director; Thomas David Williams [1947] Director

Timetoken Limited
Incorporated: 27 November 1987 *Employees:* 3
Net Worth: £14,844,072 *Total Assets:* £26,162,606
Registered Office: Lancaster House, Blackburn Street, Radcliffe, Manchester, M26 2JW
Activities: Other letting and operating of own or leased real estate
Major Shareholder: Susan Elizabeth Whitter
Officers: Sally Ann Whitter, Company Secretary; Matthew John Whitter [1978] Director; Susan Elizabeth Whitter [1952] Director/Company Secretary

Timpson Group PLC
Incorporated: 25 January 1989 *Employees:* 4,944
Net Worth: £61,180,000 *Total Assets:* £117,543,000
Registered Office: Timpson House, Claverton Road, Wythenshawe, Manchester, M23 9TT
Activities: Activities of head offices
Parent: Offerhappy Ltd
Officers: Paresh Majithia, Secretary; Roger Lane Smith [1945] Director/Solicitor; Paresh Majithia [1967] Finance Director; Stephen Peter Robertson [1954] Director General; James Timpson [1971] Managing Director; Sir William John Anthony Timpson [1943] Director

Timpson Holdings Limited
Incorporated: 6 March 1991 *Employees:* 4,944
Net Worth: £60,073,000 *Total Assets:* £115,307,000
Registered Office: Timpson House, Claverton Road, Wythenshawe, Manchester, M23 9TT
Activities: Activities of head offices
Officers: Paresh Majithia, Secretary; Roger Lane-Smith [1945] Director/Solicitor; Paresh Majithia [1967] Director; William James Timpson [1971] Director; Sir William John Anthony Timpson [1943] Director

Timpson Limited
Incorporated: 16 November 1960 *Employees:* 3,008
Net Worth: £43,802,000 *Total Assets:* £92,163,000
Registered Office: Timpson House, Claverton Road, Wythenshawe, Manchester, M23 9TT
Activities: Other retail sale of new goods in specialised stores (not commercial art galleries and opticians)
Parent: Sandymere Ltd
Officers: Paresh Majithia, Secretary; Roger Lane-Smith [1945] Director/Solicitor; Paresh Majithia [1967] Finance Director; Stephen Peter Robertson [1954] Director General; James Timpson [1971] Managing Director; Sir William John Anthony Timpson [1943] Director

Tip Holdings (UK) Limited
Incorporated: 11 March 1999
Net Worth: £200,163,040 *Total Assets:* £254,462,656
Registered Office: 3rd Floor, 1 Ashley Road, Altrincham, Cheshire, WA14 2DT
Activities: Other business support service activities n.e.c.
Officers: Paul Laurence Beadle [1969] Director; Jakob Eize de Bruin [1978] Director/VAT Manager [Dutch]; Robert Alain Fast [1956] Director [American]; Malachy McEnroe [1965] Director [Irish]

Tip Trailer Services UK Limited
Incorporated: 14 June 2013 *Employees:* 379
Net Worth: £27,525,000 *Total Assets:* £193,834,000
Registered Office: 3rd Floor, 1 Ashley Road, Altrincham, Cheshire, WA14 2DT
Activities: Renting and leasing of trucks and other heavy vehicles
Officers: Paul Laurence Beadle [1969] Director; Robert Alain Fast [1956] Director [American]; Michael Robert Furnival [1963] Director; Malachy McEnroe [1965] Director [Irish]

Tipografic Limited
Incorporated: 26 April 1989 *Employees:* 104
Net Worth: £4,672,978 *Total Assets:* £16,338,241
Registered Office: 6 Morpeth Wharf, Twelve Quays, Birkenhead, Wirral, Merseyside, CH41 1LW
Activities: Printing n.e.c.
Shareholders: Jeffrey Raymond Cornell; Stephen John Cole; Jeffrey Raymond Cornell Discretionary Settlement
Officers: Lesley Price, Secretary; Peter Benjamin Bramwell [1982] Sales and Marketing Director; Jillian Ruth Cole [1970] Director/Sales Executive; Stephen John Cole [1959] Director; Jeffrey Raymond Cornell [1951] Director; Valerie Ann Cornell [1959] Director/Teaching Assistant; Gary Davey [1967] Production Director

Titan Leisure Group Limited
Incorporated: 29 May 1948
Net Worth: £6,630,618 *Total Assets:* £6,630,618
Registered Office: Beechfield, Hollinhurst Road, Radcliffe, Manchester, M26 1JN
Activities: Activities of head offices
Parent: James Halstead PLC
Officers: David William Drillingcourt, Secretary; Mark Halstead [1957] Director; Gordon Richard Oliver [1958] Director/Chartered Accountant

Titan Telecom Limited
Incorporated: 29 December 2010 *Employees:* 2
Net Worth: £795,361 *Total Assets:* £152,463,088
Registered Office: Universal House, Longley Lane, Manchester, M22 4SY
Activities: Activities of other holding companies n.e.c.
Parent: Etihad Midco Limited
Officers: Gillian Elizabeth Hill, Secretary; Paul Doherty [1970] Director/Accountant; Christopher James Earle [1973] Director

Tithebarn Limited
Incorporated: 2 May 1935 *Employees:* 206
Net Worth: £25,845,620 *Total Assets:* £32,709,808
Registered Office: Road Five, Winsford Industrial Estate, Winsford, Cheshire, CW7 3PG
Activities: Manufacture of other food products n.e.c.
Officers: Apryl Elizabeth Biddle, Secretary; Ian Armstrong [1966] Director; Apryl Elizabeth Biddle [1963] Director; John David Melling [1971] Director; Peter Leslie Melling [1973] Director

Titleabsolute Limited
Incorporated: 28 March 2000 *Employees:* 22
Net Worth: £6,489,000 *Total Assets:* £7,603,000
Registered Office: 2nd Floor, Churchgate House, 56 Oxford Street, Manchester, M1 6EU
Activities: Activities of patent and copyright agents; other legal activities n.e.c.
Parent: Countrywide Group PLC
Officers: Gareth Rhys Williams, Secretary; Paul Robert Chapman [1969] Managing Director; James Robert Scott [1978] Director; Paul Anthony Wareham [1965] Director of Field Operations

TJA Motors Limited
Incorporated: 19 December 2001 *Employees:* 75
Net Worth: £7,838,000 *Total Assets:* £15,712,000
Registered Office: 5 Ribblesdale Place, Preston, Lancs, PR1 8BZ
Activities: Sale of new cars and light motor vehicles
Major Shareholder: Thomas James Allan McPhail
Officers: Carol Patricia McPhail, Secretary; Carol Patricia McPhail [1953] Director/Company Secretary; Thomas James Allan McPhail [1954] Director

TMD Friction Holdings (UK) Ltd
Incorporated: 6 December 2012 *Employees:* 4
Net Worth: £131,543,432 *Total Assets:* £301,074,112
Registered Office: P O Box 18, Centurion House, Centurion Way, Cleckheaton, W Yorks, BD19 3UJ
Activities: Activities of head offices
Parent: TMD Friction Holdings (Lux) S.A.R.L.
Officers: Steven Firbank, Secretary; Takaharu Dannoura [1971] Director/Chief Financial Officer [Japanese]; Steven Firbank [1972] Director/VP Finance IAM; Tetsuya Kumakawa [1968] Director/Chief Executive Officer [Japanese]

TMD Friction UK Limited
Incorporated: 28 November 2001 *Employees:* 687
Net Worth: £131,336,000 *Total Assets:* £150,936,000
Registered Office: P O Box 18, Centurion House, Centurion Way, Cleckheaton, W Yorks, BD19 3UJ
Activities: Manufacture of other parts and accessories for motor vehicles
Parent: TMD Friction Holdings (UK) Limited
Officers: Steven Firbank, Secretary; David Edward Baines [1972] Managing Director; Takaharu Dannoura [1971] Director/Chief Financial Officer [Japanese]; Ian Featherstone [1962] R&D Director; Steven Firbank [1972] Director

TMGH Limited
Incorporated: 25 May 2010 *Employees:* 49
Net Worth: £2,373,872 *Total Assets:* £9,143,232
Registered Office: 1 Oakwood Square, Cheadle Royal Business Park, Cheadle, Cheshire, SK8 3SB
Activities: Other business support service activities n.e.c.
Shareholders: Eugene McTaggart; Shankar Ramanathan
Officers: Eugene McTaggart [1957] Director [Irish]; Shankar Ramanathan [1964] Director/Banker

Together Commercial Finance Limited
Incorporated: 26 September 1986
Net Worth: £19,400,000 *Total Assets:* £1,202,200,064
Registered Office: Lake View, Lakeside, Cheadle, Cheshire, SK8 3GW
Activities: Credit granting by non-deposit taking finance houses and other specialist consumer credit grantors
Parent: Together Financial Services Limited
Officers: Sarah Elizabeth Batt, Secretary; Gary Derek Beckett [1969] Director; Wayne Bowser [1952] Director; Marc Richard Goldberg [1971] Director; Robert Michael McTighe [1953] Director; Henry Neville Moser [1949] Director; Helga Clare Taylor [1969] Finance Director

Together Financial Services Limited
Incorporated: 15 June 1994
Net Worth: £628,400,000 *Total Assets:* £2,276,100,096
Registered Office: Lake View, Lakeside, Cheadle, Cheshire, SK8 3GW
Activities: Activities of head offices
Parent: Bracken Midco2 Limited
Officers: Sarah Elizabeth Batt, Secretary; Peter Simon Ball [1968] Director; Gary Derek Beckett [1969] Director; Wayne Bowser [1952] Non-Executive Director; Marcus John Joseph Reynolds Golby [1970] Director; Marc Richard Goldberg [1971] Director; John Lowe [1972] Director; Robert Michael McTighe [1953] Director; Henry Neville Moser [1949] Director; Joseph Michael Shaoul [1940] Director/Advisor

Together Personal Finance Limited
Incorporated: 22 May 1991
Net Worth: £33,400,000 *Total Assets:* £366,700,000
Registered Office: Lake View, Lakeside, Cheadle, Cheshire, SK8 3GW
Activities: Credit granting by non-deposit taking finance houses and other specialist consumer credit grantors
Parent: Together Financial Services Limited
Officers: Sarah Elizabeth Batt, Secretary; Peter Simon Ball [1968] Director; Ronald Baxter [1951] Director; Gary Derek Beckett [1969] Director; David Jonathan Bennett [1962] Director; Wayne Bowser [1952] Director; Marcus John Joseph Reynolds Golby [1970] Executive Director; Robert Michael McTighe [1953] Director; Henry Neville Moser [1949] Non-Executive Director; Paul Antony Wilson [1971] Director

The Together Trust
Incorporated: 12 June 1935 *Employees:* 811
Net Worth: £20,276,000 *Total Assets:* £28,747,000
Registered Office: Together Trust Centre, Schools Hill, Cheadle, Cheshire, SK8 1JE
Activities: Educational support services
Officers: Mark Robinson Lee, Secretary; Paul Adams [1962] Director/Photographer; Kirsteen Ann Atkinson [1976] Director/HR Consultant; Roger Bernard Bagguley [1941] Director/Retired Schools Inspector; Wendy Coomer [1943] Director/Office Administrator; Ralph John Ellerton [1944] Director/Accountant; Giles Hugh Joynson Gaddum [1973] Business Director; Lady Paula Doone Gilbart [1955] Director/Retired Solicitor; Janet Mary Heath [1964] Director; George David Herbert [1953] Director/Retired; Roger Anthony Horne [1947] Director/Solicitor; Rosamund Mary Hughes [1968] Director/PR Consultant; Simon Christopher Lees-Jones [1966] Director; Sangam Mishra [1986] Director/Digital Transformation [Indian]; Hugh John Joseph Rylands [1954] Director; Robert John Stevenson [1952] Director/Chartered Insurance Broker

Tokyo Group Limited
Incorporated: 2 January 2008 *Employees:* 86
Net Worth: £2,761,759 *Total Assets:* £10,852,192
Registered Office: 2nd Floor, 1 City Road East, Manchester, M15 4PN
Activities: Licenced clubs
Major Shareholder: Aaron Matthew Mellor
Officers: Aaron Matthew Mellor [1970] Director

Tonrose Limited
Incorporated: 28 February 1964 *Employees:* 48
Net Worth: £2,008,661 *Total Assets:* £9,368,887
Registered Office: Unit 1 Petre Road, Clayton Business Park, Clayton-le-Moors, Accrington, Lancs, BB5 5JB
Activities: Wholesale of textiles
Shareholders: Terence Michael Sheldon; Robert Edward Sheldon
Officers: Gillian Wendy Sargeant, Secretary; Paul Court Haden [1963] Managing Director; Gillian Wendy Sargeant [1947] Director; Terence Michael Sheldon [1951] Director

Topbonus Ltd
Incorporated: 30 October 2012 *Employees:* 37
Net Worth Deficit: £122,415,088 *Total Assets:* £10,380,448
Registered Office: 3rd Floor, 1 Ashley Road, Altrincham, Cheshire, WA14 2DT
Activities: Service activities incidental to air transportation
Shareholders: Air Berlin PLC; Abu Dhabi Government

Topgrade Sportswear Limited
Incorporated: 18 December 1995 *Employees:* 119
Net Worth Deficit: £785,000 *Total Assets:* £19,820,000
Registered Office: Hollins Brook Way, Pilsworth, Bury, Lancs, BL9 8RR
Activities: Wholesale of clothing and footwear
Parent: Topgrade Sportswear Holdings Limited
Officers: Siobhan Mawdsley, Secretary; Peter Alan Cowgill [1953] Director; Ian Stuart Simpson [1958] Director; Paul Raymond Simpson [1963] Director; Brian Michael Small [1956] Director

Total Care and Support Limited
Incorporated: 5 June 2002 *Employees:* 126
Net Worth: £8,059,841 *Total Assets:* £8,574,812
Registered Office: Unit 28 Time Technology Park, Blackburn Road, Burnley, Lancs, BB12 7TW
Activities: Other business support service activities n.e.c.
Officers: Phillip Andrew Walker [1958] Director

Total Developments (NW) Ltd
Incorporated: 20 April 2015
Net Worth: £85,342 *Total Assets:* £6,832,532
Registered Office: 17 Alvaston Business Park, Middlewich Road, Nantwich, Cheshire, CW5 6PF
Activities: Other letting and operating of own or leased real estate
Shareholders: Jonathon David Beeson; Simon Chantler
Officers: Jonathon David Beeson [1978] Director; Edward Charles Chantler [1984] Director

Total Fitness Health Clubs Limited
Incorporated: 3 August 2010 *Employees:* 597
Net Worth: £7,282,000 *Total Assets:* £31,696,000
Registered Office: Total Fitness 2010 Ltd, Wilmslow Way, Handforth, Wilmslow, Cheshire, SK9 3PE
Activities: Fitness facilities
Officers: Jasvir Sanghera, Secretary; Sophie Lawler [1978] Director/Chief Executive; Jasvir Singh Sanghera [1966] Finance Director

Total Glass Holdings Limited
Incorporated: 11 July 2002 *Employees:* 194
Net Worth: £4,308,878 *Total Assets:* £9,644,747
Registered Office: Hanover Buildings, 11-13 Hanover Street, Liverpool, L1 3DN
Activities: Activities of head offices
Major Shareholder: Frank Orr Deary
Officers: Georgina Deary, Secretary; Frank Orr Deary [1962] Director; Georgina Deary [1959] Director/Company Secretary

Total Glass Limited
Incorporated: 30 January 1990 *Employees:* 213
Net Worth: £5,552,274 *Total Assets:* £13,019,811
Registered Office: Hanover Buildings, 11-13 Hanover Street, Liverpool, L1 3DN
Activities: Manufacture of other plastic products
Officers: Georgina Deary, Secretary; Frank Orr Deary [1962] Director; Georgina Deary [1959] Director/Company Secretary

Total Polyfilm (Holdings) Limited
Incorporated: 10 August 2004 *Employees:* 213
Net Worth: £13,545,000 *Total Assets:* £31,628,000
Registered Office: Unit 95 Seedlee Road, Walton Summit Industrial Estate, Preston, Lancs, PR5 8AE
Activities: Activities of head offices
Parent: Total Polyfilm Group Limited
Officers: Trevor Pilling, Secretary; Darren William Dean [1964] Director; Alastair Lloyd Murdoch [1959] Director/Accountant; Trevor Pilling [1960] Director

Total Polyfilm Group Limited
Incorporated: 27 September 2007 *Employees:* 213
Net Worth: £8,524,000 *Total Assets:* £26,607,000
Registered Office: Unit 95 Seedlee Road, Walton Summit Industrial Estate, Preston, Lancs, PR5 8AE
Activities: Activities of head offices
Shareholders: David Murray Dawson; David Grove Discretionary Will Trust
Officers: Trevor Pilling, Secretary; Darren William Dean [1964] Director; Trevor Pilling [1960] Director

Total Polyfilm Limited
Incorporated: 17 July 2001 *Employees:* 213
Net Worth: £17,700,000 *Total Assets:* £35,783,000
Registered Office: Unit 95 Seedlee Road, Walton Summit Industrial Estate, Preston, Lancs, PR5 8AE
Activities: Manufacture of plastic packing goods
Parent: Total Polyfilm (Holdings) Limited
Officers: Trevor Pilling, Secretary; Darren William Dean [1964] Director; Alastair Lloyd Murdoch [1959] Director/Accountant; Trevor Pilling [1960] Financial Director

Total Water Solutions Limited
Incorporated: 13 May 2014
Net Worth: £42,471,000 *Total Assets:* £85,208,000
Registered Office: c/o Aimia Foods Limited, Penny Lane, Haydock, St Helens, Merseyside, WA11 0QZ
Activities: Manufacture of soft drinks; production of mineral waters and other bottled waters
Shareholder: Cott Ventures UK Limited
Officers: Jason Robert Ausher [1973] Director [American]; Claire Duffy [1976] Director/Solicitor; Steven Kitching [1964] Director

Totally Local Company Limited
Incorporated: 13 June 2006 *Employees:* 748
Net Worth Deficit: £5,516,000 *Total Assets:* £16,927,000
Registered Office: Enterprise House, Oakhurst Drive, off Bird Hall Lane, Cheadle Heath, Stockport, Cheshire, SK3 0XT
Activities: Collection of non-hazardous waste
Parent: Stockport Metropolitan Borough Council
Officers: Stephen Jallands, Secretary; Katherine Helen Cowell [1952] Director; Stephen Jallands [1963] Director/Chartered Accountant; Aileen Mary McDonnell [1959] Director; Stephen Paul Morris [1952] Managing Director; Dermot Justin Power [1951] Director; Susan Webster [1950] Director

Totally Wicked Group Limited
Incorporated: 2 February 2015 *Employees:* 159
Net Worth: £16,511,477 *Total Assets:* £20,144,188
Registered Office: Stancliffe Street, Blackburn, Lancs, BB2 2QR
Activities: Activities of head offices
Major Shareholder: Fraser Brunel Nicholas Cropper
Officers: Fraser Brunel Nicholas Cropper [1966] Director

Totally Wicked Limited
Incorporated: 12 July 2012 *Employees:* 7
Net Worth: £9,007,253 *Total Assets:* £9,526,915
Registered Office: Totally Wicked, Stancliffe Street, Blackburn, Lancs, BB2 2QR
Activities: Activities of head offices
Parent: Totally Wicked Group Limited
Officers: Fraser Brunel Nicholas Cropper [1966] Managing Director; Liam Humberstone [1966] Technical Director; Stuart James Mercer [1974] Operations Director; Benjamin George Frederick Williamson [1979] Director/Chartered Accountant

Tote (Successor Company) Limited
Incorporated: 23 February 2011 *Employees:* 242
Net Worth: £67,392,000 *Total Assets:* £116,199,000
Registered Office: The Spectrum, 56-58 Benson Road, Birchwood, Warrington, Cheshire, WA3 7PQ
Activities: Gambling and betting activities
Parent: Lightcatch Limited
Officers: Michael Rodney Hamilton, Secretary; Nicola Joan Barr [1977] Finance Director; Fred Done [1943] Director/Bookmaker; Mark Warren Stebbings [1970] Managing Director

Tote Bookmakers Limited
Incorporated: 18 June 1965 *Employees:* 1,298
Net Worth: £64,873,000 *Total Assets:* £188,362,000
Registered Office: The Spectrum, 56-58 Benson Road, Birchwood, Warrington, Cheshire, WA3 7PQ
Activities: Gambling and betting activities
Parent: Tote (Successor Company) Limited
Officers: Michael Rodney Hamilton, Secretary; Nicola Joan Barr [1977] Finance Director; Fred Done [1943] Director/Bookmaker; Mark Warren Stebbings [1970] Managing Director

Tote Direct Limited
Incorporated: 17 July 1991 *Employees:* 28
Net Worth: £43,434,000 *Total Assets:* £45,311,000
Registered Office: The Spectrum, 56-58 Benson Road, Birchwood, Warrington, Cheshire, WA3 7PQ
Activities: Gambling and betting activities
Parent: Tpoolco Limited
Officers: Michael Rodney Hamilton, Secretary; Nicola Joan Barr [1977] Finance Director; Fred Done [1943] Director/Bookmaker; Mark Warren Stebbings [1970] Managing Director

Tote Media Limited
Incorporated: 22 November 2013
Net Worth Deficit: £3,289,393 *Total Assets:* £24,292,260
Registered Office: The Spectrum, Benson Road, Birchwood, Warrington, Cheshire, WA3 7PQ
Activities: Television programming and broadcasting activities
Officers: Steven Longden [1970] Director/Solicitor; Philip Zenon Sierzputowski [1952] Director

Tower Centre Hoddesdon Limited
Incorporated: 5 February 2010
Net Worth: £12,691,000 *Total Assets:* £41,362,000
Registered Office: Hilmore House, Gain Lane, Bradford, W Yorks, BD3 7DL
Activities: Development of building projects
Parent: Optimisation Developments Limited
Officers: Jonathan James Burke, Secretary; Jonathan James Burke [1966] Director; Trevor John Strain [1975] Finance Director

Tower Hill Property Investments (10) Limited
Incorporated: 25 July 1989
Net Worth: £1,015,000 *Total Assets:* £8,737,000
Registered Office: Charterhall House, Charterhall Drive, Chester, CH88 3AN
Activities: Financial intermediation not elsewhere classified
Parent: Bank of Scotland PLC
Officers: Alyson Elizabeth Mulholland, Secretary; Stuart Donald Cook [1964] Director; Laura Frances Dorey [1978] Director; Colin Graham Dowsett [1964] Director/Chartered Accountant; Christopher Alan Hastings [1969] Director/Investment Banker

Town Head Farm Products Limited
Incorporated: 24 September 2003 *Employees:* 73
Net Worth: £3,867,721 *Total Assets:* £7,411,112
Registered Office: Town Head Farm, Grassington, Skipton, N Yorks, BD23 5BL
Activities: Raising of dairy cattle
Major Shareholder: David Jonathan Oversby
Officers: James Paul Mason, Secretary; David Jonathan Oversby [1962] Director/Farmer

Trac Group Limited
Incorporated: 20 May 2002 *Employees:* 1
Net Worth: £701,000 *Total Assets:* £6,868,000
Registered Office: 9a Marshfield Bank, Crewe, Cheshire, CW2 8UY
Activities: Activities of head offices
Parent: Broomco (4266) Limited
Officers: David Kaplan, Secretary; Amanda Balog Sanders, Secretary; Paul Anthony Jerram [1964] Director/General Manager; Steven Robert Lowson [1961] Director/Vice President General Counsel and Corporate Secretary [American]

Trac Mexico Limited
Incorporated: 13 June 2008 *Employees:* 3
Net Worth Deficit: £3,342,000 *Total Assets:* £15,069,000
Registered Office: 9a Marshfield Bank Employment Park, Middlewhich Road, Wolstanwood, Crewe, Cheshire, CW2 8UY
Activities: Other manufacturing n.e.c.
Parent: Trac Group Limited
Officers: David Kaplan, Secretary; Amanda Balog Sanders, Secretary; Paul Anthony Jerram [1964] Director/General Manager; Steven Robert Lowson [1961] Director/Vice President General Counsel and Corporate Secretary [American]

Trac Precision Machining Limited
Incorporated: 19 August 2003 *Employees:* 282
Net Worth Deficit: £49,275,000 *Total Assets:* £42,893,000
Registered Office: 9a Marshfield Bank, Crewe, Cheshire, CW2 8UY
Activities: Other manufacturing n.e.c.
Parent: Trac Group Limited
Officers: David Kaplan, Secretary; Amanda Balog Sanders, Secretary; Paul Anthony Jerram [1964] Director/General Manager; Steven Robert Lowson [1961] Director/Vice President General Counsel and Corporate Secretary [American]

Trafford Housing Trust Limited
Incorporated: 14 July 2003 *Employees:* 429
Net Worth: £44,852,000 *Total Assets:* £234,340,992
Registered Office: Sale Point, 126-150 Washway Road, Sale, Manchester, M33 6AG
Activities: Renting and operating of Housing Association real estate
Officers: Brigid Burbridge, Secretary; Councillor Sean Brian Anstee [1987] Director/Councillor; Angela Bolton [1971] Director/Compliance Manager; Alastair Ian Findlay [1952] Independent Director; Matthew John Hemmings [1984] Director; John Terence Lamb [1954] Director/Consultant; Nigel Mark McGurk [1969] Director/Consultant; Edna Janet Robinson [1951] Director/Self Employed; Sheila Mary Tolley [1960] Director

Trak Global Group Limited
Incorporated: 20 September 2016
Net Worth Deficit: £11,491 *Total Assets:* £29,188,332
Registered Office: Global House, Westmere Drive, Crewe Business Park, Crewe, Cheshire, CW1 6ZD
Activities: Activities of other holding companies n.e.c.
Officers: James Hulsken, Secretary; Ivan Victor Bumstead [1973] Director/Chief Financial Officer; Nicholas Corrie [1969] Director

Tranos (UK) Limited
Incorporated: 18 July 2014 *Employees:* 1
Net Worth Deficit: £633,380 *Total Assets:* £12,843,446
Registered Office: c/o Jack Ross Chartered Accountants, Barnfield House, The Approach, Manchester, M3 7BX
Activities: Development of building projects
Officers: Benjamin William Thwaites [1983] Director

Trans - Continental Group Limited
Incorporated: 6 October 1994 *Employees:* 51
Net Worth: £3,668,392 *Total Assets:* £8,075,207
Registered Office: Transcon House, Unit 4 Amy Johnson Way, Blackpool, Lancs, FY4 2RP
Activities: Non-specialised wholesale trade
Major Shareholder: Michael Stephen Withers
Officers: Rosemary Therese Withers, Secretary; Lucy Bool [1985] Finance Director; Adam John Gregory [1989] Sales Director; Sara Louise Murray [1973] Buying Director; Michael Stephen Withers [1956] Director

Transdev PLC
Incorporated: 22 September 1992 *Employees:* 1,323
Net Worth: £10,041,000 *Total Assets:* £60,184,000
Registered Office: Cavendish House, 91-93 Cavendish Street, Keighley, W Yorks, BD21 3DG
Activities: Other passenger land transport
Parent: Transdev SA
Officers: Peter Ian Brogden, Finance Director; Loic Huet [1976] Finance Director [French]; Yann Leriche [1973] Director/Chief Performance Officer [French]; Stefano Marzio [1980] Director/Head of Legal International Business and Risk [Italian]; Ferguson Robertson-Howard [1964] Director; Bartholomeus Cornelis Schmeink [1968] Director [Dutch]

Transportation Infrastructure Group Limited
Incorporated: 5 April 2005 *Employees:* 96
Net Worth: £3,478,569 *Total Assets:* £8,271,246
Registered Office: Lowton Business Park, Newton Road, Lowton, Warrington, Cheshire, WA3 2AP
Activities: Activities of head offices
Major Shareholder: Gerard Malachy McGuinness
Officers: David Michael Smith, Secretary; Gerard Malachy McGuinness [1959] Director

Tratos (UK) Limited
Incorporated: 28 October 1980 *Employees:* 51
Net Worth: £5,146,938 *Total Assets:* £28,617,178
Registered Office: Tratos-Knowsley Factory, Randles Road, Knowsley Business Park, Prescot, Merseyside, L34 9HX
Activities: Manufacture of other electronic and electric wires and cables
Parent: Tratos Cavi S.P.A
Officers: Kevin Martin, Secretary; Albano Bragagni [1951] Director [Italian]; Germano Bragagni [1953] Director [Italian]; Maurizio Bragagni [1975] Managing Director; Elisabetta Bragagni Capaccini [1983] Director [Italian]; Dr Ennio Bragagni Capaccini [1974] Director [Italian]; Enrico Scambia [1972] Director [Italian]

Travel 2 Limited
Incorporated: 30 October 1981 *Employees:* 187
Net Worth Deficit: £8,735,000 *Total Assets:* £64,186,000
Registered Office: Glendale House, Glendale Business Park, Glendale Avenue, Sandycroft, Flintshire, CH5 2DL
Activities: Tour operator activities
Parent: Stella Travel Services (UK) Limited
Officers: Ryan James Cooke, Secretary; Paul Smith [1975] Director

Travel Counsellors Group Limited
Incorporated: 7 July 2005 *Employees:* 284
Net Worth: £59,836,000 *Total Assets:* £111,983,000
Registered Office: Venus, No 1 Old Park Lane, Trafford City, Manchester, M41 7HA
Activities: Travel agency activities
Parent: Cannes Bidco Limited
Officers: Laura Helen Anderton, Secretary; Stephen Byrne [1965] Director; Kirsten Hughes [1971] Director; Karen Morris [1962] Director; Simon Andrew Shaw [1967] Finance Director

Travel Counsellors Limited
Incorporated: 20 May 1987 *Employees:* 246
Net Worth: £39,265,512 *Total Assets:* £78,808,640
Registered Office: Venus, No 1 Old Park Lane, Trafford City, Manchester, M41 7HA
Activities: Travel agency activities
Parent: Travel Counsellors Group Limited
Officers: Laura Helen Anderton, Secretary; Stephen Byrne [1965] Managing Director; Kirsten Hughes [1971] Commercial Director; Karen Morris [1962] Operations Director; Simon Andrew Shaw [1967] Finance Director

Travelbag Limited
Incorporated: 4 July 1979 *Employees:* 154
Net Worth: £6,850,000 *Total Assets:* £94,883,000
Registered Office: Glendale House, Glendale Business Park, Glendale Avenue, Sandycroft, Flintshire, CH5 2DL
Activities: Tour operator activities
Parent: Stella Travel Services (UK) Limited
Officers: Ryan James Cooke, Secretary; Joshua Wilfrid Gubbay [1969] Director; Asif Hamza Parkar [1974] Director

Travelworld International (Manchester) Limited
Incorporated: 7 June 1991 *Employees:* 43
Net Worth: £1,002,714 *Total Assets:* £8,805,278
Registered Office: International House, 1 Church Lane, Prestwich, Manchester, M25 1AN
Activities: Travel agency activities
Major Shareholder: Paul Leslie Edge
Officers: Francine Edge, Secretary; Paul Leslie Edge [1957] Director/Travel Agent

Treedown Investments Limited
Incorporated: 20 May 2014
Net Worth: £469,700 *Total Assets:* £9,753,696
Registered Office: St Johns Chambers, Love Street, Chester, CH1 1QN
Activities: Activities of venture and development capital companies
Major Shareholder: Vivian Hugh James Bennett
Officers: Vivian Hugh James Bennett [1974] Director

Treif (UK) Limited
Incorporated: 13 September 1957
Registered Office: Genesis House, Poole Hall Industrial Estate, Poole Hall Road, Ellesmere Port, Cheshire, CH66 1ST
Activities: Non-specialised wholesale trade
Major Shareholder: Uwe Theodor Reifenhauser
Officers: Uwe Reifenhauser [1960] Director [German]

Trek Diagnostic Systems Limited
Incorporated: 18 July 1986 *Employees:* 64
Net Worth: £9,856,000 *Total Assets:* £11,301,000
Registered Office: 3rd Floor, 1 Ashley Road, Altrincham, Cheshire, WA14 2DT
Activities: Other business support service activities n.e.c.
Parent: Trek Holding Company II Limited
Officers: Rhona Gregg, Secretary; Lucie Mary Katja Grant [1976] Director/Solicitor; Nicholas Ince [1982] Director/Accountant; David John Norman [1960] Director/Chartered Accountant

Trendsetter Home Furnishings Limited
Incorporated: 15 February 1977 *Employees:* 156
Net Worth: £12,921,968 *Total Assets:* £17,920,424
Registered Office: Cobra Court, 10 Blackmore Road, Stretford, Manchester, M32 0QY
Activities: Manufacture of soft furnishings
Shareholder: Margaret Roper Black
Officers: Margaret Roper Black [1944] Director; Robert Paul Black [1943] Director/Chairman; Richard James Carryer [1966] Brand Sales Director; Nicholas William Dean [1980] Finance Director; Christopher Paul Rushby [1972] Sales Director; Claire Frances Watkin [1978] Managing Director

Trewhiddle Village Limited
Incorporated: 19 February 2007 *Employees:* 4
Net Worth Deficit: £2,545,768 *Total Assets:* £10,147,474
Registered Office: Whitecroft House, 51 Water Lane, Wilmslow, Cheshire, SK9 5BQ
Activities: Other accommodation
Officers: Timothy Dennis [1975] Director; Ewan James Kearney [1971] Director; Matthew Dawson Spence [1963] Director; Anthony Wild [1974] Director

Trigon Snacks Trading Limited
Incorporated: 30 September 2013 *Employees:* 108
Net Worth: £2,428,032 *Total Assets:* £8,096,892
Registered Office: Atherton Road, Aintree, Liverpool, L9 7AQ
Activities: Manufacture of other food products n.e.c.
Parent: T Choithram & Sons (London) Limited
Officers: Lekhraj Thakurdas Pagarani [1954] Director; Luke Pagarani [1983] Director/Merchant

Trilanco Limited
Incorporated: 6 February 2010 *Employees:* 88
Net Worth: £4,420,000 *Total Assets:* £23,781,000
Registered Office: Trilanco Ltd, Coronation Way, Mill Farm Sports Village, Wesham, Preston, Lancs, PR4 3JZ
Activities: Agents specialised in the sale of other particular products
Major Shareholder: Martin Howard Wood Balmer
Officers: Lisa Balmer [1967] Director; Martin Howard Wood Balmer [1965] Director

Trilogy (Leamington Spa) Limited
Incorporated: 6 August 2009
Net Worth: £13,399,000 *Total Assets:* £36,617,000
Registered Office: Hilmore House, Gain Lane, Bradford, W Yorks, BD3 7DL
Activities: Other business support service activities n.e.c.
Parent: Optimisation Developments Limited
Officers: Jonathan James Burke, Secretary; Jonathan James Burke [1966] Director; Trevor John Strain [1975] Finance Director

Trinity Church of England High School
Incorporated: 12 December 2011 *Employees:* 182
Net Worth: £22,960,640 *Total Assets:* £24,153,180
Registered Office: Trinity Church of England High School, Cambridge Street, Hulme, Manchester, M15 6HP
Activities: General secondary education
Officers: Jayne Langley, Secretary; The Right Reverend David Stuart Walker The Bishop of Manchester [1957] Director; Dr Admos Chimhowu [1966] Director [Zimbabwean]; Jane Elizabeth Coogan [1971] Director/Safeguarding Lead at Primary School; Peter Girvan Hilton [1946] Director; Pamela Mary Lord [1969] Director/Finance & Commercial Manager; Karen Belinda Lund [1962] Director; Prof Olwen McNamara [1950] Director/Academic; Ann Meadowcroft [1957] Director/Solicitor; David Andrew Moore [1973] Director/IT Engineer; Councillor Nigel Murphy [1972] Director; Julian Robin Nicholls [1969] Director; Adanna Lazz Onyenobi [1950] Director/Doctor of Medicine [Nigerian]; Robert David Palmer [1947] Director; Andrea Lesley Plimmer [1970] Director of Vocational Learning; Dr Peter Manley Scott [1961] Director/University Lecturer; Brian Philip Selby [1962] Director/Civil Servant; Falak Sher [1965] Director/Rector; Julie Tattersall [1957] Director; David Walker [1951] Director/Bishop of Manchester; Richard Thomas Wells [1961] Director/Teacher; Simon David Worsley [1983] Director

Trinity Enterprise Centre Limited
Incorporated: 20 December 2000 *Employees:* 3
Net Worth: £2,753,013 *Total Assets:* £7,195,045
Registered Office: Springfield House, Water Lane, Wilmslow, Cheshire, SK9 5BG
Activities: Other letting and operating of own or leased real estate
Parent: Dean Property Group Limited
Officers: Michael Edward O'Donnell, Secretary; Jonathan Charles Patrick Beever [1963] Director; Michael Edward O'Donnell [1969] Director; James Anthony Wild [1941] Director/Chartered Accountant

Trinity Hospice and Palliative Care Services Ltd
Incorporated: 7 January 1981 *Employees:* 163
Net Worth: £23,426,284 *Total Assets:* £24,323,294
Registered Office: Trinity Hospice, Low Moor Road, Bispham, Blackpool, Lancs, FY2 0BG
Activities: Hospital activities
Officers: Helena Sarah Lavin, Secretary; Christopher John Beverley [1948] Director/Solicitor; Kathryn Burn [1947] Director/Retired; Dr Stephen Doel [1954] Director/Retired; Dr Helen Grenier [1957] Director/Doctor; William Antony Holmes [1949] Director/Chemical Production Manager; Tom Inman [1948] Director/Retired; Peter Harry Jackson [1964] Director/Businessman; Andrew Keith [1954] Director/Retired; Nigel Anthony Law [1953] Director/Judge; Dr Nancy Preston [1967] Director/Lecturer; Steve Thompson [1963] Finance Director; Graham Wilkinson [1983] Director/Financial Controller

Trinity Medical Properties Limited
Incorporated: 16 November 2005 *Employees:* 7
Net Worth: £20,659,372 *Total Assets:* £128,185,872
Registered Office: The Brew House, Greenalls Avenue, Warrington, Cheshire, WA4 6HL
Activities: Other letting and operating of own or leased real estate
Parent: Assura Financing Limited
Officers: Orla Ball [1970] Director/Company Secretary; Paul Bryan Carroll [1969] Director/Accountant; Jayne Marie Cottam [1974] Finance Director; Simon Gould [1974] Director/Chartered Surveyor; Spencer Adrian Kenyon [1962] Director/Chartered Surveyor; Patrick William Lowther [1977] Director/Chartered Surveyor

Trinity School, A Church of England Academy
Incorporated: 7 July 2011 *Employees:* 176
Net Worth: £8,927,992 *Total Assets:* £13,847,184
Registered Office: Trinity School A Church of England Academy, Strand Road, Carlisle, Cumbria, CA1 1JB
Activities: General secondary education
Officers: Lorna Minns, Secretary; Susan Victoria Mary Aglionby [1945] Director/Farmer; David Brian Armstrong [1941] Director; Dr Ian Barker [1970] Director/Teacher; Dr Elizabeth Gwen Borlase [1962] Director/GP; The Reverend Mark Christopher Boyling [1952] Director/Clerk in Holy Orders; Malcolm Robert Burnes [1959] Director/Retired; Michael Carigiet [1949] Director/Chartered Surveyor; Duncan Gilchrist Carter [1971] Director; Thomas Dawson [1947] Director; Gerard Bernard Edwards [1958] Director/Facilities Manager; Sue Glendinning [1960] Director/Self Employed; Colin Jefferson [1948] Director/Retired; Karen Lesley Johnston [1960] Director; Sheila Louise Johnston [1960] Director/Co-Headteacher; Derek Kay [1958] Director/Co-Headteacher; Tom Simpson Leach [1952] Director/Solicitor; Daphne Frances Libby [1959] Director/Teacher; Michael Alan Manley [1960] Director; Stuart McDermott [1962] Director/Retail Bank Manager; Dr William David Paterson [1943] Director/Retired Physician; Rev David George Pitkeathly [1965] Director/Minister; Linda Wedderburn [1962] Director/Teacher

Trouw (UK) Limited
Incorporated: 1 September 1934 *Employees:* 148
Net Worth: £38,337,000 *Total Assets:* £114,033,000
Registered Office: Minsal Works, Wincham, Northwich, Cheshire, CW9 6DF
Activities: Marine aquaculture
Parent: Nutreco Ltd
Officers: Janine Bolton, Secretary; Janine Bolton [1965] Director/Chartered Accountant; Garth Mitchell Nicholas Boyd [1969] Managing Director; Karen Smith [1976] Director/Financial Controller; John Mark Williamson [1967] Director/General Manager

Truecommerce Holdings Limited
Incorporated: 16 June 2014 *Employees:* 112
Net Worth Deficit: £4,488,227 *Total Assets:* £26,115,230
Registered Office: Eversheds House, 70 Great Bridgewater Street, Manchester, M1 5ES
Activities: Information technology consultancy activities
Parent: True Commerce, Inc.
Officers: Michael John Cornell [1957] Director/Chief Executive Officer [American]; Edward Flint Seaton [1953] Director/Chief Financial Officer [American]

Trust Inns Limited
Incorporated: 18 January 1995 *Employees:* 122
Net Worth: £93,186,000 *Total Assets:* £199,778,000
Registered Office: Blenheim House, Ackhurst Park, Foxhole Road, Chorley, Lancs, PR7 1NY
Activities: Public houses and bars
Major Shareholder: Trevor James Hemmings
Officers: Olivia Blythe, Secretary; Lynne D'Arcy [1957] Director; John Clement Kay [1953] Director; Kathryn Revitt [1964] Director/Solicitor; Mark Lorimer Widders [1960] Finance Director

Trutex Investments Limited
Incorporated: 13 September 2010 *Employees:* 257
Net Worth: £4,659,000 *Total Assets:* £11,711,000
Registered Office: Jubilee Mill, Taylor Street, Clitheroe, Lancs, BB7 1NL
Activities: Wholesale of clothing and footwear
Shareholders: Andrew James Ducker; David Brown Manning
Officers: Andrew James Ducker [1963] Director; Matthew James Easter [1976] Director; David Brown Manning [1958] Director

Trutex Limited
Incorporated: 21 January 2010 *Employees:* 140
Net Worth: £5,007,000 *Total Assets:* £10,668,000
Registered Office: Jubilee Mill, Taylor Street, Clitheroe, Lancs, BB7 1NL
Activities: Wholesale of clothing and footwear
Parent: Trutex Investments Limited
Officers: Andrew James Ducker [1963] Director; Matthew James Easter [1976] Director; Katrina Louise Fowler [1970] Technical Director; Tim Hallas [1967] Director; John Hogan [1962] Director [Irish]; David Brown Manning [1958] Director; Tom Morley [1989] Director; Heather Walker [1953] Sales Director

TS (UK) Limited
Incorporated: 14 September 1998 *Employees:* 101
Net Worth: £5,559,740 *Total Assets:* £10,929,792
Registered Office: Unit 107 Stakehill Industrial Estate, Middleton, Manchester, M24 2SJ
Activities: Manufacture of plastic packing goods
Officers: Darren Reynolds, Secretary; Donato Castronuovo [1972] Director/Production [Italian]; Attilio Germano [1968] Director [Italian]; Darren Reynolds [1973] Managing Director; Cristian Tontarelli [1977] Director/Production Manager [Italian]; Sergio Tontarelli [1951] Director [Italian]

TSB (Investment Europe) Limited
Incorporated: 14 April 2000
Net Worth: £20,053,000 *Total Assets:* £169,804,992
Registered Office: Springfields, Salwick, Preston, Lancs, PR4 0XJ
Activities: Financial management
Parent: Westinghouse Electric UK Holdings Limited
Officers: Fiona Anne Houghton, Secretary; Linda Aylmore [1970] Director

TSC Engineering Limited
Incorporated: 30 May 2003
Net Worth: £8,961,371 *Total Assets:* £21,319,394
Registered Office: Unit E, Upper Wharf Street, Shipley, W Yorks, BD17 7DW
Activities: Other engineering activities
Parent: TSC Offshore (UK) Limited
Officers: Man Lai Chung, Secretary; Binghua Jiang [1950] Director/Chairman [American]; Menggui Zhang [1958] Director [American]

TSC Foods Group Limited
Incorporated: 29 May 2009
Net Worth: £3,007,417 *Total Assets:* £17,932,432
Registered Office: Cunard Building, Water Street, Liverpool, L3 1EL
Activities: Other business support service activities n.e.c.
Parent: Dickens 2014 Limited
Officers: David Marshall, Secretary; Simon Gamble [1961] Director; David Marshall [1961] Director; Matthew Wood [1969] Director

TSC Foods Limited
Incorporated: 8 May 1990 *Employees:* 426
Net Worth: £21,559,312 *Total Assets:* £32,043,482
Registered Office: Cunard Building, Water Street, Liverpool, L3 1EL
Activities: Production of meat and poultry meat products
Parent: Sauceinvest Limited
Officers: David Marshall, Secretary; Gary Michael Blake [1973] Director/Chief Executive Officer; Justin David Ellis [1974] Director; Richard William Lucas [1980] Director; Matthew Wood [1969] Director

TTC UK Holdings Limited
Incorporated: 4 May 2006
Net Worth: £12,449,000 *Total Assets:* £73,468,000
Registered Office: Units 2-4 Cunningham Court, Shadsworth Business Park, Blackburn, Lancs, BB1 2QX
Activities: Activities of production holding companies
Officers: Thierry Georges Yves Emile Amat [1960] Director/Chief Financial Officer [French/American]; Michael David Lawrence [1957] Director/Chief Executive Officer [American]; Luc Jozef Mechelaere [1961] Director/Executive Vice President [Belgian]

Tudorborne Limited
Incorporated: 3 February 1992 *Employees:* 96
Net Worth: £3,437,432 *Total Assets:* £8,229,193
Registered Office: 9 Coal Pit Lane, Atherton, Manchester, M46 0RY
Activities: Other specialised construction activities n.e.c.
Shareholder: Martin Neary
Officers: Nigel Philip Hooper, Secretary/Chartered Accountant; Martin Neary [1962] Director

Tullis Russell Coaters Limited
Incorporated: 8 June 1979 *Employees:* 94
Net Worth: £7,417,000 *Total Assets:* £11,065,000
Registered Office: Church Street, Bollington, Macclesfield, Cheshire, SK10 5QF
Activities: Manufacture of paper and paperboard
Parent: Tullis Russell Group Limited
Officers: Geoffrey Douglas Miller, Secretary; Frederick Alexander William Bowden [1947] Director; Julian Martyn Leek [1964] Finance Director; Geoffrey Douglas Miller [1962] Finance Director; Graeme David Milloy [1958] Managing Director; David Mark Roberts [1973] Operations Director; Hazel Jane Westwood [1976] Technology Director

Tuneside Limited
Incorporated: 11 November 1988 *Employees:* 15
Net Worth: £6,290,293 *Total Assets:* £7,630,562
Registered Office: Lace, Croxteth Drive, Sefton Park, Liverpool, L17 1AA
Activities: Construction of commercial buildings
Officers: John Paul McMahon, Secretary; The Right Reverend Peter Cookson [1939] Director/Roman Catholic Priest; Rev Sean Kirwin [1968] Director/RC Priest; Reverend Anthony O'Brien [1955] Director/Roman Catholic Priest

Turley Associates Ltd
Incorporated: 24 March 1988 *Employees:* 221
Net Worth: £7,217,036 *Total Assets:* £12,268,083
Registered Office: 1 New York Street, Manchester, M1 4HD
Activities: Urban planning and landscape architectural activities
Parent: Turley Employee Benefit Trust
Officers: Chrysta Mary Reid Poppitt, Secretary; Paul Gerard Deehan [1966] Director/Accountant; Chrysta Mary Reid Poppitt [1978] Director; David Jeffrey Trimingham [1965] Director/Town Planner

Turner Bianca PLC
Incorporated: 12 October 1949 *Employees:* 300
Net Worth: £28,314,868 *Total Assets:* £49,296,256
Registered Office: Bell Mill, Claremont Street, Hathershaw, Oldham, Lancs, OL8 3EJ
Activities: Wholesale of textiles
Major Shareholder: Jack Eddie Turner
Officers: Barbara Morrison, Secretary; Sharon Louise Batty [1973] Divisional Director; Joanne Ruth Bloomfield [1965] Director; Daniel Bullbrook [1978] Director; Richard Max Bullbrook [1953] Director; Paul John Fitzpatrick [1964] Director; Sophie Harrison [1973] Director; Leonard Pashley [1964] Director; Kevin Rutherford [1958] Director; Jack Eddie Turner [1944] Director; Luke Turner [1982] Director; Zelda Turner [1975] Director; Myles Keith Walmsley [1952] Director; James Wilson Young [1954] Director

John Turner Construction Group Ltd
Incorporated: 6 February 1989 *Employees:* 252
Net Worth: £8,072,749 *Total Assets:* £26,400,494
Registered Office: 2 Preston Road, Grimsargh, Preston, Lancs, PR2 5SD
Activities: Construction of commercial buildings
Shareholders: John Turner Group Limited; John Turner Group Limited
Officers: Michael Thomas Davies, Secretary; John Joseph Clarke [1954] Director; Pauline Mary Clarke [1958] Director [New Zealander]; Julian David Haigh [1966] Commercial Director; Nigel Andrew Sharp [1964] Director/Operations

John Turner Holdings Limited
Incorporated: 14 February 2007 *Employees:* 252
Net Worth: £5,571,489 *Total Assets:* £23,804,788
Registered Office: 2 Preston Road, Grimsargh, Preston, Lancs, PR2 5SD
Activities: Activities of head offices
Major Shareholder: John Joseph Clarke
Officers: Michael Thomas Davies, Secretary; John Joseph Clarke [1954] Director; Pauline Mary Clarke [1958] Director [New Zealander]

Turnstone Bidco 1 Limited
Incorporated: 18 January 2011
Net Worth: £214,012,000 *Total Assets:* £799,016,000
Registered Office: Europa House, Europa Trading Estate, Stoneclough Road, Kearsley, Manchester, M26 1GG
Activities: Activities of other holding companies n.e.c.
Parent: Turnstone Midco 2 Limited
Officers: Leo Damian Carroll, Secretary; Jean Michel Claude Bonnavion [1971] Director/Partner [French]; Andrew Richard Burgess [1964] Director/Investment Professional; Louis Goodman Elson [1962] Director/Managing Partner [American]; Karthic Jayaraman [1975] Director/Investment Professional; Tom Riall [1960] Director; Mohammed Omar Shafi Khan [1974] Director/Chief Financial Officer

Turnstone Equityco 1 Limited
Incorporated: 18 January 2011 *Employees:* 7,521
Net Worth Deficit: £422,372,992 *Total Assets:* £926,257,984
Registered Office: Europa House, Europa Trading Estate, Stoneclough Road, Kearsley, Manchester, M26 1GG
Activities: Activities of other holding companies n.e.c.
Officers: Leo Damian Carroll, Secretary; Jean Michel Claude Bonnavion [1971] Director/Partner [French]; Alan John Bowkett [1951] Director; Andrew Richard Burgess [1964] Director/Investment Professional; Barry Michael Cockcroft [1950] Director; Louis Goodman Elson [1962] Director/Managing Partner [American]; Karthic Jayaraman [1975] Director/Investment Professional; Tom Riall [1960] Director; Mohammed Omar Shafi Khan [1974] Director/Chief Financial Officer

Turnstone Midco 1 Limited
Incorporated: 18 January 2011
Net Worth Deficit: £225,286,000 *Total Assets:* £410,982,016
Registered Office: Europa House, Europa Trading Estate, Stoneclough Road, Kearsley, Manchester, M26 1GG
Activities: Activities of other holding companies n.e.c.
Parent: ADP Primary Care Acquisitions Limited
Officers: Leo Damian Carroll, Secretary; Jean Michel Claude Bonnavion [1971] Director/Partner [French]; Andrew Richard Burgess [1964] Director/Investment Professional; Louis Goodman Elson [1962] Director/Managing Partner [American]; Karthic Jayaraman [1975] Director/Investment Professional; Tom Riall [1960] Director; Mohammed Omar Shafi Khan [1974] Director/Chief Financial Officer

Turnstone Midco 2 Limited
Incorporated: 18 January 2011 *Employees:* 7,521
Net Worth: £210,128,992 *Total Assets:* £926,113,984
Registered Office: Europa House, Europa Trading Estate, Stoneclough Road, Kearsley, Manchester, M26 1GG
Activities: Activities of other holding companies n.e.c.
Parent: Turnstone Midco 1 Limited
Officers: Leo Damian Carroll, Secretary; Jean Michel Claude Bonnavion [1971] Director/Partner [French]; Andrew Richard Burgess [1964] Director/Investment Professional; Louis Goodman Elson [1962] Director/Managing Partner [American]; Karthic Jayaraman [1975] Director/Investment Professional; Tom Riall [1960] Director; Mohammed Omar Shafi Khan [1974] Director/Chief Financial Officer

Tustin Developments Limited
Incorporated: 11 March 1985 *Employees:* 21
Net Worth: £33,528,836 *Total Assets:* £53,613,432
Registered Office: Tustin House, Red Scar Business Park, Longridge Road, Preston, Lancs, PR2 5NE
Activities: Development of building projects
Shareholder: Gholam Hossein Ghiassi
Officers: John Andrew Roberts, Secretary; Zarrine Kate Dye [1978] Director/Accountant; Alinaghi Ghiassi [1967] Director/Attorney [American]; Gholam Hossein Ghiassi [1946] Director [Iranian]; Selina Mary Ghiassi [1949] Director; Seema Louise Ghiassi Kennedy [1974] Director/Solicitor; John Andrew Roberts [1961] Managing Director

TVS Logistics Investment UK Limited
Incorporated: 28 August 2009 *Employees:* 2,014
Net Worth: £23,099,000 *Total Assets:* £160,567,008
Registered Office: Logistics House, Buckshaw Avenue, Chorley, Lancs, PR6 7AJ
Activities: Activities of other holding companies n.e.c.
Officers: Paul John Roberts, Secretary; Arun Jayaraman [1971] Director [Indian]; Dinesh Ramachandran [1965] Director [Indian]; Paul John Roberts [1968] Director/Chartered Accountant; Ravichandran Sargunaraj [1955] Director [Indian]

TVS Supply Chain Solutions Limited
Incorporated: 21 September 1992 *Employees:* 550
Net Worth: £26,147,000 *Total Assets:* £69,554,000
Registered Office: Logistics House, Buckshaw Avenue, Chorley, Lancs, PR6 7AJ
Activities: Wholesale trade of motor vehicle parts and accessories
Parent: TVS Logistics Investment UK Ltd
Officers: Paul John Roberts, Secretary/Accountant; Andrew John Jones [1961] Managing Director; Dinesh Ramachandran [1965] Director [Indian]; Paul John Roberts [1968] Director/Chartered Accountant; Ravichandran Sargunaraj [1955] Director [Indian]

Robert Tweddle (Timber Merchant and Haulage Contractor) Limited
Incorporated: 13 October 2000 *Employees:* 16
Net Worth: £2,956,772 *Total Assets:* £8,546,419
Registered Office: 131 Kingstown Road, Carlisle, Cumbria, CA3 0AS
Activities: Freight transport by road
Shareholders: Susan Helen Tweddle; John Robert James Tweddle
Officers: Louise Dewhirst, Secretary; Louise Helen Dewhirst [1971] Director; Daniel Robert Tweddle [1984] Director; John Robert James Tweddle [1945] Director; Susan Helen Tweddle [1951] Director

TWP (Newco) 151 Limited
Incorporated: 16 July 1997 *Employees:* 113
Net Worth: £6,722,313 *Total Assets:* £13,243,121
Registered Office: Leacroft Road, Birchwood, Warrington, Cheshire, WA3 6PJ
Activities: Manufacture of lifting and handling equipment
Parent: Terberg Rosroca Group Limited
Officers: Andrew Peter Uttley, Secretary; Robert David Colby [1970] Director; Timothy James Conlon [1966] Director; William Marzano [1965] Director; Godefridus Terberg [1963] Director [Dutch]

TXM Plant Limited
Incorporated: 14 November 2011 *Employees:* 310
Net Worth: £11,971,736 *Total Assets:* £47,548,716
Registered Office: Park Lane Industrial Estates, Park Lane, off Wigan Road, Ashton in Makerfield, Wigan, Lancs, WN4 0BZ
Activities: Renting and leasing of construction and civil engineering machinery and equipment
Parent: Equipment and Track Solutions Limited
Officers: Robert Killen [1970] Director; Brian Reynolds [1971] Director/Accountant; Gareth Winfield Richardson [1966] Director

Tyco Fire & Integrated Solutions (UK) Limited
Incorporated: 3 October 1985 *Employees:* 901
Net Worth: £66,717,000 *Total Assets:* £247,256,000
Registered Office: Tyco Park, Grimshaw Lane, Newton Heath, Manchester, M40 2WL
Activities: Other service activities n.e.c.
Parent: Wormald Holdings (UK) Limited
Officers: Mark Ayre [1963] Finance Director; Deryk William Bull [1959] Financial Director; James Paul Earnshaw [1976] Finance Director; Andrew John Ellis [1961] Director; Richard Hilton Jones [1964] Director; Moosa Farook Meah [1965] Director; Peter Schieser [1967] Director [German]

Tyco Holdings (U.K.) Limited
Incorporated: 23 May 1990
Net Worth Deficit: £518,113,984 *Total Assets:* £1,044,465,024
Registered Office: Eversheds House, 70 Great Bridgewater Street, Manchester, M1 5ES
Activities: Activities of head offices
Parent: Johnson Controls International PLC
Officers: Rosalind Hilary Ben Shabat, Secretary; Mark Ayre [1963] Finance Director; Peter Schieser [1967] Director [German]

Tygavac Advanced Materials Ltd
Incorporated: 31 January 1996 *Employees:* 67
Net Worth: £33,287,984 *Total Assets:* £37,657,548
Registered Office: The Causeway, Oldham Broadway Business Park, Chadderton, Oldham, Lancs, OL9 9XD
Activities: Manufacture of other plastic products
Parent: Airtech International Inc
Officers: Alan Nixen, Secretary; Joy Carter [1963] Director [American]; Jeffrey L Dahlgren [1959] Director/Company President/CEO [American]; William R Dahlgren [1933] Director/Chairman Chief Executive Officer [American]

Typhoo Tea Limited
Incorporated: 26 September 2005 *Employees:* 287
Net Worth: £40,340,000 *Total Assets:* £130,280,000
Registered Office: Pasture Road, Moreton, Wirral, Merseyside, CH46 8XF
Activities: Tea processing
Parent: Apeejay Tea
Officers: Somnath Saha, Secretary; Nadeem Ahmed [1955] Director/Business [Indian]; Ashoke Ghosh [1956] Director/Service [Indian]; Dr. Alain Arnold Gloor [1950] Director/Lawyer [Swiss]; Issam Hamid [1975] Director; Michael David McBrien [1964] Director/Accountant; Karan Paul [1969] Director/Industrialist [Indian]; Priti Paul [1967] Director/Architect; Somnath Saha [1970] Director/Service; Maria Tapal [1979] Director [Canadian]; Ian Vyner [1937] Director; Andrew David Woodhouse [1965] Director/Chartered Accountant

Tytherington School
Incorporated: 3 March 2014 *Employees:* 109
Net Worth: £13,215,000 *Total Assets:* £15,369,000
Registered Office: Tytherington School, Manchester Road, Macclesfield, Cheshire, SK10 2EE
Activities: General secondary education
Officers: Stephen Acreman [1968] Director/Teacher; Sarah Bird [1968] Director; Emmanuel Botwe [1981] Director/Headteacher; Adam Brown [1983] Director/Teacher; Michael Charles Simon Brown [1962] Director; Jason Peter Gaunt [1987] Director; Kenneth George Gilliver [1947] Director/Retired Senior Civil Servant; Lynne Roose Jones [1959] Director; Dr David Dermot Patrick Laffan [1962] Director/Manager; Charlotte Victoria Jean Lock [1972] Director/Lead Strategist; Derek Alan Ogden [1960] Director/Chartered Certified Accountant; Dr Simon Christopher Preston [1964] Director; Dr Peter Brian Simpson [1968] Director/Science Manager; Jane Louise Stairmand [1979] Director/Transformation Programme Manager; Jane Stephens [1965] Director/Management Consultant; David Thomas Sussex [1953] Director

Tzortzis Limited
Incorporated: 27 November 2013
Net Worth: £1,081,765 *Total Assets:* £8,417,787
Registered Office: Kemple Barn, Whalley Road, Pendleton, Clitheroe, Lancs, BB7 1PP
Activities: Activities of investment trusts
Shareholders: Dieno George; Gill George
Officers: Dieno George [1956] Director; Gillian George [1959] Director

U F C Fund Management PLC
Incorporated: 29 May 1997 *Employees:* 140
Net Worth: £38,324,344 *Total Assets:* £100,292,088
Registered Office: Marlborough House, 59 Chorley New Road, Bolton, Lancs, BL1 4QP
Activities: Activities of financial services holding companies
Major Shareholder: Andrew Staley
Officers: Bernard John Leyland, Secretary; Nicholas Francis John Cooling [1964] Director; John Richard Heap [1948] Director; Bernard John Leyland [1940] Director/Chartered Accountant; Keith Ounsworth [1950] Director; Andrew Staley [1955] Managing Director

UAP Limited
Incorporated: 29 December 2000 *Employees:* 44
Net Worth: £6,340,245 *Total Assets:* £7,400,897
Registered Office: Unit 1 Block 5, Albert Close Trading Estate, Whitefield, Manchester, M45 8EH
Activities: Wholesale of household goods (other than musical instruments) n.e.c
Parent: Project Orlando Limited
Officers: Wendy Lynn Rushton, Secretary/Director; Barry Matthew Halpin [1979] Sales Director [Irish]; David Leslie Jennings [1960] Director; Mark Andrew Rushton [1976] Quality and Certification Director; Wendy Lynn Rushton [1976] Director

UBH International Limited
Incorporated: 29 March 1999 *Employees:* 74
Net Worth: £4,699,102 *Total Assets:* £6,715,416
Registered Office: Orrell Lane, Burscough, Ormskirk, Lancs, L40 0SL
Activities: Manufacture of other tanks, reservoirs and containers of metal
Parent: Baxi Partnership Limited
Officers: Malcolm John Lynch, Secretary/Solicitor; Karl Bragg [1968] Director/Accountant; Derek Thomas Doyle [1956] Director/Fitter/Welder; Allan John Goodbrand [1955] Director; Patrick Thomas Harding [1956] Sales Director; Christopher Roy Horrocks [1960] Director/Buying/Planning Engineer; John Isherwood [1955] Director/Skilled Operative; Alex McGonagle [1974] Engineering Director; Stewart Anthony Wiltshire [1969] Managing Director

UCFB College of Football Business Limited
Incorporated: 15 November 2010 *Employees:* 2
Net Worth: £1,304,248 *Total Assets:* £11,425,260
Registered Office: National Squash Centre, Rowsley Street, Manchester, M11 3FF
Activities: Other education n.e.c.
Parent: UCFB Holdings Limited
Officers: John William Banaszkiewicz [1962] Managing Director; Paul John Fletcher [1951] Director/Chief Executive and Consultant; Brendan Flood [1961] Director

UD-RD Holding Company Limited
Incorporated: 12 December 1997
Net Worth: £273,974,016 *Total Assets:* £384,497,984
Registered Office: Ocean House, Towers Business Park, Wilmslow Road, Didsbury, Manchester, M20 2LY
Activities: Other business support service activities n.e.c.
Parent: SPX Flow, Inc.
Officers: Paul Andrew Cahill [1974] Director/Accountant; Jeremy Wade Smeltser [1975] Director/CFO, SPX Flow, Inc. [American]; Stephen Tsoris [1957] Director [American]

UDP Group Limited
Incorporated: 29 July 2016 *Employees:* 38
Net Worth: £1,689,990 *Total Assets:* £9,653,810
Registered Office: UDP Group, Astor Road, Salford, M50 1BB
Activities: Activities of construction holding companies
Parent: Foresight Fund Managers Limited
Officers: Claire Alvarez [1981] Investor Director; David Atherton [1965] Director; Noel Thomas Gallagher [1956] Director; David John Hilton [1959] Director

UFP (UK) Limited
Incorporated: 12 January 1994 *Employees:* 84
Net Worth: £20,147,660 *Total Assets:* £44,503,432
Registered Office: Enterprise House, Roydsdale Way, Euroway Trading Estate, Bradford, W Yorks, BD4 6SE
Activities: Wholesale of computers, computer peripheral equipment and software
Parent: UFP International SA
Officers: Nicholas Charles Stokes, Secretary; Sajad Arshad [1970] Director/Computer Supplies Dealer; Charles Zarka [1956] Director/Dealer in Computer Accessories [French]

UK Asset Resolution Limited
Incorporated: 1 July 2010 *Employees:* 175
Net Worth: £8,531,800,064 *Total Assets:* £19,812,999,168
Registered Office: Croft Road, Crossflatts, Bingley, W Yorks, BD16 2UA
Activities: Activities of head offices
Parent: Her Majesty's Treasury
Officers: John Gornall, Secretary; Ian John Hares [1958] Finance & Investment Director; Susan Carol Langley [1963] Non-Executive Director; Brendan Paul McDonagh [1958] Director [Irish]; Keith Charles William Morgan [1963] Director; Brendan John Russell [1961] Director; John Hartley Tattersall [1952] Director; Holger Randolph Vieten [1969] Director/Head of Banking and Capital Markets [German]

UK Biobank Limited
Incorporated: 28 November 2003 *Employees:* 136
Net Worth: £15,187,290 *Total Assets:* £20,438,514
Registered Office: Units 1 & 2 Spectrum Way, Adswood, Stockport, Cheshire, SK3 0SA
Activities: Other research and experimental development on natural sciences and engineering
Officers: Jonathan Michael Holmes Sellors, Secretary; Professor Martin Bobrow [1938] Director/Retired; Professor Ruth Elisabeth Gilbert [1958] Director/Professor of Clinical Epidemiology; Professor Andrew Hattersley [1958] Director/Medical Researcher; Sir Alexander Fred Markham [1950] Director/Physician, Professor of Medicine; Sara Elizabeth Farha Marshall [1962] Director/Doctor; Dr Joseph McNamara [1958] Director/Research Manager; Professor William Ollier [1952] Director/Professor; Sir Michael Rawlins [1941] Director; Jonathan Edward Simon Tross [1949] Director/Chair IPCC Audit and Risk Committee

UK Fuels Limited
Incorporated: 20 January 1988 *Employees:* 646
Net Worth: £67,769,000 *Total Assets:* £250,243,008
Registered Office: Eurocard Centre, Herald Park, Herald Drive, Crewe, Cheshire, CW1 6EG
Activities: Wholesale of other fuels and related products
Major Shareholder: William Stanley Holmes
Officers: Adrian Stuart Rushton, Secretary; Lisa Jayne Broad [1972] Director/Certified Chartered Accountant; Lee John Everett [1974] Director; William Stanley Holmes [1964] Director

UK Pharma Impex Limited
Incorporated: 28 March 2013 *Employees:* 5
Net Worth: £120,845 *Total Assets:* £24,679,384
Registered Office: Office Suite 131, Hexagon Tower, Crumpsall Vale, Manchester, M9 8GQ
Activities: Wholesale of pharmaceutical goods
Major Shareholder: Michael Thomas Gordon
Officers: Mark Vivian Law [1965] Director/Accountant

UK Platforms Ltd
Incorporated: 15 February 2000 *Employees:* 119
Net Worth: £19,580,000 *Total Assets:* £37,753,000
Registered Office: Oakland House, 76 Talbot Road, Old Trafford, Manchester, M16 0PQ
Activities: Renting and leasing of other machinery, equipment and tangible goods n.e.c.
Parent: HSS Hire Service Group Limited
Officers: Daniel James Joll, Secretary; Stephen Ashmore [1964] Director; Paul David Quested [1970] Financial Director

UK Wood Recycling Limited
Incorporated: 11 November 2005 *Employees:* 46
Net Worth: £5,125,394 *Total Assets:* £13,309,283
Registered Office: Lumm Farm, Littlemoss, Droylsden, Manchester, M43 7LB
Activities: Recovery of sorted materials
Parent: G I Hadfield & Son Limited
Officers: Paul Darren Harrison, Secretary; Geoffrey Isaac Louis Hadfield [1955] Managing Director; Paul Darren Harrison [1968] Director; Victoria Ann Hughes [1969] Director

UK-2 Limited
Incorporated: 22 April 1998 *Employees:* 164
Net Worth: £8,700,967 *Total Assets:* £26,849,358
Registered Office: 5th Floor, Voyager House, Chicago Avenue, Manchester Airport, Manchester, M90 3DQ
Activities: Other information technology service activities
Parent: The Hut IHC Limited
Officers: James Patrick Pochin, Secretary; John Andrew Gallemore [1969] Director

UK2M Limited
Incorporated: 14 October 2016 *Employees:* 1
Net Worth: £3,619,239 *Total Assets:* £12,790,317
Registered Office: 3rd Floor, 1 Ashley Road, Altrincham, Cheshire, WA14 2DT
Activities: Wholesale of clothing and footwear
Major Shareholder: Franck Thomas Dupuis
Officers: Franck Thomas Dupuis [1973] Director [French]

UKapital Limited
Incorporated: 1 December 2015
Net Worth Deficit: £211,444 *Total Assets:* £23,398,098
Registered Office: 7th Floor, Station House, Stamford New Road, Altrincham, Cheshire, WA14 1EP
Activities: Financial intermediation not elsewhere classified
Major Shareholder: David Goldin
Officers: David Goldin [1971] Director [American]

UKFast Properties Limited
Incorporated: 22 October 2015 *Employees:* 10
Net Worth Deficit: £520,176 *Total Assets:* £7,359,741
Registered Office: UKFast Campus, Birley Fields, Manchester, M15 5QJ
Activities: Other building completion and finishing
Shareholders: Gail Suzanne Jones; Lawrence Nigel Jones
Officers: Nicola Lindsay Frost, Secretary; Gail Suzanne Jones [1977] Director; Lawrence Nigel Jones [1968] Director

UKFast.Net Limited
Incorporated: 21 September 1999 *Employees:* 269
Net Worth: £11,619,655 *Total Assets:* £46,891,560
Registered Office: UKFast Campus, Birley Fields, Manchester, M15 5QJ
Activities: Data processing, hosting and related activities
Shareholders: Lawrence Nigel Jones; Gail Suzanne Jones
Officers: Nicola Lindsay Frost, Secretary; Charlotte Marie Bentley-Crane [1987] Director of Account Management; Jonathan Bowers [1975] Communications Director; Catherine Laura Jane Greening [1971] Director; Gail Suzanne Jones [1977] Commercial Director; Lawrence Nigel Jones [1968] Director/Internet Service Provider; Neil Lathwood [1979] Technical Director; Kristina McGuirk [1987] Marketing Director; William Howard Pullman [1994] Sales Director; Joseph Donald Ryland [1986] Finance Director; Darren John Taylor [1979] Director of Research and Development

UKSV Holdings Company Ltd.
Incorporated: 1 October 2010 *Employees:* 744
Net Worth: £105,793,000 *Total Assets:* £535,091,008
Registered Office: Anfield Road, Liverpool, L4 0TH
Activities: Activities of other holding companies n.e.c.
Shareholder: John Henry
Officers: Edward J Weiss, Secretary; Gregory Edward Morris [1968] Director/Senior Vice President - Finance [American]; Edward J Weiss [1966] Director/General Counsel [American]

Ulixes Limited
Incorporated: 14 September 2007
Net Worth: £164,220,992 *Total Assets:* £252,019,008
Registered Office: Aquarius House, 6 Mid Point Business Park, Thornbury, Bradford, BD3 7AY
Activities: Activities of head offices
Parent: Univar Inc
Officers: Paul Graham Bryant [1973] Director; Jeffrey William Carr [1956] Director/Global Counsel [American]; Sabine Duyfjes [1972] Director/VP & General Counsel EMEA [German]

Ultima Acquisition GB Limited
Incorporated: 23 October 2012 *Employees:* 2
Net Worth: £56,723,000 *Total Assets:* £158,034,000
Registered Office: Mars Street, Oldham, Lancs, OL9 6LY
Activities: Financial intermediation not elsewhere classified
Parent: Ultima Holding Limited
Officers: Patrick Mathieu [1960] Managing Director [French]; Dr Max Padberg [1965] Director [German]

Ultium Business Outsourcing Group Limited
Incorporated: 14 July 2016 *Employees:* 3,437
Net Worth Deficit: £28,041,386 *Total Assets:* £154,131,056
Registered Office: Booths Park, 1 Chelford Road, Knutsford, Cheshire, WA16 8GS
Activities: Dormant company
Parent: Patron (BC) Bidco Limited
Officers: Sam Richard Del Mar [1974] Director; Frederick Karl Minturn [1956] Director [American]; Andrew David Preston [1975] Director

Ultra Finance Limited
Incorporated: 23 October 1967
Net Worth: £2,475,000 *Total Assets:* £8,189,000
Registered Office: Gateway House, Styal Road, Manchester, M22 5WY
Activities: Other business support service activities n.e.c.
Parent: Amplifon United Kingdom Limited
Officers: Vicki Clare Milton, Secretary; Giuseppe Manzo [1973] Market Director [Italian]; Vicki Clare Milton [1984] Director

Ultraframe (UK) Limited
Incorporated: 31 October 1983 *Employees:* 357
Net Worth: £27,994,000 *Total Assets:* £40,735,000
Registered Office: Enterprise Works, Salthill Road, Clitheroe, Lancs, BB7 1PE
Activities: Other manufacturing n.e.c.
Shareholders: Latium Roofing Systems Limited; Brian George Kennedy
Officers: Andrew Jonathan Crowe [1971] Operations Director; Julian Slade [1966] Managing Director; Andrew Walter McRae Thomson [1968] Director

Underground Mining Services Limited
Incorporated: 28 January 2015
Net Worth Deficit: £4,187,188 *Total Assets:* £57,899,552
Registered Office: 3rd Floor, 1 Ashley Road, Altrincham, Cheshire, WA14 2DT
Activities: Mining of other non-ferrous metal ores
Major Shareholder: Josephine Haller
Officers: Alexander Zachary Haller [1979] Director; Robin Zachary Haller [1979] Director

Underley Schools Limited
Incorporated: 26 August 1999 *Employees:* 163
Net Worth: £4,213,949 *Total Assets:* £7,613,648
Registered Office: 1 Merchant's Place, River Street, Bolton, Lancs, BL2 1BX
Activities: General secondary education
Parent: Acorn Care and Education Limited
Officers: Helen Elizabeth Lecky, Secretary; Ryan David Edwards [1977] Finance Director; Jean-Luc Emmanuel Janet [1970] Director [French]; David Jon Leatherbarrow [1969] Director/Group Chief Executive Officer

Ungerer Limited
Incorporated: 29 May 1959 *Employees:* 138
Net Worth: £29,897,000 *Total Assets:* £35,211,000
Registered Office: Sealand Road, Chester, CH1 4LP
Activities: Manufacture of other food products n.e.c.
Officers: John Graham Percy, Secretary/Director; John Graham Percy [1960] Director; Kenneth Garretson Voorhees III [1963] Sales Director [American]; Kenneth Garretson Voorhees Jr [1938] Director/President Ungerer & Company [American]

Unifrax Emission Control Europe Ltd
Incorporated: 16 January 1986 *Employees:* 145
Net Worth Deficit: £6,920,570 *Total Assets:* £19,095,490
Registered Office: Mill Lane, Rainford, St Helens, Merseyside, WA11 8LP
Activities: Other manufacturing n.e.c.
Officers: John Charles Dandolph IV [1976] Director/Chief Financial Officer [American]; Anthony Bret Greene [1959] Director/Accountant [American]; Daniel Thomas Liebel [1963] Finance Director [American]; Edward Duncan Barton Yardley [1959] Director/Senior Vice-President

Unifrax Europe Holdings Limited
Incorporated: 19 August 2003
Net Worth: £56,461,764 *Total Assets:* £141,992,560
Registered Office: Mill Lane, Rainford, St Helens, Merseyside, WA11 8LP
Activities: Activities of head offices
Officers: John Michael Tupman, Secretary; Vincent Chambon [1970] Director/Accountant [French]; John Charles Dandolph IV [1976] Director/Chief Financial Officer [American]; Anthony Bret Greene [1959] Director/Accountant [American]; Edward Duncan Barton Yardley [1959] Managing Director

Unifrax Limited
Incorporated: 2 June 2000 *Employees:* 133
Net Worth: £61,181,280 *Total Assets:* £154,347,600
Registered Office: Mill Lane, Rainford, St Helens, Merseyside, WA11 8LP
Activities: Manufacture of refractory products
Officers: John Michael Tupman, Secretary; Vincent Chambon [1970] Director/Accountant [French]; John Charles Dandolph IV [1976] Director/Chief Financial Officer [American]; Anthony Bret Greene [1959] Director/Accountant [American]; John Michael Tupman [1957] Finance Director; Edward Duncan Barton Yardley [1959] Director

Unifrax UK Holdco Limited
Incorporated: 7 August 2000
Net Worth: £5,894,056 *Total Assets:* £10,814,751
Registered Office: Mill Lane, Rainford, St Helens, Merseyside, WA11 8LP
Activities: Activities of head offices
Officers: John Michael Tupman, Secretary; Vincent Chambon [1970] Director/Accountant [French]; John Charles Dandolph IV [1976] Director/Chief Financial Officer [American]; Anthony Bret Greene [1959] Director/Accountant [American]; Edward Duncan Barton Yardley [1959] Director

Unilever PLC
Incorporated: 21 June 1894 *Employees:* 165
Net Worth: £11,920,755,712 *Total Assets:* £52,728,942,592
Registered Office: Port Sunlight, Wirral, Merseyside, CH62 4ZD
Activities: Activities of head offices
Officers: Ritva Sotamaa, Secretary; Nils Smedegaard Andersen [1958] Director [Danish]; Laura May Lung Cha [1949] Director/Deputy Chairman HSBC Asia Pacific [Chinese]; Vittorio Colao [1961] Director/CEO Vodafone Group PLC [Italian]; Dr. Marinus Emmanuel Johannes Dekkers [1957] Director [Dutch/American]; Dr Judith Hartmann [1969] Director [Austrian]; Andrea Jung [1958] Director [Canadian]; Mary Ma [1952] Director/Chairman Boyu Capital [Chinese]; Strive Masiyiwa [1961] Director [Zimbabwean]; Youngme Moon [1964] Director [American]; Graeme David Pitkethly [1966] Director/Chartered Accountant; Paulus Geradus Josephus Maria Polman [1956] Director/Chief Executive [Dutch]; John Rishton [1958] Director/CEO Rolls-Royce; Feike Sijbesma [1959] Director/CEO Royal DSM NV Netherlands [Dutch]

Union Colours Limited
Incorporated: 9 October 2003 *Employees:* 24
Net Worth Deficit: £3,011,426 *Total Assets:* £11,279,744
Registered Office: Union House, Hempshaw Lane, Stockport, Cheshire, SK1 4LG
Activities: Wholesale of chemical products
Parent: Czna Group
Officers: Bo Zhu, Secretary; Phillip Ian Myles [1968] Operations Director; Hongbo Rui [1970] Director [Chinese]; Bo Zhu [1974] Director/Company Secretary

The Union Discount Company of London Limited
Incorporated: 20 February 2002
Net Worth: £5,894,151 *Total Assets:* £10,767,850
Registered Office: Old Mills, off Whitehall Grove, Drighlington, Bradford, W Yorks, BD11 1BY
Activities: Activities of head offices
Officers: Kathryn Anne Davenport, Secretary; Peter Jan Patrik Valentin Gyllenhammar [1953] Director [Swedish]

Uniroyal Global (Europe) Limited
Incorporated: 29 June 2012 *Employees:* 219
Net Worth: £6,237,000 *Total Assets:* £19,801,000
Registered Office: West Craven Business Park, West Craven Drive, Earby, Lancs, BB18 6JZ
Activities: Activities of head offices
Officers: Oliver Janney, Secretary; Bernard Arthur Wagner, Secretary; Howard Francis Curd [1964] Director [American]; Howard Roger Curd [1939] Director [American]; Bernard Arthur Wagner [1948] Finance Director [American]

Uniroyal Global Limited
Incorporated: 25 March 2003 *Employees:* 219
Net Worth: £10,724,000 *Total Assets:* £27,193,000
Registered Office: West Craven Business Park, West Craven Drive, Earby, Lancs, BB18 6JZ
Activities: Manufacture of other plastic products
Parent: Wardle Storeys (Group) Limited
Officers: Oliver James Janney, Secretary; Bernard Arthur Wagner, Secretary; Howard Francis Curd [1964] Director [American]; Howard Roger Curd [1939] Director [American]; Edmund Creighton King [1935] Director/Financial Adviser [American]; George Sanchez [1954] Director [American]; Bernard Arthur Wagner [1948] Finance Director [American]

United Reformed Church (North Western Province) Trust Limited (The)
Incorporated: 29 June 1981 *Employees:* 4
Net Worth: £7,437,655 *Total Assets:* £7,904,109
Registered Office: Franklin Street, Patricroft, Eccles, Manchester, M30 0QZ
Activities: Activities of religious organisations
Officers: Reverend Brian Stephen Jolly, Secretary; Revd Michael Aspinal [1954] Director/Chartered Engineer; Neil Anthony Carter [1954] Director/Retired; Michael Thomas Hart [1963] Director/Management Consultant; Reverend Brian Stephen Jolly [1956] Director/Minister of Religion; Philip Frederick Jones [1952] Director/Retired; Reverend Nicholas Richard Brook Mark [1952] Director/Minister of Religion; Reverend Andrew Christopher Mills [1962] Director/Minister of Religion; Jean Claire Mullineux [1958] Director/Retired; Pamela Ward [1946] Director/Retired

United Springs Limited
Incorporated: 28 September 2000 *Employees:* 75
Net Worth: £5,701,596 *Total Assets:* £6,895,573
Registered Office: Mandale Park, Norman Road, Rochdale, Lancs, OL11 4HP
Activities: Manufacture of wire products, chain and springs
Parent: Sogefi S.P.A.
Officers: Jade Jean Law, Secretary; Franck Mauchand [1971] Director/Financial Officer [French]; Brian Pickford [1970] Director/General Manager

United Utilities Group PLC
Incorporated: 8 April 2008 *Employees:* 5,223
Net Worth: £2,950,899,968 *Total Assets:* £13,003,499,520
Registered Office: Haweswater House, Lingley Mere Business Park, Lingley Green Avenue, Great Sankey, Warrington, Cheshire, WA5 3LP
Activities: Activities of head offices
Officers: Simon Roger Gardiner, Secretary; Lord Stephen Andrew Carter [1964] Director; Mark Sydney Clare [1957] Director; Steven Richard Fraser [1975] Managing Director; Alison Jane Patricia Goligher [1965] Director; John Russell Houlden [1959] Director/Chief Financial Officer; Brian Michael May [1964] Director; Dr John David Gibson McAdam [1948] Director; Steven Lewis Mogford [1956] Director; Paulette Georgina Rowe [1966] Director; Sara Vivienne Weller [1961] Director

United Utilities International Limited
Incorporated: 7 February 1989
Net Worth: £19,158,000 *Total Assets:* £139,886,000
Registered Office: Haweswater House, Lingley Mere Business Park, Lingley Green Avenue, Great Sankey, Warrington, Cheshire, WA5 3LP
Activities: Water collection treatment and supply
Parent: United Utilities PLC
Officers: Gary Lee Baron [1981] Director/Chartered Accountant; Steven Richard Fraser [1975] Managing Director; Simon Roger Gardiner [1967] Director/Solicitor; Martin Anthony Gee [1977] Director/Chartered Accountant

United Utilities North West Limited
Incorporated: 23 January 2001 *Employees:* 3
Net Worth: £3,796,900,096 *Total Assets:* £4,409,399,808
Registered Office: Haweswater House, Lingley Mere Business Park, Lingley Green Avenue, Great Sankey, Warrington, Cheshire, WA5 3LP
Activities: Activities of head offices
Parent: United Utilities PLC
Officers: Simon Roger Gardiner, Secretary; Philip Anthony Aspin [1968] Director/Chartered Accountant; John Russell Houlden [1959] Director/Chief Financial Officer; Steven Lewis Mogford [1956] Director

United Utilities PLC
Incorporated: 1 April 1989 *Employees:* 5,223
Net Worth: £4,578,899,968 *Total Assets:* £14,702,900,224
Registered Office: Haweswater House, Lingley Mere Business Park, Lingley Green Avenue, Great Sankey, Warrington, Cheshire, WA5 3LP
Activities: Activities of head offices
Parent: United Utilities Group PLC
Officers: Simon Roger Gardiner, Secretary; Philip Anthony Aspin [1968] Director/Chartered Accountant; Steven Richard Fraser [1975] Managing Director; John Russell Houlden [1959] Director/Chief Financial Officer; Steven Lewis Mogford [1956] Director

United Utilities Property Services Limited
Incorporated: 4 May 1989
Net Worth: £20,043,000 *Total Assets:* £27,195,000
Registered Office: Haweswater House, Lingley Mere Business Park, Lingley Green Avenue, Great Sankey, Warrington, Cheshire, WA5 3LP
Activities: Buying and selling of own real estate
Parent: United Utilities PLC
Officers: Paula Marie Steer [1970] Director/Commercial Property Manager; Sian Taylor [1980] Director; Jason Robin Michael Uttley [1970] Director

United Utilities Utility Solutions (Industrial) Limited
Incorporated: 24 April 2001 *Employees:* 5
Net Worth: £8,913,000 *Total Assets:* £12,935,000
Registered Office: Haweswater House, Lingley Mere Business Park, Lingley Green Avenue, Great Sankey, Warrington, Cheshire, WA5 3LP
Activities: Other business support service activities n.e.c.
Parent: United Utilities PLC
Officers: Gary Lee Baron [1981] Director/Chartered Accountant; Simon Roger Gardiner [1967] Director/Solicitor; Martin Anthony Gee [1977] Director/Chartered Accountant; David Mark Hannon [1976] Director/Solicitor

United Utilities Utility Solutions Holdings Limited
Incorporated: 13 August 2007
Net Worth: £236,374,352 *Total Assets:* £237,597,680
Registered Office: Haweswater House, Lingley Mere Business Park, Lingley Green Avenue, Great Sankey, Warrington, Cheshire, WA5 3LP
Activities: Activities of head offices
Parent: United Utilities PLC
Officers: Gary Lee Baron [1981] Director/Chartered Accountant; Martin Anthony Gee [1977] Director/Chartered Accountant; David Mark Hannon [1976] Director/Solicitor

United Utilities Water Finance PLC
Incorporated: 19 September 2014
Net Worth: £173,000 *Total Assets:* £1,034,168,000
Registered Office: Haweswater House, Lingley Mere Business Park, Lingley Green Avenue, Great Sankey, Warrington, Cheshire, WA5 3LP
Activities: Activities of head offices
Parent: United Utilities Water Limited
Officers: Philip Anthony Aspin [1968] Director/Chartered Accountant; Simon Roger Gardiner [1967] Director/Solicitor; John Russell Houlden [1959] Director/Chief Financial Officer; Brendan Francis Murphy [1970] Director/Finance/Treasury Manager

United Utilities Water Limited
Incorporated: 1 April 1989 *Employees:* 4,964
Net Worth: £2,397,600,000 *Total Assets:* £12,622,799,872
Registered Office: Haweswater House, Lingley Mere Business Park, Lingley Green Avenue, Great Sankey, Warrington, Cheshire, WA5 3LP
Activities: Water collection, treatment and supply
Parent: United Utilities North West Limited
Officers: Simon Roger Gardiner, Secretary; Lord Stephen Andrew Carter [1964] Director; Mark Sydney Clare [1957] Director; Steven Richard Fraser [1975] Managing Director; Alison Jane Patricia Goligher [1965] Director; John Russell Houlden [1959] Director/Chief Financial Officer; Brian Michael May [1964] Director; Dr John David Gibson McAdam [1948] Director; Steven Lewis Mogford [1956] Director; Paulette Georgina Rowe [1966] Director; Sara Vivienne Weller [1961] Director

United Utilities Water Operations Holdings Limited
Incorporated: 10 August 2007
Net Worth Deficit: £36,096,848 *Total Assets:* £60,428,944
Registered Office: Haweswater House, Lingley Mere Business Park, Lingley Green Avenue, Great Sankey, Warrington, Cheshire, WA5 3LP
Activities: Activities of head offices
Parent: United Utilities Utility Solutions Holdings Limited
Officers: Gary Lee Baron [1981] Director/Chartered Accountant; Simon Roger Gardiner [1967] Director/Solicitor; Martin Anthony Gee [1977] Director/Chartered Accountant

Unity Homes Limited
Incorporated: 8 November 1990 *Employees:* 273
Net Worth: £6,895,825 *Total Assets:* £13,199,231
Registered Office: The Willows Nursing Home, 1 Murray Street, Salford, M7 2DX
Activities: Residential nursing care facilities
Shareholders: Manjit Singh Sandher; Surinder Sandher
Officers: Manjit Singh Sandher, Secretary; Manjit Singh Sandher [1960] Managing Director; Surinder Sandher [1961] Director/Company Secretary

Univar Europe Limited
Incorporated: 21 August 1973 *Employees:* 171
Net Worth: £6,408,000 *Total Assets:* £24,229,000
Registered Office: Aquarius House, 6 Mid Point Business Park, Thornbury, Bradford, BD3 7AY
Activities: Non-trading company
Parent: Univar Limited
Officers: Paul Graham Bryant [1973] Director; Jeffrey William Carr [1956] Director/Global Counsel [American]; Sabine Duyfijes [1972] Director/VP & General Counsel EMEA [German]; Richard Nigel Hayes [1969] Director/Regional Vice President - North

Univar Limited
Incorporated: 6 April 1915 *Employees:* 555
Net Worth: £46,460,000 *Total Assets:* £84,777,000
Registered Office: Aquarius House, 6 Mid Point Business Park, Thornbury, Bradford, BD3 7AY
Activities: Non-specialised wholesale trade
Parent: Univar UK Limited
Officers: Paul Graham Bryant [1973] Director; Jeffrey William Carr [1956] Director/Global Counsel [American]; Sabine Duyfjes [1972] Director/VP & General Counsel EMEA [German]; Richard Nigel Hayes [1969] Director/Regional Vice President - North

Univar Specialty Consumables Limited
Incorporated: 12 November 1970 *Employees:* 67
Net Worth: £15,032,000 *Total Assets:* £18,346,000
Registered Office: Aquarius House, 6 Mid Point Business Park, Thornbury, Bradford, BD3 7AY
Activities: Non-specialised wholesale trade
Parent: Univar Europe Limited
Officers: Paul Graham Bryant [1973] Director; Jeffrey William Carr [1956] Director/Global Counsel [American]; Sabine Duyfjes [1972] Director/VP & General Counsel EMEA [German]

Univar UK Limited
Incorporated: 7 September 2000
Net Worth: £144,294,000 *Total Assets:* £522,735,008
Registered Office: Aquarius House, 6 Mid Point Business Park, Thornbury, Bradford, BD3 7AY
Activities: Other business support service activities n.e.c.
Parent: Ulixes Limited
Officers: Paul Graham Bryant [1973] Director; Jeffrey William Carr [1956] Director/Global Counsel [American]; Sabine Duyfjes [1972] Director/VP & General Counsel EMEA [German]

Univer Manufacturing Company Ltd
Incorporated: 28 December 1987 *Employees:* 46
Net Worth: £4,352,988 *Total Assets:* £7,179,782
Registered Office: 6 Station Road, Bradford, W Yorks, BD1 4SF
Activities: Manufacture of other fabricated metal products n.e.c.
Shareholders: Michael Keith Pix; Tecnair Group Limited
Officers: Christian Pix, Secretary; Christian Pix [1981] Sales Director; Dominic Pix [1979] Director; Michael Keith Pix [1954] Director

Universal Steels and Aluminium Group Limited
Incorporated: 13 February 1997
Net Worth: £3,749,658 *Total Assets:* £6,807,773
Registered Office: Unit 7 Cranfield Road, Lostock Industrial Estate, Bolton, Lancs, BL6 4SB
Activities: Combined office administrative service activities
Shareholders: Anna Monika Kwiatkowski; Edward Wladyslaw Kwiatkowski
Officers: Antoni Pawet Kwiatkowski, Secretary; Anthony Chadwick [1960] Director; Richard Corrigan [1946] Director; Gary William Frances [1960] Director; Antoni Pawet Kwiatkowski [1977] Director; Edward Wladyslaw Kwiatkowski [1951] Director; Henry Zbigniew Kwiatkowski [1953] Director; Clive Scott [1962] Director

Universe Bidco Limited
Incorporated: 18 June 2010
Net Worth: £147,348,992 *Total Assets:* £192,395,008
Registered Office: 3rd Floor, 401 Faraday Street, Birchwood Park, Warrington, Cheshire, WA3 6GA
Activities: Activities of head offices
Parent: Universe Holdco Limited
Officers: Annette Bottaro-Walklet, Secretary; Bernice Constance Lilian Philps [1959] Director/Accountant; Bernice Constance Lilian Philps [1959] Director/Chartered Accountant; David John Price [1970] Director/Accountant

Universe Holdco Limited
Incorporated: 18 June 2010
Net Worth Deficit: £47,724,296 *Total Assets:* £221,107,344
Registered Office: 3rd Floor, 401 Faraday Street, Birchwood Park, Warrington, Cheshire, WA3 6GA
Activities: Activities of head offices
Parent: AECOM Intercontinental Holdings UK Limited
Officers: Annette Bottaro-Walklet, Secretary; Bernice Constance Lilian Philps [1959] Director/Chartered Accountant; David John Price [1970] Director/Accountant

Universities Superannuation Scheme Limited
Incorporated: 13 April 1974 *Employees:* 471
Total Assets: £49,646,000
Registered Office: Royal Liver Building, Liverpool, L3 1PY
Activities: Pension funding
Officers: Jeremy Hill, Secretary; Dr Kevin James Carter [1952] Director; Professor Sir David Stephen Eastwood [1959] Director/Vice Chancellor; Kirsten English [1960] Director/Consultant; David Guppy [1944] Director/Computer Staff; Professor Jane Hutton [1961] Director/Professor; Ian Richard Maybury [1963] Director/Actuary; Michael Ralph Merton [1951] Director/Retired; Professor Vito Antonio Muscatelli [1962] Director/Principal and Vice-Chancellor [Italian]; Professor Stuart Beaumont Palmer [1943] Director/Professor; Michael Rene Poisson [1957] Director/Pension Trustee; Stephen William Spinks [1958] Director/Registrar; Dr Steve Wharton [1962] Director/Senior Lecturer

University of Chester Academies Trust
Incorporated: 10 June 2009 *Employees:* 425
Net Worth: £38,473,000 *Total Assets:* £47,426,000
Registered Office: 164 Whitby Road, Ellesmere Port, Cheshire, CH65 6EA
Activities: General secondary education
Officers: Timothy Peter Boulton [1956] Director/Retired; Amarjit Kaur Cheema [1966] Director/Chief Executive Officer; David John Scott Cumberland [1962] Director/Deputy Dean of Education; Sharon Dempsey [1956] IT Director; Richard Huw Gill [1972] Director/Vice Chair and CEO (Education); Keith Wyn Sorrell [1955] Director/Chief Executive; David Wootton [1956] Director/Chairman and Educational Consultant

The University of Cumbria
Incorporated: 19 December 2006 *Employees:* 894
Net Worth: £57,322,000 *Total Assets:* £139,442,000
Registered Office: Fusehill Street, Carlisle, Cumbria, CA1 2HH
Activities: First-degree level higher education
Officers: Dr Jean Brown, Secretary; Fiona McPhie Aiken [1959] Director/Retired; Steven David Allen [1966] Director/Chartered Accountant; Emma Jane Bales [1974] Director/Campus Services Manager; Clive Robert James Bush [1951] Director/Chief Advisor; Reverend Cameron James Butland [1958] Director/Bishop of Carlisle's Chaplain; Professor Linda Margaret Stockwell Challis [1948] Director/Retired; Geoffrey Alan Donnelly [1949] Director; Claire Theresa Hensman [1948] Director/Retired; Jill Johnston [1969] Director/Head of HR; John Anthony Lee [1942] Director/Retired; Professor Julie Mennell [1970] Director/Vice Chancellor; Hannah Price [1995] Director/Students' Union Sabbatical Officer; Jill Stannard [1957] Director/Retired

University of Liverpool Construction Company Limited
Incorporated: 10 March 1995
Net Worth: £121,000 *Total Assets:* £14,170,000
Registered Office: The Foundation Building, 765 Brownlow Hill, Liverpool, L69 7ZX
Activities: Development of building projects
Parent: University of Liverpool
Officers: Roger Bickerstaff, Secretary/Accountant; Alex Beedle [1966] Director of Capital Projects; Nicola Davies [1973] Finance Director; Jennifer Ann Tucker [1963] Director

University of Liverpool Energy Company Limited
Incorporated: 24 September 1985
Net Worth: £3,928,000 *Total Assets:* £25,000,000
Registered Office: The Foundation Building, 765 Brownlow Hill, Liverpool, L69 7ZX
Activities: Production of electricity
Officers: Roger Bickerstaff, Secretary; Sydney John Cottle [1971] Director; Nicola Davies [1973] Finance Director; Jennifer Ann Tucker [1963] Director

The University of Manchester Innovation Centre Limited
Incorporated: 11 November 1996 *Employees:* 9
Net Worth: £13,212,085 *Total Assets:* £19,103,836
Registered Office: The Incubator Building, 48 Grafton Street, Manchester, M13 9XX
Activities: Letting and operating of conference and exhibition centres
Officers: Claire Jane McKenzie, Secretary; Jane Nicola Shelton, Secretary; Professor Luke Gregory Georghiou [1955] Director/University Vice President and Professor; Dr Luke Hakes [1980] Director/Venture Capitalist; Joanne Kelley [1959] Director; Clive Gary Rowland [1954] Director/Businessman; Professor Martin Schroder [1954] Director/University Professor; Jane Nicola Shelton [1964] Commercial Director; Jason Stockwood [1970] Director/Group CEO

The University of Manchester Worldwide Limited
Incorporated: 14 February 2003 *Employees:* 88
Net Worth: £1,258,334 *Total Assets:* £16,461,644
Registered Office: Directorate of Finance, University of Manchester, Oxford Road, Manchester, M13 9PL
Activities: First-degree level higher education
Officers: Louise Virginia Anne Bissell, Secretary; Professor Clive Thomas Agnew [1955] Director/Vice President; Stephen Benedict Dauncey [1956] Finance Director; Professor Helen Elaine Penelope Ferneley [1963] Director/Professor; Doctor Simon David Merrywest [1975] Director; Zoe Rainey [1975] Director/Financial Controller

University Technical College Warrington
Incorporated: 2 October 2013 *Employees:* 26
Net Worth: £9,825,534 *Total Assets:* £12,314,808
Registered Office: UTC Warrington, Dallam Lane, Warrington, Cheshire, WA2 7NG
Activities: Technical and vocational secondary education
Officers: Maxine Laura Ward, Secretary; Lee Michael Barber [1980] Director/Principal and Chief Executive; Ian Ramsay Cumming [1965] Director/Operations & Engineering Manager; Neil Raymond Gilligan [1976] Director/Operations Manager; Michael Houghton [1970] Director; William John McCann [1961] Director/University Lecturer; Aidan James McManus [1980] Operations Director; Stephen Park [1970] Director; John Kenneth Patterson [1968] Director/Head of Project Engineering; Rita Marie Smith [1958] Director/Senior Lecturer; Jacqueline Thomason [1971] Finance Director

Unomedical Limited
Incorporated: 13 April 1970
Net Worth: £11,649,000 *Total Assets:* £13,679,000
Registered Office: GFC Building, First Avenue, Deeside Industrial Park, Deeside, Flintshire, CH5 2NU
Activities: Wholesale of pharmaceutical goods
Parent: Unomedical Holdings Limited
Officers: Clare Jane Bates [1976] Director/Solicitor; Sarah Jane Lewis [1970] Finance Director; Christopher John Sedwell [1976] Director/Chartered Accountant; Simon James Whitfield [1966] Business Director

UP Global Sourcing Holdings PLC
Incorporated: 21 April 2005 *Employees:* 222
Net Worth: £6,793,000 *Total Assets:* £25,258,000
Registered Office: Manor Mill, Victoria Street, Chadderton, Oldham, Lancs, OL9 0DD
Activities: Activities of head offices
Parent: Pershing Nominees Limited
Officers: Graham Philip Screawn, Secretary; Robbie Ian Bell [1973] Independent Non-Executive Director; Barry Eric Franks [1946] Director; Andrew John Gossage [1971] Director; James McCarthy [1956] Director/Independent Non-Executive Chairman; Alan Rigby [1956] Senior Independent Non-Executive Director; Graham Philip Screawn [1967] Finance Director; Simon Adom Showman [1973] Director

UP Global Sourcing UK Limited
Incorporated: 22 April 1997 *Employees:* 218
Net Worth: £4,794,000 *Total Assets:* £25,208,000
Registered Office: Manor Mill, Victoria Street, Chadderton, Oldham, Lancs, OL9 0DD
Activities: Wholesale of textiles
Parent: UP Global Sourcing Holdings PLC
Officers: Graham Philip Screawn, Secretary; David Leonard Bloomfield [1966] Director; Barry Eric Franks [1946] Director; Andrew John Gossage [1971] Director; Graham Philip Screawn [1967] Director; Simon Adom Showman [1973] Director

UPL Europe Ltd
Incorporated: 13 August 1993 *Employees:* 58
Net Worth: £79,715,792 *Total Assets:* £330,768,000
Registered Office: The Centre, Birchwood Park, Birchwood, Warrington, Cheshire, WA3 6YN
Activities: Manufacture of pesticides and other agrochemical products
Officers: Mandar Jayant Kadam, Secretary; Bharat Dutia [1957] Director; Trevor John Holland [1955] Business Director

UPM Group Ltd
Incorporated: 11 April 2008
Net Worth: £8,206,779 *Total Assets:* £8,207,050
Registered Office: 8 Eastway, Sale, Cheshire, M33 4DX
Activities: Non-trading company
Major Shareholder: Dr Hakim Shalaan Elaby
Officers: Dr Hakim Shalaan Elaby [1958] Director [Iraqi]

UPM-Kymmene (UK) Holdings Limited
Incorporated: 9 June 1982
Net Worth: £101,227,000 *Total Assets:* £167,718,000
Registered Office: 6th Floor, Station House, Stamford New Road, Altrincham, Cheshire, WA14 1EP
Activities: Activities of production holding companies
Parent: UPM-Kymmene Corporation
Officers: David Graeme Chalmers, Secretary/Financial Director; David Graeme Chalmers [1958] Director & Company Secretary; Mirja Salmelin [1957] Director/Chairman [Finnish]

Upton Hall School Fcj
Incorporated: 16 February 2012 *Employees:* 126
Net Worth: £12,848,000 *Total Assets:* £14,758,000
Registered Office: Upton Hall School FCJ, Upton, Wirral, Merseyside, CH49 6LJ
Activities: General secondary education
Officers: Debra Elizabeth Chesters, Secretary; Helen Boyd [1966] Director/Receptionist; Moira Winifred Cashmore [1939] Director/Retired Headteacher; Richard Simon Duggan [1964] Director/Headmaster; Catherine Green [1962] Director/Business Manager; Sr Brigid Halligan [1941] Director/Headmistress; Philip Edward Hoskinson [1948] Director/Retired; Tammy Hughes [1975] Director/Practice Manager; Professor John Alan Hunt [1966] Director/University Lecturer; Bernard Christopher Larkin [1953] Director/Retired; Charles LEA [1971] Director; Sharon Moore [1970] Director/Business Development; David Martin Norton [1949] Director/Retired; Jay Prothero [1954] Director/Retired; Dr Elizabeth Smears [1962] Director/Lecturer; Lisa Smith [1967] Director/Teacher; Mary Claire Sykes [1944] Director/Schools Officer; Nicola Teare [1969] Director/Accountant; Helen Whitehurst [1971] Director/Exams Officer; Richard Williams [1964] Director/Engineer; Patricia Young [1954] Director/Headteacher

Uranium Asset Management Limited
Incorporated: 15 February 1996
Net Worth Deficit: £118,212,432 *Total Assets:* £105,748,336
Registered Office: Springfields, Salwick, Preston, Lancs, PR4 0XJ
Activities: Agents involved in the sale of fuels, ores, metals and industrial chemicals
Parent: Westinghouse Electric UK Holdings Limited
Officers: Fiona Anne Houghton, Secretary; Linda Aylmore [1970] Finance Director; Angela Darkey [1971] Managing Director - UAM Ltd

Urban Regen Limited
Incorporated: 6 December 2001 *Employees:* 22
Net Worth: £5,448,562 *Total Assets:* £10,079,202
Registered Office: 23 Spring Vale, Edgworth, Bolton, Lancs, BL7 0FS
Activities: Site preparation
Parent: Whitefield Brownfield Limited
Officers: Emma Louise Cowin, Secretary; Emma Louise Cowin [1976] Director; Andrew William Walker [1973] Director/Civil Engineer; Peter Graham Wilson [1961] Operations Director

Urban Splash (RWY) Limited
Incorporated: 21 February 2006
Net Worth: £10,674,006 *Total Assets:* £25,465,630
Registered Office: Timber Wharf, 16-22 Worsley Street, Castlefield, Manchester, M15 4LD
Activities: Other letting and operating of own or leased real estate
Parent: Urban Splash (RWY Investments) Limited
Officers: Kimberley Jane Essop, Secretary; Nathan James Cornish [1974] Director

Urban Splash Assets 2 Limited
Incorporated: 20 December 2012
Net Worth Deficit: £1,060,971 *Total Assets:* £16,024,184
Registered Office: Timber Wharf, 16-22 Worsley Street, Manchester, M15 4LD
Activities: Buying and selling of own real estate
Parent: Urban Splash Assets 1 Limited
Officers: Kimberley Jane Essop, Secretary; Thomas Paul Richard Bloxham [1963] Director/Company Chairman

Urban Splash Commercial 2017 Limited
Incorporated: 16 July 2016
Net Worth Deficit: £134,887 *Total Assets:* £11,409,620
Registered Office: Timber Wharf, 16-22 Worsley Street, Manchester, M15 4LD
Activities: Other letting and operating of own or leased real estate
Parent: Urban Splash Holdings Limited
Officers: Kimberley Jane Essop, Secretary; Thomas Paul Richard Bloxham [1963] Director/Property Developer

Urban Splash Developments Limited
Incorporated: 20 December 2012
Net Worth: £12,369,260 *Total Assets:* £13,996,696
Registered Office: Timber Wharf, 16-22 Worsley Street, Manchester, M15 4LD
Activities: Development of building projects
Parent: Urban Splash Investments Limited
Officers: Kimberley Jane Essop, Secretary; Thomas Paul Richard Bloxham [1963] Director/Company Chairman

Urban Splash Group Limited
Incorporated: 22 December 1995
Net Worth Deficit: £1,410,953 *Total Assets:* £24,734,864
Registered Office: Timber Wharf, 16-22 Worsley Street, Manchester, M15 4LD
Activities: Activities of head offices
Parent: Urban Splash Holdings Limited
Officers: Kimberley Jane Essop, Secretary; Thomas Paul Richard Bloxham [1963] Director; Julian Peter Curnuck [1969] Finance Director; Jonathan Mark Falkingham [1962] Director/Architect; Simon David Gawthorpe [1971] Director

Urban Splash Holdings Limited
Incorporated: 12 December 2012 *Employees:* 87
Net Worth Deficit: £5,931,825 *Total Assets:* £125,094,480
Registered Office: Timber Wharf, 16-22 Worsley Street, Manchester, M15 4LD
Activities: Activities of head offices
Major Shareholder: Thomas Paul Richard Bloxham
Officers: Kimberley Jane Essop, Secretary; Thomas Paul Richard Bloxham [1963] Director/Company Chairman; Nathan James Cornish [1974] Director/Surveyor; Julian Peter Curnuck [1969] Finance Director; Jonathan Mark Falkingham [1962] Director/Chartered Architect; Simon David Gawthorpe [1971] Managing Director

Urban Splash Work Limited
Incorporated: 24 November 1986
Net Worth: £5,141,589 *Total Assets:* £66,424,192
Registered Office: Timber Wharf, 16-22 Worsley, Street, Castlefield, Manchester, M15 4LD
Activities: Other letting and operating of own or leased real estate
Parent: Urban Splash Group Limited
Officers: Kimberley Jane Essop, Secretary; Thomas Paul Richard Bloxham [1963] Director; Julian Peter Curnuck [1969] Finance Director; Jonathan Mark Falkingham [1962] Director

Urban Vision Partnership Limited
Incorporated: 22 November 2004
Net Worth: £4,477,485 *Total Assets:* £13,386,914
Registered Office: Civic Centre, Chorley Road, Swinton, Manchester, M27 5AS
Activities: Construction of commercial buildings
Shareholders: Galliford Try Infrastructure Limited; Capita Property and Infrastructure Limited
Officers: David Bates [1960] Director; Jonathan Matthew Ellis [1970] Director; Matthew Dominic Fairweather [1979] Director; Jonathan Mark Prew [1964] Director; David Michael Seager [1966] Director; Stephen Michael Tomkins [1972] Director; Andrew Wild [1970] Director

Uren Food Group Limited
Incorporated: 18 March 1953 *Employees:* 216
Net Worth: £14,137,000 *Total Assets:* £32,250,000
Registered Office: Wood Park, Chester High Road, Neston, Cheshire, CH64 7TB
Activities: Wholesale of fruit and vegetables
Parent: Wood Park Foods Limited
Officers: Peter Nigel Barratt [1962] Director/Accountant; Paul Michael Jones [1970] Director-Juices; Robert James Laird [1973] Finance Director; Ian Ross Stewart [1963] Managing Director; Julian Laurence Wood [1968] Commercial Director

Urenco Chemplants Limited
Incorporated: 26 April 2007 *Employees:* 97
Net Worth Deficit: £415,388,000 *Total Assets:* £540,230,976
Registered Office: Capenhurst Works, Capenhurst, Chester, CH1 6ER
Activities: Manufacture of other chemical products n.e.c.
Parent: Urenco Limited
Officers: Sarah Newby, Secretary; Dr Douglas Stuart Annan [1963] Deputy Managing Director; Christopher Roy Chater [1968] Director; Thomas Michael Haeberle [1956] Director [German]; Laurent Odeh [1979] Director [French]; Ralf Ter Haar [1965] Director [Dutch]

Urenco Nuclear Stewardship Limited
Incorporated: 23 November 2000 *Employees:* 86
Net Worth: £16,802,000 *Total Assets:* £54,359,000
Registered Office: Capenhurst, Chester, CH1 6ER
Activities: Processing of nuclear fuel
Parent: Urenco Ltd
Officers: Sarah Newby, Secretary; Thomas Michael Haeberle [1956] Director [German]; Dharmendra Tony Singh Hayer [1978] Director; David John Nelligan [1959] Director; Laurent Odeh [1979] Executive Director of New Business [French]; Ralf Ter Haar [1965] Director [Dutch]

Urenco UK Limited
Incorporated: 12 November 1973 *Employees:* 370
Net Worth: £190,312,000 *Total Assets:* £940,801,984
Registered Office: Capenhurst Works, Capenhurst, Chester, CH1 6ER
Activities: Processing of nuclear fuel
Parent: Urenco Enrichment Company Limited
Officers: Sarah Newby, Secretary; Christopher Roy Chater [1968] Director; Thomas Michael Haeberle [1956] Director [German]; Lynton John Simmonds [1971] Director

Uriah Woodhead & Son Limited
Incorporated: 25 June 1936 *Employees:* 53
Net Worth: £7,134,385 *Total Assets:* £7,727,050
Registered Office: Canal Works, Canal Road, Bradford, BD1 4SD
Activities: Agents involved in the sale of timber and building materials
Major Shareholder: Paul Richard Jaggar
Officers: Paul Richard Jaggar [1967] Director/Designer

Urmston Grammar
Incorporated: 3 August 2010 *Employees:* 137
Net Worth: £18,177,000 *Total Assets:* £19,394,000
Registered Office: Urmston Grammar School, Newton Road, Urmston, Manchester, M41 5UG
Activities: General secondary education
Officers: Tracey Jayne Booth [1964] Director/Administrative Manager; Dr Kathleen Dympna Chirema [1950] Director/University Lecturer; Nicholas James Crowther [1965] Director/Senior Broadcast Journalist; Neil Edgar [1966] Director/Accountant; Sharon Mary Freeman [1972] Director/Teaching Assistant; Rebecca Louise Harding [1989] Director/Teacher; David Kirkham [1946] Director; Jane Marie Littler [1963] Director/Personal Assistant; Harry Joseph Manley [1967] Director; Peter Bernard Marks [1943] Director/Retired; Eric May [1927] Director; Andrew John McLaren [1960] Director/Accountant; Kevin Alan Procter [1958] Director/Councillor; Esther Lilian Srirangham [1973] Director/Teacher

URS Luxembourg LLP
Incorporated: 24 November 2010 *Employees:* 2
Net Worth: £258,715,536 *Total Assets:* £258,971,696
Registered Office: 3rd Floor, 401 Faraday Street, Birchwood Park, Warrington, Cheshire, WA3 6GA

USS Heritors Limited
Incorporated: 21 October 2010
Net Worth: £15,892,850 *Total Assets:* £15,892,850
Registered Office: Universities Superannuation Scheme Limited, Royal Liver Building, Liverpool, L3 1PY
Activities: Activities of open-ended investment companies
Parent: Universities Superannuation Scheme Limited
Officers: Fiona Jackelin Achola Otika, Secretary; Graham Alan Burnett [1963] Director/Fund Manager; Michael Anthony Catt [1961] Director/Senior Property Manager; Alex James Turner [1972] Director/Fund Manager

USS Investment Management Limited
Incorporated: 4 June 1997 *Employees:* 146
Net Worth: £921,000 *Total Assets:* £32,188,000
Registered Office: Royal Liver Building, Liverpool, L3 1PY
Activities: Fund management activities
Parent: Universities Superannuation Scheme Limited
Officers: Michael John Burt, Secretary; Howard James Brindle [1974] Director/Chief Operating Officer; Dr Kevin James Carter [1952] Director; William Kenny Galvin [1968] Director/Chief Executive Officer [Irish]; Roger Michael Gray [1957] Director/Investment Management [American]; Virginia Anne Holmes [1960] Director; Anthony Paul Owens [1966] Director; Michael James Powell [1972] Director/Head of Private Market Group; Christopher Paul Rowlands [1956] Director

USS Nero Limited
Incorporated: 31 October 2013
Net Worth: £66,804,268 *Total Assets:* £302,112,320
Registered Office: c/o Universities Superannuation Scheme Limited, Royal Liver Building, Liverpool, L3 1PY
Activities: Other activities auxiliary to insurance and pension funding
Parent: L3 Investment Holdings LP
Officers: Fiona Jackelin Achola Otika, Secretary; Gavin Bruce Merchant [1969] Director; Amy Laura Phakey [1982] Director/Senior Associate

Utilisoft Limited
Incorporated: 20 May 1994 *Employees:* 203
Net Worth: £4,933,549 *Total Assets:* £10,721,212
Registered Office: Utilihouse, East Terrace, Euxton Lane, Chorley, Lancs, PR7 6TE
Activities: Business and domestic software development
Parent: Utiligroup Holdings Limited
Officers: Philip Galati [1964] Director [American]; Steven Paul Gosling [1967] Director; Andrew Michael Green [1975] Director; Matthew Christopher Hirst [1977] Director

Utopia Leisure Limited
Incorporated: 27 June 1994 *Employees:* 405
Net Worth: £22,682,644 *Total Assets:* £32,123,056
Registered Office: No 1 St Pauls Square, Liverpool, L3 9SJ
Activities: Hotels and similar accommodation
Officers: Michael Thomas, Secretary; Deborah Hinchcliffe [1960] Managing Director; Peter Stuart Hinchcliffe [1947] Director

V.I.P. Computer Centre Limited
Incorporated: 26 October 1990 *Employees:* 54
Net Worth: £5,448,000 *Total Assets:* £25,702,000
Registered Office: Vip House, 4 Hardwick Grange, Woolston, Warrington, Cheshire, WA1 4RF
Activities: Wholesale of computers, computer peripheral equipment and software
Officers: Jitenderpal Singh Sahni, Secretary/Managing Director; Richard Stephen Marsden [1978] Sales Director; Avneet Kaur Sahni [1971] Director; Jitenderpal Singh Sahni [1966] Managing Director; Michael Andrew Taylor [1959] Finance Director

Vabeld UK Limited
Incorporated: 2 May 2000 *Employees:* 1
Net Worth: £6,395,818 *Total Assets:* £101,104,688
Registered Office: c/o Grant Thornton UK LLP, Royal Liver Building, Liverpool, L3 1PS
Activities: Development of building projects
Shareholders: Didier Marcel Kerckhof; Dorine Kerckhof; Danny Kerckhof
Officers: Didier Marcel Kerckhof [1978] Director/Businessman [Belgian]

Vacation Rentals (UK) Ltd
Incorporated: 4 November 1969 *Employees:* 810
Net Worth: £105,597,000 *Total Assets:* £226,308,992
Registered Office: Spring Mill, Earby, Barnoldswick, Lancs, BB94 0AA
Activities: Other accommodation
Parent: Hoseasons Limited
Officers: Garry Clark Adam [1970] Director; Simon Edward Altham [1975] Managing Director; Henry Francis John Bankes [1966] Director/Solicitor; Geoffrey John Cowley [1961] Director; Nicholas James Daniel Rudge [1961] Marketing Director

Valdeco Ltd
Incorporated: 14 January 2010 *Employees:* 124
Net Worth: £5,817,950 *Total Assets:* £18,440,476
Registered Office: Time Technology Park, Blackburn Road, Simonstone, Burnley, Lancs, BB12 7TW
Activities: Wholesale of textiles
Shareholders: Mark Anthony Mader Horne; Pascal Remi Siellet
Officers: Mark Anthony Mader-Horne [1969] Managing Director; Pascal Remi Siellet [1969] Managing Director [French]

Vale Mill (Rochdale) Limited
Incorporated: 6 February 1941 *Employees:* 315
Net Worth: £29,988,864 *Total Assets:* £36,277,768
Registered Office: Vale Mill, John Street, Rochdale, Lancs, OL16 1HR
Activities: Other manufacturing n.e.c.
Parent: Minky Group Holdings Limited
Officers: Martin John Spencer Fuchs, Secretary; Alan Stuart Donnelly [1953] Director; Julian Fuchs [1961] Managing Director; Martin John Spencer Fuchs [1963] Managing Director

Vale UK Limited
Incorporated: 8 March 1978 *Employees:* 67
Net Worth: £7,233,045 *Total Assets:* £9,161,069
Registered Office: Kitling Road, Prescot, Merseyside, L34 9JA
Activities: Other specialised construction activities n.e.c.
Shareholder: Paul Henerty
Officers: Paul Henerty [1964] Director

The Valley Printing Company, Limited
Incorporated: 2 July 1908 *Employees:* 137
Net Worth: £6,250,000 *Total Assets:* £8,330,000
Registered Office: Harden Beck Mill, Harden, Bingley, W Yorks, BD16 1BL
Activities: Printing n.e.c.
Shareholder: John Stansfield Haggas
Officers: Jonathan Simon Haggas, Secretary; James Sinclair Haggas [1966] Director; John Stansfield Haggas [1943] Director; Jonathan Simon Haggas [1970] Director

Valmet Limited
Incorporated: 10 January 2003 *Employees:* 139
Net Worth: £4,244,000 *Total Assets:* £9,378,000
Registered Office: Laneside Foundry, Manchester Road, Haslingden, Rossendale, Lancs, BB4 5SL
Activities: Repair of machinery
Parent: Valmet Corporation Oyj
Officers: Daniel Philip Miller, Secretary; Marjut Hannele Salminen [1969] Director/Vice President Finance [Finnish]; Mike Andrew Sword [1968] Director/General Operations Manager; Mika Petteri Tolvanen [1964] Director/SVP Valmet Paper [Finnish]

Valspar Powder Coatings Limited
Incorporated: 31 August 1993 *Employees:* 90
Net Worth Deficit: £3,626,251 *Total Assets:* £12,755,955
Registered Office: Valspar Powder Coatings Ltd, Goodlass Road, Speke, Liverpool, L24 9HJ
Activities: Manufacture of paints, varnishes and similar coatings, mastics and sealants
Parent: The Valspar (UK) Holding Corporation Limited
Officers: Ezio Nicola Giacomo Braggio [1956] Director/Businessman-VP Valspar Packaging Europe [Italian]; Jeffrey James Miklich [1974] Director/Business Executive [American]; Allen Joseph Mistysyn [1968] Director/Business Executive [American]

Valtris Advanced Organics Limited
Incorporated: 20 September 2012 *Employees:* 5
Net Worth: £5 685,297 *Total Assets:* £22,128,926
Registered Office: Lankro Way, Eccles, Manchester, M30 0LX
Activities: Manufacture of other organic basic chemicals
Shareholders: INEOS Enterprises Holdings Limited; INEOS Industries Holdings Limited
Officers: William John Patrick Savin, Secretary; Paul Alan Angus [1964] Director [Canadian]; Louise Jacqueline Calviou [1966] Director; Andrew Gehrlein [1970] Director [American]; Matthew Keshian [1988] Director [American]; Keval Patel [1979] Director [American]; Parashar Ranade [1980] Director [American]

Valtris Specialty Chemicals Limited
Incorporated: 1 December 1970 *Employees:* 117
Net Worth: £23,985,908 *Total Assets:* £35,106,512
Registered Office: Lankro Way, Eccles, Manchester, M30 0LX
Activities: Manufacture of other chemical products n.e.c.
Parent: Akcros Holdings Ltd
Officers: Paul Alan Angus [1964] Director [Canadian]; Andy Gehrlein [1970] Director [American]; Dr Brian William Johnson [1965] Director; Matthew Keshian [1988] Director/Private Equity Investor [American]; Keval Patel [1979] Director/Private Equity Investor [American]; Garry Walton [1963] Director/Site Manager

Value Catering Limited
Incorporated: 10 April 2003
Net Worth Deficit: £370,094 *Total Assets:* £11,518,962
Registered Office: Manchester Arena, Hunts Bank Approach, Manchester, M3 1AR
Activities: Event catering activities
Officers: John Francis Burns, Secretary; John Francis Burns [1957] Director [American]; Harold Westley [1948] Director [American]

Van Centre (West Yorkshire) Limited
Incorporated: 25 May 2004 *Employees:* 45
Net Worth: £3,681,838 *Total Assets:* £14,537,523
Registered Office: LCW House, Chain Bar Road, Cleckheaton, W Yorks, BD19 3QF
Activities: Sale of new cars and light motor vehicles
Parent: Caygill Holdings Ltd
Officers: Susan Caroline Caygill, Secretary/Director; Andrew Martin Caygill [1956] Director; Joshua Caygill [1989] Director; Lucy Walton Caygill [1983] Director; Susan Caroline Caygill [1959] Director; Howard John Marshall [1968] Director; Andrew Umpleby [1965] Director

Vanquis Bank Limited
Incorporated: 15 November 1990 *Employees:* 1,469
Net Worth: £289,300,000 *Total Assets:* £1,855,100,032
Registered Office: No 1 Godwin Street, Bradford, W Yorks, BD1 2SU
Activities: Banks
Parent: Provident Financial PLC
Officers: Gina Esposito, Secretary; Janet Connor [1964] Director; Andrew Charles Fisher [1958] Director; Andrew Thomas Gosling [1955] Director; Malcolm John Le May [1958] Director; Antoni Feliks Reczek [1953] Director [British/Polish]; Jonathan Caldwell Roe [1955] Director; Chris Sweeney [1966] Managing Director; Oliver White [1968] Finance Director

Vegetarian Express Bidco Limited
Incorporated: 29 July 2016
Net Worth Deficit: £571,359 *Total Assets:* £9,418,016
Registered Office: One St Peter's Square, Manchester, M2 3DE
Activities: Dormant company
Parent: Vegetarian Express Topco Limited
Officers: David Michael Jonas [1956] Director; Timothy Geoffrey Kelly [1957] Director; William James Matier [1968] Director; Hiten Patel [1980] Finance Director; Emma Thorne [1982] Director/Investment Manager; David Robert George Webster [1981] Commercial Director; Oliver Quentin James Wyncoll [1969] Director/Investment Manager

Veka PLC
Incorporated: 2 April 1982 *Employees:* 371
Net Worth: £4,768,000 *Total Assets:* £34,771,000
Registered Office: Farrington Road, Rossendale Road Industrial Estate, Burnley, Lancs, BB11 5DA
Activities: Manufacture of plastic plates, sheets, tubes and profiles
Parent: Veka AG
Officers: Graham Fitton, Secretary/Accountant; Paul David Armstrong [1968] Operations Director; Graham Fitton [1959] Director/Accountant; Andreas Hartleif [1966] Director/Chairman [German]; David Arthur Jones [1960] Managing Director; Michael Pattalon [1959] Director/Controller [German]; Dr Werner Schuler [1963] Director [German]

Ventcroft Limited
Incorporated: 12 April 1991 *Employees:* 27
Net Worth: £14,336,760 *Total Assets:* £23,478,274
Registered Office: Ventcroft Ltd, Faraday Road, Astmoor Industrial Estate, Runcorn, Cheshire, WA7 1PE
Activities: Manufacture of other electronic and electric wires and cables
Shareholders: Frank Beverley Rotheram; Lesley Joan Rotheram
Officers: Lesley Joan Rotheram, Secretary; Andrew Mark Groves [1970] Technical Sales Director; Karen Jones [1957] Director/Accountant; James Kennedy Malone [1957] Sales Director; Frank Beverley Rotheram [1944] Director/Engineer/Toolmaker; Ian Rotheram [1969] Director/Software Engineer

Ventgrove Limited
Incorporated: 11 April 1991
Net Worth: £9,180,937 *Total Assets:* £40,620,472
Registered Office: 6th Floor, Cardinal House, 20 St Mary's Parsonage, Manchester, M3 2LG
Activities: Real estate agencies
Officers: Joshua Halpern, Secretary/Director; Joshua Halpern [1958] Director; Samuel Halpern [1960] Director

Verastar Holdings Limited
Incorporated: 2 October 2015 *Employees:* 2
Net Worth: £97,015,000 *Total Assets:* £375,977,984
Registered Office: Longley House, Longley Lane, Manchester, M22 4SY
Activities: Activities of other holding companies n.e.c.
Parent: Etihad Acquisitions Limited
Officers: Gillian Elizabeth Hill, Secretary; Paul Doherty [1970] Director/Accountant; Christopher James Earle [1973] Director

Verastar Limited
Incorporated: 13 November 1998 *Employees:* 739
Net Worth: £32,833,000 *Total Assets:* £167,668,992
Registered Office: Longley House, Longley Lane, Manchester, M22 4SY
Activities: Other telecommunications activities
Parent: Verastar Holdings Limited
Officers: Gillian Elizabeth Hill, Secretary; Paul Doherty [1970] Director/Accountant; Christopher James Earle [1973] Director/Operations; Piotr Nowosad [1970] Director [Polish]; Janette Palmer [1968] Director/Head of CR

Verdant Leisure 2 Limited
Incorporated: 7 July 2011 *Employees:* 77
Net Worth: £5,726,000 *Total Assets:* £31,553,000
Registered Office: 10 Mannin Way, Lancaster Business Park, Lancaster, LA1 3SW
Activities: Holiday centres and villages
Parent: Palatine Private Equity LLP
Officers: Beverley Jayne Dixon [1969] Director; Graham Robert Hodgson [1960] Director; George Hope [1962] Director; Andrew Jonathan Wall [1960] Director

Verdant Leisure Limited
Incorporated: 12 October 1990 *Employees:* 95
Net Worth: £16,145,000 *Total Assets:* £21,637,000
Registered Office: 10 Mannin Way, Lancaster Business Park, Lancaster, LA1 3SW
Activities: Holiday centres and villages
Parent: Palatine Private Equity LLP
Officers: Andrew Wall, Secretary; Beverley Jayne Dixon [1969] Director; Graham Robert Hodgson [1960] Director; George Hope [1962] Director; Andrew Wall [1960] Director

Verna Group Bidco Limited
Incorporated: 28 August 2015
Net Worth Deficit: £3,847,634 *Total Assets:* £35,036,496
Registered Office: Vernacare, Folds Road, Bolton, Lancs, BL1 2TX
Activities: Manufacture of medical and dental instruments and supplies
Parent: Palatine Private Equity LLP
Officers: Matthew Kerr Miller [1956] Director; Paul Martin Wright [1961] Director

Verna Group Equityco Limited
Incorporated: 27 August 2015 *Employees:* 185
Net Worth Deficit: £2,081,627 *Total Assets:* £42,523,120
Registered Office: Vernacare, Folds Road, Bolton, Lancs, BL1 2TX
Activities: Manufacture of medical and dental instruments and supplies
Parent: Palatine Private Equity LLP
Officers: Edmund Fazakerley [1969] Director; Andrew Lees [1964] Director; Matthew Kerr Miller [1956] Director; John Andrew Walter Samuel [1952] Director/Chairman; Paul Martin Wright [1961] Director

Verna Group International Limited
Incorporated: 10 December 2007 *Employees:* 185
Net Worth: £7,488,888 *Total Assets:* £32,718,306
Registered Office: Folds Road, Bolton, Lancs, BL1 2TX
Activities: Manufacture of medical and dental instruments and supplies
Parent: Palatine Private Equity LLP
Officers: Paul Martin Wright, Secretary; Matthew Kerr Miller [1956] Director; Paul Martin Wright [1961] Director

Vernacare Limited
Incorporated: 18 March 1964 *Employees:* 167
Net Worth: £39,836,712 *Total Assets:* £45,423,068
Registered Office: Folds Road, Bolton, Lancs, BL1 2TX
Activities: Other manufacturing n.e.c.
Parent: Palatine Private Equity LLP
Officers: Paul Martin Wright, Secretary; Matthew Kerr Miller [1956] Director; Paul Martin Wright [1961] Director

Vertex Data Science Limited
Incorporated: 31 January 1996 *Employees:* 4
Net Worth: £11,298,000 *Total Assets:* £11,570,000
Registered Office: Office B223, The Heath Business & Technical Park, Runcorn, Cheshire, WA7 4QX
Activities: Activities of call centres
Parent: Vertex Group Limited
Officers: Gavin Keith James, Secretary; Gavin Keith James [1963] Director/Chief Executive Officer

Vertex Group Limited
Incorporated: 11 January 2007 *Employees:* 2,896
Net Worth: £36,916,000 *Total Assets:* £65,077,000
Registered Office: Office B223, The Heath Business & Technical Park, Runcorn, Cheshire, WA7 4QX
Activities: Activities of head offices
Parent: VTX Subco Limited
Officers: Gavin Keith James Secretary; Matthew Guenther [1969] Director/Private Equity Manager [American]; Gavin Keith James [1963] Director/Chief Executive Officer; Douglas Kaden [1971] Director/Partner of a Private Equity Firm [American]

Vet Plus Limited
Incorporated: 6 July 1995 *Employees:* 35
Net Worth: £6,620,340 *Total Assets:* £10,230,443
Registered Office: Animal House, Boundary Road, Lytham St Annes, Lancs, FY8 5LT
Activities: Other manufacturing n.e.c.
Parent: Tangerine Holdings Ltd
Officers: David Alan Haythornthwaite, Secretary; David Alan Haythornthwaite [1953] Director; Sharon Haythornthwaite [1962] Director

Vetco Group Limited
Incorporated: 8 July 2003
Net Worth: £337,355,424 *Total Assets:* £337,355,424
Registered Office: 3rd Floor, 1 Ashley Road, Altrincham, Cheshire, WA14 2DT
Activities: Activities of head offices
Parent: GE Infrastructure UK Limited
Officers: Andrew Thomas Peter Budge [1973] Director/Chartered Accountant; Akhlesh Prasad Mathur [1972] Director/Chartered Accountant

The Veterinary Defence Society Limited
Incorporated: 31 August 1987 *Employees:* 64
Net Worth: £23,520,166 *Total Assets:* £39,985,568
Registered Office: 4 Haig Court, Parkgate Industrial Estate, Knutsford, Cheshire, WA16 8XZ
Activities: Non-life insurance
Officers: Cecilia Mary Gannon, Secretary; David Hugh Black [1962] Director/Veterinary Surgeon; Brian Malcolm Hamilton Bussell [1960] Director Trevor Alan Clegg [1952] Director/Insurance Underwriter; David Scrymgeour Green [1963] Veterinary Risk Director; Howard Jeffrey Jones [1958] Finance Director; Gavin John Lawrie [1971] Director/Veterinary Surgeon; Anthony Lewis [1964] Commercial Director; Norman Allan MacFarlane [1952] Director/Chartered Accountant; Nichola Jane Paull [1956] Director/Veterinary Surgeon; Michael John Pratt [1956] Director/Chartered Accountant; Colin William Thomson [1954] Director/Veterinary Surgeon; Sarah Elizabeth Wolfensohn [1954] Director/Veterinary Surgeon

VG Systems Limited
Incorporated: 31 January 1996 *Employees:* 60
Net Worth: £27,518,000 *Total Assets:* £35,210,000
Registered Office: 3rd Floor, 1 Ashley Road, Altrincham, Cheshire, WA14 2DT
Activities: Manufacture of other fabricated metal products n.e.c.
Parent: Thermo Optek Limited
Officers: Rhona Gregg, Secretary; Lucie Mary Katja Grant [1976] Director/Solicitor; Nicholas Ince [1982] Director/Accountant; David John Norman [1960] Director/Chartered Accountant

Victor Manufacturing Limited
Incorporated: 28 October 1944 *Employees:* 109
Net Worth: £5,980,042 *Total Assets:* £7,524,692
Registered Office: Lonsdale Works, Gibson Street, Bradford, W Yorks, BD3 9TF
Activities: Manufacture of other fabricated metal products n.e.c.
Officers: Steven Robert Jamie Gordon, Secretary; Steven Robert Jamie Gordon [1965] Finance Director; Leslie Reginald Graham [1930] Director/Chairman; Michael James Inwood [1977] Director; Michael O'Shea [1960] Director; Philip Williams [1962] Operations Director

Victorguard Care PLC
Incorporated: 17 June 1996 *Employees:* 251
Net Worth: £2,368,579 *Total Assets:* £8,207,843
Registered Office: 320 Beacon Road, Wibsey, Bradford, W Yorks, BD6 3DP
Activities: Residential nursing care facilities
Shareholders: Joanne Elizabeth Walkden; Stephen John Walkden
Officers: Joanne Elizabeth Walkden, Secretary; Christopher John Eardley [1968] Director/Machinist; Jacqueline Mary Eardley [1941] Director/Retired Teacher; John Barrie Eardley [1940] Director/Retired Headmaster; Joanne Elizabeth Walkden [1966] Director; Stephen John Walkden [1965] Director/Building Contractor

Victorious Academies Trust
Incorporated: 21 November 2014 *Employees:* 28
Net Worth: £13,996,660 *Total Assets:* £14,340,435
Registered Office: Inspire Academy, Mossley Road, Ashton under Lyne, Lancs, OL6 9RU
Activities: Other business support service activities n.e.c.
Officers: Leanne Berry [1980] Director/Financial Advisor; Ruth Anne Dolan [1959] Director/Governance Consultant; Victoria Clare Samantha Hewitt-Lee [1965] Director/Headteacher; Robert Duncan Holt [1966] Group Board Director - Strategic Services; Dean McDonagh [1989] Director/Education Analyst; Tracey Summerlin [1964] Director/HR Consultant; Robert Garry White [1963] Director/Education Consultant

Victrex Manufacturing Limited
Incorporated: 16 August 1993 *Employees:* 562
Net Worth: £211,300,000 *Total Assets:* £480,100,000
Registered Office: Victrex Technology Centre, Hillhouse International, Thornton Cleveleys, Lancs, FY5 4QD
Activities: Manufacture of plastics in primary forms
Parent: Victrex PLC
Officers: Richard James Armitage [1965] Finance Director; Timothy John Cooper [1959] Director; Martin Court [1961] Director; Jakob Oskar Sigurdsson [1964] Director [Icelander]

Victrex PLC
Incorporated: 25 February 1993 *Employees:* 763
Net Worth: £478,400,000 *Total Assets:* £538,099,968
Registered Office: Victrex Technology Centre, Hillhouse International, Thornton Cleveleys, Lancs, FY5 4QD
Activities: Manufacture of plastics in primary forms
Officers: Louise Waldek, Secretary; Richard James Armitage [1965] Finance Director; Janet Elizabeth Ashdown [1959] Director; Brendan Connolly [1956] Director; Timothy John Cooper [1959] Executive Director; Martin Court [1961] Director; Dr Pamela Josephine Kirby [1953] Director; Lawrence Craig Pentz [1955] Director [American]; Jakob Oskar Sigurdsson [1964] Director [Icelander]; David Thomas [1954] Director/Accountant; Jane Elizabeth Toogood [1965] Director

Victrex USA Holdings Limited
Incorporated: 25 August 2011
Net Worth: £73,955,000 *Total Assets:* £88,860,000
Registered Office: Victrex Technology Centre, Hillhouse International, Thornton Cleveleys, Lancs, FY5 4QD
Activities: Manufacture of plastics in primary forms
Parent: Victrex PLC
Officers: Richard James Armitage [1965] Finance Director; Timothy John Cooper [1959] Director; Martin Court [1961] Director

The View Trust
Incorporated: 23 November 2016 *Employees:* 114
Net Worth: £5,354,177 *Total Assets:* £8,154,873
Registered Office: Tor View School, Clod Lane, Haslingden, Rossendale, Lancs, BB4 6LR
Activities: Primary education
Officers: Sarah Marie Hartley [1976] Director/Associate Senior Play Therapist; Angela Yvonne Holdsworth [1969] Director/Headteacher; Mary Clare Mulderrig [1963] Director/Partner in Law Firm; Janice Payne [1966] Director/Teaching Assistant; Andrew John Squire [1959] Director/Principal; Emma Jane Taylor [1978] Director/Law Teacher

VIL Holdings Limited
Incorporated: 17 March 1994 *Employees:* 89
Net Worth: £26,494,688 *Total Assets:* £31,308,676
Registered Office: Union Road, Tonge Moor, Bolton, Lancs, BL2 2DT
Activities: Activities of head offices
Officers: Philip William Richardson, Secretary; Philip William Richardson [1982] Director; Sarah Wendy Richardson [1982] Director/Accountant; Andrew Wray Wallen [1947] Director; Emma Louise Wallen [1989] Director; James Wray Wallen [1987] Director; Richard Wray Wallen [1974] Director/Manager; Sondra Lorraine Wallen [1977] Director; Wendy Wallen [1947] Director

VIL Resins Ltd.
Incorporated: 31 March 1938 *Employees:* 29
Net Worth: £5,580,062 *Total Assets:* £9,632,801
Registered Office: V I L Resins Ltd, Union Road, Bolton, Lancs, BL2 2DT
Activities: Manufacture of other chemical products n.e.c.
Parent: VIL Holdings Limited
Officers: Philip William Richardson, Secretary; Alan Lomax [1967] Production Director; Jamie Maugham [1968] Sales Director; Philip William Richardson [1982] Finance Director; Philip Mark Stonehewer [1956] Operations Director; Andrew Wray Wallen [1947] Director/Chairman; James Wray Wallen [1987] Technical Director; Richard Wray Wallen [1974] Managing Director

The Villa (Wrea Green) Limited
Incorporated: 12 March 2010
Net Worth: £1,758,202 *Total Assets:* £12,361,790
Registered Office: 4 Croft Court, Whitehills Business Park, Blackpool, Lancs, FY4 5PR
Activities: Hotels and similar accommodation
Officers: Thomas Adam Flack [1985] Finance Director; Linda Rigby [1961] Director; William Simon Rigby [1961] Director

Vimto (Out of Home) Limited
Incorporated: 29 November 2013 *Employees:* 44
Net Worth: £20,071,000 *Total Assets:* £47,891,000
Registered Office: Laurel House, Woodlands Park, Ashton Road, Newton-le-Willows, Merseyside, WA12 0HH
Activities: Wholesale of fruit and vegetable juices, mineral water and soft drinks
Parent: Nichols PLC
Officers: Timothy John Croston [1963] Finance Director; Nicholas Yates [1974] Director

Vine Mill Limited
Incorporated: 24 July 2007
Net Worth: £44,648,000 *Total Assets:* £48,844,000
Registered Office: 5400 Lakeside, Cheadle Royal Business Park, Cheadle, Cheshire, SK8 3GQ
Activities: Agents involved in the sale of furniture, household goods, hardware and ironmongery
Parent: Pulse Home Products (Holdings) Limited
Officers: Ben Hartley [1976] Director/Attorney; Dasree Vishwamaryum Ramsammy [1961] Director/Attorney [American]

Vink Holdings Limited
Incorporated: 11 June 1990
Net Worth: £12,152,000 *Total Assets:* £86,848,000
Registered Office: P O Box 1, Edmundson House, Tatton Street, Knutsford, Cheshire, WA16 6AY
Activities: Activities of head offices
Parent: Marlowe Holdings Investments Limited
Officers: Philip Graham Elsegood, Secretary; Roger David Goddard [1953] Director/Chartered Accountant; Douglas Talbot McNair [1947] Managing Director; William Sones Woof [1951] Director/Solicitor

Vinnolit Hillhouse Ltd
Incorporated: 9 March 2007 *Employees:* 55
Net Worth: £13,255,000 *Total Assets:* £19,421,000
Registered Office: Vinnolit Hillhouse Limited, Hillhouse International Site, Bourne Road, Thornton-Cleveleys, Lancs, FY5 4QD
Activities: Manufacture of other plastic products
Parent: Vinnolit GmbH & Co KG
Officers: Guy Gansfort, Secretary; Guy Gansfort [1958] Director HR & Legal [German]; Karl-Martin Schellerer [1969] Managing Director [German]

VIP (Group) Limited
Incorporated: 1 July 2014 *Employees:* 228
Net Worth: £15,193,000 *Total Assets:* £47,877,000
Registered Office: Vip House, 4 Hardwick Grange, Woolston, Warrington, Cheshire, WA1 4RF
Activities: Activities of distribution holding companies
Shareholders: Avneet Kaur Sahni; Jitenderpal Singh Sahni
Officers: Jitenderpal Singh Sahni, Secretary; David Gary Brooks [1967] Director; Avneet Kaur Sahni [1971] Director; Jitenderpal Singh Sahni [1966] Managing Director; Michael Andrew Taylor [1959] Finance Director

Virgin Wines Holding Company Limited
Incorporated: 29 February 2012 *Employees:* 156
Net Worth: £3,155,000 *Total Assets:* £23,555,000
Registered Office: 37-41 Roman Way Industrial Estate, Longridge Road, Ribbleton, Preston, Lancs, PR2 5BD
Activities: Other business support service activities n.e.c.
Officers: Justin Haschel Maltz [1969] Director/Business Consultant; Miles Daniel Otway [1983] Director/Investment Manager; Graeme David Weir [1962] Director; Jeremy Simon Wright [1969] Director

Viridis Energy (Norgen) Limited
Incorporated: 22 May 1995
Net Worth: £44,000 *Total Assets:* £22,007,000
Registered Office: 1030 Centre Park, Slutchers Lane, Warrington, Cheshire, WA1 1QL
Activities: Production of electricity
Officers: Elizabeth Alexandra Oldroyd, Secretary; John William Breckenridge [1962] Managing Director [American]; Simon Richard Eaves [1967] Managing Director; Adrian Waine Robinson [1961] Director/Chief Operating Officer; Kirsty Louise Usher [1975] Director/Accountant

Virtual Internet (UK) Limited
Incorporated: 23 May 1996 *Employees:* 13
Net Worth: £15,713,933 *Total Assets:* £18,558,026
Registered Office: 5th Floor, Voyager House, Chicago Avenue, Manchester Airport, Manchester, M90 3DQ
Activities: Data processing, hosting and related activities
Parent: Virtual Internet Holdings Limited
Officers: James Patrick Pochin, Secretary; John Andrew Gallemore [1969] Director

Visage Group Limited
Incorporated: 1 August 2005
Net Worth Deficit: £9,766,000 *Total Assets:* £30,692,000
Registered Office: Centenary House, Centenary Way, Salford, M50 1RF
Activities: Activities of head offices
Parent: Visage Holdings (2010) Limited
Officers: Robert Arthur Bacon, Secretary; Nicholas Andrew Cottrell [1960] Director; Robert Stephen Lister [1956] Director

Visage Holdings (2010) Limited
Incorporated: 17 July 1987
Net Worth Deficit: £3,874,000 *Total Assets:* £41,349,000
Registered Office: Centenary House, Centenary Way, Salford, M50 1RF
Activities: Activities of head offices
Parent: Peter Black Holdings Limited
Officers: Nicholas Andrew Cottrell [1960] Director; Robert Stephen Lister [1956] Director

Visage Limited
Incorporated: 15 June 1981 *Employees:* 238
Net Worth: £3,397,000 *Total Assets:* £79,962,000
Registered Office: Centenary House, Centenary Way, Salford, M50 1RF
Activities: Wholesale of clothing and footwear
Parent: Visage Holdings Limited
Officers: Nicholas Andrew Cottrell [1960] Director; Robert Stephen Lister [1956] Director

Vision Multi Academy Trust
Incorporated: 22 May 2017 *Employees:* 111
Net Worth: £6,037,000 *Total Assets:* £7,344,000
Registered Office: Higher Lane Primary School, Egerton Road, Whitefield, Manchester, M45 7EX
Activities: Primary education
Officers: Joan Beresford [1956] Finance Director; Sonja Butterworth [1978] Director/Education Consultant; Laurence Alan Goldberg [1943] Director/Pharmacist; David Jones [1956] Director/Retired; Ralph Harold Kelly [1953] Director/Semi Retired Sales and Management Consultant; Darryl Christopher Lester [1970] Director/Civil Servant; Carol McLachlan [1965] Director/Headteacher; Barry Thomas Minnery [1946] Director/Accountant; Colin Victor Peach [1942] Director/Retired

Vision Support Services Group Limited
Incorporated: 7 October 2005 *Employees:* 151
Net Worth: £7,546,850 *Total Assets:* £21,891,284
Registered Office: Darwen House, Walker Park, Blackburn, Lancs, BB1 2QE
Activities: Wholesale of textiles
Shareholder: Daniel Patrick Wright
Officers: Mark Thomas Doyle, Secretary; Mark Doyle [1978] Financial Director [Irish]; Michelle Louise Pegg [1971] Director; Laurie Ernest Thomas [1961] Director; Daniel Patrick Wright [1972] Director/Accountant

Vision Support Services Limited
Incorporated: 27 May 2008 *Employees:* 42
Net Worth: £4,531,364 *Total Assets:* £19,077,944
Registered Office: 2nd Floor, Darwen House, Walker Industrial Estate, Walker Road, Guide, Blackburn, Lancs, BB1 2QE
Activities: Wholesale of textiles
Parent: Vision Support Services Group Ltd
Officers: Mark Doyle [1978] Financial Director [Irish]; Michelle Louise Pegg [1971] Director; Laurie Ernest Thomas [1961] Director

Vista Engineering Limited
Incorporated: 24 July 1979 *Employees:* 61
Net Worth: £7,176,143 *Total Assets:* £11,681,752
Registered Office: Carr Brook Works, Elnor Lane, Whaley Bridge, High Peak, Derbys, SK23 7JN
Activities: Manufacture of wire products, chain and springs
Shareholders: Gillian Travis; David Travis
Officers: Gillian Travis, Secretary; David Travis [1942] Director/Engineer; Gillian Travis [1943] Director/Secretary; Philip David Travis [1969] Director; Sarah Ann Travis [1969] Director

Vita (Group) Unlimited
Incorporated: 17 February 1966 *Employees:* 3
Net Worth: £177,965,552 *Total Assets:* £478,525,248
Registered Office: Oldham Road, Middleton, Manchester, M24 2DB
Activities: Activities of head offices
Parent: Vita (Holdings) Limited
Officers: Jonathan Mark Cheele [1961] Director; Colin Michael Josephs [1963] Director; Daniel Joseph O'Riordan [1974] Director; Darren Lee Round [1963] Director; Gemma Louise Rowland [1980] Director

Vita (Holdings) Limited
Incorporated: 17 March 2005
Net Worth: £196,771,808 *Total Assets:* £651,651,200
Registered Office: Oldham Road, Middleton, Manchester, M24 2DB
Activities: Activities of other holding companies n.e.c.
Officers: Jonathan Mark Cheele [1961] Director; Colin Michael Josephs [1963] Director; Daniel Joseph O'Riordan [1974] Director; Darren Lee Round [1963] Director

Vita (Man 2) Limited
Incorporated: 18 November 2014
Net Worth: £8,891,000 *Total Assets:* £14,338,000
Registered Office: The Box, Horseshoe Lane, Alderley Edge, Cheshire, SK9 7QP
Activities: Development of building projects
Parent: Vita Ventures Ltd
Officers: Giles Peter Beswick [1974] Director; Mark Christopher Dawson [1973] Director

Vita (Sheff) 1 Limited
Incorporated: 1 October 2013
Net Worth: £1,714,000 *Total Assets:* £8,598,000
Registered Office: The Box, Horseshoe Lane, Alderley Edge, Cheshire, SK9 7QP
Activities: Development of building projects
Parent: Vita Ventures Ltd
Officers: Giles Giles Beswick, Secretary; Giles Peter Beswick [1974] Director; Mark David Stott [1972] Director

Vita Cellular Foams (UK) Limited
Incorporated: 20 February 1959 *Employees:* 566
Net Worth: £86,005,808 *Total Assets:* £124,123,664
Registered Office: Oldham Road, Middleton, Manchester, M24 2DB
Activities: Manufacture of plastics in primary forms
Parent: Vita (Group) Unlimited
Officers: Jonathan Mark Cheele [1961] Director; Gilbert James Davids [1968] Director/Accountant; Christopher David Houghton [1983] Director/Chartered Accountant; Daniel Joseph O'Riordan [1974] Director; John Christopher Skinner [1969] Director/General Manager

Vita First Street Limited
Incorporated: 13 October 2015
Net Worth: £6,909,000 *Total Assets:* £40,589,000
Registered Office: The Box, Horseshoe Lane, Alderley Edge, Cheshire, SK9 7QP
Activities: Other letting and operating of own or leased real estate
Parent: New Co (First Street) 2 Ltd
Officers: Giles Beswick, Secretary; Giles Peter Beswick [1974] Director; Mark Christopher Dawson [1973] Director; Michael Keith Slater [1974] Director; Mark David Stott [1972] Director

Vita Industrial (Lithuania) Limited
Incorporated: 3 March 2005
Net Worth: £29,858,724 *Total Assets:* £30,106,264
Registered Office: Oldham Road, Middleton, Manchester, M24 2DB
Activities: Non-trading company
Parent: Vita Industrial (UK) Limited
Officers: Jonathan Mark Cheele [1961] Director; Daniel Joseph O'Riordan [1974] Director

Vita Industrial (Poland) Limited
Incorporated: 5 December 2013
Net Worth: £31,939,660 *Total Assets:* £32,137,180
Registered Office: Oldham Road, Middleton, Manchester, M24 2DB
Activities: Non-trading company
Parent: Vita Industrial (UK) Limited
Officers: Jonathan Mark Cheele [1961] Director; Daniel Joseph O'Riordan [1974] Director

Vita Industrial (UK) Limited
Incorporated: 19 November 1971 *Employees:* 29
Net Worth: £91,449,520 *Total Assets:* £508,399,488
Registered Office: Oldham Road, Middleton, Manchester, M24 2DB
Activities: Other business support service activities n.e.c.
Parent: Vita (Group) Unlimited
Officers: Jonathan Mark Cheele [1961] Director; Colin Michael Josephs [1963] Director; Daniel Joseph O'Riordan [1974] Director; Darren Lee Round [1963] Director

Vita International Limited
Incorporated: 26 August 1949
Net Worth: £125,699,544 *Total Assets:* £212,803,520
Registered Office: Oldham Road, Middleton, Manchester, M24 2DB
Activities: Activities of head offices
Parent: Vita (Group) Unlimited
Officers: Jonathan Mark Cheele [1961] Director; Daniel Joseph O'Riordan [1974] Director; Gemma Louise Rowland [1980] Director

Vita Investments North America Limited
Incorporated: 16 October 1980
Net Worth: £7,654,006 *Total Assets:* £7,735,073
Registered Office: Oldham Road, Middleton, Manchester, M24 2DB
Activities: Other service activities n.e.c.
Parent: Vita International Limited
Officers: Jonathan Mark Cheele [1961] Director; Daniel Joseph O'Riordan [1974] Director

Vita Liquid Polymers Limited
Incorporated: 26 September 1932 *Employees:* 26
Net Worth: £1,923,177 *Total Assets:* £6,719,617
Registered Office: Oldham Road, Middleton, Manchester, M24 2DB
Activities: Manufacture of plastics in primary forms
Parent: Vita (Group) Unlimited
Officers: Jonathan Mark Cheele [1961] Director; Gilbert James Davids [1968] Director; John Hannah [1962] Director; Colin Michael Josephs [1963] Director; Daniel Joseph O'Riordan [1974] Director

Vita Lithuania (UK) Limited
Incorporated: 3 March 2005
Net Worth: £26,074,232 *Total Assets:* £26,396,496
Registered Office: Oldham Road, Middleton, Manchester, M24 2DB
Activities: Non-trading company
Parent: Vita International Limited
Officers: Jonathan Mark Cheele [1961] Director; Daniel Joseph O'Riordan [1974] Director

Vita Satellite 1 Limited
Incorporated: 16 December 2015
Net Worth: £10,448,000 *Total Assets:* £44,402,000
Registered Office: The Box, Horseshoe Lane, Alderley Edge, Cheshire, SK9 7QP
Activities: Activities of production holding companies
Parent: Vita Ventures Ltd
Officers: Giles Beswick, Secretary; Giles Peter Beswick [1974] Director; Mark Christopher Dawson [1973] Director; Kenneth John Knott [1959] Director; Michael Keith Slater [1974] Director

Vita Student Southampton Portswood Limited
Incorporated: 19 April 2016
Net Worth Deficit: £3,000 *Total Assets:* £13,648,000
Registered Office: The Box, Horseshoe Lane, Alderley Edge, Cheshire, SK9 7QP
Activities: Development of building projects
Parent: Vita Southampton Portswood Holdco 2 Limited
Officers: Giles Beswick, Secretary; Giles Peter Beswick [1974] Director; Mark Christopher Dawson [1973] Director; Mark David Stott [1972] Director

Vita Student York Holding Company Limited
Incorporated: 24 August 2015
Net Worth Deficit: £6,000 *Total Assets:* £49,541,000
Registered Office: The Box, Horseshoe Lane, Alderley Edge, Cheshire, SK9 7QP
Activities: Development of building projects
Parent: Vita Ventures Ltd
Officers: Giles Beswick, Secretary; Giles Peter Beswick [1974] Director; Mark Christopher Dawson [1973] Director; Mark David Stott [1972] Director

Vita Ventures Limited
Incorporated: 12 October 2012
Net Worth Deficit: £2,916,000 *Total Assets:* £53,175,000
Registered Office: The Box, Horseshoe Lane, Alderley Edge, Cheshire, SK9 7QP
Activities: Management of real estate on a fee or contract basis
Parent: Select Property Group (Holdings) Ltd
Officers: Giles Beswick, Secretary; Giles Peter Beswick [1974] Director; Mark Christopher Dawson [1973] Director; Trevor Philip Moore [1969] Director; Michael Keith Slater [1974] Director; Mark David Stott [1972] Director

Vita York 1 Limited
Incorporated: 14 May 2014
Net Worth Deficit: £27,000 *Total Assets:* £16,993,000
Registered Office: The Box, Horseshoe Lane, Alderley Edge, Cheshire, SK9 7QP
Activities: Buying and selling of own real estate
Parent: Vita Ventures Limited
Officers: Giles Giles Beswick, Secretary; Giles Peter Beswick [1974] Director; Mark Christopher Dawson [1973] Director; Mark David Stott [1972] Director

Vitaflo (International) Limited
Incorporated: 4 June 1997 *Employees:* 153
Net Worth: £9,151,000 *Total Assets:* £18,122,000
Registered Office: Suite 1.11 South Harrington Building, 182 Sefton Street, Brunswick Business Park, Liverpool, L3 4BQ
Activities: Other human health activities
Parent: Nestle UK Limited
Officers: Caroline Charlesworth, Secretary; Caroline Francesca Charlesworth [1961] Director; Maura O'Donnell [1958] Director

Vital Energi Solutions Limited
Incorporated: 31 October 2011 *Employees:* 12
Net Worth: £1,240,643 *Total Assets:* £11,551,834
Registered Office: Century House, Roman Road, Blackburn, Lancs, BB1 2LD
Activities: Production of electricity
Parent: Vital Holdings Limited
Officers: Stephen John Beckett, Secretary; Stephen John Beckett [1962] Director; Gary John Fielding [1955] Director; Ian Michael Whitelock [1959] Director

Vital Energi Utilities Limited
Incorporated: 9 August 2000 *Employees:* 361
Net Worth: £20,654,424 *Total Assets:* £51,666,552
Registered Office: Century House, Roman Road, Blackburn, Lancs, BB1 2LD
Activities: Steam and air conditioning supply
Parent: Vital Holdings Limited
Officers: Stephen Beckett, Finance Director; Stephen John Beckett [1962] Director/Accountant; Gary John Fielding [1955] Director; Deborah Maureen Whitelock [1960] Director; Ian Michael Whitelock [1959] Director/Chartered Surveyor

Vital Holdings Limited
Incorporated: 10 October 2007 *Employees:* 385
Net Worth: £20,529,524 *Total Assets:* £56,884,952
Registered Office: Century House, Roman Road, Blackburn, Lancs, BB1 2LD
Activities: Non-trading company
Shareholder: Gary John Fielding
Officers: Stephen John Beckett, Secretary; Stephen John Beckett [1962] Finance Director; Gary John Fielding [1955] Director; Sally Anne Fielding [1955] Director; Nicolas Gosling [1966] Director; Gary de Vinche ez Le Sueur [1970] Director; Ian Michael Whitelock [1959] Director/Chartered Surveyor

Vodafone Automotive UK Limited
Incorporated: 9 April 1999 *Employees:* 101
Net Worth: £4,801,747 *Total Assets:* £16,156,135
Registered Office: Shuttleworth House, 21 Bridgewater Close, Network 65 Business Park, Hapton, Burnley, Lancs, BB11 5TE
Activities: Other business support service activities n.e.c.
Parent: Vodafone Global Enterprise Limited
Officers: Anthony James Barbieri, Secretary; Kerry Phillip [1967] Director/Lawyer; Roberto Polli [1981] Director/Employee [Italian]; Philip Robert Skipper [1962] Director/Head of Business Development

Vogt Solar Ltd
Incorporated: 12 December 2007 *Employees:* 10
Net Worth: £633,254 *Total Assets:* £18,674,832
Registered Office: 5th Floor, One City Place, Queens Road, Chester, CH1 3BQ
Activities: Other business support service activities n.e.c.
Major Shareholder: Dagmar Vogt
Officers: Alexander Hanke, Secretary; Carl Friedrich Edler Von Braun [1965] Director [German]; Anton Charles Milner [1961] Director

Voiteq Limited
Incorporated: 29 November 1989 *Employees:* 59
Net Worth: £6,613,000 *Total Assets:* £13,084,000
Registered Office: Neptune Court, Hallam Way, Whitehills, Blackpool, Lancs, FY4 5LZ
Activities: Business and domestic software development
Parent: Centriq Group Limited
Officers: David Raymond Stanhope, Secretary; Anton Du Preez [1971] Sales Director; Isabel McCabe [1970] Managing Director; Paul Gerard Dermot Morgan [1962] Director/Accountant; David Raymond Stanhope [1964] Director

Voith Paper Limited
Incorporated: 19 July 1910 *Employees:* 108
Net Worth: £3,300,251 *Total Assets:* £13,760,902
Registered Office: P O Box 8, Apex Works, Middleton, Manchester, M24 1QT
Activities: Manufacture of machinery for paper and paperboard production
Officers: Stephan Bee, Secretary; Stephan Bee [1977] Director [German]; Robert Anthony Oshaughnessy [1971] Director/Operations Manager

VPG Systems UK Limited
Incorporated: 7 January 2002 *Employees:* 52
Net Worth: £24,484,044 *Total Assets:* £27,332,456
Registered Office: Airedale House, Canal Road, Bradford, W Yorks, BD2 1AG
Activities: Manufacture of electronic measuring, testing etc. equipment, not for industrial process control
Parent: Vishay Precision Group
Officers: Matthew John Edward Burridge [1957] Director; Robert Anthony Campbell [1958] Director/Accountant; Jonathan Jackson [1969] Director; Steven Charles Klausner [1957] Director/Treasurer [American]

VQ Developments Limited
Incorporated: 13 April 2015
Net Worth Deficit: £539,563 *Total Assets:* £15,227,860
Registered Office: 1st Floor, NQ Building, 47 Bengal Street, Ancoats, Manchester, M4 6BB
Activities: Development of building projects
Parent: XQ Developments Limited
Officers: Michael Shaw, Secretary; Daren Whitaker [1972] Director

VTX Holdings Limited
Incorporated: 31 October 2006 *Employees:* 2,896
Net Worth: £31,815,000 *Total Assets:* £59,976,000
Registered Office: Office B223, The Heath Business & Technical Park, Runcorn, Cheshire, WA7 4QX
Activities: Activities of head offices
Officers: Gavin Keith James, Secretary; Matthew Guenther [1969] Director/Private Equity Manager [American]; Gavin Keith James [1963] Director; Douglas Kaden [1971] Director/Partner of a Private Equity Firm [American]

VTX Subco Limited
Incorporated: 31 October 2006
Net Worth: £55,270,000 *Total Assets:* £55,401,000
Registered Office: Office B223, The Heath Business & Technical Park, Runcorn, Cheshire, WA7 4QX
Activities: Activities of head offices
Parent: VTX Holdings Limited
Officers: Gavin Keith James, Secretary; Matthew Guenther [1969] Director/Private Equity Manager [American]; Gavin Keith James [1963] Director; Douglas Kaden [1971] Director/Partner of a Private Equity Firm [American]

VUR Village Hotel Holdings Limited
Incorporated: 10 December 2007
Net Worth: £16,011,000 *Total Assets:* £65,458,000
Registered Office: 1st Floor, Lakeview, 600 Lakeside Drive, Centre Park, Warrington, Cheshire, WA1 1RW
Activities: Activities of other holding companies n.e.c.
Parent: VUR Village Hotels Limited
Officers: Coley James Brenan [1978] Director/Investor [American]; Gary Reginald Davis [1955] Director

VUR Village Hotels & Leisure Limited
Incorporated: 23 February 2007
Net Worth: £69,002,000 *Total Assets:* £154,620,992
Registered Office: 1st Floor, Lakeview, 600 Lakeside Drive, Centre Park, Warrington, Cheshire, WA1 1RW
Activities: Hotels and similar accommodation
Parent: VUR Village Hotel Holdings Limited
Officers: Coley James Brenan [1978] Director/Investor [American]; Gary Reginald Davis [1955] Director

VUR Village Hotels Limited
Incorporated: 11 March 1992 *Employees:* 4,108
Net Worth: £287,396,000 *Total Assets:* £897,494,976
Registered Office: 1st Floor, Lakeview, 600 Lakeside Drive, Centre Park, Warrington, Cheshire, WA1 1RW
Activities: Activities of other holding companies n.e.c.
Parent: VUR Investment (UK) Limited
Officers: Coley James Brenan [1978] Director/Investor [American]; Gary Reginald Davis [1955] Director

VUR Village Properties Limited
Incorporated: 5 March 2007 *Employees:* 2
Net Worth: £112,606,000 *Total Assets:* £418,200,992
Registered Office: 1st Floor, Lakeview, 600 Lakeside Drive, Centre Park, Warrington, Cheshire, WA1 1RW
Activities: Hotels and similar accommodation
Parent: VUR Village Holdings No 3 Limited
Officers: Coley James Brenan [1978] Director/Investor [American]; Gary Reginald Davis [1955] Director

VUR Village Trading No 1 Limited
Incorporated: 7 September 1946 *Employees:* 3,890
Net Worth: £7,934,000 *Total Assets:* £118,998,000
Registered Office: 1st Floor, Lakeview, 600 Lakeside Drive, Centre Park, Warrington, Cheshire, WA1 1RW
Activities: Hotels and similar accommodation
Parent: VUR Villiage Properties Limited
Officers: Coley James Brenan [1978] Director/Investor [American]; Gary Reginald Davis [1955] Director

Vynova Runcorn Limited
Incorporated: 7 July 2014 *Employees:* 137
Net Worth: £5,074,235 *Total Assets:* £54,007,456
Registered Office: P O Box 9, Runcorn Site HQ, South Parade, Runcorn, Cheshire, WA7 4JE
Activities: Manufacture of other organic basic chemicals
Parent: Vynova Holding SA
Officers: Janet Ann Bailey, Secretary; Luc Eduard Maria Leunis [1959] Director [Belgian]; Hans Marie Octave Mattheeuws [1962] Director [Belgian]

W A Developments Holdings Limited
Incorporated: 16 August 2006 *Employees:* 148
Net Worth Deficit: £47,482,000 *Total Assets:* £11,785,000
Registered Office: Administration Offices, Carlisle Airport, Carlisle, CA6 4NW
Activities: Non-trading company
Major Shareholder: Andrew William Tinkler
Officers: William Andrew Tinkler [1963] Director

W H Real Estate Limited
Incorporated: 20 April 2000 *Employees:* 2
Net Worth: £4,690,133 *Total Assets:* £12,361,527
Registered Office: c/o Whitaker Horton, Grampian House, 144 Deansgate, Manchester, M3 3EE
Activities: Other letting and operating of own or leased real estate
Shareholders: Robin Edward Christopher Horton; Ian Robert William Whitaker
Officers: Robin Edward Christopher Horton, Secretary/Director; Robin Edward Christopher Horton [1967] Director; Ian Robert William Whitaker [1960] Director/Surveyor

W M L Industrial Holdings Limited
Incorporated: 16 May 1986 *Employees:* 41
Net Worth: £16,215,617 *Total Assets:* £30,287,716
Registered Office: Harewood House, Union Road, Bolton, Lancs, BL2 2HE
Activities: Other business support service activities n.e.c.
Shareholders: The Joan Farnworth Life Interest Settlement; The Doug Farnworth Life Interest Settlement
Officers: John Matthew Farnworth, Secretary/Director; Douglas John Farnworth [1939] Director; Joan Farnworth [1939] Director; John Matthew Farnworth [1970] Director; Angela Clare Howe [1964] Director; Jillian Kay Turner [1962] Director

W P I Surfacing Limited
Incorporated: 15 December 1994 *Employees:* 66
Net Worth: £13,761,428 *Total Assets:* £15,881,290
Registered Office: Corpacq House, 1 Goose Green, Altrincham, Cheshire, WA14 1DW
Activities: Construction of roads and motorways
Officers: Paul Farrer [1964] Contracts Director; Benjamin David Hancock [1991] Director; Andrew William Hoose [1965] Financial Director; Katrina Marie Igoe [1984] Director/Sales Manager; Michael James Igoe [1987] Director/Engineer; Steven Michael Igoe [1979] Director; Stephen James Scott [1978] Director; Christina Margaret Stubbs [1981] Director/Accountant; Kerry Louise West [1976] Commercial Director

W W Hotels Limited
Incorporated: 22 September 2004 *Employees:* 85
Net Worth: £3,214,766 *Total Assets:* £6,975,428
Registered Office: Rendezvous Hotel, Keighley Road, Skipton, N Yorks, BD23 2TA
Activities: Hotels and similar accommodation
Shareholders: Karen Alison Weaving; Edward Malcolm Weaving
Officers: Karen Alison Weaving, Secretary; Edward Malcolm Weaving [1932] Director/Hotelier; Karen Alison Weaving [1951] Director

W2D2 Limited
Incorporated: 7 February 2011 *Employees:* 1,539
Net Worth: £5,618,000 *Total Assets:* £50,889,000
Registered Office: 4th Floor, Ridgefield House, 14 John Dalton Street, Manchester, M2 6JR
Activities: Activities of head offices
Shareholders: Steven John Walker; Sir Malcolm Conrad Walker; Tarsem Singh Dhaliwal
Officers: Peter David McCulloch, Secretary; Paul Richard Dawes [1972] Director; Tarsem Singh Dhaliwal [1963] Finance Director; Alexia Jane Gharagozlou [1975] Director; Caroline Ruth Gooding [1977] Director; Vernon James Lord [1966] Director; Sir Malcolm Conrad Walker [1946] Director/Chief Executive; Richard Malcolm Walker [1980] Director; Steven John Walker [1970] Director

Waddicar Property Limited
Incorporated: 22 July 1976 *Employees:* 6
Net Worth: £8,754,058 *Total Assets:* £16,504,883
Registered Office: 32 Derby Street, Ormskirk, Lancs, L39 2BY
Activities: Development of building projects
Shareholders: Sharon Armor; Peter Joseph Armor
Officers: Sharon Armor, Secretary; David Armor [1945] Director/Building Contractor; Peter Joseph Armor [1973] Director; Sharon Armor [1970] Director

Wain Group Holdings Limited
Incorporated: 11 July 2005 *Employees:* 265
Net Worth: £208,062,000 *Total Assets:* £325,487,008
Registered Office: Carrington Business Park, Manchester Road, Carrington, Manchester, M31 4DD
Activities: Construction of domestic buildings
Major Shareholder: William Ainscough
Officers: Andy Campbell, Secretary; William Francis Ainscough [1977] Director/Chartered Surveyor; William Ainscough [1948] Director; Andy James Campbell [1976] Director/Chartered Accountant

Wain Group Limited
Incorporated: 26 March 2001 *Employees:* 1
Net Worth: £26,269,000 *Total Assets:* £27,604,000
Registered Office: Carrington Business Park, Manchester Road, Carrington, Manchester, M31 4DD
Activities: Construction of domestic buildings
Parent: Wain Group Holdings Limited
Officers: Andy Campbell, Secretary; William Francis Ainscough [1977] Director/Chartered Surveyor; William Ainscough [1948] Director; Andy James Campbell [1976] Director/Chartered Accountant; Stephen Timothy Toghill [1966] Director/Chartered Accountant

Wainhomes (North West) Limited
Incorporated: 27 November 2003 *Employees:* 119
Net Worth: £68,313,000 *Total Assets:* £161,487,008
Registered Office: Exchange House, Kelburn Court, Birchwood, Warrington, Cheshire, WA3 6UT
Activities: Construction of domestic buildings
Parent: Wain Group Limited
Officers: Louise Mary Donaldson, Secretary; William Francis Ainscough [1977] Director; William Ainscough [1949] Director; Peter Barlow [1969] Director/Builder; Stephen Timothy Toghill [1966] Managing Director

Waitings Limited
Incorporated: 11 April 2002 *Employees:* 64
Net Worth: £8,160,312 *Total Assets:* £10,731,730
Registered Office: Moss Road, Cliburn, Penrith, Cumbria, CA10 3AL
Activities: Construction of other civil engineering projects n.e.c.
Shareholders: David Robert Waiting; Executors of Ms Victoria Louise Waiting; Christine Waiting
Officers: Adrian David Ash [1973] Director/Contract Manager; David Robert Waiting [1975] Director/Civil Engineer

Walker Fire (UK) Limited
Incorporated: 2 April 1981 *Employees:* 106
Net Worth: £6,618,845 *Total Assets:* £8,938,108
Registered Office: Unit 2 Roman Court, Roman Way, Ribbleton, Preston, Lancs, PR2 5BB
Activities: Other retail sale in non-specialised stores
Parent: Printbetter Limited
Officers: David Patrick Cosgrove, Secretary/Director; Andrew John Cosgrove [1978] Director/Accountant [Irish]; David Patrick Cosgrove [1975] Director; Julie Elizabeth Cosgrove [1976] Director [Irish]

G.Walker Properties Ltd
Incorporated: 7 April 1994 *Employees:* 3
Net Worth: £8,395,628 *Total Assets:* £12,827,012
Registered Office: Graham Walker Limited, Unit 28 Bumpers Lane, Sealand Road Industrial Estate, Chester, CH1 4NS
Activities: Development of building projects
Major Shareholder: Graham Stuart Walker
Officers: David Alyn Jones [1949] Director; Graham Stuart Walker [1948] Director

Walshaw Moor Estate Limited
Incorporated: 3 May 2002 *Employees:* 9
Net Worth: £1,067,934 *Total Assets:* £9,584,787
Registered Office: c/o Head Office, Boundary Mill Stores, Vivary Way, Colne, Lancs, BB8 9NW
Activities: Other letting and operating of own or leased real estate
Parent: Walshaw Moor Estate Holdings Ltd
Officers: Janine Elizabeth Bannister, Secretary; Richard Michael Rennie Bannister [1961] Managing Director

Wand Properties UK LLP
Incorporated: 5 July 2002 *Employees:* 3
Net Worth: £6,968,471 *Total Assets:* £11,330,193
Registered Office: c/o CHD, The Royals, Altrincham Road, Manchester, M22 4BJ
Officers: Arthur Simon Davies [1956] Member; David Andrew Warnock [1962] Member; Dawn Elizabeth Warnock [1962] Member

Warbrick Property Company Limited
Incorporated: 31 December 1982 *Employees:* 3
Net Worth: £7,861,447 *Total Assets:* £10,433,389
Registered Office: 208 Wilmslow Road, Fallowfield, Manchester, M14 6LF
Activities: Other letting and operating of own or leased real estate
Parent: DGD Properties Limited
Officers: Rachel Jane Cuthbert, Secretary; Claudia Louise Cuthbert [1979] Director; Rachel Jane Cuthbert [1974] Director/Chartered Surveyor

Warburtons 1876 Limited
Incorporated: 19 February 2013 *Employees:* 4,937
Net Worth: £374,484,000 *Total Assets:* £630,497,024
Registered Office: Back O' Th' Bank House, Hereford Street, Bolton, Lancs, BL1 8HJ
Activities: Manufacture of bread; manufacture of fresh pastry goods and cakes
Shareholders: William Ross Warburton; William Brett Warburton
Officers: John Healey, Secretary; Jonathan Warburton [1957] Director; William Ross Warburton [1958] Director; William Brett Warburton [1955] Director

Warburtons Holdings Limited
Incorporated: 12 February 2008 *Employees:* 3
Net Worth: £469,872,000 *Total Assets:* £662,222,016
Registered Office: Back O' Th' Bank House, Hereford Street, Bolton, Lancs, BL1 8HJ
Activities: Manufacture of bread; manufacture of fresh pastry goods and cakes
Parent: Warburtons 1876 Limited
Officers: John Healey, Secretary; Jonathan Warburton [1957] Director; William Ross Warburton [1958] Director; William Brett Warbuton [1955] Director

Warburtons Limited
Incorporated: 29 December 1921 *Employees:* 4,565
Net Worth: £407,569,984 *Total Assets:* £524,440,992
Registered Office: Back O' Th' Bank House, Hereford Street, Bolton, Lancs, BL1 8HJ
Activities: Manufacture of bread; manufacture of fresh pastry goods and cakes
Parent: Warburtons Holdings Limited
Officers: John Healey, Secretary; Mark Allen [1959] Director; Andrew Neil Campbell [1964] Managing Director; Nigel Wallace Boyd Dunlop [1956] Director; David Andrew Light [1964] Director; Jonathan Warburton [1957] Director; William Brett Warburton [1955] Director; William Ross Warburton [1958] Director

Warden Construction Limited
Incorporated: 8 May 1954 *Employees:* 89
Net Worth: £2,228,069 *Total Assets:* £8,527,079
Registered Office: Damar House, Richard Street, Kirkham, Preston, Lancs, PR4 2HU
Activities: Development of building projects
Officers: Richard David Kenworthy, Secretary; Alan Adrian Atkinson [1971] Director/Surveyor; Karen Browne [1968] Financial Director; Richard David Kenworthy [1972] Managing Director; Ian Francis Williams [1969] Business Development Director

Warden Holdings Limited
Incorporated: 18 December 2006 *Employees:* 81
Net Worth: £1,586,480 *Total Assets:* £7,742,213
Registered Office: Damar House, Richard Street, Kirkham, Preston, Lancs, PR4 2HU
Activities: Development of building projects
Major Shareholder: Richard David Kenworthy
Officers: Richard David Kenworthy, Secretary; Alan Adrian Atkinson [1971] Commercial Director; Karen Browne [1968] Director/FD; Richard David Kenworthy [1972] Managing Director; Ian Francis Williams [1969] Business Development Director

D Wardle (Plant) Limited
Incorporated: 3 February 1972 *Employees:* 97
Net Worth: £13,172,627 *Total Assets:* £27,884,192
Registered Office: Priory Works, Barleycastle Lane, Appleton, Warrington, Cheshire, WA4 4RE
Activities: Renting and leasing of construction and civil engineering machinery and equipment
Shareholder: David Wardle
Officers: Andrew David Wardle, Secretary; Andrew David Wardle [1968] Finance Director; David Wardle [1940] Director; Scott Wardle [1967] Director

Wardle Academy
Incorporated: 21 January 2013 *Employees:* 178
Net Worth: £5,335,000 *Total Assets:* £9,674,000
Registered Office: Wardle Academy, Birch Road, Wardle, Rochdale, Lancs, OL12 9RD
Activities: General secondary education
Officers: Julie Ashworth, Secretary; Eva Ainscough [1944] Director/H & S Consultant; Zahid Amin [1969] Director/CEO Housing [Pakistani]; Nigel George Castledine [1951] Director/Retired Headteacher; Andrew Gleave [1965] Director/Bank Manager; Howard Munson [1980] Director/Senior Manager Audit; Patrick Thomas Ottley- O'Connor [1965] Director/Educational Consultant; Linda Parker [1949] Director/Retired; Susan Taylor [1953] Director/Retired Headteacher; Gary Walczak [1953] Director/Retired

Donald Wardle and Son Limited
Incorporated: 31 March 1994
Net Worth: £19,920,000 *Total Assets:* £27,647,000
Registered Office: Merchants Warehouse, Castle Street, Manchester, M3 4LZ
Activities: Wholesale of pharmaceutical goods
Parent: Bestway Pharmacy NDC Limited
Officers: David Allen Hamilton [1974] Commercial Director; Lynette Gillian Krige [1966] Director/Chief Finance Officer [South African]; John Branson Nuttall [1963] Director/General Manager Health Care Group

Wardle Storeys (Group) Limited
Incorporated: 7 April 2003 *Employees:* 219
Net Worth: £6,752,000 *Total Assets:* £20,157,000
Registered Office: West Craven Business Park, West Craven Drive, Earby, Lancs, BB18 6JZ
Activities: Other business support service activities n.e.c.
Parent: Uniroyal Global (Europe) Limited
Officers: Oliver James Janney, Secretary; Bernard Arthur Wagner, Secretary; Howard Francis Curd [1964] Director [American]; Howard Roger Curd [1939] Director [American]; Edmund Creighton King [1935] Director/Financial Adviser [American]; George Sanchez [1954] Director [American]; Bernard Arthur Wagner [1948] Finance Director [American]

J.Wareing & Son (Wrea Green) Limited
Incorporated: 13 December 1961 *Employees:* 62
Net Worth: £7,068,710 *Total Assets:* £11,774,029
Registered Office: Whinbrick Works, Blackpool Road, Kirkham, Preston, Lancs, PR4 2RJ
Activities: Manufacture of metal structures and parts of structures
Major Shareholder: Andrew Norman Wareing
Officers: Steven John Baxendale, Secretary; Andrew Norman Wareing [1948] Director; Christopher James Wareing [1975] Director/Contract Estimator; Peter John Wareing [1943] Director/Sales Manager; Richard George Wareing [1977] Director/Engineer; Richard Neil Wareing [1974] Director/Contact Estimator; Robin Peter Wareing [1966] Director

Warmer Energy Services Limited
Incorporated: 9 August 2001 *Employees:* 145
Net Worth: £3,205,649 *Total Assets:* £7,720,493
Registered Office: Unit B2, Senator Point, South Boundary Road, Knowsley Industrial Park, Knowsley, Merseyside, L33 7RR
Activities: Plumbing, heat and air-conditioning installation
Parent: WES Energy Services Limited
Officers: Denis Joseph Hennigan [1962] Director; Charles John Seamus Mullan [1980] Director [Irish]

Warmwell Properties Limited
Incorporated: 9 November 2001 *Employees:* 6
Net Worth: £3,236,003 *Total Assets:* £7,868,384
Registered Office: Unit 11 Mold Business Park, Wrexham Road, Mold, Flintshire, CH7 1XP
Activities: Other letting and operating of own or leased real estate
Major Shareholder: Damien McGuiness
Officers: Bernard Owen McGuinness, Secretary/Property Management; Bernard Owen McGuinness [1931] Director; Damian James McGuinness [1974] Director/Property Management

Warrant Corporate Holdings Limited
Incorporated: 26 January 2011 *Employees:* 56
Net Worth: £1,791,451 *Total Assets:* £11,132,559
Registered Office: 157 Regent Road, Liverpool, L5 9TF
Activities: Other business support service activities n.e.c.
Major Shareholder: Ian Jones
Officers: Ian Jones [1969] Director; Lynsey Morrison [1980] Finance Director

Warrant Group Limited
Incorporated: 23 August 1985 *Employees:* 41
Net Worth: £7,516,903 *Total Assets:* £16,787,680
Registered Office: 157 Regent Road, Liverpool, L5 9TF
Activities: Other transportation support activities
Parent: Sunbird Shipping Limited
Officers: Ian Jones [1969] Director; Lynsey Morrison [1980] Finance Director

Warrington Community Living
Incorporated: 26 March 1991 *Employees:* 269
Net Worth: £6,748,117 *Total Assets:* £7,321,473
Registered Office: The Gateway Resource Centre, Sankey Street, Warrington, Cheshire, WA1 1SR
Activities: Other service activities n.e.c.
Officers: Sharon Lindsey Gosling, Secretary; Jane Carolan [1967] Director/Trustee; Hamish Ian Fairbrother [1948] Director/Strategic Lead; Richard James Gore [1970] Director/Trustee; Janice Preece [1950] Director/Trustee; Kathleen Robinson [1950] Director/Administrator; Hilda Ann Whitfield [1944] Director; Janice Lorraine Wycherley [1961] Director/Trustee

Warrington Primary Academy Trust
Incorporated: 16 May 2016 *Employees:* 98
Net Worth: £10 161,647 *Total Assets:* £11,395,849
Registered Office: Evelyn Street Community Primary School, Evelyn Street, Warrington, Cheshire, WA5 1BD
Activities: Primary education
Officers: Dr Carsten Kressel, Secretary; Phillip Bishop Bishop [1980] Director/Project Manager; Julie Ann Cahill [1961] Director/Training Assessor; Richard Catchpole BCS [1966] Managing Director; Penelope Ann Johnson [1954] Director/Headteacher; James Anderson Muir [1963] Director/Accountant; Audra Bernadette Ross [1970] Director/Contracts and PFI Manager; Dave Thompson [1958] Director/Chief Executive

Warrington Sports Holdings Limited
Incorporated: 10 December 1998 *Employees:* 128
Net Worth: £10,476,478 *Total Assets:* £15,371,705
Registered Office: The Halliwell Jones Stadium, Winwick Road, Warrington, Cheshire, WA2 7NE
Activities: Other sports activities
Parent: SJM Holdings North Limited
Officers: Charles Anthony Newton Agar, Secretary; Professor Steven John Broomhead [1956] Director/Chief Executive; Karl Fitzpatrick [1980] Director; Lance Norman James [1945] Director/Manager; Michael Lomax [1964] Managing Director; Stuart Middleton [1963] Director; Simon James Moran [1965] Director; Norman Summers [1948] Director/Manager

Warwick Holdings Limited
Incorporated: 17 March 1995
Net Worth: £17,997,000 *Total Assets:* £35,574,000
Registered Office: Lookers House, 3 Etchells Road, West Timperley, Altrincham, Cheshire, WA14 5XS
Activities: Activities of head offices
Parent: MB South Limited
Officers: Glenda MacGeekie, Secretary; Andrew Campbell Bruce [1965] Director; Robin Anthony Gregson [1960] Director/Chartered Accountant; Nigel John McMinn [1968] Managing Director

Washington Homes Limited
Incorporated: 27 October 1960
Net Worth: £721,083 *Total Assets:* £9,330,634
Registered Office: Workington Road, Flimby, Maryport, Cumbria, CA15 8RY
Activities: Development of building projects
Officers: Paul Armstrong, Secretary/Accountant; Paul Armstrong [1959] Director/Accountant; David Atkinson [1952] Director; John Keith Denham [1943] Managing Director

Washington Mills Electro Minerals Limited
Incorporated: 10 July 1979 *Employees:* 23
Net Worth: £4,381,741 *Total Assets:* £10,418,742
Registered Office: 64 Mosley Road, Trafford Park, Manchester, M17 1NR
Activities: Production of abrasive products
Parent: Washington Mills Group Inc
Officers: Kevin Peter Hine, Secretary; Ronald R Campbell [1944] Director/Chief Operating Officer [American]; Anne Williams [1974] Director/Executive Vice President [American]; Arthur Merrick Creagh Williams [1936] Director

Wastdale Investments Limited
Incorporated: 28 July 1960 *Employees:* 4
Net Worth: £9,843,502 *Total Assets:* £11,090,412
Registered Office: Broadhey Farm, Lower Kinnerton, Chester, CH4 9AE
Activities: Other letting and operating of own or leased real estate
Major Shareholder: Brian Eric Eaves
Officers: Pamela Joyce Eaves, Secretary; Brian Eric Eaves [1939] Director/Caravan Dealer; Karl Desmond Eaves [1963] Director/Caravan Park Manager; Pamela Joyce Eaves [1943] Director/Secretary; Richard Mark Eaves [1964] Director/Caravan Park Manager

Waterfall Catering Group Limited
Incorporated: 13 August 2014 *Employees:* 3,522
Net Worth Deficit: £3,045,417 *Total Assets:* £45,836,052
Registered Office: The Courtyard, Catherine Street, Macclesfield, Cheshire, SK11 6ET
Activities: Other manufacturing n.e.c.
Parent: Waterfall Elior Limited
Officers: James Robert Lovett [1969] Director; Vincent John Pearson [1959] Director; Catherine Margaret Roe [1960] Managing Director; Eleni Savva [1972] Finance Director

Waterfall Elior Limited
Incorporated: 16 May 2016
Net Worth: £17,417,316 *Total Assets:* £50,053,480
Registered Office: The Courtyard, Catherine Street, Macclesfield, Cheshire, SK11 6ET
Activities: Other food services
Parent: Elior UK Holdings Limited
Officers: Esther Gaide [1961] Director/Group Chief Financial Officer [French]; James Robert Lovett [1969] Director; Vincent John Pearson [1959] Director; Catherine Margaret Roe [1960] Managing Director; Eleni Savva [1972] Finance Director; Thierry Thonnier [1966] Director [French]

Waterfall Services Limited
Incorporated: 5 July 2006 *Employees:* 5
Net Worth: £1,222,696 *Total Assets:* £12,179,623
Registered Office: The Courtyard, Catherine Street, Macclesfield, Cheshire, SK11 6ET
Activities: Other manufacturing n.e.c.
Parent: Waterfall Catering Group Ltd
Officers: Jim Lovett [1969] Director; Vincent John Pearson [1959] Director; Catherine Margaret Roe [1960] Managing Director; Eleni Savva [1972] Finance Director

The Waterside Hotel and Galleon Leisure Club Limited
Incorporated: 31 March 1994 *Employees:* 43
Net Worth Deficit: £1,865,772 *Total Assets:* £9,866,735
Registered Office: Wilmslow Road, Didsbury, Manchester, M20 5WZ
Activities: Hotels and similar accommodation
Shareholders: Jamie Richard Lyne; Simon Ryan
Officers: Jamie Richard Lyne [1975] Director/Chartered Accountant; Simon James Ryan [1975] Director/Chartered Accountant

Watts Blake Bearne and Company Limited
Incorporated: 20 January 1914 *Employees:* 5
Net Worth: £50,002,300 *Total Assets:* £130,431,608
Registered Office: Brookside Hall, Congleton Road, Sandbach, Cheshire, CW11 4TF
Activities: Operation of gravel and sand pits; mining of clays and kaolin
Parent: SCR Sibelco NV
Officers: Laurence Boens [1959] Director [Belgian]; Kurt Jean-Emile Elise Decat [1965] Director/Group Chief Financial Officer Sibelco [Belgian]; Jean-Luc Andre Victor Deleersnyder [1961] Director [Belgian]; Jacques Emsens [1963] Director [Belgian]; Mark Christopher James [1959] Director; Felix Moreno Diaz [1962] Director [Spanish]; John Willem Van Put [1962] Director/Chief Executive Officer Sibelco Europe [Dutch]

Wax Lyrical Limited
Incorporated: 3 June 1980 *Employees:* 135
Net Worth: £7,083,000 *Total Assets:* £9,457,000
Registered Office: Lindal Business Park, Lindal in Furness, Ulverston, Cumbria, LA12 0LD
Activities: Other manufacturing n.e.c.
Parent: Lighthouse Holdings Limited
Officers: Moira MacDonald, Secretary; Philip Edward Atherton [1966] Director; Lawrence Frederick Bryan [1960] Director; Jacqueline Mary Gale [1963] Managing Director; Michael Trevor Raybould [1971] Finance Director

Wayne Fueling Systems UK Holdco Ltd.
Incorporated: 19 May 2014
Net Worth: £67,621,984 *Total Assets:* £174,184,016
Registered Office: The Technology Management Centre, Moss Lane View, Skelmersdale, Lancs, WN8 9TN
Activities: Support activities for petroleum and natural gas mining
Officers: Michael Wesley Hubik, Secretary; David Crouse [1964] Director/Management [American]; Michael Wesley Hubik [1966] Director [American]; William Spurgeon [1959] Director/Management [American]

WB Developments (Salford) Limited
Incorporated: 21 May 2013
Net Worth: £69 *Total Assets:* £26,669,248
Registered Office: 1st Floor, NQ Building, 47 Bengal Street, Manchester, M4 6BB
Activities: Other business support service activities n.e.c.
Parent: KQ Developments Limited
Officers: Michael Shaw, Secretary; Daren Whitaker [1972] Director

WCF Ltd.
Incorporated: 31 May 1988 *Employees:* 298
Net Worth: £29,754,000 *Total Assets:* £46,217,000
Registered Office: Crawhall, Brampton, Cumbria, CA8 1TN
Activities: Retail sale of beverages in specialised stores
Officers: Pamela Ann Murray, Secretary; Donald James Biggar [1952] Director/Farmer; Philip John Murray [1970] Director of Operations; Joanne Lesley Ritzema [1970] Director/Accountant; David Arthur Routledge [1958] Director; Martin Stuart Ward [1959] Director/Chartered Accountant

Wealth at Work Group Limited
Incorporated: 7 July 2015 *Employees:* 228
Net Worth: £52,879,000 *Total Assets:* £65,189,000
Registered Office: 5 Temple Square, Temple Street, Liverpool, L2 5RH
Activities: Other business support service activities n.e.c.
Shareholder: David Frederick Cassidy
Officers: Mark Leonard Hutchinson, Secretary; David Frederick Cassidy [1955] Director/Chief Executive Officer; Ian Copelin [1971] Director; Dominic Charles Edward Geer [1971] Director; Mark Leonard Hutchinson [1956] Director/Company Secretary; Paul Eric Morton [1969] Director; Steven Jonathan O'Hare [1975] Director; Stuart Murray Payne [1974] Finance Director; Jonathan Roy Watts-Lay [1966] Marketing and Sales Director; Alan Keith Whalley [1956] Director

Wealth at Work Holdings Limited
Incorporated: 11 May 2009
Net Worth: £28,523,000 *Total Assets:* £28,614,000
Registered Office: 5 Temple Square, Temple Street, Liverpool, L2 5RH
Activities: Other business support service activities n.e.c.
Parent: Wealth at Work Group Limited
Officers: Mark Leonard Hutchinson, Secretary; David Frederick Cassidy [1955] Director/Chief Executive Officer; Ian Copelin [1971] Director; Mark Leonard Hutchinson [1956] Director; Paul Eric Morton [1969] Director; Stuart Murray Payne [1974] Director/Accountant; Jonathan Roy Watts-Lay [1966] Marketing and Sales Director

Wealth at Work Limited
Incorporated: 8 September 2004 *Employees:* 196
Net Worth: £3,846,000 *Total Assets:* £9,091,000
Registered Office: 5 Temple Square, Temple Street, Liverpool, L2 5RH
Activities: Other business support service activities n.e.c.
Parent: Wealth at Work Midco Limited
Officers: Mark Leonard Hutchinson, Company Secretary; David Frederick Cassidy [1955] Director; Ian Copelin [1971] Director; Mark Leonard Hutchinson [1956] Director/Company Secretary; Paul Eric Morton [1969] Director; Stuart Murray Payne [1974] Director/Accountant; Jonathan Roy Watts Lay [1966] Marketing and Sales Director; Alan Keith Whalley [1956] Director

Wealth at Work Midco Limited
Incorporated: 29 April 2009
Net Worth: £28,541,000 *Total Assets:* £28,784,000
Registered Office: 5 Temple Square, Temple Street, Liverpool, L2 5RH
Activities: Other business support service activities n.e.c.
Parent: Wealth at Work Holdings Limited
Officers: Mark Leonard Hutchinson, Secretary; David Frederick Cassidy [1955] Director/Chief Executive Officer; Ian Copelin [1971] Director; Mark Leonard Hutchinson [1956] Director; Paul Eric Morton [1969] Director; Stuart Murray Payne [1974] Director/Accountant; Jonathan Roy Watts Lay [1966] Marketing and Sales Director

J.R. Webster and Company Limited
Incorporated: 23 January 1978 *Employees:* 59
Net Worth: £10,978,264 *Total Assets:* £12,209,266
Registered Office: Prince William Avenue, Sandycroft, Flintshire, CH5 2QZ
Activities: Wholesale of machine tools
Major Shareholder: John Richard Webster
Officers: John Richard Webster, Secretary; Peter Lee [1971] Managing Director; Karen Christine Walker [1957] Director/Accountant; Catherine Webster [1953] Director; John Richard Webster [1956] Director

WEC Group Limited
Incorporated: 22 June 1987 *Employees:* 320
Net Worth: £21,832,000 *Total Assets:* £31,217,000
Registered Office: Britannia House, Junction Street, Darwen, Lancs, BB3 2RB
Activities: Manufacture of metal structures and parts of structures
Parent: Burnhart Holdings Limited
Officers: Andrew Barrington Sedgley, Secretary; James Stephen Hartley [1955] Director/Welder; Wayne Tierney [1962] Director/Chartered Accountant; Wayne Anthony Wild [1967] Director/General Manager

Weightmans LLP
Incorporated: 19 February 2007 *Employees:* 1,099
Net Worth: £29,930,000 *Total Assets:* £64,908,000
Registered Office: 100 Old Hall Street, Liverpool, L3 9QJ
Officers: John Andrew Schorah [1963] Member; Sam Airey [1968] LLP Member; Philip Allen [1972] LLP Member; Dewi Glyn Ap-Thomas [1981] LLP Member; Jasmine Elizabeth Armstrong [1974] LLP Member; Carole Atkinson [1955] LLP Member; Cassandra Louise Auld [1972] LLP Member; Christopher Charles Ball [1970] LLP Member; Deborah Jayne Bannister [1974] LLP Member; Richard John Bate [1969] LLP Member; Nilesh Bathia [1977] LLP Member; William Henry Bermingham [1971] LLP Member; Anthony Craig Blakemore [1955] LLP Member; Clive Sam Romaine Bleasdale [1961] LLP Member; Rebecca Louise Blythe [1972] LLP Member; Karyn Brannigan [1970] LLP Member; Mark Timothy Brenlund [1973] LLP Member; Helen Gray Brown [1967] LLP Member; Kevin Brown [1969] LLP Member; Edward James Bryant [1968] LLP Member; Michael James Burns [1968] LLP Member; Seonaid Buchanan Busby [1967] LLP Member; James Michael Byard [1965] LLP Member; Damian Michael Carter [1971] LLP Member; Thomas James Challis [1960] LLP Member; Elaine Marie Chapman [1961] LLP Member; Andrew Neil Clarke [1975] LLP Member; Victoria Ellen Coleman [1967] LLP Member; Emma Collins [1969] LLP Member; Nicholas Dermot Collins [1958] LLP Member; Thomas Collins [1974] LLP Member; Simon John Colvin [1977] LLP Member; Sarah Jayne Conroy [1979] LLP Member; Andrew Joseph Cooper [1966] LLP Member; Richard Corran [1966] LLP Member; David John Cottam [1966] LLP Member; Andrew Archibald Dawson Cox [1966] LLP Member; Mark Christopher John Crabtree [1967] LLP Member; Ian James Critchley [1979] LLP Member; Andrew James Taylor Cromby [1967] LLP Member; Robert Crossingham [1977] LLP Member; Sean Paul Crotty [1970] LLP Member; Vasanth Benjamin Daniel [1969] LLP Member; Fiona Davidson [1973] LLP Member; Iain Alexander Davison [1967] LLP Member; Graham Michael Dean [1970] LLP Member; Paul Jonathan Debney [1967] LLP Member; James Richard Keith Denison [1978] LLP Member; Kieran Paul Donovan [1974] LLP Member; James Christopher Doran [1968] LLP Member; Sarah Jane Dowd [1965] LLP Member; Andrew Mark Dunn [1973] LLP Member; Simon Hugh Durkin [1976] LLP Member; Fiona Mary East [1957] LLP Member; Nathan Paul East [1975] LLP Member; Deborah Edwards [1963] LLP Member; Sian Evans [1966] LLP Member; Edwina Charlotte Mary Farrell [1968] LLP Member; Tristan Philippe Feunteun [1980] LLP Member; Martin James Forshaw [1967] LLP Member; Peter Phillip Forshaw [1975] LLP Member; Mickaela Louise Fox [1972] LLP Member; Quentin Joseph Fox [1957] LLP Member; Michelle Mary Garlick [1967] LLP Member; Simon Christopher Goacher [1971] LLP Member; Nicola Gonnella [1981] LLP Member; Lee David Gordon [1980] LLP Member; Christopher Henry Grady [1978] LLP Member; Michael Gerard Grant [1962] LLP Member; Christopher Barry Green [1970] LLP Member; Andrew Scott Griffiths [1979] LLP Member; Patricia Grinyer [1975] LLP Member; Oliver Graeme Harker [1979] LLP Member; Mathew Harvey [1967] LLP Member; Mark Edward John Hatfield [1956] LLP Member; Thomas Martin Henry [1954] LLP Member; Charles Beaumont Heppenstall [1972] LLP Member; Robert William Hetherington [1968] LLP Member; Mandy Higgins [1969] LLP Member; Jonathan Alan Hodgkinson [1978] LLP Member; James Manson Holman [1967] LLP Member; David Anthony Holt [1962] LLP Member; James Hough [1979] LLP Member; Sarah-Jane Howitt [1971] LLP Member; Roland Peter Hutchins [1974] LLP Member; Melanie Jane Isherwood [1962] LLP Member; Karl Jackson [1964] LLP Member; Philip C James [1969] LLP Member; Russell Michael Jarvis [1963] LLP Member; Stephen Johns [1975] LLP Member; David Johnson [1975] LLP Member; Richard Alan Jolly [1968] LLP Member; Charles Edward Jones [1955] LLP Member; Euros Jones [1967] LLP Member; Gary Robert Edmund Jones [1964] LLP Member; Keith Jones [1968] LLP Member; Kieran Mark Jones [1970] LLP Member; Robert Maurice Owen Jones [1967] LLP Member; Sandra Alison Jones [1967] LLP Member; Stuart Alexander Jones [1968] LLP Member

Weir Minerals Europe Limited
Incorporated: 4 April 1903 *Employees:* 508
Net Worth: £93,971,000 *Total Assets:* £120,758,000
Registered Office: Halifax Road, Todmorden, Lancs, OL14 5RT
Activities: Manufacture of machinery for mining
Parent: The Weir Group PLC
Officers: Gillian Kyle, Secretary; Pamela Ann Bingham [1969] Managing Director; Christopher Jonathan Martin [1968] Finance Director; Robert Fraser Pearson Park [1970] Finance Director; Carola Schulz [1953] Managing Director [German]; Cornelis Zaalberg [1955] Regional Managing Director [Dutch]

Wellacre Technology Academy Trust
Incorporated: 23 September 2010 *Employees:* 109
Net Worth: £22,060,000 *Total Assets:* £23,919,000
Registered Office: Wellacre Technology Academy, Irlam Road, Flixton, Manchester, M41 6AP
Activities: General secondary education
Officers: Paula Bailey, Secretary; Councillor Sean Brian Anstee [1987] Director/Leader of Trafford Council; Gavin Armitage [1973] Director; Natanya George [1987] Director/School Administrator; Donna Louise Harris [1970] Director/Teacher; Michael Alan Harrison [1948] Director/Governor; Javaid Khan [1963] Director/Head of Leisure Service; Rachel Slayman Platonov [1973] Director/Lecturer; Stephen Charles Tonge [1969] Director/Head of Legal Service; Julia Marie Wentlandova [1980] Director/Lawyer; John Michael Whitby [1961] Director/Chief Executive; Melanie Dawn Wicks [1975] Director/Teacher; Andrew Young [1980] Director/Strategic Planning Manager

Wellington School
Incorporated: 2 December 2010 *Employees:* 167
Net Worth: £14,914,000 *Total Assets:* £16,222,000
Registered Office: Eversheds House, 70 Great Bridgewater Street, Manchester, M1 5ES
Activities: General secondary education
Officers: Gill Aden [1955] Director/Civil Servant; Louise Bangee [1970] Director/Head of Operations; Stuart Peter Beeley [1969] Director/Teacher; Alistair Bryce-Clegg [1969] Director/Education Consultant; Alison Jane Christopher [1961] Director/Senior Manager of Francis House Children's Hospice; Matthew Robert Colledge [1974] Director; Joanne Cook [1979] Director/Teacher; Emma Louise Firth [1972] Director; Richard Fleetwood [1964] Director; Karl Myers [1976] Director/Chartered Accountant; Louise Speed [1967] Director; Peter Tarry [1962] Director/Self Employed

Wellington Shipping Services Ltd
Incorporated: 2 September 2015
Net Worth Deficit: £364,669 *Total Assets:* £6,834,037
Registered Office: Unit 42 Price Street Business Centre, Birkenhead, Merseyside, CH41 4JQ
Activities: Wholesale of clothing and footwear
Major Shareholder: Krisztian Lukacs
Officers: Krisztian Lukacs [1980] Director

Welspun Home Textiles UK Limited
Incorporated: 20 June 2006 *Employees:* 262
Net Worth: £1,082,000 *Total Assets:* £18,003,000
Registered Office: Park Square, Bird Hall Lane, Stockport, Cheshire, SK3 0XF
Activities: Activities of head offices
Parent: Welspun Holdings Private Limited
Officers: Manish Bansal, Secretary; Manish Bansal [1972] Director/Accountant [Indian]; Balkrishan Gopiram Goenka [1965] Business Director [Indian]; Dipali Balkrishan Goenka [1969] Director [Indian]; Leigh Antony Taylor [1961] Managing Director

Welspun UK Limited
Incorporated: 5 January 2000 *Employees:* 260
Net Worth: £5,062,000 *Total Assets:* £32,318,000
Registered Office: Park Square, Bird Hall Lane, Stockport, Cheshire, SK3 0XF
Activities: Wholesale of textiles
Parent: Christy Home Textiles Ltd
Officers: Manish Bansal, Secretary; Manish Bansal [1972] Director/Accountant [Indian]; Dipali Balkrishan Goenka [1969] Director [Indian]; Leigh Antony Taylor [1961] Managing Director

Weltonhurst Limited
Incorporated: 19 December 1966 *Employees:* 107
Net Worth: £3,070,608 *Total Assets:* £8,016,419
Registered Office: Centurion Way, Roman Road Industrial Estate, Blackburn, Lancs, BB1 2LD
Activities: Manufacture of other plastic products
Major Shareholder: Herbert Anthony Cann
Officers: Samantha Adele Molloy, Secretary; Herbert Anthony Cann [1939] Director/Textile Technologist; Anthony Hutchinson [1939] Director/Chartered Engineer; Paul Wareing [1963] Managing Director; Simon Robert Watts [1960] Director/Civil Engineer

Wentworth Miller Holdings Limited
Incorporated: 6 March 2015
Net Worth: £1,650,002 *Total Assets:* £16,500,002
Registered Office: 124 The Unity, Liverpool, L3 9BW
Activities: Combined office administrative service activities
Officers: Paul Bernard Hampson [1980] Director; John William Hughes [1981] Director

Werfen Limited
Incorporated: 27 January 1972 *Employees:* 69
Net Worth: £25,826,274 *Total Assets:* £40,647,524
Registered Office: 712 The Quadrant, Cavendish Avenue, Birchwood, Warrington, Cheshire, WA3 6DE
Activities: Repair of electrical equipment
Parent: Werfen Holding SL
Officers: Stephen Martin Calderbank, Secretary; Richard Hames [1977] Director/General Manager; Carles Pascual Sancho [1962] Director [Spanish]

Wesco Aircraft Europe, Ltd
Incorporated: 19 October 1984 *Employees:* 227
Net Worth: £109,528,000 *Total Assets:* £122,749,000
Registered Office: Lawrence House, Riverside Drive, Cleckheaton, W Yorks, BD19 4DH
Activities: Wholesale of other intermediate products
Parent: Wesco Aircraft Holdings, Inc.
Officers: John Holland, Secretary; Jan Alexander Dobrucki [1964] Director/Chartered Accountant; John Holland [1968] Director/Lawyer [American]; Alexander Murray [1969] Director; Alun Phennah [1968] Supply Chain Director

West and North Yorkshire Chamber of Commerce and Industry
Incorporated: 24 November 1897 *Employees:* 81
Net Worth: £10,229,561 *Total Assets:* £14,418,096
Registered Office: Devere House, Vicar Lane, Little Germany, Bradford, W Yorks, BD1 5AH
Activities: Activities of business and employers membership organisations
Officers: Julie Alexandra Snook, Secretary; Amanda Beresford [1959] Director/Partner; Andrew Mark Caton [1963] Building Society Director; Graham Philip Cooper [1958] Director; Bridget Lee Davies [1968] Managing Director; Andrew James Digwood [1976] Director/Solicitor; Paula Marie Dillon [1959] Director/Solicitor; Nicholas James Garthwaite [1957] Managing Director; Generald Robert Jennings [1957] Director/Chartered Surveyor; Sandra Needham [1955] Director; Lee Ramon Underwood [1974] Director; Victoria Wainwright [1974] Director/Chartered Accountant; Suzanne Rachel Watson [1970] Director/PR Consultant; Stephen Thomas Wright [1961] Director

West Derby School
Incorporated: 3 August 2012 *Employees:* 127
Net Worth: £24,756,336 *Total Assets:* £26,831,222
Registered Office: No 1 St Pauls Square, Liverpool, L3 9SJ
Activities: Technical and vocational secondary education
Officers: Ian Philip Andain [1947] Director/Independent Education Consultant; Jonathan Andrew Atkinson [1985] Director/Student Recruitment Officer; David Robert Barlow [1966] Director/AO Compliance Officer; Charles Birch [1960] Director/Logistics Manager; Karen Lesley Callant [1965] Director/Assistant Controller; Maureen Deakin [1964] Director/Attendance Officer; John Bernard Duncan [1959] Director/Teacher; Sian Graham [1970] Director/Headteacher; Carmel Catherine Jones [1976] Director/Assistant Headteacher; Andrew Keen [1969] Director/Headteacher; Joseph James Orme [1987] Director/Solicitor; Ann Margaret Parry [1964] Director/Housewife; Susan Poynton [1966] Director/Midday Supervisory Assistant; Susan Janet Price [1967] Director/Training & Development Administrator

John West Foods Limited
Incorporated: 1 October 1924 *Employees:* 79
Net Worth: £37,986,000 *Total Assets:* £105,623,000
Registered Office: No 1 Mann Island, Liverpool, L3 1BP
Activities: Wholesale of other food, including fish, crustaceans and molluscs
Officers: David Sankowicz, Secretary; Paul Gaskell [1957] Director/Accountant; Paul Reenan [1967] Managing Director [Irish]; Stéphane R&eacute [1974] Director [Swiss]; John Tomlinson [1961] Director/Purchasing Controller

West Hill School
Incorporated: 7 July 2011 *Employees:* 99
Net Worth: £13,911,000 *Total Assets:* £14,461,000
Registered Office: West Hill School, Thompson Cross, Stamford Street, Stalybridge, Cheshire, SK15 1LX
Activities: General secondary education
Officers: Alan Frank Harrison [1970] Director/Headteacher; John William McElwee [1953] Director; Ian Saxon [1965] Director of Operations & Neighbourhoods (Council)

West Kirby Grammar School
Incorporated: 7 July 2011 *Employees:* 114
Net Worth: £10,019,000 *Total Assets:* £12,350,000
Registered Office: West Kirby Grammar School, Graham Road, West Kirby, Wirral, Merseyside, CH48 5DP
Activities: General secondary education
Officers: Nicola McDonald, Secretary; Jeremy Charles Crighton Akehurst [1968] Director/Premises Manager; Michael Berry [1943] Director/Retired; Sophie Katherine Bevan [1970] Director/Chartered Surveyor; Lesley Broadbere [1965] Director/Businesswoman; Melissa Anne Conboy [1988] Director/Teacher; Elizabeth Davidson [1964] Director/Headteacher; Deborah Anne Favager [1953] Director/Retired; Rachel Clare Kehoe [1973] Director; Nicholas Orme Ledingham [1959] Director/Chartered Accountant; Sheila McClennon [1960] Director/Self Employed Broadcast Journalist; Alan Milne [1964] Director/Accountant; Steven Mark Rampton [1963] Director/General Manager; Elaine Sargent [1970] Director/Headteacher; Alistair Lionel Saverimutto [1970] Director; Susan Anne Talbot [1964] Director/Local Government Officer; Dr Andrew Mark Waller [1962] HR Director; Susan Erica Maria Wallis [1966] Director/Education Project Manager; Jonathan Paul Young [1979] Director/Teacher

West Kirby Residential School
Incorporated: 23 August 1924 *Employees:* 120
Net Worth: £4,828,513 *Total Assets:* £8,647,981
Registered Office: Meols Drive, West Kirby, Merseyside, CH48 5DH
Activities: Other education n.e.c.
Officers: Rachel Louise Kennedy, Secretary; Edward Billington [1966] Director; Brian Keith Boumphrey [1938] Director/Retired; Stephen Mark Dickinson [1951] Director/Lecturer; Neville George Kenyon Lumb [1934] Director; Generaldine Mary Moore [1946] Director; John Melville Wylie [1951] Director/Restaurant Owner

West Lakes Multi Academy Trust
Incorporated: 23 June 2008 *Employees:* 135
Net Worth: £23,183,000 *Total Assets:* £27,392,000
Registered Office: West Lakes Academy, Main Street, Egremont, Cumbria, CA22 2DQ
Activities: General secondary education
Officers: Stephen Kingsley Lester, Secretary; Michelle Louise Pearse [1966] Director/Quality Manager; Adrian Nicholas Thompson [1958] Director/Head of HR; Rick Wylie [1956] Director/Lecturer

West Pennine Trucks Limited
Incorporated: 22 November 1991 *Employees:* 218
Net Worth: £17,689,896 *Total Assets:* £34,463,672
Registered Office: Stakehill Industrial Park, Middleton, Manchester, M24 2RW
Activities: Sale of other motor vehicles
Parent: Ballyvesey Holdings Ltd
Officers: Alan William Thomson, Secretary; David Nigel Birkmyre [1952] Director; Stephen Mark Thomas Howard [1961] Managing Director; Harold Hugh Montgomery [1948] Director; Alan William Thomson [1972] Director/Chartered Accountant

West Wallasey Car Hire Limited
Incorporated: 3 June 1974 *Employees:* 273
Net Worth: £36,824,912 *Total Assets:* £154,926,800
Registered Office: c/o Grant Thornton, 1st Floor, Royal Liver Building, Liverpool, L3 1PS
Activities: Other business support service activities n.e.c.
Parent: Fleethire Services Limited
Officers: Jonathan Richard Darke [1961] Director; Michael Anthony Kenny [1951] Director [Irish]

West Wallasey Garages Limited
Incorporated: 24 September 2007
Net Worth: £212,477 *Total Assets:* £9,308,246
Registered Office: 75-79 Leasowe Road, Wallasey, Merseyside, CH45 8NZ
Activities: Renting and leasing of cars and light motor vehicles
Parent: Flexifleet Limited
Officers: Michael Anthony Kenny [1951] Director [Irish]

Westcliffe Holdings Limited
Incorporated: 7 October 2008 *Employees:* 85
Net Worth: £358,636 *Total Assets:* £6,925,808
Registered Office: 50 Mowbray Drive, Blackpool, Lancs, FY3 7UN
Activities: Construction of commercial buildings
Officers: Raymond John Eyre [1966] Director/Construction; Robert Wilson [1970] Director/Accountant

Western and Oriental Travel Limited
Incorporated: 10 March 2011 *Employees:* 67
Net Worth: £1,950,000 *Total Assets:* £11,667,000
Registered Office: Concorde House, Canal Street, Chester, CH1 4EJ
Activities: Tour operator activities
Shareholders: Bliss Bidco Limited; Bliss Topco Limited; Northedge Capital II GP LLP; Northedge Capital LLP; Jennifer Isobel Atkinson; ITC Luxury Travel Group Limited
Officers: Jennifer Isabel Atkinson [1975] Director/Chief Executive; Mal Barritt [1972] Director; Judith Ellis Hinkson [1970] Director; Emma Victoria Pickering [1979] Finance Director; Sarah Louise Roberts [1979] Director

Western Buses Limited
Incorporated: 24 September 1913 *Employees:* 1,038
Net Worth: £14,460,000 *Total Assets:* £52,259,000
Registered Office: c/o Stagecoach Services Limited, One Stockport Exchange, 20 Railway Road, Stockport, Cheshire, SK1 3SW
Activities: Other urban, suburban or metropolitan passenger land transport (not underground, metro or similar)
Parent: Stagecoach Bus Holdings Limited
Officers: Michael John Vaux, Secretary; Robert Gervase Andrew [1963] Director; Colin Brown [1968] Director/Accountant; Samuel Derek Greer [1968] Director

Westex (Carpets) Limited
Incorporated: 21 February 1980 *Employees:* 206
Net Worth: £12,789,000 *Total Assets:* £21,104,000
Registered Office: Castle Mills, Moorend, Cleckheaton, W Yorks, BD19 3PS
Activities: Manufacture of woven or tufted carpets and rugs
Parent: Globesign Limited
Officers: John Russell Shirt, Secretary; John Frederick Cooper [1961] Director; John Russell Shirt [1961] Director/Accountant; Geoffrey Brendon Wilding [1963] Director [New Zealander]

Westholme School Limited
Incorporated: 1 February 1968 *Employees:* 213
Net Worth: £9,755,908 *Total Assets:* £10,930,374
Registered Office: Wilmar Lodge, Meins Road, Blackburn, Lancs, BB2 6QU
Activities: General secondary education
Officers: Jonathon Norman Backhouse, Secretary; Michael Clive Abraham [1954] Director; Stephen Mark Anderson [1963] Director; Jonathon Norman Backhouse [1967] Director/Solicitor; David John Berry [1966] Director; Dr Richard David Dobrashian [1969] Director; Peter Graham Forrest [1947] Director/Chartered Surveyor; Brian Christopher Marsden [1948] Director/Chartered Accountant; Oliver John McCann [1976] Director; Julie Marie Meadows [1970] Director/Chartered Accountant; Edward Slinger [1938] Director/Circuit Judge; James Richard Yates [1945] Managing Director

Westinghouse Electric Company UK Limited
Incorporated: 26 May 2000
Net Worth Deficit: £34,090,000 *Total Assets:* £31,540,000
Registered Office: Springfields, Salwick, Preston, Lancs, PR4 0XJ
Activities: Repair of other equipment
Parent: Westinghouse Electric UK Holdings Limited
Officers: Fiona Anne Houghton, Secretary; Kirsty Amer [1970] Director NF and CM Quality and Performance Improvement; Linda Aylmore [1970] Director; Michael Robert Gornall [1964] Managing Director; John Kipling [1972] Director; David Mills [1965] Director/Head of Communications & Marketing; Brian Nixon [1976] Director

Westinghouse Electric UK Holdings Limited
Incorporated: 10 January 1990 *Employees:* 66
Net Worth: £82,633,000 *Total Assets:* £707,779,008
Registered Office: Springfields, Salwick, Preston, Lancs, PR4 0XJ
Activities: Activities of head offices
Parent: Brookfield WEC EMEA Holdings Ltd
Officers: Fiona Anne Houghton, Secretary; Michael Terrance Sweeney, Secretary; Mark Blinn [1962] Director/Consultant [American]; Ron Bloom [1955] Director/Vice Chairman and Managing Partner [American]; Jose Emeterio Gutierrez Elso [1959] Director/Chief Executive Officer [Spanish]; Denis Turcotte [1961] Director/Managing Partner [Canadian]; Mark Weinberg [1971] Director/Managing Partner [American]

Westline Investments Limited
Incorporated: 6 December 2001 *Employees:* 3
Net Worth: £32,334 *Total Assets:* £8,667,017
Registered Office: c/o Fergus and Fergus, 24 Oswald Road, Chorlton Cum Hardy, Manchester, M21 9LP
Activities: Construction of commercial buildings
Major Shareholder: Samera Abdusalam Ali Massaud
Officers: Samera Abdusalam Ali Massaud, Secretary; Abdussa Lam Massaud [1948] Director/Owner of Import/Export Business [Libyan]; Samera Abdusalam Ali Massaud [1979] Director [Libyan]

Westmorland Limited
Incorporated: 8 February 2005 *Employees:* 912
Net Worth: £27,836,000 *Total Assets:* £79,230,000
Registered Office: Westmorland Place, Orton, Penrith, Cumbria, CA10 3SB
Activities: Retail sale in non-specialised stores with food, beverages or tobacco predominating
Parent: Chapel Beck Limited
Officers: John Carter Dunning [1934] Director/Farmer; Sarah Beatrice Dunning [1970] Director/Chief Executive; Bryan Mark Gray [1953] Director; Laurence King [1962] Director; Jane Margaret Lane [1969] Director

Wetherby Building Systems Limited
Incorporated: 20 August 1998 *Employees:* 87
Net Worth: £9,182,968 *Total Assets:* £18,175,336
Registered Office: 1 Kid Glove Road, Golborne Enterprise Park, Golborne, Wigan, Lancs, WA3 3GS
Activities: Other construction installation
Major Shareholder: Robert Harold Deane
Officers: Steven John Smith, Secretary; Karen Arnold [1975] Director; Robert Harold Deane [1953] Director; Paul Kirby [1965] Director; Steven John Smith [1969] Director

WEX Europe Services (UK) Limited
Incorporated: 20 February 2014
Net Worth: £7,418,000 *Total Assets:* £39,148,000
Registered Office: Emperor Court, Emperor Way, Crewe Business Park, Crewe, Cheshire, CW1 6BD
Activities: Other business support service activities n.e.c.
Parent: WEX Europe Services Holdings Limited
Officers: William Stanley Holmes [1964] Director/Chief Executive Officer; Roberto Simon Rabanal [1974] Director/Chief Financial Officer [Spanish/American]; Hilary Ann Rapkin [1966] Director/Legal Counsel [American]

WEX Europe Services Limited
Incorporated: 7 November 2012 *Employees:* 242
Net Worth: £33,778,720 *Total Assets:* £236,192,672
Registered Office: Emperor Court, Emperor Way, Crewe Business Park, Crewe, Cheshire, CW1 6BD
Activities: Wholesale of other fuels and related products
Parent: WEX INc.
Officers: Jay W. Collins [1970] Director [American]; Bill Holmes [1964] Director Timothy Simon Oldfield [1964] Director; Scott Robert Phillips [1969] Director [American]; Roberto Simon Rabanal [1974] Director [Spanish/American]

WFEL Holdings Limited
Incorporated: 29 April 2006 *Employees:* 75
Net Worth: £28,564,000 *Total Assets:* £54,214,000
Registered Office: WFEL, Sir Richard Fairey Road, Heaton Chapel, Stockport, Cheshire, SK4 5DY
Activities: Manufacture of other fabricated metal products n.e.c.
Parent: Krauss-Maffei Wegmann GmbH & Co. KG
Officers: Patrick Neill Grady, Secretary; Ian Anderton [1965] Director; Patrick Neill Grady [1965] Finance Director; Ralf Ketzel [1959] Director [German]; Horst Rieder [1965] Director [German]; Jurgen Weber [1953] Director [German]

WFEL Limited
Incorporated: 11 February 1936 *Employees:* 72
Net Worth: £36,862,000 *Total Assets:* £56,518,000
Registered Office: WFEL, Sir Richard Fairey Road, Heaton Chapel, Stockport, Cheshire, SK4 5DY
Activities: Manufacture of other fabricated metal products n.e.c.
Parent: WFEL Holdings Limited
Officers: Patrick Neill Grady, Secretary; Ian Anderton [1965] Director; Patrick Neill Grady [1965] Finance Director; Ralf Ketzel [1959] Director [German]; Horst Rieder [1965] Director [German]; Jurgen Weber [1953] Director [German]

WGH UK Holdings Limited
Incorporated: 5 August 2003 *Employees:* 2
Net Worth Deficit: £20,126 000 *Total Assets:* £55,311,000
Registered Office: Wheelabrator House, 22 Edward Court, Broadheath, Altrincham, Cheshire, WA14 5GL
Activities: Non-trading company
Parent: WGH Holding Corp
Officers: Robert Victor Dingle, Secretary; Ian Bruce Bird [1949] Director [American]; Andrew James Matsuyama [1973] Director/Accountant [American]

WGH UK Limited
Incorporated: 5 August 2003 *Employees:* 2
Net Worth: £55,346,000 *Total Assets:* £55,346,000
Registered Office: Wheelabrator House, 22 Edward Court, Broadheath, Altrincham, Cheshire, WA14 5GL
Activities: Non-trading company
Parent: WGH UK Holdings Limited
Officers: Robert Victor Dingle, Secretary; Ian Bruce Bird [1949] Director [American]; Andrew James Matsuyama [1973] Director/Accountant [American]

What More UK Limited
Incorporated: 27 October 1999 *Employees:* 224
Net Worth: £20,885,198 *Total Assets:* £47,238,792
Registered Office: Pendle Court, 4 Mead Way, Shuttleworth Mead Business Park, Padiham, Burnley, Lancs, BB12 7NG
Activities: Manufacture of other plastic products
Officers: Josephine Dyson, Secretary; John Anthony MacAuley Grimshaw [1951] Commercial Director; Virginia Hargreaves [1968] Financial Director; Andrew Mark Holt [1964] Director; Jacqueline Mary Holt [1962] Resource and Development Director [Irish]; Garry Keith Ireland [1971] Operational Director; Andrew Riley [1963] Sales Director; Iain Sellick [1968] Production Director; Roger Stephen Tout [1960] Works Director

WHC01 Limited
Incorporated: 25 July 2016 *Employees:* 525
Net Worth: £3,291,390 *Total Assets:* £12,099,414
Registered Office: Suite A, Fernbank House, Springwood Way, Tytherington Business Park, Macclesfield, Cheshire, SK10 2XA
Activities: Other activities of employment placement agencies
Shareholder: Andrew Healing
Officers: Michael William Fell [1957] Director; Andrew Healing [1969] Director; Roger Charles Queen [1964] Director; Elaine Young [1965] Managing Director

Wheatsheaf Group Finance Company
Incorporated: 14 November 2012
Net Worth: £141,282,816 *Total Assets:* £141,282,816
Registered Office: The Quarry, Hill Road, Eccleston, Chester, CH4 9HQ
Activities: Activities of head offices
Parent: Wheatsheaf Group Limited
Officers: Geoffrey Murray Chadwick, Secretary; Fiona Jane Emmett [1982] Director/Accountant; Anthony William Searson James [1968] Director/Accountant; Graham Paul Ramsbottom [1965] Director/Surveyor

Wheatsheaf Group Limited
Incorporated: 5 July 1996 *Employees:* 331
Net Worth: £213,375,008 *Total Assets:* £223,842,000
Registered Office: The Quarry, Hill Road, Eccleston, Chester, CH4 9HQ
Activities: Activities of head offices
Shareholders: Dame Fiona Claire Reynolds; Mark Robin Preston; William Bruce Kendall; Francis Alexander Scott; Jeremy Henry Moore Newsum; Michael George Alexander McLintock
Officers: Geoffrey Murray Chadwick, Secretary; Johann Stephan Dolezalek [1956] Director/Venture Capital [American]; Peter Lawrence Doyle [1952] Director/Accountant; Anthony William Searson James [1968] Director/Accountant; William Bruce Kendall [1961] Director; Professor Clive Dylan Morris [1971] Director/Pharmaceutical Executive; Mark Robin Preston [1968] Director/Chartered Surveyor; Graham Paul Ramsbottom [1965] Director/Surveyor; Francis Alexander Scott [1959] Director

Wheelabrator Group Limited
Incorporated: 26 March 1891 *Employees:* 100
Net Worth: £24,373,000 *Total Assets:* £45,178,000
Registered Office: Wheelabrator House, 22 Edward Court, Broadheath, Altrincham, Cheshire, WA14 5GL
Activities: Manufacture of pumps
Parent: Wheelabrator Technologies Limited
Officers: Neil Christopher Moseley, Secretary/Accountant; Ian Bruce Bird [1949] Director [American]; Andrew James Matsuyama [1973] Director/Accountant [American]

Wheelabrator Technologies (UK) Limited
Incorporated: 8 September 1987
Net Worth: £33,662,000 *Total Assets:* £51,660,000
Registered Office: Wheelabrator House, 22 Edward Court, Broadheath, Altrincham, Cheshire, WA14 5GL
Activities: Activities of head offices
Parent: WGH UK Limited
Officers: Robert Victor Dingle, Secretary; Ian Bruce Bird [1949] Director [American]; Andrew James Matsuyama [1973] Director/Accountant [American]

Whelan Hotelco Limited
Incorporated: 14 June 2010 *Employees:* 132
Net Worth: £7,414,585 *Total Assets:* £13,307,800
Registered Office: Loire Drive, Robin Park, Wigan, Lancs, WN5 0UH
Activities: Hotels and similar accommodation
Major Shareholder: David Whelan
Officers: Jayne Alison Best [1962] Director; David Whelan [1936] Director; Patricia Mary Whelan [1936] Director

Dave Whelan Sports Limited
Incorporated: 13 March 2009 *Employees:* 2,508
Net Worth: £55,943,656 *Total Assets:* £211,063,424
Registered Office: Whelco Place, Enfield Industrial Estate, Enfield Street, Pemberton, Wigan, Lancs, WN5 8DB
Activities: Retail sale of clothing in specialised stores
Major Shareholder: Jayne Alison Best
Officers: Jayne Alison Best [1962] Director; Scott Barry Best [1976] Director; Daniel Andrew Cornes [1976] Director/Chartered Accountant; Matthew Joseph Sharpe [1987] Director; David Whelan [1936] Director/Retailer; Patricia Mary Whelan [1936] Director

Whinmoor Estates Limited
Incorporated: 22 March 1924 *Employees:* 6
Net Worth: £10,001,751 *Total Assets:* £12,176,900
Registered Office: 2 Friarsgate, Grosvenor Street, Chester, CH1 1XG
Activities: Other letting and operating of own or leased real estate
Officers: Nigel John Anderton [1954] Director/Chartered Surveyor; Ian James Davies [1966] Director/Chartered Surveyor; Peter James Hitchcock [1946] Director/Chartered Surveyor; Andrew Mills [1966] Director/Chartered Surveyor; Mark Guy Williams [1955] Director/Chartered Surveyor

Whiskey Jack Developments Limited
Incorporated: 29 September 2005
Net Worth: £1,003,308 *Total Assets:* £7,749,122
Registered Office: The Spectrum, 56-58 Benson Road, Birchwood, Warrington, Cheshire, WA3 7PQ
Activities: Other letting and operating of own or leased real estate
Shareholders: Peter Daniel Done; Andrea Jean Done
Officers: Andrea Done, Secretary/Architect; Andrea Done [1973] Director/Architect; Peter Daniel Done [1974] Director/Property Developer

Whispering Smith Group PLC
Incorporated: 3 January 1996 *Employees:* 140
Net Worth: £37,686,308 *Total Assets:* £41,534,004
Registered Office: The Exchange, 5 Bank Street, Bury, Lancs, BL9 0DN
Activities: Non-trading company
Shareholders: Rajan Kumar; Sanjay Kumar
Officers: Rajan Kumar, Secretary/Director; Rajan Kumar [1961] Director; Sanjay Kumar [1969] Director

Whispering Smith Limited
Incorporated: 6 September 1985 *Employees:* 140
Net Worth: £26,858,140 *Total Assets:* £36,509,232
Registered Office: The Exchange, 5 Bank Street, Bury, Lancs, BL9 0DN
Activities: Wholesale of clothing and footwear
Parent: Whispering Smith Group PLC
Officers: Rajan Kumar, Secretary; King Brian [1957] Director; Diane Heslop [1962] Finance Director; Rajan Kumar [1961] Director; Rohil Kumar [1993] Director; Rohina Kumar [1991] Director; Sanjay Kumar [1969] Director

Whitakers Chocolates Limited
Incorporated: 11 July 1961 *Employees:* 145
Net Worth: £3,473,671 *Total Assets:* £7,204,603
Registered Office: 85 Keighley Road, Skipton, N Yorks, BD23 2NA
Activities: Manufacture of cocoa and chocolate confectionery
Shareholders: Roland John Whitaker; William Reginald Whitaker
Officers: Sally Clare Thorpe, Secretary; Roland John Whitaker [1936] Director; William Reginald Whitaker [1960] Director

White Moss Horticulture Limited
Incorporated: 16 January 1951 *Employees:* 87
Net Worth Deficit: £9,619,375 *Total Assets:* £9,919,209
Registered Office: White Moss Horticulture Ltd, Simonswood Moss, North Perimeter Road, Kirkby, Merseyside, L33 3AN
Activities: Other manufacturing n.e.c.
Parent: The Minister for Public Expenditure and Reform
Officers: Anna-Marie Curry, Secretary; Michael Barry [1957] Director [Irish]; Mark Higgins [1959] Director [Irish]; Mark Gerard McGloin [1974] Director/Financial Controller [Irish]

Whitecroft Lighting Limited
Incorporated: 27 September 1999 *Employees:* 477
Net Worth: £31,851,808 *Total Assets:* £47,939,584
Registered Office: Burlington Street, Ashton under Lyne, Lancs, OL7 0AX
Activities: Manufacture of electric lighting equipment
Parent: Whitecroft Lighting Holdings Ltd
Officers: Graham Michael Daws, Secretary; Paul Anthony Cassidy [1963] Director; Graham Michael Daws [1962] Director/Accountant; Matthew John Paskin [1980] Director/Designer; David Raif Serif [1964] Director; David George Trail [1960] Director; Dr Geert Jan Van Der Meer [1965] Director/Manager [Dutch]; Michael Wood [1964] Director

Whitecross Dental Care Limited
Incorporated: 18 December 1929 *Employees:* 2,819
Net Worth: £120,799,000 *Total Assets:* £230,768,992
Registered Office: Europa House, Europa Trading Estate, Stoneclough Road, Kearsley, Manchester, M26 1GG
Activities: Dental practice activities
Parent: IDH Acquisitions Limited
Officers: Leo Damian Carroll, Secretary; Clifford Gwyn Davies [1966] Clinical Director; Sharon Patricia Letters [1975] Clinical Director; Steven Andrew Melton [1962] Managing Director - Mydentist; Bernard Moroney [1953] Clinical Director; Manish Prasad [1972] Clinical Director; Tom Riall [1960] Director; Mohammed Omar Shafi Khan [1974] Director/Chief Financial Officer; Krista Nyree Whitley [1970] Clinical Director

Whitecross Group Limited
Incorporated: 23 March 1998
Net Worth: £15,438,000 *Total Assets:* £16,938,000
Registered Office: Europa House, Europa Trading Estate, Stoneclough Road, Kearsley, Manchester, M26 1GG
Activities: Activities of head offices
Parent: Diverse Acquisitions Limited
Officers: Leo Damian Carrol , Secretary; Tom Riall [1960] Director; Mohammed Omar Shafi Khan [1974] Director/Chief Financial Officer; Krista Nyree Whitley [1970] Clinical Director

Whitecross Healthcare Limited
Incorporated: 31 January 1994
Net Worth: £2,016,000 *Total Assets:* £16,942,000
Registered Office: Europa House, Europa Trading Estate, Stoneclough Road, Kearsley, Manchester, M26 1GG
Activities: Activities of head offices
Parent: Whitecross Group Limited
Officers: Leo Damian Carroll, Secretary; Tom Riall [1960] Director; Mohammed Omar Shafi Khan [1974] Director/Chief Financial Officer; Krista Nyree Whitley [1970] Clinical Director

Whitford Limited
Incorporated: 28 July 1969 *Employees:* 109
Net Worth: £17,523,000 *Total Assets:* £21,247,000
Registered Office: 11 Stuart Road, Manor Park, Runcorn, Cheshire, WA7 1TH
Activities: Manufacture of paints, varnishes and similar coatings, mastics and sealants
Major Shareholder: David Pond Willis Jnr
Officers: David Andrew Johnson, Secretary; Martin John Garnett [1953] Managing Director; Anne Severns Willis [1962] Director [American]; David Pond Willis [1936] Director/Business Manager [American]

V.A. Whitley & Co. Limited
Incorporated: 27 October 1949 *Employees:* 84
Net Worth: £9,218,757 *Total Assets:* £11,013,765
Registered Office: Milwarc House, Fir Street, Heywood, Lancs, OL10 1NW
Activities: Wholesale of meat and meat products
Officers: Christopher Mark Rogers, Secretary; Stephen James Duxbury [1972] Director/Certified Accountant; Anthony Milward Rogers [1937] Director; Catherine Helen Rogers [1967] Director; Christopher Mark Rogers [1964] Director; Elizabeth Margaret Rogers [1938] Director; Michael Robert Wallace [1957] Director

F.G.Whitley and Sons Co.Limited
Incorporated: 19 April 1961 *Employees:* 21
Net Worth: £6,487,668 *Total Assets:* £8,904,044
Registered Office: Park House, Broncoed Busness Park, Mold, Flintshire, CH7 1FQ
Activities: Construction of domestic buildings
Shareholder: William Basil Whitley
Officers: David Thomas Humpage, Secretary; William Basil Whitley [1939] Director

Whittle Eastern Europe Logistics Ltd.
Incorporated: 26 July 1994 *Employees:* 38
Net Worth: £2,557,191 *Total Assets:* £7,906,410
Registered Office: Suites 1 & 7, The Printworks, Hey Road, Barrow, Lancs, BB7 9WA
Activities: Freight transport by road
Shareholders: Natasa Sabanovic; NMS Logistics Limited
Officers: Marko Sabanovic, Secretary; Vladimir Pasternak [1972] Operations Director [Ukrainian]; Natasa Sabanovic [1970] Managing Director

Whittle Programmed Maintenance Limited
Incorporated: 20 January 1998 *Employees:* 188
Net Worth: £3,082,597 *Total Assets:* £7,283,783
Registered Office: Cotton Place, 2 Ivy Street, Birkenhead, Merseyside, CH41 5EF
Activities: Painting
Parent: Roy Hankinson (Holdings) Limited
Officers: Stephen Roy Hankinson [1957] Director; Ivor Arthur Thomas [1960] Contracts Director

WHP Telecoms Limited
Incorporated: 21 July 1998 *Employees:* 311
Net Worth: £18,493,324 *Total Assets:* £36,780,544
Registered Office: 401 Faraday Street, Birchwood, Warrington, Cheshire, WA3 6GA
Activities: Construction of utility projects for electricity and telecommunications
Parent: WHP Holdings Ltd
Officers: Martyn James Cheyne [1970] Director/Chartered Surveyor; Paul Nicholas Hullah [1967] Director/Structural Engineer; David Christopher Humphreys [1973] Director/Chartered Accountant; Robert Michael Edward Potter [1972] Director/Chartered Certified Accountant; Christopher Tracey [1971] Operations Director

WHT Holdings Limited
Incorporated: 7 February 2007 *Employees:* 278
Net Worth: £16,645,515 *Total Assets:* £19,529,420
Registered Office: Wallwork Offices, 69 Hacking, Street, Bury, Lancs, BL9 0RG
Activities: Activities of head offices
Officers: Carole Ann Chettoe, Secretary; Ronald Peter Carpenter [1959] Director/Engineer; Simeon Peter Collins [1971] Sales Director; Ian Charles Griffin [1964] Director/Metallurgist; Hamish Andrew Wallwork [1959] Director/Metallurgist; Susan Jane Wallwork [1955] Director/Administrator

Widdop Bingham & Co. Limited
Incorporated: 10 November 1920 *Employees:* 130
Net Worth: £8,128,998 *Total Assets:* £13,217,248
Registered Office: Broadgate, Broadway Business Park, Chadderton, Oldham, Lancs, OL9 9XE
Activities: Wholesale of household goods (other than musical instruments) n.e.c
Parent: Widdop Bingham (Holdings) Ltd
Officers: Christopher John Illingworth, Secretary; Christopher John Illingworth [1958] Finance Director; Michael Andrew Illingworth [1960] Director/Manager; Robert Illingworth [1930] Director; Robert Stuart Illingworth [1957] Director/Manager; Stephen Stuart Illingworth [1983] Director/Head of Product Development & National Accounts

Widex UK Limited
Incorporated: 3 December 2009 *Employees:* 46
Net Worth: £5,299,165 *Total Assets:* £8,297,371
Registered Office: Winster House, Lakeside, Chester Business Park, Chester, CH4 9QT
Activities: Manufacture of medical and dental instruments and supplies
Officers: Robert Allen, Secretary; Henrik Skak Bender [1984] Director [Danish]; Jorgen Jensen [1968] Director/Chief Executive Officer [Danish]

Wienerberger Limited
Incorporated: 29 November 2004 *Employees:* 1,166
Net Worth: £121,773,000 *Total Assets:* £315,228,000
Registered Office: Wienerberger House, Brooks Drive, Cheadle Royal Business Park, Cheadle, Cheshire, SK8 3SA
Activities: Manufacture of bricks, tiles and construction products, in baked clay
Officers: Michael Grace, Secretary; Keith Stuart Barker [1961] Managing Director; Paul Stevenson [1959] Finance Director

Wigan and Leigh Homes Ltd
Incorporated: 15 March 2002 *Employees:* 4
Net Worth: £5,026,669 *Total Assets:* £8,362,696
Registered Office: Progress House, Westwood Park Drive, Wigan, Lancs, WN3 4HH
Activities: Management of real estate on a fee or contract basis
Parent: Wigan Council
Officers: Edward John Flanagan, Secretary; Paul Barton [1965] Director; Penny Jane McGinty [1966] Assistant Director

Wigan and Leigh Hospice
Incorporated: 10 November 1982 *Employees:* 91
Net Worth: £10,396,968 *Total Assets:* £10,799,024
Registered Office: Kildare Street, Hindley, Wigan, Lancs, WN2 3HZ
Activities: Other human health activities
Officers: Janet Anderton, Secretary; Walter Brown [1951] Director; Paul Francis Carroll [1958] Director/Retired; Margaret Sarah Evans [1951] Director/Retired; Doctor Shelagh Elaine Kenward [1960] Director/Doctor; June Christine Law [1957] Director/Retired; David Peter Mayes [1952] Director/Solicitor; Christopher Morley [1974] Finance Director; Pauline Payne [1948] Director/Retired; Mary Reid [1946] Director/Retired; Phillip Roy Williams [1947] Director/Retired

Wigan Athletic A.F.C. Limited
Incorporated: 8 November 1932 *Employees:* 160
Net Worth Deficit: £11,748,772 *Total Assets:* £10,850,155
Registered Office: DW Stadium, Loire Drive, Robin Park, Wigan, Lancs, WN5 0UZ
Activities: Activities of sport clubs
Parent: Wigan Athletic Holdings
Officers: Garry John Cook [1962] Director; Jonathan Harvey Jackson [1967] Director/Chief Executive; David James Sharpe [1991] Director/General Manager; Matthew Joseph Sharpe [1987] Director/Manager

Wigan Athletic Holdings Limited
Incorporated: 14 June 2010 *Employees:* 298
Net Worth: £28,004,508 *Total Assets:* £51,005,460
Registered Office: Loire Drive, Robin Park, Wigan, Lancs, WN5 0UH
Activities: Operation of sports facilities
Major Shareholder: David Whelan
Officers: David James Sharpe [1991] Director/General Manager; David Whelan [1936] Director; Patricia Mary Whelan [1936] Director

Wigan Boys & Girls Club
Incorporated: 25 June 2009 *Employees:* 160
Net Worth: £9,479,269 *Total Assets:* £9,534,678
Registered Office: Wigan Youth Zone, Parsons Walk, Wigan, Lancs, WN1 1RU
Activities: Other business support service activities n.e.c.
Officers: David John Fairhurst, Secretary; Martin Ainscough [1952] Director; William Ainscough [1938] Director; Alison Clare Higham [1962] Director; Anthony Hitchen [1960] Director; David Whelan [1936] Director

Wigan Football Company Limited
Incorporated: 8 December 1997 *Employees:* 138
Net Worth: £24,571,936 *Total Assets:* £30,442,462
Registered Office: Loire Drive, Robin Park, Wigan, Lancs, WN5 0UH
Activities: Operation of sports facilities
Parent: Wigan Athletic Holdings Ltd
Officers: Richard Ellis Bramwell, Secretary; Richard Ellis Bramwell [1976] Director/Accountant; Garry John Cook [1962] Director; Paul Nicholas McKevitt [1968] Director/Local Government Officer; David James Sharpe [1991] Director/General Manager; David Whelan [1936] Director

Wigan Leisure and Culture Trust
Incorporated: 23 December 2002 *Employees:* 541
Net Worth: £3,424,570 *Total Assets:* £9,842,337
Registered Office: Indoor Sports Centre, Loire Drive, Robin Park, Wigan, Lancs, WN5 0UL
Activities: Operation of arts facilities
Officers: Dawn Marie Heaton, Secretary; Della Ann Bartle [1957] Director; Gareth William Cross [1976] Director/Communications; Paul Graham Farrington [1984] Director/Senior Client Manager; David Arthur LEA [1949] Director/Retired; David William Lythgoe [1957] Director/Educational Consultant; Jennifer Brenda Meadows [1981] Managing Director; James Moodie [1956] Director/Trade Union Official; Paul Thomas Moss [1958] Finance Director; David Anthony Newman [1956] Director/Chartered Accountant; Jeremy David Charles Noott [1971] Director/Development and Delivery Specialist; Councillor Eunice Smethurst [1948] Director/Local Government Councillor; Michael Andrew Weston [1963] Director; Catherine Jane Wilks [1981] Director/Senior Data Assurance Manager

Wigan Metropolitan Development Company (Investment) Limited
Incorporated: 17 May 1984 *Employees:* 25
Net Worth: £6,210,259 *Total Assets:* £8,109,142
Registered Office: The Wigan Investment Centre, Waterside Drive, off Swan Meadow Road, Wigan, Lancs, WN3 5BA
Activities: Other letting and operating of own or leased real estate
Officers: Councillor Keith Cunliffe [1953] Director/Nurse; Penny Jane McGinty [1966] Director/Local Government Officer; Paul Nicholas McKevitt [1968] Director/Local Government Officer; Councillor David Trevor Molyneux [1954] Director/Buyer; Lord Peter Richard Charles Smith [1945] Director/Lecturer; Frederick Bown Walker [1946] Director

Wiggett Construction Group Limited
Incorporated: 22 July 1998 *Employees:* 41
Net Worth: £16,054,790 *Total Assets:* £19,757,920
Registered Office: Viking House, 449 Middleton Chadderton, Oldham, Lancs, OL9 9LB
Activities: Activities of head offices
Shareholders: Philip John Wiggett 1997 Discretionary Trust; Philip John Wiggett
Officers: Philip John Wiggett, Secretary/Director; Jennifer Claire Sutton [1985] Director; Philip John Wiggett [1954] Director; Samuel Philip John Wiggett [1982] Director/Quantity Surveyor

Wiggett Homes Limited
Incorporated: 11 December 1985 *Employees:* 2
Net Worth: £2,125,183 *Total Assets:* £14,706,321
Registered Office: Viking House, 449 Middleton Road, Chadderton, Oldham, Lancs, OL9 9LB
Activities: Construction of commercial buildings
Officers: Philip John Wiggett, Secretary; Jennifer Claire Sutton [1985] Director; Philip John Wiggett [1954] Director/Quantity Surveyor; Samuel Philip John Wiggett [1982] Director/Quantity Surveyor

Wiggins Teape Group Limited (The)
Incorporated: 1 April 1953
Net Worth Deficit: £34,226,000 *Total Assets:* £120,012,000
Registered Office: Eversheds House, 70 Great Bridgewater Street, Manchester, M1 5ES
Activities: Activities of head offices
Parent: Arjo Wiggins UK Holdings Limited
Officers: Alain Philippe Daniel Gourjon [1965] Group Accounts, Tax & Administrative Director [French]; Jonathan David Mitchell [1965] Managing Director Arjowiggins Creative Papers SAS

WIL Finco
Incorporated: 1 July 2005
Net Worth: £129,703,488 *Total Assets:* £129,703,488
Registered Office: The Quarry, Hill Road, Eccleston, Chester, CH4 9HQ
Activities: Non-trading company
Parent: Wheatsheaf Group Finance Company
Officers: Geoffrey Murray Chadwick, Secretary; Fiona Jane Emmett [1982] Director/Accountant; Anthony William Searson James [1968] Director; Graham Paul Ramsbottom [1965] Director/Surveyor

Ashley Wilde Holdings Limited
Incorporated: 12 November 1990 *Employees:* 113
Net Worth: £9,894,287 *Total Assets:* £18,226,844
Registered Office: c/o Freedman Frankl & Taylor, Reeedham House, 31 King Street West, Manchester, M3 2PJ
Activities: Non-trading company
Shareholders: Ashley Leon Brodin; Simon Dean Brodin
Officers: Simon Dean Brodin, Secretary; Ashley Leon Brodin [1945] Director

The Wilkinson Corporation Limited
Incorporated: 1 October 1979 *Employees:* 63
Net Worth: £826,811 *Total Assets:* £9,006,531
Registered Office: Shield Drive, Wardley Industrial Estate, Worsley, Manchester, M28 2WD
Activities: Wholesale of other machinery and equipment
Major Shareholder: John Arthur Wilkinson
Officers: Elaine Margaret Wilkinson, Secretary; Elaine Margaret Wilkinson [1947] Director/Company Secretary; John Arthur Wilkinson [1945] Director

Wilkinson Star Limited
Incorporated: 8 November 1983 *Employees:* 59
Net Worth: £3,725,469 *Total Assets:* £11,668,685
Registered Office: Shield Drive, Wardley Industrial Estate, Worsley, Manchester, M28 2WD
Activities: Wholesale of mining, construction and civil engineering machinery
Major Shareholder: John Arthur Wilkinson
Officers: Elaine Margaret Wilkinson, Secretary; Alan Richard Carter [1975] Finance Director; Stephen Paul Murray [1955] Managing Director; Elaine Margaret Wilkinson [1947] Director/Secretary; John Arthur Wilkinson [1945] Director; Karl Wilkinson [1968] Director; Tina Wilkinson-Bell [1969] Director

Willan Group Limited
Incorporated: 31 March 2000 *Employees:* 12
Net Worth: £19,886,964 *Total Assets:* £28,620,186
Registered Office: 2 Brooklands Road, Sale, Cheshire, M33 3SS
Activities: Activities of head offices
Shareholders: Richard James Willan; Julia Elizabeth Willan; Linda Elizabeth Willan
Officers: Alison Dawn Booth, Secretary; Keith Brian Alderson [1960] Director; Adrian Paul Stewart [1957] Construction Director; Linda Elizabeth Willan [1949] Director

Willan Investments Limited
Incorporated: 3 January 1946 *Employees:* 7
Net Worth: £11,226,128 *Total Assets:* £19,760,412
Registered Office: 2 Brooklands Road, Sale, Cheshire, M33 3SS
Activities: Other letting and operating of own or leased real estate
Shareholders: Richard James Willan; Julia Elizabeth Willan; Linda Elizabeth Willan; Willan UK Limited
Officers: Alison Dawn Booth, Secretary; Alison Dawn Booth [1977] Finance Director; Adrian Paul Stewart [1957] Director

Willan UK Limited
Incorporated: 27 October 1994 *Employees:* 4
Net Worth: £9,502,027 *Total Assets:* £17,532,252
Registered Office: 2 Brooklands Road, Sale, Manchester, M33 3SS
Activities: Activities of head offices
Shareholders: Richard James Willan; Julia Elizabeth Willan; Linda Elizabeth Willan; Willan Group Limited
Officers: Alison Dawn Booth, Secretary; Alison Dawn Booth [1977] Finance Director; Adrian Paul Stewart [1957] Director

Willem Properties Limited
Incorporated: 28 March 2007 *Employees:* 3
Net Worth: £2,620,390 *Total Assets:* £13,165,298
Registered Office: The Copper Room, The Deva Centre, Trinity Way, Manchester, M3 7BG
Activities: Buying and selling of own real estate
Shareholders: Carol Walker; Harold Walker
Officers: Emma Louise Cowin, Secretary; Emma Louise Cowin [1976] Director/Quantity Surveyor; Carol Walker [1947] Director/Housewife; Harold Walker [1945] Director/Retired

J.D. Williams & Company Limited
Incorporated: 13 December 1921 *Employees:* 2,695
Net Worth: £308,688,992 *Total Assets:* £976,641,024
Registered Office: Griffin House, 40 Lever Street, Manchester, M60 6ES
Activities: Retail sale via mail order houses or via Internet
Parent: J.D. Williams Group Limited
Officers: Theresa Casey, Secretary; Nigel Alliance [1935] Director; Alyson Tracey Fadil [1973] Director; Stephen Johnson [1972] Director; Craig Barry Lovelace [1973] Director/Accountant; Angela Lesley Spindler [1962] Director; Ann Steer [1972] Director; Ralph Eric Tucker [1974] Director; Adam John Warne [1978] Director

D P Williams Group Limited
Incorporated: 11 March 2014 *Employees:* 15
Net Worth: £12,925,096 *Total Assets:* £16,215,751
Registered Office: Brookside Works, Denbigh Road, Hendre, Mold, Flintshire, CH7 5QA
Activities: Operation of gravel and sand pits; mining of clays and kaolin
Major Shareholder: Darrell Patrick Williams
Officers: Bradley James Williams [1985] Director; Darrell Patrick Williams [1957] Director; Hazel Williams [1958] Director

J.D. Williams Group Limited
Incorporated: 19 February 1968 *Employees:* 1
Net Worth: £29,775,292 *Total Assets:* £116,778,504
Registered Office: Griffin House, 40 Lever Street, Manchester, M60 6ES
Activities: Activities of head offices
Parent: N Brown Group PLC
Officers: Daniel Michael Cropper, Secretary; Craig Barry Lovelace [1973] Director/Accountant; Ralph Eric Tucker [1974] Director

Williams Motor Co.(Holdings) Limited
Incorporated: 23 January 1958 *Employees:* 783
Net Worth: £44,734,000 *Total Assets:* £136,828,992
Registered Office: 2 Vincent Way, Raikes Lane, Bolton, Lancs, BL3 2NB
Activities: Sale of new cars and light motor vehicles
Major Shareholder: Margaret Mary Orton Williams
Officers: Alexandra Mary Cook [1971] Director/Group Head of Development; Nicholas John Cook [1952] Managing Director; Nicholas John Dunning [1962] Director; Margaret Mary Orton Williams [1939] Director/Chairman

Williams Tarr Construction Limited
Incorporated: 26 January 1918 *Employees:* 25
Net Worth: £4,205,954 *Total Assets:* £12,555,299
Registered Office: Bridge Road, Woolston, Warrington, Cheshire, WA1 4AU
Activities: Construction of commercial buildings
Officers: Christopher Frederick Carter, Secretary; Christopher Frederick Carter [1948] Director/Management Accountant; Trevor Hughes [1963] Contracts Director; Leslie Parker [1960] Contracts Director; David Michael Wilkinson [1969] Director/Chartered Accountant; John Charles Edward Wilkinson [1967] Director/Engineer Accountant

Williams Tarr Developments Limited
Incorporated: 19 April 1968
Net Worth: £626,412 *Total Assets:* £6,906,678
Registered Office: Bridge Road, Woolston, Warrington, Cheshire, WA1 4AU
Activities: Development of building projects
Officers: Christopher Frederick Carter, Secretary; Christopher Frederick Carter [1948] Director/Management Accountant; David Michael Wilkinson [1969] Director/Chartered Accountant; John Charles Edward Wilkinson [1967] Director/Engineer and Consultant

Williams Tarr Holdings Ltd
Incorporated: 10 April 1954 *Employees:* 26
Net Worth: £8,335,142 *Total Assets:* £15,534,821
Registered Office: Bridge Road, Woolston, Warrington, Cheshire, WA1 4AU
Activities: Activities of head offices
Officers: Christopher Frederick Carter, Secretary; Michael Graham Brabner [1949] Director/Solicitor; Stephen William Robson [1956] Bank Director; David Michael Wilkinson [1969] Director/Chartered Accountant; John Charles Edward Wilkinson [1967] Director/Management Accountant; Julia Ann Wilkinson [1939] Director

Ifor Williams Trailers Limited
Incorporated: 3 April 1975 *Employees:* 502
Net Worth: £16,420,484 *Total Assets:* £32,995,860
Registered Office: One St Peter's Square, Manchester, M2 3DE
Activities: Manufacture of other fabricated metal products n.e.c.
Major Shareholder: John Owen Williams
Officers: Carole Ann Williams, Secretary; John Owen Williams [1962] Director

Willow Park Housing Trust Limited
Incorporated: 4 February 1999 *Employees:* 368
Net Worth: £124,530,000 *Total Assets:* £242,342,000
Registered Office: Wythenshawe House, 8 Poundswick Lane, Wythenshawe, Manchester, M22 9TA
Activities: Renting and operating of Housing Association real estate
Officers: Shahida Latif-Haider, Secretary; Robert William Cressey [1962] Director/Accountant; Bernadette Mary Heanue [1963] Director/Events Promoter [Irish]; Sarah Jayne Judge [1990] Director/Community Organiser; Eula Maude Mesquita [1940] Director/Retired; Sarah Alison Russell [1981] Director/Solicitor; Nigel Howard Sedman [1965] Director of Investment and Regeneration; Sam Wilson [1980] Director/Systems Analyst

Willowfox Limited
Incorporated: 15 October 2004 *Employees:* 34
Net Worth: £3,389,065 *Total Assets:* £16,396,570
Registered Office: Building 2, 3rd Floor, Universal Square, Devonshire Street North, Manchester, M12 6JH
Activities: Other letting and operating of own or leased real estate
Officers: Nicholas Graham Edward Lake, Secretary; Carol Allen [1963] Director; Graham Edward Lake [1944] Director/Solicitor

Wilmslow PP Limited
Incorporated: 18 March 2010
Net Worth: £3,046,687 *Total Assets:* £9,066,418
Registered Office: Hamilton House, Church Street, Altrincham, Cheshire, WA14 4DR
Activities: Other letting and operating of own or leased real estate
Major Shareholder: Brian George Kennedy
Officers: Adrian Christopher Kirk [1961] Finance Director

Wilson & Scott (Highways) Limited
Incorporated: 12 March 1952 *Employees:* 99
Net Worth: £5,276,968 *Total Assets:* £8,942,607
Registered Office: 8 Stanhope Street, Liverpool, L8 5RQ
Activities: Other specialised construction activities n.e.c.
Officers: Rupert Sinclair Higgin [1964] Director/Self Employed; Robert Ian Shaw Meadows [1946] Director; Stephen David Scott [1952] Director; Cameron Simms [1975] Contracts Director

L.& W.Wilson (Endmoor) Limited
Incorporated: 16 June 1972 *Employees:* 126
Net Worth: £5,066,136 *Total Assets:* £11,448,025
Registered Office: Shiralee, Endmoor, Kendal, Cumbria, LA8 0HL
Activities: Construction of commercial buildings
Shareholders: Betty Hayes; Alan Wilson
Officers: Alan Wilson, Secretary; Betty Hayes [1932] Director; Alan Wilson [1957] Director/Haulage Contractor

F Wilson (Holdings) Limited
Incorporated: 4 January 2000 *Employees:* 215
Net Worth: £11,262,709 *Total Assets:* £20,517,236
Registered Office: Adlington Court, Adlington Business Park, Adlington, Macclesfield, Cheshire, SK10 4NL
Activities: Activities of financial services holding companies
Parent: F Wilson (Group) Limited
Officers: Patrick Francis McDonnell [1965] Director [Irish]; Paul Christopher Moors [1962] Director; Christopher Patterson [1971] Director

F. Wilson (Insurance Brokers) Limited
Incorporated: 28 March 1977 *Employees:* 214
Net Worth: £8,371,492 *Total Assets:* £15,479,070
Registered Office: Adlington Court, Adlington Business Park, Adlington, Macclesfield, Cheshire, SK10 4NL
Activities: Non-life insurance
Parent: F Wilson (Holdings) Limited
Officers: Patrick Francis McDonnell [1965] Director [Irish]; Paul Christopher Moors [1962] Director; Paul O'Gorman [1967] Director/Insurance Broker; Christopher Patterson [1971] Director

W.O.&J.Wilson Limited
Incorporated: 30 December 1899 *Employees:* 55
Net Worth: £15,479,067 *Total Assets:* £16,750,725
Registered Office: c/o Duncan Sheard Glass, Castle Chambers, 43 Castle Street, Liverpool, L2 9TL
Activities: Other service activities n.e.c.
Officers: Martin William Charles Bloor, Secretary; Anna Page Ashworth [1963] Director/Marketing Consultant; Ian Michael Bolton [1965] Director/Stockbroker; Martin Henry Burrill [1960] Director/Accountant; Anthony Wilson Shone [1937] Director; Peter Robert Anthony Shone [1967] Managing Director

Wilsons Contractors Limited
Incorporated: 23 July 2015
Net Worth: £101,800 *Total Assets:* £7,446,816
Registered Office: Church House Farm, Potters Lane, Samlesbury, Preston, Lancs, PR5 0UE
Activities: Support activities for crop production
Shareholders: Harry Wilson; Lynn Verona Wilson
Officers: Harry Wilson [1947] Director; Ian Wilson [1981] Director; Lynn Verona Wilson [1951] Director

Winander Group Holdings Limited
Incorporated: 19 December 1995 *Employees:* 167
Net Worth: £13,076,453 *Total Assets:* £22,783,178
Registered Office: Winander House, Glebe Road, Bowness on Windermere, Cumbria, LA23 3HE
Activities: Activities of head offices
Officers: Andrew James Simon, Secretary; William John Bewley [1945] Director; John Brockbank [1952] Director; Thomas Richard Cowherd [1933] Director; Martin Raymond Dennison [1967] Director/Engineer; Ernest George Fallowfield [1941] Director; Maureen Ann Fleming [1944] Director; Angela Rosemary Kaye Howson [1955] Director; Dawn Margaret Jackson [1987] Director; Leslie Micklethwaite [1943] Director/Business Manager; Antony Jon Rothwell [1948] Director; Sheila Sproat [1930] Director; James Roy Thompson [1947] Director; Evelyn Twaddle [1947] Director/Guest House Proprietor; Nigel Wilkinson [1964] Director/Chartered Accountant; Sharon Gillian Wilkinson [1963] Director/Nurse

Winander Leisure Limited
Incorporated: 4 October 2006 *Employees:* 21
Net Worth: £4,846,681 *Total Assets:* £10,549,857
Registered Office: Winander House, Glebe Road, Bowness on Windermere, Cumbria, LA23 3HE
Activities: Activities of head offices
Parent: Winander Group Holdings Limited
Officers: Andrew James Simon, Secretary; William John Bewley [1945] Director/Boat Proprietor; John Brockbank [1952] Director; Thomas Richard Cowherd [1933] Director/Boat Proprietor; Ernest George Fallowfield [1941] Director/Boat Proprietor; Leslie Micklethwaite [1943] Director/Boat Proprietor; Antony Jon Rothwell [1948] Director/Boat Proprietor; Andrew James Simon [1980] Director/Chartered Accountant; James Roy Thompson [1947] Director/Boat Proprietor; Nigel Wilkinson [1964] Director/Chartered Accountant; Keith Robert Wood [1955] Director

Wind Pol 2 Holding Limited
Incorporated: 19 December 2007 *Employees:* 2
Net Worth Deficit: £35,212 *Total Assets:* £7,230,316
Registered Office: Victoria House, 19-21 Ack Lane East, Bramhall, Stockport, Cheshire, SK7 2BE
Activities: Activities of head offices
Parent: Wind Pol 1 Holding Limited
Officers: Derek Patrick Stewart Henderson, Secretary; Derek Patrick Henderson [1971] Director/Financial Controller; Duncan Andrew Levie [1963] Director/General Manager [Irish]

Wind Port of Liverpool Limited
Incorporated: 12 February 2007 *Employees:* 2
Net Worth Deficit: £1,687,756 *Total Assets:* £11,840,643
Registered Office: Victoria House, 19-21 Ack Lane East, Bramhall, Stockport, Cheshire, SK7 2BE
Activities: Production of electricity
Parent: Wind Pol 2 Holding Limited
Officers: Derek Patrick Stewart Henderson, Secretary; Derek Patrick Henderson [1971] Director/Financial Controller; Duncan Andrew Levie [1963] Director/General Manager [Irish]

Windermere Aquatic Limited
Incorporated: 15 March 1928 *Employees:* 33
Net Worth: £6,228,592 *Total Assets:* £11,792,409
Registered Office: Glebe Road, Bowness on Windemere, Windermere, Cumbria, LA23 3HE
Activities: Other retail sale of new goods in specialised stores (not commercial art galleries and opticians)
Shareholders: Grahame Frederick Armer; Jill Caroline Henderson
Officers: Grahame Frederick Armer, Secretary; Grahame Frederick Armer [1954] Director; Jill Caroline Henderson [1951] Director

Windermere Educational Trust Limited
Incorporated: 8 September 1967 *Employees:* 137
Net Worth: £20,904,946 *Total Assets:* £26,166,776
Registered Office: Brow Head, Windermere, Cumbria, LA23 1NW
Activities: Primary education
Officers: Susan Ross, Secretary; Carol Julie Burrow [1961] Director; Jason Mark Peter Dearden [1972] Managing Director; Joanne Harris [1972] Director; Alison Claire Hodson [1968] Director

Windermere Lake Cruises Limited
Incorporated: 22 March 1968 *Employees:* 134
Net Worth: £10,462,936 *Total Assets:* £13,066,740
Registered Office: Winander House, Glebe Road, Bowness on Windermere, Cumbria, LA23 3HE
Activities: Inland passenger water transport
Parent: Winander Leisure Ltd
Officers: Andrew James Simon, Secretary; William John Bewley [1945] Director/Boat Proprietor; John Brockbank [1952] Director; Jennifer Cormack [1981] Sales & Marketing Director; Thomas Richard Cowherd [1933] Director/Boat Proprietor; Ernest George Fallowfield [1941] Director/Boat Proprietor; Leslie Micklethwaite [1943] Director; Andrew James Simon [1980] Director/Chartered Management Accountant; James Roy Thompson [1947] Director/Boat Proprietor; Nigel Wilkinson [1964] Director/Chartered Accountant; John Woodburn [1956] Director/Boat Operator

Windermere Marina Village Limited
Incorporated: 25 October 1946 *Employees:* 26
Net Worth: £7,334,789 *Total Assets:* £14,551,028
Registered Office: Windermere Marina Village, Bowness on Windermere, Cumbria, LA23 3JQ
Activities: Holiday centres and villages
Major Shareholder: Eileen Rebecca Ainscough
Officers: Shona Patricia Taylor, Secretary; Eileen Rebecca Ainscough [1946] Director; Jason Mark Peter Dearden [1972] Director

Windsors (Wallasey) Limited
Incorporated: 1 June 1935 *Employees:* 752
Net Worth: £5,330,106 *Total Assets:* £9,929,296
Registered Office: Harrison Drive, Wallasey, Merseyside, CH45 3HP
Activities: Sale of new cars and light motor vehicles
Major Shareholder: David Martin Tuomey
Officers: Philip John McCormick, Secretary; Philip John McCormick [1969] Director/Accountant; David Martin Tuomey [1949] Managing Director; Karen Tuomey [1953] Director

Winfield Holdings Limited
Incorporated: 13 May 2004
Net Worth: £6,879,879 *Total Assets:* £9,296,335
Registered Office: Albert Mill, Mill Street, Haslingden, Rossendale, Lancs, BB4 5JW
Activities: Activities of head offices
Major Shareholder: June Semeniuk Winfield
Officers: Janine Winfield, Secretary; Mrs June Semeniuk Winfield [1955] Director

The Wings' CE Trust
Incorporated: 7 February 2017 *Employees:* 97
Net Worth: £7,820,847 *Total Assets:* £8,352,625
Registered Office: Atherton St George's C of E Primary School, Derby Street, Atherton, Manchester, M46 0HJ
Activities: Primary education
Officers: Alice Aldred [1942] Director/Retired; Andrea Atherton [1948] Director/Retired; Rachael LeOne Coulthard [1971] Director/CEO; Revd Will Gibbons [1984] Director/Clerk in Holy Orders; Catherine Anne Hollins [1975] Director/Teacher; Vicki Lowe [1978] Director/Trustee; Rosemary Panting [1960] Director/Deputy Finance Manager; Carole Sinclair [1958] Director; Rev Reginald William Sinclair [1953] Director/Rector

Winnington CHP Limited
Incorporated: 13 June 2013
Net Worth Deficit: £5,917,000 *Total Assets:* £20,371,000
Registered Office: Mond House, Winnington, Northwich, Cheshire, CW8 4DT
Activities: Steam and air conditioning supply
Parent: Tata Chemicals Europe Limited
Officers: David Philip William Davies, Secretary; Jonathan Laurence Abbotts [1964] Director; Dr Martin John Ashcroft [1969] Operations Director; Peter Patrick Houghton [1963] Director

Wire Regeneration Limited
Incorporated: 31 October 2013 *Employees:* 6
Net Worth: £8,788,530 *Total Assets:* £9,192,500
Registered Office: St James Business Centre, Wilderspool Causeway, Warrington, Cheshire, WA4 6PS
Activities: Other letting and operating of own or leased real estate
Shareholders: Langtree Property Partners Limited; Warrington Borough Council
Officers: Neal Biddle [1975] Director; Councillor Russell Lindley Bowden [1969] Director/Nuclear Physicist; Professor Steven John Broomhead [1956] Director/Chief Executive; John Alfred Downes [1960] Director; Malcolm William Jackson [1967] Director; Councillor Terence Patrick O'Neill [1947] Director/Retired

Wireless CCTV Limited
Incorporated: 2 April 2001 *Employees:* 47
Net Worth: £2,965,732 *Total Assets:* £8,019,831
Registered Office: Charles Babbage House, Kingsway Business Park, Rochdale, OL16 4NW
Activities: Other manufacturing n.e.c.
Parent: Wireless Holdings Limited
Officers: Helen Jane Williams, Secretary; David Gilbertson [1967] Director; Adam Haworth [1976] Sales Director; Simon James Potkins [1964] Director/Chief Technology Officer; James Thornhill [1985] Director/Accountant; Timothy James Williams [1959] Director

Wireless Holdings Limited
Incorporated: 3 May 2007 *Employees:* 48
Net Worth: £2,961,550 *Total Assets:* £8,059,098
Registered Office: Charles Babbage House, Kingsway Business Park, Rochdale, OL16 4NW
Activities: Specialised design activities
Major Shareholder: Timothy James Williams
Officers: Helen Jane Williams, Secretary/HR Manager; Helen Jane Williams [1960] Director; Timothy James Williams [1959] Director

Wirral Grammar School for Boys
Incorporated: 9 August 2011 *Employees:* 94
Net Worth: £9,188,000 *Total Assets:* £11,305,000
Registered Office: Wirral Grammar School for Boys, Cross Lane, Bebington, Wirral, Merseyside, CH63 3AQ
Activities: General secondary education
Officers: Sheila Lesley Clarke Mbe [1945] Director/Retired Councillor; William Francis Davies [1939] Director/Retired; David George Elliott [1960] Director/Tax Consultant; Peter John Gordon [1970] Director/Financial Adviser; David Roger Hazeldine [1962] Director/Headteacher; Andrew Graham Lawrence [1966] Director/Self Employed Online Retailer; Dr Karen Mary Noble [1966] Director/University Lecturer in Veterinary Science; Dr Girish Dahyabhai Patel [1952] Director/Research Physicist; Dr Adrian John Pullin [1959] Director/Doctor; Edmund Paul Thomas [1971] Director/Peripatetic Music Teacher; Alison Florence Whitehead [1956] Director/Teacher; John Philip Wilson [1954] Director/Charity Officer (Chief Executive)

Wirral Hospice St John's
Incorporated: 22 September 1980 *Employees:* 163
Net Worth: £10,581,032 *Total Assets:* £11,971,754
Registered Office: Mount Road, Higher Bebington, Wirral, Merseyside, CH63 6JE
Activities: Other human health activities
Officers: John Roderick Pentland, Secretary; Stephen Burrows [1943] Director/Company Chairman; Dr Paul James Randle Cuthbertson [1940] Director/General Medical Practitioner; Marie Granby [1958] Director/Solicitor; Annie Johnson [1953] Director/Retired; Dr Hilary Margaret Leggat [1956] Director/Retired; Dr Beverly Claire Oates [1968] Director/Medical Practitioner; Christopher Miles Pope [1942] Director/Retired Stockbroker; Dr Jean Quinn [1947] Director/Retired; Graham Martin Ridgway [1958] Director/Chartered Accountant; Steve Schroeder [1951] Director/Retired

Wirral Partnership Homes Limited
Incorporated: 26 September 2003 *Employees:* 473
Net Worth: £85,982,000 *Total Assets:* £196,962,000
Registered Office: Partnership Building, Hamilton Street, Birkenhead, Merseyside, CH41 5AA
Activities: Renting and operating of Housing Association real estate
Officers: Patrick Martin McCarthy, Secretary/Deputy Chief Executive [Irish]; Geoffrey Michael Broadhead [1956] Director; Matthew Lai Huat Brown [1971] Director/Accountant; David Grove Clark [1947] Director/Retired; Stephen Foulkes [1958] Director/Research Associate; Philip Ronald Gandy [1952] Director/Retired; Nicholas Paul Gerrard [1957] Director/Consultant; Susan Joanne Goodman [1960] Director; Jeffrey Edwin Green [1957] Director/Head of Operational Transformation (VOSA); Sharon Louise Grover [1969] Director/Solicitor; Stephen Penlington [1958] Chief Executive and Director; Gordon Campbell Ronald [1960] Director of Estates; Muriel Doreen Wilkinson [1944] Director/Retired

Wise Owl Trust
Incorporated: 1 May 2012 *Employees:* 244
Net Worth: £11,321,629 *Total Assets:* £13,359,345
Registered Office: Briscoe Lane Academy, Briscoe Lane, Newton Heath, Manchester, M40 2TB
Activities: Primary education
Officers: Ian Chadwick [1964] Director/Police Community Support Officer; Emma Foster [1977] Director/Senior Manager; Graham Larder [1962] Director/Project Manager; David Savage [1958] Director/Teacher

Wise Pharmacies Limited
Incorporated: 25 September 1964 *Employees:* 65
Net Worth: £5,270,137 *Total Assets:* £9,048,397
Registered Office: 27 Aspinall Street, Rusholme, Manchester, M14 5UD
Activities: Dispensing chemist in specialised stores
Parent: Cameolord Limited
Officers: Mohammed Bashir [1956] Director/Salesman

Witherslack Group (Holdings) Limited
Incorporated: 24 November 2010 *Employees:* 958
Net Worth Deficit: £10,660,568 *Total Assets:* £81,108,952
Registered Office: Lupton Tower, Lupton, Carnforth, Lancs, LA6 2PR
Activities: Activities of other holding companies n.e.c.
Parent: Wordsworth Bidco Limited
Officers: Michael Anthony Barrow [1957] Director; Kevin Frederick Dyson [1964] Finance Director; Judith Jones [1965] Commercial Director; Philip David Jones [1962] Managing Director; Howard Charles Tennant [1963] Director

Witherslack Group Limited
Incorporated: 10 June 1998 *Employees:* 829
Net Worth: £35,114,644 *Total Assets:* £53,845,576
Registered Office: Lupton Tower, Lupton, Carnforth, Lancs, LA6 2PR
Activities: Primary education
Parent: Witherslack Group (Holdings) Limited
Officers: Kevin Frederick Dyson, Secretary; Michael Anthony Barrow [1957] Director; Kevin Frederick Dyson [1964] Finance Director; Judith Jones [1965] Commercial Director; Philip David Jones [1962] Director; Howard Charles Tennant [1963] Director

Withgill Farm Limited
Incorporated: 11 January 2002 *Employees:* 22
Net Worth: £7,740,772 *Total Assets:* £17,537,896
Registered Office: Withgill Farm, Mitton, Clitheroe, Lancs, BB7 3LW
Activities: Raising of dairy cattle
Shareholders: George Barry Barnes; David George Barnes
Officers: Graeme Robison Surtees, Secretary/Farm Manager; Ann Beverley Barnes [1965] Director/Farmer; David George Barnes [1964] Director/Farmer

C.P. Witter Limited
Incorporated: 11 April 1978 *Employees:* 134
Net Worth: £4,970,084 *Total Assets:* £9,594,012
Registered Office: Drome Road, Deeside Industrial Park, Deeside, Flintshire, CH5 2NY
Activities: Manufacture of other fabricated metal products n.e.c.
Parent: Horizon Global European Holdings Limited
Officers: Paul Charles Caruso [1957] Director/Regional Vice President [American]; Jay Samuel Goldbaum [1981] Director [American]; David Gerard Rice [1963] Director [American]

WJH Limited
Incorporated: 23 March 2005 *Employees:* 1,451
Net Worth: £93,106,000 *Total Assets:* £181,584,000
Registered Office: 7 Merseyway, Stockport, Cheshire, SK1 1PN
Activities: Non-trading company
Shareholder: John Coulter
Officers: Ann Jones, Secretary; John Coulter [1951] Director/Jeweller; Ann Jones [1954] Director/Jeweller

Wolfson Trago Limited
Incorporated: 17 September 2010 *Employees:* 865
Net Worth Deficit: £236,000 *Total Assets:* £8,543,000
Registered Office: Euro House, The Beehive Trading Park, Haslingden Road, Blackburn, Lancs, BB1 2EE
Activities: Licenced restaurants
Officers: Imraan Musa Patel, Secretary; Mohsin Issa [1971] Director; Zuber Vali Issa [1972] Director

Wolstenholme Square Developments Limited
Incorporated: 8 December 2014
Net Worth Deficit: £76,410 *Total Assets:* £39,162,352
Registered Office: 116 Duke Street, Liverpool, L1 5JW
Activities: Buying and selling of own real estate
Major Shareholder: Elliot Philip Lawless
Officers: Elliot Philip Lawless [1987] Director

Barron Wood Distribution Limited
Incorporated: 8 October 1993 *Employees:* 139
Net Worth: £6,347,201 *Total Assets:* £17,530,324
Registered Office: Brook Lane, Much Hoole, Preston, Lancs, PR4 5JB
Activities: Freight transport by road
Shareholders: David Thomas Fairbrother; John Marsh Fairbrother
Officers: John Marsh Fairbrother, Secretary; David Thomas Fairbrother [1962] Transport Director; Joanne Fairbrother [1964] Director; John Marsh Fairbrother [1961] Operations Director; Victoria Fairbrother [1970] Director; Derek John Lyon [1969] Finance Director; Raymond Fredrick McCord [1957] Director; James Stewart McDougall [1961] Director; Lucy Susan Wright [1966] Administrative Director

Wood Environment & Infrastructure Solutions UK Limited
Incorporated: 9 November 1987 *Employees:* 607
Net Worth: £54,316,000 *Total Assets:* £63,304,000
Registered Office: Booths Park, Chelford Road, Knutsford, Cheshire, WA16 8QZ
Activities: Other business support service activities n.e.c.
Parent: Entec Holdings Limited
Officers: Iain Angus Jones, Secretary; Deborah Barrow [1952] Director; Robert Philip Brown [1968] Director; Samuel Ian Cromie [1966] Director; Kendall Harris Sherrill [1957] Director [American]; Adrian Rodney Gifford Shields [1969] Director

Wood Nuclear Holdings Limited
Incorporated: 3 March 1999
Net Worth: £15,599,000 *Total Assets:* £154,826,000
Registered Office: Booths Park, Chelford Road, Knutsford, Cheshire, WA16 8QZ
Activities: Activities of head offices
Parent: AMEC Foster Wheeler Group Limited
Officers: Anthony Mark Thomas, Secretary; Grant Rae Angus [1970] Director; Nicola Jayne O'Keeffe [1971] Director

Wood Nuclear Limited
Incorporated: 28 June 1973 *Employees:* 1,020
Net Worth Deficit: £1,855,000 *Total Assets:* £83,766,000
Registered Office: Booths Park, Chelford Road, Knutsford, Cheshire, WA16 8QZ
Activities: Construction of utility projects for electricity and telecommunications
Parent: Wood Nuclear Holdings Limited
Officers: Anthony Mark Thomas, Secretary; Michael John Hughes [1962] Director/VP Commercial; Nicola Jayne Okeeffe [1971] Director/Accountant; Clive Thomas White [1962] Director

Wood Park Foods Limited
Incorporated: 14 August 2014 *Employees:* 216
Net Worth: £3,423,000 *Total Assets:* £27,841,000
Registered Office: Wood Park, Chester High Road, Neston, South Wirral, Merseyside, CH64 7TB
Activities: Activities of head offices
Shareholders: Ian Ross Stewart; Julian Laurence Wood
Officers: Peter Nigel Barratt [1962] Director/Accountant; Paul Michael Jones [1970] Director; Ian Ross Stewart [1963] Director; Julian Laurence Wood [1968] Director

Barry Wood Plant Hire Limited
Incorporated: 2 December 1994 *Employees:* 68
Net Worth: £7,062,837 *Total Assets:* £9,547,574
Registered Office: Field Farm, Batham Gate, Fairfield, Buxton, Derbys, SK17 7HS
Activities: Other specialised construction activities n.e.c.
Parent: Sustainable Quarrying and Tanker Services Group Ltd
Officers: Graham Anthony Vaughan [1965] Finance Director

Woodall Nicholson Holdings Limited
Incorporated: 30 January 2013 *Employees:* 266
Net Worth: £6,287,112 *Total Assets:* £20,543,064
Registered Office: Colmil Works, Hart Common, Wigan Road, Westhoughton, Bolton, Lancs, BL5 2EE
Activities: Activities of other holding companies n.e.c.
Officers: Brian Joseph Davidson [1963] Director; Geoffrey Kenneth Hudson [1954] Director; Warwick John Ley [1972] Director [Australian/British]; Paul Michael Newton [1964] Director; John Merrick Randerson [1973] Director; Michael Peter Rogan [1968] Director; Matthew Joseph Widdall [1972] Director/Investor

Woodall Nicholson Limited
Incorporated: 28 April 2003 *Employees:* 251
Net Worth: £10,416,227 *Total Assets:* £15,905,459
Registered Office: Colmil Works, Hart Common, Wigan Road, Westhoughton, Bolton, Lancs, BL5 2EE
Activities: Manufacture of bodies (coachwork) for motor vehicles (except caravans)
Parent: Woodall Nicholson Holdings Limited
Officers: Michael Barlow [1969] Director/Production Manager; Brian Joseph Davidson [1963] Director; Geoffrey Kenneth Hudson [1954] Director/Coachbuilder; John Merrick Randerson [1973] Director

Woodclay Limited
Incorporated: 2 December 1981 *Employees:* 130
Net Worth: £11,548,709 *Total Assets:* £14,824,865
Registered Office: Broadgate, Broadway Business Park, Chadderton, Oldham, Lancs, OL9 9XE
Activities: Wholesale of household goods (other than musical instruments) n.e.c
Officers: Christopher John Illingworth, Secretary; Christopher John Illingworth [1958] Finance Director; Michael Andrew Illingworth [1960] Sales Director; Richard Blair Illingworth [1963] Director; Robert Illingworth [1930] Director; Robert Stuart Illingworth [1957] Managing Director

Woodford Land Limited
Incorporated: 20 May 1999 *Employees:* 2
Net Worth Deficit: £18,351,570 *Total Assets:* £30,431,826
Registered Office: 8d Lockside Office Park, Lockside Road, Preston, Lancs, PR2 2YS
Activities: Development of building projects
Officers: Jason Lee William Parkinson, Secretary; Anthony Francis Lochery [1960] Director

Woodford Regeneration Limited
Incorporated: 7 June 2002
Net Worth Deficit: £2,693,944 *Total Assets:* £6,870,083
Registered Office: 8d Lockside Office Park, Lockside Road, Preston, Lancs, PR2 2YS
Activities: Construction of other civil engineering projects n.e.c.
Officers: Jason Lee William Parkinson, Secretary; Anthony Francis Lochery [1960] Director

Woodford Remediation Limited
Incorporated: 7 June 2002
Net Worth Deficit: £1,438,433 *Total Assets:* £28,892,136
Registered Office: 8d Lockside Office Park, Lockside Road, Preston, Lancs, PR2 2YS
Activities: Remediation activities and other waste management services
Officers: Jason Lee William Parkinson, Secretary; Anthony Francis Lochery [1960] Director

Woodland Assets Limited
Incorporated: 28 November 2011
Net Worth: £24,051,000 *Total Assets:* £24,077,000
Registered Office: Siddick, Workington, Cumbria, CA14 1JX
Activities: Silviculture and other forestry activities
Parent: Holmen UK Limited
Officers: Gavin Stirling Davidson [1961] Director/Head of Forestry Operations; Ulf Lennart Lofgren [1969] Director [Swedish]; Ulf Stefan Lorehn [1978] Director/Finance Manager [Swedish]; Lena Nyberg [1964] Director/Finance Manager [Swedish]; Frank Soren Olof Petersson [1969] Director [Swedish]

Woodlands Care GRP Ltd
Incorporated: 21 January 2006 *Employees:* 125
Net Worth: £1,515,500 *Total Assets:* £8,896,242
Registered Office: 22 Woodlands Drive, Atherton, Manchester, M46 9HH
Activities: Residential care activities for the elderly and disabled
Shareholders: Russell Heaton; Tracy Ann Freeman; Sam Lancaster
Officers: Russell Heaton, Secretary/Scaffolding Contractor; Tracy Ann Freeman [1964] Director/Care Home Manager; Russell Heaton [1960] Director/Scaffolding Contractor; Sam Lancaster [1952] Director/Chartered Surveyor

Woodley Sports Centre Limited
Incorporated: 10 June 2005 *Employees:* 2
Net Worth: £2,977,291 *Total Assets:* £8,103,911
Registered Office: Life Leisure, Houldsworth Village, Broadstone Road, Reddish, Stockport, Cheshire, SK5 7AT
Activities: Activities of sport clubs
Parent: Stockport Sports Trust
Officers: Valerie June Cottam [1941] Director/Retired - Former Local Government Officer; Malcolm McPhail [1967] Director/Chief Executive; Charlene Ashley Nunn [1988] Trustee/Director, Chartered Accountant

Wool Growers (Great Britain) Limited
Incorporated: 28 May 1959 *Employees:* 179
Net Worth: £10,286,000 *Total Assets:* £11,967,000
Registered Office: Wool House, Sidings Close, Canal Road, Bradford, W Yorks, BD2 1AZ
Activities: Other professional, scientific and technical activities n.e.c.
Parent: British Wool Marketing Board
Officers: Peter Anthony Baren [1960] Director/Accountant; Stephen Gawain Leigh Bradley [1978] Director; Joseph Michael Farren [1971] Director [rish]; Trevor John Richards [1953] Director/Farmer

R N Wooler & Co (Developments) Limited
Incorporated: 9 August 2000 *Employees:* 4
Net Worth: £2,324,786 *Total Assets:* £15,478,157
Registered Office: Florence House, Lawkholme Business Park, Lawkholme Lane, Keighley, W Yorks, BD21 3LA
Activities: Development of building projects
Major Shareholder: Richard Norman Wooler
Officers: Margaret Ann Wooler, Secretary; Andrew Wooler [1978] Director; Gareth David Wooler [1980] Director; Margaret Ann Wooler [1954] Director; Richard Norman Wooler [1954] Director

R.N. Wooler & Co (Holdings) Limited
Incorporated: 16 July 2002 *Employees:* 288
Net Worth: £18,934,576 *Total Assets:* £38,549,788
Registered Office: Florence House, Lawkholme Business Park, Lawkholme Lane, Keighley, W Yorks, BD21 3LA
Activities: Construction of commercial buildings
Major Shareholder: Richard Norman Wooler
Officers: Margaret Ann Wooler, Secretary; Andrew Wooler [1978] Director; Gareth David Wooler [1980] Director; Margaret Ann Wooler [1954] Director; Richard Norman Wooler [1954] Director

R.N. Wooler & Company Limited
Incorporated: 24 July 1985 *Employees:* 288
Net Worth: £11,027,373 *Total Assets:* £24,726,868
Registered Office: Florence House, Lawkholme Business Park, Lawkholme Lane, Keighley, W Yorks, BD21 3LA
Activities: Construction of commercial buildings
Major Shareholder: Richard Norman Wooler
Officers: Sheila Clarkson, Secretary; Gary Sollitt [1960] Contracts Director; Andrew Wooler [1978] Director; Gareth David Wooler [1980] Director; Margaret Ann Wooler [1954] Director; Richard Norman Wooler [1954] Director

Worcestershire Hospital SPC PLC
Incorporated: 14 October 1998
Net Worth: £5,087,000 *Total Assets:* £103,632,000
Registered Office: c/o Albany SPC Services Ltd, 3rd Floor, 3-5 Charlotte Street, Manchester, M1 4HB
Activities: Hospital activities
Parent: Worcestershire Hospital SPC Holdings Ltd
Officers: Ailison Louise Mitchell, Secretary; Alan Edward Birch [1970] Director/Chief Executive Officer; Barry Paul Millsom [1974] Director; Neil Rae [1971] Director; Peter John Sheldrake [1959] Director; Christopher Thomas Solley [1970] Director; Andrew Leslie Tennant [1958] Director

The Wordsworth Trust
Incorporated: 30 September 1997 *Employees:* 33
Net Worth: £14,535,000 *Total Assets:* £15,621,000
Registered Office: Dove Cottage, Grasmere, Cumbria, LA22 9SH
Activities: Library activities
Officers: Amanda Jane Pickup, Secretary; Professor Sir Drummond James Bone [1947] Director/Academic; Mary Chuck [1943] Director/Retired; John Spencer Collier [1945] Director/Chartered Accountant; Judith Helen Cooke [1947] Director/Public Sector Employee; David Michael Heal [1951] Director/Consultant; Diana Ruth Matthews [1946] Director; Dr Lucy Peltz [1969] Director/Museum Curator; Dr Seamus Perry [1967] Director/Academic; Dr Lynn Barbara Shepherd [1964] Director/Consultant; Jennifer Sheila Uglow [1947] Director/Publisher

Workforce Holdings Limited
Incorporated: 7 September 2016 *Employees:* 3
Net Worth Deficit: £118,699 *Total Assets:* £10,283,309
Registered Office: 16-22 Queensbrook, Bolton, Lancs, BL1 4AY
Activities: Activities of head offices
Major Shareholder: Simon Mark Hayton
Officers: Ian Kenneth Sumner Clark [1969] Director/Chief Financial Officer; Rebecca Louise Hayton [1973] Director; Simon Mark Hayton [1974] Managing Director

Workforce People Solutions Limited
Incorporated: 21 February 2006 *Employees:* 30
Net Worth: £5,304,859 *Total Assets:* £6,688,656
Registered Office: International House, Queensbrook, Spa Road, Bolton, Lancs, BL1 4AY
Activities: Other activities of employment placement agencies
Major Shareholder: Simon Mark Hayton
Officers: Ian Kenneth Sumner Clark [1969] Director/Chief Financial Officer; Rebecca Louise Hayton [1973] Director; Simon Mark Hayton [1974] Director

Workshop Properties Limited
Incorporated: 4 June 1992 *Employees:* 2
Net Worth: £6,706,785 *Total Assets:* £10,008,290
Registered Office: 47 Hilton Street, Manchester, M1 2EF
Activities: Other letting and operating of own or leased real estate
Shareholders: Abdalhaq Gillan; Iftikhar Ahmed Abdullah Gillan
Officers: Abdalhaq Atta Gillan, Secretary; Abdalhaq Atta Gillan [1948] Director; Iftikhar Ahmed Abdullah Gillan [1955] Director

Worldwide Connect Limited
Incorporated: 14 June 2007
Net Worth: £12,060,100 *Total Assets:* £12,060,100
Registered Office: Daisy House, Lindred Road Business Park, Nelson, Lancs, BB9 5SR
Activities: Non-trading company
Parent: Daisy Intermediate Holdings Limited
Officers: David Lewis McGlennon, Secretary; David Lewis McGlennon [1974] Director; Stephen Alan Smith [1963] Director

Worldwide Foods (Rochdale) Limited
Incorporated: 5 September 2000 *Employees:* 82
Net Worth: £1,686,639 *Total Assets:* £6,860,578
Registered Office: Lower Tweedale Street, Milkstone Road, Rochdale, Lancs, OL11 1HG
Activities: Other retail sale in non-specialised stores
Major Shareholder: Pervez Alam
Officers: Zahid Iqbal [1968] Director/Businessman

Worldwide Procurement Limited
Incorporated: 10 October 2016
Net Worth: £6,825,001 *Total Assets:* £6,875,001
Registered Office: Virginia House, 5-7 Great Ancoats Street, Manchester, M4 5AD
Activities: Other professional, scientific and technical activities n.e.c.
Officers: Scott Dylan [1984] Director

Worthington Mancap LLP
Incorporated: 11 February 2015
Net Worth: £12,468,202 *Total Assets:* £15,671,756
Registered Office: Brockholes Pavilion, Brockholes Way, Preston, Lancs, PR3 0PZ

Wotton House Properties Limited
Incorporated: 12 October 2006 *Employees:* 4
Net Worth Deficit: £297,000 *Total Assets:* £28,901,000
Registered Office: c/o KPMG LLP, One St Peters Square, Manchester, M2 3AE
Activities: Other letting and operating of own or leased real estate
Parent: Wotton House Properties Holdco Limited
Officers: Patrick Bour [1978] Director [French]

WPI Civil Engineering Limited
Incorporated: 11 August 1994 *Employees:* 121
Net Worth: £14,471,695 *Total Assets:* £21,260,424
Registered Office: Corpacq House, 1 Goose Green, Altrincham, Cheshire, WA14 1DW
Activities: Construction of other civil engineering projects n.e.c.
Officers: Stephen Duffy [1966] Technical Director; Jonathan Hamilton [1958] Director/Chief Engineer; Benjamin David Hancock [1991] Director; Andrew William Hoose [1965] Financial Director; Katrina Marie Igoe [1984] Director/Sales Manager; Martin Igoe [1962] Construction Director; Michael James Igoe [1987] Director/Engineer; Steven Michael Igoe [1979] Director; Stephen James Scott [1978] Director; Christina Margaret Stubbs [1981] Director/Accountant

Wrapid Group Limited
Incorporated: 24 November 2005 *Employees:* 114
Net Worth: £1,627,372 *Total Assets:* £10,171,620
Registered Office: 250 Thornton Road, Bradford, BD1 2LB
Activities: Activities of head offices
Parent: Wrapid Investments Limited
Officers: Stephen Patrick York, Secretary; James Richard Clark [1983] Director; Nicole Dillon [1977] Director; Christopher Hudson [1971] Director; Stephen Patrick York [1957] Finance Director

Wrapid Investments Limited
Incorporated: 17 February 2015 *Employees:* 111
Net Worth: £1,433 *Total Assets:* £11,987,472
Registered Office: 250 Thornton Road, Bradford, W Yorks, BD1 2LB
Activities: Activities of other holding companies n.e.c.
Officers: James Richard Clark [1983] Director; Nicole Victoria Dillon [1977] Director; Christopher Hudson [1971] Director; Stephen Patrick York [1957] Director

Wrapid Manufacturing Limited
Incorporated: 13 May 1998 *Employees:* 111
Net Worth: £1,109,531 *Total Assets:* £7,629,174
Registered Office: 250 Thornton Road, Bradford, W Yorks, BD1 2LB
Activities: Other manufacturing n.e.c.
Parent: Wrapid Holdings Limited
Officers: Stephen Patrick York, Secretary; William Peter Birkinhead [1945] Director; John Clark [1952] Director; Christopher Hudson [1971] Director; Stephen Patrick York [1957] Director

Wrather Group Limited
Incorporated: 17 March 2010 *Employees:* 2
Net Worth Deficit: £7,326,251 *Total Assets:* £30,369,512
Registered Office: 2 Mount Street, Manchester, M2 5WQ
Activities: Management of real estate on a fee or contract basis
Major Shareholder: William Harry Wrather
Officers: Paul Robert Greenlees, Secretary; Patrick Franks [1965] Director/Architect; William Harry Wrather [1939] Director

Wren Properties Limited
Incorporated: 6 July 1972 *Employees:* 18
Net Worth: £9,622,066 *Total Assets:* £22,896,928
Registered Office: 696 Wilmslow Road, Didsbury, Manchester, M20 0DN
Activities: Management of real estate on a fee or contract basis
Shareholders: Richard Robinson; Philip Robinson
Officers: Malcolm Joseph Robinson [1943] Director/Chartered Banker; Philip Robinson [1976] Director/Chartered Accountant; Richard Robinson [1973] Director/Chartered Surveyor

Wrendal Holdings Limited
Incorporated: 28 September 1959 *Employees:* 5
Net Worth: £11,144,206 *Total Assets:* £14,791,014
Registered Office: Unit 2 Second Avenue, Poynton Industrial Estate, Poynton, Cheshire, SK12 1ND
Activities: Activities of head offices
Officers: Edward Alexander Gifford Aspinall, Secretary; Edward Alexander Gifford Aspinall [1969] Director/Insurance Broker; Joanna Mary Babington Aspinall [1939] Director; Charlotte Ann Babington Kelly [1967] Director; Stephen Charles Vincent Kelly [1966] Director/Project Manager; Kate Mary Babington Titley [1966] Director

Wrengate Holdings Limited
Incorporated: 27 October 2010 *Employees:* 25
Net Worth: £24,580,480 *Total Assets:* £29,625,656
Registered Office: 10 Riverview, The Embankment, Vale Road, Heaton Mersey, Stockport, Cheshire, SK4 3GN
Activities: Activities of other holding companies n.e.c.
Shareholder: Alan Philip David Musry
Officers: Alan Philip David Musry [1963] Director/Chartered Accountant; Ronald Musry [1935] Director

Wrengate Limited
Incorporated: 6 June 1974 *Employees:* 3
Net Worth: £18,455,488 *Total Assets:* £25,526,812
Registered Office: 10 Riverview, The Embankment, Vale Road, Heaton Mersey, Stockport, Cheshire, SK4 3GN
Activities: Activities of other holding companies n.e.c.
Parent: Wrengate Holdings Limited
Officers: Alan Philip David Musry [1963] Director/Chartered Accountant; Ronald Musry [1935] Director

Robert Wright & Sons Limited
Incorporated: 24 March 2010 *Employees:* 6
Net Worth: £6,280,224 *Total Assets:* £9,058,339
Registered Office: Merscar House Farm, Merscar Lane, Scarisbrick, Ormskirk, Lancs, L40 9RL
Activities: Growing of cereals (except rice), leguminous crops and oil seeds
Shareholders: Stephen Philip Wright; Philip Robert Wright
Officers: Philip Wright [1944] Director; Stephen Wright [1972] Director

Eric Wright Civil Engineering Limited
Incorporated: 5 December 1990 *Employees:* 69
Net Worth: £1,869,436 *Total Assets:* £14,769,274
Registered Office: Sceptre House, Sceptre Way, Bamber Bridge, Preston, Lancs, PR5 6AW
Activities: Construction of commercial buildings
Parent: Eric Wright Group Limited
Officers: Manisha Kumar, Secretary; Emma Diane Bourne [1968] Director; Jeremy Peter Hartley [1965] Director/Accountant; Gavin Hulme [1974] Director; Craig William Kippax [1976] Director; Richard Eric Wright [1937] Director

Eric Wright Construction Limited
Incorporated: 25 May 1923 *Employees:* 149
Net Worth: £6,310,579 *Total Assets:* £23,212,804
Registered Office: Sceptre House, Sceptre Way, Bamber Bridge, Preston, Lancs, PR5 6AW
Activities: Construction of commercial buildings
Parent: Eric Wright Group Limited
Officers: Manisha Kumar, Secretary; James Francis Carter [1955] Director/Chartered Surveyor; James Eager [1974] Director; Daniel James Gosling [1974] Director; Jeremy Peter Hartley [1965] Director/Accountant; John Richard Hartnett [1981] Director; Steven John Reid [1975] Director; John Howard Wilson [1965] Director; Richard Eric Wright [1937] Director

Eric Wright FM Limited
Incorporated: 19 September 2002 *Employees:* 149
Net Worth: £3,231,206 *Total Assets:* £10,646,981
Registered Office: Sceptre House, Sceptre Way, Bamber Bridge, Preston, Lancs, PR5 6AW
Activities: Management of real estate on a fee or contract basis
Parent: Eric Wright Group Limited
Officers: Manisha Kumar, Secretary; James Francis Carter [1955] Director/Chartered Surveyor; Jeremy Peter Hartley [1965] Director/Accountant; Richard Eric Wright [1937] Director

Eric Wright Group Limited
Incorporated: 2 August 1993 *Employees:* 623
Net Worth: £61,251,000 *Total Assets:* £187,952,000
Registered Office: Sceptre House, Sceptre Way, Bamber Bridge, Preston, Lancs, PR5 6AW
Activities: Activities of head offices
Parent: Henmead Limited
Officers: Emma Diane Bourne [1968] Director; James Francis Carter [1955] Director/Chartered Surveyor; Gillian Chadwick [1979] Director/Chartered Accountant; Jeremy Peter Hartley [1965] Director/Chartered Accountant; Colin Hetherington [1973] Managing Director; Karen Jane Hirst [1968] Director/Chartered Surveyor; Neal David Whittle [1978] Director; John Howard Wilson [1965] Director; Christine Desiree Winstanley [1966] Managing Director; Richard Eric Wright [1937] Director

Wright's Pies (Shelton) Limited
Incorporated: 16 December 1953 *Employees:* 560
Net Worth: £22,828,496 *Total Assets:* £31,428,768
Registered Office: Weston Road, Crewe, Cheshire, CW1 6XQ
Activities: Manufacture of prepared meals and dishes
Shareholders: Peter David Wright; Alison Jane Harding
Officers: Peter David Wright, Secretary; Lisa Beard [1979] Associate Director; Helen Victoria Bowyer [1981] Associate Director; Neville Carruthers [1964] Associate Director; Alison Jane Harding [1964] Director; Peter David Wright [1964] Director; Peter James Wright [1941] Director; David Robin Douglas Yendole [1937] Director

Thomas Wright/Thorite Group Limited
Incorporated: 7 November 1921 *Employees:* 111
Net Worth: £2,520,794 *Total Assets:* £7,390,212
Registered Office: Thorite House, Laisterdyke, Bradford, BD4 8BZ
Activities: Agents involved in the sale of machinery, industrial equipment, ships and aircraft
Shareholders: Thomas Edward Wright; Stephen Thomas Wright
Officers: Stephen Thomas Wright, Secretary; Alan Donkersley [1962] Sales Director; Ross Gowler [1953] Director; Stephen Thomas Wright [1961] Director

WS Transportation Limited
Incorporated: 6 March 2014 *Employees:* 175
Net Worth Deficit: £961,121 *Total Assets:* £13,071,625
Registered Office: Unit 2 Ashville Way Industrial Estate, Sutton Weaver, Runcorn, Cheshire, WA7 3EZ
Activities: Freight transport by road
Shareholders: David Norman Cox; Edward John Stobart
Officers: David Norman Cox [1979] Director; Nigel McMullan [1979] Managing Director; Edward John Stobart [1990] Director

WSR Recycling Limited
Incorporated: 23 October 1990 *Employees:* 49
Net Worth: £3,707,307 *Total Assets:* £8,263,554
Registered Office: Ditton Road, Widnes, Cheshire, WA8 0PA
Activities: Treatment and disposal of non-hazardous waste
Parent: DM Topco Limited
Officers: Brian McCabe [1972] Director [Irish]; Eamon Waters [1960] Director [Irish]

WTH (UK) Limited
Incorporated: 12 March 2008 *Employees:* 165
Net Worth: £439,655 *Total Assets:* £26,963,976
Registered Office: The Bridge, Moorland Gate Business Park, Cowling Road, Chorley, Lancs, PR6 9FE
Activities: Travel agency activities
Parent: World Travel Holdings Inc
Officers: James Douglas Cole [1975] Director; Donald Christopher Graff [1962] Director/Travel Executive [American]; Bradley Jonathan Tolkin [1958] Director/Travel Executive [American]; Jeffrey David Tolkin [1957] Director/Travel Executive [American]

Www.Rigby LLP
Incorporated: 10 September 2008
Net Worth: £2,301,443 *Total Assets:* £7,924,782
Registered Office: 4 Croft Court, Whitehills Business Park, Blackpool, Lancs, FY4 5PR
Officers: Linda Rigby [1961] Member; William Simon Rigby [1961] Member; Victoria Jayne Rigby [1999] LLP Member

The Wythenshawe Catholic Academy Trust
Incorporated: 12 March 2013 *Employees:* 246
Net Worth: £49,230,808 *Total Assets:* £53,936,076
Registered Office: Saint Paul's Catholic High School, A Voluntary Academy and Engineering College, Firbank Rd, Newall Green, Wythenshawe, Manchester, M23 2YS
Activities: General secondary education
Officers: Michael James Fowler, Secretary; Patricia Anne Adams [1954] Director/Headteacher; Michelle Nicola Flanagan [1969] Director/Head of Retail; Matthew Alan Fox [1969] Director/IT Solutions Sales; Bernadette Hayward [1969] Director; Dominic Haird Hemington [1967] Director/Headteacher; Maria Gabrielle Higham [1965] Director/Chartered Accountant; Alex Hren [1968] Director; Sacha Humphries [1972] Director/Chief Executive; Nicholas Richard Johnson [1959] Director/Solicitor; Lisa Marie Kelly [1973] Director/Headteacher; Stephen Maricen Marciniak [1952] Director/Teacher; Alistair John Moore [1972] Director/Management Consultant; Deborah Mary Ellen Penny [1954] Director/Teacher; Maureen Sweeney [1952] Director/L & D Training Consultant

Wythenshawe Community Housing Group Limited
Incorporated: 3 September 2012 *Employees:* 538
Net Worth: £204,804,000 *Total Assets:* £387,544,992
Registered Office: Wythenshawe House, 8 Poundswick Lane, Wythenshawe, Manchester, M22 9TA
Activities: Renting and operating of Housing Association real estate
Officers: Shahida Latif-Haider, Secretary; Robert William Cressey [1962] Director/Accountant; Edward Benjamin Dyson [1975] Director/NHS Manager; Bernadette Mary Heanue [1963] Director [Irish]; Sarah Alison Russell [1981] Director/Solicitor; David Stuart Walker [1957] Director/Bishop; Sam Wilson [1980] Director/Systems Analyst

X1 Aire Leeds Limited
Incorporated: 12 June 2013 *Employees:* 1
Net Worth Deficit: £1,310,807 *Total Assets:* £22,249,900
Registered Office: 116 Duke Street, Liverpool, L1 5JW
Activities: Buying and selling of own real estate
Parent: X1 Management Limited
Officers: Lisa Mary Smith [1969] Director

X1 Developments Ltd
Incorporated: 4 November 2009 *Employees:* 41
Net Worth: £4,168,003 *Total Assets:* £14,168,276
Registered Office: 116 Duke Street, Liverpool, L1 5JW
Activities: Other business support service activities n.e.c.
Parent: Lightoak Investments Limited
Officers: Lisa Mary Smith [1969] Director/Investments

X1 Management Limited
Incorporated: 26 March 2012
Net Worth Deficit: £324,855 *Total Assets:* £9,614,742
Registered Office: 116 Duke Street, Liverpool, L1 5JW
Activities: Residents property management
Major Shareholder: Lisa Mary Smith
Officers: Lisa Mary Smith [1969] Director

X1 Manchester Waters Limited
Incorporated: 12 October 2016
Net Worth Deficit: £2,250 *Total Assets:* £8,565,247
Registered Office: 116 Duke Street, Liverpool, L1 5JW
Activities: Buying and selling of own real estate
Parent: X1 Management Limited
Officers: Lisa Mary Smith [1969] Director

X1 Media City Limited
Incorporated: 22 July 2013 *Employees:* 1
Net Worth Deficit: £2,452,316 *Total Assets:* £90,114,376
Registered Office: 116 Duke Street, Liverpool, L1 5JW
Activities: Buying and selling of own real estate
Officers: Lisa Mary Smith [1969] Director

X1 The Campus Limited
Incorporated: 24 April 2016
Net Worth Deficit: £158,871 *Total Assets:* £9,354,495
Registered Office: 116 Duke Street, Liverpool, L1 5JW
Activities: Buying and selling of own real estate
Parent: Oakmore Investments Limited
Officers: Lisa Mary Smith [1969] Director

X1 The Gateway Limited
Incorporated: 21 May 2013
Net Worth Deficit: £514,029 *Total Assets:* £17,275,498
Registered Office: 116 Duke Street, Liverpool, L1 5JW
Activities: Buying and selling of own real estate
Officers: Lisa Mary Smith [1969] Director

XLR8 Sports Limited
Incorporated: 12 April 1995 *Employees:* 134
Net Worth: £4,252,261 *Total Assets:* £7,991,594
Registered Office: Wham Farm, 155 Longmeaneygate, Midge Hall, Preston, Lancs, PR26 7TB
Activities: Other retail sale of new goods in specialised stores (not commercial art galleries and opticians)
Officers: Timothy William Noy, Secretary; Christopher David Noy [1958] Director; Iain Michael Noy [1966] Director; Mark Alan Noy [1966] Director; Timothy William Noy [1954] Director/Retailer

XYZ Building Developments Limited
Incorporated: 11 November 2015
Net Worth: £774,616 *Total Assets:* £18,373,920
Registered Office: c/o Allied London, Level 12, No 1 Spinningfields, 1 Hardman Square, Manchester, M3 3EB
Activities: Development of building projects
Parent: XYZ Building Holdco Limited
Officers: Suresh Premji Gorasia [1974] Commercial Director; Frederick Paul Graham-Watson [1957] Director; Michael Julian Ingall [1959] Director; Jonathan Raine [1981] Director

Yanco Limited
Incorporated: 19 February 1996 *Employees:* 43
Net Worth: £10,208,879 *Total Assets:* £41,634,268
Registered Office: 1 Estuary Banks, Estuary Commerce Park, Liverpool, L24 8RQ
Activities: Manufacture of pesticides and other agrochemical products
Major Shareholder: Francois Akle
Officers: Joanne Hawthorne, Secretary; James Eric Harrison [1952] Director; Joanne Hawthorne [1966] Director; Kevin Anthony Riozzi [1971] Deputy Managing Director; Valerie Roberts [1965] Director; Glen David Smith [1972] Director

A.E.Yates,Limited
Incorporated: 23 July 1946 *Employees:* 192
Net Worth: £9,445,916 *Total Assets:* £27,929,802
Registered Office: Cranfield Road, Lostock Industrial Estate, Lostock, Bolton, Lancs, BL6 4SB
Activities: Construction of roads and motorways
Major Shareholder: John Crompton Whitehead
Officers: Stephen John Harrison, Secretary; Paul Boron [1956] Director/Civil Engineer; Stephen John Harrison [1949] Director/Accountant/Company Secretary; Glen Derek Kilroy [1957] Director/Civil Engineer; Neil Duncan McLeod [1957] Director/Business Development; Timothy Peter Nield [1958] Director/Civil Engineer; John Crompton Whitehead [1945] Director/Civil Engineer; Victoria Michelle Whitehead [1971] Director/Group Solicitor and HR

Yeargate Limited
Incorporated: 7 March 1983 *Employees:* 4
Net Worth: £5,765,603 *Total Assets:* £7,470,110
Registered Office: The Gatehouse, Birch Business Park, Whittle Lane, Heywood, Lancs, OL10 2SX
Activities: Construction of commercial buildings
Parent: Yeargate SPV Limited
Officers: Lawrence Edward Smith [1956] Director; William Royston Ullathorne [1954] Director/Interim Executive

Yeargate SPV Limited
Incorporated: 5 January 2015
Net Worth: £6,107,458 *Total Assets:* £13,733,782
Registered Office: The Gatehouse, Birch Business Park, Whittle Lane, Heywood, Lancs, OL10 2SX
Activities: Buying and selling of own real estate
Major Shareholder: Harold Edward Smith
Officers: Lawrence Edward Smith [1956] Director; William Royston Ullathorne [1954] Director/Management Consultant

Harry Yearsley Limited
Incorporated: 4 November 1955 *Employees:* 1,422
Net Worth: £43,497,488 *Total Assets:* £89,163,200
Registered Office: Hareshill Road, Heywood, Lancs, OL10 2TP
Activities: Wholesale of fruit and vegetables
Officers: Philip John Whitworth, Secretary; Jonathan Carl Baker [1965] Sales Director; Ian David King [1968] Sales Director; Timothy Moran [1974] Sales Director Cold Storage; Philip John Whitworth [1962] Director/Chartered Accountant; Harry Edwin Yearsley [1966] Director; John Leonard Yearsley [1946] Director

Yemin Charitable Trust Ltd
Incorporated: 19 May 1998
Net Worth: £5,906,647 *Total Assets:* £11,489,014
Registered Office: 6th Floor, Cardinal House, 20 St Mary's Parsonage, Manchester, M3 2LG
Activities: Other social work activities without accommodation n.e.c.
Officers: Arnold Henry, Secretary/Director; Arnold Henry [1959] Director; Henry Neumann [1956] Director; Pinchas Neumann [1952] Director

Yes Car Credit (Holdings) Limited
Incorporated: 5 December 1923
Net Worth: £7,039,000 *Total Assets:* £8,847,000
Registered Office: No 1 Godwin Street, Bradford, W Yorks, BD1 2SU
Activities: Activities of financial services holding companies
Parent: Provident Financial PLC
Officers: Andrew Charles Fisher [1958] Director; Kenneth John Mullen [1958] Director/Scottish Solicitor

YKK (U.K.) Limited
Incorporated: 7 December 1966 *Employees:* 139
Net Worth Deficit: £2,145,282 *Total Assets:* £26,232,768
Registered Office: Whitehouse Industrial Estate, Runcorn, Cheshire, WA7 3BW
Activities: Manufacture of other textiles n.e.c.
Parent: YKK Holding Europe B.V
Officers: Anthony Reilly [1969] Managing Director [Irish]; Toru Yamamoto [1959] Director [Japanese]

Ylem Energy Limited
Incorporated: 3 August 1987 *Employees:* 45
Net Worth: £10,652,432 *Total Assets:* £21,027,872
Registered Office: Edison House, Daniel Adamson Road, Salford, M50 1DT
Activities: Production of electricity
Parent: Ylem Group Limited
Officers: Ian Andrew Gadsby [1964] Managing Director; Christopher John Hull [1966] Director/Chief Financial Officer; Andrew Ian MacLellan [1955] Director/Engineer; Paul Noland [1980] Director; Samantha Jane Scott [1980] Director; Timothy Hays Scott [1950] Director; Anthony Peter Roy Ward [1978] Director; Stuart Lee Watson [1967] Operations Director

Ylem Group Limited
Incorporated: 20 February 1998 *Employees:* 195
Net Worth: £31,911,000 *Total Assets:* £49,897,000
Registered Office: Edison House, Daniel Adamson Road, Salford, M50 1DT
Activities: Activities of head offices
Shareholders: Martin Lothar Ernst Hornig; Dr Thomas Martin Joseph Wilhelm
Officers: Christopher John Hull [1966] Director/Chief Financial Officer; Andrew Ian MacLellan [1955] Director/Engineer; Samantha Jane Scott [1980] Director; Timothy Hays Scott [1950] Director; Anthony Peter Roy Ward [1978] Director

Yodel Delivery Network Limited
Incorporated: 9 August 2004 *Employees:* 4,011
Net Worth: £93,474,000 *Total Assets:* £189,203,008
Registered Office: 2nd Floor, Atlantic Pavilion, Albert Dock, Liverpool, L3 4AE
Activities: Freight transport by road
Parent: Yodel Logistics Limited
Officers: Neil Henry Ashworth [1962] Commercial Director; Aidan Stuart Barclay [1956] Director; Howard Myles Barclay [1959] Director; Adrian John Harris [1966] Operations Director; Richard John Neal [1976] Director/Accountant; Andrew Michael Peeler [1963] Director; Philip Leslie Peters [1957] Director; Michael Seal [1948] Director; Stuart Andrew Winton [1964] Director

Yodel Distribution Holdings Limited
Incorporated: 19 June 2012 *Employees:* 5,106
Net Worth: £6,060,000 *Total Assets:* £256,568,000
Registered Office: 2nd Floor, Atlantic Pavilion, Albert Dock, Liverpool, L3 4AE
Activities: Other transportation support activities
Officers: Aidan Stuart Barclay [1956] Director; Howard Myles Barclay [1959] Director; Philip Leslie Peters [1957] Director/Banker; Michael Seal [1948] Director/Chartered Accountant

Yodel Logistics Limited
Incorporated: 15 February 2012 *Employees:* 5,106
Net Worth: £4,207,000 *Total Assets:* £241,279,008
Registered Office: 2nd Floor, Atlantic Pavilion, Albert Dock, Liverpool, L3 4AE
Activities: Other transportation support activities
Parent: Yodel Distribution Holdings Limited
Officers: Aidan Stuart Barclay [1956] Director; Howard Myles Barclay [1959] Director; Richard John Neal [1976] Director/Accountant; Philip Leslie Peters [1957] Director/Banker; Michael Seal [1948] Director/Chartered Accountant; Stuart Andrew Winton [1964] Director

Yodel Properties Limited
Incorporated: 28 August 2014
Net Worth: £6,855,000 *Total Assets:* £21,757,000
Registered Office: 2nd Floor, Atlantic Pavilion, Albert Dock, Liverpool, L3 4AE
Activities: Other business support service activities n.e.c.
Parent: Yodel Distribution Holdings Limited
Officers: Richard John Neal [1976] Director/Accountant; Philip Leslie Peters [1957] Director; Michael Seal [1948] Director/Chartered Accountant

Yokogawa United Kingdom Limited
Incorporated: 1 August 1986 *Employees:* 108
Net Worth: £5,633,362 *Total Assets:* £11,243,714
Registered Office: Stuart Road, Manor Park, Runcorn, Cheshire, WA7 1TR
Activities: Manufacture of electronic industrial process control equipment
Parent: Yokogawa Electric Corporation
Officers: Carl Ramsden, Secretary; Charles Nigel Bowden [1962] Managing Director; Hermanus Johannes Van Den Berg [1958] Director/President [South African]

Yorkshire Building Society Covered Bonds LLP
Incorporated: 22 September 2006
Net Worth: £6,115,000 *Total Assets:* £2,124,420,992
Registered Office: Yorkshire House, Yorkshire Drive, Bradford, W Yorks, BD5 8LJ

The Yorkshire Traction Company Limited
Incorporated: 17 October 1986 *Employees:* 1,189
Net Worth: £15,510,000 *Total Assets:* £43,541,000
Registered Office: c/o Stagecoach Services Limited, One Stockport Exchange, 20 Railway Road, Stockport, Cheshire, SK1 3SW
Activities: Other urban, suburban or metropolitan passenger land transport (not underground, metro or similar)
Parent: Stagecoach Bus Holdings Limited
Officers: Michael John Vaux, Secretary; Colin Brown [1968] Director/Accountant; Matthew Davies [1973] Managing Director; Arnold Mark Threapleton [1954] Managing Director

Yorkshire Water Services Finance Limited
Incorporated: 14 January 2003
Net Worth: £48,000 *Total Assets:* £1,614,727,040
Registered Office: Western House, Halifax Road, Bradford, BD6 2SZ
Activities: Banks
Parent: Yorkshire Water Services Limited
Officers: Kathy Smith, Secretary; Elizabeth Marian Barber [1965] Director/Accountant; Richard David Flint [1968] Director; Kathy Smith [1974] Director/Company Secretary

Yorkshire Water Services Holdings Limited
Incorporated: 10 February 2009
Net Worth: £778,318,976 *Total Assets:* £778,318,976
Registered Office: Western House, Halifax Road, Bradford, BD6 2SZ
Activities: Activities of head offices
Parent: Kelda Finance (No. 2) Limited
Officers: Kathy Smith, Secretary; Elizabeth Marian Barber [1965] Director/Accountant; Richard David Flint [1968] Director; Kathy Smith [1974] Director/Company Secretary

Yorkshire Water Services Limited
Incorporated: 1 April 1989 *Employees:* 2,605
Net Worth: £984,499,968 *Total Assets:* £9,135,899,648
Registered Office: Western House, Halifax Road, Bradford, W Yorks, BD6 2SZ
Activities: Water collection, treatment and supply
Parent: Yorkshire Water Services Holdings Limited
Officers: Kathy Smith, Secretary; Scott Auty [1978] Director/Fund Manager; Elizabeth Marian Barber [1965] Director/Accountant; Andrew James Dench [1969] Director; Pamela Jane Doherty [1969] Director; Richard David Flint [1968] Director; Nevil George Muncaster [1964] Director/Civil Engineer; Raymond O'Toole [1955] Director/Engineer; Michael Peter Francis Osborne [1980] Director; Anthony Leon Philip Rabin [1955] Director; Julia Unwin [1956] Director/Consultant; Andrew Wyllie [1962] Director

Young Foundations Limited
Incorporated: 29 January 2004 *Employees:* 157
Net Worth: £3,915,190 *Total Assets:* £8,602,534
Registered Office: 2nd Floor, Suite 1, Southwood House, Greenwood Business Centre, Regent Road, Salford, M5 4QH
Activities: Other human health activities
Parent: Mental Health Care (UK) Limited
Officers: Thomas Matthew Ellison [1970] Director of Operations; Niall Stephen Kelly [1971] Managing Director [Irish]

YPG Developments Ltd
Incorporated: 23 November 2015
Net Worth: £1,025,680 *Total Assets:* £11,928,777
Registered Office: Unit 1F, 2nd Floor, Columbus Quay, Riverside Drive, Liverpool, L3 4DB
Activities: Development of building projects
Major Shareholder: Sze Ming Yeung
Officers: Sze Ming Yeung, Secretary; Sze Ming Yeung [1967] Director

YQ Developments Limited
Incorporated: 22 August 2016
Net Worth Deficit: £287,104 *Total Assets:* £12,293,454
Registered Office: 1st Floor, NQ Building, 47 Bengal Street, Ancoats, Manchester, M4 6BB
Activities: Development of building projects
Parent: XQ Developments Limited
Officers: Michael Shaw, Secretary; Daren Whitaker [1972] Director

Ysgellog Wind Farm Limited
Incorporated: 15 September 2011
Net Worth Deficit: £728,627 *Total Assets:* £7,549,941
Registered Office: 1030 Centre Park, Slutchers Lane, Warrington, Cheshire, WA1 1QL
Activities: Production of electricity
Officers: Elizabeth Alexandra Oldroyd, Secretary; John William Breckenridge [1962] Managing Director [American]; Simon Richard Eaves [1967] Managing Director; Adrian Waine Robinson [1961] Director/Chief Operating Officer; Kirsty Louise Usher [1975] Director/Accountant

Z&D Property Investments Limited
Incorporated: 3 August 2015 *Employees:* 2
Net Worth: £7,701,439 *Total Assets:* £17,135,496
Registered Office: 1 Parkview Court, St Paul's Road, Shipley, W Yorks, BD18 3DZ
Activities: Buying and selling of own real estate
Shareholders: Zorawer Singh; Daljit Singh
Officers: Daljit Singh [1971] Director; Zorawer Singh [1965] Director

Zabaxe Limited
Incorporated: 29 April 1987 *Employees:* 1
Net Worth: £7,157,027 *Total Assets:* £8,064,351
Registered Office: Blackpool FC Stadium, Seasiders Way, Blackpool, Lancs, FY1 6JJ
Activities: Financial management
Major Shareholder: Owen John Oyston
Officers: Owen John Oyston [1934] Director; Vicki Oyston [1940] Director

Zebramarsh Limited
Incorporated: 25 November 2010
Net Worth Deficit: £38,596,524 *Total Assets:* £14,489,532
Registered Office: 7650 Daresbury Park, Daresbury, Warrington, Cheshire, WA4 4BS
Activities: Manufacture of other chemical products n.e.c.
Shareholder: Epiris Managers LLP
Officers: Steve Mark Goodwin [1961] Director/Chief Executive; Gary James Roebuck [1968] Director/C O O Sentinel Performance Solutions

Zedra Trust Company (UK) Limited
Incorporated: 1 November 1967 *Employees:* 84
Net Worth: £8,787,000 *Total Assets:* £14,950,000
Registered Office: Booths Hall, Booths Park 3, Chelford Road, Knutsford, Cheshire, WA16 8GS
Activities: Financial intermediation not elsewhere classified
Officers: Niels Nielsen [1976] Director [Danish]; Ali Reza Sarikhani [1946] Director; Alexander James Stevens [1984] Director/Chartered Accountant; Alan Victor Tidy [1954] Director

Zen Internet Limited
Incorporated: 13 September 1995 *Employees:* 433
Net Worth: £12,158,593 *Total Assets:* £35,533,320
Registered Office: Sandbrook House, Sandbrook Park, Sandbrook Way, Rochdale, Lancs, OL11 1RY
Activities: Wired telecommunications activities
Major Shareholder: Richard Tang
Officers: Emma Jayne Louise Jackson, Secretary; Matthew Martin Kay [1965] Finance Director; Shaun Parker [1961] Director; Ayshea June Robertson [1972] HR Director; Paul Lancelot Stobart [1957] Director/Chief Executive; Richard Tang [1966] Director/Chairman

Zenith International Freight Holdings Ltd
Incorporated: 24 October 2016 *Employees:* 23
Net Worth: £4,067,564 *Total Assets:* £9,857,573
Registered Office: Zenith House, Valley Court, Bradford, W Yorks, BD1 4SP
Activities: Activities of other holding companies n.e.c.
Shareholders: Catherine Anne Usher; Colin Jeffrey Usher
Officers: Colin Jeffrey Usher [1959] Director/Freight Forwarder

Zenith International Freight Limited
Incorporated: 6 July 1999 *Employees:* 23
Net Worth: £8,410,626 *Total Assets:* £12,895,635
Registered Office: Zenith House, Valley Court, Bradford, W Yorks, BD1 4SP
Activities: Operation of warehousing and storage facilities for land transport activities
Parent: Zenith International Freight Holdlings Limited
Officers: Mark Anthony Wilson, Secretary; Colin Jeffrey Usher [1959] Director/Freight Forwarder

Zep UK Limited
Incorporated: 12 June 1979 *Employees:* 43
Net Worth: £5,600,584 *Total Assets:* £9,409,107
Registered Office: P O Box 12, Tanhouse Lane, Widnes, Cheshire, WA8 0RD
Activities: Manufacture of soap and detergents
Parent: Hale Group (Widnes) Limited
Officers: Rob Novo [1957] Director [American]; Paolo Polegri [1965] Finance Director [Italian]; Peter Reilly [1964] Director [American]

Zeus Capital Limited
Incorporated: 16 April 2002 *Employees:* 59
Net Worth: £19,108,200 *Total Assets:* £21,805,180
Registered Office: 82 King Street, Manchester, M2 4WQ
Activities: Financial intermediation not elsewhere classified
Parent: Zeus Capital Investment Limited
Officers: Darren Ellis, Secretary; Michael Allen [1978] Director/Head of Research; Tremayne Anthony Ducker [1970] Director; Darren Ellis [1961] Director; John Howard Goold [1971] Director; Sir Nigel Graham Knowles [1956] Director

Zeus Group Limited
Incorporated: 16 June 2015 *Employees:* 59
Net Worth: £19,099,800 *Total Assets:* £21,796,780
Registered Office: 82 King Street, Manchester, M2 4WQ
Activities: Activities of head offices
Major Shareholder: Clare Hughes
Officers: Darren Ellis [1961] Director; John Howard Goold [1971] Director; Sir Nigel Knowles [1956] Director

Zoe Group Limited
Incorporated: 12 May 1998
Net Worth: £7,778,156 *Total Assets:* £28,556,940
Registered Office: 2nd Floor, Muskers Building, 1 Stanley Street, Liverpool, L1 6AA
Activities: Non-trading company
Shareholders: David Anastasiou; Eleftherios Eleftheriou
Officers: Aneil Kumar Singh, Secretary; David Anastasiou [1962] Director; Eleftherios Eleftheriou [1959] Director

Zoll Medical UK Limited
Incorporated: 2 June 1993 *Employees:* 40
Net Worth: £9,898,671 *Total Assets:* £12,592,494
Registered Office: 9 Seymour Court, Tudor Road, Runcorn, Cheshire, WA7 1SY
Activities: Specialists medical practice activities
Parent: Zoll Medical Corporation
Officers: David Brian Young, Secretary; Richard Andrew Knell-Moore [1976] UK Director; Mark Christopher Webster [1964] Director; A Ernest Whiton [1961] Director/Business Executive [American]

Zyex Group Limited
Incorporated: 27 July 1993 *Employees:* 27
Net Worth: £5,368,689 *Total Assets:* £7,473,694
Registered Office: Victrex Technology Centre, Hillhouse International, Thornton Cleveleys, Lancs, FY5 4QD
Activities: Other manufacturing n.e.c.
Parent: Victrex Manufacturing Limited
Officers: Richard James Armitage [1965] Finance Director; Timothy John Cooper [1959] Director; Martin Court [1961] Director

Zyex Limited
Incorporated: 21 January 1994 *Employees:* 27
Net Worth: £5,291,162 *Total Assets:* £7,473,694
Registered Office: Victrex Technolgy Centre, Hillhouse International, Thornton Cleveleys, Lancs, FY5 4QD
Activities: Manufacture of man-made fibres
Parent: Zyex Group Ltd
Officers: Richard James Armitage [1965] Finance Director; Timothy John Cooper [1959] Director; Martin Court [1961] Director

Standard Industrial Classification

01110 Growing of cereals (except rice), leguminous crops and oil seeds

Harnage Estates Limited
Love Brothers Limited
Noble Nordmann Limited
Quantil Agriculture Limited
Robert Wright & Sons Limited

01130 Growing of vegetables and melons, roots and tubers

Ivan Ambrose and Company Limited
Flavourfresh Salads Limited
Huntapac Produce Limited
Medlar Fruit Farms Ltd
Orthios Eco Parks (Anglesey) Limited

01190 Growing of other non-perennial crops

APS Produce Limited

01300 Plant propagation

Ash Lea Cottage Nurseries Limited
The Barton Grange Group Limited

01410 Raising of dairy cattle

Town Head Farm Products Limited
Withgill Farm Limited

01430 Raising of horses and other equines

Merry Fox Stud Limited

01470 Raising of poultry

Aviagen Turkeys Limited
Tom Barron Limited
A.J. Forster Limited
Mayfield Chicks Limited
Staveley's Eggs Limited

01490 Raising of other animals

Ashton Agricultural and General Limited
Boden & Davies Limited

01500 Mixed farming

Daresbury Properties Limited
Grosvenor Farms Limited
Withgill Farm Limited

01610 Support activities for crop production

Wilsons Contractors Limited

01629 Support activities for animal production (other than farm animal boarding)

Cogent Breeding Limited
Craven Cattle Marts Limited
Harrison & Hetherington Limited
Wilsons Contractors Limited

01640 Seed processing for propagation

Nuseed Europe Ltd
Nuseed Global Innovation Ltd

02100 Silviculture and other forestry activities

Noble Nordmann Limited
Woodland Assets Limited

02400 Support services to forestry

Komatsu Forest Limited
Amos Nelson,Limited

03110 Marine fishing

Mardon Public Limited Company

03210 Marine aquaculture

Nutreco Limited
Trouw (UK) Limited

03220 Freshwater aquaculture

Orthios Eco Parks (Anglesey) Limited

06100 Extraction of crude petroleum

Attock Oil Company Limited (The)
Suncor Energy UK Limited

07290 Mining of other non-ferrous metal ores

Underground Mining Services Limited

08110 Quarrying of ornamental and building stone, limestone, gypsum, chalk and slate

Burlington Slate Limited

08120 Operation of gravel and sand pits; mining of clays and kaolin

Bathgate Silica Sand Limited
Land Recovery Limited
Sibelco UK Limited
Watts Blake Bearne and Company Limited
D P Williams Group Limited

08930 Extraction of salt

British Salt Limited
Compass Minerals UK Limited

08990 Other mining and quarrying n.e.c.

Archibald Bathgate Group Limited
Armstrongs Aggregates Limited
Love Brothers Limited
Sibelco Minerals and Chemicals (Holdings) Limited

09100 Support activities for petroleum and natural gas mining

AMEC Foster Wheeler International Limited
Cuadrilla Bowland Limited
Cuadrilla Resources Limited
Cuadrilla Well Services Limited
Driver Consult Limited
Driver Group PLC
FMC Kongsberg Services Limited
FMC Technologies Limited
Fircroft Engineering Services Limited
N-Sea Offshore Ltd
Wayne Fueling Systems UK Holdco Ltd.

09900 Support activities for other mining and quarrying

ALS Testing Services (UK) Limited
AMEC Foster Wheeler Earth and Environmental (UK) Limited
H M Project Developments Ltd
Stewart Holdings Management Limited
Underground Mining Services Limited

10110 Processing and preserving of meat

Danish Crown UK Limited
Dunbia (England)

10120 Processing and preserving of poultry meat

Forresters of Cheshire Limited
Seamark PLC

10130 Production of meat and poultry meat products

Bawnbua Foods GB Ltd
Frank Bird (Poultry) Limited
Country Park Foods Limited
Deckers Restaurants Limited
Dunkleys Limited
Farmers Boy Limited
Forrester (Sales) Limited
Glendale Foods Limited
Kepak Kirkham Limited
Neerock Limited
TSC Foods Limited

10200 Processing and preserving of fish, crustaceans and molluscs

A.M. Seafoods Limited
Interfish Limited
International Seafoods Limited
MacKnight Limited
Northbay Pelagic Limited
Seamark PLC

10310 Processing and preserving of potatoes

E.Park & Sons Limited
Seabrook Crisps Limited

10390 Other processing and preserving of fruit and vegetables

F. Duerr & Sons Limited
Huntapac Produce Limited
John Morley (Importers) Limited
Wm Morrison Bananas Limited
Wm Morrison Produce Limited
R & W Scott Ltd
TSC Foods Limited

10410 Manufacture of oils and fats

BASF Pharma (Callanish) Limited
Edible Oils Ltd
Olympic Oils Limited
Roil Foods Limited

10420 Manufacture of margarine and similar edible fats

Crest Oil Holdings Ltd

10511 Liquid milk and cream production

Creamline Dairies Limited
Dewlay Cheesemakers Limited
Meadow Foods (Holdings) Limited
Meadow Foods Limited
Pakeeza Dairies Limited
Swallow Holdings Limited
Town Head Farm Products Limited

10512 Butter and cheese production

Carron Lodge Limited
Dairygold Food Ingredients (UK) Limited
The First Milk Cheese Company Limited
Glanbia Cheese Limited
Joseph Heler Limited
Singleton's Dairy Limited

10519 Manufacture of other milk products

Dale Farm (GB) Limited

10611 Grain milling

Dacsa Limited
Morning Foods,Limited
Wm. Nelstrop & Co. Ltd

10612 Manufacture of breakfast cereals and cereals-based food

Deeside Cereals I Ltd

10710 Manufacture of bread; manufacture of fresh pastry goods and cakes

Alliedtropic Limited
Bright Blue Foods Limited
Greenhalgh's Craft Bakery Limited
Guenther Bakeries UK Limited
Park Cakes Limited
Rathbone Kear Limited
Real Good Food PLC
Frank Roberts & Sons Limited
Sayers The Bakers Limited
Warburtons 1876 Limited
Warburtons Holdings Limited
Warburtons Limited

10720 Manufacture of rusks and biscuits; manufacture of preserved pastry goods and cakes

Farmhouse Biscuits Limited
Ginger Acquisition Company Limited
Hill Biscuits Limited

10810 Manufacture of sugar

J F Renshaw Ltd

10821 Manufacture of cocoa and chocolate confectionery

R & W Scott Ltd
Whitakers Chocolates Limited

10822 Manufacture of sugar confectionery

Lofthouse of Fleetwood Limited
J F Renshaw Ltd
Swizzels Matlow Limited
Tangerine Confectionery Limited

10831 Tea processing

Aimia Foods Limited
Typhoo Tea Limited

10840 Manufacture of condiments and seasonings

Aimia Foods Limited
English Provender Company Limited

10850 Manufacture of prepared meals and dishes

The Authentic Food Company Limited
The Authentic Food Group Limited
Iceland Manufacturing Limited
Laila's Fine Foods Limited
Wright's Pies (Shelton) Limited

10860 Manufacture of homogenized food preparations and dietetic food

SHS International Ltd

10890 Manufacture of other food products n.e.c.

ADM Protexin Limited
Aimia Foods Holdings Limited
Aimia Foods Limited
Bevie Partners Limited
Billington Foodservice Limited
CSM (United Kingdom) Limited
Calbee (UK) Ltd
DCC Health & Beauty Solutions Limited
Hero UK Limited
K K Fine Foods Limited
Kellogg Company of Great Britain,Limited
Kellogg Management Services (Europe) Limited
Kellogg Marketing and Sales Company (UK) Limited
Portable Foods Manufacturing Company Limited
Real Good Food PLC
Sandhof Limited
Seabrook Group Limited
Stateside Foods Limited
Sun Valley Limited
Tithebarn Limited
Trigon Snacks Trading Limited
Ungerer Limited

10910 Manufacture of prepared feeds for farm animals

Afgritech Limited
Carrs Agriculture Limited
Carrs Billington Agriculture (Operations) Limited
Carrs Billington Agriculture (Sales) Limited
Massey Bros (Feeds) Ltd.
NWF Agriculture Limited
Oakes Millers Limited
J.Stobart & Sons Limited

10920 Manufacture of prepared pet foods

GA Pet Food Partners Limited
GA Pet Food Partners Milling Limited
Pets Choice Limited

11010 Distilling, rectifying and blending of spirits

G&J Distillers Ltd.

11030 Manufacture of cider and other fruit wines

H&A Prestige Bottling Limited
Halewood International Limited
Thomas Hardy Holdings Limited
Thomas Hardy Kendal Limited

11040 Manufacture of other non-distilled fermented beverages

H&A Prestige Bottling Limited
Halewood International Limited
Thomas Hardy Holdings Limited
Thomas Hardy Kendal Limited

11050 Manufacture of beer

Thomas Hardy Holdings Limited
Thomas Hardy Kendal Limited
Joseph Holt Group Limited
Joseph Holt Limited
Hydes' Brewery Limited
J.W.Lees & Co.(Brewers) Limited
Frederic Robinson Limited
Timothy Taylor & Co.,Limited
Daniel Thwaites Public Limited Company

11070 Manufacture of soft drinks; production of mineral waters and other bottled waters

Cott Ventures UK Limited
Thomas Hardy Holdings Limited
Thomas Hardy Kendal Limited
Total Water Solutions Limited

12000 Manufacture of tobacco products

Gawith Hoggarth & Co.,Limited

13100 Preparation and spinning of textile fibres

Bulmer & Lumb Group Limited
James Dewhurst Limited
Invista Textiles (U.K.) Limited
James Robinson Fibres Limited
Standard Wool UK (Holdings) Limited

13200 Weaving of textiles

Lappet Manufacturing Company Limited
Sadaqat Global Limited

13300 Finishing of textiles

The British Millerain Company Limited
Flameproofings Limited
Fothergill Polycom Limited
Pin Croft Dyeing and Printing Co. Limited

13921 Manufacture of soft furnishings

Montgomery Tomlinson Limited
Panaz Holdings Limited
Sartex Quilts & Textiles Limited
R. Soper Limited
Trendsetter Home Furnishings Limited

13923 manufacture of household textiles

Beamfeature Limited
Comfy Quilts Limited

13931 Manufacture of woven or tufted carpets and rugs

Cavalier Carpets Limited
Flair Flooring Supplies Limited
Furlong Flooring (Central) Ltd
Milliken Industrials Limited
Penthouse Carpets Limited
Westex (Carpets) Limited

13939 Manufacture of other carpets and rugs

Flair Flooring Supplies Limited
Greenwood & Coope Limited

13950 Manufacture of non-wovens and articles made from non-wovens, except apparel

AMR Textiles Limited
Lydall Industrial Filtration Textile Manufacturing (EMEA) Limited
Nice-Pak International Limited

13960 Manufacture of other technical and industrial textiles

Albany International Limited
Amann Threads UK Limited
Andrew Industries Limited
Lydall Industrial Filtration Textile Manufacturing (EMEA) Limited
Panaz Limited
Sage Automotive Interiors Limited
Sigmatex (UK) Limited

13990 Manufacture of other textiles n.e.c.

CHA Technologies Group Public Limited Company
CHA Textiles Limited
Cosmopolitan Textile Company Limited
Fothergill Engineered Fabrics Limited
S.A.N. Limited
Sadaqat Global Limited
Robert Scott & Sons Limited
YKK (U.K.) Limited

14120 Manufacture of workwear

Alsico Laucuba Ltd
Ballyclare Limited

14131 Manufacture of other men's outerwear

Mackintosh Limited

14132 Manufacture of other women's outerwear

Mackintosh Limited
Marsylka Manufacturing Co.Limited
Q. R. I. Ltd

14142 Manufacture of women's underwear

Marsylka Manufacturing Co.Limited

14190 Manufacture of other wearing apparel and accessories n.e.c.

Emeram Urbanics Holding Ltd
Emeram Urbanics Ltd
Klash Clothing Co. Ltd
Lyon Equipment Limited
Outdoor & Sports Company Limited

14390 Manufacture of other knitted and crocheted apparel

Rowlinson Knitwear Limited

15200 Manufacture of footwear

Beaconsfield Footwear Limited
New Balance Athletic Shoes (U.K.) Limited

16100 Sawmilling and planing of wood

Archwood Limited
C & W Berry Limited
Firwood Timber & Plywood Co. Limited
Green Growth Power Ltd
Illingworth Ingham (Manchester) Limited
Irmass Company Limited
R. Plevin & Sons Limited
G E Robinson & Co Ltd
Rowlinson Garden Products Limited

16210 Manufacture of veneer sheets and wood-based panels

Bathgate Flooring Limited
Starbank Panel Products Limited
Thrislington Cubicles Limited

16230 Manufacture of other builders' carpentry and joinery

C & W Berry Limited

16240 Manufacture of wooden containers

Rowlinson Packaging Limited

16290 Manufacture of other products of wood; manufacture of articles of cork, straw and plaiting materials

W. Howard Limited
George Morgan Holdings Limited
R. Plevin & Sons Limited
Rowlinson Garden Products Limited
Rowlinson Packaging Limited

17120 Manufacture of paper and paperboard

Arjo Wiggins Fine Papers Limited
Arjowiggins Chartham Limited
Boardlink Limited
Carlson Filtration Limited
James Cropper Converting Limited
James Cropper Public Limited Company
James Cropper Speciality Papers Limited
Doric Anderton Limited
John Hargreaves,(Collyhurst and Stalybridge) Limited
Holmen UK Limited
Iggesund Paperboard (Workington) Limited
Matryx Limited
Poppies Europe Ltd
Preston Board and Packaging Limited
John Roberts Holdings Limited
Saica Flex UK Limited
Saica Paper UK Limited
Sonoco Cores and Paper Limited
Sonoco Limited
Star Tissue UK Limited
Tullis Russell Coaters Limited

17211 Manufacture of corrugated paper and paperboard, sacks and bags

Huhtamaki BCP Limited
Jiffy Packaging Company Limited
Northern Packaging Holdings Limited
Northern Packaging Limited
Ribble Investments Limited
Ribble Packaging Limited
John Roberts Ventures Limited
Smurfit Kappa Investments UK Ltd
Smurfit Kappa UK Ltd

17219 Manufacture of other paper and paperboard containers

API Foils Holdings Limited
API Foils Limited
CRP Print & Packaging Limited
Glossop Carton and Print Limited
Graphic Packaging International Bardon Limited
Graphic Packaging International Box Holdings Limited
Graphic Packaging International Europe UK Limited
Graphic Packaging International Foodservice Europe Ltd
Graphic Packaging International Gateshead Limited
Graphic Packaging International Limited
Inspirepac Limited
Kentmere Limited
Miramar Investments Limited
Preston Board and Packaging Limited
Saica Pack UK Limited
Shoo 553 Limited

17220 Manufacture of household and sanitary goods and of toilet requisites

Accrol Holdings Limited
Accrol Papers Limited
Accrol UK Limited
Northwood Tissue (Disley) Limited

17230 Manufacture of paper stationery

Heritage Envelopes Limited
Midas Paper Converters Limited
Nitecrest Limited
SG World Limited

17240 Manufacture of wallpaper

Arthouse Limited
Fine Decor Wallcoverings Limited
Graham & Brown Limited
Holden Decor Limited

17290 Manufacture of other articles of paper and paperboard n.e.c.

Billerudkorsnas Beetham Ltd
CRP Print & Packaging Holdings Limited
CRP Print & Packaging Limited
DWL (Holdings) Limited
Hollingsworth & Vose Air Filtration Limited
The Label Makers Limited
SG World Limited
J.Stell & Sons,Limited
Stell Cardboard Tubes Limited

18121 Manufacture of printed labels

Saica Flex UK Limited
Skanem UK Limited

18129 Printing n.e.c.

A.D.S. Graphics Limited
Americk Advantage Limited
Buxton Press Limited
Enesco Limited
G & H Print Services Limited
Jones & Brooks,Limited
Mayr-Melnhof Packaging UK Limited
Mediaco Limited
Spellman & Walker Group Limited
Tipografic Limited
The Valley Printing Company, Limited

19201 Mineral oil refining

Essar Oil (UK) Limited
Holt Lloyd International Limited
Ironsides Lubricants Limited (The)

19209 Other treatment of petroleum products (excluding petrochemicals manufacture)

R.S.Clare & Co.,Limited
Kerax Limited
Oil Salvage Limited

20110 Manufacture of industrial gases

Inovyn Chlorvinyls Limited
Mexichem UK Limited
Runcorn MCP Limited

20120 Manufacture of dyes and pigments

Colormatrix Europe Limited
John Hogg Technical Solutions Limited

20130 Manufacture of other inorganic basic chemicals

Airedale Chemical Company Limited
Airedale Chemical Holdings Limited
Apollo Scientific Ltd
Avocado Research Chemicals Limited
BYK Additives Limited
Dow Chemical Company Limited
INEOS Enterprises Group Limited
INEOS Fluor Limited
Innospec Limited
Inovyn Chlorvinyls Limited
Inovyn Enterprises Limited
Invista Textiles (U.K.) Limited
Lanxess Holding UK Unlimited
Lanxess Solutions UK Ltd
Magnesium Elektron Limited
Nalco Energy Services Marketing Limited
Nalco Limited
Nalco Manufacturing Ltd
PQ Silicas UK Limited
Rodol Limited
Runcorn MCP Limited
Solvay Interox Limited
Tata Chemicals Magadi Limited

20140 Manufacture of other organic basic chemicals

Avocado Research Chemicals Limited
BASF Public Limited Company
Baerlocher UK Limited
Contract Chemicals (Knowsley) Limited
Contract Chemicals Limited
FMC Chemicals Limited
INEOS Vinyls Limited
Inovyn Chlorvinyls Limited
Nalco Acquisition One
Nalco Acquisition Two Limited
Synthite Limited
Valtris Advanced Organics Limited
Vynova Runcorn Limited

20150 Manufacture of fertilizers and nitrogen compounds

CF Fertilisers UK Group Limited
CF Fertilisers UK Limited
CF Industries (UK) Limited

20160 Manufacture of plastics in primary forms

AGC Chemicals Europe, Ltd.
Abbey Masterbatch Limited
Americhem Europe Limited
Aqua Fabrications Limited
Ball & Young Limited
Basell Polyolefins UK Limited
Distrupol Limited
Hyperlast Limited
Invibio Limited
Lanxess Urethanes UK Ltd
Roydon Group PLC
A. Schulman Thermoplastic Compounds Limited
Victrex Manufacturing Limited
Victrex PLC
Victrex USA Holdings Limited
Vita Cellular Foams (UK) Limited
Vita Liquid Polymers Limited

20170 Manufacture of synthetic rubber in primary forms

Polytech International Limited

20200 Manufacture of pesticides and other agrochemical products

Calachem Ltd
Doff Portland Limited
Emerald Kalama Chemical Limited
FMC Agro Limited
Nufarm UK Limited
UPL Europe Ltd
Yanco Limited

20301 Manufacture of paints, varnishes and similar coatings, mastics and sealants

Becker Industrial Coatings Limited
Crown Paints Limited
HMG Paints Limited
Holt Lloyd International Limited
The Little Greene Paint Company Limited
Sherwin-Williams Protective & Marine Coatings
Valspar Powder Coatings Limited
Whitford Limited

20302 Manufacture of printing ink

INX Europe Limited

20411 Manufacture of soap and detergents

Acdoco Limited
Christeyns UK Ltd
Ecolab Limited
Evans Vanodine International PLC
The Holchem Group Limited
Holchem Laboratories Limited
Holt Lloyd International Limited
Robert McBride Ltd
Royal Sanders (UK) Limited
Selden Research Limited
Shorrock Trichem Limited
Stepan UK Limited
Zep UK Limited

20412 Manufacture of cleaning and polishing preparations

Astonish Holdings Limited
Evans Vanodine International PLC
The London Oil Refining Co. Limited
Robert McBride Ltd
Tetrosyl Limited

20420 Manufacture of perfumes and toilet preparations

Emerald Kalama Chemical Limited
Evans Vanodine International PLC
Fragrance Oils (International) Limited
Fragrance Oils (Purchasing) Limited
Robert McBride Ltd
Mibelle Ltd
Ungerer Limited

20510 Manufacture of explosives

Orica UK Limited

20530 Manufacture of essential oils

Emerald Kalama Chemical Limited
Ungerer Limited

20590 Manufacture of other chemical products n.e.c.

Abgene Limited
Advanced Biotechnologies Limited
Armored Auto UK Limited
Aztec Aerosols Limited
BWA Water Additives UK Limited
BYK Additives Limited
Samuel Banner & Co. Limited
Bitrez Group Limited
Bitrez Limited
Blackburn Chemicals Limited
James Briggs (Holdings) Limited
James Briggs Limited
Datac Adhesives Limited
Evans Vanodine International PLC
F2 Chemicals Limited
Faci UK Chemicals Limited
Fujifilm Imaging Colorants Limited
H.B. Fuller U.K. Manufacturing Limited
HB Fuller UK Operations Limited
Holt Lloyd International Limited
Houghton PLC
INEOS Technologies (Vinyls) Limited
Iconichem Widnes Limited
Incorez Limited
Invista Textiles (U.K.) Limited
Jacobi Carbons Limited
Kemira Chemicals (UK) Limited
M & I Materials Limited
MacDermid Canning Limited
Medimmune U.K. Limited
Metalube Ltd
Methanex (UK) Limited
National Refrigerants Ltd
Palace Chemicals Limited
Perstorp UK Ltd.
Selden Research Limited
Sentinel Performance Solutions Group Limited
Sentinel Performance Solutions Limited
Sovereign Chemicals Limited
Stepan UK Limited
Suez Water Technologies & Solutions United Kingdom
Tata Chemicals Europe Limited
Thor Specialities (UK) Limited
Tiger Tim Products Limited
UPL Europe Ltd
Urenco Chemplants Limited
VIL Resins Ltd.
Valtris Specialty Chemicals Limited
Zebramarsh Limited

20600 Manufacture of man-made fibres

IFG Drake Limited
Invista Textiles (U.K.) Limited
Shakespeare Monofilament UK Limited
Zyex Limited

21100 Manufacture of basic pharmaceutical products

Advanced Medical Solutions Limited
Allergan Biologics Limited
Bell,Sons & Co.(Druggists) Limited
Custom Powders Limited
Dechra Limited
Emerald Kalama Chemical Limited
Hologic Ltd.
Life Technologies Bpd UK Limited
Lofthouse of Fleetwood Limited
M & A Pharmachem Limited
Medlock Medical Limited
Molnlycke Health Care Limited
Nutrition Group PLC
OBG Holding Limited
Octapharma Limited
Principle Healthcare International Limited
Qiagen Manchester Limited
RSR Limited
Recipharm Limited
Sinclair Pharmaceuticals Limited
Thermo Fisher Scientific Life Holdings Limited
Thompson and Capper Limited

21200 Manufacture of pharmaceutical preparations

Calea UK Limited
Fresenius Kabi Limited
M & A Pharmachem Limited
Medlock Medical Limited
Pharmaserve (North West) Limited

22190 Manufacture of other rubber products

Armacell UK Limited
Beamfeature Limited
Berwin Industrial Polymers Limited
Berwin Rubber Company Limited
Contitech United Kingdom Limited
E3G Limited
Hexpol Tpe Ltd
Manuli Hydraulics UK Limited
Polytech International Limited
Silicone Engineering Limited
Silicone Holdings Limited

22210 Manufacture of plastic plates, sheets, tubes and profiles

API Foils Holdings Limited
API Foils Limited
API Laminates Limited
Centriforce Products Limited
Fibreforce Composites Limited
Op Acquisitions Limited
Orthoplastics Limited
Plastic Recycling Limited
Quadrant EPP UK Ltd.
Veka PLC

22220 Manufacture of plastic packing goods

Aintree Plastics Limited
Alma Products Limited
Coral Products (Mouldings) Ltd
Duo Packaging Group Limited
Duo Plastics Limited
Emballator (UK) Limited
Europlast (Blackburn) Limited
Ipackchem Limited
Jason Plastics Limited
LB Europe Limited
Marpak Extrusions Limited
Mondi UK Consumer Packaging Holding 1 Ltd
Plasto-Sac UK Limited
TS (UK) Limited
Total Polyfilm Limited

22230 Manufacture of builders ware of plastic

Building Product Design Limited
Gutterline Services Limited
Mexichem Wavin UK Ltd
Polyflor Limited
Tensar Manufacturing Limited

22290 Manufacture of other plastic products

Advanced Biotechnologies Limited
Albis (U.K.) Limited
Alpla UK Limited
Blakedale Ltd
Carpenter Limited
Checkers Safety Group UK Ltd
Colloids Limited
General All Purpose Plastics Limited
Glasdon (UK) Limited
Gradus Limited
Hubron (International) Limited
Jonesco (Preston) Limited
Kaman Composites - UK Limited
Lendlock International Ltd
Melba Products Holdings Limited
Melba Products Limited
Mexichem Dura-Line UK, Ltd
Multiplastics (Europe) Limited
Nitecrest Limited
Nova Group Limited
Patterson and Rothwell Limited
Quadrant EPP UK Ltd.
SPM Plastics U.K. Limited
SPS (EU) Limited
Sanko Gosei UK Ltd
Schoeller Allibert Limited
Stamford Products Limited
Sterilin Limited
TS (UK) Limited
Taylor Engineering & Plastics Limited
Tenmat Limited
Tensar International Limited
Thumbs-Up (Bury) Limited
Total Glass Limited
Tygavac Advanced Materials Ltd
Uniroyal Global Limited
Vinnolit Hillhouse Ltd
Weltonhurst Limited
What More UK Limited

23110 Manufacture of flat glass

Custom Glass Limited
Pilkington Automotive Limited
Pilkington Group Limited
Pilkington United Kingdom Limited
Pyroguard UK Limited

23120 Shaping and processing of flat glass

Custom Glass Limited
Regency Glass Limited
System 3 Limited

23140 Manufacture of glass fibres

Electric Glass Fiber UK, Ltd.
Knauf Insulation Limited

23200 Manufacture of refractory products

Saint-Gobain Industrial Ceramics Limited
Unifrax Limited

23320 Manufacture of bricks, tiles and construction products, in baked clay

Wienerberger Limited

23440 Manufacture of other technical ceramic products

M & I Materials Limited
Tenmat Limited

23490 Manufacture of other ceramic products n.e.c.

Thermal Ceramics UK Limited

23520 Manufacture of lime and plaster

Lhoist UK Limited

23610 Manufacture of concrete products for construction purposes

Thomas Armstrong (Concrete Blocks) Limited
William Rainford (Holdings) Limited

23620 Manufacture of plaster products for construction purposes

Promat UK Limited

23640 Manufacture of mortars

Promat UK Limited

23650 Manufacture of fibre cement

Promat UK Limited

23690 Manufacture of other articles of concrete, plaster and cement

Promat UK Limited
Stocks Bros. Limited

23910 Production of abrasive products

Icopal Limited
Washington Mills Electro Minerals Limited

23990 Manufacture of other non-metallic mineral products n.e.c.

Knauf Insulation Limited
Tenmat Limited

24310 Cold drawing of bars

Bekaert Bradford UK Limited

24320 Cold rolling of narrow strip

Bekaert Bradford UK Limited
Novelis UK Ltd

24340 Cold drawing of wire

Bekaert Bradford UK Limited

24440 Copper production

Makin Metal Powders (UK) Limited

24450 Other non-ferrous metal production

Less Common Metals Limited
Magnesium Elektron Limited
Makin Metal Powders (UK) Limited

24460 Processing of nuclear fuel

Springfields Fuels Limited
Urenco Nuclear Stewardship Limited
Urenco UK Limited

24510 Casting of iron

Ouzledale Foundry Company Limited

24520 Casting of steel

Mathers Foundry Limited
Sandusky Limited

24540 Casting of other non-ferrous metals

Metaltek International (UK) Limited
Sandusky Limited

25110 Manufacture of metal structures and parts of structures

Allmand - Smith Limited
A.C.Bacon Engineering Limited
Cellbeam Limited
Collinson PLC
FMC Technologies Limited
William Hare Limited
Hutchinson Engineering Limited
Mansell Finishes Limited
Newfield Fabrications Company Limited
Paw Structures Limited
Shawston Holdings Limited
WEC Group Limited
J.Wareing & Son (Wrea Green) Limited

25120 Manufacture of doors and windows of metal

Nova Group Limited

25290 Manufacture of other tanks, reservoirs and containers of metal

Carr's Engineering Limited
Collinson PLC
Gledhill Building Products Limited
Luxfer Gas Cylinders Limited
UBH International Limited

25500 Forging, pressing, stamping and roll-forming of metal; powder metallurgy

Flowflex Components Limited

25610 Treatment and coating of metals

Bodycote H.I.P. Limited
Bodycote Heat Treatments Limited
Bodycote Surface Technology Limited
Pipeline Induction Heat Limited
Thermal Hire Ltd

25620 Machining

Bryken Limited
Flowserve International Limited
Hyde Group Tooling Limited
Klinger Limited
Mettler-Toledo Safeline Limited
Mini-Gears (Stockport) Limited
NSG Environmental Limited
Olympus Engineering (Holdings) Limited
Olympus Engineering Limited
Presspart Manufacturing Limited
Stolle Europe Limited

25910 Manufacture of steel drums and similar containers

Greif UK Ltd
Huber Packaging Limited

25920 Manufacture of light metal packaging

Ardagh Metal Beverage UK Limited
Crown Packaging Manufacturing UK Limited
Crown Promotional Packaging UK Limited
Embalator (UK) Limited
Huber Packaging Limited
Presspart Manufacturing Limited
Specialist Anodising Company Limited

25930 Manufacture of wire products, chain and springs

Cirteq Limited
Hanson Springs Limited
Pfeifer Drako Ltd
Renold Power Transmission Limited
Renold Public Limited Company
F.D. Sims Limited
United Springs Limited
Vista Engineering Limited

25940 Manufacture of fasteners and screw machine products

Glusburn Holdings Limited
Henrob Limited

25990 Manufacture of other fabricated metal products n.e.c.

Aim Engineering Limited
Arden Dies Limited
Bodycote Surface Technology Limited
Bonfiglioli U.K. Limited
Calder Industrial Materials Limited
Cardinal Shopfitting + Systems Limited
John Chorley & Company,Limited
Denso Marston Ltd
Drive Devilbiss Sidhil Limited
Flowflex Holdings Limited
Fort Vale Engineering Limited
Gradus Limited
Graham Engineering Limited
HTA Group Limited
Hanson Springs Limited
Haynes International Ltd
Hindle Group Limited
Hutchinson Engineering Limited
Indespension Ltd
Kingspan Limited
M & I Materials Limited
MKS Instruments UK Limited
Presspart Manufacturing Limited
Produmax Limited
Renthal Limited
Rigisystems Ltd
Security Window Shutters Limited
Univer Manufacturing Company Ltd
VG Systems Limited
Victor Manufacturing Limited
WFEL Holdings Limited
WFEL Limited
Ifor Williams Trailers Limited
C.P. Witter Limited

26110 Manufacture of electronic components

Computionics Limited
Diodes Zetex Semiconductors Limited
Elstat Limited
Nexperia UK Ltd.
Oxley Developments Company Limited
Paradigm Precision Burnley Ltd
Protec Fire Detection Public Limited Company

26120 Manufacture of loaded electronic boards

C-Mac Automotive Holding Limited

26200 Manufacture of computers and peripheral equipment

CMS Computers Limited
GE Intelligent Platforms Limited
GE Transportation Systems Ltd

26301 Manufacture of telegraph and telephone apparatus and equipment

Promethean Limited

26511 Manufacture of electronic measuring, testing etc. equipment, not for industrial process control

BV PPT Holdings Ltd.
Brooks Automation Ltd
Elcometer Limited
Fives Landis Limited
Micromass UK Limited
Otter Controls Limited
Physical Properties Testing Ltd.
Thermo Electron Limited
Thermo Electron Manufacturing Limited
Thermo Onix Limited
VG Systems Limited
VPG Systems UK Limited

26512 Manufacture of electronic industrial process control equipment

Elcometer Limited
Endress + Hauser Limited
VG Systems Limited
Yokogawa United Kingdom Limited

26513 Manufacture of non-electronic measuring, testing etc. equipment, not for industrial process control

Elcometer Limited

26514 Manufacture of non-electronic industrial process control equipment

Elcometer Limited
Omega Engineering Limited

26600 Manufacture of irradiation, electromedical and electrotherapeutic equipment

Able2 UK Limited

26701 Manufacture of optical precision instruments

Laser Quantum Limited
Newport Spectra-Physics Limited

27120 Manufacture of electricity distribution and control apparatus

ABB Limited
Bilfinger Industrial Automation Services Limited
Boulting Group Limited
Morson Projects Limited
Powell (UK) Limited

27200 Manufacture of batteries and accumulators

GNB Industrial Power (UK) Limited
Spectrum Brands (UK) Limited

27320 Manufacture of other electronic and electric wires and cables

Belden UK Limited
Heat Trace Holdings Limited
Heat Trace Limited
Raydex/CDT Limited
Tratos (UK) Limited
Ventcroft Limited

27330 Manufacture of wiring devices

Ionix Aerospace Limited
Ionix Systems Limited

27400 Manufacture of electric lighting equipment

ATG Airports Limited
Crompton Lamps Limited
Ledvance Ltd
Lumenpulse Alphaled Limited
Lumenpulse UK Limited
Whitecroft Lighting Limited

27510 Manufacture of electric domestic appliances

Glen Dimplex Home Appliances Limited
Jarden Consumer Solutions (Europe) Limited
Stoves Group Ltd

27520 Manufacture of non-electric domestic appliances

Glen Dimplex Home Appliances Limited

27900 Manufacture of other electrical equipment

Anord Mardix (UK) Limited
Brooks Automation Ltd
Ingenico (UK) Limited
Mini-Cam Enterprises Limited
RMSpumptools Limited
Texecom Limited
Victor Manufacturing Limited

28110 Manufacture of engines and turbines, except aircraft, vehicle and cycle engines

ELE Advanced Technologies Limited
Gilbert Gilkes & Gordon Limited
MHI Vestas Offshore Wind UK Ltd

28120 Manufacture of fluid power equipment

APPH Limited
Husco International One Ltd
Husco International Two Ltd
PMC Fluidpower Limited

28131 Manufacture of pumps

Armstrong Integrated Limited
Armstrong Pumps Limited
Flowserve GB Limited
Gilbert Gilkes & Gordon Limited
Jetchem Systems Limited
RMI Pressure Systems Limited
Wheelabrator Group Limited

28132 Manufacture of compressors

Gardner Denver Ltd

28140 Manufacture of taps and valves

Chargepoint Technology Limited
Emerson Automation Solutions Final Control UK Ltd
Oliver Valves Limited
Oliver Valvetek Limited

28150 Manufacture of bearings, gears, gearing and driving elements

Dana Sac UK Limited
Renold Power Transmission Limited
Renold Public Limited Company

28210 Manufacture of ovens, furnaces and furnace burners

Greenbank Technology Limited

28220 Manufacture of lifting and handling equipment

Cascade (U.K.) Limited
Columbus McKinnon Corporation Limited
Granada Material Handling Limited
Joloda (International) Limited
Jost UK Limited
RMSpumptools Limited
Stolle Europe Limited
Street Crane Company Limited
TWP (Newco) 151 Limited

28250 Manufacture of non-domestic cooling and ventilation equipment

Gilberts (Blackpool) Limited
Mansfield, Pollard & Co. Limited

28290 Manufacture of other general-purpose machinery n.e.c.

Gas Control Equipment Limited
JLG Industries (United Kingdom) Limited
Univer Manufacturing Company Ltd

28302 Manufacture of agricultural and forestry machinery other than tractors

Kverneland Group UK Limited
Kverneland Holding (UK) Limited
Ifor Williams Trailers Limited

28410 Manufacture of metal forming machinery

Emerson & Renwick Limited

28490 Manufacture of other machine tools

Fives Landis Limited
Henrob Limited
Holroyd Precision Ltd

28921 Manufacture of machinery for mining

RMI Pressure Systems Limited
Weir Minerals Europe Limited

28930 Manufacture of machinery for food, beverage and tobacco processing

CarnaudMetalbox Engineering Limited
GEA Process Engineering Limited
Krones UK Limited
Mettler-Toledo Safeline Limited

28950 Manufacture of machinery for paper and paperboard production

Emerson & Renwick Limited
Kadant U.K. Limited
Saica Flex UK Limited
Voith Paper Limited

28960 Manufacture of plastics and rubber machinery

Cavitech Solutions Limited
Farrel Limited

28990 Manufacture of other special-purpose machinery n.e.c.

Belle Engineering (Sheen) Limited
Bobst Manchester Ltd
Emerson & Renwick Limited
Fives Landis Limited
Gilbert Gilkes & Gordon Limited
Hiden Analytical Limited
Hiden Instruments Limited
Hosokawa Micron Limited
Hughes Safety Showers Limited
Hutchinson Engineering Limited
Inciner8 Holdings Limited
Kratos Analytical Limited
Kunick (102) Limited
Lock Inspection Systems Limited
Matthews Environmental Solutions Limited
Pfaudler Limited
Promatic Group Limited
Promatic Holdings Limited
Promatic International Limited
Proseal UK Limited
Rotex Europe Ltd
Schilling Robotics Limited
WFEL Holdings Limited
WFEL Limited

29100 Manufacture of motor vehicles

Bentley Motors Limited
S. Cartwright & Sons (Coachbuilders) Limited
Cartwright Fleet Services Limited
Mobius Motors Limited

29201 Manufacture of bodies (coachwork) for motor vehicles (except caravans)

Artech Reduction Technologies Limited
C.P. Davidson & Sons Limited
Solomon Commercials Limited
Woodall Nicholson Limited

29202 Manufacture of trailers and semi-trailers

Cartwright Holdings Ltd
D.R.A. Ltd
I. W. T. Deeside Limited
Tiger Trailers Limited

29203 Manufacture of caravans

Lunar Caravans Limited
Pemberton Park and Leisure Homes Limited

29320 Manufacture of other parts and accessories for motor vehicles

Airbags International Limited
Borgwarner Limited
Cecuent UK Limited
ELE Advanced Technologies Limited
F-M Motorparts Limited
Federal-Mogul Limited
Federal-Mogul Valvetrain Limited
Futaba Manufacturing U.K. Limited
H.P. Chemie Pelzer (U.K.) Limited
Magna Exteriors (Liverpool) Limited
Merlin Diesel Systems Ltd
Piolax Ltd.
Setco Automotive (UK) Limited
TMD Friction UK Limited

30110 Building of ships and floating structures

Cammell Laird Shiprepairers & Shipbuilders Limited

30200 Manufacture of railway locomotives and rolling stock

Lucchini Unipart Rail Limited

30300 Manufacture of air and spacecraft and related machinery

APPH Limited
Bolton Engineering (Holdings) Limited
Safran Nacelles Limited
Silcoms Limited

30990 Manufacture of other transport equipment n.e.c.

Culimeta-Saveguard Limited
Grakon BMAC Holdings Limited
Hitachi Automotive Systems UK Ltd.

31010 Manufacture of office and shop furniture

Cardinal Shopfitting + Systems Limited
Dams Furniture Limited
Gresham Office Furniture Limited
Imperial Office Furniture Ltd
Neville Johnson Limited

31020 Manufacture of kitchen furniture

HPP Pinnacle Limited
Hill's Panel Products Limited
Tom Howley Limited

31030 Manufacture of mattresses

Silentnight Group Limited
Silentnight Holdings Limited

31090 Manufacture of other furniture

BHID Group Limited
Bespoke Home Interior Design Limited
Buoyant Upholstery Limited
Cavalier Marketing Limited
Flair Flooring Supplies Limited
Geometric Furniture Limited
Helium Sofa Group Limited
Neville Johnson Holdings Limited
Senator International Limited
Sherborne Upholstery Limited

32409 Manufacture of other games and toys, n.e.c.

James Galt & Co. Limited
HTI Toys UK Limited

32500 Manufacture of medical and dental instruments and supplies

Alere Limited
Cole-Parmer Limited
Convatec Limited
Crawford Woundcare Limited
Ferno (UK) Limited
Medicina Holdings Limited
Precision Parts UK Limited
Premaitha Health PLC
Sonova UK Limited
Thermo Shandon Limited
Verna Group Bidco Limited
Verna Group Equityco Limited
Verna Group International Limited
Widex UK Limited

33120 Repair of machinery

Electroimpact UK Limited
MAN Energy Solutions UK Limited
Valmet Limited

33130 Repair of electronic and optical equipment

FEI UK Limited

33140 Repair of electrical equipment

Pitts Wilson Limited
Powell (UK) Limited
Werfen Limited

33150 Repair and maintenance of ships and boats

Atlantic & Peninsula Marine Services Limited
Cammell Laird Shiprepairers & Shipbuilders Limited

33170 Repair and maintenance of other transport equipment n.e.c.

Faiveley Transport Birkenhead Limited
Faiveley Transport Tamworth Ltd
Stagecoach Supertram Maintenance Ltd.

33190 Repair of other equipment

Altrad NSG Limited
Carlisle Refrigeration (Holdings) Limited
Carlisle Refrigeration Limited
DBG (UK) Limited
EPTA George Barker Ltd
Electroimpact UK Limited
Furmanite 1986
Furmanite Limited
Markem-Imaje Limited
Teamfurmanite Limited
Westinghouse Electric Company UK Limited

33200 Installation of industrial machinery and equipment

AIS Projects Limited
AIS Vanguard Limited
Ainscough Wind Energy Services Limited
Airedale Catering Equipment Limited
EPTA George Barker Ltd
Markem-Imaje Limited
Nederman Limited
Pitts Wilson Limited
Powell (UK) Limited
Satake Europe Limited

35110 Production of electricity

AEE Renewables UK 31 Limited
Blencathra Hydro Limited
Boyton Solar Park Limited
Celtpower Limited
Clarke Energy Limited
Clarke Energy Operations Limited
Clarke Energy Topco Limited
Clean Energy and Infrastructure UK Limited
Clean Energy and Infrastructure UK Wind Limited
Coldham Windfarm Limited
Community Windpower Limited
Daisy No 1 Limited
East Youlstone Wind Farm Limited
Falkirk Tod Hill Wind Limited
Frodsham Wind Farm Limited
GREP1 Limited
Harthill Wind Limited
INEOS Runcorn (TPS) Holdings Limited
INEOS Runcorn (TPS) Limited
Innovative Environmental Solutions UK Ltd
KRL (LR) Hold Co Limited
KS SPV 24 Limited
Lancaster University Energy Services Ltd
Little Raith Wind Farm Limited
MSP Fairwind Limited
Mulard Renewables Limited
Nugeneration Limited
Peel Wind Farms (Sheerness) Limited
Port of Sheerness Wind Farm Limited
Red Gap Wind Farm Limited
Red Rose Infrastructure Limited
SE Bury Lane Solar Limited
SP Manweb PLC
ScottishPower (DCL) Limited
Sune Green Energy Ltd
Sune Green Holdco2 Ltd
Sune Green Holdco3 Limited
Sune Hill Farm Solar Limited
Sune Prestop Park Limited
Sune Project1 Ltd
Sune Sundorne Grove Solar Limited
Sunsave 10 (Fareham) Ltd
Sunsave 11 (Wrockwardine Farm) Limited
Sunsave 14 (Fenton) Limited
Sunsave 15 (Westwood) Limited
Sunsave 17 (Castle Combe) Limited
Sunsave 2 Limited
Sunsave 20 (Knowlton) Limited
Sunsave 31 (Horam) Limited
Sunsave 43 (Epwell) Limited
Sunsave 6 (Manston) Ltd
University of Liverpool Energy Company Limited
Viridis Energy (Norgen) Limited
Vital Energi Solutions Limited
Wilsons Contractors Limited
Wind Port of Liverpool Limited
Ylem Energy Limited
Ysgellog Wind Farm Limited

35120 Transmission of electricity

SP Manweb PLC
Seaforth Power Limited

35130 Distribution of electricity

Celtpower Limited
Electricity North West Limited
Inovyn Energy Limited

35220 Distribution of gaseous fuels through mains

Exoteric Metering Limited

35230 Trade of gas through mains

Adrian Francis Associates Ltd
Storengy UK Limited

35300 Steam and air conditioning supply

Keysource Limited
Vital Energi Solutions Limited
Vital Energi Utilities Limited
Winnington CHP Limited

36000 Water collection, treatment and supply

ACWA Services Limited
Kelda Group Limited
Peel Water Services Limited
United Utilities International Limited
United Utilities Water Limited
Yorkshire Water Services Limited

37000 Sewerage

ACWA Services Limited

38110 Collection of non-hazardous waste

Bagnall & Morris (Waste Services) Ltd
Cumbria Waste Recycling Limited
JJC Hire Limited
G & A M Lawson Limited
Metal & Waste Recycling Limited
S. Norton & Co Limited
Shorrock Trichem Limited
Totally Local Company Limited

38120 Collection of hazardous waste

Metal & Waste Recycling Limited

38210 Treatment and disposal of non-hazardous waste

P. Casey Enviro Limited
Collier Industrial Waste Limited
Cumbria Waste Management Ltd.
Earnside Energy Limited
Hadfield Wood Recyclers Limited
JWS Holdings Limited
JWS Waste & Recycling Services Limited
Mersey Bioenergy Holdings Limited
Metal & Waste Recycling Limited
Quercia Limited
South Tyne & Wear Energy Recovery Holdings Ltd
South Tyne & Wear Energy Recovery Ltd
WSR Recycling Limited

38220 Treatment and disposal of hazardous waste

Cyclife UK Ltd
Gaskells (North West) Limited
Metal & Waste Recycling Limited

38320 Recovery of sorted materials

Boden & Davies Limited
Nick Brookes Recycling Limited
Car Transplants Limited
European Metal Recycling Limited
G.I. Hadfield & Son Limited
Hadfield Wood Recyclers Limited
MLM Ltd
S. Norton & Co Limited
Preston Plastics Limited
Recycling Lives Limited
Saica Natur UK Limited
Thompsons Plant Hire Limited
UK Wood Recycling Limited

39000 Remediation activities and other waste management services

Brookshaw Developments Limited
Future Industrial Services Limited
Gaskells (North West) Limited
Greenergy Limited
Innospec Environmental Limited
Nuvia Limited
Westinghouse Electric Company UK Limited
White Moss Horticulture Limited
Woodford Remediation Limited

41202 Construction of domestic buildings

Altin Homes Limited
T.Anwyl & Son Limited
Anwyl Construction Company Limited
Anwyl Group Limited
Applethwaite Limited
Atkinson Homes Limited
Barnfield Construction Limited
B. & E. Boys Limited
Candelisa Limited
Cityblock Holdings Limited
Conlon Construction Limited
Construction Partnership UK Limited
Court Properties (Portugal) Limited
Cruden Construction Limited
Cruden Group Limited
Cubby Construction Limited
Dorbcrest Homes Limited
Eccleston Homes Limited
Herbert T. Forrest Limited
HB (HDG) Limited
Hollinwood Homes Limited
Homes By Woodford Limited
Icona Homes Limited
Jones Homes (Lancashire) Limited
Jones Homes (North West) Limited
Jones Homes (Southern) Limited
Jones Homes (Yorkshire) Limited
Kingswood Homes (UK) Ltd
P J Livesey Country Homes (Eastern) Limited
P.J. Livesey Group Limited
P.J. Livesey Holdings Limited
P J Livesey Living Space (11) Limited
P J Livesey Living Space (North) Limited
P.J. Livesey Living Space Limited
Ludgate Hill Developments Limited
Marcus Worthington and Company Limited
McGoff Construction Limited
Menta Redrow Limited
Morris Homes (Midlands) Limited
Morris Homes (North) Limited
Morris Homes Limited
Mullberry Homes Limited
New City Vision (Liverpool) Limited
Pochin Construction Limited
Qdos Developments Limited
Redrow Homes East Midlands Limited
Redrow Homes Limited
Redrow Langley Limited
Redrow PLC
Redrow Real Estate Limited
Rowland Group Limited
Rowland Homes Limited
Rowlinson Constructions Limited
Russell Armer Limited
Russell Homes (UK) Limited
Seddon Homes Limited
Skipton Properties Limited
Solicagent Investment Limited
Stirling Management Group Limited
Story Homes Limited
Wain Group Holdings Limited
Wain Group Limited
Wainhomes (North West) Limited
Warden Construction Limited
F.G.Whitley and Sons Co.Limited

42110 Construction of roads and motorways

Coffey Construction Limited
D C T Civil Engineering Limited
Dowhigh Limited
J. Hopkins (Contractors) Limited
Huyton Asphalt Holdings Limited
Huyton Asphalt Limited
Road Maintenance Services Limited
Tarways Asphalte Co. Limited
Totally Local Company Limited
Urban Vision Partnership Limited
W P I Surfacing Limited
F.G.Whitley and Sons Co.Limited
A.E.Yates,Limited

42120 Construction of railways and underground railways

Story Contracting Limited

42130 Construction of bridges and tunnels

Coffey Construction Limited
D C T Civil Engineering Limited
Merseylink (Holdings) Limited
Merseylink Limited
Underground Mining Services Limited
F.G.Whitley and Sons Co.Limited
A.E.Yates,Limited

42210 Construction of utility projects for fluids

J.N. Bentley Limited
Future Energy Group Ltd
A.E.Yates,Limited

42220 Construction of utility projects for electricity and telecommunications

Excalon Limited
Future Energy Group Ltd
Nugeneration Limited
Rongxin Power Limited
WHP Telecoms Limited
Westinghouse Electric Company UK Limited
Wood Nuclear Limited

42910 Construction of water projects

ACWA Services Limited
J.N. Bentley Limited
Cambi UK Limited
Cheetham Hill Construction Limited
D C T Civil Engineering Limited
Future Energy Group Ltd
Mott MacDonald Bentley Ltd
F.G.Whitley and Sons Co.Limited

42990 Construction of other civil engineering projects n.e.c.

Bachy Soletanche Limited
J.N. Bentley Limited
Bethell Construction Limited
Bethell Group Holdings Ltd
Bilfinger UK Limited
Chandos Civil Engineering Limited
Cheetham Hill Construction Limited
Create Construction Limited
Cubby Construction Limited
Cuerden Developments Ltd.
Cuerden Estates Ltd.
Dowhigh Limited
Drillwave Limited
Eurogold Groundworks & Civil Engineering Contractors Ltd.
Eurogold Group Limited
GPL Civil Engineering Limited
T&K Gallagher Limited
Heyrod Construction Limited
Heyrod Holdings Ltd
Huyton Asphalt Limited
Luton Engineering Services (Southwest) Limited
J.Mallinson (Ormskirk) Limited
J.Mills (Contractors) Limited
Moortown Group Limited
D. Morgan PLC
Pochin Construction Limited
Redstart Construction Limited
Soil Engineering Geoservices Limited
St. Annes (Holdings) Limited
WPI Civil Engineering Limited
Waitings Limited
Woodford Regeneration Limited
A.E.Yates,Limited

43110 Demolition

Cheetham Hill Construction Limited
S Evans & Sons Limited
G & A M Lawson Limited
PP O'Connor Group Limited
Technical Demolition Services Limited

43120 Site preparation

Cheetham Hill Construction Limited
Clive Hurt (Plant Hire) Limited
PP O'Connor Group Limited
Urban Regen Limited
L.& W.Wilson (Endmoor) Limited

43130 Test drilling and boring

LMR Drilling UK Ltd

43210 Electrical installation

ABB Limited
Ameon Limited
Bilfinger UK Limited
Boulting Group Limited
Collinson PLC
Imtech Engineering Services North Ltd
Keysource Limited
Nordex UK Limited
Piggott and Whitfield Limited
Pitts Wilson Limited
The Rosebery Group Limited
Rotary Building Services Ltd
H.E. Simm & Son Limited
John Turner Construction Group Ltd

43220 Plumbing, heat and air-conditioning installation

A. & B. Engineering (Mechanical Service Division) Limited
Ameon Limited
Coolair Equipment Limited
Gilberts (Blackpool) Limited
Imtech Engineering Services North Ltd
Liberty Gas Group Limited
The James Mercer Group Limited
Mitton Mechanical Services Limited
Piggott and Whitfield Limited
Rotary Building Services Ltd
H.E. Simm & Son Limited
Switch2 Energy Limited
Vital Energi Solutions Limited
Warmer Energy Services Limited

43290 Other construction installation

Cardinal Project Management Limited
P. Casey & Co., Limited
Infra Safety Services Labour Limited
Mansell Finishes Limited
Piggott and Whitfield Limited
Thrislington Cubicles Limited
Wetherby Building Systems Limited

43310 Plastering

Mansell Finishes Limited

43320 Joinery installation

Cubby Construction Limited
John Turner Construction Group Ltd

43330 Floor and wall covering

Arthouse Limited
Arthouse Midco Limited
Bathgate Flooring Limited
Riverside Flooring Limited

43341 Painting

Affordable Window Systems Limited
Roy Hankinson (Holdings) Limited
Taziker Industrial Limited
Whittle Programmed Maintenance Limited

43342 Glazing

H.P.A.S. Limited

43390 Other building completion and finishing

Audas Project Management Limited
Claremont Group Interiors Limited
Emerson Management Services Limited
KHILG Ltd
Knowsley Contractors Limited
L.T.D. Contractors Limited
Leisureplan Projects Limited
Mansell Finishes Limited
New Charter Building Company Limited
Polcom UK Limited
TESGL Limited
UKFast Properties Limited

43910 Roofing activities

Almire Holdings Ltd
Avonside Roofing Limited
Brand New Co (354) Limited
FK Facades Limited
Lacy Roofing Company Limited
M.A.C. (Roofing & Contracting) Limited

43991 Scaffold erection

Bilfinger UK Limited
Palmers Scaffolding UK Limited

43999 Other specialised construction activities n.e.c.

3B Construction Ltd
A & F Sprinklers Limited
A & M Energy Solutions Limited
ABS Brymar Floors Limited
AIS Projects Limited
Ainscough Crane Hire Ltd
Altrad NSG Limited
Aptus Utilities Limited
Bilfinger UK Limited
Boulting Environmental Services Limited
C J Services UK Limited
Calderdale Hospital SPC Holdings Ltd
Calderdale Hospital SPC Ltd
P.N.Daly Limited
Electricity North West (Construction and Maintenance) Limited
Emerson Management Services Limited
Engenda Group Limited
FK Facades Limited
Herbert T. Forrest Limited
G. & B. (North West) Limited
William Hare Limited
Heyrod Construction Limited
Heyrod Holdings Ltd
J.D. Hughes Group Limited
J S Fleet Services Limited
James Killelea & Company Limited
W. Maher & Sons Limited
Nightjar Sustainable Power Limited
North & Partners Technical Limited
Nuvia Limited
PP O'Connor Group Limited
O'Connor Utilities Limited
Harry Peers & Co Limited
Harry Peers Steelwork Limited
M J Quinn Integrated Services Limited
Rectella International Limited
Sheet Piling (UK) Limited
Stevens Equipment Rental Limited
Styles & Wood Limited
Survey Supplies Limited
Taziker Industrial Limited
Tudorborne Limited
Urban Vision Partnership Limited
Vale UK Limited
Vital Energi Solutions Limited
Wilson & Scott (Highways) Limited
L.& W.Wilson (Endmoor) Limited
Barry Wood Plant Hire Limited

45111 Sale of new cars and light motor vehicles

Addison Motors Limited
Colin Appleyard Limited
Bentley & Bentley Limited
Bluebell (Crewe) Limited
Bolton Car Centre Limited
Bowker Blackburn Limited
Bowker Preston Limited
Bugle Inn Motor Company Limited
Caygill Holdings Limited
Chapel House Holdings Ltd
Colebrook & Burgess Limited
Corkills Volkswagen Limited
D J Cox Limited
Cox Motor Group Limited
C.P. Davidson & Sons Limited
Drayton Group Limited
The Dutton-Forshaw Motor Company Limited
GE Financial Investments
J.F. and E. Hadwin Limited
Hadwins (Lindale) Limited
Halliwell Jones (Wilmslow) Limited
David Hayton Limited
Heaton Park Garage Limited
JCT600 (Rawdon) Limited
JCT600 (South Yorkshire) Limited
JCT600 (Yorkshire) Ltd
JCT600 Limited
JCT600 Vehicle Leasing Solutions Limited
The James Group Limited
Knights North West Limited
Lloyd Motors Limited
Lookers Birmingham Limited
Lookers Colborne Limited
Lookers Leasing Limited
Lookers Motor Group Limited
Lookers Motor Holdings Limited
Lookers PLC
M53 Motors Limited
MB South Limited
Marubeni Auto Investment (UK) Limited
The Oldham Motor Company Limited
Pye Motors,Limited
RRG (West Yorkshire) Limited
RRG Group Limited
D. Stoker Group Limited
Swansway Garages Limited
TJA Motors Limited
Thompson Motor Company (Preston) Limited
Van Centre (West Yorkshire) Limited
Williams Motor Co.(Holdings) Limited
Windsors (Wallasey) Limited

45112 Sale of used cars and light motor vehicles

Adesa Remarketing Limited
Bentley & Bentley Limited
Bluebell (Crewe) Limited
Bowker Blackburn Limited
Bowker Preston Limited
Chapel House Holdings Ltd
D J Cox Limited
Fords Cheshire Limited
Hadwins (Lindale) Limited
Halliwell Jones (Chester) Limited
Halliwell Jones (Warrington) Limited
Halliwell Jones (Wilmslow) Limited
Halliwell Jones Limited
David Hayton Limited
Heaton Park Garage Limited
Hill's Salvage & Recycling Ltd
JCT600 (Rawdon) Limited
JCT600 (South Yorkshire) Limited
JCT600 (Yorkshire) Ltd
JCT600 Limited
JCT600 Vehicle Leasing Solutions Limited
Knights North West Limited
Lookers Colborne Limited
William Loughran Limited
M53 Motors Limited
Pye Motors,Limited
RRG (West Yorkshire) Limited
Rix Motor Company Limited
Swansway Garages Limited
TJA Motors Limited
Thompson Motor Company (Preston) Limited
Williams Motor Co.(Holdings) Limited
Windsors (Wallasey) Limited

45190 Sale of other motor vehicles

Agricultural Machinery (Nantwich) Limited
Ciceley Commercials Limited
Ciceley Limited
Cornthwaite Agricultural Limited
Graham (Commercials) Limited
Thomas Hardie Commercials Limited
Haydock Commercial Vehicles Limited
JDS Trucks Limited
North West Truck Services Limited
Rickerby Limited
Solway Vehicle Distributors Limited
Spinney Garage Limited
West Pennine Trucks Limited

45200 Maintenance and repair of motor vehicles

Bluebell (Crewe) Limited
Bowker Blackburn Limited
Bowker Preston Limited
Bugle Inn Motor Company Limited
Colebrook & Burgess Limited
D J Cox Limited
Drayton Group Limited
Graham (Commercials) Limited
H.B. Panelcraft Limited
Halliwell Jones (Wilmslow) Limited
Thomas Hardie Commercials Limited
David Hayton Limited
Heatons Truck Group Ltd
Hough Green Garage Limited
JCT600 (Rawdon) Limited
JCT600 (South Yorkshire) Limited
JCT600 (Yorkshire) Ltd
JCT600 Limited
JDS Trucks Limited
Knights North West Limited
Lookers Colborne Limited
Lookers Motor Group Limited
Lookers PLC
M53 Motors Limited
MB South Limited
National Tyre Service Limited
North West Truck Services Limited
RRG (West Yorkshire) Limited
Rickerby Limited
Solway Vehicle Distributors Limited
TJA Motors Limited
Thompson Motor Company (Preston) Limited
West Pennine Trucks Limited
Williams Motor Co.(Holdings) Limited
Windsors (Wallasey) Limited

45310 Wholesale trade of motor vehicle parts and accessories

Ace Supply Company Limited (The)
The Ace Supply Holding Company Limited
Bentley & Bentley Limited
Colebrook & Burgess Limited
European Braking Systems Ltd
Exedy Clutch Europe Limited
Exide Technologies (Transportation) Limited
General Traffic Limited
JDS Trucks Limited
Jost (Great Britain) Limited
Jost UK Limited
Kirkby (Tyres) Limited
Lookers Motor Group Limited
Lookers PLC
MB South Limited
Mobiletron UK Limited
Oak Tyres UK Limited
Rickerby Limited
J. Rose (Tyres) Limited
TVS Supply Chain Solutions Limited
Tetrosyl Express Limited
West Pennine Trucks Limited

45320 Retail trade of motor vehicle parts and accessories

Bowker Blackburn Limited
Bowker Preston Limited
Thomas Hardie Commercials Limited
David Hayton Limited
Heatons Truck Group Ltd
Hill's Salvage & Recycling Ltd
JCT600 (Rawdon) Limited
JCT600 (South Yorkshire) Limited
JCT600 (Yorkshire) Ltd
JCT600 Limited
JDS Trucks Limited
Lookers Colborne Limited
M53 Motors Limited
Merlin Diesel Systems Ltd
Mitchell North West Limited
National Tyre Service Limited
North West Truck Services Limited
RRG (West Yorkshire) Limited
Rickerby Limited
Risk Technology Limited
Solway Vehicle Distributors Limited
TJA Motors Limited
West Pennine Trucks Limited
Williams Motor Co.(Holdings) Limited
Windsors (Wallasey) Limited

45400 Sale, maintenance and repair of motorcycles and related parts and accessories

2 Moto Limited
Chorley Yamaha Centre Limited
D J Cox Limited
European Braking Systems Ltd
J & S Accessories Limited
Moto GB Limited

46110 Agents selling agricultural raw materials, livestock, textile raw materials and semi-finished goods

Compass Minerals UK Holdings Limited

46120 Agents involved in the sale of fuels, ores, metals and industrial chemicals

BES Commercial Electricity Ltd
Business Energy Solutions Ltd
Crown Oil Limited
Dent Steel Services (Yorkshire) Limited
KME Yorkshire Limited
NWF Fuels Limited
Uranium Asset Management Limited

46130 Agents involved in the sale of timber and building materials

Beesley & Fildes Limited
C & C Supplies Collinson Limited
Earth's Crust Resources Limited
Firwood Timber & Plywood Co. Limited
Hardscape Products Limited
In Touch with Bricks Limited
M.Markovitz Limited
Protec International Limited
George Roberts (North West) Limited
Uriah Woodhead & Son Limited

46140 Agents involved in the sale of machinery, industrial equipment, ships and aircraft

Blue Machinery (Southern) Limited
Carrylift Materials Handling Limited
Causeway Tractors Limited
Doosan International UK Limited
Elopak UK Limited
Flintbrook Limited
Ifor Williams Trailers Limited
Thomas Wright/Thorite Group Limited

46150 Agents involved in the sale of furniture, household goods, hardware and ironmongery

Flair Flooring Supplies Limited
Pulse Home Products (Holdings) Limited
Vine Mill Limited

46160 Agents involved in the sale of textiles, clothing, fur, footwear and leather goods

Goliath Footwear Limited

46170 Agents involved in the sale of food, beverages and tobacco

Deckers Hospitality Group Limited
E-Foods Limited

46180 Agents specialised in the sale of other particular products

Builders Supply (North West) Limited
Central Glass Europe Limited
E-Foods Limited
Kondor Limited
MPM Products Limited
Protec International Limited
Talpole Limited
Trilanco Limited

46190 Agents involved in the sale of a variety of goods

E-Foods Limited

46210 Wholesale of grain, unmanufactured tobacco, seeds and animal feeds

Criddle & Co.Limited
Glasson Grain Limited
H.J. Lea Oakes Limited

46240 Wholesale of hides, skins and leather

Bradford Hide Company Limited

46310 Wholesale of fruit and vegetables

A.P.S. Salads Limited
Barton and Redman Limited
Peter Gilding & Co. Limited
Ibco Limited
J.H.F. Limited
Mercian Limited
E.Park & Sons Limited
Alfred Price & Sons,Limited
Uren Food Group Limited
Harry Yearsley Limited

46320 Wholesale of meat and meat products

Kevin Berkins Quality Meats Limited
M J Birtwistle & Co Limited
Chi Yip Group Limited
Danish Crown UK Limited
Hen House (Wholesale) Limited
J.H.F. Limited
P.F.D.(Carlisle) Limited
Sosamja Holdings Limited
V.A. Whitley & Co. Limited

46330 Wholesale of dairy products, eggs and edible oils and fats

J. S. Bailey Limited
Bradbury & Son (Buxton) Limited
Chippindale Foods Limited
Creamline Dairies Limited
Dale Farm (GB) Limited
Delamere Dairy Limited
Fayrefield Foods Limited
J.H.F. Limited
Swallow Holdings Limited
V.A. Whitley & Co. Limited

46341 Wholesale of fruit and vegetable juices, mineral water and soft drinks

Creamline Dairies Limited
Manchester Drinks Company Ltd
Swallow Holdings Limited
Vimto (Out of Home) Limited
V.A. Whitley & Co. Limited

46342 Wholesale of wine, beer, spirits and other alcoholic beverages

T. & J.T. Barton (Bottlers) Limited
Boutinot Limited
Deckers Restaurants Limited
Hammonds of Knutsford PLC
Hydes' Brewery Limited
In Vino Bidco Limited
In Vino Limited
Kingsland Drinks Group Limited
Kingsland Drinks Limited
LWC Drinks Limited
Manchester Drinks Company Ltd
Narang Wholesalers Limited
Quintessential Brands Spirit Solutions Limited

46360 Wholesale of sugar and chocolate and sugar confectionery

Fairway (G.B.) Limited
J & K Confectionery Limited

46380 Wholesale of other food, including fish, crustaceans and molluscs

All About Food Limited
Dr Schar UK Limited
Ibco Limited
Iceland Seafood Barraclough Ltd
Interfish Limited
Mardon Public Limited Company
P.F.D.(Carlisle) Limited
Royal Greenland Limited
J Sykes & Sons (Manchester) Limited
Sykes Seafoods Limited
John West Foods Limited
V.A. Whitley & Co. Limited
Harry Yearsley Limited

46390 Non-specialised wholesale of food, beverages and tobacco

Albany Products Limited
Bakers (Area 1) Limited
Carrs Foods Holdings Limited
Carrs Foods International Limited
E-Foods Limited
I.C.S. (UK) Limited
Ibco Limited
K K Fine Foods Limited
Khanjra International Foods Limited
P. & B (Foods) Limited
A.G. Parfett & Sons Limited
Princes Limited

46410 Wholesale of textiles

Adidas (U.K.) Limited
Anfield (U.K.) Limited
Arista (U.K.) Limited
Beechfield Brands Holdings Limited
Beechfield Brands Limited
Benmar Textiles Limited
Bridstock Gate Limited
Brookmann Home Manchester 1877 Ltd
Carrington Textiles Ltd
Cleland McIver Limited
Dilbag Cloth House Limited
Elias Enterprises Limited
Fabrics & Yarns (Macclesfield) Ltd
Flair Flooring Group Limited
Thomas Frederick & Company Limited
Fryett's Fabrics Limited
G.D. Yarns Limited
Haddow Group Limited
Hanes Holdings UK Limited
Richard Haworth Limited
Jessgrove Limited
M.& N.Textiles Limited
Narang Wholesalers Limited
Premier Textiles Limited
Prestigious Textiles Limited
Rectella Limited
Redwood TTM Ltd
J Rosenthal Holdings Limited
J. Rosenthal and Son Limited
S M D Textiles Limited
S.M.D. Home Limited
SMD (Holdings) Limited
Sartex Quilts & Textiles Limited
Sir Jacob Behrens & Sons,Limited
R. Soper Limited
Swiscot Textiles Limited
Tonrose Limited
Turner Bianca PLC
UP Global Sourcing UK Limited
Valdeco Ltd
Vision Support Services Group Limited
Vision Support Services Limited
Welspun UK Limited

46420 Wholesale of clothing and footwear

ASICS UK Limited
Adidas (U.K.) Limited
Albion Limited
BOI Trading Company Limited
Drew Brady & Co. Limited
Brand Search Limited
Brook Taverner Limited
Craghoppers Limited
Denim Merchants (UK) Limited
Dewhurst Dent P.L.C.
Haddow Group Limited
D. Jacobson & Sons Limited
Simon Jersey Ltd
Jo-Y-Jo International Limited
Jo-Y-Jo Limited
Kacoo Fashion Ltd
Laltex & Co.Limited
Lowe Clothing International Limited
Lyon Equipment Limited
NJK Clothing Ltd
Newstar Group Limited
Osan Limited
Regatta Ltd
Rhodi Inc. Imports Limited
Rhodi Suppliers Limited
S.R.G. Apparel PLC
Sanjeev 1979 Limited
T.A. Weatherwear Limited
Topgrade Sportswear Limited
Trutex Investments Limited
Trutex Limited
UK2M Limited
Visage Limited
Wellington Shipping Services Ltd
Whispering Smith Limited

46439 Wholesale of radio, television goods & electrical household appliances (other than records, tapes, CDs)

Adi-Gardiner Limited
Edmundson Electrical Limited
Eurosonic Group Limited
G2S Limited
GE Lighting Limited
Protec Fire and Security Group Limited
Refrigeration Norwest (Chester) Limited
SZG Europe Limited
Startech.Com Limited
UP Global Sourcing UK Limited

46450 Wholesale of perfume and cosmetics

CRM Trading Limited
ESPA International (UK) Limited
Fragrance Acquisitions Limited
Glendale S/S Limited
Per-Scent Group Limited
Per-Scent Limited
Rainbow Cosmetics (Manchester) Limited
Scent Global Ltd

46460 Wholesale of pharmaceutical goods

Bestway Pharmacy NDC Limited
C.D. Medical Limited
P & A J Cattee (Wholesale) Ltd.
Chiesi Healthcare Limited
Chiesi Limited
Dechra Veterinary Products Limited
Gee Lawson Limited
Paul Hartmann Limited
Kays Medical Limited
M & A Pharmachem Limited
Manor Drug Company (Nottingham) Limited (The)
Mawdsley-Brooks & Company Limited
Nupharm Limited
Omnicell Limited
Phoenix Healthcare Distribution Limited
Phoenix Medical Supplies Limited
Prinwest Limited
Rayburn Trading Company Limited
SSCP Blink Bidco Limited
Soho Flordis UK Limited
UK Pharma Impex Limited
Unomedical Limited
Donald Wardle and Son Limited

46470 Wholesale of furniture, carpets and lighting equipment

Furlong Flooring (Central) Ltd
Servlite U.K. Limited

46499 Wholesale of household goods (other than musical instruments) n.e.c

151 Products Limited
Ardale International Limited
Benross Marketing Limited
Black Cat Fireworks Limited
Peter Black Footwear & Accessories Limited
Brother U.K. Limited
Burg-Wachter UK Limited
Chairs Limited
Cosatto Limited
Joe Davies (Manchester) Limited
Enesco Limited
Eurosonic Group Limited
Goldcrest Distribution Ltd
Haddow Group Limited
Harper Industries PLC
J & K Henderson Enterprises Limited
Hira Company Limited (The)
KS Brands Limited
Meyer Group Limited
Qualtex UK Limited
Rayware Limited
Sambro International Limited
Searchlight Electric Limited
Silver Cross (UK) Limited
Spectrum Brands (UK) Limited
Speedy Products Limited
Status International (UK) Ltd
Supreme Imports Ltd
T.K. Components (Holdings) Limited
T.K. Components Group Limited
T.K. Components Limited
TS (UK) Limited
UAP Limited
UP Global Sourcing UK Limited
Wellington Shipping Services Ltd
Widdop Bingham & Co. Limited
Woodclay Limited

46510 Wholesale of computers, computer peripheral equipment and software

Allscripts Healthcare (IT) UK Ltd
Celestica Limited
Computer Risk Management Limited
Exertis (UK) Ltd
UFP (UK) Limited
V.I.P. Computer Centre Limited

46520 Wholesale of electronic and telecommunications equipment and parts

ABB Limited
Brother Holding (Europe) Ltd.
Brother International Europe Limited
Celestica Limited
Electric Systems Limited
Electrovision Limited
Elnur UK Limited
Ghekko Limited
T.N.Robinson Limited

46610 Wholesale of agricultural machinery, equipment and supplies

Clarke and Pulman Limited
Gunn JCB (Holdings) Limited
Lloyd Limited

46620 Wholesale of machine tools

Cutwel Limited
Entwistle & Joynt Holdings Limited
C.R. Laurence of Europe, Ltd
John Sylvester Engineering Company Limited
J.R. Webster and Company Limited

46630 Wholesale of mining, construction and civil engineering machinery

Blue Machinery (Southern) Limited
Gunn JCB (Holdings) Limited
Wilkinson Star Limited

46650 Wholesale of office furniture

Vision Support Services Group Limited

46660 Wholesale of other office machinery and equipment

Brother U.K. Limited
Canda Copying Limited
Involve Visual Collaboration Ltd

46690 Wholesale of other machinery and equipment

Ansell (Sales & Distribution) Limited
Ansell Electrical Products Limited
Brammer UK Limited
C & C Catering Equipment Limited
Carrier Transicold (UK) Limited
Corbetts Support Solutions Limited
FEI UK Limited
Gerber Technology Limited
Hilti (Gt.Britain) Limited
C.R. Laurence of Europe, Ltd
Lloyd & Jones Engineers Limited
Luton Engineering Services (Southwest) Limited
Lyon Equipment Limited
Nilfisk Ltd.
Seddons (Plant and Engineers) Limited
UK Pharma Impex Limited
The Wilkinson Corporation Limited

46711 Wholesale of petroleum and petroleum products

Hermon Hodge Limited

46719 Wholesale of other fuels and related products

Beesley Fuels Ltd
CPL Petroleum Limited
Certas Energy UK Limited
European Diesel Card Limited
Hermon Hodge Limited
David Hermon Hodge Limited
NWF Fuels Limited
Petro-Canada Europe Lubricants Limited
Radius Payment Solutions Limited
UK Fuels Limited
WEX Europe Services Limited

46720 Wholesale of metals and metal ores

Advance Uranium Asset Management Limited
The Alternative Steel Company Limited
Atlantic Steel Processing Limited
B S Stainless Limited
Barrett Steel Limited
Benteler Distribution Limited
Castle Metals UK Limited
Hall & Pickles 1812 Limited
Hillfoot Steel Limited
Lucchini Unipart Rail Limited
MRC Flangefitt Limited
MSS Products Limited
The Sebden Group Limited
Sebden Steel Service Centres Limited
Special Piping Materials (Holdings) Limited
Uranium Asset Management Limited

46730 Wholesale of wood, construction materials and sanitary equipment

Adlington Welding Supplies Limited
Beers Timber & Building Supplies Limited
C & W Berry Limited
Edwards Cheshire Company Limited
Finsa UK Limited
Firwood Timber & Plywood Co. Limited
Havwoods Limited
Irmass Company Limited
C.R. Laurence of Europe, Ltd
Rowlinson Timber Limited

46740 Wholesale of hardware, plumbing and heating equipment and supplies

C & W Berry Limited
CHP Supplies Limited
Comap UK Holdings Limited
Comap UK Limited
Firwood Timber & Plywood Co. Limited
Fluidpower Limited
James Hargreaves (Plumbers' Merchants) Limited
James Hargreaves Holdings Limited
James Hargreaves PM Limited
C.R. Laurence of Europe, Ltd
Merlyn Industries U.K. Limited
Methven UK Limited
Narang Wholesalers Limited
Penman Estates Limited
Shawston International Limited

46750 Wholesale of chemical products

Atul Europe Limited
Azelis UK Holdings Limited
Azelis UK Limited
Aztec Aerosols Limited
BASF Public Limited Company
Samuel Banner & Co. Limited
Brabant Limited
Elastomerics Limited
Euroresins UK Limited
Houghton Holdings Limited
Indace Limited
Lehvoss UK Limited
Meade-King,Robinson & Company Limited
Niokem Limited
Norkem Limited
Packed Chlorine Limited
Phenomenex Limited
Plasto-Sac UK Limited
Safic-Alcan UK Limited
Synthetic Technologies Ltd
Tennants Distribution Limited
Tetrosyl Limited
UK Pharma Impex Limited
Union Colours Limited

46760 Wholesale of other intermediate products

Budget Greeting Cards Limited
W.L. Coller Limited
Elopak UK Limited
Euro Wrap Limited
IESA Limited
KS Brands Limited
Longfield Chemicals Limited
Marchington Stone Limited
Ossur UK Limited
RMS International UK Ltd
Rodo Limited
Smith & Bateson Limited,
Smith Bateson Holdings Limited
Wesco Aircraft Europe, Ltd

46770 Wholesale of waste and scrap

JJC Hire Limited
MLM Ltd
Mantank Environmental Services Limited
Tom Martin & Company Limited
Tom Martin Metal Holdings 2011 Limited
Tom Martin Metal Holdings Limited
Maxilead Limited
John Robson (Metals) Limited

47110 Retail sale in non-specialised stores with food, beverages or tobacco predominating

E.H.Booth & Co.,Limited
Harrisons Dairies Limited
Heron Foods Limited
Lawrence Hunt & Co Limited
Iceland Foods Limited
Wm Morrison Supermarkets P L C
North East Convenience Stores Limited
Safeway (Overseas) Limited
Safeway Limited
Safeway Stores Limited
Westmorland Limited

47190 Other retail sale in non-specialised stores

Michael Abakhan Limited
Alliance Disposables Limited
Arighi Bianchi & Co.Limited
B & M Retail Limited
CT Ice Limited
Costcutter Supermarkets Group Limited
Costcutter Supermarkets Holdings Limited
J.Dixon & Son,Limited
Housing Units Group Ltd
Housing Units Limited
Lewis's Home Retail Limited
Metropolitan Cathedral Services Limited
Missguided Limited
T. J. Morris Limited
Oswaldtwistle Mills Limited
Parry's Motor Parts Limited
Quality Save Limited
Taskers PLC
Walker Fire (UK) Limited
Worldwide Foods (Rochdale) Limited

47230 Retail sale of fish, crustaceans and molluscs in specialised stores

J Sykes & Sons (Manchester) Limited

47240 Retail sale of bread, cakes, flour confectionery and sugar confectionery in specialised stores

Sayers The Bakers Limited

47250 Retail sale of beverages in specialised stores

T. & J.T. Barton (Bottlers) Limited
Inventive Service Company Limited
Revolution Bars Group PLC
Revolution Bars Limited
WCF Ltd.

47290 Other retail sale of food in specialised stores

County Milk Products Limited
Iceland International Limited
Sayers The Bakers Limited
WCF Ltd.

47300 Retail sale of automotive fuel in specialised stores

Auk Investments Limited
Euro Garages Limited
D.A. Harrison and Company Wigton
The Kay Group (UK) Limited
Ifor Williams Trailers Limited

47410 Retail sale of computers, peripheral units and software in specialised stores

Scan Computers International Limited

47510 Retail sale of textiles in specialised stores

Brookmann Home Manchester 1877 Ltd
CHT Holdings Limited
Hanes Holdings UK Limited
Libra Textiles Limited
Rectella Limited
R. Soper Limited

47520 Retail sale of hardware, paints and glass in specialised stores

Bromborough Paint & Building Supplies Limited
R.E.Dawson,Limited
Lakeland Limited

47540 Retail sale of electrical household appliances in specialised stores

AO Retail Limited
Corbetts Support Solutions Limited
Lakeland Limited

47591 Retail sale of musical instruments and scores

Dawsons Music Limited

47599 Retail of furniture, lighting, and similar (not musical instruments or scores) in specialised store

Cascade Holdings Limited
Sofology Limited
Stokers Holdings Limited
Stokers Limited
Taskers PLC

47610 Retail sale of books in specialised stores

Salts Estates Limited

47620 Retail sale of newspapers and stationery in specialised stores

Ryman Limited

47640 Retail sale of sports goods, fishing gear, camping goods, boats and bicycles

Adidas (U.K.) Limited
American Golf Discount Centre Limited
Bradley Bidco Limited
Bradley Topco Limited
Cyclesport North Limited

47710 Retail sale of clothing in specialised stores

Blacks Outdoor Retail Limited
The Bullen Healthcare Group Limited
Cotton Traders Holdings Limited
Cotton Traders Limited
Footasylum PLC
HPO1 Nominees Limited
J & S Accessories Limited
JD Sports Fashion PLC
Kukri GB Limited
Libra Textiles Limited
Matalan Retail Ltd.
Missguided Limited
R. D. Scott Limited
Tessuti Ltd
Topgrade Sportswear Limited
WCF Ltd.
Dave Whelan Sports Limited

47721 Retail sale of footwear in specialised stores

Blacks Outdoor Retail Limited
Cotton Traders Holdings Limited
Cotton Traders Limited
Courtesy Shoes Limited
Footasylum PLC
JD Sports Fashion PLC
Libra Textiles Limited
Missguided Limited
New Balance Athletic Shoes (U.K.) Limited
R. D. Scott Limited

47730 Dispensing chemist in specialised stores

Bestway National Chemists Limited
Bestway Panacea Healthcare Limited
Cameolord Limited
W.R.Evans Healthcare Limited
Famevalley Limited
Gorgemead Limited
Hollowood Chemists Limited
The Hub Pharmacy Limited
Imaan Healthcare Limited
Newbridge (Healthcare) Limited
PCT Healthcare Limited
L.Rowland & Company (Retail) Limited
Secret Potions Limited
Sykes Chemists Limited
Wise Pharmacies Limited

47749 Retail sale of medical and orthopaedic goods in specialised stores (not incl. hearing aids) n.e.c.

Charles S. Bullen Stomacare Limited

47750 Retail sale of cosmetic and toilet articles in specialised stores

G.R. & M.M. Blackledge PLC
Cartoon (Holdings) Limited
Newbridge (Healthcare) Limited
TFS Buying Limited
TFS Stores Limited

47760 Retail sale of flowers, plants, seeds, fertilizers, pet animals and pet food in specialised stores

The Barton Grange Group Limited
J. Parker Dutch Bulbs (Wholesale) Limited
Gordon Rigg (Nurseries) Limited
TGC (2015) Limited

47770 Retail sale of watches and jewellery in specialised stores

Beaverbrooks The Jewellers Ltd
LVMH Watch & Jewellery (UK) Limited
Nimogen Limited
Jon Richard Limited
David M. Robinson Limited

47789 Other retail sale of new goods in specialised stores (not commercial art galleries and opticians)

AGDC Holdings Limited
Bents Garden Centre Limited
BetterBathrooms (UK) Limited
Ellis Brigham Mountain Sports Limited
Carrs Billington Agriculture (Sales) Limited
Gordale Nurseries Limited
Harrington & Hallworth Limited
Warren James (Jewellers) Limited
Lake District Estates Company Limited
Newbank Garden Centre Limited
Pets at Home Ltd
Gordon Rigg (Nurseries) Limited
SW Golf Limited
William Strike Limited
Timpson Limited
Windermere Aquatic Limited
XLR8 Sports Limited

47799 Retail sale of other second-hand goods in stores (not incl. antiques)

Cash Converters (UK) Limited
Cash Converters UK Holdings PLC

47910 Retail sale via mail order houses or via Internet

BetterBathrooms (UK) Limited
Boohoo.Com UK Limited
Brook Taverner Limited
Chums Limited
Craghoppers Limited
Damartex UK Limited
Domu Brands Limited
Entertainment Magpie Limited
Equip4work Ltd
Express Gifts Limited
Fanatics (International) Limited
Findel Education Limited
Footasylum PLC
Freemans Grattan Holdings Limited
Freemans Public Limited Company
Grattan Public Limited Company
JD Sports Fashion PLC
Jeunesse Global (Europe) Limited
Kukri GB Limited
LRUK (Holdings) Limited
LRUK (Retail) Limited
Lakeland Limited
Limitless Digital Group Ltd
Missguided Limited
Movitex (UK) Limited
NUS Services Limited
J. Parker Dutch Bulbs (Wholesale) Limited
Shop Direct Home Shopping Limited
H C Slingsby P L C
Topgrade Sportswear Limited
UK2M Limited
J.D. Williams & Company Limited

47990 Other retail sale not in stores, stalls or markets

Alpha Flight UK Limited
Alpha LSG Limited
Barton Park Homes Limited
Blue Machinery (Central) Limited
Cend Limited
Closomat Limited
Creamline Dairies Limited
Gunn JCB Group Limited
Gunn JCB Limited
The Hut Group Limited
The Hut.Com Limited
Limitless Digital Group Ltd
MRC Transmark Limited
Petro-Canada Europe Lubricants Limited
Ralawise Limited
Swallow Holdings Limited

49100 Passenger rail transport, interurban

East Coast Main Line Company Limited
Merseyrail Electrics 2002 Limited

49200 Freight rail transport

Advance Uranium Asset Management Limited
Direct Rail Services Limited

49311 Urban and suburban passenger railway transportation by underground, metro and similar systems

South Yorkshire Supertram Limited

49319 Other urban, suburban or metropolitan passenger land transport (not underground, metro or similar)

Busways Travel Services Limited
Cambus Limited
Cheltenham and Gloucester Omnibus Company Limited
Cleveland Transit Ltd.
East Kent Road Car Company,Limited
East London Bus & Coach Company Limited
First Travel Solutions Limited
Glenvale Transport Limited
Greater Manchester Buses South Limited
Lincolnshire Road Car Company Limited
Midland Red (South) Limited
NST Transport Services Limited
National Holidays Limited
Proximo Limited
Reays Coaches Limited
Red & White Services Limited
John Shaw and Son Limited
Shearings Limited
South East London & Kent Bus Company Limited
Stagecoach (North West) Limited
Stagecoach (South) Limited
Stagecoach Devon Limited
Thames Transit Limited
Western Buses Limited
The Yorkshire Traction Company Limited

49390 Other passenger land transport

Alfa Coaches Limited
Blackpool Transport Services Limited
Eavesway Travel Limited
First Manchester Limited
First Pioneer Bus Limited
Gavin Murray Limited
National Holidays Tours Limited
Transdev PLC

49410 Freight transport by road

A & D Transport (NW) Limited
A K W Global Logistics Ltd
AKW Group Limited
Abbey Logistics Group Limited
Advance Uranium Asset Management Limited
Advanced Processing Limited
Archbold Logistics Limited
Frank Armitt & Son Limited
Thomas Armstrong (Aggregates) Limited
Ian Armstrong (Carlisle) Limited
Wm. Armstrong (Longtown) Limited
Arrow XL Limited
Atlantic Container Line UK Limited
Axle Bidco Limited
S J Bargh Group Limited
S.J.Bargh Limited
Bibby Distribution Limited
Boden & Davies Limited
Boughey Distribution Limited
W.H.Bowker Limited
Brink's Limited
Brit-European Transport Limited
Bulman's Bulk & Haulage Limited
Tyson H. Burridge Limited
Cavalier Carpets Limited
Countrywide Freight Group Limited
Dent Logistics Limited
E. C. M. (Vehicle Delivery Service) Limited
Edge Transport (Properties) Limited
European Metal Recycling Limited
Expect Distribution Limited
Expert Logistics Ltd.
Fagan & Whalley Limited
G.B.A. Services Limited
Thomas Guy,Limited
Insert Ltd
Kammac Limited
LF Logistics (UK) Limited
Lawsons Haulage Limited
Lomas Distribution Limited
R. McDowell Haulage and Distribution Limited
North West Logistics Ltd
O'Connor Container Transport Limited
M H & J Park and Son Limited
William Rainford (Holdings) Limited
Redhead Freight Limited
Rhenus Logistics Limited
Eddie Stobart Limited
Sutton and Son (St.Helens) Limited
Suttons Tankers Limited
TEF Transport Limited
Robert Tweddle (Timber Merchant and Haulage Contractor) Limited
WCF Ltd.
WS Transportation Limited
Whittle Eastern Europe Logistics Ltd.
Barron Wood Distribution Limited
Harry Yearsley Limited
Yodel Delivery Network Limited

50200 Sea and coastal freight water transport

Advance Uranium Asset Management Limited
Agility Logistics Solutions Limited
Atlantic Container Line UK Limited
Bibby Bulk Carriers Limited
Bibby Line Limited
Bibby Marine Limited
Bibby Maritime Limited
Bibby Transport Limited
Bibby Wavemaster I Limited
Birkenhead Port Limited
CMA CGM (UK) Shipping Limited
Cardinal Maritime Limited
F.T.Everard & Sons Limited
James Fisher Everard Limited
James Fisher and Sons Public Limited Company
Heysham Port Limited
M & S Logistics Limited
Mostyn Terminals Limited
Pacific Nuclear Transport Limited
The Port of Mostyn Limited
Port of Sheerness Limited
Seatruck Ferries Ltd
Seatruck Panorama Ltd
Seatruck Pennant Ltd

50300 Inland passenger water transport

The Bridgewater Canal Company Limited
Lake District Estates Company Limited
The Manchester Ship Canal Company Limited
The Mersey Docks and Harbour Company Limited
Windermere Lake Cruises Limited

51101 Scheduled passenger air transport

Brink's Limited
Doncaster Sheffield Airport Limited
Durham Tees Valley Airport Limited
Liverpool Airport Limited
Manchester Airport PLC

51102 Non-scheduled passenger air transport

Doncaster Sheffield Airport Limited
Swissport Stansted Ltd

51210 Freight air transport

Fedex Trade Networks Transport & Brokerage (UK) Limited
Kerry Logistics (UK) Limited
Swissport UK Holding Limited

52101 Operation of warehousing and storage facilities for water transport activities

Frank Armitt & Son Limited
Great Yarmouth Port Company Ltd
Thomas Guy,Limited

52102 Operation of warehousing and storage facilities for air transport activities

Tygavac Advanced Materials Ltd

52103 Operation of warehousing and storage facilities for land transport activities

AKW Group Limited
Advanced Processing Limited
Arrow XL Limited
Henry Bath & Son Limited
Bibby Distribution Limited
Boughey Distribution Limited
W.H.Bowker Limited
Brink's Limited
Cartwright Rentals Limited
Compass Minerals Storage & Archives Limited
Crampton Bros (Coopers) Ltd
Denholm UK Logistics Limited
Expert Logistics Ltd.
FDC (Holdings) Limited
Farralls Transport (Properties) Limited
Great Bear Distribution Limited
Great Bear Holdings Limited
Michael I Holdsworth Limited
Holmeswood Coaches Limited
Insert Ltd
Joda Holdings Limited
LF Logistics (UK) Limited
North West Logistics Ltd
P.J.H. Group Limited
Redhead Freight Limited
South Yorkshire Supertram Limited
Sutton and Son (St.Helens) Limited
TVS Supply Chain Solutions Limited
Harry Yearsley Limited
Zenith International Freight Limited

52211 Operation of rail freight terminals

Frank Armitt & Son Limited

52212 Operation of rail passenger facilities at railway stations

East Coast Main Line Company Limited

52219 Other service activities incidental to land transportation, n.e.c.

Arrow XL Limited
Bibby Distribution Limited
H. Dawson Sons and Company (Wool) Limited
Direct Tyre Management Limited
EG Midco Limited
Express Cargo Forwarding Limited
Parkingeye Limited
Shearings Holidays Limited
Yodel Delivery Network Limited
Zenith International Freight Limited

52220 Service activities incidental to water transportation

Great Yarmouth Port Company Ltd
Irish Ferries (U.K.) Limited

52230 Service activities incidental to air transportation

Airline Services Limited
Aviation Park Group Limited
The Manchester Airport Group PLC
Swissport GB Limited
Topbonus Ltd
Zenith International Freight Limited

52241 Cargo handling for water transport activities

Frank Armitt & Son Limited
Great Yarmouth Port Company Ltd
Ligna Biomass Limited

52242 Cargo handling for air transport activities

Brink's Global Services, Ltd.
European Metal Recycling Limited
Swissport GB Limited
Zenith International Freight Limited

52290 Other transportation support activities

AKW Group Limited
Arrow XL Limited
Banks & Lloyd (Shipping) Limited
Bridgehead Container Services Limited
Denholm Global Logistics Limited
Edge Worldwide Logistics Limited
Gogar Services Limited
Hyva (U.K.) Limited
Kerry Logistics (UK) Limited
M. & W. Freight Limited
Palletower (G.B.) Limited
SAT Business Travel Management Limited
Stagecoach Services Limited
Suttons International Limited
Warrant Group Limited
Yodel Distribution Holdings Limited
Yodel Logistics Limited

53201 Licensed carriers

CMS Network (London) Ltd
The Delivery Group Limited
Secured Express Limited

53202 Unlicensed carriers

Aramex (UK) Limited
Drop & Collect Limited

55201 Holiday centres and villages

Darwin (Cheddar Woods) Limited
Darwin (Piran Meadows) Limited
Sam Hagan Leisure (UK) Limited
Harrison Leisure UK Limited
W. & G. Harrison Limited
Holgates (Caravan Parks) Limited
The Lingholm Estate Limited
Lyons Holiday Park Limited
Morecambe Leisure 2 Limited
Project Rock Bidco Limited
Project Rock Equityco Limited
Verdant Leisure 2 Limited
Verdant Leisure Limited
Windermere Marina Village Limited

55209 Other holiday and other collective accommodation

Windermere Marina Village Limited

55300 Recreational vehicle parks, trailer parks and camping grounds

Allen (Park Foot) Limited
Barton Park Estates Limited
T G Cottam Limited
Darwin (Bath Mill) Limited
Darwin (North West) Limited
Lake District Estates Company Limited
Lakeland Leisure Estates Limited
Leisure Parks Limited
Thomas Milburn (Property) Limited
The Partington Group Limited
Partingtons Holiday Centres Limited

55900 Other accommodation

Canvas Holidays Limited
Garden State Property Management Ltd
Glencc Limited
Hewer-White Trust
Incommunities Group Limited
Leeds Independent Living Accommodation Company Limited
Natural Assets Investments Limited
Pendleton Together Operating Limited
Sustainable Communities for Leeds (Finance) PLC
Sustainable Communities for Leeds Limited
Trewhiddle Village Limited
Vacation Rentals (UK) Ltd

56101 Licenced restaurants

3Sixty Restaurants Limited
The Alchemist Bar & Restaurant Limited
Bank Restaurant Company Limited
Bispham Green Brewery Company Limited
Buttercup Bidco Limited
Buttercup Topco Limited
Christopher Bidco Limited
Christopher Midco 1 Limited
Christopher Topco Limited
City Life Projects Limited
Deckers Hospitality Group Limited
Elle R Leisure Limited
The Grosvenor - Pulford Hotel Limited
Gusto Restaurants Group Limited
Gusto Restaurants Limited
Gusto Restaurants UK Limited
Harnbury Holdings Ltd
Individual Restaurant Company Limited
Johoco 2029 Limited
New World Trading Company (UK) Holdings Limited
Northcote Hotel Limited
Northcote Leisure Group Limited
Restaurant Bar and Grill Limited
Salts Estates Limited
San Marco Limited
Daniel Thwaites Public Limited Company
Wolfson Trago Limited

56102 Unlicenced restaurants and cafes

H & S Restaurants Ltd
M C D Manchester Limited
Westmorland Limited

56103 Take-away food shops and mobile food stands

Wolfson Trago Limited

56210 Event catering activities

Alpha Flight UK Limited
Alpha LSG Limited
CGC Events Limited
Chester Race Company Limited
City Life Projects Limited
Elior UK PLC
Great Leighs Estates Limited
Value Catering Limited
Westmorland Limited

56290 Other food services

Bako North Western (Group) Limited
Bako North Western Limited
Bako South Eastern Limited
Caterplus Services Limited
Delifresh Limited
Nationwide Produce Holdings PLC
Nationwide Produce PLC
SMG (UK) Limited
Taylor Shaw Limited
Totally Local Company Limited
Waterfall Elior Limited

56301 Licenced clubs

Tokyo Group Limited

56302 Public houses and bars

Alpha Flight UK Limited
Alpha LSG Limited
Amber Taverns Limited
Bernham Ltd
Bispham Green Brewery Company Limited
Bravo Inns II Limited
Brunning and Price Limited
C2 Investment Limited
City Life Projects Limited
Dorbiere Limited
Elle R Leisure Limited
The Grosvenor - Pulford Hotel Limited
Joseph Holt Group Limited
Joseph Holt Limited
Hydes' Brewery Limited
Inns & Leisure Limited
Johoco 2029 Limited
Melli Limited
Mitchell's Brewery Limited
Mitchells of Lancaster (Brewers) Limited
New World Trading Company (UK) Limited
SPC Group Holdings Limited
Seafood Pub Company Group Limited
Daniel Thwaites Public Limited Company
Trust Inns Limited

58110 Book publishing

Coordination Group Publications Ltd

58141 Publishing of learned journals

Emerald Group Holdings Limited
Emerald Publishing Limited

58142 Publishing of consumer and business journals and periodicals

Auto Trader Limited
Newhall Group Limited (The)

58190 Other publishing activities

Allmand - Smith Limited
Hallmark Cards PLC
KVH Media Group Communication Limited

59111 Motion picture production activities

Blazing Productions Ltd

59112 Video production activities

Fresh Approach (UK) Limited
Good Night Vienna Productions Limited

59113 Television programme production activities

Good Night Vienna Productions Limited
Red Production Company Limited

59120 Motion picture, video and television programme post-production activities

Inflight Productions Ltd

59131 Motion picture distribution activities

IFE Services Limited
Inflight Productions Ltd

59133 Television programme distribution activities

IFE Services Limited
Inflight Productions Ltd
Peel Media Studios Limited

59140 Motion picture projection activities

Graves (Cumberland) Limited

60200 Television programming and broadcasting activities

Dock 10 Limited
MUTV Limited
Peel Media Studios Limited
Tote Media Limited

61100 Wired telecommunications activities

Arris International PLC
IX Reach Ltd
Jade Solutions Limited
Nexus Telecommunications Limited
M J Quinn Holdings Limited
Quinn Infrastructure Services Limited
Zen Internet Limited

61200 Wireless telecommunications activities

Anglia Telecom Centres Limited
Arris Global Ltd.
Arris International PLC
Cooper Bidco Limited
Cooper Topco Limited
Jade Solutions Limited
Nexus Telecommunications Limited
Peel Media Studios Limited
Siae Microelettronica Limited
Telesign Mobile Limited
WHP Telecoms Limited

61300 Satellite telecommunications activities

Arris Global Ltd.
Arris International PLC
Eutelsat UK Limited
Pace Distribution (Overseas) Limited
Pace Overseas Distribution Limited

61900 Other telecommunications activities

ANS Group Limited
Arris Global Ltd.
Arris International PLC
Brightstar 20:20 UK Limited
Chess Limited
Clear Business Limited
Communications Plus Ltd
Daisy Communications Ltd.
Daisy Corporate Services Limited
Daisy Corporate Services Trading Limited
Daisy Group Holdings Limited
Daisy IT Managed Services Limited
Daisy IT Services Limited
Daisy Wholesale Limited
Daisy Worldwide Limited
Elitetele.Com PLC
Elitetelecom Holdings PLC
Fleur Telecom Limited
Metronet (UK) Limited
Nesscoinvsat Limited
Noble Systems UK Limited
Nycomm Holdings Limited
Nycomm Limited
Scalable Communications Limited
Shared Access Ltd
Spiritel Mobile Limited
Verastar Limited

62011 Ready-made interactive leisure and entertainment software development

Computer Risk Management Limited
Magellan Robotech Limited
Mobica Limited
Seventh Continent Limited

62012 Business and domestic software development

Avecto Ltd
Blue Prism Group PLC
Blue Prism Limited
Blujay Solutions Group Holdings Limited
Blujay Solutions Holdings Limited
Blujay Solutions Ltd
Blujay Topco Limited
CTI Data Solutions Limited
GPC Computer Software Limited
Generis Technology Limited
K3 Business Technologies Limited
KHL Newco Limited
Kalibrate Technologies Limited
Kirona Holdings Limited
M-Hance Limited
MDS CEM Holdings Limited
MDS Global Ltd
Premaitha Health PLC
Utilisoft Limited
Voiteq Limited

62020 Information technology consultancy activities

ANS Group Limited
Acuma Solutions Limited
Adviserplus Business Solutions Limited
Business Computer Projects Limited
CTI Billing Solutions Limited
Control Circle Limited
Core Education and Consulting Solutions (UK) Ltd.
Data Intensity Limited
Datel Computing Limited
Datel Group PLC
Dovetail Systems Limited
Fircroft Engineering Services Limited
GB Group PLC
Hammer PLC
IBI Group (UK) Limited
Janson Computers PLC
K3 Business Solutions Limited
K3 Business Technologies Limited
K3 Syspro Limited
Labware Limited
M247 Ltd
NCC Group Accumuli Security Limited
NCC Group Security Services Limited
NCC Services Limited
Project Daytona Bidco Limited
Project Daytona Limited
Truecommerce Holdings Limited
Utilisoft Limited

62030 Computer facilities management activities

ANS Group Limited
Control Circle Limited
MDS Global Ltd
Micad Systems (U.K.) Limited

62090 Other information technology service activities

1st Technologies Ltd
ANS Group Limited
ASE PLC
ASM Technologies Limited
Accumuli Limited
Alphyra Payment Services Limited
Bibliotheca Limited
Brooks Automation Ltd
CDL Group Holdings Limited
Centriq Group Limited
Checkfree Solutions Limited
Cheshire Datasystems Limited
Cloud Technology Solutions Ltd
Computer Risk Management Limited
Control Circle Limited
Daisy Group Holdings Limited
Daisy IT Continuity and Resilience Services Limited
Daisy IT Managed Services Limited
Daisy IT Services Limited
Daisy Partner Services Limited
Daisy Worldwide Limited
Data Intensity Holdings Limited
Euro Options Limited
Fiserv (Europe) Limited
Fiserv UK Holding Limited
Fiserv Worldwide Holdings Limited
James Fisher Marine Services Limited
GE Capital Information Technology Solutions Limited
GE Infrastructure UK Limited
GE Transportation Systems Ltd
Hammer Group Limited
Helical Industries Ltd.
Ikonic Technology Limited
Information and Data Networks Supplies Limited
K3 Syspro Limited
Late Rooms Limited
MDS Global Ltd
MPP Global Solutions Ltd
NCC Group (Solutions) Limited
Payzone UK Limited
Pomeroy IT Solutions UK Limited
Positive Solutions Limited
Postcode Anywhere Holdings Limited
Servicepower Business Solutions Limited
Seventh Continent Limited
Telesign UK Limited
UK-2 Limited
mxData - Technologies Limited

63110 Data processing, hosting and related activities

BNN Technology PLC
Data Intensity Limited
GB Group PLC
GE Infrastructure UK Limited
IESA Limited
Intelling Group Limited
Postcode Anywhere (Europe) Limited
Sysgroup PLC
UKFast.Net Limited
Virtual Internet (UK) Limited

63990 Other information service activities n.e.c.

B.I.P. (Holdings) Limited
Bentley Global (UK) Limited
Commscare Group Limited
DBG (UK) Limited
Moneysupermarket.Com Financial Group Limited
Moneysupermarket.Com Ltd
Nextgear Capital UK Limited
PIMCO 2947 Bidco Limited
PIMCO 2947 Topco Limited
St Helens Chamber Limited
Synexus Clinical Research Midco No 2 Limited

64191 Banks

Bodycote America Treasury Limited
The Co-operative Bank P.L.C.
IGE Euro Treasury Services
Vanquis Bank Limited
Yorkshire Water Services Finance Limited

64201 Activities of agricultural holding companies

Inverco Limited
L & K Group PLC

64202 Activities of production holding companies

4L (Holdings) Limited
Anglo European Group Ltd
Angus Holdings Safety Group Limited
Angus International Safety Group Limited
Arlington Aerospace Limited
Arlington Industries Group Ltd
Arlington Management Services Ltd
CEP Biomass Energy Limited
CEP Biomass Limited
CEP Teesside Biomass Limited
Calachem Holding Limited
Clean Energy and Infrastructure UK Wind 2 Limited
The Flame Group Limited
GA Pet Food Partners Group Limited
Goodwood Holdings Limited
Hexpol Finance UK Limited
Hexpol UK Limited
The Howells Group PLC
IKO Holdings PLC
IKO U.K. Limited
Indutrade UK Limited
J M Holdings Limited
Jade Equity Limited
Jiffy (UK) Holding I Limited
Kermandine Limited
Manor Coating Systems (Holdings) Limited
Natrium Holdings Limited
Norman 1985 Limited
Novus Finance Ltd
Pacific Shelf 1809 Limited
Plastic Recycling Limited
Ruberoid International Limited
TTC UK Holdings Limited
Tangerine Confectionery Group Limited
Tangerine Confectionery Limited
Taurus 3 Limited
Taurus Bidco Limited
The Tensar Group Limited
UPM-Kymmene (UK) Holdings Limited
Vita Satellite 1 Limited

64203 Activities of construction holding companies

Aptus Group Limited
Bachy Soletanche Holdings (Europe) Limited
Bardsley Construction Holdings Limited
Bardsley Group Limited
Bruntwood Development Holdings Limited
Bunton Plant Hire Limited
CPUK Commercial Holdings Limited
The Casey Group Limited
Edge Orbital Holdings Limited
FK Group Limited
Flanagan Group Limited
Graham Heath Group Limited
Huyton Asphalt Holdings Limited
IKO Holdings PLC
IKO U.K. Limited
Leck Group Ltd
Lifting Gear UK Group Limited
Liverpool Airport Property Holdings Limited
Liverpool Airport Property Limited
Merseylink (Issuer) PLC
P I H Holdings Limited
Peel Media Development (Holdings) Limited
Peel Property Holdings Limited
Peel Property Limited
Radbourne Edge (Holdings) Limited
Road Maintenance Services (Holdings) Limited
The Rosebery Group Holdings Limited
Ruberoid International Limited
Stonewell Property Company Limited
Supremebase Limited
UDP Group Limited
R.N. Wooler & Co (Holdings) Limited

64204 Activities of distribution holding companies

Bibby Supply Chain Services Limited
Brightstar 20:20 Limited
Cardinal Maritime Holdings Limited
Fluidpower Group Limited
Fluidpower Shared Services Limited
Howgill Holdings Limited
IKO U.K. Limited
Inspirepac Holdings Limited
Lazner Holdings Limited
Medline Stellar UK Limited
Revolution Direct Ltd
Risol Imports Limited
VIP (Group) Limited

64205 Activities of financial services holding companies

The 1st Stop Group Limited
Arrow Global Accounts Management Limited
Arrow Global Finance PLC
Arrow Global Group PLC
Arrow Global One Limited
Barbican Investments Limited
Bibby FS (Holdings) Limited
Bibby Financial Services (Europe) Limited
Bibby Financial Services (UK) Limited
Bibby Financial Services Limited
Bibby Invoice Finance UK Limited
Bracken Midco1 PLC
Bracken Midco2 Limited
Chrystal Holdings Limited
Compello Holdings Limited
Connells Limited
Countrywide Assured Life Holdings Limited
T L Dallas Group Limited
Darwin Loan Solutions Limited
Dechra Finance Australia Limited
Dechra Finance Limited
Dechra Finance Sterling Limited
Diamond Resorts Financial Services Limited
Gilkes Hydro Investments Limited
Greystone Financial Services (Holdings) Limited
Griffiths & Armour Limited
HDI Holdings (UK) Limited
HSS Financing PLC
Hargreave Hale Limited
Hyde Industrial Holdings Limited
Jerrold Finco PLC
KRS Finance Ltd
Key Group Bidco Limited
Key Group Midco 1 Limited
Key Group Midco 2 Limited
LDF Group Finance Limited
LDF Group Holdco Limited
Local Pensions Partnership Ltd
Merseyside Special Investment Fund Limited
Milan Bidco Limited
Milan Midco Limited
Milan Swapco Limited
Millfield Holdings Limited
OBG Finance Holding Limited
Paymentshield Group Holdings Limited
Pershing Holdings (UK) Limited
Praetura Asset Finance (Holdings) Limited
Provident Financial PLC
Quint Holdings Ltd
Redhill Famco Limited
Skipton Group Holdings Limited
Soogen Holdings Limited
Arnold Stansby & Co. Limited
Arnold Stansby Holdings Limited
Sune Green Holdco4 Limited
Sune Green Holdco5 Limited
Sune Green Holdco7 Limited
Sune Green Holdco9 Limited
Talbot Deane Investments Limited
Taurus Acquisition Limited
Think Money Group Limited
Think Money Holdings 1 Limited
Think Money Holdings Limited
U F C Fund Management PLC
UK2M Limited
F Wilson (Holdings) Limited
Yes Car Credit (Holdings) Limited

64301 Activities of investment trusts

Axle Topco Limited
SJCF Investment Ltd
Tzortzis Limited

64303 Activities of venture and development capital companies

Ascent Ventures Limited
Campus Living Villages (Portfolio Finance) UK Limited
Treedown Investments Limited

64304 Activities of open-ended investment companies

Crossco (1317) Limited
Crossco (1318) Limited
Gweco 511 Limited
Henty Capital Limited
JPTR Bidco Limited
JPTR Midco Limited
JPTR Topco Limited
KRMCO Limited
USS Heritors Limited

64305 Activities of property unit trusts

Beauchamp Real Estate Holdings Limited

64910 Financial leasing

Bibby Asset Finance Limited
Bibby Leasing Limited
Capital Bank Leasing 3 Limited
Cardinal Health Finance
Chrystal Consulting Limited
Dobies Cumbria Finance Limited
The Funding Corporation (2) Limited
GE Capital Corporation (Leasing) Limited
GE Capital UK Limited
Haydock Asset Finance Limited
Haydock Finance Limited
Kingsley Asset Finance Limited
Kingsway Asset Finance Ltd
Kingsway Financial Group Holdings Limited
Kingsway Leasing Limited
LDF Finance No. 1 Limited
Merchant Rentals Limited
Mistral Asset Finance Limited
Praetura Asset Finance (L) Limited
Praetura Asset Finance (SB) Limited
Technology Rentals Limited

64921 Credit granting by non-deposit taking finance houses and other specialist consumer credit grantors

1st Stop Reserve Limited
Affirmative Finance Limited
Arrow Global Investments Holdings Limited
Arrow Global Limited
Arrow Global Receivables Management Limited
Bibby Trade Services Limited
Blemain Finance Limited
Borderway Finance Limited
Bridging Finance Limited
Burnley Savings and Loans Limited
CF Asset Finance Limited
Cardinal Health Finance
The Enterprise Fund Limited
Evolution Lending Limited
Ferratum UK Ltd
The Funding Corporation (2) Limited
Gemsupa Limited
Harpmanor Limited
Haydock Asset Finance Limited
International Motors Finance Limited
Oakmore Investments Limited
Provident Personal Credit Limited
Charles Street Commercial Investments Limited
Together Commercial Finance Limited
Together Personal Finance Limited

64922 Activities of mortgage finance companies

Accord Mortgages Limited
Affirmative Finance Limited
Amber Homeloans Limited
Auction Finance Limited
Bradford & Bingley PLC
Capital Bridging Finance Solutions Limited
Lowry Capital Limited
More 2 Life Ltd
Mortgage Express
North Yorkshire Mortgages Limited

64929 Other credit granting n.e.c.

Affiniture Cards Limited
Arrow Global Europe Limited
Beyond Funding (Holdco) Ltd
Business & Enterprise Finance Ltd.
CLV Finance UK Limited
Car Benefit Car Schemes Limited
Consolidated Property Wilmslow Limited
Corp Limited
Daytona Holdco Limited
Daytona JV Limited
Estuary Group Limited
Thomas Frederick & Company Limited
Goldcrest Finance Limited
Graphic Packaging International UK Finance Limited
Haslebrow Finance Limited
Haydock Finance Limited
Hindle & Walker Limited
Hope Capital Limited
LDF Finance No. 1 Limited
M.A.X. Funding Limited
Marsh Finance & Commercial Limited
Marsh Finance Limited
Rentsmart Limited
Riverside Finance PLC
Shop Direct Finance Company Limited

64991 Security dealing on own account

Bonarie Investments Limited
Countrylass Ltd
Livbeth Investco Limited
Migo Enterprises Limited
Richminster Ltd

64992 Factoring

Back Office Support Services Limited
Bibby Factors Bristol Limited
Bibby Factors International Limited
Bibby Factors Leicester Limited
Bibby Factors Limited
Bibby Factors Manchester Limited
Bibby Factors Northwest Limited
Bibby Factors Slough Limited
Bibby Factors Sussex Limited
Bibby Factors Yorkshire Limited
Bibby Invoice Discounting Limited
Bibby Trade Factors Limited
Silverburn Finance (U.K.) Limited
Skipton Business Finance Limited

65110 Life insurance

Assurant Direct Limited
Assurant Intermediary Limited
Assurant Life Limited
Bollington Insurance Brokers Limited
Countrywide Assured PLC
Monarch Assurance PLC
Prorendita Five Limited

65120 Non-life insurance

Acorn Insurance and Financial Services Limited
Ashdowns Limited
Assurant Direct Limited
Assurant General Insurance Limited
Assurant Intermediary Limited
The Bollington Group (Holdings) Limited
Bollington Insurance Brokers Limited
Bridge Insurance Brokers Limited
Car Care Plan (Holdings) Limited
Car Care Plan Limited
Chase Templeton Limited
D R & P Holdings Limited
T L Dallas & Co Limited
Financial & Legal Insurance Company Ltd
The Funding Corporation (2) Limited
Griffiths & Armour (Holdings) Limited
Guarantee Protection Insurance Limited
Integra Insurance Solutions Limited
Irwell Insurance Company Limited
Lifestyle Services Group Limited
MD Insurance Services Limited
Medicash Health Benefits Limited
Motorplus Limited
Motors Insurance Company Limited
NMU (Specialty) Ltd
Carole Nash Insurance Consultants Limited
Reich Insurance Brokers Limited
David Roberts & Partners (Insurance Brokers) Limited
South Shore Mutual Insurance Company Limited
Sovereign Health Care
Swinton Group Limited
The Veterinary Defence Society Limited
F. Wilson (Insurance Brokers) Limited

65202 Non-life reinsurance

Ashdowns Limited
Bridge Insurance Brokers Limited
Chase Templeton Limited

65300 Pension funding

Expalkan II Closed Scheme Limited
Universities Superannuation Scheme Limited

66110 Administration of financial markets

Investment Fund Services Limited

66120 Security and commodity contracts dealing activities

AJ Bell Securities Limited
Blankstone Sington Limited
James Brearley & Sons Limited
Cardinal Health Finance
Granite Finance Ltd

66190 Activities auxiliary to financial intermediation n.e.c.

AJ Bell Limited
AJ Bell Management Limited
Broker Direct PLC
GE Capital Investments
Gemini Finance Ltd
Phillips & Cohen Associates International, Ltd
Project Finland Bidco Limited
Project Finland Topco Limited
Proximo Limited
SL Mortgage Funding No 1 Limited

66220 Activities of insurance agents and brokers

Bridge Insurance Brokers Limited
Croner Taxwise Limited
Griffiths & Armour Global Risks Limited
Moneysupermarket.Com Financial Group Holdings Limited
Motorplus Limited
Caunce O'Hara & Company Limited
Schofields Limited

66290 Other activities auxiliary to insurance and pension funding

Cavalier Carpets Limited
Heathfield Holdings Limited
L1 Renewables Limited
Motorplus Limited
PSV Claims Bureau Limited
USS Nero Limited

66300 Fund management activities

Bowmore Investments Limited
Local Pensions Partnership Investments Ltd
Merseylink (Issuer) PLC
North West Business Finance Limited
Rathbone Investment Management Limited
Skirfare Investments Limited
Tearlach Limited
USS Investment Management Limited

68201 Renting and operating of Housing Association real estate

Zoe Ashton Limited
Atmore Developments Limited
Bents Property Limited
Blackburn Chemicals (Holdings) Limited
Bolling Investments Limited
Braecrest Limited
Calico Homes Limited
Cartwright Properties Limited
City South Manchester Housing Trust Limited
Eastlands Homes Partnership Limited
European Metal Recycling Limited
Four Seasons Estates Limited
GE Real Estate European Finance Limited
GE Real Estate Finance Limited
Gedling Homes
Gisburne Park Estates Limited
Granton Investments Limited
Guildford Investments Limited
Helical Industries Ltd.
Kingsoak Limited
Leasowe Community Homes
Leoron Investments Limited
Lightfooting Limited
New Charter Homes Limited
One Manchester Treasury Limited
Parkway Green Housing Trust
Peel Land and Property Investments PLC
Peelclose Properties Limited
Principal Healthcare Finance (UK) No.1 Limited
Principal Healthcare Finance (UK) No.2 Limited
Rajan Trading Co. Limited
Sandown Property Company (Liverpool) Limited
Singleton & Smart (Holdings) Limited
Southernplus Limited
Trafford Housing Trust Limited
Willow Park Housing Trust Limited
Wirral Partnership Homes Limited
Wythenshawe Community Housing Group Limited

68202 Letting and operating of conference and exhibition centres

Manchester Central Convention Complex Limited
The University of Manchester Innovation Centre Limited

68310 Real estate agencies

Adhan Developments Limited
Browntree Properties Limited
Business First Ltd
Harrison Northern Limited
Ventgrove Limited

68320 Management of real estate on a fee or contract basis

Aintree Retail Park Limited
Barlows Childcare Properties Limited
Blue Support Services Limited
Brookhouse (Ashford) Limited
Brookhouse (Hamilton) Limited
Brookhouse (Lowestoft) Limited
Brookhouse (Preston) Limited
Browntree Properties Limited
Bruntwood Management Services Limited
CLV Investments UK Limited
W & A Casement Limited
Castlefield Estates Limited
Catalyst Higher Education (Sheffield) Holdings Limited
Centrelease Limited
Community 1st Sheffield (Tranche 2) Limited
Deanbank Investments Limited
Dixondale Limited
Douglas Valley Finance Company Limited
Education Solutions Speke Limited
Emerson Developments (Holdings) Limited
Emerson Management Services Limited
Estuary Group Limited
Exchequer Partnership Holdings Limited
Exchequer Partnership PLC
Green Pastures North West Limited
Help Your Property Limited
Himor Group Limited
J T Associates Limited
JMU Property Development Company Limited
Manchester Airport Group Property Services Limited
Metropolitan Cathedral Services Limited
NDA Properties Limited
Network Space (Networkcentres) Limited
North West Portfolio Limited
Orbit Investments (Northern) Limited
Orbit Investments (Properties) Limited
Parliment Place Limited
Praedius (UK) Limited
Promenade Estates Limited
RDG Foulridge Properties Limited
Sabina Estates Group Holdings Limited
Salford Village Limited
Seamore Court Freehold Limited
Select Property Group Limited
Sigma PRS Investments II Limited
Sigma PRS Investments III Limited
Sterling Property Co. Limited
Stockport Homes Limited
Streetlands Limited
System 3 Investments Limited
Vita Ventures Limited
Wigan and Leigh Homes Ltd
Wrather Group Limited
Wren Properties Limited
Eric Wright FM Limited
Z&D Property Investments Limited

69102 Solicitors

2020 Legal Limited
BB Legal Limited
Bond Turner Limited
Co-operative Legal Services Limited
Equitas Solicitors Limited
Express Solicitors Limited
Fletchers Solicitors Limited
Michael W Halsall Solicitors Limited
Thomas Higgins Limited
Hilary Meredith Solicitors Limited
Potter Rees Limited
Ralli Ltd.
Thorneycroft Solicitors Limited

69109 Activities of patent and copyright agents; other legal activities n.e.c.

Countrywide Property Lawyers Limited
Ellis Whittam Limited
Peninsula Business Services Limited
Titleabsolute Limited

69201 Accounting and auditing activities

ASE PLC
Brookson Group Limited
Brookson Limited
Leonard Curtis Recovery Limited
Hyde Group Holdings Limited
RPG Group Limited

70210 Public relations and communications activities

Mudskipper Business Limited

70221 Financial management

Arris International IP Ltd
Arysta LifeScience U.K. EUR Limited
Arysta LifeScience U.K. Holdings Limited
Arysta LifeScience U.K. USD Limited
Channon Holdings Limited
H. Marcel Guest, Limited
Iceland BondCo PLC
Kelda Finance (No.1) Limited
Kelda Finance (No.2) Limited
Kelda Finance (No.3) PLC
Kingspan Services (UK) Limited
Manchester Airport Group Funding PLC
J & E Marshall Finance Limited
Potomac Capital Limited
Sabina Estates Group Holdings Limited
Schosween 6 Limited
Simon Family Office Limited
TSB (Investment Europe) Limited
Zabaxe Limited

70229 Management consultancy activities other than financial management

ABS Consulting Ltd.
Aidenhall Ltd
Arysta LifeScience U.K. Limited
Ashton Agricultural and General Limited
Best International Limited
Bowdon Group Limited
Byrom Public Limited Company
Carrix Limited
Chrystal Consulting Limited
Citation Limited
DBG (UK) Limited
Driver Consult Limited
Driver Group PLC
Dukefield Limited
Enterprise Solutions Holdings Limited
Flavour Warehouse Holdings Limited
Fresh Approach (UK) Holdings Limited
GM Business Support Limited
Geometric Results Holdings Limited
Global Equity Finance Ltd
Gresty Holdings Limited
HO2 Management Limited
Hoist Finance UK Limited
Inenco Group Limited
Invent and Invest
Lowe Clothing International Limited
NSG Environmental Limited
NUS Holdings Limited
NUS Services Limited
Neuven Solutions Limited
Optionis Management Limited
PTS Property Limited
Parkwood Leisure Investments Limited
Project One Consulting Limited
TFHC 2015 Limited
Transdev PLC
Vital Energi Utilities Limited
Winander Group Holdings Limited

71111 Architectural activities

Building Design Partnership Limited
IBI Group (UK) Limited
Maraq Limited
Styles & Wood Limited

71112 Urban planning and landscape architectural activities

Building Design Partnership Limited
IBI Group (UK) Limited
Turley Associates Ltd

71121 Engineering design activities for industrial process and production

ABS Consulting Ltd.
AMEC Foster Wheeler Energy Limited
Assystem UK Limited
CSA Group Testing UK Limited
Morson Projects Limited
Wood Nuclear Limited

71122 Engineering related scientific and technical consulting activities

AMEC Foster Wheeler Nuclear International Limited
Assystem UK Limited
Jeremy Benn Associates Limited
Curtins Consulting Limited
EA Technology Limited
Energy, Safety and Risk Consultants (UK) Limited
Gutteridge Haskins & Davey Limited
IBI Group (UK) Limited
JBA Group Limited
National Nuclear Laboratory Limited
Underground Mining Services Limited
Wood Nuclear Limited

71129 Other engineering activities

AMEC Services Limited
Addison Project PLC
BCW Engineering Ltd
Brinksway Tool Limited
Building Design Partnership Limited
Fichtner Consulting Engineers Limited
James Fisher Marine Services Limited
Gilbert Gilkes & Gordon Limited
Hyde Aero Products Limited
Hyde Details Limited
Hyde Group Limited
Morson Projects Limited
RM Property and Facilities Solutions Limited
S G Equipment Limited
TSC Engineering Limited
Taziker Industrial Limited
WHP Telecoms Limited

71200 Technical testing and analysis

AMEC Foster Wheeler Nuclear International Limited
CSA Group Europe Holdings Limited
EA Technology Limited
Energy, Safety and Risk Consultants (UK) Limited
NSG Environmental Limited
National Nuclear Laboratory Limited
SGS Ashby Ltd
Sonomatic Limited
Werfen Limited
Wood Nuclear Limited

72110 Research and experimental development on biotechnology

Genedrive Diagnostics Ltd
Genedrive PLC
IVCC
Nanoco Group PLC
Nuseed Global Innovation Ltd
Qiagen Manchester Limited
Redx Pharma PLC
Werfen Limited

72190 Other research and experimental development on natural sciences and engineering

Bodycote H.I.P. Limited
Concept Life Sciences Analytical & Development Services Limited
Concept Life Sciences Integrated Discovery & Development Services Limited
EA Technology Limited
Hologic Ltd.
IVCC
Innovative Technology Limited
Medicines Evaluation Unit Limited
Music Tribe Brands UK Ltd.
NSG Environmental Limited
Nanoco Group PLC
Nanoco Tech Limited
Nanoco Technologies Limited
Nufarm Crop Products UK Limited
Peakdale Molecular Limited
SmarDTV (UK) Limited
Tensar Technologies Limited
UK Biobank Limited

72200 Research and experimental development on social sciences and humanities

Liverpool School of Tropical Medicine

73110 Advertising agencies

Co-operative Brands Limited
Lagardere Sports UK Ltd
McCann Manchester Limited
McCann-Erickson Network Limited
Mediacom North Limited
Multimedia International Services Limited
Partnership Media Group Limited
Please Hold (UK) Limited

73120 Media representation services

Mediaco Limited

73200 Market research and public opinion polling

Maru Group Finance Limited
Maru Group Holdings Limited
Maru Group Limited

74100 Specialised design activities

ABS Consulting Ltd.
Tensar International Limited
Wireless Holdings Limited

74901 Environmental consulting activities

Building Design Partnership Limited
Curtins Consulting Limited
RSK Adas Limited

74909 Other professional, scientific and technical activities n.e.c.

ABS Group Ltd.
ALS Inspection UK Limited
ALS Life Sciences Limited
Agilent Technologies Lda UK Limited
Amscreen Group Limited
Assystem Group UK Limited
C J Services UK Limited
CH Holding Limited
Catalyst Healthcare (Manchester) Limited
Cheselden Limited
Concept Life Sciences (Laboratories) Limited
Concept Life Sciences Analytical & Development Services Limited
Corning Limited
Crawford Healthcare Limited
Crest Plus Operations Limited
Crosslane Investments Limited
DBG (UK) Limited
Ethika Healthcare Investments Limited
Evergreen Energy Ltd
Fishawack Communications Limited
Gecas UK Limited
Halite Energy Group Limited
Hobs Reprographics PLC
Hologic Ltd.
IESA A & D Limited
Iconix MENA Ltd
In at The Side Limited
Inception Point Systems Ltd
Inspired Energy PLC
International Nuclear Services Limited
Alfred H. Knight International Limited
Legal Marketing Services Limited
Lowri Beck Services Limited
M2 Managed Document Services Ltd
Markem-Imaje Limited
The Mines Advisory Group
NCC Group PLC
NNL Holdings Limited
Nederman Limited
Otto Simon Limited
Radioactive Waste Management Limited
Rainbow Dust Colours Limited
Risktec Solutions Limited
SGS Holding UK Ltd
SGS United Kingdom Limited
Smit Harbour Towage (UK) Limited
Sudlows Limited
Synexus Clinical Research Acquisitions Limited
Synexus Clinical Research Finance Limited
Synexus Clinical Research Limited
Synexus Clinical Research Midco No 1 Limited
Synexus Clinical Research Midco No 3 Limited
Synexus Limited
Werfen Limited
Wool Growers (Great Britain) Limited
Worldwide Procurement Limited
Yodel Delivery Network Limited
Yodel Distribution Holdings Limited
Yodel Logistics Limited

75000 Veterinary activities

Dechra Limited
Manchester and District Home for Lost Dogs Limited
North of England Zoological Society (The)

77110 Renting and leasing of cars and light motor vehicles

Birkenhead Car and Van Hire Limited
Centurion Truck Rental Ltd
Circle Leasing Limited
Direct Accident Management Limited
Easi-Drive Limited
Fleet and Plant Hire Limited
Get Motoring UK Limited
Kindertons Limited
Lex Vehicle Finance 2 Limited
Performance Car Hire Limited
Plantec Assist Limited
Regal Vehicle Rentals Limited
West Wallasey Garages Limited

77120 Renting and leasing of trucks and other heavy vehicles

Birkenhead Car and Van Hire Limited
Blakedale Ltd
Braymale Limited
Centurion Truck Rental Ltd
Firow Limited
Fleet and Plant Hire Limited
Grayrentals Limited
Hardroad Limited
Mistral Bus & Coach PLC
NRG Fleet Services Limited
Riverside Truck Rental Limited
Rowleys of Northwich Limited
Salford Van Hire Limited
Sean Louis Investments Limited
Tip Trailer Services UK Limited

77291 Renting and leasing of media entertainment equipment

ADI UK Limited
Adlib Audio Limited
HSL Group Holdings Limited

77310 Renting and leasing of agricultural machinery and equipment

J K Ashbrook Holdings Limited

77320 Renting and leasing of construction and civil engineering machinery and equipment

Abird Limited
Adlington Welding Supplies Limited
Bacchus Newco Limited
Beva Investments Limited
Blue Machinery (Southern) Limited
Boels Rental Limited
Buckhurst Plant Hire Limited
Bullen Plant Hire Limited
R. Bunton Limited
Bunton Plant Hire Limited
Cara Holdings Limited
Drillwave Limited
G.G.R. Group Ltd
Garic Limited
HSS Hire Service Group Limited
G & A M Lawson Limited
M.G.F. (Trench Construction Systems) Limited
PP O'Connor Contracting Limited
PJP (UK) Limited
Prolift Access Limited
Scotts Hire Limited
Story Contracting Limited
Supply UK Investments Limited
Survey Supplies Limited
TXM Plant Limited
D Wardle (Plant) Limited
Barry Wood Plant Hire Limited

77390 Renting and leasing of other machinery, equipment and tangible goods n.e.c.

A. V. Group Limited
Boels Rental Limited
Bullen Plant Hire Limited
Bunk-a-Bin Limited
Byworth Boiler Hire Limited
Dreambase Limited
GE Capital Sigma Holding Ltd
GE European Equipment Finance (Aircraft No. 2) Limited
Lowri Beck Services Limited
Moduleco Healthcare Limited
Multistar Container Transport Limited
Portable Offices (Hire) Limited
Red-D-Arc (UK) Limited
Red-D-Arc Limited
Scantech Offshore Limited
Speedy Asset Services Limited
Speedy Hire PLC
Speedy International Leasing Limited
Speedy Support Services Limited
Speedy Transport Limited
Supply UK Investments Limited
Tetra Pak Limited
UK Platforms Ltd
Ylem Energy Limited

77400 Leasing of intellectual property and similar products, except copyright works

Hologic IP Ltd
Tensar Technologies Limited

78109 Other activities of employment placement agencies

Air Resources Limited
Airswift Holdings Limited
Amoria Bond Limited
Braymale Limited
Heads Recruitment Limited
Oliver James Associates Limited
Kintec Recruitment Limited
N.R.L. Limited
NES Group Limited
Swift Engineering (Azerbaijan) Limited
Swift Technical (Azerbaijan) Limited
Swift Technical (Europe) Limited
Swift Technical Group Holdings Limited
Swift Technical Group Limited
Swift Technical Holdings Limited
Swift Worldwide Resources Bidco Limited
Swift Worldwide Resources Holdco Limited
Swift Worldwide Resources Midco Limited
WHC01 Limited
Workforce People Solutions Limited

78200 Temporary employment agency activities

Anderselite Ltd
Driver Hire Group Services Limited
Driver Hire Investments Limited
Fircroft Engineering Services Limited
First Technical Recruitment Limited
Heads Recruitment Limited
Health Care Resourcing Group Limited
Holt Doctors Limited
Kinetic PLC
Kinetic Recruitment Services Limited
Meridian Business Support Limited
N.R.L. Limited
NES Advantage Solutions Limited
NES Global Limited
NES Global Talent Finance Limited
NES Global Talent Holdco Limited
NES Global Talent Holdings Ltd
NES Global Talent Limited
NES Holdings Limited
NES Managed Services Limited
NES UK Limited
Paraplus (Holdings) Limited
Paystream My Max Limited
Pettra Limited
Priory Design Services Limited
Rullion Engineering Limited
Rullion IT Plus Limited
Workforce People Solutions Limited

78300 Human resources provision and management of human resources functions

Dow Chemical Services UK Limited
James Fisher Marine Services Limited
Geometric Results International Limited
MMGG Acquisition Limited
Morson Group Limited
Morson Holdings Limited
Morson Human Resources Limited
Morson Projects Limited
Rethink Professional Services Limited
Rethink Recruitment Solutions Limited

79110 Travel agency activities

Airline Network Limited
Althams Travel Services Limited
Corporate Travel Management (North) Limited
Cresta World Travel Limited
Egencia UK Ltd
Elegant Resorts Limited
The Global Travel Group Limited
Gold Medal Travel Group Limited
NST Travel Group Limited
On The Beach Beds Limited
On The Beach Bidco Limited
On The Beach Group PLC
On The Beach Limited
On The Beach Travel Limited
Scenic Tours (UK) Ltd
Stella Global UK Limited
Sunshine Cruise Holidays Limited
Travel Counsellors Group Limited
Travel Counsellors Limited
Travelworld International (Manchester) Limited
WTH (UK) Limited

79120 Tour operator activities

Alfa Travel Ltd.
Bliss Bidco Limited
Bliss Topco Limited
Carrier Ltd
Classic Collection Holidays Limited
Dnata Travel Holdings UK Limited
Elegant Resorts Limited
International Travel Connections Limited
The Portman Travel Group Limited
Sports Tours International Limited
Stella Travel Services (UK) Limited
Sunshine Cruise Holidays Limited
Travel 2 Limited
Travelbag Limited
Travelworld International (Manchester) Limited
Western and Oriental Travel Limited

79909 Other reservation service activities n.e.c.

Personalised Travel Services Limited
Sykes Cottages Ltd

80100 Private security activities

Kingdom Services Group Limited

80200 Security systems service activities

Chubb Systems Limited
Kings Security Systems Limited
RM Property and Facilities Solutions Limited
Totally Local Company Limited

81100 Combined facilities support activities

Blue Support Services Limited
Promenade Estates Limited
RM Property and Facilities Solutions Limited
SOG Limited

81210 General cleaning of buildings

Bulloughs Cleaning Services Limited
Kingdom Services Group Limited
Mantank Environmental Services Limited
RM Property and Facilities Solutions Limited

81222 Specialised cleaning services

Cavalier Carpets Limited

81299 Other cleaning services

Future Industrial Services Limited

81300 Landscape service activities

The Barton Grange Group Limited
Glendale Grounds Management Limited
The Land Restoration Trust

82110 Combined office administrative service activities

API Group Services Limited
Ardagh Metal Beverage Trading UK Limited
Bryden Capital Ltd
Lowe Clothing International Limited
MLTS Holdings Limited
Spencross Limited
T.I.M. Co. (Didsbury) Limited
Universal Steels and Aluminium Group Limited
Wentworth Miller Holdings Limited

82200 Activities of call centres

Akinika Debt Recovery Limited
Akinika UK Limited
The Contact Company Ltd
The Contact Specialists Ltd
Help Your Claim Limited
Kindertons Limited
Vertex Data Science Limited

82301 Activities of exhibition and fair organisers

Fresh Approach (UK) Limited

82302 Activities of conference organisers

Fresh Approach (UK) Limited

82911 Activities of collection agencies

Akinika Debt Recovery Limited

82920 Packaging activities

AKW Group Limited
API Foils Limited
API Group PLC
API Laminates Limited
Fisher Clinical Services UK Limited
Thomas Guy,Limited
Iforce Limited
LF Logistics (UK) Limited
Mondi Consumer Goods Packaging UK Ltd
National Flexible Limited
Nitecrest Limited
Nordic Packaging and Container (UK) Holdings Limited
Nordic Packaging and Container Holdings Limited

84110 General public administration activities

Boxwood Leisure Limited
Breckland Leisure Limited
Community Health Partnerships Limited
Penzance Leisure Limited

84220 Defence activities

James Fisher Marine Services Limited
Northern Diver (International) Ltd
Paradigm Precision Burnley Ltd

84250 Fire service activities

Northern Diver (International) Ltd
Tailored Fire & Security (London) Limited

85100 Pre-primary education

Alderley Edge School for Girls
Birkenhead School
Bradford Academy Trust
The Bury Grammar Schools Trustee Limited
Essa Foundation Academies Trust
The Fallibroome Trust
Giggleswick School
The Harmony Trust Ltd
Just Childcare Consultancy Services Limited
Just Childcare Holdings Limited
Just Childcare Limited
Kids Planet Day Nurseries Limited
Project Play Midco 1 Limited
Project Play Midco 2 Limited
The Sovereign Trust
St. Bede's College Limited
Stockport Grammar School
Stonyhurst

85200 Primary education

Alderley Edge School for Girls
Altus Education Partnership
Ashbridge School Limited
Autism Initiatives (UK)
Big Life Schools
Birkenhead School
Blackpool Multi Academy Trust
Bolton School
Bolton St Catherine's Academy
Bradford Academy Trust
Bradford Diocesan Academies Trust
Bridgewater School
Bright Tribe Trust
The Bury Grammar Schools Trustee Limited
The Challenge Academy Trust
Cheetham Church of England Community Academy
Cheshire Academies Trust
Chester Diocesan Board of Education
Children of Success Schools Trust
The Co-operative Academies Trust
Community First Academy Trust
Cranmer Education Trust
Crossacres Primary Academy
Discover Multi Academy Trust
Enhance Academy Trust
Essa Foundation Academies Trust
Exceed Academies Trust
The Fallibroome Trust
Focus Academy Trust (UK) Ltd
Fylde Coast Academy Trust
Giggleswick School
Grange School Hartford Limited (The)
The Harmony Trust Ltd
The Heath Family (North West)
IQRA Academy Education Trust
The Keys Federation
King David and Harold House Foundation
Kingfisher Learning Trust
Kirkham Grammar School
Lacey Green Primary Academy
The Learning Trust
Link Learning Trust
Liverpool College Independent School Trust
Manchester Diocesan Board of Education
Nurture Academies Trust
Oak Trees Multi Academy Trust
Oldham Hulme Grammar Schools
Pendle Education Trust
The Priestley Academy Trust
The Rowan Learning Trust
Sedbergh School
The Sovereign Trust
St. Bede's College Limited
Star Academies
Stockport Grammar School
Stonyhurst
The View Trust
Vision Multi Academy Trust
Warrington Primary Academy Trust
Windermere Educational Trust Limited
The Wings' CE Trust
Wise Owl Trust
Witherslack Group Limited

85320 Technical and vocational secondary education

AQA Education
Bolton UTC
Bright Tribe Trust
Energus
GP Strategies Holdings Limited
GP Strategies Training Limited
Genii Engineering & Technology Training Limited
North Lancs. Training Group Limited (The)
The Professional Footballers' Association Charity
Skills and Work Solutions Limited
University Technical College Warrington
West Derby School

85410 Post-secondary non-tertiary education

Altus Education Partnership
The Challenge Academy Trust
Crompton House Church of England School
The Laurus Trust
St. Ambrose College Edmund Rice Academy Trust

85421 First-degree level higher education

Liverpool Hope University
The Liverpool Institute for Performing Arts
The University of Cumbria
The University of Manchester Worldwide Limited

85422 Post-graduate level higher education

Liverpool School of Tropical Medicine
Star Academies
The University of Cumbria
The University of Manchester Worldwide Limited

85510 Sports and recreation education

The Professional Footballers' Association Charity
Sedbergh School
Stonyhurst

85590 Other education n.e.c.

AQA Education
Austin Friars
Birmingham Schools PSP Phase 1B Limited
Birmingham Schools SPC Holdings Phase 1A Ltd
Birmingham Schools SPC Holdings Phase 1B Limited
Birmingham Schools SPC Phase 1A Limited
Birmingham Schools SPC Phase 1B Limited
Birtenshaw
Bradford Diocesan Academies Trust
British Muslim Heritage Centre
Career Connect
Catalyst Higher Education (Sheffield) PLC
Cheadle Hulme School
The Christian Trust
Cidari Education Limited
Clitheroe Royal Grammar School
Education Partnership Trust
FocusEducation (Lambeth) Limited
FocusEducation (Lincolnshire) Limited
FocusEducation (Newcastle) Limited
GP Strategies Limited
Great Academies Education Trust
Lancashire Schools SPC Phase 1 Ltd
Lancashire Schools SPC Phase 2 Ltd
Lancashire Schools SPC Phase 2A Ltd
Lancashire Schools SPC Phase 3 Ltd
The David Lewis Centre
New Bridge Multi Academy Trust
The Pinnacle Learning Trust
QEGS Blackburn Academy Trust
Sandbach School
Seashell Trust
St Helens Chamber Limited
St. Catherine's Hospice (Lancashire) Limited
UCFB College of Football Business Limited
West Kirby Residential School

85600 Educational support services

The Blackburn Diocesan Board of Education
The Bolton Multi Academy Trust
Bright Tribe Trust
Concerted Academies Trust
Enhance Academy Trust
The Great Schools Trust
P H Holt Foundation
Manchester Diocesan Board of Education
New Bridge Multi Academy Trust
Star Academies
The Together Trust

86101 Hospital activities

Alder Hey Children's Charity
Alternative Futures Group Limited
Burnley General Hospital Phase V SPC Ltd
Catalyst Healthcare (Manchester) Financing PLC
Catalyst Healthcare (Romford) Financing PLC.
Catalyst Healthcare (Romford) Holdings Limited
Catalyst Healthcare (Romford) Limited
East Cheshire Hospice
Equilibrium Healthcare Limited
Making Space
Newton Abbot Health Limited
Guy Pilkington Memorial Home Limited (The)
Randomlight Limited
St George Healthcare Limited
St James's Oncology SPC Holdings Ltd
St. Ann's Hospice
Trinity Hospice and Palliative Care Services Ltd
Worcestershire Hospital SPC PLC

86102 Medical nursing home activities

The Hospital Company (Liverpool) Limited

86210 General medical practice activities

Hayes & Co Services Ltd

86220 Specialists medical practice activities

Trinity Hospice and Palliative Care Services Ltd
Zoll Medical UK Limited

86230 Dental practice activities

ADP Healthcare Acquisitions Limited
ADP Healthcare Services Limited
ADP No.1 Limited
Community Dental Centres Limited
First Choice Dental Limited
Genix Healthcare Ltd
IDH Limited
Integrated Dental Holdings Limited
KH&GW Limited
Ortho-Care (U.K.) Limited
Orthoworld 2000 Limited
Q Dental Care Limited
Whitecross Dental Care Limited

87100 Residential nursing care facilities

Alternative Futures Group Limited
Brancaster Care Homes Limited
Czajka Properties Limited
Flightcare Limited
Loven Care Homes Limited
Making Space
Marantomark Limited
Risedale Estates Limited
Salisbury Management Services Limited
Springhill House (Accrington) Limited
Stocks Hall Care Homes Limited
Unity Homes Limited
Victorguard Care PLC

87200 Residential care activities for learning difficulties, mental health and substance abuse

Alternative Futures Group Limited
L'Arche
Autism Together
Coed du Hall Limited
Czajka Properties Limited
European Care & Lifestyles (UK) Ltd
I Care Extra Care Limited
Lakeview Rest Homes Limited
The David Lewis Centre
Pathway Care Solutions Group Limited
Risedale Estates Limited

87300 Residential care activities for the elderly and disabled

Autism Initiatives (UK)
Care Worldwide (Southwell) Limited
Care Worldwide Limited
Czajka Properties Limited
European Care & Lifestyles (UK) Ltd
Federation of Jewish Services
Finbrook Limited
Flightcare Limited
The Grange Care Centre (Cheltenham) Limited
The David Lewis Centre
Loven Care Homes Limited
Making Space
Parkhaven Trust
Risedale Estates Limited
Springhill House (Accrington) Limited
Victorguard Care PLC
Woodlands Care GRP Ltd

87900 Other residential care activities n.e.c.

Bespoke Supportive Tenancies Ltd
Birtenshaw
Czajka Properties Limited
European Care & Lifestyles (UK) Ltd
Hexagon Care Services Limited
Potensial Limited
Seashell Trust
The Together Trust
Witherslack Group Limited

88100 Social work activities without accommodation for the elderly and disabled

Alternative Futures Group Limited
Health Care Resourcing Group Limited
Making Space
St. Catherine's Hospice (Lancashire) Limited

88990 Other social work activities without accommodation n.e.c.

Alliance Family Foundation Limited
L'Arche
Autism Initiatives (UK)
Beauland Limited
Bolton Lads' and Girls' Club
Brine Multi Academy Trust
Caritas Diocese of Salford
The Christian Trust
Debmar Benevolent Trust Limited
Forever Manchester
Fostering Solutions Limited
The David Lewis Centre
Liverpool Charity and Voluntary Services
Liverpool Shipbrokers Benevolent Society Incorporated
Memhay Limited
PSS (UK)
Parallel Parents Ltd
Yemin Charitable Trust Ltd

90010 Performing arts

Good Night Vienna Productions Limited
Hussein Traders Limited
The Liverpool and Merseyside Theatres Trust Limited
The Lowry Centre Trust
Royal Exchange Theatre Company Limited
Royal Liverpool Philharmonic Society (The)

90030 Artistic creation

The Bluecoat
Halle Concerts Society
Holden Decor Limited
Inflight Productions Ltd
The Lowry Centre Trust
Rayware Limited

90040 Operation of arts facilities

The Lowry Centre Trust
Wigan Leisure and Culture Trust

91011 Library activities

The Wordsworth Trust

91012 Archives activities

National Museum of Labour History (The)
The Wordsworth Trust

91020 Museums activities

The Lowry Centre Trust
National Museum of Labour History (The)
The Port Sunlight Village Trust
Wigan Leisure and Culture Trust
The Wordsworth Trust

91030 Operation of historical sites and buildings and similar visitor attractions

The Monastery of St Francis and Gorton Trust
National Museum of Labour History (The)
The Port Sunlight Village Trust
The Wordsworth Trust

91040 Botanical and zoological gardens and nature reserves activities

Grant Leisure Group Limited

92000 Gambling and betting activities

Betfred Group Limited
Done Brothers (Cash Betting) Limited
Graves (Cumberland) Limited
J. Holland & Sons Limited
IGT (UK 1) Limited
Napoleons Leisure Limited
Playnation Limited
David Pluck (North West) Limited
Tote (Successor Company) Limited
Tote Bookmakers Limited
Tote Direct Limited

93110 Operation of sports facilities

Bolton Wanderers Football & Athletic Company Limited (The)
Bradford Trident Limited
Andrew Brown Leisure Limited
Burnden Leisure Limited
Burnley FC Holdings Limited
Burnley Football & Athletic Company,Limited (The)
Chester Race Company Limited
The City of Salford Community Stadium Limited
Everton Football Club Company, Limited
Goodison Park Stadium Limited
Hale Country Club Limited
The Liverpool Football Club and Athletic Grounds Limited
Mill Farm Ventures Limited
St Helens Rugby Football Club Limited
Wigan Athletic Holdings Limited
Wigan Football Company Limited
Wigan Leisure and Culture Trust

93120 Activities of sport clubs

The Blackburn Rovers Football and Athletic Limited
Blackpool Football Club (Properties) Limited
Blackpool Football Club.Limited (The)
Burnden Leisure Limited
The City of Salford Community Stadium Limited
Formby Hall Golf Club Limited
MU Commercial Holdings Junior Limited
MU Commercial Holdings Limited
MU Finance Limited
MU RAML Limited
Manchester City Football Club Limited
Manchester City Limited
Manchester Sale Rugby Club Limited
Manchester United Football Club Limited
Manchester United Limited
Parkwood Community Leisure Limited
Parkwood Leisure Limited
Preston North End Limited
Pulse Equipment Group Limited
Red Football Holdings Limited
Red Football Junior Limited
Red Football Limited
Red Football Shareholder Limited
Wigan Athletic A.F.C. Limited
Woodley Sports Centre Limited

93130 Fitness facilities

F X Leisure Limited
Fitness First Clubs Limited
The Formby Land Trust
Linteum (Lewisham) Limited
Linteum (Willesden) Limited
Total Fitness Health Clubs Limited
The Waterside Hotel and Galleon Leisure Club Limited
Dave Whelan Sports Limited

93191 Activities of racehorse owners

Great Leighs Estates Limited

93199 Other sports activities

The British Cycling Federation
Carlisle United Association Football Club (1921) Limited
Football League Limited (The)
Ryan Giggs Limited
Imperial Corporate Events Ltd
M. Sport Limited
The Professional Footballers' Association Charity
Seashell Trust
Warrington Sports Holdings Limited

93210 Activities of amusement parks and theme parks

Blackpool Pleasure Beach Limited
Northamptonshire Leisure Estates Limited

93290 Other amusement and recreation activities n.e.c.

Billing Aquadrome Limited
The Blackpool Pier Company Limited
Blackpool Pleasure Beach (Holdings) Limited
Cavern City Tours Limited
Heritage Attractions Limited
Phil McIntyre Holdings Limited
Pure Leisure Estates Limited
S.J.M. Limited

94110 Activities of business and employers membership organisations

B&ESA Limited
North Lancs. Training Group Limited (The)
St Helens Chamber Limited
West and North Yorkshire Chamber of Commerce and Industry

94120 Activities of professional membership organisations

National Federation of Self Employed and Small Businesses Limited

94200 Activities of trade unions

The Professional Footballers' Association Charity

94910 Activities of religious organisations

Teresa Ball International Solidarity Fund
Blackburn Diocesan Board of Finance Limited
Chester Diocesan Board of Education
Chester Diocesan Board of Finance
The Christian Trust
Dawat-E-Islami UK
The Franciscan Missionaries of St Joseph
Liverpool Diocesan Board of Finance (The)
Manchester Diocesan Board of Education
Manchester Diocesan Board of Finance
New Kadampa Tradition - International Kadampa Buddhist Union
ROKPA Trust
Edmund Rice Bicentennial Trust Limited
United Reformed Church (North Western Province) Trust Limited (The)

94990 Activities of other membership organisations n.e.c.

L'Arche
The Helping Foundation
The Lancashire Wildlife Trust Ltd
Liverpool Charity and Voluntary Services
Pure Leisure Group Limited
Repic Limited

95110 Repair of computers and peripheral equipment

Flextronics Global Services (Manchester) Limited

95230 Repair of footwear and leather goods

Timpson Limited

96010 Washing and (dry-)cleaning of textile and fur products

Express Linen Services Limited
Johnson Cleaners UK Limited
Johnsons Apparelmaster Limited

96020 Hairdressing and other beauty treatment

The Grosvenor - Pulford Hotel Limited

96030 Funeral and related activities

The Avalon Trustee Company Limited
Havencare Management Limited

98000 Residents property management

J.P.S. Property Co. Limited
Six Town Housing Limited
Starcrester Properties Limited
Washington Homes Limited
X1 Management Limited

99000 Activities of extraterritorial organisations and bodies

Pendleton Together Holdings Limited

99999 Dormant company

Advanced Medical Solutions (Plymouth) Limited
Allied Filter Systems Holdings Limited
The Alternative Steel Group Limited
Bruntwood AV Holdings Limited
Bux & Co. Limited
C.U.F.C. Holdings Limited
CBL Finance (Holdings) UK Limited
CBL Finance (UK) Limited
Capital Bank Leasing 5 Limited
Capital Bank Leasing 9 Limited
Cardinal Health U.K. 418 Limited
Concept Life Sciences (Discovery) Limited
Concept Life Sciences (Environmental Consulting) Limited
Ensco 818 Limited
FQ Developments Limited
The Factory Shop Group Limited
Fircroft Technical Services UK Limited
Giti Tire Holdings (UK) Limited
Gott Agri Synergy Limited
Hamsard 3425 Limited
Holt Family (Holdings) Limited
LHS (UK) Limited
LSC Holdings Limited
LSC Investments Limited
Longfield Chemicals (Holdings) Limited
Medihealth Limited
Meridian Business Support Group PLC
NAT Flex Group Limited
PSC (Holdings) Limited
Palletower Group Holdings Limited
Partington (Holdings) Limited
Rayovac (UK) Limited
Rubix Group Midco 4 Limited
Rubix International Limited
Rural Concepts (Libya) Limited
Ultium Business Outsourcing Group Limited
Vegetarian Express Bidco Limited
Whispering Smith Group PLC

Printed in 8pt Nimbus Sans L

Designed by URW++ Design and Development GmbH

Dellam Publishing Limited

2 Heath Drive, Sutton, Surrey, SM2 5RP

Fax: 020 8770 7478 email: enquiries@dellam.com

SAN: 0177881 EAN/GLN: 5030670177882

www.ingramcontent.com/pod-product-compliance
Lightning Source LLC
LaVergne TN
LVHW082011200926
848481LV00010B/2835